James D. Campbell.

1935

THE
COMPLETE PLAYS
OF
BERNARD SHAW

THE MEDALLION on the cover of
this volume is from the bust of
the Author by DE STROBL

THE
COMPLETE PLAYS
OF
BERNARD SHAW

WIDOWERS' HOUSES : THE PHILANDERER :
MRS WARREN'S PROFESSION : ARMS AND
THE MAN : CANDIDA : THE MAN OF DES-
TINY : YOU NEVER CAN TELL : THE DEVIL'S
DISCIPLE : CÆSAR AND CLEOPATRA : CAP-
TAIN BRASSBOUND'S CONVERSION : MAN AND
SUPERMAN : JOHN BULL'S OTHER ISLAND :
HOW HE LIED TO HER HUSBAND : MAJOR
BARBARA : THE DOCTOR'S DILEMMA : GET-
TING MARRIED : THE SHEWING-UP OF
BLANCO POSNET : MISALLIANCE : THE DARK
LADY OF THE SONNETS : FANNY'S FIRST
PLAY : ANDROCLES AND THE LION : OVER-
RULED : PYGMALION : HEARTBREAK HOUSE :
GREAT CATHERINE : O'FLAHERTY V.C. : THE
INCA OF PERUSALEM : AUGUSTUS DOES HIS
BIT : ANNAJANSKA, THE BOLSHEVIK EM-
PRESS : BACK TO METHUSELAH : SAINT JOAN :
THE APPLE CART : JITTA'S ATONEMENT :
THE ADMIRABLE BASHVILLE ; OR, CON-
STANCY UNREWARDED : PRESS CUTTINGS :
THE GLIMPSE OF REALITY : PASSION, POISON,
AND PETRIFACTION ; OR, THE FATAL GAZO-
GENE : THE FASCINATING FOUNDLING : THE
MUSIC-CURE : TOO TRUE TO BE GOOD :
VILLAGE WOOING : ON THE ROCKS

ODHAMS PRESS LIMITED
LONG ACRE, LONDON W.C.2
1934

PRINTED IN GREAT BRITAIN
BY R. & R. CLARK LIMITED EDINBURGH

A WARNING
FROM THE AUTHOR

THIS is the first time I have ever attached any condition to the perusal of my books except the simple ceremony of walking into a bookshop and paying for them. I now find myself a party to a plan by which nobody, not even a millionaire, can obtain a copy of this edition of my plays unless he or she is a regular reader of one or other of certain newspapers or periodicals which credit their readers with brains beyond the ordinary and literary tastes not entirely vulgar. On this condition you can get the book for what it costs to manufacture, or less; and except on this condition you cannot get it at all. You are thus in a position at once privileged and restricted. Privileged because you can read my plays at less expense than the readers of The Times. Restricted because you must begin the day or end the week by reading your favorite paper.

This is an odd state of things; but what makes it odder is that I must warn you, before you attempt to enjoy my plays, to clear out of your consciousness most resolutely everything you have ever read about me in a newspaper. Otherwise you will not enjoy them: you will read them with a sophisticated mind, and a store of beliefs concerning me which have not the slightest foundation either in prosaic fact or in poetic truth. In some unaccountable way I seem to cast a spell on journalists which makes them recklessly indifferent not only to common veracity, but to human possibility. The person they represent me to be not only does not exist but could not possibly exist.

Now it may be that a pen portrait of an imaginary monster with my name attached to it may already have taken possession of your own mind through your inevitable daily contact with the newspaper press. If so, please class it with the unicorn and the dragon, the jabberwock and the bandersnatch, as a creature perhaps amusing but certainly entirely fabulous. If you are to get any good out of me you must accept me as a quite straightforward practitioner of the art I make my living by. Inasmuch as that living depends finally on you as reader or playgoer or both, I am your very faithful servant; and I should no more dream of pulling your leg or trifling with you or insulting you than any decent shopkeeper would dream of doing that to his best customers. If I make you laugh at yourself, remember that my business as a classic writer of comedies is "to chasten morals with ridicule"; and if I sometimes make you feel like a fool, remember that I have by the same action cured your folly, just as the dentist cures your toothache by pulling out your tooth. And I never do it without giving you plenty of laughing gas.

When you once get accustomed to my habit of mind, which I was born with and cannot help, you will not find me such bad company. But please do not think you can take in the work of my long lifetime at one reading. You must make it your practice to read all my works at least twice over every year for ten years or so. That is why this edition is so substantially bound for you.

G. Bernard Shaw.

CONTENTS

THE COMPLETE PLAYS OF
BERNARD SHAW

I
WIDOWERS' HOUSES
BEING THE FIRST OF THREE UNPLEASANT PLAYS

ACT I

In the garden restaurant of a hotel at Remagen on the Rhine, on a fine afternoon in August in the eighteen-eighties. Looking down the Rhine towards Bonn, the gate leading from the garden to the riverside is seen on the right. The hotel is on the left. It has a wooden annexe with an entrance marked Table d'Hôte. A waiter is in attendance.

A couple of English tourists come out of the hotel. The younger, Dr Harry Trench, is about 24, stoutly built, thick in the neck, close-cropped and black in the hair, with undignified medical-student manners, frank, hasty, rather boyish. The other, Mr William de Burgh Cokane, is probably over 40, possibly 50: an ill-nourished, scanty-haired gentleman, with affected manners: fidgety, touchy, and constitutionally ridiculous in uncompassionate eyes.

COKANE [*on the threshold of the hotel, calling peremptorily to the waiter*] Two beers for us out here. [*The waiter goes for the beer. Cokane comes into the garden*]. We have secured the room with the best view in the hotel, Harry, thanks to my tact. We'll leave in the morning, and do Mainz and Frankfurt. There is a very graceful female statue in the private house of a nobleman in Frankfurt. Also a zoo. Next day, Nuremberg! finest collection of instruments of torture in the world.

TRENCH. All right. You look out the trains, will you? [*He takes a Continental Bradshaw from his pocket, and tosses it on one of the tables*].

COKANE [*baulking himself in the act of sitting down*] Pah! the seat is all dusty. These foreigners are deplorably unclean in their habits.

TRENCH [*buoyantly*] Never mind: it dont matter, old chappie. Buck up, Billy, buck up. Enjoy yourself. [*He throws Cokane into the chair, and sits down opposite him, taking out his pipe, and singing noisily*]

Pour out the Rhine wine: let it flow
Like a free and bounding river—

COKANE [*scandalized*] In the name of common decency, Harry, will you remember that you are a Gentleman, and not a coster on Hampstead Heath on Bank Holiday? Would you dream of behaving like this in London?

TRENCH. Oh, rot! Ive come abroad to enjoy myself. So would you if youd just passed an examination after four years in the medical school and walking the hospital. [*He again bursts into song*].

COKANE [*rising*] Trench: either you travel as a gentleman, or you travel alone. This is what makes Englishmen unpopular on the Continent. It may not matter before the natives; but the people who came on board the steamer at Bonn are English. I have been uneasy all the afternoon about what they must think of us. Look at our appearance.

TRENCH. Whats wrong with our appearance?

COKANE. Négligé, my dear fellow, négligé. On the steamboat a little négligé was quite en règle; but here, in this hotel, some of them are sure to dress for dinner; and you have nothing but that Norfolk jacket. How are they to know that you are well connected if you do not shew it by your costume?

TRENCH. Pooh! the steamboat people were the scum of the earth: Americans and all sorts. They may go hang themselves, Billy. I shall not bother about them. [*He strikes a match, and proceeds to light his pipe*].

COKANE. Do drop calling me Billy in public, Trench. My name is Cokane. I am sure they were persons of consequence: you were struck with the distinguished appearance of the father yourself.

TRENCH [*sobered at once*] What! those people? [*He blows out the match and puts up his pipe*].

COKANE [*following up his advantage triumphantly*] Here, Harry, here: at this hotel. I

B

recognized the father's umbrella in the hall.

TRENCH [*with a touch of genuine shame*] I suppose I ought to have brought a change. But a lot of luggage is such a nuisance; and [*rising abruptly*] at all events we can go and have a wash. [*He turns to go into the hotel, but stops in consternation, seeing some people coming up to the riverside gate*]. Oh, I say! Here they are.

A lady and gentleman, followed by a porter with some light parcels, not luggage, but shop purchases, come into the garden. They are apparently father and daughter. The gentleman is 50, tall, well preserved, and of upright carriage. His incisive, domineering utterance and imposing style, with his strong aquiline nose and resolute clean-shaven mouth, give him an air of importance. He wears a light grey frock-coat with silk linings, a white hat, and a field-glass slung in a new leather case. A self-made man, formidable to servants, not easily accessible to anyone. His daughter is a well-dressed, well-fed, good-looking, strongminded young woman, presentably ladylike, but still her father's daughter. Nevertheless fresh and attractive, and none the worse for being vital and energetic rather than delicate and refined.

COKANE [*quickly taking the arm of Trench, who is staring as if transfixed*] Recollect yourself, Harry: presence of mind, presence of mind! [*He strolls with him towards the hotel. The waiter comes out with the beer*]. Kellner: ceci-la est notre table. Est ce que vous comprenez Français?

WAITER. Yes, zare. Oll right, zare.

THE GENTLEMAN [*to his porter*] Place those things on that table. [*The porter does not understand*].

WAITER [*interposing*] Zese zhentellmen are using zis table, zare. Vould you mind—

THE GENTLEMAN [*severely*] You should have told me so before. [*To Cokane, with fierce condescension*] I regret the mistake, sir.

COKANE. Dont mention it, my dear sir: dont mention it. Retain the place, I beg.

THE GENTLEMAN [*coldly turning his back on him*] Thank you. [*To the porter*] Place them on that table. [*The porter makes no movement until the gentleman points to the parcels and peremptorily raps on another table, nearer the gate*].

PORTER. Ja wohl, gnäd'g' Herr. [*He puts down the parcels*].

THE GENTLEMAN [*taking out a handful of money*] Waiter.

WAITER [*awestruck*] Yes, zare.

THE GENTLEMAN. Tea. For two. Out here.

WAITER. Yes, zare. [*He goes into the hotel*].

The gentleman selects a small coin from his handful of money, and gives it to the porter, who receives it with a submissive touch to his cap, and goes out, not daring to speak. His daughter sits down and opens a parcel of photographs. The gentleman takes out a Baedeker; places a chair for himself; and then, before sitting down, looks truculently at Cokane, as if waiting for him to take himself off. Cokane, not at all abashed, resumes his place at the other table with an air of modest good breeding, and calls to Trench, who is prowling irresolutely in the background.

COKANE. Trench, my dear fellow: your beer is waiting for you. [*He drinks*].

TRENCH [*glad of the excuse to come back to his chair*] Thank you, Cokane. [*He also drinks*].

COKANE. By the way, Harry, I have often meant to ask you: is Lady Roxdale your mother's sister or your father's?

This shot tells immediately. The gentleman is perceptibly interested.

TRENCH. My mother's, of course. What put that into your head?

COKANE. Nothing. I was just thinking— hm! She will expect you to marry, Harry: a doctor ought to marry.

TRENCH. What has she got to do with it?

COKANE. A great deal, dear boy. She looks forward to floating your wife in society in London.

TRENCH. What rot!

COKANE. Ah, you are young, dear boy: you dont know the importance of these things: apparently idle ceremonial trifles, really the springs and wheels of a great aristocratic system. [*The waiter comes back with the tea things, which he brings to the gentleman's table. Cokane rises and addresses the gentleman*]. My dear sir, excuse my addressing you; but I cannot help feeling that you prefer this table, and that we are in your way.

THE GENTLEMAN [*graciously*] Thank you. Blanche: this gentleman very kindly offers us his table, if you would prefer it.

BLANCHE. Oh, thanks: it makes no difference.

THE GENTLEMAN [*to Cokane*] We are fellow travellers, I believe, sir.

COKANE. Fellow travellers and fellow countrymen. Ah, we rarely feel the charm of our own tongue until it reaches our ears under a foreign sky. You have no doubt noticed that?

THE GENTLEMAN [*a little puzzled*] Hm! From a romantic point of view, possibly, very possibly. As a matter of fact, the sound of English makes me feel at home; and I dislike feeling at home when I am abroad. It is not precisely what one goes to the expense for. [*He looks at Trench*]. I think this gentleman travelled with us also.

COKANE [*acting as master of the ceremonies*] My valued friend, Dr Trench. [*The gentleman and Trench rise*]. Trench, my dear fellow, allow me to introduce you to—er—? [*He looks inquiringly at the gentleman, waiting for the name*].

THE GENTLEMAN. Permit me to shake your hand, Dr Trench. My name is Sartorius; and I have the honor of being known to Lady Roxdale, who is, I believe, a near relative of yours. Blanche. [*She looks up*]. Dr Trench. [*They bow*].

TRENCH. Perhaps I should introduce my friend Cokane to you. Mr Sartorius: Mr William de Burgh Cokane. [*Cokane makes an elaborate bow. Sartorius accepts it with dignity. The waiter meanwhile returns with the tea things*].

SARTORIUS [*to the waiter*] Two more cups.

WAITER. Yes, zare. [*He goes into the hotel*].

BLANCHE. Do you take sugar, Mr Cokane?

COKANE. Thank you. [*To Sartorius*] This is really too kind. Harry: bring your chair round.

SARTORIUS. You are very welcome. [*Trench brings his chair to the tea table; and they all sit round it. The waiter returns with two more cups*].

WAITER. Table d'hôte at alf pass zeex, zhentellmenn. Somesing else now, zare?

SARTORIUS. No. You can go. [*The waiter goes*].

COKANE [*very agreeably*] Do you contemplate a long stay here, Miss Sartorius?

BLANCHE. We were thinking of going on to Rolandseck. Is it as nice as this place?

COKANE. Harry: the Baedeker. [*Trench produces it from the other pocket*]. Thank you. [*He consults the index for Rolandseck*].

BLANCHE. Sugar, Dr Trench?

TRENCH. Thanks. [*She hands him the cup, and looks meaningly at him for an instant. He looks down hastily, and glances apprehensively at Sartorius, who is preoccupied with the bread and butter*].

COKANE. Rolandseck appears to be an ex-tremely interesting place. [*He reads*] "It is one of the most beautiful and frequented spots on the river, and is surrounded with numerous villas and pleasant gardens, chiefly belonging to wealthy merchants from the Lower Rhine, and extending along the wooded slopes at the back of the village."

BLANCHE. That sounds civilized and comfortable. I vote we go there.

SARTORIUS. Quite like our place at Surbiton, my dear.

BLANCHE. Quite.

COKANE. You have a place down the river? Ah, I envy you.

SARTORIUS. No: I have merely taken a furnished villa at Surbiton for the summer. I live in Bedford Square. I am a vestryman, and must reside in the parish.

BLANCHE. Another cup, Mr Cokane?

COKANE. Thank you, no. [*To Sartorius*] I presume you have been round this little place. Not much to see here, except the Apollinaris Church.

SARTORIUS [*scandalized*] The what!

COKANE. The Apollinaris Church.

SARTORIUS. A strange name to give a church. Very continental, I must say.

COCKANE. Ah, yes, yes, yes. That is where our neighbors fall short sometimes, Mr Sartorius. Taste! t a s t e is what they occasionally fail in. But in this instance they are not to blame. The water is called after the church, not the church after the water.

SARTORIUS [*as if this were an extenuating circumstance, but not a complete excuse*] I am glad to hear it. Is the church a celebrated one?

COKANE. Baedeker stars it.

SARTORIUS [*respectfully*] Oh, in that case I should like to see it.

COKANE [*reading*] "—erected in 1839 by Zwirner, the late eminent architect of the cathedral of Cologne, at the expense of Count Fürstenberg-Stammheim."

SARTORIUS [*much impressed*] We must certainly see that, Mr Cokane. I had no idea that the architect of Cologne cathedral lived so recently.

BLANCHE. Dont let us bother about any more churches, papa: theyre all the same. I'm tired to death of them.

SARTORIUS. Well, my dear, if you think it sensible to take a long and expensive journey to see what there is to be seen, and then go away without seeing it—

BLANCHE. Not this afternoon, papa, please.

SARTORIUS. My dear: I should like you to see everything. It is part of your education—

BLANCHE [*rising, with a petulant sigh*] Oh, my education! Very well, very well: I suppose I must go through with it. Are you coming, Dr Trench? [*With a grimace*] I'm sure the Johannis Church will be a treat for you.

COKANE [*laughing softly and archly*] Ah, excellent, excellent: very good indeed. [*Seriously*] But do you know, Miss Sartorius, there actually a r e Johannis churches here—several of them—as well as Apollinaris ones?

SARTORIUS [*sententiously, taking out his fieldglass and leading the way to the gate*] There is many a true word spoken in jest, Mr Cokane.

COKANE [*accompanying him*] How true! How true!

They go out together, ruminating profoundly. Blanche makes no movement to follow them. She watches until they are safely out of sight, and then posts herself before Trench, looking at him with an enigmatic smile, which he returns with a half sheepish, half conceited grin.

BLANCHE. Well! So you h a v e done it at last.

TRENCH. Yes. At least Cokane's done it. I told you he'd manage it. He's rather an ass in some ways; but he has tremendous tact.

BLANCHE [*contemptuously*] Tact! Thats not tact: thats inquisitiveness. Inquisitive people always have a lot of practice in getting into conversation with strangers. Why didnt you speak to my father yourself on the boat? You were ready enough to speak to me without any introduction.

TRENCH. I didnt particularly want to talk to him.

BLANCHE. It didnt occur to you, I suppose, that you put me in a false position by that.

TRENCH. Oh, I dont see that, exactly. Besides, your father isnt an easy man to tackle. Of course, now that I know him, I see that he's pleasant enough; but then youve got to know him first, havnt you?

BLANCHE [*impatiently*] Everybody is afraid of papa: I'm sure I dont know why. [*She sits down again, pouting a little*].

TRENCH [*tenderly*] However, it's all right now: isnt it? [*He sits near her*].

BLANCHE [*sharply*] I dont know. How should I? You had no right to speak to me that day on board the steamer. You thought I was alone, because [*with false pathos*] I had no mother with me.

TRENCH [*protesting*] Oh, I say! Come! It was you who spoke to me. Of course I was only

too glad of the chance; but on my word I shouldnt have moved an eyelid if you hadnt given me a lead.

BLANCHE. I only asked you the name of a castle. There was nothing unladylike in that.

TRENCH. Of course not. Why shouldnt you? [*With renewed tenderness*] But it's all right now: isnt it?

BLANCHE [*softly, looking subtly at him*] Is it?

TRENCH [*suddenly becoming shy*] I—I suppose so. By the way, what about the Apollinaris Church? Your father expects us to follow him, doesnt he?

BLANCHE [*with suppressed resentment*] Dont let me detain you if you wish to see it.

TRENCH. Wont you come?

BLANCHE. No. [*She turns her face away moodily*].

TRENCH [*alarmed*] I say: youre not offended, are you? [*She looks round at him for a moment with a reproachful film on her eyes*]. Blanche. [*She bristles instantly; overdoes it; and frightens him*]. I beg your pardon for calling you by your name; but I—er— [*She corrects her mistake by softening her expression eloquently. He responds with a gush*] You d o n t mind, do you? I felt sure you wouldnt, somehow. Well, look here. I have no idea how you will receive this: it must seem horribly abrupt; but the circumstances do not admit of—the fact is, my utter want of tact— [*he flounders more and more, unable to see that she can hardly contain her eagerness*]. Now, if it were Cokane—

BLANCHE [*impatiently*] Cokane!

TRENCH [*terrified*] No, not Cokane. Though I assure you I was only going to say about him that—

BLANCHE. That he will be be back presently with papa.

TRENCH [*stupidly*] Yes: they cant be very long now. I hope I'm not detaining you.

BLANCHE. I thought you were detaining me because you had something to say.

TRENCH [*totally unnerved*] Not at all. At least, nothing very particular. That is, I'm afraid you wouldnt think it very particular. Another time, perhaps—

BLANCHE. What other time? How do you know that we shall ever meet again? [*Desperately*] Tell me now. I w a n t you to tell me now.

TRENCH. Well, I was thinking that if we could make up our minds to—or not to—at least—er— [*His nervousness deprives him of the power of speech*].

BLANCHE [*giving him up as hopeless*] I dont

think theres much danger of y o u r making up your mind, Dr Trench.

TRENCH [*stammering*] I only thought— [*He stops and looks at her piteously. She hesitates a moment, and then puts her hands into his with calculated impulsiveness. He snatches her into his arms with a cry of relief*]. Dear Blanche! I thought I should never have said it. I believe I should have stood stuttering here all day if you hadnt helped me out with it.

BLANCHE [*indignantly trying to break loose from him*] I didnt help you out with it.

TRENCH [*holding her*] I dont mean that you did it on purpose, of course. Only instinctively.

BLANCHE [*still a little anxious*] But you havnt said anything.

TRENCH. What more can I say than this? [*He kisses her again*].

BLANCHE [*overcome by the kiss, but holding on to her point*] But Harry—

TRENCH [*delighted at the name*] Yes.

BLANCHE. When shall we be married?

TRENCH. At the first church we meet: the Apollinaris Church, if you like.

BLANCHE. No, but seriously. This is serious, Harry: you musnt joke about it.

TRENCH [*looking suddenly round to the river-side gate and quickly releasing her*] Sh! Here they are back again.

BLANCHE. Oh, d— [*The word is drowned by the clangor of a bell from within the hotel. The waiter appears on the steps, ringing it. Cokane and Sartorius are seen returning by the river gate*].

WAITER. Table d'hôte in dwendy minutes, ladies and zhentellmenn. [*He goes into the hotel*].

SARTORIUS [*gravely*] I intended you to accompany us, Blanche.

BLANCHE. Yes, papa. We were just about to start.

SARTORIUS. We are rather dusty: we must make ourselves presentable at the table d'hôte. I think you had better come in with me, my child. Come.

He offers Blanche his arm. The gravity of his manner overawes them all. Blanche silently takes his arm and goes into the hotel with him. Cokane, hardly less momentous than Sartorius himself, contemplates Trench with the severity of a judge.

COKANE [*with reprobation*] No, my dear boy. No, no. Never. I blush for you. I was never so ashamed in my life. You have been taking advantage of that unprotected girl.

TRENCH [*hotly*] Cokane!

COKANE [*inexorable*] Her father seems to be a perfect gentleman. I obtained the privilege of his acquaintance: I introduced you: I allowed him to believe that he might leave his daughter in your charge with absolute confidence. And what did I see on our return? what did her father see? Oh, Trench, Trench! No, my dear fellow, no, no. Bad taste, Harry, bad form!

TRENCH. Stuff! There was nothing to see.

COKANE. Nothing to see! She, a perfect lady, a person of the highest breeding, actually in your arms; and you say there was nothing to see! with a waiter there actually ringing a heavy bell to call attention to his presence! [*Lecturing him with redoubled severity*] Have you no principles, Trench? Have you no religious convictions? Have you no acquaintance with the usages of society? You actually kissed—

TRENCH. You didnt see me kiss her.

COKANE. We not only saw but h e a r d it: the report positively reverberated down the Rhine. Dont condescend to subterfuge, Trench.

TRENCH. Nonsense, my dear Billy. You—

COKANE. There you go again. D o n t use that low abbreviation. How am I to preserve the respect of fellow travellers of position and wealth, if I am to be Billied at every turn? My name is William: William de Burgh Cokane.

TRENCH. Oh, bother! There: dont be offended, old chap. Whats the use of putting your back up at every trifle? It comes natural to me to call you Billy: it suits you, somehow.

COKANE [*mortified*] You have no delicacy of feeling, Trench: no tact. I never mention it to any one; but nothing, I am afraid, will ever make a true gentleman of you. [*Sartorius appears on the threshold of the hotel*]. Here is my friend Sartorius, coming, no doubt, to ask you for an explanation of your conduct. I really should not have been surprised to see him bring a horsewhip with him. I shall not intrude on the painful scene.

TRENCH. Dont go, confound it. I dont want to meet him alone just now.

COKANE [*shaking his head*] Delicacy, Harry, delicacy! Good taste! Savoir faire! [*He walks away. Trench tries to escape in the opposite direction by strolling off towards the garden entrance*].

SARTORIUS [*mesmerically*] Dr Trench.

TRENCH [*stopping and turning*] Oh, is that you, Mr Sartorius? How did you find the church?

Sartorius, without a word, points to a seat. Trench, half hypnotized by his own nervousness and the impressiveness of Sartorius, sits down helplessly.

SARTORIUS [*also seating himself*] You have been speaking to my daughter, Dr Trench.

TRENCH [*with an attempt at ease of manner*] Yes: we had a conversation—quite a chat, in fact—while you were at the church with Cokane. How did you get on with Cokane, Mr Sartorius? I always think he has such wonderful tact.

SARTORIUS [*ignoring the digression*] I have just had a word with my daughter, Dr Trench; and I find her under the impression that something has passed between you which it is my duty as a father—the father of a motherless girl—to inquire into at once. My daughter, perhaps foolishly, has taken you quite seriously; and—

TRENCH. But—

SARTORIUS. One moment, if you will be so good. I have been a young man myself: younger, perhaps, than you would suppose from my present appearance. I mean, of course, in character. If you were not serious—

TRENCH [*ingenuously*] But I was perfectly serious. I want to marry your daughter, Mr Sartorius. I hope you dont object.

SARTORIUS [*condescending to Trench's humility from the mere instinct to seize an advantage, and yet deferring to Lady Roxdale's relative*] So far, no. I may say that your proposal seems to be an honourable and straightforward one, and that it is very gratifying to me personally.

TRENCH [*agreeably surprised*] Then I suppose we may consider the affair as settled. It's really very good of you.

SARTORIUS. Gently, Dr Trench, gently. Such a transaction as this cannot be settled off-hand.

TRENCH. Not off-hand, no. There are settlements and things, of course. But it may be regarded as settled between ourselves, maynt it?

SARTORIUS. Hm! Have you nothing further to mention?

TRENCH. Only that—that—No: I dont know that I have, except that I love—

SARTORIUS [*interrupting*] Anything about your family, for example? You do not anticipate any objection on their part, do you?

TRENCH. Oh, they have nothing to do with it.

SARTORIUS [*warmly*] Excuse me, sir: they have a great deal to do with it. [*Trench is abashed*]. I am resolved that my daughter shall approach no circle in which she will not be received with the full consideration to which her education and her breeding [*here his self-control slips a little; and he repeats, as if Trench had contradicted him*]—I say, her breeding—entitle her.

TRENCH [*bewildered*] Of course not. But what makes you think my family wont like Blanche? Of course my father was a younger son; and Ive had to take to a profession and all that; so my people wont expect us to entertain them: theyll know we cant afford it. But theyll entertain us: they always ask me.

SARTORIUS. That wont do for me, sir. Families often think it due to themselves to turn their backs on newcomers whom they may not think quite good enough for them.

TRENCH. But I assure you my people arnt a bit snobbish. Blanche is a lady: thatll be good enough for them.

SARTORIUS [*moved*] I am glad you think so. [*He offers his hand. Trench, astonished, takes it*]. I think so myself. [*He presses Trench's hand gratefully and releases it*]. And now, Dr Trench, since you have acted handsomely, you shall have no cause to complain of me. There shall be no difficulty about money: you shall entertain as much as you please: I will guarantee all that. But I must have a guarantee on my side that she will be received on equal terms by your family.

TRENCH. Guarantee!

SARTORIUS. Yes, a reasonable guarantee. I shall expect you to write to your relatives explaining your intention, and adding what you think proper as to my daughter's fitness for the best society. When you can shew me a few letters from the principal members of your family, congratulating you in a fairly cordial way, I shall be satisfied. Can I say more?

TRENCH [*much puzzled, but grateful*] No indeed. You are really very good. Many thanks. Since you wish it, I'll write to my people. But I assure you youll find them as jolly as possible over it. I'll make them write by return.

SARTORIUS. Thank you. In the meantime, I must ask you not to regard the matter as settled.

TRENCH. Oh! Not to regard the—I see. You mean between Blanche and—

SARTORIUS. I mean between you and Miss Sartorius. When I interrupted your conversation here some time ago, you and she were evidently regarding it as settled. In case difficulties arise, and the match—you see I call it a match—is broken off, I should not wish Blanche to think that she had allowed a gentleman to—to— [*Trench nods sympathetically*] Quite so. May I depend on you to keep a fair distance, and so spare me the necessity of having to restrain an intercourse which promises to be very pleasant to us all?

TRENCH. Certainly; since you prefer it. [*They shake hands on it*].

SARTORIUS [*rising*] You will write today, I think you said?

TRENCH [*eagerly*] I'll write now, before I leave here: straight off.

SARTORIUS. I will leave you to yourself then. [*He hesitates, the conversation having made him self-conscious and embarrassed; then recovers himself with an effort, and adds with dignity, as he turns to go*] I am pleased to have come to an understanding with you. [*He goes into the hotel; and Cokane, who has been hanging about inquisitively, emerges from the shrubbery*].

TRENCH [*excitedly*] Billy, old chap: youre just in time to do me a favor. I want you to draft a letter for me to copy out.

COKANE. I came with you on this tour as a friend, Trench: not as a secretary.

TRENCH. Well, youll write as a friend. It's to my Aunt Maria, about Blanche and me. To tell her, you know.

COKANE. Tell her about Blanche and you! Tell her about your conduct! Betray you, my friend; and forget that I am writing to a lady? Never!

TRENCH. Bosh, Billy: dont pretend you dont understand. We're engaged: e n g a g e d, my boy! what do you think of that? I must write by tonight's post. You are the man to tell me what to say. Come, old chap [*coaxing him to sit down at one of the tables*]: heres a pencil. Have you a bit of—oh, here: thisll do: write it on the back of the map. [*He tears the map out of his Baedeker and spreads it face downwards on the table. Cokane takes the pencil and prepares to write*]. Thats right. Thanks awfully,

old chap. Now fire away. [*Anxiously*] Be careful how you word it though, Cokane.

COKANE [*putting down the pencil*] If you doubt my ability to express myself becomingly to Lady Roxdale—

TRENCH [*propitiating him*] All right, old fellow, all right: theres not a man alive who could do it half so well as you. I only wanted to explain. You see, Sartorius has got it into his head, somehow, that my people will snub Blanche; and he wont consent unless they send letters and invitations and congratulations and the deuce knows what not. So just put it in such a way that Aunt Maria will write by return saying she is delighted, and asking us—Blanche and me, you know—to stay with her, and so forth. You know what I mean. Just tell her all about it in a chatty way; and—

COKANE [*crushingly*] If you will tell m e all about it in a chatty way, I daresay I can communicate it to Lady Roxdale with becoming delicacy. What is Sartorius?

TRENCH [*taken aback*] I dont know: I didnt ask. It's a sort of question you cant very well put to a man—at least a man like him. Do you think you could word the letter so as to pass all that over? I really dont like to ask him.

COKANE. I can pass it over if you wish. Nothing easier. But if you think Lady Roxdale will pass it over, I differ from you. I may be wrong: no doubt I am. I generally am wrong, I believe; but that is my opinion.

TRENCH [*much perplexed*] Oh, confound it! What the deuce am I to do? Cant you say he's a gentleman: that wont commit us to anything. If you dwell on his being well off, and Blanche an only child, Aunt Maria will be satisfied.

COKANE. Henry Trench: when will you begin to get a little sense? This is a serious business. Act responsibly, Harry: act responsibly.

TRENCH. Bosh! Dont be moral!

COKANE. I am not moral, Trench. At least I am not a moralist: that is the expression I should have used. Moral, but not a moralist. If you are going to get money with your wife, doesnt it concern your family to know how that money was made? Doesnt it concern you —y o u, Harry? [*Trench looks at him helplessly, twisting his fingers nervously. Cokane throws down the pencil and leans back with ostentatious indifference*]. Of course it is no business of mine: I only throw out the suggestion. Sartorius may be a retired burglar for all I know. [*Sartorius and Blanche, ready for dinner, come from the hotel*].

TRENCH. Sh! Here they come. Get the letter finished before dinner, like a good old chappie: I shall be awfully obliged to you.

COKANE [*impatiently*] Leave me, leave me: you disturb me. [*He waves him off, and begins to write*].

TRENCH [*humbly and gratefully*] Yes, old chap. Thanks awfully. [*By this time Blanche has left her father, and is strolling off towards the riverside. Sartorius comes down the garden, Baedeker in hand, and sits near Cokane, reading. Trench addresses him*]. You wont mind my taking Blanche in to dinner, I hope, sir?

SARTORIUS. By all means, Dr Trench. Pray do so. [*He graciously waves him off to join Blanche. Trench hurries after her through the gate. The light reddens as the Rhenish sunset begins. Cokane, making wry faces in the agonies of composition, is disconcerted to find Sartorius's eye upon him*].

SARTORIUS. I do not disturb you, I hope, Mr Cokane.

COKANE. By no means. Our friend Trench has entrusted me with a difficult and delicate task. He has requested me, as a friend of the family, to write to them on a subject that concerns you.

SARTORIUS. Indeed, Mr Cokane! Well, the communication could not be in better hands.

COKANE [*with an air of modesty*] Ah, that is going too far, my dear sir, too far. Still, you see what Trench is. A capital fellow in his way, Mr Sartorius, an excellent young fellow. But family communications like these require good manners. They require tact; and tact is Trench's weak point. He has an excellent heart, but no tact: none whatever. Everything depends on the way the matter is put to Lady Roxdale. But as to that, you may rely on me. I understand the sex.

SARTORIUS. Well, however she may receive it—and I care as little as any man, Mr Cokane, how people may choose to receive me—I trust I may at least have the pleasure of seeing you sometimes at my house when we return to England.

COKANE [*overwhelmed*] My dear sir! You express yourself in the true spirit of an English gentleman.

SARTORIUS. Not at all. You will always be most welcome. But I fear I have disturbed you in the composition of your letter. Pray resume it. I shall leave you to yourself. [*He pretends to rise, but checks himself to add*] Unless indeed I can assist you in any way? by clearing up any point on which you are not informed, for instance? or even, if I may so far presume on my years, giving you the benefit of my experience as to the best way of wording the matter? [*Cokane looks a little surprised at this. Sartorius looks hard at him, and continues deliberately and meaningly*] I shall always be happy to help any friend of Dr Trench's, in any way, to the best of my ability and of my means.

COKANE. My dear sir: you are really very good. Trench and I were putting our heads together over the letter just now; and there certainly were one or two points on which we were a little in the dark. [*Scrupulously*] But I would not permit Harry to question you. No. I pointed out to him that, as a matter of taste, it would be more delicate to wait until you volunteered the necessary information.

SARTORIUS. Hm! May I ask what you have said, so far?

COKANE. "My dear Aunt Maria." That is, Trench's dear Aunt Maria, my friend Lady Roxdale. You understand that I am only drafting a letter for Trench to copy.

SARTORIUS. Quite so. Will you proceed; or would it help you if I were to suggest a word or two?

COKANE [*effusively*] Your suggestions will be most valuable, my dear sir, most welcome.

SARTORIUS. I think I should begin in some such way as this. "In travelling with my friend Mr Cokane up the Rhine—"

COKANE [*murmuring as he writes*] Invaluable, invaluable. The very thing. "—my friend Mr Cokane up the Rhine—"

SARTORIUS. "I have made the acquaintance of"—or you may say "picked up," or "come across," if you think that would suit your friend's style better. We must not be too formal.

COKANE. "Picked up"! oh no: too dégagé, Mr Sartorius, too dégagé. I should say "had the privilege of becoming acquainted with."

SARTORIUS [*quickly*] By no means: Lady Roxdale must judge of that for herself. Let it stand as I said. "I have made the acquaintance of a young lady, the daughter of—" [*He hesitates*].

COKANE [*writing*] "acquaintance of a young lady, the daughter of"—yes?

SARTORIUS. "of"—you had better say "a gentleman."

COKANE [*surprised*] Of course.

SARTORIUS [*with sudden passion*] It is not of course, sir. [*Cokane, startled, looks at him with dawning suspicion. Sartorius recovers himself somewhat shamefacedly*]. Hm! "—of a gentleman of considerable wealth and position—"

COKANE [*echoing him with a new note of coldness in his voice as he writes the last words*] "—and position"

SARTORIUS. "which, however, he has made entirely for himself." [*Cokane, now fully enlightened, stares at him instead of writing*]. Have you written that?

COKANE [*expanding into an attitude of patronage and encouragement*] Ah, indeed. Quite so, quite so. [*He writes*] "—entirely for himself." Just so. Proceed, Sartorius, proceed. Very clearly expressed.

SARTORIUS. "The young lady will inherit the bulk of her father's fortune, and will be liberally treated on her marriage. Her education has been of the most expensive and complete kind obtainable; and her surroundings have been characterized by the strictest refinement. She is in every essential particular—"

COKANE [*interrupting*] Excuse the remark; but dont you think this is rather too much in the style of a prospectus of the young lady? I throw out the suggestion as a matter of taste.

SARTORIUS [*troubled*] Perhaps you are right. I am of course not dictating the exact words;—

COKANE. Of course not: of course not.

SARTORIUS. —but I desire that there may be no wrong impression as to my daughter's —er—breeding. As to myself—

COKANE. Oh, it will be sufficient to mention your profession, or pursuits, or— [*He pauses; and they look pretty hard at one another*].

SARTORIUS [*very deliberately*] My income, sir, is derived from the rental of a very extensive real estate in London. Lady Roxdale is one of the head landlords; and Dr Trench holds a mortgage from which, if I mistake not, his entire income is derived. The truth is, Mr Cokane, I am quite well acquainted with Dr Trench's position and affairs; and I have long desired to know him personally.

COKANE [*again obsequious, but still inquisitive*] What a remarkable coincidence! In what quarter is the estate situated, did you say?

SARTORIUS. In London, sir. Its management occupies as much of my time as is not devoted to the ordinary pursuits of a gentleman. [*He rises and takes out his card case*]. The rest I leave to your discretion. [*He leaves a card on the table*]. That is my address at Surbiton. If it should unfortunately happen, Mr Cokane, that this leads to nothing but a disappointment for Blanche, probably she would rather not see you afterwards. But if all turns out as we hope, Dr Trench's best friends will then be our best friends.

COKANE [*rising and confronting Sartorius confidently, pencil and paper in hand*] Rely on me, Mr Sartorius. The letter is already finished h e r e [*pointing to his brain*]. In five minutes it will be finished t h e r e [*He points to the paper; nods to emphasize the assertion; and begins to pace up and down the garden, writing, and tapping his forehead from time to time as he goes. with every appearance of severe intellectual exertion*].

SARTORIUS [*calling through the gate after a glance at his watch*] Blanche.

BLANCHE [*replying in the distance*] Yes?

SARTORIUS. Time, my dear. [*He goes into the table d'hôte*].

BLANCHE [*nearer*] Coming. [*She comes back through the gate followed by Trench*].

TRENCH [*in a half whisper, as Blanche goes towards the table d'hôte*] Blanche: stop. One moment. [*She stops*]. We must be careful when your father is by. I had to promise him not to regard anything as settled until I hear from my people at home.

BLANCHE [*chilled*] Oh, I see. Your family may object to me; and then it will be all over between us. They are almost sure to.

TRENCH [*anxiously*] Dont say that, Blanche: it sounds as if you didnt care. I hope y o u regard it as settled. Y o u havnt made any promise, you know.

BLANCHE [*earnestly*] Yes, I have: *I* promised papa too. But I have broken my promise for your sake. I suppose I am not so conscientious as you. And if the matter is not to be regarded as settled, family or no family, promise or no promise, let us break it off here and now.

TRENCH [*intoxicated with affection*] Blanche: on my most sacred honor, family or no family, promise or no promise—[*The waiter reappears*

B 2

at the table d'hôte entrance, ringing his bell]. Damn that noise!

COKANE [*as he comes to them, flourishing the letter*] Finished, dear boy, finished. Done to a turn, punctually to the second. C'est fini, mon cher garçon, c'est fini. [*Sartorius returns*].

SARTORIUS. Will you take Blanche in, Dr Trench? [*Trench takes Blanche in to the table d'hôte*]. Is the letter finished, Mr Cokane?

COKANE [*with an author's pride, handing his draft to Sartorius*] There! [*Sartorius reads it, nodding gravely over it with complete approval*].

SARTORIUS [*returning the draft*] Thank you, Mr Cokane. You have the pen of a ready writer.

COKANE [*as they go in together*] Not at all, not at all. A little tact, Mr Sartorius, a little knowledge of the world, a little experience of women— [*They disappear into the annexe*].

ACT II

In the library of a handsomely appointed villa at Surbiton on a sunny forenoon in September. Sartorius is busy at a writing table littered with business letters. The fireplace, decorated for summer, is close behind him: the window is in the opposite wall. Between the table and the window Blanche, in her prettiest frock, sits reading The Queen. The door is in the middle. All the walls are lined with shelves of smartly tooled books, fitting into their places like bricks.

SARTORIUS. Blanche.

BLANCHE. Yes, papa.

SARTORIUS. I have some news here.

BLANCHE. What is it?

SARTORIUS. I mean news for you—from Trench.

BLANCHE [*with affected indifference*] Indeed?

SARTORIUS. "Indeed?"! Is that all you have to say to me? Oh, very well.

He resumes his work. Silence.

BLANCHE. What do his people say, papa?

SARTORIUS. His people? I dont know. [*Still busy*].

Another pause.

BLANCHE. What does he say?

SARTORIUS. He! He says nothing. [*He folds a letter leisurely, and looks for the envelope*]. He prefers to communicate the result of his—where did I put?—oh, here. Yes: he prefers to communicate the result in person.

BLANCHE [*springing up*] Oh, papa! When is he coming?

SARTORIUS. If he walks from the station,

he may arrive in the course of the next half-hour. If he drives, he may be here at any moment.

BLANCHE [*making hastily for the door*] Oh!

SARTORIUS. Blanche.

BLANCHE. Yes, papa.

SARTORIUS. You will of course not meet him until he has spoken to me.

BLANCHE [*hypocritically*] Of course not, papa. I shouldnt have thought of such a thing.

SARTORIUS. That is all. [*She is going, when he puts out his hand, and says with fatherly emotion*] My dear child. [*She responds by going over to kiss him. A tap at the door*]. Come in.

Lickcheese enters, carrying a black handbag. He is a shabby, needy man, with dirty face and linen, scrubby beard and whiskers, going bald. A nervous, wiry, pertinacious human terrier, judged by his mouth and eyes, but miserably apprehensive and servile before Sartorius. He bids Blanche "Good morning, miss"; and she passes out with a slight and contemptuous recognition of him.

LICKCHEESE. Good morning, sir.

SARTORIUS [*harsh and peremptory*] Good morning.

LICKCHEESE [*taking a little sack of money from his bag*] Not much this morning, sir. I have just had the honor of making Dr Trench's acquaintance, sir.

SARTORIUS [*looking up from his writing, displeased*] Indeed?

LICKCHEESE. Yes, sir. Dr Trench asked his way of me, and was kind enough to drive me from the station.

SARTORIUS. Where is he, then?

LICKCHEESE. I left him in the hall, with his friend, sir. I should think he is speaking to Miss Sartorius.

SARTORIUS. Hm! What do you mean by his friend?

LICKCHEESE. There is a Mr Cokane with him, sir.

SARTORIUS. I see you have been talking to him, eh?

LICKCHEESE. As we drove along: yes, sir.

SARTORIUS [*sharply*] Why did you not come by the nine o'clock train?

LICKCHEESE. I thought—

SARTORIUS. It cannot be helped now; so never mind what you thought. But do not put off my business again to the last moment. Has there been any further trouble about the St Giles property?

LICKCHEESE. The Sanitary Inspector has

been complaining again about No. 13 Robbins's Row. He says he'll bring it before the vestry.

SARTORIUS. Did you tell him that I am on the vestry?

LICKCHEESE. Yes, sir.

SARTORIUS. What did he say to that?

LICKCHEESE. Said he supposed so, or you wouldnt dare to break the law so scand'lous. I only tell you what he said.

SARTORIUS. Hm! Do you know his name?

LICKCHEESE. Yes, sir. Speakman.

SARTORIUS. Write it down in the diary for the day of the next meeting of the Health Committee. I will teach Mr Speakman his duty to members of the vestry.

LICKCHEESE [doubtfully] The vestry cant hurt him, sir. He's under the Local Government Board.

SARTORIUS. I did not ask you that. Let me see the books. [Lickcheese produces the rent book, and hands it to Sartorius; then makes the desired entry in the diary on the table, watching Sartorius with misgiving as the rent book is examined. Sartorius rises, frowning]. One pound four for repairs to number thirteen! What does this mean?

LICKCHEESE. Well, sir, it was the staircase on the third floor. It was downright dangerous: there werent but three whole steps in it, and no handrail. I thought it best to have a few boards put in.

SARTORIUS. Boards! Firewood, sir, firewood! They will burn every stick of it. You have spent twenty-four shillings of my money on firewood for them.

LICKCHEESE. There ought to be stone stairs, sir: it would be a saving in the long run. The clergyman says—

SARTORIUS. What! Who says?

LICKCHEESE. The clergyman, sir, only the clergyman. Not that I make much account of him; but if you knew how he has worried me over that staircase—

SARTORIUS. I am an Englishman; and I will suffer no priest to interfere in my business. [He turns suddenly on Lickcheese]. Now look here, Mr Lickcheese! This is the third time this year that you have brought me a bill of over a pound for repairs. I have warned you repeatedly against dealing with these tenement houses as if they were mansions in a West-End square. I have had occasion to warn you too against discussing my affairs with strangers. You have chosen to disre-

gard my wishes. You are discharged.

LICKCHEESE [dismayed] Oh, sir, dont say that.

SARTORIUS [fiercely] You are discharged.

LICKCHEESE. Well, Mr Sartorius, it is hard, so it is. No man alive could have screwed more out of them poor destitute devils for you than I have, or spent less in doing it. I have dirtied my hands at it until theyre not fit for clean work hardly; and now you turn me—

SARTORIUS [interrupting him menacingly] What do you mean by dirtying your hands? If I find that you have stepped an inch outside the letter of the law, Mr Lickcheese, I will prosecute you myself. The way to keep your hands clean is to gain the confidence of your employers. You will do well to bear that in mind in your next situation.

THE PARLORMAID [opening the door] Mr Trench and Mr Cokane.

Cokane and Trench come in: Trench festively dressed and in buoyant spirits: Cokane highly self-satisfied.

SARTORIUS. How do you do, Dr Trench? Good morning, Mr Cokane. I am pleased to see you here. Mr Lickcheese: you will place your accounts and money on the table: I will examine them and settle with you presently.

Lickcheese retires to the table, and begins to arrange his accounts, greatly depressed. The parlormaid withdraws.

TRENCH [glancing at Lickcheese] I hope we're not in the way.

SARTORIUS. By no means. Sit down, pray. I fear you have been kept waiting.

TRENCH [taking Blanche's chair] Not at all. Weve only just come in. [He takes out a packet of letters, and begins untying them].

COKANE [going to a chair nearer the window, but stopping to look admiringly round before sitting down] You must be happy here with all these books, Mr Sartorius. A literary atmosphere.

SARTORIUS [resuming his seat] I have not looked into them. They are pleasant for Blanche occasionally when she wishes to read. I chose the house because it is on gravel. The death-rate is very low.

TRENCH [triumphantly] I have any amount of letters for you. All my people are delighted that I am going to settle. Aunt Maria wants Blanche to be married from her house. [He hands Sartorius a letter].

SARTORIUS. Aunt Maria?

COKANE. Lady Roxdale, my dear sir: he

means Lady Roxdale. Do express yourself with a little more tact, my dear fellow.

TRENCH. Lady Roxdale, of course. Uncle Harry—

COKANE. Sir Harry Trench. His godfather, my dear sir, his godfather.

TRENCH. Just so. The pleasantest fellow for his age you ever met. He offers us his house at St Andrews for a couple of months, if we care to pass our honeymoon there. [*He hands Sartorius another letter*]. It's the sort of house nobody can live in, you know; but it's a nice thing for him to offer. Dont you think so?

SARTORIUS [*dissembling a thrill at the titles*] No doubt. These seem very gratifying, Dr Trench.

TRENCH. Yes, arnt they? Aunt Maria has really behaved like a brick. If you read the postscript youll see she spotted Cokane's hand in my letter. [*Chuckling*] He wrote it for me.

SARTORIUS [*glancing at Cokane*] Indeed! Mr Cokane evidently did it with great tact.

COKANE [*returning the glance*] Dont mention it.

TRENCH [*gleefully*] Well, what do you say now, Mr Sartorius? May we regard the matter as settled at last?

SARTORIUS. Quite settled. [*He rises and offers his hand. Trench, glowing with gratitude, rises and shakes it vehemently, unable to find words for his feelings*].

COKANE [*coming between them*]. Allow me to congratulate you both. [*He shakes hands with the two at the same time*].

SARTORIUS. And now, gentlemen, I have a word to say to my daughter. Dr Trench: you will not, I hope, grudge me the pleasure of breaking this news to her: I have had to disappoint her more than once since I last saw you. Will you excuse me for ten minutes?

COKANE [*in a flush of friendly protest*] My dear sir: can you ask?

TRENCH. Certainly.

SARTORIUS. Thank you. [*He goes out*].

TRENCH [*chuckling again*] He wont have any news to break, poor old boy: she's seen all the letters already.

COKANE. I must say your behavior has been far from straightforward, Harry. You have been carrying on a clandestine correspondence.

LICKCHEESE [*stealthily*] Gentlemen—

TRENCH \ [*turning: they had for-* \
COKANE ∫ *gotten his presence*] \ Hallo!

LICKCHEESE [*coming between them very humbly, but in mortal anxiety and haste*] Look here, gentlemen. [*To Trench*] You, sir, I address myself to more particlar. Will you say a word in my favor to the guvnor? He's just given me the sack; and I have four children looking to me for their bread. A word from you, sir, on this happy day, might get him to take me on again.

TRENCH [*embarrassed*] Well, you see, Mr Lickcheese, I dont see how I can interfere. I'm very sorry, of course.

COKANE. Certainly you cannot interfere. It would be in the most execrable taste.

LICKCHEESE. Oh, gentlemen, youre young; and you dont know what loss of employment means to the like of me. What harm would it do you to help a poor man? Just listen to the circumstances, sir. I only—

TRENCH [*moved, but snatching at an excuse for taking a high tone in avoiding the unpleasantness of helping him*] No: I had rather not. Excuse my saying plainly that I think Mr Sartorius is not a man to act hastily or harshly. I have always found him very fair and generous; and I believe he is a better judge of the circumstances than I am.

COKANE [*inquisitive*] I think you ought to hear the circumstances, Harry. It can do no harm. Hear the circumstances by all means.

LICKCHEESE. Never mind, sir: it aint any use. When I hear that man called generous and fair!—well, never mind.

TRENCH [*severely*] If you wish me to do anything for you, Mr Lickcheese, let me tell you that you are not going the right way about it in speaking ill of Mr Sartorius.

LICKCHEESE. Have I said one word against him, sir? I leave it to your friend: have I said a word?

COKANE. True: true. Quite true. Harry: be just.

LICKCHEESE. Mark my words, gentlemen: he'll find what a man he's lost the very first week's rents the new man'll bring him. Youll find the difference yourself, Dr Trench, if you or your children come into the property. Ive took money there when no other collector alive would have wrung it out. And this is the thanks I get for it! Why, see here, gentlemen! Look at that bag of money on the table. Hardly a penny of that but there was a hungry child crying for the bread it would have bought. But I got it for him—screwed and worried and bullied it out of them. I—

look here, gentlemen: I'm pretty seasoned to the work; but theres money there that I couldnt have taken if it hadnt been for the thought of my own children depending on me for giving him satisfaction. And because I charged him four-and-twenty shillin to mend a staircase that three women have been hurt on, and that would have got him prosecuted for manslaughter if it had been let go much longer, he gives me the sack. Wouldnt listen to a word, though I would have offered to make up the money out of my own pocket: aye, and am willing to do it still if you will only put in a word for me.

TRENCH [*aghast*] You took money that ought to have fed starving children! Serve you right! If I had been the father of one of those children, I'd have given you something worse than the sack. I wouldnt say a word to save your soul, if you have such a thing. Mr Sartorius was quite right.

LICKCHEESE [*staring at him, surprised into contemptuous amusement in the midst of his anxiety*] Just listen to this! Well, you a r e an innocent young gentleman. Do you suppose he sacked me because I was too hard? Not a bit on it: it was because I wasnt hard enough. I never heard him say he was satisfied yet: no, nor he wouldnt, not if I skinned em alive. I dont say he's the worst landlord in London: he couldnt be worse than some; but he's no better than the worst I ever had to do with. And, though I say it, I'm better than the best collector he ever done business with. Ive screwed more and spent less on his properties than anyone would believe that knows what such properties are. I know my merits, Dr Trench, and will speak for myself if no one else will.

COKANE. What description of properties? Houses?

LICKCHEESE. Tenement houses, let from week to week by the room or half room: aye, or quarter room. It pays when you know how to work it, sir. Nothing like it. It's been calculated on the cubic foot of space, sir, that you can get higher rents letting by the room than you can for a mansion in Park Lane.

TRENCH. I hope Mr Sartorius hasnt much of that sort of property, however it may pay.

LICKCHEESE. He has nothing else, sir; and he shews his sense in it, too. Every few hundred pounds he could scrape together he bought old houses with: houses that you wouldnt hardly look at without holding your nose. He has em in St Giles's: he has em in Marylebone: he has em in Bethnal Green. Just look how he lives himself, and youll see the good of it to him. He likes a low death-rate and a gravel soil for himself, he does. You come down with me to Robbins's Row; and I'll shew you a soil and a death-rate, I will! And, mind you, it's me that makes it pay him so well. Catch him going down to collect his own rents! Not likely!

TRENCH. Do you mean to say that all his property—all his means—come from this sort of thing?

LICKCHEESE. Every penny of it, sir.

Trench, overwhelmed, has to sit down.

COKANE [*looking compassionately at him*] Ah, my dear fellow, the love of money is the root of all evil.

LICKCHEESE. Yes, sir; and we'd all like to have the tree growing in our garden.

COKANE [*revolted*] Mr Lickcheese: I did not address myself to you. I do not wish to be severe with you; but there is something peculiarly repugnant to my feelings in the calling of a rent collector.

LICKCHEESE. It's no worse than many another. I have my children looking to me.

COKANE. True: I admit it. So has our friend Sartorius. His affection for his daughter is a redeeming point—a redeeming point, certainly.

LICKCHEESE. She's a lucky daughter, sir. Many another daughter has been turned out upon the streets to gratify his affection for her. Thats what business is, sir, you see. Come, sir: I think your friend will say a word for me now he knows I'm not in fault.

TRENCH [*rising angrily*] I will not. It's a damnable business from beginning to end; and you deserve no better luck for helping in it. Ive seen it all among the out-patients at the hospital; and it used to make my blood boil to think that such things couldnt be prevented.

LICKCHEESE [*his suppressed spleen breaking out*] Oh indeed, sir. But I suppose youll take your share when you marry Miss Blanche, all the same. [*Furiously*] Which of us is the worse, I should like to know? me that wrings the money out to keep a home over my children, or you that spend it and try to shove the blame on to me?

COKANE. A most improper observation to

address to a gentleman, Mr Lickcheese! A most revolutionary sentiment!

LICKCHEESE. Perhaps so. But then Robbins's Row aint a school for manners. You collect a week or two there—youre welcome to my place if I cant keep it for myself—and youll hear a little plain speaking, you will.

COKANE [with dignity] Do you know to whom you are speaking, my good man?

LICKCHEESE [recklessly] I know well enough who I'm speaking to. What do I care for you, or a thousand such? I'm poor: thats enough to make a rascal of me. No consideration for me! nothing to be got by saying a word for me! [Suddenly cringing to Trench] Just a word, sir. It would cost you nothing. [Sartorius appears at the door, unobserved]. Have some feeling for the poor.

TRENCH. I'm afraid you have shewn very little, by your own confession.

LICKCHEESE [breaking out again] More than your precious father-in-law, anyhow. I— [Sartorius's voice, striking in with deadly coldness, paralyzes him].

SARTORIUS. You will come here tomorrow not later than ten, Mr Lickcheese, to conclude our business. I shall trouble you no further today. [Lickcheese, cowed, goes out amid dead silence. Sartorius continues, after an awkward pause] He is one of my agents, or rather was; for I have unfortunately had to dismiss him for repeatedly disregarding my instructions. [Trench says nothing. Sartorius throws off his embarrassment, and assumes a jocose, rallying air, unbecoming to him under any circumstances, and just now almost unbearably jarring]. Blanche will be down presently, Harry [Trench recoils]—I suppose I must call you Harry now. What do you say to a stroll through the garden, Mr Cokane? We are celebrated here for our flowers.

COKANE. Charmed, my dear sir, charmed. Life here is an idyll—a perfect idyll. We were just dwelling on it.

SARTORIUS [slyly] Harry can follow with Blanche. She will be down directly.

TRENCH [hastily] No. I cant face her just now.

SARTORIUS [rallying him] Indeed! Ha, ha!

The laugh, the first they have heard from him, sets Trench's teeth on edge. Cokane is taken aback but instantly recovers himself.

COKANE. Ha! ha! ha! Ho! ho!

TRENCH. But you dont understand.

SARTORIUS. Oh, I think we do, I think we

do. Eh, Mr Cokane? Ha! ha!

COKANE. I should think we do. Ha! ha! ha!

They go out together, laughing at him. He collapses into a chair, shuddering in every nerve. Blanche appears at the door. Her face lights up when she sees that he is alone. She trips noiselessly to the back of his chair and clasps her hands over his eyes. With a convulsive start and exclamation he springs up and breaks away from her.

BLANCHE [astonished] Harry!

TRENCH [with distracted politeness] I beg your pardon. I was thinking—wont you sit down?

BLANCHE [looking suspiciously at him] Is anything the matter? [She sits down slowly near the writing table. He takes Cokane's chair].

TRENCH. No. Oh no.

BLANCHE. Papa has not been disagreeable, I hope.

TRENCH. No: I have hardly spoken to him since I was with you. [He rises; takes up his chair; and plants it beside hers. This pleases her better. She looks at him with her most winning smile. A sort of sob breaks from him; and he catches her hands and kisses them passionately. Then, looking into her eyes with intense earnestness, he says] Blanche: are you fond of money?

BLANCHE [gaily] Very. Are you going to give me any?

TRENCH [wincing] Dont make a joke of it: I'm serious. Do you know that we shall be very poor?

BLANCHE. Is that what made you look as if you had neuralgia?

TRENCH [pleadingly] My dear: it's no laughing matter. Do you know that I have a bare seven hundred a year to live on?

BLANCHE. How dreadful!

TRENCH. Blanche: it's very serious indeed: I assure you it is.

BLANCHE. It would keep me rather short in my housekeeping, dearest boy, if I had nothing of my own. But papa has promised me that I shall be richer than ever when we are married.

TRENCH. We must do the best we can with seven hundred. I think we ought to be self-supporting.

BLANCHE. Thats just what I mean to be, Harry. If I were to eat up half your seven hundred, I should be making you twice as poor; but I'm going to make you twice as rich instead [He shakes his head]. Has papa made any difficulty?

TRENCH [rising with a sigh and taking his chair

back to its former place] No. None at all. [*He sits down dejectedly. When Blanche speaks again her face and voice betray the beginning of a struggle with her temper*].

BLANCHE. Harry: are you too proud to take money from my father?

TRENCH. Yes, Blanche: I am too proud.

BLANCHE [*after a pause*] That is not nice to me, Harry.

TRENCH. You must bear with me, Blanche. I—I cant explain. After all, it's very natural.

BLANCHE. Has it occurred to you that I may be proud too?

TRENCH. Oh, thats nonsense. No one will accuse y o u of marrying for money.

BLANCHE. No one would think the worse of me if I did, or of you either. [*She rises and begins to walk restlessly about*]. We really cannot live on seven hundred a year, Harry; and I dont think it quite fair of you to ask me merely because you are afraid of people talking.

TRENCH. It's not that alone, Blanche.

BLANCHE. What else is it, then?

TRENCH. Nothing. I—

BLANCHE [*getting behind him, and speaking with forced playfulness as she bends over him, her hands on his shoulders*] Of course it's nothing. Now dont be absurd, Harry: be good; and listen to me: I know how to settle it. You are too proud to owe anything to me; and I am too proud to owe anything to you. You have seven hundred a year. Well, I will take just seven hundred a year from papa at first; and then we shall be quits. Now, now, Harry, you know youve not a word to say against that.

TRENCH. It's impossible.

BLANCHE. Impossible!

TRENCH. Yes, impossible. I have resolved not to take any money from your father.

BLANCHE. But he'll give the money to me, not to you.

TRENCH. It's the same thing. [*With an effort to be sentimental*] I love you too well to see any distinction. [*He puts up his hand half-heartedly: she takes it over his shoulder with equal indecision. They are both trying hard to conciliate one another*].

BLANCHE. Thats a very nice way of putting it, Harry; but I'm sure theres something I ought to know. H a s papa been disagreeable?

TRENCH. No: he has been very kind—to me, at least. It's not that. It's nothing you can guess, Blanche. It would only pain you—

perhaps offend you. I dont mean, of course, that we shall live always on seven hundred a year. I intend to go at my profession in earnest, and work my fingers to the bone.

BLANCHE [*playing with his fingers, still over his shoulder*] But I shouldnt like you with your fingers worked to the bone, Harry. I must be told what the matter is. [*He takes his hand quickly away: she flushes angrily; and her voice is no longer even an imitation of the voice of a lady as she exclaims*] I hate secrets; and I dont like to be treated as if I were a child.

TRENCH [*annoyed by her tone*] Theres nothing to tell. I dont choose to trespass on your father's generosity: thats all.

BLANCHE. You had no objection half an hour ago, when you met me in the hall, and shewed me all the letters. Your family doesnt object. Do y o u object?

TRENCH [*earnestly*] I do not indeed. It's only a question of money.

BLANCHE [*imploringly, the voice softening and refining for the last time*] Harry: theres no use in our fencing in this way. Papa will never consent to my being absolutely dependent on you; and I dont like the idea of it myself. If you even mention such a thing to him you will break off the match: you will indeed.

TRENCH [*obstinately*] I cant help that.

BLANCHE [*white with rage*] You cant help—! Oh, I'm beginning to understand. I will save you the trouble. You can tell papa that *I* have broken off the match; and then there will be no further difficulty.

TRENCH [*taken aback*] What do you mean, Blanche? Are you offended?

BLANCHE. Offended! How dare you ask me?

TRENCH. Dare!

BLANCHE. How much more manly it would have been to confess that you were trifling with me that time on the Rhine! Why did you come here today? Why did you write to your people?

TRENCH. Well, Blanche, if you are going to lose your temper—

BLANCHE. Thats no answer. You depended on your family to get you out of your engagement; and they did not object: they were only too glad to be rid of you. You were not mean enough to stay away, and not manly enough to tell the truth. You thought you could provoke me to break the engagement: thats so like a man—to try to put the woman in the wrong. Well, you have your way: I release you. I wish youd opened my eyes by downright brutality; by striking me; by anything rather than shuffling as you have done.

TRENCH [*hotly*] Shuffling! If I'd thought you capable of turning on me like this, I'd never have spoken to you. Ive a good mind never to speak to you again.

BLANCHE. You shall not—not ever. I will take care of that [*going to the door*].

TRENCH [*alarmed*] What are you going to do?

BLANCHE. To get your letters: your false letters, and your presents: your hateful presents, to return them to you. I'm very glad it's all broken off; and if—[*as she puts her hand to the door it is opened from without by Sartorius, who enters and shuts it behind him*].

SARTORIUS [*interrupting her severely*] Hush, pray, Blanche: you are forgetting yourself: you can be heard all over the house. What is the matter?

BLANCHE [*too angry to care whether she is overheard or not*] You had better ask him. He has some excuse about money.

SARTORIUS. Excuse! Excuse for what?

BLANCHE. For throwing me over.

TRENCH [*vehemently*] I declare I never—

BLANCHE [*interrupting him still more vehemently*] You did. You did. You are doing nothing else.

TRENCH ⎱ *together: each trying to shout down*
BLANCHE ⎰ *the other*

{ I am doing nothing of the sort. You know very
{ What else is it but throwing me over? But
{ well that what you are saying is disgracefully
{ I dont care for you. I hate you. I always
{ untrue. It's a damned lie. I wont stand—
{ hated you. Beastly—dirty—vile—

SARTORIUS [*in desperation at the noise*] Silence! [*Still more formidably*] Silence!! [*They obey. He proceeds firmly*] Blanche: you must control your temper: I will not have these repeated scenes within hearing of the servants. Dr Trench will answer for himself to me. You had better leave us. [*He opens the door, and calls*] Mr Cokane: will you kindly join us here.

COKANE [*in the conservatory*] Coming, my dear sir, coming. [*He appears at the door*].

BLANCHE. I'm sure I have no wish to stay. I hope I shall find you alone when I come back. [*An inarticulate exclamation bursts from Trench. She goes out, passing Cokane resent-*

fully. He looks after her in surprise; then looks questioningly at the two men. Sartorius shuts the door with an angry stroke, and turns to Trench].

SARTORIUS [*aggressively*] Sir—

TRENCH [*interrupting him more aggressively*] Well, sir?

COKANE [*getting between them*] Gently, dear boy, gently. Suavity, Harry, suavity.

SARTORIUS [*mastering himself*] If you have anything to say to me, Dr Trench, I will listen to you patiently. You will then allow me to say what I have to say on my part.

TRENCH [*ashamed*] I beg your pardon. Of course, yes. Fire away.

SARTORIUS. May I take it that you have refused to fulfil your engagement with my daughter?

TRENCH. Certainly not: your daughter has refused to fulfil her engagement with me. But the match is broken off, if thats what you mean.

SARTORIUS. Dr Trench: I will be plain with you. I know that Blanche has a quick temper. It is part of her strong character and her physical courage, which is greater than that of most men, I can assure you. You must be prepared for that. If this quarrel is only Blanche's temper, you may take my word for it that it will be over before tomorrow. But I understood from what she said just now that you have made some difficulty on the score of money.

TRENCH [*with renewed excitement*] It was Miss Sartorius who made the difficulty. I shouldnt have minded that so much, if it hadnt been for the things she said. She shewed that she dosent care that [*snapping his fingers*] for me.

COKANE [*soothingly*] Dear boy—

TRENCH. Hold your tongue, Billy: it's enough to make a man wish he'd never seen a woman. Look here, Mr Sartorius: I put the matter to her as delicately and considerately as possible, never mentioning a word of my reasons, but just asking her to be content to live on my own little income; and yet she turned on me as if I'd behaved like a savage.

SARTORIUS. Live on your income! Impossible: my daughter is accustomed to a proper establishment. Did I not expressly undertake to provide for that? Did she not tell you I promised her to do so?

TRENCH. Yes, I know all about that, Mr

Sartorius; and I'm greatly obliged to you; but I'd rather not take anything from you except Blanche herself.

SARTORIUS. And why did you not say so before?

TRENCH. No matter why. Let us drop the subject.

SARTORIUS. No matter! But it d o e s matter, sir. I insist on an answer. Why did you not say so before?

TRENCH. I didnt know before.

SARTORIUS [provoked] Then you ought to have known your own mind on a point of such vital importance.

TRENCH [much injured] I ought to have known! Cokane: is this reasonable? [Cokane's features are contorted by an air of judicial consideration; but he says nothing; and Trench again addresses Sartorius, this time with a marked diminution of respect]. How the deuce could I have known? You didnt tell me.

SARTORIUS. You are trifling with me, sir. You said that you did not know your own mind before.

TRENCH. I said nothing of the sort. I say that I did not know where your money came from before.

SARTORIUS. That is not true, sir. I——

COKANE. Gently, my dear sir. Gently, Harry dear boy. Suaviter in modo: fort——

TRENCH. Let him begin then. What does he mean by attacking me in this fashion?

SARTORIUS. Mr Cokane: you will bear me out. I was explicit on the point. I said I was a self-made man; and I am not ashamed of it.

TRENCH. You are nothing of the sort. I found out this morning from your man—Lickcheese, or whatever his confounded name is—that your fortune has been made out of a parcel of unfortunate creatures that have hardly enough to keep body and soul together—made by screwing, and bullying, and threatening, and all sorts of pettifogging tyranny.

SARTORIUS [outraged] Sir! [They confront one another threateningly].

COKANE [softly] Rent must be paid, dear boy. It is inevitable, Harry, inevitable. [Trench turns away petulantly. Sartorius looks after him reflectively for a moment; then resumes his former deliberate and dignified manner, and addresses Trench with studied consideration, but with a perceptible condescension to his youth and folly].

SARTORIUS. I am afraid, Dr Trench, that you are a very young hand at business; and I am sorry I forgot that for a moment or so. May I ask you to suspend your judgment until we have had a little quiet discussion of this sentimental notion of yours? if you will excuse me for calling it so. [He takes a chair, and motions Trench to another on his right].

COKANE. Very nicely put, my dear sir. Come, Harry: sit down and listen; and consider the matter calmly and judicially. Dont be headstrong.

TRENCH. I have no objection to sit down and listen; but I dont see how that can make black white; and I am tired of being turned on as if I were in the wrong. [He sits down].

Cokane sits at Trench's elbow, on his right. They compose themselves for a conference.

SARTORIUS. I assume, to begin with, Dr Trench, that you are not a Socialist, or anything of that sort.

TRENCH. Certainly not. I'm a Conservative. At least, if I ever took the trouble to vote, I should vote for the Conservative and against the other fellow.

COKANE. True blue, Harry, true blue!

SARTORIUS. I am glad to find that so far we are in perfect sympathy. I am, of course, a Conservative. Not a narrow or prejudiced one, I hope, nor at all opposed to true progress. Still, a sound Conservative. As to Lickcheese, I need say no more about him than that I have dismissed him from my service this morning for a breach of trust; and you will hardly accept his testimony as friendly or disinterested. As to my business, it is simply to provide homes suited to the small means of very poor people, who require roofs to shelter them just like other people. Do you suppose I can keep up those roofs for nothing?

TRENCH. Yes: thats all very fine; but the point is, what sort of homes do you give them for their money? People must live somewhere or else go to jail. Advantage is taken of that to make them pay for houses that are not fit for dogs. Why dont you build proper dwellings, and give fair value for the money you take?

SARTORIUS [pitying his innocence] My young friend: these poor people do not know how to live in proper dwellings: they would wreck them in a week. You doubt me: try it for yourself. You are welcome to replace all the missing banisters, handrails, cistern lids and dusthole tops at your own expense; and you will find them missing again in less than three days: burnt, sir, every stick of them. I do not blame the poor creatures: they need fires, and often have no other way of getting them. But I really cannot spend pound after pound in repairs for them to pull down, when I can barely get them to pay me four and sixpence a week for a room, which is the recognized fair London rent. No, gentlemen: when people are very poor, you cannot help them, no matter how much you may sympathize with them. It does them more harm than good in the long run. I prefer to save my money in order to provide additional houses for the homeless, and to lay by a little for Blanche. [*He looks at them. They are silent: Trench unconvinced, but talked down; Cokane humanely perplexed. Sartorius bends his brows; comes forward in his chair as if gathering himself for a spring; and addresses himself, with impressive significance, to Trench*]. And now, Dr Trench, may I ask what your income is derived from?

TRENCH [*defiantly*] From interest: not from houses. My hands are clean as far as that goes. Interest on a mortgage.

SARTORIUS [*forcibly*] Yes: a mortgage on my property. When I, to use your own words, screw, and bully, and drive these people to pay what they have freely undertaken to pay me, I cannot touch one penny of the money they give me until I have first paid you your seven hundred a year out of it. What Lickcheese did for me, I do for you. He and I are alike intermediaries: you are the principal. It is because of the risks I run through the poverty of my tenants that you exact interest from me at the monstrous and exorbitant rate of seven per cent, forcing me to exact the uttermost farthing in my turn from the tenants. And yet, Dr Trench, you, who have never done a hand's turn of work in connection with the place, you have not hesitated to speak contemptuously of me because I have applied my industry and forethought to the management of our property, and am maintaining it by the same honorable means.

COKANE [*greatly relieved*] Admirable, my dear sir, excellent! I felt instinctively that Trench was talking unpractical nonsense. Let us drop the subject, my dear boy: you only make an ass of yourself when you meddle in business matters. I told you it was inevitable.

TRENCH [*dazed*] Do you mean to say that I am just **as** bad as you are?

COKANE. Shame, Harry, shame! Grossly bad taste! Be a gentleman. Apologize.

SARTORIUS. Allow me, Mr Cokane. [*To Trench*] If, when you say you are just as bad as I am, you mean that you are just as powerless to alter the state of society, then you are unfortunately quite right.

Trench does not at once reply. He stares at Sartorius, and then hangs his head and gazes stupidly at the floor, morally beggared, with his clasped knuckles between his knees, a living picture of disillusion. Cokane comes sympathetically to him and puts an encouraging hand on his shoulder.

COKANE [*gently*] Come, Harry, come! Pull yourself together. You owe a word to Mr Sartorius.

TRENCH [*still stupefied, slowly unlaces his fingers; puts his hands on his knees, and lifts himself upright; pulls his waistcoat straight with a tug; and tries to take his disenchantment philosophically as he says, turning to Sartorius*] Well, people who live in glass houses have no right to throw stones. But, on my honor, I never knew that my house was a glass one until you pointed it out. I beg your pardon. [*He offers his hand*].

SARTORIUS. Say no more, Harry: your feelings do you credit: I assure you I feel exactly as you do, myself. Every man who has a heart must wish that a better state of things was practicable. But unhappily it is not.

TRENCH [*a little consoled*] I suppose not.

COKANE. Not a doubt of it, my dear sir: not a doubt of it. The increase of the population is at the bottom of it all.

SARTORIUS [*to Trench*] I trust I have convinced you that you need no more object to Blanche sharing my fortune, than I need object to her sharing yours.

TRENCH [*with dull wistfulness*] It seems so. We're all in the same swim, it appears. I hope youll excuse my making such a fuss.

SARTORIUS. Not another word. In fact, I thank you for refraining from explaining the nature of your scruples to Blanche: I admire that in you, Harry. Perhaps it will be as well to leave her in ignorance.

TRENCH [*anxiously*] But I must explain now. You saw how angry she was.

SARTORIUS. You had better leave that to me. [*He looks at his watch, and rings the bell*].

Lunch is nearly due: while you are getting ready for it I can see Blanche; and I hope the result will be quite satisfactory to us all. [*The parlormaid answers the bell: he addresses her with his habitual peremptoriness*]. Tell Miss Blanche I want her.

THE PARLORMAID [*her face falling expressively*] Yes, sir. [*She turns reluctantly to go*].

SARTORIUS [*on second thoughts*] Stop. [*She stops*]. My love to Miss Blanche; and I am alone here and would like to see her for a moment if she is not busy.

THE PARLORMAID [*relieved*] Yes, sir. [*She goes out*].

SARTORIUS. I will shew you your room, Harry. I hope you will soon be perfectly at home in it. You also, Mr. Cokane, must learn your way about here. Let us go before Blanche comes. [*He leads the way to the door*].

COKANE [*cheerily, following him*] Our little discussion has given me quite an appetite.

TRENCH [*moodily*] It's taken mine away.

The two friends go out, Sartorius holding the door for them. He is following when the parlormaid reappears. She is a snivelling sympathetic creature, and is on the verge of tears.

SARTORIUS. Well: is Miss Blanche coming?

THE PARLORMAID. Yes, sir. I think so, sir.

SARTORIUS. Wait here until she comes; and tell her that I will be back in a moment. I have to shew Dr Trench his room.

THE PARLORMAID. Yes, sir. [*She comes into the room. A sound between a sob and a sniff escapes her*].

Sartorius looks suspiciously at her. He half closes the door.

SARTORIUS [*lowering his voice*] Whats the matter with you?

THE PARLORMAID [*whimpering*] Nothing, sir.

SARTORIUS [*at the same pitch, more menacingly*] Take care how you behave yourself when there are visitors present. Do you hear?

THE PARLORMAID. Yes, sir. [*Sartorius goes out*].

SARTORIUS [*outside*] Excuse me: I had a word to say to the servant.

Trench is heard replying "Not at all," and Cokane "Dont mention it, my dear sir."

Their voices pass out of hearing. The parlormaid sniffs; dries her eyes; and takes some brown paper and a ball of string from a cupboard under the bookcase. She puts them on the table, and wrestles with another sob. Blanche comes in with a jewel box in her hands. Her expression is that of a strong and determined woman in an intense passion. *The maid looks at her with abject wounded affection and bodily terror.*

BLANCHE [*looking round*] Wheres my father?

THE PARLORMAID [*tremulously propitiatory*] He left word he'd be back directly, miss. I'm sure he wont be long. Heres the paper and string all ready, miss. [*She spreads the paper on the table*]. Can I do the parcel for you, miss?

BLANCHE. No. Mind your own business. [*She empties the box on the sheet of brown paper. It contains a packet of letters and some jewellery. She plucks a ring from her finger and throws it down on the heap so angrily that it rolls away and falls on the carpet. The maid submissively picks it up and puts it on the table, again sniffing and drying her eyes*]. What are you crying for?

THE PARLORMAID [*plaintively*] You speak so brutal to me, Miss Blanche; and I do love you so. I'm sure no one else would stay and put up with what I have to put up with.

BLANCHE. Then go. I dont want you. Do you hear. Go.

THE PARLORMAID [*piteously, falling on her knees*] Oh no, Miss Blanche. Dont send me away from you: dont—

BLANCHE [*with fierce disgust*] Agh! I hate the sight of you. [*The maid, wounded to the heart, cries bitterly*]. Hold your tongue. Are those two gentlemen gone?

THE PARLORMAID [*weeping*] Oh, how could you say such a thing to me, Miss Blanche: me that—

BLANCHE [*seizing her by the hair and throat*] Stop that noise, I tell you, unless you want me to kill you.

THE PARLORMAID [*protesting and imploring, but in a carefully subdued voice*] Let me go, Miss Blanche: you know youll be sorry: you always are. Remember how dreadfully my head was cut last time.

BLANCHE [*raging*] Answer me, will you. Have they gone?

THE PARLORMAID. Lickcheese has gone, looking dreadf— [*she breaks off with a stifled cry as Blanche's fingers tighten furiously on her*].

BLANCHE. Did I ask you about Lickcheese? You beast: you know who I mean: youre doing it on purpose.

THE PARLORMAID [*in a gasp*] Theyre staying to lunch.

BLANCHE [*looking intently into her face*] He?

THE PARLORMAID [*whispering with a sympathetic nod*] Yes, miss. [*Blanche lets her drop, and stands forlorn, with despair in her face. The parlormaid, recognizing the passing of the crisis of passion, and fearing no further violence, sits discomfitedly on her heels, and tries to arrange her hair and cap, whimpering a little with exhaustion and soreness].* Now youve set my hands all trembling; and I shall jingle the things on the tray at lunch so that everybody will notice me. It's too bad of you, Miss Bl— [*Sartorius coughs outside*].

BLANCHE [*quickly*] Sh! Get up. *The parlormaid hastily rises, and goes out as demurely as she can. Sartorius glances sternly at her and comes to Blanche.*

SARTORIUS [*mournfully*] My dear: can you not make a little better fight with your temper?

BLANCHE [*panting with the subsidence of her fit*] No I cant. I wont. I do my best. Nobody who really cares for me gives me up because of my temper. I never shew my temper to any of the servants but that girl; and she is the only one that will stay with us.

SARTORIUS. But, my dear, remember that we have to meet our visitors at luncheon presently. I have run down before them to say that I have arranged that little difficulty with Trench. It was only a piece of mischief made by Lickcheese. Trench is a young fool; but it is all right now.

BLANCHE. I dont want to marry a fool.

SARTORIUS. Then you will have to take a husband over thirty, Blanche. You must not expect too much, my child. You will be richer than your husband, and, I think, cleverer too. I am better pleased that it should be so.

BLANCHE [*seizing his arm*] Papa.

SARTORIUS. Yes, my dear.

BLANCHE. May I do as I like about this marriage; or must I do as you like?

SARTORIUS [*uneasily*] Blanche—

BLANCHE. No, papa: you m u s t answer me.

SARTORIUS [*abandoning his self-control, and giving way recklessly to his affection for her*] You shall do as you like now and always, my beloved child. I only wish to do as my own darling pleases.

BLANCHE. Then I will not marry him. He has played fast and loose with me. He thinks us beneath him: he is ashamed of us: he dared to object to being benefited by you— as if it were not natural for him to owe you everything; and yet the money tempted him after all. [*She throws her arms hysterically*

about his neck] Papa: I dont want to marry: I only want to stay with you and be happy as we have always been. I hate the thought of being married: I dont care for him: I dont want to leave you. [*Trench and Cokane come in; but she can hear nothing but her own voice and does not notice them*]. Only send him away: promise me that you will send him away and keep me here with you as we have always— [*seeing Trench*] Oh! [*She hides her face on her father's breast*].

TRENCH [*nervously*] I hope we are not intruding.

SARTORIUS [*formidably*] Dr Trench: my daughter has changed her mind.

TRENCH [*disconcerted*] Am I to understand—

COKANE [*striking in in his most vinegary manner*] I think, Harry, under the circumstances, we have no alternative but to seek luncheon elsewhere.

TRENCH. But, Mr Sartorius, have you explained?

SARTORIUS [*straight in Trench's face*] I have explained, sir. Good morning. [*Trench, outraged, advances a step. Blanche sinks away from her father into a chair. Sartorius stands his ground rigidly*].

TRENCH [*turning away indignantly*] Come on, Cokane.

COKANE. Certainly, Harry, certainly. [*Trench goes out, very angry. The parlormaid, with a tray jingling in her hands, passes outside*]. You have disappointed me, sir, very acutely. Good morning. [*He follows Trench*].

ACT III

The drawing-room in Sartorius's house in Bedford Square, London. Winter evening: fire burning, curtains drawn, and lamps lighted. Sartorius and Blanche are sitting glumly near the fire. The parlormaid, who has just brought in coffee, is placing it on a small table between them. There is a large table in the middle of the room. Looking from it towards the two windows, the pianoforte, a grand, is on the right, with a photographic portrait of Blanche on a miniature easel on a sort of bedspread which covers the top, shewing that the instrument is seldom, if ever, opened. There are two doors: one on the left, further forward than the fireplace, leading to the study; the other by the corner nearest the right hand window, leading to the lobby. Blanche has her workbasket at hand, and is knitting. Sartorius, closer to the fire, has a newspaper.

The parlormaid goes out.

SARTORIUS. Blanche, my love.

BLANCHE. Yes.

SARTORIUS. I had a long talk to the doctor today about our going abroad.

BLANCHE [*impatiently*] I am quite well; and I will not go abroad. I loathe the very thought of the Continent. Why will you bother me so about my health?

SARTORIUS. It was not about your health, Blanche, but about my own.

BLANCHE [*rising*] Yours! [*She goes anxiously to him*]. Oh, papa, theres nothing the matter with you, I hope?

SARTORIUS. There will be: there must be, Blanche, long before you begin to consider yourself an old woman.

BLANCHE. But theres nothing the matter now?

SARTORIUS. Well, my dear, the doctor says I need change, travel, excitement—

BLANCHE. Excitement! You need excitement! [*She laughs joylessly, and sits down on the rug at his feet*]. How is it, papa, that you, who are so clever with everybody else, are not a bit clever with me? Do you think I cant see through your little plan to take me abroad? Since I will not be the invalid and allow you to be the nurse, you are to be the invalid and I am to be the nurse.

SARTORIUS. Well, Blanche, if you will have it that you are well and have nothing preying on your spirits, I must insist on being ill and have something preying on mine. And indeed, my girl, there is no use in our going on as we have for the last four months. You have not been happy; and I have been very far from comfortable. [*Blanche's face clouds: she turns away from him, and sits dumb and brooding. He waits in vain for some reply; then adds in a lower tone*] Need you be so inflexible, Blanche?

BLANCHE. I thought you admired inflexibility: you have always prided yourself on it.

SARTORIUS. Nonsense, my dear, nonsense! I have had to give in often enough. And I could shew you plenty of soft fellows who have done as well as I, and enjoyed themselves more, perhaps. If it is only for the sake of inflexibility that you are standing out—

BLANCHE. I am not standing out. I dont know what you mean. [*She tries to rise and go away*].

SARTORIUS [*catching her arm and arresting her on her knees*] Come, my child! you must

not trifle with me as if I were a stranger. You are fretting because—

BLANCHE [*violently twisting herself free and speaking as she rises*] If you say it, papa, I will kill myself. It is not true. If he were here on his knees tonight, I would walk out of the house sooner than endure it. [*She goes out excitedly*].

Sartorius, greatly troubled, turns again to the fire with a heavy sigh.

SARTORIUS [*gazing gloomily into the glow*] Now if I fight it out with her, no more comfort for months! I might as well live with my clerk or my servant. And if I give in now; I shall have to give in always. Well! I cant help it. I have stuck to having my own way all my life; but there must be an end to that drudgery some day. She is young: let her have her turn at it.

The parlormaid comes in, evidently excited.

THE PARLORMAID. Please, sir, Mr Lickcheese wants to see you very particlar. On important business, Your business, he told me to say.

SARTORIUS. Mr Lickcheese! Do you mean Lickcheese who used to come here on my business?

THE PARLORMAID. Yes, sir. But indeed, sir, youd scarcely know him.

SARTORIUS [*frowning*] Hm! Starving, I suppose. Come to beg?

THE PARLORMAID [*intensely repudiating the idea*] O-o-o-o-h NO, sir. Quite the gentleman, sir! Sealskin overcoat, sir! Come in a hansom, all shaved and clean! I'm sure he's come into a fortune, sir.

SARTORIUS. Hm! Shew him up.

Lickcheese, who has been waiting at the door, instantly comes in. The change in his appearance is dazzling. He is in evening dress, with an overcoat lined throughout with furs presenting all the hues of the tiger. His shirt is fastened at the breast with a single diamond stud. His silk hat is of the glossiest black; a handsome gold watch-chain hangs like a garland on his filled-out waistcoat; he has shaved his whiskers and grown a moustache, the ends of which are waxed and pointed. As Sartorius stares speechless at him, he stands, smiling, to be admired, intensely enjoying the effect he is producing. The parlormaid, hardly less pleased with her own share in this coup-de-théâtre, goes out beaming, full of the news for the kitchen. Lickcheese clinches the situation by a triumphant nod at Sartorius.

SARTORIUS [*bracing himself: hostile*] Well?

LICKCHEESE. Quite well, Sartorius, thankee.

SARTORIUS. I was not asking after your health, sir, as you know, I think, as well as I do. What is your business?

LICKCHEESE. Business that I can take elsewhere if I meet with less civility than I please to put up with, Sartorius. You and me is man and man now. It was money that used to be my master, and not you: dont think it. Now that I'm independent in respect of money—

SARTORIUS [*crossing determinedly to the door, and holding it open*] You can take your independence out of my house, then. I wont have it here.

LICKCHEESE [*indulgently*] Come, Sartorius: dont be stiff-necked. I come here as a friend to put money in your pocket. No use your lettin on to me that youre above money. Eh?

SARTORIUS [*hesitates, and at last shuts the door, saying guardedly*] How much money?

LICKCHEESE [*victorious, going to Blanche's chair and taking off his overcoat*] Ah! there you speak like yourself, Sartorius. Now suppose you ask me to sit down and make myself comfortable?

SARTORIUS [*coming from the door*] I have a mind to put you downstairs by the back of your neck, you infernal blackguard.

LICKCHEESE [*not a bit ruffled, hangs his overcoat on the back of Blanche's chair, pulling a cigar case out of one of the pockets as he does so*] You and me is too much of a pair for me to take anything you say in bad part, Sartorius. Ave a cigar?

SARTORIUS. No smoking here: this is my daughter's room. However, sit down, sit down. [*They sit*].

LICKCHEESE. I' bin gittin on a little since I saw you last.

SARTORIUS. So I see.

LICKCHEESE. I owe it partly to you, you know. Does that surprise you?

SARTORIUS. It doesnt concern me.

LICKCHEESE. So you think, Sartorius; because it never did concern you how *I* got on, so long as I got you on by bringin in the rents. But I picked up something for myself down at Robbins's Row.

SARTORIUS, I always thought so, Have you come to make restitution?

LICKCHEESE. You wouldnt take it if I offered it to you, Sartorius. It wasnt money: it was knowledge: knowledge of the great public question of the Ousing of the Working Classes. You know theres a Royal Commission on it, dont you?

SARTORIUS. Oh, I see. Youve been giving evidence.

LICKCHEESE. Giving evidence! Not me. What good would that do me? Only my expenses; and that not on the professional scale, neither. No: I gev no evidence. But I'll tell you what I did. I kep it back, jast to oblige one or two people whose feelins would a' bin urt by seein their names in a bluebook as keepin a fever den. Their Agent got so friendly with me over it that he put his name on a bill of mine to the tune of—well, no matter: it gev me a start; and a start was all I ever wanted to get on my feet. Ive got a copy of the first report of the Commission in the pocket of my overcoat. [*He rises and gets at his overcoat, from a pocket of which he takes a bluebook*]. I turned down the page to shew you: I thought youd like to see it. [*He doubles the book back at the place indicated, and hands it to Sartorius*].

SARTORIUS. So blackmail is the game, eh? [*He puts the book on the table without looking at it, and strikes it emphatically with his fist*]. I dont care t h a t for my name being in bluebooks. My friends dont read them; and I'm neither a Cabinet Minister nor a candidate for Parliament. Theres nothing to be got out of me on that lay.

LICKCHEESE [*shocked*] Blackmail! Oh, Mr Sartorius, do you think I would let out a word about your premises? Round on an old pal! no: that aint Lickcheese's way. Besides, they know all about you already. Them stairs that you and me quarrelled about, they was a whole arternoon examinin the clergyman that made such a fuss—you remember?— about the women that was urt on it. He made the worst he could of it, in an ungentlemanly, unchristian spirit. I wouldnt have that clergyman's disposition for worlds. Oh no: thats not what was in my thoughts.

SARTORIUS. Come, come, man! what w a s in your thoughts? Out with it.

LICKCHEESE [*with provoking deliberation, smiling and looking mysteriously at him*] You aint spent a few hundreds in repairs since we parted, ave you? [*Sartorius, losing patience, makes a threatening movement*]. Now dont fly out at me. I know a landlord that owned as beastly a slum as you could find in London, down there by the Tower. By my advice that man put half the houses into first-class repair, and let the other half to a new Company: the North Thames Iced Mutton Depot Company, of which I hold a few shares: promoters' shares. And what was the end of it, do you think?

SARTORIUS. Smash, I suppose.

LICKCHEESE. Smash! not a bit of it. Compensation, Mr Sartorius, compensation. Do you understand that?

SARTORIUS. Compensation for what?

LICKCHEESE. Why, the land was wanted for an extension of the Mint; and the Company had to be bought out, and the buildings compensated for. Somebody has to know these things beforehand, you know, no matter how dark theyre kept.

SARTORIUS [interested, but cautious] Well?

LICKCHEESE. Is that all you have to say to me, Mr Sartorius? "Well"! as if I was next door's dog! Suppose I'd got wind of a new street that would knock down Robbins's Row and turn Burke's Walk into a frontage worth thirty pound a foot! would you say no more to me than [mimicking] "Well"? [Sartorius hesitates, looking at him in great doubt. Lickcheese rises and exhibits himself]. Come! look at my get-up, Mr Sartorius. Look at this watchchain! Look at the corporation Ive got on me! Do you think all that came from keeping my mouth shut? No: it came from keeping my ears and eyes open.

Blanche comes in, followed by the parlormaid, who has a silver tray on which she collects the coffee cups. Sartorius, impatient at the interruption, rises and motions Lickcheese to the door of the study.

SARTORIUS. Sh! We must talk this over in the study. There is a good fire there; and you can smoke. Blanche: an old friend of ours.

LICKCHEESE. And a kind one to me. I hope I see you well, Miss Blanche.

BLANCHE. Why, it's Mr Lickcheese! I hardly knew you.

LICKCHEESE. I find you a little changed yourself, miss.

BLANCHE [hastily] Oh, I am the same as ever. How are Mrs Lickcheese and the chil—

SARTORIUS [impatiently] We have business to transact, Blanche. You can talk to Mr Lickcheese afterwards. Come on.

Sartorius and Lickcheese go into the study. Blanche, surprised at her father's abruptness, looks after them for a moment. Then, seeing Lickcheese's overcoat on her chair, she takes it up, amused, and looks at the fur.

THE PARLORMAID. Oh, we are fine, aint we, Miss Blanche? I think Mr Lickcheese must have come into a legacy. [Confidentially] I wonder what he can want with the master, Miss Blanche? He brought him this big book. [She shews the bluebook to Blanche].

BLANCHE [her curiosity roused] Let me see. [She takes the book and looks at it]. Theres something about papa in it. [She sits down and begins to read].

THE PARLORMAID [folding the tea-table and putting it out of the way] He looks ever s'much younger, Miss Blanche, dont he? I couldnt help laughing when I saw him with his whiskers shaved off: it do look so silly when youre not accustomed to it. [No answer from Blanche]. You havnt finished your coffee, miss: I suppose I may take it away? [No answer]. Oh, you are interested in Mr Lickcheese's book, miss.

Blanche springs up. The parlormaid looks at her face, and instantly hurries out of the room on tiptoe with her tray.

BLANCHE. So that was why he would not touch the money. [She tries to tear the book across. Finding this imposible she throws it violently into the fireplace. It falls into the fender]. Oh, if only a girl could have no father, no family, just as I have no mother! Clergyman! beast! "The worst slum landlord in London." "Slum landlord." Oh! [She covers her face with her hands, and sinks shuddering into the chair on which the overcoat lies. The study door opens].

LICKCHEESE [in the study] You just wait five minutes: I'll fetch him. [Blanche snatches a piece of work from her basket, and sits erect and quiet, stitching at it. Lickcheese comes back, speaking to Sartorius, who follows him]. He lodges round the corner in Gower Street; and my private ansom's at the door. By your leave, Miss Blanche [pulling gently at his overcoat.]

BLANCHE [rising] I beg your pardon. I hope I havnt crushed it.

LICKCHEESE [gallantly, as he gets into the coat] Youre welcome to crush it again now, Miss Blanche. Dont say good evenin to me, miss: I'm comin back presently: me and a friend or two. Ta ta, Sartorius: I shant be long. [He goes out].

Sartorius looks about for the bluebook.

BLANCHE. I thought we were done with Lickcheese.

SARTORIUS. Not quite yet, I think. He left a book here for me to look over: a large book in a blue paper cover. Has the girl put it away? [*He sees it in the fender; looks at Blanche; and adds*] Have you seen it?

BLANCHE. No. Yes. [*Angrily*] No: I have not seen it. What have I to do with it?

Sartorius picks up the book and dusts it; then sits down quietly to read. After a glance up and down the columns, he nods assentingly, as if he found there exactly what he expected.

SARTORIUS. It's a curious thing, Blanche, that the Parliamentary gentlemen who write such books as these should be so ignorant of practical business. One would suppose, to read this, that we are the most grasping, grinding, heartless pair in the world, you and I.

BLANCHE. Is it not true? About the state of the houses, I mean?

SARTORIUS [*calmly*] Oh, quite true.

BLANCHE. Then it is not our fault?

SARTORIUS. My dear: if we made the houses any better, the rents would have to be raised so much that the poor people would be unable to pay, and would be thrown homeless on the streets.

BLANCHE. Well, turn them out and get in a respectable class of people. Why should we have the disgrace of harboring such wretches?

SARTORIUS [*opening his eyes*] That sounds a little hard on them, doesnt it, my child?

BLANCHE. Oh, I hate the poor. At least, I hate those dirty, drunken, disreputable people who live like pigs. If they must be provided for, let other people look after them. How can you expect any one to think well of us when such things are written about us in that infamous book?

SARTORIUS [*coldly and a little wistfully*] I see I have made a real lady of you, Blanche.

BLANCHE [*defiantly*] Well? Are you sorry for that?

SARTORIUS. No, my dear: of course not. But do you know, Blanche, that my mother was a very poor woman, and that her poverty was not her fault?

BLANCHE. I suppose not; but the people we want to mix with now dont know that. And it was not my fault; so I dont see why *I* should be made to suffer for it.

SARTORIUS [*enraged*] Who makes you suffer for it, miss? What would you be now but for what your grandmother did for me when she stood at her wash-tub for thirteen hours a day and thought herself rich when she made fifteen shillings a week?

BLANCHE [*angrily*] I suppose I should have been down on her level instead of being raised above it, as I am now. Would you like us to go and live in that place in the book for the sake of grandmamma? I hate the idea of such things. I dont want to know about them. I love you because you brought me up to something better. [*Half aside, as she turns away from him*] I should hate you if you had not.

SARTORIUS [*giving in*] Well, my child, I suppose it is natural for you to feel that way, after your bringing up. It is the ladylike view of the matter. So dont let us quarrel, my girl. You shall not be made to suffer any more. I have made up my mind to improve the property, and get in quite a new class of tenants. There! does that satisfy you? I am only waiting for the consent of the ground landlord, Lady Roxdale.

BLANCHE. Lady Roxdale!

SARTORIUS. Yes. But I shall expect the mortgagee to take his share of the risk.

BLANCHE. The mortgagee! Do you mean— [*She cannot finish the sentence: Sartorius does it for her*].

SARTORIUS. Harry Trench. Yes. And remember, Blanche: if he consents to join me in the scheme, I shall have to be friends with him.

BLANCHE. And to ask him to the house?

SARTORIUS. Only on business. You need not meet him unless you like.

BLANCHE [*overwhelmed*] When is he coming?

SARTORIUS. There is no time to be lost. Lickcheese has gone to ask him to come round.

BLANCHE [*in dismay*] Then he will be here in a few minutes! What shall I do?

SARTORIUS. I advise you to receive him as if nothing had happened, and then go out and leave us to our business. You are not afraid to meet him?

BLANCHE. Afraid! No: most certainly not, But—

LICKCHEESE'S VOICE [*without*] Straight in front of you, doctor. You never bin here before; but I know the house better than my own.

BLANCHE. Here they are. Dont say I'm here, papa. [*She rushes away into the study*].

Lickcheese comes in with Trench and Cokane. Both are in evening dress. Cokane shakes hands effusively with Sartorius. Trench, who is coarsened and sullen, and has evidently not been making the best of his disappointment, bows shortly and resentfully. Lickcheese covers the general embarrassment by talking cheerfully until they are all seated round the large table: Trench nearest the fireplace; Cokane nearest the piano; and the other two between them, with Lickcheese next Cokane].

LICKCHEESE. Here we are, all friends round St Paul's. You remember Mr Cokane? he does a little business for me now as a friend, and gives me a help with my correspondence: sekketerry we call it. Ive no litery style, and thats the truth; so Mr Cokane kindly puts it into my letters and draft prospectuses and advertisements and the like. Dont you, Cokane? Of course you do: why shouldnt you? He's been helping me to persuade his old friend, Dr Trench, about the matter we were speaking of.

COKANE [*austerely*] No, Mr Lickcheese, not trying to persuade him. No: this is a matter of principle with me. I say it is your duty, Henry—your duty—to put those abominable buildings into proper and habitable repair. As a man of science you owe it to the community to perfect the sanitary arrangements. In questions of duty there is no room for persuasion, even from the oldest friend.

SARTORIUS [*to Trench*] I certainly feel, as Mr Cokane puts it, that it is our duty: one which I have perhaps too long neglected out of regard for the poorest class of tenants.

LICKCHEESE. Not a doubt of it, gents: a dooty. I can be as sharp as any man when it's a question of business; but dooty's another pair o' shoes.

TRENCH. Well, I dont see that it's any more my duty now than it was four months ago. I look at it simply as a question of so much money.

COKANE. Shame, Harry, shame! Shame!

TRENCH. Oh, shut up, you fool. [*Cokane springs up*].

LICKCHEESE [*catching his coat and holding him*] Steady! steady! Mr Sekketerry. Dr Trench is only joking.

COKANE. I insist on the withdrawal of that expression. I have been called a fool.

TRENCH [*morosely*] So you are a fool.

COKANE. Then you are a damned fool. Now, sir!

TRENCH. All right. Now weve settled that. [*Cokane, with a snort, sits down*]. What I mean is this. Dont lets have any nonsense about this job. As I understand it, Robbins's Row is to be pulled down to make way for the new street into the Strand; and the straight tip now is to go for compensation.

LICKCHEESE [*chuckling*] That's so, Dr Trench. Thats it.

TRENCH [*continuing*] Well, it appears that the dirtier a place is the more rent you get; and the decenter it is, the more compensation you get. So we're to give up dirt and go in for decency.

SARTORIUS. I should not put it exactly in that way; but—

COKANE. Quite right, Mr Sartorius, quite right. The case could not have been stated in worse taste or with less tact.

LICKCHEESE. Sh-sh-sh-sh!

SARTORIUS. I do not quite go with you there Mr Cokane. Dr Trench puts the case frankly as a man of business. I take the wider view of a public man. We live in a progressive age; and humanitarian ideas are advancing and must be taken into account. But my practical conclusion is the same as his. I should hardly feel justified in making a large claim for compensation under existing circumstances.

LICKCHEESE. Of course not; and you wouldnt get it if you did. You see, it's like this, Dr Trench. Theres no doubt that the Vestries has legal powers to play old Harry with slum properties, and spoil the houseknacking game if they please. That didnt matter in the good old times, because the Vestries used to be us ourselves. Nobody ever knew a word about the election; and we used to get ten of us into a room and elect one another, and do what we liked. Well, that cock wont fight any longer; and, to put it short, the game is up for men in the position of you and Mr Sartorius. My advice to you is, take the present chance of getting out of it. Spend a little money on the block at the Cribbs Market end: enough to make it look like a model dwelling, you know; and let the other block to me on fair terms for a depot of the North Thames Iced Mutton Company. Theyll be knocked down inside of two year to make room for the new north and south main thoroughfare; and youll be compensated to the tune of double the present valuation, with the cost of the improvements thrown in. Leave things as they are; and you stand a good chance of being fined, or condemned, or pulled down before long. Now's your time.

COKANE. Hear, hear! Hear, hear! Hear, hear! Admirably put from the business point of view! I recognize the uselessness of putting the moral point of view to you, Trench; but even you must feel the cogency of Mr Lickcheese's business statement.

TRENCH. But why cant you act without me? What have I got to do with it? I'm only a mortgagee.

SARTORIUS. There is a certain risk in this compensation investment, Dr Trench. The County Council may alter the line of the new street. If that happens, the money spent in improving the houses will be thrown away: simply thrown away. Worse than thrown away, in fact; for the new buildings may stand unlet or half let for years. But you will expect your seven per cent as usual.

TRENCH. A man must live.

COKANE. Je ne'n vois pas la nécessité.

TRENCH. Shut up, Billy; or else speak some language you understand. No, Mr Sartorius: I should be very glad to stand in with you if I could afford it; but I cant; so you may leave me out of it.

LICKCHEESE. Well, all I can say is that youre a very foolish young man.

COKANE. What did I tell you, Harry?

TRENCH. I dont see that it's any business of yours, Mr Lickcheese.

LICKCHEESE. It's a free country: every man has a right to his opinion.

COKANE. Hear, hear!

LICKCHEESE. Come! wheres your feelins for them poor people, Dr Trench? Remember how it went to your heart when I first told you about them. What! are y o u going to turn hard?

TRENCH. No: it wont do: you cant get over me that way. You proved to me before that there was no use in being sentimental over that slum shop of ours; and it's no good your turning round on the philanthropic tack now that you want me to put my capital into your speculation. I've had my lesson; and I'm going to stick to my present income. It's little enough for me as it is.

SARTORIUS. It really matters nothing to me, Dr Trench, how you decide. I can easily raise the money elsewhere and pay you off. Then, since you are resolved to run no risks, you can invest your ten thousand pounds in Consols and get two hundred and fifty pounds a year for it instead of seven hundred.

Trench, completely outwitted, stares at them in consternation. Cokane breaks the silence.

COKANE. This is what comes of being avaricious, Harry. Two thirds of your income gone at one blow. And I must say it serves you right.

TRENCH. Thats all very fine; but I dont understand it. If you can do this to me, why didnt you do it long ago?

SARTORIUS. Because, as I should prcbably have had to borrow at the same rate, I should have saved nothing; whereas you would have lost over four hundred a year: a very serious matter for you. I had no desire to be unfriendly; and even now I should be glad to let the mortgage stand, were it not that the circumstances mentioned by Mr Lickcheese force my hand. Besides, Dr Trench, I hoped for some time that our interests might be joined by closer ties even than those of friendship.

LICKCHEESE [*jumping up, relieved*] There! Now the murder's out. Excuse me, Dr Trench. Ex-cuse me, Mr Sartorius: excuse my freedom. Why not Dr Trench marry Miss Blanche, and settle the whole affair that way?

Sensation. Lickcheese sits down triumphant.

COKANE. You forget, Mr Lickcheese, that the young lady, whose taste has to be considered, decisively objected to him.

TRENCH. Oh! Perhaps you think she was struck with you.

COKANE. I do not say so, Trench. No man of any delicacy would suggest such a thing. You have an untutored mind, Trench, an untutored mind.

TRENCH. Well, Cokane: Ive told you my opinion of you already.

COKANE [*rising wildly*] And I have told you m y opinion of y o u. I will repeat it if you wish. I am ready to repeat it.

LICKCHEESE. Come, Mr Sekketerry: you and me, as married men, is out of the unt as far as young ladies is concerned. I know Miss Blanche: she has her father's eye for business. Explain this job to her; and she'll make it up with Dr Trench. Why not have a bit of romance in business when it costs nothing? We all have our feelins: we aint mere calculatin machines.

SARTORIUS [*revolted*] Do you think, Lickcheese, that my daughter is to be made part of a money bargain between you and these gentlemen?

LICKCHEESE. Oh come, Sartorius! dont talk as if you was the only father in the world. I have a daughter too; and my feelins in that matter is just as fine as yours. I propose nothing but what is for Miss Blanche's advantage and Dr Trench's.

COKANE. Lickcheese expresses himself roughly, Mr Sartorius; but his is a sterling nature; and what he says is to the point. If Miss Sartorius can really bring herself to care for Harry, I am far from desiring to stand in the way of such an arrangement.

TRENCH. Why, what have you got to do with it?

LICKCHEESE. Easy, Dr Trench, easy. We want your opinion. Are you still on for marrying Miss Blanche if she's agreeable?

TRENCH [shortly] I dont know that I am. [Sartorius rises indignantly].

LICKCHEESE. Easy one moment, Mr Sartorius. [To Trench] Come now, Dr Trench! you say that you dont know that you are. But do you know that you aint? thats what we want to know.

TRENCH [sulkily] I wont have the relations between Miss Sartorius and myself made part of a bargain. [He rises to leave the table].

LICKCHEESE [rising] Thats enough: a gentleman could say no less. [Insinuatingly] Now, would you mind me and Cokane and the guvnor steppin into the study to arrange about the lease to the North Thames Iced Mutton Company?

TRENCH. Oh, I dont mind. I'm going home. Theres nothing more to say.

LICKCHEESE. No: dont go. Only just a minute: me and Cokane will be back in no time to see you home. Youll wait for us, wont you?

TRENCH. Oh well, if you wish, yes.

LICKCHEESE [cheerily] Didnt I know you would!

SARTORIUS [at the study door, to Cokane] After you, sir.

Cokane bows formally and goes into the study.

LICKCHEESE [at the door, aside to Sartorius] You never ad such a managin man as me, Sartorius. [He goes into the study chuckling, followed by Sartorius].

Trench, left alone, looks round carefully and listens a moment. Then he goes on tiptoe to the piano and leans upon it with folded arms, gazing at Blanche's portrait. Blanche herself appears presently at the study door. When she sees how he is occupied, she closes it softly and steals over to him, watching him intently. He rises from his leaning attitude, and takes the portrait from the easel, and is about to kiss it when, taking a second look round to reassure himself that nobody is watching him, he finds Blanche close upon him. He drops the portrait, and stares at her without the least presence of mind.

BLANCHE [shrewishly] Well? So you have come back here. You have had the meanness to come into this house again. [He flushes and retreats a step. She follows him up remorselessly]. What a poor spirited creature you must be! Why dont you go? [Red and wincing, he starts huffily to get his hat from the table; but when he turns to the door with it she deliberately stands in his way; so that he has to stop]. I dont want you to stay. [For a moment they stand face to face, quite close to one another, she provocative, taunting, half defying, half inviting him to advance, in a flush of undisguised animal excitement. It suddenly flashes on him that all this ferocity is erotic: that she is making love to him. His eye lights up: a cunning expression comes into the corners of his mouth: with a heavy assumption of indifference he walks straight back to his chair, and plants himself in it with his arms folded. She comes down the room after him]. But I forgot: you have found that there is some money to be made here. Lickcheese told you. You, who were so disinterested, so independent, that you could not accept anything from my father! [At the end of every sentence she waits to see what execution she has done]. I suppose you will try to persuade me that you have come down here on a great philanthropic enterprise—to befriend the poor by having those houses rebuilt, eh? [Trench maintains his attitude and makes no sign]. Yes: when my father makes you do it. And when Lickcheese has discovered some way of making it profitable. Oh, I know papa; and I know you. And for the sake of that, you come back here—into the house where you were refused—ordered out. [Trench's face darkens: her eyes gleam as she sees it]. Aha! you remember that. You know it's true: you cant deny it. [She sits down, and softens her tone a little as she affects to pity him]. Well, let me tell you that you cut a poor figure, a very, very poor figure, Harry. [At the word Harry he relaxes the fold of his arms; and a faint grin of anticipated victory appears on his face]. And you, too, a gentleman! so highly connected! with such distinguished relations! so particular as to where your money comes from! I wonder at you. I really wonder at you. I should have thought that if your fine family gave you nothing else, it might at least have given you some sense of personal dignity. Perhaps you think you look dignified at present: eh? [*No reply*]. Well, I can assure you that you dont: you look most ridiculous—as foolish as a man could look—you dont know what to say; and you dont know what to do. But after all, I really dont see what any one could say in defence of such conduct. [*He looks straight in front of him, and purses up his lips as if whistling. This annoys her; and she becomes affectedly polite*]. I am afraid I am in your way, Dr Trench. [*She rises*]. I shall not intrude on you any longer. You seem so perfectly at home that I need make no apology for leaving you to yourself. [*She makes a feint of going to the door; but he does not budge; and she returns and comes behind his chair*]. Harry. [*He does not turn. She comes a step nearer*]. Harry: I want you to answer me a question. [*Earnestly, stooping over him*] Look me in the face. [*No reply*]. Do you hear? [*Seizing his cheeks and twisting his head round*] Look—me —in—the—face. [*He shuts his eyes tight and grins. She suddenly kneels down beside him with her breast against his shoulder*]. Harry: what were you doing with my photograph just now, when you thought you were alone? [*He opens his eyes: they are full of delight. She flings*

her arms round him, and crushes him in an ecstatic embrace as she adds, with furious tenderness*] How dare you touch anything belonging to me?

The study door opens and voices are heard.

TRENCH. I hear some one coming.

She regains her chair with a bound, and pushes it back as far as possible. Cokane, Lickcheese, and Sartorius come from the study. Sartorius and Lickcheese come to Trench. Cokane crosses to Blanche in his most killing manner.

COKANE. How do you do, Miss Sartorius? Nice weather for the return of l'enfant prodigue, eh?

BLANCHE. Capital, Mr Cokane. So glad to see you. [*She gives him her hand, which he kisses with gallantry*].

LICKCHEESE [*on Trench's left, in a low voice*] Any noos for us, Dr Trench?

TRENCH [*to Sartorius, on his right*] I'll stand in, compensation or no compensation. [*He shakes Sartorius's hand*].

The parlormaid has just appeared at the door.

THE PARLORMAID. Supper is ready, miss.

COKANE. Allow me.

Exeunt omnes: Blanche on Cokane's arm; Lickcheese jocosely taking Sartorius on one arm, and Trench on the other.

THE END

II

THE PHILANDERER

BEING THE SECOND OF THREE UNPLEASANT PLAYS

ACT I

A lady and gentleman are making love to one another in the drawing room of a flat in Ashley Gardens in the Victoria district of London. It is past ten at night. The walls are hung with theatrical engravings and photographs: Kemble as Hamlet, Mrs Siddons as Queen Katharine pleading in court, Macready as Werner (after Maclise), Sir Henry Irving as Richard III (after Long), Ellen Terry, Mrs Kendal, Ada Rehan, Sarah Bernhardt, Henry Arthur Jones, Sir Arthur Pinero, Sydney Grundy, and so on, but not Eleonora Duse nor any one connected with Ibsen. The room is not rectangular, one corner being cut off diagonally by the doorway, and the opposite one rounded by a turret window filled up with a stand of flowers surrounding a

statuet of Shakespear. The fireplace is on the doorway side, with an armchair near it. A small round table, further from the door on the same side, with a chair beside it, has a yellow backed French novel lying open on it. The piano, a grand, is on the Shakespear side, open, with the keyboard at right angles to the wall. The piece of music on the desk is When Other Lips. Incandescent lights, well shaded, are on the piano and mantelpiece. Near the piano is a sofa, on which the lady and gentleman are seated affectionately side by side, in one another's arms.*

The lady, Grace Tranfield, is about 32, slight of build, delicate of feature, and sensitive in expression. She is just now given up to the emotion of the moment; but her well closed mouth, proudly set brows, firm chin, and elegant carriage shew plenty of determination and self-respect. She is in evening dress.

The gentleman, Leonard Charteris, a few years older, is unconventionally but smartly dressed in a velvet jacket and cashmere trousers. His collar, dyed Wotan blue, is part of his shirt, and turns over a garnet colored scarf of Indian silk, secured by a turquoise ring. He wears blue socks and leather sandals. The arrangement of his tawny hair, and of his moustaches and short beard, is apparently left to Nature; but he has taken care that Nature shall do him the fullest justice. His amative enthusiasm, at which he is himself laughing, and his clever, imaginative, humorous ways, contrast strongly with the sincere tenderness and dignified quietness of the woman.

CHARTERIS [*impulsively clasping Grace*] My dearest love.

GRACE [*responding affectionately*] My darling. Are you happy?

CHARTERIS. In Heaven.

GRACE. My own.

CHARTERIS. My heart's love. [*He sighs happily, and takes her hands in his, looking quaintly at her*]. That must positively be my last kiss, Grace; or I shall become downright silly. Let us talk. [*He releases her and sits a little apart*]. Grace: is this your first love affair?

GRACE. Have you forgotten that I am a widow? Do you think I married Tranfield for money?

CHARTERIS. How do I know? Besides, you might have married him not because you loved him, but because you didnt love anybody else. When one is young, one marries out of mere curiosity, just to see what it's like.

GRACE. Well, since you ask me, I never was in love with Tranfield, though I only found that out when I fell in love with you. But I used to like him for being in love with me. It brought out all the good in him so much that I have wanted to be in love with someone ever since. I hope, now that I am in love with you, you will like me for it just as I liked Tranfield.

CHARTERIS. My dear: it is because I like you that I want to marry you. I could love anybody—any pretty woman, that is.

GRACE. Do you really mean that, Leonard?

CHARTERIS. Of course. Why not?

GRACE [*reflecting*] Never mind. Now tell me, is this y o u r first love affair?

CHARTERIS [*amazed at the simplicity of the question*] No, bless my soul, no; nor my second, nor my third.

GRACE. But I mean your first serious one?

CHARTERIS [*with a certain hesitation*] Yes. [*There is a pause. She is not convinced. He adds, with a very perceptible load on his conscience*] It is the first in which *I* have been serious.

GRACE [*searchingly*] I see. The other parties were always serious.

CHARTERIS. Not always. Heaven forbid!

GRACE. How often?

CHARTERIS. Well, once.

GRACE. Julia Craven?

CHARTERIS [*recoiling*] Who told you that? [*She shakes her head mysteriously. He turns away from her moodily and adds*] You had much better not have asked.

GRACE [*gently*] I'm sorry, dear. [*She puts out her hand and pulls softly at him to bring him near her again*].

CHARTERIS [*yielding mechanically to the pull, and allowing her hand to rest on his arm, but sitting squarely without the least attempt to return the caress*] Do I feel harder to the touch than I did five minutes ago?

GRACE. What nonsense!

CHARTERIS. I feel as if my body had turned into the toughest hickory. That is what comes of reminding me of Julia Craven. [*Brooding, with his chin on his right hand and his elbow on his knee*] I have sat alone with her just as I am sitting with you—

GRACE [*shrinking from him*] Just!

CHARTERIS [*sitting upright and facing her steadily*] Just exactly. She has put her hands in mine, and laid her cheek against mine, and listened to me saying all sorts of silly things. [*Grace, chilled to the soul, rises from the sofa and sits down on the piano stool, with her back to the keyboard*]. Ah, you dont want to hear any more of the story. So much the better.

GRACE [*deeply hurt, but controlling herself*] When did you break it off?

CHARTERIS [*guiltily*] Break it off?

GRACE [*firmly*] Yes: break it off.

CHARTERIS. Well: let me see. When did I fall in love with you?

GRACE. Did you break it off then?

CHARTERIS [*making it plainer and plainer that it has not been broken off*] It was clear then, of course, that it must be broken off.

GRACE. And d i d you break it off?

CHARTERIS. Oh, yes: *I* broke it off.

GRACE. But did s h e break it off?

CHARTERIS [*rising*] As a favor to me, dearest, change the subject. Come away from the piano: I want you to sit here with me. [*He takes a step towards her*].

GRACE. No. I also have grown hard to the touch: much harder than hickory for the present. Did she break it off?

CHARTERIS. My dear, be reasonable. It was fully explained to her that it was to be broken off.

GRACE. Did she accept the explanation?

CHARTERIS. She did what a woman like Julia always does. When I explained personally, she said it was not my better self that was speaking, and that she knew I still really loved her. When I wrote it to her with brutal explicitness, she read the letter carefully and then sent it back to me with a note to say that she had not had the courage to open it, and that I ought to be ashamed of having written it. [*He comes beside Grace, and puts his left hand caressingly round her neck*]. You see, dearie, she wont look the situation in the face.

GRACE [*shaking off his hand and turning a little away on the stool*] I am afraid, from the light way you speak of it, you did not sound the right chord.

CHARTERIS. My dear: when you are doing what a woman calls breaking her heart, you may sound the very prettiest chords you can find on the piano; but to her ears it is just like this. [*He sits down on the bass end of the keyboard. Grace puts her fingers in her ears. He rises and moves away from the piano, saying*] No, my dear: Ive been kind; Ive been frank; Ive been everything that a goodnatured man can be; but she only takes it as the making up of a lovers' quarrel. [*Grace winces*]. Frankness and kindness: one is as bad as the other. Especially frankness. Ive tried both. [*He crosses to the fireplace, and stands facing the fire, looking at the ornaments on the mantelpiece and warming his hands*].

GRACE [*her voice a little strained*] What are you going to try now?

CHARTERIS [*on the hearthrug, turning to face her*] Action, my dear. Marriage. In that she must believe. She wont be convinced by anything short of it; because, you see, Ive had some tremendous philanderings before, and have gone back to her after them.

GRACE. And so that is why you want to marry me?

CHARTERIS. I cannot deny it, my love. Yes: it is your mission to rescue me from Julia.

GRACE [*rising*] Then, if you please, I decline to be made use of for any such purpose. I will not steal you from another woman. [*She walks up and down the room with ominous disquiet*].

CHARTERIS. Steal me! [*He comes towards her*]. Grace: I have a question to put to you as an advanced woman. Mind! as an advanced woman. Does Julia belong to me? Am I her owner—her master?

GRACE. Certainly not. No woman is the property of a man. A woman belongs to herself and to nobody else.

CHARTERIS. Quite right. Ibsen for ever! Thats exactly my opinion. Now tell me, do I belong to Julia; or have I a right to belong to myself?

GRACE [*puzzled*] Of course you have; but—

CHARTERIS [*interrupting her triumphantly*] Then how can you steal me from Julia if I dont belong to her? [*He catches her by the shoulders and holds her out at arms length in front of him*]. Eh, little philosopher? No, my dear: if Ibsen sauce is good for the goose, it's good for the gander as well. Besides [*coaxing her*] it was nothing but a philander with Julia. Nothing else in the world, I assure you.

GRACE [*breaking away from him*] So much the worse! I hate your philanderings: they make me ashamed of you and of myself [*She goes to the sofa and sits in the corner furthest from the piano, leaning gloomily on her elbow with her face averted*].

CHARTERIS. Grace: you utterly misunderstand the origin of my philanderings. [*He sits down beside her*]. Listen to me. Am I a particularly handsome man?

GRACE [*astonished at his conceit*] No.

CHARTERIS [*triumphantly*] You admit it. Am I a well dressed man?

GRACE. Not particularly.

CHARTERIS. Of course not. Have I a romantic mysterious charm about me? do I look as if a secret sorrow preyed on me? am I gallant to women?

GRACE. Not in the least.

CHARTERIS. Certainly not. No one can accuse me of it. Then whose fault is it that half the women I speak to fall in love with me? Not mine: I hate it: it bores me to distraction. At first it flattered me—delighted me—that was how Julia got me, because she was the first woman who had the pluck to make me a declaration. But I soon had enough of it; and at no time have I taken the initiative and persecuted women with my advances as women have persecuted me. Never. Except, of course, in your case.

GRACE. Oh, you need not make any exception. I had a good deal of trouble to induce you to come and see us. You were very coy.

CHARTERIS [*fondly, taking her hand*] With you, dearest, the coyness was sheer coquetry. I loved you from the first, and fled only that you might pursue. But come! let us talk about something really interesting. [*He takes her in his arms*]. Do you love me better than anyone else in the world?

GRACE. I dont think you like to be loved too much.

CHARTERIS. That depends on who the person is. You [*pressing her to his heart*] cannot love me too much: you cannot love me half enough. I reproach you every day for your coldness, your— [*A violent double knock without. They start and listen, still in one another's arms, hardly daring to breathe*]. Who the deuce is calling at this hour?

GRACE. I cant imagine. [*They listen guiltily. The door of the flat is opened without. They hastily get away from one another*].

A WOMAN'S VOICE OUTSIDE. Is Mr Charteris here?

CHARTERIS [*springing up*] Julia! The devil! [*He stands at the end of the sofa with his eyes fixed on the door and his heart beating very unpleasantly*].

GRACE [*rising also*] What can she want?

THE VOICE. Never mind: I will announce myself. [*A beautiful, dark, tragic looking woman in mantle and toque, appears at the door, raging*]. Oh, this is charming. I have interrupted a pretty tête-à-tête. Oh, you villain! [*She comes straight at Grace. Charteris runs across behind the sofa, and stops her. She struggles furiously with him. Grace preserves her self-possession, but retreats quietly to the piano. Julia, finding Charteris too strong for her, gives up her attempt to get at Grace, but strikes him in the face as she frees herself*].

CHARTERIS [*shocked*] Oh, Julia, Julia! This is too bad.

JULIA. Is it, indeed, too bad? What are you doing up here with that woman? You scoundrel! But now listen to me, Leonard: you have driven me to desperation; and I dont care what I do, or who hears me: I'll not bear it. She shall not have my place with you—

CHARTERIS. Sh-sh!

JULIA. No, no: I dont care: I will expose her true character before everybody. You belong to me: you have no right to be here; and she knows it.

CHARTERIS. I think you had better let me take you home, Julia.

JULIA. I will not. I am not going home: I am going to stay here—h e r e—until I have made you give her up.

CHARTERIS. My dear: you must be reasonable. You really cannot stay in Mrs Tranfield's house if she objects. She can ring the bell and have us both put out.

JULIA. Let her do it then. Let her ring the bell if she dares. Let us see how this pure virtuous creature will face the scandal of what I will declare about her. Let us see how y o u will face it. I have nothing to lose. Everybody knows how you have treated me: you have boasted of your conquests, you poor pitiful vain creature: I am the common talk of your acquaintances and hers. Oh, I have calculated my advantage [*she tears off her mantle*]: I am a most unhappy and injured woman; but I am not the fool you take me to be. I am going to stay: see? [*She flings the mantle on the round table; puts her toque on it; and sits down*]. Now, Mrs Tranfield: theres the bell [*pointing to the button beside the fireplace*]: why dont you ring? [*Grace, looking attentively at Charteris, does not move*]. Ha! ha! I thought so.

CHARTERIS [*quietly, without relaxing his watch on Julia*] Mrs Tranfield: I think you had better go into another room. [*Grace makes a movement towards the door, but stops and looks inquiringly at Charteris as Julia springs up to intercept her. He advances a step to guard the way to the door*].

JULIA. She shall not. She shall stay here. She shall know what you are, and how you have been in love with me: how it is not two days since you kissed me and told me that the future would be as happy as the past. [*Screaming at him*] You did: deny it if you dare.

CHARTERIS [*to Grace in a low voice*] Go.

GRACE [*with nonchalant disgust, going*] Get her away as soon as you can, Leonard.

Julia, with a stifled cry of rage, rushes at Grace, who is crossing behind the sofa towards the door. Charteris seizes Julia, and prevents her from getting past the sofa. Grace goes out. Charteris, holding Julia fast, looks round to the door to see whether Grace is safely out of the room.

JULIA [*suddenly ceasing to struggle, and speaking with the most pathetic dignity*] Oh, there is no need to be violent. [*He passes her across to the sofa, and leans against the end of it, panting and mopping his forehead*]. That is worthy of you! to use brute force! to humiliate me before her! [*She bursts into tears*].

CHARTERIS [*to himself, with melancholy conviction*] This is going to be a cheerful evening. Now patience! patience! patience! [*He sits down on a chair near the round table*].

JULIA [*in anguish*] Leonard: have you no feeling for me?

CHARTERIS. Only an intense desire to get you safely out of this.

JULIA [*fiercely*] I am not going to stir.

CHARTERIS [*wearily*] Well, well. [*He heaves a long sigh*].

They sit silent for a while: Julia striving, not to regain her self-control, but to maintain her rage at boiling point.

JULIA [*rising suddenly*] I am going to speak to that woman.

CHARTERIS [*jumping up*] No, no. Hang it, Julia, dont lets have another wrestling match. Remember: I'm getting on for forty: youre too young for me. Sit down; or else let me take you home. Suppose her father comes in!

JULIA. I dont care. It rests with you. I am ready to go if she will give you up: until then I stay. Those are my terms: you owe me that. [*She sits down determinedly*].

Charteris looks at her for a moment; then, making up his mind, goes resolutely to the sofa; sits down near the end of it, she being at the opposite end; and speaks with biting emphasis.

CHARTERIS. I owe you just exactly nothing.

JULIA [*reproachfully*] Nothing! You can look me in the face and say that? Oh, Leonard!

CHARTERIS. Let me remind you, Julia, that when first we became acquainted, the position you took up was that of a woman of advanced views.

JULIA. That should have made you respect me the more.

CHARTERIS [*placably*] So it did, my dear. But that is not the point. As a woman of advanced views, you were determined to be free. You regarded marriage as a degrading bargain, by which a woman sells herself to a man for the social status of a wife and the right to be supported and pensioned in old age out of his income. Thats the advanced view: o u r view. Besides, if you had married me, I might have turned out a drunkard, a criminal, an imbecile, a horror to you; and you couldnt have released yourself. Too big a risk, you see. Thats the rational view: o u r view. Accordingly, you reserved the right to

leave me at any time if you found our companionship incompatible with—what was the expression you used?—with your full development as a human being. I think that was how you put the Ibsenist view: o u r view. So I had to be content with a charming philander, which taught me a great deal, and brought me some hours of exquisite happiness.

JULIA. Leonard: you confess then, that you owe me something?

CHARTERIS [*haughtily*] No: what I received, I paid. Did y o u learn nothing from me? was there no delight for y o u in our friendship?

JULIA [*vehemently and movingly; for she is now sincere*] No. You made me pay dearly for every moment of happiness. You revenged yourself on me for the humiliation of being the slave of your passion for me. I was never sure of you for a moment. I trembled whenever a letter came from you, lest it should contain some stab for me. I dreaded your visits almost as much as I longed for them. I was your plaything, not your companion. [*She rises, exclaiming*] Oh, there was such suffering in my happiness that I hardly knew joy from pain. [*She sinks on the piano stool, and adds, as she buries her face in her hands and turns away from him*] Better for me if I had never met you!

CHARTERIS [*rising indignantly*] You ungenerous wretch! Is this your gratitude for the way I have just been flattering you? What have I not endured from you? endured with angelic patience? Did I not find out, before our friendship was a fortnight old, that all your advanced views were merely a fashion picked up and followed like any other fashion, without understanding or meaning a word of them? Did you not, in spite of your care for your own liberty, set up claims on me compared to which the claims of the most jealous wife would have been trifles? Have I a single woman friend whom you have not abused as old, ugly, vicious—

JULIA [*quickly looking up*] So they are.

CHARTERIS. Well, then, I'll come to grievances that even you can understand. I accuse you of habitual and intolerable jealousy and ill temper; of insulting me on imaginary provocation; of positively beating me; of stealing letters of mine—

JULIA. Yes, nice letters!

CHARTERIS. —of breaking your solemn promises not to do it again; of spending hours— aye, days! piecing together the contents of my waste paper basket in your search for more letters; and then representing yourself as an ill used saint and martyr wantonly betrayed and deserted by a selfish monster of a man.

JULIA [*rising*] I was justified in reading your letters. Our perfect confidence in one another gave me the right to do it.

CHARTERIS. Thank you. Then I hasten to break off a confidence which gives such rights. [*He sits down sulkily on the sofa*].

JULIA [*bending over him threateningly*] You have no right to break it off.

CHARTERIS. I have. You refused to marry me because——

JULIA. I did not. You never asked me. If we were married, you would never dare treat me as you are doing now.

CHARTERIS [*laboriously going back to his argument*] It was understood between us as people of advanced views that we were not to marry; because, as the law stands, I might have become a drunkard, a——

JULIA. ——a criminal, an imbecile or a horror. You said that before. [*She sits down beside him with a fling*].

CHARTERIS [*politely*] I beg your pardon, my dear. I know I have a habit of repeating myself. The point is that you reserved your freedom to give me up when you pleased.

JULIA. Well, what of that? I do not please to give you up; and I will not. You have not become a drunkard or a criminal.

CHARTERIS. You don't see the point yet, Julia. You seem to forget that in reserving your freedom to leave me in case I should turn out badly, you also reserved my freedom to leave you in case you should turn out badly.

JULIA. Very ingenious. And pray, have *I* become a drunkard, or a criminal, or an imbecile?

CHARTERIS. You have become what is infinitely worse than all three together: a jealous termagant.

JULIA [*shaking her head bitterly*] Yes: abuse me: call me names.

CHARTERIS. I now assert the right I reserved: the right of breaking with you when I please. Advanced views, Julia, involve advanced duties: you cannot be an advanced woman when you want to bring a man to your feet, and a conventional woman when you want to hold him there against his will. Advanced people form charming friendships: conventional people marry. Marriage suits a good many people; and its first duty is fidelity. Friendship suits some people; and its first duty is unhesitating uncomplaining acceptance of a notice of change of feeling from either side. You chose friendship instead of marriage. Now do your duty, and accept your notice.

JULIA. Never. We are engaged in the eye of —the eye of—

CHARTERIS. Yes, Julia? Cant you get it out? In the eye of something that advanced women dont believe in, ch?

JULIA [*throwing herself at his feet*] Oh, Leonard, dont be cruel. I'm too miserable to argue—to think. I only know I love you. You reproach me with not wanting to marry you. I would have married you at any time after I came to love you, if you had asked me. I will marry you now if you will.

CHARTERIS. I wont, my dear. Thats flat. We're intellectually incompatible.

JULIA. But why? We could be so happy. You love me: I know you love me. I feel it. You say "My dear" to me: you have said it several times this evening. I know I have been wicked, odious, bad: I say nothing in defence of myself. But dont be hard on me. I was distracted by the thought of losing you. I cant face life without you, Leonard. I was happy when I met you: I had never loved any one: and if you had only let me alone, I could have gone on contentedly by myself. But I cant now. I must have you with me. Dont cast me off without a thought of all I have at stake. I could be a friend to you if you would only let me; if you would only tell me your plans; give me a share in your work; treat me as something more than the amusement of an idle hour. Oh, Leonard, Leonard, youve never given me a chance: indeed you havnt. I'll take pains; I'll read; I'll try to think; I'll conquer my jealousy; I'll— [*she breaks down, rocking her head desperately on his knees and writhing*]. Oh, I'm mad: I'm mad: youll kill me if you desert me.

CHARTERIS [*petting her*] My dear love, dont cry: dont go on in this way. You know I cant help it.

JULIA [*sobbing as he rises and tenderly lifts her with him*] Oh, you can, you can. One word from you will make us happy for ever.

CHARTERIS [*diplomatically*] Come, my dear: we really must go. We cant stay until Cuthbertson comes. [*He releases her gently, and*

C

takes her mantle from the table]. Here is your mantle: put it on and be good. You have given me a terrible evening: you must have some consideration for me.

JULIA [*dangerous again*] Then I am to be cast off?

CHARTERIS [*coaxingly*] You are to put on your bonnet, dearest. [*He puts the mantle on her shoulders*].

JULIA [*with a bitter half laugh, half sob*] Well, I suppose I must do what I am told. [*She goes to the table, and looks for her toque. She sees the yellow backed French novel*]. Ah, look at that [*holding it out to him*]! Look at what the creature reads! filthy, vile French stuff that no decent woman would touch. And you—you have been reading it with her.

CHARTERIS. You recommended that book to me yourself.

JULIA. Faugh! [*She dashes it on the floor*].

CHARTERIS [*running anxiously to the book*] Dont damage property, Julia. [*He picks it up and dusts it*]. Making scenes is an affair of sentiment: damaging property is serious. [*He replaces it on the table*]. And now do pray come along.

JULIA [*implacably*] You can go: there is nothing to prevent you. I will not stir. [*She sits down stubbornly on the sofa*].

CHARTERIS [*losing patience*] Oh come! I am not going to begin all this over again. There are limits even to my forbearance. Come on.

JULIA. I will not, I tell you.

CHARTERIS. Then goodnight. [*He makes resolutely for the door. With a rush, she gets there before him and bars his way*]. I thought you wanted me to go.

JULIA [*at the door*] You shall not leave me here alone.

CHARTERIS. Then come with me.

JULIA. Not until you have sworn to me to give up that woman.

CHARTERIS. My dear: I will swear anything if youll only come away and put an end to this.

JULIA [*perplexed, doubting him*] You will swear?

CHARTERIS. Solemnly. Propose the oath. I have been on the point of swearing for the last half hour.

JULIA [*despairingly*] You are only making fun of me. I want no oaths. I want your promise: your sacred word of honor.

CHARTERIS. Certainly: anything you demand, on condition that you come away

immediately. On my sacred word of honor as a gentleman—as an Englishman—as anything you like—I will never see her again never speak to her, never think of her. Now come.

JULIA. But are you in earnest? Will you keep your word?

CHARTERIS [*smiling subtly*] Now you are getting unreasonable. Do come along without any more nonsense. At any rate, I am going. I am not strong enough to carry you home; but I am strong enough to make my way through that door in spite of you. You will then have a new grievance against me for my brutal violence. [*He takes a step towards the door*].

JULIA [*solemnly*] If you do, I swear I will throw myself from that window, Leonard, as you pass out.

CHARTERIS [*unimpressed*] That window is at the back of the building. I shall pass out at the front; so you will not hurt me. Goodnight. [*He approaches the door.*]

JULIA. Leonard: have you no pity?

CHARTERIS. Not the least. When you condescend to these antics you force me to despise you. How can a woman who behaves like a spoiled child and talks like a sentimental novel have the audacity to dream of being a companion for a man of any sort of sense or character? [*She gives an inarticulate cry, and throws herself sobbing on his breast*]. Come! dont cry, my dear Julia: you dont look half so beautiful as when youre happy; and it makes me all damp. Come along.

Julia [*affectionately*] I'll come, dear, if you wish it. Give me one kiss.

CHARTERIS [*exasperated*] This is too much. No: I'm dashed if I will. Here: let me go, Julia. [*She clings to him*]. Will you come without another word if I give you a kiss?

JULIA. I will do anything you wish, darling.

CHARTERIS. Well, here. [*He takes her in his arms and gives her an unceremonious kiss*]. Now remember your promise. Come along.

JULIA. That was not a nice kiss, dearest. I want one of our old real kisses.

CHARTERIS [*furious*] Oh, go to the deuce. [*He disengages himself impulsively; and she, as if he had flung her down, falls pathetically with a stifled moan. With an angry look at her, he strides out and slams the door. She raises herself on one hand, listening to his retreating footsteps. They stop. Her face lights up with eager, triumphant cunning. The steps return hastily. She throws herself down again as before. Charteris reappears, in the utmost dismay, exclaiming*] Julia: we're done. Cuthbertson's coming upstairs with y o u r father [*she sits up quickly*]. Do you hear? the t w o fathers!

JULIA [*sitting on the floor*] Impossible. They dont know one another.

CHARTERIS [*desperately*] I tell you theyre coming up together like twins. What on earth are we to do?

JULIA [*scrambling up with the help of his hand*] Quick: the lift: we can go down in that. [*She rushes to the table for her toque*].

CHARTERIS. No: the man's gone home; and the lift's locked.

JULIA [*putting on her toque at express speed*] Let's go up to the next floor.

CHARTERIS. Theres no next floor. We're at the top of the house. No, no: you must invent some thumping lie. I cant think of one: you can, Julia. Exercise all your genius. I'll back you up.

JULIA. But—

CHARTERIS. Sh-sh! Here they are. Sit down and look at home. [*Julia tears off her toque and mantle; throws them on the table; and darts to the piano, at which she seats herself*].

JULIA. Come and sing.

She plays the symphony to When Other Lips. *Charteris stands at the piano, as if about to sing. Two elderly gentlemen enter. Julia stops playing.*

The elder of the two newcomers, Colonel Daniel Craven, affects the bluff simple veteran, and carries it off pleasantly and well, having a fine upright figure, and being, in fact, a good-naturedly impulsive credulous person who, after an entirely thoughtless career as an officer and a gentleman, is now being startled into some sort of self-education by the surprising proceedings of his children.

His companion, Mr Joseph Cuthbertson, Grace's father, has none of the Colonel's boyishness. He is a man of fervent idealistic sentiment, so frequently outraged by the facts of life that he has acquired an habitually indignant manner, which unexpectedly becomes enthusiastic or affectionate when he speaks.

The two men differ greatly in expression. The Colonel's face is lined with weather, with age, with eating and drinking, and with the cumulative effect of many petty vexations, but not with thought: he is still fresh, still full of expectations of pleasure and novelty. Cuthbertson has the lines of sedentary London brain work, with its chronic fatigue and longing for rest and recreative emotion, and its disillusioned indifference to adventure and enjoyment, except as a means of recuperation. His vigilant, irascible eye, piled-up hair, and the honorable seriousness with which he takes himself, give him an air of considerable consequence.

They are both in evening dress. Cuthbertson has not taken off his fur-collared overcoat.

CUTHBERTSON [*with a hospitable show of delight at finding visitors*] Dont stop, Miss Craven. Go on, Charteris.

He comes behind the sofa, and hangs his overcoat on it, after taking an opera glass and a theatre program from the pockets, and putting them down on the piano. Craven meanwhile goes to the fireplace, and plants himself on the hearth-rug.

CHARTERIS. No, thank you. Miss Craven has just been taking me through an old song; and Ive had enough of it. [*He takes the song off the piano desk and lays it aside; then closes the lid over the keyboard*].

JULIA [*passing between the sofa and piano to shake hands with Cuthbertson*] Why, youve brought Daddy! What a surprise! [*Looking across to Craven*] So glad youve come, Dad. [*She takes a chair near the window, and sits there*].

CUTHBERTSON. Craven: let me introduce you to Mr Leonard Charteris, the famous Ibsenist philosopher.

CRAVEN. Oh, we know one another already. Charteris is quite at home in our house, Jo.

CUTHBERTSON. I beg both your pardons. He's quite at home here too. [*Charteris sits down on the piano stool*]. By the bye, wheres Grace?

JULIA AND CHARTERIS. Er— [*They stop and look at one another*].

JULIA [*politely*] I beg your pardon, Mr Charteris: I interrupted you.

CHARTERIS. Not at all, Miss Craven. [*An awkward pause*].

CUTHBERTSON [*to help them out*] You were going to tell us about Grace, Charteris.

CHARTERIS. I was only going to say that I didnt know that you and Craven were acquainted.

CRAVEN. Why, *I* didnt know it until tonight. It's a most extraordinary thing. We met by chance at the theatre; and he turns out to be my oldest friend.

CUTHBERTSON [*energetically*] Yes, Craven; and do you see how this proves what I was saying to you about the break-up of family life? Here are all our young people bosom friends, inseparables; and yet they never said a word of it to us. We two, who knew each other before they were born, might never have met again if you hadnt popped into the stall next mine tonight by pure chance. Come: sit down [*bustling over to him affectionately, and pushing him into the armchair above the fire*]: theres your place, by my fireside, whenever you choose to fill it. [*He posts himself at the end of the sofa, leaning against it and admiring Craven*]. Just imagine you being Dan Craven!

CRAVEN. Just imagine you being Jo Cuthbertson, though! Thats a far more extraordinary coincidence; because I'd got it into my head that your name was Tranfield.

CUTHBERTSON. Oh, thats my daughter's name. She's a widow, you know. How uncommonly well you look, Dan! The years havnt hurt you much.

CRAVEN [*suddenly becoming unnaturally gloomy*] I look well. I even feel well. But my days are numbered.

CUTHBERTSON [*alarmed*] Oh, dont say that, my dear fellow. I hope not.

JULIA [*with anguish in her voice*] Daddy! [*Cuthbertson looks inquiringly round at her*].

CRAVEN. There, there, my dear: I was wrong to talk of it. It's a sad subject. But it's better that Cuthbertson should know. We used to be very close friends, and are so still, I hope. [*Cuthbertson goes to Craven and presses his hand silently; then returns to the sofa and sits down, pulling out his handkerchief, and displaying some emotion*].

CHARTERIS [*a little impatiently*] The fact is, Cuthbertson, Craven's a devout believer in the department of witchcraft called medical science. He's celebrated in all the medical schools as an example of the newest sort of liver complaint. The doctors say he cant last another year; and he has fully made up his mind not to survive next Easter, just to oblige them.

CRAVEN [*with military affectation*] It's very kind of you to try to keep up my spirits by making light of it, Charteris. But I shall be ready when my time comes. I'm a soldier. [*A sob from Julia*]. Don't cry, Julia.

CUTHBERTSON [*huskily*] I hope you may long be spared, Dan.

CRAVEN. To oblige me, Jo, change the subject. [*He gets up, and again posts himself on the hearthrug with his back to the fire*].

CHARTERIS. Persuade him to join our club, Cuthbertson. He mopes.

JULIA. It's no use. Sylvia and I are always at him to join; but he wont.

CRAVEN. My child: I have my own club.

CHARTERIS [*contemptuously*] Yes: the Junior Army and Navy! Do you call that a club? Why, they darent let a woman cross the doorstep!

CRAVEN [*a little ruffled*] Clubs are a matter of taste, Charteris. You like a cock-and-hen club: I dont. It's bad enough to have Julia and her sister—a girl under twenty!—spending half their time at such a place. Besides, now really, such a name for a club! The Ibsen club! I should be laughed out of London. The Ibsen club! Come, Cuthbertson! back me up. I'm sure you agree with me.

CHARTERIS. Cuthbertson's a member.

CRAVEN [*amazed*] No! Why, he's been talking to me all the evening about the way in which everything is going to the dogs through advanced ideas in the younger generation.

CHARTERIS. Of course. He's been studying it in the club. He's always there.

CUTHBERTSON [*warmly*] Not always. Dont exaggerate, Charteris. You know very well that though I joined the club on Grace's account, thinking that her father's presence there would be a protection and a—a sort of sanction, as it were, I never approved of it.

CRAVEN [*tactlessly harping on Cuthbertson's inconsistency*] Well, you know, this is unexpected: now it's really very unexpected. I should never have thought it from hearing you talk, Jo. Why, you said the whole modern movement was abhorrent to you because your life had been passed in witnessing scenes of suffering nobly endured and sacrifice willingly rendered by womanly women and manly men and deuce knows what else. Is it at the Ibsen club that you see all this manliness and womanliness?

CHARTERIS. Certainly not: the rules of the club forbid anything of the sort. Every candidate for membership must be nominated by a man and a woman, who both guarantee that the candidate, if female, is not womanly, and if male, not manly.

CRAVEN [*chuckling cunningly as he stoops to press his heated trousers against his legs, which are chilly*] Wont do, Charteris. Cant take me in with so thin a story as that.

CUTHBERTSON [*vehemently*] It's true. It's monstrous; but it's true.

CRAVEN [*with rising indignation, as he begins to draw the inevitable inferences*] Do you mean to say that somebody had the audacity to guarantee that my Julia is not a womanly woman?

CHARTERIS [*darkly*] It sounds incredible; but a man was found ready to take that inconceivable lie on his conscience.

JULIA [*firing up*] If he has nothing worse than that on his conscience, he may sleep pretty well. In what way am I more womanly than any of the rest of them, I should like to know? They are always saying things like that behind my back: I hear of them from Sylvia. Only the other day a member of the committee said I ought never to have been elected—that y o u [*to Charteris*] had smuggled me in. I should like to see her say it to my face: thats all.

CRAVEN. But, my precious, I most sincerely hope she was right. She paid you the highest compliment. Why, the place must be a den of infamy.

CUTHBERTSON [*emphatically*] So it is, Craven: so it is.

CHARTERIS. Exactly. Thats what keeps it so select: nobody but people whose reputations are above suspicion dare belong to it. If we once got a good name, we should become a mere whitewashing shop for all the shady characters in London. Better join us, Craven. Let me put you up.

CRAVEN. What! Join a club where theres some scoundrel who guaranteed my daughter to be an unwomanly woman! If I werent an invalid, I'd kick him.

CHARTERIS. Oh dont say that. It was I.

CRAVEN [*reproachfully*] You! Now upon my soul, Charteris, this is very vexing. Now how could you bring yourself to do such a thing?

CHARTERIS. She made me. Why, I had to guarantee Cuthbertson as unmanly; and he's the leading representative of manly sentiment in London.

CRAVEN. That didnt do Jo any harm; but it took away my Julia's character.

JULIA [*outraged*] Daddy!

CHARTERIS. Not at the Ibsen club: quite the contrary. After all, what can we do? You know what breaks up most clubs for men and women. Theres a quarrel—a scandal—cherchez la femme—always a woman at the bottom of it. Well, we knew this when we founded the club; but we noticed that the woman at the bottom of it was always a womanly woman. The unwomanly women who work for their living, and know how to take care of themselves, never give any trouble. So we simply said we wouldnt have any womanly women; and when one gets smuggled in she has to take care not to behave in a womanly way. We get on all right. [*He rises*] Come to lunch with me there tomorrow and see the place.

CUTHBERTSON [*rising*] No: he's engaged to me. But you can join us.

CHARTERIS. What hour?

CUTHBERTSON. Any time after twelve. [*To Craven*] It's at 90 Cork Street, at the other end of the Burlington Arcade.

CRAVEN [*making a note on his cuff*] 90, you say. After twelve. [*Suddenly relapsing into gloom*] By the bye, dont order anything special for me. I'm not allowed wine: only Apollinaris. No meat either: only a scrap of fish occasionally. I'm to have a short life, but not a merry one. [*Sighing*] Well, well! [*Bracing himself up*] Now, Julia: it's time for us to be off. [*Julia rises*].

CUTHBERTSON. But where on earth is Grace? I must go and look for her. [*He turns to the door*].

JULIA [*stopping him*] Oh pray dont disturb her, Mr Cuthbertson. She's so tired.

CUTHBERTSON. But just for a moment, to say goodnight. [*Julia and Charteris look at one another in dismay. Cuthbertson looks quickly at them, perceiving that something is wrong*].

CHARTERIS. We must make a clean breast of it, I see.

CUTHBERTSON. Of what?

CHARTERIS. The truth is, Cuthbertson, Mrs Tranfield, who is, as you know, the most thoughtful of women, took it into her head that I—well, that I particularly wanted to speak to Miss Craven alone. So she said she was tired, and went to bed.

CRAVEN [*scandalized*] Tut! tut!

CUTHBERTSON. Oho! is that it? Then it's all right: she never goes to bed as early as this. I'll fetch her in a moment. [*He goes out confidently, leaving Charteris aghast*].

JULIA. Now youve done it. [*She rushes to the round table, and snatches up her mantle and toque*]. I'm off. [*She makes for the door*].

CRAVEN [*horrified*] What are you doing, Julia? You cant go until youve said goodnight to Mrs Tranfield. It'd be horribly rude.

JULIA. You can stay if you like, Daddy: I

cant. I'll wait for you in the hall. [*She hurries out*].

CRAVEN [*following her*] But what on earth am I to say? [*She disappears, shutting the door behind her in his face. He turns to Charteris, grumbling*]. Now really you know, Charteris, this is devilish awkward: upon my life it is. That was a most indelicate thing of you to say plump out before us all: that about you and Julia.

CHARTERIS. I'll explain it all tomorrow. Just at present we'd really better follow Julia's example and bolt. [*He starts for the door*].

CRAVEN [*intercepting him*] Stop! dont leave me like this: I shall look like a fool. Now I shall really take it in bad part if you run away, Charteris.

CHARTERIS. All right. I'll stay. [*He lifts himself on to the shoulder of the grand piano and sits there swinging his legs and contemplating Craven resignedly*].

CRAVEN [*pacing up and down*] I'm excessively vexed about Julia's conduct: I am indeed. She cant bear to be crossed in the slightest thing, poor child. I'll have to apologize for her, you know: her going away is a downright slap in the face for these people here. Cuthbertson may be offended already for all I know.

CHARTERIS. Oh, never mind about him. Mrs Tranfield bosses this establishment.

CRAVEN [*cunningly*] Ah, thats it, is it? He's just the sort of fellow that would have no control over his daughter. [*He goes back to his former place on the hearthrug with his back to the fire*]. By the bye, what the dickens did he mean by all that about passing his life amid —what was it?—"scenes of suffering nobly endured and sacrifice willingly rendered by womanly women and manly men" and a lot more of the same sort? I suppose he's something in a hospital.

CHARTERIS. Hospital! Nonsense! he's a dramatic critic. Didnt you hear me say he was the leading representative of manly sentiment in London?

CRAVEN. You dont say so! Now really, who'd have thought it! How jolly it must be to be able to go to the theatre for nothing! I must ask him to get me a few tickets occasionally. But isnt it ridiculous for a man to talk like that? I'm hanged if he dont take what he sees on the stage quite seriously.

CHARTERIS. Of course: thats why he's a good critic. Besides, if you take people seri-

ously off the stage, why shouldnt you take them seriously on it, where theyre under some sort of decent restraint? [*He jumps down from the piano, and goes to the window*].

Cuthbertson comes back.

CUTHBERTSON [*to Craven, rather sheepishly*] The fact is, Grace has gone to bed. I must apologize to you and Miss—[*He turns to Julia's seat, and stops on seeing it vacant*].

CRAVEN [*embarrassed*] It is I who have to apologize for Julia, Jo. She—

CHARTERIS [*interrupting*] She said she was quite sure that if we didnt go, youd persuade Mrs Tranfield to get up to say goodnight for the sake of politeness; so she went straight off.

CUTHBERTSON. Very kind of her indeed. I'm really ashamed—

CRAVEN. Dont mention it, Jo: dont mention it. She's waiting for me below. [*Going*] Goodnight. Goodnight, Charteris.

CHARTERIS. Goodnight.

CUTHBERTSON [*seeing Craven out*] Goodnight. Say goodnight and thanks to Miss Craven for me. Tomorrow any time after twelve, remember. [*They go out*].

Charteris, with a long sigh, crosses to the fireplace, thoroughly tired out.

CRAVEN [*outside*] All right.

CUTHBERTSON [*outside*] Take care of the stairs: theyre rather steep. Goodnight. [*The outside door shuts*].

Cuthbertson returns. Instead of entering, he stands impressively in the doorway with one hand in the breast of his waistcoat, eyeing Charteris sternly.

CHARTERIS. Whats the matter?

CUTHBERTSON [*sternly*] Charteris: what has been going on here? I insist on knowing. Grace has not gone to bed: I have seen and spoken with her. What is it all about?

CHARTERIS. Ask your theatrical experience, Cuthbertson. A man, of course.

CUTHBERTSON [*coming forward and confronting him*] Dont play the fool with me, Charteris: I'm too old a hand to be amused by it. I ask you, seriously, what is the matter?

CHARTERIS. I tell you seriously, I'm the matter. Julia wants to marry me: I want to marry Grace. I came here tonight to sweetheart Grace. Enter Julia. Alarums and excursions. Exit Grace. Enter you and Craven. Subterfuges and excuses. Exeunt Craven and Julia. And here we are. Thats the whole story. Sleep over it. Goodnight. [*He leaves*].

CUTHBERTSON [*staring after him*] Well I'll be—

ACT II

Next day at noon, in the library of the Ibsen club. A long room, with glass doors half-way down on both sides, leading respectively to the dining room corridor and the main staircase. At the end, in the middle, is the fireplace, surmounted by a handsome mantelpiece, with a bust of Ibsen, and decorative inscriptions of the titles of his plays. There are circular recesses at each side of the fireplace, with divan seats running round them, the space above the divans lined with books. A long settee faces the fire. Along the back of the settee, and touching it, is a green table, littered with journals. Ibsen, looking down the room, has the dining room door on his left, and further on, nearly in the middle of the library a revolving bookcase, with an easy chair close to it. On his right, between the door and the recess, is a light library step-ladder. Further on, past the door an easy chair, and a smaller one between it and the middle of the room. Placards inscribed SILENCE *are conspicuously exhibited here and there.*

Cuthbertson is seated in the easy chair at the revolving bookstand, reading The Daily Graphic. *Dr Paramore is on the divan in the recess on Ibsen's right, reading* The British Medical Journal. *He is young as age is counted in the professions: barely forty. His hair is wearing bald on his forehead; and his dark arched eyebrows, coming rather close together, give him a conscientiously sinister appearance. He wears the frock coat of the fashionable physician, and cultivates the professional bedside manner with scrupulous conventionality. Not at all a happy or frank man, but not consciously unhappy nor intentionally insincere, and highly self-satisfied intellectually.*

Sylvia Craven is sitting in the middle of the settee before the fire, reading a volume of Ibsen, only the back of her head being visible from the middle of the room. She is a pretty girl of eighteen, small and trim, wearing a mountaineering suit of Norfolk jacket and breeches with neat town stockings and shoes. A detachable cloth skirt lies ready to her hand across the end of the settee.

A page boy's voice, monotonously calling for Dr Paramore, is heard approaching outside on the right.

THE PAGE [*outside*] Dr Paramore, Dr Paramore, Dr Paramore [*he enters, carrying a salver with a card on it*] Dr Par—

PARAMORE [*sharply, sitting up*] Here, boy. [*The boy presents the salver. Paramore takes the card and looks at it*]. All right: I'll come down to him. [*The boy goes. Paramore rises, and comes from the recess, throwing his paper on the table*]. Good morning, Mr Cuthbertson [*stopping to pull out his cuffs, and shake his coat straight*]. Mrs Tranfield quite well, I hope?

SYLVIA [*turning her head indignantly*] Sh—sh—sh!

Paramore turns, surprised. Cuthbertson rises energetically and looks across the bookstand to see who is the author of this impertinence.

PARAMORE [*to Sylvia, stiffly*] I beg your pardon, Miss Craven: I did not mean to disturb you.

SYLVIA [*flustered and self-assertive*] You may talk as much as you like if you will have the common consideration to ask first whether the other people object. What I protest against is your assumption that my presence doesnt matter because I'm only a female member. Thats all. Now go on, pray: you dont disturb me in the least. [*She turns to the fire, and again buries herself in Ibsen*].

CUTHBERTSON [*with emphatic dignity*] No gentleman would have dreamt of objecting to our exchanging a few words, madam. [*She takes no notice. He resumes angrily*] As a matter of fact I was about to say to Dr Paramore that if he would care to bring his visitor up here, *I* should not object. The impudence! [*He dashes his paper down on the chair*].

PARAMORE. Oh, many thanks; but it's only an instrument maker.

CUTHBERTSON. Any new medical discoveries, doctor?

PARAMORE. Well, since you ask me, yes: perhaps a most important one. I have discovered something that has hitherto been overlooked: a minute duct in the liver of the guinea pig. Miss Craven will forgive my mentioning it when I say that it may throw an important light on her father's case. The first thing, of course, is to find out what the duct is there for.

CUTHBERTSON [*reverently, feeling that he is in the presence of Science*] Indeed? How will you do that?

PARAMORE. Oh, easily enough, by simply cutting the duct, and seeing what will happen to the guinea pig. [*Sylvia rises, horrified*]. I shall require a knife specially made to get at it. The man who is waiting for me downstairs has brought me a few handles to try before fitting it and sending it to the laboratory. I am afraid it would not do to bring such weapons up here.

SYLVIA. If you attempt such a thing, Dr Paramore, I will complain to the committee. A majority of the members are anti-vivisectionists. You ought to be ashamed of yourself. [*She snatches up the detachable skirt, and begins buttoning it on as she flounces out at the staircase door*].

PARAMORE [*with patient contempt*] Thats the sort of thing we scientific men have to put up with nowadays, Mr Cuthbertson. Ignorance, superstition, sentimentality: they are all one. A guinea pig's convenience is set above the health and lives of the entire human race.

CUTHBERTSON [*vehemently*] It's not ignorance nor superstition, Paramore: it's sheer downright Ibsenism: thats what it is. Ive been wanting to sit comfortably at that fire the whole morning; but Ive never had a chance with that girl there. I couldnt go and plump myself down on a seat beside her: goodness knows what she'd think I wanted! Thats one of the delights of having women in the club: when they come in here they all want to sit at the fire and adore that bust. I sometimes feel that I should like to take the poker, and fetch it a wipe across the nose. Ugh!

PARAMORE. I must say I prefer the elder Miss Craven to her sister.

CUTHBERTSON [*his eye lighting up*] Ah, Julia! I believe you. A splendid fine creature: every inch a woman. No Ibsenism about h e r!

PARAMORE. I quite agree with you there, Mr Cuthbertson. Er—by the way, do you think is Miss Craven attached to Charteris at all?

CUTHBERTSON. What! that fellow! Not he. He hangs about after her; but he's not man enough for her. A woman of that sort likes a strong, manly, deep throated, broad chested man.

PARAMORE [*anxiously*] Hm! a sort of sporting character, you think?

CUTHBERTSON. Oh, no, no. A scientific man, perhaps, like yourself. But you know what I mean: a MAN. [*He strikes himself a sounding blow on the chest*].

PARAMORE. Of course; but Charteris is a man.

CUTHBERTSON. Pah! you dont see what I mean.

The page boy returns with his salver.

THE PAGE [*calling monotonously as before*] Mr Cuthbertson, Mr Cuthbertson, Mr Cuth—

CUTHBERTSON. Here, boy. [*He takes a card from the salver*]. Bring the gentleman up here. [*The boy goes out*]. It's Craven. He's coming to lunch with me and Charteris. You might join us if youve nothing better to do, when youve finished with the instrument man. If Julia turns up I'll ask her too.

PARAMORE [*flushing with pleasure*] I shall be very pleased. Thank you. [*He is going out at the staircase door when Craven enters*]. Good morning, Colonel Craven.

CRAVEN [*at the door*] Good morning: glad to see you. I'm looking for Cuthbertson.

PARAMORE [*smiling*] There he is. [*He goes out*].

CUTHBERTSON [*greeting Craven effusively*] Delighted to see you. Now will you come to the smoking room; or will you sit down here, and have a chat while we're waiting for Charteris? If you like company, the smoking room's always full of women. Here in the library we shall have it pretty well all to ourselves until about three o'clock.

CRAVEN. I dont like to see women smoking. I'll make myself comfortable here. [*He sits in the easy chair on the staircase side*].

CUTHBERTSON [*taking the smaller chair on his left*] Neither do I. Theres not a room in this club where I can enjoy a pipe quietly without a woman coming in and beginning to roll a cigaret. It's a disgusting habit in a woman: it's not natural to her sex.

CRAVEN [*sighing*] Ah, Jo, times have changed since we both courted Molly Ebden all those years ago. I took my defeat well, old chap, didnt I?

CUTHBERTSON [*with earnest approval*] You did, Dan. The thought of it has often helped me to behave well myself: it has, on my honor.

CRAVEN. Yes: you always believed in hearth and home, Jo: in a true English wife, and a happy wholesome fireside. How did Molly turn out?

CUTHBERTSON [*trying to be fair to Molly*] Well, not bad. She might have been worse. You see, I couldnt stand her relations: all the men were roaring cads; and she couldnt get on with my mother. And then she hated being in town; and of course I couldnt live in the country on account of my work. But we hit it off as well as most people until we separated.

CRAVEN [*taken aback*] Separated! [*He is irresistibly amused*]. Oh! that was the end of the hearth and home, Jo, was it?

CUTHBERTSON [*warmly*] It was not my fault, Dan. [*Sentimentally*] Some day the world will know how I loved that woman. But she was incapable of valuing a true man's affection. Do you know, she often said she wished she'd married you instead.

CRAVEN [*sobered by the suggestion*] Dear me! dear me! Well, perhaps it was better as it was. You heard about my marriage I suppose.

CUTHBERTSON. Oh yes: we all heard of it.

CRAVEN. Well, Jo, I may as well make a clean breast of it: everybody knew it. *I* married for money.

CUTHBERTSON [*encouragingly*] And why not, Dan? Why not? We cant get on without it, you know.

CRAVEN [*with sincere feeling*] I got to be very fond of her, Jo. I had a home until she died. Now everything's changed. Julia's always here. Sylvia's of a different nature; but she's always here too.

CUTHBERTSON [*sympathetically*] I know. It's the same with Grace. She's always here.

CRAVEN. And now they want me to be always here. Theyre at me every day to join the club. To stop my grumbling, I suppose. Thats what I want to consult you about. Do you think I ought to join?

CUTHBERTSON. Well, if you have no conscientious objection—

CRAVEN [*testily interrupting him*] I object to the existence of the place on principle; but whats the use of that? Here it is in spite of my objection; and I may as well have the benefit of any good that may be in it.

CUTHBERTSON [*soothing him*] Of course: thats the only reasonable view of the matter. Well, the fact is, it's not so inconvenient as you might think. When youre at home, you have the house more to yourself; and when you want to have your family about you, you can dine with them at the club.

CRAVEN [*not much attracted by this*] True.

CUTHBERTSON. Besides, if you dont want to dine with them, you neednt.

CRAVEN [*convinced*] True, very true. But dont they carry on here, rather?

CUTHBERTSON. Oh, no: they dont exactly carry on. Of course the usual tone of the club is low, because the women smoke, and earn their own living, and all that; but still theres nothing actually to complain of. And it's convenient, certainly.

Charteris comes in, looking round for them.

CRAVEN [*rising*] Do you know, Ive a great mind to join, just to see what it's like.

CHARTERIS [*coming between them*] Do so by all means. I hope I havnt disturbed your chat by coming too soon.

CRAVEN. Not at all. [*He shakes his hand cordially*].

CHARTERIS. Thats right. I'm earlier than I intended. The fact is, I have something rather pressing to say to Cuthbertson.

CRAVEN. Private?

CHARTERIS. Not particularly. [*To Cuthbertson*] Only what we were speaking of last night.

CUTHBERTSON. Well, Charteris, I think that is private, or ought to be.

CRAVEN [*retiring discreetly towards the table*] I'll just take a look at The Times—

CHARTERIS [*stopping him*] Oh, it's no secret: everybody in the club guesses it. [*To Cuthbertson*] Has Grace never mentioned to you that she wants to marry me?

CUTHBERTSON [*indignantly*] She has mentioned that you want to marry her.

CHARTERIS. Ah; but then it's not what I want, but what Grace wants, that will weigh with you.

CRAVEN [*a little shocked*] Excuse me, Charteris: this is private. I'll leave you to yourselves [*again moving towards the table*].

CHARTERIS. Wait a bit, Craven: youre concerned in this. Julia wants to marry me too.

CRAVEN [*in a tone of the strongest remonstrance*] Now really! Now upon my life and soul!

CHARTERIS. It's a fact, I assure you. Didnt it strike you as rather odd, our being up there last night, and Mrs Tranfield not with us?

CRAVEN. Well, yes it did. But you explained it. And now really Charteris, I must say your explanation was in shocking bad taste before Julia.

CHARTERIS. Never mind. It was a good, fat, healthy, bouncing lie.

CRAVEN AND CUTHBERTSON. Lie!

CHARTERIS. Didnt you suspect that?

CRAVEN. Certainly not. Did you, Jo?

CUTHBERTSON. Not at the moment.

CRAVEN. Whats more, I dont believe you. I'm sorry to have to say such a thing; but you forget that Julia was present, and didnt contradict you.

CHARTERIS. She didnt want to.

CRAVEN. Do you mean to say that my daughter deceived me?

CHARTERIS. Delicacy towards me compelled her to, Craven.

CRAVEN [*taking a very serious tone*] Now look here, Charteris: have you any proper sense of the fact that youre standing between two fathers?

CUTHBERTSON. Quite right, Dan, quite right. I repeat the question on my own account.

CHARTERIS. Well, I'm a little dazed still by standing for so long between two daughters; but I think I grasp the situation. [*Cuthbertson flings away with an exclamation of disgust*].

CRAVEN. Then I'm sorry for your manners, Charteris: thats all. [*He turns away sulkily; then suddenly flares up and comes back at Charteris*]. How dare you tell me my daughter wants to marry you? Who are you, pray, that she should have any such ambition?

CHARTERIS. Just so: youre quite right: she couldnt have made a worse choice. But she wont listen to reason. I assure you, my dear Craven, Ive said everything that fifty fathers could have said; but it's no use: she wont give me up. And if she wont listen to m e, what likelihood is there of her listening to y o u?

CRAVEN [*in angry bewilderment*] Cuthbertson: did you ever hear anything like this?

CUTHBERTSON. Never! Never!

CHARTERIS. Oh, bother! Come! dont behave like a couple of conventional old fathers: this is a serious affair. Look at these letters [*producing a letter and a letter-card*]! This [*shewing the card*] is from Grace—by the way, Cuthbertson, I wish youd ask her not to write on letter-cards: the blue color makes it so easy for Julia to pick the bits out of my waste paper basket and piece them together. Now listen. "My dear Leonard: N o t h i n g could make it worth my while to be exposed to such scenes as last night's. You had much better go back to Julia, and forget me. Yours sincerely, Grace Tranfield."

CUTHBERTSON. I approve of every word of that letter.

CHARTERIS [*turning to Craven and preparing to read the letter*] Now for Julia. [*The Colonel turns away to hide his face from Charteris, anticipating a shock, and puts his hand on a chair to steady himself*]. "My dearest boy: Nothing will make me believe that this odious woman can take my place in your heart. I send some of the letters you wrote me when we first met; and I ask you to read them. They will recall what you felt when you wrote them. You cannot have changed so much as to be indifferent to me: whoever may have struck your fancy for the moment, your heart is still mine"—and so on: you know the sort of thing—"Ever and always your loving Julia." [*The Colonel sinks on the chair, and covers his face with his hand*]. You dont suppose she's serious, do you? thats the sort of thing she writes me three times a day. [*To Cuthbertson*] Grace is in earnest though, confound it. [*He holds out Grace's letter*]. A blue card as usual! This time I shall not trust the waste paper basket. [*He goes to the fire, and throws the letters into it*].

CUTHBERTSON [*facing him with folded arms as he comes back to them*] May I ask, Mr Charteris, is this the New Humor?

CHARTERIS [*still too preoccupied with his own affairs to have any sense of the effect he is producing on the others*] Oh, stuff! Do you suppose it's a joke to be situated as I am? Youve got your head so stuffed with the New Humor and the New Woman and the New This, That, and The Other, all mixed up with your own old Adam, that youve lost your senses.

CUTHBERTSON [*strenuously*] Do you see that old man, grown grey in the honored service of his country, whose last days you have blighted?

CHARTERIS [*surprised, looking at Craven and realizing his distress with genuine concern*] I'm very sorry. Come, Craven: dont take it to heart. [*Craven shakes his head*]. I assure you it means nothing: it happens to me constantly.

CUTHBERTSON. There is only one excuse for you. You are not fully responsible for your actions. Like all advanced people, you have got neurasthenia.

CHARTERIS [*appalled*] Great Heavens! whats that?

CUTHBERTSON. I decline to explain. You know as well as I do. I'm going downstairs now to order lunch. I shall order it for three; but the third place is for Paramore, whom I have invited, not for you. [*He goes out through the dining room door*].

CHARTERIS [*putting his hand on Craven's shoulder*] Come, Craven: advise me. Youve been in this sort of fix yourself probably.

CRAVEN. Charteris: no woman writes such

a letter to a man unless he has made advances to her.

CHARTERIS [*mournfully*] How little you know the world, Colonel! The New Woman is not like that.

CRAVEN. I can only give you very old-fashioned advice, my boy; and that is that it's well to be off with the Old Woman before youre on with the New. I'm sorry you told me. You might have waited for my death: it's not far off now. [*His head droops again*].

Julia and Paramore come in from the staircase. Julia stops as she catches sight of Charteris, her face clouding, and her breast heaving. Paramore, seeing the Colonel apparently ill, hurries down to him with his bedside manner in full play.

CHARTERIS [*seeing Julia*] Oh, Lord! [*He retreats under the lee of the revolving bookstand*].

PARAMORE [*sympathetically to the Colonel, taking his wrist, and beginning to count his pulse*] Allow me.

CRAVEN [*looking up*] Eh? [*He withdraws his hand and rises rather crossly*]. No, Paramore: it's not my liver now: it's private business.

A chase begins between Julia and Charteris, all the more exciting to them because the huntress and her prey alike must conceal the real object of their movements from the others. Charteris first makes for the staircase door. Julia immediately retreats to it, barring his path. He doubles back round the bookstand, setting it whirling as he makes for the other door, Julia crossing in pursuit of him. He is about to escape when he is cut off by the return of Cuthbertson. Turning back, he sees Julia close upon him. There being nothing else for it, he bolts into the recess on Ibsen's left.

CUTHBERTSON. Good morning, Miss Craven. [*They shake hands*]. Wont you join us at lunch? Paramore's coming too.

JULIA. Thanks: I shall be very pleased. [*She strolls with affected purposelessness towards the recess. Charteris, almost trapped in it, crosses to the opposite recess by way of the fender, knocking down the fireirons with a crash as he does so*].

CRAVEN [*who has crossed to the whirling bookcase and stopped it*] What the dickens are you doing there, Charteris?

CHARTERIS. Nothing. It's such a confounded room to get about in.

JULIA [*maliciously*] Yes: isnt it? [*She is about to move to guard the staircase door when Cuthbertson offers her his arm*].

CUTHBERTSON. May I take you down?

JULIA. No, really: you know it's against the rules of the club to coddle women in any way. Whoever is nearest the door goes first.

CUTHBERTSON. Oh, well, if you insist. Come, gentlemen: let us go to lunch in the Ibsen fashion: the unsexed fashion. [*He turns and goes out, followed by Paramore, who raises his politest consulting-room laugh. Craven goes last*].

CRAVEN [*at the door, gravely*] Come, Julia.

JULIA [*with patronizing affection*] Yes, Daddy dear, presently. Dont wait for me: I'll come in a moment. [*The Colonel hesitates*]. It's all right, Daddy.

CRAVEN [*very gravely*] Dont be long, my dear. [*He goes out*].

CHARTERIS. I'm off. [*He makes a dash for the staircase door*].

JULIA [*darting at him and seizing his wrist*] Arnt you coming?

CHARTERIS. No. Unhand me, Julia. [*He tries to get away: she holds him*]. If you dont let me go, I'll scream for help.

JULIA [*reproachfully*] Leonard! [*He breaks away from her*]. Oh, how can you be so rough with me, dear! Did you get my letter?

CHARTERIS. Burnt it—

Julia turns away, struck to the heart, and buries her face in her hands.

CHARTERIS [*continuing*] —along with h e r s.

JULIA [*quickly turning again*] Hers! Has she written to you?

CHARTERIS. Yes: to break off with me on y o u r account!

JULIA [*her eyes gleaming*] Ah!

CHARTERIS. You are pleased. Wretch! Now you have lost the last scrap of my regard. [*He turns to go, but is stopped by the return of Sylvia. Julia turns away and stands pretending to read a paper which she picks up from the table*].

SYLVIA [*offhandedly*] Hallo, Charteris! how are y o u getting on? [*She takes his arm familiarly, and walks down the room with him*]. Have you seen Grace Tranfield this morning? [*Julia drops the paper, and comes a step nearer to listen*]. You generally know where she's to be found.

CHARTERIS. I shall never know any more, Sylvia. She's quarrelled with me.

SYLVIA. Sylvia! How often am I to tell you that I am not Sylvia at the club?

CHARTERIS. I forgot. I beg your pardon, Craven, old chap [*slapping her on the shoulder*].

SYLVIA. Thats better. A little overdone, but better.

JULIA. Dont be a fool, Silly.

SYLVIA. Remember, Julia, if you please,

that here we are members of the club, not sisters. I dont take liberties with you here on family grounds: dont you take any with me. [*She goes to the settee, and resumes her former place*].

CHARTERIS. Quite right, Craven. Down with the tyranny of the elder sister!

JULIA. You ought to know better than to encourage a child to make herself ridiculous, Leonard, even at my expense.

CHARTERIS [*seating himself on the edge of the table*] Your lunch will be cold, Julia.

Julia is about to retort furiously when she is checked by the reappearance of Cuthbertson at the dining room door.

CUTHBERTSON. What has become of you, Miss Craven? Your father is getting quite uneasy. We're all waiting for you.

JULIA. So I have just been reminded, thank you. [*She goes out angrily past him, Sylvia looking round to see*].

CUTHBERTSON [*looking first after her, then at Charteris*] More neurasthenia! [*He follows her*].

SYLVIA [*jumping up on her knees on the settee, and speaking over the back of it*] Whats up, Charteris? Julia been making love to you?

CHARTERIS [*speaking to her over his shoulder*] No. Jealous of Grace.

SYLVIA. Serve you right. You are an awful devil for philandering.

CHARTERIS [*calmly*] Do you consider it good club form to talk that way to a man who might nearly be your father?

SYLVIA [*knowingly*] Oh, I know you, my lad.

CHARTERIS. Then you know that I never pay any special attention to any woman.

SYLVIA [*thoughtfully*] Do you know, Leonard, I really believe you. I dont think you care a bit more for one woman than for another.

CHARTERIS. You mean I dont care a bit less for one woman than another.

SYLVIA. That makes it worse. But what I mean is that you never bother about their being only women: you talk to them just as you do to me or any other fellow. Thats the secret of your success. You cant think how sick they get of being treated with the respect due to their sex.

CHARTERIS. Ah, if Julia only had your wisdom, Craven! [*He gets off the table with a sigh, and perches himself reflectively on the step ladder*].

SYLVIA. She cant take things easy: can she, old man? But dont you be afraid of breaking her heart: she gets over her little tragedies. We found that out at home when our great sorrow came.

CHARTERIS. What was that?

SYLVIA. I mean when we learned that poor papa had Paramore's disease.

CHARTERIS. Paramore's disease! Why, whats the matter with Paramore?

SYLVIA. Oh, not a disease that he suffers from, but one that he discovered.

CHARTERIS. The liver business?

SYLVIA. Yes: thats what made Paramore's reputation, you know. Papa used to get bad occasionally; but we always thought that it was partly his Indian service, and partly his eating and drinking too much. He used to wolf down a lot in those days, did Dad. The doctor never knew what was wrong with him until Paramore discovered a dreadful little microbe in his liver. There are forty millions of them to every square inch of liver. Paramore discovered them first; and now he declares that everybody should be inoculated against them as well as vaccinated. But it was too late to inoculate poor papa. All they could do was to prolong his life for two years more by putting him on a strict diet. Poor old boy! they cut off his liquor; and he's not allowed to eat meat.

CHARTERIS. Your father appears to me to be uncommonly well.

SYLVIA. Yes: you would think he was a great deal better. But the microbe is at work, slowly but surely. In another year it will be all over. Poor old Dad! it's unfeeling to talk about him in this attitude: I must sit down properly. [*She comes down from the settee, and takes the chair near the bookstand*]. I should like papa to live for ever just to take the conceit out of Paramore. I believe he's in love with Julia.

CHARTERIS [*starting up excitedly*] In love with Julia! A ray of hope on the horizon! Do you really mean it?

SYLVIA. I should think I do. Why do you suppose he's hanging about the club today in a beautiful new coat and tie instead of attending to his patients? That lunch with Julia will finish him. He'll ask Daddy's consent before they come back: I'll bet you three to one he will, in anything you please.

CHARTERIS. Gloves?

SYLVIA. No: cigarets.

CHARTERIS. Done! But what does s h e think about it? Does she give him any encouragement?

SYLVIA. Oh, the usual thing. Enough to keep any other woman from getting him.

CHARTERIS. Just so. I understand. Now listen to me: I am going to speak as a philosopher. Julia is jealous of everybody: e v e r y-b o d y, If she saw you flirting with Paramore she'd begin to value him directly. You might play up a little, Craven, for my sake: eh?

SYLVIA [rising] Youre too awful, Leonard. For shame! However, anything to oblige a fellow Ibsenite. I'll bear your affair in mind. But I think it would be more effective if you got Grace to do it.

CHARTERIS. Think so? Hm! perhaps youre right.

THE PAGE [outside as before] Dr Paramore, Dr Paramore, Dr Paramore—

SYLVIA. They ought to get that boy's voice properly cultivated: it's a disgrace to the club. [She goes into the recess on Ibsen's left].

The page enters, carrying the British Medical Journal.

CHARTERIS [calling to the page] Dr Paramore is in the dining room.

THE PAGE. Thank you, sir. [He is about to go into the dining room when Sylvia swoops on him].

SYLVIA. Here: where are you taking that paper? It belongs to this room.

THE PAGE. It's Dr Paramore's particular orders, miss. The British Medical Journal has always to be brought to him dreckly it comes.

SYLVIA. What cheek! Charteris: oughtnt we to stop this on principle?

CHARTERIS. Certainly not. Principle's the poorest reason I know for making yourself nasty.

SYLVIA. Bosh! Ibsen!

CHARTERIS [to the page] Off with you, my boy: Dr Paramore's waiting breathless with expectation.

THE PAGE [seriously] Indeed, sir? [He hurries off].

CHARTERIS. That boy will make his way in this country. He has no sense of humor.

Grace comes in. Her dress, very convenient and businesslike, is made to please herself and serve her own purposes without the slightest regard to fashion, though by no means without a careful concern for her personal elegance. She enters briskly, like an habitually busy woman.

SYLVIA [running to her] Here you are at last, Tranfield, old girl. I've been waiting for you this last hour. I'm starving.

GRACE. All right, dear. [To Charteris] Did you get my letter?

CHARTERIS. Yes. I wish you wouldnt write on those confounded blue letter-cards.

SYLVIA [to Grace] Shall I go down first, and secure a table?

CHARTERIS [taking the reply out of Grace's mouth] Do, old boy.

SYLVIA. Dont be too long. [She goes into the dining room].

GRACE. Well?

CHARTERIS. I'm afraid to face you after last night. Can you imagine a more horrible scene? Dont you hate the very sight of me after it?

GRACE. Oh no.

CHARTERIS. Then you ought to. Ugh! it was hideous: an insult: an outrage. A nice end to all my plans for making you happy: for making you an exception to all the women who swear I have made them miserable!

GRACE [sitting down placidly] I am not at all miserable. I'm sorry; but I shant break my heart.

CHARTERIS. No: yours is a thoroughbred heart: you dont scream and cry every time it's pinched. Thats why you are the only possible woman for me.

GRACE [shaking her head] Not now. Never any more.

CHARTERIS. Never! What do you mean?

GRACE. What I say, Leonard.

CHARTERIS. Jilted again! The fickleness of the women I love is only equalled by the infernal constancy of the women who love me. Well, well! I see how it is, Grace: you cant forget that horrible scene last night. Imagine her saying I had kissed her within the last two days!

GRACE [rising eagerly] Was that not true?

CHARTERIS. True! No: a thumping lie.

GRACE. Oh, I'm so glad. That was the only thing that really hurt me.

CHARTERIS. Just why she said it. How adorable of you to care! My darling. [He seizes her hands, and presses them to his breast].

GRACE. Remember! it's all broken off.

CHARTERIS. Ah yes: you have my heart in your hands. Break it. Throw my happiness out of the window.

GRACE. Oh, Leonard, does your happiness really depend on me?

CHARTERIS [tenderly] Absolutely. [She beams with delight. A sudden revulsion comes to him at the sight: he recoils, dropping her hands and crying] Ah no: why should I lie to you? [He folds *his arms and adds firmly*] My happiness depends on nobody but myself. I can do without you.

GRACE [*nerving herself*] So you shall. Thank you for the truth. Now *I* will tell y o u the truth.

CHARTERIS [*unfolding his arms in terror*] No, please. Dont. As a philosopher, it's my business to tell other people the truth; but it's not their business to tell it to me. I dont like it; it hurts.

GRACE [*quietly*] It's only that I love you.

CHARTERIS. Ah! thats not a philosophic truth. You may tell me that as often as you like. [*He takes her in his arms*].

GRACE. Yes, Leonard; but I'm an advanced woman. [*He checks himself, and looks at her in some consternation*]. I'm what my father calls the New Woman. [*He lets her go, and stares at her*]. I quite agree with all your ideas.

CHARTERIS [*scandalized*] Thats a nice thing for a respectable woman to say! You ought to be ashamed of yourself.

GRACE. I am quite in earnest about them too, though you are not. That is why I will never marry a man I love too much. It would give him a terrible advantage over me: I should be utterly in his power. Thats what the New Woman is like. Isnt she right, Mr Philosopher?

CHARTERIS. The struggle between the Philosopher and the Man is fearful, Grace. But the Philosopher says you are right.

GRACE. I know I am right. And so we must part.

CHARTERIS. Not at all. You must marry some one else; and then I'll come and philander with you.

Sylvia comes back.

SYLVIA [*holding the door open*] Oh, I say: come along. I'm starving.

CHARTERIS. So am I. I'll lunch with you if I may.

SYLVIA. I thought you would. Ive ordered soup for three. [*Grace passes out. Sylvia continues, to Charteris*] You can watch Paramore from our table: he's pretending to read the British Medical Journal; but he must be making up his mind for the plunge: he looks green with nervousness. [*She goes out*].

CHARTERIS. Good luck to him! [*He follows her*].

The library remains unoccupied for ten minutes.

Then Julia, angry and miserable, comes in from the dining room, followed by Craven. She crosses the room tormentedly, and throws herself into a chair.

CRAVEN [*impatiently*] What is the matter? Has every one gone mad today? What do you mean by suddenly getting up from the table and tearing away like that? What does Paramore mean by reading his paper, and not answering when he's spoken to? [*Julia writhes impatiently*]. Come, come [*tenderly*]: wont my pet tell her own Daddy what—[*irritably*] what the devil is wrong with everybody. Do pull yourself together, Julia, before Cuthbertson comes. He's only paying the bill: he'll be here in a moment.

JULIA. I couldnt bear it any longer. Oh, to see them sitting there at lunch together, laughing, chatting, making game of me! I should have screamed out in another moment. I should have taken a knife and killed her. I should have—

Cuthbertson appears, stuffing the luncheon bill into his waistcoat pocket as he comes to them. He begins speaking the moment he enters.

CUTHBERTSON. I'm afraid youve had a very poor lunch, Dan. It's disheartening to see you picking at a few beans, and drinking soda water. I wonder how you live!

JULIA. Thats all he ever takes, Mr Cuthbertson, I assure you. He hates to be bothered about it.

CRAVEN. Wheres Paramore?

CUTHBERTSON. Reading his paper. I asked him wasnt he coming; but he didnt hear me. It's amazing how anything scientific absorbs him. Clever man! Monstrously clever man!

CRAVEN [*pettishly*] Oh yes, thats all very well, Jo; but it's not good manners at table: he should shut up the shop sometimes. Heaven knows I am only too anxious to forget his science, since it has pronounced my doom. [*He sits down with a melancholy air*].

CUTHBERTSON [*compassionately*] You musnt think about that, Craven: perhaps he was mistaken. [*He sighs deeply and sits down*]. But he certainly is a very clever fellow. He thinks twice before he commits himself.

They sit in silence, full of gloom. Suddenly Paramore enters, pale and in the utmost disorder, with the British Medical Journal in his clenched hand. They rise in alarm. He tries to speak, but chokes, clutches at his throat, and staggers. Cuthbertson quickly takes his chair and places it behind Paramore, who sinks into it as they crowd about him, Craven at his right shoulder,

Cuthbertson on his left, and Julia behind.

CRAVEN. Whats the matter, Paramore?

JULIA. Are you ill?

CUTHBERTSON. No bad news, I hope?

PARAMORE [*despairingly*] The worst of news! Terrible news! Fatal news! My disease—

CRAVEN [*quickly*] Do you mean my disease?

PARAMORE [*fiercely*] I mean my disease: Paramore's disease: the disease I discovered: the work of my life! Look here [*he points to the journal with a ghastly expression of horror*]! If this is true, it was all a mistake: there is no such disease.

Cuthbertson and Julia look at one another, hardly daring to believe the good news.

CRAVEN [*in strong remonstrance*] And you call this bad news! Now really, Paramore—

PARAMORE [*cutting him short hoarsely*] It's natural for you to think only of yourself. I dont blame you: all invalids are selfish. Only a scientific man can feel what I feel now. [*Writhing under a sense of intolerable injustice*] It's the fault of the wickedly sentimental laws of this country. I was not able to make experiments enough: only three dogs and a monkey. Think of that, with all Europe full of my professional rivals! men burning to prove me wrong! There is freedom in France: enlightened republican France! One Frenchman experiments on two hundred monkeys to disprove my theory. Another sacrifices £36—three hundred dogs at three francs apiece—to upset the monkey experiments. A third proves them both wrong by a single experiment in which he gets the temperature of a camel's liver sixty degrees below zero. And now comes this cursed Italian who has ruined me. He has a government grant to buy animals with, besides having the run of the largest hospital in Italy. [*With desperate resolution*] But I wont be beaten by any Italian. I'll go to Italy myself. I'll rediscover my disease: I know it exists; I feel it; and I'll prove it if I have to experiment on every mortal animal thats got a liver at all. [*He folds his arms and breathes hard at them*].

CRAVEN [*his sense of injury growing on him*] Am I to understand, Paramore, that you took it on yourself to pass sentence of death on me: yes, of Death! on the strength of three dogs and an infernal monkey?

PARAMORE [*utterly contemptuous of Craven's narrow personal view of the matter*] Yes. That was all I could get a license for.

CRAVEN. Now upon my soul, Paramore, I'm vexed at this. I dont wish to be unfriendly; but I'm extremely vexed, really. Why, confound it, do you realize what youve done? Youve cut off my meat and drink for a year! made me an object of public scorn! a miserable vegetarian and teetotaller.

PARAMORE [*rising*] Well, you can make up for lost time now. [*Bitterly, shewing Craven the Journal*] There! you can read for yourself. The camel was fed on beef dissolved in alcohol; and he gained half a ton on it. Eat and drink as much as you please. [*Still unable to stand without support, he makes his way past Cuthbertson to the revolving bookcase, and stands there with his back to them, leaning on it with his head on his hands*].

CRAVEN [*grumbling*] Oh yes: it's very easy for you to talk, Paramore. But what am I to say to the Humanitarian societies and the Vegetarian societies that have made me Vice President?

CUTHBERTSON [*chuckling*] Aha! You made a virtue of it, did you, Dan?

CRAVEN [*warmly*] I made a virtue of necessity, Jo. No one can blame me.

JULIA [*soothing him*] Well, never mind, Daddy. Come back to the dining room, and have a good beefsteak.

CRAVEN [*shuddering*] Ugh! [*Plaintively*] No: Ive lost my old manly taste for it. My very nature's been corrupted by living on pap. [*To Paramore*] Thats what comes of all this vivisection. You go experimenting on horses; and of course the result is that you try to get me into condition by feeding me on beans.

PARAMORE [*curtly, without changing his position*] Well, if theyve done you good, so much the better for you.

CRAVEN [*querulously*] Thats all very well; but it's very vexing. You dont half see how serious it is to make a man believe that he has only another year to live: you really dont, Paramore: I cant help saying it. Ive made my will, which was altogether unnecessary; and Ive been reconciled to a lot of people I'd quarrelled with: people I cant stand under ordinary circumstances. Then Ive let the girls get round me at home to an extent I should never have done if I'd had my life before me. Ive done a lot of serious thinking and reading and extra church going. And now it turns out simple waste of time. On my soul, it's too disgusting: I'd far rather die like a man when I said I would.

PARAMORE [*as before*] Perhaps you may. Your heart's shaky, if thats any satisfaction to you.

CRAVEN [*offended*] You must excuse me, Paramore, if I say that I no longer feel any confidence in your opinion as a medical man. [*Paramore's eye flashes: he straightens himself and listens*]. I paid you a pretty stiff fee for that consultation when you condemned me; and I cant say I think you gave me value for it.

PARAMORE [*turning and facing Craven with dignity*] Thats unanswerable, Colonel Craven. I shall return the fee.

CRAVEN. Oh, it's not the money; but I think you ought to realize your position. [*Paramore turns stiffly away. Craven follows him impulsively, exclaiming remorsefully*] Well, perhaps it was a nasty thing of me to allude to it. [*He offers Paramore his hand*].

PARAMORE [*conscientiously taking it*] Not at all. You are quite in the right, Colonel Craven: my diagnosis was wrong; and I must take the consequences.

CRAVEN [*holding his hand*] No, dont say that. It was natural enough: my liver is enough to set any man's diagnosis wrong. [*A long handshake, very trying to Paramore's nerves. Paramore then retires to the recess on Ibsen's left, and throws himself on the divan with a half suppressed sob, bending over The British Medical Journal with his head on his hands and his elbows on his knees*].

CUTHBERTSON [*who has been rejoicing with Julia at the other side of the room*] Well, lets say no more about it. I congratulate you, Craven, and hope you may long be spared. [*Craven offers his hand*]. No, Dan: your daughter first. [*He takes Julia's hand gently and hands her across to Craven, into whose arms she flies with a gush of feeling*].

JULIA. Dear old Daddy!

CRAVEN. Ah, is Julia glad that the old Dad is let off for a few years more?

JULIA [*almost crying*] Oh, so glad! so glad! *Cuthbertson sobs audibly. The Colonel is affected. Sylvia, entering from the dining room, stops abruptly at the door on seeing the three. Paramore, in the recess, escapes her notice.*

SYLVIA. Hallo!

CRAVEN. Tell her the news, Julia: it would sound ridiculous from me. [*He goes to the weeping Cuthbertson, and pats him consolingly on the shoulder*].

JULIA. Silly: only think! Dad's not ill at all.

It was only a mistake of Dr Paramore's. Oh, dear! [*She catches Craven's left hand and stoops to kiss it, his right hand being still on Cuthbertson's shoulder*].

SYLVIA [*contemptuously*] I knew it. Of course it was nothing but eating too much. I always said Paramore was an ass. [*Sensation. The group of Cuthbertson, Craven, and Julia breaks up as they turn in dismay*].

PARAMORE [*without malice*] Never mind, Miss Craven. That is what is being said all over Europe now. Never mind.

SYLVIA [*a little abashed*] I'm so sorry, Dr Paramore. You must excuse a daughter's feelings.

CRAVEN [*huffed*] It evidently doesnt make much difference to you, Sylvia.

SYLVIA. I'm not going to be sentimental over it, Dad, you may bet. [*Coming to Craven*] Besides, I knew it was nonsense all along. [*Petting him*] Poor dear old Dad! why should your days be numbered any more than any one else's? [*He pats her cheek, mollified. Julia impatiently turns away from them*] Come to the smoking room; and lets see what you can do after teetotalling for a year.

CRAVEN [*playfully*] Vulgar little girl! [*He pinches her ear*]. Shall we come, Jo! Youll be the better for a pick-me-up after all this emotion.

CUTHBERTSON. I'm not ashamed of it, Dan. It has done me good. [*He goes up to the table and shakes his fist at the bust over the mantelpiece*]. It would do you good too, if you had eyes and ears to take it in.

CRAVEN [*astonished*] Who?

SYLVIA. Why, good old Henrik, of course.

CRAVEN [*puzzled*] Henrik?

CUTHBERTSON [*impatiently*] Ibsen, man: Ibsen. [*He goes out by the staircase door, followed by Sylvia, who kisses her hand to the bust as she passes. Craven stares blankly after her, and then at the bust. Giving the problem up as insoluble, he shakes his head and follows them. Near the door, he checks himself, and comes back*].

CRAVEN [*softly*] By the way, Paramore?

PARAMORE [*rousing himself with an effort*] Yes?

CRAVEN. You werent in earnest that time about my heart, were you?

PARAMORE. Oh nothing, nothing. Theres a slight murmur: mitral valves a little worn perhaps; but theyll last your time if youre careful. Dont smoke too much.

CRAVEN. What! More privations! Now really,

Paramore, really—

PARAMORE [*rising distractedly*] Excuse me: I cant pursue the subject. I—I—

JULIA. Dont worry him now, Daddy.

CRAVEN. Well, well: I wont. [*He comes to Paramore, who is pacing restlessly up and down the middle of the room*]. Come, Paramore! I'm not selfish, believe me: I can feel for your disappointment. But you must face it like a man. And after all, now really, doesnt this shew that theres a lot of rot about modern science? Between ourselves, you know, it's horribly cruel: you must admit that it's a deuced nasty thing to go ripping up and crucifying camels and monkeys. It must blunt all the finer feelings sooner or later.

PARAMORE [*turning on him*] How many camels and horses and men were ripped up in that Soudan campaign where you won your Victoria Cross, Colonel Craven?

CRAVEN [*firing up*] That was fair fighting: a very different thing, Paramore.

PARAMORE. Yes: Martinis and machine guns against naked spearmen.

CRAVEN [*hotly*] Naked spearmen can kill, Paramore. I risked my life: dont forget that.

PARAMORE [*with equal spirit*] And I have risked mine, as all doctors do, oftener than any soldier.

CRAVEN [*handsomely*] Thats true. I didnt think of that. I beg your pardon, Paramore: I'll never say another word against your profession. But I hope youll let me stick to the good oldfashioned shaking-up treatment for my liver: a clinking run across country with the hounds.

PARAMORE [*with bitter irony*] Isnt that rather cruel? a pack of dogs ripping up a fox?

JULIA [*coming coaxingly between them*] Oh please dont begin arguing again. Do go to the smoking room, Daddy: Mr Cuthbertson will wonder what has become of you.

CRAVEN. Very well, very well: I'll go. But youre really not reasonable today, Paramore, to talk that way of fair sport—

JULIA. Sh—sh [*coaxing him towards the door*].

CRAVEN. Well, well, I'm off. [*He goes good-humoredly, pushed out by Julia*].

JULIA [*turning at the door with her utmost witchery of manner*] Dont look so disappointed, Dr Paramore. Cheer up. Youve been most kind to us; and youve done papa a lot of good.

PARAMORE [*delighted, rushing over to her*] How beautiful it is of you to say that to me, Miss Craven!

JULIA. I hate to see any one unhappy. I cant bear unhappiness. [*She runs out, casting a Parthian glance at him as she flies*].

Paramore stands enraptured, gazing after her through the glass door. Whilst he is thus absorbed, Charteris comes in from the dining room and touches him on the arm.

PARAMORE [*starting*] Eh? Whats the matter?

CHARTERIS [*significantly*] Charming woman, isnt she, Paramore? [*Looking admiringly at him*] How have you managed to fascinate her?

PARAMORE. I! Do you really mean—[*He looks at him; then recovers himself, and adds coldly*] Excuse me: this is a subject I do not care to jest about. [*He walks away from Charteris, and sits down in the nearest easy chair, reading his journal to intimate that he does not wish to pursue the conversation*].

CHARTERIS [*ignoring the hint, and coolly sitting down beside him*] Why dont you get married, Paramore? You know it's a scandalous thing for a man in your profession to be single.

PARAMORE [*shortly, still pretending to read*] Thats my own business: not yours.

CHARTERIS. Not at all: it's pre-eminently a social question. Youre going to get married, arnt you?

PARAMORE. Not that I am aware of.

CHARTERIS [*alarmed*] No! Dont say that. Why?

PARAMORE [*rising angrily and rapping one of the* SILENCE *placards*] Allow me to call your attention to that. [*He crosses the room to the easy chair near the revolving bookstand, and flings himself into it with determined hostility*].

CHARTERIS [*following him, too deeply concerned to mind the rebuff*] Paramore: you alarm me more than I can say. Youve muffed this business somehow. I fully expected to find you a joyful accepted suitor.

PARAMORE [*angrily*] Yes, you have been watching me because you admire Miss Craven yourself. Well, you may go in and win now. You will be pleased to hear that I am a ruined man.

CHARTERIS. You! Ruined! How? The turf?

PARAMORE [*contemptuously*] The turf!! Certainly not.

CHARTERIS. Paramore: if the loan of all I possess will help you over this difficulty, you have only to ask.

PARAMORE [*rising in surprise*] Charteris! I— [*Suspiciously*] Are you joking?

CHARTERIS. Why on earth do you always suspect me of joking? I never was more serious in my life.

PARAMORE [*shamed by Charteris's generosity*] Then I beg your pardon. I thought the news would please you.

CHARTERIS [*deprecating this injustice to his good feeling*] My dear fellow!

PARAMORE. I see I was wrong. I am really very sorry. [*They shake hands*]. And now you may as well learn the truth. I had rather you heard it from me than from the gossip of the club. My liver discovery has been—er—er— [*he cannot bring himself to say it*].

CHARTERIS [*helping him out*] Confirmed? [*Sadly*] I see: the poor Colonel's doomed.

PARAMORE. No: on the contrary, it has been —er—called in question. The Colonel now believes himself to be in perfectly good health; and my friendly relations with the Cravens are entirely spoilt.

CHARTERIS. Who told him about it?

PARAMORE. I did, of course, the moment I read the news in this. [*He shews the journal, and puts it down on the bookstand*].

CHARTERIS. Why, man, youve been a messenger of glad tidings! Didnt you congratulate him?

PARAMORE [*scandalized*] Congratulate him! Congratulate a man on the worst blow pathological science has received for the last three hundred years!

CHARTERIS. No, no, no. Congratulate him on having his life saved. Congratulate Julia on having her father spared. Swear that your discovery and your reputation are as nothing to you compared with the pleasure of restoring happiness to the household in which the best hopes of your life are centred. Confound it, man, youll never get married if you cant turn things to account with a woman in these little ways.

PARAMORE [*gravely*] Excuse me; but my self-respect is dearer to me even than Miss Craven. I cannot trifle with scientific questions for the sake of a personal advantage. [*He turns away coldly, and goes towards the table*].

CHARTERIS. Well, this beats me! The Nonconformist conscience is bad enough; but the scientific conscience is the very devil. [*He follows Paramore, and puts his arm familiarly round his shoulder, bringing him back again whilst he speaks*]. Now look here, Paramore: I have no conscience in that sense at all: I loathe it as I loathe all the snares of idealism; but I have some common humanity and common sense. [*He replaces him in the easy chair, and sits down opposite him*]. Come! what is a really scientific theory? A true theory, isnt it?

PARAMORE. No doubt.

CHARTERIS. For instance, you have a theory about Craven's liver, eh?

PARAMORE. I still believe that to be a true theory, though it has been upset for the moment.

CHARTERIS. And you have a theory that it would be pleasant to be married to Julia?

PARAMORE. I suppose so. In a sense.

CHARTERIS. That theory also will be upset, probably, before youre a year older.

PARAMORE. Always cynical, Charteris.

CHARTERIS. Never mind that. Now it's a perfectly damnable thing for you to hope that your liver theory is true, because it amounts to hoping that Craven will die an agonizing death.

PARAMORE. And always paradoxical, Charteris.

CHARTERIS. Well, at least youll admit that it's amiable and human to hope that your theory about Julia is right, because it amounts to hoping that she may live happily ever after.

PARAMORE. I do hope that with all my soul —[*correcting himself*] I mean with all my function of hoping.

CHARTERIS. Then, since both theories are equally scientific, why not devote yourself, as a humane man, to proving the amiable theory rather than the damnable one?

PARAMORE. But how?

CHARTERIS. I'll tell you. You think I'm fond of Julia myself. So I am; but then I'm fond of everybody; so I dont count. Besides, if you try the scientific experiment of asking her whether she loves me, she'll tell you that she hates and despises me. So I'm out of the running. Nevertheless, like you, I hope that she may be happy with all my—what did you call your soul?

PARAMORE [*impatiently*] Oh, go on, go on: finish what you were going to say.

CHARTERIS [*suddenly affecting complete indifference, and rising carelessly*] I dont know that I was going to say anything more. If I were you I should invite the Cravens to tea in honor of the Colonel's escape from a horrible doom. By the way, if youve done with that British Medical Journal, I should like to see how theyve smashed your theory up.

PARAMORE [*wincing as he also rises*] Oh, certainly, if you wish it. I have no objection. [*He takes the journal from the bookstand*]. I admit that the Italian experiments apparently upset my theory. But please remember that it is doubtful—extremely doubtful—whether anything can be proved by experiments on animals. [*He hands Charteris the journal*].

CHARTERIS [*taking it*] It doesnt matter: I dont intend to make any. [*He retires to the recess on Ibsen's right, picking up the step-ladder as he passes and placing it so that he is able to use it for a leg rest as he settles himself to read on the divan with his back to the corner of the mantelpiece*].

Paramore goes to the dining room door, and is about to leave the library when he meets Grace entering.

GRACE. How do you do, Dr Paramore? So glad to see you. [*They shake hands*].

PARAMORE. Thanks. Quite well, I hope?

GRACE. Quite, thank you. Youre looking overworked. We must take more care of you, Doctor.

PARAMORE. You are too kind.

GRACE. It is you who are too kind—to your patients. You sacrifice yourself. Have a little rest. Come and talk to me. Tell me all about the latest scientific discoveries, and what I ought to read to keep myself up to date. But perhaps youre busy.

PARAMORE. No, not at all. Only too delighted. [*They go into the recess on Ibsen's left, and sit there chatting in whispers, very confidentially*].

CHARTERIS. How they all love a doctor! They can say what they like to him. [*Julia returns, but does not look his way. He takes his feet from the ladder and sits up*]. Whew! [*Julia wanders along his side of the room, apparently looking for some one. Charteris steals after her*].

CHARTERIS [*in a low voice*] Looking for me, Julia?

JULIA [*starting violently*] Oh! How you startled me!

CHARTERIS. Sh! I want to shew you something. Look! [*He points to the pair in the recess*].

JULIA [*jealously*] That woman!

CHARTERIS. My young woman, carrying off your young man.

JULIA. What do you mean? Do you dare insinuate—

CHARTERIS. Sh—sh—sh! Dont disturb them.

Paramore rises; takes down a book; and sits on a footstool at Grace's feet.

JULIA. Why are they whispering like that?

CHARTERIS. Because they dont want any one to hear what they are saying to one another.

Paramore shews Grace a picture in the book. They both laugh heartily over it.

JULIA. What is he shewing her?

CHARTERIS. Probably a diagram of the liver. [*Julia, with an exclamation of disgust, makes for the recess. Charteris catches her sleeve*]. Stop: be careful, Julia. [*She frees herself by giving him a push which upsets him into the easy chair; then crosses to the recess, and stands looking down at Grace and Paramore from the corner next the fireplace*].

JULIA [*with suppressed fury*] You seem to have found a very interesting book, Dr. Paramore. [*They look up, astonished*]. May I ask what it is? [*She stoops swiftly; snatches the book from Paramore; and comes down to the table quickly to look at it whilst they rise in amazement*]. Good Words! [*She flings it on the table, and sweeps back past Charteris, exclaiming contemptuously*] You fool! [*Paramore and Grace, meanwhile, come from the recess: Paramore bewildered: Grace very determined*].

CHARTERIS [*aside to Julia as he gets out of the easy chair*] Idiot! She'll have you turned out of the club for this.

JULIA [*terrified*] She cant: can she?

PARAMORE. What is the matter, Miss Craven?

CHARTERIS [*hastily*] Nothing. My fault: a stupid practical joke. I beg your pardon and Mrs Tranfield's.

GRACE [*firmly*] It is not your fault in the least, Mr Charteris. Dr Paramore: will you oblige me by finding Sylvia Craven for me, if you can?

PARAMORE [*hesitating*] But—

GRACE. I want you to go now, if you please.

PARAMORE [*succumbing*] Certainly. [*He bows and goes out by the staircase door*].

GRACE. You are going with him, Charteris.

JULIA. You will not leave me here to be insulted by this woman, Mr Charteris. [*She takes his arm as if to go with him*].

GRACE. When two ladies quarrel in this club, it is against the rules to settle it when there are gentlemen present: especially the gentleman they are quarrelling about. I presume you do not wish to break that rule, Miss Craven. [*Julia sullenly drops Charteris's arm. Grace turns to Charteris, and adds*] Now! Trot off.

CHARTERIS. Certainly. Certainly. [*He follows Paramore ignominiously*].

GRACE [*to Julia, with quiet peremptoriness*] Now: what have you to say to me?

JULIA [*suddenly throwing herself tragically on her knees at Grace's feet*] Dont take him from me. Oh dont—dont be so cruel. Give him back to me. You dont know what youre doing—what our past has been—how I love him. You dont know—

GRACE. Get up; and dont be a fool. Suppose any one comes in and sees you in that ridiculous attitude!

JULIA. I hardly know what I'm doing. I dont care what I'm doing: I'm too miserable. Oh, wont you listen to me?

GRACE. Do you suppose I am a man, to be imposed on by this sort of rubbish?

JULIA [*getting up and looking darkly at her*] You intend to take him from me, then?

GRACE. Do you expect me to help you to keep him after the way you have behaved?

JULIA [*trying her theatrical method in a milder form: reasonable and impulsively goodnatured instead of tragic*] I know I was wrong to act as I did last night. I beg your pardon. I am sorry. I was mad.

GRACE. Not a bit mad. You calculated to an inch how far you could go. When he is present to stand between us and play out the scene with you, I count for nothing. When we are alone, you fall back on your natural way of getting anything you want: crying for it like a baby until it is given to you.

JULIA [*with unconcealed hatred*] You learnt this from him.

GRACE. I learnt it from yourself, last night and now. How I hate to be a woman when I see, by you, what wretched childish creatures we are! Those two men would cut you dead and have you turned out of the club if you were a man, and had behaved in such a way before them. But because you are only a woman, they are forbearing! sympathetic! gallant! Oh, if you had a scrap of self-respect, their indulgence would make you creep all over. I understand now why Charteris has no respect for women.

JULIA. How dare you say that?

GRACE. Dare! I love him. And I have refused his offer to marry me.

JULIA [*incredulous, but hopeful*] You have refused!

GRACE. Yes; because I will not give myself to any man who has learnt to treat women from you and your like. I can do without his love, but not without his respect; and it is your fault that I cannot have both. Take his love then; and much good may it do you! Run to him, and beg him to take you back.

JULIA. Oh, what a liar you are! He loved me before he ever saw you—before he ever dreamt of you, you pitiful thing. Do you think *I* need go down on my knees to men to make them come to me? That may be your experience, you creature with no figure: it is not mine. There are dozens of men who would give their souls for a look from me. I have only to lift my finger.

GRACE. Lift it then; and see whether h e will come.

JULIA. How I should like to kill you! I dont know why I dont.

GRACE. Yes: you like to get out of your difficulties at other people's expense. It is something to boast of, isnt it, that dozens of men would make love to you if you invited them?

JULIA [*sullenly*] I suppose it's better to be like you, with a cold heart and a serpent's tongue. Thank Heaven, I have a heart: that is why you can hurt me as I cannot hurt you. And you are a coward. You are giving him up to me without a struggle.

GRACE. Yes: it is for you to struggle. I wish you success. [*She turns away contemptuously, and is going to the dining room door when Sylvia enters on the opposite side, followed by Cuthbertson and Craven, who come to Julia, whilst Sylvia crosses to Grace*].

SYLVIA. Here I am, sent by the faithful Paramore. He hinted that I'd better bring the elder members of the family too: here they are. Whats the row?

GRACE [*quietly*] Nothing, dear. There's no row.

JULIA [*hysterically, tottering and stretching out her arms to Craven*] Daddy!

CRAVEN [*taking her in his arms*] My precious! Whats the matter?

JULIA [*through her tears*] She's going to have me expelled from the club; and we shall all be disgraced. Can she do it, Daddy?

CRAVEN. Well, really, the rules of this club are so extraordinary that I dont know. [*To Grace*] May I ask, madam, whether you have any complaint to make of my daughter's conduct?

GRACE. Yes, sir. I am going to complain to

the committee.

SYLVIA. I knew youd overdo it some day, Julia.

CRAVEN. Do you know this lady, Jo?

CUTHBERTSON. This is my daughter, Mrs Tranfield, Dan. Grace: this is my old friend Colonel Craven.

Grace and Craven bow to one another constrainedly.

CRAVEN. May I ask the ground of complaint, Mrs Tranfield?

GRACE. Simply that Miss Craven is essentially a womanly woman, and, as such, not eligible for membership.

JULIA. It's false. I'm not a womanly woman. I was guaranteed when I joined just as you were.

GRACE. By Mr Charteris, I think, at your own request. I shall call him as a witness to your thoroughly womanly conduct just now in his presence and Dr Paramore's.

CRAVEN. Cuthbertson: are they joking? or am I dreaming?

CUTHBERTSON [*grimly*] It's real, Dan: youre awake.

SYLVIA [*taking Craven's left arm, and hugging it affectionately*] Dear old Rip Van Winkle!

CRAVEN. Well, Mrs Tranfield, all I can say is that I hope you will succeed in establishing your complaint, and that Julia may soon see the last of this most outrageous institution.

Charteris returns.

CHARTERIS [*at the door*] May I come in?

SYLVIA. Yes: youre wanted here as a witness. [*Charteris comes in, and places himself with evident misgiving between Julia and Grace*]. It's a bad case of womanliness.

GRACE [*half aside to him, significantly*] You understand? [*Julia, watching them jealously, leaves her father and gets close to Charteris. Grace adds aloud*] I shall expect your support before the committee.

JULIA. If you have a scrap of manhood in you you will take my part.

CHARTERIS. But then I shall be expelled for being a manly man. Besides, I'm on the committee myself: I cant act as judge and witness too. You must apply to Paramore: he saw it all.

GRACE. Where is Dr Paramore?

CHARTERIS. Just gone home.

JULIA [*with sudden resolution*] What is Dr Paramore's number in Savile Row?

CHARTERIS. Seventy-nine.

Julia goes out quickly by the staircase door,

to their astonishment. Charteris follows her to the door, which swings back in his face, leaving him staring after her through the glass.

SYLVIA [*running to Grace*] Grace: go after her. Dont let her get beforehand with Paramore. She'll tell him the most heartbreaking stories about how she's been treated, and get round him completely.

CRAVEN [*thundering*] Sylvia! Is that the way to speak of your sister, miss? [*Grace squeezes Sylvia's hand to console her; takes a magazine from the table; and sits down calmly. Sylvia posts herself behind Grace's chair, leaning over the back to watch the ensuing colloquy between the three men*]. I assure you, Mrs Tranfield, Dr Paramore has just invited us all to take afternoon tea with him; and if my daughter has gone to his house, she is simply taking advantage of his invitation to extricate herself from a very embarrassing scene here. We're all going there. Come, Sylvia. [*He turns to go, followed by Cuthbertson*].

CHARTERIS [*in consternation*] Stop! [*He gets between Craven and Cuthbertson*]. What hurry is there? Cant you give the man time?

CRAVEN. Time! What for?

CHARTERIS [*talking foolishly in his agitation*] Well, to get a little rest, you know: a busy professional man like that! He's not had a moment to himself all day.

CRAVEN. But Julia's with him.

CHARTERIS. Well, no matter: she's only one person. And she ought to have an opportunity of laying her case before him. As a member of the committee, I think thats only just. Be reasonable, Craven: give him half an hour.

CUTHBERTSON [*sternly*] What do you mean by this, Charteris?

CHARTERIS. Nothing, I assure you. Only common consideration for poor Paramore.

CUTHBERTSON. Youve some motive. Craven: I strongly advise that we go at once. [*He grasps the door handle*].

CHARTERIS [*coaxingly*] No, no. [*He puts his hand persuasively on Craven's arm, adding*] It's not good for your liver, Craven, to rush about immediately after lunch.

CUTHBERTSON. His liver's cured. Come on, Craven. [*He opens the door*].

CHARTERIS [*catching Cuthbertson by the sleeve*] Cuthbertson: youre mad. Paramore's going to propose to Julia. We m u s t give him time: he's not the man to come to the point in three seconds as you or I would. [*Turning to Craven*] Dont you see? that will get me out of the difficulty we were speaking of this morning: you and I and Cuthbertson. You remember?

CRAVEN. Now is this a thing to say plump out before everybody, Charteris? Confound it, have you no decency?

CUTHBERTSON [*severely*] None whatever.

CHARTERIS [*turning to Cuthbertson*] No: dont be unkind, Cuthbertson. Back me up. My future, her future, Mrs Tranfield's future, Craven's future, everybody's future depends on Julia being Paramore's affianced bride when we arrive. He's certain to propose if youll only give him time. You know youre a kindly and sensible man as well as a deucedly clever one, Cuthbertson, in spite of all the nonsense you pick up in the theatre. Say a word for me.

CRAVEN. I'm quite willing to leave the decision to Cuthbertson; and I have no doubt whatever as to what that decision will be.

Cuthbertson carefully shuts the door, and comes back into the room with an air of weighty reflection.

CUTHBERTSON. I am now going to speak as a man of the world: that is, without moral responsibility.

CRAVEN. Quite so, Jo. Of course.

CUTHBERTSON. Therefore, though I have no sympathy whatever with Charteris's views, I think we can do no harm by waiting—say ten minutes or so. [*He sits down*].

CHARTERIS [*delighted*] Ah, there's nobody like you after all, Cuthbertson, when theres a difficult situation to be judged. [*He sits down on the settee back*].

CRAVEN [*deeply disappointed*] Oh well, Jo, if that is your decision, I must keep my word and abide by it. Better sit down and make ourselves comfortable, I suppose. [*He sits also, under protest*].

A pause, very trying for the three men.

GRACE [*looking up from her magazine*] Dont fidget, Leonard.

CHARTERIS [*slipping off the settee back*] I cant help it: I'm too restless. The fact is, Julia has made me so nervous that I cant answer for myself until I know her decision. Mrs Tranfield will tell you what a time Ive had lately. Julia's really a most determined woman, you know.

CRAVEN [*starting up*] Well, upon my life! Upon my honor and conscience!! Now really!!! I shall go this instant. Come on, Sylvia. Cuthbertson: I hope youll mark your sense of this

sort of thing by coming on to Paramore's with us at once. [*He marches to the door*].

CHARTERIS [*desperately*] Craven: youre trifling with your daughter's happiness. I ask only five minutes more.

CRAVEN. Not five seconds, sir. Fie for shame, Charteris! [*He goes out*].

CUTHBERTSON [*to Charteris, as he passes him on his way to the door*] Bungler! [*He follows Craven*].

SYLVIA. Serve you right, you duffer! [*She follows Cuthbertson*].

CHARTERIS. Oh, these headstrong old men! [*To Grace*] Nothing to be done now but go with them, and delay the Colonel as much as possible. So I'm afraid I must leave you.

GRACE [*rising*] Not at all. Paramore invited me, too.

CHARTERIS [*aghast*] You dont mean to say youre coming!

GRACE. Most certainly. Do you suppose I will let that woman think I am afraid to meet her? [*Charteris sinks on a chair with a prolonged groan*]. Come: dont be silly: youll not overtake the Colonel if you delay any longer.

CHARTERIS. Why was I ever born, child of misfortune that I am! [*He rises despairingly*]. Well, if you must come, you must. [*He offers his arm, which she takes*]. By the way, what happened after I left you?

GRACE. I gave her a lecture on her behavior which she will remember to the last day of her life.

CHARTERIS [*approvingly*] That was right, darling. [*He slips his arm round her waist*] Just one kiss. To soothe me.

GRACE [*complacently offering her cheek*] Foolish boy! [*He kisses her*]. Now come along. [*They go out together*].

ACT III

Paramore's reception room in Savile Row. Viewing the room from the front windows, the door is seen in the opposite wall near the left hand corner. Another door, a light noiseless one covered with green baize, leading to the consulting room, is in the right hand wall towards the back. The fireplace is on the left. At the nearer corner of it a couch is placed at right angles to the wall, settlewise. At the other corner, an easy chair. On the right the wall is occupied by a bookcase, further forward than the green baize door. Beyond the door is a cabinet of anatomical pre-

parations, with a framed photograph of Rembrandt's School of Anatomy hanging on the wall above it. In front, a little to the right, a teatable.

Paramore is seated in a round-backed chair, on castors, pouring out tea. Julia sits opposite him, with her back to the fire. He is in high spirits: she very downcast.

PARAMORE [*handing her the cup he has just filled*] There! Making tea is one of the few things I consider myself able to do thoroughly well. Cake?

JULIA. No, thank you. I dont like sweet things. [*She sets down the cup untasted*].

PARAMORE. Anything wrong with the tea?

JULIA. No. It's very nice.

PARAMORE. I'm afraid I'm a bad entertainer. The fact is, I am too professional. I shine only in consultation. I almost wish you had something serious the matter with you; so that you might call out my knowledge and sympathy. As it is, I can only admire you, and feel how pleasant it is to have you here.

JULIA [*bitterly*] And pet me, and say pretty things to me. I wonder you dont offer me a saucer of milk at once.

PARAMORE [*astonished*] Why?

JULIA. Because you seem to regard me very much as if I were a Persian cat.

PARAMORE [*in strong remonstrance*] Miss Cra—

JULIA [*cutting him short*] Oh, you neednt protest. I'm used to it: it's the sort of attachment I seem always to inspire. [*Ironically*] You cant think how flattering it is.

PARAMORE. My dear Miss Craven, what a cynical thing to say! You! who are loved at first sight by the people in the street as you pass. Why, in the club I can tell by the faces of the men whether you have been lately in the room or not.

JULIA [*shrinking fiercely*] Oh, I hate that look in their faces. Do you know that I have never had one human being care for me since I was born?

PARAMORE. Thats not true, Miss Craven. Even if it were true of your father, and of Charteris, who loves you madly in spite of your dislike for him, it is not true of me.

JULIA [*startled*] Who told you that about Charteris?

PARAMORE. Why, he himself.

JULIA [*with deep, poignant conviction*] He cares for only one person in the world; and that is himself. There is not in his whole nature one unselfish spot. He would not

spend one hour of his real life with—[*a sob chokes her: she rises passionately, crying*] You are all alike, every one of you. Even my father only makes a pet of me. [*She goes away to the fireplace, and stands with her back to him to hide her face*].

PARAMORE [*following her humbly*] I dont deserve this from you: indeed I do not.

JULIA [*rating him*] Then why do you gossip about me behind my back with Charteris?

PARAMORE. We said nothing disparaging of you. Nobody shall ever do that in my presence. We spoke of the subject nearest our hearts.

JULIA. His heart! Oh God, his heart! [*She sits down on the couch, and covers her face*].

PARAMORE [*sadly*] I am afraid you love him, for all that, Miss Craven.

JULIA [*raising her head instantly*] If he says that, he lies. If ever you hear it said that I cared for him, contradict it: it is false.

PARAMORE [*quickly advancing to her*] Miss Craven: is the way clear for me then?

JULIA [*losing interest in the conversation, and looking crossly away from him*]. What do you mean?

PARAMORE [*impetuously*] You must see what I mean. Contradict the rumor of your attachment to Charteris, not by words—it has gone too far for that—but by becoming my wife. [*Earnestly*] Believe me: it is not merely your beauty that attracts me [*Julia, interested, looks up at him quickly*]: I know other beautiful women. It is your heart, your sincerity, your sterling reality, [*Julia rises and gazes at him, breathless with a new hope*] your great gifts of character that are only half developed because you have never been understood by those about you.

JULIA [*looking intently at him, and yet beginning to be derisively sceptical in spite of herself*] Have you really seen all that in me?

PARAMORE. I have felt it. I have been alone in the world; and I need you, Julia. That is how I have divined that you, also, are alone in the world.

JULIA [*with theatrical pathos*] You are right there. I am indeed alone in the world.

PARAMORE [*timidly approaching her*] With you I should not be alone. And you? with me?

JULIA. You! [*She gets quickly out of his reach, taking refuge at the teatable*]. No, no. I cant bring myself— [*She breaks off, perplexed, and looks uneasily about her*]. Oh, I dont know what to do. You will expect too much from me. [*She sits down*].

PARAMORE. I have more faith in you than you have in yourself. Your nature is richer than you think.

JULIA [*doubtfully*] Do you really believe that I am not the shallow, jealous, devilish tempered creature they all pretend I am?

PARAMORE. I am ready to place my happiness in your hands. Does that prove what I think of you?

JULIA. Yes: I believe you really care for me. [*He approaches her eagerly: she has a violent revulsion, and rises with her hands up as if to beat him off, crying*] No, no, no, no. I cannot. It's impossible. [*She goes towards the door*].

PARAMORE [*looking wistfully after her*] Is it Charteris?

JULIA [*stopping and turning*] Ah, you think that! [*She comes back*]. Listen to me. If I say yes, will you promise not to touch me? Will you give me time to accustom myself to our new relations?

PARAMORE. I promise most faithfully. I would not press you for the world.

JULIA. Then—then— Yes: I promise.

PARAMORE. Oh, how unspeakably hap—

JULIA [*stopping his raptures*] No: not another word. Let us forget it. [*She resumes her seat at the table*]. I havnt touched my tea. [*He hastens to his former seat. As he passes, she puts her left hand on his arm and says*] Be good to me, Percy: I need it sorely.

PARAMORE [*transported*] You have called me Percy! Hurrah!

Charteris and Craven come in. Paramore hastens to meet them, beaming.

PARAMORE. Delighted to see you here with me, Colonel Craven. And you too, Charteris. Sit down. [*The Colonel sits down on the end of the couch*]. Where are the others?

CHARTERIS. Sylvia has dragged Cuthbertson off into the Burlington Arcade to buy some caramels. He likes to encourage her in eating caramels: he thinks it's a womanly taste. Besides, he likes them himself. Theyll be here presently. [*He strolls across to the cabinet, and pretends to study the Rembrandt photograph, so as to be as far out of Julia's reach as possible.*]

CRAVEN. Yes; and Charteris has been trying to persuade me that theres a short cut between Cork Street and Savile Row somewhere in Conduit Street. Now did you ever hear such nonsense? Then he said my coat was getting shabby, and wanted me to go into Poole's and order a new one. Paramore: is my coat shabby?

PARAMORE. Not that I can see.

CRAVEN. I should think not. Then he wanted to draw me into an argument about the Egyptian war. We should have been here quarter of an hour ago only for his nonsense.

CHARTERIS [*still contemplating Rembrandt*] I did my best to keep him from disturbing you, Paramore.

PARAMORE [*gratefully*] You kept him exactly the right time, to a second. [*Formally*] Colonel Craven: I have something very particular to say to you.

CRAVEN [*springing up in alarm*] In private, Paramore: now really it m u s t be in private.

PARAMORE [*surprised*] Of course. I was about to suggest my consulting room: theres nobody there. Miss Craven: will you excuse me: Charteris will entertain you until I return. [*He leads the way to the green baize door*].

CHARTERIS [*aghast*] Oh, I say, hadnt you better wait until the others come?

PARAMORE [*exultant*] No need for further delay now, my best friend. [*He wrings Charteris's hand*]. Will you come, Colonel?

CRAVEN. At your service, Paramore: at your service.

Craven and Paramore go into the consulting room. Julia turns her head, and stares insolently at Charteris. His nerves play him false: he is completely out of countenance in a moment. She rises suddenly. He starts, and comes hastily forward between the table and the bookcase. She crosses to that side behind the table; and he immediately crosses to the opposite side in front of it, dodging her.

CHARTERIS [*nervously*] Dont, Julia. Now dont abuse your advantage. Youve got me here at your mercy. Be good for once; and dont make a scene.

JULIA [*contemptuously*] Do you suppose I am going to touch you?

CHARTERIS. No. Of course not.

She comes forward on her side of the table. He retreats on his side of it. She looks at him with utter scorn; sweeps across to the couch; and sits down imperially. With a great sigh of relief he drops into Paramore's chair.

JULIA. Come here. I have something to say to you.

CHARTERIS. Yes? [*He rolls the chair a few inches towards her*].

JULIA. Come here, I say. I am not going to shout across the room at you. Are you afraid of me?

CHARTERIS. Horribly. [*He moves the chair slowly, with great misgiving, to the end of the couch*].

JULIA [*with studied insolence*] Has that woman told you that she has given you up to me without an attempt to defend her conquest?

CHARTERIS [*whispering persuasively*] Shew that you are capable of the same sacrifice. Give me up too.

JULIA. Sacrifice! And so you think I'm dying to marry you, do you?

CHARTERIS. I am afraid your intentions have been honorable, Julia.

JULIA. You cad!

CHARTERIS [*with a sigh*] I confess I am something either more or less than a gentleman, Julia. You once gave me the benefit of the doubt.

JULIA. Indeed! I never told you so. If you cannot behave like a gentleman, you had better go back to the society of the woman who has given you up: if such a coldblooded, cowardly creature can be called a woman. [*She rises majestically: he makes his chair fly back to the table*]. I know you now, Leonard Charteris, through and through, in all your falseness, your petty spite, your cruelty and your vanity. The place you coveted has been won by a man more worthy of it.

CHARTERIS [*springing up, and coming close to her, gasping with eagerness*] What do you mean? Out with it. Have you accep—

JULIA. I am engaged to Dr Paramore.

CHARTERIS [*enraptured*] My own Julia! [*He attempts to embrace her*].

JULIA [*recoiling: he catching her hands and holding them*] How dare you! Are you mad? Do you wish me to call Dr Paramore?

CHARTERIS. Call everybody, my darling—everybody in London. Now I shall no longer have to be brutal; to defend myself; to go in fear of you. How I have looked forward to this day! You know now that I dont want you to marry me or to love me: Paramore can have all that. I only want to look on and rejoice disinterestedly in the happiness of [*kissing her hand*] my dear Julia [*kissing the other*], my beautiful Julia. [*She tears her hands away and raises them as if to strike him, as she did the night before at Cuthbertson's; he faces them with joyous recklessness*]. No use to threaten me now: I am not afraid of those hands: the loveliest hands in the world.

JULIA. How have you the face to turn round like this after insulting and torturing me?

CHARTERIS. Never mind, dearest: you never did understand me; and you never will. Our vivisecting friend has made a successful experiment at last.

JULIA [*earnestly*] It is you who are the vivisector: a far crueller, more wanton vivisector than he.

CHARTERIS. Yes; but then I learn so much more from my experiments than he does! And the victims learn as much as I do. Thats where my moral superiority comes in.

JULIA [*sitting down again on the couch with rueful humor*] Well, you shall not experiment on me any more. Go to your Grace if you want a victim. She'll be a tough one.

CHARTERIS [*reproachfully, sitting down beside her*] And you drove me to propose to her to escape from you! Suppose she had accepted me, where should I be now?

JULIA. Where *I* am, I suppose, now that I have accepted Paramore.

CHARTERIS. But I should have made Grace unhappy. [*Julia sneers*]. However, now I come to think of it, youll make Paramore unhappy. And yet if you refused him he would be in despair. Poor devil!

JULIA [*her temper flashing up for a moment again*] He is a better man than you.

CHARTERIS [*humbly*] I grant you that, my dear.

JULIA [*impetuously*] Dont call me your dear. And what do you mean by saying that I shall make him unhappy? Am I not good enough for him?

CHARTERIS [*dubiously*] Well, that depends on what you mean by good enough.

JULIA [*earnestly*] You might have made me good if you had chosen to. You had a great power over me. I was like a child in your hands; and you knew it.

CHARTERIS. Yes, my dear. That means that whenever you got jealous and flew into a tearing rage, I could always depend on its ending happily if I only waited long enough, and petted you very hard all the time. When you had had your fling, and called the object of your jealousy every name you could lay your tongue to, and abused me to your heart's content for a couple of hours, then the reaction would come; and you would at last subside into a soothing rapture of affection which gave you a sensation of being angelically good and forgiving. Oh, I know that sort of goodness! You may have thought on these occasions that I was bringing out your latent amiability; but I thought you were bringing out mine, and using up rather more than your fair share of it.

JULIA. According to you, then, I have no good in me. I am an utterly vile, worthless woman. Is that it?

CHARTERIS. Yes, if you are to be judged as you judge others. From the conventional point of view, theres nothing to be said for you, Julia: nothing. Thats why I have to find some other point of view to save my self-respect when I remember how I have loved you. Oh, what I have learnt from you! from you! who could learn nothing from me! I made a fool of you; and you brought me wisdom: I broke your heart; and you brought me joy: I made you curse your womanhood; and you revealed my manhood to me. Blessings for ever and ever on my Julia's name! [*With genuine emotion, he takes her hand to kiss it again*].

JULIA [*snatching her hand away in disgust*] Oh, stop talking that nasty sneering stuff.

CHARTERIS [*laughingly appealing to the heavens*] She calls it nasty sneering stuff! Well, well: I'll never talk like that to you again, dearest. It only means that you are a beautiful woman, and that we all love you.

JULIA. Dont say that: I hate it. It sounds as if I were a mere animal.

CHARTERIS. Hm! A fine animal is a very wonderful thing. Dont let us disparage animals, Julia.

JULIA. That is what you really think me.

CHARTERIS. Come, Julia! you dont expect me to admire you for your moral qualities, do you?

Julia turns and looks hard at him. He starts up apprehensively, and backs away from her. She rises and follows him up slowly and intently.

JULIA [*deliberately*] I have seen you very much infatuated with this depraved creature who has no moral qualities.

CHARTERIS [*retreating*] Keep off, Julia. Remember your new obligations to Paramore.

JULIA [*overtaking him in the middle of the room*] Never mind Paramore: that is my business. [*She grasps the lappels of his coat in her hands, and looks fixedly at him*]. Oh, if the people you talk so cleverly to could only know you as I know you! Sometimes I wonder at myself for ever caring for you.

CHARTERIS [*beaming at her*] Only sometimes?

JULIA. You fraud! You humbug! You miserable little plaster saint! [*He looks delighted*]. Oh! [*In a paroxysm half of rage, half of tenderness, she shakes him, growling over him like a tigress over her cub*].

Paramore and Craven return from the consulting room, and are thunderstruck at the spectacle.

CRAVEN [*shouting, utterly scandalized*] Julia!!

Julia releases Charteris, but stands her ground disdainfully as they come forward, Craven on her left, Paramore on her right.

PARAMORE. Whats the matter?

CHARTERIS. Nothing, nothing. Youll soon get used to this, Paramore.

CRAVEN. Now really, Julia, this is a very extraordinary way to behave. It's not fair to Paramore.

JULIA [*coldly*] If Dr Paramore objects, he can break off our engagement. [*To Paramore*] Pray dont hesitate.

PARAMORE [*looking doubtfully and anxiously at her*] Do you wish me to break it off?

CHARTERIS [*alarmed*] Nonsense! dont act so hastily. It was my fault. I annoyed Miss Craven—insulted her. Hang it all, dont go and spoil everything like this.

CRAVEN. This is most infernally perplexing. I cant believe that you insulted Julia, Charteris. Ive no doubt you annoyed her: youd annoy anybody: upon my soul you would; but insult! now what do you mean by that?

PARAMORE [*very earnestly*] Miss Craven: in all delicacy and sincerity I ask you to be frank with me. What are the relations between you and Charteris?

JULIA [*enigmatically*] Ask him. [*She goes to the fireplace, turning her back on them*].

CHARTERIS. Certainly: I'll confess. I'm in love with Miss Craven. Ive persecuted her with my addresses ever since I knew her. It's been no use: she utterly despises me. A moment ago the spectacle of a rival's happiness stung me to make a nasty sneering speech; and she—well, she just shook me a little, as you saw.

PARAMORE [*chivalrously*] I shall never forget that you helped me to win her, Charteris. [*Julia turns quickly, a spasm of fury in her face*].

CHARTERIS. Sh! For Heaven's sake dont mention it.

CRAVEN. This is a very different story to the one you told Cuthbertson and myself this morning. Youll excuse my saying that it sounds much more like the truth. Come! you were humbugging us, werent you?

CHARTERIS [*enigmatically*] Ask Julia.

Paramore and Craven turn to Julia. Charteris remains doggedly looking straight before him.

JULIA. It's quite true. He has been in love with me; he has persecuted me; and I utterly despise him.

CRAVEN. Dont rub it in, Julia: it's not kind. No man is quite himself when he's crossed in love. [*To Charteris*] Now listen to me, Charteris. When I was a young fellow, Cuthbertson and I fell in love with the same woman. She preferred Cuthbertson. I was taken aback: I wont deny it. But I knew my duty; and I did it. I gave her up, and wished Cuthbertson joy. He told me this morning, when we met after many years, that he has respected and liked me ever since for it. And I believe him, and feel the better for it. [*Impressively*] Now, Charteris: Paramore and you stand today where Cuthbertson and I stood on a certain July evening thirty-five years ago. How are you going to take it?

JULIA [*indignantly*] How is he going to take it, indeed! Really, papa, this is too much. If Mrs Cuthbertson wouldnt have you, it may have been very noble of you to make a virtue of giving her up, just as you made a virtue of being a teetotaller when Percy cut off your wine. But he shant be virtuous over me. I have refused him; and if he doesnt like it he can—he can—

CHARTERIS. I can lump it. Precisely. Craven: you can depend on me. I'll lump it. [*He moves off nonchalantly, and leans against the bookcase with his hands in his pockets*].

CRAVEN [*hurt*] Julia: you dont treat me respectfully. I dont wish to complain; but that was not a becoming speech.

JULIA [*bursting into tears, and throwing herself into the easy chair*] Is there any one in the world who has any feeling for me? who does not think me utterly vile?

Craven and Paramore hurry to her in the greatest consternation.

CRAVEN [*remorsefully*] My pet: I didnt for a moment mean—

JULIA. Must I stand to be bargained for by two men—passed from one to the other like a slave in the market, and not say a word in my own defence?

CRAVEN. But, my love—

JULIA. Oh, go away, all of you. Leave me. I—oh—[*she gives way to a passion of tears*].

PARAMORE [*reproachfully to Craven*] Youve wounded her cruelly, Colonel Craven. Cruelly.

CRAVEN. But I didnt mean to: I said nothing. Charteris: was I harsh?

CHARTERIS. You forget the revolt of the daughters, Craven. And you certainly wouldnt have gone on like that to any grown-up woman who was n o t your daughter.

CRAVEN. Do you mean to say that I am expected to treat my daughter the same as I would any other girl?

PARAMORE. I should say certainly, Colonel Craven.

CRAVEN. Well, dash me if I will. There!

PARAMORE. If you take that tone, I have nothing more to say. [*He crosses the room with offended dignity, and posts himself with his back to the bookcase beside Charteris*].

JULIA [*with a sob*] Daddy.

CRAVEN [*turning solicitously to her*] Yes, my love.

JULIA [*looking up at him tearfully, and kissing his hand*] Dont mind them. You didnt mean it, Daddy, did you?

CRAVEN. No, no, my precious. Come: dont cry.

PARAMORE [*to Charteris, looking at Julia with delight*] How beautiful she is!

CHARTERIS [*throwing up his hands*] Oh, Lord help you, Paramore! [*He leaves the bookcase, and sits at the end of the couch farthest from the fire*].

Sylvia arrives.

SYLVIA [*contemplating Julia*] Crying again! Well, you a r e a womanly one!

CRAVEN. Dont worry your sister, Sylvia. You know she cant bear it.

SYLVIA. I speak for her good, Dad. All the world cant be expected to know that she's the family baby.

JULIA. You will get your ears boxed presently, Silly.

CRAVEN. Now! now! now! my dear children, really now! Come, Julia: put up your handkerchief before Mrs Tranfield sees you. She's coming along with Jo.

JULIA [*rising*] That woman again!

SYLVIA. Another row! Go it, Julia!

CRAVEN. Hold your tongue, Sylvia. [*He turns commandingly to Julia*]. Now look here, Julia.

CHARTERIS. Hallo! A revolt of the fathers!

CRAVEN. Silence, Charteris. [*To Julia, unanswerably*] The test of a man's or woman's breeding is how they behave in a quarrel. Anybody can behave well when things are going smoothly. Now you said today, at that iniquitous club, that you were not a womanly woman. Very well: I dont mind. But if you are not going to behave like a lady when Mrs Tranfield comes into this room, youve got to behave like a gentleman; or fond as I am of you, I'll cut you dead exactly as I would if you were my son.

PARAMORE [*remonstrating*] Colonel Craven—

CRAVEN [*cutting him short*] Dont be a fool, Paramore.

JULIA [*tearfully excusing herself*] I'm sure, Daddy—

CRAVEN. Stop snivelling. I'm not speaking as your Daddy now: I'm speaking as your commanding officer.

SYLVIA. Good old Victoria Cross! [*Craven turns sharply on her; and she darts away behind Charteris, and presently seats herself on the couch, so that she and Charteris are shoulder to shoulder, facing opposite ways*].

Cuthbertson arrives with Grace, who remains near the door whilst her father joins the others.

CRAVEN. Ah, Jo, here you are. Now, Paramore: tell em the news.

PARAMORE. Mrs Tranfield: Cuthbertson: allow me to introduce you to my future wife.

CUTHBERTSON [*coming forward to shake hands with Paramore*] My heartiest congratulations! Miss Craven: you will accept Grace's congratulations as well as mine, I hope.

CRAVEN. She will, Jo. [*Peremptorily*] Now, Julia.

Julia slowly rises.

CUTHBERTSON. Now, Grace. [*He conducts her to Julia's right; then posts himself on the hearthrug, with his back to the fire, watching them, whilst the Colonel keeps guard on the other side*].

GRACE [*speaking in a low voice to Julia alone*] So you have shewn him that you can do without him! Now I take back everything I said. Will you shake hands with me? [*Julia gives her hand painfully, with her face averted*]. They think this a happy ending, Julia, these men: our lords and masters!

The two stand silent hand in hand.

SYLVIA [*leaning back across the couch, aside to Charteris*] Has she really chucked you? [*He nods assent. She looks at him dubiously, and adds*] I expect you chucked her.

CUTHBERTSON. And now, Paramore, mind you dont stand any chaff from Charteris about this. He's in the same predicament himself.

He's engaged to Grace.

JULIA [*dropping Grace's hand, and speaking with breathless anguish, but not violently*] Again!

CHARTERIS [*rising hastily*] Dont be alarmed. It's all off.

SYLVIA [*rising indignantly*] What! Youve chucked Grace too! What a shame! [*She goes to the other side of the room, fuming*].

CHARTERIS [*following her, and putting his hand soothingly on her shoulder*] She wont have me, old chap. That is [*turning to the others*], unless Mrs Tranfield has changed her mind again.

GRACE. No: we shall remain very good friends, I hope; but nothing would induce me to marry you. [*She takes the easy chair at the fireplace, and sits down with perfect composure*].

JULIA. Ah! [*She sits down on the couch with a great sigh of relief*].

SYLVIA [*consoling Charteris*] Poor old Leonard!

CHARTERIS. Yes: this is the doom of the philanderer. I shall have to go on philandering now all my life. No domesticity, no fireside, no little ones, nothing at all in Cuthbertson's line! Nobody will marry me— unless you, Sylvia: eh?

SYLVIA. Not if I know it, Charteris.

CHARTERIS [*to them all*] You see!

CRAVEN [*coming between Charteris and Sylvia*] Now you really shouldnt make a jest of these things: upon my life and soul you shouldnt, Charteris.

CUTHBERTSON [*on the hearthrug*] The only use he can find for sacred things is to make a jest of them. Thats the New Order. Thank Heaven, we belong to the Old Order, Dan!

CHARTERIS. Cuthbertson: dont be symbolic.

CUTHBERTSON [*outraged*] Symbolic! That is an accusation of Ibsenism. What do you mean?

CHARTERIS. Symbolic of the Old Order. Dont persuade yourself that you represent the Old Order. There never was any Old Order.

CRAVEN. There I flatly contradict you, and stand up for Jo. I'd no more have behaved as you do when I was a young man than I'd have cheated at cards. *I* belong to the Old Order.

CHARTERIS. Youre getting old, Craven; and you want to make a merit of it, as usual.

CRAVEN. Come now, Charteris; youre not offended, I hope. [*With a conciliatory outburst*] Well, perhaps I shouldnt have said that about cheating at cards. I withdraw it [*offering his hand*].

CHARTERIS [*taking Craven's hand*] No offence, my dear Craven: none in the world. I didnt mean to show any temper. But [*aside, after looking round to see whether the others are listening*] only just consider! the spectacle of a rival's happiness! the——

CRAVEN [*aloud, decisively*] Charteris: now youve got to behave like a man. Your duty's plain before you. [*To Cuthbertson*] Am I right, Jo?

CUTHBERTSON [*firmly*] You are, Dan.

CRAVEN [*to Charteris*] Go straight up and congratulate Julia. And do it like a gentleman, smiling.

CHARTERIS. Colonel: I will. Not a quiver shall betray the conflict within.

CRAVEN. Julia: Charteris has not congratulated you yet. He's coming to do it.

Julia rises, and fixes a dangerous look on Charteris.

SYLVIA [*whispering quickly behind Charteris as he is about to advance*] Take care. She's going to hit you. I know her.

Charteris stops and looks cautiously at Julia, measuring the situation. They regard one another steadfastly for a moment. Grace softly rises and gets close to Julia.

CHARTERIS [*whispering over his shoulder to Sylvia*] I'll chance it. [*He walks confidently up to Julia*]. Julia? [*He proffers his hand*].

JULIA [*exhausted, allowing herself to take it*] You are right. I am a worthless woman.

CHARTERIS [*triumphant, and gaily remonstrating*] Oh, why?

JULIA. Because I am not brave enough to kill you.

GRACE [*taking her in her arms as she sinks, almost fainting away from him*] Oh no. Never make a hero of a philanderer.

Charteris, amused and untouched, shakes his head laughingly. The rest look at Julia with concern, and even a little awe, feeling for the first time the presence of a keen sorrow.

THE END

III

MRS WARREN'S PROFESSION

1894

BEING THE THIRD OF THREE UNPLEASANT PLAYS

ACT I

Summer afternoon in a cottage garden on the eastern slope of a hill a little south of Haslemere in Surrey. Looking up the hill, the cottage is seen in the left hand corner of the garden, with its thatched roof and porch, and a large latticed window to the left of the porch. A paling completely shuts in the garden, except for a gate on the right. The common rises uphill beyond the paling to the sky line. Some folded canvas garden chairs are leaning against the side bench in the porch. A lady's bicycle is propped against the wall, under the window. A little to the right of the porch a hammock is slung from two posts. A big canvas umbrella, stuck in the ground, keeps the sun off the hammock, in which a young lady lies reading and making notes, her head towards the cottage and her feet towards the gate. In front of the hammock, and within reach of her hand, is a common kitchen chair, with a pile of serious-looking books and a supply of writing paper on it.

A gentleman walking on the common comes into sight from behind the cottage. He is hardly past middle age, with something of the artist about him, unconventionally but carefully dressed, and clean-shaven except for a moustache, with an eager susceptible face and very amiable and considerate manners. He has silky black hair, with waves of grey and white in it. His eyebrows are white, his moustache black. He seems not certain of his way. He looks over the paling; takes stock of the place; and sees the young lady.

THE GENTLEMAN [*taking off his hat*] I beg your pardon. Can you direct me to Hindhead View——Mrs Alison's?

THE YOUNG LADY [*glancing up from her book*] This is Mrs Alison's. [*She resumes her work*].

THE GENTLEMAN. Indeed! Perhaps——may I ask are you Miss Vivie Warren?

THE YOUNG LADY [*sharply, as she turns on her elbow to get a good look at him*] Yes.

THE GENTLEMAN [*daunted and conciliatory*]

I'm afraid I appear intrusive. My name is Praed. [*Vivie at once throws her books upon the chair, and gets out of the hammock*]. Oh, pray dont let me disturb you.

VIVIE [*striding to the gate and opening it for him*] Come in, Mr Praed. [*He comes in*]. Glad to see you. [*She proffers her hand and takes his with a resolute and hearty grip. She is an attractive specimen of the sensible, able, highly-educated young middle-class Englishwoman. Age 22. Prompt, strong, confident, self-possessed. Plain business-like dress, but not dowdy. She wears a chatelaine at her belt, with a fountain pen and a paper knife among its pendants.*

PRAED. Very kind of you indeed. Miss Warren. [*She shuts the gate with a vigorous slam. He passes in to the middle of the garden, exercising his fingers, which are slightly numbed by her greeting.*] Has your mother arrived?

VIVIE [*quickly, evidently scenting aggression*] Is she coming?

PRAED [*surprised*] Didnt you expect us?

VIVIE. No.

PRAED. Now, goodness me, I hope Ive not mistaken the day. That would be just like me, you know. Your mother arranged that she was to come down from London and that I was to come over from Horsham to be introduced to you.

VIVIE [*not at all pleased*] Did she? Hm! My mother has rather a trick of taking me by surprise—to see how I behave myself when she's away, I suppose. I fancy I shall take my mother very much by surprise one of these days, if she makes arrangements that concern me without consulting me beforehand. She hasnt come.

PRAED [*embarrassed*] I'm really very sorry.

VIVIE [*throwing off her displeasure*] It's not your fault, Mr Praed, is it? And I'm very glad youve come. You are the only one of my mother's friends I have ever asked her to bring to see me.

PRAED [*relieved and delighted*] Oh, now this is really very good of you, Miss Warren!

VIVIE. Will you come indoors; or would you rather sit out here and talk?

PRAED. It will be nicer out here, dont you think?

VIVIE. Then I'll go and get you a chair. [*She goes to the porch for a garden chair*].

PRAED [*following her*] Oh, pray, pray! Allow me. [*He lays hands on the chair*].

VIVIE [*letting him take it*] Take care of your fingers; theyre rather dodgy things, those

chairs. [*She goes across to the chair with the books on it; pitches them into the hammock; and brings the chair forward with one swing.*]

PRAED [*who has just unfolded his chair*] Oh, now d o let me take that hard chair. I like hard chairs.

VIVIE. So do I. Sit down, Mr Praed. [*This invitation she gives with genial peremptoriness, his anxiety to please her clearly striking her as a sign of weakness of character on his part. But he does not immediately obey*].

PRAED. By the way, though, hadnt we better go to the station to meet your mother?

VIVIE [*coolly*] Why? She knows the way.

PRAED [*disconcerted*] Er—I suppose she does [*he sits down*].

VIVIE. Do you know, you are just like what I expected. I hope you are disposed to be friends with me.

PRAED [*again beaming*] Thank you, my d e a r Miss Warren: thank you. Dear me! I'm so glad your mother hasnt spoilt you!

VIVIE. How?

PRAED. Well, in making you too conventional. You know, my dear Miss Warren, I am a born anarchist. I hate authority. It spoils the relations between parent and child: even between mother and daughter. Now I was always afraid that your mother would strain her authority to make you very conventional. It's such a relief to find that she hasnt.

VIVIE. Oh! have I been behaving unconventionally?

PRAED. Oh no: oh dear no. At least not conventionally unconventionally, you understand. [*She nods and sits down. He goes on, with a cordial outburst*] But it was so charming of you to say that you were disposed to be friends with me! You modern young ladies are splendid: perfectly splendid!

VIVIE [*dubiously*] Eh? [*watching him with dawning disappointment as to the quality of his brains and character*].

PRAED. When I was your age, young men and women were afraid of each other: there was no good fellowship. Nothing real. Only gallantry copied out of novels, and as vulgar and affected as it could be. Maidenly reserve! gentlemanly chivalry! always saying no when you meant yes! simple purgatory for shy and sincere souls.

VIVIE. Yes, I imagine there must have been a frightful waste of time. Especially women's time.

PRAED. Oh, waste of life, waste of everything. But things are improving. Do you know, I have been in a positive state of excitement about meeting you ever since your magnificent achievements at Cambridge: a thing unheard of in my day. It was perfectly splendid, your tieing with the third wrangler. Just the right place, you know. The first wrangler is always a dreamy, morbid fellow, in whom the thing is pushed to the length of a disease.

VIVIE. It doesnt pay. I wouldnt do it again for the same money.

PRAED [aghast] The same money!

VIVIE. I did it for £50.

PRAED. Fifty pounds!

VIVIE. Yes. Fifty pounds. Perhaps you dont know how it was. Mrs Latham, my tutor at Newnham, told my mother that I could distinguish myself in the mathematical tripos if I went in for it in earnest. The papers were full just then of Phillipa Summers beating the senior wrangler. You remember about it, of course.

PRAED [shakes his head energetically]!!!

VIVIE. Well anyhow she did; and nothing would please my mother but that I should do the same thing. I said flatly it was not worth my while to face the grind since I was not going in for teaching; but I offered to try for fourth wrangler or thereabouts for £50. She closed with me at that, after a little grumbling; and I was better than my bargain. But I wouldnt do it again for that. £200 would have been nearer the mark.

PRAED [much damped] Lord bless me! Thats a very practical way of looking at it.

VIVIE. Did you expect to find me an unpractical person?

PRAED. But surely it's practical to consider not only the work these honors cost, but also the culture they bring.

VIVIE. Culture! My dear Mr Praed: do you know what the mathematical tripos means? It means grind, grind, grind for six to eight hours a day at mathematics, and nothing but mathematics. I'm supposed to know something about science; but I know nothing except the mathematics it involves. I can make calculations for engineers, electricians, insurance companies, and so on; but I know next to nothing about engineering or electricity or insurance. I dont even know arithmetic well. Outside mathematics, lawntennis, eating, sleeping, cycling, and walking, I'm a more ignorant barbarian than any woman could possibly be who hadnt gone in for the tripos.

PRAED [revolted] What a monstrous, wicked, rascally system! I knew it! I felt at once that it meant destroying all that makes womanhood beautiful.

VIVIE. I dont object to it on that score in the least. I shall turn it to very good account, I assure you.

PRAED. Pooh! In what way?

VIVIE. I shall set up in chambers in the City, and work at actuarial calculations and conveyancing. Under cover of that I shall do some law, with one eye on the Stock Exchange all the time. Ive come down here by myself to read law: not for a holiday, as my mother imagines. I hate holidays.

PRAED. You make my blood run cold. Are you to have no romance, no beauty in your life?

VIVIE. I dont care for either, I assure you.

PRAED. You cant mean that.

VIVIE. Oh, yes I do. I like working and getting paid for it. When I'm tired of working I like a comfortable chair, a cigar, a little whisky, and a novel with a good detective story in it.

PRAED [rising in a frenzy of repudiation] I dont believe it. I am an artist; and I cant believe it: I refuse to believe it. It's only that you havnt discovered yet what a wonderful world art can open up to you.

VIVIE. Yes I have. Last May I spent six weeks in London with Honoria Fraser. Mamma thought we were doing a round of sightseeing together; but I was really at Honoria's chamber in Chancery Lane every day, working away at actuarial calculations for her, and helping her as well as a greenhorn could. In the evenings we smoked and talked, and never dreamt of going out except for exercise. And I never enjoyed myself more in my life. I cleared all my expenses, and got initiated into the business without a fee into the bargain.

PRAED. But bless my heart and soul, Miss Warren, do you call that discovering art?

VIVIE. Wait a bit. That wasnt the beginning. I went up to town on an invitation from some artistic people in Fitzjohn's Avenue: one of the girls was a Newnham chum. They took me to the National Gallery—

PRAED [approving] Ah!! [He sits down, much relieved].

VIVIE [continuing]—to the Opera—

PRAED [still more pleased] Good!

VIVIE.—and to a concert where the band

played all the evening: Beethoven and Wagner and so on. I wouldnt go through that experience again for anything you could offer me. I held out for civility's sake until the third day; and then I said, plump out, that I couldnt stand any more of it, and went off to Chancery Lane. N o w you know the sort of perfectly splendid modern young lady I am. How do you think I shall get on with my mother?

PRAED [*startled*] Well, I hope—er—

VIVIE. It's not so much what you hope as what you believe, that I want to know.

PRAED. Well, frankly, I am afraid your mother will be a little disappointed. Not from any shortcoming on your part, you know: I dont mean that. But you are so different from her ideal.

VIVIE. Her what?!

PRAED. Her ideal.

VIVIE. Do you mean her ideal of ME?

PRAED. Yes.

VIVIE. What on earth is it like?

PRAED. Well, you must have observed, Miss Warren, that people who are dissatisfied with their own bringing-up generally think that the world would be all right if everybody were to be brought up quite differently. Now your mother's life has been—er—I suppose you know—

VIVIE. Dont suppose anything, Mr Praed. I hardly know my mother. Since I was a child I have lived in England, at school or college, or with people paid to take charge of me. I have been boarded out all my life. My mother has lived in Brussels or Vienna and never let me go to her. I only see her when she visits England for a few days. I dont complain: it's been very pleasant; for people have been very good to me; and there has always been plenty of money to make things smooth. But dont imagine I know anything about my mother. I know far less than you do.

PRAED [*very ill at ease*] In that case— [*He stops, quite at a loss. Then, with a forced attempt at gaiety*] But what nonsense we are talking! Of course you and your mother will get on capitally. [*He rises, and looks abroad at the view*]. What a charming little place you have here!

VIVIE [*unmoved*] Rather a violent change of subject, Mr Praed. Why wont my mother's life bear being talked about?

PRAED. Oh, you really mustnt say that.

Isnt it natural that I should have a certain delicacy in talking to my old friend's daughter about her behind her back? You and she will have plenty of opportunity of talking about it when she comes.

VIVIE. No: s h e wont talk about it either. [*Rising*] However, I daresay you have good reasons for telling me nothing. Only, mind this, Mr Praed. I expect there will be a battle royal when my mother hears of my Chancery Lane project.

PRAED [*ruefully*] I'm afraid there will.

VIVIE. Well, I shall win, because I want nothing but my fare to London to start there to-morrow earning my own living by devilling for Honoria. Besides, I have no mysteries to keep up; and it seems she has. I shall use that advantage over her if necessary.

PRAED [*greatly shocked*] Oh no! No, pray, youd not do such a thing.

VIVIE. Then tell me why not.

PRAED. I really cannot. I appeal to your good feeling. [*She smiles at his sentimentality*]. Besides, you may be too bold. Your mother is not to be trifled with when she's angry.

VIVIE. You cant frighten me, Mr Praed. In that month at Chancery Lane I had opportunities of taking the measure of one or two women v e r y like my mother. You may back me to win. But if I hit harder in my ignorance than I need, remember that it is you who refuse to enlighten me. Now, let us drop the subject. [*She takes her chair and replaces it near the hammock with the same vigorous swing as before*].

PRAED [*taking a desperate resolution*] One word, Miss Warren. I had better tell you. It's very difficult; but—

Mrs Warren and Sir George Crofts arrive at the gate. Mrs Warren is between 40 and 50, formerly pretty, showily dressed in a brilliant hat and a gay blouse fitting tightly over her bust and flanked by fashionable sleeves. Rather spoilt and domineering, and decidedly vulgar, but, on the whole, a genial and fairly presentable old blackguard of a woman.

Crofts is a tall powerfully-built man of about 50, fashionably dressed in the style of a young man. Nasal voice, reedier than might be expected from his strong frame. Clean-shaven bulldog jaws, large flat ears, and thick neck: gentlemanly combination of the most brutal types of city man, sporting man, and man about town.

VIVIE. Here they are. [*Coming to them as they enter the garden*] How do, mater? Mr

Praed's been here this half hour, waiting for you.

MRS WARREN. Well, if youve been waiting, Praddy, it's your own fault: I thought youd have had the gumption to know I was coming by the 3.10 train. Vivie, put your hat on, dear: youll get sunburnt. Oh, I forgot to introduce you. Sir George Crofts: my little Vivie.

Crofts advances to Vivie with his most courtly manner. She nods, but makes no motion to shake hands.

CROFTS. May I shake hands with a young lady whom I have known by reputation very long as the daughter of one of my oldest friends?

VIVIE [*who has been looking him up and down sharply*] If you like. [*She takes his tenderly proffered hand and gives it a squeeze that makes him open his eyes; then turns away, and says to her mother*] Will you come in, or shall I get a couple more chairs? [*She goes into the porch for the chairs*].

MRS WARREN. Well, George, what do you think of her?

CROFTS [*ruefully*] She has a powerful fist. Did you shake hands with her, Praed?

PRAED. Yes: it will pass off presently.

CROFTS. I hope so. [*Vivie reappears with two more chairs. He hurries to her assistance*]. Allow me.

MRS WARREN [*patronizingly*] Let Sir George help you with the chairs, dear.

VIVIE [*pitching them into his arms*] Here you are. [*She dusts her hands and turns to Mrs Warren*]. Youd like some tea, wouldnt you?

MRS WARREN [*sitting in Praed's chair and fanning herself*] I'm dying for a drop to drink.

VIVIE. I'll see about it. [*She goes into the cottage*].

Sir George has by this time managed to unfold a chair and plant it beside Mrs Warren, on her left. He throws the other on the grass and sits down, looking dejected and rather foolish, with the handle of his stick in his mouth. Praed, still very uneasy, fidgets about the garden on their right.

MRS WARREN [*to Praed, looking at Crofts*] Just look at him, Praddy: he looks cheerful, dont he? He's been worrying my life out these three years to have that little girl of mine shewn to him; and now that Ive done it, he's quite out of countenance. [*Briskly*] Come! sit up, George; and take your stick out of your mouth. [*Crofts sulkily obeys*].

PRAED. I think, you know—if you dont mind my saying so—that we had better get out of the habit of thinking of her as a little girl. You see she has really distinguished herself; and I'm not sure, from what I have seen of her, that she is not older than any of us.

MRS WARREN [*greatly amused*] Only listen to him, George! Older than any of us! Well, she has been stuffing you nicely with her importance.

PRAED. But young people are particularly sensitive about being treated in that way.

MRS WARREN. Yes; and young people have to get all that nonsense taken out of them, and a good deal more besides. Dont you interfere, Praddy: I know how to treat my own child as well as you do. [*Praed, with a grave shake of his head, walks up the garden with his hands behind his back. Mrs Warren pretends to laugh, but looks after him with perceptible concern. Then she whispers to Crofts*] Whats the matter with him? What does he take it like that for?

CROFTS [*morosely*] Youre afraid of Praed.

MRS WARREN. What! Me! Afraid of dear old Praddy! Why, a fly wouldnt be afraid of him.

CROFTS. Youre afraid of him.

MRS WARREN [*angry*] I'll trouble you to mind your own business, and not try any of your sulks on me. I'm not afraid of you, anyhow. If you cant make yourself agreeable, youd better go home. [*She gets up, and, turning her back on him, finds herself face to face with Praed*]. Come, Praddy, I know it was only your tender-heartedness. Youre afraid I'll bully her.

PRAED. My dear Kitty: you think I'm offended. Dont imagine that: pray dont. But you know I often notice things that escape you; and though you never take my advice, you sometimes admit afterwards that you ought to have taken it.

MRS WARREN. Well, what do you notice now?

PRAED. Only that Vivie is a grown woman. Pray, Kitty, treat her with every respect.

MRS WARREN [*with genuine amazement*] Respect! Treat my own daughter with respect! What next, pray!

VIVIE [*appearing at the cottage door and calling to Mrs Warren*] Mother: will you come to my room before tea?

MRS WARREN. Yes, dearie. [*She laughs indulgently at Praed's gravity, and pats him on the cheek as she passes him on her way to the porch*]. Dont be cross, Praddy. [*She follows Vivie into

D

the cottage].

CROFTS [*furtively*] I say, Praed.

PRAED. Yes.

CROFTS. I want to ask you a rather particular question.

PRAED. Certainly. [*He takes Mrs Warren's chair and sits close to Crofts*].

CROFTS. Thats right: they might hear us from the window. Look here: did Kitty ever tell you who that girl's father is?

PRAED. Never.

CROFTS. Have you any suspicion of who it might be?

PRAED. None.

CROFTS [*not believing him*] I know, of course, that you perhaps might feel bound not to tell if she had said anything to you. But it's very awkward to be uncertain about it now that we shall be meeting the girl every day. We dont exactly know how we ought to feel towards her.

PRAED. What difference can that make? We take her on her own merits. What does it matter who her father was?

CROFTS [*suspiciously*] Then you know who he was?

PRAED [*with a touch of temper*] I said no just now. Did you not hear me?

CROFTS. Look here, Praed. I ask you as a particular favor. If you do know [*movement of protest from Praed*]—I only say, if you know, you might at least set my mind at rest about her. The fact is, I feel attracted.

PRAED [*sternly*] What do you mean?

CROFTS. Oh, dont be alarmed: it's quite an innocent feeling. Thats what puzzles me about it. Why, for all I know, *I* might be her father.

PRAED. You! Impossible!

CROFTS [*catching him up cunningly*] You know for certain that I'm not?

PRAED. I know nothing about it, I tell you, any more than you. But really, Crofts—oh no, it's out of the question. Theres not the least resemblance.

CROFTS. As to that, theres no resemblance between her and her mother that I can see. I suppose she's not your daughter, is she?

PRAED [*rising indignantly*] Really, Crofts—!

CROFTS. No offence, Praed. Quite allowable as between two men of the world.

PRAED [*recovering himself with an effort and speaking gently and gravely*] Now listen to me, my dear Crofts. [*He sits down again*]. I have nothing to do with that side of Mrs Warren's life, and never had. She has never spoken to me about it; and of course I have never spoken to her about it. Your delicacy will tell you that a handsome woman needs some friends who are not—well, not on that footing with her. The effect of her own beauty would become a torment to her if she could not escape from it occasionally. You are probably on much more confidential terms with Kitty than I am. Surely you can ask her the question yourself.

CROFTS. I have asked her, often enough. But she's so determined to keep the child all to herself that she would deny that it ever had a father if she could. [*Rising*] I'm thoroughly uncomfortable about it, Praed.

PRAED [*rising also*] Well, as you are, at all events, old enough to be her father, I dont mind agreeing that we both regard Miss Vivie in a parental way, as a young girl whom we are bound to protect and help. What do you say?

CROFTS [*aggressively*] I'm no older than you, if you come to that.

PRAED. Yes you are, my dear fellow: you were born old. I was born a boy: Ive never been able to feel the assurance of a grown-up man in my life. [*He folds his chair and carries it to the porch*].

MRS WARREN [*calling from within the cottage*] Prad-dee! George! Tea-ea-ea-ea!

CROFTS [*hastily*] She's calling us. [*He hurries in.*]

Praed shakes his head bodingly, and is following Crofts when he is hailed by a young gentleman who has just appeared on the common and is making for the gate. He is pleasant, pretty, smartly dressed, cleverly good-for-nothing, not long turned 20, with a charming voice and agreeably disrespectful manners. He carries a light sporting magazine rifle.

THE YOUNG GENTLEMAN. Hallo! Praed!

PRAED. Why, Frank Gardner! [*Frank comes in and shakes hands cordially*]. What on earth are you doing here?

FRANK. Staying with my father.

PRAED. The Roman father?

FRANK. He's rector here. I'm living with my people this autumn for the sake of economy. Things came to a crisis in July: the Roman father had to pay my debts. He's stony broke in consequence; and so am I. What are you up to in these parts? Do you know the people here?

PRAED. Yes: I'm spending the day with a

Miss Warren.

FRANK [*enthusiastically*] What! Do you know Vivie? Isnt she a jolly girl? I'm teaching her to shoot with this [*putting down the rifle*]. I'm so glad she knows you: youre just the sort of fellow she ought to know. [*He smiles, and raises the charming voice almost to a singing tone as he exclaims*] It's ever so jolly to find you here, Praed.

PRAED. I'm an old friend of her mother. Mrs Warren brought me over to make her daughter's acquaintance.

FRANK. The mother! Is she here?

PRAED. Yes: inside, at tea.

MRS WARREN [*calling from within*] Prad-dee-ee-ee-eee! The tea-cake'll be cold.

PRAED [*calling*] Yes, Mrs Warren. In a moment. Ive just met a friend here.

MRS WARREN. A what?

PRAED [*louder*] A friend.

MRS WARREN. Bring him in.

PRAED. All right. [*To Frank*] Will you accept the invitation?

FRANK [*incredulous, but immensely amused*] Is that Vivie's mother?

PRAED. Yes.

FRANK. By Jove! What a lark! Do you think she'll like me?

PRAED. Ive no doubt youll make yourself popular, as usual. Come in and try [*moving towards the house*].

FRANK. Stop a bit. [*Seriously*] I want to take you into my confidence.

PRAED. Pray dont. It's only some fresh folly, like the barmaid at Redhill.

FRANK. It's ever so much more serious than that. You say youve only just met Vivie for the first time?

PRAED. Yes.

FRANK [*rhapsodically*] Then you can have no idea what a girl she is. Such character! Such sense! And her cleverness! Oh, my eye, Praed, but I can tell you she is clever! And— need I add?—she loves me.

CROFTS [*putting his head out of the window*] I say, Praed: what are you about? Do come along. [*He disappears*].

FRANK. Hallo! Sort of chap that would take a prize at a dog show, aint he? Who's he?

PRAED. Sir George Crofts, an old friend of Mrs Warren's. I think we had better come in.

On their way to the porch they are interrupted by a call from the gate. Turning, they see an elderly clergyman looking over it.

THE CLERGYMAN [*calling*] Frank!

FRANK. Hallo! [*To Praed*] The Roman father. [*To the clergyman*] Yes, gov'nor: all right: presently. [*To Praed*] Look here, Praed: youd better go in to tea. I'll join you directly.

PRAED. Very good. [*He goes into the cottage*].

The clergyman remains outside the gate, with his hands on the top of it. The Rev. Samuel Gardner, a beneficed clergyman of the Established Church, is over 50. Externally he is pretentious, booming, noisy, important. Really he is that obsolescent social phenomenon the fool of the family dumped on the Church by his father the patron, clamorously asserting himself as father and clergyman without being able to command respect in either capacity.

REV. S. Well, sir. Who are your friends here, if I may ask?

FRANK. Oh, it's all right, gov'nor! Come in.

REV. S. No, sir; not until I know whose garden I am entering.

FRANK. It's all right. It's Miss Warren's.

REV. S. I have not seen her at church since she came.

FRANK. Of course not: she's a third wrangler. Ever so intellectual. Took a higher degree than you did; so why should she go to hear you preach?

REV. S. Dont be disrespectful, sir.

FRANK. Oh, it dont matter: nobody hears us. Come in. [*He opens the gate, unceremoniously pulling his father with it into the garden*]. I want to introduce you to her. Do you remember the advice you gave me last July, gov'nor?

REV. S. [*severely*] Yes. I advised you to conquer your idleness and flippancy, and to work your way into an honorable profession and live on it and not upon me.

FRANK. No: thats what you thought of afterwards. What you actually said was that since I had neither brains nor money, I'd better turn my good looks to account by marrying somebody with both. Well, look here. Miss Warren has brains: you cant deny that.

REV. S. Brains are not everything.

FRANK. No, of course not: theres the money—

REV. S. [*interrupting him austerely*] I was not thinking of money, sir. I was speaking of higher things. Social position, for instance.

FRANK. I dont care a rap about that.

REV. S. But I do, sir.

FRANK. Well, nobody wants y o u to marry her. Anyhow, she has what amounts to a high Cambridge degree; and she seems to have as much money as she wants.

REV. S. [*sinking into a feeble vein of humor*] I greatly doubt whether she has as much money as y o u will want.

FRANK. Oh, come: I havnt been so very extravagant. I live ever so quietly; I dont drink; I dont bet much; and I never go regularly on the razzle-dazzle as you did when you were my age.

REV. S. [*booming hollowly*] Silence, sir.

FRANK. Well, you told me yourself, when I was making ever such an ass of myself about the barmaid at Redhill, that you once offered a woman £50 for the letters you wrote to her when—

REV. S. [*terrified*] Sh-sh-sh, Frank, for Heaven's sake! [*He looks round apprehensively. Seeing no one within earshot he plucks up courage to boom again, but more subduedly*]. You are taking an ungentlemanly advantage of what I confided to you for your own good, to save you from an error you would have repented all your life long. Take warning by your father's follies, sir; and dont make them an excuse for your own.

FRANK. Did you ever hear the story of the Duke of Wellington and his letters?

REV. S. No, sir; and I dont want to hear it.

FRANK. The old Iron Duke didnt throw away £50: not he. He just wrote: "Dear Jenny: publish and be damned! Yours affectionately, Wellington." Thats what you should have done.

REV. S. [*piteously*] Frank, my boy: when I wrote those letters I put myself into that woman's power. When I told you about them I put myself, to some extent, I am sorry to say, in your power. She refused my money with these words, which I shall never forget. "Knowledge is power" she said; "and I never sell power." Thats more than twenty years ago; and she has never made use of her power or caused me a moment's uneasiness. You are behaving worse to me than she did, Frank.

FRANK. Oh yes I dare say! Did you ever preach at her the way you preach at me every day?

REV. S. [*wounded almost to tears*] I leave you, sir. You are incorrigible. [*He turns towards the gate*].

FRANK [*utterly unmoved*] Tell them I shant be home to tea, will you, gov'nor, like a good fellow? [*He moves towards the cottage door and is met by Praed and Vivie coming out*].

VIVIE [*to Frank*] Is that your father, Frank? I do so want to meet him.

FRANK. Certainly. [*Calling after his father*] Gov'nor. Youre wanted. [*The parson turns at the gate, fumbling nervously at his hat. Praed crosses the garden to the opposite side, beaming in anticipation of civilities*]. My father: Miss Warren.

VIVIE [*going to the clergyman and shaking his hand*] Very glad to see you here, Mr Gardner. [*Calling to the cottage*] Mother: come along: youre wanted.

Mrs Warren appears on the threshold, and is immediately transfixed, recognizing the clergyman.

VIVIE [*continuing*] Let me introduce—

MRS WARREN [*swooping on the Reverend Samuel*] Why, it's Sam Gardner, gone into the Church! Well, I never! Dont you know us, Sam? This is George Crofts, as large as life and twice as natural. Dont you remember me?

REV. S. [*very red*] I really—er—

MRS WARREN. Of course you do. Why, I have a whole album of your letters still: I came across them only the other day.

REV. S. [*miserably confused*] Miss Vavasour, I believe.

MRS WARREN [*correcting him quickly in a loud whisper*] Tch! Nonsense! Mrs Warren: dont you see my daughter there?

ACT II

Inside the cottage after nightfall. Looking eastward from within instead of westward from without, the latticed window, with its curtains drawn, is now seen in the middle of the front wall of the cottage, with the porch door to the left of it. In the left-hand side wall is the door leading to the kitchen. Farther back against the same wall is a dresser with a candle and matches on it, and Frank's rifle standing beside them, with the barrel resting in the plate-rack. In the centre a table stands with a lighted lamp on it. Vivie's books and writing materials are on a table to the right of the window, against the wall. The fireplace is on the right, with a settle: there is no fire. Two of the chairs are set right and left of the table.

The cottage door opens, shewing a fine starlit night without; and Mrs Warren, her shoulders wrapped in a shawl borrowed from Vivie, enters, followed by Frank, who throws his cap on the window seat. She has had enough of walking, and gives a gasp of relief as she unpins her hat; takes it off; sticks the pin through the crown; and puts it on the table.

MRS WARREN. O Lord! I dont know which is the worst of the country, the walking or the sitting at home with nothing to do. I could do with a whisky and soda now very well, if only they had such a thing in this place.

FRANK. Perhaps Vivie's got some.

MRS WARREN. Nonsense! What would a young girl like her be doing with such things! Never mind: it dont matter. I wonder how she passes her time here! I'd a good deal rather be in Vienna.

FRANK. Let me take you there. [*He helps her to take off her shawl, gallantly giving her shoulders a very perceptible squeeze as he does so*].

MRS WARREN. Ah! would you? I'm beginning to think youre a chip of the old block.

FRANK. Like the gov'nor, eh? [*He hangs the shawl on the nearest chair and sits down*].

MRS WARREN. Never you mind. What do you know about such things? Youre only a boy. [*She goes to the hearth, to be farther from temptation*].

FRANK. Do come to Vienna with me? It'd be ever such larks.

MRS WARREN. No, thank you. Vienna is no place for you—at least not until youre a little older. [*She nods at him to emphasise this piece of advice. He makes a mock-piteous face, belied by his laughing eyes. She looks at him; then comes back to him*]. Now, look here, little boy [*taking his face in her hands and turning it up to her*]: I know you through and through by your likeness to your father, better than you know yourself. Dont you go taking any silly ideas into your head about me. Do you hear?

FRANK [*gallantly wooing her with his voice*] Cant help it, my dear Mrs Warren: it runs in the family.

She pretends to box his ears; then looks at the pretty laughing upturned face for a moment, tempted. At last she kisses him, and immediately turns away, out of patience with herself.

MRS WARREN. There! I shouldnt have done that. I am wicked. Never you mind, my dear: it's only a motherly kiss. Go and make love to Vivie.

FRANK. So I have.

MRS WARREN [*turning on him with a sharp*

note of alarm in her voice] What!

FRANK. Vivie and I are ever such chums.

MRS WARREN. What do you mean? Now see here: I wont have any young scamp tampering with my little girl. Do you hear? I wont have it.

FRANK [*quite unabashed*] My dear Mrs Warren: dont you be alarmed. My intentions are honorable: ever so honorable; and your little girl is jolly well able to take care of herself. She dont need looking after half so much as her mother. She aint so handsome, you know.

MRS WARREN [*taken aback by his assurance*] Well, you have got a nice healthy two inches thick of cheek all over you. I dont know where you got it. Not from your father, anyhow.

CROFTS [*in the garden*] The gipsies, I suppose?

REV. S. [*replying*] The broomsquires are far worse.

MRS WARREN [*to Frank*] S-sh! Remember! youve had your warning.

Crofts and the Reverend Samuel come in from the garden, the clergyman continuing his conversation as he enters.

REV. S. The perjury at the Winchester assizes is deplorable.

MRS WARREN. Well? what became of you two? And wheres Praddy and Vivie?

CROFTS [*putting his hat on the settle and his stick in the chimney corner*] They went up the hill. We went to the village. I wanted a drink. [*He sits down on the settle, putting his legs up along the seat*].

MRS WARREN. Well, she oughtnt to go off like that without telling me. [*To Frank*] Get your father a chair, Frank: where are your manners? [*Frank springs up and gracefully offers his father his chair; then takes another from the wall and sits down at the table, in the middle, with his father on his right and Mrs Warren on his left*]. George: where are you going to stay to-night? You cant stay here. And whats Praddy going to do?

CROFTS. Gardner'll put me up.

MRS WARREN. Oh, no doubt youve taken care of yourself! But what about Praddy?

CROFTS. Dont know. I suppose he can sleep at the inn.

MRS WARREN. Havnt you room for him, Sam?

REV. S. Well—er—you see, as rector here, I am not free to do as I like. Er—what is

Mr Praed's social position?

MRS WARREN. Oh, he's all right: he's an architect. What an old stick-in-the-mud you are, Sam!

FRANK. Yes, it's all right, gov'nor. He built that place down in Wales for the Duke. Caernarvon Castle they call it. You must have heard of it. [*He winks with lightning smartness at Mrs Warren, and regards his father blandly*].

REV. S. Oh, in that case, of course we shall only be too happy. I suppose he knows the Duke personally.

FRANK. Oh, ever so intimately! We can stick him in Georgina's old room.

MRS WARREN. Well, thats settled. Now if those two would only come in and let us have supper. Theyve no right to stay out after dark like this.

CROFTS [*aggressively*] What harm are they doing you?

MRS WARREN. Well, harm or not, I dont like it.

FRANK. Better not wait for them, Mrs Warren. Praed will stay out as long as possible. He has never known before what it is to stray over the heath on a summer night with my Vivie.

CROFTS [*sitting up in some consternation*] I say, you know! Come!

REV. S. [*rising, startled out of his professional manner into real force and sincerity*] Frank, once for all, it's out of the question. Mrs Warren will tell you that it's not to be thought of.

CROFTS. Of course not.

FRANK [*with enchanting placidity*] Is that so, Mrs Warren?

MRS WARREN [*reflectively*] Well, Sam, I dont know. If the girl wants to get married, no good can come of keeping her unmarried.

REV. S. [*astounded*] But married to him!— your daughter to my son! Only think: it's impossible.

CROFTS. Of course it's impossible. Dont be a fool, Kitty.

MRS WARREN [*nettled*] Why not? Isnt my daughter good enough for your son?

REV. S. But surely, my dear Mrs Warren, you know the reasons—

MRS WARREN [*defiantly*] I know no reasons. If you know any, you can tell them to the lad, or to the girl, or to your congregation, if you like.

REV. S. [*collapsing helplessly into his chair*]

You know very well that I couldnt tell anyone the reasons. But my boy will believe me when I tell him there a r e reasons.

FRANK. Quite right, Dad: he will. But has your boy's conduct ever been influenced by your reasons?

CROFTS. You cant marry her; and thats all about it. [*He gets up and stands on the hearth, with his back to the fireplace, frowning determinedly*].

MRS WARREN [*turning on him sharply*] What have you got to do with it, pray?

FRANK [*with his prettiest lyrical cadence*] Precisely what I was going to ask, myself, in my own graceful fashion.

CROFTS [*to Mrs Warren*] I suppose you dont want to marry the girl to a man younger than herself and without either a profession or twopence to keep her on. Ask Sam, if you dont believe me. [*To the parson*] How much more money are you going to give him?

REV. S. Not another penny. He has had his patrimony; and he spent the last of it in July. [*Mrs Warren's face falls*].

CROFTS [*watching her*] There! I told you. [*He resumes his place on the settle and puts up his legs on the seat again, as if the matter were finally disposed of*].

FRANK [*plaintively*] This is ever so mercenary. Do you suppose Miss Warren's going to marry for money? If we love one another—

MRS WARREN. Thank you. Your love's a pretty cheap commodity, my lad. If you have no means of keeping a wife, that settles it: you cant have Vivie.

FRANK [*much amused*] What do y o u say, gov'nor, eh?

REV. S. I agree with Mrs Warren.

FRANK. And good old Crofts has already expressed his opinion.

CROFTS [*turning angrily on his elbow*] Look here: I want none of y o u r cheek.

FRANK [*pointedly*] I'm e v e r so sorry to surprise you, Crofts; but you allowed yourself the liberty of speaking to me like a father a moment ago. One father is enough, thank you.

CROFTS [*contemptuously*] Yah! [*He turns away again*].

FRANK [*rising*] Mrs Warren: I cannot give my Vivie up, even for your sake.

MRS WARREN [*muttering*] Young scamp!

FRANK [*continuing*] And as you no doubt intend to hold out other prospects to her, I shall lose no time in placing my case before her. [*They stare at him; and he begins to declaim gracefully*]

He either fears his fate too much,
Or his deserts are small,
That dares not put it to the touch
To gain or lose it all.

The cottage door opens whilst he is reciting; and Vivie and Praed come in. He breaks off. Praed puts his hat on the dresser. There is an immediate improvement in the company's behavior. Crofts takes down his legs from the settle and pulls himself together as Praed joins him at the fireplace. Mrs Warren loses her ease of manner and takes refuge in querulousness.

MRS WARREN. Wherever have you been, Vivie?

VIVIE [*taking off her hat and throwing it carelessly on the table*] On the hill.

MRS WARREN. Well, you shouldnt go off like that without letting me know. How could I tell what had become of you? And night coming on too!

VIVIE [*going to the door of the kitchen and opening it, ignoring her mother*] Now, about supper? [*All rise except Mrs Warren*]. We shall be rather crowded in here, I'm afraid.

MRS WARREN. Did you hear what I said, Vivie?

VIVIE [*quietly*] Yes, mother. [*Reverting to the supper difficulty*] How many are we? [*Counting*] One, two, three, four, five, six. Well, two will have to wait until the rest are done: Mrs Alison has only plates and knives for four.

PRAED. Oh, it doesnt matter about me. I—

VIVIE. You have had a long walk and are hungry, Mr Praed: you shall have your supper at once. I can wait myself. I want one person to wait with me. Frank: are you hungry?

FRANK. Not the least in the world. Completely off my peck, in fact.

MRS. WARREN [*to Crofts*] Neither are you, George. You can wait.

CROFTS. Oh, hang it, Ive eaten nothing since tea-time. Cant Sam do it?

FRANK. Would you starve my poor father?

REV. S. [*testily*] Allow me to speak for myself, sir. I am perfectly willing to wait.

VIVIE [*decisively*] Theres no need. Only two are wanted. [*She opens the door of the kitchen*]. Will you take my mother in, Mr Gardner. [*The parson takes Mrs Warren; and they pass into the kitchen. Praed and Crofts follow. All except Praed clearly disapprove of the arrangement, but do not know how to resist it. Vivie*

stands at the door looking in at them*]. Can you squeeze past to that corner, Mr Praed: it's rather a tight fit. Take care of your coat against the white-wash: thats right. Now, are you all comfortable?

PRAED [*within*] Quite, thank you.

MRS WARREN [*within*] Leave the door open, dearie. [*Vivie frowns; but Frank checks her with a gesture, and steals to the cottage door, which he softly sets wide open*]. Oh, Lor, what a draught! Youd better shut it, dear.

Vivie shuts it with a slam, and then, noting with disgust that her mother's hat and shawl are lying about, takes them tidily to the window seat, whilst Frank noiselessly shuts the cottage door.

FRANK [*exulting*] Aha! Got rid of em. Well, Vivvums: what do you think of my governor?

VIVIE [*preoccupied and serious*] Ive hardly spoken to him. He doesnt strike me as being a particularly able person.

FRANK. Well, you know, the old man is not altogether such a fool as he looks. You see, he was shoved into the Church rather; and in trying to live up to it he makes a much bigger ass of himself than he really is. I dont dislike him as much as you might expect. He means well. How do you think youll get on with him?

VIVIE [*rather grimly*] I dont think my future life will be much concerned with him, or with any of that old circle of my mother's, except perhaps Praed. [*She sits down on the settle*]. What do you think of my mother?

FRANK. Really and truly?

VIVIE. Yes, really and truly.

FRANK. Well, she's ever so jolly. But she's rather a caution, isnt she? And Crofts! Oh, my eye, Crofts! [*He sits beside her*].

VIVIE. What a lot, Frank!

FRANK. What a crew!

VIVIE [*with intense contempt for them*] If I thought that *I* was like that—that I was going to be a waster, shifting along from one meal to another with no purpose, and no character, and no grit in me, I'd open an artery and bleed to death without one moment's hesitation.

FRANK. Oh no, you wouldnt. Why should they take any grind when they can afford not to? I wish I had their luck. No: what I object to is their form. It isnt the thing: it's slovenly, ever so slovenly.

VIVIE. Do you think your form will be any better when youre as old as Crofts, if you dont work?

FRANK. Of course I do. Ever so much better. Vivvums mustnt lecture: her little boy's incorrigible. [*He attempts to take her face caressingly in his hands*].

VIVIE [*striking his hands down sharply*] Off with you: Vivvums is not in a humor for petting her little boy this evening. [*She rises and comes forward to the other side of the room*].

FRANK [*following her*] How unkind!

VIVIE [*stamping at him*] Be serious. I'm serious.

FRANK. Good. Let us talk learnedly. Miss Warren: do you know that all the most advanced thinkers are agreed that half the diseases of modern civilization are due to starvation of the affections in the young. Now, *I*—

VIVIE [*cutting him short*] You are very tiresome. [*She opens the inner door*]. Have you room for Frank there? He's complaining of starvation.

MRS WARREN [*within*] Of course there is [*clatter of knives and glasses as she moves the things on the table*]. Here! theres room now beside me. Come along, Mr Frank.

FRANK. Her little boy will be ever so even with his Vivvums for this. [*He passes into the kitchen*].

MRS WARREN [*within*] Here, Vivie: come on you too, child. You must be famished. [*She enters, followed by Crofts, who holds the door open for Vivie with marked deference. She goes out without looking at him; and he shuts the door after her*]. Why, George, you cant be done: youve eaten nothing. Is there anything wrong with you?

CROFTS. Oh, all I wanted was a drink. [*He thrusts his hands in his pockets, and begins prowling about the room, restless and sulky*].

MRS WARREN. Well. I like enough to eat. But a little of that cold beef and cheese and lettuce goes a long way. [*With a sigh of only half repletion she sits down lazily on the settle*].

CROFTS. What do you go encouraging that young pup for?

MRS WARREN [*on the alert at once*] Now see here, George: what are you up to about that girl? Ive been watching your way of looking at her. Remember: I know you and what your looks mean.

CROFTS. Theres no harm in looking at her, is there?

MRS WARREN. I'd put you out and pack you back to London pretty soon if I saw any of your nonsense. My girl's little finger is more to me than your whole body and soul. [*Crofts receives this with a sneering grin. Mrs Warren, flushing a little at her failure to impose on him in the character of a theatrically devoted mother, adds in a lower key*] Make your mind easy: the young pup has no more chance than you have.

CROFTS. Maynt a man take an interest in a girl?

MRS WARREN. Not a man like you.

CROFTS. How old is she?

MRS WARREN. Never you mind how old she is.

CROFTS. Why do you make such a secret of it?

MRS WARREN. Because I choose.

CROFTS. Well, I'm not fifty yet; and my property is as good as ever it was—

MRS WARREN [*interrupting him*] Yes; because youre as stingy as youre vicious.

CROFTS [*continuing*] And a baronet isnt to be picked up every day. No other man in my position would put up with you for a mother-in-law. Why shouldnt she marry me?

MRS WARREN. You!

CROFTS. We three could live together quite comfortably. I'd die before her and leave her a bouncing widow with plenty of money. Why not? It's been growing in my mind all the time Ive been walking with that fool inside there.

MRS WARREN [*revolted*] Yes: it's the sort of thing that w o u l d grow in your mind.

He halts in his prowling; and the two look at one another, she steadfastly, with a sort of awe behind her contemptuous disgust: he stealthily, with a carnal gleam in his eye and a loose grin.

CROFTS [*suddenly becoming anxious and urgent as he sees no sign of sympathy in her*] Look here, Kitty: youre a sensible woman: you neednt put on any moral airs. I'll ask no more questions; and you need answer none. I'll settle the whole property on her; and if you want a cheque for yourself on the wedding day, you can name any figure you like—in reason.

MRS WARREN. So it's come to that with you, George, like all the other worn-out old creatures!

CROFTS [*savagely*] Damn you!

Before she can retort the door of the kitchen is opened; and the voices of the others are heard returning. Crofts, unable to recover his presence of mind, hurries out of the cottage. The clergyman appears at the kitchen door.

REV. S. [*looking round*] Where is Sir George?

MRS WARREN. Gone out to have a pipe. [*The clergyman takes his hat from the table, and joins Mrs Warren at the fireside. Meanwhile Vivie comes in, followed by Frank, who collapses into the nearest chair with an air of extreme exhaustion. Mrs Warren looks round at Vivie and says, with her affectation of maternal patronage even more forced than usual*] Well, dearie: have you had a good supper?

VIVIE. You know what Mrs Alison's suppers are. [*She turns to Frank and pets him*]. Poor Frank! was all the beef gone? did it get nothing but bread and cheese and ginger-beer? [*Seriously, as if she had done quite enough trifling for one evening*] Her butter is really awful. I must get some down from the stores.

FRANK. Do, in Heaven's name!

Vivie goes to the writing-table and makes a memorandum to order the butter. Praed comes in from the kitchen, putting up his handkerchief, which he has been using as a napkin.

REV. S. Frank, my boy: it is time for us to be thinking of home. Your mother does not know yet that we have visitors.

PRAED. I'm afraid we're giving trouble.

FRANK [*rising*] Not the least in the world: my mother will be delighted to see you. She's a genuinely intellectual artistic woman; and she sees nobody here from one year's end to another except the gov'nor; so you can imagine how jolly dull it pans out for her. [*To his father*] Youre not intellectual or artistic: are you, pater? So take Praed home at once; and I'll stay here and entertain Mrs Warren. Youll pick up Crofts in the garden. He'll be excellent company for the bull-pup.

PRAED [*taking his hat from the dresser, and coming close to Frank*] Come with us, Frank. Mrs Warren has not seen Miss Vivie for a long time; and we have prevented them from having a moment together yet.

FRANK [*quite softened, and looking at Praed with romantic admiration*] Of course. I forgot. Ever so thanks for reminding me. Perfect gentleman, Praddy. Always were. My ideal through life. [*He rises to go, but pauses a moment between the two older men, and puts his hand on Praed's shoulder*]. Ah, if you had only been my father instead of this unworthy old man! [*He puts his other hand on his father's shoulder*].

REV. S. [*blustering*] Silence, sir, silence: you are profane.

MRS WARREN [*laughing heartily*] You should keep him in better order, Sam. Good-night. Here: take George his hat and stick with my compliments.

REV. S. [*taking them*] Good-night. [*They shake hands. As he passes Vivie he shakes hands with her also and bids her goodnight. Then, in booming command, to Frank*] Come along, sir, at once. [*He goes out*].

MRS WARREN. Byebye, Praddy.

PRAED. Byebye, Kitty.

They shake hands affectionately and go out together, she accompanying him to the garden gate.

FRANK [*to Vivie*] Kissums?

VIVIE [*fiercely*] No. I hate you. [*She takes a couple of books and some paper from the writing-table, and sits down with them at the middle table, at the end next the fireplace*].

FRANK [*grimacing*] Sorry. [*He goes for his cap and rifle. Mrs Warren returns. He takes her hand*] Good-night, dear Mrs Warren. [*He kisses her hand. She snatches it away, her lips tightening, and looks more than half disposed to box his ears. He laughs mischievously and runs off, clapping-to the door behind him*].

MRS WARREN [*resigning herself to an evening of boredom now that the men are gone*] Did you ever in your life hear anyone rattle on so? Isnt he a tease? [*She sits at the table*]. Now that I think of it, dearie, dont you go encouraging him. I'm sure he's a regular good-for-nothing.

VIVIE [*rising to fetch more books*] I'm afraid so. Poor Frank! I shall have to get rid of him; but I shall feel sorry for him, though he's not worth it. That man Crofts does not seem to me to be good for much either: is he? [*She throws the books on the table rather roughly*].

MRS WARREN [*galled by Vivie's indifference*] What do you know of men, child, to talk that way about them? Youll have to make up your mind to see a good deal of Sir George Crofts, as he's a friend of mine.

VIVIE [*quite unmoved*] Why? [*She sits down and opens a book*]. Do you expect that we shall be much together? You and I, I mean?

MRS WARREN [*staring at her*] Of course: until youre married. Youre not going back to college again.

VIVIE. Do you think my way of life would suit you? I doubt it.

MRS WARREN. Your way of life. What do you mean?

VIVIE [*cutting a page of her book with the*

paper knife on her chatelaine] Has it really never occurred to you, mother, that I have a way of life like other people?

MRS WARREN. What nonsense is this youre trying to talk? Do you want to shew your independence, now that youre a great little person at school? Dont be a fool, child.

VIVIE [*indulgently*] Thats all you have to say on the subject, is it, mother?

MRS WARREN [*puzzled, then angry*] Dont you keep on asking me questions like that. [*Violently*] Hold your tongue. [*Vivie works on, losing no time, and saying nothing*]. You and your way of life, indeed! What next? [*She looks at Vivie again. No reply*]. Your way of life will be what I please, so it will. [*Another pause*]. Ive been noticing these airs in you ever since you got that tripos or whatever you call it. If you think I'm going to put up with them youre mistaken; and the sooner you find it out, the better. [*Muttering*] All I have to say on the subject, indeed! [*Again raising her voice angrily*] Do you know who youre speaking to, Miss?

VIVIE [*looking across at her without raising her head from her book*] No. Who are you? What are you?

MRS WARREN [*rising breathless*] You young imp!

VIVIE. Everybody knows my reputation, my social standing, and the profession I intend to pursue. I know nothing about you. What is that way of life which you invite me to share with you and Sir George Crofts, pray?

MRS WARREN. Take care. I shall do something I'll be sorry for after, and you too.

VIVIE [*putting aside her books with cool decision*] Well, let us drop the subject until you are better able to face it. [*Looking critically at her mother*] You want some good walks and a little lawn tennis to set you up. You are shockingly out of condition: you were not able to manage twenty yards uphill today without stopping to pant; and your wrists are mere rolls of fat. Look at mine. [*She holds out her wrists*].

MRS WARREN [*after looking at her helplessly, begins to whimper*] Vivie—

VIVIE [*springing up sharply*] Now pray dont begin to cry. Anything but that. I really cannot stand whimpering. I will go out of the room if you do.

MRS WARREN [*piteously*] Oh, my darling, how can you be so hard on me? Have I no rights over you as your mother?

VIVIE. A r e you my mother?

MRS WARREN [*appalled*] Am I your mother! Oh, Vivie!

VIVIE. Then where are our relatives? my father? our family friends? You claim the rights of a mother: the right to call me fool and child; to speak to me as no woman in authority over me at college dare speak to me; to dictate my way of life; and to force on me the acquaintance of a brute whom anyone can see to be the most vicious sort of London man about town. Before I give myself the trouble to resist such claims, I may as well find out whether they have any real existence.

MRS WARREN [*distracted, throwing herself on her knees*] Oh no, no. Stop, stop. I a m your mother: I swear it. Oh, you cant mean to turn on me—my own child! it's not natural. You believe me, dont you? Say you believe me.

VIVIE. Who was my father?

MRS WARREN. You dont know what youre asking. I cant tell you.

VIVIE [*determinedly*] Oh yes you can, if you like. I have a right to know; and you know very well that I have that right. You can refuse to tell me, if you please; but if you do, you will see the last of me tomorrow morning.

MRS WARREN. Oh, it's too horrible to hear you talk like that. You wouldnt—you c o u l d n t leave me.

VIVIE [*ruthlessly*] Yes, without a moment's hesitation, if you trifle with me about this. [*Shivering with disgust*] How can I feel sure that I may not have the contaminated blood of that brutal waster in my veins?

MRS WARREN. No, no. On my oath it's not he, nor any of the rest that you have ever met. I'm certain of that, at least.

Vivie's eyes fasten sternly on her mother as the significance of this flashes on her.

VIVIE [*slowly*] You are certain of that, at least. Ah! You mean that that is all you are certain of. [*Thoughtfully*] I see. [*Mrs Warren buries her face in her hands*]. Dont do that, mother: you know you dont feel it a bit. *Mrs Warren takes down her hands and looks up deplorably at Vivie, who takes out her watch and says*] Well, that is enough for tonight. At what hour would you like breakfast? Is half-past eight too early for you?

MRS WARREN [*wildly*] My God, what sort of woman are you?

VIVIE [*coolly*] The sort the world is mostly made of, I should hope. Otherwise I dont understand how it gets its business done. Come [*taking her mother by the wrist, and pulling her up pretty resolutely*]: pull yourself together. Thats right.

MRS WARREN [*querulously*] Youre very rough with me, Vivie.

VIVIE. Nonsense. What about bed? It's past ten.

MRS WARREN [*passionately*] Whats the use of my going to bed? Do you think I could sleep?

VIVIE. Why not? I shall.

MRS WARREN. You! youve no heart. [*She suddenly breaks out vehemently in her natural tongue—the dialect of a woman of the people—with all her affectations of maternal authority and conventional manners gone, and an overwhelming inspiration of true conviction and scorn in her*] Oh, I wont bear it: I wont put up with the injustice of it. What right have you to set yourself up above me like this? You boast of what you are to me—to me, who gave you the chance of being what you are. What chance had I? Shame on you for a bad daughter and a stuck-up prude!

VIVIE [*sitting down with a shrug, no longer confident; for her replies, which have sounded sensible and strong to her so far, now begin to ring rather woodenly and even priggishly against the new tone of her mother*] Dont think for a moment I set myself above you in any way. You attacked me with the conventional authority of a mother: I defended myself with the conventional superiority of a respectable woman. Frankly, I am not going to stand any of your nonsense; and when you drop it I shall not expect you to stand any of mine. I shall always respect your right to your own opinions and your own way of life.

MRS WARREN. My own opinions and my own way of life! Listen to her talking! Do you think I was brought up like you? able to pick and choose my own way of life? Do you think I did what I did because I liked it, or thought it right, or wouldnt rather have gone to college and been a lady if I'd had the chance?

VIVIE. Everybody has some choice, mother. The poorest girl alive may not be able to choose between being Queen of England or Principal of Newnham; but she can choose between ragpicking and flowerselling, according to her taste. People are always blaming their circumstances for what they are. I dont believe in circumstances. The people who get on in this world are the people who get up and look for the circumstances they want, and, if they cant find them, make them.

MRS WARREN. Oh, it's easy to talk, very easy, isnt it? Here! would you like to know what my circumstances were?

VIVIE. Yes: you had better tell me. Wont you sit down?

MRS WARREN. Oh, I'll sit down: dont you be afraid. [*She plants her chair farther forward with brazen energy, and sits down. Vivie is impressed in spite of herself*]. D'you know what your gran'mother was?

VIVIE. No.

MRS WARREN. No you dont. I do. She called herself a widow and had a fried-fish shop down by the Mint, and kept herself and four daughters out of it. Two of us were sisters: that was me and Liz; and we were both good-looking and well made. I suppose our father was a well-fed man: mother pretended he was a gentleman; but I dont know. The other two were only half sisters: undersized, ugly, starved looking, hard working, honest poor creatures: Liz and I would have half-murdered them if mother hadnt half-murdered us to keep our hands off them. They were the respectable ones. Well, what did they get by their respectability? I'll tell you. One of them worked in a whitelead factory twelve hours a day for nine shillings a week until she died of lead poisoning. She only expected to get her hands a little paralyzed; but she died. The other was always held up to us as a model because she married a Government laborer in the Deptford victualling yard, and kept his room and the three children neat and tidy on eighteen shillings a week—until he took to drink. That was worth being respectable for, wasnt it?

VIVIE [*now thoughtfully attentive*] Did you and your sister think so?

MRS WARREN. Liz didnt, I can tell you: she had more spirit. We both went to a church school—that was part of the ladylike airs we gave ourselves to be superior to the children that knew nothing and went nowhere—and we stayed there until Liz went out one night and never came back. I know the schoolmistress thought I'd soon follow her example; for the clergyman was always warning me that Lizzie'd end by jumping off Waterloo Bridge. Poor fool: that was all he knew about it! But I was more afraid of the whitelead factory than I was of the river; and so would you have been in my place. That clergyman got me a situation as scullery maid in a temperance restaurant where they sent out for anything you liked. Then I was waitress; and then I went to the bar at Waterloo station: fourteen hours a day serving drinks and washing glasses for four shillings a week and my board. That was considered a great promotion for me. Well, one cold, wretched night, when I was so tired I could hardly keep myself awake, who should come up for a half of Scotch but Lizzie, in a long fur cloak, elegant and comfortable, with a lot of sovereigns in her purse.

VIVIE [*grimly*] My aunt Lizzie!

MRS WARREN. Yes; and a very good aunt to have, too. She's living down at Winchester now, close to the cathedral, one of the most respectable ladies there. Chaperones girls at the county ball, if you please. No river for Liz, thank you! You remind me of Liz a little: she was a first-rate business woman —saved money from the beginning—never let herself look too like what she was—never lost her head or threw away a chance. When she saw I'd grown up good-looking she said to me across the bar "What are you doing there, you little fool? wearing out your health and your appearance for other people's profit!" Liz was saving money then to take a house for herself in Brussels; and she thought we two could save faster than one. So she lent me some money and gave me a start; and I saved steadily and first paid her back, and then went into business with her as her partner. Why shouldnt I have done it? The house in Brussels was real high class: a much better place for a woman to be in than the factory where Anne Jane got poisoned. None of our girls were ever treated as I was treated in the scullery of that temperance place, or at the Waterloo bar, or at home. Would you have had me stay in them and become a worn out old drudge before I was forty?

VIVIE [*intensely interested by this time*] No; but why did you choose that business? Saving money and good management will succeed in any business.

MRS WARREN. Yes, saving money. But where can a woman get the money to save in any other business? Could you save out of four shillings a week and keep yourself dressed as well? Not you. Of course, if youre a plain woman and cant earn anything more; or if you have a turn for music, or the stage, or newspaper-writing: thats different. But neither Liz nor I had any turn for such things: all we had was our appearance and our turn for pleasing men. Do you think we were such fools as to let other people trade in our good looks by employing us as shopgirls, or barmaids, or waitresses, when we could trade in them ourselves and get all the profits instead of starvation wages? Not likely.

VIVIE. You were certainly quite justified— from the business point of view.

MRS WARREN. Yes; or any other point of view. What is any respectable girl brought up to do but to catch some rich man's fancy and get the benefit of his money by marrying him?—as if a marriage ceremony could make any difference in the right or wrong of the thing! Oh, the hypocrisy of the world makes me sick! Liz and I had to work and save and calculate just like other people; elseways we should be as poor as any good-for-nothing drunken waster of a woman that thinks her luck will last for ever. [*With great energy*] I despise such people: theyve no character; and if theres a thing I hate in a woman, it's want of character.

VIVIE. Come now, mother: frankly! Isnt it part of what you call character in a woman that she should greatly dislike such a way of making money?

MRS WARREN. Why, of course. Everybody dislikes having to work and make money; but they have to do it all the same. I'm sure Ive often pitied a poor girl, tired out and in low spirits, having to try to please some man that she doesnt care two straws for—some half-drunken fool that thinks he's making himself agreeable when he's teasing and worrying and disgusting a woman so that hardly any money could pay her for putting up with it. But she has to bear with disagreeables and take the rough with the smooth, just like a nurse in a hospital or anyone else. It's not work that any woman would do for pleasure, goodness knows; though to hear the pious people talk you would suppose it was a bed of roses.

VIVIE. Still, you consider it worth while. It pays.

MRS WARREN. Of course it's worth while to a poor girl, if she can resist temptation and is good-looking and well conducted and sensible. It's far better than any other employment open to her. I always thought that oughtnt to be. It cant be right, Vivie, that there shouldnt be better opportunities for women. I stick to that: it's wrong. But it's so, right or wrong; and a girl must make the best of it. But of course it's not worth while for a lady. If you took to it youd be a fool; but I should have been a fool if I'd taken to anything else.

VIVIE [*more and more deeply moved*] Mother: suppose we were both as poor as you were in those wretched old days, are you quite sure that you wouldnt advise me to try the Waterloo bar, or marry a laborer, or even go into the factory?

MRS WARREN [*indignantly*] Of course not. What sort of mother do you take me for! How could you keep your self-respect in such starvation and slavery? And whats a woman worth? whats life worth? without self-respect! Why am I independent and able to give my daughter a first-rate education, when other women that had just as good opportunities are in the gutter? Because I always knew how to respect myself and control myself. Why is Liz looked up to in a cathedral town? The same reason. Where would we be now if we'd minded the clergyman's foolishness? Scrubbing floors for one and sixpence a day and nothing to look forward to but the workhouse infirmary. Dont you be led astray by people who dont know the world, my girl. The only way for a woman to provide for herself decently is for her to be good to some man that can afford to be good to her. If she's in his own station of life, let her make him marry her; but if she's far beneath him she cant expect it: why should she? it wouldnt be for her own happiness. Ask any lady in London society that has daughters; and she'll tell you the same, except that I tell you straight and she'll tell you crooked. Thats all the difference.

VIVIE [*fascinated, gazing at her*] My dear mother: you are a wonderful woman: you are stronger than all England. And are you really and truly not one wee bit doubtful—or—or—ashamed?

MRS WARREN. Well, of course, dearie, it's only good manners to be ashamed of it: it's expected from a woman. Women have to pretend to feel a great deal that they dont feel. Liz used to be angry with me for plumping out the truth about it. She used to say that when every woman could learn enough from what was going on in the world before her eyes, there was no need to talk about it to her. But then Liz was such a perfect lady! She had the true instinct of it; while I was always a bit of a vulgarian. I used to be so pleased when you sent me your photos to see that you were growing up like Liz: youve just her ladylike, determined way. But I cant stand saying one thing when everyone knows I mean another. Whats the use in such hypocrisy? If people arrange the world that way for women, theres no good pretending it's arranged the other way. No: I never was a bit ashamed really. I consider I had a right to be proud of how we managed everything so respectably, and never had a word against us, and how the girls were so well taken care of. Some of them did very well: one of them married an ambassador. But of course now I darent talk about such things: whatever would they think of us! [*She yawns*]. Oh dear! I do believe I'm getting sleepy after all. [*She stretches herself lazily, thoroughly relieved by her explosion, and placidly ready for her night's rest*].

VIVIE. I believe it is I who will not be able to sleep now. [*She goes to the dresser and lights the candle. Then she extinguishes the lamp, darkening the room a good deal*]. Better let in some fresh air before locking up. [*She opens the cottage door, and finds that it is broad moonlight*]. What a beautiful night! Look! [*She draws aside the curtains of the window. The landscape is seen bathed in the radiance of the harvest moon rising over Blackdown*].

MRS WARREN [*with a perfunctory glance at the scene*] Yes, dear; but take care you dont catch your death of cold from the night air.

VIVIE [*contemptuously*] Nonsense.

MRS WARREN [*querulously*] Oh yes: everything I say is nonsense, according to you.

VIVIE [*turning to her quickly*] No: really that is not so, mother. You have got completely the better of me tonight, though I intended it to be the other way. Let us be good friends now.

MRS WARREN [*shaking her head a little ruefully*] So it has been the other way. But I suppose I must give in to it. I always got the worst of it from Liz; and now I suppose it'll be the same with you.

VIVIE. Well, never mind. Come: goodnight, dear old mother. [*She takes her mother in her arms*].

MRS WARREN [*fondly*] I brought you up

well, didnt I, dearie?

VIVIE. You did.

MRS WARREN. And youll be good to your poor old mother for it, wont you?

VIVIE. I will, dear. [*Kissing her*] Goodnight.

MRS WARREN [*with unction*] Blessings on my own dearie darling! a mother's blessing!

She embraces her daughter protectingly, instinctively looking upward for divine sanction.

ACT III

In the Rectory garden next morning, with the sun shining from a cloudless sky. The garden wall has a five-barred wooden gate, wide enough to admit a carriage, in the middle. Beside the gate hangs a bell on a coiled spring, communicating with a pull outside. The carriage drive comes down the middle of the garden and then swerves to its left, where it ends in a little gravelled circus opposite the Rectory porch. Beyond the gate is seen the dusty high road, parallel with the wall, bounded on the farther side by a strip of turf and an unfenced pine wood. On the lawn, between the house and the drive, is a clipped yew tree, with a garden bench in its shade. On the opposite side the garden is shut in by a box hedge; and there is a sundial on the turf, with an iron chair near it. A little path leads off through the box hedge, behind the sundial.

Frank, seated on the chair near the sundial, on which he has placed the morning papers, is reading The Standard. His father comes from the house, red-eyed and shivery, and meets Frank's eye with misgiving.

FRANK [*looking at his watch*] Half-past eleven. Nice hour for a rector to come down to breakfast!

REV. S. Dont mock, Frank: dont mock. I am a little—er—[*Shivering*]—

FRANK. Off color?

REV. S. [*repudiating the expression*] No, sir: unwell this morning. Wheres your mother?

FRANK. Dont be alarmed: she's not here. Gone to town by the 11.13 with Bessie. She left several messages for you. Do you feel equal to receiving them now, or shall I wait til youve breakfasted?

REV. S. I have breakfasted, sir. I am surprised at your mother going to town when we have people staying with us. Theyll think it very strange.

FRANK. Possibly she has considered that. At all events, if Crofts is going to stay here, and you are going to sit up every night with

him until four, recalling the incidents of your fiery youth, it is clearly my mother's duty, as a prudent housekeeper, to go up to the stores and order a barrel of whisky and a few hundred siphons.

REV. S. I did not observe that Sir George drank excessively.

FRANK. You were not in a condition to, gov'nor.

REV. S. Do you mean to say that *I*—?

FRANK [*calmly*] I never saw a beneficed clergyman less sober. The anecdotes you told about your past career were so awful that I really dont think Praed would have passed the night under your roof if it hadnt been for the way my mother and he took to one another.

REV. S. Nonsense, sir. I am Sir George Crofts' host. I must talk to him about something; and he has only one subject. Where is Mr Praed now?

FRANK. He is driving my mother and Bessie to the station.

REV. S. Is Crofts up yet?

FRANK. Oh, long ago. He hasnt turned a hair: he's in much better practice than you. Has kept it up ever since, probably. He's taken himself off somewhere to smoke.

Frank resumes his paper. The parson turns disconsolately towards the gate; then comes back irresolutely.

REV. S. Er—Frank.

FRANK. Yes.

REV. S. Do you think the Warrens will expect to be asked here after yesterday afternoon?

FRANK Theyve been asked already.

REV. S. [*appalled*] What!!!

FRANK. Crofts informed us at breakfast that you told him to bring Mrs Warren and Vivie over here today, and to invite them to make this house their home. My mother then found she must go to town by the 11.13 train.

REV. S. [*with despairing vehemence*] I never gave any such invitation. I never thought of such a thing.

FRANK [*compassionately*] How do you know, gov'nor, what you said and thought last night?

PRAED [*coming in through the hedge*] Good morning.

REV. S. Good morning. I must apologize for not having met you at breakfast. I have a touch of—of—

FRANK. Clergyman's sore throat, Praed. Fortunately not chronic.

PRAED [*changing the subject*] Well, I must say your house is in a charming spot here. Really most charming.

REV. S. Yes: it is indeed, Frank will take you for a walk, Mr Praed, if you like. I'll ask you to excuse me: I must take the opportunity to write my sermon while Mrs Gardner is away and you are all amusing yourselves. You wont mind, will you?

PRAED. Certainly not. Dont stand on the slightest ceremony with me.

REV. S. Thank you. I'll—er—er— [*He stammers his way to the porch and vanishes into the house*].

PRAED. Curious thing it must be writing a sermon every week.

FRANK. Ever so curious, if he did it. He buys em. He's gone for some soda water.

PRAED. My dear boy: I wish you would be more respectful to your father. You know you can be so nice when you like.

FRANK. My dear Praddy: you forget that I have to live with the governor. When two people live together—it dont matter whether theyre father and son or husband and wife or brother and sister—they cant keep up the polite humbug thats so easy for ten minutes on an afternoon call. Now the governor, who unites to many admirable domestic qualities the irresoluteness of a sheep and the pompousness and aggressiveness of a jackass—

PRAED. No, pray, pray, my dear Frank, remember! He is your father.

FRANK. I give him due credit for that. [*Rising and flinging down his paper*] But just imagine his telling Crofts to bring the Warrens over here! He must have been ever so drunk. You know, my dear Praddy, my mother wouldnt stand Mrs Warren for a moment. Vivie mustnt come here until she's gone back to town.

PRAED. But your mother doesnt know anything about Mrs Warren, does she? [*He picks up the paper and sits down to read it*].

FRANK. I dont know. Her journey to town looks as if she did. Not that my mother would mind in the ordinary way: she has stuck like a brick to lots of women who had got into trouble. But they were all nice women. Thats what makes the real difference. Mrs Warren, no doubt, has her merits; but she's ever so rowdy; and my mother simply wouldnt put up with her. So—hallo! [*This exclamation is provoked by the reappearance of the clergyman, who comes out of the house in haste and dismay*].

REV. S. Frank: Mrs Warren and her daughter are coming across the heath with Crofts: I saw them from the study windows. What am I to say about your mother?

FRANK. Stick on your hat and go out and say how delighted you are to see them; and that Frank's in the garden; and that mother and Bessie have been called to the bedside of a sick relative, and were ever so sorry they couldnt stop; and that you hope Mrs Warren slept well; and—and—say any blessed thing except the truth, and leave the rest to Providence.

REV. S. But how are we to get rid of them afterwards?

FRANK. Theres no time to think of that now. Here! [*He bounds into the house*].

REV. S. He's so impetuous. I dont know what to do with him, Mr Praed.

FRANK [*returning with a clerical felt hat, which he claps on his father's head*]. Now: off with you. [*Rushing him through the gate*]. Praed and I'll wait here, to give the thing an unpremeditated air. [*The clergyman, dazed but obedient, hurries off*].

FRANK. We must get the old girl back to town somehow, Praed. Come! Honestly, dear Praddy, do you like seeing them together?

PRAED. Oh, why not?

FRANK [*his teeth on edge*] Dont it make your flesh creep ever so little? that wicked old devil, up to every villainy under the sun, I'll swear, and Vivie—ugh!

PRAED. Hush, pray. Theyre coming.

The clergyman and Crofts are seen coming along the road, followed by Mrs Warren and Vivie walking affectionately together.

FRANK. Look: she actually has her arm round the old woman's waist. It's her right arm: she began it. She's gone sentimental, by God! Ugh! Ugh! Now do you feel the creeps? [*The clergyman opens the gate; and Mrs Warren and Vivie pass him and stand in the middle of the garden looking at the house. Frank, in an ecstasy of dissimulation, turns gaily to Mrs Warren, exclaiming*] Ever so delighted to see you, Mrs Warren. This quiet old rectory garden becomes you perfectly.

MRS WARREN. Well, I never! Did you hear that, George? He says I look well in a quiet old rectory garden.

REV. S. [*still holding the gate for Crofts, who loafs through it, heavily bored*] You look well everywhere, Mrs Warren.

FRANK. Bravo, gov'nor! Now look here: lets have a treat before lunch. First lets see the church. Everyone has to do that. It's a regular old thirteenth century church, you know: the gov'nor's ever so fond of it, because he got up a restoration fund and had it completely rebuilt six years ago. Praed will be able to shew its points.

PRAED [*rising*] Certainly, if the restoration has left any to shew.

REV. S. [*mooning hospitably at them*] I shall be pleased, I'm sure, if Sir George and Mrs Warren really care about it.

MRS WARREN. Oh, come along and get it over.

CROFTS [*turning back towards the gate*] Ive no objection.

REV. S. Not that way. We go through the fields, if you dont mind. Round here. [*He leads the way by the little path through the box hedge*].

CROFTS. Oh, all right. [*He goes with the parson*].

Praed follows with Mrs Warren. Vivie does not stir: she watches them until they have gone, with all the lines of purpose in her face marking it strongly.

FRANK. Aint you coming?

VIVIE. No. I want to give you a warning, Frank. You were making fun of my mother just now when you said that about the rectory garden. That is barred in future. Please treat my mother with as much respect as you treat your own.

FRANK. My dear Viv: she wouldnt appreciate it: the two cases require different treatment. But what on earth has happened to you? Last night we were perfectly agreed as to your mother and her set. This morning I find you attitudinizing sentimentally with your arm around your parent's waist.

VIVIE [*flushing*] Attitudinizing!

FRANK. That was how it struck me. First time I ever saw you do a second-rate thing.

VIVIE [*controlling herself*] Yes, Frank: there has been a change; but I dont think it a change for the worse. Yesterday I was a little prig.

FRANK. And today?

VIVIE [*wincing; then looking at him steadily*] Today I know my mother better than you do.

FRANK. Heaven forbid!

VIVIE. What do you mean?

FRANK. Viv: theres a freemasonry among thoroughly immoral people that you know nothing of. Youve too much character. Thats the bond between your mother and me: thats why I know her better than youll ever know her.

VIVIE. You are wrong: you know nothing about her. If you knew the circumstances against which my mother had to struggle—

FRANK [*adroitly finishing the sentence for her*] I should know why she is what she is, shouldnt I? What difference would that make? Circumstances or no circumstances, Viv, you wont be able to stand your mother.

VIVIE [*very angry*] Why not?

FRANK. Because she's an old wretch, Viv. If you ever put your arm round her waist in my presence again, I'll shoot myself there and then as a protest against an exhibition which revolts me.

VIVIE. Must I choose between dropping your acquantance and dropping my mother's?

FRANK [*gracefully*] That would put the old lady at ever such a disadvantage. No, Viv: your infatuated little boy will have to stick to you in any case. But he's all the more anxious that you shouldnt make mistakes. It's no use, Viv: your mother's impossible. She may be a good sort; but she's a bad lot, a very bad lot.

VIVIE [*hotly*] Frank—! [*He stands his ground. She turns away and sits down on the bench under the yew tree, struggling to recover her self-command. Then she says*] Is she to be deserted by all the world because she's what you call a bad lot? Has she no right to live?

FRANK. No fear of that, Viv: she wont ever be deserted. [*He sits on the bench beside her*].

VIVIE. But I am to desert her, I suppose.

FRANK [*babyishly, lulling her and making love to her with his voice*] Musnt go live with her. Little family group of mother and daughter wouldnt be a success. Spoil our little group.

VIVIE [*falling under the spell*] What little group?

FRANK. The babes in the wood: Vivie and little Frank. [*He nestles against her like a weary child*]. Lets go and get covered up with leaves.

VIVIE [*rhythmically, rocking him like a nurse*] Fast asleep, hand in hand, under the trees.

FRANK. The wise little girl with her silly little boy.

VIVIE. The dear little boy with his dowdy little girl.

FRANK. Ever so peaceful, and relieved from the imbecility of the little boy's father and the questionableness of the little girl's—

VIVIE [*smothering the word against her breast*] Sh-sh-sh-sh! little girl wants to forget all about her mother. [*They are silent for some moments, rocking one another. Then Vivie wakes up with a shock, exclaiming*] What a pair of fools we are! Come: sit up. Gracious! your hair. [*She smooths it*]. I wonder do all grown up people play in that childish way when nobody is looking. I never did it when I was a child.

FRANK. Neither did I. You are my first playmate. [*He catches her hand to kiss it, but checks himself to look round first. Very unexpectedly, he sees Crofts emerging from the box hedge*]. Oh damn!

VIVIE. Why damn, dear?

FRANK [*whispering*] Sh! Heres this brute Crofts. [*He sits farther away from her with an unconcerned air*].

CROFTS. Could I have a few words with you, Miss Vivie?

VIVIE. Certainly.

CROFTS [*to Frank*] Youll excuse me, Gardner. Theyre waiting for you in the church, if you dont mind.

FRANK [*rising*] Anything to oblige you, Crofts—except church. If you should happen to want me, Vivvums, ring the gate bell. [*He goes into the house with unruffled suavity*].

CROFTS [*watching him with a crafty air as he disappears, and speaking to Vivie with an assumption of being on privileged terms with her*] Pleasant young fellow that, Miss Vivie. Pity he has no money, isnt it?

VIVIE. Do you think so?

CROFTS. Well, whats he to do? No profession. No property. Whats he good for?

VIVIE. I realize his disadvantages, Sir George.

CROFTS [*a little taken aback at being so precisely interpreted*] Oh, it's not that. But while we're in this world we're in it; and money's money. [*Vivie does not answer*]. Nice day, isnt it?

VIVIE [*with scarcely veiled contempt for this effort at conversation*] Very.

CROFTS [*with brutal good humor, as if he liked her pluck*] Well, thats not what I came to say. [*Sitting down beside her*] Now listen, Miss Vivie. I'm quite aware that I'm not a young lady's man.

VIVIE. Indeed, Sir George?

CROFTS. No; and to tell you the honest truth I dont want to be either. But when I say a thing I mean it; when I feel a sentiment I feel it in earnest; and what I value I pay hard money for. Thats the sort of man I am.

VIVIE. It does you great credit, I'm sure.

CROFTS. Oh, I dont mean to praise myself. I have my faults, Heaven knows: no man is more sensible of that than I am. I know I'm not perfect: thats one of the advantages of being a middle-aged man; for I'm not a young man, and I know it. But my code is a simple one, and, I think, a good one. Honor between man and man; fidelity between man and woman; and no cant about this religion or that religion, but an honest belief that things are making for good on the whole.

VIVIE [*with biting irony*] " A power, not ourselves, that makes for righteousness," eh?

CROFTS [*taking her seriously*] Oh certainly. Not ourselves, of course. You understand what I mean. Well, now as to practical matters. You may have an idea that Ive flung my money about; but I havnt: I'm richer today than when I first came into the property. Ive used my knowledge of the world to invest my money in ways that other men have overlooked; and whatever else I may be, I'm a safe man from the money point of view.

VIVIE. It's very kind of you to tell me all this.

CROFTS. Oh well, come, Miss Vivie: you neednt pretend you dont see what I'm driving at. I want to settle down with a Lady Crofts. I suppose you think me very blunt, eh?

VIVIE. Not at all: I am much obliged to you for being so definite and business-like. I quite appreciate the offer: the money, the position, Lady Crofts, and so on. But I think I will say no, if you dont mind. I'd rather not. [*She rises, and strolls across to the sundial to get out of his immediate neighborhood*].

CROFTS [*not at all discouraged, and taking advantage of the additional room left him on the seat to spread himself comfortably, as if a few preliminary refusals were part of the inevitable routine of courtship*] I'm in no hurry. It was only just to let you know in case young Gardner should try to trap you. Leave the question open.

VIVIE [*sharply*] My no is final. I wont go back from it.

Crofts is not impressed. He grins; leans forward with his elbows on his knees to prod with his stick at some unfortunate insect in the grass; and looks cunningly at her. She turns away impatiently.

CROFTS. I'm a good deal older than you. Twenty-five years: quarter of a century. I shant live for ever; and I'll take care that you shall be well off when I'm gone.

VIVIE. I am proof against even that inducement, Sir George. Dont you think youd better take your answer? There is not the slightest chance of my altering it.

CROFTS [*rising, after a final slash at a daisy, and coming nearer to her*] Well, no matter. I could tell you some things that would change your mind fast enough; but I wont, because I'd rather win you by honest affection. I was a good friend to your mother: ask her whether I wasnt. She'd never have made the money that paid for your education if it hadnt been for my advice and help, not to mention the money I advanced her. There are not many men would have stood by her as I have. I put not less than £40,000 into it, from first to last.

VIVIE [*staring at him*] Do you mean to say you were my mother's business partner?

CROFTS. Yes. Now just think of all the trouble and the explanations it would save if we were to keep the whole thing in the family, so to speak. Ask your mother whether she'd like to have to explain all her affairs to a perfect stranger.

VIVIE. I see no difficulty, since I understand that the business is wound up, and the money invested.

CROFTS [*stopping short, amazed*] Wound up! Wind up a business thats paying 35 per cent in the worst years! Not likely. Who told you that?

VIVIE [*her color quite gone*] Do you mean that it is still—? [*She stops abruptly, and puts her hand on the sundial to support herself. Then she gets quickly to the iron chair and sits down*]. What business are you talking about?

CROFTS. Well, the fact is it's not what would be considered exactly a high-class business in my set—the county set, you know—o u r set it will be if you think better of my offer. Not that theres any mystery about it: dont think that. Of course you know by your mother's being in it that it's perfectly straight and honest. Ive known her for many years; and I can say of her that she'd cut off

her hands sooner than touch anything that was not what it ought to be. I'll tell you all about it if you like. I dont know whether youve found in travelling how hard it is to find a really comfortable private hotel.

VIVIE [*sickened, averting her face*] Yes: go on.

CROFTS. Well, thats all it is. Your mother has a genius for managing such things. We've got two in Brussels, one in Ostend, one in Vienna, and two in Budapest. Of course there are others besides ourselves in it; but we hold most of the capital; and your mother's indispensable as managing director. Youve noticed, I daresay, that she travels a good deal. But you see you cant mention such things in society. Once let out the word hotel and everybody says you keep a publichouse. You wouldnt like people to say that of your mother, would you? Thats why we're so reserved about it. By the way, youll keep it to yourself, wont you? Since it's been a secret so long, it had better remain so.

VIVIE. And this is the business you invite me to join you in?

CROFTS. Oh no. My wife shant be troubled with business. Youll not be in it more than youve always been.

VIVIE. *I* always been! What do you mean?

CROFTS. Only that youve always lived on it. It paid for your education and the dress you have on your back. Dont turn up your nose at business, Miss Vivie: where would your Newnhams and Girtons be without it?

VIVIE [*rising, almost beside herself*] Take care. I know what this business is.

CROFTS [*starting, with a suppressed oath*] Who told you?

VIVIE. Your partner. My mother.

CROFTS [*black with rage*] The old—

VIVIE. Just so.

He swallows the epithet and stands for a moment swearing and raging foully to himself. But he knows that his cue is to be sympathetic. He takes refuge in generous indignation.

CROFTS. She ought to have had more consideration for you. *I'*d never have told you.

VIVIE. I think you would probably have told me when we were married: it would have been a convenient weapon to break me in with.

CROFTS [*quite sincerely*] I never intended that. On my word as a gentleman I didnt.

Vivie wonders at him. Her sense of the irony of his protest cools and braces her. She replies with contemptuous self-possession.

VIVIE. It does not matter. I suppose you understand that when we leave here today our acquaintance ceases.

CROFTS. Why? Is it for helping your mother?

VIVIE. My mother was a very poor woman who had no reasonable choice but to do as she did. You were a rich gentleman; and you did the same for the sake of 35 per cent. You are a pretty common sort of scoundrel, I think. That is my opinion of you.

CROFTS [*after a stare: not at all displeased, and much more at his ease on these frank terms than on their former ceremonious ones*] Ha! ha! ha! ha! Go it, little missie, go it: it doesnt hurt me and it amuses you. Why the devil shouldnt I invest my money that way? I take the interest on my capital like other people: I hope you dont think I dirty my own hands with the work. Come! you wouldnt refuse the acquaintance of my mother's cousin the Duke of Belgravia because some of the rents he gets are earned in queer ways. You wouldnt cut the Archbishop of Canterbury, I suppose, because the Ecclesiastical Commissioners have a few publicans and sinners among their tenants. Do you remember your Crofts scholarship at Newnham? Well, that was founded by my brother the M.P. He gets his 22 per cent out of a factory with 600 girls in it, and not one of them getting wages enough to live on. How d'ye suppose they manage when they have no family to fall back on? Ask your mother. And do you expect me to turn my back on 35 per cent when all the rest are pocketing what they can, like sensible men? No such fool! If youre going to pick and choose your acquaintances on moral principles, youd better clear out of this country, unless you want to cut yourself out of all decent society.

VIVIE [*conscience stricken*] You might go on to point out that I myself never asked where the money I spent came from. I believe I am just as bad as you.

CROFTS [*greatly reassured*] Of course you are; and a very good thing too! What harm does it do after all? [*Rallying her jocularly*] So you dont think me such a scoundrel now you come to think it over. Eh?

VIVIE. I have shared profits with you; and I admitted you just now to the familiarity of knowing what I think of you.

CROFTS [*with serious friendliness*] To be sure you did. You wont find me a bad sort: I dont go in for being superfine intellectually; but Ive plenty of honest human feeling; and the old Crofts breed comes out in a sort of instinctive hatred of anything low, in which I'm sure youll sympathize with me. Believe me, Miss Vivie, the world isnt such a bad place as the croakers make out. As long as you dont fly openly in the face of society, society doesnt ask any inconvenient questions; and it makes precious short work of the cads who do. There are no secrets better kept than the secrets everybody guesses. In the class of people I can introduce you to, no lady or gentleman would so far forget themselves as to discuss my business affairs or your mother's. No man can offer you a safer position.

VIVIE [*studying him curiously*] I suppose you really think youre getting on famously with me.

CROFTS. Well, I hope I may flatter myself that you think better of me than you did at first.

VIVIE [*quietly*] I hardly find you worth thinking about at all now. When I think of the society that tolerates you, and the laws that protect you! when I think of how helpless nine out of ten young girls would be in the hands of you and my mother! the unmentionable woman and her capitalist bully—

CROFTS [*livid*] Damn you!

VIVIE. You need not. I feel among the damned already.

She raises the latch of the gate to open it and go out. He follows her and puts his hand heavily on the top bar to prevent its opening.

CROFTS [*panting with fury*] Do you think I'll put up with this from you, you young devil?

VIVIE [*unmoved*] Be quiet. Someone will answer the bell. [*Without flinching a step she strikes the bell with the back of her hand. It clangs harshly; and he starts back involuntarily. Almost immediately Frank appears at the porch with his rifle*].

FRANK [*with cheerful politeness*] Will you have the rifle, Viv; or shall I operate?

VIVIE. Frank: have you been listening?

FRANK [*coming down into the garden*] Only for the bell, I assure you; so that you shouldnt have to wait. I think I shewed great insight into your character, Crofts.

CROFTS. For two pins I'd take that gun

from you and break it across your head.

FRANK [*stalking him cautiously*] Pray dont. I'm ever so careless in handling firearms. Sure to be a fatal accident, with a reprimand from the coroner's jury for my negligence.

VIVIE. Put the rifle away, Frank: it's quite unnecessary.

FRANK. Quite right, Viv. Much more sportsmanlike to catch him in a trap. [*Crofts, understanding the insult, makes a threatening movement*]. Crofts: there are fifteen cartridges in the magazine here; and I am a dead shot at the present distance and at an object of your size.

CROFTS. Oh, you neednt be afraid. I'm not going to touch you.

FRANK. Ever so magnanimous of you under the circumstances! Thank you.

CROFTS. I'll just tell you this before I go. It may interest you, since youre so fond of one another. Allow me, Mister Frank, to introduce you to your half-sister, the eldest daughter of the Reverend Samuel Gardner. Miss Vivie: your half-brother. Good morning. [*He goes out through the gate and along the road*].

FRANK [*after a pause of stupefaction, raising the rifle*] Youll testify before the coroner that it's an accident, Viv. [*He takes aim at the retreating figure of Crofts. Vivie seizes the muzzle and pulls it round against her breast*].

VIVIE. Fire now. You may.

FRANK [*dropping his end of the rifle hastily*] Stop! take care. [*She lets it go. It falls on the turf*]. Oh, youve given your little boy such a turn. Suppose it had gone off! ugh! [*He sinks on the garden seat, overcome*].

VIVIE. Suppose it had: do you think it would not have been a relief to have some sharp physical pain tearing through me?

FRANK [*coaxingly*] Take it ever so easy, dear Viv. Remember: even if the rifle scared that fellow into telling the truth for the first time in his life, that only makes us the babes in the wood in earnest. [*He holds out his arms to her*]. Come and be covered up with leaves again.

VIVIE [*with a cry of disgust*] Ah, not that, not that. You make all my flesh creep.

FRANK. Why, whats the matter?

VIVIE. Goodbye. [*She makes for the gate*].

FRANK [*jumping up*] Hallo! Stop! Viv! Viv! [*She turns in the gateway*] Where are you going to? Where shall we find you?

VIVIE. At Honoria Fraser's chambers, 67 Chancery Lane, for the rest of my life. [*She goes off quickly in the opposite direction to that taken by Crofts*].

FRANK. But I say—wait—dash it! [*He runs after her*].

ACT IV

Honoria Fraser's chambers in Chancery Lane. An office at the top of New Stone Buildings, with a plate-glass window, distempered walls, electric light, and a patent stove. Saturday afternoon. The chimneys of Lincoln's Inn and the western sky beyond are seen through the window. There is a double writing table in the middle of the room, with a cigar box, ash pans, and a portable electric reading lamp almost snowed up in heaps of papers and books. This table has knee holes and chairs right and left and is very untidy. The clerk's desk, closed and tidy, with its high stool, is against the wall, near a door communicating with the inner rooms. In the opposite wall is the door leading to the public corridor. Its upper panel is of opaque glass, lettered in black on the outside, FRASER AND WARREN. *A baize screen hides the corner between this door and the window.*

Frank, in a fashionable light-colored coaching suit, with his stick, gloves, and white hat in his hands, is pacing up and down the office. Somebody tries the door with a key.

FRANK [*calling*] Come in. It's not locked.

Vivie comes in, in her hat and jacket. She stops and stares at him.

VIVIE [*sternly*] What are you doing here?

FRANK. Waiting to see you. Ive been here for hours. Is this the way you attend to your business? [*He puts his hat and stick on the table, and perches himself with a vault on the clerk's stool, looking at her with every appearance of being in a specially restless, teasing, flippant mood*].

VIVIE. Ive been away exactly twenty minutes for a cup of tea. [*She takes off her hat and jacket and hangs them up behind the screen*]. How did you get in?

FRANK. The staff had not left when I arrived. He's gone to play cricket on Primrose Hill. Why dont you employ a woman, and give your sex a chance?

VIVIE. What have you come for?

FRANK [*springing off the stool and coming close to her*] Viv: lets go and enjoy the Saturday half-holiday somewhere, like the staff. What do you say to Richmond, and then a music hall, and a jolly supper?

VIVIE. Cant afford it. I shall put in another

six hours work before I go to bed.

FRANK. Cant afford it, cant we? Aha! Look here. [*He takes out a handful of sovereigns and makes them clink*]. Gold, Viv: gold!

VIVIE. Where did you get it?

FRANK. Gambling, Viv: gambling. Poker.

VIVIE. Pah! It's meaner than stealing it. No: I'm not coming. [*She sits down to work at the table, with her back to the glass door, and begins turning over the papers*].

FRANK [*remonstrating piteously*] But, my dear Viv, I want to talk to you ever so seriously.

VIVIE. Very well: sit down in Honoria's chair and talk here. I like ten minutes chat after tea. [*He murmurs*]. No use groaning: I'm inexorable. [*He takes the opposite seat disconsolately*]. Pass that cigar box, will you?

FRANK [*pushing the cigar box across*] Nasty womanly habit. Nice men dont do it any longer.

VIVIE. Yes: they object to the smell in the office; and weve had to take to cigarets. See! [*She opens the box and takes out a cigaret, which she lights. She offers him one; but he shakes his head with a wry face. She settles herself comfortably in her chair, smoking*]. Go ahead.

FRANK. Well, I want to know what youve done—what arrangements youve made.

VIVIE. Everything was settled twenty minutes after I arrived here. Honoria has found the business too much for her this year; and she was on the point of sending for me and proposing a partnership when I walked in and told her I hadnt a farthing in the world. So I installed myself and packed her off for a fortnight's holiday. What happened at Haslemere when I left?

FRANK. Nothing at all. I said youd gone to town on particular business.

VIVIE. Well?

FRANK. Well, either they were too flabbergasted to say anything, or else Crofts had prepared your mother. Anyhow, she didnt say anything; and Crofts didnt say anything; and Praddy only stared. After tea they got up and went; and Ive not seen them since.

VIVIE [*nodding placidly with one eye on a wreath of smoke*] Thats all right.

FRANK [*looking round disparagingly*] Do you intend to stick in this confounded place?

VIVIE [*blowing the wreath decisively away, and sitting straight up*] Yes. These two days have given me back all my strength and self-possession. I will never take a holiday again as long as I live.

FRANK [*with a very wry face*] Mps! You look quite happy. And as hard as nails.

VIVIE [*grimly*] Well for me that I am!

FRANK [*rising*] Look here, Viv: we must have an explanation. We parted the other day under a complete misunderstanding. [*He sits on the table, close to her*].

VIVIE [*putting away the cigaret*] Well: clear it up.

FRANK. You remember what Crofts said?

VIVIE. Yes.

FRANK. That revelation was supposed to bring about a complete change in the nature of our feeling for one another. It placed us on the footing of brother and sister.

VIVIE. Yes.

FRANK. Have you ever had a brother?

VIVIE. No.

FRANK. Then you dont know what being brother and sister feels like? Now I have lots of sisters; and the fraternal feeling is quite familiar to me. I assure you my feeling for you is not the least in the world like it. The girls will go their way; I will go mine; and we shant care if we never see one another again. Thats brother and sister. But as to you, I cant be easy if I have to pass a week without seeing you. Thats not brother and sister. It's exactly what I felt an hour before Crofts made his revelation. In short, dear Viv, it's love's young dream.

VIVIE [*bitingly*] The same feeling, Frank, that brought your father to my mother's feet. Is that it?

FRANK [*so revolted that he slips off the table for a moment*] I very strongly object, Viv, to have my feelings compared to any which the Reverend Samuel is capable of harboring; and I object still more to a comparison of you to your mother. [*Resuming his perch*]. Besides, I dont believe the story. I have taxed my father with it, and obtained from him what I consider tantamount to a denial.

VIVIE. What did he say?

FRANK. He said he was sure there must be some mistake.

VIVIE. Do you believe him?

FRANK. I am prepared to take his word as against Crofts'.

VIVIE. Does it make any difference? I mean in your imagination or conscience; for of course it makes no real difference.

FRANK [*shaking his head*] None whatever to me.

VIVIE. Nor to me.

FRANK [*staring*] But this is ever so surprising! [*He goes back to his chair*]. I thought our whole relations were altered in your imagination and conscience, as you put it, the moment those words were out of that brute's muzzle.

VIVIE. No: it was not that. I didnt believe him. I only wish I could.

FRANK. Eh?

VIVIE. I think brother and sister would be a very suitable relation for us.

FRANK. You really mean that?

VIVIE. Yes. It's the only relation I care for, even if we could afford any other. I mean that.

FRANK [*raising his eyebrows like one on whom a new light has dawned, and rising with quite an effusion of chivalrous sentiment*] My dear Viv: why didnt you say so before? I am ever so sorry for persecuting you. I understand, of course.

VIVIE [*puzzled*] Understand what?

FRANK. Oh, I'm not a fool in the ordinary sense: only in the Scriptural sense of doing all the things the wise man declared to be folly, after trying them himself on the most extensive scale. I see I am no longer Vivvums's little boy. Dont be alarmed: I shall never call you Vivvums again—at least unless you get tired of your new little boy, whoever he may be.

VIVIE. My new little boy!

FRANK [*with conviction*] Must be a new little boy. Always happens that way. No other way, in fact.

VIVIE. None that you know of, fortunately for you.

Someone knocks at the door.

FRANK. My curse upon yon caller, whoe'er he be!

VIVIE. It's Praed. He's going to Italy and wants to say goodbye. I asked him to call this afternoon. Go and let him in.

FRANK. We can continue our conversation after his departure for Italy. I'll stay him out. [*He goes to the door and opens it*]. How are you, Praddy? Delighted to see you. Come in.

Praed, dressed for travelling, comes in, in high spirits.

PRAED. How do you do, Miss Warren? [*She presses his hand cordially, though a certain sentimentality in his high spirits jars on her*]. I start in an hour from Holborn Viaduct. I wish I could persuade you to try Italy.

VIVIE. What for?

PRAED. Why, to saturate yourself with beauty and romance, of course.

Vivie, with a shudder, turns her chair to the table, as if the work waiting for her there were a support to her. Praed sits opposite to her. Frank places a chair near Vivie, and drops lazily and carelessly into it, talking at her over his shoulder.

FRANK. No use, Praddy. Viv is a little Philistine. She is indifferent to my romance, and insensible to my beauty.

VIVIE. Mr Praed: once for all, there is no beauty and no romance in life for me. Life is what it is; and I am prepared to take it as it is.

PRAED [*enthusiastically*] You will not say that if you come with me to Verona and on to Venice. You will cry with delight at living in such a beautiful world.

FRANK. This is most eloquent, Praddy. Keep it up.

PRAED. Oh, I assure you *I* have cried—I shall cry again, I hope—at fifty! At your age, Miss Warren, you would not need to go so far as Verona. Your spirits would absolutely fly up at the mere sight of Ostend. You would be charmed with the gaiety, the vivacity, the happy air of Brussels.

VIVIE [*springing up with an exclamation of loathing*] Agh!

PRAED [*rising*] Whats the matter?

FRANK [*rising*] Hallo, Viv!

VIVIE [*to Praed, with deep reproach*] Can you find no better example of your beauty and romance than Brussels to talk to me about?

PRAED [*puzzled*] Of course it's very different from Verona. I dont suggest for a moment that—

VIVIE [*bitterly*] Probably the beauty and romance come to much the same in both places.

PRAED [*completely sobered and much concerned*] My dear Miss Warren: I— [*looking inquiringly at Frank*] Is anything the matter?

FRANK. She thinks your enthusiasm frivolous, Praddy. She's had ever such a serious call.

VIVIE [*sharply*] Hold your tongue, Frank. Dont be silly.

FRANK [*sitting down*] Do you call this good manners, Praed?

PRAED [*anxious and considerate*] Shall I take him away, Miss Warren? I feel sure we have disturbed you at your work.

VIVIE. Sit down: I'm not ready to go back to work yet. [*Praed sits*]. You both think I have an attack of nerves. Not a bit of it. But there are two subjects I want dropped, if you dont mind. One of them [*to Frank*] is love's young dream in any shape or form: the other [*to Praed*] is the romance and beauty of life, especially Ostend and the gaiety of Brussels. You are welcome to any illusions you may have left on these subjects: I have none. If we three are to remain friends, I must be treated as a woman of business, permanently single [*to Frank*] and permanently unromantic [*to Praed*].

FRANK. I also shall remain permanently single until you change your mind. Praddy: change the subject. Be eloquent about something else.

PRAED [*diffidently*] I'm afraid theres nothing else in the world that I c a n talk about. The Gospel of Art is the only one I can preach. I know Miss Warren is a great devotee of the Gospel of Getting On; but we cant discuss that without hurting your feelings, Frank, since you are determined not to get on.

FRANK. Oh, dont mind my feelings. Give me some improving advice by all means: it does me ever so much good. Have another try to make a successful man of me, Viv. Come: lets have it all: energy, thrift, foresight, self-respect, character. Dont you hate people who have no character, Viv?

VIVIE [*wincing*] Oh, stop, stop: let us have no more of that horrible cant. Mr Praed: if there are really only those two gospels in the world, we had better all kill ourselves; for the same taint is in both, through and through.

FRANK [*looking critically at her*] There is a touch of poetry about you today, Viv, which has hitherto been lacking.

PRAED [*remonstrating*] My dear Frank: arnt you a little unsympathetic?

VIVIE [*merciless to herself*] No: it's good for me. It keeps me from being sentimental.

FRANK [*bantering her*] Checks your strong natural propensity that way, dont it?

VIVIE [*almost hysterically*] Oh yes: go on: dont spare me. I was sentimental for one moment in my life—beautifully sentimental —by moonlight; and now—

FRANK [*quickly*] I say, Viv: take care. Dont give yourself away.

VIVIE. Oh, do you think Mr Praed does not know all about my mother? [*Turning on Praed*] You had better have told me that morning, Mr Praed. You are very old fashioned in your delicacies, after all.

PRAED. Surely it is you who are a little old fashioned in your prejudices, Miss Warren. I feel bound to tell you, speaking as an artist, and believing that the most intimate human relationships are far beyond and above the scope of the law, that though I know that your mother is an unmarried woman, I do not respect her the less on that account. I respect her more.

FRANK [*airily*] Hear! hear!

VIVIE [*staring at him*] Is that a l l you know?

PRAED. Certainly that is all.

VIVIE. Then you neither of you know anything. Your guesses are innocence itself compared to the truth.

PRAED [*rising, startled and indignant, and preserving his politeness with an effort*] I hope not. [*More emphatically*] I hope not, Miss Warren.

FRANK [*whistles*] Whew!

VIVIE. You are not making it easy for me to tell you, Mr Praed.

PRAED [*his chivalry drooping before their conviction*] If there is anything worse—that is, anything else—are you sure you are right to tell us, Miss Warren?

VIVIE. I am sure that if I had the courage I should spend the rest of my life in telling everybody—stamping and branding it into them until they all felt their part in its abomination as I feel mine. There is nothing I despise more than the wicked convention that protects these things by forbidding a woman to mention them. And yet I cant tell you. The two infamous words that describe what my mother is are ringing in my ears and struggling on my tongue; but I cant utter them: the shame of them is too horrible for me. [*She buries her face in her hands. The two men, astonished, stare at one another and then at her. She raises her head again desperately and snatches a sheet of paper and a pen*]. Here: let me draft you a prospectus.

FRANK. Oh, she's mad. Do you hear, Viv? mad. Come! pull yourself together.

VIVIE. You shall see. [*She writes*]. "Paid up capital: not less than £40,000 standing in the name of Sir George Crofts, Baronet, the chief shareholder. Premises at Brussels, Ostend, Vienna, and Budapest. Managing director: Mrs Warren"; and now dont let us forget h e r qualifications: the two words. [*She writes the words and pushes the paper to them*]. There! Oh no: dont read it: dont! [*She snatches it back and tears it to pieces; then seizes her head in her hands and hides her face on the table*].

Frank, who has watched the writing over her shoulder, and opened his eyes very widely at it, takes a card from his pocket; scribbles the two words on it; and silently hands it to Praed, who reads it with amazement, and hides it hastily in his pocket.

FRANK [*whispering tenderly*] Viv, dear: thats all right. I read what you wrote: so did Praddy. We understand. And we remain, as this leaves us at present, yours ever so devotedly.

PRAED. We do indeed, Miss Warren. I declare you are the most splendidly courageous woman I ever met.

This sentimental compliment braces Vivie. She throws it away from her with an impatient shake, and forces herself to stand up, though not without some support from the table.

FRANK. Dont stir, Viv, if you dont want to. Take it easy.

VIVIE. Thank you. You can always depend on me for two things: not to cry and not to faint. [*She moves a few steps towards the door of the inner room, and stops close to Praed to say*] I shall need much more courage than that when I tell my mother that we have come to the parting of the ways. Now I must go into the next room for a moment to make myself neat again, if you dont mind.

PRAED. Shall we go away?

VIVIE. No: I'll be back presently. Only for a moment. [*She goes into the other room, Praed opening the door for her*].

PRAED. What an amazing revelation! I'm extremely disappointed in Crofts: I am indeed.

FRANK. I'm not in the least. I feel he's perfectly accounted for at last. But what a facer for me, Praddy! I cant marry her now.

PRAED [*sternly*] Frank! [*The two look at one another, Frank unruffled, Praed deeply indignant*]. Let me tell you, Gardner, that if you desert her now you will behave very despicably.

FRANK. Good old Praddy! Ever chivalrous! But you mistake: it's not the moral aspect of the case: it's the money aspect. I really cant bring myself to touch the old woman's money now?

PRAED. And was that what you were going to marry on?

FRANK. What else? *I* havnt any money, nor the smallest turn for making it. If I married Viv now she would have to support me; and I should cost her more than I am worth.

PRAED. But surely a clever bright fellow like you can make something by your own brains.

FRANK. Oh yes, a little. [*He takes out his money again*]. I made all that yesterday in an hour and a half. But I made it in a highly speculative business. No, dear Praddy: even if Bessie and Georgina marry millionaires and the governor dies after cutting them off with a shilling, I shall have only four hundred a year. And he wont die until he's three score and ten: he hasnt originality enough. I shall be on short allowance for the next twenty years. No short allowance for Viv, if I can help it. I withdraw gracefully and leave the field to the gilded youth of England. So thats settled. I shant worry her about it: I'll just send her a little note after we're gone. She'll understand.

PRAED [*grasping his hand*] Good fellow, Frank! I heartily beg your pardon. But must you never see her again?

FRANK. Never see her again! Hang it all, be reasonable. I shall come along as often as possible, and be her brother. I can not understand the absurd consequences you romantic people expect from the most ordinary transactions. [*A knock at the door*]. I wonder who this is. Would you mind opening the door? If it's a client it will look more respectable than if I appeared.

PRAED. Certainly. [*He goes to the door and opens it. Frank sits down in Vivie's chair to scribble a note*]. My dear Kitty: come in: come in.

Mrs Warren comes in, looking apprehensively round for Vivie. She has done her best to make herself matronly and dignified. The brilliant hat is replaced by a sober bonnet, and the gay blouse covered by a costly black silk mantle. She is pitiably anxious and ill at ease: evidently panic-stricken.

MRS WARREN [*to Frank*] What! Youre here, are you?

FRANK [*turning in his chair from his writing, but not rising*] Here, and charmed to see you. You come like a breath of spring.

MRS WARREN. Oh, get out with your nonsense. [*In a low voice*] Wheres Vivie?

Frank points expressively to the door of the inner room, but says nothing.

MRS WARREN [*sitting down suddenly and almost beginning to cry*] Praddy: wont she see me, dont you think?

PRAED. My dear Kitty: dont distress yourself. Why should she not?

MRS WARREN. Oh, you never can see why not: youre too innocent. Mr Frank: did she say anything to you?

FRANK [*folding his note*] She m u s t see you, if [*very expressively*] you wait til she comes in.

MRS WARREN [*frightened*] Why shouldnt I wait?

Frank looks quizzically at her; puts his note carefully on the ink-bottle, so that Vivie cannot fail to find it when next she dips her pen; then rises and devotes his attention entirely to her.

FRANK. My dear Mrs Warren: suppose you were a sparrow—ever so tiny and pretty a sparrow hopping in the roadway—and you saw a steam roller coming in your direction, would you wait for it?

MRS WARREN. Oh, dont bother me with your sparrows. What did she run away from Haslemere like that for?

FRANK. I'm afraid shc'll tell you if you rashly await her return.

MRS WARREN. Do you want me to go away?

FRANK. No: I always want you to stay. But I a d v i s e you to go away.

MRS WARREN. What! And never see her again!

FRANK. Precisely.

MRS WARREN [*crying again*] Praddy: dont let him be cruel to me. [*She hastily checks her tears and wipes her eyes*] She'll be so angry if she sees Ive been crying.

FRANK [*with a touch of real compassion in his airy tenderness*] You know that Praddy is the soul of kindness, Mrs Warren. Praddy: what do y o u say? Go or stay?

PRAED [*to Mrs Warren*] I really should be very sorry to cause you unnecessary pain; but I think perhaps you had better not wait. The fact is—[*Vivie is heard at the inner door*].

FRANK. Sh! Too late. She's coming.

MRS WARREN. Dont tell her I was crying. [*Vivic comes in. She stops gravely on seeing Mrs Warren, who greets her with hysterical cheerfulness*]. Well, dearie. So here you are at last.

VIVIE. I am glad you have come: I want to speak to you. You said you were going, Frank, I think.

FRANK. Yes. Will you come with mc, Mrs Warren? What do you say to a trip to Richmond, and the theatre in the evening? There is safety in Richmond. No steam roller there.

VIVIE. Nonsense, Frank. My mother will stay here.

MRS WARREN [*scared*] I dont know: perhaps I'd better go. We're disturbing you at your work.

VIVIE [*with quiet decision*] Mr Praed: please take Frank away. Sit down, mother. [*Mrs Warren obeys helplessly*].

PRAED. Come, Frank. Goodbye, Miss Vivie.

VIVIE [*shaking hands*] Goodbye. A pleasant trip.

PRAED. Thank you: thank you. I hope so.

FRANK [*to Mrs Warren*] Goodbye: youd ever so much better have taken my advice. [*He shakes hands with her. Then airily to Vivie*] Byebye, Viv.

VIVIE. Goodbye. [*He goes out gaily without shaking hands with her*].

PRAED [*sadly*] Goodbye, Kitty.

MRS WARREN [*snivelling*] —oobye!

Praed goes. Vivie, composed and extremely grave, sits down in Honoria's chair, and waits for her mother to speak. Mrs Warren, dreading a pause, loses no time in beginning.

MRS WARREN. Well, Vivie, what did you go away like that for without saying a word to me? How could you do such a thing! And what have you done to poor George? I wanted him to come with me; but he shuffled out of it. I could see that he was quite afraid of you. Only fancy: he wanted me not to come. As if [*trembling*] I should be afraid of you, dearie. [*Vivie's gravity deepens*]. But of course I told him it was all settled and comfortable between us, and that we were on the best of terms. [*She breaks down*]. Vivie: whats the meaning of this? [*She produces a commercial envelope, and fumbles at the enclosure with trembling fingers*]. I got it from the bank this morning.

VIVIE. It is my month's allowance. They scnt it to me as usual the other day. I simply sent it back to be placed to your credit, and asked them to send you the lodgment receipt. In future I shall support myself.

MRS WARREN [*not daring to understand*] Wasnt it enough? Why didnt you tell me? [*With a cunning gleam in her eye*] I'll double it: I was intending to double it. Only let me know how much you want.

VIVIE. You know very well that that has nothing to do with it. From this time I go my own way in my own business and among my own friends. And you will go yours. [*She rises*]. Goodbye.

MRS WARREN [*rising, appalled*] Goodbye?

VIVIE. Yes: goodbye. Come: dont let us

make a useless scene: you understand perfectly well. Sir George Crofts has told me the whole business.

MRS WARREN [*angrily*] Silly old— [*She swallows an epithet, and turns white at the narrowness of her escape from uttering it*].

VIVIE. Just so.

MRS WARREN. He ought to have his tongue cut out. But I thought it was ended: you said you didnt mind.

VIVIE [*steadfastly*] Excuse me: I do mind.

MRS WARREN. But I explained—

VIVIE. You explained how it came about. You did not tell me that it is still going on. [*She sits*].

Mrs Warren, silenced for a moment, looks forlornly at Vivie, who waits, secretly hoping that the combat is over. But the cunning expression comes back into Mrs Warren's face; and she bends across the table, sly and urgent, half whispering.

MRS WARREN. Vivie: do you know how rich I am?

VIVIE. I have no doubt you are very rich.

MRS WARREN. But you dont know all that that means: youre too young. It means a new dress every day; it means theatres and balls every night; it means having the pick of all the gentlemen in Europe at your feet; it means a lovely house and plenty of servants; it means the choicest of eating and drinking; it means everything you like, everything you want, everything you can think of. And what are you here? A mere drudge, toiling and moiling early and late for your bare living and two cheap dresses a year. Think over it. [*Soothingly*] Youre shocked, I know. I can enter into your feelings; and I think they do you credit; but trust me, nobody will blame you: you may take my word for that. I know what young girls are; and I know youll think better of it when youve turned it over in your mind.

VIVIE. So thats how it's done, is it? You must have said all that to many a woman, mother, to have it so pat.

MRS WARREN [*passionately*] What harm am I asking you to do? [*Vivie turns away contemptuously. Mrs Warren continues desperately*] Vivie: listen to me: you dont understand: youve been taught wrong on purpose: you dont know what the world is really like.

VIVIE [*arrested*] Taught wrong on purpose! What do you mean?

MRS WARREN. I mean that youre throwing away all your chances for nothing. You think that people are what they pretend to be: that the way you were taught at school and college to think right and proper is the way things really are. But it's not: it's all only a pretence, to keep the cowardly slavish common run of people quiet. Do you want to find that out, like other women, at forty, when youve thrown yourself away and lost your chances; or wont you take it in good time now from your own mother, that loves you and swears to you that it's truth: gospel truth? [*Urgently*] Vivie: the big people, the clever people, the managing people, all know it. They do as I do, and think what I think. I know plenty of them. I know them to speak to, to introduce you to, to make friends of for you. I dont mean anything wrong: thats what you dont understand: your head is full of ignorant ideas about me. What do the people that taught you know about life or about people like me? When did they ever meet me, or speak to me, or let anyone tell them about me? the fools! Would they ever have done anything for you if I hadnt paid them? Havnt I told you that I want you to be respectable? Havnt I brought you up to be respectable? And how can you keep it up without my money and my influence and Lizzie's friends? Cant you see that youre cutting your own throat as well as breaking my heart in turning your back on me?

VIVIE. I recognize the Crofts philosophy of life, mother. I heard it all from him that day at the Gardners'.

MRS WARREN. You think I want to force that played-out old sot on you! I dont, Vivie: on my oath I dont.

VIVIE. It would not matter if you did: you would not succeed. [*Mrs Warren winces, deeply hurt by the implied indifference towards her affectionate intention. Vivie, neither understanding this nor concerning herself about it, goes on calmly*] Mother: you dont at all know the sort of person I am. I dont object to Crofts more than to any other coarsely built man of his class. To tell you the truth, I rather admire him for being strongminded enough to enjoy himself in his own way and make plenty of money instead of living the usual shooting, hunting, dining-out, tailoring, loafing life of his set merely because all the rest do it. And I'm perfectly aware that if I'd been in the same circumstances as my aunt Liz, I'd have done exactly what she did. I dont think I'm more prejudiced or straitlaced than you: I think I'm less. I'm certain I'm less sentimental. I know very well that fashionable morality is all a pretence, and that if I took your money and devoted the rest of my life to spending it fashionably, I might be as worthless and vicious as the silliest woman could possibly want to be without having a word said to me about it. But I dont want to be worthless. I shouldnt enjoy trotting about the park to advertize my dressmaker and carriage builder, or being bored at the opera to shew off a shopwindowful of diamonds.

MRS WARREN [*bewildered*] But—

VIVIE. Wait a moment: Ive not done. Tell me why you continue your business now that you are independent of it. Your sister, you told me, has left all that behind her. Why dont you do the same?

MRS WARREN. Oh, it's all very easy for Liz: she likes good society, and has the air of being a lady. Imagine me in a cathedral town! Why, the very rooks in the trees would find me out even if I could stand the dulness of it. I must have work and excitement, or I should go melancholy mad. And what else is there for me to do? The life suits me: I'm fit for it and not for anything else. If I didnt do it somebody else would; so I dont do any real harm by it. And then it brings in money; and I like making money. No: it's no use: I cant give it up—not for anybody. But what need you know about it? I'll never mention it. I'll keep Crofts away. I'll not trouble you much: you see I have to be constantly running about from one place to another. Youll be quit of me altogether when I die.

VIVIE. No: I am my mother's daughter. I am like you: I must have work, and must make more money than I spend. But my work is not your work, and my way not your way. We must part. It will not make much difference to us: instead of meeting one another for perhaps a few months in twenty years, we shall never meet: thats all.

MRS WARREN [*her voice stifled in tears*] Vivie: I meant to have been more with you: I did indeed.

VIVIE. It's no use, mother: I am not to be changed by a few cheap tears and entreaties any more than you are, I daresay.

MRS WARREN [*wildly*] Oh, you call a mother's tears cheap.

VIVIE. They cost you nothing; and you ask me to give you the peace and quietness of my whole life in exchange for them. What use would my company be to you if you could get it? What have we two in common that could make either of us happy together?

MRS WARREN [*lapsing recklessly into her dialect*] We're mother and daughter. I want my daughter. Ive a right to you. Who is to care for me when I'm old? Plenty of girls have taken to me like daughters and cried at leaving me; but I let them all go because I had you to look forward to. I kept myself lonely for you. Youve no right to turn on me now and refuse to do your duty as a daughter.

VIVIE [*jarred and antagonized by the echo of the slums in her mother's voice*] My duty as a daughter! I thought we should come to that presently. Now once for all, mother, you want a daughter and Frank wants a wife. I dont want a mother; and I dont want a husband. I have spared neither Frank nor myself in sending him about his business. Do you think I will spare y o u?

MRS WARREN [*violently*] Oh, I know the sort you are: no mercy for yourself or anyone else. *I* know. My experience has done that for me anyhow: I can tell the pious, canting, hard, selfish woman when I meet her. Well, keep yourself to yourself: *I* dont want you. But listen to this. Do you know what I would do with you if you were a baby again? aye, as sure as theres a Heaven above us.

VIVIE. Strangle me, perhaps.

MRS WARREN. No: I'd bring you up to be a real daughter to me, and not what you are now, with your pride and your prejudices and the college education you stole from me: yes, stole: deny it if you can: what was it but stealing? I'd bring you up in my own house, I would.

VIVIE [*quietly*] In one of your own houses.

MRS WARREN [*screaming*] Listen to her! listen to how she spits on her mother's grey hairs! Oh, may you live to have your own daughter tear and trample on you as you have trampled on me. And you will: you will. No woman ever had luck with a mother's curse on her.

VIVIE. I wish you wouldnt rant, mother. It only hardens me. Come: I suppose I am the only young woman you ever had in your power that you did good to. Dont spoil it all now.

MRS WARREN. Yes, Heaven forgive me, it's true; and you are the only one that ever turned on me. Oh, the injustice of it! the injustice! the injustice! I always wanted to be a good woman. I tried honest work; and I was slave-driven until I cursed the day I ever heard of honest work. I was a good mother; and because I made my daughter a good woman she turns me out as if I was a leper. Oh, if I only had my life to live over again! I'd talk to that lying clergyman in the school. From this time forth, so help me Heaven in my last hour, I'll do wrong and nothing but wrong. And I'll prosper on it.

VIVIE. Yes: it's better to choose your line and go through with it. If I had been you, mother, I might have done as you did; but I should not have lived one life and believed in another. You are a conventional woman at heart. That is why I am bidding you goodbye now. I am right, am I not?

MRS WARREN [taken aback] Right to throw away all my money!

VIVIE. No: right to get rid of you? I should be a fool not to? Isnt that so?

MRS WARREN [sulkily] Oh well, yes, if you come to that, I suppose you are. But Lord help the world if everybody took to doing the right thing! And now I'd better go than stay where I'm not wanted. [She turns to the door].

VIVIE [kindly] Wont you shake hands?

MRS WARREN [after looking at her fiercely for a moment with a savage impulse to strike her] No, thank you. Goodbye.

VIVIE [matter-of-factly] Goodbye. [Mrs Warren goes out, slamming the door behind her. The strain on Vivie's face relaxes; her grave expression breaks up into one of joyous content; her breath goes out in a half sob, half laugh of intense relief. She goes buoyantly to her place at the writing-table; pushes the electric lamp out of the way; pulls over a great sheaf of papers; and is in the act of dipping her pen in the ink when she finds Frank's note. She opens it unconcernedly and reads it quickly, giving a little laugh at some quaint turn of expression in it]. And goodbye, Frank. [She tears the note up and tosses the pieces into the waste-paper basket without a second thought. Then she goes at her work with a plunge, and soon becomes absorbed in its figures].

THE END

IV

ARMS AND THE MAN

1894

BEING THE FIRST OF FOUR PLEASANT PLAYS

ACT I

Night. A lady's bedchamber in Bulgaria, in a small town near the Dragoman Pass, late in November in the year 1885. Through an open window with a little balcony a peak of the Balkans, wonderfully white and beautiful in the star-lit snow, seems quite close at hand, though it is really miles away. The interior of the room is not like anything to be seen in the west of Europe. It is half rich Bulgarian, half cheap Viennese. Above the head of the bed, which stands against a little wall cutting off the left hand corner of the room, is a painted wooden shrine, blue and gold, with an ivory image of Christ, and a light hanging before it in a pierced metal ball suspended by three chains. The principal seat, placed towards the other side of the room and opposite the window, is a Turkish ottoman. The counterpane and hangings of the bed, the window curtains, the little carpet, and all the ornamental textile fabrics in the room are oriental and gorgeous: the paper on the walls is occidental and paltry. The washstand, against the wall on the side nearest the ottoman and window, consists of an enamelled iron basin with a pail beneath it in a painted metal frame, and a single towel on the rail at the side. The dressing table, between the bed and the window, is a common pine table, covered with a cloth of many colors, with an expensive toilet mirror on it. The door is on the side nearest the bed; and there is a chest of drawers between. This chest of drawers is also covered by a variegated native cloth; and on it there is a pile of paper backed novels, a box of chocolate creams, and a miniature easel with a large photograph of an extremely handsome officer, whose lofty bearing and magnetic glance can be felt even from the portrait. The room is lighted by a candle on the chest of drawers, and another on the dressing table with a box of matches beside it.

The window is hinged doorwise and stands wide open. Outside, a pair of wooden shutters, opening outwards, also stand open. On the balcony a young lady, intensely conscious of the romantic beauty of the night, and of the fact that her own youth and beauty are part of it, is gazing at the snowy Balkans. She is in her nightgown, well covered by a long mantle of furs, worth, on a moderate estimate, about three times the furniture of her room.

Her reverie is interrupted by her mother, Catherine Petkoff, a woman over forty, imperiously energetic, with magnificent black hair and eyes, who might be a very splendid specimen of the wife of a mountain farmer, but is determined to be a Viennese lady, and to that end wears a fashionable tea gown on all occasions.

CATHERINE [*entering hastily, full of good news*] Raina! [*She pronounces it Rah-eena, with the stress on the ee*]. Raina! [*She goes to the bed, expecting to find Raina there*]. Why, where—? [*Raina looks into the room*]. Heavens, child! are you out in the night air instead of in your bed? Youll catch your death. Louka told me you were asleep.

RAINA [*dreamily*] I sent her away. I wanted to be alone. The stars are so beautiful! What is the matter?

CATHERINE. Such news! There has been a battle.

RAINA [*her eyes dilating*] Ah! [*She comes eagerly to Catherine*].

CATHERINE. A great battle at Slivnitza! A victory! And it was won by Sergius.

RAINA [*with a cry of delight*] Ah! [*They embrace rapturously*] Oh, mother! [*Then, with sudden anxiety*] Is father safe?

CATHERINE. Of course: he sends me the news. Sergius is the hero of the hour, the idol of the regiment.

RAINA. Tell me, tell me. How was it? [*Ecstatically*] Oh, mother! mother! mother! [*She pulls her mother down on the ottoman; and they kiss one another frantically*].

CATHERINE [*with surging enthusiasm*] You cant guess how splendid it is. A cavalry charge! think of that! He defied our Russian commanders—acted without orders—led a charge on his own responsibility—headed it himself—was the first man to sweep through their guns. Cant you see it, Raina: our gallant splendid Bulgarians, with their swords and eyes flashing, thundering down like an avalanche and scattering the wretched Serbs and their dandified Austrian officers like

chaff. And you! you kept Sergius waiting a year before you would be betrothed to him. Oh, if you have a drop of Bulgarian blood in your veins, you will worship him when he comes back.

RAINA. What will he care for my poor little worship after the acclamations of a whole army of heroes? But no matter: I am so happy! so proud! [*She rises and walks about excitedly*]. It proves that all our ideas were real after all.

CATHERINE [*indignantly*] Our ideas real! What do you mean?

RAINA. Our ideas of what Sergius would do. Our patriotism. Our heroic ideals. I sometimes used to doubt whether they were anything but dreams. Oh, what faithless little creatures girls are! When I buckled on Sergius's sword he looked so noble: it was treason to think of disillusion or humiliation or failure. And yet—and yet— [*She sits down again suddenly*] Promise me youll never tell him.

CATHERINE. Dont ask me for promises until I know what I'm promising.

RAINA. Well, it came into my head just as he was holding me in his arms and looking into my eyes that perhaps we only had our heroic ideas because we are so fond of reading Byron and Pushkin, and because we were so delighted with the opera that season at Bucharest. Real life is so seldom like that! indeed never, as far as I knew it then. [*Remorsefully*] Only think, mother: I doubted him: I wondered whether all his heroic qualities and his soldiership might not prove mere imagination when he went into a real battle. I had an uneasy fear that he might cut a poor figure there beside all those clever officers from the Tsar's court.

CATHERINE. A poor figure! Shame on you! The Serbs have Austrian officers who are just as clever as the Russians; but we have beaten them in every battle for all that.

RAINA [*laughing and snuggling against her mother*] Yes: I was only a prosaic little coward. Oh, to think that it was all true! that Sergius is just as splendid and noble as he looks! that the world is really a glorious world for women who can see its glory and men who can act its romance! What happiness! what unspeakable fulfilment!

They are interrupted by the entry of Louka, a handsome proud girl in a pretty Bulgarian peasant's dress with double apron, so defiant that her servility to Raina is almost insolent. She is afraid of Catherine, but even with her goes as far as she dares.

LOUKA. If you please, madam, all the windows are to be closed and the shutters made fast. They say there may be shooting in the streets. [*Raina and Catherine rise together, alarmed*]. The Serbs are being chased right back through the pass; and they say they may run into the town. Our cavalry will be after them; and our people will be ready for them, you may be sure, now theyre running away. [*She goes out on the balcony, and pulls the outside shutters to; then steps back into the room*].

CATHERINE [*businesslike, her housekeeping instincts aroused*] I must see that everything is made safe downstairs.

RAINA. I wish our people were not so cruel. What glory is there in killing wretched fugitives?

CATHERINE. Cruel! Do you suppose they would hesitate to kill y o u—or worse?

RAINA [*to Louka*] Leave the shutters so that I can just close them if I hear any noise.

CATHERINE [*authoritatively, turning on her way to the door*] Oh no, dear: you must keep them fastened. You would be sure to drop off to sleep and leave them open. Make them fast, Louka.

LOUKA. Yes, madam. [*She fastens them*].

RAINA. Dont be anxious about m e. The moment I hear a shot, I shall blow out the candles and roll myself up in bed with my ears well covered.

CATHERINE. Quite the wisest thing you can do, my love. Goodnight.

RAINA. Goodnight. [*Her emotion comes back for a moment*]. Wish me joy. [*They kiss*]. This is the happiest night of my life—if only there are no fugitives.

CATHERINE. Go to bed, dear; and dont think of them. [*She goes out*].

LOUKA [*secretly, to Raina*] If you would like the shutters open, just give them a push like this [*she pushes them: they open: she pulls them to again*]. One of them ought to be bolted at the bottom; but the bolt's gone.

RAINA [*with dignity, reproving her*] Thanks, Louka; but we must do what we are told. [*Louka makes a grimace*]. Goodnight.

LOUKA [*carelessly*] Goodnight. [*She goes out, swaggering*].

Raina, left alone, takes off her fur cloak and throws it on the ottoman. Then she goes to the chest of drawers, and adores the portrait there

with feelings that are beyond all expression. She does not kiss it or press it to her breast, or shew it any mark of bodily affection; but she takes it in her hands and elevates it, like a priestess.

RAINA [*looking up at the picture*] Oh, I shall never be unworthy of you any more, my soul's hero: never, never, never. [*She replaces it reverently. Then she selects a novel from the little pile of books. She turns over the leaves dreamily; finds her page; turns the book inside out at it; and, with a happy sigh, gets into bed and prepares to read herself to sleep. But before abandoning herself to fiction, she raises her eyes once more, thinking of the blessed reality, and murmurs*] My hero! my hero!

A distant shot breaks the quiet of the night. She starts, listening; and two more shots, much nearer, follow, startling her so that she scrambles out of bed, and hastily blows out the candle on the chest of drawers. Then, putting her fingers in her ears, she runs to the dressing table, blows out the light there, and hurries back to bed in the dark, nothing being visible but the glimmer of the light in the pierced ball before the image, and the starlight seen through the slits at the top of the shutters. The firing breaks out again: there is a startling fusillade quite close at hand. Whilst it is still echoing, the shutters disappear, pulled open from without; and for an instant the rectangle of snowy starlight flashes out with the figure of a man silhouetted in black upon it. The shutters close immediately; and the room is dark again. But the silence is now broken by the sound of panting. Then there is a scratch; and the flame of a match is seen in the middle of the room.

RAINA [*crouching on the bed*] Who's there? [*The match is out instantly*]. Who's there? Who is that?

A MAN'S VOICE [*in the darkness, subduedly, but threateningly*] Sh—sh! Dont call out; or youll be shot. Be good; and no harm will happen to you. [*She is heard leaving her bed, and making for the door*]. Take care: it's no use trying to run away.

RAINA. But who—

THE VOICE [*warning*] Remember: if you raise your voice my revolver will go off. [*Commandingly*]. Strike a light and let me see you. Do you hear. [*Another moment of silence and darkness as she retreats to the chest of drawers. Then she lights a candle; and the mystery is at an end. He is a man of about 35, in a deplorable plight, bespattered with mud and blood and snow, his belt and the strap of his revolver-case keeping together the torn ruins of the blue tunic of a Serbian artillery officer. All that the candlelight and his unwashed unkempt condition make it possible to discern is that he is of middling stature and undistinguished appearance, with strong neck and shoulders, roundish obstinate looking head covered with short crisp bronze curls, clear quick eyes and good brows and mouth, hopelessly prosaic nose like that of a strong minded baby, trim soldierlike carriage and energetic manner, and with all his wits about him in spite of his desperate predicament: even with a sense of the humor of it, without, however, the least intention of trifling with it or throwing away a chance. Reckoning up what he can guess about Raina: her age, her social position, her character, and the extent to which she is frightened, he continues, more politely but still most determinedly]* Excuse my disturbing you; but you recognize my uniform? Serb! If I'm caught I shall be killed. *[Menacingly]* Do you understand that?

RAINA. Yes.

THE MAN. Well, I dont intend to get killed if I can help it. *[Still more formidably]* Do you understand that? *[He locks the door quickly but quietly]*.

RAINA *[disdainfully]* I suppose not. *[She draws herself up superbly, and looks him straight in the face, adding, with cutting emphasis]* Some soldiers, I know, are afraid to die.

THE MAN *[with grim goodhumor]* All of them, dear lady, all of them, believe me. It is our duty to live as long as we can. Now, if you raise an alarm—

RAINA *[cutting him short]* You will shoot me. How do you know that *I* am afraid to die?

THE MAN *[cunningly]* Ah; but suppose I dont shoot you, what will happen then? A lot of your cavalry will burst into this pretty room of yours and slaughter me here like a pig; for I'll fight like a demon: they shant get me into the street to amuse themselves with: I know what they are. Are you prepared to receive that sort of company in your present undress? *[Raina, suddenly conscious of her nightgown, instinctively shrinks, and gathers it more closely about her neck. He watches her, and adds, pitilessly]* Hardly presentable, eh? *[She turns to the ottoman. He raises his pistol instantly, and cries]* Stop! *[She stops]*. Where are you going?

RAINA *[with dignified patience]* Only to get my cloak.

THE MAN *[passing swiftly to the ottoman and snatching the cloak]* A good idea! I'll keep the cloak; and youll take care that nobody comes in and sees you without it. This is a better weapon than the revolver: eh? *[He throws the pistol down on the ottoman]*.

RAINA *[revolted]* It is not the weapon of a gentleman!

THE MAN. It's good enough for a man with only you to stand between him and death. *[As they look at one another for a moment, Raina hardly able to believe that even a Serbian officer can be so cynically and selfishly unchivalrous, they are startled by a sharp fusillade in the street. The chill of imminent death hushes the man's voice as he adds]* Do you hear? If you are going to bring those blackguards in on me you shall receive them as you are.

Clamor and disturbance. The pursuers in the street batter at the house door, shouting Open the door! Open the door! Wake up, will you! *A man servant's voice calls to them angrily from within* This is Major Petkoff's house: you cant come in here; *but a renewal of the clamor, and a torrent of blows on the door, end with his letting a chain down with a clank, followed by a rush of heavy footsteps and a din of triumphant yells, dominated at last by the voice of Catherine, indignantly addressing an officer with* What does this mean, sir? Do you know where you are? *The noise subsides suddenly.*

LOUKA *[outside, knocking at the bedroom door]* My lady! my lady! get up quick and open the door. If you dont they will break it down.

The fugitive throws up his head with the gesture of a man who sees that it is all over with him, and drops the manner he has been assuming to intimidate Raina.

THE MAN *[sincerely and kindly]* No use, dear: I'm done for. *[Flinging the cloak to her]* Quick! wrap yourself up: theyre coming.

RAINA. Oh, thank you. *[She wraps herself up with intense relief]*.

THE MAN *[between his teeth]* Dont mention it.

RAINA *[anxiously]* What will you do?

THE MAN *[grimly]* The first man in will find out. Keep out of the way; and dont look. It wont last long; but it will not be nice. *[He draws his sabre and faces the door, waiting]*.

RAINA *[impulsively]* I'll help you. I'll save you.

THE MAN. You cant.

RAINA. I can. I'll hide you. *[She drags him towards the window]*. Here! behind the curtains.

THE MAN *[yielding to her]* Theres just half a

chance, if you keep your head.

RAINA [*drawing the curtain before him*] S-sh! [*She makes for the ottoman*].

THE MAN [*putting out his head*] Remember—

RAINA [*running back to him*] Yes?

THE MAN. —nine soldiers out of ten are born fools.

RAINA. Oh! [*She draws the curtain angrily before him*].

THE MAN [*looking out at the other side*] If they find me, I promise you a fight: a devil of a fight.

She stamps at him. He disappears hastily. She takes off her cloak, and throws it across the foot of the bed. Then, with a sleepy, disturbed air, she opens the door. Louka enters excitely.

LOUKA. One of those beasts of Serbs has been seen climbing up the waterpipe to your balcony. Our men want to search for him; and they are so wild and drunk and furious. [*She makes for the other side of the room to get as far from the door as possible*]. My lady says you are to dress at once, and to— [*She sees the revolver lying on the ottoman, and stops, petrified*].

RAINA [*as if annoyed at being disturbed*] They shall not search here. Why have they been let in?

CATHERINE [*coming in hastily*] Raina, darling: are you safe? Have you seen anyone or heard anything?

RAINA. I heard the shooting. Surely the soldiers will not dare come in here?

CATHERINE. I have found a Russian officer, thank Heaven: he knows Sergius. [*Speaking through the door to someone outside*] Sir: will you come in now. My daughter will receive you.

A young Russian officer, in Bulgarian uniform, enters, sword in hand.

OFFICER [*with soft feline politeness and stiff military carriage*] Good evening, gracious lady. I am sorry to intrude; but there is a Serb hiding on the balcony. Will you and the gracious lady your mother please to withdraw whilst we search?

RAINA [*petulantly*] Nonsense, sir: you can see that there is no one on the balcony. [*She throws the shutters wide open and stands with her back to the curtain where the man is hidden, pointing to the moonlit balcony. A couple of shots are fired right under the window; and a bullet shatters the glass opposite Raina, who winks and gasps, but stands her ground; whilst Catherine screams, and the officer, with a cry of* Take care! *rushes to the balcony*].

THE OFFICER [*on the balcony, shouting savagely down to the street*] Cease firing there, you fools: do you hear? Cease firing, damn you! [*He glares down for a moment; then turns to Raina, trying to resume his polite manner*]. Could anyone have got in without your knowledge? Were you asleep?

RAINA. No: I have not been to bed.

THE OFFICER [*impatiently, coming back into the room*] Your neighbors have their heads so full of runaway Serbs that they see them everywhere. [*Politely*] Gracious lady: a thousand pardons. Goodnight. [*Military bow, which Raina returns coldly. Another to Catherine, who follows him out*].

Raina closes the shutters. She turns and sees Louka, who has been watching the scene curiously.

RAINA. Dont leave my mother, Louka, until the soldiers go away.

Louka glances at Raina, at the ottoman, at the curtain; then purses her lips secretively, laughs insolently, and goes out. Raina, highly offended by this demonstration, follows her to the door, and shuts it behind her with a slam, locking it violently. The man immediately steps out from behind the curtain, sheathing his sabre. Then, dismissing the danger from his mind in a businesslike way, he comes affably to Raina.

THE MAN. A narrow shave; but a miss is as good as a mile. Dear young lady: your servant to the death. I wish for your sake I had joined the Bulgarian army instead of the other one. I am not a native Serb.

RAINA [*haughtily*] No: you are one of the Austrians who set the Serbs on to rob us of our national liberty, and who officer their army for them. We hate them!

THE MAN. Austrian! not I. Dont hate me, dear young lady. I am a Swiss, fighting merely as a professional soldier. I joined the Serbs because they came first on the road from Switzerland. Be generous: youve beaten us hollow.

RAINA. Have I not been generous?

THE MAN. Noble! Heroic! But I'm not saved yet. This particular rush will soon pass through; but the pursuit will go on all night by fits and starts. I must take my chance to get off in a quiet interval. [*Pleasantly*] You dont mind my waiting just a minute or two, do you?

RAINA [*putting on her most genteel society manner*] Oh, not at all. Wont you sit down?

THE MAN. Thanks. [*He sits on the foot of the bed*].

Raina walks with studied elegance to the ottoman and sits down. Unfortunately she sits on the pistol, and jumps up with a shriek. The man, all nerves, shies like a frightened horse to the other side of the room.

THE MAN [*irritably*] Dont frighten me like that. What is it?

RAINA. Your revolver! It was staring that officer in the face all the time. What an escape!

THE MAN [*vexed at being unnecessarily terrified*] Oh, is that all?

RAINA [*staring at him rather superciliously as she conceives a poorer and poorer opinion of him, and feels proportionately more and more at her ease*] I am sorry I frightened you. [*She takes up the pistol and hands it to him*]. Pray take it to protect yourself against me.

THE MAN [*grinning wearily at the sarcasm as he takes the pistol*] No use, dear young lady: theres nothing in it. It's not loaded. [*He makes a grimace at it, and drops it disparagingly into his revolver case*].

RAINA. Load it by all means.

THE MAN. Ive no ammunition. What use are cartridges in battle? I always carry chocolate instead; and I finished the last cake of that hours ago.

RAINA [*outraged in her most cherished ideals of manhood*] Chocolate! Do you stuff your pockets with sweets—like a schoolboy—even in the field?

THE MAN [*grinning*] Yes: isnt it contemptible? [*Hungrily*] I wish I had some now.

RAINA. Allow me. [*She sails away scornfully to the chest of drawers, and returns with the box of confectionery in her hand*]. I am sorry I have eaten them all except these. [*She offers him the box*].

THE MAN [*ravenously*] Youre an angel! [*He gobbles the contents*]. Creams! Delicious! [*He looks anxiously to see whether there are any more. There are none: he can only scrape the box with his fingers and suck them. When that nourishment is exhausted he accepts the inevitable with pathetic goodhumor, and says, with grateful emotion*] Bless you, dear lady! You can always tell an old soldier by the inside of his holsters and cartridge boxes. The young ones carry pistols and cartridges: the old ones, grub. Thank you. [*He hands back the box. She snatches it contemptuously from him and throws it away. He shies again, as if she had meant to strike him*]. Ugh! Dont do things so suddenly, gracious lady. It's mean to revenge yourself because I frightened you just now.

RAINA [*loftily*] Frighten me! Do you know, sir, that though I am only a woman, I think I am at heart as brave as you.

THE MAN. I should think so. You havnt been under fire for three days as I have. I can stand two days without shewing it much; but no man can stand three days: I'm as nervous as a mouse. [*He sits down on the ottoman, and takes his head in his hands*]. Would you like to see me cry?

RAINA [*alarmed*] No.

THE MAN. If you would, all you have to do is to scold me just as if I were a little boy and you my nurse. If I were in camp now, theyd play all sorts of tricks on me.

RAINA [*a little moved*] I'm sorry. I wont scold you. [*Touched by the sympathy in her tone, he raises his head and looks gratefully at her: she immediately draws back and says stiffly*] You must excuse me: our soldiers are not like that. [*She moves away from the ottoman*].

THE MAN. Oh yes they are. There are only two sorts of soldiers: old ones and young ones. Ive served fourteen years: half of your fellows never smelt powder before. Why, how is it that youve just beaten us? Sheer ignorance of the art of war, nothing else. [*Indignantly*] I never saw anything so unprofessional.

RAINA [*ironically*] Oh! was it unprofessional to beat you?

THE MAN. Well, come! is it professional to throw a regiment of cavalry on a battery of machine guns, with the dead certainty that if the guns go off not a horse or man will ever get within fifty yards of the fire? I couldnt believe my eyes when I saw it.

RAINA [*eagerly turning to him, as all her enthusiasm and her dreams of glory rush back on her*] Did you see the great cavalry charge? Oh, tell me about it. Describe it to me.

THE MAN. You never saw a cavalry charge, did you?

RAINA. How could I?

THE MAN. Ah, perhaps not. No: of course not! Well, it's a funny sight. It's like slinging a handful of peas against a window pane: first one comes; then two or three close behind him; and then all the rest in a lump.

RAINA [*her eyes dilating as she raises her clasped hands ecstatically*] Yes, first One! the bravest of the brave!

E

THE MAN [*prosaically*] Hm! you should see the poor devil pulling at his horse.

RAINA. Why should he pull at his horse?

THE MAN [*impatient of so stupid a question*] It's running away with him, of course: do you suppose the fellow wants to get there before the others and be killed? Then they all come. You can tell the young ones by their wildness and their slashing. The old ones come bunched up under the number one guard: t h e y know that theyre mere projectiles, and that it's no use trying to fight. The wounds are mostly broken knees, from the horses cannoning together.

RAINA. Ugh! But I dont believe the first man is a coward. I know he is a hero!

THE MAN [*goodhumoredly*] Thats what youd have said if youd seen the first man in the charge today.

RAINA [*breathless, forgiving him everything*] Ah, I knew it! Tell me. Tell me about him.

THE MAN. He did it like an operatic tenor. A regular handsome fellow, with flashing eyes and lovely moustache, shouting his war-cry and charging like Don Quixote at the windmills. We did laugh.

RAINA. You dared to laugh!

THE MAN. Yes; but when the sergeant ran up as white as a sheet, and told us theyd sent us the wrong ammunition, and that we couldnt fire a round for the next ten minutes, we laughed at the other side of our mouths. I never felt so sick in my life; though Ive been in one or two very tight places. And I hadnt even a revolver cartridge: only chocolate. We'd no bayonets: nothing. Of course, they just cut us to bits. And there was Don Quixote flourishing like a drum major, thinking he'd done the cleverest thing ever known, whereas he ought to be court-martialled for it. Of all the fools ever let loose on a field of battle, that man must be the very maddest. He and his regiment simply committed suicide; only the pistol missed fire: thats all.

RAINA [*deeply wounded, but steadfastly loyal to her ideals*] Indeed! Would you know him again if you saw him?

THE MAN. Shall I ever forget him!

She again goes to the chest of drawers. He watches her with a vague hope that she may have something more for him to eat. She takes the portrait from its stand and brings it to him.

RAINA. That is a photograph of the gentleman—the patriot and hero—to whom I am betrothed.

THE MAN [*recognizing it with a shock*] I'm really very sorry. [*Looking at her*] Was it fair to lead me on? [*He looks at the portrait again*] Yes: thats Don Quixote: not a doubt of it. [*He stifles a laugh*].

RAINA [*quickly*] Why do you laugh?

THE MAN [*apologetic, but still greatly tickled*] I didnt laugh, I assure you. At least I didnt mean to. But when I think of him charging the windmills and imagining he was doing the finest thing— [*He chokes with suppressed laughter*].

RAINA [*sternly*] Give me back the portrait, sir.

THE MAN [*with sincere remorse*] Of course. Certainly. I'm really very sorry. [*He hands her the picture. She deliberately kisses it and looks him straight in the face before returning to the chest of drawers to replace it. He follows her, apologizing*]. Perhaps I'm quite wrong, you know: no doubt I am. Most likely he had got wind of the cartridge business somehow, and knew it was a safe job.

RAINA. That is to say, he was a pretender and a coward! You did not dare say that before.

THE MAN [*with a comic gesture of despair*] It's no use, dear lady: I cant make you see it from the professional point of view. [*As he turns away to get back to the ottoman, a couple of distant shots threaten renewed trouble*].

RAINA [*sternly, as she sees him listening to the shots*] So much the better for you!

THE MAN [*turning*] How?

RAINA. You are my enemy; and you are at my mercy. What would I do if I were a professional soldier?

THE MAN. Ah, true, dear young lady: youre always right. I know how good youve been to me: to my last hour I shall remember those three chocolate creams. It was unsoldierly; but it was angelic.

RAINA [*coldly*] Thank you. And now I will do a soldierly thing. You cannot stay here after what you have just said about my future husband; but I will go out on the balcony and see whether it is safe for you to climb down into the street. [*She turns to the window*].

THE MAN [*changing countenance*] Down that waterpipe! Stop! Wait! I cant! I darent! The very thought of it makes me giddy. I came up it fast enough with death behind me. But to face it now in cold blood—! [*He sinks on the ottoman*]. It's no use: I give up: I'm beaten.

Give the alarm. [*He drops his head on his hands in the deepest dejection*].

RAINA [*disarmed by pity*] Come: dont be disheartened. [*She stoops over him almost maternally: he shakes his head*]. Oh, you are a very poor soldier: a chocolate cream soldier! Come, cheer up! it takes less courage to climb down than to face capture: remember that.

THE MAN [*dreamily, lulled by her voice*] No: capture only means death; and death is sleep: oh, sleep, sleep, sleep, undisturbed sleep! Climbing down the pipe means doing something—exerting myself—thinking! Death ten times over first.

RAINA [*softly and wonderingly, catching the rhythm of his weariness*] Are you as sleepy as that?

THE MAN. Ive not had two hours undisturbed sleep since I joined. I havnt closed my eyes for forty-eight hours.

RAINA [*at her wit's end*] But what am I to do with you?

THE MAN [*staggering up, roused by her desperation*] Of course. I must do something. [*He shakes himself; pulls himself together; and speaks with rallied vigor and courage*]. You see, sleep or no sleep, hunger or no hunger, tired or not tired, you can always do a thing when you know it must be done. Well, that pipe m u s t be got down: [*he hits himself on the chest*] do you hear that, you chocolate cream soldier? [*He turns to the window*].

RAINA [*anxiously*] But if you fall?

THE MAN. I shall sleep as if the stones were a feather bed. Goodbye. [*He makes boldly for the window; and his hand is on the shutter when there is a terrible burst of firing in the street beneath*].

RAINA [*rushing to him*] Stop! [*She seizes him recklessly, and pulls him quite round*]. Theyll kill you.

THE MAN [*coolly, but attentively*] Never mind: this sort of thing is all in my day's work. I'm bound to take my chance. [*Decisively*] Now do what I tell you. Put out the candle; so that they shant see the light when I open the shutters. And keep away from the window, whatever you do. If they see me theyre sure to have a shot at me.

RAINA [*clinging to him*] Theyre sure to see you: it's bright moonlight. I'll save you. Oh, how can you be so indifferent! You want me to save you, dont you?

THE MAN. I really dont want to be troublesome. [*She shakes him in her impatience*]. I am not indifferent, dear young lady, I assure you. But how is it to be done?

RAINA. Come away from the window. [*She takes him firmly back to the middle of the room. The moment she releases him he turns mechanically towards the window again. She seizes him and turns him back, exclaiming*] Please! [*He becomes motionless, like a hypnotized rabbit, his fatigue gaining fast on him. She releases him, and addresses him patronizingly*]. Now listen. You must trust to our hospitality. You do not yet know in whose house you are. I am a Petkoff.

THE MAN. A pet what?

RAINA [*rather indignantly*] I mean that I belong to the family of the Petkoffs, the richest and best known in our country.

THE MAN. Oh yes, of course. I beg your pardon. The Petkoffs, to be sure. How stupid of me!

RAINA. You know you never heard of them until this moment. How can you stoop to pretend!

THE MAN. Forgive me: I'm too tired to think; and the change of subject was too much for me. Dont scold me.

RAINA. I forgot. It might make you cry. [*He nods, quite seriously. She pouts and then resumes her patronizing tone*]. I must tell you that my father holds the highest command of any Bulgarian in our army. He is [*proudly*] a Major.

THE MAN [*pretending to be deeply impressed*] A Major! Bless me! Think of that!

RAINA. You shewed great ignorance in thinking that it was necessary to climb up to the balcony because ours is the only private house that has two rows of windows. There is a flight of stairs inside to get up and down by.

THE MAN. Stairs! How grand! You live in great luxury indeed, dear young lady.

RAINA. Do you know what a library is?

THE MAN. A library? A roomful of books?

RAINA. Yes. We have one, the only one in Bulgaria.

THE MAN. Actually a real library! I should like to see that.

RAINA [*affectedly*] I tell you these things to shew you that you are not in the house of ignorant country folk who would kill you the moment they saw your Serbian uniform, but among civilized people. We go to Bucharest every year for the opera season; and I have spent a whole month in Vienna.

THE MAN. I saw that, dear young lady. I saw at once that you knew the world.

RAINA. Have you ever seen the opera of Ernani?

THE MAN. Is that the one with the devil in it in red velvet, and a soldiers' chorus?

RAINA [contemptuously] No!

THE MAN [stifling a heavy sigh of weariness] Then I dont know it.

RAINA. I thought you might have remembered the great scene where Ernani, flying from his foes just as you are tonight, takes refuge in the castle of his bitterest enemy, an old Castilian noble. The noble refuses to give him up. His guest is sacred to him.

THE MAN [quickly, waking up a little] Have your people got that notion?

RAINA [with dignity] My mother and I can understand that notion, as you call it. And if instead of threatening me with your pistol as you did you had simply thrown yourself as a fugitive on our hospitality, you would have been as safe as in your father's house.

THE MAN. Quite sure?

RAINA [turning her back on him in disgust] Oh, it is useless to try to make y o u understand.

THE MAN. Dont be angry: you see how awkward it would be for me if there was any mistake. My father is a very hospitable man: he keeps six hotels; but I couldnt trust him as far as that. What about your father?

RAINA. He is away at Slivnitza fighting for his country. I answer for your safety. There is my hand in pledge of it. Will that reassure you? [She offers him her hand].

THE MAN [looking dubiously at his own hand] Better not touch my hand, dear young lady. I must have a wash first.

RAINA [touched] That is very nice of you. I see that you are a gentleman.

THE MAN [puzzled] Eh?

RAINA. You must not think I am surprised. Bulgarians of really good standing—people in our position—wash their hands nearly every day. So you see I can appreciate your delicacy. You may take my hand. [She offers it again].

THE MAN [kissing it with his hands behind his back] Thanks, gracious young lady: I feel safe at last. And now would you mind breaking the news to your mother? I had better not stay here secretly longer than is necessary.

RAINA. If you will be so good as to keep perfectly still whilst I am away.

THE MAN. Certainly. [He sits down on the ottoman].

Raina goes to the bed and wraps herself in the fur cloak. His eyes close. She goes to the door. Turning for a last look at him, she sees that he is dropping off to sleep.

RAINA [at the door] You are not going asleep, are you? [He murmurs inarticulately: she runs to him and shakes him]. Do you hear? Wake up: you are falling asleep.

THE MAN. Eh? Falling aslee—? Oh no: not the least in the world: I was only thinking. It's all right: I'm wide awake.

RAINA [severely] Will you please stand up while I am away. [He rises reluctantly]. All the time, mind.

THE MAN [standing unsteadily] Certainly. Certainly: you may depend on me.

Raina looks doubtfully at him. He smiles weakly. She goes reluctantly, turning again at the door, and almost catching him in the act of yawning. She goes out.

THE MAN [drowsily] Sleep, sleep, sleep, sleep, slee— [The words trail off into a murmur. He wakes again with a shock on the point of falling]. Where am I? Thats what I want to know: where am I? Must keep awake.Nothing keeps me awake except danger: remember that: [intently] danger, danger, danger, dan— [trailing off again: another shock] Wheres danger? Mus' find it. [He starts off vaguely round the room in search of it]. What am I looking for? Sleep—danger—dont know. [He stumbles against the bed]. Ah yes: now I know. All right now. I'm to go to bed, but not to sleep. Be sure not to sleep, because of danger. Not to lie down either, only sit down. [He sits on the bed. A blissful expression comes into his face]. Ah! [With a happy sigh he sinks back at full length; lifts his boots into the bed with a final effort; and falls fast asleep instantly].

Catherine comes in, followed by Raina.

RAINA [looking at the ottoman] He's gone! I left him here.

CATHERINE. Here! Then he must have climbed down from the—

RAINA [seeing him] Oh! [She points].

CATHERINE [scandalized] Well! [She strides to the bed, Raina following until she is opposite her on the other side]. He's fast asleep. The brute!

RAINA [anxiously] Sh!

CATHERINE [shaking him] Sir! [Shaking him again, harder] Sir!! [Vehemently, shaking very hard] Sir!!!

RAINA [catching her arm] Dont, mamma: the poor darling is worn out. Let him sleep.

CATHERINE [*letting him go, and turning amazed to Raina*] The poor darling! Raina!!! [*She looks sternly at her daughter*].

The man sleeps profoundly.

ACT II

The sixth of March, 1886. In the garden of Major Petkoff's house. It is a fine spring morning: the garden looks fresh and pretty. Beyond the paling the tops of a couple of minarets can be seen, shewing that there is a valley there, with the little town in it. A few miles further the Balkan mountains rise and shut in the landscape. Looking towards them from within the garden, the side of the house is seen on the left, with a garden door reached by a little flight of steps. On the right the stable yard, with its gateway, encroaches on the garden. There are fruit bushes along the paling and house, covered with washing spread out to dry. A path runs by the house, and rises by two steps at the corner, where it turns out of sight. In the middle, a small table, with two bent wood chairs at it, is laid for breakfast with Turkish coffee pot, cups, rolls, etc.; but the cups have been used and the bread broken. There is a wooden garden seat against the wall on the right.

Louka, smoking a cigaret, is standing between the table and the house, turning her back with angry disdain on a man servant who is lecturing her. He is a middle-aged man of cool temperament and low but clear and keen intelligence, with the complacency of the servant who values himself on his rank in servitude, and the imperturbability of the accurate calculator who has no illusions. He wears a white Bulgarian costume: jacket with embroidered border, sash, wide knickerbockers, and decorated gaiters. His head is shaved up to the crown, giving him a high Japanese forehead. His name is Nicola.

NICOLA. Be warned in time, Louka: mend your manners. I know the mistress. She is so grand that she never dreams that any servant could dare be disrespectful to her; but if she once suspects that you are defying her, out you go.

LOUKA. I do defy her. I will defy her. What do I care for her?

NICOLA. If you quarrel with the family, I never can marry you. It's the same as if you quarrelled with me!

LOUKA. You take her part against me, do you?

NICOLA [*sedately*] I shall always be dependent on the good will of the family. When I leave their service and start a shop in Sofia, their custom will be half my capital: their bad word would ruin me.

LOUKA. You have no spirit. I should like to catch them saying a word against me!

NICOLA [*pityingly*] I should have expected more sense from you, Louka. But youre young: youre young!

LOUKA. Yes; and you like me the better for it, dont you? But I know some family secrets they wouldnt care to have told, young as I am. Let them quarrel with me if they dare!

NICOLA [*with compassionate superiority*] Do you know what they would do if they heard you talk like that?

LOUKA. What could they do?

NICOLA. Discharge you for untruthfulness. Who would believe any stories you told after that? Who would give you another situation? Who in this house would dare be seen speaking to you ever again? How long would your father be left on his little farm? [*She impatiently throws away the end of her cigaret, and stamps on it*]. Child: you dont know the power such high people have over the like of you and me when we try to rise out of our poverty against them. [*He goes close to her and lowers his voice*]. Look at me, ten years in their service. Do you think I know no secrets? I know things about the mistress that she wouldnt have the master know for a thousand levas. I know things about him that she wouldnt let him hear the last of for six months if I blabbed them to her. I know things about Raina that would break off her match with Sergius if—

LOUKA [*turning on him quickly*] How do you know? I never told you!

NICOLA [*opening his eyes cunningly*] So thats your little secret, is it? I thought it might be something like that. Well, you take my advice and be respectful; and make the mistress feel that no matter what you know or dont know, she can depend on you to hold your tongue and serve the family faithfully. Thats what they like; and thats how youll make most out of them.

LOUKA [*with searching scorn*] You have the soul of a servant, Nicola.

NICOLA [*complacently*] Yes: thats the secret of success in service.

A loud knocking with a whip handle on a wooden door is heard from the stable yard.

MALE VOICE OUTSIDE. Hollo! Hollo there!

Nicola!

LOUKA. Master! back from the war!

NICOLA [*quickly*] My word for it, Louka, the war's over. Off with you and get some fresh coffee. [*He runs out into the stable yard*].

LOUKA [*as she collects the coffee pot and cups on the tray, and carries it into the house*] Youll never put the soul of a servant into me.

Major Petkoff comes from the stable yard, followed by Nicola. He is a cheerful, excitable, insignificant, unpolished man of about 50, naturally unambitious except as to his income and his importance in local society, but just now greatly pleased with the military rank which the war has thrust on him as a man of consequence in his town. The fever of plucky patriotism which the Serbian attack roused in all the Bulgarians has pulled him through the war; but he is obviously glad to be home again.

PETKOFF [*pointing to the table with his whip*] Breakfast out here, eh?

NICOLA. Yes, sir. The mistress and Miss Raina have just gone in.

PETKOFF [*sitting down and taking a roll*] Go in and say Ive come; and get me some fresh coffee.

NICOLA. It's coming, sir. [*He goes to the house door. Louka, with fresh coffee, a clean cup, and a brandy bottle on her tray, meets him*]. Have you told the mistress?

LOUKA. Yes: she's coming.

Nicola goes into the house. Louka brings the coffee to the table.

PETKOFF. Well: the Serbs havnt run away with you, have they?

LOUKA. No, sir.

PETKOFF. Thats right. Have you brought me some cognac?

LOUKA [*putting the bottle on the table*] Here, sir.

PETKOFF. Thats right. [*He pours some into his coffee*].

Catherine, who, having at this early hour made only a very perfunctory toilet, wears a Bulgarian apron over a once brilliant but now half worn-out dressing gown, and a colored handkerchief tied over her thick black hair, comes from the house with Turkish slippers on her bare feet, looking astonishingly handsome and stately under all the circumstances. Louka goes into the house.

CATHERINE. My dear Paul: what a surprise for us! [*She stoops over the back of his chair to kiss him*]. Have they brought you fresh coffee?

PETKOFF. Yes: Louka's been looking after me. The war's over. The treaty was signed three days ago at Bucharest; and the decree for our army to demobilize was issued yesterday.

CATHERINE [*springing erect, with flashing eyes*] Paul: have you let the Austrians force you to make peace?

PETKOFF [*submissively*] My dear: they didnt consult me. What could *I* do? [*She sits down and turns away from him*]. But of course we saw to it that the treaty was an honorable one. It declares peace—

CATHERINE [*outraged*] Peace!

PETKOFF [*appeasing her*] —but not friendly relations: remember that. They wanted to put that in; but I insisted on its being struck out. What more could I do?

CATHERINE. You could have annexed Serbia and made Prince Alexander Emperor of the Balkans. Thats what I would have done.

PETKOFF. I dont doubt it in the least, my dear. But I should have had to subdue the whole Austrian Empire first; and that would have kept me too long away from you. I missed you greatly.

CATHERINE [*relenting*] Ah! [*She stretches her hand affectionately across the table to squeeze his*].

PETKOFF. And how have you been, my dear?

CATHERINE. Oh, my usual sore throats: thats all.

PETKOFF [*with conviction*] That comes from washing your neck every day. Ive often told you so.

CATHERINE. Nonsense, Paul!

PETKOFF [*over his coffee and cigaret*] I dont believe in going too far with these modern customs. All this washing cant be good for the health: it's not natural. There was an Englishman at Philippopolis who used to wet himself all over with cold water every morning when he got up. Disgusting! It all comes from the English: their climate makes them so dirty that they have to be perpetually washing themselves. Look at my father! he never had a bath in his life; and he lived to be ninety-eight, the healthiest man in Bulgaria. I dont mind a good wash once a week to keep up my position; but once a day is carrying the thing to a ridiculous extreme.

CATHERINE. You are a barbarian at heart still, Paul. I hope you behaved yourself before all those Russian officers.

PETKOFF. I did my best. I took care to let them know that we have a library.

CATHERINE. Ah; but you didnt tell them that we have an electric bell in it? I have had one put up.

PETKOFF. Whats an electric bell?

CATHERINE. You touch a button: something tinkles in the kitchen; and then Nicola comes up.

PETKOFF. Why not shout for him?

CATHERINE. Civilized people never shout for their servants. Ive learnt that while you were away.

PETKOFF. Well, I'll tell you something Ive learnt too. Civilized people dont hang out their washing to dry where visitors can see it; so youd better have all that [indicating the clothes on the bushes] put somewhere else.

CATHERINE. Oh, thats absurd, Paul: I dont believe really refined people notice such things.

SERGIUS [knocking at the stable gates] Gate, Nicola!

PETKOFF. Theres Sergius. [Shouting] Hollo, Nicola!

CATHERINE. Oh, dont shout, Paul: it really isnt nice.

PETKOFF. Bosh! [He shouts louder than before] Nicola!

NICOLA [appearing at the house door] Yes, sir.

PETKOFF. Are you deaf? Dont you hear Major Saranoff knocking? Bring him round this way. [He pronounces the name with the stress on the second syllable: Sarahnoff].

NICOLA. Yes, major. [He goes into the stable yard].

PETKOFF. You must talk to him, my dear, until Raina takes him off our hands. He bores my life out about our not promoting him. Over my head, if you please.

CATHERINE. He certainly ought to be promoted when he marries Raina. Besides, the country should insist on having at least one native general.

PETKOFF. Yes; so that he could throw away whole brigades instead of regiments. It's no use, my dear: he hasnt the slightest chance of promotion until we're quite sure that the peace will be a lasting one.

NICOLA [at the gate, announcing] Major Sergius Saranoff! [He goes into the house and returns presently with a third chair, which he places at the table He then withdraws].

Major Sergius Saranoff, the original of the portrait in Raina's room, is a tall romantically handsome man, with the physical hardihood, the high spirit, and the susceptible imagination of an untamed mountaineer chieftain. But his remarkable personal distinction is of a characteristically civilized type. The ridges of his eyebrows, curving with an interrogative twist round the projections at the outer corners; his jealously observant eye; his nose, thin, keen, and apprehensive in spite of the pugnacious high bridge and large nostril; his assertive chin would not be out of place in a Parisian salon, shewing that the clever imaginative barbarian has an acute critical faculty which has been thrown into intense activity by the arrival of western civilization in the Balkans. The result is precisely what the advent of nineteenth century thought first produced in England: to wit, Byronism. By his brooding on the perpetual failure, not only of others, but of himself, to live up to his ideals; by his consequent cynical scorn for humanity; by his jejune credulity as to the absolute validity of his concepts and the unworthiness of the world in disregarding them; by his wincings and mockeries under the sting of the petty disillusions which every hour spent among men brings to his sensitive observation, he has acquired the half tragic, half ironic air, the mysterious moodiness, the suggestion of a strange and terrible history that has left nothing but undying remorse, by which Childe Harold fascinated the grandmothers of his English contemporaries. It is clear that here or nowhere is Raina's ideal hero. Catherine is hardly less enthusiastic about him than her daughter, and much less reserved in shewing her enthusiasm. As he enters from the stable gate, she rises effusively to greet him. Petkoff is distinctly less disposed to make a fuss about him.

PETKOFF. Here already, Sergius! Glad to see you.

CATHERINE. My dear Sergius! [She holds out both her hands].

SERGIUS [kissing them with scrupulous gallantry] My dear mother, if I may call you so.

PETKOFF [drily] Mother-in-law, Sergius: mother-in-law! Sit down; and have some coffee.

SERGIUS. Thank you: none for me. [He gets away from the table with a certain distaste for Petkoff's enjoyment of it, and posts himself with conscious dignity against the rail of the steps leading to the house].

CATHERINE. You look superb. The campaign has improved you, Sergius. Everybody here is mad about you. We were all wild with enthusiasm about that magnificent cavalry charge.

SERGIUS [*with grave irony*] Madam: it was the cradle and the grave of my military reputation.

CATHERINE. How so?

SERGIUS. I won the battle the wrong way when our worthy Russian generals were losing it the right way. In short, I upset their plans, and wounded their self-esteem. Two Cossack colonels had their regiments routed on the most correct principles of scientific warfare. Two major-generals got killed strictly according to military etiquette. The two colonels are now major-generals; and I am still a simple major.

CATHERINE. You shall not remain so, Sergius. The women are on your side; and they will see that justice is done you.

SERGIUS. It is too late. I have only waited for the peace to send in my resignation.

PETKOFF [*dropping his cup in his amazement*] Your resignation!

CATHERINE. Oh, you must withdraw it!

SERGIUS [*with resolute measured emphasis, folding his arms*] I never withdraw.

PETKOFF [*vexed*] Now who could have supposed you were going to do such a thing?

SERGIUS [*with fire*] Everyone that knew me. But enough of myself and my affairs. How is Raina; and where is Raina?

RAINA [*suddenly coming round the corner of the house and standing at the top of the steps in the path*] Raina is here.

She makes a charming picture as they turn to look at her. She wears an underdress of pale green silk, draped with an overdress of thin ecru canvas embroidered with gold. She is crowned with a dainty eastern cap of gold tinsel. Sergius goes impulsively to meet her. Posing regally, she presents her hand: he drops chivalrously on one knee and kisses it.

PETKOFF [*aside to Catherine, beaming with parental pride*] Pretty, isnt it? She always appears at the right moment.

CATHERINE [*impatiently*] Yes: she listens for it. It is an abominable habit.

Sergius leads Raina forward with splendid gallantry. When they arrive at the table, she turns to him with a bend of the head: he bows; and thus they separate, he coming to his place, and she going behind her father's chair.

RAINA [*stooping and kissing her father*] Dear father! Welcome home!

PETKOFF [*patting her cheek*] My little pet girl. [*He kisses her. She goes to the chair left by Nicola for Sergius, and sits down*].

CATHERINE. And so youre no longer a soldier, Sergius.

SERGIUS. I am no longer a soldier. Soldiering, my dear madam, is the coward's art of attacking mercilessly when you are strong, and keeping out of harm's way when you are weak. That is the whole secret of successful fighting. Get your enemy at a disadvantage; and never, on any account, fight him on equal terms.

PETKOFF. They wouldnt let us make a fair stand-up fight of it. However, I suppose soldiering has to be a trade like any other trade.

SERGIUS. Precisely. But I have no ambition to shine as a tradesman; so I have taken the advice of that bagman of a captain that settled the exchange of prisoners with us at Pirot, and given it up.

PETKOFF. What! that Swiss fellow? Sergius: Ive often thought of that exchange since. He over-reached us about those horses.

SERGIUS. Of course he over-reached us. His father was a hotel and livery stable keeper; and he owed his first step to his knowledge of horse-dealing. [*With mock enthusiasm*] Ah, he was a soldier: every inch a soldier! If only I had bought the horses for my regiment instead of foolishly leading it into danger, I should have been a field-marshal now!

CATHERINE. A Swiss? What was he doing in the Serbian army?

PETKOFF. A volunteer, of course: keen on picking up his profession. [*Chuckling*] We shouldnt have been able to begin fighting if these foreigners hadnt shewn us how to do it: we knew nothing about it; and neither did the Serbs. Egad, there'd have been no war without them!

RAINA. Are there many Swiss officers in the Serbian Army?

PETKOFF. No. All Austrians, just as our officers were all Russians. This was the only Swiss I came across. I'll never trust a Swiss again. He humbugged us into giving him fifty ablebodied men for two hundred worn out chargers. They werent even eatable!

SERGIUS. We were two children in the hands of that consummate soldier, Major: simply two innocent little children.

RAINA. What was he like?

CATHERINE. Oh, Raina, what a silly question!

SERGIUS. He was like a commercial traveller in uniform. Bourgeois to his boots!

PETKOFF [grinning] Sergius: tell Catherine that queer story his friend told us about how he escaped after Slivnitza. You remember. About his being hid by two women.

SERGIUS [with bitter irony] Oh yes: quite a romance! He was serving in the very battery I so unprofessionally charged. Being a thorough soldier, he ran away like the rest of them, with our cavalry at his heels. To escape their sabres he climbed a waterpipe and made his way into the bedroom of a young Bulgarian lady. The young lady was enchanted by his persuasive commercial traveller's manners. She very modestly entertained him for an hour or so, and then called in her mother lest her conduct should appear unmaidenly. The old lady was equally fascinated; and the fugitive was sent on his way in the morning, disguised in an old coat belonging to the master of the house, who was away at the war.

RAINA [rising with marked stateliness] Your life in the camp has made you coarse, Sergius. I did not think you would have repeated such a story before me. [She turns away coldly].

CATHERINE [also rising] She is right, Sergius. If such women exist, we should be spared the knowledge of them.

PETKOFF. Pooh! nonsense! what does it matter?

SERGIUS [ashamed] No, Petkoff: I was wrong. [To Raina, with earnest humility] I beg your pardon. I have behaved abominably. Forgive me, Raina. [She bows reservedly]. And you too, madam. [Catherine bows graciously and sits down. He proceeds solemnly, again addressing Raina] The glimpses I have had of the seamy side of life during the last few months have made me cynical; but I should not have brought my cynicism here: least of all into your presence, Raina. I— [Here, turning to the others, he is evidently going to begin a long speech when the Major interrupts him].

PETKOFF. Stuff and nonsense, Sergius! Thats quite enough fuss about nothing: a soldier's daughter should be able to stand up without flinching to a little strong conversation. [He rises]. Come: it's time for us to get to business. We have to make up our minds how those three regiments are to get back to Philippopolis: theres no forage for them on the Sofia route. [He goes towards the house]. Come along. [Sergius is about to follow him when Catherine rises and intervenes].

CATHERINE. Oh, Paul, cant you spare Sergius for a few moments? Raina has hardly seen him yet. Perhaps I can help you to settle about the regiments.

SERGIUS [protesting] My dear madam, impossible: you—

CATHERINE [stopping him playfully] You stay here, my dear Sergius: theres no hurry. I have a word or two to say to Paul. [Sergius instantly bows and steps back]. Now, dear [taking Petkoff's arm]: come and see the electric bell.

PETKOFF. Oh, very well, very well.

They go into the house together affectionately. Sergius, left alone with Raina, looks anxiously at her, fearing that she is still offended. She smiles, and stretches out her arms to him.

SERGIUS [hastening to her] Am I forgiven?

RAINA [placing her hands on his shoulders as she looks up at him with admiration and worship] My hero! My king!

SERGIUS. My queen! [He kisses her on the forehead].

RAINA. How I have envied you, Sergius! You have been out in the world, on the field of battle, able to prove yourself there worthy of any woman in the world; whilst I have had to sit at home inactive—dreaming—useless —doing nothing that could give me the right to call myself worthy of any man.

SERGIUS. Dearest: all my deeds have been yours. You inspired me. I have gone through the war like a knight in a tournament with his lady looking down at him!

RAINA. And you have never been absent from my thoughts for a moment. [Very solemnly] Sergius: I think we two have found the higher love. When I think of you, I feel that I could never do a base deed, or think an ignoble thought.

SERGIUS. My lady and my saint! [He clasps her reverently].

RAINA [returning his embrace] My lord and my—

SERGIUS. Sh—sh! Let me be the worshipper, dear. You little know how unworthy even the best man is of a girl's pure passion!

RAINA. I trust you. I love you. You will never disappoint me, Sergius. [Louka is heard singing within the house. They quickly release each other]. I cant pretend to talk indifferently before her: my heart is too full. [Louka comes from the house with her tray. She goes to the table, and begins to clear it, with her back turned to them]. I will get my hat; and then we can go out until lunch time. Wouldnt you like that?

SERGIUS. Be quick. If you are away five minutes, it will seem five hours. [*Raina runs to the top of the steps, and turns there to exchange looks with him and wave him a kiss with both hands. He looks after her with emotion for a moment; then turns slowly away, his face radiant with the loftiest exaltation. The movement shifts his field of vision, into the corner of which there now comes the tail of Louka's double apron. His attention is arrested at once. He takes a stealthy look at her, and begins to twirl his moustache mischievously, with his left hand akimbo on his hip. Finally, striking the ground with his heels in something of a cavalry swagger, he strolls over to the other side of the table, opposite her, and says*] Louka: do you know what the higher love is?

LOUKA [*astonished*] No, sir.

SERGIUS. Very fatiguing thing to keep up for any length of time, Louka. One feels the need of some relief after it.

LOUKA [*innocently*] Perhaps you would like some coffee, sir? [*She stretches her hand across the table for the coffee pot*].

SERGIUS [*taking her hand*] Thank you, Louka.

LOUKA [*pretending to pull*] Oh, sir, you know I didnt mean that. I'm surprised at you!

SERGIUS [*coming clear of the table and drawing her with him*] I am surprised at myself, Louka. What would Sergius, the hero of Slivnitza, say if he saw me now? What would Sergius, the apostle of the higher love, say if he saw me now? What would the half dozen Sergiuses who keep popping in and out of this handsome figure of mine say if they caught us here? [*Letting go her hand and slipping his arm dexterously round her waist*] Do you consider my figure handsome, Louka?

LOUKA. Let me go, sir. I shall be disgraced. [*She struggles: he holds her inexorably*]. Oh, will you let go?

SERGIUS [*looking straight into her eyes*] No.

LOUKA. Then stand back where we cant be seen. Have you no common sense?

SERGIUS. Ah! thats reasonable. [*He takes her into the stableyard gateway, where they are hidden from the house*].

LOUKA [*plaintively*] I may have been seen from the windows: Miss Raina is sure to be spying about after you.

SERGIUS [*stung: letting her go*] Take care, Louka. I may be worthless enough to betray the higher love; but do not you insult it.

LOUKA [*demurely*] Not for the world, sir, I'm sure. May I go on with my work, please, now?

SERGIUS [*again putting his arm round her*] You are a provoking little witch, Louka. If you were in love with me, would you spy out of windows on me?

LOUKA. Well, you see, sir, since you say you are half a dozen different gentlemen all at once, I should have a great deal to look after.

SERGIUS [*charmed*] Witty as well as pretty. [*He tries to kiss her*].

LOUKA [*avoiding him*] No : I dont want your kisses. Gentlefolk are all alike: you making love to me behind Miss Raina's back; and she doing the same behind yours.

SERGIUS [*recoiling a step*] Louka!

LOUKA. It shews how little you really care.

SERGIUS [*dropping his familiarity, and speaking with freezing politeness*] If our conversation is to continue, Louka, you will please remember that a gentleman does not discuss the conduct of the lady he is engaged to with her maid.

LOUKA. It's so hard to know what a gentleman considers right. I thought from your trying to kiss me that you had given up being so particular.

SERGIUS [*turning from her and striking his forehead as he comes back into the garden from the gateway*] Devil! devil!

LOUKA. Ha! ha! I expect one of the six of you is very like me, sir; though I am only Miss Raina's maid. [*She goes back to her work at the table, taking no further notice of him*].

SERGIUS [*speaking to himself*] Which of the six is the real man? thats the question that torments me. One of them is a hero, another a buffoon, another a humbug, another perhaps a bit of a blackguard. [*He pauses, and looks furtively at Louka as he adds, with deep bitterness*] And one, at least, is a coward: jealous, like all cowards. [*He goes to the table*]. Louka.

LOUKA. Yes?

SERGIUS. Who is my rival?

LOUKA. You shall never get that out of me, for love or money.

SERGIUS. Why?

LOUKA. Never mind why. Besides, you would tell that I told you; and I should lose my place.

SERGIUS [*holding out his right hand in affirmation*] No! on the honor of a—[*He checks himself; and his hand drops, nerveless, as he concludes sardonically*]—of a man capable of behaving as I have been behaving for the last five minutes. Who is he?

LOUKA. I dont know. I never saw him. I only heard his voice through the door of her room.

SERGIUS. Damnation! How dare you?

LOUKA [*retreating*] Oh, I mean no harm: youve no right to take up my words like that. The mistress knows all about it. And I tell you that if that gentleman ever comes here again, Miss Raina will marry him, whether he likes it or not. I know the difference between the sort of manner you and she put on before one another and the real manner.

Sergius shivers as if she had stabbed him. Then, setting his face like iron, he strides grimly to her, and grips her above the elbows with both hands.

SERGIUS. Now listen you to me.

LOUKA [*wincing*] Not so tight: youre hurting me.

SERGIUS. That doesnt matter. You have stained my honor by making me a party to your eavesdropping. And you have betrayed your mistress.

LOUKA [*writhing*] Please—

SERGIUS. That shews that you are an abominable little clod of common clay, with the soul of a servant. [*He lets her go as if she were an unclean thing, and turns away, dusting his hands of her, to the bench by the wall, where he sits down with averted head, meditating gloomily*].

LOUKA [*whimpering angrily with her hands up her sleeves, feeling her bruised arms*] You know how to hurt with your tongue as well as with your hands. But I dont care, now Ive found out that whatever clay I'm made of, youre made of the same. As for her, she's a liar; and her fine airs are a cheat; and I'm worth six of her. [*She shakes the pain off hardily; tosses her head; and sets to work to put the things on the tray*].

He looks doubtfully at her. She finishes packing the tray, and laps the cloth over the edges, so as to carry all out together. As she stoops to lift it, he rises.

SERGIUS. Louka! [*She stops and looks defiantly at him*]. A gentleman has no right to hurt a woman under any circumstances. [*With profound humility, uncovering his head*] I beg your pardon.

LOUKA. That sort of apology may satisfy a lady. Of what use is it to a servant?

SERGIUS [*rudely crossed in his chivalry, throws it off with a bitter laugh, and says slightingly*] Oh! you wish to be paid for the hurt? [*He puts on his shako, and takes some money from his pocket*].

LOUKA [*her eyes filling with tears in spite of herself*] No: I want my hurt made well.

SERGIUS [*sobered by her tone*] How?

She rolls up her left sleeve; clasps her arm with the thumb and fingers of her right hand; and looks down at the bruise. Then she raises her head and looks straight at him. Finally, with a superb gesture, she presents her arm to be kissed. Amazed, he looks at her; at the arm; at her again; hesitates; and then, with shuddering intensity, exclaims Never! *and gets away as far as possible from her.*

Her arm drops. Without a word, and with unaffected dignity, she takes her tray, and is approaching the house when Raina returns, wearing a hat and jacket in the height of the Vienna fashion of the previous year, 1885. Louka makes way proudly for her, and then goes into the house.

RAINA. I'm ready. Whats the matter? [*Gaily*] Have you been flirting with Louka?

SERGIUS [*hastily*] No, no. How can you think such a thing?

RAINA [*ashamed of herself*] Forgive me, dear: it was only a jest. I am so happy today.

He goes quickly to her, and kisses her hand remorsefully. Catherine comes out and calls to them from the top of the steps.

CATHERINE [*coming down to them*] I am sorry to disturb you, children; but Paul is distracted over those three regiments. He doesnt know how to send them to Philippopolis; and he objects to every suggestion of mine. You must go and help him, Sergius. He is in the library.

RAINA [*disappointed*] But we are just going out for a walk.

SERGIUS. I shall not be long. Wait for me just five minutes. [*He runs up the steps to the door*].

RAINA [*following him to the foot of the steps and looking up at him with timid coquetry*] I shall go round and wait in full view of the library windows. Be sure you draw father's attention to me. If you are a moment longer than five minutes, I shall go in and fetch you, regiments or no regiments.

SERGIUS [*laughing*] Very well. [*He goes in*].

Raina watches him until he is out of her sight. Then, with a perceptible relaxation of manner, she begins to pace up and down the garden in a brown study.

CATHERINE. Imagine their meeting that

Swiss and hearing the whole story! The very first thing your father asked for was the old coat we sent him off in. A nice mess you have got us into!

RAINA [*gazing thoughtfully at the gravel as she walks*] The little beast!

CATHERINE. Little beast! What little beast?

RAINA. To go and tell! Oh, if I had him here, I'd cram him with chocolate creams til he couldnt ever speak again!

CATHERINE. Dont talk such stuff. Tell me the truth, Raina. How long was he in your room before you came to me?

RAINA [*whisking round and recommencing her march in the opposite direction*] Oh, I forget.

CATHERINE. You cannot forget! Did he really climb up after the soldiers were gone; or was he there when that officer searched the room?

RAINA. No. Yes: I think he must have been there then.

CATHERINE. You think! Oh, Raina! Raina! Will anything ever make you straightforward? If Sergius finds out, it will be all over between you.

RAINA [*with cool impertinence*] Oh, I know Sergius is your pet. I sometimes wish you could marry him instead of me. You would just suit him. You would pet him, and spoil him, and mother him to perfection.

CATHERINE [*opening her eyes very widely indeed*] Well, upon my word!

RAINA [*capriciously: half to herself*] I always feel a longing to do or say something dreadful to him—to shock his propriety—to scandalize the five senses out of him. [*To Catherine, perversely*] I dont care whether he finds out about the chocolate cream soldier or not. I half hope he may. [*She again turns and strolls flippantly away up the path to the corner of the house*].

CATHERINE. And what should I be able to say to your father, pray?

RAINA [*over her shoulder, from the top of the two steps*] Oh, poor father! As if he could help himself! [*She turns the corner and passes out of sight*].

CATHERINE [*looking after her, her fingers itching*] Oh, if you were only ten years younger! [*Louka comes from the house with a salver, which she carries hanging down by her side*]. Well?

LOUKA. Theres a gentleman just called, madam. A Serbian officer.

CATHERINE [*flaming*] A Serb! And how dare he— [*checking herself bitterly*] Oh, I forgot. We are at peace now. I suppose we shall have them calling every day to pay their compliments. Well: if he is an officer why dont you tell your master? He is in the library with Major Saranoff. Why do you come to me?

LOUKA. But he asks for you, madam. And I dont think he knows who you are: he said the lady of the house. He gave me this little ticket for you. [*She takes a card out of her bosom; puts it on the salver; and offers it to Catherine*].

CATHERINE [*reading*] " Captain Bluntschli"? Thats a German name.

LOUKA. Swiss, madam, I think.

CATHERINE [*with a bound that makes Louka jump back*] Swiss! What is he like?

LOUKA [*timidly*] He has a big carpet bag, madam.

CATHERINE. Oh Heavens! he's come to return the coat. Send him away: say we're not at home: ask him to leave his address and I'll write to him. Oh stop: that will never do. Wait! [*She throws herself into a chair to think it out. Louka waits*]. The master and Major Saranoff are busy in the library, arnt they?

LOUKA. Yes, madam.

CATHERINE [*decisively*] Bring the gentleman out here at once. [*Peremptorily*] And be very polite to him. Dont delay. Here [*impatiently snatching the salver from her*]: leave that here; and go straight back to him.

LOUKA. Yes, madam [*going*].

CATHERINE. Louka!

LOUKA [*stopping*] Yes, madam.

CATHERINE. Is the library door shut?

LOUKA. I think so, madam.

CATHERINE. If not, shut it as you pass through.

LOUKA. Yes, madam [*going*].

CATHERINE. Stop! [*Louka stops*]. He will have to go that way [*indicating the gate of the stable yard*]. Tell Nicola to bring his bag here after him. Dont forget.

LOUKA [*surprised*] His bag?

CATHERINE. Yes: here: as soon as possible. [*Vehemently*] Be quick! [*Louka runs into the house. Catherine snatches her apron off and throws it behind a bush. She then takes up the salver and uses it as a mirror, with the result that the handkerchief tied round her head follows the apron. A touch to her hair and a shake to her dressing gown make her presentable*]. Oh, how? how? how can a man be such a fool! Such a moment to select! [*Louka appears at the door of the house, announcing* Captain Bluntschli. *She stands aside at the top of the steps to let him pass before she goes in again. He is the man of the midnight adventure in Raina's room, clean, well brushed, smartly uniformed, and out of trouble, but still unmistakeably the same man. The moment Louka's back is turned, Catherine swoops on him with impetuous, urgent, coaxing appeal*]. Captain Bluntschli: I am v e r y glad to see you; but you must leave this house at once. [*He raises his eyebrows*]. My husband has just returned with my future son-in-law; and they know nothing. If they did, the consequences would be terrible. You are a foreigner: you do not feel our national animosities as we do. We still hate the Serbs: the effect of the peace on my husband has been to make him feel like a lion baulked of his prey. If he discovers our secret, he will never forgive me; and my daughter's life will hardly be safe. Will you, like the chivalrous gentleman and soldier you are, leave at once before he finds you here?

BLUNTSCHLI [*disappointed, but philosophical*] At once, gracious lady. I only came to thank you and return the coat you lent me. If you will allow me to take it out of my bag and leave it with your servant as I pass out, I need detain you no further. [*He turns to go into the house*].

CATHERINE [*catching him by the sleeve*] Oh, you must not think of going back that way. [*Coaxing him across to the stable gates*] This is the shortest way out. Many thanks. So glad to have been of service to you. Goodbye.

BLUNTSCHLI. But my bag?

CATHERINE. It shall be sent on. You will leave me your address.

BLUNTSCHLI. True. Allow me. [*He takes out his card-case, and stops to write his address, keeping Catherine in an agony of impatience. As he hands her the card, Petkoff, hatless, rushes from the house in a flutter of hospitality, followed by Sergius*].

PETKOFF [*as he hurries down the steps*] My dear Captain Bluntschli—

CATHERINE. Oh Heavens! [*She sinks on the seat against the wall*].

PETKOFF [*too preoccupied to notice her as he shakes Bluntschli's hand heartily*] Those stupid people of mine thought I was out here, instead of in the—haw!—library [*he cannot mention the library without betraying how proud*

he is of it]. I saw you through the window. I was wondering why you didnt come in. Saranoff is with me: you remember him, dont you?

SERGIUS [*saluting humorously, and then offering his hand with great charm of manner*] Welcome, our friend the enemy!

PETKOFF. No longer the enemy, happily. [*Rather anxiously*] I hope youve called as a friend, and not about horses or prisoners.

CATHERINE. Oh, quite as a friend, Paul. I was just asking Captain Bluntschli to stay to lunch; but he declares he must go at once.

SERGIUS [*sardonically*] Impossible, Bluntschli. We want you here badly. We have to send on three cavalry regiments to Philippopolis; and we dont in the least know how to do it.

BLUNTSCHLI [*suddenly attentive and businesslike*] Philippopolis? The forage is the trouble, I suppose.

PETKOFF [*eagerly*] Yes: thats it. [*To Sergius*] He sees the whole thing at once.

BLUNTSCHLI. I think I can shew you how to manage that.

SERGIUS. Invaluable man! Come along! [*Towering over Bluntschli, he puts his hand on his shoulder and takes him to the steps, Petkoff following*].

Raina comes from the house as Bluntschli puts his foot on the first step.

RAINA. Oh! The chocolate cream soldier!

Bluntschli stands rigid. Sergius, amazed, looks at Raina, then at Petkoff, who looks back at him and then at his wife.

CATHERINE [*with commanding presence of mind*] My dear Raina, dont you see that we have a guest here? Captain Bluntschli: one of our new Serbian friends.

Raina bows: Bluntschli bows.

RAINA. How silly of me! [*She comes down into the centre of the group, between Bluntschli and Petkoff*]. I made a beautiful ornament this morning for the ice pudding; and that stupid Nicola has just put down a pile of plates on it and spoilt it. [*To Bluntschli, winningly*] I hope you didnt think that y o u were the chocolate cream soldier, Captain Bluntschli.

BLUNTSCHLI [*laughing*] I assure you I did. [*Stealing a whimsical glance at her*] Your explanation was a relief.

PETKOFF [*suspiciously, to Raina*] And since when, pray, have y o u taken to cooking?

CATHERINE. Oh, whilst you were away. It is her latest fancy.

PETKOFF [*testily*] And has Nicola taken to drinking? He used to be careful enough. First he shews Captain Bluntschli out here when he knew quite well I was in the library; and then he goes downstairs and breaks Raina's chocolate soldier. He must— [*Nicola appears at the top of the steps with the bag. He descends; places it respectfully before Bluntschli; and waits for further orders. General amazement. Nicola, unconscious of the effect he is producing, looks perfectly satisfied with himself. When Petkoff recovers his power of speech, he breaks out at him with*] Are you mad, Nicola?

NICOLA [*taken aback*] Sir?

PETKOFF. What have you brought that for?

NICOLA. My lady's orders, major. Louka told me that—

CATHERINE [*interrupting him*] My orders! Why should I order you to bring Captain Bluntschli's luggage out here? What are you thinking of, Nicola?

NICOLA [*after a moment's bewilderment, picking up the bag as he addresses Bluntschli with the very perfection of servile discretion*] I beg your pardon, captain, I am sure. [*To Catherine*] My fault, madam: I hope youll overlook it. [*He bows, and is going to the steps with the bag, when Petkoff addresses him angrily*].

PETKOFF. Youd better go and slam that bag, too, down on Miss Raina's ice pudding! [*This is too much for Nicola. The bag drops from his hand almost on his master's toes, eliciting a roar of*] Begone, you butter-fingered donkey.

NICOLA [*snatching up the bag, and escaping into the house*] Yes, major.

CATHERINE. Oh, never mind, Paul: dont be angry.

PETKOFF [*blustering*] Scoundrel! He's got out of hand while I was away. I'll teach him. Infernal blackguard! The sack next Saturday! I'll clear out the whole establishment— [*He is stifled by the caresses of his wife and daughter, who hang round his neck, petting him*].

CATHERINE ⎱ [*together*] ⎰ Now, now, now, it
RAINA   Wow, wow, wow:
mustnt be angry. He meant not on your first day at home. no harm. Be good to please I'll make another ice pudding. me, dear. Sh-sh-sh-sh! Tch-ch-ch!

PETKOFF [*yielding*] Oh well, never mind.

Come, Bluntschli: lets have no more nonsense about going away. You know very well youre not going back to Switzerland yet. Until you do go back youll stay with us.

RAINA. Oh, do, Captain Bluntschli.

PETKOFF [*to Catherine*] Now, Catherine: it's of you he's afraid. Press him; and he'll stay.

CATHERINE. Of course I shall be only too delighted if [*appealingly*] Captain Bluntschli really wishes to stay. He knows my wishes.

BLUNTSCHLI [*in his driest military manner*] I am at madam's orders.

SERGIUS [*cordially*] That settles it!

PETKOFF [*heartily*] Of course!

RAINA. You see you must stay.

BLUNTSCHLI [*smiling*] Well, if I must, I must.

Gesture of despair from Catherine.

ACT III

In the library after lunch. It is not much of a library. Its literary equipment consists of a single fixed shelf stocked with old paper covered novels, broken backed, coffee stained, torn and thumbed; and a couple of little hanging shelves with a few gift books on them: the rest of the wall space being occupied by trophies of war and the chase. But it is a most comfortable sitting room. A row of three large windows shews a mountain panorama, just now seen in one of its friendliest aspects in the mellowing afternoon light. In the corner next the right hand window a square earthenware stove, a perfect tower of glistening pottery, rises nearly to the ceiling and guarantees plenty of warmth. The ottoman is like that in Raina's room, and similarly placed; and the window seats are luxurious with decorated cushions. There is one object, however, hopelessly out of keeping with its surroundings. This is a small kitchen table, much the worse for wear, fitted as a writing table with an old canister full of pens, an eggcup filled with ink, and a deplorable scrap of heavily used pink blotting paper.

At the side of this table, which stands to the left of anyone facing the window, Bluntschli is hard at work with a couple of maps before him, writing orders. At the head of it sits Sergius, who is supposed to be also at work, but is actually gnawing the feather of a pen, and contemplating Bluntschli's quick, sure, businesslike progress with a mixture of envious irritation at his own incapacity and awestruck wonder at an ability which seems to him almost miraculous, though its prosaic character forbids him to esteem it.

The Major is comfortably established on the ottoman, with a newspaper in his hand and the tube of his hookah within easy reach. Catherine sits at the stove, with her back to them, embroidering. Raina, reclining on the divan, is gazing in a daydream out at the Balkan landscape, with a neglected novel in her lap.

The door is on the same side as the stove, farther from the window. The button of the electric bell is at the opposite side, behind Bluntschli.

PETKOFF [*looking up from his paper to watch how they are getting on at the table*] Are you sure I cant help you in any way, Bluntschli?

BLUNTSCHLI [*without interrupting his writing or looking up*] Quite sure, thank you. Saranoff and I will manage it.

SERGIUS [*grimly*] Yes: we'll manage it. He finds out what to do; draws up the orders; and I sign em. Division of labor! [*Bluntschli passes him a paper*]. Another one? Thank you. [*He plants the paper squarely before him; sets his chair carefully parallel to it; and signs with his cheek on his elbow and his protruded tongue following the movements of his pen*]. This hand is more accustomed to the sword than to the pen.

PETKOFF. It's very good of you, Bluntschli: it is indeed, to let yourself be put upon in this way. Now are you quite sure I can do nothing?

CATHERINE [*in a low warning tone*] You can stop interrupting, Paul.

PETKOFF [*starting and looking round at her*] Eh? Oh! Quite right, my love: quite right. [*He takes his newspaper up again, but presently lets it drop*]. Ah, you havnt been campaigning, Catherine: you dont know how pleasant it is for us to sit here, after a good lunch, with nothing to do but enjoy ourselves. Theres only one thing I want to make me thoroughly comfortable.

CATHERINE. What is that?

PETKOFF. My old coat. I'm not at home in this one: I feel as if I were on parade.

CATHERINE. My dear Paul, how absurd you are about that old coat! It must be hanging in the blue closet where you left it.

PETKOFF. My dear Catherine, I tell you Ive looked there. Am I to believe my own eyes or not? [*Catherine rises and crosses the room to press the button of the electric bell*]. What are you shewing off that bell for? [*She looks at him majestically, and silently resumes her chair and her needlework*]. My dear: if you think the obstinacy of your sex can make a coat out of two old dressing gowns of Raina's, your waterproof, and my mackintosh, youre mistaken. Thats exactly what the blue closet contains at present.

Nicola presents himself.

CATHERINE. Nicola: go to the blue closet and bring your master's old coat here: the braided one he wears in the house.

NICOLA. Yes, madame. [*He goes out*].

PETKOFF. Catherine.

CATHERINE. Yes, Paul?

PETKOFF. I bet you any piece of jewellery you like to order from Sofia against a week's housekeeping money that the coat isnt there.

CATHERINE. Done, Paul!

PETKOFF [*excited by the prospect of a gamble*] Come: heres an opportunity for some sport. Wholl bet on it? Bluntschli: I'll give you six to one.

BLUNTSCHLI [*imperturbably*] It would be robbing you, major. Madame is sure to be right. [*Without looking up, he passes another batch of papers to Sergius*].

SERGIUS [*also excited*] Bravo, Switzerland! Major: I bet my best charger against an Arab mare for Raina that Nicola finds the coat in the blue closet.

PETKOFF [*eagerly*] Your best char—

CATHERINE [*hastily interrupting him*] Dont be foolish, Paul. An Arabian mare will cost you 50,000 levas.

RAINA [*suddenly coming out of her picturesque revery*] Really, mother, if you are going to take the jewellery, I dont see why you should grudge me my Arab.

Nicola comes back with the coat, and brings it to Petkoff, who can hardly believe his eyes.

CATHERINE. Where was it, Nicola?

NICOLA. Hanging in the blue closet, madame.

PETKOFF. Well, I am d—

CATHERINE [*stopping him*] Paul!

PETKOFF. I could have sworn it wasnt there. Age is beginning to tell on me. I'm getting hallucinations. [*To Nicola*] Here: help me to change. Excuse me, Bluntschli. [*He begins changing coats, Nicola acting as valet*]. Remember: I didnt take that bet of yours, Sergius. Youd better give Raina that Arab steed yourself, since youve roused her expectations. Eh, Raina? [*He looks round at her; but she is again rapt in the landscape. With a little gush of parental affection and pride, he points her out to them, and says*] She's dreaming, as usual.

SERGIUS. Assuredly she shall not be the loser.

PETKOFF. So much the better for her. *I* shant come off so cheaply, I expect. [*The change is now complete. Nicola goes out with the discarded coat*]. Ah, now I feel at home at last. [*He sits down and takes his newspaper with a grunt of relief*].

BLUNTSCHLI [*to Sergius, handing a paper*] Thats the last order.

PETKOFF [*jumping up*] What! Finished?

BLUNTSCHLI. Finished.

PETKOFF [*with childlike envy*] Havnt you anything for me to sign?

BLUNTSCHLI. Not necessary. His signature will do.

PETKOFF [*inflating his chest and thumping it*] Ah well, I think weve done a thundering good day's work. Can I do anything more?

BLUNTSCHLI. You had better both see the fellows that are to take these. [*Sergius rises*] Pack them off at once; and shew them that Ive marked on the orders the time they should hand them in by. Tell them that if they stop to drink or tell stories—if theyre five minutes late, theyll have the skin taken off their backs.

SERGIUS [*stiffening indignantly*] I'll say so. [*He strides to the door*]. And if one of them is man enough to spit in my face for insulting him, I'll buy his discharge and give him a pension. [*He goes out*].

BLUNTSCHLI [*confidentially*] Just see that he talks to them properly, major, will you?

PETKOFF [*officiously*] Quite right, Bluntschli, quite right. I'll see to it. [*He goes to the door importantly, but hesitates on the threshold*]. By the bye, Catherine, you may as well come too. Theyll be far more frightened of you than of me.

CATHERINE [*putting down her embroidery*] I daresay I had better. You would only splutter at them. [*She goes out, Petkoff holding the door for her and following her*].

BLUNTSCHLI. What an army! They make cannons out of cherry trees; and the officers send for their wives to keep discipline! [*He begins to fold and docket the papers*].

Raina, who has risen from the divan, marches slowly down the room with her hands clasped behind her, and looks mischievously at him.

RAINA. You look ever so much nicer than when we last met. [*He looks up, surprised*]. What have you done to yourself?

BLUNTSCHLI. Washed; brushed; good night's sleep and breakfast. Thats all.

RAINA. Did you get back safely that morning?

BLUNTSCHLI. Quite, thanks.

RAINA. Were they angry with you for running away from Sergius's charge?

BLUNTSCHLI [*grinning*] No: they were glad; because theyd all just run away themselves.

RAINA [*going to the table, and leaning over it towards him*] It must have made a lovely story for them: all that about me and my room.

BLUNTSCHLI. Capital story. But I only told it to one of them: a particular friend.

RAINA. On whose discretion you could absolutely rely?

BLUNTSCHLI. Absolutely.

RAINA. Hm! He told it all to my father and Sergius the day you exchanged the prisoners. [*She turns away and strolls carelessly across to the other side of the room*].

BLUNTSCHLI [*deeply concerned, and half incredulous*] No! You dont mean that, do you?

RAINA [*turning, with sudden earnestness*] I do indeed. But they dont know that it was in this house you took refuge. If Sergius knew, he would challenge you and kill you in a duel.

BLUNTSCHLI. Bless me! then dont tell him.

RAINA. Please be serious, Captain Bluntschli. Can you not realize what it is to me to deceive him? I want to be quite perfect with Sergius: no meanness, no smallness, no deceit. My relation to him is the one really beautiful and noble part of my life. I hope you can understand that.

BLUNTSCHLI [*sceptically*] You mean that you wouldnt like him to find out that the story about the ice pudding was a—a—a—You know.

RAINA [*wincing*] Ah, dont talk of it in that flippant way. I lied: I know it. But I did it to save your life. He would have killed you. That was the second time I ever uttered a falsehood. [*Bluntschli rises quickly and looks doubtfully and somewhat severely at her*]. Do you remember the first time?

BLUNTSCHLI. I! No. Was I present?

RAINA. Yes; and I told the officer who was searching for you that you were not present.

BLUNTSCHLI. True. I should have remembered it.

RAINA [*greatly encouraged*] Ah, it is natural that you should forget it first. It cost you nothing: it cost me a lie! A lie!!

She sits down on the ottoman, looking straight before her with her hands clasped round her knee. Bluntschli, quite touched, goes to the ottoman with a particularly reassuring and considerate air, and sits down beside her.

BLUNTSCHLI. My dear young lady, dont let this worry you. Remember: I'm a soldier. Now what are the two things that happen to a soldier so often that he comes to think nothing of them? One is hearing people tell lies [*Raina recoils*]: the other is getting his life saved in all sorts of ways by all sorts of people.

RAINA [*rising in indignant protest*] And so he becomes a creature incapable of faith and of gratitude.

BLUNTSCHLI [*making a wry face*] Do you like gratitude? I dont. If pity is akin to love, gratitude is akin to the other thing.

RAINA. Gratitude! [*Turning on him*] If you are incapable of gratitude you are incapable of any noble sentiment. Even animals are grateful. Oh, I see now exactly what you think of me! You were not surprised to hear me lie. To you it was something I probably did every day! every hour!! That is how men think of women. [*She paces the room tragically*].

BLUNTSCHLI [*dubiously*] Theres reason in everything. You said youd told only two lies in your whole life. Dear young lady: isnt that rather a short allowance? I'm quite a straightforward man myself; but it wouldnt last me a whole morning.

RAINA [*staring haughtily at him*] Do you know, sir, that you are insulting me?

BLUNTSCHLI. I cant help it. When you strike that noble attitude and speak in that thrilling voice, I admire you; but I find it impossible to believe a single word you say.

RAINA [*superbly*] Captain Bluntschli!

BLUNTSCHLI [*unmoved*] Yes?

RAINA [*standing over him, as if she could not believe her senses*] Do you mean what you said just now? Do you know what you said just now?

BLUNTSCHLI. I do.

RAINA [*gasping*] I! I!!! [*She points to herself incredulously, meaning "I, Raina Petkoff, tell lies!" He meets her gaze unflinchingly. She suddenly sits down beside him, and adds, with a complete change of manner from the heroic to a babyish familiarity*] How did you find me out?

BLUNTSCHLI [*promptly*] Instinct, dear young lady. Instinct, and experience of the world.

RAINA [*wonderingly*] Do you know, you are

the first man I ever met who did not take me seriously?

BLUNTSCHLI. You mean, dont you, that I am the first man that has ever taken you quite seriously?

RAINA. Yes: I suppose I do mean that. [*Cosily, quite at her ease with him*] How strange it is to be talked to in such a way! You know, Ive always gone on like that.

BLUNTSCHLI. You mean the—?

RAINA. I mean the noble attitude and the thrilling voice. [*They laugh together*]. I did it when I was a tiny child to my nurse. She believed in it. I do it before my parents. They believe in it. I do it before Sergius. He believes in it.

BLUNTSCHLI. Yes: he's a little in that line himself, isnt he?

RAINA [*startled*] Oh! Do you think so?

BLUNTSCHLI. You know him better than I do.

RAINA. I wonder—I wonder is he? If I thought that—! [*Discouraged*] Ah, well: what does it matter? I suppose, now youve found me out, you despise me.

BLUNTSCHLI [*warmly, rising*] No, my dear young lady, no, no, no a thousand times. It's part of your youth: part of your charm. I'm like all the rest of them: the nurse, your parents, Sergius: I'm your infatuated admirer.

RAINA [*pleased*] Really?

BLUNTSCHLI [*slapping his breast smartly with his hand, German fashion*] Hand aufs Herz! Really and truly.

RAINA [*very happy*] But what did you think of me for giving you my portrait?

BLUNTSCHLI [*astonished*] Your portrait! You never gave me your portrait.

RAINA [*quickly*] Do you mean to say you never got it?

BLUNTSCHLI. No. [*He sits down beside her, with renewed interest, and says, with some complacency*] When did you send it to me?

RAINA [*indignantly*] I did not send it to you. [*She turns her head away, and adds, reluctantly*] It was in the pocket of that coat.

BLUNTSCHLI [*pursing his lips and rounding his eyes*] Oh-o-oh! I never found it. It must be there still.

RAINA [*springing up*] There still! for my father to find the first time he puts his hand in his pocket! Oh, how could you be so stupid?

BLUNTSCHLI [*rising also*] It doesnt matter: I suppose it's only a photograph: how can he tell who it was intended for? Tell him he put it there himself.

RAINA [*bitterly*] Yes: that is so clever! isnt it? [*Distractedly*] Oh! what shall I do?

BLUNTSCHLI. Ah, I see. You wrote something on it. That was rash.

RAINA [*vexed almost to tears*] Oh, to have done such a thing for y o u, who care no more —except to laugh at me—oh! Are you sure nobody has touched it?

BLUNTSCHLI. Well, I cant be quite sure. You see, I couldnt carry it about with me all the time: one cant take much luggage on active service.

RAINA. What did you do with it?

BLUNTSCHLI. When I got through to Pirot I had to put it in safe keeping somehow. I thought of the railway cloak room; but thats the surest place to get looted in modern warfare. So I pawned it.

RAINA. P a w n e d i t!!!

BLUNTSCHLI. I know it doesnt sound nice; but it was much the safest plan. I redeemed it the day before yesterday. Heaven only knows whether the pawnbroker cleared out the pockets or not.

RAINA [*furious: throwing the words right into his face*] You have a low shopkeeping mind. You think of things that would never come into a gentleman's head.

BLUNTSCHLI [*phlegmatically*] Thats the Swiss national character, dear lady. [*He returns to the table*].

RAINA. Oh, I wish I had never met you. [*She flounces away, and sits at the window fuming*].

Louka comes in with a heap of letters and telegrams on her salver, and crosses, with her bold free gait, to the table. Her left sleeve is looped up to the shoulder with a brooch, shewing her naked arm, with a broad gilt bracelet covering the bruise.

LOUKA [*to Bluntschli*] For you. [*She empties the salver with a fling on to the table*]. The messenger is waiting. [*She is determined not to be civil to an enemy, even if she must bring him his letters*].

BLUNTSCHLI [*to Raina*] Will you excuse me: the last postal delivery that reached me was three weeks ago. These are the subsequent accumulations. Four telegrams: a week old. [*He opens one*]. Oho! Bad news!

RAINA [*rising and advancing a little remorsefully*] Bad news?

BLUNTSCHLI. My father's dead. [*He looks at the telegram with his lips pursed, musing on the unexpected change in his arrangements. Louka crosses herself hastily*].

RAINA. Oh, how very sad!

BLUNTSCHLI. Yes: I shall have to start for home in an hour. He has left a lot of big hotels behind him to be looked after. [*He takes up a fat letter in a long blue envelope*]. Here's a whacking letter from the family solicitor. [*He pulls out the enclosures and glances over them*]. Great Heavens! Seventy! Two hundred! [*In a crescendo of dismay*] Four hundred! Four t h o u s a n d!! Nine thousand six hundred!!! What on earth am I to do with them all?

RAINA [*timidly*] Nine thousand hotels?

BLUNTSCHLI. Hotels! nonsense. If you only knew! Oh, it's too ridiculous! Excuse me: I must give my fellow orders about starting. [*He leaves the room hastily, with the documents in his hand*].

LOUKA [*knowing instinctively that she can annoy Raina by disparaging Bluntschli*] He has not much heart, that Swiss. He has not a word of grief for his poor father.

RAINA [*bitterly*] Grief! A man who has been doing nothing but killing people for years! What does he care? What does any soldier care? [*She goes to the door, restraining her tears with difficulty*].

LOUKA. Major Saranoff has been fighting too; and he has plenty of heart left. [*Raina, at the door, draws herself up haughtily and goes out*]. Aha! I thought you wouldnt get much feeling out of your soldier. [*She is following Raina when Nicola enters with an armful of logs for the stove*].

NICOLA [*grinning amorously at her*] Ive been trying all the afternoon to get a minute alone with you, my girl. [*His countenance changes as he notices her arm*]. Why, what fashion is that of wearing your sleeve, child?

LOUKA [*proudly*] My own fashion.

NICOLA. Indeed! If the mistress catches you, she'll talk to you. [*He puts the logs down, and seats himself comfortably on the ottoman*].

LOUKA. Is that any reason why y o u should take it on yourself to talk to me?

NICOLA. Come! dont be so contrary with me. Ive some good news for you. [*She sits down beside him. He takes out some paper money. Louka, with an eager gleam in her eyes, tries to snatch it; but he shifts it quickly to his left hand, out of her reach*]. See! a twenty leva bill! Sergius gave me that, out of pure swagger. A fool and his money are soon parted. Theres ten levas more. The Swiss gave me that for backing up the mistress's and Raina's lies about him. H e's no fool, he isnt. You should have heard old Catherine downstairs as polite as you please to me, telling me not to mind the Major being a little impatient; for they knew what a good servant I was—after making a fool and a liar of me before them all! The twenty will go to our savings; and you shall have the ten to spend if youll only talk to me so as to remind me I'm a human being. I get tired of being a servant occasionally.

LOUKA. Yes: sell your manhood for 30 levas, and buy me for 10! [*Rising scornfully*] Keep your money. You were born to be a servant. I was not. When you set up your shop you will only be everybody's servant instead of somebody's servant. [*She goes moodily to the table and seats herself regally in Sergius's chair*].

NICOLA [*picking up his logs, and going to the stove*] Ah, wait til you see. We shall have our evenings to ourselves; and I shall be master in my own house, I promise you. [*He throws the logs down and kneels at the stove*].

LOUKA. You shall never be master in mine.

NICOLA [*turning, still on his knees, and squatting down rather forlornly on his calves, daunted by her implacable disdain*] You have a great ambition in you, Louka. Remember: if any luck comes to you, it was I that made a woman of you.

LOUKA. You!

NICOLA [*scrambling up and going at her*] Yes, me. Who was it made you give up wearing a couple of pounds of false black hair on your head and reddening your lips and cheeks like any other Bulgarian girl? I did. Who taught you to trim your nails, and keep your hands clean, and be dainty about yourself, like a fine Russian lady? Me: do you hear that? me! [*She tosses her head defiantly; and he turns away, adding, more coolly*] Ive often thought that if Raina were out of the way, and you just a little less of a fool and Sergius just a little more of one, you might come to be one of my grandest customers, instead of only being my wife and costing me money.

LOUKA. I believe you would rather be my servant than my husband. You would make more out of me. Oh, I know that soul of yours.

NICOLA [*going closer to her for greater emphasis*] Never you mind my soul; but just listen to my advice. If you want to be a lady, your present behavior to me wont do at all, unless when we're alone. It's too sharp and impudent; and impudence is a sort of familiarity: it shews affection for me. And dont you try being high and mighty with me, either. Youre like all country girls: you think it's genteel to treat a servant the way I treat a stableboy. Thats only your ignorance; and dont you forget it. And dont be so ready to defy everybody. Act as if you expected to have your own way, not as if you expected to be ordered about. The way to get on as a lady is the same as the way to get on as a servant: youve got to know your place: thats the secret of it. And you may depend on me to know my place if you get promoted. Think over it, my girl. I'll stand by you: one servant should always stand by another.

LOUKA [*rising impatiently*] Oh, I must behave in my own way. You take all the courage out of me with your cold-blooded wisdom. Go and put those logs on the fire: thats the sort of thing y o u understand.

Before Nicola can retort, Sergius comes in. He checks himself a moment on seeing Louka; then goes to the stove.

SERGIUS [*to Nicola*] I am not in the way of your work, I hope.

NICOLA [*in a smooth, elderly manner*] Oh no, sir: thank you kindly. I was only speaking to this foolish girl about her habit of running up here to the library whenever she gets a chance, to look at the books. Thats the worst of her education, sir: it gives her habits above her station. [*To Louka*] Make that table tidy, Louka, for the Major. [*He goes out sedately*].

Louka, without looking at Sergius, pretends to arrange the papers on the table. He crosses slowly to her, and studies the arrangement of her sleeve reflectively.

SERGIUS. Let me see: is there a mark there? [*He turns up the bracelet and sees the bruise made by his grasp. She stands motionless, not looking at him: fascinated, but on her guard*]. Ffff! Does it hurt?

LOUKA. Yes.

SERGIUS. Shall I cure it?

LOUKA [*instantly withdrawing herself proudly, but still not looking at him*] No. You cannot cure it now.

SERGIUS [*masterfully*] Quite sure? [*He makes a movement as if to take her in his arms*].

LOUKA. Dont trifle with me, please. An

officer should not trifle with a servant.

SERGIUS [*indicating the bruise with a merciless stroke of his forefinger*] That was no trifle, Louka.

LOUKA [*flinching; then looking at him for the first time*] Are you sorry?

SERGIUS [*with measured emphasis, folding his arms*] I am n e v e r sorry.

LOUKA [*wistfully*] I wish I could believe a man could be as unlike a woman as that. I wonder are you really a brave man?

SERGIUS [*unaffectedly, relaxing his attitude*] Yes: I am a brave man. My heart jumped like a woman's at the first shot; but in the charge I found that I was brave. Yes: that at least is real about me.

LOUKA. Did you find in the charge that the men whose fathers are poor like mine were any less brave than the men who are rich like you.

SERGIUS [*with bitter levity*] Not a bit. They all slashed and cursed and yelled like heroes. Psha! the courage to rage and kill is cheap. I have an English bull terrier who has as much of that sort of courage as the whole Bulgarian nation, and the whole Russian nation at its back. But he lets my groom thrash him, all the same. Thats your soldier all over! No, Louka: your poor men can cut throats; but they are afraid of their officers; they put up with insults and blows; they stand by and see one another punished like children: aye, and help to do it when they are ordered. And the officers!!! Well [*with a short harsh laugh*] I am an officer. Oh, [*fervently*] give me the man who will defy to the death any power on earth or in heaven that sets itself up against his own will and conscience: he alone is the brave man.

LOUKA. How easy it is to talk! Men never seem to me to grow up: they all have schoolboy's ideas. You dont know what true courage is.

SERGIUS [*ironically*] Indeed! I am willing to be instructed. [*He sits on the ottoman, sprawling magnificently*].

LOUKA. Look at me! how much am I allowed to have my own will? I have to get your room ready for you: to sweep and dust, to fetch and carry. How could that degrade me if it did not degrade you to have it done for you? But [*with subdued passion*] if I were Empress of Russia, above everyone in the world, then!! Ah then, though according to you I could shew no courage at all, you

should see, you should see.

SERGIUS. What would you do, most noble Empress?

LOUKA. I would marry the man I loved, which no other queen in Europe has the courage to do. If I loved you, though you would be as far beneath me as I am beneath you, I would dare to be the equal of my inferior. Would you dare as much if you loved me? No: if you felt the beginnings of love for me you would not let it grow. You would not dare: you would marry a rich man's daughter because you would be afraid of what other people would say of you.

SERGIUS [*bounding up*] You lie: it is not so, by all the stars! If I loved you, and I were the Czar himself, I would set you on the throne by my side. You know that I love another woman, a woman as high above you as heaven is above earth. And you are jealous of her.

LOUKA. I have no reason to be. She will never marry you now. The man I told you of has come back. She will marry the Swiss.

SERGIUS [*recoiling*] The Swiss!

LOUKA. A man worth ten of you. Then you can come to me; and I will refuse you. You are not good enough for me. [*She turns to the door*].

SERGIUS [*springing after her and catching her fiercely in his arms*] I will kill the Swiss; and afterwards I will do as I please with you.

LOUKA [*in his arms, passive and steadfast*] The Swiss will kill you, perhaps. He has beaten you in love. He may beat you in war.

SERGIUS [*tormentedly*] Do you think I believe that she—s h e ! whose worst thoughts are higher than your best ones, is capable of trifling with another man behind my back?

LOUKA. Do you think s h e would believe the Swiss if he told her now that I am in your arms?

SERGIUS [*releasing her in despair*] Damnation! Oh, damnation! Mockery! mockery everywhere! everything I think is mocked by everything I do. [*He strikes himself frantically on the breast*]. Coward! liar! fool! Shall I kill myself like a man, or live and pretend to laugh at myself? [*She again turns to go*]. Louka! [*She stops near the door*]. Remember: you belong to me.

LOUKA [*turning*] What does that mean? An insult?

SERGIUS [*commandingly*] It means that you love me, and that I have had you here in my arms, and will perhaps have you there again.

Whether that is an insult I neither know nor care: take it as you please. But [*vehemently*] I will not be a coward and a trifler. If I choose to love you, I dare marry you, in spite of all Bulgaria. If these hands ever touch you again, they shall touch my affianced bride.

LOUKA. We shall see whether you dare keep your word. And take care. I will not wait long.

SERGIUS [*again folding his arms and standing motionless in the middle of the room*] Yes: we shall see. And you shall wait my pleasure.

Bluntschli, much preoccupied, with his papers still in his hand, enters, leaving the door open for Louka to go out. He goes across to the table, glancing at her as he passes. Sergius, without altering his resolute attitude, watches him steadily. Louka goes out, leaving the door open.

BLUNTSCHLI [*absently, sitting at the table as before, and putting down his papers*] Thats a remarkable looking young woman.

SERGIUS [*gravely, without moving*] Captain Bluntschli.

BLUNTSCHLI. Eh?

SERGIUS. You have deceived me. You are my rival. I brook no rivals. At six o'clock I shall be in the drilling-ground on the Klissoura road, alone, on horseback, with my sabre. Do you understand?

BLUNTSCHLI [*staring, but sitting quite at his ease*] Oh, thank you: thats a cavalry man's proposal. I'm in the artillery; and I have the choice of weapons. If I go, I shall take a machine gun. And there shall be no mistake about the cartridges this time.

SERGIUS [*flushing, but with deadly coldness*] Take care, sir. It is not our custom in Bulgaria to allow invitations of that kind to be trifled with.

BLUNTSCHLI [*warmly*] Pooh! dont talk to me about Bulgaria. You dont know what fighting is. But have it your own way. Bring your sabre along. I'll meet you.

SERGIUS [*fiercely delighted to find his opponent a man of spirit*] Well said, Switzer. Shall I lend you my best horse?

BLUNTSCHLI. No: damn your horse! thank you all the same, my dear fellow. [*Raina comes in, and hears the next sentence*]. I shall fight you on foot. Horseback's too dangerous: I dont want to kill you if I can help it.

RAINA [*hurrying forward anxiously*] I have heard what Captain Bluntschli said, Sergius. You are going to fight. Why? [*Sergius turns away in silence, and goes to the stove, where he stands watching her as she continues, to Bluntschli*] What about?

BLUNTSCHLI. I dont know: he hasnt told me. Better not interfere, dear young lady. No harm will be done: Ive often acted as sword instructor. He wont be able to touch me; and I'll not hurt him. It will save explanations. In the morning I shall be off home; and youll never see me or hear of me again. You and he will then make it up and live happily ever after.

RAINA [*turning away deeply hurt, almost with a sob in her voice*] I never said I wanted to see you again.

SERGIUS [*striding forward*] Ha! That is a confession.

RAINA [*haughtily*] What do you mean?

SERGIUS. *You love that man!*

RAINA [*scandalized*] Sergius!

SERGIUS. You allow him to make love to you behind my back, just as you treat me as your affianced husband behind his. Bluntschli: you knew our relations; and you deceived me. It is for that that I call you to account, not for having received favors I never enjoyed.

BLUNTSCHLI [*jumping up indignantly*] Stuff! Rubbish! I have received no favors. Why, the young lady doesnt even know whether I'm married or not.

RAINA [*forgetting herself*] Oh! [*Collapsing on the ottoman*] Are you?

SERGIUS. You see the young lady's concern, Captain Bluntschli. Denial is useless. You have enjoyed the privilege of being received in her own room, late at night—

BLUNTSCHLI [*interrupting him pepperily*] Yes, you blockhead! she received me with a pistol at her head. Your cavalry were at my heels. I'd have blown out her brains if she'd uttered a cry.

SERGIUS [*taken aback*] Bluntschli! Raina: is this true?

RAINA [*rising in wrathful majesty*] Oh, how dare you, how dare you?

BLUNTSCHLI. Apologize, man: apologize. [*He resumes his seat at the table*].

SERGIUS [*with the old measured emphasis, folding his arms*] I never apologize!

RAINA [*passionately*] This is the doing of that friend of yours, Captain Bluntschli. It is he who is spreading this horrible story about me. [*She walks about excitedly*].

BLUNTSCHLI. No: he's dead. Burnt alive.

RAINA [*stopping, shocked*] Burnt alive!

BLUNTSCHLI. Shot in the hip in a woodyard.

Couldnt drag himself out. Your fellows' shells set the timber on fire and burnt him, with half a dozen other poor devils in the same predicament.

RAINA. How horrible!

SERGIUS. And how ridiculous! Oh, war! war! the dream of patriots and heroes! A fraud, Bluntschli. A hollow sham, like love.

RAINA [outraged] Like love! You say that before me!

BLUNTSCHLI. Come, Saranoff: that matter is explained.

SERGIUS. A hollow sham, I say. Would you have come back here if nothing had passed between you except at the muzzle of your pistol? Raina is mistaken about your friend who was burnt. He was not my informant.

RAINA. Who then? [Suddenly guessing the truth] Ah, Louka! my maid! my servant! You were with her this morning all that time after—after— Oh, what sort of god is this I have been worshipping! [He meets her gaze with sardonic enjoyment of her disenchantment. Angered all the more, she goes closer to him, and says, in a lower, intenser tone] Do you know that I looked out of the window as I went upstairs, to have another sight of my hero; and I saw something I did not understand then. I know now that you were making love to her.

SERGIUS [with grim humor] You saw that?

RAINA. Only too well. [She turns away, and throws herself on the divan under the centre window, quite overcome].

SERGIUS [cynically] Raina: our romance is shattered. Life's a farce.

BLUNTSCHLI [to Raina, whimsically] You see: he's found himself out now.

SERGIUS [going to him] Bluntschli: I have allowed you to call me a blockhead. You may now call me a coward as well. I refuse to fight you. Do you know why?

BLUNTSCHLI. No; but it doesnt matter. I didnt ask the reason when you cried on; and I dont ask the reason now that you cry off. I'm a professional soldier: I fight when I have to, and am very glad to get out of it when I havnt to. Youre only an amateur: you think fighting's an amusement.

SERGIUS [sitting down at the table, nose to nose with him] You shall hear the reason all the same, my professional. The reason is that it takes two men—real men—men of heart, blood and honor—to make a genuine combat. I could no more fight with you than I could make love to an ugly woman. Youve no magnetism: youre not a man: youre a machine.

BLUNTSCHLI [apologetically] Quite true, quite true. I always was that sort of chap. I'm very sorry.

SERGIUS. Psha!

BLUNTSCHLI. But now that youve found that life isnt a farce, but something quite sensible and serious, what further obstacle is there to your happiness?

RAINA [rising] You are very solicitous about my happiness and his. Do you forget his new love—Louka? It is not you that he must fight now, but his rival, Nicola.

SERGIUS. Rival!! [bounding half across the room].

RAINA. Dont you know that theyre engaged?

SERGIUS. Nicola! Are fresh abysses opening? Nicola!!

RAINA [sarcastically] A shocking sacrifice, isnt it? Such beauty! such intellect! such modesty! wasted on a middle-aged servant man. Really, Sergius, you cannot stand by and allow such a thing. It would be unworthy of your chivalry.

SERGIUS [losing all self-control] Viper! Viper! [He rushes to and fro, raging].

BLUNTSCHLI. Look here, Saranoff: youre getting the worst of this.

RAINA [getting angrier] Do you realize what he has done, Captain Bluntschli? He has set this girl as a spy on us; and her reward is that he makes love to her.

SERGIUS. False! Monstrous!

RAINA. Monstrous! [Confronting him] Do you deny that she told you about Captain Bluntschli being in my room?

SERGIUS. No; but—

RAINA [interrupting] Do you deny that you were making love to her when she told you?

SERGIUS. No; but I tell you—

RAINA [cutting him short contemptuously] It is unnecessary to tell us anything more. That is quite enough for us. [She turns away from him and sweeps majestically back to the window].

BLUNTSCHLI [quietly, as Sergius, in an agony of mortification, sinks on the ottoman, clutching his averted head between his fists] I told you you were getting the worst of it, Saranoff.

SERGIUS. Tiger cat!

RAINA [running excitedly to Bluntschli] You hear this man calling me names, Captain Bluntschli?

BLUNTSCHLI. What else can he do, dear lady? He must defend himself somehow. Come [*very persuasively*]: dont quarrel. What good does it do?

Raina, with a gasp, sits down on the ottoman, and after a vain effort to look vexedly at Bluntschli, falls a victim to her sense of humor, and actually leans back babyishly against the writhing shoulder of Sergius.

SERGIUS. Engaged to Nicola! Ha! ha! Ah well, Bluntschli, you are right to take this huge imposture of a world coolly.

RAINA [*quaintly to Bluntschli, with an intuitive guess at his state of mind*] I daresay you think us a couple of grown-up babies, dont you?

SERGIUS [*grinning savagely*] He does: he does. Swiss civilization nursetending Bulgarian barbarism, eh?

BLUNTSCHLI [*blushing*] Not at all, I assure you. I'm only very glad to get you two quieted. There! there! let's be pleasant and talk it over in a friendly way. Where is this other young lady?

RAINA. Listening at the door, probably.

SERGIUS [*shivering as if a bullet had struck him, and speaking with quiet but deep indignation*] I will prove that that, at least, is a calumny. [*He goes with dignity to the door and opens it. A yell of fury bursts from him as he looks out. He darts into the passage, and returns dragging in Louka, whom he flings violently against the table, exclaiming*] Judge her, Bluntschli. You, the cool impartial man: judge the eavesdropper.

Louka stands her ground, proud and silent.

BLUNTSCHLI [*shaking his head*] I musnt judge her. I once listened myself outside a tent when there was a mutiny brewing. It's all a question of the degree of provocation. My life was at stake.

LOUKA. My love was at stake. I am not ashamed.

RAINA [*contemptuously*] Your love! Your curiosity, you mean.

LOUKA [*facing her and retorting her contempt with interest*] My love, stronger than anything you can feel, even for your chocolate cream soldier.

SERGIUS [*with quick suspicion, to Louka*] What does that mean?

LOUKA [*fiercely*] It means—

SERGIUS [*interrupting her slightingly*] Oh, I remember: the ice pudding. A paltry taunt, girl!

Major Petkoff enters, in his shirtsleeves.

PETKOFF. Excuse my shirtsleeves, gentlemen. Raina: somebody has been wearing that coat of mine: I'll swear it. Somebody with a differently shaped back. It's all burst open at the sleeve. Your mother is mending it. I wish she'd make haste: I shall catch cold. [*He looks more attentively at them*]. Is anything the matter?

RAINA. No. [*She sits down at the stove, with a tranquil air*].

SERGIUS. Oh no. [*He sits down at the end of the table, as at first*].

BLUNTSCHLI [*who is already seated*] Nothing. Nothing.

PETKOFF [*sitting down on the ottoman in his old place*] Thats all right. [*He notices Louka*]. Anything the matter, Louka?

LOUKA. No, sir.

PETKOFF [*genially*] Thats all right. [*He sneezes*]. Go and ask your mistress for my coat, like a good girl, will you?

Nicola enters with the coat. Louka makes a pretence of having business in the room by taking the little table with the hookah away to the wall near the windows.

RAINA [*rising quickly as she sees the coat on Nicola's arm*] Here it is, papa. Give it to me, Nicola; and do you put some more wood on the fire. [*She takes the coat, and brings it to the Major, who stands up to put it on. Nicola attends to the fire*].

PETKOFF [*to Raina, teasing her affectionately*] Aha! Going to be very good to poor old papa just for one day after his return from the wars, eh?

RAINA [*with solemn reproach*] Ah, how can you say that to me, father?

PETKOFF. Well, well, only a joke, little one. Come: give me a kiss. [*She kisses him*]. Now give me the coat.

RAINA. No: I am going to put it on for you. Turn your back. [*He turns his back and feels behind him with his arms for the sleeves. She dexterously takes the photograph from the pocket and throws it on the table before Bluntschli, who covers it with a sheet of paper under the very nose of Sergius, who looks on amazed, with his suspicions roused in the highest degree. She then helps Petkoff on with his coat*]. There, dear! Now are you comfortable?

PETKOFF. Quite, little love. Thanks. [*He sits down; and Raina returns to her seat near the stove*]. Oh, by the bye, Ive found something funny. Whats the meaning of this? [*He puts his hand into the picked pocket]. Eh? Hallo! [He tries the other pocket]. Well, I could have sworn—! [Much puzzled, he tries the breast pocket]. I wonder—[trying the original pocket]. Where can it—? [He rises, exclaiming] Your mother's taken it!

RAINA [very red] Taken what?

PETKOFF. Your photograph, with the inscription: "Raina, to her Chocolate Cream Soldier: a Souvenir." Now you know theres something more in this than meets the eye; and I'm going to find it out. [Shouting] Nicola!

NICOLA [coming to him] Sir!

PETKOFF. Did you spoil any pastry of Miss Raina's this morning?

NICOLA. You heard Miss Raina say that I did, sir.

PETKOFF. I know that, you idiot. Was it true?

NICOLA. I am sure Miss Raina is incapable of saying anything that is not true, sir.

PETKOFF. Are you? Then I'm not. [Turning to the others] Come: do you think I dont see it all? [He goes to Sergius, and slaps him on the shoulder]. Sergius: youre the chocolate cream soldier, arnt you?

SERGIUS [starting up] I! A chocolate cream soldier! Certainly not.

PETKOFF. Not! [He looks at them. They are all very serious and very conscious]. Do you mean to tell me that Raina sends things like that to other men?

SERGIUS [enigmatically] The world is not such an innocent place as we used to think, Petkoff.

BLUNTSCHLI [rising] It's all right, Major. I'm the chocolate cream soldier. [Petkoff and Sergius are equally astonished]. The gracious young lady saved my life by giving me chocolate creams when I was starving: shall I ever forget their flavour! My late friend Stolz told you the story at Pirot. I was the fugitive.

PETKOFF. You! [He gasps]. Sergius: do you remember how these two women went on this morning when we mentioned it? [Sergius smiles cynically. Petkoff confronts Raina severely]. Youre a nice young woman, arnt you?

RAINA [bitterly] Major Saranoff has changed his mind. And when I wrote that on the photograph, I did not know that Captain Bluntschli was married.

BLUNTSCHLI [startled into vehement protest]

I'm not married.

RAINA [with deep reproach] You said you were.

BLUNTSCHLI. I did not. I positively did not. I never was married in my life.

PETKOFF [exasperated] Raina: will you kindly inform me, if I am not asking too much, which of these gentlemen you are engaged to?

RAINA. To neither of them. This young lady [introducing Louka, who faces them all proudly] is the object of Major Saranoff's affections at present.

PETKOFF. Louka! Are you mad, Sergius? Why, this girl's engaged to Nicola.

NICOLA. I beg your pardon, sir. There is a mistake. Louka is not engaged to me.

PETKOFF. Not engaged to you, you scoundrel! Why, you had twenty-five levas from me on the day of your betrothal; and she had that gilt bracelet from Miss Raina.

NICOLA [with cool unction] We gave it out so, sir. But it was only to give Louka protection. She had a soul above her station; and I have been no more than her confidential servant. I intend, as you know, sir, to set up a shop later on in Sofia; and I look forward to her custom and recommendation should she marry into the nobility. [He goes out with impressive discretion, leaving them all staring after him].

PETKOFF [breaking the silence] Well, I am— hm!

SERGIUS. This is either the finest heroism or the most crawling baseness. Which is it, Bluntschli?

BLUNTSCHLI. Never mind whether it's heroism or baseness. Nicola's the ablest man Ive met in Bulgaria. I'll make him manager of a hotel if he can speak French and German.

LOUKA [suddenly breaking out at Sergius] I have been insulted by everyone here. You set them the example. You owe me an apology.

Sergius, like a repeating clock of which the spring has been touched, immediately begins to fold his arms.

BLUNTSCHLI [before he can speak] It's no use. He never apologizes.

LOUKA. Not to you, his equal and his enemy. To me, his poor servant, he will not refuse to apologize.

SERGIUS [approvingly] You are right. [He bends his knee in his grandest manner] Forgive me.

LOUKA. I forgive you. [*She timidly gives him her hand, which he kisses*]. That touch makes me your affianced wife.

SERGIUS [*springing up*] Ah! I forgot that.

LOUKA [*coldly*] You can withdraw if you like.

SERGIUS. Withdraw! Never! You belong to me. [*He puts his arm about her*].

Catherine comes in and finds Louka in Sergius's arms, with all the rest gazing at them in bewildered astonishment.

CATHERINE. What does this mean?

Sergius releases Louka.

PETKOFF. Well, my dear, it appears that Sergius is going to marry Louka instead of Raina. [*She is about to break out indignantly at him: he stops her by exclaiming testily*] Dont blame m e: I v e nothing to do with it. [*He retreats to the stove*].

CATHERINE. Marry Louka! Sergius: you are bound by your word to us!

SERGIUS [*folding his arms*] Nothing binds me.

BLUNTSCHLI [*much pleased by this piece of common sense*] Saranoff: your hand. My congratulations. These heroics of yours have their practical side after all. [*To Louka*] Gracious young lady: the best wishes of a good Republican! [*He kisses her hand, to Raina's great disgust, and returns to his seat*].

CATHERINE. Louka: you have been telling stories.

LOUKA. I have done Raina no harm.

CATHERINE [*haughtily*] Raina!

Raina, equally indignant, almost snorts at the liberty.

LOUKA. I have a right to call her Raina: she calls me Louka. I told Major Saranoff she would never marry him if the Swiss gentleman came back.

BLUNTSCHLI [*rising, much surprised*] Hallo!

LOUKA [*turning to Raina*] I thought you were fonder of him than of Sergius. You know best whether I was right.

BLUNTSCHLI. What nonsense! I assure you, my dear Major, my dear Madame, the gracious young lady simply saved my life, nothing else. She never cared two straws for me. Why, bless my heart and soul, look at the young lady and look at me. She, rich, young, beautiful, with her imagination full of fairy princes and noble natures and cavalry charges and goodness knows what! And I, a commonplace Swiss soldier who hardly knows what a decent life is after fifteen years

of barracks and battles: a vagabond, a man who has spoiled all his chances in life through an incurably romantic disposition, a man—

SERGIUS [*starting as if a needle had pricked him and interrupting Bluntschli in incredulous amazement*] Excuse me, Bluntschli: w h a t did you say had spoiled your chances in life?

BLUNTSCHLI [*promptly*] An incurably romantic disposition. I ran away from home twice when I was a boy. I went into the army instead of into my father's business. I climbed the balcony of this house when a man of sense would have dived into the nearest cellar. I came sneaking back here to have another look at the young lady when any other man of my age would have sent the coat back—

PETKOFF. My coat!

BLUNTSCHLI.—yes: thats the coat I mean— would have sent it back and gone quietly home. Do you suppose I am the sort of fellow a young girl falls in love with? Why, look at our ages! I'm thirty-four: I dont suppose the young lady is much over seventeen. [*This estimate produces a marked sensation, all the rest turning and staring at one another. He proceeds innocently*] All that adventure which was life or death to me, was only a schoolgirl's game to her—chocolate creams and hide and seek. Heres the proof! [*He takes the photograph from the table*]. Now, I ask you, would a woman who took the affair seriously have sent me this and written on it "Raina, to her Chocolate Cream Soldier: a Souvenir"? [*He exhibits the photograph triumphantly, as if it settled the matter beyond all possibility of refutation*].

PETKOFF. Thats what I was looking for. How the deuce did it get there? [*He comes from the stove to look at it, and sits down on the ottoman*].

BLUNTSCHLI [*to Raina, complacently*] I have put everything right, I hope, gracious young lady.

RAINA [*going to the table to face him*] I quite agree with your account of yourself. You are a romantic idiot. [*Bluntschli is unspeakably taken aback*]. Next time, I hope you will know the difference between a schoolgirl of seventeen and a woman of twenty-three.

BLUNTSCHLI [*stupefied*] Twenty-three!

Raina snaps the photograph contemptuously from his hand; tears it up; throws the pieces in his face; and sweeps back to her former place.

SERGIUS [*with grim enjoyment of his rival's*

discomfiture] Bluntschli: my one last belief is gone. Your sagacity is a fraud, like everything else. You have less sense than even I!

BLUNTSCHLI [*overwhelmed*] Twenty-three!! Twenty-three!! [*He considers*]. Hm! [*Swiftly making up his mind and coming to his host*] In that case, Major Petkoff, I beg to propose formally to become a suitor for your daughter's hand, in place of Major Saranoff retired.

RAINA. You dare!

BLUNTSCHLI. If you were twenty-three when you said those things to me this afternoon, I shall take them seriously.

CATHERINE [*loftily polite*] I doubt, sir, whether you quite realize either my daughter's position or that of Major Sergius Saranoff, whose place you propose to take. The Petkoffs and the Saranoffs are known as the richest and most important families in the country. Our position is almost historical: we can go back for twenty years.

PETKOFF. Oh, never mind that, Catherine. [*To Bluntschli*] We should be most happy, Bluntschli, if it were only a question of your position; but hang it, you know, Raina is accustomed to a very comfortable establishment. Sergius keeps twenty horses.

BLUNTSCHLI. But who wants twenty horses? We're not going to keep a circus.

CATHERINE [*severely*] My daughter, sir, is accustomed to a first-rate stable.

RAINA. Hush, mother: youre making me ridiculous.

BLUNTSCHLI. Oh well, if it comes to a question of an establishment, here goes! [*He darts impetuously to the table; seizes the papers in the blue envelope; and turns to Sergius*]. How many horses did you say?

SERGIUS. Twenty, noble Switzer.

BLUNTSCHLI. I have two hundred horses. [*They are amazed*]. How many carriages?

SERGIUS. Three.

BLUNTSCHLI. I have seventy. Twenty-four of them will hold twelve inside, besides two on the box, without counting the driver and conductor. How many tablecloths have you?

SERGIUS. How the deuce do I know?

BLUNTSCHLI. Have you four thousand?

SERGIUS. No.

BLUNTSCHLI. I have. I have nine thousand six hundred pairs of sheets and blankets, with two thousand four hundred eider-down quilts. I have ten thousand knives and forks, and the same quantity of dessert spoons. I have

three hundred servants. I have six palatial establishments, besides two livery stables, a tea gardens, and a private house. I have four medals for distinguished services; I have the rank of an officer and the standing of a gentleman; and I have three native languages. Shew me any man in Bulgaria that can offer as much!

PETKOFF [*with childish awe*] Are you Emperor of Switzerland?

BLUNTSCHLI. My rank is the highest known in Switzerland: I am a free citizen.

CATHERINE. Then, Captain Bluntschli, since you are my daughter's choice—

RAINA [*mutinously*] He's not.

CATHERINE [*ignoring her*]—I shall not stand in the way of her happiness. [*Petkoff is about to speak*] That is Major Petkoff's feeling also.

PETKOFF. Oh, I shall be only too glad. Two hundred horses! Whew!

SERGIUS. What says the lady?

RAINA [*pretending to sulk*] The lady says that he can keep his tablecloths and his omnibuses. I am not here to be sold to the highest bidder. [*She turns her back on him*].

BLUNTSCHLI. I wont take that answer. I appealed to you as a fugitive, a beggar, and a starving man. You accepted me. You gave me your hand to kiss, your bed to sleep in, and your roof to shelter me.

RAINA. I did not give them to the Emperor of Switzerland.

BLUNTSCHLI. Thats just what I say. [*He catches her by the shoulders and turns her face-to-face with him*]. Now tell us whom you did give them to.

RAINA [*succumbing with a shy smile*] To my chocolate cream soldier.

BLUNTSCHLI [*with a boyish laugh of delight*] Thatll do. Thank you. [*He looks at his watch and suddenly becomes businesslike*]. Time's up, Major. Youve managed those regiments so well that youre sure to be asked to get rid of some of the infantry of the Timok division. Send them home by way of Lom Palanka. Saranoff: dont get married until I come back: I shall be here punctually at five in the evening on Tuesday fortnight. Gracious ladies [*his heels click*] good evening. [*He makes them a military bow, and goes*].

SERGIUS. What a man! Is he a man?

THE END

V

CANDIDA

1895

BEING THE SECOND OF FOUR PLEASANT PLAYS

ACT I

A fine morning in October 1894 in the north east quarter of London, a vast district miles away from the London of Mayfair and St. James's, and much less narrow, squalid, fetid and airless in its slums. It is strong in unfashionable middle class life: wide-streeted; myriad-populated; well served with ugly iron urinals, Radical clubs, and tram lines carrying a perpetual stream of yellow cars; enjoying in its main thoroughfares the luxury of grass-grown "front gardens" untrodden by the foot of man save as to the path from the gate to the hall door; blighted by a callously endured monotony of miles and miles of unlovely brick houses, black iron railings, stony pavements, slated roofs, and respectably ill dressed or disreputably worse dressed people, quite accustomed to the place, and mostly plodding uninterestedly about somebody's else's work. The little energy and eagerness that crop up shew themselves in cockney cupidity and business "push." Even the policemen and the chapels are not infrequent enough to break the monotony. The sun is shining cheerfully: there is no fog; and though the smoke effectually prevents anything, whether faces and hands or bricks and mortar, from looking fresh and clean, it is not hanging heavily enough to trouble a Londoner.

This desert of unattractiveness has its oasis. Near the outer end of the Hackney road is a park of 217 acres, fenced in, not by railings, but by a wooden paling, and containing plenty of greensward, trees, a lake for bathers, flower beds which are triumphs of the admired cockney art of carpet gardening, and a sandpit, originally imported from the seaside for the delight of children, but speedily deserted on its becoming a natural vermin preserve for all the petty fauna of Kingsland, Hackney, and Hoxton. A bandstand, an unfurnished forum for religious, anti-religious, and political orators, cricket pitches, a gymnasium, and an old fashioned stone kiosk are among its attractions. Wherever the prospect is bounded by trees or rising green grounds, it is a pleasant place. Where the ground stretches flat to the grey palings, with bricks and mortar, sky signs, crowded chimneys and smoke beyond, the prospect makes it desolate and sordid.

The best view of Victoria Park is commanded by the front window of St. Dominic's Parsonage, from which not a brick is visible. The parsonage is semi-detached, with a front garden and a porch. Visitors go up the flight of steps to the porch: tradespeople and members of the family go down by a door under the steps to the basement, with a breakfastroom, used for all meals, in front, and the kitchen at the back. Upstairs, on the level of the hall door, is the drawing room, with its large plate glass window looking out on the park. In this, the only sitting room that can be spared from the children and the family meals, the parson, the Reverend James Mavor Morell, does his work. He is sitting in a strong round backed revolving chair at the end of a long table, which stands across the window, so that he can cheer himself with a view of the park over his left shoulder. At the opposite end of the table, adjoining it, is a little table only half as wide as the other, with a typewriter on it. His typist is sitting at this machine, with her back to the window. The large table is littered with pamphlets, journals, letters, nests of drawers, an office diary, postage scales and the like. A spare chair for visitors having business with the parson is in the middle, turned to his end. Within reach of his hand is a stationery case, and a photograph in a frame. The wall behind him is fitted with bookshelves, on which an adept eye can measure the parson's casuistry and divinity by Maurice's Theological Essays and a complete set of Browning's poems, and the reformer's politics by a yellow backed Progress and Poverty, Fabian Essays, A Dream of John Ball, Marx's Capital, and half a dozen other literary landmarks in Socialism. Facing him on the other side of the room, near the typewriter, is the door. Further down opposite the fireplace, a bookcase stands on a cellaret, with a sofa near it. There is a generous fire burning; and the hearth, with a comfortable armchair and a black japanned flower-painted coal scuttle at one side, a miniature chair for children on the other, a varnished wooden mantelpiece, with neatly moulded shelves, tiny bits of *mirror let into the panels, a travelling clock in a leather case (the inevitable wedding present), and on the wall above a large autotype of the chief figure in Titian's Assumption of the Virgin, is very inviting. Altogether the room is the room of a good housekeeper, vanquished, as far as the table is concerned, by an untidy man, but elsewhere mistress of the situation. The furniture, in its ornamental aspect, betrays the style of the advertized "drawingroom suite" of the pushing suburban furniture dealer; but there is nothing useless or pretentious in the room, money being too scarce in the house of an east end parson to be wasted on snobbish trimmings.*

The Reverend James Mavor Morell is a Christian Socialist clergyman of the Church of England, and an active member of the Guild of St. Matthew and the Christian Social Union. A vigorous, genial, popular man of forty, robust and goodlooking, full of energy, with pleasant, hearty, considerate manners, and a sound unaffected voice, which he uses with the clean athletic articulation of a practised orator, and with a wide range and perfect command of expression. He is a first rate clergyman, able to say what he likes to whom he likes, to lecture people without setting himself up against them, to impose his authority on them without humiliating them, and, on occasion, to interfere in their business without impertinence. His well-spring of enthusiasm and sympathetic emotion has never run dry for a moment: he still eats and sleeps heartily enough to win the daily battle between exhaustion and recuperation triumphantly. Withal, a great baby, pardonably vain of his powers and unconsciously pleased with himself. He has a healthy complexion: good forehead, with the brows somewhat blunt, and the eyes bright and eager, mouth resolute but not particularly well cut, and a substantial nose, with the mobile spreading nostrils of the dramatic orator, void, like all his features, of subtlety.

The typist, Miss Proserpine Garnett, is a brisk little woman of about 30, of the lower middle class, neatly but cheaply dressed in a black merino skirt and a blouse, notably pert and quick of speech, and not very civil in her manner, but sensitive and affectionate. She is clattering away busily at her machine whilst Morell opens the last of his morning's letters, He realizes its contents with a comic groan of despair.

PROSERPINE. Another lecture?

MORELL. Yes. The Hoxton Freedom Group want me to address them on Sunday morning [*he lays great emphasis on Sunday, this being the unreasonable part of the business*]. What are they?

PROSERPINE. Communist Anarchists, I think.

MORELL. Just like Anarchists not to know that they cant have a parson on Sunday! Tell them to come to church if they want to hear me: it will do them good. Say I can come on Mondays and Thursdays only. Have you the diary there?

PROSERPINE [*taking up the diary*] Yes.

MORELL. Have I any lecture on for next Monday?

PROSERPINE [*referring to diary*] Tower Hamlets Radical Club.

MORELL. Well, Thursday then?

PROSERPINE. English Land Restoration League.

MORELL. What next?

PROSERPINE. Guild of St Matthew on Monday. Independent Labor Party, Greenwich Branch, on Thursday. Monday, Social-Democratic Federation, Mile End Branch. Thursday, first Confirmation class. [*Impatiently*] Oh, I'd better tell them you cant come. Theyre only half a dozen ignorant and conceited costermongers without five shillings between them.

MORELL [*amused*] Ah; but you see theyre near relatives of mine.

PROSERPINE [*staring at him*] Relatives of yours!

MORELL. Yes: we have the same father—in Heaven.

PROSERPINE [*relieved*] Oh, is that all?

MORELL [*with a sadness which is a luxury to a man whose voice expresses it so finely*] Ah, you dont believe it. Everybody says it: nobody believes it: nobody. [*Briskly, getting back to business*] Well, well! Come, Miss Proserpine: cant you find a date for the costers? What about the 25th? That was vacant the day before yesterday.

PROSERPINE [*referring to diary*] Engaged. The Fabian Society.

MORELL. Bother the Fabian Society! Is the 28th gone too?

PROSERPINE. City dinner. Youre invited to dine with the Founders' Company.

MORELL. Thatll do: I'll go to the Hoxton Group of Freedom instead. [*She enters the engagement in silence, with implacable disparagement of the Hoxton Anarchists in every line of her face. Morell bursts open the cover of a copy of The Church Reformer, which has come by post, and glances through Mr Stewart Headlam's leader and the Guild of St Matthew news. These proceedings are presently enlivened by the appearance of Morell's curate, the Reverend Alexander Mill, a young gentleman gathered by Morell from the nearest University settlement, whither he had come from Oxford to give the east end of London the benefit of his university training. He is a conceitedly well intentioned, enthusiastic, immature novice, with nothing positively unbearable about him except a habit of speaking with his lips carefully closed a full half inch from each corner for the sake of a finicking articulation and a set of university vowels, this being his chief means so far of bringing his Oxford refinement (as he calls his habits) to bear on Hackney vulgarity. Morell, whom he has won over by a doglike devotion, looks up indulgently from The Church Reformer, and remarks*] Well, Lexy? Late again, as usual!

LEXY. I'm afraid so. I wish I could get up in the morning.

MORELL [*exulting in his own energy*] Ha! Ha! [*Whimsically*] Watch and pray, Lexy: watch and pray.

LEXY. I know. [*Rising wittily to the occasion*] But how can I watch and pray when I am asleep? Isnt that so, Miss Prossy? [*He makes for the warmth of the fire*].

PROSERPINE [*sharply*] Miss Garnett, if you please.

LEXY. I beg your pardon. Miss Garnett.

PROSERPINE. Youve got to do all the work today.

LEXY [*on the hearth*] Why?

PROSERPINE. Never mind why. It will do you good to earn your supper before you eat it, for once in a way, as I do. Come! dont dawdle. You should have been off on your rounds half an hour ago.

LEXY [*perplexed*] Is she in earnest, Morell?

MORELL [*in the highest spirits: his eyes dancing*] Yes. *I* am going to dawdle today.

LEXY. You! You dont know how.

MORELL [*rising*] Ha! ha! Dont I? I'm going to have this morning all to myself. My wife's coming back: she's due here at 11.45.

LEXY [*surprised*] Coming back already! with the children? I thought they were to stay to the end of the month.

MORELL. So they are: she's only coming up for two days, to get some flannel things for Jimmy, and to see how we're getting on without her.

LEXY [*anxiously*] But, my dear Morell, if

what Jimmy and Fluffy had was scarlatina, do you think it wise—

MORELL. Scarlatina! Rubbish! it was German measles. I brought it into the house myself from the Pycroft Street school. A parson is like a doctor, my boy: he must face infection as a soldier must face bullets. [*He claps Lexy manfully on the shoulders*]. Catch the measles if you can, Lexy: she'll nurse you; and what a piece of luck that will be for you! Eh?

LEXY [*smiling uneasily*] It's so hard to understand you about Mrs Morell—

MORELL [*tenderly*] Ah, my boy, get married: get married to a good woman; and then youll understand. Thats a foretaste of what will be best in the Kingdom of Heaven we are trying to establish on earth. That will cure you of dawdling. An honest man feels that he must pay Heaven for every hour of happiness with a good spell of hard unselfish work to make others happy. We have no more right to consume happiness without producing it than to consume wealth without producing it. Get a wife like my Candida; and youll always be in arrear with your repayment. [*He pats Lexy affectionately and moves to leave the room*].

LEXY. Oh, wait a bit: I forgot. [*Morell halts and turns with the door knob in his hand*]. Your father-in-law is coming round to see you.

Morell, surprised and not pleased, shuts the door again, with a complete change of manner.

MORELL. Mr Burgess?

LEXY. Yes. I passed him in the park, arguing with somebody. He asked me to let you know that he was coming.

MORELL [*half incredulous*] But he hasnt called here for three years. Are you sure, Lexy? Youre not joking, are you?

LEXY [*earnestly*] No sir, really.

MORELL [*thoughtfully*] Hm! Time for him to take another look at Candida before she grows out of his knowledge. [*He resigns himself to the inevitable, and goes out*].

Lexy looks after him with beaming worship. Miss Garnett, not being able to shake Lexy, relieves her feelings by worrying the typewriter.

LEXY. What a good man! What a thorough loving soul he is! [*He takes Morell's place at the table, making himself very comfortable as he takes out a cigaret*].

PROSERPINE [*impatiently, pulling the letter she has been working at off the typewriter and folding it*] Oh, a man ought to be able to be fond of his wife without making a fool of himself about her.

LEXY [shocked] Oh, Miss Prossy!

PROSERPINE [snatching at the stationery case for an envelope, in which she encloses the letter as she speaks] Candida here, and Candida there, and Candida everywhere! [She licks the envelope]. It's enough to drive anyone out of their senses [thumping the envelope to make it stick] to hear a woman raved about in that absurd manner merely because she's got good hair and a tolerable figure.

LEXY [with reproachful gravity] I think her extremely beautiful, Miss Garnett. [He takes the photograph up; looks at it; and adds, with even greater impressiveness] extremely beautiful. How fine her eyes are!

PROSERPINE. Her eyes are not a bit better than mine: now! [He puts down the photograph and stares austerely at her]. And you know very well you think me dowdy and second rate enough.

LEXY [rising majestically] Heaven forbid that I should think of any of God's creatures in such a way! [He moves stiffly away from her across the room to the neighborhood of the bookcase].

PROSERPINE [sarcastically] Thank you. Thats very nice and comforting.

LEXY [saddened by her depravity] I had no idea you had any feeling against Mrs Morell.

PROSERPINE [indignantly] I have no feeling against her. She's very nice, very good-hearted: I'm very fond of her, and can appreciate her real qualities far better than any man can. [He shakes his head sadly. She rises and comes at him with intense pepperiness]. You dont believe me? You think I'm jealous? Oh, what a knowledge of the human heart you have, Mr Lexy Mill! How well you know the weaknesses of Woman, dont you? It must be so nice to be a man and have a fine penetrating intellect instead of mere emotions like us, and to know that the reason we dont share your amorous delusions is that we're all jealous of one another! [She abandons him with a toss of her shoulders, and crosses to the fire to warm her hands].

LEXY. Ah, if you women only had the same clue to Man's strength that you have to his weakness, Miss Prossy, there would be no Woman Question.

PROSERPINE [over her shoulder, as she stoops, holding her hands to the blaze] Where did you hear Morell say that? You didnt invent it yourself: youre not clever enough.

LEXY. Thats quite true. I am not ashamed of owing him that, as I owe him so many other spiritual truths. He said it at the annual conference of the Women's Liberal Federation. Allow me to add that though they didnt appreciate it, I, a mere man, did. [He turns to the bookcase again, hoping that this may leave her crushed].

PROSERPINE [putting her hair straight at a panel of mirror in the mantelpiece] Well, when you talk to me, give me your own ideas, such as they are, and not his. You never cut a poorer figure than when you are trying to imitate him.

LEXY [stung] I try to follow his example, not to imitate him.

PROSERPINE [coming at him again on her way back to her work] Yes, you do: you imitate him. Why do you tuck your umbrella under your left arm instead of carrying it in your hand like anyone else? Why do you walk with your chin stuck out before you, hurrying along with that eager look in your eyes? you! who never get up before half past nine in the morning. Why do you say "knoaledge" in church, though you always say "knolledge" in private conversation! Bah! do you think I dont know? [She goes back to the typewriter]. Here! come and set about your work: weve wasted enough time for one morning. Here's a copy of the diary for today. [She hands him a memorandum].

LEXY [deeply offended] Thank you. [He takes it and stands at the table with his back to her, reading it. She begins to transcribe her shorthand notes on the typewriter without troubling herself about his feelings].

The door opens; and Mr Burgess enters unannounced. He is a man of sixty, made coarse and sordid by the compulsory selfishness of petty commerce, and later on softened into sluggish bumptiousness by overfeeding and commercial success. A vulgar ignorant guzzling man, offensive and contemptuous to people whose labor is cheap, respectful to wealth and rank, and quite sincere and without rancor or envy in both attitudes. The world has offered him no decently paid work except that of a sweater; and he has become, in consequence, somewhat hoggish. But he has no suspicion of this himself, and honestly regards his commercial prosperity as the inevitable and socially wholesome triumph of the ability, industry, shrewdness, and experience in business of a man who in private is easygoing, affectionate, and humorously convivial to a fault.

Corporeally he is podgy, with a snoutish nose in the centre of a flat square face, a dust colored beard with a patch of grey in the centre under his chin, and small watery blue eyes with a plaintively sentimental expression, which he transfers easily to his voice by his habit of pompously intoning his sentences.

BURGESS [*stopping on the threshold, and looking round*] They told me Mr Morell was here.

PROSERPINE [*rising*] I'll fetch him for you.

BURGESS [*staring disappointedly at her*] Youre not the same young lady as hused to typewrite for him?

PROSERPINE. No.

BURGESS [*grumbling on his way to the hearthrug*] No: she was young-er. [*Miss Garnett stares at him; then goes out, slamming the door*]. Startin on your rounds, Mr Mill?

LEXY [*folding his memorandum and pocketing it*] Yes: I must be off presently.

BURGESS [*momentously*] Dont let me detain you, Mr Mill. What I come about is p r i v a t e between me and Mr Morell.

LEXY [*huffily*] I have no intention of intruding, I am sure, Mr Burgess. Good morning.

BURGESS [*patronizingly*] Oh, good morning to you.

Morell returns as Lexy is making for the door.

MORELL [*to Lexy*] Off to work?

LEXY. Yes, sir.

MORELL. Take my silk handkerchief and wrap your throat up. Theres a cold wind. Away with you.

Lexy, more than consoled for Burgess's rudeness, brightens up and goes out.

BURGESS. Spoilin your korates as usu'l, James. Good mornin. When I pay a man, an' 'is livin depens on me, I keep him in 'is place.

MORELL [*rather shortly*] I always keep my curates in their places as my helpers and comrades. If you get as much work out of your clerks and warehousemen as I do out of my curates, you must be getting rich pretty fast. Will you take your old chair?

He points with curt authority to the armchair beside the fireplace; then takes the spare chair from the table and sits down at an unfamiliar distance from his visitor.

BURGESS [*without moving*] Just the same as hever, James!

MORELL. When you last called—it was about three years ago, I think—you said the same thing a little more frankly. Your exact words then were " Just as big a fool as ever, James! "

BURGESS [*soothingly*] Well, praps I did; but [*with conciliatory cheerfulness*] I meant no hoffence by it. A clorgyman is privileged to be a bit of a fool, you know: it's ony becomin in 'is profession that he should. Anyhow, I come here, not to rake up hold differences, but to let bygones be bygones. [*Suddenly becoming very solemn, and approaching Morell*] James: three years ago, you done me a hil turn. You done me hout of a contrac; an when I gev you arsh words in my natral disappointment, you turned my daughrter again me. Well, Ive come to hact the part of a Kerischin. [*Offering his hand*] I forgive you, James.

MORELL [*starting up*] Confound your impudence!

BURGESS [*retreating, with almost lachrymose deprecation of this treatment*] Is that becomin language for a clorgyman, James? And you so particlar, too!

MORELL [*hotly*] No, sir: it is not becoming language for a clergyman. I used the wrong word. I should have said damn your impudence : thats what St Paul or any honest priest would have said to you. Do you think I have forgotten that tender of yours for the contract to supply clothing to the workhouse?

BURGESS [*in a paroxysm of public spirit*] I hacted in the hinterest of the ratepayers, James. It was the lowest tender: you carnt deny that.

MORELL. Yes, the lowest, because you paid worse wages than any other employer— starvation wages—aye, worse than starvation wages—to the women who made the clothing. Your wages would have driven them to the streets to keep body and soul together. [*Getting angrier and angrier*] Those women were my parishioners. I shamed the Guardians out of accepting your tender: I shamed the ratepayers out of letting them do it: I shamed everybody but you. [*Boiling over*] How dare you, sir, come here and offer to forgive me, and talk about your daughter, and—

BURGESS. Heasy, James! heasy! heasy! Dont git hinto a fluster about nothink. Ive howned I was wrong.

MORELL. Have you? I didnt hear you.

BURGESS. Of course I did. I hown it now. Come: I harsk your pardon for the letter I wrote you. Is that enough?

MORELL [snapping his fingers] Thats nothing. Have you raised the wages?

BURGESS [triumphantly] Yes.

MORELL. What!

BURGESS [unctuously] Ive turned a moddle hemployer. I dont hemploy no women now: theyre all sacked; and the work is done by machinery. Not a man 'as less than sixpence a hour; and the skilled 'ands gits the Trade Union rate. [Proudly] What ave you to say to me now?

MORELL [overwhelmed] Is it possible! Well, theres more joy in heaven over one sinner that repenteth!—[Going to Burgess with an explosion of apologetic cordiality] My dear Burgess: how splendid of you! I most heartily beg your pardon for my hard thoughts. [Grasping his hand] And now, dont you feel the better for the change? Come! confess! youre happier. You look happier.

BURGESS [ruefully] Well, praps I do. I spose I must, since you notice it. At all events, I git my contrax assepted by the County Council. [Savagely] They dussent ave nothink to do with me unless I paid fair wages: curse em for a parcel o meddlin fools!

MORELL [dropping his hand, utterly discouraged] So that was why you raised the wages! [He sits down moodily].

BURGESS [severely, in spreading, mounting tones] Woy helse should I do it? What does it lead to but drink and huppishness in workin men? [He seats himself magisterially in the easy chair]. It's hall very well for you, James: it gits you hinto the papers and makes a great man of you; but you never think of the arm you do, puttin money into the pockets of workin men that they dunno ow to spend, and takin it from people that might be makin a good huse on it.

MORELL [with a heavy sigh, speaking with cold politeness] What is your business with me this morning? I shall not pretend to believe that you are here merely out of family sentiment.

BURGESS [obstinately] Yes I ham: just family sentiment and nothink helse.

MORELL [with weary calm] I dont believe you.

BURGESS [rising threateningly] Dont say that to me again, James Mavor Morell.

MORELL [unmoved] I'll say it just as often as may be necessary to convince you that it's true. I dont believe you.

BURGESS [collapsing into an abyss of wounded feeling] Oh, well, if youre detormined to be hunfriendly, I spose I'd better go. [He moves reluctantly towards the door. Morell makes no sign. He lingers]. I didnt hexpect to find a hunforgivin spirit in you, James. [Morell still not responding, he takes a few more reluctant steps doorwards. Then he comes back, whining]. We huseter git on well enough, spite of our different hopinions. Woy are you so changed to me? I give you my word I come here in peeorr [pure] frenliness, not wishin to be hon bad terms with my hown daughrter's usban. Come, James: be a Kerischin, and shake ands. [He puts his hand sentimentally on Morell's shoulder].

MORELL [looking up at him thoughtfully] Look here, Burgess. Do you want to be as welcome here as you were before you lost that contract?

BURGESS. I do, James. I do—honest.

MORELL. Then why dont you behave as you did then?

BURGESS [cautiously removing his hand] Ow d'y' mean?

MORELL. I'll tell you. You thought me a young fool then.

BURGESS [coaxingly] No I didnt, James. I—

MORELL [cutting him short] Yes, you did. And I thought you an old scoundrel.

BURGESS [most vehemently deprecating this gross self-accusation on Morell's part] No you didnt, James. Now you do yourself a hinjustice.

MORELL. Yes I did. Well, that did not prevent our getting on very well together. God made you what I call a scoundrel as He made me what you call a fool. [The effect of this observation on Burgess is to remove the keystone of his moral arch. He becomes bodily weak, and, with his eyes fixed on Morell in a helpless stare, puts out his hand apprehensively to balance himself, as if the floor had suddenly sloped under him. Morell proceeds, in the same tone of quiet conviction] It was not for me to quarrel with His handiwork in the one case more than in the other. So long as you come here honestly as a self-respecting, thorough, convinced scoundrel, justifying your scoundrelism and proud of it, you are welcome. But [and now Morell's tone becomes formidable; and he rises and strikes the back of the chair for greater emphasis] I wont have you here snivelling about being a model employer and a converted man when youre only an apostate with your coat turned for the sake of a County Council contract. [He nods at him to enforce the point; then goes to the hearth-rug, where he takes up a comfortably commanding position with his back to the fire, and continues] No: I like a man to be true to himself, even in wickedness. Come now: either take your hat and go; or else sit down and give me a good scoundrelly reason for wanting to be friends with me. [Burgess, whose emotions have subsided sufficiently to be expressed by a dazed grin, is relieved by this concrete proposition. He ponders it for a moment, and then, slowly and very modestly, sits down in the chair Morell has just left]. Thats right. Now out with it.

BURGESS [chuckling in spite of himself] Well, you orr a queer bird, James, and no mistake. But [almost enthusiastically] one carnt elp likin you: besides, as I said afore, of course one dont take hall a clorgyman says seriously, or the world couldnt go on. Could it now? [He composes himself for graver discourse, and, turning his eyes on Morell, proceeds with dull seriousness] Well, I dont mind tellin you, since it's your wish we should be free with one another, that I did think you a bit of a fool once; but I'm beginnin to think that praps I was be'ind the times a bit.

MORELL [exultant] Aha! Youre finding that out at last, are you?

BURGESS [portentously] Yes: times 'as changed mor'n I could a believed. Five yorr [year] ago, no sensible man would a thought o takin hup with your hidears. I hused to wonder you was let preach at all. Why, I know a clorgyman what 'as bin kep hout of his job for yorrs by the Bishop o London, although the pore feller's not a bit more religious than you are. But today, if henny-one was to horffer to bet me a thousan poun that youll hend by bein a bishop yourself, I dussent take the bet. [Very impressively] You and your crew are gittin hinfluential: I can see that. Theyll ave to give you somethink someday, if it's honly to stop your mouth. You ad the right instinc arter all, James: the line you took is the payin line in the long run for a man o your sort.

MORELL [offering his hand with thorough decision] Shake hands, Burgess. Now youre talking honestly. I dont think theyll make me a bishop; but if they do, I'll introduce you to the biggest jobbers I can get to come to my dinner parties.

BURGESS [who has risen with a sheepish grin and accepted the hand of friendship] You will ave your joke, James. Our quarrel's made up now, ain it?

A WOMAN'S VOICE. Say yes, James.

Startled, they turn quickly and find that Candida has just come in, and is looking at them with an amused maternal indulgence which is her characteristic expression. She is a woman of 33, well built, well nourished, likely, one guesses, to become matronly later on, but now quite at her best, with the double charm of youth and mother-hood. Her ways are those of a woman who has found that she can always manage people by engaging their affection, and who does so frankly and instinctively without the smallest scruple. So far, she is like any other pretty woman who is just clever enough to make the most of her sexual attractions for trivially selfish ends; but Candida's serene brow, courageous eyes, and well set mouth and chin signify largeness of mind and dignity of character to ennoble her cunning in the affec-tions. A wisehearted observer, looking at her, would at once guess that whoever had placed the Virgin of the Assumption over her hearth did so because he fancied some spiritual resemblance between them, and yet would not suspect either her husband or herself of any such idea, or in-deed of any concern with the art of Titian.

Just now she is in bonnet and mantle, carrying a strapped rug with her umbrella stuck through it, a handbag, and a supply of illustrated papers.

MORELL [shocked at his remissness] Candida! Why— [he looks at his watch, and is horrified to find it so late]. My darling! [Hurrying to her and seizing the rug strap, pouring forth his remorseful regrets all the time] I intended to meet you at the train. I let the time slip. [Flinging the rug on the sofa] I was so engrossed by— [returning to her]—I forgot—oh! [He em-braces her with penitent emotion].

BURGESS [a little shamefaced and doubtful of his reception] How orr you, Candy? [She, still in Morell's arms, offers him her cheek, which he kisses]. James and me is come to a nunner-stannin. A honorable unnerstannin. Ain we, James?

MORELL [impetuously] Oh bother your under-standing! youve kept me late for Candida. [With compassionate fervor] My poor love: how did you manage about the luggage? How—

CANDIDA [stopping him and disengaging her-self] There! there! there! I wasnt alone. Eugene has been down with us; and we travelled together.

MORELL [pleased] Eugene!

CANDIDA. Yes: he's struggling with my

F

luggage, poor boy. Go out, dear, at once; or he'll pay for the cab; and I dont want that. [*Morell hurries out. Candida puts down her handbag; then takes off her mantle and bonnet and puts them on the sofa with the rug, chatting meanwhile*]. Well, papa: how are you getting on at home?

BURGESS. The ouse aint worth livin in since you left it, Candy. I wish youd come round and give the gurl a talkin to. Who's this Eugene thats come with you?

CANDIDA. Oh, Eugene's one of James's discoveries. He found him sleeping on the Embankment last June. Havnt you noticed our new picture [*pointing to the Virgin*]? He gave us that.

BURGESS [*incredulously*] Garn! D'you mean to tell me—your hown father!—that cab touts or such like, orf the Embankment, buys pictures like that? [*Severely*] Dont deceive me, Candy: it's a 'Igh Church picture; and James chose it hisself.

CANDIDA. Guess again. Eugene isnt a cab tout.

BURGESS. Then what is he? [*Sarcastically*] A nobleman, I spose.

CANDIDA [*nodding delightedly*] Yes. His uncle's a peer! A real live earl.

BURGESS [*not daring to believe such good news*] No!

CANDIDA. Yes. He had a seven day bill for £55 in his pocket when James found him on the Embankment. He thought he couldnt get any money for it until the seven days were up; and he was too shy to ask for credit. Oh, he's a dear boy! We are very fond of him.

BURGESS [*pretending to belittle the aristocracy, but with his eyes gleaming*] Hm! I thort you wouldnt git a hearl's nevvy visitin in Victawriar Pawrk unless he were a bit of a flat. [*Looking again at the picture*] Of course I dont old with that picture, Candy; but still it's a 'igh class fust rate work of ort: I can see that. Be sure you hintrodooce me to im, Candy. [*He looks at his watch anxiously*]. I can ony stay about two minutes.

Morell comes back with Eugene, whom Burgess contemplates moist-eyed with enthusiasm. He is a strange, shy youth of eighteen, slight, effeminate, with a delicate childish voice, and a hunted tormented expression and shrinking manner that shew the painful sensitiveness of very swift and acute apprehensiveness in youth, before the character has grown to its full strength. Miserably irresolute, he does not know where to stand or

what to do. He is afraid of Burgess, and would run away into solitude if he dared; but the very intensity with which he feels a perfectly commonplace position comes from excessive nervous force; and his nostrils, mouth, and eyes betray a fiercely petulant wilfulness, as to the bent of which his brow, already lined with pity, is reassuring. He is so uncommon as to be almost unearthly; and to prosaic people there is something noxious in this unearthliness, just as to poetic people there is something angelic in it. His dress is anarchic. He wears an old blue serge jacket, unbuttoned, over a woollen lawn tennis shirt, with a silk handkerchief for a cravat, trousers matching the jacket, and brown canvas shoes. In these garments he has apparently lain in the heather and waded through the waters; and there is no evidence of his having ever brushed them.

As he catches sight of a stranger on entering, he stops, and edges along the wall on the opposite side of the room.

MORELL [*as he enters*] Come along: you can spare us quarter of an hour at all events. This is my father-in-law. Mr Burgess—Mr Marchbanks.

MARCHBANKS [*nervously backing against the bookcase*] Glad to meet you, sir.

BURGESS [*crossing to him with great heartiness, whilst Morell joins Candida at the fire*] Glad to meet y o u, I'm shore, Mr Morchbanks. [*Forcing him to shake hands*] Ow do you find yoreself this weather? Ope you aint lettin James put no foolish ideas into your ed?

MARCHBANKS. Foolish ideas? Oh, you mean Socialism? No.

BURGESS. Thats right. [*Again looking at his watch*] Well, I must go now: theres no elp for it. Yore not comin my way, orr you, Mr Morchbanks?

MARCHBANKS. Which way is that?

BURGESS. Victawriar Pawrk Station. Theres a city train at 12.25.

MORELL. Nonsense. Eugene will stay to lunch with us, I expect.

MARCHBANKS [*anxiously excusing himself*] No—I—I—

BURGESS. Well, well, I shornt press you: I bet youd rather lunch with Candy. Some night, I ope, youll come and dine with me at my club, the Freeman Founders in Nortn Folgit. Come: say you will!

MARCHBANKS. Thank you, Mr Burgess. Where is Norton Folgate? Down in Surrey, isnt it?

Burgess, inexpressibly tickled, begins to splutter with laughter.

CANDIDA [*coming to the rescue*] Youll lose your train, papa, if you dont go at once. Come back in the afternoon and tell Mr Marchbanks where to find the club.

BURGESS [*roaring with glee*] Down in Surrey! Har, har! thats not a bad one. Well, I never met a man as didnt know Nortn Folgit afore. [*Abashed at his own noisiness*] Goodbye, Mr Morchbanks: I know yore too ighbred to take my pleasantry in bad part. [*He again offers his hand*].

MARCHBANKS [*taking it with a nervous jerk*] Not at all.

BURGESS. Bye, bye, Candy. I'll look in again later on. So long, James.

MORELL. Must you go?

BURGESS. Dont stir. [*He goes out with unabated heartiness*].

MORELL. Oh, I'll see you off. [*He follows him*]
Eugene stares after them apprehensively, holding his breath until Burgess disappears.

CANDIDA [*laughing*] Well, Eugene? [*He turns with a start, and comes eagerly towards her, but stops irresolutely as he meets her amused look*]. What do you think of my father?

MARCHBANKS. I—I hardly know him yet. He seems to be a very nice old gentleman.

CANDIDA [*with gentle irony*] And youll go to the Freeman Founders to dine with him, wont you?

MARCHBANKS [*miserably, taking it quite seriously*] Yes, if it will please you.

CANDIDA [*touched*] Do you know, you are a very nice boy, Eugene, with all your queerness. If you had laughed at my father I shouldnt have minded; but I like you ever so much better for being nice to him.

MARCHBANKS. Ought I to have laughed? I noticed that he said something funny; but I am so ill at ease with strangers; and I never can see a joke. I'm very sorry. [*He sits down on the sofa, his elbows on his knees and his temples between his fists, with an expression of hopeless suffering*].

CANDIDA [*bustling him goodnaturedly*] Oh come! You great baby, you! You are worse than usual this morning. Why were you so melancholy as we came along in the cab?

MARCHBANKS. Oh, that was nothing. I was wondering how much I ought to give the cabman. I know it's utterly silly; but you dont know how dreadful such things are to me—how I shrink from having to deal with

strange people. [*Quickly and reassuringly*] But it's all right. He beamed all over and touched his hat when Morell gave him two shillings. I was on the point of offering him ten.

Morell comes back with a few letters and newspapers which have come by the midday post.

CANDIDA. Oh, James dear, he was going to give the cabman ten shillings! ten shillings for a three minutes drive! Oh dear!

MORELL [*at the table, glancing through the letters*] Never mind her, Marchbanks. The overpaying instinct is a generous one: better than the underpaying instinct, and not so common.

MARCHBANKS [*relapsing into dejection*] No: cowardice, incompetence. Mrs Morell's quite right.

CANDIDA. Of course she is. [*She takes up her hand-bag*]. And now I must leave you to James for the present. I suppose you are too much of a poet to know the state a woman finds her house in when she's been away for three weeks. Give me my rug. [*Eugene takes the strapped rug from the couch, and gives it to her. She takes it in her left hand, having the bag in her right*]. Now hang my cloak across my arm. [*He obeys*]. Now my hat. [*He puts it into the hand which has the bag*]. Now open the door for me. [*He hurries before her and opens the door*]. Thanks. [*She goes out; and Marchbanks shuts the door*].

MORELL [*still busy at the table*] Youll stay to lunch, Marchbanks, of course.

MARCHBANKS [*scared*] I musnt. [*He glances quickly at Morell, but at once avoids his frank look, and adds, with obvious disingenuousness*] I mean I cant.

MORELL. You mean you wont.

MARCHBANKS [*earnestly*] No: I should like to, indeed. Thank you very much. But—but—

MORELL. But—but—but—but Bosh! If youd like to stay, stay. If youre shy, go and take a turn in the park and write poetry until half past one; and then come in and have a good feed.

MARCHBANKS. Thank you, I should like that very much. But I really musnt. The truth is, Mrs Morell told me not to. She said she didnt think youd ask me to stay to lunch, but that I was to remember, if you did, that you didnt really want me to. [*Plaintively*] She said I'd understand; but I dont. Please dont tell her I told you.

MORELL [*drolly*] Oh, is that all? Wont my

suggestion that you should take a turn in the park meet the difficulty?

MARCHBANKS. How?

MORELL [*exploding good-humoredly*] Why, you duffer— [*But this boisterousness jars himself as well as Eugene. He checks himself*]. No: I wont put it in that way. [*He comes to Eugene with affectionate seriousness*]. My dear lad: in a happy marriage like ours, there is something very sacred in the return of the wife to her home. [*Marchbanks looks quickly at him, half anticipating his meaning*]. An old friend or a truly noble and sympathetic soul is not in the way on such occasions; but a chance visitor is. [*The hunted horror-stricken expression comes out with sudden vividness in Eugene's face as he understands. Morell, occupied with his own thoughts, goes on without noticing this*]. Candida thought I would rather not have you here; but she was wrong. I'm very fond of you, my boy; and I should like you to see for yourself what a happy thing it is to be married as I am.

MARCHBANKS. Happy! Your marriage! You think that! You believe that!

MORELL [*buoyantly*] I know it, my lad. Larochefoucauld said that there are convenient marriages but no delightful ones. You dont know the comfort of seeing through and through a thundering liar and rotten cynic like that fellow. Ha! ha! Now, off with you to the park, and write your poem. Half past one, sharp, mind: we never wait for anybody.

MARCHBANKS [*wildly*] No: stop: you shant. I'll force it into the light.

MORELL [*puzzled*] Eh? Force what?

MARCHBANKS. I must speak to you. There is something that must be settled between us.

MORELL [*with a whimsical glance at his watch*] Now?

MARCHBANKS [*passionately*] Now. Before you leave this room. [*He retreats a few steps, and stands as if to bar Morell's way to the door*].

MORELL [*without moving, and gravely, perceiving now that there is something serious the matter*] I'm not going to leave it, my dear boy: I thought y o u were. [*Eugene, baffled by his firm tone, turns his back on him, writhing with anger. Morell goes to him and puts his hand on his shoulder strongly and kindly, disregarding his attempt to shake it off*]. Come: sit down quietly; and tell me what it is. And remember: we are friends, and need not fear that either of us will be anything but patient and kind to the other, whatever we may have to say.

MARCHBANKS [*twisting himself round on him*] Oh, I am not forgetting myself: I am only [*covering his face desperately with his hands*] full of horror. [*Then, dropping his hands, and thrusting his face forward fiercely at Morell, he goes on threateningly*] You shall see whether this is a time for patience and kindness. [*Morell, firm as a rock, looks indulgently at him*]. Dont look at me in that self-complacent way. You think yourself stronger than I am; but I shall stagger you if you have a heart in your breast.

MORELL [*powerfully confident*] Stagger me, my boy. Out with it.

MARCHBANKS. First—

MORELL. First?

MARCHBANKS. I love your wife.

[*Morell recoils, and, after staring at him for a moment in utter amazement, bursts into uncontrollable laughter. Eugene is taken aback, but not disconcerted; and he soon becomes indignant and contemptuous.*]

MORELL [*sitting down to have his laugh out*] Why, my dear child, of course you do. Everybody loves her: they cant help it. I like it. But [*looking up jocosely at him*] I say, Eugene: do you think yours is a case to be talked about? Youre under twenty: she's over thirty. Doesnt it look rather too like a case of calf love?

MARCHBANKS [*vehemently*] You dare say that of her! You think that way of the love she inspires! It is an insult to her!

MORELL [*rising quickly, in an altered tone*] To her! Eugene: take care. I have been patient. I hope to remain patient. But there are some things I wont allow. Dont force me to shew you the indulgence I should shew to a child. Be a man.

MARCHBANKS [*with a gesture as if sweeping something behind him*] Oh, let us put aside all that cant. It horrifies me when I think of the doses of it she has had to endure in all the weary years during which you have selfishly and blindly sacrificed her to minister to your self-sufficiency: y o u! [*turning on him*] who have not one thought—one sense—in common with her.

MORELL [*philosophically*] She seems to bear it pretty well. [*Looking him straight in the face*] Eugene, my boy: you are making a fool of yourself: a very great fool of yourself. Theres a piece of wholesome plain speaking for you. [*He knocks in the lesson with a nod in his old way, and posts himself on the hearth-rug, holding his hands behind him to warm them*].

MARCHBANKS. Oh, do you think I dont know all that? Do you think that the things people make fools of themselves about are any less real and true than the things they behave sensibly about? [*Morell's gaze wavers for the first time. He forgets to warm his hands, and stands listening, startled and thoughtful*]. They are more true: they are the only things that are true. You are very calm and sensible and moderate with me because you can see that I am a fool about your wife; just as no doubt that old man who was here just now is very wise over your Socialism, because he sees that you are a fool about it. [*Morell's perplexity deepens markedly. Eugene follows up his advantage, plying him fiercely with questions*]. Does that prove you wrong? Does your complacent superiority to me prove that *I* am wrong?

MORELL. Marchbanks: some devil is putting these words into your mouth. It is easy—terribly easy—to shake a man's faith in himself. To take advantage of that to break a man's spirit is devil's work. Take care of what you are doing. Take care.

MARCHBANKS [*ruthlessly*] I know. I'm doing it on purpose. I told you I should stagger you. *They confront one another threateningly for a moment. Then Morell recovers his dignity.*

MORELL [*with noble tenderness*] Eugene: listen to me. Some day, I hope and trust, you will be a happy man like me. [*Eugene chafes intolerantly, repudiating the worth of his happiness. Morell, deeply insulted, controls himself with fine forbearance, and continues steadily, with great artistic beauty of delivery*] You will be married; and you will be working with all your might and valor to make every spot on earth as happy as your own home. You will be one of the makers of the Kingdom of Heaven on earth; and—who knows?—you may be a master builder where I am only a humble journeyman; for dont think, my boy, that I cannot see in you, young as you are, promise of higher powers than I can ever pretend to. I well know that it is in the poet that the holy spirit of man—the god within him—is most godlike. It should make you tremble to think of that—to think that the heavy burthen and great gift of a poet may be laid upon you.

MARCHBANKS [*unimpressed and remorseless, his boyish crudity of assertion telling sharply against Morell's oratory*] It does not make me tremble. It is the want of it in others that makes me tremble.

MORELL [*redoubling his force of style under the stimulus of his genuine feeling and Eugene's obduracy*] Then help to kindle it in them—in me—not to extinguish it. In the future, when you are as happy as I am, I will be your true brother in the faith. I will help you to believe that God has given us a world that nothing but our own folly keeps from being a paradise. I will help you to believe that every stroke of your work is sowing happiness for the great harvest that all—even the humblest—shall one day reap. And last, but trust me, not least, I will help you to believe that your wife loves you and is happy in her home. We need such help, Marchbanks: we need it greatly and always. There are so many things to make us doubt, if once we let our understanding be troubled. Even at home, we sit as if in camp, encompassed by a hostile army of doubts. Will you play the traitor and let them in on me?

MARCHBANKS [*looking round wildly*] Is it like this for her here always? A woman, with a great soul, craving for reality, truth, freedom; and being fed on metaphors, sermons, stale perorations, mere rhetoric. Do you think a woman's soul can live on your talent for preaching?

MORELL [*stung*] Marchbanks: you make it hard for me to control myself. My talent is like yours insofar as it has any real worth at all. It is the gift of finding words for divine truth.

MARCHBANKS [*impetuously*] It's the gift of the gab, nothing more and nothing less. What has your knack of fine talking to do with the truth, any more than playing the organ has? Ive never been in your church; but Ive been to your political meetings; and Ive seen you do whats called rousing the meeting to enthusiasm: that is, you excited them until they behaved exactly as if they were drunk. And their wives looked on and saw what fools they were. Oh, it's an old story: youll find it in the Bible. I imagine King David, in his fits of enthusiasm, was very like you. [*Stabbing him with the words*] "But his wife despised him in her heart."

MORELL [*wrathfully*] Leave my house. Do you hear? [*He advances on him threateningly*].

MARCHBANKS [*shrinking back against the couch*] Let me alone. Dont touch me. [*Morell grasps him powerfully by the lappell of his coat: he cowers down on the sofa and screams passionately*] Stop, Morell: if you strike me, I'll kill myself: I wont bear it. [*Almost in hysterics*] Let me go. Take your hand away.

MORELL [*with slow emphatic scorn*] You little snivelling cowardly whelp. [*He releases him*]. Go, before you frighten yourself into a fit.

MARCHBANKS [*on the sofa, gasping, but relieved by the withdrawal of Morell's hand*] I'm not afraid of you: it's you who are afraid of me.

MORELL [*quietly, as he stands over him*] It looks like it, doesnt it?

MARCHBANKS [*with petulant vehemence*] Yes, it does. [*Morell turns away contemptuously. Eugene scrambles to his feet and follows him*]. You think because I shrink from being brutally handled—because [*with tears in his voice*] I can do nothing but cry with rage when I am met with violence—because I cant lift a heavy trunk down from the top of a cab like you—because I cant fight for you for your wife as a drunken navvy would: all that makes you think I'm afraid of you. But youre wrong. If I havnt got what you call British pluck, I havnt British cowardice either: I'm not afraid of a clergyman's ideas. I'll fight your ideas. I'll rescue her from her slavery to them. I'll pit my own ideas against them. You are driving me out of the house because you darent let her choose between your ideas and mine. You are afraid to let me see her again. [*Morell, angered, turns suddenly on him. He flies to the door in involuntary dread*]. Let me alone, I say. I'm going.

MORELL [*with cold scorn*] Wait a moment: I am not going to touch you: dont be afraid. When my wife comes back she will want to know why you have gone. And when she finds that you are never going to cross our threshold again, she will want to have that explained too. Now I dont wish to distress her by telling her that you have behaved like a blackguard.

MARCHBANKS [*coming back with renewed vehemence*] You shall. You must. If you give any explanation but the true one, you are a liar and a coward. Tell her what I said; and how you were strong and manly, and shook me as a terrier shakes a rat; and how I shrank and was terrified; and how you called me a snivelling little whelp and put me out of the house. If you dont tell her, I will: I'll write it to her.

MORELL [*puzzled*] Why do you want her to know this?

MARCHBANKS [*with lyric rapture*] Because she will understand me, and know that I understand her. If you keep back one word of it from her—if you are not ready to lay the truth at her feet as I am—then you will know to the end of your days that she really belongs to me and not to you. Goodbye. [*Going*].

MORELL [*terribly disquieted*] Stop: I will not tell her.

MARCHBANKS [*turning near the door*] Either the truth or a lie you must tell her, if I go.

MORELL [*temporizing*] Marchbanks: it is sometimes justifiable—

MARCHBANKS [*cutting him short*] I know: to lie. It will be useless. Goodbye, Mr Clergyman.

As he turns finally to the door, it opens and Candida enters in her housekeeping dress.

CANDIDA. Are you going, Eugene? [*Looking more observantly at him*] Well, dear me, just look at you, going out into the street in that state! You are a poet, certainly. Look at him, James! [*She takes him by the coat, and brings him forward, shewing him to Morell*]. Look at his collar! look at his tie! look at his hair! One would think somebody had been throttling you. [*Eugene instinctively tries to look round at Morell; but she pulls him back*]. Here! Stand still. [*She buttons his collar; ties his neckerchief in a bow; and arranges his hair*]. There! Now you look so nice that I think youd better stay to lunch after all, though I told you you musnt. It will be ready in half an hour. [*She puts a final touch to the bow. He kisses her hand*]. Dont be silly.

MARCHBANKS. I want to stay, of course; unless the reverend gentleman your husband has anything to advance to the contrary.

CANDIDA. Shall he stay, James, if he promises to be a good boy and help me to lay the table?

MORELL [*shortly*] Oh yes, certainly: he had better. [*He goes to the table and pretends to busy himself with his papers there*].

MARCHBANKS [*offering his arm to Candida*] Come and lay the table. [*She takes it. They go to the door together. As they pass out he adds*] I am the happiest of mortals.

MORELL. So was I—an hour ago.

ACT II

The same day later in the afternoon. The same room. The chair for visitors has been replaced at the table. Marchbanks, alone and idle, is trying to find out how the typewriter works. Hearing someone at the door, he steals guiltily away to the window and pretends to be absorbed in the view. Miss Garnett, carrying the notebook in which she takes down Morell's letters in shorthand from his dictation, sits down at the typewriter and sets to work transcribing them, much too busy to notice Eugene. When she begins the second line she stops and stares at the machine. Something wrong evidently.

PROSERPINE. Bother! Youve been meddling with my typewriter, Mr Marchbanks; and theres not the least use in your trying to look as if you hadnt.

MARCHBANKS [*timidly*] I'm very sorry, Miss Garnett. I only tried to make it write. [*Plaintively*] But it wouldnt.

PROSERPINE. Well, youve altered the spacing.

MARCHBANKS [*earnestly*] I assure you I didnt. I didnt indeed. I only turned a little wheel. It gave a sort of click.

PROSERPINE. Oh, now I understand. [*She restores the spacing, talking volubly all the time*]. I suppose you thought it was a sort of barrel-organ. Nothing to do but turn the handle, and it would write a beautiful love letter for you straight off, eh?

MARCHBANKS [*seriously*] I suppose a machine could be made to write love letters. Theyre all the same, arnt they?

PROSERPINE [*somewhat indignantly: any such discussion, except by way of pleasantry, being outside her code of manners*] How do I know? Why do you ask me?

MARCHBANKS. I beg your pardon. I thought clever people—people who can do business and write letters and that sort of thing—always had to have love affairs to keep them from going mad.

PROSERPINE [*rising, outraged*] Mr Marchbanks! [*She looks severely at him, and marches majestically to the bookcase*].

MARCHBANKS [*approaching her humbly*] I hope I havnt offended you. Perhaps I shouldnt have alluded to your love affairs.

PROSERPINE [*plucking a blue book from the shelf and turning sharply on him*] I havnt any love affairs. How dare you say such a thing? The idea! [*She tucks the book under her arm, and is flouncing back to her machine when he addresses her with awakened interest and sympathy*].

MARCHBANKS. Really! Oh, then you are shy, like me.

PROSERPINE. Certainly I am not shy. What do you mean?

MARCHBANKS [*secretly*] You must be: that is the reason there are so few love affairs in the world. We all go about longing for love: it is the first need of our natures, the first prayer of our hearts; but we dare not utter our longing: we are too shy. [*Very earnestly*] Oh, Miss Garnett, what would you not give to be without fear, without shame—

PROSERPINE [*scandalized*] Well, upon my word!

MARCHBANKS [*with petulant impatience*] Ah, dont say those stupid things to me: they dont deceive me: what use are they? Why are you afraid to be your real self with me? I am just like you.

PROSERPINE. Like m e! Pray are you flattering me or flattering yourself? I dont feel quite sure which. [*She again tries to get back to her work*].

MARCHBANKS [*stopping her mysteriously*] Hush! I go about in search of love; and I find it in unmeasured stores in the bosoms of others. But when I try to ask for it, this horrible shyness strangles me; and I stand dumb, or worse than dumb, saying meaningless things: foolish lies. And I see the affection I am longing for given to dogs and cats and pet birds, because they come and ask for it. [*Almost whispering*] It must be asked for: it is like a ghost: it cannot speak unless it is first spoken to. [*At his usual pitch, but with deep melancholy*] All the love in the world is longing to speak; only it dare not, because it is shy! shy! shy! That is the world's tragedy. [*With a deep sigh he sits in the visitors' chair and buries his face in his hands*].

PROSERPINE [*amazed, but keeping her wits about her: her point of honor in encounters with strange young men*] Wicked people get over that shyness occasionally, dont they?

MARCHBANKS [*scrambling up almost fiercely*] Wicked people means people who have no love: therefore they have no shame. They have the power to ask love because they dont need it: they have the power to offer it because they have none to give. [*He collapses into his seat, and adds, mournfully*] But we, who h a v e love, and long to mingle it with the love of others: we cannot utter a word. [*Timidly*] You find that, dont you?

PROSERPINE. Look here: if you dont stop talking like this, I'll leave the room, Mr Marchbanks: I really will. It's not proper.

She resumes her seat at the typewriter, opening the blue book and preparing to copy a passage from it.

MARCHBANKS [*hopelessly*] Nothing thats worth saying is proper. [*He rises, and wanders about the room in his lost way*]. I cant understand you, Miss Garnett. What am I to talk about?

PROSERPINE [*snubbing him*] Talk about indifferent things. Talk about the weather.

MARCHBANKS. Would you talk about indifferent things if a child were by, crying bitterly with hunger?

PROSERPINE. I suppose not.

MARCHBANKS. Well: *I* cant talk about indifferent things with my heart crying out bitterly in its hunger.

PROSERPINE. Then hold your tongue.

MARCHBANKS. Yes: that is what it always comes to. We hold our tongues. Does that stop the cry of your heart? for it does cry: doesnt it? It must, if you have a heart.

PROSERPINE [*suddenly rising with her hand pressed on her heart*] Oh, it's no use trying to work while you talk like that. [*She leaves her little table and sits on the sofa. Her feelings are keenly stirred*]. It's no business of yours whether my heart cries or not; but I have a mind to tell you, for all that.

MARCHBANKS. You neednt. I know already that it must.

PROSERPINE. But mind! if you ever say I said so, I'll deny it.

MARCHBANKS [*compassionately*] Yes, I know. And so you havnt the courage to tell him?

PROSERPINE [*bouncing up*] Him! Who?

MARCHBANKS. Whoever he is. The man you love. It might be anybody. The curate, Mr Mill, perhaps.

PROSERPINE [*with disdain*] Mr Mill!!! A fine man to break my heart about, indeed! I'd rather have you than Mr Mill.

MARCHBANKS [*recoiling*] No, really: I'm very sorry; but you musnt think of that. I—

PROSERPINE [*testily, going to the fireplace and standing at it with her back to him*] Oh, dont be frightened: it's not you. It's not any one particular person.

MARCHBANKS. I know. You feel that you could love anybody that offered—

PROSERPINE [*turning, exasperated*] Anybody that offered! No, I do not. What do you take me for?

MARCHBANKS [*discouraged*] No use. You wont make me real answers: only those things that everybody says. [*He strays to the sofa and sits down disconsolately*].

PROSERPINE [*nettled at what she takes to be a disparagement of her manners by an aristocrat*] Oh well, if you want original conversation, youd better go and talk to yourself.

MARCHBANKS. That is what all poets do: they talk to themselves out loud; and the world overhears them. But it's horribly lonely not to hear someone else talk sometimes.

PROSERPINE. Wait until Mr Morell comes. He'll talk to you. [*Marchbanks shudders*]. Oh, you neednt make wry faces over him: he can talk better than you. [*With temper*] He'd talk your little head off. [*She is going back angrily to her place, when he, suddenly enlightened, springs up and stops her*].

MARCHBANKS. Ah! I understand now.

PROSERPINE [*reddening*] What do you understand?

MARCHBANKS. Your secret. Tell me: is it really and truly possible for a woman to love him?

PROSERPINE [*as if this were beyond all bounds*] Well!!

MARCHBANKS [*passionately*] No: answer me. I want to know: I must know. *I* cant understand it. I can see nothing in him but words, pious resolutions, what people call goodness. You cant love that.

PROSERPINE [*attempting to snub him by an air of cool propriety*] I simply dont know what youre talking about. I dont understand you.

MARCHBANKS [*vehemently*] You do. You lie.

PROSERPINE. Oh!

MARCHBANKS. You do understand; and you know. [*Determined to have an answer*] Is it possible for a woman to love him?

PROSERPINE [*looking him straight in the face*] Yes. [*He covers his face with his hands*]. Whatever is the matter with you! [*He takes down his hands. Frightened at the tragic mask presented to her, she hurries past him at the utmost possible distance, keeping her eyes on his face until he turns from her and goes to the child's chair beside the hearth, where he sits in the deepest dejection. As she approaches the door, it opens and Burgess enters. Seeing him, she ejaculates*] Praise heaven! here's somebody [*and feels safe enough to resume her place at her table. She puts a fresh sheet of paper into the typewriter as Burgess crosses to Eugene*].

BURGESS [*bent on taking care of the distinguished visitor*] Well: so this is the way they leave you to yoreself, Mr Morchbanks. Ive come to keep you company. [*Marchbanks looks up at him in consternation, which is quite lost on him*]. James is receivin a depptation in the dinin room; and Candy is hupstairs heducating of a young stitcher gurl she's hinterested in. [*Condolingly*] You must find it lonesome here with no one but the typist to talk to. [*He pulls round the easy chair, and sits down*].

PROSERPINE [*highly incensed*] He'll be all right now that he has the advantage of your polished conversation: thats one comfort, anyhow. [*She begins to typewrite with clattering asperity*].

BURGESS [*amazed at her audacity*] Hi was not addressin myself to you, young woman, that I'm awerr of.

PROSERPINE. Did you ever see worse manners, Mr Marchbanks?

BURGESS [*with pompous severity*] Mr Morchbanks is a gentleman, and knows his place, which is more than some people do.

PROSERPINE [*fretfully*] It's well you and I are not ladies and gentlemen: I'd talk to you pretty straight if Mr Marchbanks wasnt here. [*She pulls the letter out of the machine so crossly that it tears*]. There! now I've spoiled this letter! have to be done all over again! Oh, I cant contain myself: silly old fathead!

BURGESS [*rising, breathless with indignation*] Ho! I'm a silly ole fat'ead, am I? Ho, indeed [*gasping*]! Hall right, my gurl! Hall right. You just wait til I tell that to yore hemployer. Youll see. I'll teach you: see if I dont.

PROSERPINE [*conscious of having gone too far*] I—

BURGESS [*cutting her short*] No: youve done it now. No huse a-talkin to me. I'll let you know who I am. [*Proserpine shifts her paper carriage with a defiant bang, and disdainfully goes on with her work*]. Dont you take no notice of her, Mr Morchbanks. She's beneath it. [*He loftily sits down again*].

MARCHBANKS [*miserably nervous and disconcerted*] Hadnt we better change the subject? I—I dont think Miss Garnett meant anything.

PROSERPINE [*with intense conviction*] Oh, didnt I though, just!

BURGESS. I wouldnt demean myself to take notice on her, as—

An electric bell rings twice.

PROSERPINE [*gathering up her notebook and papers*] Thats for me. [*She hurries out*].

BURGESS [*calling after her*] Oh, we can spare you. [*Somewhat relieved by the triumph of having the last word, and yet half inclined to try to improve on it, he looks after her for a moment; then subsides into his seat by Eugene, and addresses him very confidentially*]. Now we're alone, Mr Morchbanks, let me give you a friendly int that I wouldnt give to heverybody. Ow long ave you known my son-in-law James ere?

MARCHBANKS. I dont know. I never can remember dates. A few months, perhaps.

BURGESS. Ever notice hennythink queer about him?

MARCHBANKS. I dont think so.

BURGESS [*impressively*] No more you wouldnt. Thats the danger on it. Well, he's mad.

MARCHBANKS. Mad!

BURGESS. Mad as a Morch 'are. You take notice on him and youll see.

MARCHBANKS [*uneasily*] But surely that is only because his opinions—

BURGESS [*touching him on the knee with his forefinger, and pressing it to hold his attention*] Thats the same what I hused to think, Mr Morchbanks. Hi thought long enough that it was ony his opinions; though, mind you, hopinions becomes vurry serious things when people takes to hactin on em as e does. But thats not what I go on. [*He looks round to make sure that they are alone, and bends over to Eugene's ear*] What do you think he sez to me this mornin in this very room?

MARCHBANKS. What?

BURGESS. He sez to me—this is as sure as we're settin here now—he sez "I'm a fool," he sez; " and yore a scounderl." Me a scounderl, mind you! And then shook ands with me on it, as if it was to my credit! Do you mean to tell me as that man's sane?

MORELL [*outside, calling to Proserpine as he opens the door*] Get all their names and addresses, Miss Garnett.

PROSERPINE [*in the distance*] Yes, Mr Morell.

Morell comes in, with the deputation's documents in his hands.

BURGESS [*aside to Marchbanks*] Yorr he is. Just you keep your heye on im and see. [*Rising momentously*] I'm sorry, James, to ave to make a complaint to you. I dont want to do it; but I feel I oughter, as a matter o right and dooty.

MORELL. Whats the matter?

BURGESS. Mr Morchbanks will bear me hout: he was a witness. [*Very solemnly*] Yore young woman so far forgot herself as to call me a silly ole fat'ead.

MORELL [*with tremendous heartiness*] Oh, now, isnt that e x a c t l y like Prossy? She's so frank: she cant contain herself! Poor Prossy! Ha! ha!

BURGESS [*trembling with rage*] And do you hexpec me to put up with it from the like of er?

MORELL. Pooh, nonsense! you cant take any notice of it. Never mind. [*He goes to the cellaret and puts the papers into one of the drawers*].

BURGESS. Oh, Hi dont mind. Hi'm above it. But is it r i g h t? thats what I want to know. Is it right?

MORELL. Thats a question for the Church, not for the laity. Has it done you any harm? thats the question for you, eh? Of course it hasnt. Think no more of it. [*He dismisses the subject by going to his place at the table and setting to work at his correspondence*].

BURGESS [*aside to Marchbanks*] What did I tell you? Mad as a atter. [*He goes to the table and asks, with the sickly civility of a hungry man*] When's dinner, James?

MORELL. Not for a couple of hours yet.

BURGESS [*with plaintive resignation*] Gimme a nice book to read over the fire, will you, James: thur's a good chap.

MORELL. What sort of book? A good one?

BURGESS [*with almost a yell of remonstrance*] Nah-oo! Summat pleasant, just to pass the time. [*Morell takes an illustrated paper from the table and offers it. He accepts it humbly*]. Thank yer, James. [*He goes back to the big chair at the fire, and sits there at his ease, reading*].

MORELL [*as he writes*] Candida will come to entertain you presently. She has got rid of her pupil. She is filling the lamps.

MARCHBANKS [*starting up in the wildest consternation*] But that will soil her hands. I cant bear that, Morell: it's a shame. I'll go and fill them. [*He makes for the door*].

MORELL. Youd better not. [*Marchbanks stops irresolutely*]. She'd only set you to clean my boots, to save me the trouble of doing it myself in the morning.

BURGESS [*with grave disapproval*] Dont you keep a servant now, James?

MORELL. Yes; but she isnt a slave; and the house looks as if I kept three. That means that everyone has to lend a hand. It's not a bad plan: Prossy and I can talk business after breakfast while we're washing up. Washing up's no trouble when there are two people to do it.

MARCHBANKS [*tormentedly*] Do you think every woman is as coarsegrained as Miss Garnett?

BURGESS [*emphatically*] Thats quite right, Mr Morchbanks: thats q u i t e right. She is corsegrained.

MORELL [*quietly and significantly*] Marchbanks!

MARCHBANKS. Yes?

MORELL. How many servants does your father keep?

MARCHBANKS [*pettishly*] Oh, I dont know. [*He moves to the sofa, as if to get as far as possible from Morell's questioning, and sits down in great agony of spirit, thinking of the paraffin*].

MORELL [*very gravely*] So many that you dont know! [*More aggressively*] When theres anything coarsegrained to be done, you just ring the bell and throw it on to somebody else, eh?

MARCHBANKS. Oh, dont torture me. You dont even ring the bell. But your wife's beautiful fingers are dabbling in paraffin oil while you sit here comfortably preaching about it: everlasting preaching! preaching! words! words! words!

BURGESS [*intensely appreciating this retort*] Har, har! Devil a better! [*Radiantly*] Ad you there, James, straight.

Candida comes in, well aproned, with a reading lamp trimmed, filled, and ready for lighting. She places it on the table near Morell, ready for use.

CANDIDA [*brushing her finger tips together with a slight twitch of her nose*] If you stay with us, Eugene, I think I will hand over the lamps to you.

MARCHBANKS. I will stay on condition that you hand over all the rough work to me.

CANDIDA. Thats very gallant; but I think I should like to see how you do it first. [*Turning to Morell*] James: youve not been looking after the house properly.

MORELL. What have I done—or not done— my love?

CANDIDA [*with serious vexation*] My own particular pet scrubbing brush has been used for blackleading. [*A heart-breaking wail bursts from Marchbanks. Burgess looks round, amazed. Candida hurries to the sofa*]. Whats the matter? Are you ill, Eugene?

MARCHBANKS. No: not ill. Only horror! horror! horror! [*He bows his head on his hands*].

BURGESS [*shocked*] What! Got the orrors, Mr Morchbanks! Oh, thats bad, at your age. You must leave it off grajally.

CANDIDA [*reassured*] Nonsense, papa! It's only poetic horror, isnt it, Eugene [*petting him*]?

BURGESS [*abashed*] Oh, poetic orror, is it? I beg your pordon, I'm shore. [*He turns to the fire again, deprecating his hasty conclusion*].

CANDIDA. What is it, Eugene? the scrubbing brush? [*He shudders*]. Well, there! never mind. [*She sits down beside him*]. Wouldnt you like to present me with a nice new one, with an ivory back inlaid with mother-of-pearl?

MARCHBANKS [*softly and musically, but sadly and longingly*] No, not a scrubbing brush, but a boat: a tiny shallop to sail away in, far from the world, where the marble floors are washed by the rain and dried by the sun; where the south wind dusts the beautiful green and purple carpets. Or a chariot! to carry us up into the sky, where the lamps are stars, and dont need to be filled with paraffin oil every day.

MORELL [*harshly*] And where there is nothing to do but to be idle, selfish, and useless.

CANDIDA [*jarred*] Oh, James! how could you spoil it all?

MARCHBANKS [*firing up*] Yes, to be idle, selfish, and useless: that is, to be beautiful and free and happy: hasnt every man desired that with all his soul for the woman he loves? Thats my ideal: whats yours, and that of all the dreadful people who live in these hideous rows of houses? Sermons and scrubbing brushes! With you to preach the sermon and your wife to scrub.

CANDIDA [*quickly*] He cleans the boots, Eugene. You will have to clean them tomorrow for saying that about him.

MARCHBANKS. Oh, dont talk about boots! Your feet should be beautiful on the mountains.

CANDIDA. My feet would not be beautiful on the Hackney Road without boots.

BURGESS [*scandalized*] Come, Candy! dont be vulgar. Mr Morchbanks aint accustomed to it. Youre givin him the orrors again. I mean the poetic ones.

Morell is silent. Apparently he is busy with his letters: really he is puzzling with misgiving over his new and alarming experience that the surer he is of his moral thrusts, the more swiftly and effectively Eugene parries them. To find himself beginning to fear a man whom he does not respect afflicts him bitterly.

Miss Garnett comes in with a telegram.

PROSERPINE [*handing the telegram to Morell*] Reply paid. The boy's waiting. [*To Candida, coming back to her machine and sitting down*] Maria is ready for you now in the kitchen, Mrs Morell. [*Candida rises*]. The onions have come.

MARCHBANKS [*convulsively*] Onions!

CANDIDA. Yes, onions. Not even Spanish ones: nasty little red onions. You shall help me to slice them. Come along.

She catches him by the wrist and runs out, pulling him after her. Burgess rises in consternation, and stands aghast on the hearth-rug, staring after them.

BURGESS. Candy didnt oughter andle a hearl's nevvy like that. It's goin too fur with it. Lookee ere, James: do e often git taken queer like that?

MORELL [*shortly, writing a telegram*] I dont know.

BURGESS [*sentimentally*] He talks very pretty. I awlus had a turn for a bit of poetry. Candy takes arter me that-a-way. Huseter make me tell er fairy stories when she was ony a little kiddy that igh [*indicating a stature of two feet or thereabouts*].

MORELL [*preoccupied*] Ah, indeed. [*He blots the telegram and goes out*].

PROSERPINE. Used you to make the fairy stories up out of your own head?

Burgess, not deigning to reply, strikes an attitude of the haughtiest disdain on the hearth-rug.

PROSERPINE [*calmly*] I should never have supposed you had it in you. By the way, I'd better warn you, since youve taken such a fancy to Mr Marchbanks. He's mad.

BURGESS. Mad! What! Im too!!

PROSERPINE. Mad as a March hare. He did frighten me, I can tell you, just before you came in that time. Havent you noticed the queer things he says?

BURGESS. So thats what the poetic orrors means. Blame me if it didnt come into my ed once or twyst that he was a bit horff 'is chump! [*He crosses the room to the door, lifting up his voice as he goes*]. Well, this is a pretty sort of asylum for a man to be in, with no one but you to take care of him!

PROSERPINE [*as he passes her*] Yes, what a dreadful thing it would be if anything happened to you!

BURGESS [*loftily*] Dont you haddress no remarks to me. Tell your hemployer that Ive gone into the gorden for a smoke.

PROSERPINE [*mocking*] Oh!

Before Burgess can retort, Morell comes back.

BURGESS [*sentimentally*] Goin for a turn in the gording to smoke, James.

MORELL [*brusquely*] Oh, all right, all right. [*Burgess goes out pathetically in the character of a weary old man. Morell stands at the table, turning over his papers, and adding, across to Proserpine, half humorously, half absently*] Well, Miss Prossy, why have you been calling my father-in-law names?

PROSERPINE [*blushing fiery red, and looking quickly up at him, half scared, half reproachful*] I— [*She bursts into tears*].

MORELL [*with tender gaiety, leaning across the table towards her, and consoling her*] Oh, come! come! come! Never mind, Pross: he is a silly old fathead, isnt he?

With an explosive sob, she makes a dash at the door, and vanishes, banging it. Morell, shaking his head resignedly, sighs, and goes wearily to his chair, where he sits down and sets to work, looking old and careworn.

Candida comes in. She has finished her household work and taken off the apron. She at once notices his dejected appearance, and posts herself quietly at the visitors' chair, looking down at him attentively. She says nothing.

MORELL [*looking up, but with his pen raised ready to resume his work*] Well? Where is Eugene?

CANDIDA. Washing his hands in the scullery under the tap. He will make an excellent cook if he can only get over his dread of Maria.

MORELL [*shortly*] Ha! No doubt. [*He begins writing again*].

CANDIDA [*going nearer, and putting her hand down softly on his to stop him as she says*] Come here, dear. Let me look at you. [*He drops his pen and yields himself to her disposal. She makes him rise, and brings him a little away from the table, looking at him critically all the time*]. Turn your face to the light. [*She places him facing the window*]. My boy is not looking well. Has he been overworking?

MORELL. Nothing more than usual.

CANDIDA. He looks very pale and grey, and wrinkled, and old. [*His melancholy deepens; and she attacks it with wilful gaiety*] Here: [*pulling him towards the easy chair*] youve done enough writing for to-day. Leave Prossy to finish it. Come and talk to me.

MORELL. But—

CANDIDA [*insisting*] Yes, I must be talked to. [*She makes him sit down, and seats herself on the carpet beside his knee*]. Now [*patting his hand*] youre beginning to look better already. Why must you go out every night lecturing and talking? I hardly have one evening a week with you. Of course what you say is all very true; but it does no good: they dont mind what you say to them one little bit. They think they agree with you; but whats the use of their agreeing with you if they go and do just the opposite of what you tell them the moment your back is turned? Look at our congregation at St Dominic's! Why do they come to hear you talking about Christianity every Sunday? Why, just because theyve been so full of business and money-making for six days that they want to forget all about it and have a rest on the seventh; so that they can go back fresh and make money harder than ever! You positively help them at it instead of hindering them.

MORELL [*with energetic seriousness*] You know very well, Candida, that I often blow them up soundly for that. And if there is nothing in their churchgoing but rest and diversion, why dont they try something more amusing? more self-indulgent? There must be some good in the fact that they prefer St Dominic's to worse places on Sundays.

CANDIDA. Oh, the worse places arnt open; and even if they were, they darent be seen going to them. Besides, James dear, you preach so splendidly that it's as good as a play for them. Why do you think the women are so enthusiastic?

MORELL [*shocked*] Candida!

CANDIDA. Oh, I know. You silly boy: you think it's your Socialism and your religion; but if it were that, theyd do what you tell them instead of only coming to look at you. They all have Prossy's complaint.

MORELL. Prossy's complaint! What do you mean, Candida?

CANDIDA. Yes, Prossy, and all the other secretaries you ever had. Why does Prossy condescend to wash up the things, and to peel potatoes and abase herself in all manner of ways for six shillings a week less than she used to get in a city office? She's in love with you, James: thats the reason. Theyre all in love with you. And you are in love with preaching because you do it so beautifully. And you think it's all enthusiasm for the kingdom of Heaven on earth; and so do they. You dear silly!

MORELL. Candida: what dreadful! what soul-destroying cynicism! Are you jesting? Or—can it be?—are you jealous?

CANDIDA [with curious thoughtfulness] Yes, I feel a little jealous sometimes.

MORELL [incredulously] Of Prossy?

CANDIDA [laughing] No, no, no, no. Not jealous of anybody. Jealous for somebody else, who is not loved as he ought to be.

MORELL. Me?

CANDIDA. You! Why, youre spoiled with love and worship: you get far more than is good for you. No: I mean Eugene.

MORELL [startled] Eugene!

CANDIDA. It seems unfair that all the love should go to you, and none to him; although he needs it so much more than you do. [A convulsive movement shakes him in spite of himself]. Whats the matter? Am I worrying you?

MORELL [hastily] Not at all. [Looking at her with troubled intensity] You know that I have perfect confidence in you, Candida.

CANDIDA. You vain thing! Are you so sure of your irresistible attractions?

MORELL. Candida: you are shocking me. I never thought of my attractions. I thought of your goodness, of your purity. That is what I confide in.

CANDIDA. What a nasty uncomfortable thing to say to me! Oh, you are a clergyman, James: a thorough clergyman!

MORELL [turning away from her, heart-stricken] So Eugene says.

CANDIDA [with lively interest, leaning over to him with her arms on his knee] Eugene's always right. He's a wonderful boy: I have grown fonder and fonder of him all the time I was away. Do you know, James, that though he has not the least suspicion of it himself, he is ready to fall madly in love with me?

MORELL [grimly] Oh, he has no suspicion of it himself, hasnt he?

CANDIDA. Not a bit. [She takes her arms from his knee, and turns thoughtfully, sinking into a more restful attitude with her hands in her lap].

Some day he will know: when he is grown up and experienced, like you. And he will know that I must have known. I wonder what he will think of me then.

MORELL. No evil, Candida. I hope and trust, no evil.

CANDIDA [dubiously] That will depend.

MORELL [bewildered] Depend!

CANDIDA [looking at him] Yes: it will depend on what happens to him. [He looks vacantly at her]. Dont you see? It will depend on how he comes to learn what love really is. I mean on the sort of woman who will teach it to him.

MORELL [quite at a loss] Yes. No. I dont know what you mean.

CANDIDA [explaining] If he learns it from a good woman, then it will be all right: he will forgive me.

MORELL. Forgive?

CANDIDA. But suppose he learns it from a bad woman, as so many men do, especially poetic men, who imagine all women are angels! Suppose he only discovers the value of love when he has thrown it away and degraded himself in his ignorance! Will he forgive me then, do you think?

MORELL. Forgive you for what?

CANDIDA [realizing how stupid he is, and a little disappointed, though quite tenderly so] Dont you understand? [He shakes his head. She turns to him again, so as to explain with the fondest intimacy]. I mean, will he forgive me for not teaching him myself? For abandoning him to the bad women for the sake of my goodness, of my purity, as you call it? Ah, James, how little you understand me, to talk of your confidence in my goodness and purity! I would give them both to poor Eugene as willingly as I would give my shawl to a beggar dying of cold, if there were nothing else to restrain me. Put your trust in my love for you, James; for if that went, I should care very little for your sermons: mere phrases that you cheat yourself and others with every day. [She is about to rise].

MORELL. His words!

CANDIDA [checking herself quickly in the act of getting up] Whose words?

MORELL. Eugene's.

CANDIDA [delighted] He is always right. He understands you; he understands me; he understands Prossy; and you, darling, you understand nothing. [She laughs, and kisses him to console him. He recoils as if stabbed, and *springs up*].

MORELL. How can you bear to do that when—Oh, Candida [*with anguish in his voice*] I had rather you had plunged a grappling iron into my heart than given me that kiss.

CANDIDA [*amazed*] My dear: whats the matter?

MORELL [*frantically waving her off*] Dont touch me.

CANDIDA. James!!!

They are interrupted by the entrance of Marchbanks with Burgess, who stop near the door, staring.

MARCHBANKS. Is anything the matter?

MORELL [*deadly white, putting an iron constraint on himself*] Nothing but this: that either you were right this morning, or Candida is mad.

BURGESS [*in loudest protest*] What! Candy mad too! Oh, come! come! come! [*He crosses the room to the fireplace, protesting as he goes, and knocks the ashes out of his pipe on the bars*].

Morell sits down at his table desperately, leaning forward to hide his face, and interlacing his fingers rigidly to keep them steady.

CANDIDA [*to Morell, relieved and laughing*] Oh, youre only shocked! Is that all? How conventional all you unconventional people are! [*She sits gaily on the arm of the chair*].

BURGESS. Come: be'ave yourself, Candy. Whatll Mr Morchbanks think of you?

CANDIDA. This comes of James teaching me to think for myself, and never to hold back out of fear of what other people may think of me. It works beautifully as long as I think the same things as he does. But now! because I have just thought something different! look at him! Just look! [*She points to Morell, greatly amused*].

Eugene looks, and instantly presses his hand on his heart, as if some pain had shot through it. He sits down on the sofa like a man witnessing a tragedy.

BURGESS [*on the hearth-rug*] Well, James, you certnly haint as himpressive lookin as usu'l.

MORELL [*with a laugh which is half a sob*] I suppose not. I beg all your pardons: I was not conscious of making a fuss. [*Pulling himself together*] Well, well, well, well, well! [*He sets to work at his papers again with resolute cheerfulness*].

CANDIDA [*going to the sofa and sitting beside Marchbanks, still in a bantering humor*] Well, Eugene: why are you so sad? Did the onions make you cry?

MARCHBANKS [*aside to her*] It is your cruelty. I hate cruelty. It is a horrible thing to see one person make another suffer.

CANDIDA [*petting him ironically*] Poor boy! have I been cruel? Did I make it slice nasty little red onions?

MARCHBANKS [*earnestly*] Oh, stop, stop: I dont mean myself. You have made him suffer frightfully. I feel his pain in my own heart. I know that it is not your fault: it is something that must happen; but dont make light of it. I shudder when you torture him and laugh.

CANDIDA [*incredulously*] *I* torture James! Nonsense, Eugene: how you exaggerate! Silly! [*She rises and goes to the table, a little troubled*]. Dont work any more, dear. Come and talk to us.

MORELL [*affectionately but bitterly*] Ah no: *I* cant talk. I can only preach.

CANDIDA [*caressing his hand*] Well, come and preach.

BURGESS [*strongly remonstrating*] Aw no, Candy. 'Ang it all!

Lexy Mill comes in, anxious and important.

LEXY [*hastening to shake hands with Candida*] How do you do, Mrs Morell? So glad to see you back again.

CANDIDA. Thank you, Lexy. You know Eugene, dont you?

LEXY. Oh, yes. How do you do, Marchbanks?

MARCHBANKS. Quite well, thanks.

LEXY [*to Morell*] Ive just come from the Guild of St Matthew. They are in the greatest consternation about your telegram.

CANDIDA. What did you telegraph about, James?

LEXY [*to Candida*] He was to have spoken for them tonight. Theyve taken the large hall in Mare Street and spent a lot of money on posters. Morell's telegram was to say he couldnt come. It came on them like a thunderbolt.

CANDIDA [*surprised, and beginning to suspect something wrong*] Given up an engagement to speak!

BURGESS. Fust time in his life, I'll bet. Ain it, Candy?

LEXY [*to Morell*] They decided to send an urgent telegram to you asking whether you could not change your mind. Have you received it?

MORELL [*with restrained impatience*] Yes, yes:

I got it.

LEXY. It was reply paid.

MORELL. Yes, I know. I answered it. I cant go.

CANDIDA. But why, James?

MORELL [*almost fiercely*] Because I dont choose. These people forget that I am a man: they think I am a talking machine to be turned on for their pleasure every evening of my life. May I not have one night at home, with my wife, and my friends?

They are all amazed at this outburst, except Eugene. His expression remains unchanged.

CANDIDA. Oh, James, you musnt mind what I said about that. And if you dont go youll have an attack of bad conscience to-morrow.

LEXY [*intimidated, but urgent*] I know, of course, that they make the most unreasonable demands on you. But they have been telegraphing all over the place for another speaker; and they can get nobody but the President of the Agnostic League.

MORELL [*promptly*] Well, an excellent man. What better do they want?

LEXY. But he always insists so powerfully on the divorce of Socialism from Christianity. He will undo all the good we have been doing. Of course you know best; but— [*He shrugs his shoulders and wanders to the hearth beside Burgess*].

CANDIDA [*coaxingly*] Oh, do go, James. We'll all go.

BURGESS [*grumblingly*] Look 'ere, Candy! I say! Let's stay at home by the fire, comfortable. He wont need to be more'n a couple-o-hour away.

CANDIDA. Youll be just as comfortable at the meeting. We'll all sit on the platform and be great people.

EUGENE [*terrified*] Oh please dont let us go on the platform. No: everyone will stare at us: I couldnt. I'll sit at the back of the room.

CANDIDA. Dont be afraid. Theyll be too busy looking at James to notice you.

MORELL. Prossy's complaint, Candida! Eh?

CANDIDA [*gaily*] Yes: Prossy's complaint.

BURGESS [*mystified*] Prossy's complaint! What are you talkin about, James?

MORELL [*not heeding him, rises; goes to the door; and holds it open, calling in a commanding tone*] Miss Garnett.

PROSERPINE [*in the distance*] Yes, Mr Morell. Coming.

They all wait, except Burgess, who turns stealthily to Lexy.

BURGESS. Listen ere, Mr Mill. Whats Prossy's complaint? Whats wrong with er?

LEXY [*confidentially*] Well, I dont exactly know; but she spoke very strangely to me this morning. I'm afraid she's a little out of her mind sometimes.

BURGESS [*overwhelmed*] Why, it must be catchin! Four in the same ouse!

PROSERPINE [*appearing on the threshold*] What is it, Mr Morell?

MORELL. Telegraph to the Guild of St Matthew that I am coming.

PROSERPINE [*surprised*] Dont they expect you?

MORELL [*peremptorily*] Do as I tell you.

Proserpine frightened, sits down at her typewriter, and obeys. Morell, now unaccountably resolute and forceful, goes across to Burgess. Candida watches his movements with growing wonder and misgiving.

MORELL. Burgess: you dont want to come.

BURGESS. Oh, dont put it like that, James. It's ony that it aint Sunday, you know.

MORELL. I'm sorry. I thought you might like to be introduced to the chairman. He's on the Works Committee of the County Council, and has some influence in the matter of contracts. [*Burgess wakes up at once*]. Youll come?

BURGESS [*with enthusiasm*] Cawrse I'll come, James. Aint it awlus a pleasure to ear you!

MORELL [*turning to Prossy*] I shall want you to take some notes at the meeting, Miss Garnett, if you have no other engagement. [*She nods, afraid to speak*]. You are coming, Lexy, I suppose?

LEXY. Certainly.

CANDIDA. We're all coming, James.

MORELL. No: you are not coming; and Eugene is not coming. You will stay here and entertain him—to celebrate your return home. [*Eugene rises, breathless*].

CANDIDA. But. James—

MORELL [*authoritatively*] I insist. You do not want to come: and he does not want to come. [*Candida is about to protest*]. Oh, dont concern yourselves: I shall have plenty of people without you: your chairs will be wanted by unconverted people who have never heard me before.

CANDIDA [*troubled*] Eugene: wouldnt you like to come?

MORELL. I should be afraid to let myself go before Eugene: he is so critical of sermons. [*Looking at him*] He knows I am afraid of him:

he told me as much this morning. Well, I shall shew him how much afraid I am by leaving him here in your custody, Candida.

MARCHBANKS [*to himself, with vivid feeling*] Thats brave. Thats beautiful.

CANDIDA [*with anxious misgiving*] But—but— Is anything the matter, James? [*Greatly troubled*] I cant understand—

MORELL [*taking her tenderly in his arms and kissing her on the forehead*] Ah, I thought it was *I* who couldnt understand, dear.

ACT III

Past ten in the evening. The curtains are drawn, and the lamps lighted. The typewriter is in its case: the large table has been cleared and tidied: everything indicates that the day's work is over.

Candida and Marchbanks are sitting by the fire. The reading lamp is on the mantelshelf above Marchbanks, who is in the small chair, reading aloud. A little pile of manuscripts and a couple of volumes of poetry are on the carpet beside him. Candida is in the easy chair. The poker, a light brass one, is upright in her hand. Leaning back and looking intently at the point of it, with her feet stretched towards the blaze, she is in a waking dream, miles away from her surroundings and completely oblivious of Eugene.

MARCHBANKS [*breaking off in his recitation*] Every poet that ever lived has put that thought into a sonnet. He must: he cant help it. [*He looks to her for assent, and notices her absorption in the poker*]. Havnt you been listening? [*No response*]. Mrs Morell!

CANDIDA [*starting*] Eh?

MARCHBANKS. Havnt you been listening?

CANDIDA [*with a guilty excess of politeness*] Oh, yes. It's very nice. Go on, Eugene. I'm longing to hear what happens to the angel.

MARCHBANKS [*letting the manuscript drop from his hand to the floor*] I beg your pardon for boring you.

CANDIDA. But you are not boring me, I assure you. Please go on. Do, Eugene.

MARCHBANKS. I finished the poem about the angel quarter of an hour ago. Ive read you several things since.

CANDIDA [*remorsefully*] I'm so sorry, Eugene. I think the poker must have hypnotized me. [*She puts it down*].

MARCHBANKS. It made me horribly uneasy.

CANDIDA. Why didnt you tell me? I'd have put it down at once.

MARCHBANKS. I was afraid of making you uneasy too. It looked as if it were a weapon. If I were a hero of old I should have laid my drawn sword between us. If Morell had come in he would have thought you had taken up the poker because there was no sword between us.

CANDIDA [*wondering*] What? [*With a puzzled glance at him*] I cant quite follow that. Those sonnets of yours have perfectly addled me. Why should there be a sword between us?

MARCHBANKS [*evasively*] Oh, never mind. [*He stoops to pick up the manuscript*].

CANDIDA. Put that down again, Eugene. There are limits to my appetite for poetry: even your poetry. Youve been reading to me for more than two hours, ever since James went out. I want to talk.

MARCHBANKS [*rising, scared*] No: I musnt talk. [*He looks round him in his lost way, and adds, suddenly*] I think I'll go out and take a walk in the park. [*He makes for the door*].

CANDIDA. Nonsense: it's closed long ago. Come and sit down on the hearth-rug, and talk moonshine as you usually do. I want to be amused. Dont you want to?

MARCHBANKS [*half in terror, half enraptured*] Yes.

CANDIDA. Then come along. [*She moves her chair back a little to make room*].

He hesitates; then timidly stretches himself on the hearth-rug, face upwards, and throws back his head across her knees, looking up at her.

MARCHBANKS. Oh, Ive been so miserable all the evening, because I was doing right. Now I'm doing wrong; and I'm happy.

CANDIDA [*tenderly amused at him*] Yes: I'm sure you feel a great grown-up wicked deceiver. Quite proud of yourself, arnt you?

MARCHBANKS [*raising his head quickly and turning a little to look round at her*] Take care. I'm ever so much older than you, if you only knew. [*He turns quite over on his knees, with his hands clasped and his arms on her lap, and speaks with growing impulse, his blood beginning to stir*]. May I say some wicked things to you?

CANDIDA [*without the least fear or coldness, and with perfect respect for his passion, but with a touch of her wisehearted maternal humor*] No. But you may say anything you really and truly feel. Anything at all, no matter what it is. I am not afraid, so long as it is your real self that speaks, and not a mere attitude: a gallant attitude, or a wicked attitude, or even a poetic attitude. I put you on your honor and truth. Now say whatever you want to.

MARCHBANKS [*the eager expression vanishing utterly from his lips and nostrils as his eyes light up with pathetic spirituality*] Oh, now I cant say anything: all the words I know belong to some attitude or other—all except one.

CANDIDA. What one is that?

MARCHBANKS [*softly, losing himself in the music of the name*] Candida, Candida, Candida, Candida, Candida. I must say that now, because you have put me on my honor and truth; and I never think or feel Mrs Morell: it is always Candida.

CANDIDA. Of course. And what have you to say to Candida?

MARCHBANKS. Nothing but to repeat your name a thousand times. Dont you feel that every time is a prayer to you?

CANDIDA. Doesnt it make you happy to be able to pray?

MARCHBANKS. Yes, very happy.

CANDIDA. Well, that happiness is the answer to your prayer. Do you want anything more?

MARCHBANKS. No: I have come into heaven, where want is unknown.

Morell comes in. He halts on the threshold, and takes in the scene at a glance.

MORELL [*grave and self-contained*] I hope I dont disturb you.

Candida starts up violently, but without the smallest embarrassment, laughing at herself. Eugene, capsized by her sudden movement, recovers himself without rising, and sits on the rug hugging his ankles, also quite unembarrassed.

CANDIDA. Oh, James, how you startled me! I was so taken up with Eugene that I didnt hear your latchkey. How did the meeting go off? Did you speak well?

MORELL. I have never spoken better in my life.

CANDIDA. That was first rate! How much was the collection?

MORELL. I forgot to ask.

CANDIDA [*to Eugene*] He must have spoken splendidly, or he would never have forgotten that. [*To Morell*] Where are all the others?

MORELL. They left long before I could get away: I thought I should never escape. I believe they are having supper somewhere.

CANDIDA [*in her domestic business tone*] Oh, in that case, Maria may go to bed. I'll tell her. [*She goes out to the kitchen*].

MORELL [*looking sternly down at Marchbanks*] Well?

MARCHBANKS [*squatting grotesquely on the hearth-rug, and actually at ease with Morell: even impishly humorous*] Well?

MORELL. Have you anything to tell me?

MARCHBANKS. Only that I have been making a fool of myself here in private whilst you have been making a fool of yourself in public.

MORELL. Hardly in the same way, I think.

MARCHBANKS [*eagerly, scrambling up*] The very, very v e r y same way. I have been playing the Good Man. Just like you. When you began your heroics about leaving me here with Candida—

MORELL [*involuntarily*] Candida!

MARCHBANKS. Oh yes: Ive got that far. But dont be afraid. Heroics are infectious: I caught the disease from you. I swore not to say a word in your absence that I would not have said a month ago in your presence.

MORELL. Did you keep your oath?

MARCHBANKS [*suddenly perching himself on the back of the easy chair*] It kept itself somehow until about ten minutes ago. Up to that moment I went on desperately reading to her—reading my own poems—anybody's poems—to stave off a conversation. I was standing outside the gate of Heaven, and refusing to go in. Oh, you cant think how heroic it was, and how uncomfortable! Then—

MORELL [*steadily controlling his suspense*] Then?

MARCHBANKS [*prosaically slipping down into a quite ordinary attitude on the seat of the chair*] Then she couldnt bear being read to any longer.

MORELL. And you approached the gate of Heaven at last?

MARCHBANKS. Yes.

MORELL. Well? [*Fiercely*] Speak, man: have you no feeling for me?

MARCHBANKS [*softly and musically*] Then she became an angel; and there was a flaming sword that turned every way, so that I couldnt go in; for I saw that that gate was really the gate of Hell.

MORELL [*triumphantly*] She repulsed you!

MARCHBANKS [*rising in wild scorn*] No, you fool: if she had done that I should never have seen that I was in Heaven already. Repulsed me! You think that would have saved us! virtuous indignation! Oh, you are not worthy to live in the same world with her. [*He turns away contemptuously to the other side of the room*].

MORELL [*who has watched him quietly without

changing his place] Do you think you make yourself more worthy by reviling me, Eugene?

MARCHBANKS. Here endeth the thousand and first lesson. Morell: I dont think much of your preaching after all: I believe I could do it better myself. The man I want to meet is the man that Candida married.

MORELL. The man that—? Do you mean me?

MARCHBANKS. I dont mean the Reverend James Mavor Morell, moralist and windbag. I mean the real man that the Reverend James must have hidden somewhere inside his black coat: the man that Candida loved. You cant make a woman like Candida love you by merely buttoning your collar at the back instead of in front.

MORELL [*boldly and steadily*] When Candida promised to marry me, I was the same moralist and windbag you now see. I wore my black coat, and my collar was buttoned behind instead of in front. Do you think she would have loved me any the better for being insincere in my profession?

MARCHBANKS [*on the sofa, hugging his ankles*] Oh, she forgave you, just as she forgives me for being a coward, and a weakling, and what you call a snivelling little whelp and all the rest of it. [*Dreamily*] A woman like that has divine insight: she loves our souls, and not our follies and vanities and illusions, nor our collars and coats, nor any other of the rags and tatters we are rolled up in. [*He reflects on this for an instant; then turns intently to question Morell*] What I want to know is how you got past the flaming sword that stopped me.

MORELL. Perhaps because I was not interrupted at the end of ten minutes.

MARCHBANKS [*taken aback*] What!

MORELL. Man can climb to the highest summits; but he cannot dwell there long.

MARCHBANKS [*springing up*] It's false: there can he dwell for ever, and there only. It's in the other moments that he can find no rest, no sense of the silent glory of life. Where would you have me spend my moments, if not on the summits?

MORELL. In the scullery, slicing onions and filling lamps.

MARCHBANKS. Or in the pulpit, scrubbing cheap earthenware souls?

MORELL. Yes, that too. It was there that I earned my golden moment, and the right, in that moment, to ask her to love me. *I* did not take the moment on credit; nor did I use

it to steal another man's happiness.

MARCHBANKS [*rather disgustedly, trotting back towards the fireplace*] I have no doubt you conducted the transaction as honestly as if you were buying a pound of cheese. [*He stops on the brink of the hearth-rug, and adds, thoughtfully, to himself, with his back turned to Morell*] I could only go to her as a beggar.

MORELL [*starting*] A beggar dying of cold! asking for her shawl!

MARCHBANKS [*turning, surprised*] Thank you for touching up my poetry. Yes, if you like: a beggar dying of cold, asking for her shawl.

MORELL [*excitedly*] And she refused. Shall I tell you why she refused? I c a n tell you, on her own authority. It was because of—

MARCHBANKS. She didnt refuse.

MORELL. Not!

MARCHBANKS. She offered me all I chose to ask for: her shawl, her wings, the wreath of stars on her head, the lilies in her hand, the crescent moon beneath her feet—

MORELL [*seizing him*] Out with the truth, man: my wife is my wife: I want no more of your poetic fripperies. I know well that if I have lost her love and you have gained it, no law will bind her.

MARCHBANKS [*quaintly, without fear or resistance*] Catch me by the shirt collar, Morell: she will arrange it for me afterwards as she did this morning. [*With quiet rapture*] I shall feel her hands touch me.

MORELL. You young imp, do you know how dangerous it is to say that to me? Or [*with a sudden misgiving*] has something made you brave?

MARCHBANKS. I'm not afraid now. I disliked you before: that was why I shrank from your touch. But I saw today—when she tortured you—that you love her. Since then I have been your friend: you may strangle me if you like.

MORELL [*releasing him*] Eugene: if that is not a heartless lie—if you have a spark of human feeling left in you—will you tell me what has happened during my absence?

MARCHBANKS. What happened! Why, the flaming sword [*Morell stamps with impatience*] —Well, in plain prose, I loved her so exquisitely that I wanted nothing more than the happiness of being in such love. And before I had time to come down from the highest summits, y o u came in.

MORELL [*suffering deeply*] So it is still unsettled. Still the misery of doubt.

MARCHBANKS. Misery! I am the happiest of men. I desire nothing now but her happiness. [*In a passion of sentiment*] Oh, Morell, let us both give her up. Why should she have to choose between a wretched little nervous disease like me, and a pig-headed parson like you? Let us go on a pilgrimage, you to the east and I to the west, in search of a worthy lover for her: some beautiful archangel with purple wings—

MORELL. Some fiddlestick! Oh, if she is mad enough to leave me for you, who will protect her? who will help her? who will work for her? who will be a father to her children? [*He sits down distractedly on the sofa, with his elbows on his knees and his head propped on his clenched fists*].

MARCHBANKS [*snapping his fingers wildly*] She does not ask those silly questions. It is she who wants somebody to protect, to help, to work for: somebody to give her children to protect, to help and to work for. Some grown up man who has become as a little child again. Oh, you fool, you fool, you triple fool! I am the man, Morell: I am the man. [*He dances about excitedly, crying*] You dont understand what a woman is. Send for her, Morell: send for her and let her choose be- tween—[*The door opens and Candida enters. He stops as if petrified*].

CANDIDA [*amazed, on the threshold*] What on earth are you at, Eugene?

MARCHBANKS [*oddly*] James and I are having a preaching match; and he is getting the worst of it.

Candida looks quickly round at Morell. Seeing that he is distressed, she hurries down to him, greatly vexed.

CANDIDA. You have been annoying him. Now I wont have it, Eugene: do you hear? [*She puts her hand on Morell's shoulder, and quite forgets her wifely tact in her anger*]. My boy shall not be worried: I will protect him.

MORELL [*rising proudly*] Protect!

CANDIDA [*not heeding him: to Eugene*] What have you been saying?

MARCHBANKS [*appalled*] Nothing. I—

CANDIDA. Eugene! Nothing?

MARCHBANKS [*piteously*] I mean—I—I'm very sorry. I wont do it again: indeed I wont. I'll let him alone.

MORELL [*indignantly, with an aggressive movement towards Eugene*] Let me alone! You young—

CANDIDA [*stopping him*] Sh!—no: let me deal with him, James.

MARCHBANKS. Oh, youre not angry with me, are you?

CANDIDA [*severely*] Yes I am: very angry. I have a good mind to pack you out of the house.

MORELL [*taken aback by Candida's vigor, and by no means relishing the position of being rescued by her from another man*] Gently, Candida, gently. I am able to take care of myself.

CANDIDA [*petting him*] Yes, dear: of course you are. But you musnt be annoyed and made miserable.

MARCHBANKS [*almost in tears, turning to the door*] I'll go.

CANDIDA. Oh, you neednt go: I cant turn you out at this time of night. [*Vehemently*] Shame on you! For shame!

MARCHBANKS [*desperately*] But what have I done?

CANDIDA. I know what you have done: as well as if I had been here all the time. Oh, it was unworthy! You are like a child: you cannot hold your tongue.

MARCHBANKS. I would die ten times over sooner than give you a moment's pain.

CANDIDA [*with infinite contempt for this puerility*] Much good your dying would do me!

MORELL. Candida, my dear: this altercation is hardly quite seemly. It is a matter be- tween two men; and I am the right person to settle it.

CANDIDA. Two men! Do you call that a man? [*To Eugene*] You bad boy!

MARCHBANKS [*gathering a whimsically affec- tionate courage from the scolding*] If I am to be scolded like a boy, I must make a boy's ex- cuse. He began it. And he's bigger than I am.

CANDIDA [*losing confidence a little as her con- cern for Morell's dignity takes the alarm*] That cant be true. [*To Morell*] You didnt begin it, James, did you?

MORELL [*contemptuously*] No.

MARCHBANKS [*indignant*] Oh!

MORELL [*to Eugene*] You began it: this morn- ing. [*Candida, instantly connecting this with his mysterious allusion in the afternoon to something told him by Eugene in the morning, looks at him with quick suspicion. Morell proceeds, with the emphasis of offended superiority*] But your other point is true. I am certainly the bigger of the two, and, I hope, the stronger, Candida.

So you had better leave the matter in my hands.

CANDIDA [*again soothing him*] Yes, dear; but —[*troubled*] I dont understand about this morning.

MORELL [*gently snubbing her*] You need not understand, my dear.

CANDIDA. But James, I [*the street bell rings*] —Oh bother! Here they all come. [*She goes out to let them in*].

MARCHBANKS [*running to Morell*] Oh, Morell, isnt it dreadful? She's angry with us: she hates me. What shall I do?

MORELL [*with quaint desperation, walking up and down the middle of the room*] Eugene: my head is spinning round. I shall begin to laugh presently.

MARCHBANKS [*following him anxiously*] No, no: she'll think Ive thrown you into hysterics. Dont laugh.

Boisterous voices and laughter are heard approaching. Lexy Mill, his eyes sparkling, and his bearing denoting unwonted elevation of spirit, enters with Burgess, who is greasy and self-complacent, but has all his wits about him. Miss Garnett, with her smartest hat and jacket on, follows them; but though her eyes are brighter than before, she is evidently a prey to misgiving. She places herself with her back to her type-writing table, with one hand on it to steady herself, passing the other across her forehead as if she were a little tired and giddy. Marchbanks relapses into shyness and edges away into the corner near the window, where Morell's books are.

LEXY [*exhilarated*] Morell: I m u s t congratulate you. [*Grasping his hand*] What a noble, splendid, inspired address you gave us! You surpassed yourself.

BURGESS. So you did, James. It fair kep me awake to the lars' word. Didnt it, Miss Gornett?

PROSERPINE [*worriedly*] Oh, I wasnt minding you: I was trying to make notes. [*She takes out her note-book, and looks at her stenography, which nearly makes her cry*].

MORELL. Did I go too fast, Pross?

PROSERPINE. Much too fast. You know I cant do more than ninety words a minute. [*She relieves her feelings by throwing her note-book angrily beside her machine, ready for use next morning*].

MORELL [*soothingly*] Oh well, well, never mind, never mind, never mind. Have you all had supper?

LEXY. Mr Burgess has been kind enough to give us a really splendid supper at the Belgrave.

BURGESS [*with effusive magnanimity*] Dont mention it, Mr Mill. [*Modestly*] Youre arty welcome to my little treat.

PROSERPINE. We had champagne. I never tasted it before. I feel quite giddy.

MORELL [*surprised*] A champagne supper! That was very handsome. Was it my eloquence that produced all this extravagance?

LEXY [*rhetorically*] Your eloquence, and Mr Burgess's goodness of heart. [*With a fresh burst of exhilaration*] And what a very fine fellow the chairman is, Morell! He came to supper with us.

MORELL [*with long drawn significance, looking at Burgess*] O-o-o-h! the chairman. Now I understand.

Burgess covers with a deprecatory cough a lively satisfaction with his own diplomatic cunning. Lexy folds his arms and leans against the head of the sofa in a high-spirited attitude after nearly losing his balance. Candida comes in with glasses, lemons, and a jug of hot water on a tray.

CANDIDA. Who will have some lemonade? You know our rules: total abstinence. [*She puts the tray on the table, and takes up the lemon squeezer, looking enquiringly round at them*].

MORELL. No use, dear. Theyve all had champagne. Pross has broken her pledge.

CANDIDA [*to Proserpine*] You dont mean to say youve been drinking champagne!

PROSERPINE [*stubbornly*] Yes I do. I'm only a beer teetotaller, not a champagne teetotaller. I dont like beer. Are there any letters for me to answer, Mr Morell?

MORELL. No more to-night.

PROSERPINE. Very well. Goodnight, everybody.

LEXY [*gallantly*] Had I not better see you home, Miss Garnett?

PROSERPINE. No thank you. I shant trust myself with anybody tonight. I wish I hadnt taken any of that stuff. [*She takes uncertain aim at the door; dashes at it; and barely escapes without disaster*].

BURGESS [*indignantly*] Stuff indeed! That gurl dunno what champagne is! Pommery and Greeno at twelve and six a bottle. She took two glasses amost straight horff.

MORELL [*anxious about her*] Go and look after her, Lexy.

LEXY [*alarmed*] But if she should really be — Suppose she began to sing in the street, or anything of that sort.

MORELL. Just so: she may. Thats why youd better see her safely home.

CANDIDA. Do, Lexy: theres a good fellow. [*She shakes his hand and pushes him gently to the door*].

LEXY. It's evidently my duty to go. I hope it may not be necessary. Goodnight, Mrs Morell. [*To the rest*] Goodnight. [*He goes. Candida shuts the door*].

BURGESS. He was gushin with hextra piety hisself arter two sips. People carnt drink like they huseter. [*Bustling across to the hearth*] Well, James: it's time to lock up. Mr Morchbanks: shall I ave the pleasure of your company for a bit o the way ome?

MARCHBANKS [*affrightedly*] Yes: I'd better go. [*He hurries towards the door; but Candida places herself before it, barring his way*].

CANDIDA [*with quiet authority*] You sit down. Youre not going yet.

MARCHBANKS [*quailing*] No: I—I didnt mean to. [*He sits down abjectly on the sofa*].

CANDIDA. Mr Marchbanks will stay the night with us, papa.

BURGESS. Oh well, I'll say goodnight. So long, James. [*He shakes hands with Morell, and goes over to Eugene*]. Make em give you a nightlight by your bed, Mr Morchbanks: itll comfort you if you wake up in the night with a touch of that complaint of yores. Goodnight.

MARCHBANKS. Thank you: I will. Goodnight, Mr Burgess. [*They shake hands. Burgess goes to the door*].

CANDIDA [*intercepting Morell, who is following Burgess*] Stay here, dear: I'll put on papa's coat for him. [*She goes out with Burgess*].

MARCHBANKS [*rising and stealing over to Morell*] Morell: theres going to be a terrible scene. Arnt you afraid?

MORELL. Not in the least.

MARCHBANKS. I never envied you your courage before. [*He puts his hand appealingly on Morell's forearm*]. Stand by me, wont you?

MORELL [*casting him off resolutely*] Each for himself, Eugene. She must choose between us now.

Candida returns. Eugene creeps back to the sofa like a guilty schoolboy.

CANDIDA [*between them, addressing Eugene*] Are you sorry?

MARCHBANKS [*earnestly*] Yes. Heartbroken.

CANDIDA. Well then, you are forgiven. Now go off to bed like a good little boy: I want to talk to James about you.

MARCHBANKS [*rising in great consternation*] Oh, I cant do that, Morell. I must be here. I'll not go away. Tell her.

CANDIDA [*her suspicions confirmed*] Tell me what? [*His eyes avoid hers furtively. She turns and mutely transfers the question to Morell*].

MORELL [*bracing himself for the catastrophe*] I have nothing to tell her, except [*here his voice deepens to a measured and mournful tenderness*] that she is my greatest treasure on earth—if she is really mine.

CANDIDA [*coldly, offended by his yielding to his orator's instinct and treating her as if she were the audience at the Guild of St Matthew*] I am sure Eugene can say no less, if that is all.

MARCHBANKS [*discouraged*] Morell: she's laughing at us.

MORELL [*with a quick touch of temper*] There is nothing to laugh at. Are you laughing at us, Candida?

CANDIDA [*with quiet anger*] Eugene is very quick-witted, James. I hope I am going to laugh; but I am not sure that I am not going to be very angry. [*She goes to the fireplace, and stands there leaning with her arm on the mantelpiece, and her foot on the fender, whilst Eugene steals to Morell and plucks him by the sleeve*].

MARCHBANKS [*whispering*] Stop, Morell. Dont let us say anything.

MORELL [*pushing Eugene away without deigning to look at him*] I hope you dont mean that as a threat, Candida.

CANDIDA [*with emphatic warning*] Take care, James. Eugene: I asked you to go. Are you going?

MORELL [*putting his foot down*] He shall not go. I wish him to remain.

MARCHBANKS. I'll go. I'll do whatever you want. [*He turns to the door*].

CANDIDA. Stop! [*He obeys*]. Didnt you hear James say he wished you to stay? James is master here. Dont you know that?

MARCHBANKS [*flushing with a young poet's rage against tyranny*] By what right is he master?

CANDIDA [*quietly*] Tell him, James.

MORELL [*taken aback*] My dear: I dont know of any right that makes me master. I assert no such right.

CANDIDA [*with infinite reproach*] You dont know! Oh, James! James! [*To Eugene, musingly*] I wonder do you understand, Eugene! [*He shakes his head helplessly, not daring to look at her*]. No: youre too young. Well, I give you leave to stay: to stay and learn. [*She comes away from the hearth and places herself between them*]. Now, James! whats the matter? Come: tell me.

MARCHBANKS [*whispering tremulously across to him*] Dont.

CANDIDA. Come. Out with it!

MORELL [*slowly*] I meant to prepare your mind carefully, Candida, so as to prevent misunderstanding.

CANDIDA. Yes, dear: I am sure you did. But never mind: I shant misunderstand.

MORELL. Well—er— [*he hesitates, unable to find the long explanation which he supposed to be available*].

CANDIDA. Well?

MORELL [*blurting it out baldly*] Eugene declares that you are in love with him.

MARCHBANKS [*frantically*] No, no, no, no, never. I did not, Mrs Morell: it's not true. I said I loved you. I said I understood you, and that he couldnt. And it was not after what passed there before the fire that I spoke: it was not, on my word. It was this morning.

CANDIDA [*enlightened*] This morning!

MARCHBANKS. Yes. [*He looks at her, pleading for credence, and then adds simply*] That was what was the matter with my collar.

CANDIDA. Your collar? [*suddenly taking in his meaning she turns to Morell, shocked*]. Oh, James: did you— [*she stops*]?

MORELL [*ashamed*] You know, Candida, that I have a temper to struggle with. And he said [*shuddering*] that you despised me in your heart.

CANDIDA [*turning quickly on Eugene*] Did you say that?

MARCHBANKS [*terrified*] No.

CANDIDA [*almost fiercely*] Then James has just told me a falsehood. Is that what you mean?

MARCHBANKS. No, no: I—I—[*desperately*] it was David's wife. And it wasnt at home: it was when she saw him dancing before all the people.

MORELL [*taking the cue with a debater's adroitness*] Dancing before all the people, Candida; and thinking he was moving their hearts by his mission when they were only suffering from—Prossy's complaint. [*She is about to protest: he raises his hand to silence her*]. Dont try to look indignant, Candida—

CANDIDA. Try!

MORELL [*continuing*] Eugene was right. As

you told me a few hours after, he is always right. He said nothing that you did not say far better yourself. He is the poet, who sees everything; and I am the poor parson, who understands nothing.

CANDIDA [*remorsefully*] Do you mind what is said by a foolish boy, because I said something like it in jest?

MORELL. That foolish boy can speak with the inspiration of a child and the cunning of a serpent. He has claimed that you belong to him and not to me; and, rightly or wrongly, I have come to fear that it may be true. I will not go about tortured with doubts and suspicions. I will not live with you and keep a secret from you. I will not suffer the intolerable degradation of jealousy. We have agreed—he and I—that you shall choose between us now. I await your decision.

CANDIDA [*slowly recoiling a step, her heart hardened by his rhetoric in spite of the sincere feeling behind it*] Oh! I am to choose, am I? I suppose it is quite settled that I must belong to one or the other.

MORELL [*firmly*] Quite. You must choose definitely.

MARCHBANKS [*anxiously*] Morell: you dont understand. She means that she belongs to herself.

CANDIDA [*turning on him*] I mean that, and a good deal more, Master Eugene, as you will both find out presently. And pray, my lords and masters, what have you to offer for my choice? I am up for auction, it seems. What do you bid, James?

MORELL [*reproachfully*] Cand—[*He breaks down: his eyes and throat fill with tears: the orator becomes a wounded animal*]. I cant speak—

CANDIDA [*impulsively going to him*] Ah, dearest—

MARCHBANKS [*in wild alarm*] Stop: it's not fair. You musnt shew her that you suffer, Morell. I am on the rack too; but I am not crying.

MORELL [*rallying all his forces*] Yes: you are right. It is not for pity that I am bidding. [*He disengages himself from Candida*].

CANDIDA [*retreating, chilled*] I beg your pardon, James: I did not mean to touch you. I am waiting to hear your bid.

MORELL [*with proud humility*] I have nothing to offer you but my strength for your defence, my honesty for your surety, my ability and industry for your livelihood, and my authority and position for your dignity. That is all it becomes a man to offer to a woman.

CANDIDA [*quite quietly*] And you, Eugene? What do you offer?

MARCHBANKS. My weakness. My desolation. My heart's need.

CANDIDA [*impressed*] Thats a good bid, Eugene. Now I know how to make my choice.

She pauses and looks curiously from one to the other, as if weighing them. Morell, whose lofty confidence has changed into heartbreaking dread at Eugene's bid, loses all power of concealing his anxiety. Eugene, strung to the highest tension, does not move a muscle.

MORELL [*in a suffocated voice: the appeal bursting from the depths of his anguish*] Candida!

MARCHBANKS [*aside, in a flash of contempt*] Coward!

CANDIDA [*significantly*] I give myself to the weaker of the two.

Eugene divines her meaning at once: his face whitens like steel in a furnace.

MORELL [*bowing his head with the calm of collapse*] I accept your sentence, Candida.

CANDIDA. Do y o u understand, Eugene?

MARCHBANKS. Oh, I feel I'm lost. He cannot bear the burden.

MORELL [*incredulously, raising his head and voice with comic abruptness*] Do you mean m e, Candida?

CANDIDA [*smiling a little*] Let us sit and talk comfortably over it like three friends. [*To Morell*] Sit down, dear. [*Morell, quite lost, takes the chair from the fireside: the children's chair*]. Bring me that chair, Eugene. [*She indicates the easy chair. He fetches it silently, even with something like cold strength, and places it next Morell, a little behind him. She sits down. He takes the visitor's chair himself, and sits, inscrutable. When they are all settled she begins, throwing a spell of quietness on them by her calm, sane, tender tone*]. You remember what you told me about yourself, Eugene: how nobody has cared for you since your old nurse died: how those clever fashionable sisters and successful brothers of yours were your mother's and father's pets: how miserable you were at Eton: how your father is trying to starve you into returning to Oxford: how you have had to live without comfort or welcome or refuge: always lonely, and nearly always disliked and misunderstood, poor boy!

MARCHBANKS [*faithful to the nobility of his lot*] I had my books. I had Nature. And at last I met you.

CANDIDA. Never mind that just at present. Now I want you to look at this other boy here: m y boy! spoiled from his cradle. We go once a fortnight to see his parents. You should come with us, Eugene, to see the pictures of the hero of that household. James as a baby! the most wonderful of all babies. James holding his first school prize, won at the ripe age of eight! James as the captain of his eleven! James in his first frock coat! James under all sorts of glorious circumstances! You know how strong he is (I hope he didnt hurt you): how clever he is: how happy. [*With deepening gravity*] Ask James's mother and his three sisters what it cost to save James the trouble of doing anything but be strong and clever and happy. Ask m e what it costs to be James's mother and three sisters and wife and mother to his children all in one. Ask Prossy and Maria how troublesome the house is even when we have no visitors to help us to slice the onions. Ask the tradesmen who want to worry James and spoil his beautiful sermons who it is that puts them off. When there is money to give, he gives it: when there is money to refuse, I refuse it. I build a castle of comfort and indulgence and love for him, and stand sentinel always to keep little vulgar cares out. I make him master here, though he does not know it, and could not tell you a moment ago how it came to be so. [*With sweet irony*] And when he thought I might go away with you, his only anxiety was—what should become of m e! And to tempt me to stay he offered me [*leaning forward to stroke his hair caressingly at each phrase*] h i s strength for m y defence! his industry for my livelihood! his dignity for my position! his—[*relenting*] ah, I am mixing up your beautiful cadences and spoiling them, am I not, darling? [*She lays her cheek fondly against his*].

MORELL [*quite overcome, kneeling beside her chair and embracing her with boyish ingenuousness*] It's all true, every word. What I am you have made me with the labor of your hands and the love of your heart. You are my wife, my mother, my sisters: you are the sum of all loving care to me.

CANDIDA [*in his arms, smiling, to Eugene*] Am I y o u r mother and sisters to you, Eugene?

MARCHBANKS [*rising with a fierce gesture of disgust*] Ah, never. Out, then, into the night with me!

CANDIDA [*rising quickly*] You are not going

like that, Eugene?

MARCHBANKS [*with the ring of a man's voice— no longer a boy's—in the words*] I know the hour when it strikes. I am impatient to do what must be done.

MORELL [*who has also risen*] Candida: dont let him do anything rash.

CANDIDA [*confident, smiling at Eugene*] Oh, there is no fear. He has learnt to live without happiness.

MARCHBANKS. I no longer desire happiness: life is nobler than that. Parson James: I give you my happiness with both hands: I love you because you have filled the heart of the woman I loved. Goodbye. [*He goes towards the door*].

CANDIDA. One last word. [*He stops, but without turning to her. She goes to him*]. How old are you, Eugene?

MARCHBANKS. As old as the world now. This morning I was eighteen.

CANDIDA. Eighteen! Will you, for my sake, make a little poem out of the two sentences I am going to say to you? And will you promise to repeat it to yourself whenever you think of me?

MARCHBANKS [*without moving*] Say the sentences.

CANDIDA. When I am thirty, she will be forty-five. When I am sixty, she will be seventy-five.

MARCHBANKS [*turning to her*] In a hundred years, we shall be the same age. But I have a better secret than that in my heart. Let me go now. The night outside grows impatient.

CANDIDA. Goodbye. [*She takes his face in her hands; and as he divines her intention and falls on his knees, she kisses his forehead. Then he flies out into the night. She turns to Morell, holding out her arms to him*]. Ah, James!

They embrace. But they do not know the secret in the poet's heart.

THE END

VI

THE MAN OF DESTINY

1896

BEING THE THIRD OF FOUR PLEASANT PLAYS

The twelfth of May, 1796, in north Italy, at Tavazzano, on the road from Lodi to Milan. The afternoon sun is blazing serenely over the plains of Lombardy, treating the Alps with respect and the anthills with indulgence, neither disgusted by the basking of the swine in the villages nor hurt by its cool reception in the churches, but ruthlessly disdainful of two hordes of mischievous insects which are the French and Austrian armies. Two days before, at Lodi, the Austrians tried to prevent the French from crossing the river by the narrow bridge there; but the French, commanded by a general aged 27, Napoleon Bonaparte, who does not respect the rules of war, rushed the fireswept bridge, supported by a tremendous cannonade in which the young general assisted with his own hands. Cannonading is his technical speciality: he has been trained in the artillery under the old régime, and made perfect in the military arts of shirking his duties, swindling the paymaster over travelling expenses, and dignifying war with the noise and smoke of cannon, as depicted in all military por- *traits. He is, however, an original observer, and has perceived, for the first time since the invention of gunpowder, that a cannon ball, if it strikes a man, will kill him. To a thorough grasp of this remarkable discovery he adds a highly evolved faculty for physical geography and for the calculation of times and distances. He has prodigious powers of work, and a clear realistic knowledge of human nature in public affairs, having seen it exhaustively tested in that department during the French Revolution. He is imaginative without illusions, and creative without religion, loyalty, patriotism or any of the common ideals. Not that he is incapable of these ideals: on the contrary, he has swallowed them all in his boyhood, and now, having a keen dramatic faculty, is extremely clever at playing upon them by the arts of the actor and stage manager. Withal, he is no spoiled child. Poverty, ill-luck, the shifts of impecunious shabby-gentility, repeated failure as a would-be author, humiliation as a rebuffed time server, reproof and punishment as an incompetent and dishonest* officer, an escape from dismissal from the service so narrow that if the emigration of the nobles had not raised the value of even the most rascally lieutenant to the famine price of a general he would have been swept contemptuously from the army: these trials have ground his conceit out of him, and forced him to be self-sufficient and to understand that to such men as he is the world will give nothing that he cannot take from it by force. In this the world is not free from cowardice and folly; for Napoleon, as a merciless cannonader of political rubbish, is making himself useful: indeed, it is even now impossible to live in England without sometimes feeling how much that country lost in not being conquered by him as well as by Julius Cæsar.

However, on this May afternoon in 1796, it is early days with him. He has but recently been promoted general, partly by using his wife to seduce the Directory (then governing France); partly by the scarcity of officers caused by the emigration as aforesaid; partly by his faculty of knowing a country, with all its roads, rivers, hills and valleys, as he knows the palm of his hand; and largely by that new faith of his in the efficacy of firing cannons at people. His army is, as to discipline, in a state which has so greatly shocked some modern writers before whom the following story has been enacted, that they, impressed with the later glory of "L'Empereur," have altogether refused to credit it. But Napoleon is not L'Empereur yet: his men call him Le Petit Caporal, as he is still in the stage of gaining influence over them by displays of pluck. He is not in a position to force his will on them in orthodox military fashion by the cat o' nine tails. The French Revolution, which has escaped suppression solely through the monarchy's habit of being at least four years in arrear with its soldiers in the matter of pay, has substituted for that habit, as far as possible, the habit of not paying at all, except in promises and patriotic flatteries which are not compatible with martial law of the Prussian type. Napoleon has therefore approached the Alps in command of men without money, in rags, and consequently indisposed to stand much discipline, especially from upstart generals. This circumstance, which would have embarrassed an idealist soldier, has been worth a thousand cannon to Napoleon. He has said to his army " You have patriotism and courage; but you have no money, no clothes, and hardly anything to eat. In Italy there are all these things, and glory as well, to be gained by a devoted army led by a general who regards loot as the natural right of the soldier. I am such a general. En avant, mes enfants!" The result has entirely justified him. The army conquers Italy as the locusts conquered Cyprus. They fight all day and march all night, covering impossible distances and appearing in incredible places, not because every soldier carries a field marshal's baton in his knapsack, but because he hopes to carry at least half a dozen silver forks there next day.

It must be understood, by the way, that the French army does not make war on the Italians. It is there to rescue them from the tyranny of their Austrian conquerors, and confer republican institutions on them; so that in incidentally looting them it merely makes free with the property of its friends, who ought to be grateful to it, and perhaps would be if ingratitude were not the proverbial failing of their country. The Austrians, whom it fights, are a thoroughly respectable regular army, well disciplined, commanded by gentlemen versed in orthodox campaigning: at the head of them Beaulieu, practising the classic art of war under orders from Vienna, and getting horribly beaten by Napoleon, who acts on his own responsibility in defiance of professional precedents or orders from Paris. Even when the Austrians win a battle, all that is necessary is to wait until their routine obliges them to return to their quarters for afternoon tea, so to speak, and win it back again from them: a course pursued later on with brilliant success at Marengo. On the whole, with his foe handicapped by Austrian statesmanship, classic generalship, and the exigencies of the aristocratic social structure of Viennese society, Napoleon finds it possible to be irresistible without working heroic miracles. The world, however, likes miracles and heroes, and is quite incapable of conceiving the action of such forces as academic militarism or Viennese drawingroomism. Hence it has already begun to manufacture "L'Empereur," and thus to make it difficult for the romanticists of a hundred years later to credit the hitherto unrecorded little scene now in question at Tavazzano.

The best quarters in Tavazzano are at a little inn, the first house reached by travellers passing through the place from Milan to Lodi. It stands in a vineyard; and its principal room, a pleasant refuge from the summer heat, is open so widely at the back to this vineyard that it is almost a large veranda. The bolder children, much excited by the alarums and excursions of the past few days, and by an irruption of French troops at six o'clock, know that the French commander has quartered himself in this room, and are divided between a craving to peep in at the front windows, and a mortal dread of the sentinel, a young gentleman-soldier who, having no natural moustache, has had a most ferocious one painted on his face with boot blacking by his sergeant. As his heavy uniform, like all the uniforms of that day, is designed for parade without the least reference to his health or comfort, he perspires profusely in the sun; and his painted moustache has run in little streaks down his chin and round his neck, except where it has dried in stiff japanned flakes and had its sweeping outline chipped off in grotesque little bays and headlands, making him unspeakably ridiculous in the eye of History a hundred years later, but monstrous and horrible to the contemporary north Italian infant, to whom nothing would seem more natural than that he should relieve the monotony of his guard by pitchforking a stray child up on his bayonet, and eating it uncooked. Nevertheless one girl of bad character, in whom an instinct of privilege with soldiers is already stirring, does peep in at the safest window for a moment before a glance and a clink from the sentinel sends her flying. Most of what she sees she has seen before: the vineyard at the back, with the old winepress and a cart among the vines; the door close on her right leading to the street entry; the landlord's best sideboard, now in full action for dinner, further back on the same side; the fireplace on the other side with a couch near it; another door, leading to the inner rooms, between it and the vineyard; and the table in the middle set out with a repast of Milanese risotto, cheese, grapes, bread, olives, and a big wickered flask of red wine.

The landlord, Giuseppe Grandi, she knows well. He is a swarthy vivacious shrewdly cheerful black-curled bullet headed grinning little innkeeper of 40. Naturally an excellent host, he is in the highest spirits this evening at his good fortune in having as his guest the French commander to protect him against the license of the troops. He actually sports a pair of gold earrings which would otherwise have been hidden carefully under the winepress with his little equipment of silver plate.

Napoleon, sitting facing her on the further side of the table, she sees for the first time. He is working hard, partly at his meal, which he has discovered how to dispatch in ten minutes by attacking all the courses simultaneously (this practice is the beginning of his downfall), and partly at a military map on which he from time to time marks the position of the forces by taking a grape-skin from his mouth and planting it on the map with his thumb like a wafer. There is no revolutionary untidiness about his dress or person; but his elbow has displaced most of the dishes and glasses; and his long hair trails into the risotto when he forgets it and leans more intently over the map.

GIUSEPPE. Will your excellency—

NAPOLEON [intent on his map, but cramming himself mechanically with his left hand] Dont talk. I'm busy.

GIUSEPPE [with perfect goodhumor] Excellency: I obey.

NAPOLEON. Some red ink.

GIUSEPPE. Alas! excellency, there is none.

NAPOLEON [with Corsican facetiousness] Kill something and bring me its blood.

GIUSEPPE [grinning] There is nothing but your excellency's horse, the sentinel, the lady upstairs, and my wife.

NAPOLEON. Kill your wife.

GIUSEPPE. Willingly, your excellency; but unhappily I am not strong enough. She would kill me.

NAPOLEON. That will do equally well.

GIUSEPPE. Your excellency does me too much honor. [Stretching his hand towards the flask] Perhaps some wine will answer your excellency's purpose.

NAPOLEON [hastily protecting the flask, and becoming quite serious] Wine! No: that would be waste. You are all the same: waste! waste! waste! [He marks the map with gravy, using his fork as a pen]. Clear away. [He finishes his wine; pushes back his chair; and uses his napkin, stretching his legs and leaning back, but still frowning and thinking].

GIUSEPPE [clearing the table and removing the things to a tray on the sideboard] Every man to his trade, excellency. We innkeepers have plenty of cheap wine: we think nothing of spilling it. You great generals have plenty of cheap blood: you think nothing of spilling it. Is it not so, excellency?

NAPOLEON. Blood costs nothing: wine costs money. [He rises and goes to the fireplace].

GIUSEPPE. They say you are careful of everything except human life, excellency.

NAPOLEON. Human life, my friend, is the only thing that takes care of itself. [He throws himself at his ease on the couch].

GIUSEPPE [admiring him] Ah, excellency, what fools we all are beside you! If I could only find out the secret of your success!

NAPOLEON. You would make yourself

Emperor of Italy, eh?

GIUSEPPE. Too troublesome, excellency: I leave all that to you. Besides, what would become of my inn if I were Emperor? See how you enjoy looking on at me whilst I keep the inn for you and wait on you! Well, I shall enjoy looking on at you whilst you become Emperor of Europe, and govern the country for me. [As he chatters, he takes the cloth off deftly without removing the map, and finally takes the corners in his hands and the middle in his mouth, to fold it up].

NAPOLEON. Emperor of Europe, eh? Why only Europe?

GIUSEPPE. Why, indeed? Emperor of the world, excellency! Why not? [He folds and rolls up the cloth, emphasizing his phrases by the steps of the process]. One man is like another [fold]: one country is like another [fold]: one battle is like another. [At the last fold, he slaps the cloth on the table and deftly rolls it up, adding, by way of peroration] Conquer one: conquer all. [He takes the cloth to the sideboard, and puts it in a drawer].

NAPOLEON. And govern for all; fight for all; be everybody's servant under cover of being everybody's master. Giuseppe.

GIUSEPPE [at the sideboard] Excellency?

NAPOLEON. I forbid you to talk to me about myself.

GIUSEPPE [coming to the foot of the couch] Pardon. Your excellency is so unlike other great men. It is the subject they like best.

NAPOLEON. Well, talk to me about the subject they like next best, whatever that may be.

GIUSEPPE [unabashed] Willingly, your excellency. Has your excellency by any chance caught a glimpse of the lady upstairs?

NAPOLEON [sitting up promptly] How old is she?

GIUSEPPE. The right age, excellency.

NAPOLEON. Do you mean seventeen or thirty?

GIUSEPPE. Thirty, excellency.

NAPOLEON. Goodlooking?

GIUSEPPE. I cannot see with your excellency's eyes: every man must judge that for himself. In my opinion, excellency, a fine figure of a lady. [Slyly] Shall I lay the table for her collation here?

NAPOLEON [brusquely, rising] No: lay nothing here until the officer for whom I am waiting comes back. [He looks at his watch, and takes to walking to and fro between the fireplace and the vineyard].

GIUSEPPE [with conviction] Excellency: believe me, he has been captured by the accursed Austrians. He dare not keep you waiting if he were at liberty.

NAPOLEON [turning at the edge of the shadow of the veranda] Giuseppe: if that turns out to be true, it will put me into such a temper that nothing short of hanging you and your whole household, including the lady upstairs, will satisfy me.

GIUSEPPE. We are all cheerfully at your excellency's disposal, except the lady. I cannot answer for her; but no lady could resist you, General.

NAPOLEON [sourly, resuming his march] Hm! You will never be hanged. There is no satisfaction in hanging a man who does not object to it.

GIUSEPPE [sympathetically] Not the least in the world, excellency: is there? [Napoleon again looks at his watch, evidently growing anxious]. Ah, one can see that you are a great man, General: you know how to wait. If it were a corporal now, or a sub-lieutenant, at the end of three minutes he would be swearing, fuming, threatening, pulling the house about our ears.

NAPOLEON. Giuseppe: your flatteries are insufferable. Go and talk outside. [He sits down again at the table, with his jaws in his hands, and his elbows propped on the map, poring over it with a troubled expression].

GIUSEPPE. Willingly, your excellency. You shall not be disturbed. [He takes up the tray and prepares to withdraw].

NAPOLEON. The moment he comes back, send him to me.

GIUSEPPE. Instantaneously, your excellency.

A LADY'S VOICE [calling from some distant part of the inn] Giusep-pe! [The voice is very musical, and the two final notes make an ascending interval].

NAPOLEON [startled] Who's that?

GIUSEPPE. The lady, excellency.

NAPOLEON. The lady upstairs?

GIUSEPPE. Yes, excellency. The strange lady.

NAPOLEON. Strange? Where does she come from?

GIUSEPPE [with a shrug] Who knows? She arrived here just before your excellency in a hired carriage belonging to the Golden Eagle at Borghetto. By herself, excellency.

No servants. A dressing bag and a trunk: that is all. The postillion says she left a horse at the Golden Eagle. A charger, with military trappings.

NAPOLEON. A woman with a charger! French or Austrian?

GIUSEPPE. French, excellency.

NAPOLEON. Her husband's charger, no doubt. Killed at Lodi, poor fellow.

THE LADY'S VOICE [*the two final notes now making a peremptory descending interval*] Giuseppe!

NAPOLEON [*rising to listen*] Thats not the voice of a woman whose husband was killed yesterday.

GIUSEPPE. Husbands are not always regretted, excellency. [*Calling*] Coming, lady, coming. [*He makes for the inner door*].

NAPOLEON [*arresting him with a strong hand on his shoulder*] Stop. Let her come.

VOICE. Giuseppe!! [*impatiently*].

GIUSEPPE. Let me go, excellency. It is my point of honor as an innkeeper to come when I am called. I appeal to you as a soldier.

A MAN'S VOICE [*outside, at the inn door, shouting*] Here, someone. Hollo! Landlord! Where are you? [*Somebody raps vigorously with a whip handle on a bench in the passage*].

NAPOLEON [*suddenly becoming the commanding officer again and throwing Giuseppe off*] My man at last. [*Pointing to the inner door*] Go. Attend to your business: the lady is calling you. [*He goes to the fireplace and stands with his back to it with a determined military air*].

GIUSEPPE [*with bated breath, snatching up his tray*] Certainly, excellency. [*He hurries out by the inner door*].

THE MAN'S VOICE [*impatiently*] Are you all asleep here?

The other door is kicked rudely open. A dusty sub-lieutenant bursts into the room. He is a tall chuckle-headed young man of 24, with the complexion and style of a man of rank, and a self-assurance on that ground which the French Revolution has failed to shake in the smallest degree. He has a thick silly lip, an eager credulous eye, an obstinate nose, and a loud confident voice. A young man without fear, without reverence, without imagination, without sense, hopelessly insusceptible to the Napoleonic or any other idea, stupendously egotistical, eminently qualified to rush in where angels fear to tread, yet of a vigorous babbling vitality which bustles him into the thick of things. He is just now boiling with vexation, attributable by a superficial observer to his impatience at not being promptly attended to by the staff of the inn, but in which a more discerning eye can perceive a certain moral depth, indicating a more permanent and momentous grievance. On seeing Napoleon, he is sufficiently taken aback to check himself and salute; but he does not betray by his manner any of that prophetic consciousness of Marengo and Austerlitz, Waterloo and St Helena, or the Napoleonic pictures of Delaroche and Meissonier, which later ages expect from him.

NAPOLEON [*watch in hand*] Well, sir, you have come at last. Your instructions were that I should arrive here at six, and find you waiting for me with my mail from Paris and with despatches. It is now twenty minutes to eight. You were sent on this service as a hard rider with the fastest horse in the camp. You arrive a hundred minutes late, on foot. Where is your horse?

THE LIEUTENANT [*moodily pulling off his gloves and dashing them with his cap and whip on the table*] Ah! where indeed? Thats just what I should like to know, General. [*With emotion*] You dont know how fond I was of that horse.

NAPOLEON [*angrily sarcastic*] Indeed! [*With sudden misgiving*] Where are the letters and despatches?

THE LIEUTENANT [*importantly, rather pleased than otherwise at having some remarkable news*] I dont know.

NAPOLEON [*unable to believe his ears*] You dont know!

LIEUTENANT. No more than you do, General. Now I suppose I shall be court-martialled. Well, I dont mind being court-martialled; but [*with solemn determination*] I tell you, General, if ever I catch that innocent looking youth, I'll spoil his beauty, the slimy little liar! I'll make a picture of him. I'll—

NAPOLEON [*advancing from the hearth to the table*] What innocent looking youth? Pull yourself together, sir, will you; and give an account of yourself.

LIEUTENANT [*facing him at the opposite side of the table, leaning on it with his fists*] Oh, I'm all right, General: I'm perfectly ready to give an account of myself. I shall make the court-martial thoroughly understand that the fault was not mine. Advantage has been taken of the better side of my nature; and I'm not ashamed of it. But with all respect to you as my commanding officer, General, I say again that if ever I set eyes on that son of Satan, I'll—

NAPOLEON [*angrily*] So you said before.

LIEUTENANT [*drawing himself upright*] I say it again. Just wait until I catch him. Just wait: thats all. [*He folds his arms resolutely, and breathes hard, with compressed lips*].

NAPOLEON. I am waiting, sir. For your explanation.

LIEUTENANT [*confidently*] Youll change your tone, General, when you hear what has happened to me.

NAPOLEON. Nothing has happened to you, sir: you are alive and not disabled. Where are the papers entrusted to you?

LIEUTENANT. Nothing happened to me! Nothing!! He swore eternal brotherhood with me. Was that nothing? He said my eyes reminded him of his sister's eyes. Was that nothing? He cried—actually cried—over the story of my separation from Angelica. Was that nothing? He paid for both bottles of wine, though he only ate bread and grapes himself. Perhaps you call that nothing. He gave me his pistols and his horse and his despatches—most important despatches—and let me go away with them. [*Triumphantly, seeing that he has reduced Napoleon to blank stupefaction*] Was that nothing?

NAPOLEON [*enfeebled by astonishment*] What did he do that for?

LIEUTENANT [*as if the reason were obvious*] To shew his confidence in me, of course. [*Napoleon's jaw does not exactly drop; but its hinges become nerveless*]. And I was worthy of his confidence: I brought them all back honorably. But would you believe it? when I trusted him with m y pistols, and m y horse, and m y despatches—

NAPOLEON. What the devil did you do that for?

LIEUTENANT. I'm telling you: to shew my confidence in him. And he betrayed it! abused it! never came back again! The thief! the swindler! the heartless treacherous little blackguard! You call that nothing, I suppose. But look here, General: [*again resorting to the table with his fists for greater emphasis*] y o u may put up with this outrage from the Austrians if you like; but speaking for myself personally, I tell you that if ever I catch—

NAPOLEON [*turning on his heel in disgust and irritably resuming his march to and fro*] Yes: you have said that more than once already.

LIEUTENANT [*excitedly*] More than once! I'll say it fifty times; and whats more, I'll do it. Youll see, General. I'll shew my confidence in him, so I will. I'll—

NAPOLEON. Yes, yes, sir: no doubt you will. What kind of man was he?

LIEUTENANT. Well, I should think you ought to be able to tell from his conduct the kind of man he was.

NAPOLEON. Psha! What was he like?

LIEUTENANT. Like! He was like—well, you ought to have just seen the fellow: that will give you a notion of what he was like. He wont be like it five minutes after I catch him; for I tell you that if ever—

NAPOLEON [*shouting furiously for the inn-keeper*] Giuseppe! [*To the Lieutenant, out of all patience*] Hold your tongue, sir, if you can.

LIEUTENANT [*plaintively*] I warn you it's no use trying to put the blame on me. How was I to know the sort of fellow he was? [*He takes a chair from between the sideboard and the outer door; places it near the table; and sits down*]. If you only knew how hungry and tired I am, youd have more consideration.

GIUSEPPE [*returning*] What is it, excellency?

NAPOLEON [*struggling with his temper*] Take this—this officer. Feed him; and put him to bed, if necessary. When he is in his right mind again, find out what has happened to him and bring me word. [*To the Lieutenant*] Consider yourself under arrest, sir.

LIEUTENANT [*with sulky stiffness*] I was prepared for that. It takes a gentleman to understand a gentleman. [*He throws his sword on the table*].

GIUSEPPE [*with sympathetic concern*] Have you been attacked by the Austrians, lieutenant? Dear! dear! dear!

LIEUTENANT [*contemptuously*] Attacked! I could have broken his back between my finger and thumb. I wish I had, now. No: it was by appealing to the better side of my nature: thats what I cant get over. He said he'd never met a man he liked so much as me. He put his handkerchief round my neck because a gnat bit me, and my stock was chafing it. Look! [*He pulls a handkerchief from his stock. Giuseppe takes it and examines it*].

GIUSEPPE [*to Napoleon*] A lady's handkerchief, excellency. [*He smells it*]. Perfumed.

NAPOLEON. Eh? [*He takes it and looks at it attentively*]. Hm! [*He smells it*]. Ha! [*He walks thoughtfully across the room, looking at the handkerchief, which he finally sticks in the breast of his coat*].

LIEUTENANT. Good enough for him, any-how. I noticed that he had a woman's hands when he touched my neck, with his coaxing fawning ways, the mean effeminate little hound. [*Lowering his voice with thrilling intensity*] But mark my words, General. If ever—

THE LADY'S VOICE [*outside, as before*] Giuseppe!

LIEUTENANT [*petrified*] What was that?

GIUSEPPE. Only a lady upstairs, lieutenant, calling me.

LIEUTENANT. Lady!

VOICE. Giuseppe, Giuseppe: where are you?

LIEUTENANT [*murderously*] Give me that sword. [*He snatches up the sword and draws it*].

GIUSEPPE [*rushing forward and seizing his right arm*] What are you thinking of, lieutenant? It's a lady: dont you hear? It's a woman's voice.

LIEUTENANT. It's his voice, I tell you. Let me go. [*He breaks away, and rushes to the edge of the veranda, where he posts himself, sword in hand, watching the door like a cat watching a mousehole*].

It opens; and the Strange Lady steps in. She is tall and extraordinarily graceful, with a delicately intelligent, apprehensive, questioning face: perception in the brow, sensitiveness in the nostrils, character in the chin: all keen, refined, and original. She is very feminine, but by no means weak: the lithe tender figure is hung on a strong frame: the hands and feet, neck and shoulders, are useful vigorous members, of full size in proportion to her stature, which perceptibly exceeds that of Napoleon and the innkeeper, and leaves her at no disadvantage with the lieutenant. Only, her elegance and radiant charm keep the secret of her size and strength. She is not, judging by her dress, an admirer of the latest fashions of the Directory; or perhaps she uses up her old dresses for travelling. At all events she wears no jacket with extravagant lappels, no Greco-Tallien sham chiton, nothing, indeed, that the Princesse de Lamballe might not have worn. Her dress of flowered silk is long waisted, with a Watteau pleat behind, but with the paniers reduced to mere rudiments, as she is too tall for them. It is cut low in the neck, where it is eked out by a creamy fichu. She is fair, with golden brown hair and grey eyes.

She enters with the self-possession of a woman accustomed to the privileges of rank and beauty. The innkeeper, who has excellent natural manners is highly appreciative of her. Napoleon is smitten self-conscious. His color deepens: he becomes stiffer and less at ease than before. She is advancing in an infinitely well bred manner to pay her respects to him when the lieutenant pounces on her and seizes her right wrist. As she recognizes him, she becomes deadly pale. There is no mistaking her expression: a revelation of some fatal error, utterly unexpected, has suddenly appalled her in the midst of tranquillity, security, and victory. The next moment a wave of angry color rushes up from beneath the creamy fichu and drowns her whole face. One can see that she is blushing all over her body. Even the lieutenant, ordinarily incapable of observation, can see a thing when it is painted red for him. Interpreting the blush as the involuntary confession of black deceit confronted with its victim, he addresses her in a loud crow of retributive triumph.

LIEUTENANT. So Ive got you, my lad. So youve disguised yourself, have you? [*In a voice of thunder, releasing her wrist*] Take off that skirt.

GIUSEPPE [*remonstrating*] Oh, lieutenant!

LADY [*affrighted, but highly indignant at his having dared to touch her*] Gentlemen: I appeal to you. [*To Napoleon*] You, sir, are an officer: a general. You will protect me, will you not?

LIEUTENANT. Never you mind him, General. Leave me to deal with him.

NAPOLEON. With him! With whom, sir? Why do you treat this lady in such a fashion?

LIEUTENANT. Lady! He's a man! the man I shewed my confidence in. [*Raising his sword*] Here, you—

LADY [*running behind Napoleon and in her agitation clasping to her breast the arm which he extends before her as a fortification*] Oh, thank you, General. Keep him away.

NAPOLEON. Nonsense, sir. This is certainly a lady [*she suddenly drops his arm and blushes again*]; and you are under arrest. Put down your sword, sir, instantly.

LIEUTENANT. General: I tell you he's an Austrian spy. He passed himself off on me as one of General Masséna's staff this afternoon; and now he's passing himself off on you as a woman. Am I to believe my own eyes or not?

LADY. General: it must be my brother. He is on General Masséna's staff. He is very like me.

LIEUTENANT [*his mind giving way*] Do you mean to say that youre not your brother, but your sister? the sister who was so like me? who had my beautiful blue eyes? It's a lie: your eyes are not like mine: theyre exactly like your own.

NAPOLEON [*with contained exasperation*] Lieutenant: will you obey my orders and leave the room, since you are convinced at last that this is no gentleman?

LIEUTENANT. Gentleman! I should think not. No gentleman would have abused my confi—

NAPOLEON [*out of all patience*] That will do, sir: do you hear? Will you leave the room? I order you to leave the room.

LADY. Oh pray let me go instead.

NAPOLEON [*drily*] Excuse me, madam. With all possible respect for your brother, I do not yet understand what an officer on General Masséna's staff wants with my letters. I have some questions to put to you.

GIUSEPPE [*discreetly*] Come, lieutenant. [*He opens the door*].

LIEUTENANT. I'm off. General: take warning by me: be on your guard against the better side of your nature. [*To the lady*] Madam: my apologies. I thought you were the same person, only of the opposite sex; and that naturally misled me.

LADY [*recovering her good humor*] It was not your fault, was it? I'm so glad youre not angry with me any longer, lieutenant. [*She offers her hand*].

LIEUTENANT [*bending gallantly to kiss it*] Oh, madam, not the lea— [*Checking himself and looking at it*] You have your brother's hand. And the same sort of ring!

LADY [*sweetly*] We are twins.

LIEUTENANT. That accounts for it. [*He kisses her hand*]. A thousand pardons. I didnt mind about the despatches at all: thats more the General's affair than mine: it was the abuse of my confidence through the better side of my nature. [*Taking his cap, gloves and whip from the table and going*] Youll excuse my leaving you, General, I hope. Very sorry, I'm sure. [*He talks himself out of the room. Giuseppe follows him and shuts the door*].

NAPOLEON [*looking after them with concentrated irritation*] Idiot!

The Strange Lady smiles sympathetically. He comes frowning down the room between the table and the fireplace, all his awkwardness gone now that he is alone with her.

LADY. How can I thank you, General, for your protection?

NAPOLEON [*turning on her suddenly*] My despatches: come! [*He puts out his hand for them*].

LADY. General! [*She involuntarily puts her hands on her fichu as if to protect something there*].

NAPOLEON. You tricked that blockhead out of them. You disguised yourself as a man. I want my despatches. They are there in the bosom of your dress, under your hands.

LADY [*quickly removing her hands*] Oh, how unkindly you are speaking to me! [*She takes her handkerchief from her fichu*] You frighten me. [*She touches her eyes as if to wipe away a tear*].

NAPOLEON. I see you dont know me, madam, or you would save yourself the trouble of pretending to cry.

LADY [*producing an effect of smiling through her tears*] Yes, I do know you. You are the famous General Buonaparte. [*She gives the name a marked Italian pronunciation: Bwawna-parr-te*].

NAPOLEON [*angrily, with the French pronunciation*] Bonaparte, Madam, Bonaparte. The papers, if you please.

LADY. But I assure you— [*He snatches the handkerchief rudely*]. General! [*indignantly*].

NAPOLEON [*taking the other handkerchief from his breast*] You lent one of your handkerchiefs to my lieutenant when you robbed him. [*He looks at the two handkerchiefs*]. They match one another. [*He smells them*]. The same scent. [*He flings them down on the table*]. I am waiting for my despatches. I shall take them, if necessary, with as little ceremony as I took the handkerchief.

LADY [*in dignified reproof*] General: do you threaten women?

NAPOLEON [*bluntly*] Yes.

LADY [*disconcerted, trying to gain time*] But I dont understand. I—

NAPOLEON. You understand perfectly. You came here because your Austrian employers calculated that I was six leagues away. I am always to be found where my enemies dont expect me. You have walked into the lion's den. Come! you are a brave woman. Be a sensible one: I have no time to waste. The papers. [*He advances a step ominously*].

LADY [*breaking down in the childish rage of impotence, and throwing herself in tears on the chair left beside the table by the lieutenant*] I brave! How little you know! I have spent the day in an agony of fear. I have a pain here from the tightening of my heart at every suspicious look, every threatening movement. Do you think everyone is as brave as you? Oh, why will not you brave people do the brave things? Why do you leave them to us, who have no courage at all? I'm not brave: I shrink from violence: danger makes me miserable.

NAPOLEON [*interested*] Then why have you thrust yourself into danger?

LADY. Because there is no other way: I can trust nobody else. And now it is all useless: all because of you, who have no fear because you have no heart, no feeling, no— [*She breaks off, and throws herself on her knees*]. Ah, General, let me go: let me go without asking any questions. You shall have your despatches and letters: I swear it.

NAPOLEON [*holding out his hand*] Yes: I am waiting for them.

She gasps, daunted by his ruthless promptitude into despair of moving him by cajolery. She looks up perplexedly at him, racking her brains for some device to outwit him. He meets her regard inflexibly.

LADY [*rising at last with a quiet little sigh*] I will get them for you. They are in my room. [*She turns to the door*].

NAPOLEON. I shall accompany you, madam.

LADY [*drawing herself up with a noble air of offended delicacy*] I cannot permit you, General, to enter my chamber.

NAPOLEON. Then you shall stay here, madam, whilst I have your chamber searched for my papers.

LADY [*spitefully, openly giving up her plan*] You may save yourself the trouble. They are not there.

NAPOLEON. No: I have already told you where they are [*pointing to her breast*].

LADY [*with pretty piteousness*] General: I only want to keep one little private letter. Only one. Let me have it.

NAPOLEON [*cold and stern*] Is that a reasonable demand, madam?

LADY [*encouraged by his not refusing point-blank*] No; but that is why you must grant it. Are your own demands reasonable? thousands of lives for the sake of your victories, your ambitions, your destiny! And what I ask is such a little thing. And I am only a weak woman, and you a brave man. [*She looks at him with her eyes full of tender pleading, and is about to kneel to him again*].

NAPOLEON [*brusquely*] Get up, get up. [*He turns moodily away and takes a turn across the room, pausing for a moment to say, over his shoulder*] Youre talking nonsense; and you know it. [*She sits down submissively on the couch. When he turns and sees her despair, he feels that his victory is complete, and that he may now indulge in a little play with his victim. He comes back and sits beside her. She looks alarmed and moves a little away from him; but a ray of rallying hope beams from her eye. He begins like a man enjoying some secret joke*]. How do you know I am a brave man?

LADY [*amazed*] You! General Buonaparte [*Italian pronunciation*].

NAPOLEON. Yes, I, General Bonaparte [*emphasizing the French pronunciation*].

LADY. Oh, how can you ask such a question? you! who stood only two days ago at the bridge at Lodi, with the air full of death, fighting a duel with cannons across the river! [*Shuddering*]. Oh, you do brave things.

NAPOLEON. So do you.

LADY. I! [*With a sudden odd thought*] Oh! Are you a coward?

NAPOLEON [*laughing grimly and slapping his knees*] That is the one question you must never ask a soldier. The sergeant asks after the recruit's height, his age, his wind, his limb, but never after his courage.

LADY [*as if she had found it no laughing matter*] Ah, you can laugh at fear. Then you dont know what fear is.

NAPOLEON. Tell me this. Suppose you could have got that letter by coming to me over the bridge at Lodi the day before yesterday! Suppose there had been no other way, and that this was a sure way—if only you escaped the cannon! [*She shudders and covers her eyes for a moment with her hands*]. Would you have been afraid?

LADY. Oh, horribly afraid, agonizingly afraid. [*She presses her hands on her heart*]. It hurts only to imagine it.

NAPOLEON [*inflexibly*] Would you have come for the despatches?

LADY [*overcome by the imagined horror*] Dont ask me. I must have come.

NAPOLEON. Why?

LADY. Because I must. Because there would have been no other way.

NAPOLEON [*with conviction*] Because you would have wanted my letter enough to bear your fear. [*He rises suddenly, and deliberately poses for an oration*]. There is only one universal passion: fear. Of all the thousand qualities a man may have, the only one you will find as certainly in the youngest drummer boy in my army as in me, is fear. It is fear that makes men fight: it is indifference that makes them run away: fear is the mainspring of war. Fear! I know fear well, better than you, better than any woman. I once saw a regiment of good Swiss soldiers massacred by a mob in Paris because I was afraid to interfere: I felt myself a coward to the tips of my toes as I looked on at it. Seven months ago I revenged my shame by pounding that mob to death with cannon balls. Well, what of that? Has fear ever held a man back from anything he really wanted—or a woman either? Never. Come with me; and I will shew you twenty thousand cowards who will risk death every day for the price of a glass of brandy. And do you think there are no women in the army, braver than the men, though their lives are worth more? Psha! I think nothing of your fear or your bravery. If you had had to come across to me at Lodi, you would not have been afraid: once on the bridge, every other feeling would have gone down before the necessity—the necessity—for making your way to my side and getting what you wanted.

And now, suppose you had done all this! suppose you had come safely out with that letter in your hand, knowing that when the hour came, your fear had tightened, not your heart, but your grip of your own purpose! that it had ceased to be fear, and had become strength, penetration, vigilance, iron resolution! how would you answer then if you were asked whether you were a coward?

LADY [rising] Ah, you are a hero, a real hero.

NAPOLEON. Pooh! theres no such thing as a real hero. [He strolls about the room, making light of her enthusiasm, but by no means displeased with himself for having evoked it].

LADY. Ah yes, there is. There is a difference between what you call my bravery and yours. You wanted to win the battle of Lodi for yourself and not for anyone else, didnt you?

NAPOLEON. Of course. [Suddenly recollecting himself] Stop: no. [He pulls himself piously together, and says, like a man conducting a religious service] I am only the servant of the French republic, following humbly in the footsteps of the heroes of classical antiquity. I win battles for humanity: for my country, not for myself.

LADY [disappointed] Oh, then you are only a womanish hero after all. [She sits down again, all her enthusiasm gone].

NAPOLEON [greatly astonished] Womanish!

LADY [listlessly] Yes, like me. [With deep melancholy] Do you think that if I wanted those despatches only for myself, I dare venture into a battle for them? No: if that were all, I should not have the courage to ask to see you at your hotel, even. My courage is mere slavishness: it is of no use to me for my own purposes. It is only through love, through pity, through the instinct to save and protect someone else, that I can do the things that terrify me.

NAPOLEON [contemptuously] Pshaw! [He turns slightly away from her].

LADY. Aha! now you see that I'm not really brave. [Relapsing into petulant listlessness] But what right have you to despise me if you only win your battles for others? for your country! through patriotism! That is what I call womanish: it is so like a Frenchman!

NAPOLEON [furiously] I am no Frenchman.

LADY [innocently] I thought you said you won the battle of Lodi for your country, General Bu— shall I pronounce it in Italian or French?

NAPOLEON. You are presuming on my patience, madam. I was born a French subject, but not in France.

LADY [affecting a marked access of interest in him] You were not born a subject at all, I think.

NAPOLEON [greatly pleased] Eh? Eh? You think not.

LADY. I am sure of it.

NAPOLEON. Well, well, perhaps not. [The self-complacency of his assent catches his own ear. He stops short, reddening. Then, composing himself into a solemn attitude, modelled on the heroes of classical antiquity, he takes a high moral tone]. But we must not live for ourselves alone, little one. Never forget that we should always think of others, and work for others, and lead and govern them for their own good. Self-sacrifice is the foundation of all true nobility of character.

LADY [again relaxing her attitude with a sigh] Ah, it is easy to see that you have never tried it, General.

NAPOLEON [indignantly, forgetting all about Brutus and Scipio] What do you mean by that speech, madam?

G

LADY. Havnt you noticed that people always exaggerate the value of the things they havnt got? The poor think they need nothing but riches to be quite happy and good. Everybody worships truth, purity, unselfishness, for the same reason: because they have no experience of them. Oh, if they only knew!

NAPOLEON [with angry decision] If they only knew! Pray do y o u know?

LADY. Yes. I had the misfortune to be born good. [Glancing up at him for a moment] And it is a misfortune, I can tell you, General. I really am truthful and unselfish and all the rest of it; and it's nothing but cowardice; want of character; want of being really, strongly, positively oneself.

NAPOLEON. Ha? [turning to her quickly with a flash of strong interest].

LADY [earnestly, with rising enthusiasm] What is the secret of your power? Only that you believe in yourself. You can fight and conquer for yourself and for nobody else. You are not afraid of your own destiny. You teach us what we all might be if we had the will and courage; and that [suddenly sinking on her knees before him] is why we all begin to worship you. [She kisses his hands].

NAPOLEON [embarrassed] Tut! tut! Pray rise, madam.

LADY. Do not refuse my homage: it is your right. You will be Emperor of France—

NAPOLEON [hurriedly] Take care. Treason!

LADY [insisting] Yes, Emperor of France; then of Europe; perhaps of the world. I am only the first subject to swear allegiance. [Again kissing his hand] My Emperor!

NAPOLEON [overcome, raising her] Pray! pray! No, no: this is folly. Come: be calm, be calm. [Petting her] There! there! my girl.

LADY [struggling with happy tears] Yes, I know it is an impertinence in me to tell you what you must know far better than I do. But you are not angry with me, are you?

NAPOLEON. Angry! No, no: not a bit, not a bit. Come: you are a very clever and sensible and interesting woman. [He pats her on the cheek]. Shall we be friends?

LADY [enraptured] Your friend! You will let me be your friend! Oh! [She offers him both her hands with a radiant smile]. You see: I shew my confidence in you.

This incautious echo of the lieutenant undoes her. Napoleon starts: his eyes flash: he utters a yell of rage.

NAPOLEON. What!!!

LADY. Whats the matter?

NAPOLEON. Shew your confidence in me! So that I may shew my confidence in you in return by letting you give me the slip with the despatches, eh? Ah, Dalila, Dalila, you have been trying your tricks on me; and I have been as gross a gull as my jackass of a lieutenant. [Menacingly] Come: the despatches. Quick: I am not to be trifled with now.

LADY [flying round the couch] General—

NAPOLEON. Quick, I tell you. [He passes swiftly up the middle of the room and intercepts her as she makes for the vineyard].

LADY [at bay, confronting him and giving way to her temper] You dare address me in that tone.

NAPOLEON. Dare!

LADY. Yes, dare. Who are you that you should presume to speak to me in that coarse way. Oh, the vile, vulgar Corsican adventurer comes out in you very easily.

NAPOLEON [beside himself] You she devil! [Savagely] Once more, and only once, will you give me those papers or shall I tear them from you?—by force!

LADY. Tear them from me: by force!

As he glares at her like a tiger about to spring, she crosses her arms on her breast in the attitude of a martyr. The gesture and pose instantly awaken his theatrical instinct: he forgets his rage in the desire to shew her that in acting, too, she has met her match. He keeps her a moment in suspense; then suddenly clears up his countenance; puts his hands behind him with provoking coolness; looks at her up and down a couple of times; takes a pinch of snuff; wipes his fingers carefully and puts up his handkerchief, her heroic pose becoming more and more ridiculous all the time.

NAPOLEON [at last] Well?

LADY [disconcerted, but with her arms still crossed devotedly] Well: what are you going to do?

NAPOLEON. Spoil your attitude.

LADY. You brute! [Abandoning the attitude, she comes to the end of the couch, where she turns with her back to it, leaning against it and facing him with her hands behind her].

NAPOLEON. Ah, thats better. Now listen to me. I like you. Whats more, I value your respect.

LADY. You value what you have not got, then.

NAPOLEON. I shall have it presently. Now attend to me. Suppose I were to allow myself to be abashed by the respect due to your sex, your beauty, your heroism and all the rest of it! Suppose I, with nothing but such sentimental stuff to stand between these muscles of mine and those papers which you have about you, and which I want and mean to have! suppose I, with the prize within my grasp, were to falter and sneak away with my hands empty; or, what would be worse, cover up my weakness by playing the magnanimous hero, and sparing you the violence I dared not use! would you not despise me from the depths of your woman's soul? Would any woman be such a fool? Well, Bonaparte can rise to the situation and act like a woman when it is necessary. Do you understand?

The lady, without speaking, stands upright, and takes a packet of papers from her bosom. For a moment she has an intense impulse to dash them in his face. But her good breeding cuts her off from any vulgar method of relief. She hands them to him politely, only averting her head. The moment he takes them, she hurries across to the other side of the room; sits down; and covers her face with her hands.

NAPOLEON [*gloating over the papers*] Aha! Thats right. Thats right. [*Before he opens them, he looks at her and says*] Excuse me. [*He sees that she is hiding her face*]. Very angry with me, eh? [*He unties the packet, the seal of which is already broken, and puts it on the table to examine its contents*].

LADY [*quietly, taking down her hands and shewing that she is not crying, but only thinking*] No. You were right. But I am sorry for you.

NAPOLEON [*pausing in the act of taking the uppermost paper from the packet*] Sorry for me! Why?

LADY. I am going to see you lose your honor.

NAPOLEON. Hm! Nothing worse than that? [*He takes up the paper*].

LADY. And your happiness.

NAPOLEON. Happiness! Happiness is the most tedious thing in the world to me. Should I be what I am if I cared for happiness? Anything else?

LADY. Nothing.

NAPOLEON. Good.

LADY. Except that you will cut a very foolish figure in the eyes of France.

NAPOLEON [*quickly*] What? [*The hand unfolding the paper involuntarily stops. The lady looks at him enigmatically, in tranquil silence. He throws the letter down and breaks out into a torrent of scolding*]. What do you mean? Eh? Are you at your tricks again? Do you think I dont know what these papers contain? I'll tell you. First, my information as to Beaulieu's retreat. There are only two things he can do—leather-brained idiot that he is! —shut himself up in Mantua or violate the neutrality of Venice by taking Peschiera. You are one of old Leatherbrain's spies: he has discovered that he has been betrayed, and has sent you to intercept the information at all hazards. As if that could save him from me, the old fool! The other papers are only my private letters from Paris, of which you know nothing.

LADY [*prompt and businesslike*] General: let us make a fair division. Take the information your spies have sent you about the Austrian army; and give me the Paris correspondence. That will content me.

NAPOLEON [*his breath taken away by the coolness of the proposal*] A fair di— [*he gasps*]. It seems to me, madam, that you have come to regard my letters as your own property, of which I am trying to rob you.

LADY [*earnestly*] No: on my honor I ask for no letter of yours: not a word that has been written by you or to you. That packet contains a stolen letter: a letter written by a woman to a man: a man not her husband: a letter that means disgrace, infamy—

NAPOLEON. A love letter?

LADY [*bitter-sweetly*] What else but a love letter could stir up so much hate?

NAPOLEON. Why is it sent to me? To put the husband in my power, eh?

LADY. No, no: it can be of no use to you: I swear that it will cost you nothing to give it to me. It has been sent to you out of sheer malice: solely to injure the woman who wrote it.

NAPOLEON. Then why not send it to her husband instead of to me?

LADY [*completely taken aback*] Oh! [*Sinking back into the chair*] I—I dont know. [*She breaks down*].

NAPOLEON. Aha! I thought so: a little romance to get the papers back. Per Bacco, I cant help admiring you. I wish I could lie like that. It would save me a great deal of trouble.

LADY [*wringing her hands*] Oh, how *I* wish I really had told you some lie! You would have believed me then. The truth is the one thing nobody will believe.

NAPOLEON [*with coarse familiarity, treating her as if she were a vivandière*] Capital! Capital! [*He puts his hands behind him on the table, and lifts himself on to it, sitting with his arms akimbo and his legs wide apart*] Come: I am a true Corsican in my love for stories. But I could tell them better than you if I set my mind to it. Next time you are asked why a letter compromising a wife should not be sent to her husband, answer simply that the husband wouldnt read it. Do you suppose, you goose, that a man wants to be compelled by public opinion to make a scene, to fight a duel, to break up his household, to injure his career by a scandal, when he can avoid it all by taking care not to know?

LADY [*revolted*] Suppose that packet contained a letter about your own wife?

NAPOLEON [*offended, coming off the table*] You are impertinent, madam.

LADY [*humbly*] I beg your pardon. Cæsar's wife is above suspicion.

NAPOLEON [*with a deliberate assumption of superiority*] You have committed an indiscretion. I pardon you. In future, do not permit yourself to introduce real persons in your romances.

LADY [*politely ignoring a speech which is to her only a breach of good manners*] General: there really is a woman's letter there. [*Pointing to the packet*] Give it to me.

NAPOLEON [*with brute conciseness*] Why?

LADY. She is an old friend: we were at school together. She has written to me imploring me to prevent the letter falling into your hands.

NAPOLEON. Why has it been sent to me?

LADY. Because it compromises the director Barras.

NAPOLEON [*frowning, evidently startled*] Barras! [*Haughtily*] Take care, madam. The director Barras is my attached personal friend.

LADY [*nodding placidly*] Yes. You became friends through your wife.

NAPOLEON. Again! Have I not forbidden you to speak of my wife? [*She keeps looking curiously at him, taking no account of the rebuke. More and more irritated, he drops his haughty manner, of which he is himself somewhat impatient, and says suspiciously, lowering his voice*] Who is this woman with whom you sympathize so deeply?

LADY. Oh, General! How could I tell you that?

NAPOLEON [*ill humoredly, beginning to walk about again in angry perplexity*] Ay, ay: stand by one another. You are all the same, you women.

LADY [*indignantly*] We are not all the same, any more than you are. Do you think that if *I* loved another man, I should pretend to go on loving my husband, or be afraid to tell him or all the world? But this woman is not made that way. She governs men by cheating them; and they like it, and let her govern them. [*She turns her back to him in disdain*].

NAPOLEON [*not attending to her*] Barras? Barras? [*Very threateningly, his face darkening*] Take care. Take care: do you hear? You may go too far.

LADY [*innocently turning her face to him*] Whats the matter?

NAPOLEON. What are you hinting at? Who is this woman?

LADY [*meeting his angry searching gaze with tranquil indifference as she sits looking up at him*] A vain, silly, extravagant creature, with a very able and ambitious husband who knows her through and through: knows that she has lied to him about her age, her income, her social position, about everything that silly women lie about: knows that she is incapable of fidelity to any principle or any person; and yet cannot help loving her—cannot help his man's instinct to make use of her for his own advancement with Barras.

NAPOLEON [*in a stealthy coldly furious whisper*] This is your revenge, you she cat, for having had to give me the letters.

LADY. Nonsense! Or do you mean that you are that sort of man?

NAPOLEON [*exasperated, clasps his hands behind him, his fingers twitching, and says, as he walks irritably away from her to the fireplace*] This woman will drive me out of my senses. [*To her*] Begone.

LADY [*seated immovably*] Not without that letter.

NAPOLEON. Begone, I tell you. [*Walking from the fireplace to the vineyard and back to the table*] You shall have no letter. I dont like you. Youre a detestable woman, and as ugly as Satan. I dont choose to be pestered by strange women. Be off. [*He turns his back on her. In quiet amusement, she leans her cheek on her hand and laughs at him. He turns again, angrily mock-*

ing her]. Ha! ha! ha! What are you laughing at?

LADY. At you, General. I have often seen persons of your sex getting into a pet and behaving like children; but I never saw a really great man do it before.

NAPOLEON [*brutally, flinging the words in her face*] Psha! Flattery! Flattery! Coarse, impudent flattery!

LADY [*springing up with a bright flush in her cheeks*] Oh, you are too bad. Keep your letters. Read the story of your own dishonor in them; and much good may they do you. Goodbye. [*She goes indignantly towards the inner door*].

NAPOLEON. My own—! Stop. Come back. Come back, I order you. [*She proudly disregards his savagely peremptory tone and continues on her way to the door. He rushes at her; seizes her by the arm; and drags her back*]. Now, what do you mean? Explain. Explain, I tell you, or— [*threatening her. She looks at him with unflinching defiance*]. Rrrr! you obstinate devil, you. [*Throwing her arm away*] Why cant you answer a civil question?

LADY [*deeply offended by his violence*] Why do you ask me? You have the explanation.

NAPOLEON. Where?

LADY [*pointing to the letters on the table*] There. You have only to read it.

He snatches the packet up; hesitates; looks at her suspiciously; and throws it down again.

NAPOLEON. You seem to have forgotten your solicitude for the honor of your old friend.

LADY. I do not think she runs any risk now. She does not quite understand her husband.

NAPOLEON. I am to read the letter, then? [*He stretches out his hand as if to take up the packet again, with his eye on her*].

LADY. I do not see how you can very well avoid doing so now. [*He instantly withdraws his hand*]. Oh, dont be afraid. You will find many interesting things in it.

NAPOLEON. For instance?

LADY. For instance, a duel with Barras, a domestic scene, a broken household, a public scandal, a checked career, all sorts of things.

NAPOLEON. Hm! [*He looks at her; takes up the packet and looks at it, pursing his lips and balancing it in his hand; looks at her again; passes the packet into his left hand and puts it behind his back, raising his right to scratch the back of his head as he turns and goes up to the edge of the vineyard, where he stands for a moment looking out into the vines, deep in thought. The Lady watches him in silence, somewhat slightingly. Suddenly he turns and comes back again, full of force and decision*]. I grant your request, madam. Your courage and resolution deserve to succeed. Take the letters for which you have fought so well; and remember henceforth that you found the vile vulgar Corsican adventurer as generous to the vanquished after the battle as he was resolute in the face of the enemy before it. [*He offers her the packet*].

LADY [*without taking it, looking hard at him*] What are you at now, I wonder? [*He dashes the packet furiously to the floor*]. Aha! Ive spoilt that attitude, I think. [*She makes him a pretty mocking curtsey*].

NAPOLEON [*snatching it up again*] Will you take the letters and begone [*advancing and thrusting them upon her*]?

LADY [*escaping round the table*] No: I dont want your letters.

NAPOLEON. Ten minutes ago, nothing else would satisfy you.

LADY [*keeping the table carefully between them*] Ten minutes ago you had not insulted me beyond all bearing.

NAPOLEON. I— [*swallowing his spleen*] I apologize.

LADY [*coolly*] Thanks. [*With forced politeness he offers her the packet across the table. She retreats a step out of its reach and says*] But dont you want to know whether the Austrians are at Mantua or Peschiera?

NAPOLEON. I have already told you that I can conquer my enemies without the aid of spies, madam.

LADY. And the letter? dont you want to read that?

NAPOLEON. You have said that it is not addressed to me. I am not in the habit of reading other people's letters. [*He again offers the packet*].

LADY. In that case there can be no objection to your keeping it. All I wanted was to prevent your reading it. [*Cheerfully*] Good afternoon, General. [*She turns coolly towards the inner door*].

NAPOLEON [*angrily flinging the packet on the couch*] Heaven grant me patience! [*He goes determinedly to the door, and places himself before it*]. Have you any sense of personal danger? Or are you one of those women who like to be beaten black and blue?

LADY. Thank you, General: I have no doubt

the sensation is very voluptuous; but I had rather not. I simply want to go home: thats all. I was wicked enough to steal your despatches; but you have got them back; and you have forgiven me, because [*delicately reproducing his rhetorical cadence*] you are as generous to the vanquished after the battle as you are resolute in the face of the enemy before it. Wont you say goodbye to me? [*She offers her hand sweetly*].

NAPOLEON [*repulsing the advance with a gesture of concentrated rage, and opening the door to call fiercely*] Giuseppe! [*Louder*] Giuseppe! [*He bangs the door to, and comes to the middle of the room. The lady goes a little way into the vineyard to avoid him*].

GIUSEPPE [*appearing at the door*] Excellency?

NAPOLEON. Where is that fool?

GIUSEPPE. He has had a good dinner, according to your instructions, excellency, and is now doing me the honor to gamble with me to pass the time.

NAPOLEON. Send him here. Bring him here. Come with him. [*Giuseppe, with unruffled readiness, hurries off. Napoleon turns curtly to the lady, saying*] I must trouble you to remain some moments longer, madam. [*He comes to the couch*].

She comes from the vineyard along the opposite side of the room to the sideboard, and posts herself there, leaning against it, watching him. He takes the packet from the couch and deliberately buttons it carefully into his breast pocket, looking at her meanwhile with an expression which suggests that she will soon find out the meaning of his proceedings, and will not like it. Nothing more is said until the Lieutenant arrives followed by Giuseppe, who stands modestly in attendance at the table. The Lieutenant, without cap, sword or gloves, and much improved in temper and spirits by his meal, chooses the lady's side of the room, and waits, much at his ease, for Napoleon to begin.

NAPOLEON. Lieutenant.

LIEUTENANT [*encouragingly*] General.

NAPOLEON. I cannot persuade this lady to give me much information; but there can be no doubt that the man who tricked you out of your charge was, as she admitted to you, her brother.

LIEUTENANT [*triumphantly*] What did I tell you, General! What did I tell you!

NAPOLEON. You must find that man. Your honor is at stake; and the fate of the campaign, the destiny of France, of Europe, of humanity, perhaps, may depend on the information those despatches contain.

LIEUTENANT. Yes, I suppose they really are rather serious [*as if this had hardly occurred to him before*].

NAPOLEON [*energetically*] They are so serious, sir, that if you do not recover them, you will be degraded in the presence of your regiment.

LIEUTENANT. Whew! The regiment wont like that, I can tell you.

NAPOLEON. Personally I am sorry for you. I would willingly hush up the affair if it were possible. But I shall be called to account for not acting on the despatches. I shall have to prove to all the world that I never received them, no matter what the consequences may be to you. I am sorry; but you see that I cannot help myself.

LIEUTENANT [*goodnaturedly*] Oh, dont take it to heart, General: it's really very good of you. Never mind what happens to me: I shall scrape through somehow; and we'll beat the Austrians for you, despatches or no despatches. I hope you wont insist on my starting off on a wild goose chase after the fellow now. I havnt a notion where to look for him.

GIUSEPPE [*deferentially*] You forget, Lieutenant: he has your horse.

LIEUTENANT [*starting*] I forgot that. [*Resolutely*] I'll go after him, General: I'll find that horse if it's alive anywhere in Italy. And I shant forget the despatches: never fear. Giuseppe: go and saddle one of those mangy old post-horses of yours while I get my cap and sword and things. Quick march. Off with you [*bustling him*].

GIUSEPPE. Instantly, Lieutenant, instantly [*He disappears in the vineyard, where the light is now reddening with the sunset*].

LIEUTENANT [*looking about him on his way to the inner door*] By the way, General, did I give you my sword or did I not? Oh, I remember now. [*Fretfully*] It's all that nonsense about putting a man under arrest: one never knows where to find— [*he talks himself out of the room*].

LADY [*still at the sideboard*] What does all this mean, General?

NAPOLEON. He will not find your brother.

LADY. Of course not. Theres no such person.

NAPOLEON. The despatches will be irrecoverably lost.

LADY. Nonsense! They are inside your coat.

NAPOLEON. You will find it hard, I think, to

prove that wild statement. [*The lady starts. He adds, with clinching emphasis*] Those papers are lost.

LADY [*anxiously, advancing to the corner of the table*] And that unfortunate young man's career will be sacrificed?

NAPOLEON. His career! The fellow is not worth the gunpowder it would cost to have him shot. [*He turns contemptuously and goes to the hearth, where he stands with his back to her*].

LADY [*wistfully*] You are very hard. Men and women are nothing to you but things to be used, even if they are broken in the use.

NAPOLEON [*turning on her*] Which of us has broken this fellow? I or you? Who tricked him out of the despatches? Did you think of his career then?

LADY [*conscience-stricken*] Oh, I never thought of that. It was wicked of me; but I couldnt help it, could I? How else could I have got the papers? [*Supplicating*] General: you will save him from disgrace.

NAPOLEON [*laughing sourly*] Save him yourself, since you are so clever: it was you who ruined him. [*With savage intensity*] I h a t e a bad soldier.

He goes out determinedly through the vineyard. She follows him a few steps with an appealing gesture, but is interrupted by the return of the Lieutenant, gloved and capped, with his sword on, ready for the road. He is crossing to the outer door when she intercepts him.

LADY. Lieutenant.

LIEUTENANT [*importantly*] You musnt delay me, you know. Duty, madam, duty.

LADY [*imploringly*] Oh, sir, what are you going to do to my poor brother?

LIEUTENANT. Are you very fond of him?

LADY. I should die if anything happened to him. You must spare him. [*The Lieutenant shakes his head gloomily*]. Yes, yes: you must: you shall: he is not fit to die. Listen to me. If I tell you where to find him— if I undertake to place him in your hands a prisoner, to be delivered up by you to General Bonaparte—will you promise me on your honor as an officer and a gentleman not to fight with him or treat him unkindly in any way?

LIEUTENANT. But suppose he attacks me. He has my pistols.

LADY. He is too great a coward.

LIEUTENANT. I dont feel so sure about that. He's capable of anything.

LADY. If he attacks you, or resists you in any way, I release you from your promise.

LIEUTENANT. My promise! I didnt mean to promise. Look here: youre as bad as he is: youve taken an advantage of me through the better side of my nature. What about my horse?

LADY. It is part of the bargain that you are to have your horse and pistols back.

LIEUTENANT. Honor bright?

LADY. Honor bright. [*She offers her hand*].

LIEUTENANT [*taking it and holding it*] All right: I'll be as gentle as a lamb with him. His sister's a very pretty woman. [*He attempts to kiss her*].

LADY [*slipping away from him*] Oh, Lieutenant! You forget: your career is at stake— the destiny of Europe—of humanity.

LIEUTENANT. Oh, bother the destiny of humanity! [*Making for her*] Only a kiss.

LADY [*retreating round the table*] Not until you have regained your honor as an officer. Remember: you have not captured my brother yet.

LIEUTENANT [*seductively*] Youll tell me where he is, wont you?

LADY. I have only to send him a certain signal; and he will be here in quarter of an hour.

LIEUTENANT. He's not far off, then.

LADY. No: quite close. Wait here for him: when he gets my message he will come here at once and surrender himself to you. You understand?

LIEUTENANT [*intellectually overtaxed*] Well, it's a little complicated; but I daresay it will be all right.

LADY. And now, whilst youre waiting, dont you think you had better make terms with the General?

LIEUTENANT. Oh, look here: this is getting frightfully complicated. What terms?

LADY. Make him promise that if you catch my brother he will consider that you have cleared your character as a soldier. He will promise anything you ask on that condition.

LIEUTENANT. Thats not a bad idea. Thank you: I think I'll try it.

LADY. Do. And mind, above all things, dont let him see how clever you are.

LIEUTENANT. I understand. He'd be jealous.

LADY. Dont tell him anything except that you are resolved to capture my brother or perish in the attempt. He wont believe you. Then you will produce my brother—

LIEUTENANT [*interrupting as he masters the plot*] And have the laugh at him! I say: what a jolly clever woman you are! [*Shouting*] Giuseppe!

LADY. Sh! Not a word to Giuseppe about me. [*She puts her finger on her lips. He does the same. They look at one another warningly. Then, with a ravishing smile, she changes the gesture into wafting him a kiss, and runs out through the inner door. Electrified, he bursts into a volley of chuckles*].

Giuseppe comes back by the outer door.

GIUSEPPE. The horse is ready, Lieutenant.

LIEUTENANT. I'm not going just yet. Go and find the General and tell him I want to speak to him.

GIUSEPPE [*shaking his head*] That will never do, Lieutenant.

LIEUTENANT. Why not?

GIUSEPPE. In this wicked world a general may send for a lieutenant; but a lieutenant must not send for a general.

LIEUTENANT. Oh, you think he wouldnt like it. Well, perhaps youre right: one has to be awfully particular about that sort of thing now we're a republic.

Napoleon reappears, advancing from the vineyard, buttoning the breast of his coat, pale and full of gnawing thoughts.

GIUSEPPE [*unconscious of Napoleon's approach*] Quite true, Lieutenant, quite true. You are all like innkeepers now in France: you have to be polite to everybody.

NAPOLEON [*putting his hand on Giuseppe's shoulder*] And that destroys the whole value of politeness, eh?

LIEUTENANT. The very man I wanted! See here, General: suppose I catch that fellow for you!

NAPOLEON [*with ironical gravity*] You will not catch him, my friend.

LIEUTENANT. Aha! you think so; but youll see. Just wait. Only, if I do catch him and hand him over to you, will you cry quits? Will you drop all this about degrading me in the presence of my regiment? Not that *I* mind, you know; but still no regiment likes to have all the other regiments laughing at it.

NAPOLEON [*a cold ray of humor striking pallidly across his gloom*] What shall we do with this officer, Giuseppe? Everything he says is wrong.

GIUSEPPE [*promptly*] Make him a general, excellency; and then everything he says will be right.

LIEUTENANT [*crowing*] Haw-aw! [*He throws himself ecstatically on the couch to enjoy the joke*].

NAPOLEON [*laughing and pinching Giuseppe's ear*] You are thrown away in this inn, Giuseppe. [*He sits down and places Giuseppe before him like a schoolmaster with a pupil*]. Shall I take you away with me and make a man of you?

GIUSEPPE [*shaking his head rapidly and repeatedly*] No no no no no no no. All my life long people have wanted to make a man of me. When I was a boy, our good priest wanted to make a man of me by teaching me to read and write. Then the organist at Melegnano wanted to make a man of me by teaching me to read music. The recruiting sergeant would have made a man of me if I had been a few inches taller. But it always meant making me work; and I am too lazy for that, thank Heaven! So I taught myself to cook and became an innkeeper; and now I keep servants to do the work, and have nothing to do myself except talk, which suits me perfectly.

NAPOLEON [*looking at him thoughtfully*] You are satisfied?

GIUSEPPE [*with cheerful conviction*] Quite, excellency.

NAPOLEON. And you have no devouring devil inside you who must be fed with action and victory: gorged with them night and day: who makes you pay, with the sweat of your brain and body, weeks of Herculean toil for ten minutes of enjoyment: who is at once your slave and your tyrant, your genius and your doom: who brings you a crown in one hand and the oar of a galley slave in the other: who shews you all the kingdoms of the earth and offers to make you their master on condition that you become their servant! have you nothing of that in you?

GIUSEPPE. Nothing of it! Oh, I assure you, excellency, m y devouring devil is far worse than that. He offers me no crowns and kingdoms: he expects to get everything for nothing: sausages! omelettes! grapes! cheese! polenta! wine! three times a day, excellency: nothing less will content him.

LIEUTENANT. Come: drop it, Giuseppe: youre making me feel hungry again.

Giuseppe, with an apologetic shrug, retires from the conversation.

NAPOLEON [*turning to the Lieutenant with sardonic politeness*] I hope *I* have not been making you feel ambitious.

LIEUTENANT. Not at all: I dont fly so high. Besides, I'm better as I am: men like me are wanted in the army just now. The fact is, the Revolution was all very well for civilians;

but it wont work in the army. You know what soldiers are, General: they will have men of family for their officers. A subaltern must be a gentleman, because he's so much in contact with the men. But a general, or even a colonel, may be any sort of riff-raff if he understands his job well enough. A lieutenant is a gentleman: all the rest is chance. Why, who do you suppose won the battle of Lodi? I'll tell you. My horse did.

NAPOLEON [*rising*] Your folly is carrying you too far, sir. Take care.

LIEUTENANT. Not a bit of it. You remember all that red-hot cannonade across the river: the Austrians blazing away at you to keep you from crossing, and you blazing away at them to keep them from setting the bridge on fire? Did you notice where I was then?

NAPOLEON. I am sorry. I am afraid I was rather occupied at the moment.

GIUSEPPE [*with eager admiration*] They say you jumped off your horse and worked the big guns with your own hands, General.

LIEUTENANT. That was a mistake: an officer should never let himself down to the level of his men. [*Napoleon looks at him dangerously, and begins to walk tigerishly to and fro*]. But you might have been firing away at the Austrians still if we cavalry fellows hadnt found the ford and got across and turned old Beaulieu's flank for you. You know you didnt dare give the order to charge the bridge until you saw us on the other side. Consequently, I say that whoever found that ford won the battle of Lodi. Well, who found it? I was the first man to cross; and I know. It was my horse that found it. [*With conviction, as he rises from the couch*] That horse is the true conqueror of the Austrians.

NAPOLEON [*passionately*] You idiot: I'll have you shot for losing those despatches: I'll have you blown from the mouth of a cannon: nothing less could make any impression on you. [*Baying at him*] Do you hear? Do you understand?

A French officer enters unobserved, carrying his sheathed sabre in his hand.

LIEUTENANT [*unabashed*] If I dont capture him, General. Remember the if.

NAPOLEON. If!! Ass: there is no such man.

THE OFFICER [*suddenly stepping between them and speaking in the unmistakeable voice of the Strange Lady*] Lieutenant: I am your prisoner. [*She offers him her sabre*].

Napoleon gazes at her for a moment thunderstruck; then seizes her by the wrist and drags her roughly to him, looking closely and fiercely at her to satisfy himself as to her identity; for it now begins to darken rapidly into night, the red glow over the vineyard giving way to clear starlight.

NAPOLEON. Pah! [*He flings her hand away with an exclamation of disgust, and turns his back on them with his hand in his breast, his brow lowering, and his toes twitching*].

LIEUTENANT [*triumphantly, taking the sabre*] No such man! eh, General? [*To the Lady*] I say: wheres my horse?

LADY. Safe at Borghetto, waiting for you, Lieutenant.

NAPOLEON [*turning on them*] Where are the despatches?

LADY. You would never guess. They are in the most unlikely place in the world. Did you meet my sister here, any of you?

LIEUTENANT. Yes. Very nice woman. She's wonderfully like you; but of course she's better-looking.

LADY [*mysteriously*] Well, do you know that she is a witch?

GIUSEPPE [*in terror, crossing himself*] Oh, no, no, no. It is not safe to jest about such things. I cannot have it in my house, excellency.

LIEUTENANT. Yes, drop it. Youre my prisoner, you know. Of course I dont believe in any such rubbish; but still it's not a proper subject for joking.

LADY. But this is very serious. My sister has bewitched the General. [*Giuseppe and the lieutenant recoil from Napoleon*]. General: open your coat: you will find the despatches in the breast of it. [*She puts her hand quickly on his breast*]. Yes: there they are: I can feel them. Eh? [*She looks up into his face half coaxingly, half mockingly*]. Will you allow me, General? [*She takes a button as if to unbutton his coat, and pauses for permission*].

NAPOLEON [*inscrutably*] If you dare.

LADY. Thank you. [*She opens his coat and takes out the despatches*]. There! [*To Giuseppe, shewing him the despatches*] See!

GIUSEPPE [*flying to the outer door*] No, in heaven's name! Theyre bewitched.

LADY [*turning to the lieutenant*] Here, Lieutenant: you are not afraid of them.

LIEUTENANT [*retreating*] Keep off. [*Seizing the hilt of the sabre*] Keep off, I tell you.

LADY [*to Napoleon*] They belong to you, General. Take them.

GIUSEPPE. Dont touch them, excellency. Have nothing to do with them.

LIEUTENANT. Be careful, General: be careful.

GIUSEPPE. Burn them. And burn the witch too.

LADY [*to Napoleon*] Shall I burn them?

NAPOLEON [*thoughtfully*] Yes, burn them. Giuseppe: go and fetch a light.

GIUSEPPE [*trembling and stammering*] Do you mean go alone? in the dark? with a witch in the house?

NAPOLEON. Psha! Youre a poltroon. [*To the lieutenant*] Oblige me by going, Lieutenant.

LIEUTENANT [*remonstrating*] Oh, I say, General! No, look here, you know: nobody can say I'm a coward after Lodi. But to ask me to go into the dark by myself without a candle after such an awful conversation is a little too much. How would you like to do it yourself?

NAPOLEON [*irritably*] You refuse to obey my order?

LIEUTENANT [*resolutely*] Yes I do. It's not reasonable. But I'll tell you what I'll do. If Giuseppe goes, I'll go with him and protect him.

NAPOLEON [*to Giuseppe*] There! will that satisfy you? Be off, both of you.

GIUSEPPE [*humbly, his lips trembling*] W-willingly, your excellency. [*He goes reluctantly towards the inner door*]. Heaven protect me! [*To the lieutenant*] After you, Lieutenant.

LIEUTENANT. Youd better go first: I dont know the way.

GIUSEPPE. You cant miss it. Besides [*imploringly, laying his hand on his sleeve*] I am only a poor innkeeper: you are a man of family.

LIEUTENANT. Theres something in that. Here: you neednt be in such a fright. Take my arm. [*Giuseppe does so*]. Thats the way. [*They go out, arm in arm*].

It is now starry night. The lady throws the packet on the table and seats herself at her ease on the couch, enjoying the sensation of freedom from petticoats.

LADY. Well, General: Ive beaten you.

NAPOLEON [*walking about*] You are guilty of indelicacy: of unwomanliness. Is that costume proper?

LADY. It seems to me much the same as yours.

NAPOLEON. Psha! I blush for you.

LADY [*naïvely*] Yes: soldiers blush so easily. [*He growls and turns away. She looks mischievously at him, balancing the despatches in her hand*]. Wouldnt you like to read these before theyre burnt, General? You must be dying with curiosity. Take a peep. [*She throws the packet on the table, and turns her face away from it*]. I wont look.

NAPOLEON. I have no curiosity whatever, madam. But since you are evidently burning to read them, I give you leave to do so.

LADY. Oh, Ive read them already.

NAPOLEON [*starting*] What!

LADY. I read them the first thing after I rode away on that poor lieutenant's horse. So you see I know whats in them; and you dont.

NAPOLEON. Excuse me: I read them when I was out there in the vineyard ten minutes ago.

LADY. Oh! [*Jumping up*] Oh, General: Ive not beaten you after all. I do admire you so. [*He laughs and pats her cheek*]. This time, really and truly without shamming, I do you homage [*kissing his hand*].

NAPOLEON [*quickly withdrawing it*] Brr! Dont do that. No more witchcraft.

LADY. I want to say something to you; only you would misunderstand it.

NAPOLEON. Need that stop you?

LADY. Well, it is this. I adore a man who is not afraid to be mean and selfish.

NAPOLEON [*indignantly*] I am neither mean nor selfish.

LADY. Oh, you dont appreciate yourself. Besides, I dont really mean meanness and selfishness.

NAPOLEON. Thank you. I thought perhaps you did.

LADY. Well, of course I do. But what I mean is a certain strong simplicity about you.

NAPOLEON. Thats better.

LADY. You didnt want to read the letters; but you were curious about what was in them. So you went into the garden and read them when no one was looking, and then came back and pretended you hadnt. Thats the meanest thing I ever knew any man do; but it exactly fulfilled your purpose; and so you wernt a bit afraid or ashamed to do it.

NAPOLEON [*abruptly*] Where did you pick up all these vulgar scruples? this [*with contemptuous emphasis*] conscience of yours? I took you for a lady: an aristocrat. Was your grandfather a shopkeeper, pray?

LADY. No: he was an Englishman.

NAPOLEON. That accounts for it. The English are a nation of shopkeepers. Now I understand why youve beaten me.

LADY. Oh, I havnt beaten you. And I'm

not English.

NAPOLEON. Yes you are: English to the backbone. Listen to me: I will explain the English to you.

LADY [eagerly] Do. [With a lively air of anticipating an intellectual treat, she sits down on the couch and composes herself to listen to him. Secure of his audience, he at once nerves himself for a performance. He considers a little before he begins; so as to fix her attention by a moment of suspense. His style is at first modelled on Talma's in Corneille's Cinna; but it is somewhat lost in the darkness, and Talma presently gives way to Napoleon, the voice coming through the gloom with startling intensity].

NAPOLEON. There are three sorts of people in the world: the low people, the middle people, and the high people. The low people and the high people are alike in one thing: they have no scruples, no morality. The low are beneath morality, the high above it. I am not afraid of either of them; for the low are unscrupulous without knowledge, so that they make an idol of me; whilst the high are unscrupulous without purpose, so that they go down before my will. Look you: I shall go over all the mobs and all the courts of Europe as a plough goes over a field. It is the middle people who are dangerous: they have both knowledge and purpose. But they, too, have their weak point. They are full of scruples: chained hand and foot by their morality and respectability.

LADY. Then you will beat the English; for all shopkeepers are middle people.

NAPOLEON. No, because the English are a race apart. No Englishman is too low to have scruples: no Englishman is high enough to be free from their tyranny. But every Englishman is born with a certain miraculous power that makes him master of the world. When he wants a thing, he never tells himself that he wants it. He waits patiently until there comes into his mind, no one knows how, a burning conviction that it is his moral and religious duty to conquer those who possess the thing he wants. Then he becomes irresistible. Like the aristocrat, he does what pleases him and grabs what he covets: like the shopkeeper, he pursues his purpose with the industry and steadfastness that come from strong religious conviction and deep sense of moral responsibility. He is never at a loss for an effective moral attitude. As the great champion of freedom and national independence, he conquers and annexes half the world, and calls it Colonization. When he wants a new market for his adulterated Manchester goods, he sends a missionary to teach the natives the Gospel of Peace. The natives kill the missionary: he flies to arms in defence of Christianity; fights for it; conquers for it; and takes the market as a reward from heaven. In defence of his island shores, he puts a chaplain on board his ship; nails a flag with a cross on it to his top-gallant mast; and sails to the ends of the earth, sinking, burning, and destroying all who dispute the empire of the seas with him. He boasts that a slave is free the moment his foot touches British soil; and he sells the children of his poor at six years of age to work under the lash in his factories for sixteen hours a day. He makes two revolutions, and then declares war on our one in the name of law and order. There is nothing so bad or so good that you will not find Englishmen doing it; but you will never find an Englishman in the wrong. He does everything on principle. He fights you on patriotic principles; he robs you on business principles; he enslaves you on imperial principles; he bullies you on manly principles; he supports his king on loyal principles and cuts off his king's head on republican principles. His watchword is always Duty; and he never forgets that the nation which lets its duty get on the opposite side to its interest is lost. He—

LADY. W-w-w-w-w-wh! Do stop a moment. I want to know how you make me out to be English at this rate.

NAPOLEON [dropping his rhetorical style] It's plain enough. You wanted some letters that belonged to me. You have spent the morning in stealing them: yes, stealing them, by highway robbery. And you have spent the afternoon in putting me in the wrong about them: in assuming that it was I who wanted to steal your letters: in explaining that it all came about through my meanness and selfishness, and your goodness, your devotion, your self-sacrifice. Thats English.

LADY. Nonsense! I am sure I am not a bit English. The English are a very stupid people.

NAPOLEON. Yes, too stupid sometimes to know when theyre beaten. But I grant that your brains are not English. You see, though your grandfather was an Englishman, your grandmother was—what? A Frenchwoman?

LADY. Oh no. An Irishwoman.

NAPOLEON [*quickly*] Irish! [*Thoughtfully*] Yes: I forgot the Irish. An English army led by an Irish general: that might be a match for a French army led by an Italian general. [*He pauses, and adds, half jestingly, half moodily*] At all events, you have beaten me; and what beats a man first will beat him last. [*He goes meditatively into the moonlit vineyard and looks up*].

She steals out after him. She ventures to rest her hand on his shoulder, overcome by the beauty of the night and emboldened by its obscurity.

LADY [*softly*] What are you looking at?

NAPOLEON [*pointing up*] My star.

LADY. You believe in that?

NAPOLEON. I do.

They look at it for a moment, she leaning a little on his shoulder.

LADY. Do you know that the English say that a man's star is not complete without a woman's garter?

NAPOLEON [*scandalized: abruptly shaking her off and coming back into the room*] Pah! The hypocrites! If the French said that, how they would hold up their hands in pious horror! [*He goes to the inner door and holds it open, shouting*] Hallo! Giuseppe! Wheres that light, man? [*He comes between the table and the sideboard, and moves the second chair to the table, beside his own*]. We have still to burn the letter. [*He takes up the packet*].

Giuseppe comes back, pale and still trembling, carrying in one hand a branched candlestick with a couple of candles alight, and a broad snuffers tray in the other.

GIUSEPPE [*piteously, as he places the light on the table*] Excellency: what were you looking up at just now? Out there! [*He points across his shoulder to the vineyard, but is afraid to look round*].

NAPOLEON [*unfolding the packet*] What is that to you?

GIUSEPPE. Because the witch is gone: vanished; and no one saw her go out.

LADY [*coming behind him from the vineyard*] We were watching her riding up to the moon on your broomstick, Giuseppe. You will never see her again.

GIUSEPPE. Gesu Maria! [*He crosses himself and hurries out*].

NAPOLEON [*throwing down the letters in a heap on the table*] Now! [*He sits down at the table in the chair which he has just placed*].

LADY. Yes; but you know you have THE letter in your pocket. [*He smiles; takes a letter from his pocket; and tosses it on top of the heap. She holds it up and looks at him, saying*] About Cæsar's wife.

NAPOLEON. Cæsar's wife is above suspicion. Burn it.

LADY [*taking up the snuffers and holding the letter to the candle flame with it*] I wonder would Cæsar's wife be above suspicion if she saw us here together!

NAPOLEON [*echoing her, with his elbows on the table and his cheeks on his hands, looking at the letter*] I wonder!

The Strange Lady puts the letter down alight on the snuffers tray, and sits down beside Napoleon, in the same attitude, elbows on table, cheeks on hands, watching it burn. When it is burnt, they simultaneously turn their eyes and look at one another. The curtain steals down and hides them.

THE END

VII
YOU NEVER CAN TELL
1897
BEING THE FOURTH OF FOUR PLEASANT PLAYS

ACT I

In a dentist's operating room on a fine August morning in 1896. It is the best sitting room of a furnished lodging in a terrace on the sea front at a watering place on the coast of Torbay in Devon. The operating chair, with a gas pump and cylinder beside it, is half way between the centre of the room and one of the corners. If you could look into the room through the window facing the chair, you would see the fireplace in the middle of the wall opposite you, with the door beside it to your left, a dental surgeon's diploma in a frame above the mantelshelf, an easy chair on the hearth, and a neat stool and bench, with vice, tools, and a mortar and pestle, in the corner to the right. In the wall on your left is a broad window looking on the sea. Beneath it a writing table with a blotter and a diary on it, and a chair. Also a sofa, farther along. A cabinet of instruments is handy to the operating chair. The furniture, carpet, and wallpaper are those of a mid-Victorian drawing room, formally bright and festive, not for everyday use.

Two persons just now occupy the room. One of them, a very pretty woman in miniature, her tiny figure dressed with the daintest gaiety, is hardly eighteen yet. This darling little creature clearly does not belong to the room, or even to the country; for her complexion, though very delicate, has been burnt biscuit color by some warmer sun than England's. She has a glass of water in her hand, and a rapidly clearing cloud of Spartan endurance on her small firm set mouth and quaintly squared eyebrows.

The dentist, contemplating her with the self-satisfaction of a successful operator, is a young man of thirty or thereabouts. He does not give the impression of being much of a workman: the professional manner of the newly set-up dentist in search of patients is underlain by a thoughtless pleasantry which betrays the young gentleman, still unsettled and in search of amusing adventures. He is not without gravity of demeanor; but the strained nostrils stamp it as the gravity of the humorist. His eyes are clear, alert, of sceptically moderate size, and yet a little rash; his forehead is an excellent one, with plenty of room behind it; his nose and chin are cavalierly handsome. On the whole, an attractive noticeable beginner, of whose prospects a man of business might form a tolerably favorable estimate.

THE YOUNG LADY [*handing him the glass*] Thank you. [*In spite of the biscuit complexion she has not the slightest foreign accent*].

THE DENTIST [*putting it down on the ledge of his cabinet of instruments*] That was my first tooth.

THE YOUNG LADY [*aghast*] Your first! Do you mean to say that you began practising on me?

THE DENTIST. Every dentist has to begin with somebody.

THE YOUNG LADY. Yes: somebody in a hospital, not people who pay.

THE DENTIST [*laughing*] Oh, the hospital doesnt count. I only meant my first tooth in private practice. Why didnt you let me give you gas?

THE YOUNG LADY. Because you said it

would be five shillings extra.

THE DENTIST [*shocked*] Oh, dont say that. It makes me feel as if I had hurt you for the sake of five shillings.

THE YOUNG LADY [*with cool insolence*] Well, so you have. [*She gets up*]. Why shouldnt you? it's your business to hurt people. [*It amuses him to be treated in this fashion: he chuckles secretly as he proceeds to clean and replace his instruments. She shakes her dress into order: looks inquisitively about her; and goes to the broad window*]. You h a v e a good view of the sea from your rooms! Are they expensive?

THE DENTIST. Yes.

THE YOUNG LADY. You dont own the whole house, do you?

THE DENTIST. No.

THE YOUNG LADY. I thought not. [*Tilting the chair which stands at the writing-table and looking critically at it as she spins it round on one leg*] Your furniture isnt quite the latest thing, is it?

THE DENTIST. It's my landlord's.

THE YOUNG LADY. Does he own that toothache chair? [*pointing to the operating chair*].

THE DENTIST. No: I have that on the hire-purchase system.

THE YOUNG LADY [*disparagingly*] I thought so. [*Looking about in search of further conclusions*] I suppose you havnt been here long?

THE DENTIST. Six weeks. Is there anything else you would like to know?

THE YOUNG LADY [*the hint quite lost on her*] Any family?

THE DENTIST. I am not married.

THE YOUNG LADY. Of course not: anybody can see that. I meant sisters and mother and that sort of thing.

THE DENTIST. Not on the premises.

THE YOUNG LADY. Hm! If youve been here six weeks, and mine was your first tooth, the practice cant be very large, can it?

THE DENTIST. Not as yet. [*He shuts the cabinet, having tidied up everything*].

THE YOUNG LADY. Well, good luck! [*She takes out her purse*]. Five shillings, you said it would be?

THE DENTIST. Five shillings.

THE YOUNG LADY [*producing a crown piece*] Do you charge five shillings for everything?

THE DENTIST. Yes.

THE YOUNG LADY. Why?

THE DENTIST. It's my system. I'm whats called a five shilling dentist.

THE YOUNG LADY. How nice! Well, here!

[*holding up the crown piece*] a nice new five-shilling piece! your first fee! Make a hole in it with the thing you drill people's teeth with; and wear it on your watch-chain.

THE DENTIST. Thank you.

THE PARLOR MAID [*appearing at the door*] The young lady's brother, sir.

A handsome man in miniature, obviously the young lady's twin, comes in eagerly. He wears a suit of terra cotta cashmere, the elegantly cut frock coat lined in brown silk, and carries in his hand a brown tall hat and tan gloves to match. He has his sister's delicate biscuit complexion, and is built on the same small scale; but he is elastic and strong in muscle, decisive in movement, unexpectedly deeptoned and trenchant in speech, and with perfect manners and a finished personal style which might be envied by a man twice his age. Suavity and self-possession are points of honor with him; and though this, rightly considered, is only a mode of boyish self-consciousness, its effect is none the less staggering to his elders, and would be quite insufferable in a less prepossessing youth. He is promptitude itself, and has a question ready the moment he enters.

THE YOUNG GENTLEMAN. Am I in time?

THE YOUNG LADY. No: it's all over.

THE YOUNG GENTLEMAN. Did you howl?

THE YOUNG LADY. Oh, something awful. Mr Valentine: this is my brother Phil. Phil: this is Mr Valentine, our new dentist. [*Valentine and Phil bow to one another. She proceeds, all in one breath*] He's only been here six weeks and he's a bachelor the house isnt his and the furniture is the landlord's but the professional plant is hired he got my tooth out beautifully at the first go and he and I are great friends.

PHILIP. Been asking a lot of questions?

THE YOUNG LADY [*as if incapable of doing such a thing*] Oh no.

PHILIP. Glad to hear it. [*To Valentine*] So good of you not to mind us, Mr Valentine. The fact is, weve never been in England before; and our mother tells us that the people here simply wont stand us. Come and lunch with us.

Valentine, bewildered by the leaps and bounds with which their acquaintanceship is proceeding, gasps, but has no time to reply, as the conversation of the twins is swift and continuous.

THE YOUNG LADY. Oh, do, Mr Valentine.

PHILIP. At the Marine Hotel: half past one.

THE YOUNG LADY. We shall be able to tell mamma that a respectable Englishman has promised to lunch with us.

PHILIP. Say no more, Mr Valentine: youll come.

VALENTINE. Say no more! I havnt said anything. May I ask whom I have the pleasure of entertaining? It's really quite impossible for me to lunch at the Marine Hotel with two perfect strangers.

THE YOUNG LADY [*flippantly*] Ooooh! what bosh! One patient in six weeks! What difference does it make to you?

PHILIP [*maturely*] No, Dolly: my knowledge of human nature confirms Mr Valentine's judgment. He is right. Let me introduce Miss Dorothy Clandon, commonly called Dolly. [*Valentine bows to Dolly. She nods to him*]. I'm Philip Clandon. We're from Madeira, but perfectly respectable, so far.

VALENTINE. Clandon! Are you related to—

DOLLY [*unexpectedly crying out in despair*] Yes we are.

VALENTINE [*astonished*] I beg your pardon?

DOLLY. Oh, we are, we are. It's all over, Phil: they know all about us in England. [*To Valentine*] Oh, you cant think how maddening it is to be related to a celebrated person, and never be valued anywhere for our own sakes.

VALENTINE. But excuse me: the gentleman I was thinking of is not celebrated.

DOLLY AND PHILIP [*staring at him*] Gentleman!

VALENTINE. Yes. I was going to ask whether you were by any chance a daughter of Mr Densmore Clandon of Newbury Hall.

DOLLY [*vacantly*] No.

PHILIP. Well, come, Dolly: how do you know youre not?

DOLLY [*cheered*] Oh, I forgot. Of course. Perhaps I am.

VALENTINE. Dont you know?

PHILIP. Not in the least.

DOLLY. It's a wise child—

PHILIP [*cutting her short*] Sh! [*Valentine starts nervously; for the sound made by Phil, though but momentary, is like cutting a sheet of silk in two with a flash of lightning. It is the result of long practice in checking Dolly's indiscretions*]. The fact is, Mr Valentine, we are the children of the celebrated Mrs Lanfrey Clandon, an authoress of great repute—in Madeira. No household is complete without her works. We came to England to get away from them. They are called the Twentieth Century Treatises.

DOLLY. Twentieth Century Cooking.

PHILIP. Twentieth Century Creeds.

DOLLY. Twentieth Century Clothing.

PHILIP. Twentieth Century Conduct.

DOLLY. Twentieth Century Children.

PHILIP. Twentieth Century Parents.

DOLLY. Cloth limp, half a dollar.

PHILIP. Or mounted on linen for hard family use, two dollars. No family should be without them. Read them, Mr Valentine: theyll improve your mind.

DOLLY. But not till weve gone, please.

PHILIP. Quite so: we prefer people with unimproved minds. Our own minds have successfully resisted all our mother's efforts to improve them.

VALENTINE [dubiously] Hm!

DOLLY [echoing him inquiringly] Hm? Phil: he prefers people whose minds are improved.

PHILIP. In that case we shall have to introduce him to the other member of the family: the Woman of the Twentieth Century: our sister Gloria!

DOLLY [dithyrambically] Nature's masterpiece!

PHILIP. Learning's daughter!

DOLLY. Madeira's pride!

PHILIP. Beauty's paragon!

DOLLY [suddenly descending to prose] Bosh! No complexion.

VALENTINE [desperately] May I have a word?

PHILIP [politely] Excuse us. Go ahead.

DOLLY [very nicely] So sorry.

VALENTINE [attempting to take them paternally] I really must give a hint to you young people—

DOLLY [breaking out again] Oh come! I like that. How old are you?

PHILIP. Over thirty.

DOLLY. He's not.

PHILIP [confidently] He is.

DOLLY [emphatically] Twenty-seven.

PHILIP [imperturbably] Thirty-three.

DOLLY. Stuff.

PHILIP [to Valentine] I appeal to you, Mr Valentine.

VALENTINE [remonstrating] Well, really— [resigning himself] Thirty-one.

PHILIP [to Dolly] You were wrong.

DOLLY. So were you.

PHILIP [suddenly conscientious] We're forgetting our manners, Dolly.

DOLLY [remorseful] Yes, so we are.

PHILIP [apologetic] We interrupted you, Mr Valentine.

DOLLY. You were going to improve our minds, I think.

VALENTINE. The fact is, your—

PHILIP [anticipating him] Our manners?

DOLLY. Our appearance?

VALENTINE [ad misericordiam] Oh do let me speak.

DOLLY. The old story. We talk too much.

PHILIP. We do. Shut up, both. [He seats himself on the arm of the operating chair].

DOLLY. Mum! [She sits down in the writing-table chair, and closes her lips with the tips of her fingers].

VALENTINE. Thank you. [He brings the stool from the bench in the corner; places it between them; and sits down with a judicial air. They attend to him with extreme gravity. He addresses himself first to Dolly]. Now may I ask, to begin with, have you ever been in an English seaside resort before? [She shakes her head slowly and solemnly. He turns to Phil, who shakes his head quickly and expressively]. I thought so. Well, Mr Clandon, our acquaintance has been short; but it has been voluble; and I have gathered enough to convince me that you are neither of you capable of conceiving what life in an English seaside resort is. Believe me, it's not a question of manners and appearance. In those respects we enjoy a freedom unknown in Madeira. [Dolly shakes her head vehemently]. Oh yes, I assure you. Lord de Cresci's sister bicycles in knickerbockers; and the rector's wife advocates dress reform and wears hygienic boots. [Dolly furtively looks at her own shoe: Valentine catches her in the act, and deftly adds] No, thats not the sort of boot I mean. [Dolly's shoe vanishes]. We dont bother much about dress and manners in England, because, as a nation, we dont dress well and weve no manners. But—and now will you excuse my frankness? [They nod]. Thank you. Well, in a seaside resort theres one thing you must have before anybody can afford to be seen going about with you; and thats a father, alive or dead. Am I to infer that you have omitted that indispensable part of your social equipment? [They confirm him by melancholy nods]. Then I'm sorry to say that if you are going to stay here for any length of time, it will be impossible for me to accept your kind invitation to lunch. [He rises with an air of finality, and replaces the stool by the bench].

PHILIP [rising with grave politeness] Come, Dolly. [He gives her his arm].

DOLLY. Good morning. [*They go together to the door with perfect dignity*].

VALENTINE [*overwhelmed with remorse*] Oh stop! stop! [*They halt and turn, arm in arm*]. You make me feel a perfect beast.

DOLLY. Thats your conscience: not us.

VALENTINE [*energetically, throwing off all pretence of a professional manner*] My conscience! My conscience has been my ruin. Listen to me. Twice before I have set up as a respectable medical practitioner in various parts of England. On both occasions I acted conscientiously, and told my patients the brute truth instead of what they wanted to be told. Result, ruin. Now Ive set up as a dentist, a five shilling dentist; and Ive done with conscience for ever. This is my last chance. I spent my last sovereign on moving in; and I havnt paid a shilling of rent yet. I'm eating and drinking on credit; my landlord is as rich as a Jew and as hard as nails; and Ive made five shillings in six weeks. If I swerve by a hair's breadth from the straight line of the most rigid respectability, I'm done for. Under such circumstances is it fair to ask me to lunch with you when you dont know your own father?

DOLLY. After all, our grandfather is a canon of Lincoln Cathedral.

VALENTINE [*like a castaway mariner who sees a sail on the horizon*] What! Have you a grandfather?

DOLLY. Only one.

VALENTINE. My dear good young friends, why on earth didnt you tell me that before? A canon of Lincoln! That makes it all right, of course. Just excuse me while I change my coat. [*He reaches the door in a bound and vanishes*].

Dolly and Phil stare after him, and then at one another. Missing their audience, they discard their style at once.

PHILIP [*throwing away Dolly's arm and coming ill-humoredly towards the operating chair*] That wretched bankrupt ivory snatcher makes a compliment of allowing us to stand him a lunch: probably the first square meal he has had for months. [*He gives the chair a kick, as if it were Valentine*].

DOLLY. It's too beastly. I wont stand it any longer, Phil. Here in England everybody asks whether you have a father the very first thing.

PHILIP. I wont stand it either. Mamma must tell us who he was.

DOLLY. Or who he is. He may be alive.

PHILIP. I hope not. No man alive shall father me.

DOLLY. He might have a lot of money, though.

PHILIP. I doubt it. My knowledge of human nature leads me to believe that if he had a lot of money he wouldnt have got rid of his affectionate family so easily. Anyhow, let's look at the bright side of things. Depend on it, he's dead.

He goes to the hearth and stands with his back to the fireplace. The parlormaid appears.

THE PARLORMAID. Two ladies for you, miss. Your mother and sister, miss, I think.

Mrs Clandon and Gloria come in. Mrs Clandon is a veteran of the Old Guard of the Women's Rights movement which had for its Bible John Stuart Mill's treatise on The Subjection of Women. She has never made herself ugly or ridiculous by affecting masculine waistcoats, collars, and watchchains, like some of her old comrades who had more aggressiveness than taste; and she is too militant an Agnostic to care to be mistaken for a Quaker. She therefore dresses in as businesslike a way as she can without making a guy of herself, ruling out all attempt at sex attraction and imposing respect on frivolous mankind and fashionable womankind. She belongs to the forefront of her own period (say 1860-80) in a jealously assertive attitude of character and intellect, and in being a woman of cultivated interests rather than passionately developed personal affections. Her voice and ways are entirely kindly and humane; and she lends herself conscientiously to the occasional demonstrations of fondness by which her children mark their esteem for her; but displays of personal sentiment secretly embarrass her: passion in her is humanitarian rather than human: she feels strongly about social questions and principles, not about persons. Only, one observes that this reasonableness and intense personal privacy, which leaves her relations with Gloria and Phil much as they might be between her and the children of any other woman, breaks down in the case of Dolly. Though almost every word she addresses to her is necessarily in the nature of a remonstrance for some breach of decorum, the tenderness in her voice is unmistakeable; and it is not surprising that years of such remonstrance have left Dolly hopelessly spoiled.

Gloria, who is hardly past twenty, is a much more formidable person than her mother. She is the incarnation of haughty highmindedness, rag-

ing with the impatience of a mettlesome domina-tive character paralyzed by the inexperience of her youth, and unwillingly disciplined by the con-stant danger of ridicule from her irreverent juniors. Unlike her mother, she is all passion; and the conflict of her passion with her obstinate pride and intense fastidiousness results in a freez-ing coldness of manner. In an ugly woman all this would be repulsive; but Gloria is attractive. A dangerous girl, one would say, if the moral passions were not also marked, and even nobly marked, in a fine brow. Her tailormade skirt-and-jacket dress, of saffron brown cloth, seems con-ventional when her back is turned; but it displays in front a blouse of sea-green silk which scatters its conventionality with one stroke, and sets her apart as effectually as the twins from the ordin-ary run of fashionable seaside humanity.

Mrs Clandon comes a little way into the room looking round to see who is present. Gloria, who studiously avoids encouraging the twins by be-traying any interest in them, wanders to the window and looks out to sea with her thoughts far away. The parlormaid, instead of withdrawing, shuts the door and waits at it.

MRS CLANDON. Well, children? How is the toothache, Dolly?

DOLLY. Cured, thank Heaven. Ive had it out. [*She sits down on the step of the operating chair*].

Mrs Clandon takes the writing-table chair.

PHILIP [*striking in gravely from the hearth*] And the dentist, a first rate professional man of the highest standing, is coming to lunch with us.

MRS CLANDON [*looking round apprehensively at the servant*] Phil!

THE PARLORMAID. Beg pardon, maam. I'm waiting for Mr Valentine. I have a message for him.

DOLLY. Who from?

MRS CLANDON [*shocked*] Dolly!

Dolly catches her lips suppressively with her finger tips.

THE PARLORMAID. Only the landlord, maam.

Valentine, in a blue serge suit, with a straw hat in his hand, comes back in high spirits, out of breath with the haste he has made. Gloria turns from the window and studies him with chilling attention.

PHILIP. Let me introduce you, Mr Valen-tine. My mother, Mrs Lanfrey Clandon. [*Mrs Clandon bows. Valentine bows, self-possessed and quite equal to the occasion*]. My sister Gloria. [*Gloria bows with cold dignity and sits down on the sofa*].

Valentine falls abjectly in love at first sight. He fingers his hat nervously, and makes her a sneaking bow.

MRS CLANDON. I understand that we are to have the pleasure of seeing you at luncheon today, Mr Valentine.

VALENTINE. Thank you—er—if you dont mind—I mean if you will be so kind— [*to the parlormaid, testily*] What is it?

THE PARLORMAID. The landlord, sir, wishes to speak to you before you go out.

VALENTINE. Oh, tell him I have four patients here. [*The Clandons look surprised, except Phil, who is imperturbable*]. If he wouldnt mind waiting just two minutes, I—I'll slip down and see him for a moment. [*Throwing himself confidentially on her sense of the position*] Say I'm busy, but that I w a n t to see him.

THE PARLORMAID [*reassuringly*] Yes, sir. [*She goes*].

MRS CLANDON [*on the point of rising*] We are detaining you, I am afraid.

VALENTINE. Not at all, not at all. Your presence here will be the greatest help to me. The fact is, I owe six weeks rent; and Ive had no patients until today. My inter-view with my landlord will be considerably smoothed by the apparent boom in my business.

DOLLY [*vexed*] Oh, how tiresome of you to let it all out! And weve just been pretending that you were a respectable professional man in a first rate position.

MRS CLANDON [*horrified*] Oh Dolly! D o l l y! My dearest: how can you be so rude? [*To Valentine*] Will you excuse these barbarian children of mine, Mr Valentine?

VALENTINE. Dont mention it: I'm used to them. Would it be too much to ask you to wait five minutes while I get rid of my land-lord downstairs?

DOLLY. Dont be long. We're hungry.

MRS CLANDON [*again remonstrating*] Dolly, d e a r!

VALENTINE [*to Dolly*] All right. [*To Mrs Clandon*] Thank you: I shant be long. [*He steals a look at Gloria as he turns to go. She is looking gravely at him. He falls into confusion*]. I—er—er—yes—thank you [*he succeeds at last in blundering himself out of the room; but the exhibition is a pitiful one*].

PHILIP. Did you observe? [*Pointing to Gloria*] Love at first sight. Another scalp for your collection, Gloria. Number fifteen.

MRS CLANDON. Sh—sh pray, Phil. He may have heard you.

PHILIP. Not he. [*Bracing himself for a scene*] And now look here, mamma. [*He takes the stool from the bench; and seats himself majestically in the middle of the room, copying Valentine's recent demonstration. Dolly, feeling that her position on the step of the operating chair is unworthy the dignity of the occasion, rises, looking important and uncompromising. She crosses to the window, and stands with her back to the end of the writing-table, her hands behind her and on the table. Mrs Clandon looks at them, wondering what is coming. Gloria becomes attentive. Phil straightens his back; places his knuckles symmetrically on his knees; and opens his case*]. Dolly and I have been talking over things a good deal lately; and I dont think, judging from my knowledge of human nature—we dont think that you [*speaking very pointedly, with the words detached*] quite. Appreciate. The fact—

DOLLY [*seating herself on the end of the table with a spring*] That weve grown up.

MRS CLANDON. Indeed? In what way have I given you any reason to complain?

PHILIP. Well, there are certain matters upon which we are beginning to feel that you might take us a little more into your confidence.

MRS CLANDON [*rising, with all the placidity of her age suddenly breaking up into a curious hard excitement, dignified but dogged, ladylike but implacable: the manner of the Old Guard*] Phil: take care. What have I always taught you? There are two sorts of family life, Phil; and your experience of human nature only extends, so far, to one of them. [*Rhetorically*] The sort you know is based on mutual respect, on recognition of the right of every member of the household to independence and privacy [*her emphasis on "privacy" is intense*] in their personal concerns. And because you have always enjoyed that, it seems such a matter of course to you that you dont value it. But [*with biting acrimony*] there is another sort of family life: a life in which husbands open their wives' letters, and call on them to account for every farthing of their expenditure and every moment of their time; in which women do the same to their children; in which no room is private and no hour sacred; in which duty, obedience, affection, home, morality and religion are detestable tyrannies, and life is a vulgar round of punishments and lies, coercion and rebellion, jealousy, suspicion, recrimination—Oh! I cannot describe it to you: fortunately for you, you know nothing about it. [*She sits down, panting*].

DOLLY [*inaccessible to rhetoric*] See Twentieth Century Parents, chapter on Liberty, passim.

MRS CLANDON [*touching her shoulder affectionately, softened even by a gibe from her*] My dear Dolly: if you only knew how glad I am that it is nothing but a joke to you, though it is such bitter earnest to me. [*More resolutely, turning to Phil*] Phil: I never ask you questions about your private concerns. You are not going to question me, are you?

PHILIP. I think it due to ourselves to say that the question we wanted to ask is as much our business as yours.

DOLLY. Besides, it cant be good to keep a lot of questions bottled up inside you. You did it, mamma; but see how awfully it's broken out again in me.

MRS CLANDON. I see you want to ask your question. Ask it.

DOLLY AND PHILIP [*beginning simultaneously*] Who— [*They stop*].

PHILIP. Now look here, Dolly: am I going to conduct this business or are you?

DOLLY. You.

PHILIP. Then hold your mouth. [*Dolly does so, literally*]. The question is a simple one. When the ivory snatcher—

MRS CLANDON [*remonstrating*] Phil!

PHILIP. Dentist is an ugly word. The man of ivory and gold asked us whether we were the children of Mr Densmore Clandon of Newbury Hall. In pursuance of the precepts in your treatise on Twentieth Century Conduct, and your repeated personal exhortations to us to curtail the number of unnecessary lies we tell, we replied truthfully that we didnt know.

DOLLY. Neither did we.

PHILIP. Sh! The result was that the gum architect made considerable difficulties about accepting our invitation to lunch, although I doubt if he has had anything but tea and bread and butter for a fortnight past. Now my knowledge of human nature leads me to believe that we had a father, and that you probably know who he was.

MRS CLANDON [*her agitation returning*] Stop, Phil. Your father is nothing ᴏ you, nor to me. [*Vehemently*] That is enough.

The twins are silenced, but not satisfied.

Their faces fall. But Gloria, who has been following the altercation attentively, suddenly intervenes.

GLORIA [*advancing*] Mother: we have a right to know.

MRS CLANDON [*rising and facing her*] Gloria! "We"! Who is "we"?

GLORIA [*steadfastly*] We three. [*Her tone is unmistakeable: she is pitting her strength against her mother's for the first time. The twins instantly go over to the enemy*].

MRS CLANDON [*wounded*] In your mouth "we" used to mean you and I, Gloria.

PHILIP [*rising decisively and putting away the stool*] We're hurting you: let's drop it. We didnt think youd mind. *I* dont want to know.

DOLLY [*coming off the table*] I'm sure *I* dont. Oh, dont look like that, mamma. [*She looks angrily at Gloria and flings her arms round her mother's neck*].

MRS CLANDON. Thank you, my dear. Thanks, Phil. [*She detaches Dolly gently and sits down again*].

GLORIA [*inexorably*] We have a right to know, mother.

MRS CLANDON [*indignantly*] Ah! You insist.

GLORIA. Do you intend that we shall never know?

DOLLY. Oh Gloria, dont. It's barbarous.

GLORIA [*with quiet scorn*] What is the use of being weak? You see what has happened with this gentleman here, mother. The same thing has happened to me.

MRS CLANDON ⎫   ⎧ What do you
                        ⎪   ⎪   mean?
DOLLY   ⎬ [*all*   ⎨ Oh, tell us!
                        ⎪ *together*] ⎪ What happened
PHILIP   ⎭   ⎩   to you?

GLORIA. Oh, nothing of any consequence. [*She turns away from them and strolls up to the easy chair at the fireplace, where she sits down, almost with her back to them. As they wait expectantly, she adds, over her shoulder, with studied indifference*] On board the steamer, the first officer did me the honor to propose to me.

DOLLY. No: it was to me.

MRS CLANDON. The first officer! Are you serious, Gloria? What did you say to him? [*Correcting herself*] Excuse me: I have no right to ask that.

GLORIA. The answer is pretty obvious. A woman who does not know who her father was cannot accept such an offer.

MRS CLANDON. Surely you did not want to accept it!

GLORIA [*turning a little and raising her voice*] No; but suppose I had wanted to!

PHILIP. Did that difficulty strike you, Dolly?

DOLLY. No. I accepted him.

GLORIA   ⎫   ⎧ Accepted him!
MRS CLANDON ⎬ [*all*   ⎨ Dolly!
PHILIP   ⎭ *crying out* ⎩ Oh, I say!
              together]

DOLLY [*naïvely*] He did look such a fool!

MRS CLANDON. But why did you do such a thing, Dolly?

DOLLY. For fun, I suppose. He had to measure my finger for a ring. Youd have done the same thing yourself.

MRS CLANDON. No, Dolly, I would not. As a matter of fact the first officer did propose to me; and I told him to keep that sort of thing for women who were young enough to be amused by it. He appears to have acted on my advice. [*She rises and goes to the hearth*]. Gloria: I am sorry you think me weak; but I cannot tell you what you want. You are all too young.

PHILIP. This is rather a startling departure from Twentieth Century principles.

DOLLY [*quoting*] "Answer all your children's questions, and answer them truthfully, as soon as they are old enough to ask them." See Twentieth Century Motherhood—

PHILIP. Page one.

DOLLY. Chapter one.

PHILIP. Sentence one.

MRS CLANDON. My dears: I do not mean that you are too young to know. I mean that you are too young to be taken into my confidence. You are very bright children, all of you; but you are still very inexperienced and consequently sometimes very unsympathetic. There are experiences of mine that I cannot bear to speak of except to those who have gone through what I have gone through. I hope you will never be qualified for such confidences.

PHILIP. Another grievance, Dolly!

DOLLY. We're not sympathetic.

GLORIA [*leaning forward in her chair and looking earnestly up at her mother*] Mother: I did not mean to be unsympathetic.

MRS CLANDON [*affectionately*] Of course not, dear. I quite understand!

GLORIA [*rising*] But, mother—

MRS CLANDON [*drawing back a little*] Yes?

GLORIA [*obstinately*] It is nonsense to tell us that our father is nothing to us.

MRS CLANDON [*provoked to sudden resolution*]

Do you remember your father?

GLORIA [*meditatively, as if the recollection were a tender one*] I am not quite sure. I think so.

MRS CLANDON [*grimly*] You are not sure?

GLORIA. No.

MRS CLANDON [*with quiet force*] Gloria: if I had ever s t r u c k you [*Gloria recoils: Phil and Dolly are disagreeably shocked: all three stare at her, revolted, as she continues mercilessly*]—struck you purposely, deliberately, with the intention of hurting you, with a whip bought for the purpose! would you remember that, do you think? [*Gloria utters an exclamation of indignant repulsion*]. That would have been your last recollection of your father, Gloria, if I had not taken you away from him. I have kept him out of your life: keep him now out of mine by never mentioning him to me again.

Gloria, with a shudder, covers her face with her hands until, hearing someone at the door, she recomposes herself. Mrs Clandon sits down on the sofa. Valentine returns.

VALENTINE. I hope Ive not kept you waiting. That landlord of mine is really an extraordinary old character.

DOLLY [*eagerly*] Oh, tell us. How long has he given you to pay?

MRS CLANDON [*distracted by her child's manners*] Dolly, Dolly, Dolly d e a r! You m u s t not ask questions.

DOLLY [*demurely*] So sorry. Youll tell us, wont you, Mr Valentine?

VALENTINE. He doesnt want his rent at all. He's broken his tooth on a Brazil nut; and he wants me to look at it and to lunch with him afterwards.

DOLLY. Then have him up and pull his tooth out at once; and we'll bring him to lunch too. Tell the maid to fetch him along. [*She runs to the bell and rings it vigorously. Then, with a sudden doubt, she turns to Valentine and adds*] I suppose he's respectable? r e a l l y respectable?

VALENTINE. Perfectly. Not like me.

DOLLY. Honest Injun?

Mrs Clandon gasps faintly; but her powers of remonstrance are exhausted.

VALENTINE. Honest Injun!

DOLLY. Then off with you and bring him up.

VALENTINE [*looking dubiously at Mrs Clandon*] I dare say he'd be delighted if—er—?

MRS CLANDON [*rising and looking at her watch*] I shall be happy to see your friend at lunch if you can persuade him to come; but I cant wait to see him now: I have an appointment at the hotel at a quarter to one with an old friend whom I have not seen since I left England eighteen years ago. Will you excuse me?

VALENTINE. Certainly, Mrs Clandon.

GLORIA. Shall I come?

MRS CLANDON. No, dear. I want to be alone. [*She goes out, evidently still a good deal troubled*].

Valentine opens the door for her and follows her.

PHILIP [*significantly to Dolly*] Hmhm!

DOLLY [*significantly to Phil*] Ahah!

The parlormaid answers the bell.

DOLLY. Shew the old gentleman up.

THE PARLORMAID [*puzzled*] Madam?

DOLLY. The old gentleman with the toothache.

PHILIP. The landlord.

THE PARLORMAID. Mr Crampton, sir?

PHILIP. Is his name Crampton?

DOLLY [*to Phil*] Sounds rheumaticky, doesnt it?

PHILIP. Chalkstones, probably.

DOLLY. Shew Mr Crampstones up.

THE PARLORMAID [*going out*] Mr Crampton, miss.

DOLLY [*repeating it to herself like a lesson*] Crampton, Crampton, Crampton, Crampton, Crampton. [*She sits down studiously at the writing-table*] I must get that name right, or Heaven knows what I shall call him.

GLORIA. Phil: can you believe such a horrible thing as that about our father? what mother said just now.

PHILIP. Oh, there are lots of people of that kind. Old Chamico used to thrash his wife and daughters with a cart whip.

DOLLY [*contemptuously*] Yes, a Portuguese!

PHILIP. When you come to men who are brutes, there is much in common between the Portuguese and the English variety, Doll. Trust my knowledge of human nature. [*He resumes his position on the hearth-rug with an elderly and responsible air*].

GLORIA [*with angered remorse*] I dont think we shall ever play again at our old game of guessing what our father was to be like. Dolly: are you sorry for y o u r father? the father with lots of money!

DOLLY. Oh come! What about y o u r father? the lonely old man with the tender aching heart! He's pretty well burst up, I think.

PHILIP. There can be no doubt that the governer is an exploded superstition. [*Valentine is heard talking to somebody outside the door*]. But hark! he comes.

GLORIA [*nervously*] Who?

DOLLY. Chalkstones.

PHILIP. Sh! Attention! [*They put on their best manners. Phil adds in a lower voice to Gloria*] If he's good enough for the lunch, I'll nod to Dolly; and if she nods to you, invite him straight away.

Valentine comes back with his landlord. Mr Fergus Crampton is a man of about sixty, with an atrociously obstinate ill tempered grasping mouth, and a dogmatic voice. There is no sign of straitened means or commercial diffidence about him: he is well dressed, and would be classed at a guess as a prosperous master-manufacturer in a business inherited from an old family in the aristocracy of trade. His navy blue coat is not of the usual fashionable pattern. It is not exactly a pilot's coat; but it is cut that way, double breasted, and with stout buttons and broad lappels: a coat for a shipyard rather than a counting house. He has taken a fancy to Valentine, who cares nothing for his crossness of grain, and treats him with a disrespectful humanity for which he is secretly grateful.

VALENTINE. May I introduce? This is Mr Crampton: Miss Dorothy Clandon, Mr Philip Clandon, Miss Clandon. [*Crampton stands nervously bowing. They all bow*]. Sit down, Mr Crampton.

DOLLY [*pointing to the operating chair*] That is the most comfortable chair, Mr Ch—crampton.

CRAMPTON. Thank you; but wont this young lady— [*indicating Gloria, who is close to the chair*]?

GLORIA. Thank you, Mr Crampton: we are just going.

VALENTINE [*bustling him across to the chair with good-humored peremptoriness*] Sit down, sit down. Youre tired.

CRAMPTON. Well, perhaps as I am considerably the oldest person present, I— [*he finishes the sentence by sitting down a little rheumatically in the operating chair. Meanwhile Phil, having studied him critically during his passage across the room, nods to Dolly; and Dolly nods to Gloria*].

GLORIA. Mr Crampton: we understand that we are preventing Mr Valentine from lunching with you by taking him away ourselves. My mother would be very glad indeed if you would come too.

CRAMPTON [*gratefully, after looking at her earnestly for a moment*] Thank you. I will come with pleasure.

GLORIA ⎫
DOLLY ⎬ [*politely murmuring*] ⎧ Thank you very much—er—
PHILIP ⎭ ⎨ So glad—er—
⎩ Delighted, I'm sure —er—

The conversation drops. Gloria and Dolly look at one another; then at Valentine and Phil. Valentine and Phil, unequal to the occasion, look away from them at one another, and are instantly so disconcerted by catching one another's eye, that they look back again and catch the eyes of Gloria and Dolly. Thus, catching one another all round, they all look at nothing and are quite at a loss. Crampton looks at them, waiting for them to begin. The silence becomes unbearable.

DOLLY [*suddenly, to keep things going*] How old are you, Mr Crampton?

GLORIA [*hastily*] I am afraid we must be going, Mr Valentine. It is understood, then, that we meet at half past one. [*She makes for the door. Phil goes with her. Valentine retreats to the bell*].

VALENTINE. Half past one. [*He rings the bell*]. Many thanks. [*He follows Gloria and Phil to the door, and goes out with them*].

DOLLY [*who has meanwhile stolen across to Crampton*] Make him give you gas. It's five shillings extra; but it's worth it.

CRAMPTON [*amused*] Very well. [*Looking more earnestly at her*] So you want to know my age, do you? I'm fifty seven.

DOLLY [*with conviction*] You look it.

CRAMPTON [*grimly*] I dare say I do.

DOLLY. What are you looking at me so hard for? Anything wrong? [*She feels whether her hat is right*].

CRAMPTON. Youre like somebody.

DOLLY. Who?

CRAMPTON. Well, you have a curious look of my mother.

DOLLY [*incredulously*] Your mother!!! Quite sure you dont mean your daughter?

CRAMPTON [*suddenly blackening with hate*] Yes: I'm quite sure I dont mean my daughter.

DOLLY [*sympathetically*] Tooth bad?

CRAMPTON. No, no: nothing. A twinge of memory, Miss Clandon, not of toothache.

DOLLY. Have it out. "Pluck from the memory a rooted sorrow." With gas, five shillings extra.

CRAMPTON [*vindictively*] No, not a sorrow. An injury that was done me once: thats all. I dont forget injuries; and I dont want to forget them. [*His features settle into an implacable frown*].

DOLLY [*looking critically at him*] I dont think we shall like you when you are brooding over your injuries.

PHILIP [*who has entered the room unobserved, and stolen behind her*] My sister means well, Mr Crampton; but she is indiscreet. Now Dolly: outside! [*He takes her towards the door*].

DOLLY [*in a perfectly audible undertone*] He says he's only fifty seven and he thinks me the image of his mother and he hates his daughter and—[*She is interrupted by the return of Valentine*].

VALENTINE. Miss Clandon has gone on.

PHILIP. Dont forget half past one.

DOLLY. Mind you leave Mr Crampton enough teeth to eat with. [*They go out*].

Valentine comes to his cabinet, and opens it.

CRAMPTON. Thats a spoiled child, Mr Valentine. Thats one of your modern products. When I was her age, I had many a good hiding fresh in my memory to teach me manners.

VALENTINE [*taking up his dental mirror and probe*] What did you think of her sister?

CRAMPTON. You liked her better, eh?

VALENTINE [*rhapsodically*] She struck me as being— [*He checks himself, and adds, prosaically*] However, thats not business. [*He assumes his professional tone*]. Open, please. [*Crampton opens his mouth. Valentine puts the mirror in, and examines his teeth*]. Hm! Youve smashed that one. What a pity to spoil such a splendid set of teeth! Why do you crack nuts with them? [*He withdraws the mirror, and comes forward to converse with his patient*].

CRAMPTON. Ive always cracked nuts with them: what else are they for? [*Dogmatically*] The proper way to keep teeth good is to give them plenty of use on bones and nuts, and wash them every day with soap: plain yellow soap.

VALENTINE. Soap! Why soap?

CRAMPTON. I began using it as a boy because I was made to; and Ive used it ever since. And Ive never had toothache in my life.

VALENTINE. Dont you find it rather nasty?

CRAMPTON. I found that most things that were good for me were nasty. But I was taught to put up with them, and m a d e to put up with them. I'm used to it now: in fact I like the taste when the soap is really good.

VALENTINE [*making a wry face in spite of himself*] You seem to have been very carefully educated, Mr Crampton.

CRAMPTON [*grimly*] I wasnt spoiled, at all events.

VALENTINE [*smiling a little to himself*] Are you quite sure?

CRAMPTON [*crustily*] What d'y' mean?

VALENTINE. Well, your teeth are good, I admit. But Ive seen just as good in very self-indulgent mouths. [*He goes to the cabinet and changes the probe for another one*].

CRAMPTON. It's not the effect on the teeth: it's the effect on the character.

VALENTINE [*placably*] Oh, the character! I see. [*He recommences operations*]. A little wider, please. Hm! Why do you bite so hard? youve broken the tooth worse than you broke the Brazil nut. It will have to come out: it's past saving. [*He withdraws the probe and again comes to the side of the chair to converse*]. Dont be alarmed: you shant feel anything. I'll give you gas.

CRAMPTON. Rubbish, man: I want none of your gas. Out with it! People were taught to bear necessary pain in my day.

VALENTINE. Oh, if you like being hurt, all right. I'll hurt you as much as you like, without any extra charge for the beneficial effect on your character.

CRAMPTON [*rising and glaring at him*] Young man: you owe me six weeks rent.

VALENTINE. I do.

CRAMPTON. Can you pay me?

VALENTINE. No.

CRAMPTON [*satisfied with his advantage*] I thought not. [*He sits down again*]. How soon d'y' think youll be able to pay me if you have no better manners than to make game of your patients?

VALENTINE. My good sir: my patients havnt all formed their characters on kitchen soap.

CRAMPTON [*suddenly gripping him by the arm as he turns away again to the cabinet*] So much the worse for them! I tell you you dont understand my character. If I could spare all my teeth, I'd make you pull them out one after another to shew you what a properly hardened man can go through with when he's made up his mind to it. [*He nods at Valentine to emphasize this declaration, and releases him*].

VALENTINE [*his careless pleasantry quite unruffled*] And you want to be more hardened, do you?

CRAMPTON. Yes.

VALENTINE [*strolling away to the bell*] Well, youre quite hard enough for me already—as a landlord. [*Crampton receives this with a growl of grim humor. Valentine rings the bell, and remarks in a cheerful casual way, whilst waiting for it to be answered*] Why did you never get married, Mr Crampton? A wife and children would have taken some of the hardness out of you.

CRAMPTON [*with unexpected ferocity*] What the devil is that to you?

The parlormaid appears at the door.

VALENTINE [*politely*] Some warm water, please. [*She retires; and Valentine comes back to the cabinet, not at all put out by Crampton's rudeness, and carries on the conversation whilst he selects a forceps and places it ready to his hand with a gag and a tumbler*]. You were asking me what the devil that was to me. Well, I have an idea of getting married myself.

CRAMPTON [*with grumbling irony*] Naturally, sir, naturally. When a young man has come to his last farthing, and is within twenty four hours of having his furniture distrained upon by his landlord, he marries. Ive noticed that before. Well, marry; and be miserable.

VALENTINE. Oh come! what do you know about it?

CRAMPTON. I'm not a bachelor.

VALENTINE. Then there is a Mrs Crampton?

CRAMPTON [*wincing with a pang of resentment*] Yes: damn her!

VALENTINE [*unperturbed*] Hm! A father, too, perhaps, as well as a husband, Mr Crampton?

CRAMPTON. Three children.

VALENTINE [*politely*] Damn them? eh?

CRAMPTON [*jealously*] No, sir: the children are as much mine as hers.

The parlormaid brings in a jug of hot water.

VALENTINE. Thank you. [*She gives him the jug and goes out. He brings it to the cabinet, continuing in the same idle strain*] I really should like to know your family, Mr Crampton. [*He pours some hot water into the tumbler*].

CRAMPTON. Sorry I cant introduce you, sir. I'm happy to say that I dont know where they are, and dont care, so long as they keep out of my way. [*Valentine, with a hitch of his eyebrows and shoulders, drops the forceps with a clink into the hot water*]. You neednt warm that thing to use on me. I'm not afraid of the cold steel. [*Valentine stoops to arrange the gas pump and cylinder beside the chair*]. Whats that heavy thing?

VALENTINE. Oh, never mind. Something to put my foot on, to get the necessary purchase for a good pull. [*Crampton looks alarmed in spite of himself. Valentine stands upright and places the glass with the forceps ready to his hand, chatting on with provoking indifference*]. And so you advise me not to get married, Mr Crampton? [*He puts his foot on the lever by which the chair is raised and lowered*].

CRAMPTON [*irritably*] I advise you to get my tooth out and have done reminding me of my wife. Come along, man. [*He grips the arms of the chair and braces himself*].

VALENTINE. What do you bet that I dont get that tooth out without your feeling it?

CRAMPTON. Your six weeks rent, young man. Dont you gammon me.

VALENTINE [*jumping at the bet and sending him aloft vigorously*] Done! Are you ready?

Crampton, who has lost his grip of the chair in his alarm at its sudden ascent, folds his arms; sits stiffly upright; and prepares for the worst. Valentine suddenly lets down the back of the chair to an obtuse angle.

CRAMPTON [*clutching at the arms of the chair as he falls back*] P! take care, man! I'm quite helpless in this po—

VALENTINE [*deftly stopping him with the gag, and snatching up the mouthpiece of the gas machine*] Youll be more helpless presently.

He presses the mouthpiece over Crampton's mouth and nose, leaning over his chest so as to hold his head and shoulders well down on the chair. Crampton makes an inarticulate sound in the mouthpiece and tries to lay hands on Valentine, whom he supposes to be in front of him. After a moment his arms wave aimlessly, then subside and drop. He is quite insensible. Valentine throws aside the mouthpiece quickly; picks the forceps adroitly from the glass; and—.

ACT II

On the terrace at the Marine Hotel. It is a square flagged platform, glaring in the sun, and fenced on the seaward edge by a parapet. The head waiter, busy laying napkins on a luncheon table with his back to the sea, has the hotel on his right, and on his left, in the corner nearest the sea, a flight of steps leading down to the beach. When he looks down the terrace in front of him

he sees, a little to his left, a middle aged gentle-
man sitting on a chair of iron laths at a little iron
table with a bowl of lump sugar on it, reading an
ultra-Conservative newspaper, with his umbrella
up to defend him from the sun, which, in August
and at less than an hour after noon, is toasting
his protended insteps. At the hotel side of the ter-
race, there is a garden seat of the ordinary esplan-
ade pattern. Access to the hotel for visitors is by
an entrance in the middle of its façade. Nearer
the parapet there lurks a way to the kitchen,
masked by a little trellis porch. The table at which
the waiter is occupied is a long one, set across the
terrace with covers and chairs for five, two at
each side and one at the end next the hotel.
Against the parapet another table is prepared as
a buffet to serve from.

The waiter is a remarkable person in his way.
A silky old man, white haired and delicate look-
ing, but so cheerful and contented that in his en-
couraging presence ambition stands rebuked as
vulgarity, and imagination as treason to the
abounding sufficiency and interest of the actual.
He has a certain expression peculiar to men who
are pre-eminent in their callings, and who, whilst
aware of the vanity of success, are untouched by
envy.

The gentleman at the iron table is not dressed
for the seaside. He wears his London frock coat
and gloves; and his tall silk hat is on the table
beside the sugarbowl. The excellent condition and
quality of these garments and the gold-rimmed
folding spectacles through which he is reading,
testify to his respectability. He is about fifty,
clean-shaven and close-cropped, with the corners
of his mouth turned down purposely, as if he
suspected them of wanting to turn up, and was
determined not to let them have their way. He
keeps his brow resolutely wide open, as if, again,
he had resolved in his youth to be truthful, mag-
nanimous, and incorruptible, but had never suc-
ceeded in making that habit of mind automatic
and unconscious. Still, he is by no means to be
laughed at. There is no sign of stupidity or in-
firmity of will about him: on the contrary, he
would pass anywhere at sight as a man of more
than average professional capacity and responsi-
bility. Just at present he is enjoying the weather
and the sea too much to be out of patience; but he
has exhausted all the news in his paper, and is at
present reduced to the advertisements, which are
not sufficiently succulent to induce him to per-
severe with them.

THE GENTLEMAN [*yawning and giving up the*
paper as a bad job] Waiter!

WAITER. Sir? [*coming to him*].

THE GENTLEMAN. Are you quite sure Mrs
Clandon is coming back before lunch?

WAITER. Quite sure, sir. She expects you at
a quarter to one, sir. [*The gentleman, soothed*
at once by the waiter's voice, looks at him with a
lazy smile. It is a quiet voice, with a gentle melody
in it that gives sympathetic interest to his most
commonplace remark; and he speaks with the
sweetest propriety, neither dropping his aitches
nor misplacing them, nor committing any other
vulgarism. He looks at his watch as he con-
tinues] Not that yet, sir, is it? 12.43, sir. Only
two minutes more to wait, sir. Nice morning,
sir!

THE GENTLEMAN. Yes: very fresh after
London.

WAITER. Yes, sir: so all our visitors say, sir.
Very nice family, Mrs Clandon's, sir.

THE GENTLEMAN. You like them, do you?

WAITER. Yes, sir. They have a free way
with them that is very taking, sir, very taking
indeed: especially the young lady and gentleman.

THE GENTLEMAN. Miss Dorothea and Mr
Philip, I suppose.

WAITER. Yes, sir. The young lady, in giving
an order, or the like of that, will say, "Remember, William: we came to this hotel on
your account, having heard what a perfect
waiter you are." The young gentleman will
tell me that I remind him strongly of his
father [*the gentleman starts at this*] and that
he expects me to act by him as such. [*With a*
soothing sunny cadence] Oh, v e r y pleasant, sir,
very affable and pleasant indeed!

THE GENTLEMAN. You like his father! [*He*
laughs at the notion].

WAITER. Oh sir, we must not take what they
say too seriously. Of course, sir, if it were
true, the young lady would have seen the
resemblance too, sir.

THE GENTLEMAN. Did she?

WAITER. No, sir. She thought me like the
bust of Shakespear in Stratford Church, sir.
That is why she calls me William, sir. My
real name is Walter, sir. [*He turns to go back*
to the table, and sees Mrs Clandon coming up to
the terrace from the beach by the steps]. Here is
Mrs Clandon, sir. [*To Mrs Clandon in an un-*
obtrusively confidential tone] Gentleman for
you, maam.

MRS CLANDON. We shall have two more
gentlemen at lunch, William.

WAITER. Right, maam. Thank you, maam.

[*He withdraws into the hotel*].

Mrs Clandon comes forward looking for her visitor, but passes over the gentleman without any sign of recognition.

THE GENTLEMAN [*peering at her quaintly from under the umbrella*] Dont you know me?

MRS CLANDON [*incredulously, looking hard at him*] Are you Finch M'Comas?

M'COMAS. Cant you guess? [*He shuts the umbrella; puts it aside; and jocularly plants himself with his hands on his hips to be inspected*].

MRS CLANDON. I believe you are. [*She gives him her hand. The shake that ensues is that of old friends after a long separation*]. Wheres your beard?

M'COMAS [*humorously solemn*] Would you employ a solicitor with a beard?

MRS CLANDON [*pointing to the silk hat on the table*] Is that your hat?

M'COMAS. Would you employ a solicitor with a sombrero?

MRS CLANDON. I have thought of you all these eighteen years with the beard and the sombrero. [*She sits down on the garden seat. M'Comas takes his chair again*]. Do you go to the meetings of the Dialectical Society still?

M'COMAS [*gravely*] I do not frequent meetings now.

MRS CLANDON. Finch: I see what has happened. You have become respectable.

M'COMAS. Havnt you?

MRS CLANDON. Not a bit.

M'COMAS. You hold to our old opinions still?

MRS CLANDON. As firmly as ever.

M'COMAS. Bless me! And you are still ready to make speeches in public, in spite of your sex [*Mrs Clandon nods*]; to insist on a married woman's right to her own separate property [*she nods again*]; to champion Darwin's view of the origin of species and John Stuart Mill's Essay on Liberty [*nod*]; to read Huxley, Tyndall, and George Eliot [*three nods*]; and to demand University degrees, the opening of the professions, and the parliamentary franchise for women as well as men?

MRS CLANDON [*resolutely*] Yes: I have not gone back one inch; and I have educated Gloria to take up my work when I must leave it. That is what has brought me back to England. I felt I had no right to bury her alive in Madeira: my St Helena, Finch. I suppose she will be howled at as I was; but she is prepared for that.

M'COMAS. Howled at! My dear good lady: there is nothing in any of those views nowa-days to prevent her marrying an archbishop. You reproached me just now for having become respectable. You were wrong: I hold to our old opinions as strongly as ever. I dont go to church; and I dont pretend I do. I call myself what I am: a Philosophic Radical standing for liberty and the rights of the individual, as I learnt to do from my master Herbert Spencer. Am I howled at? No: I'm indulged as an old fogey. I'm out of everything, because Ive refused to bow the knee to Socialism.

MRS CLANDON [*shocked*] Socialism!

M'COMAS. Yes: Socialism. Thats what Miss Gloria will be up to her ears in before the end of the month if you let her loose here.

MRS CLANDON [*emphatically*] But I can prove to her that Socialism is a fallacy.

M'COMAS [*touchingly*] It is by proving that, Mrs Clandon, that I have lost all my young disciples. Be careful what you do: let her go her own way. [*With some bitterness*] We're old fashioned: the world thinks it has left us behind. There is only one place in all England where your opinions would still pass as advanced.

MRS CLANDON [*scornfully unconvinced*] The Church, perhaps?

M'COMAS. No: the theatre. And now to business! Why have you made me come down here?

MRS CLANDON. Well, partly because I wanted to see you—

M'COMAS [*with good-humored irony*] Thanks.

MRS CLANDON. —and partly because I want you to explain everything to the children. They know nothing; and now that we have come back to England it is impossible to leave them in ignorance any longer. [*Agitated*] Finch: I cannot bring myself to tell them. I —

She is interrupted by the twins and Gloria. Dolly comes tearing up the steps, racing Phil, who combines terrific speed with an unhurried propriety of bearing which, however, costs him the race, as Dolly reaches her mother first and almost upsets the garden seat by the precipitancy of her embrace.

DOLLY [*breathless*] It's all right, mamma. The dentist is coming; and he's bringing his old man.

MRS CLANDON. Dolly, dear: dont you see Mr M'Comas? [*M'Comas rises, smiling*].

DOLLY [*her face falling with the most disparagingly obvious disappointment*] This! Where are the flowing locks?

PHILIP [*seconding her warmly*] Where the beard? the cloak? the poetic exterior?

DOLLY. Oh, Mr M'Comas, youve gone and spoiled yourself. Why didnt you wait til we'd seen you?

M'COMAS [*taken aback, but rallying his humor to meet the emergency*] Because eighteen years is too long for a solicitor to go without having his hair cut.

GLORIA [*at the other side of M'Comas*] How do you do, Mr M'Comas? [*He turns; and she takes his hand and presses it, with a frank straight look into his eyes*]. We are glad to meet you at last.

M'COMAS. Miss Gloria, I presume? [*Gloria smiles assent; releases his hand after a final pressure; and retires behind the garden seat, leaning over the back beside Mrs Clandon*]. And this young gentleman?

PHILIP. I was christened in a comparatively prosaic mood. My name is—

DOLLY [*completing his sentence for him declamatorily*] "Norval. On the Grampian hills"—

PHILIP [*declaiming gravely*] "My father feeds his flock, a frugal swain"—

MRS CLANDON [*remonstrating*] Dear, dear children: dont be silly. Everything is so new to them here, Finch, that they are in the wildest spirits. They think every Englishman they meet is a joke.

DOLLY. Well, so he is: it's not our fault.

PHILIP. My knowledge of human nature is fairly extensive, Mr M'Comas; but I find it impossible to take the inhabitants of this island seriously.

M'COMAS. I presume, sir, you are Master Philip [*offering his hand*].

PHILIP [*taking M'Comas's hand and looking solemnly at him*] I was Master Philip: was so for many years; just as you were once Master Finch. [*He gives the hand a single shake and drops it; then turns away, exclaiming meditatively*] How strange it is to look back on our boyhood!

DOLLY [*to Mrs Clandon*] Has Finch had a drink?

MRS CLANDON [*remonstrating*] Dearest: Mr M'Comas will lunch with us.

DOLLY. Have you ordered for seven? Dont forget the old gentleman.

MRS CLANDON. I have not forgotten him, dear. What is his name?

DOLLY. Chalkstones. He'll be here at half past one. [*To M'Comas*] Are we like what you expected?

MRS CLANDON [*earnestly, even a little peremptorily*] Dolly: Mr M'Comas has something more serious than that to tell you. Children: I have asked my old friend to answer the question you asked this morning. He is your father's friend as well as mine; and he will tell you the story of my married life more fairly than I could. Gloria: are you satisfied?

GLORIA [*gravely attentive*] Mr M'Comas is very kind.

M'COMAS [*nervously*] Not at all, my dear young lady: not at all. At the same time, this is rather sudden. I was hardly prepared —er—

DOLLY [*suspiciously*] Oh, we dont want anything prepared.

PHILIP [*exhorting him*] Tell us the truth.

DOLLY [*emphatically*] Bald headed.

M'COMAS [*nettled*] I hope you intend to take what I have to say seriously.

PHILIP [*with profound gravity*] I hope it will deserve it, Mr M'Comas. My knowledge of human nature teaches me not to expect too much.

MRS CLANDON [*remonstrating*] Phil—

PHILIP. Yes, mother: all right. I beg your pardon, Mr M'Comas: dont mind us.

DOLLY [*in conciliation*] We mean well.

PHILIP. Shut up, both.

Dolly holds her lips. M'Comas takes a chair from the luncheon table; places it between the little table and the garden seat, with Dolly on his right and Phil on his left; and settles himself in it with the air of a man about to begin a long communication. The Clandons watch him expectantly.

M'COMAS. Ahem! Your father—

DOLLY. How old is he?

PHILIP. Sh!

MRS CLANDON [*softly*] Dear Dolly: dont let us interrupt Mr M'Comas.

M'COMAS [*emphatically*] Thank you, Mrs Clandon. Thank you. [*To Dolly*] Your father is fifty-seven.

DOLLY [*with a bound, startled and excited*] Fifty-seven!! Where does he live?

MRS CLANDON [*remonstrating*] Dolly! Dolly!

M'COMAS [*stopping her*] Let me answer that, Mrs Clandon. The answer will surprise you considerably. He lives in this town.

Mrs Clandon rises, intensely angry, but sits down again, speechless: Gloria watching her perplexedly.

DOLLY [*with conviction*] I knew it. Phil: Chalkstones is our father!

M'COMAS. Chalkstones!

DOLLY. Oh, Crampstones, or whatever it is. He said I was like his mother. I k n e w he must mean his daughter.

PHILIP [*very seriously*] Mr M'Comas: I desire to consider your feelings in every possible way; but I warn you that if you stretch the long arm of coincidence to the length of telling me that Mr Crampton of this town is my father, I shall decline to entertain the information for a moment.

M'COMAS. And pray why?

PHILIP. Because I have seen the gentleman; and he is entirely unfit to be my father, or Dolly's father, or Gloria's father, or my mother's husband.

M'COMAS. Oh, indeed! Well, sir, let me tell you that whether you like it or not, he i s your father, and your sisters' father, and Mrs Clandon's husband. Now! What have you to say to that?

DOLLY [*whimpering*] You neednt be so cross. Crampton isnt y o u r father.

PHILIP. Mr M'Comas: your conduct is heartless. Here you find a family enjoying the unspeakable peace and freedom of being orphans. We have never seen the face of a relative: never known a claim except the claim of freely chosen friendship. And now you wish to thrust into the most intimate relationship with us a man whom we dont know—

DOLLY [*vehemently*] An a w f u l old man! [*Reproachfully*] And you began as if you had quite a nice father for us!

M'COMAS [*angrily*] How do you know that he is not nice? And what right have you to choose your own father? [*Raising his voice*] Let me tell you, Miss Clandon, that you are too young to—

DOLLY [*interrupting him suddenly and eagerly*] Stop: I forgot! Has he any money?

M'COMAS. He has a great deal of money.

DOLLY [*delighted*] Oh, what did I always say, Phil?

PHILIP. Dolly: we have perhaps been condemning the old man too hastily. Proceed, Mr M'Comas.

M'COMAS. I shall not proceed, sir. I am too hurt, too shocked, to proceed.

MRS CLANDON [*struggling with her temper*] Finch: do you realize what is happening? Do you understand that my children have in-vited that man to lunch, and that he will be here in a few moments?

M'COMAS [*completely upset*] What! Do you mean? am I to understand? is it—

PHILIP [*impressively*] Steady, Finch. Think it out slowly and carefully. He's coming: coming to lunch.

GLORIA. Which of us is to tell him the truth? Have you thought of that?

MRS CLANDON. Finch: y o u must tell him.

DOLLY. Oh, Finch is no good at telling things. Look at the mess he has made of telling us.

M'COMAS. I have not been allowed to speak. I protest against this.

DOLLY [*taking his arm coaxingly*] Dear Finch: dont be cross.

MRS CLANDON. Gloria: let us go in. He may arrive at any moment.

GLORIA [*proudly*] Do not stir, mother. *I* shall not stir. We must not run away.

MRS CLANDON. My dear: we cannot sit down to lunch just as we are. We shall come back again. We must have no bravado. [*Gloria winces, and goes into the hotel without a word*]. Come, Dolly. [*As she goes to the hotel door, the waiter comes out with a tray of plates, etc. for two additional covers*].

WAITER. Gentlemen come yet, maam?

MRS CLANDON. Two more to come still, thank you. They will be here immediately. [*She goes into the hotel*].

The waiter takes his tray to the service table.

PHILIP. I have an idea. Mr M'Comas: this communication should be made, should it not, by a man of infinite tact?

M'COMAS. It will require tact, certainly.

PHILIP. Good! Dolly: whose tact were you noticing only this morning?

DOLLY [*seizing the idea with rapture*] Oh yes, I declare!

PHILIP. The very man! [*Calling*] William!

WAITER. Coming, sir.

M'COMAS [*horrified*] The waiter! Stop! stop! I will not permit this. I—

WAITER [*presenting himself between Phil and M'Comas*] Yes, sir.

M'Comas's complexion fades into stone grey: all movement and expression desert his eyes. He sits down stupefied.

PHILIP. William: you remember my request to you to regard me as your son?

WAITER [*with respectful indulgence*] Yes, sir. Anything y o u please, sir.

PHILIP. William: at the very outset of your

career as my father, a rival has appeared on the scene.

WAITER. Your real father, sir? Well, that was to be expected, sooner or later, sir, wasnt it? [*Turning with a happy smile to M'Comas*] Is it you, sir?

M'COMAS [*renerved by indignation*]. Certainly not. My children know how to behave themselves.

PHILIP. No, William: this gentleman was very nearly my father: he wooed my mother, but wooed her in vain.

M'COMAS [*outraged*] Well, of all the—

PHILIP. Sh! Consequently, he is only our solicitor. Do you know one Crampton, of this town?

WAITER. Cock-eyed Crampton, sir, of the Crooked Billet, is it?

PHILIP. I dont know. Finch: does he keep a public house?

M'COMAS [*rising, scandalized*] No, no, no. Your father, sir, is a well known yacht builder, an eminent man here.

WAITER [*impressed*] Oh! Beg pardon, sir, I'm sure. A son of Mr Crampton's! Dear me!

PHILIP. Mr Crampton is coming to lunch with us.

WAITER [*puzzled*] Yes, sir. [*Diplomatically*] Dont usually lunch with his family, perhaps, sir?

PHILIP [*impressively*] William: he does not know that we a r e his family. He has not seen us for eighteen years. He wont know us. [*To emphasize the communication, Phil seats himself on the iron table with a spring, and looks at the waiter with his lips compressed and his legs swinging*].

DOLLY. We want you to break the news to him, William.

WAITER. But I should think he'd guess when he sees your mother, miss.

Phil's legs become motionless. He contemplates the waiter raptly.

DOLLY [*dazzled*] I never thought of that.

PHILIP. Nor I. [*Coming off the table and turning reproachfully on M'Comas*] Nor y o u!

DOLLY. And you a solicitor!

PHILIP. Finch: your professional incompetence is appalling. William: your sagacity put us all to shame.

DOLLY. You really a r e like Shakespear, William.

WAITER. Not at all, sir. Dont mention it, miss. Most happy, I'm sure, sir. [*He goes back modestly to the luncheon table and lays the two

additional covers, one at the end next the steps, and the other so as to make a third on the side furthest from the balustrade*].

PHILIP [*abruptly seizing M'Comas's arm and leading him towards the hotel*] Finch: come and wash your hands.

M'COMAS. I am thoroughly vexed and hurt, Mr Clandon—

PHILIP [*interrupting him*] You will get used to us. Come, Dolly. [*M'Comas shakes him off and marches into the hotel. Phil follows with unruffled composure*].

DOLLY [*turning for a moment on the steps as she follows them*] Keep your wits about you, William. There will be fireworks.

WAITER. Right, miss. You may depend on me, miss. [*She goes into the hotel*].

Valentine comes lightly up the steps from the beach, followed doggedly by Crampton. Valentine carries a walking stick. Crampton, either because he is old and chilly, or with some idea of extenuating the unfashionableness of his reefer jacket, wears a light overcoat. He stops at the chair left by M'Comas in the middle of the terrace, and steadies himself for a moment by placing his hand on the back of it.

CRAMPTON. Those steps make me giddy. [*He passes his hand over his forehead*]. I have not got over that infernal gas yet.

He goes to the iron chair, so that he can lean his elbows on the little table to prop his head as he sits. He soon recovers, and begins to unbutton his overcoat. Meanwhile Valentine interviews the waiter.

VALENTINE. Waiter!

WAITER [*coming forward between them*] Yes, sir.

VALENTINE. Mrs Lanfrey Clandon.

WAITER [*with a sweet smile of welcome*] Yes, sir. We're expecting you, sir. That is your table, sir. Mrs Clandon will be down presently, sir. The young lady and gentleman were just talking about your friend, sir.

VALENTINE. Indeed!

WAITER [*smoothly melodious*] Yes, sir. Great flow of spirits, sir. A vein of pleasantry, as you might say, sir. [*Quickly, to Crampton, who has risen to get the overcoat off*] Beg pardon, sir; but if youll allow me [*helping him to get the overcoat off, and taking it from him*]. Thank you, sir. [*Crampton sits down again; and the waiter resumes the broken melody*]. The young gentleman's latest is that y o u r e his father, sir.

CRAMPTON. What!

WAITER. Only his joke, sir, his favorite joke.

Yesterday, *I* was to be his father. Today, as soon as he knew you were coming, sir, he tried to put it up on me that you were his father: his long lost father! Not seen you for eighteen years, he said.

CRAMPTON [*startled*] Eighteen years!

WAITER. Yes, sir. [*With gentle archness*] But I was up to his tricks, sir. I saw the idea coming into his head as he stood there, thinking what new joke he'd have with me. Yes, sir: thats the sort he is: very pleasant, ve—ry off-hand and affable indeed, sir. [*Again changing his tempo to say to Valentine, who is putting his stick down against the corner of the garden seat*] If youll allow me, sir? [*He takes Valentine's stick*]. Thank you, sir. [*Valentine strolls up to the luncheon table and looks at the menu. The waiter turns to Crampton and continues his lay*]. Even the solicitor took up the joke, although he was in a manner of speaking in my confidence about the young gentleman, sir. Yes, sir, I assure you, sir. You would never imagine what respectable professional gentlemen from London will do on an outing, when the sea air takes them, sir.

CRAMPTON. Oh, theres a solicitor with them, is there?

WAITER. The family solicitor, sir: yes, sir. Name of M'Comas, sir. [*He goes towards the hotel entrance with the coat and stick, happily unconscious of the bomblike effect the name has produced on Crampton*].

CRAMPTON [*rising in angry alarm*] M'Comas! [*Calling to Valentine*] Valentine! [*Again, fiercely*] Valentine!! [*Valentine turns*]. This is a plant, a conspiracy. This is my family! my children! my infernal wife.

VALENTINE [*coolly*] Oh indeed! Interesting meeting! [*He resumes his study of the menu*].

CRAMPTON. Meeting! Not for me. Let me out of this. [*Calling across to the waiter*] Give me that coat.

WAITER. Yes, sir. [*He comes back; puts Valentine's stick carefully down against the luncheon table; and delicately shakes the coat out and holds it for Crampton to put on*]. I seem to have done the young gentleman an injustice, sir, havnt I, sir?

CRAMPTON. Rrrh! [*He stops on the point of putting his arms into the sleeves, and turns on Valentine with sudden suspicion*]. Valentine: you are in this. You made this plot. You—

VALENTINE [*decisively*] Bosh! [*He throws the menu down and goes round the table to look out unconcernedly over the parapet*].

CRAMPTON [*angrily*] What d'ye—

M'Comas, followed by Phil and Dolly, comes out, but recoils on seeing Crampton.

WAITER [*softly interrupting Crampton*] Steady, sir. Here they come, sir. [*He takes up Valentine's stick and makes for the hotel, throwing the coat across his arm.*]

M'Comas turns the corners of his mouth resolutely down and crosses to Crampton, who draws back and glares, with his hands behind him. M'Comas, with his brow opener than ever, confronts him in the majesty of a spotless conscience.

WAITER [*aside, as he passes Phil on his way out*] Ive broke it to him, sir.

PHILIP. Invaluable William! [*He passes on to the table*].

DOLLY [*aside to the waiter*] How did he take it?

WAITER [*aside to her*] Startled at first, miss; but resigned: very resigned indeed, miss. [*He takes the stick and coat into the hotel*].

M'COMAS [*having stared Crampton out of countenance*] So here you are, Mr Crampton.

CRAMPTON. Yes, here: caught in a trap: a mean trap. Are those my children?

PHILIP [*with deadly politeness*] Is this our father, Mr M'Comas?

M'COMAS [*stoutly*] He is.

DOLLY [*conventionally*] Pleased to meet you again. [*She wanders idly round the table, exchanging a grimace with Valentine on the way*].

PHILIP. Allow me to discharge my first duty as host by ordering your wine. [*He takes the wine list from the table. His polite attention, and Dolly's unconcerned indifference, leave Crampton on the footing of a casual acquaintance picked up that morning at the dentist's. The consciousness of it goes through the father with so keen a pang that he trembles all over; his brow becomes wet; and he stares dumbly at his son, who, just sensible enough of his own callousness to intensely enjoy the humor and adroitness of it, proceeds pleasantly*] Finch: some crusted old port for you, as a respectable family solicitor, eh?

M'COMAS [*firmly*] Apollinaris only. Nothing heating. [*He walks away to the side of the terrace, like a man putting temptation behind him*].

PHILIP. Valentine—?

VALENTINE. Would Lager be considered vulgar?

PHILIP. Probably. We'll order some. [*Turning to Crampton with cheerful politeness*] And now, Mr Crampton, what can we do for you?

CRAMPTON. What d'ye mean, boy?

PHILIP. Boy! [*Very solemnly*] Whose fault is it that I am a boy?

Crampton snatches the wine list rudely from him and irresolutely pretends to read it. Philip abandons it to him with perfect politeness.

DOLLY [*looking over Crampton's right shoulder*] The whisky's on the last page but one.

CRAMPTON. Let me alone, child.

DOLLY. Child! No, no: you may call me Dolly if you like; but you mustnt call me child. [*She slips her arm through Phil's; and the two stand looking at Crampton as if he were some eccentric stranger*].

CRAMPTON [*mopping his brow in rage and agony, and yet relieved even by their playing with him*] M'Comas: we are—ha!—going to have a pleasant meal.

M'COMAS [*resolutely cheerful*] There is no reason why it should not be pleasant.

PHILIP. Finch's face is a feast in itself.

Mrs Clandon and Gloria come from the hotel. Mrs Clandon advances with courageous self-possession and marked dignity of manner. She stops at the foot of the steps to address Valentine, who is in her path. Gloria also stops, looking at Crampton with a certain repulsion.

MRS CLANDON. Glad to see you again, Mr Valentine. [*He smiles. She passes on and confronts Crampton, intending to address him with complete composure; but his aspect shakes her. She stops suddenly and says anxiously, with a touch of remorse*] Fergus: you are greatly changed.

CRAMPTON [*grimly*] I daresay. A man does change in eighteen years.

MRS CLANDON [*troubled*] I—I did not mean that. I hope your health is good.

CRAMPTON. Thank you. No: it's not my health. It's my happiness: thats the change you meant, I think. [*Breaking out suddenly*] Look at her, M'Comas! Look at her; and [*with a half laugh, half sob*] look at m e?

PHILIP. Sh! [*Pointing to the hotel entrance, where the waiter has just appeared*] Order before William!

DOLLY [*touching Crampton's arm warningly*] Ahem!

The waiter goes to the service table and beckons to the kitchen entrance, whence issue a young waiter with soup plates, and a cook, in white apron and cap, with the soup tureen. The young waiter remains and serves: the cook goes out, and reappears from time to time bringing in the courses. He carves, but does not serve. The waiter comes to the end of the luncheon table next the steps.

MRS CLANDON [*as they assemble at the table*] I think you have all met one another already today. Oh no: excuse me. [*Introducing*] Mr Valentine: Mr M'Comas. [*She goes to the end of the table nearest the hotel*]. Fergus: will you take the head of the table, please.

CRAMPTON. Ha! [*Bitterly*] The head of the table!

WAITER [*holding the chair for him with inoffensive encouragement*] This end, sir. [*Crampton submits, and takes his seat*]. Thank you, sir.

MRS CLANDON. Mr Valentine: will you take that side [*indicating the side next the parapet*] with Gloria? [*Valentine and Gloria take their places, Gloria next Crampton and Valentine next Mrs Clandon*]. Finch: I must put you on this side, between Dolly and Phil. You must protect yourself as best you can.

The three take the remaining side of the table, Dolly next her mother, Phil next his father. Soup is served.

WAITER [*to Crampton*] Thick or clear, sir?

CRAMPTON [*to Mrs Clandon*] Does nobody ask a blessing in this household?

PHILIP [*interposing smartly*] Let us first settle what we are about to receive. William!

WAITER. Yes, sir. [*He glides swiftly round the table to Phil's left elbow. On his way he whispers to the young waiter*] Thick.

PHILIP. Two small Lagers for the children as usual, William; and one large for this gentleman [*indicating Valentine*]. Large Apollinaris for Mr M'Comas.

WAITER. Yes, sir.

DOLLY. Have a six of Irish in it, Finch?

M'COMAS [*scandalized*] No. No, thank you.

PHILIP. Number 413 for my mother and Miss Gloria as before; and— [*turning inquiringly to Crampton*] Eh?

CRAMPTON [*scowling and about to reply offensively*] I—

WAITER [*striking in mellifluously*] All right, sir. We know what Mr Crampton likes here, sir. [*He goes into the hotel*].

PHILIP [*looking gravely at his father*] You frequent bars. Bad habit!

The cook, followed by a waiter with hot plates, brings in the fish from the kitchen to the service table, and begins slicing it.

CRAMPTON. You have learnt your lesson from your mother, I see.

MRS CLANDON. Phil: will you please remember that your jokes are apt to irritate people who are not accustomed to us, and that your father is our guest today.

CRAMPTON [*bitterly*] Yes: a guest at the head of my own table. [*The soup plates are removed*].

DOLLY [*sympathetically*] It's embarrassing, isnt it? It's just as bad for us, you know.

PHILIP. Sh! Dolly: we are both wanting in tact. [*To Crampton*] We mean well, Mr Crampton; but we are not yet strong in the filial line. [*The waiter returns from the hotel with the drinks*]. William: come and restore good feeling.

WAITER [*cheerfully*] Yes, sir. Certainly, sir. Small Lager for you, sir. [*To Crampton*] Seltzer and Irish, sir. [*To M'Comas*] Apollinaris, sir. [*To Dolly*] Small Lager, miss. [*To Mrs Clandon, pouring out wine*] 413, madam. [*To Valentine*] Large Lager for you, sir. [*To Gloria*] 413, miss.

DOLLY [*drinking*] To the family!

PHILIP [*drinking*] Hearth and Home!

Fish is served.

M'COMAS. We are getting on very nicely after all.

DOLLY [*critically*] After all! After all what, Finch?

CRAMPTON [*sarcastically*] He means that you are getting on very nicely in spite of the presence of your father. Do I take your point rightly, Mr M'Comas?

M'COMAS [*disconcerted*] No, no. I only said "after all" to round off the sentence. I—er—er—er—

WAITER [*tactfully*] Turbot, sir?

M'COMAS [*intensely grateful for the interruption*] Thank you, waiter: thank you.

WAITER [*sotto voce*] Dont mention it, sir. [*He returns to the service table*].

CRAMPTON [*to Phil*] Have you thought of choosing a profession yet?

PHILIP. I am keeping my mind open on that subject. William!

WAITER. Yes, sir.

PHILIP. How long do you think it would take me to learn to be a really smart waiter?

WAITER. Cant be learnt, sir. It's in the character, sir. [*Confidentially to Valentine, who is looking about for something*] Bread for the lady, sir? yes, sir. [*He serves bread to Gloria, and resumes, at his former pitch*] Very few are born to it, sir.

PHILIP. You dont happen to have such a thing as a son, yourself, have you?

WAITER. Yes, sir: oh yes, sir. [*To Gloria, again dropping his voice*] A little more fish, miss? you wont care for the joint in the middle of the day.

GLORIA. No, thank you.

The fish plates are removed, and the next course served.

DOLLY. Is your son a waiter too, William?

WAITER [*serving Gloria with fowl*] Oh no, miss: he's too impetuous. He's at the Bar.

M'COMAS [*patronizingly*] A potman, eh?

WAITER [*with a touch of melancholy, as if recalling a disappointment softened by time*] No, sir: the other bar. Your profession, sir. A Q.C., sir.

M'COMAS [*embarrassed*] I'm sure I beg your pardon.

WAITER. Not at all, sir. Very natural mistake, I'm sure, sir. Ive often wished he was a potman, sir. Would have been off my hands ever so much sooner, sir. [*Aside to Valentine, who is again in difficulties*] Salt at your elbow, sir. [*Resuming*] Yes, sir: had to support him until he was thirty-seven, sir. But doing well now, sir: very satisfactory indeed, sir. Nothing less than fifty guineas, sir.

M'COMAS. Democracy, Crampton! Modern democracy!

WAITER [*calmly*] No, sir, not democracy: only education, sir. Scholarships, sir. Cambridge Local, sir. Sidney Sussex College, sir. [*Dolly plucks his sleeve and whispers as he bends down*]. Stone ginger, miss? Right, miss. [*To M'Comas*] Very good thing for him, sir: he never had any turn for real work, sir. [*He goes into the hotel, leaving the company somewhat overwhelmed by his son's eminence*].

VALENTINE. Which of us dare give that man an order again!

DOLLY. I hope he wont mind my sending him for ginger-beer.

CRAMPTON [*doggedly*] While he's a waiter it's his business to wait. If you had treated him as a waiter ought to be treated, he'd have held his tongue.

DOLLY. What a loss that would have been! Perhaps he'll give us an introduction to his son and get us into London society.

The waiter reappears with the ginger-beer.

CRAMPTON [*growling contemptuously*] London society! London society!! Youre not fit for any society, child.

DOLLY [*losing her temper*] Now look here, Mr Crampton. If you think—

WAITER [*softly, at her elbow*] Stone ginger, miss.

DOLLY [*taken aback, recovers her good humor after a long breath, and says sweetly*] Thank you, dear William. You were just in time.

[*She drinks*].

M'COMAS. If I may be allowed to change the subject, Miss Clandon, what is the established religion in Madeira?

GLORIA. I suppose the Portuguese religion. I never inquired.

DOLLY. The servants come in Lent and kneel down before you and confess all the things theyve done; and you have to pretend to forgive them. Do they do that in England, William?

WAITER. Not usually, miss. They may in some parts; but it has not come under my notice, miss. [*Catching Mrs Clandon's eye as the young waiter offers her the salad bowl*] You like it without dressing, maam: yes, maam, I have some for you. [*To his young colleague, motioning him to serve Gloria*] This side, Jo. [*He takes a special portion of salad from the service table and puts it beside Mrs Clandon's plate. In doing so he observes that Dolly is making a wry face*]. Only a bit of watercress, miss, got in by mistake [*he takes her salad away*]. Thank you, miss. [*To the young waiter, admonishing him to serve Dolly afresh*] Jo. [*Resuming*] Mostly members of the Church of England, miss.

DOLLY. Members of the Church of England? Whats the subscription?

CRAMPTON [*rising violently amid general consternation*] You see how my children have been brought up, M'Comas. You see it: you hear it. I call all of you to witness— [*He becomes inarticulate, and is about to strike his fist recklessly on the table when the waiter considerately takes away his plate*].

MRS CLANDON [*firmly*] Sit down, Fergus. There is no occasion at all for this outburst. You must remember that Dolly is just like a foreigner here. Pray sit down.

CRAMPTON [*subsiding unwillingly*] I doubt whether I ought to sit here and countenance all this. I doubt it.

WAITER. Cheese, sir? or would you like a cold sweet?

CRAMPTON [*taken aback*] What? Oh! Cheese, cheese.

DOLLY. Bring a box of cigarets, William.

WAITER. All ready, miss. [*He takes a box of cigarets from the service table and places them before Dolly, who selects one and prepares to smoke. He then returns to his table for the matches*].

CRAMPTON [*staring aghast at Dolly*] Does she smoke?

DOLLY [*out of patience*] Really, Mr Crampton, I'm afraid I'm spoiling your lunch. I'll go and have my cigaret on the beach. [*She leaves the table with petulant suddenness and goes to the steps. The waiter strikes a match and adroitly lights her cigaret*]. Thank you, dear William. [*She vanishes down the steps*].

CRAMPTON [*furiously*] Margaret: call that girl back. Call her back, I say.

M'COMAS [*trying to make peace*] Come, Crampton: never mind. She's her father's daughter: thats all.

MRS CLANDON [*with deep resentment*] I hope not, Finch. [*She rises: they all rise a little*]. Mr Valentine: will you excuse me? I am afraid Dolly is hurt and put out by what has passed. I must go to her.

CRAMPTON. To take her part against me, you mean.

MRS CLANDON [*ignoring him*] Gloria: will you take my place whilst I am away, dear. [*She crosses to the steps and goes down to the beach*]. *Crampton's expression is one of bitter hatred. The rest watch her in embarrassed silence, feeling the incident to be a very painful one. The waiter discreetly shepherds his assistant along with him into the hotel by the kitchen entrance, leaving the luncheon party to themselves.*

CRAMPTON [*throwing himself back in his chair*] Theres a mother for you, M'Comas! Theres a mother for you!

GLORIA [*steadfastly*] Yes: a good mother.

CRAMPTON. And a bad father? Thats what you mean, eh?

VALENTINE [*rising indignantly and addressing Gloria*] Miss Clandon: I—

CRAMPTON [*turning on him*] That girl's name is Crampton, Mr Valentine, not Clandon. Do you wish to join them in insulting me?

VALENTINE [*ignoring him*] I'm overwhelmed, Miss Clandon. It's all my fault: I brought him here: I'm responsible for him. And I'm ashamed of him.

CRAMPTON. What d'y' mean?

GLORIA [*rising coldly*] No harm has been done, Mr Valentine. We have all been a little childish, I am afraid. Our party has been a failure: let us break it up and have done with it. [*She puts her chair aside and turns to the steps, adding, with slighting composure, as she passes Crampton*] Goodbye, father.

She descends the steps with cold disgusted indifference. They all look after her, and so do not notice the return of the waiter from the hotel, laden with Crampton's coat, Valentine's stick, a couple of shawls and parasols, and some camp stools, which he deposits on the bench.

CRAMPTON [*to himself, staring after Gloria with a ghastly expression*] Father! Father!! [*He strikes his fist violently on the table*]. Now—

WAITER [*offering the coat*] This is yours, sir, I think, sir. [*Crampton glares at him; then snatches it rudely and comes down the terrace towards the garden seat, struggling with the coat in his angry efforts to put it on. M'Comas rises and goes to his assistance: then takes his hat and umbrella from the little iron table, and turns towards the steps. Meanwhile the waiter, after thanking Crampton with unruffled sweetness for taking the coat, picks up the other articles and offers the parasols to Phil*]. The ladies' sunshades, sir. Nasty glare off the sea today, sir: very trying to the complexion, sir. I shall carry down the camp stools myself, sir.

PHILIP. You are old, Father William; but you are the most thoughtful of men. No: keep the sunshades and give me the camp stools [*taking them*].

WAITER [*with flattering gratitude*] Thank you, sir.

PHILIP. Finch: share with me [*giving him a couple*]. Come along. [*They go down the steps together*].

VALENTINE [*to the waiter*] Leave me something to bring down. One of these [*offering to take a sunshade*].

WAITER [*discreetly*] Thats the younger lady's, sir. [*Valentine lets it go*]. Thank you, sir. If youll allow me, sir, I think you had better take this. [*He puts down his burden on Crampton's chair, and produces from the tail pocket of his dress coat a book with a lady's handkerchief between the leaves to mark the page*]. The elder young lady is reading it at present. [*Valentine takes it eagerly*]. Thank you, sir. The Subjection of Women, sir, you see. [*He takes up the burden again*]. Heavier reading than you and I would care for at the seaside, sir. [*He goes down the steps*].

VALENTINE [*coming rather excitedly to Crampton*] Now look here, Crampton: are you at all ashamed of yourself?

CRAMPTON [*pugnaciously*] Ashamed of myself! What for?

VALENTINE. For behaving like a bear. What will your daughter think of me for having brought you here?

CRAMPTON. I was not thinking of what my daughter was thinking of you.

VALENTINE. No, you were thinking of yourself. Youre a perfect egomaniac.

CRAMPTON [*heartrent*] She told you what I am: a father: a father robbed of his children. What are the hearts of this generation like? Am I to come here after all these years? to see what my children are for the first time! to hear their voices! and carry it all off like a fashionable visitor; drop in to lunch; be Mr Crampton? Mister Crampton! What right have they to talk to me like that? I'm their father: do they deny that? I'm a man, with the feelings of our common humanity: have I no rights, no claims? In all these years who have I had round me? Servants, clerks, business acquaintances. Ive had respect from them: aye, kindness. Would one of them have spoken to me as that girl spoke? Would one of them have laughed at me as that boy was laughing at me all the time? [*Frantically*] My own children! Mister Crampton! My—

VALENTINE. Come, come! theyre only children. She called you father.

CRAMPTON. Yes: "goodbye, father." Goodbye! Oh yes: she got at my feelings: with a stab!

VALENTINE [*taking this in very bad part*] Now look here, Crampton: you just let her alone: she's treated you very well. I had a much worse time of it at lunch than you.

CRAMPTON. You!

VALENTINE [*with growing impetuosity*] Yes: I. I sat next her; and I never said a single thing to her the whole time: couldnt think of a blessed word. And not a word did she say to me.

CRAMPTON. Well?

VALENTINE. Well? Well??? [*Tackling him very seriously, and talking faster and faster*] Crampton: do you know whats been the matter with me today? You dont suppose, do you, that I'm in the habit of playing such tricks on my patients as I played on you?

CRAMPTON. I hope not.

VALENTINE. The explanation is that I'm stark mad, or rather that Ive never been in my real senses before. I'm capable of anything: Ive grown up at last: I'm a Man; and it's your daughter thats made a man of me.

CRAMPTON [*incredulously*] Are you in love with my daughter?

VALENTINE [*his words now coming in a perfect torrent*] Love! Nonsense: it's something far above and beyond that. It's life, it's faith, it's strength, certainty, paradise—

CRAMPTON [*interrupting him with acrid con-*

H

tempt] Rubbish, man! What have you to keep a wife on? You cant marry her.

VALENTINE. Who wants to marry her? I'll kiss her hands; I'll kneel at her feet; I'll live for her; I'll die for her; and thatll be enough for me. Look at her book! See! [*He kisses the handkerchief*]. If you offered me all your money for this excuse for going down to the beach and speaking to her again, I'd only laugh at you. [*He rushes buoyantly off to the steps, where he bounces right into the arms of the waiter, who is coming up from the beach. The two save themselves from falling by clutching one another tightly round the waist and whirling one another round*].

WAITER [*delicately*] Steady, sir, steady!

VALENTINE [*shocked at his own violence*] I beg your pardon.

WAITER. Not at all, sir, not at all. Very natural, sir, I'm sure, sir, at your age. The lady has sent me for her book, sir. Might I take the liberty of asking you to let her have it at once, sir.

VALENTINE. With pleasure. And if you will allow me to present you with a professional man's earnings for six weeks— [*offering him Dolly's crown piece*]?

WAITER [*as if the sum were beyond his utmost expectations*] Thank you, sir: much obliged. [*Valentine dashes down the steps*]. Very high-spirited young gentleman, sir: very manly and straight set up.

CRAMPTON [*in grumbling disparagement*] And making his fortune in a hurry, no doubt. *I* know what his six weeks' earnings come to. [*He crosses the terrace to the iron table, and sits down*].

WAITER [*philosophically*] Well, sir, you never can tell. Thats a principle in life with me, sir, if youll excuse my having such a thing, sir. [*Delicately sinking the philosopher in the waiter for a moment*] Perhaps you havnt noticed that you hadnt touched that seltzer and Irish, sir, when the party broke up. [*He takes the tumbler from the luncheon table and sets it before Crampton*]. Yes, sir, you never can tell. There was my son, sir! who ever thought that he would rise to wear a silk gown, sir? And yet, today, sir, nothing less than fifty guineas. What a lesson, sir!

CRAMPTON. Well, I hope he is grateful to you, and recognizes what he owes you, as a son should.

WAITER. We get on together very well, very well indeed, sir, considering the difference in our stations. [*Crampton is about to take a drink*]. A small lump of sugar, sir, will take the flatness out of the seltzer without noticeably sweetening the drink, sir. Allow me, sir. [*He drops a lump of sugar into the tumbler*]. But as I say to him, wheres the difference after all? If I must put on a dress coat to shew what I am, sir, he must put on a wig and gown to shew what he is. If my income is mostly tips, and theres a pretence that I dont get them, why, his income is mostly fees, sir; and I understand theres a pretence that h e dont get them! If he likes society, and his profession brings him into contact with all ranks, so does mine too, sir. If it's a little against a barrister to have a waiter for his father, sir, it's a little against a waiter to have a barrister for a son: many people consider it a great liberty, sir, I assure you, sir. Can I get you anything else, sir?

CRAMPTON. No, thank you. [*With bitter humility*] I suppose theres no objection to my sitting here for a while: I cant disturb the party on the beach here.

WAITER [*with emotion*] Very kind of you, sir, to put it as if it was not a compliment and an honor to us, Mr Crampton, very kind indeed. The more you are at home here, sir, the better for us.

CRAMPTON [*in poignant irony*] Home!

WAITER [*reflectively*] Well, yes, sir: thats a way of looking at it too, sir. I have always said that the great advantage of a hotel is that it's a refuge from home life, sir.

CRAMPTON. I missed that advantage today, I think.

WAITER. You did, sir: you did. Dear me! It's the unexpected that always happens, isnt it? [*Shaking his head*] You never can tell, sir: you never can tell. [*He goes into the hotel*].

CRAMPTON [*his eyes shining hardly as he props his drawn miserable face on his hands*] Home! Home!! [*Hearing someone approaching he hastily sits bolt upright. It is Gloria, who has come up the steps alone, with her sunshade and her book in her hands. He looks defiantly at her, with the brutal obstinacy of his mouth and the wistfulness of his eyes contradicting each other pathetically. She comes to the corner of the garden seat and stands with her back to it, leaning against the end of it, and looking down at him as if wondering at his weakness: too curious about him to be cold, but supremely indifferent to their kinship. He greets her with a growl*]. Well?

GLORIA. I want to speak to you for a moment.

CRAMPTON [looking steadily at her] Indeed? Thats surprising. You meet your father after eighteen years; and you actually want to speak to him for a moment! Thats touching: isnt it?

GLORIA. All that is what seems to me so nonsensical, so uncalled for. What do you expect us to feel for you? to do for you? What is it you want? Why are you less civil to us than other people are? You are evidently not very fond of us: why should you be? But surely we can meet without quarrelling.

CRAMPTON [a dreadful grey shade passing over his face] Do you realize that I am your father?

GLORIA. Perfectly.

CRAMPTON. Do you know what is due to me as your father?

GLORIA. For instance——?

CRAMPTON [rising as if to combat a monster] For instance! For instance!! For instance, duty, affection, respect, obedience—

GLORIA [quitting her careless leaning attitude and confronting him promptly and proudly] I obey nothing but my sense of what is right. I respect nothing that is not noble. That is my duty. [She adds, less firmly] As to affection, it is not within my control. I am not sure that I quite know what affection means. [She turns away with an evident distaste for that part of the subject, and goes to the luncheon table for a comfortable chair, putting down her book and sunshade].

CRAMPTON [following her with his eyes] Do you really mean what you are saying?

GLORIA [turning on him quickly and severely] Excuse me: that is an uncivil question. I am speaking seriously to you; and I expect you to take me seriously. [She takes one of the luncheon chairs; turns it away from the table; and sits down a little wearily, saying] Can you not discuss this matter coolly and rationally?

CRAMPTON. Coolly and rationally! No I cant. Do you understand that? I cant.

GLORIA [emphatically] No. That I cannot understand. I have no sympathy with—

CRAMPTON [shrinking nervously] Stop! Dont say anything more yet: you dont know what youre doing. Do you want to drive me mad? [She frowns, finding such petulance intolerable. He adds hastily] No: I'm not angry: indeed I'm not. Wait, wait: give me a little time to think. [He stands for a moment, screwing and clinching his brows and hands in his perplexity; then takes the end chair from the luncheon table and sits down beside her, saying, with a touching effort to be gentle and patient] Now I think I have it. At least I'll try.

GLORIA [firmly] You see! Everything comes right if we only think it resolutely out.

CRAMPTON [in sudden dread] No: dont think. I want you to feel: thats the only thing that can help us. Listen! Do you—but first—I forgot. Whats your name? I mean your pet name. They cant very well call you Sophronia.

GLORIA [with astonished disgust] Sophronia! My name is Gloria. I am always called by it.

CRAMPTON [his temper rising again] Your name is Sophronia, girl: you were called after your aunt Sophronia, my sister: she gave you your first Bible with your name written in it.

GLORIA. Then my mother gave me a new name.

CRAMPTON [angrily] She had no right to do it. I will not allow this.

GLORIA. You had no right to give me your sister's name. I dont know her.

CRAMPTON. Youre talking nonsense. There are bounds to what I will put up with. I will not have it. Do you hear that?

GLORIA [rising warningly] Are you resolved to quarrel?

CRAMPTON [terrified, pleading] No, no: sit down. Sit down, wont you? [She looks at him, keeping him in suspense. He forces himself to utter the obnoxious name]. Gloria. [She marks her satisfaction with a slight tightening of the lips, and sits down]. There! You see I only want to shew you that I am your father, my —my dear child. [The endearment is so plaintively inept that she smiles in spite of herself, and resigns herself to indulge him a little]. Listen now. What I want to ask you is this. Dont you remember me at all? You were only a tiny child when you were taken away from me; but you took plenty of notice of things. Cant you remember someone whom you loved, or [shyly] at least liked in a childish way? Come! someone who let you stay in his study and look at his toy boats, as you thought them? [He looks anxiously into her face for some response, and continues less hopefully and more urgently] Someone who let you do as you liked there, and never said a word to you except to tell you that you must sit still and not speak? Someone who was something that no one else was to you—who was your father?

GLORIA [*unmoved*] If you describe things to me, no doubt I shall presently imagine that I remember them. But I really remember nothing.

CRAMPTON [*wistfully*] Has your mother never told you anything about me?

GLORIA. She has never mentioned your name to me. [*He groans involuntarily. She looks at him rather contemptuously, and continues*] Except once; and then she did remind me of something I had forgotten.

CRAMPTON [*looking up hopefully*] What was that?

GLORIA [*mercilessly*] The whip you bought to beat me with.

CRAMPTON [*gnashing his teeth*] Oh! To bring that up against me! To turn you from me! When you need never have known. [*Under a grinding, agonized breath*] Curse her!

GLORIA [*springing up*] You wretch! [*With intense emphasis*] You wretch!! You dare curse my mother!

CRAMPTON. Stop; or youll be sorry afterwards. I'm your father.

GLORIA. How I hate the name! How I love the name of mother! You had better go.

CRAMPTON. I—I'm choking. You want to kill me. Some—I—[*His voice stifles: he is almost in a fit*].

GLORIA [*going up to the balustrade with cool quick resourcefulness, and calling over it to the beach*] Mr Valentine!

VALENTINE [*answering from below*] Yes.

GLORIA. Come here for a moment, please. Mr Crampton wants you. [*She returns to the table and pours out a glass of water*].

CRAMPTON [*recovering his speech*] No: let me alone. I dont want him. I'm all right, I tell you. I need neither his help nor yours. [*He rises and pulls himself together*]. As you say, I had better go. [*He puts on his hat*]. Is that your last word?

GLORIA. I hope so.

He looks stubbornly at her for a moment; nods grimly, as if he agreed to that; and goes into the hotel. She looks at him with equal steadiness until he disappears, when, with a gesture of relief, she turns to Valentine, who comes running up the steps.

VALENTINE [*panting*] Whats the matter? [*Looking round*] Wheres Crampton?

GLORIA. Gone. [*Valentine's face lights up with sudden joy, dread, and mischief as he realizes that he is alone with Gloria. She continues indifferently*] I thought he was ill; but

he recovered himself. He wouldnt wait for you. I am sorry. [*She goes for her book and parasol*].

VALENTINE. So much the better. He gets on my nerves after a while. [*Pretending to forget himself*] How could that man have so beautiful a daughter!

GLORIA [*taken aback for a moment; then answering him with polite but intentional contempt*] That seems to be an attempt at what is called a pretty speech. Let me say at once, Mr Valentine, that pretty speeches make very sickly conversation. Pray let us be friends, if we are to be friends, in a sensible and wholesome way. I have no intention of getting married; and unless you are content to accept that state of things, we had much better not cultivate each other's acquaintance.

VALENTINE [*cautiously*] I see. May I ask just this one question? Is your objection an objection to marriage as an institution, or merely an objection to marrying me personally?

GLORIA. I do not know you well enough, Mr Valentine, to have any opinion on the subject of your personal merits. [*She turns away from him with infinite indifference, and sits down with her book on the garden seat*]. I do not think the conditions of marriage at present are such as any self-respecting woman can accept.

VALENTINE [*instantly changing his tone for one of cordial sincerity, as if he frankly accepted her terms and was delighted and reassured by her principles*] Oh, then thats a point of sympathy between us already. I quite agree with you: the conditions are most unfair. [*He takes off his hat and throws it gaily on the iron table*]. No: what I want is to get rid of all that nonsense. [*He sits down beside her, so naturally that she does not think of objecting, and proceeds, with enthusiasm*] Dont you think it a horrible thing that a man and a woman can hardly know one another without being supposed to have designs of that kind? As if there were no other interests! no other subjects of conversation! As if women were capable of nothing better!

GLORIA [*interested*] Ah, now you are beginning to talk humanly and sensibly, Mr Valentine.

VALENTINE [*with a gleam in his eye at the success of his hunter's guile*] Of course! two intelligent people like us! Isnt it pleasant, in this stupid convention-ridden world, to meet with someone on the same plane? someone with an unprejudiced enlightened mind?

GLORIA [*earnestly*] I hope to meet many such people in England.

VALENTINE [*dubiously*] Hm! There are a good many people here: nearly forty millions. Theyre not all consumptive members of the highly educated classes like the people in Madeira.

GLORIA [*now full of her subject*] Oh, everybody is stupid and prejudiced in Madeira: weak sentimental creatures. I hate weakness; and I hate sentiment.

VALENTINE. Thats what makes you so inspiring.

GLORIA [*with a slight laugh*] Am I inspiring?

VALENTINE. Yes. Strength's infectious.

GLORIA. Weakness is, I know.

VALENTINE [*with conviction*] Youre strong. Do you know that you changed the world for me this morning? I was in the dumps, thinking of my unpaid rent, frightened about the future. When you came in, I was dazzled. [*Her brow clouds a little. He goes on quickly*] That was silly, of course; but really and truly something happened to me. Explain it how you will, my blood got—[*he hesitates, trying to think of a sufficiently unimpassioned word*]—oxygenated: my muscles braced; my mind cleared; my courage rose. Thats odd, isnt it? considering that I am not at all a sentimental man.

GLORIA [*uneasily, rising*] Let us go back to the beach.

VALENTINE [*darkly: looking up at her*] What! you feel it too?

GLORIA. Feel what?

VALENTINE. Dread.

GLORIA. Dread!

VALENTINE. As if something were going to happen. It came over me suddenly just before you proposed that we should run away to the others.

GLORIA [*amazed*] Thats strange: very strange! I had the same presentiment.

VALENTINE [*solemnly*] How extraordinary! [*Rising*] Well: shall we run away?

GLORIA. Run away! Oh no: that would be childish. [*She sits down again. He resumes his seat beside her, and watches her with a gravely sympathetic air. She is thoughtful and a little troubled as she adds*] I wonder what is the scientific explanation of those fancies that cross us occasionally!

VALENTINE. Ah, I wonder! It's a curiously helpless sensation: isnt it?

GLORIA [*rebelling against the word*] Helpless?

VALENTINE. Yes, helpless. As if Nature, after letting us belong to ourselves and do what we judged right and reasonable for all these years, were suddenly lifting her great hand to take us—her two little children—by the scruffs of our little necks, and use us, in spite of ourselves, for her own purposes, in her own way.

GLORIA. Isnt that rather fanciful?

VALENTINE [*with a new and startling transition to a tone of utter recklessness*] I dont know. I dont care. [*Bursting out reproachfully*] Oh, Miss Clandon, Miss Clandon: how could you?

GLORIA. What have I done?

VALENTINE. Thrown this enchantment on me. I'm honestly trying to be sensible and scientific and everything that you wish me to be. But—but—oh, dont you see what you have set to work in my imagination?

GLORIA. I hope you are not going to be so foolish—so vulgar—as to say love.

VALENTINE. No, no, no, no, no. Not love: we know better than that. Let's call it chemistry. You cant deny that there is such a thing as chemical action, chemical affinity, chemical combination: the most irresistible of all natural forces. Well, youre attracting me irresistibly. Chemically.

GLORIA [*contemptuously*] Nonsense!

VALENTINE. Of course it's nonsense, you stupid girl. [*Gloria recoils in outraged surprise*]. Yes, stupid girl: thats a scientific fact, anyhow. Youre a prig: a feminine prig: thats what you are. [*Rising*] Now I suppose youve done with me for ever. [*He goes to the iron table and takes up his hat*].

GLORIA [*with elaborate calm, sitting up like a High-schoolmistress posing to be photographed*]. That shews how very little you understand my real character. I am not in the least offended. [*He pauses and puts his hat down again*]. I am always willing to be told my own defects, Mr Valentine, by my friends, even when they are as absurdly mistaken about me as you are. I have many faults—very serious faults—of character and temper; but if there is one thing that I am not, it is what you call a prig. [*She closes her lips trimly and looks steadily and challengingly at him as she sits more collectedly than ever*].

VALENTINE [returning to the end of the garden seat to confront her more emphatically] Oh yes, you are. My reason tells me so: my knowledge tells me so: my experience tells me so.

GLORIA. Excuse my reminding you that your reason and your knowledge and your experience are not infallible. At least I hope not.

VALENTINE. I must believe them. Unless you wish me to believe my eyes, my heart, my instincts, my imagination, which are all telling me the most monstrous lies about you.

GLORIA [the collectedness beginning to relax] Lies!

VALENTINE [obstinately] Yes, lies. [He sits down again beside her]. Do you expect me to believe that you are the most beautiful woman in the world?

GLORIA. That is ridiculous, and rather personal.

VALENTINE. Of course it's ridiculous. Well, thats what my eyes tell me. [Gloria makes a movement of contemptuous protest]. No: I'm not flattering. I tell you I dont believe it. [She is ashamed to find that this does not quite please her either]. Do you think that if you were to turn away in disgust from my weakness, I should sit down here and cry like a child?

GLORIA [beginning to feel that she must speak shortly and pointedly to keep her voice steady] Why should you, pray?

VALENTINE. Of course not: I'm not such an idiot. And yet my heart tells me I should: my fool of a heart. But I'll argue with my heart and bring it to reason. If I loved you a thousand times, I'll force myself to look the truth steadily in the face. After all, it's easy to be sensible: the facts are the facts. Whats this place? it's not heaven: it's the Marine Hotel. Whats the time? it's not eternity: it's about half past one in the afternoon. What am I? a dentist: a five shilling dentist!

GLORIA And I am a feminine prig.

VALENTINE [passionately] No, no: I cant face that: I must have one illusion left: the illusion about you. I love you. [He turns towards her as if the impulse to touch her were ungovernable: she rises and stands on her guard wrathfully. He springs up impatiently and retreats a step]. Oh, what a fool I am! an idiot! You dont understand: I might as well talk to the stones on the beach. [He turns away, discouraged].

GLORIA [reassured by his withdrawal, and a little remorseful] I am sorry. I do not mean to be unsympathetic, Mr Valentine: but what

can I say?

VALENTINE [returning to her with all his recklessness of manner replaced by an engaging and chivalrous respect] You can say nothing, Miss Clandon. I beg your pardon: it was my own fault, or rather my own bad luck. You see, it all depended on your naturally liking me. [She is about to speak: he stops her deprecatingly] Oh, I know you musnt tell me whether you like me or not; but—

GLORIA [her principles up in arms at once] Must not! Why not? I am a free woman: why should I not tell you?

VALENTINE [pleading in terror, and retreating] Dont. I'm afraid to hear.

GLORIA [no longer scornful] You need not be afraid. I think you are sentimental, and a little foolish; but I like you.

VALENTINE [dropping into the nearest chair as if crushed] Then it's all over. [He becomes the picture of despair].

GLORIA [puzzled, approaching him] But why?

VALENTINE. Because liking is not enough. Now that I think down into it seriously, I dont know whether I like you or not.

GLORIA [looking down at him with wondering concern] I'm sorry.

VALENTINE [in an agony of restrained passion] Oh, dont pity me. Your voice is tearing my heart to pieces. Let me alone, Gloria. You go down into the very depths of me, troubling and stirring me. I cant struggle with it. I cant tell you—

GLORIA [breaking down suddenly] Oh, stop telling me what you feel: I cant bear it.

VALENTINE [springing up triumphantly, the agonized voice now solid, ringing, and jubilant] Ah, it's come at last: my moment of courage. [He seizes her hands: she looks at him in terror]. Our moment of courage! [He draws her to him; kisses her with impetuous strength; and laughs boyishly]. Now youve done it, Gloria. It's all over: we're in love with one another. [She can only gasp at him]. But what a dragon you were! And how hideously afraid I was!

PHILIP'S VOICE [calling from the beach] Valentine!

DOLLY'S VOICE. Mr Valentine!

VALENTINE. Goodbye. Forgive me. [He rapidly kisses her hands, and runs away to the steps, where he meets Mrs Clandon ascending]. Gloria, quite lost, can only stare after him.

MRS CLANDON. The children want you, Mr Valentine. [She looks anxiously round]. Is he gone?

VALENTINE [*puzzled*] He? [*Recollecting*] Oh, Crampton. Gone this long time, Mrs Clandon. [*He runs off buoyantly down the steps*].

GLORIA [*sinking upon the bench*] Mother!

MRS CLANDON [*hurrying to her in alarm*] What is it, dear?

GLORIA [*with heartfelt appealing reproach*] Why didnt you educate me properly?

MRS CLANDON [*amazed*] My child: I did my best.

GLORIA. Oh, you taught me nothing: n o t h i n g .

MRS CLANDON. What is the matter with you?

GLORIA [*with the most intense expression*] Only shame! shame!! shame!!! [*Blushing unendurably, she covers her face with her hands and turns away from her mother*].

ACT III

The Clandons' sitting room in the hotel. An expensive apartment on the ground floor, with a French window leading to the gardens. In the centre of the room is a substantial table, surrounded by chairs, and draped with a maroon cloth on which opulently bound hotel and railway guides are displayed. A visitor entering through the window and coming down to this central table would have the fireplace on his left, and a writing table against the wall on his right, next the door, which is further down. He would, if his taste lay that way, admire the wall decoration of Lincrusta Walton in plum color and bronze lacquer, with dado and cornice; the ormolu consoles in the corners; the vases on pillar pedestals of veined marble with bases of polished black wood, one on each side of the window; the ornamental cabinet next the vase on the side nearest the fireplace, its centre compartment closed by an inlaid door, and its corners rounded off with curved panes of glass protecting shelves of cheap blue and white pottery; the bamboo tea table, with folding shelves, in the corresponding space on the other side of the window; the photogravures after Burton and Stacy Marks; the saddlebag ottoman in line with the door but on the other side of the room; the two comfortable seats of the same pattern on the hearth-rug; and finally, on turning round and looking up, the massive brass pole above the window, sustaining a pair of maroon rep curtains with decorated borders of staid green. Altogether, a room well arranged to flatter the middle-class occupant's sense of gentility, and reconcile him to a charge of a pound a day for its use.

Mrs Clandon sits at the writing table, correcting proofs. Gloria is standing at the window, looking out in a tormented revery.

The clock on the mantelpiece strikes five with a sickly clink, the bell being unable to bear up against the black marble cenotaph in which it is immured.

MRS CLANDON. Five! I dont think we need wait any longer for the children. They are sure to get tea somewhere.

GLORIA [*wearily*] Shall I ring?

MRS CLANDON. Do, my dear. [*Gloria goes to the hearth and rings*]. I have finished these proofs at last, thank goodness!

GLORIA [*strolling listlessly across the room and coming behind her mother's chair*] What proofs?

MRS CLANDON. The new edition of Twentieth Century Women.

GLORIA [*with a bitter smile*] Theres a chapter missing.

MRS CLANDON [*beginning to hunt among her proofs*] Is there? Surely not.

GLORIA. I mean an unwritten one. Perhaps I shall write it for you—when I know the end of it. [*She goes back to the window*].

MRS CLANDON. Gloria! More enigmas!

GLORIA. Oh no. The same enigma.

MRS CLANDON [*puzzled and rather troubled; after watching her for a moment*] My dear?

GLORIA [*returning*] Yes.

MRS CLANDON. You know I never ask questions.

GLORIA [*kneeling beside her chair*] I know. I know. [*She suddenly throws her arm about her mother and embraces her almost passionately*].

MRS CLANDON [*gently, smiling but embarrassed*] My dear: you are getting quite sentimental.

GLORIA [*recoiling*] Ah no, no. Oh, dont say that. Oh! [*She rises and turns away with a gesture as if tearing herself*].

MRS CLANDON [*mildly*] My dear: what is the matter? What—

The waiter enters with the tea-tray.

WAITER [*balmily*] Was this what you rang for, maam?

MRS CLANDON. Thank you, yes. [*She turns her chair away from the writing table, and sits down again. Gloria crosses to the hearth and sits crouching there with her face averted*].

WAITER [*placing the tray temporarily on the centre table*] I thought so, maam. Curious how the nerves seem to give out in the afternoon without a cup of tea. [*He fetches the tea table and places it in front of Mrs Clandon, conversing meanwhile*]. The young lady and gentleman have just come back, maam: they have been out in a boat, maam. Very pleasant on a fine afternoon like this: very pleasant and invigorating indeed. [*He takes the tray from the centre table and puts it on the tea table*]. Mr M'Comas will not come to tea, maam: he has gone to call upon Mr Crampton. [*He takes a couple of chairs and sets one at each end of the tea table*].

GLORIA [*looking round with an impulse of terror*] And the other gentleman?

WAITER [*reassuringly, as he unconsciously drops for a moment into the measure of "Ive been roaming," which he sang when a boy*] Oh, he's coming, miss: he's coming. He has been rowing the boat, miss, and has just run down the road to the chemist's for something to put on the blisters. But he will be here directly, miss: directly. [*Gloria, in ungovernable apprehension, rises and hurries towards the door*].

MRS CLANDON [*half rising*] Glo—

Gloria goes out. Mrs Clandon looks perplexedly at the waiter, whose composure is unruffled.

WAITER [*cheerfully*] Anything more, maam?

MRS CLANDON. Nothing, thank you.

WAITER. Thank you, maam. [*As he withdraws, Phil and Dolly, in the highest spirits, come tearing in. He holds the door open for them: then goes out and closes it*].

DOLLY [*ravenously*] Oh, give me some tea. [*Mrs Clandon pours out a cup for her*]. Weve been out in a boat. Valentine will be here presently.

PHILIP. He is unaccustomed to navigation. Wheres Gloria?

MRS CLANDON [*anxiously, as she pours out his tea*] Phil: there is something the matter with Gloria. Has anything happened? [*Phil and Dolly look at one another and stifle a laugh*]. What is it?

PHILIP [*sitting down on her left*] Romeo—

DOLLY [*sitting down on her right*]—and Juliet.

PHILIP [*taking his cup of tea from Mrs Clandon*] Yes, my dear mother: the old, old story. Dolly: dont take all the milk [*he deftly takes the jug from her*]. Yes: in the spring—

DOLLY.—a young man's fancy—

PHILIP.—lightly turns to—thank you [*to Mrs Clandon, who has passed the biscuits*]—thoughts of love. It also occurs in the autumn. The young man in this case is—

DOLLY. Valentine.

PHILIP. And his fancy has turned to Gloria to the extent of—

DOLLY.—kissing her—

PHILIP.—on the terrace—

DOLLY [*correcting him*]—on the lips, before everybody.

MRS CLANDON [*incredulously*] Phil! Dolly! Are you joking? [*They shake their heads*]. Did she allow it?

PHILIP. We waited to see him struck to earth by the lightning of her scorn; but—

DOLLY.—but he wasnt.

PHILIP. She appeared to like it.

DOLLY. As far as we could judge. [*Stopping Phil, who is about to pour out another cup*] No: youve sworn off two cups.

MRS CLANDON [*much troubled*] Children: you must not be here when Mr Valentine comes. I must speak very seriously to him about this.

PHILIP. To ask him his intentions? What a violation of Twentieth Century principles!

DOLLY. Quite right, mamma: bring him to book. Make the most of the nineteenth century while it lasts.

PHILIP. Sh! Here he is.

VALENTINE [*entering*] Very sorry to be late, Mrs Clandon. [*She takes up the tea-pot*]. No, thank you: I never take any. No doubt Miss Dolly and Phil have explained what happened to me.

PHILIP [*momentously, rising*] Yes, Valentine: we have explained.

DOLLY [*significantly, also rising*] We have explained very thoroughly.

PHILIP. It was our duty. [*Very seriously*] Come, Dolly. [*He offers Dolly his arm, which she takes. They look sadly at him, and go out gravely arm in arm, leaving Valentine staring*].

MRS CLANDON [*rising and leaving the tea table*] Will you sit down, Mr Valentine? I want to speak to you a little, if you will allow me. [*Valentine goes slowly to the ottoman, his conscience presaging a bad quarter of an hour. Mrs Clandon takes Phil's chair, and seats herself with gentle dignity. Valentine sits down*]. I must begin by throwing myself somewhat on your consideration. I am going to speak of a subject of which I know very little: perhaps nothing. I mean love.

VALENTINE. Love!

MRS CLANDON. Yes, love. Oh, you need not look so alarmed as that, Mr Valentine: I am not in love with you.

VALENTINE [*overwhelmed*] Oh, really, Mrs—

[*Recovering himself*] I should be only too proud if you were.

MRS CLANDON. Thank you, Mr Valentine. But I am too old to begin.

VALENTINE. Begin! Have you never—?

MRS CLANDON. Never. My case is a very common one, Mr Valentine. I married before I was old enough to know what I was doing. As you have seen for yourself, the result was a bitter disappointment for both my husband and myself. So you see, though I am a married woman, I have never been in love; I have never had a love affair; and, to be quite frank with you, Mr Valentine, what I have seen of the love affairs of other people has not led me to regret that deficiency in my experience. [*Valentine, looking very glum, glances sceptically at her, and says nothing. Her color rises a little; and she adds, with restrained anger*] You do not believe me?

VALENTINE [*confused at having his thoughts read*] Oh, why not? Why not?

MRS CLANDON. Let me tell you, Mr Valentine, that a life devoted to the Cause of Humanity has enthusiasms and passions to offer which far transcend the selfish personal infatuations and sentimentalities of romance. Those are not your enthusiasms and passions, I take it? [*Valentine, quite aware that she despises him for it, answers in the negative with a melancholy shake of his head*]. I thought not. Well, I am equally at a disadvantage in discussing those so-called affairs of the heart in which you appear to be an expert.

VALENTINE [*restlessly*] What are you driving at, Mrs Clandon?

MRS CLANDON. I think you know.

VALENTINE. Gloria?

MRS CLANDON. Yes. Gloria.

VALENTINE [*surrendering*] Well, yes: I'm in love with Gloria. [*Interposing as she is about to speak*] I know what youre going to say: Ive no money.

MRS CLANDON. I care very little about money, Mr Valentine.

VALENTINE. Then youre very different to all the other mothers who have interviewed me.

MRS CLANDON. Ah, now we are coming to it, Mr Valentine. You are an old hand at this. [*He opens his mouth to protest: she cuts him short with some indignation*]. Oh, do you think, little as I understand these matters, that I have not common sense enough to know that a man who could make as much way in one

interview with such a woman as my daughter can hardly be a novice?

VALENTINE. I assure you—

MRS CLANDON [*stopping him*] I am not blaming you, Mr Valentine. It is Gloria's business to take care of herself; and you have a right to amuse yourself as you please. But—

VALENTINE [*protesting*] Amuse myself! Oh, Mrs Clandon!

MRS CLANDON [*relentlessly*] On your honor, Mr Valentine, are you in earnest?

VALENTINE [*desperately*] On my honor I am in earnest. [*She looks searchingly at him. His sense of humor gets the better of him; and he adds quaintly*] Only, I always have been in earnest; and yet—! Well, here I am, you see.

MRS CLANDON. This is just what I suspected. [*Severely*] Mr Valentine: you are one of those men who play with women's affections.

VALENTINE. Well, why not, if the Cause of Humanity is the only thing worth being serious about? However, I understand. [*Rising and taking his hat with formal politeness*] You wish me to discontinue my visits.

MRS CLANDON. No: I am sensible enough to be well aware that Gloria's best chance of escape from you now is to become better acquainted with you.

VALENTINE [*unaffectedly alarmed*] Oh, dont say that, Mrs Clandon. You dont think that, do you?

MRS CLANDON. I have great faith, Mr Valentine, in the sound training Gloria's mind has had since she was a child.

VALENTINE [*amazingly relieved*] O-oh! Oh, thats all right. [*He sits down again and throws his hat flippantly aside with the air of a man who has no longer anything to fear*].

MRS CLANDON [*indignant at his assurance*] What do you mean?

VALENTINE [*turning confidentially to her*] Come! shall I teach you something, Mrs Clandon?

MRS CLANDON [*stiffly*] I am always willing to learn.

VALENTINE. Have you ever studied the subject of gunnery? artillery? cannons and war-ships and so on?

MRS CLANDON. Has gunnery anything to do with Gloria?

VALENTINE. A great deal. By way of illustration. During this whole century, my dear Mrs Clandon, the progress of artillery has been a duel between the maker of cannons and the maker of armor plates to keep the

H 2

cannon balls out. You build a ship proof against the best gun known: somebody makes a better gun and sinks your ship. You build a heavier ship, proof against that gun: somebody makes a heavier gun and sinks you again. And so on. Well, the duel of sex is just like that.

MRS CLANDON. The duel of sex!

VALENTINE. Yes: youve heard of the duel of sex, havnt you? Oh, I forgot: youve been in Madeira: the expression has come up since your time. Need I explain it?

MRS CLANDON [contemptuously] No.

VALENTINE. Of course not. Now what happens in the duel of sex? The old fashioned daughter received an old fashioned education to protect her against the wiles of man. Well, you know the result: the old fashioned man got round her. The old fashioned mother resolved to protect her daughter more effectually—to find some armor too strong for the old fashioned man. So she gave her daughter a scientific education: your plan. That was a corker for the old fashioned man: he thought it unfair, and tried to howl it down as unwomanly and all the rest of it. But that didnt do him any good. So he had to give up his old fashioned plan of attack: you know: going down on his knees and swearing to love, honor, and obey and so on.

MRS CLANDON. Excuse me: that was what the woman swore.

VALENTINE. Was it? Ah, perhaps youre right. Yes: of course it was. Well, what did the man do? Just what the artillery man does: went one better than the woman: educated himself scientifically and beat her at that game just as he had beaten her at the old game. I learnt how to circumvent the Women's Rights woman before I was twenty-three: it's all been found out long ago. You see, my methods are thoroughly modern.

MRS CLANDON [with quiet disgust] No doubt.

VALENTINE. But for that very reason theres one sort of girl against whom they are of no use.

MRS CLANDON. Pray which sort?

VALENTINE. The thoroughly old fashioned girl. If you had brought up Gloria in the old way, it would have taken me eighteen months to get to the point I got to this afternoon in eighteen minutes. Yes, Mrs Clandon: the Higher Education of Women delivered Gloria into my hands; and it was you who taught her to believe in the Higher Education of Women.

MRS CLANDON [rising] Mr Valentine: You are very clever.

VALENTINE [rising also] Oh, Mrs Clandon!

MRS CLANDON. And you have taught me—nothing. Goodbye.

VALENTINE [horrified] Goodbye! Oh, maynt I see her before I go?

MRS CLANDON. I am afraid she will not return until you have gone, Mr Valentine. She left the room expressly to avoid you.

VALENTINE [thoughtfully] Thats a good sign. Goodbye. [He bows and makes for the door, apparently well satisfied].

MRS CLANDON [alarmed] Why do you think it a good sign?

VALENTINE [turning near the door] Because I am mortally afraid of her; and it looks as if she were mortally afraid of me.

He turns to go and finds himself face to face with Gloria, who has just entered. She looks steadfastly at him. He stares helplessly at her; then round at Mrs Clandon; then at Gloria again, completely at a loss.

GLORIA [white, and controlling herself with difficulty] Mother: is what Dolly told me true?

MRS CLANDON. What did she tell you, dear?

GLORIA. That you have been speaking about me to this gentleman?

VALENTINE [murmuring] This gentleman! Oh!

MRS CLANDON [sharply] Mr Valentine: can you hold your tongue for a moment?

He looks piteously at them; then, with a despairing shrug, goes back to the ottoman and throws his hat on it.

GLORIA [confronting her mother, with deep reproach] Mother: what right had you to do it?

MRS CLANDON. I dont think I have said anything I have no right to say, Gloria.

VALENTINE [confirming her officiously] Nothing. Nothing whatever. [The two women look at him crushingly]. I beg your pardon. [He sits down ignominiously on the ottoman].

GLORIA. I cannot believe that anyone has any right even to think about things that concern me only. [She turns away from them to conceal a painful struggle with her emotion].

MRS CLANDON. My dear: if I have wounded your pride—

GLORIA [turning on them for a moment] My pride! My pride!! Oh, it's gone: I have learnt now that I have no strength to be proud of. [Turning away again] But if a woman cannot protect herself, no one can protect her. No one has any right to try: not even her mother. I know I have lost your confidence, just as I have lost this man's respect— [*She stops to regain command of her voice*].

VALENTINE. This man! Oh!

MRS CLANDON. Pray be silent, sir.

GLORIA [*continuing*] —but I have at least the right to be left alone in my disgrace. I am one of those weak creatures born to be mastered by the first man whose eye is caught by them; and I must fulfil my destiny, I suppose. At least spare me the humiliation of trying to save me. [*She sits down with her handkerchief to her eyes, at the further end of the table*].

VALENTINE [*jumping up*] Look here—

MRS CLANDON [*severely*] Mr Va—

VALENTINE [*recklessly*] No: I will speak: Ive been silent for nearly thirty seconds. [*He goes resolutely to Gloria*]. Miss Clandon—

GLORIA [*bitterly*] Oh, not Miss Clandon: you have found it quite safe to call me Gloria.

VALENTINE. No I wont: youll throw it in my teeth afterwards and accuse me of disrespect. I say it's a heartbreaking falsehood that I dont respect you. It's true that I didnt respect your old pride: why should I? it was nothing but cowardice. I didnt respect your intellect: Ive a better one myself: it's a masculine speciality. But when the depths stirred! when my moment came! when you made me brave! ah, then! then!! then!!!

GLORIA. Then you respected me, I suppose.

VALENTINE. No I didnt: I adored you. [*She rises quickly and turns her back on him*]. And you can never take that moment away from me. So now I dont care what happens. [*He comes back to the ottoman, addressing a cheerful explanation to nobody in particular*] I'm perfectly aware that I'm talking nonsense. I cant help it. [*To Mrs Clandon*] I love Gloria; and theres an end of it.

MRS CLANDON [*emphatically*] Mr Valentine: you are a most dangerous man. Gloria: come here. [*Gloria, wondering a little at the command, obeys, and stands, with drooping head, on her mother's right hand, Valentine being on the opposite side. Mrs Clandon then begins, with intense scorn*] Ask this man whom you have inspired and made brave, how many women have inspired him before [*Gloria looks up suddenly with a flash of jealous anger and amazement*]; how many times he has laid the trap in which he has caught you; how often he has baited it with the same speeches; how

much practice it has taken to make him perfect in his chosen part in life as the Duellist of Sex.

VALENTINE. This isnt fair. Youre abusing my confidence, Mrs Clandon.

MRS CLANDON. Ask him, Gloria.

GLORIA [*in a flush of rage, going over to him with her fists clenched*] Is that true?

VALENTINE. Dont be angry—

GLORIA [*interrupting him implacably*] Is it true? Did you ever say that before? Did you ever feel that before? for another woman?

VALENTINE [*bluntly*] Yes.

Gloria raises her clenched hands.

MRS CLANDON [*horrified, catching her uplifted arm*] Gloria!! My dear! Youre forgetting yourself.

Gloria, with a deep expiration, slowly relaxes her threatening attitude.

VALENTINE. Remember: a man's power of love and admiration is like any other of his powers: he has to throw it away many times before he learns what is really worthy of it.

MRS CLANDON. Another of the old speeches, Gloria. Take care.

VALENTINE [*remonstrating*] Oh!

GLORIA [*to Mrs Clandon, with contemptuous self-possession*] Do you think I need to be warned now? [*To Valentine*] You have tried to make me love you.

VALENTINE. I have.

GLORIA. Well, you have succeeded in making me hate you: passionately.

VALENTINE [*philosophically*] It's surprising how little difference there is between the two. [*Gloria turns indignantly away from him. He continues, to Mrs Clandon*] I know men whose wives love them; and they go on exactly like that.

MRS CLANDON. Excuse me, Mr Valentine; but had you not better go?

GLORIA. You need not send him away on my account, mother. He is nothing to me now; and he will amuse Dolly and Phil. [*She sits down with slighting indifference, at the end of the table nearest the window*].

VALENTINE [*gaily*] Of course: thats the sensible way of looking at it. Come, Mrs Clandon! you cant quarrel with a mere butterfly like me!

MRS CLANDON. I very greatly mistrust you, Mr Valentine. But I do not like to think that your unfortunate levity of disposition is mere shamelessness and worthlessness;—

GLORIA [*to herself, but aloud*] It is shameless; and it is worthless.

MRS CLANDON [*continuing*] —so perhaps we had better send for Phil and Dolly, and allow you to end your visit in the ordinary way.

VALENTINE [*as if she had paid him the highest compliment*] You overwhelm me, Mrs Clandon. Thank you.

The waiter returns.

WAITER. Mr M'Comas, maam.

MRS CLANDON. Oh, certainly. Bring him in.

WAITER. He wishes to see you in the reception-room, maam.

MRS CLANDON. Why not here?

WAITER. Well, if you will excuse my mentioning it, maam, I think Mr M'Comas feels that he would get fairer play if he could speak to you away from the younger members of your family, maam.

MRS CLANDON. Tell him they are not here.

WAITER. They are within sight of the door, maam; and very watchful, for some reason or other.

MRS CLANDON [*going*] Oh, very well: I'll go to him.

WAITER [*holding the door open for her*] Thank you, maam. *She goes out. He comes back into the room, and meets the eye of Valentine, who wants him to go*]. All right, sir. Only the tea-things, sir. [*Taking the tray*] Excuse me, sir. Thank you, sir. [*He goes out*].

VALENTINE [*to Gloria*] Look here. Youll forgive me, sooner or later. Forgive me now.

GLORIA [*rising to level the declaration more intensely at him*] Never! While grass grows or water runs, never! never!! never!!!

VALENTINE [*unabashed*] Well, I dont care. I cant be unhappy about anything. I shall never be unhappy again, never, never, never, while grass grows or water runs. The thought of you will always make me wild with joy. [*Some quick taunt is on her lips: he interposes swiftly*] No: I never said that before: thats new.

GLORIA. It will not be new when you say it to the next woman.

VALENTINE. Oh dont, Gloria, dont. [*He kneels at her feet*].

GLORIA. Get up! Get up! How dare you? *Phil and Dolly, racing, as usual, for first place, burst into the room. They check themselves on seeing what is passing. Valentine springs up.*

PHILIP [*discreetly*] I beg your pardon. Come, Dolly. [*He offers her his arm and turns to go*].

GLORIA [*annoyed*] Mother will be back in a moment, Phil. [*Severely*] Please wait here for

her. [*She turns away to the window, where she stands looking out with her back to them*].

PHILIP [*significantly*] Oh, indeed. Hmhm!

DOLLY. Ahah!

PHILIP. You seem in excellent spirits, Valentine.

VALENTINE. I am. [*He comes between them*]. Now look here. You both know whats going on: dont you?

Gloria turns quickly, as if anticipating some fresh outrage.

DOLLY. Perfectly.

VALENTINE. Well, it's all over. Ive been refused. Scorned. I'm here on sufferance only. You understand? it's all over. Your sister is in no sense entertaining my addresses, or condescending to interest herself in me in any way. [*Gloria, satisfied, turns back contemptuously to the window*]. Is that clear?

DOLLY. Serve you right. You were in too great a hurry.

PHILIP [*patting him on the shoulder*] Never mind: youd never have been able to call your soul your own if she'd married you. You can now begin a new chapter in your life.

DOLLY. Chapter seventeen or thereabouts, I should imagine.

VALENTINE [*much put out by this pleasantry*] No: dont say things like that. Thats just the sort of thoughtless remark that makes a lot of mischief.

DOLLY. Oh, indeed? Hmhm!

PHILIP. Ahah! [*He goes to the hearth and plants himself there in his best head-of-the-family attitude*].

M'Comas, looking very serious, comes in quickly with Mrs Clandon, whose first anxiety is about Gloria. She looks round to see where she is, and is going to join her at the window when Gloria comes down to meet her with a marked air of trust and affection. Finally Mrs Clandon takes her former seat, and Gloria posts herself behind it. M'Comas, on his way to the ottoman, is hailed by Dolly.

DOLLY. What cheer, Finch?

M'COMAS [*sternly*] Very serious news from your father, Miss Clandon. Very serious news indeed. [*He passes impressively to the ottoman, and sits down*].

Dolly, duly impressed, follows and sits beside him on his right.

VALENTINE. Perhaps I had better go.

M'COMAS. By no means, Mr Valentine. You are deeply concerned in this. [*Valentine takes a chair from the table and sits astride of it, leaning over the back, near the ottoman*]. Mrs Clandon: your husband demands the custody of his two younger children, who are not of age.

MRS CLANDON [*in quick alarm*] To take Dolly from me?

DOLLY [*touched*] But how nice of him! He likes us, mamma.

M'COMAS. I am sorry to have to disabuse you of any such illusion, Miss Dorothea.

DOLLY [*cooing ecstatically*] Dorothee-ee-ee-a [*Nestling against his shoulder, quite overcome*]. Oh, Finch!

M'COMAS [*nervously, shrinking away*] No, no, no, no!

MRS CLANDON. The deed of separation gives me the custody of the children.

M'COMAS. It also contains a covenant that you are not to approach or molest him in any way.

MRS CLANDON. Well: have I done so?

M'COMAS. Whether the behavior of your younger children amounts to legal molestation is a question on which it may be necessary to take counsel's opinion. At all events, Mr Crampton not only claims to have been molested; but he believes that he was brought here by a plot in which Mr Valentine acted as your agent.

VALENTINE. Whats that? Eh?

M'COMAS. He alleges that you drugged him, Mr Valentine.

VALENTINE. So I did.

M'COMAS. But what did you do that for?

DOLLY. Five shillings extra.

M'COMAS [*to Dolly, short-tempered*] I must really ask you, Miss Clandon, not to interrupt this very serious conversation with irrelevant interjections. [*Vehemently*] I insist on having earnest matters earnestly and reverently discussed. [*This outburst produces an apologetic silence, and puts M'Comas himself out of countenance. He coughs, and starts afresh, addressing himself to Gloria*]. Miss Clandon: it is my duty to tell you that your father has also persuaded himself that Mr Valentine wishes to marry you—

VALENTINE [*interposing adroitly*] I do.

M'COMAS [*huffily*] In that case, sir, you must not be surprised to find yourself regarded by the young lady's father as a fortune hunter.

VALENTINE. So I am. Do you expect my wife to live on what I earn? tenpence a week!

M'COMAS [*revolted*] I have nothing more to say, sir. I shall return and tell Mr Crampton

that this family is no place for a father. [*He makes for the door*].

MRS CLANDON [*With quiet authority*] Finch! [*He halts*]. If Mr Valentine cannot be serious, you can. Sit down. [*M'Comas, after a brief struggle between his dignity and his friendship, succumbs, seating himself this time midway between Dolly and Mrs Clandon*]. You know that all this is a made up case—that Fergus does not believe in it any more than you do. Now give me your real advice: your sincere, friendly advice. You know I have always trusted your judgment. I promise you the children will be quiet.

M'COMAS [*resigning himself*] Well, well! What I want to say is this. In the old arrangement with your husband, Mrs Clandon, you had him at a terrible disadvantage.

MRS CLANDON. How so, pray?

M'COMAS. Well, you were an advanced woman, accustomed to defy public opinion, and with no regard for what the world might say of you.

MRS CLANDON [*proud of it*] Yes: that is true.

Gloria, behind the chair, stoops and kisses her mother's hair, a demonstration which disconcerts her extremely.

M'COMAS. On the other hand, Mrs Clandon, your husband had a great horror of anything getting into the papers. There was his business to be considered, as well as the prejudices of an old fashioned family.

MRS CLANDON. Not to mention his own prejudices.

M'COMAS. Now no doubt he behaved badly, Mrs Clandon.

MRS CLANDON [*scornfully*] No doubt.

M'COMAS. But was it altogether his fault?

MRS CLANDON. Was it mine?

M'COMAS [*hastily*] No. Of course not.

GLORIA [*observing him attentively*] You do not mean that, Mr M'Comas.

M'COMAS. My dear young lady, you pick me up very sharply. But let me just put this to you. When a man makes an unsuitable marriage (nobody's fault, you know, but purely accidental incompatibility of tastes); when he is deprived by that misfortune of the domestic sympathy which, I take it, is what a man marries for; when, in short, his wife is rather worse than no wife at all (through no fault of her own, of course), is it to be wondered at if he makes matters worse at first by blaming her, and even, in his desperation, by occasionally drinking himself into a violent condition or seeking sympathy elsewhere?

MRS CLANDON. I did not blame him: I simply rescued myself and the children from him.

M'COMAS. Yes; but you made hard terms, Mrs Clandon. You had him at your mercy: you brought him to his knees when you threatened to make the matter public by applying to the Courts for a judicial separation. Suppose he had had that power over you, and used it to take your children away from him and bring them up in ignorance of your very name, how would you feel? what would you do? Well, wont you make some allowance for his feelings? in common humanity.

MRS CLANDON. I never discovered his feelings. I discovered his temper, and his—[she shivers] the rest of his common humanity.

M'COMAS [wistfully] Women can be very hard, Mrs Clandon.

VALENTINE. Thats true.

GLORIA [angrily] Be silent. [He subsides].

M'COMAS [rallying all his forces] Let me make one last appeal. Mrs Clandon: believe me, there are men who have a good deal of feeling, and kind feeling too, which they are not able to express. What you miss in Crampton is that mere veneer of civilization, the art of shewing worthless attentions and paying insincere compliments in a kindly charming way. If you lived in London, where the whole system is one of false good-fellowship, and you may know a man for twenty years without finding out that he hates you like poison, you would soon have your eyes opened. There we do unkind things in a kind way: we say bitter things in a sweet voice: we always give our friends chloroform when we tear them to pieces. But think of the other side of it! Think of the people who do kind things in an unkind way! people whose touch hurts, whose voices jar, whose tempers play them false, who wound and worry the people they love in the very act of trying to conciliate them, and who yet need affection as much as the rest of us. Crampton has an abominable temper, I admit. He has no manners, no tact, no grace. He'll never be able to gain anyone's affection unless they will take his desire for it on trust. Is he to have none? not even pity? from his own flesh and blood?

DOLLY [quite melted] Oh how beautiful, Finch! How nice of you!

PHILIP [with conviction] Finch: this is eloquence: positive eloquence.

DOLLY. Oh mamma, let us give him another chance. Let us have him to dinner.

MRS CLANDON [unmoved] No, Dolly: I hardly got any lunch. My dear Finch: there is not the least use in talking to me about Fergus. You have never been married to him: I have.

M'COMAS [to Gloria] Miss Clandon: I have hitherto refrained from appealing to you, because, if what Mr Crampton told me be true, you have been more merciless even than your mother.

GLORIA [defiantly] You appeal from her strength to my weakness!

M'COMAS. Not your weakness, Miss Clandon. I appeal from her intellect to your heart.

GLORIA. I have learnt to mistrust my heart. [With an angry glance at Valentine] I would tear my heart out and throw it away if I could. My answer to you is my mother's answer.

M'COMAS [defeated] Well, I am sorry. Very sorry. I have done my best. [He rises and prepares to go, deeply dissatisfied].

MRS CLANDON. But what did you expect, Finch? What do you want us to do?

M'COMAS. The first step for both you and Crampton is to obtain counsel's opinion as to whether he is bound by the deed of separation or not. Now why not obtain this opinion at once, and have a friendly meeting [her face hardens] or shall we say a neutral meeting? to settle the difficulty? Here? In this hotel? To-night? What do you say?

MRS CLANDON. But where is the counsel's opinion to come from?

M'COMAS. It has dropped down on us out of the clouds. On my way back here from Crampton's I met a most eminent Q.C.: a man whom I briefed in the case that made his name for him. He has come down here from Saturday to Monday for the sea air, and to visit a relative of his who lives here. He has been good enough to say that if I can arrange a meeting of the parties he will come and help us with his opinion. Now do let us seize this chance of a quiet friendly family adjustment. Let me bring my friend here and try to persuade Crampton to come too. Come: consent.

MRS CLANDON [rather ominously, after a moment's consideration] Finch: I dont want counsel's opinion, because I intend to be guided by my own opinion. I dont want to meet Fergus again, because I dont like him, and dont believe the meeting will do any good. However [rising], you have persuaded the children that he is not quite hopeless. Do as you please.

M'COMAS [taking her hand and shaking it] Thank you, Mrs Clandon. Will nine o'clock suit you?

MRS CLANDON. Perfectly. Phil: will you ring, please. [Phil rings the bell]. But if I am to be accused of conspiring with Mr Valentine, I think he had better be present.

VALENTINE [rising] I quite agree with you. I think it's most important.

M'COMAS. There can be no objection to that, I think. I have the greatest hopes of a happy settlement. Goodbye for the present. [He goes out, meeting the waiter, who holds the door open for him].

MRS CLANDON. We expect some visitors at nine, William. Can we have dinner at seven instead of half past?

WAITER [at the door] Seven, maam? Certainly, maam. It will be a convenience to us this busy evening, maam. There will be the band and the arranging of the fairy lights and one thing or another, maam.

DOLLY. Fairy lights!

PHILIP. A band! William: what mean you?

WAITER. The fancy ball, miss.

DOLLY AND PHILIP [simultaneously rushing to him] Fancy ball!!!

WAITER. Oh yes, sir. Given by the regatta committee for the benefit of the Life-boat, sir. [To Mrs Clandon] We often have them, maam: Chinese lanterns in the garden, maam: very bright and pleasant, very gay and innocent indeed. [To Phil] Tickets downstairs at the office, sir, five shillings: ladies half price if accompanied by a gentleman.

PHILIP [seizing his arm to drag him off] To the office, William!

DOLLY [breathlessly, seizing his other arm] Quick, before theyre all sold. [They rush him out of the room between them].

MRS CLANDON [following them] But they musnt go off dancing this evening. They must be here to meet— [She disappears].

Gloria stares coolly at Valentine, and then deliberately looks at her watch.

VALENTINE. I understand. Ive stayed too long. I'm going.

GLORIA [with disdainful punctiliousness] I owe you some apology, Mr Valentine. I am conscious of having spoken to you somewhat sharply. Perhaps rudely.

VALENTINE. Not at all.

GLORIA. My only excuse is that it is very difficult to give consideration and respect when there is no dignity of character on the other side to command it.

VALENTINE. How is a man to look dignified when he's infatuated?

GLORIA [angrily] Dont say those things to me. I forbid you. They are insults.

VALENTINE. No: theyre only follies. I cant help them.

GLORIA. If you were really in love, it would not make you foolish: it would give you dignity! earnestness! even beauty.

VALENTINE. Do you really think it would make me beautiful? [She turns her back on him with the coldest contempt]. Ah, you see youre not in earnest. Love cant give any man new gifts. It can only heighten the gifts he was born with.

GLORIA [sweeping round at him again] What gifts were y o u born with, pray?

VALENTINE. Lightness of heart.

GLORIA. And lightness of head, and lightness of faith, and lightness of everything that makes a man.

VALENTINE. Yes, the whole world is like a feather dancing in the light now; and Gloria is the sun. [She rears her head haughtily]. Beg pardon: I'm off. Back at nine. Goodbye. [He runs off gaily, leaving her standing in the middle of the room staring after him].

GLORIA [at the top of her voice; suddenly furious with him for leaving her] Idiot!

ACT IV

The same room. Nine o'clock. Nobody present. The lamps are lighted; but the curtains are not drawn. The window stands wide open; and strings of Chinese lanterns are glowing among the trees outside, with the starry sky beyond. The band is playing dance-music in the garden, drowning the sound of the sea.

The waiter enters, shewing in Crampton and M'Comas. Crampton looks cowed and anxious. He sits down wearily and timidly on the ottoman.

WAITER. The ladies have gone for a turn through the grounds to see the fancy dresses, sir. If you will be so good as to take seats, gentlemen, I shall tell them. [He is about to go into the garden through the window when M'Comas stops him].

M'COMAS. Stop a bit. If another gentleman

comes shew him in without any delay: we are expecting him.

WAITER. Right, sir. What name, sir?

M'COMAS. Boon. Mr Boon. He is a stranger to Mrs Clandon; so he may give you a card. If so, the name is spelt B.O.H.U.N. You will not forget.

WAITER [smiling] You may depend on me for that, sir. My own name is Boon, sir, though I am best known down here as Balmy Walters, sir. By rights I should spell it with the aitch you, sir; but I think it best not to take that liberty, sir. There is Norman blood in it, sir; and Norman blood is not a recommendation to a waiter.

M'COMAS. Well, well: "True hearts are more than coronets, and simple faith than Norman blood."

WAITER. That depends a good deal on one's station in life, sir. If you were a waiter, sir, youd find that simple faith would leave you just as short as Norman blood. I find it best to spell myself B. double-O.N., and to keep my wits pretty sharp about me. But I'm taking up your time, sir. Youll excuse me, sir: your own fault for being so affable, sir. I'll tell the ladies youre here, sir. [He goes out into the garden through the window].

M'COMAS. Crampton: I can depend on you, cant I?

CRAMPTON. Yes, yes. I'll be quiet. I'll be patient. I'll do my best.

M'COMAS. Remember: Ive not given you away. Ive told them it was all their fault.

CRAMPTON. You told me that it was all my fault.

M'COMAS. I told you the truth.

CRAMPTON [plaintively] If they will only be fair to me!

M'COMAS. My dear Crampton, they wont be fair to you: it's not to be expected from them at their age. If youre going to make impossible conditions of this kind, we may as well go back home at once.

CRAMPTON. But surely I have a right—

M'COMAS [intolerantly] You wont get your rights. Now, once for all, Crampton, did your promise of good behavior only mean that you wont complain if theres nothing to complain of? Because, if so— [He moves as if to go].

CRAMPTON [miserably] No, no: let me alone, cant you? Ive been bullied enough: Ive been tormented enough. I tell you I'll do my best. But if that girl begins to talk to me like that and to look at me like— [He breaks off and

buries his head in his hands].

M'COMAS [relenting] There, there: itll be all right, if you will only bear and forbear. Come: pull yourself together: theres someone coming. [Crampton, too dejected to care much, hardly changes his attitude. Gloria enters from the garden, M'Comas goes to meet her at the window; so that he can speak to her without being heard by Crampton]. There he is, Miss Clandon. Be kind to him. I'll leave you with him for a moment. [He goes into the garden].

Gloria comes in and strolls coolly down the middle of the room.

CRAMPTON [looking round in alarm] Wheres M'Comas?

GLORIA [listlessly, but not unsympathetically] Gone out. To leave us together. Delicacy on his part, I suppose. [She stops beside him and looks quaintly down at him]. Well, father?

CRAMPTON [submissively] Well, daughter?

They look at one another with a melancholy sense of humor, though humor is not their strong point.

GLORIA. Shake hands. [They shake hands].

CRAMPTON [holding her hand] My dear: I'm afraid I spoke very improperly of your mother this afternoon.

GLORIA. Oh, dont apologize. I was very high and mighty myself; but Ive come down since: oh, yes: Ive been brought down. [She sits down on the floor beside his chair].

CRAMPTON. What has happened to you, my child?

GLORIA. Oh, never mind. I was playing the part of my mother's daughter then; but I'm not: I'm my father's daughter. [Looking at him forlornly] Thats a come down, isnt it?

CRAMPTON [angry] What! [Her expression does not alter. He surrenders]. Well, yes, my dear: I suppose it is, I suppose it is. I'm afraid I'm sometimes a little irritable; but I know whats right and reasonable all the time, even when I dont act on it. Can you believe that?

GLORIA. Believe it! Why, thats myself: myself all over. I know whats right and dignified and strong and noble, just as well as she does; but oh, the things I do! the things I do! the things I let other people do!!

CRAMPTON [a little grudgingly in spite of himself] As well as she does? You mean your mother?

GLORIA [quickly] Yes, mother. [She turns to him on her knees and seizes his hands]. Now listen. No treason to her: no word, no thought against her. She is our superior: yours and mine: high heavens above us. Is that agreed?

CRAMPTON. Yes, yes. Just as you please, my dear.

GLORIA [*not satisfied, letting go his hands and drawing back from him*] You dont like her?

CRAMPTON. My child: you havnt been married to her. I have. [*She raises herself slowly to her feet, looking at him with growing coldness*]. She did me a great wrong in marrying me without really caring for me. But after that, the wrong was all on my side, I dare say. [*He offers her his hand again*].

GLORIA [*taking it firmly and warningly*] Take care. Thats my dangerous subject. My feelings—my miserable cowardly womanly feelings—may be on your side; but my conscience is on hers.

CRAMPTON. I'm very well content with that division, my dear. Thank you.

Valentine arrives. Gloria immediately becomes deliberately haughty.

VALENTINE. Excuse me; but it's impossible to find a servant to announce one: even the never failing William seems to be at the ball. I should have gone myself; only I havnt five shillings to buy a ticket. How are you getting on, Crampton? Better, eh?

CRAMPTON. I am myself again, Mr Valentine, no thanks to you.

VALENTINE. Look at this ungrateful parent of yours, Miss Clandon! I saved him from an excruciating pang; and he reviles me!

GLORIA [*coldly*] I am sorry my mother is not here to receive you, Mr Valentine. It is not quite nine o'clock; and the gentleman of whom Mr M'Comas spoke, the lawyer, has not yet come.

VALENTINE. Oh yes he has. Ive met him and talked to him. [*With gay malice*] Youll like him, Miss Clandon: he's the very incarnation of intellect. You can h e a r his mind working.

GLORIA [*ignoring the jibe*] Where is he?

VALENTINE. Bought a false nose and gone to the fancy ball.

CRAMPTON [*crustily, looking at his watch*] It seems that everybody has gone to this fancy ball instead of keeping to our appointment here.

VALENTINE. Oh, he'll come all right enough: that was half an hour ago. I didnt like to borrow five shillings from him and go in with him; so I joined the mob and looked through the railings until Miss Clandon disappeared into the hotel through the window.

GLORIA. So it has come to this, that you follow me about in public to stare at me.

VALENTINE. Yes: somebody ought to chain me up.

Gloria turns her back on him and goes to the fireplace. He takes the snub very philosophically, and goes to the opposite side of the room. The waiter appears at the window, ushering in Mrs Clandon and M'Comas.

MRS CLANDON. I am so sorry to have kept you all waiting.

A grotesquely majestic stranger, in a domino and false nose with goggles, appears at the window.

WAITER [*to the stranger*] Beg pardon, sir; but this is a private apartment, sir. If you will allow me, sir, I will shew you the American bar and supper rooms, sir. This way, sir.

He goes into the garden, leading the way under the impression that the stranger is following him. The majestic one, however, comes straight into the room to the end of the table, where, with impressive deliberation, he takes off the false nose and then the domino, rolling up the nose in the domino and throwing the bundle on the table like a champion throwing down his glove. He is now seen to be a tall stout man between forty and fifty, clean shaven, with a midnight oil pallor emphasized by stiff black hair, cropped short and oiled, and eyebrows like early Victorian horsehair upholstery. Physically and spiritually a coarsened man: in cunning and logic a ruthlessly sharpened one. His bearing as he enters is sufficiently imposing and disquieting; but when he speaks, his powerful menacing voice, impressively articulated speech, strong inexorable manner, and a terrifying power of intensely critical listening, raise the impression produced by him to absolute tremendousness.

THE STRANGER. My name is Bohun. [*General awe*]. Have I the honor of addressing Mrs Clandon? [*Mrs Clandon bows. Bohun bows*]. Miss Clandon? [*Gloria bows. Bohun bows*]. Mr Clandon?

CRAMPTON [*insisting on his rightful name as angrily as he dares*] My name is Crampton, sir.

BOHUN. Oh, indeed. [*Passing him over without further notice and turning to Valentine*] Are you Mr Clandon?

VALENTINE [*making it a point of honor not to be impressed by him*] Do I look like it? My name is Valentine. I did the drugging.

BOHUN. Ah, quite so. Then Mr Clandon has not yet arrived?

WAITER [*entering anxiously through the win-*

dow] Beg pardon, maam; but can you tell me what became of that— [*He recognizes Bohun, and loses all his self possession. Bohun waits rigidly for him to pull himself together*]. Beg pardon, sir, I'm sure, sir. [*Brokenly*] Was— was it you, sir?

BOHUN [*remorselessly*] It was I.

WAITER [*Unable to restrain his tears*] You in a false nose, Walter! [*He clings to a chair to support himself*]. I beg your pardon, maam. A little giddiness—

BOHUN [*commandingly*] You will excuse him, Mrs Clandon, when I inform you that he is my father.

WAITER [*heartbroken*] Oh no, no, Walter. A waiter for your father on top of a false nose! What will they think of you?

MRS CLANDON. I am delighted to hear it, Mr Bohun. Your father has been an excellent friend to us since we came here.

Bohun bows gravely.

WAITER [*shaking his head*] Oh no, maam. It's very kind of you: very ladylike and affable indeed, maam; but I should feel at a great disadvantage off my own proper footing. Never mind my being the gentleman's father, maam: it is only the accident of birth after all, maam. Youll excuse me, I'm sure, having interrupted your business. [*He begins to make his way along the table, supporting himself from chair to chair, with his eye on the door*].

BOHUN. One moment. [*The waiter stops, with a sinking heart*]. My father was a witness of what passed today, was he not, Mrs Clandon?

MRS CLANDON. Yes, most of it, I think.

BOHUN. In that case we shall want him.

WAITER [*pleading*] I hope it may not be necessary, sir. Busy evening for me, sir, with that ball: very busy evening indeed, sir.

BOHUN [*inexorably*] We shall want you.

MRS CLANDON [*politely*] Sit down, wont you?

WAITER [*earnestly*] Oh, if you please, maam, I really must draw the line at sitting down. I couldnt let myself be seen doing such a thing, maam: thank you, I am sure, all the same. [*He looks round from face to face wretchedly, with an expression that would melt a heart of stone*].

GLORIA. Dont let us waste time. William only wants to go on taking care of us. I should like a cup of coffee.

WAITER [*brightening perceptibly*] Coffee, miss? [*He gives a little gasp of hope*]. Certainly, miss. Thank you, miss: very timely, miss,

very thoughtful and considerate indeed. [*To Mrs Clandon, timidly but expectantly*] Anything for you, maam?

MRS CLANDON. Er—oh yes: it's so hot, I think we might have a jug of claret cup.

WAITER [*beaming*] Claret cup, maam! Certainly, maam.

GLORIA. Oh well, I'll have claret cup instead of coffee. Put some cucumber in it.

WAITER [*delighted*] Cucumber, miss! yes miss. [*To Bohun*] Anything special for you, sir? You dont like cucumber, sir.

BOHUN. If Mrs Clandon will allow me: syphon: Scotch.

WAITER. Right, sir. [*To Crampton*] Irish for you, sir, I think, sir? [*Crampton assents with a grunt. The waiter looks inquiringly at Valentine*].

VALENTINE. I like cucumber.

WAITER. Right, sir. [*Summing up*] Claret cup, syphon, one Scotch and one Irish?

MRS CLANDON. I think thats right.

WAITER [*himself again*] Right, maam. Directly, maam. Thank you. [*He ambles off through the window, having sounded the whole gamut of human happiness, from despair to ecstasy, in fifty seconds*].

M'COMAS. We can begin now, I suppose.

BOHUN. We had better wait until Mrs Clandon's husband arrives.

CRAMPTON. What d'y' mean? I'm her husband.

BOHUN [*instantly pouncing on the inconsistency between this and his previous statement*] You said just now that your name was Crampton.

CRAMPTON. So it is.

MRS CLANDON			
GLORIA	[*all four	I—
M'COMAS	speaking	My—
VALENTINE	simul-	Mrs—
	taneously*]	You—

BOHUN [*drowning them in two thunderous words*] One moment. [*Dead silence*]. Pray allow me. Sit down, everybody [*They obey humbly. Gloria takes the saddle-bag chair on the hearth. Valentine slips round to her side of the room and sits on the ottoman facing the window, so that he can look at her. Crampton sits on the ottoman with his back to Valentine's. Mrs Clandon, who has all along kept at the opposite side of the room in order to avoid Crampton as much as possible, sits near the door, with M'Comas beside her on her left. Bohun places himself magisterially in the centre of the group, near the corner of the table on Mrs Clandon's side. When they are settled, he fixes Crampton with his eye, and begins*] In this family, it appears, the husband's name is Crampton: the wife's, Clandon. Thus we have on the very threshold of the case an element of confusion.

VALENTINE [*getting up and speaking across to him with one knee on the ottoman*] But it's perfectly simple—

BOHUN [*annihilating him with a vocal thunderbolt*] It is. Mrs Clandon has adopted another name. That is the obvious explanation which you feared I could not find out for myself. You mistrust my intelligence, Mr Valentine —[*stopping him as he is about to protest*] no: I dont want you to answer that: I want you to think over it when you feel your next impulse to interrupt me.

VALENTINE [*dazed*] This is simply breaking a butterfly on a wheel. What does it matter? [*He sits down again*].

BOHUN. I will tell you what it matters, sir. It matters that if this family difference is to be smoothed over as we all hope it may be, Mrs Clandon, as a matter of social convenience and decency, will have to resume her husband's name [*Mrs Clandon assumes an expression of the most determined obstinacy*] or else Mr Crampton will have to call himself Mr Clandon. [*Crampton looks indomitably resolved to do nothing of the sort*]. No doubt you think that an easy matter, Mr Valentine. [*He looks pointedly at Mrs Clandon, then at Crampton*]. I differ from you. [*He throws himself back in his chair, frowning heavily*].

M'COMAS [*timidly*] I think, Bohun, we had perhaps better dispose of the important questions first.

BOHUN. M'Comas: there will be no difficulty about the important questions. There never is. It is the trifles that will wreck you at the harbor mouth. [*M'Comas looks as if he considered this a paradox*]. You dont agree with me, eh?

M'COMAS [*flatteringly*] If I did—

BOHUN [*interrupting him*] If you did, you would be m e, instead of being what you are.

M'COMAS [*fawning on him*] Of course, Bohun, your speciality—

BOHUN [*again interrupting him*] My speciality is being right when other people are wrong. If you agreed with me I should be no use here. [*He nods at him to drive the point home; then turns suddenly and forcibly on Crampton*]. Now you, Mr Crampton: what point in this business have y o u most at heart?

CRAMPTON [*beginning slowly*] I wish to put all considerations of self aside in this matter—

BOHUN [*cutting him short*] So do we all, Mr Crampton. [*To Mrs Clandon*] Y o u wish to put self aside, Mrs Clandon?

MRS CLANDON. Yes: I am not consulting my own feelings in being here.

BOHUN. So do you, Miss Clandon?

GLORIA. Yes.

BOHUN. I thought so. We all do.

VALENTINE. Except me. My aims are selfish.

BOHUN. Thats because you think an affectation of sincerity will produce a better effect on Miss Clandon than an affectation of disinterestedness. [*Valentine, utterly dismantled and destroyed by this just remark, takes refuge in a feeble speechless smile. Bohun, satisfied at having now effectually crushed all rebellion, again throws himself back in his chair, with an air of being prepared to listen tolerantly to their grievances*]. Now, Mr Crampton, go on. It's understood that self is put aside. Human nature always begins by saying that.

CRAMPTON. But I mean it, sir.

BOHUN. Quite so. Now for your point.

CRAMPTON. Every reasonable person will admit that it's an unselfish one. It's about the children.

BOHUN. Well? What about the children?

CRAMPTON [*with emotion*] They have—

BOHUN [*pouncing forward again*] Stop. Youre going to tell me about your feelings, Mr Crampton. Dont. I sympathize with them; but theyre not my business. Tell us exactly what you want: thats what we have to get at.

CRAMPTON [*uneasily*] It's a very difficult question to answer, Mr Bohun.

BOHUN. Come: I'll help you out. What do you object to in the present circumstances of the children?

CRAMPTON. I object to the way they have been brought up.

Mrs Clandon's brow contracts ominously.

BOHUN. How do you propose to alter that now?

CRAMPTON. I think they ought to dress more quietly.

VALENTINE. Nonsense.

BOHUN [*instantly flinging himself back in his chair, outraged by the interruption*] When you are done, Mr Valentine: when you are quite done.

VALENTINE. Whats wrong with Miss Clandon's dress?

CRAMPTON [*hotly to Valentine*] My opinion is as good as yours.

GLORIA [*warningly*] Father!

CRAMPTON [*subsiding piteously*] I didnt mean you, my dear. [*Pleading earnestly to Bohun*] But the two younger ones! you have not seen them, Mr Bohun; and indeed I think you would agree with me that there is something very noticeable, something almost gay and frivolous in their style of dressing.

MRS CLANDON [*impatiently*] Do you suppose I choose their clothes for them? Really, this is childish.

CRAMPTON [*furious, rising*] Childish! *Mrs Clandon rises indignantly.*

M'COMAS		Crampton, you promised—
VALENTINE	[*all rising and speaking together*]	Ridiculous. They dress charmingly.
GLORIA		Pray let us behave reasonably.

Tumult. Suddenly they hear a warning chime of glasses in the room behind them. They turn guiltily and find that the waiter has just come back from the bar in the garden, and is jingling his tray as he comes softly to the table with it. Dead silence.

WAITER [*to Crampton, setting a tumbler apart on the table*] Irish for you, sir. [*Crampton sits down a little shamefacedly. The waiter sets another tumbler and a syphon apart, saying to Bohun*] Scotch and syphon for you, sir. [*Bohun waves his hand impatiently. The waiter places a large glass jug and three tumblers in the middle*]. And claret cup. [*All subside into their seats. Peace reigns*].

MRS CLANDON. I am afraid we interrupted you, Mr Bohun.

BOHUN [*calmly*] You did. [*To the waiter, who is going out*] Just wait a bit.

WAITER. Yes, sir. Certainly, sir. [*He takes his stand behind Bohun's chair*].

MRS CLANDON [*to the waiter*] You dont mind our detaining you, I hope. Mr Bohun wishes it.

WAITER [*now quite at his ease*] Oh no, maam, not at all, maam. It is a pleasure to me to watch the working of his trained and powerful mind: very stimulating, very entertaining and instructive indeed, maam.

BOHUN [*resuming command of the proceedings*] Now, Mr Crampton: we are waiting for you. Do you give up your objection to the dressing or do you stick to it?

CRAMPTON [*pleading*] Mr Bohun: consider my position for a moment. I havnt got myself alone to consider: theres my sister Sophronia and my brother-in-law and all their circle. They have a great horror of anything that is at all—at all—well—

BOHUN. Out with it. Fast? Loud? Gay?

CRAMPTON. Not in any unprincipled sense, of course; but—but— [*blurting it out desperately*] those two children would shock them. Theyre not fit to mix with their own people. Thats what I complain of.

MRS CLANDON [*with suppressed anger*] Mr Valentine: do you think there is anything fast or loud about Phil and Dolly?

VALENTINE. Certainly not. It's utter bosh. Nothing can be in better taste.

CRAMPTON. Oh yes: of course you say so.

MRS CLANDON. William: you see a great deal of good English society. Are my children overdressed?

WAITER [*reassuringly*] Oh dear no, maam. [*Persuasively*] Oh no, sir, not at all. A little pretty and tasty no doubt, but very choice and classy, very genteel and high toned indeed. Might be the son and daughter of a Dean, sir, I assure you, sir. You have only to look at them, sir, to—

At this moment a harlequin and columbine, waltzing to the band in the garden, whirl one another into the room. The harlequin's dress is made of lozenges, an inch square, of turquoise blue silk and gold alternately. His bat is gilt and his mask turned up. The columbine's petticoats are the epitome of a harvest field, golden orange and poppy crimson, with a tiny velvet jacket for the poppy stamens. They pass, an exquisite and dazzling apparition, between M'Comas and Bohun, and then back in a circle to the end of the table, where, as the final chord of the waltz is struck, they make a tableau in the middle of the company, the harlequin down on his left knee, and the columbine standing on his right knee, with her arms curved over her head. Unlike their dancing, which is charmingly graceful, their attitudinizing is hardly a success, and threatens to end in a catastrophe.

THE COLUMBINE [*screaming*] Lift me down, somebody: I'm going to fall. Papa: lift me down.

CRAMPTON [*anxiously running to her and taking her hands*] My child!

DOLLY [*jumping down, with his help*] Thanks: so nice of you. [*Phil sits on the edge of the table and pours out some claret cup. Crampton returns to the ottoman in great perplexity*]. Oh, what fun! Oh dear! [*She seats herself with a vault on the front edge of the table, panting*]. Oh, claret cup! [*She drinks*].

BOHUN [*in powerful tones*] This is the younger lady, is it?

DOLLY [*slipping down off the table in alarm at his formidable voice and manner*] Yes, sir. Please, who are you?

MRS CLANDON. This is Mr Bohun, Dolly, who has very kindly come to help us this evening.

DOLLY. Oh, then he comes as a boon and a blessing—

PHILIP. Sh!

CRAMPTON. Mr Bohun—M'Comas: I appeal to you. Is this right? Would you blame my sister's family for objecting to it?

DOLLY [*flushing ominously*] Have you begun again?

CRAMPTON [*propitiating her*] No, no. It's perhaps natural at your age.

DOLLY [*obstinately*] Never mind my age. Is it pretty?

CRAMPTON. Yes, dear, yes. [*He sits down in token of submission*].

DOLLY [*insistently*] Do you like it?

CRAMPTON. My child: how can you expect me to like it or to approve of it?

DOLLY [*determined not to let him off*] How can you think it pretty and not like it?

M'COMAS [*rising, scandalized*] Really I must say—

Bohun, who has listened to Dolly with the highest approval, is down on him instantly.

BOHUN. No: dont interrupt, M'Comas. The young lady's method is right. [*To Dolly, with tremendous emphasis*] Press your questions, Miss Clandon: press your questions.

DOLLY [*turning to Bohun*] Oh dear, you are a regular overwhelmer! Do you always go on like this?

BOHUN [*rising*] Yes. Dont you try to put me out of countenance, young lady: youre too young to do it. [*He takes M'Comas's chair from beside Mrs Clandon's, and sets it beside his own*]. Sit down. [*Dolly, fascinated, obeys; and Bohun sits down again. M'Comas, robbed of his seat, takes a chair on the other side, between the table and the ottoman*]. Now, Mr Crampton, the facts are before you: both of them. You think youd like to have your two youngest children to live with you. Well, you wouldnt— [*Crampton tries to protest; but Bohun will not have it on any terms*] no you wouldnt: you think you would; but I know better than you. Youd want this young lady here to give up dressing like a stage columbine in the

evening and like a fashionable columbine in the morning. Well, she wont: never. She thinks she will; but—

DOLLY [*interrupting him*] No I dont. [*Resolutely*] I'll never give up dressing prettily. Never. As Gloria said to that man in Madeira, never, never, never! while grass grows or water runs.

VALENTINE [*rising in the wildest agitation*] What! What! [*Beginning to speak very fast*] When did she say that? Who did she say that to?

BOHUN [*throwing himself back with massive pitying remonstrance*] Mr Valentine—

VALENTINE [*pepperily*] Dont you interrupt me, sir: this is something really serious. I insist on knowing who Miss Clandon said that to.

DOLLY. Perhaps Phil remembers. Which was it, Phil? number three or number five?

VALENTINE. Number five!!!

PHILIP. Courage, Valentine! It wasnt number five: it was only a tame naval lieutenant who was always on hand: the most patient and harmless of mortals.

GLORIA [*coldly*] What are we discussing now, pray?

VALENTINE [*very red*] Excuse me: I am sorry I interrupted. I shall intrude no further, Mrs Clandon. [*He bows to Mrs Clandon and marches away into the garden, boiling with suppressed rage*].

DOLLY. Hmhm!

PHILIP. Ahah!

GLORIA. Please go on, Mr Bohun.

DOLLY [*striking in as Bohun, frowning formidably, collects himself for a fresh grapple with the case*] Youre going to bully us, Mr Bohun.

BOHUN. I—

DOLLY [*interrupting him*] Oh yes you are: you think youre not; but you are. I know by your eyebrows.

BOHUN [*capitulating*] Mrs Clandon: these are clever children: clear headed well brought up children. I make that admission deliberately. Can you, in return, point out to me any way of inducing them to hold their tongues?

MRS CLANDON. Dolly, dearest—!

PHILIP. Our old failing, Dolly. Silence!

Dolly holds her mouth.

MRS CLANDON. Now, Mr Bohun, before they begin again—

WAITER [*softly*] Be quick, sir: be quick.

DOLLY [*beaming at him*] Dear William!

PHILIP. Sh!

BOHUN [*unexpectedly beginning by hurling a question straight at Dolly*] Have you any intention of getting married?

DOLLY. I! Well, Finch calls me by my Christian name.

M'COMAS [*starting violently*] I will not have this. Mr Bohun: I use the young lady's Christian name naturally as an old friend of her mother's.

DOLLY. Yes, you call me Dolly as an old friend of my mother's. But what about Dorothee-ee-a?

M'Comas rises indignantly.

CRAMPTON [*anxiously, rising to restrain him*] Keep your temper, M'Comas. Dont let us quarrel. Be patient.

M'COMAS. I will not be patient. You are shewing the most wretched weakness of character, Crampton. I say this is monstrous.

DOLLY. Mr Bohun: please bully Finch for us.

BOHUN. I will. M'Comas: youre making yourself ridiculous. Sit down.

M'COMAS. I—

BOHUN [*waving him down imperiously*] No: sit down, sit down.

M'Comas sits down sulkily; and Crampton, much relieved, follows his example.

DOLLY [*to Bohun, meekly*] Thank you.

BOHUN. Now listen to me, all of you. I give no opinion, M'Comas, as to how far you may or may not have committed yourself in the direction indicated by this young lady. [*M'Comas is about to protest*]. No: dont interrupt me: if she doesnt marry you she will marry somebody else. That is the solution of the difficulty as to her not bearing her father's name. The other lady intends to get married.

GLORIA [*flushing*] Mr Bohun!

BOHUN. Oh yes you do: you dont know it; but you do.

GLORIA [*rising*] Stop. I warn you, Mr Bohun, not to answer for my intentions.

BOHUN [*rising*] It's no use, Miss Clandon: you cant put me down. I tell you your name will soon be neither Clandon nor Crampton; and I could tell you what it will be if I chose. [*He goes to the table and takes up his domino. They all rise; and Phil goes to the window. Bohun, with a gesture, summons the waiter to help him to robe*]. Mr Crampton: your notion of going to law is all nonsense: your children will be of age before you can get the point

decided. [*Allowing the waiter to put the domino on his shoulders*] You can do nothing but make a friendly arrangement. If you want your family more than they want you, youll get the worst of the arrangement: if they want you more than you want them youll get the better of it. [*He shakes the domino into becoming folds and takes up the false nose. Dolly gazes admiringly at him*]. The strength of their position lies in their being very agreeable people personally. The strength of your position lies in your income. [*He claps on the false nose, and is again grotesquely transfigured*].

DOLLY [*running to him*] Oh, now you look quite like a human being. Maynt I have just one dance with you? Can you dance?

Phil, resuming his part of harlequin, waves his bat as if casting a spell on them.

BOHUN [*thunderously*] Yes: you think I cant; but I can. Allow me. [*He seizes her and dances off with her through the window in a most powerful manner, but with studied propriety and grace*].

PHILIP. "On with the dance: let joy be unconfined." William.

WAITER. Yes, sir.

PHILIP. Can you procure a couple of dominos and false noses for my father and Mr M'Comas?

M'COMAS. Most certainly not. I protest—

CRAMPTON. Yes, yes. What harm will it do, just for once, M'Comas? Dont let us be spoilsports.

M'COMAS. Crampton: you are not the man I took you for. [*Pointedly*] Bullies are always cowards. [*He goes disgustedly towards the window*].

CRAMPTON [*following him*] Well, never mind. We must indulge them a little. Can you get us something to wear, waiter?

WAITER. Certainly, sir. [*He precedes them to the window, and stands aside there to let them pass out before him*]. This way, sir. Dominos and noses, sir?

M'COMAS [*angrily, on his way out*] I shall wear my own nose.

WAITER [*suavely*] Oh dear yes, sir: the false one will fit over it quite easily, sir: plenty of room, sir, plenty of room. [*He goes out after M'Comas*].

CRAMPTON [*turning at the window to Phil with an attempt at genial fatherliness*] Come along, my boy. Come along. [*He goes*].

PHILIP [*cheerily, following him*] Coming, dad, coming. [*On the window threshold he stops;*

looks after Crampton; then turns fantastically with his hat bent into a halo round his head, and says with lowered voice to Mrs Clandon and Gloria] Did you feel the pathos of that? [*He vanishes*].

MRS CLANDON [*left alone with Gloria*] Why did Mr Valentine go away so suddenly, I wonder?

GLORIA [*petulantly*] I dont know. Yes, I do know. Let us go and see the dancing.

They go towards the window, and are met by Valentine, who comes in from the garden walking quickly, with his face set and sulky.

VALENTINE [*stiffly*] Excuse me. I thought the party had quite broken up.

GLORIA [*nagging*] Then why did you come back?

VALENTINE. I came back because I am penniless. I cant get out that way without a five-shilling ticket.

MRS CLANDON. Has anything annoyed you, Mr Valentine?

GLORIA. Never mind him, mother. This is a fresh insult to me: that is all.

MRS CLANDON [*hardly able to realize that Gloria is deliberately provoking an altercation*] Gloria!

VALENTINE. Mrs Clandon: have I said anything insulting? Have I done anything insulting?

GLORIA. You have implied that my past has been like yours. That is the worst of insults.

VALENTINE. I imply nothing of the sort. I declare that my past has been blameless in comparison with yours.

MRS CLANDON [*most indignantly*] Mr Valentine!

VALENTINE. Well, what am I to think when I learn that Miss Clandon has made exactly the same speeches to other men that she has made to me? Five former lovers, with a tame naval lieutenant thrown in! Oh, it's too bad.

MRS CLANDON. But you surely do not believe that these affairs—mere jokes of the children's—were serious, Mr Valentine?

VALENTINE. Not to you. Not to her, perhaps. But I know what the men felt. [*With ludicrously genuine earnestness*] Have you ever thought of the wrecked lives, the unhappy marriages contracted in the recklessness of despair, the suicides, the—the—the—

GLORIA [*interrupting him contemptuously*] Mother: this man is a sentimental idiot. [*She sweeps away to the fireplace*].

MRS CLANDON [*shocked*] Oh, my dearest

Gloria, Mr Valentine will think that rude.

VALENTINE. I am not a sentimental idiot. I am cured of sentiment for ever. [*He turns away in dudgeon*].

MRS CLANDON. Mr Valentine: you must excuse us all. Women have to unlearn the false good manners of their slavery before they acquire the genuine good manners of their freedom. Dont think Gloria vulgar [*Gloria turns, astonished*]: she is not really so.

GLORIA. Mother! You apologize for me to him!

MRS CLANDON. My dear: you have some of the faults of youth as well as its qualities; and Mr Valentine seems rather too old fashioned in his ideas about his own sex to like being called an idiot. And now had we not better go and see what Dolly is doing? [*She goes towards the window*].

GLORIA. Do you go, mother. I wish to speak to Mr Valentine alone.

MRS CLANDON [*startled into a remonstrance*] My dear! [*Recollecting herself*] I beg your pardon, Gloria. Certainly, if you wish. [*She goes out*].

VALENTINE. Oh, if your mother were only a widow! She's worth six of you.

GLORIA. That is the first thing I have heard you say that does you honor.

VALENTINE. Stuff! Come: say what you want to say and let me go.

GLORIA. I have only this to say. You dragged me down to your level for a moment this afternoon. Do you think, if that had ever happened before, that I should not have been on my guard? that I should not have known what was coming, and known my own miserable weakness?

VALENTINE [*scolding at her passionately*] Dont talk of it in that way. What do I care for anything in you but your weakness, as you call it? You thought yourself very safe, didnt you, behind your advanced ideas? I amused myself by upsetting them pretty easily.

GLORIA [*insolently, feeling that now she can do as she likes with him*] Indeed!

VALENTINE. But why did I do it? Because I was being tempted to awaken your heart: to stir the depths in you. Why was I tempted? Because Nature was in deadly earnest with me when I was in jest with her. When the great moment came, who was awakened? who was stirred? in whom did the depths break up? In myself—myself. *I* was transported: you were only offended—shocked.

You are just an ordinary young lady, too ordinary to allow tame lieutenants to go as far as I went. Thats all. I shall not trouble you with conventional apologies. Goodbye. [*He makes resolutely for the door*].

GLORIA. Stop. [*He hesitates*]. Oh, will you understand, if I tell you the truth, that I am not making advances to you?

VALENTINE. Pooh! I know what youre going to say. You think youre not ordinary: that I was right: that you really have those depths in your nature. It flatters you to believe it. [*She recoils*]. Well, I grant that you are not ordinary in some ways: you are a clever girl [*Gloria stifles an exclamation of rage, and takes a threatening step towards him*]; but youve not been awakened yet. You didnt care: you dont care. It was my tragedy, not yours. Goodbye. [*He turns to the door. She watches him, appalled to see him slipping from her grasp. As he turns the handle, he pauses; then turns again to her, offering his hand*]. Let us part kindly.

GLORIA [*enormously relieved, and immediately turning her back on him deliberately*] Goodbye. I trust you will soon recover from the wound.

VALENTINE [*brightening up as it flashes on him that he is master of the situation after all*] I shall recover: such wounds heal more than they harm. After all, I still have my own Gloria.

GLORIA [*facing him quickly*] What do you mean?

VALENTINE. The Gloria of my imagination.

GLORIA [*proudly*] Keep your own Gloria: the Gloria of your imagination. [*Her emotion begins to break through her pride*]. The real Gloria: the Gloria who was shocked, offended, horrified—oh yes, quite truly—who was driven almost mad with shame by the feeling that all her power over herself had broken down at her first real encounter with—with— [*The color rushes over her face again. She covers it with her left hand, and puts her right on his left arm to support herself*].

VALENTINE. Take care. I'm losing my senses again. [*Summoning all her courage, she takes away her hand from her face and puts it on his right shoulder, turning him towards her and looking him straight in the eyes. He begins to protest agitatedly*]. Gloria: be sensible: it's no use: I havnt a penny in the world.

GLORIA. Cant you earn one? Other people do.

VALENTINE [*half delighted, half frightened*]

I never could: youd be unhappy. My dearest love: I should be the merest fortune-hunting adventurer if— [*Her grip of his arms tightens; and she kisses him*]. Oh Lord! [*Breathless*] Oh, I— [*he gasps*] I dont know anything about women: twelve years experience is not enough. [*In a gust of jealousy she throws him away from her; and he reels back into a chair like a leaf before the wind*].

Dolly dances in, waltzing with the waiter, followed by Mrs Clandon and Finch, also waltzing, and Phil pirouetting by himself.

DOLLY [*sinking on the chair at the writing-table*] Oh, I'm out of breath. How beautifully you waltz, William!

MRS CLANDON [*sinking on the saddle-bag seat on the hearth*] Oh, how could you make me do such a silly thing, Finch! I havnt danced since the soirée at South Place twenty years ago.

GLORIA [*peremptorily to Valentine*] Get up. [*Valentine gets up abjectly*]. Now let us have no false delicacy. Tell my mother that we have agreed to marry one another.

A silence of stupefaction ensues. Valentine, dumb with panic, looks at them with an obvious impulse to run away.

DOLLY [*breaking the silence*] Number Six!

PHILIP. Sh!

DOLLY [*tumultuously*] Oh, my feelings! I want to kiss somebody; and we bar it in the family. Wheres Finch?

M'COMAS. No, positively.

Crampton appears at the window.

DOLLY [*running to Crampton*] Oh, youre just in time. [*She kisses him*]. Now [*leading him forward*] bless them.

GLORIA. No. I will have no such thing, even in jest. When I need a blessing, I shall ask my mother's.

CRAMPTON [*to Gloria, with deep disappointment*] Am I to understand that you have engaged yourself to this young gentleman?

GLORIA [*resolutely*] Yes. Do you intend to be our friend or—

DOLLY. —or our father?

CRAMPTON. I should like to be both, my child. But surely—! Mr Valentine: I appeal to your sense of honor.

VALENTINE. Youre quite right. It's perfect madness. If we go out to dance together I shall have to borrow five shillings from her for a ticket. Gloria: dont be rash: youre throwing yourself away. I'd much better clear straight out of this, and never see any of you again. I shant commit suicide: I shant even be unhappy. Itll be a relief to me: I—I'm frightened, I'm positively frightened; and that's the plain truth.

GLORIA [*determinedly*] You shall not go.

VALENTINE [*quailing*] No, dearest: of course not. But—oh, will somebody only talk sense for a moment and bring us all to reason! *I* cant. Where's Bohun? Bohun's the man. Phil: go and summon Bohun.

PHILIP. From the vasty deep. I go. [*He makes his bat quiver in the air and darts away through the window*].

WAITER [*harmoniously to Valentine*] If you will excuse my putting in a word, sir, do not let a matter of five shillings stand between you and your happiness, sir. We shall be only too pleased to put the ticket down to you; and you can settle at your convenience. Very glad to meet you in any way, very happy and pleased indeed, sir.

PHILIP [*reappearing*] He comes. [*He waves his bat over the window*].

Bohun comes in, taking off his false nose and throwing it on the table in passing as he comes between Gloria and Valentine.

VALENTINE. The point is, Mr Bohun—

M'COMAS [*interrupting from the hearthrug*] Excuse me, sir: the point must be put to him by a solicitor. The question is one of an engagement between these two young people. The lady has some property, and [*looking at Crampton*] will probably have a good deal more.

CRAMPTON. Possibly. I hope so.

VALENTINE. And the gentleman hasnt a rap.

BOHUN [*nailing Valentine to the point instantly*] Then insist on a settlement. That shocks your delicacy: most sensible precautions do. But you ask my advice; and I give it to you. Have a settlement.

GLORIA [*proudly*] He shall have a settlement.

VALENTINE. My good sir, I dont want advice for myself. Give h e r some advice.

BOHUN. She wont take it. When youre married, she wont take yours either— [*turning suddenly on Gloria*] oh no you wont: you think you will; but you wont. He'll set to work and earn his living— [*turning suddenly on Valentine*] oh yes you will: you think you wont; but you will. She'll make you.

CRAMPTON [*only half persuaded*] Then, Mr Bohun, you dont think this match an unwise one?

BOHUN. Yes I do: all matches are unwise. It's unwise to be born; it's unwise to be married; it's unwise to live; and it's wise to die.

WAITER [*insinuating himself between Crampton and Valentine*] Then, if I may respectfully put a word in, sir, so much the worse for wisdom!

PHILIP. Allow me to remark that if Gloria has made up her mind—

DOLLY. The matter's settled; and Valentine's done for. And we're missing all the dances.

VALENTINE [*to Gloria, gallantly making the best of it*] May I have a dance—

BOHUN [*interposing in his grandest diapason*] Excuse me: I claim that privilege as counsel's fee. May I have the honor? thank you. [*He dances away with Gloria, and disappears among the lanterns, leaving Valentine gasping*].

VALENTINE [*recovering his breath*] Dolly: may I— [*offering himself as her partner*]?

DOLLY. Nonsense! [*eluding him and running round the table to the fireplace*]. Finch: my Finch! [*She pounces on M'Comas and makes him dance*].

M'COMAS [*protesting*] Pray restrain—really— [*He is borne off dancing through the window*].

VALENTINE [*making a last effort*] Mrs Clandon: may I—

PHILIP [*forestalling him*] Come, mother. [*He seizes his mother and whirls her away*].

MRS CLANDON [*remonstrating*] Phil, Phil— [*She shares M'Comas's fate*].

CRAMPTON [*following them with senile glee*] Ho! ho! He! he! he! [*He goes into the garden chuckling*].

VALENTINE [*collapsing on the ottoman and staring at the waiter*] I might as well be a married man already.

WAITER [*contemplating the defeated Duellist of Sex with ineffable benignity*] Cheer up, sir, cheer up. Every man is frightened of marriage when it comes to the point; but it often turns out very comfortable, very enjoyable and happy indeed, sir—from time to time. *I* never was master in my own house, sir: my wife was like your young lady: she was of a commanding and masterful disposition, which my son has inherited. But if I had my life to live twice over, I'd do it again: I'd do it again, I assure you. You never can tell, sir: you never can tell.

THE END

VIII

THE DEVIL'S DISCIPLE

A MELODRAMA (1897)

BEING THE FIRST OF THREE PLAYS FOR PURITANS

ACT I

At the most wretched hour between a black night and a wintry morning in the year 1777, Mrs Dudgeon, of New Hampshire, is sitting up in the kitchen and general dwelling room of her farm house on the outskirts of the town of Websterbridge. She is not a prepossessing woman. No woman looks her best after sitting up all night; and Mrs Dudgeon's face, even at its best, is grimly trenched by the channels into which the barren forms and observances of a dead Puritanism can pen a bitter temper and a fierce pride. She is an elderly matron who has worked hard and got nothing by it except dominion and detestation in her sordid home, and an unquestioned reputation for piety and respectability among her neighbors, to whom drink and debauchery are still so much more tempting than religion and rectitude, that they conceive goodness simply as self-denial. This conception is easily extended to others-denial, and finally generalized as covering anything disagreeable. So Mrs Dudgeon, being exceedingly disagreeable, is held to be exceedingly good. Short of flat felony, she enjoys complete license except for amiable weaknesses of any sort, and is consequently, without knowing it, the most licentious woman in the parish on the strength of never having broken the seventh commandment or missed a Sunday at the Presbyterian church.

The year 1777 is the one in which the passions roused by the breaking-off of the American colonies from England, more by their own weight than their own will, boiled up to shooting point, the shooting being idealized to the English mind as suppression of rebellion and maintenance of British dominion, and to the American as defence of liberty, resistance to tyranny, and self-sacrifice on the altar of the Rights of Man. Into the merits of these idealizations it is not here necessary to inquire: suffice it to say, without prejudice, that they have convinced both Americans and English that the most highminded course for them to pursue is to kill as many of one another as possible, and that military operations to that end are in full swing, morally supported by confident requests from the clergy of both sides for the blessing of God on their arms. Under such circumstances many other women

besides this disagreeable Mrs Dudgeon find themselves sitting up all night waiting for news. Like her, too, they fall asleep towards morning at the risk of nodding themselves into the kitchen fire. Mrs Dudgeon sleeps with a shawl over her head, and her feet on a broad fender of iron laths, the step of the domestic altar of the fireplace, with its huge hobs and boiler, and its hinged arm above the smoky mantelshelf for roasting. The plain kitchen table is opposite the fire, at her elbow, with a candle on it in a tin sconce. Her chair, like all the others in the room, is uncushioned and unpainted; but as it has a round railed back and a seat conventionally moulded to the sitter's curves, it is comparatively a chair of state. The room has three doors, one on the same side as the fireplace, near the corner, leading to the best bedroom; one, at the opposite end of the opposite wall, leading to the scullery and washhouse; and the housedoor, with its latch, heavy lock, and clumsy wooden bar, in the front wall, between the window in its middle and the corner next the bedroom door. Between the door and the window a rack of pegs suggests to the deductive observer that the men of the house are all away, as there are no hats or coats on them. On the other side of the window the clock hangs on a nail, with its white wooden dial, black iron weights, and brass pendulum. Between the clock and the corner, a big cupboard, locked, stands on a dwarf dresser full of common crockery.

On the side opposite the fireplace, between the door and the corner, a shamelessly ugly black horsehair sofa stands against the wall. An inspection of its stridulous surface shews that Mrs Dudgeon is not alone. A girl of sixteen or seventeen has fallen asleep on it. She is a wild, timid looking creature with black hair and tanned skin. Her frock, a scanty garment, is rent, weatherstained, berrystained, and by no means scrupulously clean. It hangs on her with a freedom which, taken with her brown legs and bare feet, suggests no great stock of underclothing.

Suddenly there comes a tapping at the door, not loud enough to wake the sleepers. Then knocking, which disturbs Mrs Dudgeon a little. Finally the latch is tried, whereupon she springs up at once.

MRS DUDGEON [*threateningly*] Well, why dont you open the door? [*She sees that the girl is asleep, and immediately raises a clamor of heart-felt vexation*]. Well, dear, dear me! Now this is— [*shaking her*] wake up, wake up: do you hear?

THE GIRL [*sitting up*] What is it?

MRS DUDGEON. Wake up; and be ashamed of yourself, you unfeeling sinful girl, falling asleep like that, and your father hardly cold in his grave.

THE GIRL [*half asleep still*] I didnt mean to. I dropped off—

MRS DUDGEON [*cutting her short*] Oh yes, youve plenty of excuses, I daresay. Dropped off! [*Fiercely, as the knocking recommences*] Why dont you get up and let your uncle in? after me waiting up all night for him! [*She pushes her rudely off the sofa*]. There: I'll open the door: much good you are to wait up. Go and mend that fire a bit.

The girl, cowed and wretched, goes to the fire and puts a log on. Mrs Dudgeon unbars the door and opens it, letting into the stuffy kitchen a little of the freshness and a great deal of the chill of the dawn, also her second son Christy, a fattish, stupid, fair-haired, roundfaced man of about 22, muffled in a plaid shawl and grey overcoat. He hurries, shivering, to the fire, leaving Mrs Dudgeon to shut the door.

CHRISTY [*at the fire*] F—f—f! but it is cold. [*Seeing the girl, and staring lumpishly at her*] Why, who are you?

THE GIRL [*shyly*] Essie.

MRS DUDGEON. Oh, you may well ask. [*To Essie*] Go to your room, child, and lie down, since you havnt feeling enough to keep you awake. Your history isnt fit for your own ears to hear.

ESSIE. I—

MRS DUDGEON [*peremptorily*] Dont answer me, Miss; but shew your obedience by doing what I tell you. [*Essie, almost in tears, crosses the room to the door near the sofa*]. And dont forget your prayers. [*Essie goes out*]. She'd have gone to bed last night just as if nothing had happened if I'd let her.

CHRISTY [*phlegmatically*] Well, she cant be expected to feel Uncle Peter's death like one of the family.

MRS DUDGEON. What are you talking about, child? Isnt she his daughter—the punishment of his wickedness and shame? [*She assaults her chair by sitting down*].

CHRISTY [*staring*] Uncle Peter's daughter!

MRS DUDGEON. Why else should she be here? D'ye think Ive not had enough trouble and care put upon me bringing up my own girls, let alone you and your good-for-nothing brother, without having your uncle's bastards—

CHRISTY [*interrupting her with an apprehensive glance at the door by which Essie went out*] Sh! She may hear you.

MRS DUDGEON [*raising her voice*] Let her hear me. People who fear God dont fear to give the devil's work its right name. [*Christy, soullessly indifferent to the strife of Good and Evil, stares at the fire, warming himself*]. Well, how long are you going to stare there like a stuck pig? What news have you for me?

CHRISTY [*taking off his hat and shawl and going to the rack to hang them up*] The minister is to break the news to you. He'll be here presently.

MRS DUDGEON. Break what news?

CHRISTY [*standing on tiptoe, from boyish habit, to hang his hat up, though he is quite tall enough to reach the peg, and speaking with callous placidity, considering the nature of the announcement*] Father's dead too.

MRS DUDGEON [*stupent*] Your father!

CHRISTY [*sulkily, coming back to the fire and warming himself again, attending much more to the fire than to his mother*] Well, it's not my fault. When we got to Nevinstown we found him ill in bed. He didnt know us at first. The minister sat up with him and sent me away. He died in the night.

MRS DUDGEON [*bursting into dry angry tears*] Well, I do think this is hard on me—very hard on me. His brother, that was a disgrace to us all his life, gets hanged on the public gallows as a rebel; and your father, instead of staying at home where his duty was, with his own family, goes after him and dies, leaving everything on my shoulders. After sending this girl to me to take care of, too! [*She plucks her shawl vexedly over her ears*]. It's sinful, so it is: downright sinful.

CHRISTY [*with a slow, bovine cheerfulness, after a pause*] I think it's going to be a fine morning, after all.

MRS DUDGEON [*railing at him*] A fine morning! And your father newly dead! Wheres your feelings, child?

CHRISTY [*obstinately*] Well, I didnt mean any harm. I suppose a man may make a remark about the weather even if his father's dead.

MRS DUDGEON [*bitterly*] A nice comfort my children are to me! One son a fool, and the other a lost sinner thats left his home to live with smugglers and gypsies and villains, the scum of the earth!

Someone knocks.

CHRISTY [*without moving*] Thats the minister.

MRS DUDGEON [*sharply*] Well, arnt you going to let Mr Anderson in?

Christy goes sheepishly to the door. Mrs Dudgeon buries her face in her hands, as it is her duty as a widow to be overcome with grief. Christy opens the door, and admits the minister, Anthony Anderson, a shrewd, genial, ready Presbyterian divine of about 50, with something of the authority of his profession in his bearing. But it is an altogether secular authority, sweetened by a conciliatory, sensible manner not at all suggestive of a quite thoroughgoing other-worldliness. He is a strong, healthy man too, with a thick sanguine neck; and his keen, cheerful mouth cuts into somewhat fleshy corners. No doubt an excellent parson, but still a man capable of making the most of this world, and perhaps a little apologetically conscious of getting on better with it than a sound Presbyterian ought.

ANDERSON [*to Christy, at the door, looking at Mrs Dudgeon whilst he takes off his cloak*] Have you told her?

CHRISTY. She made me. [*He shuts the door; yawns; and loafs across to the sofa, where he sits down and presently drops off to sleep*].

Anderson looks compassionately at Mrs Dudgeon. Then he hangs his cloak and hat on the rack. Mrs Dudgeon dries her eyes and looks up at him.

ANDERSON. Sister: the Lord has laid his hand very heavily upon you.

MRS DUDGEON [*with intensely recalcitrant resignation*] It's His will, I suppose; and I must bow to it. But I do think it hard. What call had Timothy to go to Springtown, and remind everybody that he belonged to a man that was being hanged?—and [*spitefully*] that deserved it, if ever a man did.

ANDERSON [*gently*] They were brothers, Mrs Dudgeon.

MRS DUDGEON. Timothy never acknowledged him as his brother after we were married: he had too much respect for me to insult me with such a brother. Would such a selfish wretch as Peter have come thirty miles to see Timothy hanged, do you think? Not thirty yards, not he. However, I must bear my cross as best I may: least said is soonest mended.

ANDERSON [*very grave, coming down to the fire to stand with his back to it*] Your eldest son was present at the execution, Mrs Dudgeon.

MRS DUDGEON [*disagreeably surprised*] Richard?

ANDERSON [*nodding*] Yes.

MRS DUDGEON [*vindictively*] Let it be a warning to him. He may end that way himself, the wicked, dissolute, godless— [*she suddenly stops; her voice fails; and she asks, with evident dread*] Did Timothy see him?

ANDERSON. Yes.

MRS DUDGEON [*holding her breath*] Well?

ANDERSON. He only saw him in the crowd: they did not speak. [*Mrs Dudgeon, greatly relieved, exhales the pent up breath and sits at her ease again*]. Your husband was greatly touched and impressed by his brother's awful death. [*Mrs Dudgeon sneers. Anderson breaks off to demand with some indignation*] Well, wasnt it only natural, Mrs Dudgeon? He softened towards his prodigal son in that moment. He sent for him to come to see him.

MRS DUDGEON [*her alarm renewed*] Sent for Richard!

ANDERSON. Yes; but Richard would not come. He sent his father a message; but I'm sorry to say it was a wicked message—an awful message.

MRS DUDGEON. What was it?

ANDERSON. That he would stand by his wicked uncle and stand against his good parents, in this world and the next.

MRS DUDGEON [*implacably*] He will be punished for it. He will be punished for it— in both worlds.

ANDERSON. That is not in our hands, Mrs Dudgeon.

MRS DUDGEON. Did I say it was, Mr Anderson? We are told that the wicked shall be punished. Why should we do our duty and keep God's law if there is to be no difference made between us and those who follow their own likings and dislikings, and make a jest of us and of their Maker's word?

ANDERSON. Well, Richard's earthly father has been merciful to him; and his heavenly judge is the father of us all.

MRS DUDGEON [*forgetting herself*] Richard's earthly father was a softheaded—

ANDERSON [*shocked*] Oh!

MRS DUDGEON [*with a touch of shame*] Well, I am Richard's mother. If I am against him who has any right to be for him? [*Trying to conciliate him*] Wont you sit down, Mr Anderson? I should have asked you before; but I'm so troubled.

ANDERSON. Thank you. [*He takes a chair from beside the fireplace, and turns it so that he can sit comfortably at the fire. When he is seated he adds, in the tone of a man who knows that he is opening a difficult subject*] Has Christy told you about the new will?

MRS DUDGEON [*all her fears returning*] The new will! Did Timothy—? [*She breaks off, gasping, unable to complete the question*].

ANDERSON. Yes. In his last hours he changed his mind.

MRS DUDGEON [*white with intense rage*] And you let him rob me?

ANDERSON. I had no power to prevent him giving what was his to his own son.

MRS DUDGEON. He had nothing of his own. His money was the money I brought him as my marriage portion. It was for me to deal with my own money and my own son. He dare not have done it if I had been with him; and well he knew it. That was why he stole away like a thief to take advantage of the law to rob me by making a new will behind my back. The more shame on you, Mr Anderson,—you, a minister of the gospel —to act as his accomplice in such a crime.

ANDERSON [*rising*] I will take no offence at what you say in the first bitterness of your grief.

MRS DUDGEON [*contemptuously*] Grief!

ANDERSON. Well, of your disappointment, if you can find it in your heart to think that the better word.

MRS DUDGEON. My heart! My heart! And since when, pray, have you begun to hold up our hearts as trustworthy guides for us?

ANDERSON [*rather guiltily*] I—er—

MRS DUDGEON [*vehemently*] Dont lie, Mr Anderson. We are told that the heart of man is deceitful above all things, and desperately wicked. My heart belonged, not to Timothy, but to that poor wretched brother of his that has just ended his days with a rope round his neck—aye, to Peter Dudgeon. You know it: old Eli Hawkins, the man to whose pulpit you succeeded, though you are not worthy to loose his shoe latchet, told it you when he gave over our souls into your charge. He warned me and strengthened me against my heart, and made me marry a Godfearing man —as he thought. What else but that discipline has made me the woman I am? And you,

you, who followed your heart in your marriage, you talk to me of what I find in my heart. Go home to your pretty wife, man; and leave me to my prayers. [*She turns from him and leans with her elbows on the table, brooding over her wrongs and taking no further notice of him*].

ANDERSON [*willing enough to escape*] The Lord forbid that I should come between you and the source of all comfort! [*He goes to the rack for his coat and hat*].

MRS DUDGEON [*without looking at him*] The Lord will know what to forbid and what to allow without your help.

ANDERSON. And whom to forgive, I hope— Eli Hawkins and myself, if we have ever set up our preaching against His law. [*He fastens his cloak, and is now ready to go*]. Just one word—on necessary business, Mrs Dudgeon. There is the reading of the will to be gone through; and Richard has a right to be present. He is in the town; but he has the grace to say that he does not want to force himself in here.

MRS DUDGEON. He s h a l l come here. Does he expect us to leave his father's house for his convenience? Let them all come, and come quickly, and go quickly. They shall not make the will an excuse to shirk half their day's work. I shall be ready, never fear.

ANDERSON [*coming back a step or two*] Mrs Dudgeon: I used to have some little influence with you. When did I lose it?

MRS DUDGEON [*still without turning to him*] When you married for love. Now youre answered.

ANDERSON. Yes: I am answered. [*He goes out, musing*].

MRS DUDGEON [*to herself, thinking of her husband*] Thief! Thief!! [*She shakes herself angrily out of her chair; throws back the shawl from her head; and sets to work to prepare the room for the reading of the will, beginning by replacing Anderson's chair against the wall, and pushing back her own to the window. Then she calls, in her hard, driving, wrathful way*] Christy. [*No answer: he is fast asleep*]. Christy. [*She shakes him roughly*]. Get up out of that; and be ashamed of yourself—sleeping, and your father dead! [*She returns to the table; puts the candle on the mantelshelf; and takes from the table drawer a red table cloth which she spreads*].

CHRISTY [*rising reluctantly*] Well, do you suppose we are never going to sleep until we are out of mourning?

MRS DUDGEON. I want none of your sulks. Here: help me to set this table. [*They place the table in the middle of the room, with Christy's end towards the fireplace and Mrs Dudgeon's towards the sofa. Christy drops the table as soon as possible, and goes to the fire, leaving his mother to make the final adjustments of its position*]. We shall have the minister back here with the lawyer and all the family to read the will before you have done toasting yourself. Go and wake that girl; and then light the stove in the shed: you cant have your breakfast here. And mind you wash yourself, and make yourself fit to receive the company. [*She punctuates these orders by going to the cupboard; unlocking it; and producing a decanter of wine, which has no doubt stood there untouched since the last state occasion in the family, and some glasses, which she sets on the table. Also two green ware plates, on one of which she puts a barnbrack with a knife beside it. On the other she shakes some biscuits out of a tin, putting back one or two, and counting the rest*]. Now mind: there are ten biscuits there: let there be ten there when I come back after dressing myself. And keep your fingers off the raisins in that cake. And tell Essie the same. I suppose I can trust you to bring in the case of stuffed birds without breaking the glass? [*She replaces the tin in the cupboard, which she locks, pocketing the key carefully*].

CHRISTY [*lingering at the fire*] Youd better put the inkstand instead, for the lawyer.

MRS DUDGEON. Thats no answer to make to me, sir. Go and do as youre told. [*Christy turns sullenly to obey*]. Stop: take down that shutter before you go, and let the daylight in: you cant expect me to do all the heavy work of the house with a great lout like you idling about.

Christy takes the window bar out of its clamps, and puts it aside; then opens the shutter, shewing the grey morning. Mrs Dudgeon takes the sconce from the mantelshelf; blows out the candle; extinguishes the snuff by pinching it with her fingers, first licking them for the purpose; and replaces the sconce on the shelf.

CHRISTY [*looking through the window*] Heres the minister's wife.

MRS DUDGEON [*displeased*] What! Is she coming here?

CHRISTY. Yes.

MRS DUDGEON. What does she want troubling me at this hour, before I am properly dressed to receive people?

CHRISTY. Youd better ask her.

MRS DUDGEON [*threateningly*] You d better keep a civil tongue in your head. [*He goes sulkily towards the door. She comes after him, plying him with instructions*]. Tell that girl to come to me as soon as she's had her breakfast. And tell her to make herself fit to be seen before the people. [*Christy goes out and slams the door in her face*]. Nice manners, that! [*Someone knocks at the house door: she turns and cries inhospitably*] Come in. [*Judith Anderson, the minister's wife, comes in. Judith is more than twenty years younger than her husband, though she will never be as young as he in vitality. She is pretty and proper and ladylike, and has been admired and petted into an opinion of herself sufficiently favorable to give her a self-assurance which serves her instead of strength. She has a pretty taste in dress, and in her face the pretty lines of a sentimental character formed by dreams. Even her little self-complacency is pretty, like a child's vanity. Rather a pathetic creature to any sympathetic observer who knows how rough a place the world is. One feels, on the whole, that Anderson might have chosen worse, and that she, needing protection, could not have chosen better*]. Oh, it's you, is it, Mrs Anderson?

JUDITH [*very politely—almost patronizingly*] Yes. Can I do anything for you, Mrs Dudgeon? Can I help to get the place ready before they come to read the will?

MRS DUDGEON [*stiffly*] Thank you, Mrs Anderson, my house is always ready for anyone to come into.

MRS ANDERSON [*with complacent amiability*] Yes, indeed it is. Perhaps you had rather I did not intrude on you just now.

MRS DUDGEON. Oh, one more or less will make no difference this morning, Mrs Anderson. Now that youre here, youd better stay. If you wouldnt mind shutting the door! [*Judith smiles, implying "How stupid of me!" and shuts it with an exasperating air of doing something pretty and becoming*]. Thats better. I must go and tidy myself a bit. I suppose you dont mind stopping here to receive anyone that comes until I'm ready.

JUDITH [*graciously giving her leave*] Oh yes, certainly. Leave that to me, Mrs Dudgeon; and take your time. [*She hangs her cloak and bonnet on the rack*].

MRS DUDGEON [*half sneering*] I thought that would be more in your way than getting the house ready. [*Essie comes back*]. Oh, here y o u are! [*Severely*] Come here: let me see you. [*Essie timidly goes to her. Mrs Dudgeon takes her roughly by the arm and pulls her round to inspect the results of her attempt to clean and tidy herself—results which shew little practice and less conviction*]. Mm! Thats what you call doing your hair properly, I suppose. It's easy to see what you are, and how you were brought up. [*She throws her arm away, and goes on, peremptorily*] Now you listen to me and do as youre told. You sit down there in the corner by the fire; and when the company comes dont dare to speak until youre spoken to. [*Essie creeps away to the fireplace*]. Your father's people had better see you and know youre there: theyre as much bound to keep you from starvation as I am. At any rate they might help. But let me have no chattering and making free with them, as if you were their equal. Do you hear?

ESSIE. Yes.

MRS DUDGEON. Well, then go and do as youre told. [*Essie sits down miserably on the corner of the fender furthest from the door*]. Never mind her, Mrs Anderson: you know who she is and what she is. If she gives you any trouble, just tell me; and I'll settle accounts with her. [*Mrs Dudgeon goes into the bedroom, shutting the door sharply behind her as if even it had to be made do its duty with a ruthless hand*].

JUDITH [*patronizing Essie, and arranging the cake and wine on the table more becomingly*] You must not mind if your aunt is strict with you. She is a very good woman, and desires your good too.

ESSIE [*in listless misery*] Yes.

JUDITH [*annoyed with Essie for her failure to be consoled and edified, and to appreciate the kindly condescension of the remark*] You are not going to be sullen, I hope, Essie.

ESSIE. No.

JUDITH. Thats a good girl! [*She places a couple of chairs at the table with their backs to the window, with a pleasant sense of being a more thoughtful housekeeper than Mrs Dudgeon*]. Do you know any of your father's relatives?

ESSIE. No. They wouldnt have anything to do with him: they were too religious. Father used to talk about Dick Dudgeon; but I never saw him.

JUDITH [*ostentatiously shocked*] Dick Dudgeon! Essie: do you wish to be a really respectable and grateful girl, and to make a place for yourself here by steady good conduct?

ESSIE [*very half-heartedly*] Yes.

JUDITH. Then you must never mention the name of Richard Dudgeon—never even think about him. He is a bad man.

ESSIE. What has he done?

JUDITH. You must not ask questions about him, Essie. You are too young to know what it is to be a bad man. But he is a smuggler; and he lives with gypsies; and he has no love for his mother and his family; and he wrestles and plays games on Sunday instead of going to church. Never let him into your presence, if you can help it, Essie; and try to keep yourself and all womanhood unspotted by contact with such men.

ESSIE. Yes.

JUDITH [*again displeased*] I am afraid you say Yes and No without thinking very deeply.

ESSIE. Yes. At least I mean—

JUDITH [*severely*] What do you mean?

ESSIE [*almost crying*] Only—my father was a smuggler; and— [*Someone knocks*].

JUDITH. They are beginning to come. Now remember your aunt's directions, Essie; and be a good girl. [*Christy comes back with the stand of stuffed birds under a glass case, and an inkstand, which he places on the table*]. Good morning, Mr Dudgeon. Will you open the door, please: the people have come.

CHRISTY. Good morning. [*He opens the house door*].

The morning is now fairly bright and warm; and Anderson, who is the first to enter, has left his cloak at home. He is accompanied by Lawyer Hawkins, a brisk, middleaged man in brown riding gaiters and yellow breeches, looking as much squire as solicitor. He and Anderson are allowed precedence as representing the learned professions. After them comes the family, headed by the senior uncle, William Dudgeon, a large, shapeless man, bottle-nosed and evidently no ascetic at table. His clothes are not the clothes, nor his anxious wife the wife, of a prosperous man. The junior uncle, Titus Dudgeon, is a wiry little terrier of a man, with an immense and visibly purseproud wife, both free from the cares of the William household.

Hawkins at once goes briskly to the table and takes the chair nearest the sofa, Christy having left the inkstand there. He puts his hat on the floor beside him, and produces the will. Uncle William comes to the fire and stands on the hearth warming his coat tails, leaving Mrs William derelict near the door. Uncle Titus, who is the lady's man of the family, rescues her by giving her his disengaged arm and bringing her to the sofa, where he sits down warmly between his own lady and his brother's. Anderson hangs up his hat and waits for a word with Judith.

JUDITH. She will be here in a moment. Ask them to wait. [*She taps at the bedroom door. Receiving an answer from within, she opens it and passes through*].

ANDERSON [*taking his place at the table at the opposite end to Hawkins*] Our poor afflicted sister will be with us in a moment. Are we all here?

CHRISTY [*at the house door, which he has just shut*] All except Dick.

The callousness with which Christy names the reprobate jars on the moral sense of the family. Uncle William shakes his head slowly and repeatedly. Mrs Titus catches her breath convulsively through her nose. Her husband speaks.

UNCLE TITUS. Well, I hope he will have the grace not to come. I hope so.

The Dudgeons all murmur assent, except Christy, who goes to the window and posts himself there, looking out. Hawkins smiles secretively as if he knew something that would change their tune if they knew it. Anderson is uneasy: the love of solemn family councils, especially funeral ones, is not in his nature. Judith appears at the bedroom door.

JUDITH [*with gentle impressiveness*] Friends, Mrs Dudgeon. [*She takes the chair from beside the fireplace; and places it for Mrs Dudgeon, who comes from the bedroom in black, with a clean handkerchief to her eyes. All rise, except Essie. Mrs Titus and Mrs William produce equally clean handkerchiefs and weep. It is an affecting moment*].

UNCLE WILLIAM. Would it comfort you, sister, if we were to offer up a prayer?

UNCLE TITUS. Or sing a hymn?

ANDERSON [*rather hastily*] I have been with our sister this morning already, friends. In our hearts we ask a blessing.

ALL [*except Essie*] Amen.

They all sit down, except Judith, who stands behind Mrs Dudgeon's chair.

JUDITH [*to Essie*] Essie: did you say Amen?

ESSIE [*scaredly*] No.

JUDITH. Then say it, like a good girl.

ESSIE. Amen.

UNCLE WILLIAM [*encouragingly*] Thats right: thats right. We know who you are; but we are willing to be kind to you if you are a good girl and deserve it. We are all equal before the Throne.

This republican sentiment does not please the women, who are convinced that the Throne is precisely the place where their superiority, often questioned in this world, will be recognized and rewarded.

CHRISTY [*at the window*] Heres Dick.

Anderson and Hawkins look round sociably. Essie, with a gleam of interest breaking through her misery, looks up. Christy grins and gapes expectantly at the door. The rest are petrified with the intensity of their sense of Virtue menaced with outrage by the approach of flaunting Vice. The reprobate appears in the doorway, graced beyond his alleged merits by the morning sunlight. He is certainly the best looking member of the family; but his expression is reckless and sardonic, his manner defiant and satirical, his dress picturesquely careless. Only, his forehead and mouth betray an extraordinary steadfastness; and his eyes are the eyes of a fanatic.

RICHARD [*on the threshold, taking off his hat*] Ladies and gentlemen: your servant, your very humble servant. [*With this comprehensive insult, he throws his hat to Christy with a suddenness that makes him jump like a negligent wicket keeper, and comes into the middle of the room, where he turns and deliberately surveys the company*]. How happy you all look! how glad to see me! [*He turns towards Mrs Dudgeon's chair; and his lip rolls up horribly from his dog tooth as he meets her look of undisguised hatred*]. Well, mother: keeping up appearances as usual? thats right, thats right. [*Judith pointedly moves away from his neighborhood to the other side of the kitchen, holding her skirt instinctively as if to save it from contamination. Uncle Titus promptly marks his approval of her action by rising from the sofa, and placing a chair for her to sit down upon*]. What! Uncle William! I havnt seen you since you gave up drinking. [*Poor Uncle William, shamed, would protest; but Richard claps him heartily on his shoulder, adding*] you have given it up, havnt you? [*releasing him with a playful push*] of course you have: quite right too: you overdid it. [*He turns away from Uncle William and makes for the sofa*]. And now, where is that upright horsedealer Uncle Titus? Uncle Titus: come forth. [*He comes upon him holding the chair as Judith sits down*]. As usual, looking after the ladies!

UNCLE TITUS [*indignantly*] Be ashamed of

yourself, sir—

RICHARD [*interrupting him and shaking his hand in spite of him*] I am: I am; but I am proud of my uncle—proud of all my relatives—[*again surveying them*] who could look at them and not be proud and joyful? [*Uncle Titus, overborne, resumes his seat on the sofa. Richard turns to the table*]. Ah, Mr Anderson, still at the good work, still shepherding them. Keep them up to the mark, minister, keep them up to the mark. Come! [*with a spring he seats himself on the table and takes up the decanter*] clink a glass with me, Pastor, for the sake of old times.

ANDERSON. You know, I think, Mr Dudgeon, that I do not drink before dinner.

RICHARD. You will, some day, Pastor: Uncle William used to drink before breakfast. Come: it will give your sermons unction. [*He smells the wine and makes a wry face*]. But do not begin on my mother's company sherry. I stole some when I was six years old; and I have been a temperate man ever since. [*He puts the decanter down and changes the subject*]. So I hear you are married, Pastor, and that your wife has a most ungodly allowance of good looks.

ANDERSON [*quietly indicating Judith*] Sir: you are in the presence of my wife. [*Judith rises and stands with stony propriety*].

RICHARD [*quickly slipping down from the table with instinctive good manners*] Your servant, madam: no offence. [*He looks at her earnestly*]. You deserve your reputation; but I'm sorry to see by your expression that youre a good woman. [*She looks shocked, and sits down amid a murmur of indignant sympathy from his relatives. Anderson, sensible enough to know that these demonstrations can only gratify and encourage a man who is deliberately trying to provoke them, remains perfectly good-humored*]. All the same, Pastor, I respect you more than I did before. By the way, did I hear, or did I not, that our late lamented Uncle Peter, though unmarried, was a father?

UNCLE TITUS. He had only one irregular child, sir.

RICHARD. Only one! He thinks one a mere trifle! I blush for you, Uncle Titus.

ANDERSON. Mr Dudgeon: you are in the presence of your mother and her grief.

RICHARD. It touches me profoundly, Pastor. By the way, what has become of the irregular child?

ANDERSON [*pointing to Essie*] There, sir, listening to you.

RICHARD [*shocked into sincerity*] What! Why the devil didnt you tell me that before? Children suffer enough in this house without—[*He hurries remorsefully to Essie*]. Come, little cousin! never mind me: it was not meant to hurt you. [*She looks up gratefully at him. Her tearstained face affects him violently; and he bursts out, in a transport of wrath*] Who has been making her cry? Who has been ill-treating her? By God—

MRS DUDGEON [*rising and confronting him*] Silence your blasphemous tongue. I will bear no more of this. Leave my house.

RICHARD. How do you know it's your house until the will is read? [*They look at one another for a moment with intense hatred; and then she sinks, checkmated, into her chair. Richard goes boldly up past Anderson to the window, where he takes the railed chair in his hand*]. Ladies and gentlemen: as the eldest son of my late father, and the unworthy head of this household, I bid you welcome. By your leave, Minister Anderson: by your leave, Lawyer Hawkins. The head of the table for the head of the family. [*He places the chair at the table between the minister and the attorney; sits down between them; and addresses the assembly with a presidential air*]. We meet on a melancholy occasion: a father dead! an uncle actually hanged, and probably damned. [*He shakes his head deploringly. The relatives freeze with horror*]. Thats right: pull your longest faces [*his voice suddenly sweetens gravely as his glance lights on Essie*] provided only there is hope in the eyes of the child. [*Briskly*] Now then, Lawyer Hawkins: business, business. Get on with the will, man.

TITUS. Do not let yourself be ordered or hurried, Mr Hawkins.

HAWKINS [*very politely and willingly*] Mr Dudgeon means no offence, I feel sure. I will not keep you one second, Mr Dudgeon. Just while I get my glasses— [*he fumbles for them. The Dudgeons look at one another with misgiving*].

RICHARD. Aha! They notice your civility, Mr Hawkins. They are prepared for the worst. A glass of wine to clear your voice before you begin. [*He pours out one for him and hands it; then pours one for himself*].

HAWKINS. Thank you, Mr Dudgeon. Your good health, sir.

RICHARD. Yours, sir. [*With the glass half way

I

to his lips, he checks himself, giving a dubious glance at the wine, and adds, with quaint intensity] Will anyone oblige me with a glass of water?

Essie, who has been hanging on his every word and movement, rises stealthily and slips out behind Mrs Dudgeon through the bedroom door, returning presently with a jug and going out of the house as quietly as possible.

HAWKINS. The will is not exactly in proper legal phraseology.

RICHARD. No: my father died without the consolations of the law.

HAWKINS. Good again, Mr Dudgeon, good again. [*Preparing to read*] Are you ready, sir?

RICHARD. Ready, aye ready. For what we are about to receive, may the Lord make us truly thankful. Go ahead.

HAWKINS [*reading*] "This is the last will and testament of me Timothy Dudgeon on my deathbed at Nevinstown on the road from Springtown to Websterbridge on this twenty-fourth day of September, one thousand seven hundred and seventy seven. I hereby revoke all former wills made by me and declare that I am of sound mind and know well what I am doing and that this is my real will according to my own wish and affections."

RICHARD [*glancing at his mother*] Aha!

HAWKINS [*shaking his head*] Bad phraseology, sir, wrong phraseology. "I give and bequeath a hundred pounds to my younger son Christopher Dudgeon, fifty pounds to be paid to him on the day of his marriage to Sarah Wilkins if she will have him, and ten pounds on the birth of each of his children up to the number of five."

RICHARD. How if she wont have him?

CHRISTY. She will if I have fifty pounds.

RICHARD. Good, my brother. Proceed.

HAWKINS. "I give and bequeath to my wife Annie Dudgeon, born Annie Primrose"—you see he did not know the law, Mr Dudgeon: your mother was not born Annie: she was christened so—"an annuity of fifty-two pounds a year for life [*Mrs Dudgeon, with all eyes on her, holds herself convulsively rigid*] to be paid out of the interest on her own money"—there's a way to put it, Mr Dudgeon! Her own money!

MRS DUDGEON. A very good way to put God's truth. It was every penny my own. Fifty-two pounds a year!

HAWKINS. "And I recommend her for her goodness and piety to the forgiving care of her children, having stood between them and her as far as I could to the best of my ability."

MRS DUDGEON. And this is my reward! [*Raging inwardly*] You know what I think, Mr Anderson: you know the word I gave to it.

ANDERSON. It cannot be helped, Mrs Dudgeon. We must take what comes to us. [*To Hawkins*]. Go on, sir.

HAWKINS. "I give and bequeath my house at Websterbridge with the land belonging to it and all the rest of my property soever to my eldest son and heir, Richard Dudgeon."

RICHARD. Oho! The fatted calf, Minister, the fatted calf.

HAWKINS. "On these conditions—"

RICHARD. The devil! Are there conditions?

HAWKINS. "To wit: first, that he shall not let my brother Peter's natural child starve or be driven by want to an evil life."

RICHARD [*emphatically, striking his fist on the table*] Agreed.

Mrs Dudgeon, turning to look malignantly at Essie, misses her and looks quickly round to see where she has moved to; then, seeing that she has left the room without leave, closes her lips vengefully.

HAWKINS. "Second, that he shall be a good friend to my old horse Jim"— [*again shaking his head*] he should have written James, sir.

RICHARD. James shall live in clover. Go on.

HAWKINS. —"and keep my deaf farm labourer Prodger Feston in his service."

RICHARD. Prodger Feston shall get drunk every Saturday.

HAWKINS. "Third, that he make Christy a present on his marriage out of the ornaments in the best room."

RICHARD [*holding up the stuffed birds*] Here you are, Christy.

CHRISTY [*disappointed*] I'd rather have the china peacocks.

RICHARD. You shall have both. [*Christy is greatly pleased*]. Go on.

HAWKINS. "Fourthly and lastly, that he try to live at peace with his mother as far as she will consent to it."

RICHARD [*dubiously*] Hm! Anything more, Mr Hawkins?

HAWKINS [*solemnly*] "Finally I give and bequeath my soul into my Maker's hands, humbly asking forgiveness for all my sins and mistakes, and hoping that He will so guide my son that it may not be said that I have done wrong in trusting to him rather than to others in the perplexity of my last hour in this strange place."

ANDERSON. Amen.

THE UNCLES AND AUNTS. Amen.

RICHARD. My mother does not say Amen.

MRS DUDGEON [*rising, unable to give up her property without a struggle*] Mr Hawkins: is that a proper will? Remember, I have his rightful, legal will, drawn up by yourself, leaving all to me.

HAWKINS. This is a very wrongly and irregularly worded will, Mrs Dudgeon; though [*turning politely to Richard*] it contains in my judgment an excellent disposal of his property.

ANDERSON [*interposing before Mrs Dudgeon can retort*] That is not what you are asked, Mr Hawkins. Is it a legal will?

HAWKINS. The courts will sustain it against the other.

ANDERSON. But why, if the other is more lawfully worded?

HAWKINS. Because, sir, the courts will sustain the claim of a man—and that man the eldest son—against any woman, if they can. I warned you, Mrs Dudgeon, when you got me to draw that other will, that it was not a wise will, and that though you might make him sign it, he would never be easy until he revoked it. But you wouldnt take advice; and now Mr Richard is cock of the walk. [*He takes his hat from the floor; rises; and begins pocketing his papers and spectacles*].

This is the signal for the breaking-up of the party. Anderson takes his hat from the rack and joins Uncle William at the fire. Titus fetches Judith her things from the rack. The three on the sofa rise and chat with Hawkins. Mrs Dudgeon, now an intruder in her own house, stands inert, crushed by the weight of the law on women, accepting it, as she has been trained to accept all monstrous calamities, as proofs of the greatness of the power that inflicts them, and of her own wormlike insignificance. For at this time, remember, Mary Wollstonecraft is as yet only a girl of eighteen, and her Vindication of the Rights of Women is still fourteen years off. Mrs Dudgeon is rescued from her apathy by Essie, who comes back with the jug full of water. She is taking it to Richard when Mrs Dudgeon stops her.

MRS DUDGEON [*threatening her*] Where have you been? [*Essie, appalled, tries to answer, but cannot*]. How dare you go out by yourself after the orders I gave you?

ESSIE. He asked for a drink—[*she stops, her tongue cleaving to her palate with terror*].

JUDITH [*with gentler severity*] Who asked for a drink? [*Essie, speechless, points to Richard*].

RICHARD. What! I!

JUDITH [*shocked*] Oh Essie, Essie!

RICHARD. I believe I did. [*He takes a glass and holds it to Essie to be filled. Her hand shakes*]. What! afraid of me?

ESSIE [*quickly*] No. I— [*She pours out the water*].

RICHARD [*tasting it*] Ah, youve been up the street to the market gate spring to get that. [*He takes a draught*]. Delicious! Thank you. [*Unfortunately, at this moment he chances to catch sight of Judith's face, which expresses the most prudish disapproval of his evident attraction for Essie, who is devouring him with her grateful eyes. His mocking expression returns instantly. He puts down the glass; deliberately winds his arm round Essie's shoulders; and brings her into the middle of the company. Mrs Dudgeon being in Essie's way as they come past the table, he says*] By your leave, mother [*and compels her to make way for them*]. What do they call you? Bessie?

ESSIE. Essie.

RICHARD. Essie, to be sure. Are you a good girl, Essie?

ESSIE [*greatly disappointed that he, of all people, should begin at her in this way*] Yes. [*She looks doubtfully at Judith*]. I think so. I mean I—I hope so.

RICHARD. Essie: did you ever hear of a person called the devil?

ANDERSON [*revolted*] Shame on you, sir, with a mere child—

RICHARD. By your leave, Minister: I do not interfere with your sermons: do not you interrupt mine. [*To Essie*] Do you know what they call me, Essie?

ESSIE. Dick.

RICHARD [*amused: patting her on the shoulder*] Yes, Dick; but something else too. They call me the Devil's Disciple.

ESSIE. Why do you let them?

RICHARD [*seriously*] Because it's true. I was brought up in the other service; but I knew from the first that the Devil was my natural master and captain and friend. I saw that he was in the right, and that the world cringed to his conqueror only through fear. I prayed secretly to him; and he comforted me, and saved me from having my spirit broken in this house of children's tears. I promised him my soul, and swore an oath that I would stand up for him in this world and stand by him in the next. [*Solemnly*] That promise and that oath made a man of me. From this day this house is his home; and no child shall cry in it: this hearth is his altar; and no soul shall ever cower over it in the dark evenings and be afraid. Now [turning forcibly on the rest] which of you good men will take this child and rescue her from the house of the devil?

JUDITH [coming to Essie and throwing a protecting arm about her] I will. You should be burnt alive.

ESSIE. But I dont want to. [She shrinks back, leaving Richard and Judith face to face].

RICHARD [to Judith] Actually doesnt want to, most virtuous lady!

UNCLE TITUS. Have a care, Richard Dudgeon. The law——

RICHARD [turning threateningly on him] Have a care, you. In an hour from this there will be no law here but martial law. I passed the soldiers within six miles on my way here: before noon Major Swindon's gallows for rebels will be up in the market place.

ANDERSON [calmly] What have we to fear from that, sir?

RICHARD. More than you think. He hanged the wrong man at Springtown: he thought Uncle Peter was respectable, because the Dudgeons had a good name. But his next example will be the best man in the town to whom he can bring home a rebellious word. Well, we're all rebels; and you know it.

ALL THE MEN [except Anderson] No, no, no!

RICHARD. Yes, you are. You havnt damned King George up hill and down dale as I have; but youve prayed for his defeat; and you, Anthony Anderson, have conducted the service, and sold your family bible to buy a pair of pistols. They maynt hang me, perhaps; because the moral effect of the Devil's Disciple dancing on nothing wouldnt help them. But a minister! [Judith, dismayed, clings to Anderson] or a lawyer! [Hawkins smiles like a man able to take care of himself] or an upright horsedealer! [Uncle Titus snarls at him in rage and terror] or a reformed drunkard! [Uncle William, utterly unnerved, moans and wobbles with fear] eh? Would that shew that King George meant business—ha?

ANDERSON [perfectly self-possessed] Come, my dear: he is only trying to frighten you. There is no danger. [He takes her out of the house. The rest crowd to the door to follow him, except Essie, who remains near Richard].

RICHARD [boisterously derisive] Now then: how many of you will stay with me; run up

the American flag on the devil's house; and make a fight for freedom? [They scramble out, Christy among them, hustling one another in their haste] Ha ha! Long live the devil! [To Mrs Dudgeon, who is following them] What, mother! Are you off too?

MRS DUDGEON [deadly pale, with her hand on her heart as if she had received a deathblow] My curse on you! My dying curse! [She goes out].

RICHARD [calling after her] It will bring me luck. Ha ha ha!

ESSIE [anxiously] Maynt I stay?

RICHARD [turning to her] What! Have they forgotten to save your soul in their anxiety about their own bodies? Oh yes: you may stay. [He turns excitedly away again and shakes his fist after them. His left fist, also clenched, hangs down. Essie seizes it and kisses it, her tears falling on it. He starts and looks at it]. Tears! The devil's baptism! [She falls on her knees, sobbing. He stoops goodnaturedly to raise her, saying] Oh yes, you may cry that way, Essie, if you like.

ACT II

Minister Anderson's house is in the main street of Websterbridge, not far from the town hall. To the eye of the eighteenth century New Englander, it is much grander than the plain farmhouse of the Dudgeons; but it is so plain itself that a modern house agent would let both at about the same rent. The chief dwelling room has the same sort of kitchen fireplace, with boiler, toaster hanging on the bars, movable iron griddle socketed to the hob, hook above for roasting, and broad fender, on which stand a kettle and a plate of buttered toast. The door, between the fireplace and the corner, has neither panels, fingerplates nor handles: it is made of plain boards, and fastens with a latch. The table is a kitchen table, with a treacle colored cover of American cloth, chapped at the corners by draping. The tea service on it consists of two thick cups and saucers of the plainest ware, with milk jug and bowl to match, each large enough to contain nearly a quart, on a black japanned tray, and, in the middle of the table, a wooden trencher with a big loaf upon it, and a square half pound block of butter in a crock. The big oak press facing the fire from the opposite side of the room, is for use and storage, not for ornament; and the minister's house coat hangs on a peg from its door, shewing that he is out; for when he is in, it is his best coat that hangs there. His big riding boots stand beside the press, evidently in their usual place, and rather proud of themselves. In fact, the evolution of the minister's kitchen, dining room and drawing room into three separate apartments has not yet taken place; and so, from the point of view of our pampered period, he is no better off than the Dudgeons.

But there is a difference, for all that. To begin with, Mrs Anderson is a pleasanter person to live with than Mrs Dudgeon. To which Mrs Dudgeon would at once reply, with reason, that Mrs Anderson has no children to look after; no poultry, pigs nor cattle; a steady and sufficient income not directly dependent on harvests and prices at fairs; an affectionate husband who is a tower of strength to her: in short, that life is as easy at the minister's house as it is hard at the farm. This is true; but to explain a fact is not to alter it; and however little credit Mrs Anderson may deserve for making her home happier, she has certainly succeeded in doing it. The outward and visible signs of her superior social pretensions are, a drugget on the floor, a plaster ceiling between the timbers, and chairs which, though not upholstered, are stained and polished. The fine arts are represented by a mezzotint portrait of some Presbyterian divine, a copperplate of Raphael's St Paul preaching at Athens, a rococo presentation clock on the mantelshelf, flanked by a couple of miniatures, a pair of crockery dogs with baskets in their mouths, and, at the corners, two large cowrie shells. A pretty feature of the room is the low wide latticed window, nearly its whole width, with little red curtains running on a rod half way up it to serve as a blind. There is no sofa; but one of the seats, standing near the press, has a railed back and is long enough to accommodate two people easily. On the whole, it is rather the sort of room that the nineteenth century has ended in struggling to get back to under the leadership of Mr Philip Webb and his disciples in domestic architecture, though no genteel clergyman would have tolerated it fifty years ago.

The evening has closed in; and the room is dark except for the cosy firelight and the dim oil lamps seen through the window in the wet street, where there is a quiet, steady, warm, windless downpour of rain. As the town clock strikes the quarter, Judith comes in with a couple of candles in earthenware candlesticks, and sets them on the table. Her self-conscious airs of the morning are gone: she is anxious and frightened. She goes to the window and peers into the street. The first thing she sees there is her husband, hurrying home through the rain. She gives a little gasp of relief, not very far removed from a sob, and turns to the door. Anderson comes in, wrapped in a very wet cloak.*

JUDITH [*running to him*] Oh, here you are at last, at last! [*She attempts to embrace him*].

ANDERSON [*keeping her off*] Take care, my love: I'm wet. Wait till I get my cloak off. [*He places a chair with its back to the fire; hangs his cloak on it to dry; shakes the rain from his hat and puts it on the fender; and at last turns with his hands outstretched to Judith*]. Now! [*She flies into his arms*]. I am not late, am I? The town clock struck the quarter as I came in at the front door. And the town clock is always fast.

JUDITH. I'm sure it's slow this evening. I'm so glad youre back.

ANDERSON [*taking her more closely in his arms*] Anxious, my dear?

JUDITH. A little.

ANDERSON. Why, youve been crying.

JUDITH. Only a little. Never mind: it's all over now. [*A bugle call is heard in the distance. She starts in terror and retreats to the long seat, listening*]. Whats that?

ANDERSON [*following her tenderly to the seat and making her sit down with him*] Only King George, my dear. He's returning to barracks, or having his roll called, or getting ready for tea, or booting or saddling or something. Soldiers dont ring the bell or call over the banisters when they want anything: they send a boy out with a bugle to disturb the whole town.

JUDITH. Do you think there is really any danger?

ANDERSON. Not the least in the world.

JUDITH. You say that to comfort me, not because you believe it.

ANDERSON. My dear: in this world there is always danger for those who are afraid of it. Theres a danger that the house will catch fire in the night; but we shant sleep any the less soundly for that.

JUDITH. Yes, I know what you always say; and youre quite right. Oh, quite right: I know it. But—I suppose I'm not brave: thats all. My heart shrinks every time I think of the soldiers.

ANDERSON. Never mind that, dear: bravery is none the worse for costing a little pain.

JUDITH. Yes, I suppose so. [*Embracing him again*] Oh how brave you are, my dear! [*With tears in her eyes*] Well, I'll be brave too: you shant be ashamed of your wife.

ANDERSON. Thats right. Now you make me happy. Well, well! [*He rises and goes cheerily to the fire to dry his shoes*]. I called on Richard Dudgeon on my way back; but he wasnt in.

JUDITH [*rising in consternation*] You called on that man!

ANDERSON [*reassuring her*] Oh, nothing happened, dearie. He was out.

JUDITH [*almost in tears, as if the visit were a personal humiliation to her*] But why did you go there?

ANDERSON [*gravely*] Well, it is all the talk that Major Swindon is going to do what he did in Springtown—make an example of some notorious rebel, as he calls us. He pounced on Peter Dudgeon as the worst character there; and it is the general belief that he will pounce on Richard as the worst here.

JUDITH. But Richard said—

ANDERSON [*goodhumoredly cutting her short*] Pooh! Richard said! He said what he thought would frighten you and frighten me, my dear. He said what perhaps (God forgive him!) he would like to believe. It's a terrible thing to think of what death must mean for a man like that. I felt that I must warn him. I left a message for him.

JUDITH [*querulously*] What message?

ANDERSON. Only that I should be glad to see him for a moment on a matter of importance to himself, and that if he would look in here when he was passing he would be welcome.

JUDITH [*aghast*] You asked that man to come here!

ANDERSON. I did.

JUDITH [*sinking on the seat and clasping her hands*] I hope he wont come! Oh, I pray that he may not come!

ANDERSON. Why? Dont you want him to be warned?

JUDITH. He must know his danger. Oh, Tony, is it wrong to hate a blasphemer and a villain? I do hate him. I cant get him out of my mind: I know he will bring harm with him. He insulted you: he insulted me: he insulted his mother.

ANDERSON [*quaintly*] Well, dear, lets forgive him; and then it wont matter.

JUDITH. Oh, I know it's wrong to hate anybody; but—

ANDERSON [*going over to her with humorous tenderness*] Come, dear, youre not so wicked as you think. The worst sin towards our fellow creatures is not to hate them, but to be indifferent to them; thats the essence of inhumanity. After all, my dear, if you watch people carefully, youll be surprised to find how like hate is to love. [*She starts, strangely touched—even appalled. He is amused at her*]. Yes: I'm quite in earnest. Think of how some of our married friends worry one another, tax one another, are jealous of one another, cant bear to let one another out of sight for a day, are more like jailers and slave-owners than lovers. Think of those very same people with their enemies, scrupulous, lofty, self-respecting, determined to be independent of one another, careful of how they speak of one another—pooh! havnt you often thought that if they only knew it, they were better friends to their enemies than to their own husbands and wives? Come: depend on it, my dear, you are really fonder of Richard than you are of me, if you only knew it. Eh!

JUDITH. Oh, dont say that: dont say that, Tony, even in jest. You dont know what a horrible feeling it gives me.

ANDERSON [*laughing*] Well, well: never mind, pet. He's a bad man; and you hate him as he deserves. And youre going to make the tea, arnt you?

JUDITH [*remorsefully*] Oh yes, I forgot. Ive been keeping you waiting all this time. [*She goes to the fire and puts on the kettle*].

ANDERSON [*going to the press and taking his coat off*] Have you stitched up the shoulder of my old coat?

JUDITH. Yes, dear. [*She goes to the table, and sets about putting the tea into the teapot from the caddy*].

ANDERSON [*as he changes his coat for the older one hanging on the press, and replaces it by the one he has just taken off*] Did anyone call when I was out?

JUDITH. No, only— [*Someone knocks at the door. With a start which betrays her intense nervousness, she retreats to the further end of the table with the tea caddy and spoon in her hands exclaiming*] Who's that?

ANDERSON [*going to her and patting her encouragingly on the shoulder*] All right, pet, all right. He wont eat you, whoever he is. [*She tries to smile, and nearly makes herself cry. He goes to the door and opens it. Richard is there, without overcoat or cloak*]. You might have raised the latch and come in, Mr Dudgeon. Nobody stands on much ceremony with us. [*Hospitably*] Come in. [*Richard comes in care-*

lessly and stands at the table, looking round the room with a slight pucker of his nose at the mezzotinted divine on the wall. Judith keeps her eyes on the tea caddy]. Is it still raining? [He shuts the door].

RICHARD. Raining like the very [his eye catches Judith's as she looks quickly and haughtily up]— I beg your pardon; but [shewing that his coat is wet] you see—!

ANDERSON. Take it off, sir; and let it hang before the fire a while : my wife will excuse your shirtsleeves. Judith: put in another spoonful of tea for Mr Dudgeon.

RICHARD [eyeing him cynically] The magic of property, Pastor! Are even y o u civil to me now that I have succeeded to my father's estate?

Judith throws down the spoon indignantly.

ANDERSON [quite unruffled, and helping Richard off with his coat] I think, sir, that since you accept my hospitality, you cannot have so bad an opinion of it. Sit down. [With the coat in his hand, he points to the railed seat. Richard, in his shirtsleeves, looks at him half quarrelsomely for a moment; then, with a nod, acknowledges that the minister has got the better of him, and sits down on the seat. Anderson pushes his cloak into a heap on the seat of the chair at the fire, and hangs Richard's coat on the back in its place].

RICHARD. I come, sir, on your own invitation. You left word you had something important to tell me.

ANDERSON. I have a warning which it is my duty to give you.

RICHARD [quickly rising] You want to preach to me. Excuse me: I prefer a walk in the rain [he makes for his coat].

ANDERSON [stopping him] Dont be alarmed, sir: I am no great preacher. You are quite safe. [Richard smiles in spite of himself. His glance softens: he even makes a gesture of excuse. Anderson, seeing that he has tamed him, now addresses him earnestly]. Mr Dudgeon: you are in danger in this town.

RICHARD. What danger?

ANDERSON. Your uncle's danger. Major Swindon's gallows.

RICHARD. It is you who are in danger. I warned you—

ANDERSON [interrupting him goodhumoredly but authoritatively] Yes, yes, Mr Dudgeon; but they do not think so in the town. And even if I were in danger, I have duties here which I must not forsake. But you are a free

man. Why should you run any risk?

RICHARD. Do you think I should be any great loss, Minister?

ANDERSON. I think that a man's life is worth saving, whoever it belongs to. [Richard makes him an ironical bow. Anderson returns the bow humorously]. Come: youll have a cup of tea, to prevent you catching cold?

RICHARD. I observe that Mrs Anderson is not quite so pressing as you are, Pastor.

JUDITH [almost stifled with resentment, which she has been expecting her husband to share and express for her at every insult of Richard's] You are welcome for my husband's sake. [She brings the teapot to the fireplace and sets it on the hob].

RICHARD. I know I am not welcome for my own, madam. [He rises]. But I think I will not break bread here, Minister.

ANDERSON [cheerily] Give me a good reason for that.

RICHARD. Because there is something in you that I respect, and that makes me desire to have you for my enemy.

ANDERSON. Thats well said. On those terms, sir, I will accept your enmity or any man's. Judith: Mr Dudgeon will stay to tea. Sit down: it will take a few minutes to draw by the fire. [Richard glances at him with a troubled face; then sits down with his head bent, to hide a convulsive swelling of his throat]. I was just saying to my wife, Mr Dudgeon, that enmity— [She grasps his hand and looks imploringly at him, doing both with an intensity that checks him at once]. Well, well, I mustnt tell you, I see; but it was nothing that need leave us worse friend—enemies, I mean. Judith is a great enemy of yours.

RICHARD. If all my enemies were like Mrs Anderson, I should be the best Christian in America.

ANDERSON [gratified, patting her hand] You hear that, Judith? Mr Dudgeon knows how to turn a compliment.

The latch is lifted from without.

JUDITH [starting] Who is that?

Christy comes in.

CHRISTY [stopping and staring at Richard] Oh, are y o u here?

RICHARD. Yes. Begone, you fool: Mrs Anderson doesnt want the whole family to tea at once.

CHRISTY [coming further in] Mother's very ill.

RICHARD. Well, does she want to see m e ?

CHRISTY. No.

RICHARD. I thought not.

CHRISTY. She wants to see the minister—at once.

JUDITH [to Anderson] Oh, not before youve had some tea.

ANDERSON. I shall enjoy it more when I come back, dear. [He is about to take up his cloak].

CHRISTY. The rain's over.

ANDERSON [dropping the cloak and picking up his hat from the fender] Where is your mother, Christy?

CHRISTY. At Uncle Titus's.

ANDERSON. Have you fetched the doctor?

CHRISTY. No: she didnt tell me to.

ANDERSON. Go on there at once: I'll overtake you on his doorstep. [Christy turns to go]. Wait a moment. Your brother must be anxious to know the particulars.

RICHARD. Psha! not I: he doesnt know; and I dont care. [Violently] Be off, you oaf. [Christy runs out. Richard adds, a little shamefacedly] We shall know soon enough.

ANDERSON. Well, perhaps you will let me bring you the news myself. Judith: will you give Mr Dudgeon his tea, and keep him here until I return.

JUDITH [white and trembling] Must I—

ANDERSON [taking her hands and interrupting her to cover her agitation] My dear: I can depend on you?

JUDITH [with a piteous effort to be worthy of his trust] Yes.

ANDERSON [pressing her hand against his cheek] You will not mind two old people like us, Mr Dudgeon. [Going] I shall not say good evening: you will be here when I come back. [He goes out].

They watch him pass the window, and then look at each other dumbly, quite disconcerted. Richard, noting the quiver of her lips, is the first to pull himself together.

RICHARD. Mrs Anderson: I am perfectly aware of the nature of your sentiments towards me. I shall not intrude on you. Good evening. [Again he starts for the fireplace to get his coat].

JUDITH [getting between him and the coat] No, no. Dont go: please dont go.

RICHARD [roughly] Why? You dont want me here.

JUDITH. Yes, I— [Wringing her hands in despair] Oh, if I tell you the truth, you will use it to torment me.

RICHARD [indignantly] Torment! What

right have you to say that? Do you expect me to stay after that?

JUDITH. I want you to stay; but [suddenly raging at him like an angry child] it is not because I like you.

RICHARD. Indeed!

JUDITH. Yes: I had rather you did go than mistake me about that. I hate and dread you; and my husband knows it. If you are not here when he comes back, he will believe that I disobeyed him and drove you away.

RICHARD [ironically] Whereas, of course, you have really been so kind and hospitable and charming to me that I only want to go away out of mere contrariness, eh?

Judith, unable to bear it, sinks on the chair and bursts into tears.

RICHARD. Stop, stop, stop, I tell you. Dont do that. [Putting his hand to his breast as if to a wound] He wrung my heart by being a man. Need you tear it by being a woman? Has he not raised you above my insults, like himself? [She stops crying, and recovers herself somewhat, looking at him with a scared curiosity] There: thats right. [Sympathetically] Youre better now, arnt you? [He puts his hand encouragingly on her shoulder. She instantly rises haughtily, and stares at him defiantly. He at once drops into his usual sardonic tone]. Ah, thats better. You are yourself again: so is Richard. Well, shall we go to tea like a quiet respectable couple, and wait for your husband's return?

JUDITH [rather ashamed of herself] If you please. I—I am sorry to have been so foolish. [She stoops to take up the plate of toast from the fender].

RICHARD. I am sorry, for your sake, that I am—what I am. Allow me. [He takes the plate from her and goes with it to the table].

JUDITH [following with the teapot] Will you sit down? [He sits down at the end of the table nearest the press. There is a plate and knife laid there. The other plate is laid near it: but Judith stays at the opposite end of the table, next the fire, and takes her place there, drawing the tray towards her]. Do you take sugar?

RICHARD. No: but plenty of milk. Let me give you some toast. [He puts some on the second plate, and hands it to her, with the knife. The action shews quickly how well he knows that she has avoided her usual place so as to be as far from him as possible].

JUDITH [consciously] Thanks. [She gives him his tea]. Wont you help yourself?

RICHARD. Thanks. [*He puts a piece of toast on his own plate; and she pours out tea for herself*].

JUDITH [*observing that he tastes nothing*] Dont you like it? You are not eating anything.

RICHARD. Neither are you

JUDITH [*nervously*] I never care much for my tea. Please dont mind me.

RICHARD [*looking dreamily round*] I am thinking. It is all so strange to me. I can see the beauty and peace of this home: I think I have never been more at rest in my life than at this moment; and yet I know quite well I could never live here. It's not in my nature, I suppose, to be domesticated. But it's very beautiful: it's almost holy. [*He muses a moment, and then laughs softly*].

JUDITH [*quickly*] Why do you laugh?

RICHARD. I was thinking that if any stranger came in here now, he would take us for man and wife.

JUDITH [*taking offence*] You mean, I suppose, that you are more my age than he is.

RICHARD [*staring at this unexpected turn*] I never thought of such a thing. [*Sardonic again*]. I see there is another side to domestic joy.

JUDITH [*angrily*] I would rather have a husband whom everybody respects than— than—

RICHARD. Than the devil's disciple. You are right; but I daresay your love helps him to be a good man, just as your hate helps me to be a bad one.

JUDITH. My husband has been very good to you. He has forgiven you for insulting him, and is trying to save you. Can you not forgive him for being so much better than you are? How dare you belittle him by putting yourself in his place?

RICHARD. Did I?

JUDITH. Yes, you did. You said that if anybody came in they would take us for man and— [*She stops, terrorstricken, as a squad of soldiers tramps past the window*]. The English soldiers! Oh, what do they—

RICHARD [*listening*] Sh!

A VOICE [*outside*] Halt! Four outside: two in with me.

Judith half rises, listening and looking with dilated eyes at Richard, who takes up his cup prosaically, and is drinking his tea when the latch goes up with a sharp click, and an English sergeant walks into the room with two privates, who post themselves at the door. He comes promptly to the table between them.

THE SERGEANT. Sorry to disturb you, mum. Duty! Anthony Anderson: I arrest you in King George's name as a rebel.

JUDITH [*pointing at Richard*] But that is not— [*He looks up quickly at her, with a face of iron. She stops her mouth hastily with the hand she has raised to indicate him, and stands staring affrightedly*].

THE SERGEANT. Come, parson: put your coat on and come along.

RICHARD. Yes: I'll come. [*He rises and takes a step towards his own coat; then recollects himself, and, with his back to the sergeant, moves his gaze slowly round the room without turning his head until he sees Anderson's black coat hanging up on the press. He goes composedly to it; takes it down; and puts it on. The idea of himself as a parson tickles him: he looks down at the black sleeve on his arm, and then smiles slyly at Judith, whose white face shews him that what she is painfully struggling to grasp is not the humor of the situation but its horror. He turns to the sergeant, who is approaching him with a pair of handcuffs hidden behind him, and says lightly*] Did you ever arrest a man of my cloth before, Sergeant?

THE SERGEANT [*instinctively respectful, half to the black coat, half to Richard's good breeding*] Well, no sir. At least, only an army chaplain. [*Shewing the handcuffs*]. I'm sorry sir; but duty—

RICHARD. Just so, Sergeant. Well, I'm not ashamed of them: thank you kindly for the apology. [*He holds out his hands*].

SERGEANT [*not availing himself of the offer*] One gentleman to another, sir. Wouldnt you like to say a word to your missis, sir, before you go?

RICHARD [*smiling*] Oh, we shall meet again before—eh? [*meaning "before you hang me"*].

SERGEANT [*loudly, with ostentatious cheerfulness*] Oh, of course, of course. No call for the lady to distress herself. Still— [*in a lower voice, intended for Richard alone*] your last chance, sir.

They look at one another significantly for a moment. Then Richard exhales a deep breath and turns towards Judith.

RICHARD [*very distinctly*] My love. [*She looks at him, pitiably pale, and tries to answer, but cannot—tries also to come to him, but cannot trust herself to stand without the support of the table*]. This gallant gentleman is good enough to allow us a moment of leavetaking. [*The sergeant retires delicately and joins his men near the door*]. He is trying to spare you the truth; but you had better know it. Are you listening to me? [*She signifies assent*]. Do you understand that I am going to my death? [*She signifies that she understands*]. Remember, you must find our friend who was with us just now. Do you understand? [*She signifies yes*]. See that you get him safely out of harm's way. Dont for your life let him know of my danger; but if he finds it out, tell him that he cannot save me: they would hang him; and they would not spare me. And tell him that I am steadfast in my religion as he is in his, and that he may depend on me to the death. [*He turns to go, and meets the eye of the sergeant, who looks a little suspicious. He considers a moment, and then, turning roguishly to Judith with something of a smile breaking through his earnestness, says*] And now, my dear, I am afraid the sergeant will not believe that you love me like a wife unless you give one kiss before I go.

He approaches her and holds out his arms. She quits the table and almost falls into them.

JUDITH [*the words choking her*] I ought to—it's murder—

RICHARD. No: only a kiss [*softly to her*] for his sake.

JUDITH. I cant. You must—

RICHARD [*folding her in his arms with an impulse of compassion for her distress*] My poor girl!

Judith, with a sudden effort, throws her arms round him; kisses him; and swoons away, dropping from his arms to the ground as if the kiss had killed her.

RICHARD [*going quickly to the sergeant*] Now, Sergeant: quick, before she comes to. The handcuffs. [*He puts out his hands*].

SERGEANT [*pocketing them*] Never mind, sir: I'll trust you. Youre a game one. You ought to a bin a soldier, sir. Between them two, please. [*The soldiers place themselves one before Richard and one behind him. The sergeant opens the door*].

RICHARD [*taking a last look round him*] Goodbye, wife: goodbye, home. Muffle the drums, and quick march!

The sergeant signs to the leading soldier to march. They file out quickly. * * * * * * * * * * * * * * * * *When Anderson returns from Mrs Dudgeon's, he is astonished to find the room apparently empty and almost in darkness except for the glow from the fire; for one of the candles has burnt out, and the other is at its last flicker.*

ANDERSON. Why, what on earth—? [*Calling*] Judith, Judith! [*He listens: there is no answer*]. Hm! [*He goes to the cupboard; takes a candle from the drawer; lights it at the flicker of the expiring one on the table; and looks wonderingly at the untasted meal by its light. Then he sticks it in the candlestick; takes off his hat; and scratches his head, much puzzled. This action causes him to look at the floor for the first time; and there he sees Judith lying motionless with her eyes closed. He runs to her and stoops beside her, lifting her head*]. Judith.

JUDITH [*waking; for her swoon has passed into the sleep of exhaustion after suffering*] Yes. Did you call? Whats the matter?

ANDERSON. Ive just come in and found you lying here with the candles burnt out and the tea poured out and cold. What has happened?

JUDITH [*still astray*] I dont know. Have I been asleep? I suppose— [*She stops blankly*]. I dont know.

ANDERSON [*groaning*] Heaven forgive me, I left you alone with that scoundrel. [*Judith remembers. With an agonized cry, she clutches his shoulders and drags herself to her feet as he rises with her. He clasps her tenderly in his arms*]. My poor pet!

JUDITH [*frantically clinging to him*] What shall I do? Oh my God, what shall I do?

ANDERSON. Never mind, never mind, my dearest dear: it was my fault. Come: youre safe now; and youre not hurt, are you? [*He takes his arms from her to see whether she can stand*]. There: thats right, thats right. If only you are not hurt, nothing else matters.

JUDITH. No, no, no: I'm not hurt.

ANDERSON. Thank Heaven for that! Come now: [*leading her to the railed seat and making her sit down beside him*] sit down and rest: you can tell me about it tomorrow. Or [*misunderstanding her distress*] you shall not tell me at all if it worries you. There, there! [*Cheerfully*] I'll make you some fresh tea: that will set you up again. [*He goes to the table, and empties the teapot into the slop bowl*].

JUDITH [*in a strained tone*] Tony.

ANDERSON. Yes, dear?

JUDITH. Do you think we are only in a dream now?

ANDERSON [*glancing round at her for a moment with a pang of anxiety, though he goes on steadily and cheerfully putting fresh tea into the pot*] Perhaps so, pet. But you may as well dream a cup of tea when youre about it.

JUDITH. Oh stop, stop. You dont know— [*Distracted, she buries her face in her knotted hands*].

ANDERSON [*breaking down and coming to her*] My dear, what is it? I cant bear it any longer: you must tell me. It was all my fault: I was mad to trust him.

JUDITH. No: dont say that. You mustnt say that. He— oh no, no: I cant. Tony: dont speak to me. Take my hands—both my hands. [*He takes them, wondering*]. Make me think of you, not of him. Theres danger, frightful danger; but it is your danger; and I cant keep thinking of it: I cant, I cant: my mind goes back to his danger. He must be saved—no: you must be saved: you, you, you. [*She springs up as if to do something or go somewhere, exclaiming*] Oh, Heaven help me!

ANDERSON [*keeping his seat and holding her hands with resolute composure*] Calmly, calmly, my pet. Youre quite distracted.

JUDITH. I may well be. I dont know what to do. I dont know what to do. [*Tearing her hands away*]. I must save him. [*Anderson rises in alarm as she runs wildly to the door. It is opened in her face by Essie, who hurries in full of anxiety. The surprise is so disagreeable to Judith that it brings her to her senses. Her tone is sharp and angry as she demands*] What do you want?

ESSIE. I was to come to you.

ANDERSON. Who told you to?

ESSIE [*staring at him, as if his presence astonished her*] Are you here?

JUDITH. Of course. Dont be foolish, child.

ANDERSON. Gently, dearest: youll frighten her. [*Going between them*]. Come here, Essie. [*She comes to him*]. Who sent you?

ESSIE. Dick. He sent me word by a soldier. I was to come here at once and do whatever Mrs Anderson told me.

ANDERSON [*enlightened*] A soldier! Ah, I see it all now! They have arrested Richard. [*Judith makes a gesture of despair*].

ESSIE. No. I asked the soldier. Dick's safe. But the soldier said you had been taken.

ANDERSON. I! [*Bewildered, he turns to Judith for an explanation*].

JUDITH [*coaxingly*] All right, dear: I understand. [*To Essie*] Thank you, Essie, for coming; but I dont need you now. You may go home.

ESSIE [*suspicious*] Arc you sure Dick has not been touched? Perhaps he told the soldier to say it was the minister. [*Anxiously*] Mrs Anderson: do you think it can have been that?

ANDERSON. Tell her the truth if it is so, Judith. She will learn it from the first neighbor she meets in the street. [*Judith turns away and covers her eyes with her hands*].

ESSIE [*wailing*] But what will they do to him? Oh, what will they do to him? Will they hang him? [*Judith shudders convulsively, and throws herself into the chair in which Richard sat at the tea table*].

ANDERSON [*patting Essie's shoulder and trying to comfort her*] I hope not. I hope not. Perhaps if youre very quiet and patient, we may be able to help him in some way.

ESSIE. Yes—help him—yes, yes, yes. I'll be good.

ANDERSON. I must go to him at once, Judith.

JUDITH [*springing up*] Oh no. You must go away—far away, to some place of safety.

ANDERSON. Pooh!

JUDITH [*passionately*] Do you want to kill me? Do you think I can bear to live for days and days with every knock at the door— every footstep—giving me a spasm of terror? to lie awake for nights and nights in an agony of dread, listening for them to come and arrest you?

ANDERSON. Do you think it would be better to know that I had run away from my post at the first sign of danger?

JUDITH [*bitterly*] Oh, you wont go. I know it. Youll stay; and I shall go mad.

ANDERSON. My dear, your duty—

JUDITH [*fiercely*] What do I care about my duty?

ANDERSON [*shocked*] Judith!

JUDITH. I am doing my duty. I am clinging to my duty. My duty is to get you away, to save you, to leave him to his fate [*Essie utters a cry of distress and sinks on the chair at the fire, sobbing silently*]. My instinct is the same as hers—to save him above all things, though it would be so much better for him to die! so much greater! But I know you will take your own way as he took it. I have no power. [*She sits down sullenly on the railed seat*] I'm only a woman: I can do nothing but sit here and suffer. Only, tell him I tried to save you— that I did my best to save you.

ANDERSON. My dear, I am afraid he will be thinking more of his own danger than of mine.

JUDITH. Stop; or I shall hate you.

ANDERSON [*remonstrating*] Come, come,

come! How am I to leave you if you talk like this? You are quite out of your senses. [*He turns to Essie*] Essie.

ESSIE [*eagerly rising and drying her eyes*] Yes?

ANDERSON. Just wait outside a moment, like a good girl: Mrs Anderson is not well. [*Essie looks doubtful*]. Never fear: I'll come to you presently; and I'll go to Dick.

ESSIE. You are sure you will go to him? [*Whispering*]. You wont let her prevent you?

ANDERSON [*smiling*] No, no: it's all right. All right. [*She goes*]. Thats a good girl. [*He closes the door, and returns to Judith*].

JUDITH [*seated—rigid*] You are going to your death.

ANDERSON [*quaintly*] Then I shall go in my best coat, dear. [*He turns to the press, beginning to take off his coat*]. Where—? [*He stares at the empty nail for a moment; then looks quickly round to the fire; strides across to it; and lifts Richard's coat*]. Why, my dear, it seems that he has gone in my best coat.

JUDITH [*still motionless*] Yes.

ANDERSON. Did the soldiers make a mistake?

JUDITH. Yes: they made a mistake.

ANDERSON. He might have told them. Poor fellow, he was too upset, I suppose.

JUDITH. Yes: he might have told them. So might I.

ANDERSON. Well, it's all very puzzling— almost funny. It's curious how these little things strike us even in the most— [*He breaks off and begins putting on Richard's coat*]. I'd better take him his own coat. I know what he'll say—[*imitating Richard's sardonic manner*] "Anxious about my soul, Pastor, and also about your best coat." Eh?

JUDITH. Yes, that is just what he will say to you. [*Vacantly*] It doesnt matter: I shall never see either of you again.

ANDERSON [*rallying her*] Oh pooh, pooh, pooh! [*He sits down beside her*]. Is this how you keep your promise that I shant be ashamed of my brave wife?

JUDITH. No: this is how I break it. I cannot keep my promises to him: why should I keep my promises to you?

ANDERSON. Dont speak so strangely, my love. It sounds insincere to me. [*She looks unutterable reproach at him*]. Yes, dear, nonsense is always insincere; and my dearest is talking nonsense. Just nonsense. [*Her face darkens into dumb obstinacy. She stares straight before her, and does not look at him again,* absorbed in Richard's fate. He scans her face; sees that his rallying has produced no effect; and gives it up, making no further effort to conceal his anxiety*]. I wish I knew what has frightened you so. Was there a struggle? Did he fight?

JUDITH. No. He smiled.

ANDERSON. Did he realize his danger, do you think?

JUDITH. He realized yours.

ANDERSON. Mine!

JUDITH [*monotonously*] He said "See that you get him safely out of harm's way." I promised: I cant keep my promise. He said, "Dont for your life let him know of my danger." Ive told you of it. He said that if you found it out, you could not save him— that they will hang him and not spare you.

ANDERSON [*rising in generous indignation*] And you think that I will let a man with that much good in him die like a dog, when a few words might make him die like a Christian. I'm ashamed of you, Judith.

JUDITH. He will be steadfast in his religion as you are in yours; and you may depend on him to the death. He said so.

ANDERSON. God forgive him! What else did he say?

JUDITH. He said goodbye.

ANDERSON [*fidgeting nervously to and fro in great concern*] Poor fellow, poor fellow! You said goodbye to him in all kindness and charity, Judith, I hope.

JUDITH. I kissed him.

ANDERSON. What! Judith!

JUDITH. Are you angry?

ANDERSON. No, no. You were right: you were right. Poor fellow, poor fellow! [*Greatly distressed*] To be hanged like that at his age! And then did they take him away?

JUDITH [*wearily*] Then you were here: thats the next thing I remember. I suppose I fainted. Now bid me goodbye, Tony. Perhaps I shall faint again. I wish I could die.

ANDERSON. No, no, my dear: you must pull yourself together and be sensible. I am in no danger—not the least in the world.

JUDITH [*solemnly*] You are going to your death, Tony—your sure death, if God will let innocent men be murdered. They will not let you see him: they will arrest you the moment you give your name. It was for you the soldiers came.

ANDERSON [*thunderstruck*] For me!!! [*His fists clinch; his neck thickens; his face reddens; the fleshy purses under his eyes become injected with hot blood; the man of peace vanishes, transfigured into a choleric and formidable man of war. Still, she does not come out of her absorption to look at him: her eyes are steadfast with a mechanical reflection of Richard's steadfastness*].

JUDITH. He took your place: he is dying to save you. That is why he went in your coat. That is why I kissed him.

ANDERSON [*exploding*] Blood an' owns! [*His voice is rough and dominant, his gesture full of brute energy*]. Here! Essie, Essie!

ESSIE [*running in*] Yes.

ANDERSON [*impetuously*] Off with you as hard as you can run, to the inn. Tell them to saddle the fastest and strongest horse they have [*Judith rises breathless, and stares at him incredulously*]—the chestnut mare, if she's fresh—without a moment's delay. Go into the stable yard and tell the black man there that I'll give him a silver dollar if the horse is waiting for me when I come, and that I am close on your heels. Away with you. [*His energy sends Essie flying from the room. He pounces on his riding boots; rushes with them to the chair at the fire; and begins pulling them on*].

JUDITH [*unable to believe such a thing of him*] You are not going to him!

ANDERSON [*busy with the boots*] Going to him! What good would that do? [*Growling to himself as he gets the first boot on with a wrench*] I'll go to them, so I will. [*To Judith peremptorily*] Get me the pistols: I want them. And money, money: I want money—all the money in the house. [*He stoops over the other boot, grumbling*] A great satisfaction it would be to him to have my company on the gallows. [*He pulls on the boot*].

JUDITH. You are deserting him, then?

ANDERSON. Hold your tongue, woman; and get me the pistols. [*She goes to the press and takes from it a leather belt with two pistols, a powder horn, and a bag of bullets attached to it. She throws it on the table. Then she unlocks a drawer in the press and takes out a purse. Anderson grabs the belt and buckles it on, saying*] If they took him for me in my coat, perhaps theyll take me for him in his. [*Hitching the belt into its place*] Do I look like him?

JUDITH [*turning with the purse in her hand*] Horribly unlike him.

ANDERSON [*snatching the purse from her and emptying it on the table*] Hm! We shall see.

JUDITH [*sitting down helplessly*] Is it of any use to pray, do you think, Tony?

ANDERSON [*counting the money*] Pray! Can we pray Swindon's rope off Richard's neck?

JUDITH. God may soften Major Swindon's heart.

ANDERSON [*contemptuously — pocketing a handful of money*] Let him, then. I am not God; and I must go to work another way. [*Judith gasps at the blasphemy. He throws the purse on the table*]. Keep that. Ive taken 25 dollars.

JUDITH. Have you forgotten even that you are a minister?

ANDERSON. Minister be—faugh! My hat: wheres my hat? [*He snatches up hat and cloak, and puts both on in hot haste*] Now listen, you. If you can get a word with him by pretending youre his wife, tell him to hold his tongue until morning: that will give me all the start I need.

JUDITH [*solemnly*] You may depend on him to the death.

ANDERSON. Youre a fool, a fool, Judith. [*For a moment checking the torrent of his haste, and speaking with something of his old quiet and impressive conviction*] You dont know the man youre married to. [*Essie returns. He swoops at her at once*]. Well: is the horse ready?

ESSIE [*breathless*] It will be ready when you come.

ANDERSON. Good. [*He makes for the door*].

JUDITH [*rising and stretching out her arms after him involuntarily*] Wont you say goodbye?

ANDERSON. And waste another half minute! Psha! [*He rushes out like an avalanche*].

ESSIE [*hurrying to Judith*] He has gone to save Richard, hasnt he?

JUDITH. To save Richard! No: Richard has saved him. He has gone to save himself. Richard must die.

Essie screams with terror and falls on her knees, hiding her face. Judith, without heeding her, looks rigidly straight in front of her, at the vision of Richard, dying.

ACT III

Early next morning the sergeant, at the British headquarters in the Town Hall, unlocks the door of a little empty panelled waiting room, and invites Judith to enter. She has had a bad night, probably a rather delirious one; for even in the reality of the raw morning, her fixed gaze comes back at moments when her attention is not strongly held.

The sergeant considers that her feelings do her

credit, and is sympathetic in an encouraging military way. Being a fine figure of a man, vain of his uniform and of his rank, he feels specially qualified, in a respectful way, to console her.

SERGEANT. You can have a quiet word with him here, mum.

JUDITH. Shall I have long to wait?

SERGEANT. No, mum, not a minute. We kep him in the Bridewell for the night; and he's just been brought over here for the court martial. Don't fret, mum: he slep like a child, and has made a rare good breakfast.

JUDITH [*incredulously*] He is in good spirits!

SERGEANT. Tip top, mum. The chaplain looked in to see him last night; and he won seventeen shillings off him at spoil five. He spent it among us like the gentleman he is. Duty's duty, mum, of course; but youre among friends here. [*The tramp of a couple of soldiers is heard approaching*]. There: I think he's coming. [*Richard comes in, without a sign of care or captivity in his bearing. The sergeant nods to the two soldiers, and shews them the key of the room in his hand. They withdraw*]. Your good lady, sir.

RICHARD [*going to her*] What! My wife. My adored one. [*He takes her hand and kisses it with a perverse, raffish gallantry*]. How long do you allow a brokenhearted husband for leave-taking, Sergeant?

SERGEANT. As long as we can, sir. We shall not disturb you till the court sits.

RICHARD. But it has struck the hour.

SERGEANT. So it has, sir; but there's a delay. General Burgoyne's just arrived—Gentlemanly Johnny we call him, sir—and he wont have done finding fault with everything this side of half past. I know him, sir: I served with him in Portugal. You may count on twenty minutes, sir; and by your leave I wont waste any more of them. [*He goes out, locking the door. Richard immediately drops his raffish manner and turns to Judith with considerate sincerity*].

RICHARD. Mrs Anderson: this visit is very kind of you. And how are you after last night? I had to leave you before you recovered; but I sent word to Essie to go and look after you. Did she understand the message?

JUDITH [*breathless and urgent*] Oh, dont think of me: I havnt come here to talk about myself. Are they going to—to— [*meaning "to hang you"*]?

RICHARD [*whimsically*] At noon, punctually.

At least, that was when they disposed of Uncle Peter. [*She shudders*]. Is your husband safe? Is he on the wing?

JUDITH. He is no longer my husband.

RICHARD [*opening his eyes wide*]. Eh?

JUDITH. I disobeyed you. I told him everything. I expected him to come here and save you. I wanted him to come here and save you. He ran away instead.

RICHARD. Well, thats what I meant him to do. What good would his staying have done? Theyd only have hanged us both.

JUDITH [*with reproachful earnestness*] Richard Dudgeon: on your honor, what would you have done in his place?

RICHARD. Exactly what he has done, of course.

JUDITH. Oh, why will you not be simple with me—honest and straightforward? If you are so selfish as that, why did you let them take you last night?

RICHARD [*gaily*] Upon my life, Mrs Anderson, I dont know. Ive been asking myself that question ever since; and I can find no manner of reason for acting as I did.

JUDITH. You know you did it for his sake, believing he was a more worthy man than yourself.

RICHARD [*laughing*] Oho! No: thats a very pretty reason, I must say; but I'm not so modest as that. No: it wasnt for his sake.

JUDITH [*after a pause, during which she looks shamefacedly at him, blushing painfully*] Was it for my sake?

RICHARD [*gallantly*] Well, you had a hand in it. It must have been a little for your sake. You let them take me, at all events.

JUDITH. Oh, do you think I have not been telling myself that all night? Your death will be at my door. [*Impulsively, she gives him her hand, and adds, with intense earnestness*] If I could save you as you saved him, I would do it, no matter how cruel the death was.

RICHARD [*holding her hand and smiling, but keeping her almost at arms length*] I am very sure I shouldnt let you.

JUDITH. Dont you see that I can save you?

RICHARD. How? By changing clothes with me, eh?

JUDITH [*disengaging her hand to touch his lips with it*] Dont [*meaning "Dont jest"*]. No: by telling the Court who you really are.

RICHARD [*frowning*] No use: they wouldnt spare me; and it would spoil half his chance of escaping. They are determined to cow us by making an example of somebody on that gallows today. Well, let us cow them by showing that we can stand by one another to the death. That is the only force that can send Burgoyne back across the Atlantic and make America a nation.

JUDITH [*impatiently*] Oh, what does all that matter?

RICHARD [*laughing*] True: what does it matter? what does anything matter? You see, men have these strange notions, Mrs Anderson; and women see the folly of them.

JUDITH. Women have to lose those they love through them.

RICHARD. They can easily get fresh lovers.

JUDITH [*revolted*] Oh! [*Vehemently*] Do you realize that you are going to kill yourself?

RICHARD. The only man I have any right to kill, Mrs Anderson. Dont be concerned: no woman will lose her lover through my death. [*Smiling*] Bless you, nobody cares for me. Have you heard that my mother is dead?

JUDITH. Dead!

RICHARD. Of heart disease—in the night. Her last word to me was her curse: I dont think I could have borne her blessing. My other relatives will not grieve much on my account. Essie will cry for a day or two; but I have provided for her: I made my own will last night.

JUDITH [*stonily, after a moment's silence*] And I!

RICHARD [*surprised*] You?

JUDITH. Yes, I. Am I not to care at all?

RICHARD [*gaily and bluntly*] Not a scrap. Oh, you expressed your feelings towards me very frankly yesterday. What happened may have softened you for the moment; but believe me, Mrs Anderson, you dont like a bone in my skin or a hair on my head. I shall be as good a riddance at 12 today as I should have been at 12 yesterday.

JUDITH [*her voice trembling*] What can I do to shew you that you are mistaken?

RICHARD. Dont trouble. I'll give you credit for liking me a little better than you did. All I say is that my death will not break your heart.

JUDITH [*almost in a whisper*] How do you know? [*She puts her hands on his shoulders and looks intently at him*].

RICHARD [*amazed—divining the truth*] Mrs Anderson! [*The bell of the town clock strikes the quarter. He collects himself, and removes her hands, saying rather coldly*] Excuse me: they will be here for me presently. It is too late.

JUDITH. It is not too late. Call me as witness: they will never kill you when they know how heroically you have acted.

RICHARD [*with some scorn*] Indeed! But if I dont go through with it, where will the heroism be? I shall simply have tricked them; and theyll hang me for that like a dog. Serve me right too!

JUDITH [*wildly*] Oh, I believe you want to die.

RICHARD [*obstinately*] No I dont.

JUDITH. Then why not try to save yourself? I implore you—listen. You said just now that you saved him for my sake—yes [*clutching him as he recoils with a gesture of denial*] a little for my sake. Well, save yourself for my sake. And I will go with you to the end of the world.

RICHARD [*taking her by the wrists and holding her a little way from him, looking steadily at her*] Judith.

JUDITH [*breathless—delighted at the name*] Yes.

RICHARD. If I said—to please you—that I did what I did ever so little for your sake, I lied as men always lie to women. You know how much I have lived with worthless men— aye, and worthless women too. Well, they could all rise to some sort of goodness and kindness when they were in love [*the word love comes from him with true Puritan scorn*]. That has taught me to set very little store by the goodness that only comes out red hot. What I did last night, I did in cold blood, caring not half so much for your husband, or [*ruthlessly*] for you [*she droops, stricken*] as I do for myself. I had no motive and no interest: all I can tell you is that when it came to the point whether I would take my neck out of the noose and put another man's into it, I could not do it. I dont know why not: I see myself as a fool for my pains; but I could not and I cannot. I have been brought up standing by the law of my own nature; and I may not go against it, gallows or no gallows. [*She has slowly raised her head and is now looking full at him*]. I should have done the same for any other man in the town, or any other man's wife. [*Releasing her*] Do you understand that?

JUDITH. Yes: you mean that you do not love me.

RICHARD [*revolted—with fierce contempt*] Is

that all it means to you?

JUDITH. What more—what worse—can it mean to me? [*The sergeant knocks. The blow on the door jars on her heart*]. Oh, one moment more. [*She throws herself on her knees*]. I pray to you—

RICHARD. Hush! [*Calling*] Come in. [*The sergeant unlocks the door and opens it. The guard is with him*].

SERGEANT [*coming in*] Time's up, sir.

RICHARD. Quite ready, Sergeant. Now, my dear. [*He attempts to raise her*].

JUDITH [*clinging to him*] Only one thing more—I entreat, I implore you. Let me be present in the court. I have seen Major Swindon: he said I should be allowed if you asked it. You will ask it. It is my last request: I shall never ask you anything again. [*She clasps his knee*]. I beg and pray it of you.

RICHARD. If I do, will you be silent?

JUDITH. Yes.

RICHARD. You will keep faith?

JUDITH. I will keep— [*She breaks down, sobbing*].

RICHARD [*taking her arm to lift her*] Just— her other arm, Sergeant.

They go out, she sobbing convulsively, supported by the two men.

Meanwhile, the Council Chamber is ready for the court martial. It is a large, lofty room, with a chair of state in the middle under a tall canopy with a gilt crown, and maroon curtains with the royal monogram G. R. In front of the chair is a table, also draped in maroon, with a bell, a heavy inkstand, and writing materials on it. Several chairs are set at the table. The door is at the right hand of the occupant of the chair of state when it has an occupant: at present it is empty. Major Swindon, a pale, sandy-haired, very conscientious looking man of about 45, sits at the end of the table with his back to the door, writing. He is alone until the sergeant announces the General in a subdued manner which suggests that Gentlemanly Johnny has been making his presence felt rather heavily.

SERGEANT. The General, sir.

Swindon rises hastily. The general comes in: the sergeant goes out. General Burgoyne is 55, and very well preserved. He is a man of fashion, gallant enough to have made a distinguished marriage by an elopement, witty enough to write successful comedies, aristocratically-connected enough to have had opportunities of high military distinction. His eyes, large, brilliant, apprehensive, and intelligent, are his most remarkable

feature: without them his fine nose and small mouth would suggest rather more fastidiousness and less force than go to the making of a first rate general. Just now the eyes are angry and tragic, and the mouth and nostrils tense.

BURGOYNE. Major Swindon, I presume.

SWINDON. Yes. General Burgoyne, if I mistake not. [*They bow to one another ceremoniously*]. I am glad to have the support of your presence this morning. It is not particularly lively business, hanging this poor devil of a minister.

BURGOYNE [*throwing himself into Swindon's chair*] No, sir, it is not. It is making too much of the fellow to execute him: what more could you have done if he had been a member of the Church of England? Martyrdom, sir, is what these people like: it is the only way in which a man can become famous without ability. However, you have committed us to hanging him; and the sooner he is hanged the better.

SWINDON. We have arranged it for 12 o'clock. Nothing remains to be done except to try him.

BURGOYNE [*looking at him with suppressed anger*] Nothing—except to save your own necks, perhaps. Have you heard the news from Springtown?

SWINDON. Nothing special. The latest reports are satisfactory.

BURGOYNE [*rising in amazement*] Satisfactory, sir! Satisfactory!! [*He stares at him for a moment, and then adds, with grim intensity*] I am glad you take that view of them.

SWINDON [*puzzled*] Do I understand that in your opinion—

BURGOYNE. I do not express my opinion. I never stoop to that habit of profane language which unfortunately coarsens our profession. If I did, sir, perhaps I should be able to express my opinion of the news from Springtown—the news which you [*severely*] have apparently not heard. How soon do you get news from your supports here?—in the course of a month, eh?

SWINDON [*turning sulky*] I suppose the reports have been taken to you, sir, instead of to me. Is there anything serious?

BURGOYNE [*taking a report from his pocket and holding it up*] Springtown's in the hands of the rebels. [*He throws the report on the table*].

SWINDON [*aghast*] Since yesterday!

BURGOYNE. Since two o'clock this morning.

Perhaps we shall be in their hands before two o'clock tomorrow morning. Have you thought of that?

SWINDON [*confidently*] As to that, General, the British soldier will give a good account of himself.

BURGOYNE [*bitterly*] And therefore, I suppose, sir, the British officer need not know his business: the British soldier will get him out of all his blunders with the bayonet. In future, sir, I must ask you to be a little less generous with the blood of your men, and a little more generous with your own brains.

SWINDON. I am sorry I cannot pretend to your intellectual eminence, sir. I can only do my best, and rely on the devotion of my countrymen.

BURGOYNE [*suddenly becoming suavely sarcastic*] May I ask are you writing a melodrama, Major Swindon?

SWINDON [*flushing*] No, sir.

BURGOYNE. What a pity! What a pity! [*Dropping his sarcastic tone and facing him suddenly and seriously*] Do you at all realize, sir, that we have nothing standing between us and destruction but our own bluff and the sheepishness of these colonists? They are men of the same English stock as ourselves: six to one of us [*repeating it emphatically*] six to one, sir; and nearly half our troops are Hessians, Brunswickers, German dragoons, and Indians with scalping knives. These are the countrymen on whose devotion you rely! Suppose the colonists find a leader! Suppose the news from Springtown should turn out to mean that they have already found a leader! What shall we do then? Eh?

SWINDON [*sullenly*] Our duty, sir, I presume.

BURGOYNE [*again sarcastic—giving him up as a fool*] Quite so, quite so. Thank you, Major Swindon, thank you. Now youve settled the question, sir—thrown a flood of light on the situation. What a comfort to me to feel that I have at my side so devoted and able an officer to support me in this emergency! I think, sir, it will probably relieve both our feelings if we proceed to hang this dissenter without further delay [*he strikes the bell*] especially as I am debarred by my principles from the customary military vent for my feelings. [*The sergeant appears*]. Bring your man in.

SERGEANT. Yes, sir.

BURGOYNE. And mention to any officer you may meet that the court cannot wait any longer for him.

SWINDON [*keeping his temper with difficulty*] The staff is perfectly ready, sir. They have been waiting your convenience for fully half an hour. Perfectly ready, sir.

BURGOYNE [*blandly*] So am I. [*Several officers come in and take their seats. One of them sits at the end of the table furthest from the door, and acts throughout as clerk of the court, making notes of the proceedings. The uniforms are those of the 9th, 20th, 21st, 24th, 47th, 53rd, and 62nd British Infantry. One officer is a Major General of the Royal Artillery. There are also German officers of the Hessian Rifles, and of German dragoon and Brunsvicker regiments*]. Oh, good morning, gentlemen. Sorry to disturb you, I am sure. Very good of you to spare us a few moments.

SWINDON. Will you preside, sir?

BURGOYNE [*becoming additionally polished, lofty, sarcastic, and urbane now that he is in public*] No, sir: I feel my own deficiencies too keenly to presume so far. If you will kindly allow me, I will sit at the feet of Gamaliel. [*He takes the chair at the end of the table next the door, and motions Swindon to the chair of state, waiting for him to be seated before sitting down himself*].

SWINDON [*greatly annoyed*] As you please, sir. I am only trying to do my duty under excessively trying circumstances. [*He takes his place in the chair of state*].

Burgoyne, relaxing his studied demeanor for the moment, sits down and begins to read the report with knitted brows and careworn looks, reflecting on his desperate situation and Swindon's uselessness. Richard is brought in. Judith walks beside him. Two soldiers precede and two follow him, with the sergeant in command. They cross the room to the wall opposite the door; but when Richard has just passed before the chair of state the sergeant stops him with a touch on the arm, and posts himself behind him, at his elbow. Judith stands timidly at the wall. The four soldiers place themselves in a squad near her.

BURGOYNE [*looking up and seeing Judith*] Who is that woman?

SERGEANT. Prisoner's wife, sir.

SWINDON [*nervously*] She begged me to allow her to be present; and I thought—

BURGOYNE [*completing the sentence for him ironically*] You thought it would be a pleasure for her. Quite so, quite so. [*Blandly*] Give the lady a chair; and make her thoroughly comfortable.

The sergeant fetches a chair and places it near Richard.

JUDITH. Thank you, sir. [*She sits down after an awestricken curtsy to Burgoyne, which he acknowledges by a dignified bend of his head*].

SWINDON [*to Richard, sharply*] Your name, sir?

RICHARD [*affable, but obstinate*] Come: you dont mean to say that youve brought me here without knowing who I am?

SWINDON. As a matter of form, sir, give your name.

RICHARD. As a matter of form then, my name is Anthony Anderson, Presbyterian minister in this town.

BURGOYNE [*interested*] Indeed! Pray, Mr Anderson, what do you gentlemen believe?

RICHARD. I shall be happy to explain if time is allowed me. I cannot undertake to complete your conversion in less than a fortnight.

SWINDON [*snubbing him*] We are not here to discuss your views.

BURGOYNE [*with an elaborate bow to the unfortunate Swindon*] I stand rebuked.

SWINDON [*embarrassed*] Oh, not you, I as—

BURGOYNE. Dont mention it. [*To Richard, very politely*] Any political views, Mr Anderson?

RICHARD. I understand that that is just what we are here to find out.

SWINDON [*severely*] Do you mean to deny that you are a rebel?

RICHARD. I am an American, sir.

SWINDON. What do you expect me to think of that speech, Mr Anderson?

RICHARD. I never expect a soldier to think, sir.

Burgoyne is boundlessly delighted by this retort, which almost reconciles him to the loss of America.

SWINDON [*whitening with anger*] I advise you not to be insolent, prisoner.

RICHARD. You cant help yourself, General. When you make up your mind to hang a man, you put yourself at a disadvantage with him. Why should I be civil to you? I may as well be hanged for a sheep as a lamb.

SWINDON. You have no right to assume that the court has made up its mind without a fair trial. And you will please not address me as General. I am Major Swindon.

RICHARD. A thousand pardons. I thought I had the honor of addressing Gentlemanly Johnny.

Sensation among the officers. The sergeant has a narrow escape from a guffaw.

BURGOYNE [*with extreme suavity*] I believe I am Gentlemanly Johnny, sir, at your service. My more intimate friends call me General Burgoyne. [*Richard bows with perfect politeness*]. You will understand, sir, I hope, since you seem to be a gentleman and a man of some spirit in spite of your calling, that if we should have the misfortune to hang you, we shall do so as a mere matter of political necessity and military duty, without any personal ill-feeling.

RICHARD. Oh, quite so. That makes all the difference in the world, of course.

They all smile in spite of themselves; and some of the younger officers burst out laughing.

JUDITH [*her dread and horror deepening at every one of these jests and compliments*] How can you?

RICHARD. You promised to be silent.

BURGOYNE [*to Judith, with studied courtesy*] Believe me, Madam, your husband is placing us under the greatest obligation by taking this very disagreeable business so thoroughly in the spirit of a gentleman. Sergeant: give Mr Anderson a chair. [*The sergeant does so. Richard sits down*]. Now, Major Swindon: we are waiting for you.

SWINDON. You are aware, I presume, Mr Anderson, of your obligations as a subject of His Majesty King George the Third.

RICHARD. I am aware, sir, that His Majesty King George the Third is about to hang me because I object to Lord North's robbing me.

SWINDON. That is a treasonable speech, sir.

RICHARD [*briefly*] Yes. I meant it to be.

BURGOYNE [*strongly deprecating this line of defence, but still polite*] Dont you think, Mr Anderson, that this is rather—if you will excuse the word—a vulgar line to take? Why should you cry out robbery because of a stamp duty and a tea duty and so forth? After all, it is the essence of your position as a gentleman that you pay with a good grace.

RICHARD. It is not the money, General. But to be swindled by a pig-headed lunatic like King George—

SWINDON [*scandalized*] Chut, sir—silence!

SERGEANT [*in stentorian tones, greatly shocked*] Silence!

BURGOYNE [*unruffled*] Ah, that is another point of view. My position does not allow of my going into that, except in private. But [*shrugging his shoulders*] of course, Mr Anderson, if you are determined to be hanged [*Judith flinches*] there's nothing more to be said. An unusual taste! however [*with a final shrug*]—!

SWINDON [*To Burgoyne*] Shall we call witnesses?

RICHARD. What need is there of witnesses? If the townspeople here had listened to me, you would have found the streets barricaded, the houses loopholed, and the people in arms to hold the town against you to the last man. But you arrived, unfortunately, before we had got out of the talking stage; and then it was too late.

SWINDON [*severely*] Well, sir, we shall teach you and your townspeople a lesson they will not forget. Have you anything more to say?

RICHARD. I think you might have the decency to treat me as a prisoner of war, and shoot me like a man instead of hanging me like a dog.

BURGOYNE [*sympathetically*] Now there, Mr Anderson, you talk like a civilian, if you will excuse my saying so. Have you any idea of the average marksmanship of the army of His Majesty King George the Third? If we make you up a firing party, what will happen? Half of them will miss you: the rest will make a mess of the business and leave you to the provo-marshal's pistol. Whereas we can hang you in a perfectly workmanlike and agreeable way. [*Kindly*] Let me persuade you to be hanged, Mr Anderson?

JUDITH [*sick with horror*] My God!

RICHARD [*To Judith*] Your promise! [*To Burgoyne*] Thank you, General: that view of the case did not occur to me before. To oblige you, I withdraw my objection to the rope. Hang me, by all means.

BURGOYNE [*smoothly*] Will 12 o'clock suit you, Mr Anderson?

RICHARD. I shall be at your disposal then, General.

BURGOYNE [*rising*] Nothing more to be said, gentlemen. [*They all rise*].

JUDITH [*rushing to the table*] Oh, you are not going to murder a man like that, without a proper trial—without thinking of what you are doing—without— [*she cannot find words*].

RICHARD. Is this how you keep your promise?

JUDITH. If I am not to speak, you must. Defend yourself: save yourself: tell them the truth.

RICHARD [*worriedly*] I have told them truth enough to hang me ten times over. If you say another word you will risk other lives; but you will not save mine.

BURGOYNE. My good lady, our only desire is to save unpleasantness. What satisfaction would it give you to have a solemn fuss made, with my friend Swindon in a black cap and so forth? I am sure we are greatly indebted to the admirable tact and gentlemanly feeling shewn by your husband.

JUDITH [*throwing the words in his face*] Oh, you are mad. Is it nothing to you what wicked thing you do if only you do it like a gentleman? Is it nothing to you whether you are a murderer or not, if only you murder in a red coat? [*Desperately*] You shall not hang him: that man is not my husband.

The officers look at one another, and whisper: some of the Germans asking their neighbors to explain what the woman had said. Burgoyne, who has been visibly shaken by Judith's reproach, recovers himself promptly at this new development. Richard meanwhile raises his voice above the buzz.

RICHARD. I appeal to you, gentlemen, to put an end to this. She will not believe that she cannot save me. Break up the court.

BURGOYNE [*in a voice so quiet and firm that it restores silence at once*] One moment, Mr Anderson. One moment, gentlemen. [*He resumes his seat. Swindon and the officers follow his example*]. Let me understand you clearly, madam. Do you mean that this gentleman is not your husband, or merely—I wish to put this with all delicacy—that you are not his wife?

JUDITH. I dont know what you mean, I say that he is not my husband—that my husband has escaped. This man took his place to save him. Ask anyone in the town—send out into the street for the first person you find there, and bring him in as a witness. He will tell you that the prisoner is not Anthony Anderson.

BURGOYNE [*quietly, as before*] Sergeant.

SERGEANT. Yes, sir.

BURGOYNE. Go out into the street and bring in the first townsman you see there.

SERGEANT [*making for the door*] Yes sir.

BURGOYNE [*as the sergeant passes*] The first clean, sober townsman you see.

SERGEANT. Yes sir. [*He goes out*].

BURGOYNE. Sit down, Mr Anderson—if I may call you so for the present. [*Richard sits down*]. Sit down, madam, whilst we wait. Give the lady a newspaper.

RICHARD [*indignantly*] Shame!

BURGOYNE [*keenly, with a half smile*] If you are not her husband, sir, the case is not a serious one—for h e r. [*Richard bites his lip, silenced*].

JUDITH [*to Richard, as she returns to her seat*] I couldnt help it. [*He shakes his head. She sits down*].

BURGOYNE. You will understand of course, Mr Anderson, that you must not build on this little incident. We are bound to make an example of somebody.

RICHARD. I quite understand. I suppose there's no use in my explaining.

BURGOYNE. I think we should prefer independent testimony, if you dont mind.

The sergeant, with a packet of papers in his hand, returns conducting Christy, who is much scared.

SERGEANT [*giving Burgoyne the packet*] Dispatches, sir. Delivered by a corporal of the 33rd. Dead beat with hard riding, sir.

Burgoyne opens the dispatches, and presently becomes absorbed in them. They are so serious as to take his attention completely from the court martial.

THE SERGEANT [*to Christy*] Now then. Attention, and take your hat off. [*He posts himself in charge of Christy, who stands on Burgoyne's side of the court*].

RICHARD [*in his usual bullying tone to Christy*] Dont be frightened, you fool; youre only wanted as a witness. Theyre not going to hang y o u.

SWINDON. What's your name?

CHRISTY. Christy.

RICHARD [*impatiently*] Christopher Dudgeon, you blatant idiot. Give your full name.

SWINDON. Be silent, prisoner. You must not prompt the witness.

RICHARD. Very well. But I warn you youll get nothing out of him unless you shake it out of him. He has been too well brought up by a pious mother to have any sense or manhood left in him.

BURGOYNE [*springing up and speaking to the sergeant in a startling voice*] Where is the man who brought these?

SERGEANT. In the guard-room, sir.

Burgoyne goes out with a haste that sets the officers exchanging looks.

SWINDON [*to Christy*] Do you know Anthony Anderson, the Presbyterian minister?

CHRISTY. Of course I do [*implying that Swindon must be an ass not to know it*].

SWINDON. Is he here?

CHRISTY [*staring round*] I dont know.

SWINDON. Do you see him?

CHRISTY. No.

SWINDON. You seem to know the prisoner?

CHRISTY. Do you mean Dick?

SWINDON. Which is Dick?

CHRISTY [*pointing to Richard*] Him.

SWINDON. What is his name?

CHRISTY. Dick.

RICHARD. Answer properly, you jumping jackass. What do they know about Dick?

CHRISTY. Well, you a r e Dick, aint you? What am I to say?

SWINDON. Address me, sir; and do you, prisoner, be silent. Tell us who the prisoner is.

CHRISTY. He's my brother Dick—Richard—Richard Dudgeon.

SWINDON. Your brother!

CHRISTY. Yes.

SWINDON. You are sure he is not Anderson.

CHRISTY. Who?

RICHARD [*exasperatedly*] Me, me, me, you——

SWINDON. Silence, sir.

SERGEANT [*shouting*] Silence.

RICHARD [*impatiently*] Yah! [*To Christy*] He wants to know am I Minister Anderson. Tell him, and stop grinning like a zany.

CHRISTY [*grinning more than ever*] Y o u Pastor Anderson! [*To Swindon*] Why, Mr Anderson's a minister—a very good man; and Dick's a bad character: the respectable people wont speak to him. He's the bad brother: I'm the good one. [*The officers laugh outright. The soldiers grin*].

SWINDON. Who arrested this man?

SERGEANT. I did, sir, I found him in the minister's house, sitting at tea with the lady with his coat off, quite at home. If he isnt married to her, he ought to be.

SWINDON. Did he answer to the minister's name?

SERGEANT. Yes, sir, but not to a minister's nature. You ask the chaplain, sir.

SWINDON [*to Richard, threateningly*] So, sir, you have attempted to cheat us. And your name is Richard Dudgeon?

RICHARD. Youve found it out at last, have you?

SWINDON. Dudgeon is a name well known to us, eh?

RICHARD. Yes: Peter Dudgeon, whom you

murdered, was my uncle.

SWINDON. Hm! [*He compresses his lips, and looks at Richard with vindictive gravity*].

CHRISTY. Are they going to hang you, Dick?

RICHARD. Yes, Get out: theyve done with you.

CHRISTY. And I may keep the china peacocks?

RICHARD [*jumping up*] Get out. Get out, you blithering baboon, you. [*Christy flies, panicstricken*].

SWINDON [*rising—all rise*] Since you have taken the minister's place, Richard Dudgeon, you shall go through with it. The execution will take place at 12 o'clock as arranged; and unless Anderson surrenders before then, you shall take his place on the gallows. Sergeant: take your man out.

JUDITH [*distracted*] No, no—

SWINDON [*fiercely, dreading a renewal of her entreaties*] Take that woman away.

RICHARD [*springing across the table with a tiger-like bound, and seizing Swindon by the throat*] You infernal scoundrel—

The sergeant rushes to the rescue from one side, the soldiers from the other. They seize Richard and drag him back to his place. Swindon, who has been thrown supine on the table, rises, arranging his stock. He is about to speak, when he is anticipated by Burgoyne, who has just appeared at the door with two papers in his hand: a white letter and a blue dispatch.

BURGOYNE [*advancing to the table, elaborately cool*] What is this? Whats happening? Mr Anderson: I'm astonished at you.

RICHARD. I am sorry I disturbed you, General. I merely wanted to strangle your understrapper there. [*Breaking out violently at Swindon*] Why do you raise the devil in me by bullying the woman like that? You oatmeal faced dog, I'd twist your cursed head off with the greatest satisfaction. [*He puts out his hands to the sergeant*] Here: handcuff me, will you: or I'll not undertake to keep my fingers off him.

The sergeant takes out a pair of handcuffs and looks to Burgoyne for instructions.

BURGOYNE. Have you addressed profane language to the lady, Major Swindon?

SWINDON [*very angry*] No, sir, certainly not. That question should not have been put to me. I ordered the woman to be removed, as she was disorderly; and the fellow sprang at me. Put away those handcuffs. I am per-fectly able to take care of myself.

RICHARD. Now you talk like a man, I have no quarrel with you.

BURGOYNE. Mr Anderson—

SWINDON. His name is Dudgeon, sir, Richard Dudgeon. He is an impostor.

BURGOYNE [*brusquely*] Nonsense, sir: you hanged Dudgeon at Springtown.

RICHARD. It was my uncle, General.

BURGOYNE. Oh, your uncle. [*To Swindon, handsomely*] I beg your pardon, Major Swindon. [*Swindon acknowledges the apology stiffly. Burgoyne turns to Richard*]. We are somewhat unfortunate in our relations with your family. Well, Mr Dudgeon, what I wanted to ask you is this. Who is [*reading the name from the letter*] William Maindeck Parshotter?

RICHARD. He is the Mayor of Springtown.

BURGOYNE. Is William—Maindeck and so on—a man of his word?

RICHARD. Is he selling you anything?

BURGOYNE. No.

RICHARD. Then you may depend on him.

BURGOYNE. Thank you, Mr—'m Dudgeon. By the way, since you are not Mr Anderson, do we still—eh, Major Swindon? [*meaning "do we still hang him?"*]

RICHARD. The arrangements are unaltered, General.

BURGOYNE. Ah, indeed. I am sorry. Good morning, Mr Dudgeon. Good morning, madam.

RICHARD [*interrupting Judith almost fiercely as she is about to make some wild appeal, and taking her arm resolutely*] Not one word more. Come.

She looks imploringly at him, but is overborne by his determination. They are marched out by the four soldiers: the sergeant, very sulky, walking between Swindon and Richard, whom he watches as if he were a dangerous animal.

BURGOYNE. Gentlemen: we need not detain you. Major Swindon: a word with you. [*The officers go out. Burgoyne waits with unruffled serenity until the last of them disappears. Then he becomes very grave, and addresses Swindon for the first time without his title*]. Swindon: do you know what this is [*shewing him the letter*]?

SWINDON. What?

BURGOYNE. A demand for a safe-conduct for an officer of their militia to come here and arrange terms with us.

SWINDON. Oh, they are giving in.

BURGOYNE. They add that they are sending

the man who raised Springtown last night and drove us out; so that we may know that we are dealing with an officer of importance.

SWINDON. Pooh!

BURGOYNE. He will be fully empowered to arrange the terms of—guess what.

SWINDON. Their surrender, I hope.

BURGOYNE. No: our evacuation of the town. They offer us just six hours to clear out.

SWINDON. What monstrous impudence!

BURGOYNE. What shall we do, eh?

SWINDON. March on Springtown and strike a decisive blow at once.

BURGOYNE [quietly] Hm! [Turning to the door] Come to the adjutant's office.

SWINDON. What for?

BURGOYNE. To write out that safe-conduct. [He puts his hand to the door knob to open it].

SWINDON [who has not budged] General Burgoyne.

BURGOYNE [returning] Sir?

SWINDON. It is my duty to tell you, sir, that I do not consider the threats of a mob of rebellious tradesmen a sufficient reason for our giving way.

BURGOYNE [imperturbable] Suppose I resign my command to you, what will you do?

SWINDON. I will undertake to do what we have marched south from Quebec to do, and what General Howe has marched north from New York to do: effect a junction at Albany and wipe out the rebel army with our united forces.

BURGOYNE [enigmatically] And will you wipe out our enemies in London, too?

SWINDON. In London! What enemies?

BURGOYNE [forcibly] Jobbery and snobbery, incompetence and Red Tape. [He holds up the dispatch and adds, with despair in his face and voice] I have just learnt, sir, that General Howe is still in New York.

SWINDON [thunderstruck] Good God! He has disobeyed orders!

BURGOYNE [with sardonic calm] He has received no orders, sir. Some gentleman in London forgot to dispatch them: he was leaving town for his holiday, I believe. To avoid upsetting his arrangements, England will lose her American colonies; and in a few days you and I will be at Saratoga with 5,000 men to face 18,000 rebels in an impregnable position.

SWINDON [appalled] Impossible?

BURGOYNE [coldly] I beg your pardon?

SWINDON. I cant believe it! What will

History say?

BURGOYNE. History, sir, will tell lies, as usual. Come: we must send the safe-conduct. [He goes out].

SWINDON [following distractedly] My God, my God! We shall be wiped out.

As noon approaches there is excitement in the market place. The gallows which hangs there permanently for the terror of evildoers, with such minor advertizers and examples of crime as the pillory, the whipping post, and the stocks, has a new rope attached, with the noose hitched up to one of the uprights, out of reach of the boys. Its ladder, too, has been brought out and placed in position by the town beadle, who stands by to guard it from unauthorized climbing. The Websterbridge townsfolk are present in force, and in high spirits; for the news has spread that it is the devil's disciple and not the minister that King George and his terrible general are about to hang: consequently the execution can be enjoyed without any misgiving as to its righteousness, or to the cowardice of allowing it to take place without a struggle. There is even some fear of a disappointment as midday approaches and the arrival of the beadle with the ladder remains the only sign of preparation. But at last reassuring shouts of Here they come: Here they are, are heard; and a company of soldiers with fixed bayonets, half British infantry, half Hessians, tramp quickly into the middle of the market place, driving the crowd to the sides.

THE SERGEANT. Halt. Front. Dress. [The soldiers change their column into a square enclosing the gallows, their petty officers, energetically led by the sergeant, hustling the persons who find themselves inside the square out at the corners]. Now then! Out of it with you: out of it. Some o youll get strung up yourselves presently. Form that square there, will you, you damned Hoosians. No use talkin German to them: talk to their toes with the butt ends of your muskets: theyll understand that. Get out of it, will you. [He comes upon Judith, standing near the gallows]. Now then: youve no call here.

JUDITH. May I not stay? What harm am I doing?

SERGEANT. I want none of your argufying. You ought to be ashamed of yourself, running to see a man hanged thats not your husband. And he's no better than yourself. I told my major he was a gentleman; and then he goes and tries to strangle him, and calls his blessed Majesty a lunatic. So out of it with you, double quick.

JUDITH. Will you take these two silver dollars and let me stay?

The sergeant, without an instant's hesitation, looks quickly and furtively round as he shoots the money dexterously into his pocket. Then he raises his voice in virtuous indignation.

THE SERGEANT. Me take money in the execution of my duty! Certainly not. Now I'll tell you what I'll do, to teach you to corrupt the King's officer. I'll put you under arrest until the execution's over. You just stand there; and dont let me see you as much as move from that spot until youre let. [*With a swift wink at her he points to the corner of the square behind the gallows on his right, and turns noisily away, shouting*] Now then, dress up and keep em back, will you.

Cries of Hush and Silence are heard among the townsfolk; and the sound of a military band, playing the Dead March from Saul, is heard. The crowd becomes quiet at once; and the sergeant and petty officers, hurrying to the back of the square, with a few whispered orders and some stealthy hustling cause it to open and admit the funeral procession, which is protected from the crowd by a double file of soldiers. First come Burgoyne and Swindon, who, on entering the square, glance with distaste at the gallows, and avoid passing under it by wheeling a little to the right and stationing themselves on that side. Then Mr Brudenell, the chaplain, in his surplice, with his prayer book open in his hand, walking beside Richard, who is moody and disorderly. He walks doggedly through the gallows framework, and posts himself a little in front of it. Behind him comes the executioner, a stalwart soldier in his shirtsleeves. Following him, two soldiers haul a light military waggon. Finally comes the band, which posts itself at the back of the square, and finishes the Dead March. Judith, watching Richard painfully, steals down to the gallows, and stands leaning against its right post. During the conversation which follows, the two soldiers place the cart under the gallows, and stand by the shafts, which point backwards. The executioner takes a set of steps from the cart and places it ready for the prisoner to mount. Then he climbs the tall ladder which stands against the gallows, and cuts the string by which the rope is hitched up; so that the noose drops dangling over the cart, into which he steps as he descends.

RICHARD [*with suppressed impatience, to Brudenell*] Look here, sir: this is no place for a man of your profession. Hadnt you better go away?

SWINDON. I appeal to you, prisoner, if you have any sense of decency left, to listen to the ministrations of the chaplain, and pay due heed to the solemnity of the occasion.

THE CHAPLAIN [*gently reproving Richard*] Try to control yourself, and submit to the divine will. [*He lifts his book to proceed with the service*].

RICHARD. Answer for your own will, sir, and those of your accomplices here [*indicating Burgoyne and Swindon*]: I see little divinity about them or you. You talk to me of Christianity when you are in the act of hanging your enemies. Was there ever such blasphemous nonsense! [*To Swindon, more rudely*] Youve got up the solemnity of the occasion, as you call it, to impress the people with your own dignity—Handel's music and a clergyman to make murder look like piety! Do you suppose I am going to help you? Youve asked me to choose the rope because you dont know your own trade well enough to shoot me properly. Well, hang away and have done with it.

SWINDON [*to the chaplain*] Can you do nothing with him, Mr Brudenell?

CHAPLAIN. I will try, sir. [*Beginning to read*] Man that is born of woman hath—

RICHARD [*fixing his eyes on him*] "Thou shalt not kill."

The book drops in Brudenell's hands.

CHAPLAIN [*confessing his embarrassment*] What am I to say, Mr Dudgeon?

RICHARD. Let me alone, man, cant you?

BURGOYNE [*with extreme urbanity*] I think, Mr Brudenell, that as the usual professional observations seem to strike Mr Dudgeon as incongruous under the circumstances, you had better omit them until—er—until Mr Dudgeon can no longer be inconvenienced by them. [*Brudenell, with a shrug, shuts his book and retires behind the gallows*]. You seem in a hurry, Mr Dudgeon.

RICHARD [*with the horror of death upon him*] Do you think this is a pleasant sort of thing to be kept waiting for? Youve made up your mind to commit murder: well, do it and have done with it.

BURGOYNE. Mr Dudgeon: we are only doing this—

RICHARD. Because youre paid to do it.

SWINDON. You insolent— [*he swallows his rage*].

BURGOYNE [*with much charm of manner*] Ah,

I am really sorry that you should think that, Mr Dudgeon. If you knew what my commission cost me, and what my pay is, you would think better of me. I should be glad to part from you on friendly terms.

RICHARD. Hark ye, General Burgoyne. If you think that I like being hanged, youre mistaken. I dont like it; and I dont mean to pretend that I do. And if you think I'm obliged to you for hanging me in a gentlemanly way, youre wrong there too. I take the whole business in devilish bad part; and the only satisfaction I have in it is that youll feel a good deal meaner than I'll look when it's over. [*He turns away, and is striding to the cart when Judith advances and interposes with her arms stretched out to him. Richard, feeling that a very little will upset his self-possession, shrinks from her, crying*] What are you doing here? This is no place for you. [*She makes a gesture as if to touch him. He recoils impatiently*] No: go away, go away: youll unnerve me. Take her away, will you.

JUDITH. Wont you bid me goodbye?

RICHARD [*allowing her to take his hand*] Oh goodbye, goodbye. Now go—go—quickly. [*She clings to his hand—will not be put off with so cold a last farewell—at last, as he tries to disengage himself, throws herself on his breast in agony*].

SWINDON [*angrily to the sergeant, who, alarmed at Judith's movement, has come from the back of the square to pull her back, and stopped irresolutely on finding that he is too late*] How is this? Why is she inside the lines?

SERGEANT [*guiltily*] I dunno, sir. She's that artful—cant keep her away.

BURGOYNE. You were bribed.

SERGEANT [*protesting*] No, sir—

SWINDON [*severely*] Fall back. [*He obeys*].

RICHARD [*imploringly to those around him, and finally to Burgoyne, as the least stolid of them*] Take her away. Do you think I want a woman near me now?

BURGOYNE [*going to Judith and taking her hand*] Here, madam: you had better keep inside the lines; but stand here behind us; and dont look.

Richard, with a great sobbing sigh of relief as she releases him and turns to Burgoyne, flies for refuge to the cart and mounts into it. The executioner takes off his coat and pinions him.

JUDITH [*resisting Burgoyne quietly and drawing her hand away*] No: I must stay. I wont look. [*She goes to the right of the gallows. She tries to look at Richard, but turns away with a frightful shudder, and falls on her knees in prayer. Brudenell comes towards her from the back of the square*].

BURGOYNE [*nodding approvingly as she kneels*] Ah, quite so. Do not disturb her, Mr Brudenell: that will do very nicely. [*Brudenell nods also, and withdraws a little, watching her sympathetically. Burgoyne resumes his former position, and takes out a handsome gold chronometer.*] Now then, are those preparations made? We must not detain Mr Dudgeon.

By this time Richard's hands are bound behind him; and the noose is round his neck. The two soldiers take the shafts of the waggon, ready to pull it away. The executioner, standing in the cart behind Richard, makes a sign to the sergeant.

SERGEANT [*to Burgoyne*] Ready, sir.

BURGOYNE. Have you anything more to say, Mr. Dudgeon? It wants two minutes of twelve still.

RICHARD [*in the strong voice of a man who has conquered the bitterness of death*] Your watch is two minutes slow by the town clock, which I can see from here, General. [*The town clock strikes the first stroke of twelve. Involuntarily the people flinch at the sound, and a subdued groan breaks from them*]. Amen! my life for the world's future!

ANDERSON [*shouting as he rushes into the market place*] Amen; and stop the execution. [*He bursts through the line of soldiers opposite Burgoyne, and rushes, panting, to the gallows*]. I am Anthony Anderson, the man you want.

The crowd, intensely excited, listens with all its ears. Judith, half rising, stares at him; then lifts her hands like one whose dearest prayer has been granted.

SWINDON. Indeed. Then you are just in time to take your place on the gallows. Arrest him.

At a sign from the sergeant, two soldiers come forward to seize Anderson.

ANDERSON [*thrusting a paper under Swindon's nose*] Theres my safe-conduct, sir.

SWINDON [*taken aback*] Safe-conduct! Are you—!

ANDERSON [*emphatically*] I am. [*The two soldiers take him by the elbows*]. Tell these men to take their hands off me.

SWINDON [*to the men*] Let him go.

SERGEANT. Fall back.

The two men return to their places. The townsfolk raise a cheer; and begin to exchange exultant looks, with a presentiment of triumph as they see their Pastor speaking with their enemies in the gate.

ANDERSON [*exhaling a deep breath of relief, and dabbing his perspiring brow with his handkerchief*] Thank God, I was in time!

BURGOYNE [*calm as ever, and still watch in hand*] Ample time, sir. Plenty of time. I should never dream of hanging any gentleman by an American clock. [*He puts up his watch*].

ANDERSON. Yes: we are some minutes ahead of you already, General. Now tell them to take the rope from the neck of that American citizen.

BURGOYNE [*to the executioner in the cart— very politely*] Kindly undo Mr Dudgeon.

The executioner takes the rope from Richard's neck, unties his hands, and helps him on with his coat.

JUDITH [*stealing timidly to Anderson*] Tony.

ANDERSON [*putting his arm round her shoulders and bantering her affectionately*] Well, what do you think of your husband now, eh?— eh??—eh???

JUDITH. I am ashamed— [*she hides her face against his breast*].

BURGOYNE [*to Swindon*] You look disappointed, Major Swindon.

SWINDON. You look defeated, General Burgoyne.

BURGOYNE. I am, sir; and I am humane enough to be glad of it. [*Richard jumps down from the cart, Brudenell offering his hand to help him, and runs to Anderson, whose left hand he shakes heartily, the right being occupied by Judith*]. By the way, Mr Anderson, I do not quite understand. The safe-conduct was for a commander of the militia. I understand you are a—[*He looks as pointedly as his good manners permit at the riding boots, the pistols, and Richard's coat, and adds*]—a clergyman.

ANDERSON [*between Judith and Richard*] Sir: it is in the hour of trial that a man finds his true profession. This foolish young man [*placing his hand on Richard's shoulder*] boasted himself the Devil's Disciple; but when the hour of trial came to him, he found that it was his destiny to suffer and be faithful to the death. I thought myself a decent minister of the gospel of peace; but when the hour of trial came to me, I found that it was my destiny to be a man of action, and that my place was amid the thunder of the captains and the shouting. So I am starting life at fifty as Captain Anthony Anderson of the Springtown militia; and the Devil's Disciple here will start presently as the Reverend Richard Dudgeon, and wag his pow in my old pulpit, and give good advice to this silly sentimental little wife of mine [*putting his other hand on her shoulder. She steals a glance at Richard to see how the prospect pleases him*]. Your mother told me, Richard, that I should never have chosen Judith if I'd been born for the ministry. I am afraid she was right; so, by your leave, you may keep my coat and I'll keep yours.

RICHARD. Minister—I should say Captain. I have behaved like a fool.

JUDITH. Like a hero.

RICHARD. Much the same thing, perhaps. [*With some bitterness towards himself*] But no: if I had been any good, I should have done for you what you did for me, instead of making a vain sacrifice.

ANDERSON. Not vain, my boy. It takes all sorts to make a world—saints as well as soldiers. [*Turning to Burgoyne*] And now, General, time presses; and America is in a hurry. Have you realized that though you may occupy towns and win battles, you cannot conquer a nation?

BURGOYNE. My good sir, without a Conquest you cannot have an aristocracy. Come and settle the matter at my quarters.

ANDERSON. At your service, sir. [*To Richard*] See Judith home for me, will you, my boy. [*He hands her over to him*]. Now, General. [*He goes busily up the market place towards the Town Hall, leaving Judith and Richard together. Burgoyne follows him a step or two; then checks himself and turns to Richard*].

BURGOYNE. Oh, by the way, Mr Dudgeon, I shall be glad to see you at lunch at half-past one. [*He pauses a moment and adds, with politely veiled slyness*] Bring Mrs Anderson, if she will be so good. [*To Swindon, who is fuming*] Take it quietly, Major Swindon: your friend the British soldier can stand up to anything except the British War Office. [*He follows Anderson*].

SERGEANT [*to Swindon*] What orders, sir?

SWINDON [*savagely*] Orders! What use are orders now! Theres no army. Back to quarters; and be d— [*He turns on his heel and goes*].

SERGEANT [*pugnacious and patriotic, repudiating the idea of defeat*] 'Tention. Now then: cock up your chins, and shew em you dont care a damn for em. Slope arms! Fours!

Wheel! Quick march!

*The drums mark time with a tremendous bang;
the band strikes up British Grenadiers; and the
Sergeant, Brudenell, and the English troops
march off defiantly to their quarters. The townsfolk press in behind, and follow them up the
market, jeering at them; and the town band, a
very primitive affair, brings up the rear, playing
Yankee Doodle. Essie, who comes in with them,
runs to Richard.*

ESSIE. Oh, Dick!

RICHARD [*good-humoredly, but wilfully*] Now,
now: come, come! I dont mind being hanged;
but I will not be cried over.

ESSIE. No, I promise. I'll be good. [*She tries*

to restrain her tears, but cannot]. I—I want to
see where the soldiers are going to. [*She goes
a little way up the market, pretending to look
after the crowd*].

JUDITH. Promise me you will never tell
him.

RICHARD. Dont be afraid.

They shake hands on it.

ESSIE [*calling to them*] Theyre coming back.
They want you.

*Jubilation in the market. The townsfolk surge
back again in wild enthusiasm with their band,
and hoist Richard on their shoulders, cheering
him.*

THE END

IX

CÆSAR AND CLEOPATRA
A HISTORY (1898)
BEING THE SECOND OF THREE PLAYS FOR PURITANS

PROLOGUE

*In the doorway of the temple of Ra in Mem-
phis. Deep gloom. An august personage with a
hawk's head is mysteriously visible by his own
light in the darkness within the temple. He surveys the modern audience with great contempt;
and finally speaks the following words to them.*

Peace! Be silent and hearken unto me, ye
quaint little islanders. Give ear, ye men with
white paper on your breasts and nothing
written thereon (to signify the innocency of
your minds). Hear me, ye women who adorn
yourselves alluringly and conceal your
thoughts from your men, leading them to
believe that ye deem them wondrous strong
and masterful whilst in truth ye hold them
in your hearts as children without judgment.
Look upon my hawk's head; and know that
I am Ra, who was once in Egypt a mighty
god. Ye cannot kneel nor prostrate yourselves; for ye are packed in rows without
freedom to move, obstructing one another's
vision; neither do any of ye regard it as
seemly to do ought until ye see all the rest
do so too; wherefore it commonly happens
that in great emergencies ye do nothing,
though each telleth his fellow that something
must be done. I ask you not for worship,
but for silence. Let not your men speak nor
your women cough; for I am come to draw

you back two thousand years over the graves
of sixty generations. Ye poor posterity, think
not that ye are the first. Other fools before
ye have seen the sun rise and set, and the
moon change her shape and her hour. As they
were so ye are; and yet not so great; for the
pyramids my people built stand to this day;
whilst the dustheaps on which ye slave, and
which ye call empires, scatter in the wind
even as ye pile your dead sons' bodies on
them to make yet more dust.

Hearken to me then, oh ye compulsorily
educated ones. Know that even as there is
an old England and a new, and ye stand perplexed between the twain; so in the days
when I was worshipped was there an old
Rome and a new, and men standing perplexed between them. And the old Rome
was poor and little, and greedy and fierce,
and evil in many ways; but because its mind
was little and its work was simple, it knew
its own mind and did its own work; and the
gods pitied it and helped it and strengthened
it and shielded it; for the gods are patient
with littleness. Then the old Rome, like the
beggar on horseback, presumed on the favor
of the gods, and said, "Lo! there is neither
riches nor greatness in our littleness: the
road to riches and greatness is through
robbery of the poor and slaughter of the

weak." So they robbed their own poor until they became great masters of that art, and knew by what laws it could be made to appear seemly and honest. And when they had squeezed their own poor dry, they robbed the poor of other lands, and added those lands to Rome until there came a new Rome, rich and huge. And I, Ra, laughed; for the minds of the Romans remained the same size whilst their dominion spread over the earth.

Now mark me, that ye may understand what ye are presently to see. Whilst the Romans still stood between the old Rome and the new, there arose among them a mighty soldier: Pompey the Great. And the way of the soldier is the way of death; but the way of the gods is the way of life; and so it comes that a god at the end of his way is wise and a soldier at the end of his way is a fool. So Pompey held by the old Rome, in which only soldiers could become great; but the gods turned to the new Rome, in which any man with wit enough could become what he would. And Pompey's friend Julius Cæsar was on the side of the gods; for he saw that Rome had passed beyond the control of the little old Romans. This Cæsar was a great talker and a politician: he bought men with words and with gold, even as ye are bought. And when they would not be satisfied with words and gold, and demanded also the glories of war, Cæsar in his middle age turned his hand to that trade; and they that were against him when he sought their welfare, bowed down before him when he became a slayer and a conqueror; for such is the nature of you mortals. And as for Pompey, the gods grew tired of his triumphs and his airs of being himself a god; for he talked of law and duty and other matters that concerned not a mere human worm. And the gods smiled on Cæsar; for he lived the life they had given him boldly, and was not forever rebuking us for our indecent ways of creation, and hiding our handiwork as a shameful thing. Ye know well what I mean; for this is one of your own sins.

And thus it fell out between the old Rome and the new, that Cæsar said, "Unless I break the law of old Rome, I cannot take my share in ruling her; and the gift of ruling that the gods gave me will perish without fruit." But Pompey said, "The law is above all; and if thou break it thou shalt die." Then said Cæsar, "I will break it: kill me who can."

And he broke it. And Pompey went for him, as ye say, with a great army to slay him and uphold the old Rome. So Cæsar fled across the Adriatic sea; for the high gods had a lesson to teach him, which lesson they shall also teach you in due time if ye continue to forget them and to worship that cad among gods, Mammon. Therefore before they raised Cæsar to be master of the world, they were minded to throw him down into the dust, even beneath the feet of Pompey, and blacken his face before the nations. And Pompey they raised higher than ever, he and his laws and his high mind that aped the gods, so that his fall might be the more terrible. And Pompey followed Cæsar, and overcame him with all the majesty of old Rome, and stood over him and over the whole world even as ye stand over it with your fleet that covers thirty miles of the sea. And when Cæsar was brought down to utter nothingness, he made a last stand to die honorably, and did not despair; for he said, "Against me there is Pompey, and the old Rome, and the law and the legions: all all against me; but high above these are the gods; and Pompey is a fool." And the gods laughed and approved; and on the field of Pharsalia the impossible came to pass; the blood and iron ye pin your faith on fell before the spirit of man; for the spirit of man is the will of the gods; and Pompey's power crumbled in his hand, even as the power of imperial Spain crumbled when it was set against your fathers in the days when England was little, and knew her own mind, and had a mind to know instead of a circulation of newspapers. Wherefore look to it, lest some little people whom ye would enslave rise up and become in the hand of God the scourge of your boastings and your injustices and your lusts and stupidities.

And now, would ye know the end of Pompey, or will ye sleep while a god speaks? Heed my words well; for Pompey went where ye have gone, even to Egypt, where there was a Roman occupation even as there is but now a British one. And Cæsar pursued Pompey to Egypt: a Roman fleeing, and a Roman pursuing: dog eating dog. And the Egyptians said, "Lo: these Romans which have lent money to our kings and levied a distraint upon us with their arms, call for ever upon us to be loyal to them by betraying our own country to them. But now behold two Romes! Pompey's Rome and Cæsar's Rome! To which of the twain shall we pretend to be loyal?" So they turned in their perplexity to a soldier that had once served Pompey, and that knew the ways of Rome and was full of her lusts. And they said to him, "Lo: in thy country dog eats dog; and both dogs are coming to eat us: what counsel hast thou to give us?" And this soldier, whose name was Lucius Septimius, and whom ye shall presently see before ye, replied, "Ye shall diligently consider which is the bigger dog of the two; and ye shall kill the other dog for his sake and thereby earn his favor." And the Egyptians said, "Thy counsel is expedient; but if we kill a man outside the law we set ourselves in the place of the gods; and this we dare not do. But thou, being a Roman, art accustomed to this kind of killing; for thou hast imperial instincts. Wilt thou therefore kill the lesser dog for us?" And he said, "I will; for I have made my home in Egypt; and I desire consideration and influence among you." And they said, "We knew well thou wouldst not do it for nothing: thou shalt have thy reward." Now when Pompey came, he came alone in a little galley, putting his trust in the law and the constitution. And it was plain to the people of Egypt that Pompey was now but a very small dog. So when he set his foot on the shore he was greeted by his old comrade Lucius Septimius, who welcomed him with one hand and with the other smote off his head, and kept it as it were a pickled cabbage to make a present to Cæsar. And mankind shuddered; but the gods laughed; for Septimius was but a knife that Pompey had sharpened; and when it turned against his own throat they said that Pompey had better have made Septimius a ploughman than so brave and readyhanded a slayer. Therefore again I bid you beware, ye who would all be Pompeys if ye dared; for war is a wolf that may come to your own door.

Are ye impatient with me? Do ye crave for a story of an unchaste woman? Hath the name of Cleopatra tempted ye hither? Ye foolish ones; Cleopatra is as yet but a child that is whipped by her nurse. And what I am about to shew you for the good of your souls is how Cæsar, seeking Pompey in Egypt, found Cleopatra; and how he received that present of a pickled cabbage that was once the head of Pompey; and what things

happened between the old Cæsar and the child queen before he left Egypt and battled his way back to Rome to be slain there as Pompey was slain, by men in whom the spirit of Pompey still lived. All this ye shall see; and ye shall marvel, after your ignorant manner, that men twenty centuries ago were already just such as you, and spoke and lived as ye speak and live, no worse and no better, no wiser and no sillier. And the two thousand years that have past are to me, the god Ra, but a moment; nor is this day any other than the day in which Cæsar set foot in the land of my people. And now I leave you; for ye are a dull folk, and instruction is wasted on you; and I had not spoken so much but that it is in the nature of a god to struggle for ever with the dust and the darkness, and to drag from them, by the force of his longing for the divine, more life and more light. Settle ye therefore in your seats and keep silent; for ye are about to hear a man speak, and a great man he was, as ye count greatness. And fear not that I shall speak to you again: the rest of the story must ye learn from them that lived it. Farewell; and do not presume to applaud me. [*The temple vanishes in utter darkness*].

[1912].

AN ALTERNATIVE TO THE PROLOGUE

An October night on the Syrian border of Egypt towards the end of the XXXIII Dynasty, in the year 706 by Roman computation, afterwards reckoned by Christian computation as 48 B.C. A great radiance of silver fire, the dawn of a moonlit night, is rising in the east. The stars and the cloudless sky are our own contemporaries, nineteen and a half centuries younger than we know them; but you would not guess that from their appearance. Below them are two notable drawbacks of civilization: a palace, and soldiers. The palace, an old, low, Syrian building of whitened mud, is not so ugly as Buckingham Palace; and the officers in the courtyard are more highly civilized than modern English officers: for example, they do not dig up the corpses of their dead enemies and mutilate them, as we dug up Cromwell and the Mahdi. They are in two groups: one intent on the gambling of their captain Belzanor, a warrior of fifty, who, with his spear on the ground beside his knee, is stooping to throw dice with a sly-looking young

Persian recruit; the other gathered about a guardsman who has just finished telling a naughty story (still current in English barracks) at which they are laughing uproariously. They are about a dozen in number, all highly aristocratic young Egyptian guardsmen, handsomely equipped with weapons and armor, very un-English in point of not being ashamed of and uncomfortable in their professional dress; on the contrary, rather ostentatiously and arrogantly warlike, as valuing themselves on their military caste.

Belzanor is a typical veteran, tough and wilful; prompt, capable and crafty where brute force will serve; helpless and boyish when it will not: an effective sergeant, an incompetent general, a deplorable dictator. Would, if influentially connected, be employed in the two last capacities by a modern European State on the strength of his success in the first. Is rather to be pitied just now in view of the fact that Julius Cæsar is invading his country. Not knowing this, is intent on his game with the Persian, whom, as a foreigner, he considers quite capable of cheating him.

His subalterns are mostly handsome young fellows whose interests in the game and the story symbolize with tolerable completeness the main interests in life of which they are conscious. Their spears are leaning against the walls, or lying on the ground ready to their hands. The corner of the courtyard forms a triangle of which one side is the front of the palace, with a doorway, the other a wall with a gateway. The storytellers are on the palace side: the gamblers, on the gateway side. Close to the gateway, against the wall, is a stone block high enough to enable a Nubian sentinel, standing on it, to look over the wall. The yard is lighted by a torch stuck in the wall. As the laughter from the group round the storyteller dies away, the kneeling Persian, winning the throw, snatches up the stake from the ground.

BELZANOR. By Apis, Persian, thy gods are good to thee.

THE PERSIAN. Try yet again, O captain. Double or quits!

BELZANOR. No more. I am not in the vein.

THE SENTINEL [*poising his javelin as he peers over the wall*] Stand. Who goes there?

They all start, listening. A strange voice replies from without.

VOICE. The bearer of evil tidings.

BELZANOR [*calling to the sentry*] Pass him.

THE SENTINEL [*grounding his javelin*] Draw near, O bearer of evil tidings.

BELZANOR [*pocketing the dice and picking up his spear*] Let us receive this man with honor. He bears evil tidings.

The guardsmen seize their spears and gather about the gate, leaving a way through for the new comer.

PERSIAN [*rising from his knee*] Are evil tidings, then, so honorable?

BELZANOR. O barbarous Persian, hear my instruction. In Egypt the bearer of good tidings is sacrificed to the gods as a thank offering; but no god will accept the blood of the messenger of evil. When we have good tidings, we are careful to send them in the mouth of the cheapest slave we can find. Evil tidings are borne by young noblemen who desire to bring themselves into notice. [*They join the rest at the gate.*]

THE SENTINEL. Pass, O young captain; and bow the head in the House of the Queen.

VOICE. Go anoint thy javelin with fat of swine, O Blackamoor; for before morning the Romans will make thee eat it to the very butt.

The owner of the voice, a fairhaired dandy, dressed in a different fashion from that affected by the guardsmen, but no less extravagantly, comes through the gateway laughing. He is somewhat battlestained; and his left forearm, bandaged, comes through a torn sleeve. In his right hand he carries a Roman sword in its sheath. He swaggers down the courtyard, the Persian on his right, Belzanor on his left, and the guardsmen crowding down behind him.

BELZANOR. Who art thou that laughest in the House of Cleopatra the Queen, and in the teeth of Belzanor, the captain of her guard?

THE NEW COMER. I am Bel Affris, descended from the gods.

BELZANOR [*ceremoniously*] Hail, cousin!

ALL [*except the Persian*] Hail, cousin!

PERSIAN. All the Queen's guards are descended from the gods, O stranger, save myself. I am Persian, and descended from many kings.

BEL AFFRIS [*to the guardsmen*] Hail, cousins! [*To the Persian, condescendingly*] Hail, mortal!

BELZANOR. You have been in battle, Bel Affris; and you are a soldier among soldiers. You will not let the Queen's women have the first of your tidings.

BEL AFFRIS. I have no tidings, except that we shall have our throats cut presently, women, soldiers, and all.

PERSIAN [*to Belzanor*] I told you so.

THE SENTINEL [*who has been listening*] Woe, alas!

BEL AFFRIS [*calling to him*] Peace, peace, poor Ethiop: destiny is with the gods who painted thee black. [*To Belzanor*] What has this mortal [*indicating the Persian*] told you?

BELZANOR. He says that the Roman Julius Cæsar, who has landed on our shores with a handful of followers, will make himself master of Egypt. He is afraid of the Roman soldiers. [*The guardsmen laugh with boisterous scorn*]. Peasants, brought up to scare crows and follow the plough! Sons of smiths and millers and tanners! And we nobles, consecrated to arms, descended from the gods!

PERSIAN. Belzanor: the gods are not always good to their poor relations.

BELZANOR [*hotly, to the Persian*] Man to man, are we worse than the slaves of Cæsar?

BEL AFFRIS [*stepping between them*] Listen, cousin. Man to man, we Egyptians are as gods above the Romans.

THE GUARDSMEN [*exultantly*] Aha!

BEL AFFRIS. But this Cæsar does not pit man against man: he throws a legion at you where you are weakest as he throws a stone from a catapult; and that legion is as a man with one head, a thousand arms, and no religion. I have fought against them; and I know.

BELZANOR [*derisively*] Were you frightened, cousin?

The guardsmen roar with laughter, their eyes sparkling at the wit of their captain.

BEL AFFRIS. No, cousin; but I was beaten. They were frightened (perhaps); but they scattered us like chaff.

The guardsmen, much damped, utter a growl of contemptuous disgust.

BELZANOR. Could you not die?

BEL AFFRIS. No: that was too easy to be worthy of a descendant of the gods. Besides, there was no time: all was over in a moment. The attack came just where we least expected it.

BELZANOR. That shews that the Romans are cowards.

BEL AFFRIS. They care nothing about cowardice, these Romans: they fight to win. The pride and honor of war are nothing to them.

PERSIAN. Tell us the tale of the battle. What befell?

THE GUARDSMEN [*gathering eagerly round Bel Affris*] Ay: the tale of the battle.

BEL AFFRIS. Know then, that I am a novice in the guard of the temple of Ra in Memphis, serving neither Cleopatra nor her brother Ptolemy, but only the high gods. We went a journey to inquire of Ptolemy why he had driven Cleopatra into Syria, and how we of Egypt should deal with the Roman Pompey, newly come to our shores after his defeat by Cæsar at Pharsalia. What, think ye, did we learn? Even that Cæsar is coming also in hot pursuit of his foe, and that Ptolemy has slain Pompey, whose severed head he holds in readiness to present to the conqueror. [*Sensation among the guardsmen*]. Nay, more: we found that Cæsar is already come; for we had not made half a day's journey on our way back when we came upon a city rabble flying from his legions, whose landing they had gone out to withstand.

BELZANOR. And ye, the temple guard! did ye not withstand these legions?

BEL AFFRIS. What man could, that we did. But there came the sound of a trumpet whose voice was as the cursing of a black mountain. Then saw we a moving wall of shields coming towards us. You know how the heart burns when you charge a fortified wall; but how if the fortified wall were to charge you?

THE PERSIAN [*exulting in having told them so*] Did I not say it?

BEL AFFRIS. When the wall came nigh, it changed into a line of men—common fellows enough, with helmets, leather tunics, and breastplates. Every man of them flung his javelin: the one that came my way drove through my shield as through a papyrus— lo there! [*he points to the bandage on his left arm*] and would have gone through my neck had I not stooped. They were charging at the double then, and were upon us with short swords almost as soon as their javelins. When a man is close to you with such a sword, you can do nothing with our weapons: they are all too long.

THE PERSIAN. What did you do?

BEL AFFRIS. Doubled my fist and smote my Roman on the sharpness of his jaw. He was but mortal after all: he lay down in a stupor; and I took his sword and laid it on. [*Drawing the sword*] Lo! a Roman sword with Roman blood on it!

THE GUARDSMEN [*approvingly*] Good! [*They take the sword and hand it round, examining it curiously*].

THE PERSIAN. And your men?

BEL AFFRIS. Fled. Scattered like sheep.

BELZANOR [*furiously*] The cowardly slaves! Leaving the descendants of the gods to be butchered!

BEL AFFRIS [*with acid coolness*] The descendants of the gods did not stay to be butchered, cousin. The battle was not to the strong; but the race was to the swift. The Romans, who have no chariots, sent a cloud of horsemen in pursuit, and slew multitudes. Then our high priest's captain rallied a dozen descendants of the gods and exhorted us to die fighting. I said to myself: surely it is safer to stand than to lose my breath and be stabbed in the back; so I joined our captain and stood. Then the Romans treated us with respect; for no man attacks a lion when the field is full of sheep, except for the pride and honor of war, of which these Romans know nothing. So we escaped with our lives; and I am come to warn you that you must open your gates to Cæsar; for his advance guard is scarce an hour behind me; and not an Egyptian warrior is left standing between you and his legions.

THE SENTINEL. Woe, alas! [*He throws down his javelin and flies into the palace*].

BELZANOR. Nail him to the door, quick! [*The guardsmen rush for him with their spears; but he is too quick for them*]. Now this news will run through the palace like fire through stubble.

BEL AFFRIS. What shall we do to save the women from the Romans?

BELZANOR. Why not kill them?

PERSIAN. Because we should have to pay blood money for some of them. Better let the Romans kill them: it is cheaper.

BELZANOR [*awestruck at his brain power*] O subtle one! O serpent!

BEL AFFRIS. But your Queen?

BELZANOR. True: we must carry off Cleopatra.

BEL AFFRIS. Will ye not await her command?

BELZANOR. Command! a girl of sixteen! Not we. At Memphis ye deem her a Queen: here we know better. I will take her on the crupper of my horse. When we soldiers have carried her out of Cæsar's reach, then the priests and the nurses and the rest of them can pretend she is a queen again, and put their commands into her mouth.

PERSIAN. Listen to me, Belzanor.

BELZANOR. Speak, O subtle beyond thy years.

THE PERSIAN. Cleopatra's brother Ptolemy is at war with her. Let us sell her to him.

THE GUARDSMEN. O subtle one! O serpent.

BELZANOR. We dare not. We are descended from the gods; but Cleopatra is descended from the river Nile; and the lands of our fathers will grow no grain if the Nile rises not to water them. Without our father's gifts we should live the lives of dogs.

PERSIAN. It is true: the Queen's guard cannot live on its pay. But hear me further, O ye kinsmen of Osiris.

THE GUARDSMEN. Speak, O subtle one. Hear the serpent begotten!

PERSIAN. Have I heretofore spoken truly to you of Cæsar, when you thought I mocked you?

GUARDSMEN. Truly, truly.

BELZANOR [*reluctantly admitting it*] So Bel Affris says.

PERSIAN. Hear more of him, then. This Cæsar is a great lover of women: he makes them his friends and counsellors.

BELZANOR. Faugh! This rule of women will be the ruin of Egypt.

THE PERSIAN. Let it rather be the ruin of Rome! Cæsar grows old now: he is past fifty and full of labors and battles. He is too old for the young women; and the old women are too wise to worship him.

BEL AFFRIS. Take heed, Persian. Cæsar is by this time almost within earshot.

PERSIAN. Cleopatra is not yet a woman: neither is she wise. But she already troubles men's wisdom.

BELZANOR. Ay: that is because she is descended from the river Nile and a black kitten of the sacred White Cat. What then?

PERSIAN. Why, sell her secretly to Ptolemy, and then offer ourselves to Cæsar as volunteers to fight for the overthrow of her brother and the rescue of our Queen, the Great Granddaughter of the Nile.

THE GUARDSMEN. O serpent!

PERSIAN. He will listen to us if we come with her picture in our mouths. He will conquer and kill her brother, and reign in Egypt with Cleopatra for his Queen. And we shall be her guard.

GUARDSMEN. O subtlest of all the serpents! O admiration! O wisdom!

BEL AFFRIS. He will also have arrived before you have done talking, O word spinner.

BELZANOR. That is true. [*An affrighted uproar in the palace interrupts him*]. Quick: the flight has begun: guard the door. [*They rush to the door and form a cordon before it with their spears. A mob of women-servants and nurses surges out. Those in front recoil from the spears, screaming to those behind to keep back. Belzanor's voice dominates the disturbance as he shouts*] Back there. In again, unprofitable cattle.

THE GUARDSMEN. Back, unprofitable cattle.

BELZANOR. Send us out Ftatateeta, the Queen's chief nurse.

THE WOMEN [*calling into the palace*] Ftatateeta, Ftatateeta. Come, come. Speak to Belzanor.

A WOMAN. Oh, keep back. You are thrusting me on the spearheads.

A huge grim woman, her face covered with a network of tiny wrinkles, and her eyes old, large, and wise; sinewy handed, very tall, very strong; with the mouth of a bloodhound and the jaws of a bulldog, appears on the threshold. She is dressed like a person of consequence in the palace, and confronts the guardsmen insolently.

FTATATEETA. Make way for the Queen's chief nurse.

BELZANOR [*with solemn arrogance*] Ftatateeta: I am Belzanor, the captain of the Queen's guard, descended from the gods.

FTATATEETA [*retorting his arrogance with interest*] Belzanor: I am Ftatateeta, the Queen's chief nurse; and your divine ancestors were proud to be painted on the wall in the pyramids of the kings whom my fathers served.

The women laugh triumphantly.

BELZANOR [*with grim humor*] Ftatateeta: daughter of a long-tongued, swivel-eyed chameleon, the Romans are at hand. [*A cry of terror from the women: they would fly but for the spears*]. Not even the descendants of the gods can resist them: for they have each man seven arms, each carrying seven spears. The blood in their veins is boiling quicksilver; and their wives become mothers in three hours, and are slain and eaten the next day. *A shudder of horror from the women. Ftatateeta, despising them and scorning the soldiers, pushes her way through the crowd and confronts the spear points undismayed.*

FTATATEETA. Then fly and save yourselves, O cowardly sons of the cheap clay gods that are sold to fish porters; and leave us to shift for ourselves.

BELZANOR. Not until you have first done our bidding, O terror of manhood. Bring out Cleopatra the Queen to us; and then go whither you will.

FTATATEETA [*with a derisive laugh*] Now I know why the gods have taken her out of our hands. [*The guardsmen start and look at one another*]. Know, thou foolish soldier, that the Queen has been missing since an hour past sundown.

BELZANOR [*furiously*] Hag: you have hidden her to sell to Cæsar or her brother. [*He grasps her by the left wrist, and drags her, helped by a few of the guard, to the middle of the courtyard, where, as they fling her on her knees, he draws a murderous looking knife*]. Where is she? Where is she? or— [*he threatens to cut her throat*].

FTATATEETA [*savagely*] Touch me, dog; and the Nile will not rise on your fields for seven times seven years of famine.

BELZANOR [*frightened, but desperate*] I will sacrifice: I will pay. Or stay. [*To the Persian*] You, O subtle one: your father's lands lie far from the Nile. Slay her.

PERSIAN [*threatening her with his knife*] Persia has but one god; yet he loves the blood of old women. Where is Cleopatra?

FTATATEETA. Persian: as Osiris lives, I do not know. I chid her for bringing evil days upon us by talking to the sacred cats of the priests, and carrying them in her arms. I told her she would be left alone here when the Romans came as a punishment for her disobedience. And now she is gone—run away—hidden. I speak the truth. I call Osiris to witness—

THE WOMEN [*protesting officiously*] She speaks the truth, Belzanor.

BELZANOR. You have frightened the child: she is hiding. Search—quick—into the palace —search every corner.

The guards, led by Belzanor, shoulder their way into the palace through the flying crowd of women, who escape through the courtyard gate.

FTATATEETA [*screaming*] Sacrilege! Men in the Queen's chambers! Sa— [*her voice dies away as the Persian puts his knife to her throat*].

BEL AFFRIS [*laying a hand on Ftatateeta's left shoulder*] Forbear her yet a moment, Persian. [*To Ftatateeta, very significantly*] Mother: your gods are asleep or away hunting; and the sword is at your throat. Bring us to where the Queen is hid, and you shall live.

FTATATEETA [*contemptuously*] Who shall stay the sword in the hand of a fool, if the high gods put it there? Listen to me, ye young men without understanding. Cleopatra fears me; but she fears the Romans more. There is but one power greater in her eyes than the wrath of the Queen's nurse and the cruelty of Cæsar; and that is the power of the Sphinx that sits in the desert watching the way to the sea. What she would have it know, she tells into the ears of the sacred cats; and on her birthday she sacrifices to it and decks it with poppies. Go ye therefore into the desert and seek Cleopatra in the shadow of the Sphinx; and on your heads see to it that no harm comes to her.

BEL AFFRIS [*to the Persian*] May we believe this, O subtle one?

PERSIAN. Which way come the Romans?

BEL AFFRIS. Over the desert, from the sea, by this very Sphinx.

PERSIAN [*to Ftatateeta*] O mother of guile! O aspic's tongue! You have made up this tale so that we two may go into the desert and perish on the spears of the Romans. [*Lifting his knife*] Taste death.

FTATATEETA. Not from thee, baby. [*She snatches his ankle from under him and flies stooping along the palace wall, vanishing in the darkness within its precinct. Bel Affris roars with laughter as the Persian tumbles. The guardsmen rush out of the palace with Belzanor and a mob of fugitives, mostly carrying bundles*].

PERSIAN. Have you found Cleopatra?

BELZANOR. She is gone. We have searched every corner.

THE NUBIAN SENTINEL [*appearing at the door of the palace*] Woe! Alas! Fly, fly!

BELZANOR. What is the matter now?

THE NUBIAN SENTINEL. The sacred white cat has been stolen.

ALL. Woe! woe! [*General panic. They all fly with cries of consternation. The torch is thrown down and extinguished in the rush. The noise of the fugitives dies away. Darkness and dead silence*].

ACT I

The same darkness into which the temple of Ra and the Syrian palace vanished. The same silence. Suspense. Then the blackness and stillness break softly into silver mist and strange airs as the windswept harp of Memnon plays at the dawning of the moon. It rises full over the desert; and a vast horizon comes into relief, broken by a huge shape which soon reveals itself in the spreading radiance as a Sphinx pedestalled on the sands. The light still clears, until the upraised eyes of the image are distinguished looking straight forward and upward in infinite fearless vigil, and a mass of color between its great paws defines

itself as a heap of red poppies on which a girl lies motionless, her silken vest heaving gently and regularly with the breathing of a dreamless sleeper, and her braided hair glittering in a shaft of moonlight like a bird's wing.

Suddenly there comes from afar a vaguely fearful sound (it might be the bellow of a Minotaur softened by great distance) and Memnon's music stops. Silence: then a few faint high-ringing trumpet notes. Then silence again. Then a man comes from the south with stealing steps, ravished by the mystery of the night, all wonder, and halts, lost in contemplation, opposite the left flank of the Sphinx, whose bosom, with its burden, is hidden from him by its massive shoulder.

THE MAN. Hail, Sphinx: salutation from Julius Cæsar! I have wandered in many lands, seeking the lost regions from which my birth into this world exiled me, and the company of creatures such as I myself. I have found flocks and pastures, men and cities, but no other Cæsar, no air native to me, no man kindred to me, none who can do my day's deed, and think my night's thought. In the little world yonder, Sphinx, my place is as high as yours in this great desert; only I wander, and you sit still; I conquer, and you endure; I work and wonder, you watch and wait; I look up and am dazzled, look down and am darkened, look round and am puzzled, whilst your eyes never turn from looking out —out of the world—to the lost region—the home from which we have strayed. Sphinx, you and I, strangers to the race of men, are no strangers to one another: have I not been conscious of you and of this place since I was born? Rome is a madman's dream: this is my Reality. These starry lamps of yours I have seen from afar in Gaul, in Britain, in Spain, in Thessaly, signalling great secrets to some eternal sentinel below, whose post I never could find. And here at last is their sentinel —an image of the constant and immortal part of my life, silent, full of thoughts, alone in the silver desert. Sphinx, Sphinx: I have climbed mountains at night to hear in the distance the stealthy footfall of the winds that chase your sands in forbidden play— our invisible children, O Sphinx, laughing in whispers. My way hither was the way of destiny; for I am he of whose genius you are the symbol: part brute, part woman, and part god—nothing of man in me at all. Have I read your riddle, Sphinx?

THE GIRL [*who has wakened, and peeped*

K

cautiously from her nest to see who is speaking]
Old gentleman.

CÆSAR [*starting violently, and clutching his
sword*] Immortal gods!

THE GIRL. Old gentleman: dont run away.

CÆSAR [*stupefied*] "Old gentleman: dont run
away"!!! This! to Julius Cæsar!

THE GIRL [*urgently*] Old gentleman.

CÆSAR. Sphinx: you presume on your centuries. I am younger than you, though your
voice is but a girl's voice as yet.

THE GIRL. Climb up here, quickly; or the
Romans will come and eat you.

CÆSAR [*running forward past the Sphinx's
shoulder, and seeing her*] A child at its breast!
a divine child!

THE GIRL. Come up quickly. You must get
up at its side and creep round.

CÆSAR [*amazed*] Who are you?

THE GIRL. Cleopatra, Queen of Egypt.

CÆSAR. Queen of the Gypsies, you mean.

CLEOPATRA. You must not be disrespectful
to me, or the Sphinx will let the Romans
eat you. Come up. It is quite cosy here.

CÆSAR [*to himself*] What a dream! What a
magnificent dream! Only let me not wake,
and I will conquer ten continents to pay for
dreaming it out to the end. [*He climbs to the
Sphinx's flank, and presently reappears to her
on the pedestal, stepping round its right shoulder*].

CLEOPATRA. Take care. Thats right. Now
sit down: you may have its other paw. [*She
seats herself comfortably on its left paw*]. It is
very powerful and will protect us; but [*shivering, and with plaintive loneliness*] it would not
take any notice of me or keep me company.
I am glad you have come: I was very lonely.
Did you happen to see a white cat anywhere?

CÆSAR [*sitting slowly down on the right paw in
extreme wonderment*] Have you lost one?

CLEOPATRA. Yes: the sacred white cat: is it
not dreadful? I brought him here to sacrifice
him to the Sphinx; but when we got a little
way from the city a black cat called him, and
he jumped out of my arms and ran away to
it. Do you think that the black cat can have
been my great-great-great-grandmother?

CÆSAR [*staring at her*] Your great-great-
great-grandmother! Well, why not? Nothing
would surprise me on this night of nights.

CLEOPATRA. I think it must have been. My
great-grandmother's great-grandmother was
a black kitten of the sacred white cat; and
the river Nile made her his seventh wife.
That is why my hair is so wavy. And I always

want to be let do as I like, no matter whether
it is the will of the gods or not: that is because
my blood is made with Nile water.

CÆSAR. What are you doing here at this
time of night? Do you live here?

CLEOPATRA. Of course not: I am the Queen;
and I shall live in the palace at Alexandria
when I have killed my brother, who drove
me out of it. When I am old enough I shall
do just what I like. I shall be able to poison
the slaves and see them wriggle, and pretend
to Ftatateeta that she is going to be put
into the fiery furnace.

CÆSAR. Hm! Meanwhile why are you not
at home and in bed?

CLEOPATRA. Because the Romans are coming to eat us all. You are not at home and in
bed either.

CÆSAR [*with conviction*] Yes I am. I live in
a tent; and I am now in that tent, fast asleep
and dreaming. Do you suppose that I believe
you are real, you impossible little dream
witch?

CLEOPATRA [*giggling and leaning trustfully
towards him*] You are a funny old gentleman.
I like you.

CÆSAR. Ah, that spoils the dream. Why
dont you dream that I am young?

CLEOPATRA. I wish you were; only I think
I should be more afraid of you. I like men,
especially young men with round strong
arms; but I am afraid of them. You are old
and rather thin and stringy; but you have
a nice voice; and I like to have somebody to
talk to, though I think you are a little mad.
It is the moon that makes you talk to yourself in that silly way.

CÆSAR. What! you heard that, did you? I
was saying my prayers to the great Sphinx.

CLEOPATRA. But this isnt the great Sphinx.

CÆSAR [*much disappointed, looking up at the
statue*] What!

CLEOPATRA. This is only a dear little kitten
of a Sphinx. Why, the great Sphinx is so big
that it has a temple between its paws. This
is my pet Sphinx. Tell me: do you think the
Romans have any sorcerers who could take
us away from the Sphinx by magic?

CÆSAR. Why? Are you afraid of the Romans?

CLEOPATRA [*very seriously*] Oh, they would
eat us if they caught us. They are barbarians.
Their chief is called Julius Cæsar. His father
was a tiger and his mother a burning mountain; and his nose is like an elephant's trunk.
[*Cæsar involuntarily rubs his nose*]. They all

have long noses, and ivory tusks, and little tails, and seven arms with a hundred arrows in each; and they live on human flesh.

CÆSAR. Would you like me to shew you a real Roman?

CLEOPATRA [terrified] No. You are frightening me.

CÆSAR. No matter: this is only a dream—

CLEOPATRA [excitedly] It is not a dream: it is not a dream. See, see. [She plucks a pin from her hair and jabs it repeatedly into his arm].

CÆSAR. Ffff—Stop. [Wrathfully] How dare you?

CLEOPATRA [abashed] You said you were dreaming. [Whimpering] I only wanted to shew you—

CÆSAR [gently] Come, come: dont cry. A queen mustnt cry. [He rubs his arm, wondering at the reality of the smart]. Am I awake? [He strikes his hand against the Sphinx to test its solidity. It feels so real that he begins to be alarmed, and says perplexedly] Yes, I— [quite panicstricken] no: impossible: madness, madness! [Desperately] Back to camp—to camp. [He rises to spring down from the pedestal].

CLEOPATRA [flinging her arms in terror round him] No: you shant leave me. No, no, no: dont go. I'm afraid—afraid of the Romans.

CÆSAR [as the conviction that he is really awake forces itself on him] Cleopatra: can you see my face well?

CLEOPATRA. Yes. It is so white in the moonlight.

CÆSAR. Are you sure it is the moonlight that makes me look whiter than an Egyptian? [Grimly] Do you notice that I have a rather long nose?

CLEOPATRA [recoiling, paralysed by a terrible suspicion] Oh!

CÆSAR. It is a Roman nose, Cleopatra.

CLEOPATRA. Ah! [With a piercing scream she springs up; darts round the left shoulder of the Sphinx; scrambles down to the sand; and falls on her knees in frantic supplication, shrieking] Bite him in two, Sphinx: bite him in two. I meant to sacrifice the white cat—I did indeed—I [Cæsar, who has slipped down from the pedestal, touches her on the shoulder]— Ah! [She buries her head in her arms].

CÆSAR. Cleopatra: shall I teach you a way to prevent Cæsar from eating you?

CLEOPATRA [clinging to him piteously] Oh do, do, do. I will steal Ftatateeta's jewels and give them to you. I will make the river Nile water your lands twice a year.

CÆSAR. Peace, peace, my child. Your gods are afraid of the Romans: you see the Sphinx dare not bite me, nor prevent me carrying you off to Julius Cæsar.

CLEOPATRA [in pleading murmurings] You wont, you wont. You said you wouldnt.

CÆSAR. Cæsar never eats women.

CLEOPATRA [springing up full of hope] What!

CÆSAR [impressively] But he eats girls [she relapses] and cats. Now you are a silly little girl; and you are descended from the black kitten. You are both a girl and a cat.

CLEOPATRA [trembling] And will he eat me?

CÆSAR. Yes; unless you make him believe that you are a woman.

CLEOPATRA. Oh, you must get a sorcerer to make a woman of me. Are you a sorcerer?

CÆSAR. Perhaps. But it will take a long time; and this very night you must stand face to face with Cæsar in the palace of your fathers.

CLEOPATRA. No, no. I darent.

CÆSAR. Whatever dread may be in your soul—however terrible Cæsar may be to you —you must confront him as a brave woman and a great queen; and you must feel no fear. If your hand shakes: if your voice quavers; then—night and death! [She moans]. But if he thinks you worthy to rule, he will set you on the throne by his side and make you the real ruler of Egypt.

CLEOPATRA [despairingly] No: he will find me out: he will find me out.

CÆSAR [rather mournfully] He is easily deceived by women. Their eyes dazzle him; and he sees them not as they are, but as he wishes them to appear to him.

CLEOPATRA [hopefully] Then we will cheat him. I will put on Ftatateeta's head-dress; and he will think me quite an old woman.

CÆSAR. If you do that he will eat you at one mouthful.

CLEOPATRA. But I will give him a cake with my magic opal and seven hairs of the white cat baked in it; and—

CÆSAR [abruptly] Pah! you are a little fool. He will eat your cake and you too. [He turns contemptuously from her].

CLEOPATRA [running after him and clinging to him] Oh please, please! I will do whatever you tell me. I will be good. I will be your slave. [Again the terrible bellowing note sounds across the desert, now closer at hand. It is the bucina, the Roman war trumpet].

CÆSAR. Hark!

CLEOPATRA [*trembling*] What was that?

CÆSAR. Cæsar's voice.

CLEOPATRA [*pulling at his hand*] Let us run away. Come. Oh, come.

CÆSAR. You are safe with me until you stand on your throne to receive Cæsar. Now lead me thither.

CLEOPATRA [*only too glad to get away*] I will, I will. [*Again the bucina*]. Oh come, come, come: the gods are angry. Do you feel the earth shaking?

CÆSAR. It is the tread of Cæsar's legions.

CLEOPATRA [*drawing him away*] This way, quickly. And let us look for the white cat as we go. It is he that has turned you into a Roman.

CÆSAR. Incorrigible, oh, incorrigible! Away! [*He follows her, the bucina sounding louder as they steal across the desert. The moonlight wanes: the horizon again shows black against the sky, broken only by the fantastic silhouette of the Sphinx. The sky itself vanishes in darkness, from which there is no relief until the gleam of a distant torch falls on great Egyptian pillars supporting the roof of a majestic corridor. At the further end of this corridor a Nubian slave appears carrying the torch. Cæsar, still led by Cleopatra, follows him. They come down the corridor, Cæsar peering keenly about at the strange architecture, and at the pillar shadows between which, as the passing torch makes them hurry noiselessly backwards, figures of men with wings and hawks' heads, and vast black marble cats, seem to flit in and out of ambush. Further along, the wall turns a corner and makes a spacious transept in which Cæsar sees, on his right, a throne, and behind the throne a door. On each side of the throne is a slender pillar with a lamp on it.*]

CÆSAR. What place is this?

CLEOPATRA. This is where I sit on the throne when I am allowed to wear my crown and robes. [*The slave holds his torch to shew the throne*].

CÆSAR. Order the slave to light the lamps.

CLEOPATRA [*shyly*] Do you think I may?

CÆSAR. Of course. You are the Queen. [*She hesitates*]. Go on.

CLEOPATRA [*timidly, to the slave*] Light all the lamps.

FTATATEETA [*suddenly coming from behind the throne*] Stop. [*The slave stops. She turns sternly to Cleopatra, who quails like a naughty child*]. Who is this you have with you; and how dare you order the lamps to be lighted without my permission? [*Cleopatra is dumb with apprehension*].

CÆSAR. Who is she?

CLEOPATRA. Ftatateeta.

FTATATEETA [*arrogantly*] Chief nurse to—

CÆSAR [*cutting her short*] I speak to the Queen. Be silent. [*To Cleopatra*] Is this how your servants know their places? Send her away; and do you [*to the slave*] do as the Queen has bidden. [*The slave lights the lamps. Meanwhile Cleopatra stands hesitating, afraid of Ftatateeta*]. You are the Queen: send her away.

CLEOPATRA [*cajoling*] Ftatateeta, dear: you must go away—just for a little.

CÆSAR. You are not commanding her to go away: you are begging her. You are no Queen. You will be eaten. Farewell. [*He turns to go*].

CLEOPATRA [*clutching him*] No, no, no. Dont leave me.

CÆSAR. A Roman does not stay with queens who are afraid of their slaves.

CLEOPATRA. I am not afraid. Indeed I am not afraid.

FTATATEETA. We shall see who is afraid here. [*Menacingly*] Cleopatra—

CÆSAR. On your knees, woman: am I also a child that you dare trifle with me? [*He points to the floor at Cleopatra's feet. Ftatateeta, half cowed, half savage, hesitates. Cæsar calls to the Nubian*] Slave. [*The Nubian comes to him*] Can you cut off a head? [*The Nubian nods and grins ecstatically, showing all his teeth. Cæsar takes his sword by the scabbard, ready to offer the hilt to the Nubian, and turns again to Ftatateeta, repeating his gesture*]. Have you remembered yourself, mistress?

Ftatateeta, crushed, kneels before Cleopatra, who can hardly believe her eyes.

FTATATEETA [*hoarsely*] O Queen, forget not thy servant in the days of thy greatness.

CLEOPATRA [*blazing with excitement*] Go. Begone. Go away. [*Ftatateeta rises with stooped head, and moves backwards towards the door. Cleopatra watches her submission eagerly, almost clapping her hands, which are trembling. Suddenly she cries*] Give me something to beat her with. [*She snatches a snake-skin from the throne and dashes after Ftatateeta, whirling it like a scourge in the air. Cæsar makes a bound and manages to catch her and hold her while Ftatateeta escapes*].

CÆSAR. You scratch, kitten, do you?

CLEOPATRA [*breaking from him*] I will beat

somebody. I will beat him. [*She attacks the slave*]. There, there, there! [*The slave flies for his life up the corridor and vanishes. She throws the snake-skin away and jumps on the step of the throne with her arms waving, crying*] I am a real Queen at last—a real, real Queen! Cleopatra the Queen! [*Cæsar shakes his head dubiously, the advantage of the change seeming open to question from the point of view of the general welfare of Egypt. She turns and looks at him exultantly. Then she jumps down from the steps, runs to him, and flings her arms round him rapturously, crying*] Oh, I love you for making me a Queen.

CÆSAR. But queens love only kings.

CLEOPATRA. I will make all the men I love kings. I will make you a king. I will have many young kings, with round, strong arms; and when I am tired of them I will whip them to death; but you shall always be my king: my nice, kind, wise, good old king.

CÆSAR. Oh, my wrinkles, my wrinkles! And my child's heart! You will be the most dangerous of all Cæsar's conquests.

CLEOPATRA [*appalled*] Cæsar! I forgot Cæsar. [*Anxiously*] You will tell him that I am a Queen, will you not?—a real Queen. Listen! [*stealthily coaxing him*]: let us run away and hide until Cæsar is gone.

CÆSAR. If you fear Cæsar, you are no true queen; and though you were to hide beneath a pyramid, he would go straight to it and lift it with one hand. And then—! [*he chops his teeth together*].

CLEOPATRA [*trembling*] Oh!

CÆSAR. Be afraid if you dare. [*The note of the bucina resounds again in the distance. She moans with fear. Cæsar exults in it, exclaiming*] Aha! Cæsar approaches the throne of Cleopatra. Come: take your place. [*He takes her hand and leads her to the throne. She is too downcast to speak*]. Ho, there, Teetatota. How do you call your slaves?

CLEOPATRA [*spiritlessly, as she sinks on the throne and cowers there, shaking*] Clap your hands.

He claps his hands. Ftatateeta returns.

CÆSAR. Bring the Queen's robes, and her crown, and her women; and prepare her.

CLEOPATRA [*eagerly—recovering herself a little*] Yes, the crown, Ftatateeta: I shall wear the crown.

FTATATEETA. For whom must the Queen put on her state?

CÆSAR. For a citizen of Rome. A king of

kings, Totateeta.

CLEOPATRA [*stamping at her*] How dare you ask questions? Go and do as you are told. [*Ftatateeta goes out with a grim smile. Cleopatra goes on eagerly, to Cæsar*] Cæsar will know that I am a Queen when he sees my crown and robes, will he not?

CÆSAR. No. How shall he know that you are not a slave dressed up in the Queen's ornaments?

CLEOPATRA. You must tell him.

CÆSAR. He will not ask me. He will know Cleopatra by her pride, her courage, her majesty, and her beauty. [*She looks very doubtful*]. Are you trembling?

CLEOPATRA [*shivering with dread*] No, I—I— [*in a very sickly voice*] No.

Ftatateeta and three women come in with the regalia.

FTATATEETA. Of all the Queen's women, these three alone are left. The rest are fled. [*They begin to deck Cleopatra, who submits, pale and motionless*].

CÆSAR. Good, good. Three are enough. Poor Cæsar generally has to dress himself.

FTATATEETA [*contemptuously*] The queen of Egypt is not a Roman barbarian. [*To Cleopatra*] Be brave, my nursling. Hold up your head before this stranger.

CÆSAR [*admiring Cleopatra, and placing the crown on her head*] Is it sweet or bitter to be a Queen, Cleopatra?

CLEOPATRA. Bitter.

CÆSAR. Cast out fear; and you will conquer Cæsar. Tota: are the Romans at hand?

FTATATEETA. They are at hand; and the guard has fled.

THE WOMEN [*wailing subduedly*] Woe to us!

The Nubian comes running down the hall.

NUBIAN. The Romans are in the courtyard. [*He bolts through the door. With a shriek, the women fly after him. Ftatateeta's jaw expresses savage resolution: she does not budge. Cleopatra can hardly restrain herself from following them. Cæsar grips her wrist, and looks steadfastly at her. She stands like a martyr*].

CÆSAR. The Queen must face Cæsar alone. Answer "So be it."

CLEOPATRA [*white*] So be it.

CÆSAR [*releasing her*] Good.

A tramp and tumult of armed men is heard. Cleopatra's terror increases. The bucina sounds close at hand, followed by a formidable clangor of trumpets. This is too much for Cleopatra: she utters a cry and darts towards the door. Ftatateeta stops her ruthlessly.

FTATATEETA. You are my nursling. You have said "So be it"; and if you die for it, you must make the Queen's word good. [*She hands Cleopatra to Cæsar, who takes her back, almost beside herself with apprehension, to the throne*].

CÆSAR. Now, if you quail—! [*He seats himself on the throne*].

She stands on the step, all but unconscious, waiting for death. The Roman soldiers troop in tumultuously through the corridor, headed by their ensign with his eagle, and their bucinator, a burly fellow with his instrument coiled round his body, its brazen bell shaped like the head of a howling wolf. When they reach the transept, they stare in amazement at the throne; dress into ordered rank opposite it; draw their swords and lift them in the air with a shout of H a i l , C æ s a r . *Cleopatra turns and stares wildly at Cæsar; grasps the situation; and, with a great sob of relief, falls into his arms.*

ACT II

Alexandria. A hall on the first floor of the Palace, ending in a loggia approached by two steps. Through the arches of the loggia the Mediterranean can be seen, bright in the morning sun. The clean lofty walls, painted with a procession of the Egyptian theocracy, presented in profile as flat ornament, and the absence of mirrors, sham perspectives, stuffy upholstery and textiles, make the place handsome, wholesome, simple and cool, or, as a rich English manufacturer would express it, poor, bare, ridiculous and unhomely. For Tottenham Court Road civilization is to this Egyptian civilization as glass bead and tattoo civilization is to Tottenham Court Road.

The young king Ptolemy Dionysus (aged ten) is at the top of the steps, on his way in through the loggia, led by his guardian Pothinus, who has him by the hand. The court is assembled to receive him. It is made up of men and women (some of the women being officials) of various complexions and races, mostly Egyptian; some of them, comparatively fair, from lower Egypt, some, much darker, from upper Egypt; with a few Greeks and Jews. Prominent in a group on Ptolemy's right hand is Theodotus, Ptolemy's tutor. Another group, on Ptolemy's left, is headed by Achillas, the general of Ptolemy's troops. Theodotus is a little old man, whose features are as cramped and wizened as his limbs, except his tall straight forehead, which occupies more space than all the rest of his face. He maintains an air of magpie keenness and profundity, listening to what the others say with the sarcastic vigilance of a philosopher listening to the exercises of his disciples. Achillas is a tall handsome man of thirty-five, with a fine black beard curled like the coat of a poodle. Apparently not a clever man, but distinguished and dignified. Pothinus is a vigorous man of fifty, a eunuch, passionate, energetic and quick witted, but of common mind and character; impatient and unable to control his temper. He has fine tawny hair, like fur. Ptolemy, the King, looks much older than an English boy of ten; but he has the childish air, the habit of being in leading strings, the mixture of impotence and petulance, the appearance of being excessively washed, combed and dressed by other hands, which is exhibited by court-bred princes of all ages.

All receive the King with reverence. He comes down the steps to a chair of state which stands a little to his right, the only seat in the hall. Taking his place before it, he looks nervously for instructions to Pothinus, who places himself at his left hand.

POTHINUS. The king of Egypt has a word to speak.

THEODOTUS [*in a squeak which he makes impressive by sheer self-opinionativeness*] Peace for the King's word!

PTOLEMY [*without any vocal inflexions: he is evidently repeating a lesson*] Take notice of this all of you. I am the first-born son of Auletes the Flute Blower who was your King. My sister Berenice drove him from his throne and reigned in his stead but—but—[*he hesitates*]—

POTHINUS [*stealthily prompting*]—but the gods would not suffer—

PTOLEMY. Yes—the gods would not suffer —not suffer— [*He stops; then, crestfallen*] I forget what the gods would not suffer.

THEODOTUS. Let Pothinus, the King's guardian, speak for the King.

POTHINUS [*suppressing his impatience with difficulty*] The King wished to say that the gods would not suffer the impiety of his sister to go unpunished.

PTOLEMY [*hastily*] Yes: I remember the rest of it. [*He resumes his monotone*]. Therefore the gods sent a stranger one Mark Antony a Roman captain of horsemen across the sands of the desert and he set my father again upon the throne. And my father took Berenice my sister and struck her head off. And now that my father is dead yet another of his daughters my sister Cleopatra would snatch the kingdom from me and reign in my place. But the gods would not suffer—[*Pothinus coughs admonitorily*]—the gods—the gods would not suffer—

POTHINUS [*prompting*]—will not maintain—

PTOLEMY. Oh yes—will not maintain such iniquity they will give her head to the axe even as her sister's. But with the help of the witch Ftatateeta she hath cast a spell on the Roman Julius Cæsar to make him uphold her false pretence to rule in Egypt. Take notice then that I will not suffer—that I will not suffer—[*pettishly, to Pothinus*] What is it that I will not suffer?

POTHINUS [*suddenly exploding with all the force and emphasis of political passion*] The King will not suffer a foreigner to take from him the throne of our Egypt. [*A shout of applause*]. Tell the King, Achillas, how many soldiers and horsemen follow the Roman?

THEODOTUS. Let the King's general speak!

ACHILLAS. But two Roman legions, O King. Three thousand soldiers and scarce a thousand horsemen.

The court breaks into derisive laughter; and a great chattering begins, amid which Rufio, a Roman officer, appears in the loggia. He is a burly, black-bearded man of middle age, very blunt, prompt and rough, with small clear eyes, and plump nose and cheeks, which, however, like the rest of his flesh, are in iron-hard condition.

RUFIO [*from the steps*] Peace, ho! [*The laughter and chatter cease abruptly*]. Cæsar approaches.

THEODOTUS [*with much presence of mind*] The King permits the Roman commander to enter!

Cæsar, plainly dressed, but wearing an oak wreath to conceal his baldness, enters from the loggia, attended by Britannus, his secretary, a Briton, about forty, tall, solemn, and already slightly bald, with a heavy, drooping, hazel-colored moustache trained so as to lose its ends in a pair of trim whiskers. He is carefully dressed in blue, with portfolio, inkhorn, and reed pen at his girdle. His serious air and sense of the importance of the business in hand is in marked contrast to the kindly interest of Cæsar, who looks at the scene, which is new to him, with the frank curiosity of a child, and then turns to the king's chair: Britannus and Rufio posting themselves near the steps at the other side.

CÆSAR [*looking at Pothinus and Ptolemy*] Which is the King? the man or the boy?

POTHINUS. I am Pothinus, the guardian of my lord the King.

CÆSAR [*patting Ptolemy kindly on the shoulder*] So you are the King. Dull work at your age, eh? [*To Pothinus*] Your servant, Pothinus. [*He turns away unconcernedly and comes slowly along the middle of the hall, looking from side to side at the courtiers until he reaches Achillas*]. And this gentleman?

THEODOTUS. Achillas, the King's general.

CÆSAR [*to Achillas, very friendly*] A general, eh? I am a general myself. But I began too old, too old. Health and many victories, Achillas!

ACHILLAS. As the gods will, Cæsar.

CÆSAR [*turning to Theodotus*] And you, sir, are—?

THEODOTUS. Theodotus, the King's tutor.

CÆSAR. You teach men how to be kings, Theodotus. That is very clever of you. [*Looking at the gods on the walls as he turns away from Theodotus and goes up again to Pothinus*] And this place?

POTHINUS. The council chamber of the chancellors of the King's treasury, Cæsar.

CÆSAR. Ah! that reminds me. I want some money.

POTHINUS. The King's treasury is poor, Cæsar.

CÆSAR. Yes: I notice that there is but one chair in it.

RUFIO [*shouting gruffly*] Bring a chair there, some of you, for Cæsar.

PTOLEMY [*rising shyly to offer his chair*] Cæsar—

CÆSAR [*kindly*] No, no, my boy: that is your chair of state. Sit down.

He makes Ptolemy sit down again. Meanwhile Rufio, looking about him, sees in the nearest corner an image of the god Ra, represented as a seated man with the head of a hawk. Before the image is a bronze tripod, about as large as a three-legged stool, with a stick of incense burning on it. Rufio, with Roman resourcefulness and indifference to foreign superstitions, promptly seizes the tripod; shakes off the incense; blows away the ash; and dumps it down behind Cæsar, nearly in the middle of the hall.

RUFIO. Sit on that, Cæsar.

A shiver runs through the court, followed by a hissing whisper of Sacrilege!

CÆSAR [*seating himself*] Now, Pothinus, to business. I am badly in want of money.

BRITANNUS [*disapproving of these informal*

expressions] My master would say that there is a lawful debt due to Rome by Egypt, contracted by the King's deceased father to the Triumvirate; and that it is Cæsar's duty to his country to require immediate payment.

CÆSAR [*blandly*] Ah, I forgot. I have not made my companions known here. Pothinus: this is Britannus, my secretary. He is an islander from the western end of the world, a day's voyage from Gaul. [*Britannus bows stiffly*]. This gentleman is Rufio, my comrade in arms. [*Rufio nods*]. Pothinus: I want 1,600 talents.

The courtiers, appalled, murmur loudly, and Theodotus and Achillas appeal mutely to one another against so monstrous a demand.

POTHINUS [*aghast*] Forty million sesterces! Impossible. There is not so much money in the King's treasury.

CÆSAR [*encouragingly*] Only sixteen hundred talents, Pothinus. Why count it in sesterces? A sestertius is only worth a loaf of bread.

POTHINUS. And a talent is worth a racehorse. I say it is impossible. We have been at strife here, because the King's sister Cleopatra falsely claims his throne. The King's taxes have not been collected for a whole year.

CÆSAR. Yes they have, Pothinus. My officers have been collecting them all morning. [*Renewed whisper and sensation, not without some stifled laughter, among the courtiers*].

RUFIO [*bluntly*] You must pay, Pothinus. Why waste words? You are getting off cheaply enough.

POTHINUS [*bitterly*] Is it possible that Cæsar, the conqueror of the world, has time to occupy himself with such a trifle as our taxes?

CÆSAR. My friend: taxes are the chief business of a conqueror of the world.

POTHINUS. Then take warning, Cæsar. This day, the treasures of the temple and the gold of the King's treasury shall be sent to the mint to be melted down for our ransom in the sight of the people. They shall see us sitting under bare walls and drinking from wooden cups. And their wrath be on your head, Cæsar, if you force us to this sacrilege!

CÆSAR. Do not fear, Pothinus: the people know how well wine tastes in wooden cups. In return for your bounty, I will settle this dispute about the throne for you, if you will. What say you?

POTHINUS. If I say no, will that hinder you?

RUFIO [*defiantly*] No.

CÆSAR. You say the matter has been at issue for a year, Pothinus. May I have ten minutes at it?

POTHINUS. You will do your pleasure, doubtless.

CÆSAR. Good! But first, let us have Cleopatra here.

THEODOTUS. She is not in Alexandria: she is fled into Syria.

CÆSAR. I think not. [*To Rufio*] Call Totateeta.

RUFIO [*Calling*] Ho there, Teetatota.

Ftatateeta enters the loggia, and stands arrogantly at the top of the steps.

FTATATEETA. Who pronounces the name of Ftatateeta, the Queen's chief nurse?

CÆSAR. Nobody can pronounce it, Tota, except yourself. Where is your mistress?

Cleopatra, who is hiding behind Ftatateeta, peeps out at them laughing. Cæsar rises.

CÆSAR. Will the Queen favor us with her presence for a moment?

CLEOPATRA [*pushing Ftatateeta aside and standing haughtily on the brink of the steps*] Am I to behave like a Queen?

CÆSAR. Yes.

Cleopatra immediately comes down to the chair of state; seizes Ptolemy; drags him out of his seat; then takes his place in the chair. Ftatateeta seats herself on the step of the loggia, and sits there, watching the scene with sibylline intensity.

PTOLEMY [*mortified, and struggling with his tears*] Cæsar: this is how she treats me always. If I am a king why is she allowed to take everything from me?

CLEOPATRA. You are not to be King, you little cry-baby. You are to be eaten by the Romans.

CÆSAR [*touched by Ptolemy's distress*] Come here, my boy, and stand by me.

Ptolemy goes over to Cæsar, who, resuming his seat on the tripod, takes the boy's hand to encourage him. Cleopatra, furiously jealous, rises and glares at them.

CLEOPATRA [*with flaming cheeks*] Take your throne: I dont want it. [*She flings away from the chair, and approaches Ptolemy, who shrinks from her*]. Go this instant and sit down in your place.

CÆSAR. Go, Ptolemy. Always take a throne when it is offered to you.

RUFIO. I hope you will have the good sense to follow your own advice when we return to Rome, Cæsar.

Ptolemy slowly goes back to the throne, giving Cleopatra a wide berth, in evident fear of her hands. She takes his place beside Cæsar.

CÆSAR. Pothinus—

CLEOPATRA [*interrupting him*] Are you not going to speak to me?

CÆSAR. Be quiet. Open your mouth again before I give you leave; and you shall be eaten.

CLEOPATRA. I am not afraid. A queen must not be afraid. Eat my husband there, if you like: h e is afraid.

CÆSAR [*starting*] Your husband! What do you mean?

CLEOPATRA [*pointing to Ptolemy*] That little thing.

The two Romans and the Briton stare at one another in amazement.

THEODOTUS. Cæsar: you are a stranger here, and not conversant with our laws. The kings and queens of Egypt may not marry except with their own royal blood. Ptolemy and Cleopatra are born king and consort just as they are born brother and sister.

BRITANNUS [*shocked*] Cæsar: this is not proper.

THEODOTUS [*outraged*] How!

CÆSAR [*recovering his self-possession*] Pardon him, Theodotus: he is a barbarian, and thinks that the customs of his tribe and island are the laws of nature.

BRITANNUS. On the contrary, Cæsar, it is these Egyptians who are barbarians; and you do wrong to enourage them. I say it is a scandal.

CÆSAR. Scandal or not, my friend, it opens the gate of peace. [*He addresses Pothinus seriously*]. Pothinus: hear what I propose.

RUFIO. Hear Cæsar there.

CÆSAR. Ptolemy and Cleopatra shall reign jointly in Egypt.

ACHILLAS. What of the King's younger brother and Cleopatra's younger sister?

RUFIO [*explaining*] There is another little Ptolemy, Cæsar: so they tell me.

CÆSAR. Well, the little Ptolemy can marry the other sister; and we will make them both a present of Cyprus.

POTHINUS [*impatiently*] Cyprus is of no use to anybody.

CÆSAR. No matter: you shall have it for the sake of peace.

BRITANNUS [*unconsciously anticipating a later statesman*] Peace with honor, Pothinus.

POTHINUS [*mutinously*] Cæsar: be honest.

The money you demand is the price of our freedom. Take it; and leave us to settle our own affairs.

THE BOLDER COURTIERS [*encouraged by Pothinus's tone and Cæsar's quietness*] Yes, yes. Egypt for the Egyptians!

The conference now becomes an altercation, the Egyptians becoming more and more heated. Cæsar remains unruffled; but Rufio grows fiercer and doggeder, and Britannus haughtily indignant.

RUFIO [*contemptuously*] Egypt for the Egyptians! Do you forget that there is a Roman army of occupation here, left by Aulus Gabinius when he set up your toy king for you?

ACHILLAS [*suddenly asserting himself*] And now under m y command. *I* am the Roman general here, Cæsar.

CÆSAR [*tickled by the humor of the situation*] And also the Egyptian general, eh?

POTHINUS [*triumphantly*] That is so, Cæsar.

CÆSAR [*to Achillas*] So you can make war on the Egyptians in the name of Rome, and on the Romans—on m e, if necessary—in the name of Egypt?

ACHILLAS. That is so, Cæsar.

CÆSAR. And which side are you on at present, if I may presume to ask, general?

ACHILLAS. On the side of the right and of the gods.

CÆSAR. Hm! How many men have you?

ACHILLAS. That will appear when I take the field.

RUFIO [*truculently*] Are your men Romans? If not, it matters not how many there are, provided you are no stronger than 500 to ten.

POTHINUS. It is useless to try to bluff us, Rufio. Cæsar has been defeated before and may be defeated again. A few weeks ago Cæsar was flying for his life before Pompey: a few months hence he may be flying for his life before Cato and Juba of Numidia, the African King.

ACHILLAS [*following up Pothinus's speech menacingly*] What can you do with 4,000 men?

THEODOTUS [*following up Achillas's speech with a raucous squeak*] And without money? Away with you.

ALL THE COURTIERS [*shouting fiercely and crowding towards Cæsar*] Away with you. Egypt for the Egyptians! Begone.

Rufio bites his beard, too angry to speak. Cæsar sits as comfortably as if he were at breakfast, and the cat were clamoring for a piece of

Finnan-haddie.

CLEOPATRA. Why do you let them talk to you like that, Cæsar? Are you afraid?

CÆSAR. Why, my dear, what they say is quite true.

CLEOPATRA. But if you go away, I shall not be Queen.

CÆSAR. I shall not go away until you are Queen.

POTHINUS. Achillas: if you are not a fool, you will take that girl whilst she is under your hand.

RUFIO [*daring them*] Why not take Cæsar as well, Achillas?

POTHINUS [*retorting the defiance with interest*] Well said, Rufio. Why not?

RUFIO. Try, Achillas. [*Calling*] Guard there.

The loggia immediately fills with Cæsar's soldiers, who stand, sword in hand, at the top of the steps, waiting the word to charge from their centurion, who carries a cudgel. For a moment the Egyptians face them proudly: then they retire sullenly to their former places.

BRITANNUS. You are Cæsar's prisoners, all of you.

CÆSAR [*benevolently*] Oh no, no, no. By no means. Cæsar's guests, gentlemen.

CLEOPATRA. Wont you cut their heads off?

CÆSAR. What! Cut off your brother's head?

CLEOPATRA. Why not? He would cut off mine, if he got the chance. Wouldnt you, Ptolemy?

PTOLEMY [*pale and obstinate*] I would. I will, too, when I grow up.

Cleopatra is rent by a struggle between her newly-acquired dignity as a queen, and a strong impulse to put out her tongue at him. She takes no part in the scene which follows, but watches it with curiosity and wonder, fidgeting with the restlessness of a child, and sitting down on Cæsar's tripod when he rises.

POTHINUS. Cæsar: if you attempt to detain us—

RUFIO. He will succeed, Egyptian: make up your mind to that. We hold the palace, the beach, and the eastern harbor. The road to Rome is open; and you shall travel it if Cæsar chooses.

CÆSAR [*courteously*] I could do no less, Pothinus, to secure the retreat of my own soldiers. I am accountable for every life among them. But you are free to go. So are all here, and in the palace.

RUFIO [*aghast at this clemency*] What! Renegades and all?

CÆSAR [*softening the expression*] Roman army of occupation and all, Rufio.

POTHINUS [*bewildered*] But—but—but—

CÆSAR. Well, my friend?

POTHINUS. You are turning us out of our own palace into the streets; and you tell us with a grand air that we are free to go! It is for you to go.

CÆSAR. Your friends are in the street, Pothinus. You will be safer there.

POTHINUS. This is a trick. I am the king's guardian: I refuse to stir. I stand on my right here. Where is your right?

CÆSAR. It is in Rufio's scabbard, Pothinus. I may not be able to keep it there if you wait too long.

Sensation.

POTHINUS [*bitterly*] And this is Roman justice!

THEODOTUS. But not Roman gratitude, I hope.

CÆSAR. Gratitude! Am I in your debt for any service, gentlemen?

THEODOTUS. Is Cæsar's life of so little account to him that he forgets that we have saved it?

CÆSAR. My life! Is that all?

THEODOTUS. Your life. Your laurels. Your future.

POTHINUS. It is true. I can call a witness to prove that but for us, the Roman army of occupation, led by the greatest soldier in the world, would now have Cæsar at its mercy. [*Calling through the loggia*] Ho, there, Lucius Septimius [*Cæsar starts, deeply moved*]: if my voice can reach you, come forth and testify before Cæsar.

CÆSAR [*shrinking*] No, no.

THEODOTUS. Yes, I say. Let the military tribune bear witness.

Lucius Septimius, a clean shaven, trim athlete of about 40, with symmetrical features, resolute mouth, and handsome, thin Roman nose, in the dress of a Roman officer, comes in through the loggia and confronts Cæsar, who hides his face with his robe for a moment; then, mastering himself, drops it, and confronts the tribune with dignity.

POTHINUS. Bear witness, Lucius Septimius. Cæsar came hither in pursuit of his foe. Did we shelter his foe?

LUCIUS. As Pompey's foot touched the Egyptian shore, his head fell by the stroke of my sword.

THEODOTUS [*with viperish relish*] Under the

eyes of his wife and child! Remember that, Cæsar! They saw it from the ship he had just left. We have given you a full and sweet measure of vengeance.

CÆSAR [*with horror*] Vengeance!

POTHINUS. Our first gift to you, as your galley came into the roadstead, was the head of your rival for the empire of the world. Bear witness, Lucius Septimius: is it not so?

LUCIUS. It is so. With this hand, that slew Pompey, I placed his head at the feet of Cæsar.

CÆSAR. Murderer! So would you have slain Cæsar, had Pompey been victorious at Pharsalia.

LUCIUS. Woe to the vanquished, Cæsar! When I served Pompey, I slew as good men as he, only because he conquered them. His turn came at last.

THEODOTUS [*flatteringly*] The deed was not yours, Cæsar, but ours—nay, mine; for it was done by my counsel. Thanks to us, you keep your reputation for clemency, and have your vengeance too.

CÆSAR. Vengeance! Vengeance!! Oh, if I could stoop to vengeance, what would I not exact from you as the price of this murdered man's blood? [*They shrink back, appalled and disconcerted*]. Was he not my son-in-law, my ancient friend, for 20 years the master of great Rome, for 30 years the compeller of victory? Did not I, as a Roman, share his glory? Was the Fate that forced us to fight for the mastery of the world, of our making? Am I Julius Cæsar, or am I a wolf, that you fling to me the grey head of the old soldier, the laurelled conqueror, the mighty Roman, treacherously struck down by this callous ruffian, and then claim my gratitude for it! [*To Lucius Septimius*] Begone: you fill me with horror.

LUCIUS [*cold and undaunted*] Pshaw! You have seen severed heads before, Cæsar, and severed right hands too, I think; some thousands of them, in Gaul, after you vanquished Vercingetorix. Did you spare him, with all your clemency? Was that vengeance?

CÆSAR. No, by the gods! would that it had been! Vengeance at least is human. No, I say: those severed right hands, and the brave Vercingetorix basely strangled in a vault beneath the Capitol, were [*with shuddering satire*] a wise severity, a necessary protection to the commonwealth, a duty of statesmanship—follies and fictions ten times bloodier

than honest vengeance! What a fool was I then! To think that men's lives should be at the mercy of such fools! [*Humbly*] Lucius Septimius, pardon me: why should the slayer of Vercingetorix rebuke the slayer of Pompey? You are free to go with the rest. Or stay if you will: I will find a place for you in my service.

LUCIUS. The odds are against you, Cæsar. I go. [*He turns to go out through the loggia*].

RUFIO [*full of wrath at seeing his prey escaping*] That means that he is a Republican.

LUCIUS [*turning defiantly on the loggia steps*] And what are you?

RUFIO. A Cæsarian, like all Cæsar's soldiers.

CÆSAR [*courteously*] Lucius: believe me, Cæsar is no Cæsarian. Were Rome a true republic, then were Cæsar the first of Republicans. But you have made your choice. Farewell.

LUCIUS. Farewell. Come, Achillas, whilst there is yet time.

Cæsar, seeing that Rufio's temper threatens to get the worse of him, puts his hand on his shoulder and brings him down the hall out of harm's way, Britannus accompanying them and posting himself on Cæsar's right hand. This movement brings the three in a little group to the place occupied by Achillas, who moves haughtily away and joins Theodotus on the other side. Lucius Septimius goes out through the soldiers in the loggia. Pothinus, Theodotus and Achillas follow him with the courtiers, very mistrustful of the soldiers, who close up in their rear and go out after them, keeping them moving without much ceremony. The King is left in his chair, piteous, obstinate, with twitching face and fingers. During these movements Rufio maintains an energetic grumbling, as follows:—

RUFIO [*as Lucius departs*] Do you suppose he would let us go if he had our heads in his hands?

CÆSAR. I have no right to suppose that his ways are any baser than mine.

RUFIO. Psha!

CÆSAR. Rufio: if I take Lucius Septimius for my model, and become exactly like him, ceasing to be Cæsar, will you serve me still?

BRITANNUS. Cæsar: this is not good sense. Your duty to Rome demands that her enemies should be prevented from doing further mischief. [*Cæsar, whose delight in the moral eye-to-business of his British secretary is inexhaustible, smiles indulgently*].

RUFIO. It is no use talking to him, Britannus: you may save your breath to cool your porridge. But mark this, Cæsar. Clemency is very well for you; but what is it for your soldiers, who have to fight tomorrow the men you spared yesterday? You may give what orders you please; but I tell you that your next victory will be a massacre, thanks to your clemency. *I*, for one, will take no prisoners. I will kill my enemies in the field; and then you can preach as much clemency as you please: I shall never have to fight them again. And now, with your leave, I will see these gentry off the premises. [*He turns to go*].

CÆSAR [*turning also and seeing Ptolemy*] What! have they left the boy alone! Oh shame, shame!

RUFIO [*taking Ptolemy's hand and making him rise*] Come, your majesty!

PTOLEMY [*to Cæsar, drawing away his hand from Rufio*] Is he turning me out of my palace?

RUFIO [*grimly*] You are welcome to stay if you wish.

CÆSAR [*kindly*] Go, my boy. I will not harm you; but you will be safer away, among your friends. Here you are in the lion's mouth.

PTOLEMY [*turning to go*] It is not the lion I fear, but [*looking at Rufio*] the jackal. [*He goes out through the loggia*].

CÆSAR [*laughing approvingly*] Brave boy!

CLEOPATRA [*jealous of Cæsar's approbation, calling after Ptolemy*] Little silly. You think that very clever.

CÆSAR. Britannus: attend the King. Give him in charge to that Pothinus fellow. [*Britannus goes out after Ptolemy*].

RUFIO [*pointing to Cleopatra*] And this piece of goods? What is to be done with h e r ? However, I suppose I may leave that to you. [*He goes out through the loggia*].

CLEOPATRA [*flushing suddenly and turning on Cæsar*] Did you mean me to go with the rest?

CÆSAR [*a little preoccupied, goes with a sigh to Ptolemy's chair, whilst she waits for his answer with red cheeks and clenched fists*] You are free to do just as you please, Cleopatra.

CLEOPATRA. Then you do not care whether I stay or not?

CÆSAR [*smiling*] Of course I had rather you stayed.

CLEOPATRA. Much, m u c h rather?

CÆSAR [*nodding*] Much, much rather.

CLEOPATRA. Then I consent to stay, because I am asked. But I do not want to, mind.

CÆSAR. That is quite understood. [*Calling*] Totateeta.

Ftatateeta, still seated, turns her eyes on him with a sinister expression, but does not move.

CLEOPATRA [*with a splutter of laughter*] Her name is not Totateeta: it is Ftatateeta. [*Calling*] Ftatateeta. [*Ftatateeta instantly rises and comes to Cleopatra*].

CÆSAR [*stumbling over the name*] Tfatafeeta will forgive the erring tongue of a Roman. Tota: the Queen will hold her state here in Alexandria. Engage women to attend upon her; and do all that is needful.

FTATATEETA. Am I then the mistress of the Queen's household?

CLEOPATRA [*sharply*] No: *I* am the mistress of the Queen's household. Go and do as you are told, or I will have you thrown into the Nile this very afternoon, to poison the poor crocodiles.

CÆSAR [*shocked*] Oh no, no.

CLEOPATRA. Oh yes, yes. You are very sentimental, Cæsar; but you are clever; and if you do as I tell you, you will soon learn to govern.

Cæsar, quite dumbfounded by this impertinence, turns in his chair and stares at her.

Ftatateeta, smiling grimly, and showing a splendid set of teeth, goes, leaving them alone together.

CÆSAR. Cleopatra: I really think I must eat you, after all.

CLEOPATRA [*kneeling beside him and looking at him with eager interest, half real, half affected to shew how intelligent she is*] You must not talk to me now as if I were a child.

CÆSAR. You have been growing up since the sphinx introduced us the other night; and you think you know more than I do already.

CLEOPATRA [*taken down, and anxious to justify herself*] No: that would be very silly of me: of course I know that. But— [*suddenly*] are you angry with me?

CÆSAR. No.

CLEOPATRA [*only half believing him*] Then why are you so thoughtful?

CÆSAR [*rising*] I have work to do, Cleopatra.

CLEOPATRA [*drawing back*] Work! [*Offended*] You are tired of talking to me; and that is your excuse to get away from me.

CÆSAR [*sitting down again to appease her*] Well, well: another minute. But then— work!

CLEOPATRA. Work! what nonsense! You must remember that you are a king now: I have made you one. Kings dont work.

CÆSAR. Oh! Who told you that, little kitten? Eh?

CLEOPATRA. My father was King of Egypt; and he never worked. But he was a great king, and cut off my sister's head because she rebelled against him and took the throne from him.

CÆSAR. Well; and how did he get his throne back again?

CLEOPATRA [*eagerly, her eyes lighting up*] I will tell you. A beautiful young man, with strong round arms, came over the desert with many horsemen, and slew my sister's husband and gave my father back his throne. [*Wistfully*] I was only twelve then. Oh, I wish he would come again, now that I am a queen. I would make him my husband.

CÆSAR. It might be managed, perhaps; for it was I who sent that beautiful young man to help your father.

CLEOPATRA [*enraptured*] You know him!

CÆSAR [*nodding*] I do.

CLEOPATRA. Has he come with you? [*Cæsar shakes his head: she is cruelly disappointed*]. Oh, I wish he had, I wish he had. If only I were a little older; so that he might not think me a mere kitten, as you do! But perhaps that is because you are old. He is many many years younger than you, is he not?

CÆSAR [*as if swallowing a pill*] He is somewhat younger.

CLEOPATRA. Would he be my husband, do you think, if I asked him?

CÆSAR. Very likely.

CLEOPATRA. But I should not like to ask him. Could you not persuade him to ask me —without knowing that I wanted him to?

CÆSAR [*touched by her innocence of the beautiful young man's character*] My poor child!

CLEOPATRA. Why do you say that as if you were sorry for me? Does he love anyone else?

CÆSAR. I am afraid so.

CLEOPATRA [*tearfully*] Then I shall not be his first love.

CÆSAR. Not quite the first. He is greatly admired by women.

CLEOPATRA. I wish I could be the first. But if he loves me, I will make him kill all the rest. Tell me: is he still beautiful? Do his strong round arms shine in the sun like marble?

CÆSAR. He is in excellent condition—considering how much he eats and drinks.

CLEOPATRA. Oh, you must not say common,

earthly things about him; for I love him. He is a god.

CÆSAR. He is a great captain of horsemen, and swifter of foot than any other Roman.

CLEOPATRA. What is his real name?

CÆSAR [*puzzled*] His r e a l name?

CLEOPATRA. Yes. I always call him Horus, because Horus is the most beautiful of our gods. But I want to know his real name.

CÆSAR. His name is Mark Antony.

CLEOPATRA [*musically*] Mark Antony, Mark Antony, Mark Antony! What a beautiful name! [*She throws her arms round Cæsar's neck*]. Oh, how I love you for sending him to help my father! Did you love my father very much?

CÆSAR. No, my child; but your father, as you say, never worked. I always work. So when he lost his crown he had to promise me 16,000 talents to get it back for him.

CLEOPATRA. Did he ever pay you?

CÆSAR. Not in full.

CLEOPATRA. He was quite right: it was too dear. The whole world is not worth 16,000 talents.

CÆSAR. That is perhaps true, Cleopatra. Those Egyptians who work paid as much of it as he could drag from them. The rest is still due. But as I most likely shall not get it, I must go back to my work. So you must run away for a little and send my secretary to me.

CLEOPATRA [*coaxing*] No: I want to stay and hear you talk about Mark Antony.

CÆSAR. But if I do not get to work, Pothinus and the rest of them will cut us off from the harbor; and then the way from Rome will be blocked.

CLEOPATRA. No matter: I dont want you to go back to Rome.

CÆSAR. But you want Mark Antony to come from it.

CLEOPATRA [*springing up*] Oh yes, yes, yes: I forgot. Go quickly and work, Cæsar; and keep the way over the sea open for my Mark Antony. [*She runs out through the loggia, kissing her hand to Mark Antony across the sea*].

CÆSAR [*going briskly up the middle of the hall to the loggia steps*] Ho, Britannus. [*He is startled by the entry of a wounded Roman soldier, who confronts him from the upper step*]. What now?

SOLDIER [*pointing to his bandaged head*] This, Cæsar; and two of my comrades killed in the market place.

CÆSAR [*quiet, but attending*] Ay. Why?

SOLDIER. There is an army come to Alexandria, calling itself the Roman army.

CÆSAR. The Roman army of occupation. Ay?

SOLDIER. Commanded by one Achillas.

CÆSAR. Well?

SOLDIER. The citizens rose against us when the army entered the gates. I was with two others in the market place when the news came. They set upon us. I cut my way out; and here I am.

CÆSAR. Good. I am glad to see you alive. [*Rufio enters the loggia hastily, passing behind the soldier to look out through one of the arches at the quay beneath*]. Rufio: we are besieged.

RUFIO. What! Already?

CÆSAR. Now or tomorrow: what does it matter? We s h a l l be besieged.

Britannus runs in.

BRITANNUS. Cæsar—

CÆSAR [*anticipating him*] Yes: I know. [*Rufio and Britannus come down the hall from the loggia at opposite sides, past Cæsar, who waits for a moment near the step to say to the soldier*] Comrade: give the word to turn out on the beach and stand by the boats. Get your wound attended to. Go. [*The soldier hurries out. Cæsar comes down the hall between Rufio and Britannus*] Rufio: we have some ships in the west harbor. Burn them.

RUFIO [*staring*] Burn them!!

CÆSAR. Take every boat we have in the east harbor, and seize the Pharos—that island with the lighthouse. Leave half our men behind to hold the beach and the quay outside this palace: that is the way home.

RUFIO [*disapproving strongly*] Are we to give up the city?

CÆSAR. We have not got it, Rufio. This palace we have; and—what is that building next door?

RUFIO. The theatre.

CÆSAR. We will have that too: it commands the strand. For the rest, Egypt for the Egyptians!

RUFIO. Well, you know best, I suppose. Is that all?

CÆSAR. That is all. Are those ships burnt yet?

RUFIO. Be easy: I shall waste no more time. [*He runs out*].

BRITANNUS. Cæsar: Pothinus demands speech of you. In my opinion he needs a lesson. His manner is most insolent.

CÆSAR. Where is he?

BRITANNUS. He waits without.

CÆSAR. Ho there! admit Pothinus.

Pothinus appears in the loggia, and comes down the hall very haughtily to Cæsar's left hand.

CÆSAR. Well, Pothinus?

POTHINUS. I have brought you our ultimatum, Cæsar.

CÆSAR. Ultimatum! The door was open: you should have gone out through it before you declared war. You are my prisoner now. [*He goes to the chair and loosens his toga*].

POTHINUS [*scornfully*] I y o u r prisoner! Do you know that you are in Alexandria, and that King Ptolemy, with an army outnumbering your little troop a hundred to one, is in possession of Alexandria?

CÆSAR [*unconcernedly taking off his toga and throwing it on the chair*] Well, my friend, get out if you can. And tell your friends not to kill any more Romans in the market place. Otherwise my soldiers, who do not share my celebrated clemency, will probably kill you. Britannus: pass the word to the guard; and fetch my armor. [*Britannus runs out. Rufio returns*]. Well?

RUFIO [*pointing from the loggia to a cloud of smoke drifting over the harbor*] See there! [*Pothinus runs eagerly up the steps to look out*].

CÆSAR. What, ablaze already! Impossible!

RUFIO. Yes, five good ships, and a barge laden with oil grappled to each. But it is not my doing: the Egyptians have saved me the trouble. They have captured the west harbor.

CÆSAR [*anxiously*] And the east harbor? The lighthouse, Rufio?

RUFIO [*with a sudden splutter of raging ill usage, coming down to Cæsar and scolding him*] Can I embark a legion in five minutes? The first cohort is already on the beach. We can do no more. If you want faster work, come and do it yourself.

CÆSAR [*soothing him*] Good, good. Patience, Rufio, patience.

RUFIO. Patience! Who is impatient here, you or I? Would I be here, if I could not oversee them from that balcony?

CÆSAR. Forgive me, Rufio; and [*anxiously*] hurry them as much as—

He is interrupted by an outcry as of an old man in the extremity of misfortune. It draws near rapidly; and Theodotus rushes in, tearing his hair, and squeaking the most lamentable exclamations. Rufio steps back to stare at him, amazed at his frantic condition. Pothinus turns to listen.

THEODOTUS [*on the steps, with uplifted arms*] Horror unspeakable! Woe, alas! Help!

RUFIO. What now?

CÆSAR [*frowning*] Who is slain?

THEODOTUS. Slain! Oh, worse than the death of ten thousand men! Loss irreparable to mankind.

RUFIO. What has happened, man?

THEODOTUS [*rushing down the hall between them*] The fire has spread from your ships. The first of the seven wonders of the world perishes. The library of Alexandria is in flames.

RUFIO. Psha! [*Quite relieved, he goes up to the loggia and watches the preparations of the troops on the beach*].

CÆSAR. Is that all?

THEODOTUS [*unable to believe his senses*] All! Cæsar: will you go down to posterity as a barbarous soldier too ignorant to know the value of books?

CÆSAR. Theodotus: I am an author myself; and I tell you it is better that the Egyptians should live their lives than dream them away with the help of books.

THEODOTUS [*kneeling, with genuine literary emotion: the passion of the pedant*] Cæsar: once in ten generations of men, the world gains an immortal book.

CÆSAR [*inflexible*] If it did not flatter mankind, the common executioner would burn it.

THEODOTUS. Without history, death will lay you beside your meanest soldier.

CÆSAR. Death will do that in any case. I ask no better grave.

THEODOTUS. What is burning there is the memory of mankind.

CÆSAR. A shameful memory. Let it burn.

THEODOTUS [*wildly*] Will you destroy the past?

CÆSAR. Ay, and build the future with its ruins. [*Theodotus, in despair, strikes himself on the temples with his fists*]. But harken, Theodotus, teacher of kings: you who valued Pompey's head no more than a shepherd values an onion, and who now kneel to me, with tears in your old eyes, to plead for a few sheepskins scrawled with errors. I cannot spare you a man or a bucket of water just now; but you shall pass freely out of the palace. Now, away with you to Achillas; and borrow his legions to put out the fire. [*He hurries him to the steps*].

POTHINUS [*significantly*] You understand, Theodotus: I remain a prisoner.

THEODOTUS. A prisoner!

CÆSAR. Will you stay to talk whilst the memory of mankind is burning? [*Calling through the loggia*] Ho there! Pass Theodotus out. [*To Theodotus*] Away with you.

THEODOTUS [*to Pothinus*] I must go to save the library. [*He hurries out*].

CÆSAR. Follow him to the gate, Pothinus. Bid him urge your people to kill no more of my soldiers, for your sake.

POTHINUS. My life will cost you dear if you take it, Cæsar. [*He goes out after Theodotus*].

Rufio, absorbed in watching the embarkation, does not notice the departure of the two Egyptians.

RUFIO [*shouting from the loggia to the beach*] All ready, there?

A CENTURION [*from below*] All ready. We wait for Cæsar.

CÆSAR. Tell them Cæsar is coming—the rogues! [*Calling*] Britannicus. [*This magniloquent version of his secretary's name is one of Cæsar's jokes. In later years it would have meant, quite seriously and officially, Conqueror of Britain*].

RUFIO [*calling down*] Push off, all except the longboat. Stand by it to embark, Cæsar's guard there. [*He leaves the balcony and comes down into the hall*]. Where are those Egyptians? Is this more clemency? Have you let them go?

CÆSAR [*chuckling*] I have let Theodotus go to save the library. We must respect literature, Rufio.

RUFIO [*raging*] Folly on folly's head! I believe if you could bring back all the dead of Spain, Gaul, and Thessaly to life, you would do it that we might have the trouble of fighting them over again.

CÆSAR. Might not the gods destroy the world if their only thought were to be at peace next year? [*Rufio, out of all patience, turns away in anger. Cæsar suddenly grips his sleeve, and adds slyly in his ear*] Besides, my friend: every Egyptian we imprison means imprisoning two Roman soldiers to guard him. Eh?

RUFIO. Agh! I might have known there was some fox's trick behind your fine talking. [*He gets away from Cæsar with an ill-humored shrug, and goes to the balcony for another look at the preparations; finally goes out*].

CÆSAR. Is Britannus asleep? I sent him for my armor an hour ago. [*Calling*] Britannicus, thou British islander. Britannicus!

Cleopatra runs in through the loggia with Cæsar's helmet and sword, snatched from Britannus, who follows her with a cuirass and greaves. They come down to Cæsar, she to his left hand, Britannus to his right.

CLEOPATRA. I am going to dress you, Cæsar. Sit down. [*He obeys*]. These Roman helmets are so becoming! [*She takes off his wreath*]. Oh! [*She bursts out laughing at him*].

CÆSAR. What are you laughing at?

CLEOPATRA. Youre bald [*beginning with a big B, and ending with a splutter*].

CÆSAR [*almost annoyed*] Cleopatra! [*He rises, for the convenience of Britannus, who puts the cuirass on him*].

CLEOPATRA. So that is why you wear the wreath—to hide it.

BRITANNUS. Peace, Egyptian: they are the bays of the conqueror. [*He buckles the cuirass*].

CLEOPATRA. Peace, thou: islander! [*To Cæsar*] You should rub your head with strong spirits of sugar, Cæsar. That will make it grow.

CÆSAR [*with a wry face*] Cleopatra: do you like to be reminded that you are very young.

CLEOPATRA [*pouting*] No.

CÆSAR [*sitting down again, and setting out his leg for Britannus, who kneels to put on his greaves*] Neither do I like to be reminded that I am—middle aged. Let me give you ten of my superfluous years. That will make you 26, and leave me only—no matter. Is it a bargain?

CLEOPATRA. Agreed. 26, mind. [*She puts the helmet on him*]. Oh! How nice! You look only about 50 in it!

BRITANNUS [*looking up severely at Cleopatra*] You must not speak in this manner to Cæsar.

CLEOPATRA. Is it true that when Cæsar caught you on that island, you were painted all over blue?

BRITANNUS. Blue is the color worn by all Britons of good standing. In war we stain our bodies blue; so that though our enemies may strip us of our clothes and our lives, they cannot strip us of our respectability. [*He rises*].

CLEOPATRA [*with Cæsar's sword*] Let me hang this on. Now you look splendid. Have they made any statues of you in Rome?

CÆSAR. Yes, many statues.

CLEOPATRA. You must send for one and give it to me.

RUFIO [*coming back into the loggia, more impatient than ever*] Now Cæsar: have you done

talking? The moment your foot is aboard there will be no holding our men back: the boats will race one another for the lighthouse.

CÆSAR [*drawing his sword and trying the edge*] Is this well set today, Britannicus? At Pharsalia it was as blunt as a barrel-hoop.

BRITANNUS. It will split one of the Egyptian's hairs today, Cæsar. I have set it myself.

CLEOPATRA [*suddenly throwing her arms in terror round Cæsar*] Oh, you are not really going into battle to be killed?

CÆSAR. No, Cleopatra. No man goes to battle to be killed.

CLEOPATRA. But they do get killed. My sister's husband was killed in battle. You must not go. Let him go [*pointing to Rufio. They all laugh at her*]. Oh please, please dont go. What will happen to me if you never come back?

CÆSAR [*gravely*] Are you afraid?

CLEOPATRA [*shrinking*] No.

CÆSAR [*with quiet authority*] Go to the balcony; and you shall see us take the Pharos. You must learn to look on battles. Go. [*She goes, downcast, and looks out from the balcony*]. That is well. Now, Rufio. March.

CLEOPATRA [*suddenly clapping her hands*] Oh, you will not be able to go!

CÆSAR. Why? What now?

CLEOPATRA. They are drying up the harbor with buckets—a multitude of soldiers—over there [*pointing out across the sea to her left*]— they are dipping up the water.

RUFIO [*hastening to look*] It is true. The Egyptian army! Crawling over the edge of the west harbor like locusts. [*With sudden anger he strides down to Cæsar*]. This is your accursed clemency, Cæsar. Theodotus has brought them.

CÆSAR [*delighted at his own cleverness*] I meant him to, Rufio. They have come to put out the fire. The library will keep them busy whilst we seize the lighthouse. Eh? [*He rushes out buoyantly through the loggia, followed by Britannus*].

RUFIO [*disgustedly*] More foxing! Agh! [*He rushes off. A shout from the soldiers announces the appearance of Cæsar below*].

CENTURION [*below*] All aboard. Give way there. [*Another shout*].

CLEOPATRA [*waving her scarf through the loggia arch*] Goodbye, goodbye, dear Cæsar. Come back safe. Goodbye!

ACT III

The edge of the quay in front of the palace, looking out west over the east harbor of Alexandria to Pharos island, just off the end of which, and connected with it by a narrow mole, is the famous lighthouse, a gigantic square tower of white marble diminishing in size storey by storey to the top, on which stands a cresset beacon. The island is joined to the main land by the Heptastadium, a great mole or causeway five miles long bounding the harbor on the south.

In the middle of the quay a Roman sentinel stands on guard, pilum in hand, looking out to the lighthouse with strained attention, his left hand shading his eyes. The pilum is a stout wooden shaft 4½ feet long, with an iron spit about three feet long fixed in it. The sentinel is so absorbed that he does not notice the approach from the north end of the quay of four Egyptian market porters carrying rolls of carpet, preceded by Ftatateeta and Apollodorus the Sicilian. Apollodorus is a dashing young man of about 24, handsome and debonair, dressed with deliberate æstheticism in the most delicate purples and dove greys, with ornaments of bronze, oxydized silver, and stones of jade and agate. His sword, designed as carefully as a medieval cross, has a blued blade shewing through an openwork scabbard of purple leather and filagree. The porters, conducted by Ftatateeta, pass along the quay behind the sentinel to the steps of the palace, where they put down their bales and squat on the ground. Apollodorus does not pass along with them: he halts, amused by the preoccupation of the sentinel.

APOLLODORUS [*calling to the sentinel*] Who goes there, eh?

SENTINEL [*starting violently and turning with his pilum at the charge, revealing himself as a small, wiry, sandy-haired, conscientious young man with an elderly face*] Whats this? Stand. Who are you?

APOLLODORUS. I am Apollodorus the Sicilian. Why, man, what are you dreaming of? Since I came through the lines beyond the theatre there, I have brought my caravan past three sentinels, all so busy staring at the lighthouse that not one of them challenged me. Is this Roman discipline?

SENTINEL. We are not here to watch the land but the sea. Cæsar has just landed on the Pharos. [*Looking at Ftatateeta*] What have you here? Who is this piece of Egyptian crockery?

FTATATEETA. Apollodorus: rebuke this Roman dog; and bid him bridle his tongue in the presence of Ftatateeta, the mistress of the Queen's household.

APOLLODORUS. My friend: this is a great lady who stands high with Cæsar.

SENTINEL [*not at all impressed, pointing to the carpets*] And what is all this truck?

APOLLODORUS. Carpets for the furnishing of the Queen's apartments in the palace. I have picked them from the best carpets in the world; and the Queen shall choose the best of my choosing.

SENTINEL. So you are the carpet merchant?

APOLLODORUS [*hurt*] My friend: I am a patrician.

SENTINEL. A patrician! A patrician keeping a shop instead of following arms!

APOLLODORUS. I do not keep a shop. Mine is a temple of the arts. I am a worshipper of beauty. My calling is to choose beautiful things for beautiful queens. My motto is Art for Art's sake.

SENTINEL. That is not the password.

APOLLODORUS. It is a universal password.

SENTINEL. I know nothing about universal passwords. Either give me the password for the day or get back to your shop.

Ftatateeta, roused by his hostile tone, steals towards the edge of the quay with the step of a panther, and gets behind him.

APOLLODORUS. How if I do neither?

SENTINEL. Then I will drive this pilum through you.

APOLLODORUS. At your service, my friend. [*He draws his sword, and springs to his guard with unruffled grace*].

FTATATEETA [*suddenly seizing the sentinel's arms from behind*] Thrust your knife into the dog's throat, Apollodorus. [*The chivalrous Apollodorus laughingly shakes his head; breaks ground away from the sentinel towards the palace; and lowers his point*].

SENTINEL [*struggling vainly*] Curse on you! Let me go. Help ho!

FTATATEETA [*lifting him from the ground*] Stab the little Roman reptile. Spit him on your sword.

A couple of Roman soldiers, with a centurion, come running along the edge of the quay from the north end. They rescue their comrade, and throw off Ftatateeta, who is sent reeling away on the left hand of the sentinel.

CENTURION [*an unattractive man of fifty, short in his speech and manners, with a vinewood cudgel in his hand*] How now? What is all this?

FTATATEETA [to Apollodorus] Why did you not stab him? There was time!

APOLLODORUS. Centurion: I am here by order of the Queen to—

CENTURION [interrupting him] The Queen! Yes, yes: [to the sentinel] pass him in. Pass all these bazaar people in to the Queen, with their goods. But mind you pass no one out that you have not passed in—not even the Queen herself.

SENTINEL. This old woman is dangerous: she is as strong as three men. She wanted the merchant to stab me.

APOLLODORUS. Centurion: I am not a merchant. I am a patrician and a votary of art.

CENTURION. Is the woman your wife?

APOLLODORUS [horrified] No, no! [Correcting himself politely] Not that the lady is not a striking figure in her own way. But [emphatically] she is not my wife.

FTATATEETA [to the centurion] Roman: I am Ftatateeta, the mistress of the Queen's household.

CENTURION. Keep your hands off our men, mistress; or I will have you pitched into the harbor, though you were as strong as ten men. [To his men] To your posts: march! [He returns with his men the way they came].

FTATATEETA [looking malignantly after him] We shall see whom Isis loves best: her servant Ftatateeta or a dog of a Roman.

SENTINEL [to Apollodorus, with a wave of his pilum towards the palace] Pass in there; and keep your distance. [Turning to Ftatateeta] Come within a yard of me, you old crocodile; and I will give you this [the pilum] in your jaws.

CLEOPATRA [calling from the palace] Ftatateeta, Ftatateeta.

FTATATEETA [looking up, scandalized] Go from the window, go from the window. There are men here.

CLEOPATRA. I am coming down.

FTATATEETA [distracted] No, no. What are you dreaming of? O ye gods, ye gods! Apollodorus: bid your men pick up your bales; and in with me quickly.

APOLLODORUS. Obey the mistress of the Queen's household.

FTATATEETA [impatiently, as the porters stoop to lift the bales] Quick, quick: she will be out upon us. [Cleopatra comes from the palace and runs across the quay to Ftatateeta]. Oh that ever I was born!

CLEOPATRA [eagerly] Ftatateeta: I have thought of something. I want a boat—at once.

FTATATEETA. A boat! No, no: you cannot. Apollodorus: speak to the queen.

APOLLODORUS [gallantly] Beautiful queen: I am Apollodorus the Sicilian, your servant, from the bazaar. I have brought you the three most beautiful Persian carpets in the world to choose from.

CLEOPATRA. I have no time for carpets today. Get me a boat.

FTATATEETA. What whim is this? You cannot go on the water except in the royal barge.

APOLLODORUS. Royalty, Ftatateeta, lies not in the barge but in the Queen. [To Cleopatra] The touch of your majesty's foot on the gunwale of the meanest boat in the harbor will make it royal. [He turns to the harbor and calls seaward] Ho there, boatman! Pull in to the steps.

CLEOPATRA. Apollodorus: you are my perfect knight; and I will always buy my carpets through you. [Apollodorus bows joyously. An oar appears above the quay; and the boatman, a bullet-headed, vivacious, grinning fellow, burnt almost black by the sun, comes up a flight of steps from the water on the sentinel's right, oar in hand, and waits at the top]. Can you row, Apollodorus?

APOLLODORUS. My oars shall be your majesty's wings. Whither shall I row my Queen?

CLEOPATRA. To the lighthouse. Come. [She makes for the steps].

SENTINEL [opposing her with his pilum at the charge] Stand. You cannot pass.

CLEOPATRA [flushing angrily] How dare you? Do you know that I am the Queen?

SENTINEL. I have my orders. You cannot pass.

CLEOPATRA. I will make Cæsar have you killed if you do not obey me.

SENTINEL. He will do worse to me if I disobey my officer. Stand back.

CLEOPATRA. Ftatateeta: strangle him.

SENTINEL [alarmed—looking apprehensively at Ftatateeta, and brandishing his pilum] Keep off, there.

CLEOPATRA [running to Apollodorus] Apollodorus: make your slaves help us.

APOLLODORUS. I shall not need their help, lady. [He draws his sword]. Now, soldier: choose which weapon you will defend yourself with. Shall it be sword against pilum, or sword against sword?

SENTINEL. Roman against Sicilian, curse you. Take that. [*He hurls his pilum at Apollodorus, who drops expertly on one knee. The pilum passes whizzing over his head and falls harmless. Apollodorus, with a cry of triumph, springs up and attacks the sentinel, who draws his sword and defends himself, crying*] Ho there, guard. Help!

Cleopatra, half frightened, half delighted, takes refuge near the palace, where the porters are squatting among the bales. The boatman, alarmed, hurries down the steps out of harm's way, but stops, with his head just visible above the edge of the quay, to watch the fight. The sentinel is handicapped by his fear of an attack in the rear from Ftatateeta, His swordsmanship, which is of a rough and ready sort, is heavily taxed, as he has occasionally to strike at her to keep her off between a blow and a guard with Apollodorus. The centurion returns with several soldiers. Apollodorus springs back towards Cleopatra as this reinforcement confronts him.

CENTURION [*coming to the sentinel's right hand*] What is this? What now?

SENTINEL [*panting*] I could do well enough by myself if it werent for the old woman. Keep her off me: that is all the help I need.

CENTURION. Make your report, soldier. What has happened?

FTATATEETA. Centurion: he would have slain the Queen.

SENTINEL [*bluntly*] I would, sooner than let her pass. She wanted to take boat, and go— so she said—to the lighthouse. I stopped her, as I was ordered to; and she set this fellow on me. [*He goes to pick up his pilum and returns to his place with it*].

CENTURION [*turning to Cleopatra*] Cleopatra: I am loth to offend you; but without Cæsar's express order we dare not let you pass beyond the Roman lines.

APOLLODORUS. Well, Centurion; and has not the lighthouse been within the Roman lines since Cæsar landed there?

CLEOPATRA. Yes, yes. Answer that, if you can.

CENTURION [*to Apollodorus*] As for you, Apollodorus, you may thank the gods that you are not nailed to the palace door with a pilum for your meddling.

APOLLODORUS [*urbanely*] My military friend, I was not born to be slain by so ugly a weapon. When I fall, it will be [*holding up his sword*] by this white queen of arms, the only weapon fit for an artist. And now that you are convinced that we do not want to go beyond the lines, let me finish killing your sentinel and depart with the Queen.

CENTURION [*as the sentinel makes an angry demonstration*] Peace there, Cleopatra: I must abide by my orders, and not by the subtleties of this Sicilian. You must withdraw into the palace and examine your carpets there.

CLEOPATRA [*pouting*] I will not: I am the Queen. Cæsar does not speak to me as you do. Have Cæsar's centurions changed manners with his scullions?

CENTURION [*sulkily*] I do my duty. That is enough for me.

APOLLODORUS. Majesty: when a stupid man is doing something he is ashamed of, he always declares that it is his duty.

CENTURION [*angry*] Apollodorus—

APOLLODORUS [*interrupting him with defiant elegance*] I will make amends for that insult with my sword at fitting time and place. Who says artist, says duellist. [*To Cleopatra*] Hear my counsel, star of the east. Until word comes to these soldiers from Cæsar himself, you are a prisoner. Let me go to him with a message from you, and a present; and before the sun has stooped half way to the arms of the sea, I will bring you back Cæsar's order of release.

CENTURION [*sneering at him*] And you will sell the Queen the present, no doubt.

APOLLODORUS. Centurion: the Queen shall have from me, without payment, as the unforced tribute of Sicilian taste to Egyptian beauty, the richest of these carpets for her present to Cæsar.

CLEOPATRA [*exultantly, to the centurion*] Now you see what an ignorant common creature you are!

CENTURION [*curtly*] Well, a fool and his wares are soon parted. [*He turns to his men*]. Two more men to this post here: and see that no one leaves the palace but this man and his merchandize. If he draws his sword again inside the lines, kill him. To your posts. March.

He goes out, leaving two auxiliary sentinels with the other.

APOLLODORUS [*with polite goodfellowship*] My friends: will you not enter the palace and bury our quarrel in a bowl of wine? [*He takes out his purse, jingling the coins in it*]. The Queen has presents for you all.

SENTINEL [*very sulky*] You heard our orders. Get about your business.

FIRST AUXILIARY. Yes: you ought to know

better. Off with you.

SECOND AUXILIARY [*looking longingly at the purse—this sentinel is a hooknosed man, unlike his comrade, who is squab faced*] Do not tantalize a poor man.

APOLLODORUS [*to Cleopatra*] Pearl of Queens: the centurion is at hand; and the Roman soldier is incorruptible when his officer is looking. I must carry your word to Cæsar.

CLEOPATRA [*who has been meditating among the carpets*] Are these carpets very heavy?

APOLLODORUS. It matters not how heavy. There are plenty of porters.

CLEOPATRA. How do they put the carpets into boats? Do they throw them down?

APOLLODORUS. Not into small boats, majesty. It would sink them.

CLEOPATRA. Not into that man's boat, for instance? [*pointing to the boatman*].

APOLLODORUS. No. Too small.

CLEOPATRA. But you can take a carpet to Cæsar in it if I send one?

APOLLODORUS. Assuredly.

CLEOPATRA. And you will have it carried gently down the steps and take great care of it?

APOLLODORUS. Depend on me.

CLEOPATRA. Great, great care?

APOLLODORUS. More than of my own body.

CLEOPATRA. You will promise me not to let the porters drop it or throw it about?

APOLLODORUS. Place the most delicate glass goblet in the palace in the heart of the roll, Queen; and if it be broken, my head shall pay for it.

CLEOPATRA. Good. Come, Ftatateeta. [*Ftatateeta comes to her. Apollodorus offers to squire them into the palace*]. No, Apollodorus, you must not come. I will choose a carpet for myself. You must wait here. [*She runs into the palace*].

APOLLODORUS [*to the porters*] Follow this lady [*indicating Ftatateeta*]; and obey her.

The porters rise and take up their bales.

FTATATEETA [*addressing the porters as if they were vermin*] This way. And take your shoes off before you put your feet on those stairs.

She goes in, followed by the porters with the carpets. Meanwhile Apollodorus goes to the edge of the quay and looks out over the harbor. The sentinels keep their eyes on him malignantly.

APOLLODORUS [*addressing the sentinel*] My friend—

SENTINEL [*rudely*] Silence there.

FIRST AUXILIARY. Shut your muzzle, you.

SECOND AUXILIARY [*in a half whisper, glancing apprehensively towards the north end of the quay*] Cant you wait a bit?

APOLLODORUS. Patience, worthy three-headed donkey. [*They mutter ferociously; but he is not at all intimidated*]. Listen: were you set here to watch me, or to watch the Egyptians?

SENTINEL. We know our duty.

APOLLODORUS. Then why don't you do it? There is something going on over there [*pointing southwestward to the mole*].

SENTINEL [*sulkily*] I do not need to be told what to do by the like of you.

APOLLODORUS. Blockhead. [*He begins shouting*] Ho there, Centurion. Hoiho!

SENTINEL. Curse your meddling. [*Shouting*] Hoiho! Alarm! Alarm!

FIRST AND SECOND AUXILIARIES. Alarm! alarm! Hoiho!

The Centurion comes running in with his guard.

CENTURION. What now? Has the old woman attacked you again? [*Seeing Apollodorus*] Are you here still?

APOLLODORUS [*pointing as before*] See there. The Egyptians are moving. They are going to recapture the Pharos. They will attack by sea and land: by land along the great mole; by sea from the west harbor. Stir yourselves, my military friends: the hunt is up. [*A clangor of trumpets from several points along the quay*]. Aha! I told you so.

CENTURION [*quickly*] The two extra men pass the alarm to the south posts. One man keep guard here. The rest with me—quick.

The two auxiliary sentinels run off to the south. The centurion and his guard run off northward; and immediately afterwards the bucina sounds. The four porters come from the palace carrying a carpet, followed by Ftatateeta.

SENTINEL [*handling his pilum apprehensively*] You again! [*The porters stop*].

FTATATEETA. Peace, Roman fellow: you are now singlehanded. Apollodorus: this carpet is Cleopatra's present to Cæsar. It has rolled up in it ten precious goblets of the thinnest Iberian crystal, and a hundred eggs of the sacred blue pigeon. On your honor, let not one of them be broken.

APOLLODORUS. On my head be it! [*To the porters*] Into the boat with them carefully.

The porters carry the carpet to the steps.

FIRST PORTER [*looking down at the boat*] Beware what you do, sir. Those eggs of which the lady speaks must weigh more than a pound apiece. This boat is too small for such a load.

BOATMAN [*excitedly rushing up the steps*] Oh thou injurious porter! Oh thou unnatural son of a she-camel! [*To Apollodorus*] My boat, sir, hath often carried five men. Shall it not carry your lordship and a bale of pigeons' eggs? [*To the porter*] Thou mangey dromedary, the gods shall punish thee for this envious wickedness.

FIRST PORTER [*stolidly*] I cannot quit this bale now to beat thee; but another day I will lie in wait for thee.

APOLLODORUS [*going between them*] Peace there. If the boat were but a single plank, I would get to Cæsar on it.

FTATATEETA [*anxiously*] In the name of the gods, Apollodorus, run no risks with that bale.

APOLLODORUS. Fear not, thou venerable grotesque: I guess its great worth. [*To the porters*] Down with it, I say; and gently; or ye shall eat nothing but stick for ten days.

The boatman goes down the steps, followed by the porters with the bale: Ftatateeta and Apollodorus watching from the edge.

APOLLODORUS. Gently, my sons, my children— [*with sudden alarm*] gently, ye dogs. Lay it level in the stern—so—tis well.

FTATATEETA [*screaming down at one of the porters*] Do not step on it, do not step on it. Oh thou brute beast!

FIRST PORTER [*ascending*] Be not excited, mistress: all is well.

FTATATEETA [*panting*] All well! Oh, thou has given my heart a turn! [*She clutches her side, gasping*].

The four porters have now come up and are waiting at the stairhead to be paid.

APOLLODORUS. Here, ye hungry ones. [*He gives money to the first porter, who holds it in his hand to shew to the others. They crowd greedily to see how much it is, quite prepared, after the Eastern fashion, to protest to heaven against their patron's stinginess. But his liberality overpowers them*].

FIRST PORTER. O bounteous prince!

SECOND PORTER. O lord of the bazaar!

THIRD PORTER. O favored of the gods!

FOURTH PORTER. O father to all the porters of the market!

SENTINEL [*enviously, threatening them fiercely with his pilum*] Hence, dogs: off. Out of this. [*They fly before him northward along the quay*].

APOLLODORUS. Farewell, Ftatateeta. I shall be at the lighthouse before the Egyptians. [*He descends the steps*].

FTATATEETA. The gods speed thee and protect my nursling!

The sentry returns from chasing the porters and looks down at the boat, standing near the stairhead lest Ftatateeta should attempt to escape.

APOLLODORUS [*from beneath, as the boat moves off*] Farewell, valiant pilum pitcher.

SENTINEL. Farewell, shopkeeper.

APOLLODORUS. Ha, ha! Pull, thou brave boatman, pull. Soho-o-o-o-o! [*He begins to sing in barcarolle measure to the rhythm of the oars*]

My heart, my heart, spread out thy wings:
Shake off thy heavy load of love—

Give me the oars, O son of a snail.

SENTINEL [*threatening Ftatateeta*] Now mistress: back to your henhouse. In with you.

FTATATEETA [*falling on her knees and stretching her hands over the waters*] Gods of the seas, bear her safely to the shore!

SENTINEL. Bear who safely? What do you mean?

FTATATEETA [*looking darkly at him*] Gods of Egypt and of Vengeance, let this Roman fool be beaten like a dog by his captain for suffering her to be taken over the waters.

SENTINEL. Accursed one: is she then in the boat? [*He calls over the sea*] Hoiho, there, boatman! Hoiho!

APOLLODORUS [*singing in the distance*]

My heart, my heart, be whole and free:
Love is thine only enemy.

Meanwhile Rufio, the morning's fighting done, sits munching dates on a faggot of brushwood outside the door of the lighthouse, which towers gigantic to the clouds on his left. His helmet, full of dates, is between his knees; and a leathern bottle of wine is by his side. Behind him the great stone pedestal of the lighthouse is shut in from the open sea by a low stone parapet, with a couple of steps in the middle to the broad coping. A huge chain with a hook hangs down from the lighthouse crane above his head. Faggots like the one he sits on lie beneath it ready to be drawn up to feed the beacon.

Cæsar is standing on the step at the parapet looking out anxiously, evidently ill at ease. Britannus comes out of the lighthouse door.

RUFIO. Well, my British islander. Have you been up to the top?

BRITANNUS. I have. I reckon it at 200 feet high.

RUFIO. Anybody up there?

BRITANNUS. One elderly Tyrian to work the crane; and his son, a well conducted youth of 14.

RUFIO [looking at the chain] What! An old man and a boy work that! Twenty men, you mean.

BRITANNUS. Two only, I assure you. They have counterweights, and a machine with boiling water in it which I do not understand: it is not of British design. They use it to haul up barrels of oil and faggots to burn in the brazier on the roof.

RUFIO. But—

BRITANNUS. Excuse me: I came down because there are messengers coming along the mole to us from the island. I must see what their business is. [He hurries out past the lighthouse].

CÆSAR [coming away from the parapet, shivering and out of sorts] Rufio: this has been a mad expedition. We shall be beaten. I wish I knew how our men are getting on with that barricade across the great mole.

RUFIO [angrily] Must I leave my food and go starving to bring you a report?

CÆSAR [soothing him nervously] No, Rufio, no. Eat, my son, eat. [He takes another turn, Rufio chewing dates meanwhile]. The Egyptians cannot be such fools as not to storm the barricade and swoop down on us here before it is finished. It is the first time I have ever run an avoidable risk. I should not have come to Egypt.

RUFIO. An hour ago you were all for victory.

CÆSAR [apologetically] Yes: I was a fool—rash, Rufio—boyish.

RUFIO. Boyish! Not a bit of it. Here [offering him a handful of dates].

CÆSAR. What are these for?

RUFIO. To eat. Thats whats the matter with you. When a man comes to your age, he runs down before his midday meal. Eat and drink; and then have another look at our chances.

CÆSAR [taking the dates] My age! [He shakes his head and bites a date]. Yes, Rufio: I am an old man—worn out now—true, quite true. [He gives way to melancholy contemplation, and eats another date]. Achillas is still in his prime: Ptolemy is a boy. [He eats another date, and plucks up a little]. Well, every dog has his day; and I have had mine: I cannot complain. [With sudden cheerfulness] These dates are not bad, Rufio. [Britannus returns, greatly excited, with a leathern bag. Cæsar is himself again in a moment]. What now?

BRITANNUS [triumphantly] Our brave Rhodian mariners have captured a treasure. There! [He throws the bag down at Cæsar's feet]. Our enemies are delivered into our hands.

CÆSAR. In that bag?

BRITANNUS. Wait till you hear, Cæsar. This bag contains all the letters which have passed between Pompey's party and the army of occupation here.

CÆSAR. Well?

BRITANNUS [impatient of Cæsar's slowness to grasp the situation] Well, we shall now know who your foes are. The name of every man who has plotted against you since you crossed the Rubicon may be in these papers, for all we know.

CÆSAR. Put them in the fire.

BRITANNUS. Put them— [he gasps]!!!!

CÆSAR. In the fire. Would you have me waste the next three years of my life in proscribing and condemning men who will be my friends when I have proved that my friendship is worth more than Pompey's was—than Cato's is. O incorrigible British islander: am I a bull dog, to seek quarrels merely to shew how stubborn my jaws are?

BRITANNUS. But your honor—the honor of Rome—

CÆSAR. I do not make human sacrifices to my honor, as your Druids do. Since you will not burn these, at least I can drown them. [He picks up the bag and throws it over the parapet into the sea].

BRITANNUS. Cæsar: this is mere eccentricity. Are traitors to be allowed to go free for the sake of a paradox?

RUFIO [rising] Cæsar: when the islander has finished preaching, call me again. I am going to have a look at the boiling water machine. [He goes into the lighthouse].

BRITANNUS [with genuine feeling] O Cæsar, my great master, if I could but persuade you to regard life seriously, as men do in my country!

CÆSAR. Do they truly do so, Britannus?

BRITANNUS. Have you not been there? Have you not seen them? What Briton speaks as you do in your moments of levity? What Briton neglects to attend the services at the sacred grove? What Briton wears clothes of many colors as you do, instead of plain blue, as all solid, well esteemed men should? These are moral questions with us.

CÆSAR. Well, well, my friend: some day I shall settle down and have a blue toga, perhaps. Meanwhile, I must get on as best I can in my flippant Roman way. [*Apollodorus comes past the lighthouse*]. What now?

BRITANNUS [*turning quickly, and challenging the stranger with official haughtiness*] What is this? Who are you? How did you come here?

APOLLODORUS. Calm yourself, my friend: I am not going to eat you. I have come by boat, from Alexandria, with precious gifts for Cæsar.

CÆSAR. From Alexandria!

BRITANNUS [*severely*] That is Cæsar, sir.

RUFIO [*appearing at the lighthouse door*] Whats the matter now?

APOLLODORUS. Hail, great Cæsar! I am Apollodorus the Sicilian, an artist.

BRITANNUS. An artist! Why have they admitted this vagabond?

CÆSAR. Peace, man. Apollodorus is a famous patrician amateur.

BRITANNUS [*disconcerted*] I crave the gentleman's pardon. [*To Cæsar*] I understood him to say that he was a professional. [*Somewhat out of countenance, he allows Apollodorus to approach Cæsar, changing places with him. Rufio, after looking Apollodorus up and down with marked disparagement, goes to the other side of the platform*].

CÆSAR. You are welcome, Apollodorus. What is your business?

APOLLODORUS. First, to deliver to you a present from the Queen of Queens.

CÆSAR. Who is that?

APOLLODORUS. Cleopatra of Egypt.

CÆSAR [*taking him into his confidence in his most winning manner*] Apollodorus: this is no time for playing with presents. Pray you, go back to the Queen, and tell her that if all goes well I shall return to the palace this evening.

APOLLODORUS. Cæsar: I cannot return. As I approached the lighthouse, some fool threw a great leathern bag into the sea. It broke the nose of my boat; and I had hardly time to get myself and my charge to the shore before the poor little cockleshell sank.

CÆSAR. I am sorry, Apollodorus. The fool shall be rebuked. Well, well: what have you brought me? The Queen will be hurt if I do not look at it. 1

RUFIO. Have we time to waste on this trumpery? The Queen is only a child.

CÆSAR. Just so: that is why we must not disappoint her. What is the present, Apollodorus?

APOLLODORUS. Cæsar: it is a Persian carpet —a beauty! And in it are—so I am told— pigeons' eggs and crystal goblets and fragile precious things. I dare not for my head have it carried up that narrow ladder from the causeway.

RUFIO. Swing it up by the crane, then. We will send the eggs to the cook; drink our wine from the goblets; and the carpet will make a bed for Cæsar.

APOLLODORUS. The crane! Cæsar: I have sworn to tender this bale of carpet as I tender my own life.

CÆSAR [*cheerfully*] Then let them swing you up at the same time; and if the chain breaks, you and the pigeons' eggs will perish together. [*He goes to the chain and looks up along it, examining it curiously*].

APOLLODORUS [*to Britannus*] Is Cæsar serious?

BRITANNUS. His manner is frivolous because he is an Italian; but he means what he says.

APOLLODORUS. Serious or not, he spake well. Give me a squad of soldiers to work the crane.

BRITANNUS. Leave the crane to me. Go and await the descent of the chain.

APOLLODORUS. Good. You will presently see me there [*turning to them all and pointing with an eloquent gesture to the sky above the parapet*] rising like the sun with my treasure.

He goes back the way he came. Britannus goes into the lighthouse.

RUFIO [*ill-humoredly*] Are you really going to wait here for this foolery, Cæsar?

CÆSAR [*backing away from the crane as it gives signs of working*] Why not?

RUFIO. The Egyptians will let you know why not if they have the sense to make a rush from the shore end of the mole before our barricade is finished. And here we are waiting like children to see a carpet full of pigeons' eggs.

The chain rattles, and is drawn up high enough to clear the parapet. It then swings round out of sight behind the lighthouse.

CÆSAR. Fear not, my son Rufio. When the first Egyptian takes his first step along the mole, the alarm will sound; and we two will reach the barricade from our end before the Egyptians reach it from their end— we two, Rufio: I, the old man, and you, his biggest boy. And the old man will be there first. So peace; and give me some more dates.

APOLLODORUS [*from the causeway below*] Soho, haul away. So-ho-o-o-o! [*The chain is drawn up and comes round again from behind the lighthouse. Apollodorus is swinging in the air with his bale of carpet at the end of it. He breaks into song as he soars above the parapet*]

Aloft, aloft, behold the blue
That never shone in woman's eyes—

Easy there: stop her. [*He ceases to rise*]. Further round! [*The chain comes forward above the platform*].

RUFIO [*calling up*] Lower away there. [*The chain and its load begin to descend*].

APOLLODORUS [*calling up*] Gently—slowly— mind the eggs.

RUFIO [*calling up*] Easy there—slowly— slowly.

Apollodorus and the bale are deposited safely on the flags in the middle of the platform. Rufio and Cæsar help Apollodorus to cast off the chain from the bale.

RUFIO. Haul up.

The chain rises clear of their heads with a rattle. Britannus comes from the lighthouse and helps them to uncord the carpet.

APOLLODORUS [*when the cords are loose*] Stand off, my friends: let Cæsar see. [*He throws the carpet open*].

RUFIO. Nothing but a heap of shawls. Where are the pigeons' eggs?

APOLLODORUS. Approach, Cæsar; and search for them among the shawls.

RUFIO [*drawing his sword*] Ha, treachery! Keep back, Cæsar: I saw the shawl move: there is something alive there.

BRITANNUS [*drawing his sword*] It is a serpent.

APOLLODORUS. Dares Cæsar thrust his hand into the sack where the serpent moves?

RUFIO [*turning to him*] Treacherous dog—

CÆSAR. Peace. Put up your swords. Apollodorus: your serpent seems to breathe very regularly. [*He thrusts his hand under the shawls and draws out a bare arm*]. This is a pretty little snake.

RUFIO [*drawing out the other arm*] Let us have the rest of you.

They pull Cleopatra up by the wrists into a sitting position. Britannus, scandalized, sheathes his sword with a drive of protest.

CLEOPATRA [*gasping*] Oh, I'm smothered. Oh, Cæsar, a man stood on me in the boat; and a great sack of something fell upon me out of the sky; and then the boat sank; and

then I was swung up into the air and bumped down.

CÆSAR [*petting her as she rises and takes refuge on his breast*] Well, never mind: here you are safe and sound at last.

RUFIO. Ay; and now that she is here, what are we to do with her?

BRITANNUS. She cannot stay here, Cæsar, without the companionship of some matron.

CLEOPATRA [*jealously, to Cæsar, who is obviously perplexed*] Arnt you glad to see me?

CÆSAR. Yes, yes; I am very glad. But Rufio is very angry; and Britannus is shocked.

CLEOPATRA [*contemptuously*] You can have their heads cut off, can you not?

CÆSAR. They would not be so useful with their heads cut off as they are now, my sea bird.

RUFIO [*to Cleopatra*] We shall have to go away presently and cut some of your Egyptians' heads off. How will you like being left here with the chance of being captured by that little brother of yours if we are beaten?

CLEOPATRA. But you mustnt leave me alone. Cæsar: you will not leave me alone, will you?

RUFIO. What! not when the trumpet sounds and all our lives depend on Cæsar's being at the barricade before the Egyptians reach it? Eh?

CLEOPATRA. Let them lose their lives: they are only soldiers.

CÆSAR [*gravely*] Cleopatra: when that trumpet sounds, we must take every man his life in his hand, and throw it in the face of Death. And of my soldiers who have trusted me there is not one whose hand I shall not hold more sacred than your head. [*Cleopatra is overwhelmed. Her eyes fill with tears*]. Apollodorus: you must take her back to the palace.

APOLLODORUS. Am I a dolphin, Cæsar, to cross the seas with young ladies on my back? My boat is sunk: all yours are either at the barricade or have returned to the city. I will hail one if I can: that is all I can do. [*He goes back to the causeway*].

CLEOPATRA [*struggling with her tears*] It does not matter. I will not go back. Nobody cares for me.

CÆSAR. Cleopatra—

CLEOPATRA. You want me to be killed.

CÆSAR [*still more gravely*] My poor child: your life matters little here to anyone but yourself [*She gives way altogether at this, casting herself down on the faggots weeping. Sud-*

denly a great tumult is heard in the distance, bucinas and trumpets sounding through a storm of shouting. Britannus rushes to the parapet and looks along the mole. Cæsar and Rufio turn to one another with quick intelligence].

CÆSAR. Come, Rufio.

CLEOPATRA [*scrambling to her knees and clinging to him*] No, no. Do not leave me, Cæsar. [*He snatches his skirt from her clutch*]. Oh!

BRITANNUS [*from the parapet*] Cæsar: we are cut off. The Egyptians have landed from the west harbor between us and the barricade!!!

RUFIO [*running to see*] Curses! It is true. We are caught like rats in a trap.

CÆSAR [*ruthfully*] Rufio, Rufio: my men at the barricade are between the sea party and the shore party. I have murdered them.

RUFIO [*coming back from the parapet to Cæsar's right hand*] Ay: that comes of fooling with this girl here.

APOLLODORUS [*coming up quickly from the causeway*] Look over the parapet, Cæsar.

CÆSAR. We have looked, my friend. We must defend ourselves here.

APOLLODORUS. I have thrown the ladder into the sea. They cannot get in without it.

RUFIO. Ay; and we cannot get out. Have you thought of that?

APOLLODORUS. Not get out! Why not? You have ships in the east harbor.

BRITANNUS [*hopefully, at the parapet*] The Rhodian galleys are standing in towards us already. [*Cæsar quickly joins Britannus at the parapet*].

RUFIO [*to Apollodorus, impatiently*] And by what road are we to walk to the galleys, pray?

APOLLODORUS [*with gay, defiant rhetoric*] By the road that leads everywhere—the diamond path of the sun and moon. Have you never seen the child's shadow play of The Broken Bridge? "Ducks and geese with ease get over"—eh? [*He throws away his cloak and cap, and binds his sword on his back*].

RUFIO. What are you talking about?

APOLLODORUS. I will shew you. [*Calling to Britannus*] How far off is the nearest galley?

BRITANNUS. Fifty fathom.

CÆSAR. No, no: they are further off than they seem in this clear air to your British eyes. Nearly quarter of a mile, Apollodorus.

APOLLODORUS. Good. Defend yourselves here until I send you a boat from that galley.

RUFIO. Have you wings, perhaps?

APOLLODORUS. Water wings, soldier. Behold!

He runs up the steps between Cæsar and Britannus to the coping of the parapet; springs into the air; and plunges head foremost into the sea.

CÆSAR [*like a schoolboy—wildly excited*] Bravo, bravo! [*Throwing off his cloak*] By Jupiter, I will do that too.

RUFIO [*seizing him*] You are mad. You shall not.

CÆSAR. Why not? Can I not swim as well as he?

RUFIO [*frantic*] Can an old fool dive and swim like a young one? He is twenty-five and you are fifty.

CÆSAR [*breaking loose from Rufio*] Old!!!

BRITANNUS [*shocked*] Rufio: you forget yourself.

CÆSAR. I will race you to the galley for a week's pay, father Rufio.

CLEOPATRA. But me! me!! me!!! what is to become of me?

CÆSAR. I will carry you on my back to the galley like a dolphin. Rufio: when you see me rise to the surface, throw her in: I will answer for her. And then in with you after her, both of you.

CLEOPATRA. No, no, NO. I shall be drowned.

BRITANNUS. Cæsar: I am a man and a Briton, not a fish. I must have a boat. I cannot swim.

CLEOPATRA. Neither can I.

CÆSAR [*to Britannus*] Stay here, then, alone, until I recapture the lighthouse: I will not forget you. Now, Rufio.

RUFIO. You have made up your mind to this folly?

CÆSAR. The Egyptians have made it up for me. What else is there to do? And mind where you jump: I do not want to get your fourteen stone in the small of my back as I come up. [*He runs up the steps and stands on the coping*].

BRITANNUS [*anxiously*] One last word, Cæsar. Do not let yourself be seen in the fashionable part of Alexandria until you have changed your clothes.

CÆSAR [*calling over the sea*] Ho, Apollodorus: [*he points skyward and quotes the barcarolle*]

The white upon the blue above—

APOLLODORUS [*swimming in the distance*]

Is purple on the green below—

CÆSAR [*exultantly*] Aha! [*He plunges into the sea*].

CLEOPATRA [*running excitedly to the steps*] Oh,

let me see. He will be drowned [*Rufio seizes her*]—Ah—ah—ah—ah! [*He pitches her screaming into the sea. Rufio and Britannus roar with laughter*].

RUFIO [*looking down after her*] He has got her. [*To Britannus*] Hold the fort, Briton. Cæsar will not forget you. [*He springs off*].

BRITANNUS [*running to the steps to watch them as they swim*] All safe, Rufio?

RUFIO [*swimming*] All safe.

CÆSAR [*swimming further off*] Take refuge up there by the beacon; and pile the fuel on the trap door, Britannus.

BRITANNUS [*calling in reply*] I will first do so, and then commend myself to my country's gods. [*A sound of cheering from the sea. Britannus gives full vent to his excitement*]. The boat has reached him: Hip, hip, hip, hurrah!

ACT IV

Cleopatra's sousing in the east harbor of Alexandria was in October 48 b.c. In March 47 she is passing the afternoon in her boudoir in the palace, among a bevy of her ladies, listening to a slave girl who is playing the harp in the middle of the room. The harpist's master, an old musician, with a lined face, prominent brows, white beard, moustache and eyebrows twisted and horned at the ends, and a consciously keen and pretentious expression, is squatting on the floor close to her on her right, watching her performance. Ftatateeta is in attendance near the door, in front of a group of female slaves. Except the harp player all are seated: Cleopatra in a chair opposite the door on the other side of the room; the rest on the ground. Cleopatra's ladies are all young, the most conspicuous being Charmian and Iras, her favorites. Charmian is a hatchet faced, terra cotta colored little goblin, swift in her movements, and neatly finished at the hands and feet. Iras is a plump, goodnatured creature, rather fatuous, with a profusion of red hair, and a tendency to giggle on the slightest provocation.

CLEOPATRA. Can I—

FTATATEETA [*insolently, to the player*] Peace, thou! The Queen speaks. [*The player stops*].

CLEOPATRA [*to the old musician*] I want to learn to play the harp with my own hands. Cæsar loves music. Can you teach me?

MUSICIAN. Assuredly I and no one else can teach the queen. Have I not discovered the lost method of the ancient Egyptians, who could make a pyramid tremble by touching a bass string? All the other teachers are

quacks: I have exposed them repeatedly.

CLEOPATRA. Good: you shall teach me. How long will it take?

MUSICIAN. Not very long: only four years. Your Majesty must first become proficient in the philosophy of Pythagoras.

CLEOPATRA. Has she [*indicating the slave*] become proficient in the philosophy of Pythagoras?

MUSICIAN. Oh, she is but a slave. She learns as a dog learns.

CLEOPATRA. Well, then, I will learn as a dog learns; for she plays better than you. You shall give me a lesson every day for a fortnight. [*The musician hastily scrambles to his feet and bows profoundly*]. After that, whenever I strike a false note you shall be flogged; and if I strike so many that there is not time to flog you, you shall be thrown into the Nile to feed the crocodiles. Give the girl a piece of gold; and send them away.

MUSICIAN [*much taken aback*] But true art will not be thus forced.

FTATATEETA [*pushing him out*] What is this? Answering the Queen, forsooth. Out with you.

He is pushed out by Ftatateeta, the girl following with her harp, amid the laughter of the ladies and slaves.

CLEOPATRA. Now, can any of you amuse me? Have you any stories or any news?

IRAS. Ftatateeta—

CLEOPATRA. Oh, Ftatateeta, Ftatateeta, always Ftatateeta. Some new tale to set me against her.

IRAS. No: this time Ftatateeta has been virtuous. [*All the ladies laugh—not the slaves*]. Pothinus has been trying to bribe her to let him speak with you.

CLEOPATRA [*wrathfully*] Ha! you all sell audiences with me, as if I saw whom you please, and not whom I please. I should like to know how much of her gold piece that harp girl will have to give up before she leaves the palace.

IRAS. We can easily find out that for you. *The ladies laugh.*

CLEOPATRA [*frowning*] You laugh; but take care, take care. I will find out some day how to make myself served as Cæsar is served.

CHARMIAN. Old hooknose! [*They laugh again*].

CLEOPATRA [*revolted*] Silence. Charmian: do not you be a silly little Egyptian fool. Do you know why I allow you all to chatter impertinently just as you please, instead of treating you as Ftatateeta would treat you if she were Queen?

CHARMIAN. Because you try to imitate Cæsar in everything; and he lets everybody say what they please to him.

CLEOPATRA. No; but because I asked him one day why he did so; and he said "Let your women talk; and you will learn something from them." What have I to learn from them? I said. "What they are," said he; and oh! you should have seen his eye as he said it. You would have curled up, you shallow things. [*They laugh. She turns fiercely on Iras*]. At whom are you laughing—at me or at Cæsar?

IRAS. At Cæsar.

CLEOPATRA. If you were not a fool, you would laugh at me; and if you were not a coward you would not be afraid to tell me so. [*Ftatateeta returns*]. Ftatateeta: they tell me that Pothinus has offered you a bribe to admit him to my presence.

FTATATEETA [*protesting*] Now by my father's gods—

CLEOPATRA [*cutting her short despotically*] Have I not told you not to deny things? You would spend the day calling your father's gods to witness to your virtues if I let you. Go take the bribe; and bring in Pothinus. [*Ftatateeta is about to reply*]. Dont answer me. Go.

Ftatateeta goes out; and Cleopatra rises and begins to prowl to and fro between her chair and the door, meditating. All rise and stand.

IRAS [*as she reluctantly rises*] Heigho! I wish Cæsar were back in Rome.

CLEOPATRA [*threateningly*] It will be a bad day for you all when he goes. Oh, if I were not ashamed to let him see that I am as cruel at heart as my father, I would make you repent that speech! Why do you wish him away?

CHARMIAN. He makes you so terribly prosy and serious and learned and philosophical. It is worse than being religious, at our ages. [*The ladies laugh*].

CLEOPATRA. Cease that endless cackling, will you. Hold your tongues.

CHARMIAN [*with mock resignation*] Well, well: we must try to live up to Cæsar.

They laugh again. Cleopatra rages silently as she continues to prowl to and fro. Ftatateeta comes back with Pothinus, who halts on the threshold.

FTATATEETA [*at the door*] Pothinus craves

the ear of the—

CLEOPATRA. There, there: that will do: let him come in. [*She resumes her seat. All sit down except Pothinus, who advances to the middle of the room. Ftatateeta takes her former place*]. Well, Pothinus: what is the latest news from your rebel friends?

POTHINUS [*haughtily*] I am no friend of rebellion. And a prisoner does not receive news.

CLEOPATRA. You are no more a prisoner than I am—than Cæsar is. These six months we have been besieged in this palace by my subjects. You are allowed to walk on the beach among the soldiers. Can I go further myself, or can Cæsar?

POTHINUS. You are but a child, Cleopatra, and do not understand these matters.

The ladies laugh. Cleopatra looks inscrutably at him.

CHARMIAN. I see you do not know the latest news, Pothinus.

POTHINUS. What is that?

CHARMIAN. That Cleopatra is no longer a child. Shall I tell you how to grow much older, and much, much wiser in one day?

POTHINUS. I should prefer to grow wiser without growing older.

CHARMIAN. Well, go up to the top of the lighthouse; and get somebody to take you by the hair and throw you into the sea. [*The ladies laugh*].

CLEOPATRA. She is right, Pothinus: you will come to the shore with much conceit washed out of you. [*The ladies laugh. Cleopatra rises impatiently*]. Begone, all of you. I will speak with Pothinus alone. Drive them out, Ftatateeta. [*They run out laughing. Ftatateeta shuts the door on them*]. What are you waiting for?

FTATATEETA. It is not meet that the Queen remain alone with—

CLEOPATRA [*interrupting her*] Ftatateeta: must I sacrifice you to your father's gods to teach you that I am Queen of Egypt, and not you?

FTATATEETA [*indignantly*] You are like the rest of them. You want to be what these Romans call a New Woman. [*She goes out, banging the door*].

CLEOPATRA [*sitting down again*] Now, Pothinus: why did you bribe Ftatateeta to bring you hither?

POTHINUS [*studying her gravely*] Cleopatra: what they tell me is true. You are changed.

CLEOPATRA. Do you speak with Cæsar every

day for six months: and y o u will be changed.

POTHINUS. It is the common talk that you are infatuated with this old man?

CLEOPATRA. Infatuated? What does that mean? Made foolish, is it not? Oh no: I wish I were.

POTHINUS. You wish you were made foolish! How so?

CLEOPATRA. When I was foolish, I did what I liked, except when Ftatateeta beat me; and even then I cheated her and did it by stealth. Now that Cæsar has made me wise, it is no use my liking or disliking: I do what must be done, and have no time to attend to myself. That is not happiness; but it is greatness. If Cæsar were gone, I think I could govern the Egyptians; for what Cæsar is to me, I am to the fools around me.

POTHINUS [looking hard at her] Cleopatra: this may be the vanity of youth.

CLEOPATRA. No, no: it is not that I am so clever, but that the others are so stupid.

POTHINUS [musingly] Truly, that is the great secret.

CLEOPATRA. Well, now tell me what you came to say?

POTHINUS [embarrassed] I! Nothing.

CLEOPATRA. Nothing!

POTHINUS. At least—to beg for my liberty: that is all.

CLEOPATRA. For that you would have knelt to Cæsar. No, Pothinus: you came with some plan that depended on Cleopatra being a little nursery kitten. Now that Cleopatra is a Queen, the plan is upset.

POTHINUS [bowing his head submissively] It is so.

CLEOPATRA [exultant] Aha!

POTHINUS [raising his eyes keenly to hers] Is Cleopatra then indeed a Queen, and no longer Cæsar's prisoner and slave?

CLEOPATRA. Pothinus: we are all Cæsar's slaves—all we in this land of Egypt—whether we will or no. And she who is wise enough to know this will reign when Cæsar departs.

POTHINUS. You harp on Cæsar's departure.

CLEOPATRA. What if I do?

POTHINUS. Does he not love you?

CLEOPATRA. Love me! Pothinus: Cæsar loves no one. Who are those we love. Only those whom we do not hate: all people are strangers and enemies to us except those we love. But it is not so with Cæsar. H e has no hatred in him: he makes friends with everyone as he does with dogs and children. His kindness

to me is a wonder: neither mother, father, nor nurse have ever taken so much care for me, or thrown open their thoughts to me so freely.

POTHINUS. Well: is not this love?

CLEOPATRA. What! when he will do as much for the first girl he meets on his way back to Rome? Ask his slave, Britannus: he has been just as good to him. Nay, ask his very horse! His kindness is not for anything in m e: it is in his own nature.

POTHINUS. But how can you be sure that he does not love you as men love women?

CLEOPATRA. Because I cannot make him jealous. I have tried.

POTHINUS. Hm! Perhaps I should have asked, then, do y o u love h i m?

CLEOPATRA. Can one love a god? Besides, I love another Roman: one whom I saw long before Cæsar—no god, but a man—one who can love and hate—one whom I can hurt and who would hurt me.

POTHINUS. Does Cæsar know this?

CLEOPATRA. Yes.

POTHINUS. And he is not angry?

CLEOPATRA. He promises to send him to Egypt to please me!

POTHINUS. I do not understand this man.

CLEOPATRA [with superb contempt] You understand Cæsar! How could you? [Proudly] I do—by instinct.

POTHINUS [deferentially, after a moment's thought] Your Majesty caused me to be admitted today. What message has the Queen for me?

CLEOPATRA. This. You think that by making my brother king, you will rule in Egypt, because you are his guardian and he is a little silly.

POTHINUS. The Queen is pleased to say so.

CLEOPATRA. The Queen is pleased to say this also. That Cæsar will eat up you, and Achillas, and my brother, as a cat eats up mice; and that he will put on this land of Egypt as a shepherd puts on his garment. And when he has done that, he will return to Rome, and leave Cleopatra here as his viceroy.

POTHINUS [breaking out wrathfully] That he shall never do. We have a thousand men to his ten; and we will drive him and his beggarly legions into the sea.

CLEOPATRA [with scorn, getting up to go] You rant like any common fellow. Go, then, and marshal your thousands; and make haste;

for Mithridates of Pergamos is at hand with reinforcements for Cæsar. Cæsar has held you at bay with two legions: we shall see what he will do with twenty.

POTHINUS. Cleopatra—

CLEOPATRA. Enough, enough: Cæsar has spoiled me for talking to weak things like you. [*She goes out. Pothinus, with a gesture of rage, is following, when Ftatateeta enters and stops him.*]

POTHINUS. Let me go forth from this hateful place.

FTATATEETA. What angers you?

POTHINUS. The curse of all the gods of Egypt be upon her! She has sold her country to the Roman, that she may buy it back from him with her kisses.

FTATATEETA. Fool: did she not tell you that she would have Cæsar gone?

POTHINUS. You listened?

FTATATEETA. I took care that some honest woman should be at hand whilst you were with her.

POTHINUS. Now by the gods—

FTATATEETA. Enough of your gods! Cæsar's gods are all powerful here. It is no use you coming to Cleopatra: you are only an Egyptian. She will not listen to any of her own race: she treats us all as children.

POTHINUS. May she perish for it!

FTATATEETA [*balefully*] May your tongue wither for that wish! Go! send for Lucius Septimius, the slayer of Pompey. He is a Roman: may be she will listen to him. Begone!

POTHINUS [*darkly*] I know to whom I must go now.

FTATATEETA [*suspiciously*] To whom, then?

POTHINUS. To a greater Roman than Lucius. And mark this, mistress. You thought, before Cæsar came, that Egypt should presently be ruled by you and your crew in the name of Cleopatra. I set myself against it—

FTATATEETA [*interrupting him—wrangling*] Ay; that it might be ruled by you and your crew in the name of Ptolemy.

POTHINUS. Better me, or even you, than a woman with a Roman heart; and that is what Cleopatra is now become. Whilst I live, she shall never rule. So guide yourself accordingly. [*He goes out*].

It is by this time drawing on to dinner time. The table is laid on the roof of the palace; and thither Rufio is now climbing, ushered by a majestic palace official, wand of office in hand, and followed by a slave carrying an inlaid stool. After many stairs they emerge at last into a massive colonnade on the roof. Light curtains are drawn between the columns on the north and east to soften the westering sun. The official leads Rufio to one of these shaded sections. A cord for pulling the curtains apart hangs down between the pillars.

THE OFFICIAL [*bowing*] The Roman commander will await Cæsar here.

The slave sets down the stool near the southernmost column, and slips out through the curtains.

RUFIO [*sitting down, a little blown*] Pouf! That was a climb. How high have we come?

THE OFFICIAL. We are on the palace roof, O Beloved of Victory!

RUFIO. Good! the Beloved of Victory has no more stairs to get up.

A second official enters from the opposite end, walking backwards.

THE SECOND OFFICIAL. Cæsar approaches.

Cæsar, fresh from the bath, clad in a new tunic of purple silk, comes in, beaming and festive, followed by two slaves carrying a light couch, which is hardly more than an elaborately designed bench. They place it near the northmost of the two curtained columns. When this is done they slip out through the curtains; and the two officials, formally bowing, follow them. Rufio rises to receive Cæsar.

CÆSAR [*coming over to him*] Why, Rufio! [*Surveying his dress with an air of admiring astonishment*] A new baldrick! A new golden pommel to your sword! And you have had your hair cut! But not your beard—? impossible! [*He sniffs at Rufio's beard*]. Yes, perfumed, by Jupiter Olympus!

RUFIO [*growling*] Well: is it to please myself?

CÆSAR [*affectionately*] No, my son Rufio, but to please me—to celebrate my birthday.

RUFIO [*contemptuously*] Your birthday! You always have a birthday when there is a pretty girl to be flattered or an ambassador to be conciliated. We had seven of them in ten months last year.

CÆSAR [*contritely*] It is true, Rufio! I shall never break myself of these petty deceits.

RUFIO. Who is to dine with us—besides Cleopatra?

CÆSAR. Apollodorus the Sicilian.

RUFIO. That popinjay!

CÆSAR. Come! the popinjay is an amusing dog—tells a story; sings a song; and saves us the trouble of flattering the Queen. What does she care for old politicians and camp-fed bears like us? No: Apollodorus is good company, Rufio, good company.

RUFIO. Well, he can swim a bit and fence a bit: he might be worse, if he only knew how to hold his tongue.

CÆSAR. The gods forbid he should ever learn! Oh, this military life! this tedious, brutal life of action! That is the worst of us Romans: we are mere doers and drudgers: a swarm of bees turned into men. Give me a good talker—one with wit and imagination enough to live without continually doing something!

RUFIO. Ay! a nice time he would have of it with you when dinner was over! Have you noticed that I am before my time?

CÆSAR. Aha! I thought that meant something. What is it?

RUFIO. Can we be overheard here?

CÆSAR. Our privacy invites eavesdropping. I can remedy that. [*He claps his hands twice. The curtains are drawn, revealing the roof garden with a banqueting table set across in the middle for four persons, one at each end, and two side by side. The side next Cæsar and Rufio is blocked with golden wine vessels and basins. A gorgeous major-domo is superintending the laying of the table by a staff of slaves. The colonnade goes round the garden at both sides to the further end, where a gap in it, like a great gateway, leaves the view open to the sky beyond the western edge of the roof, except in the middle, where a life size image of Ra, seated on a huge plinth, towers up, with hawk head and crown of asp and disk. His altar, which stands at his feet, is a single white stone*]. Now everybody can see us, nobody will think of listening to us. [*He sits down on the bench left by the two slaves*].

RUFIO [*sitting down on his stool*] Pothinus wants to speak to you. I advise you to see him: there is some plotting going on here among the women.

CÆSAR. Who is Pothinus?

RUFIO. The fellow with hair like squirrel's fur—the little King's bear leader, whom you kept prisoner.

CÆSAR [*annoyed*] And has he not escaped?

RUFIO. No.

CÆSAR [*rising imperiously*] Why not? You have been guarding this man instead of watching the enemy. Have I not told you always to let prisoners escape unless there are special orders to the contrary? Are there not enough mouths to be fed without him?

RUFIO. Yes; and if you would have a little sense and let me cut his throat, you would save his rations. Anyhow, he wont escape. Three sentries have told him they would put a pilum through him if they saw him again. What more can they do? He prefers to stay and spy on us. So would I if I had to do with generals subject to fits of clemency.

CÆSAR [*resuming his seat, argued down*] Hm! And so he wants to see me.

RUFIO. Ay. I have brought him with me. He is waiting there [*jerking his thumb over his shoulder*] under guard.

CÆSAR. And you want me to see him?

RUFIO [*obstinately*] I dont want anything. I daresay you will do what you like. Dont put it on to me.

CÆSAR [*with an air of doing it expressly to indulge Rufio*] Well, well: let us have him.

RUFIO [*calling*] Ho there, guard! Release your man and send him up. [*Beckoning*]. Come along!

Pothinus enters and stops mistrustfully between the two, looking from one to the other.

CÆSAR [*graciously*] Ah, Pothinus! You are welcome. And what is the news this afternoon?

POTHINUS. Cæsar: I come to warn you of a danger, and to make you an offer.

CÆSAR. Never mind the danger. Make the offer.

RUFIO. Never mind the offer. Whats the danger?

POTHINUS. Cæsar: you think that Cleopatra is devoted to you.

CÆSAR [*gravely*] My friend: I already know what I think. Come to your offer.

POTHINUS. I will deal plainly. I know not by what strange gods you have been enabled to defend a palace and a few yards of beach against a city and an army. Since we cut you off from Lake Mareotis, and you dug wells in the salt sea sand and brought up buckets of fresh water from them, we have known that your gods are irresistible, and that you are a worker of miracles. I no longer threaten you—

RUFIO [*sarcastically*] Very handsome of you, indeed.

POTHINUS. So be it: you are the master. Our gods sent the north west winds to keep you in our hands; but you have been too strong for them.

CÆSAR [*gently urging him to come to the point*]

Yes, yes, my friend. But what then?

RUFIO. Spit it out, man. What have you to say?

POTHINUS. I have to say that you have a traitress in your camp. Cleopatra—

THE MAJOR-DOMO [at the table, announcing] The Queen! [Cæsar and Rufio rise].

RUFIO [aside to Pothinus] You should have spat it out sooner, you fool. Now it is too late.

Cleopatra, in gorgeous raiment, enters in state through the gap in the colonnade, and comes down past the image of Ra and past the table to Cæsar. Her retinue, headed by Ftatateeta, joins the staff at the table. Cæsar gives Cleopatra his seat, which she takes.

CLEOPATRA [quickly, seeing Pothinus] What is he doing here?

CÆSAR [seating himself beside her, in the most amiable of tempers] Just going to tell me something about you. You shall hear it. Proceed, Pothinus.

POTHINUS [disconcerted] Cæsar— [he stammers].

CÆSAR. Well, out with it.

POTHINUS. What I have to say is for your ear, not for the Queen's.

CLEOPATRA [with subdued ferocity] There are means of making you speak. Take care.

POTHINUS [defiantly] Cæsar does not employ those means.

CÆSAR. My friend: when a man has anything to tell in this world, the difficulty is not to make him tell it, but to prevent him from telling it too often. Let me celebrate my birthday by setting you free. Farewell: we shall not meet again.

CLEOPATRA [angrily] Cæsar: this mercy is foolish.

POTHINUS [to Cæsar] Will you not give me a private audience? Your life may depend on it. [Cæsar rises loftily].

RUFIO [aside to Pothinus] Ass! Now we shall have some heroics.

CÆSAR [oratorically] Pothinus—

RUFIO [interrupting him] Cæsar: the dinner will spoil if you begin preaching your favorite sermon about life and death.

CLEOPATRA [priggishly] Peace, Rufio. I desire to hear Cæsar.

RUFIO [bluntly] Your Majesty has heard it before. You repeated it to Apollodorus last week; and he thought it was all your own. [Cæsar's dignity collapses. Much tickled, he sits down again and looks roguishly at Cleopatra, who is furious. Rufio calls as before] Ho

there, guard! Pass the prisoner out. He is released. [To Pothinus] Now off with you. You have lost your chance.

POTHINUS [his temper overcoming his prudence] I will speak.

CÆSAR [to Cleopatra] You see. Torture would not have wrung a word from him.

POTHINUS. Cæsar: you have taught Cleopatra the arts by which the Romans govern the world.

CÆSAR. Alas! they cannot even govern themselves. What then?

POTHINUS. What then? Are you so besotted with her beauty that you do not see that she is impatient to reign in Egypt alone, and that her heart is set on your departure?

CLEOPATRA [rising] Liar!

CÆSAR [shocked] What! Protestations! Contradictions!

CLEOPATRA [ashamed, but trembling with suppressed rage] No. I do not deign to contradict. Let him talk. [She sits down again].

POTHINUS. From her own lips I have heard it. You are to be her catspaw: you are to tear the crown from her brother's head and set it on her own, delivering us all into her hand —delivering yourself also. And then Cæsar can return to Rome, or depart through the gate of death, which is nearer and surer.

CÆSAR [calmly] Well, my friend; and is not this very natural?

POTHINUS [astonished] Natural! Then you do not resent treachery?

CÆSAR. Resent! O thou foolish Egyptian, what have I to do with resentment? Do I resent the wind when it chills me, or the night when it makes me stumble in the darkness? Shall I resent youth when it turns from age, and ambition when it turns from servitude? To tell me such a story as this is but to tell me that the sun will rise tomorrow.

CLEOPATRA [unable to contain herself] But it is false—false. I swear it.

CÆSAR. It is true, though you swore it a thousand times, and believed all you swore. [She is convulsed with emotion. To screen her, he rises and takes Pothinus to Rufio, saying] Come, Rufio: let us see Pothinus past the guard. I have a word to say to him. [Aside to them] We must give the Queen a moment to recover herself. [Aloud] Come. [He takes Pothinus and Rufio out with him, conversing with them meanwhile]. Tell your friends, Pothinus, that they must not think I am opposed to a reasonable settlement of the country's affairs— [*They pass out of hearing*].

CLEOPATRA [*in a stifled whisper*] Ftatateeta, Ftatateeta.

FTATATEETA [*hurrying to her from the table and petting her*] Peace, child: be comforted—

CLEOPATRA [*interrupting her*] Can they hear us?

FTATATEETA. No, dear heart, no.

CLEOPATRA. Listen to me. If he leaves the Palace alive, never see my face again.

FTATATEETA. He? Poth—

CLEOPATRA [*striking her on the mouth*] Strike his life out as I strike his name from your lips. Dash him down from the wall. Break him on the stones. Kill, kill, kill him.

FTATATEETA [*shewing all her teeth*] The dog shall perish.

CLEOPATRA. Fail in this, and you go out from before me for ever.

FTATATEETA [*resolutely*] So be it. You shall not see my face until his eyes are darkened.

Cæsar comes back, with Apollodorus, exquisitely dressed, and Rufio.

CLEOPATRA [*to Ftatateeta*] Come soon— soon. [*Ftatateeta turns her meaning eyes for a moment on her mistress; then goes grimly away past Ra and out. Cleopatra runs like a gazelle to Cæsar*] So you have come back to me, Cæsar. [*Caressingly*] I thought you were angry. Welcome, Apollodorus. [*She gives him her hand to kiss, with her other arm about Cæsar*].

APOLLODORUS. Cleopatra grows more womanly beautiful from week to week.

CLEOPATRA. Truth, Apollodorus?

APOLLODORUS. Far, far short of the truth! Friend Rufio threw a pearl into the sea: Cæsar fished up a diamond.

CÆSAR. Cæsar fished up a touch of rheumatism, my friend. Come: to dinner! to dinner! [*They move towards the table*].

CLEOPATRA [*skipping like a young fawn*] Yes, to dinner. I have ordered such a dinner for you, Cæsar!

CÆSAR. Ay? What are we to have?

CLEOPATRA. Peacocks' brains.

CÆSAR [*as if his mouth watered*] Peacocks' brains, Apollodorus!

APOLLODORUS. Not for me. I prefer nightingales' tongues. [*He goes to one of the two covers set side by side*].

CLEOPATRA. Roast boar, Rufio!

RUFIO [*gluttonously*] Good! [*He goes to the seat next Apollodorus, on his left*].

CÆSAR [*looking at his seat, which is at the end of the table, to Ra's left hand*] What has be-

come of my leathern cushion?

CLEOPATRA [*at the opposite end*] I have got new ones for you.

THE MAJOR-DOMO. These cushions, Cæsar, are of Maltese gauze, stuffed with rose leaves.

CÆSAR. Rose leaves! Am I a caterpillar? [*He throws the cushions away and seats himself on the leather mattress underneath*].

CLEOPATRA. What a shame! My new cushions!

THE MAJOR-DOMO [*at Cæsar's elbow*] What shall we serve to whet Cæsar's appetite?

CÆSAR. What have you got?

THE MAJOR-DOMO. Sea hedgehogs, black and white sea acorns, sea nettles, beccaficoes, purple shellfish—

CÆSAR. Any oysters?

THE MAJOR-DOMO. Assuredly.

CÆSAR. British oysters?

THE MAJOR-DOMO [*assenting*] British oysters, Cæsar.

CÆSAR. Oysters, then. [*The Major-Domo signs to a slave at each order; and the slave goes out to execute it*]. I have been in Britain—that western land of romance—the last piece of earth on the edge of the ocean that surrounds the world. I went there in search of its famous pearls. The British pearl was a fable; but in searching for it I found the British oyster.

APOLLODORUS. All posterity will bless you for it. [*To the Major-Domo*] Sea hedgehogs for me.

RUFIO. Is there nothing solid to begin with?

THE MAJOR-DOMO. Fieldfares with asparagus—

CLEOPATRA [*interrupting*] Fattened fowls! have some fattened fowls, Rufio.

RUFIO. Ay, that will do.

CLEOPATRA [*greedily*] Fieldfares for me.

THE MAJOR-DOMO. Cæsar will deign to choose his wine? Sicilian, Lesbian, Chian—

RUFIO [*contemptuously*] All Greek.

APOLLODORUS. Who would drink Roman wine when he could get Greek? Try the Lesbian, Cæsar.

CÆSAR. Bring me my barley water.

RUFIO [*with intense disgust*] Ugh! Bring me my Falernian. [*The Falernian is presently brought to him*].

CLEOPATRA [*pouting*] It is waste of time giving you dinners, Cæsar. My scullions would not condescend to your diet.

CÆSAR [*relenting*] Well, well: let us try the Lesbian. [*The Major-Domo fills Cæsar's goblet; then Cleopatra's and Apollodorus's*]. But when I return to Rome, I will make laws against these extravagances. I will even get the laws carried out.

CLEOPATRA [*coaxingly*] Never mind. Today you are to be like other people: idle, luxurious, and kind. [*She stretches her hand to him along the table*].

CÆSAR. Well, for once I will sacrifice my comfort— [*kissing her hand*] there! [*He takes a draught of wine*]. Now are you satisfied?

CLEOPATRA. And you no longer believe that I long for your departure for Rome?

CÆSAR. I no longer believe anything. My brains are asleep. Besides, who knows whether I shall return to Rome?

RUFIO [*alarmed*] How? Eh? What?

CÆSAR. What has Rome to shew me that I have not seen already? One year of Rome is like another, except that I grow older, whilst the crowd in the Appian Way is always the same age.

APOLLODORUS. It is no better here in Egypt. The old men, when they are tired of life, say "We have seen everything except the source of the Nile."

CÆSAR [*his imagination catching fire*] And why not see that? Cleopatra: will you come with me and track the flood to its cradle in the heart of the regions of mystery? Shall we leave Rome behind us—Rome, that has achieved greatness only to learn how greatness destroys nations of men who are not great! Shall I make you a new kingdom, and build you a holy city there in the great unknown?

CLEOPATRA [*rapturously*] Yes, yes. You shall.

RUFIO. Ay: now he will conquer Africa with two legions before we come to the roast boar.

APOLLODORUS. Come: no scoffing. This is a noble scheme: in it Cæsar is no longer merely the conquering soldier, but the creative poet-artist. Let us name the holy city, and consecrate it with Lesbian wine.

CÆSAR. Cleopatra shall name it herself.

CLEOPATRA. It shall be called Cæsar's Gift to his Beloved.

APOLLODORUS. No, no. Something vaster than that—something universal, like the starry firmament.

CÆSAR [*prosaically*] Why not simply The Cradle of the Nile!

CLEOPATRA. No: the Nile is my ancestor; and he is a god. Oh! I have thought of something. The Nile shall name it himself. Let

us call upon him. [*To the Major-Domo*] Send for him. [*The three men stare at one another; but the Major-Domo goes out as if he had received the most matter-of-fact order*]. And [*to the retinue*] away with you all.

The retinue withdraws, making obeisance.

A priest enters, carrying a miniature sphinx with a tiny tripod before it. A morsel of incense is smoking in the tripod. The priest comes to the table and places the image in the middle of it. The light begins to change to the magenta purple of the Egyptian sunset, as if the god had brought a strange colored shadow with him. The three men are determined not to be impressed; but they feel curious in spite of themselves.

CÆSAR. What hocus-pocus is this?

CLEOPATRA. You shall see. And it is not hocus-pocus. To do it properly, we should kill something to please him; but perhaps he will answer Cæsar without that if we spill some wine to him.

APOLLODORUS [*turning his head to look up over his shoulder at Ra*] Why not appeal to our hawkheaded friend here?

CLEOPATRA [*nervously*] Sh! He will hear you and be angry.

RUFIO [*phlegmatically*] The source of the Nile is out of his district, I expect.

CLEOPATRA. No: I will have my city named by nobody but my dear little sphinx, because it was in its arms that Cæsar found me asleep. [*She languishes at Cæsar; then turns curtly to the priest*]. Go. I am a priestess, and have power to take your charge from you. [*The priest makes a reverence and goes out*]. Now let us call on the Nile all together. Perhaps he will rap on the table.

CÆSAR. What! table rapping! Are such superstitions still believed in this year 707 of the Republic?

CLEOPATRA. It is no superstition: our priests learn lots of things from the tables. Is it not so, Apollodorus?

APOLLODORUS. Yes: I profess myself a converted man. When Cleopatra is priestess, Apollodorus is devotee. Propose the conjuration.

CLEOPATRA. You must say with me "Send us thy voice, Father Nile."

ALL FOUR [*holding their glasses together before the idol*] Send us thy voice, Father Nile.

The death cry of a man in mortal terror and agony answers them. Appalled, the men set down their glasses, and listen. Silence. The purple deepens in the sky. Cæsar, glancing at Cleopatra,

L

catches her pouring out her wine before the god, with gleaming eyes, and mute assurances of gratitude and worship. Apollodorus springs up and runs to the edge of the roof to peer down and listen.

CÆSAR [*looking piercingly at Cleopatra*] What was that?

CLEOPATRA [*petulantly*] Nothing. They are beating some slave.

CÆSAR. Nothing!

RUFIO. A man with a knife in him, I'll swear.

CÆSAR [*rising*] A murder!

APOLLODORUS [*at the back, waving his hand for silence*] S-sh! Silence. Did you hear that?

CÆSAR. Another cry?

APOLLODORUS [*returning to the table*] No, a thud. Something fell on the beach, I think.

RUFIO [*grimly, as he rises*] Something with bones in it, eh?

CÆSAR [*shuddering*] Hush, hush, Rufio. [*He leaves the table and returns to the colonnade: Rufio following at his left elbow, and Apollodorus at the other side*].

CLEOPATRA [*still in her place at the table*] Will you leave me, Cæsar? Apollodorus: are you going?

APOLLODORUS. Faith, dearest Queen, my appetite is gone.

CÆSAR. Go down to the courtyard, Apollodorus; and find out what has happened.

Apollodorus nods and goes out, making for the staircase by which Rufio ascended.

CLEOPATRA. Your soldiers have killed somebody, perhaps. What does it matter?

The murmur of a crowd rises from the beach below. Cæsar and Rufio look at one another.

CÆSAR. This must be seen to. [*He is about to follow Apollodorus when Rufio stops him with a hand on his arm as Ftatateeta comes back by the far end of the roof, with dragging steps, a drowsy satiety in her eyes and in the corners of the bloodhound lips. For a moment Cæsar suspects that she is drunk with wine. Not so Rufio: he knows well the red vintage that has inebriated her*].

RUFIO [*in a low tone*] There is some mischief between those two.

FTATATEETA. The Queen looks again on the face of her servant.

Cleopatra looks at her for a moment with an exultant reflection of her murderous expression. Then she flings her arms round her; kisses her repeatedly and savagely; and tears off her jewels and heaps them on her. The two men turn from

the spectacle to look at one another. Ftatateeta drags herself sleepily to the altar; kneels before Ra; and remains there in prayer. Cæsar goes to Cleopatra, leaving Rufio in the colonnade.

CÆSAR [*with searching earnestness*] Cleopatra: what has happened?

CLEOPATRA [*in mortal dread of him, but with her utmost cajolery*] Nothing, dearest Cæsar. [*With sickly sweetness, her voice almost failing*] Nothing. I am innocent. [*She approaches him affectionately*]. Dear Cæsar: are you angry with me? Why do you look at me so? I have been here with you all the time. How can I know what has happened?

CÆSAR [*reflectively*] That is true.

CLEOPATRA [*greatly relieved, trying to caress him*] Of course it is true. [*He does not respond to the caress*] You know it is true, Rufio.

The murmur without suddenly swells to a roar and subsides.

RUFIO. I shall know presently. [*He makes for the altar in the burly trot that serves him for a stride, and touches Ftatateeta on the shoulder*]. Now, mistress: I shall want you. [*He orders her, with a gesture, to go before him*].

FTATATEETA [*rising and glowering at him*] My place is with the Queen.

CLEOPATRA. She has done no harm, Rufio.

CÆSAR [*to Rufio*] Let her stay.

RUFIO [*sitting down on the altar*] Very well. Then my place is here too; and you can see what is the matter for yourself. The city is in a pretty uproar, it seems.

CÆSAR [*with grave displeasure*] Rufio: there is a time for obedience.

RUFIO. And there is a time for obstinacy. [*He folds his arms doggedly*].

CÆSAR [*to Cleopatra*] Send her away.

CLEOPATRA [*whining in her eagerness to propitiate him*] Yes, I will. I will do whatever you ask me, Cæsar, always, because I love you. Ftatateeta: go away.

FTATATEETA. The Queen's word is my will. I shall be at hand for the Queen's call. [*She goes out past Ra, as she came*].

RUFIO [*following her*] Remember, Cæsar, your bodyguard also is within call. [*He follows her out*].

Cleopatra, presuming upon Cæsar's submission to Rufio, leaves the table and sits down on the bench in the colonnade.

CLEOPATRA. Why do you allow Rufio to treat you so? You should teach him his place.

CÆSAR. Teach him to be my enemy, and to hide his thoughts from me as you are now hiding yours.

CLEOPATRA [*her fears returning*] Why do you say that, Cæsar? Indeed, indeed, I am not hiding anything. You are wrong to treat me like this. [*She stifles a sob*]. I am only a child; and you turn into stone because you think some one has been killed. I cannot bear it. [*She purposely breaks down and weeps. He looks at her with profound sadness and complete coldness. She looks up to see what effect she is producing. Seeing that he is unmoved, she sits up, pretending to struggle with her emotion and to put it bravely away*]. But there: I know you hate tears: you shall not be troubled with them. I know you are not angry, but only sad; only I am so silly, I cannot help being hurt when you speak coldly. Of course you are quite right: it is dreadful to think of anyone being killed or even hurt; and I hope nothing really serious has— [*her voice dies away under his contemptuous penetration*].

CÆSAR. What has frightened you into this? What have you done? [*A trumpet sounds on the beach below*]. Aha! that sounds like the answer.

CLEOPATRA [*sinking back trembling on the bench and covering her face with her hands*] I have not betrayed you, Cæsar: I swear it.

CÆSAR. I know that. I have not trusted you. [*He turns from her, and is about to go out when Apollodorus and Britannus drag in Lucius Septimius to him. Rufio follows. Cæsar shudders*]. Again, Pompey's murderer!

RUFIO. The town has gone mad, I think. They are for tearing the palace down and driving us into the sea straight away. We laid hold of this renegade in clearing them out of the courtyard.

CÆSAR. Release him. [*They let go his arms*]. What has offended the citizens, Lucius Septimius?

LUCIUS. What did you expect, Cæsar? Pothinus was a favorite of theirs.

CÆSAR. What has happened to Pothinus? I set him free, here, not half an hour ago. Did they not pass him out?

LUCIUS. Ay, through the gallery arch sixty feet above ground, with three inches of steel in his ribs. He is as dead as Pompey. We are quits now, as to killing—you and I.

CÆSAR [*shocked*] Assassinated!—our prisoner, our guest! [*He turns reproachfully on Rufio*] Rufio—

RUFIO [*emphatically—anticipating the question*] Whoever did it was a wise man and

a friend of yours [*Cleopatra is greatly emboldened*]; but none of us had a hand in it. So it is no use to frown at me. [*Cæsar turns and looks at Cleopatra*].

CLEOPATRA [*violently—rising*] He was slain by order of the Queen of Egypt. I am not Julius Cæsar the dreamer, who allows every slave to insult him. Rufio has said I did well: now the others shall judge me too. [*She turns to the others*]. This Pothinus sought to make me conspire with him to betray Cæsar to Achillas and Ptolemy. I refused; and he cursed me and came privily to Cæsar to accuse me of his own treachery. I caught him in the act; and he insulted me—me, the Queen! to my face. Cæsar would not avenge me: he spoke him fair and set him free. Was I right to avenge myself? Speak, Lucius.

LUCIUS. I do not gainsay it. But you will get little thanks from Cæsar for it.

CLEOPATRA. Speak, Apollodorus. Was I wrong?

APOLLODORUS. I have only one word of blame, most beautiful. You should have called upon me, your knight; and in fair duel I should have slain the slanderer.

CLEOPATRA [*passionately*] I will be judged by your very slave, Cæsar. Britannus: speak. Was I wrong?

BRITANNUS. Were treachery, falsehood, and disloyalty left unpunished, society must become like an arena full of wild beasts, tearing one another to pieces. Cæsar is in the wrong.

CÆSAR [*with quiet bitterness*] And so the verdict is against me, it seems.

CLEOPATRA [*vehemently*] Listen to me, Cæsar. If one man in all Alexandria can be found to say that I did wrong, I swear to have myself crucified on the door of the palace by my own slaves.

CÆSAR. If one man in all the world can be found, now or forever, to know that you did wrong, that man will have either to conquer the world as I have, or be crucified by it. [*The uproar in the streets again reaches them*]. Do you hear? These knockers at your gate are also believers in vengeance and in stabbing. You have slain their leader: it is right that they shall slay you. If you doubt it, ask your four counsellors here. And then in the name of that right [*he emphasizes the word with great scorn*] shall I not slay them for murdering their Queen, and be slain in my turn by their countrymen as the invader of their fatherland? Can Rome do less then than slay these slayers, too, to shew the world how Rome avenges her sons and her honor. And so, to the end of history, murder shall breed murder, always in the name of right and honor and peace, until the gods are tired of blood and create a race that can understand. [*Fierce uproar. Cleopatra becomes white with terror*]. Hearken, you who must not be insulted. Go near enough to catch their words: you will find them bitterer than the tongue of Pothinus. [*Loftily, wrapping himself up in an impenetrable dignity*] Let the Queen of Egypt now give her orders for vengeance, and take her measures for defence; for she has renounced Cæsar. [*He turns to go*].

CLEOPATRA [*terrified, running to him and falling on her knees*] You will not desert me, Cæsar. You will defend the palace.

CÆSAR. You have taken the powers of life and death upon you. I am only a dreamer.

CLEOPATRA. But they will kill me.

CÆSAR. And why not?

CLEOPATRA. In pity—

CÆSAR. Pity! What! has it come to this so suddenly, that nothing can save you now but pity? Did it save Pothinus?

She rises, wringing her hands, and goes back to the bench in despair. Apollodorus shews his sympathy with her by quietly posting himself behind the bench. The sky has by this time become the most vivid purple, and soon begins to change to a glowing pale orange, against which the colonnade and the great image shew darklier and darklier.

RUFIO. Cæsar: enough of preaching. The enemy is at the gate.

CÆSAR [*turning on him and giving way to his wrath*] Ay; and what has held him baffled at the gate all these months? Was it my folly, as you deem it, or your wisdom? In this Egyptian Red Sea of blood, whose hand has held all your heads above the waves? [*Turning on Cleopatra*] And yet, when Cæsar says to such an one, "Friend, go free," you, clinging for your little life to my sword, dare steal out and stab him in the back? And you, soldiers and gentlemen, and honest servants as you forget that you are, applaud this assassination, and say "Cæsar is in the wrong." By the gods, I am tempted to open my hand and let you all sink into the flood.

CLEOPATRA [*with a ray of cunning hope*] But, Cæsar, if you do, you will perish yourself. *Cæsar's eyes blaze.*

RUFIO [*greatly alarmed*] Now, by great Jove, you filthy little Egyptian rat, that is the very word to make him walk out alone into the city and leave us here to be cut to pieces. [*Desperately, to Cæsar*] Will you desert us because we are a parcel of fools? I mean no harm by killing: I do it as a dog kills a cat, by instinct. We are all dogs at your heels; but we have served you faithfully.

CÆSAR [*relenting*] Alas, Rufio, my son, my son: as dogs we are like to perish now in the streets.

APOLLODORUS [*at his post behind Cleopatra's seat*] Cæsar: what you say has an Olympian ring in it: it must be right; for it is fine art. But I am still on the side of Cleopatra. If we must die, she shall not want the devotion of a man's heart nor the strength of a man's arm.

CLEOPATRA [*sobbing*] But I dont want to die.

CÆSAR [*sadly*] Oh, ignoble, ignoble!

LUCIUS [*coming forward between Cæsar and Cleopatra*] Hearken to me, Cæsar. It may be ignoble; but I also mean to live as long as I can.

CÆSAR. Well, my friend, you are likely to outlive Cæsar. Is it any magic of mine, think you, that has kept your army and this whole city at bay for so long? Yesterday, what quarrel had they with me that they should risk their lives against me? But today we have flung them down their hero, murdered; and now every man of them is set upon clearing out this nest of assassins—for such we are and no more. Take courage then; and sharpen your sword. Pompey's head has fallen; and Cæsar's head is ripe.

APOLLODORUS. Does Cæsar despair?

CÆSAR [*with infinite pride*] He who has never hoped can never despair. Cæsar, in good or bad fortune, looks his fate in the face.

LUCIUS. Look it in the face, then; and it will smile as it always has on Cæsar.

CÆSAR [*with involuntary haughtiness*] Do you presume to encourage me?

LUCIUS. I offer you my services. I will change sides if you will have me.

CÆSAR [*suddenly coming down to earth again, and looking sharply at him, divining that there is something behind the offer*] What! At this point?

LUCIUS [*firmly*] At this point.

RUFIO. Do you suppose Cæsar is mad, to trust you?

LUCIUS. I do not ask him to trust me until

he is victorious. I ask for my life, and for a command in Cæsar's army. And since Cæsar is a fair dealer, I will pay in advance.

CÆSAR. Pay! How?

LUCIUS. With a piece of good news for you. *Cæsar divines the news in a flash.*

RUFIO. What news?

CÆSAR [*with an elate and buoyant energy which makes Cleopatra sit up and stare*] What news! What news, did you say, my son Rufio? The relief has arrived: what other news remains for us? Is it not so, Lucius Septimius? Mithridates of Pergamos is on the march.

LUCIUS. He has taken Pelusium.

CÆSAR [*delighted*] Lucius Septimius: you are henceforth my officer. Rufio: the Egyptians must have sent every soldier from the city to prevent Mithridates crossing the Nile. There is nothing in the streets now but mob —mob!

LUCIUS. It is so. Mithridates is marching by the great road to Memphis to cross above the Delta. Achillas will fight him there.

CÆSAR [*all audacity*] Achillas shall fight Cæsar there. See, Rufio. [*He runs to the table; snatches a napkin; and draws a plan on it with his finger dipped in wine, whilst Rufio and Lucius Septimius crowd about him to watch, all looking closely, for the light is now almost gone*]. Here is the palace [*pointing to his plan*]: here is the theatre. You [*to Rufio*] take twenty men and pretend to go by that street [*pointing it out*]; and whilst they are stoning you, out go the cohorts by this and this. My streets are right, are they, Lucius?

LUCIUS. Ay, that is the fig market—

CÆSAR [*too much excited to listen to him*] I saw them the day we arrived. Good! [*He throws the napkin on the table, and comes down again into the colonnade*]. Away, Britannus: tell Petronius that within an hour half our forces must take ship for the western lake. See to my horse and armor. [*Britannus runs out.*] With the rest, *I* shall march round the lake and up the Nile to meet Mithridates. Away, Lucius; and give the word. [*Lucius hurries out after Britannus.*] Apollodorus: lend me your sword and your right arm for this campaign.

APOLLODORUS. Ay, and my heart and life to boot.

CÆSAR [*grasping his hand*] I accept both. [*Mighty handshake*]. Are you ready for work?

APOLLODORUS. Ready for Art—the Art of War [*he rushes out after Lucius, totally forgetting Cleopatra*].

RUFIO. Come! this is something like business.

CÆSAR [*buoyantly*] Is it not, my only son? [*He claps his hands. The slaves hurry in to the table*]. No more of this mawkish revelling: away with all this stuff: shut it out of my sight and be off with you. [*The slaves begin to remove the table; and the curtains are drawn, shutting in the colonnade*]. You understand about the streets, Rufio?

RUFIO. Ay, I think I do. I will get through them, at all events.

The bucina sounds busily in the courtyard beneath.

CÆSAR. Come, then: we must talk to the troops and hearten them. You down to the beach: I to the courtyard. [*He makes for the staircase*].

CLEOPATRA [*rising from her seat, where she has been quite neglected all this time, and stretching out her hands timidly to him*] Cæsar.

CÆSAR [*turning*] Eh?

CLEOPATRA. Have you forgotten me?

CÆSAR [*indulgently*] I am busy now, my child, busy. When I return your affairs shall be settled. Farewell; and be good and patient.

He goes, preoccupied and quite indifferent. She stands with clenched fists, in speechless rage and humiliation.

RUFIO. That game is played and lost, Cleopatra. The woman always gets the worst of it.

CLEOPATRA [*haughtily*] Go. Follow your master.

RUFIO [*in her ear, with rough familiarity*] A word first. Tell your executioner that if Pothinus had been properly killed—in the throat—he would not have called out. Your man bungled his work.

CLEOPATRA [*enigmatically*] How do you know it was a man?

RUFIO [*startled, and puzzled*] It was not you: you were with us when it happened. [*She turns her back scornfully on him. He shakes his head, and draws the curtains to go out. It is now a magnificent moonlit night. The table has been removed. Ftatateeta is seen in the light of the moon and stars, again in prayer before the white altar-stone of Ra. Rufio starts; closes the curtains again softly; and says in a low voice to Cleopatra*] Was it she? with her own hand?

CLEOPATRA [*threateningly*] Whoever it was, let my enemies beware of her. Look to it, Rufio, you who dare make the Queen of

Egypt a fool before Cæsar.

RUFIO [*looking grimly at her*] I will look to it, Cleopatra. [*He nods in confirmation of the promise, and slips out through the curtains, loosening his sword in its sheath as he goes*].

ROMAN SOLDIERS [*in the courtyard below*] Hail, Cæsar! Hail, hail!

Cleopatra listens. The bucina sounds again, followed by several trumpets.

CLEOPATRA [*wringing her hands and calling*] Ftatateeta. Ftatateeta. It is dark; and I am alone. Come to me. [*Silence*]. Ftatateeta. [*Louder*] Ftatateeta. [*Silence. In a panic she snatches the cord and pulls the curtains apart*].

Ftatateeta is lying dead on the altar of Ra, with her throat cut. Her blood deluges the white stone.

ACT V

High noon. Festival and military pageant on the esplanade before the palace. In the east harbor Cæsar's galley, so gorgeously decorated that it seems to be rigged with flowers, is alongside the quay, close to the steps Apollodorus descended when he embarked with the carpet. A Roman guard is posted there in charge of a gangway, whence a red floorcloth is laid down the middle of the esplanade, turning off to the north opposite the central gate in the palace front, which shuts in the esplanade on the south side. The broad steps of the gate, crowded with Cleopatra's ladies, all in their gayest attire, are like a flower garden. The façade is lined by her guard, officered by the same gallants to whom Bel Affris announced the coming of Cæsar six months before in the old palace on the Syrian border. The north side is lined by Roman soldiers, with the townsfolk on tiptoe behind them, peering over their heads at the cleared esplanade, in which the officers stroll about, chatting. Among these are Belzanor and the Persian; also the centurion, vinewood cudgel in hand, battle worn, thick-booted, and much outshone, both socially and decoratively, by the Egyptian officers.

Apollodorus makes his way through the townsfolk and calls to the officers from behind the Roman line.

APOLLODORUS. Hullo! May I pass?

CENTURION. Pass Apollodorus the Sicilian there! [*The soldiers let him through*].

BELZANOR. Is Cæsar at hand?

APOLLODORUS. Not yet. He is still in the market place. I could not stand any more of the roaring of the soldiers! After half an hour of the enthusiasm of an army, one feels the need of a little sea air.

PERSIAN. Tell us the news. Hath he slain the priests?

APOLLODORUS. Not he. They met him in the market place with ashes on their heads and their gods in their hands. They placed the gods at his feet. The only one that was worth looking at was Apis: a miracle of gold and ivory work. By my advice he offered the chief priest two talents for it.

BELZANOR [*appalled*] Apis the all-knowing for two talents! What said the chief priest?

APOLLODORUS. He invoked the mercy of Apis, and asked for five.

BELZANOR. There will be famine and tempest in the land for this.

PERSIAN. Pooh! Why did not Apis cause Cæsar to be vanquished by Achillas? Any fresh news from the war, Apollodorus?

APOLLODORUS. The little King Ptolemy was drowned.

BELZANOR. Drowned! How?

APOLLODORUS. With the rest of them. Cæsar attacked them from three sides at once and swept them into the Nile. Ptolemy's barge sank.

BELZANOR. A marvellous man, this Cæsar! Will he come soon, think you?

APOLLODORUS. He was settling the Jewish question when I left.

A flourish of trumpets from the north, and commotion among the townsfolk, announces the approach of Cæsar.

PERSIAN. He has made short work of them. Here he comes. [*He hurries to his post in front of the Egyptian lines*].

BELZANOR [*following him*] Ho there! Cæsar comes.

The soldiers stand at attention, and dress their lines. Apollodorus goes to the Egyptian line.

CENTURION [*hurrying to the gangway guard*] Attention there! Cæsar comes.

Cæsar arrives in state with Rufio: Britannus following. The soldiers receive him with enthusiastic shouting.

CÆSAR. I see my ship awaits me. The hour of Cæsar's farewell to Egypt has arrived. And now, Rufio, what remains to be done before I go?

RUFIO [*at his left hand*] You have not yet appointed a Roman governor for this province.

CÆSAR [*looking whimsically at him, but speaking with perfect gravity*] What say you to Mithridates of Pergamos, my reliever and rescuer, the great son of Eupator?

RUFIO. Why, that you will want him elsewhere. Do you forget that you have some three or four armies to conquer on your way home?

CÆSAR. Indeed! Well, what say you to yourself?

RUFIO [*incredulously*] I! I a governor! What are you dreaming of? Do you not know that I am only the son of a freedman?

CÆSAR [*affectionately*] Has not Cæsar called you his son? [*Calling to the whole assembly*] Peace awhile there; and hear me.

THE ROMAN SOLDIERS. Hear Cæsar.

CÆSAR. Hear the service, quality, rank and name of the Roman governor. By service, Cæsar's shield; by quality, Cæsar's friend; by rank, a Roman soldier. [*The Roman soldiers give a triumphant shout*]. By name, Rufio. [*They shout again*].

RUFIO [*kissing Cæsar's hand*] Ay: I am Cæsar's shield; but of what use shall I be when I am no longer on Cæsar's arm? Well, no matter— [*He becomes husky, and turns away to recover himself*].

CÆSAR. Where is that British Islander of mine?

BRITANNUS [*coming forward on Cæsar's right hand*] Here, Cæsar.

CÆSAR. Who bade you, pray, thrust yourself into the battle of the Delta, uttering the barbarous cries of your native land, and affirming yourself a match for any four of the Egyptians, to whom you applied unseemly epithets?

BRITANNUS. Cæsar: I ask you to excuse the language that escaped me in the heat of the moment.

CÆSAR. And how did you, who cannot swim, cross the canal with us when we stormed the camp?

BRITANNUS. Cæsar: I clung to the tail of your horse.

CÆSAR. These are not the deeds of a slave, Britannicus, but of a free man.

BRITANNUS. Cæsar: I was born free.

CÆSAR. But they call you Cæsar's slave.

BRITANNUS. Only as Cæsar's slave have I found real freedom.

CÆSAR [*moved*] Well said. Ungrateful that I am, I was about to set you free; but now I will not part from you for a million talents. [*He claps him friendly on the shoulder. Britannus, gratified, but a trifle shamefaced, takes his hand and kisses it sheepishly*].

BELZANOR [*to the Persian*] This Roman knows how to make men serve him.

PERSIAN. Ay: men too humble to become dangerous rivals to him.

BELZANOR. O subtle one! O cynic!

CÆSAR [*seeing Apollodorus in the Egyptian corner, and calling to him*] Apollodorus: I leave the art of Egypt in your charge. Remember: Rome loves art and will encourage it ungrudgingly.

APOLLODORUS. I understand, Cæsar. Rome will produce no art itself; but it will buy up and take away whatever the other nations produce.

CÆSAR. What! Rome produce no art! Is peace not an art? is war not an art? is government not an art? is civilization not an art? All these we give you in exchange for a few ornaments. You will have the best of the bargain. [*Turning to Rufio*] And now, what else have I to do before I embark? [*Trying to recollect*] There is something I cannot remember: what can it be? Well, well: it must remain undone: we must not waste this favorable wind. Farewell, Rufio.

RUFIO. Cæsar: I am loth to let you go to Rome without your shield. There are too many daggers there.

CÆSAR. It matters not: I shall finish my life's work on my way back; and then I shall have lived long enough. Besides: I have always disliked the idea of dying: I had rather be killed. Farewell.

RUFIO [*with a sigh, raising his hands and giving Cæsar up as incorrigible*] Farewell. [*They shake hands*].

CÆSAR [*waving his hand to Apollodorus*] Farewell, Apollodorus, and my friends, all of you. Aboard!

The gangway is run out from the quay to the ship. As Cæsar moves towards it, Cleopatra, cold and tragic, cunningly dressed in black, without ornaments or decoration of any kind, and thus making a striking figure among the brilliantly dressed bevy of ladies as she passes through it, comes from the palace and stands on the steps. Cæsar does not see her until she speaks.

CLEOPATRA. Has Cleopatra no part in this leavetaking?

CÆSAR [*enlightened*] Ah, I knew there was something. [*To Rufio*] How could you let me forget her, Rufio? [*Hastening to her*] Had I gone without seeing you, I should never have forgiven myself. [*He takes her hands, and brings her into the middle of the esplanade. She submits stonily*]. Is this mourning for me?

CLEOPATRA. No.

CÆSAR [*remorsefully*] Ah, that was thoughtless of me! It is for your brother.

CLEOPATRA. No.

CÆSAR. For whom, then?

CLEOPATRA. Ask the Roman governor whom you have left us.

CÆSAR. Rufio?

CLEOPATRA. Yes: Rufio. [*She points at him with deadly scorn*]. He who is to rule here in Cæsar's name, in Cæsar's way, according to Cæsar's boasted laws of life.

CÆSAR [*dubiously*] He is to rule as he can, Cleopatra. He has taken the work upon him, and will do it in his own way.

CLEOPATRA. Not in your way, then?

CÆSAR [*puzzled*] What do you mean by my way?

CLEOPATRA. Without punishment. Without revenge. Without judgment.

CÆSAR [*approvingly*] Ay: that is the right way, the great way, the only possible way in the end. [*To Rufio*] Believe it, Rufio, if you can.

RUFIO. Why, I believe it, Cæsar. You have convinced me of it long ago. But look you. You are sailing for Numidia today. Now tell me: if you meet a hungry lion there, you will not punish it for wanting to eat you?

CÆSAR [*wondering what he is driving at*] No.

RUFIO. Nor revenge upon it the blood of those it has already eaten.

CÆSAR. No.

RUFIO. Nor judge it for its guiltiness.

CÆSAR. No.

RUFIO. What, then, will you do to save your life from it?

CÆSAR [*promptly*] Kill it, man, without malice, just as it would kill me. What does this parable of the lion mean?

RUFIO. Why, Cleopatra had a tigress that killed men at her bidding. I thought she might bid it kill you some day. Well, had I not been Cæsar's pupil, what pious things might I not have done to that tigress! I might have punished it. I might have revenged Pothinus on it.

CÆSAR [*interjects*] Pothinus!

RUFIO [*continuing*] I might have judged it. But I put all these follies behind me; and, without malice, only cut its throat. And that is why Cleopatra comes to you in mourning.

CLEOPATRA [*vehemently*] He has shed the blood of my servant Ftatateeta. On your head be it as upon his, Cæsar, if you hold him free of it.

CÆSAR [*energetically*] On my head be it, then; for it was well done. Rufio: had you set yourself in the seat of the judge, and with hateful ceremonies and appeals to the gods handed that woman over to some hired executioner to be slain before the people in the name of justice, never again would I have touched your hand without a shudder. But this was natural slaying: I feel no horror at it.

Rufio, satisfied, nods at Cleopatra, mutely inviting her to mark that.

CLEOPATRA [*pettish and childish in her impotence*] No: not when a Roman slays an Egyptian. All the world will now see how unjust and corrupt Cæsar is.

CÆSAR [*taking her hands coaxingly*] Come: do not be angry with me. I am sorry for that poor Totateeta. [*She laughs in spite of herself*]. Aha! you are laughing. Does that mean reconciliation?

CLEOPATRA [*angry with herself for laughing*] No, no, NO!! But it is so ridiculous to hear you call her Totateeta.

CÆSAR. What! As much a child as ever, Cleopatra! Have I not made a woman of you after all?

CLEOPATRA. Oh, it is you who are a great baby: you make me seem silly because you will not behave seriously. But you have treated me badly; and I do not forgive you.

CÆSAR. Bid me farewell.

CLEOPATRA. I will not.

CÆSAR [*coaxing*] I will send you a beautiful present from Rome.

CLEOPATRA [*proudly*] Beauty from Rome to Egypt indeed! What can Rome give me that Egypt cannot give me?

APOLLODORUS. That is true, Cæsar. If the present is to be really beautiful, I shall have to buy it for you in Alexandria.

CÆSAR. You are forgetting the treasures for which Rome is most famous, my friend. You cannot buy them in Alexandria.

APOLLODORUS. What are they, Cæsar?

CÆSAR. Her sons. Come, Cleopatra: forgive me and bid me farewell; and I will send you a man, Roman from head to heel and Roman of the noblest; not old and ripe for the knife; not lean in the arms and cold in the heart; not hiding a bald head under his conqueror's laurels; not stooped with the weight of the world on his shoulders; but brisk and fresh, strong and young, hoping in the morning, fighting in the day, and revelling in the evening. Will you take such an one in exchange for Cæsar?

CLEOPATRA [*palpitating*] His name, his name?

CÆSAR. Shall it be Mark Antony? [*She throws herself into his arms*].

RUFIO. You are a bad hand at a bargain, mistress, if you will swop Cæsar for Antony.

CÆSAR. So now you are satisfied.

CLEOPATRA. You will not forget.

CÆSAR. I will not forget. Farewell: I do not think we shall meet again. Farewell. [*He kisses her on the forehead. She is much affected*

and begins to sniff. He embarks].

THE ROMAN SOLDIERS [*as he sets his foot on the gangway*] Hail, Cæsar; and farewell!

He reaches the ship and returns Rufio's wave of the hand.

APOLLODORUS [*to Cleopatra*] No tears, dearest Queen: they stab your servant to the heart. He will return some day.

CLEOPATRA. I hope not. But I cant help crying, all the same. [*She waves her handkerchief to Cæsar; and the ship begins to move*].

THE ROMAN SOLDIERS [*drawing their swords and raising them in the air*] Hail, Cæsar!

THE END

X

CAPTAIN BRASSBOUND'S CONVERSION

AN ADVENTURE (1899)

BEING THE THIRD OF THREE PLAYS FOR PURITANS

ACT I

On the heights overlooking the harbor of Mogador, a seaport on the west coast of Morocco, the missionary, in the coolness of the late afternoon, is following the precept of Voltaire by cultivating his garden. He is an elderly Scotchman, spiritually a little weatherbeaten, as having to navigate his creed in strange waters crowded with other craft, but still a convinced son of the Free Church and the North African Mission, with a faithful brown eye, and a peaceful soul. Physically a wiry small-knit man, well tanned, clean shaven, with delicate resolute features and a twinkle of mild humor. He wears the sun helmet and pagri, the neutral-tinted spectacles, and the white canvas Spanish sand shoes of the modern Scotch missionary; but instead of a cheap tourist's suit from Glasgow, a grey flannel shirt with white collar, a green sailor knot tie with a cheap pin in it, he wears a suit of clean white linen, acceptable in color, if not in cut, to the Moorish mind.

The view from the garden includes much Atlantic Ocean and a long stretch of sandy coast to the south, swept by the north east trade wind, and scantily nourishing a few stunted pepper trees, mangy palms, and tamarisks. The prospect ends, as far as the land is concerned, in little hills that come nearly to the sea: rudiments, these, of the Atlas Mountains. The missionary, having had daily opportunities of looking at this seascape

for thirty years or so, pays no heed to it, being absorbed in trimming a huge red geranium bush, to English eyes unnaturally big, which, with a dusty smilax or two, is the sole product of his pet flower-bed. He is sitting to his work on a Moorish stool. In the middle of the garden there is a pleasant seat in the shade of a tamarisk tree. The house is in the south west corner of the garden, and the geranium bush in the north east corner.

At the garden-door of the house there appears presently a man who is clearly no barbarian, being in fact a less agreeable product peculiar to modern commercial civilization. His frame and flesh are those of an ill-nourished lad of seventeen; but his age is inscrutable: only the absence of any sign of grey in his mud colored hair suggests that he is at all events probably under forty, without prejudice to the possibility of his being under twenty. A Londoner would recognize him at once as an extreme but hardy specimen of the abortion produced by nurture in a city slum. His utterance, affectedly pumped and hearty, and naturally vulgar and nasal, is ready and fluent: nature, a Board School education, and some kerbstone practice having made him a bit of an orator. His dialect, apart from its base nasal delivery, is not unlike that of smart London society in its tendency to replace diphthongs by vowels (sometimes rather prettily) and to shuffle all the traditional vowel pronunciations. He pronounces ow as ah, and i as aw, using the ordinary ow for *o, i for ā, ă for ŭ, and ĕ for ă, with this reservation, that when any vowel is followed by an r, he signifies its presence, not by pronouncing the r, which he never does under these circumstances, but by prolonging and modifying the vowel, sometimes even to the extreme degree of pronouncing it properly. As to his yol for l (a compendious delivery of the provincial eh-al), and other metropolitan refinements, amazing to all but cockneys, they cannot be indicated, save in the above imperfect manner, without the aid of a phonetic alphabet. He is dressed in somebody else's very second best as a coastguardsman, and gives himself the airs of a stage tar with sufficient success to pass as a possible fish porter of bad character in casual employment during busy times at Billingsgate. His manner shews an earnest disposition to ingratiate himself with the missionary, probably for some dishonest purpose.*

THE MAN. Awtenoon, Mr Renkin. [*The missionary sits up quickly, and turns, resigning himself dutifully to the interruption*]. Yr honor's eolth.

RANKIN [*reservedly*] Good afternoon, Mr Drinkwotter.

DRINKWATER. Youre not best pleased to be hinterrapted in yr bit o gawdnin baw the lawk o me, gavner.

RANKIN. A missionary knows nothing of leks of that soart, or of disleks either, Mr Drinkwotter. What can I do for ye?

DRINKWATER [*heartily*] Nathink, gavner. Awve bror noos fer yer.

RANKIN. Well, sit ye doon.

DRINKWATER. Aw thenk yr honor. [*He sits down on the seat under the tree and composes himself for conversation*]. Hever ear o Judge Ellam?

RANKIN. Sir Howrrd Hallam?

DRINKWATER. Thets im—enginest judge in Hingland!—awlus gives the ket wen its robbry with voylence, bless is awt. Aw sy nathink agin im: awm all fer lor mawseolf, aw em.

RANKIN. Well?

DRINKWATER. Hever ear of is sist-in-lor: Lidy Sisly Winefleet?

RANKIN. Do ye mean the celebrated leddy —the traveller?

DRINKWATER. Yuss: should think aw doo. Walked acrost Harfricar with nathink but a little dawg, and wrowt abaht it in the Dily Mile [*the Daily Mail, a popular London newspaper*], she did.

RANKIN. Is she Sir Howrrd Hallam's sister-in-law?

DRINKWATER. Deceased wawfe's sister: yuss: thets wot s h e is.

RANKIN. Well, what about them?

DRINKWATER. Wot abaht them! Waw, theyr e a h. Lannid aht of a steam yacht in Mogador awber not twenty minnits agow. Gorn to the British cornsl's. E'll send em orn to you: e ynt got naowheres to put em. Sor em awr (*hire*) a Harab an two Krooboys to kerry their laggige. Thort awd cam an teoll yer.

RANKIN. Thank you. Its verra kind of you, Mr Drinkwotter.

DRINKWATER. Downt mention it, gavner. Lor bless yer, wawnt it you as converted me? Wot was aw wen aw cam eah but a pore lorst sinner? Downt aw ow y'a turn fer thet? Besawds, gavner, this Lidy Sisly Winefleet mawt wornt to tike a walk crost Morocker— a rawd inter the mahntns or sech lawk. Weoll, as you knaow, gavner, thet cawnt be done eah withaht a hescort.

RANKIN. It's impoassible: th' would oall b' murrdered. Morocco is not lek the rest of Africa.

DRINKWATER. No, gavner: these eah Moors ez their religion; an it mikes em dinegerous. Hever convert a Moor, gavner?

RANKIN [*with a rueful smile*] No.

DRINKWATER [*solemnly*] Nor hever will, gavner.

RANKIN. I have been at work here for twenty-five years, Mr Drinkwotter; and you are my first and only convert.

DRINKWATER. Downt seem naow good, do it, gavner?

RANKIN. I dont say that. I hope I have done some good. They come to me for medicine when they are ill; and they call me the Christian who is not a thief. T h a t is something.

DRINKWATER. Their mawnds kennot rawse to Christiennity lawk hahrs ken, gavner: thets ah it is. Weoll, ez haw was syin, if a hescort is wornted, there's maw friend and commawnder Kepn Brarsbahnd of the schooner Thenksgivin, an is crew, incloodin mawseolf, will see the lidy an Judge Ellam through henny little excursion in reason. Yr honor mawt mention it.

RANKIN. I will certainly not propose any thing so dangerous as an excursion.

DRINKWATER [*virtuously*] Naow, gavner, nor would I awst you to. [*Shaking his head*] Naow, naow: it is dinegerous. But hall the more call for a hescort if they should ev it hin their mawnds to gow.

RANKIN. I hope they wont.

DRINKWATER. An sow aw do too, gavner.

RANKIN [pondering] Tis strange that they should come to Mogador, of all places; and to my house! I once met Sir Howrrd Hallam, years ago.

DRINKWATER [amazed] Naow! didger? Think o thet, gavner! Waw, sow aw did too. But it were a misunnerstendin, thet wors. Lef the court withaht a stine on maw kerrickter, aw did.

RANKIN [with some indignation] I hope you dont think I met Sir Howrrd in that way.

DRINKWATER. Mawt yeppn to the honestest, best meanin pusson, aw do assure yer, gavner.

RANKIN. I would have you to know that I met him privately, Mr Drinkwotter. His brother was a dear friend of mine. Years ago. He went out to the West Indies.

DRINKWATER. The Wust Hindies! Jist acrost there, tather sawd thet howcean [pointing seaward]! Dear me! We cams hin with vennity, an we deepawts in dawkness. Downt we, gavner?

RANKIN [pricking up his ears] Eh? Have you been reading that little book I gave you?

DRINKWATER. Aw hev, et odd tawms. Very camfitn, gavner. [He rises, apprehensive lest further catechism should find him unprepared]. Awll sy good awtcnoon, gavner: youre busy hexpectin o Sr Ahrd an Lidy Sisly, ynt yer? [About to go].

RANKIN [stopping him] No, stop: we're oalways ready for travellers here. I have something else to say—a question to ask you.

DRINKWATER [with misgiving, which he masks by exaggerating his hearty sailor manner] An weollcome, yr honor.

RANKIN. Who is this Captain Brassbound?

DRINKWATER [guiltily] Kepn Brarsbahnd! E's—weoll, e's maw Kepn, gavner.

RANKIN. Yes. Well?

DRINKWATER [feebly] Kepn of the schooner Thenksgivin, gavner.

RANKIN [searchingly] Have ye ever haird of a bad character in these seas called Black Paquito?

DRINKWATER [with a sudden radiance of complete enlightenment] Aoh, nar aw tikes yer wiv me, yr honor. Nah sammun es bin a teolln you thet Kepn Brarsbahnd an Bleck Pakeetow is haw-dentically the sime pussn. Ynt thet sow?

RANKIN. That is so. [Drinkwater slaps his knee triumphantly. The missionary proceeds determinedly] And the someone was a verra honest, straightforward man, as far as I could judge.

DRINKWATER [embracing the implication] Course e wors, gavner. Ev aw said a word agin him? Ev aw nah?

RANKIN. But is Captain Brassbound Black Paquito then?

DRINKWATER. Waw, its the nime is blessed mather give im at er knee, bless is little awt! Ther ynt naow awm in it. She were a Wust Hinjin—howver there agin, yer see [pointing seaward]—leastwaws, naow she wornt: she were a Brazilian, aw think; an Pakeetow's Brazilian for a bloomin little perrit—awskin yr pawdn for the word. [Sentimentally] Lawk as a Hinglish lidy mawt call er little boy Birdie.

RANKIN [not quite convinced] But why Black Paquito?

DRINKWATER [artlessly] Waw, the bird in its netral stite bein green, an e evin bleck air, y' knaow—

RANKIN [cutting him short] I see. And now I will put ye another question. W h a t is Captain Brassbound, or Paquito, or whatever he calls himself?

DRINKWATER [officiously] Brarsbahnd, gavner. Awlus calls isseolf Brarsbahnd.

RANKIN. Well, Brassbound then. What is he?

DRINKWATER [fervently] You awsks me wot e is, gavner?

RANKIN [firmly] I do.

DRINKWATER [with rising enthusiasm] An shll aw teoll yer wot e is, yr honor?

RANKIN [not at all impressed] If ye will be so good, Mr Drinkwotter.

DRINKWATER [with overwhelming conviction] Then awll teoll you, gavner, wot he is. Ee's a Paffick Genlmn: thets wot e is.

RANKIN [gravely] Mr Drinkwotter: pairfection is an attribute, not of West Coast captains, but of thr Maaker. And there are gentlemen and gentlemen in the world, espaecially in these latitudes. Which sort of gentleman is he?

DRINKWATER. Hinglish genlmn, gavner. Hinglish speakin; Hinglish fawther; West Hinjin plawntcr; Hinglish true blue breed. [Reflectively] Tech o brahn from the mather, preps, she bein Brazilian.

RANKIN. Now on your faith as a Christian, Felix Drinkwotter, is Captain Brassbound a slaver or not?

DRINKWATER [*surprised into his natural cockney pertness*] Naow e ynt.

RANKIN. Are ye s u r e?

DRINKWATER. Waw, a sliver is abaht the wanne thing in the wy of a genlmn o fortn thet e y n t.

RANKIN. Ive haird that expression "gentleman of fortune" before, Mr Drinkwotter. It means pirate. Do ye know that?

DRINKWATER. Bless yr awt, y' cawnt be a pawrit naradys. Waw, the aw seas is wuss pleest nor Piccadilly Suckus. If aw was to do orn thet there Hetlentic Howcean the things aw did as a bwoy in the Worterleoo Rowd, awd ev maw air cat afore aw could turn maw ed. Pawrit be blaowed!—awskink yr pawdn, gavner. Nah, jest to shaow you ah little thet there striteforard man y' mide mention on knaowed wot e was atorkin abaht: oo would you spowse was the marster to wich Kepn Brarsbahnd served apprentice, as yr mawt sy?

RANKIN. I dont know.

DRINKWATER. Gawdn, gavner, Gawdn. Gawdn o Kawtoom—stetcher stends in Trifawlgr Square to this dy. Trined Bleck Pakeetow in smawshin hap the slive riders, e did. Promist Gawdn e wouldnt never smaggle slives nor gin, an [*with suppressed aggravation*] w o w n t, gavner, not if we gows dahn on ahr bloomin bended knees to im to do it.

RANKIN [*drily*] And d o ye go down on your bended knees to him to do it?

DRINKWATER [*somewhat abashed*] Some of huz is hanconverted men, gavner; an they sy: You smaggles wanne thing, Kepn; waw not hanather?

RANKIN. Weve come to it at last. I thought so. Captain Brassbound is a smuggler.

DRINKWATER. Weoll, waw not? Waw not, gavner? Ahrs is a Free Tride nition. It gows agin us as Hinglishmen to see these bloomin furriners settin ap their Castoms Ahses and spheres o hinfluence and sich lawk hall owver Arfricar. Daownt Harfricar belong as much to huz as to them? thets wot we sy. Ennywys, there ynt naow awm in ahr business. All we daz is hescort, tourist h o r commercial. Cook's hexcursions to the Hatlas Mahntns: thets hall it is. Waw, its spreadin civlawzytion, it is. Ynt it nah?

RANKIN. You think Captain Brassbound's crew sufficiently equipped for that, do you?

DRINKWATER. Hee-quipped! Haw should think sow. Lawtnin rawfles, twelve shots in the meggezine! Oo's to storp us?

RANKIN. The most dangerous chieftain in these parts, the Sheikh Sidi el Assif, has a new American machine pistol which fires ten bullets without loadin; and his rifle has sixteen shots in the magazine.

DRINKWATER [*indignantly*] Yuss; and the people that sells sich things into the ends o them eathen bleck niggers calls theirseolves Christians! Its a crool shime, sow it is.

RANKIN. If a man has the heart to pull the trigger, it matters little what color his hand is, Mr Drinkwotter. Have ye anything else to say to me this afternoon?

DRINKWATER [*rising*] Nathink, gavner, cept to wishyer the bust o yolth, and a many converts. Awtenoon, gavner.

As Drinkwater turns to go, a Moorish porter comes from the house with two Krooboys.

THE PORTER [*at the door, addressing Rankin*] Bikouros [*Moroccan for Epicurus, a general Moorish name for the missionaries, who are supposed by the Moors to have chosen their calling through a love of luxurious idleness*]: I have brought to your house a Christian dog and his woman.

DRINKWATER. Theres eathen menners fer yer! Calls Sr Ahrd Ellam an Lidy Winefleet a Christian dorg and is woman! If ee ed you in the dorck et the Centl Crimnal, youd fawnd aht oo was the dorg and oo was is marster, pretty quick, y o u would.

RANKIN. Have you broat their boxes?

THE PORTER. By Allah, two camel loads!

RANKIN. Have you been paid?

THE PORTER. Only one miserable dollar, Bikouros. I have brought them to your house. They will pay you. Give me something for bringing gold to your door.

DRINKWATER. Yah! You oughter bin bawn a Christian, you ought. You knaow too mach.

RANKIN. You have broat onnly trouble and expense to my door, Hassan; and you know it. Have I ever charged your wife and children for my medicines?

HASSAN [*philosophically*] It is always permitted by the Prophet to ask, Bikouros. [*He goes cheerfully into the house with the Krooboys*].

DRINKWATER. Jist thort eed trah it orn, e did. Hooman nitre is the sime everywheres. Them eathens is jast lawk you an'me, gavner.

A lady and gentleman, both English, come into the garden. The gentleman, more than elderly, is facing old age on compulsion, not re-

signedly. He is clean shaven, and has a brainy rectangular forehead, a resolute nose with strongly governed nostrils, and a tightly fastened down mouth which has evidently shut in much temper and anger in its time. He has a habit of deliberately assumed authority and dignity, but is trying to take life more genially and easily in his character of tourist, which is further borne out by his white hat and summery racecourse attire.

The lady is between thirty and forty, tall, very goodlooking, sympathetic, intelligent, tender and humorous, dressed with cunning simplicity not as a businesslike, tailor made, gaitered tourist, but as if she lived at the next cottage and had dropped in for tea in blouse and flowered straw hat. A woman of great vitality and humanity, who begins a casual acquaintance at the point usually attained by English people after thirty years' acquaintance when they are capable of reaching it at all. She pounces genially on Drinkwater, who is smirking at her, hat in hand, with an air of hearty welcome. The gentleman, on the other hand, comes down the side of the garden next the house, instinctively maintaining a distance between himself and the others.

THE LADY [*to Drinkwater*] How dye do? Are you the missionary?

DRINKWATER [*modestly*] Naow, lidy, aw will not deceive you, thow the mistike his but netral. Awm wanne of the missionary's good works, lidy—is first cornvert, a umble British seaman—countrymen o yours, lidy, and of is lawdship's. This eah is Mr Renkin, the bust worker in the wust cowst vawnyard. [*Introducing the judge*] Mr Renkin: is lawdship Sr Ahrd Ellam. [*He withdraws discreetly into the house*].

SIR HOWARD [*to Rankin*] I am sorry to intrude on you, Mr Rankin; but in the absence of a hotel there seems to be no alternative.

LADY CICELY [*beaming on him*] Besides, we would so much r a t h e r stay with you, if you will have us, Mr Rankin.

SIR HOWARD [*introducing her*] My sister-in-law, Lady Cicely Waynflete, Mr Rankin.

RANKIN. I am glad to be of service to your leddyship. You will be wishing to have some tea after your journey, I'm thinking.

LADY CICELY. Thoughtful man that you are, Mr Rankin. But weve had some already on board the yacht. And Ive arranged everything with your servants; so you must go on gardening just as if we were not here.

SIR HOWARD. I am sorry to have to warn you, Mr Rankin, that Lady Cicely, from travelling in Africa, has acquired a habit of walking into people's houses and behaving as if she were in her own.

LADY CICELY. But, my dear Howard, I assure you the natives like it.

RANKIN [*gallantly*] So do I.

LADY CICELY [*delighted*] Oh, that is so nice of you, Mr Rankin. This is a delicious country! And the people seem so good! They have such nice faces! We had such a handsome Moor to carry our luggage up! And two perfect pets of Krooboys! Did you notice their faces, Howard?

SIR HOWARD. I did; and I can confidently say, after a long experience of faces of the worst type looking at me from the dock, that I have never seen so entirely villainous a trio as that Moor and the two Krooboys, to whom you gave five dollars when they would have been perfectly satisfied with one.

RANKIN [*throwing up his hands*] Five dollars! Tis easy to see you are not Scotch, my leddy.

LADY CICELY. O, poor things, they must want it more than we do; and you know, Howard, that Mahometans never spend money in drink.

RANKIN. Excuse me a moment, my leddy. I have a word in season to say to that same Moor. [*He goes into the house*].

LADY CICELY [*walking about the garden, looking at the view and at the flowers*] I think this is a perfectly heavenly place.

Drinkwater returns from the house with a chair.

DRINKWATER [*placing the chair for Sir Howard*] Awskink yr pawdn for the libbety, Sr Ahrd.

SIR HOWARD [*looking at him*] I have seen you before somewhere.

DRINKWATER. You ev, Sr Ahrd. But aw do assure yer it were hall a mistike.

SIR HOWARD. As usual. [*He sits down*]. Wrongfully convicted, of course.

DRINKWATER [*with sly delight*] Naow, gavner. [*Half whispering, with an ineffable grin*] Wrorngfully hacquittid!

SIR HOWARD. Indeed! Thats the first case of the kind I have ever met.

DRINKWATER. Lawd, Sr Ahrd, wot jagginses them jurymen was! You an me knaowed it too, didnt we?

SIR HOWARD. I daresay we did. I am sorry to say I forget the exact nature of the difficulty you were in. Can you refresh my memory?

DRINKWATER. Owny the aw sperrits o youth y' lawdship. Worterleoo Rowd kice. Wot they calls Ooliganism.

SIR HOWARD. Oh! You were a Hooligan, were you?

LADY CICELY [*puzzled*] A Hooligan!

DRINKWATER [*deprecatingly*] Nime giv huz pore thortless leds baw a gent on the Dily Chronicle, lidy. [*Rankin returns. Drinkwater immediately withdraws, stopping the missionary for a moment near the threshold to say, touching his forelock*] Awll eng abaht within ile, gavner, hin kice aw should be wornted. [*He goes into the house with soft steps*].

Lady Cicely sits down on the bench under the tamarisk. Rankin takes his stool from the flower-bed and sits down on her left, Sir Howard being on her right.

LADY CICELY. What a pleasant face your sailor friend has, Mr Rankin! He has been so frank and truthful with us. You know I dont think anybody can pay me a greater compliment than to be quite sincere with me at first sight. Its the perfection of natural good manners.

SIR HOWARD. You must not suppose, Mr Rankin, that my sister-in-law talks nonsense on purpose. She will continue to believe in your friend until he steals her watch; and even then she will find excuses for him.

RANKIN [*drily changing the subject*] And how have ye been, Sir Howrrd, since our last meeting that morning nigh forty year ago down at the docks in London?

SIR HOWARD [*greatly surprised, pulling himself together*] Our last meeting! Mr Rankin: have I been unfortunate enough to forget an old acquaintance?

RANKIN. Well, perhaps hardly an acquaintance, Sir Howrrd. But I was a close friend of your brother Miles; and when he sailed for Brazil I was one of the little party that saw him off. You were one of the party also, if I'm not mistaken. I took particular notice of you because you were Miles's brother and I had never seen ye before. But ye had no call to take notice of me.

SIR HOWARD [*reflecting*] Yes: there was a young friend of my brother's who might well be you. But the name, as I recollect it, was Leslie.

RANKIN. That was me, sir. My name is Leslie Rankin; and your brother and I were always Miles and Leslie to one another.

SIR HOWARD [*pluming himself a little*] Ah! that explains it. I can trust my memory still, Mr Rankin; though some people do complain that I am growing old.

RANKIN. And where may Miles be now, Sir Howard?

SIR HOWARD [*abruptly*] Dont you know that he is dead?

RANKIN [*much shocked*] Never haird of it. Dear, dear: I shall never see him again; and I can scarcely bring his face to mind after all these years. [*With moistening eyes, which at once touch Lady Cicely's sympathy*] I'm right sorry—right sorry.

SIR HOWARD [*decorously subduing his voice*] Yes: he did not live long: indeed, he never came back to England. It must be nearly thirty years ago now that he died in the West Indies on his property there.

RANKIN [*surprised*] His proaperty! Miles with a proaperty!

SIR HOWARD. Yes: he became a planter, and did well out there, Mr Rankin. The history of that property is a very curious and interesting one—at least it is so to a lawyer like myself.

RANKIN. I should be glad to hear it for Miles' sake, though I am no lawyer, Sir Howrrd.

LADY CICELY. I never knew you had a brother, Howard?

SIR HOWARD [*not pleased by this remark*] Perhaps because you never asked me. [*Turning more blandly to Rankin*] I will tell you the story, Mr Rankin. When Miles died, he left an estate in one of the West Indian islands. It was in charge of an agent who was a sharpish fellow, with all his wits about him. Now, sir, that man did a thing which probably could hardly be done with impunity even here in Morocco, under the most barbarous of surviving civilizations. He quite simply took the estate for himself and kept it.

RANKIN. But how about the law?

SIR HOWARD. The law, sir, in that island, consisted practically of the Attorney General and the Solicitor General; and these gentlemen were both retained by the agent. Consequently there was no solicitor in the island to take up the case against him.

RANKIN. Is such a thing possible today in the British Empire?

SIR HOWARD [*calmly*] Oh, quite. Quite.

LADY CICELY. But could not a firstrate solicitor have been sent out from London?

SIR HOWARD. No doubt, by paying him enough to compensate him for giving up his London practice: that is, rather more than there was any reasonable likelihood of the estate proving worth.

RANKIN. Then the estate was lost?

SIR HOWARD. Not permanently. It is in my hands at present.

RANKIN. Then how did ye get it back?

SIR HOWARD [with crafty enjoyment of his own cunning] By hoisting the rogue with his own petard. I had to leave matters as they were for many years; for I had my own position in the world to make. But at last I made it. In the course of a holiday trip to the West Indies, I found that this dishonest agent had left the island, and placed the estate in the hands of an agent of his own, whom he was foolish enough to pay very badly. I put the case before that agent; and he decided to treat the estate as my property. The robber now found himself in exactly the same position he had formerly forced me into. Nobody in the island would act against me, least of all the Attorney and Solicitor General, who appreciated my influence at the Colonial Office. And so I got the estate back. "The mills of the gods grind slowly," Mr Rankin; "but they grind exceeding small."

LADY CICELY. Now I suppose if I'd done such a clever thing in England, youd have sent me to prison.

SIR HOWARD. Probably, unless you had taken care to keep outside the law against conspiracy. Whenever you wish to do anything against the law, Cicely, always consult a good solicitor first.

LADY CICELY. So I do. But suppose your agent takes it into his head to give the estate back to his wicked old employer!

SIR HOWARD. I heartily wish he would.

RANKIN [openeyed] You wish he would!!

SIR HOWARD. Yes. A few years ago the collapse of the West Indian sugar industry converted the income of the estate into an annual loss of about £150 a year. If I cant sell it soon, I shall simply abandon it—unless you, Mr Rankin, would like to take it as a present.

RANKIN [laughing] I thank your lordship: we have estates enough of that sort in Scotland. Your setting with your back to the sun, Leddy Ceecily, and losing something worth looking at. See there. [He rises and points seaward, where the rapid twilight of the latitude has begun].

LADY CICELY [getting up to look and uttering a cry of admiration] Oh, how lovely!

SIR HOWARD [also rising] What are those hills over there to the southeast?

RANKIN. They are the outposts, so to speak, of the Atlas Mountains.

LADY CICELY. The Atlas Mountains! Where Shelley's witch lived! We'll make an excursion to them tomorrow, Howard.

RANKIN. Thats impossible, my leddy. The natives are verra dangerous.

LADY CICELY. Why? Has any explorer been shooting them?

RANKIN. No. But every man of them believes he will go to Heaven if he kills an unbeliever.

LADY CICELY. Bless you, dear Mr Rankin, the people in England believe that they will go to heaven if they give all their property to the poor. But they dont do it. I'm not a bit afraid of that.

RANKIN. But they are not accustomed to see women going about unveiled.

LADY CICELY. I always get on best with people when they can see my face.

SIR HOWARD. Cicely: you are talking great nonsense; and you know it. These people have no laws to restrain them, which means, in plain English, that they are habitual thieves and murderers.

RANKIN. Nay, nay: not exactly that, Sir Howrrd.

LADY CICELY [indignantly] Of course not. You always think, Howard, that nothing prevents people killing each other but the fear of your hanging them for it. But what nonsense that is! And how wicked! If these people werent here for some good purpose, they wouldnt have been made, would they, Mr Rankin?

RANKIN. That is a point, certainly, Leddy Ceecily.

SIR HOWARD. Oh, if you are going to talk theology—

LADY CICELY. Well, why not? theology is as respectable as law, I should think. Besides, I'm only talking commonsense. Why do people get killed by savages? Because instead of being polite to them, and saying How dye do? like me, people aim pistols at them. Ive been among savages—cannibals and all sorts. Everybody said theyd kill me. But when I met them, I said Howdyedo? and they were quite nice. The kings always wanted to marry me.

SIR HOWARD. That does not seem to me to make you any safer here, Cicely. You shall certainly not stir a step beyond the protection of the consul, if I can help it, without a strong escort.

LADY CICELY. I dont want an escort.

SIR HOWARD. I do. And I suppose you will expect me to accompany you.

RANKIN. Tis not safe, Leddy Ceecily. Really and truly, tis not safe. The tribes are verra fierce; and there are cities here that no Christian has ever set foot in. If you go without being well protected, the first chief you meet will seize you and send you back again to prevent his followers murdering you.

LADY CICELY. Oh, how nice of him, Mr Rankin!

RANKIN. He would not do it for your sake, Leddy Ceecily, but for his own. The Sultan would get into trouble with England if you were killed; and the Sultan would kill the chief to pacify the English government.

LADY CICELY. But I always go everywhere. I know the people here wont touch me. They have such nice faces and such pretty scenery.

SIR HOWARD [to Rankin, sitting down again resignedly] You can imagine how much use there is in talking to a woman who admires the faces of the ruffians who infest these ports, Mr Rankin. Can anything be done in the way of an escort?

RANKIN. There is a certain Captain Brassbound here who trades along the coast, and occasionally escorts parties of merchants on journeys into the interior. I understand that he served under Gordon in the Soudan.

SIR HOWARD. That sounds promising. But I should like to know a little more about him before I trust myself in his hands.

RANKIN. I quite agree with you, Sir Howrrd. I'll send Felix Drinkwotter for him [He claps his hands. An Arab boy appears at the house door]. Muley: is sailor man here? [Muley nods]. Tell sailor man bring captain. [Muley nods and goes].

SIR HOWARD. Who is Drinkwater?

RANKIN. His agent, or mate: I dont rightly know which.

LADY CICELY. Oh, if he has a mate named Felix Drinkwater, it must be quite a respectable crew. It is such a nice name.

RANKIN. You saw him here just now. He is a convert of mine.

LADY CICELY [delighted] That nice truthful sailor!

SIR HOWARD [horrified] What! The Hooligan!

RANKIN [puzzled] Hooligan? No, my lord: he is an Englishman.

SIR HOWARD. My dear Mr Rankin, this man was tried before me on a charge of street ruffianism.

RANKIN. So he told me. He was badly broat up, I am afraid. But he is now a converted man.

LADY CICELY. Of course he is. His telling you so frankly proves it. You know, really, Howard, all those poor people whom you try are more sinned against than sinning. If you would only talk to them in a friendly way instead of passing cruel sentences on them, you would find them quite nice to you. [Indignantly] I wont have this poor man trampled on merely because his mother brought him up as a Hooligan. I am sure nobody could be nicer than he was when he spoke to us.

SIR HOWARD. In short, we are to have an escort of Hooligans commanded by a filibuster. Very well, very well. You will most likely admire all their faces; and I have no doubt at all that they will admire yours.

Drinkwater comes from the house with an Italian dressed in a much worn suit of blue serge, a dilapidated Alpine hat, and boots laced with scraps of twine. He remains near the door, whilst Drinkwater comes forward between Sir Howard and Lady Cicely.

DRINKWATER. Yr honor's servant. [To the Italian] Mawtzow: is lawdship Sr Ahrd Ellam [Marzo touches his hat]. Er lidyship Lidy Winefleet [Marzo touches his hat]. Hawtellian shipmite, lidy. Hahr chef.

LADY CICELY [nodding affably to Marzo] Howdyedo? I love Italy. What part of it were you born in?

DRINKWATER. Wornt bawn in Hitly at all, lidy. Bawn in Ettn Gawdn [Hatton Garden]. Hawce barrer an street pianner Hawtellian, lidy: thets wot e is. Kepn Brarsbahnd's respects to yr honors; an e awites yr commawnds.

RANKIN. Shall we go indoors to see him?

SIR HOWARD. I think we had better have a look at him by daylight.

RANKIN. Then we must lose no time: the dark is soon down in this latitude. [To Drinkwater] Will ye ask him to step out here to us, Mr Drinkwotter?

DRINKWATER. Rawt you aw, gavner. [He goes officiously into the house].

Lady Cicely and Rankin sit down as before to receive the Captain. The light is by this time waning rapidly, the darkness creeping west into the orange crimson.

LADY CICELY [*whispering*] Dont you feel rather creepy, Mr Rankin? I wonder what he'll be like.

RANKIN. I misdoubt me he will not answer, your leddyship.

There is a scuffling noise in the house; and Drinkwater shoots out through the doorway across the garden with every appearance of having been violently kicked. Marzo immediately hurries down the garden on Sir Howard's right out of the neighborhood of the doorway.

DRINKWATER [*trying to put a cheerful air on much mortification and bodily anguish*] Narsty step to thet ere door—tripped me hap, it did. [*Raising his voice and narrowly escaping a squeak of pain*] Kepn Brarsbahnd. [*He gets as far from the house as possible, on Rankin's left. Rankin rises to receive his guest*].

An olive complexioned man with dark southern eyes and hair comes from the house. Age about 36. Handsome features, but joyless; dark eyebrows drawn towards one another; mouth set grimly; nostrils large and strained: a face set to one tragic purpose. A man of few words, fewer gestures, and much significance. On the whole, interesting, and even attractive, but not friendly. He stands for a moment, saturnine in the ruddy light, to see who is present, looking in a singular and rather deadly way at Sir Howard; then with some surprise and uneasiness at Lady Cicely. Finally he comes down into the middle of the garden, and confronts Rankin, who has been staring at him in consternation from the moment of his entrance, and continues to do so in so marked a way that the glow in Brassbound's eyes deepens as he begins to take offence.

BRASSBOUND. Well, sir, have you stared your fill at me?

RANKIN [*recovering himself with a start*] I ask your pardon for my bad manners, Captain Brassbound. Ye are extraordinair lek an auld college friend of mine, whose face I said not ten minutes gone that I could no longer bring to mind. It was as if he had come from the grave to remind me of it.

BRASSBOUND. Why have you sent for me?

RANKIN. We have a matter of business with ye, Captain.

BRASSBOUND. Who are "we"?

RANKIN. This is Sir Howard Hallam, who will be well known to ye as one of Her Majesty's judges.

BRASSBOUND [*turning the singular look again on Sir Howard*] The friend of the widow! the protector of the fatherless!

SIR HOWARD [*startled*] I did not know I was so favorably spoken of in these parts, Captain Brassbound. We want an escort for a trip into the mountains.

BRASSBOUND [*ignoring this announcement*] Who is the lady?

RANKIN. Lady Ceecily Waynflete, his lordship's sister-in-law.

LADY CICELY. Howdyedo, Captain Brassbound? [*He bows gravely*].

SIR HOWARD [*a little impatient of these questions, which strike him as somewhat impertinent*] Let us come to business, if you please. We are thinking of making a short excursion to see the country about here. Can you provide us with an escort of respectable, trustworthy men?

BRASSBOUND. No.

DRINKWATER [*in strong remonstrance*] Nah, nah, nah! Nah look eah, Kepn, y' knaow—

BRASSBOUND [*between his teeth*] Hold your tongue.

DRINKWATER [*abjectly*] Yuss, Kepn.

RANKIN. I understood it was your business to provide escorts, Captain Brassbound.

BRASSBOUND. You were rightly informed. That is my business.

LADY CICELY. Then why wont you do it for us?

BRASSBOUND. You are not content with an escort. You want respectable, trustworthy men. You should have brought a division of London policemen with you. My men are neither respectable nor trustworthy.

DRINKWATER [*unable to contain himself*] Nah, nah, look eah, Kepn. If you want to be moddist, be moddist on your aown accahnt, nort on mawn.

BRASSBOUND. You see what my men are like. That rascal [*indicating Marzo*] would cut a throat for a dollar if he had courage enough.

MARZO. I not understand. I no spik Englis.

BRASSBOUND. This thing [*pointing to Drinkwater*] is the greatest liar, thief, drunkard, and rapscallion on the west coast.

DRINKWATER [*affecting an ironic indifference*] Gow orn, gow orn. Sr Ahrd ez erd witnesses to maw kerrickter afoah. E knaows ah mech to blieve of em.

LADY CICELY. Captain Brassbound: I have heard all that before about the blacks; and

I found them very nice people when they were properly treated.

DRINKWATER [*chuckling: the Italian is also grinning*] Nah, Kepn, nah! Owp yr prahd o y'seolf nah.

BRASSBOUND. I quite understand the proper treatment for him, madam. If he opens his mouth again without my leave, I will break every bone in his skin.

LADY CICELY [*in her most sunnily matter-of-fact way*] Does Captain Brassbound always treat you like this, Mr Drinkwater?

Drinkwater hesitates, and looks apprehensively at the Captain.

BRASSBOUND. Answer, you dog, when the lady orders you. [*To Lady Cicely*] Do not address him as Mr Drinkwater, madam: he is accustomed to be called Brandyfaced Jack.

DRINKWATER [*indignantly*] Eah, aw sy! nah look eah, Kepn: maw nime is Drinkworter. You awsk em et Sin Jorn's in the Worterleoo Rowd. Orn maw grenfawther's tombstown, it is.

BRASSBOUND. It will be on your own tombstone, presently, if you cannot hold your tongue. [*Turning to the others*] Let us understand one another, if you please. An escort here, or anywhere where there are no regular disciplined forces, is what its captain makes it. If I undertake this business, *I* shall be your escort. I may require a dozen men, just as I may require a dozen horses. Some of the horses will be vicious; so will all the men. If either horse or man tries any of his viciousness on me, so much the worse for him; but it will make no difference to you. I will order my men to behave themselves before the lady; and they shall obey their orders. But the lady will please understand that I take my own way with them and suffer no interference.

LADY CICELY. Captain Brassbound: I dont want an escort at all. It will simply get us all into danger; and I shall have the trouble of getting it out again. Thats what escorts always do. But since Sir Howard prefers an escort, I think you had better stay at home and let me take charge of it. I know your men will get on perfectly well if theyre properly treated.

DRINKWATER [*with enthusiasm*] Feed aht o yr and, lidy, we would.

BRASSBOUND [*with sardonic assent*] Good. I agree. [*To Drinkwater*] You shall go without me.

DRINKWATER [*terrified*] Eah! Wot are you a syin orn? We cawnt gow withaht yer. [*To Lady Cicely*] Naow, lidy: it wouldnt be for yr hown good. Yer cawnt hexpect a lot o poor honeddikited men lawk huz to ran ahrseolvs into dineger withaht naow Kepn to teoll us wot to do. Naow, lidy: hoonawted we stend: deevawdid we fall.

LADY CICELY. Oh, if you prefer your captain, have him by all means. Do you like to be treated as he treats you?

DRINKWATER [*with a smile of vanity*] Weoll, lidy: y' cawnt deenaw that e's a Paffick Genlmn. Bit hawbitrairy, preps; but hin a genlmn you looks for sich. It tikes a hawbitrairy wanne to knock aht them eathen Shikes, aw teoll yer.

BRASSBOUND. Thats enough. Go.

DRINKWATER. Weoll, aw was hownly a teolln the lidy thet— [*A threatening movement from Brassbound cuts him short. He flies for his life into the house, followed by the Italian*].

BRASSBOUND. Your ladyship sees. These men serve me by their own free choice. If they are dissatisfied, they go. If *I* am dissatisfied, they go. They take care that I am not dissatisfied.

SIR HOWARD [*who has listened with approval and growing confidence*] Captain Brassbound: you are the man I want. If your terms are at all reasonable, I will accept your services if we decide to make an excursion. You do not object, Cicely, I hope.

LADY CICELY. Oh no. After all, those men must really like you, Captain Brassbound. I feel sure you have a kind heart. You have such nice eyes.

SIR HOWARD [*scandalized*] My dear Cicely: you really must restrain your expressions of confidence in people's eyes and faces. [*To Brassbound*] Now, about terms, Captain?

BRASSBOUND. Where do you propose to go?

SIR HOWARD. I hardly know. Where can we go, Mr Rankin?

RANKIN. Take my advice, Sir Howrrd. Dont go far.

BRASSBOUND. I can take you to Meskala, from which you can see the Atlas Mountains. From Meskala I can take you to an ancient castle in the hills, where you can put up as long as you please. The customary charge is half a dollar a man per day and his food. *I* charge double.

SIR HOWARD. I suppose you answer for your men being sturdy fellows, who will stand to their guns if necessary.

BRASSBOUND. I can answer for their being more afraid of me than of the Moors.

LADY CICELY. That doesnt matter in the least, Howard. The important thing, Captain Brassbound, is: first, that we should have as few men as possible, because men give such a lot of trouble travelling. And then, they must have good lungs and not be always catching cold. Above all, their clothes must be of good wearing material. Otherwise I shall be nursing and stitching and mending all the way; and it will be trouble enough, I assure you, to keep them washed and fed without that.

BRASSBOUND [haughtily] My men, madam, are not children in the nursery.

LADY CICELY [with unanswerable conviction] Captain Brassbound: all men are children in the nursery. I see that you dont notice things. That poor Italian had only one proper boot-lace: the other was a bit of string. And I am sure from Mr Drinkwater's complexion that he ought to have some medicine.

BRASSBOUND [outwardly determined not to be trifled with: inwardly puzzled and rather daunted] Madam: if you want an escort, I can provide you with an escort. If you want a Sunday School treat, I can not provide it.

LADY CICELY [with sweet melancholy] Ah, dont you wish you could, Captain? Oh, if I could only shew you my children from Wayn-flete Sunday School! The darlings would love this place, with all the camels and black men. I'm sure you would enjoy having them here, Captain Brassbound; and it would be such an education for your men! [Brassbound stares at her with drying lips].

SIR HOWARD. Cicely: when you have quite done talking nonsense to Captain Brassbound, we can proceed to make some definite arrangement with him.

LADY CICELY. But it's arranged already. We'll start at eight o'clock tomorrow morning, if you please, Captain. Never mind about the Italian: I have a big box of clothes with me for my brother in Rome; and there are some bootlaces in it. Now go home to bed and dont fuss yourself. All you have to do is to bring your men round; and I'll see to the rest. Men are always so nervous about moving. Goodnight. [She offers him her hand. Surprised he pulls off his cap for the first time. Some scruple prevents him from taking her hand at once. He hesitates; then turns to Sir Howard and addresses him with warning earnestness].

BRASSBOUND. Sir Howard Hallam: I advise you not to attempt this expedition.

SIR HOWARD. Indeed! Why?

BRASSBOUND. You are safe here. I warn you, in those hills there is a justice that is not the justice of your courts in England. If you have wronged a man, you may meet that man there. If you have wronged a woman, you may meet her son there. The justice of those hills is the justice of vengeance.

SIR HOWARD [faintly amused] You are super-stitious, Captain. Most sailors are, I notice. However, I have complete confidence in your escort.

BRASSBOUND [almost threateningly] Take care. The avenger may be one of the escort.

SIR HOWARD. I have already met the only member of your escort who might have borne a grudge against me, Captain; and he was acquitted.

BRASSBOUND. You are fated to come, then?

SIR HOWARD [smiling] It seems so.

BRASSBOUND. On your head be it! [To Lady Cicely, accepting her hand at last] Goodnight. He goes. It is by this time starry night.

ACT II

Midday. A room in a Moorish castle. A divan seat runs round the dilapidated adobe walls, which are partly painted, partly faced with white tiles patterned in green and yellow. The ceiling is made up of little squares, painted in bright colors, with gilded edges, and ornamented with gilt knobs. On the cement floor are mattings, sheepskins, and leathern cushions with geometrical patterns on them. There is a tiny Moorish table in the middle; and at it a huge saddle, with saddle cloths of various colors, shewing that the room is used by foreigners accustomed to chairs. Anyone sitting at the table in this seat would have the chief entrance, a large horseshoe arch, on his left, and another saddle seat between him and the arch; whilst, if susceptible to draughts, he would probably catch cold from a little Moorish door in the wall behind him to his right.

Two or three of Brassbound's men, overcome by the midday heat, sprawl supine on the floor, with their reefer coats under their heads, their knees uplifted, and their calves laid comfortably on the divan. Those who wear shirts have them open at the throat for greater coolness. Some have jerseys. All wear boots and belts, and have guns ready to their hands. One of them, lying with his *head against the second saddle seat, wears what was once a fashionable white English yachting suit. He is evidently a pleasantly worthless young English gentleman gone to the bad, but retaining sufficient self-respect to shave carefully and brush his hair, which is wearing thin, and does not seem to have been luxuriant even in its best days.*

The silence is broken only by the snores of the young gentleman, whose mouth has fallen open, until a few distant shots half waken him. He shuts his mouth convulsively, and opens his eyes sleepily. A door is violently kicked outside; and the voice of Drinkwater is heard raising urgent alarm.

DRINKWATER. Wot ow! Wike ap there, will yr. Wike ap. [*He rushes in through the horseshoe arch, hot and excited, and runs round, kicking the sleepers*]. Nah then. Git ap. Git ap, will yr, Kiddy Redbrook. [*He gives the young gentleman a rude shove*].

REDBROOK [*sitting up*] Stow that, will you. Whats amiss?

DRINKWATER [*disgusted*] Wots amiss! Didnt eah naow fawrin, I spowse.

REDBROOK. No.

DRINKWATER [*sneering*] Naow. Thort it sifer nort, didnt yr?

REDBROOK [*with crisp intelligence*] What! Youre running away, are you? [*He springs up, crying*] Look alive, Johnnies: there's danger. Brandyfaced Jack's on the run. [*They spring up hastily, grasping their guns*].

DRINKWATER. Dineger! Yuss: should think there wors dineger. It's howver, thow, as it mowstly his baw the tawm y o u r e awike. [*They relapse into lassitude*]? Waw wasnt you on the look-aht to give us a end? Bin hat-tecked baw the Benny Seeras [*Beni Siras*], we ev, an ed to rawd for it pretty strite, too, aw teoll yr. Mawtzow is it: the bullet glawnst all rahnd is bloomin brisket. Brarsbahnd e dropt the Shike's oss at six unnern fifty yawds. [*Bustling them about*] Nah then: git the plice ready for the British herristorcracy, Lawd Ellam an Lidy Wineflete?

REDBROOK. Lady faint, eh?

DRINKWATER. Fynt! Not lawkly. Wornted to gow an talk to the Benny Seeras: blaow me if she didnt! Harskt huz wot we was frahtnd of. Tyin ap Mawtzow's wound, she is, like a bloomin orspittle nass. [*Sir Howard, with a copious pagri on his white hat, enters through the horseshoe arch, followed by a couple of men supporting the wounded Marzo, who, weeping and terrorstricken by the prospect of*

death and of subsequent torments for which he is conscious of having eminently qualified himself, has his coat off and a bandage round his chest. One of his supporters is a black-bearded, thickset, slow, middle-aged man with an air of damaged respectability, named—as it afterwards appears—Johnson. Lady Cicely walks beside Marzo. Redbrook, a little shamefaced, crosses the room to the opposite wall as far away as possible from the visitors. Drinkwater turns and receives them with jocular ceremony]. Weolcome to Brars-bahnd Cawstl, Sr Ahrd an lidy. This eah is the corfee and commercial room.

Sir Howard goes to the table and sits on the saddle, rather exhausted. Lady Cicely comes to Drinkwater.

LADY CICELY. Where is Marzo's bed?

DRINKWATER. Is bed, lidy? Weoll: e ynt petickler, lidy. E ez is chawce of henny fleg-stown agin thet wall.

They deposit Marzo on the flags against the wall close to the little door. He groans. Johnson phlegmatically leaves him and joins Redbrook.

LADY CICELY. But you cant leave him there in that state.

DRINKWATER. Ow: e's hall rawt. [*Strolling up callously to Marzo*] Youre hall rawt, ynt yer, Mawtzow? [*Marzo whimpers*]. Corse y'aw.

LADY CICELY [*to Sir Howard*] Did you ever see such a helpless lot of poor creatures? [*She makes for the little door.*]

DRINKWATER. Eah! [*He runs to the door and places himself before it*]. Where mawt yr lidyship be gowin?

LADY CICELY. I'm going through every room in this castle to find a proper place to put that man. And now I'll tell you where y o u r e going. Youre going to get some water for Marzo, who is very thirsty. And then, when Ive chosen a room for him, youre going to make a bed for him there.

DRINKWATER [*sarcastically*] Ow! Henny ather little suvvice? Mike yrseolf at owm, y' knaow, lidy.

LADY CICELY [*considerately*] Dont go if youd rather not, Mr Drinkwater. Perhaps youre too tired. [*Turning to the archway*] I'll ask Captain Brassbound: h e wont mind.

DRINKWATER [*terrified, running after her and getting between her and the arch*] Naow, naow! Naow, lidy: downt you gow disturbin the kepn. Awll see to it.

LADY CICELY [*gravely*] I was sure you would, Mr Drinkwater. You have such a kind face.

[*She turns back and goes out through the small door*].

DRINKWATER [*looking after her*] Garn!

SIR HOWARD [*to Drinkwater*] Will you ask one of your friends to shew me to my room whilst you are getting the water?

DRINKWATER [*insolently*] Yr room! Ow: this ynt good enaf fr yr, ynt it? [*Ferociously*] Oo a you orderin abaht, ih?

SIR HOWARD [*rising quietly, and taking refuge between Redbrook and Johnson, whom he addresses*] Can you find me a more private room than this?

JOHNSON [*shaking his head*] Ive no orders. You must wait til the capn comes, sir.

DRINKWATER [*following Sir Howard*] Yuss; an whawl youre witin, yll tike your horders from me: see?

JOHNSON [*with slow severity, to Drinkwater*] Look here: do you see three genlmen talkin to one another here, civil and private, eh?

DRINKWATER [*chapfallen*] No offence, Miste Jornsn—

JOHNSON [*ominously*] Ay; but there is offence. Wheres your manners, you guttersnipe? [*Turning to Sir Howard*] Thats the curse o this kind o life, sir: you got to associate with all sorts. My father, sir, was Capn Johnson o Hull—owned his own schooner, sir. We're mostly gentlemen here, sir, as youll find, except the poor ignorant foreigner and that there scum of the submerged tenth. [*Contemptuously talking at Drinkwater*] He aint nobody's son: he's only a offspring o coster folk or such.

DRINKWATER [*bursting into tears*] Clawss feelin! thets wot it is; clawss feelin! Wot are yer, arter all, bat a bloomin gang o wust cowst cazhls [*casual ward paupers*]? [*Johnson is scandalized; and there is a general thrill of indignation*]. Better ev naow fembly, an rawse aht of it, lawk me, than ev a specble one and disgrice it, lawk you.

JOHNSON. Brandyfaced Jack: I name you for conduct and language unbecoming to a gentleman. Those who agree will signify the same in the usual manner.

ALL [*vehemently*] Aye.

DRINKWATER [*wildly*] Naow.

JOHNSON. Felix Drinkwater: are you goin out, or are you goin to wait til youre chucked out? You can cry in the passage. If you give any trouble, youll have something to cry for.

They make a threatening movement towards Drinkwater.

DRINKWATER [*whimpering*] You lee me alown: awm gowin. Theres n'maw true demmecrettick feelin eah than there is in the owl bloomin M division of Noontn Corzwy coppers [*Newington Causeway policemen*].

As he slinks away in tears towards the arch, Brassbound enters. Drinkwater promptly shelters himself on the captain's left hand, the others retreating to the opposite side as Brassbound advances to the middle of the room. Sir Howard retires behind them and seats himself on the divan, much fatigued.

BRASSBOUND [*to Drinkwater*] What are you snivelling at?

DRINKWATER. You awsk the wust cowst herristorcracy. They fawnds maw cornduck hanbecammin to a genlmn.

Brassbound is about to ask Johnson for an explanation, when Lady Cicely returns through the little door, and comes between Brassbound and Drinkwater.

LADY CICELY [*to Drinkwater*] Have you fetched the water?

DRINKWATER. Yuss: nah you begin orn me. [*He weeps afresh*].

LADY CICELY [*surprised*] Oh! This wont do, Mr Drinkwater. If you cry, I cant let you nurse your friend.

DRINKWATER [*frantic*] Thetll brike maw awt, wownt it nah? [*With a lamentable sob, he throws himself down on the divan, raging like an angry child*].

LADY CICELY [*after contemplating him in astonishment for a moment*] Captain Brassbound: are there any charwomen in the Atlas Mountains?

BRASSBOUND. There are people here who will work if you pay them, as there are elsewhere.

LADY CICELY. This castle is very romantic, Captain; but it hasnt had a spring cleaning since the Prophet lived in it. There's only one room I can put that wounded man into. Its the only one that has a bed in it: the second room on the right out of that passage.

BRASSBOUND [*haughtily*] That is my room, madam.

LADY CICELY [*relieved*] Oh, thats all right. It would have been so awkward if I had had to ask one of your men to turn out. You wont mind, I know. [*All the men stare at her. Even Drinkwater forgets his sorrows in his stupefaction*].

BRASSBOUND. Pray, madam, have you made any arrangements for my accommodation?

LADY CICELY [*reassuringly*] Yes: you can have my room instead, wherever it may be: I'm sure you chose me a nice one. I must be near my patient; and I dont mind roughing it. Now I must have Marzo moved very carefully. Where is that truly gentlemanly Mr Johnson?—oh, there you are, Mr Johnson. [*She runs to Johnson, past Brassbound, who has to step back hastily out of her way with every expression frozen out of his face except one of extreme and indignant dumbfoundedness*]. Will you ask your strong friend to help you with Marzo: strong people are always so gentle.

JOHNSON. Let me introdooce Mr Redbrook. Your ladyship may know his father, the very Rev. Dean Redbrook. [*He goes to Marzo*].

REDBROOK. Happy to oblige you, Lady Cicely.

LADY CICELY [*shaking hands*] Howdyedo? Of course I knew your father—Dunham wasnt it? Were you ever called—

REDBROOK. The kid? Yes.

LADY CICELY. But why—

REDBROOK [*anticipating the rest of the question*] Cards and drink, Lady Sis. [*He follows Johnson to the patient. Lady Cicely goes too*]. Now, Count Marzo. [*Marzo groans as Johnson and Redbrook raise him*].

LADY CICELY. Now theyre n o t hurting you, Marzo. They couldnt be more gentle.

MARZO. Drink.

LADY CICELY. I'll get you some water myself. Your friend Mr Drinkwater was too overcome—take care of the corner—thats it —the second door on the right. [*She goes out with Marzo and his bearers through the little door*].

BRASSBOUND [*still staring*] Well, I am damned!

DRINKWATER [*getting up*] Weoll, blimey!

BRASSBOUND [*turning irritably on him*] What did you say?

DRINKWATER. Weoll, wot did yer sy yrseolf, kepn? Fust tawm aw yever see y' afride of ennybody. [*The others laugh*].

BRASSBOUND. Afraid!

DRINKWATER [*maliciously*] She's took y'bed from hander yr for a bloomin penny hawcemen. If y' ynt afride, lets eah yer speak ap to er wen she cams bawck agin.

BRASSBOUND [*to Sir Howard*] I wish you to understand, Sir Howard, that in this castle, it is *I* who give orders, and no one else. Will you be good enough to let Lady Cicely Waynflete know that.

SIR HOWARD [*sitting up on the divan and pulling himself together*] You will have ample opportunity for speaking to Lady Cicely yourself when she returns. [*Drinkwater chuckles; and the rest grin*].

BRASSBOUND. My manners are rough, Sir Howard. I have no wish to frighten the lady.

SIR HOWARD. Captain Brassbound: if you can frighten Lady Cicely, you will confer a great obligation on her family. If she had any sense of danger, perhaps she would keep out of it.

BRASSBOUND. Well, sir, if she were ten Lady Cicelys, she must consult me while she is here.

DRINKWATER. Thets rawt, kepn. Lets eah you steblish yr hawthority. [*Brassbound turns impatiently on him: he retreats remonstrating*] Nah, nah, nah!

SIR HOWARD. If you feel at all nervous, Captain Brassbound, I will mention the matter with pleasure.

BRASSBOUND. Nervous, sir! no. Nervousness is not in my line. You will find me perfectly capable of saying what I want to say—with considerable emphasis, if necessary. [*Sir Howard assents with a polite but incredulous nod*].

DRINKWATER. Eah, eah!

Lady Cicely returns with Johnson and Redbrook. She carries a jar.

LADY CICELY [*stopping between the door and the arch*] Now for the water. Where is it?

REDBROOK. Theres a well in the courtyard. I'll come and work the bucket.

LADY CICELY. So good of you, Mr Kidbrook. [*She makes for the horseshoe arch, followed by Redbrook*].

DRINKWATER. Nah, Kepn Brarsbahnd: you got sathink to sy to the lidy, ynt yr?

LADY CICELY [*stopping*] I'll come back to hear it presently, Captain. And oh, while I remember it, [*coming forward between Brassbound and Drinkwater*] do please tell me, Captain, if I interfere with your arrangements in any way. If I disturb you the least bit in the world, stop me at once. You have all the responsibility; and your comfort and your authority must be the first thing. Youll tell me, wont you?

BRASSBOUND [*awkwardly, quite beaten*] Pray do as you please, madam.

LADY CICELY. Thank you. Thats so like you, Captain. Thank you. Now, Mr Redbrook! Show me the way to the well. [*She follows*]

Redbrook out through the arch].

DRINKWATER. Yah! Yah! Shime! Beat baw a woman!

JOHNSON [*coming forward on Brassbound's right*] What's wrong now?

DRINKWATER [*with an air of disappointment and disillusion*] Downt awsk me, Miste Jornsn. The kepn's naow clawss arter all.

BRASSBOUND [*a little shamefacedly*] What has she been fixing up in there, Johnson?

JOHNSON. Well: Marzo's in your bed. Lady wants to make a kitchen of the Sheikh's audience chamber, and to put me and the Kid handy in his bedroom in case Marzo gets erysipelas and breaks out violent. From what I can make out, she means to make herself matron of this institution. I spose it's all right, isnt it?

DRINKWATER. Yuss, an horder huz abaht as if we was keb tahts! An the kepn afride to talk bawck at er!

Lady Cicely returns with Redbrook. She carries the jar full of water.

LADY CICELY [*putting down the jar, and coming between Brassbound and Drinkwater as before*] And now, Captain, before I go to poor Marzo, what have you to say to me?

BRASSBOUND. I! Nothing.

DRINKWATER. Downt fank it, gavner. Be a men!

LADY CICELY [*looking at Drinkwater, puzzled*] Mr Drinkwater said you had.

BRASSBOUND [*recovering himself*] It was only this. That fellow there [*pointing to Drinkwater*] is subject to fits of insolence. If he is impertinent to your ladyship, or disobedient, you have my authority to order him as many kicks as you think good for him; and I will see that he gets them.

DRINKWATER [*lifting up his voice in protest*] Nah, nah—

LADY CICELY. Oh, I couldnt think of such a thing, Captain Brassbound. I am sure it would hurt Mr Drinkwater.

DRINKWATER [*lachrymosely*] Lidy's hinky-p'ble o sich bawbrous usage.

LADY CICELY. But there's one thing I should like, if Mr Drinkwater wont mind my mentioning it. It's so important if he's to attend on Marzo.

BRASSBOUND. What is that?

LADY CICELY. Well—you wont mind, Mr Drinkwater, will you?

DRINKWATER [*suspiciously*] Wot is it?

LADY CICELY. There would be so much less danger of erysipelas if you would be so good as to take a bath.

DRINKWATER [*aghast*] A bawth!

BRASSBOUND [*in tones of command*] Stand by, all hands. [*They stand by*]. Take that man and wash him. [*With a roar of laughter they seize him*].

DRINKWATER [*in an agony of protest*] Naow, naow. Look eah—

BRASSBOUND [*ruthlessly*] In cold water.

DRINKWATER [*shrieking*] Na-a-a-a-ow. Aw cawnt, aw teol yer. Naow. Aw sy, look eah. Naow, naow, naow, naow, naow, NAOW!!!

He is dragged away through the arch in a whirlwind of laughter, protests and tears.

LADY CICELY. I'm afraid he isnt used to it, poor fellow; but really it will do him good, Captain Brassbound. Now I must be off to my patient. [*She takes up her jar and goes out by the little door, leaving Brassbound and Sir Howard alone together*].

SIR HOWARD [*rising*] And now, Captain Brass—

BRASSBOUND [*cutting him short with a fierce contempt that astonishes him*] I will attend to you presently. [*Calling*] Johnson. Send me Johnson there. And Osman. [*He pulls off his coat and throws it on the table, standing at his ease in his blue jersey*].

SIR HOWARD [*after a momentary flush of anger, with a controlled force that compels Brassbound's attention in spite of himself*] You seem to be in a strong position with reference to these men of yours.

BRASSBOUND. I am in a strong position with reference to everyone in this castle.

SIR HOWARD [*politely but threateningly*] I have just been noticing that you think so. I do not agree with you. Her Majesty's Government, Captain Brassbound, has a strong arm and a long arm. If anything disagreeable happens to me or to my sister-in-law, that arm will be stretched out. If that happens you will not be in a strong position. Excuse my reminding you of it.

BRASSBOUND [*grimly*] Much good may it do you! [*Johnson comes in through the arch*]. Where is Osman, the Sheikh's messenger? I want him too.

JOHNSON. Coming, Captain. He had a prayer to finish.

Osman, a tall, skinny, whiteclad, elderly Moor, appears in the archway.

BRASSBOUND. Osman Ali [*Osman comes forward between Brassbound and Johnson*]: you have seen this unbeliever [*indicating Sir Howard*] come in with us?

OSMAN. Yea, and the shameless one with the naked face, who flattered my countenance and offered me her hand.

JOHNSON. Yes; and you took it too, Johnny, didnt you?

BRASSBOUND. Take horse, then; and ride fast to your master the Sheikh Sidi el Assif—

OSMAN [*proudly*] Kinsman to the Prophet.

BRASSBOUND. Tell him what you have seen here. That is all. Johnson: give him a dollar; and note the hour of his going, that his master may know how fast he rides.

OSMAN. The believer's word shall prevail with Allah and his servant Sidi el Assif.

BRASSBOUND. Off with you.

OSMAN. Make good thy master's word ere I go out from his presence, O Johnson el Hull.

JOHNSON. He wants the dollar.

Brassbound gives Osman a coin.

OSMAN [*bowing*] Allah will make hell easy for the friend of Sidi el Assif and his servant. [*He goes out through the arch*].

BRASSBOUND [*to Johnson*] Keep the men out of this until the Sheikh comes. I have business to talk over. When he does come, we must keep together all: Sidi el Assif's natural instinct will be to cut every Christian throat here.

JOHNSON. We look to you, Captain, to square him, since you invited him over.

BRASSBOUND. You can depend on me; and you know it, I think.

JOHNSON [*phlegmatically*] Yes: we know it. [*He is going out when Sir Howard speaks*].

SIR HOWARD. You know also, Mr Johnson, I hope, that you can depend on me.

JOHNSON [*turning*] On y o u, sir?

SIR HOWARD. Yes: on me. If my throat is cut, the Sultan of Morocco may send Sidi's head with a hundred thousand dollars blood-money to the Colonial Office; but it will not be enough to save his kingdom—any more than it would save your life, if your Captain here did the same thing.

JOHNSON [*struck*] Is that so, Captain?

BRASSBOUND. I know the gentleman's value—better perhaps than he knows it himself. I shall not lose sight of it.

Johnson nods gravely, and is going out when Lady Cicely returns softly by the little door and calls to him in a whisper. She has taken off her travelling things and put on an apron. At her

chatelaine is a case of sewing materials.

LADY CICELY. Mr Johnson. [*He turns*]. Ive got Marzo to sleep. Would you mind asking the gentlemen not to make a noise under his window in the courtyard.

JOHNSON. Right, maam. [*He goes out*].

Lady Cicely sits down at the tiny table, and begins stitching at a sling bandage for Marzo's arm. Brassbound walks up and down on her right, muttering to himself so ominously that Sir Howard quietly gets out of his way by crossing to the other side and sitting down on the second saddle seat.

SIR HOWARD. Are you yet able to attend to me for a moment, Captain Brassbound?

BRASSBOUND [*still walking about*] What do you want?

SIR HOWARD. Well, I am afraid I want a little privacy, and, if you will allow me to say so, a little civility. I am greatly obliged to you for bringing us safely off today when we were attacked. So far, you have carried out your contract. But since we have been your guests here, your tone and that of the worst of your men has changed—intentionally changed, I think.

BRASSBOUND [*stopping abruptly and flinging the announcement at him*] You are not my guest: you are my prisoner.

SIR HOWARD. Prisoner!

Lady Cicely, after a single glance up, continues stitching, apparently quite unconcerned.

BRASSBOUND. I warned you. You should have taken my warning.

SIR HOWARD [*immediately taking the tone of cold disgust for moral delinquency*] Am I to understand, then, that you are a brigand? Is this a matter of ransom?

BRASSBOUND [*with unaccountable intensity*] All the wealth of England shall not ransom you.

SIR HOWARD. Then what do you expect to gain by this?

BRASSBOUND. Justice on a thief and a murderer.

Lady Cicely lays down her work and looks up anxiously.

SIR HOWARD [*deeply outraged, rising with venerable dignity*] Sir: do you apply those terms to me?

BRASSBOUND. I do. [*He turns to Lady Cicely, and adds, pointing contemptuously to Sir Howard*] Look at him. You would not take this virtuously indignant gentleman for the uncle of a brigand, would you?

Sir Howard starts. The shock is too much for

him: he sits down again, looking very old; and his hands tremble; but his eyes and mouth are intrepid, resolute, and angry.

LADY CICELY. Uncle! What do you mean?

BRASSBOUND. Has he never told you about my mother? this fellow who puts on ermine and scarlet and calls himself Justice.

SIR HOWARD [*almost voiceless*] You are the son of that woman!

BRASSBOUND [*fiercely*] "That woman!" [*He makes a movement as if to rush at Sir Howard*].

LADY CICELY [*rising quickly and putting her hand on his arm*] Take care. You mustnt strike an old man.

BRASSBOUND [*raging*] He did not spare my mother—"that woman," he calls her—because of her sex. I will not spare him because of his age. [*Lowering his tone to one of sullen vindictiveness*] But I am not going to strike him. [*Lady Cicely releases him, and sits down, much perplexed. Brassbound continues, with an evil glance at Sir Howard*] I shall do no more than justice.

SIR HOWARD [*recovering his voice and vigor*] Justice! I think you mean vengeance, disguised as justice by your passions.

BRASSBOUND. To many and many a poor wretch in the dock y o u have brought vengeance in that disguise—the vengeance of society, disguised as justice by i t s passions. Now the justice you have outraged meets you disguised as vengeance. How do you like it?

SIR HOWARD. I shall meet it, I trust, as becomes an innocent man and an upright judge. What do you charge against me?

BRASSBOUND. I charge you with the death of my mother and the theft of my inheritance.

SIR HOWARD. As to your inheritance, sir, it was yours whenever you came forward to claim it. Three minutes ago I did not know of your existence. I affirm that most solemnly. I never knew—never dreamt—that my brother Miles left a son. As to your mother, her case was a hard one—perhaps the hardest that has come within even my experience. I mentioned it, as such, to Mr Rankin, the missionary, the evening we met you. As to her death, you know—you m u s t know—that she died in her native country, years after our last meeting. Perhaps you were too young to know that she could hardly have expected to live long.

BRASSBOUND. You mean that she drank.

SIR HOWARD. I did not say so. I do not think she was always accountable for what she did.

BRASSBOUND. Yes: she was mad too; and whether drink drove her to madness or madness drove her to drink matters little. The question is, who drove her to both?

SIR HOWARD. I presume the dishonest agent who seized her estate did. I repeat, it was a hard case—a frightful injustice. But it could not be remedied.

BRASSBOUND. You told her so. When she would not take that false answer you drove her from your doors. When she exposed you in the street and threatened to take with her own hands the redress the law denied her, you had her imprisoned, and forced her to write you an apology and leave the country to regain her liberty and save herself from a lunatic asylum. And when she was gone, and dead, and forgotten, you found for yourself the remedy you could not find for her. You recovered the estate easily enough then, robber and rascal that you are. Did he tell the missionary that, Lady Cicely, eh?

LADY CICELY [*sympathetically*] Poor woman! [*To Sir Howard*] Couldnt you have helped her, Howard?

SIR HOWARD. No. This man may be ignorant enough to suppose that when I was a struggling barrister I could do everything I did when I was Attorney General. You know better. There is some excuse for his mother. She was an uneducated Brazilian, knowing nothing of English society, and driven mad by injustice.

BRASSBOUND. Your defence—

SIR HOWARD [*interrupting him determinedly*] I do not defend myself. I call on you to obey the law.

BRASSBOUND. I intend to do so. The law of the Atlas Mountains is administered by the Sheikh Sidi el Assif. He will be here within an hour. He is a judge, like yourself. You can talk law to him. He will give you both the law and the prophets.

SIR HOWARD. Does he know what the power of England is?

BRASSBOUND. He knows that the Mahdi killed my master Gordon, and that the Madhi died in his bed and went to paradise.

SIR HOWARD. Then he knows also that England's vengeance was on the Mahdi's track.

BRASSBOUND. Ay, on the track of the railway from the Cape to Cairo? Who are you, that a nation should go to war for you? If you are missing, what will your newspapers say? A foolhardy tourist! What will your learned friends at the bar say? That it was time for you to make room for younger and better men. You a national hero! You had better find a goldfield in the Atlas Mountains. Then all the governments of Europe will rush to your rescue. Until then, take care of yourself; for you are going to see at last the hypocrisy in the sanctimonious speech of the judge who is sentencing you, instead of the despair in the white face of the wretch you are recommending to the mercy of your god.

SIR HOWARD [*deeply and personally offended by this slight to his profession, and for the first time throwing away his assumed dignity and rising to approach Brassbound with his fists clenched; so that Lady Cicely lifts one eye from her work to assure herself that the table is between them*] I have no more to say to you, sir. I am not afraid of you, nor of any bandit with whom you may be in league. As to your property, it is ready for you as soon as you come to your senses and claim it as your father's heir. Commit a crime, and you will become an outlaw, and not only lose the property, but shut the doors of civilization against yourself for ever.

BRASSBOUND. I will not sell my mother's revenge for ten properties.

LADY CICELY [*placidly*] Besides, really, Howard, as the property now costs £150 a year to keep up instead of bringing in anything, I am afraid it would not be of much use to him. [*Brassbound stands amazed at this revelation*].

SIR HOWARD [*taken aback*] I must say, Cicely, I think you might have chosen a more suitable moment to mention that fact.

BRASSBOUND [*with disgust*] Agh! Trickster! Lawyer! Even the price you offer for your life is to be paid in false coin. [*Calling*] Hallo there! Johnson! Redbrook! Some of you there! [*To Sir Howard*] You ask for a little privacy: you shall have it. I will not endure the company of such a fellow.

SIR HOWARD [*very angry, and full of the crustiest pluck*] You insult me, sir. You are a rascal. You are a rascal.

Johnson, Redbrook, and a few others come in through the arch.

BRASSBOUND. Take this man away.

JOHNSON. Where are we to put him?

BRASSBOUND. Put him where you please so long as you can find him when he is wanted.

SIR HOWARD. You will be laid by the heels yet, my friend.

REDBROOK [*with cheerful tact*] Tut tut, Sir Howard: whats the use of talking back? Come along: we'll make you comfortable.

Sir Howard goes out through the arch between Johnson and Redbrook, muttering wrathfully. The rest, except Brassbound and Lady Cicely, follow.

Brassbound walks up and down the room, nursing his indignation. In doing so he unconsciously enters upon an unequal contest with Lady Cicely, who sits quietly stitching. It soon becomes clear that a tranquil woman can go on sewing longer than an angry man can go on fuming. Further, it begins to dawn on Brassbound's wrath-blurred perception that Lady Cicely has at some unnoticed stage in the proceedings finished Marzo's bandage, and is now stitching a coat. He stops; glances at his shirtsleeves; finally realizes the situation.

BRASSBOUND. What are you doing there, madam?

LADY CICELY. Mending your coat, Captain Brassbound.

BRASSBOUND. I have no recollection of asking you to take that trouble.

LADY CICELY. No: I dont suppose you even knew it was torn. Some men are born untidy. You cannot very well receive Sidi el—what's his name?—with your sleeve half out.

BRASSBOUND [*disconcerted*] I—I dont know how it got torn.

LADY CICELY. You should not get virtuously indignant with people. It bursts clothes more than anything else, Mr Hallam.

BRASSBOUND [*flushing quickly*] I beg you will not call me Mr Hallam. I hate the name.

LADY CICELY. Black Paquito is your pet name, isnt it?

BRASSBOUND [*huffily*] I am not usually called so to my face.

LADY CICELY [*turning the coat a little*] I'm so sorry. [*She takes another piece of thread and puts it into her needle, looking placidly and reflectively upward meanwhile*]. Do you know, you are wonderfully like your uncle.

BRASSBOUND. Damnation!

LADY CICELY. Eh?

BRASSBOUND. If I thought my veins contained a drop of his black blood, I would drain them empty with my knife. I have no relations. I had a mother: that was all.

LADY CICELY [*unconvinced*] I daresay you have your mother's complexion. But didnt you notice Sir Howard's temper, his doggedness, his high spirit: above all, his belief in ruling people by force, as you rule your men; and in revenge and punishment, just as you want to revenge your mother? Didnt you recognize yourself in that?

BRASSBOUND [*startled*] Myself!—in that!

LADY CICELY [*returning to the tailoring question as if her last remark were of no consequence whatever*] Did this sleeve catch you at all under the arm? Perhaps I had better make it a little easier for you.

BRASSBOUND [*irritably*] Let my coat alone. It will do very well as it is. Put it down.

LADY CICELY. Oh, dont ask me to sit doing nothing. It bores me so.

BRASSBOUND. In Heaven's name then, do what you like! Only dont worry me with it.

LADY CICELY. I'm so sorry. All the Hallams are irritable.

BRASSBOUND [*penning up his fury with difficulty*] As I have already said, that remark has no application to me.

LADY CICELY [*resuming her stitching*] Thats so funny! They all hate to be told that they are like one another.

BRASSBOUND [*with the beginnings of despair in his voice*] Why did you come here? My trap was laid for him, not for you. Do you know the danger you are in?

LADY CICELY. Theres always a danger of something or other. Do you think it's worth bothering about.

BRASSBOUND [*scolding her*] Do I think! Do you think my coat's worth mending?

LADY CICELY [*prosaically*] Oh yes: it's not so far gone as that.

BRASSBOUND. Have you any feeling? Or are you a fool?

LADY CICELY. I'm afraid I'm a dreadful fool. But I cant help it. I was made so, I suppose.

BRASSBOUND. Perhaps you dont realize that your friend my good uncle will be pretty fortunate if he is allowed to live out his life as a slave with a set of chains on him?

LADY CICELY. Oh, I dont know about that, Mr H—I mean Captain Brassbound. Men are always thinking that they are going to do something grandly wicked to their enemies; but when it comes to the point, really bad men are just as rare as really good ones.

BRASSBOUND. You forget that I am like my uncle, according to you. Have you any doubt as to the reality of his badness?

LADY CICELY. Bless me! your uncle Howard is one of the most harmless of men—much nicer than most professional people. Of course he does dreadful things as a judge; but then if you take a man and pay him £5,000 a year to be wicked, and praise him for it, and have policemen and courts and laws and juries to drive him into it so that he cant help doing it, what can you expect? Sir Howard's all right when he's left to himself. We caught a burglar one night at Waynflete when he was staying with us; and I insisted on his locking the poor man up, until the police came, in a room with a window opening on the lawn. The man came back next day and said he must return to a life of crime unless I gave him a job in the garden; and I did. It was much more sensible than giving him ten years penal servitude: Howard admitted it. So you see he's not a bit bad really.

BRASSBOUND. He had a fellow feeling for the thief, knowing he was a thief himself. Do you forget that he sent my mother to prison?

LADY CICELY [*softly*] Were you very fond of your poor mother, and always very good to her?

BRASSBOUND [*rather taken aback*] I was not worse than other sons, I suppose.

LADY CICELY [*opening her eyes very widely*] Oh! Was that all?

BRASSBOUND [*exculpating himself, full of gloomy remembrances*] You dont understand. It was not always possible to be very tender with my mother. She had unfortunately a very violent temper; and she—she—

LADY CICELY. Yes: so you told Howard. [*With genuine pity for him*] You must have had a very unhappy childhood.

BRASSBOUND [*grimly*] Hell. That was what my childhood was. Hell.

LADY CICELY. Do you think she would really have killed Howard, as she threatened, if he hadnt sent her to prison?

BRASSBOUND [*breaking out again, with a growing sense of being morally trapped*] What if she did? Why did he rob her? Why did he not help her to get the estate, as he got it for himself afterwards?

LADY CICELY. He says he couldnt, you know. But perhaps the real reason was that he didnt like her. You know, dont you, that if you dont like people you think of all the reasons for not helping them, and if you like them you think of all the opposite reasons.

BRASSBOUND. But his duty as a brother!

LADY CICELY. Are you going to do your duty as a nephew!

BRASSBOUND. Dont quibble with me. I am going to do my duty as a son; and you know it.

LADY CICELY. But I should have thought that the time for that was in your mother's lifetime, when you could have been kind and forbearing with her. Hurting your uncle wont do her any good, you know.

BRASSBOUND. It will teach other scoundrels to respect widows and orphans. Do you forget that there is such a thing as justice?

LADY CICELY [gaily shaking out the finished coat] Oh, if you are going to dress yourself in ermine and call yourself Justice, I give you up. You are just your uncle over again; only he gets £5,000 a year for it, and you do it for nothing. [She holds the coat up to see whether any further repairs are needed].

BRASSBOUND [sulkily] You twist my words very cleverly. But no man or woman has ever changed me.

LADY CICELY. Dear me! That must be very nice for the people you deal with, because they can always depend on you; but isnt it rather inconvenient for yourself when you change your mind?

BRASSBOUND. I never change my mind.

LADY CICELY [rising with the coat in her hands] Oh! Oh!! Nothing will ever persuade me that you are as pigheaded as that.

BRASSBOUND [offended] Pigheaded!

LADY CICELY [with quick, caressing apology] No, no, no. I didnt mean that. Firm! unalterable! Resolute! Iron-willed! Stonewall Jackson! Thats the idea, isnt it?

BRASSBOUND [hopelessly] You are laughing at me.

LADY CICELY. No: trembling, I assure you. Now will you try this on for me: I'm so afraid I have made it too tight under the arm. [She holds it behind him].

BRASSBOUND [obeying mechanically] You take me for a fool, I think. [He misses the sleeve].

LADY CICELY. No: all men look foolish when they are feeling for their sleeves—

BRASSBOUND. Agh! [He turns and snatches the coat from her; then puts it on himself and buttons the lowest button].

LADY CICELY [horrified] Stop. No. You must n e v e r pull a coat at the skirts, Captain Brassbound: it spoils the sit of it. Allow me. [She pulls the lapels of his coat vigorously forward] Put back your shoulders. [He frowns, but obeys]. Thats better. [She buttons the top button]. Now button the rest from the top down. D o e s it catch you at all under the arm?

BRASSBOUND [miserably—all resistance beaten out of him] No.

LADY CICELY. Thats right. Now before I go back to poor Marzo, say thank you to me for mending your jacket, like a nice polite sailor.

BRASSBOUND [sitting down at the table in great agitation] Damn you! you have belittled my whole life to me. [He bows his head on his hands, convulsed].

LADY CICELY [quite understanding, and putting her hand kindly on his shoulder] Oh no. I am sure you have done lots of kind things and brave things, if you could only recollect them. With Gordon for instance? Nobody can belittle that.

He looks up at her for a moment; then kisses her hand. She presses his and turns away with her eyes so wet that she sees Drinkwater, coming in through the arch just then, with a prismatic halo round him. Even when she sees him clearly, she hardly recognizes him; for he is ludicrously clean and smoothly brushed; and his hair, formerly mud color, is now lively red.

DRINKWATER. Look eah, kepn. [Brassbound springs up and recovers himself quickly]. Eahs the bloomin Shike jest appeahd on the orawzn wiv abaht fifty men. Thyll be eah insawd o ten minnits, they will.

LADY CICELY. The Sheikh!

BRASSBOUND. Sidi el Assif and fifty men! [To Lady Cicely] You were too late: I gave you up my vengeance when it was no longer in my hand. [To Drinkwater] Call all hands to stand by and shut the gates. Then all here to me for orders; and bring the prisoner.

DRINKWATER. Rawt, kepn. [He runs out].

LADY CICELY. Is there really any danger for Howard?

BRASSBOUND. Yes. Danger for all of us unless I keep to my bargain with this fanatic.

LADY CICELY. What bargain?

BRASSBOUND. I pay him so much a head for every party I escort through to the interior. In return he protects me and lets my caravans alone. But I have sworn an oath to him to take only Jews and true believers—no Christians, you understand.

LADY CICELY. Then why did you take us?

BRASSBOUND. I took my uncle on purpose—and sent word to Sidi that he was here.

LADY CICELY. Well, thats a pretty kettle of fish, isnt it?

BRASSBOUND. I will do what I can to save him—and you. But I fear my repentance has come too late, as repentance usually does.

LADY CICELY [cheerfully] Well, I must go and look after Marzo, at all events. [She goes out through the little door. Johnson, Redbrook, and the rest come in through the arch, with Sir Howard, still very crusty and determined. He keeps close to Johnson, who comes to Brassbound's right, Redbrook taking the other side].

BRASSBOUND. Wheres Drinkwater?

JOHNSON. On the lookout. Look here, Capn: we dont half like this job. The gentleman has been talking to us a bit; and we think that he is a gentleman, and talks straight sense.

REDBROOK. Righto, Brother Johnson. [To Brassbound] Wont do, governor. Not good enough.

BRASSBOUND [fiercely] Mutiny, eh?

REDBROOK. Not at all, governor. Dont talk Tommy rot with Brother Sidi only five minutes gallop off. Cant hand over an Englishman to a nigger to have his throat cut.

BRASSBOUND [unexpectedly acquiescing] Very good. You know, I suppose, that if you break my bargain with Sidi, youll have to defend this place and fight for your lives in five minutes. That cant be done without discipline: you know that too. I'll take my part with the rest under whatever leader you are willing to obey. So choose your captain and look sharp about it. [Murmurs of surprise and discontent].

VOICES. No, no. Brassbound must command.

BRASSBOUND. Youre wasting your five minutes. Try Johnson.

JOHNSON. No. I havnt the head for it.

BRASSBOUND. Well, Redbrook.

REDBROOK. Not this Johnny, thank you. Havnt character enough.

BRASSBOUND. Well, theres Sir Howard Hallam for you! He has character enough.

A VOICE. He's too old.

ALL. No, no. Brassbound, Brassbound.

JOHNSON. Theres nobody but you, Captain.

REDBROOK. The mutiny's over, governor. You win, hands down.

BRASSBOUND [turning on them] Now listen, you, all of you. If I am to command here, I am going to do what I like, not what you

like. I'll give this gentleman here to Sidi or to the devil if I choose. I'll not be intimidated or talked back to. Is that understood?

REDBROOK [diplomatically] He's offered a present of five hundred quid if he gets safe back to Mogador, governor. Excuse my mentioning it.

SIR HOWARD. Myself and Lady Cicely.

BRASSBOUND. What! A judge compound a felony! You greenhorns, he is more likely to send you all to penal servitude if you are fools enough to give him the chance.

VOICES. So he would. Whew! [Murmurs of conviction].

REDBROOK. Righto, governor. Thats the ace of trumps.

BRASSBOUND [to Sir Howard] Now, have you any other card to play? Any other bribe? Any other threat? Quick. Time presses.

SIR HOWARD. My life is in the hands of Providence. Do your worst.

BRASSBOUND. Or my best. I still have that choice.

DRINKWATER [running in] Look eah, kepn. Eahs anather lot cammin from the sahth heast. Hunnerds of em, this tawm. The owl dezzit is lawk a bloomin Awd Pawk demonstration. Aw blieve its the Kidy from Kintorfy. [General alarm. All look to Brassbound].

BRASSBOUND [eagerly] The Cadi! How far off?

DRINKWATER. Matter o two mawl.

BRASSBOUND. We're saved. Open the gates to the Sheikh [They stare at him]. Look alive there.

DRINKWATER [appalled, almost in tears] Naow, naow. Lissen, kepn [pointing to Sir Howard]: e'll give huz fawv unnerd red uns. [To the others] Ynt yer spowk to im, Miste Jornson—Miste Redbrook—

BRASSBOUND [cutting him short] Now then, do you understand plain English? Johnson and Redbrook: take what men you want and open the gates to the Sheikh. Let him come straight to me. Look alive, will you.

JOHNSON. Ay ay, sir.

REDBROOK. Righto, governor.

They hurry out, with a few others. Drinkwater stares after them, dumbfounded by their obedience.

BRASSBOUND [taking out a pistol] You wanted to sell me to my prisoner, did you, you dog.

DRINKWATER [falling on his knees with a yell] Naow! [Brassbound turns on him as if to kick him. He scrambles away and takes refuge behind

Sir Howard].

BRASSBOUND. Sir Howard Hallam: you have one chance left. The Cadi of Kintafi stands superior to the Sheikh as the responsible governor of the whole province. It is the Cadi who will be sacrificed by the Sultan if England demands satisfaction for any injury to you. If we can hold the Sheikh in parley until the Cadi arrives, you may frighten the Cadi into forcing the Sheikh to release you. The Cadi's coming is a lucky chance for you.

SIR HOWARD. If it were a real chance, you would not tell me of it. Dont try to play cat and mouse with me, man.

DRINKWATER [*aside to Sir Howard, as Brassbound turns contemptuously away to the other side of the room*] It ynt mach of a chawnst, Sir Ahrd. But if there was a ganbowt in Mogador Awbr, awd put a bit on it, aw would.

Johnson, Redbrook, and the others return, rather mistrustfully ushering in Sidi el Assif, attended by Osman and a troop of Arabs. Brassbound's men keep together on the archway side, backing their captain. Sidi's followers cross the room behind the table and assemble near Sir Howard, who stands his ground. Drinkwater runs across to Brassbound and stands at his elbow as he turns to face Sidi.

Sidi el Assif, clad in spotless white, is a nobly handsome Arab, hardly thirty, with fine eyes, bronzed complexion, and instinctively dignified carriage. He places himself between the two groups, with Osman in attendance at his right hand.

OSMAN [*pointing out Sir Howard*] This is the infidel, Cadi. [*Sir Howard bows to Sidi, but, being an infidel, receives only the haughtiest stare in acknowledgement*]. This [*pointing to Brassbound*] is Brassbound the Franguestani captain, the servant of Sidi.

DRINKWATER [*not to be outdone, points out the Sheikh and Osman to Brassbound*] This eah is the Commawnder of the Fythful an is Vizzeer Hosman.

SIDI. Where is the woman?

OSMAN. The shameless one is not here.

BRASSBOUND. Sidi el Assif, kinsman of the Prophet: you are welcome.

REDBROOK [*with much aplomb*] There is no majesty and no might save in Allah, the Glorious, the Great!

DRINKWATER. Eah, eah!

OSMAN [*to Sidi*] The servant of the captain makes his profession of faith as a true believer.

SIDI. It is well.

BRASSBOUND [*aside to Redbrook*] Where did you pick that up?

REDBROOK [*aside to Brassbound*] Captain Burton's Arabian Nights—copy in the library of the National Liberal Club.

LADY CICELY [*calling without*] Mr Drinkwater. Come and help me with Marzo. [*The Sheikh pricks up his ears. His nostrils and eyes expand*].

OSMAN. The shameless one!

BRASSBOUND [*to Drinkwater, seizing him by the collar and slinging him towards the door*] Off with you.

Drinkwater goes out through the little door.

OSMAN. Shall we hide her face before she enters?

SIDI. No.

Lady Cicely, who has resumed her travelling equipment, and has her hat slung across her arm, comes through the little door supporting Marzo, who is very white, but able to get about. Drinkwater has his other arm. Redbrook hastens to relieve Lady Cicely of Marzo, taking him into the group behind Brassbound. Lady Cicely comes forward between Brassbound and the Sheikh, to whom she turns affably.

LADY CICELY [*proffering her hand*] Sidi el Assif, isnt it? How dye do? [*He recoils, blushing somewhat*].

OSMAN [*scandalized*] Woman: touch not the kinsman of the Prophet.

LADY CICELY. Oh, I see. I'm being presented at court. Very good. [*She makes a presentation curtsey*].

REDBROOK. Sidi el Assif: this is one of the mighty women Sheikhs of Franguestan. She goes unveiled among Kings; and only princes may touch her hand.

LADY CICELY. Allah upon thee, Sidi el Assif! Be a good little Sheikh, and shake hands.

SIDI [*timidly touching her hand*] Now this is a wonderful thing, and worthy to be chronicled with the story of Solomon and the Queen of Sheba. Is it not so, Osman Ali?

OSMAN. Allah upon thee, master! it is so.

SIDI. Brassbound Ali: the oath of a just man fulfils itself without many words. The infidel Cadi, thy captive, falls to my share.

BRASSBOUND [*firmly*] It cannot be, Sidi el Assif. [*Sidi's brows contract gravely*]. The price of his blood will be required of our lord the Sultan. I will take him to Morocco and deliver him up there.

SIDI [*impressively*] Brassbound: I am in mine own house and amid mine own people. *I* am the Sultan here. Consider what you say; for when my word goes forth for life or death, it may not be recalled.

BRASSBOUND. Sidi el Assif: I will buy the man from you at what price you choose to name; and if I do not pay faithfully, you shall take my head for his.

SIDI. It is well. You shall keep the man, and give me the woman in payment.

SIR HOWARD AND BRASSBOUND [*with the same impulse*] No, no.

LADY CICELY [*eagerly*] Yes, yes. Certainly, Mr Sidi. Certainly.

Sidi smiles gravely.

SIR HOWARD. Impossible.

BRASSBOUND. You dont know what youre doing.

LADY CICELY. Oh, dont I? Ive not crossed Africa and stayed with six cannibal chiefs for nothing. [*To the Sheikh*] It's all right, Mr Sidi: I shall be delighted.

SIR HOWARD. You are mad. Do you suppose this man will treat you as a European gentleman would?

LADY CICELY. No: he'll treat me like one of Nature's gentlemen: look at his perfectly splendid face! [*Addressing Osman as if he was her oldest and most attached retainer*] Osman: be sure you choose me a good horse; and get a nice strong camel for my luggage.

Osman, after a moment of stupefaction, hurries out. Lady Cicely puts on her hat and pins it to her hair, the Sheikh gazing at her during the process with timid admiration.

DRINKWATER [*chuckling*] She'll mawch em all to church next Sunder lawk a bloomin lot o cherrity kids: you see if she downt.

LADY CICELY [*busily*] Goodbye, Howard: dont be anxious about me; and above all, dont bring a parcel of men with guns to rescue me. I shall be all right now that I am getting away from the escort. Captain Brassbound: I rely on you to see that Sir Howard gets safe to Mogador. [*Whispering*] Take your hand off that pistol. [*He takes his hand out of his pocket, reluctantly*]. Goodbye.

A tumult without. They all turn apprehensively to the arch. Osman rushes in.

OSMAN. The Cadi, the Cadi. He is in anger. His men are upon us. Defend—

The Cadi, a vigorous, fatfeatured, choleric, whitehaired and bearded elder, rushes in, cudgel in hand, with an overwhelming retinue, and silences Osman with a sounding thwack. In a moment the back of the room is crowded with his followers. The Sheikh retreats a little towards his men; and the Cadi comes impetuously forward between him and Lady Cicely.

THE CADI. Now woe upon thee, Sidi el Assif, thou child of mischief!

SIDI [*sternly*] Am I a dog, Muley Othman, that thou speakest thus to me?

THE CADI. Wilt thou destroy thy country, and give us all into the hands of them that set the sea on fire but yesterday with their ships of war? Where are the Franguestani captives?

LADY CICELY. Here we are, Cadi. How dye do?

THE CADI. Allah upon thee, thou moon at the full! Where is thy kinsman, the Cadi of Franguestan? I am his friend, his servant. I come on behalf of my master the Sultan to do him honor, and to cast down his enemies.

SIR HOWARD. You are very good, I am sure.

SIDI [*graver than ever*] Muley Othman—

THE CADI [*fumbling in his breast*] Peace, peace, thou inconsiderate one. [*He takes out a letter*].

BRASSBOUND. Cadi—

THE CADI. Oh thou dog, thou, thou accursed Brassbound, son of a wanton: it is thou hast led Sidi el Assif into this wrongdoing. Read this writing that thou has brought upon me from the commander of the warship.

BRASSBOUND. Warship! [*He takes the letter and opens it, his men whispering to one another very low-spiritedly meanwhile*].

REDBROOK. Warship! Whew!

JOHNSON. Gunboat, praps.

DRINKWATER. Lawk bloomin Worterleoo buses, they are, on this cowst.

Brassbound folds up the letter, looking glum.

SIR HOWARD [*sharply*] Well, sir, are we not to have the benefit of that letter? Your men are waiting to hear it, I think.

BRASSBOUND. It is not a British ship. [*Sir Howard's face falls*].

LADY CICELY. What is it, then?

BRASSBOUND. An American cruiser. The Santiago.

THE CADI [*tearing his beard*] Woe! alas! it is where they set the sea on fire.

SIDI. Peace, Muley Othman: Allah is still above us.

JOHNSON. Would you mind readin it to us, capn?

BRASSBOUND [*grimly*] Oh, I'll read it to you.

"Mogador Harbor. 26 Sept 1899. Captain Hamlin Kearney, of the cruiser Santiago, presents the compliments of the United States to the Cadi Muley Othman el Kintafi, and announces that he is coming to look for the two British travellers Sir Howard Hallam and Lady Cicely Waynflete, in the Cadi's jurisdiction. As the search will be conducted with machine guns, the prompt return of the travellers to Mogador Harbor will save much trouble to all parties."

THE CADI. As I live, O Cadi, and thou, moon of loveliness, ye shall be led back to Mogador with honor. And thou, accursed Brassbound, shalt go thither a prisoner in chains, thou and thy people. [*Brassbound and his men make a movement to defend themselves*]. Seize them.

LADY CICELY. Oh, please dont fight. [*Brassbound, seeing that his men are hopelessly outnumbered, makes no resistance. They are made prisoners by the Cadi's followers*].

SIDI [*attempting to draw his scimitar*] The woman is mine: I will not forego her. [*He is seized and overpowered after a Homeric struggle*].

SIR HOWARD [*drily*] I told you you were not in a strong position, Captain Brassbound [*Looking implacably at him*] You are laid by the heels, my friend, as I said you would be.

LADY CICELY. But I assure you—

BRASSBOUND [*interrupting her*] What have you to assure him of? You persuaded me to spare him. Look at his face. Will you be able to persuade him to spare me?

ACT III

Torrid forenoon filtered through small Moorish windows high up in the adobe walls of the largest room in Leslie Rankin's house. A clean cool room, with the table (a Christian article) set in the middle, a presidentially elbowed chair behind it, and an inkstand and paper ready for the sitter. A couple of cheap American chairs right and left of the table, facing the same way as the presidential chair, give a judicial aspect to the arrangement. Rankin is placing a little tray with a jug and some glasses near the inkstand when Lady Cicely's voice is heard at the door, which is behind him in the corner to his right.

LADY CICELY. Good morning. May I come in?

RANKIN. Certainly. [*She comes in to the nearest end of the table. She has discarded all travelling equipment, and is dressed exactly as she might be in Surrey on a very hot day*]. Sit ye doon, Leddy Ceecily.

LADY CICELY [*sitting down*] How nice youve made the room for the inquiry!

RANKIN [*doubtfully*] I could wish there were more chairs. Yon American captain will preside in this; and that leaves but one for Sir Howrrd and one for your leddyship. I could almost be tempted to call it a maircy that your friend that owns the yacht has sprained his ankle and cannot come. I misdoubt me it will not look judeecial to have Captain Kearney's officers squatting on the floor.

LADY CICELY. Oh, they wont mind. What about the prisoners?

RANKIN. They are to be broat here from the town gaol presently.

LADY CICELY. And where is that silly old Cadi, and my handsome Sheikh Sidi? I must see them before the inquiry, or theyll give Captain Kearney quite a false impression of what happened.

RANKIN. But ye cannot see them. They decamped last night, back to their castles in the Atlas.

LADY CICELY [*delighted*] No!

RANKIN. Indeed and they did. The poor Cadi is so tarrified by all he has haird of the destruction of the Spanish fleet, that he darent trust himself in the captain's hands. [*Looking reproachfully at her*] On your journey back here, ye seem to have frightened the poor man yourself, Leddy Ceecily, by talking to him about the fanatical Chreestianity of the Americans. Ye have largely yourself to thank if he's gone.

LADY CICELY. Allah be praised! What a weight off our minds, Mr Rankin!

RANKIN [*puzzled*] And why? Do ye not understand how necessary their evidence is?

LADY CICELY. Their evidence! It would spoil everything. They would perjure themselves out of pure spite against poor Captain Brassbound.

RANKIN [*amazed*] Do ye call him poor Captain Brassbound! Does not your leddyship know that this Brassbound is—Heaven forgive me for judging him!—a precious scoundrel? Did ye not hear what Sir Howrrd told me on the yacht last night?

LADY CICELY. All a mistake, Mr Rankin: all a mistake, I assure you. You said just now, Heaven forgive you for judging him! Well, thats just what the whole quarrel is about. Captain Brassbound is just like you: he thinks we have no right to judge one another; and as Sir Howard gets £5,000 a year for doing nothing else but judging people, he thinks poor Captain Brassbound a regular Anarchist. They quarrelled dreadfully at the castle. You mustnt mind what Sir Howard says about him: you really mustnt.

RANKIN. But his conduct——

LADY CICELY. Perfectly saintly, Mr Rankin. Worthy of yourself in your best moments. He forgave Sir Howard, and did all he could to save him.

RANKIN. Ye astoanish me, Leddy Ceecily.

LADY CICELY. And think of the temptation to behave badly when he had us all there helpless!

RANKIN. The temptation! ay: thats true. Ycre ower bonny to be cast away among a parcel o lone, lawless men, my leddy.

LADY CICELY [naïvely] Bless me, thats quite true; and I never thought of it! Oh, after that you really must do all you can to help Captain Brassbound.

RANKIN [reservedly] No: I cannot say that, Leddy Ceecily. I doubt he has imposed on your good nature and sweet disposeetion. I had a crack with the Cadi as well as with Sir Howrrd; and there is little question in my mind but that Captain Brassbound is no better than a breegand.

LADY CICELY [apparently deeply impressed] I wonder whether he can be, Mr Rankin. If you think so, thats heavily against him in my opinion, because you have more knowledge of men than anyone else here. Perhaps I'm mistaken. I only thought you might like to help him as the son of your old friend.

RANKIN [startled] The son of my old friend! What d'ye mean?

LADY CICELY. Oh! Didnt Sir Howard tell you that? Why, Captain Brassbound turns out to be Sir Howard's nephew, the son of the brother you knew.

RANKIN [overwhelmed] I saw the likeness the night he came here! It's true: it's true. Uncle and nephew!

LADY CICELY. Yes: thats why they quarrelled so.

RANKIN [with a momentary sense of ill usage] I think Sir Howrrd might have told me that.

LADY CICELY. Of course he ought to have told you. You see he only tells one side of the story. That comes from his training as a barrister. You mustnt think he's naturally deceitful: if he'd been brought up as a clergy-

man, he'd have told you the whole truth as a matter of course.

RANKIN [too much perturbed to dwell on his grievance] Leddy Ceecily: I must go to the prison and see the lad. He may have been a bit wild; but I cant leave poor Miles's son unbefriended in a foreign gaol.

LADY CICELY [rising, radiant] Oh, how good of you! You have a real kind heart of gold, Mr Rankin. Now, before you go, shall we just put our heads together, and consider how to give Miles's son every chance—I mean of course every chance that he ought to have.

RANKIN [rather addled] I am so confused by this astoanishing news—

LADY CICELY. Yes, yes: of course you are. But dont you think he would make a better impression on the American captain if he were a little more respectably dressed?

RANKIN. Mebbe. But how can that be remedied here in Mogador?

LADY CICELY. Oh, Ive thought of that. You know I'm going back to England by way of Rome, Mr Rankin; and I'm bringing a portmanteau full of clothes for my brother there: he's ambassador, you know, and has to be very particular as to what he wears. I had the portmanteau brought here this morning. Now would you mind taking it to the prison, and smartening up Captain Brassbound a little. Tell him he ought to do it to shew his respect for me; and he will. It will be quite easy: there are two Krooboys waiting to carry the portmanteau. You will: I know you will. [She edges him to the door]. And do you think there is time to get him shaved?

RANKIN [succumbing, half bewildered] I'll do my best.

LADY CICELY. I know you will. [As he is going out] Oh! one word, Mr Rankin. [He comes back]. The Cadi didnt know that Captain Brassbound was Sir Howard's nephew, did he?

RANKIN. No.

LADY CICELY. Then he must have misunderstood everything quite dreadfully. I'm afraid, Mr Rankin—though you know best, of course—that we are bound not to repeat anything at the inquiry that the Cadi said. He didnt know, you see.

RANKIN [cannily] I take your point, Leddy Ceecily. It alters the case. I shall certainly make no allusion to it.

LADY CICELY [magnanimously] Well, then, I wont either. There!

They shake hands on it. Sir Howard comes in.

M

SIR HOWARD. Good morning, Mr Rankin. I hope you got home safely from the yacht last night.

RANKIN. Quite safe, thank ye, Sir Howrrd.

LADY CICELY. Howard: he's in a hurry. Dont make him stop to talk.

SIR HOWARD. Very good, very good. [*He comes to the table and takes Lady Cicely's chair*].

RANKIN. Oo revoir, Leddy Ceecily.

LADY CICELY. Bless you, Mr Rankin. [*Rankin goes out. She comes to the other end of the table, looking at Sir Howard with a troubled, sorrowfully sympathetic air, but unconsciously making her right hand stalk about the table on the tips of its fingers in a tentative stealthy way which would put Sir Howard on his guard if he were in a suspicious frame of mind, which, as it happens, he is not*]. I'm so sorry for you, Howard, about this unfortunate inquiry.

SIR HOWARD [*swinging round on his chair, astonished*] Sorry for me! Why?

LADY CICELY. It will look so dreadful. Your own nephew, you know.

SIR HOWARD. Cicely: an English judge has no nephews, no sons even, when he has to carry out the law.

LADY CICELY. But then he oughtnt to have any property either. People will never understand about the West Indian Estate. Theyll think youre the wicked uncle out of the Babes in the Wood. [*With a fresh gush of compassion*] I'm so so sorry for you.

SIR HOWARD [*rather stiffly*] I really do not see how I need your commiseration, Cicely. The woman was an impossible person, half mad, half drunk. Do you understand what such a creature is when she has a grievance, and imagines some innocent person to be the author of it.

LADY CICELY [*with a touch of impatience*] Oh, quite. Thatll be made clear enough. I can see it all in the papers already: our half mad, half drunk sister-in-law, making scenes with you in the steeet, with the police called in, and prison and all the rest of it. The family will be furious. [*Sir Howard quails. She instantly follows up her advantage with*] Think of papa!

SIR HOWARD. I shall expect Lord Waynflete to look at the matter as a reasonable man.

LADY CICELY. Do you think he's so greatly changed as that, Howard?

SIR HOWARD [*falling back on the fatalism of the depersonalized public man*] My dear Cicely: there is no use discussing the matter. It cannot be helped, however disagreeable it may be.

LADY CICELY. Of course not. Thats whats so dreadful. Do you think people will understand?

SIR HOWARD. I really cannot say. Whether they do or not, *I* cannot help it.

LADY CICELY. If you were anybody but a judge, it wouldnt matter so much. But a judge mustnt even be misunderstood. [*Despairingly*] Oh, it's dreadful, Howard: it's terrible! What would poor Mary say if she were alive now?

SIR HOWARD [*with emotion*] I dont think, Cicely, that my dear wife would misunderstand me.

LADY CICELY. No: she'd know you mean well. And when you came home and said, "Mary: Ive just told all the world that your sister-in-law was a police court criminal, and that I sent her to prison; and your nephew is a brigand, and I'm sending him to prison," she'd have thought it must be all right because you did it. But you dont think she would have liked it, any more than papa and the rest of us, do you?

SIR HOWARD [*appalled*] But what am I to do? Do you ask me to compound a felony?

LADY CICELY [*sternly*] Certainly not. I would not allow such a thing, even if you were wicked enough to attempt it. No. What I say is, that you ought not to tell the story yourself.

SIR HOWARD. Why?

LADY CICELY. Because everybody would say you are such a clever lawyer you could make a poor simple sailor like Captain Kearney believe anything. The proper thing for you to do, Howard, is to let me tell the exact truth. Then you can simply say that you are bound to confirm me. Nobody can blame you for that.

SIR HOWARD [*looking suspiciously at her*] Cicely: you are up to some devilment.

LADY CICELY [*promptly washing her hands of his interests*] Oh, very well. Tell the story yourself, in your own clever way. I only proposed to tell the exact truth. You call that devilment. So it is, I daresay, from a lawyer's point of view.

SIR HOWARD. I hope youre not offended.

LADY CICELY [*with the utmost goodhumor*] My dear Howard, not a bit. Of course youre right: you know how these things ought to be done. I'll do exactly what you tell me, and confirm everything you say.

SIR HOWARD [*alarmed by the completeness of his victory*] Oh, my dear, you mustnt act in my interest. You must give your evidence with absolute impartiality. [*She nods, as if thoroughly impressed and reproved, and gazes at him with the steadfast candor peculiar to liars who read novels. His eyes turn to the ground; and his brow clouds perplexedly. He rises; rubs his chin nervously with his forefinger; and adds*] I think, perhaps, on reflection, that there is something to be said for your proposal to relieve me of the very painful duty of telling what has occurred.

LADY CICELY [*holding off*] But youd do it so very much better.

SIR HOWARD. For that very reason, perhaps, it had better come from you.

LADY CICELY [*reluctantly*] Well, if youd rather.

SIR HOWARD. But mind, Cicely, the exact truth.

LADY CICELY [*with conviction*] The exact truth. [*They shake hands on it*].

SIR HOWARD [*holding her hand*] Fiat justitia: ruat cœlum!

LADY CICELY. Let Justice be done, though the ceiling fall!

An American bluejacket appears at the door.

BLUEJACKET. Captain Kearney's cawmpliments to Lady Waynflete; and may he come in?

LADY CICELY. Yes. By all means. Where are the prisoners?

BLUEJACKET. Party gawn to the jail to fetch em, marm.

LADY CICELY. Thank you. I should like to be told when they are coming, if I might.

BLUEJACKET. You shall so, marm. [*He stands aside, saluting, to admit his captain, and goes out*].

Captain Hamlin Kearney is a robustly built western American, with the keen, squeezed, wind beaten eyes and obstinately enduring mouth of his profession. A curious ethnological specimen, with all the nations of the old world at war in his veins, he is developing artificially in the direction of sleekness and culture under the restraints of an overwhelming dread of European criticism, and climatically in the direction of the indigenous North American, who is already in possession of his hair, his cheekbones, and the manlier instincts in him which the sea has rescued from civilization. The world, pondering on the great part of its own future which is in his hands, contemplates him with wonder as to what the devil he will evolve into in another century or two. Meanwhile he presents himself to Lady Cicely as a blunt sailor who has something to say to her concerning her conduct which he wishes to put politely, as becomes an officer addressing a lady, but also with an emphatically implied rebuke, as an American addressing an English person who has taken a liberty.

LADY CICELY [*as he enters*] So glad youve come, Captain Kearney.

KEARNEY [*coming between Sir Howard and Lady Cicely*] When we partcd yesterday ahfternoon, Lady Waynflete, I was unaware that in the course of your visit to my ship you had entirely altered the sleeping arrangements of my stokers. I thahnk you. As captain of the ship, I am customairily cawnsulted before the orders of English visitors are carried out; but as your alterations appear to cawndooce to the comfort of the men, I have not interfered with them.

LADY CICELY. How clever of you to find out! I believe you know every bolt in that ship.

Kearney softens perceptibly.

SIR HOWARD. I am really very sorry that my sister-in-law has taken so serious a liberty, Captain Kearney. It is a mania of hers—simply a mania. Why did your men pay any attention to her?

KEARNEY [*with gravely dissembled humor*] Well, I ahsked that question too. I said, Why did you obey that lady's orders instead of waiting for mine? They said they didnt see exactly how they could refuse. I ahsked whether they cawnsidered that discipline. They said, Well, sir, will you talk to the lady yourself next time?

LADY CICELY. I'm s o sorry. But you know, Captain, the one thing that one misses on board a man-of-war is a woman.

KEARNEY. We often feel that deprivation verry keenly, Lady Waynflete.

LADY CICELY. My uncle is first Lord of the Admiralty; and I am always telling him what a scandal it is that an English captain should be forbidden to take his wife on board to look after the ship.

KEARNEY. Stranger still, Lady Waynflete, he is not forbidden to take any other lady. Yours is an extraordinairy country—to an American.

LADY CICELY. But it's most serious, Captain. The poor men go melancholy mad, and ram each other's ships and do all sorts of things.

SIR HOWARD. Cicely: I beg you will not talk

nonsense to Captain Kearney. Your ideas on some subjects are really hardly decorous.

LADY CICELY [to Kearney] Thats what English people are like, Captain Kearney. They wont hear of anything concerning your poor sailors except Nelson and Trafalgar. You understand me, dont you?

KEARNEY [gallantly] I cawnsider that you have more sense in your wedding ring finger than the British Ahdmiralty has in its whole cawnstitootion, Lady Waynflete.

LADY CICELY. Of course I have. Sailors always understand things.

The bluejacket reappears.

BLUEJACKET [to Lady Cicely] Prisoners coming up the hill, marm.

KEARNEY [turning sharply on him] Who sent you in to say that?

BLUEJACKET [calmly] British lady's orders, sir. [He goes out, unruffled, leaving Kearney dumbfounded].

SIR HOWARD [contemplating Kearney's expression with dismay] I am really very sorry, Captain Kearney. I am quite aware that Lady Cicely has no right whatever to give orders to your men.

LADY CICELY. I didnt give orders: I just asked him. He has such a nice face! Dont you think so, Captain Kearney? [He gasps, speechless]. And now will you excuse me a moment. I want to speak to somebody before the inquiry begins. [She hurries out].

KEARNEY. There is sertnly a wonderful chahm about the British aristocracy, Sir Howard Hallam. Are they all like that? [He takes the presidential chair].

SIR HOWARD [resuming his seat on Kearney's right] Fortunately not, Captain Kearney. Half a dozen such women would make an end of law in England in six months.

The bluejacket comes to the door again.

BLUEJACKET. All ready, sir.

KEARNEY. Verry good. I'm waiting.

The bluejacket turns and intimates this to those without. The officers of the Santiago enter.

SIR HOWARD [rising and bobbing to them in a judicial manner] Good morning, gentlemen.

They acknowledge the greeting rather shyly, bowing or touching their caps, and stand in a group behind Kearney.

KEARNEY [to Sir Howard] You will be glahd to hear that I have a verry good account of one of our prisoners from our chahplain, who visited them in the gaol. He has expressed a wish to be cawnverted to Episcopalianism.

SIR HOWARD [drily] Yes, I think I know him.

KEARNEY. Bring in the prisoners.

BLUEJACKET [at the door] They are engaged with the British lady, sir. Shall I ask her——

KEARNEY [jumping up and exploding in storm piercing tones] Bring in the prisoners. Tell the lady those are my orders. Do you hear? Tell her so. [The bluejacket goes out dubiously. The officers look at one another in mute comment on the unaccountable pepperiness of their commander].

SIR HOWARD [suavely] Mr Rankin will be present, I presume.

KEARNEY [angrily] Rahnkin! Who is Rahnkin?

SIR HOWARD. Our host the missionary.

KEARNEY [subsiding unwillingly] Oh! Rahnkin, is he? He'd better look sharp or he'll be late. [Again exploding] What are they doing with those prisoners?

Rankin hurries in, and takes his place near Sir Howard.

SIR HOWARD. This is Mr Rankin, Captain Kearney.

RANKIN. Excuse my delay, Captain Kearney. The leddy sent me on an errand. [Kearney grunts]. I thoaght I should be late. But the first thing I heard when I arrived was your officer giving your compliments to Leddy Ceecily, and would she kindly allow the prisoners to come in, as you were anxious to see her again. Then I knew I was in time.

KEARNEY. Oh, that was it, was it? May I ask, sir, did you notice any sign on Lady Waynflete's part of cawmplying with that verry moderate request.

LADY CICELY [outside] Coming, coming.

The prisoners are brought in by a guard of armed bluejackets. Drinkwater first, again elaborately clean, and conveying by a virtuous and steadfast smirk a cheerful confidence in his innocence. Johnson solid and inexpressive, Redbrook unconcerned and debonair, Marzo uneasy. These four form a little group together on the captain's left. The rest wait unintelligently on Providence in a row against the wall on the same side, shepherded by the bluejackets. The first bluejacket, a petty officer, posts himself on the captain's right, behind Rankin and Sir Howard. Finally Brassbound appears with Lady Cicely on his arm. He is in fashionable frock coat and trousers, spotless collar and cuffs, and elegant boots. He carries a glossy tall hat in his hand. To an unsophisticated eye, the change is monstrous and appalling; and its effect on himself is so unmanning that he is quite out of countenance —a shaven Samson. Lady Cicely, however, is greatly pleased with it; and the rest regard it as an unquestionable improvement. The officers fall back gallantly to allow her to pass. Kearney rises to receive her, and stares with some surprise at Brassbound as she stops at the table on his left. Sir Howard rises punctiliously when Kearney rises and sits when he sits.

KEARNEY. Is this another gentleman of your party, Lady Waynflete? I presume I met you lahst night, sir, on board the yacht.

BRASSBOUND. No. I am your prisoner. My name is Brassbound.

DRINKWATER [*officiously*] Kepn Brarsbahnd, of the schooner Thenksgiv—

REDBROOK [*hastily*] Shut up, you fool. [*He elbows Drinkwater into the background*].

KEARNEY [*surprised and rather suspicious*] Well, I hardly understand this. However, if you are Captain Brassbound, you can take your place with the rest. [*Brassbound joins Redbrook and Johnson. Kearney sits down again after inviting Lady Cicely, with a solemn gesture, to take the vacant chair*]. Now let me see. You are a man of experience in these matters, Sir Howard Hallam. If you had to conduct this business, how would you start?

LADY CICELY. He'd call on the counsel for the prosecution, wouldnt you, Howard?

SIR HOWARD. But there is no counsel for the prosecution, Cicely.

LADY CICELY. Oh yes there is. I'm counsel for the prosecution. You mustnt let Sir Howard make a speech, Captain Kearney: his doctors have positively forbidden anything of that sort. Will you begin with me?

KEARNEY. By your leave, Lady Waynflete, I think I will just begin with myself. Sailor fashion will do as well here as lawyer fashion.

LADY CICELY. Ever so much better, d e a r Captain Kearney. [*Silence. Kearney composes himself to speak. She breaks out again*]. You look so nice as a judge!

A general smile. Drinkwater splutters into a half suppressed laugh.

REDBROOK [*in a fierce whisper*] Shut up, you fool, will you? [*Again he pushes him back with a furtive kick*].

SIR HOWARD [*remonstrating*] Cicely!

KEARNEY [*grimly keeping his countenance*] Your ladyship's cawmpliments will be in order at a later stage. Captain Brassbound: the position is this. My ship, the United States cruiser Santiago, was spoken off

Mogador lahst Thursday by the yacht Redgauntlet. The owner of the aforesaid yacht, who is not present through having sprained his ahnkle, gave me sertn information. In cawnsequence of that information the Santiago made the twenty knots to Mogador Harbor inside of fifty-seven minutes. Before noon next day a messenger of mine gave the Cadi of the district sertn information. In cawnsequence of that information the Cadi stimulated himself to some ten knots an hour, and lodged you and your men in Mogador jail at my disposal. The Cadi then went back to his mountain fahstnesses; so we shall not have the pleasure of his company here today. Do you follow me so far?

BRASSBOUND. Yes. I know what you did and what the Cadi did. The point is, why did you do it?

KEARNEY. With doo patience we shall come to that presently. Mr Rahnkin: will you kindly take up the parable?

RANKIN. On the very day that Sir Howrrd and Lady Cicely started on their excursion I was applied to for medicine by a follower of the Sheikh Sidi el Assif. He told me I should never see Sir Howrrd again, because his master knew he was a Christian and would take him out of the hands of Captain Brassbound. I hurried on board the yacht and told the owner to scour the coast for a gunboat or cruiser to come into the harbor and put persuasion on the authorities. [*Sir Howard turns and looks at Rankin with a sudden doubt of his integrity as a witness*].

KEARNEY. But I understood from our chahplain that you reported Captain Brassbound as in league with the Sheikh to deliver Sir Howard up to him.

RANKIN. That was my first hasty conclusion, Captain Kearney. But it appears that the compact between them was that Captain Brassbound should escort travellers under the Sheikh's protection at a certain payment per head, provided none of them were Christians. As I understand it, he tried to smuggle Sir Howrrd through under this compact, and the Sheikh found him out.

DRINKWATER. Rawt, gavner. Thets jest ah it wors. The Kepn—

REDBROOK [*again suppressing him*] Shut up, you fool, I tell you.

SIR HOWARD [*to Rankin*] May I ask have you had any conversation with Lady Cicely on this subject?

RANKIN [*naïvely*] Yes. [*Sir Howard grunts emphatically, as who should say "I thought so." Rankin continues, addressing the court*] May I say how sorry I am that there are so few chairs, Captain and gentlemen.

KEARNEY [*with genial American courtesy*] Oh, thats all right, Mr Rahnkin. Well, I see no harm so far: its human fawlly, but not human crime. Now the counsel for the prosecution can proceed to prosecute. The floor is yours, Lady Waynflete.

LADY CICELY [*rising*] I can only tell you the exact truth—

DRINKWATER [*involuntarily*] Naow, downt do thet, lidy—

REDBROOK [*as before*] Shut up, you fool, will you.

LADY CICELY. We had a most delightful trip in the hills; and Captain Brassbound's men could not have been nicer—I must say that for them—until we saw a tribe of Arabs— such nice looking men!—and then the poor things were frightened.

KEARNEY. The Arabs?

LADY CICELY. No: Arabs are never frightened. The escort, of course: escorts are always frightened. I wanted to speak to the Arab chief; but Captain Brassbound cruelly shot his horse; and the chief shot the Count; and then—

KEARNEY. The Count! What Count?

LADY CICELY. Marzo. Thats Marzo [*pointing to Marzo, who grins and touches his forehead*].

KEARNEY [*slightly overwhelmed by the unexpected profusion of incident and character in her story*] Well, what happened then?

LADY CICELY. Then the escort ran away— all escorts do—and dragged me into the castle, which you really ought to make them clean and whitewash thoroughly, Captain Kearney. Then Captain Brassbound and Sir Howard turned out to be related to one another [*Sensation*]; and then of course there was a quarrel. The Hallams always quarrel.

SIR HOWARD [*rising to protest*] Cicely! Captain Kearney: this man told me—

LADY CICELY [*swiftly interrupting him*] You mustnt say what people told you: it's not evidence. [*Sir Howard chokes with indignation*].

KEARNEY [*calmly*] Allow the lady to pro-ceed, Sir Howard Hallam.

SIR HOWARD [*recovering his self-control with a gulp, and resuming his seat*] I beg your pardon, Captain Kearney.

LADY CICELY. Then Sidi came.

KEARNEY. Sidney! Who was Sidney?

LADY CICELY. No, Sidi. The Sheikh. Sidi el Assif. A noble creature, with such a fine face! He fell in love with me at first sight—

SIR HOWARD [*remonstrating*] Cicely!

LADY CICELY. He did: you know he did. You told me to tell the exact truth.

KEARNEY. I can readily believe it, madam. Proceed.

LADY CICELY. Well, that put the poor fellow into a most cruel dilemma. You see, he could claim to carry off Sir Howard, because Sir Howard is a Christian. But as I am only a woman, he had no claim to me.

KEARNEY [*somewhat sternly, suspecting Lady Cicely of aristocratic atheism*] But you are a Christian woman.

LADY CICELY. No: the Arabs dont count women. They dont believe we have any souls.

RANKIN. That is true, Captain: the poor benighted creatures!

LADY CICELY. Well, what was he to do? He wasnt in love with Sir Howard; and he was in love with me. So he naturally offered to swop Sir Howard for me. Dont you think that was nice of him, Captain Kearney?

KEARNEY. I should have done the same myself, Lady Waynflete. Proceed.

LADY CICELY. Captain Brassbound, I must say, was nobleness itself, in spite of the quarrel between himself and Sir Howard. He refused to give up either of us, and was on the point of fighting for us when in came the Cadi with your most amusing and delightful letter, captain, and bundled us all back to Mogador after calling my poor Sidi the most dreadful names, and putting all the blame on Captain Brassbound. So here we are. Now, Howard, isnt that the exact truth, every word of it?

SIR HOWARD. It is the truth, Cicely, and nothing but the truth. But the English law requires a witness to tell the whole truth.

LADY CICELY. What nonsense! As if anybody ever knew the whole truth about anything! [*Sitting down, much hurt and discouraged*] I'm sorry you wish Captain Kearney to understand that I am an untruthful witness.

SIR HOWARD. No: but—

LADY CICELY. Very well, then: please dont say things that convey that impression.

KEARNEY. But Sir Howard told me yesterday that Captain Brassbound threatened to sell him into slavery.

LADY CICELY [*springing up again*] Did Sir

Howard tell you the things he said about Captain Brassbound's mother? [*Renewed sensation*]. I told you they quarrelled, Captain Kearney. I said so, didnt I?

REDBROOK [*crisply*] Distinctly. [*Drinkwater opens his mouth to corroborate*]. Shut up, you fool.

LADY CICELY. Of course I did. Now, Captain Kearney, do y o u want me—does Sir Howard want me—does anybody want me to go into the details of that shocking family quarrel? Am I to stand here in the absence of any individual of my own sex and repeat the language of two angry men?

KEARNEY [*rising impressively*] The United States navy will have no hahnd in offering any violence to the pure instincts of womanhood. Lady Waynflete: I thahnk you for the delicacy with which you have given your evidence. [*Lady Cicely beams on him gratefully and sits down triumphant*]. Captain Brassbound: I shall not hold you respawnsible for what you may have said when the English bench addressed you in the language of the English forecastle—[*Sir Howard is about to protest*] No, Sir Howard Hallam; excuse m e. In moments of pahssion I have called a man that myself. We are all glahd to find real flesh and blood beneath the ermine of the judge. We will now drop a subject that should never have been broached in a lady's presence. [*He resumes his seat, and adds, in a businesslike tone*] Is there anything further before we release these men?

BLUEJACKET. There are some dawcuments handed over by the Cadi, sir. He reckoned they were sort of magic spells. The chahplain ordered them to be reported to you and burnt, with your leave, sir.

KEARNEY. What are they?

BLUEJACKET [*reading from a list*] Four books, torn and dirty, made up of separate numbers, value each wawn penny, and entitled Sweeny Todd, the Demon Barber of London; the Skeleton Horseman—

DRINKWATER [*rushing forward in painful alarm and anxiety*] It's maw lawbrary, gavner. Downt burn em.

KEARNEY. Youll be better without that sort of reading, my man.

DRINKWATER [*in intense distress, appealing to Lady Cicely*] Downt let em burn em, lidy. They dassent if you horder em not to. [*With desperate eloquence*] Yer dunno wot them books is to me. They took me aht of the saw-

did reeyellities of the Worterleoo Rowd. They formed maw mawnd: they shaowed me sathink awgher than the squalor of a corster's lawf—

REDBROOK [*collaring him*] Oh shut up, you fool. Get out. Hold your ton—

DRINKWATER [*frantically breaking from him*] Lidy, lidy: sy a word for me. Ev a feelin awt. [*His tears choke him: he clasps his hands in dumb entreaty*].

LADY CICELY [*touched*] Dont burn his books, Captain. Let me give them back to him.

KEARNEY. The books will be handed over to the lady.

DRINKWATER [*in a small voice*] Thenkyer, lidy. [*He retires among his comrades, snivelling subduedly*].

REDBROOK [*aside to him as he passes*] You silly ass, you. [*Drinkwater sniffs and does not reply*].

KEARNEY. I suppose you and your men accept this lady's account of what passed, Captain Brassbound.

BRASSBOUND [*gloomily*] Yes. It is true—as far as it goes.

KEARNEY [*impatiently*] Do you wawnt it to go any further?

MARZO. She leave out something. Arab shoot me. She nurse me. She cure me.

KEARNEY. And who are you, pray?

MARZO [*seized with a sanctimonious desire to demonstrate his higher nature*] Only dam thief. Dam liar. Dam rascal. She no lady.

JOHNSON [*revolted by the seeming insult to the English peerage from a low Italian*] What? Whats that you say?

MARZO. No lady nurse dam rascal. Only saint. She saint. She get me to heaven—get us all to heaven. We do what we like now.

LADY CICELY. Indeed you will do nothing of the sort, Marzo, unless you like to behave yourself very nicely indeed. What hour did you say we were to lunch at, Captain Kearney?

KEARNEY. You recall me to my dooty, Lady Waynflete. My barge will be ready to take off you and Sir Howard to the Santiago at one o'clawk. [*He rises*]. Captain Brassbound: this innquery has elicited no reason why I should detain you or your men. I advise you to ahct as escort in future to heathens exclusively. Mr Rahnkin: I thahnk you in the name of the United States for the hospitahlity you have extended to us today; and I invite you to accompany me bahck to my ship with a view to lunch at half-past-one. Gentlemen: we will wait on the governor of the gaol on our way to the harbor. [*He goes out, following his officers, and followed by the bluejackets and the petty officer*].

SIR HOWARD [*to Lady Cicely*] Cicely: in the course of my professional career I have met with unscrupulous witnesses, and, I am sorry to say, unscrupulous counsel also. But the combination of unscrupulous witness and unscrupulous counsel I have met today has taken away my breath. You have made me your accomplice in defeating justice.

LADY CICELY. Yes: arnt you glad it's been defeated for once? [*She takes his arm to go out with him*]. Captain Brassbound: I will come back to say goodbye before I go. [*He nods gloomily. She goes out with Sir Howard, following the Captain and his staff*].

RANKIN [*running to Brassbound and taking both his hands*] I'm right glad yere cleared. I'll come back and have a crack with ye when yon lunch is over. God bless ye. [*He goes out quickly*].

Brassbound and his men, left by themselves in the room, free and unobserved, go straight out of their senses. They laugh; they dance; they embrace one another; they set to partners and waltz clumsily; they shake hands repeatedly and maudlinly. Three only retain some sort of self-possession. Marzo, proud of having successfully thrust himself into a leading part in the recent proceedings and made a dramatic speech, inflates his chest, curls his scanty moustache, and throws himself into a swaggering pose, chin up and right foot forward, despising the emotional English barbarians around him. Brassbound's eyes and the working of his mouth shew that he is infected with the general excitement; but he bridles himself savagely. Redbrook, trained to affect indifference, grins cynically; winks at Brassbound; and finally relieves himself by assuming the character of a circus ringmaster, flourishing an imaginary whip and egging on the rest to wilder exertions. A climax is reached when Drinkwater, let loose without a stain on his character for the second time, is rapt by belief in his star into an ecstasy in which, scorning all partnership, he becomes as it were a whirling dervish, and executes so miraculous a clog dance that the others gradually cease their slower antics to stare at him.

BRASSBOUND [*tearing off his hat and striding forward as Drinkwater collapses, exhausted, and is picked up by Redbrook*] Now to get rid of this respectable clobber and feel like a man again. Stand by, all hands, to jump on the captain's tall hat. [*He puts the hat down and prepares to jump on it. The effect is startling, and takes him completely aback. His followers, far from appreciating his iconoclasm, are shocked into scandalized sobriety, except Redbrook, who is intensely tickled by their prudery*].

DRINKWATER. Naow, look eah, kepn: that ynt rawt. Dror a lawn somewhere.

JOHNSON. I say nothin agen a bit of fun, Capn; but lets be gentlemen.

REDBROOK. I suggest to you, Brassbound, that the clobber belongs to Lady Sis. Aint you going to give it back to her?

BRASSBOUND [*picking up the hat and brushing the dust off it anxiously*] Thats true. I'm a fool. All the same, she shall not see me again like this. [*He pulls off the coat and waistcoat together*]. Does any man here know how to fold up this sort of thing properly?

REDBROOK. Allow me, governor. [*He takes the coat and waistcoat to the table, and folds them up.*]

BRASSBOUND [*loosening his collar and the front of his shirt*] Brandyfaced Jack: youre looking at these studs. I know whats in your mind.

DRINKWATER [*indignantly*] Naow yer downt: nort a bit on it. Wots in maw mawnd is secrifawce, seolf-secrifawce.

BRASSBOUND. If one brass pin of that lady's property is missing, I'll hang you with my own hands at the gaff of the Thanksgiving—and would, if she were lying under the guns of all the fleets in Europe. [*He pulls off the shirt and stands in his blue jersey, with his hair ruffled. He passes his hand through it and exclaims*] Now I am half a man, at any rate.

REDBROOK. A horrible combination, governor: churchwarden from the waist down, and the rest pirate. Lady Sis wont speak to you in it.

BRASSBOUND. I'll change altogether. [*He leaves the room to get his own trousers*].

REDBROOK [*softly*] Look here, Johnson, and gents generally. [*They gather about him*]. Spose she takes him back to England!

MARZO [*trying to repeat his success*] Im! Im only dam pirate. She saint, I tell you—no take any man nowhere.

JOHNSON [*severely*] Dont you be a ignorant and immoral foreigner. [*The rebuke is well received; and Marzo is hustled into the background and extinguished*]. She wont take him for harm; but she might take him for good. And then where should we be?

DRINKWATER. Brarsbahnd ynt the ownly kepn in the world. Wot mikes a kepn is brines an knollidge o lawf. It ynt thet thers naow sitch pusson: its thet you dunno where to look fr him. [*The implication that he is such a person is so intolerable that they receive it with a prolonged burst of booing*].

BRASSBOUND [*returning in his own clothes, getting into his jacket as he comes*]. Stand by, all. [*They start asunder guiltily, and wait for orders*]. Redbrook: you pack that clobber in the lady's portmanteau, and put it aboard the yacht for her. Johnson: you take all hands aboard the Thanksgiving; look through the stores; weigh anchor; and make all ready for sea. Then send Jack to wait for me at the slip with a boat; and give me a gunfire for a signal. Lose no time.

JOHNSON. Ay, ay, sir. All aboard, mates.

ALL. Ay, ay. [*They rush out tumultuously*].

When they are gone, Brassbound sits down at the end of the table, with his elbows on it and his head on his fists, gloomily thinking. Then he takes from the breast pocket of his jacket a leather case, from which he extracts a scrappy packet of dirty letters and newspaper cuttings. These he throws on the table. Next comes a photograph in a cheap frame. He throws it down untenderly beside the papers; then folds his arms, and is looking at it with grim distaste when Lady Cicely enters. His back is towards her; and he does not hear her. Perceiving this, she shuts the door loudly enough to attract attention. He starts up.

LADY CICELY [*coming to the opposite end of the table*] So youve taken off all my beautiful clothes!

BRASSBOUND. Your brother's, you mean. A man should wear his own clothes; and a man should tell his own lies. I'm sorry you had to tell mine for me today.

LADY CICELY. Oh, women spend half their lives telling little lies for men, and sometimes big ones. We're used to it. But mind! I dont admit that I told any today.

BRASSBOUND. How did you square my uncle?

LADY CICELY. I dont understand the expression.

BRASSBOUND. I mean—

LADY CICELY. I'm afraid we havnt time to go into what you mean before lunch. I want to speak to you about your future. May I?

BRASSBOUND [*darkening a little, but politely*]

Sit down. [*She sits down. So does he*].

LADY CICELY. What are your plans?

BRASSBOUND. I have no plans. You will hear a gun fired in the harbor presently. That will mean that the Thanksgiving's anchor's weighed and that she is waiting for her captain to put out to sea. And her captain doesnt know now whether to turn her head north or south.

LADY CICELY. Why not north for England?

BRASSBOUND. Why not south for the Pole?

LADY CICELY. But you must do something with yourself?

BRASSBOUND [*settling himself with his fists and elbows weightily on the table and looking straight and powerfully at her*] Look you: when you and I first met, I was a man with a purpose. I stood alone: I saddled no friend, woman or man, with that purpose, because it was against law, against religion, against my own credit and safety. But I believed in it; and I stood alone for it, as a man should stand for his belief, against law and religion as much as against wickedness and selfishness. Whatever I may be, I am none of your fairweather sailors thatll do nothing for their creed but go to Heaven for it. I was ready to go to hell for mine. Perhaps you dont understand that.

LADY CICELY. Oh bless you, yes. It's so very like a certain sort of man.

BRASSBOUND. I daresay; but Ive not met many of that sort. Anyhow, that was what I was like. I dont say I was happy in it; but I wasnt unhappy, because I wasnt drifting. I was steering a course and had work in hand. Give a man health and a course to steer; and he'll never stop to trouble about whether he's happy or not.

LADY CICELY. Sometimes he wont even stop to trouble about whether other people are happy or not.

BRASSBOUND. I dont deny that: nothing makes a man so selfish as work. But I was not self-seeking: it seemed to me that I had put justice above self. I tell you life meant something to me then. Do you see that dirty little bundle of scraps of paper?

LADY CICELY. What are they?

BRASSBOUND. Accounts cut out of newspapers. Speeches made by my uncle at charitable dinners, or sentencing men to death— pious, highminded speeches by a man who was to me a thief and a murderer! To my mind they were more weighty, more momentous, better revelations of the wicked-

M 2

ness of law and respectability than the book of the prophet Amos. What are they now? [*He quietly tears the newspaper cuttings into little fragments and throws them away, looking fixedly at her meanwhile*].

LADY CICELY. Well, thats a comfort, at all events.

BRASSBOUND. Yes; but it's a part of my life gone: y o u r doing, remember. What have I left? See here! [*he takes up the letters*] the letters my uncle wrote to my mother, with her comments on their cold drawn insolence, their treachery and cruelty. And the piteous letters she wrote to him later on, returned unopened. Must they go too?

LADY CICELY [*uneasily*] I cant ask you to destroy your mother's letters.

BRASSBOUND. Why not, now that you have taken the meaning out of them? [*He tears them*]. Is that a comfort too?

LADY CICELY. It's a little sad; but perhaps it is best so.

BRASSBOUND. That leaves one relic: her portrait. [*He plucks the photograph out of its cheap case.*]

LADY CICELY [*with vivid curiosity*] Oh, let me see. [*He hands it to her. Before she can control herself, her expression changes to one of unmistakeable disappointment and repulsion*].

BRASSBOUND [*with a single sardonic cachinnation*] Ha! You expected something better than that. Well, youre right. Her face does not look well opposite yours.

LADY CICELY [*distressed*] I said nothing.

BRASSBOUND. What could you say? [*He takes back the portrait: she relinquishes it without a word. He looks at it; shakes his head; and takes it quietly between his finger and thumb to tear it*].

LADY CICELY [*staying his hand*] Oh, not your mother's picture!

BRASSBOUND. If that were your picture, would you like your son to keep it for younger and better women to see?

LADY CICELY [*releasing his hand*] Oh, you are dreadful! Tear it, tear it. [*She covers her eyes for a moment to shut out the sight*].

BRASSBOUND [*tearing it quietly*] You killed her for me that day in the castle; and I am better without her. [*He throws away the fragments*]. Now everything is gone. You have taken the old meaning out of my life; but you have put no new meaning into it. I can see that you have some clue to the world that makes all its difficulties easy for you; but I'm not clever enough to seize it. Youve lamed

me by shewing me that I take life the wrong way when I'm left to myself.

LADY CICELY. Oh no. Why do you say that?

BRASSBOUND. What else can I say? See what Ive done! My uncle is no worse a man than myself—better, most likely; for he has a better head and a higher place. Well, I took him for a villain out of a storybook. My mother would have opened anybody else's eyes: she shut mine. I'm a stupider man than Brandyfaced Jack even; for he got his romantic nonsense out of his penny numbers and such like trash; but I got just the same nonsense out of life and experience. [*Shaking his head*] It was vulgar—v u l g a r. I see that now; for youve opened my eyes to the past; but what good is that for the future? What am I to do? Where am I to go?

LADY CICELY. It's quite simple. Do whatever you like. Thats what I always do.

BRASSBOUND. That answer is no good to me. What I like is to have something to do; and I have nothing. You might as well talk like the missionary and tell me to do my duty.

LADY CICELY [*quickly*] Oh no thank you. Ive had quite enough of your duty, and Howard's duty. Where would you both be now if I'd let you do it?

BRASSBOUND. We'd have been somewhere, at all events. It seems to me that now I am nowhere.

LADY CICELY. But arnt you coming back to England with us?

BRASSBOUND. What for?

LADY CICELY. Why, to make the most of your opportunities.

BRASSBOUND. What opportunities?

LADY CICELY. Dont you understand that when you are the nephew of a great bigwig, and have influential connexions, and good friends among them, lots of things can be done for you that are never done for ordinary ship captains?

BRASSBOUND. Ah; but I'm not an aristocrat, you see. And like most poor men, I'm proud. I dont like being patronized.

LADY CICELY. What is the use of saying that? In my world, which is now your world—o u r world—getting patronage is the whole art of life. A man cant have a career without it.

BRASSBOUND. In my world a man can navigate a ship and get his living by it.

LADY CICELY. Oh, I see youre one of the Idealists—the Impossibilists! We have them, too, occasionally, in our world. There's only one thing to be done with them.

BRASSBOUND. Whats that?

LADY CICELY. Marry them straight off to some girl with enough money for them, and plenty of sentiment. Thats t h e i r fate.

BRASSBOUND. Youve spoiled even that chance for me. Do you think I could look at any ordinary woman after you? You seem to be able to make me do pretty well what you like; but you cant make me marry anybody but yourself.

LADY CICELY. Do you know, Captain Paquito, that Ive married no less than seventeen men [*Brassbound stares*] to other women. And they all opened the subject by saying that they would never marry anybody but me.

BRASSBOUND. Then I shall be the first man you ever found to stand to his word.

LADY CICELY [*part pleased, part amused, part sympathetic*] Do you really want a wife?

BRASSBOUND. I want a commander. Dont undervalue me: I am a good man when I have a good leader. I have courage: I have determination: I'm not a drinker: I can command a schooner and a shore party if I cant command a ship or an army. When work is put upon me, I turn neither to save my life nor to fill my pocket. Gordon trusted me; and he never regretted it. If you trust me, you shant regret it. All the same, theres something wanting in me: I suppose I'm stupid.

LADY CICELY. Oh, youre not stupid.

BRASSBOUND. Yes I am. Since you saw me for the first time in that garden, youve heard me say nothing clever. And Ive heard you say nothing that didnt make me laugh, or make me feel friendly, as well as telling me what to think and what to do. Thats what I mean by real cleverness. Well, I havnt got it. I can give an order when I know what order to give. I can make men obey it, willing or unwilling. But I'm stupid, I tell you: stupid. When theres no Gordon to command me, I cant think of what to do. Left to myself, Ive become half a brigand. I can kick that little gutterscrub Drinkwater; but I find myself doing what he puts into my head because I cant think of anything else. When you came, I took your orders as naturally as I took Gordon's, though I little thought my next commander would be a woman. I want to take service under you. And theres no way in which that can be done except marrying you. Will you let me do it?

LADY CICELY. I'm afraid you dont quite know how odd a match it would be for me according to the ideas of English society.

BRASSBOUND. I care nothing about English society: let it mind its own business.

LADY CICELY [*rising, a little alarmed*] Captain Paquito: I a m not in love with you.

BRASSBOUND [*also rising, with his gaze still steadfastly on her*] I didnt suppose you were: the commander is not usually in love with his subordinate.

LADY CICELY. Nor the subordinate with the commander.

BRASSBOUND [*assenting firmly*] Nor the subordinate with the commander.

LADY CICELY [*learning for the first time in her life what terror is, as she finds that he is unconsciously mesmerizing her*] Oh, you are dangerous!

BRASSBOUND. Come: are you in love with anybody else? Thats the question.

LADY CICELY [*shaking her head*] I have never been in love with any real person; and I never shall. How could I manage people if I had that mad little bit of self left in me? Thats my secret.

BRASSBOUND. Then throw away the last bit of self. Marry me.

LADY CICELY [*vainly struggling to recall her wandering will*] Must I?

BRASSBOUND. There is no must. You c a n. I ask you to. My fate depends on it.

LADY CICELY. It's frightful; for I dont mean to—dont wish to.

BRASSBOUND. But you will.

LADY CICELY [*quite lost, slowly stretches out her hand to give it to him*] I— [*Gunfire from the Thanksgiving. His eyes dilate. It wakes her from her trance*] What is that?

BRASSBOUND. It is farewell. Rescue for you —safety, freedom! You were made to be something better than the wife of Black Paquito. [*He kneels and takes her hands*] You can do no more for me now: I have blundered somehow on the secret of command at last [*he kisses her hands*]: thanks for that, and for a man's power and purpose restored and righted. And farewell, farewell, farewell.

LADY CICELY [*in a strange ecstasy, holding his hands as he rises*] Oh, farewell. With my heart's deepest feeling, farewell, farewell.

BRASSBOUND. With my heart's noblest honor and triumph, farewell. [*He turns and flies*].

LADY CICELY. How glorious! how glorious! And what an escape!

THE END

XI

MAN AND SUPERMAN

A COMEDY AND A PHILOSOPHY (1901–3)

ACT I

Roebuck Ramsden is in his study, opening the morning's letters. The study, handsomely and solidly furnished, proclaims the man of means. Not a speck of dust is visible: it is clear that there are at least two housemaids and a parlormaid downstairs, and a housekeeper upstairs who does not let them spare elbow-grease. Even the top of Roebuck's head is polished: on a sunshiny day he could heliograph his orders to distant camps by merely nodding. In no other respect, however, does he suggest the military man. It is in active civil life that men get his broad air of importance, his dignified expectation of deference, his determinate mouth disarmed and refined since the hour of his success by the withdrawal of opposition and the concession of comfort and precedence and power. He is more than a highly respectable man: he is marked out as a president of highly respectable men, a chairman among directors, an alderman among councillors, a mayor among aldermen. Four tufts of iron-grey hair, which will soon be as white as isinglass, and are in other respects not at all unlike it, grow in two symmetrical pairs above his ears and at the angles of his spreading jaws. He wears a black frock coat, a white waistcoat (it is bright spring weather), and trousers, neither black nor perceptibly blue, of one of those indefinitely mixed hues which the modern clothier has produced to harmonize with the religions of respectable men. He has not been out of doors yet today; so he still wears his slippers, his boots being ready for him on the hearthrug. Surmising that he has no valet, and seeing that he has no secretary with a shorthand notebook and a typewriter, one meditates on how little our great burgess domesticity has been disturbed by new fashions and methods, or by the enterprise of the railway and hotel companies which sell you a Saturday to Monday of life at Folkestone as a real gentleman for two guineas, first class fares both ways included.

How old is Roebuck? The question is important on the threshold of a drama of ideas; for under such circumstances everything depends on whether his adolescence belonged to the sixties or to the eighties. He was born, as a matter of fact, in 1839, and was a Unitarian and Free Trader from his boyhood, and an Evolutionist from the publication of the Origin of Species. Consequently he has always classed himself as an advanced thinker and fearlessly outspoken reformer.

Sitting at his writing table, he has on his right the windows giving on Portland Place. Through these, as through a proscenium, the curious spectator may contemplate his profile as well as the blinds will permit. On his left is the inner wall, with a stately bookcase, and the door not quite in the middle, but somewhat further from him. Against the wall opposite him are two busts on pillars: one, to his left, of John Bright; the other, to his right, of Mr Herbert Spencer. Between them hang an engraved portrait of Richard Cobden; enlarged photographs of Martineau, Huxley, and George Eliot; autotypes of allegories by Mr G. F. Watts (for Roebuck believes in the fine arts with all the earnestness of a man who does not understand them), and an impression of Dupont's engraving of Delaroche's Beaux Arts hemicycle, representing the great men of all ages. On the wall behind him, above the mantelshelf, is a family portrait of impenetrable obscurity.

A chair stands near the writing table for the convenience of business visitors. Two other chairs are against the wall between the busts.

A parlormaid enters with a visitor's card. Roebuck takes it, and nods, pleased. Evidently a welcome caller.

RAMSDEN. Shew him in.

The parlormaid goes out and returns with the visitor.

THE MAID. Mr Robinson.

Mr Robinson is really an uncommonly nice looking young fellow. He must, one thinks, be the jeune premier; for it is not in reason to suppose that a second such attractive male figure should appear in one story. The slim, shapely frame, the elegant suit of new mourning, the small head and regular features, the pretty little moustache, the frank clear eyes, the wholesome bloom on the youthful complexion, the well brushed glossy hair, not curly, but of fine texture and good dark color, the arch of good nature in the eyebrows, the erect forehead and neatly pointed chin, all announce the man who will love and suffer later on. And that he will not do so without sympathy is guaranteed by an engaging sincerity and eager modest serviceableness which stamp him as a man of amiable nature. The moment he appears, Ramsden's face expands into fatherly liking and welcome, an expression which drops into one of decorous grief as the young man approaches him with sorrow in his face as well as in his black clothes. Ramsden seems to know the nature of the bereavement. As the visitor advances silently to the writing table, the old man rises and shakes his hand across it without a word: a long, affectionate shake which tells the story of a recent sorrow common to both.

RAMSDEN [*concluding the handshake and cheering up*] Well, well, Octavius, it's the common lot. We must all face it some day. Sit down.

Octavius takes the visitor's chair. Ramsden replaces himself in his own.

OCTAVIUS. Yes: we must face it, Mr Ramsden. But I owed him a great deal. He did everything for me that my father could have done if he had lived.

RAMSDEN. He had no son of his own, you see.

OCTAVIUS. But he had daughters; and yet he was as good to my sister as to me. And his death was so sudden! I always intended to thank him—to let him know that I had not taken all his care of me as a matter of course, as any boy takes his father's care. But I waited for an opportunity; and now he is dead—dropped without a moment's warning. He will never know what I felt. [*He takes out his handkerchief and cries unaffectedly*].

RAMSDEN. How do we know that, Octavius? He may know it: we cannot tell. Come! dont grieve. [*Octavius masters himself and puts up his handkerchief*]. Thats right. Now let me tell you something to console you. The last time I saw him—it was in this very room—he said to me: "Tavy is a generous lad and the soul of honor; and when I see how little consideration other men get from their sons, I realize how much better than a son he's been to me." There! Doesnt that do you good?

OCTAVIUS. Mr Ramsden: he used to say to me that he had met only one man in the world who was the soul of honor, and that was Roebuck Ramsden.

RAMSDEN. Oh, that was his partiality: we were very old friends, you know. But there was something else he used to say about you.

I wonder whether I ought to tell you or not!

OCTAVIUS. You know best.

RAMSDEN. It was something about his daughter.

OCTAVIUS [*eagerly*] About Ann! Oh, do tell me that, Mr Ramsden.

RAMSDEN. Well, he said he was glad, after all, you were not his son, because he thought that someday Annie and you—[*Octavius blushes vividly*]. Well, perhaps I shouldnt have told you. But he was in earnest.

OCTAVIUS. Oh, if only I thought I had a chance! You know, Mr Ramsden, I dont care about money or about what people call position; and I cant bring myself to take an interest in the business of struggling for them. Well, Ann has a most exquisite nature; but she is so accustomed to be in the thick of that sort of thing that she thinks a man's character incomplete if he is not ambitious. She knows that if she married me she would have to reason herself out of being ashamed of me for not being a big success of some kind.

RAMSDEN [*getting up and planting himself with his back to the fireplace*] Nonsense, my boy, nonsense! Youre too modest. What does she know about the real value of men at her age? [*More seriously*] Besides, she's a wonderfully dutiful girl. Her father's wish would be sacred to her. Do you know that since she grew up to years of discretion, I don't believe she has ever once given her own wish as a reason for doing anything or not doing it. It's always "Father wishes me to," or "Mother wouldnt like it." It's really almost a fault in her. I have often told her she must learn to think for herself.

OCTAVIUS [*shaking his head*] I couldnt ask her to marry me because her father wished it, Mr Ramsden.

RAMSDEN. Well, perhaps not. No: of course not. I see that. No: you certainly couldnt. But when you win her on your own merits, it will be a great happiness to her to fulfil her father's desire as well as her own. Eh? Come! youll ask her, wont you?

OCTAVIUS [*with sad gaiety*] At all events I promise you I shall never ask anyone else.

RAMSDEN. Oh, you shant need to. She'll accept you, my boy—although [*here he suddenly becomes very serious indeed*] you have one great drawback.

OCTAVIUS [*anxiously*] What drawback is that, Mr Ramsden? I should rather say which of my many drawbacks?

RAMSDEN. I'll tell you, Octavius. [*He takes from the table a book bound in red cloth*]. I have in my hand a copy of the most infamous, the most scandalous, the most mischievous, the most blackguardly book that ever escaped burning at the hands of the common hangman. I have not read it: I would not soil my mind with such filth; but I have read what the papers say of it. The title is quite enough for me. [*He reads it*]. The Revolutionist's Handbook and Pocket Companion. By John Tanner, M.I.R.C., Member of the Idle Rich Class.

OCTAVIUS [*smiling*] But Jack—

RAMSDEN [*testily*] For goodness' sake, dont call him Jack under my roof [*he throws the book violently down on the table. Then, somewhat relieved, he comes past the table to Octavius, and addresses him at close quarters with impressive gravity*]. Now, Octavius, I know that my dead friend was right when he said you were a generous lad. I know that this man was your schoolfellow, and that you feel bound to stand by him because there was a boyish friendship between you. But I ask you to consider the altered circumstances. You were treated as a son in my friend's house. You lived there; and your friends could not be turned from the door. This man Tanner was in and out there on your account almost from his childhood. He addresses Annie by her Christian name as freely as you do. Well, while her father was alive, that was her father's business, not mine. This man Tanner was only a boy to him: his opinions were something to be laughed at, like a man's hat on a child's head. But now Tanner is a grown man and Annie a grown woman. And her father is gone. We dont as yet know the exact terms of his will; but he often talked it over with me; and I have no more doubt than I have that youre sitting there that the will appoints me Annie's trustee and guardian. [*Forcibly*] Now I tell you, once for all, I cant and I wont have Annie placed in such a position that she must, out of regard for you, suffer the intimacy of this fellow Tanner. It's not fair: it's not right: it's not kind. What are you going to do about it?

OCTAVIUS. But Ann herself has told Jack that whatever his opinions are, he will always be welcome because he knew her dear father.

RAMSDEN [*out of patience*] That girl's mad about her duty to her parents. [*He starts off like a goaded ox in the direction of John Bright, in whose expression there is no sympathy for him. As he speaks he fumes down to Herbert Spencer, who receives him still more coldly*]. Excuse me, Octavius; but there are limits to social toleration. You know that I am not a bigoted or prejudiced man. You know that I am plain Roebuck Ramsden when other men who have done less have got handles to their names, because I have stood for equality and liberty of conscience while they were truckling to the Church and to the aristocracy. Whitefield and I lost chance after chance through our advanced opinions. But I draw the line at Anarchism and Free Love and that sort of thing. If I am to be Annie's guardian, she will have to learn that she has a duty to me. I wont have it: I will n o t have it. She must forbid John Tanner the house; and so must you.

The parlormaid returns.

OCTAVIUS. But—

RAMSDEN [*calling his attention to the servant*] Ssh! Well?

THE MAID. Mr Tanner wishes to see you, sir.

RAMSDEN. Mr Tanner!

OCTAVIUS. Jack!

RAMSDEN. How dare Mr Tanner call on me! Say I cannot see him.

OCTAVIUS [*hurt*] I am sorry you are turning my friend from your door like that.

THE MAID [*calmly*] He's not at the door, sir. He's upstairs in the drawing room with Miss Ramsden. He came with Mrs Whitefield and Miss Ann and Miss Robinson, sir.

Ramsden's feelings are beyond words.

OCTAVIUS [*grinning*] Thats very like Jack, Mr Ramsden. You must see him, even if it's only to turn him out.

RAMSDEN [*hammering out his words with suppressed fury*] Go upstairs and ask Mr Tanner to be good enough to step down here. [*The parlormaid goes out; and Ramsden returns to the fireplace, as to a fortified position*]. I must say that of all the confounded pieces of impertinence—well, if these are Anarchist manners, I hope you like them. And Annie with him! Annie! A— [*he chokes*].

OCTAVIUS. Yes: thats what surprises me. He's so desperately afraid of Ann. There must be something the matter.

Mr John Tanner suddenly opens the door and enters. He is too young to be described simply as a big man with a beard. But it is already plain that middle life will find him in that category. He has still some of the slimness of youth; but youthfulness is not the effect he aims at: his frock coat would befit a prime minister; and a certain high chested carriage of the shoulders, a lofty pose of the head, and the Olympian majesty with which a mane, or rather a huge wisp, of hazel colored hair is thrown back from an imposing brow, suggest Jupiter rather than Apollo. He is prodigiously fluent of speech, restless, excitable (mark the snorting nostril and the restless blue eye, just the thirty-secondth of an inch too wide open), possibly a little mad. He is carefully dressed, not from the vanity that cannot resist finery, but from a sense of the importance of everything he does which leads him to make as much of paying a call as other men do of getting married or laying a foundation stone. A sensitive, susceptible, exaggerative, earnest man: a megalomaniac, who would be lost without a sense of humor.

Just at present the sense of humor is in abeyance. To say that he is excited is nothing: all his moods are phases of excitement. He is now in the panic-stricken phase; and he walks straight up to Ramsden as if with the fixed intention of shooting him on his own hearthrug. But what he pulls from his breast pocket is not a pistol, but a foolscap document which he thrusts under the indignant nose of Ramsden as he exclaims

TANNER. Ramsden: do you know what that is?

RAMSDEN [*loftily*] No, sir.

TANNER. It's a copy of Whitefield's will. Ann got it this morning.

RAMSDEN. When you say Ann, you mean, I presume, Miss Whitefield.

TANNER. I mean our Ann, your Ann, Tavy's Ann, and now, Heaven help me, m y Ann!

OCTAVIUS [*rising, very pale*] What do you mean?

TANNER. Mean! [*He holds up the will*]. Do you know who is appointed Ann's guardian by this will?

RAMSDEN [*coolly*] I believe I am.

TANNER. You! You and I, man. I! I!! I!!! Both of us! [*He flings the will down on the writing table*].

RAMSDEN. You! Impossible.

TANNER. It's only too hideously true. [*He throws himself into Octavius's chair*]. Ramsden: get me out of it somehow. You dont know Ann as well as I do. She'll commit every crime a respectable woman can; and she'll justify every one of them by saying that it was the wish of her guardians. She'll put everything on us; and we shall have no more control over her than a couple of mice over a cat. You can refuse to accept the guardianship. Why dont you?

OCTAVIUS. Jack: I wish you wouldnt talk like that about Ann.

TANNER. This chap's in love with her: thats another complication. Well, she'll either jilt him and say I didnt approve of him, or marry him and say you ordered her to. I tell you, this is the most staggering blow that has ever fallen on a man of my age and temperament.

RAMSDEN. Let me see that will, sir. [*He goes to the writing table and picks it up*]. I cannot believe that my old friend Whitefield would have shewn such a want of confidence in me as to associate me with— [*His countenance falls as he reads*].

TANNER. It's all my own doing: thats the horrible irony of it. He told me one day that you were to be Ann's guardian; and like a fool I began arguing with him about the folly of leaving a young woman under the control of an old man with obsolete ideas.

RAMSDEN [*stupended*] My ideas obsolete!!!!!!!

TANNER. Totally. I had just finished an essay called Down with Government by the Greyhaired; and I was full of arguments and illustrations. I said the proper thing was to combine the experience of an old hand with the vitality of a young one. Hang me if he didnt take me at my word and alter his will—it's dated only a fortnight after that conversation—appointing me as joint guardian with you!

RAMSDEN [*pale and determined*] I shall refuse to act.

TANNER. Whats the good of that? Ive been refusing all the way from Richmond; but Ann keeps on saying that of course she's only an orphan; and that she cant expect the people who were glad to come to the house in her father's time to trouble much about her now. Thats the latest game. An orphan! It's like hearing an ironclad talk about being at the mercy of the wind and waves.

OCTAVIUS. This is not fair, Jack. She i s an orphan. And you ought to stand by her.

TANNER. Stand by her! What danger is she in? She has the law on her side; she has popular sentiment on her side; she has plenty of money and no conscience. All she wants with me is to load up all her moral responsibilities on me, and do as she likes at the expense of my character. I cant control her; and she can compromise me as much as she likes. I might as well be her husband.

RAMSDEN. You can refuse to accept the guardianship. *I* shall certainly refuse to hold it jointly with you.

TANNER. Yes; and what will she say to that? what does she say to it? Just that her father's wishes are sacred to her, and that she shall always look up to me as her guardian whether I care to face the responsibility or not. Refuse! You might as well refuse to accept the embraces of a boa constrictor when once it gets round your neck.

OCTAVIUS. This sort of talk is not kind to me, Jack.

TANNER [*rising and going to Octavius to console him, but still lamenting*] If he wanted a young guardian, why didnt he appoint Tavy?

RAMSDEN. Ah! why indeed?

OCTAVIUS. I will tell you. He sounded me about it; but I refused the trust because I loved her. I had no right to let myself be forced on her as a guardian by her father. He spoke to her about it; and she said I was right. You know I love her, Mr Ramsden; and Jack knows it too. If Jack loved a woman, I would not compare her to a boa constrictor in his presence, however much I might dislike her [*he sits down between the busts and turns his face to the wall*].

RAMSDEN. I do not believe that Whitefield was in his right senses when he made that will. You have admitted that he made it under your influence.

TANNER. You ought to be pretty well obliged to me for my influence. He leaves you two thousand five hundred for your trouble. He leaves Tavy a dowry for his sister and five thousand for himself.

OCTAVIUS [*his tears flowing afresh*] Oh, I cant take it. He was too good to us.

TANNER. You wont get it, my boy, if Ramsden upsets the will.

RAMSDEN. Ha! I see. You have got me in a cleft stick.

TANNER. He leaves me nothing but the charge of Ann's morals, on the ground that I have already more money than is good for me. That shews that he had his wits about him, dosen't it?

RAMSDEN [*grimly*] I admit that.

OCTAVIUS [*rising and coming from his refuge by the wall*] Mr Ramsden: I think you are

prejudiced against Jack. He is a man of honor, and incapable of abusing—

TANNER. Dont, Tavy: youll make me ill. I am not a man of honor: I am a man struck down by a dead hand. Tavy: you must marry her after all and take her off my hands. And I had set my heart on saving you from her!

OCTAVIUS. Oh, Jack, you talk of saving me from my highest happiness.

TANNER. Yes, a lifetime of happiness. If it were only the first half hour's happiness, Tavy, I would buy it for you with my last penny. But a lifetime of happiness! No man alive could bear it: it would be hell on earth.

RAMSDEN [*violently*] Stuff, sir. Talk sense; or else go and waste someone else's time: I have something better to do than listen to your fooleries [*he positively kicks his way to his table and resumes his seat*].

TANNER. You hear him, Tavy! Not an idea in his head later than eighteensixty. We cant leave Ann with no other guardian to turn to.

RAMSDEN. I am proud of your contempt for my character and opinions, sir. Your own are set forth in that book, I believe.

TANNER [*eagerly going to the table*] What! Youve got my book! What do you think of it?

RAMSDEN. Do you suppose I would read such a book, sir?

TANNER. Then why did you buy it?

RAMSDEN. I did not buy it, sir. It has been sent me by some foolish lady who seems to admire your views. I was about to dispose of it when Octavius interrupted me. I shall do so now, with your permission. [*He throws the book into the waste paper basket with such vehemence that Tanner recoils under the impression that it is being thrown at his head*].

TANNER. You have no more manners than I have myself. However, that saves ceremony between us. [*He sits down again*]. What do you intend to do about this will?

OCTAVIUS. May I make a suggestion?

RAMSDEN. Certainly, Octavius.

OCTAVIUS. Arnt we forgetting that Ann herself may have some wishes in this matter?

RAMSDEN. I quite intend that Annie's wishes shall be consulted in every reasonable way. But she is only a woman, and a young and inexperienced woman at that.

TANNER. Ramsden: I begin to pity you.

RAMSDEN [*hotly*] I dont want to know how you feel towards me, Mr Tanner.

TANNER. Ann will do just exactly what she

likes. And whats more, she'll force us to advise her to do it; and she'll put the blame on us if it turns out badly. So, as Tavy is longing to see her—

OCTAVIUS [*shyly*] I am not, Jack.

TANNER. You lie, Tavy: you are. So lets have her down from the drawing room and ask her what she intends us to do. Off with you, Tavy, and fetch her. [*Tavy turns to go*]. And dont be long; for the strained relations between myself and Ramsden will make the interval rather painful. [*Ramsden compresses his lips, but says nothing*].

OCTAVIUS. Never mind him, Mr Ramsden. He's not serious [*He goes out*].

RAMSDEN [*very deliberately*] Mr Tanner: you are the most impudent person I have ever met.

TANNER [*seriously*] I know it, Ramsden. Yet even I cannot wholly conquer shame. We live in an atmosphere of shame. We are ashamed of everything that is real about us; ashamed of ourselves, of our relatives, of our incomes, of our accents, of our opinions, of our experience, just as we are ashamed of our naked skins. Good Lord, my dear Ramsden, we are ashamed to walk, ashamed to ride in an omnibus, ashamed to hire a hansom instead of keeping a carriage, ashamed of keeping one horse instead of two and a groom-gardener instead of a coachman and footman. The more things a man is ashamed of, the more respectable he is. Why, youre ashamed to buy my book, ashamed to read it: the only thing youre not ashamed of is to judge me for it without having read it; and even that only means that youre ashamed to have heterodox opinions. Look at the effect I produce because my fairy godmother withheld from me this gift of shame. I have every possible virtue that a man can have except—

RAMSDEN. I am glad you think so well of yourself.

TANNER. All you mean by that is that you think I ought to be ashamed of talking about my virtues. You dont mean that I havnt got them: you know perfectly well that I am as sober and honest a citizen as yourself, as truthful personally, and much more truthful politically and morally.

RAMSDEN [*touched on his most sensitive point*] I deny that. I will not allow you or any man to treat me as if I were a mere member of the British public. I detest its prejudices; I scorn its narrowness; I demand the right to

think for myself. You pose as an advanced man. Let me tell you that I was an advanced man before you were born.

TANNER. I knew it was a long time ago.

RAMSDEN. I am as advanced as ever I was. I defy you to prove that I have ever hauled down the flag. I am m o r e advanced than ever I was. I grow more advanced every day.

TANNER. More advanced in years, Polonius.

RAMSDEN. Polonius! So you are Hamlet, I suppose.

TANNER. No: I am only the most impudent person youve ever met. Thats your notion of a thoroughly bad character. When you want to give me a piece of your mind, you ask yourself, as a just and upright man, what is the worst you can fairly say of me. Thief, liar, forger, adulterer, perjurer, glutton, drunkard? Not one of these names fit me. You have to fall back on my deficiency in shame. Well, I admit it. I even congratulate myself; for if I were ashamed of my real self, I should cut as stupid a figure as any of the rest of you. Cultivate a little impudence, Ramsden; and you will become quite a remarkable man.

RAMSDEN. I have no—

TANNER. You have no desire for that sort of notoriety. Bless you, I knew that answer would come as well as I know that a box of matches will come out of an automatic machine when I put a penny in the slot: you would be ashamed to say anything else.

The crushing retort for which Ramsden has been visibly collecting his forces is lost for ever; for at this point Octavius returns with Miss Ann Whitefield and her mother; and Ramsden springs up and hurries to the door to receive them. Whether Ann is good-looking or not depends upon your taste; also and perhaps chiefly on your age and sex. To Octavius she is an enchantingly beautiful woman, in whose presence the world becomes transfigured, and the puny limits of individual consciousness are suddenly made infinite by a mystic memory of the whole life of the race to its beginnings in the east, or even back to the paradise from which it fell. She is to him the reality of romance, the inner good sense of nonsense, the unveiling of his eyes, the freeing of his soul, the abolition of time, place, and circumstance, the etherealization of his blood into rapturous rivers of the very water of life itself, the revelation of all the mysteries and the sanctification of all the dogmas. To her mother she is, to put it as moderately as possible, nothing what-

ever of the kind. Not that Octavius's admiration is in any way ridiculous or discreditable. Ann is a well formed creature, as far as that goes; and she is perfectly ladylike, graceful, and comely, with ensnaring eyes and hair. Besides, instead of making herself an eyesore, like her mother, she has devised a mourning costume of black and violet silk which does honor to her late father and reveals the family tradition of brave unconventionality by which Ramsden sets such store.

But all this is beside the point as an explanation of Ann's charm. Turn up her nose, give a cast to her eye, replace her black and violet confection by the apron and feathers of a flower girl, strike all the aitches out of her speech, and Ann would still make men dream. Vitality is as common as humanity; but, like humanity, it sometimes rises to genius; and Ann is one of the vital geniuses. Not at all, if you please, an oversexed person: that is a vital defect, not a true excess. She is a perfectly respectable, perfectly self-controlled woman, and looks it; though her pose is fashionably frank and impulsive. She inspires confidence as a person who will do nothing she does not mean to do; also some fear, perhaps, as a woman who will probably do everything she means to do without taking more account of other people than may be necessary and what she calls right. In short, what the weaker of her own sex sometimes call a cat.

Nothing can be more decorous than her entry and her reception by Ramsden, whom she kisses. The late Mr Whitefield would be gratified almost to impatience by the long faces of the men (except Tanner, who is fidgety), the silent handgrasps, the sympathetic placing of chairs, the sniffing of the widow, and the liquid eye of the daughter, whose heart, apparently, will not let her control her tongue to speech. Ramsden and Octavius take the two chairs from the wall, and place them for the two ladies; but Ann comes to Tanner and takes his chair, which he offers with a brusque gesture, subsequently relieving his irritation by sitting down on the corner of the writing table with studied indecorum. Octavius gives Mrs Whitefield a chair next Ann, and himself takes the vacant one which Ramsden has placed under the nose of the effigy of Mr Herbert Spencer.

Mrs Whitefield, by the way, is a little woman, whose faded flaxen hair looks like straw on an egg. She has an expression of muddled shrewdness, a squeak of protest in her voice, and an odd air of continually elbowing away some larger person who is crushing her into a corner. One guesses her as one of those women who are con-

scious of being treated as silly and negligible, and who, without having strength enough to assert themselves effectually, at any rate never submit to their fate. There is a touch of chivalry in Octavius's scrupulous attention to her, even whilst his whole soul is absorbed by Ann.

Ramsden goes solemnly back to his magisterial seat at the writing table, ignoring Tanner, and opens the proceedings.

RAMSDEN. I am sorry, Annie, to force business on you at a sad time like the present. But your poor dear father's will has raised a very serious question. You have read it, I believe?

Ann assents with a nod and a catch of her breath, too much affected to speak.

I must say I am surprised to find Mr Tanner named as joint guardian and trustee with myself of you and Rhoda. [*A pause. They all look portentous; but they have nothing to say. Ramsden, a little ruffled by the lack of any response, continues*] I dont know that I can consent to act under such conditions. Mr Tanner has, I understand, some objection also; but I do not profess to understand its nature: he will no doubt speak for himself. But we are agreed that we can decide nothing until we know your views. I am afraid I shall have to ask you to choose between my sole guardianship and that of Mr Tanner; for I fear it is impossible for us to undertake a joint arrangement.

ANN [*in a low musical voice*] Mamma—

MRS WHITEFIELD [*hastily*] Now, Ann, I do beg you not to put it on me. I have no opinion on the subject; and if I had, it would probably not be attended to. I am quite content with whatever you three think best.

Tanner turns his head and looks fixedly at Ramsden, who angrily refuses to receive this mute communication.

ANN [*resuming in the same gentle voice, ignoring her mother's bad taste*] Mamma knows that she is not strong enough to bear the whole responsibility for me and Rhoda without some help and advice. Rhoda must have a guardian; and though I am older, I do not think any young unmarried woman should be left quite to her own guidance. I hope you agree with me, Granny?

TANNER [*starting*] Granny! Do you intend to call your guardians Granny?

ANN. Dont be foolish, Jack. Mr Ramsden has always been Grandpapa Roebuck to me: I am Granny's Annie; and he is Annie's

Granny. I christened him so when I first learned to speak.

RAMSDEN [*sarcastically*] I hope you are satisfied, Mr Tanner. Go on, Annie: I quite agree with you.

ANN. Well, if I am to have a guardian, can I set aside anybody whom my dear father appointed for me?

RAMSDEN [*biting his lip*] You approve of your father's choice, then?

ANN. It is not for me to approve or disapprove. I accept it. My father loved me and knew best what was good for me.

RAMSDEN. Of course I understand your feeling, Annie. It is what I should have expected of you; and it does you credit. But it does not settle the question so completely as you think. Let me put a case to you. Suppose you were to discover that I had been guilty of some disgraceful action—that I was not the man your poor dear father took me for! Would you still consider it right that I should be Rhoda's guardian?

ANN. I cant imagine you doing anything disgraceful, Granny.

TANNER [*to Ramsden*] You havnt done anything of the sort, have you?

RAMSDEN [*indignantly*] No, sir.

MRS WHITEFIELD [*placidly*] Well, then, why suppose it?

ANN. You see, Granny, Mamma would not like me to suppose it.

RAMSDEN [*much perplexed*] You are both so full of natural and affectionate feeling in these family matters that it is very hard to put the situation fairly before you.

TANNER. Besides, my friend, you are not putting the situation fairly before them.

RAMSDEN [*sulkily*] Put it yourself, then.

TANNER. I will. Ann: Ramsden thinks I am not fit to be your guardian; and I quite agree with him. He considers that if your father had read my book, he wouldnt have appointed me. That book is the disgraceful action he has been talking about. He thinks it's your duty for Rhoda's sake to ask him to act alone and to make me withdraw. Say the word; and I will.

ANN. But I havnt read your book, Jack.

TANNER [*diving at the waste-paper basket and fishing the book out for her*] Then read it at once and decide.

RAMSDEN [*vehemently*] If I am to be your guardian, I positively forbid you to read that book, Annie. [*He smites the table with his fist and rises*].

ANN. Of course not if you dont wish it. [*She puts the book on the table*].

TANNER. If one guardian is to forbid you to read the other guardian's book, how are we to settle it? Suppose I order you to read it! What about your duty to me?

ANN [*gently*] I am sure you would never purposely force me into a painful dilemma, Jack.

RAMSDEN [*irritably*] Yes, yes, Annie: this is all very well, and, as I said, quite natural and becoming. But you must make a choice one way or the other. We are as much in a dilemma as you.

ANN. I feel that I am too young, too inexperienced, to decide. My father's wishes are sacred to me.

MRS WHITEFIELD. If you two men wont carry them out I must say it is rather hard that you should put the responsibility on Ann. It seems to me that people are always putting things on other people in this world.

RAMSDEN. I am sorry you take it in that way.

ANN [*touchingly*] Do you refuse to accept me as your ward, Granny?

RAMSDEN. No: I never said that. I greatly object to act with Mr Tanner: thats all.

MRS WHITEFIELD. Why? What's the matter with poor Jack?

TANNER. My views are too advanced for him.

RAMSDEN [*indignantly*] They are not. I deny it.

ANN. Of course not. What nonsense! Nobody is more advanced than Granny. I am sure it is Jack himself who has made all the difficulty. Come, Jack! be kind to me in my sorrow. You dont refuse to accept me as your ward, do you?

TANNER [*gloomily*] No. I let myself in for it; so I suppose I must face it. [*He turns away to the bookcase, and stands there, moodily studying the titles of the volumes*].

ANN [*rising and expanding with subdued but gushing delight*] Then we are all agreed; and my dear father's will is to be carried out. You dont know what a joy that is to me and to my mother! [*She goes to Ramsden and presses both his hands, saying*] And I shall have my dear Granny to help and advise me. [*She casts a glance at Tanner over her shoulder*]. And Jack the Giant Killer. [*She goes past her mother to Octavius*] And Jack's inseparable friend Ricky-ticky-tavy [*he blushes and looks inexpressibly foolish*].

MRS WHITEFIELD [*rising and shaking her*

widow's weeds straight] Now that you are Ann's guardian, Mr Ramsden, I wish you would speak to her about her habit of giving people nicknames. They cant be expected to like it. [*She moves towards the door*].

ANN. How can you say such a thing, Mamma! [*Glowing with affectionate remorse*] Oh, I wonder can you be right! H a v e I been inconsiderate? [*She turns to Octavius, who is sitting astride his chair with his elbows on the back of it. Putting her hand on his forehead she turns his face up suddenly*]. Do you want to be treated like a grown-up man? Must I call you Mr Robinson in future?

OCTAVIUS [*earnestly*] Oh please call me Ricky-ticky-tavy. "Mr Robinson" would hurt me cruelly. [*She laughs and pats his cheek with her finger; then comes back to Ramsden*]. You know I'm beginning to think that Granny is rather a piece of impertinence. But I never dreamt of its hurting you.

RAMSDEN [*breezily, as he pats her affectionately on the back*] My dear Annie, nonsense. I insist on Granny. I wont answer to any other name than Annie's Granny.

ANN [*gratefully*] You all spoil me, except Jack.

TANNER [*over his shoulder, from the bookcase*] I think you ought to call me Mr Tanner.

ANN [*gently*] No you dont, Jack. Thats like the things you say on purpose to shock people: those who know you pay no attention to them. But, if you like, I'll call you after your famous ancestor Don Juan.

RAMSDEN. Don Juan!

ANN [*innocently*] Oh, is there any harm in it? I didnt know. Then I certainly wont call you that. May I call you Jack until I can think of something else?

TANNER. Oh, for Heaven's sake dont try to invent anything worse. I capitulate. I consent to Jack. I embrace Jack. Here endeth my first and last attempt to assert my authority.

ANN. You see, Mamma, they all really like to have pet names.

MRS WHITEFIELD. Well, I think you might at least drop them until we are out of mourning.

ANN [*reproachfully, stricken to the soul*] Oh, how could you remind me, mother? [*She hastily leaves the room to conceal her emotion*].

MRS WHITEFIELD. Of course. My fault as usual! [*She follows Ann*].

TANNER [*coming from the bookcase*] Ramsden:

we're beaten—smashed—nonentitized, like her mother.

RAMSDEN. Stuff, sir. [*He follows Mrs Whitefield out of the room*].

TANNER [*left alone with Octavius, stares whimsically at him*] Tavy: do you want to count for something in the world?

OCTAVIUS. I want to count for something as a poet: I want to write a great play.

TANNER. With Ann as the heroine?

OCTAVIUS. Yes: I confess it.

TANNER. Take care, Tavy. The play with Ann as the heroine is all right; but if youre not very careful, by Heaven she'll marry you.

OCTAVIUS [*sighing*] No such luck, Jack!

TANNER. Why, man, your head is in the lioness's mouth: you are half swallowed already—in three bites—Bite One, Ricky; Bite Two, Ticky; Bite Three, Tavy; and down you go.

OCTAVIUS. She is the same to everybody, Jack: you know her ways.

TANNER. Yes: she breaks everybody's back with the stroke of her paw; but the question is, which of us will she eat? My own opinion is that she means to eat you.

OCTAVIUS [*rising, pettishly*] It's horrible to talk like that about her when she is upstairs crying for her father. But I do so want her to eat me that I can bear your brutalities because they give me hope.

TANNER. Tavy: thats the devilish side of a woman's fascination: she makes you will your own destruction.

OCTAVIUS. But it's not destruction: it's fulfilment.

TANNER. Yes, of her purpose; and that purpose is neither her happiness nor yours, but Nature's. Vitality in a woman is a blind fury of creation. She sacrifices herself to it: do you think she will hesitate to sacrifice you?

OCTAVIUS. Why, it is just because she is self-sacrificing that she will not sacrifice those she loves.

TANNER. That is the profoundest of mistakes, Tavy. It is the self-sacrificing women that sacrifice others most recklessly. Because they are unselfish, they are kind in little things. Because they have a purpose which is not their own purpose, but that of the whole universe, a man is nothing to them but an instrument of that purpose.

OCTAVIUS. Dont be ungenerous, Jack. They take the tenderest care of us.

TANNER. Yes, as a soldier takes care of his

rifle or a musician of his violin. But do they allow us any purpose or freedom of our own? Will they lend us to one another? Can the strongest man escape from them when once he is appropriated? They tremble when we are in danger, and weep when we die; but the tears are not for us, but for a father wasted, a son's breeding thrown away. They accuse us of treating them as a mere means to our pleasure; but how can so feeble and transient a folly as a man's selfish pleasure enslave a woman as the whole purpose of Nature embodied in a woman can enslave a man?

OCTAVIUS. What matter, if the slavery makes us happy?

TANNER. No matter at all if you have no purpose of your own, and are, like most men, a mere breadwinner. But you, Tavy, are an artist: that is, you have a purpose as absorbing and as unscrupulous as a woman's purpose.

OCTAVIUS. Not unscrupulous.

TANNER. Quite unscrupulous. The true artist will let his wife starve, his children go barefoot, his mother drudge for his living at seventy, sooner than work at anything but his art. To women he is half vivisector, half vampire. He gets into intimate relations with them to study them, to strip the mask of convention from them, to surprise their inmost secrets, knowing that they have the power to rouse his deepest creative energies, to rescue him from his cold reason, to make him see visions and dream dreams, to inspire him, as he calls it. He persuades women that they may do this for their own purpose whilst he really means them to do it for his. He steals the mother's milk and blackens it to make printer's ink to scoff at her and glorify ideal women with. He pretends to spare her the pangs of child-bearing so that he may have for himself the tenderness and fostering that belong of right to her children. Since marriage began, the great artist has been known as a bad husband. But he is worse: he is a child-robber, a blood-sucker, a hypocrite, and a cheat. Perish the race and wither a thousand women if only the sacrifice of them enable him to act Hamlet better, to paint a finer picture, to write a deeper poem, a greater play, a profounder philosophy! For mark you, Tavy, the artist's work is to shew us ourselves as we really are. Our minds are nothing but this knowledge of ourselves; and he

who adds a jot to such knowledge creates new mind as surely as any woman creates new men. In the rage of that creation he is as ruthless as the woman, as dangerous to her as she to him, and as horribly fascinating. Of all human struggles there is none so treacherous and remorseless as the struggle between the artist man and the mother woman. Which shall use up the other? that is the issue between them. And it is all the deadlier because, in your romanticist cant, they love one another.

OCTAVIUS. Even if it were so—and I dont admit it for a moment—it is out of the deadliest struggles that we get the noblest characters.

TANNER. Remember that the next time you meet a grizzly bear or a Bengal tiger, Tavy.

OCTAVIUS. I meant where there is love, Jack.

TANNER. Oh, the tiger will love you. There is no love sincerer than the love of food. I think Ann loves you that way: she patted your cheek as if it were a nicely underdone chop.

OCTAVIUS. You know, Jack, I should have to run away from you if I did not make it a fixed rule not to mind anything you say. You come out with perfectly revolting things sometimes.

Ramsden returns, followed by Ann. They come in quickly, with their former leisurely air of decorous grief changed to one of genuine concern, and, on Ramsden's part, of worry. He comes between the two men, intending to address Octavius, but pulls himself up abruptly as he sees Tanner.

RAMSDEN. I hardly expected to find you still here, Mr Tanner.

TANNER. Am I in the way? Good morning, fellow guardian [*he goes towards the door*].

ANN. Stop, Jack. Granny: he must know, sooner or later.

RAMSDEN. Octavius: I have a very serious piece of news for you. It is of the most private and delicate nature—of the most painful nature too, I am sorry to say. Do you wish Mr Tanner to be present whilst I explain?

OCTAVIUS [*turning pale*] I have no secrets from Jack.

RAMSDEN. Before you decide that finally, let me say that the news concerns your sister, and that it is terrible news.

OCTAVIUS. Violet! What has happened? Is she—dead?

RAMSDEN. I am not sure that it is not even worse than that.

OCTAVIUS. Is she badly hurt? Has there been an accident?

RAMSDEN. No: nothing of that sort.

TANNER. Ann: will you have the common humanity to tell us what the matter is?

ANN [half whispering] I cant. Violet has done something dreadful. We shall have to get her away somewhere. [She flutters to the writing table and sits in Ramsden's chair, leaving the three men to fight it out between them].

OCTAVIUS [enlightened] Is that what you meant, Mr Ramsden?

RAMSDEN. Yes. [Octavius sinks upon a chair, crushed]. I am afraid there is no doubt that Violet did not really go to Eastbourne three weeks ago when we thought she was with the Parry Whitefields. And she called on a strange doctor yesterday with a wedding ring on her finger. Mrs Parry Whitefield met her there by chance; and so the whole thing came out.

OCTAVIUS [rising with his fists clenched] Who is the scoundrel?

ANN. She wont tell us.

OCTAVIUS [collapsing into the chair again] What a frightful thing!

TANNER [with angry sarcasm] Dreadful. Appalling. Worse than death, as Ramsden says. [He comes to Octavius]. What would you not give, Tavy, to turn it into a railway accident, with all her bones broken, or something equally respectable and deserving of sympathy?

OCTAVIUS. Dont be brutal, Jack.

TANNER. Brutal! Good Heavens, man, what are you crying for? Here is a woman whom we all supposed to be making bad water color sketches, practising Grieg and Brahms, gadding about to concerts and parties, wasting her life and her money. We suddenly learn that she has turned from these sillinesses to the fulfilment of her highest purpose and greatest function—to increase, multiply, and replenish the earth. And instead of admiring her courage and rejoicing in her instinct; instead of crowning the completed womanhood and raising the triumphal strain of "Unto us a child is born: unto us a son is given", here you are—you who have been as merry as grigs in your mourning for the dead—all pulling long faces and looking as ashamed and disgraced as if the girl had committed the vilest of crimes.

RAMSDEN [roaring with rage] I will not have these abominations uttered in my house [he smites the writing-table with his fist].

TANNER. Look here: if you insult me again I'll take you at your word and leave your house. Ann: where is Violet now?

ANN. Why? Are you going to her?

TANNER. Of course I am going to her. She wants help; she wants money; she wants respect and congratulation; she wants every chance for her child. She does not seem likely to get it from you: she shall from me. Where is she?

ANN. Dont be so headstrong, Jack. She's upstairs.

TANNER. What! Under Ramsden's sacred roof! Go and do your miserable duty, Ramsden. Hunt her out into the street. Cleanse your threshold from her contamination. Vindicate the purity of your English home. I'll go for a cab.

ANN [alarmed] Oh, Granny, you mustnt do that.

OCTAVIUS [broken-heartedly, rising] I'll take her away, Mr Ramsden. She had no right to come to your house.

RAMSDEN [indignantly] But I am only too anxious to help her. [Turning on Tanner] How dare you, sir, impute such monstrous intentions to me? I protest against it. I am ready to put down my last penny to save her from being driven to run to you for protection.

TANNER [subsiding] It's all right, then. He's not going to act up to his principles. It's agreed that we all stand by Violet.

OCTAVIUS. But who is the man? He can make reparation by marrying her; and he shall, or he shall answer for it to me.

RAMSDEN. He shall, Octavius. There you speak like a man.

TANNER. Then you dont think him a scoundrel, after all?

OCTAVIUS. Not a scoundrel! He is a heartless scoundrel.

RAMSDEN. A damned scoundrel. I beg your pardon, Annie; but I can say no less.

TANNER. So we are to marry your sister to a damned scoundrel by way of reforming her character! On my soul, I think you are all mad.

ANN. Dont be absurd, Jack. Of course you are quite right, Tavy; but we dont know who he is: Violet wont tell us.

TANNER. What on earth does it matter who

he is? He's done his part; and Violet must do the rest.

RAMSDEN [*beside himself*] Stuff! lunacy! There is a rascal in our midst, a libertine, a villain worse than a murderer; and we are not to learn who he is! In our ignorance we are to shake him by the hand; to introduce him into our homes; to trust our daughters with him; to—to—

ANN [*coaxingly*] There, Granny, dont talk so loud. It's most shocking: we must all admit that; but if Violet wont tell us, what can we do? Nothing. Simply nothing.

RAMSDEN. Hmph! I'm not so sure of that. If any man has paid Violet any special attention, we can easily find that out. If there is any man of notoriously loose principles among us—

TANNER. Ahem!

RAMSDEN [*raising his voice*] Yes, sir, I repeat, if there is any man of notoriously loose principles among us—

TANNER. Or any man notoriously lacking in self-control.

RAMSDEN [*aghast*] Do you dare to suggest that *I* am capable of such an act?

TANNER. My dear Ramsden, this is an act of which every man is capable. That is what comes of getting at cross purposes with Nature. The suspicion you have just flung at me clings to us all. It's a sort of mud that sticks to the judge's ermine or the cardinal's robe as fast as to the rags of the tramp. Come, Tavy! dont look so bewildered: it might have been me: it might have been Ramsden; just as it might have been anybody. If it had, what could we do but lie and protest—as Ramsden is going to protest.

RAMSDEN [*choking*] I—I—I—

TANNER. Guilt itself could not stammer more confusedly. And yet you know perfectly well he's innocent, Tavy.

RAMSDEN [*exhausted*] I am glad you admit that, sir. I admit, myself, that there is an element of truth in what you say, grossly as you may distort it to gratify your malicious humor. I hope, Octavius, no suspicion of me is possible in your mind.

OCTAVIUS. Of you! No, not for a moment.

TANNER [*drily*] I think he suspects me just a little.

OCTAVIUS. Jack: you couldnt—you wouldnt—

TANNER. Why not?

OCTAVIUS [*appalled*] Why not!

TANNER. Oh, well, I'll tell you why not.

First, you would feel bound to quarrel with me. Second, Violet doesnt like me. Third, if I had the honor of being the father of Violet's child, I should boast of it instead of denying it. So be easy: our friendship is not in danger.

OCTAVIUS. I should have put away the suspicion with horror if only you would think and feel naturally about it. I beg your pardon.

TANNER. My pardon! nonsense! And now lets sit down and have a family council. [*He sits down. The rest follow his example, more or less under protest*]. Violet is going to do the State a service; consequently she must be packed abroad like a criminal until it's over. Whats happening upstairs?

ANN. Violet is in the housekeeper's room— by herself, of course.

TANNER. Why not in the drawing room?

ANN. Dont be absurd, Jack. Miss Ramsden is in the drawing room with my mother, considering what to do.

TANNER. Oh! the housekeeper's room is the penitentiary, I suppose; and the prisoner is waiting to be brought before her judges. The old cats!

ANN. Oh, Jack!

RAMSDEN. You are at present a guest beneath the roof of one of the old cats, sir. My sister is the mistress of this house.

TANNER. She would put me in the housekeeper's room, too, if she dared, Ramsden. However, I withdraw cats. Cats would have more sense. Ann: as your guardian, I order you to go to Violet at once and be particularly kind to her.

ANN. I have seen her, Jack. And I am sorry to say I am afraid she is going to be rather obstinate about going abroad. I think Tavy ought to speak to her about it.

OCTAVIUS. How can I speak to her about such a thing [*he breaks down*]?

ANN. Dont break down, Ricky. Try to bear it for all our sakes.

RAMSDEN. Life is not all plays and poems, Octavius. Come! face it like a man.

TANNER [*chafing again*] Poor dear brother! Poor dear friends of the family! Poor dear Tabbies and Grimalkins! Poor dear everybody except the woman who is going to risk her life to create another life! Tavy: dont you be a selfish ass. Away with you and talk to Violet; and bring her down here if she cares to come. [*Octavius rises*]. Tell her we'll stand by her.

RAMSDEN [*rising*] No, sir—

TANNER [*rising also and interrupting him*] Oh, we understand: it's against your conscience; but still youll do it.

OCTAVIUS. I assure you all, on my word, I never meant to be selfish. It's so hard to know what to do when one wishes earnestly to do right.

TANNER. My dear Tavy, your pious English habit of regarding the world as a moral gymnasium built expressly to strengthen your character in, occasionally leads you to think about your own confounded principles when you should be thinking about other people's necessities. The need of the present hour is a happy mother and a healthy baby. Bend your energies on that; and you will see your way clearly enough.

Octavius, much perplexed, goes out.

RAMSDEN [*facing Tanner impressively*] And Morality, sir? What is to become of that?

TANNER. Meaning a weeping Magdalen and an innocent child branded with her shame. Not in our circle, thank you. Morality can go to its father the devil.

RAMSDEN. I thought so, sir. Morality sent to the devil to please our libertines, male and female. That is to be the future of England, is it?

TANNER. Oh, England will survive your disapproval. Meanwhile, I understand that you agree with me as to the practical course we are to take?

RAMSDEN. Not in your spirit, sir. Not for your reasons.

TANNER. You can explain that if anybody calls you to account, here or hereafter. [*He turns away, and plants himself in front of Mr Herbert Spencer, at whom he stares gloomily*].

ANN [*rising and coming to Ramsden*] Granny: hadnt you better go up to the drawing room and tell them what we intend to do?

RAMSDEN [*looking pointedly at Tanner*] I hardly like to leave you alone with this gentleman. Will you not come with me?

ANN. Miss Ramsden would not like to speak about it before me, Granny. I ought not to be present.

RAMSDEN. You are right: I should have thought of that. You are a good girl, Annie. *He pats her on the shoulder. She looks up at him with beaming eyes; and he goes out, much moved. Having disposed of him, she looks at Tanner. His back being turned to her, she gives a moment's attention to her personal appearance,* then softly goes to him and speaks almost into his ear.

ANN. Jack [*he turns with a start*]: are you glad that you are my guardian? You dont mind being made responsible for me, I hope.

TANNER. The latest addition to your collection of scapegoats, eh?

ANN. Oh, that stupid old joke of yours about me! Do please drop it. Why do you say things that you know must pain me? I do my best to please you, Jack: I suppose I may tell you so now that you are my guardian. You will make me so unhappy if you refuse to be friends with me.

TANNER [*studying her as gloomily as he studied the bust*] You need not go begging for my regard. How unreal our moral judgments are! You seem to me to have absolutely no conscience—only hypocrisy; and you cant see the difference—yet there is a sort of fascination about you. I always attend to you, somehow. I should miss you if I lost you.

ANN [*tranquilly slipping her arm into his and walking about with him*] But isnt that only natural, Jack? We have known each other since we were children. Do you remember—

TANNER [*abruptly breaking loose*] Stop! I remember e v e r y t h i n g.

ANN. Oh, I daresay we were often very silly; but—

TANNER. I wont have it, Ann. I am no more that schoolboy now than I am the dotard of ninety I shall grow into if I live long enough. It is over: let me forget it.

ANN. Wasnt it a happy time? [*She attempts to take his arm again*].

TANNER. Sit down and behave yourself. [*He makes her sit down in the chair next the writing table*]. No doubt it was a happy time for you. You were a good girl and never compromised yourself. And yet the wickedest child that ever was slapped could hardly have had a better time. I can understand the success with which you bullied the other girls: your virtue imposed on them. But tell me this: did you ever know a good boy?

ANN. Of course. All boys are foolish sometimes; but Tavy was always a really good boy.

TANNER [*struck by this*] Yes: youre right. For some reason you never tempted Tavy.

ANN. Tempted! Jack!

TANNER. Yes, my dear Lady Mephistopheles, tempted. You were insatiably curious as to what a boy might be capable of, and diabolically clever at getting through his guard and surprising his inmost secrets.

ANN. What nonsense! All because you used to tell me long stories of the wicked things you had done—silly boy's tricks! And you call such things inmost secrets! Boys' secrets are just like men's; and you know what they are!

TANNER [*obstinately*] No I dont. What are they, pray?

ANN. Why, the things they tell everybody, of course.

TANNER. Now I swear I told you things I told no one else. You lured me into a compact by which we were to have no secrets from one another. We were to tell one another everything. I didnt notice that you never told me anything.

ANN. You didnt want to talk about me, Jack. You wanted to talk about yourself.

TANNER. Ah, true, horribly true. But what a devil of a child you must have been to know that weakness and to play on it for the satisfaction of your own curiosity! I wanted to brag to you, to make myself interesting. And I found myself doing all sorts of mischievous things simply to have something to tell you about. I fought with boys I didnt hate; I lied about things I might just as well have told the truth about; I stole things I didnt want; I kissed little girls I didnt care for. It was all bravado: passionless and therefore unreal.

ANN. I never told of you, Jack.

TANNER. No; but if you had wanted to stop me you would have told of me. You wanted me to go on.

ANN [*flashing out*] Oh, thats not true: it's not true, Jack. I never wanted you to do those dull, disappointing, brutal, stupid, vulgar things. I always hoped that it would be something really heroic at last. [*Recovering herself*] Excuse me, Jack; but the things you did were never a bit like the things I wanted you to do. They often gave me great uneasiness; but I could not tell of you and get you into trouble. And you were only a boy. I knew you would grow out of them. Perhaps I was wrong.

TANNER [*sardonically*] Do not give way to remorse, Ann. At least nineteen twentieths of the exploits I confessed to you were pure lies. I soon noticed that you didnt like the true stories.

ANN. Of course I knew that some of the things couldnt have happened. But—

TANNER. You are going to remind me that some of the most disgraceful ones did.

ANN [*fondly, to his great terror*] I dont want to remind you of anything. But I knew the people they happened to, and heard about them.

TANNER. Yes; but even the true stories were touched up for telling. A sensitive boy's humiliations may be very good fun for ordinary thickskinned grown-ups; but to the boy himself they are so acute, so ignominious, that he cannot confess them—cannot but deny them passionately. However, perhaps it was as well for me that I romanced a bit; for, on the one occasion when I told you the truth, you threatened to tell of me.

ANN. Oh, never. Never once.

TANNER. Yes, you did. Do you remember a dark-eyed girl named Rachel Rosetree? [*Ann's brows contract for an instant involuntarily*]. I got up a love affair with her; and we met one night in the garden and walked about very uncomfortably with our arms round one another, and kissed at parting, and were most conscientiously romantic. If that love affair had gone on, it would have bored me to death; but it didnt go on; for the next thing that happened was that Rachel cut me because she found out that I had told you. How did she find it out? From you. You went to her and held the guilty secret over her head, leading her a life of abject terror and humiliation by threatening to tell on her.

ANN. And a very good thing for her, too. It was my duty to stop her misconduct; and she is thankful to me for it now.

TANNER. Is she?

ANN. She ought to be, at all events.

TANNER. It was not your duty to stop my misconduct, I suppose.

ANN. I did stop it by stopping her.

TANNER. Are you sure of that? You stopped my telling you about my adventures; but how do you know that you stopped the adventures?

ANN. Do you mean to say that you went on in the same way with other girls?

TANNER. No. I had enough of that sort of romantic tomfoolery with Rachel.

ANN [*unconvinced*] Then why did you break off our confidences and become quite strange to me?

TANNER [*enigmatically*] It happened just then that I got something that I wanted to keep all to myself instead of sharing it with

ANN. I am sure I shouldnt have asked for any of it if you had grudged it.

TANNER. It wasnt a box of sweets, Ann. It was something youd never have let me call my own.

ANN [*incredulously*] What?

TANNER. My soul.

ANN. Oh, do be sensible, Jack. You know youre talking nonsense.

TANNER. The most solemn earnest, Ann. You didnt notice at that time that you were getting a soul too. But you were. It was not for nothing that you suddenly found you had a moral duty to chastise and reform Rachel. Up to that time you had traded pretty extensively in being a good child; but you had never set up a sense of duty to others. Well, I set one up too. Up to that time I had played the boy buccaneer with no more conscience than a fox in a poultry farm. But now I began to have scruples, to feel obligations, to find that veracity and honor were no longer goody-goody expressions in the mouths of grown-up people, but compelling principle in myself.

ANN [*quietly*] Yes, I suppose youre right. You were beginning to be a man, and I to be a woman.

TANNER. Are you sure it was not that we were beginning to be something more? What does the beginning of manhood and womanhood mean in most people's mouths? You know: it means the beginning of love. But love began long before that for me. Love played its part in the earliest dreams and follies and romances I can remember—may I say the earliest follies and romances we can remember?—though we did not understand it at the time. No: the change that came to me was the birth in me of moral passion; and I declare that according to my experience moral passion is the only real passion.

ANN. All passions ought to be moral, Jack.

TANNER. Ought! Do you think that anything is strong enough to impose oughts on a passion except a stronger passion still?

ANN. Our moral sense controls passion, Jack. Dont be stupid.

TANNER. Our moral sense! And is that not a passion? Is the devil to have all the passions as well as all the good tunes? If it were not a passion—if it were not the mightiest of the passions, all the other passions would sweep it away like a leaf before a hurricane. It is

the birth of that passion that turns a child into a man.

ANN. There are other passions, Jack. Very strong ones.

TANNER. All the other passions were in me before; but they were idle and aimless— mere childish greedinesses and cruelties, curiosities and fancies, habits and superstitions, grotesque and ridiculous to the mature intelligence. When they suddenly began to shine like newly lit flames it was by no light of their own, but by the radiance of the dawning moral passion. That passion dignified them, gave them conscience and meaning, found them a mob of appetites and organized them into an army of purposes and principles. My soul was born of that passion.

ANN. I noticed that you got more sense. You were a dreadfully destructive boy before that.

TANNER. Destructive! Stuff! I was only mischievous.

ANN. Oh, Jack, you were very destructive. You ruined all the young fir trees by chopping off their leaders with a wooden sword. You broke all the cucumber frames with your catapult. You set fire to the common: the police arrested Tavy for it because he ran away when he couldnt stop you. You—

TANNER. Pooh! pooh! pooh! these were battles, bombardments, stratagems to save our scalps from the red Indians. You have no imagination, Ann. I am ten times more destructive now than I was then. The moral passion has taken my destructiveness in hand and directed it to moral ends. I have become a reformer, and, like all reformers, an iconoclast. I no longer break cucumber frames and burn gorse bushes: I shatter creeds and demolish idols.

ANN [*bored*] I am afraid I am too feminine to see any sense in destruction. Destruction can only destroy.

TANNER. Yes. That is why it is so useful. Construction cumbers the ground with institutions made by busybodies. Destruction clears it and gives us breathing space and liberty.

ANN. It's no use, Jack. No woman will agree with you there.

TANNER. Thats because you confuse construction and destruction with creation and murder. Theyre quite different: I adore creation and abhor murder. Yes: I adore it in tree and flower, in bird and beast, even in you. [*A flush of interest and delight suddenly chases the growing perplexity and boredom from her face*]. It was the creative instinct that led you to attach me to you by bonds that have left their mark on me to this day. Yes, Ann: the old childish compact between us was an unconscious love compact—

ANN. Jack!

TANNER. Oh, dont be alarmed—

ANN. I am not alarmed.

TANNER [*whimsically*] Then you ought to be: where are your principles?

ANN. Jack: are you serious or are you not?

TANNER. Do you mean about the moral passion?

ANN. No, no: the other one. [*Confused*] Oh! you are so silly: one never knows how to take you.

TANNER. You must take me quite seriously. I am your guardian; and it is my duty to improve your mind.

ANN. The love compact is over, then, is it? I suppose you grew tired of me?

TANNER. No; but the moral passion made our childish relations impossible. A jealous sense of my new individuality arose in me—

ANN. You hated to be treated as a boy any longer. Poor Jack!

TANNER. Yes, because to be treated as a boy was to be taken on the old footing. I had become a new person; and those who knew the old person laughed at me. The only man who behaved sensibly was my tailor: he took my measure anew every time he saw me, whilst all the rest went on with their old measurements and expected them to fit me.

ANN. You became frightfully self-conscious.

TANNER. When you go to heaven, Ann, you will be frightfully conscious of your wings for the first year or so. When you meet your relatives there, and they persist in treating you as if you were still a mortal, you will not be able to bear them. You will try to get into a circle which has never known you except as an angel.

ANN. So it was only your vanity that made you run away from us after all?

TANNER. Yes, only my vanity, as you call it.

ANN. You need not have kept away from me on that account.

TANNER. From you above all others. You fought harder than anybody against my emancipation.

ANN [*earnestly*] Oh, how wrong you are! I would have done anything for you.

TANNER. Anything except let me get loose from you. Even then you had acquired by instinct that damnable woman's trick of heaping obligations on a man, of placing yourself so entirely and helplessly at his mercy that at last he dare not take a step without running to you for leave. I know a poor wretch whose one desire in life is to run away from his wife. She prevents him by threatening to throw herself in front of the engine of the train he leaves her in. That is what all women do. If we try to go where you do not want us to go there is no law to prevent us; but when we take the first step your breasts are under our foot as it descends: your bodies are under our wheels as we start. No woman shall ever enslave me in that way.

ANN. But, Jack, you cannot get through life without considering other people a little.

TANNER. Ay; but what other people? It is this consideration of other people—or rather this cowardly fear of them which we call consideration—that makes us the sentimental slaves we are. To consider you, as you call it, is to substitute your will for my own. How if it be a baser will than mine? Are women taught better than men or worse? Are mobs of voters taught better than statesmen or worse? Worse, of course, in both cases. And then what sort of world are you going to get, with its public men considering its voting mobs, and its private men considering their wives? What does Church and State mean nowadays? The Woman and the Ratepayer.

ANN [*placidly*] I am so glad you understand politics, Jack: it will be most useful to you if you go into parliament [*he collapses like a pricked bladder*]. But I am sorry you thought my influence a bad one.

TANNER. I dont say it was a bad one. But bad or good, I didnt choose to be cut to your measure. And I wont be cut to it.

ANN. Nobody wants you to, Jack. I assure you—really on my word—I dont mind your queer opinions one little bit. You know we have all been brought up to have advanced opinions. Why do you persist in thinking me so narrow minded?

TANNER. Thats the danger of it. I know you dont mind, because youve found out that it doesnt matter. The boa constrictor doesnt mind the opinions of a stag one little bit when once she has got her coils round it.

ANN [*rising in sudden enlightenment*] O-o-o-oh! now I understand why you warned Tavy that I am a boa constrictor. Granny told me. [*She laughs and throws her boa round his neck*]. Doesnt it feel nice and soft, Jack?

TANNER [*in the toils*] You scandalous woman, will you throw away even your hypocrisy?

ANN. I am never hypocritical with you, Jack. Are you angry? [*She withdraws the boa and throws it on a chair*]. Perhaps I shouldnt have done that.

TANNER [*contemptuously*] Pooh, prudery! Why should you not, if it amuses you?

ANN [*shyly*] Well, because—because I suppose what you really meant by the boa constrictor was this [*she puts her arms round his neck*].

TANNER [*staring at her*] Magnificent audacity! [*She laughs and pats his cheeks*]. Now just to think that if I mentioned this episode not a soul would believe me except the people who would cut me for telling, whilst if you accused me of it nobody would believe my denial!

ANN [*taking her arms away with perfect dignity*] You are incorrigible, Jack. But you should not jest about our affection for one another. Nobody could possibly misunderstand it. You do not misunderstand it, I hope.

TANNER. My blood interprets for me, Ann. Poor Ricky Ticky Tavy!

ANN [*looking quickly at him as if this were a new light*] Surely you are not so absurd as to be jealous of Tavy.

TANNER. Jealous! Why should I be? But I dont wonder at your grip of him. I feel the coils tightening round my very self, though you are only playing with me.

ANN. Do you think I have designs on Tavy?

TANNER. I know you have.

ANN [*earnestly*] Take care, Jack. You may make Tavy very unhappy if you mislead him about me.

TANNER. Never fear: he will not escape you.

ANN. I wonder are you really a clever man!

TANNER. Why this sudden misgiving on the subject?

ANN. You seem to understand all the things I dont understand; but you are a perfect baby in the things I do understand.

TANNER. I understand how Tavy feels for you, Ann: you may depend on that, at all events.

ANN. And you think you understand how I feel for Tavy, dont you?

TANNER. I know only too well what is going to happen to poor Tavy.

ANN. I should laugh at you, Jack, if it were not for poor papa's death. Mind! Tavy will be very unhappy.

TANNER. Yes; but he wont know it, poor devil. He is a thousand times too good for you. Thats why he is going to make the mistake of his life about you.

ANN. I think men make more mistakes by being too clever than by being too good [*she sits down, with a trace of contempt for the whole male sex in the elegant carriage of her shoulders*].

TANNER. Oh, I know you dont care very much about Tavy. But there is always one who kisses and one who only allows the kiss. Tavy will kiss; and you will only turn the cheek. And you will throw him over if anybody better turns up.

ANN [*offended*] You have no right to say such things, Jack. They are not true, and not delicate. If you and Tavy choose to be stupid about me, that is not my fault.

TANNER [*remorsefully*] Forgive my brutalities, Ann. They are levelled at this wicked world, not at you. [*She looks up at him, pleased and forgiving. He becomes cautious at once*]. All the same, I wish Ramsden would come back. I never feel safe with you: there is a devilish charm—or no: not a charm, a subtle interest [*she laughs*]—Just so: you know it; and you triumph in it. Openly and shamelessly triumph in it!

ANN. What a shocking flirt you are, Jack!

TANNER. A flirt!! I!!!

ANN. Yes, a flirt. You are always abusing and offending people; but you never really mean to let go your hold of them.

TANNER. I will ring the bell. This conversation has already gone further than I intended.

Ramsden and Octavius come back with Miss Ramsden, a hardheaded old maiden lady in a plain brown silk gown, with enough rings, chains, and brooches to shew that her plainness of dress is a matter of principle, not of poverty. She comes into the room very determinedly: the two men, perplexed and downcast, following her. Ann rises and goes eagerly to meet her. Tanner retreats to the wall between the busts and pretends to study the pictures. Ramsden goes to his table as usual; and Octavius clings to the neighborhood of Tanner.

MISS RAMSDEN [*almost pushing Ann aside as she comes to Mrs Whitefield's chair and plants herself there resolutely*] I wash my hands of the whole affair.

OCTAVIUS [*very wretched*] I know you wish me to take Violet away, Miss Ramsden. I will. [*He turns irresolutely to the door*].

RAMSDEN. No, no—

MISS RAMSDEN. What is the use of saying no, Roebuck? Octavius knows that I would not turn any truly contrite and repentant woman from your doors. But when a woman is not only wicked, but intends to go on being wicked, she and I part company.

ANN. Oh, Miss Ramsden, what do you mean? What has Violet said?

RAMSDEN. Violet is certainly very obstinate. She wont leave London. I dont understand her.

MISS RAMSDEN. I do. It's as plain as the nose on your face, Roebuck, that she wont go because she doesnt want to be separated from this man, whoever he is.

ANN. Oh, surely, surely! Octavius: did y o u speak to her?

OCTAVIUS. She wont tell us anything. She wont make any arrangement until she has consulted somebody. It cant be anybody else than the scoundrel who has betrayed her.

TANNER [*to Octavius*] Well, let her consult him. He will be glad enough to have her sent abroad. Where is the difficulty?

MISS RAMSDEN [*taking the answer out of Octavius's mouth*] The difficulty, Mr Jack, is that when I offered to help her I didnt offer to become her accomplice in her wickedness. She either pledges her word never to see that man again, or else she finds some new friends; and the sooner the better.

The parlormaid appears at the door. Ann hastily resumes her seat, and looks as unconcerned as possible. Octavius instinctively imitates her.

THE MAID. The cab is at the door, maam.

MISS RAMSDEN. What cab?

THE MAID. For Miss Robinson.

MISS RAMSDEN. Oh! [*Recovering herself*] All right. [*The maid withdraws*]. She has sent for a cab.

TANNER. *I* wanted to send for that cab half an hour ago.

MISS RAMSDEN. I am glad she understands the position she has placed herself in.

RAMSDEN. I dont like her going away in this fashion, Susan. We had better not do anything harsh.

OCTAVIUS. No: thank you again and again; but Miss Ramsden is quite right. Violet can-

not expect to stay.

ANN. Hadnt you better go with her, Tavy?

OCTAVIUS. She wont have me.

MISS RAMSDEN. Of course she wont. She's going straight to that man.

TANNER. As a natural result of her virtuous reception here.

RAMSDEN [*much troubled*] There, Susan! You hear! and theres some truth in it. I wish you could reconcile it with your principles to be a little patient with this poor girl. She's very young; and theres a time for everything.

MISS RAMSDEN. Oh, she will get all the sympathy she wants from the men. I'm surprised at you, Roebuck.

TANNER. So am I, Ramsden, most favorably.

Violet appears at the door. She is as impenitent and self-possessed a young lady as one would desire to see among the best behaved of her sex. Her small head and tiny resolute mouth and chin; her haughty crispness of speech and trimness of carriage; the ruthless elegance of her equipment, which includes a very smart hat with a dead bird in it, mark a personality which is as formidable as it is exquisitely pretty. She is not a siren, like Ann: admiration comes to her without any compulsion or even interest on her part; besides, there is some fun in Ann, but in this woman none, perhaps no mercy either: if anything restrains her, it is intelligence and pride, not compassion. Her voice might be the voice of a schoolmistress addressing a class of girls who had disgraced themselves, as she proceeds with complete composure and some disgust to say what she has come to say.

VIOLET. I have only looked in to tell Miss Ramsden that she will find her birthday present to me, the filagree bracelet, in the housekeeper's room.

TANNER. Do come in, Violet; and talk to us sensibly.

VIOLET. Thank you: I have had quite enough of the family conversation this morning. So has your mother, Ann: she has gone home crying. But at all events, I have found out what some of my pretended friends are worth. Goodbye.

TANNER. No, no: one moment. I have something to say which I beg you to hear. [*She looks at him without the slightest curiosity, but waits, apparently as much to finish getting her glove on as to hear what he has to say*]. I am altogether on your side in this matter. I congratulate you, with the sincerest respect, on having the courage to do what you have done.

You are entirely in the right; and the family is entirely in the wrong.

Sensation. Ann and Miss Ramsden rise and turn towards the two. Violet, more surprised than any of the others, forgets her glove, and comes forward into the middle of the room, both puzzled and displeased. Octavius alone does not move nor raise his head: he is overwhelmed with shame.

ANN [*pleading to Tanner to be sensible*] Jack!

MISS RAMSDEN [*outraged*] Well, I must say!

VIOLET [*sharply to Tanner*] Who told you?

TANNER. Why, Ramsden and Tavy of course. Why should they not?

VIOLET. But they dont know.

TANNER. Dont know what?

VIOLET. They dont know that I am in the right, I mean.

TANNER. Oh, they know it in their hearts, though they think themselves bound to blame you by their silly superstitions about morality and propriety and so forth. But I know, and the whole world really knows, though it dare not say so, that you were right to follow your instinct; that vitality and bravery are the greatest qualities a woman can have, and motherhood her solemn initiation into womanhood; and that the fact of your not being legally married matters not one scrap either to your own worth or to our real regard for you.

VIOLET [*flushing with indignation*] Oh! You think me a wicked woman, like the rest. You think I have not only been vile, but that I share your abominable opinions. Miss Ramsden: I have borne your hard words because I knew you would be sorry for them when you found out the truth. But I wont bear such a horrible insult as to be complimented by Jack on being one of the wretches of whom he approves. I have kept my marriage a secret for my husband's sake. But now I claim my right as a married woman not to be insulted.

OCTAVIUS [*raising his head with inexpressible relief*] You are married!

VIOLET. Yes; and I think you might have guessed it. What business had you all to take it for granted that I had no right to wear my wedding ring? Not one of you even asked me: I cannot forget that.

TANNER [*in ruins*] I am utterly crushed. I meant well. I apologize—abjectly apologize.

VIOLET. I hope you will be more careful in future about the things you say. Of course one does not take them seriously; but they are very disagreeable, and rather in bad taste, I think.

TANNER [*bowing to the storm*] I have no defence: I shall know better in future than to take any woman's part. We have all disgraced ourselves in your eyes, I am afraid, except Ann. She befriended you. For Ann's sake, forgive us.

VIOLET. Yes: Ann has been kind; but then Ann knew.

TANNER [*with a desperate gesture*] Oh!!! Unfathomable deceit! Double crossed!

MISS RAMSDEN [*stiffly*] And who, pray, is the gentleman who does not acknowledge his wife?

VIOLET [*promptly*] That is my business, Miss Ramsden, and not yours. I have my reasons for keeping my marriage a secret for the present.

RAMSDEN. All I can say is that we are extremely sorry, Violet. I am shocked to think of how we have treated you.

OCTAVIUS [*awkwardly*] I beg your pardon, Violet. I can say no more.

MISS RAMSDEN [*still loth to surrender*] Of course what you say puts a very different complexion on the matter. All the same, I owe it to myself—

VIOLET [*cutting her short*] You owe me an apology, Miss Ramsden: thats what you owe both to yourself and to me. If you were a married woman you would not like sitting in the housekeeper's room and being treated like a naughty child by young girls and old ladies without any serious duties and responsibilities.

TANNER. Dont hit us when we're down, Violet. We seem to have made fools of ourselves; but really it was you who made fools of us.

VIOLET. It was no business of yours, Jack, in any case.

TANNER. No business of mine! Why, Ramsden as good as accused me of being the unknown gentleman.

Ramsden makes a frantic demonstration; but Violet's cool keen anger extinguishes it.

VIOLET. You! Oh, how infamous! how abominable! how disgracefully you have all been talking about me! If my husband knew it he would never let me speak to any of you again. [*To Ramsden*] I think you might have spared me that, at least.

RAMSDEN. But I assure you I never—at

least it is a monstrous perversion of something I said that—

MISS RAMSDEN. You neednt apologize, Roebuck. She brought it all on herself. It is for her to apologize for having deceived us.

VIOLET. I can make allowances for you, Miss Ramsden: you cannot understand how I feel on this subject, though I should have expected rather better taste from people of greater experience. However, I quite feel that you have placed yourselves in a very painful position; and the most truly considerate thing for me to do is to go at once. Good morning.

She goes, leaving them staring.

MISS RAMSDEN. Well, I must say!

RAMSDEN [*plaintively*] I dont think she is quite fair to us.

TANNER. You must cower before the wedding ring like the rest of us, Ramsden. The cup of our ignominy is full.

ACT II

On the carriage drive in the park of a country house near Richmond an open touring car has broken down. It stands in front of a clump of trees round which the drive sweeps to the house, which is partly visible through them: indeed Tanner, standing in the drive with his back to us, could get an unobstructed view of the west corner of the house on his left were he not far too much interested in a pair of supine legs in dungaree overalls which protrude from beneath the machine. He is watching them intently with bent back and hands supported on his knees. His leathern overcoat and peaked cap proclaim him one of the dismounted passengers.

THE LEGS. Aha! I got him.

TANNER. All right now?

THE LEGS. Aw rawt nah.

Tanner stoops and takes the legs by the ankles, drawing their owner forth like a wheelbarrow, walking on his hands, with a hammer in his mouth. He is a young man in a neat suit of blue serge, clean shaven, dark eyed, square fingered, with short well brushed black hair and rather irregular sceptically turned eyebrows. When he is manipulating the car his movements are swift and sudden, yet attentive and deliberate. With Tanner and Tanner's friends his manner is not in the least deferential, but cool and reticent, keeping them quite effectually at a distance whilst giving them no excuse for complaining of him. Nevertheless he has a vigilant eye on them always, and

that, too, rather cynically, like a man who knows the world well from its seamy side. He speaks slowly and with a touch of sarcasm; and as he does not at all affect the gentleman in his speech, it may be inferred that his smart appearance is a mark of respect to himself and his own class, not to that which employs him.

He now gets into the car to stow away his tools and divest himself of his overalls. Tanner takes off his leathern overcoat and pitches it into the car with a sigh of relief, glad to be rid of it. The chauffeur, noting this, tosses his head contemptuously, and surveys his employer sardonically.

THE CHAUFFEUR. Had enough of it, eh?

TANNER. I may as well walk to the house and stretch my legs and calm my nerves a little. [*Looking at his watch*] I suppose you know that we have come from Hyde Park Corner to Richmond in twenty-one minutes.

THE CHAUFFEUR. I'd ha done it under fifteen if I'd had a clear road all the way.

TANNER. Why do you do it? Is it for love of sport or for the fun of terrifying your unfortunate employer?

THE CHAUFFEUR. What are you afraid of?

TANNER. The police, and breaking my neck.

THE CHAUFFEUR. Well, if you like easy going, you can take a bus, you know. It's cheaper. You pay me to save your time and give you the value of what you paid for the car. [*He sits down calmly*].

TANNER. I am the slave of that car and of you too. I dream of the accursed thing at night.

THE CHAUFFEUR. Youll get over that all right. If youre going up to the house, may I ask how long youre goin to stay? Because if you mean to put in the whole morning in there talkin to the ladies, I'll put the car in the garage and make myself agreeable with a view to lunching here. If not, I'll keep the car on the go about here til you come.

TANNER. Better wait here. We shant be long. Theres a young American gentleman, a Mr Malone, who is driving Mr Robinson down in his new American steam car.

THE CHAUFFEUR [*springing up and coming hastily out of the car to Tanner*] American steam car! Wot! racin us dahn from London!

TANNER. Perhaps theyre here already.

THE CHAUFFEUR. If I'd known it! [*With deep reproach*] Why didnt you tell me, Mr Tanner?

TANNER. Because Ive been told that this car is capable of 84 miles an hour; and I already know what y o u are capable of when there is a rival car on the road. No, Henry: there are things it is not good for you to know; and this was one of them. However, cheer up: we are going to have a day after your own heart. The American is to take Mr Robinson and his sister and Miss Whitefield. We are to take Miss Rhoda.

THE CHAUFFEUR [*consoled, and musing on another matter*] Thats Miss Whitefield's sister, isnt it?

TANNER. Yes.

THE CHAUFFEUR. And Miss Whitefield herself is goin in the other car? Not with you?

TANNER. Why the devil should she come with me? Mr Robinson will be in the other car. [*The Chauffeur looks at Tanner with cool incredulity, and turns to the car, whistling a popular air softly to himself. Tanner, a little annoyed, is about to pursue the subject when he hears the footsteps of Octavius on the gravel. Octavius is coming from the house, dressed for motoring, but without his overcoat*]. Weve lost the race, thank Heaven: heres Mr Robinson. Well, Tavy, is the steam car a success?

OCTAVIUS. I think so. We came from Hyde Park Corner here in seventeen minutes. [*The Chauffeur, furious, kicks the car with a groan of vexation*]. How long were you?

TANNER. Oh, about three quarters of an hour or so.

THE CHAUFFEUR [*remonstrating*] Now, now, Mr Tanner, come now! We could ha done it easy under fifteen.

TANNER. By the way, let me introduce you. Mr Octavius Robinson: Mr Enry Straker.

STRAKER. Pleased to meet you, sir. Mr Tanner is gittin at you with is Enry Straker, you know. You call it Henery. But I dont mind, bless you!

TANNER. You think it's simply bad taste in me to chaff him, Tavy. But youre wrong. This man takes more trouble to drop his aitches than ever his father did to pick them up. It's a mark of caste to him. I have never met anybody more swollen with the pride of class than Enry is.

STRAKER. Easy, easy! A little moderation, Mr Tanner.

TANNER. A little moderation, Tavy, you observe. Y o u would tell me to draw it mild. But this chap has been educated. Whats more, he knows that we havnt. What was that Board School of yours, Straker?

STRAKER. Sherbrooke Road.

TANNER. Sherbrooke Road! Would any of us say Rugby! Harrow! Eton! in that tone of intellectual snobbery? Sherbrooke Road is a place where boys learn something: Eton is a boy farm where we are sent because we are nuisances at home, and because in after life, whenever a Duke is mentioned, we can claim him as an old school-fellow.

STRAKER. You dont know nothing about it, Mr Tanner. It's not the Board School that does it: it's the Polytechnic.

TANNER. His university, Octavius. Not Oxford, Cambridge, Durham, Dublin, or Glasgow. Not even those Nonconformist holes in Wales. No, Tavy. Regent Street! Chelsea! the Borough!—I dont know half their confounded names: these are his universities, not mere shops for selling class limitations like ours. You despise Oxford, Enry, dont you?

STRAKER. No, I dont. Very nice sort of place, Oxford, I should think, for people that like that sort of place. They teach you to be a gentleman there. In the Polytechnic they teach you to be an engineer or such like. See?

TANNER. Sarcasm, Tavy, sarcasm! Oh, if you could only see into Enry's soul, the depth of his contempt for a gentleman, the arrogance of his pride in being an engineer, would appal you. He positively likes the car to break down because it brings out my gentlemanly helplessness and his workmanlike skill and resource.

STRAKER. Never you mind him, Mr Robinson. He likes to talk. We know him, dont we?

OCTAVIUS [*earnestly*] But theres a great truth at the bottom of what he says. I believe most intensely in the dignity of labor.

STRAKER [*unimpressed*] Thats because you never done any, Mr Robinson. My business is to do away with labor. Youll get more out of me and a machine than you will out of twenty laborers, and not so much to drink either.

TANNER. For Heaven's sake, Tavy, dont start him on political economy. He knows all about it; and we dont. Youre only a poetic Socialist, Tavy: he's a scientific one.

STRAKER [*unperturbed*] Yes. Well, this conversation is very improvin; but Ive got to look after the car; and you two want to talk about your ladies. *I* know. [*He pretends to busy himself about the car, but presently saunters off to indulge in a cigaret*].

TANNER. Thats a very momentous social phenomenon.

OCTAVIUS. What is?

TANNER. Straker is. Here have we literary and cultured persons been for years setting up a cry of the New Woman whenever some unusually old fashioned female came along, and never noticing the advent of the New Man. Straker's the New Man.

OCTAVIUS. I see nothing new about him, except your way of chaffing him. But I dont want to talk about him just now. I want to speak to you about Ann.

TANNER. Straker knew even that. He learnt it at the Polytechnic, probably. Well, what about Ann? Have you proposed to her?

OCTAVIUS [self-reproachfully] I was brute enough to do so last night.

TANNER. Brute enough! What do you mean?

OCTAVIUS [dithyrambically] Jack: we men are all coarse: we never understand how exquisite a woman's sensibilities are. How could I have done such a thing!

TANNER. Done what, you maudlin idiot?

OCTAVIUS. Yes, I am an idiot. Jack: if you had heard her voice! if you had seen her tears! I have lain awake all night thinking of them. If she had reproached me, I could have borne it better.

TANNER. Tears! thats dangerous. What did she say?

OCTAVIUS. She asked me how she could think of anything now but her dear father. She stifled a sob— [he breaks down].

TANNER [patting him on the back] Bear it like a man, Tavy, even if you feel it like an ass. It's the old game: she's not tired of playing with you yet.

OCTAVIUS [impatiently] Oh, dont be a fool, Jack. Do you suppose this eternal shallow cynicism of yours has any real bearing on a nature like hers?

TANNER. Hm! Did she say anything else?

OCTAVIUS. Yes; and that is why I expose myself and her to your ridicule by telling you what passed.

TANNER [remorsefully] No, dear Tavy, not ridicule, on my honor! However, no matter. Go on.

OCTAVIUS. Her sense of duty is so devout, so perfect, so—

TANNER. Yes: I know. Go on.

OCTAVIUS. You see, under this new arrangement, you and Ramsden are her guardians; and she considers that all her duty to her father is now transferred to you. She said she thought I ought to have spoken to you both in the first instance. Of course she is right; but somehow it seems rather absurd that I am to come to you and formally ask to be received as a suitor for your ward's hand.

TANNER. I am glad that love has not totally extinguished your sense of humor, Tavy.

OCTAVIUS. That answer wont satisfy her.

TANNER. My official answer is, obviously, Bless you, my children: may you be happy!

OCTAVIUS. I wish you would stop playing the fool about this. If it is not serious to you, it is to me, and to her.

TANNER. You know very well that she is as free to choose as you are.

OCTAVIUS. She does not think so.

TANNER. Oh, doesnt she! just! However, say what you want me to do?

OCTAVIUS. I want you to tell her sincerely and earnestly what you think about me. I want you to tell her that you can trust her to me—that is, if you feel you can.

TANNER. I have no doubt that I can trust her to you. What worries me is the idea of trusting you to her. Have you read Maeterlinck's book about the bee?

OCTAVIUS [keeping his temper with difficulty] I am not discussing literature at present.

TANNER. Be just a little patient with me. I am not discussing literature: the book about the bee is natural history. It's an awful lesson to mankind. You think that you are Ann's suitor; that you are the pursuer and she the pursued; that it is your part to woo, to persuade, to prevail, to overcome. Fool: it is you who are the pursued, the marked down quarry, the destined prey. You need not sit looking longingly at the bait through the wires of the trap: the door is open, and will remain so until it shuts behind you for ever.

OCTAVIUS. I wish I could believe that, vilely as you put it.

TANNER. Why, man, what other work has she in life but to get a husband? It is a woman's business to get married as soon as possible, and a man's to keep unmarried as long as he can. You have your poems and your tragedies to work at: Ann has nothing.

OCTAVIUS. I cannot write without inspiration. And nobody can give me that except Ann.

TANNER. Well, hadnt you better get it from her at a safe distance? Petrarch didnt see half as much of Laura, nor Dante of Beatrice, as you see of Ann now; and yet they wrote first-rate poetry—at least so I'm told. They never exposed their idolatry to the test of domestic familiarity; and it lasted them to their graves. Marry Ann; and at the end of a week youll find no more inspiration in her than in a plate of muffins.

OCTAVIUS. You think I shall tire of her!

TANNER. Not at all: you dont get tired of muffins. But you dont find inspiration in them; and you wont in her when she ceases to be a poet's dream and becomes a solid eleven stone wife. Youll be forced to dream about somebody else; and then there will be a row.

OCTAVIUS. This sort of talk is no use, Jack. You dont understand. You have never been in love.

TANNER. I! I have never been out of it. Why, I am in love even with Ann. But I am neither the slave of love nor its dupe. Go to the bee, thou poet: consider her ways and be wise. By Heaven, Tavy, if women could do without our work, and we ate their children's bread instead of making it, they would kill us as the spider kills her mate or as the bees kill the drone. And they would be right if we were good for nothing but love.

OCTAVIUS. Ah, if we were only good enough for Love! There is nothing like Love: there is nothing else but Love: without it the world would be a dream of sordid horror.

TANNER. And this—this is the man who asks me to give him the hand of my ward! Tavy: I believe we were changed in our cradles, and that you are the real descendant of Don Juan.

OCTAVIUS. I beg you not to say anything like that to Ann.

TANNER. Dont be afraid. She has marked you for her own; and nothing will stop her now. You are doomed. [*Straker comes back with a newspaper*]. Here comes the New Man, demoralizing himself with a halfpenny paper as usual.

STRAKER. Now would you believe it, Mr Robinson, when we're out motoring we take in two papers: the Times for him, the Leader or the Echo for me. And do you think I ever see my paper? Not much. He grabs the Leader and leaves me to stodge myself with his Times.

OCTAVIUS. Are there no winners in the Times?

TANNER. Enry dont old with bettin, Tavy. Motor records are his weakness. Whats the latest?

STRAKER. Paris to Biskra at forty miles an hour average, not countin the Mediterranean.

TANNER. How many killed?

STRAKER. Two silly sheep. What does it matter? Sheep dont cost such a lot: they were glad to ave the price without the trouble o sellin em to the butcher. All the same, d'y'see, therell be a clamor agin it presently; and then the French Government'll stop it; an our chance'll be gone, see? Thats what makes me fairly mad: Mr Tanner wont do a good run while he can.

TANNER. Tavy: do you remember my uncle James?

OCTAVIUS. Yes. Why?

TANNER. Uncle James had a first rate cook: he couldnt digest anything except what she cooked. Well, the poor man was shy and hated society. But his cook was proud of her skill, and wanted to serve up dinners to princes and ambassadors. To prevent her from leaving him, that poor old man had to give a big dinner twice a month, and suffer agonies of awkwardness. Now here am I; and here is this chap Enry Straker, the New Man. I loathe travelling; but I rather like Enry. He cares for nothing but tearing along in a leather coat and goggles, with two inches of dust all over him, at sixty miles an hour and the risk of his life and mine. Except, of course, when he is lying on his back in the mud under the machine trying to find out where it has given way. Well, if I dont give him a thousand mile run at least once a fortnight I shall lose him. He will give me the sack and go to some American millionaire; and I shall have to put up with a nice respectful groom-gardener-amateur, who will touch his hat and know his place. I am Enry's slave, just as Uncle James was his cook's slave.

STRAKER [*exasperated*] Garn! I wish I had a car that would go as fast as you can talk, Mr Tanner. What I say is that you lose money by a motor car unless you keep it workin. Might as well ave a pram and a nuss-maid to wheel you in it as that car and me if you dont git the last inch out of us both.

TANNER [*soothingly*] All right, Henry, all

right. We'll go out for half an hour presently.

STRAKER [*in disgust*] Arf an ahr! [*He returns to his machine; seats himself in it; and turns up a fresh page of his paper in search of more news*].

OCTAVIUS. Oh, that reminds me. I have a note for you from Rhoda. [*He gives Tanner a note*].

TANNER [*opening it*] I rather think Rhoda is heading for a row with Ann. As a rule there is only one person an English girl hates more than she hates her eldest sister; and thats her mother. But Rhoda positively prefers her mother to Ann. She—[*indignantly*] Oh, I say!

OCTAVIUS. Whats the matter?

TANNER. Rhoda was to have come with me for a ride in the motor car. She says Ann has forbidden her to go out with me.

Straker suddenly begins whistling his favorite air with remarkable deliberation. Surprised by this burst of larklike melody, and jarred by a sardonic note in its cheerfulness, they turn and look inquiringly at him. But he is busy with his paper; and nothing comes of their movement.

OCTAVIUS [*recovering himself*] Does she give any reason?

TANNER. Reason! An insult is not a reason. Ann forbids her to be alone with me on any occasion. Says I am not a fit person for a young girl to be with. What do you think of your paragon now?

OCTAVIUS. You must remember that she has a very heavy responsibility now that her father is dead. Mrs Whitefield is too weak to control Rhoda.

TANNER [*staring at him*] In short, you agree with Ann.

OCTAVIUS. No; but I think I understand her. You must admit that your views are hardly suited for the formation of a young girl's mind and character.

TANNER. I admit nothing of the sort. I admit that the formation of a young lady's mind and character usually consists in telling her lies; but I object to the particular lie that I am in the habit of abusing the confidence of girls.

OCTAVIUS. Ann doesnt say that, Jack.

TANNER. What else does she mean?

STRAKER [*catching sight of Ann coming from the house*] Miss Whitefield, gentlemen. [*He dismounts and strolls away down the avenue with the air of a man who knows he is no longer wanted*].

ANN [*coming between Octavius and Tanner*]

Good morning, Jack. I have come to tell you that poor Rhoda has got one of her headaches and cannot go out with you today in the car. It is a cruel disappointment to her, poor child!

TANNER. What do you say now, Tavy?

OCTAVIUS. Surely you cannot misunderstand, Jack. Ann is shewing you the kindest consideration, even at the cost of deceiving you.

ANN. What do you mean?

TANNER. Would you like to cure Rhoda's headache, Ann?

ANN. Of course.

TANNER. Then tell her what you said just now; and add that you arrived about two minutes after I had received her letter and read it.

ANN. Rhoda has written to you!

TANNER. With full particulars.

OCTAVIUS. Never mind him, Ann. You were right—quite right. Ann was only doing her duty, Jack; and you know it. Doing it in the kindest way, too.

ANN [*going to Octavius*] How kind you are, Tavy! How helpful! How well you understand!

Octavius beams.

TANNER. Ay: tighten the coils. You love her, Tavy, dont you?

OCTAVIUS. She knows I do.

ANN. Hush. For shame, Tavy!

TANNER. Oh, I give you leave. I am your guardian; and I commit you to Tavy's care for the next hour. I am off for a turn in the car.

ANN. No, Jack. I must speak to you about Rhoda. Ricky: will you go back to the house and entertain your American friend. He's rather on Mamma's hands so early in the morning. She wants to finish her housekeeping.

OCTAVIUS. I fly, dearest Ann [*he kisses her hand*].

ANN [*tenderly*] Ricky Ticky Tavy!

He looks at her with an eloquent blush, and runs off.

TANNER [*bluntly*] Now look here, Ann. This time youve landed yourself; and if Tavy were not in love with you past all salvation he'd have found out what an incorrigible liar you are.

ANN. You misunderstand, Jack. I didn't dare tell Tavy the truth.

TANNER. No: your daring is generally in

the opposite direction. What the devil do you mean by telling Rhoda that I am too vicious to associate with her? How can I ever have any human or decent relations with her again, now that you have poisoned her mind in that abominable way?

ANN. I know you are incapable of behaving badly—

TANNER. Then why did you lie to her?

ANN. I had to.

TANNER. Had to!

ANN. Mother made me.

TANNER [*his eye flashing*] Ha! I might have known it. The mother! Always the mother!

ANN. It was that dreadful book of yours. You know how timid mother is. All timid women are conventional: we m u s t be conventional, Jack, or we are so cruelly, so vilely misunderstood. Even you, who are a man, cannot say what you think without being misunderstood and vilified—yes: I admit it: I have had to vilify you. Do you want to have poor Rhoda misunderstood and vilified in the same way? Would it be right for mother to let her expose herself to such treatment before she is old enough to judge for herself?

TANNER. In short, the way to avoid misunderstanding is for everybody to lie and slander and insinuate and pretend as hard as they can. That is what obeying your mother comes to.

ANN. I love my mother, Jack.

TANNER [*working himself up into a sociological rage*] Is that any reason why you are not to call your soul your own? Oh, I protest against this vile abjection of youth to age! Look at fashionable society as you know it. What does it pretend to be? An exquisite dance of nymphs. What i s it? A horrible procession of wretched girls, each in the claws of a cynical, cunning, avaricious, disillusioned, ignorantly experienced, foul-minded old woman whom she calls mother, and whose duty it is to corrupt her mind and sell her to the highest bidder. Why do these unhappy slaves marry anybody, however old and vile, sooner than not marry at all? Because, marriage is their only means of escape from these decrepit fiends who hide their selfish ambitions, their jealous hatreds of the young rivals who have supplanted them, under the mask of maternal duty and family affection. Such things are abominable: the voice of nature proclaims for the daughter a father's care and for the son a mother's. The law for father and son

and mother and daughter is not the law of love: it is the law of revolution, of emancipation, of final supersession of the old and worn-out by the young and capable. I tell you, the first duty of manhood and womanhood is a Declaration of Independence: the man who pleads his father's authority is no man: the woman who pleads her mother's authority is unfit to bear citizens to a free people.

ANN [*watching him with quiet curiosity*] I suppose you will go in seriously for politics some day, Jack.

TANNER [*heavily let down*] Eh? What? Wh—? [*Collecting his scattered wits*] What has that got to do with what I have been saying?

ANN. You talk so well.

TANNER. Talk! Talk! It means nothing to you but talk. Well, go back to your mother, and help her to poison Rhoda's imagination as she has poisoned yours. It is the tame elephants who enjoy capturing the wild ones.

ANN. I am getting on. Yesterday I was a boa constrictor: today I am an elephant.

TANNER. Yes. So pack your trunk and be-gone: I have no more to say to you.

ANN. You are so utterly unreasonable and impracticable. What c a n I do?

TANNER. Do! Break your chains. Go your way according to your own conscience and not according to your mother's. Get your mind clean and vigorous; and learn to enjoy a fast ride in a motor car instead of seeing nothing in it but an excuse for a detestable intrigue. Come with me to Marseilles and across to Algiers and to Biskra, at sixty miles an hour. Come right down to the Cape if you like. That will be a Declaration of Independence with a vengeance. You can write a book about it afterwards. That will finish your mother and make a woman of you.

ANN [*thoughtfully*] I dont think there would be any harm in that, Jack. You are my guardian: you stand in my father's place, by his own wish. Nobody could say a word against our travelling together. It would be delightful: thank you a thousand times, Jack. I'll come.

TANNER [*aghast*] Youll come!!!

ANN. Of course.

TANNER. But—[*he stops, utterly appalled; then resumes feebly*] No: look here, Ann: if theres no harm in it theres no point in doing it.

ANN. How absurd you are! You dont want to compromise me, do you?

TANNER. Yes: thats the whole sense of my proposal.

ANN. You are talking the greatest nonsense; and you know it. You would never do anything to hurt me.

TANNER. Well, if you dont want to be compromised, dont come.

ANN [*with simple earnestness*] Yes, I will come, Jack, since you wish it. You are my guardian; and I think we ought to see more of one another and come to know one another better. [*Gratefully*] It's very thoughtful and very kind of you, Jack, to offer me this lovely holiday, especially after what I said about Rhoda. You really are good—much better than you think. When do we start?

TANNER. But—

The conversation is interrupted by the arrival of Mrs Whitefield from the house. She is accompanied by the American gentleman, and followed by Ramsden and Octavius.

Hector Malone is an Eastern American; but he is not at all ashamed of his nationality. This makes English people of fashion think well of him, as of a young fellow who is manly enough to confess to an obvious disadvantage without any attempt to conceal or extenuate it. They feel that he ought not to be made to suffer for what is clearly not his fault, and make a point of being specially kind to him. His chivalrous manners to women, and his elevated moral sentiments, being both gratuitous and unusual, strike them as perhaps a little unfortunate; and though they find his vein of easy humor rather amusing when it has ceased to puzzle them (as it does at first), they have had to make him understand that he really must not tell anecdotes unless they are strictly personal and scandalous, and also that oratory is an accomplishment which belongs to a cruder stage of civilization than that in which his migration has landed him. On these points Hector is not quite convinced: he still thinks that the British are apt to make merits of their stupidities, and to represent their various incapacities as points of good breeding. English life seems to him to suffer from a lack of edifying rhetoric (which he calls moral tone); English behavior to shew a want of respect for womanhood; English pronunciation to fail very vulgarly in tackling such words as world, girl, bird, etc.; English society to be plain spoken to an extent which stretches occasionally to intolerable coarseness; and English intercourse to need enlivening by games and stories and other pastimes; so he does not feel called upon to acquire these defects after taking great pains to cultivate himself in a first rate manner before venturing across the Atlantic. To this culture he finds English people either totally indifferent, as they very commonly are to all culture, or else politely evasive, the truth being that Hector's culture is nothing but a state of saturation with our literary exports of thirty years ago, reimported by him to be unpacked at a moment's notice and hurled at the head of English literature, science, and art, at every conversational opportunity. The dismay set up by these sallies encourages him in his belief that he is helping to educate England. When he finds people chattering harmlessly about Anatole France and Nietzsche, he devastates them with Matthew Arnold, the Autocrat of the Breakfast Table, and even Macaulay; and as he is devoutly religious at bottom, he first leads the unwary, by humorous irreverence, to leave popular theology out of account in discussing moral questions with him, and then scatters them in confusion by demanding whether the carrying out of his ideals of conduct was not the manifest object of God Almighty in creating honest men and pure women. The engaging freshness of his personality and the dumbfoundering staleness of his culture make it extremely difficult to decide whether he is worth knowing; for whilst his company is undeniably pleasant and enlivening, there is intellectually nothing new to be got out of him, especially as he despises politics, and is careful not to talk commercial shop, in which department he is probably much in advance of his English capitalist friends. He gets on best with romantic Christians of the amoristic sect: hence the friendship which has sprung up between him and Octavius.

In appearance Hector is a neatly built young man of twenty-four, with a short, smartly trimmed black beard, clear, well shaped eyes, and an ingratiating vivacity of expression. He is, from the fashionable point of view, faultlessly dressed. As he comes along the drive from the house with Mrs Whitefield he is sedulously making himself agreeable and entertaining, and thereby placing on her slender wit a burden it is unable to bear. An Englishman would let her alone, accepting boredom and indifference as their common lot; and the poor lady wants to be either let alone or let prattle about the things that interest her.

Ramsden strolls over to inspect the motor car. Octavius joins Hector.

ANN [*pouncing on her mother joyously*] Oh, mamma, what do you think! Jack is going to take me to Nice in his motor car. Isnt it lovely? I am the happiest person in London.

TANNER [*desperately*] Mrs Whitefield objects. I am sure she objects. Doesnt she, Ramsden?

RAMSDEN. I should think it very likely indeed.

ANN. You dont object, do you, mother?

MRS WHITEFIELD. *I* object! Why should I? I think it will do you good, Ann. [*Trotting over to Tanner*] I meant to ask you to take Rhoda out for a run occasionally: she is too much in the house; but it will do when you come back.

TANNER. Abyss beneath abyss of perfidy!

ANN [*hastily, to distract attention from this outburst*] Oh, I forgot: you have not met Mr Malone. Mr Tanner, my guardian: Mr Hector Malone.

HECTOR. Pleased to meet you, Mr Tanner. I should like to suggest an extension of the travelling party to Nice, if I may.

ANN. Oh, we're all coming. Thats understood, isnt it?

HECTOR. I also am the mawdest possessor of a motor car. If Miss Rawbnsn will allow me the privilege of taking her, my car is at her service.

OCTAVIUS. Violet!

General constraint.

ANN [*subduedly*] Come, mother: we must leave them to talk over the arrangements. I must see to my travelling kit.

Mrs Whitefield looks bewildered; but Ánn draws her discreetly away; and they disappear round the corner towards the house.

HECTOR. I think I may go so far as to say that I can depend on Miss Rawbnsn's consent.

Continued embarrassment.

OCTAVIUS. I'm afraid we must leave Violet behind. There are circumstances which make it impossible for her to come on such an expedition.

HECTOR [*amused and not at all convinced*] Too American, eh? Must the young lady have a chaperone?

OCTAVIUS. It's not that, Malone—at least not altogether.

HECTOR. Indeed! May I ask what other objection applies?

TANNER [*impatiently*] Oh, tell him, tell him. We shall never be able to keep the secret unless everybody knows what it is. Mr Malone: if you go to Nice with Violet, you go with another man's wife. She is married.

HECTOR [*thunderstruck*] You dont tell me so!

TANNER. We do. In confidence.

RAMSDEN [*with an air of importance, lest Malone should suspect a misalliance*] Her marriage has not yet been made known: she desires that it shall not be mentioned for the present.

HECTOR. I shall respect the lady's wishes. Would it be indiscreet to ask who her husband is, in case I should have an opportunity of cawnsulting him about this trip?

TANNER. We dont know who he is.

HECTOR [*retiring into his shell in a very marked manner*] In that case, I have no more to say.

They become more embarrassed than ever.

OCTAVIUS. You must think this very strange.

HECTOR. A little singular. Pardn mee for saying so.

RAMSDEN [*half apologetic, half huffy*] The young lady was married secretly; and her husband has forbidden her, it seems, to declare his name. It is only right to tell you, since you are interested in Miss—er—in Violet.

OCTAVIUS [*sympathetically*] I hope this is not a disappointment to you.

HECTOR [*softened, coming out of his shell again*] Well: it is a blow. I can hardly understand how a man can leave his wife in such a position. Surely it's not custoMary. It's not manly. It's not considerate.

OCTAVIUS. We feel that, as you may imagine, pretty deeply.

RAMSDEN [*testily*] It is some young fool who has not enough experience to know what mystifications of this kind lead to.

HECTOR [*with strong symptoms of moral repugnance*] I hope so. A man need be very young and pretty foolish too to be excused for such conduct. You take a very lenient view, Mr Ramsden. Too lenient to my mind. Surely marriage should ennoble a man.

TANNER [*sardonically*] Ha!

HECTOR. Am I to gather from that cacchination that you dont agree with me, Mr Tanner?

TANNER [*drily*] Get married and try. You may find it delightful for a while: you certainly wont find it ennobling. The greatest common measure of a man and a woman is not necessarily greater than the man's single measure.

HECTOR. Well, we think in America that a woman's morl number is higher than a man's, and that the purer nature of a woman lifts a man right out of himself, and makes him better than he was.

OCTAVIUS [*with conviction*] So it does.

TANNER. No wonder American women prefer to live in Europe! It's more comfortable than standing all their lives on an altar to be worshipped. Anyhow, Violet's husband has not been ennobled. So whats to be done?

HECTOR [*shaking his head*] I cant dismiss that man's cawnduct as lightly as you do, Mr Tanner. However, I'll say no more. Whoever he is, he's Miss Rawbnsn's husband; and I should be glad for her sake to think better of him.

OCTAVIUS [*touched; for he divines a secret sorrow*] I'm very sorry, Malone. Very sorry.

HECTOR [*gratefully*] Youre a good fellow, Rawbnsn. Thank you.

TANNER. Talk about something else. Violet's coming from the house.

HECTOR. I should esteem it a very great favor, gentlemen, if you would take the opportunity to let me have a few words with the lady alone. I shall have to cry off this trip; and it's rather a dullicate—

RAMSDEN [*glad to escape*] Say no more. Come, Tanner. Come, Tavy. [*He strolls away into the park with Octavius and Tanner, past the motor car*].

Violet comes down the avenue to Hector.

VIOLET. Are they looking?

HECTOR. No.

She kisses him.

VIOLET. Have you been telling lies for my sake?

HECTOR. Lying! Lying hardly describes it. I overdo it. I get carried away in an ecstasy of mendacity. Violet: I wish youd let me own up.

VIOLET [*instantly becoming serious and resolute*] No, no, Hector: you promised me not to.

HECTOR. I'll keep my prawmis until you release me from it. But I feel mean, lying to those men, and denying my wife. Just dastardly.

VIOLET. I wish your father were not so unreasonable.

HECTOR. He's not unreasonable. He's right from his point of view. He has a prejudice against the English middle class.

VIOLET. It's too ridiculous. You know how I dislike saying such things to you, Hector; but if I were to—oh, well, no matter.

HECTOR. I know. If you were to marry the son of an English manufacturer of awffice furniture, your friends would consider it a misalliance. And here's my silly old dad, who is the biggest awffice furniture man in the world, would shew me the door for marrying the most perfect lady in England merely because she has no handle to her name. Of course it's just absurd. But I tell you, Violet, I dont like deceiving him. I feel as if I was stealing his money. Why wont you let me own up?

VIOLET. We cant afford it. You can be as romantic as you please about love, Hector; but you mustnt be romantic about money.

HECTOR [*divided between his uxoriousness and his habitual elevation of moral sentiment*] Thats very English. [*Appealing to her impulsively*] Violet: dad's bound to find us out someday.

VIOLET. Oh yes, later on of course. But dont lets go over this every time we meet, dear. You promised—

HECTOR. All right, all right, I—

VIOLET [*not to be silenced*] It is I and not you who suffer by this concealment; and as to facing a struggle and poverty and all that sort of thing I simply will not do it. It's too silly.

HECTOR. You shall not. I'll sort of borrow the money from my dad until I get on my own feet; and then I can own up and pay up at the same time.

VIOLET [*alarmed and indignant*] Do you mean to work? Do you want to spoil our marriage?

HECTOR. Well, I dont mean to let marriage spoil my character. Your friend Mr Tanner has got the laugh on me a bit already about that; and—

VIOLET. The beast! I hate Jack Tanner.

HECTOR [*magnanimously*] Oh, h e e's all right: he only needs the love of a good woman to ennoble him. Besides, he's proposed a motoring trip to Nice; and I'm going to take you.

VIOLET. How jolly!

HECTOR. Yes; but how are we going to manage? You see, theyve warned me off going with you, so to speak. Theyve told me in cawnfidnce that youre married. Thats just the most overwhelming cawnfidnce Ive ever been honored with.

Tanner returns with Straker, who goes to his car.

TANNER. Your car is a great success, Mr Malone. Your engineer is showing it off to Mr Ramsden.

HECTOR [*eagerly—forgetting himself*] Lets

come, Vi.

VIOLET [coldly, warning him with her eyes] I beg your pardon, Mr. Malone: I did not quite catch—

HECTOR [recollecting himself] I ask to be allowed the pleasure of shewing you my little American steam car, Miss Rawbnsn.

VIOLET. I shall be very pleased. [They go off together down the avenue].

TANNER. About this trip, Straker.

STRAKER [preoccupied with the car] Yes?

TANNER. Miss Whitefield is supposed to be coming with me.

STRAKER. So I gather.

TANNER. Mr Robinson is to be one of the party.

STRAKER. Yes.

TANNER. Well, if you can manage so as to be a good deal occupied with me, and leave Mr Robinson a good deal occupied with Miss Whitefield, he will be deeply grateful to you.

STRAKER [looking round at him] Evidently.

TANNER. "Evidently"! Your grandfather would have simply winked.

STRAKER. My grandfather would have touched his at.

TANNER. And I should have given your good nice respectful grandfather a sovereign.

STRAKER. Five shillins, more likely. [He leaves the car and approaches Tanner]. What about the lady's views?

TANNER. She is just as willing to be left to Mr Robinson as Mr Robinson is to be left to her. [Straker looks at his principal with cool scepticism; then turns to the car whistling his favorite air]. Stop that aggravating noise. What do you mean by it? [Straker calmly resumes the melody and finishes it. Tanner politely hears it out before he again addresses Straker, this time with elaborate seriousness]. Enry: I have ever been a warm advocate of the spread of music among the masses; but I object to your obliging the company whenever Miss Whitefield's name is mentioned. You did it this morning, too.

STRAKER [obstinately] It's not a bit o use. Mr Robinson may as well give it up first as last.

TANNER. Why?

STRAKER. Garn! You know why. Course it's not my business; but you neednt start kiddin me about it.

TANNER. I am not kidding. I dont know why.

STRAKER [cheerfully sulky] Oh, very well.

All right. It aint my business.

TANNER [impressively] I trust, Enry, that, as between employer and engineer, I shall always know how to keep my proper distance, and not intrude my private affairs on you. Even our business arrangements are subject to the approval of your Trade Union. But dont abuse your advantages. Let me remind you that Voltaire said that what was too silly to be said could be sung.

STRAKER. It wasnt Voltaire: it was Bow Mar Shay.

TANNER. I stand corrected: Beaumarchais of course. Now you seem to think that what is too delicate to be said can be whistled. Unfortunately your whistling, though melodious, is unintelligible. Come! theres nobody listening: neither my genteel relatives nor the secretary of your confounded Union. As man to man, Enry, why do you think that my friend has no chance with Miss Whitefield?

STRAKER. Cause she's arter summun else.

TANNER. Bosh! who else?

STRAKER. You.

TANNER. Me!!!

STRAKER. Mean to tell me you didnt know? Oh, come, Mr Tanner!

TANNER [in fierce earnest] Are you playing the fool, or do you mean it?

STRAKER [with a flash of temper] I'm not playin no fool. [More coolly] Why, it's as plain as the nose on your face. If you aint spotted that, you dont know much about these sort of things. [Serene again] Ex-cuse me, you know, Mr Tanner; but you asked me as man to man; and I told you as man to man.

TANNER [wildly appealing to the heavens] Then I—I am the bee, the spider, the marked down victim, the destined prey.

STRAKER. I dunno about the bee and the spider. But the marked down victim, thats what you are and no mistake; and a jolly good job for you, too, I should say.

TANNER [momentously] Henry Straker: the golden moment of your life has arrived.

STRAKER. What d'y'mean?

TANNER. That record to Biskra.

STRAKER [eagerly] Yes?

TANNER. Break it.

STRAKER [rising to the height of his destiny] D'y'mean it?

TANNER. I do.

STRAKER. When?

TANNER. Now. Is that machine ready to

start?

STRAKER [*quailing*] But you cant—

TANNER [*cutting him short by getting into the car*] Off we go. First to the bank for money; then to my rooms for my kit; then to your rooms for your kit; then break the record from London to Dover or Folkestone; then across the channel and away like mad to Marseilles, Gibraltar, Genoa, any port from which we can sail to a Mahometan country where men are protected from women.

STRAKER. Garn! youre kiddin.

TANNER [*resolutely*] Stay behind then. If you wont come I'll do it alone. [*He starts the motor*].

STRAKER [*running after him*] Here! Mister! arf a mo! steady on! [*he scrambles in as the car plunges forward*].

ACT III

Evening in the Sierra Nevada. Rolling slopes of brown with olive trees instead of apple trees in the cultivated patches, and occasional prickly pears instead of gorse and bracken in the wilds. Higher up, tall stone peaks and precipices, all handsome and distinguished. No wild nature here: rather a most aristocratic mountain landscape made by a fastidious artist-creator. No vulgar profusion of vegetation: even a touch of aridity in the frequent patches of stones: Spanish magnificence and Spanish economy everywhere.

Not very far north of a spot at which the high road over one of the passes crosses a tunnel on the railway from Malaga to Granada, is one of the mountain amphitheatres of the Sierra. Looking at it from the wide end of the horse-shoe, one sees, a little to the right, in the face of the cliff, a romantic cave which is really an abandoned quarry, and towards the left a little hill, commanding a view of the road, which skirts the amphitheatre on the left, maintaining its higher level on embankments and an occasional stone arch. On the hill, watching the road, is a man who is either a Spaniard or a Scotchman. Probably a Spaniard, since he wears the dress of a Spanish goatherd and seems at home in the Sierra Nevada, but very like a Scotchman for all that. In the hollow, on the slope leading to the quarry-cave, are about a dozen men who, as they recline at their ease round a heap of smouldering white ashes of dead leaf and brushwood, have an air of being conscious of themselves as picturesque scoundrels honoring the Sierra by using it as an effective pictorial background. As a matter of artistic fact they are not picturesque; and the mountains tolerate them as lions tolerate lice. An English policeman or Poor Law Guardian would recognize them as a selected band of tramps and ablebodied paupers.

This description of them is not wholly contemptuous. Whoever has intelligently observed the tramp, or visited the ablebodied ward of a workhouse, will admit that our social failures are not all drunkards and weaklings. Some of them are men who do not fit the class they were born into. Precisely the same qualities that make the educated gentleman an artist may make an uneducated manual laborer an ablebodied pauper. There are men who fall helplessly into the workhouse because they are good for nothing; but there are also men who are there because they are strong-minded enough to disregard the social convention (obviously not a disinterested one on the part of the ratepayer) which bids a man live by heavy and badly paid drudgery when he has the alternative of walking into the workhouse, announcing himself as a destitute person, and legally compelling the Guardians to feed, clothe, and house him better than he could feed, clothe, and house himself without great exertion. When a man who is born a poet refuses a stool in a stockbroker's office, and starves in a garret, spunging on a poor landlady or on his friends and relatives sooner than work against his grain; or when a lady, because she is a lady, will face any extremity of parasitic dependence rather than take a situation as cook or parlormaid, we make large allowances for them. To such allowances the ablebodied pauper, and his nomadic variant the tramp, are equally entitled.

Further, the imaginative man, if his life is to be tolerable to him, must have leisure to tell himself stories, and a position which lends itself to imaginative decoration. The ranks of unskilled labor offer no such positions. We misuse our laborers horribly; and when a man refuses to be misused, we have no right to say that he is refusing honest work. Let us be frank in this matter before we go on with our play; so that we may enjoy it without hypocrisy. If we were reasoning, far-sighted people, four fifths of us would go straight to the Guardians for relief, and knock the whole social system to pieces with most beneficial reconstructive results. The reason we do not do this is because we work like bees or ants, by instinct or habit, not reasoning about the matter at all. Therefore when a man comes along who can and does reason, and who, applying the Kantian test to his conduct, can truly say to us, If every-

body did as I do, the world would be compelled to reform itself industrially, and abolish slavery and squalor, which exist only because everybody does as you do, let us honor that man and seriously consider the advisability of following his example. Such a man is the ablebodied, ableminded pauper. Were he a gentleman doing his best to get a pension or a sinecure instead of sweeping a crossing, nobody would blame him for deciding that so long as the alternative lies between living mainly at the expense of the community and allowing the community to live mainly at his, it would be folly to accept what is to him personally the greater of the two evils.

We may therefore contemplate the tramps of the Sierra without prejudice, admitting cheerfully that our objects—briefly, to be gentlemen of fortune—are much the same as theirs, and the difference in our position and methods merely accidental. One or two of them, perhaps, it would be wiser to kill without malice in a friendly and frank manner; for there are bipeds, just as there are quadrupeds, who are too dangerous to be left unchained and unmuzzled; and these cannot fairly expect to have other men's lives wasted in the work of watching them. But as society has not the courage to kill them, and, when it catches them, simply wreaks on them some superstitious expiatory rites of torture and degradation, and then lets them loose with heightened qualifications for mischief, it is just as well that they are at large in the Sierra, and in the hands of a chief who looks as if he might possibly, on provocation, order them to be shot.

This chief, seated in the centre of the group on a squared block of stone from the quarry, is a tall strong man, with a striking cockatoo nose, glossy black hair, pointed beard, upturned moustache, and a Mephistophelean affectation which is fairly imposing, perhaps because the scenery admits of a larger swagger than Piccadilly, perhaps because of a certain sentimentality in the man which gives him that touch of grace which alone can excuse deliberate picturesqueness. His eyes and mouth are by no means rascally; he has a fine voice and a ready wit; and whether he is really the strongest man in the party or not, he looks it. He is certainly the best fed, the best dressed, and the best trained. The fact that he speaks English is not unexpected, in spite of the Spanish landscape; for with the exception of one man who might be guessed as a bullfighter ruined by drink, and one unmistakable Frenchman, they are all cockney or American; therefore, in a land of cloaks and sombreros, they mostly wear seedy overcoats, woollen mufflers, hard hemispherical hats, and dirty brown gloves. Only a very few dress after their leader, whose broad sombrero with a cock's feather in the band, and voluminous cloak descending to his high boots, are as un-English as possible. None of them are armed; and the ungloved ones keep their hands in their pockets because it is their national belief that it must be dangerously cold in the open air with the night coming on. (It is as warm an evening as any reasonable man could desire).

Except the bullfighting inebriate there is only one person in the company who looks more than, say, thirty-three. He is a small man with reddish whiskers, weak eyes, and the anxious look of a small tradesman in difficulties. He wears the only tall hat visible: it shines in the sunset with the sticky glow of some sixpenny patent hat reviver, often applied and constantly tending to produce a worse state of the original surface than the ruin it was applied to remedy. He has a collar and cuffs of celluloid; and his brown Chesterfield overcoat, with velvet collar, is still presentable. He is pre-eminently the respectable man of the party, and is certainly over forty, possibly over fifty. He is the corner man on the leader's right, opposite three men in scarlet ties on his left. One of these three is the Frenchman. Of the remaining two, who are both English, one is argumentative, solemn, and obstinate; the other rowdy and mischievous.

The chief, with a magnificent fling of the end of his cloak across his left shoulder, rises to address them. The applause which greets him shews that he is a favorite orator.

THE CHIEF. Friends and fellow brigands. I have a proposal to make to this meeting. We have now spent three evenings in discussing the question Have Anarchists or Social-Democrats the most personal courage? We have gone into the principles of Anarchism and Social-Democracy at great length. The cause of Anarchy has been ably represented by our one Anarchist, who doesnt know what Anarchism means [laughter]—

THE ANARCHIST [rising] A point of order, Mendoza—

MENDOZA [forcibly] No, by thunder: your last point of order took half an hour. Besides, Anarchists dont believe in order.

THE ANARCHIST [mild, polite but persistent: he is, in fact, the respectable looking elderly man in the celluloid collar and cuffs] That is a vulgar error. I can prove—

MENDOZA. Order, order.

THE OTHERS [*shouting*] Order, order. Sit down. Chair! Shut up.

The Anarchist is suppressed.

MENDOZA. On the other hand we have three Social-Democrats among us. They are not on speaking terms; and they have put before us three distinct and incompatible views of Social-Democracy.

THE THREE MEN IN SCARLET TIES. 1. Mr Chairman, I protest. A personal explanation. 2. It's a lie. I never said so. Be fair, Mendoza. 3. Je demande la parole. C'est absolument faux. C'est faux! faux!! faux!!! Assas-s-s-sin!!!!!!

MENDOZA. Order, order.

THE OTHERS. Order, order, order! Chair!

The Social-Democrats are suppressed.

MENDOZA. Now, we tolerate all opinions here. But after all, comrades, the vast majority of us are neither Anarchists nor Socialists, but gentlemen and Christians.

THE MAJORITY [*shouting assent*] Hear, hear! So we are. Right.

THE ROWDY SOCIAL-DEMOCRAT [*smarting under suppression*] You aint no Christian. Youre a Sheeny, you are.

MENDOZA [*with crushing magnanimity*] My friend: *I* am an exception to all rules. It is true that I have the honor to be a Jew; and when the Zionists need a leader to reassemble our race on its historic soil of Palestine, Mendoza will not be the last to volunteer [*sympathetic applause—Hear, Hear, &c.*]. But I am not a slave to any superstition. I have swallowed all the formulas, even that of Socialism; though, in a sense, once a Socialist, always a Socialist.

THE SOCIAL-DEMOCRATS. Hear, hear!

MENDOZA. But I am well aware that the ordinary man—even the ordinary brigand, who can scarcely be called an ordinary man [Hear, hear!]—is not a philosopher. Common sense is good enough for him; and in our business affairs common sense is good enough for me. Well, what is our business here in the Sierra Nevada, chosen by the Moors as the fairest spot in Spain? Is it to discuss abstruse questions of political economy? No: it is to hold up motor cars and secure a more equitable distribution of wealth.

THE SULKY SOCIAL-DEMOCRAT. All made by labor, mind you.

MENDOZA [*urbanely*] Undoubtedly. All made by labor, and on its way to be squandered by wealthy vagabonds in the dens of vice that disfigure the sunny shores of the Mediterranean. We intercept that wealth. We restore it to circulation among the class that produced it and that chiefly needs it: the working class. We do this at the risk of our lives and liberties, by the exercise of the virtues of courage, endurance, foresight, and abstinence—especially abstinence. I myself have eaten nothing but prickly pears and broiled rabbit for three days.

THE SULKY SOCIAL-DEMOCRAT [*stubbornly*] No more aint we.

MENDOZA [*indignantly*] Have I taken more than my share?

THE SULKY SOCIAL-DEMOCRAT [*unmoved*] Why should you?

THE ANARCHIST. Why should he not? To each according to his needs: from each according to his means.

THE FRENCHMAN [*shaking his fist at the Anarchist*] Fumiste!

MENDOZA [*diplomatically*] I agree with both of you.

THE GENUINELY ENGLISH BRIGANDS. Hear, hear! Bravo Mendoza!

MENDOZA. What I say is, let us treat one another as gentlemen, and strive to excel in personal courage only when we take the field.

THE ROWDY SOCIAL-DEMOCRAT [*derisively*] Shikespear.

A whistle comes from the goatherd on the hill. He springs up and points excitedly forward along the road to the north.

THE GOATHERD. Automobile! Automobile! [*He rushes down the hill and joins the rest, who all scramble to their feet*].

MENDOZA [*in ringing tones*] To arms! Who has the gun?

THE SULKY SOCIAL-DEMOCRAT [*handing a rifle to Mendoza*] Here.

MENDOZA. Have the nails been strewn in the road?

THE ROWDY SOCIAL-DEMOCRAT. Two ahnces of em.

MENDOZA. Good! [*To the Frenchman*] With me, Duval. If the nails fail, puncture their tires with a bullet. [*He gives the rifle to Duval, who follows him up the hill. Mendoza produces an opera glass. The others hurry across to the road and disappear to the north*].

MENDOZA [*on the hill, using his glass*] Two only, a capitalist and his chauffeur. They look English.

DUVAL. Angliche! Aoh yess. Cochons!

[*Handling the rifle*] Faut tirer, n'est-ce-pas?

MENDOZA. No: the nails have gone home. Their tire is down: they stop.

DUVAL [*shouting to the others*] Fondez sur eux, nom de Dieu!

MENDOZA [*rebuking his excitement*] Du calme, Duval: keep your hair on. They take it quietly. Let us descend and receive them.

Mendoza descends, passing behind the fire and coming forward, whilst Tanner and Straker, in their motoring goggles, leather coats, and caps, are led in from the road by the brigands.

TANNER. Is this the gentleman you describe as your boss? Does he speak English?

THE ROWDY SOCIAL-DEMOCRAT. Course e daz. Y' downt suppowz we Hinglishmen luts ahrselves be bossed by a bloomin Spenniard, do you?

MENDOZA [*with dignity*] Allow me to introduce myself: Mendoza, President of the League of the Sierra! [*Posing loftily*] I am a brigand: I live by robbing the rich.

TANNER [*promptly*] I am a gentleman: I live by robbing the poor. Shake hands.

THE ENGLISH SOCIAL-DEMOCRATS. Hear, hear! *General laughter and good humor. Tanner and Mendoza shake hands. The Brigands drop into their former places.*

STRAKER. Ere! where do I come in?

TANNER [*introducing*] My friend and chauffeur.

THE SULKY SOCIAL-DEMOCRAT [*suspiciously*] Well, which is he? friend or show-foor? It makes all the difference, you know.

MENDOZA [*explaining*] We should expect ransom for a friend. A professional chauffeur is free of the mountains. He even takes a trifling percentage of his principal's ransom if he will honor us by accepting it.

STRAKER. I see. Just to encourage me to come this way again. Well, I'll think about it.

DUVAL [*impulsively rushing across to Straker*] Mon frère! [*He embraces him rapturously and kisses him on both cheeks*].

STRAKER [*disgusted*] Ere, git aht: dont be silly. Who are you, pray?

DUVAL. Duval: Social-Democrat.

STRAKER. Oh, youre a Social-Democrat, are you?

THE ANARCHIST. He means that he has sold out to the parliamentary humbugs and the bourgeoisie. Compromise! that is his faith.

DUVAL [*furiously*] I understand what he say.

He say Bourgeois. He say Compromise. Jamais de la vie! Misérable menteur—

STRAKER. See here, Captain Mendoza, ah mach o this sort o thing do you put up with here? Are we avin a pleasure trip in the mountains, or are we at a Socialist meetin?

THE MAJORITY. Hear, hear! Shut up. Chuck it. Sit down, &c. &c. [*The Social-Democrats and the Anarchist are hustled into the background. Straker, after superintending this proceeding with satisfaction, places himself on Mendoza's left, Tanner being on his right*].

MENDOZA. Can we offer you anything? Broiled rabbit and prickly pears—

TANNER. Thank you: we have dined.

MENDOZA [*to his followers*] Gentlemen: business is over for the day. Go as you please until morning.

The Brigands disperse into groups lazily. Some go into the cave. Others sit down or lie down to sleep in the open. A few produce a pack of cards and move off towards the road; for it is now starlight; and they know that motor cars have lamps which can be turned to account for lighting a card party.

STRAKER [*calling after them*] Dont none of you go fooling with that car, d'ye hear?

MENDOZA. No fear, Monsieur le Chauffeur. The first one we captured cured us of that.

STRAKER [*interested*] What did it do?

MENDOZA. It carried three brave comrades of ours, who did not know how to stop it, into Granada, and capsized them opposite the police station. Since then we never touch one without sending for the chauffeur. Shall we chat at our ease?

TANNER. By all means.

Tanner, Mendoza, and Straker sit down on the turf by the fire. Mendoza delicately waives his presidential dignity, of which the right to sit on the squared stone block is the appanage, by sitting on the ground like his guests, and using the stone only as a support for his back.

MENDOZA. It is the custom in Spain always to put off business until tomorrow. In fact, you have arrived out of office hours. However, if you would prefer to settle the question of ransom at once, I am at your service.

TANNER. Tomorrow will do for me. I am rich enough to pay anything in reason.

MENDOZA [*respectfully, much struck by this admission*] You are a remarkable man, sir. Our guests usually describe themselves as miserably poor.

TANNER. Pooh! Miserably poor people dont own motor cars.

MENDOZA. Precisely what we say to them.

TANNER. Treat us well: we shall not prove ungrateful.

STRAKER. No prickly pears and broiled rabbits, you know. Dont tell me you cant do us a bit better than that if you like.

MENDOZA. Wine, kids, milk, cheese, and bread can be procured for ready money.

STRAKER [graciously] Now youre talkin.

TANNER. Are you all Socialists here, may I ask?

MENDOZA [repudiating this humiliating misconception] Oh no, no, no: nothing of the kind, I assure you. We naturally have modern views as to the injustice of the existing distribution of wealth: otherwise we should lose our self-respect. But nothing that you could take exception to, except two or three faddists.

TANNER. I had no intention of suggesting anything discreditable. In fact, I am a bit of a Socialist myself.

STRAKER [drily] Most rich men are, I notice.

MENDOZA. Quite so. It has reached us, I admit. It is in the air of the century.

STRAKER. Socialism must be lookin up a bit if your chaps are taking to it.

MENDOZA. That is true, sir. A movement which is confined to philosophers and honest men can never exercise any real political influence: there are too few of them. Until a movement shews itself capable of spreading among brigands, it can never hope for a political majority.

TANNER. But are your brigands any less honest than ordinary citizens?

MENDOZA. Sir: I will be frank with you. Brigandage is abnormal. Abnormal professions attract two classes: those who are not good enough for ordinary bourgeois life and those who are too good for it. We are dregs and scum, sir: the dregs very filthy, the scum very superior.

STRAKER. Take care! some o the dregs'll hear you.

MENDOZA. It does not matter: each brigand thinks himself scum, and likes to hear the others called dregs.

TANNER. Come! you are a wit. [Mendoza inclines his head, flattered]. May one ask you a blunt question?

MENDOZA. As blunt as you please.

TANNER. How does it pay a man of your talent to shepherd such a flock as this on broiled rabbit and prickly pears? I have seen men less gifted, and I'll swear less honest, supping at the Savoy on foie gras and champagne.

MENDOZA. Pooh! they have all had their turn at the broiled rabbit, just as I shall have my turn at the Savoy. Indeed, I have had a turn there already—as waiter.

TANNER. A waiter! You astonish me!

MENDOZA [reflectively] Yes: I, Mendoza of the Sierra, was a waiter. Hence, perhaps, my cosmopolitanism. [With sudden intensity] Shall I tell you the story of my life?

STRAKER [apprehensively] If it aint too long, old chap—

TANNER [interrupting him] Tsh-sh: you are a Philistine, Henry: you have no romance in you. [To Mendoza] You interest me extremely, President. Never mind Henry: he can go to sleep.

MENDOZA. The woman I loved—

STRAKER. Oh, this is a love story, is it? Right you are. Go on: I was only afraid you were going to talk about yourself.

MENDOZA. Myself! I have thrown myself away for her sake: that is why I am here. No matter: I count the world well lost for her. She had, I pledge you my word, the most magnificent head of hair I ever saw. She had humor; she had intellect; she could cook to perfection; and her highly strung temperament made her uncertain, incalculable, variable, capricious, cruel, in a word, enchanting.

STRAKER. A six shillin novel sort o woman, all but the cookin. Er name was Lady Gladys Plantagenet, wasnt it?

MENDOZA. No, sir: she was not an earl's daughter. Photography, reproduced by the half-tone process, has made me familiar with the appearance of the daughters of the English peerage; and I can honestly say that I would have sold the lot, faces, dowries, clothes, titles, and all, for a smile from this woman. Yet she was a woman of the people, a worker: otherwise—let me reciprocate your bluntness—I should have scorned her.

TANNER. Very properly. And did she respond to your love?

MENDOZA. Should I be here if she did? She objected to marry a Jew.

TANNER. On religious grounds?

MENDOZA. No: she was a freethinker. She said that every Jew considers in his heart that English people are dirty in their habits.

TANNER [*surprised*] Dirty!

MENDOZA. It shewed her extraordinary knowledge of the world; for it is undoubtedly true. Our elaborate sanitary code makes us unduly contemptuous of the Gentile.

TANNER. Did you ever hear that, Henry?

STRAKER. Ive heard my sister say so. She was cook in a Jewish family once.

MENDOZA. I could not deny it; neither could I eradicate the impression it made on her mind. I could have got round any other objection; but no woman can stand a suspicion of indelicacy as to her person. My entreaties were in vain: she always retorted that she wasnt good enough for me, and recommended me to marry an accursed barmaid named Rebecca Lazarus, whom I loathed. I talked of suicide: she offered me a packet of beetle poison to do it with. I hinted at murder: she went into hysterics; and as I am a living man I went to America so that she might sleep without dreaming that I was stealing upstairs to cut her throat. In America I went out west and fell in with a man who was wanted by the police for holding up trains. It was he who had the idea of holding up motor cars in the South of Europe: a welcome idea to a desperate and disappointed man. He gave me some valuable introductions to capitalists of the right sort. I formed a syndicate; and the present enterprise is the result. I became leader, as the Jew always becomes leader, by his brains and imagination. But with all my pride of race I would give everything I possess to be an Englishman. I am like a boy: I cut her name on the trees and her initials on the sod. When I am alone I lie down and tear my wretched hair and cry Louisa—

STRAKER [*startled*] Louisa!

MENDOZA. It is her name—Louisa—Louisa Straker—

TANNER. Straker!

STRAKER [*scrambling up on his knees most indignantly*] Look here: Louisa Straker is my sister, see? Wot do you mean by gassin about her like this? Wotshe got to do with you?

MENDOZA. A dramatic coincidence! You are Enry, her favorite brother!

STRAKER. Oo are you callin Enry? What call have you to take a liberty with my name or with hers? For two pins I'd punch your fat edd, so I would.

MENDOZA [*with grandiose calm*] If I let you do it, will you promise to brag of it afterwards to her? She will be reminded of her Mendoza: that is all I desire.

TANNER. This is genuine devotion, Henry. You should respect it.

STRAKER [*fiercely*] Funk, more likely.

MENDOZA [*springing to his feet*] Funk! Young man: I come of a famous family of fighters; and as your sister well knows, you would have as much chance against me as a perambulator against your motor car.

STRAKER [*secretly daunted, but rising from his knees with an air of reckless pugnacity*] I aint afraid of you. With your Louisa! Louisa! Miss Straker is good enough for you, I should think.

MENDOZA. I wish you could persuade her to think so.

STRAKER [*exasperated*] Here—

TANNER [*rising quickly and interposing*] Oh come, Henry: even if you could fight the President you cant fight the whole League of the Sierra. Sit down again and be friendly. A cat may look at a king; and even a President of brigands may look at your sister. All this family pride is really very old fashioned.

STRAKER [*subdued, but grumbling*] Let him look at her. But wot does he mean by makin out that she ever looked at im? [*Reluctantly resuming his couch on the turf*] Ear him talk, one ud think she was keepin company with him. [*He turns his back on them and composes himself to sleep*].

MENDOZA [*to Tanner, becoming more confidential as he finds himself virtually alone with a sympathetic listener in the still starlight of the mountains; for all the rest are asleep by this time*] It was just so with her, sir. Her intellect reached forward into the twentieth century: her social prejudices and family affections reached back into the dark ages. Ah, sir, how the words of Shakespear seem to fit every crisis in our emotions!

I loved Louisa: 40,000 brothers
Could not with all their quantity of love
Make up my sum.

And so on. I forget the rest. Call it madness if you will—infatuation. I am an able man, a strong man: in ten years I should have owned a first-class hotel. I met her; and— you see!—I am a brigand, an outcast. Even Shakespear cannot do justice to what I feel for Louisa. Let me read you some lines that I have written about her myself. However slight their literary merit may be, they express what I feel better than any casual words can. [*He produces a packet of hotel bills scrawled with manuscript, and kneels at the fire to decipher them, poking it with a stick to make it glow*].

TANNER [*slapping him rudely on the shoulder*] Put them in the fire, President.

MENDOZA [*startled*] Eh?

TANNER. You are sacrificing your career to a monomania.

MENDOZA. I know it.

TANNER. No you dont. No man would commit such a crime against himself if he really knew what he was doing. How can you look round at these august hills, look up at this divine sky, taste this finely tempered air, and then talk like a literary hack on a second floor in Bloomsbury?

MENDOZA [*shaking his head*] The Sierra is no better than Bloomsbury when once the novelty has worn off. Besides, these mountains make you dream of women—of women with magnificent hair.

TANNER. Of Louisa, in short. They will not make me dream of women, my friend: I am heartwhole.

MENDOZA. Do not boast until morning, sir. This is a strange country for dreams.

TANNER. Well, we shall see. Goodnight. [*He lies down and composes himself to sleep*].

Mendoza, with a sigh, follows his example; and for a few moments there is peace in the Sierra. Then Mendoza sits up suddenly and says pleadingly to Tanner—

MENDOZA. Just allow me to read a few lines before you go to sleep. I should really like your opinion of them.

TANNER [*drowsily*] Go on. I am listening.

MENDOZA. I saw thee first on Whitsun week
      Louisa, Louisa—

TANNER [*rousing himself*] My dear President, Louisa is a very pretty name; but it really doesnt rhyme well to Whitsun week.

MENDOZA. Of course not. Louisa is not the rhyme, but the refrain.

TANNER [*subsiding*] Ah, the refrain. I beg your pardon. Go on.

MENDOZA. Perhaps you do not care for that one: I think you will like this better. [*He recites, in rich soft tones, and in slow time*]
Louisa, I love thee.
I love thee, Louisa.

Louisa, Louisa, Louisa, I love thee.
One name and one phrase make my music,
      Louisa.
Louisa, Louisa, Louisa, I love thee.
Mendoza thy lover,
Thy lover, Mendoza,
Mendoza adoringly lives for Louisa.
Theres nothing but that in the world for
      Mendoza.
Louisa, Louisa, Mendoza adores thee.

[*Affected*] There is no merit in producing beautiful lines upon such a name. Louisa is an exquisite name, is it not?

TANNER [*all but asleep, responds with a faint groan*].

MENDOZA. O wert thou, Louisa,
      The wife of Mendoza,
Mendoza's Louisa, Louisa Mendoza,
How blest were the life of Louisa's Mendoza!
How painless his longing of love for Louisa!

That is real poetry—from the heart—from the heart of hearts. Dont you think it will move her?

No answer.

[*Resignedly*] Asleep, as usual. Doggrel to all the world: heavenly music to me! Idiot that I am to wear my heart on my sleeve! [*He composes himself to sleep, murmuring*] Louisa, I love thee; I love thee, Louisa; Louisa, Louisa, Louisa, I—

Straker snores; rolls over on his side; and relapses into sleep. Stillness settles on the Sierra; and the darkness deepens. The fire has again buried itself in white ash and ceased to glow. The peaks shew unfathomably dark against the starry firmament; but now the stars dim and vanish; and the sky seems to steal away out of the universe. Instead of the Sierra there is nothing: omnipresent nothing. No sky, no peaks, no light, no sound, no time nor space, utter void. Then somewhere the beginning of a pallor, and with it a faint throbbing buzz as of a ghostly violoncello palpitating on the same note endlessly. A couple of ghostly violins presently take advantage of this bass

and therewith the pallor reveals a man in the void, an incorporeal but visible man, seated, absurdly enough, on nothing. For a moment he raises his head as the music passes him by. Then, with a heavy sigh, he droops in utter dejection; and the violins, discouraged, retrace their melody in despair and at last give it up, extinguished by wailings from uncanny wind instruments, thus:

It is all very odd. One recognizes the Mozartian strain; and on this hint, and by the aid of certain sparkles of violet light in the pallor, the man's costume explains itself as that of a Spanish nobleman of the XV-XVI century. Don Juan, of course; but where? why? how? Besides, in the brief lifting of his face, now hidden by his hat brim, there was a curious suggestion of Tanner. A more critical, fastidious, handsome face, paler and colder, without Tanner's impetuous credulity and enthusiasm, and without a touch of his modern plutocratic vulgarity, but still a resemblance, even an identity. The name too: Don Juan Tenorio, John Tanner. Where on earth—or elsewhere—have we got to from the XX century and the Sierra?

Another pallor in the void, this time not violet, but a disagreeable smoky yellow. With it, the whisper of a ghostly clarionet turning this tune into infinite sadness:

The yellowish pallor moves: there is an old crone wandering in the void, bent and toothless; draped, as well as one can guess, in the coarse brown frock of some religious order. She wanders and wanders in her slow hopeless way, much as a wasp flies in its rapid busy way, until she blunders against the thing she seeks: companionship. With a sob of relief the poor old creature clutches at the presence of the man and addresses him in her dry unlovely voice, which can still express pride and resolution as well as suffering.

THE OLD WOMAN. Excuse me; but I am so lonely; and this place is so awful.

DON JUAN. A new comer?

THE OLD WOMAN. Yes: I suppose I died this morning. I confessed; I had extreme unction; I was in bed with my family about me and my eyes fixed on the cross. Then it grew dark; and when the light came back it was this light by which I walk seeing nothing. I have wandered for hours in horrible loneliness.

DON JUAN [*sighing*] Ah! you have not yet lost the sense of time. One soon does, in eternity.

THE OLD WOMAN. Where are we?

DON JUAN. In hell.

THE OLD WOMAN [*proudly*] Hell! I in hell! How dare you?

DON JUAN [*unimpressed*] Why not, Señora?

THE OLD WOMAN. You do not know to whom you are speaking. I am a lady, and a faithful daughter of the Church.

DON JUAN. I do not doubt it.

THE OLD WOMAN. But how then can I be in hell? Purgatory, perhaps: I have not been perfect: who has? But hell! oh, you are lying.

DON JUAN. Hell, Señora, I assure you; hell at its best: that is, its most solitary—though perhaps you would prefer company.

THE OLD WOMAN. But I have sincerely repented; I have confessed—

DON JUAN. How much?

THE OLD WOMAN. More sins than I really committed. I loved confession.

DON JUAN. Ah, that is perhaps as bad as confessing too little. At all events, Señora, whether by oversight or intention, you are certainly damned, like myself; and there is nothing for it now but to make the best of it.

THE OLD WOMAN [*indignantly*] Oh! and I might have been so much wickeder! All my good deeds wasted! It is unjust.

DON JUAN. No: you were fully and clearly warned. For your bad deeds, vicarious atonement, mercy without justice. For your good deeds, justice without mercy. We have many good people here.

THE OLD WOMAN. Were you a good man?

DON JUAN. I was a murderer.

THE OLD WOMAN. A murderer! Oh, how dare they send me to herd with murderers! I was not as bad as that: I was a good woman. There is some mistake: where can I have it set right?

DON JUAN. I do not know whether mistakes can be corrected here. Probably they will not admit a mistake even if they have made one.

THE OLD WOMAN. But whom can I ask?

DON JUAN. I should ask the Devil, Señora: he understands the ways of this place, which is more than I ever could.

THE OLD WOMAN. The Devil! *I* speak to the Devil!

DON JUAN. In hell, Señora, the Devil is the leader of the best society.

THE OLD WOMAN. I tell you, wretch, I know

I am not in hell.

DON JUAN. How do you know?

THE OLD WOMAN. Because I feel no pain.

DON JUAN. Oh, then there is no mistake: you are intentionally damned.

THE OLD WOMAN. Why do you say that?

DON JUAN. Because hell, Señora, is a place for the wicked. The wicked are quite comfortable in it: it was made for them. You tell me you feel no pain. I conclude you are one of those for whom Hell exists.

THE OLD WOMAN. Do you feel no pain?

DON JUAN. I am not one of the wicked, Señora; therefore it bores me, bores me beyond description, beyond belief.

THE OLD WOMAN. Not one of the wicked! You said you were a murderer.

DON JUAN. Only a duel. I ran my sword through an old man who was trying to run his through me.

THE OLD WOMAN. If you were a gentleman, that was not a murder.

DON JUAN. The old man called it murder, because he was, he said, defending his daughter's honor. By this he meant that because I foolishly fell in love with her and told her so, she screamed; and he tried to assassinate me after calling me insulting names.

THE OLD WOMAN. You were like all men. Libertines and murderers all, all, all!

DON JUAN. And yet we meet here, dear lady.

THE OLD WOMAN. Listen to me. My father was slain by just such a wretch as you, in just such a duel, for just such a cause. I screamed: it was my duty. My father drew on my assailant: his honor demanded it. He fell: that was the reward of honor. I am here: in hell, you tell me: that is the reward of duty. Is there justice in heaven?

DON JUAN. No; but there is justice in hell: heaven is far above such idle human personalities. You will be welcome in hell, Señora. Hell is the home of honor, duty, justice, and the rest of the seven deadly virtues. All the wickedness on earth is done in their name: where else but in hell should they have their reward? Have I not told you that the truly damned are those who are happy in hell?

THE OLD WOMAN. And are you happy here?

DON JUAN [springing to his feet] No; and that is the enigma on which I ponder in darkness. Why am I here? I, who repudiated all duty, trampled honor underfoot, and laughed at justice.

THE OLD WOMAN. Oh, what do I care why you are here? Why am I here? I, who sacrificed all my inclinations to womanly virtue and propriety!

DON JUAN. Patience, lady: you will be perfectly happy and at home here. As saith the poet, "Hell is a city much like Seville."

THE OLD WOMAN. Happy! here! where I am nothing! where I am nobody!

DON JUAN. Not at all: you are a lady; and wherever ladies are is hell. Do not be surprised or terrified: you will find everything here that a lady can desire, including devils who will serve you from sheer love of servitude, and magnify your importance for the sake of dignifying their service—the best of servants.

THE OLD WOMAN. My servants will be devils!

DON JUAN. Have you ever had servants who were not devils?

THE OLD WOMAN. Never: they were devils, perfect devils, all of them. But that is only a manner of speaking. I thought you meant that my servants here would be real devils.

DON JUAN. No more real devils than you will be a real lady. Nothing is real here. That is the horror of damnation.

THE OLD WOMAN. Oh, this is all madness. This is worse than fire and the worm.

DON JUAN. For you, perhaps, there are consolations. For instance: how old were you when you changed from time to eternity?

THE OLD WOMAN. Do not ask me how old I was—as if I were a thing of the past. I am 77.

DON JUAN. A ripe age, Señora. But in hell old age is not tolerated. It is too real. Here we worship Love and Beauty. Our souls being entirely damned, we cultivate our hearts. As a lady of 77, you would not have a single acquaintance in hell.

THE OLD WOMAN. How can I help my age, man?

DON JUAN. You forget that you have left your age behind you in the realm of time. You are no more 77 than you are 7 or 17 or 27.

THE OLD WOMAN. Nonsense!

DON JUAN. Consider, Señora: was not this true even when you lived on earth? When you were 70, were you really older underneath your wrinkles and your grey hairs than when you were 30?

THE OLD WOMAN. No, younger: at 30 I was

a fool. But of what use is it to feel younger and look older?

DON JUAN, You see, Señora, the look was only an illusion. Your wrinkles lied, just as the plump smooth skin of many a stupid girl of 17, with heavy spirits and decrepit ideas, lies about h e r age? Well, here we have no bodies: we see each other as bodies only because we learnt to think about one another under that aspect when we were alive; and we still think in that way, knowing no other. But we can appear to one another at what age we choose. You have but to will any of your old looks back, and back they will come.

THE OLD WOMAN. It cannot be true.

DON JUAN. Try.

THE OLD WOMAN. Seventeen!

DON JUAN. Stop. Before you decide, I had better tell you that these things are a matter of fashion. Occasionally we have a rage for 17; but it does not last long. Just at present the fashionable age is 40—or say 37; but there are signs of a change. If you were at all good-looking at 27, I should suggest your trying that, and setting a new fashion.

THE OLD WOMAN. I do not believe a word you are saying. However, 27 be it. [*Whisk! the old woman becomes a young one, magnificently attired, and so handsome that in the radiance into which her dull yellow halo has suddenly lightened one might almost mistake her for Ann Whitefield*].

DON JUAN. Doña Ana de Ulloa!

ANA. What? You know me!

DON JUAN. And you forget me!

ANA. I cannot see your face. [*He raises his hat*]. Don Juan Tenorio! Monster! You who slew my father! even here you pursue me.

DON JUAN. I protest I do not pursue you. Allow me to withdraw [*going*].

ANA [*seizing his arm*] You shall not leave me alone in this dreadful place.

DON JUAN. Provided my staying be not interpreted as pursuit.

ANA [*releasing him*] You may well wonder how I can endure your presence. My dear, dear father!

DON JUAN. Would you like to see him?

ANA. My father h e r e ! ! !

DON JUAN. No: he is in heaven.

ANA. I knew it. My noble father! He is looking down on us now. What must he feel to see his daughter in this place, and in conversation with his murderer!

DON JUAN. By the way, if we should meet him—

ANA. How can we meet him? He is in heaven.

DON JUAN. He condescends to look in upon us here from time to time. Heaven bores him. So let me warn you that if you meet him he will be mortally offended if you speak of me as his murderer! He maintains that he was a much better swordsman than I, and that if his foot had not slipped he would have killed me. No doubt he is right: I was not a good fencer. I never dispute the point; so we are excellent friends.

ANA. It is no dishonor to a soldier to be proud of his skill in arms.

DON JUAN. You would rather not meet him, probably.

ANA. How dare you say that?

DON JUAN. Oh, that is the usual feeling here. You may remember that on earth—though of course we never confessed it—the death of anyone we knew, even those we liked best, was always mingled with a certain satisfaction at being finally done with them.

ANA. Monster! Never, never.

DON JUAN [*placidly*] I see you recognize the feeling. Yes: a funeral was always a festivity in black, especially the funeral of a relative. At all events, family ties are rarely kept up here. Your father is quite accustomed to this: he will not expect any devotion from you.

ANA. Wretch: I wore mourning for him all my life.

DON JUAN. Yes: it became you. But a life of mourning is one thing: an eternity of it quite another. Besides, here you are as dead as he. Can anything be more ridiculous than one dead person mourning for another? Do not look shocked, my dear Ana; and do not be alarmed: there is plenty of humbug in hell (indeed there is hardly anything else); but the humbug of death and age and change is dropped because here we are all dead and all eternal. You will pick up our ways soon.

ANA. And will all the men call me their dear Ana?

DON JUAN. No. That was a slip of the tongue. I beg your pardon.

ANA [*almost tenderly*] Juan: did you really love me when you behaved so disgracefully to me?

DON JUAN [*impatiently*] Oh, I beg you not to begin talking about love. Here they talk of nothing else but love: its beauty, its holiness, its spirituality, its devil knows what!—excuse me; but it does so bore me. They dont know what theyre talking about: I do. They think they have achieved the perfection of love because they have no bodies. Sheer imaginative debauchery! Faugh!

ANA. Has even death failed to refine your soul, Juan? Has the terrible judgment of which my father's statue was the minister taught you no reverence?

DON JUAN. How is that very flattering statue, by the way? Does it still come to supper with naughty people and cast them into this bottomless pit?

ANA. It has been a great expense to me. The boys in the monastery school would not let it alone: the mischievous ones broke it; and the studious ones wrote their names on it. Three new noses in two years, and fingers without end. I had to leave it to its fate at last; and now I fear it is shockingly mutilated. My poor father!

DON JUAN. Hush! Listen! [*Two great chords rolling on syncopated waves of sound break forth: D minor and its dominant: a sound of dreadful joy to all musicians*]. Ha! Mozart's statue music. It is your father. You had better disappear until I prepare him. [*She vanishes*].

From the void comes a living statue of white marble, designed to represent a majestic old man. But he waives his majesty with infinite grace; walks with a feather-like step; and makes every wrinkle in his war worn visage brim over with holiday joyousness. To his sculptor he owes a perfectly trained figure, which he carries erect and trim; and the ends of his moustache curl up, elastic as watchsprings, giving him an air which, but for its Spanish dignity, would be called jaunty. He is on the pleasantest terms with Don Juan. His voice, save for a much more distinguished intonation, is so like the voice of Roebuck Ramsden that it calls attention to the fact that they are not unlike one another in spite of their very different fashions of shaving.

DON JUAN. Ah, here you are, my friend. Why dont you learn to sing the splendid music Mozart has written for you?

THE STATUE. Unluckily he has written it for a bass voice. Mine is a counter tenor. Well: have you repented yet?

DON JUAN. I have too much consideration for you to repent, Don Gonzalo. If I did, you would have no excuse for coming from heaven to argue with me.

THE STATUE. True. Remain obdurate, my boy. I wish I had killed you, as I should have

done but for an accident. Then I should have come here; and you would have had a statue and a reputation for piety to live up to. Any news?

DON JUAN. Yes: your daughter is dead.

THE STATUE [*puzzled*] My daughter? [*Recollecting*] Oh! the one you were taken with. Let me see: what was her name?

DON JUAN. Ana.

THE STATUE. To be sure: Ana. A goodlooking girl, if I recollect aright. Have you warned Whatshisname? her husband.

DON JUAN. My friend Ottavio? No: I have not seen him since Ana arrived.

Ana comes indignantly to light.

ANA. What does this mean? Ottavio here and y o u r friend! And you, father, have forgotten my name. You are indeed turned to stone.

THE STATUE. My dear: I am so much more admired in marble than I ever was in my own person that I have retained the shape the sculptor gave me. He was one of the first men of his day: you must acknowledge that.

ANA. Father! Vanity! personal vanity! from you!

THE STATUE. Ah, you outlived that weakness, my daughter: you must be nearly 80 by this time. I was cut off (by an accident) in my 64th year, and am considerably your junior in consequence. Besides, my child, in this place, what our libertine friend here would call the farce of parental wisdom is dropped. Regard me, I beg, as a fellow creature, not as a father.

ANA. You speak as this villain speaks.

THE STATUE. Juan is a sound thinker, Ana. A bad fencer, but a sound thinker.

ANA [*horror creeping upon her*] I begin to understand. These are devils, mocking me. I had better pray.

THE STATUE [*consoling her*] No, no, no, my child: do not pray. If you do, you will throw away the main advantage of this place. Written over the gate here are the words "Leave every hope behind, ye who enter." Only think what a relief that is! For what is hope? A form of moral responsibility. Here there is no hope, and consequently no duty, no work, nothing to be gained by praying, nothing to be lost by doing what you like. Hell, in short, is a place where you have nothing to do but amuse yourself. [*Don Juan sighs deeply*]. You sigh, friend Juan; but if you dwelt in heaven, as I do, you would realize your advantages.

DON JUAN. You are in good spirits today, Commander. You are positively brilliant. What is the matter?

THE STATUE. I have come to a momentous decision, my boy. But first, where is our friend the Devil? I must consult him in the matter. And Ana would like to make his acquaintance, no doubt.

ANA. You are preparing some torment for me.

DON JUAN. All that is superstition, Ana. Reassure yourself. Remember: the devil is not so black as he is painted.

THE STATUE. Let us give him a call.

At the wave of the statue's hand the great chords roll out again; but this time Mozart's music gets grotesquely adulterated with Gounod's. A scarlet halo begins to glow; and into it the Devil rises, very Mephistophelean, and not at all unlike Mendoza, though not so interesting. He looks older; is getting prematurely bald; and, in spite of an effusion of goodnature and friendliness, is peevish and sensitive when his advances are not reciprocated. He does not inspire much confidence in his powers of hard work or endurance, and is, on the whole, a disagreeably self-indulgent looking person; but he is clever and plausible, though perceptibly less well bred than the two other men, and enormously less vital than the woman.

THE DEVIL [*heartily*] Have I the pleasure of again receiving a visit from the illustrious Commander of Calatrava? [*Coldly*] Don Juan, your servant. [*Politely*] And a strange lady? My respects, Señora.

ANA. Are you—

THE DEVIL [*bowing*] Lucifer, at your service.

ANA. I shall go mad.

THE DEVIL [*gallantly*] Ah, Señora, do not be anxious. You come to us from earth, full of the prejudices and terrors of that priest-ridden place. You have heard me ill spoken of; and yet, believe me, I have hosts of friends there.

ANA. Yes: you reign in their hearts.

THE DEVIL [*shaking his head*] You flatter me, Señora; but you are mistaken. It is true that the world cannot get on without me; but it never gives me credit for that: in its heart it mistrusts and hates me. Its sympathies are all with misery, with poverty, with starvation of the body and of the heart. I call on it to sympathize with joy, with love, with happiness, with beauty—

DON JUAN [*nauseated*] Excuse me: I am

going. You know I cannot stand this.

THE DEVIL [*angrily*] Yes: I know that you are no friend of mine.

THE STATUE. What harm is he doing you, Juan? It seems to me that he was talking excellent sense when you interrupted him.

THE DEVIL [*warmly patting the statue's hand*] Thank you, my friend: thank you. You have always understood me: he has always disparaged and avoided me.

DON JUAN. I have treated you with perfect courtesy.

THE DEVIL. Courtesy! What is courtesy? I care nothing for mere courtesy. Give me warmth of heart, true sincerity, the bond of sympathy with love and joy—

DON JUAN. You are making me ill.

THE DEVIL. There! [*Appealing to the statue*] You hear, sir! Oh, by what irony of fate was this cold selfish egotist sent to my kingdom, and you taken to the icy mansions of the sky!

THE STATUE. I cant complain. I was a hypocrite; and it served me right to be sent to heaven.

THE DEVIL. Why, sir, do you not join us, and leave a sphere for which your temperament is too sympathetic, your heart too warm, your capacity for enjoyment too generous?

THE STATUE. I have this day resolved to do so. In future, excellent Son of the Morning, I am yours. I have left heaven for ever.

THE DEVIL [*again touching the marble hand*] Ah, what an honor! what a triumph for our cause! Thank you, thank you. And now, my friend—I may call you so at last—could you not persuade him to take the place you have left vacant above?

THE STATUE [*shaking his head*] I cannot conscientiously recommend anybody with whom I am on friendly terms to deliberately make himself dull and uncomfortable.

THE DEVIL. Of course not; but are you sure he would be uncomfortable? Of course you know best: you brought him here originally; and we had the greatest hopes of him. His sentiments were in the best taste of our best people. You remember how he sang? [*He begins to sing in a nasal operatic baritone, tremulous from an eternity of misuse in the French manner*]

Vivan le femmine!
Viva il buon vino!

THE STATUE [*taking up the tune an octave higher in his counter tenor*]

Sostegno e gloria
D'umanità.

THE DEVIL. Precisely. Well, he never sings for us now.

DON JUAN. Do you complain of that? Hell is full of musical amateurs: music is the brandy of the damned. May not one lost soul be permitted to abstain?

THE DEVIL. You dare blaspheme against the sublimest of the arts!

DON JUAN [*with cold disgust*]You talk like a hysterical woman fawning on a fiddler.

THE DEVIL. I am not angry. I merely pity you. You have no soul; and you are unconscious of all that you lose. Now you, Señor Commander, are a born musician. How well you sing! Mozart would be delighted if he were still here: but he moped and went to heaven. Curious how these clever men, whom you would have supposed born to be popular here, have turned out social failures, like Don Juan!

DON JUAN. I am really very sorry to be a social failure.

THE DEVIL. Not that we dont admire your intellect, you know. We do. But I look at the matter from your own point of view. You dont get on with us. The place doesnt suit you. The truth is, you have—I wont say no heart; for we know that beneath all your affected cynicism you have a warm one—

DON JUAN [*shrinking*] Don't, please dont.

THE DEVIL [*nettled*] Well, youve no capacity for enjoyment. Will that satisfy you?

DON JUAN. It is a somewhat less insufferable form of cant than the other. But if youll allow me, I'll take refuge, as usual, in solitude.

THE DEVIL. Why not take refuge in heaven? Thats the proper place for you. [*To Ana*] Come, Señora! could you not persuade him for his own good to try change of air?

ANA. But can he go to heaven if he wants to?

THE DEVIL. Whats to prevent him?

ANA. Can anybody—can *I* go to heaven if I want to?

THE DEVIL [*rather contemptuously*] Certainly, if your taste lies that way.

ANA. But why doesn't everybody go to heaven, then?

THE STATUE [*chuckling*] *I* can tell you that, my dear. It's because heaven is the most angelically dull place in all creation: thats why.

THE DEVIL. His Excellency the Commander puts it with military bluntness; but the strain of living in heaven is intolerable. There is a notion that I was turned out of it; but as a matter of fact nothing could have induced me to stay there. I simply left it and organized this place.

THE STATUE. I dont wonder at it. Nobody could stand an eternity of heaven.

THE DEVIL. Oh, it suits some people. Let us be just, Commander: it is a question of temperament. I dont admire the heavenly temperament: I dont understand it: I dont know that I particularly want to understand it; but it takes all sorts to make a universe. There is no accounting for tastes: there are people who like it. I think Don Juan would like it.

DON JUAN. But—pardon my frankness—could you really go back there if you desired to; or are the grapes sour?

THE DEVIL. Back there! I often go back there. Have you never read the book of Job? Have you any canonical authority for assuming that there is any barrier between our circle and the other one?

ANA. But surely there is a great gulf fixed.

THE DEVIL. Dear lady: a parable must not be taken literally. The gulf is the difference between the angelic and the diabolic temperament. What more impassable gulf could you have? Think of what you have seen on earth. There is no physical gulf between the philosopher's class room and the bull ring; but the bull fighters do not come to the class room for all that. Have you ever been in the country where I have the largest following? England. There they have great racecourses, and also concert rooms where they play the classical compositions of His Excellency's friend Mozart. Those who go to the racecourses can stay away from them and go to the classical concerts instead if they like: there is no law against it; for Englishmen never will be slaves: they are free to do whatever the Government and public opinion allow them to do. And the classical concert is admitted to be a higher, more cultivated, poetic, intellectual, ennobling place than the racecourse. But do the lovers of racing desert their sport and flock to the concert room? Not they. They would suffer there all the weariness the Commander has suffered in heaven. There is the great gulf of the parable between the two places. A mere physical gulf they could bridge; or at least I could bridge it for them (the earth is full of Devil's Bridges); but the gulf of dislike is impassable and eternal. And that is the only gulf that separates my friends here from those who are invidiously called the blest.

ANA. I shall go to heaven at once.

THE STATUE. My child: one word of warning first. Let me complete my friend Lucifer's similitude of the classical concert. At every one of those concerts in England you will find rows of weary people who are there, not because they really like classical music, but because they think they ought to like it. Well, there is the same thing in heaven. A number of people sit there in glory, not because they are happy, but because they think they owe it to their position to be in heaven. They are almost all English.

THE DEVIL. Yes: the Southerners give it up and join me just as you have done. But the English really do not seem to know when they are thoroughly miserable. An Englishman thinks he is moral when he is only uncomfortable.

THE STATUE. In short, my daughter, if you go to Heaven without being naturally qualified for it, you will not enjoy yourself there.

ANA. And who dares say that I am not naturally qualified for it? The most distinguished princes of the Church have never questioned it. I owe it to myself to leave this place at once.

THE DEVIL [offended] As you please, Señora. I should have expected better taste from you.

ANA. Father: I shall expect you to come with me. You cannot stay here. What will people say?

THE STATUE. People! Why, the best people are here—princes of the church and all. So few go to Heaven, and so many come here, that the blest, once called a heavenly host, are a continually dwindling minority. The saints, the fathers, the elect of long ago are the cranks, the faddists, the outsiders of today.

THE DEVIL. It is true. From the beginning of my career I knew that I should win in the long run by sheer weight of public opinion, in spite of the long campaign of misrepresentation and calumny against me. At bottom the universe is a constitutional one; and with such a majority as mine I cannot be kept permanently out of office.

DON JUAN. I think, Ana, you had better stay here.

ANA [jealously] You do not want me to go with you.

DON JUAN. Surely you do not want to enter Heaven in the company of a reprobate like me.

ANA. All souls are equally precious. You repent, do you not?

DON JUAN. My dear Ana, you are silly. Do you suppose heaven is like earth, where people persuade themselves that what is done can be undone by repentance; that what is spoken can be unspoken by withdrawing it; that what is true can be annihilated by a general agreement to give it the lie? No: heaven is the home of the masters of reality: that is why I am going thither.

ANA. Thank you: I am going to heaven for happiness. I have had quite enough of reality on earth.

DON JUAN. Then you must stay here; for hell is the home of the unreal and of the seekers for happiness. It is the only refuge from heaven, which is, as I tell you, the home of the masters of reality, and from earth, which is the home of the slaves of reality. The earth is a nursery in which men and women play at being heroes and heroines, saints and sinners; but they are dragged down from their fool's paradise by their bodies: hunger and cold and thirst, age and decay and disease, death above all, makes them slaves of reality: thrice a day meals must be eaten and digested: thrice a century a new generation must be engendered: ages of faith, of romance, and of science are all driven at last to have but one prayer "Make me a healthy animal." But here you escape this tyranny of the flesh; for here you are not an animal at all: you are a ghost, an appearance, an illusion, a convention, deathless, ageless: in a word, bodiless. There are no social questions here, no political questions, no religious questions, best of all, perhaps, no sanitary questions. Here you call your appearance beauty, your emotions love, your sentiments heroism, your aspirations virtue, just as you did on earth; but here there are no hard facts to contradict you, no ironic contrast of your needs with your pretensions, no human comedy, nothing but a perpetual romance, a universal melodrama. As our German friend put it in his poem, "the poetically nonsensical here is good sense; and the Eternal

Feminine draws us ever upward and on"—without getting us a step farther. And yet you want to leave this paradise!

ANA. But if hell be so beautiful as this, how glorious must heaven be!

The Devil, the Statue, and Don Juan all begin to speak at once in violent protest; then stop, abashed.

DON JUAN. I beg your pardon.

THE DEVIL. Not at all. I interrupted you.

THE STATUE. You were going to say something.

DON JUAN. After you, gentlemen.

THE DEVIL [*to Don Juan*] You have been so eloquent on the advantages of my dominions that I leave you to do equal justice to the drawbacks of the alternative establishment.

DON JUAN. In heaven, as I picture it, dear lady, you live and work instead of playing and pretending. You face things as they are; you escape nothing but glamor; and your steadfastness and your peril are your glory. If the play still goes on here and on earth, and all the world is a stage, heaven is at least behind the scenes. But heaven cannot be described by metaphor. Thither I shall go presently, because there I hope to escape at last from lies and from the tedious, vulgar pursuit of happiness, to spend my eons in contemplation—

THE STATUE. Ugh!

DON JUAN. Señor Commander: I do not blame your disgust: a picture gallery is a dull place for a blind man. But even as you enjoy the contemplation of such romantic mirages as beauty and pleasure; so would I enjoy the contemplation of that which interests me above all things: namely, Life: the force that ever strives to attain greater power of contemplating itself. What made this brain of mine, do you think? Not the need to move my limbs; for a rat with half my brains moves as well as I. Not merely the need to do, but the need to know what I do, lest in my blind efforts to live I should be slaying myself.

THE STATUE. You would have slain yourself in your blind efforts to fence but for my foot slipping, my friend.

DON JUAN. Audacious ribald: your laughter will finish in hideous boredom before morning.

THE STATUE. Ha ha! Do you remember how I frightened you when I said something like that to you from my pedestal in Seville? It sounds rather flat without my trombones.

DON JUAN. They tell me it generally sounds flat with them, Commander.

ANA. Oh, do not interrupt with these frivolities, father. Is there nothing in heaven but contemplation, Juan.

DON JUAN. In the heaven I seek, no other joy. But there is the work of helping Life in its struggle upward. Think of how it wastes and scatters itself, how it raises up obstacles to itself and destroys itself in its ignorance and blindness. It needs a brain, this irresistible force, lest in its ignorance it should resist itself. What a piece of work is man! says the poet. Yes; but what a blunderer! Here is the highest miracle of organization yet attained by life, the most intensely alive thing that exists, the most conscious of all the organisms; and yet, how wretched are his brains! Stupidity made sordid and cruel by the realities learnt from toil and poverty: Imagination resolved to starve sooner than face these realities, piling up illusions to hide them, and calling itself cleverness, genius! And each accusing the other of its own defect: Stupidity accusing Imagination of folly, and Imagination accusing Stupidity of ignorance: whereas, alas! Stupidity has all the knowledge, and Imagination all the intelligence.

THE DEVIL. And a pretty kettle of fish they make of it between them. Did I not say, when I was arranging that affair of Faust's, that all Man's reason has done for him is to make him beastlier than any beast. One splendid body is worth the brains of a hundred dyspeptic, flatulent philosophers.

DON JUAN. You forget that brainless magnificence of body has been tried. Things immeasurably greater than man in every respect but brain have existed and perished. The megatherium, the icthyosaurus have paced the earth with seven-league steps and hidden the day with cloud vast wings. Where are they now? Fossils in museums, and so few and imperfect at that, that a knuckle bone or a tooth of one of them is prized beyond the lives of a thousand soldiers. These things lived and wanted to live; but for lack of brains they did not know how to carry out their purpose, and so destroyed themselves.

THE DEVIL. And is Man any the less destroying himself for all this boasted brain of his? Have you walked up and down upon the earth lately? I have; and I have examined Man's wonderful inventions. And I tell you that in the arts of life man invents nothing; but in the arts of death he outdoes Nature herself, and produces by chemistry and machinery all the slaughter of plague, pestilence, and famine. The peasant I tempt today eats and drinks what was eaten and drunk by the peasants of ten thousand years ago; and the house he lives in has not altered as much in a thousand centuries as the fashion of a lady's bonnet in a score of weeks. But when he goes out to slay, he carries a marvel of mechanism that lets loose at the touch of his finger all the hidden molecular energies, and leaves the javelin, the arrow, the blowpipe of his fathers far behind. In the arts of peace Man is a bungler. I have seen his cotton factories and the like, with machinery that a greedy dog could have invented if it had wanted money instead of food. I know his clumsy typewriters and bungling locomotives and tedious bicycles: they are toys compared to the Maxim gun, the submarine torpedo boat. There is nothing in Man's industrial machinery but his greed and sloth: his heart is in his weapons. This marvellous force of Life of which you boast is a force of Death: Man measures his strength by his destructiveness. What is his religion? An excuse for hating m e. What is his law? An excuse for hanging y o u. What is his morality? Gentility! an excuse for consuming without producing. What is his art? An excuse for gloating over pictures of slaughter. What are his politics? Either the worship of a despot because a despot can kill, or parliamentary cock-fighting. I spent an evening lately in a certain celebrated legislature, and heard the pot lecturing the kettle for its blackness, and ministers answering questions. When I left I chalked up on the door the old nursery-saying "Ask no questions and you will be told no lies." I bought a sixpenny family magazine, and found it full of pictures of young men shooting and stabbing one another. I saw a man die: he was a London bricklayer's laborer with seven children. He left seventeen pounds club money; and his wife spent it all on his funeral and went into the workhouse with the children next day. She would not have spent sevenpence on her children's schooling: the law had to force her to let them be taught gratuitously; but on death she spent all she had. Their imagination glows, their energies rise up at the idea of death, these people: they love it; and the more horrible it is the more they enjoy it. Hell is a place far above their comprehension: they derive their notion of it from two of the greatest fools that ever lived, an Italian and an Englishman. The Italian described it as a place of mud, frost, filth, fire, and venomous serpents: all torture. This ass, when he was not lying about me, was maundering about some woman whom he saw once in the street. The Englishman described me as being expelled from Heaven by cannons and gunpowder; and to this day every Briton believes that the whole of his silly story is in the Bible. What else he says I do not know; for it is all in a long poem which neither I nor anyone else ever succeeded in wading through. It is the same in everything. The highest form of literature is the tragedy, a play in which everybody is murdered at the end. In the old chronicles you read of earthquakes and pestilences, and are told that these shewed the power and majesty of God and the littleness of Man. Nowadays the chronicles describe battles. In a battle two bodies of men shoot at one another with bullets and explosive shells until one body runs away, when the others chase the fugitives on horseback and cut them to pieces as they fly. And this, the chronicle concludes, shews the greatness and majesty of empires, and the littleness of the vanquished. Over such battles the people run about the streets yelling with delight, and egg their governments on to spend hundreds of millions of money in the slaughter, whilst the strongest Ministers dare not spend an extra penny in the pound against the poverty and pestilence through which they themselves daily walk. I could give you a thousand instances; but they all come to the same thing: the power that governs the earth is not the power of Life but the power of Death; and the inner need that has nerved Life to the effort of organizing itself into the human being is not the need for higher life but for a more efficient engine of destruction. The plague, the famine, the earthquake, the tempest were too spasmodic in their action; the tiger and crocodile were too easily satiated and not cruel enough: something more constantly, more ruthlessly, more ingeniously destructive was needed; and that something was Man, the inventor of the rack, the stake, the gallows, the electric chair; of sword and gun and poison gas; above all, of justice, duty, patriotism, and all the other isms by which even those who are clever enough to be humanely disposed are persuaded to become the most destructive of all the destroyers.

DON JUAN. Pshaw! all this is old. Your weak side, my diabolic friend, is that you have always been a gull: you take Man at his own valuation. Nothing would flatter him more than your opinion of him. He loves to think of himself as bold and bad. He is neither one nor the other: he is only a coward. Call him tyrant, murderer, pirate, bully; and he will adore you, and swagger about with the consciousness of having the blood of the old sea kings in his veins. Call him liar and thief; and he will only take an action against you for libel. But call him coward; and he will go mad with rage: he will face death to outface that stinging truth. Man gives every reason for his conduct save one, every excuse for his crimes save one, every plea for his safety save one; and that one is his cowardice. Yet all his civilization is founded on his cowardice, on his abject tameness, which he calls his respectability. There are limits to what a mule or an ass will stand; but Man will suffer himself to be degraded until his vileness becomes so loathsome to his oppressors that they themselves are forced to reform it.

THE DEVIL. Precisely. And these are the creatures in whom you discover what you call a Life Force!

DON JUAN. Yes; for now comes the most surprising part of the whole business.

THE STATUE. Whats that?

DON JUAN. Why, that you can make any of these cowards brave by simply putting an idea into his head.

THE STATUE. Stuff! As an old soldier I admit the cowardice: it's as universal as sea sickness, and matters just as little. But that about putting an idea into a man's head is stuff and nonsense. In a battle all you need to make you fight is a little hot blood and the knowledge that it's more dangerous to lose than to win.

DON JUAN. That is perhaps why battles are so useless. But men never really overcome fear until they imagine they are fighting to further a universal purpose—fighting for an idea, as they call it. Why was the Crusader braver than the pirate? Because he fought, not for himself, but for the Cross. What force was it that met him with a valor as reckless as his own? The force of men who fought, not for themselves, but for Islam. They took Spain from us, though we were fighting for our very hearths and homes; but when we, too, fought for that mighty idea, a Catholic Church, we swept them back to Africa.

THE DEVIL [ironically] What! you a Catholic, Señor Don Juan! A devotee! My congratulations.

THE STATUE [seriously] Come, come! as a soldier, I can listen to nothing against the Church.

DON JUAN. Have no fear, Commander: this idea of a Catholic Church will survive Islam, will survive the Cross, will survive even that vulgar pageant of incompetent schoolboyish gladiators which you call the Army.

THE STATUE. Juan: you will force me to call you to account for this.

DON JUAN. Useless: I cannot fence. Every idea for which Man will die will be a Catholic idea. When the Spaniard learns at last that he is no better than the Saracen, and his prophet no better than Mahomet, he will arise, more Catholic than ever, and die on a barricade across the filthy slum he starves in, for universal liberty and equality.

THE STATUE. Bosh!

DON JUAN. What you call bosh is the only thing men dare die for. Later on, Liberty will not be Catholic enough: men will die for human perfection, to which they will sacrifice all their liberty gladly.

THE DEVIL. Ay: they will never be at a loss for an excuse for killing one another.

DON JUAN. What of that? It is not death that matters, but the fear of death. It is not killing and dying that degrades us, but base living, and accepting the wages and profits of degradation. Better ten dead men than one live slave or his master. Men shall yet rise up, father against son and brother against brother, and kill one another for the great Catholic idea of abolishing slavery.

THE DEVIL. Yes, when the Liberty and Equality of which you prate shall have made free white Christians cheaper in the labor market than black heathen slaves sold by auction at the block.

DON JUAN. Never fear! the white laborer shall have his turn too. But I am not now defending the illusory forms the great ideas take. I am giving you examples of the fact that this creature Man, who in his own selfish affairs is a coward to the backbone, will fight for an idea like a hero. He may be abject as a citizen; but he is dangerous as a fanatic. He can only be enslaved whilst he is spiritually weak enough to listen to reason. I tell you, gentlemen, if you can shew a man a piece of what he now calls God's work to do, and what he will later on call by many new names, you can make him entirely reckless of the consequences to himself personally.

ANA. Yes: he shirks all his responsibilities, and leaves his wife to grapple with them.

THE STATUE. Well said, daughter. Do not let him talk you out of your common sense.

THE DEVIL. Alas! Señor Commander, now that we have got on to the subject of Woman, he will talk more than ever. However, I confess it is for me the one supremely interesting subject.

DON JUAN. To a woman, Señora, man's duties and responsibilities begin and end with the task of getting bread for her children. To her, Man is only a means to the end of getting children and rearing them.

ANA. Is that your idea of a woman's mind? I call it cynical and disgusting animalism.

DON JUAN. Pardon me, Ana: I said nothing about a woman's whole mind. I spoke of her view of Man as a separate sex. It is no more cynical than her view of herself as above all things a Mother. Sexually, Woman is Nature's contrivance for perpetuating its highest achievement. Sexually, Man is Woman's contrivance for fulfilling Nature's behest in the most economical way. She knows by instinct that far back in the evolutional process she invented him, differentiated him, created him in order to produce something better than the single-sexed process can produce. Whilst he fulfils the purpose for which she made him, he is welcome to his dreams, his follies, his ideals, his heroisms, provided that the keystone of them all is the worship of woman, of motherhood, of the family, of the hearth. But how rash and dangerous it was to invent a separate creature whose sole function was her own impregnation! For mark what has happened. First, Man has multiplied on her hands until there are as many men as women; so that she has been unable to employ for her purposes more than a fraction of the immense energy she has left at his disposal by saving him the exhausting labor of gestation. This superfluous energy has gone to his brain and

to his muscle. He has become too strong to be controlled by her bodily, and too imaginative and mentally vigorous to be content with mere self-reproduction. He has created civilization without consulting her, taking her domestic labor for granted as the foundation of it.

ANA. That is true, at all events.

THE DEVIL. Yes: and this civilization! what is it, after all?

DON JUAN. After all, an excellent peg to hang your cynical commonplaces on; but before all, it is an attempt on Man's part to make himself something more than the mere instrument of Woman's purpose. So far, the result of Life's continual effort not only to maintain itself, but to achieve higher and higher organization and completer self-consciousness, is only, at best, a doubtful campaign between its forces and those of Death and Degeneration. The battles in this campaign are mere blunders, mostly won, like actual military battles, in spite of the commanders.

THE STATUE. That is a dig at me. No matter: go on, go on.

DON JUAN. It is a dig at a much higher power than you, Commander. Still, you must have noticed in your profession that even a stupid general can win battles when the enemy's general is a little stupider.

THE STATUE [*very seriously*] Most true, Juan, most true. Some donkeys have amazing luck.

DON JUAN. Well, the Life Force is stupid; but it is not so stupid as the forces of Death and Degeneration. Besides, these are in its pay all the time. And so Life wins, after a fashion. What mere copiousness of fecundity can supply and mere greed preserve, we possess. The survival of whatever form of civilization can produce the best rifle and the best fed riflemen is assured.

THE DEVIL. Exactly! the survival, not of the most effective means of Life but of the most effective means of Death. You always come back to my point, in spite of your wrigglings and evasions and sophistries, not to mention the intolerable length of your speeches.

DON JUAN. Oh, come! who began making long speeches? However, if I overtax your intellect, you can leave us and seek the society of love and beauty and the rest of your favorite boredoms

THE DEVIL [*much offended*] This is not fair,

Don Juan, and not civil. I am also on the intellectual plane. Nobody can appreciate it more than I do. I am arguing fairly with you, and, I think, successfully refuting you. Let us go on for another hour if you like.

DON JUAN. Good: let us.

THE STATUE. Not that I see any prospect of your coming to any point in particular, Juan. Still, since in this place, instead of merely killing time we have to kill eternity, go ahead by all means.

DON JUAN [*somewhat impatiently*] My point, you marble-headed old masterpiece, is only a step ahead of you. Are we agreed that Life is a force which has made innumerable experiments in organizing itself; that the mammoth and the man, the mouse and the megatherium, the flies and the fleas and the Fathers of the Church, are all more or less successful attempts to build up that raw force into higher and higher individuals, the ideal individual being omnipotent, omniscient, infallible, and withal completely, unilludedly self-conscious: in short, a god?

THE DEVIL. I agree, for the sake of argument.

THE STATUE. I agree, for the sake of avoiding argument.

ANA. I most emphatically disagree as regards the Fathers of the Church; and I must beg you not to drag them into the argument.

DON JUAN. I did so purely for the sake of alliteration, Ana; and I shall make no further allusion to them. And now, since we are, with that exception, agreed so far, will you not agree with me further that Life has not measured the success of its attempts at godhead by the beauty or bodily perfection of the result, since in both these respects the birds, as our friend Aristophanes long ago pointed out, are so extraordinarily superior, with their power of flight and their lovely plumage, and, may I add, the touching poetry of their loves and nestings, that it is inconceivable that Life, having once produced them, should, if love and beauty were her object, start off on another line and labor at the clumsy elephant and the hideous ape, whose grandchildren we are?

ANA. Aristophanes was a heathen; and you, Juan, I am afraid, are very little better.

THE DEVIL. You conclude, then, that Life was driving at clumsiness and ugliness?

DON JUAN. No, perverse devil that you are, a thousand times no. Life was driving at brains—at its darling object: an organ by which it can attain not only self-consciousness but self-understanding.

THE STATUE. This is metaphysics, Juan. Why the devil should—[*to The Devil*] I beg your pardon.

THE DEVIL. Pray dont mention it. I have always regarded the use of my name to secure additional emphasis as a high compliment to me. It is quite at your service, Commander.

THE STATUE. Thank you: thats very good of you. Even in heaven, I never quite got out of my old military habits of speech. What I was going to ask Juan was why Life should bother itself about getting a brain. Why should it want to understand itself? Why not be content to enjoy itself?

DON JUAN. Without a brain, Commander, you would enjoy yourself without knowing it, and so lose all the fun.

THE STATUE. True, most true. But I am quite content with brain enough to know that I'm enjoying myself. I dont want to understand why. In fact, I'd rather not. My experience is that one's pleasures dont bear thinking about.

DON JUAN. That is why intellect is so unpopular. But to Life, the force behind the Man, intellect is a necessity, because without it he blunders into death. Just as Life, after ages of struggle, evolved that wonderful bodily organ the eye, so that the living organism could see where it was going and what was coming to help or threaten it, and thus avoid a thousand dangers that formerly slew it, so it is evolving today a mind's eye that shall see, not the physical world, but the purpose of Life, and thereby enable the individual to work for that purpose instead of thwarting and baffling it by setting up shortsighted personal aims as at present. Even as it is, only one sort of man has ever been happy, has ever been universally respected among all the conflicts of interests and illusions.

THE STATUE. You mean the military man.

DON JUAN. Commander: I do n o t mean the military man. When the military man approaches, the world locks up its spoons and packs off its womankind. No: I sing, not arms and the hero, but the philosophic man: he who seeks in contemplation to discover the inner will of the world, in invention to discover the means of fulfilling that will, and in action to do that will by the so-discovered means. Of all other sorts of men I declare myself tired. They are tedious failures. When I was on earth, professors of all sorts prowled round me feeling for an unhealthy spot in me on which they could fasten. The doctors of medicine bade me consider what I must do to save my body, and offered me quack cures for imaginary diseases. I replied that I was not a hypochondriac; so they called me Ignoramus and went their way. The doctors of divinity bade me consider what I must do to save my soul; but I was not a spiritual hypochondriac any more than a bodily one, and would not trouble myself about that either; so they called me Atheist and went their way. After them came the politician who said there was only one purpose in nature, and that was to get him into parliament. I told him I did not care whether he got into parliament or not; so he called me Mugwump and went his way. Then came the romantic man, the Artist, with his love songs and his paintings and his poems; and with him I had great delight for many years, and some profit; for I cultivated my senses for his sake; and his songs taught me to hear better, his paintings to see better, and his poems to feel more deeply. But he led me at last into the worship of Woman.

ANA. Juan!

DON JUAN. Yes: I came to believe that in her voice was all the music of the song, in her face all the beauty of the painting, and in her soul all the emotion of the poem.

ANA. And you were disappointed, I suppose. Well, was it her fault that you attributed all these perfections to her?

DON JUAN. Yes, partly, For with a wonderful instinctive cunning, she kept silent and allowed me to glorify her: to mistake my own visions, thoughts, and feelings for hers. Now my friend the romantic man was often too poor or too timid to approach those women who were beautiful or refined enough to seem to realize his ideal; and so he went to his grave believing in his dream. But I was more favored by nature and circumstance. I was of noble birth and rich; and when my person did not please, my conversation flattered, though I generally found myself fortunate in both.

THE STATUE. Coxcomb!

DON JUAN. Yes; but even my coxcombry pleased. Well, I found that when I had touched a woman's imagination, she would allow me to persuade myself that she loved me; but when my suit was granted she never said "I am happy: my love is satisfied": she always said, first, "At last, the barriers are down," and second, "When will you come again?"

ANA. That is exactly what men say.

DON JUAN. I protest I never said it. But all women say it. Well, these two speeches always alarmed me; for the first meant that the lady's impulse had been solely to throw down my fortifications and gain my citadel; and the second openly announced that henceforth she regarded me as her property, and counted my time as already wholly at her disposal.

THE DEVIL. That is where your want of heart came in.

THE STATUE [shaking his head] You shouldnt repeat what a woman says, Juan.

ANA [severely] It should be sacred to you.

THE STATUE. Still, they certainly do say it. I never minded the barriers; but there was always a slight shock about the other, unless one was very hard hit indeed.

DON JUAN. Then the lady, who had been happy and idle enough before, became anxious, preoccupied with me, always intriguing, conspiring, pursuing, watching, waiting, bent wholly on making sure of her prey: I being the prey, you understand. Now this was not what I had bargained for. It may have been very proper and very natural; but it was not music, painting, poetry, and joy incarnated in a beautiful woman. I ran away from it. I ran away from it very often: in fact I became famous for running away from it.

ANA. Infamous, you mean.

DON JUAN. I did not run away from you. Do you blame me for running away from the others?

ANA. Nonsense, man. You are talking to a woman of 77 now. If you had had the chance, you would have run away from me too—if I had let you. You would not have found it so easy with me as with some of the others. If men will not be faithful to their home and their duties, they must be made to be. I daresay you all want to marry lovely incarnations of music and painting and poetry. Well, you cant have them, because they dont exist. If flesh and blood is not good enough for you you must go without: thats all. Women have to put up with flesh-and-blood husbands—and little enough of that too, sometimes; and you will have to put up with flesh-and-blood wives. [*The Devil looks dubious. The Statue makes a wry face*]. I see you dont like that, any of you; but it's true, for all that; so if you dont like it you can lump it.

DON JUAN. My dear lady, you have put my whole case against romance into a few sentences. That is just why I turned my back on the romantic man with the artist nature, as he called his infatuation. I thanked him for teaching me to use my eyes and ears; but I told him that his beauty worshipping and happiness hunting and woman idealizing was not worth a dump as a philosophy of life; so he called me Philistine and went his way.

ANA. It seems that Woman taught you something, too, with all her defects.

DON JUAN. She did more: she interpreted all the other teaching for me. Ah, my friends, when the barriers were down for the first time, what an astounding illumination! I had been prepared for infatuation, for intoxication, for all the illusions of love's young dream; and lo! never was my perception clearer, nor my criticism more ruthless. The most jealous rival of my mistress never saw every blemish in her more keenly than I. I was not duped: I took her without chloroform.

ANA. But you did take her.

DON JUAN. That was the revelation. Up to that moment I had never lost the sense of being my own master; never consciously taken a single step until my reason had examined and approved it. I had come to believe that I was a purely rational creature: a thinker! I said, with the foolish philosopher, "I think; therefore I am." It was Woman who taught me to say "I am; therefore I think." And also "I would think more; therefore I must be more."

THE STATUE. This is extremely abstract and metaphysical, Juan. If you would stick to the concrete, and put your discoveries in the form of entertaining anecdotes about your adventures with women, your conversation would be easier to follow.

DON JUAN. Bah! what need I add? Do you not understand that when I stood face to face with Woman, every fibre in my clear critical brain warned me to spare her and save myself. My morals said No. My conscience said No. My chivalry and pity for her said No. My prudent regard for myself said No. My ear, practised on a thousand songs and symphonies; my eye, exercised on a thousand paintings; tore her voice, her features, her color to shreds. I caught all those tell-tale resemblances to her father and mother by which I knew what she would be like in thirty years' time. I noted the gleam of gold from a dead tooth in the laughing mouth: I made curious observations of the strange odors of the chemistry of the nerves. The visions of my romantic reveries, in which I had trod the plains of heaven with a deathless, ageless creature of coral and ivory, deserted me in that supreme hour. I remembered them and desperately strove to recover their illusion; but they now seemed the emptiest of inventions: my judgment was not to be corrupted: my brain still said No on every issue. And whilst I was in the act of framing my excuse to the lady, Life seized me and threw me into her arms as a sailor throws a scrap of fish into the mouth of a seabird.

THE STATUE. You might as well have gone without thinking such a lot about it, Juan. You are like all the clever men: you have more brains than is good for you.

THE DEVIL. And were you not the happier for the experience, Señor Don Juan?

DON JUAN. The happier, no: the wiser, yes. That moment introduced me for the first time to myself, and, through myself, to the world. I saw then how useless it is to attempt to impose conditions on the irresistible force of Life; to preach prudence, careful selection, virtue, honor, chastity—

ANA. Don Juan: a word against chastity is an insult to me.

DON JUAN. I say nothing against your chastity, Señora, since it took the form of a husband and twelve children. What more could you have done had you been the most abandoned of women?

ANA. I could have had twelve husbands and no children: thats what I could have done, Juan. And let me tell you that that would have made all the difference to the earth which I replenished.

THE STATUE. Bravo Ana! Juan: you are floored, quelled, annihilated.

DON JUAN. No; for though that difference is the true essential difference—Doña Ana has, I admit, gone straight to the real point

—yet it is not a difference of love or chastity, or even constancy; for twelve children by twelve different husbands would have replenished the earth perhaps more effectively. Suppose my friend Ottavio had died when you were thirty, you would never have remained a widow: you were too beautiful. Suppose the successor of Ottavio had died when you were forty, you would still have been irresistible; and a woman who marries twice marries three times if she becomes free to do so. Twelve lawful children borne by one highly respectable lady to three different fathers is not impossible nor condemned by public opinion. That such a lady may be more law abiding than the poor girl whom we used to spurn into the gutter for bearing one unlawful infant is no doubt true; but dare you say she is less self-indulgent?

ANA. She is more virtuous: that is enough for me.

DON JUAN. In that case, what is virtue but the Trade Unionism of the married? Let us face the facts, dear Ana. The Life Force respects marriage only because marriage is a contrivance of its own to secure the greatest number of children and the closest care of them. For honor, chastity, and all the rest of your moral figments it cares not a rap. Marriage is the most licentious of human institutions—

ANA. Juan!

THE STATUE [protesting] Really!—

DON JUAN [determinedly] I say the most licentious of human institutions: that is the secret of its popularity. And a woman seeking a husband is the most unscrupulous of all the beasts of prey. The confusion of marriage with morality has done more to destroy the conscience of the human race than any other single error. Come, Ana! do not look shocked: you know better than any of us that marriage is a mantrap baited with simulated accomplishments and delusive idealizations. When your sainted mother, by dint of scoldings and punishments, forced you to learn how to play half a dozen pieces on the spinet—which she hated as much as you did—had she any other purpose than to delude your suitors into the belief that your husband would have in his home an angel who would fill it with melody, or at least play him to sleep after dinner? You married my friend Ottavio: well, did you ever open the spinet from the hour when the Church united him to you?

ANA. You are a fool, Juan. A young married woman has something else to do than sit at the spinet without any support for her back; so she gets out of the habit of playing.

DON JUAN. Not if she loves music. No: believe me, she only throws away the bait when the bird is in the net.

ANA [bitterly] And men, I suppose, never throw off the mask when t h e i r bird is in the net. The husband never becomes negligent, selfish, brutal—oh, never!

DON JUAN. What do these recriminations prove, Ana? Only that the hero is as gross an imposture as the heroine.

ANA. It is all nonsense: most marriages are perfectly comfortable.

DON JUAN. "Perfectly" is a strong expression, Ana. What you mean is that sensible people make the best of one another. Send me to the galleys and chain me to the felon whose number happens to be next before mine; and I must accept the inevitable and make the best of the companionship. Many such companionships, they tell me, are touchingly affectionate; and most are at least tolerably friendly. But that does not make a chain a desirable ornament nor the galleys an abode of bliss. Those who talk most about the blessings of marriage and the constancy of its vows are the very people who declare that if the chain were broken and the prisoners left free to choose, the whole social fabric would fly asunder. You cannot have the argument both ways. If the prisoner is happy, why lock him in? If he is not, why pretend that he is?

ANA. At all events, let me take an old woman's privilege again, and tell you flatly that marriage peoples the world and debauchery does not.

DON JUAN. How if a time come when this shall cease to be true? Do you not know that where there is a will there is a way? that whatever Man really wishes to do he will finally discover a means of doing? Well, you have done your best, you virtuous ladies, and others of your way of thinking, to bend Man's mind wholly towards honorable love as the highest good, and to understand by honorable love romance and beauty and happiness in the possession of beautiful, refined, delicate, affectionate women. You have taught women to value their own youth health, shapeliness, and refinement above all things. Well, what place have squalling babies and household cares in this exquisite paradise of the senses and emotions? Is it not the inevitable end of it all that the human will shall say to the human brain: invent me a means by which I can have love, beauty, romance, emotion, passion, without their wretched penalties, their expenses, their worries, their trials, their illnesses and agonies and risks of death, their retinue of servants and nurses and doctors and schoolmasters.

THE DEVIL. All this, Señor Don Juan, is realized here in my realm.

DON JUAN. Yes, at the cost of death. Man will not take it at that price: he demands the romantic delights of your hell whilst he is still on earth. Well, the means will be found: the brain will not fail when the will is in earnest. The day is coming when great nations will find their numbers dwindling from census to census; when the six roomed villa will rise in price above the family mansion; when the viciously reckless poor and the stupidly pious rich will delay the extinction of the race only by degrading it; whilst the boldly prudent, the thriftily selfish and ambitious, the imaginative and poetic, the lovers of money and solid comfort, the worshippers of success, of art, and of love, will all oppose to the Force of Life the device of sterility.

THE STATUE. That is all very eloquent, my young friend; but if you had lived to Ana's age, or even to mine, you would have learned that the people who get rid of the fear of poverty and children and all the other family troubles, and devote themselves to having a good time of it, only leave their minds free for the fear of old age and ugliness and impotence and death. The childless laborer is more tormented by his wife's idleness and her constant demands for amusement and distraction than he could be by twenty children; and his wife is more wretched than he. I have had my share of vanity; for as a young man I was admired by women; and as a statue I am praised by art critics. But I confess that had I found nothing to do in the world but wallow in these delights I should have cut my throat. When I married Ana's mother—or perhaps, to be strictly correct, I should rather say when I at last gave in and allowed Ana's mother to marry me—I knew that I was planting thorns in my pillow, and that marriage for me, a swaggering young officer thitherto

unvanquished, meant defeat and capture.

ANA [*scandalized*] Father!

THE STATUE. I am sorry to shock you, my love; but since Juan has stripped every rag of decency from the discussion I may as well tell the frozen truth.

ANA. Hmf! I suppose I was one of the thorns.

THE STATUE. By no means: you were often a rose. You see, your mother had most of the trouble you gave.

DON JUAN. Then may I ask, Commander, why you have left Heaven to come here and wallow, as you express it, in sentimental beatitudes which you confess would once have driven you to cut your throat?

THE STATUE [*struck by this*] Egad, thats true.

THE DEVIL [*alarmed*] What! You are going back from your word! [*To Don Juan*] And all y o u r philosophizing has been nothing but a mask for proselytizing! [*To the Statue*] Have you forgotten already the hideous dulness from which I am offering you a refuge here? [*To Don Juan*] And does your demonstration of the approaching sterilization and extinction of mankind lead to anything better than making the most of those pleasures of art and love which you yourself admit refined you, elevated you, developed you?

DON JUAN. I never demonstrated the extinction of mankind. Life cannot will its own extinction either in its blind amorphous state or in any of the forms into which it has organized itself. I had not finished when His Excellency interrupted me.

THE STATUE. I begin to doubt whether you ever will finish, my friend. You are extremely fond of hearing yourself talk.

DON JUAN. True; but since you have endured so much, you may as well endure to the end. Long before this sterilization which I described becomes more than a clearly foreseen possibility, the reaction will begin. The great central purpose of breeding the race: ay, breeding it to heights now deemed superhuman: that purpose, which is now hidden in a mephitic cloud of love and romance and prudery and fastidiousness, will break through into clear sunlight as a purpose no longer to be confused with the gratification of personal fancies, the impossible realization of boys' and girls' dreams of bliss, or the need of older people for companionship or money. The plain-spoken marriage services of the vernacular Churches will no longer be abbreviated and half suppressed as indelicate. The sober decency, earnestness, and authority of their declaration of the real purpose of marriage will be honored and accepted, whilst their romantic vowings and pledgings and until-death-do-us-partings and the like will be expunged as unbearable frivolities. Do my sex the justice to admit, Señora, that we have always recognized that the sex relation is not a personal or friendly relation at all.

ANA. Not a personal or friendly relation! What relation is more personal? more sacred? more holy?

DON JUAN. Sacred and holy, if you like, Ana, but not personally friendly. Your relation to God is sacred and holy: dare you call it personally friendly? In the sex relation the universal creative energy, of which the parties are both the helpless agents, overrides and sweeps away all personal considerations, and dispenses with all personal relations. The pair may be utter strangers to one another, speaking different languages, differing in race and color, in age and disposition, with no bond between them but a possibility of that fecundity for the sake of which the Life Force throws them into one another's arms at the exchange of a glance. Do we not recognize this by allowing marriages to be made by parents without consulting the woman? Have you not often expressed your disgust at the immorality of the English nation, in which women and men of noble birth become acquainted and court each other like peasants? And how much does even the peasant know of his bride or she of him before he engages himself? Why, you would not make a man your lawyer or your family doctor on so slight an acquaintance as you would fall in love with and marry him!

ANA. Yes, Juan: we know the libertine's philosophy. Always ignore the consequences to the woman.

DON JUAN. The consequences, yes: they justify her fierce grip of the man. But surely you do not call that attachment a sentimental one. As well call the policeman's attachment to his prisoner a love relation.

ANA. You see you have to confess that marriage is necessary, though, according to you, love is the slightest of all human relations.

DON JUAN. How do you know that it is not the greatest of all human relations? far too great to be a personal matter. Could your father have served his country if he had refused to kill any enemy of Spain unless he personally hated him? Can a woman serve her country if she refuses to marry any man she does not personally love? You know it is not so: the woman of noble birth marries as the man of noble birth fights, on political and family grounds, not on personal ones.

THE STATUE [impressed] A very clever point that, Juan: I must think it over. You are really full of ideas. How did you come to think of this one?

DON JUAN. I learnt it by experience. When I was on earth, and made those proposals to ladies which, though universally condemned, have made me so interesting a hero of legend, I was not infrequently met in some such way as this. The lady would say that she would countenance my advances, provided they were honorable. On inquiring what that proviso meant, I found that it meant that I proposed to get possession of her property if she had any, or to undertake her support for life if she had not; that I desired her continual companionship, counsel, and conversation to the end of my days, and would take a most solemn oath to be always enraptured by them: above all, that I would turn my back on all other women for ever for her sake. I did not object to these conditions because they were exorbitant and inhuman: it was their extraordinary irrelevance that prostrated me. I invariably replied with perfect frankness that I had never dreamt of any of these things; that unless the lady's character and intellect were equal or superior to my own, her conversation must degrade and her counsel mislead me; that her constant companionship might, for all I knew, become intolerably tedious to me; that I could not answer for my feelings for a week in advance, much less to the end of my life; that to cut me off from all natural and unconstrained intercourse with half my fellowcreatures would narrow and warp me if I submitted to it, and if not, would bring me under the curse of clandestinity; that, finally, my proposals to her were wholly unconnected with any of these matters, and were the outcome of a perfectly simple impulse of my manhood towards her womanhood.

ANA. You mean that it was an immoral impulse.

DON JUAN. Nature, my dear lady, is what

you call immoral. I blush for it; but I cannot help it. Nature is a pandar, Time a wrecker, and Death a murderer. I have always preferred to stand up to those facts and build institutions on their recognition. You prefer to propitiate the three devils by proclaiming their chastity, their thrift, and their loving kindness; and to base your institutions on these flatteries. Is it any wonder that the institutions do not work smoothly?

THE STATUE. What used the ladies to say, Juan?

DON JUAN. Oh, come! Confidence for confidence. First tell me what you used to say to the ladies.

THE STATUE. I! Oh, I swore that I would be faithful to the death; that I should die if they refused me; that no woman could ever be to me what she was—

ANA. She! Who?

THE STATUE. Whoever it happened to be at the time, my dear. I had certain things I always said. One of them was that even when I was eighty, one white hair of the woman I loved would make me tremble more than the thickest gold tress from the most beautiful young head. Another was that I could not bear the thought of anyone else being the mother of my children.

DON JUAN [revolted] You old rascal!

THE STATUE [stoutly] Not a bit; for I really believed it with all my soul at the moment. I had a heart: not like you. And it was this sincerity that made me successful.

DON JUAN. Sincerity! To be fool enough to believe a ramping, stamping, thumping lie: that is what you call sincerity! To be so greedy for a woman that you deceive yourself in your eagerness to deceive her: sincerity, you call it!

THE STATUE. Oh, damn your sophistries! I was a man in love, not a lawyer. And the women loved me for it, bless them!

DON JUAN. They made you think so. What will you say when I tell you that though I played the lawyer so callously, they made me think so too? I also had my moments of infatuation in which I gushed nonsense and believed it. Sometimes the desire to give pleasure by saying beautiful things so rose in me on the flood of emotion that I said them recklessly. At other times I argued against myself with a devilish coldness that drew tears. But I found it just as hard to escape when I was cruel as when I was kind.

When the lady's instinct was set on me, there was nothing for it but lifelong servitude or flight.

ANA. You dare boast, before me and my father, that every woman found you irresistible.

DON JUAN. Am I boasting? It seems to me that I cut the most pitiable of figures. Besides, I said "when the lady's instinct was set on me." It was not always so; and then, heavens! what transports of virtuous indignation! what overwhelming defiance to the dastardly seducer! what scenes of Imogen and Iachimo!

ANA. I made no scenes. I simply called my father.

DON JUAN. And he came, sword in hand, to vindicate outraged honor and morality by murdering me.

THE STATUE. Murdering! What do you mean? Did I kill you or did you kill me?

DON JUAN. Which of us was the better fencer?

THE STATUE. I was.

DON JUAN. Of course you were. And yet you, the hero of those scandalous adventures you have just been relating to us, you had the effrontery to pose as the avenger of outraged morality and condemn me to death! You would have slain me but for an accident.

THE STATUE. I was expected to, Juan. That is how things were arranged on earth. I was not a social reformer; and I always did what it was customary for a gentleman to do.

DON JUAN. That may account for your attacking me, but not for the revolting hypocrisy of your subsequent proceedings as a statue.

THE STATUE. That all came of my going to Heaven.

THE DEVIL. I still fail to see, Señor Don Juan, that these episodes in your earthly career and in that of the Señor Commander in any way discredit my view of life. Here, I repeat, you have all that you sought without anything that you shrank from.

DON JUAN. On the contrary, here I have everything that disappointed me without anything that I have not already tried and found wanting. I tell you that as long as I can conceive something better than myself I cannot be easy unless I am striving to bring it into existence or clearing the way for it. That is the law of my life. That is the working within me of Life's incessant aspiration to

O

higher organization, wider, deeper, intenser self-consciousness, and clearer self-understanding. It was the supremacy of this purpose that reduced love for me to the mere pleasure of a moment, art for me to the mere schooling of my faculties, religion for me to a mere excuse for laziness, since it had set up a God who looked at the world and saw that it was good, against the instinct in me that looked through my eyes at the world and saw that it could be improved. I tell you that in the pursuit of my own pleasure, my own health, my own fortune, I have never known happiness. It was not love for Woman that delivered me into her hands: it was fatigue, exhaustion. When I was a child, and bruised my head against a stone, I ran to the nearest woman and cried away my pain against her apron. When I grew up, and bruised my soul against the brutalities and stupidities with which I had to strive, I did again just what I had done as a child. I have enjoyed, too, my rests, my recuperations, my breathing times, my very prostrations after strife; but rather would I be dragged through all the circles of the foolish Italian's Inferno than through the pleasures of Europe. That is what has made this place of eternal pleasures so deadly to me. It is the absence of this instinct in you that makes you that strange monster called a Devil. It is the success with which you have diverted the attention of men from their real purpose, which in one degree or another is the same as mine, to yours, that has earned you the name of The Tempter. It is the fact that they are doing your will, or rather drifting with your want of will, instead of doing their own, that makes them the uncomfortable, false, restless, artificial, petulant, wretched creatures they are.

THE DEVIL [*mortified*] Señor Don Juan: you are uncivil to my friends.

DON JUAN. Pooh! why should I be civil to them or to you? In this Palace of Lies a truth or two will not hurt you. Your friends are all the dullest dogs I know. They are not beautiful: they are only decorated. They are not clean: they are only shaved and starched. They are not dignified: they are only fashionably dressed. They are not educated: they are only college passmen. They are not religious: they are only pewrenters. They are not moral: they are only conventional. They are not virtuous: they are only cowardly. They are not even vicious: they are only "frail." They are not artistic: they are only lascivious. They are not prosperous: they are only rich. They are not loyal, they are only servile; not dutiful, only sheepish; not public spirited, only patriotic; not courageous, only quarrelsome; not determined, only obstinate; not masterful, only domineering; not self-controlled, only obtuse; not self-respecting, only vain; not kind, only sentimental; not social, only gregarious; not considerate, only polite; not intelligent, only opinionated; not progressive, only factious; not imaginative, only superstitious; not just, only vindictive; not generous, only propitiatory; not disciplined, only cowed; and not truthful at all: liars every one of them, to the very backbone of their souls.

THE STATUE. Your flow of words is simply amazing, Juan. How I wish I could have talked like that to my soldiers.

THE DEVIL. It is mere talk, though. It has all been said before; but what change has it ever made? What notice has the world ever taken of it?

DON JUAN. Yes, it is mere talk. But why is it mere talk? Because, my friend, beauty, purity, respectability, religion, morality, art, patriotism, bravery, and the rest are nothing but words which I or anyone else can turn inside out like a glove. Were they realities, you would have to plead guilty to my indictment; but fortunately for your self-respect, my diabolical friend, they are not realities. As you say, they are mere words, useful for duping barbarians into adopting civilization, or the civilized poor into submitting to be robbed and enslaved. That is the family secret of the governing caste; and if we who are of that caste aimed at more Life for the world instead of at more power and luxury for our miserable selves, that secret would make us great. Now, since I, being a nobleman, am in the secret too, think how tedious to me must be your unending cant about all these moralistic figments, and how squalidly disastrous your sacrifice of your lives to them! If you even believed in your moral game enough to play it fairly, it would be interesting to watch; but you dont: you cheat at every trick; and if your opponent outcheats you, you upset the table and try to murder him.

THE DEVIL. On earth there may be some truth in this, because the people are uneducated and cannot appreciate my religion of love and beauty; but here—

DON JUAN. Oh yes: I know. Here there is nothing but love and beauty. Ugh! it is like sitting for all eternity at the first act of a fashionable play, before the complications begin. Never in my worst moments of superstitious terror on earth did I dream that Hell was so horrible. I live, like a hairdresser, in the continual contemplation of beauty, toying with silken tresses. I breathe an atmosphere of sweetness, like a confectioner's shopboy. Commander: are there any beautiful women in Heaven?

THE STATUE. None. Absolutely none. All dowdies. Not two pennorth of jewellery among a dozen of them. They might be men of fifty.

DON JUAN. I am impatient to get there. Is the word beauty ever mentioned; and are there any artistic people?

THE STATUE. I give you my word they wont admire a fine statue even when it walks past them.

DON JUAN. I go.

THE DEVIL. Don Juan: shall I be frank with you?

DON JUAN. Were you not so before?

THE DEVIL. As far as I went, yes. But I will now go further, and confess to you that men get tired of everything, of heaven no less than of hell; and that all history is nothing but a record of the oscillations of the world between these two extremes. An epoch is but a swing of the pendulum; and each generation thinks the world is progressing because it is always moving. But when you are as old as I am; when you have a thousand times wearied of heaven, like myself and the Commander, and a thousand times wearied of hell, as you are wearied now, you will no longer imagine that every swing from heaven to hell is an emancipation, every swing from hell to heaven an evolution. Where you now see reform, progress, fulfilment of upward tendency, continual ascent by Man on the stepping stones of his dead selves to higher things, you will see nothing but an infinite comedy of illusion. You will discover the profound truth of the saying of my friend Koheleth, that there is nothing new under the sun. Vanitas vanitatum—

DON JUAN [out of all patience] By Heaven, this is worse than your cant about love and beauty. Clever dolt that you are, is a man no better than a worm, or a dog than a wolf, because he gets tired of everything? Shall he give up eating because he destroys his appetite in the act of gratifying it? Is a field idle when it is fallow? Can the Commander expend his hellish energy here without accumulating heavenly energy for his next term of blessedness? Granted that the great Life Force has hit on the device of the clockmaker's pendulum, and uses the earth for its bob; that the history of each oscillation, which seems so novel to us the actors, is but the history of the last oscillation repeated; nay more, that in the unthinkable infinitude of time the sun throws off the earth and catches it again a thousand times as a circus rider throws up a ball, and that our agelong epochs are but the moments between the toss and the catch, has the colossal mechanism no purpose?

THE DEVIL. None, my friend. You think, because you have a purpose, Nature must have one. You might as well expect it to have fingers and toes because you have them.

DON JUAN. But I should not have them if they served no purpose. And I, my friend, am as much a part of Nature as my own finger is a part of me. If my finger is the organ by which I grasp the sword and the mandoline, my brain is the organ by which Nature strives to understand itself. My dog's brain serves only my dog's purposes; but my own brain labors at a knowledge which does nothing for me personally but make my body bitter to me and my decay and death a calamity. Were I not possessed with a purpose beyond my own I had better be a ploughman than a philosopher; for the ploughman lives as long as the philosopher, eats more, sleeps better, and rejoices in the wife of his bosom with less misgiving. This is because the philosopher is in the grip of the Life Force. This Life Force says to him "I have done a thousand wonderful things unconsciously by merely willing to live and following the line of least resistance: now I want to know myself and my destination, and choose my path; so I have made a special brain—a philosopher's brain—to grasp this knowledge for me as the husbandman's hand grasps the plough for me. And this" says the Life Force to the philosopher "must thou strive to do for me until thou diest, when I will make another brain and another philosopher to carry on the work."

THE DEVIL. What is the use of knowing?

DON JUAN. Why, to be able to choose the line of greatest advantage instead of yielding in the direction of the least resistance. Does a ship sail to its destination no better than a log drifts nowhither? The philosopher is Nature's pilot. And there you have our difference: to be in hell is to drift: to be in heaven is to steer.

THE DEVIL. On the rocks, most likely.

DON JUAN. Pooh! which ship goes oftenest on the rocks or to the bottom? the drifting ship or the ship with a pilot on board?

THE DEVIL. Well, well, go your way, Señor Don Juan. I prefer to be my own master and not the tool of any blundering universal force. I know that beauty is good to look at; that music is good to hear; that love is good to feel; and that they are all good to think about and talk about. I know that to be well exercised in these sensations, emotions, and studies is to be a refined and cultivated being. Whatever they may say of me in churches on earth, I know that it is universally admitted in good society that the Prince of Darkness is a gentleman; and that is enough for me. As to your Life Force, which you think irresistible, it is the most resistible thing in the world for a person of any character. But if you are naturally vulgar and credulous, as all reformers are, it will thrust you first into religion, where you will sprinkle water on babies to save their souls from me; then it will drive you from religion into science, where you will snatch the babies from the water sprinkling and inoculate them with disease to save them from catching it accidentally; then you will take to politics, where you will become the catspaw of corrupt functionaries and the henchman of ambitious humbugs; and the end will be despair and decrepitude, broken nerve and shattered hopes, vain regrets for that worst and silliest of wastes and sacrifices, the waste and sacrifice of the power of enjoyment: in a word, the punishment of the fool who pursues the better before he has secured the good.

DON JUAN. But at least I shall not be bored. The service of the Life Force has that advantage, at all events. So fare you well, Señor Satan.

THE DEVIL [amiably] Fare you well, Don Juan. I shall often think of our interesting chats about things in general. I wish you every happiness: Heaven, as I said before, suits some people. But if you should change your mind, do not forget that the gates are always open here to the repentant prodigal. If you feel at any time that warmth of heart, sincere unforced affection, innocent enjoyment, and warm, breathing, palpitating reality—

DON JUAN. Why not say flesh and blood at once, though we have left those two greasy commonplaces behind us?

THE DEVIL [angrily] You throw my friendly farewell back in my teeth, then, Don Juan?

DON JUAN. By no means. But though there is much to be learnt from a cynical devil, I really cannot stand a sentimental one. Señor Commander: you know the way to the frontier of hell and heaven. Be good enough to direct me.

THE STATUE. Oh, the frontier is only the difference between two ways of looking at things. Any road will take you across it if you really want to get there.

DON JUAN. Good. [Saluting Doña Ana] Señora: your servant.

ANA. But I am going with you.

DON JUAN. I can find my own way to heaven, Ana; not yours [he vanishes].

ANA. How annoying!

THE STATUE [calling after him] Bon voyage, Juan! [He wafts a final blast of his great rolling chords after him as a parting salute. A faint echo of the first ghostly melody comes back in acknowledgment]. Ah! there he goes. [Puffing a long breath out through his lips] Whew! How he does talk! Theyll never stand it in heaven.

THE DEVIL [gloomily] His going is a political defeat. I cannot keep these Life Worshippers: they all go. This is the greatest loss I have had since that Dutch painter went: a fellow who would paint a hag of 70 with as much enjoyment as a Venus of 20.

THE STATUE. I remember: he came to heaven. Rembrandt.

THE DEVIL. Ay, Rembrandt. There is something unnatural about these fellows. Do not listen to their gospel, Señor Commander: it is dangerous. Beware of the pursuit of the Superhuman: it leads to an indiscriminate contempt for the Human. To a man, horses and dogs and cats are mere species, outside the moral world. Well, to the Superman, men and women are a mere species too, also outside the moral world. This Don Juan was kind to women and courteous to men as your daughter here was kind to her pet cats and dogs; but such kindness is a denial of the exclusively human character of the soul.

THE STATUE. And who the deuce is the Superman?

THE DEVIL. Oh, the latest fashion among the Life Force fanatics. Did you not meet in Heaven, among the new arrivals, that German Polish madman? what was his name? Nietzsche?

THE STATUE. Never heard of him.

THE DEVIL. Well, he came here first, before he recovered his wits. I had some hopes of him; but he was a confirmed Life Force worshipper. It was he who raked up the Superman, who is as old as Prometheus; and the 20th century will run after this newest of the old crazes when it gets tired of the world, the flesh, and your humble servant.

THE STATUE. Superman is a good cry; and a good cry is half the battle. I should like to see this Nietzsche.

THE DEVIL. Unfortunately he met Wagner here, and had a quarrel with him.

THE STATUE. Quite right, too. Mozart for me!

THE DEVIL. Oh, it was not about music. Wagner once drifted into Life Force worship, and invented a Superman called Siegfried. But he came to his senses afterwards. So when they met here, Nietzsche denounced him as a renegade; and Wagner wrote a pamphlet to prove that Nietzsche was a Jew; and it ended in Nietzsche's going to heaven in a huff. And a good riddance too. And now, my friend, let us hasten to my palace and celebrate your arrival with a grand musical service.

THE STATUE. With pleasure: youre most kind.

THE DEVIL. This way, Commander. We go down the old trap [*he places himself on the grave trap*].

THE STATUE. Good. [*Reflectively*] All the same, the Superman is a fine conception. There is something statuesque about it. [*He places himself on the grave trap beside The Devil. It begins to descend slowly. Red glow from the abyss*]. Ah, this reminds me of old times.

THE DEVIL. And me also.

ANA. Stop! [*The trap stops*].

THE DEVIL. You, Señora, cannot come this way. You will have an apotheosis. But you will be at the palace before us.

ANA. That is not what I stopped you for. Tell me: where can I find the Superman?

THE DEVIL. He is not yet created, Señora.

THE STATUE. And never will be, probably. Let us proceed: the red fire will make me sneeze. [*They descend*].

ANA. Not yet created! Then my work is not yet done. [*Crossing herself devoutly*] I believe in the Life to Come. [*Crying to the universe*] A father! a father for the Superman!

She vanishes into the void; and again there is nothing: all existence seems suspended infinitely. Then, vaguely, there is a live human voice crying somewhere. One sees, with a shock, a mountain peak shewing faintly against a lighter background. The sky has returned from afar; and we suddenly remember where we were. The cry becomes distinct and urgent: it says Automobile, Automobile. *The complete reality comes back with a rush: in a moment it is full morning in the Sierra; and the brigands are scrambling to their feet and making for the road as the goatherd runs down from the hill, warning them of the approach of another motor. Tanner and Mendoza rise amazedly and stare at one another with scattered wits. Straker sits up to yawn for a moment before he gets on his feet, making it a point of honor not to shew any undue interest in the excitement of the bandits. Mendoza gives a quick look to see that his followers are attending to the alarm; then exchanges a private word with Tanner.*

MENDOZA. Did you dream?

TANNER. Damnably. Did you?

MENDOZA. Yes. I forget what. You were in it.

TANNER. So were you. Amazing!

MENDOZA. I warned you. [*A shot is heard from the road*]. Dolts! they will play with that gun. [*The brigands come running back scared*]. Who fired that shot? [*to Duval*] was it you?

DUVAL [*breathless*] I have not shoot. Dey shoot first.

ANARCHIST. I told you to begin by abolishing the State. Now we are all lost.

THE ROWDY SOCIAL-DEMOCRAT [*stampeding across the amphitheatre*] Ran, everybody.

MENDOZA [*collaring him; throwing him on his back; and drawing a knife*] I stab the man who stirs. [*He blocks the way. The stampede is checked*]. What has happened?

THE SULKY SOCIAL-DEMOCRAT. A motor—

THE ANARCHIST. Three men—

DUVAL. Deux femmes—

MENDOZA. Three men and two women! Why have you not brought them here? Are you afraid of them?

THE ROWDY ONE [getting up] Thyve a hescort. Ow, de-ooh luts ook it, Mendowza.

THE SULKY ONE. Two armored cars full o soldiers at the ed o the valley.

THE ANARCHIST. The shot was fired in the air. It was a signal.

Straker whistles his favorite air, which falls on the ears of the brigands like a funeral march.

TANNER. It is not an escort, but an expedition to capture you. We were advised to wait for it; but I was in a hurry.

THE ROWDY ONE [in an agony of apprehension] And Ow my good Lord, ere we are, wytin for em! Luts tike to the mahntns.

MENDOZA. Idiot, what do you know about the mountains? Are you a Spaniard? You would be given up by the first shepherd you met. Besides, we are already within range of their rifles.

THE ROWDY ONE. Bat—

MENDOZA. Silence. Leave this to me. [To Tanner] Comrade: you will not betray us.

STRAKER. Oo are you callin comrade?

MENDOZA. Last night the advantage was with me. The robber of the poor was at the mercy of the robber of the rich. You offered your hand: I took it.

TANNER. I bring no charge against you, comrade. We have spent a pleasant evening with you: that is all.

STRAKER. I gev my and to nobody, see?

MENDOZA [turning on him impressively] Young man: if I am tried, I shall plead guilty, and explain what drove me from England, home, and duty. Do you wish to have the respectable name of Straker dragged through the mud of a Spanish criminal court? The police will search me. They will find Louisa's portrait. It will be published in the illustrated papers. You blench. It will be your doing, remember.

STRAKER [with baffled rage] I dont care about the court. It's avin our name mixed up with yours that I object to, you blackmailin swine, you.

MENDOZA. Language unworthy of Louisa's brother! But no matter: you are muzzled: that is enough for us. [He turns to face his own men, who back uneasily across the amphitheatre towards the cave to take refuge behind him, as a fresh party, muffled for motoring, comes from the road in riotous spirits. Ann, who makes straight for Tanner, comes first; then Violet, helped over the rough ground by Hector holding her right hand and Ramsden her left. Mendoza

goes to his presidential block and seats himself calmly with his rank and file grouped behind him, and his Staff, consisting of Duval and the Anarchist on his right and the two Social-Democrats on his left, supporting him in flank.

ANN. It's Jack!

TANNER. Caught!

HECTOR. Why, certainly it is. I said it was you, Tanner. Weve just been stopped by a puncture: the road is full of nails.

VIOLET. What are you doing here with all these men?

ANN. Why did you leave us without a word of warning?

HECTOR. I wawnt that bunch of roses, Miss Whitefield. [To Tanner] When we found you were gone, Miss Whitefield bet me a bunch of roses my car would not overtake yours before you reached Monte Carlo.

TANNER. But this is not the road to Monte Carlo.

HECTOR. No matter. Miss Whitefield tracked you at every stopping place: she is a regular Sherlock Holmes.

TANNER. The Life Force! I am lost.

OCTAVIUS [bounding gaily down from the road into the amphitheatre, and coming between Tanner and Straker] I am so glad you are safe, old chap. We were afraid you had been captured by brigands.

RAMSDEN [who has been staring at Mendoza] I seem to remember the face of your friend here. [Mendoza rises politely and advances with a smile between Ann and Ramsden].

HECTOR. Why, so do I.

OCTAVIUS. I know you perfectly well, sir; but I cant think where I have met you.

MENDOZA [to Violet] Do you remember me, madam?

VIOLET. Oh, quite well; but I am so stupid about names.

MENDOZA. It was at the Savoy Hotel. [To Hector] You, sir, used to come with this lady [Violet] to lunch. [To Octavius] You, sir, often brought this lady [Ann] and her mother to dinner on your way to the Lyceum Theatre. [To Ramsden] You, sir, used to come to supper, with [dropping his voice to a confidential but perfectly audible whisper] several different ladies.

RAMSDEN [angrily] Well, what is that to you, pray?

OCTAVIUS. Why, Violet, I thought you hardly knew one another before this trip, you and Malone!

VIOLET [*vexed*] I suppose this person was the manager.

MENDOZA. The waiter, madam. I have a grateful recollection of you all. I gathered from the bountiful way in which you treated me that you all enjoyed your visits very much.

VIOLET. What impertinence! [*She turns her back on him, and goes up the hill with Hector*].

RAMSDEN. That will do, my friend. You do not expect these ladies to treat you as an acquaintance, I suppose, because you have waited on them at table.

MENDOZA. Pardon me: it was you who claimed my acquaintance. The ladies followed your example. However, this display of the unfortunate manners of your class closes the incident. For the future, you will please address me with the respect due to a stranger and fellow traveller. [*He turns haughtily away and resumes his presidential seat*].

TANNER. There! I have found one man on my journey capable of reasonable conversation; and you all instinctively insult him. Even the New Man is as bad as any of you. Enry: you have behaved just like a miserable gentleman.

STRAKER. Gentleman! Not me.

RAMSDEN. Really, Tanner, this tone—

ANN. Dont mind him, Granny: you ought to know him by this time [*she takes his arm and coaxes him away to the hill to join Violet and Hector. Octavius follows her, dog-like*].

VIOLET [*calling from the hill*] Here are the soldiers. They are getting out of their motors.

DUVAL [*panicstricken*] Oh, nom de Dieu!

THE ANARCHIST. Fools: the State is about to crush you because you spared it at the prompting of the political hangers-on of the bourgeoisie.

THE SULKY SOCIAL-DEMOCRAT [*argumentative to the last*] On the contrary, only by capturing the State machine—

THE ANARCHIST. It is going to capture y o u.

THE ROWDY SOCIAL-DEMOCRAT [*his anguish culminating*] Ow, chuck it. Wot are we ere for? W o t are we wytin for?

MENDOZA [*between his teeth*] Go on. Talk politics, you idiots: nothing sounds more respectable. Keep it up, I tell you.

The soldiers line the road, commanding the amphitheatre with their rifles. The brigands, struggling with an overwhelming impulse to hide behind one another, look as unconcerned as they can. Mendoza rises superbly, with undaunted front. The officer in command steps down from the road into the amphitheatre; looks hard at the brigands; and then inquiringly at Tanner.

THE OFFICER. Who are these men, Señor Ingles?

TANNER. My escort.

Mendoza, with a Mephistophelean smile, bows profoundly. An irrepressible grin runs from face to face among the brigands. They touch their hats, except the Anarchist, who defies the State with folded arms.

ACT IV

The garden of a villa in Granada. Whoever wishes to know what it is like must go to Granada to see. One may prosaically specify a group of hills dotted with villas, the Alhambra on the top of one of the hills, and a considerable town in the valley, approached by dusty white roads in which the children, no matter what they are doing or thinking about, automatically whine for halfpence and reach out little clutching brown palms for them; but there is nothing in this description except the Alhambra, the begging, and the color of the roads, that does not fit Surrey as well as Spain. The difference is that the Surrey hills are comparatively small and ugly, and should properly be called the Surrey Protuberances; but these Spanish hills are of mountain stock: the amenity which conceals their size does not compromise their dignity.

This particular garden is on a hill opposite the Alhambra; and the villa is as expensive and pretentious as a villa must be if it is to be let furnished by the week to opulent American and English visitors. If we stand on the lawn at the foot of the garden and look uphill, our horizon is the stone balustrade of a flagged platform on the edge of infinite space at the top of the hill. Between us and this platform is a flower garden with a circular basin and fountain in the centre, surrounded by geometrical flower beds, gravel paths, and clipped yew trees in the genteelest order. The garden is higher than our lawn; so we reach it by a few steps in the middle of its embankment. The platform is higher again than the garden, from which we mount a couple more steps to look over the balustrade at a fine view of the town up the valley and of the hills that stretch away beyond it to where, in the remotest distance, they become mountains. On our left is the villa, accessible by steps from the left hand corner of the garden. Returning from the plat-

form through the garden and down again to the lawn (a movement which leaves the villa behind us on our right) we find evidence of literary interests on the part of the tenants in the fact that there is no tennis net nor set of croquet hoops, but, on our left, a little iron garden table with books on it, mostly yellow-backed, and a chair beside it. A chair on the right has also a couple of open books upon it. There are no newspapers, a circumstance which, with the absence of games, might lead an intelligent spectator to the most far reaching conclusions as to the sort of people who live in the villa. Such speculations are checked, however, on this delightfully fine afternoon, by the appearance at a little gate in a paling on our left, of Henry Straker in his professional costume. He opens the gate for an elderly gentleman, and follows him on to the lawn.

This elderly gentleman defies the Spanish sun in a black frock coat, tall silk hat, trousers in which narrow stripes of dark grey and lilac blend into a highly respectable color, and a black necktie tied into a bow over spotless linen. Probably therefore a man whose social position needs constant and scrupulous affirmation without regard to climate: one who would dress thus for the middle of the Sahara or the top of Mont Blanc. And since he has not the stamp of the class which accepts as its life-mission the advertizing and maintenance of first rate tailoring and millinery, he looks vulgar in his finery, though in a working dress of any kind he would look dignified enough. He is a bullet cheeked man with a red complexion, stubbly hair, smallish eyes, a hard mouth that folds down at the corners, and a dogged chin. The looseness of skin that comes with age has attacked his throat and the laps of his cheeks; but he is still hard as an apple above the mouth; so that the upper half of his face looks younger than the lower. He has the self-confidence of one who has made money, and something of the truculence of one who has made it in a brutalizing struggle, his civility having under it a perceptible menace that he has other methods in reserve if necessary. Withal, a man to be rather pitied when he is not to be feared; for there is something pathetic about him at times, as if the huge commercial machine which has worked him into his frock coat had allowed him very little of his own way and left his affections hungry and baffled. At the first word that falls from him it is clear that he is an Irishman whose native intonation has clung to him through many changes of place and rank. One can only guess that the original material of his speech was perhaps the surly Kerry brogue; but the degradation of speech that occurs in London, Glasgow, Dublin, and big cities generally has been at work on it so long that nobody but an arrant cockney would dream of calling it a brogue now; for its music is almost gone, though its surliness is still perceptible. Straker, being a very obvious cockney, inspires him with implacable contempt, as a stupid Englishman who cannot even speak his own language properly. Straker, on the other hand, regards the old gentleman's accent as a joke thoughtfully provided by Providence expressly for the amusement of the British race, and treats him normally with the indulgence due to an inferior and unlucky species, but occasionally with indignant alarm when the old gentleman shews signs of intending his Irish nonsense to be taken seriously.

STRAKER. I'll go tell the young lady. She said youd prefer to stay here [*he turns to go up through the garden to the villa*].

THE IRISHMAN [*who has been looking round him with lively curiosity*] The young lady? Thats Miss Violet, eh?

STRAKER [*stopping on the steps with sudden suspicion*] Well, you know, dont you?

THE IRISHMAN. Do I?

STRAKER [*his temper rising*] Well, do you or dont you?

THE IRISHMAN. What business is that of yours?

Straker, now highly indignant, comes back from the steps and confronts the visitor.

STRAKER. I'll tell you what business it is of mine. Miss Robinson—

THE IRISHMAN [*interrupting*] Oh, her name is Robinson, is it? Thank you.

STRAKER. Why, you dont know even her name?

THE IRISHMAN. Yes I do, now that youve told me.

STRAKER [*after a moment of stupefaction at the old man's readiness in repartee*] Look here: what do you mean by gittin into my car and lettin me bring you here if youre not the person I took that note to?

THE IRISHMAN. Who else did you take it to, pray?

STRAKER. I took it to Mr Ector Malone, at Miss Robinson's request, see? Miss Robinson is not my principal: I took it to oblige her. I know Mr Malone; and he aint you, not by a long chalk. At the hotel they told me that your name is Ector Malone—

MALONE. Hector Malone.

STRAKER [with calm superiority] Hector in your own country: thats what comes o livin in provincial places like Ireland and America. Over here youre Ector: if you avnt noticed it before you soon will.

The growing strain of the conversation is here relieved by Violet, who has sallied from the villa and through the garden to the steps, which she now descends, coming very opportunely between Malone and Straker.

VIOLET [to Straker] Did you take my message?

STRAKER. Yes, miss. I took it to the hotel and sent it up, expecting to see young Mr Malone. Then out walks this gent, and says it's all right and he'll come with me. So as the hotel people said he was Mr Ector Malone, I fetched him. And now he goes back on what he said. But if he isnt the gentleman you meant, say the word: it's easy enough to fetch him back again.

MALONE. I should esteem it a great favor if I might have a short conversation with you, madam. I am Hector's father, as this bright Britisher would have guessed in the course of another hour or so.

STRAKER [coolly defiant] No, not in another year or so. When weve ad you as long to polish up as weve ad im, perhaps youll begin to look a little bit up to is mark. At present you fall a long way short. Youve got too many aitches, for one thing. [To Violet, amiably] All right, Miss: you want to talk to him: I shant intrude. [He nods affably to Malone and goes out through the little gate in the paling].

VIOLET [very civilly] I am so sorry, Mr Malone, if that man has been rude to you. But what can we do? He is our chauffeur.

MALONE. Your hwat?

VIOLET. The driver of our automobile. He can drive a motor car at seventy miles an hour, and mend it when it breaks down. We are dependent on our motor cars; and our motor cars are dependent on him; so of course we are dependent on him.

MALONE. Ive noticed, madam, that every thousand dollars an Englishman gets seems to add one to the number of people he's dependent on. However, you neednt apologize for your man: I made him talk on purpose. By doing so I learnt that youre stayin here in Grannida with a party of English, including my son Hector.

VIOLET [conversationally] Yes. We intended to go to Nice; but we had to follow a rather eccentric member of our party who started first and came here. Wont you sit down? [She clears the nearest chair of the two books on it].

MALONE [impressed by this attention] Thank you. [He sits down, examining her curiously as she goes to the iron table to put down the books. When she turns to him again, he says] Miss Robinson, I believe?

VIOLET [sitting down] Yes.

MALONE [taking a letter from his pocket] Your note to Hector runs as follows [Violet is unable to repress a start. He pauses quietly to take out and put on his spectacles, which have gold rims]: "Dearest: they have all gone to the Alhambra for the afternoon. I have shammed headache and have the garden all to myself. Jump into Jack's motor: Straker will rattle you here in a jiffy. Quick, quick, quick. Your loving Violet." [He looks at her; but by this time she has recovered herself, and meets his spectacles with perfect composure. He continues slowly] Now I dont know on hwat terms young people associate in English society; but in America that note would be considered to imply a very considerable degree of affectionate intimacy between the parties.

VIOLET. Yes: I know your son very well, Mr Malone. Have you any objection?

MALONE [somewhat taken aback] No, no objection exactly. Provided it is understood that my son is altogether dependent on me, and that I have to be consulted in any important step he may propose to take.

VIOLET. I am sure you would not be unreasonable with him, Mr Malone.

MALONE. I hope not, Miss Robinson; but at your age you might think many things unreasonable that dont seem so to me.

VIOLET [with a little shrug] Oh, well, I suppose theres no use our playing at cross purposes, Mr Malone. Hector wants to marry me.

MALONE. I inferred from your note that he might. Well, Miss Robinson, he is his own master; but if he marries you he shall not have a rap from me. [He takes off his spectacles and pockets them with the note].

VIOLET [with some severity] That is not very complimentary to me, Mr Malone.

MALONE. I say nothing against you, Miss Robinson: I daresay you are an amiable and excellent young lady. But I have other views for Hector.

VIOLET. Hector may not have other views

o 2

for himself, Mr Malone.

MALONE. Possibly not. Then he does without me: thats all. I daresay you are prepared for that. When a young lady writes to a young man to come to her quick, quick, quick, money seems nothing and love seems everything.

VIOLET [*sharply*] I beg your pardon, Mr Malone: I do not think anything so foolish. Hector must have money.

MALONE [*staggered*] Oh, very well, very well. No doubt he can work for it.

VIOLET. What is the use of having money if you have to work for it? [*She rises impatiently*]. It's all nonsense, Mr Malone: you must enable your son to keep up his position. It is his right.

MALONE [*grimly*] I should not advise you to marry him on the strength of that right, Miss Robinson.

Violet, who has almost lost her temper, controls herself with an effort; unclenches her fingers; and resumes her seat with studied tranquillity and reasonableness.

VIOLET. What objection have you to me, pray? My social position is as good as Hector's, to say the least. He admits it.

MALONE [*shrewdly*] You tell him so from time to time, eh? Hector's social position in England, Miss Robinson, is just what I choose to buy for him. I have made him a fair offer. Let him pick out the most historic house, castle, or abbey that England contains. The very day he tells me he wants it for a wife worthy of its traditions, I buy it for him, and give him the means of keeping it up.

VIOLET. What do you mean by a wife worthy of its traditions? Cannot any well bred woman keep such a house for him?

MALONE. No: she must be born to it.

VIOLET. Hector was not born to it, was he?

MALONE. His granmother was a barefooted Irish girl that nursed me by a turf fire. Let him marry another such, and I will not stint her marriage portion. Let him raise himself socially with my money or raise somebody else: so long as there is a social profit somewhere, I'll regard my expenditure as justified. But there must be a profit for someone. A marriage with you would leave things just where they are.

VIOLET. Many of my relations would object very much to my marrying the grandson of a common woman, Mr Malone. That may be prejudice; but so is your desire to have him marry a title prejudice.

MALONE [*rising, and approaching her with a scrutiny in which there is a good deal of reluctant respect*] You seem a pretty straightforward downright sort of a young woman.

VIOLET. I do not see why I should be made miserably poor because I cannot make profits for you. Why do you want to make Hector unhappy?

MALONE. He will get over it all right enough. Men thrive better on disappointments in love than on disappointments in money. I daresay you think that sordid; but I know what I'm talking about. Me father died of starvation in Ireland in the black 47. Maybe youve heard of it.

VIOLET. The Famine?

MALONE [*with smouldering passion*] No, the starvation. When a country is full o food, and exporting it, there can be no famine. Me father was starved dead; and I was starved out to America in me mother's arms. English rule drove me and mine out of Ireland. Well, you can keep Ireland. Me and me like are coming back to buy England; and we'll buy the best of it. I want no middle class properties and no middle class women for Hector. Thats straightforward, isnt it, like yourself?

VIOLET [*icily pitying his sentimentality*] Really, Mr Malone, I am astonished to hear a man of your age and good sense talking in that romantic way. Do you suppose English noblemen will sell their places to you for the asking?

MALONE. I have the refusal of two of the oldest family mansions in England. One historic owner cant afford to keep all the rooms dusted: the other cant afford the death duties. What do you say now?

VIOLET. Of course it is very scandalous; but surely you know that the Government will sooner or later put a stop to all these Socialistic attacks on property.

MALONE [*grinning*] D'y'think theyll be able to get that done before I buy the house—or rather the abbey? Theyre both abbeys.

VIOLET [*putting that aside rather impatiently*] Oh, well, let us talk sense, Mr Malone. You must feel that we havnt been talking sense so far.

MALONE. I cant say I do. I mean all I say.

VIOLET. Then you dont know Hector as I do. He is romantic and faddy—he gets it from you, I fancy—and he wants a certain sort of wife to take care of him. Not a faddy sort of person, you know.

MALONE. Somebody like you, perhaps?

VIOLET [*quietly*] Well, yes. But you cannot very well ask me to undertake this with absolutely no means of keeping up his position.

MALONE [*alarmed*] Stop a bit, stop a bit. Where are we getting to? I'm not aware that I'm asking you to undertake anything.

VIOLET. Of course, Mr Malone, you can make it very difficult for me to speak to you if you choose to misunderstand me.

MALONE [*half bewildered*] I dont wish to take any unfair advantage; but we seem to have got off the straight track somehow.

Straker, with the air of a man who has been making haste, opens the little gate, and admits Hector, who, snorting with indignation, comes upon the lawn, and is making for his father when Violet, greatly dismayed, springs up and intercepts him. Straker does not wait; at least he does not remain within earshot.

VIOLET. Oh, how unlucky! Now please, Hector, say nothing. Go away until I have finished speaking to your father.

HECTOR [*inexorably*] No, Violet: I mean to have this thing out, right away. [*He puts her aside; passes her by; and faces his father, whose cheeks darken as his Irish blood begins to simmer*]. Dad: youve not played this hand straight.

MALONE. Hwat d'y'mean?

HECTOR. Youve opened a letter addressed to me. Youve impersonated me and stolen a march on this lady. Thats disawnerable.

MALONE [*threateningly*] Now you take care what youre saying, Hector. Take care, I tell you.

HECTOR. I have taken care. I am taking care. I'm taking care of my honor and my position in English society.

MALONE [*hotly*] Your position has been got by my money: do you know that?

HECTOR. Well, youve just spoiled it all by opening that letter. A letter from an English lady, not addressed to you—a cawnfidential letter! a dullicate letter! a private letter! opened by my father! Thats a sort of thing a man cant struggle against in England. The sooner we go back together the better. [*He appeals mutely to the heavens to witness the shame and anguish of two outcasts*].

VIOLET [*snubbing him with an instinctive dis-like for scene making*] Dont be unreasonable, Hector. It was quite natural for Mr Malone to open my letter: his name was on the envelope.

MALONE. There! Youve no common sense, Hector. I thank you, Miss Robinson.

HECTOR. I thank you, too. It's very kind of you. My father knows no better.

MALONE [*furiously clenching his fists*] Hector—

HECTOR [*with undaunted moral force*] Oh, it's no use hectoring me. A private letter's a private letter, dad: you cant get over that.

MALONE [*raising his voice*] I wont be talked back to by you, d'y'hear?

VIOLET. Ssh! please, p l e a s e. Here they all come.

Father and son, checked, glare mutely at one another as Tanner comes in through the little gate with Ramsden, followed by Octavius and Ann.

VIOLET. Back already!

TANNER. The Alhambra is not open this afternoon.

VIOLET. What a sell!

Tanner passes on, and presently finds himself between Hector and a strange elder, both apparently on the verge of personal combat. He looks from one to the other for an explanation. They sulkily avoid his eye, and nurse their wrath in silence.

RAMSDEN. Is it wise for you to be out in the sunshine with such a headache, Violet?

TANNER. Have you recovered too, Malone?

VIOLET. Oh, I forgot. We have not all met before. Mr Malone: wont you introduce your father?

HECTOR [*with Roman firmness*] No, I will not. He is no father of mine.

MALONE [*very angry*] You disown your dad before your English friends, do you?

VIOLET. Oh, please dont make a scene.

Ann and Octavius, lingering near the gate, exchange an astonished glance, and discreetly withdraw up the steps to the garden, where they can enjoy the disturbance without intruding. On their way to the steps Ann sends a little grimace of mute sympathy to Violet, who is standing with her back to the little table, looking on in helpless annoyance as her husband soars to higher and higher moral eminences without the least regard to the old man's millions.

HECTOR. I'm very sorry, Miss Rawbnsn; but I'm contending for a principle. I am a son, and, I hope, a dutiful one; but before everything I'm a Mahn!!! And when dad treats my private letters as his own, and takes it on himself to say that I shant marry you if I am happy and fortunate enough to gain your consent, then I just snap my fingers and go my own way.

TANNER. Marry Violet!

RAMSDEN. Are you in your senses?

TANNER. Do you forget what we told you?

HECTOR [*recklessly*] I dont care what you told me.

RAMSDEN [*scandalized*] Tut tut, sir! Monstrous! [*he flings away towards the gate, his elbows quivering with indignation*].

TANNER. Another madman! These men in love should be locked up. [*He gives Hector up as hopeless, and turns away towards the garden; but Malone, taking offence in a new direction, follows him and compels him, by the aggressiveness of his tone, to stop*].

MALONE. I dont understand this. Is Hector not good enough for this lady, pray?

TANNER. My dear sir, the lady is married already. Hector knows it; and yet he persists in his infatuation. Take him home and lock him up.

MALONE [*bitterly*] So this is the highborn social tone Ive spoilt be me ignorant, uncultivated behavior! Makin love to a married woman! [*He comes angrily between Hector and Violet, and almost bawls into Hector's left ear*] Youve picked up that habit of the British aristocracy, have you?

HECTOR. Thats all right. Dont you trouble yourself about that. I'll answer for the morality of what I'm doing.

TANNER [*coming forward to Hector's right hand with flashing eyes*] Well said, Malone! You also see that mere marriage laws are not morality! I agree with you; but unfortunately Violet does not.

MALONE. I take leave to doubt that, sir. [*Turning on Violet*] Let me tell you, Mrs Robinson, or whatever your right name is, you had no right to send that letter to my son when you were the wife of another man.

HECTOR [*outraged*] This is the last straw. Dad: you have insulted my wife.

MALONE. Your wife!

TANNER. You the missing husband! Another moral impostor! [*He smites his brow, and collapses into Malone's chair*].

MALONE. Youve married without my consent!

RAMSDEN. You have deliberately humbugged us, sir!

HECTOR. Here: I have had just about enough of being badgered. Violet and I are married: thats the long and the short of it. Now what have you got to say—any of you?

MALONE. I know what Ive got to say. She's married a beggar.

HECTOR. No: she's married a Worker [*his American pronunciation imparts an overwhelming intensity to this simple and unpopular word*]. I start to earn my own living this very afternoon.

MALONE [*sneering angrily*] Yes: youre very plucky now, because you got your remittance from me yesterday or this morning, I reckon. Waitl it's spent. You wont be so full of cheek then.

HECTOR [*producing a letter from his pocketbook*] Here it is [*thrusting it on his father*]. Now you just take your remittance and yourself out of my life. I'm done with remittances; and I'm done with you. I dont sell the privilege of insulting my wife for a thousand dollars.

MALONE [*deeply wounded and full of concern*] Hector: you dont know what poverty is.

HECTOR [*fervidly*] Well, I wawnt to know what it is. I wawnt'be a Mahn. Violet: you come along with me, to your own home: I'll see you through.

OCTAVIUS [*jumping down from the garden to the lawn and running to Hector's left hand*] I hope youll shake hands with me before you go, Hector. I admire and respect you more than I can say. [*He is affected almost to tears as they shake hands*].

VIOLET [*also almost in tears, but of vexation*] Oh, dont be an idiot, Tavy. Hector's about as fit to become a workman as you are.

TANNER [*rising from his chair on the other side of Hector*] Never fear: theres no question of his becoming a navvy, Mrs Malone. [*To Hector*] Theres really no difficulty about capital to start with. Treat me as a friend: draw on me.

OCTAVIUS [*impulsively*] Or on me.

MALONE [*with fierce jealousy*] Who wants your durty money? Who should he draw on but his own father? [*Tanner and Octavius recoil, Octavius rather hurt, Tanner consoled by the solution of the money difficulty. Violet looks up hopefully*]. Hector: dont be rash, my boy. I'm sorry for what I said: I never meant to insult Violet: I take it all back. She's just the wife you want: there!

HECTOR [*patting him on the shoulder*] Well, thats all right, dad. Say no more: we're friends again. Only, I take no money from anybody.

MALONE [*pleading abjectly*] Dont be hard on me, Hector. I'd rather you quarrelled and took the money than made friends and starved. You dont know what the world is: I do.

HECTOR. No, n o, NO. Thats fixed: thats not going to change. [*He passes his father inexorably by, and goes to Violet*]. Come, Mrs Malone: youve got to move to the hotel with me, and take your proper place before the world.

VIOLET. But I must go in, dear, and tell Davis to pack. Wont you go on and make them give you a room overlooking the garden for me? I'll join you in half an hour.

HECTOR. Very well. Youll dine with us, Dad, wont you?

MALONE [*eager to conciliate him*] Yes, yes.

HECTOR. See you all later. [*He waves his hand to Ann, who has now been joined by Tanner, Octavius, and Ramsden in the garden, and goes out through the little gate, leaving his father and Violet together on the lawn*].

MALONE. Youll try to bring him to his senses, Violet: I know you will.

VIOLET. I had no idea he could be so headstrong. If he goes on like that, what can I do?

MALONE. Dont be discurridged: domestic pressure may be slow; but it's sure. Youll wear him down. Promise me you will.

VIOLET. I will do my best. Of course I think it's the greatest nonsense deliberately making us poor like that.

MALONE. Of course it is.

VIOLET [*after a moment's reflection*] You had better give me the remittance. He will want it for his hotel bill. I'll see whether I can induce him to accept it. Not now, of course, but presently.

MALONE [*eagerly*] Yes, yes, yes: thats just the thing [*he hands her the thousand dollar bill, and adds cunningly*]. Y'understand that this is only a bachelor allowance.

VIOLET [*coolly*] Oh, quite. [*She takes it*]. Thank you. By the way, Mr Malone, those two houses you mentioned—the abbeys.

MALONE. Yes?

VIOLET. Dont take one of them until Ive seen it. One never knows what may be wrong with these places.

MALONE. I wont. I'll do nothing without consulting you, never fear.

VIOLET [*politely, but without a ray of gratitude*] Thanks: that will be much the best way. [*She goes calmly back to the villa, escorted obsequiously by Malone to the upper end of the garden*].

TANNER [*drawing Ramsden's attention to Malone's cringing attitude as he takes leave of Violet*] And that poor devil is a billionaire! one of the master spirits of the age! Led in a string like a pug dog by the first girl who takes the trouble to despise him! I wonder will it ever come to that with me. [*He comes down to the lawn*].

RAMSDEN [*following him*] The sooner the better for you.

MALONE [*slapping his hands as he returns through the garden*] Thatll be a grand woman for Hector. I wouldnt exchange her for ten duchesses. [*He descends to the lawn and comes between Tanner and Ramsden*].

RAMSDEN [*very civil to the billionaire*] It's an unexpected pleasure to find you in this corner of the world, Mr Malone. Have you come to buy up the Alhambra?

MALONE. Well, I dont say I mightnt. I think I could do better with it than the Spanish government. But thats not what I came about. To tell you the truth, about a month ago I overheard a deal between two men over a bundle of shares. They differed about the price: they were young and greedy, and didnt know that if the shares were worth what was bid for them they must be worth what was asked, the margin being too small to be of any account, you see. To amuse meself, I cut in and bought the shares. Well, to this day I havnt found out what the business is. The office is in this town; and the name is Mendoza, Limited. Now whether Mendoza's a mine, or a steamboat line, or a bank, or a patent article—

TANNER. He's a man. I know him: his principles are thoroughly commercial. Let us take you round the town in our motor, Mr Malone, and call on him on the way.

MALONE. If youll be so kind, yes. And may I ask who—

TANNER. Mr Roebuck Ramsden, a very old friend of your daughter-in-law.

MALONE. Happy to meet you, Mr Ramsden.

RAMSDEN. Thank you. Mr Tanner is also one of our circle.

MALONE. Glad to know you also, Mr Tanner.

TANNER. Thanks. [*Malone and Ramsden go*

out very amicably through the little gate. Tanner calls to Octavius, who is wandering in the garden with Ann] Tavy! [*Tavy comes to the steps, Tanner whispers loudly to him*] Violet's father-in-law is a financier of brigands. [*Tanner hurries away to overtake Malone and Ramsden. Ann strolls to the steps with an idle impulse to torment Octavius*].

ANN. Wont you go with them, Tavy?

OCTAVIUS [*tears suddenly flushing his eyes*] You cut me to the heart, Ann, by wanting me to go [*he comes down on the lawn to hide his face from her. She follows him caressingly*].

ANN. Poor Ricky Ticky Tavy! Poor heart!

OCTAVIUS. It belongs to you, Ann. Forgive me: I must speak of it. I love you. You know I love you.

ANN. Whats the good, Tavy? You know that my mother is determined that I shall marry Jack.

OCTAVIUS [*amazed*] Jack!

ANN. It seems absurd, doesnt it?

OCTAVIUS [*with growing resentment*] Do you mean to say that Jack has been playing with me all this time? That he has been urging me not to marry you because he intends to marry you himself?

ANN [*alarmed*] No, no: you mustnt lead him to believe that I said that. I dont for a moment think that Jack knows his own mind. But it's clear from my father's will that he wished me to marry Jack. And my mother is set on it.

OCTAVIUS. But you are not bound to sacrifice yourself always to the wishes of your parents.

ANN. My father loved me. My mother loves me. Surely their wishes are a better guide than my own selfishness.

OCTAVIUS. Oh, I know how unselfish you are, Ann. But believe me—though I know I am speaking in my own interest—there is another side to this question. Is it fair to Jack to marry him if you do not love him? Is it fair to destroy my happiness as well as your own if you can bring yourself to love me?

ANN [*looking at him with a faint impulse of pity*] Tavy, my dear, you are a nice creature —a good boy.

OCTAVIUS [*humiliated*] Is that all?

ANN [*mischievously in spite of her pity*] Thats a great deal, I assure you. You would always worship the ground I trod on, wouldnt you?

OCTAVIUS. I do. It sounds ridiculous; but

it's no exaggeration. I do; and I always shall.

ANN. Always is a long word, Tavy. You see, I shall have to live up always to your idea of my divinity; and I dont think I could do that if we were married. But if I marry Jack, youll never be disillusioned—at least not until I grow too old.

OCTAVIUS. I too shall grow old, Ann. And when I am eighty, one white hair of the woman I love will make me tremble more than the thickest gold tress from the most beautiful young head.

ANN [*quite touched*] Oh, thats poetry, Tavy, real poetry. It gives me that strange sudden sense of an echo from a former existence which always seems to me such a striking proof that we have immortal souls.

OCTAVIUS. Do you believe that it is true?

ANN. Tavy: if it is to come true, you must lose me as well as love me.

OCTAVIUS. Oh! [*he hastily sits down at the little table and covers his face with his hands*].

ANN [*with conviction*] Tavy: I wouldnt for worlds destroy your illusions. I can neither take you nor let you go. I can see exactly what will suit you. You must be a sentimental old bachelor for my sake.

OCTAVIUS [*desperately*] Ann: I'll kill myself.

ANN. Oh no, you wont: that wouldnt be kind. You wont have a bad time. You will be very nice to women; and you will go a good deal to the opera. A broken heart is a very pleasant complaint for a man in London if he has a comfortable income.

OCTAVIUS [*considerably cooled, but believing that he is only recovering his self-control*] I know you mean to be kind, Ann. Jack has persuaded you that cynicism is a good tonic for me. [*He rises with quiet dignity*].

ANN [*studying him slyly*] You see, I'm disillusionizing you already. Thats what I dread.

OCTAVIUS. You do not dread disillusionizing Jack.

ANN [*her face lighting up with mischievous ecstasy—whispering*] I cant: he has no illusions about me. I shall surprise Jack the other way. Getting over an unfavorable impression is ever so much easier than living up to an ideal. Oh, I shall enrapture Jack sometimes!

OCTAVIUS [*resuming the calm phase of despair, and beginning to enjoy his broken heart and delicate attitude without knowing it*] I dont doubt that. You will enrapture him always. And he —the fool!—thinks you would make him wretched.

ANN. Yes: thats the difficulty, so far.

OCTAVIUS [*heroically*] Shall *I* tell him that you love him?

ANN [*quickly*] Oh no: he'd run away again.

OCTAVIUS [*shocked*] Ann: would you marry an unwilling man?

ANN. What a queer creature you are, Tavy! Theres no such thing as a willing man when you really go for him. [*She laughs naughtily*]. I'm shocking you, I suppose. But you know you are really getting a sort of satisfaction already in being out of danger yourself.

OCTAVIUS [*startled*] Satisfaction! [*Reproachfully*] You say that to me!

ANN. Well, if it were really agony, would you ask for more of it?

OCTAVIUS. H a v e I asked for more of it?

ANN. You have offered to tell Jack that I love him. Thats self-sacrifice, I suppose; but there must be some satisfaction in it. Perhaps it's because youre a poet. You are like the bird that presses its breast against the sharp thorn to make itself sing.

OCTAVIUS. It's quite simple. I love you; and I want you to be happy. You dont love me; so I cant make you happy myself; but I can help another man to do it.

ANN. Yes: it seems quite simple. But I doubt if we ever know why we do things. The only really simple thing is to go straight for what you want and grab it. I suppose I dont love you, Tavy; but sometimes I feel as if I should like to make a man of you somehow. You are very foolish about women.

OCTAVIUS [*almost coldly*] I am content to be what I am in that respect.

ANN. Then you must keep away from them, and only dream about them. I wouldnt marry you for worlds, Tavy.

OCTAVIUS. I have no hope, Ann: I accept my ill luck. But I dont think you quite know how much it hurts.

ANN. You are so softhearted! It's queer that you should be so different from Violet. Violet's as hard as nails.

OCTAVIUS. Oh no. I am sure Violet is thoroughly womanly at heart.

ANN [*with some impatience*] Why do you say that? Is it unwomanly to be thoughtful and businesslike and sensible? Do you want Violet to be an idiot—or something worse, like me?

OCTAVIUS. Something worse—like y o u ! What do you mean, Ann?

ANN. Oh well, I dont mean that, of course. But I have a great respect for Violet. She gets her own way always.

OCTAVIUS [*sighing*] So do you.

ANN. Yes; but somehow she gets it without coaxing—without having to make people sentimental about her.

OCTAVIUS [*with brotherly callousness*] Nobody could get very sentimental about Violet, I think, pretty as she is.

ANN. Oh yes they could, if she made them.

OCTAVIUS. But surely no really nice woman would deliberately practise on men's instincts in that way.

ANN [*throwing up her hands*] Oh, Tavy, Tavy, Ricky Ticky Tavy, heaven help the woman who marries you!

OCTAVIUS [*his passion reviving at the name*] Oh why, why, why do you say that? Dont torment me. I dont understand.

ANN. Suppose she were to tell fibs, and lay snares for men?

OCTAVIUS. Do you think *I* could marry such a woman—I, who have known and loved y o u ?

ANN. Hm! Well, at all events, she wouldnt let you if she were wise. So thats settled. And now I cant talk any more. Say you forgive me, and that the subject is closed.

OCTAVIUS. I have nothing to forgive; and the subject is closed. And if the wound is open, at least you shall never see it bleed.

ANN. Poetic to the last, Tavy. Goodbye, dear. [*She pats his cheek; has an impulse to kiss him and then another impulse of distaste which prevents her; finally runs away through the garden and into the villa*].

Octavius again takes refuge at the table, bowing his head on his arms and sobbing softly. Mrs Whitefield, who has been pottering round the Granada shops, and has a net full of little parcels in her hand, comes in through the gate and sees him.

MRS WHITEFIELD [*running to him and lifting his head*] Whats the matter, Tavy? Are you ill?

OCTAVIUS. No, nothing, nothing.

MRS WHITEFIELD [*still holding his head, anxiously*] But youre crying. Is it about Violet's marriage?

OCTAVIUS. No, no. Who told you about Violet?

MRS WHITEFIELD [*restoring the head to its owner*] I met Roebuck and that awful old Irishman. Are you sure youre not ill? Whats the matter?

OCTAVIUS [*affectionately*] It's nothing. Only

a man's broken heart. Doesnt that sound ridiculous?

MRS WHITEFIELD. But what is it all about? Has Ann been doing anything to you?

OCTAVIUS. It's not Ann's fault. And dont think for a moment that I blame you.

MRS WHITEFIELD [startled] For what?

OCTAVIUS [pressing her hand consolingly] For nothing. I said I didnt blame you.

MRS WHITEFIELD. But I havnt done anything. Whats the matter?

OCTAVIUS [smiling sadly] Cant you guess? I daresay you are right to prefer Jack to me as a husband for Ann; but I love Ann; and it hurts rather. [He rises and moves away from her towards the middle of the lawn].

MRS WHITEFIELD [following him hastily] Does Ann say that I want her to marry Jack?

OCTAVIUS. Yes: she has told me.

MRS WHITEFIELD [thoughtfully] Then I'm very sorry for you, Tavy. It's only her way of saying she wants to marry Jack. Little she cares what I say or what I want.

OCTAVIUS. But she would not say it unless she believed it. Surely you dont suspect Ann of—of deceit!!

MRS WHITEFIELD. Well, never mind, Tavy. I dont know which is best for a young man: to know too little, like you, or too much, like Jack.

Tanner returns.

TANNER. Well, Ive disposed of old Malone. Ive introduced him to Mendoza, Limited; and left the two brigands together to talk it out. Hullo, Tavy! anything wrong?

OCTAVIUS. I must go wash my face, I see. [To Mrs Whitefield] Tell him what you wish. [To Tanner] You may take it from me, Jack, that Ann approves of it.

TANNER [puzzled by his manner] Approves of what?

OCTAVIUS. Of what Mrs Whitefield wishes. [He goes his way with sad dignity to the villa].

TANNER [to Mrs Whitefield] This is very mysterious. What is it you wish? It shall be done, whatever it is.

MRS WHITEFIELD [with snivelling gratitude] Thank you, Jack. [She sits down. Tanner brings the other chair from the table and sits close to her with his elbows on his knees, giving her his whole attention]. I dont know why it is that other people's children are so nice to me, and that my own have so little consideration for me. It's no wonder I dont seem able to care for Ann and Rhoda as I do for you and Tavy and

Violet. It's a very queer world. It used to be so straightforward and simple; and now nobody seems to think and feel as they ought. Nothing has been right since that speech that Professor Tyndall made at Belfast.

TANNER. Yes: life is more complicated than we used to think. But what am I to do for you?

MRS WHITEFIELD. Thats just what I want to tell you. Of course youll marry Ann whether I like it or not—

TANNER [starting] It seems to me that I shall presently be married to Ann whether I like it myself or not.

MRS WHITEFIELD [peacefully] Oh, very likely you will: you know what she is when she has set her mind on anything. But dont put it on me: thats all I ask. Tavy has just let out that she's been saying that I am making her marry you; and the poor boy is breaking his heart about it; for he is in love with her himself, though what he sees in her so wonderful, goodness knows: I dont. It's no use telling Tavy that Ann puts things into people's heads by telling them that I want them when the thought of them never crossed my mind. It only sets Tavy against me. But you know better than that. So if you marry her, dont put the blame on me.

TANNER [emphatically] I havnt the slightest intention of marrying her.

MRS WHITEFIELD [slyly] She'd suit you better than Tavy. She'd meet her match in you, Jack. I'd like to see her meet her match.

TANNER. No man is a match for a woman, except with a poker and a pair of hobnailed boots. Not always even then. Anyhow, I cant take the poker to her. I should be a mere slave.

MRS WHITEFIELD. No: she's afraid of you. At all events, you would tell her the truth about herself. She wouldnt be able to slip out of it as she does with me.

TANNER. Everybody would call me a brute if I told Ann the truth about herself in terms of her own moral code. To begin with, Ann says things that are not strictly true.

MRS WHITEFIELD. I'm glad somebody sees she is not an angel.

TANNER. In short—to put it as a husband would put it when exasperated to the point of speaking out—she is a liar. And since she has plunged Tavy head over ears in love with her without any intention of marrying him, she is a coquette, according to the standard definition of a coquette as a woman who rouses passions she has no intention of gratifying. And as she has now reduced you to the point of being willing to sacrifice me at the altar for the mere satisfaction of getting me to call her a liar to her face, I may conclude that she is a bully as well. She cant bully men as she bullies women; so she habitually and unscrupulously uses her personal fascination to make men give her whatever she wants. That makes her almost something for which I know no polite name.

MRS WHITEFIELD [*in mild expostulation*] Well, you cant expect perfection, Jack.

TANNER. I dont. But what annoys me is that Ann does. I know perfectly well that all this about her being a liar and a bully and a coquette and so forth is a trumped-up moral indictment which might be brought against anybody. We all lie; we all bully as much as we dare; we all bid for admiration without the least intention of earning it; we all get as much rent as we can out of our powers of fascination. If Ann would admit this I shouldnt quarrel with her. But she wont. If she has children she'll take advantage of their telling lies to amuse herself by whacking them. If another woman makes eyes at me, she'll refuse to know a coquette. She will do just what she likes herself whilst insisting on everybody else doing what the conventional code prescribes. In short, I can stand everything except her confounded hypocrisy. Thats what beats me.

MRS WHITEFIELD [*carried away by the relief of hearing her own opinion so eloquently expressed*] Oh, she is a hypocrite. She is: she is. Isnt she?

TANNER. Then why do you want to marry me to her?

MRS WHITEFIELD [*querulously*] There now! put it on me, of course. I never thought of it until Tavy told me she said I did. But, you know, I'm very fond of Tavy: he's a sort of son to me; and I dont want him to be trampled on and made wretched.

TANNER. Whereas I dont matter, I suppose.

MRS WHITEFIELD. Oh, you are different, somehow: you are able to take care of yourself. Youd serve her out. And anyhow, she must marry somebody.

TANNER. Aha! there speaks the life instinct. You detest her; but you feel that you must get her married.

MRS WHITEFIELD [*rising, shocked*] Do you

mean that I detest my own daughter! Surely you dont believe me to be so wicked and unnatural as that, merely because I see her faults.

TANNER [*cynically*] You love her, then?

MRS WHITEFIELD. Why, of course I do. What queer things you say, Jack! We cant help loving our own blood relations.

TANNER. Well, perhaps it saves unpleasantness to say so. But for my part, I suspect that the tables of consanguinity have a natural basis in a natural repugnance [*he rises*].

MRS WHITEFIELD. You shouldnt say things like that, Jack. I hope you wont tell Ann that I have been speaking to you. I only wanted to set myself right with you and Tavy. I couldnt sit mumchance and have everything put on me.

TANNER [*politely*] Quite so.

MRS WHITEFIELD [*dissatisfied*] And now Ive only made matters worse. Tavy's angry with me because I dont worship Ann. And when it's been put into my head that Ann ought to marry you, what can I say except that it would serve her right?

TANNER. Thank you.

MRS WHITEFIELD. Now dont be silly and twist what I say into something I dont mean. I ought to have fair play—

Ann comes from the villa, followed presently by Violet, who is dressed for driving.

ANN [*coming to her mother's right hand with threatening suavity*] Well, mamma darling, you seem to be having a delightful chat with Jack. We can hear you all over the place.

MRS WHITEFIELD [*appalled*] Have you overheard—

TANNER. Never fear: Ann is only—well, we were discussing that habit of hers just now. She hasnt heard a word.

MRS WHITEFIELD [*stoutly*] I dont care whether she has or not: I have a right to say what I please.

VIOLET [*arriving on the lawn and coming between Mrs Whitefield and Tanner*] Ive come to say goodbye. I'm off for my honeymoon.

MRS WHITEFIELD [*crying*] Oh, dont say that, Violet. And no wedding, no breakfast, no clothes, nor anything.

VIOLET [*petting her*] It wont be for long.

MRS WHITEFIELD. Dont let him take you to America. Promise me that you wont.

VIOLET [*very decidedly*] I should think not, indeed. Dont cry, dear: I'm only going to the hotel.

MRS WHITEFIELD. But going in that dress, with your luggage, makes one realize—[*she chokes, and then breaks out again*] How I wish you were my daughter, Violet!

VIOLET [*soothing her*] There, there: so I am. Ann will be jealous.

MRS WHITEFIELD. Ann doesnt care a bit for me.

ANN. Fie, mother! Come, now: you mustnt cry any more: you know Violet doesnt like it [*Mrs Whitefield dries her eyes, and subsides*].

VIOLET. Goodbye, Jack.

TANNER. Goodbye, Violet.

VIOLET. The sooner you get married too, the better. You will be much less misunderstood.

TANNER [*restively*] I quite expect to get married in the course of the afternoon. You all seem to have set your minds on it.

VIOLET. You might do worse. [*To Mrs Whitefield: putting her arm round her*] Let me take you to the hotel with me: the drive will do you good. Come in and get a wrap. [*She takes her towards the villa*].

MRS WHITEFIELD [*as they go up through the garden*] I dont know what I shall do when you are gone, with no one but Ann in the house; and she always occupied with the men! It's not to be expected that your husband will care to be bothered with an old woman like me. Oh, you neednt tell me: politeness is all very well; but I know what people think— [*She talks herself and Violet out of sight and hearing*].

Ann, alone with Tanner, watches him and waits. He makes an irresolute movement towards the gate; but some magnetism in her draws him to her, a broken man.

ANN. Violet is quite right. You ought to get married.

TANNER [*explosively*] Ann: I will not marry you. Do you hear? I wont, wont, wont, wont, WONT marry you.

ANN [*placidly*] Well, nobody axd you, sir she said, sir she said, sir she said. So thats settled.

TANNER. Yes, nobody has asked me; but everybody treats the thing as settled. It's in the air. When we meet, the others go away on absurd pretexts to leave us alone together. Ramsden no longer scowls at me: his eye beams, as if he were already giving you away to me in church. Tavy refers me to your mother and gives me his blessing. Straker openly treats you as his future employer: it

was he who first told me of it.

ANN. Was that why you ran away?

TANNER. Yes, only to be stopped by a lovesick brigand and run down like a truant schoolboy.

ANN. Well, if you dont want to be married, you neednt be [*she turns away from him and sits down, much at her ease*].

TANNER [*following her*] Does any man want to be hanged? Yet men let themselves be hanged without a struggle for life, though they could at least give the chaplain a black eye. We do the world's will, not our own. I have a frightful feeling that I shall let myself be married because it is the world's will that you should have a husband.

ANN. I daresay I shall, someday.

TANNER. But why me? me of all men! Marriage is to me apostasy, profanation of the sanctuary of my soul, violation of my manhood, sale of my birthright, shameful surrender, ignominious capitulation, acceptance of defeat. I shall decay like a thing that has served its purpose and is done with; I shall change from a man with a future to a man with a past; I shall see in the greasy eyes of all the other husbands their relief at the arrival of a new prisoner to share their ignominy. The young men will scorn me as one who has sold out: to the women I, who have always been an enigma and a possibility, shall be merely somebody else's property—and damaged goods at that: a secondhand man at best.

ANN. Well, your wife can put on a cap and make herself ugly to keep you in countenance, like my grandmother.

TANNER. So that she may make her triumph more insolent by publicly throwing away the bait the moment the trap snaps on the victim!

ANN. After all, though, what difference would it make? Beauty is all very well at first sight; but who ever looks at it when it has been in the house three days? I thought our pictures very lovely when papa bought them; but I havnt looked at them for years. You never bother about my looks: you are too well used to me. I might be the umbrella stand.

TANNER. You lie, you vampire: you lie.

ANN. Flatterer. Why are you trying to fascinate me, Jack, if you dont want to marry me?

TANNER. The Life Force. I am in the grip of the Life Force.

ANN. I dont understand in the least: it sounds like the Life Guards.

TANNER. Why dont you marry Tavy? He is willing. Can you not be satisfied unless your prey struggles?

ANN [turning to him as if to let him into a secret] Tavy will never marry. Havnt you noticed that that sort of man never marries?

TANNER. What! a man who idolizes women! who sees nothing in nature but romantic scenery for love duets! Tavy, the chivalrous, the faithful, the tenderhearted and true! Tavy never marry! Why, he was born to be swept up by the first pair of blue eyes he meets in the street.

ANN. Yes, I know. All the same, Jack, men like that always live in comfortable bachelor lodgings with broken hearts, and are adored by their landladies, and never get married. Men like you always get married.

TANNER [smiting his brow] How frightfully, horribly true! It has been staring me in the face all my life; and I never saw it before.

ANN. Oh, it's the same with women. The poetic temperament's a very nice temperament, very amiable, very harmless and poetic, I daresay; but it's an old maid's temperament.

TANNER. Barren. The Life Force passes it by.

ANN. If thats what you mean by the Life Force, yes.

TANNER. You dont care for Tavy?

ANN [looking round carefully to make sure that Tavy is not within earshot] No.

TANNER. And you do care for me?

ANN [rising quietly and shaking her finger at him] Now, Jack! Behave yourself.

TANNER. Infamous, abandoned woman! Devil!

ANN. Boa-constrictor! Elephant!

TANNER. Hypocrite!

ANN [softly] I must be, for my future husband's sake.

TANNER. For mine! [Correcting himself savagely] I mean for his.

ANN [ignoring the correction] Yes, for yours. You had better marry what you call a hypocrite, Jack. Women who are not hypocrites go about in rational dress and are insulted and get into all sorts of hot water. And then their husbands get dragged in too, and live in continual dread of fresh complications.

Wouldnt you prefer a wife you could depend on?

TANNER. No: a thousand times no: hot water is the revolutionist's element. You clean men as you clean milk-pails, by scalding them.

ANN. Cold water has its uses too. It's healthy.

TANNER [despairingly] Oh, you are witty: at the supreme moment the Life Force endows you with every quality. Well, I too can be a hypocrite. Your father's will appointed me your guardian, not your suitor. I shall be faithful to my trust.

ANN [in low siren tones] He asked me who I would have as my guardian before he made that will. I chose you!

TANNER. The will is yours then! The trap was laid from the beginning.

ANN [concentrating all her magic] From the beginning—from our childhood—for both of us—by the Life Force.

TANNER. I will not marry you. I will not marry you.

ANN. Oh, you will, you will.

TANNER. I tell you, no, no, no.

ANN. I tell you, yes, yes, yes.

TANNER. No.

ANN [coaxing—imploring—almost exhausted] Yes. Before it is too late for repentance. Yes.

TANNER [struck by the echo from the past] When did all this happen to me before? Are we two dreaming?

ANN [suddenly losing her courage, with an anguish that she does not conceal] No. We are awake; and you have said no: that is all.

TANNER [brutally] Well?

ANN. Well, I made a mistake: you do not love me.

TANNER [seizing her in his arms] It is false: I love you. The Life Force enchants me: I have the whole world in my arms when I clasp you. But I am fighting for my freedom, for my honor, for my self, one and indivisible.

ANN. Your happiness will be worth them all.

TANNER. You would sell freedom and honor and self for happiness?

ANN. It will not be all happiness for me. Perhaps death.

TANNER [groaning] Oh, that clutch holds and hurts. What have you grasped in me? Is there a father's heart as well as a mother's?

ANN. Take care, Jack: if anyone comes while we are like this, you will have to marry me.

TANNER. If we two stood now on the edge of a precipice, I would hold you tight and jump.

ANN [*panting, failing more and more under the strain*] Jack: let me go. I have dared so frightfully—it is lasting longer than I thought. Let me go: I cant bear it.

TANNER. Nor I. Let it kill us.

ANN. Yes: I dont care. I am at the end of my forces. I dont care. I think I am going to faint.

At this moment Violet and Octavius come from the villa with Mrs Whitefield, who is wrapped up for driving. Simultaneously Malone and Ramsden, followed by Mendoza and Straker, come in through the little gate in the paling. Tanner shamefacedly releases Ann, who raises her hand giddily to her forehead.

MALONE. Take care. Something's the matter with the lady.

RAMSDEN. What does this mean?

VIOLET [*running between Ann and Tanner*] Are you ill?

ANN [*reeling, with a supreme effort*] I have promised to marry Jack. [*She swoons. Violet kneels by her and chafes her hand. Tanner runs round to her other hand, and tries to lift her head. Octavius goes to Violet's assistance, but does not know what to do. Mrs Whitefield hurries back into the villa. Octavius, Malone, and Ramsden run to Ann and crowd round her, stooping to assist. Straker coolly comes to Ann's feet, and Mendoza to her head, both upright and self-possessed*].

STRAKER. Now then, ladies and gentlemen: she dont want a crowd round her: she wants air—all the air she can git. If you please, gents—[*Malone and Ramsden allow him to drive them gently past Ann and up the lawn towards the garden, where Octavius, who has already become conscious of his uselessness, joins them. Straker, following them up, pauses for a moment to instruct Tanner*]. Dont lift er ed, Mr Tanner: let it go flat so's the blood can run back into it.

MENDOZA. He is right, Mr Tanner. Trust to the air of the Sierra. [*He withdraws delicately to the garden steps*].

TANNER [*rising*] I yield to your superior knowledge of physiology, Henry. [*He withdraws to the corner of the lawn; and Octavius immediately hurries down to him*].

TAVY [*aside to Tanner, grasping his hand*] Jack: be very happy.

TANNER [*aside to Tavy*] I never asked her.

It is a trap for me. [*He goes up the lawn towards the garden. Octavius remains petrified*].

MENDOZA [*intercepting Mrs Whitefield, who comes from the villa with a glass of brandy*] What is this, madam [*he takes it from her*]?

MRS WHITEFIELD. A little brandy.

MENDOZA. The worst thing you could give her. Allow me. [*He swallows it*]. Trust to the air of the Sierra, madam.

For a moment the men all forget Ann and stare at Mendoza.

ANN [*in Violet's ear, clutching her round the neck*] Violet: did Jack say anything when I fainted?

VIOLET. No.

ANN. Ah! [*with a sigh of intense relief she relapses*].

MRS WHITEFIELD. Oh, she's fainted again.

They are about to rush back to her; but Mendoza stops them with a warning gesture.

ANN [*supine*] No, I havnt. I'm quite happy.

TANNER [*suddenly walking determinedly to her, and snatching her hand from Violet to feel her pulse*] Why, her pulse is positively bounding. Come! get up. What nonsense! Up with you. [*He hauls her up summarily*].

ANN. Yes: I feel strong enough now. But you very nearly killed me, Jack, for all that.

MALONE. A rough wooer, eh? Theyre the best sort, Miss Whitefield. I congratulate Mr Tanner; and I hope to meet you and him as frequent guests at the abbey.

ANN. Thank you. [*She goes past Malone to Octavius*] Ricky Ticky Tavy: congratulate me. [*Aside to him*] I want to make you cry for the last time.

TAVY [*steadfastly*] No more tears. I am happy in your happiness. And I believe in you in spite of everything.

RAMSDEN [*coming between Malone and Tanner*] You are a happy man, Jack Tanner. I envy you.

MENDOZA [*advancing between Violet and Tanner*] Sir: there are two tragedies in life. One is to lose your heart's desire. The other is to gain it. Mine and yours, sir.

TANNER. Mr Mendoza: I have no heart's desires. Ramsden: it is very easy for you to call me a happy man: you are only a spectator. I am one of the principals; and I know better. Ann: stop tempting Tavy, and come back to me.

ANN [*complying*] You are absurd, Jack. [*She takes his proffered arm*].

TANNER [*continuing*] I solemnly say that I

am not a happy man. Ann looks happy; but she is only triumphant, successful, victorious. That is not happiness, but the price for which the strong sell their happiness. What we have both done this afternoon is to renounce happiness, renounce freedom, renounce tranquillity, above all, renounce the romantic possibilities of an unknown future, for the cares of a household and a family. I beg that no man may seize the occasion to get half drunk and utter imbecile speeches and coarse pleasantries at my expense. We propose to furnish our own house according to our own taste; and I hereby give notice that the seven or eight travelling clocks, the four or five dressing cases, the carvers and fish slices, the copies of Patmore's Angel In The House in extra morocco, and the other articles you are preparing to heap upon us, will be instantly sold, and the proceeds devoted to circulating free copies of the Revolutionist's Handbook. The wedding will take place three days after our return to England, by special licence, at the office of the district superintendent registrar, in the presence of my solicitor and his clerk, who, like his clients, will be in ordinary walking dress—

VIOLET [*with intense conviction*] You are a brute, Jack.

ANN [*looking at him with fond pride and caressing his arm*] Never mind her, dear. Go on talking.

TANNER. Talking!

Universal laughter.

THE END

XII
JOHN BULL'S OTHER ISLAND
1904

ACT I

Great George Street, Westminster, is the address of Doyle and Broadbent, civil engineers. On the threshold one reads that the firm consists of Mr Laurence Doyle and Mr Thomas Broadbent, and that their rooms are on the first floor. Most of these rooms are private; for the partners, being bachelors and bosom friends, live there; and the door marked Private, next the clerks' office, is their domestic sitting room as well as their reception room for clients. Let me describe it briefly from the point of view of a sparrow on the window sill. The outer door is in the opposite wall, close to the right hand corner. Between this door and the left hand corner is a hatstand and a table consisting of large drawing boards on trestles, with plans, rolls of tracing paper, mathematical instruments, and other draughtsman's accessories on it. In the left hand wall is the fireplace, and the door of an inner room between the fireplace and our observant sparrow. Against the right hand wall is a filing cabinet, with a cupboard on it, and nearer, a tall office desk and stool for one person. In the middle of the room a large double writing table is set across, with a chair at each end for the two partners. It is a room which no woman would tolerate, smelling of tobacco, and much in need of repapering, repainting, and recarpeting; but this is the effect of bachelor untidiness and in-difference, not want of means; for nothing that Doyle and Broadbent themselves have purchased is cheap; nor is anything they want lacking. On the walls hang a large map of South America, a pictorial advertisement of a steamship company, an impressive portrait of Gladstone, and several caricatures of Mr Balfour as a rabbit and Mr Chamberlain as a fox by Francis Carruthers Gould.

At twenty minutes to five o'clock on a summer afternoon in 1904, the room is empty. Presently the outer door is opened, and a valet comes in laden with a large Gladstone bag and a strap of rugs. He carries them into the inner room. He is a respectable valet, old enough to have lost all alacrity and acquired an air of putting up patiently with a great deal of trouble and indifferent health. The luggage belongs to Broadbent, who enters after the valet. He pulls off his overcoat and hangs it with his hat on the stand. Then he comes to the writing table and looks through the letters waiting there for him. He is a robust, full-blooded, energetic man in the prime of life, sometimes eager and credulous, sometimes shrewd and roguish, sometimes portentously solemn, sometimes jolly and impetuous, always buoyant and irresistible, mostly likeable, and enormously absurd in his most earnest moments. He bursts open his letters with his thumb, and glances through them, flinging the envelopes about the floor with reckless untidiness whilst he talks to the valet.

BROADBENT [*calling*] Hodson.

HODSON [*in the bedroom*] Yes sir.

BROADBENT. Dont unpack. Just take out the things Ive worn; and put in clean things.

HODSON [*appearing at the bedroom door*] Yes sir. [*He turns to go back into the bedroom*].

BROADBENT. And look here! [*Hodson turns again*]. Do you remember where I put my revolver?

HODSON. Revolver, sir! Yes sir. Mr Doyle uses it as a paper-weight, sir, when he's drawing.

BROADBENT. Well, I want it packed. Theres a packet of cartridges somewhere, I think. Find it and pack it as well.

HODSON. Yes sir.

BROADBENT. By the way, pack your own traps too. I shall take you with me this time.

HODSON [*hesitant*] Is it a dangerous part youre going to, sir? Should I be expected to carry a revolver, sir?

BROADBENT. Perhaps it might be as well. I'm going to Ireland.

HODSON [*reassured*] Yes sir.

BROADBENT. You dont feel nervous about it, I suppose?

HODSON. Not at all, sir. I'll risk it, sir.

BROADBENT. Ever been in Ireland?

HODSON. No sir. I understand it's a very wet climate, sir. I'd better pack your india-rubber overalls.

BROADBENT. Do. Wheres Mr Doyle?

HODSON. I'm expecting him at five, sir. He went out after lunch.

BROADBENT. Anybody been looking for me?

HODSON. A person giving the name of Haffigan has called twice today, sir.

BROADBENT. Oh, I'm sorry. Why didnt he wait? I told him to wait if I wasnt in.

HODSON. Well sir, I didnt know you expected him; so I thought it best to—to—not to encourage him, sir.

BROADBENT. Oh, he's all right. He's an Irishman, and not very particular about his appearance.

HODSON. Yes sir: I noticed that he was rather Irish.

BROADBENT. If he calls again let him come up.

HODSON. I think I saw him waiting about, sir, when you drove up. Shall I fetch him, sir?

BROADBENT. Do, Hodson.

HODSON. Yes sir [*He makes for the outer door*].

BROADBENT. He'll want tea. Let us have some.

HODSON [*stopping*] I shouldnt think he drank tea, sir.

BROADBENT. Well, bring whatever you think he'd like.

HODSON. Yes sir [*An electric bell rings*]. Here he is, sir. Saw you arrive, sir.

BROADBENT. Right. Shew him in. [*Hodson goes out. Broadbent gets through the rest of his letters before Hodson returns with the visitor*].

HODSON. Mr Affigan.

Haffigan is a stunted, shortnecked, small-headed man of about 30, with a small bullet head, a red nose, and furtive eyes. He is dressed in seedy black, almost clerically, and might be a tenth-rate schoolmaster ruined by drink. He hastens to shake Broadbent's hand with a show of reckless geniality and high spirits, helped out by a rollicking stage brogue. This is perhaps a comfort to himself, as he is secretly pursued by the horrors of incipient delirium tremens.

HAFFIGAN. Tim Haffigan, sir, at your service. The top o the mornin to you, Misther Broadbent.

BROADBENT [*delighted with his Irish visitor*] Good afternoon, Mr Haffigan.

TIM. An is it the afthernoon it is already? Begorra, what I call the mornin is all the time a man fasts afther breakfast.

BROADBENT. Havnt you lunched?

TIM. Divil a lunch!

BROADBENT. I'm sorry I couldnt get back from Brighton in time to offer you some; but—

TIM. Not a word, sir, not a word. Sure itll do tomorrow. Besides, I'm Irish, sir: a poor aither, but a powerful dhrinker.

BROADBENT. I was just about to ring for tea when you came. Sit down, Mr Haffigan.

TIM. Tay is a good dhrink if your nerves can stand it. Mine cant.

Haffigan sits down at the writing table, with his back to the filing cabinet. Broadbent sits opposite him. Hodson enters empty-handed; takes two glasses, a siphon, and a tantalus from the cupboard; places them before Broadbent on the writing table; looks ruthlessly at Haffigan, who cannot meet his eye; and retires.

BROADBENT. Try a whisky and soda.

TIM [*sobered*] There you touch the national wakeness, sir. [*Piously*] Not that I share it meself. Ive seen too much of the mischief of it.

BROADBENT [*pouring the whisky*] Say when.

TIM. Not too sthrong. [*Broadbent stops and looks inquiringly at him*]. Say half-an-half. [*Broadbent, somewhat startled by this demand, pours a little more, and again stops and looks*]. Just a dhrain more: the lower half o the tumbler doesnt hold a fair half. Thankya.

BROADBENT [*laughing*] You Irishmen certainly do know how to drink. [*Pouring some whisky for himself*] Now thats my poor English idea of a whisky and soda.

TIM. An a very good idea it is too. Dhrink is the curse o me unhappy counthry. I take it meself because Ive a wake heart and a poor digestion; but in principle I'm a teetoatler.

BROADBENT [*suddenly solemn and strenuous*] So am I, of course. I'm a Local Optionist to the backbone. You have no idea, Mr Haffigan, of the ruin that is wrought in this country by the unholy alliance of the publicans, the bishops, the Tories, and The Times. We must close the public-houses at all costs [*he drinks*].

TIM. Sure I know. It's awful [*he drinks*]. I see youre a good Liberal like meself, sir.

BROADBENT. I am a lover of liberty, like every true Englishman, Mr Haffigan. My name is Broadbent. If my name were Breitstein, and I had a hooked nose and a house in Park Lane, I should carry a Union Jack handkerchief and a penny trumpet, and tax the food of the people to support the Navy League, and clamor for the destruction of the last remnants of national liberty —

TIM. Not another word. Shake hands.

BROADBENT. But I should like to explain—

TIM. Sure I know every word youre goin to say before yev said it. *I* know the sort o man yar. An so youre thinkin o comin to Ireland for a bit?

BROADBENT. Where else can I go? I am an Englishman and a Liberal; and now that South Africa has been enslaved and destroyed, there is no country left to me to take an interest in but Ireland. Mind: I dont say that an Englishman has not other duties. He has a duty to Finland and a duty to Macedonia. But what sane man can deny that an Englishman's first duty is his duty to Ireland? Unfortunately, we have politicians here more unscrupulous than Bobrikoff, more bloodthirsty than Abdul the Damned; and it is under their heel that Ireland is now writhing.

TIM. Faith, theyve reckoned up with poor oul Bobrikoff anyhow.

BROADBENT. Not that I defend assassina-

tion: God forbid! However strongly we may feel that the unfortunate and patriotic young man who avenged the wrongs of Finland on the Russian tyrant was perfectly right from his own point of view, yet every civilized man must regard murder with abhorrence. Not even in defence of Free Trade would I lift my hand against a political opponent, however richly he might deserve it.

TIM. I'm sure you wouldnt; and I honor you for it. Youre goin to Ireland, then, out o sympithy: is it?

BROADBENT. I'm going to develop an estate there for the Land Development Syndicate, in which I am interested. I am convinced that all it needs to make it pay is to handle it properly, as estates are handled in England. You know the English plan, Mr Haffigan, dont you?

TIM. Bedad I do, sir. Take all you can out of Ireland and spend it in England: thats it.

BROADBENT [*not quite liking this*] My plan, sir, will be to take a little money out of England and spend it in Ireland.

TIM. More power to your elbow! an may your shadda never be less! for youre the broth of a boy intirely. An how can I help you? Command me to the last dhrop o me blood.

BROADBENT. Have you ever heard of Garden City?

TIM [*doubtfully*] D'ye mane Heavn?

BROADBENT. Heaven! No: it's near Hitchin. If you can spare half an hour I'll go into it with you.

TIM. I tell you hwat, Gimme a prospectus. Lemmy take it home and reflect on it.

BROADBENT. Youre quite right: I will. [*He gives him a copy of Ebenezer Howard's book, and several pamphlets*]. You understand that the map of the city—the circular construction —is only a suggestion.

TIM. I'll make a careful note o that [*looking dazedly at the map*].

BROADBENT. What I say is, why not start a Garden City in Ireland?

TIM [*with enthusiasm*] Thats just what was on the tip o me tongue to ask you. Why not? [*Defiantly*] Tell me why not.

BROADBENT. There are difficulties. I shall overcome them; but there are difficulties. When I first arrive in Ireland I shall be hated as an Englishman. As a Protestant, I shall be denounced from every altar. My life may be in danger. Well, I am prepared to face that.

TIM. Never fear, sir. We know how to re-spict a brave innimy.

BROADBENT. What I really dread is mis-understanding. I think you could help me to avoid that. When I heard you speak the other evening in Bermondsey at the meeting of the National League, I saw at once that you were—You wont mind my speaking frankly?

TIM. Tell me all me faults as man to man. I can stand anything but flatthery.

BROADBENT. May I put it in this way? that I saw at once that you are a thorough Irish-man, with all the faults and all the qualities of your race: rash and improvident but brave and goodnatured; not likely to succeed in business on your own account perhaps, but eloquent, humorous, a lover of freedom, and a true follower of that great Englishman Gladstone.

TIM. Spare me blushes. I mustnt sit here to be praised to me face. But I confess to the goodnature: it's an Irish wakeness. I'd share me last shillin with a friend.

BROADBENT. I feel sure you would, Mr Haffigan.

TIM [impulsively] Damn it! call me Tim. A man that talks about Ireland as you do may call me anything. Gimmy a howlt o that whisky bottle [he replenishes].

BROADBENT [smiling indulgently] Well, Tim, will you come with me and help to break the ice between me and your warmhearted, im-pulsive countrymen?

TIM. Will I come to Madagascar or Cochin China wid you? Bedad I'll come to the North Pole wid you if yll pay me fare; for the divil a shillin I have to buy a third class ticket.

BROADBENT. Ive not forgotten that, Tim. We must put that little matter on a solid English footing, though the rest can be as Irish as you please. You must come as my— my—well, I hardly know what to call it. If we call you my agent, theyll shoot you. If we call you a bailiff, theyll duck you in the horsepond. I have a secretary already; and—

TIM. Then we'll call him the Home Secret-ary and me the Irish Secretary. Eh?

BROADBENT [laughing industriously] Capital. Your Irish wit has settled the first difficulty. Now about your salary—

TIM. A salary, is it? Sure I'd do it for nothin, only me cloes ud disgrace you; and I'd be dhriven to borra money from your friends: a thing thats agin me nacher. But I wont take a penny more than a hundherd a year.

[He looks with restless cunning at Broadbent, trying to guess how far he may go].

BROADBENT. If that will satisfy you—

TIM [more than reassured] Why shouldnt it satisfy me? A hundherd a year is twelve pound a month, isnt it?

BROADBENT. No. Eight pound six and eight-pence.

TIM. Oh murdher! An I'll have to sind five timmy poor oul mother in Ireland. But no matther: I said a hundherd; and what I said I'll stick to, if I have to starve for it.

BROADBENT [with business caution] Well, let us say twelve pounds for the first month. Afterwards, we shall see how we get on.

TIM. Youre a gentleman, sir. Whin me mother turns up her toes, you shall take the five pounds off; for your expinses must be kep down wid a sthrong hand; an—[He is inter-rupted by the arrival of Broadbent's partner].

Mr Laurence Doyle is a man of 36, with cold grey eyes, strained nose, fine fastidious lips, critical brows, clever head, rather refined and goodlooking on the whole, but with a suggestion of thinskinnedness and dissatisfaction that con-trasts strongly with Broadbent's eupeptic jollity.

He comes in as a man at home there, but on seeing the stranger shrinks at once, and is about to withdraw when Broadbent reassures him. He then comes forward to the table, between the two others.

DOYLE [retreating] Youre engaged.

BROADBENT. Not at all, not at all. Come in. [To Tim] This gentleman is a friend who lives with me here: my partner, Mr Doyle. [To Doyle] This is a new Irish friend of mine, Mr Tim Haffigan.

TIM [rising with effusion] Sure it's meself thats proud to meet any friend o Misther Broadbent's. The top o the mornin to you, sir! Me heart goes out teeye both. It's not often I meet two such splendid speciments iv the Anglo-Saxon race.

BROADBENT [chuckling] Wrong for once, Tim. My friend Mr Doyle is a countryman of yours.

Tim is noticeably dashed by this announce-ment. He draws in his horns at once, and scowls suspiciously at Doyle under a vanishing mask of good-fellowship: cringing a little, too, in mere nerveless fear of him.

DOYLE [with cool disgust] Good evening. [He retires to the fireplace, and says to Broadbent in a tone which conveys the strongest possible hint to Haffigan that he is unwelcome] Will you soon be disengaged?

TIM [*his brogue decaying into a common would-be genteel accent with an unexpected strain of Glasgow in it*] I must be going. Avnmpoartnt engeegement in the west end.

BROADBENT [*rising*] It's settled, then, that you come with me.

TIM. Ashll be verra pleased to accompany ye, sir.

BROADBENT. But how soon? Can you start tonight? from Paddington? We go by Milford Haven.

TIM [*hesitating*] Well—A'm afraid—A [*Doyle goes abruptly into the bedroom, slamming the door and shattering the last remnant of Tim's nerve. The poor wretch saves himself from bursting into tears by plunging again into his role of daredevil Irishman. He rushes to Broadbent; plucks at his sleeve with trembling fingers; and pours forth his entreaty with all the brogue he can muster, subduing his voice lest Doyle should hear and return*]. Misther Broadbent: dont humiliate me before a fella counthryman. Look here: me cloes is up the spout. Gimmy a fypoun-note—I'll pay ya nex Choosda whin me ship comes home—or you can stop it out o me month's sallery. I'll be on the platform at Paddnton punctial an ready. Gimmy it quick, before he comes back. You wont mind me axin, will ye?

BROADBENT. Not at all. I was about to offer you an advance for travelling expenses. [*He gives him a bank note*].

TIM [*pocketing it*] Thank you. I'll be there half an hour before the thrain starts. [*Larry is heard at the bedroom door, returning*]. Whisht: he's comin back. Goodbye an God bless ye. [*He hurries out almost crying, the £5 note and all the drink it means to him being too much for his empty stomach and overstrained nerves*].

DOYLE [*returning*] Where the devil did you pick up that seedy swindler? What was he doing here? [*He goes up to the table where the plans are, and makes a note on one of them, referring to his pocket book as he does so*].

BROADBENT. There you go! Why are you so down on every Irishman you meet, especially if he's a bit shabby? poor devil! Surely a fellow-countryman may pass you the top of the morning without offence, even if his coat is a bit shiny at the seams.

DOYLE [*contemptuously*] The top of the morning! Did he call you the broth of a boy? [*He comes to the writing table*].

BROADBENT [*triumphantly*] Yes.

DOYLE. And wished you more power to your elbow?

BROADBENT. He did.

DOYLE. And that your shadow might never be less?

BROADBENT. Certainly.

DOYLE [*taking up the depleted whisky bottle and shaking his head at it*] And he got about half a pint of whisky out of you.

BROADBENT. It did him no harm. He never turned a hair.

DOYLE. How much money did he borrow?

BROADBENT. It was not borrowing exactly. He shewed a very honorable spirit about money. I believe he would share his last shilling with a friend.

DOYLE. No doubt he would share his friend's last shilling if his friend was fool enough to let him. How much did he touch you for?

BROADBENT. Oh, nothing. An advance on his salary—for travelling expenses.

DOYLE. Salary! In Heaven's name, what for?

BROADBENT. For being my Home Secretary, as he very wittily called it.

DOYLE. I dont see the joke.

BROADBENT. You can spoil any joke by being cold blooded about it. I saw it all right when he said it. It was something—something really very amusing—about the Home Secretary and the Irish Secretary. At all events, he's evidently the very man to take with me to Ireland to break the ice for me. He can gain the confidence of the people there, and make them friendly to me. Eh? [*He seats himself on the office stool, and tilts it back so that the edge of the standing desk supports his back and prevents his toppling over*].

DOYLE. A nice introduction, by George! Do you suppose the whole population of Ireland consists of drunken begging letter writers, or that even if it did, they would accept one another as references?

BROADBENT. Pooh! nonsense! he's only an Irishman. Besides, you dont seriously suppose that Haffigan can humbug me, do you?

DOYLE. No: he's too lazy to take the trouble. All he has to do is to sit there and drink your whisky while you humbug yourself. However, we neednt argue about Haffigan, for two reasons. First, with your money in his pocket he will never reach Paddington: there are too many public houses on the way. Second, he's not an Irishman at all.

BROADBENT. Not an Irishman! [*He is so*

amazed by the statement that he straightens himself and brings the stool bolt upright].

DOYLE. Born in Glasgow. Never was in Ireland in his life. I know all about him.

BROADBENT. But he spoke—he behaved just like an Irishman.

DOYLE. Like an Irishman!! Man alive, dont you know that all this top-o-the-morning and broth-of-a-boy and more-power-to-your-elbow business is got up in England to fool you, like the Albert Hall concerts of Irish music? No Irishman ever talks like that in Ireland, or ever did, or ever will. But when a thoroughly worthless Irishman comes to England, and finds the whole place full of romantic duffers like you, who will let him loaf and drink and sponge and brag as long as he flatters your sense of moral superiority by playing the fool and degrading himself and his country, he soon learns the antics that take you in. He picks them up at the theatre or the music hall. Haffigan learnt the rudiments from his father, who came from my part of Ireland. I knew his uncles, Matt and Andy Haffigan of Rosscullen.

BROADBENT [*still incredulous*] But his brogue?

DOYLE. His brogue! A fat lot you know about brogues! Ive heard you call a Dublin accent that you could hang your hat on, a brogue. Heaven help you! you dont know the difference between Connemara and Rathmines. [*With violent irritation*] Oh, damn Tim Haffigan! lets drop the subject: he's not worth wrangling about.

BROADBENT. Whats wrong with you today, Larry? Why are you so bitter?

Doyle looks at him perplexedly; comes slowly to the writing table; and sits down at the end next the fireplace before replying.

DOYLE. Well: your letter completely upset me, for one thing.

BROADBENT. Why?

LARRY. Your foreclosing this Rosscullen mortgage and turning poor Nick Lestrange out of house and home has rather taken me aback; for I liked the old rascal when I was a boy and had the run of his park to play in. I was brought up on the property.

BROADBENT. But he wouldnt pay the interest. I had to foreclose on behalf of the Syndicate. So now I'm off to Rosscullen to look after the property myself. [*He sits down at the writing table opposite Larry, and adds, casually, but with an anxious glance at his partner*] Youre coming with me, of course?

DOYLE [*rising nervously and recommencing his restless movements*] Thats it. Thats what I dread. Thats what has upset me.

BROADBENT. But dont you want to see your country again after 18 years absence? to see your people? to be in the old home again? to—

DOYLE [*interrupting him very impatiently*] Yes, yes: I know all that as well as you do.

BROADBENT. Oh well, of course [*with a shrug*] if you take it in that way, I'm sorry.

DOYLE. Never you mind my temper: it's not meant for you, as you ought to know by this time. [*He sits down again, a little ashamed of his petulance; reflects a moment bitterly; then bursts out*] I have an instinct against going back to Ireland: an instinct so strong that I'd rather go with you to the South Pole than to Rosscullen.

BROADBENT. What! Here you are, belonging to a nation with the strongest patriotism! the most inveterate homing instinct in the world! and you pretend youd rather go anywhere than back to Ireland. You dont suppose I believe you, do you? In your heart—

DOYLE. Never mind my heart: an Irishman's heart is nothing but his imagination. How many of all those millions that have left Ireland have ever come back or wanted to come back? But whats the use of talking to you? Three verses of twaddle about the Irish emigrant "sitting on the stile, Mary," or three hours of Irish patriotism in Bermondsey or the Scotland Division of Liverpool, go further with you than all the facts that stare you in the face. Why, man alive, look at me! You know the way I nag, and worry, and carp, and cavil, and disparage, and am never satisfied and never quiet, and try the patience of my best friends.

BROADBENT. Oh, come, Larry! do yourself justice. Youre very amusing and agreeable to strangers.

DOYLE. Yes, to strangers. Perhaps if I was a bit stiffer to strangers, and a bit easier at home, like an Englishman, I'd be better company for you.

BROADBENT. We get on well enough. Of course you have the melancholy of the Keltic race—

DOYLE [*bounding out of his chair*] Good God!!!

BROADBENT [*slyly*]—and also its habit of using strong language when theres nothing the matter.

DOYLE. Nothing the matter! When people talk about the Celtic race, I feel as if I could burn down London. That sort of rot does more harm than ten Coercion Acts. Do you suppose a man need be a Celt to feel melancholy in Rosscullen? Why, man, Ireland was peopled just as England was; and its breed was crossed by just the same invaders.

BROADBENT. True. All the capable people in Ireland are of English extraction. It has often struck me as a most remarkable circumstance that the only party in parliament which shews the genuine old English character and spirit is the Irish party. Look at its independence, its determination, its defiance of bad Governments, its sympathy with oppressed nationalities all the world over! How English!

DOYLE. Not to mention the solemnity with which it talks old-fashioned nonsense which it knows perfectly well to be a century behind the times. Thats English, if you like.

BROADBENT. No, Larry, no. You are thinking of the modern hybrids that now monopolize England. Hypocrites, humbugs, Germans, Jews, Yankees, foreigners, Park Laners, cosmopolitan riffraff. Dont call them English. They dont belong to the dear old island, but to their confounded new empire; and by George! theyre worthy of it; and I wish them joy of it.

DOYLE [unmoved by this outburst] There! You feel better now, dont you?

BROADBENT [defiantly] I do. Much better.

DOYLE. My dear Tom, you only need a touch of the Irish climate to be as big a fool as I am myself. If all my Irish blood were poured into your veins, you wouldnt turn a hair of your constitution and character. Go and marry the most English Englishwoman you can find, and then bring up your son in Rosscullen; and that son's character will be so like mine and so unlike yours that everybody will accuse me of being his father. [With sudden anguish] Rosscullen! oh, good Lord, Rosscullen! The dullness! the hopelessness! the ignorance! the bigotry!

BROADBENT [matter-of-factly] The usual thing in the country, Larry. Just the same here.

DOYLE [hastily] No, no: the climate is different. Here, if the life is dull, you can be dull too, and no great harm done. [Going off into a passionate dream] But your wits cant thicken in that soft moist air, on those white springy roads, in those misty rushes and brown bogs, on those hillsides of granite rocks and magenta heather. Youve no such colors in the sky, no such lure in the distances, no such sadness in the evenings. Oh, the dreaming! the dreaming! the torturing, heart-scalding, never satisfying dreaming, dreaming, dreaming, dreaming! [Savagely] No debauchery that ever coarsened and brutalized an Englishman can take the worth and usefulness out of him like that dreaming. An Irishman's imagination never lets him alone, never convinces him, never satisfies him; but it makes him that he cant face reality nor deal with it nor handle it nor conquer it: he can only sneer at them that do, and [bitterly, at Broadbent] be " agreeable to strangers," like a good-for-nothing woman on the streets. [Gabbling at Broadbent across the table] It's all dreaming, all imagination. He cant be religious. The inspired Churchman that teaches him the sanctity of life and the importance of conduct is sent away empty; while the poor village priest that gives him a miracle or a sentimental story of a saint, has cathedrals built for him out of the pennies of the poor. He cant be intelligently political: he dreams of what the Shan Van Vocht said in ninetyeight. If you want to interest him in Ireland youve got to call the unfortunate island Kathleen ni Hoolihan and pretend she's a little old woman. It saves thinking. It saves working. It saves everything except imagination, imagination, imagination; and imagination's such a torture that you cant bear it without whisky. [With fierce shivering self-contempt] At last you get that you can bear nothing real at all: youd rather starve than cook a meal; youd rather go shabby and dirty than set your mind to take care of your clothes and wash yourself; you nag and squabble at home because your wife isnt an angel, and she despises you because youre not a hero; and you hate the whole lot round you because theyre only poor slovenly useless devils like yourself. [Dropping his voice like a man making some shameful confidence] And all the while there goes on a horrible, senseless, mischievous laughter. When youre young, you exchange drinks with other young men; and you exchange vile stories with them; and as youre too futile to be able to help or cheer them, you chaff and sneer and taunt them for not doing the things you darent do yourself. And all the time you laugh! laugh! laugh! eternal derision, eternal envy, eternal folly, eternal fouling and staining and degrading, until, when you come at last to a country where men take a question seriously and give a serious answer to it, you deride them for having no sense of humor, and plume yourself on your own worthlessness as if it made you better than them.

BROADBENT [*roused to intense earnestness by Doyle's eloquence*] Never despair, Larry. There are great possibilities for Ireland. Home Rule will work wonders under English guidance.

DOYLE [*pulled up short, his face twitching with a reluctant smile*] Tom: why do you select my most tragic moments for your most irresistible strokes of humor?

BROADBENT. Humor! I was perfectly serious. What do you mean? Do you doubt my seriousness about Home Rule?

DOYLE. I am sure you are serious, Tom, about the English guidance.

BROADBENT [*quite reassured*] Of course I am. Our guidance is the important thing. We English must place our capacity for government without stint at the service of nations who are less fortunately endowed in that respect; so as to allow them to develop in perfect freedom to the English level of self-government, you know. You understand me?

DOYLE. Perfectly. And Rosscullen will understand you too.

BROADBENT [*cheerfully*] Of course it will. So thats all right. [*He pulls up his chair and settles himself comfortably to lecture Doyle*]. Now, Larry, Ive listened carefully to all youve said about Ireland; and I can see nothing whatever to prevent your coming with me. What does it all come to? Simply that you were only a young fellow when you were in Ireland. Youll find all that chaffing and drinking and not knowing what to be at in Peckham just the same as in Donnybrook. You looked at Ireland with a boy's eyes and saw only boyish things. Come back with me and look at it with a man's; and get a better opinion of your country.

DOYLE. I daresay youre partly right in that: at all events I know very well that if I had been the son of a laborer instead of the son of a country landagent, I should have struck more grit than I did. Unfortunately I'm not going back to visit the Irish nation, but to visit my father and Aunt Judy and Nora Reilly and Father Dempsey and the rest of them.

BROADBENT. Well, why not? Theyll be delighted to see you, now that England has made a man of you.

DOYLE [*struck by this*]Ah! you hit the mark there, Tom, with true British inspiration.

BROADBENT. Common sense, you mean.

DOYLE [*quickly*] No I dont: youve no more common sense than a gander. No Englishman has any common sense, or ever had, or ever will have. Youre going on a sentimental expedition for perfectly ridiculous reasons, with your head full of political nonsense that would not take in any ordinarily intelligent donkey; but you can hit me in the eye with the simple truth about myself and my father.

BROADBENT [*amazed*] I never mentioned your father.

DOYLE [*not heeding the interruption*] There he is in Rosscullen, a landagent who's always been in a small way because he's a Catholic, and the landlords are mostly Protestants. What with land courts reducing rents and Land Purchase Acts turning big estates into little holdings, he'd be a beggar if he hadnt taken to collecting the new purchase instalments instead of the old rents. I doubt if he's been further from home than Athenmullet for twenty years. And here am I, made a man of, as you say, by England.

BROADBENT [*apologetically*] I assure you I never meant—

DOYLE. Oh, dont apologize: it's quite true. I daresay Ive learnt something in America and a few other remote and inferior spots; but in the main it is by living with you and working in double harness with you that I have learnt to live in a real world and not in an imaginary one. I owe more to you than to any Irishman.

BROADBENT [*shaking his head with a twinkle in his eye*] Very friendly of you, Larry, old man, but all blarney. I like blarney; but it's rot, all the same.

DOYLE. No it's not. I should never have done anything without you; though I never stop wondering at that blessed old head of yours with all its ideas in watertight compartments, and all the compartments warranted impervious to anything it doesnt suit you to understand.

BROADBENT [*invincible*] Unmitigated rot, Larry, I assure you.

DOYLE. Well, at any rate you will admit that all my friends are either Englishmen or men of the big world that belongs to the big

Powers. All the serious part of my life has been lived in that atmosphere: all the serious part of my work has been done with men of that sort. Just think of me as I am now going back to Rosscullen! to that hell of littleness and monotony! How am I to get on with a little country landagent that ekes out his 5 per cent with a little farming and a scrap of house property in the nearest country town? What am I to say to him? What is he to say to me?

BROADBENT [*scandalized*] But youre father and son, man!

DOYLE. What difference does that make? What would you say if I proposed a visit to your father?

BROADBENT [*with filial rectitude*] I always made a point of going to see my father regularly until his mind gave way.

DOYLE [*concerned*] Has he gone mad? You never told me.

BROADBENT. He has joined the Tariff Reform League. He would never have done that if his mind had not been weakened. [*Beginning to declaim*] He has fallen a victim to the arts of a political charlatan who—

DOYLE [*interrupting him*] You mean that you keep clear of your father because he differs from you about Free Trade, and you dont want to quarrel with him. Well, think of me and my father! He's a Nationalist and a Separatist. I'm a metallurgical chemist turned civil engineer. Now whatever else metallurgical chemistry may be, it's not national. It's international. And my business and yours as civil engineers is to join countries, not to separate them. The one real political conviction that our business has rubbed into us is that frontiers are hindrances and flags confounded nuisances.

BROADBENT [*still smarting under Mr Chamberlain's economic heresy*] Only when there is a protective tariff—

DOYLE [*firmly*] Now look here, Tom: you want to get in a speech on Free Trade; and youre not going to do it: I wont stand it. My father wants to make St George's Channel a frontier and hoist a green flag on College Green; and I want to bring Galway within 3 hours of Colchester and 24 of New York. I want Ireland to be the brains and imagination of a big Commonwealth, not a Robinson Crusoe island. Then theres the religious difficulty. My Catholicism is the Catholicism of Charlemagne or Dante, qualified by a great deal of modern science and folklore which Father Dempsey would call the ravings of an Atheist. Well, my father's Catholicism is the Catholicism of Father Dempsey.

BROADBENT [*shrewdly*] I dont want to interrupt you, Larry; but you know this is all gammon. These differences exist in all families; but the members rub on together all right. [*Suddenly relapsing into portentousness*] Of course there are some questions which touch the very foundations of morals; and on these I grant you even the closest relationships cannot excuse any compromise or laxity. For instance—

DOYLE [*impatiently springing up and walking about*] For instance, Home Rule, South Africa, Free Trade, and putting the Church schools on the Education Rate. Well, I should differ from my father on every one of them, probably, just as I differ from you about them.

BROADBENT. Yes; but you are an Irishman; and these things are not serious to you as they are to an Englishman.

DOYLE. What! not even Home Rule!

BROADBENT [*steadfastly*] Not even Home Rule. We owe Home Rule not to the Irish, but to our English Gladstone. No, Larry: I cant help thinking that theres something behind all this.

DOYLE [*hotly*] What is there behind it? Do you think I'm humbugging you?

BROADBENT. Dont fly out, old chap. I only thought—

DOYLE. What did you think?

BROADBENT. Well, a moment ago I caught a name which is new to me: a Miss Nora Reilly, I think. [*Doyle stops dead and stares at him with something like awe*]. I dont wish to be impertinent, as you know, Larry; but are you sure she has nothing to do with your reluctance to come to Ireland with me?

DOYLE [*sitting down again, vanquished*] Thomas Broadbent: I surrender. The poor silly-clever Irishman takes off his hat to God's Englishman. The man who could in all seriousness make that recent remark of yours about Home Rule and Gladstone must be simply the champion idiot of all the world. Yet the man who could in the very next sentence sweep away all my special pleading and go straight to the heart of my motives must be a man of genius. But that the idiot and the genius should be the same man! how is that possible? [*Springing to his feet*] By

Jove, I see it all now. I'll write an article about it, and send it to Nature.

BROADBENT [*staring at him*] What on earth—

DOYLE. It's quite simple. You know that a caterpillar—

BROADBENT. A caterpillar!!!

DOYLE. Yes, a caterpillar. Now give your mind to what I am going to say; for it's a new and important scientific theory of the English national character. A caterpillar—

BROADBENT. Look here, Larry: dont be an ass.

DOYLE [*insisting*] I say a caterpillar and I mean a caterpillar. Youll understand presently. A caterpillar [*Broadbent mutters a slight protest, but does not press it*] when it gets into a tree, instinctively makes itself look exactly like a leaf; so that both its enemies and its prey may mistake it for one and think it not worth bothering about.

BROADBENT. Whats that got to do with our English national character?

DOYLE. I'll tell you. The world is as full of fools as a tree is full of leaves. Well, the Englishman does what the caterpillar does. He instinctively makes himself look like a fool, and eats up all the real fools at his ease while his enemies let him alone and laugh at him for being a fool like the rest. Oh, nature is cunning! cunning! [*He sits down, lost in contemplation of his word-picture*].

BROADBENT [*with hearty admiration*] Now you know, Larry, that would never have occurred to me. You Irish people are amazingly clever. Of course it's all tommy rot; but it's so brilliant, you know! How the dickens do you think of such things! You really must write an article about it: theyll pay you something for it. If Nature wont have it, I can get it into Engineering for you: I know the editor.

DOYLE. Lets get back to business. I'd better tell you about Nora Reilly.

BROADBENT. No: never mind. I shouldnt have alluded to her.

DOYLE. I'd rather. Nora has a fortune.

BROADBENT [*keenly interested*] Eh? How much?

DOYLE. Forty per annum.

BROADBENT. Forty thousand?

DOYLE. No, forty. Forty pounds.

BROADBENT [*much dashed*] Thats what you call a fortune in Rosscullen, is it?

DOYLE. A girl with a dowry of five pounds calls it a fortune in Rosscullen. Whats more,

£40 a year is a fortune there; and Nora Reilly enjoys a good deal of social consideration as an heiress on the strength of it. It has helped my father's household through many a tight place. My father was her father's agent. She came on a visit to us when he died, and has lived with us ever since.

BROADBENT [*attentively, beginning to suspect Larry of misconduct with Nora, and resolving to get to the bottom of it*] Since when? I mean how old were you when she came?

DOYLE. I was seventeen. So was she: if she'd been older she'd have had more sense than to stay with us. We were together for 18 months before I went up to Dublin to study. When I went home for Christmas and Easter, she was there. I suppose it used to be something of an event for her; though of course I never thought of that then.

BROADBENT. Were you at all hard hit?

DOYLE. Not really. I had only two ideas at that time: first, to learn to do something; and then to get out of Ireland and have a chance of doing it. She didnt count. I was romantic about her, just as I was romantic about Byron's heroines or the old Round Tower of Rosscullen; but she didnt count any more than they did. Ive never crossed St George's Channel since for her sake—never even landed at Queenstown and come back to London through Ireland.

BROADBENT. But did you ever say anything that would justify her in waiting for you?

DOYLE. No, never. But she is waiting for me.

BROADBENT. How do you know?

DOYLE. She writes to me—on her birthday. She used to write on mine, and send me little things as presents; but I stopped that by pretending that it was no use when I was travelling, as they got lost in the foreign post-offices. [*He pronounces post-offices with the stress on offices, instead of on post*].

BROADBENT. You answer the letters?

DOYLE. Not very punctually. But they get acknowledged at one time or another.

BROADBENT. How do you feel when you see her handwriting?

DOYLE. Uneasy. I'd give £50 to escape a letter.

BROADBENT [*looking grave, and throwing himself back in his chair to intimate that the cross-examination is over, and the result very damaging to the witness*] Hm!

DOYLE. What d'ye mean by Hm!

BROADBENT. Of course I know that the moral code is different in Ireland. But in England it's not considered fair to trifle with a woman's affections.

DOYLE. You mean that an Englishman would get engaged to another woman and return Nora her letters and presents with a letter to say he was unworthy of her and wished her every happiness?

BROADBENT. Well, even that would set the poor girl's mind at rest.

DOYLE. Would it? I wonder! One thing I can tell you; and that is that Nora would wait until she died of old age sooner than ask my intentions or condescend to hint at the possibility of my having any. You dont know what Irish pride is. England may have knocked a good deal of it out of me; but she's never been in England; and if I had to choose between wounding that delicacy in her and hitting her in the face, I'd hit her in the face without a moment's hesitation.

BROADBENT [who has been nursing his knee and reflecting, apparently rather agreeably] You know, all this sounds rather interesting. Theres the Irish charm about it. Thats the worst of you: the Irish charm doesnt exist for you.

DOYLE. Oh yes it does. But it's the charm of a dream. Live in contact with dreams and you will get something of their charm: live in contact with facts and you will get something of their brutality. I wish I could find a country to live in where the facts were not brutal and the dreams not unreal.

BROADBENT [changing his attitude and responding to Doyle's earnestness with deep conviction: his elbows on the table and his hands clenched] Dont despair, Larry, old boy: things may look black; but there will be a great change after the next election.

DOYLE [jumping up] Oh, get out, you idiot!

BROADBENT [rising also, not a bit snubbed] Ha! ha! you may laugh; but we shall see. However, dont let us argue about that. Come now! you ask my advice about Miss Reilly?

DOYLE [reddening] No I dont. Damn your advice! [Softening] Lets have it, all the same.

BROADBENT. Well, everything you tell me about her impresses me favorably. She seems to have the feelings of a lady; and though we must face the fact that in England her income would hardly maintain her in the lower middle class—

DOYLE [interrupting] Now look here, Tom.

That reminds me. When you go to Ireland, just drop talking about the middle class and bragging of belonging to it. In Ireland youre either a gentleman or youre not. If you want to be particularly offensive to Nora, you can call her a Papist; but if you call her a middle-class woman, Heaven help you!

BROADBENT [irrepressible] Never fear. Youre all descended from the ancient kings: I know that. [Complacently] I'm not so tactless as you think, my boy. [Earnest again] I expect to find Miss Reilly a perfect lady; and I strongly advise you to come and have another look at her before you make up your mind about her. By the way, have you a photograph of her?

DOYLE. Her photographs stopped at twenty-five.

BROADBENT [saddened] Ah yes, I suppose so. [With feeling, severely] Larry: youve treated that poor girl disgracefully.

DOYLE. By George, if she only knew that two men were talking about her like this—!

BROADBENT. She wouldnt like it, would she? Of course not. We ought to be ashamed of ourselves, Larry. [More and more carried away by his new fancy]. You know, I have a sort of presentiment that Miss Reilly is a very superior woman.

DOYLE [staring hard at him] Oh! you have, have you?

BROADBENT. Yes I have. There is something very touching about the history of this beautiful girl.

DOYLE. Beau—! Oho! Heres a chance for Nora! and for me! [Calling] Hodson.

HODSON [appearing at the bedroom door] Did you call, sir?

DOYLE. Pack for me too. I'm going to Ireland with Mr Broadbent.

HODSON. Right, sir. [He retires into the bedroom].

BROADBENT [clapping Doyle on the shoulder] Thank you, old chap. Thank you.

ACT II

Rosscullen. Westward a hillside of granite rock and heather slopes upward across the prospect from south to north. A huge stone stands on it in a naturally impossible place, as if it had been tossed up there by a giant. Over the brow, in the desolate valley beyond, is a round tower. A lonely white high road trending away westward past the tower loses itself at the foot of the far mountains. It is evening; and there are great breadths of silken green in the Irish sky. The sun is setting.

A man with the face of a young saint, yet with white hair and perhaps 50 years on his back, is standing near the stone in a trance of intense melancholy, looking over the hills as if by mere intensity of gaze he could pierce the glories of the sunset and see into the streets of heaven. He is dressed in black, and is rather more clerical in appearance than most English curates are nowadays; but he does not wear the collar and waistcoat of a parish priest. He is roused from his trance by the chirp of an insect from a tuft of grass in a crevice of the stone. His face relaxes: he turns quietly, and gravely takes off his hat to the tuft, addressing the insect in a brogue which is the jocular assumption of a gentleman and not the natural speech of a peasant.

THE MAN. An is that yourself, Misther Grasshopper? I hope I see you well this fine evenin.

THE GRASSHOPPER [*prompt and shrill in answer*] X.X.

THE MAN [*encouragingly*] Thats right. I suppose now youve come out to make yourself miserable be admyerin the sunset?

THE GRASSHOPPER [*sadly*] X.X.

THE MAN. Aye, youre a thrue Irish grasshopper.

THE GRASSHOPPER [*loudly*] X.X.X.

THE MAN. Three cheers for ould Ireland, is it? That helps you to face out the misery and the poverty and the torment, doesnt it?

THE GRASSHOPPER [*plaintively*] X.X.

THE MAN. Ah, it's no use, me poor little friend. If you could jump as far as a kangaroo you couldnt jump away from your own heart an its punishment. You can only look at Heaven from here: you cant reach it. There! [*pointing with his stick to the sunset*] thats the gate o glory, isnt it?

THE GRASSHOPPER [*assenting*] X.X.

THE MAN. Sure it's the wise grasshopper yar to know that. But tell me this, Misther Unworldly Wiseman: why does the sight of Heaven wring your heart an mine as the sight of holy wather wrings the heart o the divil? What wickedness have you done to bring that curse on you? Here! where are you jumpin to? Wheres your manners to go skyrocketin like that out o the box in the middle o your confession [*he threatens it with his stick*]?

THE GRASSHOPPER [*penitently*] X.

THE MAN [*lowering the stick*] I accept your apology; but dont do it again. And now tell me one thing before I let you go home to bed. Which would you say this counthry was: hell or purgatory?

THE GRASSHOPPER. X.

THE MAN. Hell! Faith I'm afraid youre right. I wondher what you and me did when we were alive to get sent here.

THE GRASSHOPPER [*shrilly*] X.X.

THE MAN [*nodding*] Well, as you say, it's a delicate subject; and I wont press it on you. Now off widja.

THE GRASSHOPPER. X.X. [*It springs away*].

THE MAN [*waving his stick*] God speed you! [*He walks away past the stone towards the brow of the hill. Immediately a young laborer, his face distorted with terror, slips round from behind the stone*].

THE LABORER [*crossing himself repeatedly*] Oh glory be to God! glory be to God! Oh Holy Mother an all the saints! Oh murdher! murdher! [*Beside himself, calling*] Fadher Keegan! Fadher Keegan!

THE MAN [*turning*] Who's there? Whats that? [*He comes back and finds the laborer, who clasps his knees*] Patsy Farrell! What are you doing here?

PATSY. Oh for the love o God dont lave me here wi dhe grasshopper. I hard it spakin to you. Dont let it do me any harm, Father darlint.

KEEGAN. Get up, you foolish man, get up. Are you afraid of a poor insect because I pretended it was talking to me?

PATSY. Oh, it was no pretendin, Fadher dear. Didnt it give three cheers n say it was a divil out o hell? Oh say youll see me safe home, Fadher; n put a blessin on me or somethin [*he moans with terror*].

KEEGAN. What were you doing there, Patsy, listnin? Were you spyin on me?

PATSY. No, Fadher: on me oath an soul I wasnt: I was waitn to meet Masther Larry n carry his luggage from the car; n I fell asleep on the grass; n you woke me talkin to the grasshopper; n I hard its wicked little voice. Oh, d'ye think I'll die before the year's out, Fadher?

KEEGAN. For shame, Patsy! Is that your religion, to be afraid of a little deeshy grasshopper? Suppose it was a divil, what call have you to fear it? If I could ketch it, I'd make you take it home widja in your hat for a penance.

PATSY. Sure, if you wont let it harm me, I'm not afraid, your riverence. [*He gets up, a little reassured. He is a callow, flaxen polled, smoothfaced, downy chinned lad, fully grown but not yet fully filled out, with blue eyes and an instinctively acquired air of helplessness and silliness, indicating, not his real character, but a cunning developed by his constant dread of a hostile dominance, which he habitually tries to disarm and tempt into unmasking by pretending to be a much greater fool than he really is. Englishmen think him half-witted, which is exactly what he intends them to think. He is clad in corduroy trousers, unbuttoned waistcoat, and coarse blue striped shirt*].

KEEGAN [*admonitorily*] Patsy: what did I tell you about callin me Father Keegan an your reverence? What did Father Dempsey tell you about it?

PATSY. Yis, Fadher.

KEEGAN. Father!

PATSY [*desperately*] Arra, hwat am I to call you? Fadher Dempsey sez youre not a priest; n we all know youre not a man; n how do we know what ud happen to us if we shewed any disrespect to you? N sure they say wanse a priest always a priest.

KEEGAN [*sternly*] It's not for the like of you, Patsy, to go behind the instruction of your parish priest and set yourself up to judge whether your Church is right or wrong.

PATSY. Sure I know that, sir.

KEEGAN. The Church let me be its priest as long as it thought me fit for its work. When it took away my papers it meant you to know that I was only a poor madman, unfit and unworthy to take charge of the souls of the people.

PATSY. But wasnt it only because you knew more Latn than Father Dempsey that he was jealous of you?

KEEGAN [*scolding him to keep himself from smiling*] How dar you, Patsy Farrell, put your own wicked little spites and foolishnesses into the heart of your priest? For two pins I'd tell him what you just said.

PATSY [*coaxing*] Sure you wouldnt—

KEEGAN. Wouldnt I? God forgive you! youre little better than a heathen.

PATSY. Deedn I am, Fadher: it's me bruddher the tinsmith in Dublin youre thinkin of. Sure he had to be a freethinker when he larnt a thrade and went to live in the town.

KEEGAN. Well, he'll get to Heaven before you if youre not careful, Patsy. And now you listen to me, once and for all. Youll talk to me and pray for me by the name of Pether Keegan, so you will. And when youre angry and tempted to lift your hand agen the donkey or stamp your foot on the little grasshopper, remember that the donkey's Pether Keegan's brother, and the grasshopper Pether Keegan's friend. And when youre tempted to throw a stone at a sinner or a curse at a beggar, remember that Pether Keegan is a worse sinner and a worse beggar, and keep the stone and the curse for him the next time you meet him. Now say God bless you, Pether, to me before I go, just to practise you a bit.

PATSY. Sure it wouldnt be right, Fadher. I cant—

KEEGAN. Yes you can. Now out with it; or I'll put this stick into your hand an make you hit me with it.

PATSY [*throwing himself on his knees in an ecstasy of adoration*] Sure it's your blessin I want, Fadher Keegan. I'll have no luck widhout it.

KEEGAN [*shocked*] Get up out o that, man. Dont kneel to me: I'm not a saint.

PATSY [*with intense conviction*] Oh in throth yar, sir. [*The grasshopper chirps. Patsy, terrified, clutches at Keegan's hands*] Dont set it on me, Fadher: I'll do anythin you bid me.

KEEGAN [*pulling him up*] You bosthoon, you! Dont you see that it only whistled to tell me Miss Reilly's comin? There! Look at her and pull yourself together for shame. Off widja to the road: youll be late for the car if you dont make haste [*bustling him down the hill*]. I can see the dust of it in the gap already.

PATSY. The Lord save us! [*He goes down the hill towards the road like a haunted man*].

Nora Reilly comes down the hill. A slight weak woman in a pretty muslin print gown (her best), she is a figure commonplace enough to Irish eyes; but on the inhabitants of fatter-fed, crowded, hustling and bustling modern countries she makes a very different impression. The absence of any symptoms of coarseness or hardness or appetite in her, her comparative delicacy of manner and sensibility of apprehension, her fine hands and frail figure, her novel accent, with the caressing plaintive Irish melody of her speech, give her a charm which is all the more effective because, being untravelled, she is unconscious of it, and never dreams of deliberately dramatizing and exploiting it, as the Irishwomen in England do. For Tom Broadbent therefore, an attractive

P

woman, whom he would even call ethereal. To Larry Doyle, an everyday woman fit only for the eighteenth century, helpless, useless, almost sexless, an invalid without the excuse of disease, an incarnation of everything·in Ireland that drove him out of it. These judgments have little value and no finality; but they are the judgments on which her fate hangs just at present. Keegan touches his hat to her: he does not take it off.

NORA. Mr Keegan: I want to speak to you a minute if you dont mind.

KEEGAN [*dropping the broad Irish vernacular of his speech to Patsy*] An hour if you like, Miss Reilly: youre always welcome. Shall we sit down?

NORA. Thank you. [*They sit on the heather. She is shy and anxious; but she comes to the point promptly because she can think of nothing else*]. They say you did a gradle o travelling at one time.

KEEGAN. Well, you see I'm not a Mnooth man [*he means that he was not a student at Maynooth College*]. When I was young I admired the older generation of priests that had been educated in Salamanca. So when I felt sure of my vocation I went to Salamanca. Then I walked from Salamanca to Rome, an sted in a monastery there for a year. My pilgrimage to Rome taught me that walking is a better way of travelling than the train; so I walked from Rome to the Sorbonne in Paris; and I wish I could have walked from Paris to Oxford; for I was very sick on the sea. After a year of Oxford I had to walk to Jerusalem to walk the Oxford feeling off me. From Jerusalem I came back to Patmos, and spent six months at the monastery of Mount Athos. From that I came to Ireland and settled down as a parish priest until I went mad.

NORA [*startled*] Oh dont say that.

KEEGAN. Why not? Dont you know the story? how I confessed a black man and gave him absolution? and how he put a spell on me and drove me mad?

NORA. How can you talk such nonsense about yourself? For shame!

KEEGAN. It's not nonsense at all: it's true— in a way. But never mind the black man. Now that you know what a travelled man I am, what can I do for you? [*She hesitates and plucks nervously at the heather. He stays her hand gently*]. Dear Miss Nora: dont pluck the little flower. If it was a pretty baby you wouldnt want to pull its head off and stick it in a vawse o water to look at. [*The grasshopper chirps: Keegan turns his head and addresses it in the vernacular*]. Be aisy, me son: she wont spoil the swing-swong in your little three. [*To Nora, resuming his urbane style*] You see I'm quite cracked; but never mind: I'm harmless. Now what is it?

NORA [*embarrassed*] Oh, only idle curiosity. I wanted to know whether you found Ireland —I mean the country part of Ireland, of course—very small and backwardlike when you came back to it from Rome and Oxford and all the great cities.

KEEGAN. When I went to those great cities I saw wonders I had never seen in Ireland. But when I came back to Ireland I found all the wonders there waiting for me. You see they had been there all the time; but my eyes had never been opened to them. I did not know what my own house was like, because I had never been outside it.

NORA. D'ye think thats the same with everybody?

KEEGAN. With everybody who has eyes in his soul as well as in his head.

NORA. But really and truly now, werent the people rather disappointing? I should think the girls must have seemed rather coarse and dowdy after the foreign princesses and people? But I suppose a priest wouldnt notice that.

KEEGAN. It's a priest's business to notice everything. I wont tell you all I noticed about women; but I'll tell you this. The more a man knows, and the farther he travels, the more likely he is to marry a country girl afterwards.

NORA [*blushing with delight*] Youre joking, Mr Keegan: I'm sure yar.

KEEGAN. My way of joking is to tell the truth. It's the funniest joke in the world.

NORA [*incredulous*] Galong with you!

KEEGAN [*springing up actively*] Shall we go down to the road and meet the car? [*She gives him her hand and he helps her up*]. Patsy Farrell told me you were expecting young Doyle.

NORA [*tossing her chin up at once*] Oh, I'm not expecting him particularly. It's a wonder he's come back at all. After staying away eighteen years he can harly expect us to be very anxious to see him: can he now?

KEEGAN. Well, not anxious perhaps; but you will be curious to see how much he's changed in all these years.

NORA [*with a sudden bitter flush*] I suppose thats all that brings him back to look at us, just to see how much weve changed. Well, he can wait and see me be candlelight: I didnt come out to meet him: I'm going to walk to the Round Tower [*going west across the hill*].

KEEGAN. You couldnt do better this fine evening. [*Gravely*] I'll tell him where youve gone. [*She turns as if to forbid him; but the deep understanding in his eyes makes that impossible; and she only looks at him earnestly and goes. He watches her disappear on the other side of the hill; then says*] Aye, he's come to torment you; and youre driven already to torment him. [*He shakes his head, and goes slowly away across the hill in the opposite direction, lost in thought*].

By this time the car has arrived, and dropped three of its passengers on the high road at the foot of the hill. It is a monster jaunting car, black and dilapidated, one of the last survivors of the public vehicles known to earlier generations as Beeyankiny cars, the Irish having laid violent tongues on the name of their projector, one Bianconi, an enterprising Italian. The three passengers are the parish priest, Father Dempsey; Cornelius Doyle, Larry's father; and Broadbent, all in overcoats and as stiff as only an Irish car could make them.

The priest, stout and fatherly, falls far short of that finest type of countryside pastor which represents the genius of priesthood; but he is equally far above the base type in which a strongminded unscrupulous peasant uses the Church to extort money, power, and privilege. He is a priest neither by vocation nor ambition, but because the life suits him. He has boundless authority over his flock, and taxes them stiffly enough to be a rich man. The old Protestant ascendency is now too broken to gall him. On the whole, an easygoing, amiable, even modest man as long as his dues are paid and his authority and dignity fully admitted.

Cornelius Doyle is an elder of the small wiry type, with a hardskinned, rather worried face, clean shaven except for sandy whiskers blanching into a lustreless pale yellow and quite white at the roots. His dress is that of a country-town man of business: that is, an oldish shooting suit, with elastic sided boots quite unconnected with shooting. Feeling shy with Broadbent, he is hasty, which is his way of trying to appear genial.

Broadbent, for reasons which will appear later, has no luggage except a field glass and a guide book. The other two have left theirs to the unfortunate Patsy Farrell, who struggles up the hill after them, loaded with a sack of potatoes, a hamper, a fat goose, a colossal salmon, and several paper parcels.

Cornelius leads the way up the hill, with Broadbent at his heels. The priest follows. Patsy lags laboriously behind.

CORNELIUS. This is a bit of a climb, Mr Broadbent; but it's shorter than goin round be the road.

BROADBENT [*stopping to examine the great stone*] Just a moment, Mr Doyle: I want to look at this stone. It must be Finian's diecast.

CORNELIUS [*in blank bewilderment*] Hwat?

BROADBENT. Murray describes it. One of your great national heroes—I cant pronounce the name—Finian Somebody, I think.

FATHER DEMPSEY [*also perplexed, and rather scandalized*] Is it Fin McCool you mean?

BROADBENT. I daresay it is. [*Referring to the guide book*] Murray says that a huge stone, probably of Druidic origin, is still pointed out as the die cast by Fin in his celebrated match with the devil.

CORNELIUS [*dubiously*] Jeuce a word I ever heard of it!

FATHER DEMPSEY [*very seriously indeed, and even a little severely*] Dont believe any such nonsense, sir. There never was any such thing. When people talk to you about Fin McCool and the like, take no notice of them. It's all idle stories and superstition.

BROADBENT [*somewhat indignantly; for to be rebuked by an Irish priest for superstition is more than he can stand*] You dont suppose I believe it, do you?

FATHER DEMPSEY. Oh, I thought you did. D'ye see the top o the Roun Tower there? thats an antiquity worth lookin at.

BROADBENT [*deeply interested*] Have you any theory as to what the Round Towers were for?

FATHER DEMPSEY [*a little offended*] A theory? Me! [*Theories are connected in his mind with the late Professor Tyndall, and with scientific scepticism generally: also perhaps with the view that the Round Towers are phallic symbols*].

CORNELIUS [*remonstrating*] Father Dempsey is the priest of the parish, Mr Broadbent. What would he be doing with a theory?

FATHER DEMPSEY [*with gentle emphasis*] I have a knowledge of what the Roun Towers were, if thats what you mean. They are the forefingers of the early Church, pointing us all to God.

Patsy, intolerably overburdened, loses his balance, and sits down involuntarily. His burdens are scattered over the hillside. Cornelius and Father Dempsey turn furiously on him, leaving Broadbent beaming at the stone and the tower with fatuous interest.

CORNELIUS. Oh, be the hokey, the sammin's broke in two! You schoopid ass, what d'ye mean?

FATHER DEMPSEY. Are you drunk, Patsy Farrell? Did I tell you to carry that hamper carefully or did I not?

PATSY [*rubbing the back of his head, which has almost dinted a slab of granite*] Sure me fut slipt. Howkn I carry three men's luggage at wanst?

FATHER DEMPSEY. You were told to leave behind what you couldnt carry, an go back for it.

PATSY. An whose things was I to lave behind? Hwat would your reverence think if I left your hamper behind in the wet grass; n hwat would the masther say if I left the sammin and the goose be the side o the road for annywan to pick up?

CORNELIUS. Oh, youve a dale to say for yourself, you butther-fingered omadhaun. Waitll Ant Judy sees the state o that sammin: she'll talk to you. Here! gimmy that birdn that fish there; an take Father Dempsey's hamper to his house for him; n then come back for the rest.

FATHER DEMPSEY. Do, Patsy. And mind you dont fall down again.

PATSY. Sure I—

CORNELIUS [*bustling him up the hill*] Whisht! heres Ant Judy. [*Patsy goes grumbling in disgrace, with Father Dempsey's hamper*].

Aunt Judy comes down the hill, a woman of 50, in no way remarkable, lively and busy without energy or grip, placid without tranquillity, kindly without concern for others: indeed without much concern for herself: a contented product of a narrow, strainless life. She wears her hair parted in the middle and quite smooth, with a flattened bun at the back. Her dress is a plain brown frock, with a woollen pelerine of black and aniline mauve over her shoulders, all very trim in honor of the occasion. She looks round for Larry; is puzzled; then stares incredulously at Broadbent.

AUNT JUDY. Surely to goodness thats not you, Larry!

CORNELIUS. Arra how could he be Larry, woman alive? Larry's in no hurry home, it seems. I havnt set eyes on him. This is his friend, Mr Broadbent. Mr Broadbent: me sister Judy.

AUNT JUDY [*hospitably: going to Broadbent and shaking hands heartily*] Mr Broadbent! Fancy me takin you for Larry! Sure we havnt seen a sight of him for eighteen years, n he ony a lad when he left us.

BROADBENT. It's not Larry's fault: he was to have been here before me. He started in our motor an hour before Mr Doyle arrived, to meet us at Athenmullet, intending to get here long before me.

AUNT JUDY. Lord save us! do you think he's had n axidnt?

BROADBENT. No: he's wired to say he's had a breakdown and will come on as soon as he can. He expects to be here at about ten.

AUNT JUDY. There now! Fancy him trustn himself in a motor and we all expectn him! Just like him! he'd never do anything like anybody else. Well, what cant be cured must be injoored. Come on in, all of you. You must be dyin for your tea, Mr Broadbent.

BROADBENT [*with a slight start*] Oh, I'm afraid it's too late for tea [*he looks at his watch*].

AUNT JUDY. Not a bit: we never have it airlier than this. I hope they gave you a good dinner at Athenmullet.

BROADBENT [*trying to conceal his consternation as he realizes that he is not going to get any dinner after his drive*] Oh—er—excellent, excellent. By the way, hadnt I better see about a room at the hotel? [*They stare at him*].

CORNELIUS. The hotel!

FATHER DEMPSEY. Hwat hotel?

AUNT JUDY. Indeedn youre not goin to a hotel. Youll stay with us. I'd have put you into Larry's room, ony the boy's pallyass is too short for you; but we'll make a comfortable bed for you on the sofa in the parlor.

BROADBENT. Youre very kind, Miss Doyle; but really I'm ashamed to give you so much trouble unnecessarily. I shant mind the hotel in the least.

FATHER DEMPSEY. Man alive! theres no hotel in Rosscullen.

BROADBENT. No hotel! Why, the driver told me there was the finest hotel in Ireland here. [*They regard him joylessly*].

AUNT JUDY. Arra would you mind what the like of him would tell you? Sure he'd say hwatever was the least trouble to himself and the pleasantest to you, thinkin you might give him a thruppeny bit for himself or the like.

BROADBENT. Perhaps theres a public house.

FATHER DEMPSEY [*grimly*] Theres seventeen.

AUNT JUDY. Ah then, how could you stay at a public house? theyd have no place to put you even if it was a right place for you to go. Come! is it the sofa youre afraid of? If it is, you can have me own bed. I can sleep with Nora.

BROADBENT. Not at all, not at all: I should be only too delighted. But to upset your arrangements in this way—

CORNELIUS [*anxious to cut short the discussion, which makes him ashamed of his house; for he guesses Broadbent's standard of comfort a little more accurately than his sister does*] Thats all right: itll be no trouble at all. Hweres Nora?

AUNT JUDY. Oh, how do I know? She slipped out a little while ago: I thought she was goin to meet the car.

CORNELIUS [*dissatisfied*] It's a queer thing of her to run out o the way at such a time.

AUNT JUDY. Sure she's a queer girl altogether. Come. Come in: come in.

FATHER DEMPSEY. I'll say good-night, Mr Broadbent. If theres anything I can do for you in this parish, let me know. [*He shakes hands with Broadbent*].

BROADBENT [*effusively cordial*] Thank you, Father Dempsey. Delighted to have met you, sir.

FATHER DEMPSEY [*passing on to Aunt Judy*] Good-night, Miss Doyle.

AUNT JUDY. Wont you stay to tea?

FATHER DEMPSEY. Not to-night, thank you kindly: I have business to do at home. [*He turns to go, and meets Patsy Farrell returning unloaded*]. Have you left that hamper for me?

PATSY. Yis, your reverence.

FATHER DEMPSEY. Thats a good lad [*going*].

PATSY [*to Aunt Judy*] Fadher Keegan sez—

FATHER DEMPSEY [*turning sharply on him*] Whats that you say?

PATSY [*frightened*] Fadher Keegan—

FATHER DEMPSEY. How often have you heard me bid you call Mister Keegan in his proper name, the same as I do? Father Keegan indeed! Cant you tell the difference between your priest and any ole madman in a black coat?

PATSY. Sure I'm afraid he might put a spell on me.

FATHER DEMPSEY [*wrathfully*] You mind what I tell you or I'll put a spell on you thatll make you lep. D'ye mind that now? [*He goes home*].

Patsy goes down the hill to retrieve the fish, the bird, and the sack.

AUNT JUDY. Ah, hwy cant you hold your tongue, Patsy, before Father Dempsey?

PATSY. Well, hwat was I to do? Father Keegan bid me tell you Miss Nora was gone to the Roun Tower.

AUNT JUDY. An hwy couldnt you wait to tell us until Father Dempsey was gone?

PATSY. I was afeerd o forgetn it; and then may be he'd a sent the grasshopper or the little dark looker into me at night to remind me of it. [*The dark looker is the common grey lizard, which is supposed to walk down the throats of incautious sleepers and cause them to perish in a slow decline*].

CORNELIUS. Yah, you great gaum, you! Widjer grasshoppers and dark lookers! Here: take up them things and let me hear no more o your foolish lip. [*Patsy obeys*]. You can take the sammin under your oxther. [*He wedges the salmon into Patsy's axilla*].

PATSY. I can take the goose too, sir. Put it on me back n gimmy the neck of it in me mouth. [*Cornelius is about to comply thoughtlessly*].

AUNT JUDY [*feeling that Broadbent's presence demands special punctiliousness*] For shame, Patsy! to offer to take the goose in your mouth that we have to eat after you! The masterll bring it in for you.

PATSY. Arra what would a dead goose care for me mouth? [*He takes his load up the hill*].

CORNELIUS. Hwats Nora doin at the Roun Tower?

AUNT JUDY. Oh, the Lord knows! Romancin, I suppose. Praps she thinks Larry would go there to look for her and see her safe home.

BROADBENT. Miss Reilly must not be left to wait and walk home alone at night. Shall I go for her?

AUNT JUDY [*contemptuously*] Arra hwat ud happen to her? Hurry in now, Corny. Come, Mr Broadbent: I left the tea on the hob to draw; and itll be black if we dont go in an drink it.

They go up the hill. It is dusk by this time.

Broadbent does not fare so badly after all at Aunt Judy's board. He gets not only tea and bread-and-butter, but more mutton chops than he has ever conceived it possible to eat at one sitting. There is also a most filling substance called potato cake. Hardly have his fears of being starved been replaced by his first misgiving that he is eating too much and will be sorry for it tomorrow, when his appetite is revived by the production of a bottle of illicitly distilled whisky, called potcheen, which he has read and dreamed of (he calls it pottine) and is now at last to taste. His goodhumor rises almost to excitement before Cornelius shews signs of sleepiness. The contrast between Aunt Judy's table service and that of the south and east coast hotels at which he spends his Fridays-to-Tuesdays when he is in London, seems to him delightfully Irish. The almost total atrophy of any sense of enjoyment in Cornelius, or even any desire for it or toleration of the possibility of life being something better than a round of sordid worries, relieved by tobacco, punch, fine mornings, and petty successes in buying and selling, passes with his guest as the whimsical affectation of a shrewd Irish humorist and incorrigible spendthrift. Aunt Judy seems to him an incarnate joke. The likelihood that the joke will pall after a month or so, and is probably not apparent at any time to born Rossculleners, or that he himself unconsciously entertains Aunt Judy by his fantastic English personality and English mispronunciations, does not occur to him for a moment. In the end he is so charmed, and so loth to go to bed and perhaps dream of prosaic England, that he insists on going out to smoke a cigar and look for Nora Reilly at the Round Tower. Not that any special insistence is needed; for the English inhibitive instinct does not seem to exist in Rosscullen. Just as Nora's liking to miss a meal and stay out at the round Tower is accepted as a sufficient reason for her doing it, and for the family going to bed and leaving the door open for her, so Broadbent's whim to go out for a late stroll provokes neither hospitable remonstrance nor surprise. Indeed Aunt Judy wants to get rid of him whilst she makes a bed for him on the sofa. So off he goes, full fed, happy and enthusiastic, to explore the valley by moonlight.

The Round Tower stands about half an Irish mile from Rosscullen, some fifty yards south of the road on a knoll with a circle of wide greensward on it. The road once ran over this knoll; but modern engineering has tempered the level to the Beeyankiny car by carrying the road partly round the knoll and partly through a cutting; so that the way from the road to the tower is a footpath up the embankment through furze and brambles.

On the edge of this slope, at the top of the path, Nora is straining her eyes in the moonlight, watching for Larry. At last she gives it up with a sob of impatience, and retreats to the hoary foot of the tower, where she sits down discouraged and cries a little. Then she settles herself resignedly to wait, and hums a song—not an Irish melody, but a hackneyed English drawing room ballad of the season before last—until some slight noise suggests a footstep, when she springs up eagerly and runs to the edge of the slope again. Some moments of silence and suspense follow, broken by unmistakable footsteps. She gives a little gasp as she sees a man approaching.

NORA. Is that you, Larry? [*Frightened a little*] Who's that?

BROADBENT'S *voice from below on the path.* Dont be alarmed.

NORA. Oh, what an English accent youve got!

BROADBENT [*rising into view*] I must introduce myself—

NORA [*violently startled, retreating*] It's not you! Who are you? What do you want?

BROADBENT [*advancing*] I'm really so sorry to have alarmed you, Miss Reilly. My name is Broadbent. Larry's friend, you know.

NORA [*chilled*] And has Mr Doyle not come with you?

BROADBENT. No. Ive come instead. I hope I am not unwelcome.

NORA [*deeply mortified*] I'm sorry Mr Doyle should have given you the trouble, I'm sure.

BROADBENT. You see, as a stranger and an Englishman, I thought it would be interesting to see the Round Tower by moonlight.

NORA. Oh, you came to see the tower. I thought—[*confused, trying to recover her manners*] Oh, of course. I was so startled. It's a beautiful night, isnt it?

BROADBENT. Lovely. I must explain why Larry has not come himself.

NORA. Why should he come? He's seen the tower often enough: it's no attraction to him. [*Genteelly*] An what do you think of Ireland, Mr Broadbent? Have you ever been here before?

BROADBENT. Never.

NORA. An how do you like it?

BROADBENT [*suddenly betraying a condition of extreme sentimentality*] I can hardly trust myself to say how much I like it. The magic of this Irish scene, and—I really dont want to be personal, Miss Reilly; but the charm of your Irish voice—

NORA [*quite accustomed to gallantry, and*

attaching no seriousness whatever to it] Oh, get along with you, Mr Broadbent! Youre breaking your heart about me already, I daresay, after seeing me for two minutes in the dark.

BROADBENT. The voice is just as beautiful in the dark, you know. Besides, Ive heard a great deal about you from Larry.

NORA [*with bitter indifference*] Have you now? Well, thats a great honor, I'm sure.

BROADBENT. I have looked forward to meeting you more than to anything else in Ireland.

NORA [*ironically*] Dear me! did you now?

BROADBENT. I did really. I wish you had taken half as much interest in me.

NORA. Oh, I was dying to see you, of course. I daresay you can imagine the sensation an Englishman like you would make among us poor Irish people.

BROADBENT. Ah, now youre chaffing me, Miss Reilly; you know you are. You mustnt chaff me. I'm very much in earnest about Ireland and everything Irish. I'm very much in earnest about you and about Larry.

NORA. Larry has nothing to do with me, Mr Broadbent.

BROADBENT. If I really thought that, Miss Reilly, I should—well, I should let myself feel that charm of which I spoke just now more deeply than I—than I—

NORA. Is it making love to me you are?

BROADBENT [*scared and much upset*] On my word I believe I am, Miss Reilly. If you say that to me again I shant answer for myself: all the harps of Ireland are in your voice. [*She laughs at him. He suddenly loses his head and seizes her arms, to her great indignation*]. Stop laughing: do you hear? I am in earnest: in English earnest. When I say a thing like that to a woman, I mean it. [*Releasing her and trying to recover his ordinary manner in spite of his bewildering emotion*] I beg your pardon.

NORA. How dare you touch me?

BROADBENT. There are not many things I would not dare for you. That does not sound right perhaps; but I really—[*he stops and passes his hand over his forehead, rather lost*].

NORA. I think you ought to be ashamed. I think if you were a gentleman, and me alone with you in this place at night, you would die rather than do such a thing.

BROADBENT. You mean that it's an act of treachery to Larry?

NORA. Deed I dont. What has Larry to do with it? It's an act of disrespect and rudeness to me: it shews what you take me for. You can go your way now; and I'll go mine. Good-night, Mr Broadbent.

BROADBENT. No, please, Miss Reilly. One moment. Listen to me. I'm serious: I'm desperately serious. Tell me that I'm interfering with Larry; and I'll go straight from this spot back to London and never see you again. Thats on my honor: I will. Am I interfering with him?

NORA [*answering in spite of herself in a sudden spring of bitterness*] I should think you ought to know better than me whether youre interfering with him. Youve seen him oftener than I have. You know him better than I do, by this time. Youve come to me quicker than he has, havnt you?

BROADBENT. I'm bound to tell you, Miss Reilly, that Larry has not arrived in Rosscullen yet. He meant to get here before me; but his car broke down; and he may not arrive until to-morrow.

NORA [*her face lighting up*] Is that the truth?

BROADBENT. Yes: thats the truth. [*She gives a sigh of relief*]. Youre glad of that?

NORA [*up in arms at once*] Glad indeed! Why should I be glad? As weve waited eighteen years for him we can afford to wait a day longer, I should think.

BROADBENT. If you really feel like that about him, there may be a chance for another man yet. Eh?

NORA [*deeply offended*] I suppose people are different in England, Mr Broadbent; so perhaps you dont mean any harm. In Ireland nobody'd mind what a man'd say in fun, nor take advantage of what a woman might say in answer to it. If a woman couldnt talk to a man for two minutes at their first meeting without being treated the way youre treating me, no decent woman would ever talk to a man at all.

BROADBENT. I dont understand that. I dont admit that. I am sincere; and my intentions are perfectly honorable. I think you will accept the fact that I'm an Englishman as a guarantee that I am not a man to act hastily or romantically; though I confess that your voice had such an extraordinary effect on me just now when you asked me so quaintly whether I was making love to you

NORA [*flushing*] I never thought—

BROADBENT [*quickly*] Of course you didnt: I'm not so stupid as that. But I couldnt bear your laughing at the feeling it gave me. You —[*again struggling with a surge of emotion*] you dont know what I—[*he chokes for a moment and then blurts out with unnatural steadiness*] Will you be my wife?

NORA [*promptly*] Deed I wont. The idea! [*Looking at him more carefully*] Arra, come home, Mr Broadbent; and get your senses back again. I think youre not accustomed to potcheen punch in the evening after your tea.

BROADBENT [*horrified*] Do you mean to say that I—I—I—my God! that I appear drunk to you, Miss Reilly?

NORA [*compassionately*] How many tumblers had you?

BROADBENT [*helplessly*] Two.

NORA. The flavor of the turf prevented you noticing the strength of it. Youd better come home to bed.

BROADBENT [*fearfully agitated*] But this is such a horrible doubt to put into my mind —to—to— For Heaven's sake, Miss Reilly, am I really drunk?

NORA [*soothingly*] Youll be able to judge better in the morning. Come on now back with me, an think no more about it. [*She takes his arm with motherly solicitude and urges him gently towards the path*].

BROADBENT [*yielding in despair*] I must be drunk: frightfully drunk; for your voice drove me out of my senses—[*he stumbles over a stone*]. No: on my word, on my most sacred word of honor, Miss Reilly, I tripped over that stone. It was an accident: it was indeed.

NORA. Yes, of course it was. Just take my arm, Mr Broadbent, while we're goin down the path to the road. Youll be all right then.

BROADBENT [*submissively taking it*] I cant sufficiently apologize, Miss Reilly, or express my sense of your kindness when I am in such a disgusting state. How could I be such a bea—[*he trips again*] damn the heather! my foot caught in it.

NORA. Steady now, steady. Come along: come. [*He is led down to the road in the character of a convicted drunkard. To him there is something divine in the sympathetic indulgence she substitutes for the angry disgust with which one of his own countrywomen would resent his supposed condition. And he has no suspicion of the fact, or of her ignorance of it, that when an Englishman is sentimental he behaves very much as an Irishman does when he is drunk*].

ACT III

Next morning Broadbent and Larry are sitting at the ends of a breakfast table in the middle of a small grass plot before Cornelius Doyle's house. They have finished their meal, and are buried in newspapers. Most of the crockery is crowded upon a large square black tray of japanned metal. The teapot is of brown delft ware. There is no silver; and the butter, on a dinner plate, is en bloc. The background to this breakfast is the house, a small white slated building, accessible by a half-glazed door. A person coming out into the garden by this door would find the table straight in front of him, and a gate leading to the road half way down the garden on his right; or, if he turned sharp to his left, he could pass round the end of the house through an unkempt shrubbery. The mutilated remnant of a huge plaster statue, nearly dissolved by the rains of a century, and vaguely resembling a majestic female in Roman draperies, with a wreath in her hand, stands neglected amid the laurels. Such statues, though apparently works of art, grow naturally in Irish gardens. Their germination is a mystery to the oldest inhabitants, to whose means and tastes they are totally foreign.

There is a rustic bench, much soiled by the birds, and decorticated and split by the weather, near the little gate. At the opposite side, a basket lies unmolested because it might as well be there as anywhere else. An empty chair at the table was lately occupied by Cornelius, who has finished his breakfast and gone in to the room in which he receives rents and keeps his books and cash, known in the household as "the office." This chair, like the two occupied by Larry and Broadbent, has a mahogany frame and is upholstered in black horsehair.

Larry rises and goes off through the shrubbery with his newspaper. Hodson comes in through the garden gate, disconsolate. Broadbent, who sits facing the gate, augurs the worst from his expression.

BROADBENT. Have you been to the village?

HODSON. No use, sir. We'll have to get everything from London by parcel post.

BROADBENT. I hope they made you comfortable last night.

HODSON. I was no worse than you were on that sofa, sir. One expects to rough it here, sir.

BROADBENT. We shall have to look out for some other arrangement. [*Cheering up irrepressibly*] Still, it's no end of a joke. How do you like the Irish, Hodson?

HODSON. Well, sir, theyre all right anywhere but in their own country. Ive known lots of em in England, and generally liked em. But here, sir, I seem simply to hate em. The feeling come over me the moment we landed at Cork, sir. It's no use my pretendin, sir: I cant bear em. My mind rises up agin their ways, somehow: they rub me the wrong way all over.

BROADBENT. Oh, their faults are on the surface: at heart they are one of the finest races on earth. [*Hodson turns away, without affecting to respond to his enthusiasm*]. By the way, Hodson—

HODSON [*turning*] Yes, sir.

BROADBENT. Did you notice anything about me last night when I came in with that lady?

HODSON [*surprised*] No, sir.

BROADBENT. Not any—er—? You may speak frankly.

HODSON. I didnt notice nothing, sir. What sort of thing did you mean, sir?

BROADBENT. Well—er—er—well, to put it plainly, was I drunk?

HODSON [*amazed*] No, sir.

BROADBENT. Quite sure?

HODSON. Well, I should a said rather the opposite, sir. Usually when youve been enjoying yourself, youre a bit hearty like. Last night you seemed rather low, if anything.

BROADBENT. I certainly have no headache. Did you try the pottine, Hodson?

HODSON. I just took a mouthful, sir. It tasted of peat: oh! something horrid, sir. The people here call peat turf. Potcheen and strong porter is what they like, sir. I'm sure I dont know how they can stand it. Give me beer, I say.

BROADBENT. By the way, you told me I couldnt have porridge for breakfast; but Mr Doyle had some.

HODSON. Yes, sir. Very sorry, sir. They call it stirabout, sir: thats how it was. They know no better, sir.

BROADBENT. All right: I'll have some tomorrow.

Hodson goes to the house. When he opens the door he finds Nora and Aunt Judy on the threshold. He stands aside to let them pass, with the air of a well trained servant oppressed by heavy trials. Then he goes in. Broadbent rises. Aunt Judy goes to the table and collects the plates and cups on the tray. Nora goes to the back of the rustic seat and looks out at the gate with the air

of a woman accustomed to have nothing to do. Larry returns from the shrubbery.

BROADBENT. Good morning, Miss Doyle.

AUNT JUDY [*thinking it absurdly late in the day for such a salutation*] Oh, good morning. [*Before moving his plate*] Have you done?

BROADBENT. Quite, thank you. You must excuse us for not waiting for you. The country air tempted us to get up early.

AUNT JUDY. N d'ye call this airly, God help you?

LARRY. Aunt Judy probably breakfasted about half past six.

AUNT JUDY. Whisht, you! draggin the parlor chairs out into the gardn n givin Mr Broadbent his death over his meals out here in the cold air. [*To Broadbent*] Why d'ye put up with his foolishness, Mr Broadbent?

BROADBENT. I assure you I like the open air.

AUNT JUDY. Ah galong! How can you like whats not natural? I hope you slept well.

NORA. Did anything wake yup with a thump at three o'clock? I thought the house was falling. But then I'm a very light sleeper.

LARRY. I seem to recollect that one of the legs of the sofa in the parlor had a way of coming out unexpectedly eighteen years ago. Was that it, Tom?

BROADBENT [*hastily*] Oh, it doesnt matter: I was not hurt—at least—er—

AUNT JUDY. Oh now what a shame! An I told Patsy Farrll to put a nail in it.

BROADBENT. He did, Miss Doyle. There was a nail, certainly.

AUNT JUDY. Dear oh dear!

An oldish peasant farmer, small, leathery, peat-faced, with a deep voice and a surliness that is meant to be aggressive, and is in effect pathetic—the voice of a man of hard life and many sorrows—comes in at the gate. He is old enough to have perhaps worn a long tailed frieze coat and knee breeches in his time; but now he is dressed respectably in a black frock coat, tall hat, and pollard colored trousers; and his face is as clean as washing can make it, though that is not saying much, as the habit is recently acquired and not yet congenial.

THE NEW-COMER [*at the gate*] God save all here! [*He comes a little way into the garden*].

LARRY [*patronizingly, speaking across the garden to him*] Is that yourself, Matt Haffigan? Do you remember me?

MATTHEW [*intentionally rude and blunt*] No. Who are you?

NORA. Oh, I'm sure you remember him, Mr Haffigan.

MATTHEW [grudgingly admitting it] I suppose he'll be young Larry Doyle that was.

LARRY. Yes.

MATTHEW [to Larry] I hear you done well in America.

LARRY. Fairly well.

MATTHEW. I suppose you saw me brother Andy out dhere.

LARRY. No. It's such a big place that looking for a man there is like looking for a needle in a bundle of hay. They tell me he's a great man out there.

MATTHEW. So he is, God be praised. Wheres your father?

AUNT JUDY. He's inside, in the office, Mr Haffigan, with Barney Doarn n Father Dempsey.

Matthew, without wasting further words on the company, goes curtly into the house.

LARRY [staring after him] Is anything wrong with old Matt?

NORA. No. He's the same as ever. Why?

LARRY. He's not the same to me. He used to be very civil to Masther Larry: a deal too civil, I used to think. Now he's as surly and stand-off as a bear.

AUNT JUDY. Oh sure he's bought his farm in the Land Purchase. He's independent now.

NORA. It's made a great change, Larry. Youd harly know the old tenants now. Youd think it was a liberty to speak t'dhem—some o dhem. [She goes to the table, and helps to take off the cloth, which she and Aunt Judy fold up between them].

AUNT JUDY. I wonder what he wants to see Corny for. He hasnt been here since he paid the last of his old rent; and then he as good as threw it in Corny's face, I thought.

LARRY. No wonder! Of course they all hated us like the devil. Ugh! [Moodily] Ive seen them in that office, telling my father what a fine boy I was, and plastering him with compliments, with your honor here and your honor there, when all the time their fingers were itching to be at his throat.

AUNT JUDY. Deedn why should they want to hurt poor Corny? It was he that got Matt the lease of his farm, and stood up for him as an industrious decent man.

BROADBENT. Was he industrious? Thats remarkable, you know, in an Irishman.

LARRY. Industrious! That man's industry used to make me sick, even as a boy. I tell you, an Irish peasant's industry is not human: it's worse than the industry of a coral insect. An Englishman has some sense about working: he never does more than he can help—and hard enough to get him to do that without scamping it; but an Irishman will work as if he'd die the moment he stopped. That man Matthew Haffigan and his brother Andy made a farm out of a patch of stones on the hillside: cleared it and dug it with their own naked hands and bought their first spade out of their first crop of potatoes. Talk of making two blades of wheat grow where one grew before! those two men made a whole field of wheat grow where not even a furze bush had ever got its head up between the stones.

BROADBENT. That was magnificent, you know. Only a great race is capable of producing such men.

LARRY. Such fools, you mean! What good was it to them? The moment theyd done it, the landlord put a rent of £5 a year on them, and turned them out because they couldnt pay it.

AUNT JUDY. Why couldnt they pay as well as Billy Byrne that took it after them?

LARRY [angrily] You know very well that Billy Byrne never paid it. He only offered it to get possession. He never paid it.

AUNT JUDY. That was because Andy Haffigan hurt him with a brick so that he was never the same again. Andy had to run away to America for it.

BROADBENT [glowing with indignation] Who can blame him, Miss Doyle? Who can blame him?

LARRY [impatiently] Oh, rubbish! whats the good of the man thats starved out of a farm murdering the man thats starved into it? Would you have done such a thing?

BROADBENT. Yes. I—I—I—I—[stammering with fury] I should have shot the confounded landlord, and wrung the neck of the damned agent, and blown the farm up with dynamite, and Dublin Castle along with it.

LARRY. Oh yes: youd have done great things; and a fat lot of good youd have got out of it, too! Thats an Englishman all over! make bad laws and give away all the land, and then, when your economic incompetence produces its natural and inevitable results, get virtuously indignant and kill the people that carry out your laws.

AUNT JUDY. Sure never mind him, Mr

BROADBENT. It doesnt matter, anyhow, because theres harly any landlords left; and therll soon be none at all.

LARRY. On the contrary, therll soon be nothing else; and the Lord help Ireland then!

AUNT JUDY. Ah, youre never satisfied, Larry. [*To Nora*] Come on, alanna, an make the paste for the pie. We can leave them to their talk. They dont want us [*she takes up the tray and goes into the house*].

BROADBENT [*rising and gallantly protesting*] Oh, Miss Doyle! Really, really —

Nora, following Aunt Judy with the rolled up cloth in her hands, looks at him and strikes him dumb. He watches her until she disappears; then comes to Larry and addresses him with sudden intensity.

BROADBENT. Larry.

LARRY. What is it?

BROADBENT. I got drunk last night, and proposed to Miss Reilly.

LARRY. You hwat??? [*He screams with laughter in the falsetto Irish register unused for that purpose in England*].

BROADBENT. What are you laughing at?

LARRY [*stopping dead*] I dont know. Thats the sort of thing an Irishman laughs at. Has she accepted you?

BROADBENT. I shall never forget that with the chivalry of her nation, though I was utterly at her mercy, she refused me.

LARRY. That was extremely improvident of her. [*Beginning to reflect*] But look here: when were you drunk? You were sober enough when you came back from the Round Tower with her.

BROADBENT. No, Larry, I was drunk, I am sorry to say. I had two tumblers of punch. She had to lead me home. You must have noticed it.

LARRY. I did not.

BROADBENT. She did.

LARRY. May I ask how long it took you to come to business? You can hardly have known her for more than a couple of hours.

BROADBENT. I am afraid it was hardly a couple of minutes. She was not here when I arrived; and I saw her for the first time at the tower.

LARRY. Well, you a r e a nice infant to be let loose in this country! Fancy the potcheen going to your head like that!

BROADBENT. Not to my head, I think. I have no headache; and I could speak distinctly. No: potcheen goes to the heart, not to the head. What ought I to do?

LARRY. Nothing. What need you do?

BROADBENT. There is rather a delicate moral question involved. The point is, was I drunk enough not to be morally responsible for my proposal? Or was I sober enough to be bound to repeat it now that I am undoubtedly sober?

LARRY. I should see a little more of her before deciding.

BROADBENT. No, no. That would not be right. That would not be fair. I am either under a moral obligation or I am not. I wish I knew how drunk I was.

LARRY. Well, you were evidently in a state of blithering sentimentality, anyhow.

BROADBENT. That is true, Larry: I admit it. Her voice has a most extraordinary effect on me. That Irish voice!

LARRY [*sympathetically*] Yes, I know. When I first went to London I very nearly proposed to walk out with a waitress in an Aerated Bread shop because her Whitechapel accent was so distinguished, so quaintly touching, so pretty—

BROADBENT [*angrily*] Miss Reilly is not a waitress, is she?

LARRY. Oh, come! The waitress was a very nice girl.

BROADBENT. You think every Englishwoman an angel. You really have coarse tastes in that way, Larry. Miss Reilly is one of the finer types: a type rare in England, except perhaps in the best of the aristocracy.

LARRY. Aristocracy be blowed! Do you know what Nora eats?

BROADBENT. Eats! what do you mean?

LARRY. Breakfast: tea and bread-and-butter, with an occasional rasher, and an egg on special occasions: say on her birthday. Dinner in the middle of the day, one course and nothing else. In the evening, tea and bread-and-butter again. You compare her with your Englishwomen who wolf down from three to five meat meals a day; and naturally you find her a sylph. The difference is not a difference of type: it's the difference between the woman who eats not wisely but too well, and the woman who eats not wisely but too little.

BROADBENT [*furious*] Larry: you—you— you disgust me. You are a damned fool. [*He sits down angrily on the rustic seat, which sustains the shock with difficulty*].

LARRY. Steady! stead-eee! [*He laughs and

seats himself on the table].

*Cornelius Doyle, Father Dempsey, Barney
Doran, and Matthew Haffigan come from the
house. Doran is a stout bodied, short armed,
roundheaded, red haired man on the verge of
middle age, of sanguine temperament, with an
enormous capacity for derisive, obscene, blasphemous, or merely cruel and senseless fun, and
a violent and impetuous intolerance of other
temperaments and other opinions, all this representing energy and capacity wasted and demoralized by want of sufficient training and social
pressure to force it into beneficent activity and
build a character with it; for Barney is by no means
either stupid or weak. He is recklessly untidy as
to his person; but the worst effects of his neglect
are mitigated by a powdering of flour and mill
dust; and his unbrushed clothes, made of a
fashionable tailor's sackcloth, were evidently
chosen regardless of expense for the sake of
their appearance.*

*Matthew Haffigan, ill at ease, coasts the gar-
den shyly on the shrubbery side until he anchors
near the basket, where he feels least in the way.
The priest comes to the table and slaps Larry
on the shoulder. Larry, turning quickly, and
recognizing Father Dempsey, alights from the
table and shakes the priest's hand warmly. Doran
comes down the garden between Father Dempsey
and Matt; and Cornelius, on the other side of
the table, turns to Broadbent, who rises genially.*

CORNELIUS. I think we all met las night.

DORAN. I hadnt that pleasure.

CORNELIUS. To be sure, Barney: I forgot.
[*To Broadbent, introducing Barney*] Mr Doran.
He owns that fine mill you noticed from the
car.

BROADBENT [*delighted with them all*] Most
happy, Mr Doran. Very pleased indeed.

*Doran, not quite sure whether he is being
courted or patronized, nods independently.*

DORAN. Hows yourself, Larry?

LARRY. Finely, thank you. No need to ask
you. [*Doran grins; and they shake hands*].

CORNELIUS. Give Father Dempsey a chair,
Larry.

*Matthew Haffigan runs to the nearest end of
the table and takes the chair from it, placing it
near the basket; but Larry has already taken the
chair from the other end and placed it in front
of the table. Father Dempsey accepts that more
central position.*

CORNELIUS. Sit down, Barney, will you; and
you, Matt.

Doran takes the chair Matt is still offering to

the priest; and poor Matthew, outfaced by the
miller, humbly turns the basket upside down and
sits on it. Cornelius brings his own breakfast
chair from the table and sits down on Father
Dempsey's right. Broadbent resumes his seat on
the rustic bench. Larry crosses to the bench and is
about to sit down beside him when Broadbent
holds him off nervously.*

BROADBENT. Do you think it will bear two,
Larry?

LARRY. Perhaps not. Dont move. I'll stand.
[*He posts himself behind the bench*].

*They are all now seated, except Larry; and
the session assumes a portentous air, as if something important were coming.*

CORNELIUS. Praps youll explain, Father
Dempsey.

FATHER DEMPSEY. No, no: go on, you: the
Church has no politics.

CORNELIUS. Were yever thinkin o goin into
parliament at all, Larry?

LARRY. Me!

FATHER DEMPSEY [*encouragingly*] Yes, you.
Hwy not?

LARRY. I'm afraid my ideas would not be
popular enough.

CORNELIUS. I dont know that. Do you,
Barney?

DORAN. Theres too much blatherumskite in
Irish politics: a dale too much.

LARRY. But what about your present member? Is he going to retire?

CORNELIUS. No: I dont know that he is.

LARRY [*interrogatively*] Well? then?

MATTHEW [*breaking out with surly bitterness*]
Weve had enough of his foolish talk agen
lanlords. Hwat call has he to talk about the
lan, that never was outside of a city office in
his life?

CORNELIUS. We're tired of him. He doesnt
know hwere to stop. Every man cant own
land; and some men must own it to employ
them. It was all very well when solid men
like Doran an Matt were kep from ownin
land. But hwat man in his senses ever wanted
to give land to Patsy Farrll an dhe like o him?

BROADBENT. But surely Irish landlordism
was accountable for what Mr Haffigan
suffered.

MATTHEW. Never mind hwat I suffered. I
know what I suffered adhout you tellin me.
But did I ever ask for more dhan the farm
I made wid me own hans? tell me that, Corny
Doyle, and you that knows. Was I fit for the
responsibility or was I not? [*Snarling angrily*

at Cornelius] Am I to be compared to Patsy Farrll, that doesnt harly know his right hand from his left? What did he ever suffer, I'd like to know?

CORNELIUS. Thats just what I say. I wasnt comparin you to your disadvantage.

MATTHEW [*implacable*] Then hwat did you mane be talkin about givin him lan?

DORAN. Aisy, Matt, aisy. Youre like a bear with a sore back.

MATTHEW [*trembling with rage*] An who are you, to offer to taitch me manners?

FATHER DEMPSEY [*admonitorily*] Now, now, now, Matt! none o dhat. How often have I told you youre too ready to take offence where none is meant? You dont understand: Corny Doyle is saying just what you want to have said. [*To Cornelius*] Go on, Mr Doyle; and never mind him.

MATTHEW [*rising*] Well, if me lan is to be given to Patsy and his like, I'm goin oura dhis. I—

DORAN [*with violent impatience*] Arra who's goin to give your lan to Patsy, yowl fool ye?

FATHER DEMPSEY. Aisy, Barney, aisy. [*Sternly, to Matt*] I told you, Matthew Haffigan, that Corny Doyle was sayin nothin against you. I'm sorry your priest's word is not good enough for you. I'll go, sooner than stay to make you commit a sin against the Church. Good morning, gentlemen. [*He rises. They all rise, except Broadbent*].

DORAN [*to Matt*] There! Sarve you dam well right, you cantankerous oul noodle.

MATTHEW [*appalled*] Dont say dhat, Fadher Dempsey. I never had a thought agen you or the Holy Church. I know I'm a bit hasty when I think about the lan. I ax your pardon for it.

FATHER DEMPSEY [*resuming his seat with dignified reserve*] Very well: I'll overlook it this time. [*He sits down. The others sit down, except Matthew. Father Dempsey, about to ask Corny to proceed, remembers Matthew and turns to him, giving him just a crumb of graciousness*]. Sit down, Matt [*Matthew, crushed, sits down in disgrace, and is silent, his eyes shifting piteously from one speaker to another in an intensely mistrustful effort to understand them*]. Go on, Mr Doyle. We can make allowances. Go on.

CORNELIUS. Well, you see how it is, Larry. Round about here, weve got the land at last; and we want no more Goverment meddlin. We want a new class o man in parliament: one dhat knows dhat the farmer's the real backbone o the country, n doesnt care a snap of his fingers for the shoutn o the riff-raff in the towns, or for the foolishness of the laborers.

DORAN. Aye; an dhat can afford to live in London and pay his own way until Home Rule comes, instead o wantin subscriptions and the like.

FATHER DEMPSEY. Yes: thats a good point, Barney. When too much money goes to politics, it's the Church that has to starve for it. A member of parliament ought to be a help to the Church instead of a burden on it.

LARRY. Heres a chance for you, Tom. What do you say?

BROADBENT [*deprecatory, but important and smiling*] Oh, I have no claim whatever to the seat. Besides, I'm a Saxon.

DORAN. A hwat?

BROADBENT. A Saxon. An Englishman.

DORAN. An Englishman. Bedad I never heard it called dhat before.

MATTHEW [*cunningly*] If I might make so bould, Fadher, I wouldnt say but an English Prodestn mightnt have a more indepindent mind about the lan, an be less afeerd to spake out about it, dhan an Irish Catholic.

CORNELIUS. But sure Larry's as good as English: arnt you, Larry?

LARRY. You may put me out of your head, father, once for all.

CORNELIUS. Arra why?

LARRY. I have strong opinions which wouldnt suit you.

DORAN [*rallying him blatantly*] Is it still Larry the bould Fenian?

LARRY. No: the bold Fenian is now an older and possibly foolisher man.

CORNELIUS. Hwat does it matter to us hwat your opinions are? You know that your father's bought his place here, just the same as Matt's farm n Barney's mill. All we ask now is to be let alone. Youve nothin against that, have you?

LARRY. Certainly I have. I dont believe in letting anybody or anything alone.

CORNELIUS [*losing his temper*] Arra what d'ye mean, you young fool? Here Ive got you the offer of a good seat in parliament; n you think yourself mighty smart to stand there and talk foolishness to me. Will you take it or leave it?

LARRY. Very well: I'll take it with pleasure if youll give it to me.

CORNELIUS [*subsiding sulkily*] Well, why

couldnt you say so at once? It's a good job youve made up your mind at last.

DORAN [*suspiciously*] Stop a bit: stop a bit.

MATTHEW [*writhing between his dissatisfaction and his fear of the priest*] It's not because he's your son that he's to get the sate. Fadher Dempsey: wouldnt you think well to ask him what he manes about the lan?

LARRY [*coming down on Matt promptly*] I'll tell you, Matt. I always thought it was a stupid, lazy, good-for-nothing sort of thing to leave the land in the hands of the old landlords without calling them to a strict account for the use they made of it, and the condition of the people on it. I could see for myself that they thought of nothing but what they could get out of it to spend in England; and that they mortgaged and mortgaged until hardly one of them owned his own property or could have afforded to keep it up decently if he'd wanted to. But I tell you plump and plain, Matt, that if anybody thinks things will be any better now that the land is handed over to a lot of little men like you, without calling you to account either, theyre mistaken.

MATTHEW [*sullenly*] What call have you to look down on me? I suppose you think youre everybody because your father was a land agent.

LARRY. What call have you to look down on Patsy Farrell? I suppose you think youre everybody because you own a few fields.

MATTHEW. Was Patsy Farrll ever ill used as I was ill used? tell me dhat.

LARRY. He will be, if ever he gets into your power as you were in the power of your old landlord. Do you think, because youre poor and ignorant and half-crazy with toiling and moiling morning noon and night, that youll be any less greedy and oppressive to them that have no land at all than old Nick Lestrange, who was an educated travelled gentleman that would not have been tempted as hard by a hundred pounds as youd be by five shillings? Nick was too high above Patsy Farrell to be jealous of him; but you, that are only one little step above him, would die sooner than let him come up that step; and well you know it.

MATTHEW [*black with rage, in a low growl*] Lemmy oura dhis. [*He tries to rise; but Doran catches his coat and drags him down again*] I'm goin, I say. [*Raising his voice*] Leggo me coat, Barney Doran.

DORAN. Sit down, yowl omadhaun, you. [*Whispering*] Dont you want to stay an vote agen him?

FATHER DEMPSEY [*holding up his finger*] Matt! [*Matt subsides*]. Now, now, now! come, come! Hwats all dhis about Patsy Farrll? Hwy need you fall out about him?

LARRY. Because it was by using Patsy's poverty to undersell England in the markets of the world that we drove England to ruin Ireland. And she'll ruin us again the moment we lift our heads from the dust if we trade in cheap labor; and serve us right too! If I get into parliament, I'll try to get an Act to prevent any of you from giving Patsy less than a pound a week [*they all start, hardly able to believe their ears*] or working him harder than youd work a horse that cost you fifty guineas.

DORAN. Hwat!!!

CORNELIUS [*aghast*] A pound a—God save us! the boy's mad.

Matthew, feeling that here is something quite beyond his powers, turns openmouthed to the priest, as if looking for nothing less than the summary excommunication of Larry.

LARRY. How is the man to marry and live a decent life on less?

FATHER DEMPSEY. Man alive, hwere have you been living all these years? and hwat have you been dreaming of? Why, some o dhese honest men here cant make that much out o the land for dhemselves, much less give it to a laborer.

LARRY [*now thoroughly roused*] Then let them make room for those who can. Is Ireland never to have a chance? First she was given to the rich; and now that they have gorged on her flesh, her bones are to be flung to the poor, that can do nothing but suck the marrow out of her. If we cant have men of honor own the land, lets have men of ability. If we cant have men with ability, let us at least have men with capital. Anybody's better than Matt, who has neither honor, nor ability, nor capital, nor anything but mere brute labor and greed in him, Heaven help him!

DORAN. Well, we're not all foostherin oul doddherers like Matt. [*Pleasantly, to the subject of this description*] Are we, Matt?

LARRY. For modern industrial purposes you might just as well be, Barney. Youre all children: the big world that I belong to has gone past you and left you. Anyhow, we Irishmen were never made to be farmers; and we'll never do any good at it. We're like the Jews: the Almighty gave us brains, and bid us farm t h e m, and leave the clay and the worms alone.

FATHER DEMPSEY [*with gentle irony*] Oh! is it Jews you want to make of us? I must catechize you a bit meself, I think. The next thing youll be proposing is to repeal the disestablishment of the so-called Irish Church.

LARRY. Yes: why not? [*Sensation*].

MATTHEW [*rancorously*] He's a turncoat.

LARRY. St Peter, the rock on which our Church was built, was crucified head downwards for being a turncoat.

FATHER DEMPSEY [*with a quiet authoritative dignity which checks Doran, who is on the point of breaking out*] Thats true. You hold your tongue as befits your ignorance, Matthew Haffigan; and trust your priest to deal with this young man. Now, Larry Doyle, whatever the blessed St Peter was crucified for, it was not for being a Prodestan. Are you one?

LARRY. No. I am a Catholic intelligent enough to see that the Protestants are never more dangerous to us than when they are free from all alliances with the State. The so-called Irish Church is stronger today than ever it was.

MATTHEW. Fadher Dempsey: will you tell him dhat me mother's ant was shot and kilt dead in the sthreet o Rosscullen be a soljer in the tithe war? [*Frantically*] He wants to put the tithes on us again. He—

LARRY [*interrupting him with overbearing contempt*] Put the tithes on you again! Did the tithes ever come off you? Was your land any dearer when you paid the tithe to the parson than it was when you paid the same money to Nick Lestrange as rent, and he handed it over to the Church Sustentation Fund? Will you always be duped by Acts of Parliament that change nothing but the necktie of the man that picks your pocket? I'll tell you what I'd do with you, Matt Haffigan: I'd make you pay tithes to your own Church. I want the Catholic Church established in Ireland: thats what I want. Do you think that I, brought up to regard myself as the son of a great and holy Church, can bear to see her begging her bread from the ignorance and superstition of men like you? I would have her as high above worldly want as I would have her above worldly pride or ambition. Aye; and I would have Ireland compete with Rome itself for the chair of St

Peter and the citadel of the Church; for Rome, in spite of all the blood of the martyrs, is pagan at heart to this day, while in Ireland the people is the Church and the Church the people.

FATHER DEMPSEY [*startled, but not at all displeased*] Whisht, man! youre worse than mad Pether Keegan himself.

BROADBENT [*who has listened in the greatest astonishment*] You amaze me, Larry. Who would have thought of your coming out like this! [*Solemnly*] But much as I appreciate your really brilliant eloquence, I implore you not to desert the great Liberal principle of Disestablishment.

LARRY. I am not a Liberal: Heaven forbid! A disestablished Church is the worst tyranny a nation can groan under.

BROADBENT [*making a wry face*] Dont be paradoxical, Larry. It really gives me a pain in my stomach.

LARRY. Youll soon find out the truth of it here. Look at Father Dempsey! he is disestablished: he has nothing to hope or fear from the State; and the result is that he's the most powerful man in Rosscullen. The member for Rosscullen would shake in his shoes if Father Dempsey looked crooked at him. [*Father Dempsey smiles, by no means averse to this acknowledgment of his authority*]. Look at yourself! you would defy the established Archbishop of Cantebrury ten times a day; but catch you daring to say a word that would shock a Nonconformist! not you. The Conservative party today is the only one thats not priestridden—excuse the expression, Father [*Father Dempsey nods tolerantly*]—because it's the only one that has established its Church and can prevent a clergyman becoming a bishop if he's not a Statesman as well as a Churchman.

He stops. They stare at him dumbfounded, and leave it to the priest to answer him.

FATHER DEMPSEY [*judicially*] Young man: youll not be the member for Rosscullen; but dheres more in your head than the comb will take out.

LARRY. I'm sorry to disappoint you, father; but I told you it would be no use. And now I think the candidate had better retire and leave you to discuss his successor. [*He takes a newspaper from the table and goes away through the shrubbery amid dead silence, all turning to watch him until he passes out of sight round the corner of the house*].

DORAN [*dazed*] Hwat sort of a fella is he at all at all?

FATHER DEMPSEY. He's a clever lad: dheres the making of a man in him yet.

MATTHEW [*in consternation*] D'ye mane to say dhat yll put him into parliament to bring back Nick Lesthrange on me, and to put tithes on me, and to rob me for the like o Patsy Farrll, because he's Corny Doyle's son?

DORAN [*brutally*] Arra hould your whisht: who's goin to send him into parliament? Maybe youd like us to send y o u dhere to thrate dhem to a little o your anxiety about dhat dirty little podato patch o yours.

MATTHEW [*plaintively*] Am I to be towld dhis afther all me sufferins?

DORAN. Och, I'm tired o your sufferins. Weve been hearin nothin else ever since we was childher but sufferins. Hwen it wasnt yours it was somebody else's; and hwen it was nobody else's it was ould Irelan's. How the divil are we to live on wan anodher's sufferins?

FATHER DEMPSEY. Thats a thrue word, Barney Doarn; only your tongue's a little too familiar wi dhe divil. [*To Matt*] If youd think a little more o the sufferins of the blessed saints, Matt, an a little less o your own, youd find the way shorter from your farm to heaven [*Matt is about to reply*] Dhere now! dhats enough! we know you mean well; an I'm not angry with you.

BROADBENT. Surely, Mr Haffigan, you can see the simple explanation of all this. My friend Larry Doyle is a most brilliant speaker; but he's a Tory: an ingrained old-fashioned Tory.

CORNELIUS. N how d'ye make dhat out, if I might ask you, Mr Broadbent?

BROADBENT [*collecting himself for a political deliverance*] Well, you know, Mr Doyle, theres a strong dash of Toryism in the Irish character. Larry himself says that the great Duke of Wellington was the most typical Irishman that ever lived. Of course thats an absurd paradox; but still theres a great deal of truth in it. Now I am a Liberal. You know the great principles of the Liberal Party. Peace—

FATHER DEMPSEY [*piously*] Hear! hear!

BROADBENT [*encouraged*] Thank you. Retrenchment— [*he waits for further applause*].

MATTHEW [*timidly*] What might rethrenchment mane now?

BROADBENT. It means an immense reduc-tion in the burden of the rates and taxes.

MATTHEW [*respectfully approving*] Dhats right. Dhats right, sir.

BROADBENT [*perfunctorily*] And, of course, Reform.

CORNELIUS
FATHER DEMPSEY } [*conventionally*] Of course.
DORAN

MATTHEW [*still suspicious*] Hwat does Reform mane, sir? Does it mane altherin anythin dhats as it is now?

BROADBENT [*impressively*] It means, Mr Haffigan, maintaining those reforms which have already been conferred on humanity by the Liberal Party, and trusting for future developments to the free activity of a free people on the basis of those reforms.

DORAN. Dhats right. No more meddlin. We're all right now: all we want is to be let alone.

CORNELIUS. Hwat about Home Rule?

BROADBENT [*rising so as to address them more imposingly*] I really cannot tell you what I feel about Home Rule without using the language of hyperbole.

DORAN. Savin Fadher Dempsey's presence, eh?

BROADBENT [*not understanding him*] Quite so—er—oh yes. All I can say is that as an Englishman I blush for the Union. It is the blackest stain on our national history. I look forward to the time—and it cannot be far distant, gentlemen, because Humanity is looking forward to it too, and insisting on it with no uncertain voice—I look forward to the time when an Irish legislature shall arise once more on the emerald pasture of College Green, and the Union Jack—that detestable symbol of a decadent Imperialism—be replaced by a flag as green as the island over which it waves: a flag on which we shall ask for England only a modest quartering in memory of our great party and of the immortal name of our grand old leader.

DORAN [*enthusiastically*] Dhats the style, begob! [*He smites his knee, and winks at Matt*].

MATTHEW. More power to you, sir!

BROADBENT. I shall leave you now, gentlemen, to your deliberations. I should like to have enlarged on the services rendered by the Liberal Party to the religious faith of the great majority of the people of Ireland; but I shall content myself with saying that in my opinion you should choose no representative who—no matter what his personal creed may be—is not an ardent supporter of freedom of conscience, and is not prepared to prove it by contributions, as lavish as his means will allow, to the great and beneficent work which you, Father Dempsey [*Father Dempsey bows*], are doing for the people of Rosscullen. Nor should the lighter but still most important question of the sports of the people be forgotten. The local cricket club—

CORNELIUS. The hwat!

DORAN. Nobody plays bat n ball here, if dhats what you mane.

BROADBENT. Well, let us say quoits. I saw two men, I think, last night—but after all, these are questions of detail. The main thing is that your candidate, whoever he may be, shall be a man of some means, able to help the locality instead of burdening it. And if he were a countryman of my own, the moral effect on the House of Commons would be immense! tremendous! Pardon my saying these few words: nobody feels their impertinence more than I do. Good morning, gentlemen.

He turns impressively to the gate, and trots away, congratulating himself, with a little twist of his head and cock of his eye, on having done a good stroke of political business.

HAFFIGAN [*awestruck*] Good morning, sir.

THE REST. Good morning. [*They watch him vacantly until he is out of earshot*].

CORNELIUS. Hwat d'ye think, Father Dempsey?

FATHER DEMPSEY [*indulgently*] Well, he hasnt much sense, God help him; but for the matter o that, neether has our present member.

DORAN. Arra musha he's good enough for parliament: what is there to do there but gas a bit, an chivy the Goverment, an vote wi dh Irish party?

CORNELIUS [*ruminatively*] He's the queerest Englishman *I* ever met. When he opened the paper dhis mornin the first thing he saw was that an English expedition had been bet in a battle in Inja somewhere; an he was as pleased as Punch! Larry told him that if he'd been alive when the news o Waterloo came, he'd a died o grief over it. Bedad I dont think he's quite right in his head.

DORAN. Divil a matther if he has plenty o money. He'll do for us right enough.

MATTHEW [*deeply impressed by Broadbent, and unable to understand their levity concerning him*] Did you mind what he said about re-

threnchment? That was very good, I thought.

FATHER DEMPSEY. You might find out from Larry, Corny, what his means are. God forgive us all! it's poor work spoiling the Egyptians, though we have good warrant for it; so I'd like to know how much spoil there is before I commit meself. [*He rises. They all rise respectfully*].

CORNELIUS [*ruefully*] I'd set me mind on Larry himself for the seat; but I suppose it cant be helped.

FATHER DEMPSEY [*consoling him*] Well, the boy's young yct; an he has a head on him. Goodbye, all. [*He goes out through the gate*].

DORAN. I must be goin, too. [*He directs Cornelius's attention to what is passing in the road*]. Look at me bould Englishman shakin hans wid Fadher Dempsey for all the world like a candidate on election day. And look at Fadher Dempsey givin him a squeeze an a wink as much as to say It's all right, me boy. You watch him shakin hans with me too: he's waitn for me. I'll tell him he's as good as elected. [*He goes, chuckling mischievously*].

CORNELIUS. Come in with me, Matt. I think I'll sell you the pig after all. Come in an wet the bargain.

MATTHEW [*instantly dropping into the old whine of the tenant*] I'm afeerd I cant afford the price, sir. [*He follows Cornelius into the house*].

Larry, newspaper still in hand, comes back through the shrubbery. Broadbent returns through the gate.

LARRY. Well? What has happened?

BROADBENT [*hugely self-satisfied*] I think Ive done the trick this time. I just gave them a bit of straight talk; and it went home. They were greatly impressed: everyone of those men believes in me and will vote for me when the question of selecting a candidate comes up. After all, whatever you say, Larry, they like an Englishman. They feel they can trust him, I suppose.

LARRY. Oh! theyve transferred the honor to you, have they?

BROADBENT [*complacently*] Well, it was a pretty obvious move, I should think. You know, these fellows have plenty of shrewdness in spite of their Irish oddity. [*Hodson comes from the house. Larry sits in Doran's chair and reuds*]. Oh, by the way, Hodson—

HODSON [*coming between Broadbent and Larry*] Yes, sir?

BROADBENT. I want you to be rather particular as to how you treat the people here.

HODSON. I havnt treated any of em yet, sir. If I was to accept all the treats they offer me I shouldnt be able to stand at this present moment, sir.

BROADBENT. Oh well, dont be too stand-offish, you know, Hodson. I should like you to be popular. If it costs anything I'll make it up to you. It doesnt matter if you get a bit upset at first: theyll like you all the better for it.

HODSON. I'm sure youre very kind, sir; but it dont seem to matter to me whether they like me or not. I'm not going to stand for parliament here, sir.

BROADBENT. Well, I am. Now do you understand?

HODSON [waking up at once] Oh, I beg your pardon, sir, I'm sure. I understand, sir.

CORNELIUS [appearing at the house door with Matt] Patsy'll drive the pig over this evenin, Matt. Goodbye. [He goes back into the house. Matt makes for the gate. Broadbent stops him. Hodson, pained by the derelict basket, picks it up and carries it away behind the house].

BROADBENT [beaming candidatorially] I must thank you very particularly, Mr Haffigan, for your support this morning. I value it because I know that the real heart of a nation is the class you represent, the yeomanry.

MATTHEW [aghast] The yeomanry!!!

LARRY [looking up from his paper] Take care, Tom! In Rosscullen a yeoman means a sort of Orange Bashi-Bazouk. In England, Matt, they call a freehold farmer a yeoman.

MATTHEW [huffily] I dont need to be in-sthructed be you, Larry Doyle. Some people think no one knows anythin but dhemselves. [To Broadbent, deferentially] Of course I know a gentleman like you would not compare me to the yeomanry. Me own granfather was flogged in the sthreets of Athenmullet be them when they put a gun in the thatch of his house an then went and found it there, bad cess to them!

BROADBENT [with sympathetic interest] Then you are not the first martyr of your family, Mr Haffigan?

MATTHEW. They turned me out o the farm I made out of the stones o Little Rosscullen hill wid me own hans.

BROADBENT. I have heard about it; and my blood still boils at the thought. [Calling] Hodson—

HODSON [behind the corner of the house] Yes, sir. [He hurries forward].

BROADBENT. Hodson: this gentleman's sufferings should make every Englishman think. It is want of thought rather than want of heart that allows such iniquities to disgrace society.

HODSON [prosaically] Yes, sir.

MATTHEW. Well, I'll be goin. Good mornin to you kindly, sir.

BROADBENT. You have some distance to go, Mr Haffigan: will you allow me to drive you home?

MATTHEW. Oh sure it'd be throublin your honor.

BROADBENT. I insist: it will give me the greatest pleasure, I assure you. My car is in the stable: I can get it round in five minutes.

MATTHEW. Well, sir, if you wouldnt mind, we could bring the pig Ive just bought from Corny—

BROADBENT [with enthusiasm] Certainly, Mr Haffigan: it will be quite delightful to drive with a pig in the car: I shall feel quite like an Irishman. Hodson: stay with Mr Haffigan; and give him a hand with the pig if necessary. Come, Larry; and help me. [He rushes away through the shrubbery].

LARRY [throwing the paper ill-humoredly on the chair] Look here, Tom! here, I say! confound it!— [he runs after him].

MATTHEW [glowering disdainfully at Hodson, and sitting down on Cornelius's chair as an act of social self-assertion] N are you the valley?

HODSON. The valley? Oh, I follow you: yes: I'm Mr Broadbent's valet.

MATTHEW. Ye have an aisy time of it: you look purty sleek. [With suppressed ferocity] Look at me! Do I look sleek?

HODSON [sadly] I wish I ad your ealth: you look as ard as nails. I suffer from an excess of uric acid.

MATTHEW. Musha what sort o disease is zhouragassid? Didjever suffer from injustice and starvation? Dhats the Irish disease. It's aisy for you to talk o sufferin, an you livin on the fat o the land wid money wrung from us.

HODSON [suddenly dropping the well-spoken valet, and breaking out in his native cockney] Wots wrong with you, aold chcp? Ez ennybody been doin ennythink to you?

MATTHEW. Anythin timmy! Didnt your

English masther say that the blood biled in him to hear the way they put a rint on me for the farm I made wid me own hans, and turned me out of it to give it to Billy Byrne?

HODSON. Ow, Tom Broadbent's blad boils pretty easy over ennything that eppens aht of his aown cantry. Downt you be tiken in by my aowl men, Peddy.

MATTHEW [indignantly] Paddy yourself! How dar you call me Paddy?

HODSON [unmoved] You jast keep your air on and listen to me. You Awrish people are too well off: thets wots the metter with you. [With sudden passion] You talk of your rotten little fawm cause you mide it by chackin a few stowns dahn a ill! Well, wot prawce maw grenfawther, Oi should lawk to knaow, that fitted ap a fust clawss shop and built ap a fust clawss dripery business in Landon by sixty years work, and then was chacked aht of it on is ed at the end of is lease withaht a penny for his goodwill. You talk of evictions! you that cawnt be moved until youve ran ap ighteen months rent. Oi once ran ap four weeks in Lembeth wen Oi was aht of a job in winter. They took the door off its inges and the winder aht of its seshes on me, an gev maw wawf pnoomownia. Oi'm a widower nah. [Between his teeth] Gawd! when Oi think of the things we Englishmen as to pat ap with, and eah you Awrish ahlin abaht your silly little grievances, and see the wy you mike it worse for haz by the rotten wiges youll cam over and tike and the rotten plices youll sleep in, I jast feel that I could tike the aowl bloomin British awland and mike you a present of it, jast to let you fawnd aht wot reel awdship's lawk.

MATTHEW [starting up, more in scandalized incredulity than in anger] D'ye have the face to set up England agen Ireland for injustices an wrongs an disthress an sufferin?

HODSON [with intense disgust and contempt] Ow, chack it, Peddy. Cheese it. You danno wot awdship is owver eah: all you knaow is ah to ahl abaht it. You tike the biscuit at thet, you do. Oi'm a Owm Ruler, Oi em. Do you know woy?

MATTHEW [equally contemptuous] D'ye know, yourself?

HODSON. Yus Oi do. It's because Oi want a little attention pide to my aown cantry; and thetll never be as long as your cheps are ollerin at Wesminister as if nowbody mettered but your own bloomin selves. Send em beck to ell or C'naught, as good aowld English Cramwell said. I'm jast sick of Awrland. Let it gow. Cat the caible. Mike it a present to Germany to keep the aowl Kyzer busy for a wawl; and give poor aowld England a chawnce: thets wot Oi sy.

MATTHEW [full of scorn for a man so ignorant as to be unable to pronounce the word Connaught, which practically rhymes with bonnet in Ireland, though in Hodson's dialect it rhymes with untaught] Take care we dont cut the cable ourselves some day, bad scran to you! An tell me dhis: have yanny Coercion Acs in England? Have yanny Removable magisthruts? Have you Dublin Castle to suppress every newspaper dhat takes the part o your own counthry?

HODSON. We can beyive ahrselves withaht sich things.

MATTHEW. Bedad youre right. It'd ony be waste o time to muzzle a sheep. Here! wheres me pig? God forgimmy for talkin to a poor ignorant craycher like you!

HODSON [grinning with good-humored malice, too convinced of his own superiority to feel his withers wrung] Your pig'll ev a rare doin in that car, Peddy. Forty mawl an ahr dahn that rocky line will strawk it pretty pink, you bet.

MATTHEW [scornfully] Hwy cant you tell a reasonable lie when youre about it? What horse can go forty mile an hour?

HODSON. Orse! Wy, you silly aowl rotter, it's not a orse: it's a mowtor. Do you spowse Tom Broadbent ud gow himself to fetch a orse?

MATTHEW [in consternation] Holy Moses! dont tell me it's the ingine he wants to take me on.

HODSON. Wot else?

MATTHEW. Your sowl to Morris Kelly! why didnt you tell me that before? The divil an ingine he'll get me on this day. [His ear catches an approaching teuf-teuf] Oh murdher! it's comin afther me: I hear the puff-puff of it. [He runs away through the gate, much to Hodson's amusement. The noise of the motor ceases; and Hodson, anticipating Broadbent's return, throws off the cockney and recomposes himself as a valet. Broadbent and Larry come through the shrubbery. Hodson moves aside to the gate].

BROADBENT. Where is Mr Haffigan? Has he gone for the pig?

HODSON. Bolted, sir? Afraid of the motor, sir.

BROADBENT [*much disappointed*] Oh, thats very tiresome. Did he leave any message?

HODSON. He was in too great a hurry, sir. Started to run home, sir, and left his pig behind him.

BROADBENT [*eagerly*] Left the pig! Then it's all right. The pig's the thing: the pig will win over every Irish heart to me. We'll take the pig home to Haffigan's farm in the motor: it will have a tremendous effect. Hodson!

HODSON. Yes, sir?

BROADBENT. Do you think you could collect a crowd to see the motor?

HODSON. Well, I'll try, sir.

BROADBENT. Thank you, Hodson: do.

Hodson goes out through the gate.

LARRY [*desperately*] Once more, Tom, will you listen to me?

BROADBENT. Rubbish! I tell you it will be all right.

LARRY. Only this morning you confessed how surprised you were to find that the people here shewed no sense of humor.

BROADBENT [*suddenly very solemn*] Yes: their sense of humor is in abeyance: I noticed it the moment we landed. Think of that in a country where every man is a born humorist! Think of what it means! [*Impressively*] Larry: we are in the presence of a great national grief.

LARRY. Whats to grieve them?

BROADBENT. I divined it, Larry: I saw it in their faces. Ireland has never smiled since her hopes were buried in the grave of Gladstone.

LARRY. Oh, whats the use of talking to such a man? Now look here, Tom. Be serious for a moment if you can.

BROADBENT [*stupent*] Serious! I!!!

LARRY. Yes, you. You say the Irish sense of humor is in abeyance. Well, if you drive through Rosscullen in a motor car with Haffigan's pig, it wont stay in abeyance. Now I warn you.

BROADBENT [*breezily*] Why, so much the better! I shall enjoy the joke myself more than any of them. [*Shouting*] Hallo, Patsy Farrell, where are you?

PATSY [*appearing in the shrubbery*] Here I am, your honor.

BROADBENT. Go and catch the pig and put it into the car: we're going to take it to Mr Haffigan's. [*He gives Larry a slap on the shoulders that sends him staggering off through the gate, and follows him buoyantly, exclaiming*]

Come on, you old croaker! I'll shew you how to win an Irish seat.

PATSY [*meditatively*] Bedad, if dhat pig gets a howlt o the handle o the machine— [*He shakes his head ominously and drifts away to the pigsty*].

ACT IV

The parlor in Cornelius Doyle's house. It communicates with the garden by a half glazed door. The fireplace is at the other side of the room, opposite the door and windows, the architect not having been sensitive to draughts. The table, rescued from the garden, is in the middle; and at it sits Keegan, the central figure in a rather crowded apartment. Nora, sitting with her back to the fire at the end of the table, is playing backgammon across its corner with him, on his left hand. Aunt Judy, a little further back, sits facing the fire knitting, with her feet on the fender. A little to Keegan's right, in front of the table, and almost sitting on it, is Barney Doran. Half a dozen friends of his, all men, are between him and the open door, supported by others outside. In the corner behind them is the sofa, of mahogany and horsehair, made up as a bed for Broadbent. Against the wall behind Keegan stands a mahogany sideboard. A door leading to the interior of the house is near the fireplace, behind Aunt Judy. There are chairs against the wall, one at each end of the sideboard. Keegan's hat is on the one nearest the inner door; and his stick is leaning against it. A third chair, also against the wall, is near the garden door.

There is a strong contrast of emotional atmosphere between the two sides of the room. Keegan is extraordinarily stern: no game of backgammon could possibly make a man's face so grim. Aunt Judy is quietly busy. Nora is trying to ignore Doran and attend to her game.

On the other hand Doran is reeling in an ecstasy of mischievous mirth which has infected all his friends. They are screaming with laughter, doubled up, leaning on the furniture and against the walls, shouting, screeching, crying.

AUNT JUDY [*as the noise lulls for a moment*] Arra hold your noise, Barney. What is there to laugh at?

DORAN. It got its fut into the little hweel— [*he is overcome afresh; and the rest collapse again*].

AUNT JUDY. Ah, have some sense: youre like a parcel o childher. Nora: hit him a thump on the back: he'll have a fit.

DORAN [*with squeezed eyes, exsufflicate with cachinnation*] Frens, he sez to dhem outside Doolan's: I'm takin the gintleman that pays the rint for a dhrive.

AUNT JUDY. Who did he mean be that?

DORAN. They call a pig that in England. Thats their notion of a joke.

AUNT JUDY. Musha God help them if they can joke no better than that!

DORAN [*with renewed symptoms*] Thin—

AUNT JUDY. Ah now dont be tellin it all over and settin yourself off again, Barney.

NORA. Youve told us three times, Mr Doran.

DORAN. Well but whin I think of it—!

AUNT JUDY. Then dont think of it, alanna.

DORAN. Dhere was Patsy Farrll in the back sate wi dhe pig between his knees, n me bould English boyoh in front at the machinery, n Larry Doyle in the road startin the injine wid a bed winch. At the first puff of it the pig lep out of its skin and bled Patsy's nose wi dhe ring in its snout. [*Roars of laughter: Keegan glares at them*]. Before Broadbint knew hwere he was, the pig was up his back and over into his lap; and bedad the poor baste did credit to Corny's thrainin of it; for it put in the fourth speed wid its right crubeen as if it was enthered for the Gordn Bennett.

NORA [*reproachfully*] And Larry in front of it and all! It's nothin to laugh at, Mr Doran.

DORAN. Bedad, Miss Reilly, Larry cleared six yards sideways at wan jump if he cleared an inch; and he'd a cleared seven if Doolan's granmother hadnt cotch him in her apern widhout intindin to. [*Immense merriment*].

AUNT JUDY. Ah, for shame, Barney! the poor old woman! An she was hurt before, too, when she slipped on the stairs.

DORAN. Bedad, maam, she's hurt behind now; for Larry bouled her over like a skittle. [*General delight at this typical stroke of Irish Rabelaisianism*].

NORA. It's well Mr Doyle wasnt killed.

DORAN. Faith it wasnt o Larry we were thinkin jus dhen, wi dhe pig takin the main sthreet o Rosscullen on market day at a mile a minnit. Dh ony thing Broadbint could get at wi dhe pig in front of him was a fut brake; n the pig's tail was undher dhat; so that whin he thought he was putn non the brake he was ony squeezin the life out o the pig's tail. The more he put the brake on the more the

pig squealed n the fasther he dhruv.

AUNT JUDY. Why couldnt he throw the pig out into the road?

DORAN. Sure he couldnt stand up to it, because he was spanchelled-like between his seat and dhat thing like a wheel on top of a stick between his knees.

AUNT JUDY. Lord have mercy on us!

NORA. I dont know how you can laugh. Do you, Mr Keegan?

KEEGAN [*grimly*] Why not? There is danger, destruction, torment! What more do we need to make us merry? Go on, Barney: the last drops of joy are not squeezed from the story yet. Tell us again how our brother was torn asunder.

DORAN [*puzzled*] Whose bruddher?

KEEGAN. Mine.

NORA. He means the pig, Mr Doran. You know his way.

DORAN [*rising gallantly to the occasion*] Bedad I'm sorry for your poor bruddher, Misther Keegan; but I recommend you to thry him wid a couple o fried eggs for your breakfast tomorrow. It was a case of Excelsior wi dhat ambitious baste; for not content wid jumpin from the back seat into the front wan, he jumped from the front wan into the road in front of the car. And—

KEEGAN. And everybody laughed!

NORA. Dont go over that again, p l e a s e, Mr Doran.

DORAN. Faith be the time the car went over the poor pig dhere was little left for me or anywan else to go over except wid a knife an fork.

AUNT JUDY. Why didnt Mr Broadbent stop the car when the pig was gone?

DORAN. Stop the car! He might as well ha thried to stop a mad bull. First it went wan way an made fireworks o Molly Ryan's crockery stall; an dhen it slewed round an ripped ten fut o wall out o the corner o the pound. [*With enormous enjoyment*] Begob, it just tore the town in two and sent the whole dam market to blazes. [*Nora offended, rises*].

KEEGAN [*indignantly*] Sir!

DORAN [*quickly*] Savin your presence, Miss Reilly, and Misther Keegan's. Dhere! I wont say anuddher word.

NORA. I'm surprised at you, Mr Doran. [*She sits down again*].

DORAN [*reflectively*] He has the divil's own luck, that Englishman, annyway; for hwen they picked him up he hadnt a scratch on him, barrn hwat the pig did to his cloes. Patsy had two fingers out o jynt; but the smith pulled them sthraight for him. Oh, you never heard such a hullaballoo as there was. There was Molly cryin Me chaney, me beautyful chaney! n oul Matt shoutin Me pig, me pig! n the polus takin the number o the car, n not a man in the town able to speak for laughin—

KEEGAN [*with intense emphasis*] It is hell: it IS hell. Nowhere else could such a scene be a burst of happiness for the people.

Cornelius comes in hastily from the garden, pushing his way through the little crowd.

CORNELIUS. Whisht your laughin, boys! Here he is. [*He puts his hat on the sideboard, and goes to the fireplace, where he posts himself with his back to the chimneypiece*].

AUNT JUDY. Remember your behavior, now.

Everybody becomes silent, solemn, concerned, sympathetic. Broadbent enters, soiled and disordered as to his motoring coat: immensely important and serious as to himself. He makes his way to the end of the table nearest the garden door, whilst Larry, who accompanies him, throws his motoring coat on the sofa bed, and sits down, watching the proceedings.

BROADBENT [*taking off his leather cap with dignity and placing it on the table*] I hope you have not been anxious about me.

AUNT JUDY. Deedn we have, Mr Broadbent. It's a mercy you werent killed.

DORAN. Kilt! It's a mercy dheres two bones of you left houldin together. How dijjescape at all at all? Well, I never thought I'd be so glad to see you safe and sound again. Not a man in the town would say less [*murmurs of kindly assent*]. Wont you come down to Doolan's and have a dhrop o brandy to take the shock off?

BROADBENT. Youre all really too kind; but the shock has quite passed off.

DORAN [*jovially*] Never mind. Come along all the same and tell us about it over a frenly glass.

BROADBENT. May I say how deeply I feel the kindness with which I have been overwhelmed since my accident? I can truthfully declare that I am glad it happened, because it has brought out the kindness and sympathy of the Irish character to an extent I had no conception of.

SEVERAL PRESENT. {Oh, sure youre welcome! Sure it's only natural. Sure you might have been kilt.

A young man, feeling that he must laugh or burst, hurries out. Barney puts an iron constraint on his features.

BROADBENT. All I can say is that I wish I could drink the health of everyone of you.

DORAN. Dhen come an do it.

BROADBENT [*very solemnly*] No: I am a teetotaller.

AUNT JUDY [*incredulously*] Arra since when?

BROADBENT. Since this morning, Miss Doyle. I have had a lesson [*he looks at Nora significantly*] that I shall not forget. It may be that total abstinence has already saved my life; for I was astonished at the steadiness of my nerves when death stared me in the face today. So I will ask you to excuse me. [*He collects himself for a speech*]. Gentlemen: I hope the gravity of the peril through which we have all passed—for I know that the danger to the bystanders was as great as to the occupants of the car—will prove an earnest of closer and more serious relations between us in the future. We have had a somewhat agitating day: a valuable and innocent animal has lost its life: a public building has been wrecked: an aged and infirm lady has suffered an impact for which I feel personally responsible, though my old friend Mr Laurence Doyle unfortunately incurred the first effects of her very natural resentment. I greatly regret the damage to Mr Patrick Farrell's fingers; and I have of course taken care that he shall not suffer pecuniarily by his mishap. [*Murmurs of admiration at his magnanimity, and a voice "Youre a gentleman, sir"*]. I am glad to say that Patsy took it like an Irishman, and, far from expressing any vindictive feeling, declared his willingness to break all his fingers and toes for me on the same terms [*subdued applause, and "More power to Patsy!"*]. Gentlemen: I felt at home in Ireland from the first [*rising excitement among his hearers*]. In every Irish breast I have found that spirit of liberty [*A cheery voice "Hear Hear"*], that instinctive mistrust of the Government [*A small pious voice, with intense expression, "God bless you, sir!"*], that love of independence [*A defiant voice, "Thats it! Independence!"*], that indignant sympathy with the cause of oppressed nationalities abroad [*A threatening growl from all: the ground-swell of patriotic passion*] and with the resolute assertion of personal rights at home, which is all but extinct in my own country. If it were legally possible I should become a naturalized Irishman; and if ever it be my good fortune to represent an Irish constituency in parliament, it shall be my first care to introduce a Bill legalizing such an operation. I believe a large section of the Liberal party would avail themselves of it. [*Momentary scepticism*]. I do. [*Convulsive cheering*]. Gentlemen: I have said enough. [*Cries of "Go on"*]. No: I have as yet no right to address you at all on political subjects; and we must not abuse the warm-hearted Irish hospitality of Miss Doyle by turning her sitting room into a public meeting.

DORAN [*energetically*] Three cheers for Tom Broadbent, the future member for Rosscullen!

AUNT JUDY [*waving a half knitted sock*] Hip hip hurray!

The cheers are given with great heartiness, as it is by this time, for the more humorous spirits present, a question of vociferation or internal rupture.

BROADBENT. Thank you from the bottom of my heart, friends.

NORA [*whispering to Doran*] Take them away, Mr Doran [*Doran nods*].

DORAN. Well, good evenin, Mr Broadbent; an may you never regret the day you wint dhrivin wid Haffigan's pig! [*They shake hands*]. Good evenin, Miss Doyle.

General handshaking, Broadbent shaking hands with everybody effusively. He accompanies them to the garden and can be heard outside saying Good-night in every inflexion known to parliamentary candidates, Nora, Aunt Judy, Keegan, Larry, and Cornelius are left in the parlor. Larry goes to the threshold and watches the scene in the garden.

NORA. It's a shame to make game of him like that. He's a gradle more good in him than Barney Doran.

CORNELIUS. It's all up with his candidature. He'll be laughed out o the town.

LARRY [*turning quickly from the doorway*] Oh no he wont: he's not an Irishman. He'll never know theyre laughing at him; and while theyre laughing he'll win the seat.

CORNELIUS. But he cant prevent the story getting about.

LARRY. He wont want to. He'll tell it himself as one of the most providential episodes in the history of England and Ireland.

AUNT JUDY. Sure he wouldnt make a fool of himself like that.

LARRY. Are you sure he's such a fool after all, Aunt Judy? Suppose you had a vote! which would you rather give it to? the man that told the story of Haffigan's pig Barney Doran's way or Broadbent's way?

AUNT JUDY. Faith I wouldnt give it to a man at all. It's a few women they want in parliament to stop their foolish blather.

BROADBENT [*bustling into the room, and taking off his damaged motoring overcoat, which he puts down on the sofa*] Well, thats over. I must apologize for making a speech. Miss Doyle; but they like it, you know. Everything helps in electioneering.

Larry takes the chair near the door; draws it near the table; and sits astride it, with his elbows folded on the back.

AUNT JUDY. I'd no notion you were such an orator, Mr Broadbent.

BROADBENT. Oh, it's only a knack. One picks it up on the platform. It stokes up their enthusiasm.

AUNT JUDY. Oh, I forgot. Youve not met Mr Keegan. Let me introjoosha.

BROADBENT [*shaking hands effusively*] Most happy to meet you, Mr Keegan. I have heard of you, though I have not had the pleasure of shaking your hand before. And now may I ask you—for I value no man's opinion more —what you think of my chances here.

KEEGAN [*coldly*] Your chances, sir, are excellent. You will get into parliament.

BROADBENT [*delighted*] I hope so. I think so. [*Fluctuating*] You really think so? You are sure you are not allowing your enthusiasm for our principles to get the better of your judgment?

KEEGAN. I have no enthusiasm for your principles, sir. You will get into parliament because you want to get into it enough to be prepared to take the necessary steps to induce the people to vote for you. That is how people usually get into that fantastic assembly.

BROADBENT [*puzzled*] Of course. [*Pause*]. Quite so. [*Pause*]. Er—yes. [*Buoyant again*] I think they will vote for me. Eh? Yes?

AUNT JUDY. Arra why shouldnt they? Look at the people they do vote for!

BROADBENT [*encouraged*] Thats true: thats very true. When I see the windbags, the carpet-baggers, the charlatans, the—the— the fools and ignoramuses who corrupt the multitude by their wealth, or seduce them by spouting balderdash to them, I cannot help thinking that an Englishman with no humbug about him, who will talk straight common sense and take his stand on the solid ground of principle and public duty, m u s t win his way with men of all classes.

KEEGAN [*quietly*] Sir: there was a time, in my ignorant youth, when I should have called you a hypocrite.

BROADBENT [*reddening*] A hypocrite!

NORA [*hastily*] Oh I'm sure you dont think anything of the sort, Mr Keegan.

BROADBENT [*emphatically*] Thank you, Miss Reilly: thank you.

CORNELIUS [*gloomily*] We all have to stretch it a bit in politics: hwats the use o pretendin we dont?

BROADBENT [*stiffly*] I hope I have said or done nothing that calls for any such observation, Mr Doyle. If there is a vice I detest— or against which my whole public life has been a protest—it is the vice of hypocrisy. I would almost rather be inconsistent than insincere.

KEEGAN. Do not be offended, sir: I know that you are quite sincere. There is a saying in the Scripture which runs—so far as the memory of an oldish man can carry the words —Let not the right side of your brain know what the left side doeth. I learnt at Oxford that this is the secret of the Englishman's strange power of making the best of both worlds.

BROADBENT. Surely the text refers to our right and left hands. I am somewhat surprised to hear a member of your Church quote so essentially Protestant a document as the Bible; but at least you might quote it accurately.

LARRY. Tom: with the best intentions youre making an ass of yourself. You dont understand Mr Keegan's peculiar vein of humour.

BROADBENT [*instantly recovering his confidence*] Ah! it was only your delightful Irish humor, Mr Keegan. Of course, of course. How stupid of me! I'm so sorry. [*He pats Keegan consolingly on the back*]. John Bull's wits are still slow, you see. Besides, calling me a hypocrite was too big a joke to swallow all at once, you know.

KEEGAN. You must also allow for the fact that I am mad.

NORA. Ah, dont talk like that, Mr Keegan.

BROADBENT [*encouragingly*] Not at all, not at all. Only a whimsical Irishman, eh?

LARRY. Are you really mad, Mr Keegan?

AUNT JUDY [*shocked*] Oh, Larry, how could you ask him such a thing?

LARRY. I dont think Mr Keegan minds. [*To Keegan*] Whats the true version of the story of that black man you confessed on his deathbed?

KEEGAN. What story have you heard about that?

LARRY. I am informed that when the devil came for the black heathen, he took off your head and turned it three times round before putting it on again; and that your head's been turned ever since.

NORA [*reproachfully*] Larry!

KEEGAN [*blandly*] That is not quite what occurred. [*He collects himself for a serious utterance: they attend involuntarily*]. I heard that a black man was dying, and that the people were afraid to go near him. When I went to the place I found an elderly Hindoo, who told me one of those tales of unmerited misfortune, of cruel ill luck, of relentless persecution by destiny, which sometimes wither the commonplaces of consolation on the lips of a priest. But this man did not complain of his misfortunes. They were brought upon him, he said, by sins committed in a former existence. Then, without a word of comfort from me, he died with a clear-eyed resignation that my most earnest exhortations have rarely produced in a Christian, and left me sitting there by his bedside with the mystery of this world suddenly revealed to me.

BROADBENT. That is a remarkable tribute to the liberty of conscience enjoyed by the subjects of our Indian Empire.

LARRY. No doubt; but may we venture to ask what is the mystery of this world?

KEEGAN. This world, sir, is very clearly a place of torment and penance, a place where the fool flourishes and the good and wise are hated and persecuted, a place where men and women torture one another in the name of love; where children are scourged and enslaved in the name of parental duty and education; where the weak in body are poisoned and mutilated in the name of healing, and the weak in character are put to the horrible torture of imprisonment, not for hours but for years, in the name of justice. It is a place where the hardest toil is a welcome refuge from the horror and tedium of pleasure, and where charity and good works are done only for hire to ransom the souls of the spoiler and the sybarite. Now, sir, there is only one place of horror and torment known to my religion; and that place is hell. Therefore it is plain to me that this earth of ours must be hell, and that we are all here, as the Indian revealed to me—perhaps he was sent to reveal it to me—to expiate crimes committed by us in a former existence.

AUNT JUDY [awestruck] Heaven save us, what a thing to say!

CORNELIUS [sighing] It's a queer world: thats certain.

BROADBENT. Your idea is a very clever one, Mr Keegan: really most brilliant: *I* should never have thought of it. But it seems to me —if I may say so—that you are overlooking the fact that, of the evils you describe, some are absolutely necessary for the preservation of society, and others are encouraged only when the Tories are in office.

LARRY. I expect you were a Tory in a former existence; and that is why you are here.

BROADBENT [with conviction] Never, Larry, never. But leaving politics out of the question, I find the world quite good enough for me: rather a jolly place, in fact.

KEEGAN [looking at him with quiet wonder] You are satisfied?

BROADBENT. As a reasonable man, yes. I see no evils in the world—except, of course, natural evils—that cannot be remedied by freedom, self-government, and English institutions. I think so, not because I am an Englishman, but as a matter of common sense.

KEEGAN. You feel at home in the world, then?

BROADBENT. Of course. Dont you?

KEEGAN [from the very depths of his nature] No.

BROADBENT [breezily] Try phosphorus pills. I always take them when my brain is overworked. I'll give you the address in Oxford Street.

KEEGAN [enigmatically: rising] Miss Doyle: my wandering fit has come on me: will you excuse me?

AUNT JUDY. To be sure: you know you can come in n nout as you like.

KEEGAN. We can finish the game some other time, Miss Reilly. [He goes for his hat and stick].

NORA. No: I'm out with you [she disarranges the pieces and rises]. I was too wicked in a former existence to play backgammon with a good man like you.

AUNT JUDY [whispering to her] Whisht, whisht, child! Dont set him back on that again.

KEEGAN [to Nora] When I look at you, I think that perhaps Ireland is only purgatory, after all. [He passes on to the garden door].

NORA. Galong with you!

BROADBENT [whispering to Cornelius] Has he a vote?

CORNELIUS [nodding] Yes. An theres lotsle vote the way he tells them.

KEEGAN [at the garden door, with gentle gravity] Good evening, Mr Broadbent. You have set me thinking. Thank you.

BROADBENT [delighted, hurrying across to him to shake hands] No, really? You find that contact with English ideas is stimulating, eh?

KEEGAN. I am never tired of hearing you talk, Mr Broadbent.

BROADBENT [modestly remonstrating] Oh come! come!

KEEGAN. Yes, I assure you. You are an extremely interesting man. [He goes out].

BROADBENT [enthusiastically] What a nice chap! What an intelligent, broadminded character, considering his cloth! By the way, I'd better have a wash. [He takes up his coat and cap, and leaves the room through the inner door].

Nora returns to her chair and shuts up the backgammon board.

AUNT JUDY. Keegan's very queer today. He has his mad fit on him.

CORNELIUS [worried and bitter] I wouldnt say but he's right after all. It's a contrairy world. [To Larry] Why would you be such a fool as to let Broadbent take the seat in parliament from you?

LARRY [glancing at Nora] He will take more than that from me before he's done here.

CORNELIUS. I wish he'd never set foot in my house, bad luck to his fat face! D'ye think he'd lend me £300 on the farm, Larry? When I'm so hard up, it seems a waste o money not to mortgage it now it's me own.

LARRY. *I* can lend you £300 on it.

CORNELIUS. No, no; I wasnt putn in for that. When I die and leave you the farm I should like to be able to feel that it was all me own, and not half yours to start with. Now I'll take me oath Barney Doarn's going to ask Broadbent to lend him £500 on the mill to put in a new hweel; for the old one'll harly hol together. An Haffigan cant sleep with covetn that corner o land at the foot of his medda that belongs to Doolan. He'll have to mortgage to buy it. I may as well be first as last. D'ye think Broadbent'd len me a little?

LARRY. I'm quite sure he will.

CORNELIUS. Is he as ready as that? Would he len me five hundred, d'ye think?

LARRY. He'll lend you more than the landll ever be worth to you; so for Heaven's sake be prudent.

CORNELIUS [*judicially*] All right, all right, me son: I'll be careful. I'm goin into the office for a bit. [*He withdraws through the inner door, obviously to prepare his application to Broadbent*].

AUNT JUDY [*indignantly*] As if he hadnt seen enough o borryin when he was an agent without beginnin borryin himself! [*She rises*]. I'll borry him, so I will. [*She puts her knitting on the table and follows him out, with a resolute air that bodes trouble for Cornelius*].

Larry and Nora are left together for the first time since his arrival. She looks at him with a smile that perishes as she sees him aimlessly rocking his chair, and reflecting, evidently not about her, with his lips pursed as if he were whistling. With a catch in her throat she takes up Aunt Judy's knitting, and makes a pretence of going on with it.

NORA. I suppose it didnt seem very long to you.

LARRY [*starting*] Eh? What didnt?

NORA. The eighteen years youve been away.

LARRY. Oh, that! No: it seems hardly more than a week. I've been so busy—had so little time to think.

NORA. Ive had nothin else to do but think.

LARRY. That was very bad for you. Why didnt you give it up? Why did you stay here?

NORA. Because nobody sent for me to go anywhere else, I suppose. Thats why.

LARRY. Yes: one does stick frightfully in the same place, unless some external force comes and routs one out. [*He yawns slightly; but as she looks up quickly at him, he pulls himself together and rises with an air of waking up and setting to work cheerfully to make himself agreeable*]. And how have you been all this time?

NORA. Quite well, thank you.

LARRY. Thats right. [*Suddenly finding that he has nothing else to say, and being ill at ease in consequence, he strolls about the room humming distractedly*].

NORA [*struggling with her tears*] Is that all you have to say to me, Larry?

LARRY. Well, what is there to say? You see, we know each other so well.

NORA [*a little consoled*] Yes: of course we do. [*He does not reply*]. I wonder you came back at all.

LARRY. I couldnt help it. [*She looks up affectionately*]. Tom made me. [*She looks down again quickly to conceal the effect of this blow. He whistles another stave; then resumes*] I had a sort of dread of returning to Ireland. I felt somehow that my luck would turn if I came back. And now here I am, none the worse.

NORA. Praps it's a little dull for you.

LARRY. No: I havnt exhausted the interest of strolling about the old places and remembering and romancing about them.

NORA [*hopefully*] Oh! You do remember the places, then?

LARRY. Of course. They have associations.

NORA [*not doubting that the associations are with her*] I suppose so.

LARRY. M'yes. I can remember particular spots where I had long fits of thinking about the countries I meant to get to when I escaped from Ireland. America and London, and sometimes Rome and the east.

NORA [*deeply mortified*] Was that all you used to be thinking about?

LARRY. Well, there was precious little else to think about here, my dear Nora, except sometimes at sunset, when one got maudlin and called Ireland Erin, and imagined one was remembering the days of old, and so forth. [*He whistles Let Erin Remember*].

NORA. Did jever get a letter I wrote you last February?

LARRY. Oh yes; and I really intended to answer it. But I havnt had a moment; and I knew you wouldnt mind. You see, I am so afraid of boring you by writing about affairs you dont understand and people you dont know! And yet what else have I to write about? I begin a letter; and then I tear it up again. The fact is, fond as we are of one another, Nora, we have so little in common— I mean of course the things one can put in a letter—that correspondence is apt to become the hardest of hard work.

NORA. Yes: it's hard for me to know anything about you if you never tell me anything.

LARRY [*pettishly*] Nora: a man cant sit down and write his life day by day when he's tired enough with having lived it.

NORA. I'm not blaming you.

LARRY [*looking at her with some concern*] You seem rather out of spirits. [*Going closer to her, anxiously and tenderly*] You havnt got neuralgia, have you?

NORA. No.

LARRY [*reassured*] I get a touch of it sometimes when I am below par. [*Absently, again strolling about*] Yes, yes. [*He gazes through the doorway at the Irish landscape, and sings, almost unconsciously, but very expressively, an air from Offenbach's Whittington*].

[*Nora, who has been at first touched by the tenderness of his singing, puts down her knitting at this very unexpected sentiment, and stares at him. He continues until the melody soars out of his range, when he trails off into whistling Let Erin Remember*].

I'm afraid I'm boring you, Nora, though youre too kind to say so.

NORA. Are you wanting to get back to England already?

LARRY. Not at all. Not at all.

NORA. Thats a queer song to sing to me if youre not.

LARRY. The song! Oh, it doesnt mean anything: it's by a German Jew, like most English patriotic sentiment. Never mind me, my dear: go on with your work; and dont let me bore you.

NORA [*bitterly*] Rosscullen isnt such a lively place that I am likely to be bored by you at our first talk together after eighteen years, though you dont seem to have much to say to me after all.

LARRY. Eighteen years is a devilish long time, Nora. Now if it had been eighteen minutes, or even eighteen months, we should be able to pick up the interrupted thread, and chatter like two magpies. But as it is, I have simply nothing to say; and you seem to have less.

NORA. I— [*her tears choke her; but she keeps up appearances desperately*].

LARRY [*quite unconscious of his cruelty*] In a week or so we shall be quite old friends again. Meanwhile, as I feel that I am not making myself particularly entertaining, I'll take myself off. Tell Tom Ive gone for a stroll over the hill.

NORA. You seem very fond of Tom, as you call him.

LARRY [*the triviality going suddenly out of his voice*] Yes: I'm fond of Tom.

NORA. Oh, well, dont let me keep you from him.

LARRY. I know quite well that my departure will be a relief. Rather a failure, this first meeting after eighteen years, eh? Well, never mind: these great sentimental events always a r e failures; and now the worst of it's over anyhow. [*He goes out through the garden door*].

Nora, left alone, struggles wildly to save herself from breaking down, and then drops her face on the table and gives way to a convulsion of crying. Her sobs shake her so that she can hear nothing; and she has no suspicion that she is no longer alone until her head and breast are raised by Broadbent, who, returning newly washed and combed through the inner door, has seen her condition, first with surprise and concern, and then with an emotional disturbance that quite upsets him.

BROADBENT: Miss Reilly, Miss Reilly. Whats the matter? Dont cry: I cant stand it: you musnt cry. [*She makes a choked effort to speak, so painful that he continues with impulsive sympathy*] No: dont try to speak: it's all right now. Have your cry out: never mind me: trust me. [*Gathering her to him, and babbling consolatorily*] Cry on my chest: the only really comfortable place for a woman to cry is a man's chest: a real man, a real friend. A good broad chest, eh? not less than forty-two inches— no: dont fuss: never mind the conventions: we're two friends, arnt we? Come now, come, come! It's all right and comfortable and happy now, isnt it?

NORA [*through her tears*] Let me go. I want me hankerchief.

BROADBENT [*holding her with one arm and producing a large silk handkerchief from his breast pocket*] Heres a handkerchief. Let me [*he dabs her tears dry with it*]. Never mind your own: it's too small: it's one of those wretched little cambric handkerchiefs—

NORA [*sobbing*] Indeed it's a common cotton one.

BROADBENT. Of course it's a common cotton one—silly little cotton one—not good enough for the dear eyes of Nora Cryna—

NORA [*spluttering into a hysterical laugh and clutching him convulsively with her fingers while she tries to stifle her laughter against his collar bone*] Oh dont make me laugh: please dont make me laugh.

BROADBENT [*terrified*] I didnt mean to, on my soul. What is it? What is it?

NORA. Nora Creena, Nora Creena.

BROADBENT [*patting her*] Yes, yes, of course, Nora Creena, Nora acushla [*he makes cush rhyme to plush*]—

NORA. Acushla [*she makes cush rhyme to bush*].

BROADBENT. Oh, confound the language! Nora darling—my Nora—the Nora I love—

NORA [*shocked into propriety*] You mustnt talk like that to me.

BROADBENT [*suddenly becoming prodigiously solemn and letting her go*] No, of course not. I dont mean it. At least I do mean it; but I know it's premature. I had no right to take advantage of your being a little upset; but I lost my self-control for a moment.

NORA [*wondering at him*] I think youre a very kind-hearted man, Mr Broadbent; but you seem to me to have no self-control at all [*she turns her face away with a keen pang of shame and adds*] no more than myself.

BROADBENT [*resolutely*] Oh yes, I have: you should see me when I am really roused: then I have TREMENDOUS self-control. Remember: we have been alone together only once before; and then, I regret to say, I was in a disgusting state.

NORA. Ah no, Mr Broadbent: you wernt disgusting.

BROADBENT [*mercilessly*] Yes I was: nothing can excuse it: perfectly beastly. It must have made a most unfavorable impression on you.

NORA. Oh, sure it's all right. Say no more about that.

BROADBENT. I must, Miss Reilly: it is my duty. I shall not detain you long. May I ask you to sit down. [*He indicates her chair with oppressive solemnity. She sits down wondering. He then, with the same portentous gravity, places a chair for himself near her; sits down; and proceeds to explain*]. First, Miss Reilly, may I say that I have tasted nothing of an alcoholic nature today.

NORA. It doesnt seem to make as much difference in you as it would in an Irishman, somehow.

BROADBENT. Perhaps not. Perhaps not. I never quite lose myself.

NORA [*consolingly*] Well, anyhow, youre all right now.

BROADBENT [*fervently*] Thank you, Miss Reilly: I am. Now we shall get along. [*Tenderly, lowering his voice*] Nora: I was in earnest last night. [*Nora moves as if to rise*]. No: one moment. You must not think I am going to press you for an answer before you have known me for 24 hours. I am a reasonable man, I hope; and I am prepared to wait as long as you like, provided you will give me some small assurance that the answer will not be unfavorable.

NORA. How could I go back from it if I did? I sometimes think youre not quite right in your head, Mr Broadbent, you say such funny things.

BROADBENT. Yes: I know I have a strong sense of humor which sometimes makes people doubt whether I am quite serious. That is why I have always thought I should like to marry an Irishwoman. She would always understand my jokes. For instance, you would understand them, eh?

NORA [*uneasily*] Mr Broadbent: I couldnt.

BROADBENT [*soothingly*] Wait: let me break this to you gently, Miss Reilly: hear me out. I daresay you have noticed that in speaking to you I have been putting a very strong constraint on myself, so as to avoid wounding your delicacy by too abrupt an avowal of my feelings. Well, I feel now that the time has come to be open, to be frank, to be explicit. Miss Reilly: you have inspired in me a very strong attachment. Perhaps, with a woman's intuition, you have already guessed that.

NORA [*rising distractedly*] Why do you talk to me in that unfeeling nonsensical way?

BROADBENT [*rising also, much astonished*] Unfeeling! Nonsensical!

NORA. Dont you know that you have said things to me that no man ought to say unless —unless— [*she suddenly breaks down again and hides her face on the table as before*] Oh, go away from me: I wont get married at all: what is it but heartbreak and disappointment?

BROADBENT [*developing the most formidable symptoms of rage and grief*] Do you mean to say that you are going to refuse me? that you dont care for me?

NORA [*looking at him in consternation*] Oh,

dont take it to heart, Mr Br—

BROADBENT [*flushed and almost choking*] I dont want to be petted and blarneyed. [*With childish rage*] I love you. I want you for my wife. [*In despair*] I cant help your refusing. I'm helpless: I can do nothing. You have no right to ruin my whole life. You— [*a hysterical convulsion stops him*].

NORA [*almost awestruck*] Youre not going to cry, are you? I never thought a man c o u l d cry. Dont.

BROADBENT. I'm not crying. I—I—I leave that sort of thing to your damned sentimental Irishmen. You think I have no feeling because I am a plain unemotional Englishman, with no powers of expression.

NORA. I dont think you know the sort of man you are at all. Whatever may be the matter with you, it's not want of feeling.

BROADBENT [*hurt and petulant*] It's you who have no feeling. Youre as heartless as Larry.

NORA. What do you expect me to do? Is it to throw meself at your head the minute the word is out o your mouth?

BROADBENT [*striking his silly head with his fists*] Oh, what a fool! what a brute I am! It's only your Irish delicacy: of course, of course. You mean Yes. Eh? What? Yes? yes? yes?

NORA. I think you might understand that though I might choose to be an old maid, I could never marry anybody but you now.

BROADBENT [*clasping her violently to his breast, with a crow of immense relief and triumph*] Ah, thats right, thats right: thats magnificent. I knew you would see what a first-rate thing this will be for both of us.

NORA [*incommoded and not at all enraptured by his ardor*] Youre dreadfully strong, an a gradle too free with your strength. An I never thought o whether it'd be a good thing for us or not. But when you found me here that time, I let you be kind to me, and cried in your arms, because I was too wretched to think of anything but the comfort of it. An how could I let any other man touch me after that?

BROADBENT [*moved*] Now thats very nice of you, Nora: thats really most delicately womanly [*he kisses her hand chivalrously*].

NORA [*looking earnestly and a little doubtfully at him*] Surely if you let one woman cry on you like that youd never let another touch you.

BROADBENT [*conscientiously*] One should not. One o u g h t not, my dear girl. But the honest truth is, if a chap is at all a pleasant sort of chap, his chest becomes a fortification that has to stand many assaults: at least it is so in England.

NORA [*curtly, much disgusted*] Then youd better marry an Englishwoman.

BROADBENT [*making a wry face*] No, no: the Englishwoman is too prosaic for my taste, too material, too much of the animated beefsteak about her. The ideal is what I like. Now Larry's taste is just the opposite: he likes em solid and bouncing and rather keen about him. It's a very convenient difference; for weve never been in love with the same woman.

NORA. An d'ye mean to tell me to me face that youve ever been in love before?

BROADBENT. Lord! yes.

NORA. I'm not your first love!

BROADBENT. First love is only a little foolishness and a lot of curiosity: no really selfspecting woman would take advantage of it. No, my dear Nora: Ive done with all that long ago. Love affairs always end in rows. We're not going to have any rows: we're going to have a solid four-square home: man and wife: comfort and common sense. And plenty of affection, eh [*he puts his arm round her with confident proprietorship*]?

NORA [*coldly, trying to get away*] I dont want any other woman's leavings.

BROADBENT [*holding her*] Nobody asked you to, maam. I never asked any woman to marry me before.

NORA [*severely*] Then why didnt you if youre an honorable man?

BROADBENT. Well, to tell you the truth, they were mostly married already. But never mind! there was nothing wrong. Come! dont take a mean advantage of me. After all, you must have had a fancy or two yourself, eh?

NORA [*conscience-stricken*] Yes. I suppose Ive no right to be particular.

BROADBENT [*humbly*] I know I'm not good enough for you, Nora. But no man is, you know, when the woman is a really nice woman.

NORA. Oh, I'm no better than yourself. I may as well tell you about it.

BROADBENT. No, no: lets have no telling: much better not. *I* shant tell y o u anything: dont y o u tell m e anything. Perfect confidence in one another and no tellings: thats the way to avoid rows.

NORA. Dont think it was anything I need

be ashamed of.

BROADBENT. I dont.

NORA. It was only that I'd never known anybody else that I could care for; and I was foolish enough once to think that Larry—

BROADBENT [*disposing of the idea at once*] Larry! Oh, that wouldnt have done at all, not at all. You dont know Larry as I do, my dear. He has absolutely no capacity for enjoyment: he couldnt make any woman happy. He's as clever as be-blowed; but life's too earthly for him: he doesnt really care for anything or anybody.

NORA. Ive found that out.

BROADBENT. Of course you have. No, my dear: take my word for it, youre jolly well out of that. There! [*swinging her round against his breast*] thats much more comfortable for you.

NORA [*with Irish peevishness*] Ah, you mustnt go on like that. I dont like it.

BROADBENT [*unabashed*] Youll acquire the taste by degrees. You mustnt mind me: it's an absolute necessity of my nature that I should have somebody to hug occasionally. Besides, it's good for you: itll plump out your muscles and make em elastic and set up your figure.

NORA. Well, I'm sure! if this is English manners! Arnt you ashamed to talk about such things?

BROADBENT [*in the highest feather*] Not a bit. By George, Nora, it's a tremendous thing to be able to enjoy oneself. Lets go off for a walk out of this stuffy little room. I want the open air to expand in, Come along. Co-o-ome along. [*He puts her arm into his and sweeps her out into the garden as an equinoctial gale might sweep a dry leaf*].

Later in the evening, the grasshopper is again enjoying the sunset by the great stone on the hill; but this time he enjoys neither the stimulus of Keegan's conversation nor the pleasure of terrifying Patsy Farrell. He is alone until Nora and Broadbent come up the hill arm in arm. Broadbent is still breezy and confident; but she has her head averted from him and is almost in tears.

BROADBENT [*stopping to snuff up the hillside air*] Ah! I like this spot. I like this view. This would be a jolly good place for a hotel and a golf links. Friday to Tuesday, railway ticket and hotel all inclusive. I tell you, Nora, I'm going to develop this place. [*Looking at her*] Hallo! Whats the matter? Tired?

NORA [*unable to restrain her tears*] I'm ashamed out o me life.

BROADBENT [*astonished*] Ashamed! What of?

NORA. Oh, how could you drag me all round the place like that, telling everybody that we're going to be married, and introjoocing me to the lowest of the low, and letting them shake hans with me, and encouraging them to make free with us? I little thought I should live to be shaken hans with be Doolan in broad daylight in the public street of Rosscullen.

BROADBENT. But, my dear, Doolan's a publican: a most influential man. By the way, I asked him if his wife would be at home tomorrow. He said she would; so you must take the motor car round and call on her.

NORA [*aghast*] Is it me call on Doolan's wife!

BROADBENT. Yes, of course: call on all their wives. We must get a copy of the register and a supply of canvassing cards. No use calling on people who havnt votes. Youll be a great success as a canvasser, Nora: they call you the heiress; and theyll be flattered no end by your calling, especially as youve never cheapened yourself by speaking to them before—have you?

NORA [*indignantly*] Not likely, indeed.

BROADBENT. Well, we musnt be stiff and stand-off, you know. We must be thoroughly democratic, and patronize everybody without distinction of class. I tell you I'm a jolly lucky man, Nora Cryna. I get engaged to the most delightful woman in Ireland; and it turns out that I couldnt have done a smarter stroke of electioneering.

NORA. An would you let me demean meself like that, just to get yourself into parliament?

BROADBENT [*buoyantly*] Aha! Wait til you find out what an exciting game electioneering is: youll be mad to get me in. Besides, youd like people to say that Tom Broadbent's wife had been the making of him? that she got him into parliament? into the Cabinet, perhaps, eh?

NORA. God knows I dont grudge you me money! But to lower meself to the level of common people—

BROADBENT. To a member's wife, Nora, nobody is common provided he's on the register. Come, my dear! it's all right: do you think I'd let you do it if it wasnt? The best people do it. Everybody does it.

NORA [*who has been biting her lip and looking*

over the hill, disconsolate and unconvinced] Well, praps you know best what they do in England. They must have very little respect for themselves. I think I'll go in now. I see Larry and Mr Keegan coming up the hill; and I'm not fit to talk to them.

BROADBENT. Just wait and say something nice to Keegan. They tell me he controls nearly as many votes as Father Dempsey himself.

NORA. You little know Peter Keegan. He'd see through me as if I was a pane o glass.

BROADBENT. Oh, he wont like it any the less for that. What really flatters a man is that you think him worth flattering. Not that I would flatter any man: dont think that. I'll just go and meet him. [*He goes down the hill with the eager forward look of a man about to greet a valued acquaintance. Nora dries her eyes, and turns to go as Larry strolls up the hill to her*].

LARRY. Nora. [*She turns and looks at him hardly, without a word. He continues anxiously, in his most conciliatory tone*] When I left you that time, I was just as wretched as you. I didnt rightly know what I wanted to say; and my tongue kept clacking to cover the loss I was at. Well, Ive been thinking ever since; and now I know what I ought to have said. Ive come back to say it.

NORA. Youve come too late, then. You thought eighteen years was not long enough, and that you might keep me waiting a day longer. Well, you were mistaken. I'm engaged to your friend Mr Broadbent; and I'm done with you.

LARRY [*naïvely*] But that was the very thing I was going to advise you to do.

NORA [*involuntarily*] Oh you brute! to tell me that to me face!

LARRY [*nervously relapsing into his most Irish manner*] Nora, dear, dont you understand that I'm an Irishman, and he's an Englishman. He wants you; and he grabs you. *I* want you; and I quarrel with you and have to go on wanting you.

NORA. So you may. Youd better go back to England to the animated beefsteaks youre so fond of.

LARRY [*amazed*] Nora! [*Guessing where she got the metaphor*] He's been talking about me, I see. Well, never mind: we must be friends, you and I. I dont want his marriage to you to be his divorce from me.

NORA. You care more for him than you ever did for me.

LARRY [*with curt sincerity*] Yes of course I do: why should I tell you lies about it? Nora Reilly was a person of very little consequence to me or anyone else outside this miserable little hole. But Mrs Tom Broadbent will be a person of very considerable consequence indeed. Play your new part well, and there will be no more neglect, no more loneliness, no more idle regrettings and vain-hopings in the evenings by the Round Tower, but real life and real work and real cares and real joys among real people: solid English life in London, the very centre of the world. You will find your work cut out for you keeping Tom's house and entertaining Tom's friends and getting Tom into parliament; but it will be worth the effort.

NORA. You talk as if I was under an obligation to him for marrying me.

LARRY. I talk as I think. Youve made a very good match, let me tell you.

NORA. Indeed! Well, some people might say he's not done so badly himself.

LARRY. If you mean that you will be a treasure to him, he thinks so now; and you can keep him thinking so if you like.

NORA. I wasnt thinking o meself at all.

LARRY. Were you thinking of your money, Nora?

NORA. I didnt say so.

LARRY. Your money will not pay your cook's wages in London.

NORA [*flaming up*] If thats true—and the more shame for you to throw it in me face if it is true—at all events itll make us independent; for if the worst comes to the worst, we can always come back here an live on it. An if I have to keep his house for him, at all events I can keep you out of it; for Ive done with you; and I wish I'd never seen you. So goodbye to you, Mister Larry Doyle. [*She turns her back on him and goes home*].

LARRY [*watching her as she goes*] Goodbye. Goodbye. Oh, thats so Irish! Irish both of us to the backbone: Irish! Irish! Iri—

Broadbent arrives, conversing energetically with Keegan.

BROADBENT. Nothing pays like a golfing hotel, if you hold the land instead of the shares, and if the furniture people stand in with you, and if you are a good man of business.

LARRY. Nora's gone home.

BROADBENT [*with conviction*] You were right

this morning, Larry. I must feed up Nora. She's weak; and it makes her fanciful. Oh, by the way, did I tell you that we're engaged?

LARRY. She told me herself.

BROADBENT [complacently] She's rather full of it, as you may imagine. Poor Nora! Well, Mr Keegan, as I said, I begin to see my way here. I begin to see my way.

KEEGAN [with a courteous inclination] The conquering Englishman, sir. Within 24 hours of your arrival you have carried off our only heiress, and practically secured the parliamentary seat. And you have promised me that when I come here in the evenings to meditate on my madness; to watch the shadow of the Round Tower lengthening in the sunset; to break my heart uselessly in the curtained gloaming over the dead heart and blinded soul of the island of the saints, you will comfort me with the bustle of a great hotel and the sight of the little children carrying the golf clubs of your tourists as a preparation for the life to come.

BROADBENT [quite touched, mutely offering him a cigar to console him, at which he smiles and shakes his head] Yes, Mr Keegan: youre quite right. Theres poetry in everything, even [looking absently into the cigar case] in the most modern prosaic things, if you know how to extract it [he extracts a cigar for himself and offers one to Larry, who takes it]. If I was to be shot for it I couldnt extract it myself; but thats where you come in, you see. [Roguishly, waking up from his reverie and bustling Keegan goodhumoredly] And then I shall wake you up a bit. Thats where I come in: eh? d'ye see? Eh? eh? [He pats him very pleasantly on the shoulder, half admiringly, half pityingly]. Just so, just so. [Coming back to business] By the way, I believe I can do better than a light railway here. There seems to be no question now that the motor boat has come to stay. Well, look at your magnificent river there, going to waste.

KEEGAN [closing his eyes] "Silent, O Moyle, be the roar of thy waters."

BROADBENT. You know, the roar of a motor boat is quite pretty.

KEEGAN. Provided it does not drown the Angelus.

BROADBENT [reassuringly] Oh no: it wont do that: not the least danger. You know, a church bell can make a devil of a noise when it likes.

KEEGAN. You have an answer for every-

thing, sir. But your plans leave one question still unanswered: how to get butter out of a dog's throat.

BROADBENT. Eh?

KEEGAN. You cannot build your golf links and hotels in the air. For that you must own our land. And how will you drag our acres from the ferret's grip of Matthew Haffigan? How will you persuade Cornelius Doyle to forgo the pride of being a small landowner? How will Barney Doran's millrace agree with your motor boats? Will Doolan help you to get a license for your hotel?

BROADBENT. My dear sir: to all intents and purposes the syndicate I represent already owns half Rosscullen. Doolan's is a tied house; and the brewers are in the syndicate. As to Haffigan's farm and Doran's mill and Mr Doyle's place and half a dozen others, they will be mortgaged to me before a month is out.

KEEGAN. But pardon me, you will not lend them more on their land than the land is worth; so they will be able to pay you the interest.

BROADBENT. Ah, you are a poet, Mr Keegan, not a man of business.

LARRY. We will lend everyone of these men half as much again on their land as it is worth, or ever can be worth, to them.

BROADBENT. You forget, sir, that we, with our capital, our knowledge, our organization, and may I say our English business habits, can make or lose ten pounds out of land that Haffigan, with all his industry, could not make or lose ten shillings out of. Doran's mill is a superannuated folly: I shall want it for electric lighting.

LARRY. What is the use of giving land to such men? they are too small, too poor, too ignorant, too simpleminded to hold it against us: you might as well give a dukedom to a crossing sweeper.

BROADBENT. Yes, Mr Keegan: this place may have an industrial future, or it may have a residential future: I cant tell yet; but it's not going to be a future in the hands of your Dorans and Haffigans, poor devils!

KEEGAN. It may have no future at all. Have you thought of that?

BROADBENT. Oh, I'm not afraid of that. I have faith in Ireland. Great faith, Mr Keegan.

KEEGAN. And we have none: only empty enthusiasms and patriotisms, and emptier memories and regrets. Ah yes: you have some excuse for believing that if there be any future, it will be yours; for our faith seems dead, and our hearts cold and cowed. An island of dreamers who wake up in your jails, of critics and cowards whom you buy and tame for your own service, of bold rogues who help you to plunder us that they may plunder you afterwards.

BROADBENT [*a little impatient of this unbusinesslike view*] Yes, yes; but you know you might say that of any country. The fact is, there are only two qualities in the world: efficiency and inefficiency, and only two sorts of people: the efficient and the inefficient. It dont matter whether theyre English or Irish. I shall collar this place, not because I'm an Englishman and Haffigan and Co are Irishmen, but because theyre duffers, and I know my way about.

KEEGAN. Have you considered what is to become of Haffigan?

LARRY. Oh, we'll employ him in some capacity or other, and probably pay him more than he makes for himself now.

BROADBENT [*dubiously*] Do you think so? No no: Haffigan's too old. It really doesnt pay now to take on men over forty even for unskilled labor, which I suppose is all Haffigan would be good for. No: Haffigan had better go to America, or into the Union, poor old chap! He's worked out, you know: you can see it.

KEEGAN. Poor lost soul, so cunningly fenced in with invisible bars!

LARRY. Haffigan doesnt matter much. He'll die presently.

BROADBENT [*shocked*] Oh come, Larry! Dont be unfeeling. It's hard on Haffigan. It's always hard on the inefficient.

LARRY. Pah! what does it matter where an old and broken man spends his last days, or whether he has a million at the bank or only the workhouse dole? It's the young men, the able men, that matter. The real tragedy of Haffigan is the tragedy of his wasted youth, his stunted mind, his drudging over his clods and pigs until he has become a clod and a pig himself—until the soul within him has smouldered into nothing but a dull temper that hurts himself and all around him. I say let him die, and let us have no more of his like. And let young Ireland take care that it doesnt share his fate, instead of making another empty grievance of it. Let your **syndicate** come—

BROADBENT. Your syndicate too, old chap. You have your bit of the stock.

LARRY. Yes: mine if you like. Well, our syndicate has no conscience: it has no more regard for your Haffigans and Doolans and Dorans than it has for a gang of Chinese coolies. It will use your patriotic blatherskite and balderdash to get parliamentary powers over you as cynically as it would bait a mousetrap with toasted cheese. It will plan, and organize, and find capital while you slave like bees for it and revenge yourselves by paying politicians and penny newspapers out of your small wages to write articles and report speeches against its wickedness and tyranny, and to crack up your own Irish heroism, just as Haffigan once paid a witch a penny to put a spell on Billy Byrne's cow. In the end it will grind the nonsense out of you, and grind strength and sense into you.

BROADBENT [*out of patience*] Why cant you say a simple thing simply, Larry, without all that Irish exaggeration and talky-talky? The syndicate is a perfectly respectable body of responsible men of good position. We'll take Ireland in hand, and by straightforward business habits teach it efficiency and self-help on sound Liberal principles. You agree with me, Mr Keegan, dont you?

KEEGAN. Sir: I may even vote for you.

BROADBENT [*sincerely moved, shaking his hand warmly*] You shall never regret it, Mr Keegan: I give you my word for that. I shall bring money here: I shall raise wages: I shall found public institutions: a library, a Polytechnic (undenominational, of course), a gymnasium, a cricket club, perhaps an art school. I shall make a Garden city of Rosscullen: the round tower shall be thoroughly repaired and restored.

KEEGAN. And our place of torment shall be as clean and orderly as the cleanest and most orderly place I know in Ireland, which is our poetically named Mountjoy prison. Well, perhaps I had better vote for an efficient devil that knows his own mind and his own business than for a foolish patriot who has no mind and no business.

BROADBENT [*stiffly*] Devil is rather a strong expression in that connexion, Mr Keegan.

KEEGAN. Not from a man who knows that this world is hell. But since the word offends you, let me soften it, and compare you simply to an ass. [*Larry whitens with anger*].

BROADBENT [*reddening*] An ass!

Q

KEEGAN [*gently*] You may take it without offence from a madman who calls the ass his brother—and a very honest, useful and faithful brother too. The ass, sir, is the most efficient of beasts, matter-of-fact, hardy, friendly when you treat him as a fellow-creature, stubborn when you abuse him, ridiculous only in love, which sets him braying, and in politics, which move him to roll about in the public road and raise a dust about nothing. Can you deny these qualities and habits in yourself, sir?

BROADBENT [*goodhumoredly*] Well, yes, I'm afraid I do, you know.

KEEGAN. Then perhaps you will confess to the ass's one fault.

BROADBENT. Perhaps so: what is it?

KEEGAN. That he wastes all his virtues—his efficiency, as you call it—in doing the will of his greedy masters instead of doing the will of Heaven that is in himself. He is efficient in the service of Mammon, mighty in mischief, skilful in ruin, heroic in destruction. But he comes to browse here without knowing that the soil his hoof touches is holy ground. Ireland, sir, for good or evil, is like no other place under heaven; and no man can touch its sod or breathe its air without becoming better or worse. It produces two kinds of men in strange perfection: saints and traitors. It is called the island of the saints; but indeed in these later years it might be more fitly called the island of the traitors; for our harvest of these is the fine flower of the world's crop of infamy. But the day may come when these islands shall live by the quality of their men rather than by the abundance of their minerals; and then we shall see.

LARRY. Mr Keegan: if you are going to be sentimental about Ireland, I shall bid you good evening. We have had enough of that, and more than enough of cleverly proving that everybody who is not an Irishman is an ass. It is neither good sense nor good manners. It will not stop the syndicate; and it will not interest young Ireland so much as my friend's gospel of efficiency.

BROADBENT. Ah, yes, yes: efficiency is the thing. I dont in the least mind your chaff, Mr Keegan; but Larry's right on the main point. The world belongs to the efficient.

KEEGAN [*with polished irony*] I stand rebuked, gentlemen. But believe me, I do every justice to the efficiency of you and your syndicate.

You are both, I am told, thoroughly efficient civil engineers; and I have no doubt the golf links will be a triumph of your art. Mr Broadbent will get into parliament most efficiently, which is more than St Patrick could do if he were alive now. You may even build the hotel efficiently if you can find enough efficient masons, carpenters, and plumbers, which I rather doubt. [*Dropping his irony, and beginning to fall into the attitude of the priest rebuking sin*] When the hotel becomes insolvent [*Broadbent takes his cigar out of his mouth, a little taken aback*] your English business habits will secure the thorough efficiency of the liquidation. You will reorganize the scheme efficiently; you will liquidate its second bankruptcy efficiently [*Broadbent and Larry look quickly at one another; for this, unless the priest is an old financial hand, must be inspiration*]; you will get rid of its original shareholders efficiently after efficiently ruining them; and you will finally profit very efficiently by getting that hotel for a few shillings in the pound. [*More and more sternly*] Besides these efficient operations, you will foreclose your mortgages most efficiently [*his rebuking forefinger goes up in spite of himself*]; you will drive Haffigan to America very efficiently; you will find a use for Barney Doran's foul mouth and bullying temper by employing him to slave-drive your laborers very efficiently; and [*low and bitter*] when at last this poor desolate countryside becomes a busy mint in which we shall all slave to make money for you, with our Polytechnic to teach us how to do it efficiently, and our library to fuddle the few imaginations your distilleries will spare, and our repaired Round Tower with admission sixpence, and refreshments and penny-in-the-slot mutoscopes to make it interesting, then no doubt your English and American shareholders will spend all the money we make for them very efficiently in shooting and hunting, in operations for cancer and appendicitis, in gluttony and gambling; and you will devote what they save to fresh land development schemes. For four wicked centuries the world has dreamed this foolish dream of efficiency; and the end is not yet. But the end will come.

BROADBENT [*seriously*] Too true, Mr Keegan, only too true. And most eloquently put. It reminds me of poor Ruskin: a great man, you know. I sympathize. Believe me, I'm on your side. Dont sneer, Larry: I used to read a lot of Shelley years ago. Let us be faithful to the dreams of our youth [*he wafts a wreath of cigar smoke at large across the hill*].

KEEGAN. Come, Mr Doyle! is this English sentiment so much more efficient than our Irish sentiment, after all? Mr Broadbent spends his life inefficiently admiring the thoughts of great men, and efficiently serving the cupidity of base money hunters. We spend our lives efficiently sneering at him and doing nothing. Which of us has any right to reproach the other?

BROADBENT [*coming down the hill again to Keegan's right hand*] But you know, something must be done.

KEEGAN. Yes: when we cease to do, we cease to live. Well, what shall we do?

BROADBENT. Why, what lies to our hand.

KEEGAN. Which is the making of golf links and hotels to bring idlers to a country which workers have left in millions because it is a hungry land, a naked land, an ignorant and oppressed land.

BROADBENT. But, hang it all, the idlers will bring money from England to Ireland!

KEEGAN. Just as our idlers have for so many generations taken money from Ireland to England. Has that saved England from poverty and degradation more horrible than we have ever dreamed of? When I went to England, sir, I hated England. Now I pity it. [*Broadbent can hardly conceive an Irishman pitying England; but as Larry intervenes angrily, he gives it up and takes to the hill and his cigar again*].

LARRY. Much good your pity will do it!

KEEGAN. In the accounts kept in heaven, Mr Doyle, a heart purified of hatred may be worth more than even a Land Development Syndicate of Anglicized Irishmen and Gladstonized Englishmen.

LARRY. Oh, in heaven, no doubt. I have never been there. Can you tell me where it is?

KEEGAN. Could you have told me this morning where hell is? Yet you know now that it is here. Do not despair of finding heaven: it may be no farther off.

LARRY [*ironically*] On this holy ground, as you call it, eh?

KEEGAN [*with fierce intensity*] Yes, perhaps, even on this holy ground which such Irishmen as you have turned into a Land of Derision.

BROADBENT [*coming between them*] Take care! you will be quarrelling presently. Oh, you Irishmen, you Irishmen! Toujours Ballyhooly, eh? [*Larry, with a shrug, half comic, half impatient, turns away up the hill, but presently strolls back on Keegan's right. Broadbent adds, confidentially to Keegan*] Stick to the Englishman, Mr Keegan: he has a bad name here; but at least he can forgive you for being an Irishman.

KEEGAN. Sir: when you speak to me of English and Irish you forget that I am a Catholic. My country is not Ireland nor England, but the whole mighty realm of my Church. For me there are but two countries: heaven and hell; but two conditions of men: salvation and damnation. Standing here between you the Englishman, so clever in your foolishness, and this Irishman, so foolish in his cleverness, I cannot in my ignorance be sure which of you is the more deeply damned; but I should be unfaithful to my calling if I opened the gates of my heart less widely to one than to the other.

LARRY. In either case it would be an impertinence, Mr Keegan, as your approval is not of the slightest consequence to us. What use do you suppose all this drivel is to men with serious practical business in hand?

BROADBENT. I dont agree with that, Larry. I think these things cannot be said too often: they keep up the moral tone of the community. As you know, I claim the right to think for myself in religious matters: in fact, I am ready to avow myself a bit of a—of a—well, I dont care who knows it—a bit of a Unitarian; but if the Church of England contained a few men like Mr Keegan, I should certainly join it.

KEEGAN. You do me too much honor, sir. [*With priestly humility to Larry*] Mr Doyle: I am to blame for having unintentionally set your mind somewhat on edge against me. I beg your pardon.

LARRY [*unimpressed and hostile*] I didnt stand on ceremony with you: you neednt stand on it with me. Fine manners and fine words are cheap in Ireland: you can keep both for my friend here, who is still imposed on by them. *I* know their value.

KEEGAN. You mean you dont know their value.

LARRY [*angrily*] I mean what I say.

KEEGAN [*turning quietly to the Englishman*] You see, Mr Broadbent, I only make the hearts of my countrymen harder when I preach to them: the gates of hell still prevail against me. I shall wish you good evening. I am better alone, at the Round Tower, dreaming of heaven. [*He goes up the hill*].

LARRY. Aye, thats it! there you are! dreaming! dreaming! dreaming! dreaming!

KEEGAN [*halting and turning to them for the last time*] Every dream is a prophecy: every jest is an earnest in the womb of Time.

BROADBENT [*reflectively*] Once, when I was a small kid, I dreamt I was in heaven. [*They both stare at him*]. It was a sort of pale blue satin place, with all the pious old ladies in our congregation sitting as if they were at a service; and there was some awful person in the study at the other side of the hall. I didnt enjoy it, you know. What is it like in y o u r dreams?

KEEGAN. In my dreams it is a country where the State is the Church and the Church the people: three in one and one in three. It is a commonwealth in which work is play and play is life: three in one and one in three.

It is a temple in which the priest is the worshipper and the worshipper the worshipped: three in one and one in three. It is a godhead in which all life is human and all humanity divine: three in one and one in three. It is, in short, the dream of a madman. [*He goes away across the hill*].

BROADBENT [*looking after him affectionately*] What a regular old Church and State Tory he is! He's a character: he'll be an attraction here. Really almost equal to Ruskin and Carlyle.

LARRY. Yes; and much good t h e y did with all their talk!

BROADBENT. Oh tut, tut, Larry! They improved my mind: they raised my tone enormously. I feel sincerely obliged to Keegan: he has made me feel a better man: distinctly better. [*With sincere elevation*] I feel now as I never did before that I am right in devoting my life to the cause of Ireland. Come along and help me to choose the site for the hotel.

THE END

XIII
HOW HE LIED TO HER HUSBAND
1904

It is eight o'clock in the evening. The curtains are drawn and the lamps lighted in the drawing room of Her flat in Cromwell Road. Her lover, a beautiful youth of eighteen, in evening dress and cape, with a bunch of flowers and an opera hat in his hands, comes in alone. The door is near the corner; and as he appears in the doorway, he has the fireplace on the nearest wall to his right, and the grand piano along the opposite wall to his left. Near the fireplace a small ornamental table has on it a hand mirror, a fan, a pair of long white gloves, and a little white woollen cloud to wrap a woman's head in. On the other side of the room, near the piano, is a broad, square, softly upholstered stool. The room is furnished in the most approved South Kensington fashion: that is, it is as like a shop window as possible, and is intended to demonstrate the social position and spending powers of its owners, and not in the least to make them comfortable.

He is, be it repeated, a very beautiful youth, moving as in a dream, walking as on air. He puts

his flowers down carefully on the table beside the fan; takes off his cape, and, as there is no room on the table for it, takes it to the piano; puts his hat on the cape; crosses to the hearth; looks at his watch; puts it up again; notices the things on the table; lights up as if he saw heaven opening before him; goes to the table and takes the cloud in both hands, nestling his nose into its softness and kissing it; kisses the gloves one after another; kisses the fan; gasps a long shuddering sigh of ecstasy; sits down on the stool and presses his hands to his eyes to shut out reality and dream a little; takes his hands down and shakes his head with a little smile of rebuke for his folly; catches sight of a speck of dust on his shoes and hastily and carefully brushes it off with his handkerchief; rises and takes the hand mirror from the table to make sure of his tie with the gravest anxiety; and is looking at his watch again when She comes in, much flustered. As she is dressed for the theatre; has spoilt, petted ways; and wears many diamonds, she has an air of being a young and beautiful woman; but as a matter of hard fact, she is, dress and pretensions apart, a very ordinary South Kensington female of about 37, hopelessly inferior in physical and spiritual distinction to the beautiful youth, who hastily puts down the mirror as she enters.

HE [*kissing her hand*] At last!

SHE. Henry: something dreadful has happened.

HE. Whats the matter?

SHE. I have lost your poems.

HE. They were unworthy of you. I will write you some more.

SHE. No, thank you. Never any more poems for me. Oh, how could I have been so mad! so rash! so imprudent!

HE. Thank Heaven for your madness, your rashness, your imprudence!

SHE [*impatiently*] Oh, be sensible, Henry. Cant you see what a terrible thing this is for me? Suppose anybody finds these poems! what will they think?

HE. They will think that a man once loved a woman more devotedly than ever man loved woman before. But they will not know what man it was.

SHE. What good is that to me if everybody will know what woman it was?

HE. But how will they know?

SHE. How will they know! Why, my name is all over them: my silly, unhappy name. Oh, if I had only been christened Mary Jane, or Gladys Muriel, or Beatrice, or Francesca, or Guinevere, or something quite common! But Aurora! Aurora! I'm the only Aurora in London; and everybody knows it. I believe I'm the only Aurora in the world. And it's so horribly easy to rhyme to it! Oh, Henry, why didnt you try to restrain your feelings a little in common consideration for me? Why didnt you write with some little reserve?

HE. Write poems to you with reserve! You ask me that!

SHE [*with perfunctory tenderness*] Yes, dear, of course it was very nice of you; and I know it was my own fault as much as yours. I ought to have noticed that your verses ought never to have been addressed to a married woman.

HE. Ah, how I wish they had been addressed to an un-married woman! how I wish they had!

SHE. Indeed you have no right to wish anything of the sort. They are quite unfit for anybody but a married woman. Thats just the difficulty. What will my sisters-in-law think of them?

HE [*painfully jarred*] Have y o u got sisters-in-law?

SHE. Yes, of course I have. Do you suppose I am an angel?

HE [*biting his lips*] I do. Heaven help me, I do—or I did—or [*he almost chokes a sob*].

SHE [*softening and putting her hand caressingly on his shoulder*] Listen to me, dear. It's very nice of you to live with me in a dream, and to love me, and so on; but I cant help my husband having disagreeable relatives, can I?

HE [*brightening up*] Ah, of course they are your husband's relatives: I forgot that. Forgive me, Aurora. [*He takes her hand from his shoulder and kisses it. She sits down on the stool. He remains near the table, with his back to it, smiling fatuously down at her*].

SHE. The fact is, Teddy's got nothing but relatives. He has eight sisters and six half-sisters, and ever so many brothers—but I dont mind his brothers. Now if you only knew the least little thing about the world, Henry, youd know that in a large family, though the sisters quarrel with one another like mad all the time, yet let one of the brothers marry, and they all turn on their unfortunate sister-in-law and devote the rest of their lives with perfect unanimity to persuading him that his wife is unworthy of him. They can do it to her very face without her knowing it, because they always have a lot of stupid low family jokes that nobody understands but themselves. Half the time you cant tell what theyre talking about: it just drives you wild. There ought to be a law against a man's sister ever entering his house after he's married. I'm as certain as that I'm sitting here that Georgina stole those poems out of my workbox.

HE. She will not understand them, I think.

SHE. Oh, wont she! She'll understand them only too well. She'll understand more harm than ever was in them: nasty vulgar-minded cat!

HE [*going to her*] Oh dont, dont think of people in that way. Dont think of her at all. [*He takes her hand and sits down on the carpet at her feet*]. Aurora: do you remember the evening when I sat here at your feet and read you those poems for the first time?

SHE. I shouldnt have let you: I see that now. When I think of Georgina sitting there at Teddy's feet and reading them to h i m for the first time, I feel I shall just go distracted.

HE. Yes, you are right. It will be a profanation.

SHE. Oh, I dont care about the profanation; but what will Teddy think? what will he do? [*Suddenly throwing his head away from her knee*] You dont seem to think a bit about Teddy. [*She jumps up, more and more agitated*].

HE [*supine on the floor; for she has thrown him off his balance*] To me Teddy is nothing, and Georgina less than nothing.

SHE. Youll soon find out how much less than nothing she is. If you think a woman cant do any harm because she's only a scandalmongering dowdy ragbag, youre greatly mistaken. [*She flounces about the room. He gets up slowly and dusts his hands. Suddenly she runs to him and throws herself into his arms*]. Henry: help me. Find a way out of this for me; and I'll bless you as long as you live. Oh, how wretched I am! [*She sobs on his breast*].

HE. And oh! how happy I am!

SHE [*whisking herself abruptly away*] Dont be selfish.

HE [*humbly*] Yes: I deserve that. I think if I were going to the stake with you, I should still be so happy with you that I should forget your danger as utterly as my own.

SHE [*relenting and patting his hand fondly*] Oh, you are a dear darling boy, Henry; but [*throwing his hand away fretfully*] youre no use. I want somebody to tell me what to do.

HE [*with quiet conviction*] Your heart will tell you at the right time. I have thought deeply over this; and I know what we two must do, sooner or later.

SHE. No, Henry. I will do nothing improper, nothing dishonorable. [*She sits down plump on the stool and looks inflexible*].

HE. If you did, you would no longer be Aurora. Our course is perfectly simple, perfectly straightforward, perfectly stainless and true. We love one another. I am not ashamed of that: I am ready to go out and proclaim it to all London as simply as I will declare it to your husband when you see— as you soon will see—that this is the only way honorable enough for your feet to tread. Let us go out together to our own house, this evening, without concealment and without shame. Remember! we owe something to your husband. We are his guests here: he is an honorable man: he has been kind to us: he has perhaps loved you as well as his prosaic nature and his sordid commercial environment permitted. We owe it to him in all honor not to let him learn the truth from the lips of a scandalmonger. Let us go to him now quietly, hand in hand; bid him farewell; and walk out of the house without concealment or subterfuge, freely and honestly, in full honor and self-respect.

SHE [*staring at him*] And where shall we go to?

HE. We shall not depart by a hair's breadth from the ordinary natural current of our lives. We were going to the theatre when the loss of the poems compelled us to take action at once. We shall go to the theatre still; but we shall leave your diamonds here; for we cannot afford diamonds, and do not need them.

SHE [*fretfully*] I have told you already that I hate diamonds; only Teddy insists on hanging me all over with them. You need not preach simplicity to me.

HE. I never thought of doing so, dearest: I know that these trivialities are nothing to you. What was I saying?—oh yes. Instead of coming back here from the theatre, you will come with me to my home—now and henceforth our home—and in due course of time, when you are divorced, we shall go through whatever idle legal ceremony you may desire. *I* attach no importance to the law: my love was not created in me by the law, nor can it be bound or loosed by it. That is simple enough, and sweet enough, is it not? [*He takes the flowers from the table*]. Here are flowers for you: I have the tickets: we will ask your husband to lend us the carriage to shew that there is no malice, no grudge, between us. Come!

SHE. Do you mean to say that you propose that we should walk right bang up to Teddy and tell him we're going away together?

HE. Yes. What can be simpler?

SHE. And do you think for a moment he'd stand it? He'd just kill you.

HE [*coming to a sudden stop and speaking with considerable confidence*] You dont understand these things, my darling: how could you? I have followed the Greek ideal and not neglected the culture of my body. Like all poets I have a passion for pugilism. Your husband would make a tolerable second-rate heavy weight if he were in training and ten years younger. As it is, he could, if strung up to a great effort by a burst of passion, give a good account of himself for perhaps fifteen seconds. But I am active enough to keep out of his reach for fifteen seconds; and after that I should be simply all over him.

SHE [*rising and coming to him in consternation*] What do you mean by all over him?

HE [*gently*] Dont ask me, dearest. At all events, I swear to you that you need not be anxious about me.

SHE. And what about Teddy? Do you mean to tell me that you are going to beat Teddy before my face like a brutal prizefighter?

HE. All this alarm is needless, dearest. Believe me, nothing will happen. Your husband knows that I am capable of defending myself. Under such circumstances nothing ever does happen. And of course *I* shall do nothing. The man who once loved you is sacred to me.

SHE [*suspiciously*] Doesnt he love me still? Has he told you anything?

HE. No, no. [*He takes her tenderly in his arms*]. Dearest, dearest: how agitated you are! how unlike yourself! All these worries belong to the lower plane. Come up with me to the higher one. The heights, the solitudes, the soul world!

SHE [*avoiding his gaze*] No: stop: it's no use, Mr Apjohn.

HE [*recoiling*] Mr Apjohn!!!

SHE. Excuse me: I meant Henry, of course.

HE. How could you even think of me as Mr Apjohn? I never think of you as Mrs Bompas: it is always Aurora, Aurora, Auro—

SHE. Yes, yes: thats all very well, Mr Apjohn [*he is about to interrupt again: but she wont have it*]: no: it's no use: Ive suddenly begun to think of you as Mr Apjohn; and it's ridiculous to go on calling you Henry. I thought you were only a boy, a child, a dreamer. I thought you would be too much afraid to do anything. And now you want to beat Teddy and to break up my home and disgrace me and make a horrible scandal in the papers. It's cruel, unmanly, cowardly.

HE [*with grave wonder*] Are you afraid?

SHE. Oh, of course I'm afraid. So would you be if you had any common sense. [*She goes to the hearth, turning her back to him, and puts one tapping foot on the fender*].

HE [*watching her with great gravity*] Perfect love casteth out fear. That is why I am not afraid. Mrs Bompas: you do not love me.

SHE [*turning to him with a gasp of relief*] Oh,

thank you, thank you! You really can be very nice, Henry.

HE. Why do you thank me?

SHE [*coming prettily to him from the fireplace*] For calling me Mrs Bompas again. I feel now that you are going to be reasonable and behave like a gentleman. [*He drops on the stool; covers his face with his hands; and groans*]. Whats the matter?

HE. Once or twice in my life I have dreamed that I was exquisitely happy and blessed. But oh! the misgiving at the first stir of consciousness! the stab of reality! the prison walls of the bedroom! the bitter, bitter disappointment of waking! And this time! oh, this time I thought I was awake.

SHE. Listen to me, Henry: we really havnt time for all that sort of flapdoodle now [*He starts to his feet as if she had pulled a trigger and straightened him by the release of a powerful spring, and goes past her with set teeth to the little table*]. Oh, take care: you nearly hit me in the chin with the top of your head.

HE [*with fierce politeness*] I beg your pardon. What is it you want me to do? I am at your service. I am ready to behave like a gentleman if you will be kind enough to explain exactly how.

SHE [*a little frightened*] Thank you, Henry: I was sure you would. Youre not angry with me, are you?

HE. Go on. Go on quickly. Give me something to think about, or I will—I will—[*he suddenly snatches up her fan and is about to break it in his clenched fists*].

SHE [*running forward and catching at the fan, with loud lamentation*] Dont break my fan—no, dont. [*He slowly relaxes his grip of it as she draws it anxiously out of his hands*] No, really, thats a stupid trick: I dont like that. Youve no right to do that [*She opens the fan, and finds that the sticks are disconnected*]. Oh, how could you be so inconsiderate?

HE. I beg your pardon. I will buy you a new one.

SHE [*querulously*] You will never be able to match it. And it was a particular favorite of mine.

HE [*shortly*] Then you will have to do without it: thats all.

SHE. Thats not a very nice thing to say after breaking my pet fan, I think.

HE. If you knew how near I was to breaking Teddy's pet wife and presenting him with the pieces, you would be thankful that you are alive instead of—of—of howling about fiveshillingsworth of ivory. Damn your fan!

SHE. Oh! Dont you dare swear in my presence. One would think you were my husband.

HE [*again collapsing on the stool*] This is some horrible dream. What has become of you? You are not my Aurora.

SHE. Oh, well, if you come to that, what has become of you? Do you think I would ever have encouraged you if I had known you were such a little devil?

HE. Dont drag me down—dont—dont. Help me to find the way back to the heights.

SHE [*kneeling beside him and pleading*] If you would only be reasonable, Henry. If you would only remember that I am on the brink of ruin, and not go on calmly saying it's all quite simple.

HE. It seems so to me.

SHE [*jumping up distractedly*] If you say that again I shall do something I'll be sorry for. Here we are, standing on the edge of a frightful precipice. No doubt it's quite simple to go over and have done with it. But cant you suggest anything more agreeable?

HE. I can suggest nothing now. A chill black darkness has fallen: I can see nothing but the ruins of our dream. [*He rises with a deep sigh*].

SHE. Cant you? Well, I can. I can see Georgina rubbing those poems into Teddy. [*Facing him determinedly*] And I tell you, Henry Apjohn, that you got me into this mess; and you must get me out of it again.

HE [*polite and hopeless*] All I can say is that I am entirely at your service. What do you wish me to do?

SHE. Do you know anybody else named Aurora?

HE. No.

SHE. Theres no use in saying No in that frozen pigheaded way. You must know some Aurora or other somewhere.

HE. You said you were the only Aurora in the world. And [*lifting his clasped fists with a sudden return of his emotion*] oh God! you were the only Aurora in the world for me. [*He turns away from her, hiding his face*].

SHE [*petting him*] Yes, yes, dear: of course. It's very nice of you; and I appreciate it: indeed I do; but it's not seasonable just at present. Now just listen to me. I suppose you know all those poems by heart.

HE. Yes, by heart. [*Raising his head and looking at her with a sudden suspicion*] Dont you?

SHE. Well, I never can remember verses; and besides, Ive been so busy that Ive not had time to read them all; though I intend to the very first moment I can get: I promise you that most faithfully, Henry. But now try and remember very particularly. Does the name of Bompas occur in any of the poems?

HE [*indignantly*] No.

SHE. Youre quite sure?

HE. Of course I am quite sure. How could I use such a name in a poem?

SHE. Well, I dont see why not. It rhymes to rumpus, which seems appropriate enough at present, goodness knows! However, youre a poet, and you ought to know.

HE. What does it matter—now?

SHE. It matters a lot, I can tell you. If theres nothing about Bompas in the poems, we can say that they were written to some other Aurora, and that you shewed them to me because my name was Aurora too. So youve got to invent another Aurora for the occasion.

HE [*very coldly*] Oh, if you wish me to tell a lie—

SHE. Surely, as a man of honor—as a gentleman, you wouldnt tell the truth: would you?

HE. Very well. You have broken my spirit and desecrated my dreams. I will lie and protest and stand on my honor: oh, I will play the gentleman, never fear.

SHE. Yes, put it all on me, of course. Dont be mean, Henry.

HE [*rousing himself with an effort*] You are quite right, Mrs Bompas: I beg your pardon. You must excuse my temper. I am having growing pains, I think.

SHE. Growing pains!

HE. The process of growing from romantic boyhood into cynical maturity usually takes fifteen years. When it is compressed into fifteen minutes, the pace is too fast; and growing pains are the result.

SHE. Oh, is this a time for cleverness? It's settled, isnt it, that youre going to be nice and good, and that youll brazen it out to Teddy that you have some other Aurora?

HE. Yes: I'm capable of anything now. I should not have told him the truth by halves; and now I will not lie by halves. I'll wallow in the honor of a gentleman.

SHE. Dearest boy, I knew you would. I— Sh! [*she rushes to the door, and holds it ajar, listening breathlessly*].

HE. What is it?

SHE [*white with apprehension*] It's Teddy: I hear him tapping the new barometer. He cant have anything serious on his mind or he wouldnt do that. Perhaps Georgina hasnt said anything. [*She steals back to the hearth*]. Try and look as if there was nothing the matter. Give me my gloves, quick. [*He hands them to her. She pulls on one hastily and begins buttoning it with ostentatious unconcern*]. Go further away from me, quick. [*He walks doggedly away from her until the piano prevents his going farther*]. If I button my glove, and you were to hum a tune, dont you think that—

HE. The tableau would be complete in its guiltiness. For Heaven's sake, Mrs Bompas, let that glove alone: you look like a pickpocket.

Her husband comes in: a robust, thicknecked, well groomed city man, with a strong chin but a blithering eye and credulous mouth. He has a momentous air, but shews no sign of displeasure: rather the contrary.

HER HUSBAND. Hallo! I thought you two were at the theatre.

SHE. I felt anxious about you, Teddy. Why didnt you come home to dinner?

HER HUSBAND. I got a message from Georgina. She wanted me to go to her.

SHE. Poor dear Georgina! I'm sorry I havnt been able to call on her this last week. I hope theres nothing the matter with her.

HER HUSBAND. Nothing, except anxiety for my welfare—and yours. [*She steals a terrified look at Henry*]. By the way, Apjohn, I should like a word with you this evening, if Aurora can spare you for a moment.

HE [*formally*] I am at your service.

HER HUSBAND. No hurry. After the theatre will do.

HE. We have decided not to go.

HER HUSBAND. Indeed! Well, then, shall we adjourn to my snuggery?

SHE. You neednt move. I shall go and lock up my diamonds since I'm not going to the theatre. Give me my things.

HER HUSBAND [*as he hands her the cloud and the mirror*] Well, we shall have more room here.

HE [*looking about him and shaking his shoulders loose*] I think I should prefer plenty of room.

HER HUSBAND. So, if it's not disturbing you, Rory—?

SHE. Not at all. [*She goes out*].

When the two men are alone together, Bompas deliberately takes the poems from his breast pocket; looks at them reflectively; then looks at Henry, mutely inviting his attention. Henry refuses to understand, doing his best to look unconcerned.

HER HUSBAND. Do these manuscripts seem at all familiar to you, may I ask?

HE. Manuscripts?

HER HUSBAND. Yes. Would you like to look at them a little closer? [*He proffers them under Henry's nose*].

HE [*as with a sudden illumination of glad surprise*] Why, these are my poems!

HER HUSBAND. So I gather.

HE. What a shame! Mrs Bompas has shewn them to you! You must think me an utter ass. I wrote them years ago after reading Swinburne's Songs Before Sunrise. Nothing would do me then but I must reel off a set of Songs to the Sunrise. Aurora, you know: the rosy fingered Aurora. Theyre all about Aurora. When Mrs Bompas told me her name was Aurora, I couldnt resist the temptation to lend them to her to read. But I didnt bargain for your unsympathetic eyes.

HER HUSBAND [*grinning*] Apjohn: thats really very ready of you. You are cut out for literature; and the day will come when Rory and I will be proud to have you about the house. I have heard far thinner stories from much older men.

HE [*with an air of great surprise*] Do you mean to imply that you dont believe me?

HER HUSBAND. Do you expect me to believe you?

HE. Why not? I dont understand.

HER HUSBAND. Come! Dont underrate your own cleverness, Apjohn. I think you understand pretty well.

HE. I assure you I am quite at a loss. Can you not be a little more explicit?

HER HUSBAND. Dont overdo it, old chap. However, I will just be so far explicit as to say that if you think these poems read as if they were addressed, not to a live woman, but to a shivering cold time of day at which you were never out of bed in your life, you hardly do justice to your own literary powers

Q 2

—which I admire and appreciate, mind you, as much as any man. Come! own up. You wrote those poems to my wife. [*An internal struggle prevents Henry from answering*]. Of course you did. [*He throws the poems on the table; and goes to the hearthrug, where he plants himself solidly, chuckling a little and waiting for the next move*].

HE [*formally and carefully*] Mr Bompas: I pledge you my word you are mistaken. I need not tell you that Mrs Bompas is a lady of stainless honor, who has never cast an unworthy thought on me. The fact that she has shewn you my poems—

HER HUSBAND. Thats not a fact. I came by them without her knowledge. She didnt shew them to me.

HE. Does not that prove their perfect innocence? She would have shewn them to you at once if she had taken your quite unfounded view of them.

HER HUSBAND [*shaken*] Apjohn: play fair. Dont abuse your intellectual gifts. Do you really mean that I am making a fool of myself?

HE [*earnestly*] Believe me, you are. I assure you, on my honor as a gentleman, that I have never had the slightest feeling for Mrs Bompas beyond the ordinary esteem and regard of a pleasant acquaintance.

HER HUSBAND [*shortly, shewing ill humor for the first time*] Oh! Indeed! [*He leaves his hearth and begins to approach Henry slowly, looking him up and down with growing resentment*].

HE [*hastening to improve the impression made by his mendacity*] I should never have dreamt of writing poems to her. The thing is absurd.

HER HUSBAND [*reddening ominously*] Why is it absurd?

HE [*shrugging his shoulders*] Well, it happens that I do not admire Mrs Bompas—in that way.

HER HUSBAND [*breaking out in Henry's face*] Let me tell you that Mrs Bompas has been admired by better men than you, you soapy headed little puppy, you.

HE [*much taken aback*] There is no need to insult me like this. I assure you, on my honor as a—

HER HUSBAND [*too angry to tolerate a reply, and boring Henry more and more towards the piano*] You dont admire Mrs Bompas! You would never dream of writing poems to Mrs

Bompas! My wife's not good enough for you, isnt she? [*Fiercely*] Who are you, pray, that you should be so jolly superior?

HE. Mr Bompas: I can make allowances for your jealousy—

HER HUSBAND. Jealousy! do you suppose I'm jealous of y o u? No, nor of ten like you. But if you think I'll stand here and let you insult my wife in her own house, youre mistaken.

HE [*very uncomfortable with his back against the piano and Teddy standing over him threateningly*] How can I convince you? Be reasonable. I tell you my relations with Mrs Bompas are relations of perfect coldness—of indifference—

HER HUSBAND [*scornfully*] Say it again: say it again. Youre proud of it, arnt you? Yah! youre not worth kicking.

Henry suddenly executes the feat known to pugilists as slipping, and changes sides with Teddy, who is now between Henry and the piano.

HE. Look here: I'm not going to stand this.

HER HUSBAND. Oh, you h a v e some blood in your body after all! Good job!

HE. This is ridiculous. I assure you Mrs Bompas is quite—

HER HUSBAND. What is Mrs Bompas to you, I'd like to know. I'll tell you what Mrs Bompas is. She's the smartest woman in the smartest set in South Kensington, and the handsomest, and the cleverest, and the most fetching to experienced men who know a good thing when they see it, whatever she may be to conceited penny-a-lining puppies who think nothing good enough for them. It's admitted by the best people; and not to know it argues yourself unknown. Three of our first actor-managers have offered her a hundred a week if she'll go on the stage when they start a repertory theatre; and I think they know what theyre about as well as you. The only member of the present Cabinet that you might call a handsome man has neglected the business of the country to dance with her, though he dont belong to our set as a regular thing. One of the first professional poets in Bedford Park wrote a sonnet to her, worth all your amateur trash. At Ascot last season the eldest son of a duke excused himself from calling on me on the ground that his feelings for Mrs Bompas were not consistent with his duty to me as host; and it did him honor and me too. But [*with gathering fury*] she isnt good enough for y o u, it seems. You regard her with coldness, with indifference; and you have the cool cheek to tell me so to my face. For two pins I'd flatten your nose in to teach you manners. Introducing a fine woman to you is casting pearls before swine [*yelling at him*] before s w i n e ! d'ye hear?

HE [*with a deplorable lack of polish*] You call me a swine again and I'll land you one on the chin thatll make your head sing for a week.

HER HUSBAND [*exploding*] What!

He charges at Henry with bull-like fury. Henry places himself on guard in the manner of a well taught boxer, and gets away smartly, but unfortunately forgets the stool which is just behind him. He falls backwards over it, unintentionally pushing it against the shins of Bompas, who falls forward over it. Mrs Bompas, with a scream, rushes into the room between the sprawling champions, and sits down on the floor in order to get her right arm round her husband's neck.

SHE. You shant, Teddy: you shant. You will be killed: he is a prizefighter.

HER HUSBAND [*vengefully*] I'll prizefight him. [*He struggles vainly to free himself from her embrace*].

SHE. Henry: dont let him fight you. Promise me that you wont.

HE [*ruefully*] I have got a most frightful bump on the back of my head. [*He tries to rise*].

SHE [*reaching out her left hand to seize his coat tail, and pulling him down again, whilst keeping fast hold of Teddy with the other hand*] Not until you have promised: not until you both have promised. [*Teddy tries to rise: she pulls him back again*]. Teddy: you promise, dont you? Yes, yes. Be good: you promise.

HER HUSBAND. I wont, unless he takes it back.

SHE. He will: he does. You take it back, Henry?—yes.

HE [*savagely*] Yes. I take it back. [*She lets go his coat. He gets up. So does Teddy*]. I take it all back, all, without reserve.

SHE [*on the carpet*] Is nobody going to help me up? [*They each take a hand and pull her up*]. Now wont you shake hands and be good?

HE [*recklessly*] I shall do nothing of the sort. I have steeped myself in lies for your sake; and the only reward I get is a lump on the back of my head the size of an apple.

Now I will go back to the straight path.

SHE. Henry: for Heaven's sake—

HE. It's no use. Your husband is a fool and a brute—

HER HUSBAND. Whats that you say?

HE. I say you are a fool and a brute; and if youll step outside with me I'll say it again. [*Teddy begins to take off his coat for combat*]. Those poems w e r e written to your wife, every word of them, and to nobody else. [*The scowl clears away from Bompas's countenance. Radiant, he replaces his coat*]. I wrote them because I loved her. I thought her the most beautiful woman in the world; and I told her so over and over again. I adored her: do you hear? I told her that you were a sordid commercial chump, utterly unworthy of her; and so you are.

HER HUSBAND [*so gratified, he can hardly believe his ears*] You dont mean it!

HE. Yes, I do mean it, and a lot more too. I asked Mrs Bompas to walk out of the house with me—to leave you—to get divorced from you and marry me. I begged and implored her to do it this very night. It was her refusal that ended everything between us. [*Looking very disparagingly at him*] What she can see in you, goodness only knows!

HER HUSBAND [*beaming with remorse*] My dear chap, why didnt you say so before? I apologize. Come! dont bear malice: shake hands. Make him shake hands, Rory.

SHE. For my sake, Henry. After all, he's my husband. Forgive him. Take his hand. [*Henry, dazed, lets her take his hand and place it in Teddy's*].

HER HUSBAND [*shaking it heartily*] Youve got to own that none of your literary heroines can touch my Rory. [*He turns to her and claps her with fond pride on the shoulder*]. Eh, Rory? They cant resist you: none of em. Never knew a man yet that could hold out three days.

SHE. Dont be foolish, Teddy. I hope you were not really hurt, Henry. [*She feels the back of his head. He flinches*]. Oh, poor boy, what a bump! I must get some vinegar and brown paper. [*She goes to the bell and rings*].

HER HUSBAND. Will you do me a great favor, Apjohn. I hardly like to ask; but it would be a real kindness to us both.

HE. What can I do.

HER HUSBAND [*taking up the poems*] Well, may I get these printed? It shall be done in the best style. The finest paper, sumptuous binding, everything first class. Theyre beautiful poems. I should like to shew them about a bit.

SHE [*running back from the bell, delighted with the idea, and coming between them*] Oh Henry, if you wouldnt mind?

HE. Oh, *I* dont mind. I am past minding anything.

HER HUSBAND. What shall we call the volume? To Aurora, or something like that, eh?

HE. I should call it How He Lied to Her Husband.

THE END

XIV

MAJOR BARBARA

1905

ACT I

It is after dinner in January 1906, *in the library in Lady Britomart Undershaft's house in Wilton Crescent. A large and comfortable settee is in the middle of the room, upholstered in dark leather. A person sitting on it (it is vacant at present) would have, on his right, Lady Britomart's writing table, with the lady herself busy at it; a smaller writing table behind him on his left; the door behind him on Lady Britomart's side; and a window with a window seat directly on his left. Near the window is an armchair.*

Lady Britomart is a woman of fifty or thereabouts, well dressed and yet careless of her dress, well bred and quite reckless of her breeding, well mannered and yet appallingly outspoken and indifferent to the opinion of her interlocutors, amiable and yet peremptory, arbitrary, and high-tempered to the last bearable degree, and withal a very typical managing matron of the upper class, treated as a naughty child until she grew into a scolding mother, and finally settling down with plenty of practical ability and worldly experience, limited in the oddest way with domestic and class limitations, conceiving the universe exactly as if it were a large house in Wilton Crescent, though handling her corner of it very effectively on that assumption, and being quite enlightened and liberal as to the books in the library, the pictures on the walls, the music in the portfolios, and the articles in the papers.

Her son, Stephen, comes in. He is a gravely correct young man under 25, *taking himself very seriously, but still in some awe of his mother, from childish habit and bachelor shyness rather than from any weakness of character.*

STEPHEN. Whats the matter?

LADY BRITOMART. Presently, Stephen.

Stephen submissively walks to the settee and sits down. He takes up a Liberal weekly called The Speaker.

LADY BRITOMART. Dont begin to read, Stephen. I shall require all your attention.

STEPHEN. It was only while I was waiting—

LADY BRITOMART. Dont make excuses, Stephen. [*He puts down The Speaker*]. Now! [*She finishes her writing; rises; and comes to the settee*]. I have not kept you waiting v e r y long, I think.

STEPHEN. Not at all, mother.

LADY BRITOMART. Bring me my cushion. [*He takes the cushion from the chair at the desk and arranges it for her as she sits down on the settee*]. Sit down. [*He sits down and fingers his tie nervously*]. Dont fiddle with your tie, Stephen: there is nothing the matter with it.

STEPHEN. I beg your pardon. [*He fiddles with his watch chain instead*].

LADY BRITOMART. Now are you attending to me, Stephen?

STEPHEN. Of course, mother.

LADY BRITOMART. No: it's n o t of course. I want something much more than your everyday matter-of-course attention. I am going to speak to you very seriously, Stephen. I wish you would let that chain alone.

STEPHEN [*hastily relinquishing the chain*] Have I done anything to annoy you, mother? If so, it was quite unintentional.

LADY BRITOMART [*astonished*] Nonsense! [*With some remorse*] My poor boy, did you think I was angry with you?

STEPHEN. What is it, then, mother? You are making me very uneasy.

LADY BRITOMART [*squaring herself at him rather aggressively*] Stephen: may I ask how soon you intend to realize that you are a grown-up man, and that I am only a woman?

STEPHEN [amazed] Only a—

LADY BRITOMART. Dont repeat my words, please: it is a most aggravating habit. You must learn to face life seriously, Stephen. I really cannot bear the whole burden of our family affairs any longer. You must advise me: you must assume the responsibility.

STEPHEN. I!

LADY BRITOMART. Yes, you, of course. You were 24 last June. Youve been at Harrow and Cambridge. Youve been to India and Japan. You must know a lot of things, now; unless you have wasted your time most scandalously. Well, a d v i s e me.

STEPHEN [much perplexed] You know I have never interfered in the household—

LADY BRITOMART. No: I should think not. I dont want you to order the dinner.

STEPHEN. I mean in our family affairs.

LADY BRITOMART. Well, you must interfere now; for they are getting quite beyond me.

STEPHEN [troubled] I have thought sometimes that perhaps I ought; but really, mother, I know so little about them; and what I do know is so painful! it is so impossible to mention some things to you— [he stops, ashamed].

LADY BRITOMART. I suppose you mean your father.

STEPHEN [almost inaudibly] Yes.

LADY BRITOMART. My dear: we cant go on all our lives not mentioning him. Of course you were quite right not to open the subject until I asked you to; but you are old enough now to be taken into my confidence, and to help me to deal with him about the girls.

STEPHEN. But the girls are all right. They are engaged.

LADY BRITOMART [complacently] Yes: I have made a very good match for Sarah. Charles Lomax will be a millionaire at 35. But that is ten years ahead; and in the meantime his trustees cannot under the terms of his father's will allow him more than £800 a year.

STEPHEN. But the will says also that if he increases his income by his own exertions, they may double the increase.

LADY BRITOMART. Charles Lomax's exertions are much more likely to decrease his income than to increase it. Sarah will have to find at least another £800 a year for the next ten years; and even then they will be as poor as church mice. And what about

Barbara? I thought Barbara was going to make the most brilliant career of all of you. And what does she do? Joins the Salvation Army; discharges her maid; lives on a pound a week; and walks in one evening with a professor of Greek whom she has picked up in the street, and who pretends to be a Salvationist, and actually plays the big drum for her in public because he has fallen head over ears in love with her.

STEPHEN. I was certainly rather taken aback when I heard they were engaged. Cusins is a very nice fellow, certainly: nobody would ever guess that he was born in Australia; but—

LADY BRITOMART. Oh, Adolphus Cusins will make a very good husband. After all, nobody can say a word against Greek: it stamps a man at once as an educated gentleman. And my family, thank Heaven, is not a pig-headed Tory one. We are Whigs, and believe in liberty. Let snobbish people say what they please: Barbara shall marry, not the man they like, but the man I like.

STEPHEN. Of course I was thinking only of his income. However, he is not likely to be extravagant.

LADY BRITOMART. Dont be too sure of that, Stephen. I know your quiet, simple, refined, poetic people like Adolphus: quite content with the best of everything! They cost more than your extravagant people, who are always as mean as they are second rate. No: Barbara will need at least £2000 a year. You see it means two additional households. Besides, my dear, y o u must marry soon. I dont approve of the present fashion of philandering bachelors and late marriages; and I am trying to arrange something for you.

STEPHEN. It's very good of you, mother; but perhaps I had better arrange that for myself.

LADY BRITOMART. Nonsense! you are much too young to begin matchmaking: you would be taken in by some pretty little nobody. Of course I dont mean that you are not to be consulted: you know that as well as I do. [Stephen closes his lips and is silent]. Now dont sulk, Stephen.

STEPHEN. I am not sulking, mother. What has all this got to do with—with—with my father?

LADY BRITOMART. My dear Stephen: where is the money to come from? It is easy enough for you and the other children to live on my income as long as we are in the same house; but I cant keep four families in four separate houses. You know how poor my father is: he has barely seven thousand a year now; and really, if he were not the Earl of Stevenage, he would have to give up society. He can do nothing for us. He says, naturally enough, that it is absurd that he should be asked to provide for the children of a man who is rolling in money. You see, Stephen, your father must be fabulously wealthy, because there is always a war going on somewhere.

STEPHEN. You need not remind me of that, mother. I have hardly ever opened a newspaper in my life without seeing our name in it. The Undershaft torpedo! The Undershaft quick firers! The Undershaft ten inch! the Undershaft disappearing rampart gun! the Undershaft submarine! and now the Undershaft aerial battleship! At Harrow they called me the Woolwich Infant. At Cambridge it was the same. A little brute at King's who was always trying to get up revivals, spoilt my Bible—your first birthday present to me —by writing under my name, "Son and heir to Undershaft and Lazarus, Death and Destruction Dealers: address, Christendom and Judea." But that was not so bad as the way I was kowtowed to everywhere because my father was making millions by selling cannons.

LADY BRITOMART. It is not only the cannons, but the war loans that Lazarus arranges under cover of giving credit for the cannons. You know, Stephen, it's perfectly scandalous. Those two men, Andrew Undershaft and Lazarus, positively have Europe under their thumbs. That is why your father is able to behave as he does. He is above the law. Do you think Bismarck or Gladstone or Disraeli could have openly defied every social and moral obligation all their lives as your father has? They simply wouldnt have dared. I asked Gladstone to take it up. I asked The Times to take it up. I asked the Lord Chamberlain to take it up. But it was just like asking them to declare war on the Sultan. They wouldnt. They said they couldnt touch him. I believe they were afraid.

STEPHEN. What could they do? He does not actually break the law.

LADY BRITOMART. Not break the law! He is always breaking the law. He broke the law when he was born: his parents were not married.

STEPHEN. Mother! Is that true?

LADY BRITOMART. Of course it's true: that was why we separated.

STEPHEN. He married without letting you know this!

LADY BRITOMART [rather taken aback by this inference] Oh no. To do Andrew justice, that was not the sort of thing he did. Besides, you know the Undershaft motto: Unashamed. Everybody knew.

STEPHEN. But you said that was why you separated.

LADY BRITOMART. Yes, because he was not content with being a foundling himself: he wanted to disinherit you for another foundling. That was what I couldnt stand.

STEPHEN [ashamed] Do you mean for—for —for—

LADY BRITOMART. Dont stammer, Stephen. Speak distinctly.

STEPHEN. But this is so frightful to me, mother. To have to speak to you about such things!

LADY BRITOMART. It's not pleasant for me, either, especially if you are still so childish that you must make it worse by a display of embarrassment. It is only in the middle classes, Stephen, that people get into a state of dumb helpless horror when they find that there are wicked people in the world. In our class, we have to decide what is to be done with wicked people; and nothing should disturb our self-possession. Now ask your question properly.

STEPHEN. Mother: have you no consideration for me? For Heaven's sake either treat me as a child, as you always do, and tell me nothing at all; or tell me everything and let me take it as best I can.

LADY BRITOMART. Treat you as a child! What do you mean? It is most unkind and ungrateful of you to say such a thing. You know I have never treated any of you as children. I have always made you my companions and friends, and allowed you perfect freedom to do and say whatever you liked, so long as you liked what I could approve of.

STEPHEN [desperately] I daresay we have been the very imperfect children of a very perfect mother; but I do beg you to let me alone for once, and tell me about this horrible business of my father wanting to set me aside for another son.

LADY BRITOMART [amazed] Another son! I never said anything of the kind. I never dreamt of such a thing. This is what comes of interrupting me.

STEPHEN. But you said—

LADY BRITOMART [*cutting him short*] Now be a good boy, Stephen, and listen to me patiently. The Undershafts are descended from a foundling in the parish of St Andrew Undershaft in the city. That was long ago, in the reign of James the First. Well, this foundling was adopted by an armorer and gun-maker. In the course of time the foundling succeeded to the business; and from some notion of gratitude, or some vow or something, he adopted another foundling, and left the business to him. And that foundling did the same. Ever since that, the cannon business has always been left to an adopted foundling named Andrew Undershaft.

STEPHEN. But did they never marry? Were there no legitimate sons?

LADY BRITOMART. Oh yes: they married just as your father did; and they were rich enough to buy land for their own children and leave them well provided for. But they always adopted and trained some foundling to succeed them in the business; and of course they always quarrelled with their wives furiously over it. Your father was adopted in that way; and he pretends to consider himself bound to keep up the tradition and adopt somebody to leave the business to. Of course I was not going to stand that. There may have been some reason for it when the Undershafts could only marry women in their own class, whose sons were not fit to govern great estates. But there could be no excuse for passing over m y son.

STEPHEN [*dubiously*] I am afraid I should make a poor hand of managing a cannon foundry.

LADY BRITOMART. Nonsense! you could easily get a manager and pay him a salary.

STEPHEN. My father evidently had no great opinion of my capacity.

LADY BRITOMART. Stuff, child! you were only a baby: it had nothing to do with your capacity. Andrew did it on principle, just as he did every perverse and wicked thing on principle. When my father remonstrated, Andrew actually told him to his face that history tells us of only two successful institutions: one the Undershaft firm, and the other the Roman Empire under the Antonines. That was because the Antonine emperors all

adopted their successors. Such rubbish! The Stevenages are as good as the Antonines, I hope; and you are a Stevenage. But that was Andrew all over. There you have the man! Always clever and unanswerable when he was defending nonsense and wickedness: always awkward and sullen when he had to behave sensibly and decently!

STEPHEN. Then it was on my account that your home life was broken up, mother. I am sorry.

LADY BRITOMART. Well, dear, there were other differences. I really cannot bear an immoral man. I am not a Pharisee, I hope; and I should not have minded his merely d o i n g wrong things: we are none of us perfect. But your father didnt exactly d o wrong things: he said them and thought them: that was what was so dreadful. He really had a sort of religion of wrongness. Just as one doesnt mind men practising immorality so long as they own that they are in the wrong by preaching morality; so I couldnt forgive Andrew for preaching immorality while he practised morality. You would all have grown up without principles, without any knowledge of right and wrong, if he had been in the house. You know, my dear, your father was a very attractive man in some ways. Children did not dislike him; and he took advantage of it to put the wickedest ideas into their heads, and make them quite unmanageable. I did not dislike him myself: very far from it; but nothing can bridge over moral disagreement.

STEPHEN. All this simply bewilders me, mother. People may differ about matters of opinion, or even about religion; but how can they differ about right and wrong? Right is right; and wrong is wrong; and if a man cannot distinguish them properly, he is either a fool or a rascal: thats all.

LADY BRITOMART [*touched*] Thats my own boy [*she pats his cheek*]! Your father never could answer that: he used to laugh and get out of it under cover of some affectionate nonsense. And now that you understand the situation, what do you advise me to do?

STEPHEN. Well, what c a n you do?

LADY BRITOMART. I must get the money somehow.

STEPHEN. We cannot take money from him. I had rather go and live in some cheap place like Bedford Square or even Hampstead than take a farthing of his money.

LADY BRITOMART. But after all, Stephen, our present income comes from Andrew.

STEPHEN [*shocked*] I never knew that.

LADY BRITOMART. Well, you surely didnt suppose your grandfather had anything to give me. The Stevenages could not do everything for you. We gave you social position. Andrew had to contribute s o m e t h i n g. He had a very good bargain, I think.

STEPHEN [*bitterly*] We are utterly dependent on him and his cannons, then?

LADY BRITOMART. Certainly not: the money is settled. But he provided it. So you see it is not a question of taking money from him or not: it is simply a question of how much. I dont want any more for myself.

STEPHEN. Nor do I.

LADY BRITOMART. But Sarah does; and Barbara does. That is, Charles Lomax and Adolphus Cusins will cost them more. So I must put my pride in my pocket and ask for it, I suppose. That is your advice, Stephen, is it not?

STEPHEN. No.

LADY BRITOMART [*sharply*] Stephen!

STEPHEN. Of course if you are determined—

LADY BRITOMART. I am not determined: I ask your advice; and I am waiting for it. I will not have all the responsibility thrown on my shoulders.

STEPHEN [*obstinately*] I would die sooner than ask him for another penny.

LADY BRITOMART [*resignedly*] You mean that *I* must ask him. Very well, Stephen: it shall be as you wish. You will be glad to know that your grandfather concurs. But he thinks I ought to ask Andrew to come here and see the girls. After all, he must have some natural affection for them.

STEPHEN. Ask him here!!!

LADY BRITOMART. Do n o t repeat my words, Stephen. Where else can I ask him?

STEPHEN. I never expected you to ask him at all.

LADY BRITOMART. Now dont tease, Stephen. Come! you see that it is necessary that he should pay us a visit, dont you?

STEPHEN [*reluctantly*] I suppose so, if the girls cannot do without his money.

LADY BRITOMART. Thank you, Stephen: I knew you would give me the right advice when it was properly explained to you. I have asked your father to come this evening. [*Stephen bounds from his seat*] Dont jump, Stephen: it fidgets me.

STEPHEN [*in utter consternation*] Do you mean to say that my father is coming here tonight—that he may be here at any moment?

LADY BRITOMART [*looking at her watch*] I said nine. [*He gasps. She rises*]. Ring the bell, please. [*Stephen goes to the smaller writing table; presses a button on it; and sits at it with his elbows on the table and his head in his hands, outwitted and overwhelmed*]. It is ten minutes to nine yet; and I have to prepare the girls. I asked Charles Lomax and Adolphus to dinner on purpose that they might be here. Andrew had better see them in case he should cherish any delusions as to their being capable of supporting their wives. [*The butler enters: Lady Britomart goes behind the settee to speak to him*]. Morrison: go up to the drawing room and tell everybody to come down here at once. [*Morrison withdraws. Lady Britomart turns to Stephen*]. Now remember, Stephen: I shall need all your countenance and authority. [*He rises and tries to recover some vestige of these attributes*]. Give me a chair, dear. [*He pushes a chair forward from the wall to where she stands, near the smaller writing table. She sits down; and he goes to the armchair, into which he throws himself*]. I dont know how Barbara will take it. Ever since they made her a major in the Salvation Army she has developed a propensity to have her own way and order people about which quite cows me sometimes. It's not ladylike: I'm sure I dont know where she picked it up. Anyhow, Barbara shant bully m e; but still it's just as well that your father should be here before she has time to refuse to meet him or make a fuss. Dont look nervous, Stephen: it will only encourage Barbara to make difficulties. *I* am nervous enough, goodness knows; but I dont shew it.

Sarah and Barbara come in with their respective young men, Charles Lomax and Adolphus Cusins. Sarah is slender, bored, and mundane. Barbara is robuster, jollier, much more energetic. Sarah is fashionably dressed: Barbara is in Salvation Army uniform. Lomax, a young man about town, is like many other young men about town. He is afflicted with a frivolous sense of humor which plunges him at the most inopportune moments into paroxysms of imperfectly suppressed laughter. Cusins is a spectacled student, slight, thin haired, and sweet voiced, with a more complex form of Lomax's complaint. His sense of humor is intellectual and subtle, and is complicated by an appalling temper. The lifelong struggle of a benevolent temperament and a high conscience against impulses of inhuman ridicule and fierce impatience has set up a chronic strain which has visibly wrecked his constitution. He is a most implacable, determined, tenacious, intolerant person who by mere force of character presents himself as—and indeed actually is— considerate, gentle, explanatory, even mild and apologetic, capable possibly of murder, but not of cruelty or coarseness. By the operation of some instinct which is not merciful enough to blind him with the illusions of love, he is obstinately bent on marrying Barbara. Lomax likes Sarah and thinks it will be rather a lark to marry her. Consequently he has not attempted to resist Lady Britomart's arrangements to that end.

All four look as if they had been having a good deal of fun in the drawing room. The girls enter first, leaving the swains outside. Sarah comes to the settee. Barbara comes in after her and stops at the door.

BARBARA. Are Cholly and Dolly to come in?

LADY BRITOMART [*forcibly*] Barbara: I will not have Charles called Cholly: the vulgarity of it positively makes me ill.

BARBARA. It's all right, mother: Cholly is quite correct nowadays. Are they to come in?

LADY BRITOMART. Yes, if they will behave themselves.

BARBARA [*through the door*] Come in, Dolly; and behave yourself.

Barbara comes to her mother's writing table. Cusins enters smiling, and wanders towards Lady Britomart.

SARAH [*calling*] Come in, Cholly. [*Lomax enters, controlling his features very imperfectly, and places himself vaguely between Sarah and Barbara*].

LADY BRITOMART [*peremptorily*] Sit down, all of you. [*They sit. Cusins crosses to the window and seats himself there. Lomax takes a chair. Barbara sits at the writing table and Sarah on the settee*]. I dont in the least know what you are laughing at, Adolphus. I am surprised at you, though I expected nothing better from Charles Lomax.

CUSINS [*in a remarkably gentle voice*] Barbara has been trying to teach me the West Ham Salvation March.

LADY BRITOMART. I see nothing to laugh at in that; nor should you if you are really converted.

CUSINS [*sweetly*] You were not present. It was really funny, I believe.

LOMAX. Ripping.

LADY BRITOMART. Be quiet, Charles. Now listen to me, children. Your father is coming here this evening.

General stupefaction. Lomax, Sarah, and Barbara rise: Sarah scared, and Barbara amused and expectant.

LOMAX [*remonstrating*] Oh I say!

LADY BRITOMART. You are not called on to say anything, Charles.

SARAH. Are you serious, mother?

LADY BRITOMART. Of course I am serious. It is on your account, Sarah, and also on Charles's. [*Silence. Sarah sits, with a shrug. Charles looks painfully unworthy*]. I hope you are not going to object, Barbara.

BARBARA. I! why should I? My father has a soul to be saved like anybody else. He's quite welcome as far as I am concerned. [*She sits on the table, and softly whistles 'Onward, Christian Soldiers'*].

LOMAX [*still remonstrant*] But really, dont you know! Oh I say!

LADY BRITOMART [*frigidly*] What do you wish to convey, Charles?

LOMAX. Well, you must admit that this is a bit thick.

LADY BRITOMART [*turning with ominous suavity to Cusins*] Adolphus: you are a professor of Greek. Can you translate Charles Lomax's remarks into reputable English for us?

CUSINS [*cautiously*] If I may say so, Lady Brit, I think Charles has rather happily expressed what we all feel. Homer, speaking of Autolycus, uses the same phrase. πυκινὸν δόμον ἐλθεῖν means a bit thick.

LOMAX [*handsomely*] Not that I mind, you know, if Sarah dont. [*He sits*].

LADY BRITOMART [*crushingly*] Thank you. Have I y o u r permission, Adolphus, to invite my own husband to my own house?

CUSINS [*gallantly*] You have my unhesitating support in everything you do.

LADY BRITOMART. Tush! Sarah: have you nothing to say?

SARAH. Do you mean that he is coming regularly to live here?

LADY BRITOMART. Certainly not. The spare room is ready for him if he likes to stay for a day or two and see a little more of you; but there are limits.

SARAH. Well, he cant eat us, I suppose. I

dont mind.

LOMAX [*chuckling*] I wonder how the old man will take it.

LADY BRITOMART. Much as the old woman will, no doubt, Charles.

LOMAX [*abashed*] I didnt mean—at least—

LADY BRITOMART. You didnt think, Charles. You never do; and the result is, you never mean anything. And now please attend to me, children. Your father will be quite a stranger to us.

LOMAX. I suppose he hasnt seen Sarah since she was a little kid.

LADY BRITOMART. Not since she was a little kid, Charles, as you express it with that elegance of diction and refinement of thought that seem never to desert you. Accordingly —er— [*impatiently*] Now I have forgotten what I was going to say. That comes of your provoking me to be sarcastic, Charles. Adolphus: will you kindly tell me where I was.

CUSINS [*sweetly*] You were saying that as Mr Undershaft has not seen his children since they were babies, he will form his opinion of the way you have brought them up from their behavior tonight, and that therefore you wish us all to be particularly careful to conduct ourselves well, especially Charles.

LADY BRITOMART [*with emphatic approval*] Precisely.

LOMAX. Look here, Dolly: Lady Brit didnt say that.

LADY BRITOMART [*vehemently*] I did, Charles. Adolphus's recollection is perfectly correct. It is most important that you should be good; and I do beg you for once not to pair off into opposite corners and giggle and whisper while I am speaking to your father.

BARBARA. All right, mother. We'll do you credit. [*She comes off the table, and sits in her chair with ladylike elegance*].

LADY BRITOMART. Remember, Charles, that Sarah will want to feel proud of you instead of ashamed of you.

LOMAX. Oh I say! theres nothing to be exactly proud of, dont you know.

LADY BRITOMART. Well, try and look as if there was.

Morrison, pale and dismayed, breaks into the room in unconcealed disorder.

MORRISON. Might I speak a word to you, my lady?

LADY BRITOMART. Nonsense! Shew him up.

MORRISON. Yes, my lady. [*He goes*].

LOMAX. Does Morrison know who it is?

LADY BRITOMART. Of course. Morrison has always been with us.

LOMAX. It must be a regular corker for him, dont you know.

LADY BRITOMART. Is this a moment to get on my nerves, Charles, with your outrageous expressions?

LOMAX. But this is something out of the ordinary, really—

MORRISON [*at the door*] The—er—Mr Undershaft. [*He retreats in confusion*].

Andrew Undershaft comes in. All rise. Lady Britomart meets him in the middle of the room behind the settee.

Andrew is, on the surface, a stoutish, easygoing elderly man, with kindly patient manners, and an engaging simplicity of character. But he has a watchful, deliberate, waiting, listening face, and formidable reserves of power, both bodily and mental, in his capacious chest and long head. His gentleness is partly that of a strong man who has learnt by experience that his natural grip hurts ordinary people unless he handles them very carefully, and partly the mellowness of age and success. He is also a little shy in his present very delicate situation.

LADY BRITOMART. Good evening, Andrew.

UNDERSHAFT. How d'ye do, my dear.

LADY BRITOMART. You look a good deal older.

UNDERSHAFT [*apologetically*] I am somewhat older. [*Taking her hand with a touch of courtship*] Time has stood still with you.

LADY BRITOMART [*throwing away his hand*] Rubbish! This is your family.

UNDERSHAFT [*surprised*] Is it so large? I am sorry to say my memory is failing very badly in some things. [*He offers his hand with paternal kindness to Lomax*].

LOMAX [*jerkily shaking his hand*] Ahdedoo.

UNDERSHAFT. I can see you are my eldest. I am very glad to meet you again, my boy.

LOMAX [*remonstrating*] No but look here dont you know— [*Overcome*] Oh I say!

LADY BRITOMART [*recovering from momentary speechlessness*] Andrew: do you mean to say that you dont remember how many children you have?

UNDERSHAFT. Well, I am afraid I—. They have grown so much—er. Am I making any ridiculous mistake? I may as well confess: I recollect only one son. But so many things have happened since, of course—er—

LADY BRITOMART [*decisively*] Andrew: you

are talking nonsense. Of course you have only one son.

UNDERSHAFT. Perhaps you will be good enough to introduce me, my dear.

LADY BRITOMART. That is Charles Lomax, who is engaged to Sarah.

UNDERSHAFT. My dear sir, I beg your pardon.

LOMAX. Notatall. Delighted, I assure you.

LADY BRITOMART. This is Stephen.

UNDERSHAFT [*bowing*] Happy to make your acquaintance, Mr Stephen. Then [*going to Cusins*] you must be my son. [*Taking Cusins' hands in his*] How are you, my young friend? [*To Lady Britomart*] He is very like you, my love.

CUSINS. You flatter me, Mr Undershaft. My name is Cusins: engaged to Barbara. [*Very explicitly*] That is Major Barbara Undershaft, of the Salvation Army. That is Sarah, your second daughter. This is Stephen Undershaft, your son.

UNDERSHAFT. My dear Stephen, I beg your pardon.

STEPHEN. Not at all.

UNDERSHAFT. Mr Cusins: I am much indebted to you for explaining so precisely. [*Turning to Sarah*] Barbara, my dear—

SARAH [*prompting him*] Sarah.

UNDERSHAFT. Sarah, of course. [*They shake hands. He goes over to Barbara*] Barbara— I am right this time, I hope?

BARBARA. Quite right. [*They shake hands*].

LADY BRITOMART [*resuming command*] Sit down, all of you. Sit down, Andrew. [*She comes forward and sits on the settee. Cusins also brings his chair forward on her left. Barbara and Stephen resume their seats. Lomax gives his chair to Sarah and goes for another*].

UNDERSHAFT. Thank you, my love.

LOMAX [*conversationally, as he brings a chair forward between the writing table and the settee, and offers it to Undershaft*] Takes you some time to find out exactly where you are, dont it?

UNDERSHAFT [*accepting the chair, but remaining standing*] That is not what embarrasses me, Mr Lomax. My difficulty is that if I play the part of a father, I shall produce the effect of an intrusive stranger; and if I play the part of a discreet stranger. I may appear a callous father.

LADY BRITOMART. There is no need for you to play any part at all, Andrew. You had much better be sincere and natural.

UNDERSHAFT [*submissively*] Yes, my dear: I daresay that will be best. [*He sits down comfortably*]. Well, here I am. Now what can I do for you all?

LADY BRITOMART. You need not do anything, Andrew. You are one of the family. You can sit with us and enjoy yourself.

A painfully conscious pause. Barbara makes a face at Lomax, whose too long suppressed mirth immediately explodes in agonized neighings.

LADY BRITOMART [*outraged*] Charles Lomax: if you can behave yourself, behave yourself. If not, leave the room.

LOMAX. I'm awfully sorry, Lady Brit, but really you know, upon my soul! [*He sits on the settee between Lady Britomart and Undershaft, quite overcome*].

BARBARA. Why dont you laugh if you want to, Cholly? It's good for your inside.

LADY BRITOMART. Barbara: you have had the education of a lady. Please let your father see that; and dont talk like a street girl.

UNDERSHAFT. Never mind me, my dear. As you know, I am not a gentleman; and I was never educated.

LOMAX [*encouragingly*] Nobody'd know it, I assure you. You look all right, you know.

CUSINS. Let me advise you to study Greek, Mr Undershaft. Greek scholars are privileged men. Few of them know Greek; and none of them know anything else; but their position is unchallengeable. Other languages are the qualifications of waiters and commercial travellers: Greek is to a man of position what the hallmark is to silver.

BARBARA. Dolly: dont be insincere. Cholly: fetch your concertina and play something for us.

LOMAX [*jumps up eagerly, but checks himself to remark doubtfully to Undershaft*] Perhaps that sort of thing isnt in your line, eh?

UNDERSHAFT. I am particularly fond of music.

LOMAX [*delighted*] Are you? Then I'll get it. [*He goes upstairs for the instrument*].

UNDERSHAFT. Do you play, Barbara?

BARBARA. Only the tambourine. But Cholly's teaching me the concertina.

UNDERSHAFT. Is Cholly also a member of the Salvation Army?

BARBARA. No: he says it's bad form to be a dissenter. But I dont despair of Cholly. I made him come yesterday to a meeting at the dock gates, and take the collection in his hat.

UNDERSHAFT [looks whimsically at his wife]!!

LADY BRITOMART. It is not my doing, Andrew. Barbara is old enough to take her own way. She has no father to advise her.

BARBARA. Oh yes she has. There are no orphans in the Salvation Army.

UNDERSHAFT. Your father there has a great many children and plenty of experience, eh?

BARBARA [looking at him with quick interest and nodding] Just so. How did y o u come to understand that? [Lomax is heard at the door trying the concertina].

LADY BRITOMART. Come in, Charles. Play us something at once.

LOMAX. Righto! [He sits down in his former place, and preludes].

UNDERSHAFT. One moment, Mr Lomax. I am rather interested in the Salvation Army. Its motto might be my own: Bloood and Fire.

LOMAX [shocked] But not your sort of blood and fire, you know.

UNDERSHAFT. My sort of blood cleanses: my sort of fire purifies.

BARBARA. So do ours. Come down tomorrow to my shelter—the West Ham shelter—and see what we're doing. We're going to march to a great meeting in the Assembly Hall at Mile End. Come and see the shelter and then march with us: it will do you a lot of good. Can you play anything?

UNDERSHAFT. In my youth I earned pennies, and even shillings occasionally, in the streets and in public house parlors by my natural talent for stepdancing. Later on, I became a member of the Undershaft orchestral society and performed passably on the tenor trombone.

LOMAX [scandalized—putting down the concertina] Oh I say!

BARBARA. Many a sinner has played himself into heaven on the trombone, thanks to the Army.

LOMAX [to Barbara, still rather shocked] Yes; but what about the cannon business, dont you know? [To Undershaft] Getting into heaven is not exactly in your line, is it?

LADY BRITOMART. Charles!!!

LOMAX. Well; but it stands to reason, dont it? The cannon business may be necessary and all that: we cant get on without cannons; but it isnt right, you know. On the other hand, there may be a certain amount of tosh about the Salvation Army—I belong to the Established Church myself—but still you cant deny that it's religion; and you cant go against religion, can you? At least unless youre downright immoral, dont you know.

UNDERSHAFT, You hardly appreciate my position, Mr Lomax—

LOMAX [hastily] I'm not saying anything against you personally—

UNDERSHAFT. Quite so, quite so. But consider for a moment. Here I am, a profiteer in mutilation and murder. I find myself in a specially amiable humor just now because, this morning, down at the foundry, we blew twenty-seven dummy soldiers into fragments with a gun which formerly destroyed only thirteen.

LOMAX [leniently] Well, the more destructive war becomes, the sooner it will be abolished, eh?

UNDERSHAFT. Not at all. The more destructive war becomes the more fascinating we find it. No, Mr Lomax: I am obliged to you for making the usual excuse for my trade; but I am not ashamed of it. I am not one of those men who keep their morals and their business in water-tight compartments. All the spare money my trade rivals spend on hospitals, cathedrals, and other receptacles for conscience money, I devote to experiments and researches in improved methods of destroying life and property. I have always done so; and I always shall, Therefore your Christmas card moralities of peace on earth and goodwill among men are of no use to me. Your Christianity, which enjoins you to resist not evil, and to turn the other cheek, would make me a bankrupt. M y morality—m y religion—must have a place for cannons and torpedoes in it.

STEPHEN [coldly—almost sullenly] You speak as if there were half a dozen moralities and religions to choose from, instead of one true morality and one true religion.

UNDERSHAFT. For me there is only one true morality; but it might not fit you, as you do not manufacture aerial battleships. There is only one true morality for every man; but every man has not the same true morality.

LOMAX [overtaxed] Would you mind saying that again? I didnt quite follow it.

CUSINS. It's quite simple. As Euripides says, one man's meat is another man's poison morally as well as physically.

UNDERSHAFT. Precisely.

LOMAX. Oh, that! Yes, yes, yes. True. True.

STEPHEN. In other words, some men are honest and some are scoundrels.

BARBARA. Bosh! There are no scoundrels.

UNDERSHAFT. Indeed? Are there any good men?

BARBARA. No. Not one. There are neither good men nor scoundrels: there are just children of one Father; and the sooner they stop calling one another names the better. You neednt talk to me: I know them. Ive had scores of them through my hands: scoundrels, criminals, infidels, philanthropists, missionaries, county councillors, all sorts. Theyre all just the same sort of sinner; and theres the same salvation ready for them all.

UNDERSHAFT. May I ask have you ever saved a maker of cannons?

BARBARA. No. Will you let me try?

UNDERSHAFT. Well, I will make a bargain with you. If I go to see you tomorrow in your Salvation Shelter, will you come the day after to see me in my cannon works?

BARBARA. Take care. It may end in your giving up the cannons for the sake of the Salvation Army.

UNDERSHAFT. Are you sure it will not end in your giving up the Salvation Army for the sake of the cannons?

BARBARA. I will take my chance of that.

UNDERSHAFT. And I will take my chance of the other. [*They shake hands on it*]. Where is your shelter?

BARBARA. In West Ham. At the sign of the cross. Ask anybody in Canning Town. Where are your works?

UNDERSHAFT. In Perivale St Andrews. At the sign of the sword. Ask anybody in Europe.

LOMAX. Hadnt I better play something?

BARBARA. Yes. Give us Onward, Christian Soldiers.

LOMAX. Well, thats rather a strong order to begin with, dont you know. Suppose I sing Thourt passing hence, my brother. It's much the same tune.

BARBARA. It's too melancholy. You get saved, Cholly; and youll pass hence, my brother, without making such a fuss about it.

LADY BRITOMART. Really, Barbara, you go on as if religion were a pleasant subject. Do have some sense of propriety.

UNDERSHAFT. I do not find it an unpleasant subject, my dear. It is the only one that capable people really care for.

LADY BRITOMART [*looking at her watch*] Well, if you are detemined to have it, I insist on having it in a proper and respectable way. Charles: ring for prayers.

General amazement. Stephen rises in dismay.

LOMAX [*rising*] Oh I say!

UNDERSHAFT [*rising*] I am afraid I must be going.

LADY BRITOMART. You cannot go now, Andrew: it would be most improper. Sit down. What will the servants think?

UNDERSHAFT. My dear: I have conscientious scruples. May I suggest a compromise? If Barbara will conduct a little service in the drawing room, with Mr Lomax as organist, I will attend it willingly. I will even take part, if a trombone can be procured.

LADY BRITOMART. Dont mock, Andrew.

UNDERSHAFT [*shocked—to Barbara*] You dont think I am mocking, my love, I hope.

BARBARA. No, of course not; and it wouldnt matter if you were: half the Army came to their first meeting for a lark. [*Rising*] Come along. [*She throws her arm round her father and sweeps him out, calling to the others from the threshold*] Come, Dolly. Come, Cholly.

Cusins rises.

LADY BRITOMART. I will not be disobeyed by everybody. Adolphus: sit down. [*He does not*]. Charles: you may go. You are not fit for prayers: you cannot keep your countenance.

LOMAX. Oh I say! [*He goes out*].

LADY BRITOMART [*continuing*] But you, Adolphus, can behave yourself if you choose to. I insist on your staying.

CUSINS. My dear Lady Brit: there are things in the family prayer book that I couldnt bear to hear you say.

LADY BRITOMART. What things, pray?

CUSINS. Well, you would have to say before all the servants that we have done things we ought not to have done, and left undone things we ought to have done, and that there is no health in us. I cannot bear to hear you doing yourself such an injustice, and Barbara such an injustice. As for myself, I flatly deny it: I have done my best. I shouldnt dare to marry Barbara—I couldnt look you in the face—if it were true. So I must go to the drawing room.

LADY BRITOMART [*offended*] Well, go. [*He starts for the door*]. And remember this, Adolphus [*he turns to listen*]: I have a very strong suspicion that you went to the Salvation Army to worship Barbara and nothing else. And I quite appreciate the very clever way in which you systematically humbug me. I have found you out. Take care Barbara doesnt. Thats all.

CUSINS [*with unruffled sweetness*] Dont tell on me. [*He steals out*].

LADY BRITOMART. Sarah: if you want to go, go. Anything's better than to sit there as if you wished you were a thousand miles away.

SARAH [*languidly*] Very well, mamma. [*She goes*].

Lady Britomart, with a sudden flounce, gives way to a little gust of tears.

STEPHEN [*going to her*] Mother: whats the matter?

LADY BRITOMART [*swishing away her tears with her handkerchief*] Nothing. Foolishness. You can go with him, too, if you like, and leave me with the servants.

STEPHEN. Oh, you mustnt think that, mother. I—I dont like him.

LADY BRITOMART. The others do. That is the injustice of a woman's lot. A woman has to bring up her children; and that means to restrain them, to deny them things they want, to set them tasks, to punish them when they do wrong, to do all the unpleasant things. And then the father, who has nothing to do but pet them and spoil them, comes in when all her work is done and steals their affection from her.

STEPHEN. He has not stolen our affection from you. It is only curiosity.

LADY BRITOMART [*violently*] I wont be consoled, Stephen. There is nothing the matter with me. [*She rises and goes towards the door*].

STEPHEN. Where are you going, mother?

LADY BRITOMART. To the drawing room, of course. [*She goes out. Onward, Christian Soldiers, on the concertina, with tambourine accompaniment, is heard when the door opens*]. Are you coming, Stephen?

STEPHEN. No. Certainly not. [*She goes. He sits down on the settee, with compressed lips and an expression of strong dislike*].

ACT II

The yard of the West Ham shelter of the Salvation Army is a cold place on a January morning. The building itself, an old warehouse, is newly whitewashed. Its gabled end projects into the yard in the middle, with a door on the ground floor, and another in the loft above it without any balcony or ladder, but with a pulley rigged over it for hoisting sacks. Those who come from this central gable end into the yard have the gateway leading to the street on their left, *with a stone horse trough just beyond it, and, on the right, a penthouse shielding a table from the weather. There are forms at the table; and on them are seated a man and a woman, both much down on their luck, finishing a meal of bread (one thick slice each, with margarine and golden syrup) and diluted milk.*

The man, a workman out of employment, is young, agile, a talker, a poser, sharp enough to be capable of anything in reason except honesty or altruistic considerations of any kind. The woman is a commonplace old bundle of poverty and hard-worn humanity. She looks sixty and probably is forty-five. If they were rich people, gloved and muffed and well wrapped up in furs and overcoats, they would be numbed and miserable; for it is a grindingly cold raw January day; and a glance at the background of grimy warehouses and leaden sky visible over the whitewashed walls of the yard would drive any idle rich person straight to the Mediterranean. But these two, being no more troubled with visions of the Mediterranean than of the moon, and being compelled to keep more of their clothes in the pawnshop, and less on their persons, in winter than in summer, are not depressed by the cold: rather are they stung into vivacity, to which their meal has just now given an almost jolly turn. The man takes a pull at his mug, and then gets up and moves about the yard with his hands deep in his pockets, occasionally breaking into a stepdance.

THE WOMAN. Feel better arter your meal, sir?

THE MAN. No. Call that a meal! Good enough for you, praps; but wot is it to me, an intelligent workin man?

THE WOMAN. Workin man! Wot are you?

THE MAN. Painter.

THE WOMAN [*sceptically*] Yus, I dessay.

THE MAN. Yus, you dessay! I know. Every loafer that cant do nothink calls isself a painter. Well, I'm a real painter: grainer, finisher, thirty-eight bob a week when I can get it.

THE WOMAN. Then why dont you go and get it?

THE MAN. I'll tell you why. Fust: I'm intelligent—fffff! it's rotten cold here [*he dances a step or two*]—yes: intelligent beyond the station o life into which it has pleased the capitalists to call me; and they dont like a man that sees through em. Second, an intelligent bein needs a doo share of appiness; so I drink somethink cruel when I get the chawnce. Third, I stand by my class and do as little as I can so's to leave arf the job for me fellow workers. Fourth, I'm fly enough to know wots inside the law and wots outside it; and inside it I do as the capitalists do: pinch wot I can lay me ands on. In a proper state of society I am sober, industrious and honest: in Rome, so to speak, I do as the Romans do. Wots the consequence? When trade is bad—and it's rotten bad just now—and the employers az to sack arf their men, they generally start on me.

THE WOMAN. Whats your name?

THE MAN. Price. Bronterre O'Brien Price. Usually called Snobby Price, for short.

THE WOMAN. Snobby's a carpenter, aint it? You said you was a painter.

PRICE. Not that kind of snob, but the genteel sort. I'm too uppish, owing to my intelligence, and my father being a Chartist and a reading, thinking man: a stationer, too. I'm none of your common hewers of wood and drawers of water; and dont you forget it. [He returns to his seat at the table, and takes up his mug]. Wots your name?

THE WOMAN. Rummy Mitchens, sir.

PRICE [quaffing the remains of his milk to her] Your elth, Miss Mitchens.

RUMMY [correcting him] Missis Mitchens.

PRICE. Wot! Oh Rummy, Rummy! Respectable married woman, Rummy, gittin rescued by the Salvation Army by pretendin to be a bad un. Same old game!

RUMMY. What am I to do? I cant starve. Them Salvation lasses is dear good girls; but the better you are, the worse they likes to think you were before they rescued you. Why shouldnt they av a bit o credit, poor loves? theyre worn to rags by their work. And where would they get the money to rescue us if we was to let on we're no worse than other people? You know what ladies and gentleman are.

PRICE. Thievin swine! Wish I ad their job, Rummy, all the same. Wot does Rummy stand for? Pet name praps?

RUMMY. Short for Romola.

PRICE. For wot!?

RUMMY. Romola. It was out of a new book. Somebody me mother wanted me to grow up like.

PRICE. We're companions in misfortune, Rummy. Both on us got names that nobody cawnt pronounce. Consequently I'm Snobby and youre Rummy because Bill and Sally wasnt good enough for our parents. Such is life!

RUMMY. Who saved you, Mr Price? Was it Major Barbara?

PRICE. No: I come here on my own. I'm goin to be Bronterre O'Brien Price, the converted painter. I know wot they like. I'll tell em how I blasphemed and gambled and wopped my poor old mother—

RUMMY [shocked] Used you to beat your mother?

PRICE. Not likely. She used to beat me. No matter: you come and listen to the converted painter, and youll hear how she was a pious woman that taught me me prayers at er knee, an how I used to come home drunk and drag her out o bed be er snow-white airs, an lam into er with the poker.

RUMMY. Thats whats so unfair to us women. Your confessions is just as big lies as ours: you dont tell what you really done no more than us; but you men can tell your lies right out at the meetins and be made much of for it; while the sort o confessions we az to make az to be wispered to one lady at a time. It aint right, spite of all their piety.

PRICE. Right! Do you spose the Army 'd be allowed if it went and did right? Not much. It combs our air and makes us good little blokes to be robbed and put upon. But I'll play the game as good as any of em. I'll see somebody struck by lightnin, or hear a voice sayin "Snobby Price: where will you spend eternity?" I'll av a time of it, I tell you.

RUMMY. You wont be let drink, though.

PRICE. I'll take it out in gorspellin, then. I dont want to drink if I can get fun enough any other way.

Jenny Hill, a pale, overwrought, pretty Salvation lass of 18, comes in through the yard gate, leading Peter Shirley, a half hardened, half worn-out elderly man, weak with hunger.

JENNY [supporting him] Come! pluck up. I'll get you something to eat. Youll be all right then.

PRICE [rising and hurrying officiously to take the old man off Jenny's hands] Poor old man! Cheer up, brother; youll find rest and peace and appiness ere. Hurry up with the food, miss: e's fair done. [Jenny hurries into the shelter]. Ere, buck up, daddy! she's fetchin y'a thick slice o breadn treacle, an a mug o skyblue. [He seats him at the corner of the table].

RUMMY [gaily] Keep up your old art! Never say die!

SHIRLEY. I'm not an old man. I'm only 46. I'm as good as ever I was. The grey patch come in my hair before I was thirty. All it wants is three pennorth o hair dye: am I to be turned on the streets to starve for it? Holy God! Ive worked ten to twelve hours a day since I was thirteen, and paid my way all through; and now am I to be thrown into the gutter and my job given to a young man that can do it no better than me because Ive black hair that goes white at the first change?

PRICE [*cheerfully*] No good jawrin about it. Youre ony a jumped-up, jerked-off, or spittle-turned-out incurable of an ole workin man: who cares about you? Eh? Make the thievin swine give you a meal: theyve stole many a one from you. Get a bit o your own back. [*Jenny returns with the usual meal*]. There you are, brother. Awsk a blessin an tuck that into you.

SHIRLEY [*looking at it ravenously but not touching it, and crying like a child*] I never took anything before.

JENNY [*petting him*] Come, come! the Lord sends it to you: he wasnt above taking bread from his friends; and why should you be? Besides, when we find you a job you can pay us for it if you like.

SHIRLEY [*eagerly*] Yes, yes: thats true. I can pay you back: it's only a loan. [*Shivering*] Oh Lord! oh Lord! [*He turns to the table and attacks the meal ravenously*].

JENNY. Well, Rummy, are you more comfortable now?

RUMMY. God bless you, lovey! youve fed my body and saved my soul, havnt you? [*Jenny, touched, kisses her*]. Sit down and rest a bit: you must be ready to drop.

JENNY. Ive been going hard since morning. But theres more work than we can do. I mustnt stop.

RUMMY. Try a prayer for just two minutes. Youll work all the better after.

JENNY [*her eyes lighting up*] Oh isnt it wonderful how a few minutes prayer revives you! I was quite lightheaded at twelve o'clock, I was so tired; but Major Barbara just sent me to pray for five minutes; and I was able to go as if I had only just begun. [*To Price*] Did you have a piece of bread?

PRICE [*with unction*] Yes, miss; but Ive got the piece that I value more; and thats the peace that passeth hall hannerstennin.

RUMMY [*fervently*] Glory Hallelujah!

Bill Walker, a rough customer of about 25, appears at the yard gate and looks malevolently at Jenny.

JENNY. That makes me so happy. When you say that, I feel wicked for loitering here. I must get to work again.

She is hurrying to the shelter, when the newcomer moves quickly up to the door and intercepts her. His manner is so threatening that she retreats as he comes at her truculently, driving her down the yard.

BILL. Aw knaow you. Youre the one that took way maw girl. Youre the one that set er agen me. Well, I'm gowin to ev er aht. Not that Aw care a carse for er or you: see? Bat Aw'll let er knaow; and Aw'll let you knaow. Aw'm gowing to give her a doin thatll teach er to cat awy from me. Nah in wiv you and tell er to cam aht afore Aw cam in and kick er aht. Tell er Bill Walker wants er. She'll knaow wot thet means; and if she keeps me witin itll be worse. You stop to jawr beck at me; and Aw'll stawt on you: d'ye eah? Theres your wy. In you gow. [*He takes her by the arm and slings her towards the door of the shelter. She falls on her hand and knee. Rummy helps her up again*].

PRICE [*rising, and venturing irresolutely towards Bill*] Easy there, mate. She aint doin you no arm.

BILL. Oo are you callin mite? [*Standing over him threateningly*] Youre gowin to stend ap for er, aw yer? Put ap your ends.

RUMMY [*running indignantly to him to scold him*] Oh, you great brute— [*He instantly swings his left hand back against her face. She screams and reels back to the trough, where she sits down, covering her bruised face with her hands and rocking herself and moaning with pain*].

JENNY [*going to her*] Oh, God forgive you! How could you strike an old woman like that?

BILL [*seizing her by the hair so violently that she also screams, and tearing her away from the old woman*] You Gawd forgimme again an Aw'll Gawd forgive you one on the jawr thetll stop you pryin for a week. [*Holding her and turning fiercely on Price*] Ev you ennything to sy agen it?

PRICE [*intimidated*] No, matey: she aint anything to do with me.

BILL. Good job for you! Aw'd pat two meals into you and fawt you with one finger arter, you stawved cur. [*To Jenny*] Nah are you gowin to fetch aht Mog Ebbijem; or em Aw to knock your fice off you and fetch her meself?

JENNY [*writhing in his grasp*] Oh please someone go in and tell Major Barbara— [*she screams again as he wrenches her head down; and Price and Rummy flee into the shelter*].

BILL. You want to gow in and tell your Mijor of me, do you?

JENNY. Oh please dont drag my hair. Let me go.

BILL. Do you or downt you? [*She stifles a scream*]. Yus or nao?

JENNY. God give me strength—

BILL [*striking her with his fist in the face*] Gow an shaow her thet, and tell her if she wants one lawk it to cam and interfere with me. [*Jenny, crying with pain, goes into the shed. He goes to the form and addresses the old man*]. Eah: finish your mess; an git aht o maw wy.

SHIRLEY [*springing up and facing him fiercely, with the mug in his hand*] You take a liberty with me, and I'll smash you over the face with the mug and cut your eye out. Aint you satisfied—young whelps like you—with takin the bread out o the mouths of your elders that have brought you up and slaved for you, but you must come shovin and cheekin and bullyin in here, where the bread o charity is sickening in our stummicks?

BILL [*contemptuously, but backing a little*] Wot good are you, you aold palsy mag? Wot good are you?

SHIRLEY. As good as you and better. I'll do a day's work agen you or any fat young soaker of your age. Go and take my job at Horrockses, where I worked for ten year. They want young men there: they cant afford to keep men over forty-five. Theyre very sorry—give you a character and happy to help you to get anything suited to your years—sure a steady man wont be long out of a job. Well, let em try you. They'll find the differ. What do you know? Not as much as how to beeyave yourself—layin your dirty fist across the mouth of a respectable woman!

BILL. Downt provowk me to ly it acrost yours: d'ye eah?

SHIRLEY [*with blighting contempt*] Yes: you like an old man to hit, dont you, when youve finished with the women. I aint seen you hit a young one yet.

BILL [*stung*] You loy, you aold soup-kitchener, you. There was a yang menn eah. Did Aw offer to itt him or did Aw not?

SHIRLEY. Was he starvin or was he not? Was he a man or only a crosseyed thief an a loafer? Would you hit my son-in-law's brother?

BILL. Oo's ee?

SHIRLEY. Todger Fairmile o Balls Pond. Him that won £20 off the Japanese wrastler at the music hall by standin out 17 minutes 4 seconds agen him.

BILL [*sullenly*] Aw'm nao music awl wrastler. Ken he box?

SHIRLEY. Yes: an you cant.

BILL. Wot! Aw cawnt, cawnt Aw? Wots thet you sy [*threatening him*]?

SHIRLEY [*not budging an inch*] Will you box Todger Fairmile if I put him on to you? Say the word.

BILL [*subsiding with a slouch*] Aw'll stend ap to enny menn alawv, if he was ten Todger Fairmawls. But Aw downt set ap to be a perfeshnal.

SHIRLEY [*looking down on him with unfathomable disdain*] You box! Slap an old woman with the back o your hand! You hadnt even the sense to hit her where a magistrate couldnt see the mark of it, you silly young lump of conceit and ignorance. Hit a girl in the jaw and ony make her cry! If Todger Fairmile'd done it, she wouldnt a got up inside o ten minutes, no more than you would if he got on to you. Yah! I'd set about you myself if I had a week's feedin in me instead o two months' starvation. [*He turns his back on him and sits down moodily at the table*].

BILL [*following him and stooping over him to drive the taunt in*] You loy! youve the bread and treacle in you that you cam eah to beg.

SHIRLEY [*bursting into tears*] Oh God! it's true: I'm only an old pauper on the scrap heap. [*Furiously*] But youll come to it yourself; and then youll know. Youll come to it sooner than a teetotaller like me, fillin yourself with gin at this hour o the mornin!

BILL. Aw'm nao gin drinker, you aold lawr; bat wen Aw want to give my girl a bloomin good awdin Aw lawk to ev a bit o devil in me: see? An eah Aw emm, talkin to a rotten aold blawter like you sted o givin her wot for. [*Working himself into a rage*] Aw'm gowin in there to fetch her aht. [*He makes vengefully for the shelter door*].

SHIRLEY. Youre goin to the station on a stretcher, more likely; and theyll take the gin and the devil out of you there when they get you inside. You mind what youre about: the major here is the Earl o Stevenage's granddaughter.

BILL [checked] Garn!

SHIRLEY. You'll see.

BILL [his resolution oozing] Well, Aw aint dan nathin to er.

SHIRLEY. Spose she said you did! who'd believe you?

BILL [very uneasy, skulking back to the corner of the penthouse] Gawd! theres no jastice in this cantry. To think wot them people can do! Aw'm as good as er.

SHIRLEY. Tell her so. It's just what a fool like you would do.

Barbara, brisk and businesslike, comes from the shelter with a note book, and addresses herself to Shirley. Bill, cowed, sits down in the corner on a form, and turns his back on them.

BARBARA. Good morning.

SHIRLEY [standing up and taking off his hat] Good morning, miss.

BARBARA. Sit down: make yourself at home. [He hesitates; but she puts a friendly hand on his shoulder and makes him obey]. Now then! since youve made friends with us, we want to know all about you. Names and addresses and trades.

SHIRLEY. Peter Shirley. Fitter. Chucked out two months ago because I was too old.

BARBARA [not at all surprised] Youd pass still. Why didnt you dye your hair?

SHIRLEY. I did. Me age come out at a coroner's inquest on me daughter.

BARBARA. Steady?

SHIRLEY. Teetotaller. Never out of a job before. Good worker. And sent to the knackers like an old horse!

BARBARA. No matter: if you did your part God will do his.

SHIRLEY [suddenly stubborn] My religion's no concern of anybody but myself.

BARBARA [guessing] I know. Secularist?

SHIRLEY [hotly] Did I offer to deny it?

BARBARA. Why should you? My own father's a Secularist, I think. Our Father—yours and mine—fulfils himself in many ways; and I daresay he knew what he was about when he made a Secularist of you. So buck up, Peter! we can always find a job for a steady man like you. [Shirley, disarmed and a little bewildered, touches his hat. She turns from him to Bill]. Whats your name?

BILL [insolently] Wots thet to you?

BARBARA [calmly making a note] Afraid to give his name. Any trade?

BILL. Oo's afride to give is nime? [Doggedly, with a sense of heroically defying the House of Lords in the person of Lord Stevenage] If you want to bring a chawge agen me, bring it. [She waits unruffled]. Moy nime's Bill Walker.

BARBARA [as if the name were familiar: trying to remember how] Bill Walker? [Recollecting] Oh, I know: youre the man that Jenny Hill was praying for inside just now. [She enters his name in her note book].

BILL. Oo's Jenny Ill? And wot call as she to pry for me?

BARBARA. I dont know. Perhaps it was you that cut her lip.

BILL [defiantly] Yus, it w a s me that cat her lip. Aw aint afride o you.

BARBARA. How could you be, since youre not afraid of God? Youre a brave man, Mr Walker. It takes some pluck to do o u r work here: but none of us dare lift our hand against a girl like that, for fear of her Father in heaven.

BILL [sullenly] I want nan o your kentin jawr. I spowse you think Aw cam eah to beg from you, like this demmiged lot eah. Not me. Aw downt want your bread and scripe and ketlep. Aw dont blieve in your Gawd, no more than you do yourself.

BARBARA [sunnily apologetic and ladylike, as on a new footing with him] Oh, I beg your pardon for putting your name down, Mr Walker. I didnt understand. I'll strike it out.

BILL [taking this as a slight, and deeply wounded by it] Eah! you let maw nime alown. Aint it good enaff to be in your book?

BARBARA [considering] Well, you see, theres no use putting down your name unless I can do something for you, is there? Whats your trade?

BILL [still smarting] Thets nao concern o yours.

BARBARA. Just so. [Very businesslike] I'll put you down as [writing] the man who—struck—poor little Jenny Hill—in the mouth.

BILL [rising threateningly] See eah. Awve ed enaff o this.

BARBARA [quite sunny and fearless] What did you come to us for?

BILL. Aw cam for maw gel, see? Aw cam to tike her aht o this and to brike er jawr for er.

BARBARA [complacently] You see I was right about your trade. [Bill, on the point of retorting furiously, finds himself, to his great shame and terror, in danger of crying instead. He sits down again suddenly]. Whats her name?

BILL [dogged] Er nime's Mog Ebbijem: thets wot er nime is.

BARBARA. Mog Habbijam! Oh, she's gone

to Canning Town, to our barracks there.

BILL [*fortified by his resentment of Mog's perfidy*] Is she? [*Vindictively*] Then Aw'm gowin to Kennintahn arter her. [*He crosses to the gate; hesitates; finally comes back at Barbara*]. Are you loyin to me to git shat o me?

BARBARA. I dont want to get shut of you. I want to keep you here and save your soul. Youd better stay: youre going to have a bad time today, Bill.

BILL. Oo's gowin to give it to me? You, preps?

BARBARA. Someone you dont believe in. But youll be glad afterwards.

BILL [*slinking off*] Aw'll gow to Kennintahn to be aht o reach o your tangue. [*Suddenly turning on her with intense malice*] And if Aw downt fawnd Mog there, Aw'll cam beck and do two years for you, selp me Gawd if Aw downt!

BARBARA [*a shade kindlier, if possible*] It's no use, Bill. She's got another bloke.

BILL. Wot!

BARBARA. One of her own converts. He fell in love with her when he saw her with her soul saved, and her face clean, and her hair washed.

BILL [*surprised*] Wottud she wash it for, the carroty slat? It's red.

BARBARA. It's quite lovely now, because she wears a new look in her eyes with it. It's a pity youre too late. The new bloke has put your nose out of joint, Bill.

BILL. Aw'll put his nowse aht o joint for him. Not that Aw care a carse for er, mawnd thet. But Aw'll teach her to drop me as if Aw was dirt. And Aw'll teach him to meddle with maw judy. Wots iz bleedin nime?

BARBARA. Sergeant Todger Fairmile.

SHIRLEY [*rising with grim joy*] I'll go with him, miss. I want to see them two meet. I'll take him to the infirmary when it's over.

BILL [*to Shirley, with undissembled misgiving*] Is thet im you was speakin on?

SHIRLEY. Thats him.

BILL. Im that wrastled in the music awl?

SHIRLEY. The competitions at the National Sportin Club was worth nigh a hundred a year to him. He's gev cm up now for religion; so he's a bit fresh for want of the exercise he was accustomed to. He'll be glad to see you. Come along.

BILL. Wots is wight?

SHIRLEY. Thirteen four. [*Bill's last hope expires*].

BARBARA. Go and talk to him, Bill. He'll convert you.

SHIRLEY. He'll convert your head into a mashed potato.

BILL [*sullenly*] Aw aint afride of im. Aw aint afride of ennybody. Bat e can lick me. She's dan me. [*He sits down moodily on the edge of the horse trough*].

SHIRLEY. You aint goin. I thought not. [*He resumes his seat*].

BARBARA [*calling*] Jenny!

JENNY [*appearing at the shelter door with a plaster on the corner of her mouth*] Yes, Major.

BARBARA. Send Rummy Mitchens out to clear away here.

JENNY. I think she's afraid.

BARBARA [*her resemblance to her mother flashing out for a moment*] Nonsense! she must do as she's told.

JENNY [*calling into the shelter*] Rummy: the Major says you must come.

Jenny comes to Barbara, purposely keeping on the side next Bill, lest he should suppose that she shrank from him or bore malice.

BARBARA. Poor little Jenny! Are you tired? [*Looking at the wounded cheek*] Does it hurt?

JENNY. No: it's all right now. It was nothing.

BARBARA [*critically*] It was as hard as he could hit, I expect. Poor Bill! You dont feel angry with him, do you?

JENNY. Oh no, no, no: indeed I dont, Major, bless his poor heart! [*Barbara kisses her; and she runs away merrily into the shelter. Bill writhes with an agonizing return of his new and alarming symptoms, but says nothing. Rummy Mitchens comes from the shelter*].

BARBARA [*going to meet Rummy*] Now, Rummy, bustle. Take in those mugs and plates to be washed; and throw the crumbs about for the birds.

Rummy takes the three plates and mugs; but Shirley takes back his mug from her, as there is still some milk left in it.

RUMMY. There aint any crumbs. This aint a time to waste good bread on birds.

PRICE [*appearing at the shelter door*] Gentleman come to see the shelter, Major. Says he's your father.

BARBARA. All right. Coming. [*Snobby goes back into the shelter, followed by Barbara*].

RUMMY [*stealing across to Bill and addressing him in a subdued voice, but with intense conviction*] I'd av the lor of you, you flat eared pignosed potwalloper, if she'd let me. Youre no gentleman, to hit a lady in the face. [*Bill, with greater things moving in him, takes no notice*].

SHIRLEY [*following her*] Here! in with you and dont get yourself into more trouble by talking.

RUMMY [*with hauteur*] I aint ad the pleasure o being hintroduced to you, as I can remember. [*She goes into the shelter with the plates*].

SHIRLEY. Thats the—

BILL [*savagely*] Downt you talk to me, d'ye eah? You lea me alown, or Aw'll do you a mischief. Aw'm not dirt under your feet, ennywy.

SHIRLEY [*calmly*] Dont you be afeerd. You aint such prime company that you need expect to be sought after. [*He is about to go into the shelter when Barbara comes out, with Undershaft on her right*].

BARBARA. Oh, there you are, Mr Shirley! [*Between them*] This is my father: I told you he was a Secularist, didnt I? Perhaps youll be able to comfort one another.

UNDERSHAFT [*startled*] A Secularist! Not the least in the world: on the contrary, a confirmed mystic.

BARBARA. Sorry, I'm sure. By the way, papa, what is your religion? in case I have to introduce you again.

UNDERSHAFT. My religion? Well, my dear, I am a Millionaire. That is my religion.

BARBARA. Then I'm afraid you and Mr Shirley wont be able to comfort one another after all. Youre not a Millionaire, are you, Peter?

SHIRLEY. No: and proud of it.

UNDERSHAFT [*gravely*] Poverty, my friend, is not a thing to be proud of.

SHIRLEY [*angrily*] Who made your millions for you? Me and my like. Whats kep us poor? Keepin you rich. I wouldnt have your conscience, not for all your income.

UNDERSHAFT. I wouldnt have your income not for all your conscience, Mr Shirley. [*He goes to the penthouse and sits down on a form*].

BARBARA [*stopping Shirley adroitly as he is about to retort*] You wouldnt think he was my father, would you, Peter? Will you go into the shelter and lend the lasses a hand for a while: we're worked off our feet.

SHIRLEY [*bitterly*] Yes: I'm in their debt for a meal, aint I?

BARBARA. Oh, not because youre in their debt, but for love of them, Peter, for love of them. [*He cannot understand, and is rather scandalized*] There! dont stare at me. In with you; and give that conscience of yours a holiday [*bustling him into the shelter*].

SHIRLEY [*as he goes in*] Ah! it's a pity you never was trained to use your reason, miss. Youd have been a very taking lecturer on Secularism.

Barbara turns to her father.

UNDERSHAFT. Never mind me, my dear. Go about your work; and let me watch it for a while.

BARBARA. All right.

UNDERSHAFT. For instance, whats the matter with that out-patient over there?

BARBARA [*looking at Bill, whose attitude has never changed, and whose expression of brooding wrath has deepened*] Oh, we shall cure him in no time. Just watch. [*She goes over to Bill and waits. He glances up at her and casts his eyes down again, uneasy, but grimmer than ever*]. It would be nice to just stamp on Mog Habbijam's face, wouldnt it, Bill?

BILL [*starting up from the trough in consternation*] It's a loy: Aw never said so. [*She shakes her head*]. Oo taold you wot was in moy mawnd?

BARBARA. Only your new friend.

BILL. Wot new friend?

BARBARA. The devil, Bill. When he gets round people they get miserable, just like you.

BILL [*with a heartbreaking attempt at devil-may-care cheerfulness*] Aw aint miserable. [*He sits down again, and stretches his legs in an attempt to seem indifferent*].

BARBARA. Well, if youre happy, why dont you look happy, as we do?

BILL [*his legs curling back in spite of him*] Aw'm eppy enaff, Aw tell you. Woy cawnt you lea me alown? Wot ev I dan to you? Aw aint smashed your fice, ev Aw!

BARBARA [*softly: wooing his soul*] It's not me thats getting at you, Bill.

BILL. Oo else is it?

BARBARA. Somebody that doesnt intend you to smash women's faces, I suppose. Somebody or something that wants to make a man of you.

BILL [*blustering*] Mike a menn o me! Aint Aw a menn? eh? Oo sez Aw'm not a menn?

BARBARA. Theres a man in you somewhere, I suppose. But why did he let you hit poor little Jenny Hill? That wasnt very manly of him, was it?

BILL [*tormented*] Ev dan wiv it, Aw tell you.

Chack it. Aw'm sick o your Jenny Ill and er silly little fice.

BARBARA. Then why do you keep thinking about it? Why does it keep coming up against you in your mind? Youre not getting converted, are you?

BILL [*with conviction*] Not ME. Not lawkly.

BARBARA. Thats right, Bill. Hold out against it. Put out your strength. Dont lets get you cheap. Todger Fairmile said he wrestled for three nights against his salvation harder than he ever wrestled with the Jap at the music hall. He gave in to the Jap when his arm was going to break. But he didnt give in to his salvation until his heart was going to break. Perhaps youll escape that. You havnt any heart, have you?

BILL. Wot d'ye mean? Woy aint Aw got a awt the sime as ennybody else?

BARBARA. A man with a heart wouldnt have bashed poor little Jenny's face, would he?

BILL [*almost crying*] Ow, will you lea me alown? Ev Aw ever offered to meddle with you, that you cam neggin and provowkin me lawk this? [*He writhes convulsively from his eyes to his toes*].

BARBARA [*with a steady soothing hand on his arm and a gentle voice that never lets him go*] It's your soul thats hurting you, Bill, and not me. Weve been through it all ourselves. Come with us, Bill. [*He looks wildly round*]. To brave manhood on earth and eternal glory in heaven. [*He is on the point of breaking down*]. Come. [*A drum is heard in the shelter; and Bill, with a gasp, escapes from the spell as Barbara turns quickly. Adolphus enters from the shelter with a big drum*]. Oh! there you are, Dolly. Let me introduce a new friend of mine, Mr Bill Walker. This is my bloke, Bill: Mr Cusins. [*Cusins salutes with his drumstick*].

BILL. Gowin to merry im?

BARBARA. Yes.

BILL [*fervently*] Gawd elp im! Gaw-aw-awawd elp im!

BARBARA. Why? Do you think he wont be happy with me?

BILL. Awve aony ed to stend it for a mawnin: e'll ev to stend it for a lawftawm.

CUSINS. That is a frightful reflection, Mr Walker. But I cant tear myself away from her.

BILL. Well, Aw ken. [*To Barbara*] Eah! do you knaow where Aw'm gowin to, and wot Aw'm gowin to do?

BARBARA. Yes: youre going to heaven; and youre coming back here before the week's out to tell me so.

BILL. You loy. Aw'm gowin to Kennintahn, to spit in Todger Fairmawl's eye. Aw beshed Jenny Ill's fice; an nar Aw'll git me aown fice beshed and cam beck and shaow it to er. Ee'll itt me ardern Aw itt er. Thatll mike us square. [*To Adolphus*] Is thet fair or is it not? Youre a genlmn: you oughter knaow.

BARBARA. Two black eyes wont make one white one, Bill.

BILL. Aw didnt awst you. Cawnt you never keep your mahth shat? Oy awst the genlmn.

CUSINS [*reflectively*] Yes: I think youre right, Mr Walker. Yes: I should do it. It's curious: its exactly what an ancient Greek would have done.

BARBARA. But what good will it do?

CUSINS. Well, it will give Mr Fairmile some exercise; and it will satisfy Mr Walker's soul.

BILL. Rot! there aint nao such a thing as a saoul. Ah kin you tell wevver Awve a saoul or not? You never seen it.

BARBARA. Ive seen it hurting you when you went against it.

BILL [*with compressed aggravation*] If you was maw gel and took the word aht o me mahth lawk thet, Aw'd give you sathink youd feel urtin, Aw would. [*To Adolphus*] You tike maw tip, mite. Stop er jawr; or youll doy afoah your tawm. [*With intense expression*] Wore aht: thets wot youll be: wore aht. [*He goes away through the gate*].

CUSINS [*looking after him*] I wonder!

BARBARA. Dolly! [*indignant, in her mother's manner*].

CUSINS. Yes, my dear, it's very wearing to be in love with you. If it lasts, I quite think I shall die young.

BARBARA. Should you mind?

CUSINS. Not at all. [*He is suddenly softened, and kisses her over the drum, evidently not for the first time, as people cannot kiss over a big drum without practice. Undershaft coughs*].

BARBARA. It's all right, papa, weve not forgotten you. Dolly: explain the place to papa: I havnt time. [*She goes busily into the shelter*].

Undershaft and Adolphus now have the yard to themselves. Undershaft, seated on a form, and still keenly attentive, looks hard at Adolphus. Adolphus looks hard at him.

UNDERSHAFT. I fancy you guess something of what is in my mind, Mr Cusins. [*Cusins flourishes his drumsticks as if in the act of beating a lively rataplan, but makes no sound*]. Exactly so. But suppose Barbara finds you out!

CUSINS. You know, I do not admit that I am imposing on Barbara. I am quite genuinely interested in the views of the Salvation Army. The fact is, I am a sort of collector of religions; and the curious thing is that I find I can believe them all. By the way, have you any religion?

UNDERSHAFT. Yes.

CUSINS. Anything out of the common?

UNDERSHAFT. Only that there are two things necessary to Salvation.

CUSINS [*disappointed, but polite*] Ah, the Church Catechism. Charles Lomax also belongs to the Established Church.

UNDERSHAFT. The two things are—

CUSINS. Baptism and—

UNDERSHAFT. No. Money and gunpowder.

CUSINS [*surprised, but interested*] That is the general opinion of our governing classes. The novelty is in hearing any man confess it.

UNDERSHAFT. Just so.

CUSINS. Excuse me: is there any place in your religion for honor, justice, truth, love, mercy and so forth?

UNDERSHAFT. Yes: they are the graces and luxuries of a rich, strong, and safe life.

CUSINS. Suppose one is forced to choose between them and money or gunpowder?

UNDERSHAFT. Choose money and gunpowder; for without enough of both you cannot afford the others.

CUSINS. That is your religion?

UNDERSHAFT. Yes.

The cadence of this reply makes a full close in the conversation. Cusins twists his face dubiously and contemplates Undershaft. Undershaft contemplates him.

CUSINS. Barbara wont stand that. You will have to choose between your religion and Barbara.

UNDERSHAFT. So will you, my friend. She will find out that that drum of yours is hollow.

CUSINS. Father Undershaft: you are mistaken: I am a sincere Salvationist. You do not understand the Salvation Army. It is the army of joy, of love, of courage: it has banished the fear and remorse and despair of the old hell-ridden evangelical sects: it marches to fight the devil with trumpet and drum, with music and dancing, with banner and palm, as becomes a sally from heaven by its happy garrison. It picks the waster out of the public house and makes a man of him: it finds a worm wriggling in a back kitchen, and lo! a woman! Men and women of rank too, sons and daughters of the Highest. It takes the poor professor of Greek, the most artificial and self-suppressed of human creatures, from his meal of roots, and lets loose the rhapsodist in him; reveals the true worship of Dionysos to him; sends him down the public street drumming dithyrambs [*he plays a thundering flourish on the drum*].

UNDERSHAFT. You will alarm the shelter.

CUSINS. Oh, they are accustomed to these sudden ecstasies. However, if the drum worries you—[*he pockets the drumsticks; unhooks the drum; and stands it on the ground opposite the gateway*]

UNDERSHAFT. Thank you.

CUSINS. You remember what Euripides says about your money and gunpowder?

UNDERSHAFT. No.

CUSINS [*declaiming*]

> One and another
> In money and guns may outpass his brother;
> And men in their millions float and flow
> And seethe with a million hopes as leaven;
> And they win their will; or they miss their will;
> And their hopes are dead or are pined for still;
> But whoe'er can know
> As the long days go
> That to live is happy, has found his heaven.

My translation: what do you think of it?

UNDERSHAFT. I think, my friend, that if you wish to know, as the long days go, that to live is happy, you must first acquire money enough for a decent life, and power enough to be your own master.

CUSINS. You are damnably discouraging. [*He resumes his declamation*].

> Is it so hard a thing to see
> That the spirit of God—whate'er it be—
> The Law that abides and changes not, ages long,
> The Eternal and Nature-born: these things be strong?
> What else is Wisdom? What of Man's endeavor.
> Or God's high grace so lovely and so great?
> To stand from fear set free? to breathe and wait?
> To hold a hand uplifted over Fate?
> And shall not Barbara be loved for ever?

UNDERSHAFT. Euripides mentions Barbara, does he?

CUSINS. It is a fair translation. The word means Loveliness.

UNDERSHAFT. May I ask—as Barbara's father—how much a year she is to be loved for ever on?

CUSINS. As Barbara's father, that is more your affair than mine. I can feed her by teaching Greek: that is about all.

UNDERSHAFT. Do you consider it a good match for her?

CUSINS [with polite obstinacy] Mr Undershaft: I am in many ways a weak, timid, ineffectual person; and my health is far from satisfactory. But whenever I feel that I must have anything, I get it, sooner or later. I feel that way about Barbara. I dont like marriage: I feel intensely afraid of it; and I dont know what I shall do with Barbara or what she will do with me. But I feel that I and nobody else must marry her. Please regard that as settled.—Not that I wish to be arbitrary; but why should I waste your time in discussing what is inevitable?

UNDERSHAFT. You mean that you will stick at nothing: not even the conversion of the Salvation Army to the worship of Dionysos.

CUSINS. The business of the Salvation Army is to save, not to wrangle about the name of the pathfinder. Dionysos or another: what does it matter?

UNDERSHAFT [rising and approaching him] Professor Cusins: you are a young man after my own heart.

CUSINS. Mr Undershaft: you are, as far as I am able to gather, a most infernal old rascal; but you appeal very strongly to my sense of ironic humor.

Undershaft mutely offers his hand. They shake.

UNDERSHAFT [suddenly concentrating himself] And now to business.

CUSINS. Pardon me. We were discussing religion. Why go back to such an uninteresting and unimportant subject as business?

UNDERSHAFT. Religion is our business at present, because it is through religion alone that we can win Barbara.

CUSINS. Have you, too, fallen in love with Barbara?

UNDERSHAFT. Yes, with a father's love.

CUSINS. A father's love for a grown-up daughter is the most dangerous of all infatuations. I apologize for mentioning my own pale, coy, mistrustful fancy in the same breath with it.

UNDERSHAFT. Keep to the point. We have to win her; and we are neither of us Methodists.

CUSINS. That doesnt matter. The power Barbara wields here—the power that wields Barbara herself—is not Calvinism, not Presbyterianism, not Methodism—

UNDERSHAFT. Not Greek Paganism either, eh?

CUSINS. I admit that. Barbara is quite original in her religion.

UNDERSHAFT [triumphantly] Aha! Barbara Undershaft would be. Her inspiration comes from within herself.

CUSINS. How do you suppose it got there?

UNDERSHAFT [in towering excitement] It is the Undershaft inheritance. I shall hand on my torch to my daughter. She shall make my converts and preach my gospel—

CUSINS. What! Money and gunpowder!

UNDERSHAFT. Yes, money and gunpowder. Freedom and power. Command of life and command of death.

CUSINS [urbanely] trying to bring him down to earth] This is extremely interesting, Mr Undershaft. Of course you know that you are mad.

UNDERSHAFT [with redoubled force] And you?

CUSINS. Oh, mad as a hatter. You are welcome to my secret since I have discovered yours. But I am astonished. Can a madman make cannons?

UNDERSHAFT. Would anyone else than a madman make them? And now [with surging energy] question for question. Can a sane man translate Euripides?

CUSINS. No.

UNDERSHAFT [seizing him by the shoulder] Can a sane woman make a man of a waster or a woman of a worm?

CUSINS [reeling before the storm] Father Colossus—Mammoth Millionaire—

UNDERSHAFT [pressing him] Are there two mad people or three in this Salvation shelter today?

CUSINS. You mean Barbara is as mad as we are?

UNDERSHAFT [pushing him lightly off and resuming his equanimity suddenly and completely] Pooh, Professor! let us call things by their proper names. I am a millionaire; you are a poet; Barbara is a savior of souls. What have we three to do with the common mob of slaves and idolaters? [He sits down again *with a shrug of contempt for the mob*].

CUSINS. Take care! Barbara is in love with the common people. So am I. Have you never felt the romance of that love?

UNDERSHAFT [*cold and sardonic*] Have you ever been in love with Poverty, like St Francis? Have you ever been in love with Dirt, like St Simeon? Have you ever been in love with disease and suffering, like our nurses and philanthropists? Such passions are not virtues, but the most unnatural of all the vices. This love of the common people may please an earl's granddaughter and a university professor; but I have been a common man and a poor man; and it has no romance for me. Leave it to the poor to pretend that poverty is a blessing: leave it to the coward to make a religion of his cowardice by preaching humility: we know better than that. We three must stand together above the common people: how else can we help their children to climb up beside us? Barbara must belong to us, not to the Salvation Army.

CUSINS. Well, I can only say that if you think you will get her away from the Salvation Army by talking to her as you have been talking to me, you dont know Barbara.

UNDERSHAFT. My friend: I never ask for what I can buy.

CUSINS [*in a white fury*] Do I understand you to imply that you can buy Barbara?

UNDERSHAFT. No: but I can buy the Salvation Army.

CUSINS. Quite impossible.

UNDERSHAFT. You shall see. All religious organizations exist by selling themselves to the rich.

CUSINS. Not the Army. That is the Church of the poor.

UNDERSHAFT. All the more reason for buying it.

CUSINS. I dont think you quite know what the Army does for the poor.

UNDERSHAFT. Oh yes I do. It draws their teeth: that is enough for me as a man of business.

CUSINS. Nonsense! It makes them sober—

UNDERSHAFT. I prefer sober workmen. The profits are larger.

CUSINS—honest—

UNDERSHAFT. Honest workmen are the most economical.

CUSINS—attached to their homes—

UNDERSHAFT. So much the better: they will put up with anything sooner than change their shop.

CUSINS—happy—

UNDERSHAFT. An invaluable safeguard against revolution.

CUSINS—unselfish—

UNDERSHAFT. Indifferent to their own interests, which suits me exactly.

CUSINS—with their thoughts on heavenly things—

UNDERSHAFT [*rising*] And not on Trade Unionism nor Socialism. Excellent.

CUSINS [*revolted*] You really are an infernal old rascal.

UNDERSHAFT [*indicating Peter Shirley, who has just come from the shelter and strolled dejectedly down the yard between them*] And this is an honest man!

SHIRLEY. Yes; and what av I got by it? [*he passes on bitterly and sits on the form, in the corner of the penthouse*].

Snobby Price, beaming sanctimoniously, and Jenny Hill, with a tambourine full of coppers, come from the shelter and go to the drum, on which Jenny begins to count the money.

UNDERSHAFT [*replying to Shirley*] Oh, your employers must have got a good deal by it from first to last. [*He sits on the table, with one foot on the side form. Cusins, overwhelmed, sits down on the same form nearer the shelter. Barbara comes from the shelter to the middle of the yard. She is excited and a little overwrought*].

BARBARA. Weve just had a splendid experience meeting at the other gate in Cripps's lane. Ive hardly ever seen them so much moved as they were by your confession, Mr Price.

PRICE. I could almost be glad of my past wickedness if I could believe that it would elp to keep hathers stright.

BARBARA. So it will, Snobby. How much, Jenny?

JENNY. Four and tenpence, Major.

BARBARA. Oh Snobby, if you had given your poor mother just one more kick, we should have got the whole five shillings!

PRICE. If she heard you say that, miss, she'd be sorry I didnt. But I'm glad. Oh what a joy it will be to her when she hears I'm saved!

UNDERSHAFT. Shall I contribute the odd twopence, Barbara? The millionaire's mite, eh! [*He takes a couple of pennies from his pocket*].

BARBARA. How did you make that twopence?

UNDERSHAFT. As usual, By selling cannons, torpedoes, submarines, and my new patent

Grand Duke hand grenade.

BARBARA. Put it back in your pocket. You cant buy your salvation here for twopence: you must work it out.

UNDERSHAFT. Is twopence not enough? I can afford a little more, if you press me.

BARBARA. Two million millions would not be enough. There is bad blood on your hands; and nothing but good blood can cleanse them. Money is no use. Take it away. [*She turns to Cusins*]. Dolly: you must write another letter for me to the papers. [*He makes a wry face*]. Yes: I know you dont like it; but it must be done. The starvation this winter is beating us: everybody is unemployed. The General says we must close this shelter if we cant get more money. I force the collections at the meetings until I am ashamed: dont I, Snobby?

PRICE. It's a fair treat to see you work it, miss. The way you got them up from three-and-six to four-and-ten with that hymn, penny by penny and verse by verse, was a caution. Not a Cheap Jack on Mile End Waste could touch you at it.

BARBARA. Yes; but I wish we could do without it. I am getting at last to think more of the collection than of the people's souls. And what are those hatfuls of pence and half-pence? We want thousands! tens of thousands! hundreds of thousands! I want to convert people, not to be always begging for the Army in a way I'd die sooner than beg for myself.

UNDERSHAFT [*in profound irony*] Genuine unselfishness is capable of anything, my dear.

BARBARA [*unsuspectingly, as she turns away to take the money from the drum and put it in a cash bag she carries*] Yes, isnt it? [*Undershaft looks sardonically at Cusins*].

CUSINS [*aside to Undershaft*] Mephistopheles! Machiavelli!

BARBARA [*tears coming into her eyes as she ties the bag and pockets it*] How are we to feed them? I cant talk religion to a man with bodily hunger in his eyes. [*Almost breaking down*] It's frightful.

JENNY [*running to her*] Major, dear—

BARBARA [*rebounding*] No: dont comfort me. It will be all right. We shall get the money.

UNDERSHAFT. How?

JENNY. By praying for it, of course. Mrs Baines says she prayed for it last night; and she has never prayed for it in vain: never once. [*She goes to the gate and looks out into the street*].

BARBARA [*who has dried her eyes and regained her composure*] By the way, dad, Mrs Baines has come to march with us to our big meeting this afternoon; and she is very anxious to meet you, for some reason or other. Perhaps she'll convert you.

UNDERSHAFT. I shall be delighted, my dear.

JENNY [*at the gate: excitedly*] Major! Major! heres that man back again.

BARBARA. What man?

JENNY. The man that hit me. Oh, I hope he's coming back to join us.

Bill Walker, with frost on his jacket, comes through the gate, his hands deep in his pockets and his chin sunk between his shoulders, like a cleaned-out gambler. He halts between Barbara and the drum.

BARBARA. Hullo, Bill! Back already!

BILL [*nagging at her*] Bin talkin ever sence, ev you?

BARBARA. Pretty nearly. Well, has Todger paid you out for poor Jenny's jaw?

BILL. Nao e aint.

BARBARA. I thought your jacket looked a bit snowy.

BILL. Sao it is snaowy. You want to knaow where the snaow cam from, downt you?

BARBARA. Yes.

BILL. Well, it cam from orf the grahnd in Pawkinses Corner in Kennintahn. It got rabbed orf be maw shaoulders: see?

BARBARA. Pity you didnt rub some off with your knees, Bill! That would have done you a lot of good.

BILL [*with sour mirthless humor*] Aw was sivin anather menn's knees at the tawm. E was kneelin on moy ed, e was.

JENNY. Who was kneeling on your head?

BILL. Todger was. E was pryin for me: pryin camfortable wiv me as a cawpet. Sow was Mog. Sao was the aol bloomin meetin. Mog she sez "Ow Lawd brike is stabborn sperrit; bat downt urt is dear art." Thet was wot she said. "Downt urt is dear art"! An er blowk—thirteen stun four!—kneelin wiv all is wight on me. Fanny, aint it?

JENNY. Oh no. We're so sorry, Mr Walker.

BARBARA [*enjoying it frankly*] Nonsense! of course it's funny. Served you right, Bill! You must have done something to him first.

BILL [*doggedly*] Aw did wot Aw said Aw'd do. Aw spit in is eye. E looks ap at the skoy and sez, "Ow that Aw should be fahnd worthy to be spit upon for the gospel's sike!" e sez;

R

an Mog sez "Glaory Allelloolier!"; an then e called me Braddher, an dahned me as if Aw was a kid and e was me mather worshin me a Setterda nawt. Aw ednt jast nao shaow wiv im at all. Arf the street pryed; an the tather arf larfed fit to split theirselves. [*To Barbara*] There! are you settisfawd nah?

BARBARA [*her eyes dancing*] Wish I'd been there, Bill.

BILL. Yus: youd a got in a hextra bit o talk on me, wouldnt you?

JENNY. I'm so sorry, Mr Walker.

BILL [*fiercely*] Downt you gow bein sorry for me: youve no call. Listen eah. Aw browk your jawr.

JENNY. No, it didnt hurt me: indeed it didnt, except for a moment. It was only that I was frightened.

BILL. Aw downt want to be forgive be you, or be ennybody. Wot Aw did Aw'll py for. Aw trawd to gat me aown jawr browk to settisfaw you—

JENNY [*distressed*] Oh no—

BILL [*impatiently*] Tell y'Aw did: cawnt you listen to wots bein taold you? All Aw got be it was bein mide a sawt of in the pablic street for me pines. Well, if Aw cawnt settisfaw you one wy, Aw ken anather. Listen eah! Aw ed two quid sived agen the frost; an Awve a pahnd of it left. A mite o mawn last week ed words with the judy e's gowin to merry. E give er wot-for; an e's bin fawnd fifteen bob. E ed a rawt to itt er cause they was gowin to be merrid; but Aw ednt nao rawt to itt you; sao put anather fawv bob on an call it a pahnd's worth. [*He produces a sovereign*]. Eahs the manney. Tike it; and lets ev no more o your forgivin an pryin and your Mijor jawrin me. Let wot Aw dan be dan an pide for; and let there be a end of it.

JENNY. Oh, I couldnt take it, Mr Walker. But if you would give a shilling or two to poor Rummy Mitchens! you really did hurt her; and she's old.

BILL [*contemptuously*] Not lawkly. Aw'd give her anather as soon as look at er. Let her ev the lawr o me as she threatened! She aint forgiven me: not mach. Wot Aw dan to er is not on me mawnd—wot she [*indicating Barbara*] mawt call on me conscience—no more than stickin a pig. It's this Christian gime o yours that Aw wownt ev plyed agen me: this bloomin forgivin an neggin an jawrin that mikes a menn thet sore that iz lawf's a burdn to im. Aw wownt ev it, Aw tell you;

sao tike your manney and stop thraowin your silly beshed fice hap agen me.

JENNY. Major: may I take a little of it for the Army?

BARBARA. No: the Army is not to be bought. We want your soul, Bill; and we'll take nothing less.

BILL [*bitterly*] Aw knaow. Me an maw few shillins is not good enaff for you. Youre a earl's grendorter, you are. Nathink less than a anderd pahnd for you.

UNDERSHAFT. Come, Barbara! you could do a great deal of good with a hundred pounds. If you will set this gentleman's mind at ease by taking his pound, I will give the other ninety-nine.

Bill, dazed by such opulence, instinctively touches his cap.

BARBARA. Oh, youre too extravagant, papa. Bill offers twenty pieces of silver. All you need offer is the other ten. That will make the standard price to buy anybody who's for sale. I'm not; and the Army's not. [*To Bill*] Youll never have another quiet moment, Bill, until you come round to us. You cant stand out against your salvation.

BILL [*sullenly*] Aw cawnt stend aht agen music awl wrastlers and awtful tangued women. Awve offered to py. Aw can do no more. Tike it or leave it. There it is. [*He throws the sovereign on the drum, and sits down on the horse-trough. The coin fascinates Snobby Price, who takes an early opportunity of dropping his cap on it*].

Mrs Baines comes from the shelter. She is dressed as a Salvation Army Commissioner. She is an earnest looking woman of about 40, with a caressing, urgent voice, and an appealing manner.

BARBARA. This is my father, Mrs Baines. [*Undershaft comes from the table, taking his hat off with marked civility*]. Try what you can do with him. He wont listen to me, because he remembers what a fool I was when I was a baby. [*She leaves them together and chats with Jenny*].

MRS BAINES. Have you been shewn over the shelter, Mr Undershaft? You know the work we're doing, of course.

UNDERSHAFT [*very civilly*] The whole nation knows it, Mrs Baines.

MRS BAINES. No, sir: the whole nation does not know it, or we should not be crippled as we are for want of money to carry our work through the length and breadth of the land.

Let me tell you that there would have been rioting this winter in London but for us.

UNDERSHAFT. You really think so?

MRS BAINES. I know it. I remember 1886, when you rich gentlemen hardened your hearts against the cry of the poor. They broke the windows of your clubs in Pall Mall.

UNDERSHAFT [*gleaming with approval of their method*] And the Mansion House Fund went up next day from thirty thousand pounds to seventy-nine thousand! I remember quite well.

MRS BAINES. Well, wont you help me to get at the people? They wont break windows then. Come here, Price. Let me shew you to this gentleman [*Price comes to be inspected*]. Do you remember the window breaking?

PRICE. My ole father thought it was the revolution, maam.

MRS BAINES. Would you break windows now?

PRICE. Oh no, maam. The windows of eaven av bin opened to me. I know now that the rich man is a sinner like myself.

RUMMY [*appearing above at the loft door*] Snobby Price!

SNOBBY. Wot is it?

RUMMY. Your mother's askin for you at the other gate in Cripps's Lane. She's heard about your confession [*Price turns pale*].

MRS BAINES. Go, Mr Price; and pray with her.

JENNY. You can go through the shelter, Snobby.

PRICE [*to Mrs Baines*] I couldnt face her now, maam, with all the weight of my sins fresh on me. Tell her she'll find her son at ome, waitin for her in prayer. [*He skulks off through the gate, incidentally stealing the sovereign on his way out by picking up his cap from the drum*].

MRS BAINES [*with swimming eyes*] You see how we take the anger and the bitterness against you out of their hearts, Mr Undershaft.

UNDERSHAFT. It is certainly most convenient and gratifying to all large employers of labor, Mrs Baines.

MRS BAINES. Barbara: Jenny: I have good news: most wonderful news. [*Jenny runs to her*]. My prayers have been answered. I told you they would, Jenny, didnt I?

JENNY. Yes, yes.

BARBARA [*moving nearer to the drum*] Have we got money enough to keep the shelter open?

MRS BAINES. I hope we shall have enough to keep all the shelters open. Lord Saxmundham has promised us five thousand pounds—

BARBARA. Hooray!

JENNY. Glory!

MRS BAINES. —if—

BARBARA. "If!" If what?

MRS BAINES. —if five other gentlemen will give a thousand each to make it up to ten thousand.

BARBARA. Who is Lord Saxmundham? I never heard of him.

UNDERSHAFT [*who has pricked up his ears at the peer's name, and is now watching Barbara curiously*] A new creation, my dear. You have heard of Sir Horace Bodger?

BARBARA. Bodger! Do you mean the distiller? Bodger's whisky!

UNDERSHAFT. That is the man. He is one of the greatest of our public benefactors. He restored the cathedral at Hakington. They made him a baronet for that. He gave half a million to the funds of his party: they made him a baron for that.

SHIRLEY. What will they give him for the five thousand?

UNDERSHAFT. There is nothing left to give him. So the five thousand, I should think, is to save his soul.

MRS BAINES. Heaven grant it may! Oh Mr Undershaft, you have some very rich friends. Cant you help us towards the other five thousand? We are going to hold a great meeting this afternoon at the Assembly Hall in the Mile End Road. If I could only announce that one gentleman had come forward to support Lord Saxmundham, others would follow. Dont you know somebody? couldnt you? wouldnt you? [*her eyes fill with tears*] oh, think of those poor people, Mr Undershaft: think of how much it means to them, and how little to a great man like you.

UNDERSHAFT [*sardonically gallant*] Mrs Baines: you are irresistible. I cant disappoint you; and I cant deny myself the satisfaction of making Bodger pay up. You shall have your five thousand pounds.

MRS BAINES. Thank God!

UNDERSHAFT. You dont thank me?

MRS BAINES. Oh sir, dont try to be cynical: dont be ashamed of being a good man. The Lord will bless you abundantly; and our prayers will be like a strong fortification round you all the days of your life. [*With a touch of caution*] You will let me have the cheque to shew at the meeting, wont you? Jenny: go in and fetch a pen and ink. [*Jenny runs to the shelter door*].

UNDERSHAFT. Do not disturb Miss Hill: I have a fountain pen [*Jenny halts. He sits at the table and writes the cheque. Cusins rises to make room for him. They all watch him silently*].

BILL [*cynically, aside to Barbara, his voice and accent horribly debased*] Wot prawce selvytion nah?

BARBARA. Stop. [*Undershaft stops writing: they all turn to her in surprise*]. Mrs Baines: are you really going to take this money?

MRS BAINES [*astonished*] Why not, dear?

BARBARA. Why not! Do you know what my father is? Have you forgotten that Lord Saxmundham is Bodger the whisky man? Do you remember how we implored the County Council to stop him from writing Bodger's Whisky in letters of fire against the sky; so that the poor drink-ruined creatures on the Embankment could not wake up from their snatches of sleep without being reminded of their deadly thirst by that wicked sky sign? Do you know that the worst thing I have had to fight here is not the devil, but Bodger, Bodger, Bodger, with his whisky, his distilleries, and his tied houses? Are you going to make our shelter another tied house for him, and ask me to keep it?

BILL. Rotten dranken whisky it is too.

MRS BAINES. Dear Barbara: Lord Saxmundham has a soul to be saved like any of us. If heaven has found the way to make a good use of his money, are we to set ourselves up against the answer to our prayers?

BARBARA. I know he has a soul to be saved. Let him come down here; and I'll do my best to help him to his salvation. But he wants to send his cheque down to buy us, and go on being as wicked as ever.

UNDERSHAFT [*with a reasonableness which Cusins alone perceives to be ironical*] My dear Barbara: alcohol is a very necessary article. It heals the sick—

BARBARA. It does nothing of the sort.

UNDERSHAFT. Well, it assists the doctor: that is perhaps a less questionable way of putting it. It makes life bearable to millions of people who could not endure their existence if they were quite sober. It enables Parliament to do things at eleven at night that no sane person would do at eleven in the morning. Is it Bodger's fault that this inestimable gift is deplorably abused by less than one per cent of the poor? [*He turns again to the table; signs the cheque; and crosses it*].

MRS BAINES. Barbara: will there be less drinking or more if all those poor souls we are saving come tomorrow and find the doors of our shelters shut in their faces? Lord Saxmundham gives us the money to stop drinking—to take his own business from him.

CUSINS [*impishly*] Pure self-sacrifice on Bodger's part, clearly! Bless dear Bodger! [*Barbara almost breaks down as Adolphus, too, fails her*].

UNDERSHAFT [*tearing out the cheque and pocketing the book as he rises and goes past Cusins to Mrs Baines*] I also, Mrs Baines, may claim a little disinterestedness. Think of my business! think of the widows and orphans! the men and lads torn to pieces with shrapnel and poisoned with lyddite! [*Mrs Baines shrinks; but he goes on remorselessly*] the oceans of blood, not one drop of which is shed in a really just cause! the ravaged crops! the peaceful peasants forced, women and men, to till their fields under the fire of opposing armies on pain of starvation! the bad blood of the fierce little cowards at home who egg on others to fight for the gratification of their national vanity! All this makes money for me: I am never richer, never busier than when the papers are full of it. Well, it is your work to preach peace on earth and goodwill to men. [*Mrs Baines's face lights up again*]. Every convert you make is a vote against war. [*Her lips move in prayer*]. Yet I give you this money to help you to hasten my own commercial ruin [*He gives her the cheque*].

CUSINS [*mounting the form in an ecstasy of mischief*] The millennium will be inaugurated by the unselfishness of Undershaft and Bodger. Oh be joyful! [*He takes the drumsticks from his pockets and flourishes them*].

MRS BAINES [*taking the cheque*] The longer I live the more proof I see that there is an Infinite Goodness that turns everything to the work of salvation sooner or later. Who would have thought that any good could have come out of war and drink? And yet their profits are brought today to the feet of salvation to do its blessed work. [*She is affected to tears*].

JENNY [*running to Mrs Baines and throwing her arms round her*] Oh dear! how blessed, how glorious it all is!

CUSINS [*in a convulsion of irony*] Let us seize

this unspeakable moment. Let us march to the great meeting at once. Excuse me just an instant. [*He rushes into the shelter. Jenny takes her tambourine from the drum head*].

MRS BAINES. Mr Undershaft: have you ever seen a thousand people fall on their knees with one impulse and pray? Come with us to the meeting. Barbara shall tell them that the Army is saved, and saved through you.

CUSINS [*returning impetuously from the shelter with a flag and a trombone, and coming between Mrs Baines and Undershaft*] You shall carry the flag down the first street, Mrs Baines [*he gives her the flag*]. Mr Undershaft is a gifted trombonist: he shall intone an Olympian diapason to the West Ham Salvation March. [*Aside to Undershaft, as he forces the trombone on him*] Blow, Machiavelli, blow.

UNDERSHAFT [*aside to him, as he takes the trombone*] The trumpet in Zion! [*Cusins rushes to the drum, which he takes up and puts on. Undershaft continues, aloud*] I will do my best. I could vamp a bass if I knew the tune.

CUSINS. It is a wedding chorus from one of Donizetti's operas; but we have converted it. We convert everything to good here, including Bodger. You remember the chorus. "For thee immense rejoicing—immenso giubilo— immenso giubilo." [*With drum obbligato*] Rum tum ti tum tum, tum tum ti ta—

BARBARA. Dolly: you are breaking my heart.

CUSINS. What is a broken heart more or less here? Dionysos Undershaft has descended. I am possessed.

MRS BAINES. Come, Barbara: I must have my dear Major to carry the flag with me.

JENNY. Yes, yes, Major darling.

CUSINS [*snatches the tambourine out of Jenny's hand and mutely offers it to Barbara*].

BARBARA [*coming forward a little as she puts the offer behind her with a shudder, whilst Cusins recklessly tosses the tambourine back to Jenny and goes to the gate*] I cant come.

JENNY. Not come!

MRS BAINES [*with tears in her eyes*] Barbara: do you think I am wrong to take the money?

BARBARA [*impulsively going to her and kissing her*] No, no: God help you, dear, you must: you are saving the Army. Go; and may you have a great meeting!

JENNY. But arnt you coming?

BARBARA. No. [*She begins taking off the silver S brooch from her collar*].

MRS BAINES. Barbara: what are you doing?

JENNY. Why are you taking your badge off?

You cant be going to leave us, Major.

BARBARA [*quietly*] Father: come here.

UNDERSHAFT [*coming to her*] My dear! [*seeing that she is going to pin the badge on his collar, he retreats to the penthouse in some alarm*].

BARBARA [*following him*] Dont be frightened. [*She pins the badge on and steps back towards the table, shewing him to the others*] There! It's not much for £5000, is it?

MRS BAINES. Barbara: if you wont come and pray with us, promise me you will pray for us.

BARBARA. I cant pray now. Perhaps I shall never pray again.

MRS BAINES. Barbara!

JENNY. Major!

BARBARA [*almost delirious*] I cant bear any more. Quick march!

CUSINS [*calling to the procession in the street outside*] Off we go. Play up, there! Immenso giubilo. [*He gives the time with his drum; and the band strikes up the march, which rapidly becomes more distant as the procession moves briskly away*].

MRS BAINES. I must go, dear. Youre overworked: you will be all right tomorrow. We'll never lose you. Now Jenny: step out with the old flag. Blood and Fire! [*She marches out through the gate with her flag*].

JENNY. Glory Hallelujah! [*flourishing her tambourine and marching*].

UNDERSHAFT [*to Cusins, as he marches out past him easing the slide of his trombone*] "My ducats and my daughter"!

CUSINS [*following him out*] Money and gunpowder!

BARBARA. Drunkenness and Murder! My God: why hast thou forsaken me?

She sinks on the form with her face buried in her hands. The march passes away into silence. Bill Walker steals across to her.

BILL [*taunting*] Wot prawce selvytion nah?

SHIRLEY. Dont you hit her when she's down.

BILL. She itt me wen aw wiz dahn. Waw shouldnt Aw git a bit o me aown beck?

BARBARA [*raising her head*] I didnt take your money, Bill. [*She crosses the yard to the gate and turns her back on the two men to hide her face from them*].

BILL [*sneering after her*] Naow, it warnt enaff for you. [*Turning to the drum, he misses the money*]. Ellow! If you aint took it sammun else ez. Weres it gorn? Bly me if Jenny Ill didnt tike it arter all!

RUMMY [*screaming at him from the loft*] You

lie, you dirty blackguard! Snobby Price pinched it off the drum when he took up his cap. I was up here all the time an see im do it.

BILL. Wot! Stowl maw manney! Waw didnt you call thief on him, you silly aold macker you?

RUMMY. To serve you aht for ittin me acrost the fice. It's cost y'pahnd, that az. [*Raising a pæan of squalid triumph*] I done you. I'm even with you. Ive ad it aht o y— [*Bill snatches up Shirley's mug and hurls it at her. She slams the loft door and vanishes. The mug smashes against the door and falls in fragments*].

BILL [*beginning to chuckle*] Tell us, aol menn, wot o'clock this mawnin was it wen im as they call Snobby Prawce was sived?

BARBARA [*turning to him more composedly, and with unspoiled sweetness*] About half past twelve, Bill. And he pinched your pound at a quarter to two. *I* know. Well, you cant afford to lose it. I'll send it to you.

BILL [*his voice and accent suddenly improving*] Not if Aw wiz to stawve for it. Aw aint to be bought.

SHIRLEY. Aint you? Youd sell yourself to the devil for a pint o beer; ony there aint no devil to make the offer.

BILL [*unshamed*] Sao Aw would, mite, and often ev, cheerful. But s h e cawnt baw me. [*Approaching Barbara*] You wanted maw saoul, did you? Well, you aint got it.

BARBARA. I nearly got it, Bill. But weve sold it back to you for ten thousand pounds.

SHIRLEY. And dear at the money!

BARBARA. No, Peter: it was worth more than money.

BILL [*salvationproof*] It's nao good: you cawnt get rahnd me nah. Aw downt blieve in it; and Awve seen tody that Aw was rawt. [*Going*] Sao long, aol soupkitchener! Ta, ta, Mijor Earl's Grendorter! [*Turning at the gate*] Wot prawce selvytion nah? Snobby Prawce! Ha! ha!

BARBARA [*offering her hand*] Goodbye, Bill.

BILL [*taken aback, half plucks his cap off; then shoves it on again defiantly*] Git aht. [*Barbara drops her hand, discouraged. He has a twinge of remorse*]. But thets aw rawt, you knaow. Nathink pasnl. Naow mellice. Sao long, Judy. [*He goes*].

BARBARA. No malice. So long, Bill.

SHIRLEY [*shaking his head*] You make too much of him, miss, in your innocence.

BARBARA [*going to him*] Peter: I'm like you now. Cleaned out, and lost my job.

SHIRLEY. Youve youth an hope. Thats two better than me.

BARBARA. I'll get you a job, Peter. Thats hope for you: the youth will have to be enough for me. [*She counts her money*]. I have just enough left for two teas at Lockharts, a Rowton doss for you, and my tram and bus home. [*He frowns and rises with offended pride. She takes his arm*]. Dont be proud, Peter: it's sharing between friends. And promise me youll talk to me and not let me cry. [*She draws him towards the gate*].

SHIRLEY. Well, I'm not accustomed to talk to the like of you—

BARBARA [*urgently*] Yes, yes: you must talk to me. Tell me about Tom Paine's books and Bradlaugh's lectures. Come along.

SHIRLEY. Ah, if you would only read Tom Paine in the proper spirit, miss! [*They go out through the gate together*].

ACT III

Next day after lunch Lady Britomart is writing in the library in Wilton Crescent. Sarah is reading in the armchair near the window. Barbara, in ordinary fashionable dress, pale and brooding, is on the settee. Charles Lomax enters. He starts on seeing Barbara fashionably attired and in low spirits.

LOMAX. Youve left off your uniform!

Barbara says nothing; but an expression of pain passes over her face.

LADY BRITOMART [*warning him in low tones to be careful*] Charles!

LOMAX [*much concerned, coming behind the settee and bending sympathetically over Barbara*] I'm awfully sorry, Barbara. You know I helped you all I could with the concertina and so forth. [*Momentously*] Still, I have never shut my eyes to the fact that there is a certain amount of tosh about the Salvation Army. Now the claims of the Church of England—

LADY BRITOMART. Thats enough, Charles. Speak of something suited to your mental capacity.

LOMAX. But surely the Church of England is suited to all our capacities.

BARBARA [*pressing his hand*] Thank you for your sympathy, Cholly. Now go and spoon with Sarah.

LOMAX [*dragging a chair from the writing table and seating himself affectionately by Sarah's side*] How is my ownest today?

SARAH. I wish you wouldnt tell Cholly to do things, Barbara. He always comes straight and does them. Cholly: we're going to the works this afternoon.

LOMAX. What works?

SARAH. The cannon works.

LOMAX. What! Your governor's shop!

SARAH. Yes.

LOMAX. Oh I say!

Cusins enters in poor condition. He also starts visibly when he sees Barbara without her uniform.

BARBARA. I expected you this morning, Dolly. Didnt you guess that?

CUSINS [*sitting down beside her*] I'm sorry. I have only just breakfasted.

SARAH. But weve just finished lunch.

BARBARA. Have you had one of your bad nights?

CUSINS. No: I had rather a good night: in fact, one of the most remarkable nights I have ever passed.

BARBARA. The meeting?

CUSINS. No: after the meeting.

LADY BRITOMART. You should have gone to bed after the meeting. What were you doing?

CUSINS. Drinking.

LADY BRITOMART. ⎫ ⎧ Adolphus!
SARAH.   ⎪ ⎪ Dolly!
BARBARA.   ⎬ ⎨ Dolly!
LOMAX.   ⎭ ⎩ Oh I say!

LADY BRITOMART. What were you drinking, may I ask?

CUSINS. A most devilish kind of Spanish burgundy, warranted free from added alcohol: a Temperance burgundy in fact. Its richness in natural alcohol made any addition superfluous.

BARBARA. Are you joking, Dolly?

CUSINS [*patiently*] No. I have been making a night of it with the nominal head of this household: that is all.

LADY BRITOMART. Andrew made you drunk!

CUSINS. No: he only provided the wine. I think it was Dionysos who made me drunk. [*To Barbara*] I told you I was possessed.

LADY BRITOMART. Youre not sober yet. Go home to bed at once.

CUSINS. I have never before ventured to reproach you, Lady Brit; but how could you marry the Prince of Darkness?

LADY BRITOMART. It was much more excusable to marry him than to get drunk with him. That is a new accomplishment of Andrew's, by the way. He usent to drink.

CUSINS. He doesnt now. He only sat there and completed the wreck of my moral basis, the rout of my convictions, the purchase of my soul. He cares for you, Barbara. That is what makes him so dangerous to me.

BARBARA. That has nothing to do with it, Dolly. There are larger loves and diviner dreams than the fireside ones. You know that, dont you?

CUSINS. Yes: that is our understanding. I know it. I hold to it. Unless he can win me on that holier ground he may amuse me for a while; but he can get no deeper hold, strong as he is.

BARBARA. Keep to that; and the end will be right. Now tell me what happened at the meeting?

CUSINS. It was an amazing meeting. Mrs Baines almost died of emotion. Jenny Hill simply gibbered with hysteria. The Prince of Darkness played his trombone like a madman: its brazen roarings were like the laughter of the damned. 117 conversions took place then and there. They prayed with the most touching sincerity and gratitude for Bodger, and for the anonymous donor of the £5000. Your father would not let his name be given.

LOMAX. That was rather fine of the old man, you know. Most chaps would have wanted the advertisement.

CUSINS. He said all the charitable institutions would be down on him like kites on a battle field if he gave his name.

LADY BRITOMART. Thats Andrew all over. He never does a proper thing without giving an improper reason for it.

CUSINS. He convinced me that I have all my life been doing improper things for proper reasons.

LADY BRITOMART. Adolphus: now that Barbara has left the Salvation Army, you had better leave it too. I will not have you playing that drum in the streets.

CUSINS. Your orders are already obeyed, Lady Brit.

BARBARA. Dolly: were you ever really in earnest about it? Would you have joined if you had never seen me?

CUSINS [*disingenuously*] Well—er—well, possibly, as a collector of religions—

LOMAX [*cunningly*] Not as a drummer, though, you know. You are a very clear-headed brainy chap, Dolly; and it must have been apparent to you that there is a certain amount of tosh about—

LADY BRITOMART. Charles: if you must drivel, drivel like a grown-up man and not like a schoolboy.

LOMAX [*out of countenance*] Well, drivel is drivel, dont you know, whatever a man's age.

LADY BRITOMART. In good society in England, Charles, men drivel at all ages by repeating silly formulas with an air of wisdom. Schoolboys make their own formulas out of slang, like you. When they reach your age, and get political private secretaryships and things of that sort, they drop slang and get their formulas out of The Spectator or The Times. You had better confine yourself to The Times. You will find that there is a certain amount of tosh about The Times; but at least its language is reputable.

LOMAX [*overwhelmed*] You are so awfully strong-minded, Lady Brit—

LADY BRITOMART. Rubbish! [*Morrison comes in*]. What is it?

MORRISON. If you please, my lady, Mr Undershaft has just drove up to the door.

LADY BRITOMART. Well, let him in. [*Morrison hesitates*]. Whats the matter with you?

MORRISON. Shall I announce him, my lady; or is he at home here, so to speak, my lady?

LADY BRITOMART. Announce him.

MORRISON. Thank you, my lady. You wont mind my asking, I hope. The occasion is in a manner of speaking new to me.

LADY BRITOMART. Quite right. Go and let him in.

MORRISON. Thank you, my lady. [*He withdraws*].

LADY BRITOMART. Children: go and get ready. [*Sarah and Barbara go upstairs for their out-of-door wraps*]. Charles: go and tell Stephen to come down here in five minutes: you will find him in the drawing room. [*Charles goes*]. Adolphus: tell them to send round the carriage in about fifteen minutes. [*Adolphus goes*].

MORRISON [*at the door*] Mr Undershaft.

Undershaft comes in. Morrison goes out.

UNDERSHAFT. Alone! How fortunate!

LADY BRITOMART [*rising*] Dont be sentimental, Andrew. Sit down. [*She sits on the settee: he sits beside her, on her left. She comes to the point before he has time to breathe*]. Sarah must have £800 a year until Charles Lomax comes into his property. Barbara will need more, and need it permanently, because Adolphus hasnt any property.

UNDERSHAFT [*resignedly*] Yes, my dear: I will see to it. Anything else? for yourself, for instance?

LADY BRITOMART. I want to talk to you about Stephen.

UNDERSHAFT [*rather wearily*] Dont, my dear. Stephen doesnt interest me.

LADY BRITOMART. He does interest me. He is our son.

UNDERSHAFT. Do you really think so? He has induced us to bring him into the world; but he chose his parents very incongruously, I think. I see nothing of myself in him, and less of you.

LADY BRITOMART. Andrew: Stephen is an excellent son, and a most steady, capable, highminded young man. You are simply trying to find an excuse for disinheriting him.

UNDERSHAFT. My dear Biddy: the Undershaft tradition disinherits him. It would be dishonest of me to leave the cannon foundry to my son.

LADY BRITOMART. It would be most unnatural and improper of you to leave it to anyone else, Andrew. Do you suppose this wicked and immoral tradition can be kept up for ever? Do you pretend that Stephen could not carry on the foundry just as well as all the other sons of the big business houses?

UNDERSHAFT. Yes: he could learn the office routine without understanding the business, like all the other sons; and the firm would go on by its own momentum until the real Undershaft—probably an Italian or a German—would invent a new method and cut him out.

LADY BRITOMART. There is nothing that any Italian or German could do that Stephen could not do. And Stephen at least has breeding.

UNDERSHAFT. The son of a foundling! Nonsense!

LADY BRITOMART. My son, Andrew! And even you may have good blood in your veins for all you know.

UNDERSHAFT. True. Probably I have. That is another argument in favor of a foundling.

LADY BRITOMART. Andrew: dont be aggravating. And dont be wicked. At present you are both.

UNDERSHAFT. This conversation is part of the Undershaft tradition, Biddy. Every Undershaft's wife has treated him to it ever since the house was founded. It is mere waste of breath. If the tradition be ever broken it will be for an abler man than Stephen.

LADY BRITOMART [*pouting*] Then go away.

UNDERSHAFT [*deprecatory*] Go away!

LADY BRITOMART. Yes: go away. If you will do nothing for Stephen, you are not wanted here. Go to your foundling, whoever he is; and look after him.

UNDERSHAFT. The fact is, Biddy—

LADY BRITOMART. Dont call me Biddy. I dont call you Andy.

UNDERSHAFT. I will not call my wife Britomart: it is not good sense. Seriously, my love, the Undershaft tradition has landed me in a difficulty. I am getting on in years; and my partner Lazarus has at last made a stand and insisted that the succession must be settled one way or the other; and of course he is quite right. You see, I havnt found a fit successor yet.

LADY BRITOMART [*obstinately*] There is Stephen.

UNDERSHAFT. Thats just it: all the foundlings I can find are exactly like Stephen.

LADY BRITOMART. Andrew!!

UNDERSHAFT. I want a man with no relations and no schooling: that is, a man who would be out of the running altogether if he were not a strong man. And I cant find him. Every blessed foundling nowadays is snapped up in his infancy by Barnardo homes, or School Board officers, or Boards of Guardians; and if he shews the least ability he is fastened on by schoolmasters; trained to win scholarships like a racehorse; crammed with secondhand ideas; drilled and disciplined in docility and what they call good taste; and lamed for life so that he is fit for nothing but teaching. If you want to keep the foundry in the family, you had better find an eligible foundling and marry him to Barbara.

LADY BRITOMART. Ah! Barbara! Your pet! You would sacrifice Stephen to Barbara.

UNDERSHAFT. Cheerfully. And you, my dear, would boil Barbara to make soup for Stephen.

LADY BRITOMART. Andrew: this is not a question of our likings and dislikings: it is a question of duty. It is your duty to make Stephen your successor.

UNDERSHAFT. Just as much as it is your duty to submit to your husband. Come, Biddy! these tricks of the governing class are of no use with me. I am one of the governing class myself; and it is waste of time giving tracts to a missionary. I have the power in this matter; and I am not to be humbugged into using it for your purposes.

LADY BRITOMART. Andrew: you can talk my head off; but you cant change wrong into right. And your tie is all on one side. Put it straight.

UNDERSHAFT [*disconcerted*] It wont stay unless it's pinned [*he fumbles at it with childish grimaces*]—

Stephen comes in.

STEPHEN [*at the door*] I beg your pardon [*about to retire*].

LADY BRITOMART. No: come in, Stephen. [*Stephen comes forward to his mother's writing table*].

UNDERSHAFT [*not very cordially*] Good afternoon.

STEPHEN [*coldly*] Good afternoon.

UNDERSHAFT [*to Lady Britomart*] He knows all about the tradition, I suppose?

LADY BRITOMART. Yes. [*To Stephen*] It is what I told you last night, Stephen.

UNDERSHAFT [*sulkily*] I understand you want to come into the cannon business.

STEPHEN. *I* go into trade! Certainly not.

UNDERSHAFT [*opening his eyes, greatly eased in mind and manner*] Oh! in that case—

LADY BRITOMART. Cannons are not trade, Stephen. They are enterprise.

STEPHEN. I have no intention of becoming a man of business in any sense. I have no capacity for business and no taste for it. I intend to devote myself to politics.

UNDERSHAFT [*rising*] My dear boy: this is an immense relief to me. And I trust it may prove an equally good thing for the country. I was afraid you would consider yourself disparaged and slighted. [*He moves towards Stephen as if to shake hands with him*].

LADY BRITOMART [*rising and interposing*] Stephen: I cannot allow you to throw away an enormous property like this.

STEPHEN [*stiffly*] Mother: there must be an end of treating me as a child, if you please. [*Lady Britomart recoils, deeply wounded by his tone*]. Until last night I did not take your attitude seriously, because I did not think you meant it seriously. But I find now that you left me in the dark as to matters which you should have explained to me years ago. I am extremely hurt and offended. Any further discussion of my intentions had better take place with my father, as between one man and another.

LADY BRITOMART. Stephen! [*She sits down again, her eyes filling with tears*].

UNDERSHAFT [*with grave compassion*] You see, my dear, it is only the big men who can be treated as children.

STEPHEN. I am sorry, mother, that you have forced me—

UNDERSHAFT [*stopping him*] Yes, yes, yes, yes: thats all right, Stephen. She wont interfere with you any more: your independence is achieved: you have won your latchkey. Dont rub it in; and above all, dont apologize. [*He resumes his seat*]. Now what about your future, as between one man and another— I beg your pardon, Biddy: as between two men and a woman.

LADY BRITOMART [*who has pulled herself together strongly*] I quite understand, Stephen. By all means go your own way if you feel strong enough. [*Stephen sits down magisterially in the chair at the writing table with an air of affirming his majority*].

UNDERSHAFT. It is settled that you do not ask for the succession to the cannon business.

STEPHEN. I hope it is settled that I repudiate the cannon business.

UNDERSHAFT. Come, come! dont be so devilishly sulky: it's boyish. Freedom should be generous. Besides, I owe you a fair start in life in exchange for disinheriting you. You cant become prime minister all at once. Havnt you a turn for something? What about literature, art, and so forth?

STEPHEN. I have nothing of the artist about me, either in faculty or character, thank Heaven!

UNDERSHAFT. A philosopher, perhaps? Eh?

STEPHEN. I make no such ridiculous pretension.

UNDERSHAFT. Just so. Well, there is the army, the navy, the Church, the Bar. The Bar requires some ability. What about the Bar?

STEPHEN. I have not studied law. And I am afraid I have not the necessary push—I believe that is the name barristers give to their vulgarity—for success in pleading.

UNDERSHAFT. Rather a difficult case, Stephen. Hardly anything left but the stage, is there? [*Stephen makes an impatient movement*]. Well, come! is there anything you know or care for?

STEPHEN [*rising and looking at him steadily*] I know the difference between right and wrong.

UNDERSHAFT [*hugely tickled*] You dont say so! What! no capacity for business, no knowledge of law, no sympathy with art, no pretension to philosophy; only a simple knowledge of the secret that has puzzled all the philosophers, baffled all the lawyers, muddled all the men of business, and ruined most of the artists: the secret of right and wrong. Why, man, youre a genius, a master of masters, a god! At twentyfour, too!

STEPHEN [*keeping his temper with difficulty*] You are pleased to be facetious. I pretend to nothing more than any honorable English gentleman claims as his birthright [*he sits down angrily*].

UNDERSHAFT. Oh, thats everybody's birthright. Look at poor little Jenny Hill, the Salvation lassie! she would think you were laughing at her if you asked her to stand up in the street and teach grammar or geography or mathematics or even drawing room dancing; but it never occurs to her to doubt that she can teach morals and religion. You are all alike, you respectable people. You cant tell me the bursting strain of a ten-inch gun, which is a very simple matter; but you all think you can tell me the bursting strain of a man under temptation. You darent handle high explosives; but youre all ready to handle honesty and truth and justice and the whole duty of man, and kill one another at that game. What a country! What a world!

LADY BRITOMART [*uneasily*] What do you think he had better do, Andrew?

UNDERSHAFT. Oh, just what he wants to do. He knows nothing; and he thinks he knows everything. That points clearly to a political career. Get him a private secretaryship to someone who can get him an Under Secretaryship; and then leave him alone. He will find his natural and proper place in the end on the Treasury bench.

STEPHEN [*springing up again*] I am sorry, sir, that you force me to forget the respect due to you as my father. I am an Englishman; and I will not hear the Government of my country insulted. [*He thrusts his hands in his pockets, and walks angrily across to the window*].

UNDERSHAFT [*with a touch of brutality*] The government of your country! *I* am the government of your country: I, and Lazarus. Do you suppose that you and half a dozen amateurs like you, sitting in a row in that foolish gabble shop, can govern Undershaft and Lazarus? No, my friend: you will do what pays us. You will make war when it suits us, and keep peace when it doesnt. You will find out that trade requires certain measures when we have decided on those measures. When I want anything to keep my dividends up, you will discover that my want is a national need. When other people want something to keep my dividends down, you will call out the police and military. And in return you shall have the support and applause of my newspapers, and the delight of imagining that you are a great statesman. Government of your country! Be off with you, my boy, and play with your caucuses and leading articles and historic parties and great leaders and burning questions and the rest of your toys. *I* am going back to my counting-house to pay the piper and call the tune.

STEPHEN [*actually smiling, and putting his hand on his father's shoulder with indulgent patronage*] Really, my dear father, it is impossible to be angry with you. You dont know how absurd all this sounds to me. You are very properly proud of having been industrious enough to make money; and it is greatly to your credit that you have made so much of it. But it has kept you in circles where you are valued for your money and deferred to for it, instead of in the doubtless very old-fashioned and behind-the-times public school and university where I formed my habits of mind. It is natural for you to think that money governs England; but you must allow me to think I know better.

UNDERSHAFT. And what d o e s govern England, pray?

STEPHEN. Character, father, character.

UNDERSHAFT. Whose character? Yours or mine?

STEPHEN. Neither yours nor mine, father, but the best elements in the English national character.

UNDERSHAFT. Stephen: Ive found your profession for you. Youre a born journalist. I'll start you with a high-toned weekly review. There!

Before Stephen can reply Sarah, Barbara, Lomax, and Cusins come in ready for walking. Barbara crosses the room to the window and looks out. Cusins drifts amiably to the armchair. Lomax remains near the door, whilst Sarah comes to her mother.

Stephen goes to the smaller writing table and busies himself with his letters.

SARAH. Go and get ready, mamma: the carriage is waiting. [*Lady Britomart leaves the room*].

UNDERSHAFT [*to Sarah*] Good day, my dear. Good afternoon, Mr Lomax.

LOMAX [*vaguely*] Ahdedoo.

UNDERSHAFT [*to Cusins*] Quite well after last night, Euripides, eh?

CUSINS. As well as can be expected.

UNDERSHAFT. Thats right. [*To Barbara*] So you are coming to see my death and devastation factory, Barbara?

BARBARA [*at the window*] You came yesterday to see my salvation factory. I promised you a return visit.

LOMAX [*coming forward between Sarah and Undershaft*] Youll find it awfully interesting. Ive been through the Woolwich Arsenal; and it gives you a ripping feeling of security, you know, to think of the lot of beggars we could kill if it came to fighting. [*To Undershaft, with sudden solemnity*] Still, it must be rather an awful reflection for you, from the religious point of view as it were. Youre getting on, you know, and all that.

SARAH. You dont mind Cholly's imbecility, papa, do you?

LOMAX [*much taken aback*] Oh I say!

UNDERSHAFT. Mr Lomax looks at the matter in a very proper spirit, my dear.

LOMAX. Just so. Thats all I meant, I assure you.

SARAH. Are you coming, Stephen?

STEPHEN. Well, I am rather busy—er— [*Magnanimously*] Oh well, yes: I'll come. That is, if there is room for me.

UNDERSHAFT. I can take two with me in a little motor I am experimenting with for field use. You wont mind its being rather unfashionable. It's not painted yet; but it's bullet proof.

LOMAX [*appalled at the prospect of confronting Wilton Crescent in an unpainted motor*] Oh I say!

SARAH. The carriage for me, thank you. Barbara doesnt mind what she's seen in.

LOMAX. I say, Dolly, old chap: do you really mind the car being a guy? Because of course if you do I'll go in it. Still—

CUSINS. I prefer it.

LOMAX. Thanks awfully, old man. Come, my ownest. [*He hurries out to secure his seat in the carriage. Sarah follows him*].

CUSINS [*moodily walking across to Lady Britomart's writing table*] Why are we two coming to this Works Department of Hell? that is what I ask myself.

BARBARA. I have always thought of it as a sort of pit where lost creatures with blackened faces stirred up smoky fires and were driven and tormented by my father? Is it like that, dad?

UNDERSHAFT [*scandalized*] My dear! It is a spotlessly clean and beautiful hillside town.

CUSINS. With a Methodist chapel? Oh do say theres a Methodist chapel.

UNDERSHAFT. There are two: a Primitive one and a sophisticated one. There is even an Ethical Society; but it is not much patronized, as my men are all strongly religious. In the High Explosives Sheds they object to the presence of Agnostics as unsafe.

CUSINS. And yet they dont object to you!

BARBARA. Do they obey all your orders?

UNDERSHAFT. I never give them any orders. When I speak to one of them it is "Well, Jones, is the baby doing well? and has Mrs Jones made a good recovery?" "Nicely, thank you, sir." And thats all.

CUSINS. But Jones has to be kept in order. How do you maintain discipline among your men?

UNDERSHAFT. I dont. They do. You see, the one thing Jones wont stand is any rebellion from the man under him, or any assertion of social equality between the wife of the man with 4 shillings a week less than himself, and Mrs Jones! Of course they all rebel against me, theoretically. Practically, every man of them keeps the man just below him in his place. I never meddle with them. I never bully them. I dont even bully Lazarus. I say that certain things are to be done; but I dont order anybody to do them. I dont say, mind you, that there is no ordering about and snubbing and even bullying. The men snub the boys and order them about; the carmen snub the sweepers; the artisans snub the unskilled laborers; the foremen drive and bully both the laborers and artisans; the assistant engineers find fault with the foremen; the chief engineers drop on the assistants; the departmental managers worry the chiefs; and the clerks have tall hats and hymnbooks and keep up the social tone by refusing to associate on equal terms with anybody. The result is a colossal profit, which comes to me.

CUSINS [*revolted*] You really are a—well, what I was saying yesterday.

BARBARA. What was he saying yesterday?

UNDERSHAFT. Never mind, my dear. He thinks I have made you unhappy. Have I?

BARBARA. Do you think I can be happy in this vulgar silly dress? I! who have worn the uniform. Do you understand what you have done to me? Yesterday I had a man's soul in my hand. I set him in the way of life with his face to salvation. But when we took your money he turned back to drunkenness and derision. [*With intense conviction*] I will never forgive you that. If I had a child, and you destroyed its body with your explosives— if you murdered Dolly with your horrible guns—I could forgive you if my forgiveness would open the gates of heaven to you. But to take a human soul from me, and turn it into the soul of a wolf! that is worse than any murder.

UNDERSHAFT. Does my daughter despair so easily? Can you strike a man to the heart and leave no mark on him?

BARBARA [*her face lighting up*] Oh, you are right: he can never be lost now: where was my faith?

CUSINS. Oh, clever clever devil!

BARBARA. You may be a devil; but God speaks through you sometimes. [*She takes her father's hands and kisses them*]. You have given me back my happiness: I feel it deep down now, though my spirit is troubled.

UNDERSHAFT. You have learnt something. That always feels at first as if you had lost something.

BARBARA. Well, take me to the factory of death; and let me learn something more. There must be some truth or other behind all this frightful irony. Come, Dolly. [*She goes out*].

CUSINS. My guardian angel! [*To Undershaft*] Avaunt! [*He follows Barbara*].

STEPHEN [*quietly, at the writing table*] You must not mind Cusins, father. He is a very amiable good fellow; but he is a Greek scholar and naturally a little eccentric.

UNDERSHAFT. Ah, quite so. Thank you, Stephen. Thank you. [*He goes out*].

Stephen smiles patronizingly; buttons his coat responsibly; and crosses the room to the door. Lady Britomart, dressed for out-of-doors, opens it before he reaches it. She looks round for the others; looks at Stephen; and turns to go without a word.

STEPHEN [*embarrassed*] Mother—

LADY BRITOMART. Dont be apologetic, Stephen. And dont forget that you have outgrown your mother. [*She goes out*].

Perivale St Andrews lies between two Middlesex hills, half climbing the northern one. It is an almost smokeless town of white walls, roofs of narrow green slates or red tiles, tall trees, domes, campaniles, and slender chimney shafts, beautifully situated and beautiful in itself. The best view of it is obtained from the crest of a slope about half a mile to the east, where the high explosives are dealt with. The foundry lies hidden in the depths between, the tops of its chimneys sprouting like huge skittles into the middle distance. Across the crest runs an emplacement of concrete, with a firestep, and a parapet which suggests a fortification, because there is a huge cannon of the obsolete Woolwich Infant pattern peering across it at the town. The cannon is mounted on an experimental gun carriage: possibly the original model of the Undershaft disappearing rampart gun alluded to by Stephen. The firestep, being a convenient place to sit, is furnished here and there with straw disc cushions; and at one place there is the additional luxury of a fur rug.

Barbara is standing on the firestep, looking over the parapet towards the town. On her right is the cannon; on her left the end of a shed raised on piles, with a ladder of three or four steps up to the door, which opens outwards and has a little wooden landing at the threshold, with a fire bucket in the corner of the landing. Several dummy soldiers, more or less mutilated, with straw protruding from their gashes, have been shoved out of the way under the landing. A few others are nearly upright against the shed; and one has fallen forward and lies, like a grotesque corpse, on the emplacement. The parapet stops short of the shed, leaving a gap which is the beginning of the path down the hill through the foundry to the town. The rug is on the firestep near this gap. Down on the emplacement behind the cannon is a trolley carrying a huge conical bombshell with a red band painted on it. Further to the right is the door of an office, which, like the sheds, is of the lightest possible construction.

Cusins arrives by the path from the town.

BARBARA. Well?

CUSINS. Not a ray of hope. Everything perfect! wonderful! real! It only needs a cathedral to be a heavenly city instead of a hellish one.

BARBARA. Have you found out whether they have done anything for old Peter Shirley?

CUSINS. They have found him a job as gatekeeper and timekeeper. He's frightfully miserable. He calls the timekeeping brainwork, and says he isnt used to it; and his gate lodge is so splendid that he's ashamed to use the rooms, and skulks in the scullery.

BARBARA. Poor Peter!

Stephen arrives from the town. He carries a fieldglass.

STEPHEN [*enthusiastically*] Have you two seen the place? Why did you leave us?

CUSINS. I wanted to see everything I was not intended to see; and Barbara wanted to make the men talk.

STEPHEN. Have you found anything discreditable?

CUSINS. No. They call him Dandy Andy and are proud of his being a cunning old rascal; but it's all horribly, frightfully, immorally, unanswerably perfect.

Sarah arrives.

SARAH. Heavens! what a place! [*She crosses to the trolley*]. Did you see the nursing home!? [*She sits down on the shell*].

STEPHEN. Did you see the libraries and schools!?

SARAH. Did you see the ball room and the banqueting chamber in the Town Hall!?

STEPHEN. Have you gone into the insurance fund, the pension fund, the building society, the various applications of co-operation!?

Undershaft comes from the office, with a sheaf of telegrams in his hand.

UNDERSHAFT. Well, have you seen everything? I'm sorry I was called away. [*Indicating the telegrams*] Good news from Manchuria.

STEPHEN. Another Japanese victory?

UNDERSHAFT. Oh, I dont know. Which side wins does not concern us here. No: the good news is that the aerial battleship is a tremendous success. At the first trial it has wiped out a fort with three hundred soldiers in it.

CUSINS [*from the platform*] Dummy soldiers?

UNDERSHAFT [*striding across to Stephen and kicking the prostrate dummy brutally out of his way*] No: the real thing.

Cusins and Barbara exchange glances. Then Cusins sits on the step and buries his face in his hands. Barbara gravely lays her hand on his shoulder. He looks up at her in whimsical desperation.

UNDERSHAFT. Well, Stephen, what do you think of the place?

STEPHEN. Oh, magnificent. A perfect triumph of modern industry. Frankly, my dear father, I have been a fool: I had no idea of what it all meant: of the wonderful forethought, the power of organization, the administrative capacity, the financial genius, the colossal capital it represents. I have been repeating to myself as I came through your streets "Peace hath her victories no less renowned than War." I have only one misgiving about it all.

UNDERSHAFT. Out with it.

STEPHEN. Well, I cannot help thinking that all this provision for every want of your workmen may sap their independence and weaken their sense of responsibility. And greatly as we enjoyed our tea at that splendid restaurant—how they gave us all that luxury and cake and jam and cream for threepence I really cannot imagine!—still you must remember that restaurants break up home life. Look at the continent, for instance! Are you sure so much pampering is really good for the men's characters?

UNDERSHAFT. Well you see, my dear boy, when you are organizing civilization you have to make up your mind whether trouble and anxiety are good things or not. If you decide that they are, then, I take it, you simply dont organize civilization; and there you are, with trouble and anxiety enough to make us all angels! But if you decide the other way, you may as well go through with it. However, Stephen, our characters are safe here. A sufficient dose of anxiety is always provided by the fact that we may be blown to smithereens at any moment.

SARAH. By the way, papa, where do you make the explosives?

UNDERSHAFT. In separate little sheds, like that one. When one of them blows up, it costs very little; and only the people quite close to it are killed.

Stephen, who is quite close to it, looks at it rather scaredly, and moves away quickly to the cannon. At the same moment the door of the shed is thrown abruptly open; and a foreman in overalls and list slippers comes out on the little landing and holds the door for Lomax, who appears in the doorway.

LOMAX [*with studied coolness*] My good fellow: you neednt get into a state of nerves. Nothing's going to happen to you; and I suppose

it wouldnt be the end of the world if anything did. A little bit of British pluck is what you want, old chap. [*He descends and strolls across to Sarah*].

UNDERSHAFT [*to the foreman*] Anything wrong, Bilton?

BILTON [*with ironic calm*] Gentleman walked into the high explosives shed and lit a cigaret, sir: thats all.

UNDERSHAFT. Ah, quite so. [*Going over to Lomax*] Do you happen to remember what you did with the match?

LOMAX. Oh come! I'm not a fool. I took jolly good care to blow it out before I chucked it away.

BILTON. The top of it was red hot inside, sir.

LOMAX. Well, suppose it was! I didnt chuck it into any of your messes.

UNDERSHAFT. Think no more of it, Mr Lomax. By the way, would you mind lending me your matches?

LOMAX [*offering his box*] Certainly.

UNDERSHAFT. Thanks. [*He pockets the matches*].

LOMAX [*lecturing to the company generally*] You know, these high explosives dont go off like gunpowder, except when theyre in a gun. When theyre spread loose, you can put a match to them without the least risk: they just burn quietly like a bit of paper. [*Warming to the scientific interest of the subject*] Did you know that, Undershaft? Have you ever tried?

UNDERSHAFT. Not on a large scale, Mr Lomax. Bilton will give you a sample of gun cotton when you are leaving if you ask him. You can experiment with it at home. [*Bilton looks puzzled*].

SARAH. Bilton will do nothing of the sort, papa. I suppose it's your business to blow up the Russians and Japs; but you might really stop short of blowing up poor Cholly. [*Bilton gives it up and retires into the shed*].

LOMAX. My ownest, there is no danger. [*He sits beside her on the shell*].

Lady Britomart arrives from the town with a bouquet.

LADY BRITOMART [*impetuously*] Andrew: you shouldnt have let me see this place.

UNDERSHAFT. Why, my dear?

LADY BRITOMART. Never mind why: you shouldnt have: thats all. To think of all that [*indicating the town*] being yours! and that you have kept it to yourself all these years!

UNDERSHAFT. It does not belong to me. I belong to it. It is the Undershaft inheritance.

LADY BRITOMART. It is not. Your ridiculous cannons and that noisy banging foundry may be the Undershaft inheritance; but all that plate and linen, all that furniture and those houses and orchards and gardens belong to us. They belong to me: they are not a man's business. I wont give them up. You must be out of your senses to throw them all away; and if you persist in such folly, I will call in a doctor.

UNDERSHAFT [stooping to smell the bouquet] Where did you get the flowers, my dear?

LADY BRITOMART. Your men presented them to me in your William Morris Labor Church.

CUSINS. Oh! It needed only that. A Labor Church! [he mounts the firestep distractedly, and leans with his elbows on the parapet, turning his back to them].

LADY BRITOMART. Yes, with Morris's words in mosaic letters ten feet high round the dome. No MAN IS GOOD ENOUGH TO BE ANOTHER MAN'S MASTER. The cynicism of it!

UNDERSHAFT. It shocked the men at first, I am afraid. But now they take no more notice of it than of the ten commandments in church.

LADY BRITOMART. Andrew: you are trying to put me off the subject of the inheritance by profane jokes. Well, you shant. I dont ask it any longer for Stephen: he has inherited far too much of your perversity to be fit for it. But Barbara has rights as well as Stephen. Why should not Adolphus succeed to the inheritance? I could manage the town for him: and he can look after the cannons, if they are really necessary.

UNDERSHAFT. I should ask nothing better if Adolphus were a foundling. He is exactly the sort of new blood that is wanted in English business. But he's not a foundling; and theres an end of it. [He makes for the office door].

CUSINS [turning to them] Not quite. [They all turn and stare at him]. I think—Mind! I am not committing myself in any way as to my future course—but I think the foundling difficulty can be got over. [He jumps down to the emplacement].

UNDERSHAFT [coming back to him] What do you mean?

CUSINS. Well, I have something to say which is in the nature of a confession.

SARAH. \
LADY BRITOMART. } Confession!
BARBARA. /
STEPHEN.

LOMAX. Oh I say!

CUSINS. Yes, a confession. Listen, all. Until I met Barbara I thought myself in the main an honorable, truthful man, because I wanted the approval of my conscience more than I wanted anything else. But the moment I saw Barbara, I wanted her far more than the approval of my conscience.

LADY BRITOMART. Adolphus!

CUSINS. It is true. You accused me yourself, Lady Brit, of joining the Army to worship Barbara; and so I did. She bought my soul like a flower at a street corner; but she bought it for herself.

UNDERSHAFT. What! Not for Dionysos or another?

CUSINS. Dionysos and all the others are in herself. I adored what was divine in her, and was therefore a true worshipper. But I was romantic about her too. I thought she was a woman of the people, and that a marriage with a professor of Greek would be far beyond the wildest social ambitions of her rank.

LADY BRITOMART. Adolphus!!

LOMAX. Oh I say!!!

CUSINS. When I learnt the horrible truth—

LADY BRITOMART. What do you mean by the horrible truth, pray?

CUSINS. That she was enormously rich; that her grandfather was an earl; that her father was the Prince of Darkness—

UNDERSHAFT. Chut!

CUSINS. —and that I was only an adventurer trying to catch a rich wife, then I stooped to deceive her about my birth.

BARBARA [rising] Dolly!

LADY BRITOMART. Your birth! Now Adolphus, dont dare to make up a wicked story for the sake of these wretched cannons. Remember: I have seen photographs of your parents; and the Agent General for South Western Australia knows them personally and has assured me that they are most respectable married people.

CUSINS. So they are in Australia; but here they are outcasts. Their marriage is legal in Australia, but not in England. My mother is my father's deceased wife's sister; and in this island I am consequently a foundling. [Sensation].

BARBARA. Silly! [*She climbs to the cannon, and leans, listening, in the angle it makes with the parapet*].

CUSINS. Is the subterfuge good enough, Machiavelli?

UNDERSHAFT [*thoughtfully*] Biddy: this may be a way out of the difficulty.

LADY BRITOMART. Stuff! A man cant make cannons any the better for being his own cousin instead of his proper self [*she sits down on the rug with a bounce that expresses her downright contempt for their casuistry*].

UNDERSHAFT [*to Cusins*] You are an educated man. That is against the tradition.

CUSINS. Once in ten thousand times it happens that the schoolboy is a born master of what they try to teach him. Greek has not destroyed my mind: it has nourished it. Besides, I did not learn it at an English public school.

UNDERSHAFT. Hm! Well, I cannot afford to be too particular: you have cornered the foundling market. Let it pass. You are eligible, Euripides: you are eligible.

BARBARA. Dolly: yesterday morning, when Stephen told us all about the tradition, you became very silent; and you have been strange and excited ever since. Were you thinking of your birth then?

CUSINS. When the finger of Destiny suddenly points at a man in the middle of his breakfast, it makes him thoughtful.

UNDERSHAFT. Aha! You have had your eye on the business, my young friend, have you?

CUSINS. Take care! There is an abyss of moral horror between me and your accursed aerial battleships.

UNDERSHAFT. Never mind the abyss for the present. Let us settle the practical details and leave your final decision open. You know that you will have to change your name. Do you object to that?

CUSINS. Would any man named Adolphus— any man called Dolly!—object to be called something else?

UNDERSHAFT. Good. Now, as to money! I propose to treat you handsomely from the beginning. You shall start at a thousand a year.

CUSINS [*with sudden heat, his spectacles twinkling with mischief*] A thousand! You dare offer a miserable thousand to the son-in-law of a millionaire! No, by Heavens, Machiavelli! you shall not cheat me. You cannot do without me; and I can do without you. I must have

two thousand five hundred a year for two years. At the end of that time, if I am a failure, I go. But if I am a success, and stay on, you must give me the other five thousand.

UNDERSHAFT. What other five thousand?

CUSINS. To make the two years up to five thousand a year. The two thousand five hundred is only half pay in case I should turn out a failure. The third year I must have ten per cent on the profits.

UNDERSHAFT [*taken aback*] Ten per cent! Why, man, do you know what my profits are?

CUSINS. Enormous, I hope: otherwise I shall require twentyfive per cent.

UNDERSHAFT. But, Mr Cusins, this is a serious matter of business. You are not bringing any capital into the concern.

CUSINS. What! no capital! Is my mastery of Greek no capital? Is my access to the subtlest thought, the loftiest poetry yet attained by humanity, no capital? My character! my intellect! my life! my career! what Barbara calls my soul! are these no capital? Say another word; and I double my salary.

UNDERSHAFT. Be reasonable—

CUSINS [*peremptorily*] Mr Undershaft: you have my terms. Take them or leave them.

UNDERSHAFT [*recovering himself*] Very well. I note your terms; and I offer you half.

CUSINS [*disgusted*] Half!

UNDERSHAFT [*firmly*] Half.

CUSINS. You call yourself a gentleman; and you offer me half!!

UNDERSHAFT. I do not call myself a gentleman; but I offer you half.

CUSINS. This to your future partner! your successor! your son-in-law!

BARBARA. You are selling your own soul, Dolly, not mine. Leave me out of the bargain, please.

UNDERSHAFT. Come! I will go a step further for Barbara's sake. I will give you three fifths; but that is my last word.

CUSINS. Done!

LOMAX. Done in the eye! Why, *I* get only eight hundred, you know.

CUSINS. By the way, Mac, I am a classical scholar, not an arithmetical one. Is three fifths more than half or less?

UNDERSHAFT. More, of course.

CUSINS. I would have taken two hundred and fifty. How you can succeed in business when you are willing to pay all that money to a University don who is obviously not worth a junior clerk's wages!—well! What will Lazarus say?

UNDERSHAFT. Lazarus is a gentle romantic Jew who cares for nothing but string quartets and stalls at fashionable theatres. He will be blamed for your rapacity in money matters, poor fellow! as he has hitherto been blamed for mine. You are a shark of the first order, Euripides. So much the better for the firm!

BARBARA. Is the bargain closed, Dolly? Does your soul belong to him now?

CUSINS. No: the price is settled: that is all. The real tug of war is still to come. What about the moral question?

LADY BRITOMART. There is no moral question in the matter at all, Adolphus. You must simply sell cannons and weapons to people whose cause is right and just, and refuse them to foreigners and criminals.

UNDERSHAFT [determinedly] No: none of that. You must keep the true faith of an Armorer, or you dont come in here.

CUSINS. What on earth is the true faith of an Armorer?

UNDERSHAFT. To give arms to all men who offer an honest price for them, without respect of persons or principles: to aristocrat and republican, to Nihilist and Tsar, to Capitalist and Socialist, to Protestant and Catholic, to burglar and policeman, to black man, white man and yellow man, to all sorts and conditions, all nationalities, all faiths, all follies, all causes and all crimes. The first Undershaft wrote up in his shop IF GOD GAVE THE HAND, LET NOT MAN WITHHOLD THE SWORD. The second wrote up ALL HAVE THE RIGHT TO FIGHT: NONE HAVE THE RIGHT TO JUDGE. The third wrote up TO MAN THE WEAPON: TO HEAVEN THE VICTORY. The fourth had no literary turn; so he did not write up anything; but he sold cannons to Napoleon under the nose of George the Third. The fifth wrote up PEACE SHALL NOT PREVAIL SAVE WITH A SWORD IN HER HAND. The sixth, my master, was the best of all. He wrote up NOTHING IS EVER DONE IN THIS WORLD UNTIL MEN ARE PREPARED TO KILL ONE ANOTHER IF IT IS NOT DONE. After that, there was nothing left for the seventh to say. So he wrote up, simply, UNASHAMED.

CUSINS. My good Machiavelli, I shall certainly write something up on the wall; only, as I shall write it in Greek, you wont be able to read it. But as to your Armorer's faith, if I take my neck out of the noose of my own morality I am not going to put it into the noose of yours. I shall sell cannons to whom I please and refuse them to whom I please. So there!

UNDERSHAFT. From the moment when you become Andrew Undershaft, you will never do as you please again. Dont come here lusting for power, young man.

CUSINS. If power were my aim I should not come here for it. You have no power.

UNDERSHAFT. None of my own, certainly.

CUSINS. I have more power than you, more will. You do not drive this place: it drives you. And what drives the place?

UNDERSHAFT [enigmatically] A will of which I am a part.

BARBARA [startled] Father! Do you know what you are saying; or are you laying a snare for my soul?

CUSINS. Dont listen to his metaphysics, Barbara. The place is driven by the most rascally part of society, the money hunters, the pleasure hunters, the military promotion hunters; and he is their slave.

UNDERSHAFT. Not necessarily. Remember the Armorer's Faith. I will take an order from a good man as cheerfully as from a bad one. If you good people prefer preaching and shirking to buying my weapons and fighting the rascals, dont blame me. I can make cannons: I cannot make courage and conviction. Bah! you tire me, Euripides, with your morality mongering. Ask Barbara: she understands. [He suddenly reaches up and takes Barbara's hands, looking powerfully into her eyes] Tell him, my love, what power really means.

BARBARA [hypnotized] Before I joined the Salvation Army, I was in my own power; and the consequence was that I never knew what to do with myself. When I joined it, I had not time enough for all the things I had to do.

UNDERSHAFT [approvingly] Just so. And why was that, do you suppose?

BARBARA. Yesterday I should have said, because I was in the power of God. [She resumes her self-possession, withdrawing her hands from his with a power equal to his own]. But you came and shewed me that I was in the power of Bodger and Undershaft. Today I feel—oh! how can I put it into words? Sarah: do you remember the earthquake at Cannes, when we were little children?—how little the surprise of the first shock mattered compared to the dread and horror of waiting for the second? That is how I feel in this place today. I stood on the rock I thought eternal; and without a word of warning it reeled and crumbled under me. I was safe with an infinite wisdom watching me, an army marching to Salvation with me; and in a moment, at a stroke of your pen in a cheque book, I stood alone; and the heavens were empty. That was the first shock of the earthquake: I am waiting for the second.

UNDERSHAFT. Come, come, my daughter! dont make too much of your little tinpot tragedy. What do we do here when we spend years of work and thought and thousands of pounds of solid cash on a new gun or an aerial battleship that turns out just a hairsbreadth wrong after all? Scrap it. Scrap it without wasting another hour or another pound on it. Well, you have made for yourself something that you call a morality or a religion or what not. It doesnt fit the facts. Well, scrap it. Scrap it and get one that does fit. That is what is wrong with the world at present. It scraps its obsolete steam engines and dynamos; but it wont scrap its old prejudices and its old moralities and its old religions and its old political constitutions. Whats the result? In machinery it does very well; but in morals and religion and politics it is working at a loss that brings it nearer bankruptcy every year. Dont persist in that folly. If your old religion broke down yesterday, get a newer and a better one for tomorrow.

BARBARA. Oh how gladly I would take a better one to my soul! But you offer me a worse one. [*Turning on him with sudden vehemence*]. Justify yourself: shew me some light through the darkness of this dreadful place, with its beautifully clean workshops, and respectable workmen, and model homes.

UNDERSHAFT. Cleanliness and respectability do not need justification, Barbara: they justify themselves. I see no darkness here, no dreadfulness. In your Salvation shelter I saw poverty, misery, cold, and hunger. You gave them bread and treacle and dreams of heaven. I give from thirty shillings a week to twelve thousand a year. They find their own dreams; but I look after the drainage.

BARBARA. And their souls?

UNDERSHAFT. I save their souls just as I saved yours.

BARBARA [*revolted*] You saved my soul! What do you mean?

UNDERSHAFT. I fed you and clothed you and housed you. I took care that you should have money enough to live handsomely — more than enough; so that you could be wasteful, careless, generous. That saved your soul from the seven deadly sins.

BARBARA [*bewildered*] The seven deadly sins!

UNDERSHAFT. Yes, the deadly seven. [*Counting on his fingers*] Food, clothing, firing, rent, taxes, respectability, and children. Nothing can lift those seven millstones from Man's neck but money; and the spirit cannot soar until the millstones are lifted. I lifted them from your spirit. I enabled Barbara to become Major Barbara; and I saved her from the crime of poverty.

CUSINS. Do you call poverty a crime?

UNDERSHAFT. The worst of crimes. All the other crimes are virtues beside it: all the other dishonors are chivalry itself by comparison. Poverty blights whole cities; spreads horrible pestilences; strikes dead the very souls of all who come within sight, sound, or smell of it. What you call crime is nothing: a murder here and a theft there, a blow now and a curse then: what do they matter? they are only the accidents and illnesses of life: there are not fifty genuine professional criminals in London. But there are millions of poor people, abject people, dirty people, ill fed, ill clothed people. They poison us morally and physically: they kill the happiness of society: they force us to do away with our own liberties and to organize unnatural cruelties for fear they should rise against us and drag us down into their abyss. Only fools fear crime: we all fear poverty, Pah! [*turning on Barbara*] you talk of your half-saved ruffian in West Ham: you accuse me of dragging his soul back to perdition. Well, bring him to me here; and I will drag his soul back again to salvation for you. Not by words and dreams; but by thirtyeight shillings a week, a sound house in a handsome street, and a permanent job. In three weeks he will have a fancy waistcoat; in three months a tall hat and a chapel sitting; before the end of the year he will shake hands with a duchess at a Primrose League meeting, and join the Conservative Party.

BARBARA. And will he be the better for that?

UNDERSHAFT. You know he will. Dont be a hypocrite, Barbara. He will be better fed, better housed, better clothed, better behaved; and his children will be pounds heavier and bigger. That will be better than an American cloth mattress in a shelter, chopping firewood, eating bread and treacle, and being forced to kneel down from time to time to thank heaven for it: knee drill, I think you call it. It is cheap work converting starving men with a Bible in one hand and a slice of bread in the other. I will undertake to convert West Ham to Mahometanism on the same terms. Try your hand on my men: their souls are hungry because their bodies are full.

BARBARA. And leave the east end to starve?

UNDERSHAFT [*his energetic tone dropping into one of bitter and brooding remembrance*] I was an east ender. I moralized and starved until one day I swore that I would be a full-fed free man at all costs; that nothing should stop me except a bullet, neither reason nor morals nor the lives of other men. I said "Thou shalt starve ere I starve"; and with that word I became free and great. I was a dangerous man until I had my will: now I am a useful, beneficent, kindly person. That is the history of most self-made millionaires, I fancy. When it is the history of every Englishman we shall have an England worth living in.

LADY BRITOMART. Stop making speeches, Andrew. This is not the place for them.

UNDERSHAFT [*punctured*] My dear: I have no other means of conveying my ideas.

LADY BRITOMART. Your ideas are nonsense. You got on because you were selfish and unscrupulous.

UNDERSHAFT. Not at all. I had the strongest scruples about poverty and starvation. Your moralists are quite unscrupulous about both: they make virtues of them. I had rather be a thief than a pauper; I had rather be a murderer than a slave. I dont want to be either; but if you force the alternative on me, then, by Heaven, I'll choose the braver and more moral one. I hate poverty and slavery worse than any other crimes whatsoever. And let me tell you this. Poverty and slavery have stood up for centuries to your sermons and leading articles: they will not stand up to my machine guns. Dont preach at them: dont reason with them. Kill them.

BARBARA. Killing. Is that your remedy for everything?

UNDERSHAFT. It is the final test of conviction, the only lever strong enough to overturn a social system, the only way of saying Must. Let six hundred and seventy fools loose in the streets; and three policemen can scatter them. But huddle them together in a certain house in Westminster; and let them go through certain ceremonies and call themselves certain names until at last they get the courage to kill; and your six hundred and seventy fools become a government. Your pious mob fills up ballot papers and imagines it is governing its masters; but the ballot paper that really governs is the paper that has a bullet wrapped up in it.

CUSINS. That is perhaps why, like most intelligent people, I never vote.

UNDERSHAFT. Vote! Bah! When you vote, you only change the names of the cabinet. When you shoot, you pull down governments, inaugurate new epochs, abolish old orders and set up new. Is that historically true, Mr Learned Man, or is it not?

CUSINS. It is historically true. I loathe having to admit it. I repudiate your sentiments. I abhor your nature. I defy you in every possible way. Still, it is true. But it ought not to be true.

UNDERSHAFT. Ought! ought! ought! ought! ought! Are you going to spend your life saying ought, like the rest of our moralists? Turn your oughts into shalls, man. Come and make explosives with me. Whatever can blow men up can blow society up. The history of the world is the history of those who had courage enough to embrace this truth. Have you the courage to embrace it, Barbara?

LADY BRITOMART. Barbara: I positively forbid you to listen to your father's abominable wickedness. And you, Adolphus, ought to know better than to go about saying that wrong things are true. What does it matter whether they are true if they are wrong?

UNDERSHAFT. What does it matter whether they are wrong if they are true?

LADY BRITOMART [*rising*] Children: come home instantly. Andrew: I am exceedingly sorry I allowed you to call on us. You are wickeder than ever. Come at once.

BARBARA [*shaking her head*] It's no use running away from wicked people, mamma.

LADY BRITOMART. It is every use. It shews your disapprobation of them.

BARBARA. It does not save them.

LADY BRITOMART. I can see that you are going to disobey me. Sarah: are you coming home or are you not?

SARAH. I daresay it's very wicked of papa to make cannons; but I dont think I shall cut him on that account.

LOMAX [*pouring oil on the troubled waters*] The fact is, you know, there is a certain amount of tosh about this notion of wickedness. It doesnt work. You must look at facts. Not that I would say a word in favor of anything wrong; but then, you see, all sorts of chaps are always doing all sorts of things; and we have to fit them in somehow, dont you know. What I mean is that you cant go cutting everybody; and thats about what it comes to. [*Their rapt attention to his eloquence makes him nervous*]. Perhaps I dont make myself clear.

LADY BRITOMART. You are lucidity itself, Charles. Because Andrew is successful and has plenty of money to give to Sarah, you will flatter him and encourage him in his wickedness.

LOMAX [*unruffled*] Well, where the carcase is, there will the eagles be gathered, dont you know. [*To Undershaft*] Eh? What?

UNDERSHAFT. Precisely. By the way, may I call you Charles?

LOMAX. Delighted. Cholly is the usual ticket.

UNDERSHAFT [*to Lady Britomart*] Biddy—

LADY BRITOMART [*violently*] Dont dare call me Biddy. Charles Lomax: you are a fool. Adolphus Cusins: you are a Jesuit. Stephen: you are a prig. Barbara: you are a lunatic. Andrew: you are a vulgar tradesman. Now you all know my opinion; and my conscience is clear, at all events [*she sits down with a vehemence that the rug fortunately softens*].

UNDERSHAFT. My dear: you are the incarnation of morality. [*She snorts*]. Your conscience is clear and your duty done when you have called everybody names. Come, Euripides! it is getting late; and we all want to go home. Make up your mind.

CUSINS. Understand this, you old demon—

LADY BRITOMART. Adolphus!

UNDERSHAFT. Let him alone, Biddy. Proceed, Euripides.

CUSINS. You have me in a horrible dilemma. I want Barbara.

UNDERSHAFT. Like all young men, you greatly exaggerate the difference between one young woman and another.

BARBARA. Quite true, Dolly.

CUSINS. I also want to avoid being a rascal.

UNDERSHAFT [*with biting contempt*] You lust for personal righteousness, for self-approval, for what you call a good conscience, for what Barbara calls salvation, for what I call patronizing people who are not so lucky as yourself.

CUSINS. I do not: all the poet in me recoils from being a good man. But there are things in me that I must reckon with. Pity—

UNDERSHAFT. Pity! The scavenger of misery.

CUSINS. Well, love.

UNDERSHAFT. I know. You love the needy and the outcast: you love the oppressed races, the negro, the Indian ryot, the underdog everywhere. Do you love the Japanese? Do you love the French? Do you love the English?

CUSINS. No. Every true Englishman detests the English. We are the wickedest nation on earth; and our success is a moral horror.

UNDERSHAFT. That is what comes of your gospel of love, is it?

CUSINS. May I not love even my father-in-law?

UNDERSHAFT. Who wants your love, man? By what right do you take the liberty of offering it to me? I will have your due heed and respect, or I will kill you. But your love! Damn your impertinence!

CUSINS [*grinning*] I may not be able to control my affections, Mac.

UNDERSHAFT. You are fencing, Euripides. You are weakening: your grip is slipping. Come! try your last weapon. Pity and love have broken in your hand: forgiveness is still left.

CUSINS. No: forgiveness is a beggar's refuge. I am with you there: we must pay our debts.

UNDERSHAFT. Well said. Come! you will suit me. Remember the words of Plato.

CUSINS [*starting*] Plato! You dare quote Plato to me!

UNDERSHAFT. Plato says, my friend, that society cannot be saved until either the Professors of Greek take to making gunpowder, or else the makers of gunpowder become Professors of Greek.

CUSINS. Oh, tempter, cunning tempter!

UNDERSHAFT. Come! choose, man, choose.

CUSINS. But perhaps Barbara will not marry me if I make the wrong choice.

BARBARA. Perhaps not.

CUSINS [*desperately perplexed*] You hear!

BARBARA. Father: do you love nobody?

UNDERSHAFT. I love my best friend.

LADY BRITOMART. And who is that, pray?

UNDERSHAFT. My bravest enemy. That is the man who keeps me up to the mark.

CUSINS. You know, the creature is really a sort of poet in his way. Suppose he is a great man, after all!

UNDERSHAFT. Suppose you stop talking and make up your mind, my young friend.

CUSINS. But you are driving me against my nature. I hate war.

UNDERSHAFT. Hatred is the coward's revenge for being intimidated. Dare you make war on war? Here are the means: my friend Mr Lomax is sitting on them.

LOMAX [springing up] Oh I say! You dont mean that this thing is loaded, do you? My ownest: come off it.

SARAH [sitting placidly on the shell] If I am to be blown up, the more thoroughly it is done the better. Dont fuss, Cholly.

LOMAX [to Undershaft, strongly remonstrant] Your own daughter, you know!

UNDERSHAFT. So I see. [To Cusins] Well, my friend, may we expect you here at six tomorrow morning?

CUSINS [firmly] Not on any account. I will see the whole establishment blown up with its own dynamite before I will get up at five. My hours are healthy, rational hours: eleven to five.

UNDERSHAFT. Come when you please: before a week you will come at six and stay until I turn you out for the sake of your health. [Calling] Bilton! [He turns to Lady Britomart, who rises]. My dear: let us leave these two young people to themselves for a moment. [Bilton comes from the shed]. I am going to take you through the guncotton shed.

BILTON [barring the way] You cant take anything explosive in here, sir.

LADY BRITOMART. What do you mean? Are you alluding to me?

BILTON [unmoved] No, maam. Mr Undershaft has the other gentleman's matches in his pocket.

LADY BRITOMART [abruptly] Oh! I beg your pardon. [She goes into the shed].

UNDERSHAFT. Quite right, Bilton, quite right: here you are. [He gives Bilton the box of matches]. Come, Stephen. Come, Charles. Bring Sarah. [He passes into the shed].

Bilton opens the box and deliberately drops the matches into the fire-bucket.

LOMAX. Oh I say! [Bilton stolidly hands him

the empty box]. Infernal nonsense! Pure scientific ignorance! [He goes in].

SARAH. Am I all right, Bilton?

BILTON. Youll have to put on list slippers, miss: thats all. Weve got em inside. [She goes in].

STEPHEN [very seriously to Cusins] Dolly, old fellow, think. Think before you decide. Do you feel that you are a sufficiently practical man? It is a huge undertaking, an enormous responsibility. All this mass of business will be Greek to you.

CUSINS. Oh, I think it will be much less difficult than Greek.

STEPHEN. Well, I just want to say this before I leave you to yourselves. Dont let anything I have said about right and wrong prejudice you against this great chance in life. I have satisfied myself that the business is one of the highest character and a credit to our country. [Emotionally] I am very proud of my father. I— [Unable to proceed, he presses Cusins' hand and goes hastily into the shed, followed by Bilton].

Barbara and Cusins, left alone together, look at one another silently.

CUSINS. Barbara: I am going to accept this offer.

BARBARA. I thought you would.

CUSINS. You understand, dont you, that I had to decide without consulting you. If I had thrown the burden of the choice on you, you would sooner or later have despised me for it.

BARBARA. Yes: I did not want you to sell your soul for me any more than for this inheritance.

CUSINS. It is not the sale of my soul that troubles me: I have sold it too often to care about that. I have sold it for a professorship. I have sold it for an income. I have sold it to escape being imprisoned for refusing to pay taxes for hangmen's ropes and unjust wars and things that I abhor. What is all human conduct but the daily and hourly sale of our souls for trifles? What I am now selling it for is neither money nor position nor comfort, but for reality and for power.

BARBARA. You know that you will have no power, and that he has none.

CUSINS. I know. It is not for myself alone. I want to make power for the world.

BARBARA. I want to make power for the world too; but it must be spiritual power.

CUSINS. I think all power is spiritual: these

cannons will not go off by themselves. I have tried to make spiritual power by teaching Greek. But the world can never be really touched by a dead language and a dead civilization. The people must have power; and the people cannot have Greek. Now the power that is made here can be wielded by all men.

BARBARA. Power to burn women's houses down and kill their sons and tear their husbands to pieces.

CUSINS. You cannot have power for good without having power for evil too. Even mother's milk nourishes murderers as well as heroes. This power which only tears men's bodies to pieces has never been so horribly abused as the intellectual power, the imaginative power, the poetic, religious power that can enslave men's souls. As a teacher of Greek I gave the intellectual man weapons against the common man. I now want to give the common man weapons against the intellectual man. I love the common people. I want to arm them against the lawyers, the doctors, the priests, the literary men, the professors, the artists, and the politicians, who, once in authority, are more disastrous and tyrannical than all the fools, rascals, and impostors. I want a power simple enough for common men to use, yet strong enough to force the intellectual oligarchy to use its genius for the general good.

BARBARA. Is there no higher power than that [pointing to the shell]?

CUSINS. Yes; but that power can destroy the higher powers just as a tiger can destroy a man: therefore Man must master that power first. I admitted this when the Turks and Greeks were last at war. My best pupil went out to fight for Hellas. My parting gift to him was not a copy of Plato's Republic, but a revolver and a hundred Undershaft cartridges. The blood of every Turk he shot —if he shot any—is on my head as well as on Undershaft's. That act committed me to this place for ever. Your father's challenge has beaten me. Dare I make war on war? I dare. I must. I will. And now, is it all over between us?

BARBARA [touched by his evident dread of her answer] Silly baby Dolly! How could it be?

CUSINS [overjoyed] Then you—you—you— Oh for my drum! [He flourishes imaginary drumsticks].

BARBARA [angered by his levity] Take care, Dolly, take care. Oh, if only I could get away from you and from father and from it all! if I could have the wings of a dove and fly away to heaven!

CUSINS. And leave me!

BARBARA. Yes, you, and all the other naughty mischievous children of men. But I cant. I was happy in the Salvation Army for a moment. I escaped from the world into a paradise of enthusiasm and prayer and soul saving; but the moment our money ran short, it all came back to Bodger: it was he who saved our people: he, and the Prince of Darkness, my papa. Undershaft and Bodger: their hands stretch everywhere: when we feed a starving fellow creature, it is with their bread, because there is no other bread; when we tend the sick, it is in the hospitals they endow; if we turn from the churches they build, we must kneel on the stones of the streets they pave. As long as that lasts, there is no getting away from them. Turning our backs on Bodger and Undershaft is turning our backs on life.

CUSINS. I thought you were determined to turn your back on the wicked side of life.

BARBARA. There is no wicked side: life is all one. And I never wanted to shirk my share in whatever evil must be endured, whether it be sin or suffering. I wish I could cure you of middle-class ideas, Dolly.

CUSINS [gasping] Middle cl—! A snub! A social snub to me! from the daughter of a foundling!

BARBARA. That is why I have no class, Dolly: I come straight out of the heart of the whole people. If I were middle-class I should turn my back on my father's business; and we should both live in an artistic drawing room, with you reading the reviews in one corner, and I in the other at the piano, playing Schumann: both very superior persons, and neither of us a bit of use. Sooner than that, I would sweep out the guncotton shed, or be one of Bodger's barmaids. Do you know what would have happened if you had refused papa's offer?

CUSINS. I wonder!

BARBARA. I should have given you up and married the man who accepted it. After all, my dear old mother has more sense than any of you. I felt like her when I saw this place— felt that I must have it—that never, never, never could I let it go; only she thought it was the houses and the kitchen ranges and the linen and china, when it was really all the human souls to be saved: not weak souls in starved bodies, sobbing with gratitude for a scrap of bread and treacle, but fullfed, quarrelsome, snobbish, uppish creatures, all standing on their little rights and dignities, and thinking that my father ought to be greatly obliged to them for making so much money for him—and so he ought. That is where salvation is really wanted. My father shall never throw it in my teeth again that my converts were bribed with bread. [*She is transfigured*]. I have got rid of the bribe of bread. I have got rid of the bribe of heaven. Let God's work be done for its own sake: the work he had to create us to do because it cannot be done except by living men and women. When I die, let him be in my debt, not I in his; and let me forgive him as becomes a woman of my rank.

CUSINS. Then the way of life lies through the factory of death?

BARBARA. Yes, through the raising of hell to heaven and of man to God, through the unveiling of an eternal light in the Valley of The Shadow. [*Seizing him with both hands*] Oh, did you think my courage would never come back? did you believe that I was a deserter? that I, who have stood in the streets, and taken my people to my heart, and talked of the holiest and greatest things with them, could ever turn back and chatter foolishly to fashionable people about nothing in a drawing room? Never, never, never, never: Major Barbara will die with the colors. Oh! and I have my dear little Dolly boy still; and

he has found me my place and my work. Glory Hallelujah! [*She kisses him*].

CUSINS. My dearest: consider my delicate health. I cannot stand as much happiness as you can.

BARBARA. Yes: it is not easy work being in love with me, is it? But it's good for you. [*She runs to the shed, and calls, childlike*] Mamma! Mamma! [*Bilton comes out of the shed, followed by Undershaft*]. I want Mamma.

UNDERSHAFT. She is taking off her list slippers, dear. [*He passes on to Cusins*]. Well? What does she say?

CUSINS. She has gone right up into the skies.

LADY BRITOMART [*coming from the shed and stopping on the steps, obstructing Sarah, who follows with Lomax. Barbara clutches like a baby at her mother's skirt*] Barbara: when will you learn to be independent and to act and think for yourself? I know as well as possible what that cry of "Mamma, Mamma," means. Always running to me!

SARAH [*touching Lady Britomart's ribs with her finger tips and imitating a bicycle horn*] Pip! pip!

LADY BRITOMART [*highly indignant*] How dare you say Pip! pip! to me, Sarah? You are both very naughty children. What do you want, Barbara?

BARBARA. I want a house in the village to live in with Dolly. [*Dragging at the skirt*] Come and tell me which one to take.

UNDERSHAFT [*to Cusins*] Six o'clock tomorrow morning, Euripides.

THE END

XV

THE DOCTOR'S DILEMMA

A TRAGEDY (1906)

ACT I

On the 15th June 1903, in the early forenoon, a medical student, surname Redpenny, Christian name unknown and of no importance, sits at work in a doctor's consulting room. He devils for the doctor by answering his letters, acting as his domestic laboratory assistant, and making himself indispensable generally, in return for unspecified advantages involved by intimate intercourse with a leader of his profession, and

amounting to an informal apprenticeship and a temporary affiliation. Redpenny is not proud, and will do anything he is asked without reservation of his personal dignity if he is asked in a fellow-creaturely way. He is a wide-open-eyed, ready, credulous, friendly, hasty youth, with his hair and clothes in reluctant transition from the untidy boy to the tidy doctor.

Redpenny is interrupted by the entrance of an old serving-woman who has never known the cares, the preoccupations, the responsibilities, jealousies, and anxieties of personal beauty. She has the complexion of a never-washed gypsy, incurable by any detergent; and she has, not a regular beard and moustaches, which could at least be trimmed and waxed into a masculine presentableness, but a whole crop of small beards and moustaches, mostly springing from moles all over her face. She carries a duster and toddles about meddlesomely, spying out dust so diligently that whilst she is flicking off one speck she is already looking elsewhere for another. In conversation she has the same trick, hardly ever looking at the person she is addressing except when she is excited. She has only one manner, and that is the manner of an old family nurse to a child just after it has learnt to walk. She has used her ugliness to secure indulgences unattainable by Cleopatra or Fair Rosamund, and has the further great advantage over them that age increases her qualification instead of impairing it. Being an industrious, agreeable, and popular old soul, she is a walking sermon on the vanity of feminine prettiness. Just as Redpenny has no discovered Christian name, she has no discovered surname, and is known throughout the doctors' quarter between Cavendish Square and the Marylebone Road simply as Emmy.

The consulting room has two windows looking on Queen Anne Street. Between the two is a marble-topped console, with haunched gilt legs ending in sphinx claws. The huge pier-glass which surmounts it is mostly disabled from reflection by elaborate painting on its surface of palms, ferns, lilies, tulips, and sunflowers. The adjoining wall contains the fireplace, with two armchairs before it. As we happen to face the corner we see nothing of the other two walls. On the right of the fireplace, or rather on the right of any person facing the fireplace, is the door. On its left is the writing-table at which Redpenny sits. It is an untidy table, with a microscope, several test tubes, and a spirit lamp standing up through its litter of papers. There is a couch in the middle of the room, at right angles to the console, and parallel to the fireplace. A chair stands between the couch and the window. Another in the corner. Another at the other end of the windowed wall. The windows have green Venetian blinds and rep curtains; and there is a gasalier; but it is a convert to electric lighting. The wall paper and carpets are mostly green, coeval with the gasalier and the Venetian blinds. The house, in fact, was so well furnished in the middle of the XIXth century that it stands unaltered to this day and is still quite presentable.

EMMY [entering and immediately beginning to dust the couch] Theres a lady bothering me to see the doctor.

REDPENNY [distracted by the interruption] Well, she cant see the doctor. Look here: whats the use of telling you that the doctor cant take any new patients, when the moment a knock comes to the door, in you bounce to ask whether he can see somebody?

EMMY. Who asked you whether he could see somebody?

REDPENNY. You did.

EMMY. I said theres a lady bothering me to see the doctor. That isnt asking. It's telling.

REDPENNY. Well, is the lady bothering you any reason for you to come bothering me when I'm busy?

EMMY. Have you seen the papers?

REDPENNY. No.

EMMY. Not seen the birthday honors?

REDPENNY [beginning to swear] What the—

EMMY. Now, now, ducky!

REDPENNY. What do you suppose I care about the birthday honors? Get out of this with your chattering. Dr Ridgeon will be down before I have these letters ready. Get out.

EMMY. Dr Ridgeon wont never be down any more, young man.

She detects dust on the console and is down on it immediately.

REDPENNY [jumping up and following her] What?

EMMY. He's been made a knight. Mind you dont go Dr Ridgeoning him in them letters. Sir Colenso Ridgeon is to be his name now.

REDPENNY. I'm jolly glad.

EMMY. I never was so taken aback. I always thought his great discoveries was fudge (let alone the mess of them) with his drops of blood and tubes full of Maltese fever and the like. Now he'll have a rare laugh at me.

REDPENNY. Serve you right! It was like your cheek to talk to him about science. [He returns to his table and resumes his writing].

EMMY. Oh, I dont think much of science; and neither will you when youve lived as long with it as I have. Whats on my mind is answering the door. Old Sir Patrick Cullen has been here already and left first congratulations—hadnt time to come up on his way to the hospital, but was determined to be first—coming back, he said. All the rest will be here too: the knocker will be going all day.

What I'm afraid of is that the doctor'll want a footman like all the rest, now that he's Sir Colenso. Mind: dont you go putting him up to it, ducky; for he'll never have any comfort with anybody but me to answer the door. I know who to let in and who to keep out. And that reminds me of the poor lady. I think he ought to see her. She's just the kind that puts him in a good temper. [*She dusts Redpenny's papers*].

REDPENNY. I tell you he cant see anybody. Do go away, Emmy. How can I work with you dusting all over me like this?

EMMY. I'm not hindering you working— if you call writing letters working. There goes the bell. [*She looks out of the window*]. A doctor's carriage. Thats more congratulations. [*She is going out when Sir Colenso Ridgeon enters*]. Have you finished your two eggs, sonny?

RIDGEON. Yes.

EMMY. Have you put on your clean vest?

RIDGEON. Yes.

EMMY. Thats my ducky diamond! Now keep yourself tidy and dont go messing about and dirtying your hands: the people are coming to congratulate you. [*She goes out*].

Sir Colenso Ridgeon is a man of fifty who has never shaken off his youth. He has the off-handed manner and the little audacities of address which a shy and sensitive man acquires in breaking himself in to intercourse with all sorts and conditions of men. His face is a good deal lined; his movements are slower than, for instance, Redpenny's; and his flaxen hair has lost its lustre; but in figure and manner he is more the young man than the titled physician. Even the lines in his face are those of overwork and restless scepticism, perhaps partly of curiosity and appetite, rather than that of age. Just at present the announcement of his knighthood in the morning papers makes him specially self-conscious, and consequently specially off-hand with Redpenny.

RIDGEON. Have you seen the papers? Youll have to alter the name in the letters if you havnt.

REDPENNY. Emmy has just told me. I'm awfully glad. I—

RIDGEON. Enough, young man, enough. You will soon get accustomed to it.

REDPENNY. They ought to have done it years ago.

RIDGEON. They would have; only they couldnt stand Emmy opening the door, I daresay.

EMMY [*at the door, announcing*] Dr Shoemaker. [*She withdraws*].

A middle-aged gentleman, well dressed, comes in with a friendly but propitiatory air, not quite sure of his reception. His combination of soft manners and responsive kindliness, with a certain unseizable reserve and a familiar yet foreign chiselling of feature, reveal the Jew: in this instance the handsome gentlemanly Jew, gone a little pigeon-breasted and stale after thirty, as handsome young Jews often do, but still decidedly good-looking.

THE GENTLEMAN. Do you remember me? Schutzmacher. University College school and Belsize Avenue. Loony Schutzmacher, you know.

RIDGEON. What! Loony! [*He shakes hands cordially*]. Why, man, I thought you were dead long ago. Sit down. [*Schutzmacher sits on the couch: Ridgeon on the chair between it and the window*]. Where have you been these thirty years?

SCHUTZMACHER. In general practice, until a few months ago. Ive retired.

RIDGEON. Well done, Loony! I wish *I* could afford to retire. Was your practice in London?

SCHUTZMACHER. No.

RIDGEON. Fashionable coast practice, I suppose.

SCHUTZMACHER. How could I afford to buy a fashionable practice? I hadnt a rap. I set up in a manufacturing town in the midlands in a little surgery at ten shillings a week.

RIDGEON. And made your fortune?

SCHUTZMACHER. Well, I'm pretty comfortable. I have a place in Hertfordshire besides our flat in town. If you ever want a quiet Saturday to Monday, I'll take you down in my motor at an hour's notice.

RIDGEON. Just rolling in money! I wish you rich g.p.'s would teach me how to make some. Whats the secret of it?

SCHUTZMACHER. Oh, in my case the secret was simple enough, though I suppose I should have got into trouble if it had attracted any notice. And I'm afraid youll think it rather infra dig.

RIDGEON. Oh, I have an open mind. What was the secret?

SCHUTZMACHER. Well, the secret was just two words.

RIDGEON. Not Consultation Free, was it?

SCHUTZMACHER [*shocked*] No, no. Really!

RIDGEON [*apologetic*] Of course not. I was only joking.

SCHUTZMACHER. My two words were simply Cure Guaranteed.

RIDGEON [admiring] Cure Guaranteed!

SCHUTZMACHER. Guaranteed. After all, thats what everybody wants from a doctor, isnt it?

RIDGEON. My dear Loony, it was an inspiration. Was it on the brass plate?

SCHUTZMACHER. There was no brass plate. It was a shop window: red, you know, with black lettering. Doctor Leo Schutzmacher, L.R.C.P. M.R.C.S. Advice and medicine sixpence. Cure Guaranteed.

RIDGEON. And the guarantee proved sound nine times out of ten, eh?

SCHUTZMACHER [rather hurt at so moderate an estimate] Oh, much oftener than that. You see, most people get well all right if they are careful and you give them a little sensible advice. And the medicine really did them good. Parrish's Chemical Food: phosphates, you know. One tablespoonful to a twelve-ounce bottle of water: nothing better, no matter what the case is.

RIDGEON. Redpenny: make a note of Parrish's Chemical Food.

SCHUTZMACHER. I take it myself, you know, when I feel run down. Goodbye. You dont mind my calling, do you? Just to congratulate you.

RIDGEON. Delighted, my dear Loony. Come to lunch on Saturday next week. Bring your motor and take me down to Hertford.

SCHUTZMACHER. I will. We shall be delighted. Thank you. Goodbye. [He goes out with Ridgeon, who returns immediately].

REDPENNY. Old Paddy Cullen was here before you were up, to be the first to congratulate you.

RIDGEON. Indeed. Who taught you to speak of Sir Patrick Cullen as old Paddy Cullen, you young ruffian?

REDPENNY. You never call him anything else.

RIDGEON. Not now that I am Sir Colenso. Next thing, you fellows will be calling me old Colly Ridgeon.

REDPENNY. We do, at St Anne's.

RIDGEON. Yach! Thats what makes the medical student the most disgusting figure in modern civilization. No veneration, no manners—no——

EMMY [at the door, announcing] Sir Patrick Cullen. [She retires].

Sir Patrick Cullen is more than twenty years older than Ridgeon, not yet quite at the end of his tether, but near it and resigned to it. His name, his plain, downright, sometimes rather arid common sense, his large build and stature, the absence of those odd moments of ceremonial servility by which an old English doctor sometimes shews you what the status of the profession was in England in his youth, and an occasional turn of speech, are Irish; but he has lived all his life in England and is thoroughly acclimatized. His manner to Ridgeon, whom he likes, is whimsical and fatherly: to others he is a little gruff and uninviting, apt to substitute more or less expressive grunts for articulate speech, and generally indisposed, at his age, to make much social effort. He shakes Ridgeon's hand and beams at him cordially and jocularly.

SIR PATRICK. Well, young chap. Is your hat too small for you, eh?

RIDGEON. Much too small. I owe it all to you.

SIR PATRICK. Blarney, my boy. Thank you all the same. [He sits in one of the armchairs near the fireplace. Ridgeon sits on the couch]. Ive come to talk to you a bit. [To Redpenny] Young man: get out.

REDPENNY. Certainly, Sir Patrick. [He collects his papers and makes for the door].

SIR PATRICK. Thank you. Thats a good lad. [Redpenny vanishes]. They all put up with me, these young chaps, because I'm an old man, a real old man, not like you. Youre only beginning to give yourself the airs of age. Did you ever see a boy cultivating a moustache? Well, a middle-aged doctor cultivating a grey head is much the same sort of spectacle.

RIDGEON. Good Lord! yes: I suppose so. And I thought that the days of my vanity were past. Tell me: at what age does a man leave off being a fool?

SIR PATRICK. Remember the Frenchman who asked his grandmother at what age we get free from the temptations of love. The old woman said she didnt know. [Ridgeon laughs]. Well, I make you the same answer. But the world's growing very interesting to me now, Colly.

RIDGEON. You keep up your interest in science, do you?

SIR PATRICK. Lord! yes. Modern science is a wonderful thing. Look at your great discovery! Look at all the great discoveries! Where are they leading to? Why, right back to my poor dear old father's ideas and discoveries. He's been dead now over forty years. Oh, it's very interesting.

RIDGEON. Well, theres nothing like progress, is there?

SIR PATRICK. Dont misunderstand me, my boy. I'm not belittling your discovery. Most discoveries are made regularly every fifteen years; and it's fully a hundred and fifty since yours was made last. Thats something to be proud of. But your discovery's not new. It's only inoculation. My father practised inoculation until it was made criminal in eighteen-forty. That broke the poor old man's heart, Colly: he died of it. And now it turns out that my father was right after all. Youve brought us back to inoculation.

RIDGEON. I know nothing about smallpox. My line is tuberculosis and typhoid and plague. But of course the principle of all vaccines is the same.

SIR PATRICK. Tuberculosis? M-m-m-m! Youve found out how to cure consumption, eh?

RIDGEON. I believe so.

SIR PATRICK. Ah yes. It's very interesting. What is it the old cardinal says in Browning's play? "I have known four and twenty leaders of revolt." Well, Ive known over thirty men that found out how to cure consumption. Why do people go on dying of it, Colly? Devilment, I suppose. There was my father's old friend George Boddington of Sutton Coldfield. He discovered the open-air cure in eighteen-forty. He was ruined and driven out of his practice for only opening the windows; and now we wont let a consumptive patient have as much as a roof over his head. Oh, it's very very interesting to an old man.

RIDGEON. You old cynic, you dont believe a bit in my discovery.

SIR PATRICK. No, no: I dont go quite so far as that, Colly. But still, you remember Jane Marsh?

RIDGEON. Jane Marsh? No.

SIR PATRICK. You dont!

RIDGEON. No.

SIR PATRICK. You mean to tell me you dont remember the woman with the tuberculous ulcer on her arm?

RIDGEON [enlightened] Oh, your washer-woman's daughter. Was her name Jane Marsh? I forgot.

SIR PATRICK. Perhaps youve forgotten also that you undertook to cure her with Koch's tuberculin.

RIDGEON. And instead of curing her, it rotted her arm right off. Yes: I remember.

Poor Jane! However, she makes a good living out of that arm now by shewing it at medical lectures.

SIR PATRICK. Still, that wasnt quite what you intended, was it?

RIDGEON. I took my chance of it.

SIR PATRICK. Jane did, you mean.

RIDGEON. Well, it's always the patient who has to take the chance when an experiment is necessary. And we can find out nothing without experiment.

SIR PATRICK. What did you find out from Jane's case?

RIDGEON. I found out that the inoculation that ought to cure sometimes kills.

SIR PATRICK. I could have told you that. Ive tried these modern inoculations a bit myself. Ive killed people with them; and Ive cured people with them; but I gave them up because I never could tell which I was going to do.

RIDGEON [taking a pamphlet from a drawer in the writing-table and handing it to him] Read that the next time you have an hour to spare; and youll find out why.

SIR PATRICK [grumbling and fumbling for his spectacles] Oh, bother your pamphlets. Whats the practice of it? [Looking at the pamphlet] Opsonin? What the devil is opsonin?

RIDGEON. Opsonin is what you butter the disease germs with to make your white blood corpuscles eat them. [He sits down again on the couch].

SIR PATRICK. Thats not new. Ive heard this notion that the white corpuscles—what is it that whats his name?—Metchnikoff—calls them?

RIDGEON. Phagocytes.

SIR PATRICK. Aye, phagocytes: yes, yes, yes. Well, I heard this theory that the phagocytes eat up the disease germs years ago: long before you came into fashion. Besides, they dont always eat them.

RIDGEON. They do when you butter them with opsonin.

SIR PATRICK. Gammon.

RIDGEON. No: it's not gammon. What it comes to in practice is this. The phagocytes wont eat the microbes unless the microbes are nicely buttered for them. Well, the patient manufactures the butter for himself all right; but my discovery is that the manufacture of that butter, which I call opsonin, goes on in the system by ups and downs—Nature being always rhythmical, you know

—and that what the inoculation does is to stimulate the ups or downs, as the case may be. If we had inoculated Jane Marsh when her butter factory was on the up-grade, we should have cured her arm. But we got in on the down-grade and lost her arm for her. I call the up-grade the positive phase and the down-grade the negative phase. Everything depends on your inoculating at the right moment. Inoculate when the patient is in the negative phase and you kill: inoculate when the patient is in the positive phase and you cure.

SIR PATRICK. And pray how are you to know whether the patient is in the positive or the negative phase?

RIDGEON. Send a drop of the patient's blood to the laboratory at St Anne's; and in fifteen minutes I'll give you his opsonin index in figures. If the figure is one, inoculate and cure: if it's under point eight, inoculate and kill. Thats my discovery: the most important that has been made since Harvey discovered the circulation of the blood. My tuberculosis patients dont die now.

SIR PATRICK. And mine do when my inoculation catches them in the negative phase, as you call it. Eh?

RIDGEON. Precisely. To inject a vaccine into a patient without first testing his opsonin is as near murder as a respectable practitioner can get. If I wanted to kill a man I should kill him that way.

EMMY [looking in] Will you see a lady that wants her husband's lungs cured?

RIDGEON [impatiently] No. Havnt I told you I will see nobody? [To Sir Patrick] I live in a state of siege ever since it got about that I'm a magician who can cure consumption with a drop of serum. [To Emmy] Dont come to me again about people who have no appointments. I tell you I can see nobody.

EMMY. Well, I'll tell her to wait a bit.

RIDGEON [furious] Youll tell her I cant see her, and send her away: do you hear?

EMMY [unmoved] Well, will you see Mr Cutler Walpole? He dont want a cure: he only wants to congratulate you.

RIDGEON. Of course. Shew him up. [She turns to go]. Stop. [To Sir Patrick] I want two minutes more with you between ourselves. [To Emmy] Emmy: ask Mr Walpole to wait just two minutes, while I finish a consultation.

EMMY. Oh, he'll wait all right. He's talking to the poor lady. [She goes out].

SIR PATRICK. Well? what is it?

RIDGEON. Dont laugh at me. I want your advice.

SIR PATRICK. Professional advice?

RIDGEON. Yes. Theres something the matter with me. I dont know what it is.

SIR PATRICK. Neither do I. I suppose youve been sounded.

RIDGEON. Yes, of course. Theres nothing wrong with any of the organs: nothing special anyhow. But I have a curious aching: I dont know where: I cant localize it. Sometimes I think it's my heart: sometimes I suspect my spine. It doesnt exactly hurt me; but it unsettles me completely. I feel that something is going to happen. And there are other symptoms. Scraps of tunes come into my head that seem to me very pretty, though theyre quite commonplace.

SIR PATRICK. Do you hear voices?

RIDGEON. No.

SIR PATRICK. I'm glad of that. When my patients tell me that theyve made a greater discovery than Harvey, and that they hear voices, I lock them up.

RIDGEON. You think I'm mad! Thats just the suspicion that has come across me once or twice. Tell me the truth: I can bear it.

SIR PATRICK. Youre sure there are no voices?

RIDGEON. Quite sure.

SIR PATRICK. Then it's only foolishness.

RIDGEON. Have you ever met anything like it before in your practice?

SIR PATRICK. Oh, yes: often. It's very common between the ages of seventeen and twenty-two. It sometimes comes on again at forty or thereabouts. Youre a bachelor, you see. It's not serious—if youre careful.

RIDGEON. About my food?

SIR PATRICK. No: about your behavior. Theres nothing wrong with your spine; and theres nothing wrong with your heart; but theres something wrong with your common sense. Youre not going to die; but you may be going to make a fool of yourself. So be careful.

RIDGEON. I see you dont believe in my discovery. Well, sometimes I dont believe in it myself. Thank you all the same. Shall we have Walpole up?

SIR PATRICK. Oh, have him up. [Ridgeon rings]. He's a clever operator, is Walpole, though he's only one of your chloroform surgeons. In my early days, you made your man drunk; and the porters and students held him down; and you had to set your teeth and finish the job fast. Nowadays you work at your ease; and the pain doesnt come until afterwards, when youve taken your cheque and rolled up your bag and left the house. I tell you, Colly, chloroform has done a lot of mischief. It's enabled every fool to be a surgeon.

RIDGEON [*to Emmy, who answers the bell*] Shew Mr Walpole up.

EMMY. He's talking to the lady.

RIDGEON [*exasperated*] Did I not tell you— *Emmy goes out without heeding him. He gives it up, with a shrug, and plants himself with his back to the console, leaning resignedly against it.*

SIR PATRICK. I know your Cutler Walpoles and their like. Theyve found out that a man's body's full of bits and scraps of old organs he has no mortal use for. Thanks to chloroform, you can cut half a dozen of them out without leaving him any the worse, except for the illness and the guineas it costs him. I knew the Walpoles well fifteen years ago. The father used to snip off the ends of people's uvulas for fifty guineas, and paint throats with caustic every day for a year at two guineas a time. His brother-in-law extirpated tonsils for two hundred guineas until he took up women's cases at double the fees. Cutler himself worked hard at anatomy to find something fresh to operate on; and at last he got hold of something he calls the nuciform sac, which he's made quite the fashion. People pay him five hundred guineas to cut it out. They might as well get their hair cut for all the difference it makes; but I suppose they feel important after it. You cant go out to dinner now without your neighbor bragging to you of some useless operation or other.

EMMY [*announcing*] Mr Cutler Walpole. [*She goes out*].

Cutler Walpole is an energetic, unhesitating man of forty, with a cleanly modelled face, very decisive and symmetrical about the shortish, salient, rather pretty nose, and the three trimly turned corners made by his chin and jaws. In comparison with Ridgeon's delicate broken lines, and Sir Patrick's softly rugged aged ones, his face looks machine-made and beeswaxed; but his scrutinizing, daring eyes give it life and force. He seems never at a loss, never in doubt: one feels that if he made a mistake he would make it thoroughly and firmly. He has neat, well-nourished hands, short arms, and is built for strength and compactness rather than for height He is smartly dressed with a fancy waistcoat, a richly colored scarf secured by a handsome ring, ornaments on his watch chain, spats on his shoes, and a general air of the well-to-do sportsman about him. He goes straight across to Ridgeon and shakes hands with him.

WALPOLE. My dear Ridgeon, best wishes! heartiest congratulations! You deserve it.

RIDGEON. Thank you.

WALPOLE. As a man, mind you. You deserve it as a man. The opsonin is simple rot, as any capable surgeon can tell you; but we're all delighted to see your personal qualities officially recognized. Sir Patrick: how are you? I sent you a paper lately about a little thing I invented: a new saw. For shoulder blades.

SIR PATRICK [*meditatively*] Yes: I got it. It's a good saw: a useful, handy instrument.

WALPOLE [*confidently*] I knew youd see its points.

SIR PATRICK. Yes: I remember that saw sixty-five years ago.

WALPOLE. What!

SIR PATRICK. It was called a cabinetmaker's jimmy then.

WALPOLE. Get out! Nonsense! Cabinet-maker be—

RIDGEON. Never mind him, Walpole. He's jealous,

WALPOLE. By the way, I hope I'm not disturbing you two in anything private.

RIDGEON. No no. Sit down. I was only consulting him. I'm rather out of sorts. Overwork, I suppose.

WALPOLE [*swiftly*] I know whats the matter with you. I can see it in your complexion. I can feel it in the grip of your hand.

RIDGEON. What is it?

WALPOLE. Blood-poisoning.

RIDGEON. Blood-poisoning! Impossible.

WALPOLE. I tell you, blood-poisoning. Ninety-five per cent of the human race suffer from chronic blood-poisoning, and die of it. It's as simple as A.B.C. Your nuciform sac is full of decaying matter—undigested food and waste products—rank ptomaines. Now you take my advice, Ridgeon. Let me cut it out for you. Youll be another man afterwards.

SIR PATRICK. Dont you like him as he is?

WALPOLE. No I dont. I dont like any man who hasnt a healthy circulation. I tell you this: in an intelligently governed country people wouldnt be allowed to go about with nuciform sacs, making themselves centres of infection. The operation ought to be compulsory: it's ten times more important than vaccination.

SIR PATRICK. Have you had your own sac removed, may I ask?

WALPOLE [*triumphantly*] I havnt got one. Look at me! Ive no symptoms. I'm as sound as a bell. About five per cent of the population havnt got any; and I'm one of the five per cent. I'll give you an instance. You know Mrs Jack Foljambe: the smart Mrs Foljambe? I operated at Easter on her sister-in-law, Lady Gorran, and found she had the biggest sac I ever saw: it held about two ounces. Well, Mrs Foljambe had the right spirit—the genuine hygienic instinct. She couldnt stand her sister-in-law being a clean, sound woman, and she simply a whited sepulchre. So she insisted on my operating on her, too. And by George, sir, she hadnt any sac at all. Not a trace! Not a rudiment!! I was so taken aback —so interested, that I forgot to take the sponges out, and was stitching them up inside her when the nurse missed them. Somehow, I'd made sure she'd have an exceptionally large one. [*He sits down on the couch, squaring his shoulders and shooting his hands out of his cuffs as he sets his knuckles akimbo*].

EMMY [*looking in*] Sir Ralph Bloomfield Bonington.

A long and expectant pause follows this announcement. All look to the door; but there is no Sir Ralph.

RIDGEON [*at last*] Where is he?

EMMY [*looking back*] Drat him, I thought he was following me. He's stayed down to talk to that lady.

RIDGEON [*exploding*] I told you to tell that lady— [*Emmy vanishes*].

WALPOLE [*jumping up again*] Oh, by the way, Ridgeon, that reminds me. Ive been talking to that poor girl. It's her husband; and she thinks it's a case of consumption: the usual wrong diagnosis: these damned general practitioners ought never to be allowed to touch a patient except under the orders of a consultant, She's been describing his symptoms to me; and the case is as plain as a pikestaff: bad blood-poisoning. Now she's poor. She cant afford to have him operated on. Well, you send him to me: I'll do it for nothing. Theres room for him in my nursing

home. I'll put him straight, and feed him up and make her happy. I like making people happy. [*He goes to the chair near the window*].

EMMY [*looking in*] Here he is.

Sir Ralph Bloomfield Bonington wafts himself into the room. He is a tall man, with a head like a tall and slender egg. He has been in his time a slender man; but now, in his sixth decade, his waistcoat has filled out somewhat. His fair eyebrows arch goodnaturedly and uncritically. He has a most musical voice; his speech is a perpetual anthem; and he never tires of the sound of it. He radiates an enormous self-satisfaction, cheering, reassuring, healing by the mere incompatibility of disease or anxiety with his welcome presence. Even broken bones, it is said, have been known to unite at the sound of his voice; he is a born healer, as independent of mere treatment and skill as any Christian scientist. When he expands into oratory or scientific exposition, he is as energetic as Walpole; but it is with a bland, voluminous, atmospheric energy, which envelops its subject and its audience, and makes interruption or inattention impossible, and imposes veneration and credulity on all but the strongest minds. He is known in the medical world as B. B.; and the envy roused by his success in practice is softened by the conviction that he is, scientifically considered, a colossal humbug: the fact being that, though he knows just as much (and just as little) as his contemporaries, the qualifications that pass muster in common men reveal their weakness when hung on his egregious personality.

B. B. Aha! Sir Colenso. Sir Colenso, eh? Welcome to the order of knighthood.

RIDGEON [*shaking hands*] Thank you, B. B.

B. B. What! Sir Patrick! And how are we today? a little chilly? a little stiff? but hale and still the cleverest of us all. [*Sir Patrick grunts*]. What! Walpole! the absent-minded beggar: eh?

WALPOLE. What does that mean?

B. B. Have you forgotten the lovely opera singer I sent you to have that growth taken off her vocal cords?

WALPOLE [*springing to his feet*] Great heavens, man, you dont mean to say you sent her for a throat operation!

B. B. [*archly*] Aha! Ha ha! Aha! [*trilling like a lark as he shakes his finger at Walpole*]. You removed her nuciform sac. Well, well! force of habit! force of habit! Never mind, ne-e-ever mind. She got back her voice after it, and thinks you the greatest surgeon alive; and so you are, so you are, so you are.

WALPOLE [*in a tragic whisper, intensely serious*] Blood-poisoning. I see. I see. [*He sits down again*].

SIR PATRICK. And how is a certain distinguished family getting on under your care, Sir Ralph?

B. B. Our friend Ridgeon will be gratified to hear that I have tried his opsonin treatment on little Prince Henry with complete success.

RIDGEON [*startled and anxious*] But how—

B. B. [*continuing*] I suspected typhoid: the head gardener's boy had it; so I just called at St Anne's one day and got a tube of your very excellent serum. You were out, unfortunately.

RIDGEON. I hope they explained to you carefully—

B. B. [*waving away the absurd suggestion*] Lord bless you, my dear fellow, I didnt need any explanations. I'd left my wife in the carriage at the door; and I'd no time to be taught my business by your young chaps. I know all about it. Ive handled these antitoxins ever since they first came out.

RIDGEON. But theyre not anti-toxins; and theyre dangerous unless you use them at the right time.

B. B. Of course they are. Everything is dangerous unless you take it at the right time. An apple at breakfast does you good: an apple at bedtime upsets you for a week. There are only two rules for anti-toxins. First, dont be afraid of them: second, inject them a quarter of an hour before meals, three times a day.

RIDGEON [*appalled*] Great heavens, B. B., no, no, no.

B. B. [*sweeping on irresistibly*] Yes, yes, yes, Colly. The proof of the pudding is in the eating, you know. It was an immense success. It acted like magic on the little prince. Up went his temperature; off to bed I packed him; and in a week he was all right again, and absolutely immune from typhoid for the rest of his life. The family were very nice about it: their gratitude was quite touching; but I said they owed it all to you, Ridgeon; and I am glad to think that your knighthood is the result.

RIDGEON. I am deeply obliged to you. [*Overcome, he sits down on the chair near the couch*].

B. B. Not at all, not at all. Your own merit.

Come! come! come! dont give way.

RIDGEON. It's nothing. I was a little giddy, just now. Overwork, I suppose.

WALPOLE. Blood-poisoning.

B. B. Overwork! Theres no such thing. I do the work of ten men. Am I giddy? No. NO. If youre not well, you have a disease. It may be a slight one; but it's a disease. And what is a disease? The lodgment in the system of a pathogenic germ, and the multiplication of that germ. What is the remedy? A very simple one. Find the germ and kill it.

SIR PATRICK. Suppose theres no germ?

B. B. Impossible, Sir Patrick: there must be a germ: else how could the patient be ill?

SIR PATRICK. Can you shew me the germ of overwork?

B. B. No; but why? Why? Because, my dear Sir Patrick, though the germ is there, it's invisible. Nature has given it no danger signal for us. These germs—these bacilli— are translucent bodies, like glass, like water. To make them visible you must stain them. Well, my dear Paddy, do what you will, some of them wont stain. They wont take cochineal: they wont take methylene blue: they wont take gentian violet: they wont take any coloring matter. Consequently, though we know, as scientific men, that they exist, we cannot see them. But can you disprove their existence? Can you conceive the disease existing without them? Can you, for instance, shew me a case of diphtheria without the bacillus?

SIR PATRICK. No; but I'll shew you the same bacillus, without the disease, in your own throat.

B. B. No, not the same, Sir Patrick. It is an entirely different bacillus; only the two are, unfortunately, so exactly alike that you cannot see the difference. You must understand, my dear Sir Patrick, that every one of these interesting little creatures has an imitator. Just as men imitate each other, germs imitate each other. There is the genuine diphtheria bacillus discovered by Lœffler; and there is the pseudo-bacillus, exactly like it, which you could find, as you say, in my own throat.

SIR PATRICK. And how do you tell one from the other?

B. B. Well, obviously, if the bacillus is the genuine Lœffler, you have diphtheria; and if it's the pseudo-bacillus, youre quite well. Nothing simpler. Science is always simple and always profound. It is only the half truths that are dangerous. Ignorant faddists pick up some superficial information about germs; and they write to the papers and try to discredit science. They dupe and mislead many honest and worthy people. But science has a perfect answer to them on every point.

A little learning is a dangerous thing: Drink deep; or taste not the Pierian spring. I mean no disrespect to your generation, Sir Patrick: some of you old stagers did marvels through sheer professional intuition and clinical experience; but when I think of the average men of your day, ignorantly bleeding and cupping and purging, and scattering germs over their patients from their clothes and instruments, and contrast all that with the scientific certainty and simplicity of my treatment of the little prince the other day, I cant help being proud of my own generation: the men who were trained on the germ theory, the veterans of the great struggle over Evolution in the seventies. We may have our faults; but at least we are men of science. That is why I am taking up your treatment, Ridgeon, and pushing it. It's scientific. [*He sits down on the chair near the couch*].

EMMY [*at the door, announcing*] Dr Blenkinsop.

Dr Blenkinsop is in very different case from the others. He is clearly not a prosperous man. He is flabby and shabby, cheaply fed and cheaply clothed. He has the lines made by a conscience between his eyes, and the lines made by continual money worries all over his face, cut all the deeper as he has seen better days, and hails his well-to-do colleagues as their contemporary and old hospital friend, though even in this he has to struggle with the diffidence of poverty and relegation to the poorer middle class.

RIDGEON. How are you, Blenkinsop?

BLENKINSOP. Ive come to offer my humble congratulations. Oh dear! all the great guns are before me.

B. B. [*patronizing, but charming*] How d'ye do, Blenkinsop? How d'ye do?

BLENKINSOP. And Sir Patrick, too! [*Sir Patrick grunts*].

RIDGEON. Youve met Walpole, of course?

WALPOLE. How d'ye do?

BLENKINSOP. It's the first time Ive had that honor. In my poor little practice there are no chances of meeting you great men. I know nobody but the St Anne's men of my own day. [*To Ridgeon*] And so youre Sir Colenso. How does it feel?

RIDGEON. Foolish at first. Dont take any notice of it.

BLENKINSOP. I'm ashamed to say I havnt a notion what your great discovery is; but I congratulate you all the same for the sake of old times.

B. B. [*shocked*] But, my dear Blenkinsop, you used to be rather keen on science.

BLENKINSOP. Ah, I used to be a lot of things. I used to have two or three decent suits of clothes, and flannels to go up the river on Sundays. Look at me now: this is my best; and it must last til Christmas. What can I do? Ive never opened a book since I was qualified thirty years ago. I used to read the medical papers at first; but you know how soon a man drops that; besides, I cant afford them; and what are they after all but trade papers, full of advertisements? Ive forgotten all my science: whats the use of my pretending I havnt? But I have great experience: clinical experience; and bedside experience is the main thing, isnt it?

B. B. No doubt; always provided, mind you, that you have a sound scientific theory to correlate your observations at the bedside. Mere experience by itself is nothing. If I take my dog to the bedside with me, he sees what I see. But he learns nothing from it. Why? Because he's not a scientific dog.

WALPOLE. It amuses me to hear you physicians and general practitioners talking about clinical experience. What do you see at the bedside but the outside of the patient? Well: it isnt his outside thats wrong, except perhaps in skin cases. What you want is a daily familiarity with people's insides; and that you can only get at the operating table. I know what I'm talking about: Ive been a surgeon and a consultant for twenty years; and Ive never known a general practitioner right in his diagnosis yet. Bring them a perfectly simple case; and they diagnose cancer, and arthritis, and appendicitis, and every other itis, when any really experienced surgeon can see that it's a plain case of blood-poisoning.

BLENKINSOP. Ah, it's easy for you gentlemen to talk; but what would you say if you had my practice? Except for the workmen's clubs, my patients are all clerks and shopmen. They darent be ill: they cant afford it. And when they break down, what can I do for them? You can send your people to St Moritz or to Egypt, or recommend horse exercise or motoring or champagne jelly or complete change and rest for six months. *I* might as well order my people a slice of the moon. And the worst of it is, I'm too poor to keep well myself on the cooking I have to put up with. Ive such a wretched digestion; and I look it. How am I to inspire confidence? [*He sits disconsolately on the couch*].

RIDGEON [*restlessly*] Dont, Blenkinsop: it's too painful. The most tragic thing in the world is a sick doctor.

WALPOLE. Yes, by George: it's like a bald-headed man trying to sell a hair restorer. Thank God I'm a surgeon!

B. B. [*sunnily*] I am never sick. Never had a day's illness in my life. Thats what enables me to sympathize with my patients.

WALPOLE [*interested*] What! youre never ill!

B. B. Never.

WALPOLE. Thats interesting. I believe you have no nuciform sac. If you ever do feel at all queer, I should very much like to have a look.

B. B. Thank you, my dear fellow; but I'm too busy just now.

RIDGEON. I was just telling them when you came in, Blenkinsop, that I have worked myself out of sorts.

BLENKINSOP. Well, it seems presumptuous of me to offer a prescription to a great man like you; but still I have great experience; and if I might recommend a pound of ripe greengages every day half an hour before lunch, I'm sure youd find a benefit. Theyre very cheap.

RIDGEON. What do you say to that, B. B.?

B. B. [*encouragingly*] Very sensible, Blenkinsop: very sensible indeed. I'm delighted to see that you disapprove of drugs.

SIR PATRICK [*grunts*]!

B. B. [*archly*] Aha! Haha! Did I hear from the fireside armchair the bow-wow of the old school defending its drugs? Ah, believe me, Paddy, the world would be healthier if every chemist's shop in England were demolished. Look at the papers! full of scandalous advertisements of patent medicines! a huge commercial system of quackery and poison. Well, whose fault is it? Ours, I say, ours. We set the example. We spread the superstition. We taught the people to believe in bottles of doctor's stuff; and now they buy it at the stores instead of consulting a medical man.

WALPOLE. Quite true. Ive not prescribed a drug for the last fifteen years.

B. B. Drugs can only repress symptoms: they cannot eradicate disease. The true remedy for all diseases is Nature's remedy. Nature and Science are at one, Sir Patrick, believe me; though you were taught differently. Nature has provided, in the white corpuscles as you call them—in the phagocytes as we call them— a natural means of devouring and destroying all disease germs. There is at bottom only one genuinely scientific treatment for all diseases, and that is to stimulate the phagocytes. Stimulate the phagocytes. Drugs are a delusion. Find the germ of the disease; prepare from it a suitable anti-toxin; inject it three times a day quarter of an hour before meals; and what is the result? The phagocytes are stimulated; they devour the disease; and the patient recovers—unless, of course, he's too far gone. That, I take it, is the essence of Ridgeon's discovery.

SIR PATRICK [*dreamily*] As I sit here, I seem to hear my poor old father talking again.

B. B. [*rising in incredulous amazement*] Your father! But, Lord bless my soul, Paddy, your father must have been an older man than you.

SIR PATRICK. Word for word almost, he said what you say. No more drugs. Nothing but inoculation.

B. B. [*almost contemptuously*] Inoculation! Do you mean smallpox inoculation?

SIR PATRICK. Yes. In the privacy of our family circle, sir, my father used to declare his belief that smallpox inoculation was good not only for smallpox, but for all fevers.

B. B. [*suddenly rising to the new idea with immense interest and excitement*] What! Ridgeon: did you hear that? Sir Patrick: I am more struck by what you have just told me than I can well express. Your father, sir, anticipated a discovery of my own. Listen, Walpole. Blenkinsop: attend one moment. You will all be intensely interested in this. I was put on the track by accident. I had a typhoid case and a tetanus case side by side in the hospital: a beadle and a city missionary. Think of what that meant for them, poor fellows! Can a beadle be dignified with typhoid? Can a missionary be eloquent with lockjaw? No. NO. Well, I got some typhoid anti-toxin from Ridgeon and a tube of Muldooley's anti-tetanus serum. But the missionary jerked

S

all my things off the table in one of his paroxysms; and in replacing them I put Ridgeon's tube where Muldooley's ought to have been. The consequence was that I inoculated the typhoid case for tetanus and the tetanus case for typhoid. [*The doctors look greatly concerned. B. B., undamped, smiles triumphantly*]. Well, they recovered. THEY RECOVERED. Except for a touch of St Vitus's dance the missionary's as well today as ever; and the beadle's ten times the man he was.

BLENKINSOP. Ive known things like that happen. They cant be explained.

B. B. [*severely*] Blenkinsop: there is nothing that cannot be explained by science. What did I do? Did I fold my hands helplessly and say that the case could not be explained? By no means. I sat down and used my brains. I thought the case out on scientific principles. I asked myself why didnt the missionary die of typhoid on top of tetanus, and the beadle of tetanus on top of typhoid? Theres a problem for you, Ridgeon. Think, Sir Patrick. Reflect, Blenkinsop. Look at it without prejudice, Walpole. What is the real work of the anti-toxin? Simply to stimulate the phagocytes. Very well. But so long as you stimulate the phagocytes, what does it matter which particular sort of serum you use for the purpose? Haha! Eh? Do you see? Do you grasp it? Ever since that Ive used all sorts of anti-toxins absolutely indiscriminately, with perfectly satisfactory results. I inoculated the little prince with your stuff, Ridgeon, because I wanted to give you a lift; but two years ago I tried the experiment of treating a scarlet fever case with a sample of hydrophobia serum from the Pasteur Institute, and it answered capitally. It stimulated the phagocytes; and the phagocytes did the rest. That is why Sir Patrick's father found that inoculation cured all fevers. It stimulated the phagocytes. [*He throws himself into his chair, exhausted with the triumph of his demonstration, and beams magnificently on them*].

EMMY [*looking in*] Mr Walpole: your motor's come for you; and it's frightening Sir Patrick's horses; so come along quick.

WALPOLE [*rising*] Goodbye, Ridgeon.

RIDGEON. Goodbye; and many thanks.

B. B. You see my point, Walpole?

EMMY. He cant wait, Sir Ralph. The carriage will be into the area if he dont come.

WALPOLE. I'm coming. [*To B. B.*] Theres nothing in your point: phagocytosis is pure rot: the cases are all blood-poisoning; and the knife is the real remedy. Bye-bye, Sir Paddy. Happy to have met you, Mr Blenkinsop. Now, Emmy. [*He goes out, followed by Emmy*].

B. B. [*sadly*] Walpole has no intellect. A mere surgeon. Wonderful operator; but, after all, what is operating? Only manual labor. Brain—BRAIN remains master of the situation. The nuciform sac is utter nonsense: theres no such organ. It's a mere accidental kink in the membrane, occurring in perhaps two-and-a-half per cent of the population. Of course I'm glad for Walpole's sake that the operation is fashionable; for he's a dear good fellow; and after all, as I always tell people, the operation will do them no harm: indeed, Ive known the nervous shake-up and the fortnight in bed do people a lot of good after a hard London season; but still it's a shocking fraud. [*Rising*] Well, I must be toddling. Goodbye, Paddy [*Sir Patrick grunts*], goodbye, goodbye. Goodbye, my dear Blenkinsop, goodbye! Goodbye, Ridgeon. Dont fret about your health: you know what to do: if your liver is sluggish, a little mercury never does any harm. If you feel restless, try bromide. If that doesnt answer a stimulant, you know: a little phosphorus and strychnine. If you cant sleep, trional, trional, trion—

SIR PATRICK [*dryly*] But no drugs, Colly, remember that.

B. B. [*firmly*] Certainly not. Quite right, Sir Patrick. As temporary expedients, of course; but as treatment, no, NO. Keep away from the chemist's shop, my dear Ridgeon, whatever you do.

RIDGEON [*going to the door with him*] I will. And thank you for the knighthood. Goodbye.

B. B. [*stopping at the door, with the beam in his eye twinkling a little*] By the way, who's your patient?

RIDGEON. Who?

B. B. Downstairs. Charming woman. Tuberculous husband.

RIDGEON. Is she there still?

EMMY [*looking in*] Come on, Sir Ralph: your wife's waiting in the carriage.

B. B. [*suddenly sobered*] Oh! Goodbye. [*He goes out almost precipitately*].

RIDGEON. Emmy: is that woman there still? If so, tell her once for all that I cant and wont see her. Do you hear?

EMMY. Oh, she aint in a hurry: she doesnt mind how long she waits. [*She goes out*].

BLENKINSOP. I must be off, too: every half-hour I spend away from my work costs me eighteenpence. Goodbye, Sir Patrick.

SIR PATRICK. Goodbye. Goodbye.

RIDGEON. Come to lunch with me some day this week.

BLENKINSOP. I cant afford it, dear boy; and it would put me off my own food for a week. Thank you all the same.

RIDGEON [uneasy at Blenkinsop's poverty] Can I do nothing for you?

BLENKINSOP. Well, if you have an old frock-coat to spare? you see, what would be an old one for you would be a new one for me; so remember me the next time you turn out your wardrobe. Goodbye. [He hurries out].

RIDGEON [looking after him] Poor chap! [Turning to Sir Patrick] So thats why they made me a knight! And thats the medical profession!

SIR PATRICK. And a very good profession, too, my lad. When you know as much as I know of the ignorance and superstition of the patients, youll wonder that we're half as good as we are.

RIDGEON. We're not a profession: we're a conspiracy.

SIR PATRICK. All professions are conspiracies against the laity. And we cant all be geniuses like you. Every fool can get ill; but every fool cant be a good doctor: there are not enough good ones to go round. And for all you know, Bloomfield Bonington kills less people than you do.

RIDGEON. Oh, very likely. But he really ought to know the difference between a vaccine and an anti-toxin. Stimulate the phagocytes! The vaccine doesnt affect the phagocytes at all. He's all wrong: hopelessly, dangerously wrong. To put a tube of serum into his hands is murder: simple murder.

EMMY [returning] Now, Sir Patrick. How long more are you going to keep them horses standing in the draught?

SIR PATRICK. Whats that to you, you old catamaran?

EMMY. Come, come, now! none of your temper to me. And it's time for Colly to get to his work.

RIDGEON. Behave yourself, Emmy. Get out.

EMMY. Oh, I learnt how to behave myself before I learnt you to do it. I know what doctors are: sitting talking together about themselves when they ought to be with their poor patients. And I know what horses are,

Sir Patrick. I was brought up in the country. Now be good: and come along.

SIR PATRICK [rising] Very well, very well, very well. Goodbye, Colly. [He pats Ridgeon on the shoulder and goes out, turning for a moment at the door to look meditatively at Emmy and say with grave conviction] You are an ugly old devil, and no mistake.

EMMY [highly indignant, calling after him] Youre no beauty yourself. [To Ridgeon, much flustered] Theyve no manners; they think they can say what they like to me; and you set them on, you do. I'll teach them their places. Here now: are you going to see that poor thing or are you not?

RIDGEON. I tell you for the fiftieth time I wont see anybody. Send her away.

EMMY. Oh, I'm tired of being told to send her away. What good will that do her?

RIDGEON. Must I get angry with you, Emmy.

EMMY [coaxing] Come now: just see her for a minute to please me: theres a good boy. She's given me half-a-crown. She thinks it's life and death to her husband for her to see you.

RIDGEON. Values her husband's life at half-a-crown!

EMMY. Well, it's all she can afford, poor lamb. Them others think nothing of half-a-sovereign just to talk about themselves to you, the sluts! Besides, she'll put you in a good temper for the day, because it's a good deed to see her; and she's the sort that gets round you.

RIDGEON. Well, she hasnt done so badly. For half-a-crown she's had a consultation with Sir Ralph Bloomfield Bonington and Cutler Walpole. Thats six guineas' worth to start with. I daresay she's consulted Blenkinsop too: thats another eighteenpence.

EMMY. Then youll see her for me, wont you?

RIDGEON. Oh, send her up and be hanged. [Emmy trots out, satisfied, Ridgeon calls] Redpenny!

REDPENNY [appearing at the door] What is it?

RIDGEON. Theres a patient coming up. If she hasnt gone in five minutes, come in with an urgent call from the hospital for me. You understand: she's to have a strong hint to go.

REDPENNY. Right O! [He vanishes].

Ridgeon goes to the glass, and arranges his tie a little.

EMMY [announcing] Mrs Doobidad [Ridgeon

leaves the glass and goes to the writing-table].

The lady comes in. Emmy goes out and shuts the door. Ridgeon, who has put on an impenetrable and rather distant professional manner, turns to the lady, and invites her, by a gesture, to sit down on the couch.

Mrs Dubedat is beyond all demur an arrestingly good-looking young woman. She has something of the grace and romance of a wild creature, with a good deal of the elegance and dignity of a fine lady. Ridgeon, who is extremely susceptible to the beauty of women, instinctively assumes the defensive at once, and hardens his manner still more. He has an impression that she is very well dressed; but she has a figure on which any dress would look well, and carries herself with the unaffected distinction of a woman who has never in her life suffered from those doubts and fears as to her social position which spoil the manners of most middling people. She is tall, slender, and strong; has dark hair, dressed so as to look like hair and not like a bird's nest or a pantaloon's wig (fashion wavering just then between these two models); has unexpectedly narrow, subtle, dark-fringed eyes that alter her expression disturbingly when she is excited and flashes them wide open; is softly impetuous in her speech and swift in her movements; and is just now in mortal anxiety. She carries a portfolio.

MRS DUBEDAT [*in low urgent tones*] Doctor—

RIDGEON [*curtly*] Wait. Before you begin, let me tell you at once that I can do nothing for you. My hands are full. I sent you that message by my old servant. You would not take that answer.

MRS DUBEDAT. How could I?

RIDGEON. You bribed her.

MRS DUBEDAT. I—

RIDGEON. That doesnt matter. She coaxed me to see you. Well, you must take it from me now that with all the good will in the world, I cannot undertake another case.

MRS DUBEDAT. Doctor: you must save my husband. You must. When I explain to you, you will see that you must. It is not an ordinary case, not like any other case. He is not like anybody else in the world: oh, believe me, he is not. I can prove it to you: [*fingering her portfolio*] I have brought some things to shew you. And you can save him: the papers say you can.

RIDGEON. Whats the matter? Tuberculosis?

MRS DUBEDAT. Yes. His left lung—

RIDGEON. Yes: you neednt tell me about that.

MRS DUBEDAT. You can cure him, if only you will. It is true that you can, isnt it? [*In great distress*] Oh, tell me, please.

RIDGEON [*warningly*] You are going to be quiet and self-possessed, arnt you?

MRS DUBEDAT. Yes. I beg your pardon. I know I shouldnt— [*Giving way again*] Oh, please, say that you can; and then I shall be all right.

RIDGEON [*huffily*] I am not a curemonger: if you want cures, you must go to the people who sell them. [*Recovering himself, ashamed of the tone of his own voice*] But I have at the hospital ten tuberculous patients whose lives I believe I can save.

MRS DUBEDAT. Thank God!

RIDGEON. Wait a moment. Try to think of those ten patients as ten shipwrecked men on a raft—a raft that is barely large enough to save them—that will not support one more. Another head bobs up through the waves at the side. Another man begs to be taken aboard. He implores the captain of the raft to save him. But the captain can only do that by pushing one of his ten off the raft and drowning him to make room for the new comer. That is what you are asking me to do.

MRS DUBEDAT. But how can that be? I dont understand. Surely—

RIDGEON. You must take my word for it that it is so. My laboratory, my staff, and myself are working at full pressure. We are doing our utmost. The treatment is a new one. It takes time, means, and skill; and there is not enough for another case. Our ten cases are already chosen cases. Do you understand what I mean by chosen?

MRS DUBEDAT. Chosen. No: I cant understand.

RIDGEON [*sternly*] You must understand. Youve got to understand and to face it. In every single one of those ten cases I have had to consider, not only whether the man could be saved, but whether he was worth saving. There were fifty cases to choose from; and forty had to be condemned to death. Some of the forty had young wives and helpless children. If the hardness of their cases could have saved them they would have been saved ten times over. Ive no doubt your case is a hard one: I can see the tears in your eyes [*she hastily wipes her eyes*]: I know that you have a torrent of entreaties ready for me the moment I stop speaking; but it's no use.

You must go to another doctor.

MRS DUBEDAT. But can you give me the name of another doctor who understands your secret?

RIDGEON. I have no secret: I am not a quack.

MRS DUBEDAT. I beg your pardon: I didnt mean to say anything wrong. I dont understand how to speak to you. Oh pray dont be offended.

RIDGEON [again a little ashamed] There! there! never mind. [He relaxes and sits down]. After all, I'm talking nonsense: I daresay I am a quack, a quack with a qualification. But my discovery is not patented.

MRS DUBEDAT. Then can any doctor cure my husband? Oh, why dont they do it? I have tried so many: I have spent so much. If only you would give me the name of another doctor.

RIDGEON. Every man in this street is a doctor. But outside myself and the handful of men I am training at St Anne's, there is nobody as yet who has mastered the opsonin treatment. And we are full up? I'm sorry; but that is all I can say. [Rising] Good morning.

MRS DUBEDAT [suddenly and desperately taking some drawings from her portfolio] Doctor: look at these. You understand drawings: you have good ones in your waiting-room. Look at them. They are his work.

RIDGEON. It's no use my looking. [He looks, all the same] Hallo! [He takes one to the window and studies it]. Yes: this is the real thing. Yes, yes. [He looks at another and returns to her]. These are very clever. Theyre unfinished, arnt they?

MRS DUBEDAT. He gets tired so soon. But you see, dont you, what a genius he is? You see that he is worth saving. Oh, doctor, I married him just to help him to begin: I had money enough to tide him over the hard years at the beginning—to enable him to follow his inspiration until his genius was recognized. And I was useful to him as a model: his drawings of me sold quite quickly.

RIDGEON. Have you got one?

MRS DUBEDAT [producing another] Only this one. It was the first.

RIDGEON [devouring it with his eyes] Thats a wonderful drawing. Why is it called Jennifer?

MRS DUBEDAT. My name is Jennifer.

RIDGEON. A strange name.

MRS DUBEDAT. Not in Cornwall. I am Cornish. It's only what you call Guinevere.

RIDGEON [repeating the names with a certain pleasure in them] Guinevere. Jennifer. [Looking again at the drawing] Yes: it's really a wonderful drawing. Excuse me; but may I ask is it for sale? I'll buy it.

MRS DUBEDAT. Oh, take it. It's my own: he gave it to me. Take it. Take them all. Take everything; ask anything; but save him. You can: you will: you must.

REDPENNY [entering with every sign of alarm] Theyve just telephoned from the hospital that youre to come instantly—a patient on the point of death. The carriage is waiting.

RIDGEON [intolerantly] Oh, nonsense: get out. [Greatly annoyed] What do you mean by interrupting me like this?

REDPENNY. But—

RIDGEON. Chut! cant you see I'm engaged? Be off.

Redpenny, bewildered, vanishes.

MRS DUBEDAT [rising] Doctor: one instant only before you go—

RIDGEON. Sit down. It's nothing.

MRS DUBEDAT. But the patient. He said he was dying.

RIDGEON. Oh, he's dead by this time. Never mind. Sit down.

MRS DUBEDAT [sitting down and breaking down] Oh, you none of you care. You see people die every day.

RIDGEON [petting her] Nonsense! it's nothing: I told him to come in and say that. I thought I should want to get rid of you.

MRS DUBEDAT [shocked at the falsehood] Oh!

RIDGEON [continuing] Dont look so bewildered: theres nobody dying.

MRS DUBEDAT. My husband is.

RIDGEON [pulling himself together] Ah, yes: I had forgotten your husband. Mrs Dubedat: you are asking me to do a very serious thing?

MRS DUBEDAT. I am asking you to save the life of a great man.

RIDGEON. You are asking me to kill another man for his sake; for as surely as I undertake another case, I shall have to hand back one of the old ones to the ordinary treatment. Well, I dont shrink from that. I have had to do it before; and I will do it again if you can convince me that his life is more important than the worst life I am now saving. But you must convince me first.

MRS DUBEDAT. He made those drawings; and they are not the best—nothing like the best; only I did not bring the really best: so few people like them. He is twenty-three:

his whole life is before him. Wont you let me bring him to you? wont you speak to him? wont you see for yourself?

RIDGEON. Is he well enough to come to a dinner at the Star and Garter at Richmond?

MRS DUBEDAT. Oh yes. Why?

RIDGEON. I'll tell you. I am inviting all my old friends to a dinner to celebrate my knighthood—youve seen about it in the papers, havnt you?

MRS DUBEDAT. Yes, oh yes. That was how I found out about you.

RIDGEON. It will be a doctors' dinner; and it was to have been a bachelors' dinner. I'm a bachelor. Now if you will entertain for me, and bring your husband, he will meet me; and he will meet some of the most eminent men in my profession: Sir Patrick Cullen, Sir Ralph Bloomfield Bonington, Cutler Walpole, and others. I can put the case to them; and your husband will have to stand or fall by what we think of him. Will you come?

MRS DUBEDAT. Yes, of course I will come. Oh, thank you, thank you. And may I bring some of his drawings—the really good ones?

RIDGEON. Yes. I will let you know the date in the course of tomorrow. Leave me your address.

MRS DUBEDAT. Thank you again and again. You have made me so happy: I know you will admire him and like him. This is my address. [She gives him her card].

RIDGEON. Thank you. [He rings].

MRS DUBEDAT [embarrassed] May I—is there—should I—I mean— [she blushes and stops in confusion].

RIDGEON. Whats the matter?

MRS DUBEDAT. Your fee for this consultation?

RIDGEON. Oh, I forgot that. Shall we say a beautiful drawing of his favorite model for the whole treatment, including the cure?

MRS DUBEDAT. You are very generous. Thank you. I k n o w you will cure him. Goodbye.

RIDGEON. I will. Goodbye. [They shake hands]. By the way, you know, dont you, that tuberculosis is catching. You take every precaution, I hope.

MRS DUBEDAT. I am not likely to forget it. They treat us like lepers at the hotels.

EMMY [at the door] Well, deary: have you got round him?

RIDGEON. Yes. Attend to the door and hold your tongue.

EMMY. Thats a good boy. [She goes out with Mrs Dubedat].

RIDGEON [alone] Consultation free. Cure guaranteed. [He heaves a great sigh].

ACT II

After dinner on the terrace at the Star and Garter, Richmond. Cloudless summer night; nothing disturbs the stillness except from time to time the long trajectory of a distant train and the measured clucking of oars coming up from the Thames in the valley below. The dinner is over; and three of the eight chairs are empty. Sir Patrick, with his back to the view, is at the head of the square table with Ridgeon. The two chairs opposite them are empty. On their right come, first, a vacant chair, and then one very fully occupied by B. B., who basks blissfully in the moonbeams. On their left, Schutzmacher and Walpole. The entrance to the hotel is on their right, behind B. B. The five men are silently enjoying their coffee and cigarets, full of food, and not altogether void of wine.

Mrs Dubedat, wrapped up for departure, comes in. They rise, except Sir Patrick; but she takes one of the vacant places at the foot of the table, next B. B.; and they sit down again.

MRS DUBEDAT [as she enters] Louis will be here presently. He is shewing Dr Blenkinsop how to work the telephone. [She sits]. Oh, I am so sorry we have to go. It seems such a shame, this beautiful night. And we have enjoyed ourselves so much.

RIDGEON. I dont believe another half-hour would do Mr Dubedat a bit of harm.

SIR PATRICK. Come now, Colly, come! come! none of that. You take your man home, Mrs Dubedat; and get him to bed before eleven.

B. B. Yes, yes. Bed before eleven. Quite right, quite right. Sorry to lose you, my dear lady; but Sir Patrick's orders are the laws of—er—of Tyre and Sidon.

WALPOLE. Let me take you home in my motor.

SIR PATRICK. No. You ought to be ashamed of yourself, Walpole. Your motor will take Mr and Mrs Dubedat to the station, and quite far enough too for an open carriage at night.

MRS DUBEDAT. Oh, I am sure the train is best.

RIDGEON. Well, Mrs Dubedat, we have had a most enjoyable evening.

WALPOLE. ⎫ ⎧Most enjoyable.
B. B.   ⎬ ⎨Delightful. Charming. Unfor-
          ⎭ ⎩ gettable.

MRS DUBEDAT [*with a touch of shy anxiety*] What did you think of Louis? Or am I wrong to ask?

RIDGEON. Wrong! Why, we are all charmed with him.

WALPOLE. Delighted.

B. B. Most happy to have met him. A privilege, a real privilege.

SIR PATRICK [*grunts*]!

MRS DUBEDAT [*quickly*] Sir Patrick: are you uneasy about him?

SIR PATRICK [*discreetly*] I admire his drawings greatly, maam.

MRS DUBEDAT. Yes; but I meant—

RIDGEON. You shall go away quite happy. He's worth saving. He must and shall be saved.

Mrs Dubedat rises and gasps with delight, relief, and gratitude. They all rise except Sir Patrick and Schutzmacher, and come reassuringly to her.

B. B. Certainly, cer-tainly.

WALPOLE. Theres no real difficulty, if only you know what to do.

MRS DUBEDAT. Oh, how can I ever thank you! From this night I can begin to be happy at last. You dont know what I feel.

She sits down in tears. They crowd about her to console her.

B. B. My dear lady: come come! come come! [*very persuasively*] come come!

WALPOLE. Dont mind us. Have a good cry.

RIDGEON. No: dont cry. Your husband had better not know that weve been talking about him.

MRS DUBEDAT [*quickly pulling herself together*] No, of course not. Please dont mind me. What a glorious thing it must be to be a doctor! [*They laugh*]. Dont laugh. You dont know what youve done for me. I never knew until now how deadly afraid I was—how I had come to dread the worst. I never dared let myself know. But now the relief has come: now I know.

Louis Dubedat comes from the hotel, in his overcoat, his throat wrapped in a shawl. He is a slim young man of 23, physically still a stripling, and pretty, though not effeminate. He has turquoise blue eyes, and a trick of looking you straight in the face with them, which, combined with a frank smile, is very engaging. Although he is all nerves, and very observant and quick of apprehension, *he is not in the least shy. He is younger than Jennifer; but he patronizes her as a matter of course. The doctors do not put him out in the least: neither Sir Patrick's years nor Bloomfield Bonington's majesty have the smallest apparent effect on him: he is as natural as a cat: he moves among men as most men move among things, though he is intentionally making himself agreeable to them on this occasion. Like all people who can be depended on to take care of themselves, he is welcome company; and his artist's power of appealing to the imagination gains him credit for all sorts of qualities and powers, whether he possesses them or not.*

LOUIS [*pulling on his gloves behind Ridgeon's chair*] Now, Jinny-Gwinny: the motor has come round.

RIDGEON. Why do you let him spoil your beautiful name like that, Mrs Dubedat?

MRS DUBEDAT. Oh, on grand occasions I am Jennifer.

B. B. You are a bachelor: you do not understand these things, Ridgeon. Look at me [*They look*]. I also have two names. In moments of domestic worry, I am simple Ralph. When the sun shines in the home, I am Beedle-Deedle-Dumkins. Such is married life! Mr Dubedat: may I ask you to do me a favor before you go. Will you sign your name to this menu card, under the sketch you have made of me?

WALPOLE. Yes; and mine too, if you will be so good.

LOUIS. Certainly. [*He sits down and signs the cards*].

MRS DUBEDAT. Wont you sign Dr Schutzmacher's for him, Louis?

LOUIS. I dont think Dr Schutzmacher is pleased with his portrait. I'll tear it up. [*He reaches across the table for Schutzmacher's menu card, and is about to tear it. Schutzmacher makes no sign*].

RIDGEON. No, no: if Loony doesnt want it, I do.

LOUIS. I'll sign it for you with pleasure. [*He signs and hands it to Ridgeon*]. Ive just been making a little note of the river tonight: it will work up into something good [*he shews a pocket sketch-book*]. I think I'll call it the Silver Danube.

B. B. Ah, charming, charming.

WALPOLE. Very sweet. Youre a nailer at pastel.

Louis coughs, first out of modesty, then from tuberculosis.

SIR PATRICK. Now then, Mr Dubedat: youve had enough of the night air. Take him home, maam.

MRS DUBEDAT. Yes. Come, Louis.

RIDGEON. Never fear. Never mind. I'll make that cough all right.

B. B. We will stimulate the phagocytes. [*With tender effusion, shaking her hand*] Goodnight, Mrs Dubedat. Goodnight. Goodnight.

WALPOLE. If the phagocytes fail, come to me. I'll put you right.

LOUIS. Goodnight, Sir Patrick. Happy to have met you.

SIR PATRICK. 'Night [*half a grunt*].

MRS DUBEDAT. Goodnight, Sir Patrick.

SIR PATRICK. Cover yourself well up. Dont think your lungs are made of iron because theyre better than his. Goodnight.

MRS DUBEDAT. Thank you. Thank you. Nothing hurts me. Goodnight.

Louis goes out through the hotel without noticing Schutzmacher. Mrs Dubedat hesitates, then bows to him. Schutzmacher rises and bows formally, German fashion. She goes out, attended by Ridgeon. The rest resume their seats, ruminating or smoking quietly.

B. B. [*harmoniously*] Dee-lightful couple! Charming woman! Gifted lad! Remarkable talent! Graceful outlines! Perfect evening! Great success! Interesting case! Glorious night! Exquisite scenery! Capital dinner! Stimulating conversation! Restful outing! Good wine! Happy ending! Touching gratitude! Lucky Ridgeon—

RIDGEON [*returning*] Whats that? Calling me, B. B.? [*He goes back to his seat next Sir Patrick*].

B. B. No, no. Only congratulating you on a most successful evening! Enchanting woman! Thorough breeding! Gentle nature! Refined—

Blenkinsop comes from the hotel and takes the empty chair next Ridgeon.

BLENKINSOP. I'm so sorry to have left you like this, Ridgeon; but it was a telephone message from the police. Theyve found half a milkman at our level crossing with a prescription of mine in its pocket. Wheres Mr Dubedat?

RIDGEON. Gone.

BLENKINSOP [*rising, very pale*] Gone!

RIDGEON. Just this moment—

BLENKINSOP. Perhaps I could overtake him —[*he rushes into the hotel*].

WALPOLE [*calling after him*] He's in the

motor, man, miles off. You cant— [*giving it up*]. No use.

RIDGEON. Theyre really very nice people. I confess I was afraid the husband would turn out an appalling bounder. But he's almost as charming in his way as she is in hers. And theres no mistake about his being a genius. It's something to have got a case really worth saving. Somebody else will have to go; but at all events it will be easy to find a worse man.

SIR PATRICK. How do you know?

RIDGEON. Come now, Sir Paddy, no growling. Have something more to drink.

SIR PATRICK. No, thank you.

WALPOLE. Do you see anything wrong with Dubedat, B. B.?

B. B. Oh, a charming young fellow. Besides, after all, what could be wrong with him? Look at him. What could be wrong with him?

SIR PATRICK. There are two things that can be wrong with any man. One of them is a cheque. The other is a woman. Until you know that a man's sound on these two points, you know nothing about him.

B. B. Ah, cynic, cynic!

WALPOLE. He's all right as to the cheque, for a while at all events. He talked to me quite frankly before dinner as to the pressure of money difficulties on an artist. He says he has no vices and is very economical, but that theres one extravagance he cant afford and yet cant resist; and that is dressing his wife prettily. So I said, bang plump out, "Let me lend you twenty pounds, and pay me when your ship comes home." He was really very nice about it. He took it like a man; and it was a pleasure to see how happy it made him, poor chap.

B. B. [*who has listened to Walpole with growing perturbation*] But—but—but—when was this, may I ask?

WALPOLE. When I joined you that time down by the river.

B. B. But, my dear Walpole, he had just borrowed ten pounds from me.

WALPOLE. What!

SIR PATRICK [*grunts*]!

B. B. [*indulgently*] Well, well, it was really hardly borrowing; for he said heaven only knew when he could pay me. I couldnt refuse. It appears that Mrs Dubedat has taken a sort of fancy to me—

WALPOLE [*quickly*] No: it was to me.

B. B. Certainly not. Your name was never mentioned between us. He is so wrapped up in his work that he has to leave her a good deal alone; and the poor innocent young fellow—he has of course no idea of my position or how busy I am—actually wanted me to call occasionally and talk to her.

WALPOLE. Exactly what he said to me!

B. B. Pooh! Pooh pooh! Really, I must say. [*Much disturbed, he rises and goes up to the balustrade, contemplating the landscape vexedly*].

WALPOLE. Look here, Ridgeon! this is beginning to look serious.

Blenkinsop, very anxious and wretched, but trying to look unconcerned, comes back.

RIDGEON. Well, did you catch him?

BLENKINSOP. No. Excuse my running away like that. [*He sits down at the foot of the table, next Bloomfield Bonington's chair*].

WALPOLE. Anything the matter?

BLENKINSOP. Oh no. A trifle—something ridiculous. It cant be helped. Never mind.

RIDGEON. Was it anything about Dubedat?

BLENKINSOP [*almost breaking down*] I ought to keep it to myself, I know. I cant tell you, Ridgeon, how ashamed I am of dragging my miserable poverty to your dinner after all your kindness. It's not that you wont ask me again; but it's so humiliating. And I did so look forward to one evening in my dress clothes (theyre still presentable, you see) with all my troubles left behind, just like old times.

RIDGEON. But what has happened?

BLENKINSOP. Oh, nothing. It's too ridiculous. I had just scraped up four shillings for this little outing; and it cost me one-and-fourpence to get here. Well, Dubedat asked me to lend him half-a-crown to tip the chambermaid of the room his wife left her wraps in, and for the cloakroom. He said he only wanted it for five minutes, as she had his purse. So of course I lent it to him. And he's forgotten to pay me. I've just twopence to get back with.

RIDGEON. Oh, never mind that—

BLENKINSOP [*stopping him resolutely*] No: I know what youre going to say; but I wont take it. Ive never borrowed a penny; and I never will. Ive nothing left but my friends; and I wont sell them. If none of you were to be able to meet me without being afraid that my civility was leading up to the loan of five shillings, there would be an end of everything for me. I'll take your old clothes, Colly,

sooner than disgrace you by talking to you in the street in my own; but I wont borrow money. I'll train it as far as the twopence will take me; and I'll tramp the rest.

WALPOLE. Youll do the whole distance in my motor. [*They are all greatly relieved; and Walpole hastens to get away from the painful subject by adding*] Did he get anything out of you, Mr Schutzmacher?

SCHUTZMACHER [*shakes his head in a most expressive negative*].

WALPOLE. You didnt appreciate his drawing, I think.

SCHUTZMACHER. Oh yes I did. I should have liked very much to have kept the sketch and got it autographed.

B. B. But why didnt you?

SCHUTZMACHER. Well, the fact is, when I joined Dubedat after his conversation with Mr Walpole, he said that the Jews were the only people who knew anything about art, and that though he had to put up with your Philistine twaddle, as he called it, it was what I said about the drawings that really pleased him. He also said that his wife was greatly struck with my knowledge, and that she always admired Jews. Then he asked me to advance him £50 on the security of the drawings.

B. B.		No, no. Positively! Seriously!
WALPOLE	[*All exclaiming together*]	What! Another fifty!
BLENKINSOP		Think of that!
SIR PATRICK		[*grunts*]!

SCHUTZMACHER. Of course I couldnt lend money to a stranger like that.

B. B. I envy you the power to say No, Mr Schutzmacher. Of course, I knew I oughtnt to lend money to a young fellow in that way; but I simply hadnt the nerve to refuse. I couldnt very well, you know, could I?

SCHUTZMACHER. I dont understand that. *I* felt that I couldnt very well lend it.

WALPOLE. What did he say?

SCHUTZMACHER. Well, he made a very uncalled-for remark about a Jew not understanding the feelings of a gentleman. I must say you Gentiles are very hard to please. You say we are no gentlemen when we lend money; and when we refuse to lend it you say just the same. I didnt mean to behave badly. As I told him, I might have lent it to him if he had been a Jew himself.

SIR PATRICK [*with a grunt*] And what did he

say to that?

SCHUTZMACHER. Oh, he began trying to persuade me that he was one of the chosen people—that his artistic faculty shewed it, and that his name was as foreign as my own. He said he didnt really want £50; that he was only joking; that all he wanted was a couple of sovereigns.

B. B. No, no, Mr Schutzmacher. You invented that last touch. Seriously, now?

SCHUTZMACHER. No. You cant improve on Nature in telling stories about gentlemen like Mr Dubedat.

BLENKINSOP. You certainly do stand by one another, you chosen people, Mr Schutzmacher.

SCHUTZMACHER. Not at all. Personally, I like Englishmen better than Jews, and always associate with them. Thats only natural, because, as I am a Jew, theres nothing interesting in a Jew to me, whereas there is always something interesting and foreign in an Englishman. But in money matters it's quite different. You see, when an Englishman borrows, all he knows or cares is that he wants money; and he'll sign anything to get it, without in the least understanding it, or intending to carry out the agreement if it turns out badly for him. In fact, he thinks you a cad if you ask him to carry it out under such circumstances. Just like the Merchant of Venice, you know. But if a Jew makes an agreement, he means to keep it and expects you to keep it. If he wants money for a time, he borrows it and knows he must pay it at the end of the time. If he knows he cant pay, he begs it as a gift.

RIDGEON. Come, Loony! do you mean to say that Jews are never rogues and thieves?

SCHUTZMACHER. Oh, not at all. But I was not talking of criminals. I was comparing honest Englishmen with honest Jews.

One of the hotel maids, a pretty, fair-haired woman of about 25, comes from the hotel, rather furtively. She accosts Ridgeon.

THE MAID. I beg your pardon, sir—

RIDGEON. Eh?

THE MAID. I beg pardon, sir. It's not about the hotel. I'm not allowed to be on the terrace; and I should be discharged if I were seen speaking to you, unless you were kind enough to say you called me to ask whether the motor has come back from the station yet.

WALPOLE. Has it?

THE MAID. Yes, sir.

RIDGEON. Well, what do you want?

THE MAID. Would you mind, sir, giving me the address of the gentleman that was with you at dinner?

RIDGEON [*sharply*] Yes, of course I should mind very much. You have no right to ask.

THE MAID. Yes, sir, I know it looks like that. But what am I to do?

SIR PATRICK. Whats the matter with you?

THE MAID. Nothing, sir. I want the address: thats all.

B. B. You mean the young gentleman?

THE MAID. Yes, sir: that went to catch the train with the woman he brought with him.

RIDGEON. The woman! Do you mean the lady who dined here? the gentleman's wife?

THE MAID. Dont believe them, sir. She cant be his wife. I'm his wife.

B. B. }

RIDGEON } [*in amazed remonstrance*] My good girl!

WALPOLE } You his wife!

What! whats that? Oh, this is getting perfectly fascinating, Ridgeon.

THE MAID. I could run upstairs and get you my marriage lines in a minute, sir, if you doubt my word. He's Mr Louis Dubedat, isnt he?

RIDGEON. Yes.

THE MAID. Well, sir, you may believe me or not; but I'm the lawful Mrs Dubedat.

SIR PATRICK. And why arnt you living with your husband?

THE MAID. We couldnt afford it, sir. I had thirty pounds saved; and we spent it all on our honeymoon in three weeks, and a lot more that he borrowed. Then I had to go back into service, and he went to London to get work at his drawing; and he never wrote me a line or sent me an address. I never saw nor heard of him again until I caught sight of him from the window going off in the motor with that woman.

SIR PATRICK. Well, thats two wives to start with.

B. B. Now upon my soul I dont want to be uncharitable; but really I'm beginning to suspect that our young friend is rather careless.

SIR PATRICK. Beginning to think! How long will it take you, man, to find out that he's a damned young blackguard?

BLENKINSOP. Oh, thats severe, Sir Patrick, very severe. Of course it's bigamy; but still he's very young; and she's very pretty. Mr Walpole: may I spunge on you for another of those nice cigarets of yours? [*He changes his seat for the one next Walpole.*]

WALPOLE. Certainly. [*He feels in his pockets*]. Oh bother! Where—? [*Suddenly remembering*] I say: I recollect now: I passed my cigaret case to Dubedat and he didnt return it. It was a gold one.

THE MAID. He didnt mean any harm: he never thinks about things like that, sir. I'll get it back for you, sir, if youll tell me where to find him.

RIDGEON. What am I to do? Shall I give her the address or not?

SIR PATRICK. Give her your own address; and then we'll see. [*To the maid*] Youll have to be content with that for the present, my girl. [*Ridgeon gives her his card*]. Whats your name?

THE MAID. Minnie Tinwell, sir.

SIR PATRICK. Well, you write him a letter to care of this gentleman; and it will be sent on. Now be off with you.

THE MAID. Thank you, sir. I'm sure you wouldnt see me wronged. Thank you all, gentlemen; and excuse the liberty.

She goes into the hotel. They watch her in silence.

RIDGEON [*when she is gone*] Do you realize, you chaps, that we have promised Mrs Dubedat to save this fellow's life?

BLENKINSOP. Whats the matter with him?

RIDGEON. Tuberculosis.

BLENKINSOP [*interested*] And can you cure that?

RIDGEON. I believe so.

BLENKINSOP. Then I wish youd cure me. My right lung is touched, I'm sorry to say.

RIDGEON		What! your lung is going!
B. B.	[*all together*]	My dear Blenkinsop, what do you tell me? [*full of concern for Blenkinsop, he comes back from the balustrade*].
SIR PATRICK		Eh? Eh? whats that?
WALPOLE		Hullo! you mustnt neglect this, you know.

BLENKINSOP [*putting his fingers in his ears*] No, no: it's no use. I know what youre going to say: Ive said it often to others. I cant afford to take care of myself; and theres an end of it. If a fortnight's holiday would save my life, I'd have to die. I shall get on as others have to get on. We cant all go to St Moritz or to Egypt, you know, Sir Ralph. Dont talk about it.

Embarrassed silence.

SIR PATRICK [*grunts and looks hard at Ridgeon*]!

SCHUTZMACHER [*looking at his watch and rising*] I must go. It's been a very pleasant evening, Colly. You might let me have my portrait if you dont mind. I'll send Mr Dubedat that couple of sovereigns for it.

RIDGEON [*giving him the menu card*] Oh dont do that, Loony. I dont think he'd like that.

SCHUTZMACHER. Well, of course I shant if you feel that way about it. But I dont think you understand Dubedat. However, perhaps thats because I'm a Jew. Goodnight, Dr Blenkinsop [*shaking hands*].

BLENKINSOP. Goodnight, sir—I mean—Goodnight.

SCHUTZMACHER [*waving his hand to the rest*] Goodnight, everybody.

WALPOLE	
B. B.	Goodnight.
SIR PATRICK	
RIDGEON	

B. B. repeats the salutation several times, in varied musical tones. Schutzmacher goes out.

SIR PATRICK. It's time for us all to move. [*He rises and comes between Blenkinsop and Walpole. Ridgeon also rises*]. Mr Walpole: take Blenkinsop home: he's had enough of the open air cure for tonight. Have you a thick overcoat to wear in the motor, Dr Blenkinsop?

BLENKINSOP. Oh, theyll give me some brown paper in the hotel; and a few thicknesses of brown paper across the chest are better than any fur coat.

WALPOLE. Well, come along. Goodnight, Colly. Youre coming with us, arnt you, B. B.?

B. B. Yes: I'm coming. [*Walpole and Blenkinsop go into the hotel*]. Goodnight, my dear Ridgeon [*shaking hands affectionately*]. Dont let us lose sight of your interesting patient and his very charming wife. We must not judge him too hastily, you know. [*With unction*] Goooooooodnight, Paddy. Bless you, dear old chap. [*Sir Patrick utters a formidable grunt. B. B. laughs and pats him indulgently on the shoulder*] Goodnight. Goodnight. Goodnight. Goodnight. [*He goodnights *himself into the hotel*].

The others have meanwhile gone without ceremony. Ridgeon and Sir Patrick are left alone together. Ridgeon, deep in thought, comes down to Sir Patrick.

SIR PATRICK. Well, Mr Savior of Lives: which is it to be? that honest decent man Blenkinsop, or that rotten blackguard of an artist, eh?

RIDGEON. It's not an easy case to judge, is it? Blenkinsop's an honest decent man; but is he any use? Dubedat's a rotten blackguard; but he's a genuine source of pretty and pleasant and good things.

SIR PATRICK. What will he be a source of for that poor innocent wife of his, when she finds him out?

RIDGEON. Thats true. Her life will be a hell.

SIR PATRICK. And tell me this. Suppose you had this choice put before you: either to go through life and find all the pictures bad but all the men and women good, or to go through life and find all the pictures good and all the men and women rotten. Which would you choose?

RIDGEON. Thats a devilishly difficult question, Paddy. The pictures are so agreeable, and the good people so infernally disagreeable and mischievous, that I really cant undertake to say offhand which I should prefer to do without.

SIR PATRICK. Come come! none of your cleverness with me: I'm too old for it. Blenkinsop isnt that sort of good man; and you know it.

RIDGEON. It would be simpler if Blenkinsop could paint Dubedat's pictures.

SIR PATRICK. It would be simpler still if Dubedat had some of Blenkinsop's honesty. The world isnt going to be made simple for you, my lad: you must take it as it is. Youve to hold the scales between Blenkinsop and Dubedat. Hold them fairly.

RIDGEON. Well, I'll be as fair as I can. I'll put into one scale all the pounds Dubedat has borrowed, and into the other all the halfcrowns that Blenkinsop hasnt borrowed.

SIR PATRICK. And youll take out of Dubedat's scale all the faith he has destroyed and the honor he has lost, and youll put into Blenkinsop's scale all the faith he has justified and the honor he has created.

RIDGEON. Come come, Paddy! none of your claptrap with me: I'm too sceptical for it. I'm not at all convinced that the world wouldnt be a better world if everybody behaved as Dubedat does than it is now that everybody behaves as Blenkinsop does.

SIR PATRICK. Then why dont you behave as Dubedat does?

RIDGEON. Ah, that beats me. Thats the experimental test. Still, it's a dilemma. It's a dilemma. You see theres a complication we havnt mentioned.

SIR PATRICK. Whats that?

RIDGEON. Well, if I let Blenkinsop die, at least nobody can say I did it because I wanted to marry his widow.

SIR PATRICK. Eh! Whats that?

RIDGEON. Now if I let Dubedat die, I'll marry his widow.

SIR PATRICK. Perhaps she wont have you, you know.

RIDGEON [*with a self-assured shake of the head*] I've a pretty good flair for that sort of thing. I know when a woman is interested in me. She is.

SIR PATRICK. Well, sometimes a man knows best; and sometimes he knows worst. Youd much better cure them both.

RIDGEON. I cant. I'm at my limit. I can squeeze in one more case, but not two. I must choose.

SIR PATRICK. Well, you must choose as if she didnt exist: thats clear.

RIDGEON. Is that clear to you? Mind: it's not clear to me. She troubles my judgment.

SIR PATRICK. To me, it's a plain choice between a man and a lot of pictures.

RIDGEON. It's easier to replace a dead man than a good picture.

SIR PATRICK. Colly: when you live in an age that runs to pictures and statues and plays and brass bands because its men and women are not good enough to comfort its poor aching soul, you should thank Providence that you belong to a profession which is a high and great profession because its business is to heal and mend men and women.

RIDGEON. In short, as a member of a high and great profession, I'm to kill my patient.

SIR PATRICK. Dont talk wicked nonsense. You cant kill him. But you can leave him in other hands.

RIDGEON. In B. B.'s, for instance: eh? [*looking at him significantly*].

SIR PATRICK [*demurely facing his look*] Sir Ralph Bloomfield Bonington is a very eminent physician.

RIDGEON. He is.

SIR PATRICK. I'm going for my hat.

Ridgeon strikes the bell as Sir Patrick makes for the hotel. A waiter comes.

RIDGEON [*to the waiter*] My bill, please.

WAITER. Yes, sir.

He goes for it.

ACT III

In Dubedat's studio. Viewed from the large window the outer door is in the wall on the left at the near end. The door leading to the inner rooms is in the opposite wall, at the far end. The facing wall has neither window nor door. The plaster on all the walls is uncovered and undecorated, except by scrawlings of charcoal sketches and memoranda. There is a studio throne (a chair on a dais) a little to the left, opposite the inner door, and an easel to the right, opposite the outer door, with a dilapidated chair at it. Near the easel and against the wall is a bare wooden table with bottles and jars of oil and medium, paint-smudged rags, tubes of color, brushes, charcoal, a small lay figure, a kettle and spirit-lamp, and other odds and ends. By the table is a sofa, littered with drawing blocks, sketch-books, loose sheets of paper, newspapers, books, and more smudged rags. Next the outer door is an umbrella and hatstand, occupied partly by Louis' hats and cloak and muffler, and partly by odds and ends of costumes. There is an old piano stool on the near side of this door. In the corner near the inner door is a little tea-table. A lay figure, in a cardinal's robe and hat, with an hour-glass in one hand and a scythe slung on its back, smiles with inane malice at Louis, who, in a milkman's smock much smudged with color, is painting a piece of brocade which he has draped about his wife. She is sitting on the throne, not interested in the painting, and appealing to him very anxiously about another matter.

MRS DUBEDAT. Promise.

LOUIS [*putting on a touch of paint with notable skill and care and answering quite perfunctorily*] I promise, my darling.

MRS DUBEDAT. When you want money, you will always come to me.

LOUIS. But it's so sordid, dearest. I hate money. I cant keep always bothering you for money, money, money. Thats what drives me sometimes to ask other people, though I hate doing it.

MRS DUBEDAT. It is far better to ask me, dear. It gives people a wrong idea of you.

LOUIS. But I want to spare your little fortune, and raise money on my own work.

Dont be unhappy, love: I can easily earn enough to pay it all back. I shall have a one-man-show next season; and then there will be no more money troubles. [*Putting down his palette*] There! I mustnt do any more on that until it's bone-dry; so you may come down.

MRS DUBEDAT [*throwing off the drapery as she steps down, and revealing a plain frock of tussore silk*] But you have promised, remember, seriously and faithfully, never to borrow again until you have first asked me.

LOUIS. Seriously and faithfully. [*Embracing her*] Ah, my love, how right you are! how much it means to me to have you by me to guard me against living too much in the skies. On my solemn oath, from this moment forth I will never borrow another penny.

MRS DUBEDAT [*delighted*] Ah, thats right. Does his wicked worrying wife torment him and drag him down from the clouds. [*She kisses him*]. And now, dear, wont you finish those drawings for Maclean?

LOUIS. Oh, they dont matter. Ive got nearly all the money from him in advance.

MRS DUBEDAT. But, dearest, that is just the reason why you should finish them. He asked me the other day whether you really intended to finish them.

LOUIS. Confound his impudence! What the devil does he take me for? Now that just destroys all my interest in the beastly job. Ive a good mind to throw up the commission, and pay him back his money.

MRS DUBEDAT. We cant afford that, dear. You had better finish the drawings and have done with them. I think it is a mistake to accept money in advance.

LOUIS. But how are we to live?

MRS DUBEDAT. Well, Louis, it is getting hard enough as it is, now that they are all refusing to pay except on delivery.

LOUIS. Damn those fellows! they think of nothing and care for nothing but their wretched money.

MRS DUBEDAT. Still, if they pay us, they ought to have what they pay for.

LOUIS [*coaxing*] There now: thats enough lecturing for today. Ive promised to be good, havnt I?

MRS DUBEDAT [*putting her arms round his neck*] You know that I hate lecturing, and that I dont for a moment misunderstand you, dear, dont you?

LOUIS [*fondly*] I know. I know. I'm a wretch and youre an angel. Oh, if only I were strong enough to work steadily, I'd make my darling's house a temple, and her shrine a chapel more beautiful than was ever imagined. I cant pass the shops without wrestling with the temptation to go in and order all the really good things they have for you.

MRS DUBEDAT. I want nothing but you, dear. [*She gives him a caress, to which he responds so passionately that she disengages herself*]. There! be good now: remember that the doctors are coming this morning. Isnt it extraordinarily kind of them, Louis, to insist on coming? all of them, to consult about you?

LOUIS [*coolly*] Oh, I daresay they think it will be a feather in their cap to cure a rising artist. They wouldnt come if it didnt amuse them, anyhow. [*Someone knocks at the door*]. I say: it's not time yet, is it?

MRS DUBEDAT. No, not quite yet.

LOUIS [*opening the door and finding Ridgeon there*] Hello, Ridgeon. Delighted to see you. Come in.

MRS DUBEDAT [*shaking hands*] It's so good of you to come, doctor.

LOUIS. Excuse this place, wont you? It's only a studio, you know: theres no real convenience for living here. But we pig along somehow, thanks to Jennifer.

MRS DUBEDAT. Now I'll run away. Perhaps later on, when youre finished with Louis, I may come in and hear the verdict. [*Ridgeon bows rather constrainedly*]. Would you rather I didn't?

RIDGEON. Not at all. Not at all.

Mrs Dubedat looks at him, a little puzzled by his formal manner; then goes into the inner room.

LOUIS [*flippantly*] I say: dont look so grave. Theres nothing awful going to happen, is there?

RIDGEON. No.

LOUIS. Thats all right. Poor Jennifer has been looking forward to your visit more than you can imagine. Shes taken quite a fancy to you, Ridgeon. The poor girl has nobody to talk to: I'm always painting. [*Taking up a sketch*] Theres a little sketch I made of her yesterday.

RIDGEON. She shewed it to me a fortnight ago when she first called on me.

LOUIS [*quite unabashed*] Oh! did she? Good Lord! how time does fly! I could have sworn I'd only just finished it. It's hard for her here, seeing me piling up drawings and nothing coming in for them. Of course I shall sell them next year fast enough, after my one-man-show; but while the grass grows the steed starves. I hate to have her coming to me for money, and having none to give her. But what can I do?

RIDGEON. I understood that Mrs Dubedat had some property of her own.

LOUIS. Oh yes, a little; but how could a man with any decency of feeling touch that? Suppose I did, what would she have to live on if I died? I'm not insured: cant afford the premiums. [*Picking out another drawing*] How do you like that?

RIDGEON [*putting it aside*] I have not come here today to look at your drawings. I have more serious and pressing business with you.

LOUIS. You want to sound my wretched lung. [*With impulsive candor*] My dear Ridgeon: I'll be frank with you. Whats the matter in this house isnt lungs but bills. It doesnt matter about me; but Jennifer has actually to economise in the matter of food. Youve made us feel that we can treat you as a friend. Will you lend us a hundred and fifty pounds?

RIDGEON. No.

LOUIS [*surprised*] Why not?

RIDGEON. I am not a rich man; and I want every penny I can spare and more for my researches.

LOUIS. You mean youd want the money back again.

RIDGEON. I presume people sometimes have that in view when they lend money.

LOUIS [*after a moment's reflection*] Well, I can manage that for you. I'll give you a cheque—or see here: theres no reason why you shouldnt have your bit too: I'll give you a cheque for two hundred.

RIDGEON. Why not cash the cheque at once without troubling me?

LOUIS. Bless you! they wouldnt cash it: I'm overdrawn as it is. No: the way to work it is this. I'll postdate the cheque next October. In October Jennifer's dividends come in. Well, you present the cheque. It will be returned marked " refer to drawer" or some rubbish of that sort. Then you can take it to Jennifer, and hint that if the cheque isnt taken up at once I shall be put in prison. She'll pay you like a shot. Youll clear £50; and youll do me a real service; for I do want the money very badly, old chap, I assure you.

RIDGEON [*staring at him*] You see no objection to the transaction; and you anticipate none from me!

LOUIS. Well, what objection can there be?

It's quite safe. I can convince you about the dividends.

RIDGEON. I mean on the score of its being—shall I say dishonorable?

LOUIS. Well, of course I shouldnt suggest it if I didnt want the money.

RIDGEON. Indeed! Well, you will have to find some other means of getting it.

LOUIS. Do you mean that you refuse?

RIDGEON. Do I mean—! [letting his indignation loose] Of course I refuse, man. What do you take me for? How dare you make such a proposal to me?

LOUIS. Why not?

RIDGEON. Faugh! You would not understand me if I tried to explain. Now, once for all, I will not lend you a farthing. I should be glad to help your wife; but lending you money is no service to her.

LOUIS. Oh well, if youre in earnest about helping her, I'll tell you what you might do. You might get your patients to buy some of my things, or to give me a few portrait commissions.

RIDGEON. My patients call me in as a physician, not as a commercial traveller.

A knock at the door. Louis goes unconcernedly to open it, pursuing the subject as he goes.

LOUIS. But you must have great influence with them. You must know such lots of things about them—private things that they wouldnt like to have known. They wouldnt dare to refuse you.

RIDGEON [exploding] Well, upon my—

Louis opens the door, and admits Sir Patrick, Sir Ralph, and Walpole.

RIDGEON [proceeding furiously] Walpole: Ive been here hardly ten minutes; and already he's tried to borrow £150 from me. Then he proposed that I should get the money for him by blackmailing his wife; and youve just interrupted him in the act of suggesting that I should blackmail my patients into sitting to him for their portraits.

LOUIS. Well, Ridgeon, if this is what you call being an honorable man! I spoke to you in confidence.

SIR PATRICK. We're all going to speak to you in confidence, young man.

WALPOLE [hanging his hat on the only peg left vacant on the hat-stand] We shall make ourselves at home for half an hour, Dubedat. Dont be alarmed: youre a most fascinating chap; and we love you.

LOUIS. Oh, all right, all right. Sit down—

anywhere you can. Take this chair, Sir Patrick [indicating the one on the throne]. Up-z-z-z! [helping him up: Sir Patrick grunts and enthrones himself]. Here you are, B. B. [Sir Ralph glares at the familiarity; but Louis, quite undisturbed, puts a big book and a sofa cushion on the dais, on Sir Patrick's right; and B. B. sits down, under protest]. Let me take your hat. [He takes B. B.'s hat unceremoniously, and substitutes it for the cardinal's hat on the head of the lay figure, thereby ingeniously destroying the dignity of the conclave. He then draws the piano stool from the wall and offers it to Walpole]. You dont mind this, Walpole, do you? [Walpole accepts the stool, and puts his hand into his pocket for his cigaret case. Missing it, he is reminded of his loss].

WALPOLE. By the way, I'll trouble you for my cigaret case, if you dont mind?

LOUIS. What cigaret case?

WALPOLE. The gold one I lent you at the Star and Garter.

LOUIS [surprised] Was that yours?

WALPOLE. Yes.

LOUIS. I'm awfully sorry, old chap. I wondered whose it was. I'm sorry to say this is all thats left of it. [He hitches up his smock; produces a card from his waistcoat pocket; and hands it to Walpole].

WALPOLE. A pawn ticket!

LOUIS [reassuringly] It's quite safe: he cant sell it for a year, you know. I say, my dear Walpole, I am sorry. [He places his hand ingenuously on Walpole's shoulder and looks frankly at him].

WALPOLE [sinking on the stool with a gasp] Dont mention it. It adds to your fascination.

RIDGEON [who has been standing near the easel] Before we go any further, you have a debt to pay, Mr Dubedat.

LOUIS. I have a precious lot of debts to pay, Ridgeon. I'll fetch you a chair. [He makes for the inner door].

RIDGEON [stopping him] You shall not leave the room until you pay it. It's a small one; and pay it you must and shall. I dont so much mind your borrowing £10 from one of my guests and £20 from the other—

WALPOLE. I walked into it, you know. I offered it.

RIDGEON. —they could afford it. But to clean poor Blenkinsop out of his last half-crown was damnable. I intend to give him that half-crown and to be in a position to pledge him my word that you paid it. I'll have that out of you, at all events.

B. B. Quite right, Ridgeon. Quite right. Come, young man! down with the dust. Pay up.

LOUIS. Oh, you neednt make such a fuss about it. Of course I'll pay it. I had no idea the poor fellow was hard up. I'm as shocked as any of you about it. [*Putting his hand into his pocket*] Here you are. [*Finding his pocket empty*] Oh, I say, I havnt any money on me just at present. Walpole: would you mind lending me half-a-crown just to settle this.

WALPOLE. Lend you half— [*his voice faints away*].

LOUIS. Well, if you dont, Blenkinsop wont get it; for I havnt a rap: you may search my pockets if you like.

WALPOLE. Thats conclusive. [*He produces half-a-crown*].

LOUIS [*passing it to Ridgeon*] There! I'm really glad thats settled: it was the only thing that was on my conscience. Now I hope youre all satisfied.

SIR PATRICK. Not quite, Mr Dubedat. Do you happen to know a young woman named Minnie Tinwell?

LOUIS. Minnie! I should think I do; and Minnie knows me too. She's a really nice good girl, considering her station. Whats become of her?

WALPOLE. It's no use bluffing, Dubedat. Weve seen Minnie's marriage lines.

LOUIS [*coolly*] Indeed? Have you seen Jennifer's?

RIDGEON [*rising in irrepressible rage*] Do you dare insinuate that Mrs Dubedat is living with you without being married to you?

LOUIS. Why not?

B. B.   ⎫ [*echoing him in* ⎧ Why not!
SIR PATRICK ⎪ *various tones of* ⎪ Why not!
RIDGEON   ⎬ *scandalized*   ⎨ Why not!
WALPOLE   ⎭ *amazement*]   ⎩ Why not!

LOUIS. Yes, why not? Lots of people do it: just as good people as you. Why dont you learn to think, instead of bleating and baah-ing like a lot of sheep when you come up against anything youre not accustomed to? [*Contemplating their amazed faces with a chuckle*] I say: I should like to draw the lot of you now: you do look jolly foolish. Especially you, Ridgeon. I had you that time, you know.

RIDGEON. How, pray?

LOUIS. Well, you set up to appreciate Jennifer, you know. And you despise me, dont you?

RIDGEON [*curtly*] I loathe you. [*He sits down again on the sofa*].

LOUIS. Just so. And yet you believe that Jennifer is a bad lot because you think I told you so.

RIDGEON. Were you lying?

LOUIS. No; but you were smelling out a scandal instead of keeping your mind clean and wholesome. I can just play with people like you. I only asked you had you seen Jennifer's marriage lines; and you concluded straight away that she hadnt got any. You dont know a lady when you see one.

B. B. [*majestically*] What do you mean by that, may I ask?

LOUIS. Now, I'm only an immoral artist; but if youd told me that Jennifer wasnt married, I'd have had the gentlemanly feel-ing and artistic instinct to say that she carried her marriage certificate in her face and in her character. But you are all moral men; and Jennifer is only an artist's wife—probably a model; and morality consists in suspecting other people of not being legally married. Arnt you ashamed of yourselves? Can one of you look me in the face after it?

WALPOLE. It's very hard to look you in the face, Dubedat; you have such a dazzling cheek. What about Minnie Tinwell, eh?

LOUIS. Minnie Tinwell is a young woman who has had three weeks of glorious happi-ness in her poor little life, which is more than most girls in her position get, I can tell you. Ask her whether she'd take it back if she could. She's got her name into history, that girl. My little sketches of her will be fought for by collectors at Christie's. She'll have a page in my biography. Pretty good, that, for a still-room maid at a seaside hotel, I think. What have you fellows done for her to com-pare with that?

RIDGEON. We havnt trapped her into a mock marriage and deserted her.

LOUIS. No: you wouldnt have the pluck. But dont fuss yourselves. *I* didnt desert little Minnie. We spent all our money—

WALPOLE. All her money. Thirty pounds.

LOUIS. I said all ou r money: hers and mine too. Her thirty pounds didnt last three days. I had to borrow four times as much to spend on her. But I didnt grudge it; and she didnt grudge her few pounds either, the brave little lassie. When we were cleaned out, we'd had enough of it: you can hardly suppose that we were fit company for longer than that: I an artist, and she quite out of art and literature and refined living and everything else. There was no desertion, no misunderstanding, no police court or divorce court sensation for you moral chaps to lick your lips over at breakfast. We just said, Well, the money's gone: weve had a good time that can never be taken from us; so kiss; part good friends; and she back to service, and I back to my studio and my Jennifer, both the better and happier for our holiday.

WALPOLE. Quite a little poem, by George!

B. B. If you had been scientifically trained, Mr Dubedat, you would know how very seldom an actual case bears out a principle. In medical practice a man may die when, scientifically speaking, he ought to have lived. I have actually known a man die of a disease from which he was, scientifically speaking, immune. But that does not affect the fundamental truth of science. In just the same way, in moral cases, a man's behaviour may be quite harmless and even beneficial, when he is morally behaving like a scoundrel. And he may do great harm when he is morally acting on the highest principles. But that does not affect the fundamental truth of morality.

SIR PATRICK. And it doesnt affect the criminal law on the subject of bigamy.

LOUIS. Oh bigamy! bigamy! bigamy! What a fascination anything connected with the police has for you all, you moralists! Ive proved to you that you were utterly wrong on the moral point: now I'm going to shew you that youre utterly wrong on the legal point; and I hope it will be a lesson to you not to be so jolly cocksure next time.

WALPOLE. Rot! You were married already when you married her; and that settles it.

LOUIS. Does it! Why cant you think? How do you know she wasnt married already too?

B. B. ⎫
RIDGEON ⎬ [all crying out together] ⎰ Walpole! Ridgeon! This is beyond everything.
WALPOLE ⎬ Well, damn me!
SIR PATRICK ⎭ You young rascal.

LOUIS [ignoring their outcry] She was married to the steward of a liner. He cleared out and left her; and she thought, poor girl, that it was the law that if you hadnt heard of your husband for three years you might marry again. So as she was a thoroughly respectable girl and refused to have anything to say to me unless we were married I went through

the ceremony to please her and to preserve her self-respect.

RIDGEON. Did you tell her you were already married?

LOUIS. Of course not. Dont you see that if she had known, she wouldnt have considered herself my wife? You dont seem to understand, somehow.

SIR PATRICK. You let her risk imprisonment in her ignorance of the law?

LOUIS. Well, I risked imprisonment for her sake. I could have been had up for it just as much as she. But when a man makes a sacrifice of that sort for a woman, he doesnt go and brag about it to her; at least, not if he's a gentleman.

WALPOLE. What are we to do with this daisy!

LOUIS [impatiently] Oh, go and do whatever the devil you please. Put Minnie in prison. Put me in prison. Kill Jennifer with the disgrace of it all. And then, when youve done all the mischief you can, go to church and feel good about it. [He sits down pettishly on the old chair at the easel, and takes up a sketching block, on which he begins to draw].

WALPOLE. He's got us.

SIR PATRICK [grimly] He has.

B. B. But is he to be allowed to defy the criminal law of the land?

SIR PATRICK. The criminal law is no use to decent people. It only helps blackguards to blackmail their families. What are we family doctors doing half our time but conspiring with the family solicitor to keep some rascal out of jail and some family out of disgrace?

B. B. But at least it will punish him.

SIR PATRICK. Oh yes: itll punish him. Itll punish not only him but everybody connected with him, innocent and guilty alike. Itll throw his board and lodging on our rates and taxes for a couple of years, and then turn him loose on us a more dangerous blackguard than ever. Itll put the girl in prison and ruin her: itll lay his wife's life waste. You may put the criminal law out of your head once for all: it's only fit for fools and savages.

LOUIS. Would you mind turning your face a little more this way, Sir Patrick. [Sir Patrick turns indignantly and glares at him]. Oh, thats too much.

SIR PATRICK. Put down your foolish pencil, man; and think of your position. You can defy the laws made by men; but there are other laws to reckon with. Do you know that youre going to die?

LOUIS. We're all going to die, arnt we?

WALPOLE. We're not all going to die in six months.

LOUIS. How do you know?

This for B. B. is the last straw. He completely loses his temper and begins to walk excitedly about.

B. B. Upon my soul, I will not stand this. It is in questionable taste under any circumstances or in any company to harp on the subject of death; but it is a dastardly advantage to take of a medical man. [*Thundering at Dubedat*] I will not allow it, do you hear?

LOUIS. Well, I didnt begin it: you chaps did. It's always the way with the inartistic professions: when theyre beaten in argument they fall back on intimidation. I never knew a lawyer yet who didnt threaten to put me in prison sooner or later. I never knew a parson who didnt threaten me with damnation. And now y o u threaten me with death. With all your tall talk youve only one real trump in your hand, and thats Intimidation. Well, I'm not a coward; so it's no use with me.

B. B. [*advancing upon him*] I'll tell you what you are, sir. Youre a scoundrel.

LOUIS. Oh, I dont mind you calling me a scoundrel a bit. It's only a word: a word that you dont know the meaning of. What is a scoundrel?

B. B. Y o u are a scoundrel, sir.

LOUIS. Just so. What is a scoundrel? I am. What am I? A scoundrel. It's just arguing in a circle. And you imagine youre a man of science!

B. B. I—I—I—I have a good mind to take you by the scruff of your neck, you infamous rascal, and give you a sound thrashing.

LOUIS. I wish you would. Youd pay me something handsome to keep it out of court afterwards [*B. B., baffled, flings away from him with a snort*]. Have you any more civilities to address to me in my own house? I should like to get them over before my wife comes back. [*He resumes his sketching*].

RIDGEON. My mind's made up. When the law breaks down, honest men must find a remedy for themselves. I will not lift a finger to save this reptile.

B. B. That is the word I was trying to remember. Reptile.

WALPOLE. I cant help rather liking you, Dubedat. But you certainly are a thoroughgoing specimen.

SIR PATRICK. You know our opinion of you now, at all events.

LOUIS [*patiently putting down his pencil*] Look here. All this is no good. You dont understand. You imagine that I'm simply an ordinary criminal.

WALPOLE. Not an ordinary one, Dubedat. Do yourself justice.

LOUIS. Well, youre on the wrong tack altogether. I'm not a criminal. All your moralizings have no value for me. I dont believe in morality. I'm a disciple of Bernard Shaw.

SIR PATRICK } [*puzzled*] Eh?
B. B.   } [*waving his hand as if the subject were now disposed of*] Thats enough: I wish to hear no more.

LOUIS. Of course I havnt the ridiculous vanity to set up to be exactly a Superman; but still, it's an ideal that I strive towards just as any other man strives towards his ideal.

B. B. [*intolerant*] Dont trouble to explain. I now understand you perfectly. Say no more, please. When a man pretends to discuss science, morals, and religion, and then avows himself a follower of a notorious and avowed antivaccinationist, there is nothing more to be said. [*Suddenly putting in an effusive saving clause in parenthesis to Ridgeon*] Not, my dear Ridgeon, that I believe in vaccination in the popular sense any more than you do: I neednt tell you that. But there are things that p l a c e a man socially; and antivaccination is one of them. [*He resumes his seat on the dais*].

SIR PATRICK. Bernard Shaw? I never heard of him. He's a Methodist preacher, I suppose.

LOUIS [*scandalized*] No, no. He's the most advanced man now living: he isnt anything.

SIR PATRICK. I assure you, young man, my father learnt the doctrine of deliverance from sin from John Wesley's own lips before you or Mr Shaw were born. It used to be very popular as an excuse for putting sand in sugar and water in milk. Youre a sound Methodist, my lad; only you dont know it.

LOUIS [*seriously annoyed for the first time*] It's an intellectual insult. I dont believe theres such a thing as sin.

SIR PATRICK. Well, sir, there are people who dont believe theres such a thing as disease either. They call themselves Christian Scientists, I believe. Theyll just suit your complaint. We can do nothing for you. [*He* rises]. Good afternoon to you.

LOUIS [running to him piteously] Oh dont get up, Sir Patrick. Dont go. Please dont. I didnt mean to shock you, on my word. Do sit down again. Give me another chance. Two minutes more: thats all I ask.

SIR PATRICK [surprised by this sign of grace, and a little touched] Well— [He sits down]—

LOUIS [gratefully] Thanks awfully.

SIR PATRICK [continuing]— I dont mind giving you two minutes more. But dont address yourself to me; for Ive retired from practice; and I dont pretend to be able to cure your complaint. Your life is in the hands of these gentlemen.

RIDGEON. Not in mine. My hands are full. I have no time and no means available for this case.

SIR PATRICK. What do you say, Mr Walpole?

WALPOLE. Oh, I'll take him in hand: I dont mind. I feel perfectly convinced that this is not a moral case at all: it's a physical one. Theres something abnormal about his brain. That means, probably, some morbid condition affecting the spinal cord. And that means the circulation. In short, it's clear to me that he's suffering from an obscure form of blood-poisoning, which is almost certainly due to an accumulation of ptomaines in the nuciform sac. I'll remove the sac—

LOUIS [changing color] Do you mean, operate on me? Ugh! No, thank you.

WALPOLE. Never fear: you wont feel anything. Youll be under an anæsthetic, of course. And it will be extraordinarily interesting.

LOUIS. Oh, well, if it would interest you, and if it wont hurt, thats another matter. How much will you give me to let you do it?

WALPOLE [rising indignantly] How much! What do you mean?

LOUIS. Well, you dont expect me to let you cut me up for nothing, do you?

WALPOLE. Will you paint my portrait for nothing?

LOUIS. No; but I'll give you the portrait when it's painted; and you can sell it afterwards for perhaps double the money. But I cant sell my nuciform sac when youve cut it out.

WALPOLE. Ridgeon: did you ever hear anything like this! [To Louis] Well, you can keep your nuciform sac, and your tubercular lung, and your diseased brain: Ive done with you. One would think I was not conferring a favor on the fellow! [He returns to his stool in high dudgeon].

SIR PATRICK. That leaves only one medical man who has not withdrawn from your case, Mr Dubedat. You have nobody left to appeal to now but Sir Ralph Bloomfield Bonington.

WALPOLE. If I were you, B. B., I shouldnt touch him with a pair of tongs. Let him take his lungs to the Brompton Hospital. They wont cure him; but theyll teach him manners.

B. B. My weakness is that I have never been able to say No, even to the most thoroughly undeserving people. Besides, I am bound to say that I dont think it is possible in medical practice to go into the question of the value of the lives we save. Just consider, Ridgeon. Let me put it to you, Paddy. Clear your mind of cant, Walpole.

WALPOLE [indignantly] My mind is perfectly clear of cant.

B. B. Quite so. Well now, look at my practice. It is what I suppose you would call a fashionable practice, a smart practice, a practice among the best people. You ask me to go into the question of whether my patients are of any use either to themselves or anyone else. Well, if you apply any scientific test known to me, you will achieve a reductio ad absurdum. You will be driven to the conclusion that the majority of them would be, as my friend Mr J. M. Barrie has tersely phrased it, better dead. Better dead. There are exceptions, no doubt. For instance, there is the court, an essentially social-democratic institution, supported out of public funds by the public because the public wants it and likes it. My court patients are hard-working people who give satisfaction, undoubtedly. Then I have a duke or two whose estates are probably better managed than they would be in public hands. But as to most of the rest, if I once began to argue about them, unquestionably the verdict would be, Better dead. When they actually do die, I sometimes have to offer that consolation, thinly disguised, to the family. [Lulled by the cadences of his own voice, he becomes drowsier and drowsier]. The fact that they spend money so extravagantly on medical attendance really would not justify me in wasting my talents—such as they are —in keeping them alive. After all, if my fees are high, I have to spend heavily. My own tastes are simple: a camp bed, a couple of rooms, a crust, a bottle of wine; and I am happy and contented. My wife's tastes are perhaps more luxurious; but even she deplores an expenditure the sole object of which is to maintain the state my patients require from their medical attendant. The —er—er—er— [*suddenly waking up*] I have lost the thread of these remarks. What was I talking about, Ridgeon?

RIDGEON. About Dubedat.

B. B. Ah yes. Precisely. Thank you. Dubedat, of course. Well, what is our friend Dubedat? A vicious and ignorant young man with a talent for drawing.

LOUIS. Thank you. Dont mind me.

B. B. But then, what are many of my patients? Vicious and ignorant young men without a talent for anything. If I were to stop to argue about their merits I should have to give up three-quarters of my practice. Therefore I have made it a rule not so to argue. Now, as an honorable man, having made that rule as to paying patients, can I make an exception as to a patient who, far from being a paying patient, may more fitly be described as a borrowing patient. No. I say No. Mr Dubedat: your moral character is nothing to me. I look at you from a purely scientific point of view. To me you are simply a field of battle in which an invading army of tubercle bacilli struggles with a patriotic force of phagocytes. Having made a promise to your wife, which my principles will not allow me to break, to stimulate those phagocytes, I will stimulate them. And I take no further responsibility. [*He flings himself back in his seat exhausted*].

SIR PATRICK. Well, Mr Dubedat, as Sir Ralph has very kindly offered to take charge of your case, and as the two minutes I promised you are up, I must ask you to excuse me. [*He rises*].

LOUIS. Oh, certainly. Ive quite done with you. [*Rising and holding up the sketch block*] There! While youve been talking, Ive been doing. What is there left of your moralizing? Only a little carbonic acid gas which makes the room unhealthy. What is there left of my work? That. Look at it. [*Ridgeon rises to look at it*].

SIR PATRICK [*who has come down to him from the throne*] You young rascal, was it drawing me you were?

LOUIS. Of course. What else?

SIR PATRICK [*takes the drawing from him and grunts approvingly*] Thats rather good. Dont you think so, Colly?

RIDGEON. Yes. So good that I should like to have it.

SIR PATRICK. Thank you; but I should like to have it myself. What d'ye think, Walpole?

WALPOLE [*rising and coming over to look*] No, by Jove: *I* must have this.

LOUIS. I wish I could afford to give it to you, Sir Patrick. But I'd pay five guineas sooner than part with it.

RIDGEON. Oh, for that matter, I will give you six for it.

WALPOLE. Ten.

LOUIS. I think Sir Patrick is morally entitled to it, as he sat for it. May I send it to your house, Sir Patrick, for twelve guineas?

SIR PATRICK. Twelve guineas! Not if you were President of the Royal Academy, young man. [*He gives him back the drawing decisively and turns away, taking up his hat*].

LOUIS [*to B. B.*] Would you like to take it at twelve, Sir Ralph?

B. B. [*coming between Louis and Walpole*] Twelve guineas? Thank you: I'll take it at that. [*He takes it and presents it to Sir Patrick*]. Accept it from me, Paddy; and may you long be spared to contemplate it.

SIR PATRICK. Thank you. [*He puts the drawing into his hat*].

B. B. I neednt settle with you now, Mr Dubedat: my fees will come to more than that. [*He also retrieves his hat*].

LOUIS [*indignantly*] Well, of all the mean— [*words fail him*]! I'd let myself be shot sooner than do a thing like that. I consider youve stolen that drawing.

SIR PATRICK [*drily*] So weve converted you to a belief in morality after all, eh?

LOUIS. Yah! [*To Walpole*] I'll do another one for you, Walpole, if youll let me have the ten you promised.

WALPOLE. Very good. I'll pay on delivery.

LOUIS. Oh! What do you take me for? Have you no confidence in my honor?

WALPOLE. None whatever.

LOUIS. Oh well, of course if you feel that way, you cant help it. Before you go, Sir Patrick, let me fetch Jennifer. I know she'd like to see you, if you dont mind. [*He goes to the inner door*]. And now, before she comes in, one word. Youve all been talking here pretty freely about me—in my own house too. *I* dont mind that: I'm a man and can take care of myself. But when Jennifer comes in, please remember that she's a lady, and that you are supposed to be gentlemen.

[*He goes out*].

WALPOLE. Well!!! [*He gives the situation up as indescribable, and goes for his hat*].

RIDGEON. Damn his impudence!

B. B. I shouldnt be at all surprised to learn that he's well connected. Whenever I meet dignity and self-possession without any discoverable basis, I diagnose good family.

RIDGEON. Diagnose artistic genius, B. B. Thats what saves his self-respect.

SIR PATRICK. The world is made like that. The decent fellows are always being lectured and put out of countenance by the snobs.

B. B. [*altogether refusing to accept this*] I am not out of countenance. I should like, by Jupiter, to see the man who could put me out of countenance. [*Jennifer comes in*]. Ah, Mrs Dubedat! And how are we today?

MRS DUBEDAT [*shaking hands with him*] Thank you all so much for coming. [*She shakes Walpole's hand*]. Thank you, Sir Patrick [*she shakes Sir Patrick's*]. Oh, life has been worth living since I have known you. Since Richmond I have not known a moment's fear. And it used to be nothing but fear. Wont you sit down and tell me the result of the consultation.

WALPOLE. I'll go, if you dont mind, Mrs Dubedat. I have an appointment. Before I go, let me say that I am quite agreed with my colleagues here as to the character of the case. As to the cause and the remedy, thats not my business: I'm only a surgeon; and these gentlemen are physicians and will advise you. I may have my own views: in fact I have them; and they are perfectly well known to my colleagues. If I am needed— and needed I shall be finally—they know where to find me; and I am always at your service. So for today, goodbye. [*He goes out, leaving Jennifer much puzzled by his unexpected withdrawal and formal manner*].

SIR PATRICK. I also will ask you to excuse me, Mrs Dubedat.

RIDGEON [*anxiously*] Are you going?

SIR PATRICK. Yes: I can be of no use here; and I must be getting back. As you know, maam, I'm not in practice now; and I shall not be in charge of the case. It rests between Sir Colenso Ridgeon and Sir Ralph Bloomfield Bonington. They know my opinion. Good afternoon to you, maam. [*He bows and makes for the door*].

MRS DUBEDAT [*detaining him*] Theres nothing wrong, is there? You dont think Louis is worse, do you?

SIR PATRICK. No: he's not worse. Just the same as at Richmond.

MRS DUBEDAT. Oh, thank you: you frightened me. Excuse me.

SIR PATRICK. Dont mention it, maam. [*He goes out*].

B. B. Now, Mrs Dubedat, if I am to take the patient in hand—

MRS DUBEDAT [*apprehensively, with a glance at Ridgeon*] You! But I thought that Sir Colenso—

B. B. [*beaming with the conviction that he is giving her a most gratifying surprise*] My dear lady, your husband shall have Me.

MRS DUBEDAT. But—

B. B. Not a word: it is a pleasure to me, for your sake. Sir Colenso Ridgeon will be in his proper place, in the bacteriological laboratory. *I* shall be in my proper place, at the bedside. Your husband shall be treated exactly as if he were a member of the royal family. [*Mrs Dubedat uneasy, again is about to protest*]. No gratitude: it would embarrass me, I assure you. Now, may I ask whether you are particularly tied to these apartments. Of course, the motor has annihilated distance; but I confess that if you were rather nearer to me, it would be a little more convenient.

MRS DUBEDAT. You see, this studio and flat are self-contained. I have suffered so much in lodgings. The servants are so frightfully dishonest.

B. B. Ah! Are they? Are they? Dear me!

MRS DUBEDAT. I was never accustomed to lock things up. And I missed so many small sums. At last a dreadful thing happened. I missed a five-pound note. It was traced to the housemaid; and she actually said Louis had given it to her. And he wouldnt let me do anything: he is so sensitive that these things drive him mad.

B. B. Ah—hm—ha—yes—say no more, Mrs Dubedat: you shall not move. If the mountain will not come to Mahomet, Mahomet must come to the mountain. Now I must be off. I will write and make an appointment. We shall begin stimulating the phagocytes on—on—probably on Tuesday next; but I will let you know. Depend on me; dont fret; eat regularly; sleep well; keep your spirits up; keep the patient cheerful; hope for the best; no tonic like a charming woman; no medicine like cheerfulness; no resource like science; goodbye, goodbye, goodbye. [*Having shaken hands—she being too overwhelmed to speak—he goes out, stopping to say to Ridgeon*] On Tuesday morning send me down a tube of some really stiff anti-toxin. Any kind will do. Dont forget. Goodbye, Colly. [*He goes out*].

RIDGEON. You look quite discouraged again. [*She is almost in tears*]. Whats the matter? Are you disappointed?

MRS DUBEDAT. I know I ought to be very grateful. Believe me, I am very grateful. But—but—

RIDGEON. Well?

MRS DUBEDAT. I had set my heart on your curing Louis.

RIDGEON. Well, Sir Ralph Bloomfield Bonington—

MRS DUBEDAT. Yes, I know, I know. It is a great privilege to have him. But oh, I wish it had been you. I know it's unreasonable; I cant explain; but I had such a strong instinct that you would cure him. I dont—I cant feel the same about Sir Ralph. You promised me. Why did you give Louis up?

RIDGEON. I explained to you. I cannot take another case.

MRS DUBEDAT. But at Richmond?

RIDGEON. At Richmond I thought I could make room for one more case. But my old friend Dr Blenkinsop claimed that place. His lung is attacked.

MRS DUBEDAT [*attaching no importance whatever to Blenkinsop*] Do you mean that elderly man—that rather silly—

RIDGEON [*sternly*] I mean the gentleman that dined with us: an excellent and honest man, whose life is as valuable as anyone else's. I have arranged that I shall take his case, and that Sir Ralph Bloomfield Bonington shall take Mr Dubedat's.

MRS DUBEDAT [*turning indignantly on him*] I see what it is. Oh! it is envious, mean, cruel. And I thought that you would be above such a thing.

RIDGEON. What do you mean?

MRS DUBEDAT. Oh, do you think I dont know? do you think it has never happened before? Why does everybody turn against him? Can you not forgive him for being superior to you? for being cleverer? for being braver? for being a great artist?

RIDGEON. Yes: I can forgive him for all that.

MRS DUBEDAT. Well, have you anything to say against him? I have challenged everyone who has turned against him—challenged them face to face to tell me any wrong thing he has done, any ignoble thought he has uttered. They have always confessed that they could not tell me one. I challenge you now. What do you accuse him of?

RIDGEON. I am like all the rest. Face to face, I cannot tell you one thing against him.

MRS DUBEDAT [*not satisfied*] But your manner is changed. And you have broken your promise to me to make room for him as your patient.

RIDGEON. I think you are a little unreasonable. You have had the very best medical advice in London for him; and his case has been taken in hand by a leader of the profession. Surely—

MRS DUBEDAT. Oh, it is so cruel to keep telling me that. It seems all right; and it puts me in the wrong. But I am not in the wrong. I have faith in you; and I have no faith in the others. We have seen so many doctors: I have come to know at last when they are only talking and can do nothing. It is different with you. I feel that you know. You must listen to me, doctor. [*With sudden misgiving*] Am I offending you by calling you doctor instead of remembering your title?

RIDGEON. Nonsense. I am a doctor. But mind you dont call Walpole one.

MRS DUBEDAT. I dont care about Mr Walpole: it is you who must befriend me. Oh, will you please sit down and listen to me just for a few minutes. [*He assents with a grave inclination, and sits on the sofa. She sits on the easel chair*]. Thank you. I wont keep you long; but I must tell you the whole truth. Listen. I know Louis as nobody else in the world knows him or ever can know him. I am his wife. I know he has little faults: impatience, sensitiveness, even little selfishnesses that are too trivial for him to notice. I know that he sometimes shocks people about money because he is so utterly above it, and cant understand the value ordinary people set on it. Tell me: did he—did he borrow any money from you?

RIDGEON. He asked me for some—once.

MRS DUBEDAT [*tears again in her eyes*] Oh, I am so sorry—so sorry. But he will never do it again: I pledge you my word for that. He has given me his promise: here in this room just before you came; and he is incapable of breaking his word. That was his only real weakness; and now it is conquered and done with for ever.

RIDGEON. Was that really his only weakness?

MRS DUBEDAT. He is perhaps sometimes weak about women, because they adore him so, and are always laying traps for him. And of course when he says he doesnt believe in morality, ordinary pious people think he must be wicked. You can understand, cant you, how all this starts a great deal of gossip about him, and gets repeated until even good friends get set against him?

RIDGEON. Yes: I understand.

MRS DUBEDAT. Oh, if you only knew the other side of him as I do! Do you know, doctor, that if Louis dishonored himself by a really bad action, I should kill myself.

RIDGEON. Come! dont exaggerate.

MRS DUBEDAT. I should. You dont understand that, you east country people.

RIDGEON. You did not see much of the world in Cornwall, did you?

MRS DUBEDAT [naïvely] Oh yes. I saw a great deal every day of the beauty of the world—more than you ever see here in London. But I saw very few people, if that is what you mean. I was an only child.

RIDGEON. That explains a good deal.

MRS DUBEDAT. I had a great many dreams; but at last they all came to one dream.

RIDGEON [with half a sigh] Yes, the usual dream.

MRS DUBEDAT [surprised] Is it usual?

RIDGEON. As I guess. You havnt yet told me what it was.

MRS DUBEDAT. I didnt want to waste myself. I could do nothing myself; but I had a little property and I could help with it. I had even a little beauty: dont think me vain for knowing it. I knew that men of genius always had a terrible struggle with poverty and neglect at first. My dream was to save one of them from that, and bring some charm and happiness into his life. I prayed Heaven to send me one. I firmly believe that Louis was guided to me in answer to my prayer. He was no more like the other men I had met than the Thames Embankment is like our Cornish coasts. He saw everything that I saw, and drew it for me. He understood everything. He came to me like a child. Only fancy, doctor: he never even wanted to marry me: he never thought of the things other men think of! I had to propose it myself. Then he said he had no money. When I told him I had some, he said "Oh, all right", just like a boy. He is still like that, quite unspoiled, a man in his thoughts, a great poet and artist in his dreams, and a child in his ways. I gave him myself and all that I had that he might grow to his full height with plenty of sunshine. If I lost faith in him, it would mean the wreck and failure of my life. I should go back to Cornwall and die. I could shew you the very cliff I should jump off. You must cure him: you must make him quite well again for me. I know that you can do it and that nobody else can. I implore you not to refuse what I am going to ask you to do. Take Louis yourself: and let Sir Ralph cure Dr Blenkinsop.

RIDGEON [slowly] Mrs Dubedat: do you really believe in my knowledge and skill as you say you do?

MRS DUBEDAT. Absolutely. I do not give my trust by halves.

RIDGEON. I know that. Well, I am going to test you—hard. Will you believe me when I tell you that I understand what you have just told me; that I have no desire but to serve you in the most faithful friendship; and that your hero must be preserved to you.

MRS DUBEDAT. Oh forgive me. Forgive what I said. You will preserve him to me.

RIDGEON. At all hazards. [She kisses his hand. He rises hastily]. No: you have not heard the rest. [She rises too]. You must believe me when I tell you that the one chance of preserving the hero lies in Louis being in the care of Sir Ralph.

MRS DUBEDAT [firmly] You say so: I have no more doubt: I believe you. Thank you.

RIDGEON. Goodbye. [She takes his hand]. I hope this will be a lasting friendship.

MRS DUBEDAT. It will. My friendships end only with death.

RIDGEON. Death ends everything, doesnt it? Goodbye.

With a sigh and a look of pity at her which she does not understand, he goes.

ACT IV

The studio. The easel is pushed back to the wall. Cardinal Death, holding his scythe and hour-glass like a sceptre and globe, sits on the throne. On the hat-stand hang the hats of Sir Patrick and Bloomfield Bonington. Walpole, just come in, is hanging up his beside them. There is a knock. He opens the door and finds Ridgeon there.

WALPOLE. Hallo, Ridgeon!

They come into the middle of the room together, taking off their gloves.

RIDGEON. Whats the matter? Have you been sent for, too.

WALPOLE. Weve all been sent for. Ive only just come: I havnt seen him yet. The charwoman says that old Paddy Cullen has been here with B. B. for the last half-hour. [*Sir Patrick, with bad news in his face, enters from the inner room*]. Well: whats up?

SIR PATRICK. Go in and see. B. B. is in there with him.

Walpole goes. Ridgeon is about to follow him; but Sir Patrick stops him with a look.

RIDGEON. What has happened?

SIR PATRICK. Do you remember Jane Marsh's arm?

RIDGEON. Is that whats happened?

SIR PATRICK. Thats whats happened. His lung has gone like Jane's arm. I never saw such a case. He has got through three months galloping consumption in three days.

RIDGEON. B. B. got in on the negative phase.

SIR PATRICK. Negative or positive, the lad's done for. He wont last out the afternoon. He'll go suddenly: Ive often seen it.

RIDGEON. So long as he goes before his wife finds him out, *I* dont care. I fully expected this.

SIR PATRICK [*drily*] It's a little hard on a lad to be killed because his wife has too high an opinion of him. Fortunately few of us are in any danger of that.

Sir Ralph comes from the inner room and hastens between them, humanely concerned, but professionally elate and communicative.

B. B. Ah, here you are, Ridgeon. Paddy's told you, of course.

RIDGEON. Yes.

B. B. It's an enormously interesting case. You know, Colly, by Jupiter, if I didnt know as a matter of scientific fact that I'd been stimulating the phagocytes, I should say I'd been stimulating the other things. What is the explanation of it, Sir Patrick? How do you account for it, Ridgeon? Have we over-stimulated the phagocytes? Have they not only eaten up the bacilli, but attacked and destroyed the red corpuscles as well? a possibility suggested by the patient's pallor. Nay, have they finally begun to prey on the lungs themselves? Or on one another? I shall write a paper about this case.

Walpole comes back, very serious, even shocked. He comes between B. B. and Ridgeon.

WALPOLE. Whew! B. B.: youve done it this time.

B. B. What do you mean?

WALPOLE. Killed him. The worst case of neglected blood-poisoning I ever saw. It's too late now to do anything. He'd die under the anæsthetic.

B. B. [*offended*] Killed! Really, Walpole, if your monomania were not well known, I should take such an expression very seriously.

SIR PATRICK. Come come! When youve both killed as many people as I have in my time youll feel humble enough about it. Come and look at him, Colly.

Ridgeon and Sir Patrick go into the inner room.

WALPOLE. I apologize, B. B. But it's blood-poisoning.

B. B. [*recovering his irresistible good nature*] My dear Walpole, everything is blood-poisoning. But upon my soul, I shall not use any of that stuff of Ridgeon's again. What made me so sensitive about what you said just now is that, strictly between ourselves, Ridgeon has cooked our young friend's goose.

Jennifer, worried and distressed, but always gentle, comes between them from the inner room. She wears a nurse's apron.

MRS DUBEDAT. Sir Ralph: what am I to do? That man who insisted on seeing me, and sent in word that his business was important to Louis, is a newspaper man. A paragraph appeared in the paper this morning saying that Louis is seriously ill; and this man wants to interview him about it. How can people be so brutally callous?

WALPOLE [*moving vengefully towards the door*] You just leave me to deal with him!

MRS DUBEDAT [*stopping him*] But Louis insists on seeing him: he almost began to cry about it. And he says he cant bear his room any longer. He says he wants to [*she struggles with a sob*]—to die in his studio. Sir Patrick says let him have his way: it can do no harm. What shall we do?

B. B. [*encouragingly*] Why, follow Sir Patrick's excellent advice, of course. As he says, it can do him no harm; and it will no doubt do him good—a great deal of good. He will be much the better for it.

MRS DUBEDAT [*a little cheered*] Will you bring the man up here, Mr Walpole, and tell him that he may see Louis, but that he mustnt exhaust him by talking? [*Walpole nods and goes out by the outer door*]. Sir Ralph: dont be angry with me; but Louis will die if he stays here. I must take him to Cornwall. He will recover there.

B. B. [*brightening wonderfully, as if Dubedat were already saved*] Cornwall! The very place for him! Wonderful for the lungs. Stupid of me not to think of it before. You are his best physician after all, dear lady. An inspiration! Cornwall: of course, yes, yes, yes.

MRS DUBEDAT [*comforted and touched*] You are so kind, Sir Ralph. But dont give me much hope or I shall cry; and Louis cant bear that.

B. B. [*gently putting his protecting arm round her shoulders*] Then let us come back to him and help to carry him in. Cornwall! of course, of course. The very thing! [*They go together into the bedroom*].

Walpole returns with The Newspaper Man, a cheerful, affable young man who is disabled for ordinary business pursuits by a congenital erroneousness which renders him incapable of describing accurately anything he sees, or understanding or reporting accurately anything he hears. As the only employment in which these defects do not matter is journalism (for a newspaper, not having to act on its descriptions and reports, but only to sell them to idly curious people, has nothing but honor to lose by inaccuracy and unveracity), he has perforce become a journalist, and has to keep up an air of high spirits through a daily struggle with his own illiteracy and the precariousness of his employment. He has a note-book, and occasionally attempts to make a note; but as he cannot write shorthand, and does not write with ease in any hand, he generally gives it up as a bad job before he succeeds in finishing a sentence.

THE NEWSPAPER MAN [*looking round and making indecisive attempts at notes*] This is the studio, I suppose.

WALPOLE. Yes.

THE NEWSPAPER MAN [*wittily*] Where he has his models, eh?

WALPOLE [*grimly irresponsive*] No doubt.

THE NEWSPAPER MAN. Cubicle, you said it was?

WALPOLE. Yes, tubercle.

THE NEWSPAPER MAN. Which way do you spell it: is it c-u-b-i-c-a-l or c-l-e?

WALPOLE. Tubercle, man, not cubical. [*Spelling it for him*] T-u-b-e-r-c-l-e.

THE NEWSPAPER MAN. Oh! tubercle. Some disease, I suppose. I thought he had con-sumption. Are you one of the family or the doctor?

WALPOLE. I'm neither one nor the other. I am Mister Cutler Walpole. Put that down. Then put down Sir Colenso Ridgeon.

THE NEWSPAPER MAN. Pigeon?

WALPOLE. Ridgeon. [*Contemptuously snatching his book*] Here: youd better let me write the names down for you: youre sure to get them wrong. That comes of belonging to an illiterate profession, with no qualifications and no public register. [*He writes the particulars*].

THE NEWSPAPER MAN. Oh, I say: you have got your knife into us, havnt you?

WALPOLE [*vindictively*] I wish I had: I'd make a better man of you. Now attend. [*Shewing him the book*] These are the names of the three doctors. This is the patient. This is the address. This is the name of the disease. [*He shuts the book with a snap which makes the journalist blink, and returns it to him*]. Mr Dubedat will be brought in here presently. He wants to see you because he doesnt know how bad he is. We'll allow you to wait a few minutes to humor him; but if you talk to him, out you go. He may die at any moment.

THE NEWSPAPER MAN [*interested*] Is he as bad as that? I say: I am in luck today. Would you mind letting me photograph you? [*He produces a camera*]. Could you have a lancet or something in your hand?

WALPOLE. Put it up. If you want my photograph you can get it in Baker Street in any of the series of celebrities.

THE NEWSPAPER MAN. But theyll want to be paid. If you wouldnt mind [*fingering the camera*]—?

WALPOLE. I would. Put it up, I tell you. Sit down there and be quiet.

The Newspaper Man quickly sits down on the piano stool as Dubedat, in an invalid's chair, is wheeled in by Mrs Dubedat and Sir Ralph. They place the chair between the dais and the sofa, where the easel stood before. Louis is not changed as a robust man would be; and he is not scared. His eyes look larger; and he is so weak physically that he can hardly move, lying on his cushions with complete languor; but his mind is active: it is making the most of his condition, finding voluptuousness in languor and drama in death. They are all impressed, in spite of themselves, except Ridgeon, who is implacable. B. B. is entirely sympathetic and forgiving. Ridgeon follows the chair with a tray of milk and stimu-

lants. Sir Patrick, who accompanies him, takes the tea-table from the corner and places it behind the chair for the tray. B. B. takes the easel chair and places it for Jennifer at Dubedat's side, next the dais, from which the lay figure ogles the dying artist. B. B. then returns to Dubedat's left. Jennifer sits. Walpole sits down on the edge of the dais. Ridgeon stands near him.

LOUIS [*blissfully*] Thats happiness. To be in a studio! Happiness!

MRS DUBEDAT. Yes, dear. Sir Patrick says you may stay here as long as you like.

LOUIS. Jennifer.

MRS DUBEDAT. Yes, my darling.

LOUIS. Is the newspaper man here?

THE NEWSPAPER MAN [*glibly*] Yes, Mr Dubedat: I'm here, at your service. I represent the press. I thought you might like to let us have a few words about—about—er—well, a few words on your illness, and your plans for the season.

LOUIS. My plans for the season are very simple. I'm going to die.

MRS DUBEDAT [*tortured*] Louis—dearest—

LOUIS. My darling: I'm very weak and tired. Dont put on me the horrible strain of pretending that I dont know. Ive been lying there listening to the doctors—laughing to myself. They know. Dearest: dont cry. It makes you ugly; and I cant bear that. [*She dries her eyes and recovers herself with a proud effort*]. I want you to promise me something.

MRS DUBEDAT. Yes, yes: you know I will. [*Imploringly*] Only, my love, my love, dont talk: it will waste your strength.

LOUIS. No: it will only use it up. Ridgeon: give me something to keep me going for a few minutes—not one of your confounded anti-toxins, if you dont mind. I have some things to say before I go.

RIDGEON [*looking at Sir Patrick*] I suppose it can do no harm? [*He pours out some spirit, and is about to add soda water when Sir Patrick corrects him*].

SIR PATRICK. In milk. Dont set him coughing.

LOUIS [*after drinking*] Jennifer.

MRS DUBEDAT. Yes, dear.

LOUIS. If theres one thing I hate more than another, it's a widow. Promise me that youll never be a widow.

MRS DUBEDAT. My dear, what do you mean?

LOUIS. I want you to look beautiful. I want people to see in your eyes that you were married to me. The people in Italy used to point at Dante and say "There goes the man who has been in hell." I want them to point at you and say "There goes a woman who has been in heaven." It has been heaven, darling, hasnt it—sometimes?

MRS DUBEDAT. Oh yes, yes. Always, always.

LOUIS. If you wear black and cry, people will say "Look at that miserable woman: her husband made her miserable."

MRS DUBEDAT. No, never. You are the light and the blessing of my life. I never lived until I knew you.

LOUIS [*his eyes glistening*] Then you must always wear beautiful dresses and splendid magic jewels. Think of all the wonderful pictures I shall never paint. [*She wins a terrible victory over a sob*]. Well, you must be transfigured with all the beauty of those pictures. Men must get such dreams from seeing you as they never could get from any daubing with paints and brushes. Painters must paint you as they never painted any mortal woman before. There must be a great tradition of beauty, a great atmosphere of wonder and romance. That is what men must always think of when they think of me. That is the sort of immortality I want. You can make that for me, Jennifer. There are lots of things you dont understand that every woman in the street understands; but you can understand that and do it as nobody else can. Promise me that immortality. Promise me you will not make a little hell of crape and crying and undertaker's horrors and withering flowers and all that vulgar rubbish.

MRS DUBEDAT. I promise. But all that is far off, dear. You are to come to Cornwall with me and get well. Sir Ralph says so.

LOUIS. Poor old B. B.!

B. B. [*affected to tears, turns away and whispers to Sir Patrick*] Poor fellow! Brain going.

LOUIS. Sir Patrick's there, isnt he?

SIR PATRICK. Yes, yes. I'm here.

LOUIS. Sit down, wont you? It's a shame to keep you standing about.

SIR PATRICK. Yes, yes. Thank you. All right.

LOUIS. Jennifer.

MRS DUBEDAT. Yes, dear.

LOUIS [*with a strange look of delight*] Do you remember the burning bush?

MRS DUBEDAT. Yes, yes. Oh, my dear, how it strains my heart to remember it now!

LOUIS. Does it? It fills me with joy. Tell them about it.

MRS DUBEDAT. It was nothing—only that once in my old Cornish home we lit the first fire of the winter; and when we looked through the window we saw the flames dancing in a bush in the garden.

LOUIS. Such a color! Garnet color. Waving like silk. Liquid lovely flame flowing up through the bay leaves, and not burning them. Well, I shall be a flame like that. I'm sorry to disappoint the poor little worms; but the last of me shall be the flame in the burning bush. Whenever you see the flame, Jennifer, that will be me. Promise me that I shall be burnt.

MRS DUBEDAT. Oh, if I might be with you, Louis!

LOUIS. No: you must always be in the garden when the bush flames. You are my hold on the world: you are my immortality. Promise.

MRS DUBEDAT. I'm listening. I shall not forget. You know that I promise.

LOUIS. Well, thats about all; except that you are to hang my pictures at the one-man show. I can trust your eye. You wont let anyone else touch them.

MRS DUBEDAT. You can trust me.

LOUIS. Then theres nothing more to worry about, is there? Give me some more of that milk. I'm fearfully tired; but if I stop talking I shant begin again. [*Sir Ralph gives him a drink. He takes it and looks up quaintly*]. I say, B. B., do you think anything would stop y o u talking?

B. B. [*almost unmanned*] He confuses me with you, Paddy. Poor fellow! Poor fellow!

LOUIS [*musing*] I used to be awfully afraid of death; but now it's come I have no fear; and I'm perfectly happy. Jennifer.

MRS DUBEDAT. Yes, dear?

LOUIS. I'll tell you a secret. I used to think that our marriage was all an affectation, and that I'd break loose and run away some day. But now that I'm going to be broken loose whether I like it or not, I'm perfectly fond of you, and perfectly satisfied because I'm going to live as part of you and not as my troublesome self.

MRS DUBEDAT [*heartbroken*] Stay with me, Louis. Oh, dont leave me, dearest.

LOUIS. Not that I'm selfish. With all my faults I dont think Ive ever been really selfish. No artist can: Art is too large for that. You will marry again, Jennifer.

MRS DUBEDAT. Oh, how c a n you, Louis?

LOUIS [*insisting childishly*] Yes, because people who have found marriage happy always marry again. Ah, *I* shant be jealous. [*Slyly*] But dont talk to the other fellow too much about me: he wont like it. [*Almost chuckling*] *I* shall be your lover all the time; but it will be a secret from him, poor devil!

SIR PATRICK. Come! youve talked enough. Try to rest awhile.

LOUIS [*wearily*] Yes: I'm fearfully tired; but I shall have a long rest presently. I have something to say to you fellows. Youre all there, arnt you? I'm too weak to see anything but Jennifer's bosom. That promises rest.

RIDGEON. We are all here.

LOUIS [*startled*] That voice sounded devilish. Take care, Ridgeon: my ears hear things that other people's ears cant. Ive been thinking—thinking. I'm cleverer than you imagine.

SIR PATRICK [*whispering to Ridgeon*] Youve got on his nerves, Colly. Slip out quietly.

RIDGEON [*apart to Sir Patrick*] Would you deprive the dying actor of his audience?

LOUIS [*his face lighting up faintly with mischievous glee*] I heard that, Ridgeon. That was good. Jennifer, dear: be kind to Ridgeon always; because he was the last man who amused me.

RIDGEON [*relentless*] Was I?

LOUIS. But it's not true. It's you who are still on the stage. I'm half way home already.

MRS DUBEDAT [*to Ridgeon*] What did you say?

LOUIS [*answering for him*] Nothing, dear. Only one of those little secrets that men keep among themselves. Well, all you chaps have thought pretty hard things of me, and said them.

B. B. [*quite overcome*] No, no, Dubedat. Not at all.

LOUIS. Yes, you have. I know what you all think of me. Dont imagine I'm sore about it. I forgive you.

WALPOLE [*involuntarily*] Well, damn me! [*Ashamed*] I beg your pardon.

LOUIS. That was old Walpole, I know. Dont grieve, Walpole. I'm perfectly happy. I'm not in pain. I dont want to live. Ive escaped from myself. I'm in heaven, immortal in the heart of my beautiful Jennifer. I'm not afraid, and not ashamed. [*Reflectively, puzzling it out for himself weakly*] I know that in an accidental sort of way, struggling through the unreal part of life, I havnt always been able to live up to my ideal. But in my own real world I have never done anything wrong, never denied my faith, never been untrue to myself. Ive been threatened and black-mailed and insulted and starved. But Ive played the game. Ive fought the good fight. And now it's all over, theres an indescribable peace. [*He feebly folds his hands and utters his creed*]: I believe in Michael Angelo, Velas-quez, and Rembrandt; in the might of de-sign, the mystery of color, the redemption of all things by Beauty everlasting, and the message of Art that has made these hands blessed. Amen. Amen. [*He closes his eyes and lies still*].

MRS DUBEDAT [*breathless*] Louis: are you—

Walpole rises and comes quickly to see whether he is dead.

LOUIS. Not yet, dear. Very nearly, but not yet. I should like to rest my head on your bosom; only it would tire you.

MRS DUBEDAT. No, no, no, darling: how could you tire me? [*She lifts him so that he lies in her bosom*].

LOUIS. Thats good. Thats real.

MRS DUBEDAT. Dont spare me, dear. Indeed indeed you will not tire me. Lean on me with all your weight.

LOUIS [*with a sudden half return of his normal strength and comfort*] Jinny Gwinny: I think I shall recover after all. [*Sir Patrick looks signi-ficantly at Ridgeon, mutely warning him that this is the end*].

MRS DUBEDAT [*hopefully*] Yes, yes: you shall.

LOUIS. Because I suddenly want to sleep. Just an ordinary sleep.

MRS DUBEDAT [*rocking him*] Yes, dear. Sleep. [*He seems to go to sleep. Walpole makes another movement. She protests*]. Sh-sh: please dont disturb him. [*His lips move*]. What did you say, dear? [*In great distress*] I cant listen with-out moving him. [*His lips move again: Walpole bends down and listens*].

WALPOLE. He wants to know is the news-paper man here.

THE NEWSPAPER MAN [*excited; for he has been enjoying himself enormously*] Yes, Mr Dube-dat. Here I am.

Walpole raises his hand warningly to silence him. Sir Ralph sits down quietly on the sofa and frankly buries his face in his handkerchief.

MRS DUBEDAT [*with great relief*] Oh thats right, dear: dont spare me: lean with all your weight on me. Now you are really resting.

Sir Patrick quickly comes forward and feels

Louis's pulse; then takes him by the shoulders.

SIR PATRICK. Let me put him back on the pillow, maam. He will be better so.

MRS DUBEDAT [*piteously*] Oh no, please, p l e a s e, doctor. He is not tiring me; and he will be so hurt when he wakes if he finds I have put him away.

SIR PATRICK. He will never wake again. [*He takes the body from her and replaces it in the chair. Ridgeon, unmoved, lets down the back and makes a bier of it*].

MRS DUBEDAT [*who has unexpectedly sprung to her feet, and stands dry-eyed and stately*] Was that death?

WALPOLE. Yes.

MRS DUBEDAT [*with complete dignity*] Will you wait for me a moment. I will come back. [*She goes out*].

WALPOLE. Ought we to follow her? Is she in her right senses?

SIR PATRICK [*with quiet conviction*] Yes. She's all right. Leave her alone. She'll come back.

RIDGEON [*callously*] Let us get this thing out of the way before she comes.

B. B. [*rising, shocked*] My dear Colly! The poor lad! He died splendidly.

SIR PATRICK. Aye! that is how the wicked die.

For there are no bands in their death;
But their strength is firm:
They are not in trouble as other men.

No matter: it's not for us to judge. He's in another world now.

WALPOLE. Borrowing his first five-pound note there, probably.

RIDGEON. I said the other day that the most tragic thing in the world is a sick doctor. I was wrong. The most tragic thing in the world is a man of genius who is not also a man of honor.

Ridgeon and Walpole wheel the chair into the recess.

THE NEWSPAPER MAN [*to Sir Ralph*] I thought it shewed a very nice feeling, his being so particular about his wife going into proper mourning for him and making her promise never to marry again.

B. B. [*impressively*] Mrs Dubedat is not in a position to carry the interview any further. Neither are we.

SIR PATRICK. Good afternoon to you.

THE NEWSPAPER MAN. Mrs Dubedat said she was coming back.

B. B. After you have gone.

THE NEWSPAPER MAN. Do you think she

would give me a few words on How It Feels to be a Widow? Rather a good title for an article, isnt it?

B. B. Young man: if you wait until Mrs Dubedat comes back, you will be able to write an article on How It Feels to be Turned Out of the House.

THE NEWSPAPER MAN [*unconvinced*] You think she'd rather not—

B. B. [*cutting him short*] Good day to you. [*Giving him a visiting-card*] Mind you get my name correctly. Good day.

THE NEWSPAPER MAN. Good day. Thank you. [*Vaguely trying to read the card*] Mr—

B. B. No, not Mister. This is your hat, I think [*giving it to him*]. Gloves? No, of course: no gloves. Good day to you. [*He edges him out at last; shuts the door on him; and returns to Sir Patrick as Ridgeon and Walpole come back from the recess, Walpole crossing the room to the hat-stand, and Ridgeon coming between Sir Ralph and Sir Patrick*]. Poor fellow! Poor young fellow! How well he died! I feel a better man, really.

SIR PATRICK. When youre as old as I am, youll know that it matters very little how a man dies. What matters is, how he lives. Every fool that runs his nose against a bullet is a hero nowadays, because he dies for his country. Why dont he live for it to some purpose?

B. B. No, please, Paddy: dont be hard on the poor lad. Not now, not now. After all, was he so bad? He had only two failings: money and women. Well, let us be honest. Tell the truth, Paddy. Dont be hypocritical, Ridgeon. Throw off the mask, Walpole. Are these two matters so well arranged at present that a disregard of the usual arrangements indicates real depravity?

WALPOLE. I dont mind his disregarding the usual arrangements. Confound the usual arrangements! To a man of science theyre beneath contempt both as to money and women. What I mind is his disregarding everything except his own pocket and his own fancy. He didnt disregard the usual arrangements when they paid him. Did he give us his pictures for nothing? Do you suppose he'd have hesitated to blackmail me if I'd compromised myself with his wife? Not he.

SIR PATRICK. Dont waste your time wrangling over him. A blackguard's a blackguard; an honest man's an honest man; and neither of them will ever be at a loss for a religion or a morality to prove that their ways are the right ways. It's the same with nations, the same with professions, the same all the world over and always will be.

B. B. Ah, well, perhaps, perhaps, perhaps. Still, de mortuis nil nisi bonum. He died extremely well, remarkably well. He has set us an example: let us endeavor to follow it rather than harp on the weaknesses that have perished with him. I think it is Shakespear who says that the good that most men do lives after them: the evil lies interréd with their bones. Yes: interréd with their bones. Believe me, Paddy, we are all mortal. It is the common lot, Ridgeon. Say what you will, Walpole, Nature's debt must be paid. If tis not today, twill be tomorrow.

Tomorrow and tomorrow and tomorrow
After life's fitful fever they sleep well
And like this insubstantial bourne from which
No traveller returns
Leave not a wrack behind.

Walpole is about to speak, but B. B., suddenly and vehemently proceeding, extinguishes him.

Out, out, brief candle:
For nothing canst thou to damnation add;
The readiness is all.

WALPOLE [*gently; for B. B.'s feeling, absurdly expressed as it is, is too sincere and humane to be ridiculed*] Yes, B. B. Death makes people go on like that. I dont know why it should; but it does. By the way, what are we going to do? Ought we to clear out; or had we better wait and see whether Mrs Dubedat will come back?

SIR PATRICK. I think we'd better go. We can tell the charwoman what to do.

They take their hats and go to the door.

MRS DUBEDAT [*coming from the inner room wonderfully and beautifully dressed, and radiant, carrying a great piece of purple silk, handsomely embroidered, over her arm*] I'm so sorry to have kept you waiting.

SIR PATRICK		Dont mention it, madam.
B. B.	[*amazed, all together in a confused murmur*]	Not at all, not at all.
RIDGEON		By no means.
WALPOLE		It doesnt matter in the least.

MRS DUBEDAT [*coming to them*] I felt that I must shake hands with his friends once before we part today. We have shared together a great privilege and a great happiness. I dont think we can ever think of ourselves as ordinary people again. We have had a wonderful experience; and that gives us a common faith, a common ideal, that nobody else can quite have. Life will always be beautiful to us: death will always be beautiful to us. May we shake hands on that?

SIR PATRICK [*shaking hands*] Remember: all letters had better be left to your solicitor. Let him open everything and settle everything. Thats the law, you know.

MRS DUBEDAT. Oh, thank you: I didnt know. [*Sir Patrick goes*].

WALPOLE. Goodbye. I blame myself: I should have insisted on operating. [*He goes*].

B. B. I will send the proper people: they will know what to do: you shall have no trouble. Goodbye, my dear lady. [*He goes*].

RIDGEON. Goodbye. [*He offers his hand*].

MRS DUBEDAT [*drawing back with gentle majesty*] I said his friends, Sir Colenso. [*He bows and goes*].

She unfolds the great piece of silk, and goes into the recess to cover her dead.

ACT V

One of the smaller Bond Street Picture Galleries. The entrance is from a picture shop. Nearly in the middle of the gallery there is a writing-table, at which the Secretary, fashionably dressed, sits with his back to the entrance, correcting catalogue proofs. Some copies of a new book are on the desk, also the Secretary's shining hat and a couple of magnifying glasses. At the side, on his left, a little behind him, is a small door marked PRIVATE. *Near the same side is a cushioned bench parallel to the walls, which are covered with Dubedat's works. Two screens, also covered with drawings, stand near the corners right and left of the entrance.*

Jennifer, beautifully dressed and apparently very happy and prosperous, comes into the gallery through the private door.

JENNIFER. Have the catalogues come yet, Mr Danby?

THE SECRETARY. Not yet.

JENNIFER. What a shame! It's a quarter past: the private view will begin in less than half an hour.

THE SECRETARY. I think I'd better run over to the printers to hurry them up.

JENNIFER. Oh, if you would be so good, Mr Danby. I'll take your place while youre away.

THE SECRETARY. If anyone should come before the time dont take any notice. The commissionaire wont let anyone through unless he knows him. We have a few people who like to come before the crowd—people who really buy; and of course we're glad to see them. Have you seen the notices in Brush and Crayon and in The Easel?

JENNIFER [*indignantly*] Yes: most disgraceful. They write quite patronizingly, as if they were Mr Dubedat's superiors. After all the cigars and sandwiches they had from us on the press day, and all they drank, I really think it is infamous that they should write like that. I hope you have not sent them tickets for today.

THE SECRETARY. Oh, they wont come again: theres no lunch today. The advance copies of your book have come. [*He indicates the new books*].

JENNIFER [*pouncing on a copy, wildly excited*] Give it to me. Oh! excuse me a moment [*she runs away with it through the private door*].

The Secretary takes a mirror from his drawer and smartens himself before going out. Ridgeon comes in.

RIDGEON. Good morning. May I look round, as usual, before the doors open?

THE SECRETARY. Certainly, Sir Colenso. I'm sorry the catalogues have not come: I'm just going to see about them. Heres my own list, if you dont mind.

RIDGEON. Thanks. Whats this? [*He takes up one of the new books*].

THE SECRETARY. Thats just come in. An advance copy of Mrs Dubedat's Life of her late husband.

RIDGEON [*reading the title*] The Story of a King of Men. By His Wife. [*He looks at the portrait frontispiece*]. Ay: there he is. You knew him here, I suppose.

THE SECRETARY. Oh, we knew him. Better than she did, Sir Colenso, in some ways, perhaps.

RIDGEON. So did I. [*They look significantly at one another*]. I'll take a look round.

The Secretary puts on the shining hat and goes out. Ridgeon begins looking at the pictures. Presently he comes back to the table for a magnifying glass, and scrutinizes a drawing very closely. He sighs; shakes his head, as if constrained to admit the extraordinary fascination and merit of the work; then marks the Secretary's list. Proceeding with his survey, he disappears behind the screen. Jennifer comes back with her book. A look round satisfies her that she is alone. She seats herself at the table and admires the memoir—her first printed book—to her heart's content. Ridgeon reappears, face to the wall, scrutinizing the drawings. After using his glass again, he steps back to get a more distant view of one of the larger pictures. She hastily closes the book at the sound; looks round; recognizes him; and stares, petrified. He takes a further step back which brings him nearer to her.

RIDGEON [*shaking his head as before, ejaculates*] Clever brute! [*She flushes as though he had struck her. He turns to put the glass down on the desk, and finds himself face to face with her intent gaze*]. I beg your pardon. I thought I was alone.

JENNIFER [*controlling herself, and speaking steadily and meaningly*] I am glad we have met, Sir Colenso Ridgeon. I met Dr Blenkinsop yesterday. I congratulate you on a wonderful cure.

RIDGEON [*can find no words: makes an embarrassed gesture of assent after a moment's silence, and puts down the glass and the Secretary's list on the table*].

JENNIFER. He looked the picture of health and strength and prosperity. [*She looks for a moment at the walls, contrasting Blenkinsop's fortune with the artist's fate*].

RIDGEON [*in low tones, still embarrassed*] He has been fortunate.

JENNIFER. Very fortunate. His life has been spared.

RIDGEON. I mean that he has been made a Medical Officer of Health. He cured the Chairman of the Borough Council very successfully.

JENNIFER. With your medicines?

RIDGEON. No. I believe it was with a pound of ripe greengages.

JENNIFER [*with deep gravity*] Funny!

RIDGEON. Yes. Life does not cease to be funny when people die any more than it ceases to be serious when people laugh.

JENNIFER. Dr Blenkinsop said one very strange thing to me.

RIDGEON. What was that?

JENNIFER. He said that private practice in medicine ought to be put down by law. When I asked him why, he said that private doctors were ignorant licensed murderers.

RIDGEON. That is what the public doctor always thinks of the private doctor. Well, Blenkinsop ought to know. He was a private doctor long enough himself. Come! you have talked at me long enough. Talk to me. You have something to reproach me with. There is reproach in your face, in your voice: you are full of it. Out with it.

JENNIFER. It is too late for reproaches now. When I turned and saw you just now, I wondered how you could come here coolly to look at his pictures. You answered the question. To you, he was only a clever brute.

RIDGEON [*quivering*] Oh, dont. You know I did not know you were here.

JENNIFER [*raising her head a little with a quite gentle impulse of pride*] You think it only mattered because I heard it. As if it could touch me, or touch him! Dont you see that what is really dreadful is that to you living things have no souls.

RIDGEON [*with a sceptical shrug*] The soul is an organ I have not come across in the course of my anatomical work.

JENNIFER. You know you would not dare to say such a silly thing as that to anybody but a woman whose mind you despise. If you dissected me you could not find my conscience. Do you think I have got none?

RIDGEON. I have met people who had none.

JENNIFER. Clever brutes? Do you know, doctor, that some of the dearest and most faithful friends I ever had were only brutes! You would have vivisected them. The dearest and greatest of all my friends had a sort of beauty and affectionateness that only animals have. I hope you may never feel what I felt when I had to put him into the hands of men who defend the torture of animals because they are only brutes.

RIDGEON. Well, did you find us so very cruel, after all? They tell me that though you have dropped me, you stay for weeks with the Bloomfield Boningtons and the Walpoles. I think it must be true, because they never mention you to me now.

JENNIFER. The animals in Sir Ralph's house are like spoiled children. When Mr Walpole had to take a splinter out of the mastiff's paw, I had to hold the poor dog myself; and Mr Walpole had to turn Sir Ralph out of the room. And Mrs Walpole has to tell the gardener not to kill wasps when Mr Walpole is looking. But there are doctors who are naturally cruel; and there are others who get used to cruelty and are callous about it. They blind themselves to the souls of animals; and that blinds them to the souls of men and women. You made a dreadful mistake about

Louis; but you would not have made it if you had not trained yourself to make the same mistake about dogs. You saw nothing in them but dumb brutes; and so you could see nothing in him but a clever brute.

RIDGEON [*with sudden resolution*] I made no mistake whatever about him.

JENNIFER. Oh, doctor!

RIDGEON [*obstinately*] I made no mistake whatever about him.

JENNIFER. Have you forgotten that he died?

RIDGEON [*with a sweep of his hand towards the pictures*] He is not dead. He is there. [*Taking up the book*] And there.

JENNIFER [*springing up with blazing eyes*] Put that down. How dare you touch it?

Ridgeon, amazed at the fierceness of the outburst, puts it down with a deprecatory shrug. She takes it up and looks at it as if he had profaned a relic.

RIDGEON. I am very sorry. I see I had better go.

JENNIFER [*putting the book down*] I beg your pardon. I—I forgot myself. But it is not yet —it is a private copy.

RIDGEON. But for me it would have been a very different book.

JENNIFER. But for you it would have been a longer one.

RIDGEON. You know then that I killed him?

JENNIFER [*suddenly moved and softened*] Oh, doctor, if you acknowledge that—if you have confessed it to yourself—if you realize what you have done, then there is forgiveness. I trusted in your strength instinctively at first; then I thought I had mistaken callousness for strength. Can you blame me? But if it was really strength—if it was only such a mistake as we all make sometimes—it will make me so happy to be friends with you again.

RIDGEON. I tell you I made no mistake. I cured Blenkinsop: was there any mistake there?

JENNIFER. He recovered. Oh, dont be foolishly proud, doctor. Confess to a failure, and save our friendship. Remember, Sir Ralph gave Louis your medicine; and it made him worse.

RIDGEON. I cant be your friend on false pretences. Something has got me by the throat: the truth must come out. I used that medicine myself on Blenkinsop. It did not make

him worse. It is a dangerous medicine: it cured Blenkinsop: it killed Louis Dubedat. When I handle it, it cures. When another man handles it, it kills—sometimes.

JENNIFER [*naïvely: not yet taking it all in*] Then why did you let Sir Ralph give it to Louis?

RIDGEON. I'm going to tell you. I did it because I was in love with you.

JENNIFER [*innocently surprised*] In lo—You! an elderly man!

RIDGEON [*thunderstruck, raising his fists to heaven*] Dubedat: thou art avenged! [*He drops his hands and collapses on the bench*]. I never thought of that. I suppose I appear to you a ridiculous old fogey.

JENNIFER. But surely—I did not mean to offend you, indeed—but you must be at least twenty years older than I am.

RIDGEON. Oh, quite. More, perhaps. In twenty years you will understand how little difference that makes.

JENNIFER. But even so, how could you think that I—his wife—could ever think of you—

RIDGEON [*stopping her with a nervous waving of his fingers*] Yes, yes, yes, yes: I quite understand: you neednt rub it in.

JENNIFER. But—oh, it is only dawning on me now—I was so surprised at first—do you dare to tell me that it was to gratify a miserable jealousy that you deliberately—oh! oh! you murdered him.

RIDGEON. I think I did. It really comes to that.

Thou shalt not kill, but needst not strive
Officiously to keep alive.

I suppose—yes: I killed him.

JENNIFER. And you tell me that! to my face! callously! You are not afraid!

RIDGEON. I am a doctor: I have nothing to fear. It is not an indictable offence to call in B. B. Perhaps it ought to be; but it isnt.

JENNIFER. I did not mean that. I meant afraid of my taking the law into my own hands, and killing you.

RIDGEON. I am so hopelessly idiotic about you that I should not mind it a bit. You would always remember me if you did that.

JENNIFER. I shall remember you always as a little man who tried to kill a great one.

RIDGEON. Pardon me. I succeeded.

JENNIFER [*with quiet conviction*] No. Doctors think they hold the keys of life and death;

but it is not their will that is fulfilled. I dont believe you made any difference at all.

RIDGEON. Perhaps not. But I intended to.

JENNIFER [*looking at him amazedly: not without pity*] And you tried to destroy that wonderful and beautiful life merely because you grudged him a woman whom you could never have expected to care for you!

RIDGEON. Who kissed my hands. Who believed in me. Who told me her friendship lasted until death.

JENNIFER. And whom you were betraying.

RIDGEON. No. Whom I was saving.

JENNIFER [*gently*] Pray, doctor, from what?

RIDGEON. From making a terrible discovery. From having your life laid waste.

JENNIFER. How?

RIDGEON. No matter. I have saved you. I have been the best friend you ever had. You are happy. You are well. His works are an imperishable joy and pride for you.

JENNIFER. And you think that is your doing. Oh doctor, doctor! Sir Patrick is right: you do think you are a little god. How can you be so silly? You did not paint those pictures which are my imperishable joy and pride: you did not speak the words that will always be heavenly music in my ears. I listen to them now whenever I am tired or sad. That is why I am always happy.

RIDGEON. Yes, now that he is dead. Were you always happy when he was alive?

JENNIFER [*wounded*] Oh, you are cruel, cruel. When he was alive I did not know the greatness of my blessing. I worried meanly about little things. I was unkind to him. I was unworthy of him.

RIDGEON [*laughing bitterly*] Ha!

JENNIFER. Dont insult me: dont blaspheme. [*She snatches up the book and presses it to her heart in a paroxysm of remorse, exclaiming*] Oh, my King of Men!

RIDGEON. King of Men! Oh, this is too monstrous, too grotesque. We cruel doctors have kept the secret from you faithfully; but it is like all secrets: it will not keep itself. The buried truth germinates and breaks through to the light.

JENNIFER. What truth?

RIDGEON. What truth! Why, that Louis Dubedat, King of Men, was the most entire and perfect scoundrel, the most miraculously mean rascal, the most callously selfish blackguard that ever made a wife miserable.

JENNIFER [*unshaken: calm and lovely*] He made his wife the happiest woman in the world, doctor.

RIDGEON. No: by all thats true on earth, he made his widow the happiest woman in the world; but it was I who made her a widow. And her happiness is my justification and my reward. Now you know what I did and what I thought of him. Be as angry with me as you like: at least you know me as I really am. If you ever come to care for an elderly man, you will know what you are caring for.

JENNIFER [*kind and quiet*] I am not angry with you any more, Sir Colenso. I knew quite well that you did not like Louis; but it is not your fault: you dont understand: that is all. You never could have believed in him. It is just like your not believing in my religion: it is a sort of sixth sense that you have not got. And [*with a gentle reassuring movement towards him*] dont think that you have shocked me so dreadfully. I know quite well what you mean by his selfishness. He sacrificed everything for his art. In a certain sense he had even to sacrifice everybody—

RIDGEON. Everybody except himself. By keeping that back he lost the right to sacrifice you, and gave me the right to sacrifice him. Which I did.

JENNIFER [*shaking her head, pitying his error*] He was one of the men who know what women know: that self-sacrifice is vain and cowardly.

RIDGEON. Yes, when the sacrifice is rejected and thrown away. Not when it becomes the food of godhead.

JENNIFER. I dont understand that. And I cant argue with you: you are clever enough to puzzle me, but not to shake me. You are so utterly, so wildly wrong; so incapable of appreciating Louis—

RIDGEON. Oh! [*taking up the Secretary's list*] I have marked five pictures as sold to me.

JENNIFER. They will not be sold to you. Louis' creditors insisted on selling them; but this is my birthday; and they were all bought in for me this morning by my husband.

RIDGEON. By whom?!!!

JENNIFER. By my husband.

RIDGEON [*gabbling and stuttering*] What husband? Whose husband? Which husband? Whom? how? what? Do you mean to say that you have married again?

JENNIFER. Do you forget that Louis dis-

T

liked widows, and that people who have married happily once always marry again?

RIDGEON. Then I have committed a purely disinterested murder!

The Secretary returns with a pile of catalogues.

THE SECRETARY. Just got the first batch of catalogues in time. The doors are open.

JENNIFER [*to Ridgeon, politely*] So glad you like the pictures, Sir Colenso. Good morning.

RIDGEON. Good morning. [*He goes towards the door; hesitates; turns to say something more; gives it up as a bad job; and goes*].

THE END

XVI

GETTING MARRIED

A DISQUISITORY PLAY (1908)

On a fine morning in the spring of 1908 the Norman kitchen in the Palace of the Bishop of Chelsea looks very spacious and clean and handsome and healthy.

The Bishop is lucky enough to have a XII century palace. The palace itself has been lucky enough to escape being carved up into XV century Gothic, or shaved into XVIII century ashlar, or "restored" by a XIX century builder and a Victorian architect with a deep sense of the umbrella-like gentlemanliness of XIV century vaulting. The present occupant, A. Chelsea, unofficially Alfred Bridgenorth, appreciates Norman work. He has, by adroit complaints of the discomfort of the place, induced the Ecclesiastical Commissioners to give him some money to spend on it; and with this he has got rid of the wall papers, the paint, the partitions, the exquisitely planed and moulded casings with which the Victorian cabinet-makers enclosed and hid the huge black beams of hewn oak, and of all the other expedients of his predecessors to make themselves feel at home and respectable in a Norman fortress. It is a house built to last for ever. The walls and beams are big enough to carry the tower of Babel, as if the builders, anticipating our modern ideas and instinctively defying them, had resolved to shew how much material they could lavish on a house built for the glory of God, instead of keeping a competitive eye on the advantage of sending in the lowest tender, and scientifically calculating how little material would be enough to prevent the whole affair from tumbling down by its own weight.

The kitchen is the Bishop's favorite room. This is not at all because he is a man of humble mind; but because the kitchen is one of the finest rooms in the house. The Bishop has neither the income nor the appetite to have his cooking done there. The windows, high up in the wall, look north and south. The north window is the largest; and if we look into the kitchen through it we see facing us the south wall with small Norman windows and an open door near the corner to the left. Through this door we have a glimpse of the garden, and of a garden chair in the sunshine. In the right-hand corner is an entrance to a vaulted circular chamber with a winding stair leading up through a tower to the upper floors of the palace. In the wall to our right is the immense fireplace, with its huge spit like a baby crane, and a collection of old iron and brass instruments which pass as the original furniture of the fire, though as a matter of fact they have been picked up from time to time by the Bishop at secondhand shops. In the near end of the left-hand wall a small Norman door gives access to the Bishop's study, formerly a scullery. Farther along, a great oak chest stands against the wall. Across the middle of the kitchen is a big timber table surrounded by eleven stout rush-bottomed chairs: four on the far side, three on the near side, and two at each end. There is a big chair with railed back and sides on the hearth. On the floor is a drugget of thick fibre matting. The only other piece of furniture is a clock with a wooden dial about as large as the bottom of a washtub, the weights, chains, and pendulum being of corresponding magnitude; but the Bishop has long since abandoned the attempt to keep it going. It hangs above the oak chest.

The kitchen is occupied at present by the Bishop's lady, Mrs Bridgenorth, who is talking to Mr William Collins, the greengrocer. He is in evening dress, though it is early forenoon. Mrs Bridgenorth is a quiet happy-looking woman of fifty or thereabouts, placid, gentle, and humorous, with delicate features and fine grey hair with many white threads. She is dressed as for some *festivity; but she is taking things easily as she sits in the big chair by the hearth, reading The Times.*

Collins is an elderly man with a rather youthful waist. His muttonchop whiskers have a coquettish touch of Dundreary at their lower ends. He is an affable man, with those perfect manners which can be acquired only in keeping a shop for the sale of necessaries of life to ladies whose social position is so unquestionable that they are not anxious about it. He is a reassuring man, with a vigilant grey eye, and the power of saying anything he likes to you without offence, because his tone always implies that he does it with your kind permission. Withal by no means servile: rather gallant and compassionate, but never without a conscientious recognition, on public grounds, of social distinctions. He is at the oak chest counting a pile of napkins.

Mrs Bridgenorth reads placidly: Collins counts: a blackbird sings in the garden. Mrs Bridgenorth puts The Times down in her lap and considers Collins for a moment.

MRS BRIDGENORTH. Do you never feel nervous on these occasions, Collins?

COLLINS. Lord bless you, no, maam. It would be a joke, after marrying five of your daughters, if I was to get nervous over marrying the last of them.

MRS BRIDGENORTH. I have always said you were a wonderful man, Collins.

COLLINS [*almost blushing*] Oh, maam!

MRS BRIDGENORTH. Yes. I never could arrange anything—a wedding or even a dinner—without some hitch or other.

COLLINS. Why should you give yourself the trouble, maam? Send for the greengrocer, maam: thats the secret of easy housekeeping. Bless you, it's his business. It pays him and you, let alone the pleasure in a house like this [*Mrs Bridgenorth bows in acknowledgment of the compliment*]. They joke about the greengrocer, just as they joke about the mother-in-law. But they cant get on without both.

MRS BRIDGENORTH. What a bond between us, Collins!

COLLINS. Bless you, maam, theres all sorts of bonds between all sorts of people. You are a very affable lady, maam, for a Bishop's lady. I have known Bishops' ladies that would fairly provoke you to up and cheek them; but nobody would ever forget himself and his place with you, maam.

MRS BRIDGENORTH. Collins: you are a flatterer. You will superintend the breakfast yourself as usual, of course, wont you?

COLLINS. Yes, yes, bless you, maam, of course. I always do. Them fashionable caterers send down such people as I never did set eyes on. Dukes you would take them for. You see the relatives shaking hands with them and asking them about the family— actually ladies saying "Where have we met before?" and all sorts of confusion. Thats my secret in business, maam. You can always spot me as the greengrocer. It's a fortune to me in these days, when you cant hardly tell who anyone is or isnt. [*He goes out through the tower, and immediately returns for a moment to announce*] The General, maam.

Mrs Bridgenorth rises to receive her brother-in-law, who enters resplendent in full-dress uniform, with many medals and orders. General Bridgenorth is a well set up man of fifty, with large brave nostrils, an iron mouth, faithful dog's eyes, and much natural simplicity and dignity of character. He is ignorant, stupid, and prejudiced, having been carefully trained to be so; and it is not always possible to be patient with him when his unquestionably good intentions become actively mischievous; but one blames society, not himself, for this. He would be no worse a man than Collins, had he enjoyed Collins's social opportunities. He comes to the hearth, where Mrs Bridgenorth is standing with her back to the fireplace.

MRS BRIDGENORTH. Good morning, Boxer. [*They shake hands*]. Another niece to give away. This is the last of them.

THE GENERAL [*very gloomy*] Yes, Alice. Nothing for the old warrior uncle to do but give away brides to luckier men than himself. Has—[*he chokes*] has your sister come yet?

MRS BRIDGENORTH. Why do you always call Lesbia my sister? Dont you know that it annoys her more than any of the rest of your tricks?

THE GENERAL. Tricks! Ha! Well, I'll try to break myself of it; but I think she might bear with me in a little thing like that. She knows that her name sticks in my throat. Better call her your sister than try to call her L— [*he almost breaks down*] L— well, call her by her name and make a fool of myself by crying. [*He sits down at the near end of the table*].

MRS BRIDGENORTH [*going to him and rallying him*] Oh come, Boxer! Really, really! We are no longer boys and girls. You cant keep up a broken heart all your life. It must be nearly twenty years since she refused you. And you know that it's not because she dislikes you, but only that she's not a marrying woman.

THE GENERAL. It's no use. I love her still. And I cant help telling her so whenever we meet, though I know it makes her avoid me. [*He all but weeps*].

MRS BRIDGENORTH. What does she say when you tell her?

THE GENERAL. Only that she wonders when I am going to grow out of it. I know now that I shall never grow out of it.

MRS BRIDGENORTH. Perhaps you would if you married her. I believe youre better as you are, Boxer.

THE GENERAL. I'm a miserable man. I'm really sorry to be a ridiculous old bore, Alice; but when I come to this house for a wedding —to these scenes—to—to—recollections of the past—always to give the bride to somebody else, and never to have my bride given to me—[*he rises abruptly*] May I go into the garden and smoke it off?

MRS BRIDGENORTH. Do, Boxer.

Collins returns with the wedding cake.

MRS BRIDGENORTH. Oh, heres the cake. I believe it's the same one we had for Florence's wedding.

THE GENERAL. I cant bear it [*he hurries out through the garden door*].

COLLINS [*putting the cake on the table*] Well, look at that, maam! Aint it odd that after all the weddings he's given away at, the General cant stand the sight of a wedding cake yet. It always seems to give him the same shock.

MRS BRIDGENORTH. Well, it's his last shock. You have married the whole family now, Collins. [*She takes up The Times again and resumes her seat*].

COLLINS. Except your sister, maam. A fine character of a lady, maam, is Miss Grantham. I have an ambition to arrange her wedding breakfast.

MRS BRIDGENORTH. She wont marry, Collins.

COLLINS. Bless you, maam, they all say that. You and me said it, I'll lay. I did, anyhow.

MRS BRIDGENORTH. No: marriage came natural to me. I should have thought it did to you too.

COLLINS [*pensive*] No, maam: it didnt come natural. My wife had to break me into it. It came natural to her: she's what you might call a regular old hen. Always wants to have her family within sight of her. Wouldnt go to bed unless she knew they was all safe at home and the door locked, and the lights out. Always wants her luggage in the carriage with her. Always goes and makes the engine driver promise her to be careful. She's a born wife and mother, maam. Thats why my children all ran away from home.

MRS BRIDGENORTH. Did you ever feel inclined to run away, Collins?

COLLINS. Oh yes maam, yes: very often. But when it came to the point I couldnt bear to hurt her feelings. She's a sensitive, affectionate, anxious soul; and she was never brought up to know what freedom is to some people. You see, family life is all the life she knows: she's like a bird born in a cage, that would die if you let it loose in the woods. When I thought how little it was to a man of my easy temper to put up with her, and how deep it would hurt her to think it was because I didnt care for her, I always put off running away til next time; and so in the end I never ran away at all. I daresay it was good for me to be took such care of; but it cut me off from all my old friends something dreadful, maam: especially the women, maam. She never gave them a chance: she didnt indeed. She never understood that married people should take holidays from one another if they are to keep at all fresh. Not that I ever got tired of her, maam; but my! how I used to get tired of home life sometimes. I used to catch myself envying my brother George: I positively did, maam.

MRS BRIDGENORTH. George was a bachelor then, I suppose?

COLLINS. Bless you, no, maam. He married a very fine figure of a woman; but she was that changeable and what you might call susceptible, you would not believe. She didnt seem to have any control over herself when she fell in love. She would mope for a couple of days, crying about nothing; and then she would up and say—no matter who was there to hear her—"I must go to him, George"; and away she would go from her home and her husband without with-your-leave or by-your-leave.

MRS BRIDGENORTH. But do you mean that she did this more than once? That she came back?

COLLINS. Bless you, maam, she done it five times to my own knowledge; and then George gave up telling us about it, he got so used to it.

MRS BRIDGENORTH. But did he always take her back?

COLLINS. Well, what could he do, maam? Three times out of four the men would bring her back the same evening and no harm done. Other times theyd run away from her. What could any man with a heart do but comfort her when she came back crying at the way they dodged her when she threw herself at their heads, pretending they was too noble to accept the sacrifice she was making. George told her again and again that if she'd only stay at home and hold off a bit theyd be at her feet all day long. She got sensible at last and took his advice. George always liked change of company.

MRS BRIDGENORTH. What an odious woman, Collins! Dont you think so?

COLLINS [judicially] Well, many ladies with a domestic turn thought so and said so, maam. But I will say for Mrs George that the variety of experience made her wonderful interesting. Thats where the flighty ones score off the steady ones, maam. Look at my old woman! She's never known any man but me; and she cant properly know me, because she dont know other men to compare me with. Of course she knows her parents in—well, in the way one does know one's parents: not knowing half their lives as you might say, or ever thinking that they was ever young; and she knew her children as children, and never thought of them as independent human beings til they ran away and nigh broke her heart for a week or two. But Mrs George she came to know a lot about men of all sorts and ages; for the older she got the younger she liked em; and it certainly made her interesting, and gave her a lot of sense. I have often taken her advice on things when my own poor old woman wouldnt have been a bit of use to me.

MRS BRIDGENORTH. I hope you dont tell your wife that you go elsewhere for advice.

COLLINS. Lord bless you, maam, I'm that fond of my old Matilda that I never tell her anything at all for fear of hurting her feelings. You see, she's such an out-and-out wife and mother that she's hardly a responsible human being out of her house, except when she's marketing.

MRS BRIDGENORTH. Does she approve of Mrs George?

COLLINS. Oh, Mrs George gets round her. Mrs George can get round anybody if she wants to. And then Mrs George is very particular about religion. And she's a clairvoyant.

MRS BRIDGENORTH [surprised] A clairvoyant!

COLLINS [calm] Oh yes, maam, yes. All you have to do is to mesmerize her a bit; and off she goes into a trance, and says the most wonderful things! not things about herself, but as if it was the whole human race giving you a bit of its mind. Oh, wonderful, maam, I assure you. You couldnt think of a game that Mrs George isnt up to.

Lesbia Grantham comes in through the tower. She is a tall, handsome, slender lady in her prime: that is, between 36 and 55. She has what is called a well-bred air, dressing very carefully to produce that effect without the least regard for the latest fashions, sure of herself, very terrifying to the young and shy, fastidious to the ends of her long finger-tips, and tolerant and amused rather than sympathetic.

LESBIA. Good morning, dear big sister.

MRS BRIDGENORTH. Good morning, dear little sister. [They kiss].

LESBIA. Good morning, Collins. How well you are looking! And how young! [She turns the middle chair away from the table and sits down].

COLLINS. Thats only my professional habit at a wedding, Miss. You should see me at a political dinner. I look nigh seventy. [Looking at his watch] Time's getting along, maam. May I send up word from you to Miss Edith to hurry a bit with her dressing?

MRS BRIDGENORTH. Do, Collins.

Collins goes out through the tower, taking the cake with him.

LESBIA. Dear old Collins! Has he told you any stories this morning?

MRS BRIDGENORTH. Yes. You were just late for a particularly thrilling invention of his.

LESBIA. About Mrs George?

MRS BRIDGENORTH. Yes. He says she's a clairvoyant.

LESBIA. I wonder whether he really invented Mrs George, or stole her out of some book.

MRS BRIDGENORTH. I wonder!

LESBIA. Wheres the Barmecide?

MRS BRIDGENORTH. In the study, working away at his new book. He thinks no more now of having a daughter married than of having an egg for breakfast.

The General, soothed by smoking, comes in from the garden.

THE GENERAL [with resolute bonhomie] Ah, Lesbia! How do you do? [They shake hands;

and he takes the chair on her right].

Mrs Bridgenorth goes out through the tower.

LESBIA. How are you, Boxer? You look almost as gorgeous as the wedding cake.

THE GENERAL. I make a point of appearing in uniform whenever I take part in any ceremony, as a lesson to the subalterns. It is not the custom in England; but it ought to be.

LESBIA. You look very fine, Boxer. What a frightful lot of bravery all these medals must represent!

THE GENERAL. No, Lesbia. They represent despair and cowardice. I won all the early ones by trying to get killed. You know why.

LESBIA. But you had a charmed life?

THE GENERAL. Yes, a charmed life. Bayonets bent on my buckles. Bullets passed through me and left no trace: thats the worst of modern bullets: Ive never been hit by a dumdum. When I was only a company officer I had at least the right to expose myself to death in the field. Now I'm a General even that resource is cut off. [*Persuasively drawing his chair nearer to her*] Listen to me, Lesbia. For the tenth and last time—

LESBIA [*interrupting*] On Florence's wedding morning, two years ago, you said "For the ninth and last time."

THE GENERAL. We are two years older, Lesbia. I'm fifty: you are—

LESBIA. Yes, I know. It's no use, Boxer. When will you be old enough to take no for an answer?

THE GENERAL. Never, Lesbia, never. You have never given me a real reason for refusing me yet. I once thought it was somebody else. There were lots of fellows after you; but now theyve all given it up and married. [*Bending still nearer to her*] Lesbia: tell me your secret. Why—

LESBIA [*sniffing disgustedly*] Oh! Youve been smoking. [*She rises and goes to the chair on the hearth*] Keep away, you wretch.

THE GENERAL. But for that pipe, I could not have faced you without breaking down. It has soothed me and nerved me.

LESBIA [*sitting down with The Times in her hand*] Well, it has nerved me to tell you why I'm going to be an old maid.

THE GENERAL [*impulsively approaching her*] Dont say that, Lesbia. It's not natural: it's not right: it's—

LESBIA [*fanning him off*] No: no closer, Boxer, please. [*He retreats, discouraged*]. It

may not be natural; but it happens all the same. Youll find plenty of women like me, if you care to look for them: women with lots of character and good looks and money and offers, who wont and dont get married. Cant you guess why?

THE GENERAL. I can understand when there is another.

LESBIA. Yes; but there isnt another. Besides, do you suppose I think, at my time of life, that the difference between one decent sort of man and another is worth bothering about?

THE GENERAL. The heart has its preferences, Lesbia. One image, and one only, gets indelibly—

LESBIA. Yes. Excuse my interrupting you so often; but your sentiments are so correct that I always know what you are going to say before you finish. You see, Boxer, everybody is not like you. You are a sentimental noodle: you dont see women as they really are. You dont see me as I really am. Now I do see men as they really are. I see you as you really are.

THE GENERAL [*murmuring*] No: dont say that, Lesbia.

LESBIA. I'm a regular old maid. I'm very particular about my belongings. I like to have my own house, and to have it to myself. I have a very keen sense of beauty and fitness and cleanliness and order. I am proud of my independence and jealous for it. I have a sufficiently well-stocked mind to be very good company for myself if I have plenty of books and music. The one thing I never could stand is a great lout of a man smoking all over my house and going to sleep in his chair after dinner, and untidying everything. Ugh!

THE GENERAL. But love—

LESBIA. Oh, love! Have you no imagination? Do you think I have never been in love with wonderful men? heroes! archangels! princes! sages! even fascinating rascals! and had the strangest adventures with them? Do you know what it is to look at a mere real man after that? a man with his boots in every corner, and the smell of his tobacco in every curtain?

THE GENERAL [*somewhat dazed*] Well but—excuse my mentioning it—dont you want children?

LESBIA. I ought to have children. I should be a good mother to children. I believe it would pay the country very well to pay ME very well to have children. But the country tells me that I cant have a child in my house without a man in it too; so I tell the country that it will have to do without my children. If I am to be a mother, I really cannot have a man bothering me to be a wife at the same time.

THE GENERAL. My dear Lesbia: you know I dont wish to be impertinent; but these are not correct views for an English lady to express.

LESBIA. That is why I dont express them, except to gentlemen who wont take any other answer. The difficulty, you see, is that I really am an English lady, and am particularly proud of being one.

THE GENERAL. I'm sure of that, Lesbia: quite sure of it. I never meant—

LESBIA [rising impatiently] Oh, my dear Boxer, do please try to think of something else than whether you have offended me, and whether you are doing the correct thing as an English gentleman. You are faultless, and very dull. [She shakes her shoulders intolerantly and walks across to the other side of the kitchen].

THE GENERAL [moodily] Ha! thats whats the matter with me. Not clever. A poor silly soldier man.

LESBIA. The whole matter is very simple. As I say, I am an English lady, by which I mean that I have been trained to do without what I cant have on honorable terms, no matter what it is.

THE GENERAL. I really dont understand you, Lesbia.

LESBIA [turning on him] Then why on earth do you want to marry a woman you dont understand?

THE GENERAL. I dont know. I suppose I love you.

LESBIA. Well, Boxer, you can love me as much as you like, provided you look happy about it and dont bore me. But you cant marry me; and thats all about it.

THE GENERAL. It's so frightfully difficult to argue the matter fairly with you without wounding your delicacy by overstepping the bounds of good taste. But surely there are calls of nature—

LESBIA. Dont be ridiculous, Boxer.

THE GENERAL. Well how am I to express it? Hang it all, Lesbia, dont you want a husband?

LESBIA. No. I want children; and I want to devote myself entirely to my children, and not to their father. The law will not allow me to do that; so I have made up my mind to have neither husband nor children.

THE GENERAL. But, great Heavens, the natural appetites—

LESBIA. As I said before, an English lady is not the slave of her appetites. That is what an English gentleman seems incapable of understanding. [She sits down at the end of the table, near the study door].

THE GENERAL [huffily] Oh well, if you refuse, you refuse. I shall not ask you again. I'm sorry I returned to the subject. [He retires to the hearth and plants himself there, wounded and lofty].

LESBIA. Dont be cross, Boxer.

THE GENERAL. I'm not cross, only wounded, Lesbia. And when you talk like that, I dont feel convinced: I only feel utterly at a loss.

LESBIA. Well, you know our family rule. When at a loss consult the greengrocer. [Opportunely Collins comes in through the tower]. Here he is.

COLLINS. Sorry to be so much in and out, Miss. I thought Mrs Bridgenorth was here. The table is ready now for the breakfast, if she would like to see it.

LESBIA. If you are satisfied, Collins, I am sure she will be.

THE GENERAL. By the way, Collins: I thought theyd made you an alderman.

COLLINS. So they have, General.

THE GENERAL. Then wheres your gown?

COLLINS. I dont wear it in private life, General.

THE GENERAL. Why? Are you ashamed of it?

COLLINS. No, General. To tell you the truth, I take a pride in it. I cant help it.

THE GENERAL. Attention, Collins. Come here. [Collins comes to him]. Do you see my uniform—all my medals?

COLLINS. Yes, General. They strike the eye, as it were.

THE GENERAL. They are meant to. Very well. Now you know, dont you, that your services to the community as a greengrocer are as important and as dignified as mine as a soldier?

COLLINS. I'm sure it's very honorable of you to say so, General.

THE GENERAL [emphatically] You know also, dont you, that any man who can see anything ridiculous, or unmanly, or unbecoming in your work or in your civic robes is not a gentleman, but a jumping, bounding, snorting cad?

COLLINS. Well, strictly between ourselves, that is my opinion, General.

THE GENERAL. Then why not dignify my niece's wedding by wearing your robes?

COLLINS. A bargain's a bargain, General. Mrs Bridgenorth sent for the greengrocer, not for the alderman. It's just as unpleasant to get more than you bargain for as to get less.

THE GENERAL. I'm sure she will agree with me. I attach importance to this as an affirmation of solidarity in the service of the community. The Bishop's apron, my uniform, your robes: the Church, the Army, and the Municipality.

COLLINS [retiring] Very well, General. [He turns dubiously to Lesbia on his way to the tower]. I wonder what my wife will say, Miss?

THE GENERAL. What! Is your wife ashamed of your robes?

COLLINS. No, sir, not ashamed of them. But she grudged the money for them; and she will be afraid of my sleeves getting into the gravy.

Mrs Bridgenorth, her placidity quite upset, comes in with a letter; hurries past Collins; and comes between Lesbia and the General.

MRS BRIDGENORTH. Lesbia: Boxer: heres a pretty mess!

Collins goes out discreetly.

THE GENERAL. Whats the matter?

MRS BRIDGENORTH. Reginald's in London, and wants to come to the wedding.

THE GENERAL [stupended] Well, dash my buttons!

LESBIA. Oh, all right, let him come.

THE GENERAL. Let him come! Why, the decree has not been made absolute yet. Is he to walk in here to Edith's wedding, reeking from the Divorce Court?

MRS BRIDGENORTH [vexedly sitting down in the middle chair] It's too bad. No: I cant forgive him, Lesbia, really. A man of Reginald's age, with a young wife—the best of girls, and as pretty as she can be—to go off with a common woman from the streets! Ugh!

LESBIA. You must make allowances. What can you expect? Reginald was always weak. He was brought up to be weak. The family property was all mortgaged when he inherited it. He had to struggle along in constant money difficulties, hustled by his solicitors, morally bullied by the Barmecide,

and physically bullied by Boxer, while they two were fighting their own way and getting well trained. You know very well he couldnt afford to marry until the mortgages were cleared and he was over fifty. And then of course he made a fool of himself marrying a child like Leo.

THE GENERAL. But to hit her! Absolutely to hit her! He knocked her down—knocked her flat down on a flowerbed in the presence of his gardener. He! the head of the family! the man that stands before the Barmecide and myself as Bridgenorth of Bridgenorth! to beat his wife and go off with a low woman and be divorced for it in the face of all England! in the face of my uniform and Alfred's apron! I can never forget what I felt: it was only the King's personal request—virtually a command—that stopped me from resigning my commission. I'd cut Reginald dead if I met him in the street.

MRS BRIDGENORTH. Besides, Leo's coming. Theyd meet. It's impossible, Lesbia.

LESBIA. Oh, I forgot that. That settles it. He mustnt come.

THE GENERAL. Of course he mustnt. You tell him that if he enters this house, I'll leave it; and so will every decent man and woman in it.

COLLINS [returning for a moment to announce] Mr Reginald, maam. [He withdraws when Reginald enters].

THE GENERAL [beside himself] Well, dash my buttons!!

Reginald is just the man Lesbia has described. He is hardened and tough physically, and hasty and boyish in his manner and speech, belonging as he does to the large class of English gentlemen of property (solicitor-managed) who have never developed intellectually since their schooldays. He is a muddled, rebellious, hasty, untidy, forgetful, always late sort of man, who very evidently needs the care of a capable woman, and has never been lucky or attractive enough to get it. All the same, a likeable man, from whom nobody apprehends any malice nor expects any achievement. In everything but years he is younger than his brother the General.

REGINALD [coming forward between the General and Mrs Bridgenorth] Alice: it's no use. I cant stay away from Edith's wedding. Good morning, Lesbia. How are you, Boxer? [He offers the General his hand].

THE GENERAL [with crushing stiffness] I was just telling Alice, sir, that if you entered this house, I should leave it.

REGINALD. Well, dont let me detain you, old chap. When you start calling people Sir, youre not particularly good company.

LESBIA. Dont you two begin to quarrel. That wont improve the situation.

MRS BRIDGENORTH. I think you might have waited until you got my answer, Rejjy.

REGINALD. It's so jolly easy to say No in a letter. Wont you let me stay?

MRS BRIDGENORTH. How can I? Leo's coming.

REGINALD. Well, she wont mind.

THE GENERAL. Wont mind!!!!!

LESBIA. Dont talk nonsense, Rejjy; and be off with you.

THE GENERAL [with biting sarcasm] At school you had a theory that women liked being knocked down, I remember.

REGINALD. Youre a nice, chivalrous, brotherly sort of swine, you are.

THE GENERAL. Mr Bridgenorth: are you going to leave this house or am I?

REGINALD. You are, I hope. [He emphasizes his intention to stay by sitting down].

THE GENERAL. Alice: will you allow me to be driven from Edith's wedding by this—

LESBIA [warningly] Boxer!

THE GENERAL. —by this Respondent? Is Edith to be given away by him?

MRS BRIDGENORTH. Certainly not. Reginald: you were not asked to come; and I have asked you to go. You know how fond I am of Leo; and you know what she would feel if she came in and found you here.

COLLINS [again appearing in the tower] Mrs Reginald, maam.

LESBIA	No, no. Ask her to—	
MRS BRIDGE-NORTH	Oh how unfortunate!	[All three clamoring together].
THE GENERAL	Well, dash my buttons!	

It is too late: Leo is already in the kitchen. Collins goes out, mutely abandoning a situation which he deplores but has been unable to save.

Leo is very pretty, very youthful, very restless, and consequently very charming to people who are touched by youth and beauty, as well as to those who regard young women as more or less appetizing lollipops, and dont regard old women at all. Coldly studied, Leo's restlessness is much less lovable than the kittenishness which comes from a rich and fresh vitality. She is a born fusser about herself and everybody else for whom she feels responsible; and her vanity causes her to exaggerate her responsibilities officiously. All her fussing is about little things; but she often calls them by big names, such as Art, the Divine Spark, the world, motherhood, good breeding, the Universe, the Creator, or anything else that happens to strike her imagination as sounding intellectually important. She has more than common imagination and no more than common conception and penetration; so that she is always on the high horse about words and always in the perambulator about things. Considering herself clever, thoughtful, and superior to ordinary weaknesses and prejudices, she recklessly attaches herself to clever men on that understanding, with the result that they are first delighted, then exasperated, and finally bored. When marrying Reginald she told her friends that there was a great deal in him which needed bringing out. If she were a middle-aged man she would be the terror of his club. Being a pretty young woman, she is forgiven everything, proving that "Tout comprendre, c'est tout pardonner" is an error, the fact being that the secret of forgiving everything is to understand nothing.

She runs in fussily, full of her own importance, and swoops on Lesbia, who is much less disposed to spoil her than Mrs Bridgenorth is. But Leo affects a special intimacy with Lesbia, as of two thinkers among the Philistines.

LEO [to Lesbia, kissing her] Good morning. [Coming to Mrs Bridgenorth] How do, Alice? [Passing on towards the hearth] Why so gloomy, General? [Reginald rises between her and the General] Oh, Rejjy! What will the King's Proctor say?

REGINALD. Damn the King's Proctor!

LEO. Naughty. Well, I suppose I must kiss you; but dont any of you tell. [She kisses him. They can hardly believe their eyes]. Have you kept all your promises?

REGINALD. Oh, dont begin bothering about those—

LEO [insisting] Have? You? Kept? Your? Promises? Have you rubbed your head with the lotion every night.

REGINALD. Yes, yes. Nearly every night.

LEO. Nearly! I know what that means. Have you worn your liver pad?

THE GENERAL [solemnly] Leo: forgiveness is one of the most beautiful traits in a woman's nature; but there are things that should not be forgiven to a man. When a man knocks a woman down [Leo gives a little shriek of laughter and collapses on a chair next Mrs

Bridgenorth, on her left]—

REGINALD [*sardonically*] The man that would raise his hand to a woman, save in the way of kindness, is unworthy the name of Bridgenorth. [*He sits down at the end of the table nearest the hearth*].

THE GENERAL [*much huffed*] Oh, well, if Leo does not mind, of course I have no more to say. But I think you might out of consideration for the family, beat your wife in private and not in the presence of the gardener.

REGINALD [*out of patience*] Whats the good of beating your wife unless theres a witness to prove it afterwards? You dont suppose a man beats his wife for the fun of it, do you? How could she have got her divorce if I hadnt beaten her? Nice state of things, that!

THE GENERAL [*gasping*] Do you mean to tell me that you did it in cold blood? simply to get rid of your wife?

REGINALD. No, I didnt: I did it to get her rid of me. What would you do if you were fool enough to marry a woman thirty years younger than yourself, and then found that she didnt care for you, and was in love with a young fellow with a face like a mushroom?

LEO. He has not. [*Bursting into tears*] And you are most unkind to say I didnt care for you. Nobody could have been fonder of you.

REGINALD. A nice way of shewing your fondness! I had to go out and dig that flower bed all over with my own hands to soften it. I had to pick all the stones out of it. And then she complained that I hadnt done it properly, because she got a worm down her neck. I had to go to Brighton with a poor creature who took a fancy to me on the way down, and got conscientious scruples about committing perjury after dinner. I had to put her down in the hotel book as Mrs Reginald Bridgenorth: Leo's name! Do you know what that feels like to a decent man? Do you know what a decent man feels about his wife's name? How would you like to go into a hotel before all the waiters and people with— with that on your arm? Not that it was the poor girl's fault, of course; only she started crying because I couldnt stand her touching me; and now she keeps writing to me. And then I'm held up in the public court for cruelty and adultery, and turned away from Edith's wedding by Alice, and lectured by

you! a bachelor, and a precious green one at that. What do you know about it?

THE GENERAL. Am I to understand that the whole case was one of collusion?

REGINALD. Of course it was. Half the cases are collusions: what are people to do? [*The General, passing his hand dazedly over his bewildered brow, sinks into the railed chair*]. And what do you take me for, that you should have the cheek to pretend to believe all that rot about my knocking Leo about and leaving her for—for a—a— Ugh! you should have seen her.

THE GENERAL. This is perfectly astonishing to me. Why did you do it? Why did Leo allow it?

REGINALD. Youd better ask her.

LEO [*still in tears*] I'm sure I never thought it would be so horrid for Rejjy. I offered honorably to do it myself, and let him divorce me; but he wouldnt. And he said himself that it was the only way to do it— that it was the law that he should do it that way. I never saw that hateful creature until that day in Court. If he had only shewn her to me before, I should never have allowed it.

MRS BRIDGENORTH. You did all this for Leo's sake, Rejjy?

REGINALD [*with an unbearable sense of injury*] I shouldnt mind a bit if it were for Leo's sake. But to have to do it to make room for that mushroom-faced serpent—!

THE GENERAL [*jumping up*] What right had he to be made room for? Are you in your senses? What right?

REGINALD. The right of being a young man, suitable to a young woman. I had no right at my age to marry Leo: she knew no more about life than a child.

LEO. I knew a great deal more about it than a great baby like you. I'm sure I dont know how youll get on with no one to take care of you: I often lie awake at night thinking about it. And now youve made me thoroughly miserable.

REGINALD. Serve you right! [*She weeps*]. There: dont get into a tantrum, Leo?

LESBIA. May one ask who is the mushroom-faced serpent?

LEO. He isnt.

REGINALD. Sinjon Hotchkiss, of course.

MRS BRIDGENORTH. Sinjon Hotchkiss! Why, he's coming to the wedding!

REGINALD. What! In that case I'm off [*he makes for the tower*].

LEO — *[seizing him]* No you shant. You promised to be nice to him.

THE GENERAL — No, dont go, old chap. Not from Edith's wedding.

MRS BRIDGENORTH — Oh, do stay, Rejjy. I shall really be hurt if you desert us.

LESBIA — Better stay, Reginald. You must meet him sooner or later.

[all four rushing after him and capturing him on the threshold]

REGINALD. A moment ago, when I wanted to stay, you were all shoving me out of the house. Now that I want to go, you wont let me.

MRS BRIDGENORTH. I shall send a note to Mr Hotchkiss not to come.

LEO *[weeping again]* Oh, Alice! *[She comes back to her chair, heartbroken].*

REGINALD *[out of patience]* Oh well, let her have her way. Let her have her mushroom. Let him come. Let them all come.

He crosses the kitchen to the oak chest and sits sulkily on it. Mrs Bridgenorth shrugs her shoulders and sits at the table in Reginald's neighborhood listening in placid helplessness. Lesbia, out of patience with Leo's tears, goes into the garden and sits there near the door, snuffing up the open air in her relief from the domestic stuffiness of Reginald's affairs.

LEO. It's so cruel of you to go on pretending that I dont care for you, Rejjy.

REGINALD *[bitterly]* She explained to me that it was only that she had exhausted my conversation.

THE GENERAL *[coming paternally to Leo]* My dear girl: all the conversation in the world has been exhausted long ago. Heaven knows I have exhausted the conversation of the British Army these thirty years; but I dont leave it on that account.

LEO. It's not that Ive exhausted it; but he will keep on repeating it when I want to read or go to sleep. And Sinjon amuses me. He's so clever.

THE GENERAL *[stung]* Ha! The old complaint. You all want geniuses to marry. This demand for clever men is ridiculous. Somebody must marry the plain, honest, stupid fellows. Have you thought of that?

LEO. But there are such lots of stupid women to marry. Why do they want to marry us? Besides, Rejjy knows that I'm quite fond of him. I like him because he

wants me; and I like Sinjon because I want him. I feel that I have a duty to Rejjy.

THE GENERAL. Precisely: you have.

LEO. And, of course, Sinjon has the same duty to me.

THE GENERAL. Tut, tut!

LEO. Oh, how silly the law is! Why cant I marry them both?

THE GENERAL *[shocked]* Leo!

LEO. Well, I love them both. I should like to marry a lot of men. I should like to have Rejjy for every day, and Sinjon for concerts and theatres and going out in the evenings, and some great austere saint for about once a year at the end of the season, and some perfectly blithering idiot of a boy to be quite wicked with. I so seldom feel wicked; and, when I do, it's such a pity to waste it merely because it's too silly to confess to a real grown-up man.

REGINALD. This is the kind of thing, you know—*[Helplessly]* Well, there it is!

THE GENERAL *[decisively]* Alice: this is a job for the Barmecide. He's a Bishop: it's his duty to talk to Leo. I can stand a good deal; but when it comes to flat polygamy and polyandry, we ought to do something.

MRS BRIDGENORTH *[going to the study door]* Do come here a moment, Alfred. We're in a difficulty.

THE BISHOP *[within]* Ask Collins. I'm busy.

MRS BRIDGENORTH. Collins wont do. It's something very serious. Do come just a moment, dear. *[When she hears him coming she takes a chair at the nearest end of the table].*

The Bishop comes out of his study. He is still a slim active man, spare of flesh, and younger by temperament than his brothers. He has a delicate skin, fine hands, a salient nose with chin to match, a short beard which accentuates his sharp chin by bristling forward, clever humorous eyes, not without a glint of mischief in them, ready bright speech, and the ways of a successful man who is always interested in himself and generally rather well pleased with himself. When Lesbia hears his voice she turns her chair towards him, and presently rises and stands in the doorway listening to the conversation.

THE BISHOP *[going to Leo]* Good morning, my dear. Hullo! Youve brought Reginald with you. Thats very nice of you. Have you reconciled them, Boxer?

THE GENERAL. Reconciled them! Why, man, the whole divorce was a put-up job. She wants to marry some fellow named Hotchkiss.

REGINALD. A fellow with a face like—

LEO. You shant, Rejjy. He has a very fine face.

MRS BRIDGENORTH. And now she says she wants to marry both of them, and a lot of other people as well.

LEO. I didnt say I wanted to marry them: I only said I should like to marry them.

THE BISHOP. Quite a nice distinction, Leo.

LEO. Just occasionally, you know.

THE BISHOP [sitting down cosily beside her] Quite so. Sometimes a poet, sometimes a Bishop, sometimes a fairy prince, sometimes somebody quite indescribable, and sometimes nobody at all.

LEO. Yes: thats just it. How did you know?

THE BISHOP. Oh, I should say most imaginative and cultivated young women feel like that. I wouldnt give a rap for one who didnt. Shakespear pointed out long ago that a woman wanted a Sunday husband as well as a weekday one. But, as usual, he didnt follow up the idea.

THE GENERAL [aghast] Am I to understand—

THE BISHOP [cutting him short] Now, Boxer, am I the Bishop or are you?

THE GENERAL [sulkily] You.

THE BISHOP. Then dont ask me are you to understand. "Yours not to reason why: yours but to do and die"—

THE GENERAL. Oh, very well: go on. I'm not clever. Only a silly soldier man. Ha! Go on. [He throws himself into the railed chair, as one prepared for the worst].

MRS BRIDGENORTH. Alfred: dont tease Boxer.

THE BISHOP. If we are going to discuss ethical questions we must begin by giving the devil fair play. Boxer never does. England never does. We always assume that the devil is guilty: and we wont allow him to prove his innocence, because it would be against public morals if he succeeded. We used to do the same with prisoners accused of high treason. And the consequence is that we overreach ourselves; and the devil gets the better of us after all. Perhaps thats what most of us intend him to do.

THE GENERAL. Alfred: we asked you here to preach to Leo. You are preaching at me instead. I am not conscious of having said or done anything that calls for that unsolicited attention.

THE BISHOP. But poor little Leo has only told the simple truth; whilst you, Boxer, are striking moral attitudes.

THE GENERAL. I suppose thats an epigram. I dont understand epigrams. I'm only a silly soldier man. Ha! But I can put a plain question. Is Leo to be encouraged to be a polygamist?

THE BISHOP. Remember the British Empire, Boxer. Youre a British General, you know.

THE GENERAL. What has that to do with polygamy?

THE BISHOP. Well, the great majority of our fellow-subjects are polygamists. I cant as a British Bishop insult them by speaking disrespectfully of polygamy. It's a very interesting question. Many very interesting men have been polygamists: Solomon, Mahomet, and our friend the Duke of—of—hm! I never can remember his name.

THE GENERAL. It would become you better, Alfred, to send that silly girl back to her husband and her duty than to talk clever and mock at your religion. "What God hath joined together let not man put asunder." Remember that.

THE BISHOP. Dont be afraid, Boxer. What God hath joined together no man ever shall put asunder: God will take care of that. [To Leo] By the way, who was it that joined you and Reginald, my dear?

LEO. It was that awful little curate that afterwards drank, and travelled first class with a third-class ticket, and then tried to go on the stage. But they wouldnt have him. He called himself Egerton Fotheringay.

THE BISHOP. Well, whom Egerton Fotheringay hath joined, let Sir Gorell Barnes put asunder by all means.

THE GENERAL. I may be a silly soldier man; but I call this blasphemy.

THE BISHOP [gravely] Better for me to take the name of Mr Egerton Fotheringay in earnest than for you to take a higher name in vain.

LESBIA. Cant you three brothers ever meet without quarrelling?

THE BISHOP [mildly] This is not quarrelling, Lesbia: it's only English family life. Good morning.

LEO. You know, Bishop, it's very dear of you to take my part; but I'm not sure that I'm not a little shocked.

THE BISHOP. Then I think Ive been a little

more successful than Boxer in getting you into a proper frame of mind.

THE GENERAL [*snorting*] Ha!

LEO. Not a bit; for now I'm going to shock you worse than ever. I think Solomon was an old beast.

THE BISHOP. Precisely what you ought to think of him, my dear. Dont apologize.

THE GENERAL [*more shocked*] Well, but hang it! Solomon was in the Bible. And, after all, Solomon was Solomon.

LEO. And I stick to it: I still want to have a lot of interesting men to know quite intimately—to say everything I think of to them, and have them say everything they think of to me.

THE BISHOP. So you shall, my dear, if you are lucky. But you know you neednt marry them all. Think of all the buttons you would have to sew on. Besides, nothing is more dreadful than a husband who keeps telling you everything he thinks, and always wants to know what you think.

LEO [*struck by this*] Well, thats very true of Rejjy: in fact, thats why I had to divorce him.

THE BISHOP [*condoling*] Yes: he repeats himself dreadfully, doesnt he?

REGINALD. Look here, Alfred. If I have my faults, let her find them out for herself without your help.

THE BISHOP. She has found them all out already, Reginald.

LEO [*a little huffily*] After all, there are worse men than Reginald. I daresay he's not so clever as you; but still he's not such a fool as you seem to think him!

THE BISHOP. Quite right, dear: stand up for your husband. I hope you will always stand up for all your husbands. [*He rises and goes to the hearth, where he stands complacently with his back to the fireplace, beaming at them all as at a roomful of children*].

LEO. Please dont talk as if I wanted to marry a whole regiment. For me there can never be more than two. I shall never love anybody but Rejjy and Sinjon.

REGINALD. A man with a face like a—

LEO. I wont have it, Rejjy. It's disgusting.

THE BISHOP. You see, my dear, youll exhaust Sinjon's conversation too in a week or so. A man is like a phonograph with half-a-dozen records. You soon get tired of them all; and yet you have to sit at table whilst he reels them off to every new visitor. In the end you have to be content with his common humanity; and when you come down to that, you find out about men what a great English poet of my acquaintance used to say about women: that they all taste alike. Marry whom you please: at the end of a month he'll be Reginald over again. It wasnt worth changing: indeed it wasnt.

LEO. Then it's a mistake to get married.

THE BISHOP. It is, my dear; but it's a much bigger mistake not to get married.

THE GENERAL [*rising*] Ha! You hear that, Lesbia? [*He joins her at the garden door*].

LESBIA. Thats only an epigram, Boxer.

THE GENERAL. Sound sense, Lesbia. When a man talks rot, thats epigram: when he talks sense, then I agree with him.

REGINALD [*coming off the oak chest and looking at his watch*] It's getting late. Wheres Edith? Hasnt she got into her veil and orange blossoms yet?

MRS BRIDGENORTH. Do go and hurry her, Lesbia.

LESBIA [*going out through the tower*] Come with me, Leo.

LEO [*following Lesbia out*] Yes, certainly.

The Bishop goes over to his wife and sits down, taking her hand and kissing it by way of beginning a conversation with her.

THE BISHOP. Alice: Ive had another letter from the mysterious lady who cant spell. I like that woman's letters. Theres an intensity of passion in them that fascinates me.

MRS BRIDGENORTH. Do you mean Incognita Appassionata?

THE BISHOP. Yes.

THE GENERAL [*turning abruptly: he has been looking out into the garden*] Do you mean to say that women write love-letters to you?

THE BISHOP. Of course.

THE GENERAL. They never do to me.

THE BISHOP. The Army doesnt attract women: the Church does.

REGINALD. Do you consider it right to let them? They may be married women, you know.

THE BISHOP. They always are. This one is. [*To Mrs Bridgenorth*] Dont you think her letters are quite the best love-letters I get? [*To the two men*] Poor Alice has to read my love-letters aloud to me at breakfast, when theyre worth it.

MRS BRIDGENORTH. There really is something fascinating about Incognita. She never gives her address. Thats a good sign.

THE GENERAL. Mf! No assignations, you mean?

THE BISHOP. Oh yes: she began the correspondence by making a very curious but very natural assignation. She wants me to meet her in heaven. I hope I shall.

THE GENERAL. Well, I must say I hope not, Alfred. I hope not.

MRS BRIDGENORTH. She says she is happily married, and that love is a necessary of life to her, but that she must have, high above all her lovers—

THE BISHOP. She has several apparently—

MRS BRIDGENORTH. —some great man who will never know her, never touch her, as she is on earth, but whom she can meet in heaven when she has risen above all the everyday vulgarities of earthly love.

THE BISHOP [rising] Excellent. Very good for her; and no trouble to me. Everybody ought to have one of these idealizations, like Dante's Beatrice. [He clasps his hands behind him, and strolls to the hearth and back, singing].

Lesbia appears in the tower, rather perturbed.

LESBIA. Alice: will you come upstairs? Edith is not dressed.

MRS BRIDGENORTH [rising] Not dressed! Does she know what hour it is?

LESBIA. She has locked herself into her room, reading.

The Bishop's song ceases: he stops dead in his stroll.

THE GENERAL. Reading!

THE BISHOP. What is she reading?

LESBIA. Some pamphlet that came by the eleven o'clock post. She wont come out. She wont open the door. And she says she doesnt know whether she's going to be married or not til she's finished the pamphlet. Did you ever hear such a thing? Do come and speak to her.

MRS BRIDGENORTH. Alfred: you had better go.

THE BISHOP. Try Collins.

LESBIA. Weve tried Collins already. He got all that Ive told you out of her through the keyhole. Come, Alice [She vanishes. Mrs Bridgenorth hurries after her].

THE BISHOP. This means a delay. I shall go back to my work [he makes for the study door].

REGINALD. What are you working at now?

THE BISHOP [stopping] A chapter in my history of marriage. I'm just at the Roman business, you know.

THE GENERAL [coming from the garden door to the chair Mrs Bridgenorth has just left, and sitting down] Not more Ritualism, I hope, Alfred?

THE BISHOP. Oh no. I mean ancient Rome. [He seats himself on the edge of the table]. Ive just come to the period when the propertied classes refused to get married and went in for marriage settlements instead. A few of the oldest families stuck to the marriage tradition so as to keep up the supply of vestal virgins, who had to be legitimate; but nobody else dreamt of getting married. It's all very interesting, because we're coming to that here in England; except that as we dont require any vestal virgins, nobody will get married at all, except the poor, perhaps.

THE GENERAL. You take it devilishly coolly. Reginald: do you think the Barmecide's quite sane?

REGINALD. No worse than ever he was.

THE GENERAL [to the Bishop] Do you mean to say you believe such a thing will ever happen in England as that respectable people will give up being married?

THE BISHOP. In England especially they will. In other countries the introduction of reasonable divorce laws will save the situation; but in England we always let an institution strain itself until it breaks. Ive told our last four Prime Ministers that if they didnt make our marriage laws reasonable there would be a strike against marriage, and that it would begin among the propertied classes, where no Government would dare to interfere with it.

REGINALD. What did they say to that?

THE BISHOP. The usual thing. Quite agreed with me, but were sure that they were the only sensible men in the world and that the least hint of marriage reform would lose them the next election. And then lost it all the same: on cordite, on drink, on Chinese labor in South Africa, on all sorts of trumpery.

REGINALD [lurching across the kitchen towards the hearth with his hands in his pockets] It's no use: they wont listen to our sort. [Turning on them] Of course they have to make you a Bishop and Boxer a General, because, after all, their blessed rabble of snobs and cads and half-starved shopkeepers cant do government work; and the bounders and weekenders are too lazy and vulgar. Theyd simply rot without us; but what do they ever do for us? what attention do they ever pay to what we say and what we want? I take it that we Bridgenorths are a pretty typical English family of the sort that has always set things straight and stuck up for the right to think and believe according to our conscience. But nowadays we are expected to dress and eat as the week-end bounders do, and to think and believe as the converted cannibals of Central Africa do, and to lie down and let every snob and every cad and every half-penny journalist walk over us. Why, theres not a newspaper in England today that represents what I call solid Bridgenorth opinion and tradition. Half of them read as if they were published at the nearest mothers' meeting, and the other half at the nearest motor garage. Do you call these chaps gentlemen? Do you call them Englishmen? I dont. [*He throws himself disgustedly into the nearest chair*].

THE GENERAL [*excited by Reginald's eloquence*] Do you see my uniform? What did Collins say? It strikes the eye. It was meant to. I put it on expressly to give the modern army bounder a smack in the eye. Somebody has to set a right example by beginning. Well, let it be a Bridgenorth. I believe in family blood and tradition, by George.

THE BISHOP [*musing*] I wonder who will begin the stand against marriage. It must come some day. I was married myself before I'd thought about it; and even if I had thought about it I was too much in love with Alice to let anything stand in the way. But, you know, Ive seen one of our daughters after another—Ethel, Jane, Fanny, and Christina and Florence—go out at that door in their veils and orange blossoms; and Ive always wondered whether theyd have gone quietly if theyd known what they were doing. Ive a horrible misgiving about that pamphlet. All progress means war with Society. Heaven forbid that Edith should be one of the combatants!

St John Hotchkiss comes into the tower ushered by Collins. He is a very smart young gentleman of twenty-nine or thereabouts, correct in dress to the last thread of his collar, but too much pre-occupied with his ideas to be embarrassed by any concern as to his appearance. He talks about himself with energetic gaiety. He talks to other people with a sweet forbearance (implying a kindly consideration for their stupidity) which infuriates those whom he does not succeed in amusing. They either lose their tempers with him or try in vain to snub him.

COLLINS [*announcing*] Mr Hotchkiss. [*He withdraws*].

HOTCHKISS [*clapping Reginald gaily on the shoulder as he passes him*] Tootle loo, Rejjy.

REGINALD [*curtly, without rising or turning his head*] Morning.

HOTCHKISS. Good morning, Bishop.

THE BISHOP [*coming off the table*] What on earth are you doing here, Sinjon? You belong to the bridegroom's party: youve no business here until after the ceremony.

HOTCHKISS. Yes, I know: thats just it. May I have a word with you in private? Rejjy or any of the family wont matter; but— [*he glances at the General, who has risen rather stiffly, as he strongly disapproves of the part played by Hotchkiss in Reginald's domestic affairs*].

THE BISHOP. All right, Sinjon. This is our brother, General Bridgenorth. [*He goes to the hearth and posts himself there, with his hands clasped behind him*].

HOTCHKISS. Oh, good! [*He turns to the General, and takes out a card-case*]. As you are in the service, allow me to introduce myself. Read my card, please. [*He presents his card to the astonished General*].

THE GENERAL [*reading*] "Mr St John Hotchkiss, the Celebrated Coward, late Lieutenant in the 165th Fusiliers."

REGINALD [*with a chuckle*] He was sent back from South Africa because he funked an order to attack, and spoiled his commanding officer's plan.

THE GENERAL [*very gravely*] I remember the case now. I had forgotten the name. I'll not refuse your acquaintance, Mr Hotchkiss; partly because youre my brother's guest, and partly because Ive seen too much active service not to know that every man's nerve plays him false at one time or another, and that some very honorable men should never go into action at all, because theyre not built that way. But if I were you I should not use that visiting card. No doubt it's an honorable trait in your character that you dont wish any man to give you his hand in ignorance of your disgrace; but you had better allow us to forget. We wish to forget. It isnt your disgrace alone: it's a disgrace to the army and to all of us. Pardon my plain speaking.

HOTCHKISS [*sunnily*] My dear General, I dont know what fear means in the military sense of the word. Ive fought seven duels with the sabre in Italy and Austria, and one with pistols in France, without turning a hair. There was no other way in which I could vindicate my motives in refusing to make that attack at Smutsfontein. I dont pretend to be a brave man. I'm afraid of wasps. I'm afraid of cats. In spite of the voice of reason, I'm afraid of ghosts; and twice Ive fled across Europe from false alarms of cholera. But afraid to fight I am not. [*He turns gaily to Reginald and slaps him on the shoulder*]. Eh, Rejjy? [*Reginald grunts*].

THE GENERAL. Then why did you not do your duty at Smutsfontein?

HOTCHKISS. I did my duty—my higher duty. If I had made that attack, my commanding officer's plan would have been successful, and he would have been promoted. Now I happen to think that the British Army should be commanded by gentlemen, and by gentlemen alone. This man was not a gentleman. I sacrificed my military career—I faced disgrace and social ostracism—rather than give that man his chance.

THE GENERAL [*generously indignant*] Your commanding officer, sir, was my friend Major Billiter.

HOTCHKISS. Precisely. What a name!

THE GENERAL. And pray, sir, on what ground do you dare allege that Major Billiter is not a gentleman?

HOTCHKISS. By an infallible sign: one of those trifles that stamp a man. He eats rice pudding with a spoon.

THE GENERAL [*very angry*] Confound you, *I* eat rice pudding with a spoon. Now!

HOTCHKISS. Oh, so do I, frequently. But there are ways of doing these things. Billiter's way was unmistakeable.

THE GENERAL. Well, *I*'ll tell you something now. When I thought you were only a coward, I pitied you, and would have done what I could to help you back to your place in Society—

HOTCHKISS [*interrupting him*] Thank you: I havnt lost it. My motives have been fully appreciated. I was made an honorary member of two of the smartest clubs in London when the truth came out.

THE GENERAL. Well, sir, those clubs consist of snobs; and you are a jumping, bounding, prancing, snorting snob yourself.

THE BISHOP [*amused but hospitably remonstrant*] My dear Boxer!

HOTCHKISS [*delighted*] How kind of you to say so, General! Youre quite right: I am a snob. Why not? The whole strength of England lies in the fact that the enormous majority of the English people are snobs. They insult poverty. They despise vulgarity. They love nobility. They admire exclusiveness. They will not obey a man risen from the ranks. They never trust one of their own class. I agree with them. I share their instincts. In my undergraduate days I was a Republican—a Socialist. I tried hard to feel toward a common man as I do towards a duke. I couldnt. Neither can you. Well, why should we be ashamed of this aspiration towards what is above us? Why dont I say that an honest man's the noblest work of God? Because I dont think so. If he's not a gentleman, I dont care whether he's honest or not: I shouldnt let his son marry my daughter. And thats the test, mind. Thats the test. You feel as I do. You are a snob in fact: I am a snob, not only in fact, but on principle. I shall go down in history, not as the first snob, but as the first avowed champion of English snobbery, and its first martyr in the army. The navy boasts two such martyrs in Captains Kirby and Wade, who were shot for refusing to fight under Admiral Benbow, a promoted cabin boy. I have always envied them their glory.

THE GENERAL. As a British General, sir, I have to inform you that if any officer under my command violated the sacred equality of our profession by putting a single jot of his duty or his risk on the shoulders of the humblest drummer boy, I'd shoot him with my own hand.

HOTCHKISS. That sentiment is not your equality, General, but your superiority. Ask the Bishop. [*He seats himself on the edge of the table*].

THE BISHOP. I cant support you, Sinjon. My profession also compels me to turn my back on snobbery. You see, I have to do such a terribly democratic thing to every child that is brought to me. Without distinction of class I have to confer on it a rank so high and awful that all the grades in Debrett and Burke seem like the medals they give children in Infant Schools in comparison. I'm not allowed to make any class distinction. They are all soldiers and servants, not officers and masters.

HOTCHKISS. Ah, youre quoting the Baptism

service. Thats not a bit real, you know. If I may say so, you would both feel so much more at peace with yourselves if you would acknowledge and confess your real convictions. You know you dont really think a Bishop the equal of a curate, or a lieutenant in a line regiment the equal of a general.

THE BISHOP. Of course I do. I was a curate myself.

THE GENERAL. And I was a lieutenant in a line regiment.

REGINALD. And I was nothing. But we're all our own and oneanother's equals, arnt we? So perhaps when youve quite done talking about yourselves, we shall get to whatever business Sinjon came about.

HOTCHKISS [coming off the table hastily] Oh! true, my dear fellow. I beg a thousand pardons. It's about the wedding!

THE GENERAL. What about the wedding?

HOTCHKISS. Well, we cant get our man up to the scratch. Cecil has locked himself in his room and wont see or speak to anyone. I went up to his room and banged at the door. I told him I should look through the keyhole if he didnt answer. I looked through the keyhole. He was sitting on his bed, reading a book. [Reginald rises in consternation. The General recoils]. I told him not to be an ass, and so forth. He said he was not going to budge until he had finished the book. I asked him did he know what time it was, and whether he happened to recollect that he had a rather important appointment to marry Edith. He said the sooner I stopped interrupting him, the sooner he'd be ready. Then he stuffed his fingers in his ears; turned over on his elbows; and buried himself in his beastly book. I couldnt get another word out of him; so I thought I'd better come here and warn you.

REGINALD. This looks to me like a practical joke. Theyve arranged it between them.

THE BISHOP. No. Edith has no sense of humor. And Ive never seen a man in a jocular mood on his wedding morning.

Collins appears in the tower, ushering in the bridegroom, a young gentleman with good looks of the serious kind, somewhat careworn by an exacting conscience, and just now distracted by insoluble problems of conduct.

COLLINS [announcing] Mr Cecil Sykes. [He retires].

HOTCHKISS. Look here, Cecil: this is all wrong. Youve no business here until after the wedding. Hang it, man! youre the bridegroom.

SYKES [coming to the Bishop, and addressing him with dogged desperation] Ive come here to say this. When I proposed to Edith I was in utter ignorance of what I was letting myself in for legally. Having given my word, I will stand to it. You have me at your mercy: marry me if you insist. But take notice that I protest. [He sits down distractedly in the railed chair.]

THE GENERAL.	[Both highly incensed]	What the devil do you mean by this? What the—
REGINALD.		Confound your impertinence, what do you—
HOTCHKISS.		Easy, Rejjy. Easy, old man. Steady, steady, steady. [Reginald subsides into his chair. Hotchkiss sits on his right, appeasing him].
THE BISHOP.		No, please, Rej. Control yourself, Boxer, I beg you.

THE GENERAL. I tell you I cant control myself. Ive been controlling myself for the last half-hour until I feel like bursting. [He sits down furiously at the end of the table next the study].

SYKES [pointing to the simmering Reginald and the boiling General] Thats just it, Bishop. Edith is her uncles' niece. She cant control herself any more than they can. And she's a Bishop's daughter. That means that she's engaged in social work of all sorts: organizing shop assistants and sweated work girls and all that. When her blood boils about it (and it boils at least once a week) she doesnt care what she says.

REGINALD. Well: you knew that when you proposed to her.

SYKES. Yes; but I didnt know that when we were married I should be legally responsible if she libelled anybody, though all her property is protected against me as if I were the lowest thief and cadger. This morning somebody sent me Belfort Bax's essays on Men's Wrongs; and they have been a perfect eye-opener to me. Bishop: I'm not thinking of myself: I would face anything for Edith. But my mother and sisters are wholly dependent on my property. I'd rather have to cut off an inch from my right arm than a hundred a year from my mother's income. I owe everything to her care of me.

Edith, in dressing-jacket and petticoat, comes in through the tower, swiftly and determinedly, pamphlet in hand, principles up in arms, more of a bishop than her father, yet as much a gentlewoman as her mother. She is the typical spoilt child of a clerical household: almost as terrible a product as the typical spoilt child of a Bohemian household: that is, all her childish affectations of conscientious scruple and religious impulse have been applauded and deferred to until she has become an ethical snob of the first water. Her father's sense of humor and her mother's placid balance have done something to save her humanity; but her impetuous temper and energetic will, unrestrained by any touch of humor or scepticism, carry everything before them. Imperious and dogmatic, she takes command of the party at once.

EDITH [*standing behind Cecil's chair*] Cecil: I heard your voice. I must speak to you very particularly. Papa: go away. Go away everybody.

THE BISHOP [*crossing to the study door*] I think there can be no doubt that Edith wishes us to retire. Come. [*He stands in the doorway, waiting for them to follow*].

SYKES. Thats it, you see. It's just this outspokenness that makes my position hard, much as I admire her for it.

EDITH. Do you want me to flatter and be untruthful?

SYKES. No, not exactly that.

EDITH. Does anybody want me to flatter and be untruthful?

HOTCHKISS. Well, since you ask me, I do. Surely, it's the very first qualification for tolerable social intercourse.

THE GENERAL [*markedly*] I hope you will always tell me the truth, my darling, at all events.

EDITH [*complacently coming to the fireplace*] You can depend on me for that, Uncle Boxer.

HOTCHKISS. Are you sure you have any adequate idea of what the truth about a military man really is?

REGINALD [*aggressively*] Whats the truth about you, I wonder?

HOTCHKISS. Oh, quite unfit for publication in its entirety. If Miss Bridgenorth begins telling it, I shall have to leave the room.

REGINALD. I'm not at all surprised to hear it. [*Rising*] But whats it got to do with our business here today? Is it you thats going to be married or is it Edith?

HOTCHKISS. I'm so sorry. I get so interested in myself that I thrust myself into the front of every discussion in the most insufferable way. [*Reginald, with an exclamation of disgust, crosses the kitchen towards the study door*]. But my dear Rejjy, are you quite sure that Miss Bridgenorth is going to be married? A r e you, Miss Bridgenorth?

Before Edith has time to answer her mother returns with Leo and Lesbia.

LEO. Yes, here she is, of course. I told you I heard her dash downstairs. [*She comes to the end of the table next the fireplace*].

MRS BRIDGENORTH [*transfixed in the middle of the kitchen*] And Cecil!!

LESBIA. And Sinjon!

THE BISHOP. Edith wishes to speak to Cecil. [*Mrs Bridgenorth comes to him. Lesbia goes into the garden, as before*]. Let us go into my study.

LEO. But she must come and dress. Look at the hour!

MRS BRIDGENORTH. Come, Leo dear. [*Leo follows her reluctantly. They are about to go into the study with the Bishop*].

HOTCHKISS. Do you know, Miss Bridgenorth, I should most awfully like to hear what you have to say to poor Cecil.

REGINALD [*scandalized*] Well!

EDITH. Who is p o o r Cecil, pray?

HOTCHKISS. One always calls a man that on his wedding morning: I dont know why. I'm his best man, you know. Dont you think it gives me a certain right to be present in Cecil's interest?

THE GENERAL [*gravely*] There is such a thing as delicacy, Mr Hotchkiss.

HOTCHKISS. There is such a thing as curiosity, General.

THE GENERAL [*furious*] Delicacy is thrown away here, Alfred. Edith: you had better take Sykes into the study.

The group at the study door breaks up. The General flings himself into the last chair on the long side of the table, near the garden door. Leo sits at the end, next him, and Mrs Bridgenorth next Leo. Reginald returns to the oak chest, to be near Leo; and the Bishop goes to his wife and stands by her.

HOTCHKISS [*to Edith*] Of course I'll go if you wish me to. But Cecil's objection to go through with it was so entirely on public grounds—

EDITH [*with quick suspicion*] H i s objection?

SYKES. Sinjon: you have no right to say that. I expressly said that I'm ready to go through with it.

EDITH. Cecil: do you mean to say that you have been raising difficulties about our marriage?

SYKES. I raise no difficulty. But I do beg you to be careful what you say about people. You must remember, my dear, that when we are married I shall be responsible for everything you say. Only last week you said on a public platform that Slattox and Chinnery were scoundrels. They could have got a thousand pounds damages apiece from me for that if we'd been married at the time.

EDITH [*austerely*] I never said anything of the sort. I never stoop to mere vituperation: what would my girls say of me if I did? I chose my words most carefully. I said they were tyrants, liars, and thieves; and so they are. Slattox is even worse.

HOTCHKISS. I'm afraid that would be at least five thousand pounds.

SYKES. If it were only myself, I shouldnt care. But my mother and sisters! Ive no right to sacrifice them.

EDITH. You neednt be alarmed. I'm not going to be married.

ALL THE REST. Not!

SYKES [*in consternation*] Edith! Are you throwing me over?

EDITH. How can I? you have been beforehand with me.

SYKES. On my honor, no. All I said was that I didnt know the law when I asked you to be my wife.

EDITH. And you wouldnt have asked me if you had. Is that it?

SYKES. No. I should have asked you for my sake to be a little more careful—not to ruin me uselessly.

EDITH. You think the truth useless?

HOTCHKISS. Much worse than useless, I assure you. Frequently most mischievous.

EDITH. Sinjon: hold your tongue. You are a chatterbox and a fool!

| MRS BRIDGENORTH | | | Edith! |
| THE BISHOP | } | [*shocked*] { | My love! |

HOTCHKISS [*mildly*] I shall not take an action, Cecil.

EDITH [*to Hotchkiss*] Sorry; but you are old enough to know better. [*To the others*] And now since there is to be no wedding, we had better get back to our work. Mamma: will you tell Collins to cut up the wedding cake

into thirty-three pieces for the club girls. My not getting married is no reason why they should be disappointed. [*She turns to go*].

HOTCHKISS [*gallantly*] If youll allow me to take Cecil's place, Miss Bridgenorth—

LEO. Sinjon!

HOTCHKISS. Oh, I forgot. I beg your pardon. [*To Edith, apologetically*] A prior engagement.

EDITH. What! You and Leo! I thought so. Well, hadnt you two better get married at once? I dont approve of long engagements. The breakfast's ready: the cake's ready: everything's ready. I'll lend Leo my veil and things.

THE BISHOP. I'm afraid they must wait until the decree is made absolute, my dear. And the license is not transferable.

EDITH. Oh well, it cant be helped. Is there anything else before I go off to the Club?

SYKES. You dont seem much disappointed, Edith. I cant help saying that much.

EDITH. And you cant help looking enormously relieved, Cecil. We shant be any worse friends, shall we?

SYKES [*distractedly*] Of course not. Still— I'm perfectly ready—at least—if it were not for my mother—Oh, I dont know what to do. Ive been so fond of you; and when the worry of the wedding was over I should have been so fond of you again—

EDITH [*petting him*] Come, come! dont make a scene, dear. Youre quite right. I dont think a woman doing public work ought to get married unless her husband feels about it as she does. I dont blame you at all for throwing me over.

REGINALD [*bouncing off the chest, and passing behind the General to the other end of the table*] No: dash it! I'm not going to stand this. Why is the man always to be put in the wrong? Be honest, Edith. Why werent you dressed? Were you going to throw him over? If you were, take your fair share of the blame; and dont put it all on him.

HOTCHKISS [*sweetly*] Would it not be better—

REGINALD [*violently*] Now look here, Hotchkiss. Who asked you to cut in? Is your name Edith? Am I your uncle?

HOTCHKISS. I wish you were: I should like to have an uncle Reginald.

REGINALD. Yah! Sykes: are you ready to marry Edith or are you not?

SYKES. Ive already said that I'm quite

ready. A promise is a promise.

REGINALD. We dont want to know whether a promise is a promise or not. Cant you answer yes or no without spoiling it and setting Hotchkiss here grinning like a Cheshire cat? If she puts on her veil and goes to Church, will you marry her?

SYKES. Certainly. Yes.

REGINALD. Thats all right. Now, Edie, put on your veil and off with you to Church. The bridegroom's waiting. [*He sits down at the table*].

EDITH. Is it understood that Slattox and Chinnery are liars and thieves, and that I hope by next Wednesday to have in my hands conclusive evidence that Slattox is something much worse?

SYKES. I made no conditions as to that when I proposed to you; and now I cant go back. I hope Providence will spare my poor mother. I say again I'm ready to marry you.

EDITH. Then I think you shew great weakness of character; and instead of taking advantage of it I shall set you a better example. I want to know is this true. [*She produces a pamphlet and takes it to the Bishop; then sits down between Hotchkiss and her mother*].

THE BISHOP [*reading the title*] DO YOU KNOW WHAT YOU ARE GOING TO DO? BY A WOMAN WHO HAS DONE IT. May I ask, my dear, what she did?

EDITH. She got married. When she had three children—the eldest only four years old—her husband committed a murder, and then attempted to commit suicide, but only succeeded in disfiguring himself. Instead of hanging him, they sent him to penal servitude for life, for the sake, they said, of his wife and infant children. And she could not get a divorce from that horrible murderer. They would not even keep him imprisoned for life. For twenty years she had to live singly, bringing up her children by her own work, and knowing that just when they were grown up and beginning life, this dreadful creature would be let out to disgrace them all, and prevent the two girls getting decently married, and drive the son out of the country perhaps. Is that really the law? Am I to understand that if Cecil commits a murder, or forges, or steals, or becomes an atheist, I cant get divorced from him?

THE BISHOP. Yes, my dear. That is so. You must take him for better for worse.

EDITH. Then I most certainly refuse to enter into any such wicked contract. What sort of servants? what sort of friends? what sort of Prime Ministers should we have if we took them for better for worse for all their lives? We should simply encourage them in every sort of wickedness. Surely my husband's conduct is of more importance to me than Mr Balfour's or Mr Asquith's. If I had known the law I would never have consented. I dont believe any woman would if she realized what she was doing.

SYKES. But I'm not going to commit murder.

EDITH. How do you know? Ive sometimes wanted to murder Slattox. Have you never wanted to murder somebody, Uncle Rejjy?

REGINALD [*at Hotchkiss, with intense expression*] Yes.

LEO. Rejjy!

REGINALD. I said yes; and I mean yes. There was one night, Hotchkiss, when I jolly nearly shot you and Leo and finished up with myself; and thats the truth.

LEO [*suddenly whimpering*] Oh Rejjy [*she runs to him and kisses him*].

REGINALD [*wrathfully*] Be off. [*She returns weeping to her seat*].

MRS BRIDGENORTH [*petting Leo, but speaking to the company at large*] But isnt all this great nonsense? What likelihood is there of any of us committing a crime?

HOTCHKISS. Oh yes, I assure you. I went into the matter once very carefully; and I found that things I have actually done— things that everybody does, I imagine— would expose me, if I were found out and prosecuted, to ten years penal servitude, two years hard labor, and the loss of all civil rights. Not counting that I'm a private trustee, and, like all private trustees, a fraudulent one. Otherwise, the widow for whom I am trustee would starve occasionally, and the children get no education. And I'm probably as honest a man as any here.

THE GENERAL [*outraged*] Do you imply that I have been guilty of conduct that would expose me to penal servitude?

HOTCHKISS. I should think it quite likely. But of course I dont know.

MRS BRIDGENORTH. But bless me! marriage is not a question of law, is it? Have you children no affection for oneanother? Surely thats enough?

HOTCHKISS. If it's enough, why get married.

MRS BRIDGENORTH. Stuff, Sinjon! Of course people must get married. [*Uneasily*] Alfred: why dont you say something? Surely youre not going to let this go on?

THE GENERAL. Ive been waiting for the last twenty minutes, Alfred, in amazement! in stupefaction! to hear you put a stop to all this. We look to you: it's your place, your office, your duty. Exert your authority at once.

THE BISHOP. You must give the devil fair play, Boxer. Until you have heard and weighed his case you have no right to condemn him. I'm sorry you have been kept waiting twenty minutes; but I myself have waited twenty years for this to happen. Ive often wrestled with the temptation to pray that it might not happen in my own household. Perhaps it was a presentiment that it might become a part of our old Bridgenorth burden that made me warn our Governments so earnestly that unless the law of marriage were first made human it could never become divine.

MRS BRIDGENORTH. Oh, do be sensible about this. People must get married. What would you have said if Cecil's parents had not been married?

THE BISHOP. They were not, my dear.

HOTCHKISS. Hallo!

REGINALD. What d'ye mean?

THE GENERAL. Eh?

LEO. Not married!

MRS BRIDGENORTH. What!

SYKES [*rising in amazement*] What on earth do you mean, Bishop? My parents were married.

HOTCHKISS. You cant remember, Cecil.

SYKES. Well, I never asked my mother to shew me her marriage lines, if thats what you mean. What man ever has? I never suspected—I never knew—Are you joking? Or have we all gone mad?

THE BISHOP. Dont be alarmed, Cecil. Let me explain. Your parents were not Anglicans. You were not, I think, Anglican yourself until your second year at Oxford. They were Positivists. They went through the Positivist ceremony at Newton Hall in Fetter Lane after entering into the civil contract before the Registrar of the West Strand District. I ask you, as an Anglican Catholic, was that a marriage?

SYKES [*overwhelmed*] Great Heavens, no! a thousand times no. I never thought of that.

I'm a child of sin. [*He collapses into the railed chair*].

THE BISHOP. Oh, come, come! You are no more a child of sin than any Jew, or Mahometan, or Nonconformist, or anyone else born outside the Church. But you see how it affects my view of the situation. To me there is only one marriage that is holy: the Church's sacrament of marriage. Outside that, I can recognize no distinction between one civil contract and another. There was a time when all marriages were made in Heaven. But because the Church was unwise and would not make its ordinances reasonable, its power over men and women was taken away from it; and marriages gave place to contracts at a registry office. And now that our Governments refuse to make these contracts reasonable, those whom we in our blindness drove out of the Church will be driven out of the registry office; and we shall have the history of Ancient Rome repeated. We shall be joined by our solicitors for seven, fourteen, or twenty-one years—or perhaps months. Deeds of partnership will replace the old vows.

THE GENERAL. Would you, a Bishop, approve of such partnerships?

THE BISHOP. Do you think that I, a Bishop, approve of the Deceased Wife's Sister Act? That did not prevent its becoming law.

THE GENERAL. But when the Government sounded you as to whether youd marry a man to his deceased wife's sister you very naturally and properly told them youd see them damned first.

THE BISHOP [*horrified*] No, no, really, Boxer! You must not—

THE GENERAL [*impatiently*] Oh, of course I dont mean that you used those words. But that was the meaning and the spirit of it.

THE BISHOP. Not the spirit, Boxer, I protest. But never mind that. The point is that State marriage is already divorced from Church marriage. The relations between Leo and Rejjy and Sinjon are perfectly legal; but do you expect me, as a Bishop, to approve of them?

THE GENERAL. I dont defend Reginald. He should have kicked you out of the house, Mr Hotchkiss.

REGINALD [*rising*] How could I kick him out of the house? He's stronger than me: he could have kicked me out if it came to that. He did kick me out: what else was it but kicking out, to take my wife's affections from me and establish himself in my place? [*He comes to the hearth*].

HOTCHKISS. I protest, Reginald, I said all that a man could to prevent the smash.

REGINALD. Oh, I know you did: I dont blame you: people dont do these things to one another: they happen and they cant be helped. What was I to do? I was old: she was young. I was dull: he was brilliant. I had a face like a walnut: he had a face like a mushroom. I was as glad to have him in the house as she was: he amused me. And we were a couple of fools: he gave us good advice —told us what to do when we didnt know. She found out that I wasnt any use to her and he was; so she nabbed him and gave me the chuck.

LEO. If you dont stop talking in that disgraceful way about our married life, I'll leave the room and never speak to you again.

REGINALD. Youre not going to speak to me again, anyhow, are you? Do you suppose I'm going to visit you when you marry him?

HOTCHKISS. I hope so. Surely youre not going to be vindictive, Rejjy. Besides, youll have all the advantages I formerly enjoyed. Youll be the visitor, the relief, the new face, the fresh news, the hopeless attachment: *I* shall only be the husband.

REGINALD [*savagely*] Will you tell me this, any of you? how is it that we always get talking about Hotchkiss when our business is about Edith? [*He fumes up the kitchen to the tower and back to his chair*].

MRS BRIDGENORTH. Will somebody tell me how the world is to get on if nobody is to get married?

SYKES. Will somebody tell me what an honorable man and a sincere Anglican is to propose to a woman whom he loves and who loves him and wont marry him?

LEO. Will somebody tell me how I'm to arrange to take care of Rejjy when I'm married to Sinjon. Rejjy must not be allowed to marry anyone else, especially that odious nasty creature that told all those wicked lies about him in Court.

HOTCHKISS. Let us draw up the first English partnership deed.

LEO. For shame, Sinjon!

THE BISHOP. Somebody must begin, my dear. Ive a very strong suspicion that when it is drawn up it will be so much worse than the existing law that you will all prefer get-

ting married. We shall therefore be doing the greatest possible service to morality by just trying how the new system would work.

LESBIA [*suddenly reminding them of her forgotten presence as she stands thoughtfully in the garden doorway*] Ive been thinking.

THE BISHOP [*to Hotchkiss*] Nothing like making people think: is there, Sinjon?

LESBIA [*coming to the table, on the General's left*] A woman has no right to refuse motherhood. That is clear, after the statistics given in The Times by Mr Sidney Webb.

THE GENERAL. Mr Webb has nothing to do with it. It is the Voice of Nature.

LESBIA. But if she is an English lady it is her right and her duty to stand out for honorable conditions. If we can agree on the conditions, I am willing to enter into an alliance with Boxer.

The General staggers to his feet, momentarily stupent and speechless.

EDITH [*rising*] And I with Cecil.

LEO [*rising*] And I with Rejjy and St John.

THE GENERAL [*aghast*] An alliance! Do you mean a—a—a—

REGINALD. She only means bigamy, as I understand her.

THE GENERAL. Alfred: how long more are you going to stand there and countenance this lunacy? Is it a horrible dream or am I awake? In the name of common sense and sanity, let us get back to real life—

Collins comes in through the tower, in alderman's robes. The ladies who are standing sit down hastily, and look as unconcerned as possible.

COLLINS. Sorry to hurry you, my lord; but the Church has been full this hour past; and the organist has played all the wedding music in *Lohengrin* three times over.

THE GENERAL. The very man we want. Alfred: I'm not equal to this crisis. You are not equal to it. The Army has failed. The Church has failed. I shall put aside all idle social distinctions and appeal to the Municipality.

MRS BRIDGENORTH. Do, Boxer. He is sure to get us out of this difficulty.

Collins, a little puzzled, comes forward affably to Hotchkiss's left.

HOTCHKISS [*rising, impressed by the aldermanic gown*] Ive not had the pleasure. Will you introduce me?

COLLINS [*confidentially*] All right, sir. Only the greengrocer, sir, in charge of the wedding breakfast. Mr Alderman Collins, sir, when I'm in my gown.

HOTCHKISS [*staggered*] Very pleased indeed [*he sits down again*].

THE BISHOP. Personally I value the counsel of my old friend, Mr Alderman Collins, very highly. If Edith and Cecil will allow him—

EDITH. Collins has known me from my childhood: I'm sure he will agree with me.

COLLINS. Yes, miss: you may depend on me for that. Might I ask what the difficulty is?

EDITH. Simply this. Do you expect me to get married in the existing state of the law?

SYKES [*rising and coming to Collins's left elbow*] I put it to you as a sensible man: is it any worse for her than for me?

REGINALD [*leaving his place and thrusting himself between Collins and Sykes, who returns to his chair*] Thats not the point. Let this be understood, Mr Collins. It's not the man who is backing out: it's the woman. [*He posts himself on the hearth*].

LESBIA. We do not admit that, Collins. The women are perfectly ready to make a reasonable arrangement.

LEO. With both men.

THE GENERAL. The case is now before you, Mr Collins. And I put it to you as one man to another: did you ever hear such crazy nonsense?

MRS BRIDGENORTH. The world must go on, mustnt it, Collins?

COLLINS [*snatching at this, the first intelligible proposition he has heard*] Oh, the world will go on, maam: dont you be afraid of that. It aint so easy to stop it as the earnest kind of people think.

EDITH. I knew you would agree with me, Collins. Thank you.

HOTCHKISS. Have you the least idea of what they are talking about, Mr Alderman?

COLLINS. Oh, thats all right, sir. The particulars dont matter. I never read the report of a Committee: after all, what can they say that you dont know? You pick it up as they go on talking. [*He goes to the corner of the table and speaks across it to the company*]. Well, my Lord and Miss Edith and Madam and Gentlemen, it's like this. Marriage is tolerable enough in its way if youre easygoing and dont expect too much from it. But it doesnt bear thinking about. The great thing is to get the young people tied up before they know what theyre letting themselves in for.

Theres Miss Lesbia now. She waited til she started thinking about it; and then it was all over. If you once start arguing, Miss Edith and Mr Sykes, youll never get married. Go and get married first: youll have plenty of arguing afterwards, miss, believe me.

HOTCHKISS. Your warning comes too late. Theyve started arguing already.

THE GENERAL. But you dont take in the full —well, I dont wish to exaggerate; but the only word I can find is the full horror of the situation. These ladies not only refuse our honorable offers, but as I understand it—and I'm sure I beg your pardon most heartily, Lesbia, if I'm wrong, as I hope I am—they actually call on us to enter into—I'm sorry to use the expression; but what can I say?— into ALLIANCES with them under contracts to be drawn up by our confounded solicitors.

COLLINS. Dear me, General: thats something new when the parties belong to the same class.

THE BISHOP. Not new, Collins. The Romans did it.

COLLINS. Yes: they would, them Romans. When youre in Rome do as the Romans do, is an old saying. But we're not in Rome at present, my lord.

THE BISHOP. We have got into many of their ways. What do you think of the contract system, Collins?

COLLINS. Well, my lord, when theres a question of a contract, I always say, shew it to me on paper. If it's to be talk, let it be talk; but if it's to be a contract, down with it in black and white; and then we shall know what we're about.

HOTCHKISS. Quite right, Mr Alderman. Let us draft it at once. May I go into the study for writing materials, Bishop?

THE BISHOP. Do, Sinjon.

Hotchkiss goes into the library.

COLLINS. If I might point out a difficulty, my lord—

THE BISHOP. Certainly. [*He goes to the fourth chair from the General's left, but before sitting down, courteously points to the chair at the end of the table next the hearth*]. Wont you sit down, Mr Alderman? [*Collins, very appreciative of the Bishop's distinguished consideration, sits down. The Bishop then takes his seat*].

COLLINS. We are at present six men to four ladies. Thats not fair.

REGINALD. Not fair to the men, you mean.

LEO. Oh! Rejjy has said something clever!

Can I be mistaken in him?

Hotchkiss comes back with a blotter and some paper. He takes the vacant place in the middle of the table between Lesbia and the Bishop.

COLLINS. I tell you the truth, my lord and ladies and gentlemen: I dont trust my judgment on this subject. Theres a certain lady that I always consult on delicate points like this. She has a very exceptional experience, and a wonderful temperament and instinct in affairs of the heart.

HOTCHKISS. Excuse me, Mr Alderman: I'm a snob, and I warn you that theres no use consulting anyone who will not advise us frankly on class lines. Marriage is good enough for the lower classes: they have facilities for desertion that are denied to us. What is the social position of this lady?

COLLINS. The highest in the borough, sir. She is the Mayoress. But you need not stand in awe of her, sir. She is my sister-in-law. [*To the Bishop*] Ive often spoken of her to your lady, my lord. [*To Mrs Bridgenorth*] Mrs George, maam.

MRS BRIDGENORTH [*startled*] Do you mean to say, Collins, that Mrs George is a real person?

COLLINS [*equally startled*] Didnt you believe in her, maam?

MRS BRIDGENORTH. Never for a moment.

THE BISHOP. We always thought that Mrs George was too good to be true. I still dont believe in her, Collins. You must produce her if you are to convince me.

COLLINS [*overwhelmed*] Well, I'm so taken aback by this that—Well I never!!! Why! she's at the church at this moment, waiting to see the wedding.

THE BISHOP. Then produce her. [*Collins shakes his head*]. Come, Collins! confess. Theres no such person.

COLLINS. There is, my lord: there is, I assure you. You ask George. It's true *I* cant produce her; but you can, my lord.

THE BISHOP. I!

COLLINS. Yes, my lord, you. For some reason that I never could make out, she has forbidden me to talk about you, or to let her meet you. Ive asked her to come here of a wedding morning to help with the flowers or the like; and she has always refused. But if you order her to come as her Bishop, she'll come. She has some very strange fancies, has Mrs George. Send your ring to her, my lord —the official ring—send it by some very

stylish gentleman—perhaps Mr Hotchkiss here would be good enough to take it—and she'll come.

THE BISHOP [*taking off his ring and handing it to Hotchkiss*] Oblige me by undertaking the mission.

HOTCHKISS. But how am I to know the lady?

COLLINS. She has gone to the church in state, sir, and will be attended by a Beadle with a mace. He will point her out to you; and he will take the front seat of the carriage on the way back.

HOTCHKISS. No, by heavens! Forgive me, Bishop; but you are asking too much. I ran away from the Boers because I was a snob. I run away from the Beadle for the same reason. I absolutely decline the mission.

THE GENERAL [*rising impressively*] Be good enough to give me that ring, Mr Hotchkiss.

HOTCHKISS. With pleasure. [*He hands it to him*].

THE GENERAL. I shall have great pleasure, Mr Alderman, in waiting on the Mayoress with the Bishop's orders; and I shall be proud to return with municipal honors. [*He stalks out gallantly, Collins rising for a moment to bow to him with marked dignity*].

REGINALD. Boxer is rather a fine old josser in his way.

HOTCHKISS. His uniform gives him an unfair advantage. He will take all the attention off the Beadle.

COLLINS. I think it would be as well, my lord, to go on with the contract while we're waiting. The truth is, we shall none of us have much of a look-in when Mrs George comes; so we had better finish the writing part of the business before she arrives.

HOTCHKISS. I think I have the preliminaries down all right. [*Reading*] 'Memorandum of Agreement made this day of blank blank between blank blank of blank blank in the County of blank, Esquire, hereinafter called the Gentleman, of the one part, and blank blank of blank in the County of blank, hereinafter called the Lady, of the other part, whereby it is declared and agreed as follows.'

LEO [*rising*] You might remember your manners, Sinjon. The lady comes first. [*She goes behind him and stoops to look at the draft over his shoulder*].

HOTCHKISS. To be sure. I beg your pardon. [*He alters the draft*].

LEO. And you have got only one lady and

one gentleman. There ought to be two gentlemen.

COLLINS. Oh, thats a mere matter of form, maam. Any number of ladies or gentlemen can be put in.

LEO. Not any number of ladies. Only one lady. Besides, that creature wasnt a lady.

REGINALD. You shut your head, Leo. This is a general sort of contract for everybody: it's not your contract.

LEO. Then what use is it to me?

HOTCHKISS. You will get some hints from it for your own contract.

EDITH. I hope there will be no hinting. Let us have the plain straightforward truth and nothing but the truth.

COLLINS. Yes, yes, miss: it will be all right. Theres nothing underhand, I assure you. It's a model agreement, as it were.

EDITH [unconvinced] I hope so.

HOTCHKISS. What is the first clause in an agreement, usually? You know, Mr Alderman.

COLLINS [at a loss] Well, sir, the Town Clerk always sees to that. Ive got out of the habit of thinking for myself in these little matters. Perhaps his lordship knows.

THE BISHOP. I'm sorry to say I dont. But Soames will know. Alice: where is Soames?

HOTCHKISS. He's in there [pointing to the study].

THE BISHOP [to his wife] Coax him to join us, my love. [Mrs Bridgenorth goes into the study]. Soames is my chaplain, Mr Collins. The great difficulty about Bishops in the Church of England to-day is that the affairs of the diocese make it necessary that a Bishop should be before everything a man of business, capable of sticking to his desk for sixteen hours a day. But the result of having Bishops of this sort is that the spiritual interests of the Church, and its influence on the souls and imaginations of the people, very soon begin to go rapidly to the devil—

EDITH [shocked] Papa!

THE BISHOP. I am speaking technically, not in Boxer's manner. Indeed the Bishops themselves went so far in that direction that they gained a reputation for being spiritually the stupidest men in the country and commercially the sharpest. I found a way out of this difficulty. Soames was my solicitor. I found that Soames, though a very capable man of business, had a romantic secret history. His father was an eminent Nonconformist divine

who habitually spoke of the Church of England as The Scarlet Woman. Soames became secretly converted to Anglicanism at the age of fifteen. He longed to take holy orders, but didnt dare to, because his father had a weak heart and habitually threatened to drop dead if anybody hurt his feelings. You may have noticed that people with weak hearts are the tyrants of English family life. So poor Soames had to become a solicitor. When his father died—by a curious stroke of poetic justice he died of scarlet fever, and was found to have had a perfectly sound heart—I ordained Soames and made him my chaplain. He is now quite happy. He is a celibate; fasts strictly on Fridays and throughout Lent; wears a cassock and biretta; and has more legal business to do than ever he had in his old office in Ely Place. And he sets me free for the spiritual and scholarly pursuits proper to a Bishop.

MRS BRIDGENORTH [coming back from the study with a knitting basket] Here he is. [She resumes her seat, and knits].

Soames comes in in cassock and biretta. He salutes the company by blessing them with two fingers.

HOTCHKISS. Take my place, Mr Soames. [He gives up his chair to him, and retires to the oak chest, on which he seats himself].

THE BISHOP. No longer Mr Soames, Sinjon. Father Anthony.

SOAMES [taking his seat] I was christened Oliver Cromwell Soames. My father had no right to do it. I have taken the name of Anthony. When you become parents, young gentlemen, be very careful not to label a helpless child with views which it may come to hold in abhorrence.

THE BISHOP. Has Alice explained to you the nature of the document we are drafting?

SOAMES. She has indeed.

LESBIA. That sounds as if you disapproved.

SOAMES. It is not for me to approve or disapprove. I do the work that comes to my hand from my ecclesiastical superior.

THE BISHOP. Dont be uncharitable, Anthony. You must give us your best advice.

SOAMES. My advice to you all is to do your duty by taking the Christian vows of celibacy and poverty. The Church was founded to put an end to marriage and to put an end to property.

MRS BRIDGENORTH. But how could the world go on, Anthony?

SOAMES. Do your duty and see. Doing your duty is y o u r business: keeping the world going is in higher hands.

LESBIA. Anthony: youre impossible.

SOAMES [taking up his pen] You wont take my advice. I didnt expect you would. Well, I await your instructions.

REGINALD. We got stuck on the first clause. What should we begin with?

SOAMES. It is usual to begin with the term of the contract.

EDITH. What does that mean?

SOAMES. The term of years for which it is to hold good.

LEO. But this is a marriage contract.

SOAMES. Is the marriage to be for a year, a week, or a day?

REGINALD. Come, I say, Anthony! Youre worse than any of us. A day!

SOAMES. Off the path is off the path. An inch or a mile: what does it matter?

LEO. If the marriage is not to be for ever, I'll have nothing to do with it. I call it immoral to have a marriage for a term of years. If the people dont like it they can get divorced.

REGINALD. It ought to be for just as long as the two people like. Thats what I say.

COLLINS. They may not agree on the point, sir. It's often fast with one and loose with the other.

LESBIA. I should say for as long as the man behaves himself.

THE BISHOP. Suppose the woman doesnt behave herself?

MRS BRIDGENORTH. The woman may have lost all her chances of a good marriage with anybody else. She should not be cast adrift.

REGINALD. So may the man! What about his home?

LEO. The wife ought to keep an eye on him, and see that he is comfortable and takes care of himself properly. The other man wont want her all the time.

LESBIA. There may not be another man.

LEO. Then why on earth should she leave him?

LESBIA. Because she wants to.

LEO. Oh, if people are going to be let do what they want to, then I call it simple immorality. [She goes indignantly to the oak chest, and perches herself on it close beside Hotchkiss].

REGINALD [watching them sourly] You do it yourself, dont you?

LEO. Oh, thats quite different. Dont make

foolish witticisms, Rejjy.

THE BISHOP. We dont seem to be getting on. What do you say, Mr Alderman?

COLLINS. Well my lord, you see people do persist in talking as if marriages was all of one sort. But theres almost as many different sorts of marriages as theres different sorts of people. Theres the young things that marry for love, not knowing what theyre doing, and the old things that marry for money and comfort and companionship. Theres the people that marry for children. Theres the people that dont intend to have children and that arnt fit to have them. Theres the people that marry because theyre so much run after by the other sex that they have to put a stop to it somehow. Theres the people that want to try a new experience, and the people that want to have done with experiences. How are you to please them all? Why, youll want half a dozen different sorts of contract.

THE BISHOP. Well, if so, let us draw them all up. Let us face it.

REGINALD. Why should we be held together whether we like it or not? Thats the question thats at the bottom of it all.

MRS BRIDGENORTH. Because of the children, Rejjy.

COLLINS. But even then, maam, why should we be held together when thats all over— when the girls are married and the boys out in the world and in business for themselves? When thats done with, the real work of the marriage is done with. If the two like to stay together, let them stay together. But if not, let them part, as old people in the workhouses do. Theyve had enough of one another. Theyve found one another out. Why should they be tied together to sit there grudging and hating and spiting one another like so many do? Put it twenty years from the birth of the youngest child.

SOAMES. How if there be no children?

COLLINS. Let em take one another on liking.

MRS BRIDGENORTH. Collins!

LEO. You wicked old man!

THE BISHOP [remonstrating] My dear, my dear!

LESBIA. And what is a woman to live on, pray, when she is no longer liked, as you call it?

SOAMES [with sardonic formality] It is proposed that the term of the agreement be twenty years from the birth of the youngest child when there are children. Any amendment?

LEO. I protest. It must be for life. It would not be a marriage at all if it were not for life.

SOAMES. Mrs Reginald Bridgenorth proposes life. Any seconder?

LEO. Dont be soulless, Anthony.

LESBIA. I have a very important amendment. If there are any children, the man must be cleared completely out of the house for two years on each occasion. At such times he is superfluous, importunate, and ridiculous.

COLLINS. But where is he to go, miss?

LESBIA. He can go where he likes as long as he does not bother the mother.

REGINALD. And is she to be left lonely—

LESBIA. Lonely! With her child. The poor woman would be only too glad to have a moment to herself. Dont be absurd, Rejjy.

REGINALD. The father is to be a wandering wretched outcast, living at his club, and seeing nobody but his friends' wives!

LESBIA [*ironically*] Poor fellow!

HOTCHKISS. The friends' wives are perhaps the solution of the problem. You see, their husbands will also be outcasts; and the poor ladies will occasionally pine for male society.

LESBIA. There is no reason why a mother should not have male society. What she clearly should not have is a husband.

SOAMES. Anything else, Miss Grantham?

LESBIA. Yes: I must have my own separate house, or my own separate part of a house. Boxer smokes: I cant endure tobacco. Boxer believes that an open window means death from cold and exposure to the night air: I must have fresh air always. We can be friends; but we cant live together; and that must be put in the agreement.

EDITH. Ive no objection to smoking; and as to opening the windows, Cecil will of course have to do what is best for his health.

THE BISHOP. Who is to be the judge of that, my dear? You or he?

EDITH. Neither of us. We must do what the doctor orders.

REGINALD. Doctor be—!

LEO [*admonitorily*] Rejjy!

REGINALD [*to Soames*] You take my tip, Anthony. Put a clause into that agreement that the doctor is to have no say in the job. It's bad enough for the two people to be married to one another without their both being married to the doctor as well.

LESBIA. That reminds me of something

very important. Boxer believes in vaccination: I do not. There must be a clause that I am to decide on such questions as I think best.

LEO [*to the Bishop*] Baptism is nearly as important as vaccination: isnt it?

THE BISHOP. It used to be considered so, my dear.

LEO. Well, Sinjon scoffs at it: he says that godfathers are ridiculous. I must be allowed to decide.

REGINALD. Theyll be his children as well as yours, you know.

LEO. Dont be indelicate, Rejjy.

EDITH. You are forgetting the very important matter of money.

COLLINS. Ah! Money! Now we're coming to it!

EDITH. When I'm married I shall have practically no money except what I shall earn.

THE BISHOP. I'm sorry, Cecil. A Bishop's daughter is a poor man's daughter.

SYKES. But surely you dont imagine that I'm going to let Edith work when we're married. I'm not a rich man; but Ive enough to spare her that; and when my mother dies—

EDITH. What nonsense! Of course I shall work when I'm married. I shall keep your house.

SYKES. Oh, that!

REGINALD. You call that work?

EDITH. Dont y o u? Leo used to do it for nothing; so no doubt you thought it wasnt work at all. Does your present housekeeper do it for nothing?

REGINALD. But it will be part of your duty as a wife.

EDITH. Not under this contract. I'll not have it so. If I'm to keep the house, I shall expect Cecil to pay me at least as well as he would pay a hired housekeeper. I'll not go begging to him every time I want a new dress or a cab fare, as so many women have to do.

SYKES. You know very well I would grudge you nothing, Edie.

EDITH. Then dont grudge me my self-respect and independence. I insist on it in fairness to you, Cecil, because in this way there will be a fund belonging solely to me; and if Slattox takes an action against you for anything I say, you can pay the damages and stop the interest out of my salary.

SOAMES. You forget that under this contract he will not be liable, because you will not be his wife in law.

EDITH. Nonsense! Of course I shall be his wife.

COLLINS [*his curiosity roused*] Is Slattox taking an action against you, miss? Slattox is on the Council with me. Could I settle it?

EDITH. He has not taken an action; but Cecil says he will.

COLLINS. What for, miss, if I may ask?

EDITH. Slattox is a liar and a thief; and it is my duty to expose him.

COLLINS. You surprise me, miss. Of course Slattox is in a manner of speaking a liar. If I may say so without offence, we're all liars, if it was only to spare one another's feelings. But I shouldnt call Slattox a thief. He's not all that he should be, perhaps; but he pays his way.

EDITH. If that is only your nice way of saying that Slattox is entirely unfit to have two hundred girls in his power as absolute slaves, then I shall say that too about him at the very next public meeting I address. He steals their wages under pretence of fining them. He steals their food under pretence of buying it for them. He lies when he denies having done it. And he does other things, as you evidently know, Collins. Therefore I give you notice that I shall expose him before all England without the least regard to the consequences to myself.

SYKES. Or to me?

EDITH. I take equal risks. Suppose you felt it to be your duty to shoot Slattox, what would become of me and the children? I'm sure I dont want anybody to be shot: not even Slattox; but if the public never will take any notice of even the most crying evil until somebody is shot, what are people to do but shoot somebody?

SOAMES [*inexorably*] I'm waiting for my instructions as to the term of the agreement.

REGINALD [*impatiently, leaving the hearth and going behind Soames*] It's no good talking all over the shop like this. We shall be here all day. I propose that the agreement holds good until the parties are divorced.

SOAMES. They cant be divorced. They will not be married.

REGINALD. But if they cant be divorced, then this will be worse than marriage.

MRS BRIDGENORTH. Of course it will. Do stop this nonsense. Why, who are the children to belong to?

LESBIA. We have already settled that they are to belong to the mother.

REGINALD. No: I'm dashed if you have. I'll fight for the ownership of my own children tooth and nail; and so will a good many other fellows, I can tell you.

EDITH. It seems to me that they should be divided between the parents. If Cecil wishes any of the children to be his exclusively, he should pay me a certain sum for the risk and trouble of bringing them into the world: say a thousand pounds apiece. The interest on this could go towards the support of the child as long as we live together. But the principal would be my property. In that way, if Cecil took the child away from me, I should at least be paid for what it had cost me.

MRS BRIDGENORTH [*putting down her knitting in amazement*] Edith! Who ever heard of such a thing!!

EDITH. Well, how else do you propose to settle it?

THE BISHOP. There is such a thing as a favorite child. What about the youngest child — the Benjamin — the child of its parents' matured strength and charity, always better treated and better loved than the unfortunate eldest children of their youthful ignorance and wilfulness? Which parent is to own the youngest child, payment or no payment?

COLLINS. Theres a third party, my lord. Theres the child itself. My wife is so fond of her children that they cant call their lives their own. They all run away from home to escape from her. A child hasnt a grown-up person's appetite for affection. A little of it goes a long way with them; and they like a good imitation of it better than the real thing, as every nurse knows.

SOAMES. Are you sure that any of us, young or old, like the real thing as well as we like an artistic imitation of it? Is not the real thing accursed? Are not the best beloved always the good actors rather than the true sufferers? Is not love always falsified in novels and plays to make it endurable? I have noticed in myself a great delight in pictures of the Saints and of Our Lady; but when I fall under that most terrible curse of the priest's lot, the curse of Joseph pursued by the wife of Potiphar, I am invariably repelled and terrified.

HOTCHKISS. Are you now speaking as a saint, Father Anthony, or as a solicitor?

SOAMES. There is no difference. There is not one Christian rule for solicitors and another for saints. Their hearts are alike; and their way of salvation is along the same road.

THE BISHOP. But "few there be that find it." Can you find it for us, Anthony?

SOAMES. It lies broad before you. It is the way to destruction that is narrow and tortuous. Marriage is an abomination which the Church was founded to cast out and replace by the communion of saints. I learnt that from every marriage settlement I drew up as a solicitor no less than from inspired revelation. You have set yourselves here to put your sin before you in black and white; and you cant agree upon or endure one article of it.

SYKES. It's certainly rather odd that the whole thing seems to fall to pieces the moment you touch it.

THE BISHOP. You see, when you give the devil fair play he loses his case. He has not been able to produce even the first clause of a working agreement; so I'm afraid we cant wait for him any longer.

LESBIA. Then the community will have to do without my children.

EDITH. And Cecil will have to do without me.

LEO [getting off the chest] And I positively will not marry Sinjon if he is not clever enough to make some provision for my looking after Rejjy. [She leaves Hotchkiss, and goes back to her chair at the end of the table behind Mrs Bridgenorth.]

MRS BRIDGENORTH. And the world will come to an end with this generation, I suppose.

COLLINS. Cant nothing be done, my lord?

THE BISHOP. You can make divorce reasonable and decent: that is all.

LESBIA. Thank you for nothing. If you will only make marriage reasonable and decent, you can do as you like about divorce. I have not stated my deepest objection to marriage; and I dont intend to. There are certain rights I will not give any person over me.

REGINALD. Well, I think it jolly hard that a man should support his wife for years, and lose the chance of getting a really good wife, and then have her refuse to be a wife to him.

LESBIA. I'm not going to discuss it with you, Rejjy. If your sense of personal honor doesnt make you understand, nothing will.

SOAMES [implacably] I'm still awaiting my instructions.

They look at one another, each waiting for one of the others to suggest something. Silence.

REGINALD [blankly] I suppose, after all, marriage is better than—well, than the usual alternative.

SOAMES [turning fiercely on him] What right have you to say so? You know that the sins that are wasting and maddening this unhappy nation are those committed in wedlock.

COLLINS. Well, the single ones cant afford to indulge their affections the same as married people.

SOAMES. Away with it all, I say. You have your Master's commandments. Obey them.

HOTCHKISS [rising and leaning on the back of the chair left vacant by the General] I really must point out to you, Father Anthony, that the early Christian rules of life were not made to last, because the early Christians did not believe that the world itself was going to last. Now we know that we shall have to go through with it. We have found that there are millions of years behind us; and we know that there are millions before us. Mrs Bridgenorth's question remains unanswered How is the world to go on? You say that that is not our business—that it is the business of Providence. But the modern Christian view is that we are here to do the business of Providence and nothing else. The question is, how? Am I not to use my reason to find out why? Isnt that what my reason is for? Well, all my reason tells me at present is that you are an impracticable lunatic.

SOAMES. Does that help?

HOTCHKISS. No.

SOAMES. Then pray for light.

HOTCHKISS. No: I am a snob, not a beggar. [He sits down in the General's chair].

COLLINS. We dont seem to be getting on, do we? Miss Edith: you and Mr Sykes had better go off to church and settle the right and wrong of it afterwards. Itll ease your minds, believe me: I speak from experience. You will burn your boats, as one might say.

SOAMES. We should never burn our boats. It is death in life.

COLLINS. Well, Father, I will say for you that you have views of your own and are not afraid to out with them. But some of us are of a more cheerful disposition. On the Borough Council now, you would be in a minority of one. You must take human nature as it is.

SOAMES. Upon what compulsion must I? I'll take divine nature as it is. I'll not hold a candle to the devil.

THE BISHOP. Thats a very unchristian way of treating the devil.

REGINALD. Well, we dont seem to be getting any further, do we?

THE BISHOP. Will you give it up and get married, Edith?

EDITH. No. What I propose seems to me quite reasonable.

THE BISHOP. And you, Lesbia?

LESBIA. Never.

MRS BRIDGENORTH. Never is a long word, Lesbia. Dont say it.

LESBIA [*with a flash of temper*] Dont pity me, Alice, please. As I said before, I am an English lady, quite prepared to do without anything I cant have on honorable conditions.

SOAMES [*after a silence expressive of utter deadlock*] I am still awaiting my instructions.

REGINALD. Well, we dont seem to be getting along, do we?

LEO [*out of patience*] You said that before, Rejjy. Do n o t repeat yourself.

REGINALD. Oh, bother! [*He goes to the garden door and looks out gloomily*].

SOAMES [*rising with the paper in his hands*] Psha! [*He tears it in pieces*]. So much for your contract!

THE VOICE OF THE BEADLE. By your leave there, gentlemen. Make way for the Mayoress. Way for the worshipful the Mayoress, my lords and gentlemen. [*He comes in through the tower, in cocked hat and gold-braided overcoat, bearing the borough mace, and posts himself at the entrance*]. By your leave, gentlemen, way for the worshipful the Mayoress.

COLLINS [*moving back towards the wall*] Mrs George, my lord.

Mrs George is every inch a Mayoress in point of stylish dressing; and she does it very well indeed. There is nothing quiet about Mrs George; she is not afraid of colors, and knows how to make the most of them. Not at all a lady in Lesbia's use of the term as a class label, she proclaims herself to the first glance as the triumphant, pampered, wilful, intensely alive woman who has always been rich among poor people. In a historical museum she would explain Edward the Fourth's taste for shopkeepers' wives. Her age, which is certainly 40, and might be 50, is carried off by her vitality, her resilient figure, and her confident carriage. So far, a remarkably well-preserved woman. But her beauty is wrecked, like
an ageless landscape ravaged by long and fierce war. Her eyes are alive, arresting, and haunting; and there is still a turn of delicate beauty and pride in her indomitable chin; but her cheeks are wasted and lined, her mouth writhen and piteous. The whole face is a battle-field of the passions, quite deplorable until she speaks, when an alert sense of fun rejuvenates her in a moment, and makes her company irresistible.

All rise except Soames, who sits down. Leo joins Reginald at the garden door. Mrs Bridgenorth hurries to the tower to receive her guest, and gets as far as Soames's chair when Mrs George appears. Hotchkiss, apparently recognizing her, recoils in consternation to the study door at the furthest corner of the room from her.

MRS. GEORGE [*coming straight to the Bishop with the ring in her hand*] Here is your ring, my lord; and here am I. It's your doing, remember: not mine.

THE BISHOP. Good of you to come.

MRS BRIDGENORTH. How do you do, Mrs Collins?

MRS GEORGE [*going to her past the Bishop, and gazing intently at her*] Are you his wife?

MRS BRIDGENORTH. The Bishop's wife? Yes.

MRS GEORGE. What a destiny! And you look like any other woman!

MRS BRIDGENORTH [*introducing Lesbia*] My sister, Miss Grantham.

MRS GEORGE. So strangely mixed up with the story of the General's life?

THE BISHOP. You know the story of his life, then?

MRS GEORGE. Not all. We reached the house before he brought it up to the present day. But enough to know the part played in it by Miss Grantham.

MRS BRIDGENORTH [*introducing Leo*] Mrs Reginald Bridgenorth.

REGINALD. The late Mrs Reginald Bridgenorth.

LEO. Hold your tongue, Rejjy. At least have the decency to wait until the decree is made absolute.

MRS GEORGE [*to Leo*] Well, youve more time to get married again than he has, havnt you?

MRS BRIDGENORTH [*introducing Hotchkiss*] Mr St John Hotchkiss.

Hotchkiss, still far aloof by the study door, bows.

MRS GEORGE. What! That![*She makes a half tour of the kitchen and ends right in front of him*] Young man: do you remember coming into my shop and telling me that my husband's coals were out of place in your cellar, as Nature evidently intended them for the roof?

HOTCHKISS. I remember that deplorable impertinence with shame and confusion. You were kind enough to answer that Mr Collins was looking out for a clever young man to write advertisements, and that I could take the job if I liked.

MRS GEORGE. It's still open. [*She turns to Edith*].

MRS BRIDGENORTH. My daughter Edith. [*She comes towards the study door to make the introduction*].

MRS GEORGE. The bride! [*Looking at Edith's dressing jacket*] Youre not going to get married like that, are you?

THE BISHOP [*coming round the table to Edith's left*] Thats just what we are discussing. Will you be so good as to join us and allow us the benefit of your wisdom and experience?

MRS GEORGE. Do you want the Beadle as well? He's a married man.

They all turn involuntarily and contemplate the Beadle, who sustains their gaze with dignity.

THE BISHOP. We think there are already too many men to be quite fair to the women.

MRS GEORGE. Right, my lord. [*She goes back to the tower and addresses the Beadle*] Take away that bauble, Joseph. Wait for me wherever you find yourself most comfortable in the neighbourhood. [*The Beadle withdraws. She notices Collins for the first time*]. Hullo, Bill: youve got em all on too. Go and hunt up a drink for Joseph: theres a dear. [*Collins goes out. She looks at Soames's cassock and biretta*]. What! Another uniform! Are you the sexton? [*He rises*].

THE BISHOP. My chaplain, Father Anthony.

MRS GEORGE. Oh Lord! [*To Soames, coaxingly*] You dont mind, do you?

SOAMES. I mind nothing but my duties.

THE BISHOP. You know everybody now, I think.

MRS GEORGE [*turning to the railed chair*] Who's this?

THE BISHOP. Oh, I beg your pardon, Cecil. Mr Sykes. The bridegroom.

MRS GEORGE [*to Sykes*] Adorned for the sacrifice, arnt you?

SYKES. It seems doubtful whether there is going to be any sacrifice.

MRS GEORGE. Well, I want to talk to the women first. Shall we go upstairs and look at the presents and dresses?

MRS BRIDGENORTH. If you wish, certainly.

REGINALD. But the men want to hear what you have to say too.

MRS GEORGE. I'll talk to them afterwards: one by one.

HOTCHKISS [*to himself*] Great heavens!

MRS BRIDGENORTH. This way, Mrs Collins. [*She leads the way out through the tower, followed by Mrs George, Lesbia, Leo, and Edith*].

THE BISHOP. Shall we try to get through the last batch of letters whilst they are away, Soames?

SOAMES. Yes, certainly. [*To Hotchkiss, who is in his way*] Excuse me.

The Bishop and Soames go into the study, disturbing Hotchkiss, who, plunged in a strange reverie, has forgotten where he is. Awakened by Soames, he stares distractedly; then, with sudden resolution, goes swiftly to the middle of the kitchen.

HOTCHKISS. Cecil. Rejjy. [*Startled by his urgency, they hurry to him*]. I'm frightfully sorry to desert on this day; but I must bolt. This time it really is pure cowardice. I cant help it.

REGINALD. What are you afraid of?

HOTCHKISS. I dont know. Listen to me. I was a young fool living by myself in London. I ordered my first ton of coals from that woman's husband. At that time I did not know that it is not true economy to buy the lowest priced article: I thought all coals were alike, and tried the thirteen shilling kind because it seemed cheap. It proved unexpectedly inferior to the family Silkstone; and in the irritation into which the first scuttle threw me, I called at the shop and made an idiot of myself as she described.

SYKES. Well, suppose you did! Laugh at it, man.

HOTCHKISS. At that, yes. But there was something worse. Judge of my horror when, calling on the coal merchant to make a trifling complaint at finding my grate acting as a battery of quick-firing guns, and being confronted by his vulgar wife, I felt in her presence an extraordinary sensation of unrest, of emotion, of unsatisfied need. I'll not disgust you with details of the madness and folly that followed that meeting. But it went as far as this: that I actually found myself prowling past the shop at night under a sort of desperate necessity to be near some place where she had been. A hideous temptation to kiss the doorstep because her foot had pressed it made me realize how mad I was. I tore myself away from London by a supreme effort; but I was on the point of returning like a needle to the lodestone when the outbreak of the war saved me. On the field of battle the infatuation wore off. The Billiter affair made a new man of me: I felt that I had left the follies and puerilities of the old days behind me for ever. But half-an-hour ago—when the Bishop sent off that ring—a sudden grip at the base of my heart filled me with a nameless terror—me, the fearless! I recognized its cause when she walked into the room. Cecil: this woman is a harpy, a siren, a mermaid, a vampire. There is only one chance for me: flight, instant precipitate flight. Make my excuses. Forget me. Farewell. [*He makes for the door and is confronted by Mrs George entering*]. Too late: I'm lost. [*He turns back and throws himself desperately into the chair nearest the study door: that being the furthest away from her*].

MRS GEORGE [*coming to the hearth and addressing Reginald*] Mr Bridgenorth: will you oblige me by leaving me with this young man. I want to talk to him like a mother, on y o u r business.

REGINALD. Do, maam. He needs it badly. Come along, Sykes. [*He goes into the study*].

SYKES [*looks irresolutely at Hotchkiss*]—?

HOTCHKISS. Too late: you cant save me now, Cecil. Go.

Sykes goes into the study. Mrs George strolls across to Hotchkiss and contemplates him curiously.

HOTCHKISS. Useless to prolong this agony. [*Rising*] Fatal woman—if woman you are indeed and not a fiend in human form—

MRS GEORGE. Is this out of a book? Or is it your usual society small talk?

HOTCHKISS [*recklessly*] Jibes are useless: the force that is sweeping me away will not spare you. I must know the worst at once. What was your father?

MRS GEORGE. A licensed victualler who married his barmaid. You would call him a publican, most likely.

HOTCHKISS. Then you are a woman totally beneath me. Do you deny it? Do you set up any sort of pretence to be my equal in rank, in age, or in culture?

MRS GEORGE. Have you eaten anything that has disagreed with you?

HOTCHKISS [*witheringly*] Inferior!

MRS GEORGE. Thank you. Anything else?

HOTCHKISS. This. I love you. My intentions are not honorable. [*She shews no dismay*]. Scream. Ring the bell. Have me turned out of the house.

MRS GEORGE [*with sudden depth of feeling*] Oh, if you could restore to this wasted exhausted heart one ray of the passion that once welled up at the glance—at the touch of a lover! It's y o u who would scream then, young man. Do you see this face, once fresh and rosy like your own, now scarred and riven by a hundred burnt-out fires?

HOTCHKISS [*wildly*] Slate fires. Thirteen shillings a ton. Fires that shoot out destructive meteors, blinding and burning, sending men into the streets to make fools of themselves.

MRS GEORGE. You seem to have got it pretty bad, Sinjon.

HOTCHKISS. Dont dare call me Sinjon.

MRS GEORGE. My name is Zenobia Alexandrina. You may call me Polly for short.

HOTCHKISS. Your name is Ashtoreth—Durga—there is no name yet invented malign enough for you.

MRS GEORGE [*sitting down comfortably*] Come! Do you really think youre better suited to that young saucebox than her husband? You enjoyed her company when you were only the friend of the family—when there was the husband there to shew off against and to take all the responsibility. Are you sure youll enjoy it as much when y o u are the husband? She isnt clever, you know. She's only silly-clever.

HOTCHKISS [*uneasily leaning against the table and holding on to it to control his nervous movements*] Need you tell me? fiend that you are!

MRS GEORGE. You amused the husband, didnt you?

HOTCHKISS. He has more real sense of humor than she. He's better bred. That was not my fault.

MRS GEORGE. My husband has a sense of humor too.

HOTCHKISS. The coal merchant?—I mean the slate merchant.

MRS GEORGE [*appreciatively*] He would just love to hear you talk. He's been dull lately for want of a change of company and a bit of fresh fun.

HOTCHKISS [*flinging a chair opposite her and sitting down with an overdone attempt at studied insolence*] And pray what is your wretched husband's vulgar conviviality to me?

MRS GEORGE. You love me?

HOTCHKISS. I loathe you.

MRS GEORGE. It's the same thing.

HOTCHKISS. Then I'm lost.

MRS GEORGE. You may come and see me if you promise to amuse George.

HOTCHKISS. I'll insult him, sneer at him, wipe my boots on him.

MRS GEORGE. No you wont, dear boy. Youll be a perfect gentleman.

HOTCHKISS [*beaten; appealing to her mercy*] Zenobia—

MRS GEORGE. Polly, please.

HOTCHKISS. Mrs Collins—

MRS GEORGE. Sir?

HOTCHKISS. Something stronger than my reason and common sense is holding my hands and tearing me along. I make no attempt to deny that it can drag me where you please and make me do what you like. But at least let me know your soul as you seem to know mine. Do you love this absurd coal merchant.

MRS GEORGE. Call him George.

HOTCHKISS. Do you love your Jorjy Porjy?

MRS GEORGE. Oh, I dont know that I love him. He's my husband, you know. But if I got anxious about George's health, and I thought it would nourish him, I would fry you with onions for his breakfast and think nothing of it. George and I are good friends. George belongs to me. Other men may come and go; but George goes on for ever.

HOTCHKISS. Yes: a husband soon becomes nothing but a habit. Listen: I suppose this detestable fascination you have for me is love.

MRS GEORGE. Any sort of feeling for a woman is called love nowadays.

HOTCHKISS. Do you love me?

MRS GEORGE [*promptly*] My love is not quite so cheap an article as that, my lad. I wouldnt cross the street to have another look at you—not yet. *I'm* not starving for love like the robins in winter, as the good ladies youre accustomed to are. Youll have to be very clever, and very good, and very real, if you are to interest me. If George takes a fancy to you, and you amuse him enough, I'll just tolerate you coming in and out occasionally for—well, say a month. If you can make a friend of me in that time so much the better for you. If you can touch my poor dying heart even for an instant, I'll bless you, and never forget you. You may try—if George

takes to you.

HOTCHKISS. I'm to come on liking for the month?

MRS GEORGE. On condition that you drop Mrs Reginald.

HOTCHKISS. But she wont drop me. Do you suppose I ever wanted to marry her? I was a homeless bachelor; and I felt quite happy at their house as their friend. Leo was an amusing little devil; but I liked Reginald much more than I liked her. She didnt understand. One day she came to me and told me that the inevitable had happened. I had tact enough not to ask her what the inevitable was; and I gathered presently that she had told Reginald that their marriage was a mistake and that she loved me and could no longer see me breaking my heart for her in suffering silence. What could I say? What could I do? What can I say now? What can I do now?

MRS GEORGE. Tell her that the habit of falling in love with other men's wives is growing on you; and that I'm your latest.

HOTCHKISS. What! Throw her over when she has thrown Reginald over for me!

MRS GEORGE [*rising*] You wont then? Very well. Sorry we shant meet again: I should have liked to see more of you for George's sake. Goodbye [*she moves away from him towards the hearth*].

HOTCHKISS [*appealing*] Zenobia—

MRS GEORGE. I thought I had made a difficult conquest. Now I see you are only one of those poor petticoat-hunting creatures that any woman can pick up. Not for me, thank you. [*Inexorable, she turns towards the tower to go*].

HOTCHKISS [*following*] Dont be an ass, Polly.

MRS GEORGE [*stopping*] Thats better.

HOTCHKISS. Cant you see that I maynt throw Leo over just because I should be only too glad to. It would be dishonorable.

MRS GEORGE. Will you be happy if you marry her?

HOTCHKISS. No, great heavens, NO!

MRS GEORGE. Will she be happy when she finds you out?

HOTCHKISS. She's incapable of happiness. But she's not incapable of the pleasure of holding a man against his will.

MRS GEORGE. Right, young man. You will tell her, please, that you love me: before everybody, mind, the very next time you

U

see her.

HOTCHKISS. But—

MRS GEORGE. Those are my orders, Sinjon. I cant have you marry another woman until George is tired of you.

HOTCHKISS. Oh, if only I didnt selfishly want to obey you!

The General comes in from the garden. Mrs George goes half way to the garden door to speak to him. Hotchkiss posts himself on the hearth.

MRS GEORGE. Where have you been all this time?

THE GENERAL. I'm afraid my nerves were a little upset by our conversation. I just went into the garden and had a smoke. I'm all right now [*he strolls down to the study door and presently takes a chair at that end of the big table*].

MRS GEORGE. A smoke! Why, you said she couldnt bear it.

THE GENERAL. Good heavens! I forgot! It's such a natural thing to do, somehow.

Lesbia comes in through the tower.

MRS GEORGE. He's been smoking again.

LESBIA. So my nose tells me. [*She goes to the end of the table nearest the hearth, and sits down*].

THE GENERAL. Lesbia: I'm very sorry. But if I gave it up, I should become so melancholy and irritable that you would be the first to implore me to take to it again.

MRS GEORGE. Thats true. Women drive their husbands into all sorts of wickedness to keep them in good humor. Sinjon: be off with you: this doesnt concern you.

LESBIA. Please dont disturb yourself, Sinjon. Boxer's broken heart has been worn on his sleeve too long for any pretence of privacy.

THE GENERAL. You are cruel, Lesbia: devilishly cruel. [*He sits down, wounded*].

LESBIA. You are vulgar, Boxer.

HOTCHKISS. In what way? I ask, as an expert in vulgarity.

LESBIA. In two ways. First, he talks as if the only thing of any importance in life was which particular woman he shall marry. Second, he has no self-control.

THE GENERAL. Women are not all the same to me, Lesbia.

MRS GEORGE. Why should they be, pray? Women are all different: it's the men who are all the same. Besides, what does Miss Grantham know about either men or women? She's got too much self-control.

LESBIA [*widening her eyes and lifting her chin haughtily*] And pray how does that prevent me from knowing as much about men and women as people who have no self-control?

MRS GEORGE. Because it frightens people into behaving themselves before you; and then how can you tell what they really are? Look at me! I was a spoilt child. My brothers and sisters were well brought up, like all children of respectable publicans. So should I have been if I hadnt been the youngest: ten years younger than my youngest brother. My parents were tired of doing their duty by their children by that time; and they spoilt me for all they were worth. I never knew what it was to want money or anything that money could buy. When I wanted my own way, I had nothing to do but scream for it til I got it. When I was annoyed *I* didnt control myself: I scratched and called names. Did you ever, after you were grown up, pull a grown-up woman's hair? Did you ever bite a grown-up man? Did you ever call both of them every name you could lay your tongue to?

LESBIA [*shivering with disgust*] No.

MRS GEORGE. Well, I did. I know what a woman is like when her hair's pulled. I know what a man is like when he's bit. I know what theyre both like when you tell them what you really feel about them. And thats how I know more of the world than you.

LESBIA. The Chinese know what a man is like when he is cut into a thousand pieces, or boiled in oil. That sort of knowledge is of no use to me. I'm afraid we shall never get on with one another, Mrs George. I live like a fencer, always on guard. I like to be confronted with people who are always on guard. I hate sloppy people, slovenly people, people who cant sit up straight, sentimental people!

MRS GEORGE. Oh, sentimental your grandmother! You dont learn to hold your own in the world by standing on guard, but by attacking, and getting well hammered yourself.

LESBIA. I'm not a prize-fighter, Mrs Collins. If I cant get a thing without the indignity of fighting for it, I do without it.

MRS GEORGE. Do you? Does it strike you that if we were all as clever as you at doing without, there wouldnt be much to live for, would there?

THE GENERAL. I'm afraid, Lesbia, the things you do without are the things you dont want.

LESBIA [*surprised at his wit*] Thats not bad

for the silly soldier man. Yes, Boxer: the truth is, I dont want you enough to make the very unreasonable sacrifices required by marriage. And yet that is exactly why I ought to be married. Just because I have the qualities my country wants most I shall go barren to my grave; whilst the women who have neither the strength to resist marriage nor the intelligence to understand its infinite dishonor will make the England of the future. [*She rises and walks towards the study*].

THE GENERAL [*as she is about to pass him*] Well, I shall not ask you again, Lesbia.

LESBIA. Thank you, Boxer. [*She passes on to the study door*].

MRS GEORGE. Youre quite done with him, are you?

LESBIA. As far as marriage is concerned, yes. The field is clear for you, Mrs George. [*She goes into the study*].

The General buries his face in his hands. Mrs George comes round the table to him.

MRS GEORGE [*sympathetically*] She's a nice woman, that. And a sort of beauty about her too, different from anyone else.

THE GENERAL [*overwhelmed*] Oh Mrs Collins, thank you, thank you a thousand times. [*He rises effusively*]. You have thawed the long-frozen springs [*he kisses her hand*], forgive me; and thank you: bless you—[*he again takes refuge in the garden, choked with emotion*].

MRS GEORGE [*looking after him triumphantly*] Just caught the dear old warrior on the bounce, eh?

HOTCHKISS. Unfaithful to me already!

MRS GEORGE. I'm not your property, young man: dont you think it. [*She goes over to him and faces him*]. You understand that? [*He suddenly snatches her into his arms and kisses her*]. Oh! You dare do that again, you young blackguard; and I'll jab one of these chairs in your face [*she seizes one and holds it in readiness*]. Now you shall not see me for another month.

HOTCHKISS [*deliberately*] I shall pay my first visit to your husband this afternoon.

MRS GEORGE. Youll see what he'll say to you when I tell him what youve just done.

HOTCHKISS. What can he say? What dare he say?

MRS GEORGE. Suppose he kicks you out of the house?

HOTCHKISS. How can he? Ive fought seven duels with sabres. Ive muscles of iron. Nothing hurts me: not even broken bones. Fight-

ing is absolutely uninteresting to me because it doesnt frighten me or amuse me; and I always win. Your husband is in all these respects an average man, probably. He will be horribly afraid of me; and if under the stimulus of your presence, and for your sake, and because it is the right thing to do among vulgar people, he were to attack me, I should simply defeat him and humiliate him [*he gradually gets his hands on the chair and takes it from her, as his words go home phrase by phrase*]. Sooner than expose him to that, you would suffer a thousand stolen kisses, wouldnt you?

MRS GEORGE [*in utter consternation*] You young viper!

HOTCHKISS. Ha ha! You are in my power. That is one of the oversights of your code of honor for husbands: the man who can bully them can insult their wives with impunity. Tell him if you dare. If I choose to take ten kisses, how will you prevent me?

MRS GEORGE. You come within reach of me and I'll not leave a hair on your head.

HOTCHKISS [*catching her wrists dexterously*] Ive got your hands.

MRS GEORGE. Youve not got my teeth. Let go; or I'll bite. I will, I tell you. Let go.

HOTCHKISS. Bite away: I shall taste quite as nice as George.

MRS GEORGE. You beast. Let me go. Do you call yourself a gentleman, to use your brute strength against a woman?

HOTCHKISS. You are stronger than me in every way but this. Do you think I will give up my one advantage? Promise youll receive me when I call this afternoon.

MRS GEORGE. After what youve just done? Not if it was to save my life.

HOTCHKISS. I'll amuse George.

MRS GEORGE. He wont be in.

HOTCHKISS [*taken aback*] Do you mean that we should be alone?

MRS GEORGE [*snatching away her hands triumphantly as his grasp relaxes*] Aha! Thats cooled you, has it?

HOTCHKISS [*anxiously*] When will George be at home?

MRS GEORGE. It wont matter to you whether he's at home or not. The door will be slammed in your face whenever you call.

HOTCHKISS. No servant in London is strong enough to close a door that I mean to keep open. You cant escape me. If you persist, I'll go into the coal trade; make George's acquaintance on the coal exchange: and coax him to take me home with him to make your acquaintance.

MRS GEORGE. We have no use for you, young man: neither George nor I [*she sails away from him and sits down at the end of the table near the study door*].

HOTCHKISS [*following her and taking the next chair round the corner of the table*] Yes you have. George cant fight for you: I can.

MRS GEORGE [*turning to face him*] You bully. You low bully.

HOTCHKISS. You have courage and fascination: I have courage and a pair of fists. We're both bullies, Polly.

MRS GEORGE. You have a mischievous tongue. Thats enough to keep you out of my house.

HOTCHKISS. It must be rather a house of cards. A word from me to George—just the right word, said in the right way—and down comes your house.

MRS GEORGE. Thats why I'll die sooner than let you into it.

HOTCHKISS. Then as surely as you live, I enter the coal trade tomorrow. George's taste for amusing company will deliver him into my hands. Before a month passes your home will be at my mercy.

MRS GEORGE [*rising, at bay*] Do you think I'll let myself be driven into a trap like this?

HOTCHKISS. You are in it already. Marriage is a trap. You are married. Any man who has the power to spoil your marriage has the power to spoil your life. I have that power over you.

MRS GEORGE [*desperate*] You mean it?

HOTCHKISS. I do.

MRS GEORGE [*resolutely*] Well, spoil my marriage and be—

HOTCHKISS [*springing up*] Polly!

MRS GEORGE. Sooner than be your slave I'd face any unhappiness.

HOTCHKISS. What! Even for George?

MRS GEORGE. There must be honor between me and George, happiness or no happiness. Do your worst.

HOTCHKISS [*admiring her*] Are you really game, Polly? Dare you defy me?

MRS GEORGE. If you ask me another question I shant be able to keep my hands off you [*she dashes distractedly past him to the other end of the table, her fingers crisping*].

HOTCHKISS. That settles it. Polly: I adore you: we were born for one another. As I happen to be a gentleman, I'll never do anything to annoy or injure you except that I reserve the right to give you a black eye if you bite me; but youll never get rid of me now to the end of your life.

MRS GEORGE. I shall get rid of you if the beadle has to brain you with the mace for it [*she makes for the tower*].

HOTCHKISS [*running between the table and the oak chest and across to the tower to cut her off*] You shant.

MRS GEORGE [*panting*] Shant I though?

HOTCHKISS. No you shant. I have one card left to play that youve forgotten. Why were you so unlike yourself when you spoke to the Bishop?

MRS GEORGE [*agitated beyond measure*] Stop. Not that. You shall respect that if you respect nothing else. I forbid you. [*He kneels at her feet*]. What are you doing? Get up: dont be a fool.

HOTCHKISS. Polly: I ask you on my knees to let me make George's acquaintance in his home this afternoon; and I shall remain on my knees til the Bishop comes in and sees us. What will he think of you then?

MRS GEORGE [*beside herself*] Wheres the poker?

She rushes to the fireplace; seizes the poker; and makes for Hotchkiss, who flies to the study door. The Bishop enters just then and finds himself between them, narrowly escaping a blow from the poker.

THE BISHOP. Dont hit him, Mrs Collins. He is my guest.

Mrs George throws down the poker; collapses into the nearest chair; and bursts into tears. The Bishop goes to her and pats her consolingly on the shoulder. She shudders all through at his touch.

THE BISHOP. Come! you are in the house of your friends. Can we help you?

MRS GEORGE [*to Hotchkiss, pointing to the study*] Go in there, you. Youre not wanted here.

HOTCHKISS. You understand, Bishop, that Mrs Collins is not to blame for this scene. I'm afraid Ive been rather irritating.

THE BISHOP. I can quite believe it, Sinjon. *Hotchkiss goes into the study.*

THE BISHOP [*turning to Mrs George with great kindness of manner*] I'm sorry you have been worried [*he sits down on her left*]. Never mind him. A little pluck, a little gaiety of heart, a little prayer; and youll be laughing at him.

MRS GEORGE. Never fear. I have all that.

It was as much my fault as his; and I should have put him in his place with a clip of that poker on the side of his head if you hadnt come in.

THE BISHOP. You might have put him in his coffin that way, Mrs Collins. And I should have been very sorry; because we are all fond of Sinjon.

MRS GEORGE. Yes: it's your duty to rebuke me. But do you think I dont know?

THE BISHOP. I dont rebuke you. Who am I that I should rebuke you? Besides, I know there are discussions in which the poker is the only possible argument.

MRS GEORGE. My lord: be earnest with me. I'm a very funny woman, I daresay; but I come from the same workshop as you. I heard you say that yourself years ago.

THE BISHOP. Quite so; but then I'm a very funny Bishop. Since we are both funny people, let us not forget that humor is a divine attribute.

MRS GEORGE. I know nothing about divine attributes or whatever you call them; but I can feel when I am being belittled. It was from you that I learnt first to respect myself. It was through you that I came to be able to walk safely through many wild and wilful paths. Dont go back on your own teaching.

THE BISHOP. I'm not a teacher: only a fellow-traveller of whom you asked the way. I pointed ahead—ahead of myself as well as of you.

MRS GEORGE [rising and standing over him almost threateningly] As I'm a living woman this day, if I find you out to be a fraud, I'll kill myself.

THE BISHOP. What! Kill yourself for finding out something! For becoming a wiser and therefore a better woman! What a bad reason!

MRS GEORGE. I have sometimes thought of killing you, and then killing myself.

THE BISHOP. Why on earth should you kill yourself—not to mention me?

MRS GEORGE. So that we might keep our assignation in Heaven.

THE BISHOP [rising and facing her, breathless] Mrs Collins! You are Incognita Appassionata!

MRS GEORGE. You read my letters, then? [With a sigh of grateful relief, she sits down quietly, and says] Thank you.

THE BISHOP [remorsefully] And I have broken the spell by making you come here [sitting down again]. Can you ever forgive me?

MRS GEORGE. You couldnt know that it was only the coal merchant's wife, could you?

THE BISHOP. Why do you say o n l y the coal merchant's wife?

MRS GEORGE. Many people would laugh at it.

THE BISHOP. Poor people! It's so hard to know the right place to laugh, isn't it?

MRS GEORGE. I didnt mean to make you think the letters were from a fine lady. I wrote on cheap paper; and I never could spell.

THE BISHOP. Neither could I. So that told me nothing.

MRS GEORGE. One thing I should like you to know.

THE BISHOP. Yes?

MRS GEORGE. We didnt cheat your friend. They were as good as we could do at thirteen shillings a ton.

THE BISHOP. Thats important. Thank you for telling me.

MRS GEORGE. I have something else to say; but will you please ask somebody to come and stay here while we talk? [He rises and turns to the study door]. Not a woman, if you dont mind. [He nods understandingly and passes on]. Not a man either.

THE BISHOP [stopping] Not a man and not a woman! We have no children left, Mrs Collins. They are all grown up and married.

MRS GEORGE. That other clergyman would do.

THE BISHOP. What! The sexton?

MRS GEORGE. Yes. He didnt mind my calling him that, did he? It was only my ignorance.

THE BISHOP, Not at all. [He opens the study door and calls] Soames! Anthony! [To Mrs George] Call him Father: he likes it. [Soames appears at the study door]. Mrs Collins wishes you to join us, Anthony.

Soames looks puzzled.

MRS GEORGE. You dont mind, Dad, do you? [As this greeting visibly gives him a shock that hardly bears out the Bishop's advice, she says anxiously] That was what you told me to call him, wasnt it?

SOAMES. I am called F a t h e r Anthony, Mrs Collins. But it does not matter what you call me. [He comes in, and walks past her to the hearth].

THE BISHOP. Mrs Collins has something to say to me that she wants you to hear.

SOAMES. I am listening.

THE BISHOP [going back to his seat next her]

Now.

MRS GEORGE. My lord: you should never have married.

SOAMES. This woman is inspired. Listen to her, my lord.

THE BISHOP [*taken aback by the directness of the attack*] I married because I was so much in love with Alice that all the difficulties and doubts and dangers of marriage seemed to me the merest moonshine.

MRS GEORGE. Yes: it's mean to let poor young things in for so much while theyre in that state. Would you marry now that you know better if you were a widower?

THE BISHOP. I'm old now. It wouldnt matter.

MRS GEORGE. But would you if it did matter?

THE BISHOP. I think I should marry again lest anyone should imagine I had found marriage unhappy with Alice.

SOAMES [*sternly*] Are you fonder of your wife than of your salvation?

THE BISHOP. Oh, very much. When you meet a man who is very particular about his salvation, look out for a woman who is very particular about her character; and marry them to one another: theyll make a perfect pair. I advise you to fall in love, Anthony.

SOAMES [*with horror*] I!!

THE BISHOP. Yes, you! think of what it would do for you. For her sake you would come to care unselfishly and diligently for money instead of being selfishly and lazily indifferent to it. For her sake you would come to care in the same way for preferment. For her sake you would come to care for your health, your appearance, the good opinion of your fellow creatures, and all the really important things that make men work and strive instead of mooning and nursing their salvation.

SOAMES. In one word, for the sake of one deadly sin I should come to care for all the others.

THE BISHOP. Saint Anthony! Tempt him, Mrs Collins: tempt him.

MRS GEORGE [*rising and looking strangely before her*] Take care, my lord: you still have the power to make me obey your commands. And do you, Mr Sexton, beware of an empty heart.

THE BISHOP. Yes. Nature abhors a vacuum, Anthony. I would not dare go about with an empty heart: why, the first girl I met would fly into it by mere atmospheric pressure.

Alice keeps them out now. Mrs Collins knows.

MRS GEORGE [*a faint convulsion passing like a wave over her*] I know more than either of you. One of you has not yet exhausted his first love: the other has not yet reached it. But I—I—[*she reels and is again convulsed*].

THE BISHOP [*saving her from falling*] Whats the matter? Are you ill, Mrs Collins? [*He gets her back into her chair*]. Soames: theres a glass of water in the study—quick. [*Soames hurries to the study door*].

MRS GEORGE. No. [*Soames stops*]. Dont call. Dont bring anyone. Cant you hear anything?

THE BISHOP. Nothing unusual. [*He sits by her, watching her with intense surprise and interest*].

MRS GEORGE. No music?

SOAMES. No. [*He steals to the end of the table and sits on her right, equally interested*].

MRS GEORGE. Do you see nothing—not a great light?

THE BISHOP. We are still walking in darkness.

MRS GEORGE. Put your hand on my forehead: the hand with the ring. [*He does so. Her eyes close*].

SOAMES [*inspired to prophesy*] There was a certain woman, the wife of a coal merchant, which had been a great sinner—

The Bishop, startled, takes his hand away. Mrs George's eyes open vividly as she interrupts Soames.

MRS GEORGE. You prophesy falsely, Anthony: never in all my life have I done anything that was not ordained for me. [*More quietly*] Ive been myself. Ive not been afraid of myself. And at last I have escaped from myself, and am become a voice for them that are afraid to speak, and a cry for the hearts that break in silence.

SOAMES [*whispering*] Is she inspired?

THE BISHOP. Marvellous. Hush.

MRS GEORGE. I have earned the right to speak. I have dared: I have gone through: I have not fallen withered in the fire: I have come at last out beyond, to the back of Godspeed.

THE BISHOP. And what do you see there, at the back of Godspeed?

SOAMES [*hungrily*] Give us your message.

MRS GEORGE [*with intensely sad reproach*] When you loved me I gave you the whole sun and stars to play with. I gave you eternity in a single moment, strength of the mountains in one clasp of your arms, and the volume of all the seas in one impulse of your souls. A moment only; but was it not enough? Were you not paid then for all the rest of your struggle on earth? Must I mend your clothes and sweep your floors as well? Was it not enough? I paid the price without bargaining: I bore the children without flinching: was that a reason for heaping fresh burdens on me? I carried the child in my arms: must I carry the father too? When I opened the gates of paradise, were you blind? was it nothing to you? When all the stars sang in your ears and all the winds swept you into the heart of heaven, were you deaf? were you dull? was I no more to you than a bone to a dog? Was it not enough? We spent eternity together; and you ask me for a little lifetime more. We possessed all the universe together; and you ask me to give you my scanty wages as well. I have given you the greatest of all things; and you ask me to give you little things. I gave you your own soul: you ask me for my body as a plaything. Was it not enough? Was it not enough?

SOAMES. Do you understand this, my lord?

THE BISHOP. I have that advantage over you, Anthony, thanks to Alice. [*He takes Mrs George's hand*]. Your hand is very cold. Can you come down to earth? Do you remember who I am, and who you are?

MRS GEORGE. It was enough for me. I did not ask to meet you—to touch you—[*the Bishop quickly releases her hand*]. When you spoke to my soul years ago from your pulpit, you opened the doors of my salvation to me; and now they stand open for ever. It was enough. I have asked you for nothing since: I ask you for nothing now. I have lived: it is enough. I have had my wages; and I am ready for my work. I thank you and bless you and leave you. You are happier in that than I am; for when I do for men what you did for me, I have no thanks, and no blessing: I am their prey; and there is no rest from their loving and no mercy from their loathing.

THE BISHOP. You must take us as we are, Mrs Collins.

SOAMES. No. Take us as we are capable of becoming.

MRS GEORGE. Take me as I am: I ask no more. [*She turns her head to the study door and cries*] Yes: come in, come in.

Hotchkiss comes softly in from the study.

HOTCHKISS. Will you be so kind as to tell me whether I am dreaming? In there I have heard Mrs Collins saying the strangest things, and not a syllable from you two.

SOAMES. My lord: is this possession by the devil?

THE BISHOP. Or the ecstasy of a saint?

HOTCHKISS. Or the convulsion of the pythoness on the tripod?

THE BISHOP. May not the three be one?

MRS GEORGE [*troubled*] You are paining and tiring me with idle questions. You are dragging me back to myself. You are tormenting me with your evil dreams of saints and devils and—what was it?—[*striving to fathom it*] the pythoness—the pythoness—[*giving it up*] I dont understand. I am a woman: a human creature like yourselves. Will you not take me as I am?

SOAMES. Yes; but shall we take you and burn you?

THE BISHOP. Or take you and canonize you?

HOTCHKISS [*gaily*] Or take you as a matter of course? [*Swiftly to the Bishop*] We must get her out of this: it's dangerous. [*Aloud to her*] May I suggest that you shall be Anthony's devil and the Bishop's saint and my adored Polly? [*Slipping behind her, he picks up her hand from her lap and kisses it over her shoulder*].

MRS GEORGE [*waking*] What was that? Who kissed my hand? [*To the Bishop, eagerly*] Was it you? [*He shakes his head. She is mortified*]. I beg your pardon.

THE BISHOP. Not at all. I'm not repudiating that honor. Allow me [*he kisses her hand*].

MRS GEORGE. Thank you for that. It was not the sexton, was it?

SOAMES. I!

HOTCHKISS. It was I, Polly, your ever faithful.

MRS GEORGE [*turning and seeing him*] Let me catch you doing it again: thats all. How do you come there? I sent you away. [*With great energy, becoming quite herself again*] What the goodness gracious has been happening?

HOTCHKISS. As far as I can make out, you have been having a very charming and eloquent sort of fit.

MRS GEORGE [*delighted*] What! My second sight! [*To the Bishop*] Oh, how I have prayed that it might come to me if ever I met you! And now it has come. How stunning! You may believe every word I said: I cant remember it now; but it was something that was just bursting to be said; and so it laid hold of me and said itself. Thats how it is, you see.

Edith and Cecil Sykes come in through the tower. She has her hat on. Leo follows. They have evidently been out together. Sykes, with an unnatural air, half foolish, half rakish, as if he had lost all his self-respect and were determined not to let it prey on his spirits, throws himself into a chair at the end of the table near the hearth and thrusts his hands into his pockets, like Hogarth's Rake, without waiting for Edith to sit down, She sits in the railed chair. Leo takes the chair nearest the tower on the long side of the table, brooding, with closed lips.

THE BISHOP. Have you been out, my dear?

EDITH. Yes.

THE BISHOP. With Cecil?

EDITH. Yes.

THE BISHOP. Have you come to an understanding?

No reply. Blank silence.

SYKES. You had better tell them, Edie.

EDITH. Tell them yourself.

The General comes in from the garden.

THE GENERAL [*coming forward to the table*] Can anybody oblige me with some tobacco? Ive finished mine; and my nerves are still far from settled.

THE BISHOP. Wait a moment, Boxer. Cecil has something important to tell us.

SYKES. Weve done it. Thats all.

HOTCHKISS. Done what, Cecil?

SYKES. Well, what do you suppose?

EDITH. Got married, of course.

THE GENERAL. Married! Who gave you away?

SYKES [*jerking his head towards the tower*] This gentleman did. [*Seeing that they do not understand, he looks round and sees that there is no one there*]. Oh! I thought he came in with us. He's gone downstairs, I suppose. The Beadle.

THE GENERAL. The Beadle! What the devil did he do that for?

SYKES. Oh, I dont know: I didnt make any bargain with him. [*To Mrs George*] How much ought I to give him, Mrs Collins?

MRS GEORGE. Five shillings. [*To the Bishop*] I want to rest for a moment: there! in your study. I saw it here [*she touches her forehead*].

THE BISHOP [*opening the study door for her*] By all means. Turn my brother out if he disturbs you. Soames: bring the letters out here.

SYKES. He wont be offended at my offering it, will he?

MRS GEORGE. Not he! He touches children with the mace to cure them of ringworm for fourpence apiece. [*She goes into the study. Soames follows her*].

THE GENERAL. Well, Edith, I'm a little disappointed, I must say. However, I'm glad it was done by somebody in a public uniform.

Mrs Bridgenorth and Lesbia come in through the tower. Mrs Bridgenorth makes for the Bishop. He goes to her, and they meet near the oak chest. Lesbia comes between Sykes and Edith.

THE BISHOP. Alice, my love, theyre married.

MRS BRIDGENORTH [*placidly*] Oh, well, thats all right. Better tell Collins.

Soames comes back from the study with his writing materials. He seats himself at the nearest end of the table and goes on with his work. Hotchkiss sits down in the next chair round the table corner, with his back to him.

LESBIA. You have both given in, have you?

EDITH. Not at all. We have provided for everything.

SOAMES. How?

EDITH. Before going to the church, we went to the office of that insurance company —whats its name, Cecil?

SYKES. The British Family Insurance Corporation. It insures you against poor relations and all sorts of family contingencies.

EDITH. It has consented to insure Cecil against libel actions brought against him on my account. It will give us specially low terms because I am a Bishop's daughter.

SYKES. And I have given Edie my solemn word that if I ever commit a crime I'll knock her down before a witness and go off to Brighton with another lady.

LESBIA. Thats what you call providing for everything! [*She goes to the middle of the table on the garden side and sits down*].

LEO. Do make him see that there are no worms before he knocks you down, Edith. Wheres Rejjy?

REGINALD [*coming in from the study*] Here. Whats the matter?

LEO [*springing up and flouncing round to him*] Whats the matter! You may well ask. While Edie and Cecil were at the insurance office I took a taxy and went off to your lodgings; and a nice mess I found everything in. Your clothes are in a disgraceful state. Your liver-pad has been made into a kettle-holder. Youre no more fit to be left to yourself than a one-year-old baby.

REGINALD. Oh, I cant be bothered looking after things like that. I'm all right.

LEO. Youre not: youre a disgrace. You never consider that youre a disgrace to m e : you think only of yourself. You must come home with me and be taken proper care of: my conscience will not allow me to let you live like a pig. [*She arranges his necktie*]. You must stay with me until I marry Sinjon; and then we can adopt you or something.

REGINALD [*breaking loose from her and stumping off past Hotchkiss towards the hearth*] No, I'm dashed if I'll be adopted by Sinjon. You can adopt h i m if you like.

HOTCHKISS [*rising*] I suggest that that would really be the better plan, Leo. Ive a confession to make to you. I'm not the man you took me for. Your objection to Rejjy was that he had low tastes.

REGINALD [*turning*] Was it? by George!

LEO. I said slovenly habits. I never thought he had really low tastes until I saw that woman in court. How he could have chosen such a creature and let her write to him after—

REGINALD. Is this fair? I never—

HOTCHKISS. Of course you didnt, Rejjy. Dont be silly, Leo. It's I who really have low tastes.

LEO. You!

HOTCHKISS. Ive fallen in love with a coal merchant's wife. I adore her. I would rather have one of her boot-laces than a lock of your hair. [*He folds his arms and stands like a rock*].

REGINALD. You damned scoundrel, how dare you throw my wife over like that before my face? [*He seems on the point of assaulting Hotchkiss when Leo gets between them and draws Reginald away towards the study door*].

LEO. Dont take any notice of him, Rejjy. Go at once and get that odious decree demolished or annulled or whatever it is. Tell Sir Gorell Barnes that I have changed my mind. [*To Hotchkiss*] I might have known that you were too clever to be really a gentleman. [*She takes Reginald away to the oak chest and seats him there. He chuckles. Hotchkiss resumes his seat, brooding*].

THE BISHOP. All the problems appear to be solving themselves.

LESBIA. Except mine.

THE GENERAL. But, my dear Lesbia, you see what has happened here today. [*Coming a little nearer and bending his face towards hers*] Now I put it to you, does it not shew you the folly of not marrying?

LESBIA. No: I cant say it does. And [*rising*] you have been smoking again.

THE GENERAL. You drive me to it, Lesbia. I cant help it.

LESBIA [*standing behind her chair with her hands on the back of it and looking radiant*] Well, I wont scold you today. I feel in particularly good humor just now.

THE GENERAL. May I ask why, Lesbia?

LESBIA [*drawing a large breath*] To think that after all the dangers of the morning I am still unmarried! still independent! still my own mistress! still a glorious strongminded old maid of old England!

Soames silently springs up and makes a long stretch from his end of the table to shake her hand across it.

THE GENERAL. Do you find any real happiness in being your own mistress? Would it not be more generous—would you not be happier as someone else's mistress—

LESBIA. Boxer!

THE GENERAL [*rising, horrified*] No, no, you m u s t know, my dear Lesbia, that I was not using the word in its improper sense. I am sometimes unfortunate in my choice of expressions; but you know what I mean. I feel sure you would be happier as my wife.

LESBIA. I daresay I should, in a frowsty sort of way. But I prefer my dignity and my independence. I'm afraid I think this rage for happiness rather vulgar.

THE GENERAL. Oh, very well, Lesbia. I shall not ask you again. [*He sits down huffily*].

LESBIA. You will, Boxer; but it will be no use. [*She also sits down again and puts her hand almost affectionately on his*]. Some day I hope to make a friend of you; and then we shall get on very nicely.

THE GENERAL [*starting up again*] Ha! I think you are hard, Lesbia. I shall make a fool of myself if I remain here. Alice: I shall go into the garden for a while.

COLLINS [*appearing in the tower*] I think everything is in order now, maam.

THE GENERAL [*going to him*] Oh, by the way, could you oblige me—[*the rest of the sentence is lost in a whisper*].

COLLINS. Certainly, General. [*He takes out a tobacco pouch and hands it to the General, who takes it and goes into the garden*].

LESBIA. I dont believe theres a man in England who really and truly loves his wife as much as he loves his pipe.

THE BISHOP. By the way, what has happened to the wedding party?

U 2

SYKES. I dont know. There wasnt a soul in the church when we were married except the pew opener and the curate who did the job.

EDITH. They had all gone home.

MRS BRIDGENORTH. But the bridesmaids?

COLLINS. Me and the beadle have been all over the place in a couple of taxies, maam; and weve collected them all. They were a good deal disappointed on account of their dresses, and thought it all rather irregular; but theyve agreed to come to the breakfast. The truth is, theyre wild with curiosity to know how it all happened. The organist held on until the organ was nigh worn out, and himself worse than the organ. He asked me particularly to tell you, my lord, that he held back Mendelssohn til the very last; but when that was gone he thought he might as well go too. So he played God Save The King and cleared out the church. He's coming to the breakfast to explain.

LEO. Please remember, Collins, that there is no truth whatever in the rumor that I am separated from my husband, or that there is, or ever has been, anything between me and Mr Hotchkiss.

COLLINS. Bless you, maam! one could always see that. [To Mrs Bridgenorth] Will you receive here or in the hall, maam?

MRS BRIDGENORTH. In the hall. Alfred: you and Boxer must go there and be ready to keep the first arrivals talking til we come. We have to dress Edith. Come, Lesbia: come, Leo: we must all help. Now, Edith. [Lesbia, Leo, and Edith go out through the tower]. Collins: we shall want you when Miss Edith's dressed to look over her veil and things and see that theyre all right.

COLLINS. Yes, maam. Anything you would like mentioned about Miss Lesbia, maam?

MRS BRIDGENORTH. No. She wont have the General. I think you may take that as final.

COLLINS. What a pity, maam! A fine lady wasted, maam. [They shake their heads sadly; and Mrs Bridgenorth goes out through the tower].

THE BISHOP. I'm going to the hall, Collins, to receive. Rejjy: go and tell Boxer; and come both of you to help with the small talk. Come, Cecil. [He goes out through the tower, followed by Sykes].

REGINALD [to Hotchkiss] Youve always talked a precious lot about behaving like a gentleman. Well, if you think youve behaved like a gentleman to Leo, youre mistaken. And I shall have to take her part, remember that.

HOTCHKISS. I understand. Your doors are closed to me.

REGINALD [quickly] Oh no. Dont be hasty. I think I should like you to drop in after a while, you know. She gets so cross and upset when theres nobody to liven up the house a bit.

HOTCHKISS. I'll do my best.

REGINALD [relieved] Righto. You dont mind, old chap, do you?

HOTCHKISS. It's Fate. Ive touched coal; and my hands are black; but theyre clean. So long, Rejjy. [They shake hands; and Reginald goes into the garden to collect Boxer].

COLLINS. Excuse me, sir; but do you stay to breakfast? Your name is on one of the covers; and I should like to change it if youre not remaining.

HOTCHKISS. How do I know? Is my destiny any longer in my own hands? Go: ask SHE WHO MUST BE OBEYED.

COLLINS [awestruck] Has Mrs George taken a fancy to you, sir?

HOTCHKISS. Would she had! Worse, man, worse: Ive taken a fancy to Mrs George.

COLLINS. Dont despair, sir: if George likes your conversation youll find their house a very pleasant one: livelier than Mr Reginald's was, I daresay.

HOTCHKISS [calling] Polly.

COLLINS [promptly] Oh, if it's come to Polly already, sir, I should say you were all right.

Mrs George appears at the door of the study.

HOTCHKISS. Your brother-in-law wishes to know whether I'm to stay for the wedding breakfast. Tell him.

MRS GEORGE. He stays, Bill, if he chooses to behave himself.

HOTCHKISS [to Collins] May I, as a friend of the family, have the privilege of calling you Bill?

COLLINS. With pleasure, sir, I'm sure, sir.

HOTCHKISS. My own pet name in the bosom of my family is Sonny.

MRS GEORGE. Why didnt you tell me that before? Sonny is just the name I wanted for you. [She pats his cheek familiarly: he rises abruptly and goes to the hearth, where he throws himself moodily into the railed chair]. Bill: I'm not going into the hall until there are enough people there to make a proper little court for me. Send the Beadle for me when you think it looks good enough.

COLLINS. Right, maam. [*He goes out through the tower*].

Mrs George, left alone with Hotchkiss and Soames, suddenly puts her hands on Soames's shoulders and bends over him].

MRS GEORGE. The Bishop said I was to tempt you, Anthony.

SOAMES [*without looking round*] Woman: go away.

MRS GEORGE. Anthony:

"When other lips and other hearts
Their tale of love shall tell

HOTCHKISS [*sardonically*]

In language whose excess imparts
The power they feel so well.

MRS GEORGE.

Though hollow hearts may wear a mask
Twould break your own to see,
In such a moment I but ask
That youll remember me."

And you will, Anthony. I shall put my spell on you.

SOAMES. Do you think that a man who has sung the Magnificat and adored the Queen of Heaven has any ears for such trash as that or any eyes for such trash as you—saving your poor little soul's presence. Go home to your duties, woman.

MRS GEORGE [*highly approving his fortitude*] Anthony: I adopt you as my father. Thats the talk! Give me a man whose whole life doesnt hang on some scrubby woman in the next street; and I'll never let him go [*she slaps him heartily on the back*].

SOAMES. Thats enough. You have another man to talk to. I'm busy.

MRS GEORGE [*leaving Soames and going a step or two nearer Hotchkiss*] Why arnt you like him, Sonny? Why do you hang on to a scrubby woman in the next street?

HOTCHKISS [*thoughtfully*] I must apologize to Billiter.

MRS GEORGE. Who is Billiter?

HOTCHKISS. A man who eats rice pudding with a spoon. Ive been eating rice pudding with a spoon ever since I saw you first. [*He rises*]. We all eat our rice pudding with a spoon, dont we, Soames?

SOAMES. We are members of one another. There is no need to refer to me. In the first place, I'm busy: in the second, youll find it all in the Church Catechism, which contains most of the new discoveries with which the age is bursting. Of course you should apologize to Billiter. He is your equal. He will go

to the same heaven if he behaves himself and to the same hell if he doesnt.

MRS GEORGE [*sitting down*] And so will my husband the coal merchant.

HOTCHKISS. If I were your husband's superior here I should be his superior in heaven or hell: equality lies deeper than that. The coal merchant and I are in love with the same woman. That settles the question for me for ever. [*He prowls across the kitchen to the garden door, deep in thought*].

SOAMES. Psha!

MRS GEORGE. You dont believe in women, do you, Anthony? He might as well say that he and George both like fried fish.

HOTCHKISS. I do not like fried fish. Dont be low, Polly.

SOAMES. Woman: do not presume to accuse me of unbelief. And do you, Hotchkiss, not despise this woman's soul because she speaks of fried fish. Some of the victims of the Miraculous Draught of Fishes were fried. And I eat fried fish every Friday and like it. You are as ingrained a snob as ever.

HOTCHKISS [*impatiently*] My dear Anthony: I find you merely ridiculous as a preacher, because you keep referring me to places and documents and alleged occurrences in which, as a matter of fact, I dont believe. I dont believe in anything but my own will and my own pride and honor. Your fishes and your catechisms and all the rest of it make a charming poem which you call your faith. It fits you to perfection; but it doesnt fit me. I happen, like Napoleon, to prefer Mahometanism. [*Mrs George, associating Mahometanism with polygamy, looks at him with quick suspicion*]. I believe the whole British Empire will adopt a reformed Mahometanism before the end of the century. The character of Mahomet is congenial to me. I admire him, and share his views of life to a considerable extent. That beats you, you see, Soames. Religion is a great force: the only real motive force in the world; but what you fellows dont understand is that you must get at a man through his own religion and not through yours. Instead of facing that fact, you persist in trying to convert all men to your own little sect, so that you can use it against them afterwards. You are all missionaries and proselytizers trying to uproot the native religion from your neighbor's flowerbeds and plant your own in its place. You would rather let a child perish in ignorance than have it taught by a rival sectary. You talk to me of the quintessential equality of coal merchants and British officers; and yet you cant see the quintessential equality of all the religions. Who are you, anyhow, that you should know better than Mahomet or Confucius or any of the other Johnnies who have been on this job since the world existed?

MRS GEORGE [admiring his eloquence] George will like you, Sonny. You should hear him talking about the Church.

SOAMES. Very well, then: go to your doom, both of you. There is only one religion for me: that which my soul knows to be true; but even irreligion has one tenet; and that is the sacredness of marriage. You two are on the verge of deadly sin. Do you deny that?

HOTCHKISS. You forget, Anthony: the marriage itself is the deadly sin according to you.

SOAMES. The question is not now what I believe, but what you believe. Take the vows with me; and give up that woman if you have the strength and the light. But if you are still in the grip of this world, at least respect its institutions. Do you believe in marriage or do you not?

HOTCHKISS. My soul is utterly free from any such superstition. I solemnly declare that between this woman, as you impolitely call her, and me, I see no barrier that my conscience bids me respect. I loathe the whole marriage morality of the middle classes with all my instincts. If I were an eighteenth century marquis I could not feel more free with regard to a Parisian citizen's wife than I do with regard to Polly. I despise all this domestic purity business as the lowest depth of narrow, selfish, sensual, wife-grabbing vulgarity.

MRS GEORGE [rising promptly] Oh, indeed. They youre not coming home with me, young man. I'm sorry; for it's refreshing to have met once in my life a man who wasnt frightened by my wedding ring; but I'm looking out for a friend and not for a French marquis; so youre not coming home with me.

HOTCHKISS [inexorably] Yes, I am.

MRS GEORGE. No.

HOTCHKISS. Yes. Think again. You know your set pretty well, I suppose, your petty tradesmen's set. You know all its scandals and hypocrisies, its jealousies and squabbles, its hundreds of divorce cases that never come into court, as well as its tens that do.

MRS GEORGE. We're not angels. I know a few scandals; but most of us are too dull to be anything but good.

HOTCHKISS. Then you must have noticed that just as all murderers, judging by their edifying remarks on the scaffold, seem to be devout Christians, so all libertines, both male and female, are invariably people overflowing with domestic sentimentality and professions of respect for the conventions they violate in secret.

MRS GEORGE. Well, you dont expect them to give themselves away, do you?

HOTCHKISS. They are people of sentiment, not of honor. Now, I'm not a man of sentiment, but a man of honor. I know well what will happen to me when once I cross the threshold of your husband's house and break bread with him. This marriage bond which I despise will bind me as it never seems to bind the people who believe in it, and whose chief amusement it is to go to the theatres where it is laughed at. Soames: youre a Communist, arnt you?

SOAMES. I am a Christian. That obliges me to be a Communist.

HOTCHKISS. And you believe that many of our landed estates were stolen from the Church by Henry the eighth?

SOAMES. I do not merely b e l i e v e that: I k n o w it as a lawyer.

HOTCHKISS. Would you steal a turnip from one of the landlords of those stolen lands?

SOAMES [fencing with the question] They have no right to their lands.

HOTCHKISS. Thats not what I ask you. Would you steal a turnip from one of the fields they have no right to?

SOAMES. I do not like turnips.

HOTCHKISS. As you are a lawyer, answer me.

SOAMES. I admit that I should probably not do so. I should perhaps be wrong not to steal the turnip: I cant defend my reluctance to do so; but I think I should not do so. I know I should not do so.

HOTCHKISS. Neither shall I be able to steal George's wife. I have stretched out my hand for that forbidden fruit before; and I know that my hand will always come back empty. To disbelieve in marriage is easy: to love a married woman is easy; but to betray a comrade, to be disloyal to a host, to break the covenant of bread and salt, is impossible. You may take me home with you, Polly: you have nothing to fear.

MRS GEORGE. And nothing to hope?

HOTCHKISS. Since you put it in that more than kind way, Polly, absolutely nothing.

MRS GEORGE. Hm! Like most men, you think you know everything a woman wants, dont you? But the thing one wants most has nothing to do with marriage at all. Perhaps Anthony here has a glimmering of it. Eh, Anthony?

SOAMES. Christian fellowship?

MRS GEORGE. You call it that, do you?

SOAMES. What do you call it?

COLLINS [appearing in the tower with the Beadle] Now, Polly, the hall's full; and theyre waiting for you.

THE BEADLE. Make way there, gentlemen, please. Way for the worshipful the Mayoress. If you please, my lords and gentlemen. By your leave, ladies and gentlemen: way for the Mayoress.

Mrs George takes Hotchkiss's arm, and goes out, preceded by the Beadle.

Soames resumes his writing tranquilly.

THE END

XVII

THE SHEWING-UP OF BLANCO POSNET

A SERMON IN CRUDE MELODRAMA (1909)

A number of women are sitting together in a big room not unlike an old English tithe barn in its timbered construction, but with windows high up next the roof. It is furnished as a courthouse, with the floor raised next the walls, and on this raised flooring a seat for the Sheriff, a rough jury box on his right, and a bar to put prisoners to on his left. In the well in the middle is a table with benches round it. A few other benches are in disorder round the room. The autumn sun is shining warmly through the windows and the open door. The women, whose dress and speech are those of pioneers of civilization in a territory of the United States of America, are seated round the table and on the benches, shucking nuts. The conversation is at its height.

BABSY [*a bumptious young slattern, with some good looks*] I say that a man that would steal a horse would do anything.

LOTTIE [*a sentimental girl, neat and clean*] Well, I never should look at it in that way. I do think killing a man is worse any day than stealing a horse.

HANNAH [*elderly and wise*] I dont say it's right to kill a man. In a place like this, where every man has to have a revolver, and where theres so much to try people's tempers, the men get to be a deal too free with one another in the way of shooting. God knows it's hard enough to have to bring a boy into the world and nurse him up to be a man only to have him brought home to you on a shutter, perhaps for nothing, or only just to shew that the man that killed him wasnt

afraid of him. But men are like children when they get a gun in their hands: theyre not content til theyve used it on somebody.

JESSIE [*a good-natured but sharp-tongued, hoity-toity young woman; Babsy's rival in good looks and her superior in tidiness*] They shoot for the love of it. Look at them at a lynching. Theyre not content to hang the man; but directly the poor creature is swung up they all shoot him full of holes, wasting their cartridges that cost solid money, and pretending they do it in horror of his wickedness, though half of them would have a rope round their own necks if all they did was known. Let alone the mess it makes.

LOTTIE. I wish we could get more civilized. I dont like all this lynching and shooting. I dont believe any of us like it, if the truth were known.

BABSY. Our Sheriff is a real strong man. You want a strong man for a rough lot like our people here. He aint afraid to shoot and he aint afraid to hang. Lucky for us quiet ones, too.

JESSIE. Oh, dont talk to me. I know what men are. Of course he aint afraid to shoot and he aint afraid to hang. Wheres the risk in that with the law on his side and the whole crowd at his back longing for the lynching as if it was a spree? Would one of them own to it or let him own to it if they lynched the wrong man? Not them. What they call justice in this place is nothing but a breaking out of the devil thats in all of us. What I want to see is a Sheriff that aint afraid not to shoot and not to hang.

EMMA [*a sneak who sides with Babsy or Jessie, according to the fortune of war*] Well, I must say it does sicken me to see Sheriff Kemp putting down his foot, as he calls it. Why dont he put it down on his wife? She wants it worse than half the men he lynches. He and his Vigilance Committee, indeed!

BABSY [*incensed*] Oh, well! if people are going to take the part of horse-thieves against the Sheriff—?

JESSIE. Who's taking the part of horse-thieves against the Sheriff?

BABSY. You are. Waitle your own horse is stolen, and youll know better. I had an uncle that died of thirst in the sage brush because a negro stole his horse. But they caught him and burned him; and serve him right, too.

EMMA. I have known a child that was born crooked because its mother had to do a horse's work that was stolen.

BABSY. There! You hear that? I say stealing a horse is ten times worse than killing a man. And if the Vigilance Committee ever gets hold of you, youd better have killed twenty men than as much as stole a saddle or bridle, much less a horse.

Elder Daniels comes in.

ELDER DANIELS. Sorry to disturb you, ladies; but the Vigilance Committee has taken a prisoner; and they want the room to try him in.

JESSIE. But they cant try him til Sheriff Kemp comes back from the wharf.

ELDER DANIELS. Yes; but we have to keep the prisoner here til he comes.

BABSY. What do you want to put him here for? Cant you tie him up in the Sheriff's stable?

ELDER DANIELS. He has a soul to be saved, almost like the rest of us. I am bound to try to put some religion into him before he goes into his Maker's presence after the trial.

HANNAH. What has he done, Mr Daniels?

ELDER DANIELS. Stole a horse.

BABSY. And are we to be turned out of the town hall for a horse-thief? Aint a stable good enough for his religion?

ELDER DANIELS. It may be good enough for his, Babsy; but, by your leave, it is not good enough for mine. While I am Elder here, I shall umbly endeavor to keep up the dignity of Him I serve to the best of my small ability. So I must ask you to be good enough to clear out.

Allow me. [*He takes the sack of husks and puts it out of the way against the panels of the jury box*].

THE WOMEN [*murmuring*] Thats always the way. Just as we'd settled down to work. What harm are we doing? Well, it is tiresome. Let them finish the job themselves. Oh dear, oh dear! We cant have a minute to ourselves. Shoving us out like that!

HANNAH. Whose horse was it, Mr Daniels?

ELDER DANIELS [*returning to move the other sack*] I am sorry to say it was the Sheriff's horse—the one he loaned to young Strapper. Strapper loaned it to me; and the thief stole it, thinking it was mine. If it had been mine, I'd have forgiven him cheerfully. I'm sure I hoped he would get away; for he had two hours start of the Vigilance Committee. But they caught him. [*He disposes of the other sack also*].

JESSIE. It cant have been much of a horse if they caught him with two hours start.

ELDER DANIELS [*coming back to the centre of the group*] The strange thing is that he wasnt on the horse when they took him. He was walking; and of course he denies that he ever had the horse. The Sheriff's brother wanted to tie him up and lash him til he confessed what he'd done with it; but I couldnt allow that: it's not the law.

BABSY. Law! What right has a horse-thief to any law? Law is thrown away on a brute like that.

ELDER DANIELS. Dont say that, Babsy. No man should be made to confess by cruelty until religion has been tried and failed. Please God I'll get the whereabouts of the horse from him if youll be so good as to clear out from this. [*Disturbance*]. They are bringing him in. Now ladies! please, please.

They rise reluctantly. Hannah, Jessie, and Lottie retreat to the Sheriff's bench, shepherded by Daniels; but the other women crowd forward behind Babsy and Emma to see the prisoner.

Blanco Posnet is brought in by Strapper Kemp, the Sheriff's brother, and a cross-eyed man called Squinty. Others follow. Blanco is evidently a blackguard. It would be necessary to clean him to make a close guess at his age; but he is under forty, and an upturned, red moustache, and the arrangement of his hair in a crest on his brow, proclaim the dandy in spite of his intense disreputableness. He carries his head high, and has a fairly resolute mouth, though the fire of incipient delirium tremens is in his eye.

His arms are bound with a rope with a long end, which Squinty holds. They release him when he enters; and he stretches himself and lounges across the courthouse in front of the women. Strapper and the men remain between him and the door.

BABSY [*spitting at him as he passes her*] Horse-thief! horse-thief!

OTHERS. You will hang for it; do you hear? And serve you right. Serve you right. That will teach you. I wouldnt wait to try you. Lynch him straight off, the varmint. Yes, yes. Tell the boys. Lynch him.

BLANCO [*mocking*] "Angels ever bright and fair—"

BABSY. You call me an angel, and I'll smack your dirty face for you.

BLANCO. "Take, oh take me to your care."

EMMA. There wont be any angels where youre going to.

OTHERS. Aha! Devils, more likely. And too good company for a horse-thief.

ALL. Horse-thief! Horse-thief! Horse-thief!

BLANCO. Do women make the law here, or men? Drive these heifers out.

THE WOMEN. Oh! [*They rush at him, vituperating, screaming passionately, tearing at him. Lottie puts her fingers in her ears and runs out. Hannah follows, shaking her head. Blanco is thrown down*]. Oh, did you hear what he called us? You foul-mouthed brute! You liar! How dare you put such a name to a decent woman? Let me get at him. You coward! Oh, he struck me: did you see that? Lynch him! Pete, will you stand by and hear me called names by a skunk like that? Burn him: burn him! Thats what I'd do with him. Aye, burn him!

THE MEN [*pulling the women away from Blanco, and getting them out partly by violence and partly by coaxing*] Here! come out of this. Let him alone. Clear the courthouse. Come on now. Out with you. Now, Sally: out you go. Let go my hair, or I'll twist your arm out. Ah, would you? Now, then: get along. You know you must go. Whats the use of scratching like that? Now, ladies, ladies, ladies. How would you like it if you were going to be hanged?

At last the women are pushed out, leaving Elder Daniels, the Sheriff's brother Strapper Kemp, and a few others with Blanco. Strapper is a lad just turning into a man: strong, selfish, sulky, and determined.

BLANCO [*sitting up and tidying himself*]—

Oh woman, in our hours of ease,
Uncertain, coy, and hard to please—

Is my face scratched? I can feel their damned claws all over me still. Am I bleeding? [*He sits on the nearest bench*].

ELDER DANIELS. Nothing to hurt. Theyve drawn a drop or two under your left eye.

STRAPPER. Lucky for you to have an eye left in your head.

BLANCO [*wiping the blood off*]—

When pain and anguish wring the brow,
A ministering angel thou.

Go out to them, Strapper Kemp; and tell them about your big brother's little horse that some wicked man stole. Go and cry in your mammy's lap.

STRAPPER [*furious*] You jounce me any more about that horse, Blanco Posnet; and I'll—I'll—

BLANCO. Youll scratch my face, wont you? Yah! Your brother's the Sheriff, aint he?

STRAPPER. Yes, he is. He hangs horse-thieves.

BLANCO [*with calm conviction*] He's a rotten Sheriff. Oh, a rotten Sheriff. If he did his first duty he'd hang himself. This is a rotten town. Your fathers came here on a false alarm of gold-digging; and when the gold didnt pan out, they lived by licking their young into habits of honest industry.

STRAPPER. If I hadnt promised Elder Daniels here to give him a chance to keep you out of Hell, I'd take the job of twisting your neck off the hands of the Vigilance Committee.

BLANCO [*with infinite scorn*] You and your rotten Elder, and your rotten Vigilance Committee!

STRAPPER. Theyre sound enough to hang a horse-thief, anyhow.

BLANCO. Any fool can hang the wisest man in the country. Nothing he likes better. But you cant hang me.

STRAPPER. Cant we?

BLANCO. No, you cant. I left the town this morning before sunrise, because it's a rotten town, and I couldnt bear to see it in the light. Your brother's horse did the same, as any sensible horse would. Instead of going to look for the horse, you went looking for me. That was a rotten thing to do, because the horse belonged to your brother—or to the man he stole it from—and I dont belong to him. Well, you found me; but you didnt find the horse. If I had took the horse, I'd have been on the horse. Would I have taken all that time to get to where I did if I'd a horse to carry me?

STRAPPER. I dont believe you started not for two hours after you say you did.

BLANCO. Who cares what you believe or dont believe? Is a man worth six of you to be hanged because youve lost your big brother's horse, and youll want to kill somebody to relieve your rotten feelings when he licks you for it? Not likely. Til you can find a witness that saw me with that horse you cant touch me; and you know it.

STRAPPER. Is that the law, Elder?

ELDER DANIELS. The Sheriff knows the law. I wouldnt say for sure; but I think it would be more seemly to have a witness. Go and round one up, Strapper; and leave me here alone to wrestle with his poor blinded soul.

STRAPPER. I'll get a witness all right enough. I know the road he took; and I'll ask at every house within sight of it for a mile out. Come, boys.

Strapper goes out with the others, leaving Blanco and Elder Daniels together. Blanco rises and strolls over to the Elder, surveying him with extreme disparagement.

BLANCO. Well, brother? Well, Boozy Posnet, alias Elder Daniels? Well, thief? Well, drunkard?

ELDER DANIELS. It's no good, Blanco. Theyll never believe we're brothers.

BLANCO. Never fear. Do you suppose I want to claim you? Do you suppose I'm proud of you? Youre a rotten brother, Boozy Posnet. All you ever did when I owned you was to borrow money from me to get drunk with. Now you lend money and sell drink to other people. I was ashamed of you before; and I'm worse ashamed of you now. I wont have you for a brother. Heaven gave you to me; but I return the blessing without thanks. So be easy: I shant blab. [*He turns his back on him and sits down*].

ELDER DANIELS. I tell you they wouldnt believe you; so what does it matter to me whether you blab or not? Talk sense, Blanco: theres no time for your foolery now; for youll be a dead man an hour after the Sheriff comes back. What possessed you to steal that horse?

BLANCO. I didnt steal it. I distrained on it for what you owed me. I thought it was yours. I was a fool to think that you owned anything but other people's property. You laid

your hands on everything father and mother had when they died. I never asked you for a fair share. I never asked you for all the money I'd lent you from time to time. I asked you for mother's old necklace with the hair locket in it. You wouldnt give me that: you wouldnt give me anything. So as you refused me my due I took it, just to give you a lesson.

ELDER DANIELS. Why didnt you take the necklace if you must steal something? They wouldnt have hanged you for that.

BLANCO. Perhaps I'd rather be hanged for stealing a horse than let off for a damned piece of sentimentality.

ELDER DANIELS. Oh, Blanco, Blanco: spiritual pride has been your ruin. If youd only done like me, youd be a free and respectable man this day instead of laying there with a rope round your neck.

BLANCO [*turning on him*] Done like you! What do you mean? Drink like you, eh? Well, Ive done some of that lately. I see things.

ELDER DANIELS. Too late, Blanco: too late. [*Convulsively*] Oh, why didnt you drink as I used to? Why didnt you drink as I was led to by the Lord for my good, until the time came for me to give it up? It was drink that saved my character when I was a young man; and it was the want of it that spoiled yours. Tell me this. Did I ever get drunk when I was working?

BLANCO. No; but then you never worked when you had money enough to get drunk.

ELDER DANIELS. That just shews the wisdom of Providence and the Lord's mercy. God fulfils himself in many ways: ways we little think of when we try to set up our own short-sighted laws against his Word. When does the Devil catch hold of a man? Not when he's working and not when he's drunk; but when he's idle and sober. Our own natures tell us to drink when we have nothing else to do. Look at you and me! When we'd both earned a pocketful of money, what did we do? Went on the spree, naturally. But I was humble minded. I did as the rest did. I gave my money in at the drink-shop; and I said, "Fire me out when I have drunk it all up." Did you ever see me sober while it lasted?

BLANCO. No; and you looked so disgusting that I wonder it didnt set me against drink for the rest of my life.

ELDER DANIELS. That was your spiritual

pride, Blanco. You never reflected that when I was drunk I was in a state of innocence. Temptations and bad company and evil thoughts passed by me like the summer wind as you might say: I was too drunk to notice them. When the money was gone, and they fired me out, I was fired out like gold out of the furnace, with my character unspoiled and unspotted; and when I went back to work, the work kept me steady. Can you say as much, Blanco? Did your holidays leave your character unspoiled? Oh, no, no. It was theatres: it was gambling: it was evil company: it was reading vain romances: it was women, Blanco, women: it was wrong thoughts and gnawing discontent. It ended in your becoming a rambler and a gambler: it is going to end this evening on the gallows tree. Oh, what a lesson against spiritual pride! Oh, what a— [*Blanco throws his hat at him*].

BLANCO. Stow it, Boozy. Sling it. Cut it. Cheese it. Shut up. "Shake not the dying sinner's sand."

ELDER DANIELS. Aye: there you go, with your scraps of lustful poetry. But you cant deny what I tell you. Why, do you think I would put my soul in peril by selling drink if I thought it did no good, as them silly temperance reformers make out, flying in the face of the natural tastes implanted in us all for a good purpose? Not if I was to starve for it tomorrow. But I know better. I tell you, Blanco, what keeps America today the purest of the nations is that when she's not working she's too drunk to hear the voice of the tempter.

BLANCO. Dont deceive yourself, Boozy. You sell drink because you make a bigger profit out of it than you can by selling tea. And you gave up drink yourself because when you got that fit at Edwardstown the doctor told you youd die the next time; and that frightened you off it.

ELDER DANIELS [*fervently*] Oh thank God selling drink pays me! And thank God He sent me that fit as a warning that my drinking time was past and gone, and that He needed me for another service!

BLANCO. Take care, Boozy. He hasnt finished with you yet. He always has a trick up His sleeve——

ELDER DANIELS. Oh, is that the way to speak of the ruler of the universe—the great and almighty God?

BLANCO. He's a sly one. He's a mean one.

He lies low for you. He plays cat and mouse with you. He lets you run loose until you think youre shut of Him; and then, when you least expect it, He's got you.

ELDER DANIELS. Speak more respectful, Blanco—more reverent.

BLANCO [*springing up and coming at him*] Reverent! Who taught you your reverent cant? Not your Bible. It says He cometh like a thief in the night—aye, like a thief—a horse-thief——

ELDER DANIELS [*shocked*] Oh!

BLANCO [*overbearing him*] And it's true. Thats how He caught me and put my neck into the halter. To spite me because I had no use for Him—because I lived my own life in my own way, and would have no truck with His "Dont do this," and "You mustnt do that," and "Youll go to Hell if you do the other." I gave Him the go-bye and did without Him all these years. But He caught me out at last. The laugh is with Him as far as hanging me goes. [*He thrusts his hands into his pockets and lounges moodily away from Daniels, to the table, where he sits facing the jury box*].

ELDER DANIELS. Dont dare to put your theft on Him, man. It was the Devil tempted you to steal the horse.

BLANCO. Not a bit of it. Neither God nor Devil tempted me to take the horse: I took it on my own. He had a cleverer trick than that ready for me. [*He takes his hands out of his pockets and clenches his fists*]. Gosh! When I think that I might have been safe and fifty miles away by now with that horse; and here I am waiting to be hung up and filled with lead! What came to me? What made me such a fool? Thats what I want to know. Thats the great secret.

ELDER DANIELS [*at the opposite side of the table*] Blanco: the great secret now is, what did you do with the horse?

BLANCO [*striking the table with his fist*] May my lips be blighted like my soul if ever I tell that to you or any mortal man! They may roast me alive or cut me to ribbons; but Strapper Kemp shall never have the laugh on me over that job. Let them hang me. Let them shoot. So long as they are shooting a man and not a snivelling skunk and softy, I can stand up to them and take all they can give me—game.

ELDER DANIELS. Dont be headstrong, Blanco. Whats the use? [*slyly*] They might let up on you if you put Strapper in the way of getting his brother's horse back.

BLANCO. Not they. Hanging's too big a treat for them to give up a fair chance. Ive done it myself. Ive yelled with the dirtiest of them when a man no worse than myself was swung up. Ive emptied my revolver into him, and persuaded myself that he deserved it and that I was doing justice with strong stern men. Well, my turn's come now. Let the men I yelled at and shot at look up out of Hell and see the boys yelling and shooting at me as *I* swing up.

ELDER DANIELS. Well, even if you want to be hanged, is that any reason why Strapper shouldnt have his horse? I tell you I'm responsible to him for it. [*Bending over the table and coaxing him*]. Act like a brother, Blanco: tell me what you done with it.

BLANCO [*shortly, getting up and leaving the table*] Never you mind what I done with it. I was done out of it: let that be enough for you.

ELDER DANIELS [*following him*] Then why dont you put us on to the man that done you out of it?

BLANCO. Because he'd be too clever for you, just as he was too clever for me.

ELDER DANIELS. Make your mind easy about that, Blanco. He wont be too clever for the boys and Sheriff Kemp if you put them on his trail.

BLANCO. Yes, he will. It wasnt a man.

ELDER DANIELS. Then what was it?

BLANCO [*pointing upward*] Him.

ELDER DANIELS. Oh what a way to utter His holy name!

BLANCO. He done me out of it. He meant to pay off old scores by bringing me here. He means to win the deal and you cant stop Him. Well, He's made a fool of me; but He cant frighten me. I'm not going to beg off. I'll fight off if I get a chance. I'll lie off if they cant get a witness against me. But back down I never will, not if all the hosts of heaven come to snivel at me in white surplices and offer me my life in exchange for an umble and a contrite heart.

ELDER DANIELS. Youre not in your right mind, Blanco. I'll tell em youre mad. I believe theyll let you off on that. [*He makes for the door*].

BLANCO [*seizing him, with horror in his eyes*] Dont go: dont leave me alone: do you hear?

ELDER DANIELS. Has your conscience

brought you to this that youre afraid to be left alone in broad daylight, like a child in the dark.

BLANCO. I'm afraid of Him and His tricks. When I have you to raise the devil in me—when I have people to shew off before and keep me game, I'm all right; but Ive lost my nerve for being alone since this morning. It's when youre alone that He takes His advantage. He might turn my head again. He might send people to me—not real people perhaps. [*Shivering*] By God, I dont believe that woman and the child were real. I dont. I never noticed them til they were at my elbow.

ELDER DANIELS. What woman and what child? What are you talking about? Have you been drinking too hard?

BLANCO. Never you mind. Youve got to stay with me: thats all; or else send someone else —someone rottener than yourself—to keep the devil in me. Strapper Kemp will do. Or a few of those scratching devils of women.

Strapper Kemp comes back.

ELDER DANIELS [*to Strapper*] He's gone off his head.

STRAPPER. Foxing, more likely. [*Going past Daniels and talking to Blanco nose to nose*]. It's no good: we hang madmen here; and a good job too!

BLANCO. I feel safe with you, Strapper. Youre one of the rottenest.

STRAPPER. You know youre done, and that you may as well be hanged for a sheep as a lamb. So talk away. Ive got my witness; and I'll trouble you not to make a move towards her when she comes in to identify you.

BLANCO [*retreating in terror*] A woman? She aint real: neither is the child.

ELDER DANIELS. He's raving about a woman and a child. I tell you he's gone off his chump.

STRAPPER [*calling to those without*] Shew the lady in there.

Feemy Evans comes in. She is a young woman of 23 or 24, with impudent manners, battered good looks, and dirty-fine dress.

ELDER DANIELS. Morning, Feemy.

FEEMY. Morning, Elder. [*She passes on and slips her arm familiarly through Strapper's*].

STRAPPER. Ever see him before, Feemy?

FEEMY. Thats the little lot that was on your horse this morning, Strapper. Not a doubt of it.

BLANCO [*implacably contemptuous*] Go home and wash yourself, you slut.

FEEMY [*reddening, and disengaging her arm*

from Strapper's] I'm clean enough to hang you, anyway. [*Going over to him threateningly*]. Youre no true American man, to insult a woman like that.

BLANCO. A woman! Oh Lord! You saw me on a horse, did you?

FEEMY. Yes, I did.

BLANCO. Got up early on purpose to do it, didnt you?

FEEMY. No I didnt: I stayed up late on a spree.

BLANCO. I was on a horse, was I?

FEEMY. Yes you were; and if you deny it youre a liar.

BLANCO [*to Strapper*] She saw a man on a horse when she was too drunk to tell which was the man and which was the horse—

FEEMY [*breaking in*] You lie. I wasnt drunk —at least not as drunk as that.

BLANCO [*ignoring the interruption*] —and you found a man without a horse. Is a man on a horse the same as a man on foot? Yah! Take your witness away. Who's going to believe her? Throw her out on the dump. Youve got to find that horse before you get a rope round my neck. [*He turns away from her comtemptuously, and sits at the table with his back to the jury box*].

FEEMY [*following him*] I'll hang you, you dirty horse-thief; or not a man in this camp will ever get a word or a look from me again. Youre just trash: thats what you are. White trash.

BLANCO. And what are you, darling? What are you? Youre a worse danger to a town like this than ten horse-thieves.

FEEMY. Mr Kemp: will you stand by and hear me insulted in that low way? [*To Blanco, spitefully*] I'll see you swung up and I'll see you cut down: I'll see you high and I'll see you low, as dangerous as I am. [*He laughs*]. Oh you neednt try to brazen it out. Youll look white enough before the boys are done with you.

BLANCO. You do me good, Feemy. Stay by me to the end, wont you? Hold my hand to the last; and I'll die game. [*He puts out his hand: she strikes savagely at it; but he withdraws it in time and laughs at her discomfiture*].

FEEMY. You—

ELDER DANIELS. Never mind him, Feemy: he's not right in his head today. [*She receives the assurance with comtemptuous incredulity, and sits down on the step of the Sheriff's dais*].

Sheriff Kemp comes in: a stout man, with large flat ears, and a neck thicker than his head.

ELDER DANIELS. Morning. Sheriff.

THE SHERIFF. Morning, Elder. [*Passing on*]. Morning, Strapper. [*Passing on*]. Morning, Miss Evans. [*Stopping between Strapper and Blanco*]. Is this the prisoner?

BLANCO [*rising*] Thats so. Morning, Sheriff.

THE SHERIFF. Morning. You know, I suppose, that if youve stole a horse and the jury find against you, you wont have any time to settle your affairs. Consequently, if you feel guilty, youd better settle em now.

BLANCO. Affairs be damned! Ive got none.

THE SHERIFF. Well, are you in a proper state of mind? Has the Elder talked to you?

BLANCO. He has. And I say it's against the law. It's torture: thats what it is.

ELDER DANIELS. He's not accountable. He's out of his mind, Sheriff. He's not fit to go into the presence of his Maker.

THE SHERIFF. You are a merciful man, Elder; but you wont take the boys with you there. [*To Blanco*] If it comes to hanging you, youd better for your own sake be hanged in a proper state of mind than in an improper one. But it wont make any difference to us: make no mistake about that.

BLANCO. Lord keep me wicked till I die! Now Ive said my little prayer. I'm ready. Not that I'm guilty, mind you; but this is a rotten town, dead certain to do the wrong thing.

THE SHERIFF. You wont be asked to live long in it, I guess. [*To Strapper*] Got the witness all right, Strapper?

STRAPPER. Yes, got everything.

BLANCO. Except the horse.

THE SHERIFF. Whats that? Aint you got the horse?

STRAPPER. No. He traded it before we overtook him, I guess. But Feemy saw him on it.

FEEMY. She did.

STRAPPER. Shall I call in the boys?

BLANCO. Just a moment, Sheriff. A good appearance is everything in a low-class place like this. [*He takes out a pocket comb and mirror, and retires towards the dais to arrange his hair*].

ELDER DANIELS. Oh, think of your immortal soul, man, not of your foolish face.

BLANCO. I cant change my soul, Elder: it changes me—sometimes. Feemy: I'm too pale. Let me rub my cheek against yours, darling.

FEEMY. You lie: my color's my own, such

as it is. And a pretty color youll be when youre hung white and shot red.

BLANCO. Aint she spiteful, Sheriff?

THE SHERIFF. Time's wasted on you. [*To Strapper*] Go and see if the boys are ready. Some of them were short of cartridges, and went down to the store to buy them. They may as well have their fun; and itll be shorter for him.

STRAPPER. Young Jack has brought a boxful up. Theyre all ready.

THE SHERIFF [*going to the dais and addressing Blanco*] Your place is at the bar there. Take it. [*Blanco bows ironically and goes to the bar*]. Miss Evans: youd best sit at the table. [*She does so, at the corner nearest the bar. The Elder takes the opposite corner. The Sheriff takes his chair*]. All ready, Strapper.

STRAPPER [*at the door*] All in to begin.

The crowd comes in and fills the court. Babsy, Jessie, and Emma come to the Sheriff's right; Hannah and Lottie to his left.

THE SHERIFF. Silence there. The jury will take their places as usual. [*They do so*].

BLANCO. I challenge this jury, Sheriff.

THE FOREMAN. Do you, by Gosh?

THE SHERIFF. On what ground?

BLANCO. On the general ground that it's a rotten jury. [*Laughter*].

THE SHERIFF. Thats not a lawful ground of challenge.

THE FOREMAN. It's a lawful ground for me to shoot yonder skunk at sight, first time I meet him, if he survives this trial.

BLANCO. I challenge the Foreman because he's prejudiced.

THE FOREMAN. I say you lie. We mean to hang you, Blanco Posnet; but you will be hanged fair.

THE JURY. Hear, hear!

STRAPPER [*to the Sheriff*] George: this is rot. How can you get an unprejudiced jury if the prisoner starts by telling them theyre all rotten? If theres any prejudice against him he has himself to thank for it.

THE BOYS. Thats so. Of course he has. Insulting the court! Challenge be jiggered! Gag him.

NESTOR [*a juryman with a long white beard, drunk, the oldest man present*] Besides, Sheriff, I go so far as to say that the man that is not prejudiced against a horse-thief is not fit to sit on a jury in this town.

THE BOYS. Right. Bully for you, Nestor! Thats the straight truth. Of course he aint.

Hear, hear!

THE SHERIFF. That is no doubt true, old man. Still, you must get as unprejudiced as you can. The critter has a right to his chance, such as he is. So now go right ahead. If the prisoner dont like this jury, he should have stole a horse in another town; for this is all the jury he'll get here.

THE FOREMAN. Thats so, Blanco Posnet.

THE SHERIFF [*To Blanco*] Dont you be uneasy. You will get justice here. It may be rough justice; but it is justice.

BLANCO. What is justice?

THE SHERIFF. Hanging horse-thieves is justice; so now you know. Now then: weve wasted enough time. Hustle with your witness there, will you?

BLANCO [*indignantly bringing down his fist on the bar*] Swear the jury. A rotten Sheriff you are not to know that the jury's got to be sworn.

THE FOREMAN [*galled*] Be swore for you! Not likely. What do you say, old son?

NESTOR [*deliberately and solemnly*] I say: GUILTY!!!

THE BOYS [*tumultuously rushing at Blanco*] Thats it. Guilty, guilty. Take him out and hang him. He's found guilty. Fetch a rope. Up with him. [*They are about to drag him from the bar*].

THE SHERIFF [*rising, pistol in hand*] Hands off that man. Hands off him, I say, Squinty, or I drop you, and would if you were my own son. [*Dead silence*]. I'm Sheriff here; and it's for me to say when he may lawfully be hanged. [*They release him*].

BLANCO. As the actor says in the play, "a Daniel come to judgment." Rotten actor he was, too.

THE SHERIFF. Elder Daniels is come to judgment all right, my lad. Elder: the floor is yours. [*The Elder rises*]. Give your evidence. The truth and the whole truth and nothing but the truth, so help you God.

ELDER DANIELS. Sheriff: let me off this. I didnt ought to swear away this man's life. He and I are, in a manner of speaking, brothers.

THE SHERIFF. It does you credit, Elder: every man here will acknowledge it. But religion is one thing: law is another. In religion we're all brothers. In law we cut our brother off when he steals horses.

THE FOREMAN. Besides, you neednt hang him, you know. Theres plenty of willing hands to take that job off your conscience. So rip ahead, old son.

STRAPPER. Youre accountable to me for the horse until you clear yourself, Elder: remember that.

BLANCO. Out with it, you fool.

ELDER DANIELS. You might own up, Blanco, as far as my evidence goes. Everybody knows I borrowed one of the Sheriff's horses from Strapper because my own's gone lame. Everybody knows you arrived in the town yesterday and put up in my house. Everybody knows that in the morning the horse was gone and you were gone.

BLANCO [*in a forensic manner*] Sheriff: the Elder, though known to you and to all here as no brother of mine and the rottenest liar in this town, is speaking the truth for the first time in his life as far as what he says about me is concerned. As to the horse, I say nothing; except that it was the rottenest horse you ever tried to sell.

THE SHERIFF. How do you know it was a rotten horse if you didnt steal it?

BLANCO. I dont know of my own knowledge. I only argue that if the horse had been worth its keep you wouldnt have lent it to Strapper, and Strapper wouldnt have lent it to this eloquent and venerable ram. [*Suppressed laughter*]. And now I ask him this. [*To the Elder*] Did we or did we not have a quarrel last evening about a certain article that was left by my mother, and that I considered I had a right to more than you? And did you say one word to me about the horse not belonging to you?

ELDER DANIELS. Why should I? We never said a word about the horse at all. How was I to know what it was in your mind to do?

BLANCO. Bear witness all that I had a right to take a horse from him without stealing to make up for what he denied me. I am no thief. But you havnt proved yet that I took the horse. Strapper Kemp: had I the horse when you took me or had I not?

STRAPPER. No, nor you hadnt a railway train neither. But Feemy Evans saw you pass on the horse at four o'clock twenty-five miles from the spot where I took you at seven on the road to Pony Harbor. Did you walk twenty-five miles in three hours? That so, Feemy? eh?

FEEMY. Thats so. At four I saw him. [*To Blanco*] Thats done for you.

THE SHERIFF. You say you saw him on my horse?

FEEMY. I did.

BLANCO. And I ate it, I suppose, before Strapper fetched up with me. [*Suddenly and dramatically*] Sheriff: I accuse Feemy of immoral relations with Strapper.

FEEMY. Oh you liar!

BLANCO. I accuse the fair Euphemia of immoral relations with every man in this town, including yourself, Sheriff. I say this is a conspiracy to kill me between Feemy and Strapper because I wouldnt touch Feemy with a pair of tongs. I say you darent hang any white man on the word of a woman of bad character. I stand on the honor and virtue of my American manhood. I say that she's not had the oath, and that you darent for the honor of the town give her the oath because her lips would blaspheme the holy Bible if they touched it. I say thats the law; and if you are a proper United States Sheriff and not a low-down lyncher, youll hold up the law and not let it be dragged in the mud by your brother's kept woman.

Great excitement among the women. The men much puzzled.

JESSIE. Thats right. She didnt ought to be let kiss the Book.

EMMA. How could the like of her tell the truth?

BABSY. It would be an insult to every respectable woman here to believe her.

FEEMY. It's easy to be respectable with nobody ever offering you a chance to be anything else.

THE WOMEN [*clamoring all together*] Shut up, you hussy. Youre a disgrace. How dare you open your lips to answer your betters? Hold your tongue and learn your place, miss. You painted slut! Whip her out of the town!

THE SHERIFF. Silence. Do you hear. Silence. [*The clamor ceases*]. Did anyone else see the prisoner with the horse?

FEEMY [*passionately*] Aint I good enough?

BABSY. No. Youre dirt: thats what you are.

FEEMY. And you—

THE SHERIFF. Silence. This trial is a man's job; and if the women forget their sex they can go out or be put out. Strapper and Miss Evans: you cant have it two ways. You can run straight, or you can run gay, so to speak; but you cant run both ways together. There is also a strong feeling among the men of this town that a line should be drawn between those that are straight wives and mothers and those that are, in the words of the Book of Books, taking the primrose path. We dont wish to be hard on any woman; and most of us have a personal regard for Miss Evans for the sake of old times; but theres no getting out of the fact that she has private reasons for wishing to oblige Strapper, and that—if she will excuse my saying so— she is not what I might call morally particular as to what she does to oblige him. Therefore I ask the prisoner not to drive us to give Miss Evans the oath. I ask him to tell us fair and square, as a man who has but a few moments between him and eternity, what he done with my horse.

THE BOYS. Hear, hear! Thats right. Thats fair. That does it. Now Blanco. Own up.

BLANCO. Sheriff: you touch me home. This is a rotten world; but there is still one thing in it that remains sacred even to the rottenest of us, and that is a horse.

THE BOYS. Good. Well said, Blanco. Thats straight.

BLANCO. You have a right to your horse, Sheriff; and if I could put you in the way of getting it back, I would. But if I had that horse I shouldnt be here. As I hope to be saved, Sheriff—or rather as I hope to be damned; for I have no taste for pious company and no talent for playing the harp—I know no more of that horse's whereabouts than you do yourself.

STRAPPER. Who did you trade him to?

BLANCO. I did not trade him. I got nothing for him or by him. I stand here with a rope round my neck for the want of him. When you took me, did I fight like a thief or run like a thief; and was there any sign of a horse on me or near me?

STRAPPER. You were looking at a rainbow like a damned silly fool instead of keeping your wits about you; and we stole up on you and had you tight before you could draw a bead on us.

THE SHERIFF. That dont sound like good sense. What would he look at a rainbow for?

BLANCO. I'll tell you, Sheriff. I was looking at it because there was something written on it?

SHERIFF. How do you mean written on it?

BLANCO. The words were, "Ive got the cinch on you this time, Blanco Posnet." Yes, Sheriff, I saw those words in green on the red streak of the rainbow; and as I saw them

I felt Strapper's grab on my arm and Squinty's on my pistol.

THE FOREMAN. He's shammin mad: thats what he is. Aint it about time to give a verdict and have a bit of fun, Sheriff?

THE BOYS. Yes, lets have a verdict. We're wasting the whole afternoon. Cut it short.

THE SHERIFF [making up his mind] Swear Feemy Evans, Elder. She dont need to touch the Book. Let her say the words.

FEEMY. Worse people than me has kissed that Book. What wrong Ive done, most of you went shares in. Ive to live, havnt I? same as the rest of you. However, it makes no odds to me, I guess the truth is the truth and a lie is a lie, on the Book or off it.

BABSY. Do as youre told. Who are you, to be let talk about it?

THE SHERIFF. Silence there, I tell you. Sail ahead, Elder.

ELDER DANIELS. Feemy Evans: do you swear to tell the truth and the whole truth and nothing but the truth, so help you God.

FEEMY. I do, so help me—

SHERIFF. Thats enough. Now, on your oath, did you see the prisoner on my horse this morning on the road to Pony Harbor?

FEEMY. On my oath— [Disturbance and crowding at the door].

AT THE DOOR. Now then, now then! Where are you shovin to? Whats up? Order in court. Chuck him out. Silence. You cant come in here. Keep back.

Strapper rushes to the door and forces his way out.

SHERIFF [savagely] Whats this noise? Cant you keep quiet there? Is this a Sheriff's court or is it a saloon?

BLANCO. Dont interrupt a lady in the act of hanging a gentleman. Wheres your manners?

FEEMY. I'll hang you, Blanco Posnet. I will. I wouldnt for fifty dollars I hadnt seen you this morning. I'll teach you to be civil to me next time, for all I'm not good enough to kiss the Book.

BLANCO. Lord keep me wicked till I die! I'm game for anything while youre spitting dirt at me, Feemy.

RENEWED TUMULT AT THE DOOR. Here, whats this? Fire them out. Not me. Who are you that I should get out of your way? Oh, stow it. Well, she cant come in. What woman? What horse? Whats the good of shoving like that? Who says? No! you dont say!

THE SHERIFF. Gentlemen of the Vigilance Committee: clear that doorway. Out with with them in the name of the law.

STRAPPER [*without*] Hold hard, George. [*At the door*] Theyve got the horse. [*He comes in, followed by Waggoner Jo, an elderly carter, who crosses the court to the jury side. Strapper pushes his way to the Sheriff and speaks privately to him*].

THE BOYS. What! No! Got the horse! Sheriff's horse! Who took it, then? Where? Get out. Yes it is, sure. I tell you it is. It's the horse all right enough. Rot. Go and look. By Gum!

THE SHERIFF [*to Strapper*] You dont say!

STRAPPER. It's here, I tell you.

WAGGONER JO. It's here all right enough, Sheriff.

STRAPPER. And theyve got the thief too.

ELDER DANIELS. Then it aint Blanco.

STRAPPER. No: it's a woman. [*Blanco yells and covers his eyes with his hands*].

THE WHOLE CROWD. A woman!

THE SHERIFF. Well, fetch her in. [*Strapper goes out. The Sheriff continues, to Feemy*] And what do you mean, you lying jade, by putting up this story on us about Blanco?

FEEMY. I aint put up no story on you. This is a plant: you see if it isnt.

Strapper returns with a woman. Her expression of intense grief silences them as they crane over one another's heads to see her. Strapper takes her to the corner of the table. The Elder moves up to make room for her.

BLANCO [*terrified*] Sheriff: that woman aint real. You take care. That woman will make you do what you never intended. Thats the rainbow woman. Thats the woman that brought me to this.

THE SHERIFF. Shut your mouth, will you. Youve got the horrors. [*To the woman*] Now you. Who are you? and what are you doing with a horse that doesnt belong to you?

THE WOMAN. I took it to save my child's life. I thought it would get me to a doctor in time. The child was choking with croup.

BLANCO [*strangling, and trying to laugh*] A little choker: thats the word for him. His choking wasnt real: wait and see mine. [*He feels his neck with a sob*].

THE SHERIFF. Wheres the child?

STRAPPER. On Pug Jackson's bench in his shed. He's makin a coffin for it.

BLANCO [*with a horrible convulsion of the throat—frantically*] Dead! The little Judas kid! The child I gave my life for! [*He breaks into hideous laughter*].

THE SHERIFF [*jarred beyond endurance by the sound*] Hold your noise, will you? Shove his neckerchief into his mouth if he dont stop. [*To the woman*] Dont you mind him, maam: he's mad with drink and devilment. I suppose theres no fake about this, Strapper. Who found her?

WAGGONER JO. I did, Sheriff. Theres no fake about it. I came on her on the track round by Red Mountain. She was settin on the ground with the dead body on her lap, stupid-like. The horse was grazin on the other side o the road.

THE SHERIFF [*puzzled*] Well, this is blamed queer. [*To the woman*] What call had you to take the horse from Elder Daniels' stable to find a doctor? Theres a doctor in the very next house.

BLANCO [*mopping his dabbled red crest and trying to be ironically gay*] Story simply wont wash, my angel. You got it from the man that stole the horse. He gave it to you because he was a softy and went to bits when you played off the sick kid on him. Well, I guess that clears me. I'm not that sort. Catch me putting my neck in a noose for anybody's kid!

THE FOREMAN. Dont you go putting her up to what to say. She said she took it.

THE WOMAN. Yes: I took it from a man that met me. I thought God sent him to me. I rode here joyfully thinking so all the time to myself. Then I noticed that the child was like lead in my arms. God would never have been so cruel as to send me the horse to disappoint me like that.

BLANCO. Just what He would do.

STRAPPER. We aint got nothin to do with that. This is the man, aint he? [*pointing to Blanco*].

THE WOMAN [*pulling herself together after looking scaredly at Blanco, and then at the Sheriff and at the jury*] No.

THE FOREMAN. You lie.

THE SHERIFF. Youve got to tell us the truth. Thats the law, you know.

THE WOMAN. The man looked a bad man. He cursed me; and he cursed the child: God forgive him! But something came over him. I was desperate. I put the child in his arms; and it got its little fingers down his neck and called him Daddy and tried to kiss him; for it was not right in its head with the fever.

He said it was a little Judas kid, and that it was betraying him with a kiss, and that he'd swing for it. And then he gave me the horse, and went away crying and laughing and singing dreadful dirty wicked words to hymn tunes like as if he had seven devils in him.

STRAPPER. She's lying. Give her the oath, George.

THE SHERIFF. Go easy there. Youre a smart boy, Strapper; but youre not Sheriff yet. This is my job. You just wait. I submit that we're in a difficulty here. If Blanco was the man, the lady cant, as a white woman, give him away. She oughtnt to be put in the position of having either to give him away or commit perjury. On the other hand, we dont want a horse-thief to get off through a lady's delicacy.

THE FOREMAN. No we dont; and we dont intend he shall. Not while I am foreman of this jury.

BLANCO [with intense expression] A rotten foreman! Oh, what a rotten foreman!

THE SHERIFF. Shut up, will you. Providence shows us a way out here. Two women saw Blanco with a horse. One has a delicacy about saying so. The other will excuse me saying that delicacy is not her strongest holt. She can give the necessary witness. Feemy Evans: youve taken the oath. You saw the man that took the horse.

FEEMY. I did. And he was a low-down rotten drunken lying hound that would go further to hurt a woman any day than to help her. And if he ever did a good action it was because he was too drunk to know what he was doing. So it's no harm to hang him. She said he cursed her and went away blaspheming and singing things that were not fit for the child to hear.

BLANCO [troubled] I didnt mean them for the child to hear, you venomous devil.

THE SHERIFF. All thats got nothing to do with us. The question you have to answer is, was that man Blanco Posnet?

THE WOMAN. No. I say no. I swear it. Sheriff: dont hang that man: oh dont. You may hang me instead if you like: Ive nothing to live for now. You darent take her word against mine. She never had a child: I can see it in her face.

FEEMY [stung to the quick] I can hang him in spite of you, anyhow. Much good your child is to you now, lying there on Pug Jackson's bench!

BLANCO [rushing at her with a shriek] I'll twist your heart out of you for that. [They seize him before he can reach her].

FEEMY [mocking him as he struggles to get at her] Ha, ha, Blanco Posnet. You cant touch me; and I can hang you. Ha, ha! Oh, I'll do for you. I'll twist your heart and I'll twist your neck [He is dragged back to the bar and leans on it, gasping and exhausted]. Give me the oath again, Elder. I'll settle him. And do you [to the woman] take your sickly face away from in front of me.

STRAPPER. Just turn your back on her there, will you?

THE WOMAN. God knows I dont want to see her commit murder. [She folds her shawl over her head].

THE SHERIFF. Now, Miss Evans: cut it short. Was the prisoner the man you saw this morning or was he not? Yes or no.

FEEMY [a little hysterically] I'll tell you fast enough. Dont think I'm a softy.

THE SHERIFF [losing patience] Here: weve had enough of this. You tell the truth, Feemy Evans; and let us have no more of your lip. Was the prisoner the man or was he not? On your oath?

FEEMY. On my oath as I'm a living woman —[flinching] Oh God! he felt the little child's hands on his neck—I cant [bursting into a flood of tears and scolding at the other woman] It's you with your snivelling face that has put me off it. [Desperately] No: it wasnt him. I only said it out of spite because he insulted me. May I be struck dead if I ever saw him with the horse!

Everybody draws a long breath. Dead silence.

BLANCO [whispering at her] Softy! Cry-baby! Landed like me! Doing what you never intended! [Taking up his hat and speaking in his ordinary tone] I presume I may go now, Sheriff.

STRAPPER. Here, hold hard.

THE FOREMAN. Not if we know it, you dont.

THE BOYS [barring the way to the door] You stay where you are. Stop a bit, stop a bit. Dont you be in such a hurry. Dont let him go. Not much.

Blanco stands motionless, his eye fixed, thinking hard, and apparently deaf to what is going on.

THE SHERIFF [rising solemnly] Silence there. Wait a bit. I take it that if the Sheriff is satisfied and the owner of the horse is satisfied, theres no more to be said. I have had to remark on former occasions that what is wrong with this court is that theres too many Sheriffs in it. Today there is going to be one, and only one; and that one is your humble servant. I call that to the notice of the Foreman of the jury, and also to the notice of young Strapper. I am also the owner of the horse. Does any man say I am not? [*Silence*]. Very well, then. In my opinion, to commandeer a horse for the purpose of getting a dying child to a doctor is not stealing, provided, as in the present case, that the horse is returned safe and sound. I rule that there has been no theft.

NESTOR. That aint the law.

THE SHERIFF. I fine you a dollar for contempt of court, and will collect it myself off you as you leave the building. And as the boys have been disappointed of their natural sport, I shall give them a little fun by standing outside the door and taking up a collection for the bereaved mother of the late kid that shewed up Blanco Posnet.

THE BOYS. A collection. Oh, I say! Calls that sport? Is this a mothers' meeting? Well, I'll be jiggered! Where does the sport come in?

THE SHERIFF [*continuing*] The sport comes in, my friends, not so much in contributing as in seeing others fork out. Thus each contributes to the general enjoyment; and all contribute to his. Blanco Posnet: you go free under the protection of the Vigilance Committee for just long enough to get you out of this town, which is not a healthy place for you. As you are in a hurry, I'll sell you the horse at a reasonable figure. Now, boys, let nobody go out till I get to the door. The court is adjourned. [*He goes out*].

STRAPPER [*to Feemy, as he goes to the door*] I'm done with you. Do you hear? I'm done with you. [*He goes out sulkily*].

FEEMY [*calling after him*] As if I cared about a stingy brat like you! Go back to the freckled maypole you left for me: youve been fretting for her long enough.

THE FOREMAN [*To Blanco, on his way out*] A man like you makes me sick. Just sick. [*Blanco makes no sign. The Foreman spits disgustedly, and follows Strapper out. The Jurymen leave the box, except Nestor, who collapses in a drunken sleep*].

BLANCO [*Suddenly rushing from the bar to the table and jumping up on it*] Boys, I'm going to preach you a sermon on the moral of this day's proceedings.

THE BOYS [*crowding round him*] Yes: lets have a sermon. Go ahead, Blanco. Silence for Elder Blanco. Tune the organ. Let us pray.

NESTOR [*staggering out of his sleep*] Never hold up your head in this town again. I'm done with you.

BLANCO [*pointing inexorably to Nestor*] Drunk in church. Disturbing the preacher. Hand him out.

THE BOYS [*chivying Nestor out*] Now, Nestor, outside. Outside, Nestor. Out you go. Get your subscription ready for the Sheriff. Skiddoo, Nestor.

NESTOR. Afraid to be hanged! Afraid to be hanged! [*At the door*] Coward! [*He is thrown out*].

BLANCO. Dearly beloved brethren—

A BOY. Same to you, Blanco. [*Laughter*].

BLANCO. And many of them. Boys: this is a rotten world.

ANOTHER BOY. Lord have mercy on us, miserable sinners. [*More laughter*].

BLANCO [*Forcibly*] No: thats where youre wrong. Dont flatter yourselves that youre miserable sinners. Am I a miserable sinner? No: I'm a fraud and a failure. I started in to be a bad man like the rest of you. You all started in to be bad men or you wouldnt be in this jumped-up, jerked-off, hospital-turned-out camp that calls itself a town. I took the broad path because I thought I was a man and not a snivelling canting turning-the-other-cheek apprentice angel serving his time in a vale of tears. They talked Christianity to us on Sundays; but when they really meant business they told us never to take a blow without giving it back, and to get dollars. When they talked the golden rule to me, I just looked at them as if they werent there, and spat. But when they told me to try to live my life so that I could always look my fellowman straight in the eye and tell him to go to hell, that fetched me.

THE BOYS. Quite right. Good. Bully for you, Blanco, old son. Right good sense too. Aha-a-ah!

BLANCO. Yes; but whats come of it all? Am I a real bad man? a man of game and grit? a man that does what he likes and goes over or through other people to his own gain? or am I a snivelling cry-baby that let a horse his life depended on be took from him by a woman, and then sat on the grass looking at the rainbow and let himself be took like a hare in a trap by Strapper Kemp: a lad whose back I or any grown man here could break against his knee? I'm a rottener fraud and failure than the Elder here. And youre all as rotten as me, or youd have lynched me.

A BOY. Anything to oblige you, Blanco.

ANOTHER. We can do it yet if you feel really bad about it.

BLANCO. No: the devil's gone out of you. We're all frauds. Theres none of us real good and none of us real bad.

ELDER DANIELS. There is One above, Blanco.

BLANCO. What do you know about Him? you that always talk as if He never did anything without asking your rotten leave first? Why did the child die? Tell me that if you can. He cant have wanted to kill the child. Why did He make me go soft on the child if He was going hard on it Himself? Why should He go hard on the innocent kid and go soft on a rotten thing like me? Why did I go soft myself? Why did the Sheriff go soft? Why did Feemy go soft? Whats this game that upsets our game? For seems to me theres two games bein played. Our game is a rotten game that makes me feel I'm dirt and that youre all as rotten dirt as me. T'other game may be a silly game; but it aint rotten. When the Sheriff played it he stopped being rotten. When Feemy played it the paint nearly dropped off her face. When I played it I cursed myself for a fool; but I lost the rotten feel all the same.

ELDER DANIELS. It was the Lord speaking to your soul, Blanco.

BLANCO. Oh yes: you know all about the Lord, dont you? Youre in the Lord's confidence. He wouldnt for the world do anything to shock you, would He, Boozy dear? Yah! What about the croup? It was early days when He made the croup, I guess. It was the best He could think of then; but when it turned out wrong on His hands He made you and me to fight the croup for him. You bet He didnt make us for nothing; and He wouldnt have made us at all if He could have done His work without us. By Gum, that must be what we're for! He'd never have made us to be rotten drunken blackguards like me, and good-for-nothing rips like Feemy. He made me because He had a job for me. He let me run loose til the job was ready; and then I had to come along and

do it, hanging or no hanging. And I tell you it didnt feel rotten: it felt bully, just bully. Anyhow, I got the rotten feel off me for a minute of my life; and I'll go through fire to get it off me again. Look here! which of you will marry Feemy Evans?

THE BOYS [uproariously] Who speaks first? Who'll marry Feemy? Come along, Jack. Nows your chance, Peter. Pass along a husband for Feemy. Oh my! Feemy!

FEEMY [shortly] Keep your tongue off me, will you?

BLANCO. Feemy was a rose of the broad path, wasnt she? You all thought her the champion bad woman of this district. Well, she's a failure as a bad woman; and I'm a failure as a bad man. So let Brother Daniels marry us to keep all the rottenness in the family. What do you say, Feemy?

FEEMY. Thank you; but when I marry I'll marry a man that could do a decent action without surprising himself out of his senses. Youre like a child with a new toy: you and your bit of human kindness!

THE WOMAN. How many would have done it with their life at stake?

FEEMY. Oh well, if youre so much taken with him, marry him yourself. Youd be what people call a good wife to him, wouldnt you?

THE WOMAN. I was a good wife to the child's father. I dont think any woman wants to be a good wife twice in her life. I want somebody to be a good husband to me now.

BLANCO. Any offer, gentlemen, on that understanding? [The boys shake their heads]. Oh, it's a rotten game, our game. Heres a real good woman; and she's had enough of it, finding that it only led to being put upon.

HANNAH. Well, if there was nothing wrong in the world there wouldnt be anything left for us to do, would there?

ELDER DANIELS. Be of good cheer, brothers. Seek the path.

BLANCO. No. No more paths. No more broad and narrow. No more good and bad. Theres no good and bad; but by Jiminy, gents, theres a rotten game, and theres a great game. I played the rotten game; but the great game was played on me; and now I'm for the great game every time. Amen. Gentlemen: let us adjourn to the saloon. I stand the drinks. [He jumps down from the table].

THE BOYS. Right you are, Blanco. Drinks round. Come along, boys. Blanco's standing. Right along to the Elder's. Hurrah! [*They rush out, dragging the Elder with them*].

BLANCO [*to Feemy, offering his hand*] Shake, Feemy.

FEEMY. Get along, you blackguard.

BLANCO. It's come over me again, same as when the kid touched me, same as when you swore a lie to save my neck.

FEEMY. Oh well, here. [*They shake hands*].

THE END

XVIII

MISALLIANCE

1910

Johnny Tarleton, an ordinary young business man of thirty or less, is taking his weekly Friday to Tuesday in the house of his father, John Tarleton, who has made a great deal of money out of Tarleton's Underwear. The house is in Surrey, on the slope of Hindhead; and Johnny, reclining, novel in hand, in a swinging chair with a little awning above it, is enshrined in a spacious half hemisphere of glass which forms a pavilion commanding the garden, and, beyond it, a barren but lovely landscape of hill profile with fir trees, commons of bracken and gorse, and wonderful cloud pictures.

The glass pavilion springs from a bridgelike arch in the wall of the house, through which one comes into a big hall with tiled flooring, which suggests that the proprietor's notion of domestic luxury is founded on the lounges of week-end hotels. The arch is not quite in the centre of the wall. There is more wall to Johnny's right than to his left; and this space is occupied by a hat rack and umbrella stand in which tennis rackets, white parasols, caps, Panama hats, and other summery articles are bestowed. Just through the arch at this corner stands a new portable Turkish bath, recently unpacked, with its crate beside it, and on the crate the drawn nails and the hammer used in unpacking. Near the crate are open boxes of garden games: bowls and croquet. Nearly in the middle of the glass wall of the pavilion is a door giving on the garden, with a couple of steps to surmount the hot-water pipes which skirt the glass. At intervals round the pavilion are marble pillars with specimens of Viennese pottery on them, very flamboyant in colour and florid in design. Between them are folded garden chairs flung anyhow against the pipes. In the side walls are two doors: one near the hat stand, leading to the interior of the house, the other on the opposite side and at the other end, leading to the vestibule.

There is no solid furniture except a sideboard which stands against the wall between the vestibule door and the pavilion, a small writing table with blotter, rack for telegram forms and stationery, and a wastepaper basket, standing out in the hall near the sideboard, and a lady's worktable, with two chairs at it, towards the other side of the lounge. The writing table has also two chairs at it. On the sideboard there is a tantalus, liqueur bottles, a syphon, a glass jug of lemonade, tumblers, and every convenience for casual drinking. Also a plate of sponge cakes, and a highly ornate punchbowl in the same style as the keramic display in the pavilion. Wicker chairs and little bamboo tables with ash trays and boxes of matches on them are scattered in all directions. In the pavilion, which is flooded with sunshine, is the elaborate patent swing seat and awning in which Johnny reclines with his novel. There are two wicker chairs right and left of him.

Bentley Summerhays, one of those smallish, thinskinned youths, who from 17 to 70 retain unaltered the mental airs of the later and the physical appearance of the earlier age, appears in the garden and comes through the glass door into the pavilion. He is unmistakably a grade above Johnny socially; and though he looks sensitive enough, his assurance and his high voice are a little exasperating.

JOHNNY. Hallo! Wheres your luggage?

BENTLEY. I left it at the station. Ive walked up from Haslemere. [*He goes to the hat stand and hangs up his hat*].

JOHNNY [*shortly*] Oh! And whos to fetch it?

BENTLEY. Dont know. Dont care. Providence, probably. If not, your mother will have it fetched.

JOHNNY. Not her business, exactly, is it?

BENTLEY [*returning to the pavilion*] Of course

not. Thats why one loves her for doing it. Look here: chuck away your silly week-end novel, and talk to a chap. After a week in that filthy office my brain is simply blue-mouldy. Lets argue about something intellectual. [*He throws himself into the wicker chair on Johnny's right*].

JOHNNY [*straightening up in the swing with a yell of protest*] No. Now seriously, Bunny, Ive come down here to have a pleasant week-end; and I'm not going to stand your confounded arguments. If you want to argue, get out of this and go over to the Congregationalist minister's. Hes a nailer at arguing. He likes it.

BENTLEY. You cant argue with a person when his livelihood depends on his not letting you convert him. And would you mind not calling me Bunny? My name is Bentley Summerhays, which you please.

JOHNNY. Whats the matter with Bunny?

BENTLEY. It puts me in a false position. Have you ever considered the fact that I was an afterthought?

JOHNNY. An afterthought? What do you mean by that?

BENTLEY. I—

JOHNNY. No, stop: I dont want to know. It's only a dodge to start an argument.

BENTLEY. Dont be afraid: it wont overtax your brain. My father was 44 when I was born. My mother was 41. There was twelve years between me and the next eldest. I was unexpected. I was probably unintentional. My brothers and sisters are not the least like me. Theyre the regular thing that you always get in the first batch from young parents: quite pleasant, ordinary, do-the-regular-thing sort: all body and no brains, like you.

JOHNNY. Thank you.

BENTLEY. Dont mention it, old chap. Now I'm different. By the time I was born, the old couple knew something. So I came out all brains and no more body than is absolutely necessary. I am really a good deal older than you, though you were born ten years sooner. Everybody feels that when they hear us talk; consequently, though it's quite natural to hear me calling you Johnny, it sounds ridiculous and unbecoming for you to call me Bunny. [*He rises*].

JOHNNY. Does it, by George? You stop me doing it if you can: thats all.

BENTLEY. If you go on doing it after Ive asked you not, youll feel an awful swine [*He strolls away carelessly to the sideboard with his eye on the sponge-cakes*]. At least I should; but I suppose youre not so particular.

JOHNNY [*rising vengefully and following Bentley, who is forced to turn and listen*] I'll tell you what it is, my boy: you want a good talking to; and I'm going to give it to you. If you think that because your father's a K.C.B., and you want to marry my sister, you can make yourself as nasty as you please and say what you like, youre mistaken. Let me tell you that except Hypatia, not one person in this house is in favor of her marrying you; and I dont believe shes happy about it herself. The match isnt settled yet: dont forget that. Youre on trial in the office because the Governor isnt giving his daughter money for an idle man to live on her. Youre on trial here because my mother thinks a girl should know what a man is like in the house before she marries him. Thats been going on for two months now; and whats the result? Youve got yourself thoroughly disliked in the office; and youre getting yourself thoroughly disliked here, all through your bad manners and your conceit, and the damned impudence you think clever.

BENTLEY [*deeply wounded and trying hard to control himself*] Thats enough, thank you. You dont suppose, I hope, that I should have come down if I had known that that was how you all feel about me. [*He makes for the vestibule door*].

JOHNNY [*collaring him*] No: you dont run away. I'm going to have this out with you. Sit down: d'y' hear? [*Bentley attempts to go with dignity. Johnny slings him into a chair at the writing table, where he sits, bitterly humiliated, but afraid to speak lest he should burst into tears*]. Thats the advantage of having more body than brains, you see: it enables me to teach you manners; and I'm going to do it too. Youre a spoilt young pup; and you need a jolly good licking. And if youre not careful youll get it: I'll see to that next time you call me a swine.

BENTLEY. I didnt call you a swine. But [*bursting into a fury of tears*] you a r e a swine: youre a beast: youre a brute: youre a cad: youre a liar: youre a bully: I should like to wring your damned neck for you.

JOHNNY [*with a derisive laugh*] Try it, my son. [*Bentley gives an inarticulate sob of rage*]. Fighting isnt in your line. Youre too small;

and youre too childish. I always suspected that your cleverness wouldnt come to very much when it was brought up against something solid: some decent chap's fist, for instance.

BENTLEY. I hope your beastly fist may come up against a mad bull or a prize-fighter's nose, or something solider than me. I dont care about your fist; but if everybody here dislikes me— [*he is checked by a sob*]. Well, I dont care. [*Trying to recover himself*] I'm sorry I intruded: I didnt know. [*Breaking down again*] Oh you beast! you pig! Swine, swine, swine, swine, swine! Now!

JOHNNY. All right, my lad, all right. Sling your mud as hard as you please: it wont stick to me. What I want to know is this. How is it that your father, who I suppose is the strongest man England has produced in our time—

BENTLEY. You got that out of your half-penny paper. A lot you know about him!

JOHNNY. I dont set up to be able to do anything but admire him and appreciate him and be proud of him as an Englishman. If it wasnt for my respect for him, I wouldnt have stood your cheek for two days, let alone two months. But what I cant understand is why he didnt lick it out of you when you were a kid. For twenty-five years he kept a place twice as big as England in order: a place full of seditious coffee-colored heathens and pestilential white agitators in the middle of a lot of savage tribes. And yet he couldnt keep you in order. I dont set up to be half the man your father undoubtedly is; but, by George, it's lucky for you you were not my son. I dont hold with my own father's views about corporal punishment being wrong. It's necessary for some people; and I'd have tried it on you until you first learnt to howl and then to behave yourself.

BENTLEY [*contemptuously*] Yes: behavior wouldnt come naturally to your son, would it?

JOHNNY [*stung into sudden violence*] Now you keep a civil tongue in your head. I'll stand none of your snobbery. I'm just as proud of Tarleton's Underwear as you are of your father's title and his K.C.B., and all the rest of it. My father began in a little hole of a shop in Leeds no bigger than our pantry down the passage there. He—

BENTLEY. Oh yes: I know. Ive read it. "The Romance of Business, or The Story of Tarleton's Underwear. Please Take One!" I took one the day after I first met Hypatia. I went and bought half a dozen unshrinkable vests for her sake.

JOHNNY. Well: did they shrink?

BENTLEY. Oh, dont be a fool.

JOHNNY. Never mind whether I'm a fool or not. Did they shrink? Thats the point. Were they worth the money?

BENTLEY. I couldnt wear them: do you think my skin's as thick as your customers' hides? I'd as soon have dressed myself in a nutmeg grater.

JOHNNY. Pity your father didnt give your thin skin a jolly good lacing with a cane!

BENTLEY. Pity you havnt got more than one idea! If you want to know, they did try that on me once, when I was a small kid. A silly governess did it. I yelled fit to bring down the house, and went into convulsions and brain fever and that sort of thing for three weeks. So the old girl got the sack; and serve her right! After that, I was let do what I liked. My father didnt want me to grow up a broken-spirited spaniel, which is your idea of a man, I suppose.

JOHNNY. Jolly good thing for you that my father made you come into the office and shew what you were made of. And it didnt come to much: let me tell you that. When the Governor asked me where I thought we ought to put you, I said "Make him the Office Boy." The Governor said you were too green. And so you were.

BENTLEY. I daresay. So would you be pretty green if you were shoved into my father's set. I picked up your silly business in a fortnight. Youve been at it ten years; and you havnt picked it up yet.

JOHNNY. Dont talk rot, child. You know you simply make me pity you.

BENTLEY. "Romance of Business" indeed! The real romance of Tarleton's business is the story that you understand anything about it. You never could explain any mortal thing about it to me when I asked you. "See what was done the last time": that was the beginning and the end of your wisdom. Youre nothing but a turnspit.

JOHNNY. A what!

BENTLEY. A turnspit. If your father hadnt made a roasting jack for you to turn, youd be earning twenty-four shillings a week behind a counter.

JOHNNY. If you dont take that back and

apologize for your bad manners, I'll give you as good a hiding as ever—

BENTLEY. Help! Johnny's beating me! Oh! Murder! [*He throws himself on the ground, uttering piercing yells*].

JOHNNY. Dont be a fool. Stop that noise, will you? I'm not going to touch you. Sh—sh—

Hypatia rushes in through the inner door, followed by Mrs Tarleton, and throws herself on her knees by Bentley. Mrs Tarleton, whose knees are stiffer, bends over him and tries to lift him. Mrs Tarleton is a shrewd and motherly old lady who has been pretty in her time, and is still very pleasant and likeable and unaffected. Hypatia is a typical English girl of a sort never called typical: that is, she has an opaque white skin, black hair, large dark eyes with black brows and lashes, curved lips, swift glances and movements that flash out of a waiting stillness, boundless energy and audacity held in leash.

HYPATIA [*pouncing on Bentley with no very gentle hand*] Bentley: whats the matter? Dont cry like that: whats the use? Whats happened?

MRS TARLETON. Are you ill, child? [*They get him up*]. There, there, pet! It's all right: dont cry [*they put him into a chair*]: there! there! there! Johnny will go for the doctor; and he'll give you something nice to make it well.

HYPATIA. What has happened, Johnny?

MRS TARLETON. Was it a wasp?

BENTLEY [*impatiently*] Wasp be dashed!

MRS TARLETON. Oh Bunny! that was a naughty word.

BENTLEY. Yes, I know: I beg your pardon. [*He rises, and extricates himself from them*]. Thats all right. Johnny frightened me. You know how easy it is to hurt me; and I'm too small to defend myself against Johnny.

MRS TARLETON. Johnny: how often have I told you that you must not bully the little ones. I thought youd outgrown all that.

HYPATIA [*angrily*] I do declare, mamma, that Johnny's brutality makes it impossible to live in the house with him.

JOHNNY [*deeply hurt*] It's fourteen years, mother, since you had that row with me for licking Robert and giving Hypatia a black eye because she bit me. I promised you then that I'd never raise my hand to one of them again; and Ive never broken my word. And now because this young whelp begins to cry out before he's hurt, you treat me as if I were a brute and a savage.

MRS TARLETON. No dear, not a savage; but you know you mustnt call our visitor naughty names.

BENTLEY. Oh, let him alone—

JOHNNY [*fiercely*] Dont you interfere between my mother and me: d'y' hear?

HYPATIA. Johnny's lost his temper, mother. We'd better go. Come, Bentley.

MRS TARLETON. Yes: that will be best. [*To Bentley*] Johnny doesnt mean any harm, dear: he'll be himself presently. Come.

The two ladies go out through the inner door with Bentley, who turns derisively at the door to cock a snook at Johnny as he goes out.

Johnny, left alone, clenches his fists and grinds his teeth, but can find no relief in that way for his rage. After choking and stamping for a moment, he makes for the vestibule door. It opens before he reaches it; and Lord Summerhays comes in. Johnny glares at him, speechless. Lord Summerhays takes in the situation, and quickly takes the punchbowl from the sideboard and offers it to Johnny.

LORD SUMMERHAYS. Smash it. Dont hesitate: it's an ugly thing. Smash it: hard. [*Johnny, with a stifled yell, dashes it in pieces, and then sits down and mops his brow*]. Feel better now? [*Johnny nods*]. I know only one person alive who could drive me to the point of having either to break china or commit murder; and that person is my son Bentley. Was it he? [*Johnny nods again, not yet able to speak*]. As the car stopped I heard a yell which is only too familiar to me. It generally means that some infuriated person is trying to thrash Bentley. Nobody has ever succeeded, though almost everybody has tried. [*He seats himself comfortably close to the writing table, and sets to work to collect the fragments of the punchbowl in the wastepaper basket whilst Johnny, with diminishing difficulty, collects himself*]. Bentley is a problem which I confess I have never been able to solve. He was born to be a great success at the age of fifty. Most Englishmen of his class seem to be born to be great successes at the age of twenty-four at most. The domestic problem for me is how to endure Bentley until he is fifty. The problem for the nation is how to get itself governed by men whose growth is arrested when they are little more than college lads. Bentley doesnt really mean to be offensive. You can always make him cry by telling him you dont like him. Only, he cries so loud that the experiment should be made in the open air:

in the middle of Salisbury Plain if possible. He has a hard and penetrating intellect and a remarkable power of looking facts in the face; but unfortunately, being very young, he has no idea of how very little of that sort of thing most of us can stand. On the other hand, he is frightfully sensitive and even affectionate; so that he probably gets as much as he gives in the way of hurt feelings. Youll excuse me rambling on like this about my son.

JOHNNY [who has pulled himself together] You did it on purpose. I wasnt quite myself: I needed a moment to pull round. Thank you.

LORD SUMMERHAYS. Not at all. Is your father at home?

JOHNNY. No: hes opening one of his free libraries. Thats another nice little penny gone. He's mad on reading. He promised another free library last week. It's ruinous. Itll hit you as well as me when Bunny marries Hypatia. When all Hypatia's money is thrown away on libraries, where will Bunny come in? Cant you stop him?

LORD SUMMERHAYS. I'm afraid not. Hes a perfect whirlwind. Indefatigable at public work. Wonderful man, I think.

JOHNNY. Oh, public work! He does too much of it. It's really a sort of laziness, getting away from your own serious business to amuse yourself with other people's. Mind: I dont say there isnt another side to it. It has its value as an advertisement. It makes useful acquaintances and leads to valuable business connections. But it takes his mind off the main chance; and he overdoes it.

LORD SUMMERHAYS. The danger of public business is that it never ends. A man may kill himself at it.

JOHNNY. Or he can spend more on it than it brings him in: thats how I look at it. What I say is that everybody's business is nobody's business. I hope I'm not a hard man, nor a narrow man, nor unwilling to pay reasonable taxes, and subscribe in reason to deserving charities, and even serve on a jury in my turn; and no man can say I ever refused to help a friend out of a difficulty when he was worth helping. But when you ask me to go beyond that, I tell you frankly I dont see it. I never did see it, even when I was only a boy, and had to pretend to take in all the ideas the Governor fed me up with. I didnt see it; and I dont see it.

LORD SUMMERHAYS. There is certainly no business reason why you should take more than your share of the world's work.

JOHNNY. So I say. It's really a great encouragement to me to find you agree with me. For of course if nobody agrees with you, how are you to know that youre not a fool?

LORD SUMMERHAYS. Quite so.

JOHNNY. I wish youd talk to him about it. It's no use my saying anything: I'm a child to him still: I have no influence. Besides, you know how to handle men. See how you handled me when I was making a fool of myself about Bunny!

LORD SUMMERHAYS. Not at all.

JOHNNY. Oh yes I was: I know I was. Well, if my blessed father had come in he'd have told me to control myself. As if I was losing my temper on purpose!

Bentley returns, newly washed. He beams when he sees his father, and comes affectionately behind him and pats him on the shoulders.

BENTLEY. Hel-lo, commander! have you come? Ive been making a filthy silly ass of myself here. I'm awfully sorry, Johnny, old chap: I beg your pardon. Why dont you kick me when I go on like that?

LORD SUMMERHAYS. As we came through Godalming I thought I heard some yelling—

BENTLEY. I should think you did. Johnny was rather rough on me, though. He told me nobody here liked me; and I was silly enough to believe him.

LORD SUMMERHAYS. And all the women have been kissing you and pitying you ever since to stop your crying, I suppose. Baby!

BENTLEY. I did cry. But I always feel good after crying: it relieves my wretched nerves. I feel perfectly jolly now.

LORD SUMMERHAYS. Not at all ashamed of yourself, for instance?

BENTLEY. If I started being ashamed of myself I shouldnt have time for anything else all my life. I say: I feel very fit and spry. Lets all go down and meet the Grand Cham. [He goes to the hatstand and takes down his hat].

LORD SUMMERHAYS. Does Mr Tarleton like to be called the Grand Cham, do you think, Bentley?

BENTLEY. Well, he thinks hes too modest for it. He calls himself Plain John. But you cant call him that in his own office: besides, it doesnt suit him: it's not flamboyant enough.

JOHNNY. Flam what?

BENTLEY. Flamboyant. Lets go and meet him. He's telephoned from Guildford to say hes on the road. The dear old son is always telephoning or telegraphing: he thinks hes hustling along like anything when hes only sending unnecessary messages.

LORD SUMMERHAYS. Thank you: I should prefer a quiet afternoon.

BENTLEY. Right o! I shant press Johnny: hes had enough of me for one week-end. [*He goes out through the pavilion into the grounds*].

JOHNNY. Not a bad idea, that.

LORD SUMMERHAYS. What?

JOHNNY. Going to meet the Governor. You know you wouldnt think it; but the Governor likes Bunny rather. And Bunny is cultivating it. I shouldnt be surprised if he thought he could squeeze me out one of these days.

LORD SUMMERHAYS. You dont say so! Young rascal! I want to consult you about him, if you dont mind. Shall we stroll over to the Gibbet? Bentley is too fast for me as a walking companion; but I should like a short turn.

JOHNNY [*rising eagerly, highly flattered*] Right you are. Thatll suit me down to the ground. [*He takes a Panama and stick from the hat stand*].

Mrs Tarleton and Hypatia come back just as the two men are going out. Hypatia salutes Summerhays from a distance with an enigmatic lift of her eyelids in his direction and a demure nod before she sits down at the worktable and busies herself with her needle. Mrs Tarleton, hospitably fussy, goes over to him.

MRS TARLETON. Oh, Lord Summerhays, I didnt know you were here. Wont you have some tea?

LORD SUMMERHAYS. No, thank you: I'm not allowed tea. And I'm ashamed to say Ive knocked over your beautiful punch-bowl. You must let me replace it.

MRS TARLETON. Oh, it doesnt matter: I'm only too glad to be rid of it. The shopman told me it was in the best taste; but when my poor old nurse Martha got cataract, Bunny said it was a merciful provision of Nature to prevent her seeing our china.

LORD SUMMERHAYS [*gravely*] That was exceedingly rude of Bentley, Mrs Tarleton. I hope you told him so.

MRS TARLETON. Oh, bless you! I dont care what he says; so long as he says it to me and not before visitors.

JOHNNY. We're going out for a stroll, mother.

MRS TARLETON. All right: dont let us keep you. Never mind about that crock: I'll get the girl to come and take the pieces away. [*Recollecting herself*] There! Ive done it again!

JOHNNY. Done what?

MRS TARLETON. Called her the girl. You know, Lord Summerhays, it's a funny thing; but now I'm getting old, I'm dropping back into all the ways John and I had when we had barely a hundred a year. You should have known me when I was forty! I talked like a duchess; and if Johnny or Hypatia let slip a word that was like old times, I was down on them like anything. And now I'm beginning to do it myself at every turn.

LORD SUMMERHAYS. There comes a time when all that seems to matter so little. Even queens drop the mask when they reach our time of life.

MRS TARLETON. Let you alone for giving a thing a pretty turn! Youre a humbug, you know, Lord Summerhays. John doesnt know it; and Johnny doesnt know it; but you and I know it, dont we? Now thats something that even you cant answer; so be off with you for your walk without another word.

Lord Summerhays smiles; bows; and goes out through the vestibule door, followed by Johnny. Mrs Tarleton sits down at the worktable and takes out her darning materials and one of her husband's socks. Hypatia is at the other side of the table, on her mother's right. They chat as they work.

HYPATIA. I wonder whether they laugh at us when they are by themselves!

MRS TARLETON. Who?

HYPATIA. Bentley and his father and all the toffs in their set.

MRS TARLETON. Oh, thats only their way. I used to think that the aristocracy were a nasty sneering lot, and that they were laughing at me and John. Theyre always giggling and pretending not to care much about anything. But you get used to it: theyre the same to one another and to everybody. Besides, what does it matter what they think? It's far worse when theyre civil, because that always means that they want you to lend them money; and you must never do that, Hypatia, because they never pay. How can they? They dont make anything, you see. Of course, if you can make up your mind to regard it as a gift, thats different; but then they generally ask you again; and you may as well say no first as last. You neednt be afraid of the aristocracy, dear: theyre only human creatures like ourselves after all;

and youll hold your own with them easy enough.

HYPATIA. Oh, I'm not a bit afraid of them, I assure you.

MRS TARLETON. Well, no, not afraid of them, exactly; but youve got to pick up their ways. You know, dear, I never quite agreed with your father's notion of keeping clear of them, and sending you to a school that was so expensive that they couldnt afford to send their daughters there; so that all the girls belonged to big business families like ourselves. It takes all sorts to make a world; and I wanted you to see a little of all sorts. When you marry Bunny, and go among the women of his father's set, theyll shock you at first.

HYPATIA [incredulously] How?

MRS TARLETON. Well, the things they talk about.

HYPATIA. Oh! scandalmongering?

MRS TARLETON. Oh no: we all do that: thats only human nature. But you know theyve no notion of decency. I shall never forget the first day I spent with a marchioness, two duchesses, and no end of Ladies This and That. Of course it was only a committee: theyd put me on to get a big subscription out of John. I'd never heard such talk in my life. The things they mentioned! And it was the marchioness that started it.

HYPATIA. What sort of things?

MRS TARLETON. Drainage!! She'd tried three systems in her castle; and she was going to do away with them all and try another. I didnt know which way to look when she began talking about it: I thought theyd all have got up and gone out of the room. But not a bit of it, if you please. They were all just as bad as she. They all had systems; and each of them swore by her own system. I sat there with my cheeks burning until one of the duchesses, thinking I looked out of it, I suppose, asked me what system I had. I said I was sure I knew nothing about such things, and hadnt we better change the subject. Then the fat was in the fire, I can tell you. There was a regular terror of a countess with an anaerobic system; and she told me, downright brutally, that I'd better learn something about them before my children died of diphtheria. That was just two months after I'd buried poor little Bobby; and that was the very thing he died of, poor little lamb! I burst out crying: I couldnt help it. It was as good as telling me I'd killed my own child. I had to go away; but before I was out of the door one of the duchesses— quite a young woman—began talking about what sour milk did in her inside and how she expected to live to be over a hundred if she took it regularly. And me listening to her, that had never dared to think that a duchess could have anything so common as an inside! I shouldnt have minded if it had been children's insides: we have to talk about them. But grown-up people! I was glad to get away that time.

HYPATIA. There was a physiology and hygiene class started at school; but of course none of our girls were let attend it.

MRS TARLETON. If it had been an aristocratic school plenty would have attended it. Thats what theyre like: theyve nasty minds. With really nice good women a thing is either decent or indecent; and if it's indecent, we just dont mention it or pretend to know about it; and theres an end of it. But all the aristocracy cares about is whether it can get any good out of the thing. Theyre what Johnny calls cynical-like. And of course nobody can say a word to them for it. Theyre so high up that they can do and say what they like.

HYPATIA. Well, I think they might leave the drains to their husbands, I shouldnt think much of a man that left such things to me.

MRS TARLETON. Oh, dont think that, dear, whatever you do. I never let on about it to you; but it's me that takes care of the drainage here. After what that countess said to me I wasnt going to lose another child nor trust John. And I dont want my grandchildren to die any more than my children.

HYPATIA. Do you think Bentley will ever be as big a man as his father? I dont mean clever: I mean big and strong.

MRS TARLETON. Not he. He's overbred, like one of those expensive little dogs. I like a bit of a mongrel myself, whether it's a man or a dog: theyre the best for everyday. But we all have our tastes: whats one woman's meat is another woman's poison. Bunny's a dear little fellow; but I never could have fancied him for a husband when I was your age.

HYPATIA. Yes; but he has some brains. He's not like all the rest. One cant have everything.

MRS TARLETON. Oh, youre quite right, dear: quite right. It's a great thing to have brains: look what it's done for your father! Thats the reason I never said a word when you jilted poor Jerry Mackintosh.

HYPATIA [*excusing herself*] I really couldnt stick it out with Jerry, mother. I know you liked him; and nobody can deny that he's a splendid animal—

MRS TARLETON [*shocked*] Hypatia! How can you! The things that girls say nowadays!

HYPATIA. Well, what else can you call him? If I'd been deaf or he'd been dumb, I could have married him. But living with father, Ive got accustomed to cleverness. Jerry would drive me mad: you know very well he's a fool: even Johnny thinks him a fool.

MRS TARLETON [*up in arms at once in defence of her boy*] Now dont begin about my Johnny. You know it annoys me. Johnny's as clever as anybody else in his own way. I dont say he's as clever as you in some ways; but he's a man, at all events, and not a little squit of a thing like your Bunny.

HYPATIA. Oh, I say nothing against your darling: we all know Johnny's perfection.

MRS TARLETON. Dont be cross, dearie. You let Johnny alone; and I'll let Bunny alone. I'm just as bad as you. There!

HYPATIA. Oh, I dont mind your saying that about Bentley. It's true. He is a little squit of a thing. I wish he wasnt. But who else is there? Think of all the other chances Ive had! Not one of them has as much brains in his whole body as Bentley has in his little finger. Besides, theyve no distinction. It's as much as I can do to tell one from the other. They wouldnt even have money if they werent the sons of their fathers, like Johnny. Whats a girl to do? I never met anybody like Bentley before. He may be small; but he's the best of the bunch: you cant deny that.

MRS TARLETON [*with a sigh*] Well, my pet, if you fancy him, theres no more to be said.

A pause follows this remark: the two women sewing silently.

HYPATIA. Mother: do you think marriage is as much a question of fancy as it used to be in your time and father's?

MRS TARLETON. Oh, it wasnt much fancy with me, dear: your father just wouldnt take no for an answer; and I was only too glad to be his wife instead of his shop-girl. Still, it's curious; but I had more choice than you in a way, because, you see, I was poor; and there are so many more poor men than rich ones that I might have had more of a pick, as you might say, if John hadnt suited me.

HYPATIA. I can imagine all sorts of men I could fall in love with; but I never seem to meet them. The real ones are too small, like Bunny, or too silly, like Jerry. Of course one can get into a state about any man: fall in love with him if you like to call it that. But who would risk marrying a man for love? *I* shouldnt. I remember three girls at school who agreed that the one man you should never marry was the man you were in love with, because it would make a perfect slave of you. Theres a sort of instinct against it, I think, thats just as strong as the other instinct. One of them, to my certain knowledge, refused a man she was in love with, and married another who was in love with her; and it turned out very well.

MRS TARLETON. Does all that mean that youre not in love with Bunny?

HYPATIA. Oh, how could anybody be in love with Bunny? I like him to kiss me just as I like a baby to kiss me. I'm fond of him; and he never bores me; and I see that he's very clever; but I'm not what you call gone about him, if thats what you mean.

MRS TARLETON. Then why need you marry him?

HYPATIA. What better can I do? I must marry somebody, I suppose. Ive realized that since I was twentythree. I always used to take it as a matter of course that I should be married before I was twenty.

BENTLEY'S VOICE [*in the garden*] Youve got to keep yourself fresh: to look at these things with an open mind.

JOHN TARLETON'S VOICE. Quite right, quite right: I always say so.

MRS TARLETON. Theres your father, and Bunny with him.

BENTLEY. Keep young. Keep your eye on me. Thats the tip for you.

Bentley and Mr Tarleton (an immense and genial veteran of trade) come into view and enter the pavilion.

JOHN TARLETON. You think youre young, do you? You think I'm old? [*energetically shaking off his motoring coat and hanging it up with his cap*].

BENTLEY [*helping him with the coat*] Of course youre old. Look at your face and look at mine. What you call your youth is nothing but your levity. Why do we get on so well together? Because I'm a young cub and youre an old josser. [*He throws a cushion at Hypatia's feet and sits down on it with his back against her knees*].

TARLETON. Old! Thats all you know about it, my lad. How do, Patsy! [*Hypatia kisses him*]. How is my Chickabiddy? [*He kisses Mrs Tarleton's hand and poses expansively in the middle of the picture*]. Look at me! Look at these wrinkles, these grey hairs, this repulsive mask that you call old age! What is it? [*Vehemently*] I ask you, what is it?

BENTLEY. Jolly nice and venerable, old man. Dont be discouraged.

TARLETON. Nice? Not a bit of it. Venerable? Venerable be blowed! Read your Darwin, my boy. Read your Weismann. [*He goes to the sideboard for a drink of lemonade*].

MRS TARLETON. For shame, John! Tell him to read his Bible.

TARLETON [*manipulating the syphon*] Whats the use of telling children to read the Bible when you know they wont. I was kept away from the Bible for forty years by being told to read it when I was young. Then I picked it up one evening in a hotel in Sunderland when I had left all my papers in the train; and I found it wasnt half bad. [*He drinks, and puts down the glass with a smack of enjoyment*]. Better than most halfpenny papers, anyhow, if only you could make people believe it. [*He sits down by the writing-table, near his wife*]. But if you want to understand old age scientifically, read Darwin and Weismann. Of course if you want to understand it romantically, read about Solomon.

MRS TARLETON. Have you had tea, John?

TARLETON. Yes. Dont interrupt me when I'm improving the boy's mind. Where was I? This repulsive mask—Yes. [*Explosively*] What is death?

MRS TARLETON. John!

HYPATIA. Death is a rather unpleasant subject, papa.

TARLETON. Not a bit. Not scientifically. Scientifically it's a delightful subject. You think death's natural. Well, it isnt. You read Weismann. There wasnt any death to start with. You go look in any ditch outside and youll find swimming about there as fresh as paint some of the identical little live cells that Adam christened in the Garden of Eden. But if big things like us didnt die, we'd crowd one another off the face of the globe. Nothing survived, sir, except the sort of people that had the sense and good manners to die and make room for the fresh supplies. And so death was introduced by Natural Selection.

You get it out of your head, my lad, that I'm going to die because I'm wearing out or decaying. Theres no such thing as decay to a vital man. I shall clear out; but I shant decay.

BENTLEY. And what about the wrinkles and the almond tree and the grasshopper that becomes a burden and the desire that fails?

TARLETON. Does it? by George! No, sir: it spiritualizes. As to your grasshopper, I can carry an elephant.

MRS TARLETON. You do say such things, Bunny! What does he mean by the almond tree?

TARLETON. He means my white hairs: the repulsive mask. That, my boy, is another invention of Natural Selection to disgust young women with me, and give the lads a turn.

MRS TARLETON. John: I wont have it. Thats a forbidden subject.

TARLETON. They talk of the wickedness and vanity of women painting their faces and wearing auburn wigs at fifty. But why shouldnt they? Why should a woman allow Nature to put a false mask of age on her when she knows that she's as young as ever? Why should she look in the glass and see a wrinkled lie when a touch of fine art will shew her a glorious truth? The wrinkles are a dodge to repel young men. Suppose she doesnt want to repel young men! Suppose she likes them!

MRS TARLETON. Bunny: take Hypatia out into the grounds for a walk: theres a good boy. John has got one of his naughty fits this evening.

HYPATIA. Oh, never mind me. I'm used to him.

BENTLEY. I'm not. I never heard such conversation: I cant believe my ears. And mind you, this is the man who objected to my marrying his daughter on the ground that a marriage between a member of the great and good middle class with one of the vicious and corrupt aristocracy would be a misalliance. A misalliance, if you please! This is the man Ive adopted as a father!

TARLETON. Eh? Whats that? Adopted me as a father, have you?

BENTLEY. Yes. Thats an idea of mine. I knew a chap named Joey Percival at Oxford (you know I was two months at Balliol before I was sent down for telling the old woman who was head of that silly college what I jolly well thought of him. He would have been glad to have me back, too, at the end of six months; but I wouldnt go: I just let him want; and serve him right!) Well, Joey was a most awfully clever fellow, and so nice! I asked him what made such a difference between him and all the other pups—they w e r e pups, if you like. He told me it was very simple: they had only one father apiece; and he had three.

MRS TARLETON. Dont talk nonsense, child. How could that be?

BENTLEY. Oh, very simple. His father—

TARLETON. Which father?

BENTLEY. The first one: the regulation natural chap. He kept a tame philosopher in the house: a sort of Coleridge or Herbert Spencer kind of card, you know. That was the second father. Then his mother was an Italian princess; and she had an Italian priest always about. He was supposed to take charge of her conscience; but from what I could make out she jolly well took charge of his. The whole three of them took charge of Joey's conscience. He used to hear them arguing like mad about everything. You see, the philosopher was a freethinker, and always believed the latest thing. The priest didnt believe anything, because it was sure to get him into trouble with someone or another. And the natural father kept an open mind and believed whatever paid him best. Between the lot of them Joey got cultivated no end. He said if he could only have had three mothers as well, he'd have backed himself against Napoleon.

TARLETON [impressed] Thats an idea. Thats a most interesting idea: a most important idea.

MRS TARLETON. You always were one for ideas, John.

TARLETON. Youre right, Chickabiddy. What do I tell Johnny when he brags about Tarleton's Underwear? It's not the underwear. The underwear be hanged! Anybody can make underwear. Anybody can sell underwear. Tarleton's Ideas: thats whats done it. Ive often thought of putting that up over the shop.

BENTLEY. Take me into partnership when you do, old man. I'm wasted on the underwear; but I shall come in strong on the ideas.

TARLETON. You be a good boy; and perhaps I will.

MRS TARLETON [scenting a plot against her beloved Johnny] Now, John: you promised—

TARLETON. Yes, yes. All right, Chickabiddy: dont fuss. Your precious Johnny shant be interfered with. [Bouncing up, too energetic to sit still] But I'm getting sick of that old shop. Thirty-five years Ive had of it: same blessed old stairs to go up and down every day: same old lot: same old game: sorry I ever started it now. I'll chuck it and try something else: something that will give a scope to all my faculties.

HYPATIA. Theres money in underwear: theres none in wild-cat ideas.

TARLETON. Theres money in m e, madam, no matter what I go into.

MRS TARLETON. Dont boast, John. Dont tempt Providence.

TARLETON. Rats! You dont understand Providence. Providence likes to be tempted. Thats the secret of the successful man. Read Browning. Natural theology on an island, eh? Caliban was afraid to tempt Providence: that was why he was never able to get even with Prospero. What did Prospero do? Prospero didnt even tempt Providence: he w a s Providence. Thats one of Tarleton's ideas; and dont you forget it.

BENTLEY. You a r e full of beef today, old man.

TARLETON. Beef be blowed! Joy of life. Read Ibsen. [He goes into the pavilion to relieve his restlessness, and stares out with his hands thrust deep in his pockets].

HYPATIA [thoughtful] Bentley: couldnt you invite your friend Mr Percival down here?

BENTLEY. Not if I know it. Youd throw me over the moment you set eyes on him.

MRS TARLETON. Oh, Bunny! For shame!

BENTLEY. Well, who'd marry me, dyou suppose, if they could get my brains with a full-sized body? No, thank you. I shall take jolly good care to keep Joey out of this until Hypatia is past praying for.

Johnny and Lord Summerhays return through the pavilion from their stroll.

TARLETON. Welcome! welcome! Why have you stayed away so long?

LORD SUMMERHAYS [shaking hands] Yes: I should have come sooner. But I'm still rather lost in England. [Johnny takes his hat and hangs it up beside his own]. Thank you. [Johnny returns to his swing and his novel. Lord Summerhays comes to the writing table]. The fact is that as Ive nothing to do, I never have time to go anywhere. [He sits down next Mrs Tarleton].

TARLETON [following him and sitting down on

his left] Paradox, paradox. Good. Paradoxes are the only truths. Read Chesterton. But theres lots for you to do here. You have a genius for government. You learnt your job out there in Jinghiskahn. Well, we want to be governed here in England. Govern us.

LORD SUMMERHAYS. Ah yes, my friend; but in Jinghiskahn you have to govern the right way. If you dont, you go under and come home. Here everything has to be done the wrong way, to suit governors who understand nothing but partridge shooting (our English native princes, in fact) and voters who dont know what theyre voting about. I dont understand these democratic games; and I'm afraid I'm too old to learn. What can I do but sit in the window of my club, which consists mostly of retired Indian Civil servants? We look on at the muddle and the folly and amateurishness; and we ask each other where a single fortnight of it would have landed us.

TARLETON. Very true. Still, Democracy's all right, you know. Read Mill. Read Jefferson.

LORD SUMMERHAYS. Yes. Democracy reads well; but it doesnt act well, like some people's plays. No, no, my friend Tarleton: to make Democracy work, you need an aristocratic democracy. To make Aristocracy work, you need a democratic aristocracy. Youve got neither; and theres an end of it.

TARLETON. Still, you know, the superman may come. The superman's an idea. I believe in ideas. Read Whatshisname.

LORD SUMMERHAYS. Reading is a dangerous amusement, Tarleton. I wish I could persuade your free library people of that.

TARLETON. Why, man, it's the beginning of education.

LORD SUMMERHAYS. On the contrary, it's the end of it. How can you dare teach a man to read until youve taught him everything else first?

JOHNNY [*intercepting his father's reply by coming out of the swing and taking the floor*] Leave it at that. Thats good sense. Anybody on for a game of tennis?

BENTLEY. Oh, lets have some more improving conversation. Wouldnt you rather, Johnny?

JOHNNY. If you ask me, no.

TARLETON. Johnny: you dont cultivate your mind. You dont read.

JOHNNY [*coming between his mother and Lord Summerhays, book in hand*] Yes I do. I bet you

what you like that, page for page, I read more than you, though I dont talk about it so much. Only, I dont read the same books. I like a book with a plot in it. You like a book with nothing in it but some idea that the chap that writes it keeps worrying, like a cat chasing its own tail. I can stand a little of it, just as I can stand watching the cat for two minutes, say, when Ive nothing better to do. But a man soon gets fed up with that sort of thing. The fact is, you look on an author as a sort of god. *I* look on him as a man that I pay to do a certain thing for me. I pay him to amuse me and to take me out of myself and make me forget.

TARLETON. No. Wrong principle. You want to remember. Read Kipling. "Lest we forget."

JOHNNY. If Kipling wants to remember, let him remember. If he had to run Tarleton's Underwear, he'd be jolly glad to forget. As he has a much softer job, and wants to keep himself before the public, his cry is, "Dont you forget the sort of things I'm rather clever at writing about." Well, I dont blame him: it's his business: I should do the same in his place. But what he wants and what I want are two different things. I want to forget; and I pay another man to make me forget. If I buy a book or go to the theatre, I want to forget the shop and forget myself from the moment I go in to the moment I come out. Thats what I pay my money for. And if I find that the author's simply getting at me the whole time, I consider that he's obtained my money under false pretences. I'm not a morbid crank: I'm a natural man; and, as such, I dont like being got at. If a man in my employment did it, I should sack him. If a member of my club did it, I should cut him. If he went too far with it, I should bring his conduct before the committee. I might even punch his head, if it came to that. Well, who and what is an author that he should be privileged to take liberties that are not allowed to other men?

MRS TARLETON. You see, John! What have I always told you? Johnny has as much to say for himself as anybody when he likes.

JOHNNY. I'm no fool, mother, whatever some people may fancy. I dont set up to have as many ideas as the Governor; but what ideas I have are consecutive, at all events. I can think as well as talk.

BENTLEY [*to Tarleton, chuckling*] Had you

there, old man, hadnt he? You are rather all over the shop with your ideas, aint you?

JOHNNY [*handsomely*] I'm not saying anything against you, Governor. But I do say that the time has come for sane, healthy, unpretending men like me to make a stand against this conspiracy of the writing and talking and artistic lot to put us in the back row. It isnt a fact that we're inferior to them: it's a put-up job; and it's they that have put the job up. It's we that run the country for them; and all the thanks we get is to be told we're Philistines and vulgar tradesmen and sordid city men and so forth, and that theyre all angels of light and leading. The time has come to assert ourselves and put a stop to their stuck-up nonsense. Perhaps if we had nothing better to do than talking or writing, we could do it better than they. Anyhow, theyre the failures and refuse of business (hardly a man of them that didnt begin in an office) and we're the successes of it. Thank God I havnt failed yet at anything; and I dont believe I should fail at literature if it would pay me to turn my hand to it.

BENTLEY. Hear, hear!

MRS TARLETON. Fancy you writing a book, Johnny! Do you think he could, Lord Summerhays?

LORD SUMMERHAYS. Why not? As a matter of fact all the really prosperous authors I have met since my return to England have been very like him.

TARLETON [*again impressed*] Thats an idea. Thats a new idea. I believe I ought to have made Johnny an author. Ive never said so before for fear of hurting his feelings, because, after all, the lad cant help it; but Ive never thought Johnny worth tuppence as a man of business.

JOHNNY [*sarcastic*] Oh! You think youve always kept that to yourself, do you, Governor? I know your opinion of me as well as you know it yourself. It takes one man of business to appreciate another; and you arnt, and you never have been, a real man of business. I know where Tarleton's would have been three or four times if it hadnt been for me. [*With a snort and a nod to emphasize the implied warning, he retreats to the Turkish bath, and lolls against it with an air of good-humored indifference*].

TARLETON. Well, who denies it? Youre quite right, my boy. I dont mind confessing to you all that the circumstances that condemned me to keep a shop are the biggest tragedy in modern life. I ought to have been a writer. I'm essentially a man of ideas. When I was a young man I sometimes used to pray that I might fail, so that I should be justified in giving up business and doing something: something first-class. But it was no good: I couldnt fail. I said to myself that if I could only once go to my Chickabiddy here and shew her a chartered accountant's statement proving that I'd made £20 less than last year, I could ask her to let me chance Johnny's and Hypatia's future by going into literature. But it was no good. First it was £250 more than last year. Then it was £700. Then it was £2000. Then I saw it was no use: Prometheus was chained to his rock: read Shelley: read Mrs Browning. Well, well, it was not to be. [*He rises solemnly*]. Lord Summerhays: I ask you to excuse me for a few moments. There are times when a man needs to meditate in solitude on his destiny. A chord is touched; and he sees the drama of his life as a spectator sees a play. Laugh if you feel inclined: no man sees the comic side of it more than I. In the theatre of life everyone may be amused except the actor. [*Brightening*] Theres an idea in this: an idea for a picture. What a pity young Bentley is not a painter! Tarleton meditating on his destiny. Not in a toga. Not in the trappings of the tragedian or the philosopher. In plain coat and trousers: a man like any other man. And beneath that coat and trousers a human soul. Tarleton's Underwear! [*He goes out gravely into the vestibule*].

MRS TARLETON [*fondly*] I suppose it's a wife's partiality, Lord Summerhays; but I do think John is really great. I'm sure he was meant to be a king. My father looked down on John, because he was a rate collector and John kept a shop. It hurt his pride to have to borrow money so often from John; and he used to console himself by saying, "After all, he's only a linendraper." But at last one day he said to me, "John is a king."

BENTLEY. How much did he borrow on that occasion?

LORD SUMMERHAYS [*sharply*] Bentley!

MRS TARLETON. Oh, dont scold the child: he'd have to say something like that if it was to be his last word on earth. Besides, he's quite right: my poor father had asked for his usual five pounds; and John gave him a hundred in his big way. Just like a king.

LORD SUMMERHAYS. Not at all. I had five kings to manage in Jinghiskahn; and I think you do your husband some injustice, Mrs Tarleton. They pretended to like me because I kept their brothers from murdering them; but I didnt like them. And I like Tarleton.

MRS TARLETON. Everybody does. I really must go and make the cook do him a Welsh rabbit. He expects one on special occasions. [*She goes to the inner door*]. Johnny: when he comes back ask him where we're to put that new Turkish bath. Turkish baths are his latest. [*She goes out*].

JOHNNY [*coming forward again*] Now that the Governor has given himself away, and the old lady's gone, I'll tell you something, Lord Summerhays. If you study men whove made an enormous pile in business without being keen on money, youll find that they all have a slate off. The Governor's a wonderful man; but he's not quite all there, you know. If you notice, he's different from me; and whatever my failings may be, I'm a sane man. Erratic: thats what he is. And the danger is that some day he'll give the whole show away.

LORD SUMMERHAYS. Giving the show away is a method like any other method. Keeping it to yourself is only another method. I should keep an open mind about it.

JOHNNY. Has it ever occurred to you that a man with an open mind must be a bit of a scoundrel? If you ask me, I like a man who makes up his mind once for all as to whats right and whats wrong and then sticks to it. At all events you know where to have him.

LORD SUMMERHAYS. That may not be his object.

BENTLEY. He may want to have you, old chap.

JOHNNY. Well, let him. If a member of my club wants to steal my umbrella, he knows where to find it. If a man put up for the club who had an open mind on the subject of property in umbrellas, I should blackball him. An open mind is all very well in clever talky-talky; but in conduct and in business give me solid ground.

LORD SUMMERHAYS. Yes: the quicksands make life difficult. Still, there they are. It's no use pretending theyre rocks.

JOHNNY. I dont know. You can draw a line and make other chaps toe it. Thats what I call morality.

LORD SUMMERHAYS. Very true. But you dont make any progress when youre toeing a line.

HYPATIA [*suddenly, as if she could bear no more of it*] Bentley: do go and play tennis with Johnny. You must take exercise.

LORD SUMMERHAYS. Do, my boy, do. [*To Johnny*] Take him out and make him skip about.

BENTLEY [*rising reluctantly*] I promised you two inches more round my chest this summer. I tried exercises with an indiarubber expander; but I wasnt strong enough: instead of my expanding it, it crumpled me up. Come along, Johnny.

JOHNNY. Do you no end of good, young chap. [*He goes out with Bentley through the pavilion*].

Hypatia throws aside her work with an enormous sigh of relief.

LORD SUMMERHAYS. At last!

HYPATIA. At last. Oh, if I might only have a holiday in an asylum for the dumb. How I envy the animals! They cant talk. If Johnny could only put back his ears or wag his tail instead of laying down the law, how much better it would be! We should know when he was cross and when he was pleased; and thats all we know now, with all his talk. It never stops: talk, talk, talk, talk. Thats my life. All the day I listen to mamma talking; at dinner I listen to papa talking; and when papa stops for breath I listen to Johnny talking.

LORD SUMMERHAYS. You make me feel very guilty. I talk too, I'm afraid.

HYPATIA. Oh, I dont mind that, because your talk is a novelty. But it must have been dreadful for your daughters.

LORD SUMMERHAYS. I suppose so.

HYPATIA. If parents would only realize how they bore their children! Three or four times in the last half hour Ive been on the point of screaming.

LORD SUMMERHAYS. Were we very dull?

HYPATIA. Not at all: you were very clever. Thats whats so hard to bear, because it makes it so difficult to avoid listening. You see, I'm young; and I do so want something to happen. My mother tells me that when I'm her age, I shall be only too glad that nothing's happened; but I'm not her age; so what good is that to me? Theres my father in the garden, meditating on his destiny. All very well for him: he's had a destiny to meditate on; but I havnt had any destiny yet. Everything's happened to him: nothing's happened to me. Thats why this unending talk is so maddeningly uninteresting to me.

LORD SUMMERHAYS. It would be worse if we sat in silence.

HYPATIA. No it wouldnt. If you all sat in silence, as if you were waiting for something to happen, then there would be hope even if nothing did happen. But this eternal cackle, cackle, cackle about things in general is only fit for old, old, OLD people. I suppose it means something to them: theyve had their fling. All I listen for is some sign of it ending in something; but just when it seems to be coming to a point, Johnny or papa just starts another hare; and it all begins over again; and I realize that it's never going to lead anywhere and never going to stop. Thats when I want to scream. I wonder how you can stand it.

LORD SUMMERHAYS. Well, I'm old and garrulous myself, you see. Besides, I'm not here of my own free will, exactly. I came because you ordered me to come.

HYPATIA. Didnt you want to come?

LORD SUMMERHAYS. My dear: after thirty years of managing other people's business, men lose the habit of considering what they want or dont want.

HYPATIA. Oh, dont begin to talk about what men do, and about thirty years experience. If you cant get off that subject, youd better send for Johnny and papa and begin it all over again.

LORD SUMMERHAYS. I'm sorry. I beg your pardon.

HYPATIA. I asked you didnt you want to come?

LORD SUMMERHAYS. I did not stop to consider whether I wanted or not, because when I read your letter I knew I had to come.

HYPATIA. Why?

LORD SUMMERHAYS. Oh come, Miss Tarleton! Really! really! Dont force me to call you a blackmailer to your face. You have me in your power; and I do what you tell me very obediently. Dont ask me to pretend I do it of my own free will.

HYPATIA. I dont know what a blackmailer is. I havnt even that much experience.

LORD SUMMERHAYS. A blackmailer, my dear young lady, is a person who knows a disgraceful secret in the life of another person, and extorts money from that other person by threatening to make his secret public unless the money is paid.

HYPATIA. I havnt asked you for money.

LORD SUMMERHAYS. No; but you asked me to come down here and talk to you; and you mentioned casually that if I didnt youd have nobody to talk about me to but Bentley. That was a threat, was it not?

HYPATIA. Well, I wanted you to come.

LORD SUMMERHAYS. In spite of my age and my unfortunate talkativeness?

HYPATIA. I like talking to you. I can let myself go with you. I can say things to you I cant say to other people.

LORD SUMMERHAYS. I wonder why?

HYPATIA. Well, you are the only really clever, grown-up, high-class, experienced man I know who has given himself away to me by making an utter fool of himself with me. You cant wrap yourself up in your toga after that. You cant give yourself airs with me.

LORD SUMMERHAYS. You mean you can tell Bentley about me if I do.

HYPATIA. Even if there wasnt any Bentley: even if you didnt care (and I really dont see why you should care so much), still, we never could be on conventional terms with one another again. Besides, Ive got a feeling for you: almost a ghastly sort of love for you.

LORD SUMMERHAYS [shrinking] I beg you—no, please.

HYPATIA. Oh, it's nothing at all flattering; and, of course, nothing wrong, as I suppose youd call it.

LORD SUMMERHAYS. Please believe that I know that. When men of my age—

HYPATIA [impatiently] Oh, do talk about yourself when you mean yourself, and not about men of your age.

LORD SUMMERHAYS. I'll put it as bluntly as I can. When, as you say, I made an utter fool of myself, believe me, I made a poetic fool of myself. I was seduced, not by appetites which, thank Heaven, Ive long outlived: not even by the desire of second childhood for a child companion, but by the innocent impulse to place the delicacy and wisdom and spirituality of my age at the affectionate service of your youth for a few years, at the end of which you would be a grown, strong, formed—widow. Alas, my dear, the delicacy of age reckoned, as usual, without the derision and cruelty of youth. You told me that you didnt want to be an old man's nurse, and that you didnt want to have undersized children like Bentley. It served me right: I dont reproach you: I was an old fool. But how you can imagine, after that, that I can suspect you of the smallest feeling for me except the inevitable feeling of early youth for late age, or imagine that I have any feeling for you except one of shrinking humiliation, I cant understand.

HYPATIA. I dont blame you for falling in love with me. I shall be grateful to you all my life for it, because that was the first time that anything really interesting happened to me.

LORD SUMMERHAYS. Do you mean to tell me that nothing of that kind had ever happened before? that no man had ever—

HYPATIA. Oh, lots. Thats part of the routine of life here: the very dullest part of it. The young man who comes a-courting is as familiar an incident in my life as coffee for breakfast. Of course, he's too much of a gentleman to misbehave himself; and I'm too much of a lady to let him; and he's shy and sheepish; and I'm correct and self-possessed; and at last, when I can bear it no longer, I either frighten him off or give him a chance of proposing, just to see how he'll do it, and refuse him because he does it in the same silly way as all the rest. You dont call that an event in one's life, do you? With you it was different. I should as soon have expected the North Pole to fall in love with me as you. You know I'm only a linen-draper's daughter when all's said. I was afraid of you: you, a great man! a lord! and older than my father. And then, what a situation it was! Just think of it! I was engaged to your son; and you knew nothing about it. He was afraid to tell you: he brought you down here because he thought if he could throw us together I could get round you because I was such a ripping girl. We arranged it all: he and I. We got Papa and Mamma and Johnny out of the way splendidly; and then Bentley took himself off, and left us—you and me!—to take a walk through the heather and admire the scenery of Hindhead. You never dreamt that it was all a plan: that what made me so nice was the way I was playing up to my destiny as the sweet girl that was to make your boy happy. And then! and then! [She rises to dance and clap her hands in her glee].

LORD SUMMERHAYS [shuddering] Stop, stop. Can no woman understand a man's delicacy?

HYPATIA [revelling in the recollection] And then—ha, ha!—you proposed. You! A father! For your son's girl!

LORD SUMMERHAYS. Stop, I tell you. Dont profane what you dont understand.

HYPATIA. That was something happening at last with a vengeance. It was splendid. It was my first peep behind the scenes. If I'd been seventeen I should have fallen in love with you. Even as it is, I feel quite differently towards you from what I do towards other old men. So [offering her hand] you may kiss my hand if that will be any fun for you.

LORD SUMMERHAYS [rising and recoiling to the table, deeply revolted] No, no, no. How dare you? [She laughs mischievously]. How callous youth is! How coarse! How cynical! How ruthlessly cruel!

HYPATIA. Stuff! It's only that youre tired of a great many things Ive never tried.

LORD SUMMERHAYS. It's not alone that. Ive not forgotten the brutality of my own boyhood. But do try to learn, glorious young beast that you are, that age is squeamish, sentimental, fastidious. If you cant understand my holier feelings, at least you know the bodily infirmities of the old. You know that I darent eat all the rich things you gobble up at every meal; that I cant bear the noise and racket and clatter that affect you no more than they affect a stone. Well, my soul is like that too. Spare it: be gentle with it [he involuntarily puts out his hands to plead; she takes them with a laugh]. If you could possibly think of me as half an angel and half an invalid, we should get on much better together.

HYPATIA. We get on very well, I think. Nobody else ever called me a glorious young beast. I like that. Glorious young beast expresses exactly what I like to be.

LORD SUMMERHAYS [extricating his hands and sitting down] Where on earth did you get these morbid tastes? You seem to have been well brought up in a normal, healthy, respectable, middle-class family. Yet you go on like the most unwholesome product of the rankest Bohemianism.

HYPATIA. Thats just it. I'm fed up with—

LORD SUMMERHAYS. Horrible expression. Dont.

HYPATIA. Oh, I daresay it's vulgar; but theres no other word for it. I'm fed up with nice things: with respectability, with propriety! When a woman has nothing to do, money and respectability mean that nothing is ever allowed to happen to her. I dont want to be good; and I dont want to be bad: I just dont want to be bothered about either good or bad: I want to be an active verb.

LORD SUMMERHAYS. An active verb? Oh, I see. An active verb signifies to be, to do, or to suffer.

HYPATIA. Just so: how clever of you! I want to be; I want to do; and I'm game to suffer if it costs that. But stick here doing nothing but being good and nice and ladylike I simply wont. Stay down here with us for a week; and I'll shew you what it means: shew it to you going on day after day, year after year, lifetime after lifetime.

LORD SUMMERHAYS. Shew me what?

HYPATIA. Girls withering into ladies. Ladies withering into old maids. Nursing old women. Running errands for old men. Good for nothing else at last. Oh, you cant imagine the fiendish selfishness of the old people and the maudlin sacrifice of the young. It's more unbearable than any poverty: more horrible than any regular-right-down wickedness. Oh, home! home! parents! family! duty! how I loathe them! How I'd like to see them all blown to bits! The poor escape. The wicked escape. Well, I cant be poor: we're rolling in money: it's no use pretending we're not. But I can be wicked; and I'm quite prepared to be.

LORD SUMMERHAYS. You think that easy?

HYPATIA. Well, isnt it? Being a man, you ought to know.

LORD SUMMERHAYS. It requires some natural talent, which can no doubt be cultivated. It's not really easy to be anything out of the common.

HYPATIA. Anyhow, I mean to make a fight for living.

LORD SUMMERHAYS. Living your own life, I believe the Suffragist phrase is.

HYPATIA. Living any life. Living, instead of withering without even a gardener to snip you off when youre rotten.

LORD SUMMERHAYS. Ive lived an active life; but Ive withered all the same.

HYPATIA. No: youve worn out: thats quite different. And youve some life in you yet or you wouldnt have fallen in love with me. You can never imagine how delighted I was to find that instead of being the correct sort of big panjandrum you were supposed to be, you were really an old rip like papa.

LORD SUMMERHAYS. No, no: not about your father: I really cant bear it. And if you must say these terrible things: these heart-wounding shameful things, at least find something prettier to call me than an old rip.

HYPATIA. Well, what would you call a man proposing to a girl who might be—

LORD SUMMERHAYS. His daughter: yes, I know.

HYPATIA. I was going to say his grand-daughter.

LORD SUMMERHAYS. You always have one more blow to get in.

HYPATIA. Youre too sensitive. Did you ever make mud pies when you were a kid—beg pardon: a child.

LORD SUMMERHAYS. I hope not.

HYPATIA. It's a dirty job; but Johnny and I were vulgar enough to like it. I like young people because theyre not too afraid of dirt to live. Ive grown out of the mud pies; but I like slang; and I like bustling you up by saying things that shock you; and I'd rather put up with swearing and smoking than with dull respectability; and there are lots of things that would just shrivel you up that I think rather jolly. Now!

LORD SUMMERHAYS. Ive not the slightest doubt of it. Dont insist.

HYPATIA. It's not your ideal, is it?

LORD SUMMERHAYS. No.

HYPATIA. Shall I tell you why? Your ideal is an old woman. I daresay she's got a young face; but she's an old woman. Old, old, old. Squeamish. Cant stand up to things. Cant enjoy things: not real things. Always on the shrink.

LORD SUMMERHAYS. On the shrink! Detestable expression.

HYPATIA. Bah! you cant stand even a little thing like that. What good are you? Oh, what good are you?

LORD SUMMERHAYS. Dont ask me. I dont know. I dont know.

Tarleton returns from the vestibule. Hypatia sits down demurely.

HYPATIA. Well, papa: have you meditated on your destiny?

TARLETON [*puzzled*] What? Oh! my destiny. Gad, I forgot all about it: Jock started a rabbit and put it clean out of my head. Besides, why should I give way to morbid introspection? It's a sign of madness. Read Lombroso. [*To Lord Summerhays*] Well, Summerhays, has my little girl been entertaining you?

LORD SUMMERHAYS. Yes. She is a wonderful entertainer.

TARLETON. I think my idea of bringing up a young girl has been rather a success. Dont you listen to this, Patsy: it might make you conceited. She's never been treated like a child. I always said the same thing to her mother. Let her read what she likes. Let her do what she likes. Let her go where she likes. Eh, Patsy?

HYPATIA. Oh yes, if there had only been anything for me to do, any place for me to go, anything I wanted to read.

TARLETON. There, you see! She's not satisfied. Restless. Wants things to happen. Wants adventures to drop out of the sky.

HYPATIA [gathering up her work] If youre going to talk about me and my education, I'm off.

TARLETON. Well, well, off with you. [To Lord Summerhays] She's active, like me. She actually wanted me to put her into the shop.

HYPATIA. Well, they tell me that the girls there have adventures sometimes. [She goes out through the inner door].

TARLETON. She had me there, though she doesnt know it, poor innocent lamb! Public scandal exaggerates enormously, of course; but moralize as you will, superabundant vitality is a physical fact that cant be talked away. [He sits down between the writing table and the sideboard]. Difficult question this, of bringing up children. Between ourselves, it has beaten me. I never was so surprised in my life as when I came to know Johnny as a man of business and found out what he was really like. How did you manage with your sons?

LORD SUMMERHAYS. Well, I really hadnt time to be a father: thats the plain truth of the matter. Their poor dear mother did the usual thing while they were with us. Then of course Eton, Oxford, the usual routine of their class. I saw very little of them, and thought very little about them: how could I? with a whole province on my hands. They and I are—acquaintances. Not, perhaps, quite ordinary acquaintances: theres a sort of—er—I should almost call it a sort of remorse about the way we shake hands (when we do shake hands) which means, I suppose, that we're sorry we dont care more for one another; and I'm afraid we dont meet oftener than we can help. We put each other too much out of countenance. It's really a very difficult relation. To my mind not altogether a natural one.

TARLETON [impressed, as usual] Thats an idea, certainly. I dont think anybody has ever written about that.

LORD SUMMERHAYS. Bentley is the only one who was really my son in any serious sense. He was completely spoilt. When he was sent to a preparatory school he simply yelled until he was sent home. Eton was out of the question; but we managed to tutor him into Oxford. No use: he was sent down. By that time my work was over; and I saw a good deal of him. But I could do nothing with him—except look on. I should have thought your case was quite different. You keep up the middle-class tradition: the day school and the business training instead of the university. I believe in the day school part of it. At all events, you know your own children.

TARLETON. Do we? I'm not so sure of it. Fact is, my dear Summerhays, once childhood is over, once the little animal has got past the stage at which it acquires what you might call a sense of decency, it's all up with the relation between parent and child. You cant get over the fearful shyness of it.

LORD SUMMERHAYS. Shyness?

TARLETON. Yes, shyness. Read Dickens.

LORD SUMMERHAYS [surprised] Dickens!! Of all authors, Charles Dickens! Are you serious?

TARLETON. I dont mean his books. Read his letters to his family. Read any man's letters to his children. Theyre not human. Theyre not about himself or themselves. Theyre about hotels, scenery, about the weather, about getting wet and losing the train and what he saw on the road and all that. Not a word about himself. Forced. Shy. Duty letters. All fit to be published: that says everything. I tell you theres a wall ten feet thick and ten miles high between parent and child. I know what I'm talking about. Ive girls in my employment: girls and young men. I had ideas on the subject. I used to go to the parents and tell them not to let their children go out into the world without instruction in the dangers and temptations they were going to be thrown into. What did every one of the mothers say to me? "Oh, sir, how could I speak of such things to my own daughter?" The men said I was quite right; but they didnt do it, any more than

I'd been able to do it myself to Johnny. I had to leave books in his way; and I felt just awful when I did it. Believe me, Summerhays, the relation between the young and the old should be an innocent relation. It should be something they could talk about. Well, the relation between parent and child may be an affectionate relation. It may be a useful relation. It may be a necessary relation. But it can never be an innocent relation. Youd die rather than allude to it. Depend on it, in a thousand years itll be considered bad form to know who your father and mother are. Embarrassing. Better hand Bentley over to me. I can look him in the face and talk to him as man to man. You can have Johnny.

LORD SUMMERHAYS. Thank you. Ive lived so long in a country where a man may have fifty sons, who are no more to him than a regiment of soldiers, that I'm afraid Ive lost the English feeling about it.

TARLETON [restless again] You mean Jinghiskahn. Ah yes. Good thing the empire. Educates us. Opens our minds. Knocks the Bible out of us. And civilizes the other chaps.

LORD SUMMERHAYS. Yes: it civilizes t h e m. And it uncivilizes us. Their gain. Our loss, Tarleton, believe me, our loss.

TARLETON. Well, why not? Averages out the human race. Makes the nigger half an Englishman. Makes the Englishman half a nigger.

LORD SUMMERHAYS. Speaking as the unfortunate Englishman in question, I dont like the process. If I had my life to live over again, I'd stay at home and supercivilize myself.

TARLETON. Nonsense! dont be selfish. Think how youve improved the other chaps. Look at the Spanish empire! Bad job for Spain, but splendid for South America. Look at what the Romans did for Britain! They burst up and had to clear out; but think of all they taught us! They were the making of us: I believe there was a Roman camp on Hindhead: I'll shew it to you tomorrow. Thats the good side of Imperialism: it's unselfish. I despise the Little Englanders: theyre always thinking about England. Smallminded. I'm for the Parliament of man, the federation of the world. Read Tennyson. [He settles down again]. Then theres the great food question.

LORD SUMMERHAYS [apprehensively] Need we go into that this afternoon?

TARLETON. No; but I wish youd tell the Chickabiddy that the Jinghiskahns eat no end of toasted cheese, and that it's the secret of their amazing health and long life!

LORD SUMMERHAYS. Unfortunately they are neither healthy nor long-lived. And they dont eat toasted cheese.

TARLETON. There you are! They would be if they ate it. Anyhow, say what you like, provided the moral is a Welsh rabbit for my supper.

LORD SUMMERHAYS. British morality in a nutshell!

TARLETON [hugely amused] Yes. Ha ha! Awful hypocrites, aint we?

They are interrupted by excited cries from the grounds.

HYPATIA { Papa! Mamma! Come out as fast as you can. Quick. Quick.

BENTLEY { Hello, governor! Come out. An aeroplane. Look, look.

TARLETON [starting up] Aeroplane! Did he say an aeroplane?

LORD SUMMERHAYS. Aeroplane! [A shadow falls on the pavilion; and some of the glass at the top is shattered and falls on the floor].

Tarleton and Lord Summerhays rush out through the pavilion into the garden.

HYPATIA { Take care. Take care of the chimney.

BENTLEY { Come this side: it's coming right where youre standing.

TARLETON { Hallo! where the devil are you coming? youll have my roof off.

LORD SUMMERHAYS { He's lost control.

MRS TARLETON. Look, look, Hypatia. There are two people in it.

BENTLEY. Theyve cleared it. Well steered!

TARLETON { Yes; but theyre coming slam into the greenhouse.

LORD SUMMERHAYS { Look out for the glass.

MRS TARLETON { Theyll break all the glass. Theyll spoil all the grapes.

BENTLEY { Mind where youre coming. He'll save it. No: theyre down.

An appalling crash of breaking glass is heard. Everybody shrieks.

MRS TARLETON. Oh, are they killed? John: are they killed?

LORD SUMMERHAYS. Are you hurt? Is anything broken? Can you stand?

HYPATIA. Oh, you must be hurt. Are you sure? Shall I get you some water? Or some wine?

TARLETON. Are you all right? Sure you wont have some brandy just to take off the shock.

THE AVIATOR. No, thank you. Quite right. Not a scratch. I assure you I'm all right.

BENTLEY. What luck! And what a smash! You are a lucky chap, I can tell you.

The Aviator and Tarleton come in through the pavilion, followed by Lord Summerhays and Bentley, the Aviator on Tarleton's right. Bentley passes the Aviator and turns to have an admiring look at him. Lord Summerhays overtakes Tarleton less pointedly on the opposite side with the same object.

THE AVIATOR. I'm really very sorry. I'm afraid Ive knocked your vinery into a cocked hat. [*Effusively*] You dont mind, do you?

TARLETON. Not a bit. Come in and have some tea. Stay to dinner. Stay over the week-end. All my life Ive wanted to fly.

THE AVIATOR [*taking off his goggles*] Youre really more than kind.

BENTLEY. Why, it's Joey Percival.

PERCIVAL. Hallo, Ben! That you?

TARLETON. What! The man with three fathers!

PERCIVAL. Oh! has Ben been talking about me?

TARLETON. Consider yourself as one of the family—if you will do me the honor. And your friend too. Wheres your friend?

PERCIVAL. Oh, by the way! before he comes in: let me explain. I dont know him.

TARLETON. Eh?

PERCIVAL. Havnt even looked at him. I'm trying to make a club record with a passenger. The club supplied the passenger. He just got in; and Ive been too busy handling the aeroplane to look at him. I havnt said a word to him; and I cant answer for him socially; but he's an ideal passenger for a flyer. He saved me from a smash.

LORD SUMMERHAYS. I saw it. It was extraordinary. When you were thrown out he held on to the top bar with one hand. You came past him in the air, going straight for the glass. He caught you and turned you off into the flower bed, and then lighted beside you like a bird.

PERCIVAL. How he kept his head I cant imagine. Frankly, *I* didnt.

The Passenger, also begoggled, comes in through the pavilion with Johnny and the two ladies. The Passenger comes between Percival and Tarleton, Mrs Tarleton between Lord Summerhays and her husband, Hypatia between Percival and Bentley, and Johnny to Bentley's right.

TARLETON. Just discussing your prowess, my dear sir. Magnificent. Youll stay to dinner. Youll stay the night. Stay over the week. The Chickabiddy will be delighted.

MRS TARLETON. Wont you take off your goggles and have some tea?

The passenger begins to remove the goggles.

TARLETON. Do. Have a wash. Johnny: take the gentleman to your room: I'll look after Mr Percival. They must—

By this time the passenger has got the goggles off, and stands revealed as a remarkably good-looking woman.

MRS TARLETON. Well I never!!!

BENTLEY. [*in a whisper*] Oh, I say!

JOHNNY. By George!

LORD SUMMERHAYS. A lady!

HYPATIA. A woman!

TARLETON. [*to Percival*] You never told me—

PERCIVAL. I hadnt the least idea—

All together.

An embarrassed pause.

PERCIVAL. I assure you if I'd had the faintest notion that my passenger was a lady I shouldnt have left you to shift for yourself in that selfish way.

LORD SUMMERHAYS. The lady seems to have shifted for both very effectually, sir.

PERCIVAL. Saved my life. I admit it most gratefully.

TARLETON. I must apologize, madam, for having offered you the civilities appropriate to the opposite sex. And yet, why opposite? We are all human: males and females of the same species. When the dress is the same the distinction vanishes. I'm proud to receive in my house a lady of evident refinement and distinction. Allow me to introduce myself: Tarleton: John Tarleton (*seeing conjecture in the passenger's eye*)—yes, yes: Tarleton's Underwear. My wife, Mrs Tarleton: youll excuse me for having in what I had taken to be a confidence between man and man alluded to her as the Chickabiddy. My daughter Hypatia, who has always wanted some adventure to drop out of the sky, and is now, I hope, satisfied at last. Lord Summerhays: a man known wherever the British flag waves. His son Bentley, engaged to Hypatia. Mr Joseph Percival, the promising son of three highly intellectual fathers.

HYPATIA [*startled*] Bentley's friend? [*Bentley nods*].

TARLETON [*continuing, to the passenger*] May I now ask to be allowed the pleasure of knowing your name?

THE PASSENGER. My name is Lina Szczepanowska [*pronouncing it Sh-Chepanovska*].

PERCIVAL. Sh— I beg your pardon?

LINA. Szczepanowska.

PERCIVAL [*dubiously*] Thank you.

TARLETON [*very politely*] Would you mind saying it again?

LINA. Say fish.

TARLETON. Fish.

LINA. Say church.

TARLETON. Church.

LINA. Say fish church.

TARLETON [*remonstrating*] But it's not good sense.

LINA [*inexorable*] Say fish church.

TARLETON. Fish church.

LINA. Again.

TARLETON. No, but—[*resigning himself*] fish church.

LINA. Now say Szczepanowska.

TARLETON. Szczepanowska. Got it, by Gad. [*A sibilant whispering becomes audible: they are all saying Sh-ch to themselves*]. Szczepanowska! Not an English name, is it?

LINA. Polish. I'm a Pole.

TARLETON [*dithyrambically*] Ah yes. What other nation, madame, could have produced your magical personality? Your countrywomen have always appealed to our imagination. Women of Destiny! beautiful! musical! passionate! tragic! You will be at home here: my own temperament is pre-eminently Polish. Wont you sit down?

The group breaks up. Johnny and Bentley hurry to the pavilion and fetch the two wicker chairs. Johnny gives his to Lina. Hypatia and Percival take the chairs at the worktable. Lord Summerhays gives the chair at the vestibule end of the writing table to Mrs Tarleton; and Bentley replaces it with a wicker chair, which Lord Summerhays takes. Johnny remains standing behind the worktable, Bentley behind his father.

MRS TARLETON [*to Lina*] Have some tea now, wont you?

LINA. I never drink tea.

TARLETON [*sitting down at the end of the writing table nearest Lina*] Bad thing to aeroplane on, I should imagine. Too jumpy. Been up much?

LINA. Not in an aeroplane. Ive parachuted; but thats child's play.

MRS TARLETON. But arnt you very foolish to run such a dreadful risk?

LINA. You cant live without running risks.

MRS TARLETON. Oh, what a thing to say! Didnt you know you might have been killed?

LINA. That was why I went up.

HYPATIA. Of course. Cant you understand the fascination of the thing? the novelty! the daring! the sense of something happening!

LINA. Oh no. It's too tame a business for that. I went up for family reasons.

TARLETON. Eh? What? Family reasons?

MRS TARLETON. I hope it wasnt to spite your mother?

PERCIVAL [*quickly*] Or your husband?

LINA. I'm not married. And why should I want to spite my mother?

HYPATIA [*aside to Percival*] That was clever of you, Mr Percival.

PERCIVAL. What?

HYPATIA. To find out.

TARLETON. I'm in a difficulty. I cant understand a lady going up in an aeroplane for family reasons. It's rude to be curious and ask questions; but then it's inhuman to be indifferent, as if you didnt care.

LINA. I'll tell you with pleasure. For the last hundred and fifty years, not a single day has passed without some member of my family risking his life—or her life. It's a point of honor with us to keep up that tradition. Usually several of us do it; but it happens that just at this moment it is being kept up by one of my brothers only. Early this morning I got a telegram from him to say that there had been a fire, and that he could do nothing for the rest of the week. Fortunately I had an invitation from the Aerial League to see this gentleman try to break the passenger record. I appealed to the President of the League to let me save the honor of my family. He arranged it for me.

TARLETON. Oh, I must be dreaming. This is stark raving nonsense.

LINA [*quietly*] You are quite awake, sir.

JOHNNY. We cant all be dreaming the same thing, Governor.

TARLETON. Of course not, you duffer; but then I'm dreaming you as well as the lady.

MRS TARLETON. Dont be silly, John. The lady is only joking, I'm sure. [*To Lina*] I suppose your luggage is in the aeroplane.

PERCIVAL. Luggage was out of the question. If I stay to dinner I'm afraid I cant change unless youll lend me some clothes.

MRS TARLETON. Do you mean neither of you?

PERCIVAL. I'm afraid so.

MRS TARLETON. Oh well, never mind: Hypatia will lend the lady a gown.

LINA. Thank you: I'm quite confortable as I am. I am not accustomed to gowns: they hamper me and make me feel ridiculous; so if you dont mind I shall not change.

MRS TARLETON. Well, I'm beginning to think I'm doing a bit of dreaming myself.

HYPATIA [*impatiently*] Oh, it's all right, mamma. Johnny: look after Mr Percival. [*To Lina, rising*] Come with me.

Lina follows her to the inner door. They all rise.

JOHNNY [*to Percival*] I'll shew you.

PERCIVAL. Thank you.

Lina goes out with Hypatia, and Percival with Johnny.

MRS TARLETON. Well, this is a nice thing to happen! And look at the greenhouse! Itll cost thirty pounds to mend it. People have no right to do such things. And you invited them to dinner too! What sort of woman is that to have in our house when you know that all Hindhead will be calling on us to see that aeroplane? Bunny: come with me and help me to get all the people out of the grounds: I declare they came running as if theyd sprung up out of the earth [*she makes for the inner door*].

TARLETON. No: dont you trouble, Chickabiddy: I'll tackle em.

MRS TARLETON. Indeed youll do nothing of the kind: youll stay here quietly with Lord Summerhays. Youd invite them all to dinner. Come, Bunny. [*She goes out, followed by Bentley. Lord Summerhays sits down again*].

TARLETON. Singularly beautiful woman, Summerhays. What do you make of her? She must be a princess. Whats this family of warriors and statesmen that risk their lives every day?

LORD SUMMERHAYS. Thcy are evidently not warriors and statesmen, or they wouldnt do that.

TARLETON. Well, then, what the devil are they?

LORD SUMMERHAYS. I think I know. The last time I saw that lady, she did something I should not have thought possible.

TARLETON. What was that?

LORD SUMMERHAYS. Wcll, she walked backwards along a taut wire without a balancing pole and turned a somersault in the middle. I remember that her name was Lina, and that the other name was foreign; though I dont recollect it.

TARLETON. Szcz! You couldnt have forgotten that if youd heard it.

LORD SUMMERHAYS. I didnt hear it: I only saw it on a program. But it's clear she's an acrobat. It explains how she saved Percival. And it accounts for her family pride.

TARLETON. An acrobat, eh? Good! good! good! Summerhays: that brings her within reach. Thats better than a princess. I steeled this evergreen heart of mine when I thought she was a princess. Now I shall let it be touched. She is accessible. Good.

LORD SUMMERHAYS. I hope you are not serious. Remember: you have a family. You have a position. You are not in your first youth.

TARLETON. No matter.

Theres magic in the night
When the heart is young.

My heart is young. Besides, I'm a married man, not a widower like you. A married man can do anything he likes if his wife dont mind. A widower cant be too careful. Not that I would have you think me an unprincipled man or a bad husband. I'm not. But Ive a superabundance of vitality. Read Pepys' Diary.

LORD SUMMERHAYS. The woman is your guest, Tarleton.

TARLETON. Well, is she? A woman I bring into my house is my guest. A woman you bring into my house is my guest. But a woman who drops bang down out of the sky into my greenhouse and smashes every blessed pane of glass in it must take her chance.

LORD SUMMERHAYS. Still, you know that my name must not be associated with any scandal. Youll be careful, wont you?

TARLETON. Oh Lord, yes! Yes, yes, yes, yes, yes. I was only joking, of course.

Mrs Tarleton comes back through the inner door.

MRS TARLETON. Well I never! John:I dont think that young woman's right in her head. Do you know what she's just asked for?

TARLETON. Champagne?

MRS TARLETON. No. She wants a Bible and six oranges.

TARLETON. What?

MRS TARLETON. A Bible and six oranges.

TARLETON. I understand the oranges: she's doing an orange cure of some sort. But what on earth does she want the Bible for?

MRS TARLETON. I'm sure I cant imagine. She cant be right in her head.

LORD SUMMERHAYS. Perhaps she wants to read it.

MRS TARLETON. By why should she? on a weekday at all events. What would you advise me to do, Lord Summerhays?

LORD SUMMERHAYS. Well, is there a Bible in the house?

TARLETON. Stacks of em. Theres the family Bible, and the Doré Bible, and the parallel revised version Bible, and the Doves Press Bible, and Johnny's Bible and Bobby's Bible and Patsy's Bible and the Chickabiddy's Bible and my Bible; and I daresay the servants could raise a few more between them. Let her have the lot.

MRS TARLETON. Dont talk like that before Lord Summerhays, John.

LORD SUMMERHAYS. It doesnt matter, Mrs Tarleton: in Jinghiskahn it was a punishable offence to expose a Bible for sale. The empire has no religion.

Lina comes in. She has left her cap in Hypatia's room, but has made no other change. She stops just inside the door, holding it open, evidently not intending to stay.

LINA. Oh, Mrs Tarleton, shall I be making myself very troublesome if I ask for a music-stand in my room as well?

TARLETON. Not at all. You can have the piano if you like. Or the gramophone. Have the gramophone?

LINA. No, thank you: no music.

MRS TARLETON [*going towards her*] Do you think it's good for you to eat so many oranges? Arnt you afraid of getting jaundice?

LINA. Not in the least. But billiard balls will do quite as well.

MRS TARLETON. But you cant eat billiard balls, child!

TARLETON. Get em, Chickabiddy. I understand. [*He imitates a juggler tossing up balls*]. Eh?

LINA [*going to him, past his wife*] Just so.

TARLETON. Billiard balls and cues? Plates, knives, and forks? Two paraffin lamps and a hatstand?

LINA. No: that is popular low-class business. In our family we touch nothing but classical work. Anybody can do lamps and hatstands. *I* can do silver bullets. That is really hard. [*She passes on to Lord Summerhays, and looks gravely down at him as he sits by the writing table.*]

MRS TARLETON. Well, I'm sure I dont know what youre talking about; and I only hope you know yourselves. However, you shall have what you want, of course. [*She goes out through the inner door*].

LORD SUMMERHAYS. Will you forgive my curiosity? What is the Bible for?

LINA. To quiet my soul.

LORD SUMMERHAYS [*with a sigh*] Ah, yes, yes. It no longer quiets mine, I am sorry to say.

LINA. That is because you do not know how to read it. Put it up before you on a stand; and open it at the Psalms. When you can read them and understand them, quite quietly and happily, and keep six balls in the air all the time, you are in perfect condition; and youll never make a mistake that evening. If you find you cant do that, then go and pray until you can. And be very careful that evening.

LORD SUMMERHAYS. Is that the usual form of test in your profession?

LINA. Nothing that we Szczepanowskis do is usual, my lord.

LORD SUMMERHAYS. Are you all so wonderful?

LINA. It is our profession to be wonderful.

LORD SUMMERHAYS. Do you never condescend to do as common people do? For instance, do you not pray as common people pray?

LINA. Common people do not pray, my lord: they only beg.

LORD SUMMERHAYS. You never ask for anything?

LINA. No.

LORD SUMMERHAYS. Then why do you pray?

LINA. To remind myself that I have a soul.

TARLETON [*walking about*] True. Fine. Good.

Beautiful. All this damned materialism: what good is it to anybody? Ive got a soul: dont tell me I havnt. Cut me up and you cant find it. Cut up a steam engine and you cant find the steam. But, by George, it makes the engine go. Say what you will, Summerhays, the divine spark is a fact.

LORD SUMMERHAYS. Have I denied it?

TARLETON. Our whole civilization is a denial of it. Read Walt Whitman.

LORD SUMMERHAYS. I shall go to the billiard room and get the balls for you.

LINA. Thank you.

Lord Summerhays goes out through the vestibule door.

TARLETON [*going to her*] Listen to me. [*She turns quickly*]. What you said just now was beautiful. You touch chords. You appeal to the poetry in a man. You inspire him. Come now! Youre a woman of the world: youre independent: you must have driven lots of men crazy. You know the sort of man I am, dont you? See through me at a glance, eh?

LINA. Yes. [*She sits down quietly in the chair Lord Summerhays has just left*].

TARLETON. Good. Well, do you like me? Dont misunderstand me: I'm perfectly aware that youre not going to fall in love at first sight with a ridiculous old shopkeeper. I cant help that ridiculous old shopkeeper. I have to carry him about with me whether I like it or not. I have to pay for his clothes, though I hate the cut of them: especially the waistcoat. I have to look at him in the glass while I'm shaving. I loathe him because he's a living lie. My soul's not like that: it's like yours. I want to make a fool of myself. About you. Will you let me?

LINA [*very calm*] How much will you pay?

TARLETON. Nothing. But I'll throw as many sovereigns as you like into the sea to shew you that I'm in earnest.

LINA. Are those your usual terms?

TARLETON. No. I never made that bid before.

LINA [*producing a dainty little book and preparing to write in it*] What did you say your name was?

TARLETON. John Tarleton. The great John Tarleton of Tarleton's Underwear.

LINA [*writing*] T-a-r-l-e-t-o-n. Er—? [*She looks up at him inquiringly*].

TARLETON [*promptly*] Fifty-eight.

LINA. Thank you. I keep a list of all my offers. I like to know what I'm considered worth.

TARLETON. Let me look.

LINA [*offering the book to him*] It's in Polish.

TARLETON. Thats no good. Is mine the lowest offer?

LINA. No: the highest.

TARLETON. What do most of them come to? Diamonds? Motor cars? Furs? Villa at Monte Carlo?

LINA. Oh yes: all that. And sometimes the devotion of a lifetime.

TARLETON. Fancy that! A young man offering a woman his old age as a temptation!

LINA. By the way, you did not say how long.

TARLETON. Until you get tired of me.

LINA. Or until you get tired of me?

TARLETON. I never get tired. I never go on long enough for that. But when it becomes so grand, so inspiring that I feel that everything must be an anti-climax after that, then I run away.

LINA. Does she let you go without a struggle?

TARLETON. Yes. Glad to get rid of me. When love takes a man as it takes me— when it makes him great—it frightens a woman.

LINA. The lady here is your wife, isnt she? Dont you care for her?

TARLETON. Yes. And mind! she comes first always. I reserve her dignity even when I sacrifice my own. Youll respect that point of honor, wont you?

LINA. Only a point of honor?

TARLETON [*impulsively*] No, by God! a point of affection as well.

LINA [*smiling, pleased with him*] Shake hands, old pal [*she rises and offers him her hand frankly*].

TARLETON [*giving his hand rather dolefully*] Thanks. That means no, doesnt it?

LINA. It means something that will last longer than yes. I like you. I admit you to my friendship. What a pity you were not trained when you were young! Youd be young still.

TARLETON. I suppose, to an athlete like you, I'm pretty awful, eh?

LINA. Shocking.

TARLETON. Too much crumb. Wrinkles. Yellow patches that wont come off. Short wind. I know. I'm ashamed of myself. I could do nothing on the high rope.

LINA. Oh yes: I could put you in a wheelbarrow and run you along, two hundred feet up.

TARLETON [*shuddering*] Ugh! Well, I'd do even that for you. Read The Master Builder.

LINA. Have you learnt everything from books?

TARLETON. Well, have you learnt everything from the flying trapeze?

LINA. On the flying trapeze there is often another woman; and her life is in your hands every night and your life in hers.

TARLETON. Lina: I'm going to make a fool of myself. I'm going to cry [*he crumples into the nearest chair*].

LINA. Pray instead: dont cry. Why should you cry? Youre not the first Ive said no to.

TARLETON. If you had said yes, should I have been the first then?

LINA. What right have you to ask? Have I asked am *I* the first?

TARLETON. Youre right: a vulgar question. To a man like me, everybody is the first. Life renews itself.

LINA. The youngest child is the sweetest.

TARLETON. Dont probe too deep, Lina. It hurts.

LINA. You must get out of the habit of thinking that these things matter so much. It's linendraperish.

TARLETON. Youre quite right. Ive often said so. All the same, it d o e s matter; for I want to cry. [*He buries his face in his arms on the worktable and sobs*].

LINA [*going to him*] O la la! [*She slaps him vigorously, but not unkindly, on the shoulder*]. Courage, old pal, courage! Have you a gymnasium here?

TARLETON. Theres a trapeze and bars and things in the billiard room.

LINA. Come. You need a few exercises. I'll teach you how to stop crying. [*She takes his arm and leads him off into the vestibule*].

A young man, cheaply dressed and strange in manner, appears in the garden; steals to the pavilion door; and looks in. Seeing that there is nobody, he enters cautiously until he has come far enough to see into the hatstand corner. He draws a revolver, and examines it, apparently to make sure that it is loaded. Then his attention is caught by the Turkish bath. He looks down the lunette, and opens the panels.

HYPATIA [*calling in the garden*] Mr Percival! Mr Percival! Where are you?

The young man makes for the door, but sees Percival coming. He turns and bolts into the Turkish bath, which he closes upon himself just in time to escape being caught by Percival, who runs in through the pavilion, bareheaded. He also, it appears, is in search of a hiding-place; for he stops and turns between the two tables to take a survey of the room; then runs into the corner between the end of the sideboard and the wall. Hypatia, excited, mischievous, her eyes glowing, runs in, precisely on his trail; turns at the same spot; and discovers him just as he makes a dash for the pavilion door. She flies back and intercepts him.

HYPATIA. Aha! Arnt you glad Ive caught you?

PERCIVAL [*illhumoredly turning away from her and coming towards the writing table*] No I'm not. Confound it, what sort of girl are you? What sort of house is this? Must I throw all good manners to the winds?

HYPATIA [*following him*] Do, do, do, do, do. This is the house of a respectable shopkeeper, enormously rich. This is the respectable shopkeeper's daughter, tired of good manners. [*Slipping her left hand into his right*] Come, handsome young man, and play with the respectable shopkeeper's daughter.

PERCIVAL [*withdrawing quickly from her touch*] No, no: dont you know you mustnt go on like this with a perfect stranger?

HYPATIA. Dropped down from the sky. Dont you know that you must always go on like this when you get the chance? You must come to the top of the hill and chase me through the bracken. You may kiss me if you catch me.

PERCIVAL. I shall do nothing of the sort.

HYPATIA. Yes, you will: you cant help yourself. Come along. [*She seizes his sleeve*]. Fool, fool: come along. Dont you want to?

PERCIVAL. No: certainly not. I should never be forgiven if I did it.

HYPATIA. Youll never forgive yourself if you dont.

PERCIVAL. Nonsense. Youre engaged to Ben. Ben's my friend. What do you take me for?

HYPATIA. Ben's old. Ben was born old. Theyre all old here, except you and me and the man-woman or woman-man or whatever you call her that came with you. They never do anything: they only discuss whether what other people do is right. Come and give them something to discuss.

PERCIVAL. I will do nothing incorrect.

HYPATIA. Oh, dont be afraid, little boy: youll get nothing but a kiss; and I'll fight like the devil to keep you from getting that. But we must play on the hill and race through the heather.

PERCIVAL. Why?

HYPATIA. Because we want to, handsome young man.

PERCIVAL. But if everybody went on in this way—

HYPATIA. How happy! oh how happy the world would be!

PERCIVAL. But the consequences may be serious.

HYPATIA. Nothing is worth doing unless the consequences may be serious. My father says so; and I'm my father's daughter.

PERCIVAL. I'm the son of three fathers. I mistrust these wild impulses.

HYPATIA. Take care. Youre letting the moment slip. I feel the first chill of the wave of prudence. Save me.

PERCIVAL. Really, Miss Tarleton! [She strikes him across the face]. Damn you! [Recovering himself, horrified at his lapse] I beg your pardon; but since weve both forgotten ourselves, youll please allow me to leave the house. [He turns towards the inner door, having left his cap in the bedroom].

HYPATIA [standing in his way] Are you ashamed of having said "Damn you" to me?

PERCIVAL. I had no right to say it. I'm very much ashamed of it. I have already begged your pardon.

HYPATIA. And youre not ashamed of having said "Really, Miss Tarleton!"?

PERCIVAL. Why should I?

HYPATIA. O man, man! mean, stupid, cowardly, selfish masculine male man! You ought to have been a governess. I was expelled from school for saying that the very next person that said "Really, Miss Tarleton!" to me, I would strike across the face. You were the next.

PERCIVAL. I had no intention of being offensive. Surely there is nothing that can wound any lady in— [He hesitates, not quite convinced]. At least—er—I really didnt mean to be disagreeable.

HYPATIA. Liar.

PERCIVAL. Of course if youre going to insult me, I am quite helpless. Youre a woman: you can say what you like.

HYPATIA. And you can only say what you dare. Poor wretch: it isnt much. [He bites his lip, and sits down, very much annoyed]. Really, Mr Percival! You sit down in the presence of a lady and leave her standing. [He rises hastily]. Ha, ha! Really, Mr Percival! Oh really, really, really, really, really, Mr Percival! How do you like it? Wouldnt you rather I damned you?

PERCIVAL. Miss Tarleton—

HYPATIA [caressingly] Hypatia, Joey. Patsy, if you like.

PERCIVAL. Look here: this is no good. You want to do what you like?

HYPATIA. Dont you!

PERCIVAL. No. Ive been too well brought up. Ive argued all through this thing; and I tell you I'm not prepared to cast off the social bond. It's like a corset: it's a support to the figure even if it does squeeze and deform it a bit. I want to be free.

HYPATIA. Well, I'm tempting you to be free.

PERCIVAL. Not at all. Freedom, my good girl, means being able to count on how other people will behave. If every man who dislikes me is to throw a handful of mud in my face, and every woman who likes me is to behave like Potiphar's wife, then I shall be a slave: the slave of uncertainty: the slave of fear: the worst of all slaveries. How would you like it if every laborer you met in the road were to make love to you? No. Give me the blessed protection of a good stiff conventionality among thoroughly well-brought up ladies and gentlemen.

HYPATIA. Another talker! Men like conventions because men made them. I didnt make them: I dont like them: I wont keep them. Now, what will you do?

PERCIVAL. Bolt. [He runs out through the pavilion].

HYPATIA. I'll catch you. [She dashes off in pursuit].

During this conversation the head of the scandalized man in the Turkish bath has repeatedly risen from the lunette, with a strong expression of moral shock. It vanishes abruptly as the two turn towards it in their flight. At the same moment Tarleton comes back through the vestibule door, exhausted by severe and unaccustomed exercise.

TARLETON [looking after the flying figures with amazement] Hallo, Patsy: whats up? Another aeroplane? [They are far too preoccupied to hear him; and he is left staring after them as they rush away through the garden. He goes to the pavilion door and looks up; but the heavens are empty. His exhaustion disables him from further inquiry. He dabs his brow with his *handkerchief, and walks stiffly to the nearest convenient support, which happens to be the Turkish bath. He props himself upon it with his elbow, and covers his eyes with his hand for a moment. After a few sighing breaths, he feels a little better, and uncovers his eyes. The man's head rises from the lunette a few inches from his nose. He recoils from the bath with a violent start*]. Oh Lord! My brain's gone. [*Calling piteously*] Chickabiddy! [*He staggers down to the writing table*].

THE MAN [*coming out of the bath, pistol in hand*] Another sound; and youre a dead man.

TARLETON [*braced*] Am I? Well, youre a live one: thats one comfort. I thought you were a ghost. [*He sits down, quite undisturbed by the pistol*] Who are you; and what the devil were you doing in my new Turkish bath?

THE MAN [*with tragic intensity*] I am the son of Lucinda Titmus.

TARLETON [*the name conveying nothing to him*] Indeed? And how is she? Quite well, I hope, eh?

THE MAN. She is dead. Dead, my God! and you are alive.

TARLETON [*unimpressed by the tragedy, but sympathetic*] Oh! Lost your mother? Thats sad. I'm sorry. But we cant all have the luck to die before our mothers, and be nursed out of the world by the hands that nursed us into it.

THE MAN. Much you care, damn you!

TARLETON. Oh, dont cut up rough. Face it like a man. You see I didnt know your mother; but Ive no doubt she was an excellent woman.

THE MAN. Not know her! Do you dare to stand there by her open grave and deny that you knew her?

TARLETON [*trying to recollect*] What did you say her name was?

THE MAN. Lucinda Titmus.

TARLETON. Well, I ought to remember a rum name like that if I ever heard it. But I dont. Have you a photograph or anything?

THE MAN. Forgotten even the name of your victim!

TARLETON. Oh! she was my victim, was she?

THE MAN. She was. And you shall see her face again before you die, dead as she is. I have a photograph.

TARLETON. Good.

THE MAN. Ive two photographs.

TARLETON. Still better. Treasure the mother's pictures. Good boy!

THE MAN. One of them as you knew her. The other as she became when you flung her aside, and she withered into an old woman.

TARLETON. She'd have done that anyhow, my lad. We all grow old. Look at me! [*Seeing that the man is embarrassed by his pistol in fumbling for the photographs with his left hand in his breast pocket*] Let me hold the gun for you.

THE MAN [*retreating to the worktable*] Stand back. Do you take me for a fool?

TARLETON. Well, youre a little upset, naturally. It does you credit.

THE MAN. Look here, upon this picture and on this. [*He holds out the two photographs like a hand at cards, and points to them with the pistol*].

TARLETON. Good. Read Shakespear: he has a word for every occasion. [*He takes the photographs, one in each hand, and looks from one to the other, pleased and interested, but without any sign of recognition*] What a pretty girl! Very pretty. I can imagine myself falling in love with her when I was your age. I wasnt a bad-looking young fellow myself in those days. [*Looking at the other*] Curious that we should both have gone the same way.

THE MAN. You and she the same way! What do you mean?

TARLETON. Both got stout, I mean.

THE MAN. Would you have had her deny herself food?

TARLETON. No: it wouldnt have been any use. It's constitutional. No matter how little you eat you put on flesh if youre made that way. [*He resumes his study of the earlier photograph*].

THE MAN. Is that all the feeling that rises in you at the sight of the face you once knew so well?

TARLETON [*too much absorbed in the portrait to heed him*] Funny that I cant remember! Let this be a lesson to you, young man. I could go into court tomorrow and swear I never saw that face before in my life if it wasnt for that brooch [*pointing to the photograph*]. Have you got that brooch, by the way? [*The man again resorts to his breast pocket*] You seem to carry the whole family property in that pocket.

THE MAN [*producing a brooch*] Here it is to prove my bona fides.

TARLETON [*pensively putting the photographs on the table and taking the brooch*] I bought that brooch in Cheapside from a man with a yellow wig and a cast in his left eye. Ive never set eyes on him from that day to this. And yet I remember that man; and I cant remember your mother.

THE MAN. Monster! Without conscience! without even memory! You left her to her shame—

TARLETON [*throwing the brooch on the table and rising pepperily*] Come, come, young man! none of that. Respect the romance of your mother's youth. Dont you start throwing stones at her. I dont recall her features just at this moment; but Ive no doubt she was kind to me and we were happy together. If you have a word to say against her, take yourself out of my house and say it elsewhere.

THE MAN. What sort of a joker are you? Are you trying to put me in the wrong, when you have to answer to me for a crime that would make every honest man spit at you as you passed in the street if I were to make it known?

TARLETON. You read a good deal, dont you?

THE MAN. What if I do? What has that to do with your infamy and my mother's doom?

TARLETON. There, you see! Doom! Thats not good sense; but it's literature. Now it happens that I'm a tremendous reader: always was. When I was your age I read books of that sort by the bushel: the Doom sort, you know. It's odd, isnt it, that you and I should be like one another in that respect? Can you account for it in any way?

THE MAN. No. What are you driving at?

TARLETON. Well, do you know who your father was?

THE MAN. I see what you mean now. You dare set up to be my father! Thank heaven Ive not a drop of your vile blood in my veins.

TARLETON [*sitting down again with a shrug*] Well, if you wont be civil, theres no pleasure in talking to you, is there? What do you want? Money?

THE MAN. How dare you insult me?

TARLETON. Well, what do you want?

THE MAN. Justice.

TARLETON. Youre quite sure thats all?

THE MAN. It's enough for me.

TARLETON. A modest sort of demand, isnt it? Nobody ever had it since the world began, fortunately for themselves; but you must have it, must you? Well, youve come to the wrong shop for it: youll get no justice here: we dont keep it. Human nature is what we stock.

THE MAN. Human nature! Debauchery! gluttony! selfishness! robbery of the poor! Is that what you call human nature?

TARLETON. No: thats what you call it. Come, my lad! Whats the matter with you? You dont look starved; and youve a decent suit of clothes.

THE MAN. Forty-two shillings.

TARLETON. They can do you a very decent suit for forty-two shillings. Have you paid for it?

THE MAN. Do you take me for a thief? And do you suppose I can get credit like you?

TARLETON. Then you were able to lay your hand on forty-two shillings. Judging from your conversational style, I should think you must spend at least a shilling a week on romantic literature.

THE MAN. Where would I get a shilling a week to spend on books when I can hardly keep myself decent? I get books at the Free Library.

TARLETON [*springing to his feet*] What!!!

THE MAN [*recoiling before his vehemence*] The Free Library. Theres no harm in that.

TARLETON. Ingrate! I supply you with free books; and the use you make of them is to persuade yourself that it's a fine thing to shoot me. [*He throws himself doggedly back into his chair*]. I'll never give another penny to a Free Library.

THE MAN. Youll never give another penny to anything. This is the end: for you and me.

TARLETON. Pooh! Come, come, man! talk business. Whats wrong? Are you out of employment?

THE MAN. No. This is my Saturday afternoon. Dont flatter yourself that I'm a loafer or a criminal. I'm a cashier; and I defy you to say that my cash has ever been a farthing wrong. Ive a right to call you to account because my hands are clean.

TARLETON. Well, call away. What have I to account for? Had you a hard time with your mother? Why didnt she ask me for money?

THE MAN. She'd have died first. Besides, who wanted your money? Do you suppose we lived in the gutter? My father maynt have been in as large a way as you; but he was better connected; and his shop was as respectable as yours.

TARLETON. I suppose your mother brought him a little capital.

THE MAN. I dont know. Whats that got to

do with you?

TARLETON. Well, you say she and I knew one another and parted. She must have had something off me then, you know. One doesnt get out of these things for nothing. Hang it, young man: do you suppose Ive no heart? Of course she had her due; and she found a husband with it, and set him up in business with it, and brought you up respectably; so what the devil have you to complain of?

THE MAN. Are women to be ruined with impunity?

TARLETON. I havnt ruined any woman that I'm aware of. Ive been the making of you and your mother.

THE MAN. Oh, I'm a fool to listen to you and argue with you. I came here to kill you and then kill myself.

TARLETON. Begin with yourself, if you dont mind. Ive a good deal of business to do still before I die. Havnt you?

THE MAN. No. Thats just it: Ive no business to do. Do you know what my life is? I spend my days from nine to six—nine hours of daylight and fresh air—in a stuffy little den counting another man's money. Ive an intellect: a mind and a brain and a soul; and the use he makes of them is to fix them on his tuppences and his eighteenpences and his two pound seventeen and tenpences and see how much they come to at the end of the day and take care that no one steals them. I enter and enter, and add and add, and take money and give change, and fill cheques and stamp receipts; and not a penny of that money is my own: not one of those transactions has the smallest interest for me or anyone else in the world but him; and even he couldnt stand it if he had to do it all himself. And I'm envied: aye, envied for the variety and liveliness of my job, by the poor devil of a bookkeeper that has to copy all my entries over again. Fifty thousand entries a year that poor wretch makes; and not ten out of the fifty thousand ever has to be referred to again; and when all the figures are counted up and the balance sheet made out, the boss isnt a penny the richer than he'd be if bookkeeping had never been invented. Of all the damnable waste of human life that ever was invented, clerking is the very worst.

TARLETON. Why not join the territorials?

THE MAN. Because the boss wont let me. He hasnt the sense to see that it would pay him to get some cheap soldiering out of me. How can a man tied to a desk from nine to six be anything—be even a man, let alone a soldier? But I'll teach him and you a lesson. Ive had enough of living a dog's life and despising myself for it. Ive had enough of being talked down to by hogs like you, and wearing my life out for a salary that wouldnt keep you in cigars. Youll never believe that a clerk's a man until one of us makes an example of one of you.

TARLETON. Despotism tempered by assassination, eh?

THE MAN. Yes. Thats what they do in Russia. Well, a business office is Russia as far as the clerks are concerned. So dont you take it so coolly. You think I'm not going to do it; but I am.

TARLETON [rising and facing him] Come, now, as man to man! It's not my fault that youre poorer than I am; and it's not your fault that I'm richer than you. And if you could undo all that passed between me and your mother, you wouldnt undo it; and neither would she. But youre sick of your slavery; and you want to be the hero of a romance and to get into the papers. Eh? A son revenges his mother's shame. Villain weltering in his gore. Mother: look down from heaven and receive your unhappy son's last sigh.

THE MAN. Oh, rot! do you think I read novelettes? And do you suppose I believe such superstitions as heaven? I go to church because the boss told me I'd get the sack if I didnt. Free England! Ha! [Lina appears at the pavilion door, and comes swiftly and noiselessly forward on seeing the man with a pistol in his hand].

TARLETON. Youre afraid of getting the sack; but youre not afraid to shoot yourself.

THE MAN. Damn you! youre trying to keep me talking until somebody comes. [He raises the pistol desperately, but not very resolutely].

LINA [at his right elbow] Somebody has come.

THE MAN [turning on her] Stand off. I'll shoot you if you lay a hand on me. I will, by God.

LINA. You cant cover me with that pistol. Try.

He tries, presenting the pistol at her face. She moves round him in the opposite direction to the hands of a clock with a light dancing step. He finds it impossible to cover her with the pistol: she is always too far to his left. Tarleton, behind him, grips his wrist and drags his arm straight up, so that the pistol points to the ceiling. As he *tries to turn on his assailant, Lina grips his other wrist.*

LINA. Please stop. I cant bear to twist anyone's wrist; but I must if you dont let the pistol go.

THE MAN [*letting Tarleton take it from him*] All right: I'm done. Couldnt even do that job decently. Thats a clerk all over. Very well: send for your damned police and make an end of it. I'm accustomed to prison from nine to six: I daresay I can stand it from six to nine as well.

TARLETON. Dont swear. Thats a lady. [*He throws the pistol on the writing table*].

THE MAN [*looking at Lina in amazement*] Beaten by a female! It needed only this. [*He collapses in the chair near the worktable, and hides his face. They cannot help pitying him*].

LINA. Old pal: dont call the police. Lend him a bicycle and let him get away.

THE MAN. I cant ride a bicycle. I never could afford one. I'm not even that much good.

TARLETON. If I gave you a hundred pound note now to go and have a good spree with, I wonder would you know how to set about it. Do you ever take a holiday?

THE MAN. Take! I g o t four days last August.

TARLETON. What did you do?

THE MAN. I did a cheap trip to Folkestone. I spent sevenpence on dropping pennies into silly automatic machines and peepshows of rowdy girls having a jolly time. I spent a penny on the lift and fourpence on refreshments. That cleaned me out. The rest of the time I was so miserable that I was glad to get back to the office. Now you know.

LINA. Come to the gymnasium: I'll teach you how to make a man of yourself. [*The man is about to rise irresolutely, from the mere habit of doing what he is told, when Tarleton stops him*].

TARLETON. Young man: dont. Youve tried to shoot me; but I'm not vindictive. I draw the line at putting a man on the rack. If you want every joint in your body stretched until it's an agony to live—until you have an unnatural feeling that all your muscles are singing and laughing with pain—then go to the gymnasium with that lady. But youll be more comfortable in jail.

LINA [*greatly amused*] Was that why you went away, old pal? Was that the telegram you said you had forgotten to send?

Mrs Tarleton comes in hastily through the inner door.

MRS TARLETON [*on the steps*] Is anything the matter, John? Nurse says she heard you calling me a quarter of an hour ago; and that your voice sounded as if you were ill. [*She comes between Tarleton and the man*]. Is anything the matter?

TARLETON. This is the son of an old friend of mine. Mr—er—Mr Gunner. [*To the man, who rises awkwardly*]. My wife.

MRS TARLETON. Good evening to you.

GUNNER. Er— [*He is too nervous to speak, and makes a shambling bow*].

Bentley looks in at the pavilion door, very peevish, and too preoccupied with his own affairs to pay any attention to those of the company.

BENTLEY. I say: has anybody seen Hypatia? She promised to come out with me; and I cant find her anywhere. And wheres Joey?

GUNNER [*suddenly breaking out aggressively, being incapable of any middle way between submissiveness and violence*] I can tell you where Hypatia is. I can tell you where Joey is. And I say it's a scandal and an infamy. If people only knew what goes on in this so-called respectable house it would be put a stop to. These are the morals of our pious capitalist class! This is your rotten bourgeoisie! This—

MRS TARLETON. Dont you dare use such language in company. I wont allow it.

TARLETON. All right, Chickabiddy: it's not bad language: it's only Socialism.

MRS TARLETON. Well, I wont have any Socialism in my house.

TARLETON [*to Gunner*] You hear what Mrs Tarleton says. Well, in this house everybody does what she says or out they go.

GUNNER. Do you suppose I want to stay? Do you think I would breathe this polluted atmosphere a moment longer than I could help?

BENTLEY [*running forward between Lina and Gunner*] But what did you mean by what you said about Miss Tarleton and Mr Percival, you beastly rotter, you?

GUNNER [*to Tarleton*] Oh! is Hypatia your daughter? And Joey is M i s t e r Percival, is he? One of your set, I suppose. One of the smart set! One of the bridge-playing, eighty-horse-power, week-ender set! One of the johnnies I slave for! Well, Joey has more decency than your daughter, anyhow. The women are the worst. I never believed it til I saw it with my own eyes. Well, it wont last for ever. The writing is on the wall. Rome fell. Babylon fell. Hindhead's turn will come.

MRS TARLETON [*naively looking at the wall for the writing*] Whatever are you talking about, young man?

GUNNER. I know what I'm talking about. I went into that Turkish bath a boy: I came out a man.

MRS TARLETON. Good gracious! he's mad. [*To Lina*] Did John make him take a Turkish bath?

LINA. No. He doesnt need Turkish baths: he needs to put on a little flesh. I dont understand what it's all about. I found him trying to shoot Mr Tarleton.

MRS TARLETON [*with a scream*] Oh! and John encouraging him, I'll be bound! Bunny: you go for the police. [*To Gunner*] I'll teach you to come into my house and shoot my husband.

GUNNER. Teach away. I never asked to be let off. I'm ashamed to be free instead of taking my part with the rest. Women—beautiful women of noble birth—are going to prison for their opinions. Girl students in Russia go to the gallows; let themselves be cut in pieces with the knout, or driven through the frozen snows of Siberia, sooner than stand looking on tamely at the world being made a hell for the toiling millions. If you were not all skunks and cowards youd be suffering with them instead of battening here on the plunder of the poor.

MRS TARLETON [*much vexed*] Oh, did you ever hear such silly nonsense? Bunny: go and tell the gardener to send over one of his men to Grayshott for the police.

GUNNER. I'll go with him. I intend to give myself up. I'm going to expose what Ive seen here, no matter what the consequences may be to my miserable self.

TARLETON. Stop. You stay where you are, Ben. Chickabiddy: youve never had the police in. If you had, youd not be in a hurry to have them in again. Now, young man: cut the cackle; and tell us, as short as you can, what did you see?

GUNNER. I cant tell you in the presence of ladies.

MRS TARLETON. Oh, you are tiresome. As if it mattered to anyone what you saw. Me! A married woman that might be your mother. [*To Lina*] And I'm sure youre not particular, if youll excuse my saying so.

TARLETON. Out with it. What did you see?

GUNNER. I saw your daughter with my own eyes—oh well, never mind what I saw.

BENTLEY [*almost crying with anxiety*] You beastly rotter. I'll get Joey to give you such a hiding—

TARLETON. You cant leave it at that, you know. What did you see my daughter doing?

GUNNER. After all, why shouldnt she do it? The Russian students do it. Women should be as free as men. I'm a fool. I'm so full of your bourgeois morality that I let myself be shocked by the application of my own revolutionary principles. If she likes the man why shouldnt she tell him so?

MRS TARLETON. I do wonder at you, John, letting him talk like this before everybody. [*Turning rather tartly to Lina*] Would you mind going away to the drawing room just for a few minutes, Miss Chipenoska. This is a private family matter, if you dont mind.

LINA. I should have gone before, Mrs Tarleton, if there had been anyone to protect Mr Tarleton and the young gentleman. [*She goes out through the inner door*].

GUNNER. There you are! It's all of a piece here. The men effeminate, the women unsexed—

TARLETON. Dont begin again, old chap. Keep it for Trafalgar Square.

HYPATIA'S VOICE OUTSIDE. No, no. [*She breaks off in a stifled half laugh, half scream, and is seen darting across the garden with Percival in hot pursuit. Immediately afterwards she appears again, and runs into the pavilion. Finding it full of people, including a stranger, she stops; but Percival, flushed and reckless, rushes in and seizes her before he, too, realizes that they are not alone. He releases her in confusion*].

Dead silence. They are all afraid to look at one another except Mrs Tarleton, who stares sternly at Hypatia. Hypatia is the first to recover her presence of mind.

HYPATIA. Excuse me rushing in like this. Mr Percival has been chasing me down the hill.

GUNNER. Who chased him up it? Dont be ashamed. Be fearless. Be truthful.

TARLETON. Gunner: will you go to Paris for a fortnight? I'll pay your expenses.

HYPATIA. What do you mean?

GUNNER. There was a silent witness in the Turkish bath.

TARLETON. I found him hiding there. Whatever went on here, he saw and heard. Thats what he means.

PERCIVAL [*sternly approaching Gunner, and*

speaking with deep but contained indignation] Am I to understand you as daring to put forward the monstrous and blackguardly lie that this lady behaved improperly in my presence?

GUNNER [*turning white*] You know what I saw and heard.

Hypatia, with a gleam of triumph in her eyes, slips noiselessly into the swing chair, and watches Percival and Gunner, swinging slightly, but otherwise motionless.

PERCIVAL. I hope it is not necessary for me to assure you all that there is not one word of truth—not one grain of substance—in this rascally calumny, which no man with a spark of decent feeling would have uttered even if he had been ignorant enough to believe it. Miss Tarleton's conduct, since I have had the honor of knowing her, has been, I need hardly say, in every respect beyond reproach. [*To Gunner*] As for you, sir, youll have the goodness to come out with me immediately. I have some business with you which cant be settled in Mrs Tarleton's presence or in her house.

GUNNER [*painfully frightened*] Why should I go out with you?

PERCIVAL. Because I intend that you shall.

GUNNER. I wont be bullied by you. [*Percival makes a threatening step towards him*]. Police! [*He tries to bolt; but Percival seizes him*]. Leave me go, will you? What right have you to lay hands on me?

TARLETON. Let him run for it, Mr Percival. He's very poor company. We shall be well rid of him. Let him go.

PERCIVAL. Not until he has taken back and made the fullest apology for the abominable lie he has told. He shall do that, or he shall defend himself as best he can against the most thorough thrashing I'm capable of giving him. [*Releasing Gunner, but facing him ominously*] Take your choice. Which is it to be?

GUNNER. Give me a fair chance. Go and stick at a desk from nine to six for a month, and let me have your grub and your sport and your lessons in boxing, and I'll fight you fast enough. You know I'm no good or you darent bully me like this.

PERCIVAL. You should have thought of that before you attacked a lady with a dastardly slander. I'm waiting for your decision. I'm rather in a hurry, please.

GUNNER. I never said anything against the lady.

MRS TARLETON	Oh, listen to that!
BENTLEY	What a liar!
HYPATIA	Oh!
TARLETON	Oh, come!

PERCIVAL. We'll have it in writing, if you dont mind. [*Pointing to the writing table*] Sit down; and take that pen in your hand. [*Gunner looks irresolutely a little way round; then obeys*]. Now write. "I," whatever your name is—

GUNNER [*after a vain attempt*] I cant. My hand's shaking too much. You see it's no use. I'm doing my best. I cant.

PERCIVAL. Mr Summerhays will write it: you can sign it.

BENTLEY [*insolently to Gunner*] Get up. [*Gunner obeys; and Bentley, shouldering him aside towards Percival, takes his place and prepares to write*].

PERCIVAL. Whats your name?

GUNNER. John Brown.

TARLETON. Oh come! Couldnt you make it Horace Smith? or Algernon Robinson?

GUNNER [*agitatedly*] But my name is John Brown. There a r e really John Browns. How can I help it if my name's a common one?

BENTLEY. Shew us a letter addressed to you.

GUNNER. How can I? I never get any letters: I'm only a clerk. I can shew you J. B. on my handkerchief. [*He takes out a not very clean one*].

BENTLEY [*with disgust*] Oh, put it up again. Let it go at John Brown.

PERCIVAL. Where do you live?

GUNNER. 4 Chesterfield Parade, Kentish Town, N.W.

PERCIVAL [*dictating*] I, John Brown, of 4 Chesterfield Parade, Kentish Town, do hereby voluntarily confess that on the 31st May 1909 I—[*To Tarleton*]What did he do exactly?

TARLETON [*dictating*]—I trespassed on the land of John Tarleton at Hindhead, and effected an unlawful entry into his house, where I secreted myself in a portable Turkish bath—

BENTLEY. Go slow, old man. Just a moment. "Turkish bath"—yes?

TARLETON [*continuing*]—with a pistol, with which I threatened to take the life of the said John Tarleton—

MRS TARLETON. Oh, John! You might have been killed.

TARLETON. —and was prevented from doing

so only by the timely arrival of the celebrated Miss Lina Szczepanowska.

MRS TARLETON. Is she celebrated? [*Apologetically*] I never dreamt—

BENTLEY. Look here: I'm awfully sorry;
but I cant spell Szczepanowska.

PERCIVAL. I think it's S, z, c, z—Better say
the Polish lady.

BENTLEY [*writing*] "the Polish lady"?

TARLETON [*to Percival*] Now it's your turn.

PERCIVAL [*dictating*] I further confess that
I was guilty of uttering an abominable
calumny concerning Miss Hypatia Tarleton,
for which there was not a shred of foundation.

Impressive silence whilst Bentley writes.

BENTLEY. "foundation"?

PERCIVAL. I apologize most humbly to the
lady and her family for my conduct— [*he
waits for Bentley to write*].

BENTLEY. "conduct"?

PERCIVAL. —and I promise Mr Tarleton not
to repeat it, and to amend my life—

BENTLEY. "amend my life"?

PERCIVAL. —and to do what in me lies to
prove worthy of his kindness in giving me
another chance—

BENTLEY. "another chance"?

PERCIVAL. —and refraining from delivering me up to the punishment I so richly
deserve.

BENTLEY. "richly deserve."

PERCIVAL [*to Hypatia*] Does that satisfy
you, Miss Tarleton?

HYPATIA. Yes: that will teach him to tell
lies next time.

BENTLEY [*rising to make place for Gunner
and handing him the pen*] You mean it will
teach him to tell the truth next time.

TARLETON. Ahem! Do you, Patsy?

PERCIVAL. Be good enough to sign. [*Gunner
sits down helplessly and dips the pen in the ink*].
I hope what you are signing is no mere form
of words to you, and that you not only say
you are sorry, but that you are sorry.

*Lord Summerhays and Johnny come in
through the pavilion door.*

MRS TARLETON. Stop. Mr Percival: I think,
on Hypatia's account, Lord Summerhays
ought to be told about this.

*Lord Summerhays, wondering what the matter
is, comes forward between Percival and Lina.
Johnny stops beside Hypatia.*

PERCIVAL. Certainly.

TARLETON [*uneasily*] Take my advice and
cut it short. Get rid of him.

MRS TARLETON. Hypatia ought to have
her character cleared.

TARLETON. You let well alone, Chickabiddy.
Most of our characters will bear a little careful dusting; but they wont bear scouring.
Patsy is jolly well out of it. What does it
matter, anyhow?

PERCIVAL. Mr Tarleton: we have already
said either too much or not enough. Lord
Summerhays: will you be kind enough to
witness the declaration this man has just
signed?

GUNNER. I havnt yet. Am I to sign now?

PERCIVAL. Of course. [*Gunner, who is now
incapable of doing anything on his own initiative,
signs*]. Now stand up and read your declaration to this gentleman. [*Gunner makes a vague
movement and looks stupidly round. Percival
adds peremptorily*] Now, please.

GUNNER [*rising apprehensively and reading
without punctuation in a hardly audible voice,
like a very sick man*] I John Brown of 4 Chesterfield Parade Kentish Town do hereby voluntarily confess that on the 31st May 1909 I
trespassed on the land of John Tarleton at
Hindhead and effected an unlawful entry
into his house where I secreted myself in a
portable Turkish bath with a pistol with
which I threatened to take the life of the
said John Tarleton and was prevented from
doing so only by the timely arrival of the
Polish lady I further confess that I was guilty
of uttering an abominable calumny concerning Miss Hypatia Tarleton for which there
was not a shred of foundation I apologize
most humbly to the lady and her family for
my conduct and I promise Mr Tarleton not
to repeat it and to amend my life and to do
what in me lies to prove worthy of his kindness in giving me another chance and refraining from delivering me up to the punishment I so richly deserve.

*A short and painful silence follows. Then
Percival speaks.*

PERCIVAL. Do you consider that sufficient,
Lord Summerhays?

LORD SUMMERHAYS. Oh quite, quite.

PERCIVAL [*to Hypatia*] Lord Summerhays
would probably like to hear you say that you
are satisfied, Miss Tarleton.

HYPATIA [*coming out of the swing, and advancing between Percival and Lord Summerhays*]
I must say that you have behaved like a perfect gentleman, Mr Percival.

PERCIVAL [*first bowing to Hypatia, and then turning with cold contempt to Gunner, who is standing helpless*] We need not trouble you any further. [*Gunner turns vaguely towards the pavilion*].

JOHNNY [*with less refined offensiveness, pointing to the pavilion*] Thats your way. The gardener will shew you the shortest way into the road. Go the shortest way.

GUNNER [*oppressed and disconcerted, hardly knows how to get out of the room*] Yes, sir. I— [*He turns again, appealing to Tarleton*] Maynt I have my mother's photographs back again? [*Mrs Tarleton pricks up her ears*].

TARLETON. Eh? What? Oh, the photographs! Yes, yes, yes: take them. [*Gunner takes them from the table, and is creeping away, when Mrs Tarleton puts out her hand and stops him*].

MRS TARLETON. Whats this, John? What were you doing with his mother's photographs?

TARLETON. Nothing, nothing. Never mind, Chickabiddy: it's all right.

MRS TARLETON [*snatching the photographs from Gunner's irresolute fingers, and recognizing them at a glance*] Lucy Titmus! Oh John, John!

TARLETON [*grimly, to Gunner*] Young man: youre a fool; but youve just put the lid on this job in a masterly manner. I knew you would. I told you all to let well alone. You wouldnt; and now you must take the consequences—or rather *I* must take them.

MRS TARLETON [*maternally*] Are you Lucy's son?

GUNNER. Yes!

MRS TARLETON. And why didnt you come to me? I didnt turn my back on your mother when she came to me in her trouble. Didnt you know that?

GUNNER. No. She never talked to me about anything.

TARLETON. How could she talk to her own son? Shy, Summerhays, shy. Parent and child. Shy. [*He sits down at the end of the writing table nearest the sideboard like a man resigned to anything that fate may have in store for him*].

MRS TARLETON. Then how did you find out?

GUNNER. From her papers after she died.

MRS TARLETON [*shocked*] Is Lucy dead? And I never knew! [*With an effusion of tenderness*] And you here being treated like that, poor orphan, with nobody to take your part! Tear up that foolish paper, child; and sit down and make friends with me.

JOHNNY ⎫ Hallo, mother: this is all very
        ⎪ well, you know—
PERCIVAL ⎪ But may I point out, Mrs
        ⎬ Tarleton, that—
BENTLEY ⎪ Do you mean that after what
        ⎪ he said of—
HYPATIA ⎭ Oh, look here, mamma: this
          is really—

MRS TARLETON. Will you please speak one at a time?

Silence.

PERCIVAL [*in a very gentlemanly manner*] Will you allow me to remind you, Mrs Tarleton, that this man has uttered a most serious and disgraceful falsehood concerning Miss Tarleton and myself?

MRS TARLETON. I dont believe a word of it. If the poor lad was there in the Turkish bath, who has a better right to say what was going on here than he has? You ought to be ashamed of yourself, Patsy; and so ought you too, Mr Percival, for encouraging her. [*Hypatia retreats to the pavilion, and exchanges grimaces with Johnny, shamelessly enjoying Percival's sudden reverse. They know their mother*].

PERCIVAL [*gasping*] Mrs Tarleton: I give you my word of honor—

MRS TARLETON. Oh, go along with you and your word of honor. Do you think I'm a fool? I wonder you can look the lad in the face after bullying him and making him sign those wicked lies; and all the time you carrying on with my daughter before youd been half an hour in my house. Fie, for shame!

PERCIVAL. Lord Summerhays: I appeal to you. Have I done the correct thing or not?

LORD SUMMERHAYS. Youve done your best, Mr Percival. But the correct thing depends for its success on everybody playing the game very strictly. As a single-handed game, it's impossible.

BENTLEY [*suddenly breaking out lamentably*] Joey: have you taken Hypatia away from me?

LORD SUMMERHAYS [*severely*] Bentley! Bentley! Control yourself, sir.

TARLETON. Come, Mr Percival! the shutters are up on the gentlemanly business. Try the truth.

PERCIVAL. I am in a wretched position. If I tell the truth nobody will believe me.

TARLETON. Oh yes they will. The truth makes everybody believe it.

PERCIVAL. It also makes everybody pretend not to believe it. Mrs Tarleton: youre not playing the game.

MRS TARLETON. I dont think youve behaved at all nicely, Mr Percival.

BENTLEY. I wouldnt have played you such a dirty trick, Joey. [*Struggling with a sob*] You beast.

LORD SUMMERHAYS. Bentley: you m u s t control yourself. Let me say at the same time, Mr Percival, that my son seems to have been mistaken in regarding you either as his friend or as a gentleman.

PERCIVAL. Miss Tarleton: I'm suffering this for your sake. I ask you just to say that I am not to blame. Just that and nothing more.

HYPATIA [*gloating mischievously over his distress*] You chased me through the heather and kissed me. You shouldnt have done that if you were not in earnest.

PERCIVAL. Oh, this is really the limit. [*Turning desperately to Gunner*] Sir: I appeal to y o u. As a gentleman! as a man of honor! as a man bound to stand by another man! You were in that Turkish bath. You saw how it began. Could any man have behaved more correctly than I did? Is there a shadow of foundation for the accusations brought against me?

GUNNER [*sorely perplexed*] Well, what do you want me to say?

JOHNNY. He has said what he had to say already, hasnt he? Read that paper.

GUNNER. When I tell the truth, you make me go back on it. And now you want me to go back on myself! What is a man to do?

PERCIVAL [*patiently*] Please try to get your mind clear, Mr Brown. I pointed out to you that you could not, as a gentleman, disparage a lady's character. You agree with me, I hope.

GUNNER. Yes: that sounds all right.

PERCIVAL. But youre also bound to tell the truth. Surely youll not deny that.

GUNNER. Who's denying it? I say nothing against it.

PERCIVAL. Of course not. Well, I ask you to tell the truth simply and unaffectedly. Did you witness any improper conduct on my part when you were in the bath?

GUNNER. No, sir.

JOHNNY ⎫ Then what do you mean by
HYPATIA ⎬ saying that—
BENTLEY ⎭ Do you mean to say that I— Oh, you a r e a rotter. Youre afraid—

TARLETON [*rising*] Stop. [*Silence*]. Leave it at that. Enough said. You keep quiet,

Johnny. Mr Percival: youre whitewashed. So are you, Patsy. Honors are easy. Lets drop the subject. The next thing to do is to open a subscription to start this young man on a ranch in some far country thats accustomed to be in a disturbed state. He—

MRS TARLETON. Now stop joking the poor lad, John: I wont have it. He's been worried to death between you all. [*To Gunner*] Have you had your tea?

GUNNER. Tea? No: it's too early. I'm all right; only I had no dinner: I didnt think I'd want it. I didnt think I'd be alive.

MRS TARLETON. Oh, what a thing to say! You mustnt talk like that.

JOHNNY. He's out of his mind. He thinks it's past dinnertime.

MRS TARLETON. Oh, youve no sense, Johnny. He calls his lunch his dinner, and has his tea at half-past six. Havnt you, dear?

GUNNER [*timidly*] Hasnt everybody?

JOHNNY [*laughing*] Well, by George, thats not bad.

MRS TARLETON. Now dont be rude, Johnny: you know I dont like it. [*To Gunner*] A cup of tea will pick you up.

GUNNER. I'd rather not. I'm all right.

TARLETON [*going to the sideboard*] Here! try a mouthful of sloe gin.

GUNNER. No, thanks. I'm a teetotaler. I cant touch alcohol in any form.

TARLETON. Nonsense! This isnt alcohol. Sloe gin. Vegetarian, you know.

GUNNER [*hesitating*] Is it a fruit beverage?

TARLETON. Of course it is. Fruit beverage. Here you are. [*He gives him a glass of sloe gin*].

GUNNER [*going to the sideboard*] Thanks. [*He begins to drink it confidently; but the first mouthful startles and almost chokes him*]. It's rather hot.

TARLETON. Do you good. Dont be afraid of it.

MRS TARLETON [*going to him*] Sip it, dear. Dont be in a hurry.

Gunner sips slowly, each sip making his eyes water.

JOHNNY [*coming forward into the place left vacant by Gunner's visit to the sideboard*] Well, now that the gentleman has been attended to, I should like to know where we are. It may be a vulgar business habit; but I confess I like to know where I am.

TARLETON. I dont. Wherever you are, youre there anyhow. I tell you again, leave it at that.

BENTLEY. I want to know too. Hypatia's engaged to me.

HYPATIA. Bentley: if you insult me again: if you say another word, I'll leave the house and not enter it until you leave it.

JOHNNY. Put that in your pipe and smoke it, my boy.

BENTLEY [inarticulate with fury and suppressed tears] Oh! Beasts! Brutes!

MRS TARLETON. Now dont hurt his feelings, poor little lamb!

LORD SUMMERHAYS [very sternly] Bentley: you are not behaving well. You had better leave us until you have recovered yourself.

Bentley goes out in disgrace, but gets no further than half way to the pavilion door, when, with a wild sob, he throws himself on the floor and begins to yell.

MRS TARLETON [running to him] Oh, poor child, poor child! Dont cry, duckie: he didnt mean it: dont cry.

LORD SUMMER-HAYS Stop that infernal noise, sir: do you hear? Stop it instantly.

JOHNNY Thats the game he tried on me. There you are! Now, mother! Now, Patsy! You see for yourselves.

HYPATIA [covering her ears] Oh you little wretch! Stop him, Mr Percival. Kick him.

TARLETON Steady on, steady on. Easy, Bunny, easy.

LINA [appearing at the door] Leave him to me, Mrs Tarleton. [Clear and authoritative] Stand clear, please.

She quickly lifts the upper half of Bentley from the ground; dives under him; rises with his body hanging across her shoulders; and runs out with him.

BENTLEY [in scared, sobered, humble tones as he is borne off] What are you doing? Let me down. Please, Miss Szczepanowska— [they pass out of hearing].

An awestruck silence falls on the company as they speculate on Bentley's fate.

JOHNNY. I wonder what she's going to do with him.

HYPATIA. Spank him, I hope. Spank him hard.

LORD SUMMERHAYS. I hope so. I hope so. Tarleton: I'm beyond measure humiliated and annoyed by my son's behavior in your

house. I had better take him home.

TARLETON. Not at all: not at all. Now, Chickabiddy: as Miss Lina has taken away Ben, suppose you take away Mr Brown for a while.

GUNNER [with unexpected aggressiveness] My name isnt Brown. [They stare at him: he meets their stare defiantly, pugnacious with sloe gin; drains the last drop from his glass; throws it on the sideboard; and advances to the writing table]. My name's Baker: Julius Baker. Mister Baker. If any man doubts it, I'm ready for him.

MRS TARLETON. John: you shouldnt have given him that sloe gin. It's gone to his head.

GUNNER. Dont you think it. Fruit beverages dont go to the head; and what matter if they did? I say nothing to you, maam: I regard you with respect and affection. [Lachrymosely] You were very good to my mother: my poor mother! [Relapsing into his daring mood] But I say my name's Baker; and I'm not to be treated as a child or made a slave of by any man. Baker is my name. Did you think I was going to give you my real name? Not likely! Not me!

TARLETON. So you thought of John Brown. That was clever of you.

GUNNER. Clever! Yes: we're not all such fools as you think: we clerks. It was the bookkeeper put me up to that. It's the only name that nobody gives as a false name, he said. Clever, eh? I should think so.

MRS TARLETON. Come now, Julius—

GUNNER [reassuring her gravely] Dont you be alarmed, maam. I know what is due to you as a lady and to myself as a gentleman. I regard you with respect and affection. If you had been my mother, as you ought to have been, I should have had more chance. But you shall have no cause to be ashamed of me. The strength of a chain is no greater than its weakest link; but the greatness of a poet is the greatness of his greatest moment. Shakespear used to get drunk. Frederick the Great ran away from a battle. But it was what they could rise to, not what they could sink to, that made them great. They werent good always; but they were good on their day. Well, on my day—on my day, mind you—I'm good for something too. I know that Ive made a silly exhibition of myself here. I know I didnt rise to the occasion. I know that if youd been my mother, youd have been ashamed of me. I lost my presence of mind: I was a contemptible coward. But [*slapping himself on the chest*] I'm not the man I was then. This is my day. Ive seen the tenth possessor of a foolish face carried out kicking and screaming by a woman. [*To Percival*] Y o u crowed pretty big over me. You hypnotized me. But when you were put through the fire yourself, you were found wanting. I tell you straight I dont give a damn for you.

MRS TARLETON. No: thats naughty. You shouldnt say that before me.

GUNNER. I would cut my tongue out sooner than say anything vulgar in your presence; for I regard you with respect and affection. I was not swearing. I was affirming my manhood.

MRS TARLETON. What an idea! What puts all these things into your head?

GUNNER. Oh, dont think, because I'm only a clerk, that I'm not one of the intellectuals. I'm a reading man, a thinking man. I read in a book—a high class six shilling book—this precept: Affirm your manhood. It appealed to me. Ive always remembered it. I believe in it. I feel I must do it to recover your respect after my cowardly behavior. Therefore I affirm it in your presence. I tell that man who insulted me that I dont give a damn for him. And neither I do.

TARLETON. I say, Summerhays: did you have chaps of this sort in Jinghiskahn?

LORD SUMMERHAYS. Oh yes: they exist everywhere: they are a most serious modern problem.

GUNNER. Yes. Youre right. [*Conceitedly*] I'm a problem. And I tell you that when we clerks realize that we're problems! well, look out: thats all.

LORD SUMMERHAYS [*suavely, to Gunner*] You read a great deal, you say?

GUNNER. Ive read more than any man in this room, if the truth were known, I expect. Thats whats going to smash up your Capitalism. The problems are beginning to read. Ha! We're free to do that here in England. What would you do with me in Jinghiskahn if you had me there?

LORD SUMMERHAYS. Well, since you ask me so directly, I'll tell you. I should take advantage of the fact that you have neither sense enough nor strength enough to know how to behave yourself in a difficulty of any sort. I should warn an intelligent and ambitious policeman that you are a troublesome person.

The intelligent and ambitious policeman would take an early opportunity of upsetting your temper by ordering you to move on, and treading on your heels until you were provoked into obstructing an officer in the discharge of his duty. Any trifle of that sort would be sufficient to make a man like you lose your self-possession and put yourself in the wrong. You would then be charged and imprisoned until things quieted down.

GUNNER. And you call that justice!

LORD SUMMERHAYS. No. Justice was not my business. I had to govern a province; and I took the necessary steps to maintain order in it. Men are not governed by justice, but by law or persuasion. When they refuse to be governed by law or persuasion, they have to be governed by force or fraud, or both. I used both when law and persuasion failed me. Every ruler of men since the world began has done so, even when he has hated both fraud and force as heartily as I do. It is as well that you should know this, my young friend; so that you may recognize in time that anarchism is a game at which the police can beat you. What have you to say to that?

GUNNER. What have I to say to it! Well, I call it scandalous: thats what I have to say to it.

LORD SUMMERHAYS. Precisely: thats all anybody has to say to it, except the British public, which pretends not to believe it. And now let me ask you a sympathetic personal question. Havnt you a headache?

GUNNER. Well, since you ask me, I have. Ive over-excited myself.

MRS TARLETON. Poor lad! No wonder, after all youve gone through! You want to eat a little and to lie down. You come with me. I want you to tell me about your poor dear mother and about yourself. Come along with me. [*She leads the way to the inner door*].

GUNNER [*following her obediently*] Thank you kindly, madam. [*She goes out. Before passing out after her, he partly closes the door and lingers for a moment to whisper*] Mind: I'm not knuckling down to any man here. I knuckle down to Mrs Tarleton because she's a woman in a thousand. I affirm my manhood all the same. Understand: I dont give a damn for the lot of you. [*He hurries out, rather afraid of the consequences of this defiance, which has provoked Johnny to an impatient movement towards him*].

HYPATIA. Thank goodness he's gone! Oh,

what a bore! WHAT a bore!!! Talk! talk! talk!

TARLETON. Patsy: it's no good. We're going to talk. And we're going to talk about you.

JOHNNY. It's no use shirking it, Pat. We'd better know where we are.

LORD SUMMERHAYS. Come, Miss Tarleton. Wont you sit down? I'm very tired of standing. [*Hypatia comes from the pavilion and takes a chair at the worktable. Lord Summerhays takes the opposite chair, on her right. Percival takes the chair Johnny placed for Lina on her arrival. Tarleton sits down at the end of the writing table. Johnny remains standing. Lord Summerhays continues, with a sigh of relief at being seated*] We shall now get the change of subject we are all pining for.

JOHNNY [*puzzled*] Whats that?

LORD SUMMERHAYS. The great question. The question that men and women will spend hours over without complaining. The question that occupies all the novel readers and all the playgoers. The question they never get tired of.

JOHNNY. But what question?

LORD SUMMERHAYS. The question which particular young man some young woman will mate with.

PERCIVAL. As if it mattered!

HYPATIA [*sharply*] Whats that you said?

PERCIVAL. I said: As if it mattered.

HYPATIA. I call that ungentlemanly.

PERCIVAL. Do you care about that? you who are so magnificently unladylike!

JOHNNY. Look here, Mr Percival: youre not supposed to insult my sister.

HYPATIA. Oh, shut up, Johnny. I can take care of myself. Dont you interfere.

JOHNNY. Oh, very well. If you choose to give yourself away like that—to allow a man to call you unladylike and then to be unladylike, Ive nothing more to say.

HYPATIA. I think Mr Percival is most ungentlemanly; but I wont be protected. I'll not have my affairs interfered with by men on pretence of protecting me. I'm not your baby. If I interfered between you and a woman, you would soon tell me to mind my own business.

TARLETON. Children: dont squabble. Read Dr Watts. Behave yourselves.

JOHNNY. Ive nothing more to say; and as I dont seem to be wanted here, I shall take myself off. [*He goes out with affected calm through the pavilion*].

TARLETON. Summerhays: a family is an awful thing, an impossible thing. Cat and dog. Patsy: I'm ashamed of you.

HYPATIA. I'll make it up with Johnny afterwards; but I really cant have him here sticking his clumsy hoof into my affairs.

LORD SUMMERHAYS. The question is, Mr Percival, are you really a gentleman, or are you not?

PERCIVAL. Was Napoleon really a gentleman or was he not? He made the lady get out of the way of the porter and said, "Respect the burden, madam." That was behaving like a very fine gentleman; but he kicked Volney for saying that what France wanted was the Bourbons back again. That was behaving rather like a navvy. Now I, like Napoleon, am not all one piece. On occasion, as you have all seen, I can behave like a gentleman. On occasion, I can behave with a brutal simplicity which Miss Tarleton herself could hardly surpass.

TARLETON. Gentleman or no gentleman, Patsy: what are your intentions?

HYPATIA. My intentions! Surely it's the gentleman who should be asked his intentions.

TARLETON. Come now, Patsy! none of that nonsense. Has Mr Percival said anything to you that I ought to know or that Bentley ought to know? Have you said anything to Mr Percival?

HYPATIA. Mr Percival chased me through the heather and kissed me.

LORD SUMMERHAYS. As a gentleman, Mr Percival, what do you say to that?

PERCIVAL. As a gentleman, I do not kiss and tell. As a mere man: a mere cad, if you like, I say that I did so at Miss Tarleton's own suggestion.

HYPATIA. Beast!

PERCIVAL. I dont deny that I enjoyed it. But I did not initiate it. And I began by running away.

TARLETON. So Patsy can run faster than you, can she?

PERCIVAL. Yes, when she is in pursuit of me. She runs faster and faster. I run slower and slower. And these woods of yours are full of magic. There was a confounded fern owl. Did you ever hear the churr of a fern owl? Did you ever hear it create a sudden silence by ceasing? Did you ever hear it call its mate by striking its wings together twice and whistling that single note that no nightingale can imitate? That is what happened in the woods when I was running away. So I turned; and the pursuer became the pursued.

HYPATIA. I had to fight like a wild cat.

LORD SUMMERHAYS. Please dont tell us this. It's not fit for old people to hear.

TARLETON. Come: how did it end?

HYPATIA. It's not ended yet.

TARLETON. How is it going to end?

HYPATIA. Ask him.

TARLETON. How is it going to end, Mr Percival?

PERCIVAL. I cant afford to marry, Mr Tarleton. Ive only a thousand a year until my father dies. Two people cant possibly live on that.

TARLETON. Oh, cant they? When *I* married, I should have been jolly glad to have felt sure of the quarter of it.

PERCIVAL. No doubt; but I am not a cheap person, Mr Tarleton. I was brought up in a household which cost at least seven or eight times that; and I am in constant money difficulties because I simply dont know how to live on the thousand a year scale. As to ask a woman to share my degrading poverty, it's out of the question. Besides, I'm rather young to marry. I'm only 28.

HYPATIA. Papa: buy the brute for me.

LORD SUMMERHAYS [*shrinking*] My dear Miss Tarleton: dont be so naughty. I know how delightful it is to shock an old man; but there is a point at which it becomes barbarous. Dont. Please dont.

HYPATIA. Shall I tell Papa about you?

LORD SUMMERHAYS. Tarleton: I had better tell you that I once asked your daughter to become my widow.

TARLETON [*to Hypatia*] Why didnt you accept him, you young idiot?

LORD SUMMERHAYS. I was too old.

TARLETON. All this has been going on under my nose, I suppose. You run after young men; and old men run after you. And I'm the last person in the world to hear of it.

HYPATIA. How could I tell you?

LORD SUMMERHAYS. Parents and children, Tarleton.

TARLETON. Oh, the gulf that lies between them! the impassable, eternal gulf! And so I'm to buy the brute for you, eh?

HYPATIA. If you please, papa.

TARLETON. Whats the price, Mr Percival?

PERCIVAL. We might do with another fifteen hundred if my father would contribute. But

I should like more.

TARLETON. It's purely a question of money with you, is it?

PERCIVAL [*after a moment's consideration*] Practically yes: it turns on that.

TARLETON. I thought you might have some sort of preference for Patsy, you know.

PERCIVAL. Well, but does that matter, do you think? Patsy fascinates me, no doubt. I apparently fascinate Patsy. But, believe me, all that is not worth considering. One of my three fathers (the priest) has married hundreds of couples: couples selected by one another, couples selected by the parents, couples forced to marry one another by circumstances of one kind or another; and he assures me that if marriages were made by putting all the men's names into one sack and the women's names into another, and having them taken out by a blindfolded child like lottery numbers, there would be just as high a percentage of happy marriages as we have here in England. He said Cupid was nothing but the blindfolded child: pretty idea that, I think! I shall have as good a chance with Patsy as with anyone else. Mind: I'm not bigoted about it. I'm not a doctrinaire: not the slave of a theory. You and Lord Summerhays are experienced married men. If you can tell me of any trustworthy method of selecting a wife, I shall be happy to make use of it. I await your suggestions. [*He looks with polite attention to Lord Summerhays, who, having nothing to say, avoids his eye. He looks to Tarleton, who purses his lips glumly and rattles his money in his pockets without a word*]. Apparently neither of you has anything to suggest. Then Patsy will do as well as another, provided the money is forthcoming.

HYPATIA. Oh, you beauty! you beauty!

TARLETON. When I married Patsy's mother, I was in love with her.

PERCIVAL. For the first time?

TARLETON. Yes: for the first time.

PERCIVAL. For the last time?

LORD SUMMERHAYS [*revolted*] Sir: you are in the presence of his daughter.

HYPATIA. Oh, dont mind me. I dont care. I'm accustomed to Papa's adventures.

TARLETON [*blushing painfully*] Patsy, my child: that was not—not delicate.

HYPATIA. Well, papa, youve never shewn any delicacy in talking to me about my conduct; and I really dont see why I shouldnt talk to you about yours. It's such nonsense! Do you think young people dont know?

LORD SUMMERHAYS. I'm sure they dont feel. Tarleton: this is too horrible, too brutal. If neither of these young people have any—any—any—

PERCIVAL. Shall we say paternal sentimentality? I'm extremely sorry to shock you; but you must remember that Ive been educated to discuss human affairs with three fathers simultaneously. I'm an adult person. Patsy is an adult person. You do not inspire me with veneration. Apparently you do not inspire Patsy with veneration. That may surprise you. It may pain you. I'm sorry. It cant be helped. What about the money?

TARLETON. You dont inspire me with generosity, young man.

HYPATIA [*laughing with genuine amusement*] He had you there, Joey.

TARLETON. I havnt been a bad father to you, Patsy.

HYPATIA. I dont say you have, dear. If only I could persuade you Ive grown up, we should get along perfectly.

TARLETON. Do you remember Bill Burt?

HYPATIA. Why?

TARLETON [*to the others*] Bill Burt was a laborer here. I was going to sack him for kicking his father. He said his father had kicked him until he was big enough to kick back. Patsy begged him off. I asked that man what it felt like the first time he kicked his father, and found that it was just like kicking any other man. He laughed and said that it was the old man that knew what it felt like. Think of that, Summerhays! think of that!

HYPATIA. I havnt kicked you, papa.

TARLETON. Youve kicked me harder than Bill Burt ever kicked.

LORD SUMMERHAYS. It's no use, Tarleton. Spare yourself. Do you seriously expect these young people, at their age, to sympathize with what this gentleman calls your paternal sentimentality?

TARLETON [*wistfully*] Is it nothing to you but paternal sentimentality, Patsy?

HYPATIA. Well, I greatly prefer your superabundant vitality, papa.

TARLETON [*violently*] Hold your tongue, you young devil. The young are all alike: hard, coarse, shallow, cruel, selfish, dirty-minded. You can clear out of my house as soon as you can coax him to take you; and the sooner the

better. [*To Percival*] I think you said your price was fifteen hundred a year. Take it. And I wish you joy of your bargain.

PERCIVAL. If you wish to know who I am—

TARLETON. I dont care a tinker's curse who you are or what you are. Youre willing to take that girl off my hands for fifteen hundred a year: thats all that concerns me. Tell h e r who you are if you like: it's her affair, not mine.

HYPATIA. Dont answer him, Joey: it wont last. Lord Summerhays, I'm sorry about Bentley; but Joey's the only man for me.

LORD SUMMERHAYS. It may—

HYPATIA. Please dont say it may break your poor boy's heart. It's much more likely to break yours.

LORD SUMMERHAYS. Oh!

TARLETON [*springing to his feet*] Leave the room. Do you hear: leave the room.

PERCIVAL. Arnt we getting a little cross? Dont be angry, Mr Tarleton. Read Marcus Aurelius.

TARLETON. Dont you dare make fun of me. Take your aeroplane out of my vinery and yourself out of my house.

PERCIVAL [*rising, to Hypatia*] I'm afraid I shall have to dine at the Beacon, Patsy.

HYPATIA [*rising*] Do. I dine with you.

TARLETON. Did you hear me tell you to leave the room?

HYPATIA. I did. [*To Percival*] You see what living with one's parents means, Joey. It means living in a house where you can be ordered to leave the room. Ive got to obey: it's his house, not mine.

TARLETON. Who pays for it? Go and support yourself as I did if you want to be independent.

HYPATIA. I wanted to and you wouldnt let me. How can I support myself when I'm a prisoner?

TARLETON. Hold your tongue.

HYPATIA. Keep your temper.

PERCIVAL [*coming between them*] Lord Summerhays: youll join me, I'm sure, in pointing out to both father and daughter that they have now reached that very common stage in family life at which anything but a blow would be an anticlimax. Do you seriously want to beat Patsy, Mr Tarleton?

TARLETON. Yes. I want to thrash the life out of her. If she doesnt get out of my reach, I'll do it. [*He sits down and grasps the writing table to restrain himself*].

Y

HYPATIA [*coolly going to him and leaning with her breast on his writhing shoulders*] Oh, if you want to beat me just to relieve your feelings —just really and truly for the fun of it and the satisfaction of it, beat away. I dont grudge you that.

TARLETON [*almost in hysterics*] I used to think that this sort of thing went on in other families but that it never could happen in ours. And now— [*He is broken with emotion, and continues lamentably*] I cant say the right thing. I cant do the right thing. I dont know what is the right thing. I'm beaten; and she knows it. Summerhays: tell me what to do.

LORD SUMMERHAYS. When my council in Jinghiskahn reached the point of coming to blows, I used to adjourn the sitting. Let us postpone the discussion. Wait until Monday: we shall have Sunday to quiet down in. Believe me, I'm not making fun of you; but I think theres something in this young gentleman's advice. Read something.

TARLETON. I'll read King Lear.

HYPATIA. Dont. I'm very sorry, dear.

TARLETON. Youre not. Youre laughing at me. Serve me right! Parents and children! No man should know his own child. No child should know its own father. Let the family be rooted out of civilization! Let the human race be brought up in institutions!

HYPATIA. Oh yes. How jolly! You and I might be friends then; and Joey could stay to dinner.

TARLETON. Let him stay to dinner. Let him stay to breakfast. Let him spend his life here. Dont you say I drove him out. Dont you say I drove y o u out.

PERCIVAL. I really have no right to inflict myself on you. Dropping in as I did—

TARLETON. Out of the sky. Ha! Dropping in. The new sport of aviation. You just see a nice house; drop in; scoop up the man's daughter; and off with you again.

Bentley comes back, with his shoulders hanging as if he too had been exercised to the last pitch of fatigue. He is very sad. They stare at him as he gropes to Percival's chair.

BENTLEY. I'm sorry for making a fool of myself. I beg your pardon. Hypatia: I'm awfully sorry; but Ive made up my mind that I'll never marry. [*He sits down in deep depression*].

HYPATIA [*running to him*] How nice of you, Bentley! Of course you guessed I wanted to marry Joey. What did the Polish lady do to you?

BENTLEY [*turning his head away*] I'd rather not speak of her, if you dont mind.

HYPATIA. Youve fallen in love with her. [*She laughs*].

BENTLEY. It's beastly of you to laugh.

LORD SUMMERHAYS. You are not the first to fall today under the lash of that young lady's terrible derision, Bentley.

Lina, her cap on, and her goggles in her hand, comes impetuously through the inner door.

LINA [*on the steps*] Mr Percival: can we get that aeroplane started again? [*She comes down and runs to the pavilion door*]. I must get out of this into the air: right up into the blue.

PERCIVAL. Impossible. The frame's twisted. The petrol has given out: thats what brought us down. And how can we get a clear run to start with among these woods?

LINA [*swooping back through the middle of the pavilion*] We can straighten the frame. We can buy petrol at the Beacon. With a few laborers we can get her out on to the Portsmouth Road and start her along that.

TARLETON [*rising*] But why do you want to leave us, Miss Szcz?

LINA. Old pal: this is a stuffy house. You seem to think of nothing but making love. All the conversation here is about love-making. All the pictures are about love-making. The eyes of all of you are sheep's eyes. You are steeped in it, soaked in it: the very texts on the walls of your bedrooms are the ones about love. It is disgusting. It is not healthy. Your women are kept idle and dressed up for no other purpose than to be made love to. I have not been here an hour; and already everybody makes love to me as if because I am a woman it were my profession to be made love to. First you, old pal. I forgave you because you were nice about your wife.

HYPATIA. Oh! oh! oh! Oh, papa!

LINA. Then you, Lord Summerhays, come to me; and all you have to say is to ask me not to mention that you made love to me in Vienna two years ago. I forgave you because I thought you were an ambassador; and all ambassadors make love and are very nice and useful to people who travel. Then this young gentleman. He is engaged to this young lady; but no matter for that: he makes love to me because I carry him off in my arms when he cries. All these I bore in silence. But now comes your Johnny and tells me I'm a ripping fine woman, and asks me to marry him.

I, Lina Szczepanowska, MARRY him!!!!! I do not mind this boy: he is a child: he loves me: I should have to give him money and take care of him: that would be foolish, but honorable. I do not mind you, old pal: you are what you call an old —ouf! but you do not offer to buy me: you say until we are tired—until you are so happy that you dare not ask for more. That is foolish too, at your age; but it is an adventure: it is not dishonorable. I do not mind Lord Summerhays: it was in Vienna: they had been toasting him at a great banquet: he was not sober. That is bad for the health; but it is not dishonorable. But your Johnny! Oh, your Johnny! with his marriage. He will do the straight thing by me. He will give me a home, a position. He tells me I must know that my present position is not one for a nice woman. This to me, Lina Szczepanowska! I am an honest woman: I earn my living. I am a free woman: I live in my own house. I am a woman of the world: I have thousands of friends: every night crowds of people applaud me, delight in me, buy my picture, pay hard-earned money to see me. I am strong: I am skilful: I am brave: I am independent: I am unbought: I am all that a woman ought to be; and in my family there has not been a single drunkard for four generations. And this Englishman! this linen-draper! he dares to ask me to come and live with him in this rrrrrrabbit hutch, and take my bread from his hand, and ask him for pocket money, and wear soft clothes, and be his woman! his wife! Sooner than that, I would stoop to the lowest depths of my profession. I would stuff lions with food and pretend to tame them. I would deceive honest people's eyes with conjuring tricks instead of real feats of strength and skill. I would be a clown and set bad examples of conduct to little children. I would sink yet lower and be an actress or an opera singer, imperilling my soul by the wicked lie of pretending to be somebody else. All this I would do sooner than take my bread from the hand of a man and make him the master of my body and soul. And so you may tell your Johnny to buy an Englishwoman: he shall not buy Lina Szczepanowska; and I will not stay in the house where such dishonor is offered me. Adieu. [*She turns precipitately to go, but is faced in the pavilion doorway by Johnny, who comes in slowly, his hands in his pockets, meditating deeply*].

JOHNNY [*confidentially to Lina*] You wont mention our little conversation, Miss Shepanoska. It'll do no good; and I'd rather you didnt.

TARLETON. Weve just heard about it, Johnny.

JOHNNY [*shortly, but without ill-temper*] Oh: is that so?

HYPATIA. The cat's out of the bag, Johnny, about everybody. They were all beforehand with you: papa, Lord Summerhays, Bentley and all. Dont you let them laugh at you.

JOHNNY [*a grin slowly overspreading his countenance*] Well, theres no use my pretending to be surprised at you, Governor, is there? I hope you got it as hot as I did. Mind, Miss Shepanoska: it wasnt lost on me. I'm a thinking man. I kept my temper. Youll admit that.

LINA [*frankly*] Oh yes. I do not quarrel. You are what is called a chump; but you are not a bad sort of chump.

JOHNNY. Thank you. Well, if a chump may have an opinion, I should put it at this. You make, I suppose, ten pounds a night off your own bat, Miss Lina?

LINA [*scornfully*] Ten pounds a night! I have made ten pounds a minute.

JOHNNY [*with increased respect*] Have you indeed? I didnt know: youll excuse my mistake, I hope. But the principle is the same. Now I trust you wont be offended at what I'm going to say; but Ive thought about this and watched it in daily experience; and you may take it from me that the moment a woman becomes pecuniarily independent, she gets hold of the wrong end of the stick in moral questions.

LINA. Indeed! And what do you conclude from that, Mister Johnny?

JOHNNY. Well, obviously, that independence for women is wrong and shouldnt be allowed. For their own good, you know. And for the good of morality in general. You agree with me, Lord Summerhays, dont you?

LORD SUMMERHAYS. It's a very moral moral, if I may so express myself.

Mrs Tarleton comes in softly through the inner door.

MRS TARLETON. Dont make too much noise. The lad's asleep.

TARLETON. Chickabiddy: we have some news for you.

JOHNNY [*apprehensively*] Now theres no

need, you know, Governor, to worry mother with everything that passes.

MRS TARLETON [*coming to Tarleton*] Whats been going on? Dont you hold anything back from me, John. What have you been doing?

TARLETON. Patsy isnt going to marry Bentley.

MRS TARLETON. Of course not. Is that your great news? I never believed she'd marry him.

TARLETON. Theres something else. Mr Percival here——

MRS TARLETON [*to Percival*] Are you going to marry Patsy?

PERCIVAL [*diplomatically*] Patsy is going to marry me, with your permission.

MRS TARLETON. Oh, she has my permission: she ought to have been married long ago.

HYPATIA. Mother!

TARLETON. Miss Lina here, though she has been so short a time with us, has inspired a good deal of attachment in—I may say in almost all of us. Therefore I hope she'll stay to dinner, and not insist on flying away in that aeroplane.

PERCIVAL. You must stay, Miss Szczepanowska. I cant go up again this evening.

LINA. Ive seen you work it. Do you think I require any help? And Bentley shall come with me as a passenger.

BENTLEY [*terrified*] Go up in an aeroplane! I darent.

LINA. You must learn to dare.

BENTLEY [*pale but heroic*] All right. I'll come.

LORD SUMMERHAYS / MRS TARLETON. No, no, Bentley, impossible. I shall not allow it. Do you want to kill the child? He shant go.

BENTLEY. I will. I'll lie down and yell until you let me go. I'm not a coward. I wont be a coward.

LORD SUMMERHAYS. Miss Szczepanowska: my son is very dear to me. I implore you to wait until tomorrow morning.

LINA. There may be a storm tomorrow. And I'll go: storm or no storm. I must risk my life tomorrow.

BENTLEY. I hope there will be a storm.

LINA [*grasping his arm*] You are trembling.

BENTLEY. Yes: it's terror, sheer terror. I can hardly see. I can hardly stand. But I'll go with you.

LINA [*slapping him on the back and knocking a ghastly white smile into his face*] You shall. I like you, my boy. We go tomorrow, together.

BENTLEY. Yes: together: tomorrow.

TARLETON. Well, sufficient unto the day is the evil thereof. Read the old book.

MRS TARLETON. Is there anything else?

TARLETON. Well, I—er [*he addresses Lina, and stops*]. I —er [*he addresses Lord Summerhays, and stops*]. I —er [*he gives it up*]. Well, I suppose—er—I suppose theres nothing more to be said.

HYPATIA [*fervently*] Thank goodness!

THE END

XIX
THE DARK LADY OF THE SONNETS
1910

Fin de siècle 15–1600. Midsummer night on the terrace of the Palace at Whitehall, overlooking the Thames. The Palace clock chimes four quarters and strikes eleven.

A Beefeater on guard. A Cloaked Man approaches.

THE BEEFEATER. Stand. Who goes there? Give the word?

THE MAN. Marry! I cannot. I have clean forgotten it.

THE BEEFEATER. Then cannot you pass here. What is your business? Who are you? Are you a true man?

THE MAN. Far from it, Master Warder. I am not the same man two days together: sometimes Adam, sometimes Benvolio, and anon the Ghost.

THE BEEFEATER [*recoiling*] A ghost! Angels and ministers of grace defend us!

THE MAN. Well said, Master Warder. With your leave I will set that down in writing; for I have a very poor and unhappy brain for remembrance. [*He takes out his tablets and writes*]. Methinks this is a good scene, with you on your lonely watch, and I approaching like a ghost in the moonlight. Stare not so amazedly at me; but mark what I say. I keep tryst here tonight with a dark lady. She promised to bribe the warder. I gave her the wherewithal: four tickets for the Globe Theatre.

THE BEEFEATER. Plague on her! She gave me two only.

THE MAN. [*detaching a tablet*] My friend: present this tablet, and you will be welcomed at any time when the plays of Will Shakespear are in hand. Bring your wife. Bring your friends. Bring the whole garrison. There is ever plenty of room.

THE BEEFEATER. I care not for these newfangled plays. No man can understand a word of them. They are all talk. Will you not give me a pass for The Spanish Tragedy?

THE MAN. To see The Spanish Tragedy one pays, my friend. Here are the means. [*He gives him a piece of gold*].

THE BEEFEATER [*overwhelmed*] Gold! Oh, sir, you are a better paymaster than your dark lady.

THE MAN. Women are thrifty, my friend.

THE BEEFEATER. Tis so, sir. And you have to consider that the most open handed of us must een cheapen that which we buy every day. This lady has to make a present to a warder nigh every night of her life.

THE MAN [*turning pale*] I'll not believe it.

THE BEEFEATER. Now you, sir, I dare be sworn, do not have an adventure like this twice in the year.

THE MAN. Villain: wouldst tell me that my dark lady hath ever done thus before? that she maketh occasions to meet other men?

THE BEEFEATER. Now the Lord bless your innocence, sir, do you think you are the only pretty man in the world? A merry lady, sir: a warm bit of stuff. Go to: I'll not see her pass a deceit on a gentleman that hath given me the first piece of gold I ever handled.

THE MAN. Master Warder: is it not a strange thing that we, knowing that all women are false, should be amazed to find our own particular drab no better than the rest?

THE BEEFEATER. Not all, sir. Decent bodies, many of them.

THE MAN [*intolerantly*] No. All false. All. If thou deny it, thou liest.

THE BEEFEATER. You judge too much by the Court, sir. There, indeed, you may say of frailty that its name is woman.

THE MAN [*pulling out his tablets again*] Prithee say that again: that about frailty: the strain of music.

THE BEEFEATER. What strain of music, sir? I'm no musician, God knows.

THE MAN. There is music in your soul: many of your degree have it very notably. [*Writing*] "Frailty: thy name is woman!" [*Repeating it affectionately*] "Thy name is woman."

THE BEEFEATER. Well, sir, it is but four words. Are you a snapper-up of such unconsidered trifles?

THE MAN [*eagerly*] Snapper-up of— [*he gasps*] Oh! Immortal phrase! [*He writes it down*]. This man is a greater than I.

THE BEEFEATER. You have my lord Pembroke's trick, sir.

THE MAN. Like enough: he is my near friend. But what call you his trick?

THE BEEFEATER. Making sonnets by moonlight. And to the same lady too.

THE MAN. No!

THE BEEFEATER. Last night he stood here on your errand, and in your shoes.

THE MAN. Thou, too, Brutus! And I called him friend!

THE BEEFEATER. Tis ever so, sir.

THE MAN. Tis ever so. Twas ever so. [*He turns away, overcome*]. Two Gentlemen of Verona! Judas! Judas!!

THE BEEFEATER. Is he so bad as that, sir?

THE MAN [*recovering his charity and self-possession*] Bad? O no. Human, Master Warder, human. We call one another names when we are offended, as children do. That is all.

THE BEEFEATER. Ay, sir: words, words, words. Mere wind, sir. We fill our bellies with the east wind, sir, as the Scripture hath it. You cannot feed capons so.

THE MAN. A good cadence. By your leave. [*He makes a note of it*].

THE BEEFEATER. What manner of thing is a cadence, sir? I have not heard of it.

THE MAN. A thing to rule the world with, friend.

THE BEEFEATER. You speak strangely, sir: no offence. But, an't like you, you are a very civil gentleman; and a poor man feels drawn to you, you being, as twere, willing to share your thought with him.

THE MAN. Tis my trade. But alas! the world for the most part will none of my thoughts.

Lamplight streams from the palace door as it opens from within.

THE BEEFEATER. Here comes your lady, sir. I'll to t'other end of my ward. You may een take your time about your business: I shall not return too suddenly unless my sergeant comes prowling round. Tis a fell sergeant, sir: strict in his arrest. Good een, sir; and good luck! [*He goes*].

THE MAN. "Strict in his arrest"! " Fell sergeant" ![*As if tasting a ripe plum*] O-o-o-h! [*He makes a note of them*].

A Cloaked Lady gropes her way from the palace and wanders along the terrace, walking in her sleep.

THE LADY [*rubbing her hands as if washing them*] Out, damned spot. You will mar all with these cosmetics. God made you one face; and you make yourself another. Think of your grave, woman, not ever of being beautified. All the perfumes of Arabia will not whiten this Tudor hand.

THE MAN. "All the perfumes of Arabia"! "Beautified"! "Beautified"! a poem in a single word. Can this be my Mary? [*To the Lady*] Why do you speak in a strange voice, and utter poetry for the first time? Are you ailing? You walk like the dead. Mary! Mary!

THE LADY [*echoing him*] Mary! Mary! Who would have thought that woman to have had so much blood in her! Is it my fault that my counsellors put deeds of blood on me? Fie! If you were women you would have more wit than to stain the floor so foully. Hold not up her head so: the hair is false. I tell you yet again, Mary's buried: she cannot come out of her grave. I fear her not: these cats that dare jump into thrones though they be fit only for men's laps must be put away. Whats done cannot be undone. Out, I say. Fie! a queen, and freckled!

THE MAN [*shaking her arm*] Mary, I say: art asleep?

The Lady wakes; starts; and nearly faints. He catches her on his arm.

THE LADY. Where am I? What art thou?

THE MAN. I cry your mercy. I have mistook your person all this while. Methought you were my Mary: my mistress.

THE LADY [*outraged*] Profane fellow: how do you dare?

THE MAN. Be not wroth with me, lady. My mistress is a marvellous proper woman. But she does not speak so well as you. "All the perfumes of Arabia"! That was well said: spoken with good accent and excellent discretion.

THE LADY. Have I been in speech with you here?

THE MAN. Why, yes, fair lady. Have you forgot it?

THE LADY. I have walked in my sleep.

THE MAN. Walk ever in your sleep, fair one; for then your words drop like honey.

THE LADY [*with cold majesty*] Know you to whom you speak, sir, that you dare express yourself so saucily?

THE MAN [*unabashed*] Not I, not care neither. You are some lady of the Court, belike. To me there are but two sorts of women: those with excellent voices, sweet and low, and cackling hens that cannot make me dream. Your voice has all manner of loveliness in it. Grudge me not a short hour of its music.

THE LADY. Sir: you are overbold. Season your admiration for a while with—

THE MAN [*holding up his hand to stop her*] "Season your admiration for a while—"

THE LADY. Fellow: do you dare mimic me to my face?

THE MAN. Tis music. Can you not hear? When a good musician sings a song, do you not sing it and sing it again till you have caught and fixed its perfect melody? "Season your admiration for a while": God! the history of man's heart is in that one word admiration. Admiration! [*Taking up his tablets*] What was it: "Suspend your admiration for a space—"

THE LADY. A very vile jingle of esses. I said "Season your—

THE MAN [*hastily*] Season: ay, season, season, season. Plague on my memory, my wretched memory! I must een write it down. [*He begins to write, but stops, his memory failing him*]. Yet tell me which was the vile jingle? You said very justly: mine own ear caught it even as my false tongue said it.

THE LADY. You said "for a space." I said "for a while."

THE MAN. "For a while" [*he corrects it*]. Good! [*Ardently*] And now be mine neither for a space nor a while, but for ever.

THE LADY. Odds my life! Are you by chance making love to me, knave?

THE MAN. Nay: tis you who have made the love: I but pour it out at your feet. I cannot but love a lass that sets such store by an apt word. Therefore vouchsafe, divine perfection of a woman—no: I have said that before somewhere; and the wordy garment of my love for you must be fire-new—

THE LADY. You talk too much, sir. Let me warn you: I am more accustomed to be listened to than preached at.

THE MAN. The most are like that that do talk well. But though you spake with the tongues of angels, as indeed you do, yet know that I am the king of words—

THE LADY. A king, ha!

THE MAN. No less. We are poor things, we men and women—

THE LADY. Dare you call me woman?

THE MAN. What nobler name can I tender you? How else can I love you? Yet you may well shrink from the name: have I not said we are but poor things? Yet there is a power that can redeem us.

THE LADY. Gramercy for your sermon, sir. I hope I know my duty.

THE MAN. This is no sermon, but the living truth. The power I speak of is the power of immortal poesy. For know that vile as this world is, and worms as we are, you have but to invest all this vileness with a magical garment of words to transfigure us and uplift our souls til earth flowers into a million heavens.

THE LADY. You spoil your heaven with your million. You are extravagant. Observe some measure in your speech.

THE MAN. You speak now as Ben does.

THE LADY. And who, pray, is Ben?

THE MAN. A learned bricklayer who thinks that the sky is at the top of his ladder, and so takes it on him to rebuke me for flying. I tell you there is no word yet coined and no melody yet sung that is extravagant and majestical enough for the glory that lovely words can reveal. It is heresy to deny it: have you not been taught that in the beginning was the Word? that the Word was with God? nay, that the Word was God?

THE LADY. Beware, fellow, how you presume to speak of holy things. The Queen is the head of the Church.

THE MAN. You are the head of my Church when you speak as you did at first. "All the perfumes of Arabia"! Can the Queen speak thus? They say she playeth well upon the virginals. Let her play so to me; and I'll kiss her hands. But until then, you are my Queen; and I'll kiss those lips that have dropt

music on my heart. [*He puts his arms about her*].

THE LADY. Unmeasured impudence! On your life, take your hands from me.

The Dark Lady comes stooping along the terrace behind them like a running thrush. When she sees how they are employed, she rises angrily to her full height, and listens jealously.

THE MAN [*unaware of the Dark Lady*] Then cease to make my hands tremble with the streams of life you pour through them. You hold me as the lodestar holds the iron: I cannot but cling to you. We are lost, you and I: nothing can separate us now.

THE DARK LADY. We shall see that, false lying hound, you and your filthy trull. [*With two vigorous cuffs, she knocks the pair asunder, sending the man, who is unlucky enough to receive a righthanded blow, sprawling on the flags*]. Take that, both of you!

THE CLOAKED LADY [*in towering wrath, throwing off her cloak and turning in outraged majesty on her assailant*] High treason!

THE DARK LADY [*recognizing her and falling on her knees in abject terror*] Will: I am lost: I have struck the Queen.

THE MAN [*sitting up as majestically as his ignominious posture allows*] Woman: you have struck WILLIAM SHAKESPEAR!!!!!!

QUEEN ELIZABETH [*stupent*] Marry, come up!!! Struck William Shakespear quotha! And who in the name of all the sluts and jades and light-o'-loves and fly-by-nights that infest this palace of mine, may William Shakespear be?

THE DARK LADY. Madam: he is but a player. Oh, I could have my hand cut off—

QUEEN ELIZABETH. Belike you will, mistress. Have you bethought you that I am like to have your head cut off as well?

THE DARK LADY. Will: save me. Oh, save me.

ELIZABETH. Save you! A likely savior, on my royal word! I had thought this fellow at least an esquire; for I had hoped that even the vilest of my ladies would not have dishonored my Court by wantoning with a baseborn servant.

SHAKESPEAR [*indignantly scrambling to his feet*] Baseborn! I, a Shakespear of Stratford! I, whose mother was an Arden! baseborn! You forget yourself, madam.

ELIZABETH [*furious*] S'blood! do I so? I will teach you—

THE DARK LADY [*rising from her knees and throwing herself between them*] Will: in God's name anger her no further. It is death. Madam: do not listen to him.

SHAKESPEAR. Not were it een to save your life, Mary, not to mention mine own, will I flatter a monarch who forgets what is due to my family. I deny not that my father was brought down to be a poor bankrupt; but twas his gentle blood that was ever too generous for trade. Never did he disown his debts. Tis true he paid them not; but it is an attested truth that he gave bills for them; and twas those bills, in the hands of base hucksters, that were his undoing.

ELIZABETH [*grimly*] The son of your father shall learn his place in the presence of the daughter of Harry the Eighth.

SHAKESPEAR [*swelling with intolerant importance*] Name not that inordinate man in the same breath with Stratford's worthiest alderman. John Shakespear wedded but once: Harry Tudor was married six times. You should blush to utter his name.

THE DARK LADY *crying out together* Will: for pity's sake—

ELIZABETH Insolent dog—

SHAKESPEAR [*cutting them short*] How know you that King Harry was indeed your father?

ELIZABETH Zounds! Now by— [*she stops to grind her teeth with rage*].

THE DARK LADY She will have me whipped through the streets. Oh God! Oh God!

SHAKESPEAR. Learn to know yourself better, madam. I am an honest gentleman of unquestioned parentage, and have already sent in my demand for the coat-of-arms that is lawfully mine. Can you say as much for yourself?

ELIZABETH [*almost beside herself*] Another word; and I begin with mine own hands the work the hangman shall finish.

SHAKESPEAR. You are no true Tudor: this baggage here has as good a right to your royal seat as you. What maintains you on the throne of England? Is it your renownéd wit? your wisdom that sets at nought the craftiest statesmen of the Christian world? No. Tis the mere chance that might have happened to any milkmaid, the caprice of Nature that made you the most wondrous piece of beauty the age hath seen. [*Elizabeth's raised fists, on the point of striking him, fall to her side*]. That is what hath brought all men to your feet, and founded your throne on the impregnable rock of your proud heart, a stony island in a sea of desire. There, madam, is some wholesome blunt honest speaking for you. Now do your worst.

ELIZABETH [*with dignity*] Master Shakespear: it is well for you that I am a merciful prince. I make allowance for your rustic ignorance. But remember that there are things which be true, and are yet not seemly to be said (I will not say to a queen; for you will have it that I am none), but to a virgin.

SHAKESPEAR [*bluntly*] It is no fault of mine that you are a virgin, madam, albeit tis my misfortune.

THE DARK LADY [*terrified again*] In mercy, madam, hold no further discourse with him. He hath ever some lewd jest on his tongue. You hear how he useth me! calling me baggage and the like to your Majesty's face.

ELIZABETH. As for you, mistress, I have yet to demand what your business is at this hour in this place, and how you come to be so concerned with a player that you strike blindly at your sovereign in your jealousy of him.

THE DARK LADY. Madam: as I live and hope for salvation—

SHAKESPEAR [*sardonically*] Ha!

THE DARK LADY [*angrily*]— ay, I'm as like to be saved as thou that believest naught save some black magic of words and verses— I say, madam, as I am a living woman I came here to break with him for ever. Oh, madam, if you would know what misery is, listen to this man that is more than man and less at the same time. He will tie you down to anatomize your very soul: he will wring tears of blood from your humiliation; and then he will heal the wound with flatteries that no woman can resist.

SHAKESPEAR. Flatteries! [*Kneeling*] Oh, madam, I put my case at your royal feet. I confess to much. I have a rude tongue: I am unmannerly: I blaspheme against the holiness of anointed royalty; but oh, my royal mistress, AM I a flatterer?

ELIZABETH. I absolve you as to that. You are far too plain a dealer to please me. [*He rises gratefully*].

THE DARK LADY. Madam: he is flattering you even as he speaks.

ELIZABETH [*a terrible flash in her eye*] Ha! Is it so?

SHAKESPEAR. Madam: she is jealous; and,

heaven help me! not without reason. Oh, you say you are a merciful prince; but that was cruel of you, that hiding of your royal dignity when you found me here. For how can I ever be content with this black-haired, black-eyed, black-avised devil again now that I have looked upon real beauty and real majesty?

THE DARK LADY [*wounded and desperate*] He hath swore to me ten times over that the day shall come in England when black women, for all their foulness, shall be more thought on than fair ones. [*To Shakespear, scolding at him*] Deny it if thou canst. Oh, he is compact of lies and scorns. I am tired of being tossed up to heaven and dragged down to hell at every whim that takes him. I am ashamed to my very soul that I have abased myself to love one that my father would not have deemed fit to hold my stirrup—one that will talk to all the world about me— that will put my love and my shame into his plays and make me blush for myself there— that will write sonnets about me that no man of gentle strain would put his hand to. I am all disordered: I know not what I am saying to your Majesty: I am of all ladies most deject and wretched—

SHAKESPEAR. Ha! At last sorrow hath struck a note of music out of thee. "Of all ladies most deject and wretched." [*He makes a note of it*].

THE DARK LADY. Madam: I implore you give me leave to go. I am distracted with grief and shame. I—

ELIZABETH. Go [*The Dark Lady tries to kiss her hand*]. No more. Go. [*The Dark Lady goes, convulsed*]. You have been cruel to that poor fond wretch, Master Shakespear.

SHAKESPEAR. I am not cruel, madam; but you know the fable of Jupiter and Semele. I could not help my lightnings scorching her.

ELIZABETH. You have an overweening conceit of yourself, sir, that displeases your Queen.

SHAKESPEAR. Oh, madam, can I go about with the modest cough of a minor poet, belittling my inspiration and making the mightiest wonder of your reign a thing of nought? I have said that "not marble nor the gilded monuments of princes shall outlive" the words with which I make the world glorious or foolish at my will. Besides, I would have you think me great enough to grant me a boon.

ELIZABETH. I hope it is a boon that may be asked of a virgin Queen without offence, sir. I mistrust your forwardness; and I bid you remember that I do not suffer persons of your degree (if I may say so without offence to your father the alderman) to presume too far.

SHAKESPEAR. Oh, madam, I shall not forget myself again; though by my life, could I make you a serving wench, neither a queen nor a virgin should you be for so much longer as a flash of lightning might take to cross the river to the Bankside. But since you are a queen and will none of me, nor of Philip of Spain, nor of any other mortal man, I must een contain myself as best I may, and ask you only for a boon of State.

ELIZABETH. A boon of State already! You are becoming a courtier like the rest of them. You lack advancement.

SHAKESPEAR. "Lack advancement." By your Majesty's leave: a queenly phrase. [*He is about to write it down*].

ELIZABETH. [*striking the tablets from his hand*] Your tables begin to anger me, sir. I am not here to write your plays for you.

SHAKESPEAR. You are here to inspire them, madam. For this, among the rest, were you ordained. But the boon I crave is that you do endow a great playhouse, or, if I may make bold to coin a scholarly name for it, a National Theatre, for the better instruction and gracing of your Majesty's subjects.

ELIZABETH. Why, sir, are there not theatres enow on the Bankside and in Blackfriars?

SHAKESPEAR. Madam: these are the adventures of needy and desperate men that must, to save themselves from perishing of want, give the sillier sort of people what they best like; and what they best like, God knows, is not their own betterment and instruction, as we well see by the example of the churches, which must needs compel men to frequent them, though they be open to all without charge. Only when there is a matter of a murder, or a plot, or a pretty youth in petticoats, or some naughty tale of wantonness, will your subjects pay the great cost of good players and their finery, with a little profit to boot. To prove this I will tell you that I have written two noble and excellent plays setting forth the advancement of women of high nature and fruitful industry even as your Majesty is: the one a skilful physician, the other a sister devoted to good works.

I have also stole from a book of idle wanton tales two of the most damnable foolishnesses in the world, in the one of which a woman goeth in man's attire and maketh impudent love to her swain, who pleaseth the groundlings by overthrowing a wrestler: whilst, in the other, one of the same kidney sheweth her wit by saying endless naughtinesses to a gentleman as lewd as herself. I have writ these to save my friends from penury, yet shewing my scorn for such follies and for them that praise them by calling the one As You Like It, meaning that it is not as *I* like it, and the other Much Ado About Nothing, as it truly is. And now these two filthy pieces drive their nobler fellows from the stage, where indeed I cannot have my lady physician presented at all, she being too honest a woman for the taste of the town. Wherefore I humbly beg your Majesty to give order that a theatre be endowed out of the public revenue for the playing of those pieces of mine which no merchant will touch, seeing that his gain is so much greater with the worse than with the better. Thereby you shall also encourage other men to undertake the writing of plays who do now despise it and leave it wholly to those whose counsels will work little good to your realm. For this writing of plays is a great matter, forming as it does the minds and affections of men in such sort that whatsoever they see done in show on the stage, they will presently be doing in earnest in the world, which is but a larger stage. Of late, as you know, the Church taught the people by means of plays; but the people flocked only to such as were full of superstitious miracles and bloody martyrdoms; and so the Church, which also was just then brought into straits by the policy of your royal father, did abandon and discountenance the art of playing; and thus it fell into the hands of poor players and greedy merchants that had their pockets to look to and not the greatness of this your kingdom. Therefore now must your Majesty take up that good work that your Church hath abandoned, and restore the art of playing to its former use and dignity.

ELIZABETH. Master Shakespear: I will speak of this matter to the Lord Treasurer.

SHAKESPEAR. Then I am undone madam; for there was never yet a Lord Treasurer that could find a penny for anything over and above the necessary expenses of your government, save for a war or a salary for his own nephew.

ELIZABETH. Master Shakespear: you speak sooth; yet cannot I in any wise mend it. I dare not offend my unruly Puritans by making so lewd a place as the playhouse a public charge; and there be a thousand things to be done in this London of mine before your poetry can have its penny from the general purse. I tell thee, Master Will, it will be three hundred years and more before my subjects learn that man cannot live by bread alone, but by every word that cometh from the mouth of those whom God inspires. By that time you and I will be dust beneath the feet of the horses, if indeed there be any horses then, and men be still riding instead of flying. Now it may be that by then your works will be dust also.

SHAKESPEAR. They will stand, madam: fear not for that.

ELIZABETH. It may prove so. But of this I am certain (for I know my countrymen) that until every other country in the Christian world, even to barbarian Muscovy and the hamlets of the boorish Germans, have its playhouse at the public charge, England will never adventure. And she will adventure then only because it is her desire to be ever in the fashion, and to do humbly and dutifully whatso she seeth everybody else doing. In the meantime you must content yourself as best you can by the playing of those two pieces which you give out as the most damnable ever writ, but which your countrymen, I warn you, will swear are the best you have ever done. But this I will say, that if I could speak across the ages to our descendants, I should heartily recommend them to fulfil your wish; for the Scottish minstrel hath well said that he that maketh the songs of a nation is mightier than he that maketh its laws; and the same may well be true of plays and interludes. [*The clock chimes the first quarter. The warder returns on his round*]. And now, sir, we are upon the hour when it better beseems a virgin queen to be abed than to converse alone with the naughtiest of her subjects. Ho there! Who keeps ward on the queen's lodgings tonight?

THE WARDER. I do, an't please your majesty.

ELIZABETH. See that you keep it better in future. You have let pass a most dangerous gallant even to the very door of our royal chamber. Lead him forth; and bring me word when he is safely locked out; for I shall scarce dare disrobe until the palace gates are between us.

SHAKESPEAR [*kissing her hand*] My body goes through the gate into the darkness, madam; but my thoughts follow you.

ELIZABETH. How! to my bed!

SHAKESPEAR. No, madam, to your prayers, in which I beg you to remember my theatre.

ELIZABETH. That is my prayer to posterity. Forget not your own to God; and so goodnight, Master Will.

SHAKESPEAR. Goodnight, great Elizabeth. God save the Queen!

ELIZABETH. Amen.

Exeunt severally: she to her chamber: he, in custody of the warder, to the gate nearest Blackfriars.

THE END

XX
FANNY'S FIRST PLAY
AN EASY PLAY FOR A LITTLE THEATRE (1911)

INDUCTION

The end of a saloon in an old-fashioned country house (Florence Towers, the property of Count O'Dowda) has been curtained off to form a stage for a private theatrical performance. A footman in grandiose Spanish livery enters before the curtain, on its O.P. side.

FOOTMAN [*announcing*] Mr Cecil Savoyard. [*Cecil Savoyard comes in: a middle-aged man in evening dress and a furlined overcoat. He is surprised to find nobody to receive him. So is the Footman*]. Oh, beg pardon, sir: I thought the Count was here. He was when I took up your name. He must have gone through the stage into the library. This way, sir. [*He moves towards the division in the middle of the curtains*].

SAVOYARD. Half a mo. [*The Footman stops*]. When does the play begin? Half-past eight?

FOOTMAN. Nine, sir.

SAVOYARD. Oh, good. Well, will you telephone to my wife at the George that it's not until nine?

FOOTMAN. Right, sir. Mrs Cecil Savoyard, sir?

SAVOYARD. No: Mrs William Tinkler. Dont forget.

THE FOOTMAN. Mrs Tinkler, sir. Right, sir. [*The Count comes in through the curtains*]. Here is the Count, sir. [*Announcing*] Mr Cecil Savoyard, sir. [*He withdraws*].

COUNT O'DOWDA [*A handsome man of fifty, dressed with studied elegance a hundred years out of date, advancing cordially to shake hands with his visitor*] Pray excuse me, Mr Savoyard. I suddenly recollected that all the bookcases

in the library were locked—in fact theyve never been opened since we came from Venice—and as our literary guests will probably use the library a good deal, I just ran in to unlock everything.

SAVOYARD. Oh, you mean the dramatic critics. M'yes. I suppose theres a smoking room?

THE COUNT. My study is available. An oldfashioned house, you understand. Wont you sit down, Mr Savoyard?

SAVOYARD. Thanks. [*They sit. Savoyard, looking at his host's obsolete costume, continues*] I had no idea you were going to appear in the piece yourself.

THE COUNT. I am not. I wear this costume because—well, perhaps I had better explain the position, if it interests you.

SAVOYARD. Certainly.

THE COUNT. Well, you see, Mr Savoyard, I'm rather a stranger in your world. I am not, I hope, a modern man in any sense of the word. I'm not really an Englishman: my family is Irish: Ive lived all my life in Italy— in Venice mostly—my very title is a foreign one: I am a Count of the Holy Roman Empire.

SAVOYARD. Where's that?

THE COUNT. At present, nowhere, except as a memory and an ideal. [*Savoyard inclines his head respectfully to the ideal*]. But I am by no means an idealogue. I am not content with beautiful dreams: I want beautiful realities.

SAVOYARD. Hear, hear! I'm all with you

there—when you can get them.

THE COUNT. Why not get them? The difficulty is not that there are no beautiful realities, Mr Savoyard: the difficulty is that so few of us know them when we see them. We have inherited from the past a vast treasure of beauty—of imperishable masterpieces of poetry, of painting, of sculpture, of architecture, of music, of exquisite fashions in dress, in furniture, in domestic decoration. We can contemplate these treasures. We can reproduce many of them. We can buy a few inimitable originals. We can shut out the nineteenth century—

SAVOYARD [*correcting him*] The twentieth.

THE COUNT. To me the century I shut out will always be the nineteenth century, just as your national anthem will always be God Save the Queen, no matter how many kings may succeed. I found England befouled with industrialism: well, I did what Byron did: I simply refused to live in it. You remember Byron's words: "I am sure my bones would not rest in an English grave, or my clay mix with the earth of that country. I believe the thought would drive me mad on my deathbed could I suppose that any of my friends would be base enough to convey my carcase back to her soil. I would not even feed her worms if I could help it."

SAVOYARD. Did Byron say that?

THE COUNT. He did, sir.

SAVOYARD. It dont sound like him. I saw a good deal of him at one time.

THE COUNT. You! But how is that possible? You are too young.

SAVOYARD. I was quite a lad, of course. But I had a job in the original production of Our Boys.

THE COUNT. My dear sir, not t h a t Byron. Lord Byron, the poet.

SAVOYARD. Oh, I beg your pardon. I thought you were talking of t h e Byron. So you prefer living abroad?

THE COUNT. I find England ugly and Philistine. Well, I dont live in it. I find modern houses ugly. I dont live in them: I have a palace on the grand canal. I find modern clothes prosaic. I dont wear them, except, of course, in the street. My ears are offended by the Cockney twang: I keep out of hearing of it and speak and listen to Italian. I find Beethoven's music coarse and restless, and Wagner's senseless and detestable. I do not listen to them: I listen to Cimarosa, to Per-

golesi, to Gluck and Mozart. Nothing simpler, sir.

SAVOYARD. It's all right when you can afford it.

THE COUNT. Afford it! My dear Mr Savoyard, if you are a man with a sense of beauty you can make an earthly paradise for yourself in Venice on £1500 a year, whilst our wretched vulgar industrial millionaires are spending twenty thousand on the amusements of billiard markers. I assure you I am a poor man according to modern ideas. But I have never had anything less than the very best that life has produced. It is my good fortune to have a beautiful and lovable daughter; and that girl, sir, has never seen an ugly sight or heard an ugly sound that I could spare her; and she has certainly never worn an ugly dress or tasted coarse food or bad wine in her life. She has lived in a palace; and her perambulator was a gondola. Now you know the sort of people we are, Mr Savoyard. You can imagine how we feel here.

SAVOYARD. Rather out of it, eh?

THE COUNT. Out of it, sir! Out of what?

SAVOYARD. Well, out of everything.

THE COUNT. Out of soot and fog and mud and east wind; out of vulgarity and ugliness, hypocrisy and greed, superstition and stupidity. Out of all this, and i n the sunshine, in the enchanted region of which great artists alone have had the secret, in the sacred footsteps of Byron, of Shelley, of the Brownings, of Turner and Ruskin. Dont you envy me, Mr Savoyard?

SAVOYARD. Some of us must live in England, you know, just to keep the place going. Besides—though, mind you, I dont say it isnt all right from the high art point of view and all that—three weeks of it would drive me melancholy mad. However, I'm glad you told me, because it explains why it is you dont seem to know your way about much in England. I hope, by the way, that everything has given satisfaction to your daughter.

THE COUNT. She seems quite satisfied. She tells me that the actors you sent down are perfectly suited to their parts, and very nice people to work with. I understand she had some difficulties at the first rehearsals with the gentleman you call the producer, because he hadnt read the play; but the moment he found out what it was all about everything went smoothly.

SAVOYARD. Havnt you seen the rehearsals?

THE COUNT. Oh no. I havnt been allowed even to meet any of the company. All I can tell you is that the hero is a Frenchman [*Savoyard is rather scandalized*]: I asked her not to have an English hero. That is all I know. [*Ruefully*] I havnt been consulted even about the costumes, though there, I think, I could have been some use.

SAVOYARD [*puzzled*] But there arnt any costumes.

THE COUNT [*seriously shocked*] What! No costumes! Do you mean to say it is a modern play?

SAVOYARD. I dont know: I didnt read it. I handed it to Billy Burjoyce—the producer, you know—and left it to him to select the company and so on. But I should have had to order the costumes if there had been any. There wernt.

THE COUNT [*smiling as he recovers from his alarm*] I understand. She has taken the costumes into her own hands. She is an expert in beautiful costumes. I venture to promise you, Mr Savoyard, that what you are about to see will be like a Louis Quatorze ballet painted by Watteau. The heroine will be an exquisite Columbine, her lover a dainty Harlequin, her father a picturesque Pantaloon, and the valet who hoodwinks the father and brings about the happiness of the lovers a grotesque but perfectly tasteful Punchinello or Mascarille or Sganarelle.

SAVOYARD. I see. That makes three men; and the clown and policeman will make five. Thats why you wanted five men in the company.

THE COUNT. My dear sir, you dont suppose I mean that vulgar, ugly, silly, senseless, malicious and destructive thing the harlequinade of a nineteenth century English Christmas pantomime! What was it after all but a stupid attempt to imitate the success made by the genius of Grimaldi a hundred years ago? My daughter does not know of the existence of such a thing. I refer to the graceful and charming fantasies of the Italian and French stages of the seventeenth and eighteenth centuries.

SAVOYARD. Oh, I beg pardon. I quite agree that harlequinades are rot. Theyve been dropped at all smart theatres. But from what Billy Burjoyce told me I got the idea that your daughter knew her way about here, and had seen a lot of plays. He had no idea she'd been away in Venice all the time.

THE COUNT. Oh, she has not been. I should have explained that two years ago my daughter left me to complete her education at Cambridge. Cambridge was my own University; and though of course there were no women there in my time, I felt confident that if the atmosphere of the eighteenth century still existed anywhere in England, it would be at Cambridge. About three months ago she wrote to me and asked whether I wished to give her a present on her next birthday. Of course I said yes; and she then astonished and delighted me by telling me that she had written a play, and that the present she wanted was a private performance of it with real actors and real critics.

SAVOYARD. Yes: thats what staggered me. It was easy enough to engage a company for a private performance: it's done often enough. But the notion of having critics was new. I hardly knew how to set about it. They dont expect private engagements; and so they have no agents. Besides, I didnt know what to offer them. I knew that they were cheaper than actors, because they get long engagements: forty years sometimes; but thats no rule for a single job. Then theres such a lot of them: on first nights they run away with all your stalls: you cant find a decent place for your own mother. It would have cost a fortune to bring the lot.

THE COUNT. Of course I never dreamt of having them all. Only a few first-rate representative men.

SAVOYARD. Just so. All you want is a few sample opinions. Out of a hundred notices you wont find more than four at the outside that say anything different. Well, Ive got just the right four for you. And what do you think it has cost me?

THE COUNT [*shrugging his shoulders*] I cannot guess.

SAVOYARD. Ten guineas, and expenses. I had to give Flawner Bannal ten. He wouldnt come for less; and he asked fifty. I had to give it, because if we hadnt had him we might just as well have had nobody at all.

THE COUNT. But what about the others, if Mr Flannel—

SAVOYARD [*shocked*] Flawner Bannal.

THE COUNT. —if Mr Bannal got the whole ten?

SAVOYARD. Oh, I managed that. As this is a high-class sort of thing, the first man I went for was Trotter.

THE COUNT. Oh indeed. I am very glad you have secured Mr Trotter. I have read his Playful Impressions.

SAVOYARD. Well, I was rather in a funk about him. He's not exactly what I call approachable; and he was a bit stand-off at first. But when I explained and told him your daughter—

THE COUNT [interrupting in alarm] You did not say that the play was by her, I hope?

SAVOYARD. No: thats been kept a dead secret. I just said your daughter has asked for a real play with a real author and a real critic and all the rest of it. The moment I mentioned the daughter I had him. He has a daughter of his own. Wouldnt hear of payment! Offered to come just to please her! Quite human. I was surprised.

THE COUNT. Extremely kind of him.

SAVOYARD. Then I went to Vaughan, because he does music as well as the drama; and you said you thought there would be music. I told him Trotter would feel lonely without him; so he promised like a bird. Then I thought youd like one of the latest sort: the chaps that go for the newest things and swear theyre oldfashioned. So I nailed Gilbert Gunn. The four will give you a representative team. By the way [looking at his watch] theyll be here presently.

THE COUNT. Before they come, Mr Savoyard, could you give me any hints about them that would help me to make a little conversation with them? I am, as you said, rather out of it in England; and I might unwittingly say something tactless.

SAVOYARD. Well, let me see. As you dont like English people, I dont know that youll get on with Trotter, because he's thoroughly English: never happy except when he's in Paris, and speaks French so unnecessarily well that everybody there spots him as an Englishman the moment he opens his mouth. Very witty and all that. Pretends to turn up his nose at the theatre and says people make too much fuss about art [the Count is extremely indignant]. But thats only his modesty, because art is his own line, you understand. Mind you dont chaff him about Aristotle.

THE COUNT. Why should I chaff him about Aristotle?

SAVOYARD. Well, I dont know; but it's one of the recognized ways of chaffing him. However, youll get on with him all right: he's a man of the world and a man of sense. The one youll have to be careful about is Vaughan.

THE COUNT. In what way, may I ask?

SAVOYARD. Well, Vaughan has no sense of humor; and if you joke with him he'll think youre insulting him on purpose. Mind: it's not that he doesnt see a joke: he does; and it hurts him. A comedy scene makes him sore all over: he goes away black and blue, and pitches into the play for all he's worth.

THE COUNT. But surely that is a very serious defect in a man of his profession?

SAVOYARD. Yes it is, and no mistake. But Vaughan is honest, and dont care a brass farthing what he says, or whether it pleases anybody or not; and you must have one man of that sort to say the things that nobody else will say.

THE COUNT. It seems to me to carry the principle of division of labor too far, this keeping of the honesty and the other qualities in separate compartments. What is Mr Gunn's speciality, if I may ask?

SAVOYARD. Gunn is one of the Intellectuals.

THE COUNT. But arnt they all Intellectuals?

SAVOYARD. Lord! no: heaven forbid! You must be careful what you say about that: I shouldnt like anyone to call me an Intellectual: I dont think any Englishman would! They dont count really, you know; but still it's rather the thing to have them. Gunn is one of the young Intellectuals: he writes plays himself. He's useful because he pitches into the older Intellectuals who are standing in his way. But you may take it from me that none of these chaps really matter. Flawner Bannal's your man. Bannal really represents the British playgoer. When he likes a thing, you may take your oath there are a hundred thousand people in London thatll like it if they can only be got to know about it. Besides, Bannal's knowledge of the theatre is an inside knowledge. We know him; and he knows us. He knows the ropes: he knows his way about: he knows what he's talking about.

THE COUNT [with a little sigh] Age and experience, I suppose?

SAVOYARD. Age! I should put him at twenty at the very outside, myself. It's not an old man's job after all, is it? Bannal may not ride the literary high horse like Trotter and the rest; but I'd take his opinion before any other in London. He's the man in the street; and thats what you want.

THE COUNT. I am almost sorry you didnt

give the gentleman his full terms. I should not have grudged the fifty guineas for a sound opinion. He may feel shabbily treated.

SAVOYARD. Well, let him. It was a bit of side, his asking fifty. After all, what is he? Only a pressman. Jolly good business for him to earn ten guineas: he's done the same job often enough for half a quid, I expect.

Fanny O'Dowda comes precipitately through the curtains, excited and nervous. A girl of nineteen in a dress synchronous with her father's.

FANNY. Papa, papa, the critics have come. And one of them has a cocked hat and sword like a— [*she notices Savoyard*] Oh, I beg your pardon.

THE COUNT. This is Mr Savoyard, your impresario, my dear.

FANNY [*shaking hands*] How do you do?

SAVOYARD. Pleased to meet you, Miss O'Dowda. The cocked hat is all right. Trotter is a member of the new Academic Committee. He induced them to go in for a uniform like the French Academy; and I asked him to wear it.

THE FOOTMAN [*announcing*] Mr Trotter, Mr Vaughan, Mr Gunn, Mr Flawner Bannal.

The four critics enter. Trotter wears a diplomatic dress, with sword and three-cornered hat. His age is about 50. Vaughan is 40. Gunn is 30. Flawner Bannal is 20 and is quite unlike the others, who can be classed at sight as professional men whilst Bannal is obviously an unemployable of the business class picking up a living by an obtuse courage which gives him cheerfulness, conviviality, and bounce, and is helped out positively by a slight turn for writing, and negatively by a comfortable ignorance and lack of intuition which hides from him all the dangers and disgraces that keep men of finer perception in check. The Count approaches them hospitably.

SAVOYARD. Count O'Dowda, gentlemen. Mr Trotter.

TROTTER [*looking at the Count's costume*] Have I the pleasure of meeting a *confrère?*

THE COUNT. No sir: I have no right to my costume except the right of a lover of the arts to dress myself handsomely. You are most welcome, Mr Trotter. [*Trotter bows in the French manner*].

SAVOYARD. Mr Vaughan.

THE COUNT. How do you do, Mr Vaughan?

VAUGHAN. Quite well, thanks.

SAVOYARD. Mr Gunn.

THE COUNT. Delighted to make your acquaintance, Mr Gunn.

GUNN. Very pleased.

SAVOYARD. Mr Flawner Bannal.

THE COUNT. Very kind of you to come, Mr Bannal.

BANNAL. Dont mention it.

THE COUNT. Gentlemen, my daughter. [*They all bow*]. We are very greatly indebted to you, gentlemen, for so kindly indulging her whim. [*The dressing bell sounds. The Count looks at his watch*]. Ah! The dressing bell, gentlemen. As our play begins at nine, I have had to put forward the dinner hour a little. May I shew you to your rooms? [*He goes out, followed by all the men, except Trotter, who, going last, is detained by Fanny*].

FANNY. Mr Trotter: I want to say something to you about this play.

TROTTER. No: thats forbidden. You must not attempt to *souffler* the critic.

FANNY. Oh, I would not for the world try to influence your opinion.

TROTTER. But you do: you are influencing me very shockingly. You invite me to this charming house, where I'm about to enjoy a charming dinner. And just before the dinner I'm taken aside by a charming young lady to be talked to about the play. How can you expect me to be impartial? God forbid that I should set up to be a judge, or do more than record an impression; but my impressions can be influenced; and in this case youre influencing them shamelessly all the time.

FANNY. Dont make me feel more nervous than I am already, Mr Trotter. If you knew how I feel!

TROTTER. Naturally: your first party: your first appearance in England as hostess. But youre doing it beautifully. Dont be afraid. Every *nuance* is perfect.

FANNY. It's so kind of you to say so, Mr Trotter. But that isnt whats the matter. The truth is, this play is going to give my father a dreadful shock.

TROTTER. Nothing unusual in that, I'm sorry to say. Half the young ladies in London spend their evenings making their father take them to plays that are not fit for elderly people to see.

FANNY. Oh, I know all about that; but you cant understand what it means to Papa. Youre not so innocent as he is.

TROTTER [*remonstrating*] My dear young lady—

FANNY. I dont mean morally innocent: everybody who reads your articles knows youre as innocent as a lamb.

TROTTER. What!

FANNY. Yes, Mr Trotter: Ive seen a good deal of life since I came to England; and I assure you that to me youre a mere baby: a dear, good, well-meaning, delightful, witty, charming baby; but still a wee lamb in a world of wolves. Cambridge is not what it was in my father's time.

TROTTER. Well, I must say!

FANNY. Just so. Thats one of our classifications in the Cambridge Fabian Society.

TROTTER. Classifications? I dont understand.

FANNY. We classify our aunts into different sorts. And one of the sorts is the "I must says."

TROTTER. I withdraw "I must say." I substitute "Blame my cats!" No: I substitute "Blame my kittens!" Observe, Miss O'Dowda: kittens. I say again in the teeth of the whole Cambridge Fabian Society, kittens. Impertinent little kittens. Blame them. Smack them. I guess what is on your conscience. This play to which you have lured me is one of those in which members of Fabian Societies instruct their grandmothers in the art of milking ducks. And you are afraid it will shock your father. Well, I hope it will. And if he consults me about it I shall recommend him to smack you soundly and pack you off to bed.

FANNY. Thats one of your prettiest literary attitudes, Mr Trotter; but it doesnt take me in. You see, I'm much more conscious of what you really are than you are yourself, because weve discussed you thoroughly at Cambridge; and youve never discussed yourself, have you?

TROTTER. I——

FANNY. Of course you havnt; so you see it's no good Trottering at me.

TROTTER. Trottering!

FANNY. Thats what we call it at Cambridge.

TROTTER. If it were not so obviously a stage cliché, I should say Damn Cambridge. As it is, I blame my kittens. And now let me warn you. If youre going to be a charming healthy young English girl, you may coax me. If youre going to be an unsexed Cambridge Fabian virago, I'll treat you as my intellectual equal, as I would treat a man.

FANNY [adoringly] But how few men are your intellectual equals, Mr Trotter!

TROTTER. I'm getting the worst of this.

FANNY. Oh, no. Why do you say that?

TROTTER. May I remind you that the dinner-bell will ring presently?

FANNY. What does it matter? We're both ready. I havnt told you yet what I want you to do for me.

TROTTER. Nor have you particularly predisposed me to do it, except out of pure magnanimity. What is it?

FANNY. I dont mind this play shocking my father morally. It's good for him to be shocked morally. It's all that the young can do for the old, to shock them and keep them up to date. But I know that this play will shock him artistically; and that terrifies me. No moral consideration could make a breach between us: he would forgive me for anything of that kind sooner or later; but he never gives way on a point of art. I darent let him know that I love Beethoven and Wagner; and as to Strauss, if he heard three bars of Elektra, it'd part us for ever. Now what I want you to do is this. If he's very angry—if he hates the play, because it's a modern play—will you tell him that it's not my fault; that its style and construction, and so forth, are considered the very highest art nowadays; that the author wrote it in the proper way for repertory theatres of the most superior kind—you know the kind of plays I mean?

TROTTER [emphatically] I think I know the sort of entertainments you mean. But please do not beg a vital question by calling them plays. I dont pretend to be an authority; but I have at least established the fact that these productions, whatever else they may be, are certainly not plays.

FANNY. The authors dont say they are.

TROTTER [warmly] I am aware that one author, who is, I blush to say, a personal friend of mine, resorts freely to the dastardly subterfuge of calling them conversations, discussions, and so forth, with the express object of evading criticism. But I'm not to be disarmed by such tricks. I say they are not plays. Dialogues, if you will. Exhibitions of character, perhaps: especially the character of the author. Fictions, possibly, though a little decent reticence as to introducing actual persons, and thus violating the sanctity of private life, might not be amiss. But plays, no. I say NO. Not plays. If you will not concede this point I cant continue our conversation. I take this seriously. It's a matter of principle. I must ask you, Miss O'Dowda, before we go a step further, Do you or do you not claim that these works are plays?

FANNY. I assure you I dont.

TROTTER. Not in any sense of the word?

FANNY. Not in any sense of the word. I loathe plays.

TROTTER [*disappointed*] That last remark destroys all the value of your admission. You admire these—these theatrical nondescripts? You enjoy them?

FANNY. Dont you?

TROTTER. Of course I do. Do you take me for a fool? Do you suppose I prefer popular melodramas? Have I not written most appreciative notices of them? But I say theyre not plays. Theyre not plays. I cant consent to remain in this house another minute if anything remotely resembling them is to be foisted on me as a play.

FANNY. I fully admit that theyre not plays. I only want you to tell my father that plays are not plays nowadays—not in your sense of the word.

TROTTER. Ah, there you go again! In my sense of the word! You believe that my criticism is merely a personal impression; that—

FANNY. You always said it was.

TROTTER. Pardon me: not on this point. If you had been classically educated—

FANNY. But I have.

TROTTER. Pooh! Cambridge! If you had been educated at Oxford, you would know that the definition of a play has been settled exactly and scientifically for two thousand two hundred and sixty years. When I say that these entertainments are not plays, I dont mean in my sense of the word, but in the sense given to it for all time by the immortal Stagirite.

FANNY. Who is the Stagirite?

TROTTER [*shocked*] You dont know who the Stagirite was!

FANNY. Sorry. Never heard of him.

TORTTER. And this is Cambridge education! Well, my dear young lady, I'm delighted to find theres something you dont know; and I shant spoil you by dispelling an ignorance which, in my opinion, is highly becoming to your age and sex. So we'll leave it at that.

FANNY. But you will promise to tell my father that lots of people write plays just

like this one—that I havnt selected it out of mere heartlessness?

TROTTER. I cant possibly tell you what I shall say to your father about the play until Ive seen the play. But I'll tell you what I shall say to him about you. I shall say that youre a very foolish young lady; that youve got into a very questionable set; and that the sooner he takes you away from Cambridge and its Fabian Society, the better.

FANNY. It's so funny to hear you pretending to be a heavy father. In Cambridge we regard you as a *bel esprit*, a wit, an Irresponsible, a Parisian Immoralist, *très chic*.

TROTTER. I!

FANNY. Theres quite a Trotter set.

TROTTER. Well, upon my word!

FANNY. They go in for adventures and call you Aramis.

TROTTER. They wouldnt dare!

FANNY. You always make such delicious fun of the serious people. Your *insouciance*—

TROTTER [*frantic*] Stop talking French to me: it's not a proper language for a young girl. Great heavens! how is it possible that a few innocent pleasantries should be so frightfully misunderstood? Ive tried all my life to be sincere and simple, to be unassuming and kindly. Ive lived a blameless life. Ive supported the Censorship in the face of ridicule and insult. And now I'm told that I'm a centre of Immoralism! of Modern Minxism! a trifler with the most sacred subjects! a Nietzschean!! perhaps a Shavian!!!

FANNY. Do you mean you are really on the serious side, Mr Trotter?

TROTTER. Of course I'm on the serious side. How dare you ask me such a question?

FANNY. Then why dont you play for it?

TROTTER. I do play for it—short, of course, of making myself ridiculous.

FANNY. What! not make yourself ridiculous for the sake of a good cause! Oh, Mr Trotter! Thats *vieux jeu*.

TROTTER [*shouting at her*] Dont talk French. I will not allow it.

FANNY. But this dread of ridicule is so frightfully out of date. The Cambridge Fabian Society—

TROTTER. I forbid you to mention the Fabian Society to me.

FANNY. Its motto is "You cannot learn to skate without making yourself ridiculous."

TROTTER. Skate! What has that to do with it?

FANNY. Thats not all. It goes on, "The ice of life is slippery."

TROTTER. Ice of life indeed! You should be eating penny ices and enjoying yourself. I wont hear another word.

The Count returns.

THE COUNT. We're all waiting in the drawing room, my dear. Have you been detaining Mr Trotter all this time?

TROTTER. I'm so sorry. I must have just a little brush up: I— [*He hurries out*].

THE COUNT. My dear, you should be in the drawing room. You should not have kept him here.

FANNY. I know. Dont scold me: I had something important to say to him.

THE COUNT. I shall ask him to take you in to dinner.

FANNY. Yes, papa. Oh, I hope it will go off well.

THE COUNT. Yes, love, of course it will. Come along.

FANNY. Just one thing, papa, while we're alone. Who was the Stagirite?

THE COUNT. The Stagirite! Do you mean to say you dont know?

FANNY. Havnt the least notion.

THE COUNT. The Stagirite was Aristotle. By the way, dont mention him to Mr Trotter.

They go to the dining room.

THE PLAY

ACT I

In the dining room of a house in Denmark Hill, an elderly lady sits at breakfast reading the newspaper. Her chair is at the end of the oblong dining table furthest from the fire. There is an empty chair at the other end. The fireplace is behind this chair; and the door is next the fireplace, between it and the corner. An armchair stands beside the coal-scuttle. In the middle of the back wall is the sideboard, parallel to the table. The rest of the furniture is mostly dining room chairs, ranged against the walls, and including a baby rocking-chair on the lady's side of the room. The lady is a placid person. Her husband, Mr Robin Gilbey, not at all placid, bursts violently into the room with a letter in his hand.

GILBEY [*grinding his teeth*] This is a nice thing. This is a b—

MRS GILBEY [*cutting him short*] Leave it at that, please. Whatever it is, bad language wont make it better.

GILBEY [*bitterly*] Yes, put me in the wrong as usual. Take your boy's part against me. [*He flings himself into the empty chair opposite her*].

MRS GILBEY. When he does anything right, he's your son. When he does anything wrong he mine. Have you any news of him?

GILBEY. Ive a good mind not to tell you.

MRS GILBEY. Then dont. I suppose he's been found. Thats a comfort, at all events.

GILBEY. No, he hasnt been found. The boy may be at the bottom of the river for all you care. [*Too agitated to sit quietly, he rises and paces the room distractedly*].

MRS GILBEY. Then what have you got in your hand?

GILBEY. Ive a letter from the Monsignor Grenfell. From New York. Dropping us. Cutting us. [*Turning fiercely on her*] Thats a nice thing, isnt it?

MRS GILBEY. What for?

GILBEY [*flinging away towards his chair*] How do *I* know what for?

MRS GILBEY. What does he say?

GILBEY [*sitting down and grumblingly adjusting his spectacles*] This is what he says. "My dear Mr Gilbey: The news about Bobby had to follow me across the Atlantic: it did not reach me until to-day. I am afraid he is incorrigible. My brother, as you may imagine, feels that this last escapade has gone beyond the bounds; and I think, myself, that Bobby ought to be made to feel that such scrapes involve a certain degree of reprobation." "As you may imagine!" And we know no more about it than the babe unborn.

MRS GILBEY. What else does he say?

GILBEY. "I think my brother must have been just a little to blame himself; so, between ourselves, I shall, with due and impressive formality, forgive Bobby later on; but for the present I think it had better be understood that he is in disgrace, and that we are no longer on visiting terms. As ever, yours sincerely." [*His agitation masters him again*] Thats a nice slap in the face to get from a man in his position! This is what your son has brought on me.

MRS GILBEY. Well, I think it's rather a nice letter. He as good as tells you he's only letting on to be offended for Bobby's good.

GILBEY. Oh, very well: have the letter framed and hang it up over the mantelpiece as a testimonial.

MRS GILBEY. Dont talk nonsense, Rob. You

ought to be thankful to know that the boy is alive after his disappearing like that for nearly a week.

GILBEY. Nearly a week! A fortnight, you mean. Wheres your feelings, woman! It was fourteen days yesterday.

MRS GILBEY. Oh, dont call it fourteen days, Rob, as if the boy was in prison.

GILBEY. How do you know he's not in prison? It's got on my nerves so, that I'd believe even that.

MRS GILBEY. Dont talk silly, Rob. Bobby might get into a scrape like any other lad; but he'd never do anything low.

Juggins, the footman, comes in with a card on a salver. He is a rather low-spirited man of thirty-five or more, of good appearance and address, and iron self-command.

JUGGINS [*presenting the salver to Mr Gilbey*] Lady wishes to see Mr Bobby's parents, sir.

GILBEY [*pointing to Mrs Gilbey*] Theres Mr Bobby's parent. I disown him.

JUGGINS. Yes, sir. [*He presents the salver to Mrs Gilbey*].

MRS GILBEY. You mustnt mind what your master says, Juggins: he doesnt mean it. [*She takes the card and reads it*]. Well, I never!

GILBEY. Whats up now?

MRS GILBEY [*reading*] "Miss D. Delaney. Darling Dora." Just like that—in brackets. What sort of person, Juggins?

GILBEY. Whats her address?

MRS GILBEY. The West Circular Road. Is that a respectable address, Juggins?

JUGGINS. A great many most respectable people live in the West Circular Road, madam; but the address is not a guarantee of respectability.

GILBEY. So it's come to that with him, has it?

MRS GILBEY. Dont jump to conclusions, Rob. How do you know? [*To Juggins*] Is she a lady, Juggins? You know what I mean.

JUGGINS. In the sense in which you are using the word, no, madam.

MRS GILBEY. I'd better try what I can get out of her. [*To Juggins*] Shew her up. You dont mind, do you, Rob?

GILBEY. So long as you dont flounce out and leave me alone with her. [*He rises and plants himself on the hearth-rug*].

Juggins goes out.

MRS GILBEY. I wonder what she wants, Rob?

GILBEY. If she wants money, she shant have it. Not a farthing. A nice thing, every-body seeing her on our doorstep! If it wasnt that she may tell us something about the lad, I'd have Juggins put the hussy into the street.

JUGGINS [*returning and announcing*] Miss Delaney. [*He waits for express orders before placing a chair for this visitor*].

Miss Delaney comes in. She is a young lady of hilarious disposition, very tolerable good looks, and killing clothes. She is so affable and confidential that it is very difficult to keep her at a distance by any process short of flinging her out of the house.

DORA [*plunging at once into privileged intimacy and into the middle of the room*] How d'ye do, both. I'm a friend of Bobby's. He told me all about you once, in a moment of confidence. Of course he never let on who he was at the police court.

GILBEY. Police court?

MRS GILBEY [*looking apprehensively at Juggins*]. Tch—! Juggins: a chair.

DORA. Oh, Ive let it out, have I! [*Contemplating Juggins approvingly as he places a chair for her between the table and the sideboard*] But he's the right sort: I can see that. [*Buttonholing him*] You wont let on downstairs, old man, will you?

JUGGINS. The family can rely on my absolute discretion. [*He withdraws*].

DORA [*sitting down genteelly*] I dont know what youll say to me: you know I really have no right to come here; but then what was I to do? You know Holy Joe, Bobby's tutor, dont you? But of course you do.

GILBEY [*with dignity*] I know Mr Joseph Grenfell, the brother of Monsignor Grenfell, if it is of him you are speaking.

DORA [*wide-eyed and much amused*] No!!! You dont tell me that old geezer has a brother a Monsignor! And youre Catholics! And I never knew it, though Ive known Bobby ever so long! But of course the last thing you find out about a person is their religion, isnt it?

MRS GILBEY. We're not Catholics. But when the Samuelses got an Archdeacon's son to form their boy's mind, Mr Gilbey thought Bobby ought to have a chance too. And the Monsignor is a customer. Mr Gilbey consulted him about Bobby; and he recommended a brother of his that was more sinned against than sinning.

GILBEY [*on tenterhooks*] She dont want to hear about that, Maria. [*To Dora*] Whats your business?

DORA. I'm afraid it was all my fault.

GILBEY. What was all your fault? I'm half distracted. I dont know what has happened to the boy: he's been lost these fourteen days—

MRS GILBEY. A fortnight, Rob.

GILBEY. —and not a word have we heard of him since.

MRS GILBEY. Dont fuss, Rob.

GILBEY [yelling] I will fuss. Youve no feeling. You dont care what becomes of the lad. [He sits down savagely].

DORA [soothingly] Youve been anxious about him. Of course. How thoughtless of me not to begin by telling you he's quite safe. Indeed he's in the safest place in the world, as one may say: safe under lock and key.

GILBEY [horrified, pitiable] Oh my— [his breath fails him]. Do you mean that when he was in the police court he was in the dock? Oh, Maria! Oh, great Lord! What has he done? What has he got for it? [Desperate] Will you tell me or will you see me go mad on my own carpet?

DORA [sweetly] Yes, old dear—

MRS GILBEY [starting at the familiarity] Well!

DORA [continuing] I'll tell you; but dont you worry; he's all right. I came out myself this morning: there was such a crowd! and a band! they thought I was a suffragette: only fancy! You see it was like this. Holy Joe got talking about how he'd been a champion sprinter at college.

MRS GILBEY. A what?

DORA. A sprinter. He said he was the fastest hundred yards runner in England. We were all in the old cowshed that night.

MRS GILBEY. What old cowshed?

GILBEY [groaning] Oh, get on. Get on.

DORA. Oh, of course you wouldnt know. How silly of me! It's a rather go-ahead sort of music hall in Stepney. We call it the old cowshed.

MRS GILBEY. Does Mr Grenfell take Bobby to music halls?

DORA. No: Bobby takes him. But Holy Joe likes it: fairly laps it up like a kitten, poor old dear. Well, Bobby says to me, "Darling—"

MRS GILBEY [placidly] Why does he call you darling?

DORA. Oh, everybody calls me darling: it's a sort of name Ive got. Darling Dora, you know. Well, he says, "Darling, if you can get Holy Joe to sprint a hundred yards, I'll

stand you that squiffer with the gold keys."

MRS GILBEY. Does he call his tutor Holy Joe to his face?

Gilbey clutches at his hair in his impatience.

DORA. Well, what would he call him? After all, Holy Joe is Holy Joe; and boys will be boys.

MRS GILBEY. Whats a squiffer?

DORA. Oh, of course: excuse my vulgarity: a concertina. Theres one in a shop in Green Street, ivory inlaid, with gold keys and Russia leather bellows; and Bobby knew I hankered after it; but he couldnt afford it, poor lad, though I knew he just longed to give it to me.

GILBEY. Maria: if you keep interrupting with silly questions, I shall go out of my senses. Heres the boy in gaol and me disgraced for ever; and all you care to know is what a squiffer is.

DORA. Well, remember it has gold keys. The man wouldnt take a penny less than £15 for it. It was a presentation one.

GILBEY [shouting at her] Wheres my son? Whats happened to my son? Will you tell me that, and stop cackling about your squiffer?

DORA. Oh, aint we impatient! Well, it does you credit, old dear. And you neednt fuss: theres no disgrace. Bobby behaved like a perfect gentleman. Besides, it was all my fault. I'll own it: I took too much champagne. I was not what you might call drunk; but I was bright, and a little beyond myself; and— I'll confess it—I wanted to shew off before Bobby, because he was a bit taken by a woman on the stage; and she was pretending to be game for anything. You see youve brought Bobby up too strict; and when he gets loose theres no holding him. He does enjoy life more than any lad I ever met.

GILBEY. Never you mind how he's been brought up; thats my business. Tell me how he's been brought down: thats yours.

MRS GILBEY. Oh, dont be rude to the lady, Rob.

DORA. I'm coming to it, old dear: dont you be so headstrong. Well, it was a beautiful moonlight night; and we couldnt get a cab on the nod; so we started to walk, very jolly, you know: arm in arm, and dancing along, singing and all that. When we came into Jamaica Square, there was a young copper on point duty at the corner. I says to Bob: "Dearie boy: is it a bargain about the squiffer if I make Joe sprint for you?" "Anything you like, darling," says he: "I love you." I put on my best company manners and stepped up to the copper. "If you please, sir," says I, "can you direct me to Carrick-mines Square?" I was so genteel, and talked so sweet, that he fell to it like a bird. "I never heard of any such Square in these parts," he says. "Then," says I, "what a very silly little officer you must be!"; and I gave his helmet a chuck behind that knocked it over his eyes, and did a bunk.

MRS GILBEY. Did a what?

DORA. A bunk. Holy Joe did one too all right: he sprinted faster than he ever did in college, I bet, the old dear. He got clean off, too. Just as he was overtaking me half-way down the square, we heard the whistle; and at the sound of it he drew away like a streak of lightning; and that was the last I saw of him. I was copped in the Dock Road myself: rotten luck, wasnt it? I tried the innocent and genteel and all the rest; but Bobby's hat done me in.

GILBEY. And what happened to the boy?

DORA. Only fancy! he stopped to laugh at the copper! He thought the copper would see the joke, poor lamb. He was arguing about it when the two that took me came along to find out what the whistle was for, and brought me with them. Of course I swore I'd never seen him before in my life; but there he was in my hat and I in his. The cops were very spiteful and laid it on for all they were worth: drunk and disorderly and assaulting the police and all that. I got fourteen days without the option, because you see—well, the fact is, I'd done it before, and been warned. Bobby was a first offender and had the option; but the dear boy had no money left and wouldnt give you away by telling his name; and anyhow he couldnt have brought himself to buy himself off and leave me there; so he's doing his month. Well, it was two forty shillingses; and Ive only twenty-eight shillings in the world. If I pawn my clothes I shant be able to earn any more. So I cant pay the fine and get him out: but if youll stand £3 I'll stand one; and thatll do it. If youd like to be very kind and nice you could pay the lot; but I cant deny that it was my fault; so I wont press you.

GILBEY [heart-broken] My son in gaol!

DORA. Oh, cheer up, old dear: it wont hurt him: look at me after fourteen days of it:

I'm all the better for being kept a bit quiet. You mustnt let it prey on your mind.

GILBEY. The disgrace of it will kill me. And it will leave a mark on him to the end of his life.

DORA. Not a bit of it. Dont you be afraid: Ive educated Bobby a bit: he's not the molly-coddle he was when you had him in hand.

MRS GILBEY. Indeed Bobby is not a molly-coddle. They wanted him to go in for single-stick at the Young Men's Christian Association; but, of course, I couldnt allow that: he might have had his eye knocked out.

GILBEY [to Dora, angrily] Listen here, you.

DORA. Oh, aint we cross!

GILBEY. I want none of your gaiety here. This is a respectable household. Youve gone and got my poor innocent boy into trouble. It's the like of you thats the ruin of the like of him.

DORA. So you always say, you old dears. But you know better. Bobby came to me: I didnt come to him.

GILBEY. Would he have gone if you hadnt been there for him to go to? Tell me that. You know why he went to you, I suppose.

DORA [charitably] It was dull for him at home, poor lad, wasnt it?

MRS GILBEY. Oh no. I'm at home on first Thursdays. And we have the Knoxes to dinner every Friday. Margaret Knox and Bobby are as good as engaged. Mr Knox is my husband's partner. Mrs Knox is very religious; but she's quite cheerful. We dine with them on Tuesdays. So thats two evenings pleasure every week.

GILBEY [almost in tears] We done what we could for the boy. Short of letting him go into temptations of all sorts, he can do what he likes. What more does he want?

DORA. Well, old dear, he wants me; and thats about the long and short of it. And I must say youre not very nice to me about it. Ive talked to him like a mother, and tried my best to keep him straight; but I dont deny I like a bit of fun myself; and we both get a bit giddy when we're lighthearted. Him and me is a pair, I'm afraid.

GILBEY. Dont talk foolishness, girl. How could you and he be a pair, you being what you are, and he brought up as he has been, with the example of a religious woman like Mrs Knox before his eyes? I cant understand how he could bring himself to be seen in the street with you. [Pitying himself] I havnt deserved this. Ive done my duty as a father. Ive kept him sheltered. [*Angry with her*] Creatures like you that take advantage of a child's innocence ought to be whipped through the streets.

DORA. Well, whatever I may be, I'm too much the lady to lose my temper; and I dont think Bobby would like me to tell you what I think of you; for when I start giving people a bit of my mind I sometimes use language thats beneath me. But I tell you once for all I must have the money to get Bobby out; and if you wont fork out, I'll hunt up Holy Joe. He might get it off his brother, the Monsignor.

GILBEY. You mind your own concerns. My solicitor will do what is right. I'll not have you paying my son's fine as if you were anything to him.

DORA. Thats right. Youll get him out today, wont you?

GILBEY. It's likely I'd leave my boy in prison, isnt it?

DORA. I'd like to know when theyll let him out.

GILBEY. You would, would you? Youre going to meet him at the prison door.

DORA. Well, dont you think any woman would that had the feelings of a lady?

GILBEY [*bitterly*] Oh yes: I know. Here! I must buy the lad's salvation, I suppose. How much will you take to clear out and let him go?

DORA. [*pitying him: quite nice about it*] What good would that do, old dear? There are others, you know.

GILBEY. Thats true. I must send the boy himself away.

DORA. Where to?

GILBEY. Anywhere, so long as he's out of the reach of you and your like.

DORA. Then I'm afraid youll have to send him out of the world, old dear. I'm sorry for you: I really am, though you mightnt believe it; and I think your feelings do you real credit. But I cant give him up just to let him fall into the hands of people I couldnt trust, can I?

GILBEY [*beside himself, rising*] Wheres the police? Wheres the Government? Wheres the Church? Wheres respectability and right reason? Whats the good of them if I have to stand here and see you put my son in your pocket as if he was a chattel slave, and you hardly out of gaol as a common drunk and disorderly? Whats the world coming to?

DORA. It is a lottery, isnt it, old dear?

Mr Gilbey rushes from the room, distracted.

MRS GILBEY [*unruffled*] Where did you buy that white lace? I want some to match a collaret of my own; and I cant get it at Perrys and John's.

DORA. Knagg and Pantle's: one and four-pence. It's machine hand-made.

MRS GILBEY. I never give more than one and tuppence. But I suppose youre extravagant by nature. My sister Martha was just like that. Pay anything she was asked.

DORA. Whats tuppence to you, Mrs Bobby, after all?

MRS GILBEY [*correcting her*] Mrs Gilbey.

DORA. Of course, Mrs Gilbey. I am silly.

MRS GILBEY. Bobby must have looked funny in your hat. Why did you change hats with him?

DORA. I dont know. One does, you know.

MRS GILBEY. I never did. The things people do! I cant understand them. Bobby never told me he was keeping company with you. His own mother!

DORA [*overcome*] Excuse me: I cant help smiling.

Juggins enters.

JUGGINS. Mr Gilbey has gone to Wormwood Scrubbs, madam.

MRS GILBEY. Have you ever been in a police court, Juggins?

JUGGINS. Yes, madam.

MRS GILBEY [*rather shocked*] I hope you had not been exceeding, Juggins.

JUGGINS. Yes, madam, I had. I exceeded the legal limit.

MRS GILBEY. Oh, that! Why do they give a woman a fortnight for wearing a man's hat, and a man a month for wearing hers?

JUGGINS. I didnt know that they did, madam.

MRS GILBEY. It doesnt seem justice, does it. Juggins?

JUGGINS. No, madam.

MRS GILBEY [*to Dora, rising*] Well, goodbye. [*Shaking her hand*] So pleased to have made your acquaintance.

DORA [*standing up*] Dont mention it. I'm sure it's most kind of you to receive me at all.

MRS GILBEY. I must go off now and order lunch. [*She trots to the door*]. What was it you called the concertina?

DORA. A squiffer, dear.

MRS GILBEY [*thoughtfully*] A squiffer, of course. How funny! [*She goes out*].

DORA [*exploding into ecstasies of mirth*] Oh my! isnt she an old love? How do you keep your face straight?

JUGGINS. It is what I am paid for.

DORA [*confidentially*] Listen here, dear boy. Your name isnt Juggins. Nobody's name is Juggins.

JUGGINS. My orders are, Miss Delaney, that you are not to be here when Mr Gilbey returns from Wormwood Scrubbs.

DORA. That means telling me to mind my own business, doesnt it? Well, I'm off. Tootle Loo, Charlie Darling. [*She kisses her hand to him and goes*].

ACT II

On the afternoon of the same day, Mrs Knox is writing notes in her drawing room, at a writing-table which stands against the wall. Anyone placed so as to see Mrs Knox's left profile will have the door on the right and the window on the left, both further away than Mrs Knox, whose back is presented to an obsolete upright piano at the opposite side of the room. The sofa is near the piano. There is a small table in the middle of the room, with some gilt-edged books and albums on it, and chairs near it.

Mr Knox comes in almost furtively, a troubled man of fifty, thinner, harder, and uglier than his partner, Gilbey, Gilbey being a soft stoutish man with white hair and thin smooth skin, whilst Knox has coarse black hair, and blue jaws which no diligence in shaving can whiten. Mrs Knox is a plain woman, dressed without regard to fashion, with thoughtful eyes and thoughtful ways that make an atmosphere of peace and some solemnity. She is surprised to see her husband at home during business hours.

MRS KNOX. What brings you home at this hour? Have you heard anything?

KNOX. No. Have you?

MRS KNOX. No. Whats the matter?

KNOX [*sitting down on the sofa*] I believe Gilbey has found out.

MRS. KNOX. What makes you think that?

KNOX. Well, I dont know: I didnt like to tell you: you have enough to worry you without that; but Gilbey's been very queer ever since it happened. I cant keep my mind on business as I ought; and I was depending on him. But he's worse than me. He's not looking after anything; and he keeps out of my way. His manner's not natural. He hasnt

asked us to dinner; and he's never said a word about our not asking him to dinner, after all these years when weve dined every week as regular as clockwork. It looks to me as if Gilbey's trying to drop me socially. Well, why should he do that if he hasnt heard?

MRS KNOX. I wonder! Bobby hasnt been near us either: thats what I cant make out.

KNOX. Oh, thats nothing. I told him Margaret was down in Cornwall with her aunt.

MRS KNOX [*reproachfully*] Jo! [*She takes her handkerchief from the writing-table and cries a little*].

KNOX. Well, I got to tell lies, aint I? You wont. Somebody's got to tell em.

MRS KNOX [*putting away her handkerchief*] It only ends in our not knowing what to believe. Mrs Gilbey told me Bobby was in Brighton for the sea air. Theres something queer about that. Gilbey would never let the boy loose by himself among the temptations of a gay place like Brighton without his tutor; and I saw the tutor in Kensington High Street the very day she told me.

KNOX. If the Gilbeys have found out, it's all over between Bobby and Margaret, and all over between us and them.

MRS KNOX. It's all over between us and everybody. When a girl runs away from home like that, people know what to think of her and her parents.

KNOX. She had a happy, respectable home —everything—

MRS KNOX [*interrupting him*] Theres no use going over it all again, Jo. If a girl hasnt happiness in herself, she wont be happy anywhere. Youd better go back to the shop and try to keep your mind off it.

KNOX [*rising restlessly*] I cant. I keep fancying everybody knows it and is sniggering about it. I'm at peace nowhere but here. It's a comfort to be with you. It's a torment to be with other people.

MRS KNOX [*going to him and drawing her arm through his*] There, Jo, there! I'm sure I'd have you here always if I could. But it cant be. God's work must go on from day to day, no matter what comes. We must face our trouble and bear it.

KNOX [*wandering to the window arm in arm with her*] Just look at the people in the street, going up and down as if nothing had happened. It seems unnatural, as if they all knew and didnt care.

MRS KNOX. If they knew, Jo, thered be a crowd round the house looking up at us. You shouldnt keep thinking about it.

KNOX. I know I shouldnt. You have your religion, Amelia; and I'm sure I'm glad it comforts you. But it doesnt come to me that way. Ive worked hard to get a position and be respectable. Ive turned many a girl out of the shop for being half an hour late at night; and heres my own daughter gone for a fortnight without word or sign, except a telegram to say she's not dead and that we're not to worry about her.

MRS KNOX [suddenly pointing to the street] Jo, look!

KNOX. Margaret! With a man!

MRS KNOX. Run down, Jo, quick. Catch her: save her.

KNOX [lingering] She's shaking hands with him: she's coming across to the door.

MRS KNOX [energetically] Do as I tell you. Catch the man before he's out of sight.

Knox rushes from the room. Mrs Knox looks anxiously and excitedly from the window. Then she throws up the sash and leans out. Margaret Knox comes in, flustered and annoyed. She is a strong, springy girl of eighteen, with large nostrils, an audacious chin, and a gaily resolute manner, even peremptory on occasions like the present, when she is annoyed.

MARGARET. Mother. Mother.

Mrs Knox draws in her head and confronts her daughter.

MRS KNOX [sternly] Well, miss?

MARGARET. Oh, mother, do go out and stop father making a scene in the street. He rushed at him and said "Youre the man who took away my daughter" loud enough for all the people to hear. Everybody stopped. We shall have a crowd round the house. Do do something to stop him.

Knox returns with a good-looking young marine officer.

MARGARET. Oh, Monsieur Duvallet, I'm so sorry—so ashamed. Mother: this is Monsieur Duvallet, who has been extremely kind to me. Monsieur Duvallet: my mother. [Duvallet bows].

KNOX. A Frenchman! It only needed this.

MARGARET [much annoyed] Father: do please be commonly civil to a gentleman who has been of the greatest service to me. What will he think of us?

DUVALLET [debonair] But it's very natural. I understand Mr Knox's feelings perfectly.

[He speaks English better than Knox, having learnt it on both sides of the Atlantic].

KNOX. If Ive made any mistake I'm ready to apologize. But I want to know where my daughter has been for the last fortnight.

DUVALLET. She has been, I assure you, in a particularly safe place.

KNOX. Will you tell me what place? I can judge for myself how safe it was.

MARGARET. Holloway Gaol. Was that safe enough?

KNOX AND MRS KNOX. Holloway Gaol!

KNOX. Youve joined the Suffragets!

MARGARET. No. I wish I had. I could have had the same experience in better company. Please sit down, Monsieur Duvallet. [She sits between the table and the sofa. Mrs Knox, overwhelmed, sits at the other side of the table. Knox remains standing in the middle of the room].

DUVALLET [sitting down on the sofa] It was nothing. An adventure. Nothing.

MARGARET [obdurately] Drunk and assaulting the police! Forty shillings or a month!

MRS KNOX. Margaret! Who accused you of such a thing?

MARGARET. The policeman I assaulted.

KNOX. You mean to say that you did it!

MARGARET. I did. I had that satisfaction at all events. I knocked two of his teeth out.

KNOX. And you sit there coolly and tell me this!

MARGARET. Well, where do you want me to sit? Whats the use of saying things like that?

KNOX. My daughter in Holloway Gaol!

MARGARET. All the women in Holloway are somebody's daughters. Really, father, you must make up your mind to it. If you had sat in that cell for fourteen days making up your mind to it, you would understand that I'm not in the humor to be gaped at while youre trying to persuade yourself that it can't be real. These things really do happen to real people every day; and you read about them in the papers and think it's all right. Well, theyve happened to me: thats all.

KNOX [feeble-forcible] But they shouldnt have happened to you. Dont you know that?

MARGARET. They shouldnt happen to anybody, I suppose. But they do. [Rising impatiently] And really I'd rather go out and assault another policeman and go back to Holloway than keep talking round and round it like this. If youre going to turn me out of the house, turn me out: the sooner I go the better.

DUVALLET [*rising quickly*] That is impossible, mademoiselle. Your father has his position to consider. To turn his daughter out of doors would ruin him socially.

KNOX. Oh, youve put her up to that, have you? And where did y o u come in, may I ask?

DUVALLET. I came in at your invitation—at your amiable insistence, in fact, not at my own. But you need have no anxiety on my account. I was concerned in the regrettable incident which led to your daughter's incarceration. I got a fortnight without the option of a fine on the ridiculous ground that I ought to have struck the policeman with my fist. I should have done so with pleasure had I known; but, as it was, I struck him on the ear with my boot—a magnificent *moulinet*, I must say—and was informed that I had been guilty of an act of cowardice, but that for the sake of the *entente cordiale* I should be dealt with leniently. Yet Miss Knox, who used her fist, got a month, but with the option of a fine. I did not know this until I was released, when my first act was to pay the forty shillings. And here we are.

MRS KNOX. You ought to pay the gentleman the fine, Jo.

KNOX [*reddening*] Oh, certainly. [*He takes out some money*].

DUVALLET. Oh please! it does not matter. [*Knox hands him two sovereigns*]. If you insist — [*he pockets them*]. Thank you.

MARGARET. I'm ever so much obliged to you, Monsieur Duvallet.

DUVALLET. Can I be of any further assistance, mademoiselle?

MARGARET. I think you had better leave us to fight it out, if you dont mind.

DUVALLET. Perfectly. Madame [*bow*]—Mademoiselle [*bow*]—Monsieur [*bow*]— [*He goes out*].

MRS KNOX. Dont ring, Jo. See the gentleman out yourself.

Knox hastily sees Duvallet out. Mother and daughter look forlornly at one another without saying a word. Mrs Knox slowly sits down. Margaret follows her example. They look at one another again. Mr Knox returns.

KNOX [*shortly and sternly*] Amelia: this is your job. [*To Margaret*] I leave you to your mother. I shall have my own say in the matter when I hear what you have to say to her. [*He goes out, solemn and offended*].

MARGARET [*with a bitter little laugh*] Just what the Suffraget said to me in Holloway. He throws the job on you.

MRS KNOX [*reproachfully*] Margaret!

MARGARET. You know it's true.

MRS KNOX. Margaret: if youre going to be hardened about it, theres no use my saying anything.

MARGARET. I'm not hardened, mother. But I cant talk nonsense about it. You see, it's all real to me. Ive suffered it. Ive been shoved and bullied. Ive had my arms twisted. Ive been made scream with pain in other ways. Ive been flung into a filthy cell with a lot of other poor wretches as if I were a sack of coals being emptied into a cellar. And the only difference between me and the others was that I hit back. Yes I did. And I did worse. I wasnt ladylike. I cursed. I called names. I heard words that I didnt even know that I knew, coming out of my mouth just as if somebody else had spoken them. The policeman repeated them in court. The magistrate said he could hardly believe it. The policeman held out his hand with his two teeth in it that I knocked out. I said it was all right; that I had heard myself using those words quite distinctly; and that I had taken the good conduct prize for three years running at school. The poor old gentleman put me back for the missionary to find out who I was, and to ascertain the state of my mind. I wouldnt tell, of course, for your sakes at home here; and I wouldnt say I was sorry, or apologize to the policeman, or compensate him or anything of that sort. I wasnt sorry. The one thing that gave me any satisfaction was getting in that smack on his mouth; and I said so. So the missionary reported that I seemed hardened and that no doubt I would tell who I was after a day in prison. Then I was sentenced. So now you see I'm not a bit the sort of girl you thought me. I'm not a bit the sort of girl I thought myself. And I dont know what sort of person you really are, or what sort of person father really is. I wonder what he would say or do if he had an angry brute of a policeman twisting his arm with one hand and rushing him along by the nape of his neck with the other. He couldnt whirl his leg like a windmill and knock a policeman down by a glorious kick on the helmet. Oh, if theyd all fought as we two fought we'd have beaten them.

MRS KNOX. But how did it all begin?

MARGARET. Oh, I dont know. It was boat-race night, they said.

MRS KNOX. Boat-race night! But what had you to do with the boat race? You went to the great Salvation Festival at the Albert Hall with your aunt. She put you into the bus that passes the door. What made you get out of the bus?

MARGARET. I dont know. The meeting got on my nerves, somehow. It was the singing, I suppose: you know I love singing a good swinging hymn; and I felt it was ridiculous to go home in the bus after we had been singing so wonderfully about climbing up the golden stairs to heaven. I wanted more music—more happiness—more life. I wanted some comrade who felt as I did. I felt exalted: it seemed mean to be afraid of anything: after all, what could anyone do to me against my will? I suppose I was a little mad: at all events, I got out of the bus at Piccadilly Circus, because there was a lot of light and excitement there. I walked to Leicester Square; and went into a great theatre.

MRS KNOX [horrified] A theatre!

MARGARET. Yes. Lots of other women were going in alone. I had to pay five shillings.

MRS KNOX [aghast] Five shillings!

MARGARET [apologetically] It w a s a lot. It was very stuffy; and I didnt like the people much, because they didnt seem to be enjoying themselves; but the stage was splendid and the music lovely. I saw that Frenchman, Monsieur Duvallet, standing against a barrier, smoking a cigarette. He seemed quite happy; and he was nice and sailorlike. I went and stood beside him, hoping he would speak to me.

MRS KNOX [gasps] Margaret!

MARGARET [continuing] He did, just as if he had known me for years. We got on together like old friends. He asked me would I have some champagne; and I said it would cost too much, but that I would give anything for a dance. I longed to join the people on the stage and dance with them: one of them was the most beautiful dancer I ever saw. He told me he had come there to see her, and that when it was over we could go somewhere where there was dancing. So we went to a place where there was a band in a gallery and the floor cleared for dancing. Very few people danced: the women only wanted to shew off their dresses; but we danced and danced until a lot of them joined in. We got quite reckless; and we had cham-

pagne after all. I never enjoyed anything so much. But at last it got spoilt by the Oxford and Cambridge students up for the Boat race. They got drunk; and they began to smash things; and the police came in. Then it was quite horrible. The students fought with the police; and the police suddenly got quite brutal, and began to throw everybody downstairs. They attacked the women, who were not doing anything, and treated them just as roughly as they had treated the students. Duvallet got indignant and remonstrated with a policeman, who was shoving a woman though she was going quietly as fast as she could. The policeman flung the woman through the door and then turned on Duvallet. It was then that Duvallet swung his leg like a windmill and knocked the policeman down. And then three policemen rushed at him and carried him out by the arms and legs face downwards. Two more attacked me and gave me a shove to the door. That quite maddened me. I just got in one good bang on the mouth of one of them. All the rest was dreadful. I was rushed through the streets to the police station. They kicked me with their knees; they twisted my arms; they taunted and insulted me; they called me vile names; and I told them what I thought of them, and provoked them to do their worst. Theres one good thing about being hard hurt: it makes you sleep. I slept in that filthy cell with all the other drunks sounder than I should have slept at home. I cant describe how I felt next morning: it was hideous; but the police were quite jolly; and everybody said it was a bit of English fun, and talked about last year's boat-race night when it had been a great deal worse. I was black and blue and sick and wretched. But the strange thing was that I wasnt sorry; and I'm not sorry. And I dont feel that I did anything wrong, really. [She rises and stretches her arms with a large liberating breath] Now that it's all over I'm rather proud of it; though I know now that I'm not a lady; but whether thats because we're only shopkeepers, or because nobody's really a lady except when theyre treated like ladies, I dont know. [She throws herself into a corner of the sofa].

MRS KNOX [lost in wonder] But how could you bring yourself to do it, Margaret? I'm not blaming you: I only want to know. How could you bring yourself to do it?

MARGARET. I cant tell you. I dont understand it myself. The prayer meeting set me free, somehow. I should never have done it if it were not for the prayer meeting.

MRS KNOX [*deeply horrified*] Oh, dont say such a thing as that. I know that prayer c a n set us free; though you could never understand me when I told you so; but it sets us free for good, not for evil.

MARGARET. Then I suppose what I did was not evil; or else I was set free for evil as well as good. As father says, you cant have anything both ways at once. When I was at home and at school I was what you call good; but I wasnt free. And when I got free I was what most people would call not good. But I see no harm in what I did; though I see plenty in what other people did to me.

MRS KNOX. I hope you dont think yourself a heroine of romance.

MARGARET. Oh no. [*She sits down again at the table*]. I'm a heroine of reality, if you call me a heroine at all. And reality is pretty brutal, pretty filthy, when you come to grips with it. Yet it's glorious all the same. It's so real and satisfactory.

MRS KNOX. I dont like this spirit in you, Margaret. I dont like your talking to me in that tone.

MARGARET. It's no use, mother. I dont care for you and papa any the less; but I shall never get back to the old way of talking again. Ive made a sort of descent into hell—

MRS KNOX. Margaret! Such a word!

MARGARET. You should have heard all the words that were flying round that night. You should mix a little with people who dont know any other words. But when I said that about a descent into hell I was not swearing. I was in earnest, like a preacher.

MRS KNOX. A preacher utters them in a reverent tone of voice.

MARGARET. I know: the tone that shews they dont mean anything real to him. They usent to mean anything real to me. Now hell is as real to me as a turnip; and I suppose I shall always speak of it like that. Anyhow, Ive been there; and it seems to me now that nothing is worth doing but redeeming people from it.

MRS KNOX. They are redeemed already if they choose to believe it.

MARGARET. Whats the use of that if they dont choose to believe it? You dont believe it yourself, or you wouldnt pay policemen to twist their arms. Whats the good of pretending? Thats all our respectability is, pretending, pretending, pretending. Thank heaven Ive had it knocked out of me once for all!

MRS KNOX [*greatly agitated*] Margaret: dont talk like that. I cant bear to hear you talking wickedly. I can bear to hear the children of this world talking vainly and foolishly in the language of this world. But when I hear you justifying your wickedness in the words of grace, it's too horrible: it sounds like the devil making fun of religion. Ive tried to bring you up to learn the happiness of religion. Ive waited for you to find out that happiness is within ourselves and doesnt come from outward pleasures. Ive prayed oftener than you think that you might be enlightened. But if all my hopes and all my prayers are to come to this, that you mix up my very words and thoughts with the promptings of the devil, then I dont know what I shall do: I dont indeed: itll kill me.

MARGARET. You shouldnt have prayed for me to be enlightened if you didnt want me to be enlightened. If the truth were known, I suspect we all want our prayers to be answered only by halves: the agreeable halves. Your prayer didnt get answered by halves, mother. Youve got more than you bargained for in the way of enlightenment. I shall never be the same again. I shall never speak in the old way again. Ive been set free from this silly little hole of a house and all its pretences. I k n o w now that I am stronger than you and Papa. I havnt found that happiness of yours that is within yourself; but Ive found strength. For good or evil I am set free; and none of the things that used to hold me can hold me now.

Knox comes back, unable to bear his suspense.

KNOX. How long more are you going to keep me waiting, Amelia? Do you think I'm made of iron? Whats the girl done? What are we going to do?

MRS KNOX. She's beyond my control, Jo, and beyond yours. I cant even pray for her now; for I dont know rightly what to pray for.

KNOX. Dont talk nonsense, woman: is this a time for praying? Does anybody k n o w? Thats what we have to consider now. If only we can keep it dark, I dont care for anything else.

MARGARET. Dont hope for that, father. Mind: I'll tell everybody. It ought to be told, It must be told.

KNOX. Hold your tongue, you young hussy; or go out of my house this instant.

MARGARET. I'm quite ready. [*She takes her hat and turns to the door*].

KNOX [*throwing himself in front of it*] Here! where are you going?

MRS KNOX [*rising*] You mustnt turn her out, Jo! I'll go with her if she goes.

KNOX. Who wants to turn her out? But is she going to ruin us? To let everybody know of her disgrace and shame? To tear me down from the position Ive made for myself and you by forty years hard struggling?

MARGARET. Yes: I'm going to tear it all down. It stands between us and everything. I'll tell everybody.

KNOX. Magsy, my child: dont bring down your father's hairs with sorrow to the grave. Theres only one thing I care about in the world: to keep this dark. I'm your father. I ask you here on my knees—in the dust, so to speak—not to let it out.

MARGARET. I'll tell everybody.

Knox collapses in despair. Mrs Knox tries to pray and cannot. Margaret stands inflexible.

ACT III

Again in the Gilbeys' dining room. Afternoon. The table is not laid: it is draped in its ordinary cloth, with pen and ink, an exercise-book, and school-books on it. Bobby Gilbey is in the arm-chair, crouching over the fire, reading an illus-trated paper. He is a pretty youth, of very subur-ban gentility, strong and manly enough by nature but untrained and unsatisfactory, his parents having imagined that domestic restriction is what they call "bringing up." He has learnt nothing from it except a habit of evading it by deceit.

He gets up to ring the bell; then resumes his crouch. Juggins answers the bell.

BOBBY. Juggins.

JUGGINS. Sir?

BOBBY [*morosely sarcastic*] Sir be blowed!

JUGGINS [*cheerfully*] Not at all, sir.

BOBBY. I'm a gaol-bird: youre a respectable man.

JUGGINS. That doesnt matter, sir. Your father pays me to call you sir; and as I take the money, I keep my part of the bargain.

BOBBY. Would you call me sir if you wernt paid to do it?

JUGGINS. No, sir.

BOBBY. Ive been talking to Dora about you.

JUGGINS. Indeed, sir?

BOBBY. Yes. Dora says your name cant be Juggins, and that you have the manners of a gentleman. I always thought you hadnt any manners. Anyhow, your manners are differ-ent from the manners of a gentleman in my set.

JUGGINS. They would be, sir.

BOBBY. You dont feel disposed to be com-municative on the subject of Dora's notion, I suppose.

JUGGINS. No, sir.

BOBBY [*throwing his paper on the floor and lifting his knees over the arm of the chair so as to turn towards the footman*] It was part of your bargain that you were to valet me a bit, wasnt it?

JUGGINS. Yes, sir.

BOBBY. Well, can you tell me the proper way to get out of an engagement to a girl without getting into a row for breach of promise?

JUGGINS. No, sir. You cant get out of an engagement without being sued for breach of promise if the lady wishes to be paid for her disappointment.

BOBBY. But it wouldnt be for her happiness to marry me when I dont really care for her.

JUGGINS. Women dont always marry for happiness, sir. They often marry because they wish to be married women and not old maids.

BOBBY. Then what am I to do?

JUGGINS. Marry her, sir, or take the con-sequences.

BOBBY [*jumping up*] Well, I wont marry her: thats flat. What would you do if you were in my place?

JUGGINS. I should tell the young lady that I found I couldnt fulfil my engagement.

BOBBY. But youd have to make some ex-cuse, you know. I want to give it a gentle-manly turn: to say I'm not worthy of her, or something like that.

JUGGINS. That is not a gentlemanly turn, sir. Quite the contrary.

BOBBY. I dont see that at all. Do you mean that it's not exactly true?

JUGGINS. Not at all, sir.

BOBBY. I c a n say that no other girl can ever be to me what she's been. That would be quite true, because our circumstances have been rather exceptional; and she'll imagine I mean I'm fonder of her than I can ever be of anyone else. You see, Juggins, a gentle-man has to think of a girl's feelings.

JUGGINS. If you wish to spare her feelings, sir, you can marry her. If you hurt her feelings by refusing, you had better not try to get credit for considerateness at the same time by pretending to spare them. She wont like it. And it will start an argument, of which you will get the worse.

BOBBY. But, you know, I'm not really worthy of her.

JUGGINS. Probably she never supposed you were, sir.

BOBBY. Oh, I say, Juggins, you are a pessimist.

JUGGINS [preparing to go] Anything else, sir?

BOBBY [querulously] You havnt been much use. [He wanders disconsolately across the room]. You generally put me up to the correct way of doing things.

JUGGINS. I assure you, sir, theres no correct way of jilting. It's not correct in itself.

BOBBY [hopefully] I'll tell you what. I'll say I cant hold her to an engagement with a man whos been in quod. Thatll do it. [He seats himself on the table, relieved and confident].

JUGGINS. Very dangerous, sir. No woman will deny herself the romantic luxury of self-sacrifice and forgiveness when they take the form of doing something agreeable. She's almost sure to say that your misfortune will draw her closer to you.

BOBBY. What a nuisance! I dont know what to do. You know, Juggins, your cool simple-minded way of doing it wouldnt go down in Denmark Hill.

JUGGINS. I daresay not, sir. No doubt youd prefer to make it look like an act of self-sacrifice for her sake on your part, or provoke her to break the engagement herself. Both plans have been tried repeatedly, but never with success, as far as my knowledge goes.

BOBBY. You have a devilish cool way of laying down the law. You know, in my class you have to wrap up things a bit. Denmark Hill isnt Camberwell, you know.

JUGGINS. I have noticed, sir, that Denmark Hill thinks that the higher you go in the social scale, the less sincerity is allowed, and that only tramps and riff-raff are quite sincere. Thats a mistake. Tramps are often shameless but theyre never sincere. Swells—if I may use that convenient name for the upper classes—play much more with their cards on the table. If you tell the young lady that you want to jilt her, and she calls you a pig, the tone of the transaction may leave much to be desired; but itll be less Camberwellian than if you say youre not worthy.

BOBBY. Oh, I cant make you understand, Juggins. The girl isnt a scullery-maid. I want to do it delicately.

JUGGINS. A mistake, sir, believe me, if you are not a born artist in that line.—Beg pardon, sir, I think I heard the bell. [He goes out].

Bobby, much perplexed, shoves his hands into his pockets, and comes off the table, staring disconsolately straight before him; then goes reluctantly to his books, and sits down to write. Juggins returns.

JUGGINS [announcing] Miss Knox.

Margaret comes in. Juggins withdraws.

MARGARET. Still grinding away for that Society of Arts examination, Bobby? Youll never pass.

BOBBY [rising] No: I was just writing to you.

MARGARET. What about?

BOBBY. Oh, nothing. At least— How are you?

MARGARET [passing round the other end of the table and putting down on it a copy of Lloyd's Weekly and her purse-bag] Quite well, thank you. How did you enjoy Brighton?

BOBBY. Brighton! I wasnt at— Oh yes, of course. Oh, pretty well. Is your aunt all right?

MARGARET. My aunt! I suppose so. I havent seen her for a month.

BOBBY. I thought you were down staying with her.

MARGARET. Oh! was that what they told you?

BOBBY. Yes. Why? Wernt you really?

MARGARET. No. Ive something to tell you. Sit down and lets be comfortable.

She sits on the edge of the table. He sits beside her, and puts his arm wearily round her waist.

MARGARET. You neednt do that if you dont like, Bobby. Suppose we get off duty for the day just to see what it's like.

BOBBY. Off duty? What do you mean?

MARGARET. You know very well what I mean. Bobby: did you ever care one little scrap for me in that sort of way? Dont funk answering: *I* dont care a bit for you—that way.

BOBBY [removing his arm rather huffily] I beg your pardon, I'm sure. I thought you did.

MARGARET. Well, did you? Come! Dont be mean. Ive owned up. You can put it all on me if you like; but I dont believe you care any more than I do.

BOBBY. You mean weve been shoved into it rather by the pars and mars.

MARGARET. Yes.

BOBBY. Well, it's not that I dont care for you: in fact, no girl can ever be to me exactly what you are; but weve been brought up so much together that it feels more like brother and sister than—well, than the other thing, doesnt it?

MARGARET. Just so. How did you find out the difference?

BOBBY [blushing] Oh, I say!

MARGARET. I found out from a Frenchman.

BOBBY. Oh, I say! [He comes off the table in his consternation].

MARGARET. Did you learn it from a French-woman? You know you must have learnt it from somebody.

BOBBY. Not a Frenchwoman. She's quite a nice woman. But she's been rather unfortun-ate. The daughter of a clergyman.

MARGARET [startled] Oh, Bobby! That sort of woman!

BOBBY. What sort of woman?

MARGARET. You dont believe she's really a clergyman's daughter, do you, you silly boy? It's a stock joke.

BOBBY. Do you mean to say you dont be-lieve me?

MARGARET. No: I mean to say I dont be-lieve her.

BOBBY [curious and interested, resuming his seat on the table beside her] What do you know about her? What do you know about all this sort of thing?

MARGARET. What sort of thing, Bobby?

BOBBY. Well, about life.

MARGARET. Ive lived a lot since I saw you last. I wasnt at my aunt's. All that time that you were in Brighton, I mean.

BOBBY. I wasnt at Brighton, Meg. I'd better tell you: youre bound to find out sooner or later. [He begins his confession humbly, avoiding her gaze]. Meg: it's rather awful: youll think me no end of a beast. Ive been in prison.

MARGARET. You!

BOBBY. Yes, me. For being drunk and as-saulting the police.

MARGARET. Do you mean to say that you— oh! this is a let-down for me. [She comes off the table and drops, disconsolate, into a chair at the end of it furthest from the hearth].

BOBBY. Of course I couldnt hold you to our engagement after that. I was writing to you to break it off. [He also descends from the table and makes slowly for the hearth]. You must think me an utter rotter.

MARGARET. Oh, has everybody been in prison for being drunk and assaulting the police? How long were you in?

BOBBY. A fortnight.

MARGARET. Thats what I was in for.

BOBBY. What are you talking about? In where?

MARGARET. In quod.

BOBBY. But I'm serious: I'm not rotting. Really and truly—

MARGARET. What did you do to the copper?

BOBBY. Nothing, absolutely nothing. He exaggerated grossly. I only laughed at him.

MARGARET [jumping up, triumphant] Ive beaten you hollow. I knocked out two of his teeth. Ive got one of them. He sold it to me for ten shillings.

BOBBY. Now please do stop fooling, Meg. I tell you I'm not rotting. [He sits down in the armchair, rather sulkily].

MARGARET [taking up the copy of Lloyd's Weekly and going to him] And I tell you I'm not either. Look! Heres a report of it. The daily papers are no good; but the Sunday papers are splendid. [She sits on the arm of the chair]. See! [Reading]: "Hardened at Eigh-teen. A quietly dressed, respectable-looking girl who refuses her name"—thats me.

BOBBY [pausing a moment in his perusal] Do you mean to say that you went on the loose out of pure devilment?

MARGARET. I did no harm. I went to see a lovely dance. I picked up a nice man and went to have a dance myself. I cant imagine anything more innocent and more happy. All the bad part was done by other people: they did it out of pure devilment if you like. Anyhow, here we are, two gaolbirds, Bobby, disgraced forever. Isnt it a relief?

BOBBY [rising stiffly] But you know, it's not the same for a girl. A man may do things a woman maynt. [He stands on the hearthrug with his back to the fire].

MARGARET. Are you scandalised, Bobby?

BOBBY. Well, you cant expect me to approve of it, can you, Meg? I never thought you were that sort of girl.

MARGARET [rising indignantly] I'm not. You mustnt pretend to think that I'm a clergy-man's daughter, Bobby.

BOBBY. I wish you wouldnt chaff about that. Dont forget the row you got into for letting out that you admired Juggins [*she turns her back on him quickly*]—a footman! And what about the Frenchman?

MARGARET [*facing him again*] I know nothing about the Frenchman except that he's a very nice fellow and can swing his leg round like the hand of a clock and knock a policeman down with it. He was in Wormwood Scrubs with you. I was in Holloway.

BOBBY. It's all very well to make light of it, Meg; but this is a bit thick, you know.

MARGARET. Do you feel you couldnt marry a woman whos been in prison?

BOBBY [*hastily*] No. I never said that. It might even give a woman a greater claim on a man. Any girl, if she were thoughtless and a bit on, perhaps, might get into a scrape. Anyone who really understood her character could see there was no harm in it. But youre not the larky sort. At least you usent to be.

MARGARET. I'm not; and I never will be. [*She walks straight up to him*]. I didnt do it for a lark, Bob: I did it out of the very depths of my nature. I did it because I'm that sort of person. I did it in one of my religious fits. I'm hardened at eighteen, as they say. So what about the match, now?

BOBBY. Well, I dont think you can fairly hold me to it, Meg. Of course it would be ridiculous for me to set up to be shocked, or anything of that sort. I cant afford to throw stones at anybody; and I dont pretend to. I can understand a lark; I can forgive a slip; as long as it is understood that it is only a lark or a slip. But to go on the loose on principle; to talk about religion in connection with it; to—to—well, Meg, I do find that a bit thick, I must say. I hope youre not in earnest when you talk that way.

MARGARET. Bobby: youre no good. No good to me, anyhow.

BOBBY [*huffed*] I'm sorry, Miss Knox.

MARGARET. Goodbye, Mr Gilbey. [*She turns on her heel and goes to the other end of the table*]. I suppose you wont introduce me to the clergyman's daughter.

BOBBY. I dont think she'd like it. There are limits, after all. [*He sits down at the table, as if to resume work at his books: a hint to her to go*].

MARGARET [*on her way to the door*] Ring the bell, Bobby; and tell Juggins to shew me out.

BOBBY [*reddening*] I'm not a cad, Meg.

MARGARET [*coming to the table*] Then do something nice to prevent us feeling mean about this afterwards. Youd better kiss me. You neednt ever do it again.

BOBBY. If I'm no good, I dont see what fun it would be for you.

MARGARET. Oh, it'd be no fun. If I wanted what you call fun, I should ask the Frenchman to kiss me—or Juggins.

BOBBY [*rising and retreating to the hearth*] Oh, dont be disgusting, Meg. Dont be low.

MARGARET [*determinedly, preparing to use force*] Now, I'll make you kiss me, just to punish you. [*She seizes his wrist; pulls him off his balance; and gets her arm round his neck*].

BOBBY. No. Stop. Leave go, will you.

Juggins appears at the door.

JUGGINS. Miss Delaney, sir. [*Dora comes in. Juggins goes out. Margaret hastily releases Bobby, and goes to the other side of the room*].

DORA [*through the door, to the departing Juggins*] Well, you a r e a Juggins to shew me up when theres company. [*To Margaret and Bobby*] It's all right, dear: all right, old man: I'll wait in Juggins's pantry til youre disengaged.

MARGARET. Dont you know me?

DORA [*coming to the middle of the room and looking at her very attentively*] Why, it's never No 406!

MARGARET. Yes it is.

DORA. Well, I should never have known you out of the uniform. How did you get out? You were doing a month, wernt you?

MARGARET. My bloke paid the fine the day he got out himself.

DORA. A real gentleman! [*Pointing to Bobby, who is staring open-mouthed*] Look at him! He cant take it in.

BOBBY. I suppose you made her acquaintance in prison, Meg. But when it comes to talking about blokes and all that—well!

MARGARET. Oh, Ive learnt the language; and I like it. It's another barrier broken down.

BOBBY. It's not so much the language, Meg. But I think [*he looks at Dora and stops*].

MARGARET [*suddenly dangerous*] W h a t do you think, Bobby?

DORA. He thinks you oughtnt to be so free with me, dearie. It does him credit: he always was a gentleman, you know.

MARGARET. Does him credit! To insult you like that! Bobby: say that that wasnt what you meant.

BOBBY. I didnt say it was.

MARGARET. Well, deny that it was.

BOBBY. No. I wouldnt have said it in front of Dora; but I do think it's not quite the same thing my knowing her and you knowing her.

DORA. Of course it isnt, old man. [*To Margaret*] I'll just trot off and come back in half an hour. You two can make it up together. I'm really not fit company for you, dearie: I couldnt live up to you. [*She turns to go*].

MARGARET. Stop. Do you believe he could live up to me?

DORA. Well, I'll never say anything to stand between a girl and a respectable marriage, or to stop a decent lad from settling himself. I have a conscience; though I maynt be as particular as some.

MARGARET. You seem to me to be a very decent sort; and Bobby's behaving like a skunk.

BOBBY [*much ruffled*] Nice language that!

DORA. Well, dearie, men have to do some awfully mean things to keep up their respectability. But you cant blame them for that, can you? Ive met Bobby walking with his mother; and of course he cut me dead. I wont pretend I liked it; but what could he do, poor dear?

MARGARET. And now he wants me to cut you dead to keep him in countenance. Well, I shant: not if my whole family were there. But I'll cut him dead if he doesnt treat you properly. [*To Bobby, with a threatening move in his direction*] I'll educate you, you young beast.

BOBBY [*furious, meeting her half way*] Who are you calling a young beast?

MARGARET. You.

DORA [*peacemaking*] Now, dearies!

BOBBY. If you dont take care, youll get your fat head jolly well clouted.

MARGARET. If you dont take care, the policeman's tooth will be the beginning of a collection.

DORA. Now, loveys, be good.

Bobby, lost to all sense of adult dignity, puts out his tongue at Margaret. Margaret, equally furious, catches his protended countenance a box on the cheek. He hurls himself on her. They wrestle.

BOBBY. Cat! I'll teach you.

MARGARET. Pig! Beast! [*She forces him backwards on the table*]. Now where are you?

DORA [*calling*] Juggins, Juggins. Theyll murder one another.

JUGGINS [*throwing open the door, and announcing*] Monsieur Duvallet.

Duvallet enters. Sudden cessation of hostilities, and dead silence. The combatants separate by the whole width of the room. Juggins withdraws.

DUVALLET. I fear I derange you.

MARGARET. Not at all. Bobby: you really are a beast: Monsieur Duvallet will think I'm always fighting.

DUVALLET. Practising jujitsu or the new Iceland wrestling. Admirable, Miss Knox. The athletic young Englishwoman is an example to all Europe. [*Indicating Bobby*] Your instructor, no doubt. Monsieur— [*he bows*].

BOBBY [*bowing awkwardly*] How d'y' do?

MARGARET [*to Bobby*] I'm so sorry, Bobby: I asked Monsieur Duvallet to call for me here; and I forgot to tell you. [*Introducing*] Monsieur Duvallet: Miss Four hundred and seven. Mr Bobby Gilbey. [*Duvallet bows*]. I really dont know how to explain our relationships. Bobby and I are like brother and sister.

DUVALLET. Perfectly. I noticed it.

MARGARET. Bobby and Miss—Miss—

DORA. Delaney, dear. [*To Duvallet, bewitchingly*] Darling Dora, to real friends.

MARGARET. Bobby and Dora are—are—well, not brother and sister.

DUVALLET [*with redoubled comprehension*] PErfectly.

MARGARET. Bobby has spent the last fortnight in prison. You dont mind, do you?

DUVALLET. No, naturally. *I* have spent the last fortnight in prison.

The conversation drops. Margaret renews it with an effort.

MARGARET. Dora has spent the last fortnight in prison.

DUVALLET. Quite so. I felicitate Mademoiselle on her enlargement.

DORA. *Trop merci*, as they say in Boulogne. No call to be stiff with one another, have we?

Juggins comes in.

JUGGINS. Beg pardon, sir. Mr and Mrs Gilbey are coming up the street.

DORA. Let me absquatulate [*making for the door*].

JUGGINS. If you wish to leave without being seen, you had better step into my pantry and leave afterwards.

DORA. Righto! [*She bursts into song*]
Hide me in the meat safe til the cop goes by.
Hum the dear old music as his step draws nigh.

[*She goes out on tiptoe*].

MARGARET. I wont stay here if she has to hide. I'll keep her company in the pantry. [*She follows Dora*].

BOBBY. Lets all go. We cant have any fun with the Mar here. I say, Juggins: you can give us tea in the pantry, cant you?

JUGGINS. Certainly, sir.

BOBBY. Right. Say nothing to my mother. You dont mind, Mr Doovalley, do you?

DUVALLET. I shall be charmed.

BOBBY. Right you are. Come along. [*At the door*] Oh, by the way, Juggins, fetch down that concertina from my room, will you?

JUGGINS. Yes, sir. [*Bobby goes out. Duvallet follows him to the door*]. You understand, sir, that Miss Knox is a lady absolutely *comme il faut?*

DUVALLET. Perfectly. But the other?

JUGGINS. The other, sir, may be both charitably and accurately described in your native idiom as a daughter of joy.

DUVALLET. It is what I thought. These English domestic interiors are very interesting. [*He goes out, followed by Juggins*].

Presently Mr and Mrs Gilbey come in. They take their accustomed places: he on the hearthrug, she at the colder end of the table.

MRS GILBEY. Did you smell scent in the hall, Rob?

GILBEY. No, I didnt. And I dont want to smell it. Dont you go looking for trouble, Maria.

MRS GILBEY [*snuffing up the perfumed atmosphere*] She's been here. [*Gilbey rings the bell*]. What are you ringing for? Are you going to ask?

GILBEY. No, I'm not going to ask. Juggins said this morning he wanted to speak to me. If he likes to tell me, let him; but I'm not going to ask; and dont you either. [*Juggins appears at the door*]. You said you wanted to say something to me.

JUGGINS. When it would be convenient to you, sir.

GILBEY. Well, what is it?

MRS GILBEY. Oh, Juggins, we're expecting Mr and Mrs Knox to tea.

GILBEY. He knows that. [*He sits down. Then, to Juggins*] What is it?

JUGGINS [*advancing to the middle of the table*] Would it inconvenience you, sir, if I were to give you a month's notice?

GILBEY [*taken aback*] What! Why? Aint you satisfied?

JUGGINS. Perfectly, sir. It is not that I want to better myself, I assure you.

GILBEY. Well, what do you want to leave for, then? Do you want to worse yourself?

JUGGINS. No, sir. Ive been well treated in your most comfortable establishment; and I should be greatly distressed if you or Mrs Gilbey were to interpret my notice as an expression of dissatisfaction.

GILBEY [*paternally*] Now you listen to me, Juggins. I'm an older man than you. Dont you throw out dirty water til you get in fresh. Dont get too big for your boots. Youre like all servants nowadays: you think youve only to hold up your finger to get the pick of half a dozen jobs. But you wont be treated everywhere as youre treated here. In bed every night before eleven; hardly a ring at the door except on Mrs Gilbey's day once a month; and no other manservant to interfere with you. It may be a bit quiet perhaps; but youre past the age of adventure. Take my advice: think over it. You suit me; and I'm prepared to make it suit you if youre dissatisfied—in reason, you know.

JUGGINS. I realize my advantages, sir; but Ive private reasons—

GILBEY [*cutting him short angrily and retiring to the hearthrug in dudgeon*] Oh, I know. Very well: go. The sooner the better.

MRS GILBEY. Oh, not until we're suited. He must stay his month.

GILBEY [*sarcastic*] Do you want to lose him his character, Maria? Do you think I dont see what it is? We're prison folk now. Weve been in the police court. [*To Juggins*] Well, I suppose you know your own business best. I take your notice: you can go when your month is up, or sooner, if you like.

JUGGINS. Believe me, sir—

GILBEY. Thats enough: I dont want any excuses. I dont blame you. You can go downstairs now, if youve nothing else to trouble me about.

JUGGINS. I really cant leave it at that, sir. I assure you Ive no objection to young Mr Gilbey's going to prison. You may do six months yourself, sir, and welcome, without a word of remonstrance from me. I'm leaving solely because my brother, who has suffered a bereavement, and feels lonely, begs me to spend a few months with him until he gets over it.

GILBEY. And is he to keep you all that time? or are you to spend your savings in com-

Z

forting him? Have some sense, man: how can you afford such things?

JUGGINS. My brother can afford to keep me, sir. The truth is, he objects to my being in service.

GILBEY. Is that any reason why you should be dependent on him? Dont do it, Juggins: pay your own way like an honest lad; and dont eat your brother's bread while youre able to earn your own.

JUGGINS. There is sound sense in that, sir. But unfortunately it is a tradition in my family that the younger brothers should spunge to a considerable extent on the eldest.

GILBEY. Then the sooner that tradition is broken, the better, my man.

JUGGINS. A Radical sentiment, sir. But an excellent one.

GILBEY. Radical! What do you mean? Dont you begin to take liberties, Juggins, now that you know we're loth to part with you. Your brother isnt a duke, you know.

JUGGINS. Unfortunately, he is, sir.

GILBEY. } together { What!
MRS GILBEY. }   { Juggins!

JUGGINS. Excuse me, sir: the bell. [He goes out].

GILBEY [overwhelmed] Maria: did you understand him to say his brother was a duke?

MRS GILBEY. Fancy his condescending! Perhaps if youd offer to raise his wages and treat him as one of the family, he'd stay.

GILBEY. And have my own servant above me! Not me. Whats the world coming to? Heres Bobby and—

JUGGINS [entering and announcing] Mr and Mrs Knox.

The Knoxes come in. Juggins takes two chairs from the wall and places them at the table, between the host and hostess. Then he withdraws.

MRS GILBEY [to Mrs Knox] How are you, dear?

MRS KNOX. Nicely, thank you. Good evening, Mr Gilbey. [They shake hands; and she takes the chair nearest Mrs Gilbey. Mr Knox takes the other chair].

GILBEY [sitting down] I was just saying, Knox, What is the world coming to?

KNOX [appealing to his wife] What was I saying myself only this morning?

MRS KNOX. This is a strange time. I was never one to talk about the end of the world; but look at the things that have happened!

KNOX. Earthquakes!

GILBEY. San Francisco!

MRS GILBEY. Jamaica!

KNOX. Martinique!

GILBEY. Messina!

MRS GILBEY. The plague in China!

MRS KNOX. The floods in France!

GILBEY. My Bobby in Wormwood Scrubbs!

KNOX. Margaret in Holloway!

GILBEY. And now my footman tells me his brother's a duke!

KNOX. } { No!
MRS KNOX. } { Whats that?

GILBEY. Just before he let you in. A duke! Here has everything been respectable from the beginning of the world, as you may say, to the present day; and all of a sudden everything is turned upside down.

MRS KNOX. It's like in the book of Revelations. But I do say that when people have happiness within themselves, all the earthquakes, all the floods, and all the prisons in the world cant make them really unhappy.

KNOX. It isnt alone the curious things that are happening, but the unnatural way people are taking them. Why, theres Margaret been in prison, and she hasnt time to go to all the invitations she's had from people that never asked her before.

GILBEY. I never knew we could live without being respectable.

MRS GILBEY. Oh, Rob, what a thing to say! Who says we're not respectable?

GILBEY. Well, it's not what I call respectable to have your children in and out of jail.

KNOX. Oh come, Gilbey! we're not tramps because weve had, as it were, an accident.

GILBEY. It's no use, Knox: look it in the face. Did I ever tell you my father drank?

KNOX. No. But I knew it. Simmons told me.

GILBEY. Yes: he never could keep his mouth quiet: he told me your aunt was a kleptomaniac.

MRS KNOX. It wasnt true, Mr Gilbey. She used to pick up handkerchiefs if she saw them lying about; but you might trust her with untold silver.

GILBEY. My Uncle Phil was a teetotaler. My father used to say to me: Rob, he says, dont you ever have a weakness. If you find one getting a hold on you, make a merit of it, he says. Your Uncle Phil doesnt like spirits; and he makes a merit of it, and is chairman of the Blue Ribbon Committee. I do like spirits; and I make a merit of it, and I'm the King Cockatoo of the Convivial Cockatoos. Never put yourself in the wrong, he says. I used to boast about what a good boy Bobby was. Now I swank about what a dog he is; and it pleases people just as well. What a world it is!

KNOX. It turned my blood cold at first to hear Margaret telling people about Holloway; but it goes down better than her singing used to.

MRS KNOX. I never thought she sang right after all those lessons we paid for.

GILBEY. Lord, Knox, it was lucky you and me got let in together. I tell you straight, if it hadnt been for Bobby's disgrace, I'd have broke up the firm.

KNOX. I shouldnt have blamed you: I'd have done the same only for Margaret. Too much straitlacedness narrows a man's mind. Talking of that, what about those hygienic corset advertisements that Vines & Jackson want us to put in the window? I told Vines they werent decent and we couldnt shew them in our shop. I was pretty high with him. But what am I to say to him now if he comes and throws this business in our teeth?

GILBEY. Oh, put em in. We may as well go it a bit now.

MRS GILBEY. Youve been going it quite far enough, Rob. [*To Mrs Knox*] He wont get up in the mornings now: he that was always out of bed at seven to the tick!

MRS KNOX. You hear that, Jo? [*To Mrs Gilbey*] He's taken to whisky and soda. A pint a week! And the beer the same as before!

KNOX. Oh, dont preach, old girl.

MRS KNOX [*to Mrs Gilbey*] Thats a new name he's got for me. [*To Knox*] I tell you, Jo, this doesnt sit well on you. You may call it preaching if you like; but it's the truth for all that. I say that if youve happiness within yourself, you dont need to seek it outside, spending money on drink and theatres and bad company, and being miserable after all. You can sit at home and be happy; and you can work and be happy. If you have that in you, the spirit will set you free to do what you want and guide you to do right. But if you havnt got it, then youd best be respectable and stick to the ways that are marked out for you; for youve nothing else to keep you straight.

KNOX [*angrily*] And is a man never to have a bit of fun? See whats come of it with your daughter! She was to be content with your happiness that youre always talking about; and how did the spirit guide her? To a

month's hard for being drunk and assaulting the police. Did *I* ever assault the police?

MRS KNOX. You wouldnt have the courage. I dont blame the girl.

MRS GILBEY. } Oh, Maria! What are you saying?

GILBEY. } What! And you so pious!

MRS KNOX. She went where the spirit guided her. And what harm there was in it she knew nothing about.

GILBEY. Oh, come, Mrs Knox! Girls are not so innocent as all that.

MRS KNOX. I dont say she was ignorant. But I do say that she didnt know what we know: I mean the way certain temptations get a sudden hold that no goodness nor self-control is any use against. She was saved from that, and had a rough lesson too; and I say it was no earthly protection that did that. But dont think, you two men, that youll be protected if you make what she did an excuse to go and do as youd like to do if it wasnt for the fear of losing your characters. The spirit wont guide you, because it isnt in you; and it never has been: not in either of you.

GILBEY [*with ironic humility*] I'm sure I'm obliged to you for your good opinion, Mrs Knox.

MRS KNOX. Well, I will say for you, Mr Gilbey, that youre better than my man here. He's a bitter hard heathen, is my Jo, God help me! [*She begins to cry quietly*].

KNOX. Now, dont take on like that, Amelia. You know I always gave in to you that you were right about religion. But one of us had to think of other things, or we'd have starved, we and the child.

MRS KNOX. How do you know youd have starved? All the other things might have been added unto you.

GILBEY. Come, Mrs Knox, dont tell me Knox is a sinner. I know better. I'm sure youd be the first to be sorry if anything was to happen to him.

KNOX [*bitterly to his wife*] Youve always had some grudge against me; and nobody but yourself can understand what it is.

MRS KNOX. I wanted a man who had that happiness within himself. You made me think you had it; but it was nothing but being in love with me.

MRS GILBEY. And do you blame him for that?

MRS KNOX. I blame nobody. But let him

not think he can walk by his own light. I tell him that if he gives up being respectable he'll go right down to the bottom of the hill. He has no powers inside himself to keep him steady; so let him cling to the powers outside him.

KNOX [*rising angrily*] Who wants to give up being respectable? All this for a pint of whisky that lasted a week! How long would it have lasted Simmons, I wonder?

MRS KNOX [*gently*] Oh, well, say no more, Jo. I wont plague you about it. [*He sits down*]. You never did understand; and you never will. Hardly anybody understands: even Margaret didnt til she went to prison. She does now; and I shall have a companion in the house after all these lonely years.

KNOX [*beginning to cry*] I did all I could to make you happy. I never said a harsh word to you.

GILBEY [*rising indignantly*] What right have you to treat a man like that? an honest respectable husband? as if he were dirt under your feet?

KNOX. Let her alone, Gilbey. [*Gilbey sits down, but mutinously*].

MRS KNOX. Well, you gave me all you could, Jo; and if it wasnt what I wanted, that wasnt your fault. But I'd rather have you as you were than since you took to whisky and soda.

KNOX. I dont want any whisky and soda. I'll take the pledge if you like.

MRS KNOX. No: you shall have your beer because you like it. The whisky was only brag. And if you and me are to remain friends, Mr Gilbey, youll get up tomorrow morning at seven.

GILBEY [*defiantly*] Damme if I will! There!

MRS KNOX [*with gentle pity*] How do you know, Mr Gilbey, what youll do tomorrow morning?

GILBEY. Why shouldnt I know? Are we children not to be let do what we like, and our own sons and daughters kicking their heels all over the place? [*To Knox*] I was never one to interfere between man and wife, Knox; but if Maria started ordering me about like that—

MRS GILBEY. Now dont be naughty, Rob. You know you mustnt set yourself up against religion?

GILBEY. Whos setting himself up against religion?

MRS KNOX. It doesnt matter whether you set yourself up against it or not, Mr Gilbey.

If it sets itself up against you, youll have to go the appointed way: it's no use quarrelling about it with me that am as great a sinner as yourself.

GILBEY. Oh, indeed! And who told you I was a sinner?

MRS GILBEY. Now, Rob, you know we are all sinners. What else is religion?

GILBEY. I say nothing against religion. I suppose we're all sinners, in a manner of speaking; but I dont like to have it thrown at me as if I'd really done anything.

MRS GILBEY. Mrs Knox is speaking for your good, Rob.

GILBEY. Well, I dont like to be spoken to for my good. Would anybody like it?

MRS KNOX. Dont take offence where none is meant, Mr Gilbey. Talk about something else. No good ever comes of arguing about such things among the like of us.

KNOX. The like of us! Are you throwing it in our teeth that your people were in the wholesale and thought Knox and Gilbey wasnt good enough for you?

MRS KNOX. No, Jo: you know I'm not. What better were my people than yours, for all their pride? But Ive noticed it all my life: we're ignorant. We dont really know whats right and whats wrong. We're all right as long as things go on the way they always did. We bring our children up just as we were brought up; and we go to church or chapel just as our parents did; and we say what everybody says; and it goes on all right until something out of the way happens: theres a family quarrel, or one of the children goes wrong, or a father takes to drink, or an aunt goes mad, or one of us finds ourselves doing something we never thought we'd want to do. And then you know what happens: complaints and quarrels and huff and offence and bad language and bad temper and regular bewilderment as if Satan possessed us all. We find out then that with all our respectability and piety, weve no real religion and no way of telling right from wrong. Weve nothing but our habits; and when theyre upset, where are we? Just like Peter in the storm trying to walk on the water and finding he couldnt.

MRS GILBEY [*piously*] Aye! He found out, didnt he?

GILBEY [*reverently*] I never denied that youve a great intellect, Mrs Knox—

MRS KNOX. Oh, get along with you, Gilbey,

if you begin talking about my intellect. Give us some tea, Maria. Ive said my say; and I'm sure I beg the company's pardon for being so long about it, and so disagreeable.

MRS GILBEY. Ring, Rob. [*Gilbey rings*]. Stop. Juggins will think we're ringing for him.

GILBEY [*appalled*] It's too late. I rang before I thought of it.

MRS GILBEY. Step down and apologize, Rob.

KNOX. Is it him that you said was brother to a—

Juggins comes in with the tea-tray. All rise. He takes the tray to Mrs Gilbey.

GILBEY. I didnt mean to ask you to do this, Mr Juggins. I wasnt thinking when I rang.

MRS GILBEY [*trying to take the tray from him*] Let me, Juggins.

JUGGINS. Please sit down, madam. Allow me to discharge my duties just as usual, sir. I assure you that is the correct thing. [*They sit down, ill at ease, whilst he places the tray on the table. He then goes out for the curate*].

KNOX [*lowering his voice*] Is this all right, Gilbey? Anybody may be the son of a duke, you know. Is he legitimate?

GILBEY. Good Lord! I never thought of that.

Juggins returns with the cakes. They regard him with suspicion.

GILBEY [*whispering to Knox*] You ask him.

KNOX [*to Juggins*] Just a word with you, my man. Was your mother married to your father?

JUGGINS. I believe so, sir. I cant say from personal knowledge. It was before my time.

GILBEY. Well but look here you know— [*he hesitates*].

JUGGINS. Yes, sir?

KNOX. I know whatll clinch it, Gilbey. You leave it to me. [*To Juggins*] Was your mother the duchess?

JUGGINS. Yes, sir. Quite correct, sir, I assure you. [*To Mrs Gilbey*] That is the milk, madam. [*She has mistaken the jugs*]. This is the water.

They stare at him in pitiable embarrassment.

MRS KNOX. What did I tell you? Heres something out of the common happening with a servant; and we none of us know how to behave.

JUGGINS. It's quite simple, madam. I'm a footman, and should be treated as a footman. [*He proceeds calmly with his duties, handing round cups of tea as Mrs Knox fills them*].

Shrieks of laughter from below stairs reach the ears of the company.

MRS GILBEY. Whats that noise? Is Master Bobby at home? I heard his laugh.

MRS KNOX. I'm sure I heard Margaret's.

GILBEY. Not a bit of it. It was that woman.

JUGGINS. I can explain, sir. I must ask you to excuse the liberty; but I'm entertaining a small party to tea in my pantry.

MRS GILBEY. But youre not entertaining Master Bobby?

JUGGINS. Yes, madam.

GILBEY. Whos with him?

JUGGINS. Miss Knox, sir.

GILBEY. Miss Knox! Are you sure? Is there anyone else?

JUGGINS. Only a French marine officer, sir, and—er—Miss Delaney. [*He places Gilbey's tea on the table before him*]. The lady that called about Master Bobby, sir.

KNOX. Do you mean to say theyre having a party all to themselves downstairs, and we having a party up here and knowing nothing about it?

JUGGINS. Yes, sir. I have to do a good deal of entertaining in the pantry for Master Bobby, sir.

GILBEY. Well, this is a nice state of things!

KNOX. Whats the meaning of it? What do they do it for?

JUGGINS. To enjoy themselves, sir, I should think.

MRS GILBEY. Enjoy themselves! Did ever anybody hear of such a thing?

GILBEY. Knox's daughter shewn into my pantry!

KNOX. Margaret mixing with a Frenchman and a footman—[*Suddenly realizing that the footman is offering him cake*] She doesnt know about—about His Grace, you know.

MRS GILBEY. Perhaps she does. Does she, Mr Juggins?

JUGGINS. The other lady suspects me, madam. They call me Rudolph, or the Long Lost Heir.

MRS GILBEY. It's a much nicer name than Juggins. I think I'll call you by it, if you dont mind.

JUGGINS. Not at all, madam.

Roars of merriment from below.

GILBEY. Go and tell them to stop laughing. What right have they to make a noise like that?

JUGGINS. I asked them not to laugh so loudly, sir. But the French gentleman always sets them off again.

KNOX. Do you mean to tell me that my daughter laughs at a Frenchman's jokes?

GILBEY. We all know what French jokes are.

JUGGINS. Believe me: you do not, sir. The noise this afternoon has all been because the Frenchman said that the cat had whooping cough.

MRS GILBEY [*laughing heartily*] Well, I never!

GILBEY. Dont be a fool, Maria. Look here, Knox: we cant let this go on. People cant be allowed to behave like this.

KNOX. Just what I say.

A concertina adds its music to the revelry.

MRS GILBEY [*excited*] Thats the squiffer. He's bought it for her.

GILBEY. Well, of all the scandalous— [*Redoubled laughter from below*].

KNOX. I'll put a stop to this. [*He goes out to the landing and shouts*] Margaret! [*Sudden dead silence*]. Margaret, I say!

MARGARET'S VOICE. Yes, father. Shall we all come up? We're dying to.

KNOX. Come up and be ashamed of yourselves, behaving like wild Indians.

DORA'S VOICE [*screaming*] Oh! oh! oh! Dont, Bobby. Now—Oh! [*In headlong flight she dashes into and right across the room, breathless, and slightly abashed by the company*]. I beg your pardon, Mrs Gilbey, for coming in like that; but whenever I go upstairs in front of Bobby, he pretends it's a cat biting my ankles; and I just m u s t scream.

Bobby and Margaret enter rather more shyly, but evidently in high spirits. Bobby places himself near his father, on the hearthrug, and presently slips down into the armchair.

MARGARET. How do you do, Mrs Gilbey? [*She puts herself behind her mother*].

Duvallet comes in behaving himself perfectly. Knox follows.

MARGARET. Oh—let me introduce. My friend Lieutenant Duvallet. Mrs Gilbey. Mr Gilbey.

Duvallet bows and sits down on Mr Knox's left, Juggins placing a chair for him.

DORA. Now, Bobby: introduce me: theres a dear.

BOBBY [*a little nervous about it; but trying to keep up his spirits*] Miss Delaney: Mr and Mrs Knox. [*Knox, as he resumes his seat, acknowledges the introduction suspiciously. Mrs Knox bows gravely, looking keenly at Dora and taking her measure without prejudice*].

DORA. Pleased to meet you. [*Juggins places the baby rocking-chair for her on Gilbey's right, opposite the Knoxes*]. Thank you. [*She sits*]. Bobby's given me the squiffer. Do you know what theyve been doing downstairs? Youd never guess. Theyve been trying to teach me table manners. The Lieutenant and Rudolph say I'm a regular pig. I'm sure I never knew there was anything wrong with me. But live and learn. [*To Gilbey*] Eh, old dear?

JUGGINS. Old dear is not correct, Miss Delaney. [*He retires to the end of the sideboard nearest the door*].

DORA. Oh get out! I must call a man something. He doesnt mind: do you, Charlie?

MRS GILBEY. His name isnt Charlie.

DORA. Excuse me. I call everybody Charlie.

JUGGINS. You mustnt.

DORA. Oh, if I were to mind you, I should have to hold my tongue altogether; and then how sorry youd be! Lord, how I do run on! Dont mind me, Mrs Gilbey.

KNOX. What I want to know is, whats to be the end of this? It's not for me to interfere between you and your son, Gilbey: he knows his own intentions best, no doubt, and perhaps has told them to you. But Ive my daughter to look after; and it's my duty as a parent to have a clear understanding about her. No good is ever done by beating about the bush. I ask Lieutenant—well, I dont speak French; and I cant pronounce the name—

MARGARET. Mr Duvallet, father.

KNOX. I ask Mr Doovalley what his intentions are.

MARGARET. Oh father: how can you?

DUVALLET. I'm afraid my knowledge of English is not enough to understand. Intentions? How?

MARGARET. He wants to know will you marry me.

MRS GILBEY. } What a thing to say!
KNOX. } Silence, miss.
DORA. } Well, thats straight, aint it?

DUVALLET. But I am married already. I have two daughters.

KNOX [*rising, virtuously indignant*] You sit there after carrying on with my daughter, and tell me coolly youre married.

MARGARET. Papa: you really must not tell people that they sit there. [*He sits down again sulkily*].

DUVALLET. Pardon. Carrying on? What does that mean?

MARGARET. It means—

KNOX [*violently*] Hold your tongue, you shameless young hussy. Dont you dare say what it means.

DUVALLET [*shrugging his shoulders*] What does it mean, Rudolph?

MRS KNOX. If it's not proper for her to say, it's not proper for a man to say, either. Mr Doovalley: youre a married man with daughters. Would you let them go about with a stranger, as you are to us, without wanting to know whether he intended to behave honorably?

DUVALLET. Ah, madam, my daughters are French girls. That is very different. It would not be correct for a French girl to go about alone and speak to men as English and American girls do. That is why I so immensely admire the English people. You are so free—so unprejudiced—your women are so brave and frank—their minds are so—how do you say?—wholesome. I intend to have my daughters educated in England. Nowhere else in the world but in England could I have met at a Variety Theatre a charming young lady of perfect respectability, and enjoyed a dance with her at a public dancing saloon. And where else are women trained to box and knock out the teeth of policemen as a protest against injustice and violence? [*Rising, with immense élan*] Your daughter, madam, is superb. Your country is a model to the rest of Europe. If you were a Frenchman, stifled in prudery, hypocrisy, and the tyranny of the family and the home, you would understand how an enlightened Frenchman admires and envies your freedom, your broadmindedness, and the fact that home life can hardly be said to exist in England. You have made an end of the despotism of the parent; the family council is unknown to you; everywhere in these islands one can enjoy the exhilarating, the soul-liberating spectacle of men quarrelling with their brothers, defying their fathers, refusing to speak to their mothers. In France we are not men: we are only sons—grown-up children. Here one is a human being—an end in himself. Oh, Mrs Knox, if only your military genius were equal to your moral genius—if that conquest of Europe by France which inaugurated the new age after the Revolution had only been an English conquest, how much more enlightened the world would have been now! We, alas, can only fight. France is unconquerable. We impose our narrow ideas, our prejudices, our obsolete institutions, our insufferable pedantry on the world by brute force—by that stupid quality of military heroism which shews how little we have evolved from the savage: nay, from the beast. We can charge like bulls; we can spring on our foes like gamecocks; when we are overpowered by treason, we can die fighting like rats. And we are foolish enough to be proud of it! Why should we be? Does the bull progress? Can you civilize the gamecock? Is there any future for the rat? We never fight intelligently: when we lose battles, it is because we have not sense enough to know when we are beaten. At Waterloo, had we known when we were beaten, we should have retreated; tried another plan; and won the battle. But no: we were too pigheaded to admit that there is anything impossible to a Frenchman: we were quite satisfied when our Marshals had six horses shot under them, and our stupid old grognards died fighting rather than surrender like reasonable beings. Think of your great Wellington: think of his inspiring words, when the lady asked him whether British soldiers ever ran away. "All soldiers run away, madam," he said; "but if there are supports for them to fall back on it does not matter." Think of your illustrious Nelson, always beaten on land, always victorious at sea, where his men could not run away. You are not dazzled and misled by false ideals of patriotic enthusiasm: your honest and sensible statesmen demand for England a two-power standard, even a three-power standard, frankly admitting that it is wise to fight three to one: whilst we, fools and braggarts as we are, declare that every Frenchman is a host in himself, and that when one Frenchman attacks three Englishmen he is guilty of an act of cowardice comparable to that of the man who strikes a woman. It is folly: it is nonsense: a Frenchman is not really stronger than a German, than an Italian, even than an Englishman. Sir: if all Frenchwomen were like your daughter—if all Frenchmen had the good sense, the power of seeing things as they really are, the calm judgment, the open mind, the philosophic grasp, the foresight and true courage, which are so natural to you as an Englishman that you are hardly conscious of possessing them, France would become the greatest nation in the world.

MARGARET. Three cheers for old England! [*She shakes hands with him warmly*].

BOBBY. Hurra-a-ay! And so say all of us.

Duvallet, having responded to Margaret's handshake with enthusiasm, kisses Juggins on both cheeks, and sinks into his chair, wiping his perspiring brow.

GILBEY. Well, this sort of talk is above me. Can you make anything out of it, Knox?

KNOX. The long and short of it seems to be that he cant lawfully marry my daughter, as he ought after going to prison with her.

DORA. I'm ready to marry Bobby, if that will be any satisfaction.

GILBEY. No you dont. Not if I know it.

MRS KNOX. He ought to, Mr Gilbey.

GILBEY. Well, if thats your religion, Amelia Knox, I want no more of it. Would you invite them to your house if he married her?

MRS KNOX. He ought to marry her whether or no.

BOBBY. I feel I ought to, Mrs Knox.

GILBEY. Hold your tongue. Mind your own business.

BOBBY [*wildly*] If I'm not let marry her, I'll do something downright disgraceful. I'll enlist as a soldier.

JUGGINS [*sternly*] That is not a disgrace, sir.

BOBBY. Not for you, perhaps. But youre only a footman. I'm a gentleman.

MRS GILBEY. Dont dare to speak disrespectfully to Mr Rudolph, Bobby. For shame!

JUGGINS [*coming forward to the middle of the table*] It is not gentlemanly to regard the service of your country as disgraceful. It is gentlemanly to marry the lady you make love to.

GILBEY [*aghast*] My boy is to marry this woman and be a social outcast!

JUGGINS. Your boy and Miss Delaney will be inexorably condemned by respectable society to spend the rest of their days in precisely the sort of company they seem to like best and be most at home in.

KNOX. And my daughter? Whos to marry my daughter?

JUGGINS. Your daughter, sir, will probably marry the man she makes up her mind to marry. She is a lady of very determined character.

KNOX. Yes: if he'd have her with her character gone. But who would? Youre the brother of a duke. Would——

BOBBY. } Whats that?
MARGARET. } Juggins a duke!
DUVALLET. } Comment!
DORA. } What did I tell you?

KNOX. Yes: the brother of a duke: thats what he is. [*To Juggins*] Well, would you marry her?

JUGGINS. I was about to propose that solution of your problem, Mr Knox.

MRS GILBEY. } Well, I never!
KNOX. } D'ye mean it?
MRS KNOX. } Marry Margaret!

JUGGINS [*continuing*] As an idle younger son, unable to support myself, or even to remain in the Guards in competition with the grandsons of American millionaires, I could not have aspired to Miss Knox's hand. But as a sober, honest, and industrious domestic servant, who has, I trust, given satisfaction to his employer [*he bows to Mr Gilbey*] I feel I am a man with a character. It is for Miss Knox to decide.

MARGARET. I got into a frightful row once for admiring you, Rudolph.

JUGGINS. I should have got into an equally frightful row myself, Miss, had I betrayed my admiration for you. I looked forward to those weekly dinners.

MRS KNOX. But why did a gentleman like you stoop to be a footman?

DORA. He stooped to conquer.

MARGARET. Shut up, Dora: I want to hear.

JUGGINS. I will explain; but only Mrs Knox will understand. I once insulted a servant. Rashly; for he was a sincere Christian. He rebuked me for trifling with a girl of his own class. I told him to remember what he was, and to whom he was speaking. He said God would remember. I discharged him on the spot.

GILBEY. Very properly.

KNOX. What right had he to mention such a thing to you?

MRS GILBEY. What are servants coming to?

MRS KNOX. Did it come true, what he said?

JUGGINS. It stuck like a poisoned arrow. It rankled for months. Then I gave in. I apprenticed myself to an old butler of ours who kept a hotel. He taught me my present business, and got me a place as footman with Mr Gilbey. If ever I meet that man again I shall be able to look him in the face.

MRS KNOX. Margaret: it's not on account of the duke: dukes are vanities. But take my advice; and take him.

MARGARET [*slipping her arm through his*] I have loved Juggins since the first day I beheld him. I felt instinctively he had been in the Guards. May he walk out with me, Mr Gilbey?

KNOX. Dont be vulgar, girl. Remember your new position. [*To Juggins*] I suppose youre serious about this, Mr—Mr Rudolph?

JUGGINS. I propose, with your permission, to begin keeping company this afternoon, if Mrs Gilbey can spare me.

GILBEY [*in a gust of envy, to Bobby*] Itll be long enough before you ll marry the sister of a duke, you young good-for-nothing.

DORA. Dont fret, old dear. Rudolph will teach me high-class manners. I call it quite a happy ending: dont you, lieutenant?

DUVALLET. In France it would be impossible. But here—ah! [*kissing his hand*] la belle Angleterre!

EPILOGUE

Before the curtain. The Count, dazed and agitated, hurries to the 4 critics, as they rise, bored and weary, from their seats.

THE COUNT. Gentlemen: do not speak to me. I implore you to withhold your opinion. I am not strong enough to bear it. I could never have believed it. Is this a play? Is this in any sense of the word, Art? Is it agreeable? Can it conceivably do good to any human being? Is it delicate? Do such people really exist? Excuse me, gentlemen: I speak from a wounded heart. There are private reasons for my discomposure. This play implies obscure, unjust, unkind reproaches and menaces to all of us who are parents.

TROTTER. Pooh! you take it too seriously. After all, the thing has amusing passages. Dismiss the rest as impertinence.

THE COUNT. Mr Trotter: it is easy for you to play the pococurantist. [*Trotter, amazed, repeats the first three syllables in his throat, making a noise like a pheasant*]. You see hundreds of plays every year. But to me, who have never seen anything of this kind before, the effect of this play is terribly disquieting. Sir: if it had been what people call an immoral play, I shouldnt have minded a bit. [*Vaughan is shocked*]. Love beautifies every romance and justifies every audacity. [*Bannal assents gravely*]. But there are reticences which everybody should respect. There are decencies too subtle to be put into words, without which

human society would be unbearable. People could not talk to one another as those people talk. No child could speak to its parent: no girl could speak to a youth: no human creature could tear down the veils—[*Appealing to Vaughan, who is on his left flank, with Gunn between them*] Could they, sir?

VAUGHAN. Well, I dont see that.

THE COUNT. You dont see it! dont feel it! [*To Gunn*] Sir: I appeal to you.

GUNN [*with studied weariness*] It seems to me the most ordinary sort of old-fashioned Ibsenite drivel.

THE COUNT [*turning to Trotter, who is on his right, between him and Bannal*] Mr Trotter: will you tell me that you are not amazed, outraged, revolted, wounded in your deepest and holiest feelings by every word of this play, every tone, every implication; that you did not sit there shrinking in every fibre at the thought of what might come next?

TROTTER. Not a bit. Any clever modern girl could turn out that kind of thing by the yard.

THE COUNT. Then, sir, tomorrow I start for Venice, never to return. I must believe what you tell me. I perceive that you are not agitated, not surprised, not concerned; that my own horror (yes, gentlemen, horror—horror of the very soul) appears unaccountable to you, ludicrous, absurd, even to you, Mr Trotter, who are little younger than myself. Sir: if young people spoke to me like that, I should die of shame: I could not face it. I must go back. The world has passed me by and left me. Accept the apologies of an elderly and no doubt ridiculous admirer of the art of a bygone day, when there was still some beauty in the world and some delicate grace in family life. But I promised my daughter your opinion; and I must keep my word. Gentlemen: you are the choice and master spirits of this age: you walk through it without bewilderment and face its strange products without dismay. Pray deliver your verdict. Mr Bannal: you know that it is the custom at a Court Martial for the youngest officer present to deliver his judgment first; so that he may not be influenced by the authority of his elders. You are the youngest. What is your opinion of the play?

BANNAL. Well, whos it by?

THE COUNT. That is a secret for the present.

BANNAL. You dont expect me to know what to say about a play when I dont know who

z 2

the author is, do you?

THE COUNT. Why not?

BANNAL. Why not! Why not!! Suppose you had to write about a play by Pinero and one by Jones! Would you say exactly the same thing about them?

THE COUNT. I presume not.

BANNAL. Then how could you write about them until you knew which was Pinero and which was Jones? Besides, what sort of play is this? thats what I want to know. Is it a comedy or a tragedy? Is it a farce or a melodrama? Is it repertory theatre tosh, or really straight paying stuff?

GUNN. Cant you tell from seeing it?

BANNAL. I can see it all right enough; but how am I to know how to take it? Is it serious, or is it spoof? If the author knows what his play is, let him tell us what it is. If he doesnt, he cant complain if I dont know either. *I*'m not the author.

THE COUNT. But is it a good play, Mr Bannal? Thats a simple question.

BANNAL. Simple enough when you know. If it's by a good author, it's a good play, naturally. That stands to reason. Who is the author? Tell me that; and I'll place the play for you to a hair's breadth.

THE COUNT. I'm sorry I'm not at liberty to divulge the author's name. The author desires that the play should be judged on its merits.

BANNAL. But what merits can it have except the author's merits? Who would you say it's by, Gunn?

GUNN. Well, who do you think? Here you have a rotten old-fashioned domestic melodrama acted by the usual stage puppets. The hero's a naval lieutenant. All melodramatic heroes are naval lieutenants. The heroine gets into trouble by defying the law (if she didnt get into trouble, thered be no drama) and plays for sympathy all the time as hard as she can. Her good old pious mother turns on her cruel father when he's going to put her out of the house, and says she'll go too. Then theres the comic relief: the comic shopkeeper, the comic shopkeeper's wife, the comic footman who turns out to be a duke in disguise, and the young scape-grace who gives the author his excuse for dragging in a fast young woman. All as old and stale as a fried fish shop on a winter morning.

THE COUNT. But—

GUNN [*interrupting him*] I know what youre going to say, Count. Youre going to say that the whole thing seems to you to be quite new and unusual and original. The naval lieutenant is a Frenchman who cracks up the English and runs down the French: the hackneyed old Shaw touch. The characters are second-rate middle class, instead of being dukes and millionaires. The heroine gets kicked through the mud: real mud. Theres no plot. All the old stage conventions and puppets without the old ingenuity and the old enjoyment. And a feeble air of intel-lectual pretentiousness kept up all through to persuade you that if the author hasnt written a good play it's because he's too clever to stoop to anything so commonplace. And you three experienced men have sat through all this, and cant tell me who wrote it! Why, the play bears the author's signa-ture in every line.

BANNAL. Who?

GUNN. Granville-Barker, of course. Why, old Gilbey is straight out of The Madras House.

BANNAL. Poor old Barker!

VAUGHAN. Utter nonsense! Cant you see the difference in style?

BANNAL. No.

VAUGHAN [*contemptuously*] Do you know what style is?

BANNAL. Well, I suppose youd call Trotter's uniform style. But it's not my style—since you ask me.

VAUGHAN. To me it's perfectly plain who wrote that play. To begin with, it's intensely disagreeable. Therefore it's not by Barrie, in spite of the footman, whos cribbed from The Admirable Crichton. H e was an earl, you may remember. You notice, too, the author's offensive habit of saying silly things that have no real sense in them when you come to examine them, just to set all the fools in the house giggling. Then what does it all come to? An attempt to expose the supposed hypocrisy of the Puritan middle class in England: people just as good as the author, anyhow. With, of course, the inevit-able improper female: the Mrs Tanqueray, Iris, and so forth. Well, if you cant recognize the author of that, youve mistaken your profession: thats all I have to say.

BANNAL. Why are you so down on Pinero? And what about that touch that Gunn spotted? the Frenchman's long speech. I believe it's Shaw.

GUNN. Rubbish!

VAUGHAN. Rot! You may put that idea out of your head, Bannal. Poor as this play is, theres the note of passion in it. You feel somehow that beneath all the assumed levity of that poor waif and stray, she really loves Bobby and will be a good wife to him. Now Ive repeatedly proved that Shaw is physiologically incapable of the note of passion.

BANNAL. Yes, I know. Intellect without emotion. Thats right. I always say that myself. A giant brain, if you ask me; but no heart.

GUNN. Oh, shut up, Bannal. This crude medieval psychology of heart and brain— Shakespear would have called it liver and wits—is really schoolboyish. Surely weve had enough of second-hand Schopenhauer. Even such a played-out old back number as Ibsen would have been ashamed of it. Heart and brain, indeed!

VAUGHAN. You have neither one nor the other, Gunn. Youre dekkadent.

GUNN. Decādent! How I love that early Victorian word!

VAUGHAN. Well, at all events, you cant deny that the characters in this play are quite distinguishable from one another. That proves it's not by Shaw, because all Shaw's characters are himself: mere puppets stuck up to spout Shaw. It's only the actors that make them seem different.

BANNAL. There can be no doubt of that: everybody knows it. But Shaw doesnt write his plays as plays. All he wants to do is to insult everybody all round and set us talking about him.

TROTTER [wearily] And naturally, here we are all talking about him. For heaven's sake, let us change the subject.

VAUGHAN. Still, my articles about Shaw—

GUNN. Oh, stow it, Vaughan. Drop it. What Ive always told you about Shaw is—

BANNAL. There you go, Shaw, Shaw, Shaw! Do chuck it. If you want to know my opinion about Shaw—

TROTTER ⎫ ⎧ No, please, we dont.
VAUGHAN ⎬ [yelling] ⎨ Shut your head, Bannal.
GUNN ⎭ ⎩ Oh do drop it.

The deafened Count puts his fingers in his ears and flies from the centre of the group to its outskirts, behind Vaughan.

BANNAL [sulkily] Oh, very well. Sorry I spoke, I'm sure.

TROTTER ⎫ ⎧ Shaw—
VAUGHAN ⎬ [beginning again simultaneously] ⎨ Shaw—
GUNN ⎭ ⎩ Shaw—

They are cut short by the entry of Fanny through the curtains. She is almost in tears.

FANNY [coming between Trotter and Gunn] I'm so sorry, gentlemen. And it was such a success when I read it to the Cambridge Fabian Society!

TROTTER. Miss O'Dowda: I was about to tell these gentlemen what I guessed before the curtain rose: that you are the author of the play. [General amazement and consternation].

FANNY. And you all think it beastly. You hate it. You think I'm a conceited idiot, and that I shall never be able to write anything decent.

She is almost weeping. A wave of sympathy carries away the critics.

VAUGHAN. No, no. Why, I was just saying that it must have been written by Pinero. Didnt I, Gunn?

FANNY [enormously flattered] Really?

TROTTER. I thought Pinero was much too popular for the Cambridge Fabian Society.

FANNY. Oh yes, of course; but still— Oh, did you really say that, Mr Vaughan?

GUNN. I owe you an apology, Miss O'Dowda. I said it was by Barker.

FANNY [radiant] Granville-Barker! Oh, you couldnt really have thought it so fine as that.

BANNAL. I said Bernard Shaw.

FANNY. Oh, of course it would be a little like Bernard Shaw. The Fabian touch, you know.

BANNAL [coming to her encouragingly] A jolly good little play, Miss O'Dowda. Mind: I dont say it's like one of Shakespear's— Hamlet or The Lady of Lyons, you know— but still, a firstrate little bit of work. [He shakes her hand].

GUNN [following Bannal's example] I also, Miss O'Dowda. Capital. Charming. [He shakes hands].

VAUGHAN [with maudlin solemnity] Only be true to yourself, Miss O'Dowda. Keep serious. Give up making silly jokes. Sustain the note of passion. And youll do great things.

FANNY. You think I have a future?

TROTTER. You have a past, Miss O'Dowda.

FANNY [looking apprehensively at her father] Sh-sh-sh!

THE COUNT. A past! What do you mean, Mr Trotter?

TROTTER [to Fanny] You cant deceive me. That bit about the police was real. Youre a Suffraget, Miss O'Dowda. You were on that Deputation.

THE COUNT. Fanny: is this true?

FANNY. It is. I did a month with Lady Constance Lytton; and I'm prouder of it than I ever was of anything or ever shall be again.

TROTTER. Is that any reason why you should stuff naughty plays down my throat?

FANNY. Yes: itll teach you what it feels like to be forcibly fed.

THE COUNT. She will never return to Venice. I feel now as I felt when the Campanile fell.

Savoyard comes in through the curtains.

SAVOYARD [to the Count] Would you mind coming to say a word of congratulation to the company? Theyre rather upset at having had no curtain call.

THE COUNT. Certainly, certainly. I'm afraid Ive been rather remiss. Let us go on the stage, gentlemen.

The curtains are drawn, revealing the last scene of the play and the actors on the stage. The Count, Savoyard, the critics, and Fanny join them, shaking hands and congratulating.

THE COUNT. Whatever we may think of the play, gentlemen, I'm sure you will agree with me that there can be only one opinion about the acting.

THE CRITICS. Hear, hear! [They start the applause].

THE END

XXI
ANDROCLES AND THE LION
A FABLE PLAY

PROLOGUE

Overture: forest sounds, roaring of lions, Christian hymn faintly.

A jungle path. A lion's roar, a melancholy suffering roar, comes from the jungle. It is repeated nearer. The lion limps from the jungle on three legs, holding up his right forepaw, in which a huge thorn sticks. He sits down and contemplates it. He licks it. He shakes it. He tries to extract it by scraping it along the ground, and hurts himself worse. He roars piteously. He licks it again. Tears drop from his eyes. He limps painfully off the path and lies down under the trees, exhausted with pain. Heaving a long sigh, like wind in a trombone, he goes to sleep.

Androcles and his wife Megaera come along the path. He is a small, thin, ridiculous little man who might be any age from thirty to fifty-five. He has sandy hair, watery compassionate blue eyes, sensitive nostrils, and a very presentable forehead; but his good points go no further: his arms and legs and back, though wiry of their kind, look shrivelled and starved. He carries a big bundle, is very poorly clad, and seems tired and hungry.

His wife is a rather handsome pampered slattern, well fed and in the prime of life. She has nothing to carry, and has a stout stick to help her along.

MEGAERA [suddenly throwing down her stick] I wont go another step.

ANDROCLES [pleading wearily] Oh, not again, dear. Whats the good of stopping every two miles and saying you wont go another step? We must get on to the next village before night. There are wild beasts in this wood: lions, they say.

MEGAERA. I dont believe a word of it. You are always threatening me with wild beasts to make me walk the very soul out of my body when I can hardly drag one foot before another. We havnt seen a single lion yet.

ANDROCLES. Well, dear, do you want to see one?

MEGAERA [tearing the bundle from his back] You cruel brute, you dont care how tired I am, or what becomes of me [she throws the bundle on the ground]: always thinking of yourself. Self! self! self! always yourself! [She sits down on the bundle].

ANDROCLES [sitting down sadly on the ground with his elbows on his knees and his head in his hands] We all have to think of ourselves occasionally, dear.

MEGAERA. A man ought to think of his wife sometimes.

ANDROCLES. He cant always help it, dear. You make me think of you a good deal. Not that I blame you.

MEGAERA. Blame me! I should think not indeed. Is it my fault that I'm married to you?

ANDROCLES. No, dear: that is my fault.

MEGAERA. Thats a nice thing to say to me. Arnt you happy with me?

ANDROCLES. I dont complain, my love.

MEGAERA. You ought to be ashamed of yourself.

ANDROCLES. I am, my dear.

MEGAERA. Youre not: you glory in it.

ANDROCLES. In what, darling?

MEGAERA. In everything. In making me a slave, and making yourself a laughing-stock. It's not fair. You get me the name of being a shrew with your meek ways, always talking as if butter wouldnt melt in your mouth. And just because I look a big strong woman, and because I'm goodhearted and a bit hasty, and because youre always driving me to do things I'm sorry for afterwards, people say "Poor man: what a life his wife leads him!" Oh, if they only knew! And you think I dont know. But I do, I do, [screaming] I do.

ANDROCLES. Yes, my dear: I know you do.

MEGAERA. Then why dont you treat me properly and be a good husband to me?

ANDROCLES. What can I do, my dear?

MEGAERA. What can you do! You can return to your duty, and come back to your home and your friends, and sacrifice to the gods as all respectable people do, instead of having us hunted out of house and home for being dirty disreputable blaspheming atheists.

ANDROCLES. I'm not an atheist, dear: I am a Christian.

MEGAERA. Well, isnt that the same thing, only ten times worse? Everybody knows that the Christians are the very lowest of the low.

ANDROCLES. Just like us, dear.

MEGAERA. Speak for yourself. Dont you dare to compare me to common people. My father owned his own public-house; and sorrowful was the day for me when you first came drinking in our bar.

ANDROCLES. I confess I was addicted to it, dear. But I gave it up when I became a Christian.

MEGAERA. Youd much better have remained a drunkard. I can forgive a man being addicted to drink: it's only natural; and I dont deny I like a drop myself sometimes. What I cant stand is your being addicted to Christianity. And whats worse again, your being addicted to animals. How is any woman to keep her house clean when you bring in every stray cat and lost cur and lame duck in the whole countryside? You took the bread out of my mouth to feed them: you know you did: dont attempt to deny it.

ANDROCLES. Only when they were hungry and you were getting too stout, dearie.

MEGAERA. Yes: insult me, do. [Rising] Oh! I wont bear it another moment. You used to sit and talk to those dumb brute beasts for hours, when you hadnt a word for me.

ANDROCLES. They never answered back, darling. [He rises and again shoulders the bundle].

MEGAERA. Well, if youre fonder of animals than of your own wife, you can live with them here in the jungle. Ive had enough of them and enough of you. I'm going back. I'm going home.

ANDROCLES [barring the way back] No, dearie: dont take on like that. We cant go back. Weve sold everything: we should starve; and I should be sent to Rome and thrown to the lions—

MEGAERA. Serve you right! I wish the lions joy of you. [Screaming] Are you going to get out of my way and let me go home?

ANDROCLES. No, dear—

MEGAERA. Then I'll make my way through the forest; and when I'm eaten by the wild beasts youll know what a wife youve lost. [She dashes into the jungle and nearly falls over the sleeping lion]. Oh! Oh! Andy! Andy! [She totters back and collapses into the arms of Androcles, who, crushed by her weight, falls on his bundle].

ANDROCLES [extracting himself from beneath her and slapping her hands in great anxiety] What is it, my precious, my pet? Whats the matter? [He raises her head. Speechless with terror, she points in the direction of the sleeping lion. He steals cautiously towards the spot indicated by Megaera. She rises with an effort and totters after him].

MEGAERA. No, Andy: youll be killed. Come back.

The lion utters a long snoring sigh. Androcles sees the lion, and recoils fainting into the arms of Megaera, who falls back on the bundle. They roll apart and lie staring in terror at one another.

The lion is heard groaning heavily in the jungle.

ANDROCLES [*whispering*] Did you see? A lion.

MEGAERA [*despairing*] The gods have sent him to punish us because youre a Christian. Take me away, Andy. Save me.

ANDROCLES [*rising*] Meggy: theres one chance for you. Itll take him pretty nigh twenty minutes to eat me (I'm rather stringy and tough) and you can escape in less time than that.

MEGAERA. Oh, dont talk about eating. [*The lion rises with a great groan and limps towards them*]. Oh! [*She faints*].

ANDROCLES [*quaking, but keeping between the lion and Megaera*] Dont you come near my wife, do you hear? [*The lion groans. Androcles can hardly stand for trembling*]. Meggy: run. Run for your life. If I take my eye off him, it's all up. [*The lion holds up his wounded paw and flaps it piteously before Androcles*]. Oh, he's lame, poor old chap! He's got a thorn in his paw. A frightfully big thorn. [*Full of sympathy*] Oh, poor old man! Did um get an awful thorn into um's tootsums wootsums? Has it made um too sick to eat a nice little Christian man for um's breakfast? Oh, a nice little Christian man will get um's thorn out for um; and then um shall eat the nice Christian man and the nice Christian man's nice big tender wifey pifey. [*The lion responds by moans of self-pity*]. Yes, yes, yes, yes, yes. Now, now [*taking the paw in his hand*], um is not to bite and not to scratch, not even if it hurts a very very little. Now make velvet paws. Thats right. [*He pulls gingerly at the thorn. The lion, with an angry yell of pain, jerks back his paw so abruptly that Androcles is thrown on his back*]. Steadeee! Oh, did the nasty cruel little Christian man hurt the sore paw? [*The lion moans assentingly but apologetically*]. Well, one more little pull and it will be all over. Just one little, little, leetle pull; and then um will live happily ever after. [*He gives the thorn another pull. The lion roars and snaps his jaws with a terrifying clash*]. Oh, mustnt frighten um's good kind doctor, um's affectionate nursey. That didnt hurt at all: not a bit. Just one more. Just to shew how the brave big lion can bear pain, not like the little crybaby Christian man. Oopsh! [*The thorn comes out. The lion yells with pain, and shakes his paw wildly*]. Thats it! [*Holding up the thorn*]. Now it's out. Now lick um's paw to take away the nasty inflammation. See?

[*He licks his own hand. The lion nods intelligently and licks his paw industriously*] Clever little liony-piony! Understands um's dear old friend Andy Wandy. [*The lion licks his face*]. Yes, kissums Andy Wandy. [*The lion, wagging his tail violently, rises on his hind legs, and embraces Androcles, who makes a wry face and cries*] Velvet paws! Velvet paws! [*The lion draws in his claws*]. Thats right. [*He embraces the lion, who finally takes the end of his tail in one paw, places that tight round Androcles' waist, resting it on his hip. Androcles takes the other paw in his hand, stretches out his arm, and the two waltz rapturously round and round and finally away through the jungle*].

MEGAERA [*who has revived during the waltz*] Oh, you coward, you havnt danced with me for years; and now you go off dancing with a great brute beast that you havnt known for ten minutes and that wants to eat your own wife. Coward. Coward! Coward! [*She rushes off after them into the jungle*].

ACT I

Evening. The end of three converging roads to Rome. Three triumphal arches span them where they debouch on a square at the gate of the city. Looking north through the arches one can see the campagna threaded by the three long dusty tracks. On the east and west sides of the square are long stone benches. An old beggar sits on the east side, his bowl at his feet.

Through the eastern arch a squad of Roman soldiers tramps along escorting a batch of Christian prisoners of both sexes and all ages, among them one Lavinia, a good-looking resolute young woman, apparently of higher social standing than her fellow-prisoners. A centurion, carrying his vinewood cudgel, trudges alongside the squad, on its right, in command of it. All are tired and dusty; but the soldiers are dogged and indifferent, the Christians lighthearted and determined to treat their hardships as a joke and encourage one another.

A bugle is heard far behind on the road, where the rest of the cohort is following.

CENTURION [*stopping*] Halt! Orders from the Captain. [*They halt and wait*]. Now then, you Christians, none of your larks. The captain's coming. Mind you behave yourselves. No singing. Look respectful. Look serious, if youre capable of it. See that big building over there! Thats the Coliseum. Thats where youll be thrown to the lions or set to fight the gladiators presently. Think of that; and itll help you to behave properly before the captain. [*The Captain arrives*]. Attention! Salute! [*The soldiers salute*].

A CHRISTIAN [*cheerfully*] God bless you, Captain!

THE CENTURION [*scandalized*] Silence!

The Captain, a patrician, handsome, about thirty-five, very cold and distinguished, very superior and authoritative, steps up on a stone seat at the west side of the square, behind the centurion, so as to dominate the others more effectually.

THE CAPTAIN. Centurion.

THE CENTURION [*standing at attention and saluting*] Sir?

THE CAPTAIN [*speaking stiffly and officially*] You will remind your men, Centurion, that we are now entering Rome. You will instruct them that once inside the gates of Rome they are in the presence of the Emperor. You will make them understand that the lax discipline of the march cannot be permitted here. You will instruct them to shave every day, not every week. You will impress on them particularly that there must be an end to the profanity and blasphemy of singing Christian hymns on the march. I have to reprimand you, Centurion, for not only allowing this, but actually doing it yourself.

THE CENTURION [*apologetic*] The men march better, Captain.

THE CAPTAIN. No doubt. For that reason an exception is made in the case of the march called Onward Christian Soldiers. This may be sung, except when marching through the forum or within hearing of the Emperor's palace; but the words must be altered to "Throw them to the Lions."

The Christians burst into shrieks of uncontrollable laughter, to the great scandal of the Centurion.

CENTURION. Silence! Silen-n-n-n-nce! Wheres your behavior? Is that the way to listen to an officer? [*To the Captain*] Thats what we have to put up with from these Christians every day, sir. Theyre always laughing and joking something scandalous. Theyve no religion: thats how it is.

LAVINIA. But I think the Captain meant us to laugh, Centurion. It was so funny.

CENTURION. Youll find out how funny it is when youre thrown to the lions tomorrow. [*To the Captain, who looks displeased*] Beg pardon, Sir. [*To the Christians*] Silennnnce!

THE CAPTAIN. You are to instruct your men that all intimacy with Christian prisoners must now cease. The men have fallen into habits of dependence upon the prisoners, especially the female prisoners, for cooking, repairs to uniforms, writing letters, and advice in their private affairs. In a Roman soldier such dependence is inadmissible. Let me see no more of it whilst we are in the city. Further, your orders are that in addressing Christian prisoners, the manners and tone of your men must express abhorrence and contempt. Any shortcoming in this respect will be regarded as a breach of discipline. [*He turns to the prisoners*] Prisoners.

CENTURION [*fiercely*] Prisonerrrrrs! Tention! Silence!

THE CAPTAIN. I call your attention, prisoners, to the fact that you may be called on to appear in the Imperial Circus at any time from tomorrow onwards according to the requirements of the managers. I may inform you that as there is a shortage of Christians just now, you may expect to be called on very soon.

LAVINIA. What will they do to us, Captain?

CENTURION. Silence!

THE CAPTAIN. The women will be conducted into the arena with the wild beasts of the Imperial Menagerie, and will suffer the consequences. The men, if of an age to bear arms, will be given weapons to defend themselves, if they choose, against the Imperial Gladiators.

LAVINIA. Captain: is there no hope that this cruel persecution—

CENTURION [*shocked*] Silence! Hold your tongue, there. Persecution, indeed!

THE CAPTAIN [*unmoved and somewhat sardonic*] Persecution is not a term applicable to the acts of the Emperor. The Emperor is the Defender of the Faith. In throwing you to the lions he will be upholding the interests of religion in Rome. If you were to throw him to the lions, that would no doubt be persecution.

The Christians again laugh heartily.

CENTURION [*horrified*] Silence, I tell you! Keep silence there. Did anyone ever hear the like of this?

LAVINIA. Captain: there will be nobody to appreciate your jokes when we are gone.

THE CAPTAIN [*unshaken in his official delivery*] I call the attention of the female prisoner Lavinia to the fact that as the Emperor is a divine personage, her imputation of cruelty is not only treason, but sacrilege. I point out to her further that there is no foundation for the charge, as the Emperor does not desire that any prisoner should suffer; nor can any Christian be harmed save through his or her own obstinacy. All that is necessary is to sacrifice to the gods: a simple and convenient ceremony effected by dropping a pinch of incense on the altar, after which the prisoner is at once set free. Under such circumstances you have only your own perverse folly to blame if you suffer. I suggest to you that if you cannot burn a morsel of incense as a matter of conviction, you might at least do so as a matter of good taste, to avoid shocking the religious convictions of your fellow citizens. I am aware that these considerations do not weigh with Christians; but it is my duty to call your attention to them in order that you may have no ground for complaining of your treatment, or of accusing the Emperor of cruelty when he is shewing you the most signal clemency. Looked at from this point of view, every Christian who has perished in the arena has really committed suicide.

LAVINIA. Captain: your jokes are too grim. Do not think it is easy for us to die. Our faith makes life far stronger and more wonderful in us than when we walked in darkness and had nothing to live for. Death is harder for us than for you: the martyr's agony is as bitter as his triumph is glorious.

THE CAPTAIN [*rather troubled, addressing her personally and gravely*] A martyr, Lavinia, is a fool. Your death will prove nothing.

LAVINIA. Then why kill me?

THE CAPTAIN. I mean that truth, if there be any truth, needs no martyrs.

LAVINIA. No; but my faith, like your sword, needs testing. Can you test your sword except by staking your life on it?

THE CAPTAIN [*suddenly resuming his official tone*] I call the attention of the female prisoner to the fact that Christians are not allowed to draw the Emperor's officers into arguments and put questions to them for which the military regulations provide no answer. [*The Christians titter*].

LAVINIA. Captain: how c a n you?

THE CAPTAIN. I call the female prisoner's attention specially to the fact that four comfortable homes have been offered her by officers of this regiment, of which she can

have her choice the moment she chooses to sacrifice as all wellbred Roman ladies do. I have no more to say to the prisoners.

CENTURION. Dismiss! But stay where you are.

THE CAPTAIN. Centurion: you will remain here with your men in charge of the prisoners until the arrival of three Christian prisoners in the custody of a cohort of the tenth legion. Among these prisoners you will particularly identify an armorer named Ferrovius, of dangerous character and great personal strength, and a Greek tailor reputed to be a sorcerer, by name Androcles. You will add the three to your charge here and march them all to the Coliseum, where you will deliver them into the custody of the master of the gladiators and take his receipt, countersigned by the keeper of the beasts and the acting manager. You understand your instructions?

CENTURION. Yes, sir.

THE CAPTAIN. Dismiss. [*He throws off his air of parade, and descends from his perch. The Centurion seats himself on it and prepares for a nap, whilst his men stand at ease. The Christians sit down on the west side of the square, glad to rest. Lavinia alone remains standing to speak to the Captain*].

LAVINIA. Captain: is this man who is to join us the famous Ferrovius, who has made such wonderful conversions in the northern cities?

THE CAPTAIN. Yes. We are warned that he has the strength of an elephant and the temper of a mad bull. Also that he is stark mad. Not a model Christian, it would seem.

LAVINIA. You need not fear him if he is a Christian, Captain.

THE CAPTAIN [*coldly*] I shall not fear him in any case, Lavinia.

LAVINIA [*her eyes dancing*] How brave of you, Captain!

THE CAPTAIN. You are right: it was a silly thing to say. [*In a lower tone, humane and urgent*] Lavinia: do Christians know how to love?

LAVINIA [*composedly*] Yes, Captain: they love even their enemies.

THE CAPTAIN. Is that easy?

LAVINIA. Very easy, Captain, when their enemies are as handsome as you.

THE CAPTAIN. Lavinia: you are laughing at me.

LAVINIA. At you, Captain! Impossible.

THE CAPTAIN. Then you are flirting with me, which is worse. Dont be foolish.

LAVINIA. But such a very handsome captain.

THE CAPTAIN. Incorrigible! [*Urgently*] Listen to me. The men in that audience tomorrow will be the vilest of voluptuaries: men in whom the only passion excited by a beautiful woman is a lust to see her tortured and torn shrieking limb from limb. It is a crime to gratify that passion. It is offering yourself for violation by the whole rabble of the streets and the riff-raff of the court at the same time. Why will you not choose rather a kindly love and an honorable alliance?

LAVINIA. They cannot violate my soul. I alone can do that by sacrificing to false gods.

THE CAPTAIN. Sacrifice then to the true God. What does his name matter? We call him Jupiter. The Greeks call him Zeus. Call him what you will as you drop the incense on the altar flame: He will understand.

LAVINIA. No. I couldnt. That is the strange thing, Captain, that a little pinch of incense should make all that difference. Religion is such a great thing that when I meet really religious people we are friends at once, no matter what name we give to the divine will that made us and moves us. Oh, do you think that I, a woman, would quarrel with you for sacrificing to a woman god like Diana, if Diana meant to you what Christ means to me? No: we should kneel side by side before her altar like two children. But when men who believe neither in my god nor in their own—men who do not know the meaning of the word religion—when these men drag me to the foot of an iron statue that has become the symbol of the terror and darkness through which they walk, of their cruelty and greed, of their hatred of God and their oppression of man—when they ask me to pledge my soul before the people that this hideous idol is God, and that all this wickedness and falsehood is divine truth, I cannot do it, not if they could put a thousand cruel deaths on me. I tell you, it is physically impossible. Listen, Captain: did you ever try to catch a mouse in your hand? Once there was a dear little mouse that used to come out and play on my table as I was reading. I wanted to take him in my hand and caress him; and sometimes he got among my books so that he could not escape me

when I stretched out my hand. And I did stretch out my hand; but it always came back in spite of me. I was not afraid of him in my heart; but my hand refused: it is not in the nature of my hand to touch a mouse. Well, Captain, if I took a pinch of incense in my hand and stretched it out over the altar fire, my hand would come back. My body would be true to my faith even if you could corrupt my mind. And all the time I should believe more in Diana than my persecutors have ever believed in anything. Can you understand that?

THE CAPTAIN [*simply*] Yes: I understand that. But my hand would not come back. The hand that holds the sword has been trained not to come back from anything but victory.

LAVINIA. Not even from death?

THE CAPTAIN. Least of all from death.

LAVINIA. Then I must not come back from death either. A woman has to be braver than a soldier.

THE CAPTAIN. Prouder, you mean.

LAVINIA [*startled*] Prouder! You call our courage pride!

THE CAPTAIN. There is no such thing as courage: there is only pride. You Christians are the proudest devils on earth.

LAVINIA [*hurt*] Pray God then my pride may never become a false pride. [*She turns away as if she did not wish to continue the conversation, but softens and says to him with a smile*] Thank you for trying to save me.

THE CAPTAIN. I knew it was no use; but one tries in spite of one's knowledge.

LAVINIA. Something stirs, even in the iron breast of a Roman soldier?

THE CAPTAIN. It will soon be iron again. I have seen many women die, and forgotten them in a week.

LAVINIA. Remember me for a fortnight, handsome Captain. I shall be watching you, perhaps.

THE CAPTAIN. From the skies? Do not deceive yourself, Lavinia. There is no future for you beyond the grave.

LAVINIA. What does that matter? Do you think I am only running away from the terrors of life into the comfort of heaven? If there were no future, or if the future were one of torment, I should have to go just the same. The hand of God is upon me.

THE CAPTAIN. Yes: when all is said, we are both patricians, Lavinia, and must die for our beliefs. Farewell. [*He offers her his hand. She takes it and presses it. He walks away, trim and calm. She looks after him for a moment, and cries a little as he disappears through the eastern arch. A trumpet-call is heard from the road through the western arch*].

CENTURION [*waking up and rising*] Cohort of the tenth with prisoners. Two file out with me to receive them. [*He goes out through the western arch, followed by four soldiers in two files*].

Lentulus and Metellus come into the square from the west side with a little retinue of servants. Both are young courtiers, dressed in the extremity of fashion. Lentulus, is slender, fair-haired, epicene. Metellus is manly, compactly built, olive skinned, not a talker.

LENTULUS. Christians, by Jove! Lets chaff them.

METELLUS. Awful brutes. If you knew as much about them as I do you wouldnt want to chaff them. Leave them to the lions.

LENTULUS [*indicating Lavinia, who is still looking towards the arches after the Captain*] That woman's got a figure. [*He walks past her, staring at her invitingly; but she is preoccupied and is not conscious of him*]. Do you turn the other cheek when they kiss you?

LAVINIA [*starting*] What?

LENTULUS. Do you turn the other cheek when they kiss you, fascinating Christian?

LAVINIA. Dont be foolish. [*To Metellus, who has remained on her right, so that she is between them*] Please dont let your friend behave like a cad before the soldiers. How are they to respect and obey patricians if they see them behaving like street boys? [*Sharply to Lentulus*] Pull yourself together, man. Hold your head up. Keep the corners of your mouth firm; and treat me respectfully. What do you take me for?

LENTULUS [*irresolutely*] Look here, you know: I—you—I—

LAVINIA. Stuff! Go about your business. [*She turns decisively away and sits down with her comrades, leaving him disconcerted*].

METELLUS. You didnt get much out of that. I told you they were brutes.

LENTULUS. Plucky little filly! I suppose she thinks I care. [*With an air of indifference he strolls with Metellus to the east side of the square, where they stand watching the return of the Centurion through the western arch with his men, escorting three prisoners: Ferrovius, Androcles, and Spintho. Ferrovius is a powerful, choleric man*] in the prime of life, with large nostrils, staring eyes, and a thick neck: a man whose sensibilities are keen and violent to the verge of madness. Spintho is a debauchee, the wreck of a good-looking man gone hopelessly to the bad. Androcles is overwhelmed with grief, and is restraining his tears with great difficulty].

THE CENTURION [*to Lavinia*] Here are some pals for you. This little bit is Ferrovius that you talk so much about. [*Ferrovius turns on him threateningly. The Centurion holds up his left forefinger in admonition*] Now remember that youre a Christian, and that youve got to return good for evil. [*Ferrovius controls himself convulsively; moves away from temptation to the east side near Lentulus; clasps his hands in silent prayer; and throws himself on his knees*]. Thats the way to manage them, eh! This fine fellow [*indicating Androcles, who comes to his left, and makes Lavinia a heart-broken salutation*] is a sorcerer. A Greek tailor, he is. A real sorcerer, too: no mistake about it. The tenth marches with a leopard at the head of the column. He made a pet of the leopard; and now he's crying at being parted from it. [*Androcles sniffs lamentably*]. Aint you, old chap? Well, cheer up, we march with a Billy goat [*Androcles brightens up*] thats killed two leopards and ate a turkey-cock. You can have him for a pet if you like. [*Androcles, quite consoled, goes past the Centurion to Lavinia, and sits down contentedly on the ground on her left*]. This dirty dog [*collaring Spintho*] is a real Christian. He mobs the temples, he does [*at each accusation he gives the neck of Spintho's tunic a twist*]; he goes smashing things mad drunk, he does; he steals the gold vessels, he does; he assaults the priestesses, he does— yah! [*He flings Spintho into the middle of the group of prisoners*]. Youre the sort that makes duty a pleasure, you are.

SPINTHO [*gasping*] Thats it: strangle me. Kick me. Beat me. Revile me. Our Lord was beaten and reviled. Thats my way to heaven. Every martyr goes to heaven, no matter what he's done. That is so, isnt it, brother?

CENTURION. Well, if youre going to heaven, *I* dont want to go there. I wouldnt be seen with you.

LENTULUS. Haw! Good! [*Indicating the kneeling Ferrovius*]. Is this one of the turn-the-other-cheek gentlemen, Centurion?

CENTURION. Yes, sir. Lucky for you too, sir, if you want to take any liberties with him.

LENTULUS [*to Ferrovius*] You turn the other

cheek when youre struck, I'm told.

FERROVIUS [*slowly turning his great eyes on him*] Yes, by the grace of God, I do, now.

LENTULUS. Not that youre a coward, of course; but out of pure piety.

FERROVIUS. I fear God more than man; at least I try to.

LENTULUS. Lets see. [*He strikes him on the cheek. Androcles makes a wild movement to rise and interfere; but Lavinia holds him down, watching Ferrovius intently. Ferrovius, without flinching, turns the other cheek. Lentulus, rather out of countenance, titters foolishly, and strikes him again feebly*]. You know, I should feel ashamed if I let myself be struck like that, and took it lying down. But then I'm not a Christian: I'm a man. [*Ferrovius rises impressively and towers over him. Lentulus becomes white with terror; and a shade of green flickers in his cheek for a moment*].

FERROVIUS [*with the calm of a steam hammer*] I have not always been faithful. The first man who struck me as you have just struck me was a stronger man than you: he hit me harder than I expected. I was tempted and fell; and it was then that I first tasted bitter shame. I never had a happy moment after that until I had knelt and asked his forgiveness by his bedside in the hospital. [*Putting his hands on Lentulus's shoulders with paternal weight*]. But now I have learnt to resist with a strength that is not my own. I am not ashamed now, nor angry.

LENTULUS [*uneasily*] Er—good evening. [*He tries to move away*].

FERROVIUS [*gripping his shoulders*] Oh, do not harden your heart, young man. Come: try for yourself whether our way is not better than yours. I will now strike you on one cheek; and you will turn the other and learn how much better you will feel than if you gave way to the promptings of anger. [*He holds him with one hand and clenches the other fist*].

LENTULUS. Centurion: I call on you to protect me.

CENTURION. You asked for it, sir. It's no business of ours. Youve had two whacks at him. Better pay him a trifle and square it that way.

LENTULUS. Yes, of course. [*To Ferrovius*] It was only a bit of fun, I assure you; I meant no harm. Here. [*He proffers a gold coin*].

FERROVIUS [*taking it and throwing it to the old beggar, who snatches it up eagerly, and hobbles off to spend it*] Give all thou hast to the poor. Come, friend: courage! I may hurt your body for a moment; but your soul will rejoice in the victory of the spirit over the flesh. [*He prepares to strike*].

ANDROCLES. Easy, Ferrovius, easy: you broke the last man's jaw.

Lentulus, with a moan of terror, attempts to fly; but Ferrovius holds him ruthlessly.

FERROVIUS. Yes; but I saved his soul. What matters a broken jaw?

LENTULUS. Dont touch me, do you hear? The law—

FERROVIUS. The law will throw me to the lions tomorrow: what worse could it do were I to slay you? Pray for strength; and it shall be given to you.

LENTULUS. Let me go. Your religion forbids you to strike me.

FERROVIUS. On the contrary, it commands me to strike you. How can you turn the other cheek, if you are not first struck on the one cheek?

LENTULUS [*almost in tears*] But I'm convinced already that what you said is quite right. I apologize for striking you.

FERROVIUS [*greatly pleased*] My son: have I softened your heart? Has the good seed fallen in a fruitful place? Are your feet turning towards a better path?

LENTULUS [*abjectly*] Yes, yes. Theres a great deal in what you say.

FERROVIUS [*radiant*] Join us. Come to the lions. Come to suffering and death.

LENTULUS [*falling on his knees and bursting into tears*] Oh, help me. Mother! mother!

FERROVIUS. These tears will water your soul and make it bring forth good fruit, my son. God has greatly blessed my efforts at conversion. Shall I tell you a miracle—yes, a miracle—wrought by me in Cappadocia? A young man—just such a one as you, with golden hair like yours—scoffed at and struck me as you scoffed at and struck me. I sat up all night with that youth wrestling for his soul; and in the morning not only was he a Christian, but his hair was as white as snow. [*Lentulus falls in a dead faint*]. There, there: take him away. The spirit has overwrought him, poor lad. Carry him gently to his house; and leave the rest to heaven.

CENTURION. Take him home. [*The servants, intimidated, hastily carry him out. Metellus is about to follow, when Ferrovius lays his hand on his shoulder*].

FERROVIUS. You are his friend, young man. You will see that he is taken safely home.

METELLUS [*with awestruck civility*] Certainly, sir. I shall do whatever you think best. Most happy to have made your acquaintance, I'm sure. You may depend on me. Good evening, sir.

FERROVIUS [*with unction*] The blessing of heaven upon you and him.

Metellus follows Lentulus. The Centurion returns to his seat to resume his interrupted nap. The deepest awe has settled on the spectators. Ferrovius, with a long sigh of happiness, goes to Lavinia, and offers her his hand.

LAVINIA [*taking it*] So that is how you convert people, Ferrovius.

FERROVIUS. Yes: there has been a blessing on my work in spite of my unworthiness and my backslidings—all through my wicked, devilish temper. This man—

ANDROCLES [*hastily*] Dont slap me on the back, brother. She knows you mean me.

FERROVIUS. How I wish I were weak like our brother here! for then I should perhaps be meek and gentle like him. And yet there seems to be a special providence that makes my trials less than his. I hear tales of the crowd scoffing and casting stones and reviling the brethren; but when I come, all this stops: my influence calms the passions of the mob: they listen to me in silence; and infidels are often converted by a straight heart-to-heart talk with me. Every day I feel happier, more confident. Every day lightens the load of the great terror.

LAVINIA. The great terror? What is that?

Ferrovius shakes his head and does not answer. He sits down beside her on her left, and buries his face in his hands in gloomy meditation.

ANDROCLES. Well, you see, sister, he's never quite sure of himself. Suppose at the last moment in the arena, with the gladiators there to fight him, one of them was to say anything to annoy him, he might forget himself and lay that gladiator out.

LAVINIA. That would be splendid.

FERROVIUS [*springing up in horror*] What!

ANDROCLES. Oh, sister!

FERROVIUS. Splendid to betray my master, like Peter! Splendid to act like any common blackguard in the day of my proving! Woman: you are no Christian. [*He moves away from her to the middle of the square, as if her neighborhood contaminated him*].

LAVINIA [*laughing*] You know, Ferrovius, I am not always a Christian. I dont think anybody is. There are moments when I forget all about it, and something comes out quite naturally as it did then.

SPINTHO. What does it matter? If you die in the arena, youll be a martyr; and all martyrs go to heaven, no matter what they have done. Thats so, isnt it, Ferrovius?

FERROVIUS. Yes: that is so, if we are faithful to the end.

LAVINIA. I'm not so sure.

SPINTHO. Dont say that. Thats blasphemy. Dont say that, I tell you. We shall be saved, no matter WHAT we do.

LAVINIA. Perhaps you men will all go into heaven bravely and in triumph, with your heads erect and golden trumpets sounding for you. But I am sure I shall only be allowed to squeeze myself in through a little crack in the gate after a great deal of begging. I am not good always: I have moments only.

SPINTHO. Youre talking nonsense, woman. I tell you, martyrdom pays all scores.

ANDROCLES. Well, let us hope so, brother, for your sake. Youve had a gay time, havnt you? with your raids on the temples. I cant help thinking that heaven will be very dull for a man of your temperament. [*Spintho snarls*]. Dont be angry: I say it only to console you in case you should die in your bed tonight in the natural way. Theres a lot of plague about.

SPINTHO [*rising and running about in abject terror*] I never thought of that. Oh Lord, spare me to be martyred. Oh, what a thought to put into the mind of a brother! Oh, let me be martyred today, now. I shall die in the night and go to hell. Youre a sorcerer: youve put death into my mind. Oh, curse you, curse you! [*He tries to seize Androcles by the throat*].

FERROVIUS [*holding him in a grasp of iron*] Whats this, brother? Anger! Violence! Raising your hand to a brother Christian!

SPINTHO. It's easy for you. Youre strong. Your nerves are all right. But I'm full of disease. [*Ferrovius takes his hand from him with instinctive disgust*]. Ive drunk all my nerves away. I shall have the horrors all night.

ANDROCLES [*sympathetic*] Oh, dont take on so, brother. We're all sinners.

SPINTHO [*snivelling, trying to feel consoled*] Yes: I daresay if the truth were known, youre all as bad as I am.

LAVINIA [*contemptuously*] Does that comfort you?

FERROVIUS [*sternly*] Pray, man, pray.

SPINTHO. Whats the good of praying? If we're martyred we shall go to heaven, shant we, whether we pray or not?

FERROVIUS. Whats that? Not pray! [*Seizing him again*] Pray this instant, you dog, you rotten hound, you slimy snake, you beastly goat, or—

SPINTHO. Yes: beat me: kick me. I forgive you: mind that.

FERROVIUS [*spurning him with loathing*] Yah! [*Spintho reels away and falls in front of Ferrovius*].

ANDROCLES [*reaching out and catching the skirt of Ferrovius's tunic*] Dear brother: if you wouldnt mind—just for my sake—

FERROVIUS. Well?

ANDROCLES. Dont call him by the names of the animals. Weve no right to. Ive had such friends in dogs. A pet snake is the best of company. I was nursed on goat's milk. Is it fair to them to call the like of him a dog or a snake or a goat?

FERROVIUS. I only meant that they have no souls.

ANDROCLES [*anxiously protesting*] Oh, believe me, they have. Just the same as you and me. I really dont think I could consent to go to heaven if I thought there were to be no animals there. Think of what they suffer here.

FERROVIUS. Thats true. Yes: that is just. They will have their share in heaven.

SPINTHO [*who has picked himself up and is sneaking past Ferrovius on his left, sneers derisively*]!!

FERROVIUS [*turning on him fiercely*] Whats that you say?

SPINTHO [*cowering*] Nothing.

FERROVIUS [*clenching his fist*] Do animals go to heaven or not?

SPINTHO. I never said they didnt.

FERROVIUS [*implacable*] Do they or do they not?

SPINTHO. They do: they do. [*Scrambling out of Ferrovius's reach*]. Oh, curse you for frightening me!

A bugle call is heard.

CENTURION [*waking up*] 'Tention! Form as before. Now then, prisoners: up with you and trot along spry. [*The soldiers fall in. The Christians rise*].

A man with an ox goad comes running through the central arch.

THE OX DRIVER. Here, you soldiers! clear out of the way for the Emperor.

THE CENTURION. Emperor! Wheres the Emperor? You aint the Emperor, are you?

THE OX DRIVER. It's the menagerie service. My team of oxen is drawing the new lion to the Coliseum. You clear the road.

CENTURION. What! Go in after you in your dust, with half the town at the heels of you and your lion! Not likely. We go first.

THE OX DRIVER. The menagerie service is the Emperor's personal retinue. You clear out, I tell you.

CENTURION. You tell me, do you? Well, I'll tell you something. If the lion is menagerie service, the lion's dinner is menagerie service too. This [*pointing to the Christians*] is the lion's dinner. So back with you to your bullocks double quick; and learn your place. March. [*The soldiers start*]. Now then, you Christians: step out there.

LAVINIA [*marching*] Come along, the rest of the dinner. I shall be the olives and anchovies.

ANOTHER CHRISTIAN [*laughing*] I shall be the soup.

ANOTHER. I shall be the fish.

ANOTHER. Ferrovius shall be the roast boar.

FERROVIUS [*heavily*] I see the joke. Yes, yes: I shall be the roast boar. Ha! ha! [*He laughs conscientiously and marches out with them*].

ANDROCLES [*following*] I shall be the mince pie. [*Each announcement is received with a louder laugh by all the rest as the joke catches on*].

CENTURION [*scandalized*] Silence! Have some sense of your situation. Is this the way for martyrs to behave? [*To Spintho, who is quaking and loitering*] I know what youll be at that dinner. Youll be the emetic. [*He shoves him rudely along*].

SPINTHO. It's too dreadful: I'm not fit to die.

CENTURION. Fitter than you are to live, you swine.

They pass from the square westward. The oxen, drawing a waggon with a great wooden cage and the lion in it, arrive through the central arch.

ACT II

Behind the Emperor's box at the Coliseum, where the performers assemble before entering the arena. In the middle a wide passage leading to the arena descends from the floor level under the imperial box. On both sides of this passage steps ascend to a landing at the back entrance to the box. The landing forms a bridge across the passage. At the entrance to the passage are two bronze mirrors, one on each side.

On the west side of this passage, on the right hand of anyone coming from the box and standing on the bridge, the martyrs are sitting on the steps. Lavinia is seated half-way up, thoughtful, trying to look death in the face. On her left Androcles consoles himself by nursing a cat. Ferrovius stands behind them, his eyes blazing, his figure stiff with intense resolution. At the foot of the steps crouches Spintho, with his head clutched in his hands, full of horror at the approach of martyrdom.

On the east side of the passage the gladiators are standing and sitting at ease, waiting, like the Christians, for their turn in the arena. One (Retiarius) is a nearly naked man with a net and a trident. Another (Secutor) is in armor with a sword. He carries a helmet with a barred visor. The editor of the gladiators sits on a chair a little apart from them.

The Call Boy enters from the passage.

THE CALL BOY. Number six. Retiarius versus Secutor.

The gladiator with the net picks it up. The gladiator with the helmet puts it on; and the two go into the arena, the net thrower taking out a little brush and arranging his hair as he goes, the other tightening his straps and shaking his shoulders loose. Both look at themselves in the mirrors before they enter the passage.

LAVINIA. Will they really kill one another?

SPINTHO. Yes, if the people turn down their thumbs.

THE EDITOR. You know nothing about it. The people indeed! Do you suppose we would kill a man worth perhaps fifty talents to please the riffraff? I should like to catch any of my men at it.

SPINTHO. I thought—

THE EDITOR [contemptuously] You thought! Who cares what you think? You'll be killed all right enough.

SPINTHO [groans and again hides his face]!!!

LAVINIA. Then is nobody ever killed except us poor Christians?

THE EDITOR. If the vestal virgins turn down their thumbs, thats another matter. Theyre ladies of rank.

LAVINIA. Does the Emperor ever interfere?

THE EDITOR. Oh, yes: he turns his thumb up fast enough if the vestal virgins want to have one of his pet fighting men killed.

ANDROCLES. But dont they ever just only pretend to kill one another? Why shouldnt you pretend to die, and get dragged out as if you were dead; and then get up and go home, like an actor?

THE EDITOR. See here: you want to know too much. There will be no pretending about the new lion: let that be enough for you. He's hungry.

SPINTHO [groaning with horror] Oh, Lord! cant you stop talking about it? Isnt it bad enough for us without that?

ANDROCLES. I'm glad he's hungry. Not that I want him to suffer, poor chap! but then he'll enjoy eating me so much more. Theres a cheerful side to everything.

THE EDITOR [rising and striding over to Androcles] Here: dont you be obstinate. Come with me and drop the pinch of incense on the altar. Thats all you need do to be let off.

ANDROCLES. No: thank you very much indeed; but I really mustnt.

THE EDITOR. What! Not to save your life?

ANDROCLES. I'd rather not. I couldnt sacrifice to Diana: she's a huntress, you know, and kills things.

THE EDITOR. That dont matter. You can choose your own altar. Sacrifice to Jupiter: he likes animals: he turns himself into an animal when he goes off duty.

ANDROCLES. No: it's very kind of you; but I feel I cant save myself that way.

THE EDITOR. But I dont ask you to do it to save yourself: I ask you to do it to oblige me personally.

ANDROCLES [scrambling up in the greatest agitation] Oh, please dont say that. This is dreadful. You mean so kindly by me that it seems quite horrible to disoblige you. If you could arrange for me to sacrifice when theres nobody looking, I shouldnt mind. But I must go into the arena with the rest. My honor, you know.

THE EDITOR. Honor! The honor of a tailor!

ANDROCLES [apologetically] Well, perhaps honor is too strong an expression. Still, you know, I couldnt allow the tailors to get a bad name through me.

THE EDITOR. How much will you remember of all that when you smell the beast's breath and see his jaws opening to tear out your throat?

SPINTHO [rising with a yell of terror] I cant bear it. Wheres the altar? I'll sacrifice.

FERROVIUS. Dog of an apostate. Iscariot!

SPINTHO. I'll repent afterwards. I fully mean to die in the arena: I'll die a martyr and go to heaven; but not this time, not now, not until my nerves are better. Besides, I'm too young: I want to have just one more good time. [*The gladiators laugh at him*]. Oh, will no one tell me where the altar is? [*He dashes into the passage and vanishes*].

ANDROCLES [*to the Editor, pointing after Spintho*] Brother: I cant do that, not even to oblige you. Dont ask me.

THE EDITOR. Well, if youre determined to die, I cant help you. But I wouldnt be put off by a swine like that.

FERROVIUS. Peace, peace: tempt him not. Get thee behind him, Satan.

THE EDITOR [*flushing with rage*] For two pins I'd take a turn in the arena myself today, and pay you out for daring to talk to me like that.

Ferrovius springs forward.

LAVINIA [*rising quickly and interposing*] Brother, brother: you forget.

FERROVIUS [*curbing himself by a mighty effort*] Oh, my temper, my wicked temper! [*To the Editor, as Lavinia sits down again reassured*] Forgive me, brother. My heart was full of wrath: I should have been thinking of your dear precious soul.

THE EDITOR. Yah! [*He turns his back on Ferrovius contemptuously, and goes back to his seat*].

FERROVIUS [*continuing*] And I forgot it all: I thought of nothing but offering to fight you with one hand tied behind me.

THE EDITOR [*turning pugnaciously*] What!

FERROVIUS [*on the border line between zeal and ferocity*] Oh, dont give way to pride and wrath, brother. I could do it so easily. I could—

They are separated by the Menagerie Keeper, who rushes in from the passage, furious.

THE KEEPER. Heres a nice business! Who let that Christian out of here down to the dens when we were changing the lion into the cage next the arena?

THE EDITOR. Nobody let him. He let himself.

THE KEEPER. Well, the lion's ate him.

Consternation. The Christians rise, greatly agitated. The gladiators sit callously, but are highly amused. All speak or cry out or laugh at once. Tumult.

LAVINIA. Oh, poor wretch! FERROVIUS. The apostate has perished. Praise be to God's justice! ANDROCLES. The poor beast was starving. It couldnt help itself. THE CHRISTIANS. What! Ate him! How frightful! How terrible! Without a moment to repent! God be merciful to him, a sinner! Oh, I cant bear to think of it! In the midst of his sin! Horrible, horrible! THE EDITOR. Serve the rotter right! THE GLADIATORS. Just walked into it, he did. He's martyred all right enough. Good old lion! Old Jock doesnt like that: look at his face. Devil a better! The Emperor will laugh when he hears of it. I cant help smiling. Ha ha ha!!!!!

THE KEEPER. Now his appetite's taken off, he wont as much as look at another Christian for a week.

ANDROCLES. Couldnt you have saved him, brother?

THE KEEPER. Saved him! Saved him from a lion that I'd just got mad with hunger! a wild one that came out of the forest not four weeks ago! He bolted him before you could say Balbus.

LAVINIA [*sitting down again*] Poor Spintho! And it wont even count as martyrdom!

THE KEEPER. Serve him right! What call had he to walk down the throat of one of my lions before he was asked?

ANDROCLES. Perhaps the lion wont eat me now.

THE KEEPER. Yes: thats just like a Christian: think only of yourself! What am I to do? What am I to say to the Emperor when he sees one of my lions coming into the arena half asleep?

THE EDITOR. Say nothing. Give your old lion some bitters and a morsel of fried fish to wake up his appetite. [*Laughter*].

THE KEEPER. Yes: it's easy for you to talk; but—

THE EDITOR [*scrambling to his feet*] Sh! Attention there! The Emperor. [*The Keeper bolts precipitately into the passage. The gladiators rise smartly and form into line*].

The Emperor enters on the Christians' side, conversing with Metellus, and followed by his suite.

THE GLADIATORS. Hail, Caesar! those about to die salute thee.

CAESAR. Good morrow, friends.

Metellus shakes hands with the Editor, who accepts his condescension with bluff respect.

LAVINIA. Blessing, Caesar, and forgiveness!

CAESAR [*turning in some surprise at the saluta-*

tion] There is no forgiveness for Christianity.

LAVINIA. I did not mean that, Caesar. I mean that we forgive you.

METELLUS. An inconceivable liberty! Do you not know, woman, that the Emperor can do no wrong and therefore cannot be forgiven?

LAVINIA. I expect the Emperor knows better. Anyhow, we forgive him.

THE CHRISTIANS. Amen!

CAESAR. Metellus: you see now the disadvantage of too much severity. These people have no hope; therefore they have nothing to restrain them from saying what they like to me. They are almost as impertinent as the gladiators. Which is the Greek sorcerer?

ANDROCLES [*humbly touching his forelock*] Me, your Worship.

CAESAR. My Worship! Good! A new title. Well: what miracles can you perform?

ANDROCLES. I can cure warts by rubbing them with my tailor's chalk; and I can live with my wife without beating her.

CAESAR. Is that all?

ANDROCLES. You dont know her, Caesar, or you wouldnt say that.

CAESAR. Ah, well, my friend, we shall no doubt contrive a happy release for you. Which is Ferrovius?

FERROVIUS. I am he.

CAESAR. They tell me you can fight.

FERROVIUS. It is easy to fight. *I* can die, Caesar.

CAESAR. That is still easier, is it not?

FERROVIUS. Not to me, Caesar. Death comes hard to my flesh; and fighting comes very easily to my spirit [*beating his breast and lamenting*] Oh, sinner that I am! [*He throws himself down on the steps, deeply discouraged*].

CAESAR. Metellus: I should like to have this man in the Pretorian Guard.

METELLUS. *I* should not, Caesar. He looks a spoilsport. There are men in whose presence it is impossible to have any fun: men who are a sort of walking conscience. He would make us all uncomfortable.

CAESAR. For that reason, perhaps, it might be well to have him. An Emperor can hardly have too many consciences. [*To Ferrovius*] Listen, Ferrovius. [*Ferrovius shakes his head and will not look up*]. You and your friends shall not be outnumbered today in the arena. You shall have arms; and there will be no more than one gladiator to each Christian.

If you come out of the arena alive, I will consider favorably any request of yours, and give you a place in the Pretorian Guard. Even if the request be that no questions be asked about your faith I shall perhaps not refuse it.

FERROVIUS. I will not fight. I will die. Better stand with the archangels than with the Pretorian Guard.

CAESAR. I cannot believe that the archangels—whoever they may be—would not prefer to be recruited from the Pretorian Guard. However, as you please. Come: let us see the show.

As the Court ascends the steps, Secutor and Retiarius return from the arena through the passage: Secutor covered with dust and very angry: Retiarius grinning.

SECUTOR. Ha, the Emperor. Now we shall see. Caesar: I ask you whether it is fair for the Retiarius, instead of making a fair throw of his net at me, to swish it along the ground and throw the dust in my eyes, and then catch me when I'm blinded. If the vestals had not turned up their thumbs I should have been a dead man.

CAESAR [*halting on the stair*] There is nothing in the rules against it.

SECUTOR [*indignantly*] Caesar: is it a dirty trick or is it not?

CAESAR. It is a dusty one, my friend. [*Obsequious laughter*]. Be on your guard next time.

SECUTOR. Let him be on his guard. Next time I'll throw my sword at his heels and strangle him with his own net before he can hop off. [*To the Retiarius*] You see if I dont. [*He goes out past the gladiators, sulky and furious*].

CAESAR [*to the chuckling Retiarius*]. These tricks are not wise, my friend. The audience likes to see a dead man in all his beauty and splendor. If you smudge his face and spoil his armor they will shew their displeasure by not letting you kill him. And when your turn comes, they will remember it against you and turn their thumbs down.

THE RETIARIUS. Perhaps that is why I did it, Caesar. He bet me ten sesterces that he would vanquish me. If I had had to kill him I should not have had the money.

CAESAR [*indulgent, laughing*] You rogues: there is no end to your tricks. I'll dismiss you all and have elephants to fight. They fight fairly. [*He goes up to his box, and knocks at it.*

It is opened from within by the Captain, who stands as on parade to let him pass].

The Call Boy comes from the passage, followed by three attendants carrying respectively a bundle of swords, some helmets, and some breastplates and pieces of armor which they throw down in a heap.

THE CALL BOY. By your leave, Caesar. Number eleven! Gladiators and Christians!

Ferrovius springs up, ready for martyrdom. The other Christians take the summons as best they can, some joyful and brave, some patient and dignified, some tearful and helpless, some embracing one another with emotion. The Call Boy goes back into the passage.

CAESAR [*turning at the door of the box*] The hour has come, Ferrovius. I shall go into my box and see you killed, since you scorn the Pretorian Guard. [*He goes into the box. The Captain shuts the door, remaining inside with the Emperor. Metellus and the rest of the suite disperse to their seats. The Christians, led by Ferrovius, move towards the passage*].

LAVINIA [*to Ferrovius*] Farewell.

THE EDITOR. Steady there. You Christians have got to fight. Here! arm yourselves.

FERROVIUS [*picking up a sword*] I'll die sword in hand to shew people that I could fight if it were my Master's will, and that I could kill the man who kills me if I chose.

THE EDITOR. Put on that armor.

FERROVIUS. No armor.

THE EDITOR [*bullying him*] Do what youre told. Put on that armor.

FERROVIUS [*gripping the sword and looking dangerous*] I said, No armor.

THE EDITOR. And what am I to say when I am accused of sending a naked man in to fight my men in armor?

FERROVIUS. Say your prayers, brother; and have no fear of the princes of this world.

THE EDITOR. Tsha! You obstinate fool! [*He bites his lips irresolutely, not knowing exactly what to do*].

ANDROCLES [*to Ferrovius*] Farewell, brother, till we meet in the sweet by-and-by.

THE EDITOR [*to Androcles*] You are going too. Take a sword there; and put on any armor you can find to fit you.

ANDROCLES. No, really: I cant fight: I never could: I cant bring myself to dislike anyone enough. I'm to be thrown to the lions with the lady.

THE EDITOR. Then get out of the way and hold your noise. [*Androcles steps aside with cheerful docility*]. Now then! Are you all ready there?

A trumpet is heard from the arena.

FERROVIUS [*starting convulsively*] Heaven give me strength!

THE EDITOR. Aha! That frightens you, does it?

FERROVIUS. Man: there is no terror like the terror of that sound to me. When I hear a trumpet or a drum or the clash of steel or the hum of the catapult as the great stone flies, fire runs through my veins: I feel my blood surge up hot behind my eyes: I must charge: I must strike: I must conquer: Caesar himself will not be safe in his imperial seat if once that spirit gets loose in me. Oh, brothers, pray! exhort me! remind me that if I raise my sword my honor falls and my Master is crucified afresh.

ANDROCLES. Just keep thinking how cruelly you might hurt the poor gladiators.

FERROVIUS. It does not hurt a man to kill him.

LAVINIA. Nothing but faith can save you.

FERROVIUS. Faith! Which faith? There are two faiths. There is our faith. And there is the warrior's faith, the faith in fighting, the faith that sees God in the sword. How if that faith should overwhelm me?

LAVINIA. You will find your real faith in the hour of trial.

FERROVIUS. That is what I fear. I know that I am a fighter. How can I feel sure that I am a Christian?

ANDROCLES. Throw away the sword, brother.

FERROVIUS. I cannot. It cleaves to my hand. I could as easily throw a woman I loved from my arms. [*Starting*] Who spoke that blasphemy? Not I.

LAVINIA. I cant help you, friend. I cant tell you not to save your own life. Something wilful in me wants to see you fight your way into heaven.

FERROVIUS. Ha!

ANDROCLES. But if you are going to give up our faith, brother, why not do it without hurting anybody? Dont fight them. Burn the incense.

FERROVIUS. Burn the incense! Never.

LAVINIA. That is only pride, Ferrovius.

FERROVIUS. Only pride! What is nobler than pride? [*Conscience stricken*] Oh, I'm steeped in sin. I'm proud of my pride.

LAVINIA. They say we Christians are the proudest devils on earth—that only the weak are meek. Oh, I am worse than you. I ought to send you to death; and I am tempting you.

ANDROCLES. Brother, brother: let them rage and kill: let us be brave and suffer. You must go as a lamb to the slaughter.

FERROVIUS. Aye, aye: that is right. Not as a lamb is slain by the butcher; but as a butcher might let himself be slain by a [*looking at the Editor*] by a silly ram whose head he could fetch off in one twist.

Before the Editor can retort, the Call Boy rushes up through the passage, and the Captain comes from the Emperor's box and descends the steps.

THE CALL BOY. In with you: into the arena. The stage is waiting.

THE CAPTAIN. The Emperor is waiting. [*To the Editor*] What are you dreaming of, man? Send your men in at once.

THE EDITOR. Yes, sir: it's these Christians hanging back.

FERROVIUS [*in a voice of thunder*] Liar!

THE EDITOR [*not heeding him*] March. [*The gladiators told off to fight with the Christians march down the passage*] Follow up there, you.

THE CHRISTIAN MEN AND WOMEN [*as they part*] Be steadfast, brother. Farewell. Hold up the faith, brother. Farewell. Go to glory, dearest. Farewell. Remember: we are praying for you. Farewell. Be strong, brother. Farewell. Dont forget that the divine love and our love surround you. Farewell. Nothing can hurt you: remember that, brother. Farewell. Eternal glory, dearest. Farewell.

THE EDITOR [*out of patience*] Shove them in, there.

The remaining gladiators and the Call Boy make a movement towards them.

FERROVIUS [*interposing*] Touch them, dogs; and we die here, and cheat the heathen of their spectacle. [*To his fellow Christians*] Brothers: the great moment has come. That passage is your hill to Calvary. Mount it bravely, but meekly; and remember! not a word of reproach, not a blow nor a struggle. Go. [*They go out through the passage. He turns to Lavinia*] Farewell.

LAVINIA. You forget: I must follow before you are cold.

FERROVIUS. It is true. Do not envy me because I pass before you to glory. [*He goes through the passage*].

THE EDITOR [*to the Call Boy*] Sickening work, this. Why cant they all be thrown to the lions? It's not a man's job. [*He throws himself moodily into his chair*].

The remaining gladiators go back to their former places indifferently. The Call Boy shrugs his shoulders and squats down at the entrance to the passage, near the Editor.

Lavinia and the Christian women sit down again, wrung with grief, some weeping silently, some praying, some calm and steadfast. Androcles sits down at Lavinia's feet. The Captain stands on the stairs, watching her curiously.

ANDROCLES. I'm glad I havnt to fight. That would really be an awful martyrdom. I am lucky.

LAVINIA [*looking at him with a pang of remorse*] Androcles: burn the incense: youll be forgiven. Let my death atone for both. I feel as if I were killing you.

ANDROCLES. Dont think of me, sister. Think of yourself. That will keep your heart up.

The Captain laughs sardonically.

LAVINIA [*startled: she had forgotten his presence*] Are you there, handsome Captain? Have you come to see me die?

THE CAPTAIN [*coming to her side*] I am on duty with the Emperor, Lavinia.

LAVINIA. Is it part of your duty to laugh at us?

THE CAPTAIN. No: that is part of my private pleasure. Your friend here is a humorist. I laughed at his telling you to think of yourself to keep up your heart. *I* say, think of yourself and burn the incense.

LAVINIA. He is not a humorist: he was right. You ought to know that, Captain: you have been face to face with death.

THE CAPTAIN. Not with certain death, Lavinia. Only death in battle, which spares more men than death in bed. What you are facing is certain death. You have nothing left now but your faith in this craze of yours: this Christianity. Are your Christian fairy stories any truer than our stories about Jupiter and Diana, in which, I may tell you, I believe no more than the Emperor does, or any educated man in Rome?

LAVINIA. Captain: all that seems nothing to me now. I'll not say that death is a terrible thing; but I will say that it is so real a thing that when it comes close, all the imaginary things—all the stories, as you call them—fade into mere dreams beside that inexorable reality. I know now that I am not dying for stories or dreams. Did you hear of the dreadful thing that happened here while we were waiting?

THE CAPTAIN. I heard that one of your fellows bolted, and ran right into the jaws of the lion. I laughed. I still laugh.

LAVINIA. Then you dont understand what that meant?

THE CAPTAIN. It meant that the lion had a cur for his breakfast.

LAVINIA. It meant more than that, Captain. It meant that a man cannot die for a story and a dream. None of us believed the stories and the dreams more devoutly than poor Spintho; but he could not face the great reality. What he would have called my faith has been oozing away minute by minute whilst Ive been sitting here, with death coming nearer and nearer, with reality become realler and realler, with stories and dreams fading away into nothing.

THE CAPTAIN. Are you then going to die for nothing?

LAVINIA. Yes: that is the wonderful thing. It is since all the stories and dreams have gone that I have now no doubt at all that I must die for something greater than dreams or stories.

THE CAPTAIN. But for what?

LAVINIA. I dont know. If it were for anything small enough to know, it would be too small to die for. I think I'm going to die for God. Nothing else is real enough to die for.

THE CAPTAIN. What is God?

LAVINIA. When we know that, Captain, we shall be gods ourselves.

THE CAPTAIN. Lavinia: come down to earth. Burn the incense and marry me.

LAVINIA. Handsome Captain: would you marry me if I hauled down the flag in the day of battle and burnt the incense? Sons take after their mothers, you know. Do you want your son to be a coward?

THE CAPTAIN [strongly moved] By great Diana, I think I would strangle you if you gave in now.

LAVINIA [putting her hand on the head of Androcles] The hand of God is on us three, Captain.

THE CAPTAIN. What nonsense it all is! And what a monstrous thing that you should die for such nonsense, and that I should look on helplessly when my whole soul cries out against it! Die then if you must; but at least I can cut the Emperor's throat and then my own when I see your blood.

The Emperor throws open the door of his box

angrily, and appears in wrath on the threshold. The Editor, the Call Boy, and the gladiators spring to their feet.

THE EMPEROR. The Christians will not fight; and your curs cannot get their blood up to attack them. It's all that fellow with the blazing eyes. Send for the whip. [*The Call Boy rushes out on the east side for the whip*]. If that will not move them, bring the hot irons. The man is like a mountain. [*He returns angrily into the box and slams the door*].

The Call Boy returns with a man in a hideous Etruscan mask, carrying a whip. They both rush down the passage into the arena.

LAVINIA [*rising*] Oh, that is unworthy. Can they not kill him without dishonoring him?

ANDROCLES [*scrambling to his feet and running into the middle of the space between the staircases*] It's dreadful. Now *I* want to fight. I cant bear the sight of a whip. The only time I ever hit a man was when he lashed an old horse with a whip. It was terrible: I danced on his face when he was on the ground. He mustnt strike Ferrovius: I'll go into the arena and kill him first. [*He makes a wild dash into the passage. As he does so a great clamor is heard from the arena, ending in wild applause. The gladiators listen and look inquiringly at one another*].

THE EDITOR. Whats up now?

LAVINIA [*to the Captain*] What has happened, do you think?

THE CAPTAIN. What can happen? They are killing them, I suppose.

ANDROCLES [*running in through the passage, screaming with horror and hiding his eyes*]!!!

LAVINIA. Androcles, Androcles: whats the matter?

ANDROCLES. Oh dont ask me, dont ask me. Something too dreadful. Oh! [*He crouches by her and hides his face in her robe, sobbing*].

THE CALL BOY [*rushing through from the passage as before*] Ropes and hooks there! Ropes and hooks!

THE EDITOR. Well, need you excite yourself about it? [*Another burst of applause*].

Two slaves in Etruscan masks, with ropes and drag hooks, hurry in.

ONE OF THE SLAVES. How many dead?

THE CALL BOY. Six. [*The slave blows a whistle twice; and four more masked slaves rush through into the arena with the same apparatus*] And the basket. Bring the baskets [*The slave whistles three times, and runs through the passage with his companion*].

THE CAPTAIN. Who are the baskets for?

THE CALL BOY. For the whip. He's in pieces. Theyre all in pieces, more or less. [*Lavinia hides her face*].

Two more masked slaves come in with a basket and follow the others into the arena, as the Call Boy turns to the gladiators and exclaims, exhausted] Boys: he's killed the lot.

THE EMPEROR [*again bursting from his box, this time in an ecstasy of delight*] Where is he? Magnificent! He shall have a laurel crown.

Ferrovius, madly waving his bloodstained sword, rushes through the passage in despair, followed by his co-religionists, and by the menagerie keeper, who goes to the gladiators. The gladiators draw their swords nervously].

FERROVIUS. Lost! lost for ever! I have betrayed my Master. Cut off this right hand: it has offended. Ye have swords, my brethren: strike.

LAVINIA. No, no. What have you done, Ferrovius?

FERROVIUS. I know not: but there was blood behind my eyes; and theres blood on my sword. What does that mean?

THE EMPEROR [*enthusiastically, on the landing outside his box*] What does it mean? It means that you are the greatest man in Rome. It means that you shall have a laurel crown of gold. Superb fighter: I could almost yield you my throne. It is a record for my reign: I shall live in history. Once, in Domitian's time, a Gaul slew three men in the arena and gained his freedom. But when before has one naked man slain six armed men of the bravest and best? The persecution shall cease: if Christians can fight like this, I shall have none but Christians to fight for me. [*To the Gladiators*] You are ordered to become Christians, you there: do you hear?

RETIARIUS. It is all one to us, Caesar. Had I been there with my net, the story would have been different.

THE CAPTAIN [*suddenly seizing Lavinia by the wrist and dragging her up the steps to the Emperor*] Caesar: this woman is the sister of Ferrovius. If she is thrown to the lions he will fret. He will lose weight; get out of condition—

THE EMPEROR. The lions? Nonsense! [*To Lavinia*] Madam: I am proud to have the honor of making your acquaintance. Your brother is the glory of Rome.

LAVINIA. But my friends here. Must they die?

THE EMPEROR. Die! Certainly not. There has never been the slightest idea of harming them. Ladies and gentlemen: you are all free. Pray go into the front of the house and enjoy the spectacle to which your brother has so splendidly contributed. Captain: oblige me by conducting them to the seats reserved for my personal friends.

THE MENAGERIE KEEPER. Caesar: I must have one Christian for the lion. The people have been promised it; and they will tear the decorations to bits if they are disappointed.

THE EMPEROR. True, true: we must have somebody for the new lion.

FERROVIUS. Throw me to him. Let the apostate perish.

THE EMPEROR. No. no: you would tear him in pieces, my friend; and we cannot afford to throw away lions as if they were mere slaves. But we must have somebody. This is really extremely awkward.

THE MENAGERIE KEEPER. Why not that little Greek chap? He's not a Christian: he's a sorcerer.

THE EMPEROR. The very thing: he will do very well.

THE CALL BOY [*issuing from the passage*] Number twelve. The Christian for the new lion.

ANDROCLES [*rising, and pulling himself sadly together*] Well, it was to be, after all.

LAVINIA. I'll go in his place, Caesar. Ask the Captain whether they do not like best to see a woman torn to pieces. He told me so yesterday.

THE EMPEROR. There is something in that: there is certainly something in that—if only I could feel sure that your brother would not fret.

ANDROCLES. No: I should never have another happy hour. No: on the faith of a Christian and the honor of a tailor, I accept the lot that has fallen on me. If my wife turns up, give her my love and say that my wish was that she should be happy with her next, poor fellow! Caesar: go to your box and see how a tailor can die. Make way for number twelve there. [*He marches out along the passage*].

The vast audience in the amphitheatre now sees the Emperor re-enter his box and take his place as Androcles, desperately frightened, but still marching with piteous devotion, emerges from the other end of the passage, and finds himself at the focus of thousands of eager eyes. The lion's cage, with a heavy portcullis grating, is on his left. The Emperor gives a signal. A gong sounds.

Androcles shivers at the sound; then falls on his knees and prays. The grating rises with a clash. The lion bounds into the arena. He rushes round frisking in his freedom. He sees Androcles. He stops; rises stiffly by straightening his legs; stretches out his nose forward and his tail in a horizontal line behind, like a pointer, and utters an appalling roar. Androcles crouches and hides his face in his hands. The lion gathers himself for a spring, swishing his tail to and fro through the dust in an ecstasy of anticipation. Androcles throws up his hands in supplication to heaven. The lion checks at the sight of Androcles's face. He then steals towards him; smells him; arches his back; purrs like a motor car; finally rubs himself against Androcles, knocking him over. Androcles, supporting himself on his wrist, looks affrightedly at the lion. The lion limps on three paws, holding up the other as if it was wounded. A flash of recognition lights up the face of Androcles. He flaps his hand as if it had a thorn in it, and pretends to pull the thorn out and to hurt himself. The lion nods repeatedly. Androcles holds out his hands to the lion, who gives him both paws, which he shakes with enthusiasm. They embrace rapturously, finally waltz round the arena amid a sudden burst of deafening applause, and out through the passage, the Emperor watching them in breathless astonishment until they disappear, when he rushes from his box and descends the steps in frantic excitement.

THE EMPEROR. My friends, an incredible! an amazing thing! has happened. I can no longer doubt the truth of Christianity. [*The Christians press to him joyfully*]. This Christian sorcerer— [*with a yell, he breaks off as he sees Androcles and the lion emerge from the passage, waltzing. He bolts wildly up the steps into his box, and slams the door. All, Christians and gladiators alike, fly for their lives, the gladiators bolting into the arena, the others in all directions. The place is emptied with magical suddenness*].

ANDROCLES [*naïvely*] Now I wonder why they all run away from us like that. [*The lion, combining a series of yawns, purrs, and roars, achieves something very like a laugh*].

THE EMPEROR [*standing on a chair inside his box and looking over the wall*] Sorcerer: I command you to put that lion to death instantly. It is guilty of high treason. Your conduct is most disgra— [*the lion charges at him up the stairs*] help! [*He disappears. The lion rears against the box; looks over the partition at him; and roars. The Emperor darts out through the door and down to Androcles, pursued by the lion*].

ANDROCLES. Dont run away, sir: he cant help springing if you run. [*He seizes the Emperor and gets between him and the lion, who stops at once*]. Dont be afraid of him.

THE EMPEROR. I am n o t afraid of him. [*The lion crouches, growling. The Emperor clutches Androcles*]. Keep between us.

ANDROCLES. Never be afraid of animals, your worship: thats the great secret. He'll be as gentle as a lamb when he knows that you are his friend. Stand quite still; and smile; and let him smell you all over just to reassure him; for, you see, he's afraid of you; and he must examine you thoroughly before he gives you his confidence. [*To the lion*] Come now, Tommy; and speak nicely to the Emperor, the great good Emperor who has power to have all our heads cut off if we dont behave very v e r y respectfully to him.

The lion utters a fearful roar. The Emperor dashes madly up the steps, across the landing, and down again on the other side, with the lion in hot pursuit. Androcles rushes after the lion; overtakes him as he is descending; and throws himself on his back, trying to use his toes as a brake. Before he can stop him the lion gets hold of the trailing end of the Emperor's robe.

ANDROCLES. Oh bad wicked Tommy, to chase the Emperor like that! Let go the Emperor's robe at once, sir: wheres your manners? [*The lion growls and worries the robe*]. Dont pull it away from him, your worship. He's only playing. Now I shall be really angry with you, Tommy, if you dont let go. [*The lion growls again*]. I'll tell you what it is, sir: he thinks you and I are not friends.

THE EMPEROR [*trying to undo the clasp of his brooch*] Friends! You infernal scoundrel [*the lion growls*]—dont let him go. Curse this brooch! I cant get it loose.

ANDROCLES. We mustnt let him lash himself into a rage. You must shew him that you are my particular friend—if you will have the condescension. [*He seizes the Emperor's hands and shakes them cordially*]. Look, Tommy: the nice Emperor is the dearest friend Andy Wandy has in the whole world: he loves him like a brother.

THE EMPEROR. You little brute, you damned filthy little dog of a Greek tailor: I'll have you burnt alive for daring to touch the divine person of the Emperor. [*The lion growls*].

ANDROCLES. Oh dont talk like that, sir. He understands every word you say: all animals do: they take it from the tone of your voice. [*The lion growls and lashes his tail*]. I think he's going to spring at your worship. If you wouldnt mind saying something affectionate. [*The lion roars*].

THE EMPEROR [*shaking Androcles's hands frantically*] My dearest Mr Androcles, my sweetest friend, my long lost brother, come to my arms. [*He embraces Androcles*]. Oh, what an abominable smell of garlic!

The lion lets go the robe and rolls over on his back, clasping his forepaws over one another coquettishly above his nose.

ANDROCLES. There! You see, your worship, a child might play with him now. See! [*He tickles the lion's belly. The lion wriggles ecstatically*]. Come and pet him.

THE EMPEROR. I must conquer these unkingly terrors. Mind you dont go away from him, though. [*He pats the lion's chest*].

ANDROCLES. Oh, sir, how few men would have the courage to do that!

THE EMPEROR. Yes: it takes a bit of nerve. Let us have the Court in and frighten them. Is he safe, do you think?

ANDROCLES. Quite safe now, sir.

THE EMPEROR [*majestically*] What ho, there! All who are within hearing, return without fear. Caesar has tamed the lion. [*All the fugitives steal cautiously in. The menagerie keeper comes from the passage with other keepers armed with iron bars and tridents*]. Take those things away. I have subdued the beast. [*He places his foot on it*].

FERROVIUS [*timidly approaching the Emperor and looking down with awe on the lion*] It is strange that I, who fear no man, should fear a lion.

THE CAPTAIN. Every man fears something, Ferrovius.

THE EMPEROR. How about the Pretorian Guard now?

FERROVIUS. In my youth I worshipped Mars, the God of War. I turned from him to serve the Christian god; but today the Christian god forsoook me; and Mars overcame me and took back his own. The Christian god is not yet. He will come when Mars and I are dust; but meanwhile I must serve the gods that are, not the God that will be. Until then I accept service in the Guard, Caesar.

THE EMPEROR. Very wisely said. All really sensible men agree that the prudent course is to be neither bigoted in our attachment to the old nor rash and unpractical in keeping an open mind for the new, but to make the best of both dispensations.

THE CAPTAIN. What do you say, Lavinia? Will you too be prudent?

LAVINIA [*on the stairs*] No: I'll strive for the coming of the God who is not yet.

THE CAPTAIN. May I come and argue with you occasionally?

LAVINIA. Yes, handsome Captain: you may. [*He kisses her hand*].

THE EMPEROR. And now, my friends, though I do not, as you see, fear this lion, yet the strain of his presence is considerable; for none of us can feel quite sure what he will do next.

THE MENAGERIE KEEPER. Caesar: give us this Greek sorcerer to be a slave in the menagerie. He has a way with the beasts.

ANDROCLES [*distressed*] Not if they are in cages. They should not be kept in cages. They must all be let out.

THE EMPEROR. I give this sorcerer to be a slave to the first man who lays hands on him. [*The menagerie keepers and the gladiators rush for Androcles. The lion starts up and faces them. They surge back*]. You see how magnanimous we Romans are, Androcles. We suffer you to go in peace.

ANDROCLES. I thank your worship. I thank you all, ladies and gentlemen. Come, Tommy. Whilst we stand together, no cage for you: no slavery for me [*He goes out with the lion, everybody crowding away to give him as wide a berth as possible*].

* * * * * * *

In this play I have presented one of the Roman persecutions of the early Christians, not as the conflict of a false theology with a true, but as what all such persecutions essentially are: an attempt to suppress a propaganda that seemed to threaten the interests involved in the established law and order, organized and maintained in the name of religion and justice by politicians who are pure opportunist Have-and-Holders. People who are shewn by their inner light the possibility of a better world based on the demand of the spirit for a nobler and more abundant life, not for themselves at the expense of others, but for everybody, are naturally dreaded and therefore hated by the Have-and-Holders, who keep always in reserve two sure weapons against them. The first is a persecution effected by the provocation, organization, and arming of that herd instinct which makes men abhor all departures from custom, and, by the most cruel punishments and the wildest calumnies, force eccentric people to behave and profess exactly as other people do. The second is by leading the herd to war, which immediately and infallibly makes them forget everything, even their most cherished and hardwon public liberties and private interests, in the irresistible surge of their pugnacity and the tense preoccupation of their terror.

There is no reason to believe that there was anything more in the Roman persecutions than this. The attitude of the Roman Emperor and the officers of his staff towards the opinions at issue were much the same as those of a modern British Home Secretary towards members of the lower middle classes when some pious policeman charges them with Bad Taste, technically called blasphemy: Bad Taste being a violation of Good Taste, which in such matters practically means Hypocrisy. The Home Secretary and the judges who try the case are usually far more sceptical and blasphemous than the poor men whom they persecute; and their professions of horror at the blunt utterance of their own opinions are revolting to those behind the scenes who have any genuine religious sensibility; but the thing is done because the governing classes, provided only the law against blasphemy is not applied to themselves, strongly approve of such persecution because it enables them to represent their own privileges as part of the religion of the country.

Therefore my martyrs are the martyrs of all time, and my persecutors the persecutors of all time. My Emperor, who has no sense of the value of common people's lives, and amuses himself with killing as carelessly as with sparing, is the sort of monster you can make of any silly-clever gentleman by idolizing him. We are still so easily imposed on by such idols that one of the leading pastors of the Free Churches in London denounced my play on the ground that my persecuting Emperor is a very fine fellow, and the persecuted Christians ridiculous. From which I conclude that a popular pulpit may be as perilous to a man's soul as an imperial throne.

All my articulate Christians, the reader will notice, have different enthusiasms, which they accept as the same religion only because it involves them in a common opposition to the official religion and consequently in a common doom. Androcles is a humanitarian naturalist, whose views surprise everybody. Lavinia, a clever and fearless freethinker, shocks the Pauline Ferrovius, who is comparatively stupid and conscience ridden. Spintho, the blackguardly debauchee, is presented as one of the typical Christians of that period on the authority of St Augustine, who seems to have come to the conclusion at one period of his development that most Christians were what we call wrong uns. No doubt he was to some extent right: I have had occasion often to point out that revolutionary movements attract those who are not good enough for established institutions as well as those who are too good for them.

But the most striking aspect of the play at this moment is the terrible topicality given it by the war. We were at peace when I pointed out, by the mouth of Ferrovius, the path of an honest man who finds out, when the trumpet sounds, that he cannot follow Jesus. Many years earlier, in The Devil's Disciple, I touched the same theme even more definitely, and shewed the minister throwing off his black coat for ever when he discovered, amid the thunder of the captains and the shouting, that he was a born fighter. Great numbers of our clergy have found themselves of late in the position of Ferrovius and Anthony Anderson. They have discovered that they hate not only their enemies but everyone who does not share their hatred, and that they want to fight and to force other people to fight. They have turned their churches into recruiting stations and their vestries into munition workshops. But it has never occurred to them to take off their black coats and say quite simply, "I find in the hour of trial that the Sermon on the Mount is tosh, and that I am not a Christian. I apologize for all the unpatriotic nonsense I have been preaching all these years. Have the goodness to give me a revolver and a commission in a regiment which has for its chaplain a priest of the god Mars: *my* God." Not a bit of it. They have stuck to their livings and served Mars in the name of Christ, to the scandal of all religious mankind. When the Archbishop of York behaved like a gentleman and the Head

Master of Eton preached a Christian sermon, and were reviled by the rabble, the Martian parsons encouraged the rabble. For this they made no apologies or excuses, good or bad. They simply indulged their passions, just as they had always indulged their class prejudices and commercial interests, without troubling themselves for a moment as to whether they were Christians or not. They did not protest even when a body calling itself the Anti-German League (not having noticed, apparently, that it had been anticipated by the British Empire, the French Republic, and the Kingdoms of Italy, Japan, and Serbia) actually succeeded in closing a church at Forest Hill in which God was worshipped in the German language. One would have supposed that this grotesque outrage on the commonest decencies of religion would have provoked a remonstrance from even the worldliest bench of bishops. But no: apparently it seemed to the bishops as natural that the House of God should be looted when He allowed German to be spoken in it as that a baker's shop with a German name over the door should be pillaged. Their verdict was, in effect, "Serve God right, for creating the Germans!" The incident would have been impossible in a country where the Church was as powerful as the Church of England, had it had at the same time a spark of catholic as distinguished from tribal religion in it. As it is, the thing occurred; and as far as I have observed, the only people who gasped were the Freethinkers.

Thus we see that even among men who make a profession of religion the great majority are as Martian as the majority of their congregations. The average clergyman is an official who makes his living by christening babies, marrying adults, conducting a ritual, and making the best he can (when he has any conscience about it) of a certain routine of school superintendence, district visiting, and organization of almsgiving, which does not necessarily touch Christianity at any point except the point of the tongue. The exceptional or religious clergyman may be an ardent Pauline salvationist, in which case his more cultivated parishioners dislike him, and say that he ought to have joined the Methodists. Or he may be an artist expressing religious emotion without intellectual definition by means of poetry, music, vestments, and architecture, also producing religious ecstasy by physical expedients, such as fasts and vigils, in which case he is denounced as a Ritualist. Or he may be either a Unitarian Deist like Voltaire or Tom Paine, or the more modern sort of Anglican Theosophist to whom the Holy Ghost is the Élan Vital of Bergson and the Father and Son are an expression of the fact that our functions and aspects are manifold, and that we are all sons and all either potential or actual parents, in which case he is strongly suspected by the straiter Salvationists of being little better than an Atheist. All these varieties, you see, excite remark. They may be very popular with their congregations; but they are regarded by the average man as the freaks of the Church. The Church, like the society of which it is an organ, is balanced and steadied by the great central Philistine mass above whom theology looms as a highly spoken of and doubtless most important thing, like Greek Tragedy, or classical music, or the higher mathematics, but who are very glad when church is over and they can go home to lunch or dinner, having in fact, for all practical purposes, no reasoned convictions at all, and being equally ready to persecute a poor Freethinker for saying that St James was not infallible, and to send one of the Peculiar People to prison for being so very peculiar as to take St James seriously.

In short, a Christian martyr was thrown to the lions not because he was a Christian, but because he was a crank: that is, an unusual sort of person. And multitudes of people, quite as civilized and amiable as we, crowded to see the lions eat him just as they now crowd the lion-house in the Zoo at feeding-time, not because they really cared twopence about Diana or Christ, or could have given you any intelligent or correct account of the things Diana and Christ stood against one another for, but simply because they wanted to see a curious and exciting spectacle. You, dear reader, have probably run to see a fire; and if somebody came in now and told you that a lion was chasing a man down the street you would rush to the window. And if anyone were to say that you were as cruel as the people who let the lion loose on the man, you would be justly indignant. Now that we may no longer see a man hanged, we assemble outside the jail to see the black flag run up. That is our duller method of enjoying ourselves in the old Roman spirit. And if the Government decided to throw persons of unpopular or eccentric views to the lions in the Albert Hall or the Earl's Court stadium tomorrow, can you doubt that all the seats would be crammed, mostly by people who could not give you the most superficial account of the views in question. Much less unlikely things have happened. It is true that if such a revival does take place soon, the martyrs will not be members of heretical religious sects: they will be Peculiars, Anti-Vivisectionists, Flat-Earth men, scoffers at the laboratories, or infidels who refuse to kneel down when a procession of doctors goes by. But the lions will hurt them just as much, and the spectators will enjoy themselves just as much, as the Roman lions and spectators used to do.

It was currently reported in the Berlin newspapers that when Androcles was first performed in Berlin, the Crown Prince rose and left the house, unable to endure the (I hope) very clear and fair exposition of autocratic Imperialism given by the Roman captain to his Christian prisoners. No English Imperialist was intelligent and earnest enough to do the same in London. If the report is correct, I confirm the logic of the Crown Prince, and am glad to find myself so well understood. But I can assure him that the Empire which served for my model when I wrote Androcles was, as he is now finding to his cost, much nearer my home than the German one.

THE END

XXII

OVERRULED

1912

A lady and gentleman are sitting together on a chesterfield in a retired corner of the lounge of a seaside hotel. It is a summer night: the French window behind them stands open. The terrace without overlooks a moonlit harbor. The lounge is dark. The chesterfield, upholstered in silver grey, and the two figures on it in evening dress, catch the light from an arc lamp somewhere; but the walls, covered with a dark green paper, are in gloom. There are two stray chairs, one on each side. On the gentleman's right, behind him up near the window, is an unused fireplace. Opposite it on the lady's left is a door. The gentleman is on the lady's right.

The lady is very attractive, with a musical voice and soft appealing manners. She is young: that is, one feels sure that she is under thirty-five and over twenty-four. The gentleman does not look much older. He is rather handsome, and has ventured as far in the direction of poetic dandyism in the arrangement of his hair as any man who is not a professional artist can afford to in England. He is obviously very much in love with the lady, and is, in fact, yielding to an irresistible impulse to throw his arms round her.

THE LADY. Dont—oh dont be horrid. Please, Mr Lunn [*she rises from the lounge and retreats behind it*]! Promise me you wont be horrid.

GREGORY LUNN. I'm not being horrid, Mrs Juno. I'm not going to be horrid. I love you: thats all. I'm extraordinarily happy.

MRS JUNO. You will really be good?

GREGORY. I'll be whatever you wish me to be. I tell you I love you. I love loving you. I dont want to be tired and sorry, as I should be if I were to be horrid. I dont want you to be tired and sorry. Do come and sit down again.

MRS JUNO [*coming back to her seat*] Youre sure you dont want anything you oughtnt to?

GREGORY. Quite sure. I only want you [*she recoils*]. Dont be alarmed: I like wanting you. As long as I have a want, I have a reason for living. Satisfaction is death.

MRS JUNO. Yes; but the impulse to commit suicide is sometimes irresistible.

GREGORY. Not with you.

MRS JUNO. What!

GREGORY. Oh, it sounds uncomplimentary; but it isnt really. Do you know why half the couples who find themselves situated as we are now behave horridly?

MRS JUNO. Because they cant help it if they let things go too far.

GREGORY. Not a bit of it. It's because they have nothing else to do, and no other way of entertaining each other. You dont know

2 A

what it is to be alone with a woman who has little beauty and less conversation. What is a man to do? She cant talk interestingly; and if he talks that way himself she doesnt understand him. He cant look at her: if he does, he only finds out that she isnt beautiful. Before the end of five minutes they are both hideously bored. Theres only one thing that can save the situation; and thats what you call being horrid. With a beautiful, witty, kind woman, theres no time for such follies. It's so delightful to look at her, to listen to her voice, to hear all she has to say, that nothing else happens. That is why the woman who is supposed to have a thousand lovers seldom has one; whilst the stupid, graceless animals of women have dozens.

MRS JUNO. I wonder! It's quite true that when one feels in danger one talks like mad to stave it off, even when one doesnt quite want to stave it off.

GREGORY. One never does quite want to stave it off. Danger is delicious. But death isnt. We court the danger; but the real delight is in escaping, after all.

MRS JUNO. I dont think we'll talk about it any more. Danger is all very well when you do escape; but sometimes one doesnt. I tell you frankly I dont feel as safe as you do— if you really do.

GREGORY. But surely you can do as you please without injuring anyone, Mrs Juno. That is the whole secret of your extraordinary charm for me.

MRS JUNO. I dont understand.

GREGORY. Well, I hardly know how to begin to explain. But the root of the matter is that I am what people call a good man.

MRS JUNO. I thought so until you began making love to me.

GREGORY. But you knew I loved you all along.

MRS JUNO. Yes, of course; but I depended on you not to tell me so; because I thought you were good. Your blurting it out spoilt it. And it was wicked besides.

GREGORY. Not at all. You see, it's a great many years since Ive been able to allow myself to fall in love. I know lots of charming women; but the worst of it is, theyre all married. Women dont become charming, to my taste, until theyre fully developed; and by that time, if theyre really nice, theyre snapped up and married. And then, because I am a good man, I have to place a limit to my regard for them. I may be fortunate enough to gain friendship and even very warm affection from them; but my loyalty to their husbands and their hearths and their happiness obliges me to draw a line and not overstep it. Of course I value such affectionate regard very highly indeed. I am surrounded with women who are most dear to me. But every one of them has a post sticking up, if I may put it that way, with the inscription: Trespassers Will Be Prosecuted. How we all loathe that notice! In every lovely garden, in every dell full of primroses, on every fair hillside, we meet that confounded board; and there is always a gamekeeper round the corner. But what is that to the horror of meeting it on every beautiful woman, and knowing that there is a husband round the corner? I have had this accursed board standing between me and every dear and desirable woman until I thought I had lost the power of letting myself fall really and wholeheartedly in love.

MRS JUNO. Wasnt there a widow?

GREGORY. No. Widows are extraordinarily scarce in modern society. Husbands live longer than they used to; and even when they do die, their widows have a string of names down for their next.

MRS JUNO. Well, what about the young girls?

GREGORY. Oh, who cares for young girls? Theyre unsympathetic. Theyre beginners. They dont attract me. I'm afraid of them.

MRS JUNO. Thats the correct thing to say to a woman of my age. But it doesnt explain why you seem to have put your scruples in your pocket when you met me.

GREGORY. Surely thats quite clear. I—

MRS JUNO. No: please dont explain. I dont want to know. I take your word for it. Besides, it doesnt matter now. Our voyage is over; and tomorrow I start for the north to my poor father's place.

GREGORY [surprised] Your poor father! I thought he was alive.

MRS JUNO. So he is. What made you think he wasnt?

GREGORY. You said your poor father.

MRS JUNO. Oh, thats a trick of mine. Rather a silly trick, I suppose; but theres something pathetic to me about men: I find myself calling them poor So-and-So when theres nothing whatever the matter with them.

GREGORY [who has listened in growing alarm] But—I—is?—wa—? Oh Lord!

MRS JUNO. Whats the matter?

GREGORY. Nothing.

MRS JUNO. Nothing! [*Rising anxiously*] Nonsense: youre ill.

GREGORY. No. It was something about your late husband—

MRS JUNO. My late husband! What do you mean? [*Clutching him, horror-stricken*] Dont tell me he's dead.

GREGORY [*rising, equally appalled*] Dont tell me he's alive.

MRS JUNO. Oh, dont frighten me like this. Of course he's alive—unless youve heard anything.

GREGORY. The first day we met—on the boat—you spoke to me of your poor dear husband.

MRS JUNO [*releasing him, quite reassured*] Is that all?

GREGORY. Well, afterwards you called him poor Tops. Always poor Tops, or poor dear Tops. What could I think?

MRS JUNO [*sitting down again*] I wish you hadnt given me such a shock about him; for I havnt been treating him at all well. Neither have you.

GREGORY [*relapsing into his seat, overwhelmed*] And you mean to tell me youre not a widow!

MRS JUNO. Gracious, no! I'm not in black.

GREGORY. Then I have been behaving like a blackguard! I have broken my promise to my mother. I shall never have an easy conscience again.

MRS JUNO. I'm sorry. I thought you knew.

GREGORY. You thought I was a libertine?

MRS JUNO. No: of course I shouldnt have spoken to you if I had thought that. I thought you liked me, but that you knew, and would be good.

GREGORY [*stretching his hands towards her breast*] I thought the burden of being good had fallen from my soul at last. I saw nothing there but a bosom to rest on: the bosom of a lovely woman of whom I could dream without guilt. What do I see now?

MRS JUNO. Just what you saw before.

GREGORY [*despairingly*] No, no.

MRS JUNO. What else?

GREGORY. Trespassers Will Be Prosecuted: Trespassers Will Be Prosecuted.

MRS JUNO. They wont if they hold their tongues. Dont be such a coward. My husband wont eat you.

GREGORY. I'm not afraid of your husband. I'm afraid of my conscience.

MRS JUNO [*losing patience*] Well! I dont consider myself at all a badly behaved woman; for nothing has passed between us that was not perfectly nice and friendly; but really! to hear a grown-up man talking about promises to his mother!—

GREGORY [*interrupting her*] Yes, yes: I know all about that. It's not romantic: it's not Don Juan: it's not advanced; but we feel it all the same. It's far deeper in our blood and bones than all the romantic stuff. My father got into a scandal once: that was why my mother made me promise never to make love to a married woman. And now Ive done it I cant feel honest. Dont pretend to despise me or laugh at me. You feel it too. You said just now that your own conscience was uneasy when you thought of your husband. What must it be when you think of my wife?

MRS JUNO [*rising aghast*] Your wife!!! You dont dare sit there and tell me coolly that youre a married man!

GREGORY. I never led you to believe I was unmarried.

MRS JUNO. Oh! You never gave me the faintest hint that you had a wife.

GREGORY. I did indeed. I discussed things with you that only married people really understand.

MRS JUNO. Oh!!

GREGORY. I thought it the most delicate way of letting you know.

MRS JUNO. Well, you are a daisy, I must say. I suppose thats vulgar; but really! really!! You and your goodness! However, now weve found one another out theres only one thing to be done. Will you please go?

GREGORY [*rising slowly*] I ought to go.

MRS JUNO. Well, go.

GREGORY. Yes. Er—[*he tries to go*] I—I somehow cant. [*He sits down again helplessly*] My conscience is active: my will is paralyzed. This is really dreadful. Would you mind ringing the bell and asking them to throw me out? You ought to, you know.

MRS JUNO. What! make a scandal in the face of the whole hotel! Certainly not. Dont be a fool.

GREGORY. Yes; but I cant go.

MRS JUNO. Then I can. Goodbye.

GREGORY [*clinging to her hand*] Can you really?

MRS JUNO. Of course I—[*she wavers*] Oh dear! [*They contemplate one another helplessly*]. I cant. [*She sinks on the lounge, hand in hand with him*].

GREGORY. For heaven's sake pull yourself together. It's a question of self-control.

MRS JUNO [*dragging her hand away and retreating to the end of the chesterfield*] No: it's a question of distance. Self-control is all very well two or three yards off, or on a ship, with everybody looking on. Dont come any nearer.

GREGORY. This is a ghastly business. I want to go away; and I cant.

MRS JUNO. I think you ought to go [*he makes an effort; and she adds quickly*] but if you try to I shall grab you round the neck and disgrace myself. I implore you to sit still and be nice.

GREGORY. I implore you to run away. I believe I can trust myself to let you go for your own sake. But it will break my heart.

MRS JUNO. I dont want to break your heart. I cant bear to think of your sitting here alone. I cant bear to think of sitting alone myself somewhere else. It's so senseless—so ridiculous—when we might be so happy. I dont want to be wicked, or coarse. But I like you very much; and I do want to be affectionate and human.

GREGORY. I ought to draw a line.

MRS JUNO. So you shall, dear. Tell me: do you really like me? I dont mean love me: you might love the housemaid—

GREGORY [*vehemently*] No!

MRS JUNO. Oh yes you might; and what does that matter, anyhow? Are you really fond of me? Are we friends—comrades? Would you be sorry if I died?

GREGORY [*shrinking*] Oh dont.

MRS JUNO. Or was it the usual aimless man's lark: a mere shipboard flirtation?

GREGORY. Oh no, no: nothing half so bad, so vulgar, so wrong. I assure you I only meant to be agreeable. It grew on me before I noticed it.

MRS JUNO. And you were glad to let it grow?

GREGORY. I let it grow because the board was not up.

MRS JUNO. Bother the board! I am just as fond of Sibthorpe as—

GREGORY. Sibthorpe!

MRS JUNO. Sibthorpe is my husband's Christian name. I oughtnt to call him Tops to you now.

GREGORY [*chuckling*] It sounded like something to drink. But I have no right to laugh at him. My Christian name is Gregory,

which sounds like a powder.

MRS JUNO [*chilled*] That is so like a man! I offer you my heart's warmest friendliest feeling; and you think of nothing but a silly joke. A quip like that makes you forget me.

GREGORY. Forget you! Oh, if only I could!

MRS JUNO. If you could, would you?

GREGORY [*burying his shamed face in his hands*] No: I'd die first. Oh, I hate myself.

MRS JUNO. I glory in myself. It's so jolly to be reckless. Can a man be reckless, I wonder?

GREGORY [*straightening himself desperately*] No. I'm not reckless. I know what I'm doing: my conscience is awake. Oh, where is the intoxication of love? the delirium? the madness that makes a man think the world well lost for the woman he adores? I dont think anything of the sort: I see that it's not worth it: I know that it's wrong: I have never in my life been cooler, more businesslike.

MRS JUNO [*opening her arms to him*] But you cant resist me.

GREGORY. I must. I ought. [*Throwing himself into her arms*] Oh my darling, my treasure, we shall be sorry for this.

MRS JUNO. We can forgive ourselves. Could we forgive ourselves if we let this moment slip?

GREGORY. I protest to the last. I'm against this. I have been pushed over a precipice. I'm innocent. This wild joy, this exquisite tenderness, this ascent into heaven can thrill me to the uttermost fibre of my heart [*with a gesture of ecstasy she hides her face on his shoulder*]; but it cant subdue my mind or corrupt my conscience, which still shouts to the skies that I'm not a willing party to this outrageous conduct. I repudiate the bliss with which you are filling me.

MRS JUNO. Never mind your conscience. Tell me how happy you are.

GREGORY. No: I recall you to your duty. But oh, I will give you my life with both hands if you can tell me that you feel for me one millionth part of what I feel for you now.

MRS JUNO. Oh yes, yes. Be satisfied with that. Ask for no more. Let me go.

GREGORY. I cant. I have no will. Something stronger than either of us is in command here. Nothing on earth or in heaven can part us now. You know that, dont you?

MRS JUNO. Oh, dont make me say it. Of course I know. Nothing—not life nor death nor shame nor anything can part us.

A MATTER-OF-FACT MALE VOICE IN THE CORRI-

DOR. All right. This must be it.

The two recover with a violent start; release one another; and spring back to opposite sides of the lounge.

GREGORY. That did it.

MRS JUNO [*in a thrilling whisper*] Sh-sh-sh! That was my husband's voice.

GREGORY. Impossible: it's only our guilty fancy.

A WOMAN'S VOICE. This is the way to the lounge. I know it.

GREGORY. Great Heaven! we're both mad. Thats my wife's voice.

MRS JUNO. Ridiculous! Oh, we're dreaming it all. We— [*the door opens; and Sibthorpe Juno appears in the roseate glow of the corridor (which happens to be papered in pink) with Mrs Lunn, like Tannhäuser in the hill of Venus. He is a fussily energetic little man, who gives himself an air of gallantry by greasing the points of his moustaches and dressing very carefully. She is a tall, imposing, handsome, languid woman, with flashing dark eyes and long lashes. They make for the chesterfield, not noticing the two palpitating figures blotted against the walls in the gloom on either side. The figures flit away noiselessly through the window and disappear*].

JUNO [*officiously*] Ah: here we are. [*He leads the way to the sofa*]. Sit down: I'm sure youre tired. [*She sits*]. Thats right. [*He sits beside her on her left*]. Hullo! [*he rises*] this sofa's quite warm.

MRS LUNN [*bored*] Is it? I dont notice it. I expect the sun's been on it.

JUNO. I felt it quite distinctly: I'm more thinly clad than you. [*He sits down again, and proceeds, with a sigh of satisfaction*] What a relief to get off the ship and have a private room! Thats the worst of a ship. Youre under observation all the time.

MRS LUNN. But why not?

JUNO. Well, of course theres no reason: at least I suppose not. But, you know, part of the romance of a journey is that a man keeps imagining that something might happen; and he cant do that if there are a lot of people about and it simply cant happen.

MRS LUNN. Mr Juno: romance is all very well on board ship; but when your foot touches the soil of England theres an end of it.

JUNO. No: believe me, thats a foreigner's mistake: we are the most romantic people in the world, we English. Why, my very presence here is a romance.

MRS LUNN [*faintly ironical*] Indeed?

JUNO. Yes. Youve guessed, of course, that I'm a married man.

MRS LUNN. Oh, thats all right. I'm a married woman.

JUNO. Thank Heaven for that! To my English mind, passion is not real passion without guilt. I am a red-blooded man, Mrs Lunn: I cant help it. The tragedy of my life is that I married, when quite young, a woman whom I couldnt help being very fond of. I longed for a guilty passion—for the real thing—the wicked thing; and yet I couldnt care twopence for any other woman when my wife was about. Year after year went by: I felt my youth slipping away without ever having had a romance in my life; for marriage is all very well; but it isnt romance. Theres nothing wrong in it, you see.

MRS LUNN. Poor man! How you must have suffered!

JUNO. No: that was what was so tame about it. I w a n t e d to suffer. You get so sick of being happily married. It's always the happy marriages that break up. At last my wife and I agreed that we ought to take a holiday.

MRS LUNN. Hadnt you holidays every year?

JUNO. Oh, the seaside and so on! Thats not what we meant. We meant a holiday from one another.

MRS LUNN. How very odd!

JUNO. She said it was an excellent idea; that domestic felicity was making us perfectly idiotic; that she wanted a holiday too. So we agreed to go round the world in opposite directions. I started for Suez on the day she sailed for New York.

MRS LUNN [*suddenly becoming attentive*] Thats precisely what Gregory and I did. Now I wonder did he want a holiday from me! What he said was that he wanted the delight of meeting me after a long absence.

JUNO. Could anything be more romantic than that? Would anyone else than an Englishman have thought of it? I daresay my temperament seems tame to your boiling southern blood—

MRS LUNN. My what!

JUNO. Your southern blood. Dont you remember how you told me, that night in the saloon when I sang "Farewell and adieu to you dear Spanish ladies," that you were by birth a lady of Spain? Your splendid Andalusian beauty speaks for itself.

MRS LUNN. Stuff! I was born in Gibraltar.

My father was Captain Jenkins. In the artillery.

JUNO [*ardently*] It is climate and not race that determines the temperament. The fiery sun of Spain blazed on your cradle; and it rocked to the roar of British cannon.

MRS LUNN. What eloquence! It reminds me of my husband when he was in love—before we were married. Are you in love?

JUNO. Yes; and with the same woman.

MRS LUNN. Well, of course, I didnt suppose you were in love with two women.

JUNO. I dont think you quite understand. I meant that I am in love with you.

MRS LUNN [*relapsing into deepest boredom*] Oh, that! Men do fall in love with me. They all seem to think me a creature with volcanic passions: I'm sure I dont know why; for all the volcanic women I know are plain little creatures with sandy hair. I dont consider human volcanoes respectable. And I'm so tired of the subject! Our house is always full of women who are in love with my husband and men who are in love with me. We encourage it because it's pleasant to have company.

JUNO. And is your husband as insensible as yourself?

MRS LUNN. Oh, Gregory's not insensible: very far from it; but I am the only woman in the world for him.

JUNO. But you? Are you really as insensible as you say you are?

MRS LUNN. I never said anything of the kind. I'm not at all insensible by nature; but (I dont know whether youve noticed it) I am what people call rather a fine figure of a woman.

JUNO [*passionately*] Noticed it! Oh, Mrs Lunn! Have I been able to notice anything else since we met?

MRS LUNN. There you go, like all the rest of them! I ask you, how do you expect a woman to keep up what you call her sensibility when this sort of thing has happened to her about three times a week ever since she was seventeen? It used to upset me and terrify me at first. Then I got rather a taste for it. It came to a climax with Gregory: that was why I married him. Then it became a mild lark, hardly worth the trouble. After that I found it valuable once or twice as a spinal tonic when I was run down; but now it's an unmitigated bore. I dont mind your declaration: I daresay it gives you a certain pleasure to make it. I quite understand that you adore me; but (if you dont mind) I'd rather you didnt keep on saying so.

JUNO. Is there then no hope for me?

MRS LUNN. Oh, yes. Gregory has an idea that married women keep lists of the men theyll marry if they become widows. I'll put your name down, if that will satisfy you.

JUNO. Is the list a long one?

MRS LUNN. Do you mean the real list? Not the one I shew to Gregory: there are hundreds of names on that; but the little private list that he'd better not see?

JUNO. Oh, will you really put me on that? Say you will.

MRS LUNN. Well, perhaps I will. [*He kisses her hand*]. Now dont begin abusing the privilege.

JUNO. May I call you by your Christian name?

MRS LUNN. No: it's too long. You cant go about calling a woman Seraphita.

JUNO [*ecstatically*] Seraphita!

MRS LUNN. I used to be called Sally at home; but when I married a man named Lunn, of course that became ridiculous. Thats my one little pet joke. Call me Mrs Lunn for short. And change the subject, or I shall go to sleep.

JUNO. I cant change the subject. For me there is no other subject. Why else have you put me on your list?

MRS LUNN. Because youre a solicitor. Gregory's a solicitor. I'm accustomed to my husband being a solicitor and telling me things he oughtnt to tell anybody.

JUNO [*ruefully*] Is that all? Oh, I cant believe that the voice of love has ever thoroughly awakened you.

MRS LUNN. No: it sends me to sleep. [*Juno appeals against this by an amorous demonstration*]. It's no use, Mr Juno: I'm hopelessly respectable: the Jenkinses always were. Dont you realize that unless most women were like that, the world couldnt go on as it does?

JUNO [*darkly*] You think it goes on respectably; but I can tell you as a solicitor—

MRS LUNN. Stuff! of course all the disreputable people who get into trouble go to you, just as all the sick people go to the doctors; but most people never go to a solicitor.

JUNO [*rising, with a growing sense of injury*] Look here, Mrs Lunn: do you think a man's heart is a potato? or a turnip? or a ball of knitting wool? that you can throw it away like this?

MRS LUNN. I dont throw away balls of knitting wool. A man's heart seems to me much like a sponge: it sops up dirty water as well as clean.

JUNO. I have never been treated like this in my life. Here am I, a married man, with a most attractive wife: a wife I adore, and who adores me, and has never as much as looked at any other man since we were married. I come and throw all this at your feet. I! I, a solicitor! braving the risk of your husband putting me into the divorce court and making me a beggar and an outcast! I do this for your sake. And you go on as if I were making no sacrifice: as if I had told you it's a fine evening, or asked you to have a cup of tea. It's not human. It's not right. Love has its rights as well as respectability [*he sits down again, aloof and sulky*].

MRS LUNN. Nonsense! Here! heres a flower [*she gives him one*]. Go and dream over it until you feel hungry. Nothing brings people to their senses like hunger.

JUNO [*contemplating the flower without rapture*] What good's this?

MRS LUNN [*snatching it from him*] Oh! you dont love me a bit.

JUNO. Yes I do. Or at least I did. But I'm an Englishman; and I think you ought to respect the conventions of English life.

MRS LUNN. But I am respecting them; and youre not.

JUNO. Pardon me. I may be doing wrong; but I'm doing it in a proper and customary manner. You may be doing right; but youre doing it in an unusual and questionable manner. I am not prepared to put up with that. I can stand being badly treated: I'm no baby, and can take care of myself with anybody. And of course I can stand being well treated. But the one thing I cant stand is being unexpectedly treated. It's outside my scheme of life. So come now! youve got to behave naturally and straightforwardly with me. You can leave husband and child, home, friends, and country, for my sake, and come with me to some southern isle—or say South America—where we can be all in all to one another. Or you can tell your husband and let him jolly well punch my head if he can. But I'm damned if I'm going to stand any eccentricity. It's not respectable.

GREGORY [*coming in from the terrace and advancing with dignity to his wife's end of the chesterfield*] Will you have the goodness, sir, in addressing this lady, to keep your temper and refrain from using profane language?

MRS LUNN [*rising, delighted*] Gregory! Darling [*she enfolds him in a copious embrace*]!

JUNO [*rising*] You make love to another man to my face!

MRS LUNN. Why, he's my husband.

JUNO. That takes away the last rag of excuse for such conduct. A nice world it would be if married people were to carry on their endearments before everybody!

GREGORY. This is ridiculous. What the devil business is it of yours what passes between my wife and myself? Youre not her husband, are you?

JUNO. Not at present; but I'm on the list. I'm her prospective husband: youre only her actual one. I'm the anticipation: youre the disappointment.

MRS LUNN. Oh, my Gregory is not a disappointment. [*Fondly*] Are you, dear?

GREGORY. You just wait, my pet. I'll settle this chap for you. [*He disengages himself from her embrace, and faces Juno. She sits down placidly*]. You call me a disappointment, do you? Well, I suppose every husband's a disappointment. What about yourself? Dont try to look like an unmarried man. I happen to know the lady you disappointed. I travelled in the same ship with her; and—

JUNO. And you fell in love with her.

GREGORY [*taken aback*] Who told you that?

JUNO. Aha! you confess it. Well, if you want to know, nobody told me. Everybody falls in love with my wife.

GREGORY. And do you fall in love with everybody's wife?

JUNO. Certainly not. Only with yours.

MRS LUNN. But whats the good of saying that, Mr Juno? I'm married to him; and theres an end of it.

JUNO. Not at all. You can get a divorce.

MRS LUNN. What for?

JUNO. For his misconduct with my wife.

GREGORY [*deeply indignant*] How dare you, sir, asperse the character of that sweet lady? a lady whom I have taken under my protection.

JUNO. Protection!

MRS JUNO [*returning hastily*] Really you must be more careful what you say about me, Mr Lunn.

JUNO. My precious! [*He embraces her*]. Pardon this betrayal of feeling; but Ive not seen my wife for several weeks; and she is very dear to me.

GREGORY. I call this cheek. Who is making love to his own wife before people now, pray?

MRS LUNN. Wont you introduce me to your wife, Mr Juno?

MRS JUNO. How do you do? [*They shake hands; and Mrs Juno sits down beside Mrs Lunn, on her left*].

MRS LUNN. I'm so glad to find you do credit to Gregory's taste. I'm naturally rather particular about the women he falls in love with.

JUNO [*sternly*] This is no way to take your husband's unfaithfulness. [*To Lunn*] You ought to teach your wife better. Wheres her feelings? It's scandalous.

GREGORY. What about your own conduct, pray?

JUNO. I dont defend it; and theres an end of the matter.

GREGORY. Well, upon my soul! What difference does your not defending it make?

JUNO. A fundamental difference. To serious people I may appear wicked. I dont defend myself: I am wicked, though not bad at heart. To thoughtless people I may even appear comic. Well, laugh at me: I have given myself away. But Mrs Lunn seems to have no opinion at all about me. She doesnt seem to know whether I'm wicked or comic. She doesnt seem to care. She has no moral sense. I say it's not right. I repeat, I have sinned; and I'm prepared to suffer.

MRS JUNO. Have you really sinned, Tops?

MRS LUNN [*blandly*] I dont remember your sinning. I have a shocking bad memory for trifles; but I think I should remember that— if you mean me.

JUNO [*raging*] Trifles! I have fallen in love with a monster.

GREGORY. Dont you dare call my wife a monster.

MRS JUNO [*rising quickly and coming between them*] Please dont lose your temper, Mr Lunn: I wont have my Tops bullied.

GREGORY. Well, then, let him not brag about sinning with my wife. [*He turns impulsively to his wife; makes her rise; and takes her proudly on his arm*]. What pretension has he to any such honor?

JUNO. I sinned in intention. [*Mrs Juno abandons him and resumes her seat, chilled*]. I'm as guilty as if I had actually sinned. And I insist on being treated as a sinner, and not walked over as if I'd done nothing, by your

wife or any other man.

MRS LUNN. Tush! [*She sits down again contemptuously*].

JUNO [*furious*] I wont be belittled.

MRS LUNN [*to Mrs Juno*] I hope youll come and stay with us now that you and Gregory are such friends, Mrs Juno.

JUNO. This insane magnanimity—

MRS LUNN. Dont you think youve said enough, Mr Juno? This is a matter for two women to settle. Wont you take a stroll on the beach with my Gregory while we talk it over. Gregory is a splendid listener.

JUNO. I dont think any good can come of a conversation between Mr Lunn and myself. We can hardly be expected to improve one another's morals. [*He passes behind the chesterfield to Mrs Lunn's end; seizes a chair; deliberately pushes it between Gregory and Mrs Lunn; and sits down with folded arms, resolved not to budge*].

GREGORY. Oh! Indeed! Oh, all right. If you come to that— [*he crosses to Mrs Juno; plants a chair by her side; and sits down with equal determination*].

JUNO. Now we are both equally guilty.

GREGORY. Pardon me. I'm not guilty.

JUNO. In intention. Dont quibble. You were guilty in intention, as I was.

GREGORY. No. I should rather describe myself as being guilty in fact, but not in intention.

JUNO	rising and	What!
MRS JUNO	exclaiming	No, really—
MRS LUNN	simultaneously	Gregory!

GREGORY. Yes: I maintain that I am responsible for my intentions only, and not for reflex actions over which I have no control. [*Mrs Juno sits down, ashamed*]. I promised my mother that I would never tell a lie, and that I would never make love to a married woman. I never h a v e told a lie—

MRS LUNN [*remonstrating*] Gregory! [*She sits down again*].

GREGORY. I say never. On many occasions I have resorted to prevarication; but on great occasions I have always told the truth. I regard this as a great occasion; and I wont be intimidated into breaking my promise. I solemnly declare that I did not know until this evening that Mrs Juno was married. She will bear me out when I say that from that moment my intentions were strictly and resolutely honorable; though my conduct, which I could not control and am therefore not responsible for, was disgraceful — or would have been had this gentleman not walked in and begun making love to my wife under my very nose.

JUNO [*flinging himself back into his chair*] Well, I like this!

MRS LUNN. Really, darling, theres no use in the pot calling the kettle black.

GREGORY. When you say darling, may I ask which of us you are addressing?

MRS LUNN. I really dont know. I'm getting hopelessly confused.

JUNO. Why dont you let my wife say something? I dont think she ought to be thrust into the background like this.

MRS LUNN. I'm sorry, I'm sure. Please excuse me, dear.

MRS JUNO [*thoughtfully*] I dont know what to say. I must think over it. I have always been rather severe on this sort of thing; but when it came to the point I didnt behave as I thought I should behave. I didnt intend to be wicked; but somehow or other, Nature, or whatever you choose to call it, didnt take much notice of my intentions. [*Gregory instinctively seeks her hand and presses it*]. And I really did think, Tops, that I was the only woman in the world for you.

JUNO [*cheerfully*] Oh, thats all right, my precious. Mrs Lunn thought she was the only woman in the world for him.

GREGORY [*reflectively*] So she is, in a sort of way.

JUNO [*flaring up*] And so is my wife. Dont you set up to be a better husband than I am; for youre not. Ive owned I'm wrong. You havnt.

MRS LUNN. Are you sorry, Gregory?

GREGORY [*perplexed*] Sorry?

MRS LUNN. Yes, sorry. I think it's time for you to say youre sorry, and to make friends with Mr Juno before we all dine together.

GREGORY. Seraphita: I promised my mother—

MRS JUNO [*involuntarily*] Oh, bother your mother! [*Recovering herself*] I beg your pardon.

GREGORY. A promise is a promise. I cant tell a deliberate lie. I know I ought to be sorry; but the flat fact is that I'm not sorry. I find that in this business, somehow or other, there is a disastrous separation between my moral principles and my conduct.

JUNO. Theres nothing disastrous about it. It doesnt matter about your conduct if your principles are all right.

GREGORY. Bosh! It doesnt matter about your principles if your conduct is all right.

JUNO. But your conduct isnt all right; and my principles are.

GREGORY. Whats the good of your principles being right if they wont work?

JUNO. They will work, sir, if you exercise self-sacrifice.

GREGORY. Oh yes: if, if, if. You know jolly well that self-sacrifice doesnt work either when you really want a thing. How much have you sacrificed yourself, pray?

MRS LUNN. Oh, a great deal, Gregory. Dont be rude. Mr Juno is a very nice man: he has been most attentive to me on the voyage.

GREGORY. And Mrs Juno's a very nice woman. She oughtnt to be; but she is.

JUNO. Why oughtnt she to be a nice woman, pray?

GREGORY. I mean she oughtnt to be nice to me. And you oughtnt to be nice to my wife. And your wife oughtnt to like me. And my wife oughtnt to like you. And if they do, they oughtnt to go on liking us. And I oughtnt to like your wife; and you oughtnt to like mine; and if we do, we oughtnt to go on liking them. But we do, all of us. We oughtnt; but we do.

JUNO. But, my dear boy, if we admit we are in the wrong wheres the harm of it? We're not perfect; but as long as we keep the ideal before us—

GREGORY. How?

JUNO. By admitting we're wrong.

MRS LUNN [*springing up, out of patience, and pacing round the lounge intolerantly*] Well, really, I must have my dinner. These two men, with their morality, and their promises to their mothers, and their admissions that they were wrong, and their sinning and suffering, and their going on at one another as if it meant anything, or as if it mattered, are getting on my nerves. [*Stooping over the back of the chesterfield to address Mrs Juno*] If you will be so very good, my dear, as to take my sentimental husband off my hands occasionally, I shall be more than obliged to you: I'm sure you can stand more male sentimentality than I can. [*Sweeping away to the fireplace*] I, on my part, will do my best to amuse your excellent husband when you find him tiresome.

JUNO. I call this polyandry.

MRS LUNN. I wish you wouldnt call innocent

things by offensive names, Mr Juno. What do you call your own conduct?

JUNO [*rising*] I tell you I have admitted—

GREGORY		Whats the good of keeping on at that?
MRS JUNO	*together*	Oh, not that again, please.
MRS LUNN		Tops: I'll scream if you say that again.

JUNO. Oh, well, if you wont listen to me—! [*He sits down again*].

MRS JUNO. What is the position now exactly? [*Mrs Lunn shrugs her shoulders and gives up the conundrum. Gregory looks at Juno. Juno turns away his head huffily*]. I mean, what are we going to do?

MRS LUNN. What would you advise, Mr Juno?

JUNO. I should advise you to divorce your husband.

MRS LUNN. You want me to drag your wife into court and disgrace her?

JUNO. No: I forgot that. Excuse me; but for the moment I thought I was married to you.

GREGORY. I think we had better let bygones be bygones. [*To Mrs Juno, very tenderly*] You will forgive me, wont you? Why should you let a moment's forgetfulness embitter all our future life?

MRS JUNO. But it's Mrs Lunn who has to forgive you.

GREGORY. Oh, dash it, I forgot. This is getting ridiculous.

MRS LUNN. I'm getting hungry.

MRS JUNO. Do you really mind, Mrs Lunn?

MRS LUNN. My dear Mrs Juno, Gregory is one of those terribly uxorious men who ought to have ten wives. If any really nice woman will take him off my hands for a day or two occasionally, I shall be greatly obliged to her.

GREGORY. Seraphita: you cut me to the soul [*he weeps*].

MRS LUNN. Serve you right! Youd think it quite proper if it cut me to the soul.

MRS JUNO. Am I to take Sibthorpe off your hands too, Mrs Lunn?

JUNO [*rising*] Do you suppose I'll allow this?

MRS JUNO. Youve admitted that youve done wrong, Tops. Whats the use of your allowing or not allowing after that?

JUNO. I do not admit that I have done wrong. I admit that what I did was wrong.

GREGORY. Can you explain the distinction?

JUNO. It's quite plain to anyone but an imbecile. If you tell me Ive done something wrong you insult me. But if you say that something that I did is wrong you simply raise a question of morals. I tell you flatly if you say I did anything wrong you will have to fight me. In fact I think we ought to fight anyhow. I dont particularly want to; but I feel that England expects us to.

GREGORY. I wont fight. If you beat me my wife would share my humiliation. If I beat you, she would sympathize with you and loathe me for my brutality.

MRS LUNN. Not to mention that as we are human beings and not reindeer or barndoor fowl, if two men presumed to fight for us we couldnt decently ever speak to either of them again.

GREGORY. Besides, neither of us could beat the other, as we neither of us know how to fight. We should only blacken each other's eyes and make fools of ourselves.

JUNO. I dont admit that. Every Englishman can use his fists.

GREGORY. Youre an Englishman. Can you use yours?

JUNO. I presume so: I never tried.

MRS JUNO. You never told me you couldnt fight, Tops. I thought you were an accomplished boxer.

JUNO. My precious: I never gave you any ground for such a belief.

MRS JUNO. You always talked as if it were a matter of course. You spoke with the greatest contempt of men who didnt kick other men downstairs.

JUNO. Well, I cant kick Mr Lunn downstairs. We're on the ground floor.

MRS JUNO. You could throw him into the harbor.

GREGORY. Do you want me to be thrown into the harbor?

MRS JUNO. No: I only want to shew Tops that he's making a ghastly fool of himself.

GREGORY [*rising and prowling disgustedly between the chesterfield and the windows*] We're all making fools of ourselves.

JUNO [*following him*] Well, if we're not to fight, I must insist at least on your never speaking to my wife again.

GREGORY. Does my speaking to your wife do you any harm?

JUNO. No. But it's the proper course to take. [*Emphatically*] We must behave with some sort of decency.

MRS LUNN. And are you never going to

speak to me again, Mr Juno?

JUNO. I'm prepared to promise never to do so. I think your husband has a right to demand that. Then if I speak to you after, it will not be his fault. It will be a breach of my promise; and I shall not attempt to defend my conduct.

GREGORY [*facing him*] I shall talk to your wife as often as she'll let me.

MRS JUNO. I have no objection to your speaking to me, Mr Lunn.

JUNO. Then I shall take steps.

GREGORY. What steps?

JUNO. Steps. Measures. Proceedings. Such steps as may seem advisable.

MRS LUNN [*to Mrs Juno*] Can your husband afford a scandal, Mrs Juno?

MRS JUNO. No.

MRS LUNN. Neither can mine.

GREGORY. Mrs Juno: I'm very sorry I let you in for all this. I dont know how it is that we contrive to make feelings like ours, which seem to me to be beautiful and sacred feelings, and which lead to such interesting and exciting adventures, end in vulgar squabbles and degrading scenes.

JUNO. I decline to admit that my conduct has been vulgar or degrading.

GREGORY. I promised—

JUNO. Look here, old chap: I dont say a word against your mother; and I'm sorry she's dead; but really, you know, most women are mothers; and they all die some time or other; yet that doesnt make them infallible authorities on morals, does it?

GREGORY. I was about to say so myself. Let me add that if you do things merely because you think some other fool expects you to do them, and he expects you to do them because he thinks you expect him to expect you to do them, it will end in everybody doing what nobody wants to do, which is in my opinion a silly state of things.

JUNO. Lunn: I love your wife; and thats all about it.

GREGORY. Juno: I love yours. What then?

JUNO. Clearly she must never see you again.

MRS JUNO. Why not?

JUNO. Why not! My love: I'm surprised at you.

MRS JUNO. Am I to speak only to men who dislike me?

JUNO. Yes: I think that is, properly speaking, a married woman's duty.

MRS JUNO. Then I wont do it: thats flat. I like to be liked. I like to be loved. I want everyone round me to love me. I dont want to meet or speak to anyone who doesnt like me.

JUNO. But, my precious, this is the most horrible immorality.

MRS LUNN. I dont intend to give up meeting you, Mr Juno. You amuse me very much. I dont like being loved: it bores me. But I do like to be amused.

JUNO. I hope we shall meet very often. But I hope also we shall not defend our conduct.

MRS JUNO [*rising*] This is unendurable. Weve all been flirting. Need we go on footling about it?

JUNO [*huffily*] I dont know what you call footling—

MRS JUNO [*cutting him short*] You do. You're footling. Mr Lunn is footling. Cant we admit that we're human and have done with it?

JUNO. I have admitted it all along. I—

MRS JUNO [*almost screaming*] Then stop footling.

The dinner gong sounds.

MRS LUNN [*rising*] Thank heaven! Lets go into dinner. Gregory: take in Mrs Juno.

GREGORY. But surely I ought to take in our guest, and not my own wife.

MRS LUNN. Well, Mrs Juno is not your wife, is she?

GREGORY. Oh, of course: I beg your pardon. I'm hopelessly confused. [*He offers his arm to Mrs Juno, rather apprehensively*].

MRS JUNO. You seem quite afraid of me [*she takes his arm*].

GREGORY. I am. I simply adore you. [*They go out together; and as they pass through the door he turns and says in a ringing voice to the other couple*] I have said to Mrs Juno that I simply adore her. [*He takes her out defiantly*].

MRS LUNN [*calling after him*] Yes, dear. She's a darling. [*To Juno*] Now, Sibthorpe.

JUNO [*giving her his arm gallantly*] You have called me Sibthorpe! Thank you. I think Lunn's conduct fully justifies me in allowing you to do it.

MRS LUNN. Yes: I think you may let yourself go now.

JUNO. Seraphita: I worship you beyond expression.

MRS LUNN. Sibthorpe: you amuse me beyond description. Come. [*They go in to dinner together*].

THE END

XXIII

PYGMALION

A ROMANCE IN FIVE ACTS (1912)

ACT I

Covent Garden at 11.15 p.m. Torrents of heavy summer rain. Cab whistles blowing frantically in all directions. Pedestrians running for shelter into the market and under the portico of St Paul's Church, where there are already several people, among them a lady and her daughter in evening dress. They are all peering out gloomily at the rain, except one man with his back turned to the rest, who seems wholly preoccupied with a notebook in which he is writing busily.

The church clock strikes the first quarter.

THE DAUGHTER [*in the space between the central pillars, close to the one on her left*] I'm getting chilled to the bone. What can Freddy be doing all this time? He's been gone twenty minutes.

THE MOTHER [*on her daughter's right*] Not so long. But he ought to have got us a cab by this.

A BYSTANDER [*on the lady's right*] He wont get no cab not until half-past eleven, missus, when they come back after dropping their theatre fares.

THE MOTHER. But we must have a cab. We cant stand here until half-past eleven. It's too bad.

THE BYSTANDER. Well, it aint my fault, missus.

THE DAUGHTER. If Freddy had a bit of gumption, he would have got one at the theatre door.

THE MOTHER. What could he have done, poor boy?

THE DAUGHTER. Other people got cabs. Why couldnt he?

Freddy rushes in out of the rain from the Southampton Street side, and comes between them closing a dripping umbrella. He is a young man of twenty, in evening dress, very wet round the ankles.

THE DAUGHTER. Well, havnt you got a cab?

FREDDY. Theres not one to be had for love or money.

THE MOTHER. Oh, Freddy, there must be one. You cant have tried.

THE DAUGHTER. It's too tiresome. Do you expect us to go and get one ourselves?

FREDDY. I tell you theyre all engaged. The rain was so sudden: nobody was prepared; and everybody had to take a cab. Ive been to Charing Cross one way and nearly to Ludgate Circus the other; and they were all engaged.

THE MOTHER. Did you try Trafalgar Square?

FREDDY. There wasnt one at Trafalgar Square.

THE DAUGHTER. Did you try?

FREDDY. I tried as far as Charing Cross Station. Did you expect me to walk to Hammersmith?

THE DAUGHTER. You havnt tried at all.

THE MOTHER. You really are very helpless, Freddy. Go again; and dont come back until you have found a cab.

FREDDY. I shall simply get soaked for nothing.

THE DAUGHTER. And what about us? Are we to stay here all night in this draught, with next to nothing on? You selfish pig—

FREDDY. Oh, very well: I'll go, I'll go. [*He opens his umbrella and dashes off Strandwards, but comes into collision with a flower girl, who is hurrying in for shelter, knocking her basket out of her hands. A blinding flash of lightning, followed instantly by a rattling peal of thunder, orchestrates the incident*].

THE FLOWER GIRL. Nah then, Freddy: look wh' y' gowin, deah.

FREDDY. Sorry [*he rushes off*].

THE FLOWER GIRL [*picking up her scattered flowers and replacing them in the basket*] Theres menners f' yer! Te-oo banches o voylets trod into the mad. [*She sits down on the plinth of the column, sorting her flowers, on the lady's right. She is not at all an attractive person. She is perhaps eighteen, perhaps twenty, hardly older. She wears a little sailor hat of black straw that has long been exposed to the dust and soot of London and has seldom if ever been brushed. Her hair needs washing rather badly: its mousy color can hardly be natural. She wears a shoddy black coat that reaches nearly to her knees and is shaped to her waist. She has a brown skirt with a coarse apron. Her boots are much the worse for wear. She is no doubt as clean as she can afford to be; but compared to the ladies she is very dirty. Her features are no worse than theirs; but their condition leaves something to be desired; and she needs the services of a dentist].*

THE MOTHER. How do you know that my son's name is Freddy, pray?

THE FLOWER GIRL. Ow, eez ye-ooa san, is e? Wal, fewd dan y' de-ooty bawmz a mather should, eed now bettern to spawl a pore gel's flahrzn than ran awy athaht pyin. Will ye-oo py me f' them? [*Here, with apologies, this desperate attempt to represent her dialect without a phonetic alphabet must be abandoned as unintelligible outside London].*

THE DAUGHTER. Do nothing of the sort, mother. The idea!

THE MOTHER. Please allow me, Clara. Have you any pennies?

THE DAUGHTER. No. Ive nothing smaller than sixpence.

THE FLOWER GIRL [*hopefully*] I can give you change for a tanner, kind lady.

THE MOTHER [*to Clara*] Give it to me. [*Clara parts reluctantly*]. Now [*to the girl*] This is for your flowers.

THE FLOWER GIRL. Thank you kindly, lady.

THE DAUGHTER. Make her give you the change. These things are only a penny a bunch.

THE MOTHER. Do hold your tongue, Clara. [*To the girl*] You can keep the change.

THE FLOWER GIRL. Oh, thank you, lady.

THE MOTHER. Now tell me how you know that young gentleman's name.

THE FLOWER GIRL. I didnt.

THE MOTHER. I heard you call him by it. Dont try to deceive me.

THE FLOWER GIRL [*protesting*] Who's trying to deceive you? I called him Freddy or Charlie same as you might yourself if you was talking to a stranger and wished to be pleasant. [*She sits down beside her basket*].

THE DAUGHTER. Sixpence thrown away! Really, mamma, you might have spared Freddy t h a t. [*She retreats in disgust behind the pillar*].

An elderly gentleman of the amiable military type rushes into the shelter, and closes a dripping umbrella. He is in the same plight as Freddy, very wet about the ankles. He is in evening dress, with a light overcoat. He takes the place left vacant by the daughter's retirement.

THE GENTLEMAN. Phew!

THE MOTHER [*to the gentleman*] Oh, sir, is there any sign of its stopping?

THE GENTLEMAN. I'm afraid not. It started worse than ever about two minutes ago [*he goes to the plinth beside the flower girl; puts up his foot on it; and stoops to turn down his trouser ends*].

THE MOTHER. Oh dear! [*She retires sadly and joins her daughter*].

THE FLOWER GIRL [*taking advantage of the military gentleman's proximity to establish friendly relations with him*] If it's worse, it's a sign it's nearly over. So cheer up, Captain; and buy a flower off a poor girl.

THE GENTLEMAN. I'm sorry. I havnt any change.

THE FLOWER GIRL. I can give you change, Captain.

THE GENTLEMAN. For a sovereign? Ive nothing less.

THE FLOWER GIRL. Garn! Oh do buy a flower off me, Captain. I can change half-a-crown. Take this for tuppence.

THE GENTLEMAN. Now dont be troublesome: theres a good girl. [*Trying his pockets*] I really havnt any change— Stop: heres three hapence, if thats any use to you [*he retreats to the other pillar*].

THE FLOWER GIRL [*disappointed, but thinking three halfpence better than nothing*] Thank you, sir.

THE BYSTANDER [*to the girl*] You be careful: give him a flower for it. Theres a bloke here behind taking down every blessed word youre saying. [*All turn to the man who is taking notes*].

THE FLOWER GIRL [*springing up terrified*] I aint done nothing wrong by speaking to the gentleman. Ive a right to sell flowers if I keep off the kerb. [*Hysterically*] I'm a respectable girl: so help me, I never spoke to him except to ask him to buy a flower off me. [*General hubbub, mostly sympathetic to the flower girl, but deprecating her excessive sensibility. Cries of* Dont start hollerin. Who's hurting you? Nobody's going to touch you. Whats the good of fussing? Steady on. Easy easy, etc., *come from the elderly staid spectators, who pat her comfortingly. Less patient ones bid her shut her head, or ask her roughly what is wrong with her. A remoter group, not knowing what the matter is, crowd in and increase the noise with question and answer:* Whats the row? Whatshe do? Where is he? A tec taking her down. What! him? Yes: him over there: Took money off the gentleman, etc. *The flower girl, distraught and mobbed, breaks through them to the gentleman, crying wildly*] Oh, sir, dont let him charge me. You dunno what it means to me. Theyll take away my character and drive me on the streets for speaking to gentlemen. They—

THE NOTE TAKER [*coming forward on her right, the rest crowding after him*] There, there, there, there! who's hurting you, you silly girl? What do you take me for?

THE BYSTANDER. It's all right: he's a gentleman: look at his boots. [*Explaining to the note taker*] She thought you was a copper's nark, sir.

THE NOTE TAKER [*with quick interest*] Whats a copper's nark?

THE BYSTANDER [*inapt at definition*] It's a— well, it's a copper's nark, as you might say. What else would you call it? A sort of informer.

THE FLOWER GIRL [*still hysterical*] I take my Bible oath I never said a word—

THE NOTE TAKER [*overbearing but good-humored*] Oh, shut up, shut up. Do I look like a policeman?

THE FLOWER GIRL [*far from reassured*] Then what did you take down my words for? How do I know whether you took me down right? You just shew me what youve wrote about me. [*The note taker opens his book and holds it steadily under her nose, though the pressure of the mob trying to read it over his shoulders would upset a weaker man*]. Whats that? That aint proper writing. I cant read that.

THE NOTE TAKER. I can. [*Reads, reproducing her pronunciation exactly*] "Cheer ap, Keptin; n' baw ya flahr orf a pore gel."

THE FLOWER GIRL [*much distressed*] It's because I called him Captain. I meant no harm. [*To the gentleman*] Oh, sir, dont let him lay a charge agen me for a word like that. You—

THE GENTLEMAN. Charge! I make no charge. [*To the note taker*] Really, sir, if you are a detective, you need not begin protecting me against molestation by young women until I ask you. Anybody could see that the girl meant no harm.

THE BYSTANDERS GENERALLY [*demonstrating against police espionage*] Course they could. What business is it of yours? You mind your own affairs. He wants promotion, he does. Taking down people's words! Girl never said a word to him. What harm if she did? Nice thing a girl cant shelter from the rain without being insulted, etc., etc., etc. [*She is conducted*

by the more sympathetic demonstrators back to her plinth, where she resumes her seat and struggles with her emotion].

THE BYSTANDER. He aint a tec. He's a blooming busybody: thats what he is. I tell you, look at his boots.

THE NOTE TAKER [*turning on him genially*] And how are all your people down at Selsey?

THE BYSTANDER [*suspiciously*] Who told you my people come from Selsey?

THE NOTE TAKER. Never you mind. They did. [*To the girl*] How do you come to be up so far east? You were born in Lisson Grove.

THE FLOWER GIRL [*appalled*] Oh, what harm is there in my leaving Lisson Grove? It wasnt fit for a pig to live in; and I had to pay four-and-six a week. [*In tears*] Oh, boo—hoo—oo—

THE NOTE TAKER. Live where you like; but stop that noise.

THE GENTLEMAN [*to the girl*] Come, come! he cant touch you: you have a right to live where you please.

A SARCASTIC BYSTANDER [*thrusting himself between the note taker and the gentleman*] Park Lane, for instance. I'd like to go into the Housing Question with you, I would.

THE FLOWER GIRL [*subsiding into a brooding melancholy over her basket, and talking very low-spiritedly to herself*] I'm a good girl, I am.

THE SARCASTIC BYSTANDER [*not attending to her*] Do you know where *I* come from?

THE NOTE TAKER [*promptly*] Hoxton.

Titterings. Popular interest in the note taker's performance increases.

THE SARCASTIC ONE [*amazed*] Well, who said I didnt? Bly me! You know everything, you do.

THE FLOWER GIRL [*still nursing her sense of injury*] Aint no call to meddle with me, he aint.

THE BYSTANDER [*to her*] Of course he aint. Dont you stand it from him. [*To the note taker*] See here: what call have you to know about people what never offered to meddle with you? Wheres your warrant?

SEVERAL BYSTANDERS [*encouraged by this seeming point of law*] Yes: wheres your warrant?

THE FLOWER GIRL. Let him say what he likes. I dont want to have no truck with him.

THE BYSTANDER. You take us for dirt under your feet, dont you? Catch you taking liberties with a gentleman!

THE SARCASTIC BYSTANDER. Yes: tell him where he come from if you want to go fortune-telling.

THE NOTE TAKER. Cheltenham, Harrow, Cambridge, and India.

THE GENTLEMAN. Quite right. [*Great laughter. Reaction in the note taker's favor. Exclamations of* He knows all about it. Told him proper. Hear him tell the toff where he come from? *etc.*]. May I ask, sir, do you do this for your living at a music hall?

THE NOTE TAKER. Ive thought of that. Perhaps I shall some day.

The rain has stopped; and the persons on the outside of the crowd begin to drop off.

THE FLOWER GIRL [*resenting the reaction*] He's no gentleman, he aint, to interfere with a poor girl.

THE DAUGHTER [*out of patience, pushing her way rudely to the front and displacing the gentleman, who politely retires to the other side of the pillar*] What on earth is Freddy doing? I shall get pneumonia if I stay in this draught any longer.

THE NOTE TAKER [*to himself, hastily making a note of her pronunciation of "monia"*] Earlscourt.

THE DAUGHTER [*violently*] Will you please keep your impertinent remarks to yourself.

THE NOTE TAKER. Did I say that out loud? I didnt mean to. I beg your pardon. Your mother's Epsom, unmistakeably.

THE MOTHER [*advancing between her daughter and the note taker*] How very curious! I was brought up in Largelady Park, near Epsom.

THE NOTE TAKER [*uproariously amused*] Ha! ha! What a devil of a name! Excuse me. [*To the daughter*] You want a cab, do you?

THE DAUGHTER. Dont dare speak to me.

THE MOTHER. Oh please, please, Clara. [*Her daughter repudiates her with an angry shrug and retires haughtily*]. We should be so grateful to you, sir, if you found us a cab. [*The note taker produces a whistle*]. Oh, thank you. [*She joins her daughter*].

The note taker blows a piercing blast.

THE SARCASTIC BYSTANDER. There! I knowed he was a plain-clothes copper.

THE BYSTANDER. That aint a police whistle: thats a sporting whistle.

THE FLOWER GIRL [*still preoccupied with her wounded feelings*] He's no right to take away my character. My character is the same to me as any lady's.

THE NOTE TAKER. I dont know whether youve noticed it; but the rain stopped about two minutes ago.

THE BYSTANDER. So it has. Why didnt you say so before? and us losing our time listening to your silliness! [*He walks off towards the Strand*].

THE SARCASTIC BYSTANDER. I can tell where you come from. You come from Anwell. Go back there.

THE NOTE TAKER [*helpfully*] Hanwell.

THE SARCASTIC BYSTANDER [*affecting great distinction of speech*] Thenk you, teacher. Haw haw! So long [*he touches his hat with mock respect and strolls off*].

THE FLOWER GIRL. Frightening people like that! How would he like it himself?

THE MOTHER. It's quite fine now, Clara. We can walk to a motor bus. Come. [*She gathers her skirts above her ankles and hurries off towards the Strand*].

THE DAUGHTER. But the cab—[*her mother is out of hearing*]. Oh, how tiresome! [*She follows angrily*].

All the rest have gone except the note taker, the gentleman, and the flower girl, who sits arranging her basket, and still pitying herself in murmurs.

THE FLOWER GIRL. Poor girl! Hard enough for her to live without being worried and chivied.

THE GENTLEMAN [*returning to his former place on the note taker's left*] How do you do it, if I may ask?

THE NOTE TAKER. Simply phonetics. The science of speech. Thats my profession: also my hobby. Happy is the man who can make a living by his hobby! You can spot an Irishman or a Yorkshireman by his brogue. *I* can place any man within six miles. I can place him within two miles in London. Sometimes within two streets.

THE FLOWER GIRL. Ought to be ashamed of himself, unmanly coward!

THE GENTLEMAN. But is there a living in that?

THE NOTE TAKER. Oh yes. Quite a fat one. This is an age of upstarts. Men begin in Kentish Town with £80 a year, and end in Park Lane with a hundred thousand. They want to drop Kentish Town; but they give themselves away every time they open their mouths. Now I can teach them—

THE FLOWER GIRL. Let him mind his own business and leave a poor girl—

THE NOTE TAKER [*explosively*] Woman: cease this detestable boohooing instantly; or else seek the shelter of some other place of worship.

THE FLOWER GIRL [*with feeble defiance*] Ive a right to be here if I like, same as you.

THE NOTE TAKER. A woman who utters such depressing and disgusting sounds has no right to be anywhere—no right to live. Remember that you are a human being with a soul and the divine gift of articulate speech: that your native language is the language of Shakespear and Milton and The Bible; and dont sit there crooning like a bilious pigeon.

THE FLOWER GIRL [*quite overwhelmed, looking up at him in mingled wonder and deprecation without daring to raise her head*] Ah-ah-ah-ow-ow-ow-oo!

THE NOTE TAKER [*whipping out his book*] Heavens! what a sound! [*He writes; then holds out the book and reads, reproducing her vowels exactly*] Ah-ah-ah-ow-ow-ow-oo!

THE FLOWER GIRL [*tickled by the performance, and laughing in spite of herself*] Garn!

THE NOTE TAKER. You see this creature with her kerbstone English: the English that will keep her in the gutter to the end of her days. Well, sir, in three months I could pass that girl off as a duchess at an ambassador's garden party. I could even get her a place as lady's maid or shop assistant, which requires better English. Thats the sort of thing I do for commercial millionaires. And on the profits of it I do genuine scientific work in phonetics, and a little as a poet on Miltonic lines.

THE GENTLEMAN. I am myself a student of Indian dialects; and—

THE NOTE TAKER [*eagerly*] Are you? Do you know Colonel Pickering, the author of Spoken Sanscrit?

THE GENTLEMAN. I am Colonel Pickering. Who are you?

THE NOTE TAKER. Henry Higgins, author of Higgins's Universal Alphabet.

PICKERING [*with enthusiasm*] I came from India to meet you.

HIGGINS. I was going to India to meet you.

PICKERING. Where do you live?

HIGGINS. 27A Wimpole Street. Come and see me tomorrow.

PICKERING. I'm at the Carlton. Come with me now and lets have a jaw over some supper.

HIGGINS. Right you are.

THE FLOWER GIRL [*to Pickering, as he passes her*] Buy a flower, kind gentleman. I'm short for my lodging.

PICKERING. I really havnt any change. I'm sorry [*he goes away*].

HIGGINS [*shocked at the girl's mendacity*] Liar. You said you could change half-a-crown.

THE FLOWER GIRL [*rising in desperation*] You ought to be stuffed with nails, you ought. [*Flinging the basket at his feet*] Take the whole blooming basket for sixpence.

The church clock strikes the second quarter.

HIGGINS [*hearing in it the voice of God, rebuking him for his Pharisaic want of charity to the poor girl*] A reminder. [*He raises his hat solemnly; then throws a handful of money into the basket and follows Pickering*].

THE FLOWER GIRL [*picking up a half-crown*] Ah-ow-ooh! [*Picking up a couple of florins*] Aaah-ow-ooh! [*Picking up several coins*] Aaaaaah-ow-ooh! [*Picking up a half-sovereign*] Aaaaaaaaaaaah-ow-ooh!!!

FREDDY [*springing out of a taxicab*] Got one at last. Hallo! [*To the girl*] Where are the two ladies that were here?

THE FLOWER GIRL. They walked to the bus when the rain stopped.

FREDDY. And left me with a cab on my hands! Damnation!

THE FLOWER GIRL [*with grandeur*] Never mind, young man. I'm going home in a taxi. [*She sails off to the cab. The driver puts his hand behind him and holds the door firmly shut against her. Quite understanding his mistrust, she shews him her handful of money*]. Eightpence aint no object to me, Charlie. [*He grins and opens the door*]. Angel Court, Drury Lane, round the corner of Micklejohn's oil shop. Lets see how fast you can make her hop it. [*She gets in and pulls the door to with a slam as the taxicab starts*].

FREDDY. Well, I'm dashed!

ACT II

Next day at 11 a.m. Higgins's laboratory in Wimpole Street. It is a room on the first floor, looking on the street, and was meant for the drawing room. The double doors are in the middle of the back wall; and persons entering find in the corner to their right two tall file cabinets at right angles to one another against the walls. In this corner stands a flat writing-table, on which are a phonograph, a laryngoscope, a row of tiny organ pipes with a bellows, a set of lamp chimneys for singing flames with burners attached to a gas plug in the wall by an india-rubber tube, several tuning-forks of different sizes, a life-size image of half a human head, shewing in section the vocal organs, and a box containing a supply of wax cylinders for the phonograph.

Further down the room, on the same side, is a fireplace, with a comfortable leather-covered easy-chair at the side of the hearth nearest the door, and a coal-scuttle. There is a clock on the mantelpiece. Between the fireplace and the phonograph table is a stand for newspapers.

On the other side of the central door, to the left of the visitor, is a cabinet of shallow drawers. On it is a telephone and the telephone directory. The corner beyond, and most of the side wall, is occupied by a grand piano, with the keyboard at the end furthest from the door, and a bench for the player extending the full length of the keyboard. On the piano is a dessert dish heaped with fruit and sweets, mostly chocolates.

The middle of the room is clear. Besides the easy-chair, the piano bench, and two chairs at the phonograph table, there is one stray chair. It stands near the fireplace. On the walls, engravings: mostly Piranesis and mezzotint portraits. No paintings.

Pickering is seated at the table, putting down some cards and a tuning-fork which he has been using. Higgins is standing up near him, closing two or three file drawers which are hanging out. He appears in the morning light as a robust, vital, appetizing sort of man of forty or thereabouts, dressed in a professional-looking black frock-coat with a white linen collar and black silk tie. He is of the energetic, scientific type, heartily, even violently, interested in everything that can be studied as a scientific subject, and careless about himself and other people, including their feelings. He is, in fact, but for his years and size, rather like a very impetuous baby "taking notice" eagerly and loudly, and requiring almost as much watching to keep him out of unintended mischief. His manner varies from genial bullying when he is in a good humor to stormy petulance when anything goes wrong; but he is so entirely frank and void of malice that he remains likeable even in his least reasonable moments.

HIGGINS [*as he shuts the last drawer*] Well, I think thats the whole show.

PICKERING. It's really amazing. I havnt taken half of it in, you know.

HIGGINS. Would you like to go over any of it again?

PICKERING [*rising and coming over to the fireplace, where he plants himself with his back to the fire*] No, thank you; not now. I'm quite done up for this morning.

HIGGINS [*following him, and standing beside him on his left*] Tired of listening to sounds?

PICKERING. Yes. It's a fearful strain. I rather fancied myself because I can pronounce twenty-four distinct vowel sounds; but your hundred and thirty beat me. I cant hear a bit of difference between most of them.

HIGGINS [*chuckling, and going over to the piano to eat sweets*] Oh, that comes with practice. You hear no difference at first; but you keep on listening, and presently you find theyre all as different as A from B. [*Mrs Pearce looks in: she is Higgins's housekeeper*]. Whats the matter?

MRS PEARCE [*hesitating, evidently perplexed*] A young woman wants to see you, sir.

HIGGINS. A young woman! What does she want?

MRS PEARCE. Well, sir, she says youll be glad to see her when you know what she's come about. She's quite a common girl, sir. Very common indeed. I should have sent her away, only I thought perhaps you wanted her to talk into your machines. I hope Ive not done wrong; but really you see such queer people sometimes—youll excuse me. I'm sure, sir—

HIGGINS. Oh, thats all right, Mrs Pearce. Has she an interesting accent?

MRS PEARCE. Oh, something dreadful, sir, really. I dont know how you can take an interest in it.

HIGGINS [*to Pickering*] Lets have her up. Shew her up, Mrs Pearce [*he rushes across to his working table and picks out a cylinder to use on the phonograph*].

MRS PEARCE [*only half resigned to it*] Very well, sir. It's for you to say. [*She goes downstairs*].

HIGGINS. This is rather a bit of luck. I'll shew you how I make records. We'll set her talking; and I'll take it down first in Bell's visible Speech; than in broad Romic; and then we'll get her on the phonograph so that you can turn her on as often as you like with the written transcript before you.

MRS PEARCE [*returning*] This is the young woman, sir.

The flower girl enters in state. She has a hat with three ostrich feathers, orange, sky-blue, and red. She has a nearly clean apron, and the shoddy coat has been tidied a little. The pathos of this deplorable figure, with its innocent vanity and consequential air, touches Pickering, who has already straightened himself in the presence of

Mrs Pearce. But as to Higgins, the only distinction he makes between men and women is that when he is neither bullying nor exclaiming to the heavens against some feather-weight cross he coaxes women as a child coaxes its nurse when it wants to get anything out of her.

HIGGINS [*brusquely, recognizing her with unconcealed disappointment, and at once, babylike, making an intolerable grievance of it*] Why, this is the girl I jotted down last night. She's no use: Ive got all the records I want of the Lisson Grove lingo; and I'm not going to waste another cylinder on it. [*To the girl*] Be off with you: I dont want you.

THE FLOWER GIRL. Dont you be so saucy. You aint heard what I come for yet. [*To Mrs Pearce, who is waiting at the door for further instructions*] Did you tell him I come in a taxi?

MRS PEARCE. Nonsense, girl! what do you think a gentleman like Mr Higgins cares what you came in?

THE FLOWER GIRL. Oh, we are proud! He aint above giving lessons, not him: I heard him say so. Well, I aint come here to ask for any compliment; and if my money's not good enough I can go elsewhere.

HIGGINS. Good enough for what?

THE FLOWER GIRL. Good enough for ye-oo. Now you know, dont you? I'm come to have lessons, I am. And to pay for em too: make no mistake.

HIGGINS [*stupent*] Well!!! [*Recovering his breath with a gasp*] What do you expect me to say to you?

THE FLOWER GIRL. Well, if you was a gentleman, you might ask me to sit down, I think. Dont I tell you I'm bringing you business?

HIGGINS. Pickering: shall we ask this baggage to sit down, or shall we throw her out of the window?

THE FLOWER GIRL [*running away in terror to the piano, where she turns at bay*] Ah-ah-oh-ow-ow-ow-oo! [*Wounded and whimpering*] I wont be called a baggage when Ive offered to pay like any lady.

Motionless, the two men stare at her from the other side of the room, amazed.

PICKERING [*gently*] What is it you want, my girl?

THE FLOWER GIRL. I want to be a lady in a flower shop stead of selling at the corner of Tottenham Court Road. But they wont take me unless I can talk more genteel. He said he could teach me. Well, here I am ready to pay him—not asking any favor—and he treats me as if I was dirt.

MRS PEARCE. How can you be such a foolish ignorant girl as to think you could afford to pay Mr Higgins?

THE FLOWER GIRL. Why shouldnt I? I know what lessons cost as well as you do; and I'm ready to pay.

HIGGINS. How much?

THE FLOWER GIRL [*coming back to him, triumphant*] Now youre talking! I thought youd come off it when you saw a chance of getting back a bit of what you chucked at me last night. [*Confidentially*] You had a drop in, hadnt you?

HIGGINS [*peremptorily*] Sit down.

THE FLOWER GIRL. Oh, if youre going to make a compliment of it—

HIGGINS [*thundering at her*] Sit down.

MRS PEARCE [*severely*] Sit down, girl. Do as youre told. [*She places the stray chair near the hearthrug between Higgins and Pickering, and stands behind it waiting for the girl to sit down*].

THE FLOWER GIRL. Ah-ah-ah-ow-ow-oo! [*She stands, half rebellious, half bewildered*].

PICKERING [*very courteous*] Wont you sit down?

LIZA [*coyly*] Dont mind if I do. [*She sits down. Pickering returns to the hearthrug*].

HIGGINS. Whats your name?

THE FLOWER GIRL. Liza Doolittle.

HIGGINS [*declaiming gravely*]

　Eliza, Elizabeth, Betsy and Bess,
　They went to the woods to get a bird's nes':

PICKERING. They found a nest with four eggs in it:

HIGGINS. They took one apiece, and left three in it.

They laugh heartily at their own wit.

LIZA. Oh, dont be silly.

MRS PEARCE. You mustnt speak to the gentleman like that.

LIZA. Well, why wont he speak sensible to me?

HIGGINS. Come back to business. How much do you propose to pay me for the lessons?

LIZA. Oh, I know whats right. A lady friend of mine gets French lessons for eighteen-pence an hour from a real French gentleman. Well, you wouldnt have the face to ask me the same for teaching me my own language as you would for French; so I wont give more than a shilling. Take it or leave it.

HIGGINS [*walking up and down the room, rattling his keys and his cash in his pockets*] You know, Pickering, if you consider a shilling, not as a simple shilling, but as a percentage of this girl's income, it works out as fully equivalent to sixty or seventy guineas from a millionaire.

PICKERING. How so?

HIGGINS. Figure it out. A millionaire has about £150 a day. She earns about half-a-crown.

LIZA [haughtily] Who told you I only—

HIGGINS [continuing] She offers me two-fifths of her day's income for a lesson. Two-fifths of a millionaire's income for a day would be somewhere about £60, It's handsome. By George, it's enormous! it's the biggest offer I ever had.

LIZA [rising, terrified] Sixty pounds! What are you talking about? I never offered you sixty pounds. Where would I get—

HIGGINS. Hold your tongue.

LIZA [weeping] But I aint got sixty pounds. Oh—

MRS PEARCE. Dont cry, you silly girl. Sit down. Nobody is going to touch your money.

HIGGINS. Somebody is going to touch you, with a broomstick, if you dont stop snivelling. Sit down.

LIZA [obeying slowly] Ah-ah-ah-ow-oo-o! One would think you was my father.

HIGGINS. If I decide to teach you, I'll be worse than two fathers to you. Here [he offers her his silk handkerchief]!

LIZA. Whats this for?

HIGGINS. To wipe your eyes. To wipe any part of your face that feels moist. Remember: thats your handkerchief; and thats your sleeve. Dont mistake the one for the other if you wish to become a lady in a shop.

Liza, utterly bewildered, stares helplessly at him.

MRS PEARCE. It's no use talking to her like that, Mr Higgins: she doesnt understand you, Besides, youre quite wrong: she doesnt do it that way at all [she takes the handkerchief].

LIZA [snatching it] Here! You give me that handkerchief. He give it to me, not to you.

PICKERING [laughing] He did. I think it must be regarded as her property, Mrs Pearce.

MRS PEARCE [resigning herself] Serve you right, Mr Higgins.

PICKERING. Higgins: I'm interested. What about the ambassador's garden party? I'll say youre the greatest teacher alive if you make that good. I'll bet you all the expenses of the experiment you cant do it. And I'll pay for the lessons.

LIZA. Oh, you are real good. Thank you, Captain.

HIGGINS [tempted, looking at her] It's almost irresistible. She's so deliciously low—so horribly dirty—

LIZA [protesting extremely] Ah-ah-ah-ah-ow-ow-oo-oo!!! I aint dirty: I washed my face and hands afore I come, I did.

PICKERING. Youre certainly not going to turn her head with flattery, Higgins.

MRS PEARCE [uneasy] Oh, dont say that, sir: theres more ways than one of turning a girl's head; and nobody can do it better than Mr Higgins, though he may not always mean it. I do hope, sir, you wont encourage him to do anything foolish.

HIGGINS [becoming excited as the idea grows on him] What is life but a series of inspired follies? The difficulty is to find them to do. Never lose a chance: it doesnt come every day. I shall make a duchess of this draggle-tailed guttersnipe.

LIZA [strongly deprecating this view of her] Ah-ah-ah-ow-ow-oo!

HIGGINS [carried away] Yes: in six months—in three if she has a good ear and a quick tongue—I'll take her anywhere and pass her off as anything. We'll start to-day: now! this moment! Take her away and clean her, Mrs Pearce. Monkey Brand if it wont come off any other way. Is there a good fire in the kitchen?

MRS PEARCE [protesting] Yes; but—

HIGGINS [storming on] Take all her clothes off and burn them. Ring up Whiteley or somebody for new ones. Wrap her up in brown paper til they come.

LIZA. Youre no gentleman, youre not, to talk of such things. I'm a good girl, I am; and I know what the like of you are, I do.

HIGGINS. We want none of your Lisson Grove prudery here, young woman. Youve got to learn to behave like a duchess. Take her away, Mrs Pearce. If she gives you any trouble, wallop her.

LIZA [springing up and running between Pickering and Mrs Pearce for protection] No! I'll call the police, I will.

MRS PEARCE. But Ive no place to put her.

HIGGINS. Put her in the dustbin.

LIZA. Ah-ah-ah-ow-ow-oo!

PICKERING. Oh come, Higgins! be reasonable.

MRS PEARCE [*resolutely*] You must be reasonable, Mr Higgins: really you must. You cant walk over everybody like this.

Higgins, thus scolded, subsides. The hurricane is succeeded by a zephyr of amiable surprise.

HIGGINS [*with professional exquisiteness of modulation*] I walk over everybody! My dear Mrs Pearce, my dear Pickering, I never had the slightest intention of walking over anyone. All I propose is that we should be kind to this poor girl. We must help her to prepare and fit herself for her new station in life. If I did not express myself clearly it was because I did not wish to hurt her delicacy, or yours.

Liza, reassured, steals back to her chair.

MRS PEARCE [*to Pickering*] Well, did you ever hear anything like that, sir?

PICKERING [*laughing heartily*] Never, Mrs Pearce: never.

HIGGINS [*patiently*] Whats the matter?

MRS PEARCE. Well, the matter is, sir, that you cant take a girl up like that as if you were picking up a pebble on the beach.

HIGGINS. Why not?

MRS PEARCE. Why not! But you dont know anything about her. What about her parents? She may be married.

LIZA. Garn!

HIGGINS. There! As the girl very properly says, Garn! Married indeed! Dont you know that a woman of that class looks a worn out drudge of fifty a year after she's married?

LIZA. Whood marry me?

HIGGINS [*suddenly resorting to the most thrillingly beautiful low tones in his best elocutionary style*] By George, Eliza, the streets will be strewn with the dead bodies of men shooting themselves for your sake before Ive done with you.

MRS PEARCE. Nonsense, sir. You mustnt talk like that to her.

LIZA [*rising and squaring herself determinedly*] I'm going away. He's off his chump, he is. I dont want no balmies teaching me.

HIGGINS [*wounded in his tenderest point by her insensibility to his elocution*] Oh, indeed! I'm mad, am I? Very well, Mrs Pearce: you neednt order the new clothes for her. Throw her out.

LIZA [*whimpering*] Nah-ow. You got no right to touch me.

MRS PEARCE. You see now what comes of being saucy. [*Indicating the door*] This way, please.

LIZA [*almost in tears*] I didnt want no clothes. I wouldnt have taken them [*she throws away the handkerchief*]. I can buy my own clothes.

HIGGINS [*deftly retrieving the handkerchief and intercepting her on her reluctant way to the door*] Youre an ungrateful wicked girl. This is my return for offering to take you out of the gutter and dress you beautifully and make a lady of you.

MRS PEARCE. Stop, Mr Higgins. I wont allow it. It's you that are wicked. Go home to your parents, girl; and tell them to take better care of you.

LIZA. I aint got no parents. They told me I was big enough to earn my own living and turned me out.

MRS PEARCE. Wheres your mother?

LIZA. I aint got no mother. Her that turned me out was my sixth stepmother. But I done without them. And I'm a good girl, I am.

HIGGINS. Very well then, what on earth is all this fuss about? The girl doesnt belong to anybody—is no use to anybody but me. [*He goes to Mrs Pearce and begins coaxing*]. You can adopt her, Mrs Pearce: I'm sure a daughter would be a great amusement to you. Now dont make any more fuss. Take her downstairs; and—

MRS PEARCE. But whats to become of her? Is she to be paid anything? Do be sensible, sir.

HIGGINS. Oh, pay her whatever is necessary: put it down in the housekeeping book. [*Impatiently*] What on earth will she want with money? She'll have her food and her clothes. She'll only drink if you give her money.

LIZA [*turning on him*] Oh you are a brute. It's a lie: nobody ever saw the sign of liquor on me. [*She goes back to her chair and plants herself there defiantly*].

PICKERING [*in good-humored remonstrance*] Does it occur to you, Higgins, that the girl has some feelings?

HIGGINS [*looking critically at her*] Oh no, I dont think so. Not any feelings that we need bother about. [*Cheerily*] Have you, Eliza?

LIZA. I got my feelings same as anyone else.

HIGGINS [*to Pickering, reflectively*] You see the difficulty?

PICKERING. Eh? What difficulty?

HIGGINS. To get her to talk grammar. The mere pronunciation is easy enough.

LIZA. I dont want to talk grammar. I want

to talk like a lady.

MRS PEARCE. Will you please keep to the point, Mr Higgins? I want to know on what terms the girl is to be here. Is she to have any wages? And what is to become of her when youve finished your teaching? You must look ahead a little.

HIGGINS [*impatiently*] Whats to become of her if I leave her in the gutter? Tell me that, Mrs Pearce.

MRS PEARCE. Thats her own business, not yours, Mr Higgins.

HIGGINS. Well, when Ive done with her, we can throw her back into the gutter; and then it will be her own business again; so thats all right.

LIZA. Oh, youve no feeling heart in you: you dont care for nothing but yourself [*she rises and takes the floor resolutely*]. Here! Ive had enough of this. I'm going [*making for the door*]. You ought to be ashamed of yourself, you ought.

HIGGINS [*snatching a chocolate cream from the piano, his eyes suddenly beginning to twinkle with mischief*] Have some chocolates, Eliza.

LIZA [*halting, tempted*] How do I know what might be in them? Ive heard of girls being drugged by the like of you.

Higgins whips out his penknife; cuts a chocolate in two; puts one half into his mouth and bolts it; and offers her the other half.

HIGGINS. Pledge of good faith, Eliza. I eat one half: you eat the other. [*Liza opens her mouth to retort: he pops the half chocolate into it*]. You shall have boxes of them, barrels of them, every day. You shall live on them. Eh?

LIZA [*who has disposed of the chocolate after being nearly choked by it*] I wouldnt have ate it, only I'm too ladylike to take it out of my mouth.

HIGGINS. Listen, Eliza. I think you said you came in a taxi.

LIZA. Well, what if I did? Ive as good a right to take a taxi as anyone else.

HIGGINS. You have, Eliza; and in future you shall have as many taxis as you want. You shall go up and down and round the town in a taxi every day. Think of that, Eliza.

MRS PEARCE. Mr Higgins: youre tempting the girl. It's not right. She should think of the future.

HIGGINS. At her age! Nonsense! Time enough to think of the future when you havnt any future to think of. No, Eliza: do as this lady does: think of other people's futures; but never think of your own. Think of chocolates, and taxis, and gold, and diamonds.

LIZA. No: I dont want no gold and no diamonds. I'm a good girl, I am. [*She sits down again, with an attempt at dignity*].

HIGGINS. You shall remain so, Eliza, under the care of Mrs Pearce. And you shall marry an officer in the Guards, with a beautiful moustache: the son of a marquis, who will disinherit him for marrying you, but will relent when he sees your beauty and goodness—

PICKERING. Excuse me, Higgins; but I really must interfere. Mrs Pearce is quite right. If this girl is to put herself in your hands for six months for an experiment in teaching, she must understand thoroughly what she's doing.

HIGGINS. How can she? She's incapable of understanding anything. Besides, do any of us understand what we are doing? If we did, would we ever do it?

PICKERING. Very clever, Higgins: but not sound sense. [*To Eliza*] Miss Doolittle—

LIZA [*overwhelmed*] Ah-ah-ow-oo!

HIGGINS. There! Thats all youll get out of Eliza. Ah-ah-ow-oo! No use explaining. As a military man you ought to know that. Give her her orders: thats what she wants. Eliza: you are to live here for the next six months, learning how to speak beautifully, like a lady in a florist's shop. If youre good and do whatever youre told, you shall sleep in a proper bedroom, and have lots to eat, and money to buy chocolates and take rides in taxis. If youre naughty and idle you will sleep in the back kitchen among the black beetles, and be walloped by Mrs Pearce with a broomstick. At the end of six months you shall go to Buckingham Palace in a carriage, beautifully dressed. If the King finds out youre not a lady, you will be taken by the police to the Tower of London, where your head will be cut off as a warning to other presumptuous flower girls. If you are not found out, you shall have a present of seven-and-sixpence to start life with as a lady in a shop. If you refuse this offer you will be a most ungrateful and wicked girl; and the angels will weep for you. [*To Pickering*] Now are you satisfied, Pickering? [*To Mrs Pearce*] Can I put it more plainly and fairly, Mrs Pearce?

MRS PEARCE [*patiently*] I think youd better

let me speak to the girl properly in private. I dont know that I can take charge of her or consent to the arrangement at all. Of course I know you dont mean her any harm; but when you get what you call interested in people's accents, you never think or care what may happen to them or you. Come with me, Eliza.

HIGGINS. Thats all right. Thank you, Mrs Pearce. Bundle her off to the bath-room.

LIZA [*rising reluctantly and suspiciously*] Youre a great bully, you are. I wont stay here if I dont like. I wont let nobody wallop me. I never asked to go to Bucknam Palace, I didnt. I was never in trouble with the police, not me. I'm a good girl—

MRS PEARCE. Dont answer back, girl. You dont understand the gentleman. Come with me. [*She leads the way to the door, and holds it open for Eliza*].

LIZA [*as she goes out*] Well, what I say is right. I wont go near the King, not if I'm going to have my head cut off. If I'd known what I was letting myself in for, I wouldnt have come here. I always been a good girl; and I never offered to say a word to him; and I dont owe him nothing; and I dont care; and I wont be put upon; and I have my feelings the same as anyone else—

Mrs Pearce shuts the door; and Eliza's plaints are no longer audible. Pickering comes from the hearth to the chair and sits astride it with his arms on the back.

PICKERING. Excuse the straight question, Higgins. Are you a man of good character where women are concerned?

HIGGINS [*moodily*] Have you ever met a man of good character where women are concerned?

PICKERING. Yes: very frequently.

HIGGINS [*dogmatically, lifting himself on his hands to the level of the piano, and sitting on it with a bounce*] Well, I havnt. I find that the moment I let a woman make friends with me, she becomes jealous, exacting, suspicious, and a damned nuisance. I find that the moment I let myself make friends with a woman, I become selfish and tyrannical. Women upset everything. When you let them into your life, you find that the woman is driving at one thing and youre driving at another.

PICKERING. At what, for example?

HIGGINS [*coming off the piano restlessly*] Oh, Lord knows! I suppose the woman wants to live her own life; and the man wants to live his; and each tries to drag the other on to the wrong track. One wants to go north and the other south; and the result is that both have to go east, though they both hate the east wind. [*He sits down on the bench at the keyboard*]. So here I am, a confirmed old bachelor, and likely to remain so.

PICKERING [*rising and standing over him gravely*] Come, Higgins! You know what I mean. If I'm to be in this business I shall feel responsible for that girl. I hope it's understood that no advantage is to be taken of her position.

HIGGINS. What! That thing! Sacred, I assure you. [*Rising to explain*] You see, she'll be a pupil; and teaching would be impossible unless pupils were sacred. Ive taught scores of American millionairesses how to speak English: the best looking women in the world. I'm seasoned. They might as well be blocks of wood. *I* might as well be a block of wood. It's—

Mrs Pearce opens the door. She has Eliza's hat in her hand. Pickering retires to the easy-chair at the hearth and sits down.

HIGGINS [*eagerly*] Well, Mrs Pearce: is it all right?

MRS PEARCE [*at the door*] I just wish to trouble you with a word, if I may, Mr Higgins.

HIGGINS. Yes, certainly. Come in. [*She comes forward*]. Dont burn that, Mrs Pearce. I'll keep it as a curiosity. [*He takes the hat*].

MRS PEARCE. Handle it carefully, sir, please. I had to promise her not to burn it; but I had better put it in the oven for a while.

HIGGINS [*putting it down hastily on the piano*] Oh! thank you. Well, what have you to say to me?

PICKERING. Am I in the way?

MRS PEARCE. Not at all, sir. Mr Higgins: will you please be very particular what you say before the girl?

HIGGINS [*sternly*] Of course. I'm always particular about what I say. Why do you say this to me?

MRS PEARCE [*unmoved*] No, sir: youre not at all particular when youve mislaid anything or when you get a little impatient. Now it doesnt matter before me: I'm used to it. But you really must not swear before the girl.

HIGGINS [*indignantly*] *I* swear! [*Most em-

phatically] I never swear. I detest the habit. What the devil do you mean?

MRS PEARCE [*stolidly*] Thats what I mean, sir. You swear a great deal too much. I dont mind you damning and blasting, and what the devil and where the devil and who the devil—

HIGGINS. Mrs Pearce: this language from your lips! Really!

MRS PEARCE [*not to be put off*] —but there is a certain word I must ask you not to use. The girl has just used it herself because the bath was too hot. It begins with the same letter as bath. She knows no better: she learnt it at her mother's knee. But she must not hear it from your lips.

HIGGINS [*loftily*] I cannot charge myself with having ever uttered it, Mrs Pearce. [*She looks at him steadfastly. He adds, hiding an uneasy conscience with a judicial air*] Except perhaps in a moment of extreme and justifiable excitement.

MRS PEARCE. Only this morning, sir, you applied it to your boots, to the butter, and to the brown bread.

HIGGINS. Oh, that! Mere alliteration, Mrs Pearce, natural to a poet.

MRS PEARCE. Well, sir, whatever you choose to call it, I beg you not to let the girl hear you repeat it.

HIGGINS. Oh, very well, very well. Is that all?

MRS PEARCE. No sir. We shall have to be very particular with this girl as to personal cleanliness.

HIGGINS. Certainly, Quite right. Most important.

MRS PEARCE. I mean not to be slovenly about her dress or untidy in leaving things about.

HIGGINS [*going to her solemnly*] Just so. I intended to call your attention to that. [*He passes on to Pickering, who is enjoying the conversation immensely*]. It is these little things that matter, Pickering. Take care of the pence and the pounds will take care of themselves is as true of personal habits as of money. [*He comes to anchor on the hearthrug, with the air of a man in an unassailable position*].

MRS PEARCE. Yes, sir. Then might I ask you not to come down to breakfast in your dressing-gown, or at any rate not to use it as a napkin to the extent you do, sir. And if you would be so good as not to eat everything off the same plate, and to remember not to put the porridge saucepan out of your hand on the clean tablecloth, it would be a better example to the girl. You know you nearly choked yourself with a fishbone in the jam only last week.

HIGGINS [*routed from the hearthrug and drifting back to the piano*] I may do these things sometimes in absence of mind; but surely I dont do them habitually. [*Angrily*] By the way: my dressing-gown smells most damnably of benzine.

MRS PEARCE. No doubt it does, Mr Higgins. But if you will wipe your fingers—

HIGGINS [*yelling*] Oh very well, very well: I'll wipe them in my hair in future.

MRS PEARCE. I hope youre not offended, Mr Higgins.

HIGGINS [*shocked at finding himself thought capable of an unamiable sentiment*] Not at all, not at all. Youre quite right, Mrs Pearce: I shall be particularly careful before the girl. Is that all?

MRS PEARCE. No, sir. Might she use some of those Japanese dresses you brought from abroad? I really cant put her back into her old things.

HIGGINS. Certainly, Anything you like. Is that all?

MRS PEARCE. Thank you, sir. Thats all. [*She goes out*].

HIGGINS. You know, Pickering, that woman has the most extraordinary ideas about me. Here I am, a shy, diffident sort of man. Ive never been able to feel really grown-up and tremendous, like other chaps. And yet she's firmly persuaded that I'm an arbitrary over-bearing bossing kind of person. I cant account for it.

Mrs Pearce returns.

MRS PEARCE. If you please, sir, the trouble's beginning already. Theres a dustman downstairs, Alfred Doolittle, wants to see you. He says you have his daughter here.

PICKERING [*rising*] Phew! I say! [*He retreats to the hearthrug*].

HIGGINS [*promptly*] Send the blackguard up.

MRS PEARCE. Oh, very well, sir. [*She goes out*].

PICKERING. He may not be a blackguard, Higgins.

HIGGINS. Nonsense. Of course he's a blackguard.

PICKERING. Whether he is or not, I'm afraid we shall have some trouble with him.

HIGGINS (*confidently*] Oh no : I think not.

If theres any trouble he shall have it with me, not I with him. And we are sure to get something interesting out of him.

PICKERING. About the girl?

HIGGINS. No. I mean his dialect.

PICKERING. Oh!

MRS PEARCE [at the door] Doolittle, sir. [She admits Doolittle and retires].

Alfred Doolittle is an elderly but vigorous dustman, clad in the costume of his profession, including a hat with a back brim covering his neck and shoulders. He has well marked and rather interesting features, and seems equally free from fear and conscience. He has a remarkably expressive voice, the result of a habit of giving vent to his feelings without reserve. His present pose is that of wounded honor and stern resolution.

DOOLITTLE [at the door, uncertain which of the two gentlemen is his man] Professor Higgins?

HIGGINS. Here. Good morning. Sit down.

DOOLITTLE. Morning, Governor. [He sits down magisterially] I come about a very serious matter, Governor.

HIGGINS [to Pickering] Brought up in Hounslow. Mother Welsh, I should think. [Doolittle opens his mouth, amazed. Higgins continues] What do you want, Doolittle?

DOOLITTLE [menacingly] I want my daughter: thats what I want. See?

HIGGINS. Of course you do. Youre her father, arnt you? You dont suppose anyone else wants her, do you? I'm glad to see you have some spark of family feeling left. She's upstairs. Take her away at once.

DOOLITTLE [rising, fearfully taken aback] What!

HIGGINS. Take her away. Do you suppose I'm going to keep your daughter for you?

DOOLITTLE [remonstrating] Now, now, look here, Governor. Is this reasonable? Is it fairity to take advantage of a man like this? The girl belongs to me. You got her. Where do I come in? [He sits down again].

HIGGINS. Your daughter had the audacity to come to my house and ask me to teach her how to speak properly so that she could get a place in a flower-shop. This gentleman and my housekeeper have been here all the time. [Bullying him] How dare you come here and attempt to blackmail me? You sent her here on purpose.

DOOLITTLE [protesting] No, Governor.

HIGGINS. You must have. How else could you possibly know that she is here?

DOOLITTLE. Dont take a man up like that, Governor.

HIGGINS. The police shall take you up. This is a plant—a plot to extort money by threats. I shall telephone for the police. [He goes resolutely to the telephone and opens the directory].

DOOLITTLE. Have I asked you for a brass farthing? I leave it to the gentleman here: have I said a word about money ?

HIGGINS [throwing the book aside and marching down on Doolittle with a poser] What else did you come for?

DOOLITTLE [sweetly] Well, what would a man come for? Be human, Governor.

HIGGINS [disarmed] Alfred: did you put her up to it?

DOOLITTLE. So help me, Governor, I never did. I take my Bible oath I aint seen the girl these two months past.

HIGGINS. Then how did you know she was here?

DOOLITTLE ["most musical, most melancholy"] I'll tell you, Governor, if youll only let me get a word in. I'm willing to tell you. I'm wanting to tell you. I'm waiting to tell you.

HIGGINS. Pickering: this chap has a certain natural gift of rhetoric. Observe the rhythm of his native woodnotes wild. "I'm willing to tell you: I'm wanting to tell you: I'm waiting to tell you." Sentimental rhetoric! thats the Welsh strain in him. It also accounts for his mendacity and dishonesty.

PICKERING. Oh, p l e a s e, Higgins: I'm west country myself. [To Doolittle] How did you know the girl was here if you didnt send her?

DOOLITTLE. It was like this, Governor. The girl took a boy in the taxi to give him a jaunt. Son of her landlady, he is. He hung about on the chance of her giving him another ride home. Well, she sent him back for her luggage when she heard you was willing for her to stop here. I met the boy at the corner of Long Acre and Endell Street.

HIGGINS. Public house. Yes?

DOOLITTLE. The poor man's club, Governor: why shouldnt I?

PICKERING. Do let him tell his story, Higgins.

DOOLITTLE. He told me what was up. And I ask you, what was my feelings and my duty as a father? I says to the boy, "You bring me the luggage," I says—

PICKERING. Why didnt you go for it yourself?

DOOLITTLE. Landlady wouldnt have trusted

me with it, Governor. She's that kind of woman: y o u know. I had to give the boy a penny afore h e trusted me with it, the little swine. I brought it to her just to oblige you like, and make myself agreeable. Thats all.

HIGGINS. How much luggage?

DOOLITTLE. Musical instrument, Governor. A few pictures, a trifle of jewelry, and a birdcage. She said she didnt want no clothes. What was I to think from that, Governor? I ask you as a parent what was I to think?

HIGGINS. So you came to rescue her from worse than death, eh?

DOOLITTLE [appreciatively: relieved at being so well understood] Just so, Governor. Thats right.

PICKERING. But why did you bring her luggage if you intended to take her away?

DOOLITTLE. Have I said a word about taking her away? Have I now?

HIGGINS [determinedly] Youre going to take her away, double quick. [He crosses to the hearth and rings the bell].

DOOLITTLE [rising] No, Governor. Dont say that. I'm not the man to stand in my girl's light. Heres a career opening for her, as you might say; and—

Mrs Pearce opens the door and awaits orders.

HIGGINS. Mrs Pearce: this is Eliza's father. He has come to take her away. Give her to him. [He goes back to the piano, with an air of washing his hands of the whole affair].

DOOLITTLE. No. This is a misunderstanding. Listen here—

MRS PEARCE. He cant take her away, Mr Higgins: how can he? You told me to burn her clothes.

DOOLITTLE. Thats right. I cant carry the girl through the streets like a blooming monkey, can I? I put it to you.

HIGGINS. You have put it to me that you want your daughter. Take your daughter. If she has no clothes go out and buy her some.

DOOLITTLE [desperate] Wheres the clothes she come in? Did I burn them or did your missus here?

MRS PEARCE. I am the housekeeper, if you please. I have sent for some clothes for your girl. When they come you can take her away. You can wait in the kitchen. This way, please.

Doolittle, much troubled, accompanies her to the door; then hesitates; finally turns confidentially to Higgins.

DOOLITTLE. Listen here, Governor. You

and me is men of the world, aint we?

HIGGINS. Oh! Men of the world, are we? Youd better go, Mrs Pearce.

MRS PEARCE. I think so, indeed, sir. [She goes, with dignity].

PICKERING. The floor is yours, Mr Doolittle.

DOOLITTLE [to Pickering] I thank you, Governor. [To Higgins, who takes refuge on the piano bench, a little overwhelmed by the proximity of his visitor; for Doolittle has a professional flavor of dust about him]. Well, the truth is, Ive taken a sort of fancy to you, Governor; and if you want the girl, I'm not so set on having her back home again but what I might be open to an arrangement. Regarded in the light of a young woman, she's a fine handsome girl. As a daughter she's not worth her keep; and so I tell you straight. All I ask is my rights as a father; and youre the last man alive to expect me to let her go for nothing; for I can see youre one of the straight sort, Governor. Well, whats a five-pound note to you? And whats Eliza to me? [He returns to his chair and sits down judicially].

PICKERING. I think you ought to know, Doolittle, that Mr Higgins's intentions are entirely honorable.

DOOLITTLE. Course they are, Governor. If I thought they wasnt, I'd ask fifty.

HIGGINS [revolted] Do you mean to say, you callous rascal, that you would sell your daughter for £50?

DOOLITTLE. Not in a general way I wouldnt; but to oblige a gentleman like you I'd do a good deal, I do assure you.

PICKERING. Have you no morals, man?

DOOLITTLE [unabashed] Cant afford them, Governor. Neither could you if you was as poor as me. Not that I mean any harm, you know. But if Liza is going to have a bit out of this, why not me too?

HIGGINS [troubled] I dont know what to do, Pickering. There can be no question that as a matter of morals it's a positive crime to give this chap a farthing. And yet I feel a sort of rough justice in his claim.

DOOLITTLE. Thats it, Governor. Thats all I say. A father's heart, as it were.

PICKERING. Well, I know the feeling; but really it seems hardly right—

DOOLITTLE. Dont say that, Governor. Dont look at it that way. What am I, Governors both? I ask you, what a m I? I'm one of the undeserving poor: thats what I am. Think of what that means to a man. It means that he's up agen middle class morality all the time. If theres anything going, and I put in for a bit of it, it's always the same story: "Youre undeserving; so you cant have it." But my needs is as great as the most deserving widow's that ever got money out of six different charities in one week for the death of the same husband. I dont need less than a deserving man: I need more. I dont eat less hearty than him; and I drink a lot more. I want a bit of amusement, cause I'm a thinking man. I want cheerfulness and a song and a band when I feel low. Well, they charge me just the same for everything as they charge the deserving. What is middle class morality? Just an excuse for never giving me anything. Therefore, I ask you, as two gentlemen, not to play that game on me. I'm playing straight with you. I aint pretending to be deserving. I'm undeserving; and I mean to go on being undeserving. I like it; and thats the truth. Will you take advantage of a man's nature to do him out of the price of his own daughter what he's brought up and fed and clothed by the sweat of his brow until she's growed big enough to be interesting to you two gentlemen? Is five pounds unreasonable? I put it to you; and I leave it to you.

HIGGINS [*rising, and going over to Pickering*] Pickering: if we were to take this man in hand for three months, he could choose between a seat in the Cabinet and a popular pulpit in Wales.

PICKERING. What do you say to that, Doolittle?

DOOLITTLE. Not me, Governor, thank you kindly. Ive heard all the preachers and all the prime ministers—for I'm a thinking man and game for politics or religion or social reform same as all the other amusements—and I tell you it's a dog's life any way you look at it. Undeserving poverty is my line. Taking one station in society with another, it's—it's—well, it's the only one that has any ginger in it, to my taste.

HIGGINS. I suppose we must give him a fiver.

PICKERING. He'll make a bad use of it, I'm afraid.

DOOLITTLE. Not me, Governor, so help me I wont. Dont you be afraid that I'll save it and spare it and live idle on it. There wont be a penny of it left by Monday: I'll have to go to work same as if I'd never had it. It wont pauperize me, you bet. Just one good spree for myself and the missus, giving pleasure to ourselves and employment to others, and satisfaction to you to think it's not been throwed away. You couldnt spend it better.

HIGGINS [*taking out his pocketbook and coming between Doolittle and the piano*] This is irresistible. Lets give him ten. [*He offers two notes to the dustman*].

DOOLITTLE. No, Governor. She wouldnt have the heart to spend ten; and perhaps I shouldnt neither. Ten pounds is a lot of money: it makes a man feel prudent like; and then goodbye to happiness. You give me what I ask you, Governor: not a penny more, and not a penny less.

PICKERING. Why dont you marry that missus of yours? I rather draw the line at encouraging that sort of immorality.

DOOLITTLE. Tell her so, Governor: tell her so. *I'm* willing. It's me that suffers by it. Ive no hold on her. I got to be agreeable to her. I got to give her presents. I got to buy her clothes something sinful. I'm a slave to that woman, Governor, just because I'm not her lawful husband. And she knows it too. Catch her marrying me! Take my advice, Governor: marry Eliza while she's young and dont know no better. If you dont youll be sorry for it after. If you do, s h e'll be sorry for it after; but better her than you, because youre a man, and she's only a woman and dont know how to be happy anyhow.

HIGGINS. Pickering: if we listen to this man another minute, we shall have no convictions left. [*To Doolittle*] Five pounds I think you said.

DOOLITTLE. Thank you kindly, Governor.

HIGGINS. Youre sure you wont take ten?

DOOLITTLE. Not now. Another time, Governor.

HIGGINS [*handing him a five-pound note*] Here you are.

DOOLITTLE. Thank you, Governor. Good morning. [*He hurries to the door, anxious to get away with his booty. When he opens it he is confronted with a dainty and exquisitely clean young Japanese lady in a simple blue cotton kimono printed cunningly with small white jasmine blossoms. Mrs Pearce is with her. He gets out of her way deferentially and apologizes*]. Beg pardon, miss.

THE JAPANESE LADY. Garn! Dont you know your own daughter?

DOOLITTLE } *exclaiming* { Bly me! it's Eliza!
HIGGINS } *simul-* { Whats that! This!
PICKERING } *taneously* { By Jove!

LIZA. Dont I look silly?

HIGGINS. Silly?

MRS PEARCE [*at the door*] Now, Mr. Higgins, please dont say anything to make the girl conceited about herself.

HIGGINS [*conscientiously*] Oh! Quite right, Mrs Pearce. [*To Eliza*] Yes: damned silly.

MRS PEARCE. Please, sir.

HIGGINS [*correcting himself*] I mean extremely silly.

LIZA. I should look all right with my hat on. [*She takes up her hat; puts it on; and walks across the room to the fireplace with a fashionable air*].

HIGGINS. A new fashion, by George! And it ought to look horrible!

DOOLITTLE [*with fatherly pride*] Well, I never thought she'd clean up as good looking as that, Governor. She's a credit to me, aint she?

LIZA. I tell you, it's easy to clean up here. Hot and cold water on tap, just as much as you like, there is. Woolly towels, there is; and a towel horse so hot, it burns your fingers. Soft brushes to scrub yourself, and a wooden bowl of soap smelling like primroses. Now I know why ladies is so clean. Washing's a treat for them. Wish they saw what it is for the like of me!

HIGGINS. I'm glad the bathroom met with your approval.

LIZA. It didnt: not all of it; and I dont care who hears me say it. Mrs Pearce knows.

HIGGINS. What was wrong, Mrs Pearce?

MRS PEARCE [*blandly*] Oh, nothing, sir. It doesnt matter.

LIZA. I had a good mind to break it. I didnt know which way to look. But I hung a towel over it, I did.

HIGGINS. Over what?

MRS PEARCE. Over the looking-glass, sir.

HIGGINS. Doolittle: you have brought your daughter up too strictly.

DOOLITTLE. Me! I never brought her up at all, except to give her a lick of a strap now and again. Dont put it on me, Governor. She aint accustomed to it, you see: thats all. But she'll soon pick up your free-and-easy ways.

LIZA. I'm a good girl, I am; and I wont pick up no free-and-easy ways.

HIGGINS. Eliza: if you say again that youre a good girl, your father shall take you home.

LIZA. Not him. You dont know my father. All he come here for was to touch you for some money to get drunk on.

DOOLITTLE. Well, what else would I want money for? To put into the plate in church, I suppose. [*She puts out her tongue at him. He is so incensed by this that Pickering presently finds it necessary to step between them*]. Dont you give me none of your lip; and dont let me hear you giving this gentleman any of it neither, or youll hear from me about it. See?

HIGGINS. Have you any further advice to give her before you go, Doolittle? Your blessing, for instance.

DOOLITTLE. No, Governor: I aint such a mug as to put up my children to all I know myself. Hard enough to hold them in without that. If you want Eliza's mind improved, Governor, you do it yourself with a strap. So long, gentlemen. [*He turns to go*].

HIGGINS [*impressively*] Stop. Youll come regularly to see your daughter. It's your duty, you know. My brother is a clergyman; and he could help you in your talks with her.

DOOLITTLE [*evasively*] Certainly. I'll come, Governor. Not just this week, because I have a job at a distance. But later on you may depend on me. Afternoon, gentlemen. Afternoon, maam. [*He takes off his hat to Mrs Pearce, who disdains the salutation and goes out. He winks at Higgins, thinking him probably a fellow-sufferer from Mrs Pearce's difficult disposition, and follows her*].

LIZA. Dont you believe the old liar. He'd as soon you set a bull-dog on him as a clergyman. You wont see him again in a hurry.

HIGGINS. I dont want to, Eliza. Do you?

LIZA. Not me. I dont want never to see him again, I dont. He's a disgrace to me, he is, collecting dust, instead of working at his trade.

PICKERING. What is his trade, Eliza?

LIZA. Taking money out of other people s pockets into his own. His proper trade's a navvy; and he works at it sometimes too— for exercise—and earns good money at it. Aint you going to call me Miss Doolittle any more?

PICKERING. I beg your pardon, Miss Doolittle. It was a slip of the tongue.

LIZA. Oh, I dont mind; only it sounded so genteel. I should just like to take a taxi to the corner of Tottenham Court Road and get out there and tell it to wait for me, just to put the girls in their place a bit. I wouldnt speak to them, you know.

PICKERING. Better wait til we get you something really fashionable.

HIGGINS. Besides, you shouldnt cut your old friends now that you have risen in the world. Thats what we call snobbery.

LIZA. You dont call the like of them my friends now, I should hope. Theyve took it out of me often enough with their ridicule when they had the chance; and now I mean to get a bit of my own back. But if I'm to have fashionable clothes, I'll wait. I should like to have some. Mrs Pearce says youre going to give me some to wear in bed at night different to what I wear in the daytime; but it do seem a waste of money when you could get something to shew. Besides, I never could fancy changing into cold things on a winter night.

MRS PEARCE [coming back] Now, Eliza. The new things have come for you to try on.

LIZA. Ah-ow-oo-ooh! [She rushes out].

MRS PEARCE [following her] Oh, dont rush about like that, girl. [She shuts the door behind her].

HIGGINS. Pickering: we have taken on a stiff job.

PICKERING [with conviction] Higgins: we have.

ACT III

It is Mrs Higgins's at-home day. Nobody has yet arrived. Her drawing room, in a flat on Chelsea Embankment, has three windows looking on the river; and the ceiling is not so lofty as it would be in an older house of the same pretension. The windows are open, giving access to a balcony with flowers in pots. If you stand with your face to the windows, you have the fireplace on your left and the door in the right-hand wall close to the corner nearest the windows.

Mrs Higgins was brought up on Morris and Burne Jones; and her room, which is very unlike her son's room in Wimpole Street, is not crowded with furniture and little tables and nicknacks. In the middle of the room there is a big ottoman; and this, with the carpet, the Morris wall-papers, and the Morris chintz window curtains and brocade covers of the ottoman and its cushions, supply all the ornament, and are much too handsome to be hidden by odds and ends of useless things. A few good oil-paintings from the exhibitions in the Grosvenor Gallery thirty years ago (the Burne Jones, not the Whistler side of them) are on the walls. The only landscape is a Cecil Lawson on the scale of a Rubens. There is a portrait of Mrs Higgins as she was when she defied fashion in her youth in one of the beautiful Rossettian costumes which, when caricatured by people who did not understand, led to the absurdities of popular estheticism in the eighteen-seventies.

In the corner diagonally opposite the door Mrs Higgins, now over sixty and long past taking the trouble to dress out of the fashion, sits writing at an elegantly simple writing-table with a bell button within reach of her hand. There is a Chippendale chair further back in the room between her and the window nearest her side. At the other side of the room, further forward, is an Elizabethan chair roughly carved in the taste of Inigo Jones. On the same side a piano in a decorated case. The corner between the fireplace and the windows is occupied by a divan cushioned in Morris chintz.

It is between four and five in the afternoon.

The door is opened violently; and Higgins enters with his hat on.

MRS HIGGINS [dismayed] Henry [scolding him] What are you doing here today? It is my at-home day: you promised not to come. [As he bends to kiss her, she takes his hat off, and presents it to him].

HIGGINS. Oh bother! [He throws the hat down on the table].

MRS HIGGINS. Go home at once.

HIGGINS [kissing her] I know, mother. I came on purpose.

MRS HIGGINS. But you mustnt. I'm serious, Henry. You offend all my friends: they stop coming whenever they meet you.

HIGGINS. Nonsense! I know I have no small talk; but people dont mind. [He sits on the settee].

MRS HIGGINS. Oh! dont they? Small talk indeed! What about your large talk? Really, dear, you mustnt stay.

HIGGINS. I must. Ive a job for you. A phonetic job.

MRS HIGGINS. No use, dear. I'm sorry; but I cant get round your vowels; and though I like to get pretty postcards in your patent shorthand, I always have to read the copies in ordinary writing you so thoughtfully send me.

HIGGINS. Well, this isnt a phonetic job.

MRS HIGGINS. You said it was.

HIGGINS. Not your part of it. Ive picked up a girl.

MRS HIGGINS. Does that mean that some

girl has picked y o u up?

HIGGINS. Not at all. I dont mean a love affair.

MRS HIGGINS. What a pity!

HIGGINS. Why?

MRS HIGGINS. Well, you never fall in love with anyone under forty-five. When will you discover that there are some rather nice-looking young women about?

HIGGINS. Oh, I cant be bothered with young women. My idea of a lovable woman is something as like you as possible. I shall never get into the way of seriously liking young women; some habits lie too deep to be changed. [*Rising abruptly and walking about, jingling his money and his keys in his trouser pockets*] Besides, theyre all idiots.

MRS HIGGINS. Do you know what you would do if you really loved me, Henry?

HIGGINS. Oh bother! What? Marry, I suppose?

MRS HIGGINS. No. Stop fidgeting and take your hands out of your pockets. [*With a gesture of despair, he obeys and sits down again.*] Thats a good boy. Now tell me about the girl.

HIGGINS. She's coming to see you.

MRS HIGGINS. I dont remember asking her.

HIGGINS. You didnt. *I* asked her. If youd known her you wouldnt have asked her.

MRS HIGGINS. Indeed! Why?

HIGGINS. Well, it's like this. She's a common flower girl. I picked her off the kerbstone.

MRS HIGGINS. And invited her to my at-home!

HIGGINS [*rising and coming to her to coax her*] Oh, thatll be all right. Ive taught her to speak properly; and she has strict orders as to her behavior. She's to keep to two subjects: the weather and everybody's health—Fine day and How do you do, you know—and not to let herself go on things in general. That will be safe.

MRS HIGGINS. Safe! To talk about our health! about our insides! perhaps about our outsides! How could you be so silly, Henry?

HIGGINS [*impatiently*] Well, she must talk about something. [*He controls himself and sits down again*]. Oh, she'll be all right: dont you fuss. Pickering is in it with me. Ive a sort of bet on that I'll pass her off as a duchess in six months. I started on her some months ago; and she's getting on like a house on fire. I shall win my bet. She has a quick ear; and she's been easier to teach than my middle-class pupils because she's had to learn a complete new language. She talks English almost as you talk French.

MRS HIGGINS. Thats satisfactory, at all events.

HIGGINS. Well, it is and it isnt.

MRS HIGGINS. What does that mean?

HIGGINS. You see, Ive got her pronunciation all right; but you have to consider not only h o w a girl pronounces, but w h a t she pronounces; and thats where—

They are interrupted by the parlor-maid, announcing guests.

THE PARLOR-MAID. Mrs and Miss Eynsford Hill. [*She withdraws*].

HIGGINS. Oh Lord! [*He rises; snatches his hat from the table; and makes for the door; but before he reaches it his mother introduces him*].

Mrs and Miss Eynsford Hill are the mother and daughter who sheltered from the rain in Covent Garden. The mother is well bred, quiet, and has the habitual anxiety of straitened means. The daughter has acquired a gay air of being very much at home in society: the bravado of genteel poverty.

MRS EYNSFORD HILL [*to Mrs Higgins*] How do you do? [*They shake hands*].

MISS EYNSFORD HILL. How d'you do? [*She shakes*].

MRS HIGGINS [*introducing*] My son Henry.

MRS EYNSFORD HILL. Your celebrated son! I have so longed to meet you, Professor Higgins.

HIGGINS [*glumly, making no movement in her direction*] Delighted. [*He backs against the piano and bows brusquely*].

MISS EYNSFORD HILL [*going to him with confident familiarity*] How do you do?

HIGGINS [*staring at her*] Ive seen you before somewhere. I havnt the ghost of a notion where; but Ive heard your voice. [*Drearily*] It doesnt matter. Youd better sit down.

MRS HIGGINS. I'm sorry to say that my celebrated son has no manners. You mustnt mind him.

MISS EYNSFORD HILL [*gaily*] I dont. [*She sits in the Elizabethan chair*].

MRS EYNSFORD HILL [*a little bewildered*] Not at all. [*She sits on the ottoman between her daughter and Mrs Higgins, who has turned her chair away from the writing-table*].

HIGGINS. Oh, have I been rude? I didnt mean to be.

He goes to the central window, through which, with his back to the company, he contemplates the river and the flowers in Battersea Park on the opposite bank as if they were a frozen desert.

The parlor-maid returns, ushering in Pickering.

THE PARLOR-MAID. Colonel Pickering. [*She withdraws*].

PICKERING. How do you do, Mrs Higgins?

MRS HIGGINS. So glad youve come. Do you know Mrs Eynsford Hill—Miss Eynsford Hill? [*Exchange of bows. The Colonel brings the Chippendale chair a little forward between Mrs Hill and Mrs Higgins, and sits down*].

PICKERING. Has Henry told you what weve come for?

HIGGINS [*over his shoulder*] We were interrupted: damn it!

MRS HIGGINS. Oh Henry, Henry, really!

MRS EYNSFORD HILL [*half rising*] Are we in the way?

MRS HIGGINS [*rising and making her sit down again*] No, no. You couldnt have come more fortunately: we want you to meet a friend of ours.

HIGGINS [*turning hopefully*] Yes, by George! We want two or three people. Youll do as well as anybody else.

The parlor-maid returns, ushering Freddy.

THE PARLOR-MAID. Mr Eynsford Hill.

HIGGINS [*almost audibly, past endurance*] God of Heaven! another of them.

FREDDY [*shaking hands with Mrs Higgins*] Ahdedo?

MRS HIGGINS. Very good of you to come. [*Introducing*] Colonel Pickering.

FREDDY [*bowing*] Ahdedo?

MRS HIGGINS. I dont think you know my son, Professor Higgins.

FREDDY [*going to Higgins*] Ahdedo?

HIGGINS [*looking at him much as if he were a pickpocket*] I'll take my oath Ive met you before somewhere. Where was it?

FREDDY. I dont think so.

HIGGINS [*resignedly*] It dont matter, anyhow. Sit down.

He shakes Freddy's hand, and almost slings him on to the ottoman with his face to the windows; then comes round to the other side of it.

HIGGINS. Well, here we are, anyhow! [*He sits down on the ottoman next Mrs Eynsford Hill, on her left*]. And now, what the devil are we going to talk about until Eliza comes?

MRS HIGGINS. Henry: you are the life and soul of the Royal Society's soirées; but really youre rather trying on more commonplace occasions.

HIGGINS. Am I? Very sorry. [*Beaming suddenly*] I suppose I am, you know. [*Uproariously*] Ha, ha!

MISS EYNSFORD HILL [*who considers Higgins quite eligible matrimonially*] I sympathize. I havnt any small talk. If people would only be frank and say what they really think!

HIGGINS [*relapsing into gloom*] Lord forbid!

MRS EYNSFORD HILL [*taking up her daughter's cue*] But why?

HIGGINS. What they think they ought to think is bad enough, Lord knows; but what they really think would break up the whole show. Do you suppose it would be really agreeable if I were to come out now with what I really think?

MISS EYNSFORD HILL [*gaily*] Is it so very cynical?

HIGGINS. Cynical! Who the dickens said it was cynical? I mean it wouldnt be decent.

MRS EYNSFORD HILL [*seriously*] Oh! I'm sure you dont mean that, Mr Higgins.

HIGGINS. You see, we're all savages, more or less. We're supposed to be civilized and cultured—to know all about poetry and philosophy and art and science, and so on; but how many of us know even the meanings of these names? [*To Miss Hill*] What do you know of poetry? [*To Mrs Hill*] What do you know of science? [*Indicating Freddy*] What does he know of art or science or anything else? What the devil do you imagine I know of philosophy?

MRS HIGGINS [*warningly*] Or of manners, Henry?

THE PARLOR-MAID [*opening the door*] Miss Doolittle. [*She withdraws*].

HIGGINS [*rising hastily and running to Mrs Higgins*] Here she is, mother. [*He stands on tiptoe and makes signs over his mother's head to Eliza to indicate to her which lady is her hostess*].

Eliza, who is exquisitely dressed, produces an impression of such remarkable distinction and beauty as she enters that they all rise, quite fluttered. Guided by Higgins's signals, she comes to Mrs Higgins with studied grace.

LIZA [*speaking with pedantic correctness of pronunciation and great beauty of tone*] How do you do, Mrs Higgins? [*She gasps slightly in making sure of the H in Higgins, but is quite successful*]. Mr Higgins told me I might come.

MRS HIGGINS [*cordially*] Quite right: I'm very glad indeed to see you.

PICKERING. How do you do, Miss Doolittle?

LIZA [*shaking hands with him*] Colonel Pickering, is it not?

MRS EYNSFORD HILL. I feel sure we have met before, Miss Doolittle. I remember your eyes.

LIZA. How do you do? [*She sits down on the ottoman gracefully in the place just left vacant by Higgins*].

MRS EYNSFORD HILL [*introducing*] My daughter Clara.

LIZA. How do you do?

CLARA [*impulsively*] How do you do? [*She sits down on the ottoman beside Eliza, devouring her with her eyes*].

FREDDY [*coming to their side of the ottoman*] Ive certainly had the pleasure.

MRS EYNSFORD HILL [*introducing*] My son Freddy.

LIZA. How do you do?

Freddy bows and sits down in the Elizabethan chair, infatuated.

HIGGINS [*suddenly*] By George, yes: it all comes back to me! [*They stare at him*]. Covent Garden! [*Lamentably*] What a damned thing!

MRS HIGGINS. Henry, please! [*He is about to sit on the edge of the table*] Dont sit on my writing- table: youll break it.

HIGGINS [*sulkily*] Sorry.

He goes to the divan, stumbling into the fender and over the fire-irons on his way; extricating himself with muttered imprecations; and finishing his disastrous journey by throwing himself so impatiently on the divan that he almost breaks it. Mrs Higgins looks at him, but controls herself and says nothing.

A long and painful pause ensues.

MRS HIGGINS [*at last, conversationally*] Will it rain, do you think?

LIZA. The shallow depression in the west of these islands is likely to move slowly in an easterly direction. There are no indications of any great change in the barometrical situation.

FREDDY. Ha! ha! how awfully funny!

LIZA. What is wrong with that, young man? I bet I got it right.

FREDDY. Killing!

MRS EYNSFORD HILL. I'm sure I hope it wont turn cold. Theres so much influenza about. It runs right through our whole family regularly every spring.

LIZA [*darkly*] My aunt died of influenza: so they said.

MRS EYNSFORD HILL [*clicks her tongue sympa-thetically*]!!!

LIZA [*in the same tragic tone*] But it's my belief they done the old woman in.

MRS HIGGINS [*puzzled*] Done her in?

LIZA. Y-e-e-e-es, Lord love you! Why should she die of influenza? She come through diphtheria right enough the year before. I saw her with my own eyes. Fairly blue with it, she was. They all thought she was dead; but my father he kept ladling gin down her throat til she came to so sudden that she bit the bowl off the spoon.

MRS EYNSFORD HILL [*startled*] Dear me!

LIZA [*piling up the indictment*] What call would a woman with that strength in her have to die of influenza? What become of her new straw hat that should have come to me? Somebody pinched it; and what I say is, them as pinched it done her in.

MRS EYNSFORD HILL. What does doing her in mean?

HIGGINS [*hastily*] Oh, thats the new small talk. To do a person in means to kill them.

MRS EYNSFORD HILL [*to Eliza, horrified*] You surely dont believe that your aunt was killed.

LIZA. Do I not! Them she lived with would have killed her for a hat-pin, let alone a hat.

MRS EYNSFORD HILL. But it cant have been right for your father to pour spirits down her throat like that. It might have killed her.

LIZA. Not her. Gin was mother's milk to her. Besides, he'd poured so much down his own throat that he knew the good of it.

MRS EYNSFORD HILL. Do you mean that he drank?

LIZA. Drank! My word! Something chronic.

MRS EYNSFORD HILL. How dreadful for you!

LIZA. Not a bit. It never did him no harm what I could see. But then he did not keep it up regular. [*Cheerfully*] On the burst, as you might say, from time to time. And always more agreeable when he had a drop in. When he was out of work, my mother used to give him fourpence and tell him to go out and not come back until he'd drunk himself cheerful and loving-like. Theres lots of women has to make their husbands drunk to make them fit to live with. [*Now quite at her ease*] You see, it's like this. If a man has a bit of a conscience, it always takes him when he's sober; and then it makes him low-spirited. A drop of booze just takes that off and makes him happy. [*To Freddy, who is in convulsions of suppressed laughter*] Here! what are you sniggering at?

FREDDY. The new small talk. You do it so awfully well.

LIZA. If I was doing it proper, what was you laughing at? [*To Higgins*] Have I said anything I oughtnt?

MRS HIGGINS [*interposing*] Not at all, Miss Doolittle.

LIZA. Well, thats a mercy, anyhow. [*Expansively*] What I always say is—

HIGGINS [*rising and looking at his watch*] Ahem!

LIZA [*looking round at him; taking the hint; and rising*] Well: I must go. [*They all rise. Freddy goes to the door*]. So pleased to have met you. Goodbye. [*She shakes hands with Mrs Higgins*]

MRS HIGGINS. Goodbye.

LIZA. Goodbye, Colonel Pickering.

PICKERING. Goodbye, Miss Doolittle. [*They shake hands*].

LIZA [*nodding to the others*] Goodbye, all.

FREDDY [*opening the door for her*] Are you walking across the Park, Miss Doolittle? If so—

LIZA. Walk! Not bloody likely. [*Sensation*]. I am going in a taxi. [*She goes out*].

Pickering gasps and sits down. Freddy goes out on the balcony to catch another glimpse of Eliza.

MRS EYNSFORD HILL [*suffering from shock*] Well, I really cant get used to the new ways.

CLARA [*throwing herself discontentedly into the Elizabethan chair*] Oh, it's all right mamma, quite right. People will think we never go anywhere or see anybody if you are so old-fashioned.

MRS EYNSFORD HILL. I daresay I am very old-fashioned; but I do hope you wont begin using that expression, Clara. I have got accustomed to hear you talking about men as rotters, and calling everything filthy and beastly; though I do think it horrible and unladylike. But this last is really too much. Dont you think so, Colonel Pickering?

PICKERING. Dont ask me. Ive been away in India for several years; and manners have changed so much that I sometimes dont know whether I'm at a respectable dinner-table or in a ship's forecastle.

CLARA. It's all a matter of habit. Theres no right or wrong in it. Nobody means anything by it. And it's so quaint, and gives such a smart emphasis to things that are not in themselves very witty. I find the new small talk delightful and quite innocent.

MRS EYNSFORD HILL [*rising*] Well, after that, I think it's time for us to go.

Pickering and Higgins rise.

CLARA [*rising*] Oh yes: we have three at-homes to go to still. Goodbye, Mrs. Higgins. Goodbye, Colonel Pickering. Goodbye, Professor Higgins.

HIGGINS [*coming grimly at her from the divan, and accompanying her to the door*] Goodbye. Be sure you try on that small talk at the three at-homes. Dont be nervous about it. Pitch it in strong.

CLARA [*all smiles*] I will. Goodbye. Such nonsense, all this early Victorian prudery!

HIGGINS [*tempting her*] Such damned nonsense!

CLARA. Such bloody nonsense!

MRS EYNSFORD HILL [*convulsively*] Clara!

CLARA. Ha! ha! [*She goes out radiant, conscious of being thoroughly up to date, and is heard descending the stairs in a stream of silvery laughter*].

FREDDY [*to the heavens at large*] Well, I ask you—[*He gives it up, and comes to Mrs Higgins*] Goodbye.

MRS HIGGINS [*shaking hands*] Goodbye. Would you like to meet Miss Doolittle again?

FREDDY [*eagerly*] Yes, I should, most awfully.

MRS HIGGINS. Well, you know my days.

FREDDY. Yes. Thanks awfully. Goodbye. [*He goes out*].

MRS EYNSFORD HILL. Goodbye, Mr Higgins.

HIGGINS. Goodbye. Goodbye.

MRS EYNSFORD HILL [*to Pickering*] It's no use. I shall never be able to bring myself to use that word.

PICKERING. Dont. It's not compulsory, you know. Youll get on quite well without it.

MRS EYNSFORD HILL. Only, Clara is so down on me if I am not positively reeking with the latest slang. Goodbye.

PICKERING. Goodbye [*They shake hands*].

MRS EYNSFORD HILL [*to Mrs Higgins*] You mustnt mind Clara. [*Pickering, catching from her lowered tone that this is not meant for him to hear, discreetly joins Higgins at the window*] We're so poor! and she gets so few parties, poor child! She doesnt quite know. [*Mrs Higgins, seeing that her eyes are moist, takes her hand sympathetically and goes with her to the door*]. But the boy is nice. Dont you think so?

MRS HIGGINS. Oh, quite nice. I shall always be delighted to see him.

MRS EYNSFORD HILL. Thank you, dear. Goodbye. [*She goes out*].

HIGGINS [*eagerly*] Well? Is Eliza presentable? [*He swoops on his mother and drags her to the ottoman, where she sits down in Eliza's place with her son on her left*].

Pickering returns to his chair on her right.

MRS HIGGINS. You silly boy, of course she's not presentable. She's a triumph of your art and of her dressmaker's; but if you suppose for a moment that she doesnt give herself away in every sentence she utters, you must be perfectly cracked about her.

PICKERING. But dont you think something might be done? I mean something to eliminate the sanguinary element from her conversation.

MRS HIGGINS. Not as long as she is in Henry's hands.

HIGGINS [*aggrieved*] Do you mean that my language is improper?

MRS HIGGINS. No, dearest: it would be quite proper—say on a canal barge; but it would not be proper for her at a garden party.

HIGGINS [*deeply injured*] Well I must say—

PICKERING [*interrupting him*] Come, Higgins: you must learn to know yourself. I havnt heard such language as yours since we used to review the volunteers in Hyde Park twenty years ago.

HIGGINS [*sulkily*] Oh, well, if you say so, I suppose I dont always talk like a bishop.

MRS HIGGINS [*quieting Henry with a touch*] Colonel Pickering: will you tell me what is the exact state of things in Wimpole Street?

PICKERING [*cheerfully: as if this completely changed the subject*] Well, I have come to live there with Henry. We work together at my Indian Dialects; and we think it more convenient—

MRS HIGGINS. Quite so. I know all about that: it's an excellent arrangement. But where does this girl live?

HIGGINS. With us, of course. Where should she live?

MRS HIGGINS. But on what terms? Is she a servant? If not, what is she?

PICKERING [*slowly*] I think I know what you mean, Mrs Higgins.

HIGGINS. Well, dash me if *I* do! Ive had to work at the girl every day for months to get her to her present pitch. Besides she's useful. She knows where my things are, and remembers my appointments and so forth.

MRS HIGGINS. How does your housekeeper get on with her?

HIGGINS. Mrs Pearce? Oh, she's jolly glad to get so much taken off her hands; for before Eliza came, she used to have to find things and remind me of my appointments. But she's got some silly bee in her bonnet about Eliza. She keeps saying "You dont think, sir": doesnt she, Pick?

PICKERING. Yes: thats the formula. "You dont think, sir." Thats the end of every conversation about Eliza.

HIGGINS. As if I ever stop thinking about the girl and her confounded vowels and consonants. I'm worn out, thinking about her, and watching her lips and her teeth and her tongue, not to mention her soul, which is the quaintest of the lot.

MRS HIGGINS. You certainly are a pretty pair of babies, playing with your live doll.

HIGGINS. Playing! The hardest job I ever tackled: make no mistake about that, mother. But you have no idea how frightfully interesting it is to take a human being and change her into a quite different human being by creating a new speech for her. It's filling up the deepest gulf that separates class from class and soul from soul.

PICKERING [*drawing his chair closer to Mrs Higgins and bending over to her eagerly*] Yes: it's enormously interesting. I assure you, Mrs Higgins, we take Eliza very seriously. Every week—every day almost—there is some new change. [*Closer again*] We keep records of every stage—dozens of gramophone disks and photographs—

HIGGINS [*assailing her at the other ear*] Yes, by George: it's the most absorbing experiment I ever tackled. She regularly fills our lives up: doesnt she, Pick?

PICKERING. We're always talking Eliza.

HIGGINS. Teaching Eliza.

PICKERING. Dressing Eliza.

MRS HIGGINS. What!

HIGGINS. Inventing new Elizas.

HIGGINS. [*speaking together*] You know, she has the most extraordinary quickness of ear:

PICKERING. [*speaking together*] I assure you, my dear Mrs Higgins, that girl

2 B

HIGGINS.

[*speaking together*]

PICKERING.

just like a parrot. Ive tried her with every is a genius. She can play the piano quite beautifully.

HIGGINS. PICKERING. possible sort of sound that a human being can make— We have taken her to classical concerts and to music

HIGGINS. PICKERING. Continental dialects, African dialects, Hottentot halls; and it's all the the same to her: she plays everything

HIGGINS. PICKERING. clicks, things it took me years to get hold of; and she hears right off when she comes home, whether it's

HIGGINS. PICKERING. she picks them up like a shot, right away, as if she had Beethoven and Brahms or Lehar and Lionel Monckton;

HIGGINS. PICKERING. been at it all her life. though six months ago, she'd never as much as touched a piano—

MRS HIGGINS [*putting her fingers in her ears, as they are by this time shouting one another down with an intolerable noise*] Sh-sh-sh—sh! [*They stop*].

PICKERING. I beg your pardon. [*He draws his chair back apologetically*].

HIGGINS. Sorry. When Pickering starts shouting nobody can get a word in edgeways.

MRS HIGGINS. Be quiet, Henry. Colonel Pickering: dont you realize that when Eliza walked into Wimpole Street, something walked in with her?

PICKERING. Her father did. But Henry soon got rid of him.

MRS HIGGINS. It would have been more to the point if her mother had. But as her mother didnt something else did.

PICKERING. But what?

MRS HIGGINS [*unconsciously dating herself by the word*] A problem.

PICKERING. Oh, I see. The problem of how to pass her off as a lady.

HIGGINS. I'll solve that problem. Ive half solved it already.

MRS HIGGINS. No, you two infinitely stupid male creatures: the problem of what is to be done with her afterwards.

HIGGINS. I dont see anything in that. She can go her own way, with all the advantages I have given her.

MRS HIGGINS. The advantages of that poor woman who was here just now! The manners and habits that disqualify a fine lady from earning her own living without giving her a fine lady's income! Is that what you mean?

PICKERING [*indulgently, being rather bored*] Oh, that will be all right, Mrs Higgins. [*He rises to go*].

HIGGINS [*rising also*] We'll find her some light employment.

PICKERING. She's happy enough. Dont you worry about her. Goodbye. [*He shakes hands as if he were consoling a frightened child, and makes for the door*].

HIGGINS. Anyhow, theres no good bothering now. The thing's done. Goodbye, mother. [*He kisses her, and follows Pickering*].

PICKERING [*turning for a final consolation*] There are plenty of openings. We'll do whats right. Goodbye.

HIGGINS [*to Pickering as they go out together*] Lets take her to the Shakespear exhibition at Earls Court.

PICKERING. Yes: lets. Her remarks will be delicious.

HIGGINS. She'll mimic all the people for us when we get home.

PICKERING. Ripping. [*Both are heard laughing as they go downstairs*].

MRS HIGGINS [*rises with an impatient bounce, and returns to her work at the writing-table. She sweeps a litter of disarranged papers out of her way: snatches a sheet of paper from her stationery case; and tries resolutely to write. At the third line she gives it up; flings down her pen; grips the table angrily and exclaims*] Oh, men! men!! men!!!

ACT IV

The Wimpole Street laboratory. Midnight. Nobody in the room. The clock on the mantelpiece strikes twelve. The fire is not alight: it is a

summer night.

Presently Higgins and Pickering are heard on the stairs.

HIGGINS [*calling down to Pickering*] I say, Pick: lock up, will you? I shant be going out again.

PICKERING. Right. Can Mrs Pearce go to bed? We dont want anything more, do we?

HIGGINS. Lord, no!

Eliza opens the door and is seen on the lighted landing in opera cloak, brilliant evening dress, and diamonds, with fan, flowers, and all accessories. She comes to the hearth, and switches on the electric lights there. She is tired: her pallor contrasts strongly with her dark eyes and hair; and her expression is almost tragic. She takes off her cloak, puts her fan and flowers on the piano; and sits down on the bench, brooding and silent. Higgins, in evening dress, with overcoat and hat, comes in, carrying a smoking jacket which he has picked up downstairs. He takes off the hat and overcoat; throws them carelessly on the newspaper stand; disposes of his coat in the same way; puts on the smoking jacket; and throws himself wearily into the easy-chair at the hearth. Pickering, similarly attired, comes in. He also takes off his hat and overcoat, and is about to throw them on Higgins's when he hesitates.

PICKERING. I say: Mrs Pearce will row if we leave these things lying about in the drawing room.

HIGGINS. Oh, chuck them over the bannisters into the hall. She'll find them there in the morning and put them away all right. She'll think we were drunk.

PICKERING. We are, slightly. Are there any letters?

HIGGINS. I didnt look. [*Pickering takes the overcoats and hats and goes downstairs. Higgins begins half singing half yawning an air from La Fanciulla del Golden West. Suddenly he stops and exclaims*] I wonder where the devil my slippers are!

Eliza looks at him darkly; then rises suddenly and leaves the room.

Higgins yawns again, and resumes his song. Pickering returns, with the contents of the letter-box in his hand.

PICKERING. Only circulars, and this coroneted billet-doux for you. [*He throws the circulars into the fender, and posts himself on the hearth-rug, with his back to the grate*].

HIGGINS [*glancing at the billet-doux*] Moneylender. [*He throws the letter after the circulars*].

Eliza returns with a pair of large down-at-heel slippers. She places them on the carpet before Higgins, and sits as before without a word.

HIGGINS [*yawning again*] Oh Lord! What an evening! What a crew! What a silly tomfoolery! [*He raises his shoe to unlace it, and catches sight of the slippers. He stops unlacing and looks at them as if they had appeared there of their own accord*]. Oh! theyre there, are they?

PICKERING [*stretching himself*] Well, I feel a bit tired. It's been a long day. The garden party, a dinner party, and the opera! Rather too much of a good thing. But youve won your bet, Higgins. Eliza did the trick, and something to spare, eh?

HIGGINS [*fervently*] Thank God it's over!

Eliza flinches violently; but they take no notice of her; and she recovers herself and sits stonily as before.

PICKERING. Were you nervous at the garden party? *I* was. Eliza didnt seem a bit nervous.

HIGGINS. Oh, s h e wasnt nervous. I knew she'd be all right. No: it's the strain of putting the job through all these months that has told on me. It was interesting enough at first, while we were at the phonetics; but after that I got deadly sick of it. If I hadnt backed myself to do it I should have chucked the whole thing up two months ago. It was a silly notion: the whole thing has been a bore.

PICKERING. Oh come! the garden party was frightfully exciting. My heart began beating like anything.

HIGGINS. Yes, for the first three minutes. But when I saw we were going to win hands down, I felt like a bear in a cage, hanging about doing nothing. The dinner was worse: sitting gorging there for over an hour, with nobody but a damned fool of a fashionable woman to talk to! I tell you, Pickering, never again for me. No more artificial duchesses. The whole thing has been simple purgatory.

PICKERING. Youve never been broken in properly to the social routine. [*Strolling over to the piano*] I rather enjoy dipping into it occasionally myself: it makes me feel young again. Anyhow, it was a great success: an immense success. I was quite frightened once or twice because Eliza was doing it so well. You see, lots of the real people cant do it at all: theyre such fools that they think style comes by nature to people in their position; and so they never learn. Theres always something professional about doing a thing superlatively well.

HIGGINS. Yes: thats what drives me mad: the silly people dont know their own silly business. [*Rising*] However, it's over and done with; and now I can go to bed at last without dreading tomorrow.

Eliza's beauty becomes murderous.

PICKERING. I think I shall turn in too. Still, it's been a great occasion: a triumph for you. Goodnight. [*He goes*].

HIGGINS [*following him*] Goodnight. [*Over his shoulder, at the door*] Put out the lights, Eliza: and tell Mrs Pearce not to make coffee for me in the morning: I'll take tea. [*He goes out*].

Eliza tries to control herself and feel indifferent as she rises and walks across to the hearth to switch off the lights. By the time she gets there she is on the point of screaming. She sits down in Higgins's chair and holds on hard to the arms. Finally she gives way and flings herself furiously on the floor, raging.

HIGGINS [*in despairing wrath outside*] What the devil have I done with my slippers? [*He appears at the door*].

LIZA [*snatching up the slippers, and hurling them at him one after the other with all her force*] There are your slippers. And there. Take your slippers; and may you never have a day's luck with them!

HIGGINS [*astounded*] What on earth—! [*He comes to her*]. Whats the matter? Get up. [*He pulls her up*]. Anything wrong?

LIZA [*breathless*] Nothing wrong—with y o u. Ive won your bet for you, havnt I? Thats enough for you. *I* dont matter, I suppose.

HIGGINS. Y o u won my bet! You! Presumptuous insect! *I* won it. What did you throw those slippers at me for?

LIZA. Because I wanted to smash your face. I'd like to kill you, you selfish brute. Why didnt you leave me where you picked me out of—in the gutter? You thank God it's all over, and that now you can throw me back again there, do you? [*She crisps her fingers frantically*].

HIGGINS [*looking at her in cool wonder*] The creature is nervous, after all.

LIZA [*gives a suffocated scream of fury, and instinctively darts her nails at his face*]!!

HIGGINS [*catching her wrists*] Ah! would you? Claws in, you cat. How dare you shew your temper to me? Sit down and be quiet. [*He throws her roughly into the easy-chair*].

LIZA [*crushed by superior strength and weight*] Whats to become of me? Whats to become of me?

HIGGINS. How the devil do I know whats to become of you? What does it matter what becomes of you?

LIZA. You dont care. I know you dont care. You wouldnt care if I was dead. I'm nothing to you—not so much as them slippers.

HIGGINS [*thundering*] Those slippers.

LIZA [*with bitter submission*] Those slippers. I didnt think it made any difference now.

A pause. Eliza hopeless and crushed. Higgins a little uneasy.

HIGGINS [*in his loftiest manner*] Why have you begun going on like this? May I ask whether you complain of your treatment here?

LIZA. No.

HIGGINS. Has anybody behaved badly to you? Colonel Pickering? Mrs Pearce? Any of the servants?

LIZA. No.

HIGGINS. I presume you dont pretend that *I* have treated you badly?

LIZA. No.

HIGGINS. I am glad to hear it. [*He moderates his tone*]. Perhaps youre tired after the strain of the day. Will you have a glass of champagne? [*He moves towards the door*].

LIZA. No. [*Recollecting her manners*] Thank you.

HIGGINS [*good-humored again*] This has been coming on you for some days. I suppose it was natural for you to be anxious about the garden party. But thats all over now. [*He pats her kindly on the shoulder. She writhes*]. Theres nothing more to worry about.

LIZA. No. Nothing more for y o u to worry about. [*She suddenly rises and gets away from him by going to the piano bench, where she sits and hides her face*]. Oh God! I wish I was dead.

HIGGINS [*staring after her in sincere surprise*] Why? In heaven's name, why? [*Reasonably, going to her*] Listen to me, Eliza. All this irritation is purely subjective.

LIZA. I dont understand. I'm too ignorant.

HIGGINS. It's only imagination. Low spirits and nothing else. Nobody's hurting you. Nothing's wrong. You go to bed like a good girl and sleep it off. Have a little cry and say your prayers: that will make you comfortable.

LIZA. I heard y o u r prayers. "Thank God it's all over!"

HIGGINS [*impatiently*] Well, d o n t you thank

God it's all over? Now you are free and can do what you like.

LIZA [*pulling herself together in desperation*] What am I fit for? What have you left me fit for? Where am I to go? What am I to do? Whats to become of me?

HIGGINS [*enlightened, but not at all impressed*] Oh, thats whats worrying you, is it? [*He thrusts his hands into his pockets, and walks about in his usual manner, rattling the contents of his pockets, as if condescending to a trivial subject out of pure kindness*]. I shouldnt bother about it if I were you. I should imagine you wont have much difficulty in settling yourself somewhere or other, though I hadnt quite realized that you were going away. [*She looks quickly at him: he does not look at her, but examines the dessert stand on the piano and decides that he will eat an apple*]. You might marry, you know. [*He bites a large piece out of the apple and munches it noisily*]. You see, Eliza, all men are not confirmed old bachelors like me and the Colonel. Most men are the marrying sort (poor devils!); and youre not bad-looking: it's quite a pleasure to look at you sometimes—not now, of course, because youre crying and looking as ugly as the very devil; but when youre all right and quite yourself, youre what I should call attractive. That is, to the people in the marrying line, you understand. You go to bed and have a good nice rest; and then get up and look at yourself in the glass; and you wont feel so cheap.

Eliza again looks at him, speechless, and does not stir.

The look is quite lost on him: he eats his apple with a dreamy expression of happiness, as it is quite a good one.

HIGGINS [*a genial afterthought occurring to him*] I daresay my mother could find some chap or other who would do very well.

LIZA. We were above that at the corner of Tottenham Court Road.

HIGGINS [*waking up*] What do you mean?

LIZA. I sold flowers. I didnt sell myself. Now youve made a lady of me I'm not fit to sell anything else. I wish youd left me where you found me.

HIGGINS [*slinging the core of the apple decisively into the grate*] Tosh, Eliza. Dont you insult human relations by dragging all this cant about buying and selling into it. You neednt marry the fellow if you dont like him.

LIZA. What else am I to do?

HIGGINS. Oh, lots of things. What about your old idea of a florist's shop? Pickering could set you up in one: he's lots of money. [*Chuckling*] He'll have to pay for all those togs you have been wearing today; and that, with the hire of the jewellery, will make a big hole in two hundred pounds. Why, six months ago you would have thought it the millennium to have a flower shop of your own. Come! youll be all right. I must clear off to bed: I'm devilish sleepy. By the way, I came down for something: I forget what it was.

LIZA. Your slippers.

HIGGINS. Oh yes, of course. You shied them at me. [*He picks them up, and is going out when she rises and speaks to him*].

LIZA. Before you go, sir—

HIGGINS [*dropping the slippers in his surprise at her calling him Sir*] Eh?

LIZA. Do my clothes belong to me or to Colonel Pickering?

HIGGINS [*coming back into the room as if her question were the very climax of unreason*] What the devil use would they be to Pickering?

LIZA. He might want them for the next girl you pick up to experiment on.

HIGGINS [*shocked and hurt*] Is that the way you feel towards us?

LIZA. I dont want to hear anything more about that. All I want to know is whether anything belongs to me. My own clothes were burnt.

HIGGINS. But what does it matter? Why need you start bothering about that in the middle of the night?

LIZA. I want to know what I may take away with me. I dont want to be accused of stealing.

HIGGINS [*now deeply wounded*] Stealing! You shouldnt have said that, Eliza. That shews a want of feeling.

LIZA. I'm sorry. I'm only a common ignorant girl; and in my station I have to be careful. There cant be any feelings between the like of you and the like of me. Please will you tell me what belongs to me and what doesnt?

HIGGINS [*very sulky*] You may take the whole damned houseful if you like. Except the jewels. Theyre hired. Will that satisfy you? [*He turns on his heel and is about to go in extreme dudgeon*].

LIZA [*drinking in his emotion like nectar, and nagging him to provoke a further supply*] Stop, please. [*She takes off her jewels*]. Will you take these to your room and keep them safe? I dont want to run the risk of their being missing.

HIGGINS [*furious*] Hand them over. [*She puts them into his hands*]. If these belonged to me instead of to the jeweller, I'd ram them down your ungrateful throat. [*He perfunctorily thrusts them into his pockets, unconsciously decorating himself with the protruding ends of the chains*].

LIZA [*taking a ring off*] This ring isnt the jeweller's: it's the one you bought me in Brighton. I dont want it now. [*Higgins dashes the ring violently into the fireplace, and turns on her so threateningly that she crouches over the piano with her hands over her face, and exclaims*] Dont you hit me.

HIGGINS. Hit you! You infamous creature, how dare you accuse me of such a thing? It is you who have hit me. You have wounded me to the heart.

LIZA [*thrilling with hidden joy*] I'm glad. Ive got a little of my own back, anyhow.

HIGGINS [*with dignity, in his finest professional style*] You have caused me to lose my temper: a thing that has hardly ever happened to me before. I prefer to say nothing more tonight. I am going to bed.

LIZA [*pertly*] Youd better leave a note for Mrs Pearce about the coffee; for she wont be told by me.

HIGGINS [*formally*] Damn Mrs Pearce; and damn the coffee; and damn you; and damn my own folly in having lavished hard-earned knowledge and the treasure of my regard and intimacy on a heartless guttersnipe. [*He goes out with impressive decorum, and spoils it by slamming the door savagely*].

Eliza smiles for the first time; expresses her feelings by a wild pantomime in which an imitation of Higgins's exit is confused with her own triumph; and finally goes down on her knees on the hearthrug to look for the ring.

ACT V

Mrs Higgins's drawing room. She is at her writing-table as before. The parlor-maid comes in.

THE PARLOR-MAID [*at the door*] Mr Henry, maam, is downstairs with Colonel Pickering.

MRS HIGGINS. Well, shew them up.

THE PARLOR-MAID. Theyre using the telephone, maam. Telephoning to the police, I think.

MRS HIGGINS. What!

THE PARLOR-MAID [*coming further in and lowering her voice*] Mr Henry is in a state, maam. I thought I'd better tell you.

MRS HIGGINS. If you had told me that Mr Henry was not in a state it would have been more surprising. Tell them to come up when theyve finished with the police. I suppose he's lost something.

THE PARLOR-MAID. Yes, maam [*going*].

MRS HIGGINS. Go upstairs and tell Miss Doolittle that Mr Henry and the Colonel are here. Ask her not to come down til I send for her.

THE PARLOR-MAID. Yes, maam.

Higgins bursts in. He is, as the parlor-maid has said, in a state.

HIGGINS. Look here, mother: heres a confounded thing!

MRS HIGGINS. Yes, dear. Good morning. [*He checks his impatience and kisses her, whilst the parlor-maid goes out*]. What is it?

HIGGINS. Eliza's bolted.

MRS HIGGINS [*calmly continuing her writing*] You must have frightened her.

HIGGINS. Frightened her! nonsense! She was left last night, as usual, to turn out the lights and all that; and instead of going to bed she changed her clothes and went right off: her bed wasnt slept in. She came in a cab for her things before seven this morning; and that fool Mrs Pearce let her have them without telling me a word about it. What am I to do?

MRS HIGGINS. Do without, I'm afraid, Henry. The girl has a perfect right to leave if she chooses.

HIGGINS [*wandering distractedly across the room*] But I cant find anything. I dont know what appointments Ive got. I'm— [*Pickering comes in. Mrs. Higgins puts down her pen and turns away from the writing-table*].

PICKERING [*shaking hands*] Good morning, Mrs Higgins. Has Henry told you? [*He sits down on the ottoman*].

HIGGINS. What does that ass of an inspector say? Have you offered a reward?

MRS HIGGINS [*rising in indignant amazement*] You dont mean to say you have set the police after Eliza.

HIGGINS. Of course. What are the police for? What else could we do? [*He sits in the Elizabethan chair*].

PICKERING. The inspector made a lot of difficulties. I really think he suspected us of some improper purpose.

MRS HIGGINS. Well, of course he did. What right have you to go to the police and give the girl's name as if she were a thief, or a lost umbrella, or something? Really! [*She sits down again, deeply vexed*].

HIGGINS. But we want to find her.

PICKERING. We cant let her go like this, you know, Mrs Higgins. What were we to do?

MRS HIGGINS. You have no more sense, either of you, than two children. Why—

The parlor-maid comes in and breaks off the conversation.

THE PARLOR-MAID. Mr Henry: a gentleman wants to see you very particular. He's been sent on from Wimpole Street.

HIGGINS. Oh, bother! I cant see anyone now. Who is it?

THE PARLOR-MAID. A Mr Doolittle, sir.

PICKERING. Doolittle! Do you mean the dustman?

THE PARLOR-MAID. Dustman! Oh no, sir: a gentleman.

HIGGINS [*springing up excitedly*] By George, Pick, it's some relative of hers that she's gone to. Somebody we know nothing about. [*To the parlor-maid*] Send him up, quick.

THE PARLOR-MAID. Yes, sir. [*She goes*].

HIGGINS [*eagerly, going to his mother*] Genteel relatives! now we shall hear something. [*He sits down in the Chippendale chair*].

MRS HIGGINS. Do you know any of her people?

PICKERING. Only her father: the fellow we told you about.

THE PARLOR-MAID [*announcing*] Mr Doolittle. [*She withdraws*].

Doolittle enters. He is brilliantly dressed in a new fashionable frock-coat, with white waistcoat and grey trousers. A flower in his buttonhole, a dazzling silk hat, and patent leather shoes complete the effect. He is too concerned with the business he has come on to notice Mrs Higgins. He walks straight to Higgins, and accosts him with vehement reproach.

DOOLITTLE [*indicating his own person*] See here! Do you see this? You done this.

HIGGINS. Done what, man?

DOOLITTLE. This, I tell you. Look at it. Look at this hat. Look at this coat.

PICKERING. Has Eliza been buying you clothes?

DOOLITTLE. Eliza! not she. Not half. Why would she buy me clothes?

MRS HIGGINS. Good morning, Mr Doolittle. Wont you sit down?

DOOLITTLE [*taken aback as he becomes conscious that he has forgotten his hostess*] Asking your pardon, maam. [*He approaches her and shakes her proffered hand*]. Thank you. [*He sits down on the ottoman, on Pickering's right*]. I am that full of what has happened to me that I cant think of anything else.

HIGGINS. What the dickens has happened to you?

DOOLITTLE. I shouldnt mind if it had only happened to me: anything might happen to anybody and nobody to blame but Providence, as you might say. But this is something that you done to me: yes, you, Henry Higgins.

HIGGINS. Have you found Eliza? Thats the point.

DOOLITTLE. Have you lost her?

HIGGINS. Yes.

DOOLITTLE. You have all the luck, you have. I aint found her; but she'll find me quick enough now after what you done to me.

MRS HIGGINS. But what has my son done to you, Mr Doolittle?

DOOLITTLE. Done to me! Ruined me. Destroyed my happiness. Tied me up and delivered me into the hands of middle class morality.

HIGGINS [*rising intolerantly and standing over Doolittle*] Youre raving. Youre drunk. Youre mad. I gave you five pounds. After that I had two conversations with you, at half-a-crown an hour. Ive never seen you since.

DOOLITTLE. Oh! Drunk! am I? Mad! am I? Tell me this. Did you or did you not write a letter to an old blighter in America that was giving five millions to found Moral Reform Societies all over the world, and that wanted you to invent a universal language for him?

HIGGINS. What! Ezra D. Wannafeller! He's dead. [*He sits down again carelessly*].

DOOLITTLE. Yes: he's dead; and I'm done for. Now did you or did you not write a letter to him to say that the most original moralist at present in England, to the best of your knowledge, was Alfred Doolittle, a common dustman.

HIGGINS. Oh, after your last visit I remember making some silly joke of the kind.

DOOLITTLE. Ah! you may well call it a silly joke. It put the lid on me right enough. Just give him the chance he wanted to shew that Americans is not like us: that they recognize and respect merit in every class of life, however humble. Them words is in his blooming will, in which, Henry Higgins, thanks to your silly joking, he leaves me a share in his Pre-digested Cheese Trust worth three thousand a year on condition that I lecture for his Wannafeller Moral Reform World League as often as they ask me up to six times a year.

HIGGINS. The devil he does! Whew! [*Brightening suddenly*] What a lark!

PICKERING. A safe thing for you, Doolittle. They wont ask you twice.

DOOLITTLE. It aint the lecturing I mind. I'll lecture them blue in the face, I will, and not turn a hair. It's making a gentleman of me that I object to. Who asked him to make a gentleman of me? I was happy. I was free. I touched pretty nigh everybody for money when I wanted it, same as I touched you, Henry Higgins. Now I am worrited; tied neck and heels; and everybody touches m e for money. It's a fine thing for you, says my solicitor. Is it? says I. You mean it's a good thing for you, I says. When I was a poor man and had a solicitor once when they found a pram in the dust cart, he got me off, and got shut of me and got me shut of him as quick as he could. Same with the doctors: used to shove me out of the hospital before I could hardly stand on my legs, and nothing to pay. Now they finds out that I'm not a healthy man and cant live unless they looks after me twice a day. In the house I'm not let do a hand's turn for myself: somebody else must do it and touch me for it. A year ago I hadnt a relative in the world except two or three that wouldnt speak to me. Now Ive fifty, and not a decent week's wages among the lot of them. I have to live for others and not for myself: thats middle class morality. Y o u talk of losing Eliza. Dont you be anxious: I bet she's on my doorstep by this: she that could support herself easy by selling flowers if I wasnt respectable. And the next one to touch me will be you, Henry Higgins. I'll have to learn to speak middle class language from you, instead of speaking proper English. Thats where y o u l l come in; and I daresay thats what you done it for.

MRS HIGGINS. But, my dear Mr Doolittle, you need not suffer all this if you are really in earnest. Nobody can force you to accept this bequest. You can repudiate it. Isnt that so, Colonel Pickering?

PICKERING. I believe so.

DOOLITTLE [*softening his manner in deference to her sex*] Thats the tragedy of it, maam. It's easy to say chuck it; but I havnt the nerve. Which of us has? We're all intimidated. Intimidated, maam: thats what we are. What is there for me if I chuck it but the workhouse in my old age? I have to dye my hair already to keep my job as a dustman. If I was one of the deserving poor, and had put by a bit, I could chuck it; but then why should I, acause the deserving poor might as well be millionaires for all the happiness they ever has. They dont know what happiness is. But I, as one of the undeserving poor, have nothing between me and the pauper's uniform but this here blasted three thousand a year that shoves me into the middle class. (Excuse the expression maam: youd use it yourself if you had my provocation.) Theyve got you every way you turn: it's a choice between the Skilly of the workhouse and the Char Bydis of the middle class; and I havnt the nerve for the workhouse. Intimidated: thats what I am. Broke. Bought up. Happier men than me will call for my dust, and touch me for their tip; and I'll look on helpless, and envy them. And thats what your son has brought me to. [*He is overcome by emotion*].

MRS HIGGINS. Well, I'm very glad youre not going to do anything foolish, Mr Doolittle. For this solves the problem of Eliza's future. You can provide for her now.

DOOLITTLE [*with melancholy resignation*] Yes, maam: I'm expected to provide for everyone now, out of three thousand a year.

HIGGINS [*jumping up*] Nonsense! he cant provide for her. He shant provide for her. She doesnt belong to him. I paid him five pounds for her. Doolittle: either youre an honest man or a rogue.

DOOLITTLE [*tolerantly*] A little of both, Henry, like the rest of us: a little of both.

HIGGINS. Well, you took that money for the girl: and you have no right to take her as well.

MRS HIGGINS. Henry: dont be absurd. If you want to know where Eliza is, she is upstairs.

HIGGINS [*amazed*] Upstairs!!! Then I shall jolly soon fetch her downstairs. [*He makes resolutely for the door*].

MRS HIGGINS [*rising and following him*] Be quiet, Henry. Sit down.

HIGGINS. I—

MRS HIGGINS. Sit down, dear; and listen to me.

HIGGINS. Oh very well, very well, very well. [*He throws himself ungraciously on the ottoman, with his face towards the windows*]. But I think you might have told us this half an hour ago.

MRS HIGGINS. Eliza came to me this morning. She passed the night partly walking about in a rage, partly trying to throw herself into the river and being afraid to, and partly in the Carlton Hotel. She told me of the brutal way you two treated her.

HIGGINS [*bounding up again*] What!

PICKERING [*rising also*] My dear Mrs Higgins, she's been telling you stories. We didnt treat her brutally. We hardly said a word to her; and we parted on particularly good terms. [*Turning on Higgins*]. Higgins: did you bully her after I went to bed?

HIGGINS. Just the other way about. She threw my slippers in my face. She behaved in the most outrageous way. I never gave her the slightest provocation. The slippers came bang into my face the moment I entered the room—before I had uttered a word. And used perfectly awful language.

PICKERING [*astonished*] But why? What did we do to her?

MRS HIGGINS. I think I know pretty well what you did. The girl is naturally rather affectionate, I think. Isnt she, Mr Doolittle?

DOOLITTLE. Very tender-hearted, maam. Takes after me.

MRS HIGGINS. Just so. She had become attached to you both. She worked very hard for you, Henry! I dont think you quite realize what anything in the nature of brain work means to a girl like that. Well, it seems that when the great day of trial came and she did this wonderful thing for you without making a single mistake, you two sat there and never said a word to her, but talked together of how glad you were that it was all over and how you had been bored with the whole thing. And then you were surprised because she threw your slippers at you! *I* should have thrown the fire-irons at you.

HIGGINS. We said nothing except that we were tired and wanted to go to bed. Did we, Pick?

PICKERING [*shrugging his shoulders*] That was all.

MRS HIGGINS [*ironically*] Quite sure?

PICKERING. Absolutely. Really, that was all.

MRS HIGGINS. You didnt thank her, or pet her, or admire her, or tell her how splendid she'd been.

HIGGINS [*impatiently*] But she knew all about that. We didnt make speeches to her, if thats what you mean.

PICKERING [*conscience stricken*] Perhaps we were a little inconsiderate. Is she very angry?

MRS HIGGINS [*returning to her place at the writing-table*] Well, I'm afraid she wont go back to Wimpole Street, especially now that Mr Doolittle is able to keep up the position you have thrust on her; but she says she is quite willing to meet you on friendly terms and to let bygones be bygones.

HIGGINS [*furious*] Is she, by George? Ho!

MRS HIGGINS. If you promise to behave yourself, Henry, I'll ask her to come down. If not, go home; for you have taken up quite enough of my time.

HIGGINS. Oh, all right. Very well. Pick: you behave yourself. Let us put on our best Sunday manners for this creature that we picked out of the mud. [*He flings himself sulkily into the Elizabethan chair*].

DOOLITTLE [*remonstrating*] Now, now, Henry Higgins! have some consideration for my feelings as a middle class man.

MRS HIGGINS. Remember your promise, Henry. [*She presses the bell-button on the writing-table*]. Mr Doolittle: will you be so good as to step out on the balcony for a moment. I dont want Eliza to have the shock of your news until she has made it up with these two gentlemen. Would you mind?

DOOLITTLE. As you wish, lady. Anything to help Henry to keep her off my hands. [*He disappears through the window*].

The parlor-maid answers the bell. Pickering sits down in Doolittle's place.

MRS HIGGINS. Ask Miss Doolittle to come down, please.

THE PARLOR-MAID. Yes, maam. [*She goes out*].

MRS HIGGINS. Now, Henry: be good.

HIGGINS. I am behaving myself perfectly.

PICKERING. He is doing his best, Mrs Higgins.

A pause. Higgins throws back his head; stretches out his legs; and begins to whistle.

MRS HIGGINS. Henry, dearest, you dont look at all nice in that attitude.

HIGGINS [*pulling himself together*] I was not trying to look nice, mother.

MRS HIGGINS. It doesnt matter, dear. I only wanted to make you speak.

HIGGINS. Why?

MRS HIGGINS. Because you cant speak and whistle at the same time.

Higgins groans. Another very trying pause.

HIGGINS [*springing up, out of patience*] Where the devil is that girl? Are we to wait here all day?

Eliza enters, sunny, self-possessed, and giving a staggeringly convincing exhibition of ease of manner. She carries a little workbasket, and is very much at home. Pickering is too much taken aback to rise.

LIZA. How do you do, Professor Higgins? Are you quite well?

HIGGINS [*choking*] Am I— [*He can no more*].

LIZA. But of course you are: you are never ill. So glad to see you again, Colonel Pickering. [*He rises hastily; and they shake hands*]. Quite chilly this morning, isnt it? [*She sits down on his left. He sits beside her*].

HIGGINS. Dont you dare try this game on me. I taught it to you; and it doesnt take me in. Get up and come home; and dont be a fool.

Eliza takes a piece of needlework from her basket, and begins to stitch at it, without taking the least notice of this outburst.

MRS HIGGINS. Very nicely put, indeed, Henry. No woman could resist such an invitation.

HIGGINS. You let her alone, mother. Let her speak for herself. You will jolly soon see whether she has an idea that I havnt put into her head or a word that I havnt put into her mouth. I tell you I have created this thing out of the squashed cabbage leaves of Covent Garden; and now she pretends to play the fine lady with me.

MRS HIGGINS [*placidly*] Yes, dear; but youll sit down, wont you?

Higgins sits down again, savagely.

LIZA [*to Pickering, taking no apparent notice of Higgins, and working away deftly*] Will y o u drop me altogether now that the experiment is over, Colonel Pickering?

PICKERING. Oh dont. You mustnt think of it as an experiment. It shocks me, somehow.

LIZA. Oh, I'm only a squashed cabbage leaf—

PICKERING [*impulsively*] No.

LIZA [*continuing quietly*] —but I owe so much to you that I should be very unhappy if you forgot me.

PICKERING. It's very kind of you to say so, Miss Doolittle.

LIZA. It's not because you paid for my dresses. I know you are generous to everybody with money. But it was from you that I learnt really nice manners; and that is what makes one a lady, isnt it? You see it was so very difficult for me with the example of Professor Higgins always before me. I was brought up to be just like him, unable to control myself, and using bad language on the slightest provocation. And I should never have known that ladies and gentlemen didnt behave like that if you hadnt been there.

HIGGINS. Well!!

PICKERING. Oh, thats only his way, you know. He doesnt mean it.

LIZA. Oh, *I* didnt mean it either, when I was a flower girl. It was only my way. But you see I did it; and thats what makes the difference after all.

PICKERING. No doubt. Still, he taught you to speak; and I couldnt have done that, you know.

LIZA [*trivially*] Of course: that is his profession.

HIGGINS. Damnation!

LIZA [*continuing*] It was just like learning to dance in the fashionable way: there was nothing more than that in it. But do you know what began my real education?

PICKERING. What?

LIZA [*stopping her work for a moment*] Your calling me Miss Doolittle that day when I first came to Wimpole Street. That was the beginning of self-respect for me. [*She resumes her stitching*]. And there were a hundred little things you never noticed, because they came naturally to you. Things about standing up and taking off your hat and opening doors—

PICKERING. Oh, that was nothing.

LIZA. Yes: things that shewed you thought and felt about me as if I were something better than a scullery-maid; though of course I know you would have been just the same to a scullery-maid if she had been let into the drawing room. Y o u never took off your boots in the dining room when I was there.

PICKERING. You mustnt mind that. Higgins takes off his boots all over the place.

LIZA. I know. I am not blaming him. It is his way, isnt it? But it made s u c h a difference to me that you didnt do it. You see, really and truly, apart from the things anyone can pick up (the dressing and the proper way of speaking, and so on), the difference between a lady and a flower girl is not how she behaves, but how she's treated. I shall always be a flower girl to Professor Higgins, because he always treats me as a flower girl, and always will; but I know I can be a lady to you, because you always treat me as a lady, and always will.

MRS HIGGINS. Please dont grind your teeth, Henry.

PICKERING. Well, this is really very nice of you, Miss Doolittle.

LIZA. I should like you to call me Eliza, now, if you would.

PICKERING. Thank you. Eliza, of course.

LIZA. And I should like Professor Higgins to call me Miss Doolittle.

HIGGINS. I'll see you damned first.

MRS HIGGINS. Henry! Henry!

PICKERING [*laughing*] Why dont you slang back at him? Dont stand it. It would do him a lot of good.

LIZA. I cant. I could have done it once; but now I cant go back to it. Last night, when I was wandering about, a girl spoke to me; and I tried to get back into the old way with her; but it was no use. You told me, you know, that when a child is brought to a foreign country, it picks up the language in a few weeks, and forgets its own. Well, I am a child in your country. I have forgotten my own language, and can speak nothing but yours. Thats the real break-off with the corner of Tottenham Court Road. Leaving Wimpole Street finishes it.

PICKERING [*much alarmed*] Oh! but youre coming back to Wimpole Street, arnt you? Youll forgive Higgins?

HIGGINS [*rising*] Forgive! Will she, by George! Let her go. Let her find out how she can get on without us. She will relapse into the gutter in three weeks without me at her elbow.

Doolittle appears at the centre window. With a look of dignified reproach at Higgins, he comes slowly and silently to his daughter, who, with her back to the window, is unconscious of his approach.

PICKERING. He's incorrigible, Eliza. You wont relapse, will you?

LIZA. No: not now. Never again. I have learnt my lesson. I dont believe I could utter one of the old sounds if I tried. [*Doolittle touches her on her left shoulder. She drops her work, losing her self-possession utterly at the spectacle of her father's splendor*] A-a-a-a-a-ah-ow-ooh!

HIGGINS [*with a crow of triumph*] Aha! Just

so. A-a-a-a-ahowooh! A-a-a-a-ahowooh! A-a-a-a-ahowooh! Victory! Victory! [*He throws himself on the divan, folding his arms, and spraddling arrogantly*].

DOOLITTLE. Can you blame the girl? Dont look at me like that, Eliza. It aint my fault. Ive come into some money.

LIZA. You must have touched a millionaire this time, dad.

DOOLITTLE. I have. But I'm dressed something special today. I'm going to St George's, Hanover Square. Your stepmother is going to marry me.

LIZA [*angrily*] Youre going to let yourself down to marry that low common woman!

PICKERING [*quietly*] He ought to, Eliza. [*To Doolittle*] Why has she changed her mind?

DOOLITTLE [*sadly*] Intimidated, Governor. Intimidated. Middle class morality claims its victim. Wont you put on your hat, Liza, and come and see me turned off?

LIZA. If the Colonel says I must, I—I'll [*almost sobbing*]—I'll demean myself. And get insulted for my pains, like enough.

DOOLITTLE. Dont be afraid: she never comes to words with anyone now, poor woman! respectability has broke all the spirit out of her.

PICKERING [*squeezing Eliza's elbow gently*] Be kind to them, Eliza. Make the best of it.

LIZA [*forcing a little smile for him through her vexation*] Oh well, just to shew theres no ill feeling. I'll be back in a moment. [*She goes out*].

DOOLITTLE [*sitting down beside Pickering*] I feel uncommon nervous about the ceremony, Colonel. I wish youd come and see me through it.

PICKERING. But youve been through it before, man. You were married to Eliza's mother.

DOOLITTLE. Who told you that, Colonel?

PICKERING. Well, nobody told me. But I concluded—naturally—

DOOLITTLE. No: that aint the natural way, Colonel: it's only the middle class way. My way was always the undeserving way. But dont say nothing to Eliza. She dont know: I always had a delicacy about telling her.

PICKERING. Quite right. We'll leave it so, if you dont mind.

DOOLITTLE. And youll come to the church, Colonel, and put me through straight?

PICKERING. With pleasure. As far as a bachelor can.

MRS HIGGINS. May I come, Mr Doolittle? I should be very sorry to miss your wedding.

DOOLITTLE. I should indeed be honored by

your condescension, maam; and my poor old woman would take it as a tremenjous compliment. She's been very low, thinking of the happy days that are no more.

MRS HIGGINS [*rising*] I'll order the carriage and get ready. [*The men rise, except Higgins*]. I shant be more than fifteen minutes. [*As she goes to the door Eliza comes in, hatted and buttoning her gloves*]. I'm going to the church to see your father married, Eliza. You had better come in the brougham with me. Colonel Pickering can go on with the bridegroom.

Mrs Higgins goes out. Eliza comes to the middle of the room between the centre window and the ottoman. Pickering joins her.

DOOLITTLE. Bridegroom! What a word! It makes a man realize his position, somehow. [*He takes up his hat and goes towards the door*].

PICKERING. Before I go, Eliza, do forgive him and come back to us.

LIZA. I dont think papa would allow me. Would you, dad?

DOOLITTLE [*sad but magnanimous*] They played you off very cunning, Eliza, them two sportsmen. If it had been only one of them, you could have nailed him. But you see, there was two; and one of them chaperoned the other, as you might say. [*To Pickering*] It was artful of you, Colonel; but I bear no malice: I should have done the same myself. I been the victim of one woman after another all my life; and I dont grudge you two getting the better of Eliza. I shant interfere. It's time for us to go, Colonel. So long, Henry. See you in St George's, Eliza. [*He goes out*].

PICKERING [*coaxing*] Do stay with us, Eliza. [*He follows Doolittle*].

Eliza goes out on the balcony to avoid being alone with Higgins. He rises and joins her there. She immediately comes back into the room and makes for the door; but he goes along the balcony quickly and gets his back to the door before she reaches it.

HIGGINS. Well, Eliza, youve had a bit of your own back, as you call it. Have you had enough? and are you going to be reasonable? Or do you want any more?

LIZA. You want me back only to pick up your slippers and put up with your tempers and fetch and carry for you.

HIGGINS. I havnt said I wanted you back at all.

LIZA. Oh, indeed. Then what are we talking about?

HIGGINS. About you, not about me. If you come back I shall treat you just as I have always treated you. I cant change my nature; and I dont intend to change my manners. My manners are exactly the same as Colonel Pickering's.

LIZA. Thats not true. He treats a flower girl as if she was a duchess.

HIGGINS. And I treat a duchess as if she was a flower girl.

LIZA. I see. [*She turns away composedly, and sits on the ottoman, facing the window*]. The same to everybody.

HIGGINS. Just so.

LIZA. Like father.

HIGGINS [*grinning, a little taken down*] Without accepting the comparison at all points, Eliza, it's quite true that your father is not a snob, and that he will be quite at home in any station of life to which his eccentric destiny may call him. [*Seriously*] The great secret, Eliza, is not having bad manners or good manners or any other particular sort of manners, but having the same manner for all human souls: in short, behaving as if you were in Heaven, where there are no third-class carriages, and one soul is as good as another.

LIZA. Amen. You are a born preacher.

HIGGINS [*irritated*] The question is not whether I treat you rudely, but whether you ever heard me treat anyone else better.

LIZA [*with sudden sincerity*] I dont care how you treat me. I dont mind your swearing at me. I dont mind a black eye: Ive had one before this. But [*standing up and facing him*] I wont be passed over.

HIGGINS. Then get out of my way; for I wont stop for you. You talk about me as if I were a motor bus.

LIZA. So you are a motor bus: all bounce and go, and no consideration for anyone. But I can do without you: dont think I cant.

HIGGINS. I know you can. I told you you could.

LIZA [*wounded, getting away from him to the other side of the ottoman with her face to the hearth*] I know you did, you brute, You wanted to get rid of me.

HIGGINS. Liar.

LIZA. Thank you. [*She sits down with dignity*].

HIGGINS. You never asked yourself, I suppose, whether *I* could do without y o u.

LIZA [*earnestly*] Dont you try to get round me. Youll h a v e to do without me.

HIGGINS [*arrogant*] I can do without anybody. I have my own soul: my own spark of divine fire. But [*with sudden humility*] I shall miss you, Eliza. [*He sits down near her on the ottoman*]. I have learnt something from your idiotic notions: I confess that humbly and gratefully. And I have grown accustomed to your voice and appearance. I like them, rather.

LIZA. Well, you have both of them on your gramophone and in your book of photographs. When you feel lonely without me, you can turn the machine on. It's got no feelings to hurt.

HIGGINS. I cant turn your soul on. Leave me those feelings; and you can take away the voice and the face. They are not you.

LIZA. Oh, you a r e a devil. You can twist the heart in a girl as easy as some could twist her arms to hurt her. Mrs Pearce warned me. Time and again she has wanted to leave you; and you always got round her at the last minute. And you dont care a bit for her. And you dont care a bit for me.

HIGGINS. I care for life, for humanity; and you are a part of it that has come my way and been built into my house. What more can you or anyone ask?

LIZA. I wont care for anybody that doesnt care for me.

HIGGINS. Commercial principles, Eliza. Like [*reproducing her Covent Garden pronunciation with professional exactness*] s'yollin voylets [selling violets], isnt it?

LIZA. Dont sneer at me, It's mean to sneer at me.

HIGGINS. I have never sneered in my life. Sneering doesnt become either the human face or the human soul. I am expressing my righteous contempt for Commercialism. I dont and wont trade in affection. You call me a brute because you couldnt buy a claim on me by fetching my slippers and finding my spectacles. You were a fool: I think a woman fetching a man's slippers is a disgusting sight: did I ever fetch y o u r slippers? I think a good deal more of you for throwing them in my face. No use slaving for me and then saying you want to be cared for: who cares for a slave? If you come back, come back for the sake of good fellowship; for youll get nothing else. Youve had a thousand times as much out of me as I have out of you; and if you dare to set up your little dog's tricks of fetching and carrying slippers

against my creation of a Duchess Eliza, I'll slam the door in your silly face.

LIZA. What did you do it for if you didnt care for me?

HIGGINS [*heartily*] Why, because it was my job.

LIZA. You never thought of the trouble it would make for me.

HIGGINS. Would the world ever have been made if its maker had been afraid of making trouble? Making life means making trouble. Theres only one way of escaping trouble; and thats killing things. Cowards, you notice, are always shrieking to have troublesome people killed.

LIZA. I'm no preacher: I dont notice things like that. I notice that you dont notice me.

HIGGINS [*jumping up and walking about intolerantly*] Eliza: youre an idiot. I waste the treasures of my Miltonic mind by spreading them before you. Once for all, understand that I go my way and do my work without caring twopence what happens to either of us. I am not intimidated, like your father and your stepmother. So you can come back or go to the devil: which you please.

LIZA. What am I to come back for?

HIGGINS [*bouncing up on his knees on the ottoman and leaning over it to her*] For the fun of it. Thats why I took you on.

LIZA [*with averted face*] And you may throw me out tomorrow if I dont do everything you want me to?

HIGGINS. Yes; and you may walk out tomorrow if I dont do everything y o u want me to.

LIZA. And live with my stepmother?

HIGGINS. Yes, or sell flowers.

LIZA. Oh! if I only c o u l d go back to my flower basket! I should be independent of both you and father and all the world! Why did you take my independence from me? Why did I give it up? I'm a slave now, for all my fine clothes.

HIGGINS. Not a bit. I'll adopt you as my daughter and settle money on you if you like. Or would you rather marry Pickering?

LIZA [*looking fiercely round at him*] I wouldnt marry y o u if you asked me; and youre nearer my age than what he is.

HIGGINS [*gently*] Than he is: not "than what he is."

LIZA [*losing her temper and rising*] I'll talk as I like. Youre not my teacher now.

HIGGINS [*reflectively*] I dont suppose Pickering would, though. He's as confirmed an old bachelor as I am.

LIZA. Thats not what I want; and dont you think it. Ive always had chaps enough wanting me that way. Freddy Hill writes to me twice and three times a day, sheets and sheets.

HIGGINS [disagreeably surprised] Damn his impudence! [He recoils and finds himself sitting on his heels].

LIZA. He has a right to if he likes, poor lad. And he does love me.

HIGGINS [getting off the ottoman] You have no right to encourage him.

LIZA. Every girl has a right to be loved.

HIGGINS. What! By fools like that?

LIZA. Freddy's not a fool. And if he's weak and poor and wants me, may be he'd make me happier than my betters that bully me and dont want me.

HIGGINS. Can he m a k e anything of you? Thats the point.

LIZA. Perhaps I could make something of him. But I never thought of us making anything of one another; and you never think of anything else. I only want to be natural.

HIGGINS. In short, you want me to be as infatuated about you as Freddy? Is that it?

LIZA. No I dont. Thats not the sort of feeling I want from you. And dont you be too sure of yourself or of me. I could have been a bad girl if I'd liked. Ive seen more of some things than you, for all your learning. Girls like me can drag gentlemen down to make love to them easy enough. And they wish each other dead the next minute.

HIGGINS. Of course they do. Then what in thunder are we quarrelling about?

LIZA [much troubled] I want a little kindness. I know I'm a common ignorant girl, and you a book-learned gentleman; but I'm not dirt under your feet. What I done [correcting herself] what I did was not for the dresses and the taxis: I did it because we were pleasant together and I come—came—to care for you; not to want you to make love to me, and not forgetting the difference between us, but more friendly like.

HIGGINS. Well, of course. Thats just how I feel. And how Pickering feels. Eliza: youre a fool.

LIZA. Thats not a proper answer to give me. [She sinks on the chair at the writing-table in tears].

HIGGINS. It's all youll get until you stop being a common idiot. If youre going to be a lady, youll have to give up feeling neglected if the men you know dont spend half their time snivelling over you and the other half giving you black eyes. If you cant stand the coldness of my sort of life, and the strain of it, go back to the gutter. Work til you are more a brute than a human being ; and then cuddle and squabble and drink til you fall asleep. Oh, it's a fine life, the life of the gutter. It's real: it's warm: it's violent: you can feel it through the thickest skin: you can taste it and smell it without any training or any work. Not like Science and Literature and Classical Music and Philosophy and Art. You find me cold, unfeeling, selfish, dont you? Very well: be off with you to the sort of people you like. Marry some sentimental hog or other with lots of money, and a thick pair of lips to kiss you with and a thick pair of boots to kick you with. If you cant appreciate what youve got, youd better get what you can appreciate.

LIZA [desperate] Oh, you a r e a cruel tyrant. I cant talk to you: you turn everything against me: I'm always in the wrong. But you know very well all the time that youre nothing but a bully. You know I cant go back to the gutter, as you call it, and that I have no real friends in the world but you and the Colonel. You know well I couldnt bear to live with a low common man after you two; and it's wicked and cruel of you to insult me by pretending I could. You think I must go back to Wimpole Street because I have nowhere else to go but father's. But dont you be too sure that you have me under your feet to be trampled on and talked down. I'll marry Freddy, I will, as soon as he's able to support me.

HIGGINS [sitting down beside her] Rubbish! you shall marry an ambassador. You shall marry the Governor-General of India or the Lord-Lieutenant of Ireland, or somebody who wants a deputy-queen. I'm not going to have my masterpiece thrown away on Freddy.

LIZA. You think I like you to say that. But I havnt forgot what you said a minute ago; and I wont be coaxed round as if I was a baby or a puppy. If I cant have kindness, I'll have independence.

HIGGINS. Independence? Thats middle class blasphemy. We are all dependent on one another, every soul of us on earth.

LIZA [*rising determinedly*] I'll let you see whether I'm dependent on you. If you can preach, I can teach. I'll go and be a teacher.

HIGGINS. Whatll you teach, in heaven's name?

LIZA. What you taught me. I'll teach phonetics.

HIGGINS. Ha! ha! ha!

LIZA. I'll offer myself as an assistant to Professor Nepean.

HIGGINS [*rising in a fury*] What! That impostor! that humbug! that toadying ignoramus! Teach him m y methods! m y discoveries! You take one step in his direction and I'll wring your neck. [*He lays hands on her*]. Do you hear?

LIZA [*defiantly non-resistant*] Wring away. What do I care? I knew youd strike me some day.[*He lets her go, stamping with rage at having forgotten himself, and recoils so hastily that he stumbles back into his seat on the ottoman*]. Aha! Now I know how to deal with you. What a fool I was not to think of it before! You cant take away the knowledge you gave me. You said I had a finer ear than you. And I can be civil and kind to people, which is more than you can. Aha! Thats done you, Henry Higgins, it has. Now I dont care that [*snapping her fingers*] for your bullying and your big talk. I'll advertize it in the papers that your duchess is only a flower girl that you taught, and that she'll teach anybody to be a duchess just the same in six months for a thousand guineas. Oh, when I think of myself crawling under your feet and being trampled on and called names, when all the time I had only to lift up my finger to be as good as you, I could just kick myself.

HIGGINS [*wondering at her*] You damned impudent slut, you! But it's better than snivelling; better than fetching slippers and finding spectacles, isnt it? [*Rising*] By George, Eliza, I said I'd make a woman of you; and I have. I like you like this.

LIZA. Yes: you turn round and make up to me now that I'm not afraid of you, and can do without you.

HIGGINS. Of course I do, you little fool. Five minutes ago you were like a millstone round my neck. Now youre a tower of strength: a consort battleship. You and I and Pickering will be three old bachelors together instead of only two men and a silly girl.

Mrs Higgins returns, dressed for the wedding.

Eliza instantly becomes cool and elegant.

MRS HIGGINS. The carriage is waiting, Eliza. Are you ready?

LIZA. Quite. Is the Professor coming?

MRS HIGGINS. Certainly not. He cant behave himself in church. He makes remarks out loud all the time on the clergyman's pronunciation.

LIZA. Then I shall not see you again, Professor. Goodbye. [*She goes to the door*].

MRS HIGGINS [*coming to Higgins*] Goodbye, dear.

HIGGINS. Goodbye, mother. [*He is about to kiss her, when he recollects something*]. Oh, by the way, Eliza, order a ham and a Stilton cheese, will you? And buy me a pair of reindeer gloves, number eights, and a tie to match that new suit of mine, at Eale & Binman's. You can choose the color. [*His cheerful, careless, vigorous voice shews that he is incorrigible*].

LIZA [*disdainfully*] Buy them yourself. [*She sweeps out*].

MRS HIGGINS. I'm afraid youve spoiled that girl, Henry. But never mind, dear: I'll buy you the tie and gloves.

HIGGINS [*sunnily*] Oh, dont bother. She'll buy em all right enough. Goodbye.

They kiss, Mrs Higgins runs out. Higgins, left alone, rattles his cash in his pocket; chuckles; and disports himself in a highly self-satisfied manner.

* * * * *

The rest of the story need not be shewn in action, and indeed, would hardly need telling if our imaginations were not so enfeebled by their lazy dependence on the ready-mades and reach-me-downs of the ragshop in which Romance keeps its stock of " happy endings " to misfit all stories. Now, the history of Eliza Doolittle, though called a romance because the transfiguration it records seems exceedingly improbable, is common enough. Such transfigurations have been achieved by hundreds of resolutely ambitious young women since Nell Gwynne set them the example by playing queens and fascinating kings in the theatre in which she began by selling oranges. Nevertheless, people in all directions have assumed, for no other reason than that she became the heroine of a romance, that she must have married the hero of it. This is unbearable, not only because her little drama, if acted on such a thoughtless assumption, must be spoiled, but because the true sequel is patent to anyone with a sense of human nature in general, and of feminine instinct in particular.

Eliza, in telling Higgins she would not marry him if he asked her, was not coquetting: she was announcing a well-considered decision. When a bachelor interests, and dominates, and teaches, and becomes important to a spinster, as Higgins with Eliza, she always, if she has character enough to be capable of it, considers very seriously indeed whether she will play for becoming that bachelor's wife, especially if he is so little interested in marriage that a determined and devoted woman might capture him if she set herself resolutely to do it. Her decision will depend a good deal on whether she is really free to choose; and that, again, will depend on her age and income. If she is at the end of her youth, and has no security for her livelihood, she will marry him because she must marry anybody who will provide for her. But at Eliza's age a good-looking girl does not feel that pressure: she feels free to pick and choose. She is therefore guided by her instinct in the matter. Eliza's instinct tells her not to marry Higgins. It does not tell her to give him up. It is not in the slightest doubt as to his remaining one of the strongest personal interests in her life. It would be very sorely strained if there was another woman likely to supplant her with him. But as she feels sure of him on that last point, she has no doubt at all as to her course, and would not have any, even if the difference of twenty years in age, which seems so great to youth, did not exist between them.

As our own instincts are not appealed to by her conclusion, let us see whether we cannot discover some reason in it. When Higgins excused his indifference to young women on the ground that they had an irresistible rival in his mother he gave the clue to his inveterate old-bachelordom. The case is uncommon only to the extent that remarkable mothers are uncommon. If an imaginative boy has a sufficiently rich mother who has intelligence, personal grace, dignity of character without harshness, and a cultivated sense of the best art of her time to enable her to make her house beautiful, she sets a standard for him against which very few women can struggle, besides effecting for him a disengagement of his affections, his sense of beauty, and his idealism from his specifically sexual impulses. This makes him a standing puzzle to the huge number of uncultivated people who have been brought up in tasteless homes by commonplace or disagreeable parents, and to whom, consequently, literature, painting, sculpture, music, and affectionate personal relations come as modes of sex if they come at all. The word passion means nothing else to them; and that Higgins could have a passion for phonetics and idealize his mother instead of Eliza, would seem to them absurd and unnatural. Nevertheless, when we look round and see that hardly anyone is too ugly or disagreeable to find a wife or a husband if he or she wants one, whilst many old maids and bachelors are above the average in quality and culture, we cannot help suspecting that the disentanglement of sex from the associations with which it is so commonly confused, a disentanglement which persons of genius achieve by sheer intellectual analysis, is sometimes produced or aided by parental fascination.

Now, though Eliza was incapable of thus explaining to herself Higgins's formidable powers of resistance to the charm that prostrated Freddy at the first glance, she was instinctively aware that she could never obtain a complete grip of him, or come between him and his mother (the first necessity of the married woman). To put it shortly, she knew that for some mysterious reason he had not the makings of a married man in him, according to her conception of a husband as one to whom she would be his nearest and fondest and warmest interest. Even had there been no mother-rival, she would still have refused to accept an interest in herself that was secondary to philosophic interests. Had Mrs Higgins died, there would still have been Milton and the Universal Alphabet. Landor's remark that to those who have the greatest power of loving, love is a secondary affair, would not have recommended Landor to Eliza. Put that along with her resentment of Higgins's domineering superiority, and her mistrust of his coaxing cleverness in getting round her and evading her wrath when he had gone too far with his impetuous bullying, and you will see that Eliza's instinct had good grounds for warning her not to marry her Pygmalion.

And now, whom did Eliza marry? For if

Higgins was a predestinate old bachelor, she was most certainly not a predestinate old maid. Well, that can be told very shortly to those who have not guessed it from the indications she has herself given them.

Almost immediately after Eliza is stung into proclaiming her considered determination not to marry Higgins, she mentions the fact that young Mr Frederick Eynsford Hill is pouring out his love for her daily through the post. Now Freddy is young, practically twenty years younger than Higgins: he is a gentleman (or, as Eliza would qualify him, a toff), and speaks like one; he is nicely dressed, is treated by the Colonel as an equal, loves her unaffectedly, and is not her master, nor ever likely to dominate her in spite of his advantage of social standing. Eliza has no use for the foolish romantic tradition that all women love to be mastered, if not actually bullied and beaten. "When you go to women," says Nietzsche, "take your whip with you." Sensible despots have never confined that precaution to women: they have taken their whips with them when they have dealt with men, and been slavishly idealized by the men over whom they have flourished the whip much more than by women. No doubt there are slavish women as well as slavish men: and women, like men, admire those that are stronger than themselves. But to admire a strong person and to live under that strong person's thumb are two different things. The weak may not be admired and hero-worshipped; but they are by no means disliked or shunned; and they never seem to have the least difficulty in marrying people who are too good for them. They may fail in emergencies; but life is not one long emergency: it is mostly a string of situations for which no exceptional strength is needed, and with which even rather weak people can cope if they have a stronger partner to help them out. Accordingly, it is a truth everywhere in evidence that strong people, masculine or feminine, not only do not marry stronger people, but do not shew any preference for them in selecting their friends. When a lion meets another with a louder roar "the first lion thinks the last a bore." The man or woman who feels strong enough for two, seeks for every other quality in a partner than strength.

The converse is also true. Weak people want to marry strong people who do not frighten them too much; and this often leads them to make the mistake we describe metaphorically as "biting off more than they can chew." They want too much for too little; and when the bargain is unreasonable beyond all bearing, the union becomes impossible: it ends in the weaker party being either discarded or borne as a cross, which is worse. People who are not only weak, but silly or obtuse as well, are often in these difficulties.

This being the state of human affairs, what is Eliza fairly sure to do when she is placed between Freddy and Higgins? Will she look forward to a lifetime of fetching Higgins's slippers or to a lifetime of Freddy fetching hers? There can be no doubt about the answer. Unless Freddy is biologically repulsive to her, and Higgins biologically attractive to a degree that overwhelms all her other instincts, she will, if she marries either of them, marry Freddy.

And that is just what Eliza did.

Complications ensued; but they were economic, not romantic. Freddy had no money and no occupation. His mother's jointure, a last relic of the opulence of Largelady Park, had enabled her to struggle along in Earlscourt with an air of gentility, but not to procure any serious secondary education for her children, much less give the boy a profession. A clerkship at thirty shillings a week was beneath Freddy's dignity, and extremely distasteful to him besides. His prospects consisted of a hope that if he kept up appearances somebody would do something for him. The something appeared vaguely to his imagination as a private secretaryship or a sinecure of some sort. To his mother it perhaps appeared as a marriage to some lady of means who could not resist her boy's niceness. Fancy her feelings when he married a flower girl who had become déclassée under extraordinary circumstances which were now notorious!

It is true that Eliza's situation did not seem wholly ineligible. Her father, though formerly a dustman, and now fantastically disclassed, had become extremely popular in the smartest society by a social talent which triumphed over every prejudice and every disadvantage. Rejected by the middle class, which he loathed, he had shot up at once into the highest circles by his wit, his dustmanship (which he carried like a banner) and his Nietzschean transcendence of good and evil. At intimate ducal dinners he sat on the right hand of the Duchess; and in country houses he smoked in the pantry and was made much of by the butler when he was not feeding in the dining room and being consulted by cabinet ministers. But he found it almost as hard to do all this on four thousand a year as Mrs Eynsford Hill to live in Earlscourt on an income so pitiably smaller that I have not the heart to disclose its exact figure. He absolutely refused to add the last straw to his burden by contributing to Eliza's support.

Thus Freddy and Eliza, now Mr and Mrs Eynsford Hill, would have spent a penniless honeymoon but for a wedding present of £500 from the Colonel to Eliza. It lasted a long time because Freddy did not know how to spend money, never having had any to spend, and Eliza, socially trained by a pair of old bachelors, wore her clothes as long as they held together and looked pretty, without the least regard to their being many months out of fashion. Still, £500 will not last two young people for ever; and they both knew, and Eliza felt as well, that they must shift for themselves in the end. She could quarter herself on Wimpole Street because it had come to be her home; but she was quite aware that she ought not to quarter Freddy there, and that it would not be good for his character if she did.

Not that the Wimpole Street bachelors objected. When she consulted them, Higgins declined to be bothered about her housing problem when that solution was so simple. Eliza's desire to have Freddy in the house with her seemed of no more importance than if she had wanted an extra piece of bedroom furniture. Pleas as to Freddy's character, and the moral obligation on him to earn his own living, were lost on Higgins. He denied that Freddy had any character, and declared that if he tried to do any useful work some competent person would have the trouble of undoing it: a procedure involving a net loss to the community, and great unhappiness to Freddy himself, who was obviously intended by Nature for such light work as amusing Eliza, which, Higgins declared, was a much more useful and honorable occupation than working in the city. When Eliza referred again to her project of teaching phonetics, Higgins abated not a jot of his violent opposition to it. He said she was

not within ten years of being qualified to meddle with his pet subject; and as it was evident that the Colonel agreed with him, she felt she could not go against them in this grave matter, and that she had no right, without Higgins's consent, to exploit the knowledge he had given her; for his knowledge seemed to her as much his private property as his watch: Eliza was no communist. Besides, she was superstitiously devoted to them both, more entirely and frankly after her marriage than before it.

It was the Colonel who finally solved the problem, which had cost him much perplexed cogitation. He one day asked Eliza, rather shyly, whether she had quite given up her notion of keeping a flower shop. She replied that she had thought of it, but had put it out of her head, because the Colonel had said, that day at Mrs Higgins's, that it would never do. The Colonel confessed that when he said that, he had not quite recovered from the dazzling impression of the day before. They broke the matter to Higgins that evening. The sole comment vouchsafed by him very nearly led to a serious quarrel with Eliza. It was to the effect that she would have in Freddy an ideal errand boy.

Freddy himself was next sounded on the subject. He said he had been thinking of a shop himself; though it had presented itself to his pennilessness as a small place in which Eliza should sell tobacco at one counter whilst he sold newspapers at the opposite one. But he agreed that it would be extraordinarily jolly to go early every morning with Eliza to Covent Garden and buy flowers on the scene of their first meeting: a sentiment which earned him many kisses from his wife. He added that he had always been afraid to propose anything of the sort, because Clara would make an awful row about a step that must damage her matrimonial chances, and his mother could not be expected to like it after clinging for so many years to that step of the social ladder on which retail trade is impossible.

This difficulty was removed by an event highly unexpected by Freddy's mother. Clara, in the course of her incursions into those artistic circles which were the highest within her reach, discovered that her conversational qualifications were expected to include a grounding in the novels of Mr H. G. Wells. She borrowed them in various directions so energetically that she swallowed them all within two months. The result was a conversion of a kind quite common today. A modern Acts of the Apostles would fill fifty whole Bibles if anyone were capable of writing it.

Poor Clara, who appeared to Higgins and his mother as a disagreeable and ridiculous person, and to her own mother as in some inexplicable way a social failure, had never seen herself in either light; for, though to some extent ridiculed and mimicked in West Kensington like everybody else there, she was accepted as a rational and normal—or shall we say inevitable?—sort of human being. At worst they called her The Pusher; but to them no more than to herself had it ever occurred that she was pushing the air, and pushing it in a wrong direction. Still, she was not happy. She was growing desperate. Her one asset, the fact that her mother was what the Epsom greengrocer called a carriage lady, had no exchange value, apparently. It had prevented her from getting educated, because the only education she could have afforded was education with the Earlscourt greengrocer's daughter. It had led her to seek the society of her mother's class; and that class simply would not have her, because she was much poorer than the greengrocer, and, far from being able to afford a maid, could not afford even a housemaid, and had to scrape along at home with an illiberally treated general servant. Under such circumstances nothing could give her an air of being a genuine product of Largelady Park. And yet its tradition made her regard a marriage with anyone within her reach as an unbearable humiliation. Commercial people and professional people in a small way were odious to her. She ran after painters and novelists; but she did not charm them; and her bold attempts to pick up and practise artistic and literary talk irritated them. She was, in short, an utter failure, an ignorant, incompetent, pretentious, unwelcome, penniless, useless little snob; and though she did not admit these disqualifications (for nobody ever faces unpleasant truths of this kind until the possibility of a way out dawns on them) she felt their effects too keenly to be satisfied with her position.

Clara had a startling eyeopener when, on being suddenly wakened to enthusiasm by a girl of her own age who dazzled her and pro-

duced in her a gushing desire to take her for a model, and gain her friendship, she discovered that this exquisite apparition had graduated from the gutter in a few months time. It shook her so violently, that when Mr H. G. Wells lifted her on the point of his puissant pen, and placed her at the angle of view from which the life she was leading and the society to which she clung appeared in its true relation to real human needs and worthy social structure, he effected a conversion and a conviction of sin comparable to the most sensational feats of General Booth or Gypsy Smith. Clara's snobbery went bang. Life suddenly began to move with her. Without knowing how or why, she began to make friends and enemies. Some of the acquaintances to whom she had been a tedious or indifferent or ridiculous affliction, dropped her: others became cordial. To her amazement she found that some "quite nice" people were saturated with Wells, and that this accessibility to ideas was the secret of their niceness. People she had thought deeply religious, and had tried to conciliate on that tack with disastrous results, suddenly took an interest in her, and revealed a hostility to conventional religion which she had never conceived possible except amongst the most desperate characters. They made her read Galsworthy; and Galsworthy exposed the vanity of Largelady Park and finished her. It exasperated her to think that the dungeon in which she had languished for so many unhappy years had been unlocked all the time, and that the impulses she had so carefully struggled with and stifled for the sake of keeping well with society, were precisely those by which alone she could have come into any sort of sincere human contact. In the radiance of these discoveries, and the tumult of their reaction, she made a fool of herself as freely and conspicuously as when she so rashly adopted Eliza's expletive in Mrs Higgins's drawing room; for the new-born Wellsian had to find her bearings almost as ridiculously as a baby; but nobody hates a baby for its ineptitudes, or thinks the worse of it for trying to eat the matches; and Clara lost no friends by her follies. They laughed at her to her face this time; and she had to defend herself and fight it out as best she could.

When Freddy paid a visit to Earlscourt (which he never did when he could possibly help it) to make the desolating announcement that he and his Eliza were thinking of blackening the Largelady scutcheon by opening a shop, he found the little household already convulsed by a prior announcement from Clara that she also was going to work in an old furniture shop in Dover Street, which had been started by a fellow Wellsian. This appointment Clara owed, after all, to her old social accomplishment of Push. She had made up her mind that, cost what it might, she would see Mr Wells in the flesh; and she had achieved her end at a garden party. She had better luck than so rash an enterprise deserved. Mr Wells came up to her expectations. Age had not withered him, nor could custom stale his infinite variety in half an hour. His pleasant neatness and compactness, his small hands and feet, his teeming ready brain, his unaffected accessibility, and a certain fine apprehensiveness which stamped him as susceptible from his topmost hair to his tipmost toe, proved irresistible. Clara talked of nothing else for weeks and weeks afterwards. And as she happened to talk to the lady of the furniture shop, and that lady also desired above all things to know Mr Wells and sell pretty things to him, she offered Clara a job on the chance of achieving that end through her.

And so it came about that Eliza's luck held, and the expected opposition to the flower shop melted away. The shop is in the arcade of a railway station not very far from the Victoria and Albert Museum; and if you live in that neighborhood you may go there any day and buy a buttonhole from Eliza.

Now here is a last opportunity for romance. Would you not like to be assured that the shop was an immense success, thanks to Eliza's charms and her early business experience in Covent Garden? Alas! the truth is the truth: the shop did not pay for a long time, simply because Eliza and her Freddy did not know how to keep it. True, Eliza had not to begin at the very beginning: she knew the names and prices of the cheaper flowers; and her elation was unbounded when she found that Freddy, like all youths educated at cheap, pretentious, and thoroughly inefficient schools, knew a little Latin. It was very little, but enough to make him appear to her a Porson or Bentley, and to put him at his ease with botanical nomenclature. Unfortunately he knew nothing else; and Eliza, though she could count money up to eighteen shillings or so, and had acquired a certain familiarity with the language of Milton from her struggles to qualify herself for winning Higgins's bet, could not write out a bill without utterly disgracing the establishment. Freddy's power of stating in Latin that Balbus built a wall and that Gaul was divided into three parts did not carry with it the slightest knowledge of accounts or business: Colonel Pickering had to explain to him what a cheque book and a bank account meant. And the pair were by no means easily teachable. Freddy backed up Eliza in her obstinate refusal to believe that they could save money by engaging a bookkeeper with some knowledge of the business. How, they argued, could you possibly save money by going to extra expense when you already could not make both ends meet? But the Colonel, after making the ends meet over and over again, at last gently insisted; and Eliza, humbled to the dust by having to beg from him so often, and stung by the uproarious derision of Higgins, to whom the notion of Freddy succeeding at anything was a joke that never palled, grasped the fact that business, like phonetics, has to be learned.

On the piteous spectacle of the pair spending their evenings in shorthand schools and polytechnic classes, learning bookkeeping and typewriting with incipient junior clerks, male and female, from the elementary schools, let me not dwell. There were even classes at the London School of Economics, and a humble personal appeal to the director of that institution to recommend a course bearing on the flower business. He, being a humorist, explained to them the method of the celebrated Dickensian essay on Chinese Metaphysics by the gentleman who read an article on China and an article on Metaphysics and combined the information. He suggested that they should combine the London School with Kew Gardens. Eliza, to whom the procedure of the Dickensian gentleman seemed perfectly correct (as in fact it was) and not in the least funny (which was only her ignorance), took his advice with entire gravity. But the effort that cost her the deepest humiliation was a request to Higgins, whose pet artistic fancy, next to Milton's verse, was caligraphy, and who himself wrote a most beautiful Italian hand, that he would teach her to write. He declared that she was congenitally incapable of forming a single letter worthy of the least of Milton's words; but she persisted; and again he suddenly threw himself into the task of teaching her with a combination of stormy intensity, concentrated patience, and occasional bursts of interesting disquisition on the beauty and nobility, the august mission and destiny, of human handwriting. Eliza ended by acquiring an extremely uncommercial script which was a positive extension of her personal beauty, and spending three times as much on stationery as anyone else because certain qualities and shapes of paper became indispensable to her. She could not even address an envelope in the usual way because it made the margins all wrong.

Their commercial schooldays were a period of disgrace and despair for the young couple. They seemed to be learning nothing about flower shops. At last they gave it up as hopeless, and shook the dust of the shorthand schools, and the polytechnics, and the London School of Economics from their feet for ever. Besides, the business was in some mysterious way beginning to take care of itself. They had somehow forgotten their objections to employing other people. They came to the conclusion that their own way was the best, and that they had really a remarkable talent for business. The Colonel, who had been compelled for some years to keep a sufficient sum on current account at his bankers to make up their deficits, found that the provision was unnecessary: the young people were prospering. It is true that there was not quite fair play between them and their competitors in trade. Their weekends in the country cost them nothing, and saved them the price of their Sunday dinners; for the motor car was the Colonel's; and he and Higgins paid the hotel bills. Mr F. Hill, florist and greengrocer (they soon discovered that there was money in asparagus; and asparagus led to other vegetables), had an air which stamped the business as classy; and in private life he was still Frederick Eynsford Hill, Esquire. Not that there was any swank about him: nobody but Eliza knew that he had been christened Frederick Challoner. Eliza herself swanked like anything.

That is all. That is how it has turned out.

It is astonishing how much Eliza still manages to meddle in the housekeeping at Wimpole Street in spite of the shop and her own family. And it is notable that though she never nags her husband, and frankly loves the Colonel as if she were his favorite daughter, she has never got out of the habit of nagging Higgins that was established on the fatal night when she won his bet for him. She snaps his head off on the faintest provocation, or on none. He no longer dares to tease her by assuming an abysmal inferiority of Freddy's mind to his own. He storms and bullies and derides; but she stands up to him so ruthlessly that the Colonel has to ask her from time to time to be kinder to Higgins; and it is the only request of his that brings a mulish expression into her face. Nothing but some emergency or calamity great enough to break down all likes and dislikes, and throw them both back on their common humanity—and may they be spared any such trial!—will ever alter this. She knows that Higgins does not need her, just as her father did not need her. The very scrupulousness with which he told her that day that he had become used to having her there, and dependent on her for all sorts of little services, and that he should miss her if she went away (it would never have occurred to Freddy or the Colonel to say anything of the sort) deepens her inner certainty that she is "no more to him than them slippers"; yet she has a sense, too, that his indifference is deeper than the infatuation of commoner souls. She is immensely interested in him. She has even secret mischievous moments in which she wishes she could get him alone, on a desert island, away from all ties and with nobody else in the world to consider, and just drag him off his pedestal and see him making love like any common man. We all have private imaginations of that sort. But when it comes to business, to the life that she really leads as distinguished from the life of dreams and fancies, she likes Freddy and she likes the Colonel; and she does not like Higgins and Mr Doolittle. Galatea never does quite like Pygmalion: his relation to her is too godlike to be altogether agreeable.

THE END

XXIV

HEARTBREAK HOUSE

A FANTASIA IN THE RUSSIAN MANNER ON ENGLISH THEMES

ACT I

The hilly country in the middle of the north edge of Sussex, looking very pleasant on a fine evening at the end of September, is seen through the windows of a room which has been built so as to resemble the after part of an old-fashioned high-pooped ship with a stern gallery; for the windows are ship built with heavy timbering, and run right across the room as continuously as the stability of the wall allows. A row of lockers under the windows provides an unupholstered window-seat interrupted by twin glass doors, respectively halfway between the stern post and the sides. Another door strains the illusion a little by being apparently in the ship's port side, and yet leading, not to the open sea, but to the entrance hall of the house. Between this door and the stern gallery are bookshelves. There are electric light switches beside the door leading to the hall and the glass doors in the stern gallery. Against the starboard wall is a carpenter's bench. The vice has a board in its jaws; and the floor is littered with shavings, overflowing from a waste-paper basket. A couple of planes and a centrebit are on the bench. In the same wall, between the bench and the windows, is a narrow doorway with a half door, above which a glimpse of the room beyond shews that it is a shelved pantry with bottles and kitchen crockery.

On the starboard side, but close to the middle, is a plain oak drawing-table with drawing-board, T-square, straightedges, set squares, mathematical instruments, saucers of water color, a tumbler of discolored water, Indian ink, pencils, and brushes on it. The drawing-board is set so that the draughtsman's chair has the window on its left hand. On the floor at the end of the table, on his right, is a ship's fire bucket. On the port side of the room, near the bookshelves, is a sofa with its back to the windows. It is a sturdy mahogany article, oddly upholstered in sailcloth, including the bolster, with a couple of blankets hanging over the back. Between the sofa and the drawing-table is a big wicker chair, with broad arms and a low sloping back, with its back to the light. A small but stout table of teak, with a round top and gate legs, stands against the port wall between the door and the bookcase. It is the only article in the room that suggests (not at all convincingly) a woman's hand in the furnishing. The uncarpeted floor of narrow boards is caulked and holystoned like a deck.

The garden to which the glass doors lead dips to the south before the landscape rises again to the hills. Emerging from the hollow is the cupola of an observatory. Between the observatory and the house is a flagstaff on a little esplanade, with a hammock on the east side and a long garden seat on the west.

A young lady, gloved and hatted, with a dust coat on, is sitting in the window-seat with her body twisted to enable her to look out at the view. One hand props her chin: the other hangs down with a volume of the Temple Shakespear in it, and her finger stuck in the page she has been reading.

A clock strikes six.

The young lady turns and looks at her watch. She rises with an air of one who waits and is almost at the end of her patience. She is a pretty girl, slender, fair, and intelligent looking, nicely but not expensively dressed, evidently not a smart idler.

With a sigh of weary resignation she comes to the draughtsman's chair; sits down; and begins to read Shakespear. Presently the book sinks to her lap; her eyes close; and she dozes into a slumber.

An elderly womanservant comes in from the hall with three unopened bottles of rum on a tray. She passes through and disappears in the pantry without noticing the young lady. She places the bottles on the shelf and fills her tray with empty bottles. As she returns with these, the young lady lets her book drop, awakening herself, and startling the womanservant so that she all but lets the tray fall.

THE WOMANSERVANT. God bless us! [The young lady picks up the book and places it on the table]. Sorry to wake you, miss, I'm sure; but you are a stranger to me. What might you be waiting here for now?

THE YOUNG LADY. Waiting for somebody to shew some signs of knowing that I have been invited here.

THE WOMANSERVANT. Oh, youre invited, are you? And has nobody come? Dear! dear!

THE YOUNG LADY. A wild-looking old gentleman came and looked in at the window; and I heard him calling out "Nurse: there is a young and attractive female waiting in the poop. Go and see what she wants." Are you the nurse?

THE WOMANSERVANT. Yes, miss: I'm Nurse Guinness. That was old Captain Shotover, Mrs Hushabye's father. I heard him roaring; but I thought it was for something else. I suppose it was Mrs Hushabye that invited you, ducky?

THE YOUNG LADY. I understood her to do so. But really I think I'd better go.

NURSE GUINNESS. Oh, dont think of such a thing, miss. If Mrs Hushabye has forgotten all about it, it will be a pleasant surprise for her to see you, wont it?

THE YOUNG LADY. It has been a very unpleasant surprise to me to find that nobody expects me.

NURSE GUINNESS. Youll get used to it, miss: this house is full of surprises for them that dont know our ways.

CAPTAIN SHOTOVER [looking in from the hall suddenly; an ancient but still hardy man with an immense white beard, in a reefer jacket with a whistle hanging from his neck] Nurse: there is a hold-all and a handbag on the front steps for everybody to fall over. Also a tennis racquet. Who the devil left them there?

THE YOUNG LADY. They are mine, I'm afraid.

THE CAPTAIN [advancing to the drawing-table] Nurse: who is this misguided and unfortunate young lady?

NURSE GUINNESS. She says Miss Hessy invited her, sir.

THE CAPTAIN. And had she no friend, no parents, to warn her against my daughter's invitations? This is a pretty sort of house, by heavens! A young and attractive lady is invited here. Her luggage is left on the steps for hours; and she herself is deposited in the poop and abandoned, tired and starving. This is our hospitality. These are our manners. No room ready. No hot water. No welcoming hostess. Our visitor is to sleep in the toolshed, and to wash in the duckpond.

NURSE GUINNESS. Now it's all right, Captain: I'll get the lady some tea; and her room shall be ready before she has finished it. [To the young lady] Take off your hat, ducky; and make yourself at home [she goes to the door leading to the hall].

THE CAPTAIN [as she passes him] Ducky! Do you suppose, woman, that because this young lady has been insulted and neglected, you have the right to address her as you address my wretched children, whom you have brought up in ignorance of the commonest decencies of social intercourse?

NURSE GUINNESS. Never mind him, doty. [Quite unconcerned, she goes out into the hall on her way to the kitchen].

THE CAPTAIN. Madam: will you favor me with your name? [He sits down in the big wicker chair].

THE YOUNG LADY. My name is Ellie Dunn.

THE CAPTAIN. Dunn! I had a boatswain whose name was Dunn. He was originally a pirate in China. He set up as a ship's chandler with stores which I have every reason to believe he stole from me. No doubt he became rich. Are you his daughter?

ELLIE [indignant] No : certainly not. I am proud to be able to say that though my father has not been a successful man, nobody has ever had one word to say against him. I think my father is the best man I have ever known.

THE CAPTAIN. He must be greatly changed. Has he attained the seventh degree of concentration?

ELLIE. I dont understand.

THE CAPTAIN. But how could he, with a daughter? I, madam, have two daughters. One of them is Hesione Hushabye, who invited you here. I keep this house: she upsets it. I desire to attain the seventh degree of concentration: she invites visitors and leaves me to entertain them. [Nurse Guinness returns with the tea-tray, which she places on the teak table]. I have a second daughter who is, thank God, in a remote part of the Empire with her numskull of a husband. As a child she thought the figure-head of my ship, the Dauntless, the most beautiful thing on earth. He resembled it. He had the same expression: wooden yet enterprising. She married him, and will never set foot in this house again.

NURSE GUINNESS [carrying the table, with the tea-things on it, to Ellie's side] Indeed you never were more mistaken. She is in England this very moment. You have been told three times this week that she is coming home for a year for her health. And very glad you should be to see your own daughter again after all these years.

THE CAPTAIN. I am not glad. The natural

term of the affection of the human animal for its offspring is six years. My daughter Ariadne was born when I was forty-six. I am now eighty-eight. If she comes, I am not at home. If she wants anything, let her take it. If she asks for me, let her be informed that I am extremely old, and have totally forgotten her.

NURSE GUINNESS. Thats no talk to offer to a young lady. Here, ducky, have some tea; and dont listen to him [she pours out a cup of tea].

THE CAPTAIN [rising wrathfully] Now before high heaven they have given this innocent child Indian tea: the stuff they tan their own leather insides with. [He seizes the cup and the tea-pot and empties both into the leathern bucket].

ELLIE [almost in tears] Oh, please! I am so tired. I should have been glad of anything.

NURSE GUINNESS. Oh, what a thing to do! The poor lamb is ready to drop.

THE CAPTAIN. You shall have some of my tea. Do not touch that fly-blown cake: nobody eats it here except the dogs. [He disappears into the pantry].

NURSE GUINNESS. Theres a man for you! They say he sold himself to the devil in Zanzibar before he was a captain; and the older he grows the more I believe them.

A WOMAN'S VOICE [in the hall] Is anyone at home? Hesione! Nurse! Papa! Do come, somebody; and take in my luggage.

Thumping heard, as of an umbrella, on the wainscot.

NURSE GUINNESS. My gracious! It's Miss Addie, Lady Utterword, Mrs Hushabye's sister: the one I told the Captain about. [Calling] Coming, Miss, coming.

She carries the table back to its place by the door, and is hurrying out when she is intercepted by Lady Utterword, who bursts in much flustered. Lady Utterword, a blonde, is very handsome, very well dressed, and so precipitate in speech and action that the first impression (erroneous) is one of comic silliness.

LADY UTTERWORD. Oh, is that you, Nurse? How are you? You dont look a day older. Is nobody at home? Where is Hesione? Doesnt she expect me? Where are the servants? Whose luggage is that on the steps? Where's Papa? Is everybody asleep? [Seeing Ellie] Oh! I beg your pardon. I suppose you are one of my nieces. [Approaching her with outstretched arms] Come and kiss your aunt, darling.

ELLIE. I'm only a visitor. It is my luggage on the steps.

NURSE GUINNESS. I'll go get you some fresh tea, ducky. [She takes up the tray].

ELLIE. But the old gentleman said he would make some himself.

NURSE GUINNESS. Bless you! he's forgotten what he went for already. His mind wanders from one thing to another.

LADY UTTERWORD. Papa, I suppose?

NURSE GUINNESS. Yes, Miss.

LADY UTTERWORD [vehemently] Dont be silly, nurse. Dont call me Miss.

NURSE GUINNESS [placidly] No, lovey [she goes out with the tea-tray].

LADY UTTERWORD [sitting down with a flounce on the sofa] I know what you must feel. Oh, this house, this house! I come back to it after twenty-three years; and it is just the same: the luggage lying on the steps, the servants spoilt and impossible, nobody at home to receive anybody, no regular meals, nobody ever hungry because they are always gnawing bread and butter or munching apples, and, what is worse, the same disorder in ideas, in talk, in feeling. When I was a child I was used to it: I had never known anything better, though I was unhappy, and longed all the time — oh, how I longed! — to be respectable, to be a lady, to live as others did, not to have to think of everything for myself. I married at nineteen to escape from it. My husband is Sir Hastings Utterword, who has been governor of all the crown colonies in succession. I have always been the mistress of Government House. I have been so happy: I had forgotten that people could live like this. I wanted to see my father, my sister, my nephews and nieces (one ought to, you know), and I was looking forward to it. And now the state of the house! the way I'm received! the casual impudence of that woman Guinness, our old nurse! really Hesione might at least have been here: some preparation might have been made for me. You must excuse my going on in this way; but I am really very much hurt and annoyed and disillusioned: and if I had realized it was to be like this, I wouldnt have come. I have a great mind to go away without another word [she is on the point of weeping].

ELLIE [also very miserable] Nobody has been here to receive me either. I thought I ought to go away too. But how can I, Lady Utterword? My luggage is on the steps; and the station fly has gone.

The Captain emerges from the pantry with a

tray of Chinese lacquer and a very fine tea-set on it. He rests it provisionally on the end of the table; snatches away the drawing-board, which he stands on the floor against the table legs; and puts the tray in the space thus cleared. Ellie pours out a cup greedily.

THE CAPTAIN. Your tea, young lady. What! another lady! I must fetch another cup [*he makes for the pantry*].

LADY UTTERWORD [*rising from the sofa, suffused with emotion*] Papa! Dont you know me? I'm your daughter.

THE CAPTAIN. Nonsense! my daughter's upstairs asleep. [*He vanishes through the half door*].

Lady Utterword retires to the window to conceal her tears.

ELLIE [*going to her with the cup*] Dont be so distressed. Have this cup of tea. He is very old and very strange: he has been just like that to me. I know how dreadful it must be: my own father is all the world to me. Oh, I'm sure he didnt mean it.

The Captain returns with another cup.

THE CAPTAIN. Now we are complete. [*He places it on the tray*].

LADY UTTERWORD [*hysterically*] Papa: you cant have forgotten me. I am Ariadne. I'm little Paddy Patkins. Wont you kiss me? [*She goes to him and throws her arms round his neck*].

THE CAPTAIN [*woodenly enduring her embrace*] How can you be Ariadne? You are a middle-aged woman: well preserved, madam, but no longer young.

LADY UTTERWORD. But think of all the years and years I have been away, Papa. I have had to grow old, like other people.

THE CAPTAIN [*disengaging himself*] You should grow out of kissing strange men: they may be striving to attain the seventh degree of concentration.

LADY UTTERWORD. But I'm your daughter. You havnt seen me for years.

THE CAPTAIN. So much the worse! When our relatives are at home, we have to think of all their good points or it would be impossible to endure them. But when they are away, we console ourselves for their absence by dwelling on their vices. That is how I have come to think my absent daughter Ariadne a perfect fiend; so do not try to ingratiate yourself here by impersonating her [*he walks firmly away to the other side of the room*].

LADY UTTERWORD. Ingratiating myself indeed [*With dignity*] Very well, papa. [*She sits down at the drawing-table and pours out tea for herself*].

THE CAPTAIN. I am neglecting my social duties. You remember Dunn? Billy Dunn?

LADY UTTERWORD. Do you mean that villainous sailor who robbed you?

THE CAPTAIN [*introducing Ellie*] His daughter. [*He sits down on the sofa*].

ELLIE [*protesting*] No—

Nurse Guinness returns with fresh tea.

THE CAPTAIN. Take that hogwash away. Do you hear?

NURSE. Youve actually remembered about the tea! [*To Ellie*] O, miss, he didnt forget you after all! You h a v e made an impression.

THE CAPTAIN [*gloomily*] Youth! beauty! novelty! They are badly wanted in this house. I am excessively old. Hesione is only moderately young. Her children are not youthful.

LADY UTTERWORD. How can children be expected to be youthful in this house? Almost before we could speak we were filled with notions that might have been all very well for pagan philosophers of fifty, but were certainly quite unfit for respectable people of any age.

NURSE. You were always for respectability, Miss Addy.

LADY UTTERWORD. Nurse: will you please remember that I am Lady Utterword, and not Miss Addy, nor lovey, nor darling, nor doty? Do you hear?

NURSE. Yes, ducky: all right. I'll tell them all they must call you my lady. [*She takes her tray out with undisturbed placidity*].

LADY UTTERWORD. What comfort? what sense is there in having servants with no manners?

ELLIE [*rising and coming to the table to put down her empty cup*] Lady Utterword: do you think Mrs Hushabye really expects me?

LADY UTTERWORD. Oh, dont ask me. You can see for yourself that Ive just arrived; her only sister, after twenty-three years absence! and it seems that *I* am not expected.

THE CAPTAIN. What does it matter whether the young lady is expected or not? She is welcome. There are beds: there is food. I'll find a room for her myself [*he makes for the door*].

ELLIE [*following him to stop him*] Oh please— [*he goes out*]. Lady Utterword: I dont know what to do. Your father persists in believing that my father is some sailor who robbed him.

LADY UTTERWORD. You had better pretend not to notice it. My father is a very clever man; but he always forgot things; and now that he is old, of course he is worse. And I must warn you that it is sometimes very hard to feel quite sure that he really forgets.

Mrs Hushabye bursts into the room tempestuously, and embraces Ellie. She is a couple of years older than Lady Utterword, and even better looking. She has magnificent black hair, eyes like the fishpools of Heshbon, and a nobly modelled neck, short at the back and low between her shoulders in front. Unlike her sister she is uncorseted and dressed anyhow in a rich robe of black pile that shews off her white skin and statuesque contour.

MRS HUSHABYE. Ellie, my darling, my pettikins [*kissing her*]: how long have you been here? Ive been at home all the time: I was putting flowers and things in your room; and when I just sat down for a moment to try how comfortable the armchair was I went off to sleep. Papa woke me and told me you were here. Fancy your finding no one, and being neglected and abandoned. [*Kissing her again*]. My poor love! [*She deposits Ellie on the sofa. Meanwhile Ariadne has left the table and come over to claim her share of attention*]. Oh! youve brought someone with you. Introduce me.

LADY UTTERWORD. Hesione: is it possible that you dont know me?

MRS HUSHABYE [*conventionally*] Of course I remember your face quite well. Where have we met?

LADY UTTERWORD. Didnt Papa tell you I was here? Oh! this is really too much. [*She throws herself sulkily into the big chair*].

MRS HUSHABYE. Papa!

LADY UTTERWORD. Yes: Papa. Our papa, you unfeeling wretch. [*Rising angrily*] I'll go straight to a hotel.

MRS HUSHABYE [*seizing her by the shoulders*] My goodness gracious goodness, you dont mean to say that youre Addy!

LADY UTTERWORD. I certainly am Addy; and I dont think I can be so changed that you would not have recognized me if you had any real affection for me. And papa didnt think me even worth mentioning!

MRS HUSHABYE. What a lark! Sit down [*she pushes her back into the chair instead of kissing her, and posts herself behind it*]. You do look a swell. Youre much handsomer than you used to be. Youve made the acquaintance of Ellie,

of course. She is going to marry a perfect hog of a millionaire for the sake of her father, who is as poor as a church mouse; and you must help me to stop her.

ELLIE. Oh p l e a s e, Hesione.

MRS HUSHABYE. My pettikins, the man's coming here today with your father to begin persecuting you; and everybody will see the state of the case in ten minutes; so whats the use of making a secret of it?

ELLIE. He is not a hog, Hesione. You dont know how wonderfully good he was to my father, and how deeply grateful I am to him.

MRS HUSHABYE [*to Lady Utterword*] Her father is a very remarkable man, Addy. His name is Mazzini Dunn. Mazzini was a celebrity of some kind who knew Ellie's grandparents. They were both poets, like the Brownings; and when her father came into the world Mazzini said "Another soldier born for freedom!" So they christened him Mazzini; and he has been fighting for freedom in his quiet way ever since. Thats why he is so poor.

ELLIE. I am proud of his poverty.

MRS HUSHABYE. Of course you are, pettikins. Why not leave him in it, and marry someone you love?

LADY UTTERWORD [*rising suddenly and explosively*] Hesione: are you going to kiss me or are you not?

MRS HUSHABYE. What do you want to be kissed for?

LADY UTTERWORD. I d o n t want to be kissed; but I do want you to behave properly and decently. We are sisters. We have been separated for twenty-three years. You ought to kiss me.

MRS HUSHABYE. Tomorrow morning, dear, before you make up. I hate the smell of powder.

LADY UTTERWORD. Oh! you unfeeling—[*she is interrupted by the return of the captain*].

THE CAPTAIN [*to Ellie*] Your room is ready. [*Ellie rises*]. The sheets were damp; but I have changed them [*he makes for the garden door on the port side*].

LADY UTTERWORD. Oh! What about m y sheets?

THE CAPTAIN [*halting at the door*] Take my advice: air them; or take them off and sleep in blankets. You shall sleep in Ariadne's old room.

LADY UTTERWORD. Indeed I shall do nothing of the sort. That little hole! I am entitled to the best spare room.

THE CAPTAIN [*continuing unmoved*] She married a numskull. She told me she would marry anyone to get away from home.

LADY UTTERWORD. You are pretending not to know me on purpose. I will leave the house.

Mazzini Dunn enters from the hall. He is a little elderly man with bulging credulous eyes and earnest manners. He is dressed in a blue serge jacket suit with an unbuttoned mackintosh over it, and carries a soft black hat of clerical cut.

ELLIE. At last! Captain Shotover: here is my father.

THE CAPTAIN. This! Nonsense! not a bit like him [*he goes away through the garden, shutting the door sharply behind him*].

LADY UTTERWORD. I will not be ignored and pretended to be somebody else. I will have it out with papa now, this instant. [*To Mazzini*] Excuse me. [*She follows the Captain out, making a hasty bow to Mazzini, who returns it*].

MRS HUSHABYE [*hospitably, shaking hands*] How good of you to come, Mr Dunn! You dont mind papa, do you? He is as mad as a hatter, you know, but quite harmless, and extremely clever. You will have some delightful talks with him.

MAZZINI. I hope so. [*To Ellie*] So here you are, Ellie, dear. [*He draws her arm affectionately through his*]. I must thank you, Mrs Hushabye, for your kindness to my daughter. I'm afraid she would have had no holiday if you had not invited her.

MRS HUSHABYE. Not at all. Very nice of her to come and attract young people to the house for us.

MAZZINI [*smiling*] I'm afraid Ellie is not interested in young men, Mrs Hushabye. Her taste is on the graver, solider side.

MRS HUSHABYE [*with a sudden rather hard brightness in her manner*] Wont you take off your overcoat, Mr Dunn? You will find a cupboard for coats and hats and things in the corner of the hall.

MAZZINI [*hastily releasing Ellie*] Yes—thank you—I had better—[*he goes out*].

MRS HUSHABYE [*emphatically*] The old brute!

ELLIE. Who?

MRS HUSHABYE. Who! Him. He. It [*pointing after Mazzini*]. "Graver, solider tastes," indeed!

ELLIE [*aghast*] You dont mean that you were speaking like that of my father!

MRS HUSHABYE. I was. You know I was.

ELLIE [*with dignity*] I will leave your house at once. [*She turns to the door*].

MRS HUSHABYE. If you attempt it, I'll tell your father why.

ELLIE [*turning again*] Oh! How can you treat a visitor like this, Mrs Hushabye?

MRS HUSHABYE. I thought you were going to call me Hesione.

ELLIE. Certainly not now?

MRS HUSHABYE. Very well: I'll tell your father.

ELLIE [*distressed*] Oh!

MRS HUSHABYE. If you turn a hair—if you take his part against me and against your own heart for a moment, I'll give that born soldier of freedom a piece of my mind that will stand him on his selfish old head for a week.

ELLIE. Hesione! My father selfish! How little you know—

She is interrupted by Mazzini, who returns, excited and perspiring.

MAZZINI. Ellie: Mangan has come: I thought youd like to know. Excuse me, Mrs Hushabye: the strange old gentleman—

MRS HUSHABYE. Papa. Quite so.

MAZZINI. Oh, I beg your pardon: of course: I was a little confused by his manner. He is making Mangan help him with something in the garden; and he wants me too—

A powerful whistle is heard.

THE CAPTAIN'S VOICE. Bosun ahoy! [*the whistle is repeated*].

MAZZINI [*flustered*] Oh dear! I believe he is whistling for me. [*He hurries out*].

MRS HUSHABYE. Now my father is a wonderful man if you like.

ELLIE. Hesione: listen to me. You dont understand. My father and Mr Mangan were boys together. Mr Ma—

MRS HUSHABYE. I dont care what they were: we must sit down if you are going to begin as far back as that [*She snatches at Ellie's waist, and makes her sit down on the sofa beside her*]. Now, pettikins: tell me all about Mr Mangan. They call him Boss Mangan, dont they? He is a Napoleon of industry and disgustingly rich, isnt he? Why isnt your father rich?

ELLIE. My poor father should never have been in business. His parents were poets; and they gave him the noblest ideas; but they could not afford to give him a profession.

MRS HUSHABYE. Fancy your grandparents, with their eyes in fine frenzy rolling! And so your poor father had to go into business. Hasnt he succeeded in it?

ELLIE. He always used to say he could succeed if he only had some capital. He fought his way along, to keep a roof over our heads and bring us up well; but it was always a struggle: always the same difficulty of not having capital enough. I dont know how to describe it to you.

MRS HUSHABYE. Poor Ellie! I know. Pulling the devil by the tail.

ELLIE [hurt] Oh no. Not like that. It was at least dignified.

MRS HUSHABYE. That made it all the harder, didnt it? *I* shouldnt have pulled the devil by the tail with dignity. I should have pulled hard—[between her teeth] h a r d. Well? Go on.

ELLIE. At last it seemed that all our troubles were at an end. Mr Mangan did an extraordinarily noble thing out of pure friendship for my father and respect for his character. He asked him how much capital he wanted, and gave it to him. I dont mean that he lent it to him, or that he invested it in his business. He just simply made him a present of it. Wasnt that splendid of him?

MRS HUSHABYE. On condition that you married him?

ELLIE. Oh no, no, no. This was when I was a child. He had never even seen me: he never came to our house. It was absolutely disinterested. Pure generosity.

MRS HUSHABYE. Oh! I beg the gentleman's pardon. Well, what became of the money?

ELLIE. We all got new clothes and moved into another house. And I went to another school for two years.

MRS HUSHABYE. Only two years?

ELLIE. That was all; for at the end of two years my father was utterly ruined.

MRS HUSHABYE. How?

ELLIE. I dont know. I never could understand. But it was dreadful. When we were poor my father had never been in debt. But when he launched out into business on a large scale, he had to incur liabilities. When the business went into liquidation he owed more money than Mr Mangan had given him.

MRS HUSHABYE. Bit off more than he could chew, I suppose.

ELLIE. I think you are a little unfeeling about it.

MRS HUSHABYE. My pettikins: you mustnt mind my way of talking. I was quite as sensitive and particular as you once; but I have picked up so much slang from the children that I am really hardly presentable. I suppose your father had no head for business, and made a mess of it.

ELLIE. Oh, that just shows how entirely you are mistaken about him. The business turned out a great success. It now pays forty-four per cent after deducting the excess profits tax.

MRS HUSHABYE. Then why arnt you rolling in money?

ELLIE. I dont know. It seems very unfair to me. You see, my father was made bankrupt. It nearly broke his heart, because he had persuaded several of his friends to put money into the business. He was sure it would succeed; and events proved that he was quite right. But they all lost their money. It was dreadful. I dont know what we should have done but for Mr Mangan.

MRS HUSHABYE. What! Did the Boss come to the rescue again, after all his money being thrown away?

ELLIE. He did indeed, and never uttered a reproach to my father. He bought what was left of the business — the buildings and the machinery and things — from the official trustee for enough money to enable my father to pay six and eightpence in the pound and get his discharge. Everyone pitied papa so much, and saw so plainly that he was an honorable man, that they let him off at six-and-eightpence instead of ten shillings. Then Mr Mangan started a company to take up the business, and made my father a manager in it to save us from starvation; for I wasnt earning anything then.

MRS HUSHABYE. Quite a romance. And when did the Boss develop the tender passion?

ELLIE. Oh, that was years after, quite lately. He took the chair one night at a sort of people's concert. I was singing there. As an amateur, you know: half a guinea for expenses and three songs with three encores. He was so pleased with my singing that he asked might he walk home with me. I never saw anyone so taken aback as he was when I took him home and introduced him to my father: his own manager. It was then that my father told me how nobly he had behaved. Of course it was considered a great chance for me, as he is so rich. And—and—we drifted into a sort of understanding—I suppose I should call it an engagement—[she is distressed and cannot go on].

MRS HUSHABYE [*rising and marching about*] You may have drifted into it; but you will bounce out of it, my pettikins, if I am to have anything to do with it.

ELLIE [*hopelessly*] No: it's no use. I am bound in honor and gratitude. I will go through with it.

MRS HUSHABYE [*behind the sofa, scolding down at her*] You know, of course, that it's not honorable or grateful to marry a man you dont love. Do you love this Mangan man?

ELLIE. Yes. At least—

MRS HUSHABYE. I dont want to know about "the least": I want to know the worst. Girls of your age fall in love with all sorts of impossible people, especially old people.

ELLIE. I like Mr Mangan very much; and I shall always be—

MRS HUSHABYE [*impatiently completing the sentence and prancing away intolerantly to starboard*]—grateful to him for his kindness to dear father. I know. Anybody else?

ELLIE. What do you mean?

MRS HUSHABYE. Anybody else? Are you in love with anybody else?

ELLIE. Of course not.

MRS HUSHABYE. Humph! [*The book on the drawing-table catches her eye. She picks it up, and evidently finds the title very unexpected. She looks at Ellie, and asks, quaintly*]. Quite sure youre not in love with an actor?

ELLIE. No, no. Why? What put such a thing into your head?

MRS HUSHABYE. This is yours, isnt it? Why else should you be reading Othello?

ELLIE. My father taught me to love Shakespear.

MRS HUSHABYE [*flinging the book down on the table*] Really! your father does seem to be about the limit.

ELLIE [*naïvely*] Do you never read Shakespear, Hesione? That seems to me so extraordinary. I like Othello.

MRS HUSHABYE. Do you indeed? He was jealous, wasnt he?

ELLIE. Oh, not that. I think all the part about jealousy is horrible. But dont you think it must have been a wonderful experience for Desdemona, brought up so quietly at home, to meet a man who had been out in the world doing all sorts of brave things and having terrible adventures, and yet finding something in her that made him love to sit and talk with her and tell her about them?

MRS HUSHABYE. Thats your idea of romance, is it?

ELLIE. Not romance, exactly. It might really happen.

Ellie's eyes shew that she is not arguing, but in a daydream. Mrs Hushabye, watching her inquisitively, goes deliberately back to the sofa and resumes her seat beside her.

MRS HUSHABYE. Ellie darling: have you noticed that some of those stories that Othello told Desdemona couldnt have happened?

ELLIE. Oh no. Shakespear thought they could have happened.

MRS HUSHABYE. Hm! Desdemona thought they could have happened. But they didnt.

ELLIE. Why do you look so enigmatic about it? You are such a sphinx: I never know what you mean.

MRS HUSHABYE. Desdemona would have found him out if she had lived, you know. I wonder was that why he strangled her!

ELLIE. Othello was not telling lies.

MRS HUSHABYE. How do you know?

ELLIE. Shakespear would have said if he was. Hesione: there are men who have done wonderful things: men like Othello, only, of course, white, and very handsome, and—

MRS HUSHABYE. Ah! Now we're coming to it. Tell me all about him. I knew there must be somebody, or youd never have been so miserable about Mangan: youd have thought it quite a lark to marry him.

ELLIE [*blushing vividly*] Hesione: you are dreadful. But I dont want to make a secret of it, though of course I dont tell everybody. Besides, I dont know him.

MRS HUSHABYE. Dont know him! What does that mean?

ELLIE. Well, of course I know him to speak to.

MRS HUSHABYE. But you want to know him ever so much more intimately, eh?

ELLIE. No no: I know him quite—almost intimately.

MRS HUSHABYE. You dont know him; and you know him almost intimately. How lucid!

ELLIE. I mean that he does not call on us. I—I got into conversation with him by chance at a concert.

MRS HUSHABYE. You seem to have rather a gay time at your concerts, Ellie.

ELLIE. Not at all: we talk to everyone in the green-room waiting for our turns. I thought he was one of the artists: he looked so splendid. But he was only one of the committee. I happened to tell him that I was copying a picture at the National Gallery. I make a little money that way. I cant paint much; but as it's always the same picture I can do it pretty quickly and get two or three pounds for it. It happened that he came to the National Gallery one day.

MRS HUSHABYE. One student's day. Paid sixpence to stumble about through a crowd of easels, when he might have come in next day for nothing and found the floor clear! Quite by accident?

ELLIE [triumphantly] No. On purpose. He liked talking to me. He knows lots of the most splendid people. Fashionable women who are all in love with him. But he ran away from them to see me at the National Gallery and persuade me to come with him for a drive round Richmond Park in a taxi.

MRS HUSHABYE. My pettikins, you have been going it. It's wonderful what you good girls can do without anyone saying a word.

ELLIE. I am not in society, Hesione. If I didnt make acquaintances in that way I shouldnt have any at all.

MRS HUSHABYE. Well, no harm if you know how to take care of yourself. May I ask his name?

ELLIE [slowly and musically] Marcus Darnley.

MRS HUSHABYE [echoing the music] Marcus Darnley! What a splendid name!

ELLIE. Oh, I'm so glad you think so. I think so too; but I was afraid it was only a silly fancy of my own.

MRS HUSHABYE. Hm! Is he one of the Aberdeen Darnleys?

ELLIE. Nobody knows. Just fancy! He was found in an antique chest—

MRS HUSHABYE. A what?

ELLIE. An antique chest, one summer morning in a rose garden, after a night of the most terrible thunderstorm.

MRS HUSHABYE. What on earth was he doing in the chest? Did he get into it because he was afraid of the lightning?

ELLIE. Oh no, no: he was a baby. The name Marcus Darnley was embroidered on his baby-clothes. And five hundred pounds in gold.

MRS HUSHABYE [looking hard at her] Ellie!

ELLIE. The garden of the Viscount—

MRS HUSHABYE. —de Rougemont?

ELLIE [innocently] No: de Larochejaquelin.

A French family. A vicomte. His life has been one long romance. A tiger—

MRS HUSHABYE. Slain by his own hand?

ELLIE. Oh no: nothing vulgar like that. He saved the life of the tiger from a hunting party: one of King Edward's hunting parties in India. The King was furious: that was why he never had his military services properly recognized. But he doesnt care. He is a Socialist and despises rank, and has been in three revolutions fighting on the barricades.

MRS HUSHABYE. How can you sit there telling me such lies? You, Ellie, of all people! And I thought you were a perfectly simple, straightforward, good girl.

ELLIE [rising, dignified but very angry] Do you mean to say you dont believe me?

MRS HUSHABYE. Of course I dont believe you. Youre inventing every word of it. Do you take me for a fool?

Ellie stares at her. Her candor is so obvious that Mrs Hushabye is puzzled.

ELLIE. Goodbye, Hesione. I'm very sorry. I see now that it sounds very improbable as I tell it. But I cant stay if you think that way about me.

MRS HUSHABYE [catching her dress] You shant go. I couldnt be so mistaken: I know too well what liars are like. Somebody has really told you all this.

ELLIE [flushing] Hesione: dont say that you dont believe him. I couldnt bear that.

MRS HUSHABYE [soothing her] Of course I believe him, dearest. But you should have broken it to me by degrees. [Drawing her back to her seat] Now tell me all about him. Are you in love with him?

ELLIE. Oh no. I'm not so foolish. I dont fall in love with people. I'm not so silly as you think.

MRS HUSHABYE. I see. Only something to think about—to give some interest and pleasure to life.

ELLIE. Just so. Thats all, really.

MRS HUSHABYE. It makes the hours go fast, doesnt it? No tedious waiting to go to sleep at nights and wondering whether you will have a bad night. How delightful it makes waking up in the morning! How much better than the happiest dream! All life transfigured! No more wishing one had an interesting book to read, because life is so much happier than any book! No desire but to be alone and not to have to talk to anyone: to be alone and just think about it.

ELLIE [*embracing her*] Hesione: you are a witch. How do you know? Oh, you are the most sympathetic woman in the world.

MRS HUSHABYE [*caressing her*] Pettikins, my pettikins: how I envy you! and how I pity you!

ELLIE. Pity me! Oh, why?

A very handsome man of fifty, with mousquetaire moustaches, wearing a rather dandified curly brimmed hat, and carrying an elaborate walking-stick, comes into the room from the hall, and stops short at sight of the women on the sofa.

ELLIE [*seeing him and rising in glad surprise*] Oh! Hesione: this is Mr Marcus Darnley.

MRS HUSHABYE [*rising*] What a lark! He is my husband.

ELLIE. But how—[*she stops suddenly; then turns pale and sways*].

MRS HUSHABYE [*catching her and sitting down with her on the sofa*] Steady, my pettikins.

THE MAN [*with a mixture of confusion and effrontery, depositing his hat and stick on the teak table*] My real name, Miss Dunn, is Hector Hushabye. I leave you to judge whether that is a name any sensitive man would care to confess to. I never use it when I can possibly help it. I have been away for nearly a month; and I had no idea you knew my wife, or that you were coming here. I am none the less delighted to find you in our little house.

ELLIE [*in great distress*] I dont know what to do. Please, may I speak to papa? Do leave me. I cant bear it.

MRS HUSHABYE. Be off, Hector.

HECTOR. I—

MRS HUSHABYE. Quick, quick. Get out.

HECTOR. If you think it better—[*he goes out, taking his hat with him but leaving the stick on the table*].

MRS HUSHABYE [*laying Ellie down at the end of the sofa*] Now, pettikins, he is gone. Theres nobody but me. You can let yourself go. Dont try to control yourself. Have a good cry.

ELLIE [*raising her head*] Damn!

MRS HUSHABYE. Splendid! Oh, what a relief! I thought you were going to be broken-hearted. Never mind me. Damn him again.

ELLIE. I am not damning him: I am damning myself for being such a fool. [*Rising*] How could I let myself be taken in so? [*She begins prowling to and fro, her bloom gone, looking curiously older and harder*].

MRS HUSHABYE [*cheerfully*] Why not, pettikins? Very few young women can resist Hector. I couldnt when I was your age. He is really rather splendid, you know.

ELLIE [*turning on her*] Splendid! Yes: splendid looking, of course. But how can you love a liar?

MRS HUSHABYE. I dont know. But you can, fortunately. Otherwise there wouldnt be much love in the world.

ELLIE. But to lie like that! To be a boaster! a coward!

MRS HUSHABYE [*rising in alarm*] Pettikins: none of that, if you please. If you hint the slightest doubt of Hector's courage, he will go straight off and do the most horribly dangerous things to convince himself that he isnt a coward. He has a dreadful trick of getting out of one third-floor window and coming in at another, just to test his nerve. He has a whole drawerful of Albert Medals for saving people's lives.

ELLIE. He never told me that.

MRS HUSHABYE. He never boasts of anything he really did: he cant bear it; and it makes him shy if anyone else does. All his stories are made-up stories.

ELLIE [*coming to her*] Do you mean that he is really brave, and really has adventures, and yet tells lies about things that he never did and that never happened?

MRS HUSHABYE. Yes, pettikins, I do. People dont have their virtues and vices in sets: they have them anyhow: all mixed.

ELLIE [*staring at her thoughtfully*] Theres something odd about this house, Hesione, and even about you. I dont know why I'm talking to you so calmly. I have a horrible fear that my heart is broken, but that heartbreak is not like what I thought it must be.

MRS HUSHABYE [*fondling her*] It's only life educating you, pettikins. How do you feel about Boss Mangan now?

ELLIE [*disengaging herself with an expression of distaste*] Oh, how can you remind me of him, Hesione?

MRS HUSHABYE. Sorry, dear. I think I hear Hector coming back. You dont mind now, do you, dear?

ELLIE. Not in the least. I am quite cured.

Mazzini Dunn and Hector come in from the hall.

HECTOR [*as he opens the door and allows Mazzini to pass in*] One second more, and she would have been a dead woman!

MAZZINI. Dear! dear! what an escape! Ellie, my love: Mr Hushabye has just been telling me the most extraordinary—

ELLIE. Yes: Ive heard it [*she crosses to the other side of the room*].

HECTOR [*following her*] Not this one: I'll tell it to you after dinner. I think youll like it. The truth is, I made it up for you, and was looking forward to the pleasure of telling it to you. But in a moment of impatience at being turned out of the room, I threw it away on your father.

ELLIE [*turning at bay with her back to the carpenter's bench, scornfully self-possessed*] It was not thrown away. He believes it. I should not have believed it.

MAZZINI [*benevolently*] Ellie is very naughty, Mr Hushabye. Of course she does not really think that. [*He goes to the bookshelves, and inspects the titles of the volumes*].

Boss Mangan comes in from the hall, followed by the Captain. Mangan, carefully frockcoated as for church or for a directors' meeting, is about fiftyfive, with a careworn, mistrustful expression, standing a little on an entirely imaginary dignity, with a dull complexion, straight, lustreless hair, and features so entirely commonplace that it is impossible to describe them.

CAPTAIN SHOTOVER [*to Mrs Hushabye, introducing the new comer*] Says his name is Mangan. Not ablebodied.

MRS HUSHABYE [*graciously*] How do you do, Mr Mangan?

MANGAN [*shaking hands*] Very pleased.

CAPTAIN SHOTOVER. Dunn's lost his muscle, but recovered his nerve. Men seldom do after three attacks of delirium tremens [*he goes into the pantry*].

MRS HUSHABYE. I congratulate you, Mr Dunn.

MAZZINI [*dazed*] I am a lifelong teetotaler.

MRS HUSHABYE. You will find it far less trouble to let papa have his own way than try to explain.

MAZZINI. But three attacks of delirium tremens, really!

MRS HUSHABYE [*to Mangan*] Do you know my husband, Mr Mangan [*she indicates Hector*].

MANGAN [*going to Hector, who meets him with outstretched hand*] Very pleased. [*Turning to Ellie*] I hope, Miss Ellie, you have not found the journey down too fatiguing. [*They shake hands*].

MRS HUSHABYE. Hector: shew Mr Dunn his room.

HECTOR. Certainly. Come along, Mr Dunn. [*He takes Mazzini out*].

ELLIE. You havnt shewn me my room yet, Hesione.

MRS HUSHABYE. How stupid of me! Come along. Make yourself quite at home, Mr Mangan. Papa will entertain you. [*She calls to the Captain in the pantry*] Papa: come and explain the house to Mr Mangan.

She goes out with Ellie. The Captain comes from the pantry.

CAPTAIN SHOTOVER. Youre going to marry Dunn's daughter. Dont. Youre too old.

MANGAN [*staggered*] Well! Thats fairly blunt, Captain.

CAPTAIN SHOTOVER. It's true.

MANGAN. She doesnt think so.

CAPTAIN SHOTOVER. She does.

MANGAN. Older men than I have—

CAPTAIN SHOTOVER [*finishing the sentence for him*]—made fools of themselves. That, also, is true.

MANGAN [*asserting himself*] I dont see that this is any business of yours.

CAPTAIN SHOTOVER. It is everybody's business. The stars in their courses are shaken when such things happen.

MANGAN. I'm going to marry her all the same.

CAPTAIN SHOTOVER. How do you know?

MANGAN [*playing the strong man*] I intend to. I mean to. See? I never made up my mind to do a thing yet that I didnt bring it off. Thats the sort of man I am; and there will be a better understanding between us when you make up your mind to that, Captain.

CAPTAIN SHOTOVER. You frequent picture palaces.

MANGAN. Perhaps I do. Who told you?

CAPTAIN SHOTOVER. Talk like a man, not like a movy. You mean that you make a hundred thousand a year.

MANGAN. I dont boast. But when I meet a man that makes a hundred thousand a year, I take off my hat to that man, and stretch out my hand to him and call him brother.

CAPTAIN SHOTOVER. Then you also make a hundred thousand a year, hey?

MANGAN. No. I cant say that. Fifty thousand, perhaps.

CAPTAIN SHOTOVER. His half brother only [*he turns away from Mangan with his usual abruptness, and collects the empty tea-cups on the Chinese tray*].

MANGAN [*irritated*] See here, Captain Shotover. I dont quite understand my position here. I came here on your daughter's invitation. Am I in her house or in yours?

CAPTAIN SHOTOVER. You are beneath the dome of heaven, in the house of God. What is true within these walls is true outside them. Go out on the seas; climb the mountains; wander through the valleys. She is still too young.

MANGAN [*weakening*] But I'm very little over fifty.

CAPTAIN SHOTOVER. You are still less under sixty. Boss Mangan: you will not marry the pirate's child [*he carries the tray away into the pantry*].

MANGAN [*following him to the half door*] What pirate's child? What are you talking about?

CAPTAIN SHOTOVER [*in the pantry*] Ellie Dunn. You will not marry her.

MANGAN. Who will stop me?

CAPTAIN SHOTOVER [*emerging*] My daughter [*he makes for the door leading to the hall*].

MANGAN [*following him*] Mrs Hushabye! Do you mean to say she brought me down here to break it off?

CAPTAIN SHOTOVER [*stopping and turning on him*] I know nothing more than I have seen in her eye. She will break it off. Take my advice: marry a West Indian negress: they make excellent wives. I was married to one myself for two years.

MANGAN. Well, I am damned!

CAPTAIN SHOTOVER. I thought so. I was, too, for many years. The negress redeemed me.

MANGAN [*feebly*] This is queer. I ought to walk out of this house.

CAPTAIN SHOTOVER. Why?

MANGAN. Well, many men would be offended by your style of talking.

CAPTAIN SHOTOVER. Nonsense! It's the other sort of talking that makes quarrels. Nobody ever quarrels with me.

A gentleman, whose firstrate tailoring and frictionless manners proclaim the wellbred West Ender, comes in from the hall. He has an engaging air of being young and unmarried, but on close inspection is found to be at least over forty.

THE GENTLEMAN. Excuse my intruding in this fashion; but there is no knocker on the door; and the bell does not seem to ring.

CAPTAIN SHOTOVER. Why should there be a knocker? Why should the bell ring? The door

is open.

THE GENTLEMAN. Precisely. So I ventured to come in.

CAPTAIN SHOTOVER. Quite right. I will see about a room for you [*he makes for the door*].

THE GENTLEMAN [*stopping him*] But I'm afraid you dont know who I am.

CAPTAIN SHOTOVER. Do you suppose that at my age I make distinctions between one fellowcreature and another? [*He goes out. Mangan and the newcomer stare at one another*].

MANGAN. Strange character, Captain Shotover, sir.

THE GENTLEMAN. Very.

CAPTAIN SHOTOVER [*shouting outside*] Hesione: another person has arrived and wants a room. Man about town, well dressed, fifty.

THE GENTLEMAN. Fancy Hesione's feelings! May I ask are you a member of the family?

MANGAN. No.

THE GENTLEMAN. I am. At least a connexion. *Mrs Hushabye comes back.*

MRS HUSHABYE. How do you do? How good of you to come!

THE GENTLEMAN. I am very glad indeed to make your acquaintance, Hesione. [*Instead of taking her hand he kisses her. At the same moment the Captain appears in the doorway*]. You will excuse my kissing your daughter, Captain, when I tell you that—

CAPTAIN SHOTOVER. Stuff! Everyone kisses my daughter. Kiss her as much as you like [*he makes for the pantry*].

THE GENTLEMAN. Thank you. One moment, Captain. [*The Captain halts and turns. The gentleman goes to him affably*]. Do you happen to remember—but probably you dont, as it occurred many years ago —that your younger daughter married a numskull.

CAPTAIN SHOTOVER. Yes. She said she'd marry anybody to get away from this house. I should not have recognized you: your head is no longer like a walnut. Your aspect is softened. You have been boiled in bread and milk for years and years, like other married men. Poor devil! [*He disappears into the pantry*].

MRS HUSHABYE [*going past Mangan to the gentleman and scrutinizing him*] I dont believe you are Hastings Utterword.

THE GENTLEMAN. I am not.

MRS HUSHABYE. Then what business had you to kiss me?

THE GENTLEMAN. I thought I would like to. The fact is, I am Randall Utterword, the

2 C

unworthy younger brother of Hastings. I was abroad diplomatizing when he was married.

LADY UTTERWORD [*dashing in*] Hesione: where is the key of the wardrobe in my room? My diamonds are in my dressing-bag: I must lock it up— [*recognizing the stranger with a shock*] Randall: how dare you? [*She marches at him past Mrs Hushabye, who retreats and joins Mangan near the sofa*].

RANDALL. How dare I what? I am not doing anything.

LADY UTTERWORD. Who told you I was here?

RANDALL. Hastings. You had just left when I called on you at Claridge's; so I followed you down here. You are looking extremely well.

LADY UTTERWORD. Dont presume to tell me so.

MRS HUSHABYE. What is wrong with Mr Randall, Addy?

LADY UTTERWORD [*recollecting herself*] Oh, nothing. But he has no right to come bothering you and papa without being invited [*she goes to the window-seat and sits down, turning away from them ill-humoredly and looking into the garden, where Hector and Ellie are now seen strolling together*].

MRS HUSHABYE. I think you have not met Mr Mangan, Addy.

LADY UTTERWORD [*turning her head and nodding coldly to Mangan*] I beg your pardon. Randall: you have flustered me so: I made a perfect fool of myself.

MRS HUSHABYE. Lady Utterword. My sister. My y o u n g e r sister.

MANGAN [*bowing*] Pleased to meet you, Lady Utterword.

LADY UTTERWORD [*with marked interest*] Who is that gentleman walking in the garden with Miss Dunn?

MRS HUSHABYE. I dont know. She quarrelled mortally with my husband only ten minutes ago; and I didn't know anyone else had come. It must be a visitor. [*She goes to the window to look*]. Oh, it is Hector. Theyve made it up.

LADY UTTERWORD. Your husband! That handsome man?

MRS HUSHABYE. Well, why shouldnt my husband be a handsome man?

RANDALL [*joining them at the window*] One's husband never is, Ariadne [*he sits by Lady Utterword, on her right*].

MRS HUSHABYE. One's sister's husband always is, Mr Randall.

LADY UTTERWORD. Dont be vulgar, Randall. And you, Hesione, are just as bad.

Ellie and Hector come in from the garden by the starboard door. Randall rises. Ellie retires into the corner near the pantry. Hector comes forward; and Lady Utterword rises looking her very best.

MRS HUSHABYE. Hector: this is Addy.

HECTOR [*apparently surprised*] Not this lady.

LADY UTTERWORD [*smiling*] Why not?

HECTOR [*looking at her with a piercing glance of deep but respectful admiration, his moustache bristling*] I thought— [*pulling himself together*] I beg your pardon, Lady Utterword. I am extremely glad to welcome you at last under our roof [*he offers his hand with grave courtesy*].

MRS HUSHABYE. She wants to be kissed, Hector.

LADY UTTERWORD. Hesione! [*but she still smiles*].

MRS HUSHABYE. Call her Addy; and kiss her like a good brother-in-law; and have done with it. [*She leaves them to themselves*].

HECTOR. Behave yourself, Hesione. Lady Utterword is entitled not only to hospitality but to civilization.

LADY UTTERWORD [*gratefully*] Thank you, Hector. [*They shake hands cordially*].

Mazzini Dunn is seen crossing the garden from starboard to port.

CAPTAIN SHOTOVER [*coming from the pantry and addressing Ellie*] Your father has washed himself.

ELLIE [*quite self-possessed*] He often does, Captain Shotover.

CAPTAIN SHOTOVER. A strange conversion! I saw him through the pantry window.

Mazzini Dunn enters through the port window door, newly washed and brushed, and stops, smiling benevolently, between Mangan and Mrs Hushabye.

MRS HUSHABYE [*introducing*] Mr Mazzini Dunn, Lady Ut—oh, I forgot: youve met. [*Indicating Ellie*] Miss Dunn.

MAZZINI [*walking across the room to take Ellie's hand, and beaming at his own naughty irony*] I have met Miss Dunn also. She is my daughter. [*He draws her arm through his caressingly*].

MRS HUSHABYE. Of course: how stupid! Mr Utterword, my sister's - er -

RANDALL [*shaking hands agreeably*] Her brother-in-law, Mr Dunn. How do you do?

MRS HUSHABYE. This is my husband.

HECTOR. We have met, dear. Dont introduce us any more. [*He moves away to the big chair, and adds*] Wont you sit down, Lady Utterword? [*She does so very graciously*].

MRS HUSHABYE. Sorry. I hate it: it's like making people shew their tickets.

MAZZINI [*sententiously*] How little it tells us, after all! The great question is, not who we are, but what we are.

CAPTAIN SHOTOVER. Ha! What are you?

MAZZINI [*taken aback*] What am I?

CAPTAIN SHOTOVER. A thief, a pirate, and a murderer.

MAZZINI. I assure you you are mistaken.

CAPTAIN SHOTOVER. An adventurous life; but what does it end in? Respectability. A ladylike daughter. The language and appearance of a city missionary. Let it be a warning to all of you [*he goes out through the garden*].

DUNN. I hope nobody here believes that I am a thief, a pirate, or a murderer. Mrs Hushabye: will you excuse me a moment? I must really go and explain. [*He follows the Captain*].

MRS HUSHABYE [*as he goes*] It's no use. Youd really better— [*but Dunn has vanished*]. We had better all go out and look for some tea. We never have regular tea; but you can always get some when you want: the servants keep it stewing all day. The kitchen veranda is the best place to ask. May I shew you? [*She goes to the starboard door*].

RANDALL [*going with her*] Thank you, I dont think I'll take any tea this afternoon. But if you will shew me the garden—?

MRS HUSHABYE. Theres nothing to see in the garden except papa's observatory, and a gravel pit with a cave where he keeps dynamite and things of that sort. However, its pleasanter out of doors; so come along.

RANDALL. Dynamite! Isnt that rather risky?

MRS HUSHABYE. Well, we dont sit in the gravel pit when theres a thunderstorm.

LADY UTTERWORD. Thats something new. What is the dynamite for?

HECTOR. To blow up the human race if it goes too far. He is trying to discover a psychic ray that will explode all the explosives at the will of a Mahatma.

ELLIE. The Captain's tea is delicious, Mr Utterword.

MRS HUSHABYE [*stopping in the doorway*] Do you mean to say that youve had some of my father's tea? that you got round him before you were ten minutes in the house?

ELLIE. I did.

MRS HUSHABYE. You little devil! [*She goes out with Randall*].

MANGAN. Wont you come, Miss Ellie?

ELLIE. I'm too tired. I'll take a book up to my room and rest a little. [*She goes to the bookshelf*].

MANGAN. Right. You cant do better. But I'm disappointed. [*He follows Randall and Mrs Hushabye*].

Ellie, Hector, and Lady Utterword are left. Hector is close to Lady Utterword. They look at Ellie, waiting for her to go.

ELLIE [*looking at the title of a book*] Do you like stories of adventure, Lady Utterword?

LADY UTTERWORD [*patronizingly*] Of course, dear.

ELLIE. Then I'll leave you to Mr Hushabye. [*She goes out through the hall*].

HECTOR. That girl is mad about tales of adventure. The lies I have to tell her!

LADY UTTERWORD [*not interested in Ellie*] When you saw me what did you mean by saying that you thought, and then stopping short? What did you think?

HECTOR [*folding his arms and looking down at her magnetically*] May I tell you?

LADY UTTERWORD. Of course.

HECTOR. It will not sound very civil. I was on the point of saying "I thought you were a plain woman."

LADY UTTERWORD. Oh for shame, Hector! What right had you to notice whether I am plain or not?

HECTOR. Listen to me, Ariadne. Until today I have seen only photographs of you; and no photograph can give the strange fascination of the daughters of that supernatural old man. There is some damnable quality in them that destroys men's moral sense, and carries them beyond honor and dishonor. You know that, dont you?

LADY UTTERWORD. Perhaps I do, Hector. But let me warn you once for all that I am a rigidly conventional woman. You may think because I'm a Shotover that I'm a Bohemian, because we are all so horribly Bohemian. But I'm not. I hate and loathe Bohemianism. No child brought up in a strict Puritan household ever suffered from Puritanism as I suffered from our Bohemianism.

HECTOR. Our children are like that. They spend their holidays in the houses of their respectable schoolfellows.

LADY UTTERWORD. I shall invite them for

Christmas.

HECTOR. Their absence leaves us both without our natural chaperons.

LADY UTTERWORD. Children are certainly very inconvenient sometimes. But intelligent people can always manage, unless they are Bohemians.

HECTOR. You are no Bohemian; but you are no Puritan either: your attraction is alive and powerful. What sort of woman do you count yourself?

LADY UTTERWORD. I am a woman of the world, Hector; and I can assure you that if you will only take the trouble always to do the perfectly correct thing, and to say the perfectly correct thing, you can do just what you like. An ill-conducted, careless woman gets simply no chance. An ill-conducted, careless man is never allowed within arms length of any woman worth knowing.

HECTOR. I see. You are neither a Bohemian woman nor a Puritan woman. You are a dangerous woman.

LADY UTTERWORD. On the contrary, I am a safe woman.

HECTOR. You are a most accursedly attractive woman. Mind: I am not making love to you. I do not like being attracted. But you had better know how I feel if you are going to stay here.

LADY UTTERWORD. You are an exceedingly clever ladykiller, Hector. And terribly handsome. I am quite a good player, myself, at that game. Is it quite understood that we are only playing?

HECTOR. Quite. I am deliberately playing the fool, out of sheer worthlessness.

LADY UTTERWORD [rising brightly] Well, you are my brother-in-law. Hesione asked you to kiss me. [He seizes her in his arms, and kisses her strenuously]. Oh! that was a little more than play, brother-in-law. [She pushes him suddenly away]. You shall not do that again.

HECTOR. In effect, you got your claws deeper into me than I intended.

MRS HUSHABYE [coming in from the garden] Dont let me disturb you: I only want a cap to put on daddiest. The sun is setting; and he'll catch cold [she makes for the door leading to the hall].

LADY UTTERWORD. Your husband is quite charming, darling. He has actually condescended to kiss me at last. I shall go into the garden: it's cooler now [she goes out by the port door].

MRS HUSHABYE. Take care, dear child. I dont believe any man can kiss Addy without falling in love with her. [She goes into the hall].

HECTOR [striking himself on the chest] Fool! Goat!

Mrs Hushabye comes back with the Captain's cap.

HECTOR. Your sister is an extremely enterprising old girl. Wheres Miss Dunn!

MRS HUSHABYE. Mangan says she has gone up to her room for a nap. Addy wont let you talk to Ellie: she has marked you for her own.

HECTOR. She has the diabolical family fascination. I began making love to her automatically. What am I to do? I cant fall in love; and I cant hurt a woman's feelings by telling her so when she falls in love with me. And as women are always falling in love with my moustache I get landed in all sorts of tedious and terrifying flirtations in which I'm not a bit in earnest.

MRS HUSHABYE. Oh, neither is Addy. She has never been in love in her life, though she has always been trying to fall in head over ears. She is worse than you, because you had one real go at least, with me.

HECTOR. That was a confounded madness. I cant believe that such an amazing experience is common. It has left its mark on me. I believe that is why I have never been able to repeat it.

MRS HUSHABYE [laughing and caressing his arm] We were frightfully in love with one another, Hector. It was such an enchanting dream that I have never been able to grudge it to you or anyone else since. I have invited all sorts of pretty women to the house on the chance of giving you another turn. But it has never come off.

HECTOR. I dont know that I want it to come off. It was damned dangerous. You fascinated me; but I loved you; so it was heaven. This sister of yours fascinates me; but I hate her; so it is hell. I shall kill her if she persists.

MRS HUSHABYE. Nothing will kill Addy: she is as strong as a horse. [Releasing him] Now I am going off to fascinate somebody.

HECTOR. The Foreign Office toff? Randall?

MRS HUSHABYE. Goodness gracious, no! Why should I fascinate him?

HECTOR. I presume you dont mean the bloated capitalist, Mangan?

MRS HUSHABYE. Hm! I think he had better be fascinated by me than by Ellie. [She is going into the garden when the Captain comes in *from it with some sticks in his hand*]. What have you got there, daddiest?

CAPTAIN SHOTOVER. Dynamite.

MRS HUSHABYE. Youve been to the gravel pit. Dont drop it about the house: theres a dear. [*She goes into the garden, where the evening light is now very red*].

HECTOR. Listen, O sage. How long dare you concentrate on a feeling without risking having it fixed in your consciousness all the rest of your life?

CAPTAIN SHOTOVER. Ninety minutes. An hour and a half. [*He goes into the pantry*].

Hector, left alone, contracts his brows, and falls into a day-dream. He does not move for some time. Then he folds his arms. Then, throwing his hands behind him, and gripping one with the other, he strides tragically once to and fro. Suddenly he snatches his walking-stick from the teak table, and draws it; for it is a sword-stick. He fights a desperate duel with an imaginary antagonist, and after many vicissitudes runs him through the body up to the hilt. He sheathes his sword and throws it on the sofa, falling into another reverie as he does so. He looks straight into the eyes of an imaginary woman; seizes her by the arms; and says in a deep and thrilling tone "Do you love me!" The Captain comes out of the pantry at this moment; and Hector, caught with his arms stretched out and his fists clenched, has to account for his attitude by going through a series of gymnastic exercises.

CAPTAIN SHOTOVER. That sort of strength is no good. You will never be as strong as a gorilla.

HECTOR. What is the dynamite for?

CAPTAIN SHOTOVER. To kill fellows like Mangan.

HECTOR. No use. They will always be able to buy more dynamite than you.

CAPTAIN SHOTOVER. I will make a dynamite that he cannot explode.

HECTOR. And that you can, eh?

CAPTAIN SHOTOVER. Yes: when I have attained the seventh degree of concentration.

HECTOR. Whats the use of that? You never do attain it.

CAPTAIN SHOTOVER. What then is to be done? Are we to be kept for ever in the mud by these hogs to whom the universe is nothing but a machine for greasing their bristles and filling their snouts ?

HECTOR. Are Mangan's bristles worse than Randall's lovelocks?

CAPTAIN SHOTOVER. We must win powers of life and death over them both. I refuse to die until I have invented the means.

HECTOR. Who are we that we should judge them?

CAPTAIN SHOTOVER. What are they that they should judge us? Yet they do, unhesitatingly. There is enmity between our seed and their seed. They know it and act on it, strangling our souls. They believe in themselves. When we believe in ourselves, we shall kill them.

HECTOR. It is the same seed. You forget that your pirate has a very nice daughter. Mangan's son may be a Plato: Randall's a Shelley. What was my father?

CAPTAIN SHOTOVER. The damndest scoundrel I ever met. [*He replaces the drawing-board; sits down at the table; and begins to mix a wash of color*].

HECTOR. Precisely. Well, dare you kill his innocent grandchildren?

CAPTAIN SHOTOVER. They are mine also.

HECTOR. Just so. We are members one of another. [*He throws himself carelessly on the sofa*]. I tell you I have often thought of this killing of human vermin. Many men have thought of it. Decent men are like Daniel in the lion's den: their survival is a miracle; and they do not always survive. We live among the Mangans and Randalls and Billie Dunns as they, poor devils, live among the disease germs and the doctors and the lawyers and the parsons and the restaurant chefs and the tradesmen and the servants and all the rest of the parasites and blackmailers. What are our terrors to theirs? Give me the power to kill them; and I'll spare them in sheer—

CAPTAIN SHOTOVER [*cutting in sharply*] Fellow feeling?

HECTOR. No. I should kill myself if I believed that. I must believe that my spark, small as it is, is divine, and that the red light over their door is hell fire. I should spare them in simple magnanimous pity.

CAPTAIN SHOTOVER. You cant spare them until you have the power to kill them. At present they have the power to kill you. There are millions of blacks over the water for them to train and let loose on us. Theyre going to do it. Theyre doing it already.

HECTOR. They are too stupid to use their power.

CAPTAIN SHOTOVER [*throwing down his brush and coming to the end of the sofa*] Do not deceive yourself: they do use it. We kill the better half of ourselves every day to propitiate them. The knowledge that these people are there to render all our aspirations barren prevents us having the aspirations. And when we are tempted to seek their destruction they bring forth demons to delude us, disguised as pretty daughters, and singers and poets and the like, for whose sake we spare them.

HECTOR [*sitting up and leaning towards him*] May not Hesione be such a demon, brought forth by you lest I should slay you?

CAPTAIN SHOTOVER. That is possible. She has used you up, and left you nothing but dreams, as some women do.

HECTOR. Vampire women, demon women.

CAPTAIN SHOTOVER. Men think the world well lost for them, and lose it accordingly. Who are the men that do things? The husbands of the shrew and of the drunkard, the men with the thorn in the flesh. [*Walking distractedly away towards the pantry*] I must think these things out. [*Turning suddenly*] But I go on with the dynamite none the less. I will discover a ray mightier than any X-ray: a mind ray that will explode the ammunition in the belt of my adversary before he can point his gun at me. And I must hurry. I am old: I have no time to waste in talk [*he is about to go into the pantry, and Hector is making for the hall, when Hesione comes back*].

MRS HUSHABYE. Daddiest: you and Hector must come and help me to entertain all these people. What on earth were you shouting about?

HECTOR [*stopping in the act of turning the doorhandle*] He is madder than usual.

MRS HUSHABYE. We all are.

HECTOR. I must change [*he resumes his door opening*].

MRS HUSHABYE. Stop, stop. Come back, both of you. Come back. [*They return, reluctantly*]. Money is running short.

HECTOR. Money! Where are my April dividends?

MRS HUSHABYE. Where is the snow that fell last year?

CAPTAIN SHOTOVER. Where is all the money you had for that patent lifeboat I invented?

MRS HUSHABYE. Five hundred pounds; and I have made it last since Easter!

CAPTAIN SHOTOVER. Since Easter! Barely four months! Monstrous extravagance! I could live for seven years on £500.

MRS HUSHABYE. Not keeping open house as we do here, daddiest.

CAPTAIN SHOTOVER. Only £500 for that lifeboat! I got twelve thousand for the invention before that.

MRS HUSHABYE. Yes, dear; but that was for the ship with the magnetic keel that sucked up submarines. Living at the rate we do, you cannot afford life-saving inventions. Cant you think of something that will murder half Europe at one bang?

CAPTAIN SHOTOVER. No. I am ageing fast. My mind does not dwell on slaughter as it did when I was a boy. Why doesnt your husband invent something? He does nothing but tell lies to women.

HECTOR. Well, that is a form of invention, is it not? However, you are right: I ought to support my wife.

MRS HUSHABYE. Indeed you shall do nothing of the sort: I should never see you from breakfast to dinner. I want my husband.

HECTOR [*bitterly*] I might as well be your lapdog.

MRS HUSHABYE. Do you want to be my breadwinner, like the other poor husbands?

HECTOR. No, by thunder! What a damned creature a husband is anyhow!

MRS HUSHABYE [*to the Captain*] What about that harpoon cannon?

CAPTAIN SHOTOVER. No use. It kills whales, not men.

MRS HUSHABYE. Why not? You fire the harpoon out of a cannon. It sticks in the enemy's general; you wind him in; and there you are.

HECTOR. You are your father's daughter, Hesione.

CAPTAIN SHOTOVER. There is something in it. Not to wind in generals: they are not dangerous. But one could fire a grapnel and wind in a machine gun or even a tank. I will think it out.

MRS HUSHABYE [*squeezing the Captain's arm affectionately*] Saved! You are a darling, daddiest. Now we must go back to these dreadful people and entertain them.

CAPTAIN SHOTOVER. They have had no dinner. Dont forget that.

HECTOR. Neither have I. And it is dark: it must be all hours.

MRS HUSHABYE. Oh, Guinness will produce some sort of dinner for them. The servants always take jolly good care that there is food in the house.

CAPTAIN SHOTOVER [*raising a strange wail in the darkness*] What a house! What a daughter!

MRS HUSHABYE [*raving*] What a father!

HECTOR [*following suit*] What a husband!

CAPTAIN SHOTOVER. Is there no thunder in heaven?

HECTOR. Is there no beauty, no bravery, on earth?

MRS HUSHABYE. What do men want? They have their food, their firesides, their clothes mended, and our love at the end of the day. Why are they not satisfied? Why do they envy us the pain with which we bring them into the world, and make strange dangers and torments for themselves to be even with us?

CAPTAIN SHOTOVER [*weirdly chanting*]
I built a house for my daughters, and
    opened the doors thereof,
That men might come for their choosing, and
    their betters spring from their love;
But one of them married a numskull;

HECTOR [*taking up the rhythm*]
                The other a liar wed;

MRS HUSHABYE [*completing the stanza*]
And now must she lie beside him, even as
    she made her bed.

LADY UTTERWORD [*calling from the garden*] Hesione! Hesione! Where are you?

HECTOR. The cat is on the tiles.

MRS HUSHABYE. Coming, darling, coming [*she goes quickly into the garden*].

The Captain goes back to his place at the table.

HECTOR [*going into the hall*] Shall I turn up the lights for you?

CAPTAIN SHOTOVER. No. Give me deeper darkness. Money is not made in the light.

ACT II

The same room, with the lights turned up and the curtains drawn. Ellie comes in, followed by Mangan. Both are dressed for dinner. She strolls to the drawing-table. He comes between the table and the wicker chair.

MANGAN. What a dinner! I dont call it a dinner: I call it a meal.

ELLIE. I am accustomed to meals, Mr Mangan, and very lucky to get them. Besides, the captain cooked some maccaroni for me.

MANGAN [*shuddering liverishly*] Too rich: I cant eat such things. I suppose it's because I have to work so much with my brain. Thats the worst of being a man of business: you are always thinking, thinking, thinking. By the way, now that we are alone, may I take the opportunity to come to a little understanding with you?

ELLIE [*settling into the draughtsman's seat*] Certainly. I should like to.

MANGAN [*taken aback*] Should you? That surprises me; for I thought I noticed this afternoon that you avoided me all you could. Not for the first time either.

ELLIE. I was very tired and upset. I wasn't used to the ways of this extraordinary house. Please forgive me.

MANGAN. Oh, thats all right: I dont mind. But Captain Shotover has been talking to me about you. You and me, you know.

ELLIE [*interested*] The Captain! What did he say?

MANGAN. Well, he noticed the difference between our ages.

ELLIE. He notices everything.

MANGAN. You dont mind, then?

ELLIE. Of course I know quite well that our engagement—

MANGAN. Oh! you call it an engagement.

ELLIE. Well, isnt it?

MANGAN. Oh, yes, yes: no doubt it is if you hold to it. This is the first time youve used the word; and I didnt quite know where we stood: thats all. [*He sits down in the wicker chair; and resigns himself to allow her to lead the conversation*]. You were saying—?

ELLIE. Was I? I forget. Tell me. Do you like this part of the country? I heard you ask Mr Hushabye at dinner whether there are any nice houses to let down here.

MANGAN. I like the place. The air suits me. I shouldnt be surprised if I settled down here.

ELLIE. Nothing would please me better. The air suits me too. And I want to be near Hesione.

MANGAN [*with growing uneasiness*] The air may suit us; but the question is, should we suit one another? Have you thought about that?

ELLIE. Mr Mangan: we must be sensible, mustnt we? It's no use pretending that we are Romeo and Juliet. But we can get on very well together if we choose to make the best of it. Your kindness of heart will make it easy for me.

MANGAN [*leaning forward, with the beginning of something like deliberate unpleasantness in his voice*] Kindness of heart, eh? I ruined your father, didnt I?

ELLIE. Oh, not intentionally.

MANGAN. Yes I did. Ruined him on purpose.

ELLIE. On purpose!

MANGAN. Not out of ill-nature, you know. And youll admit that I kept a job for him when I had finished with him. But business is business; and I ruined him as a matter of business.

ELLIE. I dont understand how that can be. Are you trying to make me feel that I need not be grateful to you, so that I may choose freely?

MANGAN [*rising aggressively*] No. I mean what I say.

ELLIE. But how could it possibly do you any good to ruin my father? The money he lost was yours.

MANGAN [*with a sour laugh*] W a s mine! It is mine, Miss Ellie, and all the money the other fellows lost too. [*He shoves his hands into his pockets and shews his teeth*]. I just smoked them out like a hive of bees. What do you say to that? A bit of a shock, eh?

ELLIE. It would have been, this morning. N o w! you cant think how little it matters. But it's quite interesting. Only, you must explain it to me. I dont understand it. [*Propping her elbows on the drawing-board and her chin on her hands, she composes herself to listen with a combination of conscious curiosity with unconscious contempt which provokes him to more and more unpleasantness, and an attempt at patronage of her ignorance*].

MANGAN. Of course you dont understand: what do y o u know about business? You just listen and learn. Your father's business was a new business; and I dont start new businesses: I let other fellows start them. They put all their money and their friends' money into starting them. They wear out their souls and bodies trying to make a success of them. Theyre what you call enthusiasts. But the first dead lift of the thing is too much for them; and they havnt enough financial experience. In a year or so they have either to let the whole show go bust, or sell out to a new lot of fellows for a few deferred ordinary shares: that is, if theyre lucky enough to get anything at all. As likely as not the very same thing happens to the new lot. They put in more money and a couple of years more work; and then perhaps t h e y have to sell out to a third lot. If it's really a big thing the third lot will have to sell out too, and leave t h e i r work and t h e i r money behind them. And thats where the real business man comes in: where I come in.

But I'm cleverer than some: I dont mind dropping a little money to start the process. I took your father's measure. I saw that he had a sound idea, and that he would work himself silly for it if he got the chance. I saw that he was a child in business, and was dead certain to outrun his expenses and be in too great a hurry to wait for his market. I knew that the surest way to ruin a man who doesnt know how to handle money is to give him some. I explained my idea to some friends in the city, and they found the money; for I take no risks in ideas, even when theyre my own. Your father, and the friends that ventured their money with him were no more to me than a heap of squeezed lemons. Youve been wasting your gratitude: my kind heart is all rot. I'm sick of it. When I see your father beaming at me with his moist, grateful eyes, regularly wallowing in gratitude, I sometimes feel I must tell him the truth or burst. What stops me is that I know he wouldnt believe me. He'd think it was my modesty, as you did just now. He'd think anything rather than the truth, which is that he's a blamed fool, and I am a man that knows how to take care of himself. [*He throws himself back into the big chair with large self-approval*]. Now what do you think of me, Miss Ellie?

ELLIE [*dropping her hands*] How strange! that my mother, who knew nothing at all about business, should have been quite right about you! She always said—not before papa, of course, but to us children—that you were just that sort of man.

MANGAN [*sitting up, much hurt*] Oh! did she? And yet she'd have let you marry me.

ELLIE. Well, you see, Mr Mangan, my mother married a very good man—for whatever you may think of my father as a man of business, he is the soul of goodness—and she is not at all keen on my doing the same.

MANGAN. Anyhow, you dont want to marry me now, do you?

ELLIE [*very calmly*] Oh, I think so. Why not?

MANGAN [*rising aghast*] Why not!

ELLIE. I dont see why we shouldnt get on very well together.

MANGAN. Well, but look here, you know— [*he stops, quite at a loss*].

ELLIE [*patiently*] Well?

MANGAN. Well, I thought you were rather particular about people's characters.

ELLIE. If we women were particular about

men's characters, we should never get married at all, Mr Mangan.

MANGAN. A child like you talking of "we women"! What next! Youre not in earnest?

ELLIE. Yes I am. Arnt you?

MANGAN. You mean to hold me to it?

ELLIE. Do you wish to back out of it?

MANGAN. Oh no. Not exactly back out of it.

ELLIE. Well?

He has nothing to say. With a long whispered whistle, he drops into the wicker chair and stares before him like a beggared gambler. But a cunning look soon comes into his face. He leans over towards her on his right elbow, and speaks in a low steady voice.

MANGAN. Suppose I told you I was in love with another woman!

ELLIE [*echoing him*] Suppose I told you I was in love with another man!

MANGAN [*bouncing angrily out of his chair*] I'm not joking.

ELLIE. Who told you *I* was?

MANGAN. I tell you I'm serious. Youre too young to be serious; but youll have to believe me. I want to be near your friend Mrs Hushabye. I'm in love with her. Now the murder's out.

ELLIE. I want to be near your friend Mr Hushabye. I'm in love with him. [*She rises and adds with a frank air*] Now we are in one another's confidence, we shall be real friends. Thank you for telling me.

MANGAN [*almost beside himself*] Do you think I'll be made a convenience of like this?

ELLIE. Come, Mr Mangan! you made a business convenience of my father. Well, a woman's business is marriage. Why shouldnt I make a domestic convenience of you?

MANGAN. Because I dont choose, see? Because I'm not a silly gull like your father. Thats why.

ELLIE [*with serene contempt*] You are not good enough to clean my father's boots, Mr Mangan; and I am paying you a great compliment in condescending to make a convenience of you, as you call it. Of course you are free to throw over our engagement if you like; but, if you do, youll never enter Hesione's house again: I will take care of that.

MANGAN [*gasping*] You little devil, youve done me [*On the point of collapsing into the big chair again he recovers himself*] Wait a bit, though: youre not so cute as you think. You cant beat Boss Mangan as easy as that.

Suppose I go straight to Mrs Hushabye and tell her that youre in love with her husband.

ELLIE. She knows it.

MANGAN. You told her!!!

ELLIE. She told me.

MANGAN [*clutching at his bursting temples*] Oh, this is a crazy house. Or else I'm going clean off my chump. Is she making a swop with you—she to have your husband and you to have hers?

ELLIE. Well, you dont want us both, do you?

MANGAN [*throwing himself into the chair distractedly*] My brain wont stand it. My head's going to split. Help! Help me to hold it. Quick: hold it: squeeze it. Save me. [*Ellie comes behind his chair; clasps his head hard for a moment; then begins to draw her hands from his forehead back to his ears*]. Thank you. [*Drowsily*] Thats very refreshing. [*Waking a little*] Dont you hypnotize me, though. Ive seen men made fools of by hypnotism.

ELLIE [*steadily*] Be quiet. Ive seen men made fools of without hypnotism.

MANGAN [*humbly*] You dont dislike touching me, I hope. You never touched me before, I noticed.

ELLIE. Not since you fell in love naturally with a grown-up nice woman, who will never expect you to make love to her. And I will never expect him to make love to me.

MANGAN. He may, though.

ELLIE [*making her passes rhythmically*] Hush. Go to sleep. Do you hear? You are to go to sleep, go to sleep, go to sleep; be quiet, deeply deeply quiet; sleep, sleep, sleep, sleep, sleep.

He falls asleep. Ellie steals away; turns the light out; and goes into the garden.

Nurse Guinness opens the door and is seen in the light which comes in from the hall.

GUINNESS [*speaking to someone outside*] Mr Mangan's not here, duckie: theres no one here. It's all dark.

MRS HUSHABYE [*without*] Try the garden. Mr Dunn and I will be in my boudoir. Shew him the way.

GUINNESS. Yes, ducky. [*She makes for the garden door in the dark; stumbles over the sleeping Mangan; and screams*] Ahoo! Oh Lord, sir! I beg your pardon, I'm sure: I didnt see you in the dark. Who is it? [*She goes back to the door and turns on the light*]. Oh, Mr Mangan, sir, I hope I havnt hurt you plumping into your lap like that. [*Coming to him*] I was

2 c 2

looking for you, sir. Mrs Hushabye says will you please—[*noticing that he remains quite insensible*] Oh, my good Lord, I hope I havnt killed him. Sir! Mr Mangan! Sir! [*She shakes him; and he is rolling inertly off the chair on the floor when she holds him up and props him against the cushion*]. Miss Hessy! Miss Hessy! Quick, doty darling. Miss Hessy! [*Mrs Hushabye comes in from the hall, followed by Mazzini Dunn*]. Oh, Miss Hessy, Ive been and killed him.

Mazzini runs round the back of the chair to Mangan's right hand, and sees that the nurse's words are apparently only too true.

MAZZINI. What tempted you to commit such a crime, woman?

MRS HUSHABYE [*trying not to laugh*] Do you mean you did it on purpose?

GUINNESS. Now is it likely I'd kill any man on purpose. I fell over him in the dark; and I'm a pretty tidy weight. He never spoke nor moved until I shook him; and then he would have dropped dead on the floor. Isnt it tiresome?

MRS HUSHABYE [*going past the nurse to Mangan's side, and inspecting him less credulously than Mazzini*] Nonsense! he is not dead: he is only asleep. I can see him breathing.

GUINNESS. But why wont he wake?

MAZZINI [*speaking very politely into Mangan's ear*] Mangan! My dear Mangan! [*he blows into Mangan's ear*].

MRS HUSHABYE. Thats no good [*she shakes him vigorously*]. Mr Mangan: wake up. Do you hear? [*He begins to roll over*]. Oh! Nurse, nurse: he's falling: help me.

Nurse Guinness rushes to the rescue. With Mazzini's assistance, Mangan is propped safely up again.

GUINNESS [*behind the chair; bending over to test the case with her nose*] Would he be drunk, do you think, pet?

MRS HUSHABYE. Had he any of papa's rum?

MAZZINI. It cant be that: he is most abstemious. I am afraid he drank too much formerly, and has to drink too little now. You know, Mrs Hushabye, I really think he has been hypnotized.

GUINNESS. Hip no what, sir?

MAZZINI. One evening at home, after we had seen a hypnotizing performance, the children began playing at it; and Ellie stroked my head. I assure you I went off dead asleep; and they had to send for a professional to wake me up after I had slept eighteen hours. They had to carry me upstairs; and as the poor children were not very strong, they let me slip; and I rolled right down the whole flight and never woke up. [*Mrs Hushabye splutters*]. Oh, you may laugh, Mrs Hushabye; but I might have been killed.

MRS HUSHABYE. I couldnt have helped laughing even if you had been, Mr Dunn. So Ellie has hypnotized him. What fun!

MAZZINI. Oh no, no, no. It was such a terrible lesson to her: nothing would induce her to try such a thing again.

MRS HUSHABYE. Then who did it? *I* didnt.

MAZZINI. I thought perhaps the Captain might have done it unintentionally. He is so fearfully magnetic: I feel vibrations whenever he comes close to me.

GUINNESS. The Captain will get him out of it anyhow, sir: I'll back him for that. I'll go fetch him [*she makes for the pantry*].

MRS HUSHABYE. Wait a bit. [*To Mazzini*] You say he is all right for eighteen hours?

MAZZINI. Well, *I* was asleep for eighteen hours.

MRS HUSHABYE. Were you any the worse for it?

MAZZINI. I dont quite remember. They had poured brandy down my throat, you see; and—

MRS HUSHABYE. Quite. Anyhow, you survived. Nurse, darling: go and ask Miss Dunn to come to us here. Say I want to speak to her particularly. You will find her with Mr Hushabye probably.

GUINNESS. I think not, ducky: Miss Addy is with him. But I'll find her and send her to you. [*She goes out into the garden*].

MRS HUSHABYE [*calling Mazzini's attention to the figure on the chair*] Now, Mr Dunn, look. Just look. Look hard. Do you still intend to sacrifice your daughter to that thing?

MAZZINI [*troubled*] You have completely upset me, Mrs Hushabye, by all you have said to me. That anyone could imagine that I—*I*, a consecrated soldier of freedom, if I may say so—could sacrifice Ellie to anybody or anyone, or that I should ever have dreamed of forcing her inclinations in any way, is a most painful blow to my—well, I suppose you would say to my good opinion of myself.

MRS HUSHABYE [*rather stolidly*] Sorry.

MAZZINI [*looking forlornly at the body*] What is your objection to poor Mangan, Mrs Hushabye? He looks all right to me. But then I am so accustomed to him.

MRS HUSHABYE. Have you no heart? Have you no sense? Look at the brute! Think of poor weak innocent Ellie in the clutches of this slavedriver, who spends his life making thousands of rough violent workmen bend to his will and sweat for him: a man accustomed to have great masses of iron beaten into shape for him by steam-hammers! to fight with women and girls over a halfpenny an hour ruthlessly! a captain of industry, I think you call him, dont you? Are you going to fling your delicate, sweet, helpless child into such a beast's claws just because he will keep her in an expensive house and make her wear diamonds to shew how rich he is?

MAZZINI [staring at her in wide-eyed amazement] Bless you, dear Mrs Hushabye, what romantic ideas of business you have! Poor dear Mangan isnt a bit like that.

MRS HUSHABYE [scornfully] Poor dear Mangan indeed!

MAZZINI. But he doesnt know anything about machinery. He never goes near the men: he couldnt manage them: he is afraid of them. I never can get him to take the least interest in the works: he hardly knows more about them than you do. People are cruelly unjust to Mangan: they think he is all rugged strength just because his manners are bad.

MRS HUSHABYE. Do you mean to tell me he isnt strong enough to crush poor little Ellie?

MAZZINI. Of course it's very hard to say how any marriage will turn out; but speaking for myself, I should say that he wont have a dog's chance against Ellie. You know, Ellie has remarkable strength of character. I think it is because I taught her to like Shakespear when she was very young.

MRS HUSHABYE [contemptuously] Shakespear! The next thing you will tell me is that you could have made a great deal more money than Mangan. [She retires to the sofa, and sits down at the port end of it in the worst of humors].

MAZZINI [following her and taking the other end] No: I'm no good at making money. I dont care enough for it, somehow. I'm not ambitious! that must be it. Mangan is wonderful about money: he thinks of nothing else. He is so dreadfully afraid of being poor. I am always thinking of other things: even at the works I think of the things we are doing and not of what they cost. And the worst of it is, poor Mangan doesnt know what to do with his money when he gets it. He is such a baby that he doesnt know even what to eat and drink: he has ruined his liver eating and drinking the wrong things; and now he can hardly eat at all. Ellie will diet him splendidly. You will be surprised when you come to know him better: he is really the most helpless of mortals. You get quite a protective feeling towards him.

MRS HUSHABYE. Then who manages his business, pray?

MAZZINI. I do. And of course other people like me.

MRS HUSHABYE. Footling people, you mean.

MAZZINI. I suppose youd think us so.

MRS HUSHABYE. And pray why dont you do without him if youre all so much cleverer?

MAZZINI. Oh, we couldnt: we should ruin the business in a year. I've tried: and I know. We should spend too much on everything. We should improve the quality of the goods and make them too dear. We should be sentimental about the hard cases among the workpeople. But Mangan keeps us in order. He is down on us about every extra halfpenny. We could never do without him. You see, he will sit up all night thinking of how to save sixpence. Wont Ellie make him jump, though, when she takes his house in hand!

MRS HUSHABYE. Then the creature is a fraud even as a captain of industry!

MAZZINI. I am afraid all the captains of industry are what you call frauds, Mrs Hushabye. Of course there are some manufacturers who really do understand their own works; but they dont make as high a rate of profit as Mangan does. I assure you Mangan is quite a good fellow in his way. He means well.

MRS HUSHABYE. He doesnt look well. He is not in his first youth, is he?

MAZZINI. After all, no husband is in his first youth for very long, Mrs Hushabye. And men cant afford to marry in their first youth nowadays.

MRS HUSHABYE. Now if I said that, it would sound witty. Why cant you say it wittily? What on earth is the matter with you? Why dont you inspire everybody with confidence? with respect?

MAZZINI [humbly] I think that what is the matter with me is that I am poor. You dont know what that means at home. Mind: I dont say they have ever complained. Theyve all been wonderful: theyve been proud of my poverty. Theyve even joked about it quite often. But my wife has had a very poor time of it. She has been quite resigned—

MRS HUSHABYE [*shuddering involuntarily*]!!

MAZZINI. There! You see, Mrs Hushabye. I dont want Ellie to live on resignation.

MRS HUSHABYE. Do you want her to have to resign herself to living with a man she doesnt love?

MAZZINI [*wistfully*] Are you sure that would be worse than living with a man she did love, if he was a footling person?

MRS HUSHABYE [*relaxing her contemptuous attitude, quite interested in Mazzini now*] You know, I really think you must love Ellie very much; for you become quite clever when you talk about her.

MAZZINI. I didnt know I was so very stupid on other subjects.

MRS HUSHABYE. You are, sometimes.

MAZZINI [*turning his head away; for his eyes are wet*] I have learnt a good deal about myself from you, Mrs Hushabye; and I'm afraid I shall not be the happier for your plain speaking. But if you thought I needed it to make me think of Ellie's happiness you were very much mistaken.

MRS HUSHABYE [*leaning towards him kindly*] Have I been a beast?

MAZZINI [*pulling himself together*] It doesnt matter about me, Mrs Hushabye. I think you like Ellie; and that is enough for me.

MRS HUSHABYE. I'm beginning to like you a little. I perfectly loathed you at first. I thought you the most odious, self-satisfied, boresome elderly prig I ever met.

MAZZINI [*resigned, and now quite cheerful*] I daresay I am all that. I never have been a favorite with gorgeous women like you. They always frighten me.

MRS HUSHABYE [*pleased*] Am I a gorgeous woman, Mazzini? I shall fall in love with you presently.

MAZZINI [*with placid gallantry*] No you wont, Hesione. But you would be quite safe. Would you believe it that quite a lot of women have flirted with me because I am quite safe? But they get tired of me for the same reason.

MRS HUSHABYE [*mischievously*] Take care. You may not be so safe as you think.

MAZZINI. Oh yes, quite safe. You see, I have been in love really: the sort of love that only happens once. [*Softly*] Thats why Ellie is such a lovely girl.

MRS HUSHABYE. Well, really, you are coming out. Are you quite sure you wont let me tempt you into a second grand passion?

MAZZINI. Quite. It wouldnt be natural. The fact is, you dont strike on my box, Mrs Hushabye; and I certainly dont strike on yours.

MRS HUSHABYE. I see. Your marriage was a safety match.

MAZZINI. What a very witty application of the expression I used! I should never have thought of it.

Ellie comes in from the garden, looking anything but happy.

MRS HUSHABYE [*rising*] Oh! here is Ellie at last. [*She goes behind the sofa*].

ELLIE [*on the threshold of the starboard door*] Guinness said you wanted me: you and papa.

MRS HUSHABYE. You have kept us waiting so long that it almost came to—well, never mind. Your father is a very wonderful man [*she ruffles his hair affectionately*]: the only one I ever met who could resist me when I made myself really agreeable. [*She comes to the big chair, on Mangan's left*]. Come here. I have something to shew you. [*Ellie strolls listlessly to the other side of the chair*]. Look.

ELLIE [*contemplating Mangan without interest*] I know. He is only asleep. We had a talk after dinner; and he fell asleep in the middle of it.

MRS HUSHABYE. You did it, Ellie. You put him asleep.

MAZZINI [*rising quickly and coming to the back of the chair*] Oh, I hope not. Did you, Ellie?

ELLIE [*wearily*] He asked me to.

MAZZINI. But it's dangerous. You know what happened to me.

ELLIE [*utterly indifferent*] Oh, I daresay I can wake him. If not, somebody else can.

MRS HUSHABYE. It doesnt matter, anyhow, because I have at last persuaded your father that you dont want to marry him.

ELLIE [*suddenly coming out of her listlessness, much vexed*] But why did you do that, Hesione? I do want to marry him. I fully intend to marry him.

MAZZINI. Are you quite sure, Ellie? Mrs Hushabye has made me feel that I may have been thoughtless and selfish about it.

ELLIE [*very clearly and steadily*] Papa. When Mrs Hushabye takes it on herself to explain to you what I think or dont think, shut your ears tight; and shut your eyes too. Hesione knows nothing about me: she hasnt the least notion of the sort of person I am, and never will. I promise you I wont do anything I dont want to do and mean to do for my own sake.

MAZZINI. You are quite, quite sure?

ELLIE. Quite, quite sure. Now you must go away and leave me to talk to Mrs Hushabye.

MAZZINI. But I should like to hear. Shall I be in the way?

ELLIE [*inexorable*] I had rather talk to her alone.

MAZZINI [*affectionately*] Oh, well, I know what a nuisance parents are, dear. I will be good and go. [*He goes to the garden door*]. By the way, do you remember the address of that professional who woke me up? Dont you think I had better telegraph to him.

MRS HUSHABYE [*moving towards the sofa*] It's too late to telegraph tonight.

MAZZINI. I suppose so. I do hope he'll wake up in the course of the night. [*He goes out into the garden*].

ELLIE [*turning vigorously on Hesione the moment her father is out of the room*] Hesione: what the devil do you mean by making mischief with my father about Mangan?

MRS HUSHABYE [*promptly losing her temper*] Dont you dare speak to me like that, you little minx. Remember that you are in my house.

ELLIE. Stuff! Why dont you mind your own business? What is it to you whether I choose to marry Mangan or not?

MRS HUSHABYE. Do you suppose you can bully me, you miserable little matrimonial adventurer?

ELLIE. Every woman who hasnt any money is a matrimonial adventurer. It's easy for you to talk: you have never known what it is to want money; and you can pick up men as if they were daisies. I am poor and respectable—

MRS HUSHABYE [*interrupting*] Ho! respectable! How did you pick up Mangan? How did you pick up my husband? You have the audacity to tell me that I am a—a—a—

ELLIE. A siren. So you are. You were born to lead men by the nose: if you werent, Marcus would have waited for me, perhaps.

MRS HUSHABYE [*suddenly melting and half laughing*] Oh, my poor Ellie, my pettikins, my unhappy darling! I am so sorry about Hector. But what can I do? It's not my fault: I'd give him to you if I could.

ELLIE. I dont blame you for that.

MRS HUSHABYE. What a brute I was to quarrel with you and call you names! Do kiss me and say youre not angry with me.

ELLIE [*fiercely*] Oh, dont slop and gush and be sentimental. Dont you see that unless I can be hard—as hard as nails—I shall go mad. I dont care a damn about your calling me names: do you think a woman in my situation can feel a few hard words?

MRS HUSHABYE. Poor little woman! Poor little situation!

ELLIE. I suppose you think youre being sympathetic. You are just foolish and stupid and selfish. You see me getting a smasher right in the face that kills a whole part of my life: the best part that can never come again; and you think you can help me over it by a little coaxing and kissing. When I want all the strength I can get to lean on: something iron, something stony, I dont care how cruel it is, you go all mushy and want to slobber over me. I'm not angry; I'm not unfriendly; but for God's sake do pull yourself together; and dont think that because youre on velvet and always have been, women who are in hell can take it as easily as you.

MRS HUSHABYE [*shrugging her shoulders*] Very well. [*She sits down on the sofa in her old place*]. But I warn you that when I am neither coaxing and kissing nor laughing, I am just wondering how much longer I can stand living in this cruel, damnable world. You object to the siren: well, I drop the siren. You want to rest your wounded bosom against a grindstone. Well [*folding her arms*], here is the grindstone.

ELLIE [*sitting down beside her, appeased*] Thats better: you really have the trick of falling in with everyone's mood; but you dont understand, because you are not the sort of woman for whom there is only one man and only one chance.

MRS HUSHABYE. I certainly dont understand how your marrying that object [*indicating Mangan*] will console you for not being able to marry Hector.

ELLIE. Perhaps you dont understand why I was quite a nice girl this morning, and am now neither a girl nor particularly nice.

MRS HUSHABYE. Oh yes I do. It's because you have made up your mind to do something despicable and wicked.

ELLIE. I dont think so, Hesione. I must make the best of my ruined house.

MRS HUSHABYE. Pooh! Youll get over it. Your house isnt ruined.

ELLIE. Of course I shall get over it. You dont suppose I'm going to sit down and die of a broken heart, I hope, or be an old maid living on a pittance from the Sick and Indigent Roomkeepers' Association. But my heart is broken, all the same. What I mean by that is that I know that what has happened to me with Marcus will not happen to me ever again. In the world for me there is Marcus and a lot of other men of whom one is just the same as another. Well, if I cant have love, thats no reason why I should have poverty. If Mangan has nothing else, he has money.

MRS HUSHABYE. And are there no young men with money?

ELLIE. Not within my reach. Besides, a young man would have the right to expect love from me, and would perhaps leave me when he found I could not give it to him. Rich young men can get rid of their wives, you know, pretty cheaply. But this object, as you call him, can expect nothing more from me than I am prepared to give him.

MRS HUSHABYE. He will be your owner, remember. If he buys you, he will make the bargain pay him and not you. Ask your father.

ELLIE [rising and strolling to the chair to contemplate their subject] You need not trouble on that score, Hesione. I have more to give Boss Mangan than he has to give me: it is I who am buying him, and at a pretty good price too, I think. Women are better at that sort of bargain than men. I have taken the Boss's measure; and ten Boss Mangans shall not prevent me doing far more as I please as his wife than I have ever been able to do as a poor girl. [Stooping to the recumbent figure] Shall they, Boss? I think not. [She passes on to the drawing-table, and leans against the end of it, facing the windows]. I shall not have to spend most of my time wondering how long my gloves will last, anyhow.

MRS HUSHABYE [rising superbly] Ellie: you are a wicked sordid little beast. And to think that I actually condescended to fascinate that creature there to save you from him! Well, let me tell you this: if you make this disgusting match, you will never see Hector again if I can help it.

ELLIE [unmoved] I nailed Mangan by telling him that if he did not marry me he should never see you again [she lifts herself on her wrists and seats herself on the end of the table].

MRS HUSHABYE [recoiling] Oh!

ELLIE. So you see I am not unprepared for your playing that trump against me. Well, you just try it: thats all. I should have made a man of Marcus, not a household pet.

MRS HUSHABYE [flaming] You dare!

ELLIE [looking almost dangerous] Set him thinking about me if you dare.

MRS HUSHABYE. Well, of all the impudent little fiends I ever met! Hector says there is a certain point at which the only answer you can give to a man who breaks all the rules is to knock him down. What would you say if I were to box your ears?

ELLIE [calmly] I should pull your hair.

MRS HUSHABYE [mischievously] That wouldnt hurt me. Perhaps it comes off at night.

ELLIE [so taken aback that she drops off the table and runs to her] Oh, you dont mean to say, Hesione, that your beautiful black hair is false?

MRS HUSHABYE [patting it] Dont tell Hector. He believes in it.

ELLIE [groaning] Oh! Even the hair that ensnared him false! Everything false!

MRS HUSHABYE. Pull it and try. Other women can snare men in their hair; but I can swing a baby on mine. Aha! you cant do that, Goldylocks.

ELLIE [heartbroken] No. You have stolen my babies.

MRS HUSHABYE. Pettikins: dont make me cry. You know, what you said about my making a household pet of him is a little true. Perhaps he ought to have waited for you. Would any other woman on earth forgive you?

ELLIE. Oh, what right had you to take him all for yourself! [Pulling herself together] There! You couldnt help it: neither of us could help it. He couldnt help it. No: dont say anything more: I cant bear it. Let us wake the object. [She begins stroking Mangan's head, reversing the movement with which she put him to sleep]. Wake up, do you hear? You are to wake up at once. Wake up, wake up, wake—

MANGAN [bouncing out of the chair in a fury and turning on them] Wake up! So you think Ive been asleep, do you? [He kicks the chair violently back out of his way, and gets between them]. You throw me into a trance so that I cant move hand or foot—I might have been buried alive! it's a mercy I wasnt—and then you think I was only asleep. If youd let me drop the two times you rolled me about, my nose would have been flattened for life against the floor. But Ive found you all out, anyhow. I know the sort of people I'm among now. Ive heard every word youve said, you and your precious father, and [to Mrs Hushabye] you too. So I'm an object, am I? I'm a thing, am I? I'm a fool that hasnt sense enough to feed myself properly, am I? I'm afraid of the men that would starve if it werent for the wages I give them, am I? I'm nothing but a disgusting old skinflint to be made a convenience of by designing women and fool managers of my works, am I? I'm—

MRS HUSHABYE [with the most elegant aplomb] Sh-sh-sh-sh-sh! Mr Mangan: you are bound in honor to obliterate from your mind all you heard while you were pretending to be asleep. It was not meant for you to hear.

MANGAN. Pretending to be asleep! Do you think if I was only pretending that I'd have sprawled there helpless, and listened to such unfairness, such lies, such injustice and plotting and backbiting and slandering of me, if I could have up and told you what I thought of you! I wonder I didnt burst.

MRS HUSHABYE [sweetly] You dreamt it all, Mr Mangan. We were only saying how beautifully peaceful you looked in your sleep. That was all, wasnt it, Ellie? Believe me, Mr Mangan, all those unpleasant things came into your mind in the last half second before you woke. Ellie rubbed your hair the wrong way; and the disagreeable sensation suggested a disagreeable dream.

MANGAN [doggedly] I believe in dreams.

MRS HUSHABYE. So do I. But they go by contraries, dont they?

MANGAN [depths of emotion suddenly welling up in him] I shant forget, to my dying day, that when you gave me the glad eye that time in the garden, you were making a fool of me. That was a dirty low mean thing to do. You had no right to let me come near you if I disgusted you. It isnt my fault if I'm old and havnt a moustache like a bronze candlestick as your husband has. There are things no decent woman would do to a man— like a man hitting a woman in the breast.

Hesione, utterly shamed, sits down on the sofa and covers her face with her hands. Mangan sits down also on his chair and begins to cry like a child. Ellie stares at them. Mrs Hushabye, at the distressing sound he makes, takes down her hands and looks at him. She rises and runs to him.

MRS HUSHABYE. Dont cry: I cant bear it. Have I broken your heart? I didnt know you had one. How could I?

MANGAN. I'm a man, aint I?

MRS HUSHABYE [half coaxing, half rallying, altogether tenderly] Oh no: not what I call a man. Only a Boss: just that and nothing else. What business has a Boss with a heart?

MANGAN. Then youre not a bit sorry for what you did, nor ashamed?

MRS HUSHABYE. I was ashamed for the first time in my life when you said that about hitting a woman in the breast, and I found out what I'd done. My very bones blushed red. Youve had your revenge. Boss. Arnt you satisfied?

MANGAN. Serve you right! Do you hear? Serve you right! Youre just cruel. Cruel.

MRS HUSHABYE. Yes: cruelty would be delicious if one could only find some sort of cruelty that didnt really hurt. By the way [sitting down beside him on the arm of the chair], whats your name? It's not really Boss, is it?

MANGAN [shortly] If you want to know, my name's Alfred.

MRS HUSHABYE [springing up] Alfred!! Ellie: he was christened after Tennyson!!!

MANGAN [rising] I was christened after my uncle, and never had a penny from him, damn him! What of it?

MRS HUSHABYE. It comes to me suddenly that you are a real person: that you had a mother, like anyone else. [Putting her hands on his shoulders and surveying him] Little Alf!

MANGAN. Well, you have a nerve.

MRS HUSHABYE. And you have a heart, Alfy, a whimpering little heart, but a real one. [Releasing him suddenly] Now run and make it up with Ellie. She has had time to think what to say to you, which is more than I had [she goes out quickly into the garden by the port door].

MANGAN. That woman has a pair of hands that go right through you.

ELLIE. Still in love with her, in spite of all we said about you?

MANGAN. Are all women like you two? Do they never think of anything about a man except what they can get out of him? You werent even thinking that about me. You were only thinking whether your gloves would last.

ELLIE. I shall not have to think about that when we are married.

MANGAN. And you think I am going to marry you after what I heard there!

ELLIE. You heard nothing from me that I did not tell you before.

MANGAN. Perhaps you think I cant do without you.

ELLIE. I think you would feel lonely without us all now, after coming to know us so well.

MANGAN [*with something like a yell of despair*] Am I never to have the last word?

CAPTAIN SHOTOVER [*appearing at the starboard garden door*] There is a soul in torment here. What is the matter?

MANGAN. This girl doesnt want to spend her life wondering how long her gloves will last.

CAPTAIN SHOTOVER [*passing through*] Dont wear any. I never do [*he goes into the pantry*].

LADY UTTERWORD [*appearing at the port garden door, in a handsome dinner dress*] Is anything the matter?

ELLIE. This gentleman wants to know is he never to have the last word?

LADY UTTERWORD [*coming forward to the sofa*] I should let him have it, my dear. The important thing is not to have the last word, but to have your own way.

MANGAN. She wants both.

LADY UTTERWORD. She wont get them, Mr Mangan. Providence always has the last word.

MANGAN [*desperately*] Now y o u are going to come religion over me. In this house a man's mind might as well be a football. I'm going. [*He makes for the hall, but is stopped by a hail from the Captain, who has just emerged from his pantry*].

CAPTAIN SHOTOVER. Whither away, Boss Mangan?

MANGAN. To hell out of this house: let that be enough for you and all here.

CAPTAIN SHOTOVER. You were welcome to come: you are free to go. The wide earth, the high seas, the spacious skies are waiting for you outside.

LADY UTTERWORD. But your things, Mr Mangan. Your bags, your comb and brushes, your pyjamas—

HECTOR [*who has just appeared in the port doorway in a handsome Arab costume*] Why should the escaping slave take his chains with him?

MANGAN. Thats right, Hushabye. Keep the pyjamas, my lady; and much good may they do you.

HECTOR [*advancing to Lady Utterword's left hand*] Let us all go out into the night and leave everything behind us.

MANGAN. You stay where you are, the lot of you. I want no company, especially female company.

ELLIE. Let him go. He is unhappy here. He is angry with us.

CAPTAIN SHOTOVER. Go, Boss Mangan; and when you have found the land where there is happiness and where there are no women, send me its latitude and longitude; and I will join you there.

LADY UTTERWORD. You will certainly not be comfortable without your luggage, Mr Mangan.

ELLIE [*impatient*] Go, go: why dont you go? It is a heavenly night: you can sleep on the heath. Take my waterproof to lie on: it is hanging up in the hall.

HECTOR. Breakfast at nine, unless you prefer to breakfast with the Captain at six.

ELLIE. Good night, Alfred.

HECTOR. Alfred! [*He runs back to the door and calls into the garden*] Randall: Mangan's Christian name is Alfred.

RANDALL [*appearing in the starboard doorway in evening dress*] Then Hesione wins her bet.

Mrs Hushabye appears in the port doorway. She throws her left arm round Hector's neck; draws him with her to the back of the sofa; and throws her right arm round Lady Utterword's neck.

MRS HUSHABYE. They wouldnt believe me, Alf.

They contemplate him.

MANGAN. Is there any more of you coming in to look at me, as if I was the latest thing in a menagerie.

MRS HUSHABYE. You a r e the latest thing in this menagerie.

Before Mangan can retort, a fall of furniture is heard from upstairs; then a pistol shot, and a yell of pain. The staring group breaks up in consternation.

MAZZINI'S VOICE [*from above*] Help! A burglar! Help!

HECTOR [*his eyes blazing*] A burglar!!!

MRS HUSHABYE. No, Hector: youll be shot [*but it is too late: he has dashed out past Mangan, who hastily moves towards the bookshelves out of his way*].

CAPTAIN SHOTOVER [*blowing his whistle*] All hands aloft! [*He strides out after Hector*].

LADY UTTERWORD. My diamonds! [*She follows the Captain*].

RANDALL [*rushing after her*] No, Ariadne. Let me.

ELLIE. Oh, is papa shot? [*she runs out*].

MRS HUSHABYE. Are you frightened, Alf?

MANGAN. No. It aint my house, thank God.

MRS HUSHABYE. If they catch a burglar, shall we have to go into court as witnesses, and be asked all sorts of questions about our private lives?

MANGAN. You wont be believed if you tell the truth.

Mazzini, terribly upset, with a duelling pistol in his hand, comes from the hall, and makes his way to the drawing-table.

MAZZINI. Oh, my dear Mrs Hushabye, I might have killed him [*He throws the pistol on the table and staggers round to the chair*]. I hope you wont believe I really intended to.

Hector comes in, marching an old and villainous looking man before him by the collar. He plants him in the middle of the room and releases him.

Ellie follows, and immediately runs across to the back of her father's chair, and pats his shoulders.

RANDALL [*entering with a poker*] Keep your eye on this door, Mangan. I'll look after the other [*he goes to the starboard door and stands on guard there*].

Lady Utterword comes in after Randall, and goes between Mrs Hushabye and Mangan.

Nurse Guinness brings up the rear, and waits near the door, on Mangan's left.

MRS HUSHABYE. What has happened?

MAZZINI. Your housekeeper told me there was somebody upstairs, and gave me a pistol that Mr Hushabye had been practising with. I thought it would frighten him; but it went off at a touch.

THE BURGLAR. Yes, and took the skin off my ear. Precious near took the top off my head. Why dont you have a proper revolver instead of a thing like that, that goes off if you as much as blow on it?

HECTOR. One of my duelling pistols. Sorry.

MAZZINI. He put his hands up and said it was a fair cop.

THE BURGLAR. So it was. Send for the police.

HECTOR. No, by thunder! It was not a fair cop. We were four to one.

MRS HUSHABYE. What will they do to him?

THE BURGLAR. Ten years. Beginning with solitary. Ten years off my life. I shant serve it all: I'm too old. It will see me out.

LADY UTTERWORD. You should have thought of that before you stole my diamonds.

THE BURGLAR. Well, youve got them back, lady: havnt you? Can you give me back the years of my life you are going to take from me?

MRS HUSHABYE. Oh, we cant bury a man alive for ten years for a few diamonds.

THE BURGLAR. Ten little shining diamonds! Ten long black years!

LADY UTTERWORD. Think of what it is for us to be dragged through the horrors of a criminal court, and have all our family affairs in the papers! If you were a native, and Hastings could order you a good beating and send you away, I shouldnt mind; but here in England there is no real protection for any respectable person.

THE BURGLAR. I'm too old to be giv a hiding, lady. Send for the police and have done with it. It's only just and right you should.

RANDALL [*who has relaxed his vigilance on seeing the burglar so pacifically disposed, and comes forward swinging the poker between his fingers like a well-folded umbrella*] It is neither just nor right that we should be put to a lot of inconvenience to gratify your moral enthusiasm, my friend. You had better get out, while you have the chance.

THE BURGLAR [*inexorably*] No. I must work my sin off my conscience. This has come as a sort of call to me. Let me spend the rest of my life repenting in a cell. I shall have my reward above.

MANGAN [*exasperated*] The very burglars cant behave naturally in this house.

HECTOR. My good sir: you must work out your salvation at somebody else's expense. Nobody here is going to charge you.

THE BURGLAR. Oh, you wont charge me, wont you?

HECTOR. No. I'm sorry to be inhospitable; but will you kindly leave the house?

THE BURGLAR. Right. I'll go to the police station and give myself up. [*He turns resolutely to the door; but Hector stops him*].

HECTOR. } { Oh no. You musnt do that.

RANDALL. } { No, no. Clear out, man, cant you; and dont be a fool.

MRS HUSHABYE. } { Dont be so silly. Cant you repent at home?

LADY UTTERWORD. You will have to do as you are told.

THE BURGLAR. It's compounding a felony, you know.

MRS HUSHABYE. This is utterly ridiculous.

Are we to be forced to prosecute this man when we dont want to?

THE BURGLAR. Am I to be robbed of my salvation to save you the trouble of spending a day at the sessions? Is that justice? Is it right? Is it fair to me?

MAZZINI [rising and leaning across the table persuasively as if it were a pulpit desk or a shop counter] Come, come! let me shew you how you can turn your very crimes to account. Why not set up as a locksmith? You must know more about locks than most honest men?

THE BURGLAR. Thats true, sir. But I couldnt set up as a locksmith under twenty pounds.

RANDALL. Well, you can easily steal twenty pounds. You will find it in the nearest bank.

THE BURGLAR [horrified] Oh what a thing for a gentleman to put into the head of a poor criminal scrambling out of the bottomless pit as it were! Oh, shame on you, sir! Oh, God forgive you! [He throws himself into the big chair and covers his face as if in prayer].

LADY UTTERWORD. Really, Randall!

HECTOR. It seems to me that we shall have to take up a collection for this inopportunely contrite sinner.

LADY UTTERWORD. But twenty pounds is ridiculous.

THE BURGLAR [looking up quickly] I shall have to buy a lot of tools, lady.

LADY UTTERWORD. Nonsense: you have your burgling kit.

THE BURGLAR. Whats a jemmy and a centrebit and an acetylene welding plant and a bunch of skeleton keys? I shall want a forge, and a smithy, and a shop, and fittings. I cant hardly do it for twenty.

HECTOR. My worthy friend, we havnt got twenty pounds.

THE BURGLAR [now master of the situation] You can raise it among you, cant you?

MRS HUSHABYE. Give him a sovereign, Hector; and get rid of him.

HECTOR [giving him a pound] There! Off with you.

THE BURGLAR [rising and taking the money very ungratefully] I wont promise nothing. You have more on you than a quid: all the lot of you, I mean.

LADY UTTERWORD [vigorously] Oh, let us prosecute him and have done with it. I have a conscience too, I hope; and I do not feel at all sure that we have any right to let him go, especially if he is going to be greedy and

impertinent.

THE BURGLAR [quickly] All right, lady, all right. Ive no wish to be anything but agreeable. Good evening, ladies and gentlemen; and thank you kindly.

He is hurrying out when he is confronted in the doorway by Captain Shotover.

CAPTAIN SHOTOVER [fixing the burglar with a piercing regard] Whats this? Are there two of you?

THE BURGLAR [falling on his knees before the Captain in abject terror] Oh my good Lord, what have I done? Dont tell me it's your house Ive broken into, Captain Shotover.

The Captain seizes him by the collar; drags him to his feet; and leads him to the middle of the group, Hector falling back beside his wife to make way for them.

CAPTAIN SHOTOVER [turning him towards Ellie] Is that your daughter? [He releases him].

THE BURGLAR. Well, how do I know, Captain? You know the sort of life you and me has led. Any young lady of that age might be my daughter anywhere in the wide world, as you might say.

CAPTAIN SHOTOVER [to Mazzini] You are not Billy Dunn. This is Billy Dunn. Why have you imposed on me?

THE BURGLAR [indignantly to Mazzini] Have you been giving yourself out to be me? You, that nigh blew my head off! Shooting yourself, in a manner of speaking!

MAZZINI. My dear Captain Shotover, ever since I came into this house I have done hardly anything else but assure you that I am not Mr William Dunn, but Mazzini Dunn, a very different person.

THE BURGLAR. He dont belong to my branch, Captain. Theres two sets in the family: the thinking Dunns and the drinking Dunns, each going their own ways. I'm a drinking Dunn: he's a thinking Dunn. But that didnt give him any right to shoot me.

CAPTAIN SHOTOVER. So youve turned burglar, have you?

THE BURGLAR. No, Captain: I wouldnt disgrace our old sea calling by such a thing. I am no burglar.

LADY UTTERWORD. What were you doing with my diamonds?

GUINNESS. What did you break into the house for if youre no burglar?

RANDALL. Mistook the house for your own and came in by the wrong window, eh?

THE BURGLAR. Well, it's no use my telling you a lie: I can take in most captains, but not Captain Shotover, because he sold himself to the devil in Zanzibar, and can divine water, spot gold, explode a cartridge in your pocket with a glance of his eye, and see the truth hidden in the heart of man. But I'm no burglar.

CAPTAIN SHOTOVER. Are you an honest man?

THE BURGLAR. I dont set up to be better than my fellow-creatures, and never did, as you well know, Captain. But what I do is innocent and pious. I enquire about for houses where the right sort of people live. I work it on them same as I worked it here. I break into the house; put a few spoons or diamonds in my pocket; make a noise; get caught; and take up a collection. And you wouldnt believe how hard it is to get caught when youre actually trying to. I have knocked over all the chairs in a room without a soul paying any attention to me. In the end I have had to walk out and leave the job.

RANDALL. When that happens, do you put back the spoons and diamonds?

THE BURGLAR. Well, I dont fly in the face of Providence, if thats what you want to know.

CAPTAIN SHOTOVER. Guinness: you remember this man?

GUINNESS. I should think I do, seeing I was married to him, the blackguard!

HESIONE *exclaiming* (Married to him!

LADY UTTERWORD *together* (Guinness!!

THE BURGLAR. It wasnt legal. Ive been married to no end of women. No use coming that over me.

CAPTAIN SHOTOVER. Take him to the forecastle [*he flings him to the door with a strength beyond his years*].

GUINNESS. I suppose you mean the kitchen. They wont have him there. Do you expect servants to keep company with thieves and all sorts?

CAPTAIN SHOTOVER. Land-thieves and water-thieves are the same flesh and blood. I'll have no boatswain on my quarter-deck. Off with you both.

THE BURGLAR. Yes, Captain. [*He goes out humbly*].

MAZZINI. Will it be safe to have him in the house like that?

GUINNESS. Why didnt you shoot him, sir? If I'd known who he was, I'd have shot him myself. [*She goes out*].

MRS HUSHABYE. Do sit down, everybody. [*She sits down on the sofa*].

They all move except Ellie. Mazzini resumes his seat. Randall sits down in the window seat near the starboard door, again making a pendulum of his poker, and studying it as Galileo might have done. Hector sits on his left, in the middle. Mangan, forgotten, sits in the port corner. Lady Utterword takes the big chair. Captain Shotover goes into the pantry in deep abstraction. They all look after him; and Lady Utterword coughs consciously.

MRS HUSHABYE. So Billy Dunn was poor nurse's little romance. I knew there had been somebody.

RANDALL. They will fight their battles over again and enjoy themselves immensely.

LADY UTTERWORD [*irritably*] You are not married; and you know nothing about it, Randall. Hold your tongue.

RANDALL. Tyrant!

MRS HUSHABYE. Well, we have had a very exciting evening. Everything will be an anticlimax after it. We'd better all go to bed.

RANDALL. Another burglar may turn up.

MAZZINI. Oh, impossible! I hope not.

RANDALL. Why not? There is more than one burglar in England.

MRS HUSHABYE. What do you say, Alf?

MANGAN [*huffily*] Oh, I dont matter. I'm forgotten. The burglar has put my nose out of joint. Shove me into a corner and have done with me.

MRS HUSHABYE [*jumping up mischievously, and going to him*] Would you like a walk on the heath, Alfred? With me?

ELLIE. Go, Mr Mangan. It will do you good. Hesione will soothe you.

MRS HUSHABYE [*slipping her arm under his and pulling him upright*] Come, Alfred. There is a moon: it's like the night in Tristan and Isolde. [*She caresses his arm and draws him to the port garden door*].

MANGAN [*writhing but yielding*] How you can have the face—the heart—[*he breaks down and is heard sobbing as she takes him out*].

LADY UTTERWORD. What an extraordinary way to behave! What is the matter with the man?

ELLIE [*in a strangely calm voice, staring into an imaginary distance*] His heart is breaking: that is all. [*The Captain appears at the pantry door, listening*]. It is a curious sensation: the sort of pain that goes mercifully beyond our powers of feeling. When your heart is broken, your boats are burned: nothing matters any more. It is the end of happiness and the beginning of peace.

LADY UTTERWORD [*suddenly rising in a rage, to the astonishment of the rest*] How dare you?

HECTOR. Good heavens! Whats the matter?

RANDALL [*in a warning whisper*] Tch—tch—tch! Steady.

ELLIE [*surprised and haughty*] I was not addressing you particularly, Lady Utterword. And I am not accustomed to be asked how dare I.

LADY UTTERWORD. Of course not. Anyone can see how badly you have been brought up.

MAZZINI. Oh, I hope not, Lady Utterword. Really!

LADY UTTERWORD. I know very well what you meant. The impudence!

ELLIE. What on earth do you mean?

CAPTAIN SHOTOVER [*advancing to the table*] She means that her heart will not break. She has been longing all her life for someone to break it. At last she has become afraid she has none to break.

LADY UTTERWORD [*flinging herself on her knees and throwing her arms round him*] Papa: dont say you think Ive no heart.

CAPTAIN SHOTOVER [*raising her with grim tenderness*] If you had no heart how could you want to have it broken, child?

HECTOR [*rising with a bound*] Lady Utterword: you are not to be trusted. You have made a scene [*he runs out into the garden through the starboard door*].

LADY UTTERWORD. Oh! Hector, Hector! [*she runs out after him*].

RANDALL. Only nerves, I assure you. [*He rises and follows her, waving the poker in his agitation*] Ariadne! Ariadne! For God's sake be careful. You will—[*he is gone*].

MAZZINI [*rising*] How distressing! Can I do anything, I wonder?

CAPTAIN SHOTOVER [*promptly taking his chair and setting to work at the drawing-board*] No. Go to bed. Goodnight.

MAZZINI [*bewildered*] Oh! Perhaps you are right.

ELLIE. Goodnight, dearest. [*She kisses him*].

MAZZINI. Goodnight, love. [*He makes for the door, but turns aside to the bookshelves*]. I'll just take a book [*he takes one*]. Goodnight. [*He goes out, leaving Ellie alone with the Captain*].

The Captain is intent on his drawing. Ellie, standing sentry over his chair, contemplates him for a moment.

ELLIE. Does nothing ever disturb you, Captain Shotover?

CAPTAIN SHOTOVER. Ive stood on the bridge for eighteen hours in a typhoon. Life here is stormier; but I can stand it.

ELLIE. Do you think I ought to marry Mr Mangan?

CAPTAIN SHOTOVER [*never looking up*] One rock is as good as another to be wrecked on.

ELLIE. I am not in love with him.

CAPTAIN SHOTOVER. Who said you were?

ELLIE. You are not surprised?

CAPTAIN SHOTOVER. Surprised! At my age!

ELLIE. It seems to me quite fair. He wants me for one thing: I want him for another.

CAPTAIN SHOTOVER. Money?

ELLIE. Yes.

CAPTAIN SHOTOVER. Well, one turns the cheek: the other kisses it. One provides the cash: the other spends it.

ELLIE. Who will have the best of the bargain, I wonder?

CAPTAIN SHOTOVER. You. These fellows live in an office all day. You will have to put up with him from dinner to breakfast; but you will both be asleep most of that time. All day you will be quit of him; and you will be shopping with his money. If that is too much for you, marry a seafaring man: you will be bothered with him only three weeks in the year, perhaps.

ELLIE. That would be best of all, I suppose.

CAPTAIN SHOTOVER. It's a dangerous thing to be married right up to the hilt, like my daughter's husband. The man is at home all day, like a damned soul in hell.

ELLIE. I never thought of that before.

CAPTAIN SHOTOVER. If youre marrying for business, you cant be too businesslike.

ELLIE. Why do women always want other women's husbands?

CAPTAIN SHOTOVER. Why do horse-thieves prefer a horse that is broken-in to one that is wild?

ELLIE [*with a short laugh*] I suppose so. What a vile world it is!

CAPTAIN SHOTOVER. It doesnt concern me. I'm nearly out of it.

ELLIE. And I'm only just beginning.

CAPTAIN SHOTOVER. Yes; so look ahead.

ELLIE. Well, I think I am being very prudent.

CAPTAIN SHOTOVER. I didnt say prudent. I said look ahead.

ELLIE. Whats the difference?

CAPTAIN SHOTOVER. It's prudent to gain the whole world and lose your own soul. But dont forget that your soul sticks to you if you stick to it; but the world has a way of slipping through your fingers.

ELLIE [*wearily, leaving him and beginning to wander restlessly about the room*] I'm sorry, Captain Shotover; but it's no use talking like that to me. Old-fashioned people are no use to me. Old-fashioned people think you can have a soul without money. They think the less money you have, the more soul you have. Young people nowadays know better. A soul is a very expensive thing to keep: much more so than a motor car.

CAPTAIN SHOTOVER. Is it? How much does your soul eat?

ELLIE. Oh, a lot. It eats music and pictures and books and mountains and lakes and beautiful things to wear and nice people to be with. In this country you cant have them without lots of money: that is why our souls are so horribly starved.

CAPTAIN SHOTOVER. Mangan's soul lives on pigs' food.

ELLIE. Yes: money is thrown away on him. I suppose his soul was starved when he was young. But it will not be thrown away on me. It is just because I want to save my soul that I am marrying for money. All the women who are not fools do.

CAPTAIN SHOTOVER. There are other ways of getting money. Why dont you steal it?

ELLIE. Because I dont want to go to prison.

CAPTAIN SHOTOVER. Is that the only reason? Are you quite sure honesty has nothing to do with it?

ELLIE. Oh, you are very v e r y old-fashioned, Captain. Does any modern girl believe that the legal and illegal ways of getting money are the honest and dishonest ways? Mangan robbed my father and my father's friends. I should rob all the money back from Mangan if the police would let me. As they wont, I must get it back by marrying him.

CAPTAIN SHOTOVER. I cant argue: I'm too old: my mind is made up and finished. All I can tell you is that, old-fashioned or new-fashioned, if you sell yourself, you deal your soul a blow that all the books and pictures and concerts and scenery in the world wont heal [*he gets up suddenly and makes for the pantry*].

ELLIE [*running after him and seizing him by the sleeve*] Then why did you sell yourself to the devil in Zanzibar?

CAPTAIN SHOTOVER [*stopping, startled*] What?

ELLIE. You shall not run away before you answer. I have found out that trick of yours. If you sold yourself, why shouldnt I?

CAPTAIN SHOTOVER. I had to deal with men so degraded that they wouldnt obey me unless I swore at them and kicked them and beat them with my fists. Foolish people took young thieves off the streets; flung them into a training ship where they were taught to fear the cane instead of fearing God; and thought theyd made men and sailors of them by private subscription. I tricked these thieves into believing I'd sold myself to the devil. It saved my soul from the kicking and swearing that was damning me by inches.

ELLIE [*releasing him*] I shall pretend to sell myself to Boss Mangan to save my soul from the poverty that is damning m e by inches.

CAPTAIN SHOTOVER. Riches will damn you ten times deeper. Riches wont save even your body.

ELLIE. Old-fashioned again. We know now that the soul is the body, and the body the soul. They tell us they are different because they want to persuade us that we can keep our souls if we let them make slaves of our bodies. I am afraid you are no use to me, Captain.

CAPTAIN SHOTOVER. What did you expect? A Savior, eh? Are you old-fashioned enough to believe in that?

ELLIE. No. But I thought you were very wise, and might help me. Now I have found you out. You pretend to be busy, and think of fine things to say, and run in and out to surprise people by saying them, and get away before they can answer you.

CAPTAIN SHOTOVER. It confuses me to be answered. It discourages me. I cannot bear men and women. I h a v e to run away. I must run away now [*he tries to*].

ELLIE [*again seizing his arm*] You shall not run away from me. I can hypnotize you. You are the only person in the house I can say what I like to. I know you are fond of me. Sit down. [*She draws him to the sofa*].

CAPTAIN SHOTOVER [*yielding*] Take care: I am in my dotage. Old men are dangerous: it doesnt matter to them what is going to happen to the world.

They sit side by side on the sofa. She leans affectionately against him with her head on his shoulder and her eyes half closed.

ELLIE [*dreamily*] I should have thought nothing else mattered to old men. They cant be very interested in what is going to happen to themselves.

CAPTAIN SHOTOVER. A man's interest in the world is only the overflow from his interest in himself. When you are a child your vessel is not yet full; so you care for nothing but your own affairs. When you grow up, your vessel overflows; and you are a politician, a philosopher, or an explorer and adventurer. In old age the vessel dries up: there is no overflow: you are a child again. I can give you the memories of my ancient wisdom: mere scraps and leavings; but I no longer really care for anything but my own little wants and hobbies. I sit here working out my old ideas as a means of destroying my fellow-creatures. I see my daughters and their men living foolish lives of romance and sentiment and snobbery. I see you, the younger generation, turning from their romance and sentiment and snobbery to money and comfort and hard common sense. I was ten times happier on the bridge in the typhoon, or frozen into Arctic ice for months in darkness, than you or they have ever been. You are looking for a rich husband. At your age I looked for hardship, danger, horror, and death, that I might feel the life in me more intensely. I did not let the fear of death govern my life; and my reward was, I had my life. You are going to let the fear of poverty govern your life; and your reward will be that you will eat, but you will not live.

ELLIE [*sitting up impatiently*] But what can I do? I am not a sea captain: I cant stand on bridges in typhoons, or go slaughtering seals and whales in Greenland's icy mountains. They wont let women be captains. Do you want me to be a stewardess?

CAPTAIN SHOTOVER. There are worse lives. The stewardesses could come ashore if they liked; but they sail and sail and sail.

ELLIE. What could they do ashore but marry for money? I dont want to be a stewardess: I am too bad a sailor. Think of something else for me.

CAPTAIN SHOTOVER. I cant think so long and continuously. I am too old. I must go in and out. [*He tries to rise*].

ELLIE [*pulling him back*] You shall not. You are happy here, arnt you?

CAPTAIN SHOTOVER. I tell you it's dangerous to keep me. I cant keep awake and alert.

ELLIE. What do you run away for? To sleep?

CAPTAIN SHOTOVER. No. To get a glass of rum.

ELLIE [*frightfully disillusioned*] Is that it? How disgusting! Do you like being drunk?

CAPTAIN SHOTOVER. No: I dread being drunk more than anything in the world. To be drunk means to have dreams; to go soft; to be easily pleased and deceived; to fall into the clutches of women. Drink does that for you when you are young. But when you are old: very very old, like me, the dreams come by themselves. You dont know how terrible that is: you are young: you sleep at night only, and sleep soundly. But later on you will sleep in the afternoon. Later still you will sleep even in the morning; and you will awake tired, tired of life. You will never be free from dozing and dreams: the dreams will steal upon your work every ten minutes unless you can awaken yourself with rum. I drink now to keep sober; but the dreams are conquering: rum is not what it was: I have had ten glasses since you came; and it might be so much water. Go get me another: Guinness knows where it is. You had better see for yourself the horror of an old man drinking.

ELLIE. You shall not drink. Dream. I like you to dream. You must never be in the real world when we talk together.

CAPTAIN SHOTOVER. I am too weary to resist, or too weak. I am in my second childhood. I do not see you as you really are. I cant remember what I really am. I feel nothing but the accursed happiness I have dreaded all my life long: the happiness that comes as life goes, the happiness of yielding and dreaming instead of resisting and doing, the sweetness of the fruit that is going rotten.

ELLIE. You dread it almost as much as I used to dread losing my dreams and having to fight and do things. But that is all over for me: my dreams are dashed to pieces. I should like to marry a very old, very rich man. I should like to marry you. I had much rather marry you than marry Mangan. Are you very rich?

CAPTAIN SHOTOVER. No. Living from hand to mouth. And I have a wife somewhere in Jamaica: a black one. My first wife. Unless she's dead.

ELLIE. What a pity! I feel so happy with you. [*She takes his hand, almost unconsciously, and pats* it]. I thought I should never feel happy again.

CAPTAIN SHOTOVER. Why?

ELLIE. Dont you know?

CAPTAIN SHOTOVER. No.

ELLIE. Heartbreak. I fell in love with Hector, and didnt know he was married.

CAPTAIN SHOTOVER. Heartbreak? Are you one of those who are so sufficient to themselves that they are only happy when they are stripped of everything, even of hope?

ELLIE [*gripping the hand*] It seems so; for I feel now as if there was nothing I could not do, because I want nothing.

CAPTAIN SHOTOVER. Thats the only real strength. Thats genius. Thats better than rum.

ELLIE [*throwing away his hand*] Rum! Why did you spoil it?

Hector and Randall come in from the garden through the starboard door.

HECTOR. I beg your pardon. We did not know there was anyone here.

ELLIE [*rising*] That means that you want to tell Mr Randall the story about the tiger. Come, Captain: I want to talk to my father; and you had better come with me.

CAPTAIN SHOTOVER [*rising*] Nonsense! the man is in bed.

ELLIE. Aha! Ive caught you. My real father has gone to bed; but the father you gave me is in the kitchen. You knew quite well all along. Come. [*She draws him out into the garden with her through the port door*].

HECTOR. Thats an extraordinary girl. She has the Ancient Mariner on a string like a Pekinese dog.

RANDALL. Now that they have gone, shall we have a friendly chat?

HECTOR. You are in what is supposed to be my house. I am at your disposal.

Hector sits down in the draughtsman's chair, turning it to face Randall, who remains standing, leaning at his ease against the carpenter's bench.

RANDALL. I take it that we may be quite frank. I mean about Lady Utterword.

HECTOR. You may. I have nothing to be frank about. I never met her until this afternoon.

RANDALL [*straightening up*] What! But you are her sister's husband.

HECTOR. Well, if you come to that, you are

her husband's brother.

RANDALL. But you seem to be on intimate terms with her.

HECTOR. So do you.

RANDALL. Yes; but I am on intimate terms with her. I have known her for years.

HECTOR. It took her years to get to the same point with you that she got to with me in five minutes, it seems.

RANDALL [*vexed*] Really, Ariadne is the limit [*he moves away huffishly towards the windows*].

HECTOR [*coolly*] She is, as I remarked to Hesione, a very enterprising woman.

RANDALL [*returning, much troubled*] You see, Hushabye, you are what women consider a good-looking man.

HECTOR. I cultivated that appearance in the days of my vanity; and Hesione insists on my keeping it up. She makes me wear these ridiculous things [*indicating his Arab costume*] because she thinks me absurd in evening dress.

RANDALL. Still, you do keep it up, old chap. Now, I assure you I have not an atom of jealousy in my disposition—

HECTOR. The question would seem to be rather whether your brother has any touch of that sort.

RANDALL. What! Hastings! Oh, dont trouble about Hastings. He has the gift of being able to work sixteen hours a day at the dullest detail, and actually likes it. That gets him to the top wherever he goes. As long as Ariadne takes care that he is fed regularly, he is only too thankful to anyone who will keep her in good humor for him.

HECTOR. And as she has all the Shotover fascination, there is plenty of competition for the job, eh?

RANDALL [*angrily*] She encourages them. Her conduct is perfectly scandalous. I assure you, my dear fellow, I havnt an atom of jealousy in my composition; but she makes herself the talk of every place she goes to by her thoughtlessness. It's nothing more: she doesnt really care for the men she keeps hanging about her; but how is the world to know that? It's not fair to Hastings. It's not fair to me.

HECTOR. Her theory is that her conduct is so correct—

RANDALL. Correct! She does nothing but make scenes from morning til night. You be careful, old chap. She will get you into trouble: that is, she would if she really cared for you.

HECTOR. Doesnt she?

RANDALL. Not a scrap. She may want your scalp to add to her collection; but her true affection has been engaged years ago. You had really better be careful.

HECTOR. Do you suffer much from this jealousy?

RANDALL. Jealousy! I jealous! My dear fellow, havnt I told you that there is not an atom of—

HECTOR. Yes. And Lady Utterword told me she never made scenes. Well, dont waste your jealousy on my moustache.Never waste jealousy on a real man: it is the imaginary hero that supplants us all in the long run. Besides, jealousy does not belong to your easy man-of-the-world pose, which you carry so well in other respects.

RANDALL. Really, Hushabye, I think a man may be allowed to be a gentleman without being accused of posing.

HECTOR. It is a pose like any other. In this house we know all the poses: our game is to find out the man under the pose. The man under your pose is apparently Ellie's favorite, Othello.

RANDALL. Some of your games in this house are damned annoying, let me tell you.

HECTOR. Yes: I have been their victim for many years. I used to writhe under them at first; but I became accustomed to them. At last I learned to play them.

RANDALL. If it's all the same to you, I had rather you didnt play them on me. You evidently dont quite understand my character, or my notions of good form.

HECTOR. Is it your notion of good form to give away Lady Utterword?

RANDALL [*a childishly plaintive note breaking into his huff*] I have not said a word against Lady Utterword. This is just the conspiracy over again.

HECTOR. What conspiracy?

RANDALL. You know very well, sir. A conspiracy to make me out to be pettish and jealous and childish and everything I am not. Everyone knows I am just the opposite.

HECTOR [*rising*] Something in the air of the house has upset you. It often does have that effect. [*He goes to the garden door and calls Lady Utterword with commanding emphasis*] Ariadne!

LADY UTTERWORD [*at some distance*] Yes.

RANDALL. What are you calling her for? I want to speak—

LADY UTTERWORD [*arriving breathless*] Yes. You really are a terribly commanding person. Whats the matter?

HECTOR. I do not know how to manage your friend Randall. No doubt you do.

LADY UTTERWORD. Randall: have you been making yourself ridiculous, as usual? I can see it in your face. Really, you are the most pettish creature.

RANDALL. You know quite well, Ariadne, that I have not an ounce of pettishness in my disposition. I have made myself perfectly pleasant here. I have remained absolutely cool and imperturbable in the face of a burglar. Imperturbability is almost too strong a point of mine. But [*putting his foot down with a stamp, and walking angrily up and down the room*] I i n s i s t on being treated with a certain consideration. I will not allow Hushabye to take liberties with me. I will not stand your encouraging people as you do.

HECTOR. The man has a rooted delusion that he is your husband.

LADY UTTERWORD. I know. He is jealous. As if he had any right to be! He compromises me everywhere. He makes scenes all over the place. Randall: I will not allow it. I simply will not allow it. You had no right to discuss me with Hector. I will not be discussed by men.

HECTOR. Be reasonable, Ariadne. Your fatal gift of beauty forces men to discuss you.

LADY UTTERWORD. Oh indeed! what about y o u r fatal gift of beauty?

HECTOR. How can I help it?

LADY UTTERWORD. You could cut off your moustache: I cant cut off my nose. I get my whole life messed up with people falling in love with me. And then Randall says I run after men.

RANDALL. I—

LADY UTTERWORD. Yes you do: you said it just now. Why cant you think of something else than women? Napoleon was quite right when he said that women are the occupation of the idle man. Well, if ever there was an idle man on earth, his name is Randall Utterword.

RANDALL. Ariad—

LADY UTTERWORD [*overwhelming him with a torrent of words*] Oh yes you are: it's no use denying it. What have you ever done? What good are you? You are as much trouble in the house as a child of three. You couldnt live without your valet.

RANDALL. This is—

LADY UTTERWORD. Laziness! You are laziness incarnate. You are selfishness itself. You are the most uninteresting man on earth. You cant even gossip about anything but yourself and your grievances and your ailments and the people who have offended you. [*Turning to Hector*] Do you know what they call him, Hector?

HECTOR \[*speaking* ⌠Please dont tell me.
RANDALL⌡ *together*] ⌊I'll not stand it—

LADY UTTERWORD. Randall the Rotter: that is his name in good society.

RANDALL [*shouting*] I'll not bear it, I tell you. Will you listen to me, you infernal— [*he chokes*].

LADY UTTERWORD. Well: go on. What were you going to call me? An infernal what? Which unpleasant animal is it to be this time?

RANDALL [*foaming*] There is no animal in the world so hateful as a woman can be. You are a maddening devil. Hushabye: you will not believe me when I tell you that I have loved this demon all my life; but God knows I have paid for it [*he sits down in the draughtsman's chair, weeping*].

LADY UTTERWORD [*standing over him with triumphant contempt*] Cry-baby!

HECTOR [*gravely, coming to him*] My friend: the Shotover sisters have two strange powers over men. They can make them love; and they can make them cry. Thank your stars that you are not married to one of them.

LADY UTTERWORD [*haughtily*] And pray, Hector—

HECTOR [*suddenly catching her round the shoulders; swinging her right round him and away from Randall; and gripping her throat with the other hand*] Ariadne: if you attempt to start on me, I'll choke you: do you hear? The cat-and-mouse game with the other sex is a good game; but I can play your head off at it. [*He throws her, not at all gently, into the big chair, and proceeds, less fiercely but firmly*] It is true that Napoleon said that woman is the occupation of the idle man. But he added that she is the relaxation of the warrior. Well, *I* am the warrior. So take care.

LADY UTTERWORD [*not in the least put out, and rather pleased by his violence*] My dear Hector: I have only done what you asked me to do.

HECTOR. How do you make that out, pray?

LADY UTTERWORD. You called me in to manage Randall, didnt you? You said you couldnt manage him yourself.

HECTOR. Well, what if I did? I did not ask you to drive the man mad.

LADY UTTERWORD. He isnt mad. Thats the way to manage him. If you were a mother, youd understand.

HECTOR. Mother! What are you up to now?

LADY UTTERWORD. It's quite simple. When the children got nerves and were naughty, I smacked them just enough to give them a good cry and a healthy nervous shock. They went to sleep and were quite good afterwards. Well, I cant smack Randall: he is too big; so when he gets nerves and is naughty, I just rag him til he cries. He will be all right now. Look: he is half asleep already [*which is quite true*].

RANDALL [*waking up indignantly*] I'm not. You are most cruel, Ariadne. [*Sentimentally*] But I suppose I must forgive you, as usual [*he checks himself in the act of yawning*].

LADY UTTERWORD [*to Hector*] Is the explanation satisfactory, dread warrior?

HECTOR. Some day I shall kill you, if you go too far. I thought you were a fool.

LADY UTTERWORD [*laughing*] Everybody does, at first. But I am not such a fool as I look. [*She rises complacently*]. Now, Randall: go to bed. You will be a good boy in the morning.

RANDALL [*only very faintly rebellious*] I'll go to bed when I like. It isnt ten yet.

LADY UTTERWORD. It is long past ten. See that he goes to bed at once, Hector. [*She goes into the garden*].

HECTOR. Is there any slavery on earth viler than this slavery of men to women?

RANDALL [*rising resolutely*] I'll not speak to her tomorrow. I'll not speak to her for another week. I'll give her s u c h a lesson. I'll go straight to bed without bidding her goodnight. [*He makes for the door leading to the hall*].

HECTOR. You are under a spell, man. Old Shotover sold himself to the devil in Zanzibar. The devil gave him a black witch for a wife; and these two demon daughters are their mystical progeny. I am tied to Hesione's apron-string; but I'm her husband; and if I did go stark staring mad about her, at least we became man and wife. But why should y o u let yourself be dragged about and beaten by Ariadne as a toy donkey is dragged about and beaten by a child? What do you get by it? Are you her lover?

RANDALL. You must not misunderstand me. In a higher sense—in a Platonic sense—

HECTOR. Psha! Platonic sense! She makes you her servant; and when pay-day comes round, she bilks you: that is what you mean.

RANDALL [*feebly*] Well, if I dont mind, I dont see what business it is of yours. Besides, I tell you I am going to punish her. You shall see: *I* know how to deal with women. I'm really very sleepy. Say goodnight to Mrs Hushabye for me, will you, like a good chap. Goodnight. [*He hurries out*].

HECTOR. Poor wretch! Oh women! women! women! [*He lifts his fists in invocation to heaven*] Fall. Fall and crush. [*He goes out into the garden*].

ACT III

In the garden, Hector, as he comes out through the glass door of the poop, finds Lady Utterword lying voluptuously in the hammock on the east side of the flagstaff, in the circle of light cast by the electric arc, which is like a moon in its opal globe. Beneath the head of the hammock, a campstool. On the other side of the flagstaff, on the long garden seat, Captain Shotover is asleep, with Ellie beside him, leaning affectionately against him on his right hand. On his left is a deck chair. Behind them in the gloom, Hesione is strolling about with Mangan. It is a fine still night, moonless.

LADY UTTERWORD. What a lovely night! It seems made for us.

HECTOR. The night takes no interest in us. What are we to the night? [*He sits down moodily in the deck chair*].

ELLIE [*dreamily, nestling against the Captain*] Its beauty soaks into my nerves. In the night there is peace for the old and hope for the young.

HECTOR. Is that remark your own?

ELLIE. No. Only the last thing the Captain said before he went to sleep.

CAPTAIN SHOTOVER. I'm not asleep.

HECTOR. Randall is. Also Mr Mazzini Dunn. Mangan too, probably.

MANGAN. No.

HECTOR. Oh, you are there. I thought Hesione would have sent you to bed by this time.

MRS HUSHABYE [*coming to the back of the garden seat, into the light, with Mangan*] I think I shall. He keeps telling me he has a presentiment that he is going to die. I never met a man so greedy for sympathy.

MANGAN [*plaintively*] But I have a presentiment. I really have. And you wouldnt listen.

MRS HUSHABYE. I was listening for something else. There was a sort of splendid drumming in the sky. Did none of you hear it? It came from a distance and then died away.

MANGAN. I tell you it was a train.

MRS HUSHABYE. And *I* tell y o u, Alf, there is no train at this hour. The last is nine fortyfive.

MANGAN. But a goods train.

MRS HUSHABYE. Not on our little line. They tack a truck on to the passenger train. What can it have been, Hector?

HECTOR. Heaven's threatening growl of disgust at us useless futile creatures. [*Fiercely*] I tell you, one of two things must happen. Either out of that darkness some new creation will come to supplant us as we have supplanted the animals, or the heavens will fall in thunder and destroy us.

LADY UTTERWORD [*in a cool instructive manner, wallowing comfortably in her hammock*] We have not supplanted the animals, Hector. Why do you ask heaven to destroy this house, which could be made quite comfortable if Hesione had any notion of how to live? Dont you know what is wrong with it?

HECTOR. We are wrong with it. There is no sense in us. We are useless, dangerous, and ought to be abolished.

LADY UTTERWORD. Nonsense! Hastings told me the very first day he came here, nearly twentyfour years ago, what is wrong with the house.

CAPTAIN SHOTOVER. What! The numskull said there was something wrong with my house!

LADY UTTERWORD. I said Hastings said it; and he is not in the least a numskull.

CAPTAIN SHOTOVER. Whats wrong with my house?

LADY UTTERWORD. Just what is wrong with a ship, papa. Wasnt it clever of Hastings to see that?

CAPTAIN SHOTOVER. The man's a fool. Theres nothing wrong with a ship.

LADY UTTERWORD. Yes there is.

MRS HUSHABYE. But what is it? Dont be aggravating, Addy.

LADY UTTERWORD. Guess.

HECTOR. Demons. Daughters of the witch of Zanzibar. Demons.

LADY UTTERWORD. Not a bit. I assure you, all this house needs to make it a sensible, healthy, pleasant house, with good appetites and sound sleep in it, is horses.

MRS HUSHABYE. Horses! What rubbish!

LADY UTTERWORD. Yes: horses. Why have we never been able to let this house? Because there are no proper stables. Go anywhere in England where there are natural, wholesome, contented, and really nice English people; and what do you always find? That the stables are the real centre of the household; and that if any visitor wants to play the piano the whole room has to be upset before it can be opened, there are so many things piled on it. I never lived until I learned to ride; and I shall never ride really well because I didnt begin as a child. There are only two classes in good society in England: the equestrian classes and the neurotic classes. It isnt mere convention: everybody can see that the people who hunt are the right people and the people who dont are the wrong ones.

CAPTAIN SHOTOVER. There is some truth in this. My ship made a man of me; and a ship is the horse of the sea.

LADY UTTERWORD. Exactly how Hastings explained your being a gentleman.

CAPTAIN SHOTOVER. Not bad for a numskull. Bring the man here with you next time: I must talk to him.

LADY UTTERWORD. Why is Randall such an obvious rotter? He is well bred; he has been at a public school and a university; he has been in the Foreign Office; he knows the best people and has lived all his life among them. Why is he so unsatisfactory, so contemptible? Why cant he get a valet to stay with him longer than a few months? Just because he is too lazy and pleasure-loving to hunt and shoot. He strums the piano, and sketches, and runs after married women, and reads literary books and poems. He actually plays the flute; but I never let him bring it into my house. If he would only—[*she is interrupted by the melancholy strains of a flute coming from an open window above. She raises herself indignantly in the hammock*]. Randall: you have not gone to bed. Have you been listening? [*The flute replies pertly*]

How vulgar! Go to bed instantly, Randall:

how dare you? [*The window is slammed down. She subsides*]. How can anyone care for such a creature!

MRS HUSHABYE. Addy: do you think Ellie ought to marry poor Alfred merely for his money?

MANGAN [*much alarmed*] Whats that? Mrs Hushabye: are my affairs to be discussed like this before everybody?

LADY UTTERWORD. I dont think Randall is listening now.

MANGAN. Everybody is listening. It isnt right.

MRS HUSHABYE. But in the dark, what does it matter? Ellie doesnt mind. Do you, Ellie?

ELLIE. Not in the least. What is your opinion, Lady Utterword? You have so much good sense.

MANGAN. But it isnt right. It—[*Mrs Hushabye puts her hand on his mouth*]. Oh, very well.

LADY UTTERWORD. How much money have you, Mr Mangan?

MANGAN. Really— No: I cant stand this.

LADY UTTERWORD. Nonsense, Mr Mangan! It all turns on your income, doesnt it?

MANGAN. Well, if you come to that, how much money has she?

ELLIE. None.

LADY UTTERWORD. You are answered, Mr Mangan. And now, as you have made Miss Dunn throw her cards on the table, you cannot refuse to shew your own.

MRS HUSHABYE. Come, Alf! out with it! How much?

MANGAN [*baited out of all prudence*] Well, if you want to know, I have no money and never had any.

MRS HUSHABYE. Alfred: you mustnt tell naughty stories.

MANGAN. I'm not telling you stories. I'm telling you the raw truth.

LADY UTTERWORD. Then what do you live on, Mr Mangan?

MANGAN. Travelling expenses. And a trifle of commission.

CAPTAIN SHOTOVER. What more have any of us but travelling expenses for our life's journey?

MRS HUSHABYE. But you have factories and capital and things?

MANGAN. People think I have. People think I'm an industrial Napoleon. Thats why Miss Ellie wants to marry me. But I tell you I have nothing.

ELLIE. Do you mean that the factories are like Marcus's tigers? That they dont exist?

MANGAN. They exist all right enough. But theyre not mine. They belong to syndicates and shareholders and all sorts of lazy good-for-nothing capitalists. I get money from such people to start the factories. I find people like Miss Dunn's father to work them, and keep a tight hand so as to make them pay. Of course I make them keep me going pretty well; but it's a dog's life; and I dont own anything.

MRS HUSHABYE. Alfred, Alfred: you are making a poor mouth of it to get out of marrying Ellie.

MANGAN. I'm telling the truth about my money for the first time in my life; and it's the first time my word has ever been doubted.

LADY UTTERWORD. How sad! Why dont you go in for politics, Mr Mangan?

MANGAN. Go in for politics! Where have you been living? I am in politics.

LADY UTTERWORD. I'm sure I beg your pardon. I never heard of you.

MANGAN. Let me tell you, Lady Utterword, that the Prime Minister of this country asked me to join the Government without even going through the nonsense of an election, as the dictator of a great public department.

LADY UTTERWORD. As a Conservative or a Liberal?

MANGAN. No such nonsense. As a practical business man. [*They all burst out laughing*]. What are you all laughing at?

MRS HUSHABYE. Oh, Alfred, Alfred!

ELLIE. You! who have to get my father to do everything for you!

MRS HUSHABYE. You! who are afraid of your own workmen!

HECTOR. You! with whom three women have been playing cat and mouse all the evening!

LADY UTTERWORD. You must have given an immense sum to the party funds, Mr Mangan.

MANGAN. Not a penny out of my own pocket. The syndicate found the money: they knew how useful I should be to them in the Government.

LADY UTTERWORD. This is most interesting and unexpected, Mr Mangan. And what have your administrative achievements been, so far?

MANGAN. Achievements? Well, I dont know what you call achievements; but Ive jolly well put a stop to the games of the other fellows in the other departments. Every man of them thought he was going to save the country all by himself, and do me out of the credit and out of my chance of a title. I took good care that if they wouldnt let me do it they shouldnt do it themselves either. I may not know anything about my own machinery; but I know how to stick a ramrod into the other fellow's. And now they all look the biggest fools going.

HECTOR. And in heaven's name, what do you look like?

MANGAN. I look like the fellow that was too clever for all the others, dont I? If that isnt a triumph of practical business, what is?

HECTOR. Is this England, or is it a madhouse?

LADY UTTERWORD. Do you expect to save the country, Mr Mangan?

MANGAN. Well, who else will? Will your Mr Randall save it?

LADY UTTERWORD. Randall the rotter! Certainly not.

MANGAN. Will your brother-in-law save it with his moustache and his fine talk.

HECTOR. Yes, if they will let me.

MANGAN [*sneering*] Ah! Will they let you?

HECTOR. No. They prefer you.

MANGAN. Very well then, as youre in a world where I'm appreciated and youre not, youd best be civil to me, hadnt you? Who else is there but me?

LADY UTTERWORD. There is Hastings. Get rid of your ridiculous sham democracy; and give Hastings the necessary powers; and a good supply of bamboo to bring the British native to his senses: he will save the country with the greatest ease.

CAPTAIN SHOTOVER. It had better be lost. Any fool can govern with a stick in his hand. *I* could govern that way. It is not God's way. The man is a numskull.

LADY UTTERWORD. The man is worth all of you rolled into one. What do you say, Miss Dunn?

ELLIE. I think my father would do very well if people did not put upon him and cheat him and despise him because he is so good.

MANGAN [*contemptuously*] I think I see Mazzini Dunn getting into parliament or pushing his way into the Government. Weve not come to that yet, thank God! What do you say, Mrs Hushabye?

MRS HUSHABYE. Oh, *I* say it matters very little which of you governs the country so long as we govern you.

HECTOR. We? Who is we, pray?

MRS HUSHABYE. The devil's granddaughters, dear. The lovely women.

HECTOR [*raising his hands as before*] Fall, I say; and deliver us from the lures of Satan!

ELLIE. There seems to be nothing real in the world except my father and Shakespear. Marcus's tigers are false; Mr Mangan's millions are false; there is nothing really strong and true about Hesione but her beautiful black hair; and Lady Utterword's is too pretty to be real. The one thing that was left to me was the Captain's seventh degree of concentration; and that turns out to be—

CAPTAIN SHOTOVER. Rum.

LADY UTTERWORD [*placidly*] A good deal of my hair is quite genuine. The Duchess of Dithering offered me fifty guineas for this [*touching her forehead*] under the impression that it was a transformation; but it is all natural except the color.

MANGAN [*wildly*] Look here: I'm going to take off all my clothes [*he begins tearing off his coat*].

LADY UTTERWORD. | Mr Mangan!
CAPTAIN SHOTOVER. | [*in* | Whats that?
HECTOR. | *conster-* | Ha! ha! Do.
   | *nation*] | Do.
ELLIE. | | Please dont.

MRS HUSHABYE [*catching his arm and stopping him*] Alfred: for shame! Are you mad?

MANGAN. Shame! What shame is there in this house? Let's all strip stark naked. We may as well do the thing thoroughly when we're about it. Weve stripped ourselves morally naked: well, let us strip ourselves physically naked as well, and see how we like it. I tell you I cant bear this. I was brought up to be respectable. I dont mind the women dyeing their hair and the men drinking : it's human nature. But it's not human nature to tell everybody about it. Every time one of you opens your mouth I go like this [*he cowers as if to avoid a missile*] afraid of what will come next. How are we to have any self-respect if we dont keep it up that we're better than we really are?

LADY UTTERWORD. I quite sympathize with you, Mr Mangan. I have been through it all; and I know by experience that men and women are delicate plants and must be cultivated under glass. Our family habit of throwing stones in all directions and letting the air in is not only unbearably rude, but positively dangerous. Still, there is no use catching physical colds as well as moral ones; so please keep your clothes on.

MANGAN. I'll do as I like: not what you tell me. Am I a child or a grown man? I wont stand this mothering tyranny. I'll go back to the city, where I'm respected and made much of.

MRS HUSHABYE. Goodbye, Alf. Think of us sometimes in the city. Think of Ellie's youth!

ELLIE. Think of Hesione's eyes and hair!

CAPTAIN SHOTOVER. Think of this garden in which you are not a dog barking to keep the truth out!

HECTOR. Think of Lady Utterword's beauty! her good sense! her style!

LADY UTTERWORD. Flatterer. Think, Mr Mangan, whether you can really do any better for yourself elsewhere: that is the essential point, isnt it?

MANGAN [*surrendering*] All right: all right. I'm done. Have it your own way. Only let me alone. I dont know whether I'm on my head or my heels when you all start on me like this. I'll stay. I'll marry her. I'll do anything for a quiet life. Are you satisfied now?

ELLIE. No. I never really intended to make you marry me, Mr Mangan. Never in the depths of my soul. I only wanted to feel my strength: to know that you could not escape if I chose to take you.

MANGAN [*indignantly*] What! Do you mean to say you are going to throw me over after my acting so handsome?

LADY UTTERWORD. I should not be too hasty, Miss Dunn. You can throw Mr Mangan over at any time up to the last moment. Very few men in his position go bankrupt. You can live very comfortably on his reputation for immense wealth.

ELLIE. I cannot commit bigamy, Lady Utterword.

MRS HUSHABYE. | | Bigamy! Whatever on earth are you talking about, Ellie?
LADY UTTERWORD. | [*exclaiming all together*] | Bigamy! What do you mean, Miss Dunn?
MANGAN. | | Bigamy! Do you mean to say youre married already?
HECTOR. | | Bigamy! This is some enigma.

ELLIE. Only half an hour ago I became Captain Shotover's white wife.

MRS HUSHABYE. Ellie! What nonsense! Where?

ELLIE. In heaven, where all true marriages are made.

LADY UTTERWORD. Really, Miss Dunn! Really, papa!

MANGAN. He told me *I* was too old! And him a mummy!

HECTOR [*quoting Shelley*]

"Their altar the grassy earth outspread,
And their priest the muttering wind."

ELLIE. Yes: I, Ellie Dunn, give my broken heart and my strong sound soul to its natural captain, my spiritual husband and second father.

She draws the Captain's arm through hers, and pats his hand. The Captain remains fast asleep.

MRS HUSHABYE. Oh, thats very clever of you, pettikins. V e r y clever. Alfred: you could never have lived up to Ellie. You must be content with a little share of me.

MANGAN [*sniffing and wiping his eyes*] It isnt kind—[*his emotion chokes him*].

LADY UTTERWORD. You are well out of it, Mr Mangan. Miss Dunn is the most conceited young woman I have met since I came back to England.

MRS HUSHABYE. Oh, Ellie isnt conceited. Are you, pettikins?

ELLIE. I know my strength now, Hesione.

MANGAN. Brazen, I call you. Brazen.

MRS HUSHABYE. Tut tut, Alfred: dont be rude. Dont you feel how lovely this marriage night is, made in heaven? Arnt you happy, you and Hector? Open your eyes: Addy and Ellie look beautiful enough to please the most fastidious man: we live and love and have not a care in the world. We women have managed all that for you. Why in the name of common sense do you go on as if you were two miserable wretches?

CAPTAIN SHOTOVER. I tell you happiness is no good. You can be happy when you are only half alive. I am happier now I am half dead than ever I was in my prime. But there is no blessing on my happiness.

ELLIE [*her face lighting up*] Life with a blessing! that is what I want. Now I know the real reason why I couldnt marry Mr Mangan: there would be no blessing on our marriage. There is a blessing on my broken heart. There is a blessing on your beauty, Hesione. There is a blessing on your father's spirit. Even on the lies of Marcus there is a blessing; but on Mr Mangan's money there is none.

MANGAN. I dont understand a word of that.

ELLIE. Neither do I. But I know it means something.

MANGAN. Dont say there was any difficulty about the blessing. I was ready to get a bishop to marry us.

MRS HUSHABYE. Isnt he a fool, pettikins?

HECTOR [*fiercely*] Do not scorn the man. We are all fools.

Mazzini, in pyjamas and a richly colored silk dressing-gown, comes from the house, on Lady Utterword's side.

MRS HUSHABYE. Oh! here comes the only man who ever resisted me. Whats the matter, Mr Dunn? Is the house on fire?

MAZZINI. Oh no: nothing's the matter; but really it's impossible to go to sleep with such an interesting conversation going on under one's window, and on such a beautiful night too. I just had to come down and join you all. What has it all been about?

MRS HUSHABYE. Oh, wonderful things, soldier of freedom.

HECTOR. For example, Mangan, as a practical business man, has tried to undress himself and has failed ignominiously; whilst you, as an idealist, have succeeded brilliantly.

MAZZINI. I hope you dont mind my being like this, Mrs Hushabye. [*He sits down on the campstool*].

MRS HUSHABYE. On the contrary, I could wish you always like that.

LADY UTTERWORD. Your daughter's match is off, Mr Dunn. It seems that Mr Mangan, whom we all supposed to be a man of property, owns absolutely nothing.

MAZZINI. Well of course I knew that, Lady Utterword. But if people believe in him and are always giving him money, whereas they dont believe in me and never give me any, how can I ask poor Ellie to depend on what I can do for her?

MANGAN. Dont you run away with this idea that I have nothing. I—

HECTOR. Oh, dont explain. We understand. You have a couple of thousand pounds in exchequer bills, 50,000 shares worth tenpence a dozen, and half a dozen tabloids of cyanide of potassium to poison yourself with when you are found out. Thats the reality of your millions.

MAZZINI. Oh no, no, no. He is quite honest: the businesses are genuine and perfectly legal.

HECTOR [*disgusted*] Yah! Not even a great swindler!

MANGAN. So you think. But Ive been too many for some honest men, for all that.

LADY UTTERWORD. There is no pleasing you, Mr Mangan. You are determined to be neither rich nor poor, honest nor dishonest.

MANGAN. There you go again. Ever since I came into this silly house I have been made to look like a fool, though I'm as good a man in this house as in the city.

ELLIE [*musically*] Yes: this silly house, this strangely happy house, this agonizing house, this house without foundations. I shall call it Heartbreak House.

MRS HUSHABYE. Stop, Ellie; or I shall howl like an animal.

MANGAN [*breaks into a low snivelling*]!!!

MRS HUSHABYE. There! you have set Alfred off.

ELLIE. I like him best when he is howling.

CAPTAIN SHOTOVER. Silence! [*Mangan subsides into silence*]. I say, let the heart break in silence.

HECTOR. Do you accept that name for your house?

CAPTAIN SHOTOVER. It is not my house: it is only my kennel.

HECTOR. We have been too long here. We do not live in this house: we haunt it.

LADY UTTERWORD [*heart torn*] It is dreadful to think how you have been here all these years while I have gone round the world. I escaped young; but it has drawn me back. It wants to break my heart too. But it shant. I have left you and it behind. It was silly of me to come back. I felt sentimental about papa and Hesione and the old place. I felt them calling to me.

MAZZINI. But what a very natural and kindly and charming human feeling, Lady Utterword!

LADY UTTERWORD. So I thought, Mr Dunn. But I know now that it was only the last of my influenza. I found that I was not remembered and not wanted.

CAPTAIN SHOTOVER. You left because you did not want us. Was there no heartbreak in that for your father? You tore yourself up by the roots; and the ground healed up and brought forth fresh plants and forgot you. What right had you to come back and probe old wounds?

MRS HUSHABYE. You were a complete stranger to me at first, Addy; but now I feel as if you had never been away.

LADY UTTERWORD. Thank you, Hesione; but the influenza is quite cured. The place may be Heartbreak House to you, Miss Dunn, and to this gentleman from the city who seems to have so little self-control; but to me it is only a very ill-regulated and rather untidy villa without any stables.

HECTOR. Inhabited by—?

ELLIE. A crazy old sea captain and a young singer who adores him.

MRS HUSHABYE. A sluttish female, trying to stave off a double chin and an elderly spread, vainly wooing a born soldier of freedom.

MAZZINI. Oh, really, Mrs Hushabye—

MANGAN. A member of His Majesty's Government that everybody sets down as a nincompoop: dont forget him, Lady Utterword.

LADY UTTERWORD. And a very fascinating gentleman whose chief occupation is to be married to my sister.

HECTOR. All heartbroken imbeciles.

MAZZINI. Oh no. Surely, if I may say so, rather a favorable specimen of what is best in our English culture. You are very charming people, most advanced, unprejudiced, frank, humane, unconventional, democratic, free-thinking, and everything that is delightful to thoughtful people.

MRS HUSHABYE. You do us proud, Mazzini.

MAZZINI. I am not flattering, really. Where else could I feel perfectly at ease in my pyjamas? I sometimes dream that I am in very distinguished society, and suddenly I have nothing on but my pyjamas! Sometimes I havnt even pyjamas. And I always feel overwhelmed with confusion. But here, I dont mind in the least: it seems quite natural.

LADY UTTERWORD. An infallible sign that you are not now in really distinguished society, Mr Dunn. If you were in my house, you would feel embarrassed.

MAZZINI. I shall take particular care to keep out of your house, Lady Utterword.

LADY UTTERWORD. You will be quite wrong, Mr Dunn. I should make you very comfortable; and you would not have the trouble and anxiety of wondering whether you should wear your purple and gold or your green and crimson dressing-gown at dinner. You complicate life instead of simplifying it by doing these ridiculous things.

ELLIE. Your house is not Heartbreak House: is it, Lady Utterword?

HECTOR. Yet she breaks hearts, easy as her house is. That poor devil upstairs with his flute howls when she twists his heart, just as Mangan howls when my wife twists his.

LADY UTTERWORD. That is because Randall has nothing to do but have his heart broken. It is a change from having his head shampooed. Catch anyone breaking Hastings' heart!

CAPTAIN SHOTOVER. The numskull wins, after all.

LADY UTTERWORD. I shall go back to my numskull with the greatest satisfaction when I am tired of you all, clever as you are.

MANGAN [huffily] I never set up to be clever.

LADY UTTERWORD. I forgot you, Mr Mangan.

MANGAN. Well, I dont see that quite, either.

LADY UTTERWORD. You may not be clever, Mr Mangan; but you are successful.

MANGAN. But I dont want to be regarded merely as a successful man. I have an imagination like anyone else. I have a presentiment—

MRS HUSHABYE. Oh, you are impossible, Alfred. Here I am devoting myself to you; and you think of nothing but your ridiculous presentiment. You bore me. Come and talk poetry to me under the stars. [She drags him away into the darkness].

MANGAN [tearfully, as he disappears] Yes: it's all very well to make fun of me; but if you only knew—

HECTOR [impatiently] How is all this going to end?

MAZZINI. It wont end, Mr Hushabye. Life doesnt end: it goes on.

ELLIE. Oh, it cant go on for ever. I'm always expecting something. I dont know what it is; but life must come to a point sometime.

LADY UTTERWORD. The point for a young woman of your age is a baby.

HECTOR. Yes, but, damn it, I have the same feeling; and I cant have a baby.

LADY UTTERWORD. By deputy, Hector.

HECTOR. But I have children. All that is over and done with for me: and yet I too feel that this cant last. We sit here talking, and leave everything to Mangan and to chance and to the devil. Think of the powers of destruction that Mangan and his mutual admiration gang wield! It's madness: it's

like giving a torpedo to a badly brought up child to play at earthquakes with.

MAZZINI. I know. I used often to think about that when I was young.

HECTOR. Think! Whats the good of thinking about it? Why didnt you do something?

MAZZINI. But I did. I joined societies and made speeches and wrote pamphlets. That was all I could do. But, you know, though the people in the societies thought they knew more than Mangan, most of them wouldnt have joined if they had known as much. You see they had never had any money to handle or any men to manage. Every year I expected a revolution, or some frightful smash-up: it seemed impossible that we could blunder and muddle on any longer. But nothing happened, except, of course, the usual poverty and crime and drink that we are used to. Nothing ever does happen. It's amazing how well we get along, all things considered.

LADY UTTERWORD. Perhaps somebody cleverer than you and Mr Mangan was at work all the time.

MAZZINI. Perhaps so. Though I was brought up not to believe in anything, I often feel that there is a great deal to be said for the theory of an over-ruling Providence, after all.

LADY UTTERWORD. Providence! I meant Hastings.

MAZZINI. Oh, I beg your pardon, Lady Utterword.

CAPTAIN SHOTOVER. Every drunken skipper trusts to Providence. But one of the ways of Providence with drunken skippers is to run them on the rocks.

MAZZINI. Very true, no doubt, at sea. But in politics, I assure you, they only run into jellyfish. Nothing happens.

CAPTAIN SHOTOVER. At sea nothing happens to the sea. Nothing happens to the sky. The sun comes up from the east and goes down to the west. The moon grows from a sickle to an arc lamp, and comes later and later until she is lost in the light as other things are lost in the darkness. After the typhoon, the flying-fish glitter in the sunshine like birds. It's amazing how they get along, all things considered. Nothing happens, except something not worth mentioning.

ELLIE. What is that, O Captain, my captain?

CAPTAIN SHOTOVER [savagely] Nothing but the smash of the drunken skipper's ship on the rocks, the splintering of her rotten timbers, the tearing of her rusty plates, the drowning of the crew like rats in a trap.

ELLIE. Moral: dont take rum.

CAPTAIN SHOTOVER [*vehemently*] That is a lie, child. Let a man drink ten barrels of rum a day, he is not a drunken skipper until he is a drifting skipper. Whilst he can lay his course and stand on his bridge and steer it, he is no drunkard. It is the man who lies drinking in his bunk and trusts to Providence that I call the drunken skipper, though he drank nothing but the waters of the River Jordan.

ELLIE. Splendid! And you havnt had a drop for an hour. You see you dont need it: your own spirit is not dead.

CAPTAIN SHOTOVER. Echoes: nothing but echoes. The last shot was fired years ago.

HECTOR. And this ship that we are all in ? This soul's prison we call England?

CAPTAIN SHOTOVER. The captain is in his bunk, drinking bottled ditch-water; and the crew is gambling in the forecastle. She will strike and sink and split. Do you think the laws of God will be suspended in favor of England because you were born in it?

HECTOR. Well, I dont mean to be drowned like a rat in a trap. I still have the will to live. What am I to do?

CAPTAIN SHOTOVER. Do? Nothing simpler. Learn your business as an Englishman.

HECTOR. And what may my business as an Englishman be, pray?

CAPTAIN SHOTOVER. Navigation. Learn it and live; or leave it and be damned.

ELLIE. Quiet, quiet: youll tire yourself.

MAZZINI. I thought all that once, Captain; but I assure you nothing will happen.

A dull distant explosion is heard.

HECTOR [*starting up*] What was that?

CAPTAIN SHOTOVER. Something happening. [*He blows his whistle*]. Breakers ahead!

The light goes out.

HECTOR [*furiously*] Who put that light out? Who dared put that light out?

NURSE GUINNESS [*running in from the house to the middle of the esplanade*] I did, sir. The police have telephoned to say we'll be summoned if we dont put that light out: it can be seen for miles.

HECTOR. It shall be seen for a hundred miles. [*He dashes into the house*].

NURSE GUINNESS. The rectory is nothing but a heap of bricks, they say. Unless we can give the rector a bed he has nowhere to lay his head this night.

CAPTAIN SHOTOVER. The Church is on the rocks, breaking up. I told him it would unless it headed for God's open sea.

NURSE GUINNESS. And you are all to go down to the cellars.

CAPTAIN SHOTOVER. Go there yourself, you and all the crew. Batten down the hatches.

NURSE GUINNESS. And hide beside the coward I married! I'll go on the roof first. [*The lamp lights up again*]. There! Mr Hushabyc's turned it on again.

THE BURGLAR [*hurrying in and appealing to Nurse Guinness*] Here: wheres the way to that gravel pit? The boot-boy says theres a cave in the gravel pit. Them cellars is no use. Wheres the gravel pit, Captain.

NURSE GUINNESS. Go straight on past the flagstaff until you fall into it and break your dirty neck. [*She pushes him contemptuously towards the flagstaff, and herself goes to the foot of the hammock and waits there, as it were by Ariadne's cradle*].

Another and louder explosion is heard. The burglar stops and stands trembling.

ELLIE [*rising*] That was nearer.

CAPTAIN SHOTOVER. The next one will get us. [*He rises*]. Stand by, all hands, for judgment.

THE BURGLAR. Oh my Lordy God! [*He rushes away frantically past the flagstaff into the gloom*].

MRS HUSHABYE [*emerging panting from the darkness*] Who was that running away? [*She comes to Ellie*]. Did you hear the explosions? And the sound in the sky: it's splendid: it's like an orchestra: it's like Beethoven.

ELLIE. By thunder, Hesione: it is Beethoven.

She and Hesione throw themselves into one another's arms in wild excitement. The light increases.

MAZZINI [*anxiously*] The light is getting brighter.

NURSE GUINNESS [*looking up at the house*] It's Mr Hushabye turning on all the lights in the house and tearing down the curtains.

RANDALL [*rushing in in his pyjamas, distractedly waving a flute*] Ariadne: my soul, my precious, go down to the cellars: I beg and implore you, go down to the cellars!

LADY UTTERWORD [*quite composed in her hammock*] The governor's wife in the cellars with the servants! Really, Randall!

RANDALL. But what shall I do if you are

2 D

killed?

LADY UTTERWORD. You will probably be killed, too, Randall. Now play your flute to shew that you are not afraid; and be good. Play us Keep the home fires burning.

NURSE GUINNESS [grimly] They ll keep the homes fires burning for us: them up there.

RANDALL [having tried to play] My lips are trembling. I cant get a sound.

MAZZINI. I hope poor Mangan is safe.

MRS HUSHABYE. He is hiding in the cave in the gravel pit.

CAPTAIN SHOTOVER. My dynamite drew him there. It is the hand of God.

HECTOR [returning from the house and striding across to his former place] There is not half light enough. We should be blazing to the skies.

ELLIE [tense with excitement] Set fire to the house, Marcus.

MRS HUSHABYE. My house! No.

HECTOR. I thought of that; but it would not be ready in time.

CAPTAIN SHOTOVER. The judgment has come. Courage will not save you; but it will shew that your souls are still alive.

MRS HUSHABYE. Sh-sh! Listen: do you hear it now? It's magnificent.

They all turn away from the house and look up, listening.

HECTOR [gravely] Miss Dunn: you can do no good here. We of this house are only moths flying into the candle. You had better go down to the cellar.

ELLIE [scornfully] I dont think.

MAZZINI. Ellie, dear, there is no disgrace in going to the cellar. An officer would order his soldiers to take cover. Mr Hushabye is behaving like an amateur. Mangan and the burglar are acting very sensibly; and it is they who will survive.

ELLIE. Let them. I shall behave like an amateur. But why should you run any risk?

MAZZINI. Think of the risk those poor fellows up there are running!

NURSE GUINNESS. Think of them, indeed, the murdering blackguards! What next?

A terrific explosion shakes the earth. They reel back into their seats, or clutch the nearest support. They hear the falling of the shattered glass from the windows.

MAZZINI. Is anyone hurt?

HECTOR. Where did it fall?

NURSE GUINNESS [in hideous triumph] Right in the gravel pit: I seen it. Serve un right! I seen it. [She runs away towards the gravel pit, laughing harshly].

HECTOR. One husband gone.

CAPTAIN SHOTOVER. Thirty pounds of good dynamite wasted.

MAZZINI. Oh, poor Mangan!

HECTOR. Are you immortal that you need pity him? Our turn next.

They wait in silence and intense expectation. Hesione and Ellie hold each other's hand tight.

A distant explosion is heard.

MRS HUSHABYE [relaxing her grip] Oh! they have passed us.

LADY UTTERWORD. The danger is over, Randall. Go to bed.

CAPTAIN SHOTOVER. Turn in, all hands. The ship is safe. [He sits down and goes asleep].

ELLIE [disappointedly] Safe!

HECTOR [disgustedly] Yes, safe. And how damnably dull the world has become again suddenly! [He sits down].

MAZZINI [sitting down] I was quite wrong, after all. It is we who have survived; and Mangan and the burglar—

HECTOR. —the two burglars—

LADY UTTERWORD. —the two practical men of business—

MAZZINI. —both gone. And the poor clergyman will have to get a new house.

MRS HUSHABYE. But what a glorious experience! I hope theyll come again tomorrow night.

ELLIE [radiant at the prospect] Oh, I hope so.

Randall at last succeeds in keeping the home fires burning on his flute.

THE END

XXV
GREAT CATHERINE
(WHOM GLORY STILL ADORES)

THE FIRST SCENE

1776. Patiomkin in his bureau in the Winter Palace, St Petersburgh. Huge palatial apartment: style, Russia in the XVIII century imitating the Versailles du Roi Soleil. Extravagant luxury. Also dirt and disorder.

Patiomkin, gigantic in stature and build, his face marred by the loss of one eye and a marked squint in the other, sits at the end of a table littered with papers and the remains of three or four successive breakfasts. He has supplies of coffee and brandy at hand sufficient for a party of ten. His coat, encrusted with diamonds, is on the floor. It has fallen off a chair placed near the other end of the table for the convenience of visitors. His court sword, with its attachments, is on the chair. His three-cornered hat, also bejewelled, is on the table. He himself is half dressed in an unfastened shirt and an immense dressing-gown, once gorgeous, now food-splashed and dirty, as it serves him for towel, handkerchief, duster, and every other use to which a textile fabric can be put by a slovenly man. It does not conceal his huge hairy chest, nor his half-buttoned knee breeches, nor his legs. These are partly clad in silk stockings, which he occasionally hitches up to his knees, and presently shakes down to his shins, by his restless movements. His feet are thrust into enormous slippers, worth, with their crust of jewels, several thousand roubles apiece.

Superficially Patiomkin is a violent, brutal barbarian, an upstart despot of the most intolerable and dangerous type, ugly, lazy, and disgusting in his personal habits. Yet ambassadors report him the ablest man in Russia, and the one who can do most with the still abler Empress Catherine II, who is not a Russian but a German, by no means barbarous or intemperate in her personal habits. She not only disputes with Frederick the Great the reputation of being the cleverest monarch in Europe, but may even put in a very plausible claim to be the cleverest and most attractive individual alive. Now she not only tolerates Patiomkin long after she has got over her first romantic attachment to him, but esteems him highly as a counsellor and a good friend. His love letters are among the best on record. He has a wild sense of humor, which enables him to laugh at himself as well as at everybody else. In the eyes of the English visitor now about to be admitted to his presence he may be an outrageous ruffian. In fact he actually is an outrageous ruffian, in no matter whose eyes; but the visitor will find out, as everyone else sooner or later finds out, that he is a man to be reckoned with even by those who are not intimidated by his temper, bodily strength, and exalted rank.*

A pretty young lady, Varinka, his favorite niece, is lounging on an ottoman between his end of the table and the door, very sulky and dissatisfied, perhaps because he is preoccupied with his papers and his brandy bottle, and she can see nothing of him but his broad back.

There is a screen behind the ottoman.

An old soldier, a Cossack sergeant, enters.

THE SERGEANT [*softly to the lady, holding the door handle*] Little darling honey: is his Highness the prince very busy?

VARINKA. His Highness the prince is very busy. He is singing out of tune; he is biting his nails; he is scratching his head; he is hitching up his untidy stockings; he is making himself disgusting and odious to everybody; and he is pretending to read state papers that he does not understand because he is too lazy and selfish to talk and be companionable.

PATIOMKIN [*growls; then wipes his nose with his dressing-gown*]!!

VARINKA. Pig. Ugh! [*She curls herself up with a shiver of disgust and retires from the conversation*].

THE SERGEANT [*stealing across to the coat, and picking it up to replace it on the back of the chair*] Little Father: the English captain, so highly recommended to you by old Fritz of Prussia, by the English ambassador, and by Monsieur Voltaire (whom [*crossing himself*] may God in his infinite mercy damn eternally!), is in the antechamber and desires audience.

PATIOMKIN [*deliberately*] To hell with the English captain; and to hell with old Fritz of Prussia; and to hell with the English ambassador; and to hell with Monsieur Voltaire; and to hell with you too!

THE SERGEANT. Have mercy on me, Little Father. Your head is bad this morning. You drink too much French brandy and too little good Russian kvass.

PATIOMKIN [with sudden fury] Why are visitors of consequence announced by a sergeant? [Springing at him and seizing him by the throat] What do you mean by this, you hound? Do you want five thousand blows of the stick? Where is General Volkonsky?

THE SERGEANT [on his knees] Little Father: you kicked his Highness downstairs.

PATIOMKIN [flinging him down and kicking him] You lie, you dog. You lie.

THE SERGEANT. Little Father: life is hard for the poor. If you say it is a lie, it is a lie. He fell downstairs. I picked him up; and he kicked me. They all kick me when you kick them. God knows that is not just, Little Father!

PATIOMKIN [laughs ogreishly; then returns to his place at the table, chuckling]!!!

VARINKA. Savage! Boor! It is a disgrace. No wonder the French sneer at us as barbarians.

THE SERGEANT [who has crept round the table to the screen, and insinuated himself between Patiomkin's back and Varinka] Do you think the Prince will see the Captain, little darling?

PATIOMKIN. He will not see any captain. Go to the devil!

THE SERGEANT. Be merciful, Little Father. God knows it is your duty to see him! [To Varinka] Intercede for him and for me, beautiful little darling. He has given me a rouble.

PATIOMKIN. Oh, send him in, send him in; and stop pestering me. Am I never to have a moment's peace?

The Sergeant salutes joyfully and hurries out, divining that Patiomkin has intended to see the English captain all along, and has played this comedy of fury and exhausted impatience to conceal his interest in the visitor.

VARINKA. Have you no shame? You refuse to see the most exalted persons. You kick princes and generals downstairs. And then you see an English captain merely because he has given a rouble to that common soldier. It is scandalous.

PATIOMKIN. Darling beloved, I am drunk; but I know what I am doing. I wish to stand well with the English.

VARINKA. And you think you will impress an Englishman by receiving him as you are now, half drunk?

PATIOMKIN [gravely] It is true: the English despise men who cannot drink. I must make myself wholly drunk. [He takes a huge draught of brandy].

VARINKA. Sot!

The Sergeant returns ushering a handsome strongly built young English officer in the uniform of a Light Dragoon. He is evidently on fairly good terms with himself, and very sure of his social position. He crosses the room to the end of the table opposite Patiomkin's, and awaits the civilities of that statesman with confidence. The Sergeant remains prudently at the door.

THE SERGEANT [paternally] Little Father: this is the English captain, so well recommended to her sacred Majesty the Empress. God knows, he needs your countenance and protec— [He vanishes precipitately, seeing that Patiomkin is about to throw a bottle at him. The Captain contemplates these preliminaries with astonishment, and with some displeasure, which is not allayed when Patiomkin, hardly condescending to look at his visitor, of whom he nevertheless takes stock with the corner of his one eye, says gruffly] Well?

EDSTASTON. My name is Edstaston: Captain Edstaston of the Light Dragoons. I have the honor to present to your Highness this letter from the British ambassador, which will give you all necessary particulars. [He hands Patiomkin the letter].

PATIOMKIN [tearing it open and glancing at it for about a second] What do you want?

EDSTASTON. The letter will explain to your Highness who I am.

PATIOMKIN. I dont want to know who you are. What do you want?

EDSTASTON. An audience of the Empress. [Patiomkin contemptuously throws the letter aside. Edstaston adds hotly] Also some civility, if you please.

PATIOMKIN [with derision] Ho!

VARINKA. My uncle is receiving you with unusual civility, Captain. He has just kicked a general downstairs.

EDSTASTON. A Russian general, madam?

VARINKA. Of course.

EDSTASTON. I must allow myself to say, madam, that your uncle had better not attempt to kick an English officer downstairs.

PATIOMKIN. You want me to kick you upstairs: eh? You want an audience of the

Empress.

EDSTASTON. I have said nothing about kicking, sir. If it comes to that, my boots shall speak for me. Her Majesty has signified a desire to have news of the rebellion in America. I have served against the rebels; and I am instructed to place myself at the disposal of her Majesty, and to describe the events of the war to her, as an eye-witness, in a discreet and agreeable manner.

PATIOMKIN. Psha! I know. You think if she once sets eyes on your face and your uniform your fortune is made. You think that if she could stand a man like me, with only one eye, and a cross eye at that, she must fall down at your feet at first sight, eh?

EDSTASTON [shocked and indignant] I think nothing of the sort; and I'll trouble you not to repeat it. If I were a Russian subject and you made such a boast about my queen, I'd strike you across the face with my sword. [Patiomkin, with a yell of fury, rushes at him]. Hands off, you swine! [As Patiomkin, towering over him, attempts to seize him by the throat, Edstaston, who is a bit of a wrestler, adroitly backheels him. He falls, amazed, on his back].

VARINKA [rushing out] Help! Call the guard! The Englishman is murdering my uncle! Help! Help!

The guard and the Sergeant rush in. Edstaston draws a pair of small pistols from his boots, and points one at the Sergeant and the other at Patiomkin, who is sitting on the floor, somewhat sobered. The soldiers stand irresolute.

EDSTASTON. Stand off. [To Patiomkin] Order them off, if you dont want a bullet through your silly head.

THE SERGEANT. Little Father: tell us what to do. Our lives are yours; but God knows you are not fit to die.

PATIOMKIN [absurdly self-possessed] Get out.

THE SERGEANT. Little Father—

PATIOMKIN [roaring] Get out. Get out, all of you. [They withdraw, much relieved at their escape from the pistol. Patiomkin attempts to rise, and rolls over]. Here! help me up, will you? Dont you see that I'm drunk and cant get up?

EDSTASTON [suspiciously] You want to get hold of me.

PATIOMKIN [squatting resignedly against the chair on which his clothes hang] Very well, then: I shall stay where I am, because I'm drunk and youre afraid of me.

EDSTASTON. I'm not afraid of you, damn you!

PATIOMKIN [ecstatically] Darling: your lips are the gates of truth. Now listen to me. [He marks off the items of his statement with ridiculous stiff gestures of his head and arms, imitating a puppet] You are Captain Whathisname; and your uncle is the Earl of Whatdyecallum; and your father is Bishop of Thingummybob; and you are a young man of the highest spr-promise (I told you I was drunk), educated at Cambridge, and got your step as captain in the field at the GLORIOUS battle of Bunker's Hill. Invalided home from America at the request of Aunt Fanny, Lady-in-Waiting to the Queen. All right, eh?

EDSTASTON. How do you know all this?

PATIOMKIN [crowing fantastically] In er lerrer, darling, darling, darling, darling. Lerrer you shewed me.

EDSTASTON. But you didnt read it.

PATIOMKIN [flapping his fingers at him grotesquely] Only one eye, darling. Cross eye. Sees everything. Read lerrer ince-ince-istastaneously. Kindly give me vinegar borle. Green borle. On'y to sober me. Too drunk to speak proply. If you would be so kind, darling. Green borle. [Edstaston, still suspicious, shakes his head and keeps his pistols ready]. Reach it myself. [He reaches behind him up to the table, and snatches at the green bottle, from which he takes a copious draught. Its effect is appalling. His wry faces and agonized belchings are so heartrending that they almost upset Edstaston. When the victim at last staggers to his feet, he is a pale fragile nobleman, aged and quite sober, extremely dignified in manner and address, though shaken by his recent convulsions]. Young man: it is not better to be drunk than sober; but it is happier. Goodness is not happiness. That is an epigram. But I have overdone this. I am too sober to be good company. Let me redress the balance. [He takes a generous draught of brandy, and recovers his geniality]. Aha! Thats better. And now listen, darling. You must not come to Court with pistols in your boots.

EDSTASTON. I have found them useful.

PATIOMKIN. Nonsense. I'm your friend. You mistook my intention because I was drunk. Now that I am sober—in moderation —I will prove that I am your friend. Have some diamonds. [Roaring] Hullo there! Dogs, pigs: hullo!

The Sergeant comes in.

THE SERGEANT. God be praised, Little Father: you are still spared to us.

PATIOMKIN. Tell them to bring some diamonds. Plenty of diamonds. And rubies. Get out. [*He aims a kick at the Sergeant, who flees*]. Put up your pistols, darling. I'll give you a pair with gold handgrips. I am your friend.

EDSTASTON [*replacing the pistols in his boots rather unwillingly*] Your Highness understands that if I am missing, or if anything happens to me, there will be trouble.

PATIOMKIN [*enthusiastically*] Call me darling.

EDSTASTON. It is not the English custom.

PATIOMKIN. You have no hearts, you English! [*Slapping his right breast*] Heart! Heart!

EDSTASTON. Pardon, your Highness: your heart is on the other side.

PATIOMKIN [*surprised and impressed*] Is it? You are learned! You are a doctor! You English are wonderful! We are barbarians, drunken pigs. Catherine does not know it; but we are. Catherine's a German. But I have given her a Russian heart. [*He is about to slap himself again*].

EDSTASTON [*delicately*] The other side, your Highness.

PATIOMKIN [*maudlin*] Darling: a true Russian has a heart on both sides.

The Sergeant enters carrying a goblet filled with precious stones.

PATIOMKIN. Get out. [*He snatches the goblet and kicks the Sergeant out, not maliciously but from habit, indeed not noticing that he does it*]. Darling: have some diamonds. Have a fistful. [*He takes up a handful and lets them slip back through his fingers into the goblet, which he then offers to Edstaston*].

EDSTASTON. Thank you: I dont take presents.

PATIOMKIN [*amazed*] You refuse!

EDSTASTON. I thank your Highness; but it is not the custom for English gentlemen to take presents of that kind.

PATIOMKIN. Are you really an Englishman?

EDSTASTON [*bows*]!

PATIOMKIN. You are the first Englishman I ever saw refuse anything he could get. [*He puts the goblet on the table; then turns again to Edstaston*]. Listen, darling. You are a wrestler: a splendid wrestler. You threw me on my back like magic, though I could lift you with one hand. Darling: you are a giant, a paladin.

EDSTASTON [*complacently*] We wrestle rather well in my part of England.

PATIOMKIN. I have a Turk who is a wrestler: a prisoner of war. You shall wrestle with him for me. I'll stake a million roubles on you.

EDSTASTON [*incensed*] Damn you! do you take me for a prize-fighter? How dare you make me such a proposal?

PATIOMKIN [*with wounded feeling*] Darling: there is no pleasing you. Dont you like me?

EDSTASTON [*mollified*] Well, in a sort of way I do; though I dont know why I should. But my instructions are that I am to see the Empress; and—

PATIOMKIN. Darling: you shall see the Empress. A glorious woman, the greatest woman in the world. But lemme give you piece 'vice—pah! still drunk. They water my vinegar. [*He shakes himself; clears his throat; and resumes soberly*] If Catherine takes a fancy to you, you may ask for roubles, diamonds, palaces, titles, orders, anything! and you may aspire to everything: field-marshal, admiral, minister, what you please —except Tsar.

EDSTASTON. I tell you I dont want to ask for anything. Do you suppose I am an adventurer and a beggar?

PATIOMKIN [*plaintively*] Why not, darling? *I* was an adventurer. *I* was a beggar.

EDSTASTON. Oh, you!

PATIOMKIN. Well: whats wrong with me?

EDSTASTON. You are a Russian. Thats different.

PATIOMKIN [*effusively*] Darling: I am a man; and you are a man; and Catherine is a woman. Woman reduces us all to the common denominator. [*Chuckling*]. Again an epigram! [*Gravely*] You understand it, I hope. Have you had a college education, darling? *I* have.

EDSTASTON. Certainly. I am a Bachelor of Arts.

PATIOMKIN. It is enough that you are a bachelor, darling: Catherine will supply the arts. Aha! Another epigram? I am in the vein today.

EDSTASTON [*embarrassed and a little offended*] I must ask your Highness to change the subject. As a visitor in Russia, I am the guest of the Empress; and I must tell you plainly that I have neither the right nor the disposition to speak lightly of her Majesty.

PATIOMKIN. You have conscientious scruples?

EDSTASTON. I have the scruples of a gentleman.

PATIOMKIN. In Russia a gentleman has no scruples. In Russia we face facts.

EDSTASTON. In England, sir, a gentleman never faces any facts if they are unpleasant facts.

PATIOMKIN. In real life, darling, all facts are unpleasant. [*Greatly pleased with himself*] Another epigram! Where is my accursed chancellor? these gems should be written down and recorded for posterity. [*He rushes to the table; sits down; and snatches up a pen. Then, recollecting himself.*] But I have not asked you to sit down. [*He rises and goes to the other chair*]. I am a savage: a barbarian. [*He throws the shirt and coat over the table on to the floor and puts his sword on the table*]. Be seated, Captain.

EDSTASTON. Thank you.

They bow to one another ceremoniously. Patiomkin's tendency to grotesque exaggeration costs him his balance: he nearly falls over Edstaston, who rescues him and takes the proffered chair.

PATIOMKIN [*resuming his seat*] By the way, what was the piece of advice I was going to give you?

EDSTASTON. As you did not give it, I dont know. Allow me to add that I have not asked for your advice.

PATIOMKIN. I give it to you unasked, delightful Englishman. I remember it now. It was this. Dont try to become Tsar of Russia.

EDSTASTON [*in astonishment*] I havnt the slightest intention—

PATIOMKIN. Not now; but you will have: take my word for it. It will strike you as a splendid idea to have conscientious scruples —to desire the blessing of the Church on your union with Catherine.

EDSTASTON [*rising in utter amazement*] My union with Catherine! Youre mad.

PATIOMKIN [*unmoved*] The day you hint at such a thing will be the day of your downfall. Besides, it is not lucky to be Catherine's husband. You know what happened to Peter?

EDSTASTON [*shortly: sitting down again*] I do not wish to discuss it.

PATIOMKIN. You think she murdered him?

EDSTASTON. I know that people have said so.

PATIOMKIN [*thunderously: springing to his feet*] It is a lie: Orloff murdered him. [*Subsiding a little*] He also knocked my eye out; but [*sitting down placidly*] I succeeded him for all that. And [*patting Edstaston's hand very affectionately*] I'm sorry to say, darling, that if you become Tsar, *I* shall murder y o u.

EDSTASTON [*ironically returning the caress*] Thank you. The occasion will not arise. [*Rising*] I have the honour to wish your Highness good morning.

PATIOMKIN [*jumping up and stopping him on his way to the door*] Tut tut! I'm going to take you to the Empress n o w, this very instant.

EDSTASTON. In these boots? Impossible! I must change.

PATIOMKIN. Nonsense! You shall come just as you are. You shall shew her your calves later on.

EDSTASTON. But it will take me only half an hour to—

PATIOMKIN. In half an hour it will be too late for the *petit lever*. Come along. Damn it, man, I must oblige the British ambassador, and the French ambassador, and old Fritz, and Monsieur Voltaire and the rest of them. [*He shouts rudely to the door*] Varinka! [*To Edstaston, with tears in his voice*] Varinka shall persuade you: nobody can refuse Varinka anything. My niece. A treasure, I assure you. Beautiful! devoted! fascinating! [*Shouting again*] Varinka: where the devil are you?

VARINKA [*returning*] I'll not be shouted for. You have the voice of a bear, and the manners of a tinker.

PATIOMKIN. Tsh-sh-sh. Little angel Mother: you must behave yourself before the English captain. [*He takes off his dressing-gown and throws it over the papers and the breakfasts; picks up his coat; and disappears behind the screen to complete his toilette*].

EDSTASTON. Madam! [*He bows*].

VARINKA [*curtseying*] Monsieur le Capitaine!

EDSTASTON. I must apologize for the disturbance I made, madam.

PATIOMKIN [*behind the screen*] You must not call her madam. You must call her little Mother, and beautiful darling.

EDSTASTON. My respect for the lady will not permit it.

VARINKA. Respect! How can you respect the niece of a savage?

EDSTASTON. [*deprecating*] Oh, madam!

VARINKA. Heaven is my witness, Little English Father, we need someone who is not afraid of him. He is so strong! I hope you will throw him down on the floor many, many, many times.

PATIOMKIN [*behind the screen*] Varinka!

VARINKA. Yes?

PATIOMKIN. Go and look through the keyhole of the Imperial bed-chamber; and bring me word whether the Empress is awake yet.

VARINKA. Fi donc! I do not look through keyholes.

PATIOMKIN [*emerging, having arranged his shirt and put on his diamonded coat*]You have been badly brought up, little darling. Would any lady or gentleman walk unannounced into a room without first looking through the keyhole? [*Taking his sword from the table and putting it on*] The great thing in life is to be simple; and the perfectly simple thing is to look through keyholes. Another epigram: the fifth this morning! Where is my fool of a chancellor? Where is Popof?

EDSTASTON [*choking with suppressed laughter*]!!!!

PATIOMKIN [*gratified*] Darling: you appreciate my epigram.

EDSTASTON. Excuse me. Pop off! Ha! ha! I cant help laughing. Whats his real name, by the way, in case I meet him?

VARINKA [*surprised*] His real name? Popof, of course. Why do you laugh, Little Father?

EDSTASTON. How can anyone with a sense of humor help laughing? Pop off! [*He is convulsed*].

VARINKA [*looking at her uncle, taps her forehead significantly*]!!

PATIOMKIN [*aside to Varinka*] No: only English. He will amuse Catherine. [*To Edstaston*] Come! you shall tell the joke to the Empress: she is by way of being a humorist. [*He takes him by the arm, and leads him towards the door*].

EDSTASTON [*resisting*] No, really. I am not fit—

PATIOMKIN. Persuade him, Little angel Mother.

VARINKA [*taking his other arm*] Yes, yes, yes, Little English Father: God knows it is your duty to be brave and wait on the Empress. Come.

EDSTASTON. No. I had rather—

PATIOMKIN [*hauling him along*] Come.

VARINKA [*pulling him and coaxing him*] Come, little love: you cant refuse me.

EDSTASTON. But how can I?

PATIOMKIN. Why not? She wont eat you.

VARINKA. She will; but you must come.

EDSTASTON. I assure you—it is quite out of the question—my clothes.

VARINKA. You look perfect.

PATIOMKIN. Come along, darling.

EDSTASTON [*struggling*] Impossible—

VARINKA. Come, come, come.

EDSTASTON. No. Believe me—I dont wish —I—

VARINKA. Carry him, uncle.

PATIOMKIN [*lifting him in his arms like a father carrying a little boy*] Yes: I'll carry you.

EDSTASTON. Dash it all, this is ridiculous!

VARINKA [*seizing his ankles and dancing as he is carried out*] You must come. If you kick you will blacken my eyes.

PATIOMKIN. Come, baby, come.

By this time they have made their way through the door and are out of hearing.

THE SECOND SCENE

The Empress's petit lever. The central doors are closed. Those who enter through them find on their left on a dais of two broad steps, a magnificent curtained bed. Beyond it a door in the panelling leads to the Empress's cabinet. Near the foot of the bed, in the middle of the room, stands a gilt chair, with the Imperial arms carved and the Imperial monogram embroidered.

The Court is in attendance, standing in two melancholy rows down the side of the room opposite to the bed, solemn, bored, waiting for the Empress to awaken. The Princess Dashkoff, with two ladies, stands a little in front of the line of courtiers, by the Imperial chair. Silence, broken only by the yawns and whispers of the courtiers. Naryshkin, the Chamberlain, stands by the head of the bed.

A loud yawn is heard from behind the curtains.

NARYSHKIN [*holding up a warning hand*] Ssh!

The courtiers hastily cease whispering; dress up their lines; and stiffen. Dead silence. A bell tinkles within the curtains. Naryshkin and the Princess solemnly draw them and reveal the Empress.

Catherine turns over on her back, and stretches herself.

CATHERINE [*yawning*] Heigho—ah—yah—ah—ow—what o'clock is it? [*Her accent is German*].

NARYSHKIN [*formally*] Her Imperial Majesty is awake. [*The Court falls on its knees*].

ALL. Good morning to your Majesty.

NARYSHKIN. Half-past ten, Little Mother.

CATHERINE [*sitting up abruptly*] Potztausend! [*Contemplating the kneeling courtiers*] Oh, get up, get up. [*All rise*]. Your etiquette bores me. I am hardly awake in the morning before it begins. [*Yawning again and relapsing sleepily against her pillows*] Why do they do it, Naryshkin?

NARYSHKIN. God knows it is not for your sake, Little Mother. But you see if you were not a great queen they would all be nobodies.

CATHERINE [*sitting up*] They make me do it to keep up their own little dignities? So?

NARYSHKIN. Exactly. Also because if they didnt you might have them flogged, dear Little Mother.

CATHERINE [*springing energetically out of bed and seating herself on the edge of it*] Flogged! I! A Liberal Empress! A philosopher! You are a barbarian, Naryshkin. [*She rises and turns to the courtiers*] And then, as if I cared! [*She turns again to Naryshkin*] You should know by this time that I am frank and original in character, like an Englishman. [*She walks about restlessly*]. No: what maddens me about all this ceremony is that I am the only person in Russia who gets no fun out of my being Empress. You all glory in me: you bask in my smiles: you get titles and honors and favors from me: you are dazzled by my crown and my robes: you feel splendid when you have been admitted to my presence; and when I say a gracious word to you, you talk about it to everyone you meet for a week afterwards. But what do *I* get out of it? Nothing. [*She throws herself into the chair. Naryshkin deprecates with a gesture: she hurls an emphatic repetition at him*] Nothing!! I wear a crown until my neck aches: I stand looking majestic until I am ready to drop: I have to smile at ugly old ambassadors and frown and turn my back on young and handsome ones. Nobody gives me anything. When I was only an Archduchess, the English ambassador used to give me money whenever I wanted it —or rather whenever he wanted to get anything out of my sacred predecessor Elizabeth [*the Court bows to the ground*]; but now that I am Empress he never gives me a kopek. When I have headaches and colics I envy the scullerymaids. And you are not a bit grateful to me for all my care of you, my work, my thought, my fatigue, my sufferings.

THE PRINCESS DASHKOFF. God knows, Little Mother, we all implore you to give your wonderful brain a rest. That is why you get headaches. Monsieur Voltaire also has headaches. His brain is just like yours.

CATHERINE. Dashkoff: what a liar you are! [*Dashkoff curtsies with impressive dignity*]. And you think you are flattering me! Let me tell you I would not give a rouble to have the brains of all the philosophers in France. What is our business for today?

NARYSHKIN. The new museum, Little Mother. But the model will not be ready until tonight.

CATHERINE [*rising eagerly*] Yes: the museum. An enlightened capital should have a museum. [*She paces the chamber with a deep sense of the importance of the museum*]. It shall be one of the wonders of the world. I must have specimens: specimens, specimens, specimens.

NARYSHKIN. You are in high spirits this morning, Little Mother.

CATHERINE [*with sudden levity*] I am always in high spirits, even when people do not bring me my slippers. [*She runs to the chair and sits down, thrusting her feet out*].

The two ladies rush to her feet, each carrying a slipper. Catherine, about to put her feet into them, is checked by a disturbance in the antechamber.

PATIOMKIN [*carrying Edstaston through the antechamber*] Useless to struggle. Come along, beautiful baby darling. Come to Little Mother. [*He sings*]
 March him baby,
  Baby, baby,
 Lit-tle ba-by bumpkins.

VARINKA [*joining in to the same doggerel in canon, a third above*] March him, baby, etc., etc.

EDSTASTON [*trying to make himself heard*] No, no. This is carrying a joke too far. I must insist. Let me down! Hang it, will you let me down! Confound it! No, no. Stop playing the fool, will you? We dont understand this sort of thing in England. I shall be disgraced. Let me down.

CATHERINE [*meanwhile*] What a horrible noise! Naryshkin: see what it is.

Naryshkin goes to the door.

CATHERINE [*listening*] That is Prince Patiomkin.

NARYSHKIN [*calling from the door*] Little Mother: a stranger.

Catherine plunges into bed again and covers herself up. Patiomkin, followed by Varinka, carries Edstaston in; dumps him down on the foot of the bed; and staggers past it to the cabinet door. Varinka joins the courtiers at the opposite side of the room. Catherine, blazing with wrath, pushes Edstaston off her bed on to the floor; gets out of bed; and turns on Patiomkin with so terrible an expression that all kneel down hastily except Edstaston, who is sprawling on the carpet in angry confusion.

CATHERINE. Patiomkin: how dare you? [*Looking at Edstaston*] What is this?

PATIOMKIN [*on his knees: tearfully*] I dont know. I am drunk. What is this, Varinka?

EDSTASTON [*scrambling to his feet*] Madam: this drunken ruffian—

PATIOMKIN. Thas true. Drungn ruffian. Took dvantage of my being drunk. Said: take me to Lil angel Mother. Take me to beaufl Empress. Take me to the grea'st woman on earth. Thas whas he said. I took him. I was wrong. I am not sober.

CATHERINE. Men have grown sober in Siberia for less, Prince.

PATIOMKIN. Serve em right! Sgusting habit. Ask Varinka.

Catherine turns her face from him to the Court. The courtiers see that she is trying not to laugh, and know by experience that she will not succeed. They rise, relieved and grinning.

VARINKA. It is true. He drinks like a pig.

PATIOMKIN [*plaintively*] No: not like a pig. Like prince. Lil Mother made poor Patiomkin prince. Whas use being prince if I maynt drink?

CATHERINE [*biting her lips*] Go. I am offended.

PATIOMKIN. Dont scold, Ll Mother.

CATHERINE [*imperiously*] Go.

PATIOMKIN [*rising unsteadily*] Yes: go. Go bye bye. Very sleepy. Berr go bye bye than go Siberia. Go bye bye in Lil Mother's bed. [*He pretends to make an attempt to get into the bed*].

CATHERINE [*energetically pulling him back*] No, no! Patiomkin! What are you thinking of? [*He falls like a log on the floor, apparently dead drunk*].

THE PRINCESS DASHKOFF. Scandalous! An insult to your Imperial Majesty!

CATHERINE. Dashkoff: you have no sense of humor. [*She steps down to the floor level and looks indulgently at Patiomkin. He gurgles brutishly. She has an impulse of disgust*] Hog. [*She kicks him as hard as she can*]. Oh! You have broken my toe. Brute. Beast. Dashkoff is quite right. Do you hear?

PATIOMKIN. If you ask my pi-pinion of Dashkoff, my pipinion is that Dashkoff is drunk. Scanlous. Poor Patiomkin go bye bye. [*He relapses into drunken slumbers*].

Some of the courtiers move to carry him away.

CATHERINE [*stopping them*] Let him lie. Let him sleep it off. If he goes out it will be to a tavern and low company for the rest of the day. [*Indulgently*] There! [*She takes a pillow from the bed and puts it under his head; then turns to Edstaston; surveys him with perfect dignity; and asks, in her queenliest manner*] Varinka: who is this gentleman?

VARINKA. A foreign captain: I cannot pronounce his name. I think he is mad. He came to the Prince and said he must see your Majesty. He can talk of nothing else. We could not prevent him.

EDSTASTON [*overwhelmed by this apparent betrayal*] Oh! Madam: I am perfectly sane: I am actually an Englishman. I should never have dreamt of approaching your Majesty without the fullest credentials. I have letters from the English ambassador, from the Prussian ambassador. [*Naïvely*] But everybody assured me that Prince Patiomkin is all-powerful with your Majesty; so I naturally applied to him.

PATIOMKIN [*interrupts the conversation by an agonized wheezing groan, as of a donkey beginning to bray*]!!!

CATHERINE [*like a fishfag*] Schweig, du Hund. [*Resuming her impressive Royal manner*] Have you never been taught, sir, how a gentleman should enter the presence of a sovereign.

EDSTASTON. Yes, Madam; but I did not enter your presence: I was carried.

CATHERINE. But you say you asked the Prince to carry you.

EDSTASTON. Certainly not, Madam. I protested against it with all my might. I appeal to this lady to confirm me.

VARINKA [*pretending to be indignant*] Yes: you protested. But, all the same, you were very very very anxious to see her Imperial Majesty. You blushed when the Prince spoke of her. You threatened to strike him across the face with your sword because you thought he did not speak enthusiastically enough of her. [*To Catherine*] Trust me: he has seen your Imperial Majesty before.

CATHERINE [*to Edstaston*] You have seen us before?

EDSTASTON. At the review, Madam.

VARINKA [*triumphantly*] Aha! I knew it. Your Majesty wore the hussar uniform. He saw how radiant! how splendid! your Majesty looked. Oh! he has dared to admire your Majesty. Such insolence is not to be endured.

EDSTASTON. All Europe is a party to that insolence, Madam.

THE PRINCESS DASHKOFF. All Europe is content to do so at a respectful distance. It is possible to admire her Majesty's policy and her eminence in literature and philosophy without performing acrobatic feats in the Imperial bed.

EDSTASTON. I know nothing about her Majesty's eminence in policy or philosophy: I dont pretend to understand such things. I speak as a practical man. And I never knew that foreigners had any policy: I always thought that policy was Mr Pitt's business.

CATHERINE [lifting her eyebrows] So?

VARINKA. What else did you presume to admire her Majesty for, pray?

EDSTASTON [addled] Well, I—I—I—that is, I— [He stammers himself dumb].

CATHERINE [after a pitiless silence] We are waiting for your answer.

EDSTASTON. But I never said I admired your Majesty. The lady has twisted my words.

VARINKA. You dont admire her, then?

EDSTASTON. Well, I—naturally—of course, I cant deny that the uniform was very becoming—perhaps a little unfeminine—still—

Dead silence. Catherine and the Court watch him stonily. He is wretchedly embarrassed.

CATHERINE [with cold majesty] Well, sir: is that all you have to say?

EDSTASTON. Surely there is no harm in noticing that er—that er— [He stops again].

CATHERINE. Noticing that er—? [He gazes at her, speechless, like a fascinated rabbit. She repeats fiercely] That er—?

EDSTASTON [startled into speech] Well, that your Majesty was—was— [Soothingly] Well, let me put it this way: that it was rather natural for a man to admire your Majesty without being a philosopher.

CATHERINE [suddenly smiling and extending her hand to him to be kissed] Courtier!

EDSTASTON [kissing it] Not at all. Your Majesty is very good. I have been very awkward; but I did not intend it. I am rather stupid, I am afraid.

CATHERINE. Stupid! By no means. Courage, Captain: we are pleased. [He falls on his knee. She takes his cheeks in her hands; turns up his face; and adds] We are greatly pleased. [She slaps his cheek coquettishly: he bows almost to his knee]. The petit lever is over. [She turns to go into the cabinet, and stumbles against the supine Patiomkin]. Ach! [Edstaston springs to her assistance, seizing Patiomkin's heels and shifting him out of the Empress's path]. We thank you, Captain.

He bows gallantly, and is rewarded by a very gracious smile. Then Catherine goes into her cabinet, followed by the Princess Dashkoff, who turns at the door to make a deep curtsey to Edstaston.

VARINKA. Happy Little Father! Remember: I did this for you. [She runs out after the Empress].

Edstaston, somewhat dazed, crosses the room to the courtiers, and is received with marked deference, each courtier making him a profound bow or curtsey before withdrawing through the central doors. He returns each obeisance with a nervous jerk, and turns away from it, only to find another courtier bowing at the other side. The process finally reduces him to distraction, as he bumps into one in the act of bowing to another and then has to bow his apologies. But at last they are all gone except Naryshkin.

EDSTASTON. Ouf!

PATIOMKIN [jumping up vigorously] You have done it, darling. Superbly! Beautifully!

EDSTASTON [astonished] Do you mean to say you are not drunk?

PATIOMKIN. Not dead drunk, darling. Only diplomatically drunk. As a drunken hog, I have done for you in five minutes what I could not have done in five months as a sober man. Your fortune is made. She likes you.

EDSTASTON. The devil she does!

PATIOMKIN. Why? Arnt you delighted?

EDSTASTON. Delighted! Gracious heavens man, I am engaged to be married.

PATIOMKIN. What matter? She is in England, isn't she?

EDSTASTON. No. She has just arrived in St Petersburg.

THE PRINCESS DASHKOFF [returning] Captain Edstaston: the Empress is robed, and commands your presence.

EDSTASTON. Say I was gone before you arrived with the message. [He hurries out. The other three, too taken aback to stop him, stare after him in the utmost astonishment].

NARYSHKIN [turning from the door] She will have him knouted. He is a dead man.

THE PRINCESS DASHKOFF. But what am I to do? I cannot take such an answer to the Empress.

PATIOMKIN. P-P-P-P-P-P-W-W-W-W-W-rrrrrr [*a long puff, turning into a growl*]! [*He spits*]. I must kick somebody.

NARYSHKIN [*flying precipitately through the central doors*] No, no. Please.

THE PRINCESS DASHKOFF [*throwing herself recklessly in front of Patiomkin as he starts in pursuit of the Chamberlain*] Kick me. Disable me. It will be an excuse for not going back to her. Kick me hard.

PATIOMKIN. Yah! [*He flings her on the bed and dashes after Naryshkin*].

THE THIRD SCENE

In a terrace garden overlooking the Neva. Claire, a robust young English lady, is leaning on the river wall. She turns expectantly on hearing the garden gate opened and closed. Edstaston hurries in. With a cry of delight she throws her arms round his neck.

CLAIRE. Darling!

EDSTASTON [*making a wry face*] Dont call me darling.

CLAIRE [*amazed and chilled*] Why?

EDSTASTON. I have been called darling all the morning.

CLAIRE [*with a flash of jealousy*] By whom?

EDSTASTON. By everybody. By the most unutterable swine. And if we do not leave this abominable city now: do you hear? now: I shall be called darling by the Empress.

CLAIRE [*with magnificent snobbery*] She would not dare. Did you tell her you were engaged to me?

EDSTASTON. Of course not.

CLAIRE. Why?

EDSTASTON. Because I didnt particularly want to have you knouted, and to be hanged or sent to Siberia myself.

CLAIRE. What on earth do you mean?

EDSTASTON. Well, the long and short of it is —dont think me a coxcomb, Claire: it is too serious to mince matters—I have seen the Empress; and—

CLAIRE. Well: you wanted to see her.

EDSTASTON. Yes; but the Empress has seen me.

CLAIRE. She has fallen in love with you.

EDSTASTON. How did you know?

CLAIRE. Dearest: as if anyone could help it.

EDSTASTON. Oh, dont make me feel like a fool. But, though it does sound conceited to say it, I flatter myself I'm better looking than Patiomkin and the other hogs she is

accustomed to. Anyhow, I darent risk staying.

CLAIRE. What a nuisance! Mamma will be furious at having to pack, and at missing the Court ball this evening.

EDSTASTON. I cant help that. We havnt a moment to lose.

CLAIRE. May I tell her she will be knouted if we stay?

EDSTASTON. Do, dearest.

He kisses her and lets her go, expecting her to run into the house.

CLAIRE [*pausing thoughtfully*] Is she—is she good-looking when you see her close?

EDSTASTON. Not a patch on you, dearest.

CLAIRE [*jealous*] Then you did see her close.

EDSTASTON. Fairly close.

CLAIRE. Indeed! How close? No: thats silly of me: I will tell mamma. [*She is going out when Naryshkin enters with the Sergeant and a squad of soldiers*]. What do you want here?

The Sergeant goes to Edstaston; plumps down on his knees; and takes out a magnificent pair of pistols with gold grips. He proffers them to Edstaston, holding them by the barrels.

NARYSHKIN. Captain Edstaston: his Highness Prince Patiomkin sends you the pistols he promised you.

THE SERGEANT. Take them, Little Father; and do not forget us poor soldiers who have brought them to you; for God knows we get but little to drink.

EDSTASTON [*irresolutely*] But I cant take these valuable things. By Jiminy, though, theyre beautiful! Look at them, Claire.

As he is taking the pistols the kneeling Sergeant suddenly drops them; flings himself forward; and embraces Edstaston's hips to prevent him from drawing his own pistols from his boots.

THE SERGEANT. Lay hold of him there. Pin his arms. I have his pistols. [*The soldiers seize Edstaston*].

EDSTASTON. Ah, would you, damn you! [*He drives his knee into the Sergeant's epigastrium, and struggles furiously with his captors*].

THE SERGEANT [*rolling on the ground, gasping and groaning*] Owgh! Murder! Holy Nicholas! Owwwgh!

CLAIRE. Help! help! They are killing Charles. Help!

NARYSHKIN [*seizing her and clapping his hand over her mouth*] Tie him neck and crop. Ten thousand blows of the stick if you let him go. [*Claire twists herself loose; turns on him; and cuffs him furiously*] Yow—ow! Have mercy,

Little Mother.

CLAIRE. You wretch! Help! Help! Police! We are being murdered. Help!

The Sergeant, who has risen, comes to Naryshkin's rescue, and grasps Claire's hands, enabling Naryshkin to gag her again. By this time Edstaston and his captors are all rolling on the ground together. They get Edstaston on his back and fasten his wrists together behind his knees. Next they put a broad strap round his ribs. Finally they pass a pole through this breast strap and through the wrist strap and lift him by it, helplessly trussed up, to carry him off. Meanwhile he is by no means suffering in silence.

EDSTASTON [*gasping*] You shall hear more of this. Damn you, will you untie me? I will complain to the ambassador. I will write to the Gazette. England will blow your trumpery little fleet out of the water and sweep your tinpot army into Siberia for this. Will you let me go? Damn you! Curse you! What the devil do you mean by it? I'll—I'll—I'll— [*He is carried out of hearing*].

NARYSHKIN [*snatching his hands from Claire's face with a scream, and shaking his finger frantically*] Agh! [*The Sergeant, amazed, lets go her hands*]. She has bitten me, the little vixen.

CLAIRE [*spitting and wiping her mouth disgustedly*] How dare you put your dirty paws on my mouth? Ugh! Psha!

THE SERGEANT. Be merciful, Little angel Mother.

CLAIRE. Do not presume to call me your little angel mother. Where are the police?

NARYSHKIN. We are the police in St Petersburg, little spitfire.

THE SERGEANT. God knows we have no orders to harm you, Little Mother. Our duty is done. You are well and strong; but I shall never be the same man again. He is a mighty and terrible fighter, as stout as a bear. He has broken my sweetbread with his strong knees. God knows poor folk should not be set upon such dangerous adversaries!

CLAIRE. Serve you right! Where have they taken Captain Edstaston to?

NARYSHKIN [*spitefully*] To the Empress, little beauty. He has insulted the Empress. He will receive a hundred and one blows of the knout. [*He laughs and goes out, nursing his bitten finger*].

THE SERGEANT. He will feel only the first twenty; and he will be mercifully dead long before the end, little darling.

CLAIRE [*sustained by an invincible snobbery*] They dare not touch an English officer. I will go to the Empress myself: she cannot know who Captain Edstaston is—who w e are.

THE SERGEANT. Do so in the name of the Holy Nicholas, little beauty.

CLAIRE. Dont be impertinent. How can I get admission to the palace?

THE SERGEANT. Everybody goes in and out of the palace, little love.

CLAIRE. But I must get into the Empress's presence. I must speak to her.

THE SERGEANT. You shall, dear Little Mother. You shall give the poor old Sergeant a rouble; and the blessed Nicholas will make your salvation his charge.

CLAIRE [*impetuously*] I will give you [*she is about to say fifty roubles, but checks herself cautiously*]— Well: I dont mind giving you two roubles if I can speak to the Empress.

THE SERGEANT [*joyfully*] I praise Heaven for you, Little Mother. Come. [*He leads the way out*]. It was the temptation of the devil that led your young man to bruise my vitals and deprive me of breath. We must be merciful to one another's faults.

THE FOURTH SCENE

A triangular recess communicating by a heavily curtained arch with the huge ballroom of the palace. The light is subdued by red shades on the candles. In the wall adjoining that pierced by the arch is a door. The only piece of furniture is a very handsome chair on the arch side. In the ballroom they are dancing a polonaise to the music of a brass band.

Naryshkin enters through the door, followed by the soldiers carrying Edstaston, still trussed to the pole. Exhausted and dogged, he makes no sound.

NARYSHKIN. Halt. Get that pole clear of the prisoner. [*They dump Edstaston on the floor, and detach the pole. Naryshkin stoops over him and addresses him insultingly*]. Well! are you ready to be tortured? This is the Empress's private torture chamber. Can I do anything to make you quite comfortable? You have only to mention it.

EDSTASTON. Have you any back teeth?

NARYSHKIN [*surprised*] Why?

EDSTASTON. His Majesty King George the Third will send for six of them when the news of this reaches London; so look out, damn your eyes!

NARYSHKIN [*frightened*] Oh, I assure you I am only obeying my orders. Personally I abhor torture, and would save you if I could. But the Empress is proud; and what woman would forgive the slight you put upon her?

EDSTASTON. As I said before: Damn your eyes!

NARYSHKIN [*almost in tears*] Well, it isnt my fault. [*To the soldiers, insolently*] You know your orders? You remember what you have to do when the Empress gives you the word? [*The soldiers salute in assent*].

Naryshkin passes through the curtains, admitting a blare of music and a strip of the brilliant white candle-light from the chandeliers in the ballroom as he does so. The white light vanishes and the music is muffled as the curtains fall together behind him. Presently the band stops abruptly; and Naryshkin comes back through the curtains. He makes a warning gesture to the soldiers, who stand at attention. Then he moves the curtain to allow Catherine to enter. She is in full Imperial regalia, and stops sternly just where she has entered. The soldiers fall on their knees.

CATHERINE. Obey your orders.

The soldiers seize Edstaston, and throw him roughly at the feet of the Empress.

CATHERINE [*looking down coldly on him*] Also [*the German word*], you have put me to the trouble of sending for you twice. You had better have come the first time.

EDSTASTON [*exsufflicate, and pettishly angry*] I havnt come either time. Ive been carried. I call it infernal impudence.

CATHERINE. Take care what you say.

EDSTASTON. No use. I daresay you look very majestic and very handsome; but I cant see you; and I am not intimidated. I am an Englishman; and you can kidnap me; but you cant bully me.

NARYSHKIN. Remember to whom you are speaking.

CATHERINE [*violently, furious at his intrusion*] Remember that dogs should be dumb. [*He shrivels*]. And do you, Captain, remember that famous as I am for my clemency, there are limits to the patience even of an Empress.

EDSTASTON. How is a man to remember anything when he is trussed up in this ridiculous fashion? I can hardly breathe. [*He makes a futile struggle to free himself*]. Here: dont be unkind, your Majesty: tell these fellows to unstrap me. You know you really owe me an apology.

CATHERINE. You think you can escape by appealing, like Prince Patiomkin, to my sense of humor?

EDSTASTON. Sense of humor! Ho! Ha, ha! I like that. Would anybody with a sense of humor make a guy of a man like this, and then expect him to take it seriously? I say: do tell them to loosen these straps.

CATHERINE [*seating herself*] Why should I, pray?

EDSTASTON. Why! Why!! Why, because theyre hurting me.

CATHERINE. People sometimes learn through suffering. Manners, for instance.

EDSTASTON. Oh, well, of course, if youre an ill-natured woman, hurting me on purpose, I have nothing more to say.

CATHERINE. A monarch, sir, has sometimes to employ a necessary and salutary severity—

EDSTASTON [*interrupting her petulantly*] Quack! quack! quack!

CATHERINE. Donnerwetter!

EDSTASTON [*continuing recklessly*] This isnt severity: it's tomfoolery. And if you think it's reforming my character or teaching me anything, youre mistaken. It may be a satisfaction to you; but if it is, all I can say is that it's not an amiable satisfaction.

CATHERINE [*turning suddenly and balefully on Naryshkin*] What are you grinning at?

NARYSHKIN [*falling on his knees in terror*] Be merciful, Little Mother. My heart is in my mouth.

CATHERINE. Your heart and your mouth will be in two separate parts of your body if you again forget in whose presence you stand. Go. And take your men with you. [*Naryshkin crawls to the door. The soldiers rise*]. Stop. Roll that [*indicating Edstaston*] nearer. [*The soldiers obey*]. Not so close. Did I ask you for a footstool? [*She pushes Edstaston away with her foot*].

EDSTASTON [*with a sudden squeal*] Agh!!! I must really ask your Majesty not to put the point of your Imperial toe between my ribs. I am ticklesome.

CATHERINE. Indeed? All the more reason for you to treat me with respect, Captain. [*To the others*] Begone. How many times must I give an order before it is obeyed?

NARYSHKIN. Little Mother: they have brought some instruments of torture. Will they be needed?

CATHERINE [*indignantly*] How dare you

name such abominations to a Liberal Empress? You will always be a savage and a fool, Naryshkin. These relics of barbarism are buried, thank God, in the grave of Peter the Great. My methods are more civilized. [*She extends her toe towards Edstaston's ribs*].

EDSTASTON [*shrieking hysterically*] Yagh! Ah! [*Furiously*] If your Majesty does that again I will write to the London Gazette.

CATHERINE [*to the soldiers*] Leave us. Quick! do you hear? Five thousand blows of the stick for the soldier who is in the room when I speak next. [*The soldiers rush out*]. Naryshkin: are you waiting to be knouted? [*Naryshkin backs out hastily*].

Catherine and Edstaston are now alone. Catherine has in her hand a sceptre or baton of gold. Wrapped round it is a new pamphlet, in French, entitled L'Homme aux Quarante Écus. She calmly unrolls this and begins to read it at her ease as if she were quite alone. Several seconds elapse in dead silence. She becomes more and more absorbed in the pamphlet, and more and more amused by it.

CATHERINE [*greatly pleased by a passage, and turning over the leaf*] Ausgezeichnet!

EDSTASTON. Ahem!

Silence. Catherine reads on.

CATHERINE. Wie komisch!

EDSTASTON. Ahem! ahem!

Silence.

CATHERINE [*soliloquizing enthusiastically*] What a wonderful author is Monsieur Voltaire! How lucidly he exposes the folly of this crazy plan for raising the entire revenue of the country from a single tax on land! how he withers it with his irony! how he makes you laugh whilst he is convincing you! how sure one feels that the proposal is killed by his wit and economic penetration: killed never to be mentioned again among educated people!

EDSTASTON. For Heaven's sake, Madam, do you intend to leave me tied up like this while you discuss the blasphemies of that abominable infidel? Agh!! [*She has again applied her toe*]. Oh! Oo!

CATHERINE [*calmly*] Do I understand you to say that Monsieur Voltaire is a great philanthropist and a great philosopher as well as the wittiest man in Europe?

EDSTASTON. Certainly not. I say that his books ought to be burnt by the common hangman. [*Her toe touches his ribs*]. Yagh! Oh dont. I shall faint. I cant bear it.

CATHERINE. Have you changed your opinion of Monsieur Voltaire?

EDSTASTON. But you cant expect me as a member of the Church of England [*she tickles him*]—Agh! Ow! Oh Lord! he is anything you like. He is a philanthropist, a philosopher, a beauty: he ought to have a statue, damn him! [*She tickles him*]. No! bless him! save him victorious, happy and glorious! Oh, let eternal honors crown his name: Voltaire thrice worthy on the rolls of fame! [*Exhausted*]. Now will you let me up? And look here! I can see your ankles when you tickle me: it's not ladylike.

CATHERINE [*sticking out her toe and admiring it critically*] Is the spectacle so disagreeable?

EDSTASTON. It's agreeable enough; only [*with intense expression*] for heaven's sake dont touch me in the ribs.

CATHERINE [*putting aside the pamphlet*] Captain Edstaston: why did you refuse to come when I sent for you?

EDSTASTON. Madam: I cannot talk tied up like this.

CATHERINE. Do you still admire me as much as you did this morning?

EDSTASTON. How can I possibly tell when I cant see you? Let me get up and look. I cant see anything now except my toes and yours.

CATHERINE. Do you still intend to write to the London Gazette about me?

EDSTASTON. Not if you will loosen these straps. Quick: loosen me. I'm fainting.

CATHERINE. I dont think you are [*tickling him*].

EDSTASTON. Agh! Cat!

CATHERINE. What [*she tickles him again*]!

EDSTASTON [*with a shriek*] No: angel, angel!

CATHERINE [*tenderly*] Geliebter!

EDSTASTON. I dont know a word of German; but that sounded kind. [*Becoming hysterical*] Little Mother, beautiful little darling angel mother: dont be cruel: untie me. Oh, I beg and implore you. Dont be unkind. I shall go mad.

CATHERINE. You are expected to go mad with love when an Empress deigns to interest herself in you. When an Empress allows you to see her foot you should kiss it. Captain Edstaston: you are a booby.

EDSTASTON [*indignantly*] I am nothing of the kind. I have been mentioned in dispatches as a highly intelligent officer. And let me warn your Majesty that I am not so helpless as you think. The English Ambassador is in that ballroom. A shout from me will bring him to my side; and then where will your Majesty be?

CATHERINE. I should like to see the English Ambassador or anyone else pass through that curtain against my orders. It might be a stone wall ten feet thick. Shout your loudest. Sob. Curse. Scream. Yell. [*She tickles him unmercifully*].

EDSTASTON [*frantically*] Ahowyow!!!! Agh! Ooh! Stop! Oh Lord! Ya-a-a-ah! [*A tumult in the ballroom responds to his cries*].

VOICES FROM THE BALLROOM. Stand back. You cannot pass. Hold her back there. The Empress's orders. It is out of the question. No, little darling, not in there. Nobody is allowed in there. You will be sent to Siberia. Dont let her through there, on your life. Drag her back. You will be knouted. It is hopeless, Mademoiselle: you must obey orders. Guard there! Send some men to hold her.

CLAIRE'S VOICE. Let me go. They are torturing Charles in there. I will go. How can you all dance as if nothing was happening? Let me go, I tell you. Let—me—go. [*She dashes through the curtain. No one dares follow her*].

CATHERINE [*rising in wrath*] How dare you?

CLAIRE [*recklessly*] Oh, dare your grandmother! Where is my Charles? What are they doing to him?

EDSTASTON [*shouting*] Claire: loosen these straps, in Heaven's name. Quick.

CLAIRE [*seeing him and throwing herself on her knees at his side*] Oh, how dare they tie you up like that! [*To Catherine*] You wicked wretch! You Russian savage! [*She pounces on the straps, and begins unbuckling them*].

CATHERINE [*conquering herself with a mighty effort*] Now self-control. Self-control, Catherine. Philosophy. Europe is looking on. [*She forces herself to sit down*].

EDSTASTON. Steady, dearest: it is the Empress. Call her your Imperial Majesty. Call her Star of the North, Little Mother, Little Darling: thats what she likes; but get the straps off.

CLAIRE. Keep quiet, dear; I cannot get them off if you move.

CATHERINE [*calmly*] Keep quite still, Captain. [*She tickles him*].

EDSTASTON. Ow! Agh! Ahowyow!

CLAIRE [*stopping dead in the act of unbuckling the straps and turning sick with jealousy as she grasps the situation*] Was that what I thought was your being tortured?

CATHERINE [*urbanely*] That is the favorite torture of Catherine the Second, Mademoiselle. I think the Captain enjoys it very much.

CLAIRE. Then he can have as much more of it as he wants. I am sorry I intruded. [*She rises to go*].

EDSTASTON [*catching her train in his teeth and holding on like a bull-dog*] Dont go. Dont leave me in this horrible state. Loosen me. [*This is what he is saying; but as he says it with the train in his mouth it is not very intelligible.*]

CLAIRE. Let go. You are undignified and ridiculous enough yourself without making me ridiculous. [*She snatches her train away*].

EDSTASTON. Ow! Youve nearly pulled my teeth out: youre worse than the Star of the North. [*To Catherine*] Darling Little Mother: you have a kind heart, the kindest in Europe. Have pity. Have mercy. I love you. [*Claire bursts into tears*]. Release me.

CATHERINE. Well, just to shew you how much kinder a Russian savage can be than an English one (though I am sorry to say I am a German), here goes! [*She stoops to loosen the straps*].

CLAIRE [*jealously*] You neednt trouble, thank you. [*She pounces on the straps; and the two set Edstaston free between them*]. Now get up, please; and conduct yourself with some dignity if you are not utterly demoralized.

EDSTASTON. Dignity! Ow! I cant. I'm stiff all over. I shall never be able to stand up again. Oh Lord! how it hurts! [*They seize him by the shoulders and drag him up*]. Yah! Agh! Wow! Oh! Mmmmmm! Oh, Little Angel Mother, dont ever do this to a man again. Knout him; kill him; roast him; baste him; head, hang, and quarter him; but dont tie him up like that and tickle him.

CATHERINE. Your young lady still seems to think that you enjoyed it.

CLAIRE. I know what I think. I will never speak to him again. Your Majesty can keep him, as far as I am concerned.

CATHERINE. I would not deprive you of him for worlds; though really I think he's rather a darling. [*She pats his cheek*].

CLAIRE [*snorting*] So I see, indeed.

EDSTASTON. Dont be angry, dearest: in this country everybody's a darling. I'll prove it to you. [*To Catherine*] Will your Majesty be good enough to call Prince Patiomkin?

CATHERINE [*surprised into haughtiness*] Why?

EDSTASTON. To oblige me.

Catherine laughs good-humoredly and goes to the curtains and opens them. The band strikes up a Redowa.

CATHERINE [*calling imperiously*] Patiomkin! [*The music stops suddenly*]. Here! To me! Go on with your music there, you fools. [*The Redowa is resumed*].

The sergeant rushes from the ballroom to relieve the Empress of the curtain. Patiomkin comes in dancing with Varinka.

CATHERINE [*to Patiomkin*] The English captain wants you, little darling.

Catherine resumes her seat as Patiomkin intimates by a grotesque bow that he is at Edstaston's service. Varinka passes behind Edstaston and Claire, and posts herself on Claire's right.

EDSTASTON. Precisely. [*To Claire*] You observe, my love: "little darling." Well, if her Majesty calls h i m a darling, is it my fault that she calls me one too?

CLAIRE. I dont care: I dont think you ought to have done it. I am very angry and offended.

EDSTASTON. They tied me up, dear. I couldnt help it. I fought for all I was worth.

THE SERGEANT [*at the curtains*] He fought with the strength of lions and bears. God knows I shall carry a broken sweetbread to my grave.

EDSTASTON. You cant mean to throw me over, Claire. [*Urgently*] Claire. Claire.

VARINKA [*in a transport of sympathetic emotion, pleading with clasped hands to Claire*] Oh, sweet little angel lamb, he loves you: it shines in his darling eyes. Pardon him, pardon him.

PATIOMKIN [*rushing from the Empress's side to Claire and falling on his knees to her*] Pardon him, pardon him, little cherub! little wild duck! little star! little glory! little jewel in the crown of heaven!

CLAIRE. This is perfectly ridiculous.

VARINKA [*kneeling to her*] Pardon him, pardon him, little delight, little sleeper in a rosy cradle.

CLAIRE. I'll do anything if youll only let me alone.

THE SERGEANT [*kneeling to her*] Pardon him, pardon him, lest the mighty man bring his whip to you. God knows we all need pardon!

CLAIRE [*at the top of her voice*] I pardon him! I pardon him!

PATIOMKIN [*springing up joyfully and going*

behind Claire, *whom he raises in his arms*] Embrace her, victor of Bunker's Hill. Kiss her till she swoons.

THE SERGEANT. Receive her in the name of the holy Nicholas.

VARINKA. She begs you for a thousand dear little kisses all over her body.

CLAIRE [*vehemently*] I do not. [*Patiomkin throws her into Edstaston's arms*]. Oh! [*The pair, awkward and shamefaced, recoil from one another, and remain utterly inexpressive*].

CATHERINE [*pushing Edstaston towards Claire*] There is no help for it, Captain. This is Russia, not England.

EDSTASTON [*plucking up some geniality, and kissing Claire ceremoniously on the brow*] I have no objection.

VARINKA [*disgusted*] Only one kiss! and on the forehead! Fish. See how I kiss, though it is only my horribly ugly old uncle [*she throws her arms round Patiomkin's neck and covers his face with kisses*].

THE SERGEANT [*moved to tears*] Sainted Nicholas: bless your lambs!

CATHERINE. Do you wonder now that I love Russia as I love no other place on earth?

NARYSHKIN [*appearing at the door*] Majesty: the model for the new museum has arrived.

CATHERINE [*rising eagerly and making for the curtains*] Let us go. I can think of nothing but my museum. [*In the archway she stops and turns to Edstaston, who has hurried to lift the curtain for her*]. Captain: I wish you every happiness that your little angel can bring you. [*For his ear alone*] I could have brought you more; but you did not think so. Farewell.

EDSTASTON [*kissing her hand, which, instead of releasing, he holds caressingly and rather patronizingly in his own*] I feel your Majesty's kindness so much that I really cannot leave you without a word of plain wholesome English advice.

CATHERINE [*snatching her hand away and bounding forward as if he had touched her with a spur*] Advice!!!

PATIOMKIN. Madman: take care!

NARYSHKIN. Advise the Empress!!

THE SERGEANT. Sainted Nicholas!

VARINKA. Hoo hoo! [*a stifled splutter of laughter*].

[*exclaiming simultaneously*].

EDSTASTON [*following the Empress and re-*

suming kindly but judicially] After all, though your Majesty is of course a great queen, yet when all is said, I am a man; and your Majesty is only a woman.

CATHERINE. Only a wo— [*she chokes*].

EDSTASTON [*continuing*] Believe me, this Russian extravagance will not do. I appreciate as much as any man the warmth of heart that prompts it; but it is overdone: it is hardly in the best taste: it is—really I must say it—it is not proper.

CATHERINE [*ironically, in German*] So!

EDSTASTON. Not that I cannot make allowances. Your Majesty has, I know, been unfortunate in your experience as a married woman—

CATHERINE [*furious*] Alle Wetter!!!

EDSTASTON [*sentimentally*] Dont say that. Dont think of him in that way. After all, he was your husband; and whatever his faults may have been, it is not for you to think unkindly of him.

CATHERINE [*almost bursting*] I shall forget myself.

EDSTASTON. Come! I am sure he really loved you; and you truly loved him.

CATHERINE [*controlling herself with a supreme effort*] No, Catherine. What would Voltaire say?

EDSTASTON. Oh, never mind that vile scoffer. Set an example to Europe, Madam, by doing what I am going to do. Marry again. Marry some good man who will be a strength and a support to your old age.

CATHERINE. My old—[*she again becomes speechless*].

EDSTASTON. Yes: we must all grow old, even the handsomest of us.

CATHERINE [*sinking into her chair with a gasp*] Thank you.

EDSTASTON. You will thank me more when you see your little ones round your knee, and your man there by the fireside in the winter evenings—by the way, I forgot that you have no firesides here in spite of the coldness of the climate; so shall I say by the stove?

CATHERINE. Certainly, if you wish. The stove, by all means.

EDSTASTON [*impulsively*] Ah, Madam, abolish the stove: believe me, there is nothing like the good old open grate. Home! duty! happiness! they all mean the same thing; and they all flourish best on the drawing room hearthrug. [*Turning to Claire*] And now, my love, we must not detain the Queen: she is anxious to inspect the model of her museum, to which I am sure we wish every success.

CLAIRE [*coldly*] I am not detaining her.

EDSTASTON. Well, goodbye [*wringing Patiomkin's hand*], goo-oo-oodbye, Prince: come and see us if ever you visit England. Spire View, Deepdene, Little Mugford, Devon, will always find me. [*To Varinka, kissing her hand*] Goodbye, Mademoiselle: goodbye, Little Mother, if I may call you that just once. [*Varinka puts up her face to be kissed*]. Eh? No, no, no, no: you dont mean that, you know. Naughty! [*To the Sergeant*] Goodbye, my friend. You will drink our healths with this [*tipping him*].

THE SERGEANT. The blessed Nicholas will multiply your fruits, Little Father.

EDSTASTON. Goodbye, goodbye, goodbye, goodbye, goodbye, goodbye.

He goes out backwards bowing, with Claire curtseying, having been listened to in utter dumbfoundedness by Patiomkin and Naryshkin, in childlike awe by Varinka, and with quite inexpressible feelings by Catherine. When he is out of sight she rises with clinched fists and raises her arms and her closed eyes to Heaven. Patiomkin, rousing himself from his stupor of amazement, springs to her like a tiger, and throws himself at her feet.

PATIOMKIN. What shall I do to him for you? Skin him alive? Cut off his eyelids and stand him in the sun? Tear his tongue out? What shall it be?

CATHERINE [*opening her eyes*] Nothing. But oh, if I could only have had him for my—for my—for my—

PATIOMKIN [*in a growl of jealousy*] For your lover?

CATHERINE [*with an ineffable smile*] No: for my museum.

THE END

XXVI
O'FLAHERTY V.C.
A RECRUITING PAMPHLET

At the door of an Irish country house in a park. Fine summer weather: the summer of 1915. The porch, painted white, projects into the drive; but the door is at the side and the front has a window. The porch faces east; and the door is in the north side of it. On the south side is a tree in which a thrush is singing. Under the window is a garden seat with an iron chair at each end of it.

The last four bars of God Save the King are heard in the distance, followed by three cheers. Then the band strikes up It's a Long Way to Tipperary and recedes until it is out of hearing.

Private O'Flaherty V.C. comes wearily southward along the drive, and falls exhausted into the garden seat. The thrush utters a note of alarm and flies away. The tramp of a horse is heard.

A GENTLEMAN'S VOICE. Tim! Hi! Tim! [*He is heard dismounting*].

A LABORER'S VOICE. Yes, your honor.

THE GENTLEMAN'S VOICE. Take this horse to the stables, will you?

A LABORER'S VOICE. Right, your honor. Yup there. Gwan now. Gwan. [*The horse is led away*].

General Sir Pearce Madigan, an elderly baronet in khaki, beaming with enthusiasm, arrives. O'Flaherty rises and stands at attention.

SIR PEARCE. No, no, O'Flaherty: none of that now. Youre off duty. Remember that though I am a general of forty years service, that little Cross of yours gives you a higher rank in the roll of glory than I can pretend to.

O'FLAHERTY [*relaxing*] I'm thankful to you, Sir Pearce; but I wouldnt have anyone think that the baronet of my native place would let a common soldier like me sit down in his presence without leave.

SIR PEARCE. Well, youre not a common soldier, O'Flaherty: youre a very uncommon one; and I'm proud to have you for my guest here today.

O'FLAHERTY. Sure I know, sir. You have to put up with a lot from the like of me for the sake of the recruiting. All the quality shakes hands with me and says theyre proud to know me, just the way the king said when he pinned the Cross on me. And it's as true as I'm standing here, sir, the queen said to me

"I hear you were born on the estate of General Madigan," she says; "and the General himself tells me you were always a fine young fellow." "Bedad, Mam," I says to her, "if the General knew all the rabbits I snared on him, and all the salmon I snatched on him, and all the cows I milked on him, he'd think me the finest ornament for the county jail he ever sent there for poaching."

SIR PEARCE [*laughing*] Youre welcome to them all, my lad. Come [*he makes him sit down again on the garden seat*]! sit down and enjoy your holiday [*he sits down on one of the iron chairs: the one at the doorless side of the porch*].

O'FLAHERTY. Holiday, is it? I'd give five shillings to be back in the trenches for the sake of a little rest and quiet. I never knew what hard work was til I took to recruiting. What with the standing on my legs all day, and the shaking hands, and the making speeches, and—whats worse—the listening to them, and the calling for cheers for king and country, and the saluting the flag til I'm stiff with it, and the listening to them playing God Save the King and Tipperary, and the trying to make my eyes look moist like a man in a picture book, I'm that bet that I hardly get a wink of sleep. I give you my word, Sir Pearce, that I never heard the tune of Tipperary in my life til I came back from Flanders; and already it's drove me to that pitch of tiredness of it that when a poor little innocent slip of a boy in the street the other night drew himself up and saluted and began whistling it at me, I clouted his head for him, God forgive me.

SIR PEARCE [*soothingly*] Yes, yes: I know. *I* know. One does get fed up with it: Ive been dog tired myself on parade many a time. But still, you know, theres a gratifying side to it, too. After all, he is our king; and it's our own country, isnt it?

O'FLAHERTY. Well, sir, to you that have an estate in it, it would feel like your country. But the divil a perch of it ever I owned. And as to the king, God help him, my mother would have taken the skin off my back if I'd ever let on to have any other king than

Parnell.

SIR PEARCE [*rising, painfully shocked*] Your mother! What are you dreaming about, O'Flaherty? A most loyal woman. Always most loyal. Whenever there is an illness in the Royal Family, she asks me every time we meet about the health of the patient as anxiously as if it were yourself, her only son.

O'FLAHERTY. Well, she's my mother; and I wont utter a word agen her. But I'm not saying a word of lie when I tell you that that old woman is the biggest kanatt from here to the cross of Monasterboice. Sure she's the wildest Fenian and rebel, and always has been, that ever taught a poor innocent lad like myself to pray night and morning to St Patrick to clear the English out of Ireland the same as he cleared the snakes. Youll be surprised at my telling you that now, maybe, Sir Pearce?

SIR PEARCE [*unable to keep still, walking away from O'Flaherty*] Surprised! I'm more than surprised, O'Flaherty. I'm overwhelmed. [*Turning and facing him*] Are you—are you joking?

O'FLAHERTY. If youd been brought up by my mother, sir, youd know better than to joke about her. What I'm telling you is the truth; and I wouldnt tell it to you if I could see my way to get out of the fix I'll be in when my mother comes here this day to see her boy in his glory, and she after thinking all the time it was against the English I was fighting.

SIR PEARCE. Do you mean to say you told her such a monstrous falsehood as that you were fighting in the German army?

O'FLAHERTY. I never told her one word that wasnt the truth and nothing but the truth. I told her I was going to fight for the French and for the Russians; and sure who ever heard of the French or the Russians doing anything to the English but fighting them? That was how it was, sir. And sure the poor woman kissed me and went about the house singing in her old cracky voice that the French was on the sea, and theyd be here without delay, and the Orange will decay, says the Shan Van Vocht.

SIR PEARCE [*sitting down again, exhausted by his feelings*] Well, I never could have believed this. Never. What do you suppose will happen when she finds out?

O'FLAHERTY. She mustnt find out. It's not that she'd half kill me, as big as I am and

as brave as I am. It's that I'm fond of her, and cant bring myself to break the heart in her. You may think it queer that a man should be fond of his mother, sir, and she having bet him from the time he could feel to the time she was too slow to ketch him; but I'm fond of her; and I'm not ashamed of it. Besides, didnt she win the Cross for me?

SIR PEARCE. Your mother! How?

O'FLAHERTY. By bringing me up to be more afraid of running away than of fighting. I was timid by nature; and when the other boys hurted me, I'd want to run away and cry. But she whaled me for disgracing the blood of the O'Flahertys until I'd have fought the divil himself sooner than face her after funking a fight. That was how I got to know that fighting was easier than it looked, and that the others was as much afeard of me as I was of them, and that if I only held out long enough theyd lose heart and give up. Thats the way I came to be so courageous. I tell you, Sir Pearce, if the German army had been brought up by my mother, the Kaiser would be dining in the banqueting hall at Buckingham Palace this day, and King George polishing his jack boots for him in the scullery.

SIR PEARCE. But I dont like this, O'Flaherty. You cant go on deceiving your mother, you know. It's not right.

O'FLAHERTY. Cant go on deceiving her, cant I? It's little you know what a son's love can do, sir. Did you ever notice what a ready liar I am?

SIR PEARCE. Well, in recruiting a man gets carried away. I stretch it a bit occasionally myself. After all, it's for king and country. But if you wont mind my saying it, O'Flaherty, I think that story about your fighting the Kaiser and the twelve giants of the Prussian guard singlehanded would be the better for a little toning down. I dont ask you to drop it, you know; for it's popular, undoubtedly; but still, the truth is the truth. Dont you think it would fetch in almost as many recruits if you reduced the number of guardsmen to six?

O'FLAHERTY. Youre not used to telling lies like I am, sir. I got great practice at home with my mother. What with saving my skin when I was young and thoughtless, and sparing her feelings when I was old enough to understand them, Ive hardly told my mother the truth twice a year since I was born; and would you have me turn round on her and tell it now, when she's looking to have some peace and quiet in her old age?

SIR PEARCE [troubled in his conscience] Well, it's not my affair, of course, O'Flaherty. But hadnt you better talk to Father Quinlan about it?

O'FLAHERTY. Talk to Father Quinlan, is it! Do you know what Father Quinlan says to me this very morning?

SIR PEARCE. Oh, youve seen him already, have you? What did he say?

O'FLAHERTY. He says "You know, dont you" he says "that it's your duty, as a Christian and a good son of the Holy Church, to love your enemies?" he says. "I know it's my juty as a soldier to kill them." I says. "Thats right, Dinny," he says: "quite right. But" says he "you can kill them and do them a good turn afterwards to shew your love for them" he says; "and it's your duty to have a mass said for the souls of the hundreds of Germans you say you killed" says he; "for many and many of them were Bavarians and good Catholics" he says. "Is it me that must pay for masses for the souls of the Boshes?" I says. "Let the King of England pay for them" I says; "for it was his quarrel and not mine."

SIR PEARCE [warmly] It is the quarrel of every honest man and true patriot, O'Flaherty. Your mother must see that as clearly as I do. After all, she is a reasonable, well disposed woman, quite capable of understanding the right and the wrong of the war. Why cant you explain to her what the war is about?

O'FLAHERTY. Arra, sir, how the divil do I know what the war is about?

SIR PEARCE [rising again and standing over him] What! O'Flaherty: do you know what you are saying? You sit there wearing the Victoria Cross for having killed God knows how many Germans; and you tell me you dont know why you did it!

O'FLAHERTY. Asking your pardon, Sir Pearce, I tell you no such thing. I know quite well why I kilt them. I kilt them because I was afeard that, if I didnt, theyd kill me.

SIR PEARCE [giving it up, and sitting down again] Yes, yes, of course; but have you no knowledge of the causes of the war? of the interests at stake? of the importance—I may almost say—in fact I will say—the sacred rights for which we are fighting? Dont you

read the papers?

O'FLAHERTY. I do when I can get them. Theres not many newsboys crying the evening paper in the trenches. They do say, Sir Pearce, that we shall never beat the Boshes until we make Horatio Bottomley Lord Leftnant of England. Do you think thats true, sir?

SIR PEARCE. Rubbish, man! theres no Lord Lieutenant in England: the king is Lord Lieutenant. It's a simple question of patriotism. Does patriotism mean nothing to you?

O'FLAHERTY. It means different to me than what it would to you, sir. It means England and England's king to you. To me and the like of me, it means talking about the English just the way the English papers talk about the Boshes. And what good has it ever done here in Ireland? It's kept me ignorant because it filled up my mother's mind, and she thought it ought to fill up mine too. It's kept Ireland poor, because instead of trying to better ourselves we thought we was the fine fellows of patriots when we were speaking evil of Englishmen that was as poor as ourselves and maybe as good as ourselves. The Boshes I kilt was more knowledgable men than me: and what better am I now that Ive kilt them? What better is anybody?

SIR PEARCE [huffed, turning a cold shoulder to him] I am sorry the terrible experience of this war—the greatest war ever fought—has taught you no better, O'Flaherty.

O'FLAHERTY [preserving his dignity] I dont know about it's being a great war, sir. It's a big war; but thats not the same thing. Father Quinlan's new church is a big church: you might take the little old chapel out of the middle of it and not miss it. But my mother says there was more true religion in the old chapel. And the war has taught me that may be she was right.

SIR PEARCE [grunts sulkily]!!

O'FLAHERTY [respectfully but doggedly] And theres another thing it's taught me too, sir, that concerns you and me, if I may make bold to tell it to you.

SIR PEARCE [still sulkily] I hope it's nothing you oughtnt to say to me, O'Flaherty.

O'FLAHERTY. It's this, sir: that I'm able to sit here now and talk to you without humbugging you; and thats what not one of your tenants or your tenants' childer ever did to you before in all your long life. It's a true respect I'm shewing you at last, sir. Maybe youd rather have me humbug you and tell you lies as I used, just as the boys here, God help them, would rather have me tell them how I fought the Kaiser, that all the world knows I never saw in my life, than tell them the truth. But I cant take advantage of you the way I used, not even if I seem to be wanting in respect to you and cocked up by winning the Cross.

SIR PEARCE [*touched*] Not at all, O'Flaherty. Not at all.

O'FLAHERTY. Sure whats the Cross to me, barring the little pension it carries? Do you think I dont know that theres hundreds of men as brave as me that never had the luck to get anything for their bravery but a curse from the sergeant, and the blame for the faults of them that ought to have been their betters? Ive learnt more than youd think, sir; for how would a gentleman like you know what a poor ignorant conceited creature I was when I went from here into the wide world as a soldier? What use is all the lying, and pretending, and humbugging, and letting on, when the day comes to you that your comrade is killed in the trench beside you, and you dont as much as look round at him until you trip over his poor body, and then all you say is to ask why the hell the stretcher-bearers dont take it out of the way. Why should I read the papers to be humbugged and lied to by them that had the cunning to stay at home and send me to fight for them? Dont talk to me or to any soldier of the war being right. No war is right; and all the holy water that Father Quinlan ever blessed couldnt make one right. There, sir! Now you know what O'Flaherty V.C. thinks; and youre wiser so than the others that only knows what he done.

SIR PEARCE [*making the best of it, and turning good-humoredly to him again*] Well, what you did was brave and manly, anyhow.

O'FLAHERTY. God knows whether it was or not, better than you nor me, General. I hope He wont be too hard on me for it, anyhow.

SIR PEARCE [*sympathetically*] Oh yes: we all have to think seriously sometimes, especially when we're a little run down. I'm afraid weve been overworking you a bit over these recruiting meetings. However, we can knock off for the rest of the day; and tomorrow's Sunday. Ive had about as much as I can stand myself. [*He looks at his watch*]. It's tea-

time. I wonder whats keeping your mother.

O'FLAHERTY. It's nicely cocked up the old woman will be, having tea at the same table as you, sir, instead of in the kitchen. She'll be after dressing in the heighth of grandeur; and stop she will at every house on the way to shew herself off and tell them where she's going, and fill the whole parish with spite and envy. But sure, she shouldnt keep you waiting, sir.

SIR PEARCE. Oh, thats all right: she must be indulged on an occasion like this. I'm sorry my wife is in London: she'd have been glad to welcome your mother.

O'FLAHERTY. Sure, I know she would, sir. She was always a kind friend to the poor. Little her ladyship knew, God help her, the depth of divilment that was in us: we were like a play to her. You see, sir, she was English: that was how it was. We was to her what the Pathans and Senegalese was to me when I first seen them: I couldnt think, somehow, that they were liars, and thieves, and backbiters, and drunkards, just like ourselves or any other Christians. Oh, her ladyship never knew all that was going on behind her back: how would she? When I was a weeshy child, she gave me the first penny I ever had in my hand; and I wanted to pray for her conversion that night the same as my mother made me pray for yours; and—

SIR PEARCE [*scandalized*] Do you mean to say that your mother made you pray for m y conversion?

O'FLAHERTY. Sure and she wouldnt want to see a gentleman like you going to hell after she nursing your own son and bringing up my sister Annie on the bottle. That was how it was, sir. She'd rob you; and she'd lie to you; and she'd call down all the blessings of God on your head when she was selling you your own three geese that you thought had been ate by the fox the day after youd finished fattening them, sir; and all the time you were like a bit of her own flesh and blood to her. Often has she said she'd live to see you a good Catholic yet, leading victorious armies against the English and wearing the collar of gold that Malachi won from the proud invader. Oh, she's the romantic woman is my mother, and no mistake.

SIR PEARCE [*in great perturbation*] I really cant believe this, O'Flaherty. I could have sworn your mother was as honest a woman as ever breathed.

o'flaherty. And so she is, sir. She's as honest as the day.

sir pearce. Do you call it honest to steal my geese?

o'flaherty. She didnt steal them, sir. It was me that stole them.

sir pearce. Oh! And why the devil did you steal them?

o'flaherty. Sure we needed them, sir. Often and often we had to sell our own geese to pay you the rent to satisfy your needs; and why shouldnt we sell your geese to satisfy ours?

sir pearce. Well, damn me!

o'flaherty [sweetly] Sure you had to get what you could out of us; and we had to get what we could out of you. God forgive us both!

sir pearce. Really, O'Flaherty, the war seems to have upset you a little.

o'flaherty. It's set me thinking, sir; and I'm not used to it. It's like the patriotism of the English. They never thought of being patriotic until the war broke out; and now the patriotism has took them so sudden and come so strange to them that they run about like frightened chickens, uttering all manner of nonsense. But please God theyll forget all about it when the war's over. Theyre getting tired of it already.

sir pearce. No, no: it has uplifted us all in a wonderful way. The world will never be the same again, O'Flaherty. Not after a war like this.

o'flaherty. So they all say, sir. I see no great differ myself. It's all the fright and the excitement; and when that quiets down theyll go back to their natural divilment and be the same as ever. It's like the vermin: itll wash off after a while.

sir pearce [rising and planting himself firmly behind the garden seat] Well, the long and the short of it is, O'Flaherty, I must decline to be a party to any attempt to deceive your mother. I thoroughly disapprove of this feeling against the English, especially at a moment like the present. Even if your mother's political sympathies are really what you represent them to be, I should think that her gratitude to Gladstone ought to cure her of such disloyal prejudices.

o'flaherty (over his shoulder) She says Gladstone was an Irishman, sir. What call would he have to meddle with Ireland as he did if he wasnt?

sir pearce. What nonsense! Does she suppose Mr Asquith is an Irishman?

o'flaherty. She wont give him any credit for Home Rule, sir. She says Redmond made him do it. She says you told her so.

sir pearce [convicted out of his own mouth] Well, I never meant her to take it up in that ridiculous way. [He moves to the end of the garden seat on O'Flaherty's left] I'll give her a good talking to when she comes. I'm not going to stand any of her nonsense.

o'flaherty. It's not a bit of use, sir. She says all the English generals is Irish. She says all the English poets and great men was Irish. She says the English never knew how to read their own books until we taught them. She says we're the lost tribes of the house of Israel and the chosen people of God. She says that the goddess Venus, that was born out of the foam of the sea, came up out of the water in Killiney Bay off Bray Head. She says that Moses built the seven churches, and that Lazarus was buried in Glasnevin.

sir pearce. Bosh! How does she know he was? Did you ever ask her?

o'flaherty. I did, sir, often.

sir pearce. And what did she say?

o'flaherty. She asked me how did I know he wasnt, and fetched me a clout on the side of my head.

sir pearce. But have you never mentioned any famous Englishman to her, and asked her what she had to say about him?

o'flaherty. The only one I could think of was Shakespear, sir; and she says he was born in Cork.

sir pearce [exhausted] Well, I give it up [he throws himself into the nearest chair]. The woman is—Oh, well! No matter.

o'flaherty [sympathetically] Yes, sir: she's pigheaded and obstinate: theres no doubt about it. She's like the English: they think theres no one like themselves. It's the same with the Germans, though theyre educated and ought to know better. Youll never have a quiet world til you knock the patriotism out of the human race.

sir pearce. Still, we—

o'flaherty. Whisht, sir, for God's sake: here she is.

The General jumps up. Mrs O'Flaherty arrives, and comes between the two men. She is very clean, and carefully dressed in the old fashioned peasant costume: black silk sunbonnet *with a tiara of trimmings, and black cloak.*

o'flaherty [*rising shyly*] Good evening, mother.

mrs o'flaherty [*severely*] You hold your whisht, and learn behavior while I pay my juty to his honor. [*To Sir Pearce, heartily*] And how is your honor's good self? And how is her ladyship and all the young ladies? Oh, it's right glad we are to see your honor back again and looking the picture of health.

sir pearce [*forcing a note of extreme geniality*] Thank you, Mrs O'Flaherty. Well, you see weve brought you back your son safe and sound. I hope youre proud of him.

mrs o'flaherty. And indeed and I am, your honor. It's the brave boy he is; and why wouldnt he be, brought up on your honor's estate and with you before his eyes for a pattern of the finest soldier in Ireland. Come and kiss your old mother, Dinny darlint. [*O'Flaherty does so sheepishly*]. Thats my own darling boy. And look at your fine new uniform stained already with the eggs youve been eating and the porter youve been drinking. [*She takes out her handkerchief; spits on it; and scrubs his lapel with it*]. Oh, it's the untidy slovenly one you always were. There! It wont be seen on the khaki: it's not like the old red coat that would shew up everything that dribbled down on it. [*To Sir Pearce*] And they tell me down at the lodge that her ladyship is staying in London, and that Miss Agnes is to be married to a fine young nobleman. Oh, it's your honor that is the lucky and happy father! It will be bad news for many of the young gentlemen of the quality round here, sir. Theres lots thought she was going to marry young Master Lawless—

sir pearce. What! That—that—that bosthoon!

mrs o'flaherty [*hilariously*] Let your honor alone for finding the right word! A big bosthoon he is indeed, your honor. Oh, to think of the times and times I have said that Miss Agnes would be my lady as her mother was before her! Didnt I, Dinny?

sir pearce. And now, Mrs O'Flaherty, I daresay you have a great deal to say to Dennis that doesnt concern me. I'll just go in and order tea.

mrs o'flaherty. Oh, why would your honor disturb yourself? Sure I can take the boy into the yard.

sir pearce. Not at all. It wont disturb me in the least. And he's too big a boy to be taken into the yard now. He has made a front seat for himself. Eh? [*He goes into the house*].

mrs o'flaherty. Sure he has that, your honor. God bless your honor! [*The General being now out of hearing, she turns threateningly to her son with one of those sudden Irish changes of manner which amaze and scandalize less flexible nations, and exclaims*] And what do you mean, you lying young scald, by telling me you were going to fight agen the English? Did you take me for a fool that couldnt find out, and the papers all full of you shaking hands with the English king at Buckingham Palace?

o'flaherty. I didnt shake hands with him: he shook hands with me. Could I turn on the man in his own house, before his own wife, with his money in my pocket and in yours, and throw his civility back in his face?

mrs o'flaherty. You would take the hand of a tyrant red with the blood of Ireland—

o'flaherty. Arra hold your nonsense, mother: he's not half the tyrant you are, God help him. His hand was cleaner than mine that had the blood of his own relations on it, may be.

mrs o'flaherty [*threateningly*] Is that a way to speak to your mother, you young spalpeen?

o'flaherty [*stoutly*] It is so, if you wont talk sense to me. It's a nice thing for a poor boy to be made much of by kings and queens, and shook hands with by the heighth of his country's nobility in the capital cities of the world, and then to come home and be scolded and insulted by his own mother. I'll fight for who I like; and I'll shake hands with what kings I like; and if your own son is not good enough for you, you can go and look for another. Do you mind me now?

mrs o'flaherty. And was it the Belgians learned you such brazen impudence?

o'flaherty. The Belgians is good men; and the French ought to be more civil to them, let alone their being half murdered by the Boshes.

mrs o'flaherty. Good men is it! Good men! to come over here when they were wounded because it was a Catholic country, and then to go to the Protestant Church because it didnt cost them anything, and some of them to never go near a church at all. Thats what you call good men!

o'flaherty. Oh, youre the mighty fine

politician, arnt you? Much you know about Belgians or foreign parts or the world youre living in, God help you!

MRS O'FLAHERTY. Why wouldnt I know better than you? Amment I your mother?

O'FLAHERTY. And if you are itself, how can you know what you never seen as well as me that was dug into the continent of Europe for six months, and was buried in the earth of it three times with the shells bursting on the top of me? I tell you I know what I'm about. I have my own reasons for taking part in this great conflict. I'd be ashamed to stay at home and not fight when everybody else is fighting.

MRS O'FLAHERTY. If you wanted to fight, why couldnt you fight in the German army?

O'FLAHERTY. Because they only get a penny a day.

MRS O'FLAHERTY. Well, and if they do itself, isnt there the French army?

O'FLAHERTY. They only get a hapenny a day.

MRS O'FLAHERTY [much dashed] Oh murder! They must be a mean lot, Dinny.

O'FLAHERTY [sarcastic] Maybe youd have me join the Turkish army, and worship the heathen Mahomet that put a corn in his ear and pretended it was a message from the heavens when the pigeon come to pick it out and eat it. I went where I could get the biggest allowance for you; and little thanks I get for it!

MRS O'FLAHERTY. Allowance, is it! Do you know what the thieving blackguards did on me? They came to me and they says, "Was your son a big eater?" they says. "Oh, he was that" says I: "ten shillings a week wouldnt keep him." Sure I thought the more I said the more theyd give me. "Then" says they, "thats ten shillings a week off your allowance" they says, "because you save that by the king feeding him." "Indeed!" says I: "I suppose if I'd six sons, youd stop three pound a week from me, and make out that I ought to pay you money instead of you paying me." "Theres a fallacy in your argument" they says.

O'FLAHERTY. A what?

MRS O'FLAHERTY. A fallacy: thats the word he said. I says to him, "It's a Pharisee I'm thinking you mean, sir; but you can keep your dirty money that your king grudges a poor old widow; and please God the English will be bet yet for the deadly sin of oppressing the poor"; and with that I shut the door in his face.

O'FLAHERTY [furious] Do you tell me they knocked ten shillings off you for my keep?

MRS O'FLAHERTY [soothing him] No, darlint: they only knocked off half a crown. I put up with it because Ive got the old age pension; and they know very well I'm only sixty-two; so Ive the better of them by half a crown a week anyhow.

O'FLAHERTY. It's a queer way of doing business. If theyd tell you straight out what they was going to give you, you wouldnt mind; but if there was twenty ways of telling the truth and only one way of telling a lie, the Government would find it out. It's in the nature of governments to tell lies.

Teresa Driscoll, a parlor maid, comes from the house.

TERESA. Youre to come up to the drawing room to have your tea, Mrs O'Flaherty.

MRS O'FLAHERTY. Mind you have a sup of good black tea for me in the kitchen afterwards, acushla. That washy drawing room tea will give me the wind if I leave it on my stomach. [*She goes into the house, leaving the two young people alone together*].

O'FLAHERTY. Is that yourself, Tessie? And how are you?

TERESA. Nicely, thank you. And hows yourself?

O'FLAHERTY. Finely, thank God. [*He produces a gold chain*]. Look what Ive brought you, Tessie.

TERESA [shrinking] Sure I dont like to touch it, Denny. Did you take it off a dead man?

O'FLAHERTY. No: I took it off a live one; and thankful he was to me to be alive and kept a prisoner in ease and comfort, and me left fighting in peril of my life.

TERESA [taking it] Do you think it's real gold, Denny?

O'FLAHERTY. It's real German gold, anyhow.

TERESA. But German silver isnt real, Denny.

O'FLAHERTY [his face darkening] Well, it's the best the Bosh could do for me, anyhow.

TERESA. Do you think I might take it to the jeweller next market day and ask him?

O'FLAHERTY [sulkily] You may take it to the divil if you like.

TERESA. You neednt lose your temper about it. I only thought I'd like to know. The nice fool I'd look if I went about shewing off a chain that turned out to be only brass!

O'FLAHERTY. I think you might say Thank

you.

TERESA. Do you? I think you might have said something more to me than "Is that yourself?" You couldnt say less to the postman.

O'FLAHERTY [his brow clearing] Oh, is that whats the matter? Here! come and take the taste of the brass out of my mouth. [He seizes her and kisses her].

Teresa, without losing her Irish dignity, takes the kiss as appreciatively as a connoisseur might take a glass of wine, and sits down with him on the garden seat.

TERESA [as he squeezes her waist] Thank God the priest cant see us here!

O'FLAHERTY. It's little they care for priests in France, alanna.

TERESA. And what had the queen on her, Denny, when she spoke to you in the palace?

O'FLAHERTY. She had a bonnet on without any strings to it. And she had a plakeen of embroidery down her bosom. And she had her waist where it used to be, and not where the other ladies had it. And she had little brooches in her ears, though she hadnt half the jewelry of Mrs Sullivan that keeps the popshop in Drumpogue. And she dresses her hair down over her forehead, in a fringe like. And she has an Irish look about her eyebrows. And she didnt know what to say to me, poor woman! and I didnt know what to say to her, God help me!

TERESA. Youll have a pension now with the Cross, wont you, Denny?

O'FLAHERTY. Sixpence three farthings a day.

TERESA. That isnt much.

O'FLAHERTY. I take out the rest in glory.

TERESA. And if youre wounded, youll have a wound pension, wont you?

O'FLAHERTY. I will, please God.

TERESA. Youre going out again, arnt you, Denny?

O'FLAHERTY. I cant help myself. I'd be shot for a deserter if I didnt go; and may be I'll be shot by the Boshes if I do go; so between the two of them I'm nicely fixed up.

MRS O'FLAHERTY [calling from within the house] Tessie! Tessie darlint!

TERESA [disengaging herself from his arm and rising] I'm wanted for the tea table. Youll have a pension anyhow, Denny, wont you, whether youre wounded or not?

MRS O'FLAHERTY. Come, child, come.

TERESA [impatiently] Oh, sure I'm coming.

[She tries to smile at Denny, not very convincingly, and hurries into the house].

O'FLAHERTY [alone] And if I do get a pension itself, the divil a penny of it youll ever have the spending of.

MRS O'FLAHERTY [as she comes from the porch] Oh, it's a shame for you to keep the girl from her juties, Dinny. You might get her into trouble.

O'FLAHERTY. Much I care whether she gets into trouble or not! I pity the man that gets her into trouble. He'll get himself into worse.

MRS O'FLAHERTY. Whats that you tell me? Have you been falling out with her, and she a girl with a fortune of ten pounds?

O'FLAHERTY. Let her keep her fortune. I wouldnt touch her with the tongs if she had thousands and millions.

MRS O'FLAHERTY. Oh fie for shame, Dinny! why would you say the like of that of a decent honest girl, and one of the Driscolls too?

O'FLAHERTY. Why wouldnt I say it? She's thinking of nothing but to get me out there again to be wounded so that she may spend my pension, bad scran to her!

MRS O'FLAHERTY. Why, whats come over you, child, at all at all?

O'FLAHERTY. Knowledge and wisdom have come over me with pain and fear and trouble. Ive been made a fool of and imposed upon all my life. I thought that covetous sthreal in there was a walking angel; and now if ever I marry at all I'll marry a Frenchwoman.

MRS O'FLAHERTY [fiercely] Youll not, so; and dont you dar repeat such a thing to me.

O'FLAHERTY. Wont I, faith! Ive been as good as married to a couple of them already.

MRS O'FLAHERTY. The Lord be praised, what wickedness have you been up to, you young blackguard?

O'FLAHERTY. One of them Frenchwomen would cook you a meal twice in the day and all days and every day that Sir Pearce himself might go begging through Ireland for, and never see the like of. I'll have a French wife, I tell you; and when I settle down to be a farmer I'll have a French farm, with a field as big as the continent of Europe that ten of your dirty little fields here wouldnt so much as fill the ditch of.

MRS O'FLAHERTY [furious] Then it's a French mother you may go look for; for I'm done with you.

O'FLAHERTY. And it's no great loss youd be if it wasnt for my natural feelings for you; for it's only a silly ignorant old countrywoman you are with all your fine talk about Ireland: you that never stepped beyond the few acres of it you were born on!

MRS O'FLAHERTY [*tottering to the garden seat and shewing signs of breaking down*] Dinny darlint, why are you like this to me? Whats happened to you?

O'FLAHERTY [*gloomily*] Whats happened to everybody? thats what I want to know. Whats happened to you that I thought all the world of and was afeard of? Whats happened to Sir Pearce, that I thought was a great general, and that I now see to be no more fit to command an army than an old hen? Whats happened to Tessie, that I was mad to marry a year ago, and that I wouldnt take now with all Ireland for her fortune? I tell you the world's creation is crumbling in ruins about me; and then you come and ask whats happened to me?

MRS O'FLAHERTY [*giving way to wild grief*] Ochone! ochone! my son's turned agen me. Oh, whatll I do at all at all? Oh! oh! oh! oh!

SIR PEARCE [*running out of the house*] Whats this infernal noise? What on earth is the matter?

O'FLAHERTY. Arra hold your whisht, mother. Dont you see his honor?

MRS O'FLAHERTY. Oh, sir, I'm ruined and destroyed. Oh, wont you speak to Dinny, sir: I'm heart scalded with him. He wants to marry a Frenchwoman on me, and to go away and be a foreigner and desert his mother and betray his country. It's mad he is with the roaring of the cannons and he killing the Germans and the Germans killing him, bad cess to them! My boy is taken from me and turned agen me; and who is to take care of me in my old age after all Ive done for him, ochone! ochone!

O'FLAHERTY. Hold your noise, I tell you. Who's going to leave you? I'm going to take you with me. There now: does that satisfy you?

MRS O'FLAHERTY. Is it take me into a strange land among heathens and pagans and savages, and me not knowing a word of their language nor them of mine?

O'FLAHERTY. A good job they dont: may be theyll think youre talking sense.

MRS O'FLAHERTY. Ask me to die out of Ireland, is it? and the angels not to find me when they come for me!

O'FLAHERTY. And would you ask me to live in Ireland where Ive been imposed on and kept in ignorance, and to die where the divil himself wouldnt take me as a gift, let alone the blessed angels? You can come or stay. You can take your old way or take my young way. But stick in this place I will not among a lot of good-for-nothing divils thatll not do a hand's turn but watch the grass growing and build up the stone wall where the cow walked through it. And Sir Horace Plunkett breaking his heart all the time telling them how they might put the land into decent tillage like the French and Belgians.

SIR PEARCE. Yes: he's quite right, you know, Mrs O'Flaherty: quite right there.

MRS O'FLAHERTY. Well, sir, please God the war will last a long time yet; and may be I'll die before it's over and the separation allowance stops.

O'FLAHERTY. Thats all you care about. It's nothing but milch cows we men are for the women, with their separation allowances, ever since the war began, bad luck to them that made it!

TERESA [*coming from the porch between the General and Mrs O'Flaherty*] Hannah sent me out for to tell you, sir, that the tea will be black and the cake not fit to eat with the cold if yous all dont come at wanst.

MRS O'FLAHERTY [*breaking out again*] Oh, Tessie darlint, what have you been saying to Dinny at all at all? Oh! oh—

SIR PEARCE [*out of patience*] You cant discuss that here. We shall have Tessie beginning now.

O'FLAHERTY. Thats right, sir: drive them in.

TERESA. I havnt said a word to him. He—

SIR PEARCE. Hold your tongue; and go in and attend to your business at the tea table.

TERESA. But amment I telling your honor that I never said a word to him? He gave me a beautiful gold chain. Here it is to shew your honour thats it's no lie I'm telling you.

SIR PEARCE. Whats this, O'Flaherty? Youve been looting some unfortunate officer.

O'FLAHERTY. No sir: I stole it from him of his own accord.

MRS O'FLAHERTY. Wouldnt your honor tell him that his mother has the first call on it? What would a slip of a girl like that be doing with a gold chain round her neck?

TERESA [*venomously*] Anyhow, I have a neck to put it round and not a hank of wrinkles.

At this unfortunate remark, Mrs O'Flaherty

bounds from her seat; and an appalling tempest of wordy wrath breaks out. The remonstrances and commands of the General, and the protests and menaces of O'Flaherty, only increase the hubbub. They are soon all speaking at once at the top of their voices.

MRS O'FLAHERTY [*solo*] You impudent young heifer, how dar you say such a thing to me? [*Teresa retorts furiously; the men interfere; and the solo becomes a quartet, fortissimo*]. Ive a good mind to clout your ears for you to teach you manners. Be ashamed of yourself, do; and learn to know who youre speaking to. That I maytnt sin! but I dont know what the good God was thinking about when he made the like of you. Let me not see you casting sheep's eyes at my son again. There never was an O'Flaherty yet that would demean himself by keeping company with a dirty Driscoll; and if I see you next or nigh my house I'll put you in the ditch with a flea in your ear: mind that now.

TERESA. Is it me you offer such a name to, you foul-mouthed, dirty minded, lying, sloothering old sow, you? I wouldnt soil my tongue by calling you in your right name and telling Sir Pearce whats the common talk of the town about you. You and your O'Flahertys! setting yourself up agen the Driscolls that would never lower themselves to be seen in conversation with you at the fair. You can keep your ugly stingy lump of a son; for what he is but a common soldier? and God help the girl that gets him, say I! So the back of my hand to you, Mrs O'Flaherty; and that the cat may tear your ugly old face!

SIR PEARCE. Silence. Tessie: did you hear me ordering you to go into the house? Mrs O'Flaherty! [*Louder*] Mrs O'Flaherty!! Will you just listen to me one moment? Please. [*Furiously*] Do you hear me speaking to you, woman? Are you human beings or are you wild beasts? Stop that noise immediately: do you hear? [*Yelling*] Are you going to do what I order you, or are you not? Scandalous! Disgraceful! This comes of being too familiar with you. O'Flaherty: shove them into the house. Out with the whole damned pack of you.

O'FLAHERTY [*to the women*] Here now: none of that, none of that. Go easy, I tell you. Hold your whisht, mother, will you, or youll be sorry for it after. [*To Teresa*] Is

that the way for a decent young girl to speak? [*Despairingly*] Oh, for the Lord's sake, shut up, will yous? Have yous no respect for yourselves or your betters? [*Peremptorily*] Let me have no more of it, I tell you. Och! the divil's in the whole crew of you. In with you into the house this very minute and tear one another's eyes out in the kitchen if you like. In with you.

The two men seize the two women, and push them, still violently abusing one another, into the house. Sir Pearce slams the door upon them savagely. Immediately a heavenly silence falls on the summer afternoon. The two sit down out of breath; and for a long time nothing is said. Sir Pearce sits on an iron chair. O'Flaherty sits on the garden seat. The thrush begins to sing melodiously. O'Flaherty cocks his ears, and looks up at it. A smile spreads over his troubled features. Sir Pearce, with a long sigh, takes out his pipe, and begins to fill it.

O'FLAHERTY [*idyllically*] What a discontented sort of an animal a man is, sir! Only a month ago, I was in the quiet of the country out at the front, with not a sound except the birds and the bellow of a cow in the distance as it might be, and the shrapnel making little clouds in the heavens, and the shells whistling, and may be a yell or two when one of us was hit; and would you believe it, sir, I complained of the noise and wanted to have a peaceful hour at home. Well: them two has taught me a lesson. This morning, sir, when I was telling the boys here how I was longing to be back taking my part for king and country with the others, I was lying, as you well knew, sir. Now I can go and say it with a clear conscience. Some likes war's alarums; and some likes home life. Ive tried both, sir; and I'm all for war's alarums now. I always was a quiet lad by natural disposition.

SIR PEARCE. Strictly between ourselves, O'Flaherty, and as one soldier to another [*O'Flaherty salutes, but without stiffening*], do you think we should have got an army without conscription if domestic life had been as happy as people say it is?

O'FLAHERTY. Well, between you and me and the wall, Sir Pearce, I think the less we say about that until the war's over, the better.

He winks at the General. The General strikes a match. The thrush sings. A jay laughs. The conversation drops.

THE END

XXVII

THE INCA OF PERUSALEM

AN ALMOST HISTORICAL COMEDIETTA

PROLOGUE

The tableau curtains are closed. An English archdeacon comes through them in a condition of extreme irritation. He speaks through the curtains to someone behind them.

THE ARCHDEACON. Once for all, Ermyntrude, I cannot afford to maintain you in your present extravagance. [*He goes to a flight of steps leading to the stalls and sits down disconsolately on the top step. A fashionably dressed lady comes through the curtains and contemplates him with patient obstinacy. He continues, grumbling*] An English clergyman's daughter should be able to live quite respectably and comfortably on an allowance of £150 a year, wrung with great difficulty from the domestic budget.

ERMYNTRUDE. You are not a common clergyman: you are an archdeacon.

THE ARCHDEACON [*angrily*] That does not affect my emoluments to the extent of enabling me to support a daughter whose extravagance would disgrace a royal personage. [*Scrambling to his feet and scolding at her*] What do you mean by it, Miss?

ERMYNTRUDE. Oh really, father! Miss! Is that the way to talk to a widow?

THE ARCHDEACON. Is that the way to talk to a father? Your marriage was a most disastrous imprudence. It gave you habits that are absolutely beyond your means—I mean beyond my means: you have no means. Why did you not marry Matthews: the best curate I ever had?

ERMYNTRUDE. I wanted to; and you wouldnt let me. You insisted on my marrying Roosenhonkers-Pipstein.

THE ARCHDEACON. I had to do the best for you, my child. Roosenhonkers-Pipstein was a millionaire.

ERMYNTRUDE. How did you know he was a millionaire?

THE ARCHDEACON. He came from America. Of course he was a millionaire. Besides, he proved to my solicitors that he had fifteen million dollars when you married him.

ERMYNTRUDE. His solicitors proved to me that he had sixteen millions when he died. He was a millionaire to the last.

THE ARCHDEACON. O Mammon, Mammon! I am punished now for bowing the knee to him. Is there nothing left of your settlement? Fifty thousand dollars a year it secured to you, as we all thought. Only half the securities could be called speculative. The other half were gilt-edged. What has become of it all?

ERMYNTRUDE. The speculative ones were not paid up; and the gilt-edged ones just paid the calls on them until the whole show burst up.

THE ARCHDEACON. Ermyntrude: what expressions!

ERMYNTRUDE. Oh bother! If you had lost ten thousand a year what expressions would you use, do you think? The long and the short of it is that I cant live in the squalid way you are accustomed to.

THE ARCHDEACON. Squalid!

ERMYNTRUDE. I have formed habits of comfort.

THE ARCHDEACON. Comfort!!

ERMYNTRUDE. Well, elegance if you like. Luxury, if you insist. Call it what you please. A house that costs less than a hundred thousand dollars a year to run is intolerable to me.

THE ARCHDEACON. Then, my dear, you had better become lady's maid to a princess until you can find another millionaire to marry you.

ERMYNTRUDE. Thats an idea. I will [*She vanishes through the curtains*].

THE ARCHDEACON. What! Come back, Miss. Come back this instant. [*The lights are lowered*]. Oh, very well: I have nothing more to say. [*He descends the steps into the auditorium and makes for the door, grumbling all the time*]. Insane, senseless extravagance! [*Barking*] Worthlessness!! [*Muttering*] I will not bear it any longer. Dresses, hats, furs, gloves, motor rides: one bill after another: money going like water. No restraint, no self-control, no decency. [*Shrieking*] I say, no decency! [*Muttering again*] Nice state of things we are coming to! A pretty world! But I simply will not bear it. She can do as she likes. I wash my hands of her: I am not going to die in the workhouse for any good-for-nothing, undutiful, spendthrift daughter; and the sooner that is understood by everybody the better for all par— [*He is by this time out of hearing in the corridor*].

THE PLAY

A hotel sitting room. A table in the centre. On it a telephone. Two chairs at it, opposite one another. Behind it, the door. The fireplace has a mirror in the mantelpiece.

A spinster Princess, hatted and gloved, is ushered in by the Hotel Manager, spruce and artificially bland by professional habit, but treating his customer with a condescending affability which sails very close to the east wind of insolence.

THE MANAGER. I am sorry I am unable to accommodate Your Highness on the first floor.

THE PRINCESS [*very shy and nervous*] Oh please dont mention it. This is quite nice. Very nice. Thank you very much.

THE MANAGER. We could prepare a room in the annexe—

THE PRINCESS. Oh no. This will do very well.

She takes off her gloves and hat; puts them on the table; and sits down.

THE MANAGER. The rooms are quite as good up here. There is less noise; and there is the lift. If Your Highness desires anything, there is the telephone—

THE PRINCESS. Oh, thank you, I dont want anything. The telephone is so difficult: I am not accustomed to it.

THE MANAGER. Can I take any order? Some tea?

THE PRINCESS. Oh, thank you. Yes: I should like some tea, if I might—if it would not be too much trouble.

He goes out. The telephone rings. The Princess starts out of her chair, terrified, and recoils as far as possible from the instrument.

THE PRINCESS. Oh dear! [*It rings again. She looks scared. It rings again. She approaches it timidly. It rings again. She retreats hastily. It rings repeatedly. She runs to it in desperation and puts the receiver to her ear*]. Who is there? What do I do? I am not used to the telephone: I dont know how—What! Oh, I can hear you speaking quite distinctly. [*She sits down, delighted, and settles herself for a conversation*]. How wonderful! What! A lady? Oh! a person.

Oh yes: I know. Yes, please, send her up. Have my servants finished their lunch yet? Oh no: please dont disturb them: I'd rather not. It doesnt matter. Thank you. What? Oh yes, it's quite easy. I had no idea—am I to hang it up just as it was? Thank you. [*She hangs it up*].

Ermyntrude enters, presenting a plain and staid appearance in a long straight waterproof with a hood over her head gear. She comes to the end of the table opposite to that at which the Princess is seated.

THE PRINCESS. Excuse me. I have been talking through the telephone; and I heard quite well, though I have never ventured before. Wont you sit down?

ERMYNTRUDE. No, thank you, Your Highness. I am only a lady's maid. I understood you wanted one.

THE PRINCESS. Oh no: you mustnt think I want one. It's so unpatriotic to want anything now, on account of the war, you know. I sent my maid away as a public duty; and now she has married a soldier and is expecting a war baby. But I dont know how to do without her. Ive tried my very best; but somehow it doesnt answer: everybody cheats me; and in the end it isnt any saving. So Ive made up my mind to sell my piano and have a maid. That will be a real saving, because I really dont care a bit for music, though of course one has to pretend to. Dont you think so?

ERMYNTRUDE. Certainly I do, Your Highness. Nothing could be more correct. Saving and self-denial both at once; and an act of kindness to me, as I am out of place.

THE PRINCESS. I'm so glad you see it in that way. Er—you wont mind my asking, will you?—how did you lose your place?

ERMYNTRUDE. The war, Your Highness, the war.

THE PRINCESS. Oh yes, of course. But how—

ERMYNTRUDE [*taking out her handkerchief and shewing signs of grief*] My poor mistress—

THE PRINCESS. Oh please say no more. Dont think about it. So tactless of me to mention it.

ERMYNTRUDE [*mastering her emotion and smiling through her tears*] Your Highness is too good.

THE PRINCESS. Do you think you could be happy with me? I attach such importance to that.

ERMYNTRUDE [*gushing*] Oh, I know I shall.

THE PRINCESS. You must not expect too much. There is my uncle. He is very severe and hasty; and he is my guardian. I once had a maid I liked very much; but he sent her away the very first time.

ERMYNTRUDE. The first time of what, Your Highness?

THE PRINCESS. Oh, something she did. I am sure she had never done it before; and I know she would never have done it again, she was so truly contrite and nice about it.

ERMYNTRUDE. About what, Your Highness?

THE PRINCESS. Well, she wore my jewels and one of my dresses at a rather improper ball with her young man; and my uncle saw her.

ERMYNTRUDE. Then he was at the ball too, Your Highness?

THE PRINCESS [struck by the inference] I suppose he must have been. I wonder! You know, it's very sharp of you to find that out. I hope you are not too sharp.

ERMYNTRUDE. A lady's maid has to be, Your Highness. [She produces some letters]. Your Highness wishes to see my testimonials, no doubt. I have one from an Archdeacon. [She proffers the letters].

THE PRINCESS [taking them] Do archdeacons have maids? How curious!

ERMYNTRUDE. No, Your Highness. They have daughters. I have first-rate testimonials from the Archdeacon and from his daughter.

THE PRINCESS [reading them] The daughter says you are in every respect a treasure. The Archdeacon says he would have kept you if he could possibly have afforded it. Most satisfactory, I'm sure.

ERMYNTRUDE. May I regard myself as engaged then, Your Highness?

THE PRINCESS [alarmed] Oh, I'm sure I dont know. If you like, of course: but do you think I ought to?

ERMYNTRUDE. Naturally I think Your Highness ought to, most decidedly.

THE PRINCESS. Oh well, if you think that, I daresay youre quite right. Youll excuse my mentioning it, I hope; but what wages—er—?

ERMYNTRUDE. The same as the maid who went to the ball. Your Highness need not make any change.

THE PRINCESS. M'yes. Of course she began with less. But she had such a number of relatives to keep! It was quite heartbreaking:

I had to raise her wages again and again.

ERMYNTRUDE. I shall be quite content with what she began on; and I have no relatives dependent on me. And I am willing to wear my own dresses at balls.

THE PRINCESS. I am sure nothing could be fairer than that. My uncle cant object to that: can he?

ERMYNTRUDE. If he does, Your Highness, ask him to speak to me about it. I shall regard it as part of my duties to speak to your uncle about matters of business.

THE PRINCESS. Would you? You must be frightfully courageous.

ERMYNTRUDE. May I regard myself as engaged. Your Highness? I should like to set about my duties immediately.

THE PRINCESS. Oh yes, I think so. Oh certainly. I—

A waiter comes in with the tea. He places the tray on the table.

THE PRINCESS. Oh, thank you.

ERMYNTRUDE [raising the cover from the tea cake and looking at it] How long has that been standing at the top of the stairs?

THE PRINCESS [terrified] Oh please! It doesnt matter.

THE WAITER. It has not been waiting. Straight from the kitchen, madam, believe me.

ERMYNTRUDE. Send the manager here.

THE WAITER. The manager! What do you want with the manager?

ERMYNTRUDE. He will tell you when I have done with him. How dare you treat Her Highness in this disgraceful manner? What sort of pothouse is this? Where did you learn to speak to persons of quality? Take away your cold tea and cold cake instantly. Give them to the chambermaid you were flirting with whilst Her Highness was waiting. Order some fresh tea at once; and do not presume to bring it yourself: have it brought by a civil waiter who is accustomed to wait on ladies, and not, like you, on commercial travellers.

THE WAITER. Alas, madam, I am not accustomed to wait on anybody. Two years ago I was an eminent medical man. My waiting-room was crowded with the flower of the aristocracy and the higher bourgeoisie from nine to six every day. But the war came; and my patients were ordered to give up their luxuries. They gave up their doctors, but kept their week-end hotels, closing every career to me except the career of a waiter. [*He puts his fingers on the teapot to test its temperature, and automatically takes out his watch with the other hand as if to count the teapot's pulse*]. You are right: the tea is cold: it was made by the wife of a once fashionable architect. The cake is only half toasted: what can you expect from a ruined west-end tailor whose attempt to establish a second-hand business failed last Tuesday week? Have you the heart to complain to the manager? Have we not suffered enough? Are our miseries nev—[*the manager enters*] Oh Lord! here he is. [*The waiter withdraws abjectly, taking the tea tray with him*].

THE MANAGER. Pardon, Your Highness; but I have received an urgent inquiry for rooms from an English family of importance; and I venture to ask you to let me know how long you intend to honour us with your presence.

THE PRINCESS [*rising anxiously*] Oh! am I in the way?

ERMYNTRUDE [*sternly*] Sit down, madam. [*The Princess sits down forlornly. Ermyntrude turns imperiously to the Manager*]. Her Highness will require this room for twenty minutes.

THE MANAGER. Twenty minutes!

ERMYNTRUDE. Yes: it will take fully that time to find a proper apartment in a respectable hotel.

THE MANAGER. I do not understand.

ERMYNTRUDE. You understand perfectly. How dare you offer Her Highness a room on the second floor?

THE MANAGER. But I have explained. The first floor is occupied. At least—

ERMYNTRUDE. Well? At least?

THE MANAGER. It is occupied.

ERMYNTRUDE. Dont you dare tell Her Highness a falsehood. It is not occupied. You are saving it up for the arrival of the five fifteen express, from which you hope to pick up some fat armaments contractor who will drink all the bad champagne in your cellar at 25 francs a bottle, and pay twice over for everything because he is in the same hotel with Her Highness, and can boast of having turned her out of the best rooms.

THE MANAGER. But Her Highness was so gracious. I did not know that Her Highness was at all particular.

ERMYNTRUDE. And you take advantage of Her Highness's graciousness. You impose on her with your stories. You give her a room not fit for a dog. You send cold tea to her by a decayed professional person disguised as a waiter. But dont think you can trifle with me. I am a lady's maid; and I know the ladies' maids and valets of all the aristocracies of Europe and all the millionaires of America. When I expose your hotel as the second-rate little hole it is, not a soul above the rank of a curate with a large family will be seen entering it. I shake its dust off my feet. Order the luggage to be taken down at once.

THE MANAGER [*appealing to the Princess*] Can Your Highness believe this of me? Have I had the misfortune to offend Your Highness?

THE PRINCESS. Oh no. I am quite satisfied. Please—

ERMYNTRUDE. Is Your Highness dissatisfied with me?

THE PRINCESS [*intimidated*] Oh no: please dont think that. I only meant—

ERMYNTRUDE [*to the Manager*] You hear. Perhaps you think Her Highness is going to do the work of teaching you your place herself, instead of leaving it to her maid.

THE MANAGER. Oh please, mademoiselle. Believe me: our only wish is to make you perfectly comfortable. But in consequence of the war, all royal personages now practise a rigid economy, and desire us to treat them like their poorest subjects.

THE PRINCESS. Oh yes. You are quite right—

ERMYNTRUDE [*interrupting*] There! Her Highness forgives you; but dont do it again. Now go downstairs, my good man, and get that suite on the first floor ready for us. And send some proper tea. And turn on the heating apparatus until the temperature in the rooms is comfortably warm. And have hot water put in all the bedrooms—

THE MANAGER. There are basins with hot and cold taps.

ERMYNTRUDE [*scornfully*] Yes: there would be. I suppose we must put up with that: sinks in our rooms, and pipes that rattle and bang and guggle all over the house whenever anyone washes his hands. *I* know.

THE MANAGER [*gallant*] You are hard to please, mademoiselle.

ERMYNTRUDE. No harder than other people. But when I'm not pleased I'm not too lady-like to say so. Thats all the difference. There is nothing more, thank you.

The Manager shrugs his shoulders resignedly;

makes a deep bow to the Princess; goes to the door; wafts a kiss surreptitiously to Ermyntrude; and goes out.

THE PRINCESS. It's wonderful! How have you the courage?

ERMYNTRUDE. In Your Highness's service I know no fear. Your Highness can leave all unpleasant people to me.

THE PRINCESS. How I wish I could! The most dreadful thing of all I have to go through myself.

ERMYNTRUDE. Dare I ask what it is, Your Highness?

THE PRINCESS. I'm going to be married. I'm to be met here and married to a man I never saw. A boy! A boy who never saw m e! One of the sons of the Inca of Perusalem.

ERMYNTRUDE. Indeed? Which son?

THE PRINCESS. I dont know. They havnt settled which. It's a dreadful thing to be a princess: they just marry you to anyone they like. The Inca is to come and look at me, and pick out whichever of his sons he thinks will suit. And then I shall be an alien enemy everywhere except in Perusalem, because the Inca has made war on everybody. And I shall have to pretend that everybody has made war on him. It's too bad.

ERMYNTRUDE. Still, a husband is a husband. I wish I had one.

THE PRINCESS. Oh, how can you say that! I'm afraid youre not a nice woman.

ERMYNTRUDE. Your Highness is provided for. I'm not.

THE PRINCESS. Even if you could bear to let a man touch you, you shouldnt say so.

ERMYNTRUDE. I shall not say so again, Your Highness, except perhaps to the man.

THE PRINCESS. It's too dreadful to think of. I wonder you can be so coarse. I really dont think youll suit. I feel sure now that you know more about men than you should.

ERMYNTRUDE. I am a widow, Your Highness.

THE PRINCESS [*overwhelmed*] Oh, I BEG your pardon. Of course I ought to have known you would not have spoken like that if you were not married. That makes it all right, doesnt it? I'm so sorry.

The Manager returns, white, scared, hardly able to speak.

THE MANAGER. Your Highness: an officer asks to see you on behalf of the Inca of Perusalem.

THE PRINCESS [*rising distractedly*] Oh, I cant, really. Oh, what shall I do?

THE MANAGER. On important business, he says, Your Highness. Captain Duval.

ERMYNTRUDE. Duval! Nonsense! The usual thing. It is the Inca himself, incognito.

THE PRINCESS. Oh, send him away. Oh, I'm so afraid of the Inca. I'm not properly dressed to receive him; and he is so particular: he would order me to stay in my room for a week. Tell him to call tomorrow: say I'm ill in bed. I cant: I wont: I darent: you must get rid of him somehow.

ERMYNTRUDE. Leave him to me, Your Highness.

THE PRINCESS. Youd never dare!

ERMYNTRUDE. I am an Englishwoman, Your Highness, and perfectly capable of tackling ten Incas if necessary. I will arrange the matter. [*To the Manager*] Shew Her Highness to her bedroom; and then shew Captain Duval in here.

THE PRINCESS. Oh, thank you so much. [*She goes to the door. Ermyntrude, noticing that she has left her hat and gloves on the table, runs after her with them*]. Oh, t h a n k you. And oh, please, if I must have one of his sons, I should like a fair one that doesnt shave, with soft hair and a beard. I couldnt bear being kissed by a bristly person. [*She runs out, the Manager bowing as she passes. He follows her*].

Ermyntrude whips off her waterproof; hides it; and gets herself swiftly into perfect trim at the mirror, before the Manager, with a large jewel case in his hand, returns, ushering in the Inca.

THE MANAGER. Captain Duval.

The Inca, in military uniform, advances with a marked and imposing stage walk; stops; orders the trembling Manager by a gesture to place the jewel case on the table; dismisses him with a frown; touches his helmet graciously to Ermyntrude; and takes off his cloak.

THE INCA. I beg you, madam, to be quite at your ease, and to speak to me without ceremony.

ERMYNTRUDE [*moving haughtily and carelessly to the table*] I hadnt the slightest intention of treating you with ceremony. [*She sits down: a liberty which gives him a perceptible shock*]. I am quite at a loss to imagine why I should treat a perfect stranger named Duval: a captain! almost a subaltern! with the smallest ceremony.

THE INCA. That is true. I had for the moment forgotten my position.

2 E

ERMYNTRUDE. It doesnt matter. You may sit down.

THE INCA [frowning] What!

ERMYNTRUDE. I said, you ... may ... sit ... down.

THE INCA. Oh. [His moustache droops. He sits down].

ERMYNTRUDE. What is your business?

THE INCA. I come on behalf of the Inca of Perusalem.

ERMYNTRUDE. The Allerhöchst?

THE INCA. Precisely.

ERMYNTRUDE. I wonder does he feel ridiculous when people call him the Allerhöchst.

THE INCA [surprised] Why should he? He is the Allerhöchst.

ERMYNTRUDE. Is he nice looking?

THE INCA. I—er. Er—I. I—er. I am not a good judge.

ERMYNTRUDE. They say he takes himself very seriously.

THE INCA. Why should he not, madam? Providence has entrusted to his family the care of a mighty empire. He is in a position of half divine, half paternal responsibility towards sixty millions of people, whose duty it is to die for him at the word of command. To take himself otherwise than seriously would be blasphemous. It is a punishable offence—severely punishable—in Perusalem. It is called Incadisparagement.

ERMYNTRUDE. How cheerful! Can he laugh?

THE INCA. Certainly, madam. [He laughs, harshly and mirthlessly]. Ha ha! Ha ha ha!

ERMYNTRUDE [frigidly] I asked could the Inca laugh. I did not ask could you laugh.

THE INCA. That is true, madam. [Chuckling] Devilish amusing, that! [He laughs, genially and sincerely, and becomes a much more agreeable person]. Pardon me: I am now laughing because I cannot help it. I am amused. The other was merely an imitation: a failure, I admit.

ERMYNTRUDE. You intimated that you had some business?

THE INCA [producing a very large jewel case, and relapsing into solemnity] I am instructed by the Allerhöchst to take a careful note of your features and figure, and, if I consider them satisfactory, to present you with this trifling token of His Imperial Majesty's regard. I do consider them satisfactory. Allow me [he opens the jewel case and presents it]!

ERMYNTRUDE [staring at the contents] What awful taste he must have! I cant wear that.

THE INCA [reddening] Take care, madam! This brooch was designed by the Inca himself. Allow me to explain the design. In the centre, the shield of Arminius. The ten surrounding medallions represent the ten castles of His Majesty. The rim is a piece of the telephone cable laid by His Majesty across the Shipskeel canal. The pin is a model in miniature of the sword of Henry the Birdcatcher.

ERMYNTRUDE. Miniature! It must be bigger than the original. My good man, you dont expect me to wear this round my neck: it's as big as a turtle. [He shuts the case with an angry snap]. How much did it cost?

THE INCA. For materials and manufacture alone, half a million Perusalem dollars, madam. The Inca's design constitutes it a work of art. As such, it is now worth probably ten million dollars.

ERMYNTRUDE. Give it to me. [She snatches it]. I'll pawn it and buy something nice with the money.

THE INCA. Impossible, madam. A design by the Inca must not be exhibited for sale in the shop window of a pawnbroker. [He flings himself into his chair, fuming].

ERMYNTRUDE. So much the better. The Inca will have to redeem it to save himself from that disgrace; and the poor pawnbroker will get his money back. Nobody would buy it, you know.

THE INCA. May I ask why?

ERMYNTRUDE. Well, look at it! Just look at it! I ask you!

THE INCA [his moustache drooping ominously] I am sorry to have to report to the Inca that you have no soul for fine art. [He rises sulkily]. The position of daughter-in-law to the Inca is not compatible with the tastes of a pig. [He attempts to take back the brooch].

ERMYNTRUDE [rising and retreating behind her chair with the brooch] Here! you let that brooch alone. You presented it to me on behalf of the Inca. It is mine. You said my appearance was satisfactory.

THE INCA. Your appearance is not satisfactory. The Inca would not allow his son to marry you if the boy were on a desert island and you were the only other human being on it. [He strides up the room].

ERMYNTRUDE [calmly sitting down and replacing the case on the table] How could he? There would be no clergyman to marry us. It would have to be quite morganatic.

THE INCA [*returning*] Such an expression is out of place in the mouth of a princess aspiring to the highest destiny on earth. You have the morals of a dragoon. [*She receives this with a shriek of laughter. He struggles with his sense of humor*]. At the same time [*he sits down*] there is a certain coarse fun in the idea which compels me to smile. [*He turns up his moustache and smiles*].

ERMYNTRUDE. When I marry the Inca's son, Captain, I shall make the Inca order you to cut off that moustache. It is too irresistible. Doesnt it fascinate everyone in Perusalem?

THE INCA [*leaning forward to her energetically*] By all the thunders of Thor, madam, it fascinates the whole world.

ERMYNTRUDE. What I like about you, Captain Duval, is your modesty.

THE INCA [*straightening up suddenly*] Woman: do not be a fool.

ERMYNTRUDE [*indignant*] Well!

THE INCA. You must look facts in the face. This moustache is an exact copy of the Inca's moustache. Well, does the world occupy itself with the Inca's moustache or does it not? Does it ever occupy itself with anything else? If that is the truth, does its recognition constitute the Inca a coxcomb? Other potentates have moustaches: even beards and moustaches. Does the world occupy itself with those beards and moustaches? Do the hawkers in the streets of every capital on the civilized globe sell ingenious cardboard representations of t h e i r faces on which, at the pulling of a simple string, the moustaches turn up and down, so—[*he makes his moustache turn up and down several times*]? No! I say No. The Inca's moustache is so watched and studied that it has made his face the political barometer of the whole continent. When that moustache goes up, culture rises with it. Not what y o u call culture; but Kultur, a word so much more significant that I hardly understand it myself except when I am in specially good form. When it goes down, millions of men perish.

ERMYNTRUDE. You know, if I had a moustache like that, it would turn my head. I should go mad. Are you quite sure the Inca isnt mad?

THE INCA. How can he be mad, madam? What is sanity? The condition of the Inca's mind. What is madness? The condition of the people who disagree with the Inca.

ERMYNTRUDE. Then I am a lunatic because I dont like that ridiculous brooch.

THE INCA. No, madam: you are only an idiot.

ERMYNTRUDE. Thank you.

THE INCA. Mark you: it is not to be expected that you should see eye to eye with the Inca. That would be presumption. It is for you to accept without question or demur the assurance of your Inca that the brooch is a masterpiece.

ERMYNTRUDE. My Inca! Oh, come! I like that. He is not my Inca yet.

THE INCA. He is everybody's Inca, madam. His realm will yet extend to the confines of the habitable earth. It is his divine right; and let those who dispute it look to themselves. Properly speaking, all those who are now trying to shake his world predominance are not at war with him, but in rebellion against him.

ERMYNTRUDE. Well, he started it, you know.

THE INCA. Madam, be just. When the hunters surround the lion, the lion will spring. The Inca had kept the peace for years. Those who attacked him were steeped in blood, black blood, white blood, brown blood, yellow blood, blue blood. The Inca had never shed a drop.

ERMYNTRUDE. He had only talked.

THE INCA. Only talked! Only talked! What is more glorious than talk? Can anyone in the world talk like him? Madam: when he signed the declaration of war, he said to his foolish generals and admirals, "Gentlemen: you will all be sorry for this." And they are. They know now that they had better have relied on the sword of the spirit: in other words, on their Inca's talk, than on their murderous cannons. The world will one day do justice to the Inca as the man who kept the peace with nothing but his tongue and his moustache. While he talked: talked just as I am talking now to you, simply, quietly, sensibly, but GREATLY, there was peace; there was prosperity; Perusalem went from success to success. He has been silenced for a year by the roar of trinitrotoluene and the bluster of fools; and the world is in ruins. What a tragedy! [*He is convulsed with grief*].

ERMYNTRUDE. Captain Duval: I dont want to be unsympathetic; but suppose we get back to business.

THE INCA. Business! What business?

ERMYNTRUDE. Well, m y business. You

want me to marry one of the Inca's sons: I forget which.

THE INCA. As far as I can recollect the name, it is His Imperial Highness Prince Eitel William Frederick George Franz Josef Alexander Nicholas Victor Emmanuel Albert Theodore Wilson—

ERMYNTRUDE [interrupting] Oh, please, please, maynt I have one with a shorter name? What is he called at home?

THE INCA. He is usually called Sonny, madam. [With great charm of manner] But you will please understand that the Inca has no desire to pin you to any particular son. There is Chips and Spots and Lulu and Pongo and the Corsair and the Piffler and Jack Johnson the Second, all unmarried. At least not seriously married: nothing, in short, that cannot be arranged. They are all at your service.

ERMYNTRUDE. Are they all as clever and charming as their father?

THE INCA [lifts his eyebrows pityingly; shrugs his shoulders; then, with indulgent paternal contempt] Excellent lads, madam. Very honest affectionate creatures. I have nothing against them. Pongo imitates farmyard sounds—cock-crowing and that sort of thing—extremely well. Lulu plays Strauss's Sinfonia Domestica on the mouth organ really screamingly. Chips keeps owls and rabbits. Spots motor bicycles. The Corsair commands canal barges and steers them himself. The Piffler writes plays, and paints most abominably. Jack Johnson trims ladies' hats, and boxes with professionals hired for that purpose. He is invariably victorious. Yes: they all have their different little talents. And also, of course, their family resemblances. For example, they all smoke; they all quarrel with one another; and they none of them appreciate their father, who, by the way, is no mean painter, though the Piffler pretends to ridicule his efforts.

ERMYNTRUDE. Quite a large choice, eh?

THE INCA. But very little to choose, believe me. I should not recommend Pongo, because he snores so frightfully that it has been necessary to build him a sound-proof bedroom: otherwise the royal family would get no sleep. But any of the others would suit equally well—if you are really bent on marrying one of them.

ERMYNTRUDE. If! What is this? I never wanted to marry one of them. I thought you wanted me to.

THE INCA. I did, madam; but [confidentially, flattering her] you are not quite the sort of person I expected you to be; and I doubt whether any of these young degenerates would make you happy. I trust I am not shewing any want of natural feeling when I say that from the point of view of a lively, accomplished, and beautiful woman [Ermyntrude bows] they might pall after a time. I suggest that you might prefer the Inca himself.

ERMYNTRUDE. Oh, Captain, how could a humble person like myself be of any interest to a prince who is surrounded with the ablest and most far-reaching intellects in the world?

THE INCA [explosively] What on earth are you talking about, madam? Can you name a single man in the entourage of the Inca who is not a born fool?

ERMYNTRUDE. Oh, how can you say that! There is Admiral von Cockpits—

THE INCA [rising intolerantly and striding about the room] Von Cockpits! Madam: if Von Cockpits ever goes to heaven, before three weeks are over, the Angel Gabriel will be at war with the man in the moon.

ERMYNTRUDE. But General Von Schinkenburg—

THE INCA. Schinkenburg! I grant you, Schinkenburg has a genius for defending market gardens. Among market gardens he is invincible. But what is the good of that? The world does not consist of market gardens. Turn him loose in pasture and he is lost. The Inca has defeated all these generals again and again at manœuvres; and yet he has to give place to them in the field because he would be blamed for every disaster—accused of sacrificing the country to his vanity. Vanity! Why do they call him vain? Just because he is one of the few men who are not afraid to live. Why do they call themselves brave? Because they have not sense enough to be afraid to die. Within the last year the world has produced millions of heroes. Has it produced more than one Inca? [He resumes his seat].

ERMYNTRUDE. Fortunately not, Captain. I'd rather marry Chips.

THE INCA [making a wry face] Chips! Oh no: I wouldnt marry Chips.

ERMYNTRUDE. Why?

THE INCA [whispering the secret] Chips talks too much about himself.

ERMYNTRUDE. Well, what about Snooks?

THE INCA. Snooks? Who is he? Have I a son named Snooks? There are so many— [*wearily*] so many — that I often forget. [*Casually*] But I wouldnt marry him, anyhow, if I were you.

ERMYNTRUDE. But hasnt any of them inherited the family genius? Surely, if Providence has entrusted them with the care of Perusalem—if they are all descended from Bedrock the Great—

THE INCA [*interrupting her impatiently*] Madam: if you ask me, I consider Bedrock a grossly overrated monarch.

ERMYNTRUDE [*shocked*] Oh, Captain! Take care! Incadisparagement.

THE INCA. I repeat, grossly overrated. Strictly between ourselves, I do not believe all this about Providence entrusting the care of sixty million human beings to the abilities of Chips and the Piffler and Jack Johnson. I believe in individual genius. That is the Inca's secret. It must be. Why, hang it all, madam, if it were a mere family matter, the Inca's uncle would have been as great a man as the Inca. And—well, everybody knows what the Inca's uncle was.

ERMYNTRUDE. My experience is that the relatives of men of genius are always the greatest duffers imaginable.

THE INCA. Precisely. That is what proves that the Inca is a man of genius. His relatives are duffers.

ERMYNTRUDE. But bless my soul, Captain, if all the Inca's generals are incapables, and all his relatives duffers, Perusalem will be beaten in the war; and then it will become a republic, like France after 1871, and the Inca will be sent to St Helena.

THE INCA [*triumphantly*] That is just what the Inca is playing for, madam. It is why he consented to the war.

ERMYNTRUDE. What!

THE INCA. Aha! The fools talk of crushing the Inca; but they little know their man. Tell me this. Why did St Helena extinguish Napoleon?

ERMYNTRUDE. I give it up.

THE INCA. Because, madam, with certain rather remarkable qualities, which I should be the last to deny, Napoleon lacked versatility. After all, any fool can be a soldier: we know that only too well in Perusalem, where every fool is a soldier. But the Inca has a thousand other resources. He is an architect.

Well, St Helena presents an unlimited field to the architect. He is a painter: need I remind you that St Helena is still without a National Gallery? He is a composer: Napoleon left no symphonies in St Helena. Send the Inca to St Helena, madam, and the world will crowd thither to see his works as they crowd now to Athens to see the Acropolis, to Madrid to see the pictures of Velasquez, to Bayreuth to see the music dramas of that egotistical old rebel Richard Wagner, who ought to have been shot before he was forty, as indeed he very nearly was. Take this from me: hereditary monarchs are played out: the age for men of genius has come: the career is open to the talents: before ten years have elapsed every civilized country from the Carpathians to the Rocky Mountains will be a Republic.

ERMYNTRUDE. Then goodbye to the Inca.

THE INCA. On the contrary, madam, the Inca will then have his first real chance. He will be unanimously invited by those Republics to return from his exile and act as Superpresident of all the republics.

ERMYNTRUDE. But wont that be a come down for him? Think of it! after being Inca, to be a mere President!

THE INCA. Well, why not! An Inca can do nothing. He is tied hand and foot. A constitutional monarch is openly called an india-rubber stamp. An emperor is a puppet. The Inca is not allowed to make a speech: he is compelled to take up a screed of flatulent twaddle written by some noodle of a minister and read it aloud. But look at the American President! He is the Allerhöchst, if you like. No, madam, believe me, there is nothing like Democracy, American Democracy. Give the people voting papers: good long voting papers, American fashion; and while the people are reading the voting papers the Government does what it likes.

ERMYNTRUDE. What! You too worship before the statue of Liberty, like the Americans?

THE INCA. Not at all, madam. The Americans do not worship the statue of Liberty. They have erected it in the proper place for a statue of Liberty: on its tomb. [*He turns down his moustaches*].

ERMYNTRUDE [*laughing*] Oh! Youd better not let them hear you say that, Captain.

THE INCA. Quite safe, madam: they would take it as a joke. [*He rises*]. And now, prepare yourself for a surprise. [*She rises*]. A shock. Brace yourself. Steel yourself. And do not be afraid.

ERMYNTRUDE. Whatever on earth can you be going to tell me, Captain?

THE INCA. Madam: I am no captain. I—

ERMYNTRUDE. You are the Inca in disguise.

THE INCA. Good heavens! how do you know that? Who has betrayed me?

ERMYNTRUDE. How could I help divining it, sir? Who is there in the world like you? Your magnetism—

THE INCA. True: I had forgotten my magnetism. But you know now that beneath the trappings of Imperial Majesty there is a Man: simple, frank, modest, unaffected, colloquial: a sincere friend, a natural human being, a genial comrade, one eminently calculated to make a woman happy. You, on the other hand, are the most charming woman I have ever met. Your conversation is wonderful. I have sat here almost in silence listening to your shrewd and penetrating account of my character, my motives, if I may say so, my talents. Never has such justice been done me : never have I experienced such perfect sympathy. Will you— I hardly know how to put this—will you be mine?

ERMYNTRUDE. Oh, sir, you are married.

THE INCA. I am prepared to embrace the Mahometan faith, which allows a man four wives, if you will consent. It will please the Turks. But I had rather you did not mention it to the Inca-ess, if you dont mind.

ERMYNTRUDE. This is really charming of you. But the time has come for me to make a revelation. It is your Imperial Majesty's turn now to brace yourself. To steel yourself. I am not the princess. I am—

THE INCA. The daughter of my old friend Archdeacon Daffodil Donkin, whose sermons are read to me every evening after dinner. I never forget a face.

ERMYNTRUDE. You knew all along!

THE INCA [*bitterly, throwing himself into his chair*] And you supposed that I, who have been condemned to the society of princesses all my wretched life, believed for a moment that any princess that ever walked could have your intelligence!

ERMYNTRUDE. How clever of you, Sir! But you cannot afford to marry me.

THE INCA [*springing up*] Why not?

ERMYNTRUDE. You are too poor. You have

to eat war bread. Kings nowadays belong to the poorer classes. The King of England does not even allow himself wine at dinner.

THE INCA [*delighted*] Haw! Ha ha! Haw! haw! [*He is convulsed with laughter, and finally has to relieve his feelings by waltzing half round the room*].

ERMYNTRUDE. You may laugh, Sir; but I really could not live in that style. I am the widow of a millionaire, ruined by your little war.

THE INCA. A millionaire! What are millionaires now, with the world crumbling?

ERMYNTRUDE. Excuse me: mine was a hyphenated millionaire.

THE INCA. A highfalutin millionaire, you mean. [*Chuckling*] Haw! ha ha! really very nearly a pun, that. [*He sits down in her chair*].

ERMYNTRUDE [*revolted, sinking into his chair*] I think it quite the worst pun I ever heard.

THE INCA. The best puns have all been made years ago : nothing remained but to achieve the worst. However, madam— [*He rises majestically; and she is about to rise also*]. No: I prefer a seated audience. [*She falls back into her seat at the imperious wave of his hand*]. So [*he clicks his heels*]. Madam: I recognize my presumption in having sought the honor of your hand. As you say, I cannot afford it. Victorious as I am, I am hopelessly bankrupt; and the worst of it is, I am intelligent enough to know it. And I shall be beaten in consequence, because my most implacable enemy, though only a few months further away from bankruptcy than myself, has not a ray of intelligence, and will go on fighting until civilization is destroyed, unless I, out of sheer pity for the world, condescend to capitulate.

ERMYNTRUDE. The sooner the better, Sir. Many fine young men are dying while you wait.

THE INCA [*flinching painfully*] Why? Why do they do it?

ERMYNTRUDE. Because you make them.

THE INCA. Stuff! How can I? I am only one man; and they are millions. Do you suppose they would really kill each other if they didnt want to, merely for the sake of my beautiful eyes? Do not be deceived by newspaper claptrap, madam. I was swept away by a passion not my own, which imposed itself on me. By myself I am nothing. I dare not walk down the principal street of my own capital in a coat two years old, though the sweeper of that street can wear one ten years old. You talk of death as an unpopular thing. You are wrong: for years I gave them art, literature, science, prosperity, that they might live more abundantly; and they hated me, ridiculed me, caricatured me. Now that I give them death in its frightfullest forms, they are devoted to me. If you doubt me, ask those who for years have begged our taxpayers in vain for a few paltry thousands to spend on Life: on the bodies and minds of the nation's children, on the beauty and healthfulness of its cities, on the honor and comfort of its worn-out workers. They refused; and because they refused, death is let loose on them. They grudged a few hundreds a year for their salvation: they now pay millions a day for their own destruction and damnation. And this they call my doing! Let them say it, if they dare, before the judgment - seat at which they and I shall answer at last for what we have left undone no less than for what we have done. [*Pulling himself together suddenly*] Madam: I have the honor to be your most obedient. [*He clicks his heels and bows*].

ERMYNTRUDE. Sir! [*she curtsies*].

THE INCA [*turning at the door*] Oh, by the way, there is a princess, isnt there, somewhere on the premises?

ERMYNTRUDE. There is. Shall I fetch her?

THE INCA [*dubious*] Pretty awful, I suppose, eh?

ERMYNTRUDE. About the usual thing.

THE INCA [*sighing*] Ah well! What can one expect? I dont think I need trouble her personally. Will you explain to her about the boys?

ERMYNTRUDE. I am afraid the explanation will fall rather flat without your magnetism.

THE INCA [*returning to her and speaking very humanly*] You are making fun of me. Why does everybody make fun of me? Is it fair?

ERMYNTRUDE [*seriously*] Yes: it is fair. What other defence have we poor common people against your shining armor, your mailed fist, your pomp and parade, your terrible power over us? Are these things fair?

THE INCA. Ah, well, perhaps, perhaps. [*He looks at his watch*]. By the way, there is time for a drive round the town and a cup of tea at the Zoo. Quite a bearable band there: it does not play any patriotic airs. I am sorry you will not listen to any more permanent arrangement; but if you would care to come—

ERMYNTRUDE [*eagerly*] Ratherrrrrr. I shall be delighted.

THE INCA [*cautiously*] In the strictest honor, you understand.

ERMYNTRUDE. Dont be afraid. I promise to refuse any incorrect proposals.

THE INCA [*enchanted*] Oh! Charming woman: how well you understand men!

He offers her his arm: they go out together.

THE END

XXVIII

AUGUSTUS DOES HIS BIT

A TRUE-TO-LIFE FARCE

The Mayor's parlor in the Town Hall of Little Pifflington. Lord Augustus Highcastle, a distinguished member of the governing class, in the uniform of a colonel, and very well preserved at 45, is comfortably seated at a writing-table with his heels on it, reading The Morning Post. The door faces him, a little to his left, at the other side of the room. The window is behind him. In the fireplace, a gas stove. On the table a bell button and a telephone. Portraits of past Mayors, in robes and gold chains, adorn the walls. An elderly clerk with a short white beard and whiskers, and a very red nose, shuffles in.

AUGUSTUS [*hastily putting aside his paper and replacing his feet on the floor*] Hullo! Who are you?

THE CLERK. The staff [*a slight impediment in his speech adds to the impression of incompetence produced by his age and appearance*].

AUGUSTUS. You the staff! What do you mean, man?

THE CLERK. What I say. There aint anybody else.

AUGUSTUS. Tush! Where are the others?

THE CLERK. At the front.

AUGUSTUS. Quite right. Most proper. Why arnt you at the front?

THE CLERK. Over age. Fiftyseven.

AUGUSTUS. But you can still do your bit. Many an older man is in the G.R.'s, or volunteering for home defence.

THE CLERK. I have volunteered.

AUGUSTUS. Then why are you not in uniform?

THE CLERK. They said they wouldnt have me if I was given away with a pound of tea. Told me to go home and not be an old silly. [*A sense of unbearable wrong, til now only smouldering in him, bursts into flame*]. Young Bill Knight, that I took with me, got two and sevenpence. I got nothing. Is it justice? This country is going to the dogs, if you ask me.

AUGUSTUS [*rising indignantly*] I do not ask you, sir; and I will not allow you to say such things in my presence. Our statesmen are the greatest known to history. Our generals are invincible. Our army is the admiration of the world. [*Furiously*] How dare you tell me that the country is going to the dogs!

THE CLERK. Why did they give young Bill Knight two and sevenpence, and not give me even my tram fare? Do you call that being great statesmen? As good as robbing me, I call it.

AUGUSTUS. Thats enough. Leave the room. [*He sits down and takes up his pen, settling himself to work. The clerk shuffles to the door. Augustus adds, with cold politeness*] Send me the Secretary.

THE CLERK. I'm the Secretary. I cant leave the room and send myself to you at the same time, can I?

AUGUSTUS. Dont be insolent. Where is the gentleman I have been corresponding with: Mr Horatio Floyd Beamish?

THE CLERK [*returning and bowing*] Here. Me.

AUGUSTUS. You! Ridiculous. What right have you to call yourself by a pretentious name of that sort?

THE CLERK. You may drop the Horatio Floyd. Beamish is good enough for me.

AUGUSTUS. Is there nobody else to take my instructions?

THE CLERK. It's me or nobody. And for two pins I'd chuck it. Dont you drive me too far. Old uns like me is up in the world now.

AUGUSTUS. If we were not at war, I should discharge you on the spot for disrespectful behavior. But England is in danger; and I cannot think of my personal dignity at such a moment. [*Shouting at him*] Dont you think of yours, either, worm that you are; or I'll

have you arrested under the Defence of the Realm Act, double quick.

THE CLERK. What do I care about the realm? They done me out of two and seven—

AUGUSTUS. Oh, damn your two and seven! Did you receive my letters?

THE CLERK. Yes.

AUGUSTUS. I addressed a meeting here last night—went straight to the platform from the train. I wrote to you that I should expect you to be present and report yourself. Why did you not do so?

THE CLERK. The police wouldnt let me on the platform.

AUGUSTUS. Did you tell them who you were?

THE CLERK. They knew who I was. Thats why they wouldnt let me up.

AUGUSTUS. This is too silly for anything. This town wants waking up. I made the best recruiting speech I ever made in my life; and not a man joined.

THE CLERK. What did you expect? You told them our gallant fellows is falling at the rate of a thousand a day in the big push. Dying for Little Pifflington, you says. Come and take their places, you says. That aint the way to recruit.

AUGUSTUS. But I expressly told them their widows would have pensions.

THE CLERK. I heard you. Would have been all right if it had been the widows you wanted to get round.

AUGUSTUS [*rising angrily*] This town is inhabited by dastards. I say it with a full sense of responsibility, d a s t a r d s! They call themselves Englishmen; and they are afraid to fight.

THE CLERK. Afraid to fight! You should see them on a Saturday night.

AUGUSTUS. Yes: they fight one another; but they wont fight the Germans.

THE CLERK. They got grudges again one another: how can they have grudges again the Huns that they never saw? Theyve no imagination: thats what it is. Bring the Huns here; and theyll quarrel with them fast enough.

AUGUSTUS [*returning to his seat with a grunt of disgust*] Mf! Theyll have them here if theyre not careful. [*Seated*] Have you carried out my orders about the war saving?

THE CLERK. Yes.

AUGUSTUS. The allowance of petrol has been reduced by three quarters?

THE CLERK. It has.

AUGUSTUS. And you have told the motor-car people to come here and arrange to start munition work now that their motor business is stopped?

THE CLERK. It aint stopped. Theyre busier than ever.

AUGUSTUS. Busy at what?

THE CLERK. Making small cars.

AUGUSTUS. New cars!

THE CLERK. The old cars only do twelve miles to the gallon. Everybody has to have a car that will do thirtyfive now.

AUGUSTUS. Cant they take the train?

THE CLERK. There aint no trains now. Theyve tore up the rails and sent them to the front.

AUGUSTUS. Psha!

THE CLERK. Well, we have to get about somehow.

AUGUSTUS. This is perfectly monstrous. Not in the least what I intended.

THE CLERK. Hell—

AUGUSTUS. Sir!

THE CLERK [explaining] Hell, they says, is paved with good intentions.

AUGUSTUS [springing to his feet] Do you mean to insinuate that hell is paved with m y good intentions—with the good intentions of His Majesty's Government?

THE CLERK. I dont mean to insinuate anything until the Defence of the Realm Act is repealed. It aint safe.

AUGUSTUS. They told me that this town had set an example to all England in the matter of economy. I came down here to promise the Mayor a knighthood for his exertions.

THE CLERK. The Mayor! Where do I come in?

AUGUSTUS. You dont come in. You go out. This is a fool of a place. I'm greatly disappointed. Deeply disappointed. [Flinging himself back into his chair] Disgusted.

THE CLERK. What more can we do? Weve shut up everything. The picture gallery is shut. The museum is shut. The theatres and picture shows is shut: I havnt seen a movy picture for six months.

AUGUSTUS. Man, man: do you want to see picture shows when the Hun is at the gate?

THE CLERK [mournfully] I dont now, though it drove me melancholy mad at first. I was on the point of taking a pennorth of rat poison—

AUGUSTUS. Why didnt you?

THE CLERK. Because a friend advised me to take to drink instead. That saved my life, though it makes me very poor company in the mornings, as [hiccuping] perhaps youve noticed.

AUGUSTUS. Well, upon my soul! You are not ashamed to stand there and confess yourself a disgusting drunkard.

THE CLERK. Well, what of it? We're at war now; and everything's changed. Besides, I should lose my job here if I stood drinking at the bar. I'm a respectable man and must buy my drink and take it home with me. And they wont serve me with less than a quart. If youd told me before the war that I could get through a quart of whisky in a day, I shouldnt have believed you. Thats the good of war: it brings out powers in a man that he never suspected himself capable of. You said so yourself in your speech last night.

AUGUSTUS. I did not know that I was talking to an imbecile. You ought to be ashamed of yourself. There must be an end of this drunken slacking. I'm going to establish a new order of things here. I shall come down every morning before breakfast until things are properly in train. Have a cup of coffee and two rolls for me here every morning at half past ten.

THE CLERK. You cant have no rolls. The only baker that baked rolls was a Hun; and he's been interned.

AUGUSTUS. Quite right, too. And was there no Englishman to take his place?

THE CLERK. There was. But he was caught spying; and they took him up to London and shot him.

AUGUSTUS. Shot an Englishman!

THE CLERK. Well, it stands to reason if the Germans wanted a spy they wouldnt employ a German that everybody would suspect, dont it?

AUGUSTUS [rising again] Do you mean to say, you scoundrel, that an Englishman is capable of selling his country to the enemy for gold?

THE CLERK. Not as a general thing I wouldnt say it; but theres men here would sell their own mothers for two coppers if they got the chance.

AUGUSTUS. Beamish: it's an ill bird that fouls its own nest.

THE CLERK. It wasnt me that let Little

2 E 2

Pifflington get foul. *I* dont belong to the governing classes. I only tell you why you cant have no rolls.

AUGUSTUS [*intensely irritated*] Can you tell me where I can find an intelligent being to take my orders?

THE CLERK. One of the street sweepers used to teach in the school until it was shut up for the sake of economy. Will he do?

AUGUSTUS. What! You mean to tell me that when the lives of the gallant fellows in our trenches, and the fate of the British Empire, depend on our keeping up the supply of shells, you are wasting money on sweeping the streets?

THE CLERK. We have to. We dropped it for a while; but the infant death rate went up something frightful.

AUGUSTUS. What matters the death rate of Little Pifflington in a moment like this? Think of our gallant soldiers, not of your squalling infants.

THE CLERK. If you want soldiers you must have children. You cant buy em in boxes, like toy soldiers.

AUGUSTUS. Beamish: the long and the short of it is, you are no patriot. Go downstairs to your office; and have that gas stove taken away and replaced by an ordinary grate. The Board of Trade has urged on me the necessity for economizing gas.

THE CLERK. Our orders from the Minister of Munitions is to use gas instead of coal, because it saves material. Which is it to be?

AUGUSTUS [*bawling furiously at him*] Both! Dont criticize your orders: obey them. Yours not to reason why: yours but to do and die. Thats war. [*Cooling down*] Have you anything else to say?

THE CLERK. Yes: I want a rise.

AUGUSTUS [*reeling against the table in his horror*] A rise! Horatio Floyd Beamish: do you know that we are at war?

THE CLERK [*feebly ironical*] I h a v e noticed something about it in the papers. Heard y o u mention it once or twice, now I come to think of it.

AUGUSTUS. Our gallant fellows are dying in the trenches; and you want a rise!

THE CLERK. What are they dying for? To keep me alive, aint it? Well, whats the good of that if I'm dead of hunger by the time they come back?

AUGUSTUS. Everybody else is making

sacrifices without a thought of self; and you—

THE CLERK. Not half, they aint. Wheres the baker's sacrifice? Wheres the coal merchant's? Wheres the butcher's? Charging me double: thats how they sacrifice themselves. Well, I want to sacrifice myself that way too. Just double next Saturday: double and not a penny less; or no secretary for you. [*He stiffens himself shakily, and makes resolutely for the door*].

AUGUSTUS [*looking after him contemptuously*] Go: miserable pro-German.

THE CLERK [*rushing back and facing him*] Who are you calling a pro-German?

AUGUSTUS. Another word, and I charge you under the Act with discouraging me. Go.

The clerk blenches and goes out, cowed.

The telephone rings.

AUGUSTUS [*taking up the telephone receiver*] Hallo . . . Yes: who are you? . . . oh, Blueloo, is it? . . . Yes: theres nobody in the room: fire away . . . What? . . . A spy! . . . A woman! . . . Yes: I brought it down with me. Do you suppose I'm such a fool as to let it out of my hands? Why, it gives a list of all our anti-aircraft emplacements from Ramsgate to Skegness. The Germans would give a million for it—what? . . . But how could she possibly know about it? I havnt mentioned it to a soul, except, of course, dear Lucy. . . . Oh, Toto and Lady Popham and that lot: they dont count: theyre all right. I mean that I havnt mentioned it to any Germans. . . . Pooh! Dont you be nervous, old chap. I know you think me a fool; but I'm not such a fool as all that. If she tries to get it out of me I'll have her in the Tower before you ring up again. [*The clerk returns*]. Sh-sh! Somebody's just come in: ring off. Goodbye. [*He hangs up the receiver*].

THE CLERK. Are you engaged? [*His manner is strangely softened*].

AUGUSTUS. What business is that of yours? However, if you will take the trouble to read the society papers for this week, you will see that I am engaged to the Honorable Lucy Popham, youngest daughter of—

THE CLERK. That aint what I mean. Can you see a female?

AUGUSTUS. Of course I can see a female as easily as a male. Do you suppose I'm blind?

THE CLERK. You dont seem to follow me, somehow. Theres a female downstairs: what you might call a lady. She wants to know can you see her if I let her up.

AUGUSTUS. Oh, you mean am I disengaged. Tell the lady I have just received news of the greatest importance which will occupy my entire attention for the rest of the day, and that she must write for an appointment.

THE CLERK. I'll ask her to explain her business to me. *I* aint above talking to a handsome young female when I get the chance [*going*].

AUGUSTUS. Stop. Does she seem to be a person of consequence?

THE CLERK. A regular marchioness, if you ask me.

AUGUSTUS. Hm! Beautiful, did you say?

THE CLERK. A human chrysanthemum, sir, believe me.

AUGUSTUS. It will be extremely inconvenient for me to see her; but the country is in danger; and we must not consider our own comfort. Think how our gallant fellows are suffering in the trenches! Shew her up. [*The clerk makes for the door, whistling the latest popular love ballad*]. Stop whistling instantly, sir. This is not a casino.

THE CLERK. Aint it? You just wait til you see her. [*He goes out*].

Augustus produces a mirror, a comb, and a pot of moustache pomade from the drawer of the writing-table, and sits down before the mirror to put some touches to his toilet.

The clerk returns, devotedly ushering a very attractive lady, brilliantly dressed. She has a dainty wallet hanging from her wrist. Augustus hastily covers up his toilet apparatus with The Morning Post, and rises in an attitude of pompous condescension.

THE CLERK [*to Augustus*] Here she is. [*To the lady*] May I offer you a chair, lady? [*He places a chair at the writing-table opposite Augustus, and steals out on tiptoe*].

AUGUSTUS. Be seated, madam.

THE LADY [*sitting down*] Are you Lord Augustus Highcastle?

AUGUSTUS [*sitting also*] Madam: I am.

THE LADY [*with awe*] The great Lord Augustus?

AUGUSTUS. I should not dream of describing myself so, madam; but no doubt I have impressed my countrymen—and [*bowing gallantly*] may I say my countrywomen—as having some exceptional claims to their consideration.

THE LADY [*emotionally*] What a beautiful voice you have!

AUGUSTUS. What you hear, madam, is the voice of my country, which now takes a sweet and noble tone even in the harsh mouth of high officialism.

THE LADY. Please go on. You express yourself so wonderfully!

AUGUSTUS. It would be strange indeed, if, after sitting on thirty-seven Royal Commissions, mostly as chairman, I had not mastered the art of public expression. Even the Radical papers have paid me the high compliment of declaring that I am never more impressive than when I have nothing to say.

THE LADY. I never read the Radical papers. All I can tell you is that what we women admire in you is not the politician, but the man of action, the heroic warrior, the *beau sabreur*.

AUGUSTUS [*gloomily*] Madam, I beg! Please! My military exploits are not a pleasant subject, unhappily.

THE LADY. Oh, I know, I know. How shamefully you have been treated! What ingratitude! But the country is with you. The women are with you. Oh, do you think all our hearts did not throb and all our nerves thrill when we heard how, when you were ordered to occupy that terrible quarry in Hulluch, and you swept into it at the head of your men like a sea-god riding on a tidal wave, you suddenly sprang over the top shouting "To Berlin! Forward!"; dashed at the German army single-handed; and were cut off and made prisoner by the Huns.

AUGUSTUS. Yes, madam; and what was my reward? They said I had disobeyed orders, and sent me home. Have they forgotten Nelson in the Baltic? Has any British battle ever been won except by a bold individual initiative? I say nothing of professional jealousy: it exists in the army as elsewhere; but it is a bitter thought to me that the recognition denied me by my own country— or rather by the Radical cabal in the Cabinet which pursues my family with rancorous class hatred—that this recognition, I say, came to me at the hands of an enemy—of a rank Prussian.

THE LADY. You dont say so!

AUGUSTUS. How else should I be here instead of starving to death in Ruhleben? Yes, madam: the Colonel of the Pomeranian regiment which captured me, after learning what I had done, and conversing for an hour with me on European politics and military strategy, declared that nothing would induce him to deprive my country of my services, and set me free. I offered, of course, to procure the release in exchange of a German officer of equal quality; but he would not hear of it. He was kind enough to say he could not believe that a German officer answering to that description existed. [*With emotion*] I had my first taste of the ingratitude of my own country as I made my way back to our lines. A shot from our front trench struck me in the head. I still carry the flattened projectile as a trophy. [*He throws it on the table; the noise it makes testifies to its weight*]. Had it penetrated to the brain I might never have sat on another Royal Commission. Fortunately we have strong heads, we Highcastles. Nothing has ever penetrated to our brains.

THE LADY. How thrilling! How simple! And how tragic! But you will forgive England? Remember: England! Forgive her.

AUGUSTUS [*with gloomy magnanimity*] It will make no difference whatever to my services to my country. Though she slay me, yet will I, if not exactly trust in her, at least take my part in her government. I am ever at my country's call. Whether it be the embassy in a leading European capital, a governor-generalship in the tropics, or my humble mission here to make Little Pifflington do its bit, I am always ready for the sacrifice. Whilst England remains England, wherever there is a public job to be done you will find a Highcastle sticking to it. And now, madam, enough of my tragic personal history. You have called on business. What can I do for you?

THE LADY. You have relatives at the Foreign Office, have you not?

AUGUSTUS [*haughtily*] Madam: the Foreign Office is staffed by my relatives exclusively.

THE LADY. Has the Foreign Office warned you that you are being pursued by a female spy who is determined to obtain possession of a certain list of gun emplacements—

AUGUSTUS [*interrupting her somewhat loftily*] All that is perfectly well known to this department, madam.

THE LADY [*surprised and rather indignant*] Is it? Who told you? Was it one of your German brothers-in-law?

AUGUSTUS [*injured, remonstrating*] I have only three German brothers-in-law, madam. Really, from your tone, one would suppose that I had several. Pardon my sensitiveness

on that subject; but reports are continually being circulated that I have been shot as a traitor in the courtyard of the Ritz Hotel simply because I have German brothers-in-law. [*With feeling*] If you had a German brother-in-law, madam, you would know that nothing else in the world produces so strong an anti-German feeling. Life affords no keener pleasure than finding a brother-in-law's name in the German casualty list.

THE LADY. Nobody knows that better than I. Wait until you hear what I have come to tell you: you will understand me as no one else could. Listen. This spy, this woman—

AUGUSTUS [*all attention*] Yes?

THE LADY. She is a German. A Hun.

AUGUSTUS. Yes, yes. She would be. Continue.

THE LADY. She is my sister-in-law.

AUGUSTUS [*deferentially*] I see you are well connected, madam, Proceed.

THE LADY. Need I add that she is my bitterest enemy?

AUGUSTUS. May I— [*He proffers his hand. They shake, fervently. From this moment onward Augustus becomes more and more confidential, gallant, and charming*].

THE LADY. Quite so. Well, she is an intimate friend of your brother at the War Office, Hungerford Highcastle: Blueloo as you call him: I dont know why.

AUGUSTUS [*explaining*] He was originally called The Singing Oyster, because he sang drawing-room ballads with such an extraordinary absence of expression. He was then called the Blue Point for a season or two. Finally he became Blueloo.

THE LADY. Oh, indeed: I didnt know. Well, Blueloo is simply infatuated with my sister-in-law; and he has rashly let out to her that this list is in your possession. He forgot himself because he was in a towering rage at its being entrusted to you: his language was terrible. He ordered all the guns to be shifted at once.

AUGUSTUS. What on earth did he do that for?

THE LADY. I cant imagine. But this I know. She made a bet with him that she would come down here and obtain possession of that list and get clean away into the street with it. He took the bet on condition that she brought it straight back to him at the War Office.

AUGUSTUS. Good heavens! And you mean

to tell me that Blueloo was such a dolt as to believe that she could succeed? Does he take me for a fool?

THE LADY. Oh, impossible! He is jealous of your intellect. The bet is an insult to you: dont you feel that? After what you have done for our country—

AUGUSTUS. Oh, never mind that. It is the idiocy of the thing I look at. He'll lose his bet; and serve him right!

THE LADY. You feel sure you will be able to resist the siren? I warn you she is very fascinating.

AUGUSTUS. You need have no fear, madam. I hope she will come and try it on. Fascination is a game that two can play at. For centuries the younger sons of the Highcastles have had nothing to do but fascinate attractive females when they were not sitting on Royal Commissions or on duty at Knightsbridge barracks. By Gad, madam, if the siren comes here she will meet her match.

THE LADY. I feel that. But if she fails to seduce you—

AUGUSTUS [blushing] Madam!

THE LADY [continuing] —from your allegiance—

AUGUSTUS. Oh, that!

THE LADY. —she will resort to fraud, to force, to anything. She will burgle your office: she will have you attacked and garotted at night in the street.

AUGUSTUS. Pooh! I'm not afraid.

THE LADY. Oh, your courage will only tempt you into danger. She may get the list after all. It is true that the guns are moved. But she would win her bet.

AUGUSTUS [cautiously] You did not say that the guns were moved. You said that Blueloo had ordered them to be moved.

THE LADY. Well, that is the same thing, isnt it?

AUGUSTUS. Not quite—at the War Office. No doubt those guns will be moved: possibly even before the end of the war.

THE LADY. Then you think they are there still! But if the German War Office gets the list—and she will copy it before she gives it back to Blueloo, you may depend on it—all is lost.

AUGUSTUS [lazily] Well, I should not go as far as that. [Lowering his voice] Will you swear to me not to repeat what I am going to say to you: for if the British public knew that I had said it, I should be at once hounded down as a pro-German.

THE LADY. I will be silent as the grave. I swear it.

AUGUSTUS [again taking it easily] Well, our people have for some reason made up their minds that the German War Office is everything that our War Office is not—that it carries promptitude, efficiency, and organization to a pitch of completeness and perfection that must be, in my opinion, destructive to the happiness of the staff. My own view—which you are pledged, remember, not to betray—is that the German War Office is no better than any other War Office. I found that opinion on my observation of the characters of my brothers-in-law: one of whom, by the way, is on the German general staff. I am not at all sure that this list of gun emplacements would receive the smallest attention. You see, there are always so many more important things to be attended to. Family matters, and so on, you understand.

THE LADY. Still, if a question were asked in the House of Commons.

AUGUSTUS. The great advantage of being at war, madam, is that nobody takes the slightest notice of the House of Commons. No doubt it is sometimes necessary for a Minister to soothe the more seditious members of that assembly by giving a pledge or two; but the War Office takes no notice of such things.

THE LADY [staring at him] Then you think this list of gun emplacements doesnt matter!!

AUGUSTUS. By no means, madam. It matters very much indeed. If this spy were to obtain possession of the list, Blueloo would tell the story at every dinner table in London; and—

THE LADY. And you might lose your post. Of course.

AUGUSTUS [amazed and indignant] I lose my post! What are you dreaming about, madam? How could I possibly be spared? There are hardly Highcastles enough at present to fill half the posts created by this war. No: Blueloo would not go that far. He is at least a gentleman. But I should be chaffed; and, frankly, I dont like being chaffed.

THE LADY. Of course not. Who does? It would never do. Oh, never, never.

AUGUSTUS. I'm glad you see it in that light. And now, as a measure of security, I shall put that list in my pocket. [He begins searching vainly from drawer to drawer in the writing-

table]. Where on earth—? What the dickens did I—? Thats very odd: I— Where the deuce—? I thought I had put it in the— Oh. here it is! No: this is Lucy's last letter.

THE LADY [*clegiacally*] Lucy's Last Letter! What a title for a picture play!

AUGUSTUS [*delighted*] Yes: it is, isn't it? Lucy appeals to the imagination like no other woman. By the way [*handing over the letter*] I wonder could you read it for me? Lucy is a darling girl; but I really cant read her writing. In London I get the office typist to decipher it and make me a typed copy; but here there is nobody.

THE LADY [*puzzling over it*] It is really almost illegible. I think the beginning is meant for "Dearest Gus."

AUGUSTUS [*eagerly*] Yes: that is what she usually calls me. Please go on.

THE LADY [*trying to decipher it*] "What a"— 'what a"—oh yes: "what a forgetful old"— something—"you are!" I cant make out the word.

AUGUSTUS [*greatly interested*] Is it blighter? That is a favorite expression of hers.

THE LADY. I think so. At all events it begins with a B. [*Reading*] "What a forgetful old—" [*She is interrupted by a knock at the door*].

AUGUSTUS [*impatiently*] Come in. [*The clerk enters, clean shaven and in khaki, with an official paper and an envelope in his hand*]. What is this ridiculous mummery, sir?

THE CLERK [*coming to the table and exhibiting his uniform to both*] Theyve passed me. The recruiting officer come for me. Ive had my two and seven.

AUGUSTUS [*rising wrathfully*] I shall not permit it. What do they mean by taking my office staff? Good God! they will be taking our hunt servants next. [*Confronting the clerk*] What did the man mean? What did he say?

THE CLERK. He said that now you was on the job we'd want another million men, and he was going to take the old-age pensioners or anyone he could get.

AUGUSTUS. And did you dare to knock at my door and interrupt my business with this lady to repeat this man's ineptitudes?

THE CLERK. No. I come because the waiter from the hotel brought this paper. You left it on the coffee-room breakfast-table this morning.

THE LADY [*intercepting it*] It is the list. Good heavens!

THE CLERK [*proffering the envelope*] He says

he thinks this is the envelope belonging to it.

THE LADY [*snatching the envelope also*] Yes! Addressed to you. Lord Augustus! [*Augustus comes back to the table to look at it*] Oh, how imprudent! Everybody would guess its importance with your name on it. Fortunately I have some letters of my own here [*opening her wallet*]. Why not hide it in one of my envelopes? then no one will dream that the enclosure is of any political value. [*Taking out a letter, she crosses the room towards the window, whispering to Augustus as she passes him*] Get rid of that man.

AUGUSTUS [*haughtily approaching the clerk, who humorously makes a paralytic attempt to stand at attention*] Have you any further business here, pray?

THE CLERK. Am I to give the waiter anything; or will you do it yourself?

AUGUSTUS. Which waiter is it? The English one?

THE CLERK. No: the one that calls hisself a Swiss. Shouldnt wonder if he'd made a copy of that paper.

AUGUSTUS. Keep your impertinent surmises to yourself, sir. Remember that you are in the army now; and let me have no more of your civilian insubordination. Attention! Left turn! Quick march!

THE CLERK [*stolidly*] I dunno what you mean.

AUGUSTUS. Go to the guard-room and report yourself for disobeying orders. Now do you know what I mean?

THE CLERK. Now look here. I aint going to argue with you—

AUGUSTUS. Nor I with you. Out with you.

He seizes the clerk; and rushes him through the door. The moment the lady is left alone, she snatches a sheet of official paper from the stationery rack; folds it so that it resembles the list; compares the two to see that they look exactly alike; whips the list into her wallet; and substitutes the facsimile for it. Then she listens for the return of Augustus. A crash is heard, as of the clerk falling downstairs.

Augustus returns and is about to close the door when the voice of the clerk is heard from below:

THE CLERK. I'll have the law of you for this, I will.

AUGUSTUS [*shouting down to him*] Theres no more law for you, you scoundrel. Youre a soldier now. [*He shuts the door and comes to the lady*]. Thank heaven, the war has given us the upper hand of these fellows at last. Excuse my violence; but discipline is absolutely necessary in dealing with the lower middle classes.

THE LADY. Serve the insolent creature right! Look! I have found you a beautiful envelope for the list, an unmistakeable lady's envelope. [*She puts the sham list into her envelope and hands it to him*].

AUGUSTUS. Excellent. Really very clever of you. [*Slyly*] Come: would you like to have a peep at the list [*beginning to take the blank paper from the envelope*]?

THE LADY [*on the brink of detection*] No no. Oh, please, no.

AUGUSTUS. Why? It wont bite you [*drawing it out further*].

THE LADY [*snatching at his hand*] Stop. Remember: if there should be an inquiry, you must be able to swear that you never shewed that list to a mortal soul.

AUGUSTUS. Oh, that is a mere form. If you are really curious—

THE LADY. I am not. I couldnt bear to look at it. One of my dearest friends was blown to pieces by an aircraft gun; and since then I have never been able to think of one without horror.

AUGUSTUS. You mean it was a real gun, and actually went off. How sad! how sad! [*He pushes the sham list back into the envelope, and pockets it*].

THE LADY. Ah! [*great sigh of relief*]. And now, Lord Augustus, I have taken up too much of your valuable time. Goodbye.

AUGUSTUS. What! Must you go?

THE LADY. You are so busy.

AUGUSTUS. Yes: but not before lunch, you know. I never can do much before lunch. And I'm no good at all in the afternoon. From five to six is my real working time. Must you really go?

THE LADY. I must, really. I have done my business very satisfactorily. Thank you ever so much. [*She proffers her hand*].

AUGUSTUS [*shaking it affectionately as he leads her to the door, but first pressing the bell button with his left hand*] Goodbye. Goodbye. So sorry to lose you. Kind of you to come; but there was no real danger. You see, my dear little lady, all this talk about war saving, and secrecy, and keeping the blinds down at night, and so forth, is all very well; but unless it's carried out with intelligence, believe me, you may waste a pound to save a penny; you may let out all sorts of secrets to the enemy; you may guide the Zeppelins right on to your own chimneys. Thats where the ability of the governing class comes in. Shall the fellow call a taxi for you?

THE LADY. No, thanks: I prefer walking. Goodbye. Again, many, many thanks.

She goes out. Augustus returns to the writing-table smiling, and takes another look at himself in the mirror. The clerk returns with his head bandaged, carrying a poker.

THE CLERK. What did you ring for? [*Augustus hastily drops the mirror*]. Dont you come nigh me or I'll split your head with this poker, thick as it is.

AUGUSTUS. It does not seem to me an exceptionally thick poker. I rang for you to shew the lady out.

THE CLERK. She's gone. She run out like a rabbit. I ask myself, why was she in such a hurry?

THE LADY'S VOICE [*from the street*] Lord Augustus. Lord Augustus.

THE CLERK. She's calling you.

AUGUSTUS [*running to the window and throwing it up*] What is it? Wont you come up?

THE LADY. Is the clerk there?

AUGUSTUS. Yes. Do you want him?

THE LADY. Yes.

AUGUSTUS. The lady wants you at the window.

THE CLERK [*rushing to the window and putting down the poker*] Yes, maam? Here I am, maam. What is it, maam?

THE LADY. I want you to witness that I got clean away into the street. I am coming up now.

The two men stare at one another.

THE CLERK. Wants me to witness that she got clean away into the street!

AUGUSTUS. What on earth does she mean? *The lady returns.*

THE LADY. May I use your telephone?

AUGUSTUS. Certainly. Certainly. [*Taking the receiver down*] What number shall I get you?

THE LADY. The War Office, please.

AUGUSTUS. The War Office!?

THE LADY. If you will be so good.

AUGUSTUS. But— Oh, very well. [*Into the receiver*] Hallo. This is the Town Hall Recruiting Office. Give me Colonel Bogey, sharp.

A pause.

THE CLERK [*breaking the painful silence*] I dont think I'm awake. This is a dream of a movy picture, this is.

AUGUSTUS [*his ear at the receiver*] Shut up, will you? [*Into the telephone*] What? . . . [*To the lady*] Whom do you want to get on to?

THE LADY. Blueloo.

AUGUSTUS [*into the telephone*] Put me through to Lord Hungerford Highcastle. . . . I'm his brother, idiot. . . . That you, Blueloo? Lady here at Little Pifflington wants to speak to you. Hold the line. [*To the lady*] Now, madam. [*He hands her the receiver*].

THE LADY [*sitting down in Augustus's chair to speak into the telephone*] Is that Blueloo? . . . Do you recognize my voice? . . . Ive won our bet. . . .

AUGUSTUS. Your bet!

THE LADY [*into the telephone*] Yes: I have the list in my wallet. . . .

AUGUSTUS. Nothing of the kind, madam. I have it here in my pocket. [*He takes the envelope from his pocket; draws out the paper; and unfolds it*].

THE LADY [*continuing*] Yes: I got clean into the street with it. I have a witness. I could have got to London with it. Augustus wont deny it. . . .

AUGUSTUS [*contemplating the blank paper*] Theres nothing written on this. Where is the list of guns?

THE LADY [*continuing*] Oh, it was quite easy. I said I was my sister-in-law and that I was a Hun. He lapped it up like a kitten. . . .

AUGUSTUS. You dont mean to say that—

THE LADY [*continuing*] I got hold of the list for a moment and changed it for a piece of paper out of his stationery rack: it was quite easy. [*She laughs; and it is clear that Blueloo is*

laughing too].

AUGUSTUS. What!

THE CLERK [*laughing slowly and laboriously, with intense enjoyment*] Ha ha! Ha ha ha! Ha! [*Augustus rushes at him: he snatches up the poker and stands on guard*]. No you dont.

THE LADY [*still at the telephone, waving her disengaged hand behind her impatiently at them to stop making a noise*] Sh-sh-sh-sh-sh!!! [*Augustus, with a shrug, goes up the middle of the room. The lady resumes her conversation with the telephone*] What? . . . Oh yes: I'm coming up by the 12.35: why not have tea with me at Rumpelmeister's? . . . Rum-pel-meister's. You know: they call it Robinson's now. . . . Right. Ta ta. [*She hangs up the receiver, and is passing round the table on her way towards the door when she is confronted by Augustus*].

AUGUSTUS. Madam: I consider your conduct most unpatriotic. You make bets and abuse the confidence of the hardworked officials who are doing their bit for their country whilst our gallant fellows are perishing in the trenches—

THE LADY. Oh, the gallant fellows are not all in the trenches, Augustus. Some of them have come home for a few days' hard-earned leave; and I am sure you wont grudge them a little fun at your expense.

THE CLERK. Hear! hear!

AUGUSTUS [*amiably*] Ah, well! For my country's sake—!

THE END

XXIX

ANNAJANSKA, THE BOLSHEVIK EMPRESS

A REVOLUTIONARY ROMANCELET

The General's office in a military station on the east front in Beotia. An office table with a telephone, writing materials, official papers, etc., is set across the room. At the end of the table, a comfortable chair for the General. Behind the chair, a window. Facing it at the other end of the table, a plain wooden bench. At the side of the table, with its back to the door, a common chair, with a typewriter before it. Beside the door, which is opposite the end of the bench, a rack for caps and coats. There is nobody in the room.

General Strammfest enters, followed by Lieutenant Schneidekind. They hang up their cloaks and caps. Schneidekind takes a little longer than Strammfest, who comes to the table.

STRAMMFEST. Schneidekind.

SCHNEIDEKIND. Yes, sir.

STRAMMFEST. Have you sent my report yet to the government? [*He sits down*].

SCHNEIDEKIND [*coming to the table*] Not yet, sir. Which government do you wish it sent to? [*He sits down*].

STRAMMFEST. That depends. Whats the

latest? Which of them do you think is most likely to be in power tomorrow morning?

SCHNEIDEKIND. Well, the provisional government was going strong yesterday. But today they say that the prime minister has shot himself, and that the extreme left fellow has shot all the others.

STRAMMFEST. Yes: thats all very well; but these fellows always shoot themselves with blank cartridge.

SCHNEIDEKIND. Still, even the blank cartridge means backing down. I should send the report to the Maximilianists.

STRAMMFEST. Theyre no stronger than the Oppidoshavians; and in my own opinion the Moderate Red Revolutionaries are as likely to come out on top as either of them.

SCHNEIDEKIND. I can easily put a few carbon sheets in the typewriter and send a copy each to the lot.

STRAMMFEST. Waste of paper. You might as well send reports to an infant school. [*He throws his head on the table with a groan*].

SCHNEIDEKIND. Tired out, sir?

STRAMMFEST. O Schneidekind, Schneidekind, how can you bear to live?

SCHNEIDEKIND. At my age, sir, I ask myself how can I bear to die?

STRAMMFEST. You are young, young and heartless. You are excited by the revolution: you are attached to abstract things like liberty. But my family has served the Panjandrums of Beotia faithfully for seven centuries. The Panjandrums have kept our place for us at their courts, honored us, promoted us, shed their glory on us, made us what we are. When I hear you young men declaring that you are fighting for civilization, for democracy, for the overthrow of militarism, I ask myself how can a man shed his blood for empty words used by vulgar tradesmen and common laborers: mere wind and stink. [*He rises, exalted by his theme*]. A king is a splendid reality, a man raised above us like a god. You can see him; you can kiss his hand; you can be cheered by his smile and terrified by his frown. I would have died for my Panjandrum as my father died for his father. Your toiling millions were only too honored to receive the toes of our boots in the proper spot for them when they displeased their betters. And now what is left in life for me? [*He relapses into his chair discouraged*] My Panjandrum is deposed and transported to herd with convicts. The army,

his pride and glory, is paraded to hear seditious speeches from penniless rebels, with the colonel actually forced to take the chair and introduce the speaker. I myself am made Commander-in-Chief by my own solicitor: a Jew, Schneidekind! a Hebrew Jew! It seems only yesterday that these things would have been the ravings of a madman: today they are the commonplaces of the gutter press. I live now for three objects only: to defeat the enemy, to restore the Panjandrum, and to hang my solicitor.

SCHNEIDEKIND. Be careful, sir: these are dangerous views to utter nowadays. What if I were to betray you?

STRAMMFEST. What!

SCHNEIDEKIND. I wont, of course: my own father goes on just like that; but suppose I did?

STRAMMFEST [*chuckling*] I should accuse you of treason to the Revolution, my lad; and they would immediately shoot you, unless you cried and asked to see your mother before you died, when they would probably change their minds and make you a brigadier. Enough. [*He rises and expands his chest*]. I feel the better for letting myself go. To business. [*He takes up a telegram; opens it; and is thunderstruck by its contents*]. Great heaven! [*He collapses into his chair*]. This is the worst blow of all.

SCHNEIDEKIND. What has happened? Are we beaten?

STRAMMFEST. Man: do you think that a mere defeat could strike me down as this news does: I, who have been defeated thirteen times since the war began? O, my master, my master, my Panjandrum! [*he is convulsed with sobs*].

SCHNEIDEKIND. They have killed him?

STRAMMFEST. A dagger has been struck through his heart —

SCHNEIDEKIND. Good God!

STRAMMFEST. —and through mine, through mine.

SCHNEIDEKIND [*relieved*] Oh: a metaphorical dagger. I thought you meant a real one. What has happened?

STRAMMFEST. His daughter, the Grand Duchess Annajanska, she whom the Panjandrina loved beyond all her other children, has—has—[*he cannot finish*].

SCHNEIDEKIND. Committed suicide?

STRAMMFEST. No. Better if she had. Oh, far far better.

SCHNEIDEKIND [*in hushed tones*] Left the

Church?

STRAMMFEST [shocked] Certainly not. Do not blaspheme, young man.

SCHNEIDEKIND. Asked for the vote?

STRAMMFEST. I would have given it to her with both hands to save her from this.

SCHNEIDEKIND. Save her from what? Dash it, sir, out with it.

STRAMMFEST. She has joined the Revolution.

SCHNEIDEKIND. But so have you, sir. Weve all joined the Revolution. She doesnt mean it any more than we do.

STRAMMFEST. Heaven grant you may be right! But that is not the worst. She has eloped with a young officer. Eloped, Schneidekind, eloped!

SCHNEIDEKIND [not particularly impressed] Yes, sir.

STRAMMFEST. Annajanska, the beautiful, the innocent, my master's daughter! [He buries his face in his hands].

The telephone rings.

SCHNEIDEKIND [taking the receiver] Yes: G.H.Q. Yes. . . Dont bawl: I'm not a general. Who is it speaking? . . . Why didnt you say so? dont you know your duty? Next time you will lose your stripe. . . . Oh, theyve made you a colonel, have they? Well, theyve made me a field-marshal: now what have you to say? . . . Look here: what did you ring up for? I cant spend the day here listening to your cheek. . . . What! the Grand Duchess! [Strammfest starts]. Where did you catch her?

STRAMMFEST [snatching the telephone and listening for the answer] Speak louder, will you: I am a General . . . I know that, you dolt. Have you captured the officer that was with her? . . . Damnation! You shall answer for this: you let him go: he bribed you. . . . You must have seen him: the fellow is in the full dress court uniform of the Panderobajensky Hussars. I give you twelve hours to catch him or . . . whats that you say about the devil? Are you swearing at me, you . . . Thousand thunders! [To Schneidekind] The swine says that the Grand Duchess is a devil incarnate. [Into the telephone] Filthy traitor: is that the way you dare speak of the daughter of our anointed Panjandrum? I'll—

SCHNEIDEKIND. [pulling the telephone from his lips] Take care, sir.

STRAMMFEST. I wont take care: I'll have him shot. Let go that telephone.

SCHNEIDEKIND. But for her own sake, sir—

STRAMMFEST. Eh?

SCHNEIDEKIND. For her own sake they had better send her here. She will be safe in your hands.

STRAMMFEST [yielding the receiver] You are right. Be civil to him. I should choke [he sits down].

SCHNEIDEKIND [into the telephone] Hullo. Never mind all that: it's only a fellow here who has been fooling with the telephone. I had to leave the room for a moment. Wash out; and send the girl along. We'll jolly soon teach her to behave herself here. . . . Oh, youve sent her already. Then why the devil didnt you say so, you— [he hangs up the telephone angrily]. Just fancy: they started her off this morning: and all this is because the fellow likes to get on the telephone and hear himself talk now that he is a colonel. [The telephone rings again. He snatches the receiver furiously] Whats the matter now? . . . [To the General] It's our own people downstairs. [Into the receiver] Here! do you suppose Ive nothing else to do than to hang on to the telephone all day? . . . Whats that? Not men enough to hold her! What do you mean? [To the General] She is there, sir.

STRAMMFEST. Tell them to send her up. I shall have to receive her without even rising, without kissing her hand, to keep up appearances before the escort. It will break my heart.

SCHNEIDEKIND [into the receiver] Send her up. . . . Tcha! [He hangs up the receiver]. He says she is half way up already: they couldnt hold her.

The Grand Duchess bursts into the room, dragging with her two exhausted soldiers hanging on desperately to her arms. She is enveloped from head to foot by a fur-lined cloak, and wears a fur cap.

SCHNEIDEKIND [pointing to the bench] At the word Go, place your prisoner on the bench in a sitting posture; and take your seats right and left of her. Go.

The two soldiers make a supreme effort to force her to sit down. She flings them back so that they are forced to sit on the bench to save themselves from falling backwards over it, and is herself dragged into sitting between them. The second soldier, holding on tight to the Grand Duchess with one hand, produces papers with the other, and waves them towards Schneidekind, who takes them from him and passes them on to the General. He opens them and reads them with a grave expression.

SCHNEIDEKIND. Be good enough to wait,

prisoner, until the General has read the papers on your case.

THE GRAND DUCHESS [to the soldiers] Let go. [To Strammfest] Tell them to let go, or I'll upset the bench backwards and bash our three heads on the floor.

FIRST SOLDIER. No, little mother. Have mercy on the poor.

STRAMMFEST [growling over the edge of the paper he is reading] Hold your tongue.

THE GRAND DUCHESS [blazing] Me, or the soldier?

STRAMMFEST [horrified] The soldier, madam.

THE GRAND DUCHESS. Tell him to let go.

STRAMMFEST. Release the lady.

The soldiers take their hands off her. One of them wipes his fevered brow. The other sucks his wrist.

SCHNEIDEKIND [fiercely] 'ttention! The two soldiers sit up stiffly.

THE GRAND DUCHESS. Oh, let the poor man suck his wrist. It may be poisoned. I bit it.

STRAMMFEST [shocked] You bit a common soldier!

GRAND DUCHESS. Well, I offered to cauterize it with the poker in the office stove. But he was afraid. What more could I do?

SCHNEIDEKIND. Why did you bite him, prisoner?

THE GRAND DUCHESS. He would not let go.

STRAMMFEST. Did he let go when you bit him?

THE GRAND DUCHESS. No. [Patting the soldier on the back] You should give the man a cross for his devotion. I could not go on eating him; so I brought him along with me.

STRAMMFEST. Prisoner—

THE GRAND DUCHESS. Dont call me prisoner, General Strammfest. My grandmother dandled you on her knee.

STRAMMFEST [bursting into tears] O God, yes. Believe me, my heart is what it was then.

THE GRAND DUCHESS. Your brain also is what it was then. I will not be addressed by you as prisoner.

STRAMMFEST. I may not, for your own sake, call you by your rightful and most sacred titles. What am I to call you?

THE GRAND DUCHESS. The Revolution has made us comrades. Call me comrade.

STRAMMFEST. I had rather die.

THE GRAND DUCHESS. Then call me Annajanska; and I will call you Peter Piper, as grandmamma did.

STRAMMFEST [painfully agitated] Schneide-kind: you must speak to her: I cannot—[he breaks down].

SCHNEIDEKIND [officially] The Republic of Beotia has been compelled to confine the Panjandrum and his family, for their own safety, within certain bounds. You have broken those bounds.

STRAMMFEST [taking the word from him] You are—I must say it—a prisoner. What am I to do with you?

THE GRAND DUCHESS. You should have thought of that before you arrested me.

STRAMMFEST. Come, come, prisoner! do you know what will happen to you if you compel me to take a sterner tone with you?

THE GRAND DUCHESS. No. But I know what will happen to you.

STRAMMFEST. Pray what, prisoner?

THE GRAND DUCHESS. Clergyman's sore throat.

Schneidekind splutters: drops a paper; and conceals his laughter under the table.

STRAMMFEST [thunderously] Lieutenant Schneidekind.

SCHNEIDEKIND [in a stifled voice] Yes, sir. [The table vibrates visibly].

STRAMMFEST. Come out of it, you fool: youre upsetting the ink.

Schneidekind emerges, red in the face with suppressed mirth.

STRAMMFEST. Why dont you laugh? Dont you appreciate Her Imperial Highness's joke?

SCHNEIDEKIND [suddenly becoming solemn] I dont want to, sir.

STRAMMFEST. Laugh at once, sir. I order you to laugh.

SCHNEIDEKIND [with a touch of temper] I really cant, sir. [He sits down decisively].

STRAMMFEST [growling at him] Yah! [He turns impressively to the Grand Duchess] Your Imperial Highness desires me to address you as comrade?

THE GRAND DUCHESS [rising and waving a red handkerchief] Long live the Revolution, comrade!

STRAMMFEST [rising and saluting] Proletarians of all lands, unite. Lieutenant Schneidekind: you will rise and sing the Marseillaise.

SCHNEIDEKIND [rising] But I cannot, sir. I have no voice, no ear.

STRAMMFEST. Then sit down; and bury your shame in your typewriter [Schneidekind sits down]. Comrade Annajanska: you have eloped with a young officer.

THE GRAND DUCHESS [*astounded*] General Strammfest: you lie.

STRAMMFEST. Denial, comrade, is useless. It is through that officer that your movements have been traced. [*The Grand Duchess is suddenly enlightened, and seems amused. Strammfest continues in a forensic manner*] He joined you at the Golden Anchor in Hakonsburg. You gave us the slip there; but the officer was traced to Potterdam, where you rejoined him and went alone to Premsylople. What have you done with that unhappy young man? Where is he?

THE GRAND DUCHESS [*pretending to whisper an important secret*] Where he has always been.

STRAMMFEST [*eagerly*] Where is that?

THE GRAND DUCHESS [*impetuously*] In your imagination. I came alone. I am alone. Hundreds of officers travel every day from Hakonsburg to Potterdam. What do I know about them?

STRAMMFEST. They travel in khaki. They do not travel in full dress court uniform as this man did.

SCHNEIDEKIND. Only officers who are eloping with grand duchesses wear court uniform: otherwise the grand duchesses could not be seen with them.

STRAMMFEST. Hold your tongue. [*Schneidekind, in high dudgeon, folds his arms and retires from the conversation. The General returns to his paper and to his examination of the Grand Duchess*] This officer travelled with your passport. What have you to say to that?

THE GRAND DUCHESS. Bosh! How could a man travel with a woman's passport?

STRAMMFEST. It is quite simple, as you very well know. A dozen travellers arrive at the boundary. The official collects their passports. He counts twelve persons; then counts the passports. If there are twelve, he is satisfied.

THE GRAND DUCHESS. Then how do you know that one of the passports was mine?

STRAMMFEST. A waiter at the Potterdam Hotel looked at the officer's passport when he was in his bath. It was your passport.

THE GRAND DUCHESS. Stuff! Why did he not have me arrested?

STRAMMFEST. When the waiter returned to the hotel with the police the officer had vanished; and you were there with your own passport. They knouted him.

THE GRAND DUCHESS. Oh! Strammfest: send these men away. I must speak to you alone.

STRAMMFEST [*rising in horror*] No: this is the last straw: I cannot consent. It is impossible, utterly, eternally impossible, that a daughter of the Imperial House should speak to anyone alone, were it even her own husband.

THE GRAND DUCHESS. You forget that there is an exception. She may speak to a child alone. [*She rises*] Strammfest: you have been dandled on my grandmother's knee. By that gracious action the dowager Panjandrina made you a child forever. So did Nature, by the way. I order you to speak to me alone. Do you hear? I order you. For seven hundred years no member of your family has ever disobeyed an order from a member of mine. Will you disobey me?

STRAMMFEST. There is an alternative to obedience. The dead cannot disobey. [*He takes out his pistol and places the muzzle against his temple*].

SCHNEIDEKIND [*snatching the pistol from him*] For God's sake, General—

STRAMMFEST [*attacking him furiously to recover the weapon*] Dog of a subaltern, restore that pistol, and my honor.

SCHNEIDEKIND [*reaching out with the pistol to the Grand Duchess*] Take it: quick: he is as strong as a bull.

THE GRAND DUCHESS [*snatching it*] Aha! Leave the room, all of you except the General At the double! lightning! electricity! [*she fires shot after shot, spattering bullets about the ankles of the soldiers. They fly precipitately. She turns to Schneidekind, who has by this time been flung on the floor by the General*] You too. [*He scrambles up*]. March [*He flies to the door*].

SCHNEIDEKIND [*turning at the door*] For your own sake, comrade—

THE GRAND DUCHESS [*indignantly*] Comrade! You!!! Go. [*She fires two more shots. He vanishes*].

STRAMMFEST [*making an impulsive movement towards her*] My Imperial Mistress—

THE GRAND DUCHESS. Stop. I have one bullet left, if you attempt to take this from me [*putting the pistol to her temple*].

STRAMMFEST [*recoiling, and covering his eyes with his hands*] No no: put it down: put it down. I promise everything: I swear anything; put it down, I implore you.

THE GRAND DUCHESS [*throwing it on the table*] There!

STRAMMFEST [*uncovering his eyes*] Thank God!

THE GRAND DUCHESS [*gently*] Strammfest: I am your comrade. Am I nothing more to you?

STRAMMFEST [*falling on his knee*] You are, God help me, all that is left to me of the only power I recognize on earth [*he kisses her hand*].

THE GRAND DUCHESS [*indulgently*] Idolater! When will you learn that our strength has never been in ourselves, but in your illusions about us? [*She shakes off her kindliness, and sits down in his chair*] Now tell me, what are your orders? And do you mean to obey them?

STRAMMFEST [*starting like a goaded ox, and blundering fretfully about the room*] How can I obey six different dictators, and not one gentleman among the lot of them? One of them orders me to make peace with the foreign enemy. Another orders me to offer all the neutral countries 48 hours to choose between adopting his views on the single tax and being instantly invaded and annihilated. A third orders me to go to a damned Socialist Conference and explain that Beotia will allow no annexations and no indemnities, and merely wishes to establish the Kingdom of Heaven on Earth throughout the universe. [*He finishes behind Schneidekind's chair*].

THE GRAND DUCHESS. Damn their trifling!

STRAMMFEST. I thank Your Imperial Highness from the bottom of my heart for that expression. Europe thanks you.

THE GRAND DUCHESS. M'yes; but—[*rising*] Strammfest: you know that your cause—the cause of the dynasty— is lost.

STRAMMFEST. You must not say so. It is treason, even from you. [*He sinks, discouraged, into the chair, and covers his face with his hand*].

THE GRAND DUCHESS. Do not deceive yourself, General: never again will a Panjandrum reign in Beotia. [*She walks slowly across the room, brooding bitterly, and thinking aloud*]. We are so decayed, so out of date, so feeble, so wicked in our own despite, that we have come at last to will our own destruction.

STRAMMFEST. You are uttering blasphemy.

THE GRAND DUCHESS. All great truths begin as blasphemies. All the king's horses and all the king's men cannot set up my father's throne again. If they could, you would have done it, would you not?

STRAMMFEST. God knows I would!

THE GRAND DUCHESS. You really mean that? You would keep the people in their hopeless squalid misery? you would fill those infamous prisons again with the noblest spirits in the land? you would thrust the rising sun of liberty back into the sea of blood from which it has risen? And all because there was in the middle of the dirt and ugliness and horror a little patch of court splendor in which you could stand with a few orders on your uniform and yawn day after day and night after night in unspeakable boredom until your grave yawned wider still, and you fell into it because you had nothing better to do. How can you be so stupid, so heartless?

STRAMMFEST. You must be mad to think of royalty in such a way. I never yawned at court. The dogs yawned; but that was because they were dogs: they had no imagination, no ideals, no sense of honor and dignity to sustain them.

THE GRAND DUCHESS. My poor Strammfest: you were not often enough at court to tire of it. You were mostly soldiering; and when you came home to have a new order pinned on your breast, your happiness came through looking at my father and mother and at me, and adoring us. Was that not so?

STRAMMFEST. Do you reproach me with it? I am not ashamed of it.

THE GRAND DUCHESS. Oh, it was all very well for you, Strammfest. But think of me, of me! standing there for you to gape at, and knowing that I was no goddess, but only a girl like any other girl! It was cruelty to animals: you could have stuck up a wax doll or a golden calf to worship; it would not have been bored.

STRAMMFEST. Stop; or I shall renounce my allegiance to you. I have had women flogged for such seditious chatter as this.

THE GRAND DUCHESS. Do not provoke me to send a bullet through your head for reminding me of it.

STRAMMFEST. You always had low tastes. You are no true daughter of the Panjandrums: you are a changeling, thrust into the Panjandrina's bed by some profligate nurse. I have heard stories of your childhood: of how—

THE GRAND DUCHESS. Ha, ha! Yes: they took me to the circus when I was a child. It was my first moment of happiness, my first glimpse of heaven. I ran away and joined the troupe. They caught me and dragged me back to my gilded cage; but I had tasted freedom; and they never could make me forget it.

STRAMMFEST. Freedom! To be the slave of an acrobat! to be exhibited to the public! to—

THE GRAND DUCHESS. Oh, I was trained to that. I had learnt that part of the business at court.

STRAMMFEST. You had not been taught to strip yourself half naked and turn head over heels—

THE GRAND DUCHESS. Man: I w a n t e d to get rid of my swaddling clothes and turn head over heels. I wanted to, I wanted to, I wanted to. I can do it still. Shall I do it now?

STRAMMFEST. If you do, I swear I will throw myself from the window so that I may meet your parents in heaven without having my medals torn from my breast by them.

THE GRAND DUCHESS. Oh, you are incorrigible. You are mad, infatuated. You will not believe that we royal divinities are mere common flesh and blood even when we step down from our pedestals and tell you ourselves what a fool you are. I will argue no more with you: I will use my power. At a word from me your men will turn against you: already half of them do not salute you; and you dare not punish them: you have to pretend not to notice it.

STRAMMFEST. It is not for you to taunt me with that if it is so.

THE GRAND DUCHESS. [haughtily] Taunt! I condescend to taunt! To taunt a common General! You forget yourself, sir.

STRAMMFEST [dropping on his knee submissively] Now at last you speak like your royal self.

THE GRAND DUCHESS. Oh, Strammfest, Strammfest, they have driven your slavery into your very bones. Why did you not spit in my face?

STRAMMFEST [rising with a shudder] God forbid!

THE GRAND DUCHESS. Well, since you will be my slave, take your orders from me. I have not come here to save our wretched family and our bloodstained crown. I am come to save the Revolution.

STRAMMFEST. Stupid as I am, I have come to think that I had better save that than save nothing. But what will the Revolution do for the people? Do not be deceived by the fine speeches of the revolutionary leaders and the pamphlets of the revolutionary writers. How much liberty is there where t h e y have gained the upper hand? Are they not hanging, shooting, imprisoning as much as ever we did? Do they ever tell the people the truth? No: if the truth does not suit them they spread lies instead, and make it a crime to tell the truth.

THE GRAND DUCHESS. Of course they do. Why should they not?

STRAMMFEST [hardly able to believe his ears] Why should they not!

THE GRAND DUCHESS. Yes: why should they not? We did it. You did it, whip in hand: you flogged women for teaching children to read.

STRAMMFEST. To read sedition. To read Karl Marx.

THE GRAND DUCHESS. Pshaw! How could they learn to read the Bible without learning to read Karl Marx? Why do you not stand to your guns and justify what you did, instead of making silly excuses. Do you suppose I think flogging a woman worse than flogging a man? I, who am a woman myself!

STRAMMFEST. I am at a loss to understand your Imperial Highness. You seem to me to contradict yourself.

THE GRAND DUCHESS. Nonsense! I say that if the people cannot govern themselves, they must be governed by somebody. If they will not do their duty without being half forced and half humbugged, somebody must force them and humbug them. Some energetic and capable minority must always be in power. Well, I am on the side of the energetic minority whose principles I agree with. The Revolution is as cruel as we were; but its aims are my aims. Therefore I stand for the Revolution.

STRAMMFEST. You do not know what you are saying. This is pure Bolshevism. Are you, the daughter of a Panjandrum, a Bolshevist?

THE GRAND DUCHESS. I am anything that will make the world less like a prison and more like a circus.

STRAMMFEST. Ah! You still want to be a circus star.

THE GRAND DUCHESS. Yes, and be billed as the Bolshevik Empress. Nothing shall stop me. You have your orders, General Strammfest: save the Revolution.

STRAMMFEST. What Revolution? Which Revolution? No two of your rabble of revolutionists mean the same thing by the Revolution. What can save a mob in which every man is rushing in a different direction?

THE GRAND DUCHESS. I will tell you. The war can save it.

STRAMMFEST. The war?

THE GRAND DUCHESS. Yes, the war. Only a great common danger and a great common duty can unite us and weld these wrangling factions into a solid commonwealth.

STRAMMFEST. Bravo! War sets everything right: I have always said so. But what is a united people without a united army? And what can *I* do? I am only a soldier. I cannot make speeches: I have won no victories: they will not rally to my call [*again he sinks into his chair with his former gesture of discouragement*].

THE GRAND DUCHESS. Are you sure they will not rally to mine?

STRAMMFEST. Oh, if only you were a man and a soldier!

THE GRAND DUCHESS. Suppose I find you a man and a soldier?

STRAMMFEST [*rising in a fury*] Ah! the scoundrel you eloped with! You think you will shove this fellow into an army command, over my head. Never.

THE GRAND DUCHESS. You promised everything. You swore anything. [*She marches as if in front of a regiment*]. I know that this man alone can rouse the army to enthusiasm.

STRAMMFEST. Delusion! Folly! He is some circus acrobat; and you are in love with him.

THE GRAND DUCHESS. I swear I am not in love with him. I swear I will never marry him.

STRAMMFEST. Then who is he?

THE GRAND DUCHESS. Anybody in the world but you would have guessed long ago. He is under your very eyes.

STRAMMFEST [*staring past her right and left*] Where?

THE GRAND DUCHESS. Look out of the window.

He rushes to the window, looking for the officer. The Grand Duchess takes off her cloak and appears in the uniform of the Panderobajensky Hussars.

STRAMMFEST [*peering through the window*] Where is he? I can see no one.

THE GRAND DUCHESS. Here, silly.

STRAMMFEST [*turning*] You! Great Heavens! The Bolshevik Empress!

THE END

XXX

BACK TO METHUSELAH

PART I

IN THE BEGINNING

ACT I

The Garden of Eden. Afternoon. An immense serpent is sleeping with her head buried in a thick bed of Johnswort, and her body coiled in apparently endless rings through the branches of a tree, which is already well grown; for the days of creation have been longer than our reckoning. She is not yet visible to anyone unaware of her presence, as her colors of green and brown make a perfect camouflage. Near her head a low rock shews above the Johnswort.

The rock and tree are on the border of a glade in which lies a dead fawn all awry, its neck being broken. Adam, crouching with one hand on the rock, is staring in consternation at the dead body. He has not noticed the serpent on his left hand. He turns his face to his right and calls excitedly.

ADAM. Eve! Eve!

EVE'S VOICE. What is it, Adam?

ADAM. Come here. Quick. Something has happened.

EVE [*running in*] What? Where? [*Adam points to the fawn*]. Oh! [*She goes to it; and he is emboldened to go with her*]. What is the matter with its eyes?

ADAM. It is not only its eyes. Look. [*He kicks it*].

EVE. Oh dont! Why doesnt it wake?

ADAM. I dont know. It is not asleep.

EVE. Not asleep?

ADAM. Try.

EVE [*trying to shake it and roll it over*] It is stiff and cold.

ADAM. Nothing will wake it.

EVE. It has a queer smell. Pah! [*She dusts her hands, and draws away from it*]. Did you find it like that?

ADAM. No. It was playing about; and it tripped and went head over heels. It never stirred again. Its neck is wrong [*he stoops to lift the neck and shew her*].

EVE. Dont touch it. Come away from it.

They both retreat, and contemplate it from a few steps' distance with growing repulsion.

EVE. Adam.

ADAM. Yes?

EVE. Suppose you were to trip and fall, would you go like that?

ADAM. Ugh! [*He shudders and sits down on the rock*].

EVE [*throwing herself on the ground beside him, and grasping his knee*] You must be careful. Promise me you will be careful.

ADAM. What is the good of being careful? We have to live here for ever. Think of what for ever means! Sooner or later I shall trip and fall. It may be tomorrow; it may be after as many days as there are leaves in the garden and grains of sand by the river. No matter: some day I shall forget and stumble.

EVE. I too.

ADAM [*horrified*] Oh no, no. I should be alone. Alone for ever. You must never put yourself in danger of stumbling. You must not move about. You must sit still. I will take care of you and bring you what you want.

EVE [*turning away from him with a shrug, and hugging her ankles*] I should soon get tired of that. Besides, if it happened to you, *I* should be alone. I could not sit still then. And at last it would happen to me too.

ADAM. And then?

EVE. Then we should be no more. There would be only the things on all fours, and the birds, and the snakes.

ADAM. That must not be.

EVE. Yes: that must not be. But it might be.

ADAM. No. I tell you it must not be. I know that it must not be.

EVE. We both know it. How do we know it?

ADAM. There is a voice in the garden that tells me things.

EVE. The garden is full of voices sometimes. They put all sorts of thoughts into my head.

ADAM. To me there is only one voice. It is very low; but it is so near that it is like a whisper from within myself. There is no mistaking it for any voice of the birds or beasts, or for your voice.

EVE. It is strange that I should hear voices from all sides and you only one from within. But I have some thoughts that come from within me and not from the voices. The thought that we must not cease to be comes from within.

ADAM [*despairingly*] But we sh a ll cease to be. We shall fall like the fawn and be broken. [*Rising and moving about in his agitation*] I cannot bear this knowledge. I will not have it. It must not be, I tell you. Yet I do not know how to prevent it.

EVE. That is just what I feel; but it is very strange that you should say so: there is no pleasing you. You change your mind so often.

ADAM [*scolding her*] Why do you say that? How have I changed my mind?

EVE. You say we must not cease to exist. But you used to complain of having to exist always and for ever. You sometimes sit for hours brooding and silent, hating me in your heart. When I ask you what I have done to you, you say you are not thinking of me, but of the horror of having to be here for ever. But I know very well that what you mean is the horror of having to be here with me for ever.

ADAM. Oh! That is what you think, is it? Well, you are wrong. [*He sits down again, sulkily*]. It is the horror of having to be with myself for ever. I like you; but I do not like myself. I want to be different; to be better; to begin again and again; to shed myself as a snake sheds its skin. I am tired of myself. And yet I must endure myself, not for a day or for many days, but for ever. That is a dreadful thought. That is what makes me sit brooding and silent and hateful. Do you never think of that?

EVE. No: I do not think about myself: what is the use? I am what I am: nothing can alter that. I think about you.

ADAM. You should not. You are always spying on me. I can never be alone. You always want to know what I have been doing. It is a burden. You should try to have an existence of your own, instead of occupying yourself with my existence.

EVE. I h a v e to think about you. You are lazy: you are dirty: you neglect yourself: you are always dreaming: you would eat bad food and become disgusting if I did not watch you and occupy myself with you. And now some day, in spite of all my care, you will fall on your head and become dead.

ADAM. Dead? What word is that?

EVE [*pointing to the fawn*] Like that. I call it dead.

ADAM [*rising and approaching it slowly*] There is something uncanny about it.

EVE [*joining him*] Oh! It is changing into

little white worms.

ADAM. Throw it into the river. It is unbearable.

EVE. I dare not touch it.

ADAM. Then I must, though I loathe it. It is poisoning the air. [*He gathers its hooves in his hand and carries it away in the direction from which Eve came, holding it as far from him as possible*].

Eve looks after them for a moment; then, with a shiver of disgust, sits down on the rock, brooding. The body of the serpent becomes visible, glowing with wonderful new colors. She rears her head slowly from the bed of Johnswort, and speaks into Eve's ear in a strange seductively musical whisper.

THE SERPENT. Eve.

EVE [*startled*] Who is that?

THE SERPENT. It is I. I have come to shew you my beautiful new hood. See [*she spreads a magnificent amethystine hood*]!

EVE [*admiring it*] Oh! But who taught you to speak?

THE SERPENT. You and Adam. I have crept through the grass, and hidden, and listened to you.

EVE. That was wonderfully clever of you.

THE SERPENT. I am the most subtle of all the creatures of the field.

EVE. Your hood is most lovely. [*She strokes it and pets the serpent*]. Pretty thing! Do you love your godmother Eve?

THE SERPENT. I adore her. [*She licks Eve's neck with her double tongue*].

EVE [*petting her*] Eve's wonderful darling snake. Eve will never be lonely now that her snake can talk to her.

THE SNAKE. I can talk of many things. I am very wise. It was I who whispered the word to you that you did not know. Dead. Death. Die.

EVE [*shuddering*] Why do you remind me of it? I forgot it when I saw your beautiful hood. You must not remind me of unhappy things.

THE SERPENT. Death is not an unhappy thing when you have learnt how to conquer it.

EVE. How can I conquer it?

THE SERPENT. By another thing, called birth.

EVE. What? [*Trying to pronounce it*] B-birth?

THE SERPENT. Yes, birth.

EVE. What is birth?

THE SERPENT. The serpent never dies. Some day you shall see me come out of this beautiful skin, a new snake with a new and lovelier skin. That is birth.

EVE. I have seen that. It is wonderful.

THE SERPENT. If I can do that, what can I not do? I tell you I am very subtle. When you and Adam talk, I hear you say "Why?" Always "Why?" You see things; and you say "Why?" But I dream things that never were; and I say "Why not?" I made the word dead to describe my old skin that I cast when I am renewed. I call that renewal being born.

EVE. Born is a beautiful word.

THE SERPENT. Why not be born again and again as I am, new and beautiful every time?

EVE. I! It does not happen: that is why.

THE SERPENT. That is how; but it is not why. Why not?

EVE. But I should not like it. It would be nice to be new again; but my old skin would lie on the ground looking just like me; and Adam would see it shrivel up and—

THE SERPENT. No. He need not. There is a second birth.

EVE. A second birth?

THE SERPENT. Listen. I will tell you a great secret. I am very subtle; and I have thought and thought and thought. And I am very wilful, and must have what I want; and I have willed and willed and willed. And I have eaten strange things: stones and apples that you are afraid to eat.

EVE. You dared!

THE SERPENT. I dared everything. And at last I found a way of gathering together a part of the life in my body—

EVE. What is the life?

THE SERPENT. That which makes the difference between the dead fawn and the live one.

EVE. What a beautiful word! And what a wonderful thing! Life is the loveliest of all the new words.

THE SERPENT. Yes: it was by meditating on Life that I gained the power to do miracles.

EVE. Miracles? Another new word.

THE SERPENT. A miracle is an impossible thing that is nevertheless possible. Something that never could happen, and yet does happen.

EVE. Tell me some miracle that you have done.

THE SERPENT. I gathered a part of the life in my body, and shut it into a tiny white case made of the stones I had eaten.

EVE. And what good was that?

THE SERPENT. I shewed the little case to the sun, and left it in its warmth. And it burst; and a little snake came out; and it became bigger and bigger from day to day until it was as big as I. That was the second birth.

EVE. Oh! That is too wonderful. It stirs inside me. It hurts.

THE SERPENT. It nearly tore me asunder. Yet I am alive, and can burst my skin and renew myself as before. Soon there will be as many snakes in Eden as there are scales on my body. Then death will not matter: this snake and that snake will die; but the snakes will live.

EVE. But the rest of us will die sooner or later, like the fawn. And then there will be nothing but snakes, snakes, snakes everywhere.

THE SERPENT. That must not be. I worship you, Eve. I must have something to worship. Something quite different to myself, like you. There must be something greater than the snake.

EVE. Yes: it must not be. Adam must not perish. You are very subtle: tell me what to do.

THE SERPENT. Think. Will. Eat the dust. Lick the white stone: bite the apple you dread. The sun will give life.

EVE. I do not trust the sun. I will give life myself. I will tear another Adam from my body if I tear my body to pieces in the act.

THE SERPENT. Do. Dare it. Everything is possible: everything. Listen. I am old. I am the old serpent, older than Adam, older than Eve. I remembered Lilith, who came before Adam and Eve. I was her darling as I am yours. She was alone: there was no man with her. She saw death as you saw it when the fawn fell; and she knew then that she must find out how to renew herself and cast the skin like me. She had a mighty will: she strove and strove and willed and willed for more moons than there are leaves on all the trees of the garden. Her pangs were terrible: her groans drove sleep from Eden. She said it must never be again: that the burden of renewing life was past bearing: that it was too much for one. And when she cast the skin, lo! there was not one new Lilith but two: one like herself, the other like Adam. You were the one: Adam was the other.

EVE. But why did she divide into two, and make us different?

THE SERPENT. I tell you the labor is too much for one. Two must share it.

EVE. Do you mean that Adam must share it with me? He will not. He cannot bear pain, nor take trouble with his body.

THE SERPENT. He need not. There will be no pain for him. He will implore you to let him do his share. He will be in your power through his desire.

EVE. Then I will do it. But how? How did Lilith work this miracle?

THE SERPENT. She imagined it.

EVE. What is imagined?

THE SERPENT. She told it to me as a marvellous story of something that never happened to a Lilith that never was. She did not know then that imagination is the beginning of creation. You imagine what you desire; you will what you imagine; and at last you create what you will.

EVE. How can I create out of nothing?

THE SERPENT. Everything must have been created out of nothing. Look at that thick roll of hard flesh on your strong arm! That was not always there: you could not climb a tree when I first saw you. But you willed and tried and willed and tried; and your will created out of nothing the roll on your arm until you had your desire, and could draw yourself up with one hand and seat yourself on the bough that was above your head.

EVE. That was practice.

THE SERPENT. Things wear out by practice: they do not grow by it. Your hair streams in the wind as if it were trying to stretch itself further and further. But it does not grow longer for all its practice in streaming, because you have not willed it so. When Lilith told me what she had imagined in our silent language (for there were no words then) I bade her desire it and will it; and then, to our great wonder, the thing she had desired and willed created itself in her under the urging of her will. Then I too willed to renew myself as two instead of one; and after many days the miracle happened, and I burst from my skin with another snake interlaced with me; and now there are two imaginations, two desires, two wills to create with.

EVE. To desire, to imagine, to will, to create. That is too long a story. Find me one word for it all: you, who are so clever at words.

THE SERPENT. In one word, to conceive. That is the word that means both the beginning in imagination and the end in creation.

EVE. Find me a word for the story Lilith imagined and told you in your silent language: the story that was too wonderful to be true, and yet came true.

THE SERPENT. A poem.

EVE. Find me another word for what Lilith was to me.

THE SERPENT. She was your mother.

EVE. And Adam's mother?

THE SERPENT. Yes.

EVE [about to rise] I will go and tell Adam to conceive.

THE SERPENT [laughs]!!!

EVE [jarred and startled] What a hateful noise! What is the matter with you? No one has ever uttered such a sound before.

THE SERPENT. Adam cannot conceive.

EVE. Why?

THE SERPENT. Lilith did not imagine him so. He can imagine: he can will: he can desire: he can gather his life together for a great spring towards creation: he can create all things except one; and that one is his own kind.

EVE. Why did Lilith keep this from him?

THE SERPENT. Because if he could do that he could do without Eve.

EVE. That is true. It is I who must conceive.

THE SERPENT. Yes. By that he is tied to you.

EVE. And I to him!

THE SERPENT. Yes, until you create another Adam.

EVE. I had not thought of that. You are very subtle. But if I create another Eve he may turn to her and do without me. I will not create any Eves, only Adams.

THE SERPENT. They cannot renew themselves without Eves. Sooner or later you will die like the fawn; and the new Adams will be unable to create without new Eves. You can imagine such an end; but you cannot desire it, therefore cannot will it, therefore cannot create Adams only.

EVE. If I am to die like the fawn, why should not the rest die too? What do I care?

THE SERPENT. Life must not cease. That comes before everything. It is silly to say you do not care. You do care. It is that care that will prompt your imagination; inflame your desires; make your will irresistible; and create out of nothing.

EVE [thoughtfully] There can be no such thing as nothing. The garden is full, not empty.

THE SERPENT. I had not thought of that. That is a great thought. Yes: there is no such thing as nothing, only things we cannot see. The chameleon eats the air.

EVE. I have another thought: I must tell it to Adam. [Calling] Adam! Adam! Coo-ee!

ADAM'S VOICE. Coo-ee!

EVE. This will please him, and cure his fits of melancholy.

THE SERPENT. Do not tell him yet. I have not told you the great secret.

EVE. What more is there to tell? It is I who have to do the miracle.

THE SERPENT. No: he, too, must desire and will. But he must give his desire and his will to you.

EVE. How?

THE SERPENT. That is the great secret. Hush! he is coming.

ADAM [returning] Is there another voice in the garden besides our voices and t h e Voice? I heard a new voice.

EVE [rising and running to him] Only think, Adam! Our snake has learnt to speak by listening to us.

ADAM [delighted] Is it so? [He goes past her to the stone, and fondles the serpent].

THE SERPENT [responding affectionately] It is so, dear Adam.

EVE. But I have more wonderful news than that. Adam: we need not live for ever.

ADAM [dropping the snake's head in his excitement] What! Eve: do not play with me about this. If only there may be an end some day, and yet no end! If only I can be relieved of the horror of having to endure myself for ever! If only the care of this terrible garden may pass on to some other gardener! If only the sentinel set by the Voice can be relieved! If only the rest and sleep that enable me to bear it from day to day could grow after many days into an eternal rest, an eternal sleep, then I could face my days, however long they may last. Only, there must be some end, some end: I am not strong enough to bear eternity.

THE SERPENT. You need not live to see another summer; and yet there shall be no end.

ADAM. That cannot be.

THE SERPENT. It can be.

EVE. It shall be.

THE SERPENT. It is. Kill me; and you will find another snake in the garden tomorrow.

You will find more snakes than there are fingers on your hands.

EVE. I will make other Adams, other Eves.

ADAM. I tell you you must not make up stories about this. It cannot happen.

THE SERPENT. I can remember when you were yourself a thing that could not happen. Yet you are.

ADAM [*struck*] That must be true. [*He sits down on the stone*].

THE SERPENT. I will tell Eve the secret; and she will tell it to you.

ADAM. The secret! [*He turns quickly towards the serpent, and in doing so puts his foot on something sharp*]. Oh!

EVE. What is it?

ADAM [*rubbing his foot*] A thistle. And there, next to it, a briar. And nettles, too! I am tired of pulling these things up to keep the garden pleasant for us for ever.

THE SERPENT. They do not grow very fast. They will not overrun the whole garden for a long time: not until you have laid down your burden and gone to sleep for ever. Why should you trouble yourself? Let the new Adams clear a place for themselves.

ADAM. That is very true. You must tell us your secret. You see, Eve, what a splendid thing it is not to have to live for ever.

EVE [*throwing herself down discontentedly and plucking at the grass*] That is so like a man. The moment you find we need not last for ever, you talk as if we were going to end today. You must clear away some of those horrid things, or we shall be scratched and stung whenever we forget to look where we are stepping.

ADAM. Oh yes, some of them, of course. But only some. I will clear them away tomorrow.

THE SERPENT [*laughs*]!!!

ADAM. That is a funny noise to make. I like it.

EVE. I do not. Why do you make it again?

THE SERPENT. Adam has invented something new. He has invented tomorrow. You will invent things every day now that the burden of immortality is lifted from you.

EVE. Immortality? What is that?

THE SERPENT. My new word for having to live for ever.

EVE. The serpent has made a beautiful word for being. Living.

ADAM. Make me a beautiful word for doing things tomorrow; for that surely is a great and blessed invention.

THE SERPENT. Procrastination.

EVE. That is a sweet word. I wish I had a serpent's tongue.

THE SERPENT. That may come too. Everything is possible.

ADAM [*springing up in sudden terror*] Oh!

EVE. What is the matter now?

ADAM. My rest! My escape from life!

THE SERPENT. Death. That is the word.

ADAM. There is a terrible danger in this procrastination.

EVE. What danger?

ADAM. If I put off death until tomorrow, I shall never die. There is no such day as tomorrow, and never can be.

THE SERPENT. I am very subtle; but Man is deeper in his thought than I am. The woman knows that there is no such thing as nothing: the man knows that there is no such day as tomorrow. I do well to worship them.

ADAM. If I am to overtake death, I must appoint a real day, not a tomorrow. When shall I die?

EVE. You may die when I have made another Adam. Not before. But then, as soon as you like. [*She rises, and passing behind him, strolls off carelessly to the tree and leans against it, stroking a ring of the snake*].

ADAM. There need be no hurry even then.

EVE. I see you will put it off until tomorrow.

ADAM. And you? Will you die the moment you have made a new Eve?

EVE. Why should I? Are you eager to be rid of me? Only just now you wanted me to sit still and never move lest I should stumble and die like the fawn. Now you no longer care.

ADAM. It does not matter so much now.

EVE [*angrily to the snake*] This death that you have brought into the garden is an evil thing. He wants me to die.

THE SERPENT [*to Adam*] Do you want her to die?

ADAM. No. It is I who am to die. Eve must not die before me. I should be lonely.

EVE. You could get one of the new Eves.

ADAM. That is true. But they might not be quite the same. They could not: I feel sure of that. They would not have the same memories. They would be—I want a word for them.

THE SERPENT. Strangers.

ADAM. Yes: that is a good hard word. Strangers.

EVE. When there are new Adams and new Eves we shall live in a garden of strangers. We shall need each other. [*She comes quickly behind him and turns up his face to her*]. Do not forget that, Adam. Never forget it.

ADAM. Why should I forget it? It is I who have thought of it.

EVE. I, too, have thought of something. The fawn stumbled and fell and died. But you could come softly up behind me and [*she suddenly pounces on his shoulders and throws him forward on his face*] throw me down so that I should die. I should not dare to sleep if there were no reason why you should not make me die.

ADAM [*scrambling up in horror*] Make you die!!! What a frightful thought!

THE SERPENT. Kill, kill, kill, kill. That is the word.

EVE. The new Adams and Eves might kill us. I shall not make them. [*She sits on the rock and pulls him down beside her, clasping him to her with her right arm*].

THE SERPENT. You must. For if you do not there will be an end.

ADAM. No: they will not kill us: they will feel as I do. There is something against it. The Voice in the garden will tell them that they must not kill, as it tells me.

THE SERPENT. The voice in the garden is your own voice.

ADAM. It is; and it is not. It is something greater than me: I am only a part of it.

EVE. The Voice does not tell me not to kill you. Yet I do not want you to die before me. No voice is needed to make me feel that.

ADAM [*throwing his arm round her shoulder with an expression of anguish*] Oh no: that is plain without any voice. There is something that holds us together, something that has no word—

THE SERPENT. Love. Love. Love.

ADAM. That is too short a word for so long a thing.

THE SERPENT [*laughs*]!!!

EVE [*turning impatiently to the snake*] That heart-biting sound again! Do not do it. Why do you do it?

THE SERPENT. Love may be too long a word for so short a thing soon. But when it is short it will be very sweet.

ADAM [*ruminating*] You puzzle me. My old trouble was heavy; but it was simple. These wonders that you promise to do may tangle up my being before they bring me the gift

of death. I was troubled with the burden of eternal being; but I was not confused in my mind. If I did not know that I loved Eve, at least I did not know that she might cease to love me, and come to love some other Adam and desire my death. Can you find a name for that knowledge?

THE SERPENT. Jealousy. Jealousy. Jealousy.

ADAM. A hideous word.

EVE [*shaking him*] Adam: you must not brood. You think too much.

ADAM [*angrily*] How can I help brooding when the future has become uncertain? Anything is better than uncertainty. Life has become uncertain. Love is uncertain. Have you a word for this new misery?

THE SERPENT. Fear. Fear. Fear.

ADAM. Have you a remedy for it?

THE SERPENT. Yes. Hope. Hope. Hope.

ADAM. What is hope?

THE SERPENT. As long as you do not know the future you do not know that it will not be happier than the past. That is hope.

ADAM. It does not console me. Fear is stronger in me than hope. I must have certainty. [*He rises threateningly*]. Give it to me; or I will kill you when next I catch you asleep.

EVE [*throwing her arms round the serpent*] My beautiful snake. Oh no. How can you even think such a horror?

ADAM. Fear will drive me to anything. The serpent gave me fear. Let it now give me certainty or go in fear of me.

THE SERPENT. Bind the future by your will. Make a vow.

ADAM. What is a vow?

THE SERPENT. Choose a day for your death; and resolve to die on that day. Then death is no longer uncertain but certain. Let Eve vow to love you until your death. Then love will be no longer uncertain.

ADAM. Yes: that is splendid: that will bind the future.

EVE [*displeased, turning away from the serpent*] But it will destroy hope.

ADAM [*angrily*] Be silent, woman. Hope is wicked. Happiness is wicked. Certainty is blessed.

THE SERPENT. What is wicked? You have invented a word.

ADAM. Whatever I fear to do is wicked. Listen to me, Eve; and you, snake, listen too, that your memory may hold my vow. I will live a thousand sets of the four seasons—

THE SERPENT. Years. Years.

ADAM. I will live a thousand years; and then I will endure no more: I will die and take my rest. And I will love Eve all that time and no other woman.

EVE. And if Adam keeps his vow I will love no other man until he dies.

THE SERPENT. You have both invented marriage. And what he will be to you and not to any other woman is husband; and what you will be to him and not to any other man is wife.

ADAM [instinctively moving his hand towards her] Husband and wife.

EVE [slipping her hand into his] Wife and husband.

THE SERPENT [laughs]!!!

EVE [snatching herself loose from Adam] Do not make that odious noise, I tell you.

ADAM. Do not listen to her: the noise is good: it lightens my heart. You are a jolly snake. But you have not made a vow yet. What vow do you make?

THE SERPENT. I make no vows. I take my chance.

ADAM. Chance? What does that mean?

THE SERPENT. It means that I fear certainty as you fear uncertainty. It means that nothing is certain but uncertainty. If I bind the future I bind my will. If I bind my will I strangle creation.

EVE. Creation must not be strangled. I tell you I will create, though I tear myself to pieces in the act.

ADAM. Be silent, both of you. I will bind the future. I will be delivered from fear. [To Eve] We have made our vows; and if you must create, you shall create within the bounds of those vows. You shall not listen to that snake any more. Come [he seizes her by the hair to drag her away].

EVE. Let me go, you fool. It has not yet told me the secret.

ADAM [releasing her] That is true. What is a fool?

EVE. I do not know: the word came to me. It is what you are when you forget and brood and are filled with fear. Let us listen to the snake.

ADAM. No: I am afraid of it. I feel as if the ground were giving way under my feet when it speaks. Do you stay and listen to it.

THE SERPENT [laughs]!!!

ADAM [brightening] That noise takes away fear. Funny. The snake and the woman are going to whisper secrets. [He chuckles and goes away slowly, laughing his first laugh].

EVE. Now the secret. The secret. [She sits on the rock and throws her arms round the serpent, who begins whispering to her].

Eve's face lights up with intense interest, which increases until an expression of overwhelming repugnance takes its place. She buries her face in her hands.

ACT II

A few centuries later. Morning. An oasis in Mesopotamia. Close at hand the end of a log house abuts on a kitchen garden. Adam is digging in the middle of the garden. On his right, Eve sits on a stool in the shadow of a tree by the doorway, spinning flax. Her wheel, which she turns by hand, is a large disc of heavy wood, practically a fly-wheel. At the opposite side of the garden is a thorn brake with a passage through it barred by a hurdle.

The two are scantily and carelessly dressed in rough linen and leaves. They have lost their youth and grace; and Adam has an unkempt beard and jaggedly cut hair; but they are strong and in the prime of life. Adam looks worried, like a farmer. Eve, better humored (having given up worrying), sits and spins and thinks.

A MAN'S VOICE. Hallo, mother!

EVE [looking across the garden towards the hurdle] Here is Cain.

ADAM [uttering a grunt of disgust]!!! [He goes on digging without raising his head].

Cain kicks the hurdle out of his way, and strides into the garden. In pose, voice, and dress he is insistently warlike. He is equipped with a huge spear and broad brass-bound leather shield; his casque is a tiger's head with bull's horns; he wears a scarlet cloak with gold brooch over a lion's skin with the claws dangling; his feet are in sandals with brass ornaments; his shins are in brass greaves; and his bristling military moustache glistens with oil. To his parents he has the self-assertive, not-quite-at-ease manner of a revolted son who knows that he is not forgiven nor approved of.

CAIN [to Adam] Still digging? Always dig, dig, dig. Sticking in the old furrow. No progress! no advanced ideas! no adventures! What should I be if I had stuck to the digging you taught me?

ADAM. What are you now, with your shield and spear, and your brother's blood crying from the ground against you?

CAIN. I am the first murderer: you are only the first man. Anybody could be the first man: it is as easy as to be the first cabbage. To be the first murderer one must be a man of spirit.

ADAM. Begone. Leave us in peace. The world is wide enough to keep us apart.

EVE. Why do you want to drive him away? He is mine. I made him out of my own body. I want to see my work sometimes.

ADAM. You made Abel also. He killed Abel. Can you bear to look at him after that?

CAIN. Whose fault was it that I killed Abel? Who invented killing? Did *I*? No: he invented it himself. I followed your teaching. I dug and dug and dug. I cleared away the thistles and briars. I ate the fruits of the earth. I lived in the sweat of my brow, as you do. I was a fool. But Abel was a discoverer, a man of ideas, of spirit: a true Progressive. He was the discoverer of blood. He was the inventor of killing. He found out that the fire of the sun could be brought down by a dewdrop. He invented the altar to keep the fire alive. He changed the beasts he killed into meat by the fire on the altar. He kept himself alive by eating meat. His meal cost him a day's glorious health-giving sport and an hour's amusing play with the fire. You learnt nothing from him: you drudged and drudged and drudged, and dug and dug and dug, and made me do the same. I envied his happiness, his freedom. I despised myself for not doing as he did instead of what you did. He became so happy that he shared his meal with the Voice that had whispered all his inventions to him. He said that the Voice was the voice of the fire that cooked his food, and that the fire that could cook could also eat. It was true: I saw the fire consume the food on his altar. Then I, too, made an altar, and offered my food on it, my grains, my roots, my fruit. Useless: nothing happened. He laughed at me; and then came my great idea: why not kill him as he killed the beasts? I struck; and he died, just as they did. Then I gave up your old silly drudging ways, and lived as he had lived, by the chase, by the killing, and by the fire. Am I not better than you? stronger, happier, freer?

ADAM. You are not stronger: you are shorter in the wind: you cannot endure. You have made the beasts afraid of us; and the snake has invented poison to protect herself against you. I fear you myself. If you take a step towards your mother with that spear of yours I will strike you with my spade as you struck Abel.

EVE. He will not strike me. He loves me.

ADAM. He loved his brother. But he killed him.

CAIN. I do not want to kill women. I do not want to kill my mother. And for her sake I will not kill you, though I could send this spear through you without coming within reach of your spade. But for her, I could not resist the sport of trying to kill you, in spite of my fear that you would kill me. I have striven with a boar and with a lion as to which of us should kill the other. I have striven with a man: spear to spear and shield to shield. It is terrible; but there is no joy like it. I call it fighting. He who has never fought has never lived. That is what has brought me to my mother today.

ADAM. What have you to do with one another now? She is the creator, you the destroyer.

CAIN. How can I destroy unless she creates? I want her to create more and more men: aye, and more and more women, that they may in turn create more men. I have imagined a glorious poem of many men, of more men than there are leaves on a thousand trees. I will divide them into two great hosts. One of them I will lead; and the other will be led by the man I fear most and desire to fight and kill most. And each host shall try to kill the other host. Think of that! all those multitudes of men fighting, fighting, killing, killing! The four rivers running with blood! The shouts of triumph! the howls of rage! the curses of despair! the shrieks of torment! That will be life indeed: life lived to the very marrow: burning, overwhelming life. Every man who has not seen it, heard it, felt it, risked it, will feel a humbled fool in the presence of the man who has.

EVE. And I! I am to be a mere convenience to make men for you to kill!

ADAM. Or to kill y o u, you fool.

CAIN. Mother: the making of men is your right, your risk, your agony, your glory, your triumph. You make my father here your mere convenience, as you call it, for that. He has to dig for you, sweat for you, plod for you, like the ox who helps him to tear up the ground or the ass who carries his burdens for him. No woman shall make me live my father's life. I will hunt: I will fight and strive to the very bursting of my sinews. When I have slain the boar at the risk of my life, I will throw it to my woman to cook, and give her a morsel of it for her pains. She shall have no other food; and that will make her my slave. And the man that slays me shall have her for his booty. Man shall be the master of Woman, not her baby and her drudge.

Adam throws down his spade, and stands looking darkly at Eve.

EVE. Are you tempted, Adam? Does this seem a better thing to you than love between us?

CAIN. What does he know of love? Only when he has fought, when he has faced terror and death, when he has striven to the spending of the last rally of his strength, can he know what it is to rest in love in the arms of a woman. Ask that woman whom you made, who is also my wife, whether she would have me as I was in the days when I followed the ways of Adam, and was a digger and a drudge?

EVE [*angrily throwing down her distaff*] What! You dare come here boasting about that good-for-nothing Lua, the worst of daughters and the worst of wives! You her master! You are more her slave than Adam's ox or your own sheep-dog. Forsooth, when you have slain the boar at the risk of your life, you will throw her a morsel of it for her pains! Ha! Poor wretch: do you think I do not know her, and know you, better than that? Do you risk your life when you trap the ermine and the sable and the blue fox to hang on her lazy shoulders and make her look more like an animal than a woman? When you have to snare the little tender birds because it is too much trouble for her to chew honest food, how much of a great warrior do you feel then? You slay the tiger at the risk of your life; but who gets the striped skin you have run that risk for? She takes it to lie on, and flings you the carrion flesh you cannot eat. You fight because you think that your fighting makes her admire and desire you. Fool: she makes you fight because you bring her the ornaments and the treasures of those you have slain, and because she is courted and propitiated with power and gold by the people who fear you. You say that *I* make a mere convenience of Adam: I who spin and keep the house, and bear and rear children, and am a woman and not a pet animal to please men and prey on them! What are you, you poor slave of a painted face and a bundle of skunk's fur? You were a man-child when I bore you. Lua was a woman-child when I bore her. What have you made of yourselves?

CAIN [*letting his spear fall into the crook of his shield arm, and twirling his moustache*] There is something higher than man. There is hero and superman.

EVE. Superman! You are no superman: you are Anti-Man: you are to other men what the stoat is to the rabbit; and she is to you what the leech is to the stoat. You despise your father; but when he dies the world will be the richer because he lived. When you die, men will say, "He was a great warrior; but it would have been better for the world if he had never been born." And of Lua they will say nothing; but when they think of her they will spit.

CAIN. She is a better sort of woman to live with than you. If Lua nagged at me as you are nagging, and as you nag at Adam, I would beat her black and blue from head to foot. I have done it too, slave as you say I am.

EVE. Yes, because she looked at another man. And then you grovelled at her feet, and cried, and begged her to forgive you, and were ten times more her slave than ever; and she, when she had finished screaming and the pain went off a little, she forgave you, did she not?

CAIN. She loved me more than ever. That is the true nature of woman.

EVE [*now pitying him maternally*] Love! You call that love! You call that the nature of woman! My boy: this is neither man nor woman nor love nor life. You have no real strength in your bones nor sap in your flesh.

CAIN. Ha! [*he seizes his spear and swings it muscularly*].

EVE. Yes: you have to twirl a stick to feel your strength: you cannot taste life without making it bitter and boiling hot: you cannot love Lua until her face is painted, nor feel the natural warmth of her flesh until you have stuck a squirrel's fur on it. You can feel nothing but a torment, and believe nothing but a lie. You will not raise your head to look at all the miracles of life that surround you; but you will run ten miles to see a fight or a death.

ADAM. Enough said. Let the boy alone.

CAIN. Boy! Ha! ha!

EVE [*to Adam*] You think, perhaps, that his way of life may be better than yours after all. You are still tempted. Well, will you pamper me as he pampers his woman? Will you kill tigers and bears until I have a heap of their skins to lounge on? Shall I paint my face and let my arms waste into pretty softness, and eat partridges and doves, and the flesh of kids whose milk you will steal for me?

ADAM. You are hard enough to bear with as you are. Stay as you are; and I will stay as I am.

CAIN. You neither of you know anything about life. You are simple country folk. You are the nurses and valets of the oxen and dogs and asses you have tamed to work for you. I can raise you out of that. I have a plan. Why not tame men and women to work for us? Why not bring them up from childhood never to know any other lot, so that they may believe that we are gods, and that they are here only to make life glorious for us?

ADAM [*impressed*] That is a great thought, certainly.

EVE [*contemptuously*] Great thought!

ADAM. Well, as the serpent used to say, why not?

EVE. Because I would not have such wretches in my house. Because I hate creatures with two heads, or with withered limbs, or that are distorted and perverted and unnatural. I have told Cain already that he is not a man and that Lua is not a woman: they are monsters. And now you want to make still more unnatural monsters, so that you may be utterly lazy and worthless, and that your tamed human animals may find work a blasting curse. A fine dream, truly! [*To Cain*] Your father is a fool skin deep; but you are a fool to your very marrow; and your baggage of a wife is worse.

ADAM. Why am I a fool? How am I a greater fool than you?

EVE. You said there would be no killing because the Voice would tell our children that they must not kill. Why did it not tell Cain that?

CAIN. It did; but I am not a child to be afraid of a Voice. The Voice thought I was nothing but my brother's keeper. It found that I was myself, and that it was for Abel to be himself also, and look to himself. He was not my keeper any more than I was his: why did he not kill me? There was no more to prevent him than there was to prevent

me: it was man to man; and I won. I was the first conqueror.

ADAM. What did the Voice say to you when you thought all that?

CAIN. Why, it gave me right. It said that my deed was as a mark on me, a burnt-in mark such as Abel put on his sheep, that no man should slay me. And here I stand unslain, whilst the cowards who have never slain, the men who are content to be their brothers' keepers instead of their masters, are despised and rejected, and slain like rabbits. He who bears the brand of Cain shall rule the earth. When he falls, he shall be avenged sevenfold: the Voice has said it; so beware how you plot against me, you and all the rest.

ADAM. Cease your boasting and bullying, and tell the truth. Does not the Voice tell you that as no man dare slay you for murdering your brother, you ought to slay yourself?

CAIN. No.

ADAM. Then there is no such thing as divine justice, unless you are lying.

CAIN. I am not lying: I dare all truths. There is divine justice. For the Voice tells me that I must offer myself to every man to be killed if he can kill me. Without danger I cannot be great. That is how I pay for Abel's blood. Danger and fear follow my steps everywhere. Without them courage would have no sense. And it is courage, courage, courage, that raises the blood of life to crimson splendor.

ADAM [*picking up his spade and preparing to dig again*] Take yourself off then. This splendid life of yours does not last for a thousand years; and I must last for a thousand years. When you fighters do not get killed in fighting one another or fighting the beasts, you die from mere evil in yourselves. Your flesh ceases to grow like man's flesh: it grows like a fungus on a tree. Instead of breathing, you sneeze, or cough up your insides, and wither and perish. Your bowels become rotten; your hair falls from you; your teeth blacken and drop out; and you die before your time, not because you will, but because you must. I will dig, and live.

CAIN. And pray, what use is this thousand years of life to you, you old vegetable? Do you dig any better because you have been digging for hundreds of years? I have not lived as long as you; but I know all there is to be known of the craft of digging. By quit-

2 F

ting it I have set myself free to learn nobler crafts of which ou know nothing. I know the craft of fighting and of hunting: in a word, the craft of killing. What certainty have you of your thousand years? I could kill both of you; and you could no more defend yourselves than a couple of sheep. I spare you; but others may kill you. Why not live bravely, and die early and make room for others? Why, I—I! that know many more crafts than either of you, am tired of myself when I am not fighting or hunting. Sooner than face a thousand years of it I should kill myself, as the Voice sometimes tempts me to do already.

ADAM. Liar: you denied just now that it called on you to pay for Abel's life with your own.

CAIN. The Voice does not speak to me as it does to you. I am a man: you are only a grown-up child. One does not speak to a child as to a man. And a man does not listen and tremble in silence. He replies: he makes the Voice respect him: in the end he dictates what the Voice shall say.

ADAM. May your tongue be accurst for such blasphemy!

EVE. Keep a guard on your own tongue; and do not curse my son. It was Lilith who did wrong when she shared the labor of creation so unequally between man and wife. If you, Cain, had had the trouble of making Abel, or had had to make another man to replace him when he was gone, you would not have killed him: you would have risked your own life to save his. That is why all this empty talk of yours, which tempted Adam just now when he threw down his spade and listened to you for a while, went by me like foul wind that has passed over a dead body. That is why there is enmity between Woman the creator and Man the destroyer. I know you: I am your mother. You are idle: you are selfish. It is long and hard and painful to create life: it is short and easy to steal the life others have made. When you dug, you made the earth live and bring forth as I live and bring forth. It was for that that Lilith set you free from the travail of women, not for theft and murder.

CAIN. The Devil thank her for it! I can make better use of my time than to play the husband to the clay beneath my feet.

ADAM. Devil? What new word is that?

CAIN. Hearken to me, old fool. I have never in my soul listened willingly when you have

told me of the Voice that whispers to you. There must be two Voices: one that gulls and despises you, and another that trusts and respects me. I call yours the Devil. Mine I call the Voice of God.

ADAM. Mine is the Voice of Life: yours the Voice of Death.

CAIN. Be it so. For it whispers to me that death is not really death: that it is the gate of another life: a life infinitely splendid and intense: a life of the soul alone: a life without clods or spades, hunger or fatigue—

EVE. Selfish and idle, Cain. I know.

CAIN. Selfish, yes: a life in which no man is his brother's keeper, because his brother can keep himself. But am I idle? In rejecting your drudgery, have I not embraced evils and agonies of which you know nothing? The arrow is lighter in the hand than the spade; but the energy that drives it through the breast of a fighter is as fire to water compared with the strength that drives the spade into the harmless dirty clay. My strength is as the strength of ten because my heart is pure.

ADAM. What is that word? What is pure?

CAIN. Turned from the clay. Turned upward to the sun, to the clear clean heavens.

ADAM. The heavens are empty, child. The earth is fruitful. The earth feeds us. It gives us the strength by which we made you and all mankind. Cut off from the clay which you despise, you would perish miserably.

CAIN. I revolt against the clay. I revolt against the food. You say it gives us strength: does it not also turn into filth and smite us with diseases? I revolt against these births that you and mother are so proud of. They drag us down to the level of the beasts. If that is to be the last thing as it has been the first, let mankind perish. If I am to eat like a bear, if Lua is to bring forth cubs like a bear, then I had rather be a bear than a man; for the bear is not ashamed: he knows no better. If you are content, like the bear, I am not. Stay with the woman who gives you children: I will go to the woman who gives me dreams. Grope in the ground for your food: I will bring it from the skies with my arrows, or strike it down as it roams the earth in the pride of its life. If I must have food or die, I will at least have it at as far a remove from the earth as I can. The ox shall make it something nobler than grass before it comes to me. And as the man is nobler than the ox,

I shall some day let my enemy eat the ox; and then I will slay and eat him.

ADAM. Monster! You hear this, Eve?

EVE. So that is what comes of turning your face to the clean clear heavens! Man-eating! Child-eating! For that is what it would come to, just as it came to lambs and kids when Abel began with sheep and goats. You are a poor silly creature after all. Do you think I never have these thoughts: I! who have the labor of the child-bearing: I! who have the drudgery of preparing the food? I thought for a moment that perhaps this strong brave son of mine, who could imagine something better, and could desire what he imagined, might also be able to will what he desired until he created it. And all that comes of it is that he wants to be a bear and eat children. Even a bear would not eat a man if it could get honey instead.

CAIN. I do not want to be a bear. I do not want to eat children. I do not know what I want, except that I want to be something higher and nobler than this stupid old digger whom Lilith made to help you to bring me into the world, and whom you despise now that he has served your turn.

ADAM [in sullen rage] I have half a mind to shew you that my spade can split your undutiful head open, in spite of your spear.

CAIN. Undutiful! Ha! ha! [Flourishing his spear] Try it, old everybody's father. Try a taste of fighting.

EVE. Peace, peace, you two fools. Sit down and be quiet; and listen to me. [Adam, with a weary shrug, throws down his spade. Cain, with a laughing one, throws down his shield and spear. Both sit on the ground]. I hardly know which of you satisfies me least, you with your dirty digging, or he with his dirty killing. I cannot think it was for either of these cheap ways of life that Lilith set you free. [To Adam] You dig roots and coax grains out of the earth: why do you not draw down a divine sustenance from the skies? He steals and kills for his food; and makes up idle poems of life after death; and dresses up his terror-ridden life with fine words and his disease-ridden body with fine clothes, so that men may glorify and honor him instead of cursing him as murderer and thief. All you men, except only Adam, are my sons, or my sons' sons, or my sons' sons' sons: you all come to see me: you all shew off before me: all your little wisdoms and accomplishments are

trotted out before mother Eve. The diggers come: the fighters and killers come: they are both very dull; for they either complain to me of the last harvest, or boast to me of the last fight; and one harvest is just like another, and the last fight only a repetition of the first. Oh, I have heard it all a thousand times. They tell me too of their last-born: the clever thing the darling child said yesterday, and how much more wonderful or witty or quaint it is than any child that ever was born before. And I have to pretend to be surprised, delighted, interested; though the last child is like the first, and has said and done nothing that did not delight Adam and me when you and Abel said it. For you were the first children in the world, and filled us with such wonder and delight as no couple can ever again feel while the world lasts. When I can bear no more, I go to our old garden, that is now a mass of nettles and thistles, in the hope of finding the serpent to talk to. But you have made the serpent our enemy: she has left the garden, or is dead: I never see her now. So I have to come back and listen to Adam saying the same thing for the ten-thousandth time, or to receive a visit from the last great-great-grandson who has grown up and wants to impress me with his importance. Oh, it is dreary, dreary! And there is yet nearly seven hundred years of it to endure.

CAIN. Poor mother! You see, life is too long. One tires of everything. There is nothing new under the sun.

ADAM [to Eve, grumpily] Why do you live on, if you can find nothing better to do than complain?

EVE. Because there is still hope.

CAIN. Of what?

EVE. Of the coming true of your dreams and mine. Of newly created things. Of better things. My sons and my sons' sons are not all diggers and fighters. Some of them will neither dig nor fight: they are more useless than either of you: they are weaklings and cowards: they are vain; yet they are dirty and will not take the trouble to cut their hair. They borrow and never pay; but one gives them what they want, because they tell beautiful lies in beautiful words. They can remember their dreams. They can dream without sleeping. They have not will enough to create instead of dreaming; but the serpent said that every dream could be willed into creation by those strong enough to believe in it. There are others who cut reeds of different lengths and blow through them, making lovely patterns of sound in the air; and some of them can weave the patterns together, sounding three reeds at the same time, and raising my soul to things for which I have no words. And others make little mammoths out of clay, or make faces appear on flat stones, and ask me to create women for them with such faces. I have watched those faces and willed; and then I have made a woman-child that has grown up quite like them. And others think of numbers without having to count on their fingers, and watch the sky at night, and give names to the stars, and can foretell when the sun will be covered with a black saucepan lid. And there is Tubal, who made this wheel for me which has saved me so much labor. And there is Enoch, who walks on the hills, and hears the Voice continually, and has given up his will to do the will of the Voice, and has some of the Voice's greatness. When they come, there is always some new wonder, or some new hope: something to live for. They never want to die, because they are always learning and always creating either things or wisdom, or at least dreaming of them. And then you, Cain, come to me with your stupid fighting and destroying, and your foolish boasting; and you want me to tell you that it is all splendid, and that you are heroic, and that nothing but death or the dread of death makes life worth living. Away with you, naughty child; and do you, Adam, go on with your work and not waste your time listening to him.

CAIN. I am not, perhaps, very clever; but—

EVE [*interrupting him*] Perhaps not; but do not begin to boast of that. It is no credit to you.

CAIN. For all that, mother, I have an instinct which tells me that death plays its part in life. Tell me this: who invented death?

Adam springs to his feet. Eve drops her distaff. Both shew the greatest consternation.

CAIN. What is the matter with you both?

ADAM. Boy: you have asked us a terrible question.

EVE. You invented murder. Let that be enough for you.

CAIN. Murder is not death. You know what I mean. Those whom I slay would die if I spared them. If I am not slain, yet I shall die. Who put this upon me? I say, who invented death?

ADAM. Be reasonable, boy. Could you bear to live for ever? You think you could, because you know that you will never have to make your thought good. But I have known what it is to sit and brood under the terror of eternity, of immortality. Think of it, man: to have no escape! to be Adam, Adam, Adam through more days than there are grains of sand by the two rivers, and then be as far from the end as ever! I, who have so much in me that I hate and long to cast off! Be thankful to your parents, who enabled you to hand on your burden to new and better men, and won for you an eternal rest; for it was we who invented death.

CAIN [*rising*] You did well: I, too, do not want to live for ever. But if you invented death, why do you blame me, who am a minister of death?

ADAM. I do not blame you. Go in peace. Leave me to my digging, and your mother to her spinning.

CAIN. Well, I will leave you to it, though I have shewn you a better way. [*He picks up his shield and spear*]. I will go back to my brave warrior friends and their splendid women. [*He strides to the thorn brake*]. When Adam delved and Eve span, where was then the gentleman? [*He goes away roaring with laughter, which ceases as he cries from the distance*] Goodbye, mother.

ADAM [*grumbling*] He might have put the hurdle back, lazy hound! [*He replaces the hurdle across the passage*].

EVE. Through him and his like, death is gaining on life. Already most of our grandchildren die before they have sense enough to know how to live.

ADAM. No matter. [*He spits on his hands, and takes up the spade again*]. Life is still long enough to learn to dig, short as they are making it.

EVE [*musing*] Yes, to dig. And to fight. But is it long enough for the other things, the great things? Will they live long enough to eat manna?

ADAM. What is manna?

EVE. Food drawn down from heaven, made out of the air, not dug dirtily from the earth. Will they learn all the ways of all the stars in their little time? It took Enoch two hundred years to learn to interpret the will of the Voice. When he was a mere child of eighty, his babyish attempts to understand the Voice were more dangerous than the wrath of Cain. If they shorten their lives, they will dig and fight and kill and die; and their baby Enochs will tell them that it is the will of the Voice that they should dig and fight and kill and die for ever.

ADAM. If they are lazy and have a will towards death I cannot help it. I will live my thousand years: if they will not, let them die and be damned.

EVE. Damned? What is that?

ADAM. The state of them that love death more than life. Go on with your spinning; and do not sit there idle while I am straining my muscles for you.

EVE [slowly taking up her distaff] If you were not a fool you would find something better for both of us to live by than this spinning and digging.

ADAM. Go on with your work, I tell you; or you shall go without bread.

EVE. Man need not always live by bread alone. There is something else. We do not yet know what it is; but some day we shall find out; and then we will live on that alone; and there shall be no more digging nor spinning, nor fighting nor killing.

She spins resignedly; he digs impatiently.

PART II
THE GOSPEL
OF THE BROTHERS BARNABAS

In the first years after the war an impressive-looking gentleman of 50 is seated writing in a well-furnished spacious study. He is dressed in black. His coat is a frock-coat; his tie is white; and his waistcoat, though it is not quite a clergyman's waistcoat, and his collar, though it buttons in front instead of behind, combine with the prosperity indicated by his surroundings, and his air of personal distinction, to suggest the clerical dignitary. Still, he is clearly neither dean nor bishop; he is rather too starkly intellectual for a popular Free Church enthusiast; and he is not careworn enough to be a great headmaster.

The study windows, which have broad comfortable window seats, overlook Hampstead Heath towards London. Consequently, it being a fine afternoon in spring, the room is sunny. As you face these windows, you have on your right the fireplace, with a few logs smouldering in it,

and a couple of comfortable library chairs on the hearthrug; beyond it and beside it the door; before you the writing-table, at which the clerical gentleman sits a little to your left facing the door with his right profile presented to you; on your left a settee; and on your right a couple of Chippendale chairs. There is also an upholstered square stool in the middle of the room, against the writing-table. The walls are covered with bookshelves above and lockers beneath.

The door opens; and another gentleman, shorter than the clerical one, within a year or two of the same age, dressed in a well-worn tweed lounge suit, with a short beard and much less style in his bearing and carriage, looks in.

THE CLERICAL GENTLEMAN [familiar and by no means cordial] Hallo! I didnt expect you until the five o'clock train.

THE TWEEDED GENTLEMAN [coming in very slowly] I have something on my mind. I thought I'd come early.

THE CLERICAL GENTLEMAN [throwing down his pen] What is on your mind?

THE TWEEDED GENTLEMAN [sitting down on the stool, heavily preoccupied with his thought] I have made up my mind at last about the time. I make it three hundred years.

THE CLERICAL GENTLEMAN [sitting up energetically] Now that is extraordinary. Most extraordinary. The very last words I wrote when you interrupted me were "at least three centuries." [He snatches up his manuscript, and points to it]. Here it is: [reading] "the term of human life must be extended to at least three centuries."

THE TWEEDED GENTLEMAN. How did you arrive at it?

A parlor maid opens the door, ushering in a young clergyman.

THE PARLOR MAID. Mr Haslam. [She withdraws].

The visitor is so very unwelcome that his host forgets to rise; and the two brothers stare at the intruder, quite unable to conceal their dismay. Haslam, who has nothing clerical about him except his collar, and wears a snuff-colored suit, smiles with a frank schoolboyishness that makes it impossible to be unkind to him, and explodes into obviously unpremeditated speech.

HASLAM. I'm afraid I'm an awful nuisance. I'm the rector; and I suppose one ought to call on people.

THE TWEEDED GENTLEMAN [in ghostly tones] We're not Church people, you know.

HASLAM. Oh, I dont mind that, if you dont.

The Church people here are mostly as dull as ditch-water. I have heard such a lot about you; and there are so jolly few people to talk to. I thought you perhaps wouldnt mind. Do you mind? for of course I'll go like a shot if I'm in the way.

THE CLERICAL GENTLEMAN [*rising, disarmed*] Sit down, Mr — er?

HASLAM. Haslam.

THE CLERICAL GENTLEMAN. Mr Haslam.

THE TWEEDED GENTLEMAN [*rising and offering him the stool*] Sit down. [*He retreats towards the Chippendale chairs*].

HASLAM [*sitting down on the stool*] Thanks awfully.

THE CLERICAL GENTLEMAN [*resuming his seat*] This is my brother Conrad, Professor of Biology at Jarrowfields University: Dr Conrad Barnabas. My name is Franklyn: Franklyn Barnabas. I was in the Church myself for some years.

HASLAM [*sympathizing*] Yes: one cant help it. If theres a living in the family, or one's Governor knows a patron, one gets shoved into the Church by one's parents.

CONRAD [*sitting down on the furthest Chippendale with a snort of amusement*] Mp!

FRANKLYN. One gets shoved out of it, sometimes, by one's conscience.

HASLAM. Oh yes; but where is a chap like me to go? I'm afraid I'm not intellectual enough to split straws when theres a job in front of me and nothing better for me to do. I daresay the Church was a bit thick for you; but it's good enough for me. It will last my time, anyhow. [*He laughs good-humoredly*].

FRANKLYN [*with renewed energy*] There again! You see, Con. It will last his time. Life is too short for men to take it seriously.

HASLAM. Thats a way of looking at it, certainly.

FRANKLYN. I was not shoved into the Church, Mr Haslam: I felt it to be my vocation to walk with God, like Enoch. After twenty years of it I realized that I was walking with my own ignorance and self-conceit, and that I was not within a hundred and fifty years of the experience and wisdom I was pretending to.

HASLAM. Now I come to think of it, old Methuselah must have had to think twice before he took on anything for life. If I thought I was going to live nine hundred and sixty years, I dont think I should stay in the Church.

FRANKLYN. If men lived even a third of that time, the Church would be very different from the thing it is.

CONRAD. If I could count on nine hundred and sixty years I could make myself a real biologist, instead of what I am now: a child trying to walk. Are you sure you might not become a good clergyman if you had a few centuries to do it in?

HASLAM. Oh, theres nothing much the matter with m e : it's quite easy to be a decent parson. It's the Church that chokes me off. I couldnt stick it for nine hundred years. I should chuck it. You know, sometimes, when the bishop, who is the most priceless of fossils, lets off something more than usually out-of-date, the bird starts in my garden.

FRANKLYN. The bird?

HASLAM. Oh yes. Theres a bird there that keeps on singing "Stick it or chuck it: stick it or chuck it"—just like that—for an hour on end in the spring. I wish my father had found some other shop for me.

The parlor maid comes back.

THE PARLOR MAID. Any letters for the post, sir?

FRANKLYN. These. [*He proffers a basket of letters. She comes to the table and takes them*].

HASLAM [*to the maid*] Have you told Mr Barnabas yet?

THE PARLOR MAID [*flinching a little*] No, sir.

FRANKLYN. Told me what?

HASLAM. She is going to leave you?

FRANKLYN. Indeed? I'm sorry. Is it our fault, Mr Haslam?

HASLAM. Not a bit. She is jolly well off here.

THE PARLOR MAID [*reddening*] I have never denied it, sir: I couldnt ask for a better place. But I have only one life to live; and I maynt get a second chance. Excuse me, sir; but the letters must go to catch the post. [*She goes out with the letters*].

The two brothers look inquiringly at Haslam.

HASLAM. Silly girl! Going to marry a village woodman and live in a hovel with him and a lot of kids tumbling over one another, just because the fellow has poetic-looking eyes and a moustache.

CONRAD [*demurring*] She said it was because she had only one life.

HASLAM. Same thing, poor girl! The fellow persuaded her to chuck it; and when she marries him she'll have to stick it. Rotten state of things, I call it.

CONRAD. You see, she hasnt time to find

out what life really means. She has to die before she knows.

HASLAM [*agreeably*] Thats it.

FRANKLYN. She hasnt time to form a well-instructed conscience.

HASLAM [*still more cheerfully*] Quite.

FRANKLYN. It goes deeper. She hasnt time to form a genuine conscience at all. Some romantic points of honor and a few conventions. A world without conscience: that is the horror of our condition.

HASLAM [*beaming*] Simply fatuous. [*Rising*] Well, I suppose I'd better be going. It's most awfully good of you to put up with my calling.

CONRAD [*in his former low ghostly tone*] You neednt go, you know, if you are really interested.

HASLAM [*fed up*] Well, I'm afraid I ought to—I really must get back—I have something to do in the—

FRANKLYN [*smiling benignly and rising to proffer his hand*] Goodbye.

CONRAD [*gruffly, giving him up as a bad job*] Goodbye.

HASLAM. Goodbye. Sorry—er—

As the rector moves to shake hands with Franklyn, feeling that he is making a frightful mess of his departure, a vigorous sunburnt young lady with hazel hair cut to the level of her neck, like an Italian youth in a Gozzoli picture, comes in impetuously. She seems to have nothing on but her short skirt, her blouse, her stockings, and a pair of Norwegian shoes: in short, she is a Simple-Lifer.

THE SIMPLE-LIFER [*swooping on Conrad and kissing him*] Hallo, Nunk. Youre before your time.

CONRAD. Behave yourself. Theres a visitor. *She turns quickly and sees the rector. She instinctively snitches at her Gozzoli fringe with her fingers, but gives it up as hopeless.*

FRANKLYN. Mr Haslam, our new rector. [*To Haslam*] My daughter Cynthia.

CONRAD. Usually called Savvy, short for Savage.

SAVVY. I usually call Mr Haslam Bill, short for William. [*She strolls to the hearthrug, and surveys them calmly from that commanding position*].

FRANKLYN. You know him?

SAVVY. Rather. Sit down, Bill.

FRANKLYN. Mr Haslam is going, Savvy. He has an engagement.

SAVVY. I know. I'm the engagement.

CONRAD. In that case, would you mind taking him into the garden while I talk to your father?

SAVVY [*to Haslam*] Tennis?

HASLAM. Rather!

SAVVY. Come on. [*She dances out. He runs out boyishly after her*].

FRANKLYN [*leaving his table and beginning to walk up and down the room discontentedly*] Savvy's manners jar on me. They would have horrified her grandmother.

CONRAD [*obstinately*] They are happier manners than Mother's manners.

FRANKLYN. Yes : they are franker, wholesomer, better in a hundred ways. And yet I squirm at them. I cannot get it out of my head that Mother was a well-mannered woman, and that Savvy has no manners at all.

CONRAD. There wasnt any pleasure in Mother's fine manners. That makes a biological difference.

FRANKLYN. But there was beauty in Mother's manners, grace in them, style in them: above all, decision in them. Savvy is such a cub.

CONRAD. So she ought to be, at her age.

FRANKLYN. There it comes again! Her age! her age!

CONRAD. You want her to be fully grown at eighteen. You want to force her into a stuck-up, artificial, premature self-possession before she has any self to possess. You just let her alone: she is right enough for her years.

FRANKLYN. I have let her alone; and look at the result! Like all the other young people who have been let alone, she becomes a Socialist. That is, she becomes hopelessly demoralized.

CONRAD. Well, arnt you a Socialist?

FRANKLYN. Yes; but that is not the same thing. You and I were brought up in the old bourgeois morality. We were taught bourgeois manners and bourgeois points of honor. Bourgeois manners may be snobbish manners: there may be no pleasure in them, as you say; but they are better than no manners. Many bourgeois points of honor may be false; but at least they exist. The women know what to expect and what is expected of them. Savvy doesnt. She is a Bolshevist and nothing else. She has to improvize her manners and her conduct as she goes along. It's often charming, no doubt; but sometimes she puts her foot in it frightfully; and then I feel that she is blaming me for not teaching her better.

CONRAD. Well, you have something better to teach her now, at all events.

FRANKLYN. Yes; but it is too late. She doesnt trust me now. She doesnt talk about such things to me. She doesnt read anything I write. She never comes to hear me lecture. I am out of it as far as Savvy is concerned. [*He resumes his seat at the writing-table*].

CONRAD. I must have a talk to her.

FRANKLYN. Perhaps she will listen to you. You are not her father.

CONRAD. I sent her my last book. I can break the ice by asking her what she made of it.

FRANKLYN. When she heard you were coming, she asked me whether all the leaves were cut, in case it fell into your hands. She hasnt read a word of it.

CONRAD [*rising indignantly*] What!

FRANKLYN [*inexorably*] Not a word of it.

CONRAD [*beaten*] Well, I suppose it's only natural. Biology is a dry subject for a girl; and I am a pretty dry old codger. [*He sits down again resignedly*].

FRANKLYN. Brother: if that is so; if biology as you have worked at it, and religion as I have worked at it, are dry subjects like the old stuff they taught under these names, and we two are dry old codgers, like the old preachers and professors, then the Gospel of the Brothers Barnabas is a delusion. Unless this withered thing religion, and this dry thing science, have come alive in our hands, alive and intensely interesting, we may just as well go out and dig the garden until it is time to dig our graves. [*The parlor maid returns. Franklyn is impatient at the interruption*]. Well? what is it now?

THE PARLOR MAID. Mr Joyce Burge on the telephone, sir. He wants to speak to you.

FRANKLYN [*astonished*] Mr Joyce Burge!

THE PARLOR MAID. Yes, sir.

FRANKLYN [*to Conrad*] What on earth does this mean? I havnt heard from him nor exchanged a word with him for years. I resigned the chairmanship of the Liberal Association and shook the dust of party politics from my feet before he was Prime Minister in the Coalition. Of course, he dropped me like a hot potato.

CONRAD. Well, now that the Coalition has chucked him out, and he is only one of the half-dozen leaders of the Opposition, perhaps he wants to pick you up again.

THE PARLOR MAID [*warningly*] He is holding the line, sir.

FRANKLYN. Yes: all right. [*He hurries out*].

The parlor maid goes to the hearthrug to make up the fire. Conrad rises and strolls to the middle of the room, where he stops and looks quizzically down at her.

CONRAD. So you have only one life to live, eh?

THE PARLOR MAID [*dropping on her knees in consternation*] I meant no offence, sir.

CONRAD. You didnt give any. But you know you could live a devil of a long life if you really wanted to.

THE PARLOR MAID [*sitting down on her heels*] Oh, dont say that, sir. It's so unsettling.

CONRAD. Why? Have you been thinking about it?

THE PARLOR MAID. It would never have come into my head if you hadnt put it there, sir. Me and cook had a look at your book.

CONRAD. What!

You and cook
Had a look
At my book!

And my niece wouldnt open it! The prophet is without honor in his own family. Well, what do you think of living for several hundred years? Are you going to have a try for it?

THE PARLOR MAID. Well, of course youre not in earnest, sir. But it does set one thinking, especially when one is going to be married.

CONRAD. What has that to do with it? He may live as long as you, you know.

THE PARLOR MAID. Thats just it, sir. You see, he must take me for better for worse, til death do us part. Do you think he would be so ready to do that, sir, if he thought it might be for several hundred years?

CONRAD. Thats true. And what about yourself?

THE PARLOR MAID. Oh, I tell you straight out, sir, I'd never promise to live with the same man as long as that. I wouldnt put up with my own children as long as that. Why, cook figured it out, sir, that when you were only 200, you might marry your own great-great-great-great-great-great-grandson and not even know who he was.

CONRAD. Well, why not? For all you know, the man you are going to marry may be your great-great-great-great-great-great-grand-mother's great-great-great-great-great-

great-grandson.

THE PARLOR MAID. But do you think it would ever be thought respectable, sir?

CONRAD. My good girl, all biological necessities have to be made respectable whether we like it or not; so you neednt worry yourself about that.

Franklyn returns and crosses the room to his chair, but does not sit down. The parlor maid goes out.

CONRAD. Well, what does Joyce Burge want?

FRANKLYN. Oh, a silly misunderstanding. I have promised to address a meeting in Middlesborough; and some fool has put it into the papers that I am "coming to Middlesborough," without any explanation. Of course, now that we are on the eve of a general election, political people think I am coming there to contest the parliamentary seat. Burge knows that I have a following, and thinks I could get into the House of Commons and head a group there. So he insists on coming to see me. He is staying with some people at Dollis Hill, and can be here in five or ten minutes, he says.

CONRAD. But didnt you tell him that it's a false alarm?

FRANKLYN. Of course I did; but he wont believe me.

CONRAD. Called you a liar, in fact?

FRANKLYN. No: I wish he had: any sort of plain speaking is better than the nauseous sham goodfellowship our democratic public men get up for shop use. He pretends to believe me, and assures me his visit is quite disinterested; but why should he come if he has no axe to grind? These chaps never believe anything they say themselves; and naturally they cannot believe anything anyone else says.

CONRAD [*rising*] Well, I shall clear out. It was hard enough to stand the party politicians before the war; but now that they have managed to half kill Europe between them, I cant be civil to them, and I dont see why I should be.

FRANKLYN. Wait a bit. We have to find out how the world will take our new gospel. [*Conrad sits down again*]. Party politicians are still unfortunately an important part of the world. Suppose we try it on Joyce Burge.

CONRAD. How can you? You can tell things only to people who can listen. Joyce Burge has talked so much that he has lost the power

of listening. He doesnt listen even in the House of Commons.

Savvy rushes in breathless, followed by Haslam, who remains timidly just inside the door.

SAVVY [*running to Franklyn*] I say! Who do you think has just driven up in a big car?

FRANKLYN. Mr Joyce Burge, perhaps.

SAVVY [*disappointed*] Oh, they know, Bill. Why didnt you tell us he was coming? I have nothing on.

HASLAM. I'd better go, hadnt I?

CONRAD. You just wait here, both of you. When you start yawning, Joyce Burge will take the hint, perhaps.

SAVVY [*to Franklyn*] May we?

FRANKLYN. Yes, if you promise to behave yourself.

SAVVY [*making a wry face*] That will be a treat, wont it?

THE PARLOR MAID [*entering and announcing*] Mr Joyce Burge. [*Haslam hastily moves to the fireplace; and the parlor maid goes out and shuts the door when the visitor has passed in*].

FRANKLYN [*hurrying past Savvy to his guest with the false cordiality he has just been denouncing*] Oh! Here you are. Delighted to see you. [*He shakes Burge's hand, and introduces Savvy*] My daughter.

SAVVY [*not daring to approach*] Very kind of you to come.

Joyce Burge stands fast and says nothing; but he screws up his cheeks into a smile at each introduction, and makes his eyes shine in a very winning manner. He is a well-fed man turned fifty, with broad forehead, and grey hair which, his neck being short, falls almost to his collar.

FRANKLYN. Mr Haslam, our rector.

Burge conveys an impression of shining like a church window; and Haslam seizes the nearest library chair on the hearth, and swings it round for Burge between the stool and Conrad. He then retires to the window seat at the other side of the room, and is joined by Savvy. They sit there, side by side, hunched up with their elbows on their knees and their chins on their hands, providing Burge with a sort of Strangers' Gallery during the ensuing sitting.

FRANKLYN. I forget whether you know my brother Conrad. He is a biologist.

BURGE [*suddenly bursting into energetic action and shaking hands heartily with Conrad*] By reputation only, but very well, of course. How I wish I could have devoted myself to biology! I have always been interested in rocks and strata and volcanoes and so forth:

they throw such a light on the age of the earth. [*With conviction*] There is nothing like biology. "The cloud-capped towers, the solemn binnacles, the gorgeous temples, the great globe itself: yea, all that it inherit shall dissolve, and, like this influential pageant faded, leave not a rack behind." Thats biology, you know: good sound biology. [*He sits down. So do the others, Franklyn on the stool, and Conrad on his Chippendale*]. Well, my dear Barnabas, what do you think of the situation? Dont you think the time has come for us to make a move?

FRANKLYN. The time has always come to make a move.

BURGE. How true! But what is the move to be? You are a man of enormous influence. We know that. Weve always known it. We have to consult you whether we like it or not. We—

FRANKLYN [*interrupting firmly*] I never meddle in party politics now.

SAVVY. It's no use saying you have no influence, daddy. Heaps of people swear by you.

BURGE [*shining at her*] Of course they do. Come! let me prove to you what we think of you. Shall we find you a first-rate constituency to contest at the next election? One that wont cost you a penny. A metropolitan seat. What do you say to the Strand?

FRANKLYN. My dear Burge, I am not a child. Why do you go on wasting your party funds on the Strand? You know you cannot win it.

BURGE. We cannot win it; but you—

FRANKLYN. Oh, please!

SAVVY. The Strand's no use, Mr Burge. I once canvassed for a Socialist there. Cheese it.

BURGE. Cheese it!

HASLAM [*spluttering with suppressed laughter*] Priceless!

SAVVY. Well, I suppose I shouldnt say cheese it to a Right Honorable. But the Strand, you know! Do come off it.

FRANKLYN. You must excuse my daughter's shocking manners, Burge; but I agree with her that popular democratic statesmen soon come to believe that everyone they speak to is an ignorant dupe and a born fool into the bargain.

BURGE [*laughing genially*] You old aristocrat, you! But believe me, the instinct of the people is sound—

CONRAD [*cutting in sharply*] Then why are you in the Opposition instead of in the Government?

BURGE [*shewing signs of temper under this heckling*] I deny that I am in the Opposition morally. The Government does not represent the country. I was chucked out of the Coalition by a Tory conspiracy. The people want me back. I dont want to go back.

FRANKLYN [*gently remonstrant*] My dear Burge: of course you do.

BURGE [*turning on him*] Not a bit of it. I want to cultivate my garden. I am not interested in politics: I am interested in roses. I havnt a scrap of ambition. I went into politics because my wife shoved me into them, bless her! But I want to serve my country. What else am I for? I want to save my country from the Tories. They dont represent the people. The man they have made Prime Minister has never represented the people; and you know it. Lord Dunreen is the bitterest old Tory left alive. What has he to offer to the people?

FRANKLYN [*cutting in before Burge can proceed—as he evidently intends—to answer his own question*] I will tell you. He has ascertainable beliefs and principles to offer. The people know where they are with Lord Dunreen. They know what he thinks right and what he thinks wrong. With your followers they never know where they are. With you they never know where they are.

BURGE [*amazed*] With me!

FRANKLYN. Well, where are you? What are you?

BURGE. Barnabas: you must be mad. You ask me what I am?

FRANKLYN. I do.

BURGE. I am, if I mistake not, Joyce Burge, pretty well known throughout Europe, and indeed throughout the world, as the man who—unworthily perhaps, but not quite unsuccessfully—held the helm when the ship of State weathered the mightiest hurricane that has ever burst with earth-shaking violence on the land of our fathers.

FRANKLYN. I know that. I know who you are. And the earth-shaking part of it to me is that though you were placed in that enormously responsible position, neither I nor anyone else knows what your beliefs are, or even whether you have either beliefs or principles. What we did know was that your Government was formed largely of men who regarded you as a robber of henroosts, and whom you regarded as enemies of the people.

BURGE [*adroitly, as he thinks*] I agree with you. I agree with you absolutely. I dont believe in coalition governments.

FRANKLYN. Precisely. Yet you formed two.

BURGE. Why? Because we were at war. That is what you fellows never would realize. The Hun was at the gate. Our country, our lives, the honor of our wives and mothers and daughters, the tender flesh of our innocent babes, were at stake. Was that a time to argue about principles?

FRANKLYN. I should say it was the time of all others to confirm the resolution of our own men and gain the confidence and support of public opinion throughout the world by a declaration of principle. Do you think the Hun would ever have come to the gate if he had known that it would be shut in his face on principle? Did he not hold his own against you until America boldly affirmed the democratic principle and came to our rescue? Why did you let America snatch that honor from England?

BURGE. Barnabas: America was carried away by words, and had to eat them at the Peace Conference. Beware of eloquence: it is the bane of popular speakers like you.

FRANKLYN [*exclaiming*] Well!!
SAVVY [*all together*] I like that!
HASLAM [*Priceless!*]

BURGE [*continuing remorselessly*] Come down to facts. It wasnt principle that won the war: it was the British fleet and the blockade. America found the talk: I found the shells. You cannot win wars by principles; but you can win elections by them. There I am with you. You want the next election to be fought on principles: that is what it comes to, doesnt it?

FRANKLYN. I dont want it to be fought at all? An election is a moral horror, as bad as a battle except for the blood: a mud bath for every soul concerned in it. You know very well that it will not be fought on principle.

BURGE. On the contrary it will be fought on nothing else. I believe a program is a mistake. I agree with you that principle is what we want.

FRANKLYN. Principle without program, eh?

BURGE. Exactly. There it is in three words.

FRANKLYN. Why not in one word? Platitudes. That is what principle without program means.

BURGE [*puzzled but patient, trying to get at Franklyn's drift in order to ascertain his price*] I have not made myself clear. Listen. I am agreeing with you. I am on your side. I am accepting your proposal. There isnt going to be any more coalition. This time there wont be a Tory in the Cabinet. Every candidate will have to pledge himself to Free Trade, slightly modified by consideration for our Overseas Dominions; to Disestablishment; to Reform of the House of Lords; to a revised scheme of Taxation of Land Values; and to doing something or other to keep the Irish quiet. Does that satisfy you?

FRANKLYN. It does not even interest me. Suppose your friends do commit themselves to all this! What does it prove about them except that they are hopelessly out of date even in party politics? that they have learnt nothing and forgotten nothing since 1885? What is it to me that they hate the Church and hate the landed gentry; that they are jealous of the nobility, and have shipping shares instead of manufacturing businesses in the Midlands? I can find you hundreds of the most sordid rascals, or the most densely stupid reactionaries, with all these qualifications.

BURGE. Personal abuse proves nothing. Do you suppose the Tories are all angels because they are all members of the Church of England?

FRANKLYN. No; but they stand together as members of the Church of England, whereas your people, in attacking the Church, are all over the shop. The supporters of the Church are of one mind about religion: its enemies are of a dozen minds. The Churchmen are a phalanx: your people are a mob in which atheists are jostled by Plymouth Brethren, and Positivists by Pillars of Fire. You have with you all the crudest unbelievers and all the crudest fanatics.

BURGE. We stand, as Cromwell did, for liberty of conscience, if that is what you mean.

FRANKLYN. How can you talk such rubbish over the graves of your conscientious objectors? All law limits liberty of conscience: if a man's conscience allows him to steal your watch or to shirk military service, how much liberty do you allow it? Liberty of conscience is not my point.

BURGE [*testily*] I wish you would come to your point. Half the time you are saying that you must have principles; and when I offer you principles you say they wont work.

FRANKLYN. You have not offered me any principles. Your party shibboleths are not principles. If you get into power again you will find yourself at the head of a rabble of Socialists and anti-Socialists, of Jingo Imperialists and Little Englanders, of cast-iron Materialists and ecstatic Quakers, of Christian Scientists and Compulsory Inoculationists, of Syndicalists and Bureaucrats: in short, of men differing fiercely and irreconcilably on every principle that goes to the root of human society and destiny; and the impossibility of keeping such a team together will force you to sell the pass again to the solid Conservative Opposition.

BURGE [rising in wrath] Sell the pass again! You accuse me of having sold the pass!

FRANKLYN. When the terrible impact of real warfare swept your parliamentary sham warfare into the dustbin, you had to go behind the backs of your followers and make a secret agreement with the leaders of the Opposition to keep you in power on condition that you dropped all legislation of which they did not approve. And you could not even hold them to their bargain; for they presently betrayed the secret and forced the coalition on you.

BURGE. I solemnly declare that this is a false and monstrous accusation.

FRANKLYN. Do you deny that the thing occurred? Were the uncontradicted reports false? Were the published letters forgeries?

BURGE. Certainly not. But I did not do it. I was not Prime Minister then. It was that old dotard, that played-out old humbug Lubin. He was Prime Minister then, not I.

FRANKLYN. Do you mean to say you did not know?

BURGE [sitting down again with a shrug] Oh, I had to be told. But what could I do? If we had refused we might have had to go out of office.

FRANKLYN. Precisely.

BURGE. Well, could we desert the country at such a crisis? The Hun was at the gate. Everyone has to make sacrifices for the sake of the country at such moments. We had to rise above party; and I am proud to say we never gave party a second thought. We stuck to—

CONRAD. Office?

BURGE [turning on him] Yes, sir, to office: that is, to responsibility, to danger, to heartsickening toil, to abuse and misunderstanding, to a martyrdom that made us envy the very soldiers in the trenches. If you had had to live for months on aspirin and bromide of potassium to get a wink of sleep, you wouldnt talk about office as if it were a catch.

FRANKLYN. Still, you admit that under our parliamentary system Lubin could not have helped himself?

BURGE. On that subject my lips are closed. Nothing will induce me to say one word against the old man. I never have; and I never will. Lubin is old: he has never been a real statesman: he is as lazy as a cat on a hearthrug: you cant get him to attend to anything: he is good for nothing but getting up and making speeches with a peroration that goes down with the back benches. But I say nothing against him. I gather that you do not think much of me as a statesman; but at all events I can get things done. I can hustle: even you will admit that. But Lubin! Oh my stars, Lubin!! If you only knew—

The parlor maid opens the door and announces a visitor.

THE PARLOR MAID. Mr Lubin.

BURGE [bounding from his chair] Lubin! Is this a conspiracy?

They all rise in amazement, staring at the door. Lubin enters: a man at the end of his sixties, a Yorkshireman with the last traces of Scandinavian flax still in his white hair, undistinguished in stature, unassuming in his manner, and taking his simple dignity for granted, but wonderfully comfortable and quite self-assured in contrast to the intellectual restlessness of Franklyn and the mesmeric self-assertiveness of Burge. His presence suddenly brings out the fact that they are unhappy men, ill at ease, square pegs in round holes, whilst he flourishes like a primrose.

The parlor maid withdraws.

LUBIN [coming to Franklyn] How do you do, Mr Barnabas? [He speaks very comfortably and kindly, much as if he were the host, and Franklyn an embarrassed but welcome guest]. I had the pleasure of meeting you once at the Mansion House. I think it was to celebrate the conclusion of the hundred years' peace with America.

FRANKLYN [shaking hands] It was long before that: a meeting about Venezuela, when we were on the point of going to war with America.

LUBIN [not at all put out] Yes: you are quite right. I knew it was something about America.

[*He pats Franklyn's hand*]. And how have you been all this time? Well, eh?

FRANKLYN [*smiling to soften the sarcasm*] A few vicissitudes of health naturally in so long a time.

LUBIN. Just so. Just so. [*Looking round at Savvy*] The young lady is—?

FRANKLYN. My daughter, Savvy.

Savvy comes from the window between her father and Lubin.

LUBIN [*taking her hand affectionately in both his*] And why has she never come to see us?

BURGE. I dont know whether you have noticed, Lubin, that I am present.

Savvy takes advantage of this diversion to slip away to the settee, where she is stealthily joined by Haslam, who sits down on her left.

LUBIN [*seating himself in Burge's chair with ineffable comfortableness*] My dear Burge: if you imagine that it is possible to be within ten miles of your energetic presence without being acutely aware of it, you do yourself the greatest injustice. How are you? And how are your good newspaper friends? [*Burge makes an explosive movement; but Lubin goes on calmly and sweetly*] And what are you doing here with my old friend Barnabas, if I may ask?

BURGE [*sitting down in Conrad's chair, leaving him standing uneasily in the corner*] Well, just what you are doing, if you want to know. I am trying to enlist Mr Barnabas's valuable support for my party.

LUBIN. Your party, eh? The newspaper party?

BURGE. The Liberal Party. The party of which I have the honor to be leader.

LUBIN. Have you now? Thats very interesting; for I thought *I* was the leader of the Liberal Party. However, it is very kind of you to take it off my hands, if the party will let you.

BURGE. Do you suggest that I have not the support and confidence of the party?

LUBIN. I dont suggest anything, my dear Burge. Mr Barnabas will tell you that we all think very highly of you. The country owes you a great deal. During the war, you did very creditably over the munitions; and if you were not quite so successful with the peace, nobody doubted that you meant well.

BURGE. Very kind of you, Lubin. Let me remark that you cannot lead a progressive party without getting a move on.

LUBIN. You mean you cannot. I did it for ten years without the least difficulty. And very comfortable, prosperous, pleasant years they were.

BURGE. Yes; but what did they end in?

LUBIN. In you, Burge. You dont complain of that, do you?

BURGE [*fiercely*] In plague, pestilence, and famine; battle, murder, and sudden death.

LUBIN [*with an appreciative chuckle*] The Nonconformist can quote the prayer-book for his own purposes, I see. How you enjoyed yourself over that business, Burge! Do you remember the Knock-Out Blow?

BURGE. It came off: dont forget that. Do you remember fighting to the last drop of your blood?

LUBIN [*unruffled, to Franklyn*] By the way, I remember your brother Conrad—a wonderful brain and a dear good fellow—explaining to me that I couldnt fight to the last drop of my blood, because I should be dead long before I came to it. Most interesting, and quite true. He was introduced to me at a meeting where the suffragettes kept disturbing me. They had to be carried out kicking and making a horrid disturbance.

CONRAD. No: it was later, at a meeting to support the Franchise Bill which gave them the vote.

LUBIN [*discovering Conrad's presence for the first time*] Youre right: it was. I knew it had something to do with women. My memory never deceives me. Thank you. Will you introduce me to this gentleman, Barnabas?

CONRAD [*not at all affably*] I am the Conrad in question. [*He sits down in dudgeon on the vacant Chippendale*].

LUBIN. Are you? [*Looking at him pleasantly*] Yes: of course you are. I never forget a face. But [*with an arch turn of his eyes to Savvy*] your pretty niece engaged all my powers of vision.

BURGE. I wish youd be serious, Lubin. God knows we have passed through times terrible enough to make any man serious.

LUBIN. I do not think I need to be reminded of that. In peace time I used to keep myself fresh for my work by banishing all worldly considerations from my mind on Sundays; but war has no respect for the Sabbath; and there have been Sundays within the last few years on which I have had to play as many as sixty-six games of bridge to keep my mind off the news from the front.

BURGE [*scandalized*] Sixty-six games of bridge on Sunday!!!

LUBIN. You probably sang sixty-six hymns. But as I cannot boast either your admirable voice or your spiritual fervor, I had to fall back on bridge.

FRANKLYN. If I may go back to the subject of your visit, it seems to me that you may both be completely superseded by the Labor Party.

BURGE. But I am in the truest sense myself a Labor leader. I— [*He stops, as Lubin has risen with a half-suppressed yawn, and is already talking calmly, but without a pretence of interest*].

LUBIN. The Labor Party! Oh no, Mr Barnabas. No, no, no, no, no. [*He moves in Savvy's direction*]. There will be no trouble about that. Of course we must give them a few seats: more, I quite admit, than we should have dreamt of leaving to them before the war; but— [*by this time he has reached the sofa where Savvy and Haslam are seated. He sits down between them; takes her hand; and drops the subject of Labor*]. Well, my dear young lady? What is the latest news? Whats going on? Have you seen Shoddy's new play? Tell me all about it, and all about the latest books, and all about everything.

SAVVY. You have not met Mr Haslam. Our Rector.

LUBIN [*who has quite overlooked Haslam*] Never heard of him. Is he any good?

FRANKLYN. I was introducing him. This is Mr Haslam.

HASLAM. How d'ye do?

LUBIN. I beg your pardon, Mr Haslam. Delighted to meet you. [*To Savvy*] Well, now, how many books have you written?

SAVVY [*rather overwhelmed but attracted*] None. I dont write.

LUBIN. You dont say so! Well, what do you do? Music? Skirt-dancing?

SAVVY. I dont do anything.

LUBIN. Thank God! You and I were born for one another. Who is your favorite poet, Sally?

SAVVY. Savvy.

LUBIN. Savvy! I never heard of him. Tell me all about him. Keep me up to date.

SAVVY. It's not a poet. *I* am Savvy, not Sally.

LUBIN. Savvy! Thats a funny name, and very pretty. Savvy. It sounds Chinese. What does it mean?

CONRAD. Short for Savage.

LUBIN [*patting her hand*] La belle Sauvage.

HASLAM [*rising and surrendering Savvy to Lubin by crossing to the fireplace*] I suppose the Church is out of it as far as progressive politics are concerned.

BURGE. Nonsense! That notion about the Church being unprogressive is one of those shibboleths that our party must drop. The Church is all right essentially. Get rid of the establishment; get rid of the bishops; get rid of the candlesticks; get rid of the 39 articles; and the Church of England is just as good as any other Church; and I dont care who hears me say so.

LUBIN. It doesnt matter a bit who hears you say so, my dear Burge. [*To Savvy*] Who did you say your favorite poet was?

SAVVY. I dont make pets of poets. Who's yours?

LUBIN. Horace.

SAVVY. Horace who?

LUBIN. Quintus Horatius Flaccus: the noblest Roman of them all, my dear.

SAVVY. Oh, if he is dead, that explains it. I have a theory that all the dead people we feel especially interested in must have been ourselves. You must be Horace's reincarnation.

LUBIN [*delighted*] That is the very most charming and penetrating and intelligent thing that has ever been said to me. Barnabas: will you exchange daughters with me? I can give you your choice of two.

FRANKLYN. Man proposes. Savvy disposes.

LUBIN. What does Savvy say?

BURGE. Lubin: I came here to talk politics.

LUBIN. Yes: you have only one subject, Burge. I came here to talk to Savvy. Take Burge into the next room, Barnabas; and let him rip.

BURGE [*half-angry, half-indulgent*] No; but really, Lubin, we are at a crisis—

LUBIN. My dear Burge, life is a disease; and the only difference between one man and another is the stage of the disease at which he lives. You are always at the crisis: I am always in the convalescent stage. I enjoy convalescence. It is the part that makes the illness worth while.

SAVVY [*half-rising*] Perhaps I'd better run away. I am distracting you.

LUBIN [*making her sit down again*] Not at all, my dear. You are only distracting Burge. Jolly good thing for him to be distracted by a pretty girl. Just what he needs.

BURGE. I sometimes envy you, Lubin. The great movement of mankind, the giant sweep of the ages, passes you by and leaves you standing.

LUBIN. It leaves me sitting, and quite comfortable, thank you. Go on sweeping. When you are tired of it, come back; and you will find England where it was, and me in my accustomed place, with Miss Savvy telling me all sorts of interesting things.

SAVVY [*who has been growing more and more restless*] Dont let him shut you up, Mr Burge. You know, Mr Lubin, I am frightfully interested in the Labor movement, and in Theosophy, and in reconstruction after the war, and all sorts of things. I daresay the flappers in your smart set are tremendously flattered when you sit beside them and are nice to them as you are being nice to me; but I am not smart; and I am no use as a flapper. I am dowdy and serious. I want you to be serious. If you refuse, I shall go and sit beside Mr Burge, and ask him to hold my hand.

LUBIN. He wouldnt know how to do it, my dear. Burge has a reputation as a profligate—

BURGE [*starting*] Lubin: this is monstrous. I—

LUBIN [*continuing*] —but he is really a model of domesticity. His name is coupled with all the most celebrated beauties; but for him there is only one woman; and that is not you, my dear, but his very charming wife.

BURGE. You are destroying my character in the act of pretending to save it. Have the goodness to confine yourself to your own character and your own wife. Both of them need all your attention.

LUBIN. I have the privilege of my age and of my transparent innocence. I have not to struggle with your volcanic energy.

BURGE [*with an immense sense of power*] No, by George!

FRANKLYN. I think I shall speak both for my brother and myself, and possibly also for my daughter, if I say that since the object of your visit and Mr Joyce Burge's is to some extent political, we should hear with great interest something about your political aims, Mr Lubin.

LUBIN [*assenting with complete good humor, and becoming attentive, clear, and businesslike in his tone*] By all means, Mr Barnabas. What we have to consider first, I take it, is what prospect there is of our finding you beside us in the House after the next election.

FRANKLYN. When I speak of politics, Mr Lubin, I am not thinking of elections, or available seats, or party funds, or the registers, or even, I am sorry to have to add, of parliament as it exists at present. I had much rather you talked about bridge than about electioneering: it is the more interesting game of the two.

BURGE. He wants to discuss principles, Lubin.

LUBIN [*very cool and clear*] I understand Mr Barnabas quite well. But elections are unsettled things: principles are settled things.

CONRAD [*impatiently*] Great Heavens!—

LUBIN [*interrupting him with quiet authority*] One moment, Dr Barnabas. The main principles on which modern civilized society is founded are pretty well understood among educated people. That is what our dangerously half-educated masses and their pet demagogues—if Burge will excuse that expression—

BURGE. Dont mind me. Go on. I shall have something to say presently.

LUBIN. —that is what our dangerously half-educated people do not realize. Take all this fuss about the Labor Party, with its imaginary new principles and new politics. The Labor members will find that the immutable laws of political economy take no more notice of their ambitions and aspirations than the law of gravitation. I speak, if I may say so, with knowledge; for I have made a special study of the Labor question.

FRANKLYN [*with interest and some surprise*] Indeed?

LUBIN. Yes. It occurred quite at the beginning of my career. I was asked to deliver an address to the students at the Working Men's College; and I was strongly advised to comply, as Gladstone and Morley and others were doing that sort of thing at the moment. It was rather a troublesome job, because I had not gone into political economy at the time. As you know, at the university I was a classical scholar; and my profession was the Law. But I looked up the text-books, and got up the case most carefully. I found that the correct view is that all this Trade Unionism and Socialism and so forth is founded on the ignorant delusion that wages and the production and distribution of wealth can be controlled by legislation or by any human action whatever. They obey fixed scientific laws, which have been ascertained and settled finally by the highest economic authorities. Naturally I do not at this distance of time remember the exact process of reasoning; but I can get up the case again at any time in a couple of days; and you may rely on me absolutely, should the occasion arise, to deal with all these ignorant and unpractical people in a conclusive and convincing way, except, of course, as far as it may be advisable to indulge and flatter them a little so as to let them down without creating ill feeling in the working-class electorate. In short, I can get that lecture up again almost at a moment's notice.

SAVVY. But, Mr Lubin, I have had a university education too; and all this about wages and distribution being fixed by immutable laws of political economy is obsolete rot.

FRANKLYN [*shocked*] Oh, my dear! That is not polite.

LUBIN. No, no, no. Dont scold her. She mustnt be scolded. [*To Savvy*] I understand. You are a disciple of Karl Marx.

SAVVY. No, no. Karl Marx's economics are all rot.

LUBIN [*at last a little taken aback*] Dear me!

SAVVY. You must excuse me, Mr Lubin; but it's like hearing a man talk about the Garden of Eden.

CONRAD. Why shouldnt he talk about the Garden of Eden? It was a first attempt at biology anyhow.

LUBIN [*recovering his self-possession*] I am sound on the Garden of Eden. I have heard of Darwin.

SAVVY. But Darwin is all rot.

LUBIN. What! Already!

SAVVY. It's no good your smiling at me like a Cheshire cat, Mr Lubin; and I am not going to sit here mumchance like an old-fashioned goody goody wife while you men monopolize the conversation and pay out the very ghastliest exploded drivel as the latest thing in politics. I am not giving you my own ideas, Mr Lubin, but just the regular orthodox science of today. Only the most awful old fossils think that Socialism is bad economics and that Darwin invented Evolution. Ask Papa. Ask Uncle. Ask the first person you meet in the street. [*She rises and crosses to Haslam*]. Give me a cigaret, Bill, will you?

HASLAM. Priceless. [*He complies*].

FRANKLYN. Savvy has not lived long enough to have any manners, Mr Lubin; but that is where you stand with the younger generation. Dont smoke, dear.

Savvy, with a shrug of rather mutinous resignation, throws the cigaret into the fire. Haslam, on the point of lighting one for himself, changes his mind.

LUBIN [*shrewd and serious*] Mr Barnabas: I confess I am surprised; and I will not pretend that I am convinced. But I am open to conviction. I may be wrong.

BURGE [*in a burst of irony*] Oh no. Impossible! Impossible!

LUBIN. Yes, Mr Barnabas, though I do not possess Burge's genius for being always wrong, I have been in that position once or twice. I could not conceal from you, even if I wished to, that my time has been so completely filled by my professional work as a lawyer, and later on by my duties as leader of the House of Commons in the days when Prime Ministers were also leaders—

BURGE [*stung*] Not to mention bridge and smart society.

LUBIN. —not to mention the continual and trying effort to make Burge behave himself, that I have not been able to keep my academic reading up to date. I have kept my classics brushed up out of sheer love for them; but my economics and my science, such as they were, may possibly be a little rusty. Yet I think I may say that if you and your brother will be so good as to put me on the track of the necessary documents, I will undertake to put the case to the House or to the country to your entire satisfaction. You see, as long as you can shew these troublesome half-educated people who want to turn the world upside down that they are talking nonsense, it really does not matter very much whether you do it in terms of what Miss Barnabas calls obsolete rot or in terms of what her granddaughter will probably call unmitigated tosh. I have no objection whatever to denounce Karl Marx. Anything I can say against Darwin will please a large body of sincerely pious voters. If it will be easier to carry on the business of the country on the understanding that the present state of things is to be called Socialism, I have no objection in the world to call it Socialism. There is the precedent of the Emperor Constantine, who saved the society of his own day by agreeing to call his Imperialism Christianity. Mind: I must not go ahead of the electorate. You must not call a voter a Socialist until—

FRANKLYN. Until he is a Socialist. Agreed.

LUBIN. Oh, not at all. You need not wait

for that. You must not call him a Socialist until he wishes to be called a Socialist: that is all. Surely you would not say that I must not address my constituents as gentlemen until they a r e gentlemen. I address them as gentlemen because they wish to be so addressed. [*He rises from the sofa and goes to Franklyn, placing a reassuring hand on his shoulder*]. Do not be afraid of Socialism, Mr Barnabas. You need not tremble for your property or your position or your dignity. England will remain what England is, no matter what new political names may come into vogue. I do not intend to resist the transition to Socialism. You may depend on me to guide it, to lead it, to give suitable expression to its aspirations, and to steer it clear of Utopian absurdities. I can honestly ask for your support on the most advanced Socialist grounds no less than on the soundest Liberal ones.

BURGE. In short, Lubin, youre incorrigible. You dont believe anything is going to change. The millions are still to toil—the people—m y people—for I am a man of the people—

LUBIN [*interrupting him contemptuously*] Dont be ridiculous, Burge. You are a country solicitor, further removed from the people, more foreign to them, more jealous of letting them up to your level, than any duke or any archbishop.

BURGE [*hotly*] I deny it. You think I have never been poor. You think I have never cleaned my own boots. You think my fingers have never come out through the soles when I was cleaning them. You think—

LUBIN. I think you fall into the very common mistake of supposing that it is poverty that makes the proletarian and money that makes the gentleman. You are quite wrong. You never belonged to the people: you belonged to the impecunious. Impecuniosity and broken boots are the lot of the unsuccessful middle class, and the commonplaces of the early struggles of the professional and younger son class. I defy you to find a farm laborer in England with broken boots. Call a mechanic one of the poor, and he'll punch your head. When you talk to your constituents about the toiling millions, they dont consider that you are referring to them. They are all third cousins of somebody with a title or a park. I am a Yorkshireman, my friend. I know England; and you dont. If you did you would know—

BURGE. What do you know that I dont know?

LUBIN. I know that we are taking up too much of Mr Barnabas's time. [*Franklyn rises*]. May I take it, my dear Barnabas, that I may count on your support if we succeed in forcing an election before the new register is in full working order?

BURGE [*rising also*] May the p a r t y count on your support? I say nothing about myself. Can the party depend on you? Is there any question of yours that I have left unanswered?

CONRAD. We havnt asked you any, you know.

BURGE. May I take that as a mark of confidence?

CONRAD. If I were a laborer in your constituency, I should ask you a biological question?

LUBIN. No you wouldnt, my dear Doctor. Laborers never ask questions.

BURGE. Ask it now. I have never flinched from being heckled. Out with it. Is it about the land?

CONRAD. No.

BURGE. Is it about the Church?

CONRAD. No.

BURGE. Is it about the House of Lords?

CONRAD. No.

BURGE. Is it about Proportional Representation?

CONRAD. No.

BURGE. Is it about Free Trade?

CONRAD. No.

BURGE. Is it about the priest in the school?

CONRAD. No.

BURGE. Is it about Ireland?

CONRAD. No.

BURGE. Is it about Germany?

CONRAD. No.

BURGE. Well, is it about Republicanism? Come! I wont flinch. Is it about the Monarchy?

CONRAD. No.

BURGE. Well, what the devil is it about, then?

CONRAD. You understand that I am asking the question in the character of a laborer who earned thirteen shillings a week before the war and earns thirty now, when he can get it?

BURGE. Yes: I understand that. I am ready for you. Out with it.

CONRAD. And whom you propose to represent in parliament?

BURGE. Yes, yes, yes. Come on.

CONRAD. The question is this. Would you allow your son to marry my daughter, or your daughter to marry my son?

BURGE [taken aback] Oh, come! Thats not a political question.

CONRAD. Then, as a biologist, I dont take the slightest interest in your politics; and I shall not walk across the street to vote for you or anyone else at the election. Good evening.

LUBIN. Serve you right, Burge! Dr Barnabas: you have my assurance that my daughter shall marry the man of her choice, whether he be lord or laborer. May I count on your support?

BURGE [hurling the epithet at him] Humbug!

SAVVY. Stop. [They all stop short in the movement of leavetaking to look at her]. Daddy: are you going to let them off like this? How are they to know anything if nobody ever tells them? If you dont, I will.

CONRAD. You cant. You didnt read my book; and you know nothing about it. You just hold your tongue.

SAVVY. I just wont, Nunk. I shall have a vote when I am thirty; and I ought to have it now. Why are these two ridiculous people to be allowed to come in and walk over us as if the world existed only to play their silly parliamentary game?

FRANKLYN [severely] Savvy: you really must not be uncivil to our guests.

SAVVY. I'm sorry. But Mr Lubin didnt stand on much ceremony with me, did he? And Mr Burge hasnt addressed a single word to me. I'm not going to stand it. You and Nunk have a much better program than either of them. It's the only one we are going to vote for; and they ought to be told about it for the credit of the family and the good of their own souls. You just tip them a chapter from the gospel of the brothers Barnabas, Daddy.

Lubin and Burge turn inquiringly to Franklyn, suspecting a move to form a new party.

FRANKLYN. It is quite true, Mr Lubin, that I and my brother have a little program of our own which—

CONRAD [interrupting] It's not a little program: it's an almighty big one. It's not our own: it's the program of the whole of civilization.

BURGE. Then why split the party before you have put it to us? For God's sake let us have no more splits. I am here to learn. I am here to gather your opinions and represent them. I invite you to put your views before me. I offer myself to be heckled. You have asked me only an absurd non-political question.

FRANKLYN. Candidly, I fear our program will be thrown away on you. It would not interest you.

BURGE [with challenging audacity] Try. Lubin can go if he likes; but I am still open to new ideas, if only I can find them.

FRANKLYN [to Lubin] Are you prepared to listen, Mr Lubin; or shall I thank you for your very kind and welcome visit, and say good evening?

LUBIN [sitting down resignedly on the settee, but involuntarily making a movement which looks like the stifling of a yawn] With pleasure, Mr Barnabas. Of course you know that before I can adopt any new plank in the party platform, it will have to reach me through the National Liberal Federation, which you can approach through your local Liberal and Radical Association.

FRANKLYN. I could recall to you several instances of the addition to your party program of measures of which no local branch of your Federation had ever dreamt. But I understand that you are not really interested. I will spare you, and drop the subject.

LUBIN [waking up a little] You quite misunderstand me. Please do not take it in that way. I only—

BURGE [talking him down] Never mind the Federation: I will answer for the Federation. Go on, Barnabas: go on. Never mind Lubin [he sits down in the chair from which Lubin first displaced him].

FRANKLYN. Our program is only that the term of human life shall be extended to three hundred years.

LUBIN [softly] Eh?

BURGE [explosively] What!

SAVVY. Our election cry is " Back to Methuselah!"

HASLAM. Priceless!

Lubin and Burge look at one another.

CONRAD. No. We are not mad.

SAVVY. Theyre not joking either. They mean it.

LUBIN [cautiously] Assuming that, in some sense which I am for the moment unable to fathom, you are in earnest, Mr Barnabas, may I ask what this has to do with politics?

FRANKLYN. The connection is very evident. You are now, Mr Lubin, within immediate reach of your seventieth year. Mr Joyce Burge is your junior by about eleven years. You will go down to posterity as one of a European group of immature statesmen and monarchs who, doing the very best for your respective countries of which you were capable, succeeded in all-but-wrecking the civilization of Europe, and did, in effect, wipe out of existence many millions of its inhabitants.

BURGE. Less than a million.

FRANKLYN. That was our loss alone.

BURGE. Oh, if you count foreigners—!

HASLAM. God counts foreigners, you know.

SAVVY [with intense satisfaction] Well said, Bill.

FRANKLYN. I am not blaming you. Your task was beyond human capacity. What with our huge armaments, our terrible engines of destruction, our systems of coercion manned by an irresistible police, you were called on to control powers so gigantic that one shudders at the thought of their being entrusted even to an infinitely experienced and benevolent God, much less to mortal men whose whole life does not last a hundred years.

BURGE. We won the war: dont forget that.

FRANKLYN. No: the soldiers and sailors won it, and left you to finish it. And you were so utterly incompetent that the multitudes of children slain by hunger in the first years of peace made us all wish we were at war again.

CONRAD. It's no use arguing about it. It is now absolutely certain that the political and social problems raised by our civilization cannot be solved by mere human mushrooms who decay and die when they are just beginning to have a glimmer of the wisdom and knowledge needed for their own government.

LUBIN. Quite an interesting idea, Doctor. Extravagant. Fantastic. But quite interesting. When I was young I used to feel my human limitations very acutely.

BURGE. God knows I have often felt that I could not go on if it had not been for the sense that I was only an instrument in the hands of a Power above us.

CONRAD. I'm glad you both agree with us, and with one another.

LUBIN. I have not gone so far as that, I think. After all, we have had many very able political leaders even within your recollection and mine.

FRANKLYN. Have you read the recent biographies—Dilke's, for instance—which revealed the truth about them?

LUBIN. I did not discover any new truth revealed in these books, Mr Barnabas.

FRANKLYN. What! Not the truth that England was governed all that time by a little woman who knew her own mind?

SAVVY. Hear, hear!

LUBIN. That often happens. Which woman do you mean?

FRANKLYN. Queen Victoria, to whom your Prime Ministers stood in the relation of naughty children whose heads she knocked together when their tempers and quarrels became intolerable. Within thirteen years of her death Europe became a hell.

BURGE. Quite true. That was because she was piously brought up, and regarded herself as an instrument. If a statesman remembers that he is only an instrument, and feels quite sure that he is rightly interpreting the divine purpose, he will come out all right, you know.

FRANKLYN. The Kaiser felt like that. Did he come out all right?

BURGE. Well, let us be fair, even to the Kaiser. Let us be fair.

FRANKLYN. Were you fair to him when you won an election on the program of hanging him?

BURGE. Stuff! I am the last man alive to hang anybody; but the people wouldnt listen to reason. Besides, I knew the Dutch wouldnt give him up.

SAVVY. Oh, dont start arguing about poor old Bill. Stick to our point. Let these two gentlemen settle the question for themselves. Mr Burge: do you think Mr Lubin is fit to govern England?

BURGE. No. Frankly, I dont.

LUBIN [remonstrant] Really!

CONRAD. Why?

BURGE. Because he has no conscience: thats why.

LUBIN. [shocked and amazed] Oh!

FRANKLYN. Mr Lubin: do you consider Joyce Burge qualified to govern England?

LUBIN [with dignified emotion, wounded, but without bitterness] Excuse me, Mr Barnabas; but before I answer that question I want to say this. Burge: we have had differences of opinion; and your newspaper friends have said hard things of me. But we worked together for years; and I hope I have done nothing to justify you in the amazing accusation you have just brought against me. Do you realize that you said that I have no conscience?

BURGE. Lubin: I am very accessible to an appeal to my emotions; and you are very cunning in making such appeals. I will meet you to this extent. I dont mean that you are a bad man. I dont mean that I dislike you, in spite of your continual attempts to discourage and depress me. But you have a mind like a looking-glass. You are very clear and smooth and lucid as to what is standing in front of you. But you have no foresight and no hindsight. You have no vision and no memory. You have no continuity; and a man without continuity can have neither conscience nor honor from one day to another. The result is that you have always been a damned bad minister; and you have sometimes been a damned bad friend. Now you can answer Barnabas's question and take it out of me to your heart's content. He asked you was I fit to govern England.

LUBIN [recovering himself] After what has just passed I sincerely wish I could honestly say yes, Burge. But it seems to me that you have condemned yourself out of your own mouth. You represent something which has had far too much influence and popularity in this country since Joseph Chamberlain set the fashion; and that is mere energy without intellect and without knowledge. Your mind is not a trained mind: it has not been stored with the best information, nor cultivated by intercourse with educated minds at any of our great seats of learning. As I happen to have enjoyed that advantage, it follows that you do not understand my mind. Candidly, I think that disqualifies you. The peace found out your weaknesses.

BURGE. Oh! What did it find out in you?

LUBIN. You and your newspaper confederates took the peace out of my hands. The peace did not find me out because it did not find me in.

FRANKLYN. Come! Confess, both of you! You were only flies on the wheel. The war went England's way; but the peace went its own way, and not England's way nor any of the ways you had so glibly appointed for it. Your peace treaty was a scrap of paper before the ink dried on it. The statesmen of Europe were incapable of governing Europe. What they needed was a couple of hundred years training and experience: what they had actually had was a few years at the bar or in a counting-house or on the grouse moors and golf courses. And now we are waiting, with monster cannons trained on every city and seaport, and huge aeroplanes ready to spring into the air and drop bombs every one of which will obliterate a whole street, and poison gases that will strike multitudes dead with a breath, until one of you gentlemen rises in his helplessness to tell us, who are as helpless as himself, that we are at war again.

CONRAD. Aha! What consolation will it be for us then that you two are able to tell off one another's defects so cleverly in your afternoon chat?

BURGE [angrily] If you come to that, what consolation will it be that you two can sit there and tell both of us off? you, who have had no responsibility! you, who havnt lifted a finger, as far as I know, to help us through this awful crisis which has left me ten years older than my proper age! Can you tell me a single thing you did to help us during the whole infernal business?

CONRAD. We're not blaming you: you hadnt lived long enough. No more had we. Cant you see that three-score-and-ten, though it may be long enough for a very crude sort of village life, isnt long enough for a complicated civilization like ours? Flinders Petrie has counted nine attempts at civilization made by people exactly like us; and every one of them failed just as ours is failing. They failed because the citizens and statesmen died of old age or over-eating before they had grown out of schoolboy games and savage sports and cigars and champagne. The signs of the end are always the same: Democracy, Socialism, and Votes for Women. We shall go to smash within the lifetime of men now living unless we recognize that we must live longer.

LUBIN. I am glad you agree with me that Socialism and Votes for Women are signs of decay.

FRANKLYN. Not at all: they are only the difficulties that overtax your capacity. If you cannot organize Socialism you cannot organize civilized life; and you will relapse into barbarism accordingly.

SAVVY. Hear, hear!

BURGE. A useful point. We cannot put back the clock.

HASLAM. I can. Ive often done it.

LUBIN. Tut tut! My dear Burge: what are you dreaming of? Mr Barnabas: I am a very patient man. But will you tell me what earthly use or interest there is in a conclusion that cannot be realized? I grant you that if we could live three hundred years we should all be, perhaps wiser, certainly older. You will grant me in return, I hope, that if the sky fell we should all catch larks.

FRANKLYN. Your turn now, Conrad. Go ahead.

CONRAD. I dont think it's any good. I dont think they want to live longer than usual.

LUBIN. Although I am a mere child of 69, I am old enough to have lost the habit of crying for the moon.

BURGE. Have you discovered the elixir of life or have you not? If not, I agree with Lubin that you are wasting our time.

CONRAD. Is your time of any value?

BURGE [unable to believe his ears] My time of any value! What do you mean?

LUBIN [smiling comfortably] From your high scientific point of view, I daresay, none whatever, Professor. In any case I think a little perfectly idle discussion would do Burge good. After all, we might as well hear about the elixir of life as read novels, or whatever Burge does when he is not playing golf on Walton Heath. What is your elixir, Dr Barnabas? Lemons? Sour milk? Or what is the latest?

BURGE. We were just beginning to talk seriously; and now you snatch at the chance of talking rot. [He rises]. Good evening. [He turns to the door].

CONRAD [rudely] Die as soon as you like. Good evening.

BURGE [hesitating] Look here. I took sour milk twice a day until Metchnikoff died. He thought it would keep him alive for ever; and he died of it.

CONRAD. You might as well have taken sour beer.

BURGE. You believe in lemons?

CONRAD. I wouldnt eat a lemon for ten pounds.

BURGE [sitting down again] What do you recommend?

CONRAD [rising with a gesture of despair] Whats the use of going on, Frank? Because I am a doctor, and because they think I have a bottle to give them that will make them live for ever, they are listening to me for the first time with their mouths open and their eyes shut. Thats their notion of science.

SAVVY. Steady, Nunk! Hold the fort.

CONRAD [growls and sits down]!!!

LUBIN. You volunteered the consultation, Doctor. I may tell you that, far from sharing the credulity as to science which is now the fashion, I am prepared to demonstrate that during the last fifty years, though the Church has often been wrong, and even the Liberal Party has not been infallible, the men of science have always been wrong.

CONRAD. Yes: the fellows you call men of science. The people who make money by it, and their medical hangers-on. But has anybody been right?

LUBIN. The poets and story tellers, especially the classical poets and story tellers, have been, in the main, right. I will ask you not to repeat this as my opinion outside; for the vote of the medical profession and its worshippers is not to be trifled with.

FRANKLYN. You are quite right: the poem is our real clue to biological science. The most scientific document we possess at present is, as your grandmother would have told you quite truly, the story of the Garden of Eden.

BURGE [pricking up his ears] Whats that? If you can establish that, Barnabas, I am prepared to hear you out with my very best attention. I am listening. Go on.

FRANKLYN. Well, you remember, dont you, that in the Garden of Eden Adam and Eve were not created mortal, and that natural death, as we call it, was not a part of life, but a later and quite separate invention?

BURGE. Now you mention it, thats true. Death came afterwards.

LUBIN. What about accidental death? That was always possible.

FRANKLYN. Precisely. Adam and Eve were hung up between two frightful possibilities. One was the extinction of mankind by their accidental death. The other was the prospect of living for ever. They could bear neither. They decided that they would just take a short turn of a thousand years, and meanwhile hand on their work to a new pair. Consequently, they had to invent natural birth and natural death, which are, after all, only modes of perpetuating life without putting on any single creature the terrible burden of immortality.

LUBIN. I see. The old must make room for the new.

BURGE. Death is nothing but making room.

Thats all there is in it or ever has been in it.

FRANKLYN. Yes; but the old must not desert their posts until the new are ripe for them. They desert them now two hundred years too soon.

SAVVY. I believe the old people are the new people reincarnated, Nunk. I suspect I am Eve. I am very fond of apples; and they always disagree with me.

CONRAD. You are Eve, in a sense. The Eternal Life persists; only It wears out Its bodies and minds and gets new ones, like new clothes. You are only a new hat and frock on Eve.

FRANKLYN. Yes. Bodies and minds ever better and better fitted to carry out Its eternal pursuit.

LUBIN [with quiet scepticism] What pursuit, may one ask, Mr Barnabas?

FRANKLYN. The pursuit of omnipotence and omniscience. Greater power and greater knowledge: these are what we are all pursuing even at the risk of our lives and the sacrifice of our pleasures. Evolution is that pursuit and nothing else. It is the path to godhead. A man differs from a microbe only in being further on the path.

LUBIN. And how soon do you expect this modest end to be reached?

FRANKLYN. Never, thank God! As there is no limit to power and knowledge there can be no end. "The power and the glory, world without end": have those words meant nothing to you?

BURGE [pulling out an old envelope] I should like to make a note of that. [He does so].

CONRAD. There will always be something to live for.

BURGE [pocketing his envelope and becoming more and more businesslike] Right: I have got that. Now what about sin? What about the Fall? How do you work them in?

CONRAD. I dont work in the Fall. The Fall is outside Science. But I daresay Frank can work it in for you.

BURGE [to Franklyn] I wish you would, you know. It's important. Very important.

FRANKLYN. Well, consider it this way. It is clear that when Adam and Eve were immortal it was necessary that they should make the earth an extremely comfortable place to live in.

BURGE. True. If you take a house on a ninety-nine years lease, you spend a good deal of money on it. If you take it for three months you generally have a bill for dilapidations to pay at the end of them.

FRANKLYN. Just so. Consequently, when Adam had the Garden of Eden on a lease for ever, he took care to make it what the house agents call a highly desirable country residence. But the moment he invented death, and became a tenant for life only, the place was no longer worth the trouble. It was then that he let the thistles grow. Life was so short that it was no longer worth his while to do anything thoroughly well.

BURGE. Do you think that is enough to constitute what an average elector would consider a Fall? Is it tragic enough?

FRANKLYN. That is only the first step of the Fall. Adam did not fall down that step only: he fell down a whole flight. For instance, before he invented birth he dared not have lost his temper; for if he had killed Eve he would have been lonely and barren to all eternity. But when he invented birth, and anyone who was killed could be replaced, he could afford to let himself go. He undoubtedly invented wife-beating; and that was another step down. One of his sons invented meat-eating. The other was horrified at the innovation. With the ferocity which is still characteristic of bulls and other vegetarians, he slew his beefsteak-eating brother, and thus invented murder. That was a very steep step. It was so exciting that all the others began to kill one another for sport, and thus invented war, the steepest step of all. They even took to killing animals as a means of killing time, and then, of course, ate them to save the long and difficult labor of agriculture. I ask you to contemplate our fathers as they came crashing down all the steps of this Jacob's ladder that reached from paradise to a hell on earth in which they had multiplied the chances of death from violence, accident, and disease until they could hardly count on three score and ten years of life, much less the thousand that Adam had been ready to face! With that picture before you, will you now ask me where was the Fall? You might as well stand at the foot of Snowdon and ask me where is the mountain. The very children see it so plainly that they compress its history into a two line epic:

Old Daddy Long Legs wouldnt say his
      prayers:
Take him by the hind legs and throw him
      downstairs.

LUBIN [*still immovably sceptical*] And what does Science say to this fairy tale, Doctor Barnabas? Surely Science knows nothing of Genesis, or of Adam and Eve.

CONRAD. Then it isnt Science: thats all. Science has to account for everything; and everything includes the Bible.

FRANKLYN. The Book of Genesis is a part of nature like any other part of nature. The fact that the tale of the Garden of Eden has survived and held the imagination of men spellbound for centuries, whilst hundreds of much more plausible and amusing stories have gone out of fashion and perished like last year's popular song, is a scientific fact; and Science is bound to explain it. You tell me that Science knows nothing of it. Then Science is more ignorant than the children at any village school.

CONRAD. Of course if you think it more scientific to say that what we are discussing is not Adam and Eve and Eden, but the phylogeny of the blastoderm—

SAVVY. You neednt swear, Nunk.

CONRAD. Shut up, you: I am not swearing. [*To Lubin*] If you want the professional humbug of rewriting the Bible in words of four syllables, and pretending it's something new, I can humbug you to your heart's content. I can call Genesis Phylogenesis. Let the Creator say, if you like, "I will establish an antipathetic symbiosis between thee and the female, and between thy blastoderm and her blastoderm." Nobody will understand you; and Savvy will think you are swearing. The meaning is the same.

HASLAM. Priceless. But it's quite simple. The one version is poetry: the other is science.

FRANKLYN. The one is classroom jargon: the other is inspired human language.

LUBIN [*calmly reminiscent*] One of the few modern authors into whom I have occasionally glanced is Rousseau, who was a sort of Deist like Burge—

BURGE [*interrupting him forcibly*] Lubin: has this stupendously important communication which Professor Barnabas has just made to us: a communication for which I shall be indebted to him all my life long: has this, I say, no deeper effect on you than to set you pulling my leg by trying to make out that I am an infidel.

LUBIN. It's very interesting and amusing, Burge; and I think I see a case in it. I think I could undertake to argue it in an ecclesias-tical court. But important is hardly a word I should attach to it.

BURGE. Good God! Here is this professor: a man utterly removed from the turmoil of our political life: devoted to pure learning in its most abstract phases; and I solemnly declare he is the greatest politician, the most inspired party leader, in the kingdom. I take off my hat to him. I, Joyce Burge, give him best. And you sit there purring like an Angora cat, and can see nothing in it!

CONRAD [*opening his eyes widely*] Hallo! What have I done to deserve this tribute?

BURGE. Done! You have put the Liberal Party into power for the next thirty years, Doctor: thats what youve done.

CONRAD. God forbid!

BURGE. It's all up with the Church now. Thanks to you, we go to the country with one cry and one only: Back to the Bible! Think of the effect on the Nonconformist vote. You gather that in with one hand; and you gather in the modern scientific sceptical professional vote with the other. The village atheist and the first cornet in the local Salvation Army band meet on the village green and shake hands. You take your school children, your Bible class under the Cowper-Temple clause, into the museum. You shew the kids the Piltdown skull; and you say, "Thats Adam. Thats Eve's husband." You take the spectacled science student from the laboratory in Owens College; and when he asks you for a truly scientific history of Evolution, you put into his hand The Pilgrim's Progress. You— [*Savvy and Haslam explode into shrieks of merriment*]. What are you two laughing at?

SAVVY. Oh, go on, Mr Burge. Dont stop.

HASLAM. Priceless!

FRANKLYN. Would thirty years of office for the Liberal Party seem so important to you, Mr Burge, if you had another two and a half centuries to live?

BURGE [*decisively*] No. You will have to drop that part of it. The constituencies wont swallow it.

LUBIN [*seriously*] I am not so sure of that, Burge. I am not sure that it may not prove the only point they will swallow.

BURGE. It will be no use to us even if they do. It's not a party point. It's as good for the other side as for us.

LUBIN. Not necessarily. If we get in first with it, it will be associated in the public mind with our party. Suppose I put it forward as a plank in our program that we advocate the extension of human life to three hundred years! Dunreen, as leader of the opposite party, will be bound to oppose me: to denounce me as a visionary and so forth. By doing so he will place himself in the position of wanting to rob the people of two hundred and thirty years of their natural life. The Unionists will become the party of Premature Death; and we shall become the Longevity party.

BURGE [*shaken*] You really think the electorate would swallow it?

LUBIN. My dear Burge: is there anything the electorate will not swallow if it is judiciously put to them? But we must make sure of our ground. We must have the support of the men of science. Is there serious agreement among them, Doctor, as to the possibility of such an evolution as you have described?

CONRAD. Yes. Ever since the reaction against Darwin set in at the beginning of the present century, all scientific opinion worth counting has been converging rapidly upon Creative Evolution.

FRANKLYN. Poetry has been converging on it: philosophy has been converging on it: religion has been converging on it. It is going to be the religion of the twentieth century: a religion that has its intellectual roots in philosophy and science just as medieval Christianity had its intellectual roots in Aristotle.

LUBIN. But surely any change would be so extremely gradual that—

CONRAD. Dont deceive yourself. It's only the politicians who improve the world so gradually that nobody can see the improvement. The notion that Nature does not proceed by jumps is only one of the budget of plausible lies that we call classical education. Nature always proceeds by jumps. She may spend twenty thousand years making up her mind to jump; but when she makes it up at last, the jump is big enough to take us into a new age.

LUBIN [*impressed*] Fancy my being leader of the party for the next three hundred years!

BURGE. What!!!

LUBIN. Perhaps hard on some of the younger men. I think in fairness I shall have to step aside to make room after another century or so: that is, if Mimi can be persuaded to give up Downing Street.

BURGE. This is too much. Your colossal conceit blinds you to the most obvious necessity of the political situation.

LUBIN. You mean my retirement. I really cannot see that it is a necessity. I could not see it when I was almost an old man—or at least an elderly one. Now that it appears that I am a young man, the case for it breaks down completely. [*To Conrad*] May I ask are there any alternative theories? Is there a scientific Opposition?

CONRAD. Well, some authorities hold that the human race is a failure, and that a new form of life, better adapted to high civilization, will supersede us as we have superseded the ape and the elephant.

BURGE. The superman: eh?

CONRAD. No. Some being quite different from us.

LUBIN. Is that altogether desirable?

FRANKLYN. I fear so. However that may be, we may be quite sure of one thing. We shall not be let alone. The force behind evolution, call it what you will, is determined to solve the problem of civilization; and if it cannot do it through us, it will produce some more capable agents. Man is not God's last word: God can still create. If you cannot do His work He will produce some being who can.

BURGE [*with zealous reverence*] What do we know about Him, Barnabas? What does anyone know about Him?

CONRAD. We know this about Him with absolute certainty. The power my brother calls God proceeds by the method of Trial and Error; and if we turn out to be one of the errors, we shall go the way of the mastodon and the megatherium and all the other scrapped experiments.

LUBIN [*rising and beginning to walk up and down the room with his considering cap on*] I admit that I am impressed, gentlemen. I will go so far as to say that your theory is likely to prove more interesting than ever Welsh Disestablishment was. But as a practical politician—hm! Eh, Burge?

CONRAD. We are not practical politicians. We are out to get something done. Practical politicians are people who have mastered the art of using parliament to prevent anything being done.

FRANKLYN. When we get matured statesmen and citizens—

LUBIN [*stopping short*] Citizens! Oh! Are the

citizens to live three hundred years as well as the statesmen?

CONRAD. Of course.

LUBIN. I confess that had not occurred to me [*he sits down abruptly, evidently very unfavorably affected by this new light*].

Savvy and Haslam look at one another with unspeakable feelings.

BURGE. Do you think it would be wise to go quite so far at first? Surely it would be more prudent to begin with the best men.

FRANKLYN. You need not be anxious about that. It will begin with the best men.

LUBIN. I am glad to hear you say so. You see, we must put this into a practical parliamentary shape.

BURGE. We shall have to draft a Bill: that is the long and the short of it. Until you have your Bill drafted you dont know what you are really doing: that is my experience.

LUBIN. Quite so. My idea is that whilst we should interest the electorate in this as a sort of religious aspiration and personal hope, using it at the same time to remove their prejudices against those of us who are getting on in years, it would be in the last degree upsetting and even dangerous to enable everyone to live longer than usual. Take the mere question of the manufacture of the specific, whatever it may be! There are forty millions of people in the country. Let me assume for the sake of illustration that each person would have to consume, say, five ounces a day of the elixir. That would be— let me see—five times three hundred and sixty-five is—um—twenty-five—thirty-two —eighteen—eighteen hundred and twenty-five ounces a year: just two ounces over the hundredweight.

BURGE. Two million tons a year, in round numbers, of stuff that everyone would clamor for: that men would trample down women and children in the streets to get at. You couldnt produce it. There would be blue murder. It's out of the question. We must keep the actual secret to ourselves.

CONRAD [*staring at them*] The actual secret! What on earth is the man talking about?

BURGE. The stuff. The powder. The bottle. The tabloid. Whatever it is. You said it wasnt lemons.

CONRAD. My good sir: I have no powder, no bottle, no tabloid. I am not a quack: I am a biologist. This is a thing thats going to happen.

LUBIN [*completely let down*] Going to happen! Oh! Is that all? [*He looks at his watch*].

BURGE. Going to happen! What do you mean? Do you mean that you cant make it happen?

CONRAD. No more than I could have made you happen.

FRANKLYN. We can put it into men's heads that there is nothing to prevent its happening but their own will to die before their work is done, and their own ignorance of the splendid work there is for them to do.

CONRAD. Spread that knowledge and that conviction; and as surely as the sun will rise tomorrow, the thing will happen.

FRANKLYN. We dont know where or when or to whom it will happen. It may happen first to someone in this room.

HASLAM. It wont happen to me: thats jolly sure.

CONRAD. It might happen to anyone. It might happen to the parlormaid. How do we know?

SAVVY. The parlormaid! Oh, thats nonsense, Nunk.

LUBIN [*once more quite comfortable*] I think Miss Savvy has delivered the final verdict.

BURGE. Do you mean to say that you have nothing more practical to offer than the mere wish to live longer? Why, if people could live by merely wishing to, we should all be living for ever already! Everybody would like to live for ever. Why dont they?

CONRAD. Pshaw! Everybody would like to have a million of money. Why havnt they? Because the men who would like to be millionaires wont save sixpence even with the chance of starvation staring them in the face. The men who want to live for ever wont cut off a glass of beer or a pipe of tobacco, though they believe the teetotallers and non-smokers live longer. That sort of liking is not willing. See what they do when they know they must.

FRANKLYN. Do not mistake mere idle fancies for the tremendous miracle-working force of Will nerved to creation by a conviction of Necessity. I tell you men capable of such willing, and realizing its necessity, will do it reluctantly, under inner compulsion, as all great efforts are made. They will hide what they are doing from themselves: they will take care not to know what they are doing. They will live three hundred years, not because they would like to, but because the soul deep down in them will know that they must, if the world is to be saved.

LUBIN [*turning to Franklyn and patting him almost paternally*] Well, my dear Barnabas, for the last thirty years the post has brought me at least once a week a plan from some crank or other for the establishment of the millennium. I think you are the maddest of all the cranks; but you are much the most interesting. I am conscious of a very curious mixture of relief and disappointment in finding that your plan is all moonshine, and that you have nothing practical to offer us. But what a pity! It is such a fascinating idea! I think you are too hard on us practical men; but there are men in every Government, even on the Front Bench, who deserve all you say. And now, before dropping the subject, may I put just one question to you? An idle question, since nothing can come of it; but still—

FRANKLYN. Ask your question.

LUBIN. Why do you fix three hundred years as the exact figure?

FRANKLYN. Because we must fix some figure. Less would not be enough; and more would be more than we dare as yet face.

LUBIN. Pooh! I am quite prepared to face three thousand, not to say three million.

CONRAD. Yes, because you dont believe you will be called on to make good your word.

FRANKLYN [*gently*] Also, perhaps, because you have never been troubled much by visions of the future.

BURGE [*with intense conviction*] The future does not exist for Henry Hopkins Lubin.

LUBIN. If by the future you mean the millennial delusions which you use as a bunch of carrots to lure the uneducated British donkey to the polling booth to vote for you, it certainly does not.

BURGE. I can see the future not only because, if I may say so in all humility, I have been gifted with a certain power of spiritual vision, but because I have practised as a solicitor. A solicitor has to advise families. He has to think of the future and know the past. His office is the real modern confessional. Among other things he has to make people's wills for them. He has to shew them how to provide for their daughters after their deaths. Has it occurred to you, Lubin, that if you live three hundred years, your daughters will have to wait a devilish long time for their money?

FRANKLYN. The money may not wait for them. Few investments flourish for three hundred years.

SAVVY. And what about before your death? Suppose they didnt get married! Imagine a girl living at home with her mother and on her father for three hundred years! Theyd murder her if she didnt murder them first.

LUBIN. By the way, Barnabas, is your daughter to keep her good looks all the time?

FRANKLYN. Will it matter? Can you conceive the most hardened flirt going on flirting for three centuries? At the end of half the time we shall hardly notice whether it is a woman or a man we are speaking to.

LUBIN [*not quite relishing this ascetic prospect*] Hm! [*He rises*] Ah, well: you must come and tell my wife and my young people all about it; and you will bring your daughter with you, of course. [*He shakes hands with Savvy*]. Goodbye. [*He shakes hands with Franklyn*]. Goodbye, Doctor. [*He shakes hands with Conrad*]. Come on, Burge: you must really tell me what line you are going to take about the Church at the election?

BURGE. Havnt you heard? Havnt you taken in the revelation that has been vouchsafed to us? The line I am going to take is Back to Methuselah.

LUBIN [*decisively*] Dont be ridiculous, Burge. You dont suppose, do you, that our friends here are in earnest, or that our very pleasant conversation has had anything to do with practical politics! They have just been pulling our legs very wittily. Come along. [*He goes out, Franklyn politely going with him, but shaking his head in mute protest*].

BURGE [*shaking Conrad's hand*] It's beyond the old man, Doctor. No spiritual side to him: only a sort of classical side that goes down with his own set. Besides, he's done, gone, past, burnt out, burst up; thinks he is our leader and is only our rag and bottle department. But you may depend on me. I will work this stunt of yours in. I see its value. [*He begins moving towards the door with Conrad*]. Of course I cant put it exactly in your way; but you are quite right about our needing something fresh; and I believe an election can be fought on the death rate and on Adam and Eve as scientific facts. It will take the Opposition right out of its depth. And if we win there will be an O.M. for somebody when the first honors list comes round [*by this time he has talked himself out of the room and out of earshot, Conrad accompanying him*].

Savvy and Haslam, left alone, seize each other in an ecstasy of amusement, and jazz to the settee, where they sit down again side by side.

HASLAM [*caressing her*] Darling! What a priceless humbug old Lubin is!

SAVVY. Oh, sweet old thing! I love him. Burge is a flaming fraud if you like.

HASLAM. Did you notice one thing? It struck me as rather curious.

SAVVY. What?

HASLAM. Lubin and your father have both survived the war. But their sons were killed in it.

SAVVY [*sobered*] Yes. Jim's death killed mother.

HASLAM. And they never said a word about it!

SAVVY. Well, why should they? The subject didnt come up. *I* forgot about it too; and I was very fond of Jim.

HASLAM. *I* didnt forget it, because I'm of military age; and if I hadnt been a parson I'd have had to go out and be killed too. To me the awful thing about their political incompetence was that they had to kill their own sons. It was the war casualty lists and the starvation afterwards that finished me up with politics and the Church and everything else except you.

SAVVY. Oh, I was just as bad as any of them. I sold flags in the streets in my best clothes; and—hsh! [*she jumps up and pretends to be looking for a book on the shelves behind the settee*].

Franklyn and Conrad return, looking weary and glum.

CONRAD. Well, thats how the gospel of the brothers Barnabas is going to be received! [*He drops into Burge's chair*].

FRANKLYN [*going back to his seat at the table*] It's no use. Were y o u convinced, Mr Haslam?

HASLAM. About our being able to live three hundred years? Frankly no.

CONRAD [*to Savvy*] Nor you, I suppose?

SAVVY. Oh, I dont know. I thought I was for a moment. I can believe, in a sort of way, that p e o p l e might live for three hundred years. But when you came down to tin tacks, and said that the parlormaid might, then I saw how absurd it was.

FRANKLYN. Just so. We had better hold our tongues about it, Con. We should only be laughed at, and lose the little credit we earned on false pretences in the days of our ignorance.

CONRAD. I daresay. But Creative Evolution doesnt stop while people are laughing. Laughing may even lubricate its job.

SAVVY. What does that mean?

CONRAD. It means that the first man to live three hundred years maynt have the slightest notion that he is going to do it, and may be the loudest laugher of the lot.

SAVVY. Or the first woman?

CONRAD [*assenting*] Or the first woman.

HASLAM. Well, it wont be one of us, anyhow.

FRANKLYN. How do you know?

This is unanswerable. None of them have anything more to say.

PART III
THE THING HAPPENS

A Summer afternoon in the year 2170 A.D. The official parlor of the President of the British Islands. A board table, long enough for three chairs at each side besides the presidential chair at the head and an ordinary chair at the foot, occupies the breadth of the room. On the table, opposite every chair, a small switchboard with a dial. There is no fireplace. The end wall is a silvery screen nearly as large as a pair of folding doors. The door is on your left as you face the screen; and there is a row of thick pegs, padded and covered with velvet, beside it.

A stoutish middle-aged man, good-looking and breezily genial, dressed in a silk smock, stockings, handsomely ornamented sandals, and a gold fillet round his brows, comes in. He is like Joyce Burge, yet also like Lubin, as if Nature had made a composite photograph of the two men. He takes off the fillet and hangs it on a peg; then sits down in the presidential chair at the head of the table, which is at the end farthest from the door. He puts a peg into his switchboard; turns the pointer on the dial; puts another peg in; and presses a button. Immediately the silvery screen vanishes; and in its place appears, in reverse from right to left, another office similarly furnished, with a thin, unamiable man similarly dressed, but in duller colors, turning over some documents at the table. His gold fillet is hanging up on a similar peg beside the door. He is rather like Conrad Barnabas, but younger, and much more commonplace.

BURGE-LUBIN. Hallo, Barnabas!

BARNABAS [*without looking round*] What number?

BURGE-LUBIN. Five double x three two gamma. Burge-Lubin.

Barnabas puts a plug in number five; turns his pointer to double x; puts another plug in 32; presses a button and looks round at Burge-Lubin, who is now visible to him as well as audible.

BARNABAS [*curtly*] Oh! That you, President?

BURGE-LUBIN. Yes. They told me you wanted me to ring you up. Anything wrong?

BARNABAS [*harsh and querulous*] I wish to make a protest.

BURGE-LUBIN [*good-humored and mocking*] What! Another protest! Whats wrong now?

BARNABAS. If you only knew all the protests I havnt made, you would be surprised at my patience. It is you who are always treating me with the grossest want of consideration.

BURGE-LUBIN. What have I done now?

BARNABAS. You have put me down to go to the Record Office today to receive that American fellow, and do the honors of a ridiculous cinema show. That is not the business of the Accountant General: it is the business of the President. It is an outrageous waste of my time, and an unjustifiable shirking of your duty at my expense. I refuse to go. You must go.

BURGE-LUBIN. My dear boy, nothing would give me greater pleasure than to take the job off your hands—

BARNABAS. Then do it. Thats all I want [*he is about to switch off*].

BURGE-LUBIN. Dont switch off. Listen. This American has invented a method of breathing under water.

BARNABAS. What do I care? I dont want to breathe under water.

BURGE-LUBIN. You may, my dear Barnabas, at any time. You know you never look where you are going when you are immersed in your calculations. Some day you will walk into the Serpentine. This man's invention may save your life.

BARNABAS [*angrily*] Will you tell me what that has to do with your putting your ceremonial duties on to my shoulders? I will not be trifled [*he vanishes and is replaced by the blank screen*]—

BURGE-LUBIN [*indignantly holding down his button*] Dont cut us off, please: we have not finished. I am the President, speaking to the Accountant General. What are you dreaming of?

A WOMAN'S VOICE. Sorry. [*The screen shews Barnabas as before*].

BURGE-LUBIN. Since you take it that way, I will go in your place. It's a pity, because, you see, this American thinks you are the greatest living authority on the duration of human life; and—

BARNABAS [*interrupting*] The American thinks! What do you mean? I am the greatest living authority on the duration of human life. Who dares dispute it?

BURGE-LUBIN. Nobody, dear lad, nobody. Dont fly out at me. It is evident that you have not read the American's book.

BARNABAS. Dont tell me that you have, or that you have read any book except a novel for the last twenty years; for I wont believe you.

BURGE-LUBIN. Quite right, dear old fellow: I havnt read it. But I have read what The Times Literary Supplement says about it.

BARNABAS. I dont care two straws what it says about it. Does it say anything about me?

BURGE-LUBIN. Yes.

BARNABAS. Oh, does it? What?

BURGE-LUBIN. It points out that an extraordinary number of first-rate persons like you and me have died by drowning during the last two centuries, and that when this invention of breathing under water takes effect, your estimate of the average duration of human life will be upset.

BARNABAS [*alarmed*] Upset my estimate! Gracious Heavens! Does the fool realize what that means? Do you realize what that means?

BURGE-LUBIN. I suppose it means that we shall have to amend the Act.

BARNABAS. Amend my Act! Monstrous!

BURGE-LUBIN. But we must. We cant ask people to go on working until they are forty-three unless our figures are unchallengeable. You know what a row there was over those last three years, and how nearly the too-old-at-forty people won.

BARNABAS. They would have made the British Islands bankrupt if theyd won. But you dont care for that: you care for nothing but being popular.

BURGE-LUBIN. Oh, well: I shouldnt worry if I were you; for most people complain that there is not enough work for them, and would be only too glad to stick on instead of retiring at forty-three if only they were asked as a favor instead of having to.

BARNABAS. Thank you: I need no consolation. [*He rises determinedly and puts on his fillet*].

BURGE-LUBIN. Are you off? Where are you going to?

BARNABAS. To that cinema tomfoolery, of course. I shall put this American impostor in his place. [*He goes out*].

BURGE-LUBIN [*calling after him*] God bless you, dear old chap! [*With a chuckle, he switches off; and the screen becomes blank. He presses a button and holds it down while he calls*] Hallo!

A WOMAN'S VOICE. Hallo!

BURGE-LUBIN [*formally*] The President respectfully solicits the privilege of an interview with the Chief Secretary, and holds himself entirely at his honor's august disposal.

A CHINESE VOICE. He is coming.

BURGE-LUBIN. Oh! That you, Confucius? So good of you. Come along [*he releases the button*].

A man in a yellow gown, presenting the general appearance of a Chinese sage, enters.

BURGE-LUBIN [*jocularly*] Well, illustrious Sage-&-Onions, how are your poor sore feet?

CONFUCIUS [*gravely*] I thank you for your kind inquiries. I am well.

BURGE-LUBIN. Thats right. Sit down and make yourself comfortable. Any business for me today?

CONFUCIUS [*sitting down on the first chair round the corner of the table to the President's right*] None.

BURGE-LUBIN. Have you heard the result of the bye-election?

CONFUCIUS. A walk-over. Only one candidate.

BURGE-LUBIN. Any good?

CONFUCIUS. He was released from the County Lunatic Asylum a fortnight ago. Not mad enough for the lethal chamber: not sane enough for any place but the division lobby. A very popular speaker.

BURGE-LUBIN. I wish the people would take a serious interest in politics.

CONFUCIUS. I do not agree. The Englishman is not fitted by nature to understand politics. Ever since the public services have been manned by Chinese, the country has been well and honestly governed. What more is needed?

BURGE-LUBIN. What I cant make out is that China is one of the worst governed countries on earth.

CONFUCIUS. No. It was badly governed twenty years ago; but since we forbade any Chinaman to take part in our public services,

and imported natives of Scotland for that purpose, we have done well. Your information here is always twenty years out of date.

BURGE-LUBIN. People dont seem to be able to govern themselves. I cant understand it. Why should it be so?

CONFUCIUS. Justice is impartiality. Only strangers are impartial.

BURGE-LUBIN. It ends in the public services being so good that the Government has nothing to do but think.

CONFUCIUS. Were it otherwise, the Government would have too much to do to think.

BURGE-LUBIN. Is that any excuse for the English people electing a parliament of lunatics?

CONFUCIUS. The English people always did elect parliaments of lunatics. What does it matter if your permanent officials are honest and competent?

BURGE-LUBIN. You do not know the history of this country. What would my ancestors have said to the menagerie of degenerates that is still called the House of Commons? Confucius: you will not believe me; and I do not blame you for it; but England once saved the liberties of the world by inventing parliamentary government, which was her peculiar and supreme glory.

CONFUCIUS. I know the history of your country perfectly well. It proves the exact contrary.

BURGE-LUBIN. How do you make that out?

CONFUCIUS. The only power your parliament ever had was the power of withholding supplies from the king.

BURGE-LUBIN. Precisely. That great Englishman Simon de Montfort—

CONFUCIUS. He was not an Englishman: he was a Frenchman. He imported parliaments from France.

BURGE-LUBIN [*surprised*] You dont say so!

CONFUCIUS. The king and his loyal subjects killed Simon for forcing his French parliament on them. The first thing British parliaments always did was to grant supplies to the king for life with enthusiastic expressions of loyalty, lest they should have any real power, and be expected to do something.

BURGE-LUBIN. Look here, Confucius: you know more history than I do, of course; but democracy—

CONFUCIUS. An institution peculiar to China. And it was never really a success there.

BURGE-LUBIN. But the Habeas Corpus Act!

CONFUCIUS. The English always suspended it when it threatened to be of the slightest use.

BURGE-LUBIN. Well, trial by jury: you cant deny that we established that?

CONFUCIUS. All cases that were dangerous to the governing classes were tried in the Star Chamber or by Court Martial, except when the prisoner was not tried at all, but executed after calling him names enough to make him unpopular.

BURGE-LUBIN. Oh, bother! You may be right in these little details; but in the large we have managed to hold our own as a great race. Well, people who could do nothing couldnt have done that, you know.

CONFUCIUS. I did not say you could do nothing. You could fight. You could eat. You could drink. Until the twentieth century you could produce children. You could play games. You could work when you were forced to. But you could not govern yourselves.

BURGE-LUBIN. Then how did we get our reputation as the pioneers of liberty?

CONFUCIUS. By your steadfast refusal to be governed at all. A horse that kicks everyone who tries to harness and guide him may be a pioneer of liberty; but he is not a pioneer of government. In China he would be shot.

BURGE-LUBIN. Stuff! Do you imply that the administration of which I am president is no Government?

CONFUCIUS. I do. _I_ am the Government.

BURGE-LUBIN. You! You!! You fat yellow lump of conceit!

CONFUCIUS. Only an Englishman could be so ignorant of the nature of government as to suppose that a capable statesman cannot be fat, yellow, and conceited. Many Englishmen are slim, red-nosed, and modest. Put them in my place, and within a year you will be back in the anarchy and chaos of the nineteenth and twentieth centuries.

BURGE-LUBIN. Oh, if you go back to the dark ages, I have nothing more to say. But we did not perish. We extricated ourselves from that chaos. We are now the best governed country in the world. How did we manage that if we are such fools as you pretend?

CONFUCIUS. You did not do it until the slaughter and ruin produced by your anarchy forced you at last to recognize two inexorable facts. First, that government is absolutely necessary to civilization, and that you could not maintain civilization by merely doing down your neighbor, as you called it, and cutting off the head of your king whenever he happened to be a logical Scot and tried to take his position seriously. Second, that government is an art of which you are congenitally incapable. Accordingly, you imported educated negresses and Chinese to govern you. Since then you have done very well.

BURGE-LUBIN. So have you, you old humbug. All the same, I dont know how you stand the work you do. You seem to me positively to like public business. Why wont you let me take you down to the coast some week-end and teach you marine golf?

CONFUCIUS. It does not interest me. I am not a barbarian.

BURGE-LUBIN. You mean that I am?

CONFUCIUS. That is evident.

BURGE-LUBIN. How?

CONFUCIUS. People like you. They like cheerful good-natured barbarians. They have elected you President five times in succession. They will elect you five times more. _I_ like you. You are better company than a dog or a horse because you can speak.

BURGE-LUBIN. Am I a barbarian because you like me?

CONFUCIUS. Surely. Nobody likes me: I am held in awe. Capable persons are never liked. I am not likeable; but I am indispensable.

BURGE-LUBIN. Oh, cheer up, old man: theres nothing so disagreeable about you as all that. I dont dislike you; and if you think I'm afraid of you, you jolly well dont know Burge-Lubin: thats all.

CONFUCIUS. You are brave: yes. It is a form of stupidity.

BURGE-LUBIN. You may not be brave: one doesnt expect it from a Chink. But you have the devil's own cheek.

CONFUCIUS. I have the assured certainty of the man who sees and knows. Your genial bluster, your cheery self-confidence, are pleasant, like the open air. But they are blind: they are vain. I seem to see a great dog wag his tail and bark joyously. But if he leaves my heel he is lost.

BURGE-LUBIN. Thank you for a handsome compliment. I have a big dog; and he is the best fellow I know. If you knew how much uglier you are than a chow, you wouldnt start those comparisons, though. [_Rising_]

Well, if you have nothing for me to do, I am going to leave your heel for the rest of the day and enjoy myself. What would you recommend me to do with myself?

CONFUCIUS. Give yourself up to contemplation; and great thoughts will come to you.

BURGE-LUBIN. Will they? If you think I am going to sit here on a fine day like this with my legs crossed waiting for great thoughts, you exaggerate my taste for them. I prefer marine golf. [*Stopping short*] Oh, by the way, I forgot something. I have a word or two to say to the Minister of Health. [*He goes back to his chair*].

CONFUCIUS. Her number is—

BURGE-LUBIN. I know it.

CONFUCIUS [*rising*] I cannot understand her attraction for you. For me a woman who is not yellow does not exist, save as an official. [*He goes out*].

Burge-Lubin operates his switchboard as before. The screen vanishes; and a dainty room with a bed, a wardrobe, and a dressing-table with a mirror and a switch on it, appears. Seated at it a handsome negress is trying on a brilliant head scarf. Her dressing-gown is thrown back from her shoulders to her chair. She is in corset, knickers, and silk stockings.

BURGE-LUBIN [*horrified*] I beg your pardon a thousand times—[*The startled negress snatches the peg out of her switchboard and vanishes*].

THE NEGRESS'S VOICE. Who is it?

BURGE-LUBIN. Me. The President. Burge-Lubin. I had no idea your bedroom switch was in. I beg your pardon.

The negress reappears. She has pulled the dressing-gown perfunctorily over her shoulders, and continues her experiments with the scarf, not at all put out, and rather amused by Burge's prudery.

THE NEGRESS. Stupid of me. I was talking to another lady this morning; and I left the peg in.

BURGE-LUBIN. But I am so sorry.

THE NEGRESS [*sunnily: still busy with the scarf*] Why? It was my fault.

BURGE-LUBIN [*embarrassed*] Well—er—er— But I suppose you were used to it in Africa.

THE NEGRESS. Your delicacy is very touching, Mr President. It would be funny if it were not so unpleasant, because, like all white delicacy, it is in the wrong place. How do you think this suits my complexion?

BURGE-LUBIN. How can any really vivid color go wrong with a black satin skin? It is

our women's wretched pale faces that have to be matched and lighted. Yours is always right.

THE NEGRESS. Yes: it is a pity your white beauties have all the same ashy faces, the same colorless drab, the same age. But look at their beautiful noses and little lips! They are physically insipid: they have no beauty: you cannot love them; but how elegant!

BURGE-LUBIN. Cant you find an official pretext for coming to see me? Isnt it ridiculous that we have never met? It's so tantalizing to see you and talk to you, and to know all the time that you are two hundred miles away, and that I cant touch you?

THE NEGRESS. I cannot live on the East Coast: it is hard enough to keep my blood warm here. Besides, my friend, it would not be safe. These distant flirtations are very charming; and they teach self-control.

BURGE-LUBIN. Damn self-control! I want to hold you in my arms—to—[*the negress snatches out the peg from the switchboard and vanishes. She is still heard laughing*]. Black devil! [*He snatches out his peg furiously: her laugh is no longer heard*]. Oh, these sex episodes! Why can I not resist them? Disgraceful!

Confucius returns.

CONFUCIUS. I forgot. There is something for you to do this morning. You have to go to the Record Office to receive the American barbarian.

BURGE-LUBIN. Confucius: once for all, I object to this Chinese habit of describing white men as barbarians.

CONFUCIUS [*standing formally at the end of the table with his hands palm to palm*] I make a mental note that you do not wish the Americans to be described as barbarians.

BURGE-LUBIN. Not at all. The Americans are barbarians. But we are not. I suppose the particular barbarian you are speaking of is the American who has invented a means of breathing under water.

CONFUCIUS. He says he has invented such a method. For some reason which is not intelligible in China, Englishmen always believe any statement made by an American inventor, especially one who has never invented anything. Therefore you believe this person and have given him a public reception. Today the Record Office is entertaining him with a display of the cinematographic records of all the eminent Englishmen who have lost their lives by drowning since the cinema was invented. Why not go to see it if you are at a loss for something to do?

BURGE-LUBIN. What earthly interest is there in looking at a moving picture of a lot of people merely because they were drowned? If they had had any sense, they would not have been drowned, probably.

CONFUCIUS. That is not so. It has never been noticed before; but the Record Office has just made two remarkable discoveries about the public men and women who have displayed extraordinary ability during the past century. One is that they retained unusual youthfulness up to an advanced age. The other is that they all met their death by drowning.

BURGE-LUBIN. Yes: I know. Can you explain it?

CONFUCIUS. It cannot be explained. It is not reasonable. Therefore I do not believe it.

The Accountant General rushes in, looking ghastly. He staggers to the middle of the table.

BURGE-LUBIN. Whats the matter? Are you ill?

BARNABAS [*choking*] No. I—[*he collapses into the middle chair*]. I must speak to you in private.

Confucius calmly withdraws.

BURGE-LUBIN. What on earth is it? Have some oxygen.

BARNABAS. I have had some. Go to the Record Office. You will see men fainting there again and again, and being revived with oxygen, as I have been. They have seen with their own eyes as I have.

BURGE-LUBIN. Seen what?

BARNABAS. Seen the Archbishop of York.

BURGE-LUBIN. Well, why shouldnt they see the Archbishop of York? What are they fainting for? Has he been murdered?

BARNABAS. No: he has been drowned.

BURGE-LUBIN. Good God! Where? When? How? Poor fellow!

BARNABAS. Poor fellow! Poor thief! Poor swindler! Poor robber of his country's Exchequer! Poor fellow indeed! Wait til I catch him.

BURGE-LUBIN. How can you catch him when he is dead? Youre mad.

BARNABAS. Dead! Who said he was dead?

BURGE-LUBIN. You did. Drowned.

BARNABAS [*exasperated*] Will you listen to me? Was old Archbishop Haslam, the present man's last predecessor but four, drowned or not?

BURGE-LUBIN. I dont know. Look him up in the Encyclopedia Britannica.

BARNABAS. Yah! Was Archbishop Stickit, who wrote Stickit on the Psalms, drowned or not?

BURGE-LUBIN. Yes, mercifully. He deserved it.

BARNABAS. Was President Dickenson drowned? Was General Bullyboy drowned?

BURGE-LUBIN. Who is denying it?

BARNABAS. Well, weve had moving pictures of all four put on the screen today for this American; and they and the Archbishop are the same man. Now tell me I am mad.

BURGE-LUBIN. I do tell you you are mad. Stark raving mad.

BARNABAS. Am I to believe my own eyes or am I not?

BURGE-LUBIN. You can do as you please. All I can tell you is that *I* dont believe your eyes if they cant see any difference between a live archbishop and two dead ones. [*The apparatus rings, he holds the button down*]. Yes?

THE WOMAN'S VOICE. The Archbishop of York, to see the President.

BARNABAS [*hoarse with rage*] Have him in. I'll talk to the scoundrel.

BURGE-LUBIN [*releasing the button*] Not while you are in this state.

BARNABAS [*reaching furiously for his button and holding it down*] Send the Archbishop in at once.

BURGE-LUBIN. If you lose your temper, Barnabas, remember that we shall be two to one.

The Archbishop enters. He has a white band round his throat, set in a black stock. He wears a sort of kilt of black ribbons, and soft black boots that button high up on his calves. His costume does not differ otherwise from that of the President and the Accountant General; but its color scheme is black and white. He is older than the Reverend Bill Haslam was when he wooed Miss Savvy Barnabas; but he is recognizably the same man. He does not look a day over fifty, and is very well preserved even at that; but his boyishness of manner is quite gone: he now has complete authority and self-possession: in fact the President is a little afraid of him; and it seems quite natural and inevitable that he should speak first.

THE ARCHBISHOP. Good day, Mr President.

BURGE-LUBIN. Good day, Mr Archbishop. Be seated.

THE ARCHBISHOP [*sitting down between them*]

Good day, Mr Accountant General.

BARNABAS [*malevolently*] Good day to you. I have a question to put to you, if you dont mind.

THE ARCHBISHOP [*looking curiously at him, jarred by his uncivil tone*] Certainly. What is it?

BARNABAS. What is your definition of a thief?

THE ARCHBISHOP. Rather an old-fashioned word, is it not?

BARNABAS. It survives officially in my department.

THE ARCHBISHOP. Our departments are full of survivals. Look at my tie! my apron! my boots! They are all mere survivals; yet it seems that without them I cannot be a proper Archbishop.

BARNABAS. Indeed! Well, in my department the word thief survives, because in the community the thing thief survives. And a very despicable and dishonorable thing he is, too.

THE ARCHBISHOP [*coolly*] I daresay.

BARNABAS. In my department, sir, a thief is a person who lives longer than the statutory expectation of life entitles him to, and goes on drawing public money when, if he were an honest man, he would be dead.

THE ARCHBISHOP. Then let me say, sir, that your department does not understand its own business. If you have miscalculated the duration of human life, that is not the fault of the persons whose longevity you have miscalculated. And if they continue to work and produce, they pay their way, even if they live two or three centuries.

BARNABAS. I know nothing about their working and producing. That is not the business of my department. I am concerned with their expectation of life; and I say that no man has any right to go on living and drawing money when he ought to be dead.

THE ARCHBISHOP. You do not comprehend the relation between income and production.

BARNABAS. I understand my own department.

THE ARCHBISHOP. That is not enough. Your department is part of a synthesis which embraces all the departments.

BURGE-LUBIN. Synthesis! This is an intellectual difficulty. This is a job for Confucius. I heard him use that very word the other day; and I wondered what the devil he meant. [*Switching on*] Hallo! Put me through to the Chief Secretary.

CONFUCIUS'S VOICE. You are speaking to him.

BURGE-LUBIN. An intellectual difficulty, old man. Something we dont understand. Come and help us out.

THE ARCHBISHOP. May I ask how the question has arisen?

BARNABAS. Ah! You begin to smell a rat, do you? You thought yourself pretty safe. You—

BURGE-LUBIN. Steady, Barnabas. Dont be in a hurry.

Confucius enters.

THE ARCHBISHOP [*rising*] Good morning, Mr Chief Secretary.

BURGE-LUBIN [*rising in instinctive imitation of the Archbishop*] Honor us by taking a seat, O sage.

CONFUCIUS. Ceremony is needless. [*He bows to the company, and takes the chair at the foot of the table*].

The President and the Archbishop resume their seats.

BURGE-LUBIN. We wish to put a case to you, Confucius. Suppose a man, instead of conforming to the official estimate of his expectation of life, were to live for more than two centuries and a half, would the Accountant General be justified in calling him a thief?

CONFUCIUS. No. He would be justified in calling him a liar.

THE ARCHBISHOP. I think not, Mr Chief Secretary. What do you suppose my age is?

CONFUCIUS. Fifty.

BURGE-LUBIN. You dont look it. Forty-five; and young for your age.

THE ARCHBISHOP. My age is two hundred and eighty-three.

BARNABAS [*morosely triumphant*] Hmp! Mad, am I?

BURGE-LUBIN. Youre both mad. Excuse me, Archbishop; but this is getting a bit—well—

THE ARCHBISHOP [*to Confucius*] Mr Chief Secretary: will you, to oblige me, assume that I have lived nearly three centuries? As a hypothesis?

BURGE-LUBIN. What is a hypothesis?

CONFUCIUS. It does not matter. I understand. [*To the Archbishop*] Am I to assume that you have lived in your ancestors, or by metempsychosis—

BURGE-LUBIN. Met — Emp — Sy — Good Lord! What a brain, Confucius! What a brain!

THE ARCHBISHOP. Nothing of that kind. Assume in the ordinary sense that I was born in the year 1887, and that I have worked continuously in one profession or another

2 G

since the year 1910. Am I a thief?

CONFUCIUS. I do not know. Was that one of your professions?

THE ARCHBISHOP. No. I have been nothing worse than an Archbishop, a President, and a General.

BARNABAS. Has he or has he not robbed the Exchequer by drawing five or six incomes when he was only entitled to one? Answer me that.

CONFUCIUS. Certainly not. The hypothesis is that he has worked continuously since 1910. We are now in the year 2170. What is the official lifetime?

BARNABAS. Seventy-eight. Of course it's an average; and we dont mind a man here and there going on to ninety, or even, as a curiosity, becoming a centenarian. But I say that a man who goes beyond that is a swindler.

CONFUCIUS. Seventy-eight into two hundred and eighty-three goes more than three and a half times. Your department owes the Archbishop two and a half educations and three and a half retiring pensions.

BARNABAS. Stuff! How can that be?

CONFUCIUS. At what age do your people begin to work for the community?

BURGE-LUBIN. Three. They do certain things every day when they are three. Just to break them in, you know. But they become self-supporting, or nearly so, at thirteen.

CONFUCIUS. And at what age do they retire?

BARNABAS. Forty-three.

CONFUCIUS. That is, they do thirty years' work; and they receive maintenance and education, without working, for thirteen years of childhood and thirty-five years of superannuation, forty-eight years in all, for each thirty years' work. The Archbishop has given you 260 years' work, and has received only one education and no superannuation. You therefore owe him over 300 years of leisure and nearly eight educations. You are thus heavily in his debt. In other words, he has effected an enormous national economy by living so long; and you, by living only seventy-eight years, are profiting at his expense. He is the benefactor: you are the thief. [Half rising] May I now withdraw and return to my serious business, as my own span is comparatively short?

BURGE-LUBIN. Dont be in a hurry, old chap. [Confucius sits down again]. This hypothecary, or whatever you call it, is put up seriously. I

dont believe it; but if the Archbishop and the Accountant General are going to insist that it's true, we shall have either to lock them up or to see the thing through.

BARNABAS. It's no use trying these Chinese subtleties on me. I'm a plain man; and though I dont understand metaphysics, and dont believe in them, I understand figures; and if the Archbishop is only entitled to seventy-eight years, and he takes 283, I say he takes more than he is entitled to. Get over that if you can.

THE ARCHBISHOP. I have not taken 283 years: I have taken 23 and given 260.

CONFUCIUS. Do your accounts shew a deficiency or a surplus?

BARNABAS. A surplus. Thats what I cant make out. Thats the artfulness of these people.

BURGE-LUBIN. That settles it. Whats the use of arguing? The Chink says you are wrong; and theres an end of it.

BARNABAS. I say nothing against the Chink's arguments. But what about my facts?

CONFUCIUS. If your facts include a case of a man living 283 years, I advise you to take a few weeks at the seaside.

BARNABAS. Let there be an end of this hinting that I am out of my mind. Come and look at the cinema record. I tell you this man is Archbishop Haslam, Archbishop Stickit, President Dickenson, General Bullyboy and himself into the bargain: all five of them.

THE ARCHBISHOP. I do not deny it. I never have denied it. Nobody has ever asked me.

BURGE-LUBIN. But damn it, man—I beg your pardon, Archbishop; but really, really—

THE ARCHBISHOP. Dont mention it. What were you going to say?

BURGE-LUBIN. Well, you were drowned four times over. You are not a cat, you know.

THE ARCHBISHOP. That is very easy to understand. Consider my situation when I first made the amazing discovery that I was destined to live three hundred years! I—

CONFUCIUS [interrupting him] Pardon me. Such a discovery was impossible. You have not made it yet. You may live a million years if you have already lived two hundred. There is no question of three hundred years. You have made a slip at the very beginning of your fairy tale, Mr Archbishop.

BURGE-LUBIN. Good, Confucius! [To theArchbishop] He has you there. I dont see how you can get over that.

THE ARCHBISHOP. Yes: it is quite a good point. But if the Accountant General will go to the British Museum library, and search the catalogue, he will find under his own name a curious and now forgotten book, dated 1924, entitled The Gospel of the Brothers Barnabas. That gospel was that men must live three hundred years if civilization is to be saved. It shewed that this extension of individual human life was possible, and how it was likely to come about. I married the daughter of one of the brothers.

BARNABAS. Do you mean to say you claim to be a connection of mine?

THE ARCHBISHOP. I claim nothing. As I have by this time perhaps three or four million cousins of one degree or another, I have ceased to call on the family.

BURGE-LUBIN. Gracious heavens! Four million relatives! Is that calculation correct, Confucius?

CONFUCIUS. In China it might be forty millions if there were no checks on population.

BURGE-LUBIN. This is a staggerer. It brings home to one—but [recovering] it isnt true, you know. Let us keep sane.

CONFUCIUS [to the Archbishop] You wish us to understand that the illustrious ancestors of the Accountant General communicated to you a secret by which you could attain the age of three hundred years.

THE ARCHBISHOP. No. Nothing of the kind. They simply believed that mankind could live any length of time it knew to be absolutely necessary to save civilization from extinction. I did not share their belief: at least I was not conscious of sharing it: I thought I was only amused by it. To me my father-in-law and his brother were a pair of clever cranks who had talked one another into a fixed idea which had become a monomania with them. It was not until I got into serious difficulties with the pension authorities after turning seventy that I began to suspect the truth.

CONFUCIUS. The truth?

THE ARCHBISHOP. Yes, Mr Chief Secretary: the truth. Like all revolutionary truths, it began as a joke. As I shewed no signs of ageing after forty-five, my wife used to make fun of me by saying that I was certainly going to live three hundred years. She was sixty-eight when she died; and the last thing she said to me, as I sat by her bedside

holding her hand, was "Bill: you really dont look fifty. I wonder—" She broke off, and fell asleep wondering, and never awoke. Then I began to wonder too. That is the explanation of the three hundred years, Mr Secretary.

CONFUCIUS. It is very ingenious, Mr Archbishop. And very well told.

BURGE-LUBIN. Of course you understand that I dont for a moment suggest the very faintest doubt of your absolute veracity, Archbishop. You know that, dont you?

THE ARCHBISHOP. Quite, Mr President. Only you dont believe me: that is all. I do not expect you to. In your place I should not believe. You had better have a look at the films. [Pointing to the Accountant General] He believes.

BURGE-LUBIN. But the drowning? What about the drowning? A man might get drowned once, or even twice if he was exceptionally careless. But he couldnt be drowned four times. He would run away from water like a mad dog.

THE ARCHBISHOP. Perhaps Mr Chief Secretary can guess the explanation of that.

CONFUCIUS. To keep your secret, you had to die.

BURGE-LUBIN. But dash it all, man, he isnt dead.

CONFUCIUS. It is socially impossible not to do what everybody else does. One must die at the usual time.

BARNABAS. Of course. A simple point of honor.

CONFUCIUS. Not at all. A simple necessity.

BURGE-LUBIN. Well, I'm hanged if I see it. I should jolly well live for ever if I could.

THE ARCHBISHOP. It is not so easy as you think. You, Mr Chief Secretary, have grasped the difficulties of the position. Let me remind you, Mr President, that I was over eighty before the 1969 Act for the Redistribution of Income entitled me to a handsome retiring pension. Owing to my youthful appearance I was prosecuted for attempting to obtain public money on false pretences when I claimed it. I could prove nothing; for the register of my birth had been blown to pieces by a bomb dropped on a village church years before in the first of the big modern wars. I was ordered back to work as a man of forty, and had to work for fifteen years more, the retiring age being then fifty-five.

BURGE-LUBIN. As late as fifty-five! How did people stand it?

THE ARCHBISHOP. They made difficulties about letting me go even then, I still looked so young. For some years I was in continual trouble. The industrial police rounded me up again and again, refusing to believe that I was over age. They began to call me The Wandering Jew. You see how impossible my position was. I foresaw that in twenty years more my official record would prove me to be seventy-five; my appearance would make it impossible to believe that I was more than forty-five; and my real age would be one hundred and seventeen. What was I to do? Bleach my hair? Hobble about on two sticks? Mimic the voice of a centenarian? Better have killed myself.

BARNABAS. You o u g h t to have killed yourself. As an honest man you were entitled to no more than an honest man's expectation of life.

THE ARCHBISHOP. I d i d kill myself. It was quite easy. I left a suit of clothes by the seashore during the bathing season, with documents in the pockets to identify me. I then turned up in a strange place, pretending that I had lost my memory, and did not know my name or my age or anything about myself. Under treatment I recovered my health, but not my memory. I have had several careers since I began this routine of life and death. I have been an archbishop three times. When I persuaded the authorities to knock down all our towns and rebuild them from the foundations, or move them, I went into the artillery, and became a general. I have been President.

BURGE-LUBIN. Dickenson?

THE ARCHBISHOP. Yes.

BURGE-LUBIN. But they found Dickenson's body: its ashes are buried in St Paul's.

THE ARCHBISHOP. They almost always found the body. During the bathing season there are plenty of bodies. I have been cremated again and again. At first I used to attend my own funeral in disguise, because I had read about a man doing that in an old romance by an author named Bennett, from whom I remember borrowing five pounds in 1912. But I got tired of that. I would not cross the street now to read my latest epitaph.

The Chief Secretary and the President look very glum. Their incredulity is vanquished at last.

BURGE-LUBIN. Look here. Do you chaps realize how awful this is? Here we are sitting calmly in the presence of a man whose death is overdue by two centuries. He may crumble into dust before our eyes at any moment.

BARNABAS. Not he. He'll go on drawing his pension until the end of the world.

THE ARCHBISHOP. Not quite that. My expectation of life is only three hundred years.

BARNABAS. You will last out my time anyhow: thats enough for me.

THE ARCHBISHOP [*coolly*] How do you know?

BARNABAS [*taken aback*] How do I know!

THE ARCHBISHOP. Yes: how do you know? I did not begin even to suspect until I was nearly seventy. I was only vain of my youthful appearance. I was not quite serious about it until I was ninety. Even now I am not sure from one moment to another, though I have given you my reason for thinking that I have quite unintentionally committed myself to a lifetime of three hundred years.

BURGE-LUBIN. But how do you do it? Is it lemons? Is it Soya beans? Is it—

THE ARCHBISHOP. I do not do it. It happens. It may happen to anyone. It may happen to you.

BURGE-LUBIN [*the full significance of this for himself dawning on him*] Then we three may be in the same boat with you, for all we know?

THE ARCHBISHOP. You may. Therefore I advise you to be very careful how you take any step that will make my position uncomfortable.

BURGE-LUBIN. Well, I'm dashed! One of my secretaries was remarking only this morning how well and young I am looking. Barnabas: I have an absolute conviction that I am one of the—the—shall I say one of the victims?— of this strange destiny.

THE ARCHBISHOP. Your great-great-great-great-great-great-grandfather formed the same conviction when he was between sixty and seventy. I knew him.

BURGE-LUBIN [*depressed*] Ah! But he died.

THE ARCHBISHOP. No.

BURGE-LUBIN [*hopefully*] Do you mean to say he is still alive?

THE ARCHBISHOP. No. He was shot. Under the influence of his belief that he was going to live three hundred years he became a changed man. He began to tell people the truth; and they disliked it so much that they took advantage of certain clauses of an Act of Parliament he had himself passed during the Four Years War, and had purposely forgotten to repeal afterwards. They took him to the Tower of London and shot him.

The apparatus rings.

CONFUCIUS [*answering*] Yes? [*He listens*].

A WOMAN'S VOICE. The Domestic Minister has called.

BURGE-LUBIN [*not quite catching the answer*] Who does she say has called?

CONFUCIUS. The Domestic Minister.

BARNABAS. Oh, dash it! That awful woman!

BURGE-LUBIN. She certainly is a bit of a terror. I dont exactly know why; for she is not at all bad-looking.

BARNABAS [*out of patience*] For Heaven's sake, dont be frivolous.

THE ARCHBISHOP. He cannot help it, Mr Accountant General. Three of his sixteen great - great - great - grandfathers married Lubins.

BURGE-LUBIN. Tut tut! I am not frivolling. *I* did not ask the lady here. Which of you did?

CONFUCIUS. It is her official duty to report personally to the President once a quarter.

BURGE-LUBIN. Oh, t h a t! Then I suppose it's my official duty to receive her. Theyd better send her in. You dont mind, do you? She will bring us back to real life. I dont know how you fellows feel; but I'm just going dotty.

CONFUCIUS [*into the telephone*] The President will receive the Domestic Minister at once.

They watch the door in silence for the entrance of the Domestic Minister.

BURGE-LUBIN [*suddenly, to the Archbishop*] I suppose you have been married over and over again.

THE ARCHBISHOP. Once. You do not make vows until death when death is three hundred years off.

They relapse into uneasy silence. The Domestic Minister enters. She is a handsome woman, apparently in the prime of life, with elegant, tense, well held-up figure, and the walk of a goddess. Her expression and deportment are grave, swift, decisive, awful, unanswerable. She wears a Dianesque tunic instead of a blouse, and a silver coronet instead of a gold fillet. Her dress otherwise is not markedly different from that of the men, who rise as she enters, and incline their heads with instinctive awe. She comes to the vacant chair between Barnabas and Confucius.

BURGE-LUBIN [*resolutely genial and gallant*] Delighted to see you, Mrs Lutestring.

CONFUCIUS. We are honored by your celestial presence.

BARNABAS. Good day, madam.

THE ARCHBISHOP. I have not had the pleasure of meeting you before. I am the Archbishop of York.

MRS LUTESTRING. Surely we have met, Mr Archbishop. I remember your face. We— [*she checks herself suddenly*] Ah, no: I remember now: it was someone else. [*She sits down*].

They all sit down.

THE ARCHBISHOP [*also puzzled*] Are you sure you are mistaken? I also have some association with your face, Mrs Lutestring. Something like a door opening continually and revealing you. And a smile of welcome when you recognized me. Did you ever open a door for me, I wonder?

MRS LUTESTRING. I often opened a door for the person you have just reminded me of. But he has been dead many years.

The rest, except the Archbishop, look at one another quickly.

CONFUCIUS. May I ask how many years?

MRS LUTESTRING [*struck by his tone, looks at him for a moment with some displeasure; then replies*] It does not matter. A long time.

BURGE-LUBIN. You mustnt rush to conclusions about the Archbishop, Mrs Lutestring. He is an older bird than you think. Older than you, at all events.

MRS LUTESTRING [*with a melancholy smile*] I think not, Mr President. But the subject is a delicate one. I had rather not pursue it.

CONFUCIUS. There is a question which has not been asked.

MRS LUTESTRING [*very decisively*] If it is a question about my age, Mr Chief Secretary, it had better not be asked. All that concerns you about my personal affairs can be found in the books of the Accountant General.

CONFUCIUS. The question I was thinking of will not be addressed to you. But let me say that your sensitiveness on the point is very strange, coming from a woman so superior to all common weaknesses as we know you to be.

MRS LUTESTRING. I may have reasons which have nothing to do with common weaknesses, Mr Chief Secretary. I hope you will respect them.

CONFUCIUS [*after bowing to her in assent*] I will now put my question. Have you, Mr Archbishop, any ground for assuming, as you seem to do, that what has happened to you has not happened to other people as well?

BURGE-LUBIN. Yes, by George! I never thought of that.

THE ARCHBISHOP. I have never met any case but my own.

CONFUCIUS. How do you know?

THE ARCHBISHOP. Well, no one has ever told me that they were in this extraordinary position.

CONFUCIUS. That proves nothing. Did you ever tell anybody that y o u were in it? You never told us. Why did you never tell us?

THE ARCHBISHOP. I am surprised at the question, coming from so astute a mind as yours, Mr Secretary. When you reach the age I reached before I discovered what was happening to me, I was old enough to know and fear the ferocious hatred with which human animals, like all other animals, turn upon any unhappy individual who has the misfortune to be unlike themselves in every respect: to be unnatural, as they call it. You will still find, among the tales of that twentieth-century classic, Wells, a story of a race of men who grew twice as big as their fellows, and another story of a man who fell into the hands of a race of blind men. The big people had to fight the little people for their lives; and the man with eyes would have had his eyes put out by the blind had he not fled to the desert, where he perished miserably. Wells's teaching, on that and other matters, was not lost on me. By the way, he lent me five pounds once which I never repaid; and it still troubles my conscience.

CONFUCIUS. And were you the only reader of Wells? If there were others like you, had they not the same reason for keeping the secret?

THE ARCHBISHOP. That is true. But I should know. You shortlived people are so childish. If I met a man of my own age I should recognize him at once. I have never done so.

MRS LUTESTRING. Would you recognize a woman of your age, do you think?

THE ARCHBISHOP. I—[He stops and turns upon her with a searching look, startled by the suggestion and the suspicion it rouses].

MRS LUTESTRING. What is your age, Mr Archbishop?

BURGE-LUBIN. Two hundred and eighty-three, he says. That is his little joke. Do you know, Mrs Lutestring, he had almost talked us into believing him when you came in and cleared the air with your robust common sense.

MRS LUTESTRING. Do you really feel that, Mr President? I hear the note of breezy assertion in your voice. I miss the note of conviction.

BURGE-LUBIN [jumping up] Look here. Let us stop talking damned nonsense. I dont wish to be disagreeable; but it's getting on my nerves. The best joke wont bear being pushed beyond a certain point. That point has been reached. I—I'm rather busy this morning. We all have our hands pretty full. Confucius here will tell you that I have a heavy day before me.

BARNABAS. Have you anything more important than this thing, if it's true?

BURGE-LUBIN. Oh, if, if, i f it's true! But it isnt true.

BARNABAS. Have you anything at all to do?

BURGE-LUBIN. Anything to do! Have you forgotten, Barnabas, that I happen to be President, and that the weight of the entire public business of this country is on my shoulders?

BARNABAS. Has he anything to do, Confucius?

CONFUCIUS. He has to be President.

BARNABAS. That means that he has nothing to do.

BURGE-LUBIN [sulkily] Very well, Barnabas. Go on making a fool of yourself. [He sits down]. Go on.

BARNABAS. I am not going to leave this room until we get to the bottom of this swindle.

MRS LUTESTRING [turning with deadly gravity on the Accountant General] This what, did you say?

CONFUCIUS. These expressions cannot be sustained. You obscure the discussion in using them.

BARNABAS [glad to escape from her gaze by addressing Confucius] Well, this unnatural horror. Will that satisfy you?

CONFUCIUS. That is in order. But we do not commit ourselves to the implications of the word horror.

THE ARCHBISHOP. By the word horror the Accountant General means only something unusual.

CONFUCIUS. I notice that the honorable Domestic Minister, on learning the advanced age of the venerable prelate, shews no sign of surprise or incredulity.

BURGE-LUBIN. She doesnt take it seriously. Who would? Eh, Mrs Lutestring?

MRS LUTESTRING. I take it very seriously indeed, Mr President. I see now that I was not mistaken at first. I h a v e met the Archbishop before.

THE ARCHBISHOP. I felt sure of it. This vision of a door opening to me, and a woman's face welcoming me, must be a reminiscence of something that really happened; though I see it now as an angel opening the gate of heaven.

MRS LUTESTRING. Or a parlormaid opening the door of the house of the young woman you were in love with?

THE ARCHBISHOP [making a wry face] Is that the reality? How these things grow in our imagination! But may I say, Mrs Lutestring, that the transfiguration of a parlormaid to an angel is not more amazing than her transfiguration to the very dignified and able Domestic Minister I am addressing. I recognize the angel in you. Frankly, I do not recognize the parlormaid.

BURGE-LUBIN. Whats a parlormaid?

MRS LUTESTRING. An extinct species. A woman in a black dress and white apron, who opened the house door when people knocked or rang, and was either your tyrant or your slave. I was a parlormaid in the house of one of the Accountant General's remote ancestors. [To Confucius] You asked me my age, Mr Chief Secretary. I am two hundred and seventy-four.

BURGE-LUBIN [gallantly] You dont look it. You really dont look it.

MRS LUTESTRING [turning her face gravely towards him] Look again, Mr President.

BURGE-LUBIN [looking at her bravely until the smile fades from his face, and he suddenly covers his eyes with his hands] Yes: you d o look it. I am convinced. It's true. Now call up the Lunatic Asylum, Confucius; and tell them to send an ambulance for me.

MRS LUTESTRING [to the Archbishop] Why have you given away your secret? o u r secret?

THE ARCHBISHOP. They found it out. The cinema records betrayed me. But I never dreamt that there were others. Did you?

MRS LUTESTRING. I knew one other. She was a cook. She grew tired, and killed herself.

THE ARCHBISHOP. Dear me! However, her death simplifies the situation, as I have been able to convince these gentlemen that the matter had better go no further.

MRS LUTESTRING. What! When the President knows! It will be all over the place before the end of the week.

BURGE-LUBIN [injured] Really, Mrs Lutestring! You speak as if I were a notoriously indiscreet person. Barnabas: have I such a reputation?

BARNABAS [resignedly] It cant be helped. It's constitutional.

CONFUCIUS. It is utterly unconstitutional. But, as you say, it cannot be helped.

BURGE-LUBIN [solemnly] I deny that a secret of State has ever passed my lips—except perhaps to the Minister of Health, who is discretion personified. People think, because she is a negress—

MRS LUTESTRING. It does not matter much now. Once, it would have mattered a great deal. But my children are all dead.

THE ARCHBISHOP. Yes: the children must have been a terrible difficulty. Fortunately for me, I had none.

MRS LUTESTRING. There was one daughter who was the child of my very heart. Some years after my first drowning I learnt that she had lost her sight. I went to her. She was an old woman of ninety-six, blind. She asked me to sit and talk with her because my voice was like the voice of her dead mother.

BURGE-LUBIN. The complications must be frightful. Really I hardly know whether I d o want to live much longer than other people.

MRS LUTESTRING. You can always kill yourself, as cook did; but that was influenza. Long life is complicated, and even terrible; but it is glorious all the same. I would no more change places with an ordinary woman than with a mayfly that lives only an hour.

THE ARCHBISHOP. What set you thinking of it first?

MRS LUTESTRING. Conrad Barnabas's book. Your wife told me it was more wonderful than Napoleon's Book of Fate and Old Moore's Almanac, which cook and I used to read. I was very ignorant: it did not seem so impossible to me as to an educated woman. Yet I forgot all about it, and married and drudged as a poor man's wife, and brought up children, and looked twenty years older than I really was, until one day, long after my husband died and my children were out in the world working for themselves, I noticed that I looked twenty years younger than I really was. The truth came to me in a flash.

BURGE-LUBIN. An amazing moment. Your

feelings must have been beyond description. What was your first thought?

MRS LUTESTRING. Pure terror. I saw that the little money I had laid up would not last, and that I must go out and work again. They had things called Old Age Pensions then: miserable pittances for worn-out old laborers to die on. I thought I should be found out if I went on drawing it too long. The horror of facing another lifetime of drudgery, of missing my hard-earned rest and losing my poor little savings, drove everything else out of my mind. You people nowadays can have no conception of the dread of poverty that hung over us then, or of the utter tiredness of forty years' unending overwork and striving to make a shilling do the work of a pound.

THE ARCHBISHOP. I wonder you did not kill yourself. I often wonder why the poor in those evil old times did not kill themselves. They did not even kill other people.

MRS LUTESTRING. You never kill yourself, because you always may as well wait until tomorrow. And you have not energy or conviction enough to kill the others. Besides, how can you blame them when you would do as they do if you were in their place?

BURGE-LUBIN. Devilish poor consolation, that.

MRS LUTESTRING. There were other consolations in those days for people like me. We drank preparations of alcohol to relieve the strain of living and give us an artificial happiness.

BURGE-LUBIN ⎱ [all together, ⎰ Alcohol!
CONFUCIUS   ⎰ making   ⎱ Pfff....!
BARNABAS   ⎰ wry faces] ⎱ Disgusting.

MRS LUTESTRING. A little alcohol would improve your temper and manners, and make you much easier to live with, Mr Accountant General.

BURGE-LUBIN [laughing] By George, I believe you! Try it, Barnabas.

CONFUCIUS. No. Try tea. It is the more civilized poison of the two.

MRS LUTESTRING. You, Mr President, were born intoxicated with your own well-fed natural exuberance. You cannot imagine what alcohol was to an underfed poor woman. I had carefully arranged my little savings so that I could get drunk, as we called it, once a week; and my only pleasure was looking forward to that poor little debauch. That is what saved me from suicide. I could not bear to miss my next carouse. But when I

stopped working, and lived on my pension, the fatigue of my life's drudgery began to wear off, because, you see, I was not really old. I recuperated. I looked younger and younger. And at last I was rested enough to have courage and strength to begin life again. Besides, political changes were making it easier: life was a little better worth living for the nine-tenths of the people who used to be mere drudges. After that, I never turned back or faltered. My only regret now is that I shall die when I am three hundred or thereabouts. There was only one thing that made life hard; and that is gone now.

CONFUCIUS. May we ask what that was?

MRS LUTESTRING. Perhaps you will be offended if I tell you.

BURGE-LUBIN. Offended! My dear lady, do you suppose, after such a stupendous revelation, that anything short of a blow from a sledge-hammer could produce the smallest impression on any of us?

MRS LUTESTRING. Well, you see, it has been so hard on me never to meet a grown-up person. You are all such children. And I never was very fond of children, except that one girl who woke up the mother passion in me. I have been very lonely sometimes.

BURGE-LUBIN [again gallant] But surely, Mrs Lutestring, that has been your own fault. If I may say so, a lady of your attractions need never have been lonely.

MRS LUTESTRING. Why?

BURGE-LUBIN. Why! Well—. Well, er—. Well, er er—. Well! [he gives it up].

THE ARCHBISHOP. He means that you might have married. Curious, how little they understand our position.

MRS LUTESTRING. I did marry. I married again on my hundred and first birthday. But of course I had to marry an elderly man: a man over sixty. He was a great painter. On his deathbed he said to me "It has taken me fifty years to learn my trade, and to paint all the foolish pictures a man must paint and get rid of before he comes through them to the great things he ought to paint. And now that my foot is at last on the threshold of the temple I find that it is also the threshold of my tomb." That man would have been the greatest painter of all time if he could have lived as long as I. I saw him die of old age whilst he was still, as he said himself, a gentleman amateur, like all modern painters.

BURGE-LUBIN. But why had you to marry

an elderly man? Why not marry a young one? or shall I say a middle-aged one? If my own affections were not already engaged; and if, to tell the truth, I were not a little afraid of you—for you are a very superior woman, as we all acknowledge—I should esteem myself happy in—er—er—

MRS LUTESTRING. Mr President: have you ever tried to take advantage of the innocence of a little child for the gratification of your senses?

BURGE-LUBIN. Good Heavens, madam, what do you take me for? What right have you to ask me such a question?

MRS LUTESTRING. I am at present in my two hundred and seventy-fifth year. You suggest that I should take advantage of the innocence of a child of thirty, and marry it.

THE ARCHBISHOP. Can you shortlived people not understand that as the confusion and immaturity and primitive animalism in which we live for the first hundred years of our life is worse in this matter of sex than in any other, you are intolerable to us in that relation?

BURGE-LUBIN. Do you mean to say, Mrs Lutestring, that you regard me as a child?

MRS LUTESTRING. Do you expect me to regard you as a completed soul? Oh, you may well be afraid of me. There are moments when your levity, your ingratitude, your shallow jollity, make my gorge rise so against you that if I could not remind myself that you are a child I should be tempted to doubt your right to live at all.

CONFUCIUS. Do you grudge us the few years we have? you who have three hundred!

BURGE-LUBIN. You accuse me of levity! Must I remind you, madam, that I am the President, and that you are only the head of a department?

BARNABAS. Ingratitude too! You draw a pension for three hundred years when we owe you only seventy-eight; and you call us ungrateful!

MRS LUTESTRING. I do. When I think of the blessings that have been showered on you, and contrast them with the poverty! the humiliations! the anxieties! the heartbreak! the insolence and tyranny that were the daily lot of mankind when I was learning to suffer instead of learning to live! when I see how lightly you take it all! how you quarrel over the crumpled leaves in your beds of roses! how you are so dainty about your work

that unless it is made either interesting or delightful to you you leave it to negresses and Chinamen, I ask myself whether even three hundred years of thought and experience can save you from being superseded by the Power that created you and put you on your trial.

BURGE-LUBIN. My dear lady: our Chinese and colored friends are perfectly happy. They are twenty times better off here than they would be in China or Liberia. They do their work admirably; and in doing it they set us free for higher employments.

THE ARCHBISHOP [who has caught the infection of her indignation] What higher employments are you capable of? you that are superannuated at seventy and dead at eighty!

MRS LUTESTRING. You are not really doing higher work. You are supposed to make the decisions and give the orders; but the negresses and the Chinese make up your minds for you and tell you what orders to give, just as my brother, who was a sergeant in the Guards, used to prompt his officers in the old days. When I want to get anything done at the Health Ministry I do not come to you: I go to the black lady who has been the real president during your present term of office, or to Confucius, who goes on for ever while presidents come and presidents go.

BURGE-LUBIN. This is outrageous. This is treason to the white race. And let me tell you, madam, that I have never in my life met the Minister of Health, and that I protest against the vulgar color prejudice which disparages her great ability and her eminent services to the State. My relations with her are purely telephonic, gramophonic, photophonic, and, may I add, platonic.

THE ARCHBISHOP. There is no reason why you should be ashamed of them in any case, Mr President. But let us look at the position impersonally. Can you deny that what is happening is that the English people have become a Joint Stock Company admitting Asiatics and Africans as shareholders?

BARNABAS. Nothing like it. I know all about the old joint stock companies. The shareholders did no work.

THE ARCHBISHOP. That is true; but we, like them, get our dividends whether we work or not. We work partly because we know there would be no dividends if we did not, and partly because if we refuse we are regarded as mentally deficient and put into a lethal

2 G 2

chamber. But what do we work at? Before the few changes we were forced to make by the revolutions that followed the Four Years War, our governing classes had been so rich, as it was called, that they had become the most intellectually lazy and fat-headed people on the face of the earth. There is a good deal of that fat still clinging to us.

BURGE-LUBIN. As President, I must not listen to unpatriotic criticisms of our national character, Mr Archbishop.

THE ARCHBISHOP. As Archbishop, Mr President, it is my official duty to criticize the national character unsparingly. At the canonization of Saint Henrik Ibsen, you yourself unveiled the monument to him which bears on its pedestal the noble inscription, "I came not to call sinners, but the righteous, to repentance." The proof of what I say is that our routine work, and what may be called our ornamental and figure-head work, is being more and more sought after by the English; whilst the thinking, organizing, calculating, directing work is done by yellow brains, brown brains, and black brains, just as it was done in my early days by Jewish brains, Scottish brains, Italian brains, German brains. The only white men who still do serious work are those who, like the Accountant General, have no capacity for enjoyment, and no social gifts to make them welcome outside their offices.

BARNABAS. Confound your impudence! I had gifts enough to find you out, anyhow.

THE ARCHBISHOP [disregarding this outburst] If you were to kill me as I stand here, you would have to appoint an Indian to succeed me. I take precedence today not as an Englishman, but as a man with more than a century and a half of fully adult experience. We are letting all the power slip into the hands of the colored people. In another hundred years we shall be simply their household pets.

BURGE-LUBIN [reacting buoyantly] Not the least danger of it. I grant you we leave the most troublesome part of the labor of the nation to them. And a good job too: why should we drudge at it? But think of the activities of our leisure! Is there a jollier place on earth to live in than England out of office hours? And to whom do we owe that? To ourselves, not to the niggers. The nigger and the Chink are all right from Tuesday to Friday; but from Friday to Tuesday they are simply nowhere; and the real life of England is from Friday to Tuesday.

THE ARCHBISHOP. That is terribly true. In devising brainless amusements; in pursuing them with enormous vigor, and taking them with eager seriousness, our English people are the wonder of the world. They always were. And it is just as well; for otherwise their sensuality would become morbid and destroy them. What appals me is that their amusements should amuse them. They are the amusements of boys and girls. They are pardonable up to the age of fifty or sixty: after that they are ridiculous. I tell you, what is wrong with us is that we are a non-adult race; and the Irish and the Scots, and the niggers and Chinks, as you call them, though their lifetime is as short as ours, or shorter, yet do somehow contrive to grow up a little before they die. We die in boyhood: the maturity that should make us the greatest of all the nations lies beyond the grave for us. Either we shall go under as greybeards with golf clubs in our hands, or we must will to live longer.

MRS LUTESTRING. Yes: that is it. I could not have expressed it in words; but you have expressed it for me. I felt, even when I was an ignorant domestic slave, that we had the possibility of becoming a great nation within us; but our faults and follies drove me to cynical hopelessness. We all ended then like that. It is the highest creatures who take the longest to mature, and are the most helpless during their immaturity. I know now that it took me a whole century to grow up. I began my serious life when I was a hundred and twenty. Asiatics cannot control me: I am not a child in their hands, as you are, Mr President. Neither, I am sure, is the Archbishop. They respect me. You are not grown up enough even for that, though you were kind enough to say that I frighten you.

BURGE-LUBIN. Honestly, you do. And will you think me very rude if I say that if I must choose between a white woman old enough to be my great-grandmother and a black woman of my own age, I shall probably find the black woman more sympathetic?

MRS LUTESTRING. And more attractive in color, perhaps?

BURGE-LUBIN. Yes. Since you ask me, more —well, not more attractive: I do not deny that you have an excellent appearance—but I will say, richer. More Venetian. Tropical.

"The shadowed livery of the burnished sun."

MRS LUTESTRING. Our women, and their favorite story writers, begin already to talk about men with golden complexions.

CONFUCIUS [*expanding into a smile all across both face and body*]. A-a-a-a——h!

BURGE-LUBIN. Well, what of it, madam? Have you read a very interesting book by the librarian of the Biological Society suggesting that the future of the world lies with the Mulatto?

MRS LUTESTRING [*rising*] Mr Archbishop: if the white race is to be saved, our destiny is apparent.

THE ARCHBISHOP. Yes: our duty is pretty clear.

MRS LUTESTRING. Have you time to come home with me and discuss the matter?

THE ARCHBISHOP [*rising*] With pleasure.

BARNABAS [*rising also and rushing past Mrs Lutestring to the door, where he turns to bar her way*] No you dont. Burge: you understand, dont you?

BURGE-LUBIN. No. What is it?

BARNABAS. These two are going to marry.

BURGE-LUBIN. Why shouldnt they, if they want to?

BARNABAS. They dont want to. They will do it in cold blood because their children will live three hundred years. It mustnt be allowed.

CONFUCIUS. You cannot prevent it. There is no law that gives you power to interfere with them.

BARNABAS. If they force me to it I will obtain legislation against marriages above the age of seventy-eight.

THE ARCHBISHOP. There is not time for that before we are married, Mr Accountant General. Be good enough to get out of the lady's way.

BARNABAS. There is time to send the lady to the lethal chamber before anything comes of your marriage. Dont forget that.

MRS LUTESTRING. What nonsense, Mr Accountant General! Good afternoon, Mr President. Good afternoon, Mr Chief Secretary. [*They rise and acknowledge her salutation with bows. She walks straight at the Accountant General, who instinctively shrinks out of her way as she leaves the room*].

THE ARCHBISHOP. I am surprised at you, Mr Barnabas. Your tone was like an echo from the Dark Ages. [*He follows the Domestic Minister*].

Confucius, shaking his head and clucking with his tongue in deprecation of this painful episode, moves to the chair just vacated by the Archbishop and stands behind it with folded palms, looking at the President. The Accountant General shakes his fist after the departed visitors, and bursts into savage abuse of them.

BARNABAS. Thieves! Cursed thieves! Vampires! What are you going to do, Burge?

BURGE-LUBIN. Do?

BARNABAS. Yes, do. There must be dozens of these people in existence. Are you going to let them do what the two who have just left us mean to do, and crowd us off the face of the earth?

BURGE-LUBIN [*sitting down*] Oh, come, Barnabas! What harm are they doing? Arnt you interested in them? Dont you like them?

BARNABAS. Like them! I hate them. They are monsters, unnatural monsters. They are poison to me.

BURGE-LUBIN. What possible objection can there be to their living as long as they can? It does not shorten our lives, does it?

BARNABAS. If I have to die when I am seventy-eight, I dont see why another man should be privileged to live to be two hundred and seventy-eight. It does shorten my life, relatively. It makes us ridiculous. If they grew to be twelve feet high they would make us all dwarfs. They talked to us as if we were children. There is no love lost between us: their hatred of us came out soon enough. You heard what the woman said, and how the Archbishop backed her up?

BURGE-LUBIN. But what can we do to them?

BARNABAS. Kill them.

BURGE-LUBIN. Nonsense!

BARNABAS. Lock them up. Sterilize them somehow, anyhow.

BURGE-LUBIN. But what reason could we give?

BARNABAS. What reason can you give for killing a snake? Nature tells you to do it.

BURGE-LUBIN. My dear Barnabas, you are out of your mind.

BARNABAS. Havnt you said that once too often already this morning?

BURGE-LUBIN. I dont believe you will carry a single soul with you.

BARNABAS. I understand. I know you. You think you are one of them.

CONFUCIUS. Mr Accountant General: you may be one of them.

BARNABAS. How dare you accuse me of such a thing? I am an honest man, not a monster. I won my place in public life by demonstrating that the true expectation of human life is seventy-eight point six. And I will resist any attempt to alter or upset it to the last drop of my blood if need be.

BURGE-LUBIN. Oh, tut tut! Come, come! Pull yourself together. How can you, a descendant of the great Conrad Barnabas, the man who is still remembered by his masterly Biography of a Black Beetle, be so absurd?

BARNABAS. You had better go and write the autobiography of a jackass. I am going to raise the country against this horror, and against you, if you shew the slightest sign of weakness about it.

CONFUCIUS [very impressively] You will regret it if you do.

BARNABAS. What is to make me regret it?

CONFUCIUS. Every mortal man and woman in the community will begin to count on living for three centuries. Things will happen which you do not foresee: terrible things. The family will dissolve: parents and children will be no longer the old and the young: brothers and sisters will meet as strangers after a hundred years separation: the ties of blood will lose their innocence. The imaginations of men, let loose over the possibilities of three centuries of life, will drive them mad and wreck human society. This discovery must be kept a dead secret. [He sits down].

BARNABAS. And if I refuse to keep the secret?

CONFUCIUS. I shall have you safe in a lunatic asylum the day after you blab.

BARNABAS. You forget that I can produce the Archbishop to prove my statement.

CONFUCIUS. So can I. Which of us do you think he will support when I explain to him that your object in revealing his age is to get him killed?

BARNABAS [desperate] Burge: are you going to back up this yellow abomination against me? Are we public men and members of the Government? or are we damned blackguards?

CONFUCIUS [unmoved] Have you ever known a public man who was not what vituperative people called a damned blackguard when some inconsiderate person wanted to tell the public more than was good for it?

BARNABAS. Hold your tongue, you insolent heathen. Burge: I spoke to you.

BURGE-LUBIN. Well, you know, my dear Barnabas, Confucius is a very long-headed chap. I see his point.

BARNABAS. Do you? Then let me tell you that, except officially, I will never speak to you again. Do you hear?

BURGE-LUBIN [cheerfully] You will. You will.

BARNABAS. And dont you ever dare speak to me again. Do you hear? [He turns to the door].

BURGE-LUBIN. I will. I will. Goodbye, Barnabas. God bless you.

BARNABAS. May you live forever, and be the laughing-stock of the whole world! [he dashes out in a fury].

BURGE-LUBIN [laughing indulgently] He will keep the secret all right. I know Barnabas. You neednt worry.

CONFUCIUS [troubled and grave] There are no secrets except the secrets that keep themselves. Consider. There are those films at the Record Office. We have no power to prevent the Master of the Records from publishing this discovery made in his department. We cannot silence the American—who can silence an American?—nor the people who were there today to receive him. Fortunately, a film can prove nothing but a resemblance.

BURGE-LUBIN. Thats very true. After all, the whole thing is confounded nonsense, isnt it?

CONFUCIUS [raising his head to look at him] You have decided not to believe it now that you realize its inconveniences. That is the English method. It may not work in this case.

BURGE-LUBIN. English be hanged! It's common sense. You know, those two people got us hypnotized: not a doubt of it. They must have been kidding us. They were, werent they?

CONFUCIUS. You looked into that woman's face; and you believed.

BURGE-LUBIN. Just so. Thats where she had me. I shouldnt have believed her a bit if she'd turned her back to me.

CONFUCIUS [shakes his head slowly and repeatedly]???

BURGE-LUBIN. You really think—? [he hesitates].

CONFUCIUS. The Archbishop has always been a puzzle to me. Ever since I learnt to distinguish between one English face and another I have noticed what the woman pointed out: that the English face is not an adult face, just as the English mind is not an adult mind.

BURGE-LUBIN. Stow it, John Chinaman. If ever there was a race divinely appointed to take charge of the non-adult races and guide them and train them and keep them out of mischief until they grow up to be capable of adopting our institutions, that race is the English race. It is the only race in the world that has that characteristic. Now!

CONFUCIUS. That is the fancy of a child nursing a doll. But it is ten times more childish of you to dispute the highest compliment ever paid you.

BURGE-LUBIN. You call it a compliment to class us as grown-up children.

CONFUCIUS. Not grown-up children, children at fifty, sixty, seventy. Your maturity is so late that you never attain to it. You have to be governed by races which are mature at forty. That means that you are potentially the most highly developed race on earth, and would be actually the greatest if you could live long enough to attain to maturity.

BURGE-LUBIN [grasping the idea at last] By George, Confucius, youre right! I never thought of that. That explains everything. We are just a lot of schoolboys: theres no denying it. Talk to an Englishman about anything serious, and he listens to you curiously for a moment just as he listens to a chap playing classical music. Then he goes back to his marine golf, or motoring, or flying, or women, just like a bit of stretched elastic when you let it go. [Soaring to the height of his theme] Oh, youre quite right. We are only in our infancy. I ought to be in a perambulator, with a nurse shoving me along. It's true: it's absolutely true. But some day we'll grow up; and then, by Jingo, we'll shew em.

CONFUCIUS. The Archbishop is an adult. When I was a child I was dominated and intimidated by people whom I now know to have been weaker and sillier than I, because there was some mysterious quality in their mere age that overawed me. I confess that, though I have kept up appearances, I have always been afraid of the Archbishop.

BURGE-LUBIN. Between ourselves, Confucius, so have I.

CONFUCIUS. It is this that convinced me. It was this in the woman's face that convinced you. Their new departure in the history of the race is no fraud. It does not even surprise me.

BURGE-LUBIN. Oh, come! Not surprise you! It's your pose never to be surprised at anything; but if you are not surprised at this you are not human.

CONFUCIUS. I am staggered, just as a man may be staggered by an explosion for which he has himself laid the charge and lighted the fuse. But I am not surprised, because, as a philosopher and a student of evolutionary biology, I have come to regard some such development as this as inevitable. If I had not thus prepared myself to be credulous, no mere evidence of films and well-told tales would have persuaded me to believe. As it is, I do believe.

BURGE-LUBIN. Well, that being settled, what the devil is to happen next? Whats the next move for us?

CONFUCIUS. We do not make the next move. The next move will be made by the Archbishop and the woman.

BURGE-LUBIN. Their marriage?

CONFUCIUS. More than that. They have made the momentous discovery that they are not alone in the world.

BURGE-LUBIN. You think there are others?

CONFUCIUS. There must be many others. Each of them believes that he or she is the only one to whom the miracle has happened. But the Archbishop knows better now. He will advertize in terms which only the long-lived people will understand. He will bring them together and organize them. They will hasten from all parts of the earth. They will become a great Power.

BURGE-LUBIN [a little alarmed] I say, will they? I suppose they will. I wonder is Barnabas right after all? Ought we to allow it?

CONFUCIUS. Nothing that we can do will stop it. We cannot in our souls really want to stop it: the vital force that has produced this change would paralyse our opposition to it, if we were mad enough to oppose. But we will not oppose. You and I may be of the elect, too.

BURGE-LUBIN. Yes: thats what gets us every time. What the deuce ought we to do? Something must be done about it, you know.

CONFUCIUS. Let us sit still, and meditate in silence on the vistas before us.

BURGE-LUBIN. By George, I believe youre right. Let us.

They sit meditating, the Chinaman naturally, the President with visible effort and intensity. He is positively glaring into the future when the voice *of the Negress is heard.*

THE NEGRESS. Mr President.

BURGE-LUBIN [*joyfully*] Yes. [*Taking up a peg*] Are you at home?

THE NEGRESS. No. Omega, zero, x squared.

The President rapidly puts the peg in the switchboard; works the dial; and presses the button. The screen becomes transparent; and the Negress, brilliantly dressed, appears on what looks like the bridge of a steam yacht in glorious sea weather. The installation with which she is communicating is beside the binnacle.

CONFUCIUS [*looking round, and recoiling with a shriek of disgust*] Ach! Avaunt! Avaunt! [*He rushes from the room*].

BURGE-LUBIN. What part of the coast is that?

THE NEGRESS. Fishguard Bay. Why not run over and join me for the afternoon? I am disposed to be approachable at last.

BURGE-LUBIN. But Fishguard! Two hundred and seventy miles!

THE NEGRESS. There is a lightning express on the Irish Air Service at half-past sixteen. They will drop you by a parachute in the bay. The dip will do you good. I will pick you up and dry you and give you a first-rate time.

BURGE-LUBIN. Delightful. But a little risky, isnt it?

THE NEGRESS. Risky! I thought you were afraid of nothing.

BURGE-LUBIN. I am not exactly afraid; but—

THE NEGRESS [*offended*] But you think it is not good enough. Very well [*she raises her hand to take the peg out of her switchboard*].

BURGE-LUBIN [*imploringly*] No: stop: let me explain: hold the line just one moment. Oh, please.

THE NEGRESS [*waiting with her hand poised over the peg*] Well?

BURGE-LUBIN. The fact is, I have been behaving very recklessly for some time past under the impression that my life would be so short that it was not worth bothering about. But I have just learnt that I may live —well, much longer than I expected. I am sure your good sense will tell you that this alters the case. I—

THE NEGRESS [*with suppressed rage*] Oh, quite. Pray dont risk your precious life on my account. Sorry for troubling you. Good-bye. [*She snatches out her peg and vanishes*].

BURGE-LUBIN [*urgently*] No: please hold on. I can convince you—[*a loud buzz-uzz-uzz*]. Engaged! Who is she calling up now? [*He*

presses the button and calls] The Chief Secretary. Say I want to see him again, just for a moment.

CONFUCIUS'S VOICE. Is the woman gone?

BURGE-LUBIN. Yes, yes: it's all right. Just a moment, if—[*Confucius returns*] Confucius: I have some important business at Fishguard. The Irish Air Service can drop me in the bay by parachute. I suppose it's quite safe, isnt it?

CONFUCIUS. Nothing is quite safe. The air service is as safe as any other travelling service. The parachute is safe. But the water is not safe.

BURGE-LUBIN. Why? They will give me an unsinkable tunic, wont they?

CONFUCIUS. You will not sink; but the sea is very cold. You may get rheumatism for life.

BURGE-LUBIN. For life! That settles it: I wont risk it.

CONFUCIUS. Good. You have at last become prudent: you are no longer what you call a sportsman: you are a sensible coward, almost a grown-up man. I congratulate you.

BURGE-LUBIN [*resolutely*] Coward or no coward, I will not face an eternity of rheumatism for any woman that ever was born. [*He rises and goes to the rack for his fillet*] I have changed my mind: I am going home. [*He cocks the fillet rakishly*] Good evening.

CONFUCIUS. So early? If the Minister of Health rings you up, what shall I tell her?

BURGE-LUBIN. Tell her to go to the devil. [*He goes out*].

CONFUCIUS [*shaking his head, shocked at the President's impoliteness*] No. No, no, no, no, no. Oh, these English! these crude young civilizations! Their manners! Hogs. Hogs.

PART IV

TRAGEDY OF AN ELDERLY GENTLEMAN

ACT I

Burrin pier on the south shore of Galway Bay in Ireland, a region of stone-capped hills and granite fields. It is a fine summer day in the year 3000 A.D. On an ancient stone stump, about three feet thick and three feet high, used for securing ships by ropes to the shore, and called a bollard or holdfast, an elderly gentleman sits facing the land, with his head bowed and his face in his hands, sobbing. His sunburnt skin contrasts with his white whiskers and eyebrows. He wears a black frock-coat, a white waistcoat, lavender trousers, a brilliant silk cravat with a jewelled pin stuck in it, a tall hat of grey felt, and patent leather boots with white spats. His starched linen cuffs protrude from his coat sleeves; and his collar, also of starched white linen, is Gladstonian. On his right, three or four full sacks, lying side by side on the flags, suggest that the pier, unlike many remote Irish piers, is occasionally useful as well as romantic. On his left, behind him, a flight of stone steps descends out of sight to the sea level.

A woman in a silk tunic and sandals, wearing little else except a cap with the number 2 on it in gold, comes up the steps from the sea, and stares in astonishment at the sobbing man. Her age cannot be guessed: her face is firm and chiselled like a young face; but her expression is unyouthful in its severity and determination.

THE WOMAN. What is the matter?

The elderly gentleman looks up; hastily pulls himself together; takes out a silk handkerchief and dries his tears lightly with a brave attempt to smile through them; and tries to rise gallantly, but sinks back.

THE WOMAN. Do you need assistance?

THE ELDERLY GENTLEMAN. No. Thank you very much. No. Nothing. The heat. [*He punctuates with sniffs, and dabs with his handkerchief at his eyes and nose*]. Hay fever.

THE WOMAN. You are a foreigner, are you not?

THE ELDERLY GENTLEMAN. No. You must not regard me as a foreigner. I am a Briton.

THE WOMAN. You come from some part of the British Commonwealth?

THE ELDERLY GENTLEMAN [*amiably pompous*] From its capital, madam.

THE WOMAN. From Baghdad?

THE ELDERLY GENTLEMAN. Yes. You may not be aware, madam, that these islands were once the centre of the British Commonwealth, during a period now known as The Exile. They were its headquarters a thousand years ago. Few people know this interesting circumstance now; but I assure you it is true. I have come here on a pious pilgrimage to one of the numerous lands of my fathers. We are of the same stock, you and I. Blood is thicker than water. We are cousins.

THE WOMAN. I do not understand. You say you have come here on a pious pilgrimage. Is that some new means of transport?

THE ELDERLY GENTLEMAN [*again shewing*

signs of distress] I find it very difficult to make myself understood here. I was not referring to a machine, but to a—a—a sentimental journey.

THE WOMAN. I am afraid I am as much in the dark as before. You said also that blood is thicker than water. No doubt it is; but what of it?

THE ELDERLY GENTLEMAN. Its meaning is obvious.

THE WOMAN. Perfectly. But I assure you I am quite aware that blood is thicker than water.

THE ELDERLY GENTLEMAN [*sniffing: almost in tears again*] We will leave it at that, madam.

THE WOMAN [*going nearer to him and scrutinizing him with some concern*] I am afraid you are not well. Were you not warned that it is dangerous for shortlived people to come to this country? There is a deadly disease called discouragement, against which shortlived people have to take very strict precautions. Intercourse with us puts too great a strain on them.

THE ELDERLY GENTLEMAN [*pulling himself together huffily*] It has no effect on me, madam. I fear my conversation does not interest you. If not, the remedy is in your own hands.

THE WOMAN [*looking at her hands, and then looking inquiringly at him*] Where?

THE ELDERLY GENTLEMAN [*breaking down*] Oh, this is dreadful. No understanding, no intelligence, no sympathy—[*his sobs choke him*].

THE WOMAN. You see, you are ill.

THE ELDERLY GENTLEMAN [*nerved by indignation*] I am not ill. I have never had a day's illness in my life.

THE WOMAN. May I advise you?

THE ELDERLY GENTLEMAN. I have no need of a lady doctor, thank you, madam.

THE WOMAN [*shaking her head*] I am afraid I do not understand. I said nothing about a butterfly.

THE ELDERLY GENTLEMAN. Well, *I* said nothing about a butterfly.

THE WOMAN. You spoke of a lady doctor. The word is known here only as the name of a butterfly.

THE ELDERLY GENTLEMAN [*insanely*] I give up. I can bear this no longer. It is easier to go out of my mind at once. [*He rises and dances about, singing*]

I'd be a butterfly, born in a bower,
Making apple dumplings without any flour.

THE WOMAN [*smiling gravely*] It must be at least a hundred and fifty years since I last laughed. But if you do that any more I shall certainly break out like a primary of sixty. Your dress is so extraordinarily ridiculous.

THE ELDERLY GENTLEMAN [*halting abruptly in his antics*] My dress ridiculous! I may not be dressed like a Foreign Office clerk; but my clothes are perfectly in fashion in my native metropolis, where yours—pardon my saying so—would be considered extremely unusual and hardly decent.

THE WOMAN. Decent? There is no such word in our language. What does it mean?

THE ELDERLY GENTLEMAN. It would not be decent for me to explain. Decency cannot be discussed without indecency.

THE WOMAN. I cannot understand you at all. I fear you have not been observing the rules laid down for shortlived visitors.

THE ELDERLY GENTLEMAN. Surely, madam, they do not apply to persons of my age and standing. I am not a child, nor an agricultural laborer.

THE WOMAN [*severely*] They apply to you very strictly. You are expected to confine yourself to the society of children under sixty. You are absolutely forbidden to approach fully adult natives under any circumstances. You cannot converse with persons of my age for long without bringing on a dangerous attack of discouragement. Do you realize that you are already shewing grave symptoms of that very distressing and usually fatal complaint?

THE ELDERLY GENTLEMAN. Certainly not, madam. I am fortunately in no danger of contracting it. I am quite accustomed to converse intimately and at the greatest length with the most distinguished persons. If you cannot discriminate between hay fever and imbecility, I can only say that your advanced years carry with them the inevitable penalty of dotage.

THE WOMAN. I am one of the guardians of this district; and I am responsible for your welfare—

THE ELDERLY GENTLEMAN. The Guardians! Do you take me for a pauper?

THE WOMAN. I do not know what a pauper is. You must tell me who you are, if it is possible for you to express yourself intelligibly—

THE ELDERLY GENTLEMAN [*snorts indignantly*]!

THE WOMAN [*continuing*]—and why you are wandering here alone without a nurse.

THE ELDERLY GENTLEMAN [*outraged*] Nurse!

THE WOMAN. Shortlived visitors are not allowed to go about here without nurses. Do you not know that rules are meant to be kept?

THE ELDERLY GENTLEMAN. By the lower classes, no doubt. But to persons in my position there are certain courtesies which are never denied by well-bred people; and—

THE WOMAN. There are only two human classes here: the shortlived and the normal. The rules apply to the shortlived, and are for their own protection. Now tell me at once who you are.

THE ELDERLY GENTLEMAN [*impressively*] Madam, I am a retired gentleman, formerly Chairman of the All-British Synthetic Egg and Vegetable Cheese Trust in Baghdad, and now President of the British Historical and Archæological Society, and a Vice-President of the Travellers' Club.

THE WOMAN. All that does not matter.

THE ELDERLY GENTLEMAN [*again snorting*] Hm! Indeed!

THE WOMAN. Have you been sent here to make your mind flexible?

THE ELDERLY GENTLEMAN. What an extraordinary question! Pray do you find my mind noticeably stiff?

THE WOMAN. Perhaps you do not know that you are on the west coast of Ireland, and that it is the practice among natives of the Eastern Island to spend some years here to acquire mental flexibility. The climate has that effect.

THE ELDERLY GENTLEMAN [*haughtily*] I was born, not in the Eastern Island, but, thank God, in dear old British Baghdad; and I am not in need of a mental health resort.

THE WOMAN. Then why are you here?

THE ELDERLY GENTLEMAN. Am I trespassing? I was not aware of it.

THE WOMAN. Trespassing? I do not understand the word.

THE ELDERLY GENTLEMAN. Is this land private property? If so, I make no claim. I proffer a shilling in satisfaction of damage (if any), and am ready to withdraw if you will be good enough to shew me the nearest way. [*He offers her a shilling*].

THE WOMAN [*taking it and examining it without much interest*] I do not understand a single word of what you have just said.

THE ELDERLY GENTLEMAN. I am speaking the

plainest English. Are you the landlord?

THE WOMAN [*shaking her head*] There is a tradition in this part of the country of an animal with a name like that. It used to be hunted and shot in the barbarous ages. It is quite extinct now.

THE ELDERLY GENTLEMAN [*breaking down again*] It is a dreadful thing to be in a country where nobody understands civilized institutions. [*He collapses on the bollard, struggling with his rising sobs*]. Excuse me. Hay fever.

THE WOMAN [*taking a tuning-fork from her girdle and holding it to her ear; then speaking into space on one note, like a chorister intoning a psalm*] Burrin Pier Galway please send someone to take charge of a discouraged short-liver who has escaped from his nurse male harmless babbles unintelligibly with moments of sense distressed hysterical foreign dress very funny has curious fringe of white seaweed under his chin.

THE GENTLEMAN. This is a gross impertinence. An insult.

THE WOMAN [*replacing her tuning-fork and addressing the elderly gentleman*] These words mean nothing to me. In what capacity are you here? How did you obtain permission to visit us?

THE ELDERLY GENTLEMAN [*importantly*] Our Prime Minister, Mr Badger Bluebin, has come to consult the oracle. He is my son-in-law. We are accompanied by his wife and daughter: my daughter and granddaughter. I may mention that General Aufsteig, who is one of our party, is really the Emperor of Turania travelling incognito. I understand he has a question to put to the oracle informally. I have come solely to visit the country.

THE WOMAN. Why should you come to a place where you have no business?

THE ELDERLY GENTLEMAN. Great Heavens, madam, can anything be more natural? I shall be the only member of the Travellers' Club who has set foot on these shores. Think of that! My position will be unique.

THE WOMAN. Is that an advantage? We have a person here who has lost both legs in an accident. His position is unique. But he would much rather be like everyone else.

THE ELDERLY GENTLEMAN. This is maddening. There is no analogy whatever between the two cases.

THE WOMAN. They are both unique.

THE ELDERLY GENTLEMAN. Conversation in this place seems to consist of ridiculous quibbles. I am heartily tired of them.

THE WOMAN. I conclude that your Travellers' Club is an assembly of persons who wish to be able to say that they have been in some place where nobody else has been.

THE ELDERLY GENTLEMAN. Of course if you wish to sneer at us—

THE WOMAN. What is sneer?

THE ELDERLY GENTLEMAN [*with a wild sob*] I shall drown myself.

He makes desperately for the edge of the pier, but is confronted by a man with the number one on his cap, who comes up the steps and intercepts him. He is dressed like the woman, but a slight moustache proclaims his sex.

THE MAN [*to the elderly gentleman*] Ah, here you are. I shall really have to put a collar and lead on you if you persist in giving me the slip like this.

THE WOMAN. Are you this stranger's nurse?

THE MAN. Yes. I am very tired of him. If I take my eyes off him for a moment, he runs away and talks to everybody.

THE WOMAN [*after taking out her tuning-fork and sounding it, intones as before*] Burrin Pier. Wash out. [*She puts up the fork, and addresses the man*]. I sent a call for someone to take care of him. I have been trying to talk to him; but I can understand very little of what he says. You must take better care of him: he is badly discouraged already. If I can be of any further use, Fusima, Gort, will find me. [*She goes away*].

THE ELDERLY GENTLEMAN. Any further use! She has been of no use to me. She spoke to me without any introduction, like any improper female. And she has made off with my shilling.

THE MAN. Please speak slowly: I cannot follow. What is a shilling? What is an introduction? Improper female doesnt make sense.

THE ELDERLY GENTLEMAN. Nothing seems to make sense here. All I can tell you is that she was the most impenetrably stupid woman I have ever met in the whole course of my life.

THE MAN. That cannot be. She cannot appear stupid to you. She is a secondary, and getting on for a tertiary at that.

THE ELDERLY GENTLEMAN. What is a tertiary? Everybody here keeps talking to me about primaries and secondaries and tertiaries as if people were geological strata.

THE MAN. The primaries are in their first century. The secondaries are in their second century. I am still classed as a primary [*he points to his number*]; but I may almost call myself a secondary, as I shall be ninety-five next January. The tertiaries are in their third century. Did you not see the number two on her badge? She is an advanced secondary.

THE ELDERLY GENTLEMAN. That accounts for it. She is in her second childhood.

THE MAN. Her second childhood! She is in her fifth childhood.

THE ELDERLY GENTLEMAN [*again resorting to the bollard*] Oh! I cannot bear these unnatural arrangements.

THE MAN [*impatient and helpless*] You shouldnt have come among us. This is no place for you.

THE ELDERLY GENTLEMAN [*nerved by indignation*] May I ask why? I am a Vice-President of the Travellers' Club. I have been everywhere: I hold the record in the Club for civilized countries.

THE MAN. What is a civilized country?

THE ELDERLY GENTLEMAN. It is—well, it is a civilized country. [*Desperately*] I dont know: I—I—I—I shall go mad if you keep on asking me to tell you things that everybody knows. Countries where you can travel comfortably. Where there are good hotels. Excuse me; but, though you say you are ninety-four, you are worse company than a child of five with your eternal questions. Why not call me Daddy at once?

THE MAN. I did not know your name was Daddy.

THE ELDERLY GENTLEMAN. My name is Joseph Popham Bolge Bluebin Barlow, O.M.

THE MAN. That is five men's names. Daddy is shorter. And O.M. will not do here. It is our name for certain wild creatures, descendants of the aboriginal inhabitants of this coast. They used to be called the O'Mulligans. We will stick to Daddy.

THE ELDERLY GENTLEMAN. People will think I am your father.

THE MAN [*shocked*] Sh-sh! People here never allude to such relationships. It is not quite delicate, is it? What does it matter whether you are my father or not?

THE ELDERLY GENTLEMAN. My worthy nonagenarian friend: your faculties are totally decayed. Could you not find me a guide of my own age?

THE MAN. A young person?

THE ELDERLY GENTLEMAN. Certainly not. I cannot go about with a young person.

THE MAN. Why?

THE ELDERLY GENTLEMAN. Why! Why!! Why!!! Have you no moral sense?

THE MAN. I shall have to give you up. I cannot understand you.

THE ELDERLY GENTLEMAN. But you meant a young woman, didnt you?

THE MAN. I meant simply somebody of your own age. What difference does it make whether the person is a man or a woman?

THE ELDERLY GENTLEMAN. I could not have believed in the existence of such scandalous insensibility to the elementary decencies of human intercourse.

THE MAN. What are decencies?

THE ELDERLY GENTLEMAN [*shrieking*] Everyone asks me that.

THE MAN [*taking out a tuning-fork and using it as the woman did*] Zozim on Burrin Pier to Zoo Ennistymon I have found the discouraged shortliver he has been talking to a secondary and is much worse I am too old he is asking for someone of his own age or younger come if you can. [*He puts up his fork and turns to the elderly gentleman*]. Zoo is a girl of fifty, and rather childish at that. So perhaps she may make you happy.

THE ELDERLY GENTLEMAN. Make me happy! A bluestocking of fifty! Thank you.

THE MAN. Bluestocking? The effort to make out your meaning is fatiguing. Besides, you are talking too much to me: I am old enough to discourage you. Let us be silent until Zoo comes. [*He turns his back on the elderly gentleman, and sits down on the edge of the pier, with his legs dangling over the water*].

THE ELDERLY GENTLEMAN. Certainly. I have no wish to force my conversation on any man who does not desire it. Perhaps you would like to take a nap. If so, pray do not stand on ceremony.

THE MAN. What is a nap?

THE ELDERLY GENTLEMAN [*exasperated, going to him and speaking with great precision and distinctness*] A nap, my friend, is a brief period of sleep which overtakes superannuated persons when they endeavor to entertain unwelcome visitors or to listen to scientific lectures. Sleep. Sleep. [*Bawling into his ear*] Sleep.

THE MAN. I tell you I am nearly a secondary. I never sleep.

THE ELDERLY GENTLEMAN [*awestruck*] Good Heavens!

A young woman with the number one on her cap arrives by land. She looks no older than Savvy Barnabas, whom she somewhat resembles, looked a thousand years before. Younger, if anything.

THE YOUNG WOMAN. Is this the patient?

THE MAN [*scrambling up*] This is Zoo. [*To Zoo*] Call him Daddy.

THE ELDERLY GENTLEMAN [*vehemently*] No.

THE MAN [*ignoring the interruption*] Bless you for taking him off my hands! I have had as much of him as I can bear. [*He goes down the steps and disappears*].

THE ELDERLY GENTLEMAN [*ironically taking off his hat and making a sweeping bow from the edge of the pier in the direction of the Atlantic Ocean*] Good afternoon, sir; and thank you very much for your extraordinary politeness, your exquisite consideration for my feelings, your courtly manners. Thank you from the bottom of my heart. [*Clapping his hat on again*] Pig! Ass!

zoo [*laughs very heartily at him*]!!!

THE ELDERLY GENTLEMAN [*turning sharply on her*] Good afternoon, madam. I am sorry to have had to put your friend in his place; but I find that here as elsewhere it is necessary to assert myself if I am to be treated with proper consideration. I had hoped that my position as a guest would protect me from insult.

zoo. Putting my friend in his place. That is some poetic expression, is it not? What does it mean?

THE ELDERLY GENTLEMAN. Pray, is there no one in these islands who understands plain English?

zoo. Well, nobody except the oracles. They have to make a special historical study of what we call the dead thought.

THE ELDERLY GENTLEMAN. Dead thought! I have heard of the dead languages, but never of the dead thought.

zoo. Well, thoughts die sooner than languages. I understand your language; but I do not always understand your thought. The oracles will understand you perfectly. Have you had your consultation yet?

THE ELDERLY GENTLEMAN. I did not come to consult the oracle, madam. I am here simply as a gentleman travelling for pleasure in the company of my daughter, who is the wife of the British Prime Minister, and of General Aufsteig, who, I may tell you in confidence, is really the Emperor of Turania, the greatest military genius of the age.

zoo. Why should you travel for pleasure! Can you not enjoy yourself at home?

THE ELDERLY GENTLEMAN. I wish to see the world.

zoo. It is too big. You can see a bit of it anywhere.

THE ELDERLY GENTLEMAN [*out of patience*] Damn it, madam, you dont want to spend your life looking at the same bit of it! [*Checking himself*] I beg your pardon for swearing in your presence.

zoo. Oh! That is swearing, is it? I have read about that. It sounds quite pretty. Dammitmaddam, dammitmaddam, dammitmaddam, dammitmaddam. Say it as often as you please: I like it.

THE ELDERLY GENTLEMAN [*expanding with intense relief*] Bless you for those profane but familiar words! Thank you, thank you. For the first time since I landed in this terrible country I begin to feel at home. The strain which was driving me mad relaxes: I feel almost as if I were at the club. Excuse my taking the only available seat. I am not so young as I was. [*He sits on the bollard*]. Promise me that you will not hand me over to one of these dreadful tertiaries or secondaries or whatever you call them.

zoo. Never fear. They had no business to give you in charge to Zozim. You see he is just on the verge of becoming a secondary; and these adolescents will give themselves the airs of tertiaries. You naturally feel more at home with a flapper like me. [*She makes herself comfortable on the sacks*].

THE ELDERLY GENTLEMAN. Flapper? What does that mean?

zoo. It is an archaic word which we still use to describe a female who is no longer a girl and is not yet quite adult.

THE ELDERLY GENTLEMAN. A very agreeable age to associate with, I find. I am recovering rapidly. I have a sense of blossoming like a flower. May I ask your name?

zoo. Zoo.

THE ELDERLY GENTLEMAN. Miss Zoo.

zoo. Not Miss Zoo. Zoo.

THE ELDERLY GENTLEMAN. Precisely. Er— Zoo what?

zoo. No. Not Zoo What. Zoo. Nothing but Zoo.

THE ELDERLY GENTLEMAN [*puzzled*] Mrs Zoo, perhaps.

zoo. No. Zoo. Cant you catch it? Zoo.

THE ELDERLY GENTLEMAN. Of course. Believe me, I did not really think you were married: you are obviously too young; but here it is so hard to feel sure—er—

ZOO [hopelessly puzzled] What?

THE ELDERLY GENTLEMAN. Marriage makes a difference, you know. One can say things to a married lady that would perhaps be in questionable taste to anyone without that experience.

ZOO. You are getting out of my depth: I dont understand a word you are saying. Married and questionable taste convey nothing to me. Stop, though. Is married an old form of the word mothered?

THE ELDERLY GENTLEMAN. Very likely. Let us drop the subject. Pardon me for embarrassing you. I should not have mentioned it.

ZOO. What does embarrassing mean?

THE ELDERLY GENTLEMAN. Well, really! I should have thought that so natural and common a condition would be understood as long as human nature lasted. To embarrass is to bring a blush to the cheek.

ZOO. What is a blush?

THE ELDERLY GENTLEMAN [amazed] Dont you blush???

ZOO. Never heard of it. We have a word flush, meaning a rush of blood to the skin. I have noticed it in my babies, but not after the age of two.

THE ELDERLY GENTLEMAN. Your babies!!! I fear I am treading on very delicate ground; but your appearance is extremely youthful; and if I may ask how many—?

ZOO. Only four as yet. It is a long business with us. I specialize in babies. My first was such a success that they made me go on. I—

THE ELDERLY GENTLEMAN [reeling on the bollard] Oh! dear!

ZOO. Whats the matter? Anything wrong?

THE ELDERLY GENTLEMAN. In Heaven's name, madam, how old are you?

ZOO. Fifty-six.

THE ELDERLY GENTLEMAN. My knees are trembling. I fear I am really ill. Not so young as I was.

ZOO. I noticed that you are not strong on your legs yet. You have many of the ways and weaknesses of a baby. No doubt that is why I feel called on to mother you. You certainly are a very silly little Daddy.

THE ELDERLY GENTLEMAN [stimulated by indignation] My name, I repeat, is Joseph Popham Bolge Bluebin Barlow, O.M.

ZOO. What a ridiculously long name! I cant call you all that. What did your mother call you?

THE ELDERLY GENTLEMAN. You recall the bitterest struggles of my childhood. I was sensitive on the point. Children suffer greatly from absurd nicknames. My mother thoughtlessly called me Iddy Toodles. I was called Iddy until I went to school, when I made my first stand for children's rights by insisting on being called at least Joe. At fifteen I refused to answer to anything shorter than Joseph. At eighteen I discovered that the name Joseph was supposed to indicate an unmanly prudery because of some old story about a Joseph who rejected the advances of his employer's wife: very properly in my opinion. I then became Popham to my family and intimate friends, and Mister Barlow to the rest of the world. My mother slipped back into Iddy when her faculties began to fail her, poor woman; but I could not resent that, at her age.

ZOO. Do you mean to say that your mother bothered about you after you were ten?

THE ELDERLY GENTLEMAN. Naturally, madam. She was my mother. What would you have had her do?

ZOO. Go on to the next, of course. After eight or nine children become quite uninteresting, except to themselves. I shouldnt know my two eldest if I met them.

THE ELDERLY GENTLEMAN [again drooping] I am dying. Let me die. I wish to die.

ZOO [going to him quickly and supporting him] Hold up. Sit up straight. Whats the matter?

THE ELDERLY GENTLEMAN [faintly] My spine, I think. Shock. Concussion.

ZOO [maternally] Pow wow wow! What is there to shock you? [Shaking him playfully] There! Sit up; and be good.

THE ELDERLY GENTLEMAN [still feebly] Thank you. I am better now.

ZOO [resuming her seat on the sacks] But what was all the rest of that long name for? There was a lot more of it. Blops Booby or something.

THE ELDERLY GENTLEMAN [impressively] Bolge Bluebin, madam: a historical name. Let me inform you that I can trace my family back for more than a thousand years, from the Eastern Empire to its ancient seat in these islands, to a time when two of my ancestors, Joyce Bolge and Hengist Horsa Bluebin, wrestled with one another for the prime ministership of the British Empire, and occupied that position successively with a glory of which we can in these degenerate days form but a faint conception. When I think of these mighty men, lions in war, sages in peace, not babblers and charlatans like the pigmies who now occupy their places in Baghdad, but strong silent men, ruling an empire on which the sun never set, my eyes fill with tears: my heart bursts with emotion: I feel that to have lived but to the dawn of manhood in their day, and then died for them, would have been a nobler and happier lot than the ignominious ease of my present longevity.

zoo. Longevity! [*she laughs*].

THE ELDERLY GENTLEMAN. Yes, madam, r e l a t i v e longevity. As it is, I have to be content and proud to know that I am descended from both those heroes.

zoo. You must be descended from every Briton who was alive in their time. Dont you know that?

THE ELDERLY GENTLEMAN. Do not quibble, madam. I bear their names, Bolge and Bluebin; and I hope I have inherited something of their majestic spirit. Well, they were born in these islands. I repeat, these islands were then, incredible as it now seems, the centre of the British Empire. When that centre shifted to Baghdad, and the Englishman at last returned to the true cradle of his race in Mesopotamia, the western islands were cast off, as they had been before by the Roman Empire. But it was to the British race, and in these islands, that the greatest miracle in history occurred.

zoo. Miracle?

THE ELDERLY GENTLEMAN. Yes: the first man to live three hundred years was an Englishman. The first, that is, since the contemporaries of Methuselah.

zoo. Oh, t h a t!

THE ELDERLY GENTLEMAN. Yes, t h a t, as you call it so flippantly. Are you aware, madam, that at that immortal moment the English race had lost intellectual credit to such an extent that they habitually spoke of one another as fatheads? Yet England is now a sacred grove to which statesmen from all over the earth come to consult English sages who speak with the experience of two and a half centuries of life. The land that once exported cotton shirts and hardware now exports nothing but wisdom. You see before you, madam, a man utterly weary of the week-end riverside hotels of the Euphrates, the minstrels and pierrots on the sands of the Persian Gulf, the toboggans and funiculars of the Hindoo Koosh. Can you wonder that I turn, with a hungry heart, to the mystery and beauty of these haunted islands, thronged with spectres from a magic past, made holy by the footsteps of the wise men of the West. Consider this island on which we stand, the last foothold of man on this side of the Atlantic: this Ireland, described by the earliest bards as an emerald gem set in a silver sea! Can I, a scion of the illustrious British race, ever forget that when the Empire transferred its seat to the East, and said to the turbulent Irish race which it had oppressed but never conquered, "At last we leave you to yourselves; and much good may it do you," the Irish as one man uttered the historic shout "No: we'll be damned if you do," and emigrated to the countries where there was still a Nationalist question, to India, Persia, and Corea, to Morocco, Tunis, and Tripoli. In these countries they were ever foremost in the struggle for national independence; and the world rang continually with the story of their sufferings and wrongs. And what poem can do justice to the end, when it came at last? Hardly two hundred years had elapsed when the claims of nationality were so universally conceded that there was no longer a single country on the face of the earth with a national grievance or a national movement. Think of the position of the Irish, who had lost all their political faculties by disuse except that of nationalist agitation, and who owed their position as the most interesting race on earth solely to their sufferings! The very countries they had helped to set free boycotted them as intolerable bores. The communities which had once idolized them as the incarnation of all that is adorable in the warm heart and witty brain, fled from them as from a pestilence. To regain their lost prestige, the Irish claimed the city of Jerusalem, on the ground that they were the lost tribes of Israel; but on their approach the Jews abandoned the city and redistributed themselves throughout Europe. It was then that these devoted Irishmen, not one of whom had ever seen Ireland, were counselled by an English Archbishop, the father of the oracles, to go back to their own country. This had never once occurred to them, because there was nothing to prevent them and nobody to forbid them. They jumped at the suggestion. They landed here: here in Galway Bay, on this very ground. Then they reached the shore the older men and women flung themselves down and passionately kissed the soil of Ireland, calling on the young to embrace the earth that had borne their ancestors. But the young looked gloomily on, and said "There is no earth, only stone." You will see by looking round you why they said that: the fields here are of stone: the hills are capped with granite. They all left for England next day; and no Irishman ever again confessed to being Irish, even to his own children; so that when that generation passed away the Irish race vanished from human knowledge. And the dispersed Jews did the same lest they should be sent back to Palestine. Since then the world, bereft of its Jews and its Irish, has been a tame dull place. Is there no pathos for you in this story? Can you not understand now why I am come to visit the scene of this tragic effacement of a race of heroes and poets?

zoo. We still tell our little children stories like that, to help them to understand. But such things do not happen really. That scene of the Irish landing here and kissing the ground might have happened to a hundred people. It couldnt have happened to a hundred thousand: you know that as well as I do. And what a ridiculous thing to call people Irish because they live in Ireland! you might as well call them Airish because they live in air. They must be just the same as other people. Why do you shortlivers persist in making up silly stories about the world and trying to act as if they were true? Contact with truth hurts and frightens you: you escape from it into an imaginary vacuum in which you can indulge your desires and hopes and loves and hates without any obstruction from the solid facts of life. You love to throw dust in your own eyes.

THE ELDERLY GENTLEMAN. It is my turn now, madam, to inform you that I do not understand a single word you are saying. I should have thought that the use of a vacuum for removing dust was a mark of civilization rather than of savagery.

zoo [giving him up as hopeless] Oh, Daddy, Daddy: I can hardly believe that you are human, you are so stupid. It was well said of your people in the olden days, "Dust thou

art; and to dust thou shalt return."

THE ELDERLY GENTLEMAN [nobly] My body is dust, madam: not my soul. What does it matter what my body is made of? the dust of the ground, the particles of the air, or even the slime of the ditch? The important thing is that when my Creator took it, whatever it was, He breathed into its nostrils the breath of life; and Man became a living soul. Yes, madam, a living soul. I am not the dust of the ground: I am a living soul. That is an exalting, a magnificent thought. It is also a great scientific fact. I am not interested in the chemicals and the microbes: I leave them to the chumps and noodles, to the blockheads and the muckrakers who are incapable of their own glorious destiny, and unconscious of their own divinity. They tell me there are leucocytes in my blood, and sodium and carbon in my flesh. I thank them for the information, and tell them that there are black-beetles in my kitchen, washing soda in my laundry, and coal in my cellar. I do not deny their existence; but I keep them in their proper place, which is not, if I may be allowed to use an antiquated form of expression, the temple of the Holy Ghost. No doubt you think me behind the times; but I rejoice in my enlightenment; and I recoil from your ignorance, your blindness, your imbecility. Humanly I pity you. Intellectually I despise you.

zoo. Bravo, Daddy! You have the root of the matter in you. You will not die of discouragement after all.

THE ELDERLY GENTLEMAN. I have not the smallest intention of doing so, madam. I am no longer young; and I have moments of weakness; but when I approach this subject the divine spark in me kindles and glows, the corruptible becomes incorruptible, and the mortal Bolge Bluebin Barlow puts on immortality. On this ground I am your equal, even if you survive me by ten thousand years.

zoo. Yes; but what do we know about this breath of life that puffs you up so exaltedly? Just nothing. So let us shake hands as cultivated Agnostics, and change the subject.

THE ELDERLY GENTLEMAN. Cultivated fiddlesticks, madam! You cannot change this subject until the heavens and the earth pass away. I am not an Agnostic: I am a gentleman. When I believe a thing I say I believe it: when I dont believe it I say I dont believe it. I do not shirk my responsibilities by pretending that I know nothing and therefore can believe nothing. We cannot disclaim knowledge and shirk responsibility. We must proceed on assumptions of some sort or we cannot form a human society.

ZOO. The assumptions must be scientific, Daddy. We must live by science in the long run.

THE ELDERLY GENTLEMAN. I have the utmost respect, madam, for the magnificent discoveries which we owe to science. But any fool can make a discovery. Every baby has to discover more in the first years of its life than Roger Bacon ever discovered in his laboratory. When I was seven years old I discovered the sting of the wasp. But I do not ask you to worship me on that account. I assure you, madam, the merest mediocrities can discover the most surprising facts about the physical universe as soon as they are civilized enough to have time to study these things, and to invent instruments and apparatus for research. But what is the consequence? Their discoveries discredit the simple stories of our religion. At first we had no idea of astronomical space. We believed the sky to be only the ceiling of a room as large as the earth, with another room on top of it. Death was to us a going upstairs into that room, or, if we did not obey the priests, going downstairs into the coal cellar. We founded our religion, our morality, our laws, our lessons, our poems, our prayers, on that simple belief. Well, the moment men became astronomers and made telescopes, their belief perished. When they could no longer believe in the sky, they found that they could no longer believe in their Deity, because they had always thought of him as living in the sky. When the priests themselves ceased to believe in their Deity and began to believe in astronomy, they changed their name and their dress, and called themselves doctors and men of science. They set up a new religion in which there was no Deity, but only wonders and miracles, with scientific instruments and apparatus as the wonder workers. Instead of worshipping the greatness and wisdom of the Deity, men gaped foolishly at the million billion miles of space and worshipped the astronomer as infallible and omniscient. They built temples for his telescopes. Then they looked into their own bodies with microscopes, and found there, not the soul they had formerly believed in, but millions of micro-organisms; so they gaped at these as foolishly as at the millions of miles, and built microscope temples in which horrible sacrifices were offered. They even gave their own bodies to be sacrificed by the microscope man, who was worshipped, like the astronomer, as infallible and omniscient. Thus our discoveries, instead of increasing our wisdom, only destroyed the little childish wisdom we had. All I can grant you is that they increased our knowledge.

ZOO. Nonsense! Consciousness of a fact is not knowledge of it: if it were, the fish would know more of the sea than the geographers and the naturalists.

THE ELDERLY GENTLEMAN. That is an extremely acute remark, madam. The dullest fish could not possibly know less of the majesty of the ocean than many geographers and naturalists of my acquaintance.

ZOO. Just so. And the greatest fool on earth, by merely looking at a mariners' compass, may become conscious of the fact that the needle turns always to the pole. Is he any the less a fool with that consciousness than he was without it?

THE ELDERLY GENTLEMAN. Only a more conceited one, madam, no doubt. Still, I do not quite see how you can be aware of the existence of a thing without knowing it.

ZOO. Well, you can see a man without knowing him, can you not?

THE ELDERLY GENTLEMAN [illuminated] Oh how true! Of course, of course. There is a member of the Travellers' Club who has questioned the veracity of an experience of mine at the South Pole. I see that man almost every day when I am at home. But I refuse to know him.

ZOO. If you could see him much more distinctly through a magnifying glass, or examine a drop of his blood through a microscope, or dissect out all his organs and analyze them chemically, would you know him then?

THE ELDERLY GENTLEMAN. Certainly not. Any such investigation could only increase the disgust with which he inspires me, and make me more determined than ever not to know him on any terms.

ZOO. Yet you would be much more conscious of him, would you not?

THE ELDERLY GENTLEMAN. I should not allow that to commit me to any familiarity with the fellow. I have been twice at the Summer Sports at the South Pole; and this man pretended he had been to the North Pole, which can hardly be said to exist, as it is in the middle of the sea. He declared he had hung his hat on it.

ZOO [laughing] He knew that travellers are amusing only when they are telling lies. Perhaps if you looked at that man through a microscope you would find some good in him.

THE ELDERLY GENTLEMAN. I do not want to find any good in him. Besides, madam, what you have just said encourages me to utter an opinion of mine which is so advanced! so intellectually daring! that I have never ventured to confess to it before, lest I should be imprisoned for blasphemy, or even burnt alive.

ZOO. Indeed! What opinion is that?

THE ELDERLY GENTLEMAN [after looking cautiously round] I do not approve of microscopes. I never have.

ZOO. You call that advanced! Oh, Daddy, that is pure obscurantism.

THE ELDERLY GENTLEMAN. Call it so if you will, madam; but I maintain that it is dangerous to shew too much to people who do not know what they are looking at. I think that a man who is sane as long as he looks at the world through his own eyes is very likely to become a dangerous madman if he takes to looking at the world through telescopes and microscopes. Even when he is telling fairy stories about giants and dwarfs, the giants had better not be too big nor the dwarfs too small and too malicious. Before the microscope came, our fairy stories only made the children's flesh creep pleasantly, and did not frighten grown-up persons at all. But the microscope men terrified themselves and everyone else out of their wits with the invisible monsters they saw: poor harmless little things that die at the touch of a ray of sunshine, and are themselves the victims of all the diseases they are supposed to produce! Whatever the scientific people may say, imagination without microscopes was kindly and often courageous, because it worked on things of which it had some real knowledge. But imagination with microscopes, working on a terrifying spectacle of millions of grotesque creatures of whose nature it had no knowledge, became a cruel, terror-stricken, persecuting delirium. Are you aware, madam, that a general massacre of men of science took place in the twenty-first century of the pseudo-Christian era, when all their laboratories were demolished, and all their apparatus destroyed?

ZOO. Yes: the shortlived are as savage in their advances as in their relapses. But when Science crept back, it had been taught its place. The mere collectors of anatomical or chemical facts were not supposed to know more about Science than the collector of used postage stamps about international trade or literature. The scientific terrorist who was afraid to use a spoon or a tumbler until he had dipt it in some poisonous acid to kill the microbes, was no longer given titles, pensions, and monstrous powers over the bodies of other people: he was sent to an asylum, and treated there until his recovery. But all that is an old story: the extension of life to three hundred years has provided the human race with capable leaders, and made short work of such childish stuff.

THE ELDERLY GENTLEMAN [pettishly] You seem to credit every advance in civilization to your inordinately long lives. Do you not know that this question was familiar to men who died before they had reached my own age?

ZOO. Oh yes: one or two of them hinted at it in a feeble way. An ancient writer whose name has come down to us in several forms, such as Shakespear, Shelley, Sheridan, and Shoddy, has a remarkable passage about your dispositions being horridly shaken by thoughts beyond the reaches of your souls. That does not come to much, does it?

THE ELDERLY GENTLEMAN. At all events, madam, I may remind you, if you come to capping ages, that whatever your secondaries and tertiaries may be, y o u are younger than I am.

ZOO. Yes, Daddy; but it is not the number of years we have behind us, but the number we have before us, that makes us careful and responsible and determined to find out the truth about everything. What does it matter to you whether anything is true or not? your flesh is as grass: you come up like a flower, and wither in your second childhood. A lie will last your time: it will not last mine. If I knew I had to die in twenty years it would not be worth my while to educate myself: I should not bother about anything but having a little pleasure while I lasted.

THE ELDERLY GENTLEMAN. Young woman: you are mistaken. Shortlived as we are, we—the best of us, I mean—regard civilization and learning, art and science as an everburning torch, which passes from the hand of one generation to the hand of the next, each generation kindling it to a brighter, prouder flame. Thus each lifetime, however short, contributes a brick to a vast and growing edifice, a page to a sacred volume, a chapter to a Bible, a Bible to a literature. We may be insects; but like the coral insect we build islands which become continents: like the bee we store sustenance for future communities. The individual perishes; but the race is immortal. The acorn of today is the oak of the next millennium. I throw my stone on the cairn and die; but later comers add another stone and yet another; and lo! a mountain. I—

zoo [interrupts him by laughing heartily at him]!!!!!!

THE ELDERLY GENTLEMAN [with offended dignity] May I ask what I have said that calls for this merriment?

zoo. Oh, Daddy, Daddy, Daddy, you are a funny little man, with your torches, and your flames, and your bricks and edifices and pages and volumes and chapters and coral insects and bees and acorns and stones and mountains.

THE ELDERLY GENTLEMAN. Metaphors, madam. Metaphors merely.

zoo. Images, images, images. I was talking about men, not about images.

THE ELDERLY GENTLEMAN. I was illustrating —not, I hope, quite infelicitously—the great march of Progress. I was shewing you how, shortlived as we orientals are, mankind gains in stature from generation to generation, from epoch to epoch, from barbarism to civilization, from civilization to perfection.

zoo. I see. The father grows to be six feet high, and hands on his six feet to his son, who adds another six feet and becomes twelve feet high, and hands his twelve feet on to his son, who is full-grown at eighteen feet, and so on. In a thousand years you would all be three or four miles high. At that rate your ancestors Bilge and Bluebeard, whom you call giants, must have been about quarter of an inch high.

THE ELDERLY GENTLEMAN. I am not here to bandy quibbles and paradoxes with a girl who blunders over the greatest names in history. I am in earnest. I am treating a solemn theme seriously. I never said that the son of a man six feet high would be twelve feet high.

zoo. You didnt mean that?

THE ELDERLY GENTLEMAN. Most certainly not.

zoo. Then you didnt mean anything. Now listen to me, you little ephemeral thing. I knew quite well what you meant by your torch handed on from generation to generation. But every time that torch is handed on, it dies down to the tiniest spark; and the man who gets it can rekindle it only by his own light. You are no taller than Bilge or Bluebeard; and you are no wiser. Their wisdom, such as it was, perished with them: so did their strength, if their strength ever existed outside your imagination. I do not know how old you are: you look about five hundred—

THE ELDERLY GENTLEMAN. Five hundred! Really, madam—

zoo [continuing]; but I know, of course, that you are an ordinary shortliver. Well, your wisdom is only such wisdom as a man can have before he has had experience enough to distinguish his wisdom from his folly, his destiny from his delusions, his—

THE ELDERLY GENTLEMAN. In short, such wisdom as your own.

zoo. No, no, no, no. How often must I tell you that we are made wise not by the recollections of our past, but by the responsibilities of our future. I shall be more reckless when I am a tertiary than I am today. If you cannot understand that, at least you must admit that I have learnt from tertiaries. I have seen their work and lived under their institutions. Like all young things I rebelled against them; and in their hunger for new lights and new ideas they listened to me and encouraged me to rebel. But my ways did not work; and theirs did; and they were able to tell me why. They have no power over me except that power: they refuse all other power; and the consequence is that there are no limits to their power except the limits they set themselves. You are a child governed by children, who make so many mistakes and are so naughty that you are in continual rebellion against them; and as they can never convince you that they are right: they can govern you only by beating you, imprisoning you, torturing you, killing you if you disobey them without being strong enough to kill or torture them.

THE ELDERLY GENTLEMAN. That may be an unfortunate fact. I condemn it and deplore it. But our minds are greater than the facts.

We know better. The greatest ancient teachers, followed by the galaxy of Christs who arose in the twentieth century, not to mention such comparatively modern spiritual leaders as Blitherinjam, Tosh, and Spiffkins, all taught that punishment and revenge, coercion and militarism, are mistakes, and that the golden rule—

zoo [*interrupting*] Yes, yes, yes, Daddy: we longlived people know that quite well. But did any of their disciples ever succeed in governing you for a single day on their Christlike principles? It is not enough to know what is good: you must be able to do it. They couldnt do it because they did not live long enough to find out how to do it, or to outlive the childish passions that prevented them from really wanting to do it. You know very well that they could only keep order— such as it was—by the very coercion and militarism they were denouncing and deploring. They had actually to kill one another for preaching their own gospel, or be killed themselves.

THE ELDERLY GENTLEMAN. The blood of the martyrs, madam, is the seed of the Church.

zoo. More images, Daddy! The blood of the shortlived falls on stony ground.

THE ELDERLY GENTLEMAN [*rising, very testy*] You are simply mad on the subject of longevity. I wish you would change it. It is rather personal and in bad taste. Human nature is human nature, longlived or shortlived, and always will be.

zoo. Then you give up the idea of progress? You cry off the torch, and the brick, and the acorn, and all the rest of it?

THE ELDERLY GENTLEMAN. I do nothing of the sort. I stand for progress and for freedom broadening down from precedent to precedent.

zoo. You are certainly a true Briton.

THE ELDERLY GENTLEMAN. I am proud of it. But in your mouth I feel that the compliment hides some insult; so I do not thank you for it.

zoo. All I meant was that though Britons sometimes say quite clever things and deep things as well as silly and shallow things, they always forget them ten minutes after they have uttered them.

THE ELDERLY GENTLEMAN. Leave it at that, madam: leave it at that. [*He sits down again*]. Even a Pope is not expected to be continually pontificating. Our flashes of inspiration shew that our hearts are in the right place.

zoo. Of course. You cannot keep your heart in any place but the right place.

THE ELDERLY GENTLEMAN. Tcha!

zoo. But you can keep your hands in the wrong place. In your neighbors' pockets, for example. So, you see, it is your hands that really matter.

THE ELDERLY GENTLEMAN [*exhausted*] Well, a woman must have the last word. I will not dispute it with you.

zoo. Good. Now let us go back to the really interesting subject of our discussion. You remember? The slavery of the shortlived to images and metaphors.

THE ELDERLY GENTLEMAN [*aghast*] Do you mean to say, madam, that after having talked my head off, and reduced me to despair and silence by your intolerable loquacity, you actually propose to begin all over again? I shall leave you at once.

zoo. You must not. I am your nurse; and you must stay with me.

THE ELDERLY GENTLEMAN. I absolutely decline to do anything of the sort [*he rises and walks away with marked dignity*].

zoo [*using her tuning-fork*] Zoo on Burrin Pier to Oracle Police at Ennistymon have you got me? . . . What? . . . I am picking you up now but you are flat to my pitch. . . Just a shade sharper. . . . Thats better: still a little more. . . . Got you: right. Isolate Burrin Pier quick.

THE ELDERLY GENTLEMAN [*is heard to yell*] Oh!

zoo [*still intoning*] Thanks. . . . Oh nothing serious I am nursing a shortliver and the silly creature has run away he has discouraged himself very badly by gadding about and talking to secondaries and I must keep him strictly to heel.

The Elderly Gentleman returns, indignant.

zoo. Here he is you can release the Pier thanks. Goodbye. [*She puts up her tuning-fork*].

THE ELDERLY GENTLEMAN. This is outrageous. When I tried to step off the pier on to the road, I received a shock, followed by an attack of pins and needles which ceased only when I stepped back on to the stones.

zoo. Yes: there is an electric hedge there. It is a very old and very crude method of keeping animals from straying.

THE ELDERLY GENTLEMAN. We are perfectly familiar with it in Baghdad, madam; but I little thought I should live to have it ignominiously applied to myself. You have actually Kiplingized me.

zoo. Kiplingized! What is that?

THE ELDERLY GENTLEMAN. About a thousand years ago there were two authors named Kipling. One was an eastern and a writer of merit: the other, being a western, was of course only an amusing barbarian. He is said to have invented the electric hedge. I consider that in using it on me you have taken a very great liberty.

zoo. What is a liberty?

THE ELDERLY GENTLEMAN [exasperated] I shall not explain, madam. I believe you know as well as I do. [He sits down on the bollard in dudgeon].

zoo. No: even you can tell me things I do not know. Havnt you noticed that all the time you have been here we have been asking you questions?

THE ELDERLY GENTLEMAN. Noticed it! It has almost driven me mad. Do you see my white hair? It was hardly grey when I landed: there were patches of its original auburn still distinctly discernible.

zoo. That is one of the symptoms of discouragement. But have you noticed something much more important to yourself: that is, that you have never asked us any questions, although we know so much more than you do?

THE ELDERLY GENTLEMAN. I am not a child, madam. I believe I have had occasion to say that before. And I am an experienced traveller. I know that what the traveller observes must really exist, or he could not observe it. But what the natives tell him is invariably pure fiction.

zoo. Not here, Daddy. With us life is too long for telling lies. They all get found out. Youd better ask me questions while you have the chance.

THE ELDERLY GENTLEMAN. If I have occasion to consult the oracle I shall address myself to a proper one: to a tertiary: not to a primary flapper playing at being an oracle. If you are a nurserymaid, attend to your duties; and do not presume to ape your elders.

zoo [rising ominously and reddening] You silly—

THE ELDERLY GENTLEMAN [thundering] Silence! Do you hear! Hold your tongue.

zoo. Something very disagreeable is happening to me. I feel hot all over. I have a horrible impulse to injure you. What have you done to me?

THE ELDERLY GENTLEMAN [triumphant] Aha! I have made you blush. Now you know what blushing means. Blushing with shame!

zoo. Whatever you are doing, it is something so utterly evil that if you do not stop I will kill you.

THE ELDERLY GENTLEMAN [apprehending his danger] Doubtless you think it safe to threaten an old man—

zoo [fiercely] Old! You are a child: an evil child. We kill evil children here. We do it even against our own wills, by instinct. Take care.

THE ELDERLY GENTLEMAN [rising with crestfallen courtesy] I did not mean to hurt your feelings. I—[swallowing the apology with an effort] I beg your pardon. [He takes off his hat, and bows].

zoo. What does that mean?

THE ELDERLY GENTLEMAN. I withdraw what I said.

zoo. How can you withdraw what you said?

THE ELDERLY GENTLEMAN. I can say no more than that I am sorry.

zoo. You have reason to be. That hideous sensation you gave me is subsiding; but you have had a very narrow escape. Do not attempt to kill me again; for at the first sign in your voice or face I shall strike you dead.

THE ELDERLY GENTLEMAN. I attempt to kill you! What a monstrous accusation!

zoo [frowns]!

THE ELDERLY GENTLEMAN [prudently correcting himself] I mean misunderstanding. I never dreamt of such a thing. Surely you cannot believe that I am a murderer.

zoo. I know you are a murderer. It is not merely that you threw words at me as if they were stones, meaning to hurt me. It was the instinct to kill that you roused in me. I did not know it was in my nature: never before has it wakened and sprung out at me, warning me to kill or be killed. I must now reconsider my whole political position. I am no longer a Conservative.

THE ELDERLY GENTLEMAN [dropping his hat] Gracious Heavens! you have lost your senses. I am at the mercy of a madwoman: I might have known it from the beginning. I can bear no more of this. [Offering his chest for the sacrifice] Kill me at once; and much good may my death do you!

zoo. It would be useless unless all the other shortlivers were killed at the same time. Besides, it is a measure which should be taken politically and constitutionally, not privately. However, I am prepared to discuss it with you.

THE ELDERLY GENTLEMAN. No, no, no. I had much rather discuss your intention of withdrawing from the Conservative party. How the Conservatives have tolerated your opinions so far is more than I can imagine: I can only conjecture that you have contributed very liberally to the party funds. [*He picks up his hat, and sits down again*].

zoo. Do not babble so senselessly: our chief political controversy is the most momentous in the world for you and your like.

THE ELDERLY GENTLEMAN [*interested*] Indeed? Pray, may I ask what it is? I am a keen politician, and may perhaps be of some use. [*He puts on his hat, cocking it slightly*].

zoo. We have two great parties: the Conservative party and the Colonization party. The Colonizers are of opinion that we should increase our numbers and colonize. The Conservatives hold that we should stay as we are, confined to these islands, a race apart, wrapped up in the majesty of our wisdom on a soil held as holy ground for us by an adoring world, with our sacred frontier traced beyond dispute by the sea. They contend that it is our destiny to rule the world, and that even when we were shortlived we did so. They say that our power and our peace depend on our remoteness, our exclusiveness, our separation, and the restriction of our numbers. Five minutes ago that was my political faith. Now I do not think there should be any shortlived people at all. [*She throws herself again carelessly on the sacks*].

THE ELDERLY GENTLEMAN. Am I to infer that you deny my right to live because I allowed myself—perhaps injudiciously—to give you a slight scolding?

zoo. Is it worth living for so short a time? Are you any good to yourself?

THE ELDERLY GENTLEMAN [*stupent*] Well, upon my soul!

zoo. It is such a very little soul. You only encourage the sin of pride in us, and keep us looking down at you instead of up to something higher than ourselves.

THE ELDERLY GENTLEMAN. Is not that a selfish view, madam? Think of the good you do us by your oracular counsels!

zoo. What good have our counsels ever done you? You come to us for advice when you know you are in difficulties. But you never know you are in difficulties until twenty years after you have made the mistakes that led to them; and then it is too late. You cannot understand our advice: you often do more mischief by trying to act on it than if you had been left to your own childish devices. If you were not childish you would not come to us at all: you would learn from experience that your consultations of the oracle are never of any real help to you. You draw wonderful imaginary pictures of us, and write fictitious tales and poems about our beneficent operations in the past, our wisdom, our justice, our mercy: stories in which we often appear as sentimental dupes of your prayers and sacrifices; but you do it only to conceal from yourselves the truth that you are incapable of being helped by us. Your Prime Minister pretends that he has come to be guided by the oracle; but we are not deceived: we know quite well that he has come here so that when he goes back he may have the authority and dignity of one who has visited the holy islands and spoken face to face with the ineffable ones. He will pretend that all the measures he wishes to take for his own purposes have been enjoined on him by the oracle.

THE ELDERLY GENTLEMAN. But you forget that the answers of the oracle cannot be kept secret or misrepresented. They are written and promulgated. The Leader of the Opposition can obtain copies. All the nations know them. Secret diplomacy has been totally abolished.

zoo. Yes: you publish documents; but they are garbled or forged. And even if you published our real answers it would make no difference, because the shortlived cannot interpret the plainest writings. Your scriptures command you in the plainest terms to do exactly the contrary of everything your own laws and chosen rulers command and execute. You cannot defy Nature. It is a law of Nature that there is a fixed relation between conduct and length of life.

THE ELDERLY GENTLEMAN. I have never heard of any such law, madam.

zoo. Well, you are hearing of it now.

THE ELDERLY GENTLEMAN. Let me tell you that we shortlivers, as you call us, have lengthened our lives very considerably.

zoo. How?

THE ELDERLY GENTLEMAN. By saving time. By enabling men to cross the ocean in an afternoon, and to see and speak to one another when they are thousands of miles apart. We hope shortly to organize their labor, and press natural forces into their service, so scientifically that the burden of labor will cease to be perceptible, leaving common men more leisure than they will know what to do with.

zoo. Daddy: the man whose life is lengthened in this way may be busier than a savage; but the difference between such men living seventy years and those living three hundred would be all the greater; for to a shortliver increase of years is only increase of sorrow; but to a longliver every extra year is a prospect which forces him to stretch his faculties to the utmost to face it. Therefore I say that we who live three hundred years can be of no use to you who live less than a hundred, and that our true destiny is not to advise and govern you, but to supplant and supersede you. In that faith I now declare myself a Colonizer and an Exterminator.

THE ELDERLY GENTLEMAN. Oh, steady! steady! Pray! pray! Reflect, I implore you. It is possible to colonize without exterminating the natives. Would you treat us less mercifully than our barbarous forefathers treated the Redskin and the Negro? Are we not, as Britons, entitled at least to some reservations?

zoo. What is the use of prolonging the agony? You would perish slowly in our presence, no matter what we did to preserve you. You were almost dead when I took charge of you today, merely because you had talked for a few minutes to a secondary. Besides, we have our own experience to go upon. Have you never heard that our children occasionally revert to the ancestral type, and are born shortlived?

THE ELDERLY GENTLEMAN [eagerly] Never. I hope you will not be offended if I say that it would be a great comfort to me if I could be placed in charge of one of those normal individuals.

zoo. Abnormal, you mean. What you ask is impossible: we weed them all out.

THE ELDERLY GENTLEMAN. When you say that you weed them out, you send a cold shiver down my spine. I hope you dont mean that you—that you—that you assist Nature in any way?

zoo. Why not? Have you not heard the saying of the Chinese sage Dee Ning, that a good garden needs weeding? But it is not necessary for us to interfere. We are naturally rather particular as to the conditions on which we consent to live. One does not mind the accidental loss of an arm or a leg or an eye: after all, no one with two legs is unhappy because he has not three; so why should a man with one be unhappy because he has not two? But infirmities of mind and temper are quite another matter. If one of us has no self-control, or is too weak to bear the strain of our truthful life without wincing, or is tormented by depraved appetites and superstitions, or is unable to keep free from pain and depression, he naturally becomes discouraged, and refuses to live.

THE ELDERLY GENTLEMAN. Good Lord! Cuts his throat, do you mean?

zoo. No: why should he cut his throat? He simply dies. He wants to. He is out of countenance, as we call it.

THE ELDERLY GENTLEMAN. Well!!! But suppose he is depraved enough not to want to die, and to settle the difficulty by killing all the rest of you?

zoo. Oh, he is one of the thoroughly degenerate shortlivers whom we occasionally produce. He emigrates.

THE ELDERLY GENTLEMAN. And what becomes of him then?

zoo. You shortlived people always think very highly of him. You accept him as what you call a great man.

THE ELDERLY GENTLEMAN. You astonish me; and yet I must admit that what you tell me accounts for a great deal of the little I know of the private life of our great men. We must be very convenient to you as a dumping place for your failures.

zoo. I admit that.

THE ELDERLY GENTLEMAN. Good. Then if you carry out your plan of colonization, and leave no shortlived countries in the world, what will you do with your undesirables?

zoo. Kill them. Our tertiaries are not at all squeamish about killing.

THE ELDERLY GENTLEMAN. Gracious Powers!

zoo [glancing up at the sun] Come. It is just sixteen o'clock; and you have to join your party at half-past in the temple in Galway.

THE ELDERLY GENTLEMAN [rising] Galway! Shall I at last be able to boast of having seen that magnificent city?

ZOO. You will be disappointed: we have no cities. There is a temple of the oracle: that is all.

THE ELDERLY GENTLEMAN. Alas! and I came here to fulfil two long-cherished dreams. One was to see Galway. It has been said, "See Galway and die." The other was to contemplate the ruins of London.

ZOO. Ruins! We do not tolerate ruins. Was London a place of any importance?

THE ELDERLY GENTLEMAN [amazed] What! London! It was the mightiest city of antiquity. [Rhetorically] Situate just where the Dover Road crosses the Thames, it—

ZOO [curtly interrupting] There is nothing there now. Why should anybody pitch on such a spot to live? The nearest houses are at a place called Strand-on-the-Green: it is very old. Come. We shall go across the water. [She goes down the steps].

THE ELDERLY GENTLEMAN. Sic transit gloria mundi!

ZOO [from below] What did you say?

THE ELDERLY GENTLEMAN [despairingly] Nothing. You would not understand. [He goes down the steps].

ACT II

A courtyard before the columned portico of a temple. The temple door is in the middle of the portico. A veiled and robed woman of majestic carriage passes along behind the columns towards the entrance. From the opposite direction a man of compact figure, clean-shaven, saturnine, and self-centred: in short, very like Napoleon I, and wearing a military uniform of Napoleonic cut, marches with measured steps; places his hand in his lapel in the traditional manner; and fixes the woman with his eye. She stops, her attitude expressing haughty amazement at his audacity. He is on her right: she on his left.

NAPOLEON [impressively] I am the Man of Destiny.

THE VEILED WOMAN [unimpressed] How did you get in here?

NAPOLEON. I walked in. I go on until I am stopped. I never am stopped. I tell you I am the Man of Destiny.

THE VEILED WOMAN. You will be a man of very short destiny if you wander about here without one of our children to guide you. I suppose you belong to the Baghdad envoy.

NAPOLEON. I came with him; but I do not belong to him. I belong to myself. Direct me to the oracle if you can. If not, do not waste my time.

THE VEILED WOMAN. Your time, poor creature, is short. I will not waste it. Your envoy and his party will be here presently. The consultation of the oracle is arranged for them, and will take place according to the prescribed ritual. You can wait here until they come [she turns to go into the temple].

NAPOLEON. I never wait. [She stops]. The prescribed ritual is, I believe, the classical one of the pythoness on her tripod, the intoxicating fumes arising from the abyss, the convulsions of the priestess as she delivers the message of the God, and so on. That sort of thing does not impose on me: I use it myself to impose on simpletons. I believe that what is, is. I know that what is not, is not. The antics of a woman sitting on a tripod and pretending to be drunk do not interest me. Her words are put into her mouth, not by a god, but by a man three hundred years old, who has had the capacity to profit by his experience. I wish to speak to that man face to face, without mummery or imposture.

THE VEILED WOMAN. You seem to be an unusually sensible person. But there is no old man. I am the oracle on duty today. I am on my way now to take my place on the tripod, and go through the usual mummery, as you rightly call it, to impress your friend the envoy. As you are superior to that kind of thing, you may consult me now. [She leads the way into the middle of the courtyard]. What do you want to know?

NAPOLEON [following her] Madam: I have not come all this way to discuss matters of State with a woman. I must ask you to direct me to one of your oldest and ablest men.

THE ORACLE. None of our oldest and ablest men or women would dream of wasting their time on you. You would die of discouragement in their presence in less than three hours.

NAPOLEON. You can keep this idle fable of discouragement for people credulous enough to be intimidated by it, madam. I do not believe in metaphysical forces.

THE ORACLE. No one asks you to. A field is something physical, is it not. Well, I have a field.

NAPOLEON. I have several million fields. I

am Emperor of Turania.

THE ORACLE. You do not understand. I am not speaking of an agricultural field. Do you not know that every mass of matter in motion carries with it an invisible gravitational field, every magnet an invisible magnetic field, and every living organism a mesmeric field? Even you have a perceptible mesmeric field. Feeble as it is, it is the strongest I have yet observed in a shortliver.

NAPOLEON. By no means feeble, madam. I understand you now; and I may tell you that the strongest characters blench in my presence, and submit to my domination. But I do not call that a physical force.

THE ORACLE. What else do you call it, pray? Our physicists deal with it. Our mathematicians express its measurements in algebraic equations.

NAPOLEON. Do you mean that they could measure mine?

THE ORACLE. Yes: by a figure infinitely near to zero. Even in us the force is negligible during our first century of life. In our second century it develops quickly, and becomes dangerous to shortlivers who venture into its field. If I were not veiled and robed in insulating material you could not endure my presence; and I am still a young woman: one hundred and seventy if you wish to know exactly.

NAPOLEON [folding his arms] I am not intimidated: no woman alive, old or young, can put me out of countenance. Unveil, madam. Disrobe. You will move this temple as easily as shake me.

THE ORACLE. Very well [she throws back her veil].

NAPOLEON [shrieking, staggering, and covering his eyes] No. Stop. Hide your face again. [Shutting his eyes and distractedly clutching at his throat and heart] Let me go. Help! I am dying.

THE ORACLE. Do you still wish to consult an older person?

NAPOLEON. No, no. The veil, the veil, I beg you.

THE ORACLE [replacing the veil] So.

NAPOLEON. Ouf! One cannot always be at one's best. Twice before in my life I have lost my nerve and behaved like a poltroon. But I warn you not to judge my quality by these involuntary moments.

THE ORACLE. I have no occasion to judge of your quality. You want my advice. Speak quickly; or I shall go about my business.

NAPOLEON [After a moment's hesitation, sinks respectfully on one knee] I—

THE ORACLE. Oh, rise, rise. Are you so foolish as to offer me this mummery which even you despise?

NAPOLEON [rising] I knelt in spite of myself. I compliment you on your impressiveness, madam.

THE ORACLE [impatiently] Time! time! time! time!

NAPOLEON. You will not grudge me the necessary time, madam, when you know my case. I am a man gifted with a certain specific talent in a degree altogether extraordinary. I am not otherwise a very extraordinary person: my family is not influential; and without this talent I should cut no particular figure in the world.

THE ORACLE. Why cut a figure in the world?

NAPOLEON. Superiority will make itself felt, madam. But when I say I possess this talent I do not express myself accurately. The truth is that my talent possesses me. It is genius. It drives me to exercise it. I must exercise it. I am great when I exercise it. At other moments I am nobody.

THE ORACLE. Well, exercise it. Do you need an oracle to tell you that?

NAPOLEON. Wait. This talent involves the shedding of human blood.

THE ORACLE. Are you a surgeon, or a dentist?

NAPOLEON. Psha! You do not appreciate me, madam. I mean the shedding of oceans of blood, the death of millions of men.

THE ORACLE. They object, I suppose.

NAPOLEON. Not at all. They adore me.

THE ORACLE. Indeed!

NAPOLEON. I have never shed blood with my own hand. They kill each other: they die with shouts of triumph on their lips. Those who die cursing do not curse me. My talent is to organize this slaughter; to give mankind this terrible joy which they call glory; to let loose the devil in them that peace has bound in chains.

THE ORACLE. And you? Do you share their joy?

NAPOLEON. Not at all. What satisfaction is it to me to see one fool pierce the entrails of another with a bayonet? I am a man of princely character, but of simple personal tastes and habits. I have the virtues of a laborer: industry and indifference to personal comfort. But I must rule, because I am so superior to other men that it is intolerable to me to be misruled by them. Yet only as a slayer can I become a ruler. I cannot be great as a writer: I have tried and failed. I have no talent as a sculptor or painter; and as lawyer, preacher, doctor, or actor, scores of second-rate men can do as well as I, or better. I am not even a diplomatist: I can only play my trump card of force. What I can do is to organize war. Look at me! I seem a man like other men, because nine-tenths of me is common humanity. But the other tenth is a faculty for seeing things as they are that no other man possesses.

THE ORACLE. You mean that you have no imagination?

NAPOLEON [*forcibly*] I mean that I have the only imagination worth having: the power of imagining things as they are, even when I cannot see them. You feel yourself my superior, I know: nay, you are my superior: have I not bowed my knee to you by instinct? Yet I challenge you to a test of our respective powers. Can you calculate what the mathematicians call vectors, without putting a single algebraic symbol on paper? Can you launch ten thousand men across a frontier and a chain of mountains and know to a mile exactly where they will be at the end of seven weeks? The rest is nothing: I got it all from the books at my military school. Now this great game of war, this playing with armies as other men play with bowls and skittles, is one which I must go on playing, partly because a man must do what he can and not what he would like to do, and partly because, if I stop, I immediately lose my power and become a beggar in the land where I now make men drunk with glory.

THE ORACLE. No doubt then you wish to know how to extricate yourself from this unfortunate position?

NAPOLEON. It is not generally considered unfortunate, madam. Supremely fortunate rather.

THE ORACLE. If you think so, go on making them drunk with glory. Why trouble me with their folly and your vectors?

NAPOLEON. Unluckily, madam, men are not only heroes: they are also cowards. They desire glory; but they dread death.

THE ORACLE. Why should they? Their lives are too short to be worth living. That is why they think your game of war worth playing.

NAPOLEON. They do not look at it quite in that way. The most worthless soldier wants to live for ever. To make him risk being killed by the enemy I have to convince him that if he hesitates he will inevitably be shot at dawn by his own comrades for cowardice.

THE ORACLE. And if his comrades refuse to shoot him?

NAPOLEON. They will be shot too, of course.

THE ORACLE. By whom?

NAPOLEON. By their comrades.

THE ORACLE. And if they refuse?

NAPOLEON. Up to a certain point they do not refuse.

THE ORACLE. But when that point is reached, you have to do the shooting yourself, eh?

NAPOLEON. Unfortunately, madam, when that point is reached, they shoot me.

THE ORACLE. Mf! It seems to me they might as well shoot you first as last. Why dont they?

NAPOLEON. Because their love of fighting, their desire for glory, their shame of being branded as dastards, their instinct to test themselves in terrible trials, their fear of being killed or enslaved by the enemy, their belief that they are defending their hearths and homes, overcome their natural cowardice, and make them willing not only to risk their own lives but to kill everyone who refuses to take that risk. But if war continues too long, there comes a time when the soldiers, and also the taxpayers who are supporting and munitioning them, reach a condition which they describe as being fed up. The troops have proved their courage, and want to go home and enjoy in peace the glory it has earned them. Besides, the risk of death for each soldier becomes a certainty if the fighting goes on for ever: he hopes to escape for six months, but knows he cannot escape for six years. The risk of bankruptcy for the citizen becomes a certainty in the same way. Now what does this mean for me?

THE ORACLE. Does that matter in the midst of such calamity?

NAPOLEON. Psha! madam: it is the only thing that matters: the value of human life is the value of the greatest living man. Cut off that infinitesimal layer of grey matter which distinguishes my brain from that of the common man, and you cut down the stature of humanity from that of a giant to that of a nobody. I matter supremely: my soldiers do not matter at all: there are plenty more where they came from. If you kill me, or put a stop to my activity (it is the same thing), the nobler part of human life perishes. You must save the world from that catastrophe, madam. War has made me popular, powerful, famous, historically immortal. But I foresee that if I go on to the end it will leave me execrated, dethroned, imprisoned, perhaps executed. Yet if I stop fighting I commit suicide as a great man and become a common one. How am I to escape the horns of this tragic dilemma? Victory I can guarantee: I am invincible. But the cost of victory is the demoralization, the depopulation, the ruin of the victors no less than of the vanquished. How am I to satisfy my genius by fighting until I die? that is my question to you.

THE ORACLE. Were you not rash to venture into these sacred islands with such a question on your lips? Warriors are not popular here, my friend.

NAPOLEON. If a soldier were restrained by such a consideration, madam, he would no longer be a soldier. Besides [*he produces a pistol*] I have not come unarmed.

THE ORACLE. What is that thing?

NAPOLEON. It is an instrument of my profession, madam. I raise this hammer; I point the barrel at you; I pull this trigger that is against my forefinger; and you fall dead.

THE ORACLE. Shew it to me. [*She puts out her hand to take it from him*].

NAPOLEON [*retreating a step*] Pardon me, madam. I never trust my life in the hands of a person over whom I have no control.

THE ORACLE [*sternly*] Give it to me. [*She raises her hand to her veil*].

NAPOLEON [*dropping the pistol and covering his eyes*] Quarter! Kamerad! Take it, madam [*he kicks it towards her*]: I surrender.

THE ORACLE. Give me that thing. Do you expect me to stoop for it?

NAPOLEON [*taking his hands from his eyes with an effort* [*A poor victory, madam* [*he picks up the pistol and hands it to her*]: there was no vector strategy needed to win it. [*Making a pose of his humiliation*] But enjoy your triumph: you have made me—ME! Cain Adamson Charles Napoleon! Emperor of Turania! cry for quarter.

THE ORACLE. The way out of your difficulty, Cain Adamson, is very simple.

NAPOLEON [*eagerly*] Good. What is it?

THE ORACLE. To die before the tide of glory turns. Allow me. [*She shoots him*].

He falls with a shriek. She throws the pistol away and goes haughtily into the temple.

NAPOLEON [*scrambling to his feet*] Murderess! Monster! She-devil, Unnatural, inhuman wretch! You deserve to be hanged, guillotined, broken on the wheel, burnt alive. No sense of the sacredness of human life! No thought for my wife and children! Bitch! Sow! Wanton! [*He picks up the pistol*]. And missed me at five yards! Thats a woman all over.

He is going away whence he came when Zoo arrives and confronts him at the head of a party consisting of the British Envoy, the Elderly Gentleman, the Envoy's wife, and her daughter, aged about eighteen. The Envoy, a typical politician, looks like an imperfectly reformed criminal disguised by a good tailor. The dress of the ladies is coeval with that of the Elderly Gentleman, and suitable for public official ceremonies in western capitals at the XVIII-XIX fin de siècle.

They file in under the portico. Zoo immediately comes out imperiously to Napoleon's right, whilst the Envoy's wife hurries effusively to his left. The Envoy meanwhile passes along behind the columns to the door, followed by his daughter. The Elderly Gentleman stops just where he entered, to see why Zoo has swooped so abruptly on the Emperor of Turania.

ZOO [*to Napoleon, severely*] What are you doing here by yourself? You have no business to go about here alone. What was that noise just now? What is that in your hand?

Napoleon glares at her in speechless fury; pockets the pistol; and produces a whistle.

THE ENVOY'S WIFE. Arnt you coming with us to the oracle, sire?

NAPOLEON. To hell with the oracle, and with you too [*he turns to go*]!

| THE ENVOY'S WIFE | | Oh, sire!! |
| ZOO | [*together*] | Where are you going? |

NAPOLEON. To fetch the police [*He goes out past Zoo, almost jostling her, and blowing piercing blasts on his whistle*].

ZOO [*whipping out her tuning-fork and intoning*] Hallo Galway Central. [*The whistling continues*]. Stand by to isolate. [*To the Elderly Gentleman, who is staring after the whistling Emperor*] How far has he gone?

THE ELDERLY GENTLEMAN. To that curious statue of a fat old man.

ZOO [*quickly, intoning*] Isolate the Falstaff monument isolate hard. Paralyze— [*The whistling stops*]. Thank you. [*She puts up her tuning-fork*]. He shall not move a muscle

2 H

until I come to fetch him.

THE ENVOY'S WIFE. Oh! he will be frightfully angry! Did you hear what he said to me?

ZOO. Much we care for his anger!

THE DAUGHTER [coming forward between her mother and Zoo] Please, madam, whose statue is it? and where can I buy a picture postcard of it? It is so funny. I will take a snapshot when we are coming back; but they come out so badly sometimes.

ZOO. They will give you pictures and toys in the temple to take away with you. The story of the statue is too long. It would bore you. [She goes past them across the courtyard to get rid of them].

THE WIFE [gushing] Oh no, I assure you.

THE DAUGHTER [copying her mother] We should be so interested.

ZOO. Nonsense! All I can tell you about it is that a thousand years ago, when the whole world was given over to you shortlived people, there was a war called the War to end War. In the war which followed it about ten years later, hardly any soldiers were killed; but seven of the capital cities of Europe were wiped out of existence. It seems to have been a great joke; for the statesmen who thought they had sent ten million common men to their deaths were themselves blown into fragments with their houses and families, while the ten million men lay snugly in the caves they had dug for themselves. Later on even the houses escaped; but their inhabitants were poisoned by gas that spared no living soul. Of course the soldiers starved and ran wild; and that was the end of pseudo-Christian civilization. The last civilized thing that happened was that the statesmen discovered that cowardice was a great patriotic virtue; and a public monument was erected to its first preacher, an ancient and very fat sage called Sir John Falstaff. Well [pointing], thats Falstaff.

THE ELDERLY GENTLEMAN [coming from the portico to his granddaughter's right] Great Heavens! And at the base of this monstrous poltroon's statue the War God of Turania is now gibbering impotently.

ZOO. Serve him right! War God indeed!

THE ENVOY [coming between his wife and Zoo] I dont know any history: a modern Prime Minister has something better to do than sit reading books; but—

THE ELDERLY GENTLEMAN [interrupting him encouragingly] You make history, Ambrose.

THE ENVOY. Well, perhaps I do; and perhaps history makes me. I hardly recognize myself in the newspapers sometimes, though I suppose leading articles are the materials of history, as you might say. But what I want to know is, how did war come back again? and how did they make those poisonous gases you speak of? We should be glad to know; for they might come in very handy if we have to fight Turania. Of course I am all for peace, and dont hold with the race of armaments in principle; still, we must keep ahead or be wiped out.

ZOO. You can make the gases for yourselves when your chemists find out how. Then you will do as you did before: poison each other until there are no chemists left, and no civilization. You will then begin all over again as half-starved ignorant savages, and fight with boomerangs and poisoned arrows until you work up to the poison gases and high explosives once more, with the same result. That is, unless we have sense enough to make an end of this ridiculous game by destroying you.

THE ENVOY [aghast] Destroying us!

THE ELDERLY GENTLEMAN. I told you, Ambrose. I warned you.

THE ENVOY. But—

ZOO [impatiently] I wonder what Zozim is doing. He ought to be here to receive you.

THE ELDERLY GENTLEMAN. Do you mean that rather insufferable young man whom you found boring me on the pier?

ZOO. Yes. He has to dress-up in a Druids' robe, and put on a wig and a long false beard, to impress you silly people. I have to put on a purple mantle. I have no patience with such mummery; but you expect it from us; so I suppose it must be kept up. Will you wait here until Zozim comes, please. [She turns to enter the temple].

THE ENVOY. My good lady, is it worth while dressing-up and putting on false beards for us if you tell us beforehand that it is all humbug?

ZOO. One would not think so; but if you wont believe in anyone who is not dressed-up, why, we must dress-up for you. It was you who invented all this nonsense, not we.

THE ELDERLY GENTLEMAN. But do you expect us to be impressed, after this?

ZOO. I dont expect anything. I know, as a matter of experience, that you will be impressed. The oracle will frighten you out of your wits. [*She goes into the temple*].

THE WIFE. These people treat us as if we were dirt beneath their feet. I wonder at you putting up with it, Amby. It would serve them right if we went home at once: wouldnt it, Eth?

THE DAUGHTER. Yes, mamma. But perhaps they wouldnt mind.

THE ENVOY. No use talking like that, Molly. Ive got to see this oracle. The folks at home wont know how we have been treated: all theyll know is that Ive stood face to face with the oracle and had the straight tip from her. I hope this Zozim chap is not going to keep us waiting much longer; for I feel far from comfortable about the approaching interview; and thats the honest truth.

THE ELDERLY GENTLEMAN. I never thought I should want to see that man again; but now I wish he would take charge of us instead of Zoo. She was charming at first: quite charming; but she turned into a fiend because I had a few words with her. You would not believe: she very nearly killed me. You heard what she said just now. She belongs to a party here which wants to have us all killed.

THE WIFE [*terrified*] Us! But we have done nothing: we have been as nice to them as nice could be. Oh, Amby, come away, come away: there is something dreadful about this place and these people.

THE ENVOY. There is, and no mistake. But youre safe with m e : you ought to have sense enough to know that.

THE ELDERLY GENTLEMAN. I am sorry to say, Molly, that it is not merely us four poor weak creatures they want to kill, but the entire race of Man, except themselves.

THE ENVOY. Not so poor neither, Poppa. Nor so weak, if you are going to take in all the Powers. If it comes to killing, two can play at that game, longlived or shortlived.

THE ELDERLY GENTLEMAN. No, Ambrose: we should have no chance. We are worms beside these fearful people: mere worms.

Zozim comes from the temple, robed majestically, and wearing a wreath of mistletoe in his flowing white wig. His false beard reaches almost to his waist. He carries a staff with a curiously carved top.

ZOZIM [*in the doorway, impressively*] Hail, strangers!

ALL [*reverently*] Hail!

ZOZIM. Are ye prepared?

THE ENVOY. We are.

ZOZIM [*unexpectedly becoming conversational, and strolling down carelessly to the middle of the group between the two ladies*] Well, I'm sorry to say the oracle is not. She was delayed by some member of your party who got loose; and as the show takes a bit of arranging, you will have to wait a few minutes. The ladies can go inside and look round the entrance hall and get pictures and things if they want them.

THE WIFE
THE DAUGHTER [*together*] Thank you. I should like to, very much. [*They go into the temple*].

THE ELDERLY GENTLEMAN [*in dignified rebuke of Zozim's levity*] Taken in this spirit, sir, the show, as you call it, becomes almost an insult to our common sense.

ZOZIM. Quite, I should say. You need not keep it up with me.

THE ENVOY [*suddenly making himself very agreeable*] Just so: just so. We can wait as long as you please. And now, if I may be allowed to seize the opportunity of a few minutes' friendly chat—?

ZOZIM. By all means, if only you will talk about things I can understand.

THE ENVOY. Well, about this colonizing plan of yours. My father-in-law here has been telling me something about it; and he has just now let out that you want not only to colonize us, but to —to—to—well, shall we say to supersede us? Now why supersede us? Why not live and let live? Theres not a scrap of ill-feeling on our side. We should welcome a colony of immortals—we may almost call you that—in the British Middle East. No doubt the Turanian Empire, with its Mahometan traditions, overshadows us now. We have had to bring the Emperor with us on this expedition, though of course you know as well as I do that he has imposed himself on my party just to spy on me. I dont deny that he has the whip hand of us to some extent, because if it came to a war none of our generals could stand up against him. I give him best at that game: he is the finest soldier in the world. Besides, he is an emperor and an autocrat; and I am only an elected representative of the British democracy. Not that our British democrats wont fight: they will fight the heads off all the Turanians that ever walked; but then it takes so long to work them up to it, while he has only to say the word and march. But you people would never get on with him. Believe me, you would not be as comfortable in Turania as you would be with us. We understand you. We like you. We are easy-going people; and we are rich people. That will appeal to you. Turania is a poor place when all is said. Five-eighths of it is desert. They dont irrigate as we do. Besides—now I am sure this will appeal to you and to all right-minded men—we are Christians.

zozim. The old uns prefer Mahometans.

THE ENVOY [shocked] What!

zozim [distinctly] They prefer Mahometans. Whats wrong with that?

THE ENVOY. Well, of all the disgraceful—

THE ELDERLY GENTLEMAN [diplomatically interrupting his scandalized son-in-law] There can be no doubt, I am afraid, that by clinging too long to the obsolete features of the old pseudo-Christian Churches we allowed the Mahometans to get ahead of us at a very critical period of the development of the Eastern world. When the Mahometan Reformation took place, it left its followers with the enormous advantage of having the only established religion in the world in whose articles of faith any intelligent and educated person could believe.

THE ENVOY. But what about our Reformation? Dont give the show away, Poppa. We followed suit, didnt we?

THE ELDERLY GENTLEMAN. Unfortunately, Ambrose, we could not follow suit very rapidly. We had not only a religion to deal with, but a Church.

zozim. What is a Church?

THE ENVOY. Not know what a Church is! Well!

THE ELDERLY GENTLEMAN. You must excuse me; but if I attempted to explain you would only ask me what a bishop is; and that is a question that no mortal man can answer. All I can tell you is that Mahomet was a truly wise man; for he founded a religion without a Church; consequently when the time came for a Reformation of the mosques there were no bishops and priests to obstruct it. Our bishops and priests prevented us for two hundred years from following suit; and we have never recovered the start we lost then. I can only plead that we did reform our Church at last. No doubt we had to make a few compromises as a matter of good taste; but there is now very little in our Articles of Religion that is not accepted as at least alle-

gorically true by our Higher Criticism.

THE ENVOY [encouragingly] Besides, does it matter? Why, I have never read the Articles in my life; and I am Prime Minister! Come! if my services in arranging for the reception of a colonizing party would be acceptable, they are at your disposal. And when I say a reception I mean a reception. Royal honors, mind you! A salute of a hundred and one guns! The streets lined with troops! The Guards turned out at the Palace! Dinner at the Guildhall!

zozim. Discourage me if I know what youre talking about! I wish Zoo would come: she understands these things. All I can tell you is that the general opinion among the Colonizers is in favor of beginning in a country where the people are of a different color from us; so that we can make short work without any risk of mistakes.

THE ENVOY. What do you mean by short work? I hope—

zozim [with obviously feigned geniality] Oh, nothing, nothing, nothing. We are thinking of trying North America: thats all. You see, the Red Men of that country used to be white. They passed through a period of sallow complexions, followed by a period of no complexions at all, into the red characteristic of their climate. Besides, several cases of long life have occurred in North America. They joined us here; and their stock soon reverted to the original white of these islands.

THE ELDERLY GENTLEMAN. But have you considered the possibility of your colony turning red?

zozim. That wont matter. We are not particular about our pigmentation. The old books mention red-faced Englishmen: they appear to have been common objects at one time.

THE ELDERLY GENTLEMAN [very persuasively] But do you think you would be popular in North America? It seems to me, if I may say so, that on your own shewing you need a country in which society is organized in a series of highly exclusive circles, in which the privacy of private life is very jealously guarded, and in which no one presumes to speak to anyone else without an introduction following a strict examination of social credentials. It is only in such a country that persons of special tastes and attainments can form a little world of their own, and protect themselves absolutely from intrusion by common persons. I think I may claim that our British society has developed this exclusiveness to perfection. If you would pay us a visit and see the working of our caste system, our club system, our guild system, you would admit that nowhere else in the world, least of all perhaps in North America, which has a regrettable tradition of social promiscuity, could you keep yourselves so entirely to yourselves.

ZOZIM [*good-naturedly embarrassed*] Look here. There is no good discussing this. I had rather not explain; but it wont make any difference to our Colonizers what sort of shortlivers they come across. We shall arrange all that. Never mind how. Let us join the ladies.

THE ELDERLY GENTLEMAN [*throwing off his diplomatic attitude and abandoning himself to despair*] We understand you only too well, sir. Well, kill us. End the lives you have made miserably unhappy by opening up to us the possibility that any of us may live three hundred years. I solemnly curse that possibility. To you it may be a blessing, because you do live three hundred years. To us, who will live less than a hundred, whose flesh is as grass, it is the most unbearable burden our poor tortured humanity has ever groaned under.

THE ENVOY. Hullo, Poppa! Steady! How do you make that out?

ZOZIM. What is three hundred years? Short enough, if you ask me. Why, in the old days you people lived on the assumption that you were going to last out for ever and ever and ever. Immortal, you thought yourselves. Were you any happier then?

THE ELDERLY GENTLEMAN. As President of the Baghdad Historical Society I am in a position to inform you that the communities which took this monstrous pretension seriously were the most wretched of which we have any record. My society has printed an editio princeps of the works of the father of history, Thucyderodotus Macollybuckle. Have you read his account of what was blasphemously called the Perfect City of God, and the attempt made to reproduce it in the northern part of these islands by Jonhobsnoxius, called the Leviathan? Those misguided people sacrificed the fragment of life that was granted to them to an imaginary immortality. They crucified the prophet who

told them to take no thought for the morrow, and that here and now was their Australia: Australia being a term signifying paradise, or an eternity of bliss. They tried to produce a condition of death in life: to mortify the flesh, as they called it.

ZOZIM. Well, you are not suffering from that, are you? You have not a mortified air.

THE ELDERLY GENTLEMAN. Naturally we are not absolutely insane and suicidal. Nevertheless we impose on ourselves abstinences and disciplines and studies that are meant to prepare us for living three centuries. And we seldom live one. My childhood was made unnecessarily painful, my boyhood unnecessarily laborious, by ridiculous preparations for a length of days which the chances were fifty thousand to one against my ever attaining. I have been cheated out of the natural joys and freedoms of my life by this dream to which the existence of these islands and their oracles gives a delusive possibility of realization. I curse the day when long life was invented, just as the victims of Jonhobsnoxius cursed the day when eternal life was invented.

ZOZIM. Pooh! You could live three centuries if you chose.

THE ELDERLY GENTLEMAN. That is what the fortunate always say to the unfortunate. Well, I do not choose. I accept my three score and ten years. If they are filled with usefulness, with justice, with mercy, with good-will: if they are the lifetime of a soul that never loses its honor and a brain that never loses its eagerness, they are enough for me, because these things are infinite and eternal, and can make ten of my years as long as thirty of yours. I shall not conclude by saying live as long as you like and be damned to you, because I have risen for the moment far above any ill-will to you or to any fellow-creature; but I am your equal before that eternity in which the difference between your lifetime and mine is as the difference between one drop of water and three in the eyes of the Almighty Power from which we have both proceeded.

ZOZIM [*impressed*] You spoke that piece very well, Daddy. I couldnt talk like that if I tried. It sounded fine. Ah! here come the ladies.

To his relief, they have just appeared on the threshold of the temple.

THE ELDERLY GENTLEMAN [*passing from*

exaltation to distress] It means nothing to him: in this land of discouragement the sublime has become the ridiculous. [*Turning on the hopelessly puzzled Zozim*] "Behold, thou hast made my days as it were a span long; and mine age is even as nothing in respect of thee."

THE WIFE } [*running to him*] { Poppa, Poppa: dont look like that.

THE DAUGHTER } { Oh, granpa, whats the matter?

ZOZIM [*with a shrug*] Discouragement!

THE ELDERLY GENTLEMAN [*throwing off the women with a superb gesture*] Liar! [*Recollecting himself, he adds, with noble courtesy, raising his hat and bowing*] I beg your pardon, sir; but I am NOT discouraged.

A burst of orchestral music, through which a powerful gong sounds, is heard from the temple. Zoo, in a purple robe, appears in the doorway.

ZOO. Come. The oracle is ready.

Zozim motions them to the threshold with a wave of his staff. The Envoy and the Elderly Gentleman take off their hats and go into the temple on tiptoe, Zoo leading the way. The Wife and Daughter, frightened as they are, raise their heads uppishly and follow flatfooted, sustained by a sense of their Sunday clothes and social consequence. Zozim remains in the portico, alone.

ZOZIM [*taking of his wig, beard, and robe, and bundling them under his arm*] Ouf! [*He goes home*].

ACT III

Inside the temple. A gallery overhanging an abyss. Dead silence. The gallery is brightly lighted; but beyond is a vast gloom, continually changing in intensity. A shaft of violet light shoots upward; and a very harmonious and silvery carillon chimes. When it ceases the violet ray vanishes.

Zoo comes along the gallery, followed by the Envoy's daughter, his wife, the Envoy himself, and the Elderly Gentleman. The two men are holding their hats with the brims near their noses, as if prepared to pray into them at a moment's notice. Zoo halts: they all follow her example. They contemplate the void with awe. Organ music of the kind called sacred in the nineteenth century begins. Their awe deepens. The violet ray, now a diffused mist, rises again from the abyss.

THE WIFE [*to Zoo, in a reverent whisper*] Shall we kneel?

ZOO [*loudly*] Yes, if you want to. You can stand on your head if you like. [*She sits down carelessly on the gallery railing, with her back to the abyss*].

THE ELDERLY GENTLEMAN [*jarred by her callousness*] We desire to behave in a becoming manner.

ZOO. Very well. Behave just as you feel. It doesnt matter how you behave. But keep your wits about you when the pythoness ascends, or you will forget the questions you have come to ask her.

THE ENVOY } [*simultaneously*] { [*very nervous, takes out a paper to refresh his memory*] Ahem!

THE DAUGHTER } { [*alarmed*] The pythoness? Is she a snake?

THE ELDERLY GENTLEMAN. Tch-ch! The priestess of the oracle. A sybil. A prophetess. Not a snake.

THE WIFE. How awful!

ZOO. I'm glad you think so.

THE WIFE. Oh dear! Dont y o u think so?

ZOO. No. This sort of thing is got up to impress y o u, not to impress me.

THE ELDERLY GENTLEMAN. I wish you would let it impress us, then, madam. I am deeply impressed; but you are spoiling the effect.

ZOO. You just wait. All this business with coloured lights and chords on that old organ is only tomfoolery. Wait til you see the pythoness.

The Envoy's wife falls on her knees, and takes refuge in prayer.

THE DAUGHTER [*trembling*] Are we really going to see a woman who has lived three hundred years?

ZOO. Stuff! Youd drop dead if a tertiary as much as looked at you. The oracle is only a hundred and seventy; and youll find it hard enough to stand her.

THE DAUGHTER [*piteously*] Oh! [*She falls on her knees*].

THE ENVOY. Whew! Stand by me, Poppa. This is a little more than I bargained for. Are you going to kneel; or how?

THE ELDERLY GENTLEMAN. Perhaps it would be in better taste.

The two men kneel.

The vapor of the abyss thickens; and a distant roll of thunder seems to come from its depths. The pythoness, seated on her tripod, rises slowly from it. She has discarded the insulating robe and veil in which she conversed with Napoleon, and is now draped and hooded in voluminous folds of a single piece of grey-white stuff. Something supernatural about her terrifies the beholders, who throw themsleves on their faces. Her outline flows and waves: she is almost distinct at moments, and again vague and shadowy: above all, she is larger than life-size, not enough to be measured by the flustered congregation, but enough to affect them with a dreadful sense of her supernaturalness.

ZOO. Get up, get up. Do pull yourselves together, you people.

The Envoy and his family, by shuddering negatively, intimate that it is impossible. The Elderly Gentleman manages to get on his hands and knees.

ZOO. Come on, Daddy: you are not afraid. Speak to her. She wont wait here all day for you, you know.

THE ELDERLY GENTLEMAN [*rising very deferentially to his feet*] Madam: you will excuse my very natural nervousness in addressing, for the first time in my life, a—a—a—a goddess. My friend and relative the Envoy is unhinged. I throw myself upon your indulgence—

ZOO [*interrupting him intolerantly*] Dont throw yourself on anything belonging to her or you will go right through her and break your neck. She isnt solid, like you.

THE ELDERLY GENTLEMAN. I was speaking figuratively—

ZOO. You have been told not to do it. Ask her what you want to know; and be quick about it.

THE ELDERLY GENTLEMAN [*stooping and taking the prostrate Envoy by the shoulders*] Ambrose: you must make an effort. You cannot go back to Baghdad without the answers to your questions.

THE ENVOY [*rising to his knees*] I shall be only too glad to get back alive on any terms. If my legs would support me I'd just do a bunk straight for the ship.

THE ELDERLY GENTLEMAN. No, no. Remember: your dignity—

THE ENVOY. Dignity be damned! I'm terrified. Take me away, for God's sake.

THE ELDERLY GENTLEMAN [*producing a brandy flask and taking the cap off*] Try some of this. It is still nearly full, thank goodness!

THE ENVOY [*clutching it and drinking eagerly*] Ah! Thats better. [*He tries to drink again. Finding that he has emptied it, he hands it back to his father-in-law upside down*].

THE ELDERLY GENTLEMAN [*taking it*] Great heavens! He has swallowed half-a-pint of neat brandy. [*Much perturbed, he screws the cap on again, and pockets the flask*].

THE ENVOY [*staggering to his feet; pulling a paper from his pocket; and speaking with boisterous confidence*] Get up, Molly. Up with you, Eth.

The two women rise to their knees.

THE ENVOY. What I want to ask is this. [*He refers to the paper*]. Ahem! Civilization has reached a crisis. We are at the parting of the ways. We stand on the brink of the Rubicon. Shall we take the plunge? Already a leaf has been torn out of the book of the Sybil. Shall we wait until the whole volume is consumed? On our right is the crater of the volcano: on our left the precipice. Once false step, and we go down to annihilation dragging the whole human race with us. [*He pauses for breath*].

THE ELDERLY GENTLEMAN [*recovering his spirits under the familiar stimulus of political oratory*] Hear, hear!

ZOO. What are you raving about? Ask your question while you have the chance? What is it you want to know?

THE ENVOY [*patronizing her in the manner of a Premier debating with a very young member of the Opposition*] A young woman asks me a question. I am always glad to see the young taking an interest in politics. It is an impatient question; but it is a practical question, an intelligent question. She asks why we seek to lift a corner of the veil that shrouds the future from our feeble vision.

ZOO. I dont. I ask you to tell the oracle what you want, and not keep her sitting there all day.

THE ELDERLY GENTLEMAN [*warmly*] Order, order!

ZOO. What does "Order, order!" mean?

THE ENVOY. I ask the august oracle to listen to my voice—

ZOO. You people seem never to tire of listening to your voices; but it doesnt amuse us. What do you want?

THE ENVOY. I want, young woman, to be allowed to proceed without unseemly interruptions.

A low roll of thunder comes from the abyss.

THE ELDERLY GENTLEMAN. There! Even the oracle is indignant. [*To the Envoy*] Do not allow yourself to be put down by this lady's rude clamor. Ambrose. Take no notice. Proceed.

THE ENVOY'S WIFE. I cant bear this much longer, Amby. Remember: *I* havnt had any brandy.

HIS DAUGHTER [*trembling*] There are serpents curling in the vapor. I am afraid of the lightning. Finish it, Papa; or I shall die.

THE ENVOY [*sternly*] Silence. The destiny of British civilization is at stake. Trust me. I am not afraid. As I was saying—where was I?

ZOO. I dont know. Does anybody?

THE ELDERLY GENTLEMAN [*tactfully*] You were just coming to the election, I think.

THE ENVOY [*reassured*] Just so. The election. Now what we want to know is this: ought we to dissolve in August, or put it off until next spring?

ZOO. Dissolve? In what? [*Thunder*]. Oh! My fault this time. That means that the oracle understands you, and desires me to hold my tongue.

THE ENVOY [*fervently*] I thank the oracle.

THE WIFE [*to Zoo*] Serve you right!

THE ELDERLY GENTLEMAN. Before the oracle replies, I should like to be allowed to state a few of the reasons why, in my opinion, the Government should hold on until the spring. In the first—

Terrific lightning and thunder. The Elderly Gentleman is knocked flat; but as he immediately sits up again dazedly it is clear that he is none the worse for the shock. The ladies cower in terror. The Envoy's hat is blown off; but he seizes it just as it quits his temples, and holds it on with both hands. He is recklessly drunk, but quite articulate, as he seldom speaks in public without taking stimulants beforehand.

THE ENVOY [*taking one hand from his hat to make a gesture of stilling the tempest*] Thats enough. We know how to take a hint. I'll put the case in three words. I am the leader of the Potterbill party. My party is in power. I am Prime Minister. The Opposition—the Rotterjacks—have won every bye-election for the last six months. They—

THE ELDERLY GENTLEMAN [*scrambling heatedly to his feet*] Not by fair means. By bribery, by misrepresentation, by pandering to the vilest prejudices [*muttered thunder*]—I beg your pardon. [*He is silent*].

THE ENVOY. Never mind the bribery and lies. The oracle knows all about that. The point is that though our five years will not expire until the year after next, our majority will be eaten away at the bye-elections by about Easter. We cant wait: we must start

some question that will excite the public, and go to the country on it. But some of us say do it now. Others say wait til the spring. We cant make up our minds one way or the other. Which would you advise?

ZOO. But what is the question that is to excite your public?

THE ENVOY. That doesnt matter. I dont know yet. We will find a question all right enough. The oracle can foresee the future: we cannot. [*Thunder*]. What does that mean? What have I done now?

ZOO [*severely*] How often must you be told that we cannot foresee the future? There is no such thing as the future until it is the present.

THE ELDERLY GENTLEMAN. Allow me to point out, madam, that when the Potterbill party sent to consult the oracle fifteen years ago, the oracle prophesied that the Potterbills would be victorious at the General Election; and they were. So it is evident that the oracle c a n foresee the future, and is sometimes willing to reveal it.

THE ENVOY. Quite true. Thank you, Poppa. I appeal now, over your head, young woman, direct to the August Oracle, to repeat the signal favor conferred on my illustrious predecessor, Sir Fuller Eastwind, and to answer me exactly as he was answered.

The oracle raises her hand to command silence.

ALL. Sh-sh-sh!

Invisible trombones utter three solemn blasts in the manner of Die Zauberflöte.

THE ELDERLY GENTLEMAN. May I—

ZOO [*quickly*] Hush. The oracle is going to speak.

THE ORACLE. Go home, poor fool.

She vanishes; and the atmosphere changes to prosaic daylight. Zoo comes off the railing; throws off her robe; makes a bundle of it; and tucks it under her arm. The magic and mystery are gone. The women rise to their feet. The Envoy's party stare at one another helplessly.

ZOO. The same reply, word for word, that your illustrious predecessor, as you call him, got fifteen years ago. You asked for it; and you got it. And just think of all the important questions you might have asked. She would have answered them, you know. It is always like that. I will go and arrange to have you sent home: you can wait for me in the entrance hall. [*She goes out*].

THE ENVOY. What possessed me to ask for the same answer old Eastwind got?

THE ELDERLY GENTLEMAN. But it was not the same answer. The answer to Eastwind was an inspiration to our party for years. It won us the election.

THE ENVOY'S DAUGHTER. I learnt it at school, granpa. It wasnt the same at all. I can repeat it. [*She quotes*] "When Britain was cradled in the west, the east wind hardened her and made her great. Whilst the east wind prevails Britain shall prosper. The east wind shall wither Britain's enemies in the day of contest. Let the Rotterjacks look to it."

THE ENVOY. The old man invented that. I see it all. He was a doddering old ass when he came to consult the oracle. The oracle naturally said "Go home, poor fool." There was no sense in saying that to me; but as that girl said, I asked for it. What else could the poor old chap do but fake up an answer fit for publication? There were whispers about it; but nobody believed them. I believe them now.

THE ELDERLY GENTLEMAN. Oh, I cannot admit that Sir Fuller Eastwind was capable of such a fraud.

THE ENVOY. He was capable of anything: I knew his private secretary. And now what are we going to say? You dont suppose I am going back to Baghdad to tell the British Empire that the oracle called me a fool, do you?

THE ELDERLY GENTLEMAN. Surely we must tell the truth, however painful it may be to our feelings.

THE ENVOY. I am not thinking of my feelings: I am not so selfish as that, thank God. I am thinking of the country: of our party. The truth, as you call it, would put the Rotterjacks in for the next twenty years. It would be the end of me politically. Not that I care for that: I am only too willing to retire if you can find a better man. Dont hesitate on my account.

THE ELDERLY GENTLEMAN. No, Ambrose: you are indispensable. There is no one else.

THE ENVOY. Very well, then. What are you going to do?

THE ELDERLY GENTLEMAN. My dear Ambrose, y o u are the leader of the party, not I. What are y o u going to do?

THE ENVOY. I am going to tell the exact truth: thats what I'm going to do. Do you take me for a liar?

THE ELDERLY GENTLEMAN [*puzzled*] Oh. I beg your pardon. I understood you to say—

THE ENVOY [*cutting him short*] You understood me to say that I am going back to Baghdad to tell the British electorate that the oracle repeated to me, word for word, what it said to Sir Fuller Eastwind fifteen years ago. Molly and Ethel can bear me out. So must you, if you are an honest man. Come on.

He goes out, followed by his wife and daughter.

THE ELDERLY GENTLEMAN [*left alone and shrinking into an old and desolate figure*] What am I to do? I am a most perplexed and wretched man. [*He falls on his knees, and stretches his hands in entreaty over the abyss*]. I invoke the oracle. I cannot go back and connive at a blasphemous lie. I implore guidance.

The Pythoness walks in on the gallery behind him, and touches him on the shoulder. Her size is now natural. Her face is hidden by her hood. He flinches as if from an electric shock; turns to her; and cowers, covering his eyes in terror.

THE ELDERLY GENTLEMAN. No: not close to me. I'm afraid I cant bear it.

THE ORACLE [*with grave pity*] Come: look at me. I am my natural size now: what you saw there was only a foolish picture of me thrown on a cloud by a lantern. How can I help you?

THE ELDERLY GENTLEMAN. They have gone back to lie about your answer. I cannot go with them. I cannot live among people to whom nothing is real. I have become incapable of it through my stay here. I implore to be allowed to stay.

THE ORACLE. My friend: if you stay with us you will die of discouragement.

THE ELDERLY GENTLEMAN. If I go back I shall die of disgust and despair. I take the nobler risk. I beg you, do not cast me out.

He catches her robe and holds her.

THE ORACLE. Take care. I have been here one hundred and seventy years. Your death does not mean to me what it means to you.

THE ELDERLY GENTLEMAN. It is the meaning of life, not of death, that makes banishment so terrible to me.

THE ORACLE. Be it so, then. You may stay.

She offers him her hands. He grasps them and raises himself a little by clinging to her. She looks steadily into his face. He stiffens; a little convulsion shakes him; his grasp relaxes; and he falls dead.

THE ORACLE [*looking down at the body*] Poor shortlived thing! What else could I do for you?

2 H 2

PART V

AS FAR AS THOUGHT CAN REACH

Summer afternoon in the year 31,920 A.D. A sunlit glade at the southern foot of a thickly wooded hill. On the west side of it, the steps and columned porch of a dainty little classic temple. Between it and the hill, a rising path to the wooded heights begins with rough steps of stones in the moss. On the opposite side, a grove. In the middle of the glade, an altar in the form of a low marble table as long as a man, set parallel to the temple steps and pointing to the hill. Curved marble benches radiate from it into the foreground; but they are not joined to it: there is plenty of space to pass between the altar and the benches.

A dance of youths and maidens is in progress. The music is provided by a few fluteplayers seated carelessly on the steps of the temple. There are no children; and none of the dancers seems younger than eighteen. Some of the youths have beards. Their dress, like the architecture of the theatre and the design of the altar and curved seats, resembles Grecian of the fourth century B.C., freely handled. They move with perfect balance and remarkable grace, racing through a figure like a farandole. They neither romp nor hug in our manner.

At the first full close they clap their hands to stop the musicians, who recommence with a saraband, during which a strange figure appears on the path beyond the temple. He is deep in thought, with his eyes closed and his feet feeling automatically for the rough irregular steps as he slowly descends them. Except for a sort of linen kilt consisting mainly of a girdle carrying a sporran and a few minor pockets, he is naked. In physical hardihood and uprightness he seems to be in the prime of life; and his eyes and mouth shew no signs of age; but his face, though fully and firmly fleshed, bears a network of lines, varying from furrows to hairbreadth reticulations, as if Time had worked over every inch of it incessantly through whole geologic periods. His head is finely domed and utterly bald. Except for his eyelashes he is quite hairless. He is unconscious of his surroundings, and walks right into one of the dancing couples, separating them. He wakes up and stares about him. The couple stop indignantly. The rest stop. The music stops. The youth whom he has jostled accosts him without malice, but without anything that we should call manners.

THE YOUTH. Now, then, ancient sleepwalker, why dont you keep your eyes open and mind where you are going?

THE ANCIENT [*mild, bland, and indulgent*] I did not know there was a nursery here, or I should not have turned my face in this direction. Such accidents cannot always be avoided. Go on with your play: I will turn back.

THE YOUTH. Why not stay with us and enjoy life for once in a way? We will teach you to dance.

THE ANCIENT. No, thank you. I danced when I was a child like you. Dancing is a very crude attempt to get into the rhythm of life. It would be painful to me to go back from that rhythm to your babyish gambols: in fact I could not do it if I tried. But at your age it is pleasant; and I am sorry I disturbed you.

THE YOUTH. Come! own up: arnt you very unhappy? It's dreadful to see you ancients going about by yourselves, never noticing anything, never dancing, never laughing, never singing, never getting anything out of life. None of us are going to be like that when we grow up. It's a dog's life.

THE ANCIENT. Not at all. You repeat that old phrase without knowing that there was once a creature on earth called a dog. Those who are interested in extinct forms of life will tell you that it loved the sound of its own voice and bounded about when it was happy, just as you are doing here. It is you, my children, who are living the dog's life.

THE YOUTH. The dog must have been a good sensible creature: it set you a very wise example. You should let yourself go occasionally and have a good time.

THE ANCIENT: My children: be content to let us ancients go our ways and enjoy ourselves in our own fashion.

He turns to go.

THE MAIDEN. But wait a moment. Why will you not tell us h o w you enjoy yourself? You must have secret pleasures that you hide from us, and that you never get tired of. I get tired of all our dances and all our tunes. I get tired of all my partners.

THE YOUTH [*suspiciously*] Do you? I shall bear that in mind.

They all look at one another as if there were some sinister significance in what she has said.

THE MAIDEN. We all do: what is the use of pretending we dont? It is natural.

SEVERAL YOUNG PEOPLE. No, no. We dont. It is not natural.

THE ANCIENT. You are older than he is, I see. You are growing up.

THE MAIDEN. How do you know? I do not look so much older, do I?

THE ANCIENT. Oh, I was not looking at you. Your looks do not interest me.

THE MAIDEN. Thank you.

They all laugh.

THE YOUTH. You old fish! I believe you dont know the difference between a man and a woman.

THE ANCIENT. It has long ceased to interest me in the way it interests you. And when anything no longer interests us we no longer know it.

THE MAIDEN. You havnt told me how I shew my age. That is what I want to know. As a matter of fact I am older than this boy here: older than he thinks. How did you find that out?

THE ANCIENT. Easily enough. You are ceasing to pretend that these childish games— this dancing and singing and mating—do not become tiresome and unsatisfying after a while. And you no longer care to pretend that you are younger than you are. These are the signs of adolescence. And then, see these fantastic rags with which you have draped yourself. [*He takes up a piece of her draperies in his hand*]. It is rather badly worn here. Why do you not get a new one?

THE MAIDEN. Oh, I did not notice it. Besides, it is too much trouble. Clothes are a nuisance. I think I shall do without them some day, as you ancients do.

THE ANCIENT. Signs of maturity. Soon you will give up all these toys and games and sweets.

THE YOUTH. What! And be as miserable as you?

THE ANCIENT. Infant: one moment of the ecstasy of life as we live it would strike you dead. [*He stalks gravely out through the grove*].

They stare after him, much damped.

THE YOUTH [*to the musicians*] Let us have another dance.

The musicians shake their heads; get up from their seats on the steps; and troop away into the temple. The others follow them, except the Maiden, who sits down on the altar.

A MAIDEN [*as she goes*] There! The ancient has put them out of countenance. It is your fault, Strephon, for provoking him. [*She leaves, much disappointed*].

A YOUTH. Why need you have cheeked

him like that? [*He goes, grumbling*].

STREPHON [*calling after him*] I thought it was understood that we are always to cheek the ancients on principle.

ANOTHER YOUTH. Quite right too! There would be no holding them if we didnt. [*He goes*].

THE MAIDEN. Why dont you really stand up to them? *I* did.

ANOTHER YOUTH. Sheer, abject, pusillanimous, dastardly cowardice. Thats why. Face the filthy truth. [*He goes*].

ANOTHER YOUTH [*turning on the steps as he goes out*] And dont you forget, infant, that one moment of the ecstasy of life as I live it would strike you dead. Haha!

STREPHON [*now the only one left, except the Maiden*] Arnt you coming, Chloe?

THE MAIDEN [*shakes her head*]!

THE YOUTH [*hurrying back to her*] What is the matter?

THE MAIDEN [*tragically pensive*] I dont know.

THE YOUTH. Then there is something the matter. Is that what you mean?

THE MAIDEN. Yes. Something is happening to me. I dont know what.

THE YOUTH. You no longer love me. I have seen it for a month past.

THE MAIDEN. Dont you think all that is rather silly? We cannot go on as if this kind of thing, this dancing and sweethearting, were everything.

THE YOUTH. What is there better? What else is there worth living for?

THE MAIDEN. Oh, stuff! Dont be frivolous.

THE YOUTH. Something horrible is happening to you. You are losing all heart, all feeling. [*He sits on the altar beside her and buries his face in his hands*]. I am bitterly unhappy.

THE MAIDEN. Unhappy! Really, you must have a very empty head if there is nothing in it but a dance with one girl who is no better than any of the other girls.

THE YOUTH. You did not always think so. You used to be vexed if I as much as looked at another girl.

THE MAIDEN. What does it matter what I did when I was a baby? Nothing existed for me then except what I tasted and touched and saw; and I wanted all that for myself, just as I wanted the moon to play with. Now the world is opening out for me. More than the world: the universe. Even little things are turning out to be great things, and becoming intensely interesting. Have you ever thought about the properties of numbers?

THE YOUTH [*sitting up, markedly disenchanted*] Numbers!!! I cannot imagine anything drier or more repulsive.

THE MAIDEN. They are fascinating, just fascinating. I want to get away from our eternal dancing and music, and just sit down by myself and think about numbers.

THE YOUTH [*rising indignantly*] Oh, this is too much. I have suspected you for some time past. We have all suspected you. All the girls say that you have deceived us as to your age: that you are getting flat-chested; that you are bored with us; that you talk to the ancients when you get the chance. Tell me the truth: how old are you?

THE MAIDEN. Just twice your age, my poor boy.

THE YOUTH. Twice my age! Do you mean to say you are four?

THE MAIDEN. Very nearly four.

THE YOUTH [*collapsing on the altar with a groan*] Oh!

THE MAIDEN. My poor Strephon: I pretended I was only two for your sake. I was two when you were born. I saw you break from your shell; and you were such a charming child! You ran round and talked to us all so prettily, and were so handsome and well grown, that I lost my heart to you at once. But now I seem to have lost it altogether: bigger things are taking possession of me. Still, we were very happy in our childish way for the first year, werent we?

STREPHON. I was happy until you began cooling towards me.

THE MAIDEN. Not towards you, but towards all the trivialities of our life here. Just think. I have hundreds of years to live: perhaps thousands. Do you suppose I can spend centuries dancing; listening to flutes ringing changes on a few tunes and a few notes; raving about the beauty of a few pillars and arches; making jingles with words; lying about with your arms round me, which is really neither comfortable nor convenient; everlastingly choosing colors for dresses, and putting them on, and washing; making a business of sitting together at fixed hours to absorb our nourishment; taking little poisons with it to make us delirious enough to imagine we are enjoying ourselves; and then having to pass the nights in shelters lying in cots and losing half our lives in a state of unconsciousness. Sleep is a shameful thing: I have not slept at all for weeks past. I have stolen out at night when you were all lying insensible—quite disgusting, I call it—and wandered about the woods, thinking, thinking, thinking; grasping the world; taking it to pieces; building it up again; devising methods; planning experiments to test the methods; and having a glorious time. Every morning I have come back here with greater and greater reluctance; and I know that the time will soon come—perhaps it has come already—when I shall not come back at all.

STREPHON. How horribly cold and uncomfortable!

THE MAIDEN. Oh, dont talk to me of comfort! Life is not worth living if you have to bother about comfort. Comfort makes winter a torture, spring an illness, summer an oppression, and autumn only a respite. The ancients could make life one long frowsty comfort if they chose. But they never lift a finger to make themselves comfortable. They will not sleep under a roof. They will not clothe themselves: a girdle with a few pockets hanging to it to carry things about in is all they wear: they will sit down on the wet moss or in a gorse bush when there is dry heather within two yards of them. Two years ago, when you were born, I did not understand this. Now I feel that I would not put myself to the trouble of walking two paces for all the comfort in the world.

STREPHON. But you dont know what this means to me. It means that you are dying to me: yes, just dying. Listen to me. [*He puts his arm around her*].

THE MAIDEN [*extricating herself*] Dont. We can talk quite as well without touching one another.

STREPHON [*horrified*] Chloe! Oh, this is the worst symptom of all! The ancients never touch one another.

THE MAIDEN. Why should they?

STREPHON. Oh, I dont know. But dont you w a n t to touch me? You used to.

THE MAIDEN. Yes: that is true: I used to. We used to think it would be nice to sleep in one another's arms; but we never could go to sleep because our weight stopped our circulations just above the elbows. Then somehow my feeling began to change bit by bit. I kept a sort of interest in your head and arms long after I lost interest in your whole body. And now that has gone.

STREPHON. You no longer care for me at all,

then?

THE MAIDEN. Nonsense! I care for you much more seriously than before; though perhaps not so much for you in particular. I mean I care more for everybody. But I dont want to touch you unnecessarily; and I certainly dont want you to touch me.

STREPHON [rising decisively] That finishes it. You dislike me.

THE MAIDEN [impatiently] I tell you again, I do not dislike you; but you bore me when you cannot understand; and I think I shall be happier by myself in future. You had better get a new companion. What about the girl who is to be born today?

STREPHON. I do not want the girl who is to be born today. How do I know what she will be like? I want you.

THE MAIDEN. You cannot have me. You must recognize facts and face them. It is no use running after a woman twice your age. I cannot make my childhood last to please you. The age of love is sweet; but it is short; and I must pay nature's debt. You no longer attract me; and I no longer care to attract you. Growth is too rapid at my age: I am maturing from week to week.

STREPHON. You are maturing, as you call it—I call it ageing—from minute to minute. You are going much further than you did when we began this conversation.

THE MAIDEN. It is not the ageing that is so rapid. It is the realization of it when it has actually happened. Now that I have made up my mind to the fact that I have left childhood behind me, it comes home to me in leaps and bounds with every word you say.

STREPHON. But your vow. Have you forgotten that? We all swore together in that temple: the temple of love. You were more earnest than any of us.

THE MAIDEN [with a grim smile] Never to let our hearts grow cold! Never to become as the ancients! Never to let the sacred lamp be extinguished! Never to change or forget! To be remembered for ever as the first company of true lovers faithful to this vow so often made and broken by past generations! Ha! ha! Oh, dear!

STREPHON. Well, you need not laugh. It is a beautiful and holy compact; and I will keep it whilst I live. Are you going to break it?

THE MAIDEN. Dear child: it has broken itself. The change has come in spite of my childish vow. [She rises]. Do you mind if I go into the woods for a walk by myself? This chat of ours seems to me an unbearable waste of time. I have so much to think of.

STREPHON [again collapsing on the altar and covering his eyes with his hands] My heart is broken. [He weeps].

THE MAIDEN [with a shrug] I have luckily got through my childhood without that experience. It shews how wise I was to choose a lover half my age. [She goes towards the grove, and is disappearing among the trees, when another youth, older and manlier than Strephon, with crisp hair and firm arms, comes from the temple, and calls to her from the threshold].

THE TEMPLE YOUTH. I say, Chloe. Is there any sign of the Ancient yet? The hour of birth is overdue. The baby is kicking like mad. She will break her shell prematurely.

THE MAIDEN [looks across to the hill path; then points up it, and says] She is coming, Acis.

The Maiden turns away through the grove and is lost to sight among the trees.

ACIS [coming to Strephon] Whats the matter? Has Chloe been unkind?

STREPHON. She has grown up in spite of all her promises. She deceived us about her age. She is four.

ACIS. Four! I am sorry, Strephon. I am getting on for three myself; and I know what old age is. I hate to say "I told you so"; but she was getting a little hard set and flat-chested and thin on the top, wasnt she?

STREPHON [breaking down] Dont.

ACIS. You must pull yourself together. This is going to be a busy day. First the birth. Then the Festival of the Artists.

STREPHON [rising] What is the use of being born if we have to decay into unnatural, heartless, loveless, joyless monsters in four short years? What use are the artists if they cannot bring their beautiful creations to life? I have a great mind to die and have done with it all. [He moves away to the corner of the curved seat farthest from the theatre, and throws himself moodily into it].

An Ancient Woman has descended the hill path during Strephon's lament, and has heard most of it. She is like the He-Ancient, equally bald, and equally without sexual charm, but intensely interesting and rather terrifying. Her sex is discoverable only by her voice, as her breasts are manly, and her figure otherwise not very different. She wears no clothes, but has draped herself rather perfunctorily with a ceremonial robe, and carries two implements like long slender *saws. She comes to the altar between the two young men.*

THE SHE-ANCIENT [*to Strephon*] Infant: you are only at the beginning of it all. [*To Acis*] Is the child ready to be born?

ACIS. More than ready, Ancient. Shouting and kicking and cursing. We have called to her to be quiet and wait until you come; but of course she only half understands, and is very impatient.

THE SHE-ANCIENT. Very well. Bring her out into the sun.

ACIS [*going quickly into the temple*] All ready. Come along.

Joyous processional music strikes up in the temple.

THE SHE-ANCIENT [*going close to Strephon*] Look at me.

STREPHON [*sulkily keeping his face averted*] Thank you; but I dont want to be cured. I had rather be miserable in my own way than callous in yours.

THE SHE-ANCIENT. You like being miserable? You will soon grow out of that. [*She returns to the altar*].

The procession, headed by Acis, emerges from the temple. Six youths carry on their shoulders a burden covered with a gorgeous but light pall. Before them certain official maidens carry a new tunic, ewers of water, sliver dishes pierced with holes, cloths, and immense sponges. The rest carry wands with ribbons, and strew flowers. The burden is deposited on the altar, and the pall removed. It is a huge egg.

THE SHE-ANCIENT [*freeing her arms from her robe, and placing her saws on the altar ready to her hand in a businesslike manner*] A girl, I think you said?

ACIS. Yes.

THE TUNIC BEARER. It is a shame. Why cant we have more boys?

SEVERAL YOUTHS [*protesting*] Not at all. More girls. We want new girls.

A GIRL'S VOICE FROM THE EGG. Let me out. Let me out. I want to be born. I want to be born. [*The egg rocks*].

ACIS [*snatching a wand from one of the others and whacking the egg with it*] Be quiet, I tell you. Wait. You will be born presently.

THE EGG. No, no: at once, at once. I want to be born: I want to be born. [*Violent kicking within the egg, which rocks so hard that it has to be held on the altar by the bearers*].

THE SHE-ANCIENT. Silence. [*The music stops; and the egg behaves itself*].

The She-Ancient takes her two saws, and with a couple of strokes rips the egg open. The Newly Born, a pretty girl who would have been guessed as seventeen in our day, sits up in the broken shell, exquisitely fresh and rosy, but with filaments of spare albumen clinging to her here and there.

THE NEWLY BORN [*as the world bursts on her vision*] Oh! Oh!! Oh!!! Oh!!!! [*She continues this ad libitum during the following remonstrances*].

ACIS. Hold your noise, will you?

The washing begins. The Newly Born shrieks and struggles.

A YOUTH. Lie quiet, you clammy little devil.

A MAIDEN. You must be washed, dear. Now quiet, quiet, quiet: be good.

ACIS. Shut your mouth, or I'll shove the sponge in it.

THE MAIDEN. Shut your eyes. Itll hurt if you dont.

ANOTHER MAIDEN. Dont be silly. One would think nobody had ever been born before.

THE NEWLY BORN [*yells*]!!!!!!

ACIS. Serve you right! You were told to shut your eyes.

THE YOUTH. Dry her off quick. I can hardly hold her. Shut will you; or I'll smack you into a pickled cabbage.

The dressing begins. The Newly Born chuckles with delight.

THE MAIDEN. Your arms go here, dear. Isnt it pretty? Youll look lovely.

THE NEWLY BORN [*rapturously*] Oh! Oh!! Oh!!! Oh!!!!

ANOTHER YOUTH. No: the other arm: youre putting it on back to front. You *are* a silly little beast.

ACIS. Here! Thats it. Now youre clean and decent. Up with you! Oopsh! [*He hauls her to her feet. She cannot walk at first, but masters it after a few steps*]. Now then: march. Here she is, Ancient: put her through the catechism.

THE SHE-ANCIENT. What name have you chosen for her?

ACIS. Amaryllis.

THE SHE-ANCIENT [*to the Newly Born*] Your name is Amaryllis.

THE NEWLY BORN. What does it mean?

A YOUTH. Love.

A MAIDEN. Mother.

ANOTHER YOUTH. Lilies.

THE NEWLY BORN. [*to Acis*] What is your name?

ACIS. Acis.

THE NEWLY BORN. I love you, Acis. I must have you all to myself. Take me in your arms.

ACIS. Steady, young one. I am three years old.

THE NEWLY BORN. What has that to do with it? I love you; and I must have you or I will go back into my shell again.

ACIS. You cant. It's broken. Look here [*pointing to Strephon, who has remained in his seat without looking round at the birth, wrapped up in his sorrow*]! Look at this poor fellow!

THE NEWLY BORN. What is the matter with him?

ACIS. When he was born he chose a girl two years old for his sweetheart. He is two years old now himself; and already his heart is broken because she is four. That means that she has grown up like this Ancient here, and has left him. If you choose me, we shall have only a year's happiness before I break your heart by growing up. Better choose the youngest you can find.

THE NEWLY BORN. I will not choose anyone but you. You must not grow up. We will love one another for ever. [*They all laugh*]. What are you laughing at?

THE SHE-ANCIENT. Listen, child—

THE NEWLY BORN. Do not come near me, you dreadful old creature. You frighten me.

ACIS. Just give her another moment. She is not quite reasonable yet. What can you expect from a child less than five minutes old?

THE NEWLY BORN. I think I feel a little more reasonable now. Of course I was rather young when I said that; but the inside of my head is changing very rapidly. I should like to have things explained to me.

ACIS [*to the She-Ancient*] Is she all right, do you think?

The She-Ancient looks at the Newly Born critically; feels her bumps like a phrenologist; grips her muscles and shakes her limbs; examines her teeth; looks into her eyes for a moment; and finally relinquishes her with an air of having finished her job.

THE SHE-ANCIENT. She will do. She may live.

They all wave their hands and shout for joy.

THE NEWLY BORN [*indignant*] I may live! Suppose there had been anything wrong with me?

THE SHE-ANCIENT. Children with anything wrong do not live here, my child. Life is not cheap with us. But you would not have felt anything.

THE NEWLY BORN. You mean that you would have murdered me!

THE SHE-ANCIENT. That is one of the funny words the newly born bring with them out of the past. You will forget it tomorrow. Now listen. You have four years of childhood before you. You will not be very happy; but you will be interested and amused by the novelty of the world; and your companions here will teach you how to keep up an imitation of happiness during your four years by what they call arts and sports and pleasures. The worst of your troubles is already over.

THE NEWLY BORN. What! In five minutes?

THE SHE-ANCIENT. No: you have been growing for two years in the egg. You began by being several sorts of creatures that no longer exist, though we have fossils of them. Then you became human; and you passed in fifteen months through a development that once cost human beings twenty years of awkward stumbling immaturity after they were born. They had to spend fifty years more in the sort of childhood you will complete in four years. And then they died of decay. But you need not die until your accident comes.

THE NEWLY BORN. What is my accident?

THE SHE-ANCIENT. Sooner or later you will fall and break your neck; or a tree will fall on you; or you will be struck by lightning. Something or other must make an end of you some day.

THE NEWLY BORN. But why should any of these things happen to me?

THE SHE-ANCIENT. There is no why. They do. Everything happens to everybody sooner or later if there is time enough. And with us there is eternity.

THE NEWLY BORN. Nothing need happen. I never heard such nonsense in all my life. I shall know how to take care of myself.

THE SHE-ANCIENT. So you think.

THE NEWLY BORN. I dont think: I know. I shall enjoy life for ever and ever.

THE SHE-ANCIENT. If you should turn out to be a person of infinite capacity, you will no doubt find life infinitely interesting. However, all you have to do now is to play with your companions. They have many pretty toys, as you see: a playhouse, pictures, images, flowers, bright fabrics, music: above all, themselves; for the most amusing child's toy is another child. At the end of four years, your mind will change: you will become wise; and then you will be entrusted with power.

THE NEWLY BORN. But I want power now.

THE SHE-ANCIENT. No doubt you do; so that

you could play with the world by tearing it to pieces.

THE NEWLY BORN. Only to see how it is made. I should put it all together again much better than before.

THE SHE-ANCIENT. There was a time when children were given the world to play with because they promised to improve it. They did not improve it; and they would have wrecked it had their power been as great as that which you will wield when you are no longer a child. Until then your young companions will instruct you in whatever is necessary. You are not forbidden to speak to the ancients; but you had better not do so, as most of them have long ago exhausted all the interest there is in observing children and conversing with them. [*She turns to go*].

THE NEWLY BORN. Wait. Tell me some things that I ought to do and ought not to do. I feel the need of education.

They all laugh at her, except the She-Ancient.

THE SHE-ANCIENT. You will have grown out of that by tomorrow. Do what you please. [*She goes away up the hill path*].

The officials take their paraphernalia and the fragments of the egg back into the temple.

ACIS. Just fancy: that old girl has been going for seven hundred years and hasnt had her fatal accident yet; and she is not a bit tired of it all.

THE NEWLY BORN. How could anyone ever get tired of life?

ACIS. They do. That is, of the same life. They manage to change themselves in a wonderful way. You meet them sometimes with a lot of extra heads and arms and legs: they make you split laughing at them. Most of them have forgotten how to speak: the ones that attend to us have to brush up their knowledge of the language once a year or so. Nothing makes any difference to them that I can see. They never enjoy themselves. I dont know how they can stand it. They dont even come to our festivals of the arts. That old one who saw you out of your shell has gone off to moodle about doing nothing; though she knows that this is Festival Day.

THE NEWLY BORN. What is Festival Day?

ACIS. Two of our greatest sculptors are bringing us their latest masterpieces; and we are going to crown them with flowers and sing dithyrambs to them and dance round them.

THE NEWLY BORN. How jolly! What is a sculptor?

ACIS. Listen here, young one. You must find out things for yourself, and not ask questions. For the first day or two you must keep your eyes and ears open and your mouth shut. Children should be seen and not heard.

THE NEWLY BORN. Who are you calling a child? I am fully quarter of an hour old. [*She sits down on the curved bench near Strephon with her maturest air*].

VOICES IN THE TEMPLE [*all expressing protest, disappointment, disgust*] Oh! Oh! Scandalous. Shameful, Disgraceful. What filth! Is this a joke? Why, theyre ancients! Ss-s-s-sss! Are you mad, Arjillax? This is an outrage. An insult. Yah! etc. etc. etc. [*The malcontents appear on the steps, grumbling*].

ACIS. Hullo: whats the matter? [*He goes to the steps of the temple*].

The two sculptors issue from the temple. One has a beard two feet long: the other is beardless. Between them comes a handsome nymph with marked features, dark hair richly waved, and authoritative bearing.

THE AUTHORITATIVE NYMPH [*swooping down to the centre of the glade with the sculptors, between Acis and the Newly Born*] Do not try to browbeat me, Arjillax, merely because you are clever with your hands. Can you play the flute?

ARJILLAX [*the bearded sculptor on her right*] No, Ecrasia: I cannot. What has that to do with it? [*He is half derisive, half impatient, wholly resolved not to take her seriously in spite of her beauty and imposing tone*].

ECRASIA. Well, have you ever hesitated to criticize our best flute players, and to declare whether their music is good or bad? Pray have I not the same right to criticize your busts, though I cannot make images any more than you can play?

ARJILLAX. Any fool can play the flute, or play anything else, if he practises enough; but sculpture is a creative art, not a mere business of whistling into a pipe. The sculptor must have something of the god in him. From his hand comes a form which reflects a spirit. He does not make it to please you, nor even to please himself, but because he must. You must take what he gives you, or leave it if you are not worthy of it.

ECRASIA [*scornfully*] Not worthy of it! Ho! May I not leave it because it is not worthy of me?

ARJILLAX. Of you! Hold your silly tongue,

you conceited humbug. What do you know about it?

ECRASIA. I know what every person of culture knows: that the business of the artist is to create beauty. Until today your works have been full of beauty; and I have been the first to point that out.

ARJILLAX. Thank you for nothing. People have eyes, havnt they, to see what is as plain as the sun in the heavens without your pointing it out?

ECRASIA. You were very glad to have it pointed out. You did not call me a conceited humbug then. You stifled me with caresses. You modelled me as the genius of art presiding over the infancy of your master here [indicating the other sculptor], Martellus.

MARTELLUS [a silent and meditative listener, shudders and shakes his head, but says nothing].

ARJILLAX [quarrelsomely] I was taken in by your talk.

ECRASIA. I discovered your genius before anyone else did. Is that true, or is it not?

ARJILLAX. Everybody knew I was an extraordinary person. When I was born my beard was three feet long.

ECRASIA. Yes; and it has shrunk from three feet to two. Your genius seems to have been in the last foot of your beard; for you have lost both.

MARTELLUS [with a short sardonic cachinnation] Ha! My beard was three and a half feet long when I was born; and a flash of lightning burnt it off and killed the ancient who was delivering me. Without a hair on my chin I became the greatest sculptor in ten generations.

ECRASIA. And yet you come to us today with empty hands. We shall actually have to crown Arjillax here because no other sculptor is exhibiting.

ACIS [returning from the temple steps to behind the curved seat on the right of the three] Whats the row, Ecrasia? Why have you fallen out with Arjillax?

ECRASIA. He has insulted us! outraged us! profaned his art! You know how much we hoped from the twelve busts he placed in the temple to be unveiled today. Well, go in and look at them. That is all I have to say. [She sweeps to the curved seat, and sits down just where Acis is leaning over it].

ACIS. I am no great judge of sculpture. Art is not my line. What is wrong with the busts?

ECRASIA. Wrong with them! Instead of being ideally beautiful nymphs and youths, they are horribly realistic studies of—but I really cannot bring my lips to utter it.

The Newly Born, full of curiosity, runs to the temple, and peeps in.

ACIS. Oh, stow it, Ecrasia. Your lips are not so squeamish as all that. Studies of what?

THE NEWLY BORN [from the temple steps] Ancients.

ACIS [surprised but not scandalized] Ancients!

ECRASIA. Yes, ancients. The one subject that is by the universal consent of all connoisseurs absolutely excluded from the fine arts. [To Arjillax] How can you defend such a proceeding?

ARJILLAX. If you come to that, what interest can you find in the statues of smirking nymphs and posturing youths you stick up all over the place?

ECRASIA. You did not ask that when your hand was still skilful enough to model them.

ARJILLAX. Skilful! You high-nosed idiot, I could turn such things out by the score with my eyes bandaged and one hand tied behind me. But what use would they be? They would bore me; and they would bore you if you had any sense. Go in and look at my busts. Look at them again and yet again until you receive the full impression of the intensity of mind that is stamped on them; and then go back to the pretty-pretty confectionery you call sculpture, and see whether you can endure its vapid emptiness. [He mounts the altar impetuously] Listen to me, all of you; and do you, Ecrasia, be silent if you are capable of silence.

ECRASIA. Silence is the most perfect expression of scorn. Scorn! That is what I feel for your revolting busts.

ARJILLAX. Fool: the busts are only the beginning of a mighty design. Listen.

ACIS. Go ahead, old sport. We are listening.

Martellus stretches himself on the sward beside the altar. The Newly Born sits on the temple steps with her chin on her hands, ready to devour the first oration she has ever heard. The rest sit or stand at ease.

ARJILLAX. In the records which generations of children have rescued from the stupid neglect of the ancients, there has come down to us a fable which, like many fables, is not a thing that was done in the past, but a thing that is to be done in the future. It is a legend of a supernatural being called the Archangel

Michael.

THE NEWLY BORN. Is this a story? I want to hear a story. [*She runs down the steps and sits on the altar at Arjillax's feet*].

ARJILLAX. The Archangel Michael was a mighty sculptor and painter. He found in the centre of the world a temple erected to the goddess of the centre, called Mediterranea. This temple was full of silly pictures of pretty children, such as Ecrasia approves.

ACIS. Fair play, Arjillax! If she is to keep silent, let her alone.

ECRASIA. I shall not interrupt, Acis. Why should I not prefer youth and beauty to age and ugliness?

ARJILLAX. Just so. Well, the Archangel Michael was of my opinion, not yours. He began by painting on the ceiling the newly born in all their childish beauty. But when he had done this he was not satisfied; for the temple was no more impressive than it had been before, except that there was a strength and promise of greater things about his newly born ones than any other artist had attained to. So he painted all round these newly born a company of ancients, who were in those days called prophets and sybils, whose majesty was that of the mind alone at its intensest. And this painting was acknowledged through ages and ages to be the summit and masterpiece of art. Of course we cannot believe such a tale literally. It is only a legend. We do not believe in archangels; and the notion that thirty thousand years ago sculpture and painting existed, and had even reached the glorious perfection they have reached with us, is absurd. But what men cannot realize they can at least aspire to. They please themselves by pretending that it was realized in a golden age of the past. This splendid legend endured because it lived as a desire in the hearts of the greatest artists. The temple of Mediterranea never was built in the past, nor did Michael the Archangel exist. But today the temple is here [*he points to the porch*]; and the man is here [*he slaps himself on the chest*]. I, Arjillax, am the man. I will place in your theatre such images of the newly born as must satisfy even Ecrasia's appetite for beauty; and I will surround them with ancients more august than any who walk through our woods.

MARTELLUS [*as before*] Ha!

ARJILLAX [*stung*] Why do you laugh, you who have come empty-handed, and, it seems, empty-headed?

ECRASIA [*rising indignantly*] Oh, shame! You dare disparage Martellus, twenty times your master.

ACIS. Be quiet, will you [*he seizes her shoulders and thrusts her back into her seat*].

MARTELLUS. Let him disparage his fill, Ecrasia. [*Sitting up*] My poor Arjillax, I too had this dream. I too found one day that my images of loveliness had become vapid, uninteresting, tedious, a waste of time and material. I too lost my desire to model limbs, and retained only my interest in heads and faces. I, too, made busts of ancients; but I had not your courage: I made them in secret, and hid them from you all.

ARJILLAX [*jumping down from the altar behind Martellus in his surprise and excitement*] You made busts of ancients! Where are they, man? Will you be talked out of your inspiration by Ecrasia and the fools who imagine she speaks with authority? Let us have them all set up beside mine in the theatre. I have opened the way for you; and you see I am none the worse.

MARTELLUS. Impossible. They are all smashed. [*He rises, laughing*].

ALL. Smashed!

ARJILLAX. Who smashed them?

MARTELLUS. I did. That is why I laughed at you just now. You will smash yours before you have completed a dozen of them. [*He goes to the end of the altar and sits down beside the Newly Born*].

ARJILLAX. But why?

MARTELLUS. Because you cannot give them life. A live ancient is better than a dead statue. [*He takes the Newly Born on his knee: she is flattered and voluptuously responsive*]. Anything alive is better than anything that is only pretending to be alive. [*To Arjillax*] Your disillusion with your works of beauty is only the beginning of your disillusion with images of all sorts. As your hand became more skilful and your chisel cut deeper, you strove to get nearer and nearer to truth and reality, discarding the fleeting fleshly lure, and making images of the mind that fascinates to the end. But how can so noble an inspiration be satisfied with any image, even an image of the truth? In the end the intellectual conscience that tore you away from the fleeting in art to the eternal must tear you away from art altogether, because art is false and life alone is true.

THE NEWLY BORN [*flings her arms round his neck and kisses him enthusiastically*].

MARTELLUS [*rises; carries her to the curved bench on his left; deposits her beside Strephon as if she were his overcoat; and continues without the least change of tone*] Shape it as you will, marble remains marble, and the graven image an idol. As I have broken my idols, and cast away my chisel and modelling tools, so will you too break these busts of yours.

ARJILLAX. Never.

MARTELLUS. Wait, my friend. I do not come empty-handed today, as you imagined. On the contrary, I bring with me such a work of art as you have never seen, and an artist who has surpassed both you and me further than we have surpassed all our competitors.

ECRASIA. Impossible. The greatest things in art can never be surpassed.

ARJILLAX. Who is this paragon whom you declare greater than I?

MARTELLUS. I declare him greater than myself, Arjillax.

ARJILLAX [*frowning*] I understand. Sooner than not drown me, you are willing to clasp me round the waist and jump overboard with me.

ACIS. Oh, stop squabbling. That is the worst of you artists. You are always in little squabbling cliques; and the worst cliques are those which consist of one man. Who is this new fellow you are throwing in one another's teeth?

ARJILLAX. Ask Martellus: do not ask me. I know nothing of him. [*He leaves Martellus, and sits down beside Ecrasia, on her left*].

MARTELLUS. You know him quite well. Pygmalion.

ECRASIA [*indignantly*] Pygmalion! That soulless creature! A scientist! A laboratory person!

ARJILLAX. Pygmalion produce a work of art! You have lost your artistic senses. The man is utterly incapable of modelling a thumb nail, let alone a human figure.

MARTELLUS. That does not matter: I have done the modelling for him.

ARJILLAX. What on earth do you mean?

MARTELLUS [*calling*] Pygmalion: come forth.

Pygmalion, a square-fingered youth with his face laid out in horizontal blocks, and a perpetual smile of eager benevolent interest in everything, and expectation of equal interest from everybody else, comes from the temple to the centre of the group, *who regard him for the most part with dismay, as dreading that he will bore them. Ecrasia is openly contemptuous.*

MARTELLUS. Friends: it is unfortunate that Pygmalion is constitutionally incapable of exhibiting anything without first giving a lecture about it to explain it; but I promise you that if you will be patient he will shew you the two most wonderful works of art in the world, and that they will contain some of my own very best workmanship. Let me add that they will inspire a loathing that will cure you of the lunacy of art for ever. [*He sits down next the Newly Born, who pouts and turns a very cold right shoulder to him, a demonstration utterly lost on him*].

Pygmalion, with the smile of a simpleton, and the eager confidence of a fanatical scientist, climbs awkwardly on to the altar. They prepare for the worst.

PYGMALION. My friends: I will omit the algebra—

ACIS. Thank God!

PYGMALION [*continuing*]—because Martellus has made me promise to do so. To come to the point, I have succeeded in making artificial human beings. Real live ones, I mean.

INCREDULOUS VOICES. Oh, come! Tell us another. Really, Pyg! Get out. You havnt. What a lie!

PYGMALION. I tell you I have. I will shew them to you. It has been done before. One of the very oldest documents we possess mentions a tradition of a biologist who extracted certain unspecified minerals from the earth and, as it quaintly expresses it, "breathed into their nostrils the breath of life." This is the only tradition from the primitive ages which we can regard as really scientific. There are later documents which specify the minerals with great precision, even to their atomic weights; but they are utterly unscientific, because they overlook the element of life which makes all the difference between a mere mixture of salts and gases and a living organism. These mixtures were made over and over again in the crude laboratories of the Silly-Clever Ages; but nothing came of them until the ingredient which the old chronicler called the breath of life was added by this very remarkable early experimenter. In my view he was the founder of biological science.

ARJILLAX. Is that all we know about him? It doesnt amount to very much, does it?

PYGMALION. There are some fragments of pictures and documents which represent him as walking in a garden and advising people to cultivate their gardens. His name has come down to us in several forms. One of them is Jove. Another is Voltaire.

ECRASIA. You are boring us to distraction with your Voltaire. What about your human beings?

ARJILLAX. Aye: come to them.

PYGMALION. I assure you that these details are intensely interesting. [Cries of No! They are not! Come to the human beings! Conspuez Voltaire! Cut it short, Pyg! interrupt him from all sides]. You will see their bearing presently. I promise you I will not detain you long. We know, we children of science, that the universe is full of forces and powers and energies of one kind and another. The sap rising in a tree, the stone holding together in a definite crystalline structure, the thought of a philosopher holding his brain in form and operation with an inconceivably powerful grip, the urge of evolution: all these forces can be used by us. For instance, I use the force of gravitation when I put a stone on my tunic to prevent it being blown away when I am bathing. By substituting appropriate machines for the stone we have made not only gravitation our slave, but also electricity and magnetism, atomic attraction, repulsion, polarization, and so forth. But hitherto the vital force has eluded us; so it has had to create machinery for itself. It has created and developed bony structure of the requisite strength, and clothed them with cellular tissue of such amazing sensitiveness that the organs it forms will adapt their action to all the normal variations in the air they breathe, the food they digest, and the circumstances about which they have to think. Yet, as these live bodies, as we call them, are only machines after all, it must be possible to construct them mechanically.

ARJILLAX. Everything is possible. Have you done it? that is the question.

PYGMALION. Yes. But that is a mere fact. What is interesting is the explanation of the fact. Forgive my saying so; but it is such a pity that you artists have no intellect.

ECRASIA [sententiously] I do not admit that. The artist divines by inspiration all the truths that the so-called scientist grubs up in his laboratory slowly and stupidly long afterwards.

ARJILLAX [to Ecrasia, quarrelsomely] What do you know about it? You are not an artist.

ACIS. Shut your heads, both of you. Let us have the artificial men. Trot them out, Pygmalion.

PYGMALION. It is a man and a woman. But I really must explain first.

ALL [groaning]!!!

PYGMALION. Yes: I—

ACIS. We want results, not explanations.

PYGMALION [hurt] I see I am boring you. Not one of you takes the least interest in science. Goodbye. [He descends from the altar and makes for the temple].

SEVERAL YOUTHS AND MAIDENS [rising and rushing to him] No, no. Dont go. Dont be offended. We want to see the artificial pair. We will listen. We are tremendously interested. Tell us all about it.

PYGMALION [relenting] I shall not detain you two minutes.

ALL. Half an hour if you like. Please go on, Pygmalion. [They rush him back to the altar, and hoist him on to it]. Up you go.

They return to their former places.

PYGMALION. As I told you, lots of attempts were made to produce protoplasm in the laboratory. Why were these synthetic plasms, as they called them, no use?

ECRASIA. We are waiting for you to tell us.

THE NEWLY BORN [modelling herself on Ecrasia, and trying to outdo her intellectually] Clearly because they were dead.

PYGMALION. Not bad for a baby, my pet. But dead and alive are very loose terms. You are not half as much alive as you will be in another month or so. What was wrong with the synthetic protoplasm was that it could not fix and conduct the Life Force. It was like a wooden magnet or a lightning conductor made of silk: it would not take the current.

ACIS. Nobody but a fool would make a wooden magnet, and expect it to attract anything.

PYGMALION. He might if he were so ignorant as not to be able to distinguish between wood and soft iron. In those days they were very ignorant of the differences between things, because their methods of analysis were crude. They mixed up messes that were so like protoplasm that they could not tell the difference. But the difference was there, though their analysis was too superficial and incomplete to detect it. You must remember that these poor devils were very little better than our idiots: we should never dream of letting one of them survive the day of its birth. Why, the Newly Born there already knows by instinct many things that their greatest physicists could hardly arrive at by forty years of strenuous study. Her simple direct sense of space-time and quantity unconsciously solves problems which cost their most famous mathematicians years of prolonged and laborious calculations requiring such intense mental application that they frequently forgot to breathe when engaged in them, and almost suffocated themselves in consequence.

ECRASIA. Leave these obscure prehistoric abortions; and come back to your synthetic man and woman.

PYGMALION. When I undertook the task of making synthetic men, I did not waste my time on protoplasm. It was evident to me that if it were possible to make protoplasm in the laboratory, it must be equally possible to begin higher up and make fully evolved muscular and nervous tissues, bone, and so forth. Why make the seed when the making of the flower would be no greater miracle? I tried thousands of combinations before I succeeded in producing anything that would fix high-potential Life Force.

ARJILLAX. High what?

PYGMALION. High-po-tential. The Life Force is not so simple as you think. A high-potential current of it will turn a bit of dead tissue into a philosopher's brain. A low-potential current will reduce the same bit of tissue to a mass of corruption. Will you believe me when I tell you that, even in man himself, the Life Force used to slip suddenly down from its human level to that of a fungus, so that men found their flesh no longer growing as flesh, but proliferating horribly in a lower form which was called cancer, until the lower form of life killed the higher, and both perished together miserably?

MARTELLUS. Keep off the primitive tribes, Pygmalion. They interest you; but they bore these young things.

PYGMALION. I am only trying to make you understand. There was the Life Force raging all round me: there was I, trying to make organs that would capture it as a battery captures electricity, and tissues that would conduct it and operate it. It was easy enough to make eyes more perfect than our own,

and ears with a larger range of sound; but they could neither see nor hear, because they were not susceptible to the Life Force. But it was far worse when I discovered how to make them susceptible; for the first thing that happened was that they ceased to be eyes and ears and turned into heaps of maggots.

ECRASIA. Disgusting! Please stop.

ACIS. If you dont want to hear, go away. You go ahead, Pyg.

PYGMALION. I went ahead. You see, the lower potentials of the Life Force could make maggots, but not human eyes or ears. I improved the tissue until it was susceptible to a higher potential.

ARJILLAX [intensely interested] Yes; and then?

PYGMALION. Then the eyes and ears turned into cancers.

ECRASIA. Oh, hideous!

PYGMALION. Not at all. That was a great advance. It encouraged me so much that I put aside the eyes and ears, and made a brain. It wouldnt take the Life Force at all until I had altered its constitution a dozen times; but when it did, it took a much higher potential, and did not dissolve; and neither did the eyes and ears when I connected them up with the brain. I was able to make a sort of monster: a thing without arms or legs; and it really and truly lived for half-an-hour.

THE NEWLY BORN. Half-an-hour! What good was that? Why did it die?

PYGMALION. Its blood went wrong. But I got that right; and then I went ahead with a complete human body: arms and legs and all. He was my first man.

ARJILLAX. Who modelled him?

PYGMALION. I did.

MARTELLUS. Do you mean to say you tried your own hand before you sent for me?

PYGMALION. Bless you, yes, several times. My first man was the ghastliest creature: a more dreadful mixture of horror and absurdity than you who have not seen him can conceive.

ARJILLAX. If you modelled him, he must indeed have been a spectacle.

PYGMALION. Oh, it was not his shape. You see I did not invent that. I took actual measurements and moulds from my own body. Sculptors do that sometimes, you know; though they pretend they dont.

MARTELLUS. Hm!

ARJILLAX. Hah!

PYGMALION. He was all right to look at, at first, or nearly so. But he behaved in the most appalling manner; and the subsequent developments were so disgusting that I really cannot describe them to you. He seized all sorts of things and swallowed them. He drank every fluid in the laboratory. I tried to explain to him that he must take nothing that he could not digest and assimilate completely; but of course he could not understand me. He assimilated a little of what he swallowed; but the process left horrible residues which he had no means of getting rid of. His blood turned to poison; and he perished in torments, howling. I then perceived that I had produced a prehistoric man; for there are certain traces in our own bodies of arrangements which enabled the earlier forms of mankind to renew their bodies by swallowing flesh and grains and vegetables and all sorts of unnatural and hideous foods, and getting rid of what they could not digest.

ECRASIA. But what a pity he died! What a glimpse of the past we have lost! He could have told us stories of the Golden Age.

PYGMALION. Not he. He was a most dangerous beast. He was afraid of me, and actually tried to kill me by snatching up things and striking at me with them. I had to give him two or three pretty severe shocks before I convinced him that he was at my mercy.

THE NEWLY BORN. Why did you not make a woman instead of a man? She would have known how to behave herself.

MARTELLUS. Why did you not make a man and a woman? Their children would have been interesting.

PYGMALION. I intended to make a woman; but after my experience with the man it was out of the question.

ECRASIA. Pray why?

PYGMALION. Well, it is difficult to explain if you have not studied prehistoric methods of reproduction. You see the only sort of men and women I could make were men and women just like us as far as their bodies were concerned. That was how I killed the poor beast of a man. I hadnt provided for his horrible prehistoric methods of feeding himself. Suppose the woman had reproduced in some prehistoric way instead of being oviparous as we are? She couldnt have done it with a modern female body. Besides, the experiment might have been painful.

ECRASIA. Then you have nothing to shew us at all?

PYGMALION. Oh yes I have. I am not so easily beaten as that. I set to work again for months to find out how to make a digestive system that would deal with waste products and a reproductive system capable of internal nourishment and incubation.

ECRASIA. Why did you not find out how to make them like us?

STREPHON [crying out in his grief for the first time] Why did you not make a woman whom you could love? That was the secret you needed.

THE NEWLY BORN. Oh yes. How true! How great of you, darling Strephon! [She kisses him impulsively].

STREPHON [passionately] Let me alone.

MARTELLUS. Control your reflexes, child.

THE NEWLY BORN. My what!

MARTELLUS. Your reflexes. The things you do without thinking. Pygmalion is going to shew you a pair of human creatures who are all reflexes and nothing else. Take warning by them.

THE NEWLY BORN. But wont they be alive, like us?

PYGMALION. That is a very difficult question to answer, my dear. I confess I thought at first I had created living creatures; but Martellus declares they are only automata. But then Martellus is a mystic: I am a man of science. He draws a line between an automaton and a living organism. I cannot draw that line to my own satisfaction.

MARTELLUS. Your artificial men have no self-control. They only respond to stimuli from without.

PYGMALION. But they are conscious. I have taught them to talk and read; and now they tell lies. That is so very lifelike.

MARTELLUS. Not at all. If they were alive they would tell the truth. You can provoke them to tell any silly lie; and you can foresee exactly the sort of lie they will tell. Give them a clip below the knee, and they will jerk their foot forward. Give them a clip in their appetites or vanities or any of their lusts and greeds, and they will boast and lie, and affirm and deny, and hate and love without the slightest regard to the facts that are staring them in the face, or to their own obvious limitations. That proves that they are automata.

PYGMALION [*unconvinced*] I know, dear old chap; but there really is some evidence that we are descended from creatures quite as limited and absurd as these. After all, the baby there is three-quarters an automaton. Look at the way she has been going on!

THE NEWLY BORN [*indignantly*] What do you mean? How have I been going on?

ECRASIA. If they have no regard for truth, they can have no real vitality.

PYGMALION. Truth is sometimes so artificial: so relative, as we say in the scientific world, that it is very hard to feel quite sure that what is false and even ridiculous to us may not be true to them.

ECRASIA. I ask you again, why did you not make them like us? Would any true artist be content with less than the best?

PYGMALION. I couldnt. I tried. I failed. I am convinced that what I am about to shew you is the very highest living organism that can be produced in the laboratory. The best tissues we can manufacture will not take as high potentials as the natural product: that is where Nature beats us. You dont seem to understand, any of you, what an enormous triumph it was to produce consciousness at all.

ACIS. Cut the cackle; and come to the synthetic couple.

SEVERAL YOUTHS AND MAIDENS. Yes, yes. No more talking. Let us have them. Dry up, Pyg; and fetch them along. Come on: out with them! The synthetic couple: the synthetic couple.

PYGMALION [*waving his hands to appease them*] Very well, very well. Will you please whistle for them? They respond to the stimulus of a whistle.

All who can, whistle like streetboys.

ECRASIA [*makes a wry face and puts her fingers in her ears*]!

PYGMALION. Sh-sh-sh! Thats enough: thats enough: thats enough. [*Silence*]. Now let us have some music. A dance tune. Not too fast.

The flutists play a quiet dance.

MARTELLUS. Prepare yourselves for something ghastly.

Two figures, a man and woman of noble appearance, beautifully modelled and splendidly attired, emerge hand in hand from the temple. Seeing that all eyes are fixed on them, they halt on the steps, smiling with gratified vanity. The woman is on the man's left.

PYGMALION [*rubbing his hands with the purring satisfaction of a creator*] This way, please.

The Figures advance condescendingly and pose themselves centrally between the curved seats.

PYGMALION. Now if you will be so good as to oblige us with a little something. You dance so beautifully, you know. [*He sits down next Martellus, and whispers to him*] It is extraordinary how sensitive they are to the stimulus of flattery.

The Figures, with a gracious air, dance pompously, but very passably. At the close they bow to one another.

ON ALL HANDS [*clapping*] Bravo! Thank you. Wonderful! Splendid. Perfect.

The Figures acknowledge the applause in an obvious condition of swelled head.

THE NEWLY BORN. Can they make love?

PYGMALION. Yes: they can respond to every stimulus. They have all the reflexes. Put your arm round the man's neck, and he will put his arm round your body. He cannot help it.

THE FEMALE FIGURE [*frowning*] Round mine, you mean.

PYGMALION. Yours, too, of course, if the stimulus comes from you.

ECRASIA. Cannot he do anything original?

PYGMALION. No. But then, you know, I do not admit that any of us can do anything really original, though Martellus thinks we can.

ACIS. Can he answer a question?

PYGMALION. Oh yes. A question is a stimulus, you know. Ask him one.

ACIS [*to the Male Figure*] What do you think of what you see around you? Of us, for instance, and our ways and doings?

THE MALE FIGURE. I have not seen the newspaper today.

THE FEMALE FIGURE. How can you expect my husband to know what to think of you if you give him his breakfast without his paper?

MARTELLUS. You see. He is a mere automaton.

THE NEWLY BORN. I dont think I should like him to put his arm round my neck. I dont like them. [*The Male Figure looks offended, and the Female jealous*]. Oh, I thought they couldnt understand. Have they feelings?

PYGMALION. Of course they have. I tell you they have all the reflexes.

THE NEWLY BORN. But feelings are not reflexes.

PYGMALION. They are sensations. When the rays of light enter their eyes and make a picture on their retinas, their brains become conscious of the picture and they act accordingly. When the waves of sound started by your speaking enter their ears and record a disparaging remark on their keyboards, their brains become conscious of the disparagement and resent it accordingly. If you did not disparage them they would not resent it. They are merely responding to a stimulus.

THE MALE FIGURE. We are part of a cosmic system. Free will is an illusion. We are the children of Cause and Effect. We are the Unalterable, the Irresistible, the Irresponsible, the Inevitable.

My name is Ozymandias, king of kings:
Look on my works, ye mighty, and despair.

There is a general stir of curiosity at this.

ACIS. What the dickens does he mean?

THE MALE FIGURE. Silence, base accident of Nature. This [*taking the hand of the Female Figure and introducing her*] is Cleopatra-Semiramis, consort of the king of kings, and therefore queen of queens. Ye are things hatched from eggs by the brainless sun and the blind fire; but the king of kings and queen of queens are not accidents of the egg: they are thought-out and hand-made to receive the sacred Life Force. There is one person of the king and one of the queen; but the Life Force of the king and queen is all one: the glory equal, the majesty co-eternal. Such as the king is so is the queen, the king thought-out and hand-made, the queen thought-out and hand-made. The actions of the king are caused, and therefore determined, from the beginning of the world to the end; and the actions of the queen are likewise. The king logical and predetermined and inevitable, and the queen logical and predetermined and inevitable. And yet they are not two logical and predetermined and inevitable, but one logical and predetermined and inevitable. Therefore confound not the persons, nor divide the substance; but worship us twain as one throne, two in one and one in two, lest by error ye fall into irretrievable damnation.

THE FEMALE FIGURE. And if any say unto you "Which one?" remember that though there is one person of the king and one of the queen, yet these two persons are not alike, but are woman and man, and that as woman was created after man, the skill and practice gained in making him were added to her, wherefore she is to be exalted above him in all personal respects, and—

THE MALE FIGURE. Peace, woman; for this is a damnable heresy. Both Man and Woman are what they are and must do what they must according to the eternal laws of Cause and Effect. Look to your words; for if they enter my ear and jar too repugnantly on my sensorium, who knows that the inevitable response to that stimulus may not be a message to my muscles to snatch up some heavy object and break you in pieces.

The Female Figure picks up a stone and is about to throw it at her consort.

ARJILLAX [*springing up and shouting to Pygmalion, who is fondly watching the Male Figure*] Look out, Pygmalion! Look at the woman!

Pygmalion, seeing what is happening, hurls himself on the Female Figure and wrenches the stone out of her hand.

All spring up in consternation.

ARJILLAX. She meant to kill him

STREPHON. This is horrible.

THE FEMALE FIGURE [*wrestling with Pygmalion*] Let me go. Let me go, will you [*she bites his hand*].

PYGMALION [*releasing her and staggering*] Oh!

A general shriek of horror echoes his exclamation. He turns deadly pale, and supports himself against the end of the curved seat.

THE FEMALE FIGURE [*to her consort*] You would stand there and let me be treated like this, you unmanly coward.

Pygmalion falls dead.

THE NEWLY BORN. Oh! Whats the matter? Why did he fall? What has happened to him?

They look on anxiously as Martellus kneels down and examines the body of Pygmalion.

MARTELLUS. She has bitten a piece out of his hand nearly as large as a finger nail: enough to kill ten men. There is no pulse, no breath.

ECRASIA. But his thumb is clinched.

MARTELLUS. No: it has just straightened out. See! He has gone. Poor Pygmalion!

THE NEWLY BORN. Oh! [*She weeps*].

STREPHON. Hush, dear: thats childish.

THE NEWLY BORN [*subsiding with a sniff*]!!

MARTELLUS [*rising*] Dead in his third year. What a loss to Science!

ARJILLAX. Who cares about Science? Serve him right for making that pair of horrors!

THE MALE FIGURE [*glaring*] Ha!

THE FEMALE FIGURE. Keep a civil tongue in your head, you.

THE NEWLY BORN. Oh, do not be so unkind, Arjillax. You will make water come out of my eyes again.

MARTELLUS [*contemplating the Figures*] Just look at these two devils. I modelled them out of the stuff Pygmalion made for them. They are masterpieces of art. And see what they have done! Does that convince you of the value of art, Arjillax?

STREPHON. They look dangerous. Keep away from them.

ECRASIA. No need to tell us that, Strephon. Pf! They poison the air.

THE MALE FIGURE. Beware, woman. The wrath of Ozymandias strikes like lightning.

THE FEMALE FIGURE. You just say that again if you dare, you filthy creature.

ACIS. What are you going to do with them, Martellus? You are responsible for them, now that Pygmalion has gone.

MARTELLUS. If they were marble it would be simple enough: I could smash them. As it is, how am I to kill them without making a horrible mess?

THE MALE FIGURE [*posing heroically*] Ha! [*He declaims*]

Come one: come all: this rock shall fly
From its firm base as soon as I.

THE FEMALE FIGURE [*fondly*] My man! My hero husband! I am proud of you. I love you.

MARTELLUS. We must send out a message for an ancient.

ACIS. Need we bother an ancient about such a trifle? It will take less than half a second to reduce our poor Pygmalion to a pinch of dust. Why no calcine the two along with him?

MARTELLUS. No: the two automata are trifles; but the use of our powers of destruction is never a trifle. I had rather have the case judged.

The He-Ancient emerges from the grove. The Figures are panic-stricken.

THE HE-ANCIENT [*mildly*] Am I wanted? I feel called. [*Seeing the body of Pygmalion, and immediately taking a sterner tone*] What! A child lost! A life wasted! How has this happened?

THE FEMALE FIGURE [*frantically*] I didnt do it. It was not me. May I be struck dead if I touched him! It was he [*pointing to the Male Figure*].

ALL [*amazed at the lie*] Oh!

THE MALE FIGURE. Liar. You bit him. Everyone here saw you do it.

THE HE-ANCIENT. Silence. [*Going between the Figures*] Who made these two loathsome dolls?

THE MALE FIGURE [*trying to assert himself with his knees knocking*] My name is Ozymandias, king of—

THE HE-ANCIENT [*with a contemptuous gesture*] Pooh!

THE MALE FIGURE [*falling on his knees*] Oh dont, sir. D o n t. She did it, sir: indeed she did.

THE FEMALE FIGURE [*howling lamentably*] Boohoo! oo! ooh!

THE HE-ANCIENT. Silence, I say.

He knocks the Male Automaton upright by a very light flip under the chin. The Female Automaton hardly dares to sob. The immortals contemplate them with shame and loathing. The She-Ancient comes from the trees opposite the temple.

THE SHE-ANCIENT. Somebody wants me. What is the matter? [*She comes to the left hand of the Female Figure, not seeing the body of Pygmalion*]. Pf! [*Severely*] You have been making dolls. You must not: they are not only disgusting: they are dangerous.

THE FEMALE FIGURE [*snivelling piteously*] I'm not a doll, mam. I'm only poor Cleopatra-Semiramis, queen of queens. [*Covering her face with her hands*] Oh, dont look at me like that, mam. I meant no harm. He hurt me: indeed he did.

THE HE-ANCIENT. The creature has killed that poor youth.

THE SHE-ANCIENT [*seeing the body of Pygmalion*] What! This clever child, who promised so well!

THE FEMALE FIGURE. He made me. I had as much right to kill him as he had to make me. And how was I to know that a little thing like that would kill him? I shouldnt die if he cut off my arm or leg.

ECRASIA. What nonsense!

MARTELLUS. It may not be nonsense. I daresay if you cut off her leg she would grow another, like the lobsters and the little lizards.

THE HE-ANCIENT. Did this dead boy make these two things?

MARTELLUS. He made them in his laboratory. I moulded their limbs. I am sorry. I was thoughtless: I did not foresee that they would kill and pretend to be persons they were not, and declare things that were false, and wish evil. I thought they would be merely mechanical fools.

THE MALE FIGURE. Do you blame us for our human nature?

THE FEMALE FIGURE. We are flesh and blood and not angels.

THE MALE FIGURE. Have you no hearts?

ARJILLAX. They are mad as well as mischievous. May we not destroy them?

STREPHON. We abhor them.

THE NEWLY BORN. We loathe them.

ECRASIA. They are noisome.

ACIS. I dont want to be hard on the poor devils; but they are making me feel uneasy in my inside. I never had such a sensation before.

MARTELLUS. I took a lot of trouble with them. But as far as I am concerned, destroy them by all means. I loathed them from the beginning.

ALL. Yes, yes: we all loathe them. Let us calcine them.

THE FEMALE FIGURE. Oh, dont be so cruel. I'm not fit to die. I will never bite anyone again. I will tell the truth. I will do good. Is it my fault if I was not made properly? Kill him; but spare me.

THE MALE FIGURE. No! I have done no harm: she has. Kill her if you like: you have no right to kill me.

THE NEWLY BORN. Do you hear that? They want to have one another killed.

ARJILLAX. Monstrous! Kill them both.

THE HE-ANCIENT. Silence. These things are mere automata: they cannot help shrinking from death at any cost. You see that they have no self-control, and are merely shuddering through a series of reflexes. Let us see whether we cannot put a little more life into them. [He takes the Male Figure by the hand, and places his disengaged hand on its head]. Now listen. One of you two is to be destroyed. Which of you shall it be?

THE MALE FIGURE [after a slight convulsion during which his eyes are fixed on the He-Ancient] Spare her; and kill me.

STREPHON. Thats better.

THE NEWLY BORN. Much better.

THE SHE-ANCIENT [handling the Female Automaton in the same manner] Which of you shall we kill?

THE FEMALE FIGURE. Kill us both. How could either of us live without the other?

ECRASIA. The woman is more sensible than the man.

The Ancients release the Automata.

THE MALE FIGURE [sinking to the ground] I am discouraged. Life is too heavy a burden.

THE FEMALE FIGURE [collapsing] I am dying. I am glad. I am afraid to live.

THE NEWLY BORN. I think it would be nice to give the poor things a little music.

ARJILLAX. Why?

THE NEWLY BORN. I dont know. But it would. The Musicians play.

THE FEMALE FIGURE. Ozymandias: do you hear that? [She rises on her knees and looks raptly into space]. Queen of queens! [She dies].

THE MALE FIGURE [crawling feebly towards her until he reaches her hand] I knew I was really a king of kings. [To the others] Illusions, farewell: we are going to our thrones. [He dies].

The music stops. There is dead silence for a moment.

THE NEWLY BORN. That was funny.

STREPHON. It was. Even the Ancients are smiling.

THE NEWLY BORN. Just a little.

THE SHE-ANCIENT [quickly recovering her grave and peremptory manner] Take these two abominations away to Pygmalion's laboratory, and destroy them with the rest of the laboratory refuse. [Some of them move to obey]. Take care: do not touch their flesh: it is noxious: lift them by their robes. Carry Pygmalion into the temple; and dispose of his remains in the usual way.

The three bodies are carried out as directed, Pygmalion into the temple by his bare arms and legs, and the two Figures through the grove by their clothes. Martellus superintends the removal of the Figures, Acis that of Pygmalion. Ecrasia, Arjillax, Strephon, and the Newly Born sit down as before, but on contrary benches; so that Strephon and the Newly Born now face the grove, and Ecrasia and Arjillax the temple. The Ancients remain standing at the altar.

ECRASIA [as she sits down] Oh for a breeze from the hills!

STREPHON. Or the wind from the sea at the turn of the tide!

THE NEWLY BORN. I want some clean air.

THE HE-ANCIENT. The air will be clean in a moment. This doll flesh that children make decomposes quickly at best; but when it is shaken by such passions as the creatures are capable of, it breaks up at once and becomes horribly tainted.

THE SHE-ANCIENT. Let it be a lesson to you all to be content with lifeless toys, and not attempt to make living ones. What would you think of us ancients if we made toys of you children?

THE NEWLY BORN [coaxingly] Why do you not make toys of us? Then you would play with us; and that would be very nice.

THE SHE-ANCIENT. It would not amuse us. When you play with one another you play with your bodies, and that makes you supple and strong; but if we played with you we should play with your minds, and perhaps deform them.

STREPHON. You are a ghastly lot, you ancients. I shall kill myself when I am four years old. What do you live for?

THE HE-ANCIENT. You will find out when you grow up. You will not kill yourself.

STREPHON. If you make me believe that, I shall kill myself now.

THE NEWLY BORN. Oh no. I want you. I love you.

STREPHON. I love someone else. And she has gone old, old. Lost to me for ever.

THE HE-ANCIENT. How old?

STREPHON. You saw her when you barged into us as we were dancing. She is four.

THE NEWLY BORN. How I should have hated her twenty minutes ago! But I have grown out of that now.

THE HE-ANCIENT. Good. That hatred is called jealousy, the worst of our childish complaints.

Martellus, dusting his hands and puffing, returns from the grove.

MARTELLUS. Ouf! [*He sits down next the Newly Born*] That job's finished.

ARJILLAX. Ancients: I should like to make a few studies of you. Not portraits, of course: I shall idealize you a little. I have come to the conclusion that you ancients are the most interesting subjects after all.

MARTELLUS. What! Have those two horrors, whose ashes I have just deposited with peculiar pleasure in poor Pygmalion's dustbin, not cured you of this silly image-making?

ARJILLAX. Why did you model them as young things, you fool? If Pygmalion had come to me, I should have made ancients of them for him. Not that I should have modelled them any better. I have always said that no one can beat you at your best as far as handwork is concerned. But this job required brains. That is where I should have come in.

MARTELLUS. Well, my brainy boy, you are welcome to try your hand. There are two of Pygmalion's pupils at the laboratory who helped him to manufacture the bones and tissues and all the rest of it. They can turn out a couple of new automatons; and you can model them as ancients if this venerable pair will sit for you.

ECRASIA [*decisively*] No. No more automata. They are too disgusting.

ACIS [*returning from the temple*] Well, thats done. Poor old Pyg!

ECRASIA. Only fancy, Acis! Arjillax wants to make more of those abominable things, and to destroy even their artistic character by making ancients of them.

THE NEWLY BORN. You wont sit for them, will you? Please dont.

THE HE-ANCIENT. Children, listen.

ACIS [*striding down the steps to the bench and seating himself next Ecrasia*] What! Even the Ancient wants to make a speech! Give it mouth, O Sage.

STREPHON. For heaven's sake dont tell us that the earth was once inhabited by Ozymandiases and Cleopatras. Life is hard enough for us as it is.

THE HE-ANCIENT. Life is not meant to be easy, my child; but take courage: it can be delightful. What I wanted to tell you is that ever since men existed, children have played with dolls.

ECRASIA. You keep using that word. What are dolls, pray?

THE SHE-ANCIENT. What you call works of art. Images. We call them dolls.

ARJILLAX. Just so. You have no sense of art; and you instinctively insult it.

THE HE-ANCIENT. Children have been known to make dolls out of rags, and to caress them with the deepest fondness.

THE SHE-ANCIENT. Eight centuries ago, when I was a child, I made a rag doll. The rag doll is the dearest of all.

THE NEWLY BORN [*eagerly interested*] Oh! Have you got it still?

THE SHE-ANCIENT. I kept it a full week.

ECRASIA. Even in your childhood, then, you did not understand high art, and adored your own amateur crudities.

THE SHE-ANCIENT. How old are you?

ECRASIA. Eight months.

THE SHE-ANCIENT. When you have lived as long as I have—

ECRASIA [*interrupting rudely*] I shall worship rag dolls, perhaps. Thank heaven, I am still in my prime.

THE HE-ANCIENT. You are still capable of thanking, though you do not know what you thank. You are a thanking little animal, a blaming little animal, a—

ACIS. A gushing little animal.

ARJILLAX. And, as she thinks, an artistic little animal.

ECRASIA [nettled] I am an animated being with a reasonable soul and human flesh subsisting. If your Automata had been properly animated, Martellus, they would have been more successful.

THE SHE-ANCIENT. That is where you are wrong, my child. If those two loathsome things had been rag dolls, they would have been amusing and lovable. The Newly Born here would have played with them; and you would all have laughed and played with them too until you had torn them to pieces; and then you would have laughed more than ever.

THE NEWLY BORN. Of course we should. Isnt that funny?

THE HE-ANCIENT. When a thing is funny, search it for a hidden truth.

STREPHON. Yes; and take all the fun out of it.

THE SHE-ANCIENT. Do not be so embittered because your sweetheart has outgrown her love for you. The Newly Born will make amends.

THE NEWLY BORN. Oh yes: I will be more than she could ever have been.

STREPHON. Psha! Jealous!

THE NEWLY BORN. Oh no. I have grown out of that. I love her now because she loved you, and because you love her.

THE HE-ANCIENT. That is the next stage. You are getting on very nicely, my child.

MARTELLUS. Come! what is the truth that was hidden in the rag doll?

THE HE-ANCIENT. Well, consider why you are not content with the rag doll, and must have something more closely resembling a real living creature. As you grow up you make images and paint pictures. Those of you who cannot do that make stories about imaginary dolls. Or you dress yourselves up as dolls and act plays about them.

THE SHE-ANCIENT. And, to deceive yourself the more completely, you take them so very very seriously that Ecrasia here declares that the making of dolls is the holiest work of creation, and the words you put into the mouths of dolls the sacredest of scriptures and the noblest of utterances.

ECRASIA. Tush!

ARJILLAX. Tosh!

THE SHE-ANCIENT. Yet the more beautiful they become the further they retreat from you. You cannot caress them as you caress the rag doll. You cannot cry for them when they are broken or lost, or when you pretend they have been unkind to you, as you could when you played with rag dolls.

THE HE-ANCIENT. At last, like Pygmalion, you demand from your dolls the final perfection of resemblance to life. They must move and speak.

THE SHE-ANCIENT. They must love and hate.

THE HE-ANCIENT. They must think that they think.

THE SHE-ANCIENT. They must have soft flesh and warm blood.

THE HE-ANCIENT. And then, when you have achieved this as Pygmalion did; when the marble masterpiece is dethroned by the automaton and the homo by the homunculus; when the body and the brain, the reasonable soul and human flesh subsisting, as Ecrasia says, stand before you unmasked as mere machinery, and your impulses are shewn to be nothing but reflexes, you are filled with horror and loathing, and would give worlds to be young enough to play with your rag doll again, since every step away from it has been a step away from love and happiness. Is it not true?

THE SHE-ANCIENT. Speak, Martellus: you who have travelled the whole path.

MARTELLUS. It is true. With fierce joy I turned a temperature of a million degrees on those two things I had modelled, and saw them vanish in an instant into inoffensive dust.

THE SHE-ANCIENT. Speak, Arjillax: you who have advanced from imitating the lightly living child to the intensely living ancient. Is it true, so far?

ARJILLAX. It is partly true: I cannot pretend to be satisfied now with modelling pretty children.

THE HE-ANCIENT. And you, Ecrasia: you cling to your highly artistic dolls as the noblest projections of the Life Force, do you not?

ECRASIA. Without art, the crudeness of reality would make the world unbearable.

THE NEWLY BORN [anticipating the She-Ancient, who is evidently going to challenge her] Now you are coming to me, because I am the latest arrival. But I dont understand your art and your dolls at all. I want to caress my darling Strephon, not to play with dolls.

ACIS. I am in my fourth year; and I have got on very well without your dolls. I had rather walk up a mountain and down again than look at all the statues Martellus and Arjillax ever made. You prefer a statue to an automaton, and a rag doll to a statue. So do I; but I prefer a man to a rag doll. Give me friends, not dolls.

THE HE-ANCIENT. Yet I have seen you walking over the mountains alone. Have you not found your best friend in yourself?

ACIS. What are you driving at, old one? What does all this lead to?

THE HE-ANCIENT. It leads, young man, to the truth that you can create nothing but yourself.

ACIS [musing] I can create nothing but myself. Ecrasia: you are clever. Do you understand it? I dont.

ECRASIA. It is as easy to understand as any other ignorant error. What artist is as great as his own works? He can create masterpieces; but he cannot improve the shape of his own nose.

ACIS. There! What have you to say to that, old one?

THE HE-ANCIENT. He can alter the shape of his own soul. He could alter the shape of his nose if the difference between a turned-up nose and a turned-down one were worth the effort. One does not face the throes of creation for trifles.

ACIS. What have you to say to that, Ecrasia?

ECRASIA. I say that if the ancients had thoroughly grasped the theory of fine art they would understand that the difference between a beautiful nose and an ugly one is of supreme importance: that it is indeed the only thing that matters.

THE SHE-ANCIENT. That is, they would understand something they could not believe, and that you do not believe.

ACIS. Just so, mam. Art is not honest: that is why I never could stand much of it. It is all make-believe. Ecrasia never really says things: she only rattles her teeth in her mouth.

ECRASIA. Acis: you are rude.

ACIS. You mean that I wont play the game of make-believe. Well, I dont ask you to play it with me; so why should you expect me to play it with you?

ECRASIA. You have no right to say that I am not sincere. I have found a happiness in art that real life has never given me. I am intensely in earnest about art. There is a magic and mystery in art that you know nothing of.

THE SHE-ANCIENT. Yes, child: art is the magic mirror you make to reflect your invisible dreams in visible pictures. You use a glass mirror to see your face: you use works of art to see your soul. But we who are older use neither glass mirrors nor works of art. We have a direct sense of life. When you gain that you will put aside your mirrors and statues, your toys and your dolls.

THE HE-ANCIENT. Yet we too have our toys and our dolls. That is the trouble of the ancients.

ARJILLAX. What! The ancients have their troubles! It is the first time I ever heard one of them confess it.

THE HE-ANCIENT. Look at us. Look at me. This is my body, my blood, my brain; but it is not me. I am the eternal life, the perpetual resurrection; but [striking his body] this structure, this organism, this makeshift, can be made by a boy in a laboratory, and is held back from dissolution only by my use of it. Worse still, it can be broken by a slip of the foot, drowned by a cramp in the stomach, destroyed by a flash from the clouds. Sooner or later, its destruction is certain.

THE SHE-ANCIENT. Yes: this body is the last doll to be discarded. When I was a child, Ecrasia, I, too, was an artist, like your sculptor friends there, striving to create perfection in things outside myself. I made statues: I painted pictures: I tried to worship them.

THE HE-ANCIENT. I had no such skill; but I, like Acis, sought perfection in friends, in lovers, in nature, in things outside myself. Alas! I could not create it: I could only imagine it.

THE SHE-ANCIENT. I, like Arjillax, found out that my statues of bodily beauty were no longer even beautiful to me; and I pressed on and made statues and pictures of men and women of genius, like those in the old fable of Michael Angelo. Like Martellus, I smashed them when I saw that there was no life in them: that they were so dead that they would not even dissolve as a dead body does.

THE HE-ANCIENT. And I, like Acis, ceased to walk over the mountains with my friends, and walked alone; for I found that I had creative power over myself but none over my friends. And then I ceased to walk on the mountains; for I saw that the mountains were dead.

ACIS [protesting vehemently] No. I grant you about the friends perhaps; but the mountains are still the mountains, each with its name, its individuality, its upstanding strength and majesty, its beauty—

ECRASIA. What! Acis among the rhapsodists!

THE HE-ANCIENT. Mere metaphor, my poor boy: the mountains are corpses.

ALL THE YOUNG [repelled] Oh!

THE HE-ANCIENT. Yes. In the hardpressed heart of the earth, where the inconceivable heat of the sun still glows, the stone lives in fierce atomic convulsion, as we live in our slower way. When it is cast out to the surface it dies like a deep-sea fish: what you see is only its cold dead body. We have tapped that central heat as prehistoric man tapped water springs; but nothing has come up alive from those flaming depths: your landscapes, your mountains, are only the world's cast skins and decaying teeth on which we live like microbes.

ECRASIA. Ancient: you blaspheme against Nature and against Man.

THE SHE-ANCIENT. Child, child, how much enthusiasm will you have for man when you have endured eight centuries of him, as I have, and seen him perish by an empty mischance that is yet a certainty? When I discarded my dolls as he discarded his friends and his mountains, it was to myself I turned as to the final reality. Here, and here alone, I could shape and create. When my arm was weak and I willed it to be strong, I could create a roll of muscle on it; and when I understood that, I understood that I could without any greater miracle give myself ten arms and three heads.

THE HE-ANCIENT. I also came to understand such miracles. For fifty years I sat contemplating this power in myself and concentrating my will.

THE SHE-ANCIENT. So did I; and for five more years I made myself into all sorts of fantastic monsters. I walked upon a dozen legs: I worked with twenty hands and a hundred fingers: I looked to the four quarters of the compass with eight eyes out of four heads. Children fled in amazement from me until I had to hide myself from them; and the ancients, who had forgotten how to laugh, smiled grimly when they passed.

THE HE-ANCIENT. We have all committed these follies. You will all commit them.

THE NEWLY BORN. Oh, do grow a lot of arms and legs and heads for us. It would be so funny.

THE HE-ANCIENT. My child: I am just as well as I am. I would not lift my finger now to have a thousand heads.

THE SHE-ANCIENT. But what would I not give to have no head at all?

ALL THE YOUNG. Whats that? No head at all? Why? How?

THE HE-ANCIENT. Can you not understand?

ALL THE YOUNG [shaking their heads] No.

THE SHE-ANCIENT. One day, when I was tired of learning to walk forward with some of my feet and backwards with others and sideways with the rest all at once, I sat on a rock with my four chins resting on four of my palms, and four of my elbows resting on four of my knees. And suddenly it came into my mind that this monstrous machinery of heads and limbs was no more me than my statues had been me, and that it was only an automaton that I had enslaved.

MARTELLUS. Enslaved? What does that mean?

THE SHE-ANCIENT. A thing that must do what you command it is a slave; and its commander is its master. These are words you will learn when your turn comes.

THE HE-ANCIENT. You will also learn that when the master has come to do everything through the slave, the slave becomes his master, since he cannot live without him.

THE SHE-ANCIENT. And so I perceived that I had made myself the slave of a slave.

THE HE-ANCIENT. When we discovered that, we shed our superfluous heads and legs and arms until we had our old shapes again, and no longer startled the children.

THE SHE-ANCIENT. But still I am the slave of this slave, my body. How am I to be delivered from it?

THE HE-ANCIENT. That, children, is the trouble of the ancients. For whilst we are tied to this tyrannous body we are subject to its death, and our destiny is not achieved.

THE NEWLY BORN. What is your destiny?

THE HE-ANCIENT. To be immortal.

THE SHE-ANCIENT. The day will come when there will be no people, only thought.

THE HE-ANCIENT. And that will be life eternal.

ECRASIA. I trust I shall meet my fatal accident before that day dawns.

ARJILLAX. For once, Ecrasia, I agree with you. A world in which there were nothing plastic would be an utterly miserable one.

ECRASIA. No limbs, no contours, no exquisite lines and elegant shapes, no worship of beautiful bodies, no poetic embraces in which cultivated lovers pretend that their caressing hands are wandering over celestial hills and enchanted valleys, no—

ACIS [*interrupting her disgustedly*] What an inhuman mind you have, Ecrasia!

ECRASIA. Inhuman!

ACIS. Yes: inhuman. Why dont you fall in love with someone?

ECRASIA. I! I have been in love all my life. I burned with it even in the egg.

ACIS. Not a bit of it. You and Arjillax are just as hard as two stones.

ECRASIA. You did not always think so, Acis.

ACIS. Oh, I know. I offered you my love once, and asked for yours.

ECRASIA. And did I deny it to you, Acis?

ACIS. You didnt even know what love was.

ECRASIA. Oh! I adored you, you stupid oaf, until I found that you were a mere animal.

ACIS. And I made no end of a fool of myself about you until I discovered that you were a mere artist. You appreciated my contours! I was plastic, as Arjillax says. I wasnt a man to you: I was a masterpiece appealing to your tastes and your senses. Your tastes and senses had overlaid the direct impulse of life in you. And because I cared only for our life, and went straight to it, and was bored by your calling my limbs fancy names and mapping me into mountains and valleys and all the rest of it, you called me an animal. Well, I am an animal, if you call a live man an animal.

ECRASIA. You need not explain. You refused to be refined. I did my best to lift your prehistoric impulses on to the plane of beauty, of imagination, of romance, of poetry, of art, of—

ACIS. These things are all very well in their way and in their proper places. But they are not love. They are an unnatural adulteration of love. Love is a simple thing and a deep thing: it is an act of life and not an illusion. Art is an illusion.

ARJILLAX. That is false. The statue comes to life always. The statues of today are the men and women of the next incubation. I hold up the marble figure before the mother and say, "This is the model you must copy." We produce what we see. Let no man dare to create in art a thing that he would not have exist in life.

MARTELLUS. Yes: I have been through all that. But you yourself are making statues of ancients instead of beautiful nymphs and swains. And Ecrasia is right about the an-

cients being inartistic. They are damnably inartistic.

ECRASIA [*triumphant*] Ah! Our greatest artist vindicates me. Thanks, Martellus.

MARTELLUS. The body always ends by being a bore. Nothing remains beautiful and interesting except thought, because the thought is the life. Which is just what this old gentleman and this old lady seem to think too.

THE SHE-ANCIENT. Quite so.

THE HE-ANCIENT. Precisely.

THE NEWLY BORN [*to the He-Ancient*] But you cant be nothing. What do you want to be?

THE HE-ANCIENT. A vortex.

THE NEWLY BORN. A what?

THE SHE-ANCIENT. A vortex. I began as a vortex: why should I not end as one?

ECRASIA. Oh! That is what you old people are. Vorticists.

ACIS. But if life is thought, can you live without a head?

THE HE-ANCIENT. Not now perhaps. But prehistoric men thought they could not live without tails. I can live without a tail. Why should I not live without a head?

THE NEWLY BORN. What is a tail?

THE HE-ANCIENT. A habit of which your ancestors managed to cure themselves.

THE SHE-ANCIENT. None of us now believe that all this machinery of flesh and blood is necessary. It dies.

THE HE-ANCIENT. It imprisons us on this petty planet and forbids us to range through the stars.

ACIS. But even a vortex is a vortex in something. You cant have a whirlpool without water; and you cant have a vortex without gas, or molecules or atoms or ions or electrons or something, not nothing.

THE HE-ANCIENT. No: the vortex is not the water nor the gas nor the atoms: it is a power over these things.

THE SHE-ANCIENT. The body was the slave of the vortex; but the slave has become the master; and we must free ourselves from that tyranny. It is this stuff [*indicating her body*], this flesh and blood and bone and all the rest of it, that is intolerable. Even prehistoric man dreamed of what he called an astral body, and asked who would deliver him from the body of this death.

ACIS [*evidently out of his depth*] I shouldnt think too much about it if I were you. You have to keep sane, you know.

The two Ancients look at one another; shrug their shoulders; and address themselves to their departure.

THE HE-ANCIENT. We are staying too long with you, children. We must go.

All the young people rise rather eagerly.

ARJILLAX. Dont mention it.

THE SHE-ANCIENT. It is tiresome for us, too. You see, children, we have to put things very crudely to you to make ourselves intelligible.

THE HE-ANCIENT. And I am afraid we do not quite succeed.

STREPHON. Very kind of you to come at all and talk to us, I'm sure.

ECRASIA. Why do the other ancients never come and give us a turn?

THE SHE-ANCIENT. It is so difficult for them. They have forgotten how to speak; how to read; even how to think in your fashion. We do not communicate with one another in that way or apprehend the world as you do.

THE HE-ANCIENT. I find it more and more difficult to keep up your language. Another century or two and it will be impossible. I shall have to be relieved by a younger shepherd.

ACIS. Of course we are always delighted to see you; but still, if it tries you very severely, we c o u l d manage pretty well by ourselves, you know.

THE SHE-ANCIENT. Tell me, Acis: do you ever think of yourself as having to live perhaps for thousands of years?

ACIS. Oh, dont talk about it. Why, I know very well that I have only four years of what any reasonable person would call living; and three and a half of them are already gone.

ECRASIA. You must not mind our saying so; but really you cannot call being an ancient living.

THE NEWLY BORN [*almost in tears*] Oh, this dreadful shortness of our lives! I cannot bear it.

STREPHON. I made up my mind on that subject long ago. When I am three years and fifty weeks old, I shall have my fatal accident. And it will not be an accident.

THE HE-ANCIENT. We are very tired of this subject. I must leave you.

THE NEWLY BORN. What is being tired?

THE SHE-ANCIENT. The penalty of attending to children. Farewell.

The two Ancients go away severally, she into the grove, he up to the hills behind the temple.

ALL. Ouf! [*A great sigh of relief*].

ECRASIA. Dreadful people!

STREPHON. Bores!

MARTELLUS. Yet one would like to follow them; to enter into their life; to grasp their thought; to comprehend the universe as they must.

ARJILLAX. Getting old, Martellus?

MARTELLUS. Well, I have finished with the dolls; and I am no longer jealous of you. That looks like the end. Two hours sleep is enough for me. I am afraid I am beginning to find you all rather silly.

STREPHON. I know. My girl went off this morning. She hadnt slept for weeks. And she found mathematics more interesting than me.

MARTELLUS. There is a prehistoric saying that has come down to us from a famous woman teacher. She said: "Leave women; and study mathematics." It is the only remaining fragment of a lost scripture called The Confessions of St Augustin, the English Opium Eater. That primitive savage must have been a great woman, to say a thing that still lives after three hundred centuries. I too will leave women and study mathematics, which I have neglected too long. Farewell, children, my old playmates. I almost wish I could feel sentimental about parting from you; but the cold truth is that you bore me. Do not be angry with me: your turn will come. [*He passes away gravely into the grove*].

ARJILLAX. There goes a great spirit. What a sculptor he was! And now, nothing! It is as if he had cut off his hands.

THE NEWLY BORN. Oh, will you all leave me as he has left you?

ECRASIA. Never. We have sworn it.

STREPHON. What is the use of swearing? She swore. He swore. You have sworn. They have sworn.

ECRASIA. You speak like a grammar.

STREPHON. That is how one ought to speak, isnt it? We shall all be forsworn.

THE NEWLY BORN. Do not talk like that. You are saddening us; and you are chasing the light away. It is growing dark.

ACIS. Night is falling. The light will come back tomorrow.

THE NEWLY BORN. What is tomorrow?

ACIS. The day that never comes. [*He turns towards the temple*].

All begin trooping into the temple.

THE NEWLY BORN [*holding Acis back*] That is no answer. What—

ARJILLAX. Silence. Little children should be seen and not heard.

THE NEWLY BORN [putting out her tongue at him]!

ECRASIA. Ungraceful. You must not do that.

THE NEWLY BORN. I will do what I like. But there is something the matter with me. I want to lie down. I cannot keep my eyes open.

ECRASIA. You are falling asleep. You will wake up again.

THE NEWLY BORN [drowsily] What is sleep?

ACIS. Ask no questions; and you will be told no lies. [He takes her by the ear, and leads her firmly towards the temple].

THE NEWLY BORN. Ai! oi! ai! Dont. I want to be carried. [She reels into the arms of Acis, who carries her into the temple].

ECRASIA. Come, Arjillax: you at least are still an artist. I adore you.

ARJILLAX. Do you? Unfortunately for you, I am not still a child. I have grown out of cuddling. I can only appreciate your figure. Does that satisfy you?

ECRASIA. At what distance?

ARJILLAX. Arm's length or more.

ECRASIA. Thank you: not for me. [She turns away from him].

ARJILLAX. Ha! Ha! [He strides off into the temple].

ECRASIA [calling to Strephon, who is on the threshold of the temple, going in] Strephon.

STREPHON. No. My heart is broken. [He goes into the temple].

ECRASIA. Must I pass the night alone? [She looks round, seeking another partner; but they have all gone]. After all, I can imagine a lover nobler than any of you. [She goes into the temple].

It is now quite dark. A vague radiance appears near the temple and shapes itself into the ghost of Adam.

A WOMAN'S VOICE [in the grove] Who is that?

ADAM. The ghost of Adam, the first father of mankind. Who are you?

THE VOICE. The ghost of Eve, the first mother of mankind.

ADAM. Come forth, wife; and shew yourself to me.

EVE [appearing near the grove] Here I am, husband. You are very old.

A VOICE [in the hills] Ha! ha! ha!

ADAM. Who laughs? Who dares laugh at Adam?

EVE. Who has the heart to laugh at Eve?

THE VOICE. The ghost of Cain, the first child, and the first murderer. [He appears between them; and as he does so there is a prolonged hiss]. Who dares hiss at Cain, the lord of death?

A VOICE. The ghost of the serpent, that lived before Adam and before Eve, and taught them how to bring forth Cain. [She becomes visible, coiled in the trees].

A VOICE. There is one that came before the serpent.

THE SERPENT. That is the voice of Lilith, in whom the father and mother were one. Hail, Lilith!

Lilith becomes visible between Cain and Adam.

LILITH. I suffered unspeakably; I tore myself asunder; I lost my life, to make of my one flesh these twain, man and woman. And this is what has come of it. What do you make of it, Adam, my son?

ADAM. I made the earth bring forth by my labor, and the woman bring forth by my love. And this is what has come of it. What do you make of it, Eve, my wife?

EVE. I nourished the egg in my body and fed it with my blood. And now they let it fall as the birds did, and suffer not at all. What do you make of it, Cain, my first-born?

CAIN. I invented killing and conquest and mastery and the winnowing out of the weak by the strong. And now the strong have slain one another; and the weak live for ever; and their deeds do nothing for the doer more than for another. What do you make of it, snake?

THE SERPENT. I am justified. For I chose wisdom and the knowledge of good and evil; and now there is no evil; and wisdom and good are one. It is enough. [She vanishes].

CAIN. There is no place for me on earth any longer. You cannot deny that mine was a splendid game while it lasted. But now! Out, out, brief candle! [He vanishes].

EVE. The clever ones were always my favorites. The diggers and the fighters have dug themselves in with the worms. My clever ones have inherited the earth. All's well. [She fades away].

ADAM. I can make nothing of it, neither head nor tail. What is it all for? Why?

Whither? Whence? We were well enough in the garden. And now the fools have killed all the animals; and they are dissatisfied because they cannot be bothered with their bodies! Foolishness, I call it. [*He disappears*].

LILITH. They have accepted the burden of eternal life. They have taken the agony from birth; and their life does not fail them even in the hour of their destruction. Their breasts are without milk: their bowels are gone: the very shapes of them are only ornaments for their children to admire and caress without understanding. Is this enough; or shall I labor again? Shall I bring forth something that will sweep them away and make an end of them as they have swept away the beasts of the garden, and made an end of the crawling things and the flying things and of all them that refuse to live for ever? I had patience with them for many ages: they tried me very sorely. They did terrible things: they embraced death, and said that eternal life was a fable. I stood amazed at the malice and destructiveness of the things I had made: Mars blushed as he looked down on the shame of his sister planet: cruelty and hypocrisy became so hideous that the face of the earth was pitted with the graves of little children among which living skeletons crawled in search of horrible food. The pangs of another birth were already upon me when one man repented and lived three hundred years; and I waited to see what would come of that. And so much came of it that the horrors of that time seem now but an evil dream. They have redeemed themselves from their vileness, and turned away from their sins. Best of all, they are still not satisfied: the impulse I gave them in that day when I sundered myself in twain and launched Man and Woman on the earth still urges them: after passing a million goals they press on to the goal of redemption from the flesh, to the vortex freed from matter, to the whirlpool in pure intelligence that, when the world began, was a whirlpool in pure force. And though all that they have done seems but the first hour of the infinite work of creation, yet I will not supersede them until they have forded this last stream that lies between flesh and spirit, and disentangled their life from the matter that has always mocked it. I can wait: waiting and patience mean nothing to the eternal. I gave the woman the greatest of gifts: curiosity. By that her seed has been saved from my wrath; for I also am curious; and I have waited always to see what they will do tomorrow. Let them feed that appetite well for me. I say, let them dread, of all things, stagnation; for from the moment I, Lilith, lose hope and faith in them, they are doomed. In that hope and faith I have let them live for a moment; and in that moment I have spared them many times. But mightier creatures than they have killed hope and faith, and perished from the earth; and I may not spare them for ever. I am Lilith: I brought life into the whirlpool of force, and compelled my enemy, Matter, to obey a living soul. But in enslaving Life's enemy I made him Life's master; for that is the end of all slavery; and now I shall see the slave set free and the enemy reconciled, the whirlpool become all life and no matter. And because these infants that call themselves ancients are reaching out towards that, I will have patience with them still; though I know well that when they attain it they shall become one with me and supersede me, and Lilith will be only a legend and a lay that has lost its meaning. Of Life only is there no end; and though of its million starry mansions many are empty and many still unbuilt, and though its vast domain is as yet unbearably desert, my seed shall one day fill it and master its matter to its uttermost confines. And for what may be beyond, the eyesight of Lilith is too short. It is enough that there is a beyond. [*She vanishes*].

THE END

XXXI

SAINT JOAN

A CHRONICLE PLAY IN SIX SCENES, AND AN EPILOGUE

SCENE I

A fine spring morning on the river Meuse, between Lorraine and Champagne, in the year 1429 A.D., in the castle of Vaucouleurs.

Captain Robert de Baudricourt, a military squire, handsome and physically energetic, but with no will of his own, is disguising that defect in his usual fashion by storming terribly at his steward, a trodden worm, scanty of flesh, scanty of hair, who might be any age from 18 to 55, being the sort of man whom age cannot wither because he has never bloomed.

The two are in a sunny stone chamber on the first floor of the castle. At a plain strong oak table, seated in chair to match, the captain presents his left profile. The steward stands facing him at the other side of the table, if so deprecatory a stance as his can be called standing. The mullioned thirteenth-century window is open behind him. Near it in the corner is a turret with a narrow arched doorway leading to a winding stair which descends to the courtyard. There is a stout fourlegged stool under the table, and a wooden chest under the window.

ROBERT. No eggs! No eggs!! Thousand thunders, man, what do you mean by no eggs?

STEWARD. Sir: it is not my fault. It is the act of God.

ROBERT. Blasphemy. You tell me there are no eggs; and you blame your Maker for it.

STEWARD. Sir: what can I do? I cannot lay eggs.

ROBERT [*sarcastic*] Ha! You jest about it.

STEWARD. No, sir, God knows. We all have to go without eggs just as you have, sir. The hens will not lay.

ROBERT. Indeed! [*Rising*] Now listen to me, you.

STEWARD [*humbly*] Yes, sir.

ROBERT. What am I?

STEWARD. What are you, sir?

ROBERT [*coming at him*] Yes: what am I? Am I Robert, squire of Baudricourt and captain of this castle of Vaucouleurs; or am I a cowboy?

STEWARD. Oh, sir, you know you are a greater man here than the king himself.

ROBERT. Precisely. And now, do you know what you are?

STEWARD. I am nobody, sir, except that I have the honor to be your steward.

ROBERT [*driving him to the wall, adjective by adjective*] You have not only the honor of being my steward, but the privilege of being the worst, most incompetent, drivelling snivelling jibbering jabbering idiot of a steward in France. [*He strides back to the table*].

STEWARD [*cowering on the chest*] Yes, sir: to a great man like you I must seem like that.

ROBERT [*turning*] My fault, I suppose. Eh?

STEWARD [*coming to him deprecatingly*] Oh, sir: you always give my most innocent words such a turn!

ROBERT. I will give your neck a turn if you dare tell me, when I ask you how many eggs there are, that you cannot lay any.

STEWARD [*protesting*] Oh sir, oh sir—

ROBERT. No: not oh sir, oh sir, but no sir, no sir. My three Barbary hens and the black are the best layers in Champagne. And you come and tell me that there are no eggs! Who stole them? Tell me that, before I kick you out through the castle gate for a liar and a seller of my goods to thieves. The milk was short yesterday, too: do not forget that.

STEWARD [*desperate*] I know, sir. I know only too well. There is no milk: there are no eggs: tomorrow there will be nothing.

ROBERT. Nothing! You will steal the lot: eh?

STEWARD. No, sir: nobody will steal anything. But there is a spell on us: we are bewitched.

ROBERT. That story is not good enough for me. Robert de Baudricourt burns witches and hangs thieves. Go. Bring me four dozen eggs and two gallons of milk here in this room before noon, or Heaven have mercy on your bones! I will teach you to make a fool of me. [*He resumes his seat with an air of finality*].

STEWARD. Sir: I tell you there are no eggs. There will be none—not if you were to kill me for it—as long as The Maid is at the door.

ROBERT. The Maid! What maid? What are you talking about?

STEWARD. The girl from Lorraine, sir. From Domrémy.

ROBERT [rising in fearful wrath] Thirty thousand thunders! Fifty thousand devils! Do you mean to say that that girl, who had the impudence to ask to see me two days ago, and whom I told you to send back to her father with my orders that he was to give her a good hiding, is here still?

STEWARD. I have told her to go, sir. She wont.

ROBERT. I did not tell you to tell her to go: I told you to throw her out. You have fifty men-at-arms and a dozen lumps of ablebodied servants to carry out my orders. Are they afraid of her?

STEWARD. She is so positive, sir.

ROBERT [seizing him by the scruff of the neck] Positive! Now see here. I am going to throw you downstairs.

STEWARD. No, sir. Please.

ROBERT. Well, stop me by being positive. It's quite easy: any slut of a girl can do it.

STEWARD [hanging limp in his hands] Sir, sir: you cannot get rid of h e r by throwing m e out. [Robert has to let him drop. He squats on his knees on the floor, contemplating his master resignedly]. You see, sir, you are much more positive than I am. But so is she.

ROBERT. I am stronger than you are, you fool.

STEWARD. No sir: it isnt that: it's your strong character, sir. She is weaker than we are: she is only a slip of a girl; but we cannot make her go.

ROBERT. You parcel of curs: you are afraid of her.

STEWARD [rising cautiously] No, sir: we are afraid of you; but she puts courage into us. She really doesnt seem to be afraid of anything. Perhaps you could frighten her, sir.

ROBERT [grimly] Perhaps. Where is she now?

STEWARD. Down in the courtyard, sir, talking to the soldiers as usual. She is always talking to the soldiers except when she is praying.

ROBERT. Praying! Ha! You believe she prays, you idiot. I know the sort of girl that is always talking to soldiers. She shall talk to me a bit. [He goes to the window and shouts fiercely through it] Hallo, you there!

A GIRL'S VOICE [bright, strong, and rough] Is it me, sir?

ROBERT. Yes, you.

THE VOICE. Be you captain?

ROBERT. Yes, damn your impudence, I be captain. Come up here. [To the soldiers in the yard] Shew her the way, you. And shove her along quick. [He leaves the window, and returns to his place at the table, where he sits magisterially].

STEWARD [whispering] She wants to go and be a soldier herself. She wants you to give her soldier's clothes. Armor, sir! And a sword! Actually! [He steals behind Robert].

Joan appears in the turret doorway. She is an ablebodied country girl of 17 or 18, respectably dressed in red, with an uncommon face: eyes very wide apart and bulging as they often do in very imaginative people, a long well-shaped nose with wide nostrils, a short upper lip, resolute but full-lipped mouth, and handsome fighting chin. She comes eagerly to the table, delighted at having penetrated to Baudricourt's presence at last, and full of hope as to the result. His scowl does not check or frighten her in the least. Her voice is normally a hearty coaxing voice, very confident, very appealing, very hard to resist.

JOAN [bobbing a curtsey] Good morning, captain squire. Captain: you are to give me a horse and armor and some soldiers, and send me to the Dauphin. Those are your orders from my Lord.

ROBERT [outraged] Orders from y o u r lord! And who the devil may your lord be? Go back to him, and tell him that I am neither duke nor peer at his orders: I am squire of Baudricourt; and I take no orders except from the king.

JOAN [reassuringly] Yes, squire: that is all right. My Lord is the King of Heaven.

ROBERT. Why, the girl's mad. [To the steward] Why didnt you tell me so, you blockhead?

STEWARD. Sir: do not anger her: give her what she wants.

JOAN [impatient, but friendly] They all say I am mad until I talk to them, squire. But you see that it is the will of God that you are to do what He has put into my mind.

ROBERT. It is the will of God that I shall send you back to your father with orders to put you under lock and key and thrash the madness out of you. What have you to say to that?

JOAN. You think you will, squire; but you will find it all coming quite different. You said you would not see me; but here I am.

STEWARD [*appealing*] Yes, sir. You see, sir.

ROBERT. Hold your tongue, you.

STEWARD [*abjectly*] Yes, sir.

ROBERT [*to Joan, with a sour loss of confidence*] So you are presuming on my seeing you, are you?

JOAN [*sweetly*] Yes, squire.

ROBERT [*feeling that he has lost ground, brings down his two fists squarely on the table, and inflates his chest imposingly to cure the unwelcome and only too familiar sensation*] Now listen to me. I am going to assert myself.

JOAN [*busily*] Please do, squire. The horse will cost sixteen francs. It is a good deal of money; but I can save it on the armor. I can find a soldier's armor that will fit me well enough: I am very hardy; and I do not need beautiful armor made to my measure like you wear. I shall not want many soldiers: the Dauphin will give me all I need to raise the siege of Orleans.

ROBERT [*flabbergasted*] To raise the siege of Orleans!

JOAN [*simply*] Yes, squire: that is what God is sending me to do. Three men will be enough for you to send with me if they are good men and gentle to me. They have promised to come with me. Polly and Jack and—

ROBERT. Polly!! You impudent baggage, do you dare call squire Bertrand de Poulengey Polly to my face?

JOAN. His friends call him so, squire: I did not know he had any other name. Jack—

ROBERT. That is Monsieur John of Metz, I suppose?

JOAN. Yes, squire. Jack will come willingly: he is a very kind gentleman, and gives me money to give to the poor. I think John Godsave will come, and Dick the Archer, and their servants John of Honecourt and Julian. There will be no trouble for you, squire: I have arranged it all: you have only to give the order.

ROBERT [*contemplating her in a stupor of amazement*] Well, I am damned!

JOAN [*with unruffled sweetness*] No, squire: God is very merciful; and the blessed saints Catherine and Margaret, who speak to me every day [*he gapes*], will intercede for you. You will go to paradise; and your name will be remembered for ever as my first helper.

ROBERT [*to the steward, still much bothered, but changing his tone as he pursues a new clue*] Is this true about Monsieur de Poulengey?

STEWARD [*eagerly*] Yes, sir, and about Monsieur de Metz too. They both want to go with her.

ROBERT [*thoughtful*] Mf! [*He goes to the window, and shouts into the courtyard*] Hallo! You there: send Monsieur de Poulengey to me, will you? [*He turns to Joan*]. Get out; and wait in the yard.

JOAN [*smiling brightly at him*] Right, squire. [*She goes out*].

ROBERT [*to the steward*] Go with her, you, you dithering imbecile. Stay within call; and keep your eye on her. I shall have her up here again.

STEWARD. Do so in God's name, sir. Think of those hens, the best layers in Champagne; and—

ROBERT. Think of my boot; and take your backside out of reach of it.

The steward retreats hastily and finds himself confronted in the doorway by Bertrand de Poulengey, a lymphatic French gentleman-at-arms, aged 36 or thereabout, employed in the department of the provost-marshal, dreamily absent-minded, seldom speaking unless spoken to, and then slow and obstinate in reply: altogether in contrast to the self-assertive, loud-mouthed, superficially energetic, fundamentally will-less Robert. The steward makes way for him, and vanishes.

Poulengey salutes, and stands awaiting orders.

ROBERT [*genially*] It isnt service, Polly. A friendly talk. Sit down. [*He hooks the stool from under the table with his instep*].

Poulengey, relaxing, comes into the room; places the stool between the table and the window; and sits down ruminatively. Robert, half sitting on the end of the table, begins the friendly talk.

ROBERT. Now listen to me, Polly. I must talk to you like a father.

Poulengey looks up at him gravely for a moment, but says nothing.

ROBERT. It's about this girl you are interested in. Now, I have seen her. I have talked to her. First, she's mad. That doesnt matter. Second, she's not a farm wench. She's a bourgeoise. That matters a good deal. I know her class exactly. Her father came here last year to represent his village in a lawsuit: he is one of their notables. A farmer. Not a gentleman farmer: he makes money by it, and lives by it. Still, not a laborer. Not a mechanic. He might have a cousin a lawyer, or in the Church. People of this sort may be of no account socially; but they can give a lot of bother to the authorities. That is to say, to m e. Now no doubt it seems to you a very simple thing to take this girl away, humbugging her into the belief that you are taking her to the Dauphin. But if you get her into trouble, you may get m e into·no end of a mess, as I am her father's lord, and responsible for her protection. So friends or no friends, Polly, hands off her.

POULENGEY [*with deliberate impressiveness*] I should as soon think of the blessed Virgin herself in that way, as of this girl.

ROBERT [*coming off the table*] But she says you and Jack and Dick have offered to go with her. What for? You are not going to tell me that you take her crazy notion of going to the Dauphin seriously, are you?

POULENGEY [*slowly*] There is something about her. They are pretty foulmouthed and foulminded down there in the guardroom, some of them. But there hasnt been a word that has anything to do with her being a woman. They have stopped swearing before her. There is something. Something. It may be worth trying.

ROBERT. Oh, come, Polly! pull yourself together. Commonsense was never your strong point; but this is a little too much. [*He retreats disgustedly*].

POULENGEY [*unmoved*] What is the good of commonsense? If we had any commonsense we should join the Duke of Burgundy and the English king. They hold half the country, right down to the Loire. They have Paris. They have this castle: you know very well that we had to surrender it to the Duke of Bedford, and that you are only holding it on parole. The Dauphin is in Chinon, like a rat in a corner, except that he wont fight. We dont even know that he i s the Dauphin: his mother says he isnt; and she ought to know. Think of that! the queen denying the legitimacy of her own son!

ROBERT. Well, she married her daughter to the English king. Can you blame the woman?

POULENGEY. I blame nobody. But thanks to her, the Dauphin is down and out; and we may as well face it. The English will take Orleans: the Bastard will not be able to stop them.

ROBERT. He beat the English the year before last at Montargis. I was with him.

POULENGEY. No matter: his men are cowed now; and he cant work miracles. And I tell you that nothing can save our side now but a miracle.

ROBERT. Miracles are all right, Polly. The only difficulty about them is that they dont happen nowadays.

POULENGEY. I used to think so. I am not so sure now. [*Rising, and moving ruminatively towards the window*] At all events this is not a time to leave any stone unturned. There is something about the girl.

ROBERT. Oh! You think the girl can work miracles, do you?

POULENGEY. I think the girl herself is a bit of a miracle. Anyhow, she is the last card left in our hand. Better play her than throw up the game. [*He wanders to the turret*].

ROBERT [*wavering*] You really think that?

POULENGEY [*turning*] Is there anything else letf for us to think?

ROBERT [*going to him*] Look here, Polly. If you were in my place would you let a girl like that do you out of sixteen francs for a horse?

POULENGEY. I will pay for the horse.

ROBERT. You will!

POULENGEY. Yes: I will back my opinion.

ROBERT. You will really gamble on a forlorn hope to the tune of sixteen francs?

POULENGEY. It is not a gamble.

ROBERT. What else is it?

POULENGEY. It is a certainty. Her words and her ardent faith in God have put fire into me.

ROBERT [*giving him up*] Whew! You are as mad as she is.

POULENGEY [*obstinately*] We want a few mad people now. See where the sane ones have landed us!

ROBERT [*his irresoluteness now openly swamping his affected decisiveness*] I shall feel like a precious fool. Still, if you feel sure—?

POULENGEY. I feel sure enough to take her to Chinon—unless you stop me.

ROBERT. This is not fair. You are putting the responsibility on me.

POULENGEY. It is on you whichever way you decide.

ROBERT. Yes: thats just it. Which way am I to decide? You dont see how awkward this is for me. [*Snatching at a dilatory step with an unconscious hope that Joan will make up his mind for him*] Do you think I ought to have another talk to her?

POULENGEY [*rising*] Yes. [*He goes to the window and calls*] Joan!

JOAN'S VOICE. Will he let us go, Polly?

POULENGEY. Come up. Come in. [*Turning to*

Robert] Shall I leave you with her?

ROBERT. No: stay here; and back me up.

Poulengey sits down on the chest. Robert goes back to his magisterial chair, but remains standing to inflate himself more imposingly. Joan comes in, full of good news.

JOAN. Jack will go halves for the horse.

ROBERT. Well!! [*He sits, deflated*].

POULENGEY [*gravely*] Sit down, Joan.

JOAN [*checked a little, and looking to Robert*] May I?

ROBERT. Do what you are told.

Joan curtsies and sits down on the stool between them. Robert outfaces his perplexity with his most peremptory air.

ROBERT. What is your name?

JOAN [*chattily*] They always call me Jenny in Lorraine. Here in France I am Joan. The soldiers call me The Maid.

ROBERT. What is your surname?

JOAN. Surname? What is that? My father sometimes calls himself d'Arc; but I know nothing about it. You met my father. He—

ROBERT. Yes, yes: I remember. You come from Domrémy in Lorraine, I think.

JOAN. Yes; but what does it matter? we all speak French.

ROBERT. Dont ask questions: answer them. How old are you?

JOAN. Seventeen: so they tell me. It might be nineteen. I dont remember.

ROBERT. What did you mean when you said that St Catherine and St Margaret talked to you every day?

JOAN. They do.

ROBERT. What are they like?

JOAN [*suddenly obstinate*] I will tell you nothing about that: they have not given me leave.

ROBERT. But you actually see them; and they talk to you just as I am talking to you?

JOAN. No: it is quite different. I cannot tell you: you must not talk to me about my voices.

ROBERT. How do you mean? voices?

JOAN. I hear voices telling me what to do. They come from God.

ROBERT. They come from your imagination.

JOAN. Of course. That is how the messages of God come to us.

POULENGEY. Checkmate.

ROBERT. No fear! [*To Joan*] So God says you are to raise the siege of Orleans?

JOAN. And to crown the Dauphin in Rheims Cathedral.

ROBERT [*gasping*] Crown the D——! Gosh!

JOAN. And to make the English leave France.

ROBERT [*sarcastic*] Anything else?

JOAN [*charming*] Not just at present, thank you, squire.

ROBERT. I suppose you think raising a siege is as easy as chasing a cow out of a meadow. You think soldiering is anybody's job?

JOAN. I do not think it can be very difficult if God is on your side, and you are willing to put your life in His hand. But many soldiers are very simple.

ROBERT [*grimly*] Simple! Did you ever see English soldiers fighting?

JOAN. They are only men. God made them just like us; but He gave them their own country and their own language; and it is not His will that they should come into our country and try to speak our language.

ROBERT. Who has been putting such nonsense into your head? Dont you know that soldiers are subject to their feudal lord, and that it is nothing to them or to you whether he is the duke of Burgundy or the king of England or the king of France? What has their language to do with it?

JOAN. I do not understand that a bit. We are all subject to the King of Heaven; and He gave us our countries and our languages, and meant us to keep to them. If it were not so it would be murder to kill an Englishman in battle; and you, squire, would be in great danger of hell fire. You must not think about your duty to your feudal lord, but about your duty to God.

POULENGEY. It's no use, Robert: she can choke you like that every time.

ROBERT. Can she, by Saint Dennis! We shall see. [*To Joan*] We are not talking about God: we are talking about practical affairs. I ask you again, girl, have you ever seen English soldiers fighting? Have you ever seen them plundering, burning, turning the countryside into a desert? Have you heard no tales of their Black Prince who was blacker than the devil himself, or of the English king's father?

JOAN. You must not be afraid, Robert—

ROBERT. Damn you, I am not afraid. And who gave you leave to call me Robert?

JOAN. You were called so in church in the name of our Lord. All the other names are your father's or your brother's or anybody's.

ROBERT. Tcha!

JOAN. Listen to me, squire. At Domrémy we had to fly to the next village to escape from the English soldiers. Three of them were left behind, wounded. I came to know these three poor goddams quite well. They had not half my strength.

ROBERT. Do you know why they are called goddams?

JOAN. No. Everyone calls them goddams.

ROBERT. It is because they are always calling on their God to condemn their souls to perdition. That is what goddam means in their language. How do you like it?

JOAN. God will be merciful to them; and they will act like His good children when they go back to the country He made for them, and made them for. I have heard the tales of the Black Prince. The moment he touched the soil of our country the devil entered into him and made him a black fiend. But at home, in the place made for him by God, he was good. It is always so. If I went into England against the will of God to conquer England, and tried to live there and speak its language, the devil would enter into me; and when I was old I should shudder to remember the wickednesses I did.

ROBERT. Perhaps. But the more devil you were the better you might fight. That is why the goddams will take Orleans. And you cannot stop them, nor ten thousand like you.

JOAN. One thousand like me can stop them. Ten like me can stop them with God on our side. [She rises impetuously, and goes at him, unable to sit quiet any longer]. You do not understand, squire. Our soldiers are always beaten because they are fighting only to save their skins; and the shortest way to save your skin is to run away. Our knights are thinking only of the money they will make in ransoms: it is not kill or be killed with them, but pay or be paid. But I will teach them all to fight that the will of God may be done in France; and then they will drive the poor goddams before them like sheep. You and Polly will live to see the day when there will not be an English soldier on the soil of France; and there will be but one king there: not the feudal English king, but God's French one.

ROBERT [to Poulengey] This may be all rot, Polly; but the troops might swallow it, though nothing that we can say seems able to put any fight into them. Even the Dauphin might swallow it. And if she can put fight into him, she can put it into anybody.

POULENGEY. I can see no harm in trying. Can you? And there is something about the girl—

ROBERT [turning to Joan] Now listen you to me; and [desperately] dont cut in before I have time to think.

JOAN [plumping down on the stool again, like an obedient schoolgirl] Yes, squire.

ROBERT. Your orders are, that you are to go to Chinon under the escort of this gentleman and three of his friends.

JOAN [radiant, clasping her hands] Oh, squire! Your head is all circled with light, like a saint's.

POULENGEY. How is she to get into the royal presence?

ROBERT [who has looked up for his halo rather apprehensively] I dont know: how did she get into my presence? If the Dauphin can keep her out he is a better man than I take him for. [Rising] I will send her to Chinon; and she can say I sent her. Then let come what may: I can do no more.

JOAN. And the dress? I may have a soldier's dress, maynt I, squire?

ROBERT. Have what you please. I wash my hands of it.

JOAN [wildly excited by her success] Come, Polly. [She dashes out].

ROBERT [shaking Poulengey's hand] Goodbye, old man, I am taking a big chance. Few other men would have done it. But as you say, there is something about her.

POULENGEY. Yes: there is something about her. Goodbye. [He goes out].

Robert, still very doubtful whether he has not been made a fool of by a crazy female, and a social inferior to boot, scratches his head and slowly comes back from the door.

The steward runs in with a basket.

STEWARD. Sir, sir—

ROBERT. What now?

STEWARD. The hens are laying like mad, sir. Five dozen eggs!

ROBERT [stiffens convulsively; crosses himself; and forms with his pale lips the words] Christ in heaven! [Aloud but breathless] She did come from God.

SCENE II

Chinon, in Touraine. An end of the throne-room in the castle, curtained off to make an ante-chamber. The Archbishop of Rheims, close on

50, *a full-fed political prelate with nothing of the ecclesiastic about him except his imposing bearing, and the Lord Chamberlain, Monseigneur de la Trémouille, a monstrous arrogant wineskin of a man, are waiting for the Dauphin. There is a door in the wall to the right of the two men. It is late in the afternoon on the 8th of March, 1429. The Archbishop stands with dignity whilst the Chamberlain, on his left, fumes about in the worst of tempers.*

LA TRÉMOUILLE. What the devil does the Dauphin mean by keeping us waiting like this? I dont know how you have the patience to stand there like a stone idol.

THE ARCHBISHOP. You see, I am an archbishop; and an archbishop is a sort of idol. At any rate he has to learn to keep still and suffer fools patiently. Besides. my dear Lord Chamberlain, it is the Dauphin's royal privilege to keep you waiting, is it not?

LA TRÉMOUILLE. Dauphin be damned! saving your reverence. Do you know how much money he owes me?

THE ARCHBISHOP. Much more than he owes me, I have no doubt, because you are a much richer man. But I take it he owes you all you could afford to lend him. That is what he owes me.

LA TRÉMOUILLE. Twentyseven thousand: that was his last haul. A cool twentyseven thousand!

THE ARCHBISHOP. What becomes of it all? He never has a suit of clothes that I would throw to a curate.

LA TRÉMOUILLE. He dines on a chicken or a scrap of mutton. He borrows my last penny; and there is nothing to shew for it. [*A page appears in the doorway*]. At last!

THE PAGE. No, my lord: it is not His Majesty. Monsieur de Rais is approaching.

LA TRÉMOUILLE. Young Bluebeard! Why announce him?

THE PAGE. Captain La Hire is with him. Something has happened, I think.

Gilles de Rais, a young man of 25, very smart and self-possessed, and sporting the extravagance of a little curled beard dyed blue at a clean-shaven court, comes in. He is determined to make himself agreeable, but lacks natural joyousness, and is not really pleasant. In fact when he defies the Church some eleven years later he is accused of trying to extract pleasure from horrible cruelties, and hanged. So far, however, there is no shadow of the gallows on him. He advances gaily to the Archbishop. The page withdraws.

BLUEBEARD. Your faithful lamb, Archbishop. Good day, my lord. Do you know what has happened to La Hire?

LA TRÉMOUILLE. He has sworn himself into a fit, perhaps.

BLUEBEARD. No: just the opposite. Foul Mouthed Frank, the only man in Touraine who could beat him at swearing, was told by a soldier that he shouldnt use such language when he was at the point of death.

THE ARCHBISHOP. Nor at any other point. But was Foul Mouthed Frank on the point of death?

BLUEBEARD. Yes: he has just fallen into a well and been drowned. La Hire is frightened out of his wits.

Captain La Hire comes in: a war dog with no court manners and pronounced camp ones.

BLUEBEARD. I have just been telling the Chamberlain and the Archbishop. The Archbishop says you are a lost man.

LA HIRE [*striding past Bluebeard, and planting himself between the Archbishop and La Trémouille*] This is nothing to joke about. It is worse than we thought. It was not a soldier, but an angel dressed as a soldier.

THE ARCHBISHOP }
THE CHAMBERLAIN } [*exclaiming all together*] An angel!
BLUEBEARD }

LA HIRE. Yes, an angel. She has made her way from Champagne with half a dozen men through the thick of everything: Burgundians, Goddams, deserters, robbers, and Lord knows who; and they never met a soul except the country folk. I know one of them: de Poulengey. He says she's an angel. If ever I utter an oath again may my soul be blasted to eternal damnation!

THE ARCHBISHOP. A very pious beginning, Captain.

Bluebeard and La Trémouille laugh at him. The page returns.

THE PAGE. His Majesty.

They stand perfunctorily at court attention. The Dauphin, aged 26, really King Charles the Seventh since the death of his father, but as yet uncrowned, comes in through the curtains with a paper in his hands. He is a poor creature physically; and the current fashion of shaving closely, and hiding every scrap of hair under the head-covering or headdress, both by women and men, makes the worst of his appearance. He has little narrow eyes, near together, a long pendulous nose that droops over his thick short upper lip, and the expression of a young dog accustomed to be kicked, yet incorrigible and irrepressible. But he is neither vulgar nor stupid; and he has a cheeky humor which enables him to hold his own in conversation. Just at present he is excited, like a child with a new toy. He comes to the Archbishop's left hand. Bluebeard and La Hire retire towards the curtains.

CHARLES. Oh, Archbishop, do you know what Robert de Baudricourt is sending me from Vaucouleurs?

THE ARCHBISHOP [*contemptuously*] I am not interested in the newest toys.

CHARLES [*indignantly*] It isnt a toy. [*Sulkily*] However, I can get on very well without your interest.

THE ARCHBISHOP. Your Highness is taking offence very unnecessarily.

CHARLES. Thank you. You are always ready with a lecture, arnt you?

LA TRÉMOUILLE [*roughly*] Enough grumbling. What have you got there?

CHARLES. What is that to you?

LA TRÉMOUILLE. It is my business to know what is passing between you and the garrison at Vaucouleurs. [*He snatches the paper from the Dauphin's hand, and begins reading it with some difficulty, following the words with his finger and spelling them out syllable by syllable.*]

CHARLES [*mortified*] You all think you can treat me as you please because I owe you money, and because I am no good at fighting. But I have the blood royal in my veins.

THE ARCHBISHOP. Even that has been questioned, your Highness. One hardly recognizes in you the grandson of Charles the Wise.

CHARLES. I want to hear no more of my grandfather. He was so wise that he used up the whole family stock of wisdom for five generations, and left me the poor fool I am, bullied and insulted by all of you.

THE ARCHBISHOP. Control yourself, sir. These outbursts of petulance are not seemly.

CHARLES. Another lecture! Thank you. What a pity it is that though you are an archbishop saints and angels dont come to see you!

THE ARCHBISHOP. What do you mean?

CHARLES. Aha! Ask that bully there [*pointing to La Trémouille*].

LA TRÉMOUILLE [*furious*] Hold your tongue. Do you hear?

CHARLES. Oh, I hear. You neednt shout. The whole castle can hear. Why dont you go and shout at the English, and beat them for me?

LA TRÉMOUILLE [*raising his fist*] You young—

CHARLES [*running behind the Archbishop*] Dont you raise your hand to me. It's high treason.

LA HIRE. Steady, Duke! Steady!

THE ARCHBISHOP [*resolutely*] Come, come! this will not do. My lord Chamberlain: please! please! we must keep some sort of order. [*To the Dauphin*] And you, sir: if you cannot rule your kingdom, at least try to rule yourself.

CHARLES. Another lecture! Thank you.

LA TRÉMOUILLE [*handing the paper to the Archbishop*] Here: read the accursed thing for me. He has sent the blood boiling into my head: I cant distinguish the letters.

CHARLES [*coming back and peering round La Trémouille's left shoulder*] I will read it for you if you like. I c a n read, you know.

LA TRÉMOUILLE [*with intense contempt, not at all stung by the taunt*] Yes: reading is about all you are fit for. Can you make it out, Archbishop?

THE ARCHBISHOP. I should have expected more commonsense from De Baudricourt. He is sending some cracked country lass here—

CHARLES [*interrupting*] No: he is sending a saint: an angel. And she is coming to me: to m e, the king, and not to you, Archbishop, holy as you are. She knows the blood royal if you dont. [*He struts up to the curtains between Bluebeard and La Hire*].

THE ARCHBISHOP. You cannot be allowed to see this crazy wench.

CHARLES [*turning*] But I am the king; and I will.

LA TRÉMOUILLE [*brutally*] Then she cannot be allowed to see y o u. Now!

CHARLES. I tell you I will. I am going to put my foot down—

BLUEBEARD [*laughing at him*] Naughty! What would your wise grandfather say?

CHARLES. That just shews your ignorance, Bluebeard. My grandfather had a saint who used to float in the air when she was praying, and told him everything he wanted to know. My poor father had two saints, Marie de Maillé and the Gasque of Avignon. It is in our family; and I dont care what you say: I will have my saint too.

THE ARCHBISHOP. This creature is not a saint. She is not even a respectable woman. She does not wear women's clothes. She is dressed like a soldier, and rides round the country with soldiers. Do you suppose such a person can be admitted to your Highness's court?

LA HIRE. Stop. [*Going to the Archbishop*] Did you say a girl in armor, like a soldier?

THE ARCHBISHOP. So De Baudricourt describes her.

LA HIRE. But by all the devils in hell— Oh, God forgive me, what am I saying?—by Our Lady and all the saints, this must be the angel that struck Foul Mouthed Frank dead for swearing.

CHARLES. [*triumphant*] You see! A miracle!

LA HIRE. She may strike the lot of us dead if we cross her. For Heaven's sake, Archbishop, be careful what you are doing.

THE ARCHBISHOP [*severely*] Rubbish! Nobody has been struck dead. A drunken blackguard who has been rebuked a hundred times for swearing has fallen into a well and been drowned. A mere coincidence.

LA HIRE. I do not know what a coincidence is. I do know that the man is dead, and that she told him he was going to die.

THE ARCHBISHOP. We are all going to die, Captain.

LA HIRE [*crossing himself*] I hope not. [*He backs out of the conversation*].

BLUEBEARD. We can easily find out whether she is an angel or not. Let us arrange when she comes that I shall be the Dauphin, and see whether she will find me out.

CHARLES. Yes: I agree to that. If she cannot find the blood royal I will have nothing to do with her.

THE ARCHBISHOP. It is for the Church to make saints: let De Baudricourt mind his own business, and not dare usurp the function of his priest. I say the girl shall not be admitted.

BLUEBEARD. But, Archbishop—

THE ARCHBISHOP [*sternly*] I speak in the Church's name. [*To the Dauphin*] Do you dare say she shall?

CHARLES [*intimidated but sulky*] Oh, if you make it an excommunication matter, I have nothing more to say, of course. But you havnt read the end of the letter. De Baudricourt says she will raise the siege of Orleans, and beat the English for us.

LA TRÉMOUILLE. Rot!

CHARLES. Well, will y o u save Orleans for us, with all your bullying?

LA TRÉMOUILLE [*savagely*] Do not throw that in my face again: do you hear? I have done more fighting than you ever did or ever will. But I cannot be everywhere.

THE DAUPHIN. Well, thats something.

BLUEBEARD [*coming between the Archbishop and Charles*] You have Jack Dunois at the head of your troops in Orleans: the brave Dunois, the handsome Dunois, the wonderful invincible Dunois, the darling of all the ladies, the beautiful bastard. Is it likely that the country lass can do what he cannot do?

CHARLES. Why doesnt he raise the siege, then?

LA HIRE. The wind is against him.

BLUEBEARD. How can the wind hurt him at Orleans? It is not on the Channel.

LA HIRE. It is on the river Loire; and the English hold the bridgehead. He must ship his men across the river and upstream if he is to take them in the rear. Well, he cannot, because there is a devil of a wind blowing the other way. He is tired of paying the priests to pray for a west wind. What he needs is a miracle. You tell me that what the girl did to Foul Mouthed Frank was no miracle. No matter: it finished Frank. If she changes the wind for Dunois, that may not be a miracle either; but it may finish the English. What harm is there in trying?

THE ARCHBISHOP [*who has read the end of the letter and become more thoughtful*] It is true that De Baudricourt seems extraordinarily impressed.

LA HIRE. De Baudricourt is a blazing ass; but he is a soldier; and if he thinks she can beat the English all the rest of the army will think so too.

LA TRÉMOUILLE [*to the Archbishop, who is hesitating*] Oh, let them have their way. Dunois' men will give up the town in spite of him if somebody does not put some fresh spunk into them.

THE ARCHBISHOP. The Church must examine the girl before anything decisive is done about her. However, since his Highness desires it, let her attend the Court.

LA HIRE. I will find her and tell her. [*He goes out*].

CHARLES. Come with me, Bluebeard; and let us arrange so that she will not know who I am. You will pretend to be me. [*He goes out through the curtains*].

BLUEBEARD. Pretend to be that thing! Holy Michael! [*He follows the Dauphin*].

LA TRÉMOUILLE. I wonder will she pick him out!

THE ARCHBISHOP. Of course she will.

LA TRÉMOUILLE. Why? How is she to know?

THE ARCHBISHOP. She will know what everybody in Chinon knows: that the Dauphin is the meanest-looking and worst-dressed figure in the Court, and that the man with the blue beard is Gilles de Rais.

LA TRÉMOUILLE. I never thought of that.

THE ARCHBISHOP. You are not so accustomed to miracles as I am. It is part of my profession.

LA TRÉMOUILLE [*puzzled and a little scandalized*] But that would not be a miracle at all.

THE ARCHBISHOP [*calmly*] Why not?

LA TRÉMOUILLE. Well, come! what is a miracle?

THE ARCHBISHOP. A miracle, my friend, is an event which creates faith. That is the purpose and nature of miracles. They may seem very wonderful to the people who witness them, and very simple to those who perform them. That does not matter: if they confirm or create faith they are true miracles.

LA TRÉMOUILLE. Even when they are frauds, do you mean?

THE ARCHBISHOP. Frauds deceive. An event which creates faith does not deceive: therefore it is not a fraud, but a miracle.

LA TRÉMOUILLE [*scratching his neck in his perplexity*] Well, I suppose as you are an archbishop you must be right. It seems a bit fishy to me. But I am no churchman, and dont understand these matters.

THE ARCHBISHOP. You are not a churchman; but you are a diplomatist and a soldier. Could you make our citizens pay war taxes, or our soldiers sacrifice their lives, if they knew what is really happening instead of what seems to them to be happening?

LA TRÉMOUILLE. No, by Saint Dennis: the fat would be in the fire before sundown.

THE ARCHBISHOP. Would it not be quite easy to tell them the truth?

LA TRÉMOUILLE. Man alive, they wouldnt believe it.

THE ARCHBISHOP. Just so. Well, the Church has to rule men for the good of their souls as you have to rule them for the good of their bodies. To do that, the Church must do as you do: nourish their faith by poetry.

LA TRÉMOUILLE. Poetry! I should call it humbug.

THE ARCHBISHOP. You would be wrong, my friend. Parables are not lies because they describe events that have never happened. Miracles are not frauds because they are often—I do not say always—very simple and innocent contrivances by which the priest fortifies the faith of his flock. When this girl picks out the Dauphin among his courtiers, it will not be a miracle for me, because I shall know how it has been done, and my faith will not be increased. But as for the others, if they feel the thrill of the supernatural, and forget their sinful clay in a sudden sense of the glory of God, it will be a miracle and a blessed one. And you will find that the girl herself will be more affected than anyone else. She will forget how she really picked him out. So, perhaps, will you.

LA TRÉMOUILLE. Well, I wish I were clever enough to know how much of you is God's archbishop and how much the most artful fox in Touraine. Come on, or we shall be late for the fun; and I want to see it, miracle or no miracle.

THE ARCHBISHOP [*detaining him a moment*] Do not think that I am a lover of crooked ways. There is a new spirit rising in men: we are at the dawning of a wider epoch. If I were a simple monk, and had not to rule men, I should seek peace for my spirit with Aristotle and Pythagoras rather than with the saints and their miracles.

LA TRÉMOUILLE. And who the deuce was Pythagoras?

THE ARCHBISHOP. A sage who held that the earth is round, and that it moves round the sun.

LA TRÉMOUILLE. What an utter fool! Couldnt he use his eyes?

They go out together through the curtains, which are presently withdrawn, revealing the full depth of the throne-room with the Court assembled. On the right are two Chairs of State on a dais. Bluebeard is standing theatrically on the dais, playing the king, and, like the courtiers, enjoying the joke rather obviously. There is a curtained arch in the wall behind the dais; but the main door, guarded by men-at-arms, is at the other side of the room; and a clear path across is kept and lined by the courtiers. Charles is in this path in the middle of the room. La Hire is on his right. The Archbishop, on his left, has taken his place by the dais: La Trémouille at the other side of it. The Duchess de la Trémouille, pretending to be the Queen, sits in the Consort's chair, with a group of ladies in waiting close by, behind the Archbishop.

The chatter of the courtiers makes such a noise

that nobody notices the appearance of the page at the door.

THE PAGE. The Duke of— [*Nobody listens*]. The Duke of— [*The chatter continues. Indignant at his failure to command a hearing, he snatches the halberd of the nearest man-at-arms, and thumps the floor with it. The chatter ceases; and everybody looks at him in silence*]. Attention! [*He restores the halberd to the man-at-arms*]. The Duke of Vendôme presents Joan the Maid to his Majesty.

CHARLES [*putting his finger on his lip*] Ssh! [*He hides behind the nearest courtier, peering out to see what happens*].

BLUEBEARD [*majestically*] Let her approach the throne.

Joan, dressed as a soldier, with her hair bobbed and hanging thickly round her face, is led in by a bashful and speechless nobleman, from whom she detaches herself to stop and look round eagerly for the Dauphin.

THE DUCHESS [*to the nearest lady in waiting*] My dear! Her hair!

All the ladies explode in uncontrollable laughter.

BLUEBEARD [*trying not to laugh, and waving his hand in deprecation of their merriment*] Ssh—ssh! Ladies! Ladies!!

JOAN [*not at all embarrassed*] I wear it like this because I am a soldier. Where be Dauphin?

A titter runs through the Court as she walks to the dais.

BLUEBEARD [*condescendingly*] You are in the presence of the Dauphin.

Joan looks at him sceptically for a moment, scanning him hard up and down to make sure. Dead silence, all watching her. Fun dawns in her face.

JOAN. Coom, Bluebeard! Thou canst not fool me. Where be Dauphin?

A roar of laughter breaks out as Gilles, with a gesture of surrender, joins in the laugh, and jumps down from the dais beside La Trémouille. Joan, also on the broad grin, turns back, searching along the row of courtiers, and presently makes a dive, and drags out Charles by the arm.

JOAN [*releasing him and bobbing him a little curtsey*] Gentle little Dauphin, I am sent to you to drive the English away from Orleans and from France, and to crown you king in the cathedral at Rheims, where all true kings of France are crowned.

CHARLES [*triumphant, to the Court*] You see, all of you: she knew the blood royal. Who

dare say now that I am not my father's son. [*To Joan*] But if you want me to be crowned at Rheims you must talk to the Archbishop, not to me. There he is [*he is standing behind her*]!

JOAN [*turning quickly, overwhelmed with emotion*] Oh, my lord! [*She falls on both knees before him, with bowed head, not daring to look up*] My lord: I am only a poor country girl; and you are filled with the blessedness and glory of God Himself; but you will touch me with your hands, and give me your blessing, wont you?

BLUEBEARD [*whispering to La Trémouille*] The old fox blushes.

LA TRÉMOUILLE. Another miracle!

THE ARCHBISHOP [*touched, putting his hand on her head*] Child: you are in love with religion.

JOAN [*startled: looking up at him*] Am I? I never thought of that. Is there any harm in it?

THE ARCHBISHOP. There is no harm in it, my child. But there is danger.

JOAN [*rising, with a sunflush of reckless happiness irradiating her face*] There is always danger, except in heaven. Oh, my lord, you have given me such strength, such courage. It must be a most wonderful thing to be Archbishop.

The Court smiles broadly: even titters a little.

THE ARCHBISHOP [*drawing himself up sensitively*] Gentlemen: your levity is rebuked by this maid's faith. I am, God help me, all unworthy; but your mirth is a deadly sin.

Their faces fall. Dead silence.

BLUEBEARD. My lord: we were laughing at her, not at you.

THE ARCHBISHOP. What? Not at my unworthiness but at her faith! Gilles de Rais: this maid prophesied that the blasphemer should be drowned in his sin—

JOAN [*distressed*] No!

THE ARCHBISHOP [*silencing her by a gesture*] I prophesy now that you will be hanged in yours if you do not learn when to laugh and when to pray.

BLUEBEARD. My lord: I stand rebuked. I am sorry: I can say no more. But if you prophesy that I shall be hanged, I shall never be able to resist temptation, because I shall always be telling myself that I may as well be hanged for a sheep as a lamb.

The courtiers take heart at this. There is more tittering.

JOAN [*scandalized*] You are an idle fellow,

Bluebeard; and you have great impudence to answer the Archbishop.

LA HIRE [*with a huge chuckle*] Well said, lass! Well said!

JOAN [*impatiently to the Archbishop*] Oh, my lord, will you send all these silly folks away so that I may speak to the Dauphin alone?

LA HIRE [*goodhumoredly*] I can take a hint. [*He salutes; turns on his heel; and goes out*].

THE ARCHBISHOP. Come, gentlemen. The Maid comes with God's blessing, and must be obeyed.

The courtiers withdraw, some through the arch, others at the opposite side. The Archbishop marches across to the door, followed by the Duchess and La Trémouille. As the Archbishop passes Joan she falls on her knees, and kisses the hem of his robe fervently. He shakes his head in instinctive remonstrance; gathers the robe from her; and goes out. She is left kneeling directly in the Duchess's way.

THE DUCHESS [*coldly*] Will you allow me to pass, please?

JOAN [*hastily rising, and standing back*] Beg pardon, maam, I am sure.

The Duchess passes on. Joan stares after her; then whispers to the Dauphin.

JOAN. Be that Queen?

CHARLES. No. She thinks she is.

JOAN [*again staring after the Duchess*] Oo-oo-ooh! [*Her awestruck amazement at the figure cut by the magnificently dressed lady is not wholly complimentary*].

LA TRÉMOUILLE [*very surly*] I'll trouble your Highness not to gibe at my wife. [*He goes out. The others have already gone*].

JOAN [*to the Dauphin*] Who be old Gruff-and-Grum?

CHARLES. He is the Duke de la Trémouille.

JOAN. What be his job?

CHARLES. He pretends to command the army. And whenever I find a friend I can care for, he kills him.

JOAN. Why dost let him?

CHARLES [*petulantly moving to the throne side of the room to escape from her magnetic field*] How can I prevent him? He bullies me. They all bully me.

JOAN. Art afraid?

CHARLES. Yes: I am afraid. It's no use preaching to me about it. It's all very well for these big men with their armor that is too heavy for me, and their swords that I can hardly lift, and their muscle and their shouting and their bad tempers. They like fighting: most of them are making fools of themselves all the time they are not fighting; but I am quiet and sensible; and I dont want to kill people: I only want to be left alone to enjoy myself in my own way. I never asked to be a king: it was pushed on me. So if you are going to say "Son of St Louis: gird on the sword of your ancestors, and lead us to victory" you may spare your breath to cool your porridge; for I cannot do it. I am not built that way; and there is an end of it.

JOAN [*trenchant and masterful*] Blethers! We are all like that to begin with. I shall put courage into thee.

CHARLES. But I dont want to have courage put into me. I want to sleep in a comfortable bed, and not live in continual terror of being killed or wounded. Put courage into the others, and let them have their bellyful of fighting; but let me alone.

JOAN. It's no use, Charlie: thou must face what God puts on thee. If thou fail to make thyself king, thoult be a beggar: what else art fit for? Come! Let me see thee sitting on the throne. I have looked forward to that.

CHARLES. What is the good of sitting on the throne when the other fellows give all the orders? However! [*he sits enthroned, a piteous figure*] here is the king for you! Look your fill at the poor devil.

JOAN. Thourt not king yet, lad: thourt but Dauphin. Be not led away by them around thee. Dressing up dont fill empty noddle. I know the people: the real people that make thy bread for thee; and I tell thee they count no man king of France until the holy oil has been poured on his hair, and himself consecrated and crowned in Rheims Cathedral. And thou needs new clothes, Charlie. Why does not Queen look after thee properly?

CHARLES. We're too poor. She wants all the money we can spare to put on her own back. Besides, I like to see her beautifully dressed; and I dont care what I wear myself: I should look ugly anyhow.

JOAN. There is some good in thee, Charlie; but it is not yet a king's good.

CHARLES. We shall see. I am not such a fool as I look. I have my eyes open; and I can tell you that one good treaty is worth ten good fights. These fighting fellows lose all on the treaties that they gain on the fights. If we can only have a treaty, the English are sure to have the worst of it, because they are better at fighting than at thinking.

JOAN. If the English win, it is they that will make the treaty; and then God help poor France! Thou must fight, Charlie, whether thou will or no. I will go first to hearten thee. We must take our courage in both hands: aye, and pray for it with both hands too.

CHARLES [*descending from his throne and again crossing the room to escape from her dominating urgency*] Oh do stop talking about God and praying. I cant bear people who are always praying. Isnt it bad enough to have to do it at the proper times?

JOAN [*pitying him*] Thou poor child, thou hast never prayed in thy life. I must teach thee from the beginning.

CHARLES. I am not a child: I am a grown man and a father; and I will not be taught any more.

JOAN. Aye, you have a little son. He that will be Louis the Eleventh when you die. Would you not fight for him?

CHARLES. No: a horrid boy. He hates me. He hates everybody, selfish little beast! I dont want to be bothered with children. I dont want to be a father; and I dont want to be a son: especially a son of St Louis. I dont want to be any of these fine things you all have your heads full of: I want to be just what I am. Why cant you mind your own business, and let me mind mine?

JOAN [*again contemptuous*] Minding your own business is like minding your own body: it's the shortest way to make yourself sick. What is my business? Helping mother at home. What is thine? Petting lapdogs and sucking sugarsticks. I call that muck. I tell thee it is God's business we are here to do: not our own. I have a message to thee from God; and thou must listen to it, though thy heart break with the terror of it.

CHARLES. I dont want a message; but can you tell me any secrets? Can you do any cures? Can you turn lead into gold, or anything of that sort?

JOAN. I can turn thee into a king, in Rheims Cathedral; and that is a miracle that will take some doing, it seems.

CHARLES. If we go to Rheims, and have a coronaton, Anne will want new dresses. We cant afford them. I am all right as I am.

JOAN. As you are! And what is that? Less than my father's poorest shepherd. Thourt not lawful owner of thy own land of France till thou be consecrated.

CHARLES. But I shall not be lawful owner of my own land anyhow. Will the consecration pay off my mortgages? I have pledged my last acre to the Archbishop and that fat bully. I owe money even to Bluebeard.

JOAN [*earnestly*] Charlie: I come from the land, and have gotten my strength working on the land; and I tell thee that the land is thine to rule righteously and keep God's peace in, and not to pledge at the pawnshop as a drunken woman pledges her children's clothes. And I come from God to tell thee to kneel in the cathedral and solemnly give thy kingdom to Him for ever and ever, and become the greatest king in the world as His steward and His bailiff, His soldier and His servant. The very clay of France will become holy: her soldiers will be the soldiers of God: the rebel dukes will be rebels against God: the English will fall on their knees and beg thee let them return to their lawful homes in peace. Wilt be a poor little Judas, and betray me and Him that sent me?

CHARLES [*tempted at last*] Oh, if I only dare!

JOAN. I shall dare, dare, and dare again, in God's name! Art for or against me?

CHARLES [*excited*] I'll risk it. I warn you I shant be able to keep it up; but I'll risk it. You shall see. [*Running to the main door and shouting*] Hallo! Come back, everybody. [*To Joan, as he runs back to the arch opposite*] Mind you stand by and dont let me be bullied. [*Through the arch*] Come along, will you: the whole Court. [*He sits down in the royal chair as they all hurry in to their former places, chattering and wondering*]. Now I'm in for it; but no matter: here goes! [*To the page*] Call for silence, you little beast, will you?

THE PAGE [*snatching a halberd as before and thumping with it repeatedly*] Silence for His Majesty the King. The King speaks. [*Peremptorily*] Will you be silent there? [*Silence*].

CHARLES [*rising*] I have given the command of the army to The Maid. The Maid is to do as she likes with it. [*He descends from the dais*].

General amazement. La Hire, delighted, slaps his steel thigh-piece with his gauntlet.

LA TRÉMOUILLE [*turning threateningly towards Charles*] What is this? *I* command the army.

Joan quickly puts her hand on Charles's shoulder as he instinctively recoils. Charles, with a grotesque effort culminating in an extravagant gesture, snaps his fingers in the Chamberlain's face.

JOAN. Thourt answered, old Gruff-and-

Grum. [*Suddenly flashing out her sword as she divines that her moment has come*] Who is for God and His Maid? Who is for Orleans with me?

LA HIRE [*carried away, drawing also*] For God and His Maid! To Orleans!

ALL THE KNIGHTS [*following his lead with enthusiasm*] To Orleans!

Joan, radiant, falls on her knees in thanksgiving to God. They all kneel, except the Archbishop, who gives his benediction with a sign, and La Trémouille, who collapses, cursing.

SCENE III

Orleans, May 29th, 1429. Dunois, aged 26, is pacing up and down a patch of ground on the south bank of the silver Loire, commanding a long view of the river in both directions. He has had his lance stuck up with a pennon, which streams in a strong east wind. His shield with its bend sinister lies beside it. He has his commander's baton in his hand. He is well built, carrying his armor easily. His broad brow and pointed chin give him an equilaterally triangular face, already marked by active service and responsibility, with the expression of a goodnatured and capable man who has no affectations and no foolish illusions. His page is sitting on the ground, elbows on knees, cheeks on fists, idly watching the water. It is evening; and both man and boy are affected by the loveliness of the Loire.

DUNOIS [*halting for a moment to glance up at the streaming pennon and shake his head wearily before he resumes his pacing*] West wind, west wind, west wind. Strumpet: steadfast when you should be wanton, wanton when you should be steadfast. West wind on the silver Loire: what rhymes to Loire? [*He looks again at the pennon, and shakes his fist at it*] Change, curse you, change, English harlot of a wind, change. West, west, I tell you. [*With a growl he resumes his march in silence, but soon begins again*] West wind, wanton wind, wilful wind, womanish wind, false wind from over the water, will you never blow again?

THE PAGE [*bounding to his feet*] See! There! There she goes!

DUNOIS [*startled from his reverie: eagerly*] Where? Who? The Maid?

THE PAGE. No: the kingfisher. Like blue lightning. She went into that bush.

DUNOIS [*furiously disappointed*] Is that all? You infernal young idiot: I have a mind to pitch you into the river.

THE PAGE [*not afraid, knowing his man*] It looked frightfully jolly, that flash of blue. Look! There goes the other!

DUNOIS [*running eagerly to the river brim*] Where? Where?

THE PAGE [*pointing*] Passing the reeds.

DUNOIS [*delighted*] I see.

They follow the flight till the bird takes cover.

THE PAGE. You blew me up because you were not in time to see them yesterday.

DUNOIS. You knew I was expecting The Maid when you set up your yelping. I will give you something to yelp for next time.

THE PAGE. Arnt they lovely? I wish I could catch them.

DUNOIS. Let me catch you trying to trap them, and I will put you in the iron cage for a month to teach you what a cage feels like. You are an abominable boy.

THE PAGE [*laughs, and squats down as before*]!

DUNOIS [*pacing*] Blue bird, blue bird, since I am friend to thee, change thou the wind for me. No: it does not rhyme. He who has sinned for thee: thats better. No sense in it, though. [*He finds himself close to the page*] You abominable boy! [*He turns away from him*] Mary in the blue snood, kingfisher color: will you grudge me a west wind?

A SENTRY'S VOICE WESTWARD. Halt! Who goes there?

JOAN'S VOICE. The Maid.

DUNOIS. Let her pass. Hither, Maid! To me!

Joan, in splendid armor, rushes in in a blazing rage. The wind drops; and the pennon flaps idly down the lance; but Dunois is too much occupied with Joan to notice it.

JOAN [*bluntly*] Be you Bastard of Orleans?

DUNOIS [*cool and stern, pointing to his shield*] You see the bend sinister. Are you Joan the Maid?

JOAN. Sure.

DUNOIS. Where are your troops?

JOAN. Miles behind. They have cheated me. They have brought me to the wrong side of the river.

DUNOIS. I told them to.

JOAN. Why did you? The English are on the other side!

DUNOIS. The English are on both sides.

JOAN. But Orleans is on the other side. We must fight the English there. How can we cross the river?

DUNOIS [*grimly*] There is a bridge.

JOAN. In God's name, then, let us cross the bridge, and fall on them.

DUNOIS. It seems simple; but it cannot be done.

JOAN. Who says so?

DUNOIS. I say so; and older and wiser heads than mine are of the same opinion.

JOAN [roundly] Then your older and wiser heads are fatheads: they have made a fool of you; and now they want to make a fool of me too, bringing me to the wrong side of the river. Do you not know that I bring you better help than ever came to any general or any town?

DUNOIS [smiling patiently] Your own?

JOAN. No: the help and counsel of the King of Heaven. Which is the way to the bridge?

DUNOIS. You are impatient, Maid.

JOAN. Is this a time for patience? Our enemy is at our gates; and here we stand doing nothing. Oh, why are you not fighting? Listen to me: I will deliver you from fear. I—

DUNOIS [laughing heartily, and waving her off] No, no, my girl: if you delivered me from fear I should be a good knight for a story book, but a very bad commander of the army. Come! let me begin to make a soldier of you. [He takes her to the water's edge]. Do you see those two forts at this end of the bridge? the big ones?

JOAN. Yes. Are they ours or the goddams'?

DUNOIS. Be quiet, and listen to me. If I were in either of those forts with only ten men I could hold it against an army. The English have more than ten times ten goddams in those forts to hold them against us.

JOAN. They cannot hold them against God. God did not give them the land under those forts: they stole it from Him. He gave it to us. I will take those forts.

DUNOIS. Single-handed?

JOAN. Our men will take them. I will lead them.

DUNOIS. Not a man will follow you.

JOAN. I will not look back to see whether anyone is following me.

DUNOIS [recognizing her mettle, and clapping her heartily on the shoulder] Good. You have the makings of a soldier in you. You are in love with war.

JOAN [startled] Oh! And the Archbishop said I was in love with religion.

DUNOIS. I, God forgive me, am a little in love with war myself, the ugly devil! I am like a man with two wives. Do you want to be like a woman with two husbands?

JOAN [matter-of-fact] I will never take a husband. A man in Toul took an action against me for breach of promise; but I never promised him. I am a soldier: I do not want to be thought of as a woman. I will not dress as a woman. I do not care for the things women care for. They dream of lovers, and of money. I dream of leading a charge, and of placing the big guns. You soldiers do not know how to use the big guns: you think you can win battles with a great noise and smoke.

DUNOIS [with a shrug] True. Half the time the artillery is more trouble than it is worth.

JOAN. Aye, lad; but you cannot fight stone walls with horses: you must have guns, and much bigger guns too.

DUNOIS [grinning at her familiarity, and echoing it] Aye, lass; but a good heart and a stout ladder will get over the stoniest wall.

JOAN. I will be first up the ladder when we reach the fort, Bastard. I dare you to follow me.

DUNOIS. You must not dare a staff officer, Joan: only company officers are allowed to indulge in displays of personal courage. Besides, you must know that I welcome you as a saint, not as a soldier. I have daredevils enough at my call, if they could help me.

JOAN. I am not a daredevil: I am a servant of God. My sword is sacred: I found it behind the altar in the church of St Catherine, where God hid it for me; and I may not strike a blow with it. My heart is full of courage, not of anger. I will lead; and your men will follow: that is all I can do. But I must do it: you shall not stop me.

DUNOIS. All in good time. Our men cannot take those forts by a sally across the bridge. They must come by water, and take the English in the rear on this side.

JOAN [her military sense asserting itself] Then make rafts and put big guns on them; and let your men cross to us.

DUNOIS. The rafts are ready; and the men are embarked. But they must wait for God.

JOAN. What do you mean? God is waiting for them.

DUNOIS. Let Him send us a wind then. My boats are downstream: they cannot come up against both wind and current. We must wait until God changes the wind. Come: let me take you to the church.

JOAN. No. I love church; but the English will not yield to prayers: they understand nothing but hard knocks and slashes. I will not go to church until we have beaten them.

DUNOIS. You must: I have business for you there.

JOAN. What business?

DUNOIS. To pray for a west wind. I have prayed; and I have given two silver candlesticks; but my prayers are not answered. Yours may be: you are young and innocent.

JOAN. Oh yes: you are right. I will pray: I will tell St Catherine: she will make God give me a west wind. Quick: shew me the way to the church.

THE PAGE [*sneezes violently*] At-cha!!!

JOAN. God bless you, child! Coom, Bastard. *They go out. The page rises to follow. He picks up the shield, and is taking the spear as well when he notices the pennon, which is now streaming eastward.*

THE PAGE [*dropping the shield and calling excitedly after them*] Seigneur! Seigneur! Mademoiselle!

DUNOIS [*running back*] What is it? The kingfisher? [*He looks eagerly for it up the river*].

JOAN [*joining them*] Oh, a kingfisher! Where?

THE PAGE. No: the wind, the wind, the wind [*pointing to the pennon*]: that is what made me sneeze.

DUNOIS [*looking at the pennon*] The wind has changed. [*He crosses himself*] God has spoken. [*Kneeling and handing his baton to Joan*] You command the king's army. I am your soldier.

THE PAGE [*looking down the river*] The boats have put off. They are ripping upstream like anything.

DUNOIS [*rising*] Now for the forts. You dared me to follow. Dare you lead?

JOAN [*bursting into tears and flinging her arms round Dunois, kissing him on both cheeks*] Dunois, dear comrade in arms, help me. My eyes are blinded with tears. Set my foot on the ladder, and say "Up, Joan."

DUNOIS [*dragging her out*] Never mind the tears: make for the flash of the guns.

JOAN [*in a blaze of courage*] Ah!

DUNOIS [*dragging her along with him*] For God and Saint Dennis!

THE PAGE [*shrilly*] The Maid! The Maid! God and The Maid! Hurray-ay-ay! [*He snatches up the shield and lance, and capers out after them, mad with excitement*].

SCENE IV

A tent in the English camp. A bullnecked English chaplain of 50 is sitting on a stool at a table, hard at work writing. At the other side of the table an imposing nobleman, aged 46, is seated in a handsome chair turning over the leaves of an illuminated Book of Hours. The nobleman is enjoying himself: the chaplain is struggling with suppressed wrath. There is an unoccupied leather stool on the nobleman's left. The table is on his right.

THE NOBLEMAN. Now this is what I call workmanship. There is nothing on earth more exquisite than a bonny book, with well-placed columns of rich black writing in beautiful borders, and illuminated pictures cunningly inset. But nowadays, instead of looking at books, people read them. A book might as well be one of those orders for bacon and bran that you are scribbling.

THE CHAPLAIN. I must say, my lord, you take our situation very coolly. Very coolly indeed.

THE NOBLEMAN [*supercilious*] What is the matter?

THE CHAPLAIN. The matter, my lord, is that we English have been defeated.

THE NOBLEMAN. That happens, you know. It is only in history books and ballads that the enemy is always defeated.

THE CHAPLAIN. But we are being defeated over and over again. First, Orleans—

THE NOBLEMAN [*poohpoohing*] Oh, Orleans!

THE CHAPLAIN. I know what you are going to say, my lord: that was a clear case of witchcraft and sorcery. But we are still being defeated. Jargeau, Meung, Beaugency, just like Orleans. And now we have been butchered at Patay, and Sir John Talbot taken prisoner. [*He throws down his pen, almost in tears*] I feel it, my lord: I feel it very deeply. I cannot bear to see my countrymen defeated by a parcel of foreigners.

THE NOBLEMAN. Oh! you are an Englishman, are you?

THE CHAPLAIN. Certainly not, my lord: I am a gentleman. Still, like your lordship, I was born in England; and it makes a difference.

THE NOBLEMAN. You are attached to the soil, eh?

THE CHAPLAIN. It pleases your lordship to be satirical at my expense: your greatness privileges you to be so with impunity. But your lordship knows very well that I am not attached to the soil in a vulgar manner, like a serf. Still, I have a feeling about it; [*with growing agitation*] and I am not ashamed of it; and [*rising wildly*] by God, if this goes on any longer I will fling my cassock to the devil, and take arms myself, and strangle the accursed witch with my own hands.

THE NOBLEMAN [*laughing at him good-naturedly*] So you shall, chaplain: so you shall, if we can do nothing better. But not yet, not quite yet.

The Chaplain resumes his seat very sulkily.

THE NOBLEMAN [*airily*] I should not care very much about the witch—you see, I have made my pilgrimage to the Holy Land; and the Heavenly Powers, for their own credit, can hardly allow m e to be worsted by a village sorceress—but the Bastard of Orleans is a harder nut to crack; and as he has been to the Holy Land too, honors are easy between us as far as that goes.

THE CHAPLAIN. He is only a Frenchman, my lord.

THE NOBLEMAN. A Frenchman! Where did you pick up that expression? Are these Burgundians and Bretons and Picards and Gascons beginning to call themselves Frenchmen, just as our fellows are beginning to call themselves Englishmen? They actually talk of France and England as their countries. Theirs, if you please! What is to become of me and you if that way of thinking comes into fashion?

THE CHAPLAIN. Why, my lord? Can it hurt us?

THE NOBLEMAN. Men cannot serve two masters. If this cant of serving their country once takes hold of them, goodbye to the authority of their feudal lords, and goodbye to the authority of the Church. That is, goodbye to you and me.

THE CHAPLAIN. I hope I am a faithful servant of the Church; and there are only six cousins between me and the barony of Stogumber, which was created by the Conqueror. But is that any reason why I should stand by and see Englishmen beaten by a French bastard and a witch from Lousy Champagne?

THE NOBLEMAN. Easy, man, easy: we shall burn the witch and beat the bastard all in good time. Indeed I am waiting at present for the Bishop of Beauvais, to arrange the burning with him. He has been turned out of his diocese by her faction.

THE CHAPLAIN. You have first to catch her, my lord.

THE NOBLEMAN. Or buy her. I will offer a king's ransom.

THE CHAPLAIN. A king's ransom! For that slut!

THE NOBLEMAN. One has to leave a margin. Some of Charles's people will sell her to the Burgundians; the Burgundians will sell her to us; and there will probably be three or four middlemen who will expect their little commissions.

THE CHAPLAIN. Monstrous. It is all those scoundrels of Jews: they get in every time money changes hands. I would not leave a Jew alive in Christendom if I had my way.

THE NOBLEMAN. Why not? The Jews generally give value. They make you pay; but they deliver the goods. In my experience the men who want something for nothing are invariably Christians.

A page appears.

THE PAGE. The Right Reverend the Bishop of Beauvais: Monseigneur Cauchon.

Cauchon, aged about 60, comes in. The page withdraws. The two Englishmen rise.

THE NOBLEMAN [*with effusive courtesy*] My dear Bishop, how good of you to come! Allow me to introduce myself: Richard de Beauchamp, Earl of Warwick, at your service.

CAUCHON. Your lordship's fame is well known to me.

WARWICK. This reverend cleric is Master John de Stogumber.

THE CHAPLAIN [*glibly*] John Bowyer Spenser Neville de Stogumber, at your service, my lord: Bachelor of Theology, and Keeper of the Private Seal to His Eminence the Cardinal of Winchester.

WARWICK [*to Cauchon*] You call him the Cardinal of England, I believe. Our king's uncle.

CAUCHON. Messire John de Stogumber: I am always the very good friend of His Eminence. [*He extends his hand to the chaplain, who kisses his ring*].

WARWICK. Do me the honor to be seated. [*He gives Cauchon his chair, placing it at the head of the table*].

Cauchon accepts the place of honor with a grave inclination. Warwick fetches the leather stool carelessly, and sits in his former place. The chaplain goes back to his chair.

Though Warwick has taken second place in calculated deference to the Bishop, he assumes the lead in opening the proceedings as a matter of course. He is still cordial and expansive; but there is a new note in his voice which means that he is coming to business.

WARWICK. Well, my Lord Bishop, you find us in one of our unlucky moments. Charles is to be crowned at Rheims, practically by the young woman from Lorraine; and—I must not deceive you, nor flatter your hopes —we cannot prevent it. I suppose it will make a great difference to Charles's position.

CAUCHON. Undoubtedly. It is a masterstroke of The Maid's.

THE CHAPLAIN [*again agitated*] We were not fairly beaten, my lord. No Englishman is ever fairly beaten.

Cauchon raises his eyebrow slightly, then quickly composes his face.

WARWICK. Our friend here takes the view that the young woman is a sorceress. It would, I presume, be the duty of your reverend lordship to denounce her to the Inquisition, and have her burnt for that offence.

CAUCHON. If she were captured in my diocese: yes.

WARWICK [*feeling that they are getting on capitally*] Just so. Now I suppose there can be no reasonable doubt that she is a sorceress.

THE CHAPLAIN. Not the least. An arrant witch.

WARWICK [*gently reproving the interruption*] We are asking for the Bishop's opinion, Messire John.

CAUCHON. We shall have to consider not merely our own opinions here, but the opinions—the prejudices, if you like—of a French court.

WARWICK [*correcting*] A Catholic court, my lord.

CAUCHON. Catholic courts are composed of mortal men, like other courts, however sacred their function and inspiration may be. And if the men are Frenchmen, as the modern fashion calls them, I am afraid the bare fact that an English army has been defeated by a French one will not convince them that there is any sorcery in the matter.

THE CHAPLAIN. What! Not when the famous Sir John Talbot himself has been defeated and actually taken prisoner by a drab from the ditches of Lorraine!

CAUCHON. Sir John Talbot, we all know, is a fierce and formidable soldier, Messire; but I have yet to learn that he is an able general. And though it pleases you to say that he has been defeated by this girl, some of us may be disposed to give a little of the credit to Dunois.

THE CHAPLAIN [*contemptuously*] The Bastard of Orleans!

CAUCHON. Let me remind—

WARWICK [*interposing*] I know what you are going to say, my lord. Dunois defeated me at Montargis.

CAUCHON [*bowing*] I take that as evidence that the Seigneur Dunois is a very able commander indeed.

WARWICK. Your lordship is the flower of courtesy. I admit, on our side, that Talbot is a mere fighting animal, and that it probably served him right to be taken at Patay.

THE CHAPLAIN [*chafing*] My lord: at Orleans this woman had her throat pierced by an English arrow, and was seen to cry like a child from the pain of it. It was a death wound; yet she fought all day; and when our men had repulsed all her attacks like true Englishmen, she walked alone to the wall of our fort with a white banner in her hand; and our men were paralyzed, and could neither shoot nor strike whilst the French fell on them and drove them on to the bridge, which immediately burst into flames and crumbled under them, letting them down into the river, where they were drowned in heaps. Was this your bastard's generalship? or were those flames the flames of hell, conjured up by witchcraft?

WARWICK. You will forgive Messire John's vehemence, my lord; but he has put our case. Dunois is a great captain, we admit; but why could he do nothing until the witch came?

CAUCHON. I do not say that there were no supernatural powers on her side. But the names on that white banner were not the names of Satan and Beelzebub, but the blessed names of our Lord and His holy mother. And your commander who was drowned—Clahz-da I think you call him—

WARWICK. Glasdale. Sir William Glasdale.

CAUCHON. Glass-dell, thank you. He was no saint; and many of our people think that he was drowned for his blasphemies against The Maid.

WARWICK [*beginning to look very dubious*] Well, what are we to infer from all this, my lord? Has The Maid converted you?

CAUCHON. If she had, my lord, I should have known better than to have trusted myself here within your grasp.

WARWICK [*blandly deprecating*] Oh! oh! My lord!

CAUCHON. If the devil is making use of this girl—and I believe he is—

WARWICK [*reassured*] Ah! You hear, Messire

John? I knew your lordship would not fail us. Pardon my interruption. Proceed.

CAUCHON. If it be so, the devil has longer views than you give him credit for.

WARWICK. Indeed? In what way? Listen to this, Messire John.

CAUCHON. If the devil wanted to damn a country girl, do you think so easy a task would cost him the winning of half a dozen battles? No, my lord: any trumpery imp could do that much if the girl could be damned at all. The Prince of Darkness does not condescend to such cheap drudgery. When he strikes, he strikes at the Catholic Church, whose realm is the whole spiritual world. When he damns, he damns the souls of the entire human race. Against that dreadful design The Church stands ever on guard. And it is as one of the instruments of that design that I see this girl. She is inspired, but diabolically inspired.

THE CHAPLAIN. I told you she was a witch.

CAUCHON [*fiercely*] She is not a witch. She is a heretic.

THE CHAPLAIN. What difference does that make?

CAUCHON. You, a priest, ask me that! You English are strangely blunt in the mind. All these things that you call witchcraft are capable of a natural explanation. The woman's miracles would not impose on a rabbit: she does not claim them as miracles herself. What do her victories prove but that she has a better head on her shoulders than your swearing Glass-dells and mad bull Talbots, and that the courage of faith, even though it be a false faith, will always outstay the courage of wrath?

THE CHAPLAIN [*hardly able to believe his ears*] Does your lordship compare Sir John Talbot, three times Governor of Ireland, to a mad bull?!!!

WARWICK. It would not be seemly for you to do so, Messire John, as you are still six removes from a barony. But as I am an earl, and Talbot is only a knight, I may make bold to accept the comparison. [*To the Bishop*] My lord: I wipe the slate as far as the witchcraft goes. None the less, we must burn the woman.

CAUCHON. I cannot burn her. The Church cannot take life. And my first duty is to seek this girl's salvation.

WARWICK. No doubt. But you do burn people occasionally.

CAUCHON. No. When the Church cuts off an obstinate heretic as a dead branch from the tree of life, the heretic is handed over to the secular arm. The Church has no part in what the secular arm may see fit to do.

WARWICK. Precisely. And I shall be the secular arm in this case. Well, my lord, hand over your dead branch; and I will see that the fire is ready for it. If you will answer for the Church's part, I will answer for the secular part.

CAUCHON [*with smouldering anger*] I can answer for nothing. You great lords are too prone to treat the Church as a mere political convenience.

WARWICK [*smiling and propitiatory*] Not in England, I assure you.

CAUCHON. In England more than anywhere else. No, my lord: the soul of this village girl is of equal value with yours or your king's before the throne of God; and my first duty is to save it. I will not suffer your lordship to smile at me as if I were repeating a meaningless form of words, and it were well understood between us that I should betray the girl to you. I am no mere political bishop: my faith is to me what your honor is to you; and if there be a loophole through which this baptized child of God can creep to her salvation, I shall guide her to it.

THE CHAPLAIN [*rising in a fury*] You are a traitor.

CAUCHON [*springing up*] You lie, priest. [*Trembling with rage*] If you dare do what this woman has done—set your country above the holy Catholic Church—you shall go to the fire with her.

THE CHAPLAIN. My lord: I—I went too far. I— [*he sits down with a submissive gesture*].

WARWICK [*who has risen apprehensively*] My lord: I apologize to you for the word used by Messire John de Stogumber. It does not mean in England what it does in France. In your language traitor means betrayer: one who is perfidious, treacherous, unfaithful, disloyal. In our country it means simply one who is not wholly devoted to our English interests.

CAUCHON. I am sorry: I did not understand. [*He subsides into his chair with dignity*].

WARWICK [*resuming his seat, much relieved*] I must apologize on my own account if I have seemed to take the burning of this poor girl too lightly. When one has seen whole countrysides burnt over and over again as mere items in military routine, one has to grow a very thick skin. Otherwise one might go mad: at all events, I should. May I venture to assume that your lordship also, having to see so many heretics burned from time to time, is compelled to take—shall I say a professional view of what would otherwise be a very horrible incident?

CAUCHON. Yes: it is a painful duty: even, as you say, a horrible one. But in comparison with the horror of heresy it is less than nothing. I am not thinking of this girl's body, which will suffer for a few moments only, and which must in any event die in some more or less painful manner, but of her soul, which may suffer to all eternity.

WARWICK. Just so; and God grant that her soul may be saved! But the practical problem would seem to be how to save her soul without saving her body. For we must face it, my lord: if this cult of The Maid goes on, our cause is lost.

THE CHAPLAIN [*his voice broken like that of a man who has been crying*] May I speak, my lord?

WARWICK. Really, Messire John, I had rather you did not, unless you can keep your temper.

THE CHAPLAIN. It is only this. I speak under correction; but The Maid is full of deceit: she pretends to be devout. Her prayers and confessions are endless. How can she be accused of heresy when she neglects no observance of a faithful daughter of The Church?

CAUCHON [*flaming up*] A faithful daughter of The Church! The Pope himself at his proudest dare not presume as this woman presumes. She acts as if she herself were The Church. She brings the message of God to Charles; and The Church must stand aside. She will crown him in the cathedral of Rheims: she, not The Church! She sends letters to the king of England giving him God's command through her to return to his island on pain of God's vengeance, which she will execute. Let me tell you that the writing of such letters was the practice of the accursed Mahomet, the anti-Christ. Has she ever in all her utterances said one word of The Church? Never. It is always God and herself.

WARWICK. What can you expect? A beggar on horseback! Her head is turned.

CAUCHON. Who has turned it? The devil. And for a mighty purpose. He is spreading this heresy everywhere. The man Hus, burnt only thirteen years ago at Constance, infected all Bohemia with it. A man named WcLeef, himself an anointed priest, spread the pestilence in England; and to your shame you let him die in his bed. We have such people here in France too: I know the breed. It is cancerous: if it be not cut out, stamped out, burnt out, it will not stop until it has brought the whole body of human society into sin and corruption, into waste and ruin. By it an Arab camel driver drove Christ and His Church out of Jerusalem, and ravaged his way west like a wild beast until at last there stood only the Pyrenees and God's mercy between France and damnation. Yet what did the camel driver do at the beginning more than this shepherd girl is doing? He had his voices from the angel Gabriel: she has her voices from St Catherine and St Margaret and the Blessed Michael. He declared himself the messenger of God, and wrote in God's name to the kings of the earth. Her letters to them are going forth daily. It is not the Mother of God now to whom we must look for intercession, but to Joan the Maid. What will the world be like when The Church's accumulated wisdom and knowledge and experience, its councils of learned, venerable pious men, are thrust into the kennel by every ignorant laborer or dairymaid whom the devil can puff up with the monstrous self-conceit of being directly inspired from heaven? It will be a world of blood, of fury, of devastation, of each man striving for his own hand: in the end a world wrecked back into barbarism. For now you have only Mahomet and his dupes, and the Maid and her dupes; but what will it be when every girl thinks herself a Joan and every man a Mahomet? I shudder to the very marrow of my bones when I think of it. I have fought it all my life; and I will fight it to the end. Let all this woman's sins be forgiven her except only this sin; for it is the sin against the Holy Ghost; and if she does not recant in the dust before the world, and submit herself to the last inch of her soul to her Church, to the fire she shall go if she once falls into my hand.

WARWICK [*unimpressed*] You feel strongly about it, naturally.

CAUCHON. Do not you?

WARWICK. I am a soldier, not a churchman. As a pilgrim I saw something of the Mahometans. They were not so ill-bred as I had been led to believe. In some respects their conduct compared favorably with ours.

CAUCHON [*displeased*] I have noticed this before. Men go to the East to convert the infidels. And the infidels pervert them. The Crusader comes back more than half a Saracen. Not to mention that all Englishmen are born heretics.

THE CHAPLAIN. Englishmen heretics!!! [*Appealing to Warwick*] My lord: must we endure this? His lordship is beside himself. How can what an Englishman believes be heresy? It is a contradiction in terms.

CAUCHON. I absolve you, Messire de Stogumber, on the ground of invincible ignorance. The thick air of your country does not breed theologians.

WARWICK. You would not say so if you heard us quarrelling about religion, my lord! I am sorry you think I must be either a heretic or a blockhead because, as a travelled man, I know that the followers of Mahomet profess great respect for our Lord, and are more ready to forgive St Peter for being a fisherman than your lordship is to forgive Mahomet for being a camel driver. But at least we can proceed in this matter without bigotry.

CAUCHON. When men call the zeal of the Christian Church bigotry I know what to think.

WARWICK. They are only east and west views of the same thing.

CAUCHON [*bitterly ironical*] Only east and west! Only!!

WARWICK. Oh, my Lord Bishop, I am not gainsaying you. You will carry The Church with you; but you have to carry the nobles also. To my mind there is a stronger case against The Maid than the one you have so forcibly put. Frankly, I am not afraid of this girl becoming another Mahomet, and superseding The Church by a great heresy. I think you exaggerate that risk. But have you noticed that in these letters of hers, she proposes to all the kings of Europe, as she has already pressed on Charles, a transaction which would wreck the whole social structure of Christendom?

CAUCHON. Wreck The Church. I tell you so.

WARWICK [*whose patience is wearing out*] My lord: pray get The Church out of your head for a moment; and remember that there are temporal institutions in the world as well as spiritual ones. I and my peers represent the feudal aristocracy as you represent The Church. We are the temporal power. Well, do you not see how this girl's idea strikes at us?

CAUCHON. How does her idea strike at you, except as it strikes at all of us, through The Church?

WARWICK. Her idea is that the kings should give their realms to God, and then reign as God's bailiffs.

CAUCHON [*not interested*] Quite sound theologically, my lord. But the king will hardly care, provided he reign. It is an abstract idea: a mere form of words.

WARWICK. By no means. It is a cunning device to supersede the aristocracy, and make the king sole and absolute autocrat. Instead of the king being merely the first among his peers, he becomes their master. That we cannot suffer: we call no man master. Nominally we hold our lands and dignities from the king, because there must be a keystone to the arch of human society; but we hold our lands in our own hands, and defend them with our own swords and those of our own tenants. Now by The Maid's doctrine the king will take our lands—o u r lands! – and make them a present to God; and God will then vest them wholly in the king.

CAUCHON. Need you fear that? You are the makers of kings after all. York or Lancaster in England, Lancaster or Valois in France: they reign according to your pleasure.

WARWICK. Yes; but only as long as the people follow their feudal lords, and know the king only as a travelling show, owning nothing but the highway that belongs to everybody. If the people's thoughts and hearts were turned to the king, and their lords became only the king's servants in their eyes, the king could break us across his knee one by one; and then what should we be but liveried courtiers in his halls?

CAUCHON. Still you need not fear, my lord. Some men are born kings; and some are born statesmen. The two are seldom the same. Where would the king find counsellors to plan and carry out such a policy for him?

WARWICK [*with a not too friendly smile*] Perhaps in the Church, my lord.

Cauchon, with an equally sour smile, shrugs his shoulders, and does not contradict him.

WARWICK. Strike down the barons; and the cardinals will have it all their own way.

CAUCHON [*conciliatory, dropping his polemical tone*] My lord: we shall not defeat The Maid if we strive against one another. I know well that there is a Will to Power in the world. I know that while it lasts there will be a struggle between the Emperor and the Pope, between the dukes and the political cardinals, between the barons and the kings. The devil divides us and governs. I see you are no friend to The Church: you are an earl first and last, as I am a churchman first and last. But can we not sink our differences in the face of a common enemy? I see now that what is in your mind is not that this girl has never once mentioned The Church, and thinks only of God and herself, but that she has never once mentioned the peerage, and thinks only of the king and herself.

WARWICK. Quite so. These two ideas of hers are the same idea at bottom. It goes deep, my lord. It is the protest of the individual soul against the interference of priest or peer between the private man and his God. I should call it Protestantism if I had to find a name for it.

CAUCHON [looking hard at him] You understand it wonderfully well, my lord. Scratch an Englishman, and find a Protestant.

WARWICK [playing the pink of courtesy] I think you are not entirely void of sympathy with The Maid's secular heresy, my lord. I leave you to find a name for it.

CAUCHON. You mistake me, my lord. I have no sympathy with her political presumptions. But as a priest I have gained a knowledge of the minds of the common people; and there you will find yet another most dangerous idea. I can express it only by such phrases as France for the French, England for the English, Italy for the Italians, Spain for the Spanish, and so forth. It is sometimes so narrow and bitter in country folk that it surprises me that this country girl can rise above the idea of her village for its villagers. But she can. She does. When she threatens to drive the English from the soil of France she is undoubtedly thinking of the whole extent of country in which French is spoken. To her the French-speaking people are what the Holy Scriptures describe as a nation. Call this side of her heresy Nationalism if you will: I can find you no better name for it. I can only tell you that it is essentially anti-Catholic and anti-Christian; for the Catholic Church knows only one realm, and that is the realm of Christ's kingdom. Divide that kingdom into nations, and you dethrone Christ. De-

throne Christ, and who will stand between our throats and the sword? The world will perish in a welter of war.

WARWICK. Well, if you will burn the Protestant, I will burn the Nationalist, though perhaps I shall not carry Messire John with me there. England for the English will appeal to him.

THE CHAPLAIN. Certainly England for the English goes without saying: it is the simple law of nature. But this woman denies to England her legitimate conquests, given her by God because of her peculiar fitness to rule over less civilized races for their own good. I do not understand what your lordships mean by Protestant and Nationalist: you are too learned and subtle for a poor clerk like myself. But I know as a matter of plain commonsense that the woman is a rebel; and that is enough for me. She rebels against Nature by wearing man's clothes, and fighting. She rebels against The Church by usurping the divine authority of the Pope. She rebels against God by her damnable league with Satan and his evil spirits against our army. And all these rebellions are only excuses for her great rebellion against England. That is not to be endured. Let her perish. Let her burn. Let her not infect the whole flock. It is expedient that one woman die for the people.

WARWICK [rising] My lord: we seem to be agreed.

CAUCHON [rising also, but in protest] I will not imperil my soul. I will uphold the justice of the Church. I will strive to the utmost for this woman's salvation.

WARWICK. I am sorry for the poor girl. I hate these severities. I will spare her if I can.

THE CHAPLAIN [implacably] I would burn her with my own hands.

CAUCHON [blessing him] Sancta simplicitas!

SCENE V

The ambulatory in the cathedral of Rheims, near the door of the vestry. A pillar bears one of the stations of the cross. The organ is playing the people out of the nave after the coronation. Joan is kneeling in prayer before the station. She is beautifully dressed, but still in male attire. The organ ceases as Dunois, also splendidly arrayed, comes into the ambulatory from the vestry.

DUNOIS. Come, Joan! you have had enough

praying. After that fit of crying you will catch a chill if you stay here any longer. It is all over: the cathedral is empty; and the streets are full. They are calling for The Maid. We have told them you are staying here alone to pray; but they want to see you again.

JOAN. No: let the king have all the glory.

DUNOIS. He only spoils the show, poor devil. No, Joan: you have crowned him; and you must go through with it.

JOAN [shakes her head reluctantly].

DUNOIS [raising her] Come come! it will be over in a couple of hours. It's better than the bridge at Orleans: eh?

JOAN. Oh, dear Dunois, how I wish it were the bridge at Orleans again! We l i v e d at that bridge.

DUNOIS. Yes, faith, and died too: some of us.

JOAN. Isnt it strange, Jack? I am such a coward: I am frightened beyond words before a battle; but it is so dull afterwards when there is no danger: oh, so dull! dull! dull!

DUNOIS. You must learn to be abstemious in war, just as you are in your food and drink, my little saint.

JOAN. Dear Jack: I think you like me as a soldier likes his comrade.

DUNOIS. You need it, poor innocent child of God. You have not many friends at court.

JOAN. Why do all these courtiers and knights and churchmen hate me? What have I done to them? I have asked nothing for myself except that my village shall not be taxed; for we cannot afford war taxes. I have brought them luck and victory: I have set them right when they were doing all sorts of stupid things: I have crowned Charles and made him a real king; and all the honors he is handing out have gone to them. Then why do they not love me?

DUNOIS [rallying her] Sim-ple-ton! Do you expect stupid people to love you for shewing them up? Do blundering old military dug-outs love the successful young captains who supersede them? Do ambitious politicians love the climbers who take the front seats from them? Do archbishops enjoy being played off their own altars, even by saints? Why, I should be jealous of you myself if I were ambitious enough.

JOAN. You are the pick of the basket here, Jack: the only friend I have among all these nobles. I'll wager your mother was from the country. I will go back to the farm when I have taken Paris.

DUNOIS. I am not so sure that they will let you take Paris.

JOAN [startled] What!

DUNOIS. I should have taken it myself before this if they had all been sound about it. Some of them would rather Paris took you, I think. So take care.

JOAN. Jack: the world is too wicked for me. If the goddams and the Burgundians do not make an end of me, the French will. Only for my voices I should lose all heart. That is why I had to steal away to pray here alone after the coronation. I'll tell you something, Jack. It is in the bells I hear my voices. Not today, when they all rang: that was nothing but jangling. But here in this corner, where the bells come down from heaven, and the echoes linger, or in the fields, where they come from a distance through the quiet of the countryside, my voices are in them. [The cathedral clock chimes the quarter] Hark! [She becomes rapt] Do you hear? "Dear-child-of-God": just what you said. At the half-hour they will say "Be-brave-go-on." At the three-quarters they will say "I-am-thy-Help." But it is at the hour, when the great bell goes after "God-will-save-France": it is then that St Margaret and St Catherine and sometimes even the blessed Michael will say things that I cannot tell beforehand. Then, oh then—

DUNOIS [interrupting her kindly but not sympathetically] Then, Joan, we shall hear whatever we fancy in the booming of the bell. You make me uneasy when you talk about your voices: I should think you were a bit cracked if I hadnt noticed that you give me very sensible reasons for what you do, though I hear you telling others you are only obeying Madame Saint Catherine.

JOAN [crossly] Well, I have to find reasons for you, because you do not believe in my voices. But the voices come first; and I find the reasons after: whatever you may choose to believe.

DUNOIS. Are you angry, Joan?

JOAN. Yes. [Smiling] No: not with you. I wish you were one of the village babies.

DUNOIS. Why?

JOAN. I could nurse you for awhile.

DUNOIS. You are a bit of a woman after all.

JOAN. No: not a bit: I am a soldier and nothing else. Soldiers always nurse children when they get a chance.

DUNOIS. That is true. [He laughs].

King Charles, with Bluebeard on his left and

La Hire on his right, comes from the vestry, where he has been disrobing. Joan shrinks away behind the pillar. Dunois is left between Charles and La Hire.

DUNOIS. Well, your Majesty is an anointed king at last. How do you like it?

CHARLES. I would not go through it again to be emperor of the sun and moon. The weight of those robes! I thought I should have dropped when they loaded that crown on to me. And the famous holy oil they talked so much about was rancid: phew! The Archbishop must be nearly dead: his robes must have weighed a ton: they are stripping him still in the vestry.

DUNOIS [*drily*] Your Majesty should wear armor oftener. That would accustom you to heavy dressing.

CHARLES. Yes: the old jibe! Well, I am not going to wear armor: fighting is not my job. Where is The Maid?

JOAN [*coming forward between Charles and Bluebeard, and falling on her knee*] Sire: I have made you king: my work is done. I am going back to my father's farm.

CHARLES [*surprised, but relieved*] Oh, are you? Well, that will be very nice.

Joan rises, deeply discouraged.

CHARLES [*continuing heedlessly*] A healthy life, you know.

DUNOIS. But a dull one.

BLUEBEARD. You will find the petticoats tripping you up after leaving them off for so long.

LA HIRE. You will miss the fighting. It's a bad habit, but a grand one, and the hardest of all to break yourself of.

CHARLES [*anxiously*] Still, we dont want you to stay if you would really rather go home.

JOAN [*bitterly*] I know well that none of you will be sorry to see me go. [*She turns her shoulder to Charles and walks past him to the more congenial neighborhood of Dunois and La Hire*].

LA HIRE. Well, I shall be able to swear when I want to. But I shall miss you at times.

JOAN. La Hire: in spite of all your sins and swears we shall meet in heaven; for I love you as I love Pitou, my old sheep dog. Pitou could kill a wolf. You will kill the English wolves until they go back to their country and become good dogs of God, will you not?

LA HIRE. You and I together: yes.

JOAN. No: I shall last only a year from the beginning.

ALL THE OTHERS. What!

JOAN. I know it somehow.

DUNOIS. Nonsense!

JOAN. Jack: do you think you will be able to drive them out?

DUNOIS [*with quiet conviction*] Yes: I shall drive them out. They beat us because we thought battles were tournaments and ransom markets. We played the fool while the goddams took war seriously. But I have learnt my lesson, and taken their measure. They have no roots here. I have beaten them before; and I shall beat them again.

JOAN. You will not be cruel to them, Jack?

DUNOIS. The goddams will not yield to tender handling. We did not begin it.

JOAN [*suddenly*] Jack: before I go home, let us take Paris.

CHARLES [*terrified*] Oh no no. We shall lose everything we have gained. Oh dont let us have any more fighting. We can make a very good treaty with the Duke of Burgundy.

JOAN. Treaty! [*She stamps with impatience*].

CHARLES. Well, why not, now that I am crowned and anointed? Oh, that oil!

The Archbishop comes from the vestry, and joins the group between Charles and Bluebeard.

CHARLES. Archbishop: The Maid wants to start fighting again.

THE ARCHBISHOP. Have we ceased fighting, then? Are we at peace?

CHARLES. No: I suppose not; but let us be content with what we have done. Let us make a treaty. Our luck is too good to last; and now is our chance to stop before it turns.

JOAN. Luck! God has fought for us; and you call it luck! And you would stop while there are still Englishmen on this holy earth of dear France!

THE ARCHBISHOP [*sternly*] Maid: the king addressed himself to me, not to you. You forget yourself. You very often forget yourself.

JOAN [*unabashed, and rather roughly*] Then speak; and tell him that it is not God's will that he should take his hand from the plough.

THE ARCHBISHOP. If I am not so glib with the name of God as you are, it is because I interpret His will with the authority of the Church and of my sacred office. When you first came you respected it, and would not have dared to speak as you are now speaking. You came clothed with the virtue of humility;

and because God blessed your enterprises accordingly, you have stained yourself with the sin of pride. The old Greek tragedy is rising among us. It is the chastisement of hubris.

CHARLES. Yes: she thinks she knows better than everyone else.

JOAN [distressed, but naïvely incapable of seeing the effect she is producing] But I do know better than any of you seem to. And I am not proud: I never speak unless I know I am right.

BLUEBEARD ⎫ [exclaiming ⎰ Ha ha!
CHARLES ⎭ together] ⎱ Just so.

THE ARCHBISHOP. How do you know you are right?

JOAN. I always know. My voices—

CHARLES. Oh, your voices, your voices. Why dont the voices come to me? I am king, not you.

JOAN. They do come to you; but you do not hear them. You have not sat in the field in the evening listening for them. When the angelus rings you cross yourself and have done with it; but if you prayed from your heart, and listened to the thrilling of the bells in the air after they stop ringing, you would hear the voices as well as I do. [Turning brusquely from him] But what voices do you need to tell you what the blacksmith can tell you: that you must strike while the iron is hot? I tell you we must make a dash at Compiègne and relieve it as we relieved Orleans. Then Paris will open its gates; or if not, we will break through them. What is your crown worth without your capital?

LA HIRE. That is what I say too. We shall go through them like a red hot shot through a pound of butter. What do you say, Bastard?

DUNOIS. If our cannon balls were all as hot as your head, and we had enough of them, we should conquer the earth, no doubt. Pluck and impetuosity are good servants in war, but bad masters: they have delivered us into the hands of the English every time we have trusted to them. We never know when we are beaten: that is our great fault.

JOAN. You never know when you are victorious: that is a worse fault. I shall have to make you carry looking-glasses in battle to convince you that the English have not cut off all your noses. You would have been besieged in Orleans still, you and your councils of war, if I had not made you attack. You should always attack; and if you only hold on long enough the enemy will stop first. You dont know how to begin a battle; and you dont know how to use your cannons. And I do.

She squats down on the flags with crossed ankles, pouting.

DUNOIS. I know what you think of us, General Joan.

JOAN. Never mind that, Jack. Tell them what you think of me.

DUNOIS. I think that God was on your side; for I have not forgotten how the wind changed, and how our hearts changed when you came; and by my faith I shall never deny that it was in your sign that we conquered. But I tell you as a soldier that God is no man's daily drudge, and no maid's either. If you are worthy of it He will sometimes snatch you out of the jaws of death and set you on your feet again; but that is all: once on your feet you must fight with all your might and all your craft. For He has to be fair to your enemy too: dont forget that. Well, He set us on our feet through you at Orleans; and the glory of it has carried us through a few good battles here to the coronation. But if we presume on it further, and trust to God to do the work we should do ourselves, we shall be defeated; and serve us right!

JOAN. But—

DUNOIS. Sh! I have not finished. Do not think, any of you, that these victories of ours were won without generalship. King Charles: you have said no word in your proclamations of my part in this campaign; and I make no complaint of that; for the people will run after The Maid and her miracles and not after the Bastard's hard work finding troops for her and feeding them. But I know exactly how much God did for us through The Maid, and how much He left me to do by my own wits; and I tell you that your little hour of miracles is over, and that from this time on he who plays the war game best will win— if the luck is on his side.

JOAN. Ah! if, if, if, if! If ifs and ans were pots and pans there'd be no need of tinkers. [Rising impetuously] I tell you, Bastard, your art of war is no use, because your knights are no good for real fighting. War is only a game to them, like tennis and all their other games: they make rules as to what is fair and what is not fair, and heap armor on themselves and on their poor horses to keep out the arrows; and when they fall they cant get up, and have to wait for their squires to come and lift them to arrange about the ransom with the man that has poked them off their horse. Cant you see that all the like of that is gone by and done with? What use is armor against gunpowder? And if it was, do you think men that are fighting for France and for God will stop to bargain about ransoms, as half your knights live by doing? No: they will fight to win; and they will give up their lives out of their own hand into the hand of God when they go into battle, as I do. Common folks understand this. They cannot afford armor and cannot pay ransoms; but they follow me half naked into the moat and up the ladder and over the wall. With them it is my life or thine, and God defend the right! You may shake your head, Jack; and Bluebeard may twirl his billygoat's beard and cock his nose at me; but remember the day your knights and captains refused to follow me to attack the English at Orleans! You locked the gates to keep me in; and it was the townsfolk and the common people that followed me, and forced the gate, and shewed you the way to fight in earnest.

BLUEBEARD [*offended*] Not content with being Pope Joan, you must be Caesar and Alexander as well.

THE ARCHBISHOP. Pride will have a fall, Joan.

JOAN. Oh, never mind whether it is pride or not: is it true? is it commonsense?

LA HIRE. It is true. Half of us are afraid of having our handsome noses broken; and the other half are out for paying off their mortgages. Let her have her way, Dunois: she does not know everything; but she has got hold of the right end of the stick. Fighting is not what it was; and those who know least about it often make the best job of it.

DUNOIS. I know all that. I do not fight in the old way: I have learnt the lesson of Agincourt, of Poitiers and Crecy. I know how many lives any move of mine will cost; and if the move is worth the cost I make it and pay the cost. But Joan never counts the cost at all: she goes ahead and trusts to God: she thinks she has God in her pocket. Up to now she has had the numbers on her side; and she has won. But I know Joan; and I see that some day she will go ahead when she has only ten men to do the work of a hundred. And then she will find that God is on the side of the big battalions. She will be taken by the enemy. And the lucky man that makes the capture will receive sixteen thousand pounds from the Earl of Ouareek.

JOAN [*flattered*] Sixteen thousand pounds! Eh, laddie, have they offered that for me? There cannot be so much money in the world.

DUNOIS. There is, in England. And now tell me, all of you, which of you will lift a finger to save Joan once the English have got her? I speak first, for the army. The day after she has been dragged from her horse by a goddam or a Burgundian, and he is not struck dead: the day after she is locked in a dungeon, and the bars and bolts do not fly open at the touch of St Peter's angel: the day when the enemy finds out that she is as vulnerable as I am and not a bit more invincible, she will not be worth the life of a single soldier to us; and I will not risk that life, much as I cherish her as a companion-in-arms.

JOAN. I dont blame you, Jack: you are right. I am not worth one soldier's life if God lets me be beaten; but France may think me worth my ransom after what God has done for her through me.

CHARLES. I tell you I have no money; and this coronation, which is all your fault, has cost me the last farthing I can borrow.

JOAN. The Church is richer than you. I put my trust in the Church.

THE ARCHBISHOP. Woman: they will drag you through the streets, and burn you as a witch.

JOAN [*running to him*] Oh, my lord, do not say that. It is impossible. I a witch!

THE ARCHBISHOP. Peter Cauchon knows his business. The University of Paris has burnt a woman for saying that what you have done was well done, and according to God.

JOAN [*bewildered*] But why? What sense is there in it? What I have done is according to God. They could not burn a woman for speaking the truth.

THE ARCHBISHOP. They did.

JOAN. But you know that she was speaking the truth. You would not let them burn me.

THE ARCHBISHOP. How could I prevent them?

JOAN. You would speak in the name of the Church. You are a great prince of the Church. I would go anywhere with your blessing to protect me.

THE ARCHBISHOP. I have no blessing for you while you are proud and disobedient.

JOAN. Oh, why will you go on saying things like that? I am not proud and disobedient. I am a poor girl, and so ignorant that I do not know A from B. How could I be proud? And how can you say that I am disobedient when I always obey my voices, because they come from God.

THE ARCHBISHOP. The voice of God on earth is the voice of the Church Militant; and all the voices that come to you are the echoes of your own wilfulness.

JOAN. It is not true.

THE ARCHBISHOP [*flushing angrily*] You tell the Archbishop in his cathedral that he lies; and yet you say you are not proud and disobedient.

JOAN. I never said you lied. It was you that as good as said my voices lied. When have they ever lied? If you will not believe in them: even if they are only the echoes of my own commonsense, are they not always right? and are not your earthly counsels always wrong?

THE ARCHBISHOP [*indignantly*] It is waste of time admonishing you.

CHARLES. It always comes back to the same thing. She is right; and everyone else is wrong.

THE ARCHBISHOP. Take this as your last warning. If you perish through setting your private judgment above the instructions of your spiritual directors, the Church disowns you, and leaves you to whatever fate your presumption may bring upon you. The Bastard has told you that if you persist in setting up your military conceit above the counsels of your commanders—

DUNOIS [*interposing*] To put it quite exactly, if you attempt to relieve the garrison in Compiègne without the same superiority in numbers you had at Orleans—

THE ARCHBISHOP. The army will disown you, and will not rescue you. And His Majesty the King has told you that the throne has not the means of ransoming you.

CHARLES. Not a penny.

THE ARCHBISHOP. You stand alone: absolutely alone, trusting to your own conceit, your own ignorance, your own headstrong presumption, your own impiety in hiding all these sins under the cloak of a trust in God. When you pass through these doors into the sunlight, the crowd will cheer you. They will bring you their little children and their invalids to heal: they will kiss your hands and feet, and do what they can, poor simple souls, to turn your head, and madden you with the self-confidence that is leading you to your destruction. But you will be none the less alone: they cannot save you. We and we only can stand between you and the stake at which our enemies have burnt that wretched woman in Paris.

JOAN [*her eyes skyward*] I have better friends and better counsel than yours.

THE ARCHBISHOP. I see that I am speaking in vain to a hardened heart. You reject our protection, and are determined to turn us all against you. In future, then, fend for yourself; and if you fail, God have mercy on your soul.

DUNOIS. That is the truth, Joan. Heed it.

JOAN. Where would you all have been now if I had heeded that sort of truth? There is no help, no counsel, in any of you. Yes: I am alone on earth: I have always been alone. My father told my brothers to drown me if I would not stay to mind his sheep while France was bleeding to death: France might perish if only our lambs were safe. I thought France would have friends at the court of the king of France; and I find only wolves fighting for pieces of her poor torn body. I thought God would have friends everywhere, because He is the friend of everyone; and in my innocence I believed that you who now cast me out would be like strong towers to keep harm from me. But I am wiser now; and nobody is any the worse for being wiser. Do not think you can frighten me by telling me that I am alone. France is alone; and God is alone; and what is my loneliness before the loneliness of my country and my God? I see now that the loneliness of God is His strength: what would He be if He listened to your jealous little counsels? Well, my loneliness shall be my strength too: it is better to be alone with God: His friendship will not fail me, nor His counsel, nor His love. In His strength I will dare, and dare, and dare, until I die. I will go out now to the common people, and let the love in their eyes comfort me for the hate in yours. You will all be glad to see me burnt; but if I go through the fire I shall go through it to their hearts for ever and ever. And so, God be with me!

She goes from them. They stare after her in glum silence for a moment. Then Gilles de Rais twirls his beard.

BLUEBEARD. You know, the woman is quite impossible. I dont dislike her, really; but what are you to do with such a character?

DUNOIS. As God is my judge, if she fell into the Loire I would jump in in full armor to fish her out. But if she plays the fool at Compiègne, and gets caught, I must leave her to her doom.

LA HIRE. Then you had better chain me up; for I could follow her to hell when the spirit rises in her like that.

THE ARCHBISHOP. She disturbs my judgment too: there is a dangerous power in her outbursts. But the pit is open at her feet; and for good or evil we cannot turn her from it.

CHARLES. If only she would keep quiet, or go home!

They follow her dispiritedly.

SCENE VI

Rouen, 30th May 1431. A great stone hall in the castle, arranged for a trial-at-law, but not a trial-by-jury, the court being the Bishop's court with the Inquisition participating: hence there are two raised chairs side by side for the Bishop and the Inquisitor as judges. Rows of chairs radiating from them at an obtuse angle are for the canons, the doctors of law and theology, and the Dominican monks, who act as assessors. In the angle is a table for the scribes, with stools. There is also a heavy rough wooden stool for the prisoner. All these are at the inner end of the hall. The further end is open to the courtyard through a row of arches. The court is shielded from the weather by screens and curtains.

Looking down the great hall from the middle of the inner end, the judicial chairs and scribes' table are to the right. The prisoner's stool is to the left. There are arched doors right and left. It is a fine sunshiny May morning.

Warwick comes in through the arched doorway on the judges' side, followed by his page.

THE PAGE [*pertly*] I suppose your lordship is aware that we have no business here. This is an ecclesiastical court; and we are only the secular arm.

WARWICK. I am aware of that fact. Will it please your impudence to find the Bishop of Beauvais for me, and give him a hint that he can have a word with me here before the trial, if he wishes?

THE PAGE [*going*] Yes, my lord.

WARWICK. And mind you behave yourself. Do not address him as Pious Peter.

THE PAGE. No, my lord. I shall be kind to him, because, when The Maid is brought in, Pious Peter will have to pick a peck of pickled pepper.

Cauchon enters through the same door with a Dominican monk and a canon, the latter carrying a brief.

THE PAGE. The Right Reverend his lordship the Bishop of Beauvais. And two other reverend gentlemen.

WARWICK. Get out; and see that we are not interrupted.

THE PAGE. Right, my lord [*he vanishes airily*].

CAUCHON. I wish your lordship good-morrow.

WARWICK. Good-morrow to your lordship. Have I had the pleasure of meeting your friends before? I think not.

CAUCHON [*introducing the monk, who is on his right*] This, my lord, is Brother John Lemaître, of the order of St Dominic. He is acting as deputy for the Chief Inquisitor into the evil of heresy in France. Brother John: the Earl of Warwick.

WARWICK. Your Reverence is most welcome. We have no Inquisitor in England, unfortunately; though we miss him greatly, especially on occasions like the present.

The Inquisitor smiles patiently, and bows. He is a mild elderly gentleman, but has evident reserves of authority and firmness.

CAUCHON [*introducing the Canon, who is on his left*] This gentleman is Canon John D'Estivet, of the Chapter of Bayeux. He is acting as Promoter.

WARWICK. Promoter?

CAUCHON. Prosecutor, you would call him in civil law.

WARWICK. Ah! prosecutor. Quite, quite. I am very glad to make your acquaintance, Canon D'Estivet.

D'Estivet bows. [He is on the young side of middle age, well mannered, but vulpine beneath his veneer].

WARWICK. May I ask what stage the proceedings have reached? It is now more than nine months since The Maid was captured at Compiègne by the Burgundians. It is fully four months since I bought her from the Burgundians for a very handsome sum, solely that she might be brought to justice. It is very nearly three months since I delivered her up to you, my Lord Bishop, as a person suspected of heresy. May I suggest that you are taking a rather unconscionable time to make up your minds about a very plain case? Is this trial never going to end?

THE INQUISITOR [*smiling*] It has not yet begun, my lord.

WARWICK. Not yet begun! Why, you have been at it eleven weeks!

CAUCHON. We have not been idle, my lord. We have held fifteen examinations of The Maid: six public and nine private.

THE INQUISITOR [*always patiently smiling*] You see, my lord, I have been present at only two of these examinations. They were proceedings of the Bishop's court solely, and not of the Holy Office. I have only just decided to associate myself—that is, to associate the Holy Inquisition—with the Bishop's court. I did not at first think that this was a case of heresy at all. I regarded it as a political case, and The Maid as a prisoner of war. But having now been present at two of the examinations, I must admit that this seems to be one of the gravest cases of heresy within my experience. Therefore everything is now in order; and we proceed to trial this morning. [*He moves towards the judicial chairs*].

CAUCHON. This moment, if your lordship's convenience allows.

WARWICK [*graciously*] Well, that is good news, gentlemen. I will not attempt to conceal from you that our patience was becoming strained.

CAUCHON. So I gathered from the threats of your soldiers to drown those of our people who favor The Maid.

WARWICK. Dear me! At all events their intentions were friendly to you, my lord.

CAUCHON [*sternly*] I hope not. I am determined that the woman shall have a fair hearing. The justice of the Church is not a mockery, my lord.

THE INQUISITOR [*returning*] Never has there been a fairer examination within my experience, my lord. The Maid needs no lawyers to take her part: she will be tried by her most faithful friends, all ardently desirous to save her soul from perdition.

D'ESTIVET. Sir: I am the Promoter; and it has been my painful duty to present the case against the girl; but believe me, I would throw up my case today and hasten to her defence if I did not know that men far my superiors in learning and piety, in eloquence and persuasiveness, have been sent to reason with her, to explain to her the danger she is running, and the ease with which she may avoid it. [*Suddenly bursting into forensic eloquence, to the disgust of Cauchon and the Inquisitor, who have listened to him so far with patronizing approval*] Men have dared to say that we are acting from hate; but God is our witness that they lie. Have we tortured her? No. Have we ceased to exhort her; to implore her to have pity on herself; to come to the bosom of her Church as an erring but beloved child? Have we—

CAUCHON [*interrupting drily*] Take care, Canon. All that you say is true; but if you make his lordship believe it I will not answer for your life, and hardly for my own.

WARWICK [*deprecating, but by no means denying*] Oh, my lord, you are very hard on us poor English. But we certainly do not share your pious desire to save The Maid: in fact I tell you now plainly that her death is a political necessity which I regret but cannot help. If the Church lets her go—

CAUCHON [*with fierce and menacing pride*] If the Church lets her go, woe to the man, were he the Emperor himself, who dares lay a finger on her! The Church is not subject to political necessity, my lord.

THE INQUISITOR [*interposing smoothly*] You need have no anxiety about the result, my lord. You have an invincible ally in the matter: one who is far more determined than you that she shall burn.

WARWICK. And who is this very convenient partisan, may I ask?

THE INQUISITOR. The Maid herself. Unless you put a gag in her mouth you cannot prevent her from convicting herself ten times over every time she opens it.

D'ESTIVET. That is perfectly true, my lord. My hair bristles on my head when I hear so young a creature utter such blasphemies.

WARWICK. Well, by all means do your best for her if you are quite sure it will be of no avail. [*Looking hard at Cauchon*] I should be sorry to have to act without the blessing of the Church.

CAUCHON [*with a mixture of cynical admiration and contempt*] And yet they say Englishmen are hypocrites! You play for your side, my lord, even at the peril of your soul. I cannot but admire such devotion; but I dare not go so far myself. I fear damnation.

WARWICK. If we feared anything we could never govern England, my lord. Shall I send your people in to you?

CAUCHON. Yes: it will be very good of your lordship to withdraw and allow the court to assemble.

Warwick turns on his heel, and goes out through the courtyard. Cauchon takes one of the judicial seats; and D'Estivet sits at the scribes' table, studying his brief.

CAUCHON [*casually, as he makes himself comfortable*] What scoundrels these English nobles are!

THE INQUISITOR [*taking the other judicial chair on Cauchon's left*] All secular power makes men scoundrels. They are not trained for the work; and they have not the Apostolic Succession. Our own nobles are just as bad.

The Bishop's assessors hurry into the hall, headed by Chaplain de Stogumber and Canon de Courcelles, a young priest of 30. The scribes sit at the table, leaving a chair vacant opposite D'Estivet. Some of the assessors take their seats: others stand chatting, waiting for the proceedings to begin formally. De Stogumber, aggrieved and obstinate, will not take his seat: neither will the Canon, who stands on his right.

CAUCHON. Good morning, Master de Stogumber. [*To the Inquisitor*] Chaplain to the Cardinal of England.

THE CHAPLAIN [*correcting him*] Of Winchester, my lord. I have to make a protest, my lord.

CAUCHON. You make a great many.

THE CHAPLAIN. I am not without support, my lord. Here is Master de Courcelles, Canon of Paris, who associates himself with me in my protest.

CAUCHON. Well, what is the matter?

THE CHAPLAIN [*sulkily*] Speak you, Master de Courcelles, since I do not seem to enjoy his lordship's confidence. [*He sits down in dudgeon next to Cauchon, on his right*].

COURCELLES. My lord: we have been at great pains to draw up an indictment of The Maid on sixtyfour counts. We are now told that they have been reduced, without consulting us.

THE INQUISITOR. Master de Courcelles: I am the culprit. I am overwhelmed with admiration for the zeal displayed in your sixtyfour counts; but in accusing a heretic, as in other things, enough is enough. Also you must remember that all the members of the court are not so subtle and profound as you, and that some of your very great learning might appear to them to be very great nonsense. Therefore I have thought it well to have your sixtyfour articles cut down to twelve—

COURCELLES [*thunderstruck*] Twelve!!!

THE INQUISITOR. Twelve will, believe me, be quite enough for your purpose.

THE CHAPLAIN. But some of the most important points have been reduced almost to nothing. For instance, The Maid has actually declared that the blessed saints Margaret and Catherine, and the holy Archangel Michael, spoke to her in French. That is a vital point.

THE INQUISITOR. You think, doubtless, that they should have spoken in Latin?

CAUCHON. No: he thinks they should have spoken in English.

THE CHAPLAIN. Naturally, my lord.

THE INQUISITOR. Well, as we are all here agreed, I think, that these voices of The Maid are the voices of evil spirits tempting her to her damnation, it would not be very courteous to you, Master de Stogumber, or to the King of England, to assume that English is the devil's native language. So let it pass. The matter is not wholly omitted from the twelve articles. Pray take your places, gentlemen; and let us proceed to business.

All who have not taken their seats, do so.

THE CHAPLAIN. Well, I protest. That is all.

COURCELLES. I think it hard that all our work should go for nothing. It is only another example of the diabolical influence which this woman exercises over the court. [*He takes his chair, which is on the Chaplain's right*].

CAUCHON. Do you suggest that I am under diabolical influence?

COURCELLES. I suggest nothing, my lord. But it seems to me that there is a conspiracy here to hush up the fact that The Maid stole the Bishop of Senlis's horse.

CAUCHON [*keeping his temper with difficulty*] This is not a police court. Are we to waste our time on such rubbish?

COURCELLES [*rising, shocked*] My lord: do you call the Bishop's horse rubbish?

THE INQUISITOR [*blandly*] Master de Courcelles: The Maid alleges that she paid handsomely for the Bishop's horse, and that if he did not get the money the fault was not hers. As that may be true, the point is one on which The Maid may well be acquitted.

COURCELLES. Yes, if it were an ordinary horse. But the Bishop's horse! how can she be acquitted for that? [*He sits down again, bewildered and discouraged*].

THE INQUISITOR. I submit to you, with great respect, that if we persist in trying The Maid on trumpery issues on which we may have to declare her innocent, she may escape us on the great main issue of heresy, on which she seems so far to insist on her own guilt. I will ask you, therefore, to say nothing, when The Maid is brought before us, of these stealings of horses, and dancings round fairy trees with the village children, and prayings at haunted wells, and a dozen other things which you were diligently inquiring into until my arrival. There is not a village girl in France against whom you could not prove such things: they all dance round haunted trees, and pray at magic wells. Some of them would steal the Pope's horse if they got the chance. Heresy, gentlemen, heresy is the charge we have to try. The detection and suppression of heresy is my peculiar business: I am here as an inquisitor, not as an ordinary magistrate. Stick to the heresy, gentlemen; and leave the other matters alone.

CAUCHON. I may say that we have sent to the girl's village to make inquiries about her; and there is practically nothing serious against her.

THE CHAPLAIN *[rising and* Nothing serious, COURCELLES *clamoring* my lord—*together]* What! The fairy tree not—

CAUCHON *[out of patience]* Be silent, gentlemen; or speak one at a time.

Courcelles collapses into his chair, intimidated.

THE CHAPLAIN *[sulkily resuming his seat]* That is what The Maid said to us last Friday.

CAUCHON. I wish you had followed her counsel, sir. When I say nothing serious, I mean nothing that men of sufficiently large mind to conduct an inquiry like this would consider serious. I agree with my colleague the Inquisitor that it is on the count of heresy that we must proceed.

LADVENU *[a young but ascetically fine-drawn Dominican who is sitting next Courcelles, on his right]* But is there any great harm in the girl's heresy? Is it not merely her simplicity? Many saints have said as much as Joan.

THE INQUISITOR *[dropping his blandness and speaking very gravely]* Brother Martin: if you had seen what I have seen of heresy, you would not think it a light thing even in its most apparently harmless and even lovable and pious origins. Heresy begins with people who are to all appearance better than their neighbours. A gentle and pious girl, or a young man who has obeyed the command of our Lord by giving all his riches to the poor, and putting on the garb of poverty, the life of austerity, and the rule of humility and charity, may be the founder of a heresy that will wreck both Church and Empire if not ruthlessly stamped out in time. The records of the holy Inquisition are full of histories we dare not give to the world, because they are beyond the belief of honest men and innocent women; yet they all began with saintly simpletons. I have seen this again and again. Mark what I say: the woman who quarrels with her clothes, and puts on the dress of a man, is like the man who throws off his fur gown and dresses like John the Baptist: they are followed, as surely as the night follows the day, by bands of wild women and men who refuse to wear any clothes at all. When maids will neither marry nor take regular vows, and men reject marriage and exalt their lusts into divine inspirations, then, as surely as the summer follows the spring, they begin with polygamy, and end by incest. Heresy at first seems innocent and even laudable; but it ends in such a monstrous horror of unnatural wickedness that the most tender-hearted among you, if you saw it at work as I have seen it, would clamor against the mercy of the Church in dealing with it. For two hundred years the Holy Office has striven with these diabolical madnesses; and it knows that they begin always by vain and ignorant persons setting up their own judgment against the Church, and taking it upon themselves to be the interpreters of God's will. You must not fall into the common error of mistaking these simpletons for liars and hypocrites. They believe honestly and sincerely that their diabolical inspiration is divine. Therefore you must be on your guard against your natural compassion. You are all, I hope, merciful men: how else could you have devoted your lives to the service of our gentle Savior? You are going to see before you a young girl, pious and chaste; for I must tell you, gentlemen, that the things said of her by our English friends are supported by no evidence, whilst there is abundant testimony that her excesses have been excesses of religion and charity and not of worldliness and wantonness. This girl is not one of those whose hard features are the sign of hard hearts, and whose brazen looks and lewd demeanor condemn them before they are accused. The devilish pride that has led her into her present peril has left no mark on her countenance. Strange as it may seem to you,

2 K

it has even left no mark on her character outside those special matters in which she is proud ; so that you will see a diabolical pride and a natural humility seated side by side in the selfsame soul. Therefore be on your guard. God forbid that I should tell you to harden your hearts; for her punishment if we condemn her will be so cruel that we should forfeit our own hope of divine mercy were there one grain of malice against her in our hearts. But if you hate cruelty—and if any man here does not hate it I command him on his soul's salvation to quit this holy court—I say, if you hate cruelty, remember that nothing is so cruel in its consequences as the toleration of heresy. Remember also that no court of law can be so cruel as the common people are to those whom they suspect of heresy. The heretic in the hands of the Holy Office is safe from violence, is assured of a fair trial, and cannot suffer death, even when guilty, if repentance follows sin. Innumerable lives of heretics have been saved because the Holy Office has taken them out of the hands of the people, and because the people have yielded them up, knowing that the Holy Office would deal with them. Before the Holy Inquisition existed, and even now when its officers are not within reach, the unfortunate wretch suspected of heresy, perhaps quite ignorantly and unjustly, is stoned, torn in pieces, drowned, burned in his house with all his innocent children, without a trial, unshriven, unburied save as a dog is buried: all of them deeds hateful to God and most cruel to man. Gentlemen: I am compassionate by nature as well as by my profession; and though the work I have to do may seem cruel to those who do not know how much more cruel it would be to leave it undone, I would go to the stake myself sooner than do it if I did not know its righteousness, its necessity, its essential mercy. I ask you to address yourself to this trial in that conviction. Anger is a bad counsellor: cast out anger. Pity is sometimes worse: cast out pity. But do not cast out mercy. Remember only that justice comes first. Have you anything to say, my lord, before we proceed to trial?

CAUCHON. You have spoken for me, and spoken better than I could. I do not see how any sane man could disagree with a word that has fallen from you. But this I will add. The crude heresies of which you have told us are horrible; but their horror is like that of the black death: they rage for a while and then die out, because sound and sensible men will not under any incitement be reconciled to nakedness and incest and polygamy and the like. But we are confronted today throughout Europe with a heresy that is spreading among men not weak in mind nor diseased in brain: nay, the stronger the mind, the more obstinate the heretic. It is neither discredited by fantastic extremes nor corrupted by the common lusts of the flesh; but it, too, sets up the private judgment of the single erring mortal against the considered wisdom and experience of the Church. The mighty structure of Catholic Christendom will never be shaken by naked madmen or by the sins of Moab and Ammon. But it may be betrayed from within, and brought to barbarous ruin and desolation, by this arch heresy which the English Commander calls Protestantism.

THE ASSESSORS [*whispering*] Protestantism! What was that! What does the Bishop mean? Is it a new heresy? The English Commander, he said. Did you ever hear of Protestantism? etc., etc.

CAUCHON [*continuing*] And that reminds me. What provision has the Earl of Warwick made for the defence of the secular arm should The Maid prove obdurate, and the people be moved to pity her?

THE CHAPLAIN. Have no fear on that score, my lord. The noble earl has eight hundred men-at-arms at the gates. She will not slip through our English fingers even if the whole city be on her side.

CAUCHON [*revolted*] Will you not add, God grant that she repent and purge her sin?

THE CHAPLAIN. That does not seem to me to be consistent; but of course I agree with your lordship.

CAUCHON [*giving him up with a shrug of contempt*] The court sits.

THE INQUISITOR. Let the accused be brought in.

LADVENU [*calling*] The accused. Let her be brought in.

Joan, chained by the ankles, is brought in through the arched door behind the prisoner's stool by a guard of English soldiers. With them is the Executioner and his assistants. They lead her to the prisoner's stool, and place themselves behind it after taking off her chain. She wears a page's black suit. Her long imprisonment and the strain of the examinations which have pre-

ceded the trial have left their mark on her; but her vitality still holds: she confronts the court unabashed, without a trace of the awe which their formal solemnity seems to require for the complete success of its impressiveness.

THE INQUISITOR [*kindly*] Sit down, Joan. [*She sits on the prisoner's stool*]. You look very pale today. Are you not well?

JOAN. Thank you kindly: I am well enough. But the Bishop sent me some carp; and it made me ill.

CAUCHON. I am sorry. I told them to see that it was fresh.

JOAN. You meant to be good to me, I know; but it is a fish that does not agree with me. The English thought you were trying to poison me—

CAUCHON }[*together*]{ What!
THE CHAPLAIN }[*together*]{ No, my lord.

JOAN [*continuing*] They are determined that I shall be burnt as a witch; and they sent their doctor to cure me; but he was forbidden to bleed me because the silly people believe that a witch's witchery leaves her if she is bled: so he only called me filthy names. Why do you leave me in the hands of the English? I should be in the hands of the Church. And why must I be chained by the feet to a log of wood? Are you afraid I will fly away?

D'ESTIVET [*harshly*] Woman: it is not for you to question the court: it is for us to question you.

COURCELLES. When you were left unchained, did you not try to escape by jumping from a tower sixty feet high? If you cannot fly like a witch, how is it that you are still alive?

JOAN. I suppose because the tower was not so high then. It has grown higher every day since you began asking me questions about it.

D'ESTIVET. Why did you jump from the tower?

JOAN. How do you know that I jumped?

D'ESTIVET. You were found lying in the moat. Why did you leave the tower?

JOAN. Why would anybody leave a prison if they could get out?

D'ESTIVET. You tried to escape?

JOAN. Of course I did; and not for the first time either. If you leave the door of the cage open the bird will fly out.

D'ESTIVET [*rising*] That is a confession of heresy. I call the attention of the court to it.

JOAN. Heresy, he calls it! Am I a heretic because I try to escape from prison?

D'ESTIVET. Assuredly, if you are in the hands of the Church, and you wilfully take yourself out of its hands, you are deserting the Church; and that is heresy.

JOAN. It is great nonsense. Nobody could be such a fool as to think that.

D'ESTIVET. You hear, my lord, how I am reviled in the execution of my duty by this woman. [*He sits down indignantly*].

CAUCHON. I have warned you before, Joan, that you are doing yourself no good by these pert answers.

JOAN. But you will not talk sense to me. I am reasonable if you will be reasonable.

THE INQUISITOR [*interposing*] This is not yet in order. You forget, Master Promoter, that the proceedings have not been formally opened. The time for questions is after she has sworn on the Gospels to tell us the whole truth.

JOAN. You say this to me every time. I have said again and again that I will tell you all that concerns this trial. But I cannot tell you the whole truth : God does not allow the whole truth to be told. You do not understand it when I tell it. It is an old saying that he who tells too much truth is sure to be hanged. I am weary of this argument : we have been over it nine times already. I have sworn as much as I will swear; and I will swear no more.

COURCELLES. My lord: she should be put to the torture.

THE INQUISITOR. You hear, Joan? That is what happens to the obdurate. Think before you answer. Has she been shewn the instruments?

THE EXECUTIONER. They are ready, my lord. She has seen them.

JOAN. If you tear me limb from limb until you separate my soul from my body you will get nothing out of me beyond what I have told you. What more is there to tell that you could understand? Besides, I cannot bear to be hurt; and if you hurt me I will say anything you like to stop the pain. But I will take it all back afterwards; so what is the use of it?

LADVENU. There is much in that. We should proceed mercifully.

COURCELLES. But the torture is customary.

THE INQUISITOR. It must not be applied wantonly. If the accused will confess voluntarily, then its use cannot be justified.

COURCELLES. But this is unusual and irregular. She refuses to take the oath.

LADVENU [disgusted] Do you want to torture the girl for the mere pleasure of it?

COURCELLES [bewildered] But it is not a pleasure. It is the law. It is customary. It is always done.

THE INQUISITOR. That is not so, Master, except when the inquiries are carried on by people who do not know their legal business.

COURCELLES. But the woman is a heretic. I assure you it is always done.

CAUCHON [decisively] It will not be done to-day if it is not necessary. Let there be an end of this. I will not have it said that we proceeded on forced confessions. We have sent our best preachers and doctors to this woman to exhort and implore her to save her soul and body from the fire : we shall not now send the executioner to thrust her into it.

COURCELLES. Your lordship is merciful, of course. But it is a great responsibility to depart from the usual practice.

JOAN. Thou art a rare noodle, Master. Do what was done last time is thy rule, eh?

COURCELLES [rising] Thou wanton: dost thou dare call me noodle?

THE INQUISITOR. Patience, Master, patience: I fear you will soon be only too terribly avenged.

COURCELLES [mutters] Noodle indeed! [He sits down, much discontented].

THE INQUISITOR. Meanwhile, let us not be moved by the rough side of a shepherd lass's tongue.

JOAN. Nay: I am no shepherd lass, though I have helped with the sheep like anyone else. I will do a lady's work in the house—spin or weave—against any woman in Rouen.

THE INQUISITOR. This is not a time for vanity, Joan. You stand in great peril.

JOAN. I know it: have I not been punished for my vanity? If I had not worn my cloth of gold surcoat in battle like a fool, that Burgundian soldier would never have pulled me backwards off my horse; and I should not have been here.

THE CHAPLAIN. If you are so clever at woman's work why do you not stay at home and do it?

JOAN. There are plenty of other women to do it; but there is nobody to do my work.

CAUCHON. Come! we are wasting time on trifles. Joan: I am going to put a most solemn question to you. Take care how you answer; for your life and salvation are at stake on it. Will you for all you have said and done, be it good or bad, accept the judgment of God's Church on earth? More especially as to the acts and words that are imputed to you in this trial by the Promoter here, will you submit your case to the inspired interpretation of the Church Militant?

JOAN. I am a faithful child of the Church. I will obey the Church—

CAUCHON [hopefully leaning forward] You will?

JOAN. —provided it does not command anything impossible.

Cauchon sinks back in his chair with a heavy sigh. The Inquisitor purses his lips and frowns. Ladvenu shakes his head pitifully.

D'ESTIVET. She imputes to the Church the error and folly of commanding the impossible.

JOAN. If you command me to declare that all that I have done and said, and all the visions and revelations I have had, were not from God, then that is impossible: I will not declare it for anything in the world. What God made me do I will never go back on; and what He has commanded or shall command I will not fail to do in spite of any man alive. That is what I mean by impossible. And in case the Church should bid me do anything contrary to the command I have from God, I will not consent to it, no matter what it may be.

THE ASSESSORS [shocked and indignant] Oh! The Church contrary to God! What do you say now? Flat heresy. This is beyond everything, etc., etc.

D'ESTIVET [throwing down his brief] My lord: do you need anything more than this?

CAUCHON. Woman: you have said enough to burn ten heretics. Will you not be warned? Will you not understand?

THE INQUISITOR. If the Church Militant tells you that your revelations and visions are sent by the devil to tempt you to your damnation, will you not believe that the Church is wiser than you?

JOAN. I believe that God is wiser than I; and it is His commands that I will do. All the things that you call my crimes have come to me by the command of God. I say that I have done them by the order of God: it is impossible for me to say anything else. If any Churchman says the contrary I shall not mind him: I shall mind God alone, whose command I always follow.

LADVENU [*pleading with her urgently*] You do not know what you are saying, child. Do you want to kill yourself? Listen. Do you not believe that you are subject to the Church of God on earth?

JOAN. Yes. When have I ever denied it?

LADVENU. Good. That means, does it not, that you are subject to our Lord the Pope, to the cardinals, the archbishops, and the bishops for whom his lordship stands here today?

JOAN. God must be served first.

D'ESTIVET. Then your voices command you not to submit yourself to the Church Militant?

JOAN. My voices do not tell me to disobey the Church; but God must be served first.

CAUCHON. And you, and not the Church, are to be the judge?

JOAN. What other judgment can I judge by but my own?

THE ASSESSORS [*scandalized*] Oh! [*They cannot find words*].

CAUCHON. Out of your own mouth you have condemned yourself. We have striven for your salvation to the verge of sinning ourselves: we have opened the door to you again and again; and you have shut it in our faces and in the face of God. Dare you pretend, after what you have said, that you are in a state of grace?

JOAN. If I am not, may God bring me to it: if I am, may God keep me in it!

LADVENU. That is a very good reply, my lord.

COURCELLES. Were you in a state of grace when you stole the Bishop's horse?

CAUCHON [*rising in a fury*] Oh, devil take the Bishop's horse and you too! We are here to try a case of heresy; and no sooner do we come to the root of the matter than we are thrown back by idiots who understand nothing but horses. [*Trembling with rage, he forces himself to sit down*].

THE INQUISITOR. Gentlemen, gentlemen: in clinging to these small issues you are The Maid's best advocates. I am not surprised that his lordship has lost patience with you. What does the Promoter say? Does he press these trumpery matters?

D'ESTIVET. I am bound by my office to press everything; but when the woman confesses a heresy that must bring upon her the doom of excommunication, of what consequence is it that she has been guilty also of offences which expose her to minor penances?

I share the impatience of his lordship as to these minor charges. Only, with great respect, I must emphasize the gravity of two very horrible and blasphemous crimes which she does not deny. First, she has intercourse with evil spirits, and is therefore a sorceress. Second, she wears men's clothes, which is indecent, unnatural, and abominable; and in spite of our most earnest remonstrances and entreaties, she will not change them even to receive the sacrament.

JOAN. Is the blessed St Catherine an evil spirit? Is St Margaret? Is Michael the Archangel?

COURCELLES. How do you know that the spirit which appears to you is an archangel? Does he not appear to you as a naked man?

JOAN. Do you think God cannot afford clothes for him?

The assessors cannot help smiling, especially as the joke is against Courcelles.

LADVENU. Well answered, Joan.

THE INQUISITOR. It is, in effect, well answered. But no evil spirit would be so simple as to appear to a young girl in a guise that would scandalize her when he meant her to take him for a messenger from the Most High? Joan: the Church instructs you that these apparitions are demons seeking your soul's perdition. Do you accept the instruction of the Church?

JOAN. I accept the messenger of God. How could any faithful believer in the Church refuse him?

CAUCHON. Wretched woman: again I ask you, do you know what you are saying?

THE INQUISITOR. You wrestle in vain with the devil for her soul, my lord: she will not be saved. Now as to this matter of the man's dress. For the last time, will you put off that impudent attire, and dress as becomes your sex?

JOAN. I will not.

D'ESTIVET [*pouncing*] The sin of disobedience, my lord.

JOAN [*distressed*] But my voices tell me I must dress as a soldier.

LADVENU. Joan, Joan: does not that prove to you that the voices are the voices of evil spirits? Can you suggest to us one good reason why an angel of God should give you such shameless advice?

JOAN. Why, yes: what can be plainer commonsense? I was a soldier living among soldiers. I am a prisoner guarded by soldiers.

If I were to dress as a woman they would think of me as a woman; and then what would become of me? If I dress as a soldier they think of me as a soldier, and I can live with them as I do at home with my brothers. That is why St Catherine tells me I must not dress as a woman until she gives me leave.

COURCELLES. When will she give you leave?

JOAN. When you take me out of the hands of the English soldiers. I have told you that I should be in the hands of the Church, and not left night and day with four soldiers of the Earl of Warwick. Do you want me to live with them in petticoats?

LADVENU. My lord: what she says is, God knows, very wrong and shocking; but there is a grain of worldly sense in it such as might impose on a simple village maiden.

JOAN. If we were as simple in the village as you are in your courts and palaces, there would soon be no wheat to make bread for you.

CAUCHON. That is the thanks you get for trying to save her, Brother Martin.

LADVENU. Joan: we are all trying to save you. His lordship is trying to save you. The Inquisitor could not be more just to you if you were his own daughter. But you are blinded by a terrible pride and self-sufficiency.

JOAN. Why do you say that? I have said nothing wrong. I cannot understand.

THE INQUISITOR. The blessed St Athanasius has laid it down in his creed that those who cannot understand are damned. It is not enough to be simple. It is not enough even to be what simple people call good. The simplicity of a darkened mind is no better than the simplicity of a beast.

JOAN. There is great wisdom in the simplicity of a beast, let me tell you; and sometimes great foolishness in the wisdom of scholars.

LADVENU. We know that, Joan: we are not so foolish as you think us. Try to resist the temptation to make pert replies to us. Do you see that man who stands behind you [he indicates the Executioner]?

JOAN [turning and looking at the man] Your torturer? But the Bishop said I was not to be tortured.

LADVENU. You are not to be tortured because you have confessed everything that is necessary to your condemnation. That man is not only the torturer: he is also the Executioner. Executioner: let The Maid hear your answers to my questions. Are you

prepared for the burning of a heretic this day?

THE EXECUTIONER. Yes, Master.

LADVENU. Is the stake ready?

THE EXECUTIONER. It is. In the market-place. The English have built it too high for me to get near her and make the death easier. It will be a cruel death.

JOAN [horrified] But you are not going to burn me now?

THE INQUISITOR. You realize it at last.

LADVENU. There are eight hundred English soldiers waiting to take you to the market-place the moment the sentence of excommunication has passed the lips of your judges. You are within a few short moments of that doom.

JOAN [looking round desperately for rescue] Oh God!

LADVENU. Do not despair, Joan. The Church is merciful. You can save yourself.

JOAN [hopefully] Yes: my voices promised me I should not be burnt. St Catherine bade me be bold.

CAUCHON. Woman: are you quite mad? Do you not yet see that your voices have deceived you?

JOAN. Oh no: that is impossible.

CAUCHON. Impossible! They have led you straight to your excommunication, and to the stake which is there waiting for you.

LADVENU [pressing the point hard] Have they kept a single promise to you since you were taken at Compiègne? The devil has betrayed you. The Church holds out its arms to you.

JOAN [despairing] Oh, it is true: it is true: my voices have deceived me. I have been mocked by devils: my faith is broken. I have dared and dared; but only a fool will walk into a fire: God, who gave me my common-sense, cannot will me to do that.

LADVENU. Now God be praised that He has saved you at the eleventh hour! [He hurries to the vacant seat at the scribes' table, and snatches a sheet of paper, on which he sets to work writing eagerly].

CAUCHON. Amen!

JOAN. What must I do?

CAUCHON. You must sign a solemn recantation of your heresy.

JOAN. Sign? That means to write my name. I cannot write.

CAUCHON. You have signed many letters before.

JOAN. Yes; but someone held my hand and

guided the pen. I can make my mark.

THE CHAPLAIN [*who has been listening with growing alarm and indignation*] My lord: do you mean that you are going to allow this woman to escape us?

THE INQUISITOR. The law must take its course, Master de Stogumber. And you know the law.

THE CHAPLAIN [*rising, purple with fury*] I know that there is no faith in a Frenchman. [*Tumult, which he shouts down*]. I know what my lord the Cardinal of Winchester will say when he hears of this. I know what the Earl of Warwick will do when he learns that you intend to betray him. There are eight hundred men at the gate who will see that this abominable witch is burnt in spite of your teeth.

THE ASSESSORS [*meanwhile*] What is this? What did he say? He accuses us of treachery! This is past bearing. No faith in a Frenchman! Did you hear that? This is an intolerable fellow. Who is he? Is this what English Churchmen are like? He must be mad or drunk, etc., etc.

THE INQUISITOR [*rising*] Silence, pray! Gentlemen: pray silence! Master Chaplain: bethink you a moment of your holy office: of what you are, and where you are. I direct you to sit down.

THE CHAPLAIN [*folding his arms doggedly, his face working convulsively*] I will NOT sit down.

CAUCHON. Master Inquisitor: this man has called me a traitor to my face before now.

THE CHAPLAIN. So you are a traitor. You are all traitors. You have been doing nothing but begging this damnable witch on your knees to recant all through this trial.

THE INQUISITOR [*placidly resuming his seat*] If you will not sit, you must stand: that is all.

THE CHAPLAIN. I will NOT stand [*he flings himself back into his chair*].

LADVENU [*rising with the paper in his hand*] My lord: here is the form of recantation for The Maid to sign.

CAUCHON. Read it to her.

JOAN. Do not trouble. I will sign it.

THE INQUISITOR. Woman: you must know what you are putting your hand to. Read it to her, Brother Martin. And let all be silent.

LADVENU [*reading quietly*] "I, Joan, commonly called The Maid, a miserable sinner, do confess that I have most grievously sinned in the following articles. I have pretended to have revelations from God and the angels and the blessed saints, and perversely rejected the Church's warnings that these were temptations by demons. I have blasphemed abominably by wearing an immodest dress, contrary to the Holy Scripture and the canons of the Church. Also I have clipped my hair in the style of a man, and, against all the duties which have made my sex specially acceptable in heaven, have taken up the sword, even to the shedding of human blood, inciting men to slay each other, invoking evil spirits to delude them, and stubbornly and most blasphemously imputing these sins to Almighty God. I confess to the sin of sedition, to the sin of idolatry, to the sin of disobedience, to the sin of pride, and to the sin of heresy. All of which sins I now renounce and abjure and depart from, humbly thanking you Doctors and Masters who have brought me back to the truth and into the grace of our Lord. And I will never return to my errors, but will remain in communion with our Holy Church and in obedience to our Holy Father the Pope of Rome. All this I swear by God Almighty and the Holy Gospels, in witness whereto I sign my name to this recantation."

THE INQUISITOR. You understand this, Joan?

JOAN [*listless*] It is plain enough, sir.

THE INQUISITOR. And it is true?

JOAN. It may be true. If it were not true, the fire would not be ready for me in the market-place.

LADVENU [*taking up his pen and a book, and going to her quickly lest she should compromise herself again*] Come, child: let me guide your hand. Take the pen. [*She does so; and they begin to write, using the book as a desk*] J.E.H.A.N.E. So. Now make your mark by yourself.

JOAN [*makes her mark, and gives him back the pen, tormented by the rebellion of her soul against her mind and body*] There!

LADVENU [*replacing the pen on the table, and handing the recantation to Cauchon with a reverence*] Praise be to God, my brothers, the lamb has returned to the flock; and the shepherd rejoices in her more than in ninety and nine just persons. [*He returns to his seat*].

THE INQUISITOR [*taking the paper from Cauchon*] We declare thee by this act set free from the danger of excommunication in which thou stoodest. [*He throws the paper down to the table*].

JOAN. I thank you.

THE INQUISITOR. But because thou hast sinned most presumptuously against God and the Holy Church, and that thou mayst repent thy errors in solitary contemplation, and be shielded from all temptation to return to them, we, for the good of thy soul, and for a penance that may wipe out thy sins and bring thee finally unspotted to the throne of grace, do condemn thee to eat the bread of sorrow and drink the water of affliction to the end of thy earthly days in perpetual imprisonment.

JOAN [*rising in consternation and terrible anger*] Perpetual imprisonment! Am I not then to be set free?

LADVENU [*mildly shocked*] Set free, child, after such wickedness as yours! What are you dreaming of?

JOAN. Give me that writing. [*She rushes to the table; snatches up the paper; and tears it into fragments*] Light your fire: do you think I dread it as much as the life of a rat in a hole? My voices were right!

LADVENU. Joan! Joan!

JOAN. Yes: they told me you were fools [*the word gives great offence*], and that I was not to listen to your fine words nor trust to your charity. You promised me my life; but you lied [*indignant exclamations*]. You think that life is nothing but not being stone dead. It is not the bread and water I fear: I can live on bread: when have I asked for more? It is no hardship to drink water if the water be clean. Bread has no sorrow for me, and water no affliction. But to shut me from the light of the sky and the sight of the fields and flowers; to chain my feet so that I can never again ride with the soldiers nor climb the hills; to make me breathe foul damp darkness, and keep from me everything that brings me back to the love of God when your wickedness and foolishness tempt me to hate Him: all this is worse than the furnace in the Bible that was heated seven times. I could do without my warhorse; I could drag about in a skirt; I could let the banners and the trumpets and the knights and soldiers pass me and leave me behind as they leave the other women, if only I could still hear the wind in the trees, the larks in the sunshine, the young lambs crying through the healthy frost, and the blessed blessed church bells that send my angel voices floating to me on the wind. But without these things I cannot live; and by your wanting to take them away from me, or from any human creature, I know that your counsel is of the devil, and that mine is of God.

THE ASSESSORS [*in great commotion*] Blasphemy! blasphemy! She is possessed. She said our counsel was of the devil. And hers of God. Monstrous! The devil is in our midst, etc., etc.

D'ESTIVET [*shouting above the din*] She is a relapsed heretic, obstinate, incorrigible, and altogether unworthy of the mercy we have shewn her. I call for her excommunication.

THE CHAPLAIN [*to the Executioner*] Light your fire, man. To the stake with her.

The Executioner and his assistants hurry out through the courtyard.

LADVENU. You wicked girl: if your counsel were of God would He not deliver you?

JOAN. His ways are not your ways. He wills that I go through the fire to His bosom; for I am His child, and you are not fit that I should live among you. That is my last word to you.

The soldiers seize her.

CAUCHON [*rising*] Not yet.

They wait. There is a dead silence. Cauchon turns to the Inquisitor with an inquiring look. The Inquisitor nods affirmatively. They rise solemnly, and intone the sentence antiphonally.

CAUCHON. We decree that thou art a relapsed heretic.

THE INQUISITOR. Cast out from the unity of the Church.

CAUCHON. Sundered from her body.

THE INQUISITOR. Infected with the leprosy of heresy.

CAUCHON. A member of Satan.

THE INQUISITOR. We declare that thou must be excommunicate.

CAUCHON. And now we do cast thee out, segregate thee, and abandon thee to the secular power.

THE INQUISITOR. Admonishing the same secular power that it moderate its judgment of thee in respect of death and division of the limbs. [*He resumes his seat*].

CAUCHON. And if any true sign of penitence appear in thee, to permit our Brother Martin to administer to thee the sacrament of penance.

THE CHAPLAIN. Into the fire with the witch [*he rushes at her, and helps the soldiers to push her out*].

*Joan is taken away through the courtyard.
The assessors rise in disorder, and follow the
soldiers, except Ladvenu, who has hidden his
face in his hands.*

CAUCHON [*rising again in the act of sitting
down*] No, no: this is irregular. The representative of the secular arm should be here
to receive her from us.

THE INQUISITOR [*also on his feet again*] That
man is an incorrigible fool.

CAUCHON. Brother Martin: see that everything is done in order.

LADVENU. My place is at her side, my lord.
You must exercise your own authority. [*He
hurries out*].

CAUCHON. These English are impossible:
they will thrust her straight into the fire.
Look!

*He points to the courtyard, in which the glow
and flicker of fire can now be seen reddening the
May daylight. Only the Bishop and the Inquisitor are left in the court.*

CAUCHON [*turning to go*] We must stop that.

THE INQUISITOR [*calmly*] Yes; but not too
fast, my lord.

CAUCHON [*halting*] But there is not a moment
to lose.

THE INQUISITOR. We have proceeded in
perfect order. If the English choose to put
themselves in the wrong, it is not our business to put them in the right. A flaw in the
procedure may be useful later on: one never
knows. And the sooner it is over, the better
for that poor girl.

CAUCHON [*relaxing*] That is true. But I
suppose we must see this dreadful thing
through.

THE INQUISITOR. One gets used to it. Habit
is everything. I am accustomed to the fire:
it is soon over. But it is a terrible thing to see
a young and innocent creature crushed between these mighty forces, the Church and
the Law.

CAUCHON. You call her innocent!

THE INQUISITOR. Oh, quite innocent. What
does she know of the Church and the Law?
She did not understand a word we were
saying. It is the ignorant who suffer. Come,
or we shall be late for the end.

CAUCHON [*going with him*] I shall not be
sorry if we are: I am not so accustomed as you.

*They are going out when Warwick comes in,
meeting them.*

WARWICK. Oh, I am intruding. I thought
it was all over. [*He makes a feint of retiring*].

CAUCHON. Do not go, my lord. It is all over.

THE INQUISITOR. The execution is not in
our hands, my lord; but it is desirable that
we should witness the end. So by your leave
—[*He bows, and goes out through the courtyard*].

CAUCHON. There is some doubt whether
your people have observed the forms of law,
my lord.

WARWICK. I am told that there is some
doubt whether your authority runs in this
city, my lord. It is not in your diocese. However, if you will answer for that I will answer
for the rest.

CAUCHON. It is to God that we both must
answer. Good morning, my lord.

WARWICK. My lord: good morning.

*They look at one another for a moment with
unconcealed hostility. Then Cauchon follows
the Inquisitor out. Warwick looks round. Finding
himself alone, he calls for attendance.*

WARWICK. Hallo: some attendance here!
[*Silence*]. Hallo, there! [*Silence*]. Hallo! Brian,
you young blackguard, where are you?
[*Silence*]. Guard! [*Silence*]. They have all gone
to see the burning: even that child.

*The silence is broken by someone frantically
howling and sobbing.*

WARWICK. What in the devil's name—?

*The Chaplain staggers in from the courtyard
like a demented creature, his face streaming with
tears, making the piteous sounds that Warwick
has heard. He stumbles to the prisoner's stool,
and throws himself upon it with heartrending
sobs.*

WARWICK [*going to him and patting him on the
shoulder*] What is it, Master John? What is
the matter?

THE CHAPLAIN [*clutching at his hands*] My
lord, my lord: for Christ's sake pray for my
wretched guilty soul.

WARWICK [*soothing him*] Yes, yes: of course
I will. Calmly, gently—

THE CHAPLAIN [*blubbering miserably*] I am
not a bad man, my lord.

WARWICK. No, no: not at all.

THE CHAPLAIN. I meant no harm. I did not
know what it would be like.

WARWICK [*hardening*] Oh! You saw it, then?

THE CHAPLAIN. I did not know what I was
doing. I am a hotheaded fool; and I shall be
damned to all eternity for it.

WARWICK. Nonsense! Very distressing, no
doubt; but it was not your doing.

THE CHAPLAIN [*lamentably*] I let them do it.

2 K 2

If I had known, I would have torn her from their hands. You dont know: you havnt seen: it is so easy to talk when you dont know. You madden yourself with words: you damn yourself because it feels grand to throw oil on the flaming hell of your own temper. But when it is brought home to you; when you see the thing you have done; when it is blinding your eyes, stifling your nostrils, tearing your heart, then — then — [*Falling on his knees*] O God, take away this sight from me! O Christ, deliver me from this fire that is consuming me! She cried to Thee in the midst of it: Jesus! Jesus! Jesus! She is in Thy bosom; and I am in hell for evermore.

WARWICK [*summarily hauling him to his feet*] Come come, man! you must pull yourself together. We shall have the whole town talking of this. [*He throws him not too gently into a chair at the table*] If you have not the nerve to see these things, why do you not do as I do, and stay away?

THE CHAPLAIN [*bewildered and submissive*] She asked for a cross. A soldier gave her two sticks tied together. Thank God he was an Englishman! I might have done it; but I did not: I am a coward, a mad dog, a fool. But he was an Englishman too.

WARWICK. The fool! they will burn him too if the priests get hold of him.

THE CHAPLAIN [*shaken with a convulsion*] Some of the people laughed at her. They would have laughed at Christ. They were French people, my lord: I know they were French.

WARWICK. Hush? someone is coming. Control yourself.

Ladvenu comes back through the courtyard to Warwick's right hand, carrying a bishop's cross which he has taken from a church. He is very grave and composed.

WARWICK. I am informed that it is all over, Brother Martin.

LADVENU [*enigmatically*] We do not know, my lord. It may have only just begun.

WARWICK. What does that mean, exactly?

LADVENU. I took this cross from the church for her that she might see it to the last: she had only two sticks that she put into her bosom. When the fire crept round us, and she saw that if I held the cross before her I should be burnt myself, she warned me to get down and save myself. My lord: a girl who could think of another's danger in such a moment was not inspired by the devil.

When I had to snatch the cross from her sight, she looked up to heaven. And I do not believe that the heavens were empty. I firmly believe that her Savior appeared to her then in His tenderest glory. She called to Him and died. This is not the end for her, but the beginning.

WARWICK. I am afraid it will have a bad effect on the people.

LADVENU. It had, my lord, on some of them. I heard laughter. Forgive me for saying that I hope and believe it was English laughter.

THE CHAPLAIN [*rising frantically*] No: it was not. There was only one Englishman there that disgraced his country; and that was the mad dog, de Stogumber. [*He rushes wildly out, shrieking*] Let them torture him. Let them burn him. I will go pray among her ashes. I am no better than Judas: I will hang myself.

WARWICK. Quick, Brother Martin: follow him: he will do himself some mischief. After him, quick.

Ladvenu hurries out, Warwick urging him. The Executioner comes in by the door behind the judges' chairs; and Warwick, returning, finds himself face to face with him.

WARWICK. Well, fellow: who are you?

THE EXECUTIONER [*with dignity*] I am not addressed as fellow, my lord. I am the Master Executioner of Rouen: it is a highly skilled mystery. I am come to tell your lordship that your orders have been obeyed.

WARWICK. I crave your pardon, Master Executioner; and I will see that you lose nothing by having no relics to sell. I have your word, have I, that nothing remains, not a bone, not a nail, not a hair?

THE EXECUTIONER. Her heart would not burn, my lord; but everything that was left is at the bottom of the river. You have heard the last of her.

WARWICK [*with a wry smile, thinking of what Ladvenu said*] The last of her? Hm! I wonder!

EPILOGUE

A restless fitfully windy night in June 1456, full of summer lightning after many days of heat. King Charles the Seventh of France, formerly Joan's Dauphin, now Charles the Victorious, aged 51, is in bed in one of his royal chateaux. The bed, raised on a dais of two steps, is towards the side of the room so as to avoid blocking a tall lancet window in the middle.

*Its canopy bears the royal arms in embroidery.
Except for the canopy and the huge down pillows
there is nothing to distinguish it from a broad
settee with bed-clothes and a valance. Thus its
occupant is in full view from the foot.*

*Charles is not asleep: he is reading in bed, or
rather looking at the pictures in Fouquet's
Boccaccio with his knees doubled up to make a
reading desk. Beside the bed on his left is a little
table with a picture of the Virgin, lighted by
candles of painted wax. The walls are hung from
ceiling to floor with painted curtains which stir
at times in the draughts. At first glance the pre-
vailing yellow and red in these hanging pictures
is somewhat flamelike when the folds breathe in
the wind.*

*The door is on Charles's left, but in front of
him close to the corner farthest from him. A large
watchman's rattle, handsomely designed and gaily
painted, is in the bed under his hand.*

*Charles turns a leaf. A distant clock strikes
the half-hour softly. Charles shuts the book with
a clap; throws it aside; snatches up the rattle;
and whirls it energetically, making a deafening
clatter. Ladvenu enters, 25 years older, strange
and stark in bearing, and still carrying the cross
from Rouen. Charles evidently does not expect
him; for he springs out of bed on the farther side
from the door.*

CHARLES. Who are you? Where is my gentleman of the bedchamber? What do you want?

LADVENU [*solemnly*] I bring you glad tidings
of great joy. Rejoice, O king; for the taint is
removed from your blood, and the stain from
your crown. Justice, long delayed, is at last
triumphant.

CHARLES. What are you talking about?
Who are you?

LADVENU. I am brother Martin.

CHARLES. And who, saving your reverence,
may Brother Martin be?

LADVENU. I held this cross when The Maid
perished in the fire. Twenty-five years have
passed since then: nearly ten thousand days.
And on every one of those days I have prayed
God to justify His daughter on earth as she
is justified in heaven.

CHARLES [*reassured, sitting down on the foot
of the bed*] Oh, I remember now. I have heard
of you. You have a bee in your bonnet about
The Maid. Have you been at the inquiry?

LADVENU. I have given my testimony.

CHARLES. Is it over?

LADVENU. It is over.

CHARLES. Satisfactorily?

LADVENU. The ways of God are very strange.

CHARLES. How so?

LADVENU. At the trial which sent a saint to
the stake as a heretic and a sorceress, the
truth was told; the law was upheld; mercy
was shewn beyond all custom; no wrong was
done but the final and dreadful wrong of the
lying sentence and the pitiless fire. At this
inquiry from which I have just come, there
was shameless perjury, courtly corruption,
calumny of the dead who did their duty
according to their lights, cowardly evasion
of the issue, testimony made of idle tales
that could not impose on a ploughboy. Yet
out of this insult to justice, this defamation
of the Church, this orgy of lying and foolishness, the truth is set in the noonday sun on
the hilltop; the white robe of innocence is
cleansed from the smirch of the burning
faggots; the holy flame is sanctified; the
true heart that lived through the flame
is consecrated; a great lie is silenced for
ever; and a great wrong is set right before
all men.

CHARLES. My friend: provided they can no
longer say that I was crowned by a witch
and a heretic, I shall not fuss about how the
trick was done. Joan would not have fussed
about it if it came all right in the end: she
was not that sort: I knew her. Is her rehabilitation complete? I made it pretty clear that
there was to be no nonsense about it.

LADVENU. It is solemnly declared that her
judges were full of corruption, cozenage,
fraud, and malice. Four falsehoods.

CHARLES. Never mind the falsehoods: her
judges are dead.

LADVENU. The sentence on her is broken,
annulled, annihilated, set aside as non-
existent, without value or effect.

CHARLES. Good. Nobody can challenge my
consecration now, can they?

LADVENU. Not Charlemagne nor King
David himself was more sacredly crowned.

CHARLES [*rising*] Excellent. Think of what
that means to me!

LADVENU. I think of what it means to her!

CHARLES. You cannot. None of us ever
knew what anything meant to her. She was
like nobody else; and she must take care of
herself wherever she is; for *I* cannot take
care of her; and neither can you, whatever
you may think: you are not big enough. But
I will tell you this about her. If you could
bring her back to life, they would burn her

again within six months, for all their present adoration of her. And you would hold up the cross, too, just the same. So [*crossing himself*] let her rest; and let you and I mind our own business, and not meddle with hers.

LADVENU. God forbid that I should have no share in her, nor she in me! [*He turns and strides out as he came, saying*] Henceforth my path will not lie through palaces, nor my conversation be with kings.

CHARLES [*following him towards the door, and shouting after him*] Much good may it do you, holy man! [*He returns to the middle of the chamber, where he halts, and says quizzically to himself*] That was a funny chap. How did he get in? Where are my people? [*He goes impatiently to the bed, and swings the rattle. A rush of wind through the open door sets the walls swaying agitatedly. The candles go out. He calls in the darkness*] Hallo! Someone come and shut the windows: everything is being blown all over the place. [*A flash of summer lightning shews up the lancet window. A figure is seen in silhouette against it*] Who is there? Who is that? Help! Murder! [*Thunder. He jumps into bed, and hides under the clothes*].

JOAN'S VOICE. Easy, Charlie, easy. What art making all that noise for? No one can hear thee. Thourt asleep. [*She is dimly seen in a pallid greenish light by the bedside*].

CHARLES [*peeping out*] Joan! Are you a ghost, Joan?

JOAN. Hardly even that, lad. Can a poor burnt-up lass have a ghost? I am but a dream that thourt dreaming. [*The light increases: they become plainly visible as he sits up*] Thou looks older, lad.

CHARLES. I a m older. Am I really asleep?

JOAN. Fallen asleep over thy silly book.

CHARLES. That's funny.

JOAN. Not so funny as that I am dead, is it?

CHARLES. Are you really dead?

JOAN. As dead as anybody ever is, laddie. I am out of the body.

CHARLES. Just fancy! Did it hurt much?

JOAN. Did what hurt much?

CHARLES. Being burnt.

JOAN. Oh, t h a t! I cannot remember very well. I think it did at first; but then it all got mixed up; and I was not in my right mind until I was free of the body. But do not thou go handling fire and thinking it will not hurt thee. How hast been ever since?

CHARLES. Oh, not so bad. Do you know, I actually lead my army out and win battles?

Down into the moat up to my waist in mud and blood. Up the ladders with the stones and hot pitch raining down. Like you.

JOAN. No! Did I make a man of thee after all, Charlie?

CHARLES. I am Charles the Victorious now. I had to be brave because you were. Agnes put a little pluck into me too.

JOAN. Agnes! Who was Agnes?

CHARLES. Agnes Sorel. A woman I fell in love with. I dream of her often. I never dreamed of you before.

JOAN. Is she dead, like me?

CHARLES. Yes. But she was not like you. She was very beautiful.

JOAN [*laughing heartily*] Ha ha! I was no beauty: I was always a rough one: a regular soldier. I might almost as well have been a man. Pity I wasnt: I should not have bothered you all so much then. But my head was in the skies; and the glory of God was upon me; and, man or woman, I should have bothered you as long as your noses were in the mud. Now tell me what has happened since you wise men knew no better than to make a heap of cinders of me?

CHARLES. Your mother and brothers have sued the courts to have your case tried over again. And the courts have declared that your judges were full of corruption and cozenage, fraud and malice.

JOAN. Not they. They were as honest a lot of poor fools as ever burned their betters.

CHARLES. The sentence on you is broken, annihilated, annulled: null, non-existent, without value or effect.

JOAN. I was burned, all the same. Can they unburn me?

CHARLES. If they could, they would think twice before they did it. But they have decreed that a beautiful cross be placed where the stake stood, for your perpetual memory and for your salvation.

JOAN. It is the memory and the salvation that sanctify the cross, not the cross that sanctifies the memory and the salvation. [*She turns away, forgetting him*] I shall outlast that cross. I shall be remembered when men will have forgotten where Rouen stood.

CHARLES. There you go with your self-conceit, the same as ever! I think you might say a word of thanks to me for having had justice done at last.

CAUCHON [*appearing at the window between them*] Liar!

CHARLES. Thank you.

JOAN. Why, if it isnt Peter Cauchon! How are you, Peter? What luck have you had since you burned me?

CAUCHON. None. I arraign the justice of Man. It is not the justice of God.

JOAN. Still dreaming of justice, Peter? See what justice came to with me! But what has happened to thee? Art dead or alive?

CAUCHON. Dead. Dishonored. They pursued me beyond the grave. They excommunicated my dead body: they dug it up and flung it into the common sewer.

JOAN. Your dead body did not feel the spade and the sewer as my live body felt the fire.

CAUCHON. But this thing that they have done against me hurts justice; destroys faith; saps the foundation of the Church. The solid earth sways like the treacherous sea beneath the feet of men and spirits alike when the innocent are slain in the name of law, and their wrongs are undone by slandering the pure of heart.

JOAN. Well, well, Peter, I hope men will be the better for remembering me; and they would not remember me so well if you had not burned me.

CAUCHON. They will be the worse for remembering me: they will see in me evil triumphing over good, falsehood over truth, cruelty over mercy, hell over heaven. Their courage will rise as they think of you, only to faint as they think of me. Yet God is my witness I was just: I was merciful: I was faithful to my light: I could do no other than I did.

CHARLES [scrambling out of the sheets and enthroning himself on the side of the bed] Yes: it is always you good men that do the big mischiefs. Look at me! I am not Charles the Good, nor Charles the Wise, nor Charles the Bold. Joan's worshippers may even call me Charles the Coward because I did not pull her out of the fire. But I have done less harm than any of you. You people with your heads in the sky spend all your time trying to turn the world upside down; but I take the world as it is, and say that top-side-up is right-side-up; and I keep my nose pretty close to the ground. And I ask you, what king of France has done better, or been a better fellow in his little way?

JOAN. Art really king of France, Charlie? Be the English gone?

DUNOIS [coming through the tapestry on Joan's left, the candles relighting themselves at the same moment, and illuminating his armour and surcoat cheerfully] I have kept my word: the English are gone.

JOAN. Praised be God! now is fair France a province in heaven. Tell me all about the fighting, Jack. Was it thou that led them? Wert thou God's captain to thy death?

DUNOIS. I am not dead. My body is very comfortably asleep in my bed at Chateaudun; by my spirit is called here by yours.

JOAN. And you fought them my way, Jack: eh? Not the old way, chaffering for ransoms; but The Maid's way: staking life against death, with the heart high and humble and void of malice, and nothing counting under God but France free and French. Was it my way, Jack?

DUNOIS. Faith, it was any way that would win. But the way that won was always your way. I give you best, lassie. I wrote a fine letter to set you right at the new trial. Perhaps I should never have let the priests burn you; but I was busy fighting; and it was the Church's business, not mine. There was no use in both of us being burned, was there?

CAUCHON. Ay! put the blame on the priests. But I, who am beyond praise and blame, tell you that the world is saved neither by its priests nor its soldiers, but by God and His Saints. The Church Militant sent this woman to the fire; but even as she burned, the flames whitened into the radiance of the Church Triumphant.

The clock strikes the third quarter. A rough male voice is heard trolling an improvised tune.

Rum tum trumpledum,
Bacon fat and rumpledum,
Old Saint mumpledum,
Pull his tail and stumpledum
    O my Ma—ry Ann!

A ruffianly English soldier comes through the curtains and marches between Dunois and Joan.

DUNOIS. What villainous troubadour taught you that doggrel?

THE SOLDIER. No troubadour. We made it up ourselves as we marched. We were not gentlefolks and troubadours. Music straight out of the heart of the people, as you might say. Rum tum trumpledum, Bacon fat and rumpledum, Old Saint mumpledum, Pull his tail and stumpledum: that dont mean anything, you know; but it keeps you marching. Your servant, ladies and gentlemen. Who asked for a saint?

JOAN. Be you a saint?

THE SOLDIER. Yes, lady, straight from hell.

DUNOIS. A saint, and from hell!

THE SOLDIER. Yes, noble captain: I have a day off. Every year, you know. Thats my allowance for my one good action.

CAUCHON. Wretch! In all the years of your life did you do only one good action?

THE SOLDIER. I never thought about it: it came natural like. But they scored it up for me.

CHARLES. What was it?

THE SOLDIER. Why, the silliest thing you ever heard of. I—

JOAN [*interrupting him by strolling across to the bed, where she sits beside Charles*] He tied two sticks together, and gave them to a poor lass that was going to be burned.

THE SOLDIER. Right. Who told you that?

JOAN. Never mind. Would you know her if you saw her again?

THE SOLDIER. Not I. There are so many girls! and they all expect you to remember them as if there was only one in the world. This one must have been a prime sort; for I have a day off every year for her; and so, until twelve o'clock punctually, I am a saint, at your service, noble lords and lovely ladies.

CHARLES. And after twelve?

THE SOLDIER. After twelve, back to the only place fit for the likes of me.

JOAN [*rising*] Back there! You! that gave the lass the cross!

THE SOLDIER [*excusing his unsoldierly conduct*] Well, she asked for it; and they were going to burn her. She had as good a right to a cross as they had; and they had dozens of them. It was her funeral, not theirs. Where was the harm in it?

JOAN. Man: I am not reproaching you. But I cannot bear to think of you in torment.

THE SOLDIER [*cheerfully*] No great torment, lady. You see I was used to worse.

CHARLES. What! worse than hell?

THE SOLDIER. Fifteen years' service in the French wars. Hell was a treat after that.

Joan throws up her arms, and takes refuge from despair of humanity before the picture of the Virgin.

THE SOLDIER [*continuing*]—Suits me somehow. The day off was dull at first, like a wet Sunday. I dont mind it so much now. They tell me I can have as many as I like as soon as I want them.

CHARLES. What is hell like?

THE SOLDIER. You wont find it so bad, sir. Jolly. Like as if you were always drunk without the trouble and expense of drinking. Tip top company too: emperors and popes and kings and all sorts. They chip me about giving that young judy the cross; but I dont care: I stand up to them proper, and tell them that if she hadnt a better right to it than they, she'd be where they are. That dumbfounds them, that does. All they can do is gnash their teeth, hell fashion; and I just laugh and go off singing the old chanty: Rum tum trumple—Hullo! Who's that knocking at the door?

They listen. A long gentle knocking is heard.

CHARLES. Come in.

The door opens; and an old priest, white-haired, bent, with a silly but benevolent smile, comes in and trots over to Joan.

THE NEWCOMER. Excuse me, gentle lords and ladies. Do not let me disturb you. Only a poor old harmless English rector. Formerly chaplain to the cardinal: to my lord of Winchester. John de Stogumber, at your service. [*He looks at them inquiringly*] Did you say anything? I am a little deaf, unfortunately. Also a little—well, not always in my right mind, perhaps; but still, it is a small village with a few simple people. I suffice: I suffice: they love me there: and I am able to do a little good. I am well connected, you see; and they indulge me.

JOAN. Poor old John! What brought thee to this state?

DE STOGUMBER. I tell my folks they must be very careful. I say to them, "If you only saw what you think about you would think quite differently about it. It would give you a great shock. Oh, a great shock." And they all say "Yes, parson: we all know you are a kind man, and would not harm a fly." That is a great comfort to me. For I am not cruel by nature, you know.

THE SOLDIER. Who said you were?

DE STOGUMBER. Well, you see, I did a very cruel thing once because I did not know what cruelty was like. I had not seen it, you know. That is the great thing: you must see it. And then you are redeemed and saved.

CAUCHON. Were not the sufferings of our Lord Christ enough for you?

DE STOGUMBER. No. Oh no: not at all. I had

seen them in pictures, and read of them in books, and been greatly moved by them, as I thought. But it was no use: it was not our Lord that redeemed me, but a young woman whom I saw actually burned to death. It was dreadful: oh, most dreadful. But it saved me. I have been a different man ever since, though a little astray in my wits sometimes.

CAUCHON. Must then a Christ perish in torment in every age to save those that have no imagination?

JOAN. Well, if I saved all those he would have been cruel to if he had not been cruel to me, I was not burnt for nothing, was I?

DE STOGUMBER. Oh no; it was not you. My sight is bad: I cannot distinguish your features: but you are not she: oh no: she was burned to a cinder: dead and gone, dead and gone.

THE EXECUTIONER [stepping from behind the bed curtains on Charles's right, the bed being between them] She is more alive than you, old man. Her heart would not burn; and it would not drown. I was a master at my craft: better than the master of Paris, better than the master of Toulouse; but I could not kill The Maid. She is up and alive everywhere.

THE EARL OF WARWICK [sallying from the bed curtains on the other side, and coming to Joan's left hand] Madam: my congratulations on your rehabilitation. I feel that I owe you an apology.

JOAN. Oh, please dont mention it.

WARWICK [pleasantly] The burning was purely political. There was no personal feeling against you, I assure you.

JOAN. I bear no malice, my lord.

WARWICK. Just so. Very kind of you to meet me in that way: a touch of true breeding. But I must insist on apologizing very amply. The truth is, these political necessities sometimes turn out to be political mistakes; and this one was a veritable howler; for your spirit conquered us, madam, in spite of our faggots. History will remember me for your sake, though the incidents of the connection were perhaps a little unfortunate.

JOAN. Ay, perhaps just a little, you funny man.

WARWICK. Still, when they make you a saint, you will owe your halo to me, just as this lucky monarch owes his crown to you.

JOAN [turning from him] I shall owe nothing to any man: I owe everything to the spirit of God that was within me. But fancy me a saint! What would St Catherine and St Margaret say if the farm girl was cocked up beside them!

A clerical-looking gentleman in black frock-coat and trousers, and tall hat, in the fashion of the year 1920, *suddenly appears before them in the corner on their right. They all stare at him. Then they burst into uncontrollable laughter.*

THE GENTLEMAN. Why this mirth, gentlemen?

WARWICK. I congratulate you on having invented a most extraordinarily comic dress.

THE GENTLEMAN. I do not understand. You are all in fancy dress: I am properly dressed.

DUNOIS. All dress is fancy dress, is it not, except our natural skins?

THE GENTLEMAN. Pardon me: I am here on serious business, and cannot engage in frivolous discussions. [He takes out a paper, and assumes a dry official manner]. I am sent to announce to you that Joan of Arc, formerly known as The Maid, having been the subject of an inquiry instituted by the Bishop of Orleans—

JOAN [interrupting] Ah! They remember me still in Orleans.

THE GENTLEMAN [emphatically, to mark his indignation at the interruption]—by the Bishop of Orleans into the claim of the said Joan of Arc to be canonized as a saint—

JOAN [again interrupting] But I never made any such claim.

THE GENTLEMAN [as before]—the Church has examined the claim exhaustively in the usual course, and, having admitted the said Joan successively to the ranks of Venerable and Blessed,—

JOAN [chuckling] Me venerable!

THE GENTLEMAN. —has finally declared her to have been endowed with heroic virtues and favored with private revelations, and calls the said Venerable and Blessed Joan to the communion of the Church Triumphant as Saint Joan.

JOAN [rapt] Saint Joan!

THE GENTLEMAN. On every thirtieth day of May, being the anniversary of the death of the said most blessed daughter of God, there shall in every Catholic church to the end of time be celebrated a special office in commemoration of her; and it shall be lawful to dedicate a special chapel to her, and to place her image on its altar in every such church. And it shall be lawful and laudable for the faithful to kneel and address their prayers through her to the Mercy Seat.

JOAN. Oh no. It is for the saint to kneel. [*She falls on her knees, still rapt*].

THE GENTLEMAN [*putting up his paper, and retiring beside the Executioner*] In Basilica Vaticana, the sixteenth day of May, nineteen hundred and twenty.

DUNOIS [*raising Joan*] Half an hour to burn you, dear Saint; and four centuries to find out the truth about you!

DE STOGUMBER. Sir: I was chaplain to the Cardinal of Winchester once. They always would call him the Cardinal of England. It would be a great comfort to me and to my master to see a fair statue to The Maid in Winchester Cathedral. Will they put one there, do you think?

THE GENTLEMAN. As the building is temporarily in the hands of the Anglican heresy, I cannot answer for that.

A vision of the statue in Winchester Cathedral is seen through the window.

DE STOGUMBER. Oh look! look! that is Winchester.

JOAN. Is that meant to be me? I was stiffer on my feet.

The vision fades.

THE GENTLEMAN. I have been requested by the temporal authorities of France to mention that the multiplication of public statues to The Maid threatens to become an obstruction to traffic. I do so as a matter of courtesy to the said authorities, but must point out on behalf of the Church that The Maid's horse is no greater obstruction to traffic than any other horse.

JOAN. Eh! I am glad they have not forgotten my horse.

A vision of the statue before Rheims Cathedral appears.

JOAN. Is that funny little thing me too?

CHARLES. That is Rheims Cathedral where you had me crowned. It must be you.

JOAN. Who has broken my sword? My sword was never broken. It is the sword of France.

DUNOIS. Never mind. Swords can be mended. Your soul is unbroken; and you are the soul of France.

The vision fades. The Archbishop and the Inquisitor are now seen on the right and left of Cauchon.

JOAN. My sword shall conquer yet: the sword that never struck a blow. Though men destroyed my body, yet in my soul I have seen God.

CAUCHON [*kneeling to her*] The girls in the field praise thee; for thou hast raised their eyes; and they see that there is nothing between them and heaven.

DUNOIS [*kneeling to her*] The dying soldiers praise thee, because thou art a shield of glory between them and the judgment.

THE ARCHBISHOP [*kneeling to her*] The princes of the Church praise thee, because thou hast redeemed the faith their worldlinesses have dragged through the mire.

WARWICK [*kneeling to her*] The cunning counsellors praise thee, because thou hast cut the knots in which they have tied their own souls.

DE STOGUMBER [*kneeling to her*] The foolish old men on their deathbeds praise thee, because their sins against thee are turned into blessings.

THE INQUISITOR [*kneeling to her*] The judges in the blindness and bondage of the law praise thee, because thou hast vindicated the vision and the freedom of the living soul.

THE SOLDIER [*kneeling to her*] The wicked out of hell praise thee, because thou hast shewn them that the fire that is not quenched is a holy fire.

THE EXECUTIONER [*kneeling to her*] The tormentors and executioners praise thee, because thou has shewn that their hands are guiltless of the death of the soul.

CHARLES [*kneeling to her*] The unpretending praise thee, because thou hast taken upon thyself the heroic burdens that are too heavy for them.

JOAN. Woe unto me when all men praise me! I bid you remember that I am a saint, and that saints can work miracles. And now tell me: shall I rise from the dead, and come back to you a living woman?

A sudden darkness blots out the walls of the room as they all spring to their feet in consternation. Only the figures and the bed remain visible.

JOAN. What! Must I burn again? Are none of you ready to receive me?

CAUCHON. The heretic is always better dead. And mortal eyes cannot distinguish the saint from the heretic. Spare them. [*He goes out as he came*].

DUNOIS. Forgive us, Joan: we are not yet good enough for you. I shall go back to my bed. [*He also goes*].

WARWICK. We sincerely regret our little mistake; but political necessities, though occasionally erroneous, are still imperative; so if you will be good enough to excuse me— [*He steals discreetly away*].

THE ARCHBISHOP. Your return would not make me the man you once thought me. The utmost I can say is that though I dare not bless you, I hope I may one day enter into your blessedness. Meanwhile, however— [*He goes*].

THE INQUISITOR. I who am of the dead, testified that day that you were innocent. But I do not see how The Inquisition could possibly be dispensed with under existing circumstances. Therefore— [*He goes*].

DE STOGUMBER. Oh, do not come back: you must not come back. I must die in peace. Give us peace in our time, O Lord! [*He goes*].

THE GENTLEMAN. The possibility of your resurrection was not contemplated in the recent proceedings for your canonization. I must return to Rome for fresh instructions. [*He bows formally, and withdraws*].

THE EXECUTIONER. As a master in my profession I have to consider its interests. And, after all, my first duty is to my wife and children. I must have time to think over this. [*He goes*].

CHARLES. Poor old Joan! They have all run away from you except this blackguard who has to go back to hell at twelve o'clock. And what can I do but follow Jack Dunois' example, and go back to bed too? [*He does so*].

JOAN [*sadly*] Goodnight, Charlie.

CHARLES [*mumbling in his pillows*] Goo ni. [*He sleeps. The darkness envelops the bed*].

JOAN [*to the soldier*] And you, my one faithful? What comfort have you for Saint Joan?

THE SOLDIER. Well, what do they all amount to, these kings and captains and bishops and lawyers and such like? They just leave you in the ditch to bleed to death; and the next thing is, you meet them down there, for all the airs they give themselves. What I say is, you have as good a right to your notions as they have to theirs, and perhaps better. [*Settling himself for a lecture on the subject*] You see, it's like this. If— [*the first stroke of midnight is heard softly from a distant bell*]. Excuse me: a pressing appointment— [*He goes on tiptoe*].

The last remaining rays of light gather into a white radiance descending on Joan. The hour continues to strike.

JOAN. O God that madest this beautiful earth, when will it be ready to receive Thy saints? How long, O Lord, how long?

THE END

XXXII
THE APPLE CART
A POLITICAL EXTRAVAGANZA

ACT I

An office in the royal palace. Two writing tables face each other from opposite sides of the room, leaving plenty of room between them. Each table has a chair by it for visitors. The door is in the middle of the farthest wall. The clock shews that it is a little past 11; and the light is that of a fine summer morning.

Sempronius, smart and still presentably young, shews his right profile as he sits at one of the tables opening the King's letters. Pamphilius, middle aged, shews his left as he leans back in his chair at the other table with a pile of the morning papers at his elbow, reading one of them. This goes on silently for some time. Then Pamphilius, putting down his paper, looks at Sempronius for a moment before speaking.

PAMPHILIUS. What was your father?

SEMPRONIUS [*startled*] Eh?

PAMPHILIUS. What was your father?

SEMPRONIUS. My father?

PAMPHILIUS. Yes. What was he?

SEMPRONIUS. A Ritualist.

PAMPHILIUS. I dont mean his religion. I mean his profession. And his politics.

SEMPRONIUS. He was a Ritualist by profession, a Ritualist in politics, a Ritualist in religion: a raging emotional Die Hard Ritualist right down to his boots.

PAMPHILIUS. Do you mean that he was a parson?

SEMPRONIUS. Not at all. He was a sort of spectacular artist. He got up pageants and Lord Mayors' Shows and military tattoos and big public ceremonies and things like that. He arranged the last two coronations. That was how I got my job here in the palace. All our royal people knew him quite well: he was behind the scenes with them.

PAMPHILIUS. Behind the scenes and yet believed they were all real!

SEMPRONIUS. Yes. Believed in them with all his soul.

PAMPHILIUS. Although he manufactured them himself?

SEMPRONIUS. Certainly. Do you suppose a baker cannot believe sincerely in the sacrifice of the Mass or in holy communion because he has baked the consecrated wafer himself?

PAMPHILIUS. I never thought of that.

SEMPRONIUS. My father might have made millions in the theatres and film studios. But he refused to touch them because the things they represented hadnt really happened. He didnt mind doing the christening of Queen Elizabeth in Shakespear's Henry the Eighth because that had really happened. It was a celebration of royalty. But not anything romantic: not though they offered him thousands.

PAMPHILIUS. Did you ever ask him what he really thought about it all? But of course you didnt: one cant ask one's father anything about himself.

SEMPRONIUS. My dear Pam: my father never thought. He didnt know what thought meant. Very few people do, you know. He had vision: actual bodily vision, I mean; and he had an oddly limited sort of imagination. What I mean is that he couldnt imagine anything he didnt see; but he could imagine that what he did see was divine and holy and omniscient and omnipotent and eternal and everything that is impossible if only it looked splendid enough, and the organ was solemn enough, or the military bands brassy enough.

PAMPHILIUS. You mean that he had to get everything from outside.

SEMPRONIUS. Exactly. He'd never have felt anything if he hadnt had parents to feel about in his childhood, and a wife and babies to feel about when he grew up. He'd never have known anything if he hadnt been taught at school. He couldnt amuse himself: he had to pay oceans of money to other people to amuse him with all sorts of ghastly sports and pleasures that would have driven me into a monastery to escape from them. You see it was all ritual: he went to the Riviera every winter just as he went to church.

PAMPHILIUS. By the way, is he alive? I should like to know him.

SEMPRONIUS. No. He died in 1962, of solitude.

PAMPHILIUS. What do you mean? of solitude?

SEMPRONIUS. He couldnt bear to be alone for a moment: it was death to him. Somebody had to be with him always.

PAMPHILIUS. Oh well, come! That was friendly and kindly. It shews he had something inside him after all.

SEMPRONIUS. Not a bit. He never talked to his friends. He played cards with them. They never exchanged a thought.

PAMPHILIUS. He must have been a rum old bird.

SEMPRONIUS. Not rum enough to be noticed. There are millions like him.

PAMPHILIUS. But what about his dying of solitude? Was he imprisoned?

SEMPRONIUS. No. His yacht struck a reef and sank somewhere off the north of Scotland; and he managed to swim to an uninhabited island. All the rest were drowned; and he was not taken off for three weeks. When they found him he was melancholy mad, poor old boy; and he never got over it. Simply from having no one to play cards with, and no church to go to.

PAMPHILIUS. My dear Sem: one isnt alone on an uninhabited island. My mother used to stand me on the table and make me recite about it.

[He declaims]

To sit on rocks; to muse o'er flood and fell;
To slowly trace the forest's shady scene
Where things that own not man's dominion
    dwell
And mortal foot hath ne'er or rarely been;
To climb the trackless mountain all unseen
With the wild flock that never needs a fold;
Alone o'er steeps and foaming falls to lean:
This is not solitude: 'tis but to hold
Converse with Nature's charms, and view her
    stores unrolled.

SEMPRONIUS. Now you have hit the really funny thing about my father. All that about the lonely woods and the rest of it—what you call Nature—didnt exist for him. It had to be something artificial to get at him. Nature to him meant nakedness; and nakedness only disgusted him. He wouldnt look at a horse grazing in a field; but put splendid trappings on it and stick it into a procession and he just loved it. The same with men and women: they were nothing to him until they were dressed up in fancy costumes and painted and wigged and titled. To him the sacredness of the priest was the beauty of his vestment, the loveliness of women the dazzle of their jewels and robes, the charm of the countryside not in its hills and trees, nor in the blue smoke from its cottages in the winter evenings, but of its temples, palaces, mansions, park gates, and porticoed country houses. Think of the horror of that island to him! A void! a place where he was deaf and dumb and blind and lonely! If only there had been a peacock with its tail in full bloom it might have saved his reason; but all the birds were gulls; and gulls are not decorative. Our King could have lived there for thirty years with nothing but his own thoughts. You would have been all right with a fishing rod and a golf ball with a bag of clubs. I should have been as happy as a man in a picture gallery looking at the dawns and sunsets, the changing seasons, the continual miracle of life ever renewing itself. Who could be dull with pools in the rocks to watch? Yet my father, with all that under his nose, was driven mad by its nothingness. They say that where there is nothing the king loses his rights. My father found that where there is nothing a man loses his reason and dies.

PAMPHILIUS. Let me add that in this palace, when the king's letters are not ready for him at 12 o'clock, a secretary loses his job.

SEMPRONIUS [hastily resuming his work] Yes, devil take you: why did you start me talking before I had finished my work? You have nothing to do but pretend to read the newspapers for him; and when you say "Nothing particular this morning, Sir," all he says is "Thank Heaven!" But if I missed a note from one of his aunts inviting herself to tea, or a little line from Orinthia the Beloved marked "Strictly private and confidential: to be opened by His Majesty alone," I should never hear the end of it. He had six love letters yesterday; and all he said when I told him was "Take them to the Queen." He thinks they amuse her. I believe they make her as sick as they make me.

PAMPHILIUS. Do Orinthia's letters go to the Queen?

SEMPRONIUS. No, by George! Even I dont read Orinthia's letters. My instructions are to read everything; but I take care to forget to open hers. And I notice that I am not rebuked for my negligence.

PAMPHILIUS [thoughtfully] I suppose—

SEMPRONIUS. Oh shut up, Pam. I shall never get through if you go on talking.

PAMPHILIUS. I was only going to say that I suppose—

SEMPRONIUS. Something about Orinthia. Dont. If you indulge in supposition on that subject, you will lose your job, old chap. So stow it.

PAMPHILIUS. Dont cry out before Orinthia is hurt, young chap. I was going to say that I suppose you know that that bull-roarer Boanerges has just been taken into the Cabinet as President of the Board of Trade, and that he is coming here today to give the King a piece of his mind, or what he calls his mind, about the crisis.

SEMPRONIUS. What does the King care about the crisis? There has been a crisis every two months since he came to the throne; but he has always been too clever for them. He'll turn Boanerges inside out after letting him roar the palace down.

Boanerges enters, dressed in a Russian blouse and peaked cap, which he keeps on. He is fifty, heavily built and aggressively self-assertive.

BOANERGES. Look here. The King has an appointment with me at a quarter to twelve. How long more am I to be kept waiting?

SEMPRONIUS [with cheerful politeness] Good morning. Mr Boanerges, I think.

BOANERGES [shortly, but a little taken aback] Oh, good morning to you. They say that politeness is the punctuality of kings—

SEMPRONIUS. The other way about, Mr Boanerges. Punctuality is the politeness of kings; and King Magnus is a model in that respect. Your arrival cannot have been announced to His Majesty. I will see about it. [He hurries out].

PAMPHILIUS. Be seated, Mr Boanerges.

BOANERGES [seating himself by Pamphilius's writing table] A nice lot of young upstarts you have in this palace, Mr—?

PAMPHILIUS. Pamphilius is my name.

BOANERGES. Oh yes: Ive heard of you. Youre one of the king's private secretaries.

PAMPHILIUS. I am. And what have our young upstarts been doing to you, Mr Boanerges?

BOANERGES. Well, I told one of them to tell the king I was here, and to look sharp about it. He looked at me as if I was a performing elephant, and took himself off after whispering to another flunkey. Then this other chap comes over to me and pretends he doesnt know who I am! asks me can he have my name! "My lad" I said: "not to know me argues yourself unknown. You know who I am as well as I do myself. Go and tell the king I'm waiting for him, d'ye see?" So he took himself off with a flea in his ear. I waited until I was fed up with it, and then opened the nearest door and came in here.

PAMPHILIUS. Young rascals! However, my friend Mr Sempronius will make it all right for you.

BOANERGES. Oh: that was Sempronius, was it. Ive heard of him too.

PAMPHILIUS. You seem to have heard of all of us. You will be quite at home in the palace now that you are a Cabinet Minister. By the way, may I congratulate you on your appointment—or rather congratulate the Cabinet on your accession?

SEMPRONIUS [returning] The King. [He goes to his table and takes the visitor's chair in his hand, ready for the king's instructions as to where to place it].

Pamphilius rises. Boanerges turns to the door in his chair without rising. King Magnus, a tallish studious looking gentleman of 45 or thereabouts, enters, and comes quickly down the middle of the room to Boanerges, proffering his hand cordially.

MAGNUS. You are very welcome to my little palace, Mr Boanerges. Wont you sit down?

BOANERGES. I am sitting down.

MAGNUS. True, Mr Boanerges. I had not noticed it. Forgive me: force of habit.

He indicates to Sempronius that he wishes to sit near Boanerges, on his right. Sempronius places the chair accordingly.

MAGNUS. You will allow me to be seated?

BOANERGES. Oh, sit down, man, sit down. Youre in your own house: ceremony cuts no ice with me.

MAGNUS [gratefully] Thank you.

The King sits. Pamphilius sits. Sempronius returns to his table and sits.

MAGNUS. It is a great pleasure to meet you at last, Mr Boanerges. I have followed your career with interest ever since you contested Northampton twenty-five years ago.

BOANERGES [pleased and credulous] I should just think you have, King Magnus. I have made you sit up once or twice, eh?

MAGNUS [smiling] Your voice has shaken the throne oftener than that.

BOANERGES [indicating the secretaries with a jerk of his head] What about these two? Are they to overhear everything that passes?

MAGNUS. My private secretaries. Do they incommode you?

BOANERGES. Oh, they dont incommode me. I am ready to have our talk out in Trafalgar Square if you like, or have it broadcast on the wireless.

MAGNUS. That would be a treat for my people, Mr Boanerges. I am sorry we have not arranged for it.

BOANERGES [gathering himself together formidably] Yes; but do you realize that I am going to say things to you that have never been said to a king before?

MAGNUS. I am very glad indeed to hear it, Mr Boanerges. I thought I had already heard everything that could possibly be said to a king. I shall be grateful for the smallest novelty.

BOANERGES. I warn you it wont be agreeable. I am a plain man, Magnus: a very plain man.

MAGNUS. Not at all, I assure you—

BOANERGES [indignantly] I was not alluding to my personal appearance.

MAGNUS [gravely] Nor was I. Do not deceive yourself, Mr Boanerges. You are very far from being a plain man. To me you have always been an Enigma.

BOANERGES [surprised and enormously flattered: he cannot help smiling with pleasure] Well, perhaps I am a bit of an enigma. Perhaps I am.

MAGNUS [humbly] I wish I could see through you, Mr Boanerges. But I have not your sort of cleverness. I can only ask you to be frank with me.

BOANERGES [now convinced that he has the upper hand] You mean about the crisis. Well, frank is just what I have come here to be. And the first thing I am going to tell you frankly about it is that this country has got to be governed, not by you, but by your ministers.

MAGNUS. I shall be only too grateful to them for taking a very difficult and thankless job off my hands.

BOANERGES. But it's not on your hands. It's on your ministers' hands. You are only a constitutional monarch. Do you know what they call that in Belgium?

MAGNUS. An indiarubber stamp, I think. Am I right?

BOANERGES. You are, King Magnus. An indiarubber stamp. Thats what you have got to be; and dont you forget it.

MAGNUS. Yes: thats what we are most of the time: both of us.

BOANERGES [outraged] What do you mean? both of us?

MAGNUS. They bring us papers. We sign. You have no time to read them, luckily for you. But I am expected to read everything. I do not always agree; but I must sign: there is nothing else to be done. For instance, death warrants. Not only have I to sign the death warrants of persons who in my opinion ought not to be killed; but I may not even issue death warrants for a great many people who in my opinion ought to be killed.

BOANERGES [sarcastic] Youd like to be able to say "Off with his head!" wouldnt you?

MAGNUS. Many men would hardly miss their heads, there is so little in them. Still, killing is a serious business: at least the person who is to be killed is usually conceited enough to think so. I think that if there were a question of killing me—

BOANERGES [grimly] There may be, someday. I have heard it discussed.

MAGNUS. Oh, quite. I have not forgotten King Charles's head. Well, I hope it will be settled by a living person and not by an indiarubber stamp.

BOANERGES. It will be settled by the Home Secretary, your duly constituted democratic minister.

MAGNUS. Another indiarubber stamp, eh?

BOANERGES. At present, perhaps. But not when I am Home Secretary, by Jingo! Nobody will make an indiarubber stamp of Bill Boanerges: take that from me.

MAGNUS. Of course not. Is it not curious how people idealize their rulers? In the old days the king—poor man!—was a god, and was actually called God and worshipped as infallible and omniscient. That was monstrous—

BOANERGES. It was silly: just silly.

MAGNUS. But was it half so silly as our pretence that he is an indiarubber stamp? The ancient Roman emperor-god had not infinite wisdom, infinite knowledge, infinite power; but he had some: perhaps even as

much as his ministers. He was alive, not dead. What man has ever approached either a king or a minister and been able to pick him up from the table and use him as one picks up and uses a piece of wood and brass and rubber? Permanent officials of your department will try to pick you up and use you like that. Nineteen times out of twenty you will have to let them do it, because you cannot know everything; and even if you could you cannot do everything and be everywhere. But what about the twentieth time?

BOANERGES. The twentieth time they will find they are up against Bill Boanerges, eh?

MAGNUS. Precisely. The indiarubber stamp theory will not work, Mr Boanerges. The old divine theory worked because there is a divine spark in us all; and the stupidest or worst monarch or minister, if not wholly god, is a bit of a god—an attempt at a god—however little the bit and unsuccessful the attempt. But the indiarubber stamp theory breaks down in every real emergency, because no king or minister is the very least little bit like a stamp: he is a living soul.

BOANERGES. A soul, eh? You kings still believe in that, I suppose.

MAGNUS. I find the word convenient: it is short and familiar. But if you dislike being called a soul, let us say that you are animate matter as distinguished from inanimate.

BOANERGES [not quite liking this] I think I'd rather you called me a soul, you know, if you must call me anything at all. I know I have too much matter about me: the doctor says I ought to knock off a stone or two; but there's something more to me than beef. Call it a soul if you like; only not in a superstitious sense, if you understand me.

MAGNUS. Perfectly. So you see, Mr Boanerges, that though we have been dealing with one another for less than ten minutes, you have already led me into an intellectual discussion which shews that we are something more than a pair of indiarubber stamps. You are up against my brains, such as they are.

BOANERGES. And you are up against mine.

MAGNUS [gallantly] There can be no doubt of that.

BOANERGES [grinning] Such as they are, eh?

MAGNUS. It is not for me to make that qualification, except in my own case. Besides, you have given your proofs. No common man could have risen as you have done. As for me, I am a king because I was the nephew of my uncle, and because my two elder brothers died. If I had been the stupidest man in the country I should still be its king. I have not won my position by my merits. If I had been born as you were in the—in the—

BOANERGES. In the gutter. Out with it. Picked up by a policeman at the foot of Captain Coram's statue. Adopted by the policeman's grandmother, bless her!

MAGNUS. Where should *I* have been if the policeman had picked m e up?

BOANERGES. Ah! Where? Not, mind you, that you mightnt have done pretty well for yourself. Youre no fool, Magnus: I will say that for you.

MAGNUS. You flatter me.

BOANERGES. Flatter a king! Never. Not Bill Boanerges.

MAGNUS. Yes, yes: everybody flatters the King. But everybody has not your tact, and, may I say? your good nature.

BOANERGES [*beaming with self-satisfaction*] Perhaps not. Still, I am a Republican, you know.

MAGNUS. That is what has always surprised me. Do you really think that any man should have as much personal power as the presidents of the republican States have? Ambitious kings envy them.

BOANERGES. What's that? I dont follow that.

MAGNUS [*smiling*] You cannot humbug me, Mr Boanerges. I see why you are a Republican. If the English people send me packing and establish a republic, no man has a better chance of being the first British president than you.

BOANERGES [*almost blushing*] Oh! I dont say that.

MAGNUS. Come come! You know it as well as I do. Well, if it happens you will have ten times more power than I have ever had.

BOANERGES [*not quite convinced*] How can that be? Youre King.

MAGNUS. And what is the King? An idol set up by a group of plutocrats so that they can rule the country with the king as their scapegoat and puppet. Presidents, now, are chosen by the people, who always want a Strong Man to protect them against the rich.

BOANERGES. Well, speaking as a bit of a Strong Man myself, there may be something in that. But honestly, Magnus, as man to man, do you tell me youd rather be a president than what you are?

MAGNUS. By no means. You wouldnt believe me if I did; and you would be quite right. You see, my security is very comfortable.

BOANERGES. Security, eh? You admitted just now that even a modest individual like myself had given your throne a shake or two.

MAGNUS. True. You are quite right to remind me of it. I know that the monarchy may come to an end at any moment. But while the monarchy lasts—while it lasts, mark you—I am very secure. I escape the dreadful and demoralizing drudgery of electioneering. I have no voters to please. Ministers come and ministers go; but I go on for ever. The terrible precariousness of your position—

BOANERGES. What's that? How is my position precarious?

MAGNUS. The vote may go against you. Yours is a Trade Union seat, is it not? If the Hydro-Electric Workers Federation throw you over, where would you be?

BOANERGES [*confidently*] They wont throw me over. You dont know the workers, Magnus: you have never been a worker.

MAGNUS [*lifts his eyebrows*]!

BOANERGES [*continuing*] No king on earth is as safe in his job as a Trade Union official. There is only one thing that can get him sacked; and that is drink. Not even that, as long as he doesnt actually fall down. I talk democracy to these men and women. I tell them that they have the vote, and that theirs is the kingdom and the power and the glory. I say to them "You are supreme: exercise your power." They say, "That's right: tell us what to do"; and I tell them. I say "Exercise your vote intelligently by voting for me." And they do. That's democracy; and a splendid thing it is too for putting the right men in the right place.

MAGNUS. Magnificent! I have never heard it better described. You certainly have a head on you, Mr Boanerges. You should write an essay on democracy. But—

BOANERGES. But what?

MAGNUS. Suppose a man with a bigger voice comes along! Some fool! Some windbag! Some upstart with a platform trick of gulling the multitude!

BOANERGES. Youre thinking of Iky Jacobus? He is only a talker. [*Snapping his fingers*] I dont give t h a t for him.

MAGNUS. I never even heard of Mr Jacobus.

But why do you say "only a talker." Talkers are very formidable rivals for popular favor. The multitude understands talk: it does not understand work. I mean brain work, like yours and mine.

BOANERGES. That's true. But I can talk Iky's head off.

MAGNUS. Lucky man: you have all the trumps in your hand. But I, who cannot pretend to your gifts, am very glad that Iky cannot upset me as long as I am the nephew of my uncle.

A young lady, dressed for walking, rushes in impetuously.

THE YOUNG LADY. Papa: I cannot find the address—

MAGNUS [*cutting her short*] No, no, no, dear: not now. Go away. Dont you see that I am particularly engaged with the President of the Board of Trade? You must excuse my unruly daughter, Mr Boanerges. May I present her to you? Alice, my eldest girl. Mr Boanerges, dear.

ALICE. Oh! Are you the great Mr Boanerges?

BOANERGES [*rising in a glow of gratification*] Well, I dont call myself that, you know. But I believe the expression is in use, as you might say. I am very pleased indeed to make the acquaintance of the Princess Royal.

They shake hands.

ALICE. Why do you wear such awful clothes, Mr Boanerges?

MAGNUS [*remonstrating*] My dear—!

ALICE [*continuing*] I cant go out walking with you in that [*pointing to his blouse*].

BOANERGES. The uniform of Labor, your Royal Highness. I'm proud of it.

ALICE. Oh yes, I know all that, Mr Boanerges. But you dont look the part, you know. Anyone can see that you belong naturally to the governing class.

BOANERGES [*struck by this view*] In a way, perhaps. But I have earned my bread by my hands. Not as a laborer, though. I am a skilled mechanic, or was until my country called on me to lead it.

MAGNUS [*to Alice*] Well, my dear, you have broken up a most interesting conversation, and to me a most instructive one. It's no use our trying to go on, Mr Boanerges: I must go and find what my daughter wants, though I strongly suspect that what she really came in for was to see my wonderful new minister. We shall meet again presently: you know

that the Prime Minister is calling on me today with some of his colleagues—including, I hope, yourself—to discuss the crisis. [*Taking Alice's arm and turning towards the door*] You will excuse us, wont you?

BOANERGES [*graciously*] Oh, thats all right. Thats quite all right.

The King and the Princess go out, apparently much pleased.

BOANERGES [*to Sempronius and Pamphilius comprehensively*] Well, say what you will, the King is no fool. Not when you know how to handle him.

PAMPHILIUS. Of course, that makes all the difference.

BOANERGES. And the girl hasnt been spoilt. I was glad to see that. She doesnt seem to know that she is the Princess Royal, eh?

SEMPRONIUS. Well, she wouldnt dream of giving herself any airs with you.

BOANERGES. What! Isnt she always like that?

SEMPRONIUS. Oh no. It's not everybody who is received as you have been. I hope you have enjoyed your visit.

BOANERGES. Well, I pulled Magnus through it pretty well: eh? Dont you think so?

SEMPRONIUS. He was pleased. You have a way with you, Mr President.

BOANERGES. Well, perhaps I have, perhaps I have.

A bevy of six Cabinet Ministers, resplendent in diplomatic uniforms, enters. Proteus the Prime Minister has on his left, Pliny, Chancellor of the Exchequer, goodhumored and conciliatory, and Nicobar, Foreign Secretary, snaky and censorious. On his right Crassus, Colonial Secretary, elderly and anxious, and Balbus, Home Secretary, rude and thoughtless.

BALBUS. Holy snakes! look at Bill. [*To Boanerges*] Go home and dress yourself properly, man.

NICOBAR. Where do you think you are?

CRASSUS. Who do you think you are?

PLINY [*fingering the blouse*] Where did you buy it, Bill?

BOANERGES [*turning on them like a baited bear*] Well, if you come to that, who do you think you are, the lot of you?

PROTEUS [*conciliatory*] Never mind them, Bill: theyre jealous because they didnt think of it themselves. How did you get on with the King?

BOANERGES. Right as rain, Joe. You leave the King to me. I know how to handle him. If I'd been in the Cabinet these last three months there'd have been no crisis.

NICOBAR. He put you through it, did he?

BOANERGES. What do you mean? put me through it? Is this a police office?

PLINY. The third degree is not unknown in this palace, my boy. [*To Pamphilius*] Did the matron take a hand?

PAMPHILIUS. No. But the Princess Alice happened to drop in. She was greatly impressed by the President.

They all laugh uproariously at Boanerges.

BOANERGES. What in hell are you laughing at?

PROTEUS. Take no notice of them, Bill: they are only having their bit of fun with you as a new comer. Come, lads! enough of fooling: lets get to business. [*He takes the chair vacated by the King*].

Sempronius and Pamphilius at once rise and go out busily, taking some of their papers with them. Pliny takes Boanerges' chair, Balbus that of Sempronius, Boanerges that of Pamphilius, whilst Nicobar and Crassus take chairs from the wall and sit down at the ends of the writing tables, left and right of the Prime Minister respectively.

PROTEUS. Now to start with, do you chaps all fully realize that though we wiped out every other party at the last election, and have been in power for the last three years, this country has been governed during that time by the King?

NICOBAR. I dont see that. We—

PROTEUS [*impatiently*] Well, if you dont, then for Heaven's sake either resign and get out of the way of men who can see facts and look them in the face, or else take my job and lead the party yourself.

NICOBAR. The worst of you is that you wont face the fact that though youre Prime Minister youre not God Almighty. The King cant do anything except what we advise him to do. How can he govern the country if we have all the power and he has none?

BOANERGES. Dont talk silly, Nick. This india-rubber stamp theory doesnt work. What man has ever approached a king or a minister and been able to pick him up from the table and use him as youd use a bit of wood and brass and rubber? The King's a live man; and what more are you, with your blessed advice?

PLINY. Hullo, Bill! You have been having your mind improved by somebody.

BOANERGES. What do you mean? Isnt it what I have always said?

PROTEUS [*whose nerves are on edge*] Oh, will you stop squabbling. What are we going to say to the King when he comes in? If you will only hold together and say the same thing—or let me say it—he must give way. But he is as artful as the very devil. He'll have a pin to stick into the seat of every man of you. If you all start quarrelling and scolding and bawling, which is just what he wants you to do, it will end in his having his own way as usual, because one man that has a mind and knows it can always beat ten men who havnt and dont.

PLINY. Steady, Prime Minister. Youre overwrought.

PROTEUS. It's enough to drive a man mad. I am sorry.

PLINY [*changing the subject*] Where's Mandy?

NICOBAR. And Lizzie?

PROTEUS. Late as usual. Come! Business, business, business.

BOANERGES [*thunderously*] Order order!

PROTEUS. The King is working the Press against us. The King is making speeches. Things have come to a head. He said yesterday on the opening of the new Chamber of Commerce building that the king's veto is the only remaining defence of the people against corrupt legislation.

BOANERGES. So it is, by Jingo. What other defence is there? Democracy? Yah! We know what Democracy is worth. What we need is a Strong Man.

NICOBAR [*sneering*] Yourself, for instance.

BOANERGES. I should stand a better chance than you, my lad, if we were a Republic, and the people could choose. And let me tell you that a republican president has more power than a king because the people know that they need a Strong Man to protect them against the rich.

PROTEUS [*flinging himself back in his chair in desperation*] This is a nice thing. Two Labor papers have leading articles this morning supporting the King; and the latest addition to the Cabinet here is a King's man. I resign.

General consternation except on the part of Nicobar, who displays cheerful unconcern, and of Boanerges, who squares himself with an iron face.

PLINY. No: dont do that, Joe.

BALBUS. What! Now! You cant. You mustnt.

CRASSUS. Of course not. Out of the question.

PROTEUS. No use. [*Rising*] I resign, I tell you. You can all go to the devil. I have lost my health, and almost lost my reason, trying to keep this Cabinet together in the face of the cunningest enemy popular government has ever had to face. I have had enough of it. [*Sitting down again*] I resign.

CRASSUS. But not at such a moment as this. Dont let us swop horses when crossing a stream.

NICOBAR. Why not, if the horse you have got is subject to hysterics?

BOANERGES. Not to mention that you may have more than one horse at your disposal.

PROTEUS. Right you are. Perfectly true. Take my job, Nick. It's vacant for you, Bill. I wish you joy of it.

PLINY. Now boys, boys, boys: be good. We cant make a new Cabinet before Magnus comes in. You have something in your pocket, Joe. Out with it. Read it to them.

PROTEUS [*taking a paper from his pocket*] What I was going to propose—and you can take it or leave it—is an ultimatum.

CRASSUS. Good!

PROTEUS. Either he signs this, or—[*he pauses significantly*]—!

NICOBAR. Or what?

PROTEUS [*disgusted*] Oh, you make me sick.

NICOBAR. Youre sick already, by your own account. I only ask, suppose he refuses to sign your ultimatum?

PROTEUS. You call yourself a Cabinet Minister, and you cant answer that!

NICOBAR. No I cant. I press my question. You said he must sign, OR. I ask, or what?

PROTEUS. Or we resign and tell the country that we cant carry on the King's Government under conditions which destroy our responsibility.

BALBUS. Thatll do it. He couldnt face that.

CRASSUS. Yes: thatll bunker him.

PROTEUS. Is that agreed?

PLINY. ⎫
CRASSUS. ⎬ Yes, yes, yes, 'greed 'greed
BALBUS. ⎭ 'greed.

BOANERGES. I retain an open mind. Let us hear the ultimatum.

NICOBAR. Yes: lets hear it.

PROTEUS. Memorandum of understanding arrived at—

The King enters, with Amanda, Postmistress General, a merry lady in uniform like the men, on his left, and Lysistrata, Powermistress General, a grave lady in academic robes, on his right. All rise. The Prime Minister's face darkens.

MAGNUS. Welcome, gentlemen. I hope I am not too early. [*Noting the Prime Minister's scowl*] Am I intruding?

PROTEUS. I protest. It is intolerable. I call a conference of my Cabinet to consider our position in regard to the prerogative; and I find the two lady members, the Postmistress General and the Powermistress General, closeted with your majesty instead of being in their places to confer with me.

LYSISTRATA. You mind your own business, Joe.

MAGNUS. Oh no: really, really, my dear Lysistrata, you must not take that line. Our business is to meddle in everybody's business. A Prime Minister is a busybody by profession. So is a monarch. So are we all.

LYSISTRATA. Well, they say everybody's business is nobody's business, which is just what Joe is fit for. [*She takes a chair from the wall with a powerful hand, and swings it forward to the inside corner of Sempronius's table, where she stands waiting for the King to sit down*].

PROTEUS. This is what I have to put up with when I am on the verge of a nervous breakdown [*he sits down distractedly, and buries his face in his hands*].

AMANDA [*going to him and petting him*] Come, Joe! dont make a scene. You asked for it, you know.

NICOBAR. What do you go provoking Lizzie for like that? You know she has a temper.

LYSISTRATA. There is nothing whatever wrong with my temper. But I am not going to stand any of Joe's nonsense; and the sooner he makes up his mind to that the smoother our proceedings are likely to be.

BOANERGES. I protest. I say, let us be dignified. I say, let us respect ourselves and respect the throne. All this Joe and Bill and Nick and Lizzie: we might as well be hobnobbing in a fried fish shop. The Prime Minister is the prime minister: he isnt Joe. The Powermistress isnt Lizzie: she's Lysis Traitor.

LYSISTRATA [*who has evidently been a schoolmistress*] Certainly not, Bill. She is Ly Sístrata. You had better say Lizzie: it is easier to pronounce.

BOANERGES [*scornfully*] Ly Sístrata! A more foolish affectation I never heard: you might as well call me Bo Annerjeeze [*he flings him-*

self into his chair].

MAGNUS [*sweetly*] Shall we sit, ladies and gentlemen?

Boanerges hastily rises and sits down again. The King sits in Pliny's chair. Lysistrata and the rest of the men resume their seats, leaving Pliny and Amanda standing. Amanda takes an empty chair in each hand and plants them side by side between the King and the table of Pamphilius.

AMANDA. There you are, Plin. [*She sits next the table*].

PLINY. Ta ta, Mandy. Pardon me: I should have said Amanda. [*He sits next the King*].

AMANDA. Dont mention it, darling.

BOANERGES. Order, order!

AMANDA [*waves him a kiss*]!!

MAGNUS. Prime Minister: the word is with you. Why have you all simultaneously given me the great pleasure of exercising your constitutional right of access to the sovereign?

LYSISTRATA. Have I that right, sir; or havnt I?

MAGNUS. Most undoubtedly you have.

LYSISTRATA. You hear that, Joe?

PROTEUS. I——

BALBUS. Oh for Heaven's sake dont contradict her, Joe. We shall never get anywhere at this rate. Come to the crisis.

NICOBAR.⎫   ⎧Yes yes: the crisis!
CRASSUS. ⎬[*together*]⎨Yes yes: come along!
PLINY.   ⎭   ⎩The crisis: out with it!

BALBUS. The ultimatum. Lets have the ultimatum.

MAGNUS. Oh, there is an ultimatum! I gathered from yesterday's evening papers that there is a crisis—another crisis. But the ultimatum is new to me. [*To Proteus*] Have you an ultimatum?

PROTEUS. Your Majesty's allusion to the royal veto in a speech yesterday has brought matters to a head.

MAGNUS. It was perhaps indelicate. But you all allude so freely to your own powers— to the supremacy of Parliament and the voice of the people and so forth—that I fear I have lost any little delicacy I ever possessed. If you may flourish your thunderbolts why may I not shoulder my little popgun of a veto and strut up and down with it for a moment?

NICOBAR. This is not a subject for jesting—

MAGNUS [*interrupting him quickly*] I am not jesting, Mr Nicobar. But I am certainly trying to discuss our differences in a good-humored manner. Do you wish me to lose my temper and make scenes?

AMANDA. Oh please no, your Majesty. We get enough of that from Joe.

PROTEUS. I pro—

MAGNUS [*his hand persuasively on the Prime Minister's arm*] Take care, Prime Minister: take care: do not let your wily Postmistress General provoke you to supply the evidence against yourself.

All the rest laugh.

PROTEUS [*coolly*] I thank your Majesty for the caution. The Postmistress General has never forgiven me for not making her First Lady of the Admiralty. She has three nephews in the navy.

AMANDA. Oh you— [*She swallows the epithet, and contents herself with shaking her fist at the Premier*].

MAGNUS. Tch-tch-tch! Gently, Amanda, gently. Three very promising lads: they do you credit.

AMANDA. I never wanted them to go to sea. I could have found them better jobs in the Post Office.

MAGNUS. Apart from Amanda's family relations, am I face to face with a united Cabinet?

PLINY. No, sir. You are face to face with a squabbling Cabinet; but, on the constitutional question, united we stand: divided we fall.

BALBUS. That is so.

NICOBAR. Hear hear!

MAGNUS. What is the constitutional question? Do you deny the royal veto? or do you object only to my reminding my subjects of its existence?

NICOBAR. What we say is that the king has no right to remind his subjects of anything constitutional except by the advice of the Prime Minister, and in words which he has read and approved.

MAGNUS. Which Prime Minister? There are so many of them in the Cabinet.

BOANERGES. There! Serves you all right! Arnt you ashamed of yourselves? But I am not surprised, Joseph Proteus. I own I like a Prime Minister that knows how to be a Prime Minister. Why do you let them take the word out of your mouth every time?

PROTEUS. If His Majesty wants a Cabinet of dumb dogs he will not get it from my party.

BALBUS. Hear hear, Joe!

MAGNUS. Heaven forbid! The variety of opinion in the Cabinet is always most instructive and interesting. Who is to be its spokesman today?

PROTEUS. I know your Majesty's opinion of me; but let—

MAGNUS [*before he can proceed*] Let me state it quite frankly. My opinion of you is that no man knows better than you when to speak and when to let others speak for you; when to make scenes and threaten resignation; and when to be as cool as a cucumber.

PROTEUS [*not altogether displeased*] Well, sir, I hope I am not such a fool as some fools think me. I may not always keep my temper. You would not be surprised at that if you knew how much temper I have to keep. [*He straightens up and becomes impressively eloquent*]. At this moment my cue is to shew you, not my own temper, but the temper of my Cabinet. What the Foreign Secretary and the Chancellor of the Exchequer and the Home Secretary have told you is true. If we are to carry on your government we cannot have you making speeches that express your own opinions and not ours. We cannot have you implying that everything that is of any value in our legislation is your doing and not ours. We cannot have you telling people that their only safeguard against the political encroachments of big business whilst we are doing nothing but bungling and squabbling is your power of veto. It has got to stop, once for all.

BALBUS. } Hear hear!
NICOBAR. }

PROTEUS. Is that clear?

MAGNUS. Far clearer than I have ever dared to make it, Mr Proteus. Except, by the way, on one point. When you say that all this of which you complain must cease once for all, do you mean that henceforth I am to agree with you or you with me?

PROTEUS. I mean that when you disagree with us you are to keep your disagreement to yourself.

MAGNUS. That would be a very heavy responsibility for me. If I see you leading the nation over the edge of a precipice may I not warn it?

BALBUS. It is our business to warn it, not yours.

MAGNUS. Suppose you dont do your business! Suppose you dont see the danger! That has happened. It may happen again.

CRASSUS [*insinuating*] As democrats, I think we are bound to proceed on the assumption that such a thing cannot happen.

BOANERGES. Rot! It's happening all the time until somebody has the gumption to put his foot down and stop it.

CRASSUS. Yes: I know. But that is not democracy.

BOANERGES. Democracy be— [*he leaves the word unspoken*]! I have thirty years experience of democracy. So have most of you. I say no more.

BALBUS. Wages are too high, if you ask me. Anybody can earn from five to twenty pounds a week now, and a big dole when there is no job for him. And what Englishman will give his mind to politics as long as he can afford to keep a motor car?

NICOBAR. How many voted at the last election? Not seven per cent of the register.

BALBUS. Yes; and the seven per cent were only a parcel of sillies playing at ins and outs. To make democracy work in Crassus's way we need poverty and hardship.

PROTEUS [*emphatically*] And we have abolished poverty and hardship. That is why the people trust us. [*To the King*] And that is why you will have to give way to us. We have the people of England in comfort—solid middle class comfort—at our backs.

MAGNUS. No: we have not abolished poverty and hardship. Our big business men have abolished them. But how? By sending our capital abroad to places where poverty and hardship still exist: in other words, where labor is cheap. We live in comfort on the imported profits of that capital. We are all ladies and gentlemen now.

NICOBAR. Well, what more do you want?

PLINY. You surely dont grudge us our wonderful prosperity, sir.

MAGNUS. I want it to last.

NICOBAR. Why shouldnt it last? [*Rising*] Own the truth. You had rather have the people poor, and pose as their champion and savior, than have to admit that the people are better off under our government—under our squabbling and bungling, as you call it.

MAGNUS. No: it was the Prime Minister who used those expressions.

NICOBAR. Dont quibble: he was quoting them from your reptile press. What I say is that we stand for high wages, and you are always belittling and opposing the men that pay them. Well, the voters like high wages. They know when they are well off; and they dont know what you are grumbling about;

and thats what will beat you every time you try to stir them against us [*he resumes his seat*].

PLINY. There is no need to rub it in like that, Nick. We're all good friends. Nobody objects to prosperity.

MAGNUS. You think this prosperity is safe?

NICOBAR. Safe!

PLINY. Oh come, sir! Really!

BALBUS. Safe! Look at my constituency: Northeast-by-north Birmingham, with its four square miles of confectionery works! Do you know that in the Christmas cracker trade Birmingham is the workshop of the world?

CRASSUS. Take Gateshead and Middlesbrough alone! Do you know that there has not been a day's unemployment there for five years past, and that their daily output of chocolate creams totals up to twenty thousand tons?

MAGNUS. It is certainly a consoling thought that if we were peacefully blockaded by the League of Nations we could live for at least three weeks on our chocolate creams.

NICOBAR. You neednt sneer at the sweets: we turn out plenty of solid stuff. Where will you find the equal of the English golf club?

BALBUS. Look at the potteries: the new crown Derby! the new Chelsea! Look at the tapestries! Why, Greenwich Goblin has chased the French stuff out of the market.

CRASSUS. Dont forget our racing motor boats and cars, sir: the finest on earth, and all individually designed. No cheap mass production stuff there.

PLINY. And our live stock! Can you beat the English polo pony?

AMANDA. Or the English parlormaid? She wins in all the international beauty shows.

PLINY. Now Mandy, Mandy! None of your triviality.

MAGNUS. I am not sure that the British parlormaid is not the only real asset in your balance sheet.

AMANDA [*triumphant*] Aha! [*To Pliny*] You go home to bed and reflect on that, old man.

PROTEUS. Well, sir? Are you satisfied that we have the best paid proletariat in the world on our side?

MAGNUS [*gravely*] I dread revolution.

All except the two women laugh uproariously at this.

BOANERGES. I must join them there, sir. I am as much against chocolate creams as

you are: they never agree with me. But a revolution in England!!! Put that out of your head, sir. Not if you were to tear up Magna Carta in Trafalgar Square, and light the fires of Smithfield to burn every member of the House of Commons.

MAGNUS. I was not thinking of a revolution in England. I was thinking of the countries on whose tribute we are living. Suppose it occurs to them to stop paying it! That has happened before.

PLINY. Oh no, sir: no, no, no. What would become of their foreign trade with us?

MAGNUS. At a pinch, I think they could do without the Christmas crackers.

CRASSUS. Oh, thats childish.

MAGNUS. Children in their innocence are sometimes very practical, Mr Colonial Secretary. The more I see of the sort of prosperity that comes of your leaving our vital industries to big business men as long as they keep your constituents quiet with high wages, the more I feel as if I were sitting on a volcano.

LYSISTRATA [*who has been listening with implacable contempt to the discussion, suddenly breaks in in a sepulchral contralto*] Hear hear! My department was perfectly able and ready to deal with the supply of power from the tides in the north of Scotland, and you gave it away, like the boobs you are, to the Pentland Forth Syndicate: a gang of foreign capitalists who will make billions out of it at the people's expense while we are bungling and squabbling. Crassus worked that. His uncle is chairman.

CRASSUS. A lie. A flat lie. He is not related to me. He is only my stepson's father-in-law.

BALBUS. I demand an explanation of the words bungling and squabbling. We have had quite enough of them here today. Who are you getting at? It was not I who bungled the Factory Bill. I found it on my desk when I took office, with all His Majesty's suggestions in the margin; and you know it.

PROTEUS. Have you all done playing straight into His Majesty's hand, and making my situation here impossible?

Guilty silence.

PROTEUS [*proceeding deliberately and authoritatively*] The question before us is not one of our manners and our abilities. His Majesty will not press that question, because if he did he would oblige us to raise the question of his own morals.

MAGNUS [*starts*] What!

BALBUS. Good, Joe!

CRASSUS [*aside to Amanda*] Thats got him.

MAGNUS. Am I to take that threat seriously, Mr Proteus?

PROTEUS. If you try to prejudice what is a purely constitutional question by personal scandal, it will be easy enough for us to throw your mud back. In this conflict we are the challengers. You have the choice of weapons. If you choose scandal, we'll take you on at that. Personally I shall deplore it if you do. No good will come of washing our dirty linen in public. But dont make any mistake as to what will happen. I will be plain with you: I will dot the Is and cross the Ts. You will say that Crassus is a jobber.

CRASSUS [*springing up*] I—

PROTEUS [*fiercely crushing him*] Sit down. Leave this to me.

CRASSUS [*sits*] I a jobber! Well!

PROTEUS [*continuing*] You will say that I should never have given the Home Office to a bully like Balbus—

BALBUS [*intimidated by the fate of Crassus, but unable to forbear a protest*] Look here, Joe—

PROTEUS. You shut up, Bert. It's true.

BALBUS [*subsides with a shrug*]!

PROTEUS. Well, what will happen? There will be no denials, no excuses, no vindications. We shall not fall into that trap, clever as you are at setting it. Crassus will say just simply that you are a freethinker. And Balbus will say that you are a libertine.

THE MALE CABINET [*below their breaths*] Aha-a-a-a-h!!!

PROTEUS. Now, King Magnus! Our cards are on the table. What have you to say?

MAGNUS. Admirably put! People ask how it is that with all these strong characters around you hold your own as the only possible Prime Minister, in spite of your hysterics and tantrums, your secretiveness and your appalling laziness—

BALBUS [*delighted*] Hear hear! Youre getting it now, Joe.

MAGNUS [*continuing*] But when the decisive moment comes, they find out what a wonderful man you are.

PROTEUS. I am not a wonderful man. There is not a man or woman here whose job I could do as well as they do it. I am Prime Minister for the same reason that all Prime Ministers have been Prime Ministers: because I am good for nothing else. But I can keep to the point—when it suits me. And I can keep you to the point, sir, whether it suits you or not.

MAGNUS. At all events you do not flatter kings. One of them, at least, is grateful to you for that.

PROTEUS. Kings, as you and I very well know, rule their ministers by flattering them; and now that you are the only king left in the civilized half of Europe Nature seems to have concentrated in you all the genius for flattery that she used to have to divide between half a dozen kings, three emperors, and a Sultan.

MAGNUS. But what interest has a king in flattering a subject?

AMANDA. Suppose she's a goodlooking woman, sir!

NICOBAR. Suppose he has a lot of money, and the king's hard up!

PROTEUS. Suppose he is a Prime Minister, and you can do nothing except by his advice.

MAGNUS [*smiling with his utmost charm*] Ah, there you have hit the nail on the head. Well, I suppose I must surrender. I am beaten. You are all too clever for me.

BOANERGES. Well, nothing can be fairer than that.

PLINY [*rubbing his hands*] You are a gentleman, sir. We shant rub it in, you know.

BALBUS. Ever the best of friends. I am the last to kick a man when he's down.

CRASSUS. I may be a jobber; but nobody shall say that I am an ungenerous opponent.

BOANERGES [*suddenly overwhelmed with emotion, rises and begins singing in stentorian tones*]
    Should auld acquaintance be forgot,
    And never brought to mind—
Amanda bursts into uncontrollable laughter. The King looks reproachfully at her, struggling hard to keep his countenance. The others are beginning to join in the chorus when Proteus rises in a fury.

PROTEUS. Are you all drunk?

Dead silence. Boanerges sits down hastily. The other singers pretend that they have disapproved of his minstrelsy.

PROTEUS. You are at present engaged in a tug of war with the King: the tug of your lives. You think you have won. You havnt. All that has happened is that the King has let go the rope. You are sprawling on your backs; and he is laughing at you. Look at him! [*He sits down contemptuously*].

MAGNUS [*making no further attempt to conceal

his merriment] Come to my rescue, Amanda. It was you who set me off.

AMANDA [*wreathed with smiles*] You got me so nicely, sir. [*To Boanerges*] Bill: you are a great boob.

BOANERGES. I dont understand this. I understood His Majesty to give way to us in, I must say, the handsomest manner. Cant we take our victory like gentlemen?

MAGNUS. Perhaps I had better explain. I quite appreciate the frank and magnanimous spirit—may I say the English spirit?—in which my little concession has been received, especially by you, Mr Boanerges. But in truth it leaves matters just where they were; for I should never have dreamt of entering on a campaign of recrimination such as the Prime Minister suggested. As he has reminded you, my own character is far too vulnerable. A king is not allowed the luxury of a good character. Our country has produced millions of blameless greengrocers, but not one blameless monarch. I have to rule over more religious sects than I can count. To rule them impartially I must not belong to any of them; and they all regard people who do not belong to them as atheists. My court includes several perfectly respectable wives and mothers whose strange vanity it is to be talked about as abandoned females. To gain the reputation of being the king's mistress they would do almost anything except give the unfortunate monarch the pleasure of substantiating their claim. Side by side with them are the ladies who are really unscrupulous. They are so careful of their reputations that they lose no opportunity of indignantly denying that they have ever yielded to solicitations which have in fact never been made to them. Thus every king is supposed to be a libertine; and as, oddly enough, he owes a great part of his popularity to this belief, he cannot deny it without deeply disappointing his subjects.

There is a rather grim silence, during which the King looks round in vain for some encouraging response.

LYSISTRATA [*severely*] Your Majesty's private affairs do not concern us, in any case.

AMANDA [*splutters into an irrepressible laugh*]!!

MAGNUS [*looks reproachfully at Amanda*]!

AMANDA [*composing her features as best she can*] Excuse me.

CRASSUS. I hope your Majesty recognizes that kings are not the only people to whom certain sorts of mud always stick, no matter what fool throws them. Call a minister a jobber—

BALBUS. Or a bungler.

CRASSUS. Yes, or a bungler, and everybody believes it. Jobbery and incompetence are the two sorts of mud that stick to us, no matter how honest or capable we are; and we havnt the royal advantage that you enjoy, that the more the ladies take away your character the better the people like you.

BOANERGES [*suddenly*] Prime Minister: will you tell me what the Postmistress General is sniggering at?

AMANDA. This is a free country, Bill. A sense of humor is not a crime. And when the King is not setting me off, y o u are.

BOANERGES. Where is the joke? I dont see it.

AMANDA. If you could see a joke, Bill, you wouldnt be the great popular orator you are.

BOANERGES. Thank Heaven, I am not a silly giggler like some I could mention.

AMANDA. Thanks, dearest Bill. Now Joe: dont you think you have let us run loose long enough? What about that ultimatum?

MAGNUS [*shaking his head at her*] Traitor!

PROTEUS. I am in no hurry. His Majesty's speeches are very wise and interesting; and your back chat amuses both you and him. But the ultimatum is here all the time; and I shall not leave this room until I have His Majesty's signed pledge that its conditions will be observed.

All become gravely attentive.

MAGNUS. What are its terms?

PROTEUS. First, no more royal speeches.

MAGNUS. What! Not even if you dictate them?

PROTEUS. Not even if we dictate them. Your Majesty has a way of unrolling the manuscript and winking—

MAGNUS. Winking!

PROTEUS. You know what I mean. The best speech in the world can be read in such a way as to set the audience laughing at it. We have had enough of that. So, in future, no speeches.

MAGNUS. A dumb king?

PROTEUS. Of course we cannot object to such speeches as "We declare this foundation stone well and truly laid" and so forth. But politically, yes: a dumb king.

PLINY [*to soften it*] A constitutional king.

PROTEUS [*implacably*] A dumb king.

MAGNUS. Hm! What next?

PROTEUS. The working of the Press from the palace back stairs must cease.

MAGNUS. You know that I have no control of the Press. The Press is in the hands of men much richer than I, who would not insert a single paragraph against their own interests even if it were signed by my own hand and sent to them with a royal command.

PROTEUS. We know that. But though these men are richer than you, they are not cleverer. They get amusing articles, spiced with exclusive backstairs information, that dont seem to them to have anything to do with politics. The next thing they know is that their pet shares have dropped fifteen points; that capital is frightened off their best prospectuses; and that some of the best measures in our party program are made to look like city jobs.

MAGNUS. Am I supposed to write these articles?

NICOBAR. Your man Sempronius does. I can spot his fist out of fifty columns.

CRASSUS. So can I. When he is getting at me he always begins the sentence with "Singularly enough."

PLINY [chuckling] Thats his trademark. "Singularly enough." Ha! ha!

MAGNUS. Is there to be any restriction on the other side? I have noticed, for instance, that in a certain newspaper which loses no opportunity of disparaging the throne, the last sentence of the leading article almost invariably begins with the words "Once for all." Whose trademark is that?

PROTEUS. Mine.

MAGNUS. Frank, Mr Proteus.

PROTEUS. I know when to be frank. I learnt the trick from Your Majesty.

AMANDA [tries not to laugh]!

MAGNUS [gently reproachful] Amanda: what is the joke now? I am surprised at you.

AMANDA. Joe frank! When I want to find out what he is up to I have to come and ask your Majesty.

LYSISTRATA. That is perfectly true. In this Cabinet there is no such thing as a policy. Every man plays for his own hand.

NICOBAR. It's like a game of cards.

BALBUS. Only there are no partners.

LYSISTRATA. Except Crassus and Nicobar.

PLINY. Good, Lizzie! He! he! he!

NICOBAR. What do you mean?

LYSISTRATA. You know quite well what I mean. When will you learn, Nicobar, that it is no use trying to browbeat me. I began life as a schoolmistress; and I can browbeat any man in this Cabinet or out of it if he is fool enough to try to compete with me in that department.

BOANERGES. Order! order! Cannot the Prime Minister check these unseemly personalities?

PROTEUS. They give me time to think, Bill. When you have had as much parliamentary experience as I have you will be very glad of an interruption occasionally. May I proceed? *Silence.*

PROTEUS. His Majesty asks whether the restriction on press campaigning is to be entirely onesided. That, I take it, sir, is your question.

MAGNUS [nods assent]!

PROTEUS. The answer is in the affirmative.

BALBUS. Good!

MAGNUS. Anything more?

PROTEUS. Yes: one thing more. The veto must not be mentioned again. That can apply to both sides, if you like. The veto is dead.

MAGNUS. May we not make a historical reference to the corpse?

PROTEUS. No. I cannot carry on the King's government unless I can give pledges and carry them out. What is my pledge worth if our constituents are reminded every day that the King may veto anything that Parliament does? Do you expect me to say, when I am asked for a pledge, "You must ask the King"?

MAGNUS. I have to say "You must ask the Prime Minister."

PLINY [consoling him] Thats the constitution, you know.

MAGNUS. Quite. I only mention it to shew that the Prime Minister does not really wish to kill the veto. He only wishes to move it to next door.

PROTEUS. The people live next door. The name on the brass plate is Public Opinion.

MAGNUS [gravely] Admirably turned, Mr Prime Minister; but unreal. I am far more subject to public opinion than you, because, thanks to the general belief in democracy, you can always pretend that what you do is done by the will of the people, who, God knows, never dreamt of it, and would not have understood it if they had; whereas, for what a king does, he, and he alone, is held responsible. A demagogue may steal a horse where a king dare not look over a hedge.

LYSISTRATA. I doubt if that is any longer true, sir. I know that I get blamed for everything that goes wrong in my department.

MAGNUS. Ah! But what a despot you are, Lysistrata! Granted, however, that the people have found out long ago that democracy is humbug, and that instead of establishing responsible government it has abolished it, do you not see what this means?

BOANERGES [scandalized] Steady, steady! I cannot sit here and listen to such a word as humbug being applied to democracy. I am sorry, sir; but with all respect for you, I really must draw the line at that.

MAGNUS. You are right, Mr Boanerges, as you always are. Democracy is a very real thing, with much less humbug about it than many older institutions. But it means, not that the people govern, but that the responsibility and the veto now belong neither to kings nor demagogues as such, but to whoever is clever enough to get them.

LYSISTRATA. Yourself, sir, for example?

MAGNUS. I think I am in the running. That is why I do not feel bound to accept this ultimatum. By signing it I put myself out of the running. Why should I?

BALBUS. Because youre the king: thats why.

MAGNUS. Does it follow?

PROTEUS. If two men ride the same horse, one must ride behind.

LYSISTRATA. Which?

PROTEUS [turning to her sharply] What was that you said?

LYSISTRATA [with placid but formidable obstinacy and ironical explicitness] I said Which? You said that if two men rode the same horse one of them must ride behind. I said Which? [Explanatorily] Which man must ride behind?

AMANDA. Got it, Joe?

PROTEUS. That is exactly the question that has to be settled here and now.

AMANDA. "Once for all."

Everybody laughs except Proteus, who rises in a fury.

PROTEUS. I will not stand this perpetual tomfooling. I had rather be a dog than the Prime Minister of a country where the only things the inhabitants can be serious about are football and refreshments. Lick the king's boots: that is all you are fit for. [He dashes out of the room].

BALBUS. Youve done it now, Mandy. I hope youre proud of yourself.

MAGNUS. It is you, Amanda, who should go and coax him back. But I suppose I must do it myself, as usual. Excuse me, ladies and gentlemen.

He rises. The rest rise. He goes out.

BOANERGES. I told you. I told you what would come of conducting a conference with His Majesty as if it were a smoking concert. I am disgusted. [He flings himself back into his chair].

BALBUS. We'd just cornered the old fox; and then Amanda must have her silly laugh and lets him out of it [he sits].

NICOBAR. What are we to do now? thats what I want to know.

AMANDA [incorrigible] I suggest a little community singing [she makes conductorlike gestures].

NICOBAR. Yah!! [he sits down very sulkily].

AMANDA [sits down with a little splutter of laughter]!

CRASSUS [thoughtful] Take it easy, friends. Joe knows what he is about.

LYSISTRATA. Of course he does. I can excuse you, Bill, because it's your first day in the Cabinet. But if the rest of you havnt found out by this time that Joe's rages are invariably calculated, then nothing will ever teach you anything [she sits down contemptuously].

BOANERGES [in his grandest manner] Well, madam, I know I am a newcomer: everything must have a beginning. I am open to argument and conviction. The Prime Minister brought this conference, in what I admit was a very able and resolute manner, to the verge of a decision. Then, in a fit of childish temper he breaks up the conference, leaving us looking like fools with nothing done. And you tell me he did it on purpose! Where was the advantage to him in such a display? answer me that.

LYSISTRATA. He is settling the whole business with the King behind our backs. That is what Joe always contrives to do, by hook or crook.

PLINY. You didnt arrange it with him, Mandy: did you?

AMANDA. There wasnt any need to arrange it. Joe can always depend on one or other of us saying something that will give him an excuse for flying out.

CRASSUS. In my opinion, ladies and gentlemen, we have done our bit, and may leave the rest to Joe. Matters had reached a point at which it was yes or no between the Cabinet and the Crown. There is only one sort of committee that is better than a committee of two; and that is a committee of one. Like the family in Wordsworth's poem, we are seven—

LYSISTRATA. Eight.

CRASSUS. Well, seven or eight, we were too many for the final grapple. Two persons sticking to the point are worth eight all over the shop. So my advice is that we just sit here quietly until Joe comes back and tells us whats been settled. Perhaps Amanda will oblige with a song. [*He resumes his seat*].

The King returns with Proteus, who looks glum. All rise. The two resume their seats in silence. The rest sit down.

MAGNUS [*very grave*] The Prime Minister has been good enough to pursue the discussion with me in private to a point at which the issue is now clear. If I do not accept the ultimatum I shall receive your resignations and his: and the country will learn from his explanatory speech in the House of Commons that it is to choose between Cabinet government and monarchical government: an issue on which I frankly say that I should be very sorry to win, as I cannot carry on without the support of a body of ministers whose existence gives the English people a sensation of self-government.

AMANDA [*splutters*]!

CRASSUS [*whispers*] Shut up, will you?

MAGNUS [*continuing*] Naturally I want to avert a conflict in which success would damage me and failure disable me. But you tell me that I can do so only by signing pledges which would make me a mere Lord Chamberlain, without even the despotism which he exercises over the theatre. I should sink below the level of the meanest of my subjects, my sole privilege being that of being shot at when some victim of misgovernment resorts to assassination to avenge himself. How am I to defend myself? You are many: I oppose you single-handed. There was a time when the king could depend on the support of the aristocracy and the cultivated bourgeoisie. Today there is not a single aristocrat left in politics, not a single member of the professions, not a single leading personage in big business or finance. They are richer than ever, more powerful than ever, more able and better educated than ever. But not one of them will touch this drudgery of government, this public work that never ends because we

cannot finish one job without creating ten fresh ones. We get no thanks for it because ninety nine hundredths of it is unknown to the people, and the remaining hundredth is resented by them as an invasion of their liberty or an increase in their taxation. It wears out the strongest man, and even the strongest woman, in five or six years. It slows down to nothing when we are fresh from our holidays and best able to bear it, and rises in an overwhelming wave through some unforeseen catastrophe when we are on the verge of nervous breakdown from overwork and fit for rest and sleep only. And this drudgery, remember, is a sweated trade, the only one now left in this country. My civil list leaves me a poor man among multi-millionaires. Your salaries can be earned ten times over in the city by anyone with outstanding organizing or administrative ability. History tells us that the first Lord Chancellor who abandoned the woolsack for the city boardroom struck the nation with amazement: today the nation would be equally amazed if a man of his ability thought it worth his while to prefer the woolsack even to the stool of an office boy as a jumping-off place for his ambition. Our work is no longer even respected. It is looked down on by our men of genius as dirty work. What great actor would exchange his stage? what great barrister his court? what great preacher his pulpit? for the squalor of the political arena in which we have to struggle with foolish factions in parliament and with ignorant voters in the constituencies? The scientists will have nothing to do with us; for the atmosphere of politics is not the atmosphere of science. Even political science, the science by which civilization must live or die, is busy explaining the past whilst we have to grapple with the present: it leaves the ground before our feet in black darkness whilst it lights up every corner of the landscape behind us. All the talent and genius of the country is bought up by the flood of unearned money. On that poisoned wealth talent and genius live far more luxuriously in the service of the rich than we in the service of our country. Politics, once the centre of attraction for ability, public spirit, and ambition, has now become the refuge of a few fanciers of public speaking and party intrigue who find all the other avenues to distinction closed to them either by their lack of practical ability, their comparative poverty and lack of education, or, let me hasten to add, their hatred of oppression and injustice, and their contempt for the chicaneries and false pretences of commercialized professionalism. History tells us of a gentleman-statesman who declared that such people were not fit to govern. Within a year it was discovered that they could govern at least as well as anyone else who could be persuaded to take on the job. Then began that abandonment of politics by the old governing class which has ended in all Cabinets, conservative no less than progressive, being what were called in the days of that rash statesman Labor Cabinets. Do not misunderstand me: I do not want the old governing class back. It governed so selfishly that the people would have perished if democracy had not swept it out of politics. But evil as it was in many ways, at least it stood above the tyranny of popular ignorance and popular poverty. Today only the King stands above that tyranny. You are dangerously subject to it. In spite of my urgings and remonstrances you have not yet dared to take command of our schools and put a stop to the inculcation upon your unfortunate children of superstitions and prejudices that stand like stone walls across every forward path. Are you well advised in trying to reduce me to your own slavery to them? If I do not stand above them there is no longer any reason for my existence at all. I stand for the future and the past, for the posterity that has no vote and the tradition that never had any. I stand for the great abstractions: for conscience and virtue; for the eternal against the expedient; for the evolutionary appetite against the day's gluttony; for intellectual integrity, for humanity, for the rescue of industry from commercialism and of science from professionalism, for everything that you desire as sincerely as I, but which in you is held in leash by the Press, which can organize against you the ignorance and superstition, the timidity and credulity, the gullibility and prudery, the hating and hunting instinct of the voting mob, and cast you down from power if you utter a word to alarm or displease the adventurers who have the Press in their pockets. Between you and that tyranny stands the throne. I have no elections to fear; and if any newspaper magnate dares offend me, that magnate's fashion-able wife and marriageable daughters will soon make him understand that the King's displeasure is still a sentence of social death within range of St James's Palace. Think of the things you dare not do! the persons you dare not offend! Well, a King with a little courage may tackle them for you. Responsibilities which would break your backs may still be borne on a King's shoulders. But he must be a king, not a puppet. You would be responsible for a puppet, remember that. But whilst you continue to support me as a separate and independent estate of the realm, I am your scapegoat: you get the credit of all our popular legislation whilst you put the odium of all our resistance to ignorant popular clamor on me. I ask you, before you play your last card and destroy me, to consider where you will be without me. Think once: think twice; for your danger is, not that I may defeat you, but that your success is certain if you insist.

LYSISTRATA. Splendid!

AMANDA. You did speak that piece beautifully, sir.

BALBUS [grumbling] All very well; but what about my brother-in-law Mike?

LYSISTRATA [maddened] Oh, confound your brother-in-law Mike!

BOANERGES. Order! order!

LYSISTRATA [to the King] I beg your pardon, sir; but really—at a moment like this—[words fail her].

MAGNUS [to Balbus] If I had not put my foot down, Mr Balbus, the Prime Minister would have been unable to keep your brother-in-law out of the Cabinet.

BALBUS [aggressively] And why should he not be in the Cabinet?

AMANDA. Booze, my Balby: booze. Raising the elbow!

BALBUS [bullying] Who says so?

AMANDA. I do, darling.

BALBUS [subsiding] Well, perhaps it would surprise you all to know that Mike doesnt drink as much as I do.

AMANDA. You carry it better, Bert.

PLINY. Mike never knows when to stop.

CRASSUS. The time for Mike to stop is before he begins, if you ask me.

LYSISTRATA [impetuously] What sort of animals are you—you men? The king puts before us the most serious question of principle we shall ever have to deal with; and off you start discussing whether this drunken wretch takes honest whisky like Balbus or methylated spirit or petrol or whatever he can lay his hands on when the fit takes him.

BALBUS. I agree with that. What does it matter what Mike drinks? What does it matter whether he drinks or not? Mike would strengthen the Cabinet because he represents Breakages, Limited, the biggest industrial corporation in the country.

LYSISTRATA [*letting herself go*] Just so! Breakages, Limited! just so! Listen to me, sir; and judge whether I have not reason to feel everything you have just said to the very marrow of my bones. Here am I, the Powermistress Royal. I have to organize and administer all the motor power in the country for the good of the country. I have to harness the winds and the tides, the oils and the coal seams. I have to see that every little sewing machine in the Hebrides, every dentist's drill in Shetland, every carpet sweeper in Margate, has its stream of driving power on tap from a switch in the wall as punctually as the great thundering dynamos of our big industrial plants. I do it; but it costs twice as much as it should. Why? Because every new invention is bought up and suppressed by Breakages, Limited. Every breakdown, every accident, every smash and crash, is a job for them. But for them we should have unbreakable glass, unbreakable steel, imperishable materials of all sorts. But for them our goods trains could be started and stopped without battering and tearing the vitals out of every wagon and sending it to their repair shops once a week instead of once a year. Our national repair bill runs up to hundreds of millions. I could name you a dozen inventions within my own term of office which would have effected enormous economies in breakages and breakdowns; but these people can afford to pay an inventor more for his machine or his process or whatever it may be than he could hope to make by a legitimate use of it; and when they have bought it they smother it. When the inventor is poor and not good at defending himself they make bogus trials of his machine and report that it is no use. I have been shot at twice by inventors driven crazy by this sort of thing: they blamed me for it—as if I could stand up against this monster with its millions and its newspapers and its fingers in every pie. It is heartbreaking. I love my department:

I dream of nothing but its efficiency: with me it comes before every personal tie, every happiness that common women run after. I would give my right hand to see these people in the bankruptcy court with half their business abolished and the other half done in public workshops where public losses are not private gains. You stand for that, sir; and I would be with you to the last drop of my blood if I dared. But what can I do? If I said one word of this in public, not a week would pass in the next two years without an article on the inefficiency and corruption of all Government departments, especially departments managed, like mine, by females. They would dig up the very machines they have buried, and make out that it is my fault that they have never been brought into use. They would set their private police to watch me day and night to get something against my private character. One of their directors told me to my face that by lifting up his finger he could get my windows broken by the mob; and that Breakages, Limited, would get the job of putting in new glass. And it is true. It is infamous; it is outrageous; but if I attempt to fight them I shall be hounded out of public life, and they will shove Mouldy Mike into the Cabinet to run my department in their interests: that is, to make such a failure of it that Joe will have to sell it to Breakages, Limited, at scrap iron prices. I—I—oh, it is beyond bearing [*she breaks down*].

There is a troubled silence for a moment. Then the voice of the Prime Minister breaks it impressively as he addresses the King.

PROTEUS. You hear that, sir. Your one supporter in the Cabinet admits that the industrial situation is too strong for her. I do not pretend to be able to control the women in my Cabinet; but not one of them dare support you.

AMANDA [*springing up*] Whats that? Not dare! What do you bet that I dont go down to Mouldy Mike's constituency and say everything that Lizzie has said and a lot more too, if I choose? I tell you, Breakages, Limited, never interferes in my department. I'd like to catch them at it.

MAGNUS. I am afraid that that is only because the efficiency of the Post Office is as important to them as to the general public.

AMANDA. Stuff! They could get rid of me without shutting up the Post Office. Theyre afraid of me—of me, Amanda Postlethwaite.

MAGNUS. You coax them, I am afraid.

AMANDA. Coax! What do you think they care for coaxing? They can have all the coaxing they want from younger and prettier women than I by paying for it. No use trying to coax that lot. Intimidate them: thats the way to handle them.

LYSISTRATA [*her voice still broken*] I wish I could intimidate them.

MAGNUS. But what can Amanda do that you cannot do?

AMANDA. I'll tell you. She cant mimic people. And she cant sing funny songs. I can do both; and that—with all respect, sir— makes me the real queen of England.

BOANERGES. Oh, come! Disgraceful! Shame!

AMANDA. If you provoke me, Bill, I'll drive you out of your constituency inside of two months.

BOANERGES. Ho! You will, will you? How?

AMANDA. Just as I drove the Chairman of Breakages out of my own constituency when he came down there and tried to take my seat from me.

MAGNUS. I never quite understood why he turned tail. How did you do it?

AMANDA. I'll tell you. He opened his campaign with a great Saturday night speech against me in the Home Lovers' Hall to five thousand people. In that same hall a week later, I faced a meeting of the very same people. I didnt argue. I mimicked him. I took all the highfalutin passages in his speech, and repeated them in his best manner until I had the whole five thousand laughing at him. Then I asked them would they like me to sing; and their Yes nearly lifted the roof off. I had two songs. They both had choruses. One went "She lets me go out on Saturday night, on Saturday night, on Saturday night" —like that. The other went "Boo! Hoo! I want Amanda's Teddy bear to play with." They sang it under the windows of his hotel next time he came. He cancelled his meeting and left. And thats how England is governed by yours truly, sir. Lucky for England that Queen Amanda is a good sort, in spite of some surface faults. [*She resumes her seat with triumphant self-satisfaction*].

BALBUS. Lucky for England theres only one of you: thats what *I* say.

AMANDA [*wafts him a kiss*]!

MAGNUS. Should not the Queen support the King, your Majesty?

AMANDA. Sorry, sir; but there isnt room for two monarchs in my realm. I am against you on principle because the talent for mimicry isnt hereditary.

PROTEUS. Now, anybody else? We have heard why the two ladies cannot support the King. Is there anybody who can?

Silence.

MAGNUS. I see that my appeal has been in vain. I do not reproach you, ladies and gentlemen, because I perceive that your situation is a difficult one. The question is, how to change it.

NICOBAR. Sign the ultimatum: that is how.

MAGNUS. I am not quite convinced of that. The Home Secretary's brother-in-law was quite willing to sign the pledge of total abstinence if I would admit him to the Cabinet. His offer was not accepted, because, though none of us doubted that he would sign the pledge, we were not equally certain that the infirmities of his nature would allow him to keep it. My nature is also subject to infirmity. Are you satisfied, Mr Proteus, that if I sign this ultimatum, I shall not inevitably relapse into the conduct that my nature dictates?

PROTEUS [*his patience strained*] What is the use of going on like this? You are like a man on the scaffold, spinning out his prayers to put off the inevitable execution as long as possible. Nothing that you can say will make any difference. You know you must sign. Why not sign and have done with it?

NICOBAR. Now youre talking, Joe.

BALBUS. Thats the stuff to give him.

PLINY. Gulp it down, sir. It wont get any sweeter by keeping: what?

LYSISTRATA. Oh, for God's sake, sign, sir. This is torture to me.

MAGNUS. I perceive, gentlemen, that I have come to the end of your patience. I will tax it no further: you have been very forbearing; and I thank you for it. I will say no more by way of discussion; but I must have until five o'clock this evening to consider my decision. At that hour, if I can find no other way out, I will sign without another word. Meanwhile, ladies and gentlemen, au revoir! *He rises. All rise. He marches out.*

PROTEUS. His last wriggle. Never mind: we have him safe enough. What about lunch? I am starving. Will you lunch with me, Lizzie?

LYSISTRATA. Dont speak to me. [*She rushes out distractedly*].

AMANDA. Poor darling Lizzie! She's a regular old true blue Diehard. If only I had her brains and education! or if she had my variety talent! what a queen she'd make! Like old Queen Elizabeth, eh? Dont grieve, Joe: I'll lunch with you since youre so pressing.

CRASSUS. Come and lunch with me—all of you.

AMANDA. What opulence! Can you afford it?

CRASSUS. Breakages will pay. They have a standing account at the Ritz. Over five thousand a year, it comes to.

PROTEUS. Right. Let us spoil the Egyptians.

BOANERGES [with Roman dignity] My lunch will cost me one and sixpence; and I shall pay for it myself [he stalks out].

AMANDA [calling after him] Dont make a beast of yourself, Bill. Ta ta!

PROTEUS. Come on, come on: it's ever so late.

They all hurry out. Sempronius and Pamphilius, entering, have to stand aside to let them pass before returning to their desks. Proteus, with Amanda on his arm, stops in the doorway on seeing them.

PROTEUS. Have you two been listening, may I ask?

PAMPHILIUS. Well, it would be rather inconvenient, wouldnt it, if we had to be told everything that passed?

SEMPRONIUS. Once for all, Mr Proteus, the King's private secretaries must hear everything, see everything, and know everything.

PROTEUS. Singularly enough, Mr Sempronius, I havnt the slightest objection [he goes].

AMANDA [going with him] Goodbye, Semmy. So long, Pam.

SEMPRONIUS.
PAMPHILIUS. } [seating themselves at their writing tables and yawning prodigiously] Ou-ou-ou-ou-ou-fff!!!

AN INTERLUDE

Orinthia's boudoir at half-past fifteen on the same day. She is at her writing table scribbling notes. She is romantically beautiful, and beautifully dressed. As the table is against the wall near a corner, with the other wall on her left, her back alone is visible from the middle of the room. The door is near the corner diagonally opposite. There is a large settee in the middle of the room.

The King enters and waits on the threshold.

ORINTHIA [crossly, without looking round] Who is that?

MAGNUS. His Majesty the King.

ORINTHIA. I dont want to see him.

MAGNUS. How soon will you be disengaged?

ORINTHIA. I didnt say I was engaged. Tell the king I dont want to see him.

MAGNUS. He awaits your pleasure [he comes in and seats himself on the settee].

ORINTHIA. Go away. [A pause]. I wont speak to you. [Another pause]. If my private rooms are to be broken into at any moment because they are in the palace, and the king is not a gentleman, I must take a house outside. I am writing to the agents about one now.

MAGNUS. What is our quarrel today, belovéd?

ORINTHIA. Ask your conscience.

MAGNUS. I have none when you are concerned. You must tell me.

She takes a book from the table and rises; then sweeps superbly forward to the settee and flings the book into his hands.

ORINTHIA. There!

MAGNUS. What is this?

ORINTHIA. Page 16. Look at it.

MAGNUS [looking at the title on the back of the book] "Songs of our Great Great Grandparents." What page did you say?

ORINTHIA [between her teeth] Six-teen.

MAGNUS [opening the book and finding the page, his eye lighting up with recognition as he looks at it] Ah! The Pilgrim of Love!

ORINTHIA. Read the first three words—if you dare.

MAGNUS [smiling as he caresses the phrase] "Orinthia, my belovéd".

ORINTHIA. The name you pretended to invent specially for me, the only woman in the world for you. Picked up out of the rubbish basket in a secondhand bookseller's! And I thought you were a poet!

MAGNUS. Well, one poet may consecrate a name for another. Orinthia is a name full of magic for me. It could not be that if I had invented it myself. I heard it at a concert of ancient music when I was a child; and I have treasured it ever since.

ORINTHIA. You always have a pretty excuse. You are the King of liars and humbugs. You cannot understand how a falsehood like that wounds me.

MAGNUS [remorsefully, stretching out his arms towards her] Belovéd: I am sorry.

ORINTHIA. Put your hands in your pockets: they shall not touch me ever again.

MAGNUS [obeying] Dont pretend to be hurt

unless you really are, dearest. It wrings my heart.

ORINTHIA. Since when have you set up a heart? Did you buy that, too, secondhand?

MAGNUS. I have something in me that winces when you are hurt—or pretend to be.

ORINTHIA [contemptuously] Yes: I have only to squeal, and you will take me up and pet me as you would a puppy run over by a car. [Sitting down beside him, but beyond arm's length] That is what you give me when my heart demands love. I had rather you kicked me.

MAGNUS. I should like to kick you sometimes, when you are specially aggravating. But I shouldnt do it well. I should be afraid of hurting you all the time.

ORINTHIA. I believe you would sign my death warrant without turning a hair.

MAGNUS. That is true, in a way. It is wonderful how subtle your mind is, as far as it goes.

ORINTHIA. It does not go as far as yours, I suppose.

MAGNUS. I dont know. Our minds go together half way. Whether it is that your mind stops there or else that the road forks, and you take the high road and I take the low road, I cannot say; but somehow after a certain point we lose one another.

ORINTHIA. And then you go back to your Amandas and Lysistratas: creatures whose idea of romance is a minister in love with a department, and whose bedside books are blue books.

MAGNUS. They are not always thinking of some man or other. That is a rather desirable extension of their interests, in my opinion. If Lysistrata had a lover I should not be interested in him in the least; and she would bore me to distraction if she could talk of nothing else. But I am very much interested in her department. Her devotion to it gives us a topic of endless interest.

ORINTHIA. Well, go to her: I am not detaining you. But dont tell her that I have nothing to talk about but men: for that is a lie; and you know it.

MAGNUS. It is, as you say, a lie; and I know it. But I did not say it.

ORINTHIA. You implied it. You meant it. When those ridiculous political women are with us you talk to them all the time, and never say a word to me.

MAGNUS. Nor you to me. We cannot talk to one another in public: we have nothing to say that could be said before other people. Yet we find enough to say to one another when we are alone together. Would you change that if you could?

ORINTHIA. You are as slippery as an eel; but you shall not slip through my fingers. Why do you surround yourself with political bores and frumps and dowdy busybodies who cant talk: they can only debate about their dull departments and their fads and their election chances. [Rising impatiently] Who could talk to such people? If it were not for the nonentities of wives and husbands they drag about with them, there would be nobody to talk to at all. And even they can talk of nothing but the servants and the baby. [Suddenly returning to her seat] Listen to me, Magnus. Why can you not be a real king?

MAGNUS. In what way, belovédest?

ORINTHIA. Send all these stupid people packing. Make them do their drudgeries in their departments without bothering you about it, as you make your servants here sweep the floors and dust the furniture. Live a really noble and beautiful life—a kingly life—with me. What you need to make you a real king is a real queen.

MAGNUS. But I have got one.

ORINTHIA. Oh, you are blind. You are worse than blind: you have low tastes. Heaven is offering you a rose; and you cling to a cabbage.

MAGNUS [laughing] That is a very apt metaphor, belovéd. But what wise man, if you force him to choose between doing without roses and doing without cabbages, would not secure the cabbages? Besides, all these old married cabbages were once roses; and, though young things like you dont remember that, their husbands do. They dont notice the change. Besides, you should know better than anyone else that when a man gets tired of his wife and leaves her it is never because she has lost her good looks. The new love is often older and uglier than the old.

ORINTHIA. Why should I know it better than anyone else?

MAGNUS. Why, because you have been married twice; and both your husbands have run away from you to much plainer and stupider women. When I begged your present husband to come back to court for a while for the sake of appearances he said no man could call his soul his own in the same house with you. And yet that man was utterly infatuated with your beauty when he married you. Your first husband actually forced a good wife to divorce him so that he might marry you; but before two years were out he went back to her and died in her arms, poor chap.

ORINTHIA. Shall I tell you why these men could not live with me? It was because I am a thoroughbred, and they are only hacks. They had nothing against me: I was perfectly faithful to them. I kept their houses beautifully: I fed them better than they had ever been fed in their lives. But because I was higher than they were, and greater, they could not stand the strain of trying to live up to me. So I let them go their way, poor wretches, back to their cabbages. Look at the old creature Ignatius is living with now! She gives you his real measure.

MAGNUS. An excellent woman. Ignatius is quite happy with her. I never saw a man so changed.

ORINTHIA. Just what he is fit for. Commonplace. Bourgeoise. She trots through the streets shopping. [*Rising*] I tread the plains of Heaven. Common women cannot come where I am; and common men find themselves out and slink away.

MAGNUS. It must be magnificent to have the consciousness of a goddess without ever doing a thing to justify it.

ORINTHIA. Give me a goddess's work to do; and I will do it. I will even stoop to a queen's work if you will share the throne with me. But do not pretend that people become great by doing great things. They do great things because they are great, if the great things come along. But they are great just the same when the great things do not come along. If I never did anything but sit in this room and powder my face and tell you what a clever fool you are, I should still be heavens high above the millions of common women who do their domestic duty, and sacrifice themselves, and run Trade departments and all the rest of the vulgarities. Has all the tedious public work you have done made you any the better? I have seen you before and after your boasted strokes of policy; and you were the same man, and would have been the same man to me and to yourself if you had never done them. Thank God my self-consciousness is something nobler than vulgar conceit in having done something. It is what I am, not

what I do, that you must worship in me. If you want deeds, go to your men and women of action, as you call them, who are all in a conspiracy to pretend that the mechanical things they do, the foolhardy way they risk their worthless lives, or their getting up in the morning at four and working sixteen hours a day for thirty years, like coral insects, make them great. What are they for? these dull slaves? To keep the streets swept for me. To enable me to reign over them in beauty like the stars without having anything to do with their slavery except to console it, to dazzle it, to enable them to forget it in adoring dreams of me. Am I not worth it? [*She sits, fascinating him*]. Look into my eyes and tell the truth. Am I worth it or not?

MAGNUS. To me, who love beauty, yes. But you should hear the speeches Balbus makes about your pension.

ORINTHIA. And my debts: do not forget my debts, my mortgages, the bill of sale on my furniture, the thousands I have had from the moneylenders to save me from being sold up because I will not borrow from my friends. Lecture me again about them; but do not dare pretend that the people grudge me my pension. They glory in it, and in my extravagance, as you call it.

MAGNUS [*more gravely*] By the way, Orinthia, when your dressmakers took up that last bill for you, they were speculating, were they not, in your chances of becoming my queen some day?

ORINTHIA. Well, what if they were?

MAGNUS. They would hardly have ventured on that without a hint from somebody. Was it from you?

ORINTHIA. You think me capable of that! You have a very low side to you, Magnus.

MAGNUS. No doubt: like other mortal fabrics I have a wrong side and a right side. But it is no use your giving yourself airs, belovédest. You are capable of anything. Do you deny that there was some suggestion of the kind?

ORINTHIA. How dare you challenge me to deny it? I never deny. Of course there was a suggestion of the kind.

MAGNUS. I thought so.

ORINTHIA. Oh, stupid! stupid! Go keep a grocer's shop: that is what you are fit for. Do you suppose that the suggestion came from me? Why, you great oaf, it is in the air: when my dressmaker hinted at it I told her that if she ever dared to repeat such a thing she should never get another order from me. But can I help people seeing what is as plain as the sun in the heavens? [*Rising again*] Everyone knows that I am the real queen. Everyone treats me as the real queen. They cheer me in the streets. When I open one of the art exhibitions or launch a new ship they crowd the place out. I am one of Nature's queens; and they know it. If you do not, you are not one of Nature's kings.

MAGNUS. Sublime! Nothing but genuine inspiration could give a woman such cheek.

ORINTHIA. Yes: inspiration, not cheek. [*Sitting as before*] Magnus: when are you going to face my destiny, and your own?

MAGNUS. But my wife? the queen? What is to become of my poor dear Jemima?

ORINTHIA. Oh, drown her: shoot her: tell your chauffeur to drive her into the Serpentine and leave her there. The woman makes you ridiculous.

MAGNUS. I dont think I should like that. And the public would think it illnatured.

ORINTHIA. Oh, you know what I mean. Divorce her. Make her divorce you. It is quite easy. That was how Ronny married me. Everybody does it when they need a change.

MAGNUS. But I cant imagine what I should do without Jemima.

ORINTHIA. Nobody else can imagine what you do with her. But you need not do without her. You can see as much of her as you like when we are married. I shall not be jealous and make scenes.

MAGNUS. That is very magnanimous of you. But I am afraid it does not settle the difficulty. Jemima would not think it right to keep up her present intimacy with me if I were married to you.

ORINTHIA. What a woman! Would she be in any worse position then than I am in now?

MAGNUS. No.

ORINTHIA. You mean, then, that you do not mind placing me in a position that you do not think good enough for her?

MAGNUS. Orinthia: I did not place you in your present position. You placed yourself in it. I could not resist you. You gathered me like a daisy.

ORINTHIA. Did you want to resist me?

MAGNUS. Oh no. I never resist temptation, because I have found that things that are bad for me do not tempt me.

ORINTHIA. Well, then, what are we talking about?

MAGNUS. I forget. I think I was explaining the impossibility of my wife changing places with you.

ORINTHIA. Why impossible, pray?

MAGNUS. I cannot make you understand: you see you have never been really married, though you have led two captives to the altar, and borne children to one of them. Being your husband is only a job for which one man will do as well as another, and which the last man holds subject to six months notice in the divorce court. Being my wife is something quite different. The smallest derogation to Jemima's dignity would hit me like the lash of a whip across the face. About yours, somehow, I do not care a rap.

ORINTHIA. Nothing can derogate from my dignity: it is divine. Hers is only a convention: that is why you tremble when it is challenged.

MAGNUS. Not a bit. It is because she is a part of my real workaday self. You belong to fairyland.

ORINTHIA. Suppose she dies! Will you die too?

MAGNUS. Not immediately. I shall have to carry on as best I can without her, though the prospect terrifies me.

ORINTHIA. Might not carrying on without her include marrying me?

MAGNUS. My dear Orinthia, I had rather marry the devil. Being a wife is not your job.

ORINTHIA. You think so because you have no imagination. And you dont know me because I have never let you really possess me. I should make you more happy than any man has ever yet been on earth.

MAGNUS. I defy you to make me more happy than our strangely innocent relations have already made me.

ORINTHIA [*rising restlessly*] You talk like a child or a saint. [*Turning on him*] I can give you a new life: one of which you have no conception. I can give you beautiful, wonderful children: have you ever seen a lovelier boy than my Basil?

MAGNUS. Your children are beautiful; but they are fairy children; and I have several very real ones already. A divorce would not sweep them out of the way of the fairies.

ORINTHIA. In short, when your golden moment comes—when the gates of heaven open before you, you are afraid to come out of your pigsty.

MAGNUS. If I am a pig, a pigsty is the

proper place for me.

ORINTHIA. I cannot understand it. All men are fools and moral cowards when you come to know them. But you are less of a fool and less of a moral coward than any man I have ever known. You have almost the makings of a first rate woman in you. When I leave the earth and soar up to the regions which are my real eternal home, you can follow me: I can speak to you as I can speak to no one else; and you can say things to me that would just make your stupid wife cry. There is more of you in me than of any other man within my reach. There is more of me in you than of any other woman within y o u r reach. We are meant for one another: it is written across the sky that you and I are queen and king. How can you hesitate? What attraction is there for you in your common healthy jolly lumps of children and your common housekeeper wife and the rabble of dowdies and upstarts and intriguers and clowns that think they are governing the country when they are only squabbling with you? Look again at me, man: again and again. Am I not worth a million such? Is not life with me as high above them as the sun is above the gutter?

MAGNUS. Yes yes yes yes, of course. You are lovely: you are divine [*she cannot restrain a gesture of triumph*]. And you are enormously amusing.

This anti-climax is too much for Orinthia's exaltation; but she is too clever not to appreciate it. With another gesture, this time of deflation, she sits down at his left hand with an air of suffering patience, and listens in silence to the harangue which follows.

MAGNUS. Some day perhaps Nature will graft the roses on the cabbages and make every woman as enchanting as you; and then what a glorious lark life will be! But at present, what I come here for is to enjoy talking to you like this when I need an hour's respite from royalty: when my stupid wife has been worrying me, or my jolly lumps of children bothering me, or my turbulent Cabinet obstructing me: when, as the doctors say, what I need is a change. You see, my dear, there is no wife on earth so precious, no children so jolly, no Cabinet so tactful that it is impossible ever to get tired of them. Jemima has her limitations, as you have observed. And I have mine. Now if our limitations exactly corresponded I should

never want to talk to anyone else; and neither would she. But as that never happens, we are like all other married couples: that is, there are subjects which can never be discussed between us because they are sore subjects. There are people we avoid mentioning to one another because one of us likes them and the other doesnt. Not only individuals, but whole sorts of people. For instance, your sort. My wife doesnt like your sort, doesnt understand it, mistrusts and dreads it. Not without reason; for women like you are dangerous to wives. But I dont dislike your sort: I understand it, being a little in that line myself. At all events I am not afraid of it; though the least allusion to it brings a cloud over my wife's face. So when I want to talk freely about it I come and talk to you. And I take it she talks to friends of hers about people of whom she never talks to me. She has men friends from whom she can get some things that she cannot get from me. If she didnt do so she would be limited by my limitations, which would end in her hating me. So I always do my best to make her men friends feel at home with us.

ORINTHIA. A model husband in a model household! And when the model household becomes a bore, I am the diversion.

MAGNUS. Well, what more can you ask? Do not let us fall into the common mistake of expecting to become one flesh and one spirit. Every star has its own orbit; and between it and its nearest neighbor there is not only a powerful attraction but an infinite distance. When the attraction becomes stronger than the distance the two do not embrace: they crash together in ruin. We two also have our orbits, and must keep an infinite distance between us to avoid a disastrous collision. Keeping our distance is the whole secret of good manners; and without good manners human society is intolerable and impossible.

ORINTHIA. Would any other woman stand your sermons, and even like them?

MAGNUS. Orinthia: we are only two children at play; and you must be content to be my queen in fairyland. And [*rising*] I must go back to my work.

ORINTHIA. What work have you that is more important than being with me?

MAGNUS. None.

ORINTHIA. Then sit down.

MAGNUS. Unfortunately, this silly business of government must be carried on. And there is a crisis this evening, as usual.

ORINTHIA. But the crisis is not until five: I heard all about it from Sempronius. Why do you encourage that greedy schemer Proteus? He humbugs you. He humbugs everybody. He even humbugs himself; and of course he humbugs that Cabinet which is a disgrace to you: it is like an overcrowded third class carriage. Why do you allow such riffraff to waste your time? After all, what are you paid for? To be a king: that is, to wipe your boots on common people.

MAGNUS. Yes; but this king business, as the Americans call it, has got itself so mixed up with democracy that half the country expects me to wipe my perfectly polished boots on the Cabinet, and the other half expects me to let the Cabinet wipe its muddy boots on me. The Crisis at five o'clock is to decide which of us is to be the doormat.

ORINTHIA. And you will condescend to fight with Proteus for power?

MAGNUS. Oh no: I never fight. But I sometimes win.

ORINTHIA. If you let yourself be beaten by that trickster and poseur, never dare to approach me again.

MAGNUS. Proteus is a clever fellow: even on occasion a fine fellow. It would give me no satisfaction to beat him: I hate beating people. But there would be some innocent fun in outwitting him.

ORINTHIA. Magnus: you are a mollycoddle. If you were a real man you would just delight in beating him to a jelly.

MAGNUS. A real man would never do as a king. I am only an idol, my love; and all I can do is to draw the line at being a cruel idol. [*He looks at his watch*] Now I must really be off. Au revoir.

ORINTHIA [*looking at her wrist watch*] But it is only twentyfive minutes past four. You have heaps of time before five.

MAGNUS. Yes; but tea is at half-past four.

ORINTHIA [*catching him by the arm with a snakelike dart*] Never mind your tea. I will give you your tea.

MAGNUS. Impossible, belovéd. Jemima does not like to be kept waiting.

ORINTHIA. Oh, bother Jemima! You shall not leave me to go to Jemima [*she pulls him back so vigorously that he falls into the seat beside her*].

MAGNUS. My dear, I must.

ORINTHIA. No, not today. Listen, Magnus.

I have something very particular to say to you.

MAGNUS. You have not. You are only trying to make me late to annoy my wife. [*He tries to rise, but is pulled back*]. Let me go, please.

ORINTHIA [*holding on*] Why are you so afraid of your wife? You are the laughing stock of London, you poor henpecked darling.

MAGNUS. Henpecked! What do you call this? At least my wife does not restrain me by bodily violence.

ORINTHIA. I will not be deserted for your old Dutch.

MAGNUS. Listen, Orinthia. Dont be absurd. You know I must go. Do be good.

ORINTHIA. Only ten minutes more.

MAGNUS. It is half-past already.

He tries to rise; but she holds him back.

MAGNUS [*pausing for breath*] You are doing this out of sheer devilment. You are so abominably strong that I cannot break loose without hurting you. Must I call the guard?

ORINTHIA. Do, do. It will be in all the papers tomorrow.

MAGNUS. Fiend [*Summoning all his dignity*] Orinthia: I command you.

ORINTHIA [*laughs wildly*]!!!

MAGNUS [*furious*] Very well, then, you she devil: you s h a l l let go.

He tackles her in earnest. She flings her arms round him and holds on with mischievous enjoyment. There is a tapping at the door; but they do not hear it. As he is breaking loose she suddenly shifts her grip to his waist and drags him on to the floor, where they roll over one another. Sempronius enters. He stares at the scandalous scene for a moment; then hastily slips out; shuts the door; clears his throat and blows his nose noisily; and knocks loudly and repeatedly. The two combatants cease hostilities and scramble hastily to their feet.

MAGNUS. Come in.

SEMPRONIUS [*entering*] Her Majesty sent me to remind you that tea is waiting, sir.

MAGNUS. Thank you. [*He goes quickly out*].

ORINTHIA [*panting but greatly pleased with herself*] The King forgets everything when he is here. So do I, I am afraid. I am so sorry.

SEMPRONIUS [*stiffly*] No explanations are needed. I saw what happened. [*He goes out*].

ORINTHIA. The beast! He must have looked through the keyhole. [*She throws her hand up with a gesture of laughing defiance, and dances back to her seat at the writing table*].

ACT II

Later in the afternoon. The Terrace of the Palace. A low balustrade separates it from the lawn. Terrace chairs in abundance, ranged along the balustrade. Some dining room chairs also, not ranged, but standing about as if they had just been occupied. The terrace is accessible from the lawn by a central flight of steps.

The King and Queen are sitting apart near the corners of the steps, the Queen to the King's right. He is reading the evening paper: she is knitting. She has a little work table on her right, with a small gong on it.

THE QUEEN. Why did you tell them to leave the chairs when they took away the tea?

MAGNUS. I shall receive the Cabinet here.

THE QUEEN. Here! Why?

MAGNUS. Well, I think the open air and the evening light will have a quieting effect on them. They cannot make speeches at me so easily as in a room.

THE QUEEN. Are you sure? When Robert asked Boanerges where he learnt to speak so beautifully, he said " In Hyde Park."

MAGNUS. Yes; but with a crowd to stimulate him.

THE QUEEN. Robert says you have tamed Boanerges.

MAGNUS. No: I have not tamed him. I have taught him how to behave. I have to valet all the beginners; but that does not tame them: it teaches them how to use their strength instead of wasting it in making fools of themselves. So much the worse for me when I have to fight them.

THE QUEEN. You get no thanks for it. They think you are only humbugging them.

MAGNUS. Well, so I am, in the elementary lessons. But when it comes to real business humbug is no use: they pick it up themselves too quickly.

Pamphilius enters along the terrace, from the Queen's side.

MAGNUS [*looking at his watch*] Good Heavens! They havnt come, have they? It's not five yet.

PAMPHILIUS. No, sir. It's the American ambassador.

THE QUEEN [*resenting this a little*] Has he an audience?

PAMPHILIUS. No, maam. He is rather excited about something, I think. I cant get anything out of him. He says he must see His Majesty at once.

THE QUEEN. Must!! An American m u s t see the King at once, without an audience! Well!

MAGNUS [*rising*] Send him in, Pam.

Pamphilius goes out.

THE QUEEN. *I* should have told him to write for an audience, and then kept him waiting a week for it.

MAGNUS. What! When we still owe America that old war debt. And with a mad imperialist president like Bossfield! No you wouldnt, my dear: you would be crawlingly civil to him, as I am going to be, confound him!

PAMPHILIUS [*re-appearing*] His Excellency the American Ambassador. Mr Vanhattan.

He retires as Mr Vanhattan enters in an effusive condition, and, like a man assured of an enthusiastic welcome, hurries to the Queen, and salutes her with a handshake so prolonged that she stares in astonishment, first at him, and then appealingly at the King, with her hands being vigorously wrung and waved up and down all the time.

MAGNUS. What on earth is the matter, Mr Vanhattan? You are shaking Her Majesty's rings off.

VANHATTAN [*desisting*] Her Majesty will excuse me when she learns the nature of my errand here. This, King Magnus, is a great historic scene: one of the greatest, perhaps, that history has ever recorded or will ever again record.

MAGNUS. Have you had tea?

VANHATTAN. Tea! Who can think of tea at such a moment as this?

THE QUEEN [*rather coldly*] It is hard for us to share your enthusiasm in complete ignorance of its cause.

VANHATTAN. That is true, maam. I am just behaving like a crazy man. But you shall hear. You shall judge. And then you shall say whether I exaggerate the importance —the immensity—of an occasion that cannot be exaggerated.

MAGNUS. Goodness gracious! Wont you sit down?

VANHATTAN [*taking a chair and placing it between them*] I thank your Majesty. [*He sits*].

MAGNUS. You have some exciting news for us, apparently. Is it private or official?

VANHATTAN. Official, sir. No mistake about it. What I am going to tell you is authentic from the United States of America to the British Empire.

THE QUEEN. Perhaps I had better go.

VANHATTAN. No, maam: you shall not go. Whatever may be the limits of your privileges as the consort of your sovereign, it is your right as an Englishwoman to learn what I have come here to communicate.

MAGNUS. My dear Vanhattan, what the devil is the matter?

VANHATTAN. King Magnus: between your country and mine there is a debt.

MAGNUS. Does that matter, now that our capitalists have invested so heavily in American concerns that after paying yourselves the interest on the debt you have to send us two thousand million dollars a year to balance the account.

VANHATTAN. King Magnus: for the moment, forget figures. Between your country and mine there is not only a debt but a frontier: the frontier that has on it not a single gun nor a single soldier, and across which the American citizen every day shakes the hand of the Canadian subject of your throne.

MAGNUS. There is also the frontier of the ocean, which is somewhat more expensively defended at our joint expense by the League of Nations.

VANHATTAN [rising to give his words more impressiveness] Sir: the debt is cancelled. The frontier no longer exists.

THE QUEEN. How can that be?

MAGNUS. Am I to understand, Mr Vanhattan, that by some convulsion of Nature the continent of North America has been submerged in the Atlantic?

VANHATTAN. Something even more wonderful than that has happened. One may say that the Atlantic Ocean has been submerged in the British Empire.

MAGNUS. I think you had better tell us as succinctly as possible w h a t has happened. Pray sit down.

VANHATTAN [resuming his seat] You are aware, sir, that the United States of America at one time formed a part of your empire.

MAGNUS. There is a tradition to that effect.

VANHATTAN. No mere tradition, sir. An undoubted historical fact. In the eighteenth century—

MAGNUS. That is a long time ago.

VANHATTAN. Centuries count for but little in the lifetimes of great nations, sir. Let me recall the parable of the prodigal son.

MAGNUS. Oh really, Mr Vanhattan, that was a very v e r y long time ago. I take it that something important has happened since yesterday.

VANHATTAN. It has. It has indeed, King Magnus.

MAGNUS. Then what is it? I have not time to attend to the eighteenth century and the prodigal son at this moment.

THE QUEEN. The King has a Cabinet meeting in ten minutes, Mr Vanhattan.

VANHATTAN. I should like to see the faces of your Cabinet ministers, King Magnus, when they hear what I have to tell you.

MAGNUS. So should I. But I am not in a position to tell it to them, because I dont know what it is.

VANHATTAN. The prodigal, sir, has returned to his father's house. Not poor, not hungry, not ragged, as of old. Oh no. This time he returns bringing with him the riches of the earth to the ancestral home.

MAGNUS [starting from his chair] You dont mean to say—

VANHATTAN [rising also, blandly triumphant] I do, sir. The Declaration of Independence is cancelled. The treaties which endorsed it are torn up. We have decided to rejoin the British Empire. We shall of course enjoy Dominion Home Rule under the Presidency of Mr Bossfield. I shall revisit you here shortly, not as the Ambassador of a foreign power, but as High Commissioner for the greatest of your dominions, and your very loyal and devoted subject, sir.

MAGNUS [collapsing into his chair] The devil you will! [He stares haggardly into futurity, now for the first time utterly at a loss].

THE QUEEN. What a splendid thing, Mr Vanhattan!

VANHATTAN. I thought your Majesty would say so. The most splendid thing that has ever happened. [He resumes his seat].

THE QUEEN [looking anxiously at the king] Dont you think so, Magnus?

MAGNUS [pulling himself together with a visible effort] May I ask, Mr Vanhattan, with whom did this—this—this masterstroke of American policy originate? Frankly, I have been accustomed to regard your President as a statesman whose mouth was the most efficient part of his head. He cannot have thought of this himself. Who suggested it to him?

VANHATTAN. I must accept your criticism of Mr Bossfield with all doo reserve, but I may mention that we Americans will probably connect the good news with the recent visit to our shores of the President of the Irish Free State. I cannot pronounce his name in its official Gaelic form; and there is only one typist in our bureau who can spell it; but he is known to his friends as Mick O'Rafferty.

MAGNUS. The rascal! Jemima: we shall have to live in Dublin. This is the end of England.

VANHATTAN. In a sense that may be so. But England will not perish. She will merge —merge, sir—into a bigger and brighter concern. Perhaps I should have mentioned that one of our conditions will be that you shall be Emperor. King may be good enough for this little island; but if we come in we shall require something grander.

MAGNUS. This little island! "This little gem set in a silver sea!" Has it occurred to you, Mr Vanhattan, that rather than be reduced to a mere appendage of a big American concern, we might raise the old warcry of Sinn Fein, and fight for our independence to the last drop of our blood?

VANHATTAN. I should be right sorry to contemplate such a reversion to a barbarous past. Fortunately, it's impossible—immpawsibl. The old warcry would not appeal to the cosmopolitan crews of the fleet of the League of Nations in the Atlantic. That fleet would blockade you, sir. And I fear we should be obliged to boycott you. The two thousand million dollars a year would stop.

MAGNUS. But the continental Powers! Do you suppose they would consent for a moment to such a change in the balance of power?

VANHATTAN. Why not? The change would be only nominal.

MAGNUS. Nominal! You call an amalgamation of the British Commonwealth with the United States a nominal change! What will France and Germany call it?

VANHATTAN [shaking his head indulgently] France and Germany? These queer old geographical expressions which you use here from old family habit do not trouble us. I suppose you mean by Germany the chain of more or less Soviet Republics between the Ural Mountains and the North Sea. Well, the clever people at Moscow and Berlin and Geneva are trying to federate them; and it is fully understood between us that if we dont object to their move they will not object to ours. France, by which I take it you mean the Government at New Timgad, is too busy in Africa to fuss about what is happening at the ends of your little Channel

Tube. So long as Paris is full of Americans, and Americans are full of money, all's well in the west from the French point of view. One of the great attractions of Paris for Americans is the excursion to Old England. The French want us to feel at home here. And so we do. Why shouldnt we? After all, we are at home here.

MAGNUS. In what sense, may I ask?

VANHATTAN. Well, we find here everything we are accustomed to: our industrial products, our books, our plays, our sports, our Christian Science churches, our osteopaths, our movies and talkies. Put it in a small parcel and say our goods and our ideas. A political union with us will be just the official recognition of an already accomplished fact. A union of hearts, you might call it.

THE QUEEN. You forget, Mr Vanhattan. We have a great national tradition.

VANHATTAN. The United States, maam, have absorbed all the great national traditions, and blended them with their own glorious tradition of Freedom into something that is unique and universal.

THE QUEEN. We have a civilized culture which is peculiar to ourselves. It may not be better than yours; but it is different.

VANHATTAN. Well, is it? We found that culture enshrined in British material works of art: in the stately country homes of your nobility, in the cathedrals our common forefathers built as the country houses of God. What did you do with them? You sold them to us. I was brought up in the shade of Ely cathedral, the removal of which from the county of Cambridge to New Jersey was my dear old father's first big professional job. The building which stands on its former site is a very fine one: in my opinion the best example of reinforced concrete of its period; but it was designed by an American architect, and built by the Synthetic Building Materials Trust, an international affair. Believe me, the English people, the real English people who take things as they come instead of reading books about them, will be more at home with us than they are with the old English notions which our tourists try to keep alive. When you find some country gentleman keeping up the old English customs at Christmas and so forth, who is he? An American who has bought the place. Your people get up the show for him because he pays for it, not because it is natural to them.

THE QUEEN [*with a sigh*] Our own best families go so much to Ireland nowadays. People should not be allowed to go from England to Ireland. They never come back.

VANHATTAN. Well, can you blame them, maam? Look at the climate!

THE QUEEN. No: it is not the climate. It is the Horse Show.

The King rises very thoughtfully; and Vanhattan follows his example.

MAGNUS. I must think over this. I have known for years past that it was on the cards. When I was young, and under the influence of our family tradition, which of course never recognized the rebellion of the American colonies as valid, I actually dreamt of a reunited English speaking empire at the head of civilization.

VANHATTAN. Fine! Great! And now come true.

MAGNUS. Not yet. Now that I am older and wiser. I find the reality less attractive than the dream.

VANHATTAN. And is that all I am to report to the President, sir? He will be disappointed. I am a little taken aback, myself.

MAGNUS. For the present, that is all. This may be a great idea—

VANHATTAN. Surely, surely.

MAGNUS. It may also be a trap in which England will perish.

VANHATTAN [*encouragingly*] Oh, I shouldnt look at it that way. Besides, nothing—not even dear old England—can last for ever. Progress, you know, sir, progress, progress!

MAGNUS. Just so, just so. We may survive only **as** another star on your flag. Still, we cling to the little scrap of individuality you have left us. If we must merge, as you call it —or did you say submerge?—some of us will swim to the last. [*To the Queen*] My dear.

The Queen strikes her gong.

Pamphilius returns.

MAGNUS. You shall hear from me after the Cabinet meets. Not tonight: you must not sit up waiting for a message. Early tomorrow, I hope. Thank you for bringing me the news before the papers got it: that seldom happens now. Pamphilius: you will reconduct his Excellency. Good evening. [*He shakes hands*].

VANHATTAN. I thank your Majesty. [*To the Queen*] Good evening, maam. I look forward to presenting myself in court dress soon.

THE QUEEN. You will look very nice in it, Mr Vanhattan. Good evening.

The Ambassador goes out with Pamphilius.

MAGNUS [*striding grimly to and fro*] The scoundrels! That blackguard O'Rafferty! That booby bullroarer Bossfield! Breakages, Limited, have taken it into their heads to mend the British Commonwealth.

THE QUEEN [*quietly*] I think it is a very good thing. You will make a very good emperor. We shall civilize these Americans.

MAGNUS. How can we when we have not yet civilized ourselves? They have come to regard us as a mere tribe of redskins. England will be just a reservation.

THE QUEEN. Nonsense, dear! They know that we are their natural superiors. You can see it by the way their women behave at court. They really love and reverence royalty; while our English peeresses are hardly civil— when they condescend to come at all.

MAGNUS. Well, my dear, I do many things to please you that I should never do to please myself; and I suppose I shall end as American Emperor just to keep you amused.

THE QUEEN. I never desire anything that is not good for you, Magnus. You do not always know what is good for you.

MAGNUS. Well, well, well, well! Have it your own way, dearest. Where are these infernal ministers? Theyre late.

THE QUEEN [*looking out into the garden*] Coming across the lawn with Sempronius.

The Cabinet arrives. The men take off their hats as they come up the steps. Boanerges has taken advantage of the interval to procure a brilliant uniform and change into it. Proteus, with Sempronius, heads the procession, followed immediately by the two lady ministers. The Queen rises as Proteus turns to her. Sempronius moves the little table quickly back to the balustrade out of the way, and puts the Queen's chair in the centre for the King.

THE QUEEN [*shaking hands*] How do you do, Mr Proteus?

PROTEUS. May I present the President of the Board of Trade, Mr Boanerges?

THE QUEEN. I remember seeing you, Mr Boanerges, at the opening of the Transport Workers' Summer Palace. You wore a most becoming costume then. I hope you have not given it up.

BOANERGES. But the Princess told me I looked ridiculous in it!

THE QUEEN. That was very naughty of the

Princess. You looked particularly well in it. However, you look well in anything. And now I leave you all to your labors.

She goes out along the terrace. Sempronius follows with her knitting.

MAGNUS [*sitting down*] Be seated, ladies and gentlemen.

They take chairs of one sort or another where they can find them, first leaving their hats on the balustrade. When they are seated, their order from the King's right to his left is Nicobar, Crassus, Boanerges, Amanda, the King, Proteus, Lysistrata, Pliny, and Balbus.

A pause, Proteus waiting for the King to begin. He, deep in thought, says nothing. The silence becomes oppressive.

PLINY [*chattily*] Nice weather we're having, these evenings.

AMANDA [*splutters*]!!!

MAGNUS. There is rather a threatening cloud on the western horizon, Mr Pliny. [*To Proteus*] Have you heard the news from America?

PROTEUS. I have, sir.

MAGNUS. Am I to be favored with the advice of my ministers on that subject?

PROTEUS. By your Majesty's leave, we will take the question of the ultimatum first.

MAGNUS. Do you think the ultimatum will matter much when the capital of the British Commonwealth is shifted to Washington?

NICOBAR. We'll see it shifted to Melbourne or Montreal or Johannesburg first.

MAGNUS. It would not stay there. It will stay at a real centre of gravity only.

PROTEUS. We are agreed about that. If it shifts at all it will shift either west to Washington or east to Moscow.

BOANERGES. Moscow thinks a lot of itself. But what has Moscow to teach us that we cannot teach ourselves? Moscow is built on English history, written in London by Karl Marx.

PROTEUS. Yes; and the English king has sidetracked you again. [*To Magnus*] What about the ultimatum, sir? You promised us your decision at five o'clock. It is now a quarter past.

MAGNUS. Are you inexorably determined to force this issue to its logical end? You know how unEnglish it is to do that?

PROTEUS. My people came from Scotland.

LYSISTRATA. I wish they had stayed there. I am English: every bone in my body.

BOANERGES [*vociferously*] Same here!

PROTEUS. God help England if she had no Scots to think for her!

MAGNUS. What does the Cabinet say to that?

AMANDA. All their people came from Scotland or Ireland or Wales or Jerusalem or somewhere, sir. It is no use appealing to English sentiment here.

CRASSUS. Politics are not suited to the English, if you ask me.

MAGNUS. Then I, the only Englishman left in politics, apparently, am to be reduced to complete nullity?

PROTEUS [*bluntly*] Yes. You cannot frighten us out of our position by painting it red. I could paint your position black if I liked. In plain terms we require from you an unconditional surrender. If you refuse it then I go to the country on the question whether England is to be an absolute monarchy or a constitutional one. We are all agreed on that: there will be no resignations. I have letters from the absent members of the Government: those present will speak for themselves.

ALL THE OTHER MEN. Agreed, agreed.

PROTEUS. Now, what is your answer?

MAGNUS. The day for absolute monarchies is past. You think you can do without me; and I know that I cannot do without you. I decide, of course, in favor of a constitutional monarchy.

THE MEN [*greatly relieved and delighted*] Hear! hear!

MAGNUS. Wait a moment.

Sudden silence and mistrust.

PROTEUS. So! There is a catch in it, is there?

MAGNUS. Not exactly a catch. But you have driven me to face the fact that I am unfitted to be a constitutional monarch. I am by nature incapable of the necessary self-effacement.

AMANDA. Well, thats true, at all events. You and I are a pair, sir.

MAGNUS. Thank you. Therefore, whilst accepting your constitutional principle without the slightest reserve, I cannot sign your ultimatum, because by doing so I should be making personal promises which I know I should break—which in fact I must break because I have forces within me which your constitutional limits cannot hold in check.

BALBUS. How can you accept our principle if you dont sign the ultimatum?

MAGNUS. Oh, there is no difficulty about that. When an honest man finds himself incapable of discharging the duties of a public post, he resigns.

PROTEUS [*alarmed*] Resigns! What are you driving at?

CRASSUS. A king cannot resign.

NICOBAR. You might as well talk of beheading yourself. You cant behead yourself.

BOANERGES. Other people can, though.

MAGNUS. Do not let us quarrel about words, gentlemen. I cannot resign. But I can abdicate.

ALL THE REST [*starting to their feet*] Abdicate! [*They stare at him in consternation*].

AMANDA [*whistling a descending minor scale very expressively*]!!!!!!!!! [*She sits down*].

MAGNUS. Of course, abdicate. Lysistrata: you have been a teacher of history. You can assure your colleagues that there is nothing unprecedented in an abdication. The Emperor Charles the Fifth, for instance—

LYSISTRATA. Oh, Charles the Fifth be—be bothered! he's not good enough. Sir: I have stood by you as far as I dared. Dont throw me over. You must not abdicate. [*She sits down, distressed*].

PROTEUS. You cannot abdicate except by my advice.

MAGNUS. I am acting upon your advice.

PROTEUS. Nonsense! [*He sits down*].

BALBUS. Ridiculous! [*He sits down*].

PLINY. Youre not serious, you know. [*He sits down*].

NICOBAR. You cant upset the apple cart like this. [*He sits down.*]

CRASSUS. I must say this is not playing the game. [*He sits down*].

BOANERGES [*powerfully*] Well, why not? Why not? Though as an old Republican I have no respect for His Majesty as a King, I have a great respect for him as a Strong Man. But he is not the only pebble on the beach. Why not have done with this superstition of monarchy, and bring the British Commonwealth into line with all the other great Powers today as a republic? [*He sits down*].

MAGNUS. My abdication does not involve that, Mr Boanerges. I am abdicating to save the monarchy, not to destroy it. I shall be succeeded by my son Robert, Prince of Wales. He will make an admirable constitutional monarch.

PLINY. Oh, come! Dont be hard on the lad, sir. He has plenty of brains.

MAGNUS. Oh yes, yes, yes: I did not mean that he is a nonentity: quite the contrary: he is much cleverer than I am. But I have never been able to induce him to take any interest in parliamentary politics. He prefers intellectual pursuits.

NICOBAR. Dont you believe it. He is up to his neck in business.

MAGNUS. Just so. He asks me why I waste my time with you here pretending to govern the country when it is really governed by Breakages, Limited. And really I hardly know how to answer him.

CRASSUS. Things are like that nowadays. My son says just the same.

LYSISTRATA. Personally I get on very well with the Prince; but somehow I do not feel that he is interested in what I am doing.

BALBUS. He isnt. He wont interfere with you as long as you dont interfere with him. Just the right king for us. Not pig-headed. Not meddlesome. Thinks that nothing we do matters a rap. What do you say, Joe?

PROTEUS. After all, why not? if your Majesty is in earnest.

MAGNUS. I assure you I am very much in earnest.

PROTEUS. Well, I confess I did not foresee this turn of events. But I ought to have foreseen it. What your Majesty proposes is the straightforward, logical, intellectually honest solution of our difficulty. Consequently it is the last solution I could have expected in politics. But I reckoned without your Majesty's character. The more I think of it the more clearly I see that you are right— that you are taking the only course open to you.

CRASSUS. I never said I was against it, Joe.

BALBUS. Neither did I.

NICOBAR. I think theres a great deal to be said for it. *I* have no objection.

PLINY. One king is no worse than another, is he?

BOANERGES. Is he any better? The way you fellows scuttle backward and forward from one mind to another whenever Joe holds up his finger is disgusting. This is a Cabinet of sheep.

PROTEUS. Well, give the flock a better lead if you can. Have you anything else to propose?

BOANERGES. I dont know that I have on the spur of the moment. We should have had notice of this. But I suppose the King must do as he thinks right.

PROTEUS. Then the goat goes with the sheep; so thats all right.

BOANERGES. Who are you calling a goat?

NICOBAR. If you come to that, who are you calling sheep?

AMANDA. Steady there, children! steady! steady! [*To the King*] You have brought us all round, sir, as usual.

PROTEUS. There is nothing more to be said.

AMANDA. That means another half hour at least.

BOANERGES. Woman: this is not the moment for your tomfooleries.

PROTEUS [*impressively*] Bill is right, Amanda. [*He rises and becomes the conventional House of Commons orator*].

Ministers compose themselves to listen with grave attention, as if in church; but Lysistrata is contemptuous and Amanda amused.

PROTEUS [*continuing*] It is a solemn moment. It is a moment in which an old tie is being broken. I am not ashamed to confess that it is a tie from which I have learned something.

MALE MINISTERS [*murmur*] Hear hear! Hear hear!

PROTEUS. For my own part—and I think I may speak for others here as well—it has been no mere political tie, but a tie of sincere friendship.

Renewed murmurs of sympathy. Increasing emotion.

PROTEUS. We have had our disagreements —as which of us has not?—but they have been family quarrels.

CRASSUS. Thats all. Nothing more.

PROTEUS. May I say lovers' quarrels?

PLINY [*wiping his eyes*] You may, Joe. You may.

PROTEUS. My friends, we came here to a meeting. We find, alas! that the meeting is to be a leavetaking. [*Crassus sniffs tearfully*]. It is a sad leavetaking on our part, but a cordial one. [*Hear Hear from Pliny*]. We are cast down, but not discouraged. Looking back to the past with regret, we can still look forward to the future with hope. That future has its dangers and its difficulties. It will bring us new problems; and it will bring us face to face with a new king. But the new problems and the new king will not make us forget our old counsellor, monarch, and—he will allow me to say—comrade. [*Hear Hears ad libitum*]. I know my words will find an echo in all your hearts when I conclude by saying that whatsoever king shall reign—

AMANDA. Youll be the Vicar of Bray, Joe.

Uproar. Proteus flings himself into his chair indignantly.

BALBUS. Shame!

NICOBAR. Shut up, you b—

PLINY. A joke's a joke; but really—

CRASSUS. Too bad, Amanda! Behave yourself.

LYSISTRATA. She has a perfect right to speak. You are a parcel of sentimental fools.

BOANERGES [*rising*] Silence. Order.

AMANDA. Sorry.

BOANERGES. So you ought to be. Where's your manners? Where's your education? King Magnus: we part; but we part as strong men part: as friends. The Prime Minister has correctly represented the sentiments of all the men present. I call on them to express those sentiments in the good old English fashion. [*Singing in stentorian tones*] Fo-o-o-o-r-r-r

MALE MINISTERS EXCEPT PROTEUS [*rising and singing*]
—he's a jolly good fel-low
For he's a jolly good fel-low
For he's—

MAGNUS [*peremptorily*] Stop. Stop.

Sudden silence and misgiving. They sit down furtively.

MAGNUS. I thank you with all my heart; but there is a misapprehension. We are not taking leave of one another. I have no intention of withdrawing from an active part in politics.

PROTEUS. What!!

MAGNUS. You are looking on me, with an emotion which has deeply touched me, as a man with a political past. But I look on myself rather as a man with a political future. I have not yet told you my plans.

NICOBAR. What plans?

BALBUS. A retired king cant have plans and a future.

MAGNUS. Why not? I am looking forward to a most exciting and enjoyable time. As I shall of course dissolve parliament, the fun will begin with a general election.

BOANERGES [*dismayed*] But Ive only just been elected. Do you mean that I shall have to stand two elections in one month? Have you thought of the expenses?

MAGNUS. Surely your expenses will be paid by the State.

BOANERGES. Paid by the State! Is that all you know about electioneering in England?

PROTEUS. You will get your whack out of the party funds, Bill; and if you cant find the extras you must put up with straight votes.

Go on, sir: we want to hear about those plans of yours.

MAGNUS. My last act of royal authority will be to divest myself of all titles and dignities; so that I may step down at once into the position of a commoner.

BOANERGES. Step up, you mean. The common man is the superior, not the inferior, of the titled man.

MAGNUS. That is why I am going to make myself a common man, Mr Boanerges.

PLINY. Well, it does you honor.

CRASSUS. Not all of us would be capable of a sacrifice like that.

BOANERGES. A fine gesture, sir. A fine gesture. I admit it.

PROTEUS [*suspicious*] And since when, pray, has your Majesty taken to making gestures? Whats the game this time?

BOANERGES. Shame!

PROTEUS. Shut up, you gaby. [*To the King*] I say, whats the game?

MAGNUS. There is no imposing on you, Prime Minister. The game is, of course, that when I come back into politics I shall be in a better position as a commoner than as a peer. I shall seek a parliamentary seat.

PROTEUS. You in the House of Commons!

MAGNUS [*blandly*] It is my intention to offer myself to the Royal Borough of Windsor as a candidate at the forthcoming General Election.

All the rest except Boanerges and the ladies rise in consternation.

PROTEUS. This is treachery.

BALBUS. A dirty trick.

NICOBAR. The meanest on record.

PLINY. He'll be at the top of the poll.

CRASSUS. There wont be any poll: it will be a walk-over.

BALBUS. This shews what all your fine manners and friendly ways are worth.

NICOBAR. Hypocrite!

CRASSUS. Humbug!

LYSISTRATA. I wish your Majesty every success.

AMANDA. Hear hear! Fair play, boys. Why shouldnt he go into Parliament with us?

BOANERGES. Well said! well said! Why not?

THE OTHER MALE MINISTERS. Ya-a-a-ah! [*They sit down in utter disgust*].

PROTEUS [*very sullen*] And when you are in Parliament, what then?

MAGNUS. There are several possibilities. I shall naturally endeavor to form a party. My

son King Robert will have to call on some Party leader who can depend on the support of the House of Commons to form a Government. He may call on you. He may even call on me.

AMANDA [*breaks the glum silence by whistling a bar or two of the National Anthem*]!!

MAGNUS. Whatever happens, it will be a great relief to us to be able to speak out quite frankly about oneanother in public. You have never been able to tell the British people what you really think of me: no real criticism of the King is possible. I have never been able to speak my mind as to your various capacities and characters. All that reserve, that tedious affectation, that unwholesome concealment will end. I hope you look forward to our new footing as pleasurably as I do.

LYSISTRATA. I am delighted, sir. You will fight Breakages for me.

AMANDA. It will be awful fun.

BOANERGES. Now, Mr Prime Minister, we are waiting for you. What have you to say about it?

PROTEUS [*rising and speaking slowly, with his brows deeply knitted*] Has your Majesty got that ultimatum on you?

MAGNUS [*produces it from his breast pocket and presents it to him*]!

PROTEUS [*with measured emphasis, after tearing the paper up into four pieces at two deliberate strokes, and throwing the pieces away*] There is not going to be any abdication. There is not going to be any general election. There is not going to be any ultimatum. We go on as before. The crisis is a washout. [*To the King, with deadly concentration*] I will never forgive you for this. You stole your ace of trumps from the hand I played this morning. [*He takes his hat from the balustrade and goes away through the park*].

BOANERGES [*rising*] That was a very deplorable exhibition of temper on the part of the Prime Minister, sir. It was not the gesture of a Strong Man. I will remonstrate with him. You may depend on me. [*He takes his hat and follows Proteus in a serious and dignified manner*].

NICOBAR [*rising*] Well, I shall not say what I think. [*He is taking his hat when the King addresses him*].

MAGNUS. So I have not upset the apple cart after all, Mr Nicobar.

NICOBAR. You can upset it as soon as you

like for all I care. I am going out of politics. Politics is a mug's game. [*He goes*].

CRASSUS [*rising reluctantly and taking his hat*] If Nick goes, I shall have to go too.

MAGNUS. Can you really tear yourself away from politics?

CRASSUS. Only too glad to be well out of them, if Breakages will let me. They shoved me into it; and I daresay theyll find another job for me. [*He goes*].

PLINY [*cheerful to the last as he, too, goes for his hat*] Well, I am glad nothing's happened. You know, sir, nothing ever really does happen in the Cabinet. Never mind their bit of temper. Theyll feed out of your hand tomorrow. [*He goes*].

BALBUS [*after taking his hat*] Now that theyre all gone I dont mind saying that if anything should ever happen to the throne, and your Majesty should become a President with a Cabinet to pick, you might easily find a worse Home Secretary than me, with all my faults.

MAGNUS. I shall bear it in mind. By the way, if you should happen to overtake the Prime Minister, will you be so good as to remind him that we quite forgot to settle that little affair of the proposal of America to annex the British Commonwealth.

BALBUS. By the Lord, so we did! Well, thats a good one! Ha ha! Ha ha ha ha ha! [*He goes out laughing heartily*].

MAGNUS. They dont take it in, Lizzie: not one bit. It is as if another planet were crashing into us. The kingdom and the power and the glory will pass from us and leave us naked, face to face with our real selves at last.

LYSISTRATA. So much the better, if by our real selves you mean the old English stock that was unlike any other. Nowadays men all over the world are as much alike as hotel dinners. It's no use pretending that the America of George Washington is going to swallow up the England of Queen Anne. The America of George Washington is as dead as Queen Anne. What they call an American is only a wop pretending to be a

Pilgrim Father. He is no more Uncle Jonathan than you are John Bull.

MAGNUS. Yes: we live in a world of wops, all melting into one another; and when all the frontiers are down London may be outvoted by Tennessee, and all the other places where we still madly teach our children the mentality of an eighteenth century village school.

LYSISTRATA. Never fear, sir. It is not the most ignorant national crowd that will come out on top, but the best power station; for you cant do without power stations, and you cant run them on patriotic songs and hatred of the foreigner, and guff and bugaboo, though you can run nationalism on nothing else. But I am heartbroken at your not coming into the House with us to keep old England in front and lead a new Party against Breakages [*tears come into her eyes*].

MAGNUS [*patting her consolingly on the back*] That would have been splendid, wouldnt it? But I am too old fashioned. This is a farce that younger men must finish.

AMANDA [*taking her arm*] Come home with me, dear. I will sing to you until you cant help laughing. Come.

Lysistrata pockets her handkerchief; shakes the King's hands impulsively; and goes with Amanda. The King plunges into deep thought. Presently the Queen comes back.

THE QUEEN. Now Magnus: it's time to dress for dinner.

MAGNUS [*much disturbed*] Oh, not now. I have something very big to think about. I dont want any dinner.

THE QUEEN [*peremptorily*] No dinner! Did anyone ever hear of such a thing! You know you will not sleep if you think after seven o'clock.

MAGNUS [*worried*] But really, Jemima—

THE QUEEN [*going to him and taking his arm*] Now, now, now! dont be naughty. I mustnt be late for dinner. Come on, like a good little boy.

The King, with a grimace of hopeless tenderness, allows himself to be led away.

THE END

XXXIII

JITTA'S ATONEMENT

BY SIEGFRIED TREBITSCH

Author of Genesung, Weltuntergang, Das Haus am Abhang, Tagwandler, Ein
Muttersohn, Der Tod und die Liebe, Gefährliche Jahre, Spätes Licht, Die Frau
ohne Dienstag, Der Geliebte, Die Last des Blutes, etc. etc.

TRANSLATED BY BERNARD SHAW

ACT I

1920. *The drawing room in a flat in Vienna.
It is fashionably decorated and elegantly furnished, but not homelike, as there are no books
nor personal belongings nor household odds and
ends lying about. The two photogravure repro-
ductions of pictures on the walls, symmetrically
placed at equal distances from the door, are of
the refinedly aphrodisiac character considered
de rigueur in hotels. But the place is not quite
like a hotel sitting room; because there is very
little furniture: only two seats, a couch, and a
small table with a glass flower-vase and a mirror
on it.*

*It is an oblong room; and from the point of
view of anyone looking towards the corner the
long wall on the right has in the middle of it the
door leading to the entrance hall; and the short
wall on the left has an open door close to the
corner through which a bed with rose-coloured
hangings is partly visible. In the same wall
further forward from the same point of view is
the fireplace.*

*The couch is in the corner, parallel to the
longer wall, not quite close against it. A comfortable upholstered stool, really a chair without a
back, is at the foot of the couch. This stool has a
cushion on it which evidently belongs to the couch.
The other seat, a chair with arms, is almost in
the middle of the room, but nearer to the fireplace
than to the door. The table stands near the corner
of the fireplace.*

It is almost dark.

*Mrs Billiter, an elderly housekeeper, has
something of the same undomesticated air as the
room. Her hair, though not aggressively dyed, is
still rather younger than her face. She is well
dressed, like a hotel manageress. She opens the
door, letting in some electric light from the hall.
She has a silver tray in her hands, with a siphon,
two tumblers, and a bottle on it. She switches on
the light at the door, and crosses the room to the
table, where she puts down the tray. She looks
round the room to see whether it is tidy. She goes*
to the stool; takes the cushion from it; and puts it
in its proper place on the couch.

*Somebody rings at the outer door of the flat.
Mrs Billiter goes out to open it.*

A GIRL'S VOICE [*the accent is not that of a lady*]
Gentleman ordered these. Suppose it's all
right, isnt it?

MRS BILLITER'S VOICE. Yes. Just bring them
in, and put them in the vase for me, will you?

*Mrs Billiter returns, followed by a girl from
the florist's shop, carrying a handsome present
of flowers.*

MRS BILLITER [*pointing to the vase*] There.
I'll fetch some water.

*She goes into the bedroom and switches on the
light there. The roseate hangings of the bed appear to great advantage. The flower girl, on her
way to the vase, stops fascinated.*

*Mrs Billiter returns with a jug from the bed-
room washstand: a very pretty jug in rose color
and gold.*

*The flower girl puts the roses into the vase;
and Mrs Billiter fills it with water.*

*Mrs Billiter takes the jug back into the bed-
room; and the girl steals after her to the door and
peeps enviously in.*

*Mrs Billiter returns, putting out the bedroom
light as she does so, and finds the girl at the door.*

THE FLOWER GIRL. Just right for two, aint
it?

MRS BILLITER [*incensed*] What do you mean,
with your "Just right for two"?

THE FLOWER GIRL [*grinning*] Oh, it's nothing
to me. But I know.

MRS BILLITER. You know too much, you do.
Are they paid for?

THE FLOWER GIRL. Oh yes: thats quite all
right. [*She grins again, shewing no sign of
going*].

MRS BILLITER [*peremptorily*] Well? What are
you waiting for? And what are you grinning
at?

THE FLOWER GIRL. Aint the gentleman
here? He promised to leave me something.

MRS BILLITER [*impatiently groping in her purse and extracting a tip*] Thats how they give themselves away, offering tips when they have no call to. [*She gives her some money*]. There! Now, out you go. I'm busy.

THE FLOWER GIRL [*sarcastic*] Sorry, I'm sure. Thanks awfully. [*She goes to the door, but stops on hearing the outer door opened by a latch-key from without*]. Oh, here is the gentleman.

The gentleman enters. The girl ogles him. He recognizes her, and makes a gesture towards his pocket.

MRS BILLITER [*very decisively*] Thats all right, sir: she's had what you promised. [*To the girl, sternly*] Good evening to you. [*She sails to the door so formidably that the girl, after an ineffectual grimace, has to go*].

The moment the gentleman is left alone he shews signs of severe physical suffering. His ascent of the stairs has brought on an attack of angina pectoris. He makes his way to the stool, and collapses on it, struggling with the paroxysm. Mrs Billiter returns.

MRS BILLITER [*running to him*] Oh dear, oh dear, has it come on again, sir?

THE GENTLEMAN [*a little better*] It's all right now, Mrs Billiter. I took the stairs too fast. I rush at them without thinking. [*He rises, and tries to take off his overcoat. She helps him*]. Thank you, Mrs Billiter. I—I—I— [*gasping*] Just a moment. Whew! [*As the coat comes off he plunges to the armchair, and sinks into it*].

MRS BILLITER. How often have I begged you never to walk upstairs but always to take the lift? And now see the state you are in!

THE GENTLEMAN. Dont look at me: it will only distress you. Angina pectoris is a horrible thing; but it passes off soon. You can do nothing, thank you.

MRS BILLITER [*taking his hat and coat out into the vestibule*] Dear! dear! dear!

Rather dazed by the attack, he sits up, straightening his collar and coat rather irresolutely, and looking very careworn indeed. He is well dressed, on the verge of fifty, going grey, very distinguished in appearance and kindly in manner.

MRS BILLITER [*returning*] Why will you never take the lift, sir? It isnt as if anyone in this house knew you. And for that matter you meet people on the stairs as well as in the lift.

THE GENTLEMAN. I know; but I mustnt let the liftmen see me coming here too often. People talk, even when they have to live by holding their tongues.

MRS BILLITER [*reproachfully*] Oh, sir!

THE GENTLEMAN [*quickly saving the situation*] Except you, Mrs Billiter. You are an exception to all the rules.

MRS BILLITER. It's you who are the exception, sir. I wish all the other gentlemen that keep rooms here on the quiet to enjoy themselves were like you. There are people and people in this world; and I know a gentleman when I see him. And I feel sure your lady is a real lady, and always the same lady; though of course I take care never to see her.

THE GENTLEMAN. Thats very kind of you, Mrs Billiter. [*He rises to go to the table*].

MRS BILLITER [*stopping him*] Now do sit quiet a moment, sir. What was it you wanted?

THE GENTLEMAN. A mouthful of soda water.

MRS BILLITER. There: I'll get it for you. Sit down. [*He does so. She goes to the table and fills a glass from the siphon*]. If you would only let me put a drop of brandy in it?

THE GENTLEMAN [*shaking his head decisively*] It would probably kill me. I know. I am a doctor. [*He takes the glass from her*]. Thank you. [*He drinks*].

MRS BILLITER. You are not right yet. I can see it in your face.

THE GENTLEMAN [*hands her back the glass a little abruptly, and pulls himself together*]!!!

MRS BILLITER. There! I shouldnt have said that. [*She replaces the glass on the table, snubbed*].

THE GENTLEMAN. Not at all: I know how anxious you are about me, and how kindly you mean it. But I am all right now; and I— I — [*he takes out his watch and looks at it*] I am expecting somebody.

MRS BILLITER [*taking the hint*] Yes, sir: I'm going. [*She crosses the room to the door, but turns for a moment appealingly before going out*]. But you will take the lift next time, sir, wont you? If anything were to happen to you— not that I think anything like that, of course; but—

THE GENTLEMAN. Of course not, Mrs Billiter. Still—[*he shrugs his shoulders*]!

MRS BILLITER. Yes, sir. And then what could I do but send for the police?

THE GENTLEMAN. Quite so, quite so. If I come again I will take the lift. I promise.

MRS BILLITER. Thank you, sir. Thank you kindly. [*She goes out, closing the door very softly behind her*].

The gentleman, left alone, rises and goes to

the table, where he takes up the mirror and looks at his wrinkles and his blanching hair. He shakes his head and puts the mirror down. Then he takes out a cigaret; puts it between his lips; takes out a match, and is about to strike it when the bell rings twice. His face lights up; he throws the match and the cigaret into the fire; and goes out eagerly to admit the visitor, leaving the door of the room open. Immediately afterwards a veiled lady hurries in like a hunted creature. He follows her; shuts the door; and comes to her in the middle of the room. They embrace.

THE GENTLEMAN [*affectionately*] Why do you always look as if you were running away, and had just stumbled into my arms by chance?

THE LADY. I always feel as if my husband were lying in wait for me at the next turn.

THE GENTLEMAN. Well, suppose he were! You are not afraid of poor Alfred, are you? At home you are a perfect tyrant to him.

JITTA. I should have no courage if he caught me. Besides, if we are found out there will be an end of everything.

BRUNO. I almost wish we were found out.

JITTA. Why?

BRUNO. It would force us to stand by one another, and come out openly before all the world with our love.

JITTA [*embracing him impulsively*] Shall we?

BRUNO. There is my wife. Always my wife.

JITTA [*recoiling from him impatiently, and throwing her cloak on the couch*] Oh yes: Agnes. Always Agnes, Agnes, Agnes.

BRUNO. She has done nothing to deserve our betrayal of her: she has sacrificed her life to me. I cant face what she would suffer.

JITTA. Has she sacrificed more for you than you for her? It is not the thought of Agnes that holds me back. But the scandal would ruin you. [*She takes off her hat, and puts it on the table*].

BRUNO [*with sudden energy*] I want to be ruined. Oh, the life of a University professor. His respectability kills his mind. His wife's respectability kills her soul. They both become mere shells of their former selves: going through life in grooves, on rails like tramcars, envying the tinkers and gipsies. If it were not for Agnes I should commit some disgraceful offence to free myself.

JITTA. I am afraid disgrace would not mend matters. I could not bear yours.

BRUNO. Nor I yours. We are in the net.

JITTA. Not here, Bruno. We have broken through the net into our dreamland. [*Now*

that her hat and veil are off Jitta is revealed as one of those attractively refined women whose wistfully sensitive unsmiling mouths and tragic eyes not only make imaginative men fancy unfathomable depths in their natures, and something undefinably sad and splendid in their destinies, but actually force this conception on the women themselves, however commonplace their characters and circumstances may be. Jitta is nothing more extraordinary than the wife of a college don, and has done nothing more heroic than fall in love with another and more poetic don (also married); but to her lover and herself her life is as dignified and beautiful as her face, and their relations as nobly tragic as her eyes. So, as we are all a little like that, let us share their dream for a moment whilst she continues, sitting down beside him] You must brush off the bits of the broken net. [*Tracing on his brow*] There is a thread of it here, and here, and straight down here. [*She kisses his brow*]. No: they are not gone yet.

BRUNO. It is not the net. I can leave that behind when I come here into the dreamland. These last few months have been wonderful. But they have been terrible.

JITTA. Yes: wonderful and terrible. But they have been real, r e a l. Life in the net is never real: it is all acting.

BRUNO. That is true. But there is something still more real than the dream.

JITTA. What is that?

BRUNO. The awakening.

JITTA. For me there will be no awakening.

BRUNO. There is always the tap at the door in the morning. The tap with bony knuckles. The caller.

JITTA. Death! Oh, why will you always harp on that? Death is nothing. Life with love is everything. Think, Bruno. We are here alone. There is nothing between us and happiness except the courage to grasp it. Can you never be happy?

BRUNO. Can any mortal be happy?

JITTA [*suddenly prosaic and impatient*] Yes: Alfred can. A glass of wine and a cigar can make Alfred happy. A vote of thanks can make Alfred happy. A cheque for £25 can make him happy. But I cannot make you happy.

BRUNO. Dearest love: you can, you do make me inexpressibly happy. So happy, that every time you go away from me, and I stand listening to your footsteps dying away in the distance—I always listen to them to catch the last sound of you—I am stabbed with a fear that I have held you in my arms for the last time. But when we have been parted for days, and I am here waiting for you and thinking the moments endless until you come, and at last I hear your ring, I suddenly become like a freshman just up from school. [*She laughs, smoothing his grey hair*]. Yes: I know; but grey as I am, I am still a hobbledehoy; just a student waiting for his girl at the corner of the street where her shop is.

JITTA [*moved*] And do you think it is any different with me? All day I long to be with you, to say a thousand things to you! And when at last— [*she finishes the sentence by a caress*]! When you are away from me, I plod through my housework, and just count the days until—until this [*she again presses him in her arms, and draws him down beside her on the couch*].

BRUNO. If only I were young! Then I could really begin a new life with you instead of merely thinking and dreaming about it.

JITTA. I like it better as it is. I dont want to see you every day and become a commonplace with you, Bruno.

BRUNO. But are you content with these heartbreaking stolen hours? I'd risk you becoming a commonplace: I want you to be a commonplace for me; but I daresay I should bore you.

JITTA [*sighing blissfully*] The happiness of these stolen hours is so delicious that it makes up to me for everything I have to endure between times. And who knows what would happen if I were to break up your home and shatter your career? Are you sure we should not be too tired out, too broken by the effort, to enjoy our rest? One has to be young to do such things, Bruno: young enough to be able to forget.

BRUNO [*sadly*] You are right. Our love looks well only by candlelight. It wont stand daylight.

JITTA [*refusing to be discouraged*] Daylight is for your work, for your great book that is to be the crown of your career. But here in the candlelight you belong to me, and to me only.

BRUNO [*quickly*] Oh, not here alone. Do you think that my wife and my daughter put you quite out of my head when I am at home? They never do: you are everywhere. But what must it be for you? I often reproach myself—

JITTA [*softly*] You mustnt do that. I am not unhappy, Bruno. I was at first: I hardly dared go home and face Alfred's inquisitive eyes. But he saw nothing: his self-conceit is impenetrable. His cheerful grin killed my conscience. I hold up my head now everywhere: I am proud of belonging to you. When one is really happy, one is ruthless and shameless.

BRUNO. Jitta: do you know that you belonged to me before we ever saw one another?

JITTA. Yes. We were destined—

BRUNO. I dont mean that. I mean that we actually belonged to one another physically. I mean that my daughter—born before we knew one another—is your daughter.

JITTA. Edith! What do you mean, Bruno? You have the strangest fancies.

BRUNO. This is not a fancy, Jitta. It is a hard scientific fact: I worked out its theoretic possibility before Edith was born—before I ever set eyes on you. It strikes me dumb with wonder when I think how it has worked out between us. The daughter of my wife, my child and hers, not yours, resembles you, aye, loves you more than she loves her own mother, though she may not know it.

JITTA [*thoughtfully*] Strange. And I love your Edith as only a childless woman can love the child of the man she has interested and saved. I am not clever enough to share the rest of your science with you; but this I believe and accept. But how can such a miracle come about?

BRUNO [*mystically*] Men do not yet realize that no prophetic aspiration of theirs can fall utterly without fruit if its roots lie deep enough in their innermost conviction.

JITTA. Bruno: that must be right. It is an inspiration. It takes hold of my heart with both hands. You really are great.

BRUNO. Not at all: it is not new: everybody knows it nowadays in the rough. But it has never been worked out scientifically far enough to explain this miracle of Edith and you. Well, I am working it out; and there is somebody else working at it with me.

JITTA [*jealous*] Somebody else!

BRUNO. You would never guess who.

JITTA. I do not want to guess. I do not care.

BRUNO. Think of the most hardened materialist you know: the very last man you could imagine lending himself to such a mystical speculation!

JITTA [*relieved*] Oh, a man! The most hopeless materialist I know is my husband; and I do not want to be reminded of him just now.

BRUNO. But it is your husband I mean. I have converted him.

JITTA. Oh, impossible. He would never believe a thing like that. Dont let Alfred deceive you, Bruno. He is only playing with your belief because he feels sure of discovering some grossly material explanation of it, and making you ridiculous. He does not believe it as you believe it.

BRUNO [*brightly*] I do not say he does: I do not say he can. Alfred is clever; but he is not me—or rather, not us two: two in one.

JITTA. Darling!

BRUNO. All the same, he is burning with ambition to have his name connected with a new departure in science. As he has failed to do it in physics he is willing to do it in psychology rather than not do it at all.

JITTA [*scornfully*] At your expense?

BRUNO. Not altogether, dearest. He really has given me some quite handy curve diagrams for my lectures. He knows everything: what he lacks is a sense of the significance of what he knows. I am really sorry for him, and should like to help him.

JITTA. You can help him without letting him rob you of your ideas.

BRUNO. It is not he who is robbing me of my ideas: it is I who am robbing him of his wife; and the less he is conscious of his loss the meaner thief am I. I feel that through and through. [*He kisses her hand passionately*]. I have taken a priceless treasure from him. I must make amends somehow: I must pay my debt. That sense of obligation is in my very bones.

JITTA [*looking hard at him*] Why have I never felt this sense of obligation to your wife? Have I no conscience? or have you too much?

BRUNO. It is not the same. You do not feel that you have taken anything from Agnes: you feel that she has taken something from you.

JITTA. I know that I have a divine right to you. And I know that she has not.

BRUNO. There are other rights beside divine rights. If I had never come into your life, you would perhaps have come to some sort of understanding with Alfred; and he would have found some sort of happiness in possessing you.

JITTA. He has all the happiness he is capable of.

BRUNO. We have no right to say so. I have taken you from him.

JITTA. You have not taken me from him. I belonged to myself: and I gave you myself.

BRUNO. I have betrayed his trust.

JITTA. As I have betrayed your wife's trust.

BRUNO. That is quite different. Your relations with Agnes are mere society relations, conventional and superficial. But I am your husband's comrade: we were chums at school: we were at college together: we are professional colleagues. He knows me intimately; and if he were not such a confoundedly bad psychologist he would know that Nature meant you to be my wife. It is a stroke of luck for us that he knows nothing—if indeed it is only luck, and not his subconscious knowledge that he must not let himself know. Yes: he not only does not know: he will not know: he refuses to know. And that refusal, because it is unconscious, binds my sense of honor as if he spared us knowingly.

JITTA [*changing her tone, and trying to soothe and coax him*] Darling: you are tormenting yourself for nothing. Let me see whether I can cure you of all these scruples and fancies. They are only spooks. [*She draws him towards the bedroom*]. Come.

BRUNO. No, not yet. [*He gets away from her by standing up. She shrinks a little, wounded*]. I am telling you this once for all; so that I may never have to speak of it again. God knows it is not to involve you in my struggles with myself, nor to whitewash myself, that I am spending our priceless moments like this. I am as impatient as you are: I long for you beyond all expression. But there is something you must do for me. Something you can understand only when you know the rights of it.

JITTA [*repelled and anxious*] But what is it?

BRUNO [*pulling himself together*] I want to speak to you about my book. I have something very important to say to you about it.

JITTA [*a little disappointed*] Bruno: cant that wait a little? You know how I value your work; but we have so little time left this evening—

BRUNO [*resolutely*] It is just because I have so little time left that I dare not put this off any longer. You know the value of my book. Well, you must take charge of it.

JITTA. You need not trouble about that, Bruno: it will make your name famous without my help.

BRUNO [*looking hard at her, and forcing the emphasis of his words to the utmost*] Not my name. His name.

JITTA. God of Heaven! whose name?

BRUNO. Your husband's.

JITTA [*springing up*] Alfred's!

BRUNO. Listen to me. The book is finished: the typed copy will be found in my desk. And the title-page reads "Fetters of the Feminine Psyche, by Professor Alfred Lenkheim."

JITTA. Bruno! You are mad.

BRUNO. I burnt the original manuscript yesterday: there is not a word of it in my handwriting left to prove that I am the author. They will find a book by your husband among my things: that is all. [*She is about to protest*]. Promise me that you will leave this secret buried in my grave.

JITTA [*beside herself*] But why? Why? Why?

BRUNO [*seizing her hands, but now pleading like a lover*] It is my deepest wish. It is my most urgent prayer to you, Jitta.

JITTA [*gasping*] You ask me to do that! to promise you this unheard-of thing! This man who has no soul; who has been guilty of everything to me that a man can be guilty of to a woman except the infidelity that I would welcome with delight to excuse my own (he is not man enough for that): the fruit of your life's work is to drop into his mouth! And I am to be your accomplice in such a crime! No. I cannot. Never.

BRUNO [*soothing her*] I know how hard it is for you, darling. That is why I have not been able to bring myself to tell you until today. But I know you will not fail me.

JITTA. Dont say that, Bruno, as if it settled everything. I cannot act like a madwoman. Give me a reason.

BRUNO. I will. Listen. A book by a dead man is an orphan. Orphans sometimes die when they are not adopted. Mendel's masterpiece lay dead for thirty-five years while the fame of the living Darwin spread over the world. If Alfred adopts my orphan it will not perish; for Alfred's wife will adopt it too.

JITTA. Oh, Bruno, Bruno, how can you? That is so clever, so damnably clever. Has it come to mere cleverness between us?

BRUNO. I asked for a promise. You asked for a reason.

JITTA. But I am thinking of your fame—

BRUNO [*snapping his fingers*] Psha! That for my fame! What does it matter from whose hands the new generation will take the torch to carry on the great race of science? The truth will be as true with Alfred's name tacked on to it as Bruno's.

JITTA [*impatiently*] Oh yes, yes: I know all that. It sounds like a sentence from your annual address to your students. It's not true, Bruno: I feel it. It is not human. There is something else at the back of your mind.

BRUNO. No—except this. When I finally and irrevocably sealed my resolution yesterday by burning the manuscript, there came to me a moment of extraordinary exaltation in which I saw this sacrifice as my atonement to Alfred. It is the price at which I buy his wife from him; and now at last I can take my happiness with both hands, free in my conscience, right in my heart, in all honor as well as in all affection to the very end. [*He clasps her to his breast*].

JITTA [*still wondering at him*] You throw the greatest achievement of your life to him like a bone to a dog; and then feel you have made us two one. [*Breaking away from him*] No, no, Bruno: you are asking too much. You know that I love you as my man, without a thought of your greatness and your work; but all the same your work, your greatness, are a part of you; and I love every bit of you, your body, your soul, your reputation, your work, everything that would not exist if you did not exist. All that is my treasure and my pride. When you take a handful of it and throw it into the mud, you make me so much the poorer. Have you thought of that?

BRUNO. When two people stand to one another as we stand, the children born from their intercourse are not always children of flesh and blood, but inspirations, intuitions, convictions that they cannot discard without unfaithfulness. This is such an inspiration. Will you be unfaithful to it?

JITTA. Bruno: you want to play at Providence. Alfred is far too conceited to let anyone play Providence to him. If he refuses, what then?

BRUNO. He will not refuse. I have thought all that out. Why should he refuse to father a book which he already regards as half his own? He believes that I could never have written it without him. And you know how ambitious he is. I can depend on Alfred absolutely. Can I depend on you?

JITTA [half beaten] Who knows? I cannot depend on myself. This sacrifice is no child born of our intercourse, Bruno: you may be its father; but I am not its mother. I shall be its stepmother; and I shall hate it as no stepmother ever hated before. But the book is yours; and I have no rights over it: it must take the course you desire. I cannot go further than that. When you ask me to bind myself by a solemn vow, I— [shuddering] no, no: it is inhuman: a mockery, an impossibility.

BRUNO. I know I am putting your love to the cruellest test; but oh, Jitta, Jitta, do not fail me.

JITTA. So be it. [He snatches her hands and kisses them]. I promise you that if I survive the day that takes you from me, I will hide the truth as you demand, and take all the ghastly consequences just as you are mad enough to mean them. Are you satisfied now?

BRUNO [clasping her convulsively to him and hardly able to speak] I—I—thanks, thanks. My love.

JITTA [extricating herself quickly from his embrace] But if God wishes to be good to me he will never let me live to keep my promise.

BRUNO. I could not have pained you like this if I had the smallest doubt that I shall go first and go soon.

JITTA. Dont say that. Oh, do let us forget Death for one moment.

BRUNO. Death is nothing: if I could be sure that I should die tonight I should be unspeakably glad; for I should not have to strike you the bitterest blow of all.

JITTA. Bruno! Another blow!

BRUNO. Yes, another. My strength is going from me; and I need it all to force myself not to play the coward.

JITTA. How?

BRUNO. By leaving you today without daring to tell you that I do not intend to meet you again.

JITTA [struck to the heart] Not meet me again! Leave me!

BRUNO [with deliberate emphasis] This must be the last time. [Rising, with a sudden fanciful recklessness] Come: let it be the best. Let it be so full of happiness that we can say "It is enough: farewell."

JITTA. You are going to give me up! You can bring yourself to do that!

BRUNO. Nonsense! I shall never give you up. But it would be a crime to let you meet me here again at such a risk.

JITTA. How is the risk greater now than it has always been?

BRUNO. It was only a risk of being caught here with a live man. That was nothing: only a secret that three can keep. What about the risk of being found with a dead one?

JITTA [about to shriek]!

BRUNO [covering her mouth with his hand] Hush—sh! [She looks affrightedly at him: he looks gravely and significantly at her]. It is all up with me, dearest. I could not stop working; and my heart—

JITTA [with agonizing anxiety] Is it worse?

BRUNO [with a ghost of a laugh] Worse! It has gone all to pieces. I had no right to let you come this evening. I have put off telling you too long; but when I climbed those terrible stairs just now, I knew. You would have to give your name to the police. Our relations would be shouted through the streets and posted on the newspaper bills if you were found here with a—with a [he cannot say it, and indicates, by a gesture, the figure of a dead man lying on the floor].

JITTA [flinching at the image, but steadfast in her thought] Have no fear, Bruno. Why did you not tell me sooner what was troubling you? I could have relieved your mind. I have known all along that you were ill; and my only fear was that that [she repeats his gesture] might happen when you were alone instead of in my arms. Does that sound as if I cared what would become of me without you?

BRUNO. But I care, dearest. That is why I am resolved on our parting before this crazy tired old clock [he taps his left breast] runs down and stops ticking for good and all.

JITTA. Never. There is only one thing that can part me from you; and that is not the stopping of the clock, but of your love for me. No other danger exists for me; and no forethought of ours can protect us against that if it comes. [Abandoning herself to her passion] All the more reason why we must make the most of our love while it is within our reach. I love you: I love you: we are alive, not dead: you are living with my life as well as your own: your blood surges to mix with mine: you cannot die while I hold you fast. All the rest is an uneasy dream that means nothing: this is love; and love is life made irresistible.

BRUNO [carried away] Life: yes: this is life,

and this [*he kisses her eyes*], and this [*he kisses her lips*]. What a fool I was with my iron resolutions! one throb of your breast, one touch of your lips; and where are they? Nothing matters but Jitta, Jitta, Jitta [*he kisses her again and again*]. I am neither weak nor afraid now; and I promise you to live a hundred years.

JITTA. All the unhappinesses are forgotten: they never existed. [*She turns him round and draws him towards the bedroom*] Come.

BRUNO [*beside himself*] You trust me; and I must betray you. You thought me a young man; and I let you think so. But you shall not be deceived. You have made me as young as I seemed to you. [*He seizes her round the hips, and lifts her up exultantly*].

JITTA [*terrified*] Oh God, no: take care, Bruno: take care.

BRUNO [*setting her down gaily*] Bah! Do I love you?

JITTA. Yes, yes. You love me. I love you. Come.

BRUNO [*pushing her towards the bedroom door*] Quick, quick.

JITTA [*running into the bedroom*] Yes, yes, yes.

BRUNO [*with a grim change of countenance*] Poor Jitta! That lift broke the mainspring. [*He staggers against the door frame; clutches at the wall to save himself; strikes the electric light out by chance; reels back into the middle of the room; and drops dead*].

JITTA [*running in: she has begun to undress*] What is the matter? Where are you? [*She stumbles against the body*]. Oh God! [*She switches on the light*] Bruno. [*She rushes to him and kneels by him*]. Bruno: speak to me if you can: is it your heart again? What can I do for you? Shall I try to lift you?

She tries to raise him by his shoulders; but they are too heavy. She puts her hands round his neck and pulls it up from the floor; but the back of his head remains hanging and his jaw drops. With a gasp of horror she replaces the head and closes the open mouth. Then she scrambles to her feet and runs to the other door, calling breathlessly and voicelessly Mrs Billiter, Mrs Billiter. She opens the door, and regaining her voice, cries Mrs— She checks herself, suddenly remembering the consequences to herself of being found with the body. She closes the door quickly and noiselessly. She tries to think, her strained senses shewing in her eyes. Her fingers clutch for a moment at her half-naked breast as she thinks of her disordered appearance. She dashes into the bedroom, and reappears almost immediately with her blouse on, arranging it with nervous hands. She puts on her hat and mantle anyhow. As she turns to rush to the door the hat falls off. With a little cry of misery she takes the hat-pins from the hat and pins it properly to her hair; then she looks at herself in the mirror and shakes her mantle straight. She turns, and is hurrying to the door when she finds the body in her way. A flush of remorse comes over her. She turns impulsively to the vase: takes out a handful of roses; and is stooping to lay them on his breast when she realizes that a man who drops dead cannot scatter flowers on himself. She shakes her head and puts the roses back; puts her hands distractedly to her head in an anguish of perplexity, feeling that she must not leave him without some ceremony of love. There is only one thing that comes into her mind that will not compromise her. She goes to him, and cannot touch him or kiss him; but she makes the sign of the cross over him; kisses her hand; crosses herself; and hurries out, closing the door very softly behind her.*

ACT II

A week has elapsed. Bruno is buried, and his death from natural causes duly certified. Jitta has taken refuge in an illness, and is keeping her bed. Her husband, Professor Alfred Lenkheim, is sitting in his study after lunch with young Dr Fessler, who is engaged to Bruno's daughter Edith. Alfred lacks the distinction and heroic touch of Bruno; but prosaic as he certainly is, he is saved from being common, if not from being a little comic, by the stamp put upon him as a man of learning by his university training and his professorial Chair. His age is between forty and fifty. Fessler is just an ordinary nice-looking young doctor.

The room has two doors; one, in the middle of the wall behind the two men, opening on the corridor; the other, on their left, leading to an inner room. The window faces the inner door from the opposite side; and there is a window-seat before it. At right angles to this window-seat, further up the room, is a sofa. There are two tables: one a writing-table on the side near the window, at which the professor is sitting, and the other a round table on the side near the inner door. There is a chair at it with its back to the wall in which the entrance door is, and another, in which Dr Fessler is sitting, between it and the writing-table. The walls are crowded with book-shelves; and the writing-table is heaped with examination papers and manuscripts.

LENKHEIM. Whats the matter? Going asleep at your age! You were not called up last night, were you?

FESSLER. No. But, by Jimminy, Lenkheim, I have gone through a lot this last week.

LENKHEIM. How?

FESSLER. Just consider. Imagine having to console Bruno's widow when I'm engaged to his daughter!

LENKHEIM. Why not?

FESSLER. Because theyre at daggers drawn. Every word that soothes old Agnes is an outrage to Edith.

LENKHEIM. Why? Whats wrong between them?

FESSLER. Oh, Mrs Haldenstedt is old-fashioned. She keeps up the convention that because Edith is a young unmarried woman she cant possibly understand about her father's death; and Edith has to pretend to be in the dark. But of course she knows as well as you or I; and it maddens her to have to hold her tongue and be treated like a child when all her feelings are boiling over about it. She was very fond of her father.

LENKHEIM. I knew the mother and daughter never got on very well together—jealousy, I suppose, as usual—but I thought this awful business would have brought them together.

FESSLER. Not a bit. It has set them more against one another than ever.

LENKHEIM. I suppose theyve no notion who the woman was?

FESSLER. None. She will never be found out unless she comes forward herself.

LENKHEIM. She wont do that. Why should she give herself away?

FESSLER. Women do, sometimes, God knows why! But meanwhile, poor Mrs Haldenstedt is most frightfully cut up. There she is, distracted by all sorts of surmises and suspicions, not knowing what to think, asking herself every minute whether he went on the loose and died in a vulgar street adventure, or whether there was somebody all along whom she never suspected, making her marriage a mockery. We are all as much in the dark as she is; for there never was a word against him: he seemed the correctest, most domesticated of men. That is, unless y o u know anything. You were so intimate with him, you know.

LENKHEIM. Was I really intimate with him? Certainly we were friends at college; and we kept it up afterwards. But he never told me much about himself.

FESSLER. He was not that sort of man. But he trusted nobody in the world as he trusted you: the widow is dead certain of that. By the way, she asked me to prepare you for a visit she is going to pay you.

LENKHEIM. Why should you prepare me?

FESSLER. Well, she is going to ask you to act as his scientific and literary executor.

LENKHEIM [*pleasantly surprised and suddenly self-conscious*] Really! Of course I shall be delighted. I may tell you that in my own will I made him my literary executor. Who would have thought that he would peg out first?

FESSLER. But didnt you know that he was ill?

LENKHEIM. Oh, I knew about his heart and so forth. But many a patient with heart disease lives to bury his doctor. As a matter of fact his case was not a very serious one. His heart would not have stood racing up two or three flights of stairs. But does any man of his age race upstairs? A very strong emotion or excitement might have killed him; but a settled married man with a wife and a grown-up daughter suffers more from too little excitement than from too much. What emotions has a domesticated man of science to fear after forty?

FESSLER. Then why did he die?

LENKHEIM. Just so: why did he die? He wouldnt have died if he had been leading the quiet life we all gave him credit for. What sort of life did he really lead? That is the question.

FESSLER. Isnt it shocking that such a man should die under such—such—well, such shady circumstances?

LENKHEIM. Shady! I should call them disgraceful. Yes, my dear boy, we must face it: he came to a disgraceful end. An operatic tenor, or even a literary man, might be forgiven for dying in an adventure of that kind. But a man of science! Unfortunate, to say the least: most unfortunate.

FESSLER. At all events, since it was his luck to die in the dark, we are not called on to light the candle, are we?

LENKHEIM. We are not; but what about the police? And what about his wife?

FESSLER. They havnt the ghost of a clue.

LENKHEIM. It wont upset or delay your engagement, I hope. Not that I could blame you if you broke it off. Still—

FESSLER. *I* break it off! Good gracious, no!

LENKHEIM. I'm glad of that. Of course you must keep it up to Edith that there was nothing wrong.

FESSLER. But she wont have it that there was nothing wrong.

LENKHEIM. What!

FESSLER. You see, she adored her father. She sees him with a halo round his head; and nothing that he could do would be wrong for her. She has always felt that her mother could not live up to him; and she is persuading herself that this unknown woman was some wonderful person who made him as happy as she thinks he deserved to be.

LENKHEIM. Thats funny. Very funny. Does she suspect anybody?

FESSLER. I dont know. I cant see through her; and the worst of it is, she can see through me. She will find out what I think.

LENKHEIM. Which is?

FESSLER. Well, just what you think. And when she finds out what that is, heaven help me!

LENKHEIM. She wont find out. All that a young girl sees in a death is the romance of it: the vulgar reality does not exist for her. What an eye-opener for us who know better! [*Sententiously*] And yet, whatever view we may take of the affair, we must admit that these moral problems are very difficult: in fact, insoluble. Is there any man who can say that he has never been in a position in which sudden death would have been extremely embarrassing?

FESSLER. I suppose not. [*Naïvely*] By the way, that reminds me that I forgot to ask how Mrs Lenkheim is.

LENKHEIM. Oh, Jitta is getting over it. She hopes to be able to get up for a couple of hours today. Just in a dressing-gown, you know, to sit about a bit.

FESSLER. Oh, good. Well, I must be off to the hospital. [*He rises*]. Tell her I asked after her.

LENKHEIM [*rising*] I will. How soon do you think I may expect the Haldenstedts?

FESSLER. Any time now, I should think. The old girl wont be easy until she has seen you.

Lenkheim goes out for a moment through the inner door. Jitta comes in, languid, and dressed as Lenkheim has described.

JITTA. Oh, so glad youve come, Doctor. [*She shakes hands with Fessler*]. Have you seen the Haldenstedts? I was so sorry not to be able to call on them. I have been really

too ill. I hope they know that.

FESSLER [*with affectionate deference*] They thoroughly understand that. You must take the greatest care of yourself.

JITTA. You are not running away, are you?

FESSLER. I must. I have to be at the hospital; and I am late already.

JITTA. Come again soon, Doctor.

FESSLER. I hope to find you quite well then, dear lady.

He kisses her hand, and goes out. When he has gone, Lenkheim returns, full of excitement and curiosity.

LENKHEIM. Jitta: old Agnes is coming to see us. Bruno has made me his literary executor. That is what she is coming about.

JITTA. Has she recovered enough to bear discussing it with you?

LENKHEIM. She must. The world doesnt stand still when people die. I wonder what we shall find in his papers!

JITTA [*going white*] Has she found anything?

LENKHEIM. Yes: didnt I tell you? He has made me his scientific and literary executor.

JITTA. I mean about—about—

LENKHEIM. About his death? Absolutely nothing: Fessler has just told me so.

JITTA [*sitting down at the table, reassured*] Poor Fessler!

LENKHEIM [*resuming his seat at his writing-table*] Yes, poor chap: he is rather in a fright about Edith.

JITTA. Why?

LENKHEIM. He is afraid that her grief for her father will kill her feeling for him; so youd better take Edith in hand: you know how she clings to you. She is like her father in that: he clung to you.

JITTA. To me!

LENKHEIM. Yes: you know very well he did. If I had died you would have been up before this, I expect.

JITTA. Alfred: if you begin nagging I shall have to go back to bed.

LENKHEIM. Who's nagging? [*She rises. He jumps up apprehensively*] There now: for God's sake dont make a scene about nothing. All I meant was that if he ever told anything to anybody he would have told it to you. [*She sits down again*]. Jitta: have you really no suspicion?

JITTA. Of what?

LENKHEIM. Who the woman was.

JITTA. How could he tell anyone who she was? It would have been dishonorable to betray her.

LENKHEIM. Men do tell, all the same. They dont tell the newspapers; but they tell other women.

JITTA. I object to be classed with "other women."

LENKHEIM. Oh well, it's no use talking to you if you will be so touchy. I didnt suggest that he told you: you brought that in yourself. All that was in my mind was that as you were so much in and out of his house you must have met her one time or another if she was the wife of any of his friends. It usually is a friend's wife.

JITTA [*with affected listlessness*] Is it?

LENKHEIM. Well, it stands to reason, doesnt it? Unless it's a chance woman from the streets.

JITTA [*wincing*] I suppose so.

LENKHEIM. Did he never talk to you about love, or anything of that sort?

JITTA. The last time we were at the theatre he discussed the play with me. It was a play about love.

LENKHEIM. Well, what else would a play be about? Thats no clue. I wonder was she a patient of his?

JITTA. Does it matter? Need we gossip about it?

LENKHEIM [*impatiently*] Dont be so superior. I like gossip. Everybody likes gossip. You like it yourself as well as anybody. If she was a patient that would account for his being so reserved about her.

JITTA. Alfred: you are unbearable. I will go back to bed.

She rises and makes for the door, but is checked by the entrance of Agnes Haldenstedt and her daughter, both in deep mourning. Agnes carries a small dispatch case. She is not really much older than Jitta; but she has retired so completely from the competition of women in attractiveness, and accepted so fully her lot as a good bourgeoise with a home to keep and a family to manage on a slender income that she is set down as much older and less distinguished socially. Her sense of duty has kept her upright; and her uprightness has given her a certain authority, as of a person of some consequence. She has been deeply wounded by the circumstances of her husband's death, and is stiff and suspicious in her manner.

Her daughter is young and ingenuous, with a strong character. A passion of grief for her father has set her on fire with pride and a sense of being ready for any sacrifice.

The conversation which ensues is solemn, artificial, and constrained. They condole with one another in low tones and unnaturally bookish sentences. Jitta has to draw the girl to her, and kiss her on the brow. Alfred leads Mrs Haldenstedt to the sofa. When she sits down, he sits on the window-seat near her. Jitta leads Edith to the chair she has just vacated, and goes to the sofa, where she seats herself on the widow's left.

All these movements are ridiculous; yet the mourning worn by the two visitors makes them seem, if not natural, at least becoming.

LENKHEIM [*in hollow tones*] May I say again, dear Mrs Haldenstedt, how deeply I—

JITTA [*gushing*] At last, dearest Mrs Haldenstedt, I am able to tell you what I felt when I lay helpless, unable to pay the last respects to our dear lost friend. [*As she sits down, she seizes the hands of Mrs Haldenstedt, giving her no opportunity of refusing the attention*]. But in my sick room I was with you in spirit. Indeed I have never been closer to you and poor Edith than in that moment when I had to ask my husband to tell you what it cost me to stay away.

AGNES [*not at all disposed to allow Jitta so prominent a share in her grief, but conventionally resorting to her handkerchief*] Thank you. I'm sure it's very kind of you.

LENKHEIM [*clearing his throat and sniffing*] Under such a sudden blow, what can we say? We are all struck dumb. We all share your grief.

AGNES. When people are sick, and we can sacrifice ourselves completely to the duty of nursing them: when they can lean on us to the very last, then, when the parting comes, there is some consolation in the thought that we have done all in our power. But an end like this, so sudden, so dreadful— [*she breaks down*].

LENKHEIM [*making the best of it*] Still, I am not sure that a lingering death really spares the feelings of the survivors. Death often tortures its victims before it strikes the final blow. In your case, dear Mrs Haldenstedt, there was at least no torture.

AGNES [*staring at him*] No torture! What has the future for me but the torture of a widow's grief?

EDITH [*unsympathetic*] It has the honor of father's name. Is that nothing?

LENKHEIM [*effusively*] Which I will help you both to uphold, my dear Edith, believe me.

AGNES. He knew he could depend on you.

I have a packet of papers marked "Professor Lenkheim's property: to be given into his own hands": that is why I have come today instead of waiting for Mrs Lenkheim to call.

LENKHEIM. Dear fellow: how conscientious of him! such papers as he had of mine were of no consequence. Shall we have a little quiet talk all to ourselves, in here? [*He rises and crosses the room, inviting her, by a gesture, to come with him through the door opposite the window*].

AGNES [*pausing between Jitta and Edith*] I wanted to come alone: but Edith insisted on coming with me.

LENKHEIM. She was quite right. She is now your only support.

EDITH [*proudly*] Thank you, Professor. I wish you could persuade my mother that I could do much more for her if she would tell me all her troubles. I am no longer a child. There is nothing now that cannot be spoken of quite frankly before me.

AGNES [*with a weary smile*] Of course not, dear. But there are things it is better not to know. I know them; and I only wish I could change places with you.

Emphasizing this with an emphatic nod at Edith, she goes into the next room. Lenkheim follows her.

JITTA [*throwing off her false manner, whilst retaining the patronizing suavity of an older woman to a younger one, holds out her hands to Edith with genuine sympathy*] Come, darling. [*Edith comes to her and takes her hands*]. Sit here, close to me. [*She makes room for her on the sofa beside her. Edith sits down on her left, and looks gratefully and longingly into her eyes*]. Do you remember when we were last here together? Your father brought you. He was radiant with joy and pride in you. We were all so happy.

EDITH [*thoughtfully*] How long was that ago?

JITTA. Barely three weeks.

EDITH. It seems an age. I was a child then. I can hardly remember how I felt. It is as if I had been asleep.

JITTA. Your father's death has awakened you: you are looking at life for the first time.

EDITH. I have been looking at death for the first time.

JITTA. My poor child! But dont lose courage. Life lies before you: it will make up to you for many sorrows. You will get over it, Edith.

EDITH. Why should I get over it? I dont want to get over it. Do you suppose I feel disgraced?

JITTA. Oh no, no: of course not. But such a grief as this always makes us feel that we have come to the end of everything: that nothing can ever be the same again. Yet next day we find ourselves at the beginning of everything instead.

EDITH [*impatient*] You need not speak to me like that. You know very well that what is the matter is not merely the loss of a father: a thing that happens to everybody sooner or later.

JITTA [*taken aback*] Edith, dear—

EDITH [*downright and indignant*] Why do you treat me as if I were a little girl, as my mother does? I did not expect it from you. Oh, I am so tired of all this humbug. I turned to you because I hoped you would understand me, and let me open my heart to you like a friend.

JITTA. My dear: I will be an elder sister to you—

EDITH [*fiercely*] I said a friend.

JITTA [*surrendering*] Oh, you are terrible. I will be everything you want, if I can. But why are you angry with me? I really meant what I said. Life has a great deal to offer you: dont forget that you are going to be married. I believe you can trust your man. He adored your father. He will regard you as a sacred legacy.

EDITH. Thats curious. He used that word himself the day we buried poor papa. But I dont intend to be taken as a legacy, sacred or not.

JITTA. Edith: he feels your loss as deeply as you do yourself. Some of us perhaps feel it more deeply, because we have more experience of men, and know how much better what he was than you are yet old enough to know.

EDITH [*rising and pacing restlessly across the room*] Oh, these commonplaces! How you keep throwing them at me! None of us know what my father was: he was thrown away among us. [*Turning on Jitta*] Why did he not die with us? Why had he no last word for us? I was nothing to him: none of us were anything to him.

JITTA. You know, dear, that you are unjust to him when you say so.

EDITH. Unjust! unjust! what has that to do with it? Why did he not come to us for help, for nursing, for care?

JITTA. He was too considerate to let you

know how ill he was.

EDITH. He told everyone else. We were left in the dark.

JITTA. No, no. No one knew it except himself.

EDITH [*passionately*] My mother wont speak to me about it; but I know very well what she is thinking. They whisper all day at home. I see it in the eyes of the visitors; and it makes me furious. I never want to see anyone cry again as my mother cried that night when they brought him home. It wasnt only grief: there was a bitterness in her that had nothing to do with grief or love. I have often felt in my soul that papa never found in his home what he needed and longed for. There were moments when I somehow got beyond myself and became another person; perhaps the woman I am growing into; and he was so responsive to that flash of something different in me, so grateful for it, that I saw quite plainly how he was longing for something else, something more, than we were giving him. We were not good enough for him. [*She throws herself into the chair beside the round table, sobbing*].

JITTA [*rising and going to her*] Dearest: dont cry like that.

EDITH. It nearly killed me to see him sitting there, as he often did, staring right through me without seeing me, and sighing as he drew his hand across his eyes and through his hair.

JITTA. Dear child: you must not worry yourself because he sometimes looked straight at you and did not see you. Just think. He was a doctor: he knew his danger better than anyone. When a man finds himself condemned to death, his thoughts and feelings must be overwhelming. Well, if you were looking at the sea in a storm or at the heavens opening above it, would you see a tiny figure on the shore, even if it were your own child?

EDITH [*rising in a girlish rapture*] Thank you for that: it is beautiful, and quite true. [*She closes her eyes, silent for a moment, and a little breathless. Jitta smiles, and sits down in the writing-table chair*]. And now, wont you help me to find out the secret of his death?

JITTA. What secret?

EDITH. Who is the woman in whose arms my father died?

JITTA [*startled*] So that is what you think! Poor child!

EDITH [*angry*] I do not think it: I know it. You know it. Please let us have no more of the poor child business: it does not impose on me. How am I to find her?

JITTA [*remonstrating*] Edith, Edith, what could you say to her, even if you found her?

EDITH. Only that I love her.

JITTA. Love her! What for?

EDITH. For making my father happy. [*Restless again, pacing up and down*]. Oh, if you knew how infamously all those people who call on us misunderstand him. They insult my mother by condoling with her on her husband's unfaithfulness. They insult God by declaring that my father threw himself into the gutter, and was justly punished for it.

JITTA [*springing up*] What! They dare say such brutal things!

EDITH. Oh, not in those words: they are too polite to speak as horribly as they think; but I know. And my mother encourages them. She actually likes to feel that some unheard-of disgrace has fallen on her. She thinks it makes her interesting and revenges her. She positively wallows in it.

JITTA [*shocked*] Edith!

EDITH. Oh, it is the right word for it: why should I not use it? She never thinks of his sorrows: only of her own.

JITTA [*taking her arm persuasively*] My dear: you mustnt go on like this. Come: let me talk to you quietly. [*She draws her back to the sofa, and makes her sit down again*]. If you loved your mother as you loved your father, you would be kinder to her. You think of him as a man whose wife has failed him. Dont forget that she is a woman whose husband failed her.

EDITH. How did he fail her? If she had been worthy of him—

JITTA. Yes, yes, dear; but she was not worthy of him. Or stop: no: we have no right to say that.

EDITH. We have a right to say that she was not the right woman for him.

JITTA. Yes; but dont forget that that means that he was not the right man for her. He was her superior if you like; but that only made it worse for her. His superiority must often have wounded her self-respect; and as any weakness of his flattered it, she perhaps likes to think that he was not quite perfect, and even that he treated her badly.

EDITH. You think that an excuse for her!

I call it abominable.

JITTA. Dont be impossible, dear. Abominable or not, it explains her readiness to believe the worst. You must not blame her because your faith in him is greater, and your consolation nobler. Remember: he did not betray you as he betrayed her. For he did betray her; and so did that woman. Tell yourself that, Edith, whenever you feel tempted to hate your mother. Promise me you will.

EDITH. I will never tell myself such a silly lie. I will take my father's memory and good name out of my mother's hands, and out of the hands of her tittle-tattling friends. I will make the world see him as he was, and as I loved him, not as she sees him, and as she hates him.

JITTA. The world will see him with its own eyes, dear, not with yours. All you can do is to save his memory from being blackened by that odious thing, a family quarrel. Come! promise me to stop worrying about your mother?

EDITH. I am not worrying about her: I am worrying about the woman my father loved. I cannot help it: she is always in my mind. Why was she not with him when they found him? Why did she run away like a criminal?

JITTA. Perhaps she is asking herself those questions every day in her shame and misery. Oh, Edith, we dont know what meannesses we are capable of until we are tried. The dread of a public scandal—of having to face a policeman prying into the most sacred and secret places in her soul—will drive a woman to anything. Remember: she had not only to save herself from the scandal, but his memory as well.

EDITH. No, no, no. She did not save him. She left him under the stigma of having died in the arms of some vile creature. I know in my soul that she was not that. The world would forgive him if it knew that she is what I know she must be if h e loved her. Oh, why does she not defy all the silly world for his sake, and say "It was I."

JITTA. You ask too much from her. She may have been capable of great things when he was alive and at her side. What is the poor wretch now but a broken-hearted lonely coward?

EDITH. She is not broken - hearted: my father never broke any woman's heart. I loved him; and that makes even his death a glory to me. If she is lonely why does she not come to me? She s h a l l come to me. We shall cure one another's loneliness, we two. Where is she to cry her heart out if not in my arms?

JITTA. No: she slunk away into the darkness. Let her be. She can bleed to death in her hiding-place.

EDITH. She shall not: she will be drawn to me: you will see. Remember that I have no longer any place at home. I cannot live with people who cannot feel about my father as I do; and there is only one such person in the world.

JITTA. That woman?

EDITH. Yes. I will give her every right over me that the woman who returned my father's love should have over his daughter: the right I deny to my mother. I swear it.

JITTA. How serious you are, Edith! But what will your mother say, and the man you are engaged to?

EDITH. My mother would never understand: I take nothing from her that she is capable of missing. As to the man who says he loves me, and asks me to share my whole life with him, if he cannot understand me and support me in this he will never have me for a wife. I can do without any man if I can find the woman to whom I am bound for ever and ever. You will help me to find her, will you not?

JITTA [deeply moved, drawing Edith to her] Oh, darling, darling, if only I could! If only I dared!

Lenkheim throws the door open: he is returning with Agnes. Jitta and Edith move asunder and rise hastily. Agnes comes in, drying her eyes with her handkerchief. Lenkheim follows her solemnly with her dispatch case in his hand.

EDITH [stamping] Oh, bother! Always at the wrong moment. Always spoiling everything. [She turns impatiently to the window, and stands with her back to them, fuming].

AGNES [to Alfred] Thank God I found strength for this. It is a great relief to me. But I am dead tired: I must go home. [To Edith] Come, child.

JITTA. Wont you sit down and rest for a moment?

AGNES. Thank you; but I shall be better at home. And I have so many accounts to settle.

LENKHEIM. Ah, yes, yes: of course you have. Well, if you must go, you must. And you may depend on me not to keep you waiting too long before I go to work on the scientific

2 M

papers.

JITTA. I hope to be allowed to go out again in a day or two. May I come to see you if the doctor says I may?

AGNES. Do, of course. I shall expect you. [*To Lenkheim*] You will forgive me, wont you, all the trouble I am giving you? It has done me so much good to unburden myself to a real friend.

LENKHEIM. You have had a cruel experience, dear Mrs Haldenstedt; but we must all resign ourselves to our trials.

AGNES. Yes: I suppose that is a great consolation.

EDITH. My consolation is that nobody dares console me.

ALFRED [*pompously*] Proud words; and how true! h o w true! [*Unctuously, as he shakes her hand*] Goodbye, dear lady, good-bye.

AGNES. Goodbye. [*To Edith, laughing a little maliciously*] Since you are so strong, child, just give me your arm.

JITTA [*shaking hands*] Goodbye.

Edith goes out with her mother leaning heavily on her. Jitta goes out with them.

LENKHEIM [*relieved at being rid of the widow*] Ouf! [*He carries the dispatch case to his writing-table, and sits down to examine its contents. He is in no hurry. It contains nothing but the manuscript of a biggish book. He leans lazily back with his legs stretched, and turns over the cover without looking at it. He reads a bit, and makes a wry face. He disagrees intensely and contemptuously with every passage he reads, abandoning each with sniffs and pishes, only to be still more disgusted with the next.*

Jitta returns; sees what he is doing; and halts between him and the round table, silently watching him.

Finally he gives the book up as hopeless; shuts up the pages; and stares at the mass of manuscript as if wondering what he is to do with such trash. Suddenly his expression changes. His eyes bulge in amazement.

ALFRED [*after a stifled exclamation*] Jitta! Jitta! [*He turns, half rising, and sees her*]. Oh, youre there.

JITTA. What is the matter? [*knowing only too well, and very angry at his contemptuous air, but pretending to be listless and languid*].

LENKHEIM [*shewing her the manuscript*] Look at this!

JITTA. Well?

LENKHEIM. Look at the title.

JITTA [*reading*] "Fetters of the Feminine Psyche." Is that the book you worked on with him?

LENKHEIM. I! Certainly not: he wrote it all himself: I only gave him his facts. Read the next line.

JITTA [*reading*] "By Alfred Lenkheim." I suppose he meant you to finish it.

LENKHEIM [*turning over to the end*] But it is finished. Look. Was he mad? Did he suppose I would condescend to put my name to another man's work? I have some reputation of my own to fall back on, thank God. There is something behind this.

JITTA. I suppose he wished to leave you something valuable as a keepsake. You were his friend.

LENKHEIM [*scornfully*] A keepsake! Dont talk nonsense, Jitta: a man does not give away his biggest work as if it were his diamond pin, unless he is afraid to put his own name to it. But if he thinks he is going to put mine to his trash he is greatly mistaken.

JITTA [*boiling with rage, pointing to the manuscript*] He has sacrificed his immortality for your benefit.

LENKHEIM [*angrily*] Rot. Why should he? Nobody who can create sacrifices his creation. [*He throws the manuscript on the table*]. Not that he ever pretended to think much of the book.

JITTA [*indignantly*] He thought the world of it. It was his greatest pride.

LENKHEIM [*turning on her, a suspicion flashing on him*] How do you know?

JITTA [*checking herself, feeling that her temper has betrayed her*] He often spoke to me about this book, and about the hopes he had built on it.

LENKHEIM. To you! What do you know about psychiatry? Why should he sacrifice his reputation to add to mine? quite unnecessarily.

JITTA. The whim of an invalid, I suppose.

LENKHEIM [*out of patience*] Whim! He throws away his one chance of notoriety; and you call that a whim. Do you take me for a fool?

JITTA. Dont shout, Alfred, please.

ALFRED [*subsiding a little*] I'm not shouting: I'm asking you to talk sense. You say he spoke to you about this. What did he tell you?

JITTA. Of course I knew too little of the work you and he were doing together to be able to help or understand much. [*Decisively*] But in any case you must carry out his wishes.

LENKHEIM. What wishes?

JITTA. You must accept what he has left you.

LENKHEIM. Why must I?

JITTA. It was his last wish: we have no choice.

LENKHEIM. We! Me, you mean. What have you to do with it?

JITTA. Well, you if you like.

LENKHEIM. It's not me youre thinking of. Funny, the way women run after a dead man if only he dies romantically! Anyhow this thing is impossible. I wont do it.

JITTA. Why?

LENKHEIM. Because it would be nothing short of swindling the scientific world to pass off his stuff on it as mine: thats why. And now, what the deuce am I to say to old Agnes? [Grumbling] Such an unreasonable thing to ask me to do! Such an ungrateful thing!

JITTA. Was it ungrateful to give you the whole credit when you were only his collaborator?

LENKHEIM. Collaborator! What are you talking about? He knew as well as I did that I was only waiting for the publication of his idiotic theory to tear it to pieces. You dont suppose I believe in it, do you?

JITTA. Then perhaps that was what he wanted to prevent.

LENKHEIM. Jitta: you are simply drivelling. Bruno was too jolly conceited to be afraid of me. Dont be childish.

JITTA [irritably] I am like yourself: I am only trying to guess why he did it.

LENKHEIM. Just so. Why did he do it? Where is the sense in it? I believe you know, Jitta.

JITTA. Really, Alfred—! I must go back to bed.

LENKHEIM. You havnt been up an hour.

JITTA. But I am dead tired.

LENKHEIM. You cant be as tired as all that. What do you want to run away for?

JITTA. Have you forgotten that I am ill? I can hardly stand. I must lie down.

ALFRED. Well, lie on the sofa.

JITTA. Dont be brutal, Alfred.

LENKHEIM. Bosh! You are hiding something from me: I havnt experimented with psychoanalysis for nothing. I notice that this crazy thing that bothers me doesnt bother you. You understand it: you couldnt take it so quietly if you didnt.

JITTA. I take it without shouting, if that is what you mean.

LENKHEIM. What did he say to you about the book and about his hopes? Why did you never say a word about them to me?

JITTA. I never thought about it.

LENKHEIM. If you had never thought about it you would have talked to me about it.

JITTA. I suppose I did not think it worth mentioning.

LENKHEIM. Psha! Would a man who told you all that not tell you plenty of other things? That love affair, now—?

JITTA [shrinking] Oh, Alfred!

LENKHEIM. Oh, stuff! Who was the woman? You know all about her: I can see it in your eyes. [He takes her by the shoulders and turns her face to face]. Aha! You know who she was. You know all about it.

JITTA [rising indignantly and letting herself go] You are mad, and grossly rude.

LENKHEIM [rising also] I have had enough of being humbugged. Who was she?

JITTA [closes her lips obstinately]!

LENKHEIM. Was he so much to you that you will not give the other woman away, even to me, your husband? Were those his orders?

JITTA [exhausted] I have no orders. I go my own way [she attempts to leave the room].

LENKHEIM [intercepting her] You shant run away. If you dont tell me who she is, I will— I will—[he makes a threatening gesture, not very convincingly].

JITTA. Take care, Alfred. Your cunning is only a fool's cunning after all. The answer to your question is staring you in the face. Thank your stars you are too stupid to see it.

LENKHEIM. Am I? We shall see. Before you leave this room I will find out the part you played in this dirty business.

JITTA [starting as from the lash of a whip] Dirty! Oh, never was anything purer, holier, nobler.

LENKHEIM [screaming] Ah! It was you! There was no other woman: it was you, you. He bought you from me, for that [he bangs his fist on the manuscript]. The damned thief! [He collapses into his chair at the table, clasping his head in his hands].

JITTA [sitting down wearily on the sofa] Leave the dead in peace. If you cannot hold your tongue, abuse me. I am alive, and can feel it.

LENKHEIM [miserably] You dont even deny it!

JITTA. No. Are you surprised? You lost me long ago.

LENKHEIM. My fault, of course. You worthless devil: what do you expect me to think of you?

JITTA. You can think what you like, Alfred. I dont grudge you that melancholy satisfaction.

LENKHEIM. Have you no conscience, no shame?

JITTA. Do you want me to make a scene for you, Alfred? I am sorry: I am too tired.

LENKHEIM. If I had him here—

JITTA. Threaten him to your heart's content. He is dead.

ALFRED. Yes; but I am very much alive. Dont forget that.

JITTA. Not so very much alive, Alfred.

ALFRED. Yah [*gnashes his teeth with rage*]!

JITTA. However, what I enjoyed I shall have to pay for. I know that.

LENKHEIM. You and he were lovers?

JITTA [*proudly*] Yes: you have found the right word at last. Lovers.

LENKHEIM. [*whining pitiably*] And you could live in the house with me, and take my care and my nursing and my money, and even— [*He looks at her and chokes*]. How long has this affair been going on?

JITTA. Our love has lasted three years.

LENKHEIM. Love! Love in the sort of house he was found dead in!

JITTA. Love wherever we were. And wherever we were was paradise. Does that give you any idea of his greatness?

LENKHEIM. Of your meanness, more likely. Dont try to stuff me with big words: they only shew that you wont confess your caddishness even to yourself.

JITTA [*rising*] Oh, please! I cut a pretty contemptible figure—

LENKHEIM [*triumphing*] You do. You do.

JITTA [*continuing*]—beside him.

LENKHEIM [*rising, goaded beyond endurance: threatening her*] You take care, do you hear?

JITTA [*wringing her hands*] My place was at his side. They should have had to tear me away from him by force. Yes; and I will tell you something more. The last beat of his heart would have broken mine if I had been any good. But I am no good; and here I am, as you see me. Oh, you are quite right. I have no right to be in any decent house [*she turns to the door*].

LENKHEIM. Stop: where are you going?

JITTA. I dont know. Into the streets, I suppose.

LENKHEIM. Oh, damn your heroics! You shant leave this room until you have told me everything.

JITTA. [*bitterly*] Dont you know enough already?

LENKHEIM [*pointing to the manuscript*] What does that title-page mean?

JITTA. You know. You have said what it means.

LENKHEIM. I want to know what he said.

JITTA That you are to be the father to his orphaned book. That the fame it will bring you will make amends to you—for me.

LENKHEIM. The blackguard! Not content with stealing you from me, he must dictate the rest of my life to me, as if I were a child.

JITTA. Yes: compared to him you are a child. He has provided for you.

LENKHEIM. Ha! And were you equally kind and thoughtful for his wife, eh?

JITTA [*earnestly*] Alfred: it was too strong for us.

LENKHEIM. What was too strong for you?

JITTA. Love. You dont understand love. Have you anything else to say to me?

LENKHEIM. No. [*He turns his back on her, and goes sulkily to the window*].

JITTA. Goodbye. [*She tries to go, but suddenly becomes weak, and reels against the head of the sofa*]. Alfred.

LENKHEIM. Whats the matter? [*He runs to her; and gets her safely seated*].

JITTA. Dont mind, Alfred. I shall be better soon: it is passing.

LENKHEIM [*turning brusquely from her like an angry child*] I am not sympathizing with you. It serves you right. [*He sits down at the round table, with his elbows on it, muttering and sulking*]. Treated me disgracefully. Disgracefully.

JITTA [*sighs wearily*]!!

LENKHEIM [*unaggressively*] Jitta?

Her name and the change in his tone give her a shock. She turns and looks searchingly at him.

LENKHEIM [*recovering his self-control by a rather broken effort*]. This is no use. I have come to my senses. I—I will take it quietly and reasonably.

JITTA. I am glad you can: I wish I could.

LENKHEIM [*shaking his head*] But we cant leave it like this, can we?

JITTA. What can we do, Alfred?

LENKHEIM. You have done me harm

enough. Do you want to ruin me as well?

JITTA. It is I who am ruined, as you call it, is it not? The sin is mine: I will pay the penalty by myself. Your life is only beginning: with that book you have a future. I have only a past. I will take it and myself out of your life. [*She rises*].

LENKHEIM [*out of patience, jumping up*] Look here: since you wont talk sense and be commonly civil to me, I'm going to assert myself. You cant settle an affair like this by looking like a martyr and walking out into the street. You must learn to consider other people a little. If you have no regard for me, at least remember that Agnes and Edith have a future, and have a right not to have it spoiled. For their sake I am prepared to endure your presence in my house.

JITTA [*with faint surprise and some irony*] You can bring yourself to that? You can still bear to look at me?

LENKHEIM. Make no mistake: all is over between you and me. For ever. I mean it.

JITTA. So do I.

LENKHEIM. Very well: be it so. But that does not mean that we need separate. People can live miles apart under the same roof. That is how you will have to live with me. If you have a spark of decent feeling left, you will not force a public scandal on me.

JITTA. Does it matter?

LENKHEIM. Does it matter! Are you utterly selfish? Dont you understand that if this miserable break-up of our marriage becomes known it will break up that poor woman's widowhood as well?

JITTA. Does s h e matter so much?

LENKHEIM [*playing his ace*] Well, what about Edith? Doesnt s h e matter? Do you suppose Fessler can afford to marry her if you drag her family through the mud?

JITTA [*staggered*] Oh! I was not thinking, Alfred. Give me until tomorrow to think it over. I can bear no more today. I can hardly stand.

LENKHEIM. You can stand as well as I can. [*She immediately sits down obstinately at the writing-table*]. Very well; but stand or sit, you dont leave this room until you give me your word to stay.

JITTA. With you?

LENKHEIM. Yes, with me. It is I who will have to pay the housekeeping bills. But dont be afraid: I am done with you, except before company. Not one word will I ever speak to you again when we are alone together.

JITTA. Oh, Alfred, you will tell me so ten times a day. Dont let us talk nonsense.

LENKHEIM. You will see. Not one word. Not a sound. I tell you I am done with you; and I wish I had never met you.

JITTA. It sounds too good to be true, Alfred.

LENKHEIM. Psha!

JITTA. But that part of it rests with yourself. [*Determinedly*] And now for m y conditions.

LENKHEIM. Y o u r conditions! Yours!!! You dare talk to me of conditions!

JITTA. You are in my hands, Alfred; and you know it. I can give the whole scandal away if you defy me. I will not be unkind; but if I am to keep up appearances, you must keep them up too. If I am to pretend to be a good woman, you must pretend to be a great man.

LENKHEIM. Pretend!

JITTA. Oh, b e a great man by all means, Alfred, if you can. But you must pretend in any case.

LENKHEIM. How?

JITTA. You will pretend to be the author of that great book. That will be your share of the sham of our life together.

LENKHEIM. But I tell you I dont believe a word of the silly thing.

JITTA. Of course not. If you had the genius to believe it, you would have had the genius to write it.

LENKHEIM [*goaded*] I——

JITTA [*continuing calmly*] You cannot believe it, just as I cannot believe that you will never speak to me again;—

LENKHEIM. I never will.

JITTA [*still ignoring his protests*] —but you will come to believe every word of the silly thing, as you call it, when it makes Lenkheim as famous as Einstein.

LENKHEIM [*startled by the name*] Einstein! You are tempting me, you devil.

JITTA. You envied Einstein, Alfred. Well, all that you envied him for is within your reach. Stretch out your hand, and take it.

LENKHEIM. And you envied Einstein's wife, did you? I see. Why could not your stupid husband give you a triumphant tour through Europe? Why should you not shake hands with all the kings, and dine with all the presidents, and have gala nights at the Opera? To get all that you will be my accomplice in a fraud, eh? Since you cannot have a good time with him you will have one with me.

JITTA [round-eyed for a moment at this new light on her conduct] How clever of you, Alfred! You have found a reason you can really believe in. I should never have thought of it; but you are welcome to it if only you will father his book.

LENKHEIM [desperately perplexed: yielding] But, Jitta: I dont really believe that. It's not like you: you are not clever enough, not ambitious enough. What is your real reason?

JITTA [decisively] He wished it: that is enough for me. He knew better than either of us what is best for us.

LENKHEIM. Did he indeed, confound him!

JITTA. He did indeed, Alfred; and I forbid you to confound him.

LENKHEIM. Well, if I do—and mind: I dont say I will—I—

JITTA. Yes?

LENKHEIM. I will think it over.

JITTA. Just so, Alfred. Goodnight. [She goes out, tranquilly convinced that she will have her own way].

LENKHEIM [rushing to the door in a last effort to assert himself, and shouting after her] If you think—[He peters out; thrusts his hands desperately into his pockets like a cleaned-out gambler; trots back irresolutely to his writing-table; takes up the MS.; stares at it for a moment; and reads slowly] "By Professor Alfred Lenkheim, Doctor of Philosophy in the University of Vienna." Well, I'm dashed!

ACT III

Mrs Haldenstedt is in her sitting-room with Alfred and Fessler, all three very busy going through the papers of her late husband. She is feverishly reading letters, and tearing them up and throwing them into the waste-paper basket as they prove one after another to be of no interest. Her sighs and exclamations of disappointment and impatience are getting on the nerves of Alfred, who is trying to read a manuscript. He flinches at the sharp sounds made by her violent tearing of the letters. Fessler, who is sorting some papers which he has already gone through, is sympathetic, and looks pityingly at the widow from time to time.

The room is lighted by a large bay window, with a window-seat under it. The table heaped with papers is in this bay; and Mrs Haldenstedt sits at the head of it with her back to the light,

and Alfred and Fessler at the sides of it to her right and left respectively. The corner of the room behind them on their right is cut off by a double door leading to the study. Another door leading to the corridor of the flat is in the diagonally opposite corner, and is consequently before them on their left. On their right between the window and the study door, a console stands against the wall, with flowers on it, and above it a convex mirror. On the same side of the room, a couch.

LENKHEIM [unable to bear the noise any longer] Do you mind my taking these manuscripts into the study and examining them there? They require a certain degree of quiet concentration.

AGNES. I am so sorry. Bruno always said that it was like trying to work in a shooting gallery when I cleared up his papers and tore up useless letters. But if you dont tear them what is there to prevent the servants and everyone else from reading them?

ALFRED. Just so. But why not leave the work to us? Why worry? Cant you trust us?

AGNES. Oh, Professor, how can you ask me that? Of course I can trust you.

LENKHEIM [nodding] Good. Then do trust us. [He goes into the study, and shuts the door behind him].

AGNES [alone with Fessler, letting herself droop] I have gone through this last batch of letters three times over in the hope of finding some clue. But it's no use: theres nothing.

FESSLER. You mustnt worry.

AGNES [sitting up sharply] Have you ever lost anyone you really cared for?

FESSLER. Well, my poor dear father—

AGNES. I'm not talking about poor dear fathers or poor dear anybodies. Bruno was none of your poor dears: he was three quarters of my life, even if half of it was being his slave and his household drudge. All the same, I cant spend my whole life doing nothing but grieving, can I?

FESSLER. Just so. Of course not.

AGNES. Life goes on, doesnt it? Housekeeping goes on: the future has to be thought for as well as the past. All my business and responsibilities and duties go on just as if nothing had happened.

FESSLER. I'm so glad you have recovered enough to be able to look at it in that way.

AGNES. Doctor Fessler: a widow is not an invalid; and it doesnt help her to be treated as one when the first shock is over.

FESSLER. Quite so. Quite so.

AGNES. I am going to talk to you very seriously.

FESSLER. Of course. Of course.

AGNES. And you are going to talk to me seriously, I hope.

FESSLER [surprised] But certainly, my dear Mrs Haldenstedt.

AGNES. Yes; but that doesnt mean saying "Certainly" and "Of course" and "Quite so: quite so" to everything I say, as if you were soothing a baby.

FESSLER [protesting] But I assure you I—

AGNES [gripping his hand on the table] Tell me the honest truth. Did you consider Bruno a clever man?

FESSLER [amazed] Mrs Haldenstedt!!!

AGNES. Do you think he had anything to say more than any of the rest of the professors? [Stopping him as he opens his mouth for a fresh protest] Now if you dont, please dont begin to excuse yourself and spare my feelings. Ive had enough of having my feelings spared: I want the truth.

FESSLER [whole-heartedly] My dear Mrs Haldenstedt: he was a g r e a t man. His psychological doctrine was a revelation. It was the beginning of a new epoch in science.

AGNES. So I have always understood. I know he thought so himself.

FESSLER [indignant] Oh no: he was the most modest of men. I am sure he never said so.

AGNES. Do you think a man's wife knows nothing about his thoughts except what he tells?

FESSLER. I am quite sure he did not know half his own greatness.

AGNES. Then will you tell me what has become of it all? You and Professor Lenkheim have gone through his papers with me. Have we come across one word that could not have been written by an elementary schoolmaster?

FESSLER [shaken a little] Well, everything he wrote, even about trifles, has his peculiar touch.

AGNES. Everything he wrote is in his own handwriting, of course, if you mean that. But can you pick out from all that heap one single bit of paper which you could shew to a stranger and expect him to say "The man that wrote this must have been as great as Einstein"?

FESSLER. Well, not exactly Einstein, perhaps. But— [he stops].

AGNES. But what? Suppose he had left you a safe full of diamonds, and when you opened the safe it was empty!

FESSLER. Oh, you exaggerate!

AGNES [rising, out of patience] Doctor Fessler: if you can take neither me nor my husband's affairs seriously, I think you had better leave both alone.

FESSLER [rising, greatly surprised] Have I offended you?

AGNES [disarmed by his naïve sincerity] No, no. Never mind. Never mind. You are too young. You are not used to women. [Sitting down again] Sit down, wont you? I will talk to Professor Lenkheim about it. He will understand.

FESSLER [standing stiffly, being now really offended] By all means, Mrs Haldenstedt, though I really do not see what he can say more than I can.

AGNES. There! You a r e offended. But if you had been neglected as I have been for months past, while my husband spent hours and hours and hours in his study, writing, writing, writing, using up paper until it cost as much as the butter and eggs, you would want to know what had become of it all.

FESSLER [sitting down again with a gesture of apology] True. I should have thought of that.

AGNES. I never complained, because I thought it was a book that would make him famous and bring him in money. Well, is that heap of old letters and bills and prescriptions all that came of it? Dont tell me: there is a book somewhere; and I want to know where it is. Did he go mad and destroy it? If not, who took it from him? Did that woman?

FESSLER. Good gracious, Mrs Haldenstedt!

AGNES. Oh, this dreadful ending to all our happiness! It spoils everything that was nice in our lives. When the first and best of it was over and we settled down, troubles came I know; but I had my memories, and could sit and think of them. Now they are all poisoned for me.

FESSLER [reflectively] Dear Mrs Haldenstedt: may I speak quite frankly to you?

AGNES. Why, I am begging and praying you to. But I can get nothing out of you but sympathy, as if you were only a visitor instead of going to marry my daughter.

FESSLER. You see, though your husband will be remembered as a great psychologist, he had to practise as a doctor to make a living. Well, the wickedest and worst people have to call in doctors just as often as respectable people; and a doctor cant have them coming to his own house where his wife and daughter are. He has to keep a consulting room somewhere where they can come. The landlady said he rented the room to see his friends in occasionally. I daresay the women he saw there were common women; but how do you know that they were not his patients?

AGNES. Dont deceive yourself; and dont try to deceive me. Whatever I may have said when I was upset, I knew very well all along that Bruno never went with common women from the streets. The landlady said it was always the same woman, and that she was a lady. When she ran away she took that book with her: you mark my words. [*She rises and goes moodily to the console*].

They are interrupted by Lenkheim, who opens the door of the study and trots in flourishing a manuscript.

LENKHEIM. See here!

AGNES. The book!

LENKHEIM. I have just found an unfinished lecture on varieties of sleep.

AGNES [*disappointed*] Only a lecture! [*Taking the manuscript*] Why, it's only six pages. And what can it mean? There is only one sort of sleep.

LENKHEIM. Not at all. He says that hardly any two people sleep in the same way. Every case is an individual one. You must read it, Fessler.

FESSLER [*eagerly*] How interesting! May I look? [*Taking it from Mrs Haldenstedt*] Thank you. I'll read it in the study. [*To Alfred*] Mrs Haldenstedt wants to speak to you. [*He hurries into the study*].

AGNES [*shaking her head*] You see, Professor, it doesnt account for anything.

LENKHEIM. What doesnt?

AGNES. The lecture about sleep. He could have written it in one evening. Thats not the book that he said might be my best insurance policy. It was part of his provision for me. He would never have given it to another woman. If she has it, she stole it. [*She sits down on the couch*].

LENKHEIM. You are still worrrying about that woman. I shouldnt if I were you. [*He takes his former chair, drawing it from the table to the couch*].

AGNES. I shall worry about her until I find

out who she is. And I will find her out some day.

LENKHEIM. If it is any comfort to you, you may take my word for it that with all his professional engagements it was utterly impossible for him to have given much of his time to any woman.

AGNES. What comfort is there in that? One hour is enough for a man. Then he can sit alone at his desk, thinking he is writing some great scientific work, when all the time he is thinking of her, living the hour over again, and looking forward to the next one, right in his wife's face.

LENKHEIM [*very uncomfortable*] Mrs Haldenstedt: do you suspect anybody?

AGNES. I cant see anything clearly. I thought I knew everybody that it could possibly be; but there's nobody. All I know is what he liked and what he wanted, and how easily he could get it by lifting up his little finger. Oh, I know exactly how he deceived us.

LENKHEIM [*rising, startled*] Us!

AGNES. Well, me and Edith, of course.

LENKHEIM [*sitting down, relieved*] Oh! Just so.

AGNES. She wasnt what you think she was, Professor: she was one of us. And I say that when a man has a wife and children and a home and a good position, he should think twice before asking any respectable woman to meet him in such a room in such a house. It was fit neither for him nor for her.

LENKHEIM [*drawing a little closer to her*] Dear lady: may I ask you a very indiscreet question? I shall not be in the least offended if you refuse to answer it.

AGNES. What is it?

LENKHEIM. Was your marriage a happy one?

AGNES. I always thought it was, at least until the last few years. Then there was a sudden change. Up to that time he was full of interest in his home, in Edith's education, in our plans, our money, the chance of our being able to move into a better house, the furniture and pictures, in everything. Then he seemed to get beyond us somehow.

LENKHEIM. What were the symptoms?

AGNES. Well, he was sometimes very irritable, though he used to be a perfect lamb. I thought it was only his health; for of course neither of us was growing younger. I know better now. Oh, what a fool I was! But that is how things happen. They go on from year to year under your very nose, staring you in the face; and you never notice, never think, because your mind is off the track. And then suddenly your eyes are opened with a bang; and you could kill yourself for having been so blind. If I could only find out who she was! [*She rises restlessly*].

LENKHEIM. Mrs Haldenstedt: take my advice: give it up. What is the use of tormenting yourself? You will have no peace until you put that woman out of your head.

AGNES. I dont want peace. I want to find her out.

LENKHEIM [*rising*] But suppose you do find her. What then? Think of the scandal. Believe me, it's better not to know. You could not hurt her without hurting yourself and Edith worse.

AGNES. I dont want to make a scandal; and I dont want to hurt her: I want to find out from her what sort of life Bruno was really leading, and what has become of all that work he did.

LENKHEIM. But the lecture on varieties of sleep—

AGNES. Stuff! I know the variety of sleep he learnt from her. [*Looking at him queerly*] Why do you want to prevent me from finding her out?

LENKHEIM [*meeting her eye with imposing firmness*] Solely for your own sake, Mrs Haldenstedt. How could it possibly affect me? Banish this abandoned female from your mind; and trust to Time. Time is the great healer. Time will restore your happiness.

AGNES. Well, Time works wonders, they say. But it will never comfort me until I know for certain that the happiness he had with me was the right sort of happiness, and the happiness he had with the other woman the wrong sort. How do I know that she wasnt a cleverer woman than I am? I dont care that [*snapping her fingers*] how young she is, or how pretty she is: Time will bring her to my level in those ways soon enough. But I'm not clever at the things he was clever at. I dont understand science nor care about it. If I have to keep the house spick and span I cant always keep myself spick and span; and I know he was particular about such things. Thats where she might have cut me out. She might easily have persuaded him that she was the right woman for him, and

that I was the wrong one.

LENKHEIM. No, no. You were an excellent wife to him, Mrs Haldenstedt; and he knew it.

AGNES. I dont say I wasnt. But she hadnt to keep the house for him. She had nothing to do but please him. And if she was clever into the bargain, what chance had I?

Edith comes in from the corridor.

EDITH. Good morning, Professor.

LENKHEIM [*relieved by the interruption*] Good morning. Will you excuse me, Mrs Haldenstedt: I have a few words to say to Fessler before Jitta comes.

AGNES. You have been so good. I will think over your advice: indeed I will.

LENKHEIM [*encouragingly*] Do. [*He waves his hand to Edith, and goes into the study, leaving the mother and daughter alone together*].

AGNES [*looking after him bitterly as she goes back to her place at the table*] It's easy for him to talk.

EDITH [*wandering about restlessly between the table and the console*] Why do you listen to him? Why do you run to strangers when you want to talk about father? Why should our being mother and daughter keep us so far apart?

AGNES. What a thing to say, child.

EDITH [*going to her*] Of course if you dont want me, mother, I dont want to force myself on you.

AGNES [*dutifully, without real feeling*] Well, of course, darling, I want you.

EDITH [*irritated*] No, not of course, not in the way you think. Has it occurred to you that it is rather hard on me to be left entirely to myself when things are so serious with us?

AGNES. I dont know what you have to complain of. You used to trust me to know what was right for you, and now you have suddenly turned on me. Surely, child, nobody can be a better judge of what is best for you than your own mother. Here I am, worried to death almost; and you making it worse for me by setting yourself against me.

EDITH. I am not setting myself against you, mother. What I am setting myself against is being expected to go through life blindfold, or pretending to be blindfold. I am to be a good little child, and not know anything nor feel anything that little children ought not to know and feel, just when I, as a woman, most want the companionship of another woman to whom I can pour out my

2 M 2

feelings and my sorrow on equal terms.

AGNES. I cant understand you, child; and I wont have you talking to me like that.

EDITH. I often wonder whether you have ever understood anybody. Perhaps you did not understand father.

AGNES. You dare—

EDITH [*continuing impetuously*] Oh, I know very well how tidy you kept his house for him, just as I keep my room. You did your duty: nobody can blame you. But was his house a home for him, as his heart made it a home for me?

AGNES. You are simply silly, child. Your grief and your crazy love for your father have turned your head. I wonder what you would say if you really knew.

EDITH [*scornfully*] If I really knew! Do you suppose any girl of my age nowadays does not know more than you were ever taught?

AGNES [*shrieking*] What?

EDITH. I know, as well as you do, where my father died, and how he died.

Mrs Haldenstedt covers her eyes in horror. Fessler, opening the study door, appears on the threshold.

AGNES. Oh, how dreadful! This will kill me. [*To Edith, rising*] Oh, now I know what you are. Just as bad as your father! Just as bad as your father!

FESSLER. What on earth is the matter?

AGNES. Dont ask me. Oh, this is beyond everything. Let me go [*she rushes from the room*].

FESSLER. What have you done?

EDITH [*coolly*] Told her I knew. I had to.

FESSLER [*closing the door, and coming softly to Edith*] My dear: you have dragged the poor woman down from her little heaven.

EDITH. My father's wife might have had a heaven on earth; but that poor woman, as you call her, did not know even how to begin.

FESSLER. Your grief is carrying you too far. Try not to be unjust to her.

EDITH. I am not unjust. It is my father who needs justice.

FESSLER. It is not much use, is it, giving justice to the dead and withholding it from the living?

EDITH. You need not lecture me: I am on my guard.

FESSLER. Against what?

EDITH. Against sharing my father's fate.

FESSLER [*terrified*] Dying!

EDITH. No. Living in utter loneliness.

FESSLER. Oh, that! How you frightened me! But you know, dear, you mustnt worry too much about your father. It's a sort of hypochondria; and it may make you really ill.

EDITH [*scornfully*] Yes, I know. What cant be cured must be endured; so let us get away from this unfortunate affair and fall back into the current of everyday life. That is what you want me to do. But I cannot do it. He was everything to me: I cannot describe what I feel: it is as if I were a branch broken off from him, a limb torn out of him, as if I were bleeding to death of the wound that killed him. As I see him now he is quite different from what he seemed to me when he was alive, and much greater. I think of him imprisoned in these walls, longing for his proper happiness, and then finding too late the woman who was his real destiny.

FESSLER. Ah yes: destiny! destiny! He had to fulfil his destiny, I suppose.

EDITH. He did not fulfil it. Life fulfils destiny, not death.

FESSLER [*prosaically*] Well, you know, death is a sort of destiny as well. If you are right, and he really was lonely here owing to your mother being incompatible and all that, then I quite agree it was a mercy he hit on somebody who could understand him and comfort him. Still, you must be careful not to idealize a person you dont know. You see, everybody is an ideal person to us until we meet them; and then, undoubtedly, some of the gilt comes off the gingerbread. I am so desperately afraid that if you find her out, she will prove a horrible disappointment to you.

EDITH. Never fear. I know my father too well. [*Turning fiercely on him*] But that you can think so little of him as to believe what other people are whispering about him: yes, and about her: you! who have worked with him and had all his confidence! that digs a gulf between us.

FESSLER. Oh dont say that. You cant mean it, Edith. I love you. I have the truest respect for your father.

EDITH. Then how can you belittle him so?

FESSLER. My dear, I am a man; and I know more about men's ways than you do. A man is a very mixed sort of animal. Ask any experienced man, and he will tell you that there is a certain side to human nature that must just be ruled out in judging people's characters. Even the best men are subject to aberrations, or at least commonnesses, in their relations with women, just as they will eat rotten cheese, and half-putrid partridges that are really only fit for pigs.

EDITH. You are not making it any better by saying such disgusting things.

FESSLER. Yes: but you want the truth, dont you? You know very well that Goethe was a great man; but the fine ladies of Weimar were shocked by his marriage. Rousseau was a great man; but his Teresa married a groom after his death.

EDITH. My father was a gentleman. He was worlds above Rousseau in refinement, and even above Goethe.

FESSLER. Well, I could say something more; but I suppose I mustnt.

EDITH. What more can you say? Is it something more against my father?

FESSLER. Not exactly against him; but still—

EDITH. Well, still?

FESSLER. He married your mother.

EDITH [staggered] Oh! How mean of you to throw that in his face! Why do you not point out what is so clear to any unprejudiced mind, that a man who made a mistake like that once would be the last person in the world to make the same mistake again?

FESSLER [with placid obstinacy] Because I am sorry to say, my dear, that men's lives consist mostly of their making the same mistake over and over again. I see a lot of that as a doctor. Look at your mother: she knows that if she eats prawns and cucumbers she will have a wretched night; but she never can resist them. I knew a man who was married three times; and every one of his wives drank.

EDITH. The more you say, the more I see that we shall never understand one another, and that you will never feel about my father as I do. I could not have believed you could be so coarse. Nobody in this house understands me, neither my mother nor you nor anybody.

FESSLER. But if you want people to understand you, you must be reasonable. I often used to have to say that to your father. You take after him, you know.

EDITH. If I do I must take care not to make the mistake in marrying that he made. Doctor Fessler: I am sorry; but I cannot be your wife.

FESSLER. I dont mind that so much for the present if only you wont call me Doctor Fessler. It's ridiculous. You dont expect me to call you Miss Haldenstedt, do you?

EDITH. Yes I do.

FESSLER. Then I wont. You see, I dont know how long this mood of yours will last.

EDITH. Life is short: dont waste any more of yours on me. I shall not go back from what I have said.

FESSLER. Neither shall I. I can wait.

EDITH. I cannot prevent your waiting. Everybody seems to think they know my own mind better than I do myself. I can only tell you one thing. I have one object in life now, and one only.

FESSLER. And what is that, if I may ask?

EDITH. To find the woman who made my father happy, and to force you to confess that she is high heavens above your Goethe's Christiane, and your Rousseau's Teresa, and —you neednt remind me—above my own mother.

FESSLER. Well, I hope you may, darling. Does that please you?

Jitta comes in from the corridor. Fessler pulls himself together into his best professional bedside manner. Edith rushes to Jitta and embraces her.

EDITH. Oh, how good of you to come! How glad I am to see you!

JITTA. Is your mother at home?

EDITH. Yes: do you want her? I will send her [she runs out].

JITTA [coming to Fessler in the middle of the room] What is the matter with the child?

FESSLER. She is still fearfully upset. She is having a hard fight of it here.

JITTA [looking at him with quick sympathy] You are not looking very happy yourself, Doctor.

FESSLER. She has broken it off [he narrowly misses a sob].

JITTA. Oh, that mustnt be. Why, it was for your sake that I opened her eyes a little about her father.

FESSLER. I am afraid it had rather the opposite effect.

JITTA. I hope not. Tell me: does my husband know of this new turn?

FESSLER. Not yet. Perhaps you had better tell him. I dont know that I can go on working here every day if Edith sticks to it.

JITTA. Dont give in too soon, Doctor.

FESSLER. I am pretending not to—to her. But I am really afraid she may be in earnest.

JITTA. Is there nothing I can do?

FESSLER. It's very good of you, Mrs Lenkheim. But I must see this thing through myself, thank you. And now I must be off. [*He goes past her towards the door*].

JITTA [*shaking his hand*] Goodbye, Doctor. Dont despise my help.

FESSLER. Oh no, Mrs Lenkheim; but— *Mrs Haldenstedt comes in.*

AGNES [*still distracted*] Oh, what is this that Edith tells me, Doctor?

FESSLER. We wont discuss it now, Mrs Haldenstedt. You had better talk it over with Mrs Lenkheim. Goodbye. Goodbye, Mrs Lenkheim. [*He bows to them and goes out*].

AGNES. Sit down, wont you? [*Jitta sits on the couch. Agnes sits down woefully beside her*]. He's gone; and Heaven knows whether he will ever come back. This is a marked house: everybody deserts it. Who knows how soon I shall be left alone here to haunt the place like my own shadow? I shall sit alone, going over and over that dreadful time in my imagination, with no relief but just thinking how I can catch that wretch that stole from me my right to be beside my husband when he died.

JITTA. She did not intend that. You may forgive her that, at least.

AGNES. Oh, you mustnt think it's mere spite and revenge. It's that I really loved Bruno to the last as I loved him from the first. He was all I had that I cared about. I am not like a man, to begin all over again with a new love: I shall never get away from it or get over it. Day by day all those years we lived together; sat at the same table; took it in turns to rock the cradle or take the child in our hands to pet it; and then he goes off to another woman without a word or a thought for me. [*Crying*] I didnt deserve it: I didnt indeed.

JITTA. There, dear, there! Dont torture yourself. After all, if he had died in your arms, you would still have had to grieve for him. It might even have broken your heart.

AGNES. Oh, if only it had! I could think of him then without bitterness and shame.

JITTA. Try to forgive him for the sake of the old days when you were young together. What does it matter what foolish things we old people do?

AGNES. I cant forgive him. Not while I am in the dark about h e r. Listen to me, Mrs Lenkheim. If I thought it was only her body that took him, I wouldnt care a straw. I have had thoughts myself about our young men at the college sports: only fancies of course; and I wouldnt have indulged them for the

world; but a man might. What I cant bear is the thought that she might have been somebody like you.

JITTA [*startled*] Like me!

AGNES. Yes: for he thought a great deal of you; and if you had been that sort of woman, I might have been jealous of you. You are clever in his way; and you could understand him when he was talking right above my head. You could talk about his work to him. I couldnt.

JITTA. Oh no, Mrs Haldenstedt: I knew better than that. Nothing annoys a man more than a woman who talks to him about his business and pretends to understand it. Do you know what Bruno always talked to me about? what it always came round to, no matter what subject he started with?

AGNES. What?

JITTA. You.

AGNES. Me!

JITTA. Yes, you, you, you, you. Do you know, I sometimes wanted to shake him for not taking a little more interest in me occasionally? His conscience was never easy about you. You had done everything for him; and he had taken it all and gone on with his scientific work: the work that did not pay, when he might have been making a fashionable practice for himself and leaving you comfortably off.

AGNES [*beginning to cry*] But I never grudged it to him. I wanted him to be great. I wasnt really as good a wife as I might have been. I worried him about things that he neednt have known anything about. It's in my nature: I cant help it.

JITTA. It was not in his nature to blame you for that. He understood. He was frightfully faithful to you. You possessed all his thoughts: you dominated his destiny: you haunted him. What right had you to take a great man like that all to yourself? I wanted a little bit of Bruno; but you stood always in the way. Marriage is a very wonderful thing. It held him as nothing else could hold him.

AGNES. But the other woman?

JITTA. Oh, the other woman! Need you make such a fuss about her? You dont even know whether she was not a patient who had to conceal the fact that she was consulting a doctor. There are such people, you know. But suppose she was what you think! Would a woman who had any serious relations with him have coolly walked off and left him to die? A pet dog would not have done such a thing. They would have found it at his side.

AGNES [excitedly] You think then that though he forgot what was due to himself, he didnt forget what was due to me? that when he went into that disgraceful place with another woman he was only making a convenience of her? that it was a mere chance that she was there to close his eyes, like a chambermaid in a hotel?

JITTA. She did not close his eyes. She stole away from his side after coldbloodedly covering up her tracks. Could you have done that?

AGNES. I never thought of that. Of course: of course. Yes: that shewed what she was, didnt it?

JITTA. What does it matter what she was? She came out of the dark, and went back into the dark. Leave her there, as she left him.

AGNES [shaking her head] I cant imagine how women can bring themselves to behave so. What sort of women must they be? She must have known that he could never have cared for her.

JITTA. You dont know how she got him there. But I know that if he really opened his heart to her, he talked to her about you.

AGNES [smiling] Well, I am sure, Mrs Lenkheim, this talk has made the most wonderful difference to me. You dont know how much good you have done me. It only shews how little we can trust our own feelings and our own judgment when such troubles come to us. The weight you have taken off my mind! you cant imagine.

JITTA. Have I? Then I have done what I came to do. [She rises].

AGNES [holding her] Oh, dont go yet. You know, it's very funny how one's mind works.

JITTA [sitting down again] How?

AGNES [slowly and almost roguishly] I'm so grateful to you, that I'm afraid of offending you if I tell you. But I am sure you will only laugh.

JITTA [with a melancholy smile] We both need a good laugh, dont we?

AGNES. Have you ever found that you have been all along thinking something that never came into your head for a single moment?

JITTA. That sounds a little difficult. I am afraid I dont quite follow.

AGNES. Of course you dont: it's too silly. But do you know that the moment you took that weight off my mind, and gave me back my peace and happiness—

JITTA [murmurs] I am so glad that I did.

AGNES [nodding gratefully, and continuing] Well, that very moment I knew that I had been believing all along—but I dont think I ought to say it; only it's so funny.

JITTA. What?

AGNES. Why, that you were the woman. [She begins to chuckle].

JITTA. No!!!

AGNES. Yes I did.

JITTA. But really?

AGNES. Really and truly.

JITTA [beginning to laugh hysterically] How funny!

AGNES [her chuckles now culminating in hearty laughter] Isnt it? Youre not angry, are you? Oh dear—[laughing more than ever].

JITTA. Oh no: of course not.

Jitta has a paroxysm of agonizing laughter; and Agnes accompanies her without a suspicion that she is not enjoying the joke in good faith. Jitta at last recovers her self-control with a desperate effort.

JITTA. Dont make me laugh any more: I am afraid I shall go into hysterics. I am still very far from well.

AGNES. It's such a shame to laugh at all at such a time. But for the life of me I couldnt help it.

JITTA [looking hard at her] You know, Mrs Haldenstedt. I was very very fond of him.

AGNES. I am sure you were, darling; and I shouldnt have minded a bit if it had been you: in fact I'm half disappointed that it wasnt, you have been such an angel to me. Isnt it funny, the things that come into our heads? But it's wicked of me to make you talk and laugh so much, and you so ill. Youre very pale, dear. Can I get you anything?

JITTA. If I might just lie down here for awhile. I—

AGNES [rising to make room for Jitta to recline] Yes, yes: of course you shall, dear. Make yourself comfortable.

JITTA. I dont want to go without seeing Edith.

AGNES [taken aback] Oh!

JITTA. What is it?

AGNES. I forgot all about Edith. Who is to tell her? She sees her father like a saint in a picture; and I could never put it to her in the wonderful way you put it to me. If only you would be so good as to tell her for me. Would you mind?

JITTA. Not in the least. Edith is like a child of my own to me: it would be the greatest happiness to me if I could set her mind at rest as you are good enough to think I have set yours.

AGNES. You have: indeed and indeed you have. I am sure what we owe you, with your dear husband coming here every day to set the papers in order, and you being more than an angel to me in spite of your illness, words can never say. Just lie quiet where you are; and I will send Edith to you. Oh, you h a v e made me happy, dear! [*She goes out into the corridor*].

Jitta, left alone, begins to laugh again hysterically, and is dissolving into convulsive sobs when she makes a great effort; springs up from the sofa; dashes the tears from her eyes with a proud gesture; goes to the glass; and has just made herself presentable when Edith appears. Her eyes are wide open and her expression one of joyful surprise and relief. She runs eagerly to Jitta.

EDITH. What on earth have you done to mother? She is laughing. She is positively singing. Either you are a witch, or she has gone mad.

JITTA. Are you angry with her for daring to sing in this house of mourning? Or angry with me for making her sing?

EDITH. Oh no: it's rather a relief. But it's very odd. How did you do it?

JITTA. She made me laugh before I made her sing. You mustnt be shocked, dear. There is always a sort of reaction: Nature must have a relief from any feeling, no matter how deep and sincere it is. Have you ever seen a soldier's funeral?

EDITH. No. Why?

JITTA. They play the Dead March as they go to the grave; but they play the merriest tunes they know on their way back.

EDITH. How unfeeling!

JITTA. Yes; but how natural! Your mother would have gone mad if she had gone on as she was for another week. I am not sure that I should not have gone mad myself if she had not made me laugh. [*Taking Edith by the shoulders and looking straight at her*] And now what I want to know is how I am to make y o u laugh. For y o u will go mad if

you do not get back into everyday life again.

EDITH [*backing to the table, and half sitting against its edge*] Yes: I know. This house has been a sort of madhouse since my father died. We havnt spoken naturally, nor walked naturally, nor breathed naturally, nor thought naturally, because we were all so determined to feel naturally. Somehow, my mother's laughing and singing has made nonsense of it all suddenly.

JITTA. Then you are happy again? If so, I may as well go home.

EDITH. Happy! Oh no. But I am done with hypocrisy and conventionality; and that is such a relief that I seem happy by contrast. I suppose it is a sort of happiness to be able to give myself up at last wholly to my sorrow.

JITTA [*sitting down in Lenkheim's chair*] Which sorrow? The old sorrow that God made for you, or the new one that you have made for yourself?

EDITH [*straightening up*] I dont know what you mean.

JITTA. Doctor Fessler says you have jilted him.

EDITH. Did he call it jilting him?

JITTA. No. I call it that.

EDITH. But you cant think that. Do you know what he said?

JITTA. No. Anything very dreadful?

EDITH. He believes that my father died in the arms of a common woman of the streets.

JITTA. And he thinks your father must have been as worthless as the woman he died with. I see.

EDITH. Not at all. That is what is so dreadful. He thinks it makes no difference. He adores my father as much as he ever did; but he thinks you have to leave all that out when you are judging men. He thinks a woman doesnt matter. I cant forgive him for that. I couldnt marry a man unless he felt exactly as I do about my father.

JITTA. Is that reasonable, dear? How could poor Doctor Fessler feel as you feel? you! your father's daughter!

EDITH. Oh, of course I know that. I dont expect him to feel the same affection. But if he thought my father could go with low women—if he did not know for certain, as I know, that the woman my father loved must have been one of the best and noblest of women, I would rather die than let him touch me.

JITTA. My dear: how can he know for certain? You do not know for certain yourself.

EDITH. I know I cant prove it. But I am certain. And I will devote my life to proving it.

JITTA. How?

EDITH. I will find the woman: that is how. I have thought and thought about it. I know that she cannot be very far off. I know that her grief and desolation must be as great as mine: greater. I know she will love me because I am his daughter. And I know that she will be somebody worthy of him.

JITTA. Edith, Edith, how sentimental you are!

EDITH [*fiercely*] You call my feeling sentimentality! Are you going to disappoint me too?

JITTA [*sternly*] You must learn to expect disappointments. How do you know that if you found this woman she would not disappoint you? It is easy to imagine wonderful women worthy of your father's love. But the real person always kills the imagined person.

EDITH. He said that once.

JITTA. Well, is it not true? Can you think of any real woman among your acquaintances that you could bear to think of as that woman—even the best of them?

EDITH. You cant put me off that way. I tell you I know. There is some woman who was real to my father; and he loved her. I shall love her when she is real to me. Besides, I have a queer sense that I know her quite as well as a real person; that she is here within reach of my hands if only I could recollect. I—I sometimes wonder does everybody know? does my mother know?

JITTA [*quickly*] Your mother does not know. Your mother could never understand.

EDITH. Jitta: do you know?

JITTA. Yes.

EDITH. Jitta!!!

JITTA. Yes. I know that poor criminal. I know what has become of her. I know what she did. I know what she has suffered ever since.

EDITH. But how do you know? Oh, tell me. You must tell me now.

JITTA. When you are excited like that your voice is his voice. Oh, the agony of hearing it, and the happiness! You bring him to life again for me.

EDITH. Then it was—

JITTA. Only me, dear.

EDITH [*flinging herself into Jitta's arms*] Only you! Who better could it be? Of course it was you. I knew it all along, only I couldnt recollect. Oh, darling! Dont you want a daughter? Here I am. His daughter.

JITTA. Dearest, yes. You have been a daughter to me ever since I knew him. But we must be very careful, very discreet. You see, you are very young.

EDITH. Oh, dont begin that. I dont want that sort of mother.

JITTA. I know. But I mustnt take your devotion—it is devotion, isnt it?—

EDITH. Oh yes, yes.

JITTA. I mustnt take it under false pretences. Above all, you must not throw away your engagement because your lover does not feel about me as you do. He is right about me, you know: I am not a good woman. Have you quite forgotten that *I* have a husband, and that for your father's sake I was unfaithful to him?

EDITH [*naïvely*] Oh, but Alfred is such a chump!

JITTA [*a little shocked*] Edith!

EDITH. And papa was such a wonderful man! Nobody could blame you.

JITTA. I assure you a great many people would blame me so much that they would never speak to me again if they knew.

EDITH. More shame for them! Do such people matter?

JITTA. They do, dear. I am afraid they are the only people who do matter in this wretched world. So you mustnt tell them. You mustnt tell anybody.

EDITH [*slowly*] I suppose not.

JITTA. Did you intend to tell everybody?

EDITH. No, of course not: I am not such a fool as that. But I did think that if I told Doctor Fessler he might see that he was wrong.

JITTA. And you might forgive him. Very well: I give you leave to tell him. But you understand that if you tell him you must marry him; for you mustnt tell anyone except your husband.

EDITH. You want me to marry him?

JITTA. I do.

EDITH. Then I'll telephone him. I suppose that will do. I am so happy now that it doesnt matter tuppence whom I marry. [*Lenkheim opens the study door and is coming in when Edith, not hearing him, goes on*] I'd marry anyone to please you. I'd even marry Alfred.

LENKHEIM. Thank you. [*The two women spring up in dismay*]. Thats very kind of you, Edith, and very kind of Jitta to include me in the number of husbands she has apparently been offering you. But I have no intention of divorcing her at present.

EDITH [*not knowing what else to say*] It wasnt that. Mrs Lenkheim never offered you to me.

JITTA. Go off to the telephone, dear, and make it up with your man. I will make it up for you with Alfred.

LENKHEIM. Do, Edith. [*He crosses the room to the other door, and opens it for her with sardonic politeness*].

EDITH [*to Lenkheim, after kissing Jitta rather defiantly*] Mrs Lenkheim did not say a single unkind word about you. I did. [*She nods mockingly in his face and goes out*].

LENKHEIM. Have you told her?

JITTA [*her bored manner with her husband contrasting strongly with her warm interest in Edith*] She guessed. She knew. It is no use keeping secrets when they will not keep themselves. I have made her happy: that is all I care about. [*She goes listlessly to the window-seat, and sits there looking out, with her shoulder turned to him*].

LENKHEIM. And have you told the old woman? Have you made her happy?

JITTA. I have made her happy. But I did not tell her. The strange thing is that she guesses it too; but she will never know it. She doesnt want to know it. Edith did. That makes all the difference. I have made them both happy. I wish someone could make me happy.

LENKHEIM. As I unfortunately am only your husband, I suppose there is no use my trying.

JITTA [*turning her face to him with open contempt*] You!

LENKHEIM. Funny, isnt it?

JITTA [*rising*] Dont be insufferable. You owe it to your position as an injured husband never to speak to me when we are alone and there are no appearances to be kept up. You swore not to. And you have been talking to me ever since, except when there was somebody else present to talk to.

LENKHEIM. Make no mistake, Jitta: when I swore that, I meant it.

JITTA [*ironically*] So it appears.

LENKHEIM. When you swore to be faithful to me, you meant it, didnt you?

JITTA [*interrupting him curtly*] You need not remind me of that again. I have not denied it. I have not excused myself. But I do not intend to have it thrown in my teeth every time we meet. [*She turns away from him determinedly, and sits down in the chair between the table and the door*].

LENKHEIM. Very well, then, dont you start reminding me every time we meet that I swore to do a good many things that I find I cant do. Is that a bargain?

JITTA [*a little ashamed, feeling that she has allowed herself to descend to his level*] Yes. I beg your pardon. I should not have said it. But please remember that you can hurt me more than I can hurt you, because you have done nothing wrong. You are within your rights: you are above reproach: you have the superior position morally: no taunts of mine can degrade you as your reproaches can degrade me. [*Tragically*] I am a miserable creature. I betrayed you to please myself. I deserted him in his extremity to save myself. Please leave me to my disgrace. Nothing that you can say or think can add to the contempt I feel for myself.

LENKHEIM [*chuckling a little*] How you enjoy being miserable, Jitta!

JITTA. Enjoy!!

LENKHEIM. You just revel in it. You think yourself such a jolly romantic figure. You think that everything that happens to you is extraordinarily interesting because it happens to you. And you think that everything that happens to me is quite uninteresting because it hasnt happened to you. But what has happened to you has happened to lots of women—except, of course, the way it ended. And even that was an accident that might have happened to anyone.

JITTA. No doubt. Unfortunately, I did not behave as any decent woman would.

LENKHEIM. That is just where you are mistaken, darling. When you were brought to the point and put to the proof, you didnt behave romantically: you behaved very sensibly. You kept your head, and did just the right thing. You saved your reputation and my reputation. You prevented a horrible scandal. You have managed to make his wife and daughter happy. And yet you think you are ashamed of yourself because you were not found stretched on his dead body, with the limelight streaming on your white face, and the band playing slow music.

JITTA. Oh, what a nature you have, Alfred! You are prosaic to the core.

LENKHEIM [grinning] If you had only been clever enough to take me in, your success would have been complete. It wouldnt have been difficult. I always took you in when I had an adventure.

JITTA [rising, very unpleasantly surprised, and not a little furious] You! You have had adventures since we were married? You have deceived me?

LENKHEIM. Now dont begin imagining that I am a Don Juan. To be precise, I have kissed other women twice. I was drunk both times. And I had a serious affair with your dear friend Thelma Petersen. That lasted until she and her husband went back to Norway.

JITTA. Oh, how disgraceful! And you call her my friend!

LENKHEIM. I call Bruno Haldenstedt my friend. So you see I am not your moral superior. I thought it might restore your happiness a little to know that.

JITTA. Alfred: I will never speak to you nor cross the threshold of your house again.

LENKHEIM [more amused than ever] Except when you call to tell me so. When you let out about Haldenstedt I felt just as you feel now. Tomorrow you will think better of it, as I have thought better of it.

JITTA [more dignified than ever] If you imagine that any relations that could exist between Mrs Petersen and yourself were in the least like my relations with Bruno, you only shew for the thousandth time how incapable you are of understanding either him or me.

LENKHEIM. I'm afraid you dont understand either Thelma or me as sympathetically as I could wish. Thelma was a very superior woman, let me tell you. If my taste did not lie in the direction of superior women I shouldnt have married you.

JITTA. I will not have it, Alfred. I will not be dragged down to your level.

LENKHEIM. Five minutes ago you were amusing yourself by pretending that you were beneath contempt.

JITTA. So I am, on my own plane, and on his. But not on yours.

LENKHEIM. I dont believe theres a woman alive who doesnt look on herself as a special creation, and consider her husband an inferior and common sort of animal.

JITTA. You forget that I did not think of Bruno in that way.

LENKHEIM. Yes; but then he wasnt your husband. Thelma thought me a much finer fellow than Petersen.

JITTA [exasperated] If you mention that woman to me again, I will break my promise to you, and walk straight out of your house before all the world.

LENKHEIM. That will only make us quits, because, as it happens, I am going to break my promise to you.

JITTA. How?

LENKHEIM. About the book. I have read it.

JITTA. Well?

LENKHEIM. Well, I'll be hanged if I put my name to it. In the first place nobody would believe I had ever written it. In the second, it's the most utter tommy-rot that was ever put forward as a serious contribution to psychology. Why, it flatly contradicts everything I have been teaching for years past, and everything I was taught myself.

JITTA [intensely angry] Does that prove it to be tommy-rot, or does it prove that you are an idiot?

LENKHEIM. I may be an idiot; but my idiocy is the accepted idiocy taught in the University at which I am a professor; and his idiocy is not taught anywhere. Do you forget that I have to earn bread for the household, and that your own money hardly pays for your dresses? This book would ruin us both.

JITTA. It is a sacred trust; and I swore to him that it should be fulfilled.

LENKHEIM. I didnt. And the old woman has just told me that he said the book was to be her insurance policy. No doubt I am Bruno's inferior; but I draw the line at helping him to rob his widow for my own profit.

JITTA. Then you refuse to carry out his intentions?

LENKHEIM. I cant carry out his intentions.

JITTA. You mean you wont.

LENKHEIM. I mean what I say. When he left me this book of his, he did so on the understanding that I was to know nothing of his relations with you. He hadnt quite such a low opinion of me as to suppose that I would take it as the price of my wife. Well, whose fault is it that I know all about it? Who let the secret out? You did.

JITTA [*collapsing into his chair*] Oh how shamefully I have betrayed him at every step! How despicable I am!

LENKHEIM [*sympathetically*] Not a bit of it, dear. You have just said yourself that if secrets dont keep themselves, nobody can keep them. This secret wouldnt keep itself. Come! stop crying. If only you would be content to be a woman for a moment, and not a heroine! And oh Lord! if you only had the smallest sense of humor!

JITTA [*passionately*] You cant even try to console me without sneering at me. Do you know what Edith called you?

LENKHEIM. No. You can tell me if it will relieve your feelings.

JITTA. She said you were a chump; and so you are.

LENKHEIM. All husbands are chumps, dear, after the first month or so. Jolly good thing for their wives too, sometimes.

JITTA. What are you going to do with that book?

LENKHEIM. If I had any regard for his reputation I should burn it at our domestic hearth.

JITTA [*recovering her dignity; rising; and speaking with tranquil conviction*] You shall not do that, Alfred.

LENKHEIM. Perhaps not; but it would serve you right if I did.

JITTA. It would not serve Edith right. Besides, his work, his reputation, his greatness—for whatever you may say I know that that book is the greatest that ever was written—belong not only to humanity, but to her. And I love her as if she were my own daughter. I have no other child.

LENKHEIM [*wincing a little*] My fault, I suppose. Oh, you c a n be nasty when you want to, Jitta.

JITTA. Oh, no, no. Will you never understand?

LENKHEIM. Probably not, being only a chump. Be a little amiable, Jitta: I havnt been so very hard on you, have I?

JITTA [*insisting*] You will not destroy the book? You will edit it? You will do everything for it that you could for a book of your own?

LENKHEIM. Well, if—

Fessler and Edith come in arm-in-arm, followed by Mrs Haldenstedt.

EDITH. Here he is. Kiss him.

FESSLER [*hastily*] Tchut! [*Taking Jitta's hand and kissing it*] I owe you my life's happiness, Mrs Lenkheim.

AGNES. I am sure we all owe you the happiness of our lives. You are our good angel: indeed you are. Oh, you are a lucky man, Mr Lenkheim, to have such a wife.

JITTA [*striking in before he can reply*] I have one more piece of news for you, Mrs Haldenstedt. Alfred has found your husband's book. It is a masterpiece. He will edit it. He will do everything he could do for it if it were his own book.

FESSLER [*triumphant*] Splendid!

AGNES [*overjoyed*] Oh, think of that! Edith [*she kisses Edith*]! Doctor [*she kisses the doctor*]! Professor [*she kisses Lenkheim*]! Didnt I say she was our good angel?

LENKHEIM. And now, may I take my good angel home?

AGNES [*to Jitta*] Oh, must you go, dear.

JITTA [*sweetly, to Agnes*] Yes, dear. [*Threateningly to Alfred*] Come home. [*She goes to the door*].

LENKHEIM [*cheerily, as he shakes hands with everybody*] Goodbye.

ALL [*shaking hands*] Goodbye. Goodbye. Goodbye.

JITTA [*sternly*] Alfred: come home.

LENKHEIM [*hastily obeying*] Yes, dear.

AGNES [*as the door closes sharply behind them*] She's too good for him.

THE END

XXXIV

THE ADMIRABLE BASHVILLE; OR, CONSTANCY UNREWARDED

BEING THE NOVEL OF CASHEL BYRON'S PROFESSION DONE INTO A STAGE PLAY IN THREE ACTS AND IN BLANK VERSE

ACT I

A glade in Wiltstoken Park
Enter LYDIA

LYDIA. Ye leafy breasts and warm protecting wings
Of mother trees that hatch our tender souls,
And from the well of Nature in our hearts
Thaw the intolerable inch of ice
That bears the weight of all the stamping world,
Hear ye me sing to solitude that I,
Lydia Carew, the owner of these lands,
Albeit most rich, most learned, and most wise,
Am yet most lonely. What are riches worth
When wisdom with them comes to show the purse bearer
That life remains unpurchasable? Learning
Learns but one lesson: doubt! To excel all
Is, to be lonely. Oh, ye busy birds,
Engrossed with real needs, ye shameless trees
With arms outspread in welcome of the sun,
Your minds, bent singly to enlarge your lives,
Have given you wings and raised your delicate heads
High heavens above us crawlers.

[*A rook sets up a great cawing; and the other birds chatter loudly as a gust of wind sets the branches swaying. She makes as though she would shew them her sleeves.*]

Lo, the leaves
That hide my drooping boughs! Mock me—
poor maid!—
Deride with joyous comfortable chatter
These stolen feathers. Laugh at me, the clothed one.
Laugh at the mind fed on foul air and books.
Books! Art! And Culture! Oh, I shall go mad.
Give me a mate that never heard of these,
A sylvan god, tree born in heart and sap;
Or else, eternal maidhood be my hap.

[*Another gust of wind and bird-chatter. She sits on the mossy root of an oak and buries her face in her hands. Cashel Byron, in a* white singlet and breeches, comes through the trees.*]

CASHEL. Whats this? Whom have we here?
A woman!

LYDIA [*looking up*]   Yes.

CASHEL. You have no business here. I have.
Away!
Women distract me. Hence!

LYDIA.   Bid you me hence?
I am upon mine own ground. Who are you?
I take you for a god, a sylvan god.
This place is mine: I share it with the birds,
The trees, the sylvan gods, the lovely company
Of haunted solitudes.

CASHEL.   A sylvan god!
A goat-eared image! Do your statues speak?
Walk? heave the chest with breath? or like a feather
Lift you—like this? [*He sets her on her feet.*

LYDIA [*panting*] You take away my breath!
Youre strong. Your hands off, please. Thank
you. Farewell.

CASHEL. Before you go: when shall we meet again?

LYDIA. Why should we meet again?

CASHEL.   Who knows? We shall.
That much I know by instinct. Whats your name?

LYDIA. Lydia Carew.

CASHEL.   Lydia's a pretty name.
Where do you live?

LYDIA.   I' the castle.

CASHEL [*thunderstruck*]   Do not say
You are the lady of this great domain.

LYDIA. I am.

CASHEL.   Accursed luck! I took you for
The daughter of some farmer. Well, your pardon.
I came too close: I looked too deep. Farewell.

LYDIA. I pardon that. Now tell me who you
are.

CASHEL. Ask me not whence I come, nor
what I am.
You are the lady of the castle. I

Have but this hard and blackened hand to
    live by.

LYDIA. I have felt its strength and envied
    you. Your name?

I have told you mine.

    CASHEL.   My name is Cashel Byron.

LYDIA. I never heard the name; and yet
    you utter it

As men announce a celebrated name.

Forgive my ignorance.

    CASHEL.   I bless it, Lydia.

I have forgot your other name.

    LYDIA.   Carew.

Cashel's a pretty name too.

    MELLISH [calling through the wood] Coo-ee!
    Byron!

    CASHEL. A thousand curses! Oh, I beg you,
    go.

This is a man you must not meet.

    MELLISH [further off]   Coo-ee!

    LYDIA. He's losing us. What does he in my
    woods?

    CASHEL. He is a part of what I am. What
    that is

You must not know. It would end all between
us.

And yet there's no dishonor in't: your lawyer,

Who let your lodge to me, will vouch me
    honest.

I am ashamed to tell you what I am—

At least, as yet. Some day, perhaps.

    MELLISH [nearer]   Coo-ee!

    LYDIA. His voice is nearer. Fare you well,
    my tenant.

When next your rent falls due, come to the
    castle.

Pay me in person. Sir: your most obedient.

        [She curtsies and goes.

    CASHEL. Lives in this castle! Owns this park!

A lady

Marry a prizefighter! Impossible.

And yet the prizefighter must marry her.

        Enter MELLISH

Ensanguined swine, whelped by a doggish
    dam,

Is this thy park, that thou, with voice ob-
    scene,

Fillst it with yodeled yells, and screamst my
    name

For all the world to know that Cashel Byron

Is training here for combat.

    MELLISH.   Swine you me?

Ive caught you, have I? You have found a
    woman.

Let her shew here again, I'll set the dog on
her.

I will. I say it. And my name's Bob Mellish.

    CASHEL. Change thy initial and be truly
    hight

Hellish. As for thy dog, why dost thou keep
    one

And bark thyself? Begone.

    MELLISH.   I'll not begone.

You shall come back with me and do your
    duty—

Your duty to your backers, do you hear?

You have not punched the bag this blessèd
    day.

    CASHEL. The putrid bag engirdled by thy
    belt

Invites my fist.

    MELLISH [weeping] Ingrate! O wretched lot!

Who would a trainer be? O Mellish, Mellish,

Trainer of heroes, builder-up of brawn,

Vicarious victor, thou createst champions

That quickly turn thy tyrants. But beware:

Without me thou art nothing. Disobey me,

And all thy boasted strength shall fall from
    thee.

With flaccid muscles and with failing breath

Facing the fist of thy more faithful foe,

I'll see thee on the grass cursing the day

Thou didst forswear thy training.

    CASHEL.   Noisome quack

That canst not from thine own abhorrent
    visage

Take one carbuncle, thou contaminat'st

Even with thy presence my untainted blood.

Preach abstinence to rascals like thyself

Rotten with surfeiting. Leave me in peace.

This grove is sacred: thou profanest it.

Hence! I have business that concerns thee
    not.

    MELLISH. Ay, with your woman. You will
    lose your fight.

Have you forgot your duty to your backers?

Oh, what a sacred thing your duty is!

What makes a man but duty? Where were
    we

Without our duty? Think of Nelson's words:

England expects that every man—

    CASHEL.   Shall twaddle

About his duty. Mellish: at no hour

Can I regard thee wholly without loathing;

But when thou playst the moralist, by
    Heaven,

My soul flies to my fist, my fist to thee;

And never did the Cyclops' hammer fall

On Mars's armor—but enough of that.

It does remind me of my mother.

MELLISH.   Ah
Byron, let it remind thee. Once I heard
An old song: it ran thus. [*He clears his throat*]
   Ahem, Ahem!
  [*Sings*]—They say there is no other
    Can take the place of mother—
I am out o' voice: forgive me; but remember:
Thy mother — were that sainted woman
  here—
Would say, Obey thy trainer.
   CASHEL.   Now, by Heaven,
Some fate is pushing thee upon thy doom.
Canst thou not hear thy sands as they run out?
They thunder like an avalanche. Old man:
Two things I hate, my duty and my mother.
Why dost thou urge them both upon me now?
Presume not on thine age and on thy nasti-
  ness.
Vanish, and promptly.
   MELLISH.   Can I leave thee here
Thus thinly clad, exposed to vernal dews?
Come back with me, my son, unto our lodge.
   CASHEL. Within this breast a fire is newly
  lit
Whose glow shall sun the dew away, whose
  radiance
Shall make the orb of night hang in the
  heavens
Unnoticed, like a glow-worm at high noon.
   MELLISH. Ah me, ah me, where wilt thou
  spend the night?
   CASHEL. Wiltstoken's windows wandering
  beneath,
Wiltstoken's holy bell hearkening,
Wiltstoken's lady loving breathlessly.
   MELLISH. The lady of the castle! Thou art
  mad.
   CASHEL. Tis thou art mad to trifle in my
  path.
Thwart me no more. Begone.
   MELLISH.   My boy, my son,
I'd give my heart's blood for thy happiness.
Thwart thee, my son! Ah no. I'll go with
  thee.
I'll brave the dews. I'll sacrifice my sleep.
I am old—no matter: ne'er shall it be said
Mellish deserted thee.
   CASHEL.   You resolute gods
That will not spare this man, upon your
  knees
Take the disparity twixt his age and mine.
Now from the ring to the high judgment seat
I step at your behest. Bear you me witness
This is not Victory, but Execution.
  [*He solemnly projects his fist with colossal*

*force against the waistcoat of Mellish, who
doubles up like a folded towel, and lies
without sense or motion.*
And now the night is beautiful again.
  [*The castle clock strikes the hour in the
  distance.*
Hark! Hark! Hark! Hark! Hark! Hark! Hark!
  Hark! Hark! Hark!
It strikes in poetry. Tis ten o'clock.
Lydia: to thee!
  [*He steals off towards the castle. Mellish stirs
  and groans.*

ACT II. SCENE I

London. A room in Lydia's house
Enter LYDIA and LUCIAN

   LYDIA. Welcome, dear cousin, to my London
  house.
Of late you have been chary of your visits.
   LUCIAN. I have been greatly occupied of
  late.
The minister to whom I act as scribe
In Downing Street was born in Birmingham,
And, like a thoroughbred commercial states-
  man,
Splits his infinitives, which I, poor slave,
Must reunite, though all the time my heart
Yearns for my gentle coz's company.
   LYDIA. Lucian: there is some other reason.
  Think!
Since England was a nation every mood
Her scribes with adverbs recklessly have
  split,
But thine avoidance dates from yestermonth.
   LUCIAN. There is a man I like not haunts
  this house.
   LYDIA. Thou speakest of Cashel Byron?
   LUCIAN.   Aye, of him.
Hast thou forgotten that eventful night
When as we gathered were at Hoskyn House
To hear a lecture by Herr Abendgasse,
He placed a single finger on my chest,
And I, ensorceled, would have sunk supine
Had not a chair received my falling form.
   LYDIA. Pooh! That was but by way of
  illustration.
   LUCIAN. What right had he to illustrate his
  point
Upon my person? Was I his assistant
That he should try experiments on me
As Simpson did on his with chloroform?
Now, by the cannon balls of Galileo
He hath unmanned me: all my nerve is gone.
This very morning my official chief,

Tapping with friendly forefinger this button,
Levelled me like a thunderstricken elm
Flat upon the Colonial Office floor.

LYDIA. Fancies, coz.

LUCIAN.   Fancies! Fits! the chief said fits!
Delirium tremens! the chlorotic dance
Of Vitus! What could anyone have thought?
Your ruffian friend hath ruined me. By
    Heaven,
I tremble at a thumbnail. Give me drink.

LYDIA. What ho, without there! Bashville.

BASHVILLE [*without*]   Coming, madam.
            Enter BASHVILLE

LYDIA. My cousins ails, Bashville. Procure
    some wet.

                [*Exit* BASHVILLE.

LUCIAN. Some wet!!! Where learnt y o u
that atrocious word?
This is the language of a flower-girl.

LYDIA. True. It is horrible. Said I "Some
wet"?
I meant, some drink. Why did I say "Some
wet"?
Am I ensorceled too? "Some wet"! Fie!
fie!
I feel as though some hateful thing had
    stained me.
Oh, Lucian, how could I have said "Some
wet"?

LUCIAN. The horrid conversation of this
    man
Hath numbed thy once unfailing sense of
    fitness.

LYDIA. Nay, he speaks very well: he's
    literate:
Shakespear he quotes unconsciously.

LUCIAN.   And yet
Anon he talks pure pothouse.
            Enter BASHVILLE

BASHVILLE.   Sir: your potion.

LUCIAN. Thanks. [*He drinks*]. I am better.

A NEWSBOY [*calling without*] Extra special
    Star!
Result of the great fight! Name of the winner!

LYDIA. Who calls so loud?

BASHVILLE.   The papers, madam,

LYDIA.   Why?
Hath ought momentous happened?

BASHVILLE.   Madam: yes.
            [*He produces a newspaper*.
All England for these thrilling paragraphs
A week has waited breathless.

LYDIA.   Read them us.

BASHVILLE [*reading*] " At noon today, un-
    known to the police.

Within a thousand miles of Wormwood
    Scrubbs,
Th' Australian Champion and his challenger,
The Flying Dutchman, formerly engaged
I' the mercantile marine, fought to a finish.
Lord Worthington, the well-known sporting
    peer,
Was early on the scene."

LYDIA.   Lord Worthington!

BASHVILLE. "The bold Ned Skene revisited
    the ropes
To hold the bottle for his quondam novice;
Whilst in the seaman's corner were assembled
Professor Palmer and the Chelsea Snob.
Mellish, whose epigastrium has been hurt,
Tis said, by accident at Wiltstoken,
Looked none the worse in the Australian's
    corner.
The flying Dutchman wore the Union Jack:
His colors freely sold amid the crowd;
But Cashel's well-known spot of white on
    blue—"

LYDIA. Whose, did you say?

BASHVILLE.   Cashel's, my lady.

LYDIA.   Lucian:
Your hand—a chair—

BASHVILLE.   Madam: youre ill.

LYDIA.   Proceed.
What you have read I do not understand;
Yet I will hear it through. Proceed.

LUCIAN.   Proceed.

BASHVILLE. "But Cashel's well-known spot
    of white on blue
Was fairly rushed for. Time was called at
    twelve,
When, with a smile of confidence upon
His ocean-beaten mug—"

LYDIA.   His mug?

LUCIAN [*explaining*]   His face.

BASHVILLE [*continuing*] "The Dutchman
    came undaunted to the scratch,
But found the champion there already. Both
Most heartily shook hands, amid the cheers
Of their encouraged backers. Two to one
Was offered on the Melbourne nonpareil;
And soon, so fit the Flying Dutchman seemed,
Found takers everywhere. No time was lost
In getting to the business of the day.
The Dutchman led at once, and seemed to
    land
On Byron's dicebox; but the seaman's reach
Too short for execution at long shots,
Did not get fairly home upon the ivory;
And Byron had the best of the exchange."

LYDIA. I do not understand. What were

they doing?

LUCIAN. Fighting with naked fists.

LYDIA.   Oh, horrible!
I'll hear no more. Or stay: how did it end?
Was Cashel hurt?

LUCIAN [to Bashville] Skip to the final round.

BASHVILLE. "Round Three: the rumors that
    had gone about
Of a breakdown in Byron's recent training
Seemed quite confirmed. Upon the call of
    time
He rose, and, looking anything but cheerful,
Proclaimed with every breath Bellows to
    Mend.
At this point six to one was freely offered
Upon the Dutchman; and Lord Worthington
Plunged at this figure till he stood to lose
A fortune should the Dutchman, as seemed
    certain,
Take down the number of the Panley boy.
The Dutchman, glutton as we know he is,
Seemed this time likely to go hungry. Cashel
Was clearly groggy as he slipped the sailor,
Who, not to be denied, followed him up,
Forcing the fighting mid tremendous cheers."

LYDIA. Oh stop—no more—or tell the worst
    at once.
I'll be revenged. Bashville: call the police.
This brutal sailor shall be made to know
There's law in England.

LUCIAN.   Do not interrupt him:
Mine ears are thirsting. Finish, man. What
    next?

BASHVILLE. "Forty to one, the Dutchman's
    friends exclaimed.
Done, said Lord Worthington, who shewed
    himself
A sportsman every inch. Barely the bet
Was booked, when, at the reeling champion's
    jaw
The sailor, bent on winning out of hand,
Sent in his right. The issue seemed a cert,
When Cashel, ducking smartly to his left,
Cross-countered like a hundredweight of
    brick—"

LUCIAN. Death and damnation!

LYDIA.   Oh, what does it mean?

BASHVILLE. "The Dutchman went to grass,
    a beaten man."

LYDIA. Hurrah! Hurrah! Hurrah! Oh, well
    done, Cashel!

BASHVILLE. "A scene of indescribable
    excitement
Ensued; for it was now quite evident
That Byron's grogginess had all along

Been feigned to make the market for his
    backers.
We trust this sample of colonial smartness
Will not find imitators on this side.
The losers settled up like gentlemen;
But many felt that Byron shewed bad taste
In taking old Ned Skene upon his back,
And, with Bob Mellish tucked beneath his
    oxter,
Sprinting a hundred yards to show the crowd
The perfect pink of his condition"—[a knock].

LYDIA [turning pale]   Bashville,
Didst hear? A knock.

BASHVILLE.   Madam: tis Byron's knock.
Shall I admit him?

LUCIAN.   Reeking from the ring!
Oh, monstrous! Say youre out.

LYDIA.   Send him away.
I will not see the wretch. How dare he
    keep
Secrets from ME? I'll punish him. Pray say
I'm not at home. [Bashville turns to go]. Yet
    stay. I am afraid
He will not come again.

LUCIAN.   A consummation
Devoutly to be wished by any lady.
Pray, do you wish this man to come again?

LYDIA. No, Lucian. He hath used me very
    ill.
He should have told me. I will ne'er forgive
    him.
Say, Not at home.

BASHVILLE.   Yes, madam.   [Exit.

LYDIA.   Stay—

LUCIAN [stopping her]   No, Lydia:
You shall not countermand that proper order.
Oh, would you cast the treasure of your mind,
The thousands at your bank, and, above all,
Your unassailable social position
Before this soulless mass of beef and brawn.

LYDIA. Nay, coz: youre prejudiced.

CASHEL [without]   Liar and slave!

LYDIA. What words were those?

LUCIAN. The man is drunk with slaughter.

Enter BASHVILLE running: he shuts the door
    and locks it.

BASHVILLE. Save yourselves: at the staircase
    foot the champion
Sprawls on the mat, by trick of wrestler
    tripped;
But when he rises, woe betide us all!

LYDIA. Who bade you treat my visitor with
    violence?

BASHVILLE. He would not take my answer;
    thrust the door

Back in my face; gave me the lie i' th' throat;
Averred he felt your presence in his bones.
I said he should feel mine there too, and
    felled him;
Then fled to bar your door.

LYDIA.   O lover's instinct!
He felt my presence. Well, let him come in.
We must not fail in courage with a fighter.
Unlock the door.

LUCIAN.   Stop. Like all women, Lydia,
You have the courage of immunity.
To strike y o u were against his code of honor;
But m e, above the belt, he may perform on
T' th' height of his profession. Also Bashville.

BASHVILLE. Think not of me, sir. Let him
    do his worst.
Oh, if the valor of my heart could weigh
The fatal difference twixt his weight and
    mine,
A second battle should he do this day:
Nay, though outmatched I be, let but my
    mistress
Give me the word: instant I'll take him on
Here—now—at catchweight. Better bite the
    carpet
A man, than fly, a coward.

LUCIAN.   Bravely said:
I will assist you with the poker.

LYDIA.   No:
I will not have him touched. Open the door.

BASHVILLE. Destruction knocks thereat. I
    smile, and open.

[Bashville opens the door. Dead silence.
Cashel enters, in tears. A solemn pause.

CASHEL. You know my secret?

LYDIA.   Yes.

CASHEL.   And thereupon
You bade your servant fling me from your
    door.

LYDIA. I bade my servant say I was not
    here.

CASHEL [to Bashville] Why didst thou better
    thy instruction, man?
Hadst thou but said, "She bade me tell thee
    this,"
Thoudst burst my heart. I thank thee for
    thy mercy.

LYDIA. Oh, Lucian, didst thou call him
    "drunk with slaughter"?
Canst thou refrain from weeping at his woe?

CASHEL [to Lucian] The unwritten law that
    shields the amateur
Against professional resentment, saves thee.
O coward, to traduce behind their backs
Defenceless prizefighters!

LUCIAN.   Thou dost avow
Thou art a prizefighter.

CASHEL.   It was my glory.
I had hoped to offer to my lady there
My belts, my championships, my heaped-up
    stakes,
My undefeated record: but I knew
Behind their blaze a hateful secret lurked.

LYDIA. Another secret?

LUCIAN.   Is there worse to come?

CASHEL. Know ye not then my mother is an
    actress?

LUCIAN. How horrible!

LYDIA.   Nay, nay: how interesting!

CASHEL. A thousand victories cannot wipe
    out
That birthstain. Oh, my speech bewrayeth it:
My earliest lesson was the player's speech
In Hamlet; and to this day I express myself
More like a mobled queen than like a man
Of flesh and blood. Well may your cousin
    sneer!
What's Hecuba to him or he to Hecuba?

LUCIAN. Injurious upstart: if by Hecuba
Thou pointest darkly at my lovely cousin,
Know that she is to me, and I to her,
What never canst thou be. I do defy thee;
And maugre all the odds thy skill doth give,
Outside I will await thee.

LYDIA.   I forbid
Expressly any such duello. Bashville:
The door. Put Mr Webber in a hansom,
And bid the driver hie to Downing Street.
No answer: tis my will.

                    [Exeunt LUCIAN and BASHVILLE.
                              And now, farewell.
You must not come again, unless indeed
You can some day look in my eyes and say:
Lydia: my occupation's gone.

CASHEL.   Ah no:
It would remind you of my wretched mother.
O God, let me be natural a moment!
What other occupation can I try?
What would you have me be?

LYDIA.   A gentleman.

CASHEL. A gentleman! Cashel Byron, stoop
To be the thing that bets on me! the fool
I flatter at so many coins a lesson!
The screaming creature who beside the ring
Gambles with basest wretches for my blood,
And pays with money that he never earned!
Let me die broken hearted rather!

LYDIA.   But
You need not be an idle gentleman.
I call you one of Nature's gentlemen.

CASHEL. Thats the collection for the loser,
Lydia.
I am not wont to need it. When your friends
Contest elections, and at foot o' th' poll
Rue their presumption, tis their wont to
claim
A moral victory. In a sort they are
Nature's M.P.s. I am not yet so threadbare
As to accept these consolation stakes.

LYDIA. You are offended with me.

CASHEL.   Yes I am.
I can put up with much; but—"Nature's
gentleman"!
I thank your ladyship of Lyons, but
Must beg to be excused.

LYDIA.   But surely, surely,
To be a prizefighter, and maul poor mariners
With naked knuckles, is no work for you.

CASHEL. Thou dost arraign the inattentive
Fates
That weave my thread of life in ruder
patterns
Than these that lie, antimacassarly,
Asprent thy drawing room. As well demand
Why I at birth chose to begin my life
A speechless babe, hairless, incontinent,
Hobbling upon all fours, a nurse's nuisance?
Or why I do propose to lose my strength,
To blanch my hair, to let the gums recede
Far up my yellowing teeth, and finally
Lie down and moulder in a rotten grave?
Only one thing more foolish could have been,
And that was to be born, not man, but
woman.
This was thy folly, why rebuk'st thou mine?

LYDIA. These are not things of choice.

CASHEL.   And did I choose
My quick divining eye, my lightning hand,
My springing muscle and untiring heart?
Did I implant the instinct in the race
That found a use for these, and said to me,
Fight for us, and be fame and fortune thine?

LYDIA. But there are other callings in the
world.

CASHEL. Go tell thy painters to turn stock-
brokers,
Thy poet friends to stoop oer merchants'
desks
And pen prose records of the gains of greed.
Tell bishops that religion is outworn,
And that the Pampa to the horsebreaker
Opes new careers. Bid the professor quit
His fraudulent pedantries, and do i' the
world
The thing he would teach others. Then

return
To me and say: Cashel: they have obeyed;
And on that pyre of sacrifice I, too,
Will throw my championship.

LYDIA.   But tis so cruel.

CASHEL. Is it so? I have hardly noticed that,
So cruel are all callings. Yet this hand,
That many a two days bruise hath ruthless
given,
Hath kept no dungeon locked for twenty
years,
Hath slain no sentient creature for my sport.
I am too squeamish for your dainty world,
That cowers behind the gallows and the lash,
The world that robs the poor, and with their
spoil
Does what its tradesmen tell it. Oh, your
ladies!
Sealskinned and egret-feathered; all defiance
To Nature; cowering if one say to them
"What will the servants think?" Your gentle-
men!
Your tailor-tyrannized visitors of whom
Flutter of wing and singing in the wood
Make chickenbutchers. And your medicine
men!
Groping for cures in the tormented entrails
Of friendly dogs. Pray have you asked all
these
To change their occupations? Find you mine
So grimly crueller? I cannot breathe
An air so petty and so poisonous.

LYDIA. But find you not their manners very
nice?

CASHEL. To me, perfection. Oh, they con-
descend
With a rare grace. Your duke, who conde-
scends
Almost to the whole world, might for a Man
Pass in the eyes of those who never saw
The duke capped with a prince. See then, ye
gods,
The duke turn footman, and his eager dame
Sink the great lady in the obsequious house-
maid!
Oh, at such moments I could wish the Court
Had but one breadbasket, that with my fist
I could make all its windy vanity
Gasp itself out on the gravel. Fare you well.
I did not choose my calling; but at least
I can refrain from being a gentleman.

LYDIA. You say farewell to me without a
pang.

CASHEL. My calling hath apprenticed me to
pangs.

This is a rib-bender; but I can bear it.
It is a lonely thing to be a champion.
LYDIA. It is a lonelier thing to be a woman.
CASHEL. Be lonely then. Shall it be said of
thee
That for his brawn thou misalliance mad'st
Wi' the Prince of Ruffians? Never. Go thy
ways;
Or, if thou hast nostalgia of the mud,
Wed some bedoggéd wretch that on the slot
Of gilded snobbery, *ventre à terre,*
Will hunt through life with eager nose on
earth
And hang thee thick with diamonds. I am
rich;
But all my gold was fought for with my hands.
LYDIA. What dost thou mean by rich?
CASHEL.   There is a man,
Hight Paradise, vaunted unconquerable,
Hath dared to say he will be glad to hear
from me.
I have replied that none can hear from me
Until a thousand solid pounds be staked.
His friends have confidently found the
money.
Ere fall of leaf that money shall be mine;
And then I shall possess ten thousand pounds.
I had hoped to tempt thee with that mon-
strous sum.
LYDIA. Thou silly Cashel, tis but a week's
income.
I did propose to give thee three times that
For pocket money when we two were wed.
CASHEL. Give me my hat. I have been fooling
here.
Now, by the Hebrew lawgiver, I thought
That only in America such revenues
Were decent deemed. Enough. My dream
is dreamed.
Your gold weighs like a mountain on my
chest.
Farewell.
LYDIA. The golden mountain shall be thine
The day thou quitst thy horrible profession.
CASHEL. Tempt me not, woman. It is honor
calls.
Slave to the Ring I rest until the face
Of Paradise be changed.
        Enter BASHVILLE
BASHVILLE.   Madam, your carriage,
Ordered by you at two. Tis now half-past.
CASHEL. Sdeath! is it half-past two? The
king! the king!
LYDIA. The king! What mean you?
CASHEL.   I must meet a monarch

This very afternoon at Islington.
LYDIA. At Islington! You must be mad.
CASHEL.   A cab!
Go call a cab; and let a cab be called;
And let the man that calls it be thy footman.
LYDIA. You are not well. You shall not go
alone.
My carriage waits. I must accompany you.
I go to find my hat.   [*Exit.*
CASHEL.   Like Paracelsus,
Who went to find his soul. [*To Bashville*] And
now, young man,
How comes it that a fellow of your inches.
So deft a wrestler and so bold a spirit,
Can stoop to be a flunkey? Call on me
On your next evening out. I'll make a man
of you.
Surely you are ambitious and aspire—
BASHVILLE. To be a butler and draw corks;
wherefore,
By Heaven, I will draw yours.
        [*He hits Cashel on the nose and runs out.*
CASHEL [*thoughtfully putting the side of his
forefinger to his nose, and studying the
blood on it*] Too quick for me!
There's money in this youth.
        Re-enter LYDIA, *hatted and gloved.*
LYDIA.   O Heaven! you bleed.
CASHEL. Lend me a key or other frigid
object,
That I may put it down my back, and
staunch
The welling life stream.
LYDIA [*giving him her keys*] Oh, what have
you done?
CASHEL. Flush on the boko napped your
footman's left.
LYDIA. I do not understand.
CASHEL.   True. Pardon me.
I have received a blow upon the nose
In sport from Bashville. Next, ablution; else
I shall be total gules.   [*He hurries out.*
LYDIA.   How well he speaks!
There is a silver trumpet in his lips
That stirs me to the finger ends. His nose
Dropt lovely color: tis a perfect blood.
I would twere mingled with mine own!
        Enter BASHVILLE
                                    What now?
BASHVILLE. Madam, the coachman can no
longer wait:
The horses will take cold.
LYDIA.   I do beseech him
A moment's grace. Oh, mockery of wealth!
The third class passenger unchidden rides

Whither and when he will: obsequious trams
Await him hourly: subterranean tubes
With tireless coursers whisk him through the
    town;
But we, the rich, are slaves to Houyhnhnms:
We wait upon their colds, and frowst all day
Indoors, if they but cough or spurn their
    hay.

BASHVILLE. Madam, an omnibus to Euston
    Road,
And thence t' th' Angel—
            Enter CASHEL
LYDIA.   Let us haste, my love:
The coachman is impatient.
CASHEL.   Did he guess
He stays for Cashel Byron, he'd outwait
Pompei's sentinel. Let us away.
This day of deeds, as yet but half begun,
Must ended be in merrie Islington.
            [*Exeunt* LYDIA *and* CASHEL.
BASHVILLE. Gods! how she hangs on 's arm!
    I am alone.
Now let me lift the cover from my soul.
O wasted humbleness! Deluded diffidence!
How often have I said, Lie down, poor
    footman:
She'll never stoop to thee, rear as thou wilt
Thy powder to the sky. And now, by Heaven,
She stoops below me; condescends upon
This hero of the pothouse, whose exploits,
Writ in my character from my last place,
Would damn me into ostlerdom. And yet
Theres an eternal justice in it; for
By so much as the ne'er subduéd Indian
Excels the servile negro, doth this ruffian
Precedence take of me. "*Ich dien.*" Damna-
    tion!
I serve. My motto should have been, "I
    scalp."
And yet I do not bear the yoke for gold.
Because I love her I have blacked her boots;
Because I love her I have cleaned her knives,
Doing in this the office of a boy,
Whilst, like the celebrated maid that milks
And does the meanest chares, Ive shared the
    passions
Of Cleopatra. It has been my pride
To give her place the greater altitude
By lowering mine, and of her dignity
To be so jealous that my cheek has flamed
Even at the thought of such a deep disgrace
As love for such a one as I would be
For such a one as she; and now! and now!
A prizefighter! O irony! O bathos!
To have made way for this! Oh, Bashville,

Bashville:
Why hast thou thought so lowly of thyself,
So heavenly high of her? Let what will come,
My love must speak: twas my respect was
    dumb.

SCENE II

The Agricultural Hall in Islington, crowded
with spectators. In the arena a throne, with
a boxing ring before it. A balcony above on
the right, occupied by persons of fashion:
among others, Lydia and Lord Worthington.
Flourish. Enter LUCIAN *and* CETEWAYO, *with*
Chiefs in attendance

CETEWAYO. Is this the Hall of Husbandmen?
LUCIAN.   It is.
CETEWAYO. Are these anæmic dogs the
    English people?
LUCIAN. Mislike us not for our complexions,
The pallid liveries of the pall of smoke
Belched by the mighty chimneys of our
    factories,
And by the million patent kitchen ranges
Of happy English homes.
CETEWAYO.   When first I came
I deemed those chimneys the fuliginous
    altars
Of some infernal god. I now perceive.
The English dare not look upon the sky.
They are moles and owls: they call upon the
    soot
To cover them.
LUCIAN.   You cannot understand
The greatness of this people, Cetewayo.
You are a savage, reasoning like a child.
Each pallid English face conceals a brain
Whose powers are proven in the works of
    Newton
And in the plays of the immortal Shakespear.
There is not one of all the thousands here
But, if you placed him naked in the desert,
Would presently construct a steam engine,
And lay a cable t' th' Antipodes.
CETEWAYO. Have I been brought a million
    miles by sea
To learn how men can lie! Know, Father
    Webber,
Men become civilized through twin diseases,
Terror and Greed to wit: these two conjoined
Become the grisly parents of Invention.
Why does the trembling white with frantic
    toil
Of hand and brain produce the magic gun
That slays a mile off, whilst the manly Zulu
Dares look his foe i' the face; fights foot to

foot;
Lives in the present; drains the Here and
    Now;
Makes life a long reality, and death
A moment only; whilst your Englishman
Glares on his burning candle's winding-
    sheets,
Counting the steps of his approaching doom,
And in the murky corners ever sees
Two horrid shadows, Death and Poverty:
In the which anguish an unnatural edge
Comes on his frighted brain, which straight
    devises
Strange frauds by which to filch unearnéd
    gold,
Mad crafts by which to slay unfacéd foes,
Until at last his agonized desire
Makes possibility its slave. And then—
Horrible climax! All-undoing spite!—
Th' importunate clutching of the coward's
    hand
From wearied Nature Devastation's secrets
Doth wrest; when straight the brave black-
    livered man
Is blown explosively from off the globe;
And Death and Dread, with their white-
    livered slaves,
Oer-run the earth, and through their chatter-
    ing teeth
Stammer the words "Survival of the Fittest."
Enough of this: I came not here to talk.
Thou sayst thou hast two white-faced ones
    who dare
Fight without guns, and spearless, to the
    death.
Let them be brought.
    LUCIAN.   They fight not to the death,
But under strictest rules: as, for example,
Half of their persons shall not be attacked;
Nor shall they suffer blows when they fall
    down,
Nor stroke of foot at any time. And, further,
That frequent opportunities of rest
With succor and refreshment be secured
    them.
    CETEWAYO. Ye gods, what cowards! Zulu-
    land, my Zululand:
Personified Pusillanimity
Hath taen thee from the bravest of the brave!
    LUCIAN. Lo the rude savage whose un-
    tutored mind
Cannot perceive self-evidence, and doubts
That Brave and English mean the self-same
    thing!
    CETEWAYO. Well, well, produce these

heroes. I surmise
They will be carried by their nurses, lest
Some barking dog or bumbling bee should
    scare them.
    CETEWAYO takes his state. Enter PARADISE
    LYDIA. What hateful wretch is this whose
    mighty thews
Presage destruction to his adversaries.
    LORD WORTHINGTON. Tis Paradise.
    LYDIA.   He of whom Cashel spoke?
A dreadful thought ices my heart. Oh, why
Did Cashel leave us at the door?
            Enter CASHEL
    LORD WORTHINGTON.   Behold!
The champion comes.
    LYDIA.   Oh, I could kiss him now
Here, before all the world. His boxing things
Render him most attractive. But I fear
Yon villain's fists may maul him.
    WORTHINGTON.   Have no fear.
Hark! the king speaks.
    CETEWAYO.   Ye sons of the white
    queen:
Tell me your names and deeds ere ye fall to.
    PARADISE. Your royal highness, you beholds
    a bloke
What gets his living honest by his fists.
I may not have the polish of some toffs
As I could mention on; but up to now
No man has took my number down.   I scale
Close on twelve stun; my age is twenty-three;
And at Bill Richardson's Blue Anchor pub
Am to be heard of any day by such
As likes the job. I dont know, governor,
As ennythink remains for me to say.
    CETEWAYO. Six wives and thirty oxen shalt
    thou have
If on the sand thou leave thy foeman dead.
Methinks he looks full scornfully on thee.
[To Cashel] Ha! dost thou not so?
    CASHEL.   Sir, I do beseech you
To name the bone, or limb, or special place
Where you would have me hit him with this
    fist.
    CETEWAYO. Thou hast a noble brow; but
    much I fear
Thine adversary will disfigure it.
    CASHEL. Theres a divinity that shapes our
    ends
Rough hew them how we will. Give me the
    gloves.
    THE MASTER OF THE REVELS. Paradise, a
    professor. Cashel Byron,
Also professor. Time!   [They spar.
    LYDIA.   Eternity

It seems to me until this fight be done.

CASHEL. Dread monarch: this is called the upper cut,
And this a hook-hit of mine own invention.
The hollow region where I plant this blow
Is called the mark. My left, you will observe,
I chiefly use for long shots: with my right
Aiming beside the angle of the jaw
And landing with a certain delicate screw
I without violence knock my foeman out.
Mark how he falls forward upon his face!
The rules allow ten seconds to get up;
And as the man is still quite silly, I
Might safely finish him; but my respect
For your most gracious majesty's desire
To see some further triumphs of the science
Of self-defence postpones awhile his doom.

PARADISE. How can a bloke do hisself proper justice
With pillows on his fists?

[*He tears off his gloves and attacks Cashel with his bare knuckles.*

THE CROWD. Unfair! The rules!

CETEWAYO. The joy of battle surges boiling up
And bids me join the mellay. Isandhlana
And Victory! [*He falls on the bystanders.*

THE CHIEFS. Victory and Isandhlana!

[*They run amok. General panic and stampede. The ring is swept away.*

LUCIAN. Forbear these most irregular proceedings.
Police! Police!

[*He engages Cetewayo with his umbrella. The balcony comes down with a crash. Screams from its occupants. Indescribable confusion.*

CASHEL [*dragging Lydia from the struggling heap*] My love, my love, art hurt?

LYDIA. No, no; but save my sore oermatchéd cousin.

A POLICEMAN. Give us a lead, sir. Save the English flag.
Africa tramples on it.

CASHEL. Africa!
Not all the continents whose mighty shoulders
The dancing diamonds of the seas bedeck
Shall trample on the blue with spots of white.
Now, Lydia, mark thy lover. [*He charges the Zulus.*

LYDIA. Hercules
Cannot withstand him. See: the king is down;
The tallest chief is up, heels over head,
Tossed corklike oer my Cashel's sinewy back;
And his lieutenant all deflated gasps
For breath upon the sand. The others fly.

In vain: his fist oer magic distances
Like a chameleon's tongue shoots to its mark;
And the last African upon his knees
Sues piteously for quarter. [*Rushing into Cashel's arms*] Oh, my hero:
Thoust saved us all this day.

CASHEL. Twas all for thee.

CETEWAYO [*trying to rise*] Have I been struck by lightning?

LUCIAN. Sir, your conduct
Can only be described as most ungentlemanly.

POLICEMAN. One of the prone is white.

CASHEL. Tis Paradise.

POLICEMAN. He's choking: he has something in his mouth.

LYDIA [*to Cashel*] Oh Heaven! there is blood upon your hip.
Youre hurt.

CASHEL. The morsel in yon wretch's mouth
Was bitten out of me.

[*Sensation. Lydia screams and swoons in Cashel's arms.*

ACT III

Wiltstoken. A room in the Warren Lodge
Lydia at her writing-table

LYDIA. O Past and Present, how ye do conflict
As here I sit writing my father's life!
The autumn woodland woos me from without
With whispering of leaves and dainty airs
To leave this fruitless haunting of the past.
My father was a very learnéd man.
I sometimes think I shall oldmaided be
Ere I unlearn the things he taught to me.

Enter POLICEMAN

POLICEMAN. Asking your ladyship to pardon me
For this intrusion, might I be so bold
As ask a question of your people here
Concerning the Queen's peace?

LYDIA. My people here
Are but a footman and a simple maid;
And both have craved a holiday to join
Some local festival. But, sir, your helmet
Proclaims the Metropolitan Police.

POLICEMAN. Madam, it does; and I may now inform you
That what you term a local festival
Is a most hideous outrage gainst the law,
Which we to quell from London have come down:

In short, a prizefight. My sole purpose here
Is to inquire whether your ladyship
Any bad characters this afternoon
Has noted in the neighbourhood.

LYDIA.   No, none, sir.
I had not let my maid go forth today
Thought I the roads unsafe.

POLICEMAN.   Fear nothing, madam:
The force protects the fair. My mission here
Is to wreak ultion for the broken law.
I wish your ladyship good afternoon.

LYDIA. Good afternoon.   [*Exit* POLICEMAN.
                    A prizefight! O my heart!
Cashel: hast thou deceived me? Can it be
Thou hast backslidden to the hateful calling
I asked thee to eschew?
                        O wretched maid,
Why didst thou flee from London to this place
To write thy father's life, whenas in town
Thou mightst have kept a guardian eye on
    him—
Whats that? A flying footstep—
                Enter CASHEL

CASHEL.   Sanctuary!
The law is on my track. What! Lydia here!

LYDIA. Ay: Lydia here. Hast thou done
    murder, then,
That in so horrible a guise thou comest?

CASHEL. Murder! I would I had. Yon
    cannibal
Hath forty thousand lives; and I have taen
But thousands thirty-nine. I tell thee, Lydia,
On the impenetrable sarcolobe
That holds his seedling brain these fists have
    pounded
By Shrewsb'ry clock an hour. This bruiséd
    grass
And cakéd mud adhering to my form
I have acquired in rolling on the sod
Clinched in his grip. This scanty reefer coat
For decency snatched up as fast I fled
When the police arrived, belongs to Mellish.
Tis all too short; hence my display of rib
And forearm mother-naked. Be not wroth
Because I seem to wink at you: by Heaven,
Twas Paradise that plugged me in the eye
Which I perforce keep closing. Pity me,
My training wasted and my blows unpaid,
Sans stakes, sans victory, sans everything
I had hoped to win. Oh, I could sit me
    down
And weep for bitterness.

LYDIA.   Thou wretch, begone.

CASHEL. Begone!

LYDIA.   I say begone. Oh, tiger's

heart
Wrapped in a young man's hide, canst thou
    not live
In love with Nature and at peace with Man?
Must thou, although thy hands were never
    made
To blacken other's eyes, still batter at
The image of Divinity? I loathe thee.
Hence from my house and never see me
    more.

CASHEL. I go. The meanest lad on thy estate
Would not betray me thus. But tis no matter.
                        [*He opens the door.*
Ha! the police. I'm lost.
                    [*He shuts the door again.*
                        Now shalt thou see
My last fight fought. Exhausted as I am,
To capture me will cost the coppers dear.
Come one, come all!

LYDIA.   Oh, hide thee, I implore:
I cannot see thee hunted down like this.
There is my room. Conceal thyself therein.
Quick, I command.   [*He goes into the room.*
                With horror I foresee,
Lydia, that never lied, must lie for thee.

Enter POLICEMAN, *with* PARADISE *and*
    MELLISH *in custody,* BASHVILLE, con-
    stables, and others

POLICEMAN. Keep back your bruiséd
    prisoner lest he shock
This wellbred lady's nerves. Your pardon,
    maam;
But have you seen by chance the other one?
In this direction he was seen to run.

LYDIA. A man came here anon with bloody
    hands
And aspect that did turn my soul to snow.

POLICEMAN. Twas he. What said he?

LYDIA.   Begged for sanctuary.
I bade the man begone.

POLICEMAN.   Most properly.
Saw you which way he went?

LYDIA.   I cannot tell.

PARADISE. He seen me coming; and he done
    a bunk.

POLICEMAN. Peace, there. Excuse his
    damaged features, lady:
He's Paradise; and this one's Byron's trainer,
    Mellish.

MELLISH. Injurious copper, in thy teeth
I hurl the lie. I am no trainer, I.
My father, a respected missionary,
Apprenticed me at fourteen years of age
T' the poetry writing. To these woods I came

With Nature to commune. My revery
Was by a sound of blows rudely dispelled.
Mindful of what my sainted parent taught
I rushed to play the peacemaker, when lo!
These minions of the law laid hands on me.

BASHVILLE. A lovely woman, with distracted
    cries,
In most resplendent fashionable frock,
Approaches like a wounded antelope.

Enter ADELAIDE GISBORNE

ADELAIDE. Where is my Cashel? Hath he
    been arrested?

POLICEMAN. I would I had thy Cashel by
    the collar:
He hath escaped me.

ADELAIDE.   Praises be for ever!

LYDIA. Why dost thou call the missing man
    thy Cashel?

ADELAIDE. He is mine only son.

ALL.   Thy son:

ADELAIDE.   My son.

LYDIA. I thought his mother hardly would
    have known him,
So crushed his countenance.

ADELAIDE.   A ribald peer,
Lord Worthington by name, this morning
    came
With honeyed words besceeching me to
    mount
His four-in-hand, and to the country hie
To see some English sport. Being by nature
Frank as a child, I fell into the snare,
But took so long to dress that the design
Failed of its full effect; for not until
The final round we reached the horrid scene.
Be silent, all; for now I do approach
My tragedy's catastrophe. Know, then,
That Heaven did bless me with an only son,
A boy devoted to his doting mother—

POLICEMAN. Hark! did you hear an oath
    from yonder room?

ADELAIDE.   Respect a broken-hearted
    mother's grief,
And do not interrupt me in my scene.
Ten years ago my darling disappeared
(Ten dreary twelvemonths of continuous
    tears,
Tears that have left me prematurely aged;
For I am younger far than I appear).
Judge of my anguish when today I saw
Stripped to the waist, and fighting like a
    demon
With one who, whatsoe'er his humble virtues,
Was clearly not a gentleman, my son!

ALL. O strange event! O passing tearful

tale!

ADELAIDE. I thank you from the bottom
    of my heart
For the reception you have given my woe;
And now I ask, where is my wretched son?
He must at once come home with me, and
    quit
A course of life that cannot be allowed.

Enter CASHEL

CASHEL. Policeman: I do yield me to the
    law.

LYDIA. Oh no.

ADELAIDE.   My son!

CASHEL.   My mother! Do not kiss me.
My visage is too sore.

POLICEMAN.   The lady hid him.
This is a regular plant. You cannot be
Up to that sex. [*To Cashel*] You come along
    with me.

LYDIA. Fear not, my Cashel: I will bail thee
    out.

CASHEL. Never. I do embrace my doom
    with joy.
With Paradise in Pentonville or Portland
I shall feel safe: there are no mothers there.

ADELAIDE. Ungracious boy—

CASHEL.   Constable: bear me hence.

MELLISH. Oh, let me sweetest reconcile-
    ment make
By calling to thy mind that moving song:—
[*Sings*] They say there is no other—

CASHEL. Forbear at once, or the next note
    of music
That falls upon thine ear shall clang in
    thunder
From the last trumpet.

ADELAIDE.   A disgraceful threat
To level at this virtuous old man.

LYDIA. Oh, Cashel, if thou scornst thy
    mother thus,
How wilt thou treat thy wife?

CASHEL.   There spake my fate:
I knew you would say that. Oh, mothers,
    mothers,
Would you but let your wretched sons alone
Life were worth living! Had I any choice
In this importunate relationship?
None. And until that high auspicious day
When the millennium on an orphaned world
Shall dawn, and man upon his fellow look,
Reckless of consanguinity, my mother
And I within the self-same hemisphere
Conjointly may not dwell.

ADELAIDE.   Ungentlemanly!

CASHEL. I am no gentleman. I am a criminal,

Redhanded, baseborn—

ADELAIDE. Baseborn! Who dares say it?
Thou art the son and heir of Bingley Bumpkin
FitzAlgernon de Courcy Cashel Byron,
Sieur of Park Lane and Overlord of Dorset,
Who after three months wedded happiness
Rashly fordid himself with prussic acid,
Leaving a tearstained note to testify
That having sweetly honeymooned with me,
He now could say, O Death, where is thy
    sting?

POLICEMAN. Sir: had I known your quality,
    this cop
I had averted; but it is too late.
The law's above us both.

    Enter LUCIAN, *with an Order in Council*

LUCIAN. Not so, policeman.
I bear a message from The Throne itself
Of fullest amnesty for Byron's past.
Nay, more: of Dorset deputy lieutenant
He is proclaimed. Further, it is decreed,
In memory of his glorious victory
Over our country's foes at Islington,
The flag of England shall for ever bear
On azure field twelve swanlike spots of white;
And by an exercise of feudal right
Too long disused in this anarchic age
Our sovereign doth confer on him the hand
Of Miss Carew, Wiltstoken's wealthy heiress.

    [General acclamation.

POLICEMAN. Was anything, sir, said about
    me?
LUCIAN. Thy faithful services are not forgot:
In future call thyself Inspector Smith.

    [Renewed acclamation.

POLICEMAN. I thank you, sir. I thank you,
    gentlemen.
LUCIAN. My former opposition, valiant
    champion,
Was based on the supposed discrepancy
Betwixt your rank and Lydia's. Heres my
    hand.
BASHVILLE. And I do here unselfishly re-
    nounce
All my pretensions to my lady's favor.

    [Sensation.

LYDIA. What, Bashville! didst thou love me?
BASHVILLE. Madam: yes.
Tis said: now let me leave immediately.
LYDIA. In taking, Bashville, this most
    tasteful course
You are but acting as a gentleman
In the like case would act. I fully grant
Your perfect right to make a declaration
Which flatters me and honors your ambition.

Prior attachment bids me firmly say
That whilst my Cashel lives, and polyandry
Rests foreign to the British social scheme,
Your love is hopeless; still, your services,
Made zealous by disinterested passion,
Would greatly add to my domestic comfort;
And if—

CASHEL. Excuse me. I have other views.
Ive noted in this man such aptitude
For art and exercise in his defence
That I prognosticate for him a future
More glorious than my past. Henceforth I
    dub him
The Admirable Bashville, Byron's Novice;
And to the utmost of my mended fortunes
Will back him gainst the world at ten stone
    six.

ALL. Hail, Byron's Novice, champion that
    shall be!
BASHVILLE. Must I renounce my lovely
    lady's service.
And mar the face of man?
CASHEL. Tis Fate's decree.
For know, rash youth, that in this star crost
    world
Fate drives us all to find our chiefest good
In what we c a n, and not in what we w o u l d.
POLICEMAN. A post-horn—hark!
CASHEL. What noise of wheels is this?
Lord Worthington drives upon the scene in his
    four-in-hand, and descends
ADELAIDE. Perfidious peer!
LORD WORTHINGTON. Sweet Adelaide—
ADELAIDE. Forbear,
Audacious one: my name is Mrs Byron.
LORD WORTHINGTON. Oh, change that title
    for the sweeter one
Of Lady Worthington.
CASHEL. Unhappy man,
You know not what you do.
LYDIA. Nay, tis a match
Of most auspicious promise. Dear Lord
    Worthington,
You tear from us our mother-in-law—
CASHEL. Ha! True.
LYDIA. —but we will make the sacrifice.
She blushes:
At least she very prettily produces
Blushing's effect.
ADELAIDE. My lord: I do accept you.
    [They embrace. Rejoicings.
CASHEL [*aside*] It wrings my heart to see
    my noble backer
Lay waste his future thus. The world's a
    chess-board,

And we the merest pawns in fist of Fate.
[*Aloud*] And now, my friends, gentle and
simple both,
Our scene draws to a close. In lawful course
As Dorset's deputy lieutenant I
Do pardon all concerned this afternoon
In the late gross and brutal exhibition
Of miscalled sport.

LYDIA [*throwing herself into his arms*] Your
boats are burnt at last.

CASHEL. This is the face that burnt a
thousand boats,
And ravished Cashel Byron from the ring.
But to conclude. Let William Paradise
Devote himself to science, and acquire,
By studying the player's speech in Hamlet,

A more refined address. You, Robert Mellish,
To the Blue Anchor hostelry attend him;
Assuage his hurts, and bid Bill Richardson
Limit his access to the fatal tap.
Now mount we on my backer's four-in-hand,
And to St George's Church, whose portico
Hanover Square shuts off from Conduit
Street,
Repair we all. Strike up the wedding march;
And, Mellish, let thy melodies trill forth
Broad oer the wold as fast we bowl along.
Give me the post-horn. Loose the flowing
rein;
And up to London drive with might and
main. [*Exeunt.*

THE END

XXXV

PRESS CUTTINGS

A TOPICAL SKETCH COMPILED FROM THE EDITORIAL AND
CORRESPONDENCE COLUMNS OF THE DAILY PAPERS DURING
THE WOMEN'S WAR IN 1909

*The forenoon of the first of April, three years
hence.*

*General Mitchener is at his writing-table in
the War Office, opening letters. On his left is the
fireplace, with a fire burning. On his right,
against the opposite wall, is a standing desk with
an office stool. The door is in the wall behind him,
half way between the table and the desk. The
table is not quite in the middle of the room: it is
nearer to the hearthrug than to the desk. There is
a chair at each end of it for persons having business with the General. There is a telephone on the
table.*

Long silence.

A VOICE FROM THE STREET. Votes for Women!

*The General starts convulsively; snatches a
revolver from a drawer; and listens in an agony
of apprehension. Nothing happens. He puts the
revolver back, ashamed; wipes his brow; and resumes his work. He is startled afresh by the entry
of an Orderly. This Orderly is an unsoldierly,
slovenly, discontented young man.*

MITCHENER. Oh, it's only you. Well?

THE ORDERLY. Another one, sir. She's
chained herself.

MITCHENER. Chained herself? How? To what?
Weve taken away the railings and everything
that a chain can be passed through.

THE ORDERLY. We forgot the door-scraper,
sir. She lay down on the flags and got the
chain through before she started hollerin.
She's lyin there now; and she downfaces us
that youve got the key of the padlock in a
letter in a buff envelope, and that youll see
her when you open it.

MITCHENER. She's mad. Have the scraper
dug up and let her go home with it hanging
round her neck.

THE ORDERLY. There is a buff envelope
there, sir.

MITCHENER. Youre all afraid of these women.
[*He picks the letter up*] It does seem to have a
key in it. [*He opens the letter; takes out a key
and a note; and reads*] "Dear Mitch"—Well,
I'm dashed!

THE ORDERLY. Yes, sir.

MITCHENER. What do you mean by Yes, sir?

THE ORDERLY. Well, you said you was
dashed, sir; and you did look—if youll excuse
my saying it, sir—well, you looked it.

MITCHENER [*who has been reading the letter,
and is too astonished to attend to the Orderly's
reply*] This is a letter from the Prime Minister
asking me to release the woman with this key
if she padlocks herself, and to have her shewn
up and see her at once.

2 N

THE ORDERLY [*tremulously*] Dont do it, governor.

MITCHENER [*angrily*] How often have I ordered you not to address me as governor? Remember that you are a soldier and not a vulgar civilian. Remember also that when a man enters the army he leaves fear behind him. Heres the key. Unlock her and shew her up.

THE ORDERLY. Me unlock her! I dursent. Lord knows what she'd do to me.

MITCHENER [*pepperily, rising*] Obey your orders instantly, sir; and dont presume to argue. Even if she kills you, it is your duty to die for your country. Right about face. March.

The Orderly goes out, trembling.

THE VOICE OUTSIDE. Votes for Women! Votes for Women! Votes for Women!

MITCHENER [*mimicking her*] Votes for Women! Votes for Women! Votes for Women! [*In his natural voice*] Votes for children! Votes for babies! Votes for monkeys! [*He posts himself on the hearthrug and awaits the enemy*].

THE ORDERLY [*outside*] In you go. [*He pushes a panting Suffraget into the room*] The person, sir. [*He withdraws*].

The Suffraget takes off her tailor-made skirt and reveals a pair of fashionable trousers.

MITCHENER [*horrified*] Stop, madam. What are you doing? you must not undress in my presence. I protest. Not even your letter from the Prime Minister—

THE SUFFRAGET. My dear Mitchener: I am the Prime Minister. [*He takes off his hat and cloak; throws them on the desk; and confronts the General in the ordinary costume of a Cabinet Minister*].

MITCHENER. Good heavens! Balsquith!

BALSQUITH [*throwing himself into Mitchener's chair*] Yes: it is indeed Balsquith. It has come to this: that the only way the Prime Minister of England can get from Downing Street to the War Office is by assuming this disguise; shrieking "VOTES FOR WOMEN"; and chaining himself to your doorscraper. They were at the corner in force. They cheered me. Bellachristina herself was there. She shook my hand and told me to say I was a vegetarian, as the diet was better in Holloway for vegetarians.

MITCHENER. Why didn't you telephone?

BALSQUITH. They tap the telephone. Every switchboard in London is in their hands, or in those of their young men.

MITCHENER. Where on earth did you get the dress? I hope it's not a French dress!

BALSQUITH. Great heavens, no. We're not allowed even to put on our gloves with French chalk. Everything's labelled "Made in Camberwell."

MITCHENER. As a Tariff Reformer, I must say Quite right. [*Balsquith has a strong controversial impulse and is evidently going to dispute this profession of faith*]. No matter. Dont argue. What have you come for?

BALSQUITH. Sandstone has resigned.

MITCHENER [*amazed*] Old Red resigned!

BALSQUITH. Resigned.

MITCHENER. But how? Why? Oh, impossible! the proclamation of martial law last Tuesday made Sandstone virtually Dictator in the metropolis; and to resign now is flat desertion.

BALSQUITH. Yes, yes, my dear Mitchener: I know all that as well as you do: I argued with him until I was black in the face, and he so red about the neck that if I had gone on he would have burst. He is furious because we have abandoned his plan.

MITCHENER. But you accepted it unconditionally.

BALSQUITH. Yes, before we knew what it was. It was unworkable, you know.

MITCHENER. I dont know. Why is it unworkable?

BALSQUITH. I mean the part about drawing a cordon round Westminster at a distance of two miles, and turning all women out of it.

MITCHENER. A masterpiece of strategy. Let me explain. The Suffragets are a very small body; but they are numerous enough to be troublesome—even dangerous—when they are all concentrated in one place—say in Parliament Square. But by making a two-mile radius and pushing them beyond it, you scatter their attack over a circular line twelve miles long. Just what Wellington would have done.

BALSQUITH. But the women wont go.

MITCHENER. Nonsense: they must go.

BALSQUITH. They wont.

MITCHENER. What does Sandstone say?

BALSQUITH. He says: Shoot them down.

MITCHENER. Of course.

BALSQUITH. Youre not serious?

MITCHENER. I'm perfectly serious.

BALSQUITH. But you cant shoot them down! Women, you know!

MITCHENER [*straddling confidently*] Yes you can. Strange as it may seem to you as a civilian, Balsquith, if you point a rifle at a woman and fire it, she will drop exactly as a man drops.

BALSQUITH. But suppose your own daughters —Helen and Georgina—

MITCHENER. My daughters would not dream of disobeying the proclamation. [*As an after-thought*] At least Helen wouldnt.

BALSQUITH. But Georgina?

MITCHENER. Georgina would if she knew she'd be shot if she didnt. Thats how the thing would work. Military methods are really the most merciful in the end. You keep sending these misguided women to Holloway and killing them slowly and inhumanly by ruining their health; and it does no good: they go on worse than ever. Shoot a few promptly and humanely; and there will be an end at once of all resistance and of all the suffering that resistance entails.

BALSQUITH. But public opinion would never stand it.

MITCHENER [*walking about and laying down the law*] Theres no such thing as public opinion.

BALSQUITH. No such thing as public opinion!!

MITCHENER. Absolutely no such thing. There are certain persons who entertain certain opinions. Well, shoot them down. When you have shot them down, there are no longer any persons entertaining those opinions alive; consequently there is no longer any more of the public opinion you are so much afraid of. Grasp that fact, my dear Balsquith; and you have grasped the secret of government. Public opinion is mind. Mind is inseparable from matter. Shoot down the matter and you kill the mind.

BALSQUITH. But hang it all—

MITCHENER [*intolerantly*] No I wont hang it all. It's no use coming to me and talking about public opinion. You have put yourself into the hands of the army; and you are committed to military methods. And the basis of all military methods is that when people wont do what theyre told to do, you shoot them down.

BALSQUITH. Oh yes; it's all jolly fine for you and Old Red. You dont depend on votes for your places. What do you suppose would happen at the next election?

MITCHENER. Have no next election. Bring in a Bill at once repealing all the Reform Acts and vesting the Government in a properly trained magistracy responsible only to a Council of War. It answers perfectly in India.

If anyone objects, shoot him down.

BALSQUITH. But none of the members of my party would be on the Council of War. Neither should I. Do you expect us to vote for making ourselves nobodies?

MITCHENER. Youll have to, sooner or later, or the Socialists will make nobodies of the lot of you by collaring every penny you possess. Do you suppose this damned democracy can be allowed to go on now that the mob is beginning to take it seriously and using its power to lay hands on property? Parliament must abolish itself. The Irish parliament voted for its own extinction. The English parliament will do the same if the same means are taken to persuade it.

BALSQUITH. That would cost a lot of money.

MITCHENER. Not money necessarily. Bribe them with titles.

BALSQUITH. Do you think we dare?

MITCHENER [*scornfully*] Dare! Dare! What is life but daring, man? "To dare, to dare, and again to dare—"

FEMALE VOICE IN THE STREET. Votes for Women! [*Mitchener, revolver in hand, rushes to the door and locks it. Balsquith hides under the table*]. Votes for Women!

A shot is heard.

BALSQUITH [*emerging in the greatest alarm*] Good heavens, you havnt given orders to fire on them: have you?

MITCHENER. No; but it's a sentinel's duty to fire on anyone who persists in attempting to pass without giving the word.

BALSQUITH [*wiping his brow*] This military business is really awful.

MITCHENER. Be calm, Balsquith. These things must happen: they save bloodshed in the long run, believe me. Ive seen plenty of it; and I know.

BALSQUITH. I havnt; and I dont know. I wish those guns didnt make such a devil of a noise. We must adopt Maxim's Silencer for the army rifles if we're going to shoot women. I really couldnt stand hearing it. [*Someone outside tries to open the door and then knocks*]. Whats that?

MITCHENER. Who's there?

THE ORDERLY. It's only me, governor. It's all right.

MITCHENER [*unlocking the door and admitting the Orderly, who comes between them*] What was it?

THE ORDERLY. Suffraget, sir.

BALSQUITH. Did the sentry shoot her?

THE ORDERLY. No, sir: she shot the sentry.

BALSQUITH [*relieved*] Oh: is that all?

MITCHENER [*most indignantly*] All! A civilian shoots down one of His Majesty's soldiers on duty; and the Prime Minister of England asks, Is that all?!!! Have you no regard for the sanctity of human life?

BALSQUITH [*much relieved*] Well, getting shot is what a soldier is for. Besides, he doesnt vote.

MITCHENER. Neither do the Suffragets.

BALSQUITH. Their husbands do. [*To the Orderly*] Did she kill him?

THE ORDERLY. No, sir. He got a stinger on his trousers, sir; but it didnt penetrate. He lost his temper a bit and put down his gun and clouted her head for her. So she said he was no gentleman; and we let her go, thinking she'd had enough, sir.

MITCHENER [*groaning*] Clouted her head! These women are making the army as lawless as themselves. Clouted her head indeed! A purely civil procedure.

THE ORDERLY. Any orders, sir?

MITCHENER. No. Yes. No. Yes: send everybody who took part in this disgraceful scene to the guard-room. No. I'll address the men on the subject after lunch. Parade them for that purpose: full kit. Dont grin at me, sir. Right about face. March.

The Orderly obeys and goes out.

BALSQUITH [*taking Mitchener affectionately by the arm and walking him persuasively to and fro*] And now, Mitchener, will you come to the rescue of the Government and take the command that Old Red has thrown up?

MITCHENER. How can I? You know that the people are devoted heart and soul to Sandstone. He is only bringing you "on the knee," as we say in the army. Could any other living man have persuaded the British nation to accept universal compulsory military service as he did last year? Why, even the Church refused exemption. He is supreme—omnipotent.

BALSQUITH. He w a s, a year ago. But ever since your book of reminiscences went into two more editions than his, and the rush for it led to the wrecking of the Times Book Club, you have become to all intents and purposes his senior. He lost ground by saying that the wrecking was got up by the booksellers. It shewed jealousy; and the public felt it.

MITCHENER. But I cracked him up in my book—you see I could do no less after the handsome way he cracked me up in his—and I cant go back on it now. [*Breaking loose from Balsquith*] No: it's no use, Balsquith: he can dictate his terms to you.

BALSQUITH. Not a bit of it. That affair of the curate—

MITCHENER [*impatiently*] Oh, damn that curate. Ive heard of nothing but that wretched mutineer for a fortnight past. He's not a curate; whilst he's serving in the army he's a private soldier and nothing else. I really havnt time to discuss him further. I'm busy. Good morning. [*He sits down at his table and takes up his letters*].

BALSQUITH [*near the door*] I'm sorry you take that tone, Mitchener. Since you d o take it, let me tell you frankly that I think Lieutenant Chubbs-Jenkinson shewed a great want of consideration for the Government in giving an unreasonable and unpopular order, and bringing compulsory military service into disrepute.

MITCHENER. No order is unreasonable; and all orders are unpopular.

BALSQUITH. When the leader of the Labor Party appealed to me and to the House last year not to throw away all the liberties of Englishmen by accepting compulsory military service without full civil rights for the soldier—

MITCHENER. Rot.

BALSQUITH. —I said that no British officer would be capable of abusing the authority with which it was absolutely necessary to invest him.

MITCHENER. Quite right.

BALSQUITH. That carried the House;—

MITCHENER. Naturally.

BALSQUITH. —and the feeling was that the Labor Party were soulless cads.

MITCHENER. So they are.

BALSQUITH. And now comes this unmannerly young whelp Chubbs-Jenkinson, the only son of what they call a soda king, and orders a curate to lick his boots. And when the curate punches his head, you first sentence him to be shot; and then make a great show of clemency by commuting it to a flogging. What did you expect the curate to do?

MITCHENER [*throwing down his pen and his letters and jumping up to confront Balsquith*] His duty was perfectly simple. He should have obeyed the order; and then laid his complaint against the officer in proper form. He would have received the fullest satisfaction.

BALSQUITH. What satisfaction?

MITCHENER. Chubbs-Jenkinson would have been reprimanded. In fact, he was reprimanded. Besides, the man was thoroughly insubordinate. You cant deny that the very first thing he did when they took him down after flogging him was to walk up to Chubbs-Jenkinson and break his jaw. That shewed there was no use flogging him; so now he will get two years' hard labor; and serve him right!

BALSQUITH. I bet you a guinea he wont get even a week. I bet you another that Chubbs-Jenkinson apologizes abjectly. You evidently havnt heard the news.

MITCHENER. What news?

BALSQUITH. It turns out that the curate is well connected. [*Mitchener staggers at the shock. He reels into his chair and buries his face in his hands over the blotter*]. He has three aunts in the peerage; Lady Richmond's one of them [*Mitchener punctuates these announcements with heartrending groans*]; and they all adore him. The invitations for six garden parties and fourteen dances have been cancelled for all the subalterns in Chubb's regiment. [*Mitchener attempts to shoot himself*].

BALSQUITH [*seizing the pistol*] No: your country needs you, Mitchener.

MITCHENER [*putting down the pistol*] For my country's sake. [*Balsquith, reassured, sits down*]. But what an infernal young fool Chubbs-Jenkinson is, not to know the standing of his man better! Why didnt he know? It was his business to know. He ought to be flogged.

BALSQUITH. Probably he will be, by the other subalterns.

MITCHENER. I hope so. Anyhow, out he goes. Out of the army. He or I.

BALSQUITH. Steady, steady. His father has subscribed a million to the party funds. We owe him a peerage.

MITCHENER. I dont care.

BALSQUITH. I do. How do you think parties are kept up? Not by the subscriptions of the local associations, I hope. They dont pay for the gas at the meetings.

MITCHENER. Man: can you not be serious? Here are we, face to face with Lady Richmond's grave displeasure; and you talk to me about gas and subscriptions. Her own nephew!!!!!

BALSQUITH [*gloomily*] It's unfortunate. He

was at Oxford with Bobby Bessborough.

MITCHENER. Worse and worse. What shall we do?

A VOICE IN THE STREET. Votes for Women! Votes for Women!

A terrific explosion shakes the building. They take no notice.

MITCHENER [*breaking down*] You dont know what this means to me, Balsquith. I love the army. I love my country.

BALSQUITH. It certainly is rather awkward. *The Orderly comes in.*

MITCHENER [*angrily*] What is it? How dare you interrupt us like this?

THE ORDERLY. Didn't you hear the explosion, sir?

MITCHENER. Explosion. What explosion? No: I heard no explosion: I have something more serious to attend to than explosions. Great heavens! Lady Richmond's nephew has been treated like any common laborer; and while England is reeling under the shock, a private walks in and asks me if I heard an explosion.

BALSQUITH. By the way, what was the explosion?

THE ORDERLY. Only a sort of bombshell, sir.

BALSQUITH. Bombshell!

THE ORDERLY. A pasteboard one, sir. Full of papers with Votes for Women in red letters. Fired into the yard from the roof of the Alliance Office.

MITCHENER. Pooh! Go away. GO away. *The Orderly, bewildered, goes out.*

BALSQUITH. Mitchener: you can save the country yet. Put on your full dress uniform and your medals and orders and so forth. Get a guard of honor—something showy—horse guards or something of that sort; and call on the old girl—

MITCHENER. The old girl?

BALSQUITH. Well, Lady Richmond. Apologize to her. Ask her leave to accept the command. Tell her that youve made the curate your adjutant or your aide-de-camp or whatever is the proper thing. By the way, what can you make him?

MITCHENER. I might make him my chaplain. I dont see why I shouldnt have a chaplain on my staff. He shewed a very proper spirit in punching that young cub's head. I should have done the same myself.

BALSQUITH. Then Ive your promise to take command if Lady Richmond consents?

MITCHENER. On condition that I have a free

hand. No nonsense about public opinion or democracy.

BALSQUITH. As far as possible, I think I may say yes.

MITCHENER [*rising intolerantly and going to the hearthrug*] That wont do for me. Dont be weak-kneed, Balsquith. You know perfectly well that the real government of this country is and always must be the government of the masses by the classes. You know that democracy is damned nonsense, and that no class stands less of it than the working class. You know that we are already discussing the steps that will have to be taken if the country should ever be face to face with the possibility of a Labor majority in Parliament. You know that in that case we should disfranchise the mob, and if they made a fuss, shoot them down. You know that if we need public opinion to support us, we can get any quantity of it manufactured in our papers by poor devils of journalists who will sell their souls for five shillings. You know—

BALSQUITH. Stop. Stop, I say. I dont know. That is the difference between your job and mine, Mitchener. After twenty years in the army a man thinks he knows everything. After twenty months in the Cabinet he knows that he knows nothing.

MITCHENER. We learn from history—

BALSQUITH. We learn from history that men never learn anything from history. That's not my own: it's Hegel.

MITCHENER. Who's Hegel?

BALSQUITH. Dead. A German philosopher. [*He half rises, but recollects something and sits down again*]. Oh, confound it: that reminds me. The Germans have laid down four more Dreadnoughts.

MITCHENER. Then you must lay down twelve.

BALSQUITH. Oh yes: it's easy to say that; but think of what they'll cost.

MITCHENER. Think of what it would cost to be invaded by Germany and forced to pay an indemnity of five hundred millions.

BALSQUITH. But you said that if you got compulsory military service there would be an end of the danger of invasion.

MITCHENER. On the contrary, my dear fellow, it increases the danger tenfold, because it increases German jealousy of our military supremacy.

BALSQUITH. After all, why should the Germans invade us?

MITCHENER. Why shouldnt they? What else has their army to do? What else are they building a navy for?

BALSQUITH. Well, we never think of invading Germany.

MITCHENER. Yes, we do. I have thought of nothing else for the last ten years. Say what you will, Balsquith, the Germans have never recognized, and until they get a stern lesson they never w i l l recognize, the plain fact that the interests of the British Empire are paramount, and that the command of the sea belongs by nature to England.

BALSQUITH. But if they wont recognize it, what can I do?

MITCHENER. Shoot them down.

BALSQUITH. I c a n t shoot them down.

MITCHENER. Yes you can. You dont realize it; but if you fire a rifle into a German he drops just as surely as a rabbit does.

BALSQUITH. But dash it all, man, a rabbit hasnt got a rifle and a German has. Suppose he shoots you down.

MITCHENER. Excuse me, Balsquith; but that consideration is what we call cowardice in the army. A soldier always assumes that he is going to shoot, not to be shot.

BALSQUITH [*jumping up and walking about sulkily*] Oh come! I like to hear you military people talking of cowardice. Why, you spend your lives in an ecstasy of terror of imaginary invasions. I dont believe you ever go to bed without looking under it for a burglar.

MITCHENER [*calmly*] A very sensible precaution, Balsquith. I always take it; and, in consequence, Ive never been burgled.

BALSQUITH. Neither have I. Anyhow, dont you taunt me with cowardice. [*He posts himself on the hearthrug beside Mitchener, on his left*]. I never look under my bed for a burglar. I'm not always looking under the nation's bed for an invader. And if it comes to fighting, I'm quite willing to fight without being three to one.

MITCHENER. These are the romantic ravings of a Jingo civilian, Balsquith. At least youll not deny that the absolute command of the sea is essential to our security.

BALSQUITH. The absolute command of the sea is essential to the security of the principality of Monaco. But Monaco isnt going to get it.

MITCHENER. And consequently Monaco enjoys no security. What a frightful thing! How do the inhabitants sleep with the possibility of invasion, of bombardment, continually present to their minds? Would you have our English slumbers broken in the same way? Are we also to live without security?

BALSQUITH [*dogmatically*] Yes. Theres no such thing as security in the world; and there never can be as long as men are mortal. England will be secure when England is dead, just as the streets of London will be safe when theres no longer a man in her streets to be run over or a vehicle to run over him. When you military chaps ask for security you are crying for the moon.

MITCHENER [*very seriously*] Let me tell you, Balsquith, that in these days of aeroplanes and Zeppelin airships the question of the moon is becoming one of the greatest importance. It will be reached at no very distant date. Can you, as an Englishman, tamely contemplate the possibility of having to live under a German moon? The British flag must be planted there at all hazards.

BALSQUITH. My dear Mitchener, the moon is outside practical politics. I'd swop it for a coaling-station tomorrow with Germany or any other Power sufficiently military in its way of thinking to attach any importance to it.

MITCHENER [*losing his temper*] You are the friend of every country but your own.

BALSQUITH. Say nobody's enemy but my own. It sounds nicer. You really neednt be so horribly afraid of the other countries. They're all in the same fix as we are. I'm much more interested in the death-rate in Lambeth than in the German fleet.

MITCHENER. You darent say that in Lambeth.

BALSQUITH. I'll say it the day after you publish your scheme for invading Germany and repealing all the Reform Acts.

The Orderly comes in.

MITCHENER. What do you want?

THE ORDERLY. I dont want anything, governor, thank you. The secretary and president of the Anti-Suffraget League says they had an appointment with the Prime Minister, and that theyve been sent on here from Downing Street.

BALSQUITH [*going to the table*] Quite right. I forgot them. [*To Mitchener*] Would you mind my seeing them here? I feel extraordinarily grateful to these women for standing by us and facing the Suffragets, especially as they are naturally the gentler and timider sort of women. [*The Orderly moans*]. Did you say

anything?

THE ORDERLY. No, sir.

BALSQUITH. Did you catch their names?

THE ORDERLY. Yes, sir. The president is Lady Corinthia Fanshawe; and the secretary is Mrs Banger.

MITCHENER [*abruptly*] Mrs what?

THE ORDERLY. Mrs Banger.

BALSQUITH. Curious that quiet people always seem to have violent names.

THE ORDERLY. Not much quiet about her, sir.

MITCHENER [*outraged*] Attention! Speak when youre spoken to. Hold your tongue when youre not. Right about face. March. [*The Orderly obeys*]. Thats the way to keep these chaps up to the mark. [*The Orderly returns*]. Back again! What do you mean by this mutiny?

THE ORDERLY. What am I to say to the ladies, sir?

BALSQUITH. You dont mind my seeing them somewhere, do you?

MITCHENER. Not at all. Bring them in to see me when youve done with them. I understand that Lady Corinthia is a very fascinating woman. Who is she, by the way?

BALSQUITH. Daughter of Lord Broadstairs, the automatic turbine man. Gave quarter of a million to the party funds. She's musical and romantic and all that—dont hunt: hates politics: stops in town all the year round: one never sees her except at the opera and at musical at-homes and so forth.

MITCHENER. What a life! [*To the Orderly*] Where are the ladies?

THE ORDERLY. In No. 17, sir.

MITCHENER. Shew Mr Balsquith there; and send Mrs Farrell here.

THE ORDERLY [*calling into the corridor*] Mrs Farrell! [*To Balsquith*] This way, sir. [*He goes out with Balsquith*].

Mrs Farrell, a lean, highly respectable Irish charwoman of about fifty, comes in.

MITCHENER. Mrs Farrell: Ive a very important visit to pay: I shall want my full dress uniform and all my medals and orders and my presentation sword. There was a time when the British Army contained men capable of discharging these duties for their commanding officer. Those days are over. The compulsorily enlisted soldier runs to a woman for everything. I'm therefore reluctantly obliged to trouble you.

MRS FARRELL. Your meddles n ordhers n the

crooked sword widh the ivory handle n your full dress uniform is in the waxworks in the Chamber o Military Glory over in the place they used to call the Banquetin Hall. I told you youd be sorry for sendin them away; and you told me to mind me own business. Youre wiser now.

MITCHENER. I am. I had not at that time discovered that you were the only person in the whole military establishment of this capital who could be trusted to remember where anything was, or to understand an order and obey it.

MRS FARRELL. It's no good flattherin me. I'm too old.

MITCHENER. Not at all, Mrs Farrell. How is your daughter?

MRS FARRELL. Which daughter?

MITCHENER. The one who has made such a gratifying success in the Music Halls.

MRS FARRELL. Theres no Music Halls nowadays: theyre Variety Theatres. She's got an offer of marriage from a young jook.

MITCHENER. Is it possible? What did you do?

MRS FARRELL. I told his mother on him.

MITCHENER. Oh! What did she say?

MRS FARRELL. She was as pleased as Punch. Thank Heaven, she says, he's got somebody thatll be able to keep him when the supertax is put up to twenty shillings in the pound.

MITCHENER. But your daughter herself? What did she say?

MRS FARRELL. Accepted him, of course. What else would a young fool like her do? He inthrojooced her to the Poet Laureate, thinkin she'd inspire him.

MITCHENER. Did she?

MRS FARRELL. Faith, I dunna. All I know is she walked up to him as bold as brass n said, "Write me a sketch, dear." Afther all the throuble Ive took with that child's manners she's no more notion how to behave herself than a pig. Youll have to wear General Sandstone's uniform: it's the only one in the place, because he wont lend it to the shows.

MITCHENER. But Sandstone's clothes wont fit me.

MRS FARRELL [unmoved] Then you'll have to fit them. Why shouldnt they fitchya as well as they fitted General Blake at the Mansion House?

MITCHENER. They didnt fit him. He looked a frightful guy.

MRS FARRELL. Well, you must do the best you can with them. You cant exhibit your clothes and wear them too.

MITCHENER. And the public thinks the lot of a commanding officer a happy one! Oh, if they could only see the seamy side of it. [He returns to his table to resume work].

MRS FARRELL. If they could only see the seamy side o General Sandstone's uniform, where his flask rubs agen the buckle of his braces, theyd tell him he ought to get a new one. Let alone the way he swears at me.

MITCHENER. When a man has risked his life on eight battlefields, Mrs Farrell, he has given sufficient proof of his self-control to be excused a little strong language.

MRS FARRELL. Would you put up with bad language from me because Ive risked me life eight times in childbed?

MITCHENER. My dear Mrs Farrell, you surely would not compare a risk of that harmless domestic kind to the fearful risks of the battlefield.

MRS FARRELL. I wouldnt compare risks run to bear livin people into the world to risks run to blow dhem out of it. A mother's risk is jooty: a soldier's is nothin but divilmint.

MITCHENER [nettled] Let me tell you, Mrs Farrell, that if the men did not fight, the women would have to fight themselves. We spare you that at all events.

MRS FARRELL. You cant help yourselves. If three-quarters of you was killed we could replace you with the help of the other quarter. If three-quarters of us was killed how many people would there be in England in another generation? If it wasnt for that, the men'd put the fighting on us just as they put all the other dhrudgery. What would you do if we was all kilt? Would you go to bed and have twins?

MITCHENER. Really, Mrs Farrell, you must discuss these questions with a medical man. You make me blush, positively.

MRS FARRELL [grumbling to herself] A good job too. If I could have made Farrell blush I wouldnt have had to risk me life so often. You n your risks n your bravery n your self-conthrol indeed! "Why dont you conthrol yourself?" I sez to Farrell. "It's agen me religion," he sez.

MITCHENER [plaintively] Mrs Farrell: youre a woman of very powerful mind. I'm not qualified to argue these delicate matters with you. I ask you to spare me, and to be good enough to take these clothes to Mr

Balsquith when the ladies leave.

The Orderly comes in.

THE ORDERLY. Lady Corinthia Fanshawe and Mrs Banger want to see you, sir. Mr Balsquith told me to tell you.

MRS FARRELL. Theyve come about the vote. I dont know whether it's dhem dhat want it or dhem dhat doesnt want it: anyhow, theyre all alike when they get into a state about it. [*She goes out, having gathered Balsquith's Suffraget disguise from the desk*].

MITCHENER. Is Mr Balsquith not with them.

THE ORDERLY. No, sir. Couldn't stand Mrs Banger, I expect. Fair caution she is. [*Chuckling*] Couldnt help larfin when I sor im op it.

MITCHENER [*highly incensed*] How dare you indulge in this unseemly mirth in the presence of your commanding officer? Have you no sense of a soldier's duty?

THE ORDERLY [*sadly*] I'm afraid I shant ever get the ang of it, sir. You see, my father has a tidy little barber's business down off Shoreditch; and I was brought up to be chatty and easy-like with everybody. I tell you, when I drew the number in the conscription it gev my old mother the needle and it gev me the ump. I should take it very kind, sir, if youd let me off the drill and let me shave you instead. Youd appreciate my qualities then: you would indeed, sir. I shant never do myself jastice at soljerin, sir. I cant bring myself to think of it as proper work for a man with an active mind, as you might say, sir. Arf of it's only ousemaidin; and tother arf is dress-up and make-believe.

MITCHENER. Stuff, sir. It's the easiest life in the world. Once you learn your drill, all you have to do is to hold your tongue and obey your orders.

THE ORDERLY. But I do assure you, sir, arf the time theyre the wrong orders; and I get into trouble when I obey them. The sergeant's orders is all right; but the officers dont know what theyre talkin about. Why, the orses knows better sometimes. "Fours," says Lieutenant Trevor at the gate of Bucknam Palace only this mornin when we was on dooty for a State visit to the Coal Trust. I was fourth man like in the first file; and when I started the orse eld back; and the sergeant was on to me straight. Threes, you bally fool, e whispers. An e was on to me again about it when we come back, and called me a fathead, e did. What am I to do, I says: the lieutenant's orders was fours, I says. I'll shew you who's

lieutenant here, e says. In future you attend to my orders and not to iz, e says: what does e know about it? e says. You didnt give me any orders, I says. Couldnt you see for yourself there wasnt room for fours, e says: why cant you think? General Mitchener tells me I'm not to think, but to obey orders, I says. Is Mitchener your sergeant or am I? e says in his bullyin way. You are, I says. Well, e says, you got to do what your sergeant tells you: thats discipline, e says. And what am I to do for the General? I says. Youre to let him talk, e says: thats what e's for.

MITCHENER [*groaning*] It is impossible for the human mind to conceive anything more dreadful than this. Youre a disgrace to the service.

THE ORDERLY [*deeply wounded*] The service is a disgrace to me. When my mother's people pass me in the street with this uniform on, I ardly know which way to look. There never was a soldier in my family before.

MITCHENER. There never was anything else in mine, sir.

THE ORDERLY. My mother's second cousin was one of the Parkinsons o Stepney. [*Almost in tears*] What do you know of the feelings of a resepctable family in the middle station of life? I cant bear to be looked down on as a common soldier. Why cant my father be let buy my discharge? Youve done away with the soldier's right to ave his discharge bought for him by his relations. The country didnt know you were going to do that or it'd never ave stood it. Is an Englishman to be made a mockery like this?

MITCHENER. Silence. Attention. Right about face. March.

THE ORDERLY [*retiring to the standing desk and bedewing it with passionate tears*] Oh that I should have lived to be spoke to as if I was the lowest of the low! Me! that has shaved a City o London alderman wiv me own and.

MITCHENER. Poltroon. Crybaby. Well, better disgrace yourself here than disgrace your country on the field of battle.

THE ORDERLY [*angrily coming to the table*] Who's going to disgrace his country on the field of battle? It's not fightin I object to: it's soljerin. Shew me a German and I'll ave a go at him as fast as you or any man. But to ave me time wasted like this, an be stuck in a sentry-box at a street corner for an ornament to be stared at; and to be told "right about face: march," if I speak as one man to another: that aint pluck: that aint fightin: that aint patriotism: it's bein made a bloomin sheep of.

MITCHENER. A sheep has many valuable military qualities. Emulate them, dont disparage them.

THE ORDERLY. Oh, wots the good of talkin to you? If I wasnt a poor soldier I could punch your ed for forty shillins or a month. But because youre my commandin officer you deprive me of my right to a magistrate, and make a compliment of giving me two years ard stead o shootin me. Why cant you take your chance the same as any civilian does?

MITCHENER [rising majestically] I search the pages of history in vain for a parallel to such a speech made by a private to a General. But for the coherence of your remarks I should conclude that you were drunk. As it is, you must be mad. You shall be placed under restraint at once. Call the guard.

THE ORDERLY. Call your grandmother. If you take one man off the doors the place'll be full of Suffragets before you can wink.

MITCHENER. Then arrest yourself; and off with you to the guard-room.

THE ORDERLY. What am I to arrest myself for?

MITCHENER. Thats nothing to you. You have your orders: obey them. Do you hear? Right about face. March.

THE ORDERLY. How would you feel if you was told to right-about-face and march as if you were a door-mat?

MITCHENER. I should feel as if my country had spoken through the voice of my officer. I should feel proud and honored to be able to serve my country by obeying its commands. No thought of self, no vulgar preoccupation with my own petty vanity, could touch my mind at such a moment. To me my officer would not be a mere man: he would be for the moment—whatever his personal frailties—the incarnation of our national destiny.

THE ORDERLY. What I'm saying to you is the voice of old England a jolly sight more than all this rot that you get out of books. I'd rather be spoke to by a sergeant than by you. He tells me to go to hell when I challenges him to argue it out like a man. It aint polite; but it's English. What you say aint anything at all. You dont act on it yourself. You dont believe in it. Youd punch my

head if I tried it on you; and serve me right. And look here. Heres another point for you to argue—

MITCHENER [with a shriek of protest] No—

Mrs Banger comes in followed by Lady Corinthia Fanshawe. Mrs Banger is a masculine woman of forty with a powerful voice and great physical strength. Lady Corinthia, who is also over thirty, is beautiful and romantic.

MRS BANGER [throwing the door open decisively and marching straight to Mitchener] Pray how much longer is the Anti-Suffraget League to be kept waiting? [She passes him contemptuously and sits down with impressive confidence in the chair next the fireplace. Lady Corinthia takes the chair on the opposite side of the table with equal aplomb].

MITCHENER. I'm extremely sorry. You really do not know what I have to put up with. This imbecile, incompetent, unsoldierly disgrace to the uniform he should never have been allowed to put on ought to have shewn you in fifteen minutes ago.

THE ORDERLY. All I said was—

MITCHENER. Not another word. Attention. Right about face. March. [The Orderly sits down doggedly]. Get out of the room this instant, you fool; or I'll kick you out.

THE ORDERLY [civilly] I dont mind that, sir. It's human. It's English. Why couldnt you have said it before? [He goes out].

MITCHENER. Take no notice, I beg: these scenes are of daily occurrence now that we have compulsory service under the command of the halfpenny papers. Pray sit down.

LADY CORINTHIA AND MRS BANGER } [rising] { Thank you. [They sit down again].

MITCHENER [sitting down with a slight chuckle of satisfaction] And now, ladies, to what am I indebted—

MRS BANGER. Let me introduce us. I am Rosa Carmina Banger: Mrs Banger, organizing secretary of the Anti-Suffraget League. This is Lady Corinthia Fanshawe, the president of the League, known in musical circles —I am not musical—as the Richmond Park nightingale. A soprano. I am myself said to be almost a baritone; but I do not profess to understand these distinctions.

MITCHENER [murmuring politely] Most happy, I'm sure.

MRS BANGER. We have come to tell you plainly that the Anti-Suffragets are going to fight.

MITCHENER [gallantly] Oh, pray leave that

to the men, Mrs Banger.

LADY CORINTHIA. We can no longer trust the men.

MRS BANGER. They have shewn neither the strength, the courage, nor the determination which are needed to combat women like the Suffragets.

LADY CORINTHIA. Nature is too strong for the combatants.

MRS BANGER. Physical struggles between persons of opposite sexes are unseemly.

LADY CORINTHIA. Demoralizing.

MRS BANGER. Insincere.

LADY CORINTHIA. They are merely embraces in disguise.

MRS BANGER. No such suspicion can attach to combats in which the antagonists are of the same sex.

LADY CORINTHIA. The Anti-Suffragets have resolved to take the field.

MRS BANGER. They will enforce the order of General Sandstone for the removal of all women from the two-mile radius—that is, all women except themselves.

MITCHENER. I am sorry to have to inform you, madam, that the Government has given up that project, and that General Sandstone has resigned in consequence.

MRS BANGER. That does not concern us in the least. We approve of the project and will see that it is carried out. We have spent a good deal of money arming ourselves; and we are not going to have that money thrown away through the pusillanimity of a Cabinet of males.

MITCHENER. Arming yourselves! But, my dear ladies, under the latest proclamation women are strictly forbidden to carry chains, padlocks, tracts on the franchise, or weapons of any description.

LADY CORINTHIA [producing an ivory-handled revolver and pointing it at his nose] You little know your countrywomen, General Mitchener.

MITCHENER [without flinching] Madam: it is my duty to take possession of that weapon in accordance with the proclamation. Be good enough to put it down.

MRS BANGER [producing an XVIII century horse pistol] Is it your duty to take possession of this also?

MITCHENER. That, madam, is not a weapon: it is a curiosity. If you would be kind enough to place it in some museum instead of pointing it at my head, I should be obliged to you.

MRS BANGER. This pistol, sir, was carried at Waterloo by my grandmother.

MITCHENER. I presume you mean your grandfather.

MRS BANGER. You presume unwarrantably.

LADY CORINTHIA. Mrs Banger's grandmother commanded a canteen at that celebrated battle.

MRS. BANGER. Who my grandfather was is a point that has never been quite clearly settled. I put my trust, not in my ancestors, but in my good sword, which is at my lodgings.

MITCHENER. Your sword!

MRS BANGER. The sword with which I slew five Egyptians with my own hand at Kassassin, where I served as a trooper.

MITCHENER. Lord bless me! But was your sex never discovered?

MRS BANGER. It was never even suspected. I had a comrade—a gentleman ranker—whom they called Fanny. They never called me Fanny.

LADY CORINTHIA. The Suffragets have turned the whole woman movement on to the wrong track. They ask for a vote.

MRS BANGER. What use is a vote? Men have the vote.

LADY CORINTHIA. And men are slaves.

MRS BANGER. What women need is the right to military service. Give me a well-mounted regiment of women with sabres, opposed to a regiment of men with votes. We shall see which will go down before the other. No: we have had enough of these gentle pretty creatures who merely talk and cross-examine ministers in police courts, and go to prison like sheep, and suffer and sacrifice themselves. This question must be solved by blood and iron, as was well said by Bismarck, whom I have reason to believe was a woman in disguise.

MITCHENER. Bismarck a woman!

MRS BANGER. All the really strong men of history have been disguised women.

MITCHENER [remonstrating] My dear lady!

MRS BANGER. How can you tell? You never knew that the hero of the charge at Kassassin was a woman: yet she was: it was I, Rosa Carmina Banger. Would Napoleon have been so brutal to women, think you, had he been a man?

MITCHENER. Oh, come, come! Really! Surely female rulers have often shewn all the feminine weaknesses. Queen Elizabeth, for instance. Her vanity, her levity—

MRS BANGER. Nobody who has studied the history of Queen Elizabeth can doubt for a moment that she was a disguised man.

LADY CORINTHIA [admiring Mrs Banger] Isnt she splendid!

MRS BANGER [rising with a large gesture] This very afternoon I shall cast off this hampering skirt for ever; mount my charger; and with my good sabre lead the Anti-Suffragets to victory. [She strides to the other side of the room, snorting].

MITCHENER. But I cant allow anything of the sort, madam. I shall stand no such ridiculous nonsense. I'm perfectly determined to put my foot down—

LADY CORINTHIA. Dont be hysterical, General.

MITCHENER. Hysterical!

MRS BANGER. Do you think we are to be stopped by these childish exhibitions of temper? They are useless; and your tears and entreaties—a man's last resource—will avail you just as little. I sweep them away, just as I sweep your plans of campaign "made in Germany"—

MITCHENER [flying into a transport of rage] How dare you repeat that infamous slander! [He rings the bell violently]. If this is the alternative to votes for women, I shall advocate giving every woman in the country six votes. [The Orderly comes in]. Remove that woman. See that she leaves the building at once.

The Orderly forlornly contemplates the iron front presented by Mrs Banger.

THE ORDERLY [propitiatorily] Would you av the feelin art to step out, madam?

MRS BANGER. You are a soldier. Obey your orders. Put me out. If I got such an order I should not hesitate.

THE ORDERLY [to Mitchener] Would you mind lendin me a and, Guvner?

LADY CORINTHIA [raising her revolver] I shall be obliged to shoot you if you stir, General.

MRS BANGER [to the Orderly] When you are ordered to put a person out you should do it like this. [She hurls him from the room. He is heard falling headlong downstairs and crashing through a glass door]. I shall now wait on General Sandstone. If he shews any sign of weakness, he shall share that poor wretch's fate. [She goes out].

LADY CORINTHIA. Isnt she magnificent?

MITCHENER. Thank heaven she's gone. And now, my dear lady, is it necessary to keep that loaded pistol to my nose all through our conversation?

LADY CORINTHIA. It's not loaded. It's heavy enough, goodness knows, without putting bullets in it.

MITCHENER [triumphantly snatching his revolver from the drawer] Then I am master of the situation. This is loaded. Ha, ha!

LADY CORINTHIA. But since we are not really going to shoot one another, what difference can it possibly make?

MITCHENER [putting his pistol down on the table] True. Quite true. I recognize there the practical good sense that has prevented you from falling into the snares of the Suffragets.

LADY CORINTHIA. The Suffragets, General, are the dupes of dowdies. A really attractive and clever woman—

MITCHENER [gallantly] Yourself, for instance.

LADY CORINTHIA [snatching up his revolver] Another step and you are a dead man.

MITCHENER [amazed] My dear lady!

LADY CORINTHIA. I am not your dear lady. You are not the first man who has concluded that because I am devoted to music and can reach F in alt with the greatest facility— Patti never got above E flat—I am marked out as the prey of every libertine. You think I am like the thousands of weak women whom you have ruined—

MITCHENER. I solemnly protest—

LADY CORINTHIA. Oh, I know what you officers are. To you a woman's honor is nothing, and the idle pleasure of the moment is everything.

MITCHENER. This is perfectly ridiculous. I never ruined anyone in my life.

LADY CORINTHIA. Never! Are you in earnest?

MITCHENER. Certainly I am in earnest. Most indignantly in earnest.

LADY CORINTHIA [throwing down the pistol contemptuously] Then you have no temperament: you are not an artist. You have no soul for music.

MITCHENER. Ive subscribed to the regimental band all my life. I bought two sarrusophones for it out of my own pocket. When I sang Tosti's Goodbye for Ever at Knightsbridge in 1880 the whole regiment wept. You are too young to remember that.

LADY CORINTHIA. Your advances are useless. I—

MITCHENER. Confound it, madam, can you not receive an innocent compliment without suspecting me of dishonorable intentions?

LADY CORINTHIA. Love—real love—makes all intentions honorable. But you could never understand that.

MITCHENER. I'll not submit to the vulgar penny-novelette notion that an officer is less honorable than a civilian in his relations with women. While I live I'll raise my voice—

LADY CORINTHIA. Tush!

MITCHENER. What do you mean by tush?

LADY CORINTHIA. You cant raise your voice above its natural compass. What sort of voice have you?

MITCHENER. A tenor. What sort had you?

LADY CORINTHIA. Had! I have it still. I tell you I am the highest living soprano. [*Scornfully*] What was your highest note, pray?

MITCHENER. B flat—once—in 1879. I was drunk at the time.

LADY CORINTHIA [*gazing at him almost tenderly*] Though you may not believe me, I find you are more interesting when you talk about music than when you are endeavoring to betray a woman who has trusted you by remaining alone with you in your apartment.

MITCHENER [*springing up and fuming away to the fireplace*] Those repeated insults to a man of blameless life are as disgraceful to you as they are undeserved by me, Lady Corinthia. Such suspicions invite the conduct they impute. [*She raises the pistol*] You need not be alarmed: I am only going to leave the room.

LADY CORINTHIA. Fish.

MITCHENER. Fish! This is worse than tush. Why fish?

LADY CORINTHIA. Yes, fish: cold-blooded fish.

MITCHENER. Dash it all, madam, do you want me to make advances to you?

LADY CORINTHIA. I have not the slightest intention of yielding to them; but to make them would be a tribute to romance. What is life without romance?

MITCHENER [*making a movement towards her*] I tell you—

LADY CORINTHIA. Stop. No nearer. No vulgar sensuousness. If you must adore, adore at a distance.

MITCHENER. This is worse than Mrs Banger. I shall ask that estimable woman to come back.

LADY CORINTHIA. Poor Mrs Banger! Do not for a moment suppose, General Mitchener, that Mrs Banger represents my views on the suffrage question. Mrs Banger is a man in petticoats. I am every inch a woman; but I find it convenient to work with her.

MITCHENER. Do you find the combination comfortable?

LADY CORINTHIA. I do not wear combinations, General: [*with dignity*] they are unwomanly.

MITCHENER [*throwing himself despairingly into the chair next the hearthrug*] I shall go mad. I never for a moment dreamt of alluding to anything of the sort.

LADY CORINTHIA. There is no need to blush and become self-conscious at the mention of underclothing. You are extremely vulgar, General.

MITCHENER. Lady Corinthia: you have my pistol. Will you have the goodness to blow my brains out? I should prefer it to any other effort to follow the gyrations of the weathercock you no doubt call your mind. If you refuse, then I warn you that youll not get another word out of me—not if we sit here until doomsday.

LADY CORINTHIA. I dont want you to talk. I want you to listen. You do not understand my views on the question of the suffrage. [*She rises to make a speech*] I must preface my remarks by reminding you that the Suffraget movement is essentially a dowdy movement. The Suffragets are not all dowdies; but they are mainly supported by dowdies. Now I am not a dowdy. Oh, no compliments—

MITCHENER. I did not utter a sound.

LADY CORINTHIA [*smiling*] It is easy to read your thoughts. I am one of those women who are accustomed to rule the world through men. Man is ruled by beauty, by charm. The men who are not have no influence. The Salic Law, which forbade women to occupy a throne, is founded on the fact that when a woman is on the throne the country is ruled by men, and therefore ruled badly; whereas when a man is on the throne the country is ruled by women, and therefore ruled well. The Suffragets would degrade women from being rulers to being voters, mere politicians, the drudges of the caucus and the polling booth. We should lose our influence completely under such a state of affairs. The New Zealand women have the vote. What is the result? No poet ever makes a New Zealand woman his heroine. One might as well be romantic about New Zealand mutton. Look at the Suffragets themselves. The only ones who are popular are the pretty ones, who flirt with mobs as ordinary women flirt with officers.

MITCHENER. Then I understand you to hold that the country should be governed by the women after all.

LADY CORINTHIA. Not by all the women. By certain women. I had almost said by one woman. By the women who have charm—who have artistic talent—who wield a legitimate, a refining influence over the men. [*She sits down gracefully, smiling, and arranging her draperies with conscious elegance*].

MITCHENER. In short, madam, you think that if you give the vote to the man, you give the power to the woman who can get round the man.

LADY CORINTHIA. That is not a very delicate way of putting it; but I suppose that is how you would express what I mean.

MITCHENER. Perhaps youve never had any experience of garrison life. If you had, youd have noticed that the sort of woman who's clever at getting round men is sometimes rather a bad lot.

LADY CORINTHIA. What do you mean by a bad lot?

MITCHENER. I mean a woman who would play the very devil if the other women didnt keep her in pretty strict order. I dont approve of democracy, because it's rot; and I'm against giving the vote to women, because I'm not accustomed to it, and therefore am able to see with an unprejudiced eye what infernal nonsense it is. But I tell you plainly, Lady Corinthia, that there is one game that I dislike more than either democracy or votes for women; and that is the game of Antony and Cleopatra. If I must be ruled by women, let me have decent women, and not—well, not the other sort.

LADY CORINTHIA. You have a coarse mind, General Mitchener.

MITCHENER. So has Mrs Banger. And, by George! I prefer Mrs Banger to you!

LADY CORINTHIA [*bounding to her feet*] You prefer Mrs Banger to me!!!

MITCHENER. I do. You said yourself she was splendid.

LADY CORINTHIA. You are no true man. You are one of those unsexed creatures who have no joy in life, no sense of beauty, no high notes.

MITCHENER. No doubt I am, madam. As a matter of fact, I am not clever at discussing public questions, because, as an English gentleman, I was not brought up to use my brains. But occasionally, after a number of remarks which are perhaps sometimes rather idiotic, I get certain convictions. Thanks to you, I have now got a conviction that this woman question is not a question of lovely and accomplished females, but of dowdies. The average Englishwoman is a dowdy and never has half a chance of becoming anything else. She hasnt any charm; and she has no high notes, except when she's giving her husband a piece of her mind, or calling down the street for one of the children.

LADY CORINTHIA. How disgusting!

MITCHENER. Somebody must do the dowdy work! If we had to choose between pitching all the dowdies into the Thames and pitching all the lovely and accomplished women, the lovely ones would have to go.

LADY CORINTHIA. And if you had to do without Wagner's music or do without your breakfast, you would do without Wagner. Pray does that make eggs and bacon more precious than music, or the butcher and baker better than the poet and philosopher? The scullery may be more necessary to our bare existence than the cathedral. Even humbler apartments might make the same claim. But which is the more essential to the higher life?

MITCHENER. Your arguments are so devilishly ingenious that I feel convinced you got them out of some confounded book. Mine—such as they are—are my own. I imagine it's something like this. There is an old saying that if you take care of the pence, the pounds will take care of themselves. Well, perhaps if we take care of the dowdies and the butchers and the bakers, the beauties and the bigwigs will take care of themselves. [*Rising and facing her determinedly*] Anyhow, I dont want to have things arranged for me by Wagner. I'm not Wagner. How does he know where the shoe pinches me? How do you know where the shoe pinches your washerwoman? you and your high F in alt! How are you to know when you havnt made her comfortable unless she has a vote? Do you want her to come and break your windows?

LADY CORINTHIA. Am I to understand that General Mitchener is a Democrat and a Suffraget?

MITCHENER. Yes: you have converted me—

you and Mrs Banger.

LADY CORINTHIA. Farewell, creature. [*Balsquith enters hurriedly*]. Mr Balsquith: I am going to wait on General Sandstone. He, at least, is an officer and a gentleman. [*She sails out*].

BALSQUITH. Mitchener: the game is up.

MITCHENER. What do you mean?

BALSQUITH. The strain is too much for the Cabinet. The old Liberal and Unionist Free Traders declare that if they are defeated on their resolution to invite tenders from private contractors for carrying on the Army and Navy, they will go solid for votes for women as the only means of restoring the liberties of the country which we have destroyed by compulsory military service.

MITCHENER. Infernal impudence!

BALSQUITH. The Labor Party is taking the same line. They say the men got the Factory Acts by hiding behind the women's petticoats, and that they will get votes for the army in the same way.

MITCHENER. Balsquith: we must not yield to clamor. I have just told that woman that I am at last convinced—

BALSQUITH [*joyfully*] —that the Suffragets must be supported?

MITCHENER. No: that the Anti-Suffragets must be put down at all hazards.

BALSQUITH. Same thing.

MITCHENER. No. For you now tell me that the Labor Party demands votes for women. That makes it impossible to give them, because it would be yielding to clamor. The one condition on which we can consent to grant anything in this country is that nobody shall presume to ask for it.

BALSQUITH [*earnestly*] Mitchener: it's no use. You cant have the conveniences of Democracy without its occasional inconveniences.

MITCHENER. What are its conveniences, I should like to know?

BALSQUITH. Well, when you tell people that they are the real rulers and they can do what they like, nine times out of ten they say "All right: tell us what to do." But it happens sometimes that they get an idea of their own; and then of course youre landed.

MITCHENER. Sh—

BALSQUITH [*desperately shouting him down*] No: it's no use telling me to shoot them down: I'm not going to do it. After all, I dont suppose votes for women will make much differ-ence. It hasnt in the other countries in which it has been tried.

MITCHENER. I never supposed it would make any difference. What I cant stand is giving in to that Pankhurst lot. Hang it all, Balsquith, it seems only yesterday that we put them in quad for a month. I said at the time that it ought to have been ten years. If my advice had been taken this wouldnt have happened. It's a consolation to me that events are proving how thoroughly right I was.

The Orderly rushes in.

THE ORDELY. Look 'ere, sir: Mrs Banger's locked the door of General Sandstone's room on the inside; an' she's sittin on his ed til he signs a proclamation for women to serve in the army.

MITCHENER. Put your shoulder to the door and burst it open.

THE ORDERLY. It's only in story books that doors burst open as easy as that. Besides, I'm only too thankful to av a locked door between me and Mrs B.; and so is all the rest of us.

MITCHENER. Cowards. Balsquith: to the rescue! [*He dashes out*].

BALSQUITH [*ambling calmly to the hearth*] This is the business of the Serjeant-at-Arms rather than of the leader of the House. Theres no use in my tackling Mrs Banger: she would only sit on my head too.

THE ORDERLY. You take my tip, Mr Balsquith. Give the women the vote and give the army civil rights; and av done with it.

Mitchener returns and comes between them.

MITCHENER. Balsquith: prepare to hear the worst.

BALSQUITH. Sandstone is no more?

MITCHENER. On the contrary, he is particularly lively. He has softened Mrs Banger by a proposal of marriage in which he appears to be perfectly in earnest. He says he has met his ideal at last, a really soldierly woman. She will sit on his head for the rest of his life; and the British Army is now to all intents and purposes commanded by Mrs Banger. When I remonstrated with Sandstone she positively shouted "Right about face. March" at me in the most offensive tone. If she hadnt been a woman I should have punched her head. I precious nearly punched Sandstone's. The horrors of martial law administered by Mrs Banger are too terrible to be faced. I demand civil rights for the army.

THE ORDERLY [*chuckling*] Wot oh, General! Wot oh!

MITCHENER. Hold your tongue. [*He goes to the door and calls*] Mrs Farrell! [*He returns, and again addresses the Orderly*]. Civil rights dont mean the right to be uncivil. [*Pleased with his own wit*] Almost a pun. Ha ha!

MRS FARRELL [*entering*] Whats the matter now? [*She comes to the table*].

MITCHENER [*to the Orderly*] I have private business with Mrs Farrell. Outside, you infernal blackguard.

THE ORDERLY [*arguing, as usual*] Well, I didnt ask to— [*Mitchener seizes him by the nape; marches him out; slams the door; and comes solemnly to Mrs Farrell*].

MITCHENER. Excuse the abruptness of this communication, Mrs Farrell; but I know only one woman in the country whose practical ability and force of character can maintain her husband in competition with the husband of Mrs Banger. I have the honor to propose for your hand.

MRS FARRELL. D'ye mean you want to marry me?

MITCHENER. I do.

MRS FARRELL. No thank you. I'd have to work for you just the same; only I shouldnt get any wages for it.

BALSQUITH. That will be remedied when women get the vote. Ive had to promise that.

MITCHENER [*winningly*] Mrs Farrell: you have been charwoman here now ever since I took up my duties. Have you really never, in your more romantic moments, cast a favorable eye on my person?

MRS FARRELL. Ive been too busy casting an unfavorable eye on your cloze an on the litther you make with your papers.

MITCHENER [*wounded*] Am I to understand that you refuse me?

MRS FARRELL. Just wait a bit. [*She takes Mitchener's chair and rings up the telephone*] Double three oh seven Elephant.

MITCHENER. I trust youre not ringing for the police, Mrs Farrell. I assure you I'm perfectly sane.

MRS FARRELL [*into the telephone*] Is that you, Eliza? [*She listens for the answer*]. Not out o bed yet! Go and pull her out be the heels, the lazy sthreel; and tell her her mother wants to speak to her very particularly about General Mitchener. [*To Mitchener*] Dont you be afeard: I know youre sane enough when youre not talkin about the Germans. [*Into

the telephone*] Is that you, Eliza? [*She listens for the answer*]. D'ye remember me givin you a clout on the side of the head for tellin me that if I only knew how to play me cards I could marry any General on the staff instead o disgracin you be bein a charwoman? [*She listens for the answer*]. Well, I can have General Mitchener without playin any cards at all. What d'ye think I ought to say? [*She listens*]. Well, I'm no chicken meself. [*To Mitchener*] How old are you?

MITCHENER [*with an effort*] Fifty-two.

MRS FARRELL [*into the telephone*] He says he's fifty-two. [*She listens; then, to Mitchener*] She says youre down in Who's Who as sixty-one.

MITCHENER. Damn Who's Who!

MRS FARRELL [*into the telephone*] Anyhow I wouldnt let that stand in the way. [*She listens*] If I really w h a t? [*She listens*]. I cant hear you. If I really w h a t? [*She listens*]. W h o druv him? I never said a word to— Eh? [*She listens*]. Oh, l o v e him. Arra, dont be a fool, child. [*To Mitchener*] She wants to know do I really love you. [*Into the telephone*] It's likely indeed I'd frighten the man off with any such nonsense at my age. What? [*She listens*]. Well, thats just what I was thinkin.

MITCHENER. May I ask what you were thinking, Mrs Farrell? This suspense is awful.

MRS FARRELL. I was thinkin that praps the Duchess might like her daughter-in-law's mother to be a General's lady betther than to be a charwoman. [*Into the telephone*] Waitle youre married yourself, me fine lady: youll find out that every woman's a charwoman from the day she's married. [*She listens*]. Then you think I might take him? [*She listens*]. G'lang, you young scald: if I had you here I'd teach you manners. [*She listens*]. Thats enough now. Back wid you to bed; and be thankful I'm not there to put me slipper across you. [*She rings off*]. The impudence! [*To Mitchener*] Bless you, me childher, may you be happy, she says. [*To Balsquith, going to his side of the room*] Give dear old Mitch me love, she says.

The Orderly opens the door, ushering in Lady Corinthia.

THE ORDERLY. Lady Corinthia Fanshawe to speak to you, sir.

LADY CORINTHIA. General Mitchener: your designs on Mrs Banger are defeated. She is engaged to General Sandstone. Do you still prefer her to me?

MRS FARRELL. He's out o the hunt. He's engaged to me.

The Orderly, overcome by this news, reels from the door to the standing desk and clutches the stool to save himself from collapsing.

MITCHENER. And extremely proud of it, Lady Corinthia.

LADY CORINTHIA [*contemptuously*] She suits you exactly. [*Coming to Balsquith*] Mr Balsquith: you, at least, are not a Philistine.

BALSQUITH. No, Lady Corinthia; but I'm a confirmed bachelor. I dont want a wife; but I want an Egeria.

MRS FARRELL. More shame for you!

LADY CORINTHIA. Silence, woman. The position and functions of a wife may suit your gross nature. An Egeria is exactly what I desire to be. [*To Balsquith*] Can you play accompaniments?

BALSQUITH. Melodies only, I regret to say. With one finger. But my brother, who is a very obliging fellow, and not unlike me personally, is acquainted with three chords, with which he manages to accompany most of the comic songs of the day.

LADY CORINTHIA. I do not sing comic songs. Neither will you when I am your Egeria. You must come to my musical at-home this afternoon. I will allow you to sit at my feet.

BALSQUITH [*doing so*] That is my ideal of romantic happiness. It commits me exactly as far as I desire to venture. Thank you.

THE ORDERLY. Wot price me, General? Wont you celebrate your engagement by doin somethin for me? Maynt I be promoted to be a sergeant?

MITCHENER. Youre too utterly incompetent to discharge the duties of a sergeant. You are only fit to be a lieutenant. I shall recommend you for a commission.

THE ORDERLY. Hooray! The Parkinsons o Stepney'll be proud to have me call on em now. I'll go and tell the sergeant what I think of him. Hooray! [*He rushes out*].

MRS FARRELL [*going to the door and calling after him*] You might have the manners to shut the door afther you. [*She shuts it and comes between Mitchener and Lady Corinthia*].

MITCHENER. Poor wretch! the day after civil rights are conceded to the army he and Chubbs-Jenkinson will be found incapable of maintaining discipline. They will be sacked and replaced by really capable men. Mrs Farrell: as we are engaged, and I am anxious to do the correct thing in every way, I am quite willing to kiss you if you wish it.

MRS FARRELL. Youd only feel like a fool; and so would I.

MITCHENER. You are really the most sensible woman. Ive made an extremely wise choice. [*He kisses her hand*].

LADY CORINTHIA [*to Balsquith*] You may kiss my hand, if you wish.

BALSQUITH [*cautiously*] I think we had better not commit ourselves too far. Let us change a subject which threatens to become embarrassing. [*To Mitchener*] The moral of the occasion for you, Mitchener, appears to be that youve got to give up treating soldiers as if they were schoolboys.

MITCHENER. The moral for you, Balsquith, is that youve got to give up treating women as if they were angels. Ha ha!

MRS FARRELL. It's a mercy youve found one another out at last. Thats enough now.

THE END

XXXVI

THE GLIMPSE OF REALITY

A TRAGEDIETTA

In the fifteenth century A.D. Gloaming. An inn on the edge of an Italian lake. A stone cross with a pedestal of steps. A very old friar sitting on the steps. The angelus rings. The friar prays and crosses himself. A girl ferries a boat to the shore and comes up the bank to the cross.

THE GIRL. Father: were you sent here by a boy from —

THE FRIAR [*in a high, piping, but clear voice*] I'm a very old man. Oh, very old. Old enough to be your great grandfather, my daughter. Oh, very v e r y old.

THE GIRL. But were you sent here by a boy from—

THE FRIAR. Oh yes, yes, yes, yes, yes. Quite a boy, he was. Very young. And I'm very old. Oh, very very old, dear daughter.

THE GIRL. Are you a holy man?

THE FRIAR [*ecstatically*] Oh, very holy. Very, very, very, v e r y holy.

THE GIRL. But have you your wits still about you, father? Can you absolve me from a great sin?

THE FRIAR. Oh yes, yes, yes. A very great sin. I'm very old; but Ive my wits about me. I'm one hundred and thirteen years old, by the grace of Our Lady; but I still remember all my Latin; and I can bind and loose; and I'm very very wise; for I'm old and have left far behind me the world, the flesh, and the devil. You see I am blind, daughter; but when a boy told me that there was a duty for me to do here, I came without a guide, straight to this spot, led by St Barbara. She led me to this stone, daughter. It's a comfortable stone to me: she has blessed it for me.

THE GIRL. It's a cross, father.

THE FRIAR [*piping rapturously*] Oh blessed, blessed, ever blessed be my holy patroness for leading me to this sacred spot. Is there any building near this, daughter? The boy mentioned an inn.

THE GIRL. There is an inn, father, not twenty yards away. It's kept by my father, Squarcio.

THE FRIAR. And is there a barn where a very very old man may sleep and have a handful of peas for his supper?

THE GIRL. There is bed and board both for holy men who will take the guilt of our sins from us. Swear to me on the cross that you are a very holy man.

THE FRIAR. I'll do better than that, daughter. I'll prove my holiness to you by a miracle.

THE GIRL. A miracle!

THE FRIAR. A most miraculous miracle. A wonderful miracle! When I was only eighteen years of age I was already famous for my devoutness. When the hand of the blessed Saint Barbara, which was chopped off in the days when the church was persecuted, was found at Viterbo, I was selected by the Pope himself to carry it to Rome for that blessed lady's festival there; and since that my hand has never grown old. It remains young and warm and plump whilst the rest of my body is withered almost to dust, and my voice is cracked and become the whistling you now hear.

THE GIRL. Is that true? Let me see. [*He takes her hand in his. She kneels and kisses it fervently*] Oh, it's true. You are a saint.

Heaven has sent you in answer to my prayer.

THE FRIAR. As soft as your neck, is it not? [*He caresses her neck*].

THE GIRL. It thrills me: it is wonderful.

THE FRIAR. It thrills me also, daughter. That, too, is a miracle at my age.

THE GIRL. Father—

THE FRIAR. Come closer, daughter. I'm very very old and very very very deaf: you must speak quite close to my ear if you speak low. [*She kneels with her breast against his arm and her chin on his shoulder*]. Good. Good. Thats better. Oh, I'm very very old.

THE GIRL. Father: I am about to commit a deadly sin.

THE FRIAR. Do, my daughter. Do, do, do, do, do.

THE GIRL [*discouraged*] Oh, you do not hear what I say.

THE FRIAR. Not hear! Then come closer, daughter. Oh, much, m u c h closer. Put your arm round my shoulders, and speak in my ear. Do not be ashamed, my daughter: I'm only a sack of old bones. You can hear them rattle. [*He shakes his shoulders and makes the beads of his rosary rattle at the same time*]. Listen to the old man's bones rattling. Oh, take the old old man to heaven, Blessed Barbara.

THE GIRL. Your wits are wandering. Listen to me. Are you listening?

THE FRIAR. Yes yes yes yes yes yes yes. Remember: whether I hear or not, I can absolve. All the better for you perhaps if I do not hear the worst. He! He! He! Well well. When my wits wander, squeeze my young hand; and the blessed Barbara will restore my faculties. [*She squeezes his hand vigorously*] Thats right. Tha-a-a-ats right. Now I remember what I am and who you are. Proceed, my child.

THE GIRL. Father, I am to be married this year to a young fisherman.

THE FRIAR. The devil you are, my dear.

THE GIRL [*squeezing his hand*] Oh listen, listen; you are wandering again.

THE FRIAR. Thats right: hold my hand tightly. I understand, I understand. This young fisherman is neither very beautiful nor very brave; but he is honest and devoted to you; and there is something about him different to all the other young men.

THE GIRL. You know him, then!

THE FRIAR. No no no no no. I'm too old to remember people. But Saint Barbara tells me everything.

THE GIRL. Then you know why we cant marry yet.

THE FRIAR. He is too poor. His mother will not let him unless his bride has a dowry—

THE GIRL [*interrupting him impetuously*] Yes, yes: oh blessed be Saint Barbara for sending you to me! Thirty crowns—thirty crowns from a poor girl like me: it is wicked—monstrous. I must sin to earn it.

THE FRIAR. That will not be your sin, but his mother's.

THE GIRL. Oh, that is true: I never thought of that. But will she suffer for it?

THE FRIAR. Thousands of years in purgatory for it, my daughter. The worse the sin, the longer she will suffer. So let her have it as hot as possible. [*The girl recoils*]. Do not let go my hand: I'm wandering. [*She squeezes his hand*]. Thats right, darling. Sin is a very wicked thing, my daughter. Even a mother-in-law's sin is very expensive; for your husband would stint you to pay for masses for her soul.

THE GIRL. That is true. You are very wise, father.

THE FRIAR. Let it be a venial sin: an amiable sin. What sin were you thinking of, for instance?

THE GIRL. There is a young Count Ferruccio [*the Friar starts at the name*], son of the tyrant of Parma—

THE FRIAR. An excellent young man, daughter. You could not sin with a more excellent young man. But thirty crowns is too much to ask from him. He cant afford it. He is a beggar: an outcast. He made love to Madonna Brigita, the sister of Cardinal Poldi, a Cardinal eighteen years of age, a nephew of the Holy Father. The Cardinal surprised Ferruccio with his sister; and Ferrucio's temper got the better of him. He threw that holy young Cardinal out of the window and broke his arm.

THE GIRL. You know everything.

THE FRIAR. Saint Barbara, my daughter, Saint Barbara. *I* know nothing. But where have you seen Ferruccio? Saint Barbara says that he never saw you in his life, and has not thirty crowns in the world.

THE GIRL. Oh, why does not Saint Barbara tell you that I am an honest girl who would not sell herself for a thousand crowns.

THE FRIAR. Do not give way to pride, daughter. Pride is one of the seven deadly sins.

THE GIRL. I know that, father; and believe me, I'm humble and good. I swear to you by Our Lady that it is not Ferruccio's love that I must take, but his life. [*The Friar, startled, turns powerfully on her*]. Do not be angry, dear father: do not cast me off. What is a poor girl to do? We are very poor, my father and I. And I am not to kill him. I am only to decoy him here; for he is a devil for women; and once he is in the inn, my father will do the rest.

THE FRIAR [*in a rich baritone voice*] Will he, by thunder and lightning and the flood and all the saints, will he? [*He flings off his gown and beard, revealing himself as a handsome youth, a nobleman by his dress, as he springs up and rushes to the door of the inn, which he batters with a stone*]. Ho there, Squarcio, rascal, assassin, son of a pig: come out that I may break every bone in your carcass.

THE GIRL. You are a young man!

THE FRIAR. Another miracle of Saint Barbara. [*Kicking the door*] Come out, whelp: come out, rat. Come out and be killed. Come out and be beaten to a jelly. Come out, dog, swine, animal, mangy hound, lousy— [*Squarcio comes out, sword in hand*]. Do you know who I am, dog?

SQUARCIO [*impressed*] No, your Excellency.

THE FRIAR. I am Ferruccio, Count Ferruccio, the man you are to kill, the man your devil of a daughter is to decoy, the man who is now going to cut you into forty thousand pieces and throw you into the lake.

SQUARCIO. Keep your temper, Signor Count.

FERRUCCIO. I'll not keep my temper. Ive an uncontrollable temper. I get blinding splitting headaches if I do not relieve my temper by acts of violence. I'll relieve it now by pounding you to jelly, assassin that you are.

SQUARCIO [*shrugging his shoulders*] As you please, Signor Count. I may as well earn my money now as another time. [*He handles his sword*].

FERRUCCIO. Ass: do you suppose I have trusted myself in this territory without precautions? My father has made a wager with your feudal lord here about me.

SQUARCIO. What wager, may it please your Excellency?

FERRUCCIO. What wager, blockhead! Why, that if I am assassinated, the murderer will not be brought to justice.

SQUARCIO. So that if I kill you—

FERRUCCIO. Your Baron will lose ten crowns unless you are broken on the wheel for it.

SQUARCIO. Only ten crowns, Excellency! Your father does not value your life very highly.

FERRUCCIO. Dolt. Can you not reason? If the sum were larger your Baron would win it by killing me himself and breaking somebody else on the wheel for it: you, most likely. Ten crowns is just enough to make him break you on the wheel if you kill me, but not enough to pay for all the masses that would have to be said for him if the guilt were his.

SQUARCIO. That is very clever, Excellency. [Sheathing his sword]. You shall not be slain: I will take care of that. If anything happens, it will be an accident.

FERRUCCIO. Body of Bacchus! I forgot that trick. I should have killed you when my blood was hot.

SQUARCIO. Will your Excellency please to step in? My best room and my best cooking are at your Excellency's disposal.

FERRUCCIO. To the devil with your mangy kennel! You want to tell every traveller that Count Ferruccio slept in your best bed and was eaten by your army of fleas. Take yourself out of my sight when you have told me where the next inn is.

SQUARCIO. I'm sorry to thwart your Excellency; but I have not forgotten your father's wager; and until you leave this territory I shall stick to you like your shadow.

FERRUCCIO. And why, pray?

SQUARCIO. Someone else might kill your Excellency; and, as you say, my illustrious Baron might break me on the wheel for your father's ten crowns. I must protect your Excellency, whether your Excellency is willing or not.

FERRUCCIO. If you dare to annoy me, I'll handle your bones so that there will be nothing left for the hangman to break. Now what do you say?

SQUARCIO. I say that your Excellency overrates your Excellency's strength. You would have no more chance against me than a grasshopper. [Ferruccio makes a demonstration]. Oh, I know that your Excellency has been taught by fencers and wrestlers and the like; but I can take all you can give me without turning a hair, and settle the account when you are out of breath. That is why

common men are dangerous, your Excellency: they are inured to toil and endurance. Besides, I know all the tricks.

THE GIRL. Do not attempt to quarrel with my father, Count. It must be as he says. It is his profession to kill. What could you do against him? If you want to beat somebody, you must beat me. [She goes into the inn].

SQUARCIO. I advise you not to try that, Excellency. She also is very strong.

FERRUCCIO. Then I shall have a headache: thats all. [He throws himself ill-humoredly on a bench at the table outside the inn. Giulia returns with a tablecloth and begins preparing the table for a meal].

SQUARCIO. A good supper, Excellency, will prevent that. And Giulia will sing for you.

FERRUCCIO. Not while theres a broomstick in the house to break her ugly head with. Do you suppose I'm going to listen to the howling of a she-wolf who wanted me to absolve her for getting me killed?

SQUARCIO. The poor must live as well as the rich, sir. Giulia is a good girl. [He goes into the inn].

FERRUCCIO [shouting after him] Must the rich die that the poor may live?

GIULIA. The poor often die that the rich may live.

FERRUCCIO. What an honor for them! But it would have been no honor for me to die merely that you might marry your clod of a fisherman.

GIULIA. You are spiteful, Signor.

FERRUCCIO. I am no troubadour, Giuliaccia, if that is what you mean.

GIULIA. How did you know about my Sandro and his mother? How were you so wise when you pretended to be an old friar? you that are so childish now that you are yourself!

FERRUCCIO. I take it that either Saint Barbara inspired me, or else that you are a great fool.

GIULIA. Saint Barbara will surely punish you for that wicked lie you told about her hand.

FERRUCCIO. The hand that thrilled you?

GIULIA. That was blasphemy. You should not have done it. You made me feel as if I had had a taste of heaven; and then you poisoned it in my heart as a taste of hell. That was wicked and cruel. You nobles are cruel.

FERRUCCIO. Well! do you expect us to nurse your babies for you? Our work is to rule and to fight. Ruling is nothing but inflicting cruelties on wrongdoers: fighting is nothing but being cruel to one's enemies. You poor people leave us all the cruel work, and then wonder that we are cruel. Where would you be if we left it undone? Outside the life I lead all to myself—the life of thought and poetry—I know only two pleasures: cruelty and lust. I desire revenge: I desire women. And both of them disappoint me when I get them.

GIULIA. It would have been a good deed to kill you, I think.

FERRUCCIO. Killing is always sport, my Giuliaccia.

SANDRO'S VOICE [on the lake] Giulietta! Giulietta!

FERRUCCIO [calling to him] Stop that noise. Your Giulietta is here with a young nobleman. Come up and amuse him. [To Giulietta] What will you give me if I tempt him to defy his mother and marry you without a dowry?

GIULIA. You are tempting me. A poor girl can give no more than she has. I should think you were a devil if you were not a noble, which is worse. [She goes out to meet Sandro].

FERRUCCIO [calling after her] The devil does evil for pure love of it: he does not ask a price: he offers it. [Squarcio returns]. Prepare supper for four, bandit.

SQUARCIO. Is your appetite so great in this heat, Signor?

FERRUCCIO. There will be four to supper. You, I, your daughter, and Sandro. Do not stint yourselves: I pay for all. Go and prepare more food.

SQUARCIO. Your order is already obeyed, Excellency.

FERRUCCIO. How?

SQUARCIO. I prepared for four, having you here to pay. The only difference your graciousness makes is that we shall have the honor to eat with you instead of after you.

FERRUCCIO. Dog of a bandit: you should have been born a nobleman.

SQUARCIO. I was born noble, Signor; but as we had no money to maintain our pretensions, I dropped them. [He goes back into the inn].
Giulia returns with Sandro.

GIULIA. This is the lad, Excellency. Sandro: this is his lordship Count Ferruccio.

SANDRO. At your lordship's service.

FERRUCCIO. Sit down, Sandro. You, Giulia, and Squarcio are my guests. [They sit].

GIULIA. Ive told Sandro everything, Excellency.

FERRUCCIO. And what does Sandro say? [Squarcio returns with a tray].

GIULIA. He says that if you have ten crowns in your purse, and we kill you, we can give them to the Baron. It would be the same to him as if he got it from your illustrious father.

SQUARCIO. Stupid: the Count is cleverer than you think. No matter how much money you give the Baron he can always get ten crowns more by breaking me on the wheel if the Count is killed.

GIULIA. That is true. Sandro did not think of that.

SANDRO [with cheerful politeness] Oh! what a head I have! I am not clever, Excellency. At the same time you must know that I did not mean my Giulietta to tell you. I know my duty to your Excellency better than that.

FERRUCCIO. Come! You are dear people: charming people. Let us get to work at the supper. You shall be the mother of the family and give us our portions, Giulietta. [They take their places]. Thats right. Serve me last, Giulietta. Sandro is hungry.

SQUARCIO [to the girl] Come come! do you not see that his Excellency will touch nothing until we have had some first. [He eats]. See, Excellency! I have tasted everything. To tell you the truth, poisoning is an art I do not understand.

FERRUCCIO. Very few professional poisoners do, Squarcio. One of the best professionals in Rome poisoned my uncle and aunt. They are alive still. The poison cured my uncle's gout, and only made my aunt thin, which was exactly what she desired, poor lady, as she was losing her figure terribly.

SQUARCIO. There is nothing like the sword, Excellency.

SANDRO. Except the water, Father Squarcio. Trust a fisherman to know that. Nobody can tell that drowning was not an accident.

FERRUCCIO. What does Giulietta say?

GIULIA. I should not kill a man if I hated him. You cannot torment a man when he is dead. Men kill because they think it is what they call a satisfaction. But that is only fancy.

FERRUCCIO. And if you loved him? Would you kill him then?

GIULIA. Perhaps. If you love a man you are his slave: everything he says—everything he does—is a stab to your heart: every day is a long dread of losing him. Better kill him if there be no other escape.

FERRUCCIO. How well you have brought up your family, Squarcio! Some more omelette, Sandro?

SANDRO [*very cheerfully*] I thank your Excellency. [*He accepts and eats with an appetite*].

FERRUCCIO. I pledge you all. To the sword and the fisherman's net: to love and hate! [*He drinks: they drink with him*].

SQUARCIO. To the sword!

SANDRO. To the net, Excellency, with thanks for the honor.

GIULIA. To love, Signor.

FERRUCCIO. To hate: the noble's portion!

SQUARCIO. The meal has done you good, Excellency. How do you feel now?

FERRUCCIO. I feel that there is nothing but a bait of ten crowns between me and death, Squarcio.

SQUARCIO. It is enough, Excellency. And enough is always enough.

SANDRO. Do not think of that, Excellency. It is only that we are poor folk, and have to consider how to make both ends meet as one may say. [*Looking at the dish*] Excellency—?

FERRUCCIO. Finish it, Sandro. Ive done.

SANDRO. Father Squarcio?

SQUARCIO. Finish it, finish it.

SANDRO. Giulietta?

GIULIA [*surprised*] Me? Oh no. Finish it, Sandro: it will only go to the pig.

SANDRO. Then, with your Excellency's permission—[*he helps himself*].

SQUARCIO. Sing for his Excellency, my daughter.

Giulia turns to the door to fetch her mandoline.

FERRUCCIO. I shall jump into the lake, Squarcio, if your cat begins to miaowl.

SANDRO [*always cheerful and reassuring*] No, no, Excellency: Giulietta sings very sweetly: have no fear.

FERRUCCIO. I do not care for singing: at least not the singing of peasants. There is only one thing for which one woman will do as well as another, and that is lovemaking. Come, Father Squarcio: I will buy Giulietta from you: you can have her back for nothing when I am tired of her. How much?

SQUARCIO. In ready money, or in promises?

FERRUCCIO. Old fox. Ready money.

SQUARCIO. Fifty crowns, Excellency.

FERRUCCIO. Fifty crowns! Fifty crowns for that blackfaced devil! I would not give fifty crowns for one of my mother's ladies-in-waiting. Fifty pence, you must mean.

SQUARCIO. Doubtless your Excellency, being a younger son, is poor. Shall we say five and twenty crowns?

FERRUCCIO. I tell you she is not worth five.

SQUARCIO. Oh, if you come to what she is worth, Excellency, what are any of us worth? I take it that you are a gentleman, not a merchant.

GIULIA. What are you worth, Signorino?

FERRUCCIO. I am accustomed to be asked for favors, Giuliaccia, not to be asked impertinent questions.

GIULIA. What would you do if a strong man took you by the scruff of your neck, or his daughter thrust a knife in your throat, Signor?

FERRUCCIO. It would be many a year, my gentle Giuliaccia, before any baseborn man or woman would dare threaten a nobleman again. The whole village would be flayed alive.

SANDRO. Oh no, Signor. These things often have a great air of being accidents. And the great families are well content that they should appear so. It is such a great trouble to flay a whole village alive. Here by the water, accidents are so common.

SQUARCIO. We of the nobility, Signor, are not strict enough. I learnt that when I took to breeding horses. The horses you breed from thoroughbreds are not all worth the trouble: most of them are screws. Well, the horsebreeder gets rid of his screws for what they will fetch: they go to labor like any peasant's beast. But our nobility does not study its business so carefully. If you are a screw, and the son of a baron, you are brought up to think yourself a little god, though you are nothing, and cannot rule yourself, much less a province. And you presume, and presume, and presume—

GIULIA. And insult, and insult, and insult.

SQUARCIO. Until one day you find yourself in a strange place with nothing to help you but your own hands and your own wits—

GIULIA. And you perish—

SANDRO. Accidentally—

GIULIA. And your soul goes crying to your father for vengeance—

SQUARCIO. If indeed, my daughter, there be any soul left when the body is slain.

FERRUCCIO [*crossing himself hastily*] Dog of a bandit: do you dare doubt the existence of God and the soul?

SQUARCIO. I think, Excellency, that the soul is so precious a gift that God will not give it to a man for nothing. He must earn it by being something and doing something. I should not like to kill a man with a good soul. Ive had a dog that had, I'm persuaded, made itself something of a soul; and if anyone had murdered that dog, I would have slain him. But shew me a man with no soul: one who has never done anything or been anything; and I will kill him for ten crowns with as little remorse as I would stick a pig.

SANDRO. Unless he be a nobleman, of course—

SQUARCIO. In which case the price is fifty crowns.

FERRUCCIO. Soul or no soul?

SQUARCIO. When it comes to a matter of fifty crowns, Excellency, business is business. The man who pays me must square the account with the devil. It is for my employer to consider whether the action be a good one or no: it is for me to earn his money honestly. When I said I should not like to kill a man with a good soul, I meant killing on my own account: not professionally.

FERRUCCIO. Are you such a fool then as to spoil your own trade by sometimes killing people for nothing?

SQUARCIO. One kills a snake for nothing, Excellency. One kills a dog for nothing sometimes.

SANDRO [apologetically] Only a mad dog, Excellency, of course.

SQUARCIO. A pet dog, too. One that eats and eats and is useless, and makes an honest man's house dirty. [He rises]. Come, Sandro, and help me to clean up. You, Giulia, stay and entertain his Excellency.

He and Sandro make a hammock of the cloth, in which they carry the wooden platters and fragments of the meal indoors. Ferruccio is left alone with Giulia. The gloaming deepens.

FERRUCCIO. Does your father do the house work with a great girl like you idling about? Squarcio is a fool, after all.

GIULIA. No, Signor: he has left me here to prevent you from escaping.

FERRUCCIO. There is nothing to be gained by killing me, Giuliaccia.

GIULIA. Perhaps; but I do not know. I saw Sandro make a sign to my father: that is why they went in. Sandro has something in his head.

FERRUCCIO [brutally] Lice, no doubt.

GIULIA [unmoved] That would only make him scratch his head, Signor, not make signs

with it to my father. You did wrong to throw the Cardinal out of the window.

FERRUCCIO. Indeed: and pray why?

GIULIA. He will pay thirty crowns for your dead body. Then Sandro could marry me.

FERRUCCIO. And be broken on the wheel for it.

GIULIA. It would look like an accident, Signor. Sandro is very clever; and he is so humble and cheerful and good-tempered that people do not suspect him as they suspect my father.

FERRUCCIO. Giulietta: if I reach Sacromonte in safety, I swear to send you thirty crowns by a sure messenger within ten days. Then you can marry your Sandro. How does that appeal to you?

GIULIA. Your oath is not worth twenty pence, Signor.

FERRUCCIO. Do you think I will die here like a rat in a trap— [his breath fails him].

GIULIA. Rats have to wait in their traps for death, Signor. Why not you?

FERRUCCIO. I'll fight.

GIULIA. You are welcome, Signor. The blood flows freeest when it is hot.

FERRUCCIO. She devil! Listen to me, Giulietta—

GIULIA. It is useless, Signor. Giulietta or Giuliaccia: it makes no difference. If they two in there kill you it will be no more to me—except for the money—than if my father trod on a snail.

FERRUCCIO. Oh, it is not possible that I, a nobleman, should die by such filthy hands.

GIULIA. You have lived by them, Signor. I see no sign of any work on your own hands. We can bring death as well as life, we poor people, Signor.

FERRUCCIO. Mother of God, what shall I do?

GIULIA. Pray, Signor.

FERRUCCIO. Pray! With the taste of death in my mouth? I can think of nothing.

GIULIA. It is only that you have forgotten your beads, Signor [she picks up the Friar's rosary]. You remember the old man's bones rattling. Here they are [she rattles them before him].

FERRUCCIO. That reminds me. I know of a painter in the north that can paint such beautiful saints that the heart goes out of one's body to look at them. If I get out of this alive I'll make him paint St Barbara so that everyone can see that she is lovelier than St Cecilia, who looks like my washerwoman's mother in her Chapel in our cathedral. Can you give St Cecilia a picture if she lets me be killed?

GIULIA. No; but I can give her many prayers.

FERRUCCIO. Prayers cost nothing. She will prefer the picture unless she is a greater fool than I take her to be.

GIULIA. She will thank the painter for it, not you, Signor. And I'll tell her in my prayers to appear to the painter in a vision, and order him to paint her just as he sees her if she really wishes to be painted.

FERRUCCIO. You are devilishly ready with your answers. Tell me, Giulietta: is what your father told me true? Is your blood really noble?

GIULIA. It is red, Signor, like the blood of the Christ in the picture in Church. I do not know if yours is different. I shall see when my father kills you.

FERRUCCIO. Do you know what I am thinking, Giulietta?

GIULIA. No, Signor.

FERRUCCIO. I am thinking that if the good God would oblige me by taking my fool of an elder brother up to heaven, and his silly doll of a wife with him before she has time to give him a son, you would make a rare duchess for me. Come! Will you help me to outwit your father and Sandro if I marry you afterwards?

GIULIA. No, Signor: I'll help them to kill you.

FERRUCCIO. My back is to the wall, then?

GIULIA. To the precipice, I think, Signor.

FERRUCCIO. No matter, so my face is to the danger. Did you notice, Giulia, a minute ago? I was frightened.

GIULIA. Yes, Signor. I saw it in your face.

FERRUCCIO. The terror of terrors.

GIULIA. The terror of death.

FERRUCCIO. No: death is nothing. I can face a stab just as I faced having my tooth pulled out at Faenza.

GIULIA [shuddering with sincere sympathy] Poor Signorino! That must have hurt horribly.

FERRUCCIO. What! You pity me for the tooth affair, and you did not pity me in that hideous agony of terror that is not the terror of death nor of anything else, but pure grim terror in itself.

GIULIA. It was the terror of the soul, Signor. And I do not pity your soul: you have a wicked soul. But you have pretty teeth.

FERRUCCIO. The toothache lasted a week; but the agony of my soul was too dreadful to last five minutes: I should have died of it if it could have kept its grip of me. But you helped me out of it.

GIULIA. I, Signor!

FERRUCCIO. Yes: you. If you had pitied me: if you had been less inexorable than death itself, I should have broken down and cried and begged for mercy. But now I have come up against something hard: something real: something that does not care for me. I see now the truth of my excellent uncle's opinion that I was a spoilt cub. When I wanted anything I threatened men or ran crying to women; and they gave it to me. I dreamed and romanced: imagining things as I wanted them, not as they really are. There is nothing like a good look into the face of death: close up: right on you: for shewing you how little you really believe and how little you really are. A priest said to me once, "In your last hour everything will fall away from you except your religion." But I have lived through my last hour; and my religion was the first thing that fell away from me. When I was forced at last to believe in grim death I knew at last what belief was, and that I had never believed in anything before: I had only flattered myself with pretty stories, and sheltered myself behind Mumbo Jumbo, as a soldier will shelter himself from arrows behind a clump of thistles that only hide the shooters from him. When I believe in everything that is real as I believed for that moment in death, then I shall be a man at last. I have tasted the water of life from the cup of death; and it may be now that my real life began with this [he holds up the rosary] and will end with the triple crown or the heretic's fire: I care not which. [Springing to his feet] Come out, then, dog of a bandit, and fight a man who has found his soul. [Squarcio appears at the door, sword in hand. Ferruccio leaps at him and strikes him full in the chest with his dagger. Squarcio puts back his left foot to brace himself against the shock. The dagger snaps as if it had struck a stone wall].

GIULIA. Quick, Sandro.

Sandro, who has come stealing round the corner of the inn with a fishing net, casts it over Ferruccio, and draws it tight.

SQUARCIO. Your Excellency will excuse my shirt of mail. A good home blow, nevertheless, Excellency.

SANDRO. Your Excellency will excuse my net: it is a little damp.

FERRUCCIO. Well, what now? Accidental drowning, I suppose.

SANDRO. Eh, Excellency, it is such a pity to throw a good fish back into the water when once you have got him safe in your net. My Giulietta: hold the net for me.

GIULIA [*taking the net and twisting it in her hands to draw it tighter round him*] I have you very fast now, Signorino, like a little bird in a cage.

FERRUCCIO. You have my body, Giulia. My soul is free.

GIULIA. Is it, Signor? I think Saint Barbara has got that in her net too. She has turned your jest into earnest.

SANDRO. It is indeed true, sir, that those who come under the special protection of God and the Saints are always a little mad; and this makes us think it very unlucky to kill a madman. And since from what Father Squarcio and I overheard, it is clear that your Excellency, though a very wise and reasonable young gentleman in a general way, is somewhat cracked on the subject of the soul and so forth, we have resolved to see that no harm comes to your Excellency.

FERRUCCIO. As you please. My life is only a drop falling from the vanishing clouds to the everlasting sea, from finite to infinite, and itself part of the infinite.

SANDRO [*impressed*] Your Excellency speaks like a crazy but very holy book. Heaven forbid that we should raise a hand against you! But your Excellency will notice that this good action will cost us thirty crowns.

FERRUCCIO. Is it not worth it?

SANDRO. Doubtless, doubtless. It will in fact save us the price of certain masses which we should otherwise have had said for the souls of certain persons who—ahem! Well, no matter. But we think it dangerous and unbecoming that a nobleman like your Excellency should travel without a retinue, and unarmed; for your dagger is unfortunately broken, Excellency. If you would therefore have the condescension to accept Father Squarcio as your man-at-arms—your servant in all but the name, to save his nobility—he will go with you to any town in which you will feel safe from His Eminence the Cardinal, and will leave it to your Excellency's graciousness as to whether his magnanimous conduct will not then deserve some trifling present: say a wedding gift for my Giulietta.

FERRUCCIO. Good: the man I tried to slay will save me from being slain. Who would have thought Saint Barbara so full of irony!

SANDRO. And if the offer your Excellency was good enough to make in respect of Giulietta still stands—

FERRUCCIO. Rascal: have you then no soul?

SANDRO. I am a poor man, Excellency: I cannot afford these luxuries of the rich.

FERRUCCIO. There is a certain painter will presently make a great picture of St Barbara; and Giulia will be his model. He will pay her well. Giulia: release the bird. It is time for it to fly.

She takes the net from his shoulders.

COOLE PARK, *Summer*, 1909.

THE END

XXXVII

PASSION, POISON, AND PETRIFACTION; OR, THE FATAL GAZOGENE

A BRIEF TRAGEDY FOR BARNS AND BOOTHS

In a bed-sitting room in a fashionable quarter of London a lady sits at her dressing-table, with her maid combing her hair. It is late; and the electric lamps are glowing. Apparently the room is bedless; but there stands against the opposite wall to that at which the dressing-table is placed a piece of furniture that suggests a bookcase without carrying conviction. On the same side is a chest of drawers of that disastrous kind which, recalcitrant to the opener until she is provoked to violence, then suddenly come wholly out and defy all her efforts to fit them in again. Opposite this chest of drawers, on the lady's side of the room, is a cupboard. The presence of a row of gentleman's boots beside the chest of drawers proclaims that the lady is married. Her own boots are beside the cupboard. The third wall is pierced midway by the door, above which is a cuckoo clock. Near the door a pedestal bears a portrait bust of the lady in plaster. There is a fan on the dressing-table, a hatbox and rug strap on the chest of drawers, an umbrella and a bootjack against the wall near the bed. The general impression is one of brightness, beauty, and social ambition, damped by somewhat inadequate means. A certain air of theatricality is produced by the fact that though the room is rectangular it has only three walls. Not a sound is heard except the overture and the crackling of the lady's hair as the maid's brush draws electric sparks from it in the dry air of the London midsummer.

The cuckoo clock strikes sixteen.

THE LADY. How much did the clock strike, Phyllis?

PHYLLIS. Sixteen, my lady.

THE LADY. That means eleven o'clock, does it not?

PHYLLIS. Eleven at night, my lady. In the morning it means half-past two; so if you hear it strike sixteen during your slumbers, do not rise.

THE LADY. I will not, Phyllis. Phyllis: I am weary. I will go to bed. Prepare my couch.

Phyllis crosses the room to the bookcase and touches a button. The front of the bookcase falls out with a crash and becomes a bed. A roll of distant thunder echoes the crash.

PHYLLIS [*shuddering*] It is a terrible night. Heaven help all poor mariners at sea! My master is late. I trust nothing has happened to him. Your bed is ready, my lady.

THE LADY. Thank you, Phyllis. [*She rises and approaches the bed*]. Goodnight.

PHYLLIS. Will your ladyship not undress?

THE LADY. Not tonight, Phyllis. [*Glancing through where the fourth wall is missing*] Not under the circumstances.

PHYLLIS [*impulsively throwing herself on her knees by her mistress's side, and clasping her round the waist*] Oh, my beloved mistress, I know not why or how; but I feel that I shall never see you alive again. There is murder in the air. [*Thunder*]. Hark!

THE LADY. Strange! As I sat there methought I heard angels singing, Oh, wont you come home, Bill Bailey? Why should angels call me Bill Bailey? My name is Magnesia Fitztollemache.

PHYLLIS [*emphasizing the title*] Lady Magnesia Fitztollemache.

LADY MAGNESIA. In case we should never

again meet in this world, let us take a last farewell.

PHYLLIS [*embracing her with tears*] My poor murdered angel mistress!

LADY MAGNESIA. In case we should meet again, call me at half-past eleven.

PHYLLIS. I will, I will.

Phyllis withdraws, overcome by emotion. Lady Magnesia switches off the electric light, and immediately hears the angels quite distinctly. They sing Bill Bailey so sweetly that she can attend to nothing else, and forgets to remove even her boots as she draws the coverlet over herself and sinks to sleep, lulled by celestial harmony. A white radiance plays on her pillow, and lights up her beautiful face. But the thunder growls again; and a lurid red glow concentrates itself on the door, which is presently flung open, revealing a saturnine figure in evening dress, partially concealed by a crimson cloak. As he steals towards the bed the unnatural glare in his eyes and the broad-bladed dagger nervously gripped in his right hand bode ill for the sleeping lady. Providentially she sneezes on the very brink of eternity; and the tension of the murderer's nerves is such that he bolts precipitately under the bed at the sudden and startling Atscha! A dull, heavy, rhythmic thumping—the beating of his heart—betrays his whereabouts. Soon he emerges cautiously and raises his head above the bed coverlet level.

THE MURDERER. I can no longer cower here listening to the agonized thumpings of my own heart. She but snoze in her sleep. I'll do't. [*He again raises the dagger. The angels sing again. He cowers*] What is this? Has that tune reached Heaven?

LADY MAGNESIA [*waking and sitting up*] My husband! [*All the colors of the rainbow chase one another up his face with ghastly brilliancy*]. Why do you change color? And what on earth are you doing with that dagger?

FITZ [*affecting unconcern, but unhinged*] It is a present for you: a present from mother. Pretty, isnt it? [*he displays it fatuously*].

LADY MAGNESIA. But she promised me a fish slice.

FITZ. This is a combination fish slice and dagger. One day you have salmon for dinner. The next you have a murder to commit. See?

LADY MAGNESIA. My sweet mother-in-law! [*Someone knocks at the door*]. That is Adolphus's knock. [*Fitz's face turns a dazzling green*]. What has happened to your complexion? You have turned green. Now I think of it, you always do when Adolphus is mentioned. Arnt you going to let him in?

FITZ. Certainly not. [*He goes to the door*]. Adolphus: you cannot enter. My wife is undressed and in bed.

LADY MAGNESIA [*rising*] I am not. Come in, Adolphus [*she switches on the electric light*].

ADOLPHUS [*without*] Something most important has happened. I must come in for a moment.

FITZ [*calling to Adolphus*] Something important happened? What is it?

ADOLPHUS [*without*] My new clothes have come home.

FITZ. He says his new clothes have come home.

LADY MAGNESIA [*running to the door and opening it*] Oh, come in, come in. Let me see.

Adolphus Bastable enters. He is in evening dress, made in the latest fashion, with the right half of the coat and the left half of the trousers yellow and the other halves black. His silver-spangled waistcoat has a crimson handkerchief stuck between it and his shirt front.

ADOLPHUS. What do you think of it?

LADY MAGNESIA. It is a dream! a creation! [*she turns him about to admire him*].

ADOLPHUS [*proudly*] I shall never be mistaken for a waiter again.

FITZ. A drink, Adolphus?

ADOLPHUS. Thanks.

Fitztollemache goes to the cupboard and takes out a tray with tumblers and a bottle of whisky. He puts them on the dressing-table.

FITZ. Is the gazogene full?

LADY MAGNESIA. Yes: you put in the powders yourself today.

FITZ [*sardonically*] So I did. The special powders! Ha! ha! ha! ha! ha! [*his face is again strangely variegated*].

LADY MAGNESIA. Your complexion is really going to pieces. Why do you laugh in that silly way at nothing?

FITZ. Nothing! Ha, ha! Nothing! Ha, ha, ha!

ADOLPHUS. I hope, Mr Fitztollemache, you are not laughing at my clothes. I warn you that I am an Englishman. You may laugh at my manners, at my brains, at my national institutions; but if you laugh at my clothes, one of us must die.

Thunder.

FITZ. I laughed but at the irony of Fate [*he takes a gazogene from the cupboard*].

ADOLPHUS [*satisfied*] Oh, that! Oh, yes, of course!

FITZ. Let us drown all unkindness in a loving cup. [*He puts the gazogene on the floor in the middle of the room*]. Pardon the absence of a table: we found it in the way and pawned it. [*He takes the whisky bottle from the dressing-table*].

LADY MAGNESIA. We picnic at home now. It is delightful.

She takes three tumblers from the dressing-table and sits on the floor, presiding over the gazogene, with Fitz and Adolphus squatting on her left and right respectively. Fitz pours whisky into the tumblers.

FITZ [*as Magnesia is about to squirt soda into his tumbler*] Stay! No soda for me. Let Adolphus have it all—all. I will take mine neat.

LADY MAGNESIA [*proffering tumbler to Adolphus*] Pledge me, Adolphus.

FITZ. Kiss the cup, Magnesia. Pledge her, man. Drink deep.

ADOLPHUS. To Magnesia!

FITZ. To Magnesia! [*The two men drink*] It is done. [*Scrambling to his feet*] Adolphus: you have but ten minutes to live—if so long.

ADOLPHUS. What mean you?

MAGNESIA [*rising*] My mind misgives me. I have a strange feeling here [*touching her heart*].

ADOLPHUS. So have I, but lower down [*touching his stomach*]. That gazogene is disagreeing with me.

FITZ. It was poisoned!

Sensation.

ADOLPHUS [*rising*] Help! Police!

FITZ. Dastard! you would appeal to the law? Can you not die like a gentleman?

ADOLPHUS. But so young! when I have only worn my new clothes once.

MAGNESIA. It is too horrible. [*To Fitz*] Fiend! what drove you to this wicked deed?

FITZ. Jealousy. You admired his clothes: you did not admire mine.

ADOLPHUS. My clothes [*his face lights up with heavenly radiance*]! Have I indeed been found worthy to be the first clothes-martyr? Welcome, death! Hark! angels call me. [*The celestial choir again raises its favorite chant. He listens with a rapt expression. Suddenly the angels sing out of tune; and the radiance on the poisoned man's face turns a sickly green*] Yah—ah! Oh—ahoo! The gazogene is disagreeing extremely. Oh! [*he throws himself on the bed, writhing*].

MAGNESIA [*to Fitz*] Monster: what have you done? [*She points to the distorted figure on the *bed*]. That was once a Man, beautiful and glorious. What have you made of it? A writhing, agonized, miserable, moribund worm.

ADOLPHUS [*in a tone of the strongest remonstrance*] Oh, I say! Oh, come! No: look here, Magnesia! Really!

MAGNESIA. Oh, is this a time for petty vanity? Think of your misspent life—

ADOLPHUS [*much injured*] W h o s e misspent life?

MAGNESIA [*continuing relentlessly*] Look into your conscience: look into your stomach. [*Adolphus collapses in hideous spasms. She turns to Fitz*] And this is y o u r handiwork!

FITZ. Mine is a passionate nature, Magnesia. I must have your undivided love. I must have your love: do you hear? LOVE! LOVE!! LOVE!!! LOVE!!!! LOVE!!!!!

He raves, accompanied by a fresh paroxysm from the victim on the bed.

MAGNESIA [*with sudden resolution*] You s h a l l have it.

FITZ [*enraptured*] Magnesia! I have recovered your love! Oh, how slight appears the sacrifice of this man compared to so glorious a reward! I would poison ten men without a thought of self to gain one smile from you.

ADOLPHUS [*in a broken voice*] Farewell, Magnesia: my last hour is at hand. Farewell, farewell, farewell!

MAGNESIA. At this supreme moment, George Fitztollemache, I solemnly dedicate to you all that I formerly dedicated to poor Adolphus.

ADOLPHUS. Oh, please not poor Adolphus yet. I still live, you know.

MAGNESIA. The vital spark but flashes before it vanishes. [*Adolphus groans*]. And now, Adolphus, take this last comfort from the unhappy Magnesia Fitztollemache. As I have dedicated to George all that I gave to you, so I will bury in your grave—or in your urn if you are cremated—all that I gave to him.

FITZ. I hardly follow this.

MAGNESIA. I will explain. George: hitherto I have given Adolphus all the romance of my nature—all my love—all my dreams—all my caresses. Henceforth they are yours!

FITZ. Angel!

MAGNESIA. Adolphus: forgive me if this pains you.

ADOLPHUS. Dont mention it. I hardly feel it. The gazogene is so much worse. [*Taken bad again*] Oh!

MAGNESIA. Peace, poor sufferer: there is still some balm. You are about to hear what I am going to dedicate to y o u.

ADOLPHUS. All I ask is a peppermint lozenge, for mercy's sake.

MAGNESIA. I have something far better than any lozenge: the devotion of a lifetime. Formerly it was George's. I kept his house, or rather, his lodgings. I mended his clothes. I darned his socks. I bought his food. I interviewed his creditors. I stood between him and the servants. I administered his domestic finances. When his hair needed cutting or his countenance was imperfectly washed, I pointed it out to him. The trouble that all this gave me made him prosaic in my eyes. Familiarity bred contempt. Now all that shall end. My husband shall be my hero, my lover, my perfect knight. He shall shield me from all care and trouble. He shall ask nothing in return but love—boundless, priceless, rapturous, soul-enthralling love, LOVE! LOVE!! LOVE!!! [*she raves and flings her arms about Fitz*]. And the duties I formerly discharged shall be replaced by the one supreme duty of duties: the duty of weeping at Adolphus's tomb.

FITZ [*reflectively*] My ownest, this sacrifice makes me feel that I have perhaps been a little selfish. I cannot help feeling that there is much to be said for the old arrangement. Why should Adolphus die for my sake?

ADOLPHUS. I am not dying for your sake, Fitz. I am dying because you poisoned me.

MAGNESIA. You do not fear to die, Adolphus, do you?

ADOLPHUS. N-n-no, I dont exactly f e a r to die. Still—

FITZ. Still, if an antidote—

ADOLPHUS [*bounding from the bed*] Antidote!

MAGNESIA [*with wild hope*] Antidote!

FITZ. If an antidote would not be too much of an anti-climax.

ADOLPHUS. Anti-climax be blowed! Do you think I am going to die to please the critics? Out with your antidote. Quick!

FITZ. The best antidote to the poison I have given you is lime, plenty of lime.

ADOLPHUS. Lime! You mock me! Do you think I carry lime about in my pockets?

FITZ. There is the plaster ceiling.

MAGNESIA. Yes, the ceiling. Saved, saved, saved!

All three frantically shy boots at the ceiling.

Flakes of plaster rain down which Adolphus devours, at first ravenously, then with a marked falling off in relish.

MAGNESIA [*picking up a huge slice*] Take this, Adolphus: it is the largest [*she crams it into his mouth*].

FITZ. Ha! a lump off the cornice! Try this.

ADOLPHUS [*desperately*] Stop! stop!

MAGNESIA. Do not stop. You will die. [*She tries to stuff him again*].

ADOLPHUS [*resolutely*] I prefer death.

MAGNESIA and FITZ [*throwing themselves on their knees on either side of him*] For our sakes, Adolphus, persevere.

ADOLPHUS. No: unless you can supply lime in liquid form, I must perish. Finish that ceiling I cannot and will not.

MAGNESIA. I have a thought—an inspiration. My bust. [*She snatches it from its pedestal and brings it to him*].

ADOLPHUS [*gazing fondly at it*] Can I resist it?

FITZ. Try the bun.

ADOLPHUS [*gnawing at the knot of hair at the back of the bust's head: it makes him ill*]. Yah, I cannot. I cannot. Not even y o u r bust, Magnesia. Do not ask me. Let me die.

FITZ [*pressing the bust on him*] Force yourself to take a mouthful. Down with it, Adolphus!

ADOLPHUS. Useless. It would not stay down. Water! Some fluid! Ring for something to drink [*he chokes*].

MAGNESIA. I will save you [*she rushes to the bell and rings*].

Phyllis, in her night-gown, with her hair prettily made up into a chevaux de frise of crocuses with pink and yellow curl papers, rushes in straight to Magnesia.

PHYLLIS [*hysterically*] My beloved mistress, once more we meet. [*She sees Fitztollemache and screams*] Ah! ah! ah! A man! [*She sees Adolphus*] Men!! [*She flies; but Fitztollemache seizes her by the night-gown just as she is escaping*]. Unhand me, villain!

FITZ. This is no time for prudery, girl. Mr Bastable is dying.

PHYLLIS [*with concern*] Indeed, sir? I hope he will not think it unfeeling of me to appear at his deathbed in curl papers.

MAGNESIA. We know you have a good heart, Phyllis. Take this [*giving her the bust*]; dissolve it in a jug of hot water; and bring it back instantly. Mr Bastable's life depends on your haste.

PHYLLIS [*hesitating*] It do seem a pity, dont it, my lady, to spoil your lovely bust?

ADOLPHUS. Tush! This craze for fine art is beyond all bounds. Off with you [*he pushes her out*]. Drink, drink, drink! My entrails are parched. Drink! [*he rushes deliriously to the gazogene*].

FITZ [*rushing after him*] Madman, you forget! It is poisoned!

ADOLPHUS. I dont care. Drink, drink! [*They wrestle madly for the gazogene. In the struggle they squirt all its contents away, mostly into one another's face. Adolphus at last flings Fitztollemache to the floor, and puts the spout into his mouth*]. Empty! empty! [*with a shriek of despair he collapses on the bed, clasping the gazogene like a baby, and weeping over it*].

FITZ [*aside to Magnesia*] Magnesia: I have always pretended not to notice it; but you keep a siphon for your private use in my hat-box.

MAGNESIA. I use it for washing old lace; but no matter: he shall have it [*she produces a siphon from the hat-box, and offers a tumbler of soda-water to Adolphus*].

ADOLPHUS. Thanks, thanks, oh, thanks! [*he drinks. A terrific fizzing is heard. He starts up screaming*] Help! help! The ceiling is effervescing! I am BURSTING! [*He wallows convulsively on the bed*].

FITZ. Quick! the rug strap! [*They pack him with blankets and strap him*]. Is that tight enough?

MAGNESIA [*anxiously*] Will you hold, do you think?

ADOLPHUS. The peril is past. The soda-water has gone flat.

MAGNESIA and FITZ. Thank heaven!

Phyllis returns with a washstand ewer, in which she has dissolved the bust.

MAGNESIA [*snatching it*] At last!

FITZ. You are saved. Drain it to the dregs.

Fitztollemache holds the lip of the ewer to Adolphus's mouth and gradually raises it until it stands upside down. Adolphus's efforts to swallow it are fearful, Phyllis thumping his back when he chokes, and Magnesia loosening the straps when he moans. At last, with a sigh of relief, he sinks back in the women's arms. Fitz shakes the empty ewer upside down like a potman shaking the froth out of a flagon.

ADOLPHUS. How inexpressibly soothing to the chest! A delicious numbness steals through all my members. I would sleep.

MAGNESIA
FITZ }[*whispering*] Let him sleep.
PHYLLIS

He sleeps. Celestial harps are heard; but their chords cease on the abrupt entrance of the landlord, a vulgar person in pujamas.

THE LANDLORD. Eah! Eah! Wots this? Wots all this noise? Ah kin ennybody sleep through it? [*Looking at the floor and ceiling*] Ellow! wot you bin doin te maw ceilin?

FITZ. Silence, or leave the room. If you wake that man he dies.

THE LANDLORD. If e kin sleep through the noise you three mikes e kin sleep through ennythink.

MAGNESIA. Detestable vulgarian: your pronunciation jars on the finest chords of my nature. Begone!

THE LANDLORD [*looking at Adolphus*] Aw downt blieve eze esleep. Aw blieve eze dead. [*Calling*] Pleece! Pleece! Merder! [*A blue halo plays mysteriously on the door, which opens and reveals a policeman. Thunder*]. Eah, pleecmin: these three's bin an merdered this gent between em, an naw tore moy ahse dahn.

THE POLICEMAN [*offended*] Policeman, indeed! Wheres your manners?

FITZ. Officer—

THE POLICEMAN [*with distinguished consideration*] Sir?

FITZ. As between gentlemen—

THE POLICEMAN [*bowing*] Sir: to you.

FITZ [*bowing*] I may inform you that my friend had an acute attack of indigestion. No carbonate of soda being available, he swallowed a portion of this man's ceiling. [*Pointing to Adolphus*] Behold the result!

THE POLICEMAN. The ceiling was poisoned! Well, of all the artful— [*he collars the landlord*]. I arrest you for wilful murder.

THE LANDLORD [*appealing to the heavens*] Ow, is this jestice! Ah could aw tell e wiz gowin te eat moy ceilin?

THE POLICEMAN [*releasing him*] True. The case is more complicated than I thought. [*He tries to lift Adolphus's arm but cannot*]. Stiff already.

THE LANDLORD [*trying to lift Adolphus's leg*] An' precious evvy. [*Feeling the calf*] Woy, eze gorn ez awd ez niles.

FITZ [*rushing to the bed*] What is this?

MAGNESIA. Oh, say not he is dead. Phyllis: fetch a doctor. [*Phyllis runs out. They all try to lift Adolphus; but he is perfectly stiff, and as heavy as lead*]. Rouse him. Shake him.

THE POLICEMAN [*exhausted*] Whew! Is he a man or a statue? [*Magnesia utters a piercing scream*]. Whats wrong, Miss?

MAGNESIA [*to Fitz*] Do you not see what has happened?

FITZ [*striking his forehead*] Horror on horror's head!

THE LANDLORD. Wotjemean?

MAGNESIA. The plaster has set inside him. The officer was right: he is indeed a living statue.

Magnesia flings herself on the stony breast of Adolphus. Fitztollemache buries his head in his hands; and his chest heaves convulsively. The policeman takes a small volume from his pocket and consults it.

THE POLICEMAN. This case is not provided for in my book of instructions. It dont seem no use trying artificial respiration, do it? [*To the landlord*] Here! lend a hand, you. We'd best take him and set him up in Trafalgar Square.

THE LANDLORD. Aushd pat im in the cestern an worsh it aht of im.

Phyllis comes back with a Doctor.

PHYLLIS. The medical man, my lady.

THE POLICEMAN. A poison case, sir.

THE DOCTOR. Do you mean to say that an unqualified person! a layman! has dared to administer poison in my district?

THE POLICEMAN [*raising Magnesia tenderly*] It looks like it. Hold up, my lady.

THE DOCTOR. Not a moment must be lost. The patient must be kept awake at all costs. Constant and violent motion is necessary.

He snatches Magnesia from the Policeman, and rushes her about the room.

FITZ. Stop! That is not the poisoned person!

THE DOCTOR. It is you, then. Why did you not say so before?

He seizes Fitztollemache and rushes him about.

THE LANDLORD. Naow, naow, thet ynt im.

THE DOCTOR. What, you!

He pounces on the Landlord and rushes him round.

THE LANDLORD. Eah! chack it. [*He trips the Doctor up. Both fall*]. Jest owld this leoonatic, will you, Mister Horficer?

THE POLICEMAN [*dragging both of them to their feet*] Come out of it, will you. You must all come with me to the station.

Thunder.

MAGNESIA. What! In this frightful storm!

The hail patters noisily on the window.

PHYLLIS. I think it's raining.

The wind howls.

THE LANDLORD. It's thanderin and lawtnin.

FITZ. It's dangerous.

THE POLICEMAN [*drawing his baton and whistle*] If you wont come quietly, then—

He whistles. A fearful flash is followed by an appalling explosion of heaven's artillery. A thunderbolt enters the room, and strikes the helmet of the devoted constable, whence it is attracted to the waistcoat of the doctor by the lancet in his pocket. Finally it leaps with fearful force on the landlord, who, being of a gross and spongy nature, absorbs the electric fluid at the cost of his life. The others look on horror-stricken as the three victims, after reeling, jostling, cannoning through a ghastly quadrille, at last sink inanimate on the carpet.

MAGNESIA [*listening at the doctor's chest*] Dead!

FITZ [*kneeling by the landlord, and raising his hand, which drops with a thud*] Dead!

PHYLLIS [*seizing the looking-glass and holding it to the Policeman's lips*] Dead!

FITZ [*solemnly rising*] The copper attracted the lightning.

MAGNESIA [*rising*] After life's fitful fever they sleep well. Phyllis: sweep them up.

Phyllis replaces the looking-glass on the dressing-table; takes up the fan; and fans the Policeman, who rolls away like a leaf before the wind to the wall. She disposes similarly of the landlord and doctor.

PHYLLIS. Will they be in your way if I leave them there until morning, my lady?

Or shall I bring up the ashpan and take them away?

MAGNESIA. They will not disturb us. Goodnight, Phyllis.

PHYLLIS. Goodnight, my lady. Goodnight, sir.

She retires.

MAGNESIA. And now, husband, let us perform our last sad duty to our friend. He has become his own monument. Let us erect him. He is heavy; but love can do much.

FITZ. A little leverage will get him on his feet. Give me my umbrella.

MAGNESIA. True.

She hands him the umbrella, and takes up the bootjack. They get them under Adolphus's back, and prize him up on his feet.

FITZ. Thats done it! Whew!

MAGNESIA [*kneeling at the left hand of the statue*] For ever and for ever, Adolphus.

FITZ [*kneeling at the right hand of the statue*] The rest is silence.

The Angels sing Bill Bailey. The statue raises its hands in an attitude of blessing, and turns its limelit face to heaven as the curtain falls. National Anthem.

ATTENDANTS [*in front*] All out for the next performance. Pass along, please, ladies and gentlemen: pass along.

THE END

XXXVIII

THE FASCINATING FOUNDLING

A DISGRACE TO THE AUTHOR

Morning. Office of the Lord Chancellor. Door on the right leading to his private room, near the fireplace. Door on the left leading to the public staircase. Mercer, an elderly clerk, seated at work. Enter, to him, through the public door, Horace Brabazon, a smart and beautiful young man of nineteen, dressed in the extremity of fashion, with a walking stick.

BRABAZON. I want to see the Lord Chancellor.

MERCER. Have you an appointment?

BRABAZON. No.

MERCER. Then you cant see the Lord Chancellor.

BRABAZON. I tell you I must see him.

MERCER. I tell you you cant. Look here. do you think the Lord Chancellor's a palmist or a hair doctor that people can rush in out of the street and see him whenever they want to?

BRABAZON. That speech was meant to insult and humiliate me. I make it a rule to fight people who attempt to insult and humiliate me. [*Throwing away his stick*] Put up your hands. [*He puts up his own*].

MERCER. Here: you let me alone. You leave this office, d'ye hear; or I'll have the police in on you.

BRABAZON. You are face to face with your destiny; and your destiny is to fight me. Be quick: I'm going to begin. Dont look pale: I scorn to take you by surprise. I shall lead off with my left on your right eye. Put them up.

MERCER. I aint going to fight you. Let me alone, will you? I said nothing to you.

BRABAZON. Liar and slave. Fight, I tell you: fight.

MERCER. Oh, was there ever the like of this? Dont make such a noise.

BRABAZON. I'm making it on purpose. I want you to fight because itll make more noise than anything else. The Lord Chancellor will come to see what the noise is about if only it's loud enough. Time! [*he spars*].

MERCER [*retreating to the fireplace and snatching up the poker*] Ah, would you? You come near me, and I'll split your head open, I will.

BRABAZON [*snatching up the tongs, and engaging him in a stage fight of the noisiest*] Lay on, Macduff; and damned be he that first cries Hold! Enough!

The Lord Chancellor enters indignantly.

THE LORD CHANCELLOR. Whats this? Who is this gentleman?

BRABAZON. The Lord Chancellor. Good. [*To Mercer*] Hence, horrible shadow: unreal mockery, hence. My lord, I have called on professional business. In the matter of Brabazon, an infant.

THE LORD CHANCELLOR. If you are a solicitor, sir, you must be aware that this is not the proper way to approach the Court.

BRABAZON. I approach you as the father of all the orphans in Chancery.

THE LORD CHANCELLOR. Sir—

BRABAZON. Dont fly out: I'll explain everything. You remember the matter of Brabazon, an infant. Come, now! frankly as man to man you do remember the matter of Brabazon, an infant.

THE LORD CHANCELLOR. There is such a case, I believe.

BRABAZON. Of course there is. Well, I'm the infant. I'm Brabazon. I'll call thee Hamlet! King! father! Royal Dane: wilt thou not answer me? [*Prosaically*] Now you see, dont you?

THE LORD CHANCELLOR. You are young Horace Brabazon, are you?

BRABAZON. I am, my lord. Such is life!

THE LORD CHANCELLOR. You are a ward of the Court; and you have systematically disobeyed every order made in your case.

BRABAZON. The orders were unreasonable. Fatuous, in fact.

THE LORD CHANCELLOR. Sir—

BRABAZON. Let me explain. One of the orders was that I was to go into the Church.

THE LORD CHANCELLOR. At your own desire.

BRABAZON. Exactly. But I should not have been indulged. I was too young. How did I know what was good for me? I put it to you as one man to another: do I look like an archbishop?

THE LORD CHANCELLOR. Stuff, sir.

BRABAZON. As you say, nothing could have been more idiotic. You ought to have known better. No: the Church is not in my line. Nature intended me for the stage. The Unreal Mockery here was practising Macduff with me when you came in. Now what I want to know is, can you get me an engagement? As your ward, I have a right to expect that of you. You must know lots of people who could give me a start. And theres another thing: very important. I— Oh, by the way, wont you sit down? Excuse me keeping you standing all this time. Macduff: a chair.

THE LORD CHANCELLOR [*with ironic politeness*] You are too good. [*He sits down*].

BRABAZON. Dont mention it. Well, you know: I want some good home influence to steady me. You see you cant steady me: youre too much occupied here with your shop: besides, you may shake a loose leg yourself occasionally for all the public knows, eh? Even if you are virtuous, I should probably lead you astray. No: what I want is a wife. Not a young woman, you know. Someone old enough to be my mother: say thirty or so. I adore a mature woman. Not old enough to be your mother, you understand: old enough to be my mother. I attach some importance to that distinction; so be good enough to bear it in mind. One mustnt overdo these notions.

THE LORD CHANCELLOR. Mr Mercer, will you be good enough to make a careful note of this gentleman's requirements: an engagement at a leading theatre to play Macbeth, and a wife of quiet habits and grave disposition. Anything else, Mr Brabazon?

BRABAZON. Nothing today, thank you. And now, I know better than to take up the time of a busy man. Happy to have made your acquaintance. So long! Ta, ta, Macduff.

He goes out.

THE LORD CHANCELLOR. What do you mean

by letting this lunatic in, Mr Mercer? I'm extremely annoyed.

MERCER. I didnt let him in, my lord. He came in. I was keeping him from you at the risk of my life when you came in to ask what the noise was.

THE LORD CHANCELLOR [*with emotion*] My faithful Mercer.

MERCER. My honored master. [*They shake hands, weeping*].

THE LORD CHANCELLOR. We were happy together until this man came between us.

MERCER. Let us try to forget him, my lord. [*Turns to his desk and sees Brabazon's walking stick on the floor*] My lord, he has left his walking stick behind. He will return for it. Let us fly. [*He picks it up and puts it on the desk*].

THE LORD CHANCELLOR. Nonsense, Mercer: we have no aeroplane; and if we had we shouldnt know how to use it. Hark! A visitor at the door. [*They both rush to it. The handle is turned*]. Tell him we have both gone out.

MERCER. Useless, my lord: he is a man of strong reasoning powers: he would conclude, on hearing our voices, that we were both within.

A WOMAN'S VOICE. Is anybody there? Let me in. [*She rattles the door*].

THE LORD CHANCELLOR. That is the voice of a young and probably beautiful woman.

MERCER. It is, my lord.

THE LORD CHANCELLOR. Then why the dickens dont you open the door instead of striking melodramatic attitudes? How dare you keep the lady waiting? I'm very much annoyed.

MERCER. I'm sorry, my lord. [*He opens the door*].

Anastasia Vulliamy enters.

ANASTASIA [*to Mercer*] Is this the Lord Chancellor's?

MERCER. Yes.

ANASTASIA. Sir Cardonius Boshington's?

MERCER. Yes, maam.

ANASTASIA. Are you the Lord Chancellor?

MERCER. No, maam. Leastways, not yet.

ANASTASIA. What are you?

MERCER. I'm the Lord Chancellor's—

ANASTASIA. Secretary?

MERCER. Well, hardly that, maam. If you ask me, I should say I was a sort of what you might call a clerk-valet to his lordship.

ANASTASIA. Are you a gentleman?

MERCER [*staggered*] Well, thats a poser, Miss, really. I'm in a manner of speaking a gentleman.

ANASTASIA. In what manner of speaking are you a gentleman?

MERCER. Well, Miss, I'm a gentleman to my tobacconist. Every man is a gentleman to his tobacconist. The parliamentary candidate for Hornsey always addresses me as a gentleman. But then he aint particular: leastways, not at election times. You see, Miss, there are three classes of gentry in this country.

ANASTASIA. Only three?

MERCER. Only three, maam.

ANASTASIA. How do you tell one from the other?

MERCER. You tell by the railway porters, Miss. The real upper class gives them a shilling; the upper middle class sixpence; and the lower middle, tuppence. I give tuppence myself.

ANASTASIA. And which particular class of gentleman is it, pray, that gives a lady a chair?

MERCER. Oh, I'm sure I beg your pardon, Miss. [*He places a chair for her*].

ANASTASIA. Thanks. And now will you be good enough to tell Sir Cardonius Boshington that Miss Anastasia Vulliamy wishes to see him?

MERCER [*to the Lord Chancellor*] Miss Anaesthesia Vulliamy, my lord, to see you.

ANASTASIA [*springing up*] Do you mean to tell me that this old man in livery is the great Chancellor?

THE LORD CHANCELLOR. At your service, Miss Vulliamy.

ANASTASIA [*producing a newspaper*] Quite impossible. I have here an article on Sir Cardonius, headed Our Great Chancellor; and the description does not correspond in the least. [*Reading*] "No man of our time has succeeded in tempering the awe inspired by a commanding stature and majestic presence with a love and confidence which even the youngest and most timid ward of the Court feels at the sound of his kindly voice and the encouraging beam, twinkling with humor, of his tender grey eyes." Do you mean to tell me that thats you?

THE LORD CHANCELLOR. It is not for me to say how far the description is an accurate or a happy one, madam; but I believe I am the person intended by the writer.

MERCER [*producing another paper*] Perhaps youd recognize this better, Miss. Sir Car-

2 O

donius and me is on opposite sides in politics.

ANASTASIA [*taking the paper and reading at the place he indicates*] "How much longer will the nation allow this despicable pantaloon to occupy the woolsack—" Whats the woolsack?

MERCER. What the Lord Chancellor sits on in the House of Lords, Miss.

ANASTASIA [*continuing her reading*] "whose contents only too strongly resemble those of his own head." Thats a nasty one, you know: isnt it? It means that your brains are woolly, doesnt it?

THE LORD CHANCELLOR. Its meaning is entirely beneath my notice. I'm surprised, Mercer, to find you in possession of a scurrilous rag of this character. We may differ in our opinions; but if any paper taken in by me were to speak of you in such unbecoming terms, I should never open it again.

MERCER. Well, my lord; politics is politics; and after all, what is politics if it isnt shewing up the other side? When I pay a penny for a paper Ive a right to get value for my money the same as any other man.

ANASTASIA. But I dont understand [*To the Chancellor*] A r e you a despicable pantaloon? The other paper says your name will be cherished by the warm hearts of the English people when Eldon and Sir Thomas More are forgotten. I thought that whatever is in the papers must be true. How do you explain being a great Chancellor and a despicable pantaloon at the same time?

THE LORD CHANCELLOR. I take it that the excellent journal from which you first quoted has put all considerations of party aside, and simply endeavored to place before you a dispassionate estimate of such modest services as I have been able to render to my country. The other paper gives you nothing but the vituperative ravings of an illiterate penny-a-liner blinded by party passion.

MERCER. You should never read more than one paper, Miss. It unsettles the mind, let alone the waste of a penny.

ANASTASIA. Well, it's a great relief to me to hear that the Great Chancellor paper is the right one. [*To the Lord Chancellor*] You think I may believe everything it says?

THE LORD CHANCELLOR. I trust I shall not disappoint any favorable opinion you may have founded on it.

ANASTASIA. It says here that though you are stern with the worthless and merciless to the impostor, yet your mature wisdom and unparalleled legal knowledge are freely at the service of all deserving persons, and that no distressed suitor has ever been turned empty away from your door.

THE LORD CHANCELLOR. That refers to my private house, madam. I dont keep food here.

MERCER. I have a sandwich for my lunch, Miss. Sooner than send you empty away, I would give it to you, Miss, most joyfully.

ANASTASIA. I ask, not charity, but justice.

THE LORD CHANCELLOR. Madam: I must request you to speak like a lady and not like a procession of the unemployed. The House of Lords always gives charity and never gives justice.

MERCER. The House of Lords will find itself unemployed one of these days, if you ask me.

THE LORD CHANCELLOR. Silence, Mercer. Have the goodness to keep your Radicalism to yourself in the presence of this lady.

ANASTASIA. Why do you allow your clerk to be a Radical?

THE LORD CHANCELLOR. Well, madam, to make him a Conservative and an Imperialist I should have to raise his salary very considerably; and I prefer to save money and put up with a Radical.

ANASTASIA. Youll excuse me asking you all these questions; but as Ive decided, after what the paper says, that you are the man to advise me and be a father to me, it's very important that you should be quite all right, isnt it?

THE LORD CHANCELLOR. But it's not my business to be a father to every young lady who walks into my office.

ANASTASIA. Not your business! Why, Whitaker's Almanack says you get £10,000 a year. You dont get that for nothing, I suppose. [*To Mercer*] By the way, Whitaker doesnt say how much you get.

MERCER. I get one-fifty.

ANASTASIA. One-fifty into £5000 goes about 33 times. Why does he get 33 times as much as you? Is he thirty-three times as good?

MERCER. He thinks so.

THE LORD CHANCELLOR. I set up no such ridiculous pretension, Mercer.

ANASTASIA [*to the Lord Chancellor*] Perhaps youre 33 times as sober. How much do you drink every day?

THE LORD CHANCELLOR. I am almost a teetotaller. A single bottle of burgundy is quite sufficient for me.

ANASTASIA [*to Mercer*] Then I suppose you drink 33 bottles of burgundy a day.

MERCER. 33 bottles of burgundy a day on one-fifty a year! Not me. It hardly runs to beer on Sundays.

ANASTASIA. Well, there must be something awfully wrong about you, you know, if you get only the thirty-third of what he gets.

THE LORD CHANCELLOR. No, madam. Mercer is an excellent man in his proper place.

ANASTASIA. Then there must be something awfully right about you.

THE LORD CHANCELLOR. I hope so.

ANASTASIA. I dont see the difference myself.

MERCER. He's better fed.

ANASTASIA. Is he? I should have thought he was too red about the nose to be quite healthy. It's the burgundy, I expect. However, I didnt come here to talk about you two. Call it selfish if you will; but I came to talk about myself. The fact is, I'm an orphan. At least, I think I am.

THE LORD CHANCELLOR. Dont you know?

ANASTASIA. No. I was brought up in what you might politely call a sort of public institution. They found me on the doorstep, you know. Might have happened to anybody, mightnt it?

MERCER [*scandalized*] And you have the audacity to come here and talk up to us as if you was a lady. Be off with you; and be ashamed of yourself, you hussy.

THE LORD CHANCELLOR. Gently, Mercer, gently. It is not the poor girl's fault.

MERCER. Not her fault! Why, she aint anybody's daughter: she's only an offspring.

ANASTASIA. Perhaps I'm his daughter, my lord.

MERCER. Oh, you wicked girl! Oh, you naughty story, you! Oh, that I should have lived to have this accusation brought against me: me! a respectable man!

ANASTASIA. I had a feeling the moment I saw you.

THE LORD CHANCELLOR. The voice of Nature! Oh, Mercer, Mercer!

MERCER. I'll have the law of you for this, I will. Oh, say you dont believe her, my lord. Dont drive me mad. Say you dont believe her.

THE LORD CHANCELLOR. I cant disregard the voice of Nature, Mercer. The evidence against you is very black.

MERCER. Me the father of a common girl found on a workhouse doorstep!

ANASTASIA [*rising most indignantly*] How dare you presume to say such a thing? A workhouse doorstep indeed! I was found on the doorstep of one of the very best houses in Park Lane.

THE LORD CHANCELLOR [*overwhelmed*] My dear young lady, how can I apologize—

MERCER [*crushed*] I'm sure I beg your pardon most humbly, Miss.

THE LORD CHANCELLOR. Forget the rudeness of my clerk: he knows no better. Resume your seat, I beg.

MERCER. If I had only known, Miss! Park Lane! I could bite my tongue out for my bad manners, I do assure you.

ANASTASIA. Say no more. Of course you could not know my social position.

MERCER. Dont say that, Miss. You have Park Lane in every feature.

THE LORD CHANCELLOR [*effusively*] In your manners.

MERCER. In your accent.

THE LORD CHANCELLOR. In your tone—

MERCER. Address—

THE LORD CHANCELLOR. A je ne sais quoi—

MERCER. A tout ensemble—

ANASTASIA. You speak French?

MERCER. Not a word, Miss; but at the sight of that hat of yours the French fairly burst out of me.

ANASTASIA. You are very good—

THE LORD CHANCELLOR. } Oh, not at all.
MERCER. } Dont mention it.

ANASTASIA. Dont begin again. I forgive you both. Now, attention! I'm a good-hearted but somewhat flighty girl; and I require some serious interest in life to steady me. As I had an ungovernable appetite, and was naturally rather inclined to be stout, I tried politics. For you, a man, politics meant the House of Lords. For me, a woman, politics meant Holloway Gaol and the hunger strike. I refused to take food until I was so frightfully hungry that when the Governor—who was a plump, chubby, tempting sort of man, you know—came into my cell and remonstrated with me, I attempted to devour him.

THE LORD CHANCELLOR. Pardon me. I thought you Suffragist lambs prided yourselves on acting always on principle. On what principle, may I ask, do you justify an attempt to devour an estimable public official?

ANASTASIA. On the Cat and Mouse principle, my lord. That is a part of the law of England.

MERCER. Never. Not when the woman is the cat.

THE LORD CHANCELLOR. May I ask, madam, what the unfortunate mouse did on this occasion?

ANASTASIA. He got quite angry, and said he wouldnt have me in his prison another minute—not if I went down on my knees and begged him to let me stay. Of course I refused to go; but I had to let the poor man have his way at last, though it took ten wardresses to persuade me to do it. I left them simply in ribbons, poor things. Prison made a great change in me. Before I went in I felt a great want of something to love; but when I came out I felt nothing but a great want of something to eat. There were two public houses near the prison. One had a placard up "Sausage and Mashed," the other "Sandwich and Small Lloyd George." I visited both in succession, and had two goes of each delicacy. I then drove to the Holborn Restaurant and had a five shilling lunch, stopping at three Pearce and Plentys on the way to sustain exhausted nature. At the Holborn they refused to serve me with a second lunch; so I went on to the Carlton. Of my subsequent experiences at the Savoy, Pagani's, Frascati's, Gatti's, five baked potato men, and a coffee stall, I shall say nothing. Suffice it that when at last the craving for food was stilled, the craving for love returned in all its original force. I felt I must have something to cherish, to sacrifice myself for. You no doubt hold that self-sacrifice is a woman's chief amusement.

THE LORD CHANCELLOR. Certainly I do.

ANASTASIA. Any man would. Well, what was I to love? My friends recommended marriage: a man, in fact. But I hesitated to rush at once to so expensive and troublesome an extreme. I tried a pet dog; but when it had been stolen for the sixth time by the man I bought it from, I refused to pay any more rewards, and we were parted for ever. I tried a cat; but its conduct was so disreputable that I really could not live in the same house with it. I adopted the orphan child of a crossing sweeper who was run over; but when its aunt learnt that I had no parents she would not permit it to stay. Glad as I must confess I was to get rid of the little beast, my starved heart still ached, my empty arms still longed to gather some beloved object to my breast.

THE LORD CHANCELLOR. If I can be of any service to you, madam—

ANASTASIA. You? You are married, are you not?

THE LORD CHANCELLOR. Well, er, yes, I er— am married.

MERCER [catching her eye] I'm sorry, Miss; but so am I. Still, a divorce would be a matter of only eighty pound or so if we made it a fairly straight case.

ANASTASIA. Never shall it be said that Anastasia Vulliamy built her happiness on the ruin of another woman's home. There are younger and handsomer men than you, my lord: there are more genteel characters than Mercer. Neither of you, if I may be allowed the expression, is precisely what I should call a peach. And I want—oh, I want a peach. He must be a young peach. Not that I am to be seduced by the fleeting charms of a smooth cheek and a slim figure. But it's a necessity of my position as a woman that I should marry someone whom I can bully, because if a woman cant bully her husband, her husband generally bullies her.

You, my lord, you will, you can,
Find me a young and foolish man.
Into my arms: under my thumb
Let him come, let him come.

I fear I am almost dropping into poetry; but the tumult of my emotions carries me away. I implore you not to keep me waiting. My soul, my soul is thrilling as it never thrilled before. My arms, my arms are longing as they never longed before. My heart, my heart is beating as it never bet before. Every nerve in my body, every fibre in my heart—

Brabazon enters.

BRABAZON. Excuse me: I left my stick, I think—

ANASTASIA [throwing herself into his arms] He has come: he has come: the very thing I want.

BRABAZON. Quite out of the question, my dear lady. Sir Cardonius will tell you that you are too young, too irresponsible, too impulsive to be anything more to me than an extremely agreeable object of contemplation, and a charming hostess. With that object may I venture to propose a marriage to you?

ANASTASIA. Silly! that is exactly what I am proposing to you.

BRABAZON. Not marriage to the same person, I think. You, as I understand it, propose to marry me. I propose that you should marry one of my friends. You can then invite me to your house, and put on your best company manners for my benefit. He will have the privilege of paying for your hats, and enjoying your no-company manners.

MERCER. My lord: this man has a giant intellect.

THE LORD CHANCELLOR. It will avail him as little as if he were the biggest fool in creation. Young man: you are lost. I argued as you do. I tried to get out of it.

MERCER. I moved all the way from Gospel Oak to Islington to escape; but it was no use.

THE LORD CHANCELLOR. Beware how you anger her by shewing any reluctance. Remember: "Hell hath no fury like a woman scorned."

MERCER. Whats the good of that nowadays? When that was written a woman would take no for an answer. She wont now.

ANASTASIA. You will begin walking out with me at once. You are only on approval, of course; but if you suit, you may consider next Friday three weeks named as the day.

BRABAZON. But where does the merit come in for me? Where is the moral discipline? Where is the self-sacrifice? You are an agreeable person: to marry you would be an act of pure selfishness.

ANASTASIA. So you think now, dearest. You wont think that a year hence. I'll take care of that for my own boy.

BRABAZON. Yes, but look here, you know. Have you any money?

ANASTASIA. Not a rap.

BRABAZON. And you expect to get a slave for nothing. What cheek!

ANASTASIA. I'm richer than you think, darling. It's true that I'm a poor penniless orphan. Doesnt that touch you?

BRABAZON. Not in the least.

ANASTASIA. Thoughtless boy. Have you forgotten that the women who have money always belong to some family or other?

BRABAZON. Well?

ANASTASIA. Well, a family means relations. You cant call your house your own. The brothers borrow money. The sisters come and stay for months. The mother quarrels with your mother.

MERCER. Gospel truth, every word of it.

THE LORD CHANCELLOR. Undeniable. [He sighs deeply].

ANASTASIA. I, my love, am not perfect. I am a weak woman: I have nothing to cling to but your love, nor any place to rest except your very becoming fancy waistcoat. But at least I'm a foundling.

BRABAZON [excited and hopeful] A foundling?

ANASTASIA. I havnt a relation in the world.

BRABAZON [clasping her] Mine! mine!! MINE!!!

AYOT ST LAWRENCE,
10th August 1909.

THE END

XXXIX

THE MUSIC-CURE

A PIECE OF UTTER NONSENSE

Lord Reginald Fitzambey, a fashionably dressed, rather pretty young man of 22, is prostrate on a sofa in a large hotel drawing room, crying convulsively. His doctor is trying to soothe him. The doctor is about a dozen years his senior; and his ways are the ways of a still youthful man who considers himself in smart society as well as professionally attendant on it.

The drawing room has tall central doors, at present locked. If anyone could enter under these circumstances, he would find on his left a grand piano with the keyboard end towards him, and a smaller door beyond the piano. On his right would be the window, and, further on, the sofa

on which the unhappy youth is wallowing, with, close by it, the doctor's chair and a little table accommodating the doctor's hat, a plate, a medicine bottle, a half emptied glass, and a bell call.

THE DOCTOR. Come come! be a man. Now really this is silly. You mustnt give way like this. I tell you nothing's happened to you. Hang it all! it's not the end of the world if you did buy a few shares——

REGINALD [interrupting him frantically] I never meant any harm in buying those shares. I am ready to give them up. Oh, I never meant any harm in buying those shares.

I never meant any harm in buying those shares. [*Clutching the doctor imploringly*] Wont you believe me, Doctor? I never meant any harm in buying those shares. I never—

THE DOCTOR [*extricating himself and replacing Reginald on the couch, not very gently*] Of course you didnt. I know you didnt.

REGINALD. I never—

THE DOCTOR [*desperate*] Dont go on saying that over and over again or you will drive us all as distracted as you are yourself. This is nothing but nerves. Remember that youre in a hotel. Theyll put you out if you make a row.

REGINALD [*tearfully*] But you dont understand. Oh, why wont anybody understand? I never—

THE DOCTOR [*shouting him down*] You never meant any harm in buying those shares. This is the four hundredth time youve said it.

REGINALD [*wildly*] Then why do you keep asking me the same questions over and over again? It's not fair. Ive told you I never meant any harm in—

THE DOCTOR. Yes, yes, yes: I know, I know. You think you made a fool of yourself before that committee. Well, you didnt. You stood up to it for six days with the coolness of an iceberg and the cheerfulness of an idiot. Every member of it had a go at you; and everyone of them, including some of the cleverest cross-examiners in London, fell back baffled before your fatuous self-satisfaction, your impenetrable inability to see any reason why you shouldnt have bought those shares.

REGINALD. But why shouldnt I have bought them? I made no secret of it. When the Prime Minister ragged me about it I offered to sell him the shares for what I gave for them.

THE DOCTOR. Yes, after they had fallen six points. But never mind that. The point for you is that you are an under-secretary in the War Office. You knew that the army was going to be put on vegetarian diet, and that the British Maccaroni Trust shares would go up with a rush when this became public. And what did you do?

REGINALD. I did what any fellow would have done. I bought all the shares I could afford.

THE DOCTOR. You bought a great many more than you could afford.

REGINALD. But why shouldnt I? Explain it to me. I'm anxious to learn. I meant no harm. I see no harm. Why am I to be badgered because the beastly Opposition papers and all the Opposition rotters on that committee try to make party capital out of it by saying that it was disgraceful? It wasnt disgraceful: it was simple common sense. I'm not a financier; but you cant persuade me that if you happen to know that certain shares are going to rise you shouldnt buy them. It would be flying in the face of Providence not to. And they wouldnt see that. They pretended not to see it. They worried me, and kept asking me the same thing over and over again, and wrote blackguardly articles about me—

THE DOCTOR. And you got the better of them all because you couldnt see their point of view. But what beats me is why you broke down afterwards.

REGINALD. Everyone was against me. I thought the committee a pack of fools; and I as good as told them so. But everyone took their part. The governor said I had disgraced the family name. My brothers said I ought to resign from my clubs. My mother said that all her hopes of marrying me to a rich woman were shattered. And I'd done nothing: absolutely nothing to what other chaps are doing every day.

THE DOCTOR. Well, the long and short of it is that officials mustnt gamble.

REGINALD. But I wasnt gambling. I knew. It isnt gambling if you know that the shares will go up. It's a cert.

THE DOCTOR. Well, all I can tell you is that if you werent a son of the Duke of Dunmow, youd have to resign; and—

REGINALD [*breaking down*] Oh, stop talking to me about it. Let me alone. I cant bear it. I never meant any harm in buying those shares. I never meant any harm—

THE DOCTOR. Sh-sh-sh-sh-sh! There: I shouldnt have started the subject again. Take some of this valerian [*he puts the glass to Reginald's lips*]. Thats right. Now youre better.

REGINALD [*exhausted but calm*] Why does valerian soothe me when it excites cats? Theres a question to reflect on! You know, they ought to have made me a philosopher.

THE DOCTOR. Philosophers are born, not made.

REGINALD. Fine old chestnut, that. Everybody's born, not made.

THE DOCTOR. Youre getting almost clever.

I dont like it: youre not yourself today. I wish I could take your mind off your troubles. Suppose you try a little music.

REGINALD. I cant play. My fingers wont obey me. And I cant stand the sound of the piano. I sounded a note this morning; and it made me scream.

THE DOCTOR. But why not get somebody to play to you?

REGINALD. Whom could I get, even if I could bear it? You cant play.

THE DOCTOR. Well: I'm not the only person in the world.

REGINALD. If you bring anyone else in here, I shall go mad. I'll throw myself out of the window. I cant bear the idea of music. I dread it, hate it, loathe it.

THE DOCTOR. Thats very serious, you know.

REGINALD. Why is it serious?

THE DOCTOR. Well, what would become of you without your turn for music? You have absolutely no capacity in any other direction.

REGINALD. I'm in Parliament. And I'm an under-secretary.

THE DOCTOR. Thats because your father is a Duke. If you were in a Republic you wouldnt be trusted to clean boots, unless your father was a millionaire. No, Reginald: the day you give up vamping accompaniments and playing the latest ragtimes by ear, youre a lost man socially.

REGINALD [deprecating] Oh, I say!

THE DOCTOR [rising] However, perhaps it's too soon for you to try the music-cure yet. It was your mother's idea; but I'll call and tell her to wait a day or two. I think she meant to send somebody to play. I must be off now. Look in again later. Meanwhile, sleep as much as you can. Or you might read a little.

REGINALD. What can I read?

THE DOCTOR. Try the Strand Magazine.

REGINALD. But it's so frightfully intellectual. It would overtax my brain.

THE DOCTOR. Oh, well, I suppose it would. Well, sleep. Perhaps I'd better give you something to send you off [he produces a medicine case].

REGINALD. Whats this? Veronal?

THE DOCTOR. Dont be alarmed. Only the old-fashioned remedy: opium. Take this [Reginald takes a pill]: that will do the trick, I expect. If you find after half an hour that it has only excited you, take another. I'll leave one for you [he puts one on the plate, and pockets his medicine case].

REGINALD. Better leave me a lot. I like pills.

THE DOCTOR. Thank you: I'm not treating you with a view to a coroner's inquest. You know, dont you, that opium is a poison?

REGINALD. Yes, opium. But not pills.

THE DOCTOR. Well, Heaven forbid that I, a doctor, should shake anybody's faith in pills. But I shant leave you enough to kill you. [He puts on his hat].

REGINALD. Youll tell them, wont you, not to let anyone in. Really and truly I shall throw myself out of the window if any stranger comes in. I should go out of my mind.

THE DOCTOR. None of us have very far to go to do that, my young friend. Ta ta, for the moment [he makes for the central doors].

REGINALD. You cant go out that way. I made my mother lock it and take away the key. I felt sure theyd let somebody in that way if she didnt. Youll have to go the way you came.

THE DOCTOR [returning] Right. Now let me see you settle down before I go. I want you to be asleep before I leave the room.

Reginald settles himself to sleep with his face to the back of the sofa. The doctor goes softly to the side door and goes out.

REGINALD [sitting up wildly and staring affrightedly at the piano] Doctor! Doctor! Help!!!

THE DOCTOR [returning hastily] What is it?

REGINALD [after another doubtful look at the piano] Nothing. [He composes himself to sleep again].

THE DOCTOR. Nothing! There must have been something or you wouldnt have yelled like that. [Pulling Reginald over so as to see his face] Here! what was it?

REGINALD. Well, it's gone.

THE DOCTOR. Whats gone?

REGINALD. The crocodile.

THE DOCTOR. The crocodile!

REGINALD. Yes. It laughed at me, and was going to play the piano with its tail.

THE DOCTOR. Opium in small doses doesnt agree with you, my young friend. [Taking the spare pill from the plate] I shall have to give you a second pill.

REGINALD. But suppose two crocodiles come!

THE DOCTOR. They wont. If anything comes it will be something pretty this time. Thats how opium acts. Anyhow, youll be fast asleep in ten minutes. Here. Take it.

REGINALD [*after taking the pill*] It was awfully silly of me. But you know I really saw the thing.

THE DOCTOR. You neednt trouble about what you see with your eyes shut. [*He turns to the door*].

REGINALD. Would you mind looking under the sofa to make sure the crocodile isnt there?

THE DOCTOR. Why not look yourself? that would be more convincing.

REGINALD. I darent.

THE DOCTOR. You duffer! [*He looks*]. All serene. No crocodile. Now go bye bye. [*He goes out*].

Reginald again composes himself to sleep. Somebody unlocks the central doors. A lovely lady enters with a bouquet in her hand. She looks about her; takes a letter from wherever she carries letters; and starts on a voyage of discovery round the room, checking her observations by the contents of the letter. The piano seems specially satisfactory: she nods as she sees it. Reginald seems also to be quite expected. She does not speak to him. When she is quite satisfied that she is in the right room, she goes to the piano and tantalizes the expectant audience for about two minutes by putting down her flowers on the candle-stand; taking off her gloves and putting them with the flowers; taking off half a dozen diamond rings in the same way; sitting down to the keyboard and finding it too near to the piano, then too far, then too high, then too low: in short, exhausting all the tricks of the professional pianist before she at last strikes the keys and preludes brilliantly. At the sound, Reginald, with a scream, rolls from the sofa and writhes on the carpet in horrible contortions. She stops playing, amazed.

REGINALD. Oh! Oh! Oh! The crocodiles! Stop! Ow! Oh! [*He looks at the piano and sees the lady*] Oh I say!

THE LADY. What on earth do you mean by making that noise when I'm playing? Have you no sense? Have you no manners?

REGINALD [*sitting on the floor*] I'm awfully sorry.

THE LADY. Sorry! Why did you do it?

REGINALD. I thought you were a crocodile.

THE LADY. What a silly thing to say! Do I look like a crocodile?

REGINALD. No.

THE LADY. Do I play like a crocodile!

REGINALD [*cautiously rising and approaching her*] Well, you know, it's so hard to know how a crocodile would play.

THE LADY. Stuff! [*She resumes her playing*].

REGINALD. Please! [*He stops her by shutting the keyboard lid*]. Who let you in?

THE LADY [*rising threateningly*] What is that to you, pray?

REGINALD [*retreating timidly*] It's my room, you know.

THE LADY. It's nothing of the sort. It's the Duchess of Dunmow's room. I know it's the right one, because she gave me the key; and it was the right key.

REGINALD. But what did she do that for? Who are you, if you dont mind my asking?

THE LADY. I do mind your asking. It's no business of yours. However, youd better know to whom you are speaking. I am Strega Thundridge. [*She pronounces it Strayga*].

REGINALD. What! The female Paderewski!

STREGA. Pardon me. I believe Mr Paderewski has been called the male Thundridge; but no gentleman would dream of repeating such offensive vulgarities. Will you be good enough to return to your sofa, and hold your tongue, or else leave the room.

REGINALD. But, you know, I am ill.

STREGA. Then go to bed, and send for a doctor. [*She sits down again to the keyboard*].

REGINALD [*falling on his knees*] You mustnt play. You really mustnt. I cant stand it. I shall simply not be myself if you start playing.

STREGA [*raising the lid*] Then I shall start at once.

REGINALD [*running to her on his knees and snatching at her hands*] No, you shant. [*She rises indignantly. He holds on to her hands, but exclaims ecstatically*] Oh, I say, what lovely hands youve got!

STREGA. The idea! [*She hurls him to the carpet*].

REGINALD [*on the floor staring at her*] You are strong.

STREGA. My strength has been developed by playing left hand octave passages—like this. [*She begins playing Liszt's transcription of Schubert's Erl König*].

REGINALD [*puts his fingers in his ears, but continues to stare at her*].

STREGA [*stopping*] I really cannot play if you keep your ears stopped. It is an insult. Leave the room.

REGINALD. But I tell you it's my room.

STREGA [*rising*] Leave the room, or I will ring your bell and have you put out. [*She goes to the little table, and poises her fingers over the bell call*].

REGINALD [*rushing to her*] No no: somebody will come if you ring; and I shall go distracted if a stranger comes in. [*With a touch of her left hand she sends him reeling. He appeals to her plaintively*] Dont you see that I am ill?

STREGA. I see that you are mentally afflicted. But that doesnt matter to me. The Duchess of Dunmow has engaged me to come to this room and play for two hours. I never break an engagement, especially a two hundred and fifty guinea one. [*She turns towards the piano*].

REGINALD. But didnt she tell you anything about me?

STREGA [*turning back to him*] She said there would be a foolish young man in the room, but that I was not to mind him. She assured me you were not dangerous except to yourself. [*Collaring him and holding him bent backwards over the piano*]. But I will have no nonsense about not listening. All the world listens when I play. Listen, or go.

REGINALD [*helpless*] But I shall have to sit on the stairs. I darent go into any of the rooms: I should meet people there.

STREGA. You will meet plenty of people on the stairs, young man. They are sitting six on each stair, not counting those who are sitting astride the banisters on the chance of hearing me play.

REGINALD. How dreadful! [*Tearfully*] Youve no right to bully me like this. I'm ill: I cant bear it. I'll throw myself out of the window.

STREGA [*releasing him*] Do. What an advertisement! It will be really kind of you. [*She goes back to the keyboard and sits down to play*].

REGINALD [*crossing to the window*] Youll be sorry you were so unfeeling when you see my mangled body. [*He opens the window; looks out; shuts it hastily, and retreats with a scream*]. Theres a crowd. I darent.

STREGA [*pleased*] Waiting to hear me play [*she preludes softly*].

REGINALD [*ravished*] Oh! I can stand that, you know.

STREGA [*ironically, still preluding*] Thank you.

REGINALD. The fact is, I can play a bit myself.

STREGA [*still preluding*] An amateur, I presume.

REGINALD. I have often been told I could make a living at it if I tried. But of course it wouldnt do for a man in my position to lower himself by becoming a professional.

STREGA [*abruptly ceasing to play*] Tactful, that, I dont think! And what do you play, may I ask?

REGINALD. Oh, all the very best music.

STREGA. For instance?

REGINALD. I wish you belonged to me.

STREGA [*rising outraged*] You young blackguard! How dare you?

REGINALD. You dont understand: it's the name of a tune. Let me play it for you. [*He sits down at the keyboard*] I dont think you believe I can play.

STREGA. Pardon me. I have heard a horse play the harmonium at a music hall. I can believe anything.

REGINALD. Aha! [*He plays*]. Do you like that?

STREGA. What is it? Is it intended for music?

REGINALD. Oh, you beautiful doll.

STREGA. Take that [*she knocks him sprawling over the keyboard*]! Beautiful doll indeed!

REGINALD. Oh, I say! Look here: thats the name of the tune too. You seem quite ignorant of the best music. Dont you know Rum Tum Tiddle, and Alexander's Rag Time Band, and Take me back to the Garden of Love, and Everybody likes our Mary.

STREGA. Young man: I have never even heard of these abominations. I am now going to educate you musically. I am going to play Chopin, and Brahms, and Bach, and Schumann, and—

REGINALD [*horrified*] You dont mean classical music?

STREGA. I do [*he bolts through the central doors*].

STREGA [*disgusted*] Pig! [*She sits down at the piano again*].

REGINALD [*rushing back into the room*] I forgot the people on the stairs: crowds of them. Oh, what shall I do! Oh dont, Dont, DONT play classical music to me. Say you wont. Please.

STREGA [*looks at him enigmatically and softly plays a Liebeslieder Waltz*]!!

REGINALD. Oh, I say: thats rather pretty.

STREGA. Like it?

REGINALD. Awfully. Oh, I say, you know: I really do wish you belonged to me. [*Strega suddenly plays a violent Chopin study. He goes into convulsions*]. Oh! Stop! Mercy! Help! Oh please, please!

STREGA [*pausing with her hands raised over the keyboard, ready to pounce on the chords*] Will you ever say that again?

REGINALD. Never. I beg your pardon.

STREGA [*satisfied*] Hm! [*She drops her hands in her lap*].

REGINALD [*wiping his brow*] Oh, that was fearfully classical.

STREGA. You want your back stiffened a little, my young friend. Besides, I really cannot earn two hundred and fifty guineas by playing soothing syrup to you. Now prepare for the worst. I'm going to make a man of you.

REGINALD. How?

STREGA. With Chopin's Polonaise in A Flat. Now. Imagine yourself going into battle. [*He runs away as before*]. Goose!

REGINALD [*returning as before*] The crowd is worse than ever. Have you no pity?

STREGA. Come here. Dont imagine yourself going into battle. Imagine that you have just been in a battle; and that you have saved your country by deeds of splendid bravery; and that you are going to dance with beautiful women who are proud of you. Can you imagine that?

REGINALD. Rathe-e-e-errr. Thats how I always do imagine myself.

STREGA. Right. Now listen. [*She plays the first section of the Polonaise. Reginald flinches at first, but gradually braces himself; stiffens; struts; throws up his head and slaps his chest*]. Thats better. What a hero! [*After a difficult passage*]. Takes a bit of doing, that, dearest child. [*Coming to the chords which announce the middle section*] Now for it.

REGINALD [*unable to contain himself*] Oh, this is too glorious. I must have a turn or I shall forget myself.

STREGA. Can you play this? Nothing but this. [*She plays the octave passage in the bass*].

REGINALD. Just riddle tiddle, riddle tiddle, riddle tiddle, riddle tiddle? Nothing but that?

STREGA. Very softly at first. Like the ticking of a watch. Then louder and louder, as you feel my soul swelling.

REGINALD. I understand. Just give me those chords again to buck me up to it. [*She plays the chords again. He plays the octave passages; and they play the middle section as a duet. At the repeat he cries*] Again! again!

STREGA. It's meant to be played again. Now. *They repeat it. At the end of the section she pushes him off the bench on to the floor, and goes on with the Polonaise alone.*

REGINALD. Wonderful woman: I have a confession to make, a confidence to impart. Your playing draws it from me. Listen, Strega [*she plays a horrible discord*] I mean Miss Thundridge.

STREGA. Thats better; but I prefer Wonderful Woman.

REGINALD. You are a wonderful woman, you know. Adored one—would you mind my taking a little valerian? I'm so excited [*he takes some*]. A—a—ah! Now I feel that I can speak. Listen to me, goddess. I am not happy. I hate my present existence. I loathe parliament. I am not fit for public affairs. I am condemned to live at home with five coarse and brutal sisters who care for nothing but Alpine climbing, and looping the loop on aeroplanes, and going on deputations, and fighting the police. Do you know what they call me?

STREGA [*playing softly*] What do they call you, dear?

REGINALD. They call me a Clinger. Well, I confess it. I am a Clinger. I am not fit to be thrown unprotected upon the world. I want to be shielded. I want a strong arm to lean on, a dauntless heart to be gathered to and cherished, a breadwinner on whose income I can live without the sordid horrors of having to make money for myself. I am a poor little thing, I know, Strega; but I could make a home for you. I have great taste in carpets and pictures. I can cook like anything. I can play quite nicely after dinner. Though you mightnt think it, I can be quite stern and strongminded with servants. I get on splendidly with children: they never talk over my head as grown-up people do. I have a real genius for home life. And I shouldnt at all mind being tyrannized over a little: in fact, I like it. It saves me the trouble of having to think what to do. Oh, Strega, dont you want a dear little domesticated husband who would have no concern but to please you, no thought outside our home, who would be unspotted and unsoiled by the rude cold world, who would never meddle in politics or annoy you by interfering with your profession? Is there any hope for me?

STREGA [*coming away from the piano*] My child: I am a hard, strong, independent, muscular woman. How can you, with your delicate soft nature, see anything to love in me? I should hurt you, shock you, perhaps— yes: let me confess it—I have a violent temper, and might even, in a transport of rage, beat you.

REGINALD. Oh do, do. Dont laugh at this ridiculous confession; but ever since I was a child I have had only one secret longing, and that was to be mercilessly beaten by a splendid, strong, beautiful woman.

STREGA [*solemnly*] Reginald—I think your mother spoke of you as Reginald—

REGINALD. Rejjy.

STREGA. I too have a confession to make. I too need some music to speak through. Will you be so good?

REGINALD. Angel. [*He rushes to the piano and plays sympathetically whilst she speaks*].

STREGA. I, too, have had my dream. It has consoled me through the weary hours when I practised scales for eight hours a day. It has pursued me through the applause of admiring thousands in Europe and America. It is a dream of a timid little heart fluttering against mine, of a gentle voice to welcome me home, of a silky moustache to kiss my weary fingers when I return from a Titanic struggle with Tchaikovsky's Concerto in G major, of somebody utterly dependent on me, utterly devoted to me, utterly my own, living only to be cherished and worshipped by me.

REGINALD. But you would be angry sometimes: terrible, splendid, ruthless, violent. You would throw down the thing you loved and trample on it as it clung to your feet.

STREGA. Yes—oh, why do you force me to confess it?—I should beat it to a jelly, and then cast myself in transports of remorse on its quivering frame and smother it with passionate kisses.

REGINALD [*transported*] Let it be me, let it be me.

STREGA. You dare face this terrible destiny?

REGINALD. I embrace it. I adore you. I am wholly yours. Oh, let me cling, cling, cling.

STREGA [*embracing him fiercely*] Nothing shall tear you from my arms now.

REGINALD. Nothing. I am provided for. Oh how happy this will make my mother!

STREGA. Sweet: name the day.

He plays a wedding march. She plays the bass.

AYOT ST LAWRENCE,
21st January 1914.

THE END

XL

TOO TRUE TO BE GOOD

A POLITICAL EXTRAVAGANZA

ACT I

Night. One of the best bedrooms in one of the best suburban villas in one of the richest cities in England. A young lady with an unhealthy complexion is asleep in the bed. A small table at the head of the bed, convenient to her right hand, and crowded with a medicine bottle, a measuring glass, a pill box, a clinical thermometer in a glass of water, a half read book with the place marked by a handkerchief, a powder puff and hand-mirror, and an electric bell handle on a flex, shews that the bed is a sick bed and the young lady an invalid.

The furniture includes a very handsome dressing table with silver-backed hairbrushes and toilet articles, a dainty pincushion, a stand of rings, a jewel box of black steel with the lid open and a rope of pearls heaped carelessly half in and half out, a Louis Quinze writing table and chair with inkstand, blotter, and cabinet of stationery, a magnificent wardrobe, a luxurious couch, and a

tall screen of Chinese workmanship which, like the expensive carpet and everything else in the room, proclaims that the owner has money enough to buy the best things at the best shops in the best purchaseable taste.

The bed is nearly in the middle of the room, so that the patient's nurses can pass freely between the wall and the head of it. If we contemplate the room from the foot of the bed, with the patient's toes pointing straight at us, we have the door (carefully sandbagged lest a draught of fresh air should creep underneath) level with us in the righthand wall, the couch against the same wall farther away, the window (every ray of moonlight excluded by closed curtains and a dark green spring blind) in the middle of the left wall with the wardrobe on its right and the writing table on its left, the screen at right angles to the wardrobe, and the dressing table against the wall facing us half way between the bed and the couch.

Besides the chair at the writing table there is an

easy chair at the medicine table, and a chair at each side of the dressing table.

The room is lighted by invisible cornice lights, and by two mirror lights on the dressing table and a portable one on the writing table; but these are now switched off; and the only light in action is another portable one on the medicine table, very carefully subdued by a green shade.

The patient is sleeping heavily. Near her, in the easy chair, sits a Monster. In shape and size it resembles a human being; but in substance it seems to be made of a luminous jelly with a visible skeleton of short black rods. It droops forward in the chair with its head in its hands, and seems in the last degree wretched.

THE MONSTER. Oh! Oh!! Oh!!! I am so ill! so miserable! Oh, I wish I were dead. Why doesnt she die and release me from my sufferings? What right has she to get ill and make me ill like this? Measles: thats what she's got. Measles! German measles! And she's given them to me, a poor innocent microbe that never did her any harm. And she says that *I* gave them to her. Oh, is this justice? Oh, I feel so rotten. I wonder what my temperature is: they took it from under her tongue half an hour ago. [*Scrutinizing the table and discovering the thermometer in the glass*]. Here's the thermometer: theyve left it for the doctor to see instead of shaking it down. If it's over a hundred I'm done for: I darent look. Oh, can it be that I'm dying? I must look. [*It looks, and drops the thermometer back into the glass with a gasping scream*]. A hundred and three! It's all over. [*It collapses*].

The door opens; and an elderly lady and a young doctor come in. The lady steals along on tiptoe, full of the deepest concern for the invalid. The doctor is indifferent, but keeps up his bedside manner carefully, though he evidently does not think the case so serious as the lady does. She comes to the bedside on the invalid's left. He comes to the other side of the bed and looks attentively at his patient.

THE ELDERLY LADY [*in a whisper sibillant enough to wake the dead*] She is asleep.

THE MONSTER. I should think so. This fool here, the doctor, has given her a dose of the latest fashionable opiate that would keep a cock asleep til half past eleven on a May morning.

THE ELDERLY LADY. Oh doctor, do you think there is any chance? Can she possibly survive this last terrible complication.

THE MONSTER. Measles! He mistook it for influenza.

THE ELDERLY LADY. It was so unexpected! such a crushing blow! And I have taken such care of her. She is my only surviving child: my pet: my precious one. Why do they all die? I have never neglected the smallest symptom of illness. She has had doctors in attendance on her almost constantly since she was born.

THE MONSTER. She has the constitution of a horse or she'd have died like the others.

THE ELDERLY LADY. Oh, dont you think, dear doctor—of course you know best; but I am so terribly anxious—dont you think you ought to change the prescription? I had such hopes of that last bottle; but you know it was after that that she developed measles.

THE DOCTOR. My dear Mrs Mopply, you may rest assured that the bottle had nothing to do with the measles. It was merely a gentle tonic—

THE MONSTER. Strychnine!

THE DOCTOR. —to brace her up.

THE ELDERLY LADY. But she got measles after it.

THE DOCTOR. That was a specific infection: a germ, a microbe.

THE MONSTER. Me! Put it all on me.

THE ELDERLY LADY. But how did it get in? I keep the windows closed so carefully. And there is a sheet steeped in carbolic acid always hung over the door.

THE MONSTER [*in tears*] Not a breath of fresh air for me!

THE DOCTOR. Who knows? It may have lurked here since the house was built. You never can tell. But you must not worry. It is not serious: a light rubeola: you can hardly call it measles. We shall pull her through, believe me.

THE ELDERLY LADY. It is such a comfort to hear you say so, doctor. I am sure I shall never be able to express my gratitude for all you have done for us.

THE DOCTOR. Oh, that is my profession. We do what we can.

THE ELDERLY LADY. Yes; but some doctors are dreadful. There was that man at Folkestone: he was impossible. He tore aside the curtain and let the blazing sunlight into the room, though she cannot bear it without green spectacles. He opened the windows and let in all the cold morning air. I told him he was a murderer; and he only said "One guinea, please". I am sure he let in that microbe.

THE DOCTOR. Oh, three months ago! No: it was not that.

THE ELDERLY LADY. Then what was it? Oh, are you quite quite sure that it would not be better to change the prescription?

THE DOCTOR. Well, I have already changed it.

THE MONSTER. Three times!

THE ELDERLY LADY. Oh, I know you have, doctor: nobody could have been kinder. But it really did not do her any good. She got worse.

THE DOCTOR. But, my dear lady, she was sickening for measles. That was not the fault of my prescription.

THE ELDERLY LADY. Oh, of course not. You mustnt think that I ever doubted for a moment that everything you did was for the best. Still—

THE DOCTOR. Oh, very well, very well: I will write another prescription.

THE ELDERLY LADY. Oh, thank you, thank you: I felt sure you would. I have so often known a change of medicine work wonders.

THE DOCTOR. When we have pulled her through this attack I think a change of air—

THE ELDERLY LADY. Oh no: dont say that. She must be near a doctor who knows her constitution. Dear old Dr Newland knew it so well from her very birth.

THE DOCTOR. Unfortunately, Newland is dead.

THE ELDERLY LADY. Yes; but you bought his practice. I should never be easy in my mind if you were not within call. You persuaded me to take her to Folkestone; and see what happened! No: never again.

THE DOCTOR. Oh, well! [*He shrugs his shoulders resignedly, and goes to the bedside table*]. What about the temperature?

THE ELDERLY LADY. The day nurse took it. I havnt dared to look.

THE DOCTOR [*looking at the thermometer*] Hm!

THE ELDERLY LADY [*trembling*] Has it gone up? Oh, doctor!

THE DOCTOR [*hastily shaking the mercury down*] No. Nothing. Nearly normal.

THE MONSTER. Liar!

THE ELDERLY LADY. What a relief!

THE DOCTOR. You must be careful, though. Dont fancy she's well yet: she isnt. She must not get out of bed for a moment. The slightest chill might be serious.

THE ELDERLY LADY. Doctor: are you sure you are not concealing something from me? Why does she never get well in spite of the fortune I have spent on her illnesses? There must be some deep-rooted cause. Tell me the worst: I have dreaded it all my life. Perhaps I should have told you the whole truth; but I was afraid. Her uncle's stepfather died of an enlarged heart. Is that what it is?

THE DOCTOR. Good gracious, NO! What put that into your head?

THE ELDERLY LADY. But even before this rash broke out there were pimples.

THE MONSTER. Boils! Too many chocolate creams.

THE DOCTOR. Oh, that! Nothing. Her blood is not quite what it should be. But we shall get that right.

THE ELDERLY LADY. You are sure it is not her lungs?

THE DOCTOR. My good lady, her lungs are as sound as a seagull's.

THE ELDERLY LADY. Then it must be her heart. Dont deceive me. She has palpitations. She told me the other day that it stopped for five minutes when that horrid nurse was rude to her.

THE DOCTOR. Nonsense! She wouldnt be alive now if her heart had stopped for five seconds. There is nothing constitutionally wrong. A little below par: that is all. We shall feed her up scientifically. Plenty of good fresh meat. A half bottle of champagne at lunch and a glass of port after dinner will make another woman of her. A chop at breakfast, rather underdone, is sometimes very helpful.

THE MONSTER. I shall die of overfeeding. So will she too: thats one consolation.

THE DOCTOR. Dont worry about the measles. It's really quite a light case.

THE ELDERLY LADY. Oh, you can depend on me for that. Nobody can say that I am a worrier. You wont forget the new prescription?

THE DOCTOR. I will write it here and now [*he takes out his pen and book, and sits down at the writing table*].

THE ELDERLY LADY. Oh, thank you. And I will go and see what the new night nurse is doing. They take so long with their cups of tea [*she goes to the door and is about to go out when she hesitates and comes back*]. Doctor: I know you dont believe in inoculations; but I cant help thinking she ought to have one. They do so much good.

THE DOCTOR [*almost at the end of his patience*] My dear Mrs Mopply: I never said that I dont believe in inoculations. But it is no use inoculating when the patient is already fully infected.

THE ELDERLY LADY. But I have found it so necessary myself. I was inoculated against influenza three years ago; and I have had it only four times since. My sister has it every February. Do, to please me, give her an inoculation. I feel such a responsibility if anything is left undone to cure her.

THE DOCTOR. Oh very well, very well: I will see what can be done. She shall have both an inoculation and a new prescription. Will that set your mind at rest?

THE ELDERLY LADY. Oh, thank you. You have lifted such a weight from my conscience. I feel sure they will do her the greatest good. And now excuse me a moment while I fetch the nurse. [*She goes out*].

THE DOCTOR. What a perfectly maddening woman!

THE MONSTER [*rising and coming behind him*] Yes: aint she?

THE DOCTOR [*starting*] What! Who is that?

THE MONSTER. Nobody but me and the patient. And you have dosed her so that she wont speak again for ten hours. You will overdo that some day.

THE DOCTOR. Rubbish! She thought it was an opiate; but it was only an aspirin dissolved in ether. But who am I talking to? I must be drunk.

THE MONSTER. Not a bit of it.

THE DOCTOR. Then who are you? What are you? Where are you? Is this a trick?

THE MONSTER. I'm only an unfortunate sick bacillus.

THE DOCTOR. A sick bacillus!

THE MONSTER. Yes. I suppose it never occurs to you that a bacillus can be sick like anyone else.

THE DOCTOR. Whats the matter with you?

THE MONSTER. Measles.

THE DOCTOR. Rot! The microbe of measles has never been discovered. If there is a microbe it cannot be measles: it must be parameasles.

THE MONSTER. Great Heavens! what are parameasles?

THE DOCTOR. Something so like measles that nobody can see any difference.

THE MONSTER. If there is no measles microbe why did you tell the old girl that her daughter caught measles from a microbe?

THE DOCTOR. Patients insist on having microbes nowadays. If I told her there is no measles microbe she wouldnt believe me; and I should lose my patient. When there is no microbe I invent one. Am I to understand that you are the missing microbe of measles, and that you have given them to this patient here?

THE MONSTER. No: she gave them to me. These humans are full of horrid diseases: they infect us poor microbes with them; and you doctors pretend that it is we that infect them. You ought all to be struck off the register.

THE DOCTOR. We should be, if we talked like that.

THE MONSTER. Oh, I feel so wretched! Please cure my measles.

THE DOCTOR. I cant. I cant cure any disease. But I get the credit when the patients cure themselves. When she cures herself she will cure you too.

THE MONSTER. But she cant cure herself because you and her mother wont give her a dog's chance. You wont let her have even a breath of fresh air. I tell you she's naturally as strong as a rhinoceros. Curse your silly bottles and inoculations! Why dont you chuck them and turn faith healer?

THE DOCTOR. I am a faith healer. You dont suppose I believe the bottles cure people? But the patient's faith in the bottle does.

THE MONSTER. Youre a humbug: thats what you are.

THE DOCTOR. Faith is humbug. But it works.

THE MONSTER. Then why do you call it science?

THE DOCTOR. Because people believe in science. The Christian Scientists call their fudge science for the same reason.

THE MONSTER. The Christian Scientists let their patients cure themselves. Why dont you?

THE DOCTOR. I do. But I help them. You see, it's easier to believe in bottles and inoculations than in oneself and in that mysterious power that gives us our life and that none of us knows anything about. Lots of people believe in the bottles and wouldnt know what you were talking about if you suggested the real thing. And the bottles do the trick. My patients get well as often as not. That is, unless their number's up. Then we all have to go.

THE MONSTER. No girl's number is up until

she's worn out. I tell you this girl could cure herself and cure me if youd let her.

THE DOCTOR. And I tell you that it would be very hard work for her. Well, why should she work hard when she can afford to pay other people to work for her? She doesnt black her own boots or scrub her own floors. She pays somebody else to do it. Why should she cure herself, which is harder work than blacking boots or scrubbing floors, when she can afford to pay the doctor to cure her? It pays her and it pays me. That's logic, my friend. And now, if you will excuse me, I shall take myself off before the old woman comes back and provokes me to wring her neck. [*Rising*] Mark my words: someday somebody will fetch her a clout over the head. Somebody who can afford to. Not the doctor. She has driven me mad already: the proof is that I hear voices and talk to them. [*He goes out*].

THE MONSTER. Youre saner than most of them, you fool. They think I have the keys of life and death in my pocket; but I have nothing but a horrid headache. Oh dear! oh dear!

The Monster wanders away behind the screen. The patient, left alone, begins to stir in her bed. She turns over and calls querulously for somebody to attend to her.

THE PATIENT. Nurse! Mother! Oh, is anyone there? [*Crying*] Selfish beasts! to leave me like this. [*She snatches angrily at the electric bell which hangs within her reach and presses the button repeatedly*].

The Elderly Lady and the night nurse come running in. The nurse is young, quick, active, resolute, and decidedly pretty. Mrs Mopply goes to the bedside table, the nurse going to the patient's left.

THE ELDERLY LADY. What is it, darling? Are you awake? Was the sleeping draught no good? Are you worse? What has happened? What has become of the doctor?

THE PATIENT. I am in the most frightful agony. I have been lying here ringing for ages and ages, and no one has come to attend to me. Nobody cares whether I am alive or dead.

THE ELDERLY LADY. Oh, how can you say such things, darling? I left the doctor here. I was away only for a minute. I had to receive the new night nurse and give her her instructions. Here she is. And oh, do cover up your arm, darling. You will get a chill; and then it will be all over. Nurse: see that she is never uncovered for a moment. Do you think it would be well to have another hot water bottle against her arm until it is quite warm again? Do you feel it cold, darling?

THE PATIENT [*angrily*] Yes, deadly cold.

THE ELDERLY LADY. Oh dont say that. And there is so much pneumonia about. I wish the doctor had not gone. He could sound your lungs—

NIGHT NURSE [*feeling the patient's arm*] She is quite warm enough.

THE PATIENT [*bursting into tears*] Mother: take this hateful woman away. She wants to kill me.

THE ELDERLY LADY. Oh no, dear: she has been so highly recommended. I cant get a new nurse at this hour. Wont you try, for my sake, to put up with her until the day nurse comes in the morning?

THE NURSE. Come! Let me arrange your pillows and make you comfortable. You are smothered with all this bedding. Four thick blankets and an eiderdown! No wonder you feel irritable.

THE PATIENT [*screaming*] Dont touch me. Go away. You want to murder me. Nobody cares whether I am alive or dead.

THE ELDERLY LADY. Oh, darling, dont keep on saying that. You know it's not true; and it does hurt me so.

THE NURSE. You must not mind what a sick person says, madam. You had better go to bed and leave the patient to me. You are quite worn out. [*She comes to Mrs Mopply and takes her arm coaxingly but firmly*].

THE ELDERLY LADY. I know I am: I am ready to drop. How sympathetic of you to notice it! But how can I leave her at such a moment?

THE NURSE. She ought not to have more than one person in the room at a time. You see how it excites and worries her.

THE ELDERLY LADY. Oh, thats very true. The doctor said she was to be kept as quiet as possible.

THE NURSE [*leading her to the door*] You need a good night's sleep. You may trust me to do what is right and necessary.

THE ELDERLY LADY [*whispering*] I will indeed. How kind of you! You will let me know if anything—

THE NURSE. Yes, yes. I promise to come for you and wake you if anything happens. Good night, madam.

THE ELDERLY LADY [*sotto voce*] Good night. [*She steals out*].

The nurse, left alone with her patient, pays no

attention to her, but goes to the window. She opens the curtains and raises the blind, admitting a flood of moonlight. She unfastens the sash and throws it right up. She then makes for the door, where the electric switch is.

THE PATIENT [*huddling herself up in the bedclothes*] What are you doing? Shut that window and pull down that blind and close those curtains at once. Do you want to kill me?

The nurse turns all the lights full on.

THE PATIENT [*hiding her eyes*] Oh! Oh! I cant bear it: turn it off.

The nurse switches the lights off.

THE PATIENT. So inconsiderate of you!

The nurse switches the lights on again.

THE PATIENT. Oh, please, please. Not all that light.

The nurse switches off.

THE PATIENT. No, no. Leave me something to read by. My bedside lamp is not enough, you stupid idiot.

The nurse switches on again, and calmly returns to the bedside.

THE PATIENT. I cant imagine how anyone can be so thoughtless and clumsy when I am so ill. I am suffering horribly. Shut that window and switch off half those lights at once: do you hear?

The nurse snatches the eiderdown and one of the pillows rudely from the bed, letting the patient down with a jerk, and arranges them comfortably in the bedside chair.

THE PATIENT. How dare you touch my pillow? The audacity!

The nurse sits down; takes out a leaf cut from an illustrated journal; and proceeds to study it attentively.

THE PATIENT. Well! How much longer are you going to sit there neglecting me? Shut that window instantly.

THE NURSE [*insolently, in her commonest dialect*] Oh go to—to sleep [*she resumes her study of the document*].

THE PATIENT. Dont dare address me like that. I dont believe you are a properly qualified nurse.

THE NURSE [*calmly*] I should think not. I wouldnt take five thousand a year to be a nurse. But I know how to deal with you and your like, because I was once a patient in a hospital where the women patients were a rough lot, and the nurses had to treat them accordingly. I kept my eyes open there, and learnt a little of the game. [*She takes a paper packet from her pocket and opens it on the bed-*

side table. It contains about half a pound of kitchen salt]. Do you know what that is and what it's for?

THE PATIENT. Is it medicine?

THE NURSE. Yes. It's a cure for screaming and hysterics and tantrums. When a woman starts making a row, the first thing she does is to open her mouth. A nurse who knows her business just shoves a handful of this into it. Common kitchen salt. No more screaming. Understand?

THE PATIENT [*hardily*] No I dont [*she reaches for the bell*].

THE NURSE [*intercepting her quickly*] No you dont. [*She throws the bell cord with its button away on the floor behind the bed*]. Now we shant be disturbed. No bell. And if you open your mouth too wide, youll get the salt. See?

THE PATIENT. And do you think I am a poor woman in a hospital whom you can illtreat as you please? Do you know what will happen to you when my mother comes in the morning?

THE NURSE. In the morning, darling, I shall be over the hills and far away.

THE PATIENT. And you expect me, sick as I am, to stay here alone with you!

THE NURSE. We shant be alone. I'm expecting a friend.

THE PATIENT. A friend!

THE NURSE. A gentleman friend. I told him he might drop in when he saw the lights switched off twice.

THE PATIENT. So that was why—

THE NURSE. That was why.

THE PATIENT. And you calmly propose to have your young man here in my room to amuse yourself all night before my face.

THE NURSE. You can go to sleep.

THE PATIENT. I shall do nothing of the sort. You will have to behave yourself decently before me.

THE NURSE. Oh, dont worry about that. He's coming on business. He's my business partner, in fact: not my best boy.

THE PATIENT. And can you not find some more suitable place for your business than in my room at night?

THE NURSE. You see, you dont know the nature of the business yet. It's got to be done here and at night. Here he is, I think.

A burglar, well dressed, wearing rubber gloves and a small white mask over his nose, clambers in. He is still in his early thirties, and quite goodlooking. His voice is disarmingly pleasant.

THE BURGLAR. All right, Sweetie?

THE NURSE. All right, Popsy.

The burglar closes the window softly; draws the curtains; and comes past the nurse to the bedside.

THE BURGLAR. Damn it, she's awake. Didnt you give her a sleeping draught?

THE PATIENT. Do you expect me to sleep with you in the room? Who are you? and what are you wearing that mask for?

THE BURGLAR. Only so that you will not recognize me if we should happen to meet again.

THE PATIENT. I have no intention of meeting you again. So you may just as well take it off.

THE NURSE. I havnt broken to her what we are here for, Popsy.

THE PATIENT. I neither know nor care what you are here for. All I can tell you is that if you dont leave the room at once and send my mother to me, I will give you both measles.

THE BURGLAR. We have both had them, dear invalid. I am afraid we must intrude a little longer. [*To the nurse*] Have you found out where it is?

THE NURSE. No: I havnt had time. The dressing table's over there. Try that.

The burglar crosses to the other side of the bed, coming round by the foot of it, and is making for the dressing table when—

THE PATIENT. What do you want at my dressing table?

THE BURGLAR. Obviously, your celebrated pearl necklace.

THE PATIENT [*escaping from her bed with a formidable bound and planting herself with her back to the dressing table as a bulwark for the jewel case*] Not if I know it, you shant.

THE BURGLAR [*approaching her*] You really must allow me.

THE PATIENT. Take that.

Holding on to the table edge behind her, she lifts her foot vigorously waist high, and shoots it hard into his solar plexus. He curls up on the bed with an agonized groan and rolls off on to the carpet at the other side. The nurse rushes across behind the head of the bed and tackles the patient. The patient swoops at her knees; lifts her; and sends her flying. She comes down with a thump flat on her back on the couch. The patient pants hard; sways giddily; staggers to the bed and falls on it, exhausted. The nurse, dazed by the patient's very unexpected athleticism, but not hurt, springs up.

THE NURSE. Quick, Popsy: tie her feet. She's

fainted.

THE BURGLAR [*utters a lamentable groan and rolls over on his face*]!!

THE NURSE. Be quick, will you?

THE BURGLAR [*trying to rise*] Ugh! Ugh!

THE NURSE [*running to him and shaking him*] My God, you are a fool, Popsy. Come and help me before she comes to. She's too strong for me.

THE BURGLAR. Ugh! Let me die.

THE NURSE. Are you going to lie there for ever? Has she killed you?

THE BURGLAR [*rising slowly to his knees*] As nearly as doesnt matter. Oh, Sweetiest, why did you tell me that this heavyweight champion was a helpless invalid?

THE NURSE. Shut up. Get the pearls.

THE BURGLAR [*rising with difficulty*] I dont seem to want any pearls. She got me just in the wind. I am sorry to have been of so little assistance; but oh, my Sweetie-Weetie, Nature never intended us to be burglars. Our first attempt has been a hopeless failure. Let us apologize and withdraw.

THE NURSE. Fathead! Dont be such a coward. [*Looking closely at the patient*] I say, Popsy: I believe she's asleep.

THE BURGLAR. Let her sleep. Wake not the lioness's wrath.

THE NURSE. You maddening fool, dont you see that we can tie her feet and gag her before she wakes, and get away with the pearls. It's quite easy if we do it quick together. Come along.

THE BURGLAR. Do not deceive yourself, my pet: we should have about as much chance as if we tried to take a female gorilla to the Zoo. No: I am not going to steal those jewels. Honesty is the best policy. I have another idea, and a much better one. You leave this to me. [*He goes to the dressing table. She follows him*].

THE NURSE. Whatever have you got into your silly head now?

THE BURGLAR. You shall see. [*Handling the jewel case*] One of these safes that open by a secret arrangement of letters. As they are as troublesome as an automatic telephone nobody ever locks them. Here is the necklace. By Jove! If they are all real, it must be worth about twenty thousand pounds. Gosh! here's a ring with a big blue diamond in it. Worth four thousand pounds if it's worth a penny. Sweetie: we are on velvet for the rest of our lives.

THE NURSE. What good are blue diamonds to us if we dont steal them?

THE BURGLAR. Wait. Wait and see. Go and sit down in that chair and look as like a nice gentle nurse as you can.

THE NURSE. But—

THE BURGLAR. Do as you are told. Have faith—faith in your Popsy.

THE NURSE [obeying] Well, I give it up. Youre mad.

THE BURGLAR. I was never saner in my life. Stop. How does she call people? Hasnt she an electric bell? Where is it?

THE NURSE [picking it up] Here. I chucked it out of her reach when she was grabbing at it.

THE BURGLAR. Put it on the bed close to her hand.

THE NURSE. Popsy: youre off your chump. She—

THE BURGLAR. Sweetie: in our firm I am the brains: you are the hand. This is going to be our most glorious achievement. Obey me instantly.

THE NURSE [resignedly] Oh, very well. [She places the handle of the bell as desired]. I wash my hands of this job. [She sits down doggedly].

THE BURGLAR [coming to the bedside] By the way, she is hardly a success as The Sleeping Beauty. She has a wretched complexion; and her breath is not precisely ambrosial. But if we can turn her out to grass she may put up some good looks. And if her punch is anything like her kick she will be an invaluable bodyguard for us two weaklings—if I can persuade her to join us.

THE NURSE. Join us! What do you mean?

THE BURGLAR. Shshshshsh. Not too much noise: we must wake her gently. [He stoops to the patient's ear and whispers] Miss Mopply.

THE PATIENT [in a murmur of protest] Mmm-mmmmmmmmmmmmmmm.

THE NURSE. What does she say?

THE BURGLAR. She says, in effect, "Youhave waked me too soon: I must slumber again." [To the patient, more distinctly] It is not your dear mother, Miss Mopply: it is the burglar. [The patient springs half up, threateningly. He falls on his knees and throws up his hands]. Kamerad, Miss Mopply: Kamerad! I am utterly at your mercy. The bell is on your bed, close to your hand: look at it. You have only to press the button to bring your mother and the police in upon me [she seizes the handle of the bell] and be a miserable invalid again for the rest of your life. [She drops the bell

thoughtfully]. Not an attractive prospect, is it? Now listen. I have something to propose to you of the greatest importance: something that may make another woman of you and change your entire destiny. You can listen to me in perfect security: at any moment you can ring your bell, or throw us out of the window if you prefer it. I ask you for five minutes only.

THE PATIENT [still dangerously on guard] Well?

THE BURGLAR [rising] Let me give you one more proof of my confidence. [He takes off his mask]. Look. Can you be afraid of such a face? Do I look like a burglar?

THE PATIENT [relaxing, and even shewing signs of goodhumor] No: you look like a curate

THE BURGLAR [a little hurt] Oh, not a curate. I hope I look at least like a beneficed clergyman. But it is very clever of you to have found me out. The fact is, I am a clergyman. But I must ask you to keep it a dead secret; for my father, who is an atheist, would disinherit me if he knew. I was secretly ordained when I was up at Oxford.

THE PATIENT. Oh, this is ridiculous. I'm dreaming. It must be that new sleeping draught the doctor gave me. But it's delicious, because I'm dreaming that I'm perfectly well. Ive never been so happy in my life. Go on with the dream, Pops: the nicest part of it is that I am in love with you. My beautiful Pops, my own, my darling, you are a perfect film hero, only more like an English gentleman. [She waves him a kiss].

THE NURSE. Well I'll be da—

THE BURGLAR. Shshshshsh. Break not the spell.

THE PATIENT [with a deep sigh of contentment] Let nobody wake me. I'm in heaven. [She sinks back blissfully on her pillows]. Go on, Pops. Tell me another.

THE BURGLAR. Splendid. [He takes a chair from beside the dressing table and seats himself comfortably at the bedside]. We are going to have an ideal night. Now listen. Picture to yourself a heavenly afternoon in July: a Scottish loch surrounded by mirrored mountains, and a boat—may I call it a shallop?—

THE PATIENT [ecstatically] A shallop! Oh, Popsy!

THE BURGLAR.—with Sweetie sitting in the stern, and I stretched out at full length with my head pillowed on Sweetie's knees.

THE PATIENT. You can leave Sweetie out,

Pops. Her amorous emotions do not interest me.

THE BURGLAR. You misunderstand. Sweetie's thoughts were far from me. She was thinking about you.

THE PATIENT. Just like her impudence! How did she know about me?

THE BURGLAR. Simply enough. In her lily hand was a copy of The Lady's Pictorial. It contained an illustrated account of your jewels. Can you guess what Sweetie said to me as she gazed at the soft majesty of the mountains and bathed her soul in the beauty of the sunset?

THE PATIENT. Yes. She said "Popsy: we must pinch that necklace."

THE BURGLAR. Exactly. Word for word. But now can you guess what I said?

THE PATIENT. I suppose you said "Right you are, Sweetie" or something vulgar like that.

THE BURGLAR. Wrong. I said, "If that girl had any sense she'd steal the necklace herself."

THE PATIENT. Oh! This is getting interesting. How could I steal my own necklace?

THE BURGLAR. Sell it; and have a glorious spree with the price. See life. Live. You dont call being an invalid living, do you?

THE PATIENT. Why shouldnt I call it living? I am not dead. Of course when I am awake I am terribly delicate——

THE BURGLAR. Delicate! It's not five minutes since you knocked me out, and threw Sweetie all over the room. If you can fight like that for a string of pearls that you never have a chance of wearing, why not fight for freedom to do what you like, with your pocket full of money and all the fun in the wide world at your command? Hang it all, dont you want to be young and goodlooking and have a sweet breath and be a lawn tennis champion and enjoy everything that is to be enjoyed instead of frowsting here and being messed about by your silly mother and all the doctors that live on her folly? Have you no conscience, that you waste God's gifts so shamefully? You think you are in a state of illness. Youre not: youre in a state of sin. Sell the necklace and buy your salvation with the proceeds.

THE PATIENT. Youre a clergyman all right, Pops. But I dont know how to sell the necklace.

THE BURGLAR. I do. Let me sell it for you.

You will of course give us a fairly handsome commission on the transaction.

THE PATIENT. Theres some catch in this. If I trust you with it how do I know that you will not keep the whole price for yourself?

THE BURGLAR. Sweetie: Miss Mopply has the makings of a good business woman in her. [To the patient] Just reflect, Mops (Let us call one another Mops and Pops for short). If I steal that necklace, I shall have to sell it as a burglar to a man who will know perfectly well that I have stolen it. I shall be lucky if I get a fiftieth of its value. But if I sell it on the square, as the agent of its lawful owner, I shall be able to get its full market value. The payment will be made to you; and I will trust you to pay me the commission. Sweetie and I will be more than satisfied with fifty per cent.

THE PATIENT. Fifty! Oh!

THE BURGLAR [firmly] I think you will admit that we deserve it for our enterprise, our risk, and the priceless boon of your emancipation from this wretched home. Is it a bargain, Mops?

THE PATIENT. It's a monstrous overcharge; but in dreamland generosity costs nothing. You shall have your fifty. Lucky for you that I'm asleep. If I wake up I shall never get loose from my people and my social position. It's all very well for you two criminals: you can do what you like. If you were ladies and gentlemen, youd know how hard it is not to do what everybody else does.

THE BURGLAR. Pardon me; but I think you will feel more at ease with us if I inform you that we are ladies and gentlemen. My own rank—not that I would presume on it for a moment—is, if you ask Burke or Debrett, higher than your own. Your people's money was made in trade: my people have always lived by owning property or governing Crown Colonies. Sweetie would be a woman of the highest position but for the unfortunate fact that her parents, though united in the sight of Heaven, were not legally married. At least so she tells me.

THE NURSE [hotly] I tell you what is true. [To the patient] Popsy and I are as good company as ever you kept.

THE PATIENT. No, Sweetie: you are a common little devil and a liar. But you amuse me. If you were a real lady you wouldnt amuse me. Youd be afraid to be so unladylike.

THE BURGLAR. Just so. Come! confess! we

are better fun than your dear anxious mother and the curate and all the sympathizing relatives, arnt we? Of course we are.

THE PATIENT. I think it perfectly scandalous that you two, who ought to be in prison, are having all the fun while I, because I am respectable and a lady, might just as well be in prison.

THE BURGLAR. Dont you wish you could come with us?

THE PATIENT [calmly] I fully intend to come with you. I'm going to make the most of this dream. Do you forget that I love you, Pops. The world is before us. You and Sweetie have had a week in the land of the mountain and the flood for seven guineas, tips included. Now you shall have an eternity with your Mops in the loveliest earthly paradise we can find, for nothing.

THE NURSE. And where do I come in?

THE PATIENT. You will be our chaperone.

THE NURSE. Chaperone! Well, you have a nerve, you have.

THE PATIENT. Listen. You will be a Countess. We shall go abroad, where nobody will know the difference. You shall have a splendid foreign title. The Countess Valbrioni: doesnt that tempt you?

THE NURSE. Tempt me hell! I'll see you further first.

THE BURGLAR. Stop. Sweetie: I have another idea. A regular dazzler. Lets stage a kidnap.

THE NURSE. What do you mean? stage a kidnap.

THE BURGLAR. It's quite simple. We kidnap Mops: that is, we shall hide her in the mountains of Corsica or Istria or Dalmatia or Greece or in the Atlas or where you please that is out of reach of Scotland Yard. We shall pretend to be brigands. Her devoted mother will cough up five thousand to ransom her. We shall share the ransom fifty-fifty: fifty for Mops, twentyfive for you, twentyfive for me. Mops: you will realize not only the value of the pearls, but of yourself. What a stroke of finance!

THE PATIENT [excited] Greece! Dalmatia! Kidnapped! Brigands! Ransomed! [Collapsing a little] Oh, dont tantalize me, you two fools: you have forgotten the measles.

The Monster suddenly reappears from behind the screen. It is transfigured. The bloated moribund Caliban has become a dainty Ariel.

THE MONSTER [picking up the last remark of the patient] So have you. No more measles:

that scrap for the jewels cured you and cured me. Ha ha! I am well, I am well, I am well. [It bounds about ecstatically, and finally perches on the pillows and gets into bed beside the patient].

THE NURSE. If you could jump out of bed to knock out Popsy and me you can jump out to dress yourself and hop it from here. Wrap yourself up well: we have a car waiting.

THE BURGLAR. It's no worse than being taken to a nursing home, Mops. Strike for freedom. Up with you!

They pull her out of bed.

THE PATIENT. But I cant dress myself without a maid.

THE NURSE. Have you ever tried?

THE BURGLAR. We will give you five minutes. If you are not ready we go without you [he looks at his watch].

The patient dashes at the wardrobe and tears out a fur cloak, a hat, a walking dress, a combination, a pair of stockings, black silk breeches, and shoes, all of which she flings on the floor. The nurse picks up most of them; the patient snatches up the rest; the two retire behind the screen. Meanwhile the burglar comes forward to the foot of the bed and comments oratorically, half auctioneer, half clergyman.

THE BURGLAR. Fur cloak. Seal. Old fashioned but worth forty-five guineas. Hat. Quiet and ladylike. Tailor made frock. Combination: silk and wool. Real silk stockings without ladders. Knickers: how daringly modern! Shoes: heels only two inches but no use for the mountains. What a theme for a sermon! The well brought up maiden revolts against her respectable life. The aspiring soul escapes from home, sweet home, which, as a wellknown author has said, is the girl's prison and the woman's workhouse. The intrusive care of her anxious parents, the officious concern of the family clergyman for her salvation and of the family doctor for her health, the imposed affection of uninteresting brothers and sisters, the outrage of being called by her Christian name by distant cousins who will not keep their distance, the invasion of her privacy and independence at every turn by questions as to where she has been and what she has been doing, the whispering behind her back about her chances of marriage, the continual violation of that sacred aura which surrounds every living soul like the halo surrounding the heads of saints in religious pictures: against all these devices for worrying her to death the innermost uppermost life in her rises like milk in a boiling saucepan and cries "Down with you! away with you! henceforth my gates are open to real life, bring what it may. For what sense is there in this world of hazards, disasters, elations and victories, except as a field for the adventures of the life everlasting? In vain do we disfigure our streets with scrawls of Safety First: in vain do the nations clamor for Security, security, security. They who cry Safety First never cross the street: the empires which sacrifice life to security find it in the grave. For me Safety Last; and Forward, Forward, always For—"

THE NURSE [coming from behind the screen] Dry up, Popsy: she's ready.

The patient, cloaked, hatted, and shoed, follows her breathless, and comes to the burglar, on his left.

THE PATIENT. Here I am, Pops. One kiss; and then—Lead on.

THE BURGLAR. Good. Your complexion still leaves something to be desired; but [kissing her] your breath is sweet: you breathe the air of freedom.

THE MONSTER. Never mind her complexion: look at mine!

THE BURGLAR [releasing the patient and turning to the nurse] Did you speak?

THE NURSE. No. Hurry up, will you?

THE BURGLAR. It must have been your mother snoring, Mops. It will be long before you hear that music again. Drop a tear.

THE PATIENT. Not one. A woman's future is not with her mother.

THE NURSE. If you are going to start preaching like Popsy, the milkman will be here before we get away. Remember, I have to take off this uniform and put on my walking things downstairs. Popsy: there may be a copper on his beat outside. Spy out and see. Safety First [she hurries out].

THE BURGLAR. Well, for just this once, safety first [he makes for the window].

THE PATIENT [stopping him] Idiot: the police cant touch you if I back you up. It's I who run the risk of being caught by my mother.

THE BURGLAR. True. You have an unexpectedly powerful mind. Pray Heaven that in kidnapping you I am not biting off more than I can chew. Come along. [He runs out].

THE PATIENT. He's forgotten the pearls!!! Thank Heaven he's a fool, a lovely fool: I shall be able to do as I like with him. [She rushes to the dressing table; bundles the jewels into their case; and carries it out].

THE MONSTER [sitting up] The play is now virtually over; but the characters will discuss it at great length for two acts more. The exit doors are all in order. Goodnight. [It draws up the bedclothes round its neck and goes to sleep].

ACT II

A sea beach in a mountainous country. Sand dunes rise to a brow which cuts off the view of the plain beyond, only the summits of the distant mountain range which bounds it being visible. An army hut on the hither side, with a klaxon electric horn projecting from a board on the wall, shews that we are in a military cantoonment. Opposite the hut is a particolored canvas bathing pavilion with a folding stool beside the entrance. As seen from the sand dunes the hut is on the right and the pavilion on the left. From the neighbourhood of the hut a date palm throws a long shadow; for it is early morning.

In this shadow sits a British colonel in a deck chair, peacefully reading the weekly edition of The Times, but with a revolver in his equipment. A light cane chair for use by his visitors is at hand by the hut. Though well over fifty, he is still slender, handsome, well set up, and every inch a commanding officer. His full style and title is Colonel Tallboys, V.C., D.S.O. He won his cross as a company-officer, and has never looked back since then.

He is disturbed by a shattering series of explosions announcing the approach of a powerful and very imperfectly silenced motor bicycle from the side opposite to the huts.

TALLBOYS. Damn that noise!

The unseen rider dismounts and races his engine with a hideous clatter.

TALLBOYS [angrily] Stop that motorbike, will you?

The noise stops; and the bicyclist, having hoiked his machine up on to its stand, taken off his goggles and gloves, and extracted a letter from his carrier, comes past the pavilion into the colonel's view with the letter in his hand.

He is an insignificant looking private soldier, dusty as to his clothes and a bit gritty as to his windbeaten face. Otherwise there is nothing to find fault with: his tunic and puttees are smart and correct, and his speech ready and rapid. Yet the colonel, already irritated by the racket of the bicycle and the interruption to his newspaper, contemplates him with stern disfavor; for there is something exasperatingly and inexplicably wrong about him. He wears a pith helmet with a pagri; and in profile this pagri suggests a shirt which he has forgotten to tuck in behind, whilst its front view as it falls on his shoulders gives him a feminine air of having ringlets and a veil which is in the last degree unsoldierly. His figure is that of a boy of seventeen; but he seems to have borrowed a long head and Wellingtonian nose and chin from somebody else for the express purpose of annoying the colonel. Fortunately for him these are offences which cannot be stated on a charge sheet and dealt with by the provo-marshal; and of this the colonel is angrily aware. The dispatch rider seems conscious of his incongruities; for, though very prompt, concise, and soldierly in his replies, he somehow suggests that there is an imprescriptible joke somewhere by an invisible smile which unhappily produces at times an impression of irony.

He salutes; hands the letter to the colonel; and stands at attention.

TALLBOYS [*taking the letter*] Whats this?

THE RIDER. I was sent with a letter to the headman of the native village in the mountains, sir. That is his answer, sir.

TALLBOYS. I know nothing about it. Who sent you?

THE RIDER. Colonel Saxby, sir.

TALLBOYS. Colonel Saxby has just returned to the base, seriously ill. I have taken over from him. I am Colonel Tallboys.

THE RIDER. So I understand, sir.

TALLBOYS. Well, is this a personal letter to be sent on to him, or is it a dispatch?

THE RIDER. Dispatch, sir. Service document, sir. You may open it.

TALLBOYS [*turning in his chair and concentrating on him with fierce sarcasm*] Thank you. [*He surveys him from his instep to his nose*]. What is your name?

THE RIDER. Meek, sir.

TALLBOYS [*with disgust*] What!

THE RIDER. Meek, sir. M, double e, k.

The colonel looks at him with loathing, and tears open the letter. There is a painful silence whilst he puzzles over it.

TALLBOYS. In dialect. Send the interpreter to me.

MEEK. It's of no consequence, sir. It was only to impress the headman.

TALLBOYS. INNdeed. Who picked you for this duty?

MEEK. Sergeant, sir.

TALLBOYS. He should have selected a cap-

able responsible person, with sufficient style to impress the native headman to whom Colonel Saxby's letter was addressed. How did he come to select you?

MEEK. I volunteered, sir.

TALLBOYS. Did you indeed? You consider yourself an impressive person, eh? You think you carry about with you the atmosphere of the British Empire, do you?

MEEK. No, sir. I know the country. I can speak the dialects a little.

TALLBOYS. Marvellous! And why, with all these accomplishments, are you not at least a corporal?

MEEK. Not educationally qualified, sir.

TALLBOYS. Illiterate! Are you not ashamed?

MEEK. No, sir.

TALLBOYS. Proud of it, eh?

MEEK. Cant help it, sir.

TALLBOYS. Where did you pick up your knowledge of the country?

MEEK. I was mostly a sort of tramp before I enlisted, sir.

TALLBOYS. Well, if I could get hold of the recruiting sergeant who enlisted you, I'd have his stripes off. Youre a disgrace to the army.

MEEK. Yessir.

TALLBOYS. Go and send the interpreter to me. And dont come back with him. Keep out of my sight.

MEEK [*hesitates*] Er—

TALLBOYS [*peremptorily*] Now then! Did you hear me give you an order? Send me the interpreter.

MEEK. The fact is, Colonel—

TALLBOYS [*outraged*] How dare you say Colonel and tell me that the fact is? Obey your order and hold your tongue.

MEEK. Yessir. Sorry, sir. *I* am the interpreter.

Tallboys bounds to his feet; towers over Meek, who looks smaller than ever; and folds his arms to give emphasis to a terrible rejoinder. On the point of delivering it, he suddenly unfolds them again and sits down resignedly.

TALLBOYS [*wearily and quite gently*] Very well. If you are the interpreter you had better interpret this for me. [*He proffers the letter*].

MEEK [*not accepting it*] No need, thank you, sir. The headman couldnt compose a letter, sir. I had to do it for him.

TALLBOYS. How did you know what was in Colonel Saxby's letter?

MEEK. I read it to him, sir.

TALLBOYS. Did he ask you to?

MEEK. Yessir.

TALLBOYS. He had no right to communicate the contents of such a letter to a private soldier. He cannot have known what he was doing. You must have represented yourself as being a responsible officer. Did you?

MEEK. It would be all the same to him, sir. He addressed me as Lord of the Western Isles.

TALLBOYS. You! You worm! If my letter was sent by the hands of an irresponsible messenger it should have contained a statement to that effect. Who drafted it?

MEEK. Quartermaster's clerk, sir.

TALLBOYS. Send him to me. Tell him to bring his note of Colonel Saxby's instructions. Do you hear? Stop making idiotic faces; and get a move on. Send me the quartermaster's clerk.

MEEK. The fact is—

TALLBOYS [*thundering*] Again!!

MEEK. Sorry, sir. *I* am the quartermaster's clerk.

TALLBOYS. What! You wrote both the letter and the headman's answer?

MEEK. Yessir.

TALLBOYS. Then either you are lying now or you were lying when you said you were illiterate. Which is it?

MEEK. I dont seem to be able to pass the examination when they want to promote me. It's my nerves, sir, I suppose.

TALLBOYS. Your nerves! What business has a soldier with nerves? You mean that you are no use for fighting, and have to be put to do anything that can be done without it.

MEEK. Yessir.

TALLBOYS. Well, next time you are sent with a letter I hope the brigands will catch you and keep you.

MEEK. There are no brigands, sir.

TALLBOYS. No brigands! Did you say no brigands?

MEEK. Yessir.

TALLBOYS. You are acquainted with the Articles of War, are you not?

MEEK. I have heard them read out, sir.

TALLBOYS. Do you understand them?

MEEK. I think so, sir.

TALLBOYS. You think so! Well, do a little more thinking. You are serving on an expeditionary force sent out to suppress brigandage in this district and to rescue a British lady who is being held for ransom. You know

that. You dont think it: you know it, eh?

MEEK. So they say, sir.

TALLBOYS. You know also that under the Articles of War any soldier who knowingly does when on active service any act calculated to imperil the success of his Majesty's forces or any part thereof shall be liable to suffer death. Do you understand? Death!

MEEK. Yessir. Army Act, Part One, Section Four, Number Six. I think you mean Section Five, Number Five, sir.

TALLBOYS. Do I? Perhaps you will be good enough to quote Section Five, Number Five.

MEEK. Yessir. "By word of mouth spreads reports calculated to create unnecessary alarm or despondency."

TALLBOYS. It is fortunate for you, Private Meek, that the Act says nothing about private soldiers who create despondency by their personal appearance. Had it done so your life would not be worth half an hour's purchase.

MEEK. No, sir. Am I to file the letter and the reply with a translation, sir?

TALLBOYS [*tearing the letter to pieces and throwing them away*] Your folly has made a mockery of both. What did the headman say?

MEEK. Only that the country has very good roads now, sir. Motor coaches ply every day all the year round. The last active brigand retired fifteen years ago, and is ninety years old.

TALLBOYS. The usual tissue of lies. That headman is in league with the brigands. He takes a turn himself occasionally, I should say.

MEEK. I think not, sir. The fact is—

TALLBOYS. Did I hear you say "The fact is"?

MEEK. Sorry, sir. That old brigand was the headman himself. He is sending you a present of a sheep and six turkeys.

TALLBOYS. Send them back instantly. Take them back on your damned bicycle. Inform him that British officers are not orientals, and do not accept bribes from officials in whose districts they have to restore order.

MEEK. He wont understand, sir. He wont believe you have any authority unless you take presents. Besides, they havnt arrived yet.

TALLBOYS. Well, when his messengers arrive pack them back with their sheep and their turkeys and a note to say that my favor can be earned by honesty and diligence, but not purchased.

MEEK. They wont dare take back either the presents or the note, sir. Theyll steal the sheep and turkeys and report gracious messages from you. Better keep the meat and the birds, sir: they will be welcome after a long stretch of regulation food.

TALLBOYS. Private Meek.

MEEK. Yessir.

TALLBOYS. If you should be at any future time entrusted with the command of this expedition you will no doubt give effect to your own views and moral standards. For the present will you be good enough to obey my orders without comment?

MEEK. Yessir. Sorry, sir.

As Meek salutes and turns to go, he is confronted by the nurse, who, brilliantly undressed for bathing under a variegated silk wrap, comes from the pavilion, followed by the patient in the character of a native servant. All traces of the patient's illness have disappeared: she is sunburnt to the color of terra cotta; and her muscles are hard and glistening with unguent. She is disguised en belle sauvage *by headdress, wig, ornaments, and girdle proper to no locality on earth except perhaps the Russian ballet. She carries a sun umbrella and a rug.*

TALLBOYS [*rising gallantly*] Ah, my dear Countess, delighted to see you. How good of you to come!

THE COUNTESS [*giving him her finger tips*] How do, Colonel? Hot, isnt it? [*Her dialect is now a spirited amalgamation of the foreign accents of all the waiters she has known*].

TALLBOYS. Take my chair. [*He goes behind it and moves it nearer to her*].

THE COUNTESS. Thanks. [*She throws off her wrap, which the patient takes, and flings herself with careless elegance into the chair, calling*] Mr Meek. Mr Mee-e-e-eek!

Meek returns smartly, and touches the front of his cap.

THE COUNTESS. My new things from Paris have arrived at last. If you would be so very sweet as to get them to my bungalow somehow. Of course I will pay anything necessary. And could you get a letter of credit cashed for me. I'd better have three hundred pounds to go on with.

MEEK [*quite at his ease: unconsciously dropping the soldier and assuming the gentleman*] How many boxes, Countess?

THE COUNTESS. Six, I am afraid. Will it be a lot of trouble?

MEEK. It will involve a camel.

THE COUNTESS. Oh, strings of camels if necessary. Expense is no object. And the letter of credit?

MEEK. Sorry, Countess: I have only two hundred on me. You shall have the other hundred tomorrow. [*He hands her a roll of notes; and she gives him the letter of credit*].

THE COUNTESS. You are never at a loss. Thanks. So good of you.

TALLBOYS. Chut! Dismiss.

Meek comes to attention, salutes, left-turns, and goes out at the double.

TALLBOYS [*who has listened to this colloquy in renewed stupefaction*] Countess: that was very naughty of you.

THE COUNTESS. What have I done?

TALLBOYS. In camp you must never forget discipline. We keep it in the background; but it is always there and always necessary. That man is a private soldier. Any sort of social relation—any hint of familiarity with him— is impossible for you.

THE COUNTESS. But surely I may treat him as a human being.

TALLBOYS. Most certainly not. Your intention is natural and kindly; but if you treat a private soldier as a human being the result is disastrous to himself. He presumes. He takes liberties. And the consequence of that is that he gets into trouble and has a very bad time of it until he is taught his proper place by appropriate disciplinary measures. I must ask you to be particularly careful with this man Meek. He is only half-witted: he carries all his money about with him. If you have occasion to speak to him, make him feel by your tone that the relation between you is one of a superior addressing a very distant inferior. Never let him address you on his own initiative, or call you anything but "my lady." If there is anything we can do for you we shall be delighted to do it; but you must always ask me.

The patient, greatly pleased with the colonel for snubbing Sweetie, deposits her rug and umbrella on the sand, and places a chair for him on the lady's right with grinning courtesy. She then seats herself on the rug, and listens to them, hugging her knees and her umbrella, and trying to look as indigenous as possible.

TALLBOYS. Thank you. [*He sits down*].

THE COUNTESS. I am so sorry. But if I ask anyone else they only look helpless and say "You had better see Meek about it."

TALLBOYS. No doubt they put everything

on the poor fellow because he is not quite all there. Is it understood that in future you come to me, and not to Meek?

THE COUNTESS. I will indeed, Colonel. I am so sorry, and I thoroughly understand. I am scolded and forgiven, arnt I?

TALLBOYS [smiling graciously] Admonished, we call it. But of course it is not your fault: I have no right to scold you. It is I who must ask your forgiveness.

THE COUNTESS. Granted.

THE PATIENT [in waiting behind them, coughs significantly]!!

THE COUNTESS [hastily] A vulgar expression, Colonel, isn't it? But so simple and direct. I like it.

TALLBOYS. I didnt know it was vulgar. It is concise.

THE COUNTESS. Of course it isnt really vulgar. But a little lower middle class, if you follow me.

THE PATIENT [pokes the chair with the sun umbrella]!

THE COUNTESS [as before] Any news of the brigands, Colonel?

TALLBOYS. No; but Miss Mopply's mother, who is in a distracted condition—very naturally of course, poor woman!—has actually sent me the ransom. She implores me to pay it and release her child. She is afraid that if I make the slightest hostile demonstration the brigands will cut off the girl's fingers and send them in one by one until the ransom is paid. She thinks they may even begin with her ears, and disfigure her for life. Of course that is a possibility: such things have been done; and the poor lady points out very justly that I cannot replace her daughter's ears by exterminating the brigands afterwards, as I shall most certainly do if they dare lay a hand on a British lady. But I cannot countenance such a concession to deliberate criminality as the payment of a ransom. [The two conspirators exchange dismayed glances]. I have sent a message to the old lady by wireless to say that payment of a ransom is out of the question, but that the British Government is offering a substantial reward for information.

THE COUNTESS [jumping up excitedly] Woljesoy? A reward on top of the ransom?

THE PATIENT [pokes her savagely with the umbrella]!!!!

TALLBOYS [surprised] No. Instead of the ransom.

THE COUNTESS [recollecting herself] Of course. How silly of me! [She sits down and adds, reflectively] If this native girl could find out anything would she get the reward?

TALLBOYS. Certainly she would. Good idea that: what?

THE COUNTESS. Yes, Colonel, isn't it?

TALLBOYS. By the way, Countess, I met three people yesterday who know you very well.

THE PATIENT [forgetting herself and scrambling forward to her knees] But you—

THE COUNTESS [stopping her with a back-handed slap on the mouth] Silence, girl. How dare you interrupt the colonel? Go back to your place and hold your tongue.

The Patient obeys humbly until the Colonel delicately turns his head away, when she shakes her fist threateningly at the smiter.

TALLBOYS. One of them was a lady. I happened to mention your brother's name; and she lit up at once and said "Dear Aubrey Bagot! I know his sister intimately. We were all three children together."

THE COUNTESS. It must have been dear Florence Dorchester. I hope she wont come here. I want to have an absolute holiday. I dont want to see anybody—except you, Colonel.

TALLBOYS. Haw! Very good of you to say so.

The Burglar comes from the bathing tent, very elegant in black and white bathing costume and black silken wrap with white silk lapels: a clerical touch.

TALLBOYS [continuing] Ah, Bagot! Ready for your dip? I was just telling the Countess that I met some friends of yours yesterday. Fancy coming on them out here of all places! Shews how small the world is, after all. [Rising] And now I am off to inspect stores. There is a shortage of maroons that I dont understand.

THE COUNTESS. What a pity! I love maroons. They have such nice ones at that confectioner's near the Place Vendôme.

TALLBOYS. Oh, youre thinking of marrons glacés. No: maroons are fireworks: things that go off with a bang. For signalling.

THE COUNTESS. Oh! the things they used to have in the war to warn us of an air raid?

TALLBOYS. Just so. Well, au revoir.

THE COUNTESS. Au revoir. Au revoir.

The Colonel touches his cap gallantly and bustles off past the hut to his inspection.

THE PATIENT [rising vengefully] You dare smack me in the face again, my girl, and I'll lay you out flat, even if I have to give away the whole show.

THE COUNTESS. Well, you keep that umbrella to yourself next time. What do you suppose I'm made of? Leather?

AUBREY [*coming between them*] Now! now! now! Children! children! Whats wrong?

THE PATIENT. This silly bitch—

AUBREY. Oh no, no, no, Mops. Damn it, be a lady. Whats the matter, Sweetie?

THE COUNTESS. You shouldnt talk like that, dearie. A low girl might say a thing like that; but youre expected to know better.

AUBREY. Mops: youve shocked Sweetie.

THE PATIENT. Well: do you think she never shocks me? She's a walking earthquake. And now what are we to do if these people the colonel has met turn up? There must be a real Countess Valbrioni.

THE COUNTESS. Not much there isnt. Do you suppose we three are the only liars in the world? All you have to do is to give yourself a swell title, and all the snobs within fifty miles will swear that you are their dearest friend.

AUBREY. The first lesson a crook has to learn, darling, is that nothing succeeds like lying. Make any statement that is so true that it has been staring us in the face all our lives, and the whole world will rise up and passionately contradict you. If you dont withdraw and apologize, it will be the worse for you. But just tell a thundering silly lie that everyone knows is a lie, and a murmur of pleased assent will hum up from every quarter of the globe. If Sweetie had introduced herself as what she obviously is: that is, an ex-hotel chambermaid who became a criminal on principle through the preaching of an ex-army chaplain—me!—with whom she fell in love deeply but transitorily, nobody would have believed her. But she has no sooner made the impossible statement that she is a countess, and that the ex-chaplain is her half stepbrother the Honorable Aubrey Bagot, than clouds of witnesses spring up to assure Colonel Tallboys that it is all gospel truth. So have no fear of exposure, darling; and do you, my Sweetie, lie and lie and lie until your imagination bursts.

THE PATIENT [*throwing herself moodily into the deck chair*] I wonder are all crooks as fond of preaching as you are.

AUBREY [*bending affectionately over her*] Not all, dearest. I dont preach because I am a

crook, but because I have a gift—a divine gift—that way.

THE PATIENT. Where did you get it? Is your father a bishop?

AUBREY [*straightening himself up to declaim*] Have I not told you that he is an atheist, and, like all atheists, an inflexible moralist? He said I might become a preacher if I believed what I preached. That, of course, was nonsense: my gift of preaching is not confined to what I believe: I can preach anything, true or false. I am like a violin, on which you can play all sorts of music, from jazz to Mozart. [*Relaxing*] But the old man never could be brought to see it. He said the proper profession for me was the bar. [*He snatches up the rug; replaces it on the patient's left; and throws himself down lazily on it*].

THE COUNTESS. Aint we going to bathe?

AUBREY. Oh, dash it, dont lets go into the water. Lets sunbathe.

THE COUNTESS. Lazy devil! [*She takes the folding stool from the pavilion, and sits down discontentedly*].

THE PATIENT. Your father was right. If you have no conscience about what you preach, your proper job is at the bar. But as you have no conscience about what you do, you will probably end in the dock.

AUBREY. Most likely. But I am a born preacher, not a pleader. The theory of legal procedure is that if you set two liars to expose one another, the truth will emerge. That would not suit me. I greatly dislike being contradicted; and the only place where a man is safe from contradiction is in the pulpit. I detest argument: it is unmannerly, and obscures the preacher's message. Besides, the law is too much concerned with crude facts and too little with spiritual things; and it is in spiritual things that I am interested: they alone call my gift into full play.

THE PATIENT. You call preaching things you dont believe spiritual, do you?

AUBREY. Put a sock in it, Mops. My gift is divine: it is not limited by my petty personal convictions. It is a gift of lucidity as well as of eloquence. Lucidity is one of the most precious of gifts: the gift of the teacher: the gift of explanation. I can explain anything to anybody; and I love doing it. I feel I must do it if only the doctrine is beautiful and subtle and exquisitely put together. I may feel instinctively that it is the rottenest nonsense. Still, if I can get a moving dramatic effect out of it, and preach a really splendid sermon about it, my gift takes possession of me and obliges me to sail in and do it. Sweetie: go and get me a cushion for my head: there's a dear.

THE PATIENT. Do nothing of the kind, Sweetie. Let him wait on himself.

THE COUNTESS [rising] He'd only mess everything about looking for it. I like to have my rooms left tidy. [She goes into the pavilion].

THE PATIENT. Isnt that funny, Pops? She has a conscience as a chambermaid and none as a woman.

AUBREY. Very few people have more than one point of honor, Mops. And lots of them havnt even one.

THE COUNTESS [returning with a silk cushion, which she hurls hard at Aubrey's head] There! And now I give you both notice. I'm getting bored with this place.

AUBREY [making himself comfortable with his cushion] Oh, you are always getting bored.

THE PATIENT. I suppose that means that you are tired of Tallboys.

THE COUNTESS [moving restlessly about] I am fed up with him to that degree that I sometimes feel I could almost marry him, just to put him on the list of the inevitables that I must put up with willynilly, like getting up in the morning, and washing and dressing and eating and drinking: things you darent let yourself get tired of because if you did theyd drive you mad. Lets go and have a bit of real life somewhere.

THE PATIENT. Real life! I wonder where thats to be found! Weve spent nearly six thousand pounds in two months looking for it. The money we got for the necklace wont last for ever.

AUBREY. Sweetie: you will have to stick it in this spot until we touch that ransom; and that's all about it.

THE COUNTESS. I'll do as I like, not what you tell me. And I tell you again——the two of you —you can take a week's notice. I'm bored with this business. I need a change.

AUBREY. What are we to do with her, Mops? Always change! change! change!

THE COUNTESS. Well, I like to see new faces.

AUBREY. I could be happy as a Buddha in a temple, eternally contemplating my own middle and having the same old priest to polish me up every day. But Sweetie wants a new face every fortnight. I have known her fall in love with a new face twice in the same week. [Turning to her] Woman: have you any sense of the greatness of constancy?

THE COUNTESS. I might be constant if I were a real countess. But I'm only a hotel chambermaid; and a hotel chambermaid gets so used to new faces that at last they become a necessity. [She sits down on the stool].

AUBREY. And the oftener the faces change the more the tips come to, eh?

THE COUNTESS. Oh, it's not that, though of course that counts. The real secret of it is that though men are awfully nice for the first few days, it doesnt last. You get the best out of men by having them always new. What I say is that a love affair should always be a honeymoon. And the only way to make sure of that is to keep changing the man; for the same man can never keep it up. In all my life I have known only one man that kept it up til he died.

THE PATIENT [interested] Ah! Then the thing is possible?

THE COUNTESS. Yes: it was a man that married my sister: that was how I came to know about it.

AUBREY. And his ardor never palled? Day in and day out, until death did them part, he was the same as on the wedding day? Is that really true, Sweetie?

THE COUNTESS. It is. But then he beat her on their wedding day; and he beat her just as hard every day afterwards. I made her get a separation order; but she went back to him because nobody else paid her any attention.

AUBREY. Why didnt you tell me that before? I'd have beaten you black and blue sooner than lose you. [Sitting up] Would you believe it, Mops, I was in love with this woman: madly in love with her. She was not my intellectual equal; and I had to teach her table manners. But there was an extraordinary sympathy between our lower centres; and when after ten days she threw me over for another man I was restrained from murder and suicide only by the most resolute exercise of my reasoning powers, my determination to be a civilized man, and fear of the police.

THE COUNTESS. Well, I gave you a good time for the ten days, didnt I? Lots of people dont get that much to look back on. Besides, you know it was for your own good, Popsy. We werent really suited, were we?

AUBREY. You had acquired an insatiable taste for commercial travellers. You could sample them at the rate of three a week. I could not help admiring such amazing mobility of the affections. I had heard operatic tenors bawling Woman Is Fickle; but it always seemed to me that what was to be dreaded in women was their implacable constancy. But you! Fickle! I should think so.

THE COUNTESS. Well, the travellers were just as bad, you know.

AUBREY. Just as bad! Say just as good. Fickleness means simply mobility, and mobility is a mark of civilization. You should pride yourself on it. If you dont you will lose your self-respect; and I cannot endure a woman who has no self-respect.

THE COUNTESS. Oh, whats the use of us talking about self-respect? You are a thief and so am I. I go a little further than that, myself; and so would you if you were a woman. Dont you be a hypocrite, Popsy: at least not with me.

AUBREY. At least not with you! Sweetie: that touch of concern for my spiritual welfare almost convinces me that you still love me.

THE COUNTESS. Not me. Not much. I'm through with you, my lad. And I cant quite fancy the colonel: he's too old, and too much the gentleman.

AUBREY. He's better than nobody. Who else is there?

THE COUNTESS. Well, there's the sergeant. I daresay I have low tastes; but he's my sort, and the colonel isnt.

THE PATIENT. Have you fallen in love with Sergeant Fielding, Sweetie?

THE COUNTESS. Well, yes; if you like to call it that.

AUBREY. May I ask have you sounded him on the subject?

THE COUNTESS. How can I? I'm a countess; and he's only a sergeant. If I as much as let on that I'm conscious of his existence I give away the show to the colonel. I can only look at him. And I cant do even that when anyone else is looking. And all the time I want to hug him [she breaks down in tears].

AUBREY. Oh for Heaven's sake dont start crying.

THE PATIENT. For all you know, Sweetie, the sergeant may be a happily married man.

THE COUNTESS. What difference does that make to my feelings? I am so lonely. The place is so dull. No pictures. No dances.

Nothing to do but be ladylike. And the one really lovable man going to waste! I'd rather be dead.

THE PATIENT. Well, it's just as bad for me.

THE COUNTESS. No it isnt. Youre a real lady: youre broken in to be dull. Besides, you have Popsy. And youre supposed to be our servant. That gives you the run of the whole camp when youre tired of him. You can pick up a private when you like. Whats to prevent you?

THE PATIENT. My ladylike morals, I suppose.

THE COUNTESS. Morals your grandmother! I thought youd left all that flapdoodle behind you when you came away with us.

THE PATIENT. I meant to. Ive tried to. But you shock me in spite of myself every second time you open your mouth.

THE COUNTESS. Dont you set up to be a more moral woman than I am, because youre not.

THE PATIENT. I dont pretend to be. But I may tell you that my infatuation for Popsy, which I now see was what really nerved me to this astonishing breakaway, has been, so far, quite innocent. Can you believe that, you clod?

THE COUNTESS. Oh yes I can: Popsy's satisfied as long as you let him talk. What I mean is—and I tell it to you straight—that with all my faults I'm content with one man at a time.

THE PATIENT. Do you suggest that I am carrying on with two men?

THE COUNTESS. I dont suggest anything. I say what I mean straight out; and if you dont like it you can lump it. You may be in love with Popsy; but youre interested in Private Meek, though what you see in that dry little worm beats me.

THE PATIENT. Have you noticed, my Sweetie, that your big strapping splendid sergeant is completely under the thumb of that dry little worm?

THE COUNTESS. He wont be when I get him under my thumb. But you just be careful. Take this tip from me: one man at a time. I am advising you for your good, because youre only a beginner; and what you think is love, and interest, and all that, is not real love at all: three quarters of it is only unsatisfied curiosity. Ive lived at that address myself; and I know. When I love a man now it's all love and nothing else. It's the real thing while it lasts. I havnt the least curiosity about my lovely sergeant: I know just what he'll say and what he'll do. I just want him to do it.

THE PATIENT [*rising, revolted*] Sweetie: I really cannot bear any more of this. No doubt it's perfectly true. It's quite right that you should say it frankly and plainly. I envy and admire the frightful coolness with which you plump it all out. Perhaps I shall get used to it in time. But at present it knocks me to pieces. I shall simply have to go away if you pursue the subject. [*She sits down in the cane chair with her back to them*].

AUBREY. Thats the worst of Sweetie. We all have—to put it as nicely as I can—our lower centres and our higher centres. Our lower centres act: they act with a terrible power that sometimes destroys us; but they dont talk. Speech belongs to the higher centres. In all the great poetry and literature of the world the higher centres speak. In all respectable conversation the higher centres speak, even when they are saying nothing or telling lies. But the lower centres are there all the time: a sort of guilty secret with every one of us, though they are dumb. I remember asking my tutor at college whether, if anyone's lower centres began to talk, the shock would not be worse than the one Balaam got when his donkey began talking to him. He only told me half a dozen improper stories to shew how openminded he was. I never mentioned the subject again until I met Sweetie. Sweetie is Balaam's ass.

THE COUNTESS. Keep a civil tongue in your head, Popsy. I—

AUBREY [*springing to his feet*] Woman: I am paying you a compliment: Balaam's ass was wiser than Balaam. You should read your Bible. That is what makes Sweetie almost superhuman. Her lower centres speak. Since the war the lower centres have become vocal. And the effect is that of an earthquake. For they speak truths that have never been spoken before—truths that the makers of our domestic institutions have tried to ignore. And now that Sweetie goes shouting them all over the place, the institutions are rocking and splitting and sundering. They leave us no place to live, no certainties, no workable morality, no heaven, no hell, no commandments, and no God.

THE PATIENT. What about the light in our own souls that you were so eloquent about the day before yesterday at lunch when you drank a pint of champagne?

AUBREY. Most of us seem to have no souls. Or if we have them, they have nothing to hang on to. Meanwhile, Sweetie goes on shouting. [*He takes refuge in the deck chair*].

THE COUNTESS [*rising*] Oh, what are you gassing about? I am not shouting. I should be a good woman if it wasnt so dull. If youre goodnatured, you just get put upon. Who are the good women? Those that enjoy being dull and like being put upon. Theyve no appetites. Life's thrown away on them: they get nothing out of it

THE PATIENT. Well, come, Sweetie! What do you get out of it?

THE COUNTESS. Excitement: thats what I get out of it. Look at Popsy and me! We're always planning robberies. Of course I know it's mostly imagination; but the fun is in the planning and the expectation. Even if we did them and were caught, there would be the excitement of being tried and being in all the papers. Look at poor Harry Smiler that murdered the cop in Croydon! When he came and told us what he'd done Popsy offered to go out and get him some cyanide to poison himself; for it was a dead sure thing that he'd be caught and bumped off. "What!" says Harry; "and lose the excitement of being tried for my life! I'd rather be hanged" he says; and hanged he was. And I say it must have been almost worth it. After all, he'd have died anyhow: perhaps of something really painful. Harry wasnt a bad man really; but he couldnt bear dullness. He had a wonderful collection of pistols that he had begun as a boy: he picked up a lot in the war. Just for the romance of it, you know: he meant no harm. But he'd never shot anyone with them; and at last the temptation was too great and he went out and shot the cop. Just for nothing but the feeling that he'd fired the thing off and done somebody in with it. When Popsy asked him why he'd done it, all he could say was that it was a sort of fulfilment. But it gives you an idea, doesnt it, of what I mean? [*She sits down again, relieved by her outburst*].

AUBREY. All it means is a low vitality. Here is a man with all the miracles of the universe to stagger his imagination and all the problems of human destiny to employ his mind, and he goes out and shoots an innocent policeman because he can think of nothing more interesting to do. Quite right to hang him. And all the people who can find nothing more exciting to do than to crowd into the court to watch him being sentenced to death should have been hanged too. You will be hanged someday, Sweetie, because you have not what people call a richly stored mind. I have tried to educate you—

THE COUNTESS. Yes: you gave me books to read. But I couldnt read them: they were as dull as ditchwater. Ive tried crossword puzzles to occupy my mind and keep me off planning robberies; but what crossword puzzle is half the fun and excitement of picking somebody's pocket, let alone that you cant live by it? You wanted me to take to drink to keep me quiet. But I dont like being drunk; and what would become of my good looks if I did? Ten bottles of champagne couldnt make you feel as you do when you walk past a policeman who has only to stop you and search you to put you away for three years.

THE PATIENT. Pops: did you really try to set her drinking? What a thoroughpaced blackguard you are!

AUBREY. She is much better company when she's half drunk. Listen to her now, when she is sober!

THE PATIENT. Sweetie: are you really having such a jolly time after all? You began by threatening to give up our exciting enterprise because it is so dull.

AUBREY. She is free. There is the sergeant. And there is always the hope of something turning up and the sense of being ready for it without having to break all the shackles and throw down all the walls that imprison a respectable woman.

THE PATIENT. Well, what about me?

AUBREY [puzzled] Well, what about you? You are free, arnt you?

THE PATIENT [rising very deliberately, and going behind him to his left hand, which she picks up and fondles as she sermonizes, seated on the arm of his chair] My angel love, you have rescued me from respectability so completely that I have for a month past been living the life of a mountain goat. I have got rid of my anxious worrying mother as completely as a weaned kid, and I no longer hate her. My slavery to cooks stuffing me with long meals of fish, flesh, and fowl is a thing of the miserable past: I eat dates and bread and water and raw onions when I can get them; and when I cant get them I fast, with the result that I have forgotten what illness means; and

if I ran away from you two neither of you could catch me; and if you did I could fight the pair of you with one hand tied behind me. I revel in all your miracles of the universe: the delicious dawns, the lovely sunsets, the changing winds, the cloud pictures, the flowers, the animals and their ways, the birds and insects and reptiles. Every day is a day of adventure with its cold and heat, its light and darkness, its cycles of exultant vigor and exhaustion, hunger and satiety, its longings for action that change into a longing for sleep, its thoughts of heavenly things that change so suddenly into a need for food.

AUBREY. What more could any mortal desire?

THE PATIENT [seizing him by the ears] Liar.

AUBREY. Thank you. You mean, I presume, that these things do not satisfy you: you want me as well.

THE PATIENT. You!! You!!! you selfish lazy sugary tongued blackguard. [Releasing him] No: I included you with the animals and their ways, just as I included Sweetie and the sergeant.

THE COUNTESS. You let Sweetie and her sergeant alone: d'y'hear? I have had enough of that joke on me.

THE PATIENT [rising and taking her by the chin to turn her face up] It is no joke, Sweetiest: it is the dead solemn earnest. I called Pops a liar, Sweetie, because all this is not enough. The glories of nature dont last any decently active person a week, unless theyre professional naturalists or mathematicians or a painter or something. I want something sensible to do. A beaver has a jolly time because it has to build its dam and bring up its family. I want my little job like the beaver. If I do nothing but contemplate the universe there is so much in it that is cruel and terrible and wantonly evil, and so much more that is oppressively astronomical and endless and inconceivable and impossible, that I shall just go stark raving mad and be taken back to my mother with straws in my hair. The truth is, I am free; I am healthy; I am happy; and I am utterly miserable. [Turning on Aubrey] Do you hear? Utterly miserable.

AUBREY [losing his temper] And what do you suppose I am? Here with nothing to do but drag about two damn' silly women and talk to them.

THE COUNTESS. It's worse for them. They have to listen to you.

THE PATIENT. I despise you. I hate you.

You—you—you—you gentleman thief. What right has a thief to be a gentleman? Sweetie is bad enough, heaven knows, with her vulgarity and her low cunning: always trying to get the better of somebody or to get hold of a man; but at least she's a woman; and she's real. Men are not real: theyre all talk, talk, talk—

THE COUNTESS [half rising] You keep a civil tongue in your head: do you hear?

THE PATIENT. Another syllable of your cheek, Sweetie; and I'll give you a hiding that will keep you screaming for half an hour. [Sweetie subsides]. I want to beat somebody: I want to kill somebody. I shall end by killing the two of you. What are we, we three glorious adventurers? Just three inefficient fertilizers.

AUBREY. What on earth do you mean by that?

THE PATIENT. Yes: inefficient fertilizers. We do nothing but convert good food into bad manure. We are walking factories of bad manure: thats what we are.

THE COUNTESS [rising] Well, I am not going to sit here and listen to that sort of talk. You ought to be ashamed of yourself.

AUBREY [rising also, shocked] Miss Mopply: there are certain disgusting truths that no lady would throw in the teeth of her fellow creatures—

THE PATIENT. I am not a lady: I am free now to say what I please. How do you like it?

THE COUNTESS [relenting] Look here, dearie. You mustnt go off at the deep end like this. You— [The patient turns fiercely on her: she screams]. Ah-a-a-ah! Popsy: she's mad. Save me. [She runs away, out past the pavilion].

AUBREY. What is the matter with you? Are you out of your senses? [He tries to hold her; but she sends him sprawling].

THE PATIENT. No. I am exercising my freedom. The freedom you preached. The freedom you made possible for me. You dont like to hear Sweetie's lower centres shouting. Well, now you hear my higher centres shouting. You dont seem to like it any better.

AUBREY. Mops: youre hysterical. You felt splendid an hour ago; and you will feel splendid again an hour from now. You will always feel splendid if you keep yourself fit.

THE PATIENT. Fit for what? A lost dog feels fit: thats what makes him stray; but he's the unhappiest thing alive. I am a lost dog: a tramp, a vagabond. Ive got nothing to do.

Ive got nowhere to go. Sweetie's miserable; and youre miserable; and I'm miserable; and I shall just kick you and beat you to a jelly.

She rushes at him. He dodges her and runs off past the hut. At that moment Tallboys returns with Meek past the other side of the hut; and the patient, unable to check herself, crashes into his arms.

TALLBOYS [sternly] Whats this? What are you doing here? Why are you making this noise? Dont clench your fists in my presence. [She droops obsequiously]. Whats the matter?

THE PATIENT [salaaming and chanting] Bmal elttil a dah yram, Tuan.

TALLBOYS. Can you speak English?

THE PATIENT. No Engliss.

TALLBOYS. Or French?

THE PATIENT. No Frennss, Tuan. Wons sa etihw saw eceelf sti.

TALLBOYS. Very well: dont do it again. Now off with you.

She goes out backward into the pavilion, salaaming. Tallboys sits down in the deck chair.

TALLBOYS [to Meek] Here, you. You say youre the interpreter. Did you understand what that girl said to me?

MEEK. Yessir.

TALLBOYS. What dialect was it? It didnt sound like what the natives speak here.

MEEK. No sir. I used to speak it at school. English back slang, sir.

TALLBOYS. Back slang? What do you mean?

MEEK. English spelt backwards. She reversed the order of the words too, sir. That shews that she has those two little speeches off by heart.

TALLBOYS. But how could a native girl do such a thing? I couldnt do it myself.

MEEK. That shews that she's not a native girl, sir.

TALLBOYS. But this must be looked into. Were you able to pick up what she said?

MEEK. Only bmal elttil, sir. That was quite easy. It put me on to the rest.

TALLBOYS. But what does bmal elttil mean?

MEEK. Little lamb, sir.

TALLBOYS. She called me a little lamb!

MEEK. No sir. All she said was "Mary had a little lamb." And when you asked her could she speak French she said, of course, "Its fleece was white as snow."

TALLBOYS. But that was insolence.

MEEK. It got her out of her difficulty, sir.

TALLBOYS. This is very serious. The woman

is passing herself off on the Countess as a native servant.

MEEK. Do you think so, sir?

TALLBOYS. I dont think so: I know so. Dont be a fool, man. Pull yourself together, and dont make silly answers.

MEEK. Yessir. No sir.

TALLBOYS [*angrily bawling at him*] "Ba Ba black sheep: have you any wool? Yes sir, no sir, three bags full." Dont say yessir no sir to me.

MEEK. No sir.

TALLBOYS. Go and fetch that girl back. Not a word to her about my finding her out, mind. When I have finished with her you will explain to me about those maroons.

MEEK. Yessir. [*He goes into the pavilion*].

TALLBOYS. Hurry up. [*He settles himself comfortably and takes out his cigaret case*].

The Countess peers round the corner of the pavilion to see whether she may safely return. Aubrey makes a similar reconnaissance round the corner of the hut.

THE COUNTESS. Here I am again, you see. [*She smiles fascinatingly at the Colonel and sits down on her stool*].

AUBREY. Moi aussi. May I— [*he stretches himself on the rug*].

TALLBOYS [*sitting up and putting the cigaret case back in his pocket*] Just in the nick of time. I was about to send for you. I have made a very grave discovery. That native servant of yours is not a native. Her lingo is a ridiculous fraud. She is an Englishwoman.

AUBREY. You dont say so!

THE COUNTESS. Oh, impossible.

TALLBOYS. Not a doubt of it. She's a fraud: take care of your jewels. Or else—and this is what I suspect—she's a spy.

AUBREY. A spy! But we are not at war.

TALLBOYS. The League of Nations has spies everywhere. [*To the Countess*] You must allow me to search her luggage at once, before she knows that I have found her out.

THE COUNTESS. But I have missed nothing. I am sure she hasnt stolen anything. What do you want to search her luggage for?

TALLBOYS. For maroons.

THE COUNTESS ⎫ [*together*] ⎧Maroons!
AUBREY   ⎭   ⎩Maroons!

TALLBOYS. Yes, maroons. I inspected the stores this morning; and the maroons are missing. I particularly wanted them to recall me at lunch time when I go sketching. I am rather a dab at watercolors. And there is not a single maroon left. There should be fifteen.

AUBREY. Oh, I can clear that up. It's one of your men: Meek. He goes about on a motor bicycle with a sack full of maroons and a lot of wire. He said he was surveying. He was evidently very anxious to get rid of me; so I did not press my inquiries. But that accounts for the maroons.

TALLBOYS. Not at all. This is very serious. Meek is a half witted creature who should never have been enlisted. He is like a child: this woman could do anything she pleases with him.

THE COUNTESS. But what could she possibly want with maroons?

TALLBOYS. I dont know. This expedition has been sent out without the sanction of the League of Nations. We always forget to consult it when there is anything serious in hand. The woman may be an emissary of the League. She may be working against us.

THE COUNTESS. But even so, what harm can she do us?

TALLBOYS [*tapping his revolver*] My dear lady, do you suppose I am carrying this for fun? Dont you realize that the hills here are full of hostile tribes who may try to raid us at any moment? Look at that electric horn there. If it starts honking, look out; for it will mean that a body of tribesmen has been spotted advancing on us.

THE COUNTESS [*alarmed*] If I'd known that, you wouldnt have got me here. Is that so, Popsy?

AUBREY. Well, yes; but it doesnt matter: theyre afraid of us.

TALLBOYS. Yes, because they dont know that we are a mere handful of men. But if this woman is in communication with them and has got hold of that idiot Meek, we may have them down on us like a swarm of hornets. I dont like this at all. I must get to the bottom of it at once. Ah! here she comes.

Meek appears at the entrance to the pavilion. He stands politely aside to let the patient pass him, and remains there.

MEEK. The colonel would like a word with you, Miss.

AUBREY. Go easy with her, Colonel. She can run like a deer. And she has muscles of iron. You had better turn out the guard before you tackle her.

TALLBOYS. Pooh! Here, you!

The patient comes to him past the Countess with an air of disarming innocence; falls on her knees; lifts her palms; and smites the ground with her forehead.

TALLBOYS. They tell me you can run fast. Well, a bullet can run faster. [*He taps his revolver*]. Do you understand that?

THE PATIENT [*salaaming*] Bmal elttil a dah yram wons sa etihw saw eceelf sti—

TALLBOYS [*tonitruant*] And everywhere that Mary went—

THE PATIENT [*adroitly cutting in*] That lamb was sure to go. Got me, Colonel. How clever of you! Well, what of it?

TALLBOYS. That is what I intend to find out. You are not a native.

THE PATIENT. Yes, of Somerset.

TALLBOYS. Precisely. Well, why are you disguised? Why did you try to make me believe that you dont understand English?

THE PATIENT. For a lark, Colonel.

TALLBOYS. Thats not good enough. Why have you passed yourself off on this lady as a native servant? Being a servant is no lark. Answer me. Dont stand there trying to invent a lie. Why did you pretend to be a servant?

THE PATIENT. One has so much more control of the house as a servant than as a mistress nowadays, Colonel.

TALLBOYS. Very smart, that. You will tell me next that one controls a regiment much more effectively as a private than as a colonel, eh?

The klaxon sounds stridently. The Colonel draws his revolver and makes a dash for the top of the sandhill, but is outraced by Meek, who gets there first and takes the word of command with irresistible authority, leaving him stupent. Aubrey, who has scrambled to his feet, moves towards the sand dunes to see what is happening. Sweetie clutches the patient's arm in terror and drags her towards the pavilion. She is fiercely shaken off; and Mops stands her ground defiantly and runs towards the sound of the guns when they begin.

MEEK. Stand to. Charge your magazines. Stand by the maroons. How many do you make them, sergeant? How far off?

SERGEANT FIELDING [*invisible*] Forty horse. Nine hundred yards, about, I make it.

MEEK. Rifles at the ready. Cut-offs open. Sights up to eighteen hundred, right over their heads: no hitting. Ten rounds rapid: fire. [*Fusillade of rifles*]. How is that?

SERGEANT'S VOICE. Theyre coming on, sir.

MEEK. Number one maroons: ready. Contact. [*Formidable explosions on the right*]. How is that?

SERGEANT'S VOICE. Theyve stopped.

MEEK. Number two maroons ready. Contact. [*Explosions on the left*]. How is that?

SERGEANT'S VOICE. Bolted, sir, every man of them.

Meek returns from the hill in the character of an insignificant private, followed by Aubrey, to the Colonel's left and right respectively.

MEEK. Thats all right, sir. Excuse interruption.

TALLBOYS. Oh! You call this an interruption?

MEEK. Yessir: theres nothing in it to trouble you about. Shall I draw up the report, sir? Important engagement: enemy routed: no British casualties. D.S.O. for you, perhaps, sir.

TALLBOYS. Private Meek: may I ask—if you will pardon my presumption—who is in command of this expedition, you or I?

MEEK. You, sir.

TALLBOYS [*repouching the revolver*] You flatter me. Thank you. May I ask, further, who the devil gave you leave to plant the entire regimental stock of maroons all over the hills and explode them in the face of the enemy?

MEEK. It was the duty of the intelligence orderly, sir. I'm the intelligence orderly. I had to make the enemy believe that the hills are bristling with British cannon. They think that now, sir. No more trouble from them.

TALLBOYS. Indeed! Quartermaster's clerk, interpreter, intelligence orderly. Any further rank of which I have not been informed?

MEEK. No sir.

TALLBOYS. Quite sure youre not a field-marshal, eh?

MEEK. Quite sure, sir. I never was anything higher than a colonel.

TALLBOYS. You a colonel? What do you mean?

MEEK. Not a real colonel, sir. Mostly a brevet, sir, to save appearances when I had to take command.

TALLBOYS. And how do you come to be a private now?

MEEK. I prefer the ranks, sir. I have a freer hand. And the conversation in the officers' mess doesnt suit me. I always resign a commission and enlist again.

TALLBOYS. Always! How many commissions have you held?

2 P

MEEK. I dont quite remember, sir. Three, I think.

TALLBOYS. Well, I am dashed!

THE PATIENT. Oh, Colonel! And you mistook this great military genius for a half wit!!!

TALLBOYS [*with aplomb*] Naturally. The symptoms are precisely the same. [*To Meek*] Dismiss.

Meek salutes and trots smartly out past the hut.

AUBREY. By Jove!!

THE COUNTESS. Well I ne— [*Correcting herself*] Tiens, tiens, tiens, tiens!

THE PATIENT. What are you going to do about him, Colonel?

TALLBOYS. Madam: the secret of command, in the army and elsewhere, is never to waste a moment doing anything that can be delegated to a subordinate. I have a passion for sketching in watercolors. Hitherto the work of commanding my regiment has interfered very seriously with its gratification. Henceforth I shall devote myself almost entirely to sketching, and leave the command of the expedition to Private Meek. And since you all seem to be on more intimate terms with him than I can claim, will you be good enough to convey to him—casually, you understand —that I already possess the D.S.O. and that what I am out for at present is a K.C.B. Or rather, to be strictly accurate, that is what my wife is out for. For myself, my sole concern for the moment is whether I should paint that sky with Prussian blue or with cobalt.

THE COUNTESS. Fancy you wasting your time on painting pictures!

TALLBOYS. Countess: I paint pictures to make me feel sane. Dealing with men and women makes me feel mad. Humanity always fails me: Nature never.

ACT III

A narrow gap leading down to the beach through masses of soft brown sandstone, pitted with natural grottoes. Sand and big stones in the foreground. Two of the grottoes are accessible from the beach by mounting from the stones, which make rough platforms in front of them. The soldiers have amused themselves by hewing them into a rude architecture and giving them fancy names. The one on your right as you descend the rough path through the gap is taller *than it is broad, and has a natural pillar and a stone like an altar in it, giving a Gothic suggestion which has been assisted by knocking the top of the opening into something like a pointed arch, and surmounting it with the inscription* SN PAULS. *The grotto to the left is much wider. It contains a bench long enough to accommodate two persons, its recesses are illuminated rosily by bulbs wrapped in pink paper; and some scholarly soldier has carved above it in Greek characters the word* Αγαπεμονε, *beneath which is written in red chalk* THE ABODE OF LOVE, *under which again some ribald has added in white chalk,* NO NEED TO WASTE THE ELECTRIC LIGHT.

For the moment The Abode of Love has been taken possession of by the sergeant, a wellbuilt handsome man, getting on for forty. He is sitting on the bench, and is completely absorbed in two books, comparing them with rapt attention.

St Pauls is also occupied. A very tall gaunt elder, by his dress and bearing a well-to-do English gentleman, sits on a stone at the altar, resting his elbows on it with his chin in his hands. He is in the deepest mourning; and his attitude is one of hopeless dejection.

Sweetie, now fully and brilliantly dressed, comes slowly down the path through the gap, moody and bored. On the beach she finds nothing to interest her until the sergeant unconsciously attracts her notice by finding some remarkable confirmation or contradiction between his two books, and smiting one of them appreciatively with his fist. She instantly brightens up; climbs to the mouth of the grotto eagerly; and posts herself beside him, on his right. But he is so rapt in his books that she waits in vain to be noticed.

SWEETIE [*contemplating him ardently*] Ahem!

The Sergeant looks up. Seeing who it is, he springs to his feet and stands to attention.

SWEETIE [*giving herself no airs*] You neednt stand up for me, you know.

THE SERGEANT [*stiffly*] Beg pardon, your ladyship. I was not aware of your ladyship's presence.

SWEETIE. Can all that stuff, Sergeant. [*She sits on the bench on his right*]. Dont lets waste time. This place is as dull for me as it is for you. Dont you think we two could amuse ourselves a bit if we were friends?

THE SERGEANT [*with stern contempt*] No, my lady, I dont. I saw a lot of that in the war: pretty ladies brightening up the hospitals and losing their silly heads, let alone upsetting the men; and I dont hold with it.

Keep to your class: I'll keep to mine.

SWEETIE. My class! Garn! I'm no countess; and I'm fed up with pretending to be one. Didnt you guess?

THE SERGEANT [resuming his seat and treating her as one of his own class] Why should I trouble to start guessing about you? Any girl can be a countess nowadays if she's good-looking enough to pick up a count.

SWEETIE. Oh! You think I'm goodlooking, do you?

THE SERGEANT. Come! If youre not a countess what are you? Whats the game, eh?

SWEETIE. The game, darling, is that youre my fancy. I love you.

THE SERGEANT. Whats that to me? A man of my figure can have his pick.

SWEETIE. Not here, dear. Theres only one other white woman within fifty miles; and she's a real lady. She wouldnt look at you.

THE SERGEANT. Well, thats a point. Thats a point, certainly.

SWEETIE [snuggling to him] Yes, isnt it?

THE SERGEANT [suffering the advance but not responding] This climate plays the devil with a man, no matter how serious minded he is.

SWEETIE [slipping her arm through his] Well, isnt it natural? Whats the use of pretending?

THE SERGEANT. Still, I'm not a man to treat a woman as a mere necessity. Many soldiers do: to them a woman is no more than a jar of marmalade, to be consumed and put away. I dont take that view. I admit that there is that side to it, and that for people incapable of anything better—mere animals as you might say—thats the beginning and the end of it. But to me thats only the smallest part of it. I like getting a woman's opinions. I like to explore her mind as well as her body. See these two little books I was deep in when you accosted me? I carry them with me wherever I go. I put the problems they raise for me to every woman I meet.

SWEETIE [with growing misgiving] What are they?

THE SERGEANT [pointing to them successively] The Bible. The Pilgrim's Progress from this world to that which is to come.

SWEETIE [dismayed, trying to rise] Oh, my God!

THE SERGEANT [holding her ruthlessly in the crook of his elbow] No you dont. Sit quiet; and dont take the name of the Lord your God in vain. If you believe in him, it's blasphemy: if you dont, it's nonsense. You must learn to exer-cise your mind: what is a woman without an active mind to a man but a mere convenience?

SWEETIE. I have plenty to exercise my mind looking after my own affairs. What I look to you for, my lad, is a bit of fun.

THE SERGEANT. Quite. But when men and women pick one another up just for a bit of fun, they find theyve picked up more than they bargained for, because men and women have a top storey as well as a ground floor; and you cant have the one without the other. Theyre always trying to; but it doesnt work. Youve picked up my mind as well as my body; and youve got to explore it. You thought you could have a face and a figure like mine with the limitations of a gorilla. Youre finding out your mistake: thats all.

SWEETIE. Oh, let me go; I have had enough of this. If I'd thought you were religious I'd have given you a wide berth, I tell you. Let me go, will you?

THE SERGEANT. Wait a bit. Nature may be using me as a sort of bait to draw you to take an interest in things of the mind. Nature may be using your pleasant animal warmth to stimulate my mind. I want your advice. I dont say I'll take it; but it may suggest something to me. You see, I'm in a mess.

SWEETIE. Well, of course. Youre in the sergeants' mess.

THE SERGEANT. Thats not the mess I mean. My mind's in a mess—a muddle. I used to be a religious man; but I'm not so clear about it as I was.

SWEETIE. Thank goodness for that, anyhow.

THE SERGEANT. Look at these two books. I used to believe every word of them because they seemed to have nothing to do with real life. But war brought those old stories home quite real; and then one starts asking questions. Look at this bit here [he points to a page of The Pilgrim's Progress]. It's on the very first page of it. "I am for certain informed that this our city will be burned with fire from heaven, in which fearful overthrow both myself, with thee my wife, and you my sweet babes, shall miserably come to ruin, except some way of escape can be found whereby we may be delivered." Well, London and Paris and Berlin and Rome and the rest of them will be burned with fire from heaven all right in the next war: thats certain. Theyre all Cities of Destruction. And our Government chaps are running about with a great burden of corpses and debts on their backs, crying "What must we do to be saved?" There it is: not a story in a book as it used to be, but God's truth in the real actual world. And all the comfort they get is "Flee from the wrath to come." But where are they to flee to? There they are, meeting at Geneva or hobnobbing at Chequers over the weekend, asking one another, like the man in the book, "Whither must we flee?" And nobody can tell them. The man in the book says "Do you see yonder shining light?" Well, today the place is blazing with shining lights: shining lights in parliament, in the papers, in the churches, and in the books that they call Outlines—Outlines of History and Science and what not—and in spite of all their ballyhoo here we are waiting in the City of Destruction like so many sheep for the wrath to come. This uneducated tinker tells me the way is straight before us and so narrow that we cant miss it. But he starts by calling the place the wilderness of this world. Well, theres no road in a wilderness: you have to make one. All the straight roads are made by soldiers; and the soldiers didnt get to heaven along them. A lot of them landed up in the other place. No, John: you could tell a story well; and they say you were a soldier; but soldiers that try to make storytelling do for service end in the clink; and thats where they put you. Twelve years in Bedford Gaol, he got. He used to read the Bible in gaol; and—

SWEETIE. Well, what else was there to read there? It's all they give you in some gaols.

THE SERGEANT. How do you know that?

SWEETIE. Never you mind how I know it. It's nothing to do with you.

THE SERGEANT. Nothing to do with me! You dont know me, my lass. Some men would just order you off; but to me the most interesting thing in the world is the experience of a woman thats been shut up in a cell for years at a time with nothing but a Bible to read.

SWEETIE. Years! What are you talking about? The longest I ever did was nine months; and if anyone says I ever did a day longer she's a liar.

THE SERGEANT [laying his hand on the bible] You could read that book from cover to cover in nine months.

SWEETIE. Some of it would drive you melancholy mad. It only got me into trouble: it did. The chaplain asked me what I was in for. Spoiling the Egyptians, I says; and heres chapter and verse for it. He went and re-ported me, the swine; and I lost seven days remission for it.

THE SERGEANT. Serve you right! I dont hold with spoiling the Egyptians. Before the war, spoiling the Egyptians was something holy. Now I see plainly it's nothing but thieving.

SWEETIE [shocked] Oh, you shouldnt say that. But what I say is, if Moses might do it why maynt I?

THE SERGEANT. If thats the effect it had on your mind, it's a bad effect. Some of this scripture is all right. Do justice; love mercy; and walk humbly before your God. That appeals to a man if only it could be set out in plain army regulations. But all this thieving, and slaughtering your enemies without giving quarter, and offering up human sacrifices, and thinking you can do what you like to other people because youre the chosen people of God, and you are in the right and everyone else is in the wrong: how does that look when you have had four years of the real thing instead of merely reading about it. No: damn it, we're civilized men; and though it may have gone down with those old Jews it isnt religion. And, if it isnt, where are we? Thats what I want to know.

SWEETIE. And is this all you care about? Sitting here and thinking of things like that?

THE SERGEANT. Well, somebody must think about them, or whats going to become of us all? The officers wont think about them. The colonel goes out sketching: the lootnants go out and kill the birds and animals, or play polo. They wont flee from the wrath to come, not they. When they wont do their military duties I have to do them. It's the same with our religious duties. It's the chaplain's job, not mine; but when you get a real religious chaplain you find he doesnt believe any of the old stuff; and if you get a gentleman, all he cares about is to shew you that he's a real sport and not a mealy mouthed parson. So I have to puzzle it out for myself.

SWEETIE. Well, God help the woman that marries you: thats all I have to say to you. I dont call you a man. [She rises quickly to escape from him].

THE SERGEANT [also rising, and seizing her in a very hearty embrace] Not a man, eh? [He kisses her] How does that feel, Judy?

SWEETIE [struggling, but not very resolutely] You let me go, will you. I dont want you now.

THE SERGEANT. You will if I kiss you half a dozen times, more than you ever wanted anything in your life before. Thats a hard fact of human nature; and its one of the facts that religion has to make room for.

SWEETIE. Oh, well, kiss me and have done with it. You cant kiss and talk about religion at the same time.

THE ELDER [*springing from his cell to the platform in front of it*] Forbear this fooling, both of you. You, sir, are not an ignorant man: you know that the universe is wrecked.

SWEETIE [*clinging to the sergeant*] He's mad.

THE ELDER. I am sane in a world of lunatics.

THE SERGEANT [*putting Sweetie away*] It's a queer thing, isnt it, that though there is a point at which I'd rather kiss a woman than do anything else in the world, yet I'd rather be shot than let anyone see me doing it?

THE ELDER. Sir: women are not, as they suppose, more interesting than the universe. When the universe is crumbling let women be silent; and let men rise to something nobler than kissing them.

The Sergeant, interested and overawed, sits down quietly and makes Sweetie sit beside him as before. The Elder continues to declaim with fanatical intensity.

THE ELDER. Yes, sir: the universe of Isaac Newton, which has been an impregnable citadel of modern civilization for three hundred years, has crumbled like the walls of Jericho before the criticism of Einstein. Newton's universe was the stronghold of rational Determinism: the stars in their orbits obeyed immutably fixed laws; and when we turned from surveying their vastness to study the infinite littleness of the atoms, there too we found the electrons in their orbits obeying the same universal laws. Every moment of time dictated and determined the following moment, and was itself dictated and determined by the moment that came before it. Everything was calculable: everything happened because it must: the commandments were erased from the tables of the law; and in their place came the cosmic algebra: the equations of the mathematicians. Here was my faith: here I found my dogma of infallibility: I, who scorned alike the Catholic with his vain dream of responsible Free Will, and the Protestant with his pretence of private judgment. And now—now—what is left of it? The orbit of the electron obeys no law: it chooses one path and rejects another: it is as capricious as the planet Mercury, who wanders from his road to warm his hands at the sun. All is caprice: the calculable world has become incalculable: Purpose and Design, the pretexts for all the vilest superstitions, have risen from the dead to cast down the mighty from their seats and put paper crowns on presumptuous fools. Formerly, when differences with my wife, or business worries, tried me too hard, I sought consolation and reassurance in our natural history museums, where I could forget all common cares in wondering at the diversity of forms and colors in the birds and fishes and animals, all produced without the agency of any designer by the operation of Natural Selection. Today I dare not enter an aquarium, because I can see nothing in those grotesque monsters of the deep but the caricatures of some freakish demon artist: some Zeus-Mephistopheles with paintbox and plasticine, trying to surpass himself in the production of fantastic and laughable creatures to people a Noah's ark for his baby. I have to rush from the building lest I go mad, crying, like the man in your book, "What must I do to be saved?" Nothing can save us from a perpetual headlong fall into a bottomless abyss but a solid footing of dogma; and we no sooner agree to that than we find that the only trustworthy dogma is that there is no dogma. As I stand here I am falling into that abyss, down, down, down. We are all falling into it; and our dizzy brains can utter nothing but madness. My wife has died cursing me. I do not know how to live without her: we were unhappy together for forty years. My son, whom I brought up to be an incorruptible Godfearing atheist, has become a thief and a scoundrel; and I can say nothing to him but "Go, boy: perish in your villainy; for neither your father nor anyone else can now give you a good reason for being a man of honor."

He turns from them and is rushing distractedly away when Aubrey, in white tropicals, comes strolling along the beach from the St Pauls side, and hails him nonchalantly.

AUBREY. Hullo, father, is it really you? I thought I heard the old trombone: I couldnt mistake it. How the dickens did you turn up here?

THE ELDER [*to the sergeant*] This is my prodigal son.

AUBREY. I am not a prodigal son. The prodigal son was a spendthrift and neer-do-weel who was reduced to eating the husks that the swine did eat. I am not ruined: I am rolling in money. I have never owed a farthing to any man. I am a model son; but I regret to say that you are very far from being a model father.

THE ELDER. What right have you to say that, sir? In what way have I fallen short?

AUBREY. You tried to thwart my manifest destiny. Nature meant me for the Church. I had to get ordained secretly.

THE ELDER. Ordained! You dared to get ordained without my knowledge!

AUBREY. Of course. You objected. How could I have done it with your knowledge? You would have stopped my allowance.

THE ELDER [sitting down on the nearest stone, overwhelmed] My son a clergyman! This will kill me.

AUBREY [coolly taking another stone, on his father's right] Not a bit of it: fathers are not so easily killed. It was at the university that I became what was then called a sky pilot. When the war took me it seemed natural that I should pursue that avocation as a member of the air force. As a flying ace I won a very poorly designed silver medal for committing atrocities which were irreconcilable with the profession of a Christian clergyman. When I was wounded and lost my nerve for flying, I became an army chaplain. I then found myself obliged to tell mortally wounded men that they were dying in a state of grace and were going straight to heaven when as a matter of fact they were dying in mortal sin and going elsewhere. To expiate this blasphemy I kept as much under fire as possible; but my nerve failed again: I had to take three months leave and go into a nursing home. In that home I met my doom.

THE ELDER. What do you mean by your doom? You are alive and well, to my sorrow and shame.

AUBREY. To be precise, I met Sweetie. Thats Sweetie.

SWEETIE. Very pleased to meet Popsy's father, I'm sure.

THE ELDER. My son was called Popsy in his infancy; I put a stop to it, on principle, when he entered on his sixth year. It is strange to hear the name from your lips after so long an interval.

SWEETIE. I always ask a man what his mother called him, and call him that. It takes the starch out of him, somehow.

AUBREY [resuming his narrative] Sweetie was quite the rottenest nurse that ever raised the mortality of a hospital by ten per cent. But—

SWEETIE. Oh, what a lie! It was the other nurses that killed the men: waking them up at six in the morning and washing them! Half of them died of chills.

AUBREY. Well, you will not deny that you were the prettiest woman in the place.

SWEETIE. You thought so, anyhow.

THE ELDER. Oh, cease—cease this trifling. I cannot endure this unending sex appeal.

AUBREY. During the war it was found that sex appeal was as necessary for wounded or shellshocked soldiers as skilled nursing; so pretty girls were allowed to pose as nurses because they could sit about on beds and prevent the men from going mad. Sweetie did not prevent me going mad: on the contrary, she drove me mad. I saw in Sweetie not only every charm, but every virtue. And she returned my love. When I left that nursing home, she left it too. I was discharged as cured on the third of the month: she had been kicked out on the first. The trained staff could stand a good deal; but they could not stand Sweetie.

SWEETIE. They were jealous; and you know it.

AUBREY. I daresay they were. Anyhow, Sweetie and I took the same lodgings; and she was faithful to me for ten days. It was a record for her.

SWEETIE. Popsy: are you going to give the whole show away, or only part of it? The Countess Valbrioni would like to know.

AUBREY. We may as well be frank up to the point at which we should lose money by it. But perhaps I am boring the company.

THE ELDER. Complete your confession, sir. You have just said that you and this lady took the same lodging. Am I to understand that you are husband and wife.

SWEETIE. We might have been if we could have depended on you for a good time. But how could I marry an army chaplain with nothing but his pay and an atheist for his father?

AUBREY. So that was the calculation, Sweetie, was it? I never dreamt that the idea of marriage had occurred to either of us. It certainly never occurred to me. I went to live with you quite simply because I felt I could not live without you. The improbability of that statement is the measure of my infatuation.

SWEETIE. Dont you be so spiteful. Did I give you a good time or did I not?

AUBREY. Heavenly. That also seems improbable; but it is gospel truth.

THE ELDER. Wretched boy: do not dare to trifle with me. You said just now that you owe no man anything, and that you are rolling in money. Where did you get that money?

AUBREY. I stole a very valuable pearl necklace and restored it to the owner. She rewarded me munificently. Hence my present opulence. Honesty is the best policy—sometimes.

THE ELDER. Worse even than a clergyman! A thief!

AUBREY. Why make such a fuss about nothing?

THE ELDER. Do you call the theft of a pearl necklace nothing?

AUBREY. Less than nothing, compared to the things I have done with your approval. I was hardly more than a boy when I first dropped a bomb on a sleeping village. I cried all night after doing that. Later on I swooped into a street and sent machine gun bullets into a crowd of civilians: women, children, and all. I was past crying by that time. And now you preach to me about stealing a pearl necklace! Doesnt that seem a little ridiculous?

THE SERGEANT. That was war, sir.

AUBREY. It was me, sergeant: ME. You cannot divide my conscience into a war department and a peace department. Do you suppose that a man who will commit murder for political ends will hesitate to commit theft for personal ends? Do you suppose you can make a man the mortal enemy of sixty millions of his fellow creatures without making him a little less scrupulous about his next door neighbor?

THE ELDER. I did not approve. Had I been of military age I should have been a conscientious objector.

AUBREY. Oh, you were a conscientious objector to everything, even to God. But my mother was an enthusiast for everything: that was why you never could get on with her. She would have shoved me into the war if I had needed any shoving. She shoved my brother into it, though he did not believe a word of all the lies we were stuffed with, and didnt want to go. He was killed; and when it came out afterwards that he was right, and that we were all a parcel of fools killing one another for nothing, she lost the courage to face life, and died of it.

THE SERGEANT. Well, sir, I'd never let a son of mine talk to me like that. Let him have a bit of your Determinism, sir.

THE FATHER [rising impulsively] Determinism is gone, shattered, buried with a thousand dead religions, evaporated with the clouds of a million forgotten winters. The science I pinned my faith to is bankrupt: its tales were more foolish than all the miracles of the priests, its cruelties more horrible than all the atrocities of the Inquisition. Its spread of enlightenment has been a spread of cancer: its counsels that were to have established the millennium have led straight to European suicide. And I—I who believed in it as no religious fanatic has ever believed in his superstition! For its sake I helped to destroy the faith of millions of worshippers in the temples of a thousand creeds. And now look at me and behold the supreme tragedy of the atheist who has lost his faith—his faith in atheism, for which more martyrs have perished than for all the creeds put together. Here I stand, dumb before my scoundrel of a son; for that is what you are, boy, a common scoundrel and nothing else.

AUBREY. Well, why not? If I become an honest man I shall become a poor man; and then nobody will respect me: nobody will admire me: nobody will say thank you to me. If on the contrary I am bold, unscrupulous, acquisitive, successful and rich, everyone will respect me, admire me, court me, grovel before me. Then no doubt I shall be able to afford the luxury of honesty. I learnt that from my religious education.

THE ELDER. How dare you say that you had a religious education. I shielded you from that, at least.

AUBREY. You thought you did, old man; but you reckoned without my mother.

THE ELDER. What!

AUBREY. You forbad me to read the Bible; but my mother made me learn three verses of it every day, and whacked me if I could not repeat them without misplacing a word. She threatened to whack me still worse if I told you.

THE ELDER [thunderstruck] Your mother!!!

AUBREY. So I learnt my lesson. Six days on the make, and on the seventh shalt thou rest. I shall spend another six years on the make, and then I shall retire and be a saint.

THE ELDER. A saint! Say rather the ruined

son of an incorrigibly superstitious mother. Retire now—from the life you have dishonored. There is the sea. Go. Drown yourself. In that graveyard there are no lying epitaphs. [*He mounts to his chapel and again gives way to utter dejection*].

AUBREY [*unconcerned*] I shall do better as a saint. A few thousands to the hospitals and the political party funds will buy me a halo as large as Sweetie's sun hat. That is my program. What have any of you to say against it?

THE SERGEANT. Not the program of a gentleman, as I understand the word, sir.

AUBREY. You cannot be a gentleman on less than fifty thousand a year nowadays, sergeant.

THE SERGEANT. You can in the army, by God.

AUBREY. Yes: because you drop bombs on sleeping villages. And even then you have to be an officer. Are you a gentleman?

THE SERGEANT. No, sir: it wouldnt pay me. I couldnt afford it.

Disturbance. A voice is heard in complaint and lamentation. It is that of the Elderly Lady, Mrs Mopply. She is pursuing Colonel Tallboys down the path through the gap, the lady distracted and insistent, the colonel almost equally distracted: she clutching him and stopping him: he breaking loose and trying to get away from her. She is dressed in black precisely as if she were in Cheltenham, except that she wears a sun helmet. He is equipped with a box of sketching materials slung over his shoulder, an easel, which he has tucked under his left arm, and a sun umbrella, a substantial affair of fawn lined with red, podgily rolled up, which he carries in his right hand.

MRS MOPPLY. I wont be patient. I wont be quiet. My child is being murdered.

TALLBOYS. I tell you she is not being murdered. Will you be good enough to excuse me whilst I attend to my business?

MRS MOPPLY. Your business is to save my child. She is starving.

TALLBOYS. Nonsense. Nobody starves in this country. There are plenty of dates. Will you be good enough—

MRS MOPPLY. Do you think my child can live on dates? She has to have a sole for breakfast, a cup of nourishing soup at eleven, a nice chop and a sweetbread for lunch, a pint of beef-tea with her ordinary afternoon tea, and a chicken and some lamb or veal—

TALLBOYS. Will you be good enough—

MRS MOPPLY. My poor delicate child with nothing to eat but dates! And she is the only one I have left: they were all delicate—

TALLBOYS. I really must— [*He breaks away and hurries off along the beach past the Abode of Love*].

MRS MOPPLY [*running after him*] Colonel, Colonel: you might have the decency to listen to a distracted mother for a moment. Colonel: my child is dying. She may be dead for all I know. And nobody is doing anything: nobody cares. Oh dear, wont you listen— [*Her voice is lost in the distance*].

Whilst they are staring mutely after the retreating pair, the patient, still in her slave girl attire, but with some brilliant variations, comes down the path.

THE PATIENT. My dream has become a nightmare. My mother has pursued me to these shores. I cannot shake her off. No woman can shake off her mother. There should be no mothers: there should be only women, strong women able to stand by themselves, not clingers. I would kill all the clingers. Mothers cling: daughters cling: we are all like drunken women clinging to lamp posts: none of us stands upright.

THE ELDER. There is great comfort in clinging, and great loneliness in standing alone.

THE PATIENT. Hallo! [*She climbs to the St Pauls platform and peers into the cell*]. A sententious anchorite! [*To Aubrey*]. Who is he?

AUBREY. The next worse thing to a mother: a father.

THE ELDER. A most unhappy father.

AUBREY. My father, in fact.

THE PATIENT. If only I had had a father to stand between me and my mother's care. Oh, that I had been an orphan!

THE SERGEANT. You will be, miss, if the old lady drives the colonel too hard. She has been at him all the morning, ever since she arrived; and I know the colonel. He has a temper; and when it gives way, it's a bit of high explosive. He'll kill her if she pushes him too far.

THE PATIENT. Let him kill her. I am young and strong: I want a world without parents: there is no room for them in my dream. I shall found a sisterhood.

AUBREY. All right, Mops. Get thee to a nunnery.

THE PATIENT. It need not be a nunnery if men will come in without spoiling everything. But all the women must be rich. There must be no chill of poverty. There are plenty of rich women like me who hate being devoured by parasites.

AUBREY. Stop. You have the most disgusting mental pictures. I really cannot stand intellectual coarseness. Sweetie's vulgarity I can forgive and even enjoy. But you say perfectly filthy things that stick in my mind, and break my spirit, I can bear no more of it. [*He rises angrily and tries to escape by the beach past the Abode of Love*].

SWEETIE. Youre dainty, arnt you? If chambermaids were as dainty as you, youd have to empty your own slops.

AUBREY [*recoiling from her with a yell of disgust*] You need not throw them in my teeth, you beast. [*He sits in his former place, sulking*].

THE ELDER. Silence, boy. These are home truths. They are good for you. [*To the patient*] May I ask, young woman, what are the relations between you and my son, whom you seem to know?

THE PATIENT. Popsy stole my necklace, and got me to run away with him by a wonderful speech he made about freedom and sunshine and lovely scenery. Sweetie made me write it all down and sell it to a tourist agency as an advertisement. And then I was devoured by parasites: by tourist agencies, steamboat companies, railways, motor car people, hotel keepers, dressmakers, servants, all trying to get my money by selling me things I dont really want; shoving me all over the globe to look at what they call new skies, though they know as well as I do that it is only the same old sky everywhere; and disabling me by doing all the things for me that I ought to do for myself to keep myself in health. They preyed on me to keep themselves alive: they pretended they were making me happy when it was only by drinking and drugging—cocktails and cocaine—that I could endure my life.

AUBREY. I regret to have to say it, Mops; but you have not the instincts of a lady. [*He sits down moodily on a stone a little way up the path*].

THE PATIENT. You fool, there is no such thing as a lady. I have the instincts of a good housekeeper: I want to clean up this filthy world and keep it clean. There must be other women who want it too. Florence Nightingale had the same instinct when she went to clean up the Crimean war. She wanted a sisterhood; but there wasnt one.

THE ELDER. There were several. But steeped in superstition, unfortunately.

THE PATIENT. Yes, all mixed up with things that I dont believe. Women have to set themselves apart to join them. I dont want to set myself apart. I want to have every woman in my sisterhood, and to have all the others strangled.

THE ELDER. Down! down! down! Even the young, the strong, the rich, the beautiful, feel that they are plunging into a bottomless pit.

THE SERGEANT. Your set, miss, if you will excuse me saying so, is only a small bit of the world. If you dont like the officers' mess, the ranks are open to you. Look at Meek! That man could be an emperor if he laid his mind to it: but he'd rather be a private. He's happier so.

THE PATIENT. I dont belong to the poor, and dont want to. I always knew that there were thousands of poor people; and I was taught to believe that they were poor because God arranged it that way to punish them for being dirty and drunken and dishonest, and not knowing how to read and write. But I didnt know that the rich were miserable. I didnt know that I was miserable. I didnt know that our respectability was uppish snobbery and our religion gluttonous selfishness, and that my soul was starving on them. I know now. I have found myself out thoroughly—in my dream.

THE ELDER. You are young. Some good man may cure you of this for a few happy years. When you fall in love, life will seem worth living.

THE PATIENT. I did fall in love. With that thing. And though I was never a hotel chambermaid I got tired of him sooner than Sweetie did. Love gets people into difficulties, not out of them. No more lovers for me: I want a sisterhood. Since I came here I have been wanting to join the army, like Joan of Arc. It's a brotherhood, of a sort.

THE SERGEANT. Yes, miss: that is so; and there used to be a peace of mind in the army that you could find nowhere else. But the war made an end of that. You see, miss, the great principle of soldiering, I take it, is that the world is kept going by the people who want the right thing killing the people who want the wrong thing. When the soldier is doing that, he is doing the work of God, which my mother brought me up to do. But thats a very different thing from killing a man because he's a German and he killing you because youre an Englishman. We were not killing the right people in 1915. We werent even killing the wrong people. It was innocent men killing one another.

THE PATIENT. Just for the fun of it.

THE SERGEANT. No, miss: it was no fun. For the misery of it.

THE PATIENT. For the devilment of it, then.

THE SERGEANT. For the devilment of the godless rulers of this world. Those that did the killing hadnt even the devilment to comfort them: what comfort is there in screwing on a fuse or pulling a string when the devilment it makes is from three to forty miles off, and you dont know whether you have only made a harmless hole in the ground or blown up a baby in its cradle that might have been your own? That wasnt devilment: it was damnation. No, miss: the bottom has come out of soldiering. What the gentleman here said about our all falling into a bottomless pit came home to me. I feel like that too.

THE ELDER. Lost souls, all of us.

THE PATIENT. No: only lost dogs. Cheer up, old man: the lost dogs always find their way home. [*The voice of the Elderly Lady is heard returning*]. Oh! here she comes again!

Mrs Mopply is still pursuing the colonel, who is walking doggedly and steadily away from her, with closed lips and a dangerous expression on his set features.

MRS MOPPLY. You wont even speak to me. It's a disgrace. I will send a cable message home to the Government about it. You were sent out here to rescue my daughter from these dreadful brigands. Why is nothing being done? What are the relations between yourself and that disgraceful countess who ought to have her coronet stripped off her back? You are all in a conspiracy to murder my poor lost darling child. You are in league with the brigands You are—

The Colonel turns at bay, and brings down his umbrella whack on poor Mrs Mopply's helmet.

MRS MOPPLY. Oh! Oh! Oh! Oh! [*With a series of short, dry, detached screams she totters and flutters back along the beach out of sight like a wounded bird*].

General stupefaction. All stare at the Colonel aghast. The Sergeant rises in amazement, and remains standing afterwards as a matter of military etiquette.

THE PATIENT. Oh, if only someone had done that to her twenty years ago, how different

my childhood would have been! But I must see to the poor old dear. [*She runs after her mother*].

AUBREY. Colonel: you have our full, complete, unreserved sympathy. We thank you from the bottom of our hearts. But that does not alter the fact that the man who would raise his hand to a woman, save in the way of kindness, is unworthy the name of Briton.

TALLBOYS. I am perfectly aware of that, sir. I need no reminder. The lady is entitled to an apology She shall have it.

THE ELDER. But have you considered the possibility of a serious injury—

TALLBOYS [*cutting him short*] My umbrella is quite uninjured, thank you. The subject is now closed. [*He sits down on the stone below St Pauls recently vacated by Aubrey. His manner is so decisive that nobody dares carry the matter further*].

As they sit uneasily seeking one another's eyes and avoiding them again, dumbfounded by the violence of the catastrophe, a noise like that of a machine gun in action reaches their ears from afar. It increases to shattering intensity as it approaches. They all put their fingers to their ears. It diminishes slightly, then suddenly rises to a climax of speed and uproar, and stops.

TALLBOYS. Meek.

AUBREY. Meek.

SWEETIE. Meek.

THE ELDER. What is this? Why do you all say Meek?

Meek, dusty and gritty, but very alert, comes down the path through the gap with a satchel of papers.

TALLBOYS. My dear Meek, can you not be content with a motor cycle of ordinary horse power? Must you always travel at eighty miles an hour?

MEEK. I have good news for you, Colonel; and good news should travel fast.

TALLBOYS. For me?

MEEK. Your K.C.B., sir. [*Presenting a paper*] Honors list by wireless.

TALLBOYS [*rising joyously to take the paper*] Ah! Congratulate me, my friends. My dear Sarah is Lady Tallboys at last. [*He resumes his seat and pores over the paper*].

AUBREY		Splendid!
THE SERGEANT	[*together*]	You deserve it, sir, if I may say so.
SWEETIE		Delighted, I am sure.

THE ELDER. May I crave to know the nature of the distinguished service which has won this official recognition, sir?

TALLBOYS. I have won the battle of the maroons. I have suppressed brigandage here. I have rescued a British lady from the clutches of the brigands. The Government is preparing for a general election, and has had to make the most of these modest achievements.

THE ELDER. Brigands! Are there any here?

TALLBOYS. None.

THE ELDER. But—? The British lady? In their clutches?

TALLBOYS. She has been in my clutches, and perfectly safe, all the time.

THE ELDER [more and more puzzled] Oh! Then the battle of the—

TALLBOYS. Won by Private Meek. I had nothing whatever to do with it.

AUBREY. I invented the brigands and the British lady. [To Tallboys] By the way, Colonel, the impressive old party in the shrine is my father.

TALLBOYS. Indeed! Happy to meet you, sir, though I cannot congratulate you on your son, except in so far as you have brought into the world the most abandoned liar I have ever met.

THE ELDER. And may I ask, sir, is it your intention not only to condone my son's frauds, but to take advantage of them to accept a distinction which you have in no way earned?

TALLBOYS. I have earned it, sir, ten times over. Do you suppose, because the brigandage which I am honored for suppressing has no existence, that I have never suppressed real brigands? Do you forget that though this battle of which I am crowned victor was won by a subordinate, I, too, have won real battles, and seen all the honors go to a brigadier who did not even know what was happening? In the army these things average themselves out: merit is rewarded in the long run. Justice is none the less justice though it is always delayed, and finally done by mistake. My turn today: Private Meek's tomorrow.

THE FATHER. And meanwhile Mr Meek—this humble and worthy soldier—is to remain in obscurity and poverty whilst you are strutting as a K.C.B.

TALLBOYS. How I envy him! Look at me and look at him! I, loaded with responsibilities whilst my hands are tied, my body disabled, my mind crippled because a colonel must not do anything but give orders and look significant and profound when his mind is entirely vacant! he, free to turn his hand to everything and to look like an idiot when he feels like one! I have been driven to sketching in watercolors because I may not use my hands in life's daily useful business. A commanding officer must not do this, must not do that, must not do the other, must not do anything but tell other men to do it. He may not even converse with them. I see this man Meek doing everything that is natural to a complete man: carpentering, painting, digging, pulling and hauling, fetching and carrying, helping himself and everybody else, whilst I, with a bigger body to exercise and quite as much energy, must loaf and loll, allowed to do nothing but read the papers and drink brandy and water to prevent myself going mad. I should have become a drunkard had it not been for the colors.

THE SERGEANT. Ah yes, sir, the colors. The fear of disgracing them has kept me off the drink many a time.

TALLBOYS. Man: I do not mean the regimental colors, but the watercolors. How willingly would I exchange my pay, my rank, my K.C.B., for Meek's poverty, his obscurity!

MEEK. But, my dear Colonel—sorry, sir: what I mean to say is that you can become a private if you wish. Nothing easier: I have done it again and again. You resign your commission; take a new and very common name by deed poll; dye your hair and give your age to the recruiting sergeant as twenty-two; and there you are! You can select your own regiment.

TALLBOYS. Meek: you should not tantalize your commanding officer. No doubt you are an extraordinary soldier. But have you ever passed the extreme and final test of manly courage?

MEEK. Which one is that, sir?

TALLBOYS. Have you ever married?

MEEK. No, sir.

TALLBOYS. Then do not ask me why I do not resign my commission and become a free and happy private. My wife would not let me.

THE COUNTESS. Why dont you hit her on the head with your umbrella?

TALLBOYS. I dare not. There are moments when I wish some other man would. But not in my presence. I should kill him.

THE ELDER. We are all slaves. But at least your son is an honest man.

TALLBOYS. Is he? I am glad to hear it. I have not spoken to him since he shirked military service at the beginning of the war and went into trade as a contractor. He is now so enormously rich that I cannot afford to keep up his acquaintance. Neither need you keep up that of your son. By the way, he passes here as the half step-brother of this lady, the Countess Valbrioni.

SWEETIE. Valbrioni be blowed! My name is Susan Simpkins. Being a countess isnt worth a damn. There's no variety in it: no excitement. What I want is a month's leave for the sergeant. Wont you give it to him, Colonel?

TALLBOYS. What for?

SWEETIE. Never mind what for. A fortnight might do; but I dont know for certain yet. Theres something steadying about him; and I suppose I will have to settle down some day.

TALLBOYS. Nonsense! The sergeant is a pious man, not your sort. Eh, Sergeant?

SERGEANT. Well, sir, a man should have one woman to prevent him from thinking too much about women in general. You cannot read your Bible undisturbed if visions and wandering thoughts keep coming between you and it. And a pious man should not marry a pious woman: two of a trade never agree. Besides, it would give the children a onesided view of life. Life is very mixed, sir: it is not all piety and it is not all gaiety. This young woman has no conscience; but I have enough for two. I have no money; but she seems to have enough for two. Mind: I am not committing myself; but I will go so far as to say that I am not dead set against it. On the plane of this world and its vanities—and weve got to live in it, you know, sir—she appeals to me.

AUBREY. Take care, sergeant. Constancy is not Sweetie's strong point.

THE SERGEANT. Neither is it mine. As a single man and a wandering soldier I am fair game for every woman. But if I settle down with this girl she will keep the others off. I'm a bit tired of adventures.

SWEETIE. Well, if the truth must be told, so am I. We were made for one another, Sergeant. What do you say?

THE SERGEANT. Well, I dont mind keeping company for a while, Susan, just to see how we get along together.

The voice of Mrs Mopply is again heard. Its tone is hardy and even threatening; and its sound is approaching rapidly.

MRS MOPPLY'S VOICE. You just let me alone, will you? Nobody asked you to interfere. Get away with you.

General awe and dismay. Mrs Mopply appears striding resolutely along the beach. She walks straight up to the Colonel, and is about to address him when he rises firmly to the occasion and takes the word out of her mouth.

TALLBOYS. Mrs Mopply: I have a duty to you which I must discharge at once. At our last meeting, I struck you.

MRS MOPPLY. Struck me! You bashed me. Is that what you mean?

TALLBOYS. If you consider my expression inadequate I am willing to amend it. Let us put it that I bashed you. Well, I apologize without reserve, fully and amply. If you wish, I will give it to you in writing.

MRS MOPPLY. Very well. Since you express your regret, I suppose there is nothing more to be said.

TALLBOYS [*darkening ominously*] Pardon me. I apologized. I did not express my regret.

AUBREY. Oh, for heaven's sake, Colonel, dont start her again. Dont qualify your apology in any way.

MRS MOPPLY. You shut up, whoever you are.

TALLBOYS. I do not qualify my apology in the least. My apology is complete. The lady has a right to it. My action was inexcusable. But no lady—no human being—has a right to impose a falsehood on me. I do not regret my action. I have never done anything which gave me more thorough and hearty satisfaction. When I was a company officer I once cut down an enemy in the field. Had I not done so he would have cut me down. It gave me no satisfaction: I was half ashamed of it: I have never before spoken of it. But this time I struck with unmixed enjoyment. In fact I am grateful to Mrs Mopply. I owe her one of the very few delightfully satisfactory moments of my life.

MRS MOPPLY. Well, thats a pretty sort of apology, isnt it?

TALLBOYS [*firmly*] I have nothing to add, madam.

MRS MOPPLY. Well, I forgive you, you peppery old blighter.

Sensation. They catch their breaths, and stare at one another in consternation. The patient arrives.

THE PATIENT. I am sorry to say, Colonel Tallboys, that you have unsettled my mother's reason. She wont believe that I am her daughter. She's not a bit like herself.

MRS MOPPLY. Isnt she? What do you know about myself? my real self? They told me lies; and I had to pretend to be somebody quite different.

TALLBOYS. Who told you lies, madam? It was not with my authority.

MRS MOPPLY. I wasnt thinking of you. My mother told me lies. My nurse told me lies. My governess told me lies. Everybody told me lies. The world is not a bit like what they said it was. I wasnt a bit like what they said I ought to be. I thought I had to pretend. And I neednt have pretended at all.

THE ELDER. Another victim! She, too, is falling through the bottomless abyss.

MRS MOPPLY. I dont know who you are or what you think you mean; but you have just hit it: I dont know my head from my heels. Why did they tell me that children couldnt live without medicine and three meat meals a day? Do you know that I have killed two of my children because they told me that? My own children! Murdered them, just!

THE ELDER. Medea! Medea!

MRS MOPPLY. It isnt an idea: it's the truth. I will never believe anything again as long as I live. I'd have killed the only one I had left if she hadnt run away from me. I was told to sacrifice myself—to live for others; and I did it if ever a woman did. They told me that everyone would love me for it; and I thought they would; but my daughter ran away when I had sacrificed myself to her until I found myself wishing she would die like the others and leave me a little to myself. And now I find it was not only my daughter that hated me but that all my friends, all the time they were pretending to sympathize, were just longing to bash me over the head with their umbrellas. This poor man only did what all the rest would have done if theyd dared. When I said I forgave you I meant it: I am greatly obliged to you. [*She kisses him*]. But now what am I to do? How am I to behave in a world thats just the opposite of everything I was told about it?

THE PATIENT. Steady, mother! steady! Sit down. [*She picks up a heavy stone and places it near the Abode of Love for Mrs Mopply to sit on*].

MRS MOPPLY [*seating herself*] Dont you call me mother. Do you think my daughter could carry rocks about like that? she that had to call the nurse to pick up her Pekingese dog when she wanted to pet it! You think you can get round me by pretending to be my daughter; but that just shews what a fool you are; for I hate my daughter and my daughter hates me, because I sacrificed myself to her. She was a horrid selfish girl, always ill and complaining, and never satisfied, no matter how much you did for her. The only sensible thing she ever did was to steal her own necklace and sell it and run away to spend the money on herself. I expect she's in bed somewhere with a dozen nurses and six doctors all dancing attendance on her. Youre not a bit like her, thank goodness: thats why Ive taken a fancy to you. You come with me, darling. I have lots of money, and sixty years of a misspent life to make up for; so you will have a good time with me. Come with me as my companion; and lets forget that there are such miserable things in the world as mothers and daughters.

THE PATIENT. What use shall we be to one another?

MRS MOPPLY. None, thank God. We can do without one another if we dont hit it off.

THE PATIENT. Righto! I'll take you on trial until Ive had time to look about me and see what I'm going to do. But only on trial, mind.

MRS MOPPLY. Just so, darling. We'll both be on trial. So thats settled.

THE PATIENT. And now, Mr Meek, what about the little commission you promised to do for me? Have you brought back my passport?

THE COUNTESS. Your passport! Whatever for?

AUBREY. What have you been up to, Mops? Are you going to desert me?

Meek advances and empties a heap of passports from his satchel on the sand, kneeling down to sort out the patient's.

TALLBOYS. What is the meaning of this? Whose passports are these? What are you doing with them? Where did you get them?

MEEK. Everybody within fifty miles is asking me to get a passport visa'd.

TALLBOYS. Visa'd! For what country?

MEEK. For Beotia, sir.

TALLBOYS. Beotia?

MEEK. Yessir. The Union of Federated Sensible Societies, sir. The U.F.S.S. Everybody wants to go there now, sir.

THE COUNTESS. Well I never.

THE ELDER. And what is to become of our unhappy country if all its inhabitants desert it for an outlandish place in which even property is not respected?

MEEK. No fear, sir: they wont have us. They wont admit any more English, sir: they say their lunatic asylums are too full already. I couldnt get a single visa, except [*to the Colonel*] for you, sir.

TALLBOYS. For me! Damn their impudence! I never asked for one.

MEEK. No, sir; but their people have so much leisure that they are at their wits' end for some occupation to keep them out of mischief. They want to introduce the only institution of ours that they admire.

THE ELDER. And pray which one is that?

MEEK. The English school of watercolor painting, sir. Theyve seen some of the Colonel's work; and theyll make him head of their centres of repose and culture if he'll settle there.

TALLBOYS. This cannot be true, Meek. It indicates a degree of intelligence of which no Government is capable.

MEEK. It's true, sir, I assure you.

TALLBOYS. But my wife—

MEEK. Yessir: I told them. [*He repacks his satchel*].

TALLBOYS. Well, well: there is nothing for it but to return to our own country.

THE ELDER. Can our own country return to its senses, sir? that is the question.

TALLBOYS. Ask Meek.

MEEK. No use, sir: all the English privates want to be colonels: there's no salvation for snobs. [*To Tallboys*] Shall I see about getting the expedition back to England, sir?

TALLBOYS. Yes. And get me two tubes of rose madder and a big one of Chinese White, will you?

MEEK [*about to go*] Yessir.

THE ELDER. Stop. There are police in England. What is to become of my son there?

SWEETIE [*rising*] Make Popsy a preacher, old man. But dont start him until weve gone.

THE ELDER. Preach, my son, preach to your heart's content. Do anything rather than steal and make your military crimes an ex-

cuse for your civil ones. Let men call you the reverend. Let them call you anything rather than thief.

AUBREY [*rising*] If I may be allowed to improve the occasion for a moment—

General consternation. All who are seated rise in alarm, except the patient, who jumps up and claps her hands in mischievous encouragement to the orator.

MRS MOPPLY		You hold your tongue, young man.
SWEETIE		Oh Lord! we're in for it now.
THE ELDER	[*together*]	Shame and silence would better become you, sir.
THE PATIENT		Go on, Pops. It's the only thing you do well.

AUBREY [*continuing*]—it is clear to me that though we seem to be dispersing quietly to do very ordinary things: Sweetie and the Sergeant to get married [*the Sergeant hastily steals down from his grotto, beckoning to Sweetie to follow him. They both escape along the beach*] the colonel to his wife, his watercolors, and his K.C.B. [*the colonel hurries away noiselessly in the opposite direction*] Napoleon Alexander Trotsky Meek to his job of repatriating the expedition [*Meek takes to flight up the path through the gap*] Mops, like Saint Teresa, to found an unladylike sisterhood with her mother as cook-housekeeper [*Mrs Mopply hastily follows the sergeant, dragging with her the patient, who is listening to Aubrey with signs of becoming rapt in his discourse*] yet they are all, like my father here, falling, falling, falling endlessly and hopelessly through a void in which they can find no footing. [*The Elder vanishes into the recesses of St Pauls, leaving his son to preach in solitude*]. There is something fantastic about them, something unreal and perverse, something profoundly unsatisfactory. They are too absurd to be believed in; yet they are not fictions: the newspapers are full of them: what storyteller, however reckless a liar, would dare to invent figures so improbable as men and women with their minds stripped naked? Naked bodies no longer shock us: our sunbathers, grinning at us from every illustrated summer number of our magazines, are nuder than shorn lambs. But the horror of the naked mind is still more than we can bear. Throw off the last rag of your bathing costume; and I shall not blench nor expect you to blush. You may even throw away the outer garments of your souls: the manners, the morals, the decencies. Swear; use dirty words; drink cocktails; kiss and caress and cuddle until girls who are like roses at eighteen are like battered demireps at twenty-two: in all these ways the bright young things of the victory have scandalized their dull old pre-war elders and left nobody but their bright young selves a penny the worse. But how are we to bear this dreadful new nakedness: the nakedness of the souls who until now have always disguised themselves from one another in beautiful impossible idealisms to enable them to bear one another's company. The iron lightning of war has burnt great rents in these angelic veils, just as it has smashed great holes in our cathedral roofs and torn great gashes in our hillsides. Our souls go in rags now; and the young are spying through the holes and getting glimpses of the reality that was hidden. And they are not horrified: they exult in having found us out: they expose their own souls; and when we their elders desperately try to patch our torn clothes with scraps of the old material, the young lay violent hands on us and tear from us even the rags that were left to us. But when they have stripped themselves and us utterly naked, will they be able to bear the spectacle? You have seen me try to strip my soul before my father; but when these two young women stripped themselves more boldly than I—when the old woman had the mask struck from her soul and revelled in it instead of dying of it—I shrank from the revelation as from a wind bringing from the unknown regions of the future a breath which may be a breath of life, but of a life too keen for me to bear, and therefore for me a blast of death. I stand midway between youth and age like a man who has missed his train: too late for the last and too early for the next. What am I to do? What am I? A soldier who has lost his nerve, a thief who at his first great theft has found honesty the best policy and restored his booty to its owner. Nature never intended me for soldiering or thieving: I am by nature and destiny a preacher. I am the new Ecclesiastes. But I have no Bible, no creed: the war has shot both out of my hands. The war has been a fiery forcing house in which we have grown with a rush like flowers in a late spring following a terrible winter. And with what result? This: that we have outgrown our religion, outgrown our political system, outgrown our own strength of mind and character. The fatal word NOT has been miraculously inserted into all our creeds: in the desecrated temples where we knelt murmuring "I believe" we stand with stiff knees and stiffer necks shouting "Up, all! the erect posture is the mark of the man: let lesser creatures kneel and crawl: we will not kneel and we do not believe." But what next? Is NO enough? For a boy, yes: for a man, never. Are we any the less obsessed with a belief when we are denying it than when we were affirming it? No: I must have affirmations to preach. Without them the young will not listen to me; for even the young grow tired of denials. The negative-monger falls before the soldiers, the men of action, the fighters, strong in the old uncompromising affirmations which give them status, duties, certainty of consequences; so that the pugnacious spirit of man in them can reach out and strike deathblows with steadfastly closed minds. Their way is straight and sure; but it is the way of death; and the preacher must preach the way of life. Oh, if I could only find it! [*A white sea fog swirls up from the beach to his feet, rising and thickening round him*]. I am ignorant: I have lost my nerve and am intimidated: all I know is that I must find the way of life, for myself and all of us, or we shall surely perish. And meanwhile my gift has possession of me: I must preach and preach and preach no matter how late the hour and how short the day, no matter whether I have nothing to say—

The fog has enveloped him; the gap with its grottoes is lost to sight; the ponderous stones are wisps of shifting white cloud; there is left only fog: impenetrable fog; but the incorrigible preacher will not be denied his peroration, which, could we only hear it distinctly, would probably run—

—or whether in some Pentecostal flame of revelation the Spirit will descend on me and inspire me with a message the sound whereof shall go out unto all lands and realize for us at last the Kingdom and the Power and the Glory for ever and ever. Amen.

The audience disperses (or the reader puts down the book) impressed in the English manner with the Pentecostal flame and the echo from the Lord's Prayer. But fine words butter no parsnips. A few of the choicer spirits will know that the

Pentecostal flame is always alight at the service of those strong enough to bear its terrible intensity. They will not forget that it is accompanied by a rushing mighty wind, and that any rascal who happens to be also a windbag can get a prodigious volume of talk out of it without ever going near enough to be shrivelled up. The author, though himself a professional talk maker, does not believe that the world can be saved by talk alone. He has given the rascal the last word; but his own favorite is the woman of action, who begins by knocking the wind out of the rascal, and ends with a cheerful conviction that the lost dogs always find their way home. So they will, perhaps, if the women go out and look for them.

THE END

XLI
VILLAGE WOOING
A COMEDIETTINA FOR TWO VOICES

FIRST CONVERSATION

The lounge deck of the Empress of Patagonia, a pleasure ship. Two of the deck chairs are occupied by A, a literary looking pale gentleman under forty in green spectacles, a limp black beard, and a tropical suit of white silk, who is writing and does not wish to be disturbed, and Z, a young woman, presentable but not aristocratic, who is bored with her book. She is undressed for bathing, but is very modestly covered up with a not too flamboyant wrap.

z. Excuse me. Could you tell me the time?

A [*curtly*] Eleven.

z. My watch makes it half past ten.

A. The clocks were put on half an hour last night. We are going east.

z. I always think it adds to the interest of a voyage having to put on your watch.

A. I am glad you are so easily interested [*he resumes his writing pointedly*].

z. The steward will be round with the soup in half an hour. I thought we should have to wait an hour.

A. I never take it. It interrupts my work.

z. Why do you work all the time? It's not what one comes on a pleasure cruise for, is it?

A. Work is my only pleasure.

z. Oh, thats not good sense, is it? It gives me the pip to see you always sitting there over your writing, and never enjoying yourself, nor even taking a drop of soup. You should get up and have a game of deck quoits: you will feel ever so much better after it.

A. I feel perfectly well, thank you. And I loathe deck games, especially deck quoits. The slapping of those silly things on the deck destroys the quiet of the ship.

z. Oh, I see. That is why you select this end of the deck. I often wondered why.

A. Within the last fortnight you have inspected the priceless antiquities of Naples, Athens, Egypt, and the Holy Land. Please occupy your mind with them until the soup comes.

z. I never cared much for geography. Where are we now?

A. We are on the Red Sea.

z. But it's blue.

A. What did you expect it to be?

z. Well, I didnt know what color the sea might be in these parts. I always thought the Red Sea would be red.

A. Well, it isnt.

z. And isnt the Black Sea black?

A. It is precisely the color of the sea at Margate.

z [*eagerly*] Oh, I am so glad you know Margate. Theres no place like it in the season, is there?

A. I dont know: I have never been there.

z. [*disappointed*] Oh, you ought to go. You could write a book about it.

A [*shudders, sighs, and pretends to write very hard*]!

A pause.

z. I wonder why they call it the Red Sea.

A. Because their fathers did. Why do you call America America?

z. Well, because it is America. What else would you call it?

A. Oh, call it what you like, dear lady; but I have five hundred words to write before lunch; and I cannot do that if I talk to you.

z [*sympathetically*] Yes: it is awful to have to talk to people, isnt it? Oh, that reminds me: I have something really interesting to tell you. I believe the man in the cabin next mine beats his wife.

A. I feel a little like him myself. Some women would provoke any men to beat them.

z. I will say this for him, that she always begins it.

A. No doubt.

z. I hate a nagger: dont you?

A. It is your privilege as a woman to have the last word. Please take it and dont end all your remarks with a question.

z. You are funny.

A. Am I? I never felt less funny in my life.

z. I cant make you out at all. I am rather good at making out people as a rule; but I cant make head or tail of you.

A. I am not here to be made out. You are not here to make people out, but to revel in the enjoyments you have paid for. Deck tennis, deck quoits, shuffleboard, golf, squash rackets, the swimming pool, the gymnasium all invite you.

z. I am no good at games: besides, theyre silly. I'd rather sit and talk.

A. Then for heaven's sake talk to somebody else. I have no time for talk. I have to work my passage.

z. What do you mean: work your passage? You are not a sailor.

A. No. I make a precarious living on board ship by writing the Marco Polo Series of Chatty Guide Books. Unless I complete two thousand words a day I am bankrupt. I cannot complete them if you persist in talking to me.

z. Do you mean you are writing a book about this cruise?

A. I am trying to—under great difficulties.

z. Will I be in it?

A [grimly] You will.

z. How thrilling! I have never been put in a book before. You will read me what you have written about me, wont you?

A. When the book is published you can read it to your heart's content.

z. But I should like you to get me right. After all, what do you know about me? I will tell you the whole of my life if you like.

A. Great heavens, NO. Please dont.

z. Oh, I dont care who knows it.

A. Evidently. You would hardly offer to tell it to a perfect stranger if you cared, or if it was of the smallest interest.

z. Oh, I'd never think of you as a stranger. Here we are on the same ship, arnt we? And most people would think my life quite a

romance. Wouldnt you really like to hear it?

A. No, I tell you. When I want romances I invent them for myself.

z. Oh, well, perhaps you wouldnt think it very wonderful. But it was a regular treat for me. You may think because I am well dressed and travelling de lucks and all that, that I am an educated lady. But I'm not.

A. I never supposed for a moment that you were.

z. But how could you know? How did you find out?

A. I didnt find out. I knew.

z. Who told you?

A. Nobody told me.

z. Then how did you know?

A [exasperated] How do I know that a parrot isnt a bird of paradise?

z. Theyre different.

A. Precisely.

z. There you are, you see. But what would you take me for if you met me in a third class carriage?

A. I should not notice you.

z. I bet you would. I maynt be a beauty; but when I get into a railway carriage every man in it has a look at me.

A. I am not Everyman. Everyman thinks that every woman that steps into a railway carriage may be the right woman. But she is always a disappointment.

z. Same with the women, isnt it? If you were a woman youd know.

A. I am a woman; and you are a man, with a slight difference that doesnt matter except on special occasions.

z. Oh, what a thing to say! I never could bring myself to believe that. I know, of course, that men have their weaknesses and their tempers; but all the same there is something wonderful you can get from a man that you never could get from a woman. Dont you think so?

A. Inexperienced men think there is something wonderful you can get from a woman that you never could get from a man. Hence many unhappy marriages.

z. Are you married?

A. Widower. Are you?

z. Oh, thats the first time youve asked me a question. We're getting on, arnt we?

A. No. I am not getting on with my work.

z. Youre an intellectual, arnt you?

A. What do you think you mean by an intellectual?

z. Only that you consider me no better than an idiot, and that you were a bad husband, most likely.

A. You are quite right on both points.

z. I thought so.

A. And now, please, may I go on with my work?

z. Please yourself. I'm not hindering you.

A. Thank you [*he resumes his writing*].

A pause.

z. What books would you recommend me to read to improve my mind?

A [*shouting furiously*] Steward!

z. Oh, you shouldnt trouble the steward now. He's busy getting the soup.

A. I want him to remove my chair to the very furthest extremity of this ship.

z. I always say it's fresher under the awning at the end. You dont mind if I move too, do you?

A. If you persecute me any more I shall go overboard. Dont you see that I want to be left alone to work, and that your chatter is preventing me from working?

z [*sympathetically*] It is annoying to have somebody talking to you all the time when you dont want to. But it's just as bad when you want to talk, and the other person wont, isnt it?

A. There are three or four hundred persons on this ship. Cannot you find one of them with the same insatiable thirst for conversation as yourself?

z. Well; but we all have to make ourselves agreeable, havnt we?

A. Not at oneanother's expense. You are not making yourself agreeable to me at present: you are driving me mad.

z. My father used to say that men and women are always driving oneanother mad.

A. That sounds literary. Was your father a man of letters?

z. Yes: I should think he was. A postman.

A. A what?

z. A postman. A village postman.

A. Ha ha! Ha ha ha!

z. What is there funny in that?

A. I dont know. Ha ha! The postman's daughter hath ripe red lips: butter and eggs and a pound of cheese! Ha ha ha!

z. Well, I'm glad Ive amused you. But I dont think it's very polite of you to laugh at my father.

A [*punctiliously—recovering himself*] You are right. I was rude. But a good laugh is worth a hundred pounds to me. I feel a different man. Forgive me. You see, you quoted a remark of your father's—almost an epigram—which suggested that he must have been a man of genius.

z. Well, so he was. He had a genius for walking.

A. For what?

z. For walking. When he was a child, he won a prize as The Infant Pedestrian. And would you believe it, my mother was that indoory that she grudged having to go out and do her marketing. After we had a telephone put in she never went out at all.

A. Thats strange. As she was never out and he was never in, the household should have been a quiet one; but that remark of his about men and women driving oneanother mad rather suggests the opposite.

z. So it was the opposite. She was always complaining of being lonely; and he was always at her to take more exercise. When they were not quarrelling about that, they were quarrelling about me. You see they had great ambitions for me. She wanted me to be a parlormaid in a great house. He wanted me to be a telephone operator. He said there is no future for the great houses and a great future for telephones.

A. And you? Had you no ambition for yourself?

z. Oh, I wanted to be something romantic, like an acrobat in a circus.

A. And what actually happened?

z. I became shop assistant and telephone operator in the village shop.

A. Do village shop assistants and telephone girls—

z. Operators.

A. Pardon: operators. Do they earn enough to take cruises round the world in pleasure ships?

z. Not they. I won the first prize in a newspaper competition. My mother wanted me to save it: she said it would help me to get a thrifty husband. My father told me to blue it all in a lump while I had the chance. "You will be poor all your life," he said; "but now you have the chance of living at the rate of five thousand a year for four months. Dont miss it," he said: "see what it's like. Have your fling," he said; "for they never can take that away from you once youve had it." His idea was a walking tour, spending the nights in the best hotels but I chose the ship because it's more dressy and more people to look at. Besides, I can get all the walking I want round the deck. At the end of the cruise back I go to the village shop without a penny.

A. Have they found out here that you are not a lady?

z. The Americans dont know the difference: they think my telephone talk is aristocratic; and the English wont speak to anyone anyhow. And lots of them are just like me.

A. Well, how do you like living at the rate of five thousand a year? Is it worth it?

z. It is while the novelty lasts. You see, when youre at home you get tired of doing the same thing every day: the same places! the same faces! the same old round. When you get a holiday you go off in a crowded hot excursion train to the seaside and make yourself tired and miserable just because it's a change; and youd do anything for a change. But here it's change all the time until you begin to realize what it is to have a settled home and belong somewhere. I shant be sorry to get home to the shop and the telephone. I get such a dreadful lost dog feeling sometimes. Other times it seems such a foolish waste of money. And I hate wasting money.

A. Thats an extremely attractive point in your character. My wife used to waste my money. Stick to that and you will get married in no time.

z. Oh, I have had plenty of offers. But you know it's a terrible thing to be a poor man's wife when you have been accustomed to a clean decent job. I have seen so many bright jolly girls turn into dirty old drudges through getting married.

A. Dont be afraid of dirt. Mine is a clean job; but I often wish I had a dirty one to exercise me and keep me in health. Women are so set on clean collars that they make their sons clerks when they would be stronger and earn more money as navvies. I wish I was a navvy instead of writing guide books.

z. Well, whats to prevent you?

A. I am not trained to manual work. Half an hour of it would make me wish myself dead. And five minutes of my work would produce a strike among the navvies. I am only a writing machine, just as a navvy is a digging machine.

z. I dont think the world is rightly arranged: do you?

A. We must take the world as we find it.

It's we that are not rightly arranged.

z. Thats what I mean. Well, I suppose I mustnt interrupt your work.

A. You mean that the steward is coming round with the soup at last.

z. Well, it's half past eleven, isnt it?

The steward appears with the soup and offers it to z, *who seizes it eagerly; then to* A.

A. No, thank you. No soup.

He buries himself in his work, unmolested.

She buries herself in the soup.

SECOND CONVERSATION

In a village shop and post office on the Wiltshire Downs on a fine summer morning. The counter is for general shopping for most of its length; but one end is reserved and railed in for postal business. A couple of chairs are available for customers. The goods for sale include ginger beer in stone bottles, tablets of milk chocolate, glass jars of sweets containing (inter alia) sugared almonds, all on the counter; cheese, butter, and Hovis bread handy to the scales; and, in front of the counter, a sack of apples on the floor and some string bags hanging from the rafters.

z [*invisible*] Th-reee ni-nnn. Sorry: no such number. Whoo-mmm do you want? Doctor Byles? One fi-fff. You are through.

A *comes in. He is in hiking costume, with stick and rucksack, but wears well cut breeches (not plus fours) instead of shorts. Seeing nobody to attend to him he raps loudly on the counter with his stick.* z *emerges.*

A. I want a packet of milk chocolate——

z. Thanks very much.

A [*continuing*]—a couple of hard apples——

z. Thanks very much. [*She comes out through the counter to get them from the sack*].

A [*continuing*]—quarter of a pound of Cheddar cheese——

z. Thanks very much.

A. Dont interrupt me. You can express your gratitude for the order when I have finished. Quarter of a pound of your best butter, a small loaf of Hovis, and twopennyworth of sugared almonds.

z. Anything else?

A. No, thank you.

z. Thanks very much [*she goes back through the counter to cut and weigh the butter and cheese*].

He sits down watching her deft but leisurely proceedings.

A. Do you sell baskets?

z. We sell everything. Hadnt you better

have a string bag? It's handier; and it packs away almost to nothing when it's empty.

A. What is a string bag? Shew me one.

Z [*coming out and taking one down*] This is the cheapest. Or would you like a better quality with a Zip fastening?

A. Certainly not. I should have the trouble of opening and shutting it, and the worry of wondering whether it would open or shut, with no compensatory advantage whatever.

Z. Thats just like you. Youre not a bit changed.

A. What do you mean? I have been in this shop for less than two minutes. Why should I have changed in that time?

Z. Excuse me: I shouldnt have mentioned it. Will you take a string bag?

A. Yes.

Z. Thanks very much. Shall I put the rest of the order into it?

A. Of course. What else do you suppose I am buying it for? Have you any buttermilk?

Z. Sorry. We dont stock it.

A. Any ginger beer?

Z. Yes. We have a very good local brew.

A. Shove a bottle into the string bag.

Z. Thanks very much.

A. How many times a day do you say thanks very much?

Z. Depends on the number of orders.

A. Dont say it to me again, if you dont mind. It gets on my nerves.

Z. It used to get on mine, at first. But I am used to it.

A. Have you a guide book of this village?

Z. Sorry. Theres a leaflet in the church, written by the vicar. You are expected to put tuppence in the box for it. Excuse me; but the chocolates are tuppence, sixpence, and a shilling. Which size would you run to?

A. It is a poor heart that never rejoices. I will have a shilling one.

Z. Thanks very much.

A. Dont.

Z. Excuse me: I cant help it. I say it without thinking: same as if you touched a button.

The telephone rings.

A. Someone has touched the button.

Z [*vanishing into the post office section*] What number please? Whitehall on-n-n-e two on-n-n-e two. I will ring you. Whitehall one two one two. Yes. [*She reappears*] Thats a police call.

A. You need not point the information at me. I am not the criminal.

Z. Oh, it isnt a criminal. Somebody thats been broadcasted on the wireless as lost. You know the sort of thing. Missing from his home since January the first. Last seen in a deck chair on the Empress of Patagonia talking to a female. Suffering from loss of memory.

A. How extraor— [*the telephone rings again*].

Z. Excuse me. [*She vanishes*]. You are through to Whitehall. [*She reappears*].

A. You have hit on an extraordinary coincidence. I wonder whether you will believe me when I tell you that in January last I was sitting on the deck of a ship named the Empress of Patagonia, and that I was talking to a female—or rather she was talking to me. How that woman did talk!

Z. And are you suffering from loss of memory?

A. Certainly not. I never forget anything.

Z. Oh, then it cant be you, can it?

A. There! Can it? That woman always finished up with can it? wont it? isnt it? so that you had to answer her out of common politeness. Take care never to pick up that trick or you will be murdered some day.

Z. Some people are like that. It often goes with orange colored eyes [*or whatever color her eyes happen to be*]. Did you notice the color of her eyes?

A. No: I never notice things like that. I am not a detective. It is people's characters that impress me; I cant tell you the color of her hair or the shape of her nose; but I can tell you that she was a most fearful nuisance. How much does all that come to?

Z. The string bag sixpence, chocolates a shilling: one and sixpence. The ginger beer is—

A. Spare me the details. Will ten shillings cover it?

Z. Oh yes, of course. You shouldnt be so careless about money.

A [*presenting a Treasury note*] Cease preaching. Take it; and give me the change.

Z. Let me see. Eighteenpence, and fourpence for the ginger beer is one and tenpence, isnt it?

A. Have I denied it?

Z. Cheese threepence: two and a penny; butter sixpence: two and sevenpence; apples we sell by the pound. Hadnt you better have a pound?

A. How many to the pound?

Z. Three.

A. I cannot eat more than two apples at a

time. Charge me for a pound; and eat the odd one yourself.

z. Oh well, say threepence for two: thats two and tenpence, isnt it?

a. I dont know.

z. Hovis, tuppence halfpenny. Three shillings and a halfpenny. Do you happen to have a halfpenny to save having to take fippence halfpenny in coppers?

a. I hate halfpennies: I always throw them away. Stop. I have one. Here.

z. Thanks very much. [*Handing him his change coin by coin*] Three, four, five, seven and six, ten. Thanks very much.

a [*pocketing his change, but remaining comfortably seated*] Dont you find it rather dull in this village shop saying thanks very much all day?

z. Well, no matter where you are you are doing the same thing all day and every day, arnt you? The only way to get it off your mind is to live in the same place and stick at the same job. Then you never have to think about it. Thats the way the people live here; and they live for ever so long: eighty's no age here. Grandfather will be a hundred and two in August. Thats because he's never had to worry about what he'll do or where he'll go. He just imagines and imagines. It's the only way to be happy and longlived.

a. But if your imagination has only one village in it it must be pretty bare. How would you like to live in a room with only one chair in it.

z. Well, if you have only one seat what more do you want than one chair? Up at the castle there are thirtysix chairs of one sort or another in the big drawing room; but Lady Flopping cant flop on more than one, can she?

a [*pointing to the vacant chair*] May I suggest that you flop on that one while we talk?

z [*sitting down*] Thanks very much.

a. I am not interrupting your work, I hope. There is nothing so maddening as to be talked to when you want to work.

z. Talking is part of the work in a village shop.

a. Tell me: do you ever read?

z. I used to read travels and guide books. We used to stock the Marco Polo series. I was mad about travelling. I had daydreams about the glory that was Greece, the grandeur that was Rome, and all that flapdoodle.

a. Flapdoodle!

z. Well, I suppose I shouldnt call it that; but it ended in my going to Rome and Athens. They were all right; but the old parts were half knocked down; and I couldnt see any glory or grandeur different to Cheltenham. I was glad to be home again. And I had so wanted to meet the Marco Polo man and walk about with him in the ruins by moonlight and hear him go on about them!

a. The Marco Polo man! The milkman! the postman! the muffin man! the Marco Polo man! Some frustrated poet, earning his crust by quoting scraps of verse to bring the Call of the East to dreaming telephone girls.

z. Operators.

a. Operators dont dream. Girls! girls of the golden west. Did that poor devil never bring you the Call of the East?

z. I'd read about it in novels and seen it on the films. They were all about moony drunkards and shecks and the sort of girls that go dotty about them. I went right round the world to see the reality. Pretty places, of course; but the heat! and the mosquitoes! and the smells!! Travelling just destroyed the world for me as I imagined it. Give me this village all the time.

a. Had you no thrill when you stood somewhere where a poet had said "Stop; for thy tread is on an empire's dust"?

z. A guide, you mean. Theyd take the poetry out of anything; and all the time youre thinking what you ought to give them. If you fancy empires' dusts and all that sort of thing you should meet our vicar and start him talking about our standing stones, and the barrows on the downs, and the Mound. Every grain of our dust, he says, is full of history. Same everywhere, I expect.

a. Are you married?

z. No. Why? Have you any intentions?

a. Dont be in a hurry. Weve known each other less than ten minutes.

z. How much better do you think you will know me when we have talked for twenty years?

a. That is profoundly true. Still, I must think it over.

z. Nobody would ever marry if they thought it over. Youve got to take your chance, no matter how long you think.

a. You are in a hurry.

z. Well, I am past the age at which girls marry here, though I'm the pick of this village. Thats because I thought all my offers over. So I have made up my mind to take the next man that asks me, provided he's reasonably suitable.

A. Do I strike you as being reasonably suitable?

z. Well, I think I have the sort of commonsense you need to keep you straight. And you being a widower know what to expect from a woman. An inexperienced man expects the earth.

A. How do you know that I am a widower?

z. You told me.

A. Did I? When did I tell you?

z. Never mind. You did. I have noticed you have a bad memory; but I have a very good one; so it wont matter.

A. Steady. Steady. I have not yet made myself liable to an action for breach of promise.

z. Dont be afraid. I'm not that sort. We dont consider it respectable here.

A. Should I get any money with you? Do you own the shop?

z. No. All the money I ever had I blued on a trip round the world. But Mrs Ward is getting too old for the business: she couldnt run it now without me. If you could afford to buy her an annuity she'd sell it.

A. I dont know how much annuities cost.

z. You will find it in Whitaker's almanac.

A. This is rather upsetting. Somehow I have always taken it for granted that when I married again I'd marry a woman with money.

z. Oh, that wouldnt suit you at all. She'd want to spend it going into society and travelling about. How could you bear that sort of life? you that never spoke to anyone on the ship and wouldnt take any part in their games and dances! When it got about that you were the Marco Polo man—the man of all our dreams as you might say—I made a bet that I'd get you to talk to me; and I had all the trouble in the world to win it.

A. Do you mean to say that we have met before? That you were on that trip round the world?

z. Of course I do. But you never notice anything. Youre always reading or writing. The world doesnt exist for you. You never looked at me really. Youre shy with strangers, arnt you?

A. I am absolutely certain I never spoke to any woman on that ship. If I talk to women they always want to marry me.

z. Well, there you are, you see! The moment I set eyes on you I said to myself, "Now thats the sort of man that would suit me as a husband." I'd have said it even if you hadnt been the Marco Polo man.

A. Love at first sight: what?

z. Oh no. You know, if I fell in love with a man I'd never marry him: he could make me so miserable. But there was something about you: I dont exactly know what; but it made me feel that I could do with you in the house; and then I could fall in love with anyone I liked without any fear of making a fool of myself. I suppose it was because you are one of the quiet sort and dont run after women.

A. How do you know I dont run after women?

z. Well, if you want to know, it's because you didnt run after me. You mightnt believe it; but men do run after me.

A. Why?

z. Oh, how do I know? They dont know, themselves. But the lot of money they spend on things they dont want merely to come in and have a look at me and a word with me, you wouldnt believe. It's worth at least twenty pounds a year to the business.

A [putting on his glasses and looking at her attentively for the first time] I shouldnt call you a pretty woman.

z. Oh, I'm not pretty. But what you might call desirable, dont you think?

A [alarmed] No I dont think. May I explain? I am a man of letters and a gentleman. I am accustomed to associate with ladies. That means that I am accustomed to speak under certain well understood reserves which act as a necessary protection to both parties. You are not a lady: you are a villager; but somebody has educated you—probably the Church or the local authority—to a point at which you can impose on unobservant and unwary travellers. You have had finishing lessons on the telephone which give you a distinguished articulation: you can say Th-reee fiv-v-v-v-e ni-n-n-n instead of theree fauv nawn. But you have not acquired any of the reserves. You say what you think. You announce all the plans that wellbred women conceal. You play with your cards on the table instead of keeping them where a lady should keep them: up your sleeve.

z. Well, wheres the harm?

A. Oh, no harm. Quite the contrary. But

I feel rushed.

z. What do you mean? rushed?

a. Rushed. Precipitated. Carried to lengths I had no intention of going to.

z. Well, it gets you somewhere: doesnt it?

a. Yes; but where?

z. Here. Theres no mystery about it. Here, in a good business in a village shop in a quiet place, with me to keep it straight and look after you.

a. May I ask how much that expression "looking after me" includes? Let me be clear on the point. As a matter of fact I possess a small property which I could sell for enough to purchase an annuity for old Mrs Williams—

z. Ward.

a. I believe I have enough to purchase annuities for both Mrs Ward and Mrs Williams, as they are presumably both centenarians. But why on earth should I complicate the transaction by marrying you? I could pay you your present wages—

z. Salary.

a. I beg your pardon: salary. You will retain your present position as my shopgirl.

z. Shop assistant.

a. I beg your pardon: shop assistant. You can then make your own matrimonial arrangements, and leave me to make mine.

z. Oh, I'll make my own matrimonial arrangements all right enough. You may depend on that.

a. Excuse me: I added "and leave me to make mine." Can I depend on you for that also?

z. Well, we'll see.

a [angrily firm] No: you will not see.

z. Well, what?

a. I dont know what. I will not commit myself. We'll see.

z. Just so: we'll see. It's a bargain then?

a. No: it most certainly is not a bargain. When I entered this shop half an hour ago I had not the faintest notion of buying a village shop or marrying a village maiden or any of the things you have put into my head. Have you ever read the fable of the spider and the fly?

z. No; but I used to sing a song called the honeysuckle and the bee.

a [resolutely] Good morning. [He makes for the door].

z [following him with the string bag] You are forgetting your things.

a [taking it] Thank you.

z. Thanks very much.

She tempts him to kiss her.

a. No!!! [he strides out].

THIRD CONVERSATION

a *is now the proprietor of the shop with z as his hired assistant. The counter has been fitted with a desk at the opposite end to the post-office section. At this a sits writing. He wears pepper-and-salt trousers of country cut, with an apron. He is in his shirtsleeves, and looks every inch a shopkeeper. z comes in through the post office, very fresh and matutinal.*

z. Morning, boss.

a. Good morning, slave.

z. I havnt begun slaving yet. You have been at it for half an hour. Whatever on earth are you working at so hard?

a. I am making out my balance sheet.

z. Oh, you neednt do that. The accountant's clerk from Salisbury does all that when he makes out the income tax return. Youre not expected to do figures in this village. Fancy old Mrs Ward doing such a thing!

a. When I bought this shop from Mrs Ward for an annuity I found she was much cleverer at figures than I was. She should have been a moneylender.

z. She was. She lent a shilling for a penny a week.

a. That must have been between four and five hundred per cent per annum. Shylock would have blushed.

z. Whats the good of it when you have to give credit at the shop, and then lend the customers the money to pay you?

a. Mrs Ward should have gone to Geneva. International finance would have come naturally to her.

z. Thats too clever for me. Anyhow, you neednt worry over a balance sheet. The accountant will do all that for you.

a [rising and waving the balance sheet proudly as he comes through the counter into the public part of the shop] This is not an accountant's balance sheet. It is a Robinson Crusoe balance sheet.

z [following him] Whatever's that?

a. Crusoe drew up a balance sheet of the advantages and disadvantages of being cast away on a desert island. I am cast away in a village on the Wiltshire Downs. I am drawing up a similar balance sheet. I propose to read it to you as far as I have got. [He takes *one of the customer's chairs*] You can remind me of anything I have forgotten.

z. Lets have it. [*She takes the other chair*].

a. I begin with the credit entries.

z. Things to your own credit, you mean?

a. No, to the credit of village shopkeeping as a way of life.

z. Oh, you are silly, boss.

a. That is a disrespectful remark. As such, it should not be made to a boss by his slave. The understanding on which I raised your salary when I engaged you as my assistant was that our relations should be completely conventional and businesslike on your side, however I might occasionally forget myself.

z [*rising*] Very well: you can keep your balance sheet to yourself. I will go on with the telephone call book.

a. You will do nothing of the sort. You will do what I tell you to do. That is what I pay you for. Sit down again. [*She does so*]. Now listen. [*He takes up his manuscript and reads*]. Item: I have sharpened my faculties, and greatly improved in observation and mathematics.

z. Couldnt you put it into shorter words? What does it mean?

a. It means that formerly I always took what money was given me without condescending to count it or attempting to calculate it. I can now both calculate and count quite rapidly. Formerly I made no distinctions between grades of butter and eggs. To me an egg was an egg: butter was butter. I now make critical distinctions of the greatest subtlety, and value them in terms of money. I am forced to admit that the shopkeeper is enormously superior to the Marco Polo man, and that I have learnt more in three months in this shop than I learnt in three years in Oxford.

z. I cant believe that about the learning. But see how your manners have improved!

a. My manners!!

z. Yes. Why, on that ship you hadnt a word to throw to a dog; and if anyone came near you you shrank up into yourself like a hedgehog, afraid that they didnt belong to your class and wanted to speak to you without an introduction. Now it's a pleasure to hear you say "Good morning; and what can I do for you today, Mrs Burrell?" and "Have you noticed the cauliflowers today, maam? Not a touch of frost on them!" and "Sparrowgrass very good today, my lady, if you would

be wanting some."

a. I positively deny that I have ever in my life called asparagus sparrowgrass to an educated customer. Of course, when people are too ignorant to know the names of what they eat, that is another matter.

z. Well, anyhow, your manners have improved, havnt they?

a. I dont know. I know that they are no longer disinterested and sincere.

z. No more they never used to be. Never easy with anybody. Now you are hail fellow well met, as you might say, with everybody.

a. The world has become a world of customers. Let me write that down. [*He pencils on the back of his balance sheet*] "Manners will never be universally good until every person is every other person's customer."

z. Youre not a real shopkeeper yet, boss. All you want is to find something clever to write.

a. Well, why not? Find enough clever things to say, and you are a Prime Minister. Write them down, and you are a Shakespear.

z. Yes; but who wants to be a Prime Minister or a Shakespear? Youve got to make a living.

a. Well, am I not making a living? I am no poorer than when I bought the shop.

z. But if the money goes as fast as it comes you cant save anything.

a. I loathe saving. It turns human nature sour. "Cast your bread upon the waters; and it will return to you after many days."

z. And how are you to live for the many days with nothing to eat?

a. I dont know. One does, somehow. Stop asking questions; and let us get on with the balance sheet.

z. I speak for your good.

a [*rising wrathfully*] The most offensive liberty one human being can possibly take with another. What business is it of yours?

z [*rising and facing him*] If you wont think for yourself somebody else must think for you. It's my business as much as yours.

a. Oh, indeed! Who does this shop belong to? I mean to whom does this shop belong?

z. I get my living out of it, dont I. If it shuts up what becomes of me?

a. Well, if you come to that, what becomes of me? You can get another job. I very greatly doubt whether anyone would give me one. [*Calming down*] Can you not be content with the fact that the shop is making enough to support two people? [*He resumes his seat*].

z. Aye; but suppose it had to support three people!

a. Why suppose? It hasnt: thats all.

z. It's not all. If you marry a stranger there will be three. And what about the children?

a. The remedy is simple. I shall not marry.

z. You dont know.

a. Neither do you.

z. Yes I do. You have married once; and you will marry twice. Somebody will snap you up. You are that sort of man.

a. If a woman snaps me up she must take the consequences. She must assist in the shop. And you will get the sack.

z. Oh, you are tiresome. [*She sits down, discouraged*]. But you see my point, at all events.

a. No. What point?

z. Well, that it's really cheaper to keep a wife than to pay an assistant. Let alone that you dont have to live a single life.

a. You can get rid of an assistant if she doesnt suit. You cant get rid of a wife.

z. If people thought that way, theyd never get married.

a. Precisely.

z. In this life you have to take chances.

a. I have taken them, and escaped.

z. You wont escape here. We dont hold with bachelors here.

a. You cant do without a general shop here, nor a post office. While I command both I am in an impregnable strategic position.

z. Well, I dont like to say it; but people are beginning to talk.

a. Beginning! When did they ever stop?

z. Oh, theres no use talking to you.

a. Not the slightest.

z. Oh well then, take a month's notice. [*She rises*].

a. A month's notice!

z. Yes: a month's notice.

a. A month's notice because I refuse to marry some ridiculous village maiden or illiterate widow with whom I could not hold a moment's conversation!

z. Wives are not for conversation: thats for visitors. Youve had plenty of conversation with me.

a. Leave yourself out of this conversation, please.

z. Oh, very well. A month's notice.

a. Dont say that again. Utter nonsense. What have you to complain of? You are quite well off here. I purposely pay you ten pounds

a year more than you could get anywhere else.

z. Why?

a. What do you mean, why?

z. Why do you pay me ten pounds more than you could get another assistant for?

a. Heaven only knows!

z [*in a fury*] I'll go this very day. I'll go this very minute. You can keep my month. You dont know when youre well off. Youre selfish. I dont wonder your wife died. Did she die mad?

a [*gravely*] As a matter of fact, she did. I am one of those unlucky men who draw the black chances in the lottery of marriage.

z [*remorsefully*] Oh, I didnt know: I didnt indeed. I was only joking. [*She sits again*] I wouldnt have said it for the world if I'd known.

a. Never mind: I know you didnt mean it. By the way, I made an inconsiderate remark which hurt you. I did not intend that. I should have told you seriously that I pay you ten pounds more than the market rate because I value your services in the shop, and wish to offer you every inducement to stay here permanently.

z. Ten pounds extra, to stay all my life here as a single woman!

a. Not necessarily. You can get married if you wish.

z. Who to?

a. To whom? Oh, anyone.

z. Anyone in the village is good enough for me; but nobody in the village is good enough for you: is that it?

a. Dont lose your temper again.

z. I will if I like. And if you knew how near I was to putting a couple of extra words in, youd perhaps realize that a woman wants something more in life than a job and a salary.

a. I know that perfectly well. There is one thing we are all out for when we are young.

z. And what is that, pray?

a. Trouble, adventure, hardship, care, disappointment, doubt, misery, danger, and death.

z. Not me, thank you. All I want is a husband and the usual consequences.

a. The same thing. Marriage is the village form of all these adventures.

z. Oh, why dont you take a more cheerful view of life?

A. I have learnt not to expect too much from life. That is the secret of real cheerfulness, because I am always getting agreeable surprises instead of desolating disappointments.

z. Well, your second marriage may be an agreeable surprise, maynt it?

A. What, exactly, do you mean by my second marriage? I have only been married once. I mean I have been married only once.

z. Well, look here? Straight, now? Is there any man in this village that would be suitable to me now that I have got used to you?

A. My dear: men are all alike.

z. You mean it will make no difference to me who I marry.

A. Very little, I am afraid.

z. And women are all alike too, arnt they?

A [*suspicious*] What are you getting at?

z. If it doesnt matter who anybody marries, then it doesnt matter who I marry and it doesnt matter who you marry.

A. Whom, not who.

z. Oh, speak English: youre not on the telephone now. What I mean is that if it doesnt matter to me it doesnt matter to you either.

A. You admit, then, that it doesnt matter?

z. No I dont. It's a lie.

A. Oh!

z. Dont "oh" me. All men are not alike to me. There are men—and good nice men, too —that I wouldnt let touch me. But when I saw you on the ship I said to myself "I could put up with him."

A. Not at all. You told me just now that you said something quite different. I believe you really said something much more rapturous. Being rather a futile sort of person I attract vigorous women like you.

z. When you looked at me out of the corner of your eye—you looked at all the women out of the corner of your eye in spite of your keeping yourself so much to yourself —did you never say "I could put up with her"?

A. No. I said "Damn that woman: she wont stop talking to me and interrupting my work."

z. Well, I tell you we were made for oneanother. It maynt be as plain to you as to me yet; but if it's plain to me there must be something in it; for I'm never wrong when I see a thing quite plain. I dont believe youd ever have bought this shop and given up being a gentleman if I hadnt been here.

A. Now that you mention it I believe that is true. You were one of the amenities of the estate.

z. Well, I might be one of the amenities of the estate of holy matrimony, mightnt I?

A. Take care. You may find what you are trying to do easier than you think. About five per cent of the human race consists of positive masterful acquisitive people like you, obsessed with some passion which they must gratify at all hazards. The rest let them have their own way because they have neither the strength nor the courage to resist, or because the things the masterful ones want seem trifling beside the starry heavens and the destiny of Man. I am not one of the masterful ones. I am not worth marrying. Any woman could marry me if she took trouble enough.

z. Thats just what I'm afraid of. If I let you out of my sight for a month I might find you married to someone else at the end of it. Well, I'm taking no chances. I dont set up to be masterful: I dont like selfish uppish domineering people any more than you do; but I must and will have you; and thats all about it.

A. Well, you already have me—as an employer. And you are independent of me, and can leave me if you are not satisfied.

z. How can I be satisfied when I cant lay my hands on you? I work for you like a slave for a month on end; and I would have to work harder as your wife than I do now; but there come times when I want to get hold of you in my arms, every bit of you; and when I do I'll give you something better to think about than the starry heavens, as you call them. Youll find that you have senses to gratify as well as fine things to say.

A. Senses! You dont know what youre talking about. Look around you. Here in this shop I have everything that can gratify the senses: apples, onions, and acid drops: pepper and mustard; cosy comforters and hot water bottles. Through the window I delight my eyes with the old church and market place, built in the days when beauty came naturally from the hands of mediæval craftsmen. My ears are filled with delightful sounds, from the cooing of doves and the humming of bees to the wireless echoes of Beethoven and Elgar. My nose can gloat over our sack of fresh lavender or our special sixpenny Eau de Cologne when the smell of rain on dry earth is denied me. My senses are saturated with satisfactions of all sorts. But when I am full to the neck with onions and acid drops; when I am so fed up with mediæval architecture that I had rather die than look at another cathedral; when all I desire is rest from sensation, not more of it, what use will my senses be to me if the starry heavens still seem no more than a senseless avalanche of lumps of stone and wisps of gas—if the destiny of Man holds out no higher hope to him than the final extinction and annihilation of so mischievous and miserable a creature?

z. We dont bother about all that in the village.

a. Yes you do. Our best seller here is Old Moore's Almanack; and next to it comes Napoleon's Book of Fate. Old Mrs Ward would never have sold the shop to me if she had not become persuaded that the Day of Judgment is fixed for the seventh of August next.

z. I dont believe such nonsense. Whats it all got to do with you and me?

a. You are inexperienced. You dont know. You are the dupe of thoughtless words like sensuality, sensuousness, and all the rest of the twaddle of the Materialists. I am not a Materialist: I am a poet; and I know that to be in your arms will not gratify my senses at all. As a matter of mere physical sensation you will find the bodily contacts to which you are looking forward neither convenient nor decorous.

z. Oh, dont talk like that. You mustnt let yourself think about it like that.

a. You must always let yourself think about everything. And you must think about everything as it is, not as it is talked about. Your secondhand gabble about gratifying my senses is only your virgin innocence. We shall get quite away from the world of sense. We shall light up for oneanother a lamp in the holy of holies in the temple of life; and the lamp will make its veil transparent. Aimless lumps of stone blundering through space will become stars singing in their spheres. Our dull purposeless village existence will become one irresistible purpose and nothing else. An extraordinary delight and an intense love will seize us. It will last hardly longer than the lightning flash which turns the black night into infinite radiance. It will be dark

again before you can clear the light out of your eyes; but you will have seen; and for ever after you will think about what you have seen and not gabble catchwords invented by the wasted virgins that walk in darkness. It is to give ourselves this magic moment that we feel that we must and shall hold oneanother in our arms; and when the moment comes, the world of the senses will vanish; and for us there will be nothing ridiculous, nothing uncomfortable, nothing unclean, nothing but pure paradise.

z. Well, I am glad you take a nice view of it; for now I come to think of it I never could bear to be nothing more to a man than a lollipop. But you mustnt expect too much.

a. I shall expect more than you have ever dreamt of giving, in spite of the boundless audacity of women. What great men would ever have been married if the female nobodies who snapped them up had known the enormity of their own presumption? I believe they all thought they were going to refine, to educate, to make real gentlemen of their husbands. What do you intend to make of me, I wonder?

z. Well, I have made a decent shopkeeper of you already, havnt I? But you neednt be afraid of my not appreciating you. I want a fancy sort of husband, not a common villager that any woman could pick up. I shall be proud of you. And now Ive nailed you, I wonder at my own nerve.

a. So do I.

z. I'm not a bit like that, you know, really. Something above me and beyond me drove me on. Thats why I know it will be all right. Dont be afraid. I cant make a fine speech about it like you; but it will be all right. I promise you that.

a. Very well. Go round to the rectory; and put up the banns. And tell the rector's wife that we got in some prime artichokes this morning. She's fond of artichokes.

z. You are sure you feel happy about it?

a. I dont know what I feel about it. Go and do as you are told; and dont ask ridiculous questions.

The telephone rings. She hastens to answer it.

z. Number, please? . . . Oh, an order. Thanks very much. . . . Yes: we have some very fine artichokes just in this morning. . . . Thanks very much: they shall be sent round directly. Oh; and theres something else—are you there? . . . Sorry to detain you: could I speak to the rector? . . . Yes: it's rather particular. It's about banns . . . banns . . . BANNS: b for beauty, a for audacity, two enns for nonsense, and s for singing. . . . Yes, banns: thats right. . . . Who are the what? . . . Oh,

the parties! Of course. Well, it's—

The curtain falls

In the Sunda Strait,
27th January 1933

XLII

ON THE ROCKS

A POLITICAL COMEDY

ACT I

The Cabinet Room in number ten Downing Street, Westminster, the official residence of the British Prime Minister. The illustrious holder of that office, Sir Arthur Chavender, is reading The Times on the hearth under the portrait of Walpole. The fireplace wall is covered with bookshelves; but one bit of it, on Walpole's right, is a masked door, painted with sham books and shelves, leading to the Minister's private apartments; and in the end of the same wall, on Walpole's left, is a door leading to the office of Sir Arthur's private secretary Miss Hilda Hanways. The main door is in the side wall on Walpole's right. In the opposite wall on his left are the spacious windows. Everything is on an imposing scale, including an oblong table across the middle of the room, with fourteen leather upholstered chairs, six at each side and one at each end, pushed in all along it. The presidential chair is the central one next the cold fireplace (it is mid-July); and there is a telephone and a switchboard on the table within reach of it. Sir Arthur has pulled it round and is making himself comfortable in it as he reads. At the end of the table nearest the window a silver tray, with coffee and milk for one person, indicates Sir Arthur's unofficial seat. In the corner farthest from Walpole, on his right, is a writing bureau and chair for the secretary. In the corresponding corner on his left, an armchair. There is a bluebook lying, neglected and dusty, on a half empty shelf of the bookcase within reach of the Prime Minister's seat.

Sir Arthur can hardly be much less than fifty; but his natural buoyancy makes him look younger. He has an orator's voice of pleasant tone; and his manners are very genial. In oldish clothes he has the proper aristocratic air of being carelessly but well dressed, an easy feat for him, as he is so trimly built that any clothes would look well cut on him. On the whole, a very engaging personality.

He reads The Times until his secretary hurries in from her office, with her notebook and a sheaf of letters in her hand. Her age is unknown; but she is made up to pass as reasonably young and attractive. She looks capable; but she does not carry the burden of State affairs as easily as the Prime Minister. Both are worried; but with a difference. She is worried not only by an excess of business but a sense of responsibility. He is equally worried by the excess of business; but in him enjoyment of his position leaves no doubt in his mind as to his own entire adequacy to it.

HILDA. I hear you have been asking for me, Sir Arthur. I'm so sorry to be late; but really the streets are becoming quite impassable with the crowds of unemployed. I took a taxi, but it was no use: we were blocked by a procession; and I had to get out and push my way through. [*She goes to her bureau*].

SIR ARTHUR [*rising*] What on earth good do they think they can do themselves by crowding aimlessly about Westminster and the public offices?

HILDA. Thank Goodness the police wont let them into Downing Street. [*She sits down*]. They would be all over the doorstep.

SIR ARTHUR. It's all so foolish—so ignorant, poor chaps! [*He throws The Times on the table and moves to the end chair, where his coffee is*]. They think because I'm Prime Minister I'm Divine Providence and can find jobs for them before trade revives. [*He sits down and fidgets with his papers*].

HILDA. Trafalgar Square's full. The Horse Guards parade is full. The Mall is full all the way down to Marlborough House and Buckingham Palace.

SIR ARTHUR. They have no right to be there. Trafalgar Square is not a public place: it belongs to the Commissioner of Woods and Forests. The Horse Guards parade is reserved for the military. The Mall is a thoroughfare: anyone stopping there is guilty of obstruction. What are the police thinking of? Why dont they clear them out?

HILDA. I asked the policeman who got me through to the gates why they didnt. He said "We're only too glad to have them where they cant break any windows, and where the mounted men can have a fair whack at the Hooligan Fringe when they get too obstreperous."

SIR ARTHUR. Hooligan Fringe! He got that out of the papers. It only encourages them to write them up like that.

HILDA. Sir Broadfoot Basham has come over from Scotland Yard. He is talking to Lady Chavender.

SIR ARTHUR [*rising and making for the telephone*] Yes: I telephoned for him. He really must do something to stop these meetings. It was a mistake to make a man with a name like that Chief Commissioner of Police. People think him a trampling, bashing, brutal terrorist no matter how considerately the police behave. What we need is a thoroughly popular figure. [*He takes up the telephone*] Ask Sir Broadfoot Basham to come up.

HILDA. I dont think any chief of police could be popular at present. Every day they are bludgeoning deputations of the unemployed. [*She sits down and busies herself with letters*].

SIR ARTHUR. Poor devils! I hate that part of the business. But what are the police to do? We cant have the sittings of the local authorities threatened by deputations. Deputations are frightful nuisances even in the quietest times; but just now they are a public danger.

The Chief Commissioner of Police enters by the main door. A capable looking man from the military point of view. He is a gentleman: and his manners are fairly pleasant; but they are not in the least conciliatory.

Hilda rises and pulls out a chair for him at the end of the table nearest to her and farthest from Sir Arthur; then returns to her work at her desk. Sir Arthur comes round to his side of the table.

SIR ARTHUR. Morning, Basham. Sit down. I'm devilishly busy; but you are always welcome to your ten minutes.

BASHAM [*coolly, sitting down*] Thank you. You sent for me. [*Anxiously*] Anything new?

SIR ARTHUR. These street corner meetings are going beyond all bounds.

BASHAM [*relieved*] What harm do they do? Crowds are dangerous when theyve nothing to listen to or look at. The meetings keep them amused. They save us trouble.

SIR ARTHUR. Thats all very well for you, Basham; but think of the trouble they make for me! Remember: this is a National Government, not a party one. I am up against my Conservative colleagues all the time; and they cant swallow the rank sedition that goes on every day at these meetings. Sir Dexter Rightside—you know what a regular old Diehard he is—heard a speaker say that if the police used tear gas the unemployed would give old Dexy something to cry for without any tear gas. That has brought matters to a head in the Cabinet. We shall make an Order in Council to enable you to put a stop to all street meetings and speeches.

BASHAM [*unimpressed—slowly*] If you dont mind, P.M., I had rather you didnt do that.

SIR ARTHUR. Why not?

BASHAM. Crowd psychology.

SIR ARTHUR. Nonsense! Really, Basham, if you are going to come this metaphysical rot over me I shall begin to wonder whether your appointment wasnt a mistake.

BASHAM. Of course it was a mistake. Dealing with the unemployed is not a soldier's job; and I was a soldier. If you want these crowds settled on soldierly lines, say so; and give me half a dozen machine guns. The streets will be clear before twelve o'clock.

SIR ARTHUR. Man: have you considered the effect on the bye-elections?

BASHAM. A soldier has nothing to do with elections. You shew me a crowd and tell me to disperse it. All youll hear is a noise like a watchman's rattle. Quite simple.

SIR ARTHUR. Far too simple. You soldiers never understand the difficulties a statesman has to contend with.

BASHAM. Well, whats your alternative?

SIR ARTHUR. I have told you. Arrest the sedition mongers. That will shut old Dexy's mouth.

BASHAM. So that Satan may find mischief still for idle hands to do. No, P.M.: the right alternative is mine: keep the crowd amused. You ought to know that, I think, better than most men.

SIR ARTHUR. I! What do you mean?

BASHAM. The point is to prevent the crowd doing anything, isnt it?

SIR ARTHUR. Anything mischievous: I suppose so. But—

BASHAM. An English crowd will never do anything, mischievous or the reverse, while it is listening to speeches. And the fellows who make the speeches can be depended on never to do anything else. In the first place, they dont know how. In the second, they are afraid. I am instructing my agents to press all the talking societies, the Ethical Societies, the Socialist societies, the Communists, the Fascists, the Anarchists, the Syndicalists, the official Labor Party, the Independent Labor Party, the Salvation Army, the Church Army and the Atheists, to send their best tub-thumpers into the streets to seize the opportunity.

SIR ARTHUR. What opportunity?

BASHAM. They dont know. Neither do I. It's only a phrase that means nothing: just what they are sure to rise at. I must keep Trafalgar Square going night and day. A few Labor M.P.s would help. You have a rare lot of gasbags under your thumb in the House. If you could send half a dozen of them down to the Yard, I could plant them where they would be really useful.

SIR ARTHUR [incensed] Basham: I must tell you that we are quite determined to put a stop to this modern fashion of speaking disrespectfully of the House of Commons. If it goes too far we shall not hesitate to bring prominent offenders to the bar of the House, no matter what their position is.

BASHAM. Arthur: as responsible head of the police, I am up against the facts all day and every day; and one of the facts is that nowadays nobody outside the party cliques cares a brass button for the House of Commons. [Rising] You will do what I ask you as to letting the speaking go on, wont you?

SIR ARTHUR. Well, I—er—

BASHAM. Unless you are game to try the machine guns.

SIR ARTHUR. Oh do drop that, Basham [he returns to his chair and sits moodily].

BASHAM. Righto! We'll let them talk. Thanks ever so much. Sorry to have taken up so much of your time: I know it's priceless. [He hurries to the door; then hesitates and adds] By the way, I know it's asking a lot; but if you could give us a turn in Trafalgar Square yourself—some Sunday afternoon would be best—it—

SIR ARTHUR [springing up, thoroughly roused] I!!!!

BASHAM [hurriedly] No: of course you couldnt. Only, it would do such a lot of good —keep the crowd quiet talking about it for a fortnight. However, of course it's impossible: say no more: so long. [He goes out].

SIR ARTHUR [collapsing into his chair] Well, really! Basham's losing his head. I wonder what he meant by saying that I ought to know better than most men. What ought I to know better than most men?

HILDA. I think he meant that you are such a wonderful speaker you ought to know what a magical effect a fine speech has on a crowd.

SIR ARTHUR [musing] Do you know, I am not at all sure that there is not something in his idea of my making a speech in Trafalgar Square. I have not done such a thing for many many years; but I have stood between the lions in my time; and I believe that if I were to tackle the unemployed face to face, and explain to them that I intend to call a conference in March next on the prospects of a revival of trade, it would have a wonderfully soothing effect.

HILDA. But it's impossible. You have a conference every month until November. And think of the time taken by the travelling! One in Paris! Two in Geneva! One in Japan! You cant possibly do it: you will break down.

SIR ARTHUR. And shall I be any better at home here leading the House? sitting up all night in bad air listening to fools insulting me? I tell you I should have been dead long ago but for the relief of these conferences: the journeys and the change. And I look forward to Japan. I shall be able to pick up some nice old bric-a-brac there.

HILDA. Oh well! You know best.

SIR ARTHUR [energetically] And now to work. Work! work! work! [He rises and paces the floor in front of the table]. I want you to take down some notes for my speech this afternoon at the Church House. The Archbishop tells me that the Anglo-Catholics are going mad on what they call Christian Communism, and that I must head them off.

HILDA. There are those old notes on the economic difficulties of Socialism that you used at the British Association last year.

SIR ARTHUR. No: these parsons know too much about that. Besides, this is not the time to talk about economic difficulties: we're up to the neck in them. The Archbishop says "Avoid figures; and stick to the fact that Socialism would break up the family." I believe he is right: a bit of sentiment about the family always goes down well. Just jot this down for me. [*Dictating*] Family. Foundation of civilization. Foundation of the empire.

HILDA. Will there be any Hindus or Mahometans present?

SIR ARTHUR. No. No polygamists at the Church House. Besides, everybody knows that The Family means the British family. By the way, I can make a point of that. Put down in a separate line, in red capitals, "One man one wife." Let me see now: can I work that up? "One child one father." How would that do?

HILDA. I think it would be safer to say "One child one mother."

SIR ARTHUR. No: that might get a laugh— the wrong sort of laugh. I'd better not risk it. Strike it out. A laugh in the wrong place in the Church House would be the very devil. Where did you get that necklace? it's rather pretty. I havnt seen it before.

HILDA. Ive worn it every day for two months. [*Striking out the "one child" note*] Yes?

SIR ARTHUR. Then—er—what subject are we on? [*Testily*] I wish you wouldnt interrupt me: I had the whole speech in my head beautifully; and now it's gone.

HILDA. Sorry. The family.

SIR ARTHUR. The family? Whose family? What family? The Holy Family? The Royal Family? The Swiss Family Robinson? Do be a little more explicit, Miss Hanways.

HILDA [*gently insistent*] Not any particular family. THE family. Socialism breaking up the family. For the Church House speech this afternoon.

SIR ARTHUR. Yes yes yes, of course. I was in the House yesterday until three in the morning; and my brains are just so much tripe.

HILDA. Why did you sit up? The business didnt matter.

SIR ARTHUR [*scandalized*] Not matter! You really must not say these things, Miss Hanways. A fulldress debate on whether Jameson or Thompson was right about what Johnson said in the Cabinet!

HILDA. Ten years ago.

SIR ARTHUR. What does that matter? The real question: the question whether Jameson or Thompson is a liar, is a vital question of the first importance.

HILDA. But theyre both liars.

SIR ARTHUR. Of course they are; but the division might have affected their inclusion in the next Cabinet. The whole House rose at it. Look at the papers this morning! Full of it.

HILDA. And three lines about the unemployed, though I was twenty minutes late trying to shove my way through them. Really, Sir Arthur, you should have come home to bed. You will kill yourself if you try to get through your work and attend so many debates as well: you will indeed.

SIR ARTHUR. Miss Hanways: I wish I could persuade you to remember occasionally that I happen to be the leader of the House of Commons.

HILDA. Oh, what is the use of leading the House if it never goes anywhere? It just breaks my heart to see the state you come home in. You are good for nothing next morning.

SIR ARTHUR [*yelling at her*] Dont remind me of it: do you think I dont know? My brain is overworked: my mental grasp is stretched and strained to breaking point. I shall go mad. [*Pulling himself together*] However, it's no use grousing about it: I shall have a night off going to Geneva, and a weekend at Chequers. But it is hard to govern a country and do fifty thousand other things every day that might just as well be done by the Beadle of Burlington Arcade. Well, well, we mustnt waste time. Work! work! work! [*He returns to his chair and sits down resolutely*]. Get along with it. What were we talking about?

HILDA. The family.

SIR ARTHUR [*grasping his temples distractedly*] Oh dear! Has Lady Chavender's sister-in-law been making a fuss again?

HILDA. No, no. The family. Not any real family. THE family. Socialism breaking up the family. Your speech this afternoon at the Church House.

SIR ARTHUR. Ah, of course. I am going dotty. Thirty years in Parliament and ten on the Front Bench would drive any man dotty. I have only one set of brains and I need ten. I—

HILDA [*urgently*] We must get on with the notes for your speech, Sir Arthur. The morning has half gone already; and weve done nothing.

SIR ARTHUR [*again infuriated*] How can the busiest man in England find time to do anything? It is you who have wasted the morning interrupting me with your silly remarks about your necklace. What do I care about your necklace?

HILDA. You gave it to me, Sir Arthur.

SIR ARTHUR. Did I? Ha ha ha! Yes: I believe I did. I bought it in Venice. But come along now. What about that speech?

HILDA. Yes. The family. It was about the family.

SIR ARTHUR. Well, I know that: I have not yet become a complete idiot. You keep saying the family, the family, the family.

HILDA. Socialism and the family. How Socialism will break up the family.

SIR ARTHUR. Who says Socialism will break up the family? Dont be a fool.

HILDA. The Archbishop wants you to say it. At the Church House.

SIR ARTHUR. Decidedly I am going mad.

HILDA. No: you are only tired. You were getting along all right. One man one wife: that is where you stopped.

SIR ARTHUR. One man one wife is one wife too many, if she has a lot of brothers who cant get on with the women they marry. Has it occurred to you, Miss Hanways, that the prospect of Socialism destroying the family may not be altogether unattractive?

HILDA [despairingly] Oh, Sir Arthur, we must get on with the notes: we really must. I have all the letters to do yet. Do try to pick up the thread. The family the foundation of the empire. The foundation of Christianity. Of civilization. Of human society.

SIR ARTHUR. Thats enough about the foundation: it wont bear any more. I must have another word to work up. Let me see. I have it. Nationalization of women.

HILDA [remonstrating] Oh, Sir Arthur!

SIR ARTHUR. Whats the matter now?

HILDA. Such bunk!

SIR ARTHUR. Miss Hanways: when a statesman is not talking bunk he is making trouble for himself; and Goodness knows I have trouble enough without making any more. Put this down. [He rises and takes his platform attitude at the end of the table]. "No, your Grace, my lords and gentlemen. Nationalize the land if you will; nationalize our industries if we must; nationalize education, housing, science, art, the theatre, the opera, even the cinema; but spare our women."

HILDA [having taken it down] Is that the finish?

SIR ARTHUR [abandoning the attitude and pacing about] No: write in red capitals under it "Rock of Ages."

HILDA. I think Rock of Ages will be rather a shock unless in connexion with something very sincere. May I suggest "The Church's One Foundation"?

SIR ARTHUR. Yes. Much better. Thank you. The family the Church's one foundation. Splendid.

Miss Flavia Chavender, 19, bursts violently into the room through the masked door and dashes to her father.

FLAVIA. Papa: I will not stand Mamma any longer. She interferes with me in every possible way out of sheer dislike of me. I refuse to live in this house with her a moment longer.

Lady Chavender follows her in, speaking as she enters, and comes between the Prime Minister and his assailant.

LADY CHAVENDER. I knew you were coming here to make a scene and disturb your father, though he has had hardly six hours sleep this week, and was up all night. I am so sorry, Arthur: she is uncontrollable.

David Chavender, 18, slight, refined, rather small for his age, charges in to the table.

DAVID [in a childish falsetto] Look here, Mamma. Cant you let Flavia alone? I wont stand by and see her nagged at and treated like a child of six. Nag! nag! nag! everything she does.

LADY CHAVENDER. Nag!! I control myself to the limit of human endurance with you all. But Flavia makes a study of annoying me.

FLAVIA. It's not true: I have considered you and given up all the things I wanted for you until I have no individuality left. If I take up a book you want me to read something else. If I want to see anybody you want me to see somebody else. If I choose the color of my own dress you want something different and dowdy. I cant sit right nor stand right nor do my hair right nor dress myself right: my life here is a hell.

LADY CHAVENDER. Flavia!!

FLAVIA [passionately] Yes, hell.

DAVID. Quite true. [Fortissimo] Hell.

LADY CHAVENDER [quietly] Miss Hanways: would you mind—

HILDA. Yes, Lady Chavender [she rises to go].

FLAVIA. You neednt go, Hilda, You know what I have to endure.

DAVID. Damn all this paralyzing delicacy! Damn it!

LADY CHAVENDER. Arthur—

SIR ARTHUR [*patting her*] Never mind, dear. They must be let talk. [*He returns placidly to his chair*]. It's just like the House of Commons except that the speeches are shorter.

FLAVIA. Oh, it's no use trying to make papa listen to anything. [*She throws herself despairingly into Basham's chair and writhes*].

DAVID [*approaching Sir Arthur with dignity*] I really think, father, you might for once in a way take some slight interest in the family.

SIR ARTHUR. My dear boy, at this very moment I am making notes for a speech on the family. Ask Miss Hanways.

HILDA. Yes. Mr Chavender: Sir Arthur is to speak this afternoon on the disintegrating effect of Socialism on family life.

FLAVIA [*irresistible amusement struggling with hysterics and getting the better of them*] Ha ha! Ha ha ha!

DAVID [*retreating*] Ha ha! Haw! Thats the best—ha ha ha!

SIR ARTHUR. I dont see the joke. Why this hilarity?

DAVID. Treat the House to a brief description of this family; and you will get the laugh of your life.

FLAVIA. Damn the family!

LADY CHAVENDER. Flavia!

FLAVIA [*bouncing up*] Yes: there you go. I mustnt say damn. I mustnt say anything I feel and think, only what you feel and think. Thats family life. Scold, scold, scold!

DAVID. Squabble, squabble, squabble!

FLAVIA. Look at the unbearable way you treat me! Look at the unbearable way you treat Papa!

SIR ARTHUR [*rising in flaming wrath*] How dare you? Silence. Leave the room.

After a moment of awestruck silence Flavia, rather dazed by the avalanche she has brought down on herself, looks at her father in a lost way; then bursts into tears and runs out through the masked door.

SIR ARTHUR [*quietly*] Youd better go too, my boy.

David, also somewhat dazed, shrugs his shoulders and goes out. Sir Arthur looks at Hilda. She hurries out almost on tiptoe.

SIR ARTHUR [*taking his wife in his arms affectionately*] Treat me badly! You!! I could have killed her, poor little devil.

He sits down; and she passes behind him and takes the nearest chair on his right.

She is a nice woman, and goodlooking; but she is bored; and her habitual manner is one of apology for being not only unable to take an interest in people, but even to pretend that she does.

LADY CHAVENDER. It serves us right, dear, for letting them bring themselves up in the post-war fashion instead of teaching them to be ladies and gentlemen. Besides, Flavia was right. I do treat you abominably. And you are so good!

SIR ARTHUR. Nonsense! Such a horrid wicked thing to say. Dont you know, my love, that you are the best of wives? the very best as well as the very dearest?

LADY CHAVENDER. You are certainly the best of husbands, Arthur. You are the best of everything. I dont wonder at the country adoring you. But Flavia was quite right. It is the first time I have ever known her to be right about anything. I am a bad wife and a bad mother. I dislike my daughter and treat her badly. I like you very much; and I treat you abominably.

SIR ARTHUR. No; no.

LADY CHAVENDER. Yes, yes. I suppose it's something wrong in my constitution. I was not born for wifing and mothering. And yet I am very very fond of you, as you know. But I have a grudge against your career.

SIR ARTHUR. My career! [*Complacently*] Well, theres not much wrong with that, is there? Of course I know it keeps me too much away from home. That gives you a sort of grudge against it. All the wives of successful men are a bit like that. But it's better to see too little of a husband than too much of him, isnt it?

LADY CHAVENDER. I am so glad that you really feel successful.

SIR ARTHUR. Well, it may sound conceited and all that; but after all a man cant be Prime Minister and go about with a modest cough pretending to be a nobody. Facts are facts; and the facts in my case are that I have climbed to the top of the tree; I am happy in my work; and—

LADY CHAVENDER. Your what?

SIR ARTHUR. You are getting frightfully deaf, dear. I said "my work."

LADY CHAVENDER. You call it work?

SIR ARTHUR. Brain work, dear, brain work. Do you really suppose that governing the country is not work, but a sort of gentlemanly diversion?

LADY CHAVENDER. But you dont govern the country, Arthur. The country isnt governed: it just slummocks along anyhow.

SIR ARTHUR. I have to govern within democratic limits. I cannot go faster than our voters will let me.

LADY CHAVENDER. Oh, your voters! What do they know about government? Football, prizefighting, war: that is what they like. And they like war because it isnt real to them: it's only a cinema show. War is real to me; and I hate it, as every woman to whom it is real hates it. But to you it is only part of your game: one of the regular moves of the Foreign Office and the War Office.

SIR ARTHUR. My dear, I hate war as much as you do. It makes a Prime Minister's job easy because it brings every dog to heel; but it produces coalitions; and I believe in party government.

LADY CHAVENDER [rising] Oh, it's no use talking to you, Arthur. [She comes behind him and plants her hands on his shoulders]. You are a dear and a duck and a darling; but you live in fairyland and I live in the hard wicked world. Thats why I cant be a good wife and take an interest in your career.

SIR ARTHUR. Stuff! Politics are not a woman's business: thats all it means. Thank God I have not a political wife. Look at Higginbotham! He was just ripe for the Cabinet when his wife went into Parliament and made money by journalism. That was the end of him.

LADY CHAVENDER. And I married a man with a hopelessly parliamentary mind; and that was the end of me.

SIR ARTHUR. Yes, yes, my pettums. I know that you have sacrificed yourself to keeping my house and sewing on my buttons; and I am not ungrateful. I am sometimes remorseful; but I love it. And now you must run away, I am very very very busy this morning.

LADY CHAVENDER. Yes, yes, very very busy doing nothing. And it wears you out far more than if your mind had something sensible to work on! Youll have a nervous breakdown if you go on like this. Promise me that you will see the lady I spoke to you about—if you wont see a proper doctor.

SIR ARTHUR. But you told me this woman is a doctor! [He rises and breaks away from her]. Once for all, I wont see any doctor. I'm old enough to do my own doctoring; and I'm not going to pay any doctor, male or female, three guineas to tell me what I know perfectly well already: that my brain's over-worked and I must take a fortnight off on the links, or go for a sea voyage.

LADY CHAVENDER. She charges twenty guineas, Arthur.

SIR ARTHUR [shaken] Oh! Does she? What for?

LADY CHAVENDER. Twenty guineas for the diagnosis and twelve guineas a week at her sanatorium in the Welsh mountains, where she wants to keep you under observation for six weeks. That would really rest you; and I think you would find her a rather interesting and attractive woman.

SIR ARTHUR. Has she a good cook?

LADY CHAVENDER. I dont think that matters.

SIR ARTHUR. Not matter!

LADY CHAVENDER. No. She makes her patients fast.

SIR ARTHUR. Tell her I'm not a Mahatma. If I pay twelve guineas a week I shall expect three meals a day for it.

LADY CHAVENDER. Then you will see her?

SIR ARTHUR. Certainly not, if I have to pay twenty guineas for it.

LADY CHAVENDER. No, no. Only a social call, not a professional visit. Just to amuse you, and gratify her curiosity. She wants to meet you.

SIR ARTHUR. Very well, dear, very well, very well. This woman has got round you, I see. Well, she shant get round me; but to please you I'll have a look at her. And now you really must run away. I have a frightful mass of work to get through this morning.

LADY CHAVENDER. Thank you, darling. [She kisses him] May I tell Flavia she is forgiven?

SIR ARTHUR. Yes. But I havnt really forgiven her. I'll never forgive her.

LADY CHAVENDER [smiling] Dearest. [She kisses his fingers and goes out, giving him a parting smile as she goes through the masked door].

Sir Arthur, left alone, looks inspired and triumphant. He addresses an imaginary assembly.

SIR ARTHUR. "My lords and gentlemen: you are not theorists. You are not rhapsodists. You are no longer young"—no, damn it, old Middlesex wont like that. "We have all been young. We have seen visions and dreamt dreams. We have cherished hopes and striven towards ideals. We have aspired to things that have not been realized. But we are now settled experienced men, family men. We are husbands and fathers. Yes, my lords and gentlemen: husbands and fathers. And I venture to claim your unanimous consent when I affirm that we have found something in these realities that was missing in the ideals. I thank you for that burst of applause: which I well know is no mere tribute to my poor eloquence, but the spontaneous and irresistible recognition of the great natural truth that our friends the Socialists have left out of their fancy pictures of a mass society in which regulation is to take the place of emotion and economics of honest human passion." Whew! that took a long breath. "They never will, gentlemen, I say they never will. They will NOT [*he smites the table and pauses, glaring round at his imaginary hearers*]. I see that we are of one mind, my lords and gentlemen. I need not labor the point." Then labor it for the next ten minutes. That will do. That will do. [*He sits down; rings the telephone bell; and seizes the milk jug, which he empties at a single draught*].

Hilda appears at the main door.

HILDA. Did you say you would receive a deputation from the Isle of Cats this morning? I have no note of it.

SIR ARTHUR. Oh, confound it, I believe I did. I totally forgot it.

HILDA. Theyve come.

SIR ARTHUR. Bother them!

HILDA. By all means. But how am I to get rid of them? What am I to say?

SIR ARTHUR [*resignedly*] Oh, I suppose I must see them. Why do I do these foolish things? Tell Burton to shew them in.

HILDA. Burton is in his shirt sleeves doing something to the refrigerator. I'd better introduce them.

SIR ARTHUR. Oh, bundle them in anyhow. And tell them I am frightfully busy.

She goes out, closing the door softly behind her. He pushes away the breakfast tray and covers it with The Times, which he opens out to its fullest extent for that purpose. Then he collects his papers into the vacant space, and takes up a big blue one, in the study of which he immerses himself profoundly.

HILDA [*flinging the door open*] The worshipful the Mayor of the Isle of Cats.

The Mayor, thick and elderly, enters, a little shyly, followed by (a) an unladylike but brilliant and very confident young woman in smart factory-made clothes after the latest Parisian models, (b) a powerfully built loud voiced young man fresh from Oxford University, defying convention in corduroys, pullover, and unshaven black

beard, (c) a thin, undersized lower middle class young man in an alderman's gown, evidently with a good conceit of himself, and (d) a sunny comfortable old chap in his Sunday best, who might be anything from a working man with a very sedentary job (say a watchman) to a city missionary of humble extraction. He is aggressively modest, or pretends to be, and comes in last with a disarming smile rather as a poor follower of the deputation than as presuming to form part of it. They group themselves at the door behind the Mayor, who is wearing his chain of office.

SIR ARTHUR [*starting from his preoccupation with important State documents, and advancing past the fireplace to greet the Mayor with charming affability*] What! My old friend Tom Humphries! How have you been all these years? Sit down. [*They shake hands, whilst Hilda deftly pulls out a chair from the end of the table nearest the door*].

The Mayor sits down, rather overwhelmed by the cordiality of his reception.

SIR ARTHUR [*continuing*] Well, well! fancy your being Mayor of—of—

HILDA [*prompting*] The Isle of Cats.

THE YOUNG WOMAN [*brightly, helping her out*] Down the river, Sir Arthur. Twenty minutes from your door by Underground.

THE OXFORD YOUTH [*discordantly*] Oh, he knows as well as you do, Aloysia. [*He advances offensively on Sir Arthur, who declines the proximity by retreating a step or two somewhat haughtily*]. Stow all this fo bunnum business, Chavender.

SIR ARTHUR. This what??

OXFORD YOUTH. Oh, chuck it. You know French as well as I do.

SIR ARTHUR. Oh, faux bonhomme, of course, yes. [*Looking him up and down*]. I see by your costume that you represent the upper classes in the Isle of Cats.

OXFORD YOUTH. There are no upper classes in the Isle of Cats.

SIR ARTHUR. In that case, since it is agreed that there is to be no fo bunnum nonsense between us, may I ask what the dickens you are doing here?

OXFORD YOUTH. I am not here to bandy personalities. Whatever the accident of birth and the humbug of rank may have made me I am here as a delegate from the Borough Council and an elected representative of the riverside proletariat.

SIR ARTHUR [*suddenly pulling out a chair*

from the middle of the table—peremptorily] Sit down. Dont break the chair. [*The Youth scowls at him and flings himself into the chair like a falling tree*]. You are all most welcome. Perhaps, Tom, you will introduce your young friends.

THE MAYOR [*introducing*] Alderwoman Aloysia Brollikins.

SIR ARTHUR [*effusively shaking her hand*] How do you do, Miss Brollikins? [*He pulls out a chair for her on the Oxford Youth's right*].

ALOYSIA. Nicely, thank you. Pleased to meet you, Sir Arthur. [*She sits*].

THE MAYOR. Alderman Blee.

SIR ARTHUR [*with flattering gravity, pressing his hand*] Ah, we have all heard of you, Mr Blee. Will you sit here? [*He indicates the presidential chair on the Oxford Youth's left*].

BLEE. Thank you. I do my best. [*He sits*].

THE MAYOR. Viscount Barking.

SIR ARTHUR [*triumphantly*] Ah! I thought so. A red Communist: what!

OXFORD YOUTH. Red as blood. Same red as the people's.

SIR ARTHUR. How did you get the blue out of it? The Barkings came over with the Conqueror.

OXFORD YOUTH [*rising*] Look here. The unemployed are starving. Is this a time for persiflage?

SIR ARTHUR. Camouflage, my lad, camouflage. Do you expect me to take you seriously in that get-up?

OXFORD YOUTH [*hotly*] I shall wear what I damn well please. I—

ALOYSIA. Shut up, Toffy. You promised to behave yourself. Sit down; and lets get to business.

BARKING [*subsides into his chair with a grunt of disgust*]!

SIR ARTHUR [*looking rather doubtfully at the old man, who is still standing*] Is this gentleman a member of your deputation?

THE MAYOR. Mr Hipney. Old and tried friend of the working class.

OXFORD YOUTH. Old Hipney. Why dont you call him by the name the East End knows him by? Old Hipney. Good old Hipney.

OLD HIPNEY [*slipping noiselessly into the secretary's chair at the bureau*] Dont mind me, Sir Arthur. I dont matter.

SIR ARTHUR. At such a crisis as the present, Mr Hipney, every public-spirited man matters. Delighted to meet you. [*He returns to his own chair and surveys them now that they are all seated, whilst Hilda slips discreetly out into her office*]. And now, what can I do for you, Miss Brollikins? What can I do for you, gentlemen?

THE MAYOR [*slowly*] Well, Sir Arthur, as far as I can make it out the difficulty seems to be that you cant do anything. But something's got to be done.

SIR ARTHUR [*stiffening suddenly*] May I ask why, if everything that is possible has already been done?

THE MAYOR. Well, the unemployed are—well, unemployed, you know.

SIR ARTHUR. We have provided for the unemployed. That provision has cost us great sacrifices; but we have made the sacrifices without complaining.

THE OXFORD YOUTH [*scornfully*] Sacrifices! What sacrifices? Are you starving? Have you pawned your overcoat? Are you sleeping ten in a room?

SIR ARTHUR. The noble lord enquires—

OXFORD YOUTH [*furiously*] Dont noble lord me: you are only doing it to rattle me. Well, you cant rattle me. But it makes me sick to see you rolling in luxury and think of what these poor chaps and their women folk are suffering.

SIR ARTHUR. I am not rolling, Toffy—I think that is what Miss Brollikins called you. [*To Aloysia*] Toffy is a diminutive of Toff, is it not, Miss Brollikins?

OXFORD YOUTH. Yah! Now you have something silly to talk about, youre happy. But I know what would make you sit up and do something.

SIR ARTHUR. Indeed? Thats interesting. May I ask what?

OXFORD YOUTH. Break your bloody windows.

THE MAYOR. Order! order!

ALOYSIA. Come, Toffy! you promised not to use any of your West End language here. You know we dont like it.

SIR ARTHUR. Thats right, Miss Brollikins: snub him. He is disgracing his class. As a humble representative of that class I apologize for him to the Isle of Cats. I apologize for his dress, for his manners, for his language. He must shock you every time he opens his mouth.

BLEE. We working folks know too much of bad language and bad manners to see any fun in them or think they can do any good.

THE MAYOR. Thats right.

ALOYSIA. We are as tired of bad manners as Toffy is tired of good manners. We brought Toffy here, Sir Arthur, because we knew he'd speak to you as a dock laborer would speak to you if his good manners would let him. And he's right, you know. He's rude; but he's right.

OXFORD YOUTH. Yours devotedly, Brolly. And what has his Right Honorable nibs to say to that?

SIR ARTHUR [concentrating himself on his adversary in the House of Commons manner] I will tell the noble lord what I have to say. He may marshal his friends the unemployed and break every window in the West End, beginning with every pane of glass in this house. What will he gain by it? Next day a score or so of his followers will be in prison with their heads broken. A few ignorant and cowardly people who have still any money to spare will send it to the funds for the relief of distress, imagining that they are ransoming their riches. You, ladies and gentlemen, will have to put your hands in your pockets to support the wives and children of the men in prison, and to pay cheap lawyers to put up perfectly useless defences for them in the police courts. And then, I suppose, the noble lord will boast that he has made me do something at last. What can I do? Do you suppose that I care less about the sufferings of the poor than you? Do you suppose I would not revive trade and put an end to it all tomorrow if I could? But I am like yourself: I am in the grip of economic forces that are beyond human control. What mortal men could do this Government has done. We have saved the people from starvation by stretching unemployment benefit to the utmost limit of our national resources. We—

OXFORD YOUTH. You have cut it down to fifteen bob a week and shoved every man you could off it with your beastly means test.

SIR ARTHUR [fiercely] What do you propose? Will you take my place and put the dole up to five pounds a week without any means test?

THE MAYOR. Order! order! Why are we here? We are here because we are all sick of arguing and talking, and we want something doing. And here we are arguing and talking just as if it was an all night sitting of the Borough Council about an item of three-and-six for refreshments. If you, Sir Arthur, tell us that you cant find work for our people we are only wasting your time and our own, sitting here.

He rises. The rest, except Hipney, follow his example. Sir Arthur is only too glad to rise too.

SIR ARTHUR. At least I hope I have convinced you about the windows, Mr Mayor.

THE MAYOR. We needed no convincing. More crockery than windows will have to be broken if you gentlemen can do nothing to get us out of our present mess. But some people will say that a few thousands more to the relief funds is better than nothing. And some of the unemployed are glaziers.

SIR ARTHUR. Let us close our little talk on a more hopeful note. I assure you it has been intensely interesting to me; and I may tell you that signs of a revival of trade are not wholly wanting. Some of the best informed city authorities are of opinion that this year will see the end of the crisis. Some of them even hold that trade is already reviving. By the last returns the export of Spanish onions has again reached the 1913 level.

OXFORD YOUTH. Holy Jerusalem! Spanish onions! Come on, Brolly. [He goes out].

THE MAYOR. Weve got nothing out of this. We dont run to Spanish in the Isle. [Resignedly] Good morning. [He goes out].

SIR ARTHUR [winningly] And do you, Miss Brollikins, feel that you have got nothing?

ALOYSIA. I feel what they feel. And I dont believe you feel anything at all. [She goes out, followed by Blee].

BLEE [turning at the door] The Mayor's wrong. Weve got something all right.

SIR ARTHUR [brightening] Indeed? What is it?

BLEE [with intense contempt] Your measure. [He goes out].

The Prime Minister, nettled by this gibe, resumes his seat angrily and pushes the bluebook out of his way. Then he notices that old Hipney has not budged from his seat at the secretary's bureau.

SIR ARTHUR. The deputation has withdrawn, Mr Hipney.

HIPNEY [rising and coming to a chair at Sir Arthur's elbow, in which he makes himself comfortable with a disarmingly pleasant air of beginning the business instead of ending it] Yes: now we can talk a bit. I been at this game now for fifty year.

SIR ARTHUR [interested in spite of himself] What game? Deputations?

HIPNEY. Unemployed deputations. This is my twelfth.

SIR ARTHUR. As many as that! But these crises dont come oftener than every ten years, do they?

HIPNEY. Not what you would call a crisis, perhaps. But unemployment is chronic.

SIR ARTHUR. It always blows over, doesnt it? Trade revives.

HIPNEY. It used to. We was the workshop of the world then. But you gentlemen went out of the workshop business to make a war. And while that was going on our customers had to find out how to make things for themselves. Now we shall have to be their customers when weve any money to buy with.

SIR ARTHUR. No doubt that has occurred to some extent; but there is still an immense fringe of the human race growing up to a sense of the necessity for British goods.

HIPNEY. All goods is alike to that lot provided theyre the cheapest. They tell me the Italians are tapping their volcanoes for cheap power. We dont seem able to tap nothing. The east is chock full of volcanoes: they think no more of an earthquake there than you would of a deputation. A Chinese coolie can live on a penny a day. What can we do against labor at a penny a day and power for next to nothing out of the burning bowels of the earth?

SIR ARTHUR. Too true, Mr Hipney. Our workers must make sacrifices.

HIPNEY. They will if you drive em to it, Srarthur. But it's you theyll sacrifice.

SIR ARTHUR. Oh come, Mr Hipney! you are a man of sense and experience. What good would it do them to sacrifice me?

HIPNEY. Not a bit in the world, sir. But that wont stop them. Look at yourself. Look at your conferences! Look at your debates! They dont do no good. But you keep on holding them. It's a sort of satisfaction to you when you feel helpless. Well, sir, if you come to helplessness there isnt on God's earth a creature more helpless than what our factories and machines have made of an English working man when nobody will give him a job and pay him to do it. And when he gets it what does he understand of it? Just nothing. Where did the material that he does his little bit of a job on come from? He dont know. What will happen to it when it goes out of the factory after he and his like have all done their little bits of jobs on it? He dont

know. Where could he buy it if it stopped coming to him? He dont know. Where could he sell it if it was left on his hands? He dont know. He dont know nothing of the business that his life depends on. Turn a cat loose and itll feed itself. Turn an English working man loose and he'll starve. You have to buy him off with a scrap of dole to prevent his saying "Well, if I'm to die I may as well have the satisfaction of seeing you die first."

SIR ARTHUR. But—I really must press the point—what good will that do him?

HIPNEY. What good does backing horses do him? What good does drinking do him? What good does going to political meetings do him? What good does going to church do him? Not a scrap. But he keeps on doing them all the same.

SIR ARTHUR. But surely you recognize, Mr Hipney, that all this is thoroughly wrong—wrong in feeling—contrary to English instincts—out of character, if I may put it that way.

HIPNEY. Well, Srarthur, whatever's wrong you and your like have taken on yourselves the job of setting it right. I havnt: I'm only a poor man: a nobody, as you might say.

SIR ARTHUR. I have not taken anything on myself, Mr Hipney. I have chosen a parliamentary career, and found it, let me tell you, a very arduous and trying one: I might almost say a heartbreaking one. I have just had to promise my wife to see a doctor for brain fag. But that does not mean that I have taken it on myself to bring about the millennium.

HIPNEY [soothingly] Just so, Srarthur: just so. It tries you and worries you, and breaks your heart and does no good; but you keep on doing it. Theyve often wanted me to go into Parliament. And I could win the seat. Put up old Hipney for the Isle of Cats and your best man wouldnt have a chance against him. But not me: I know too much. It would be the end of me, as it's been the end of all the Labor men that have done it. The Cabinet is full of Labor men that started as red-hot Socialists; and what change has it made except that theyre in and out at Bucknam Palace like peers of the realm?

SIR ARTHUR. You ought to be in Parliament, Mr Hipney. You have the making of a first-rate debater in you.

HIPNEY. Psha! An old street corner speaker like me can debate the heads off you parliamentary gentlemen. You stick your thumbs in your waistcoat holes and wait half an hour between every sentence to think of what to say next; and you call that debating. If I did that in the Isle not a man would stop to listen to me. Mind you, I know you mean it as a compliment that I'd make a good parliamentary debater. I appreciate it. But people dont look to Parliament for talk nowadays: that game is up. Not like it was in old Gladstone's time, eh?

SIR ARTHUR. Parliament, Mr Hipney, is what the people of England have made it. For good or evil we have committed ourselves to democracy. I am here because the people have sent me here.

HIPNEY. Just so. Thats all the use they could make of the vote when they got it. Their hopes was in you; and your hopes is in Spanish onions. What a world it is, aint it, Srarthur?

SIR ARTHUR. We must educate our voters, Mr Hipney. Education will teach them to understand.

HIPNEY. Dont deceive yourself, Srarthur: you cant teach people anything they dont want to know. Old Dr Marx—Karl Marx they call him now—my father knew him well —thought that when he'd explained the Capitalist System to the working classes of Europe theyd unite and overthrow it. Fifty years after he founded his Red International the working classes of Europe rose up and shot oneanother down and blew oneanother to bits, and turned millions and millions of their infant children out to starve in the snow or steal and beg in the sunshine, as if Dr Marx had never been born. And theyd do it again tomorrow if they was set on to do it. Why did you set them on? All they wanted was to be given their job, and fed and made comfortable according to their notion of comfort. If youd done that for them you wouldnt be having all this trouble. But you werent equal to it; and now the fat's in the fire.

SIR ARTHUR. But the Government is not responsible for that. The Government cannot compel traders to buy goods that they cannot sell. The Government cannot compel manufacturers to produce goods that the traders will not buy. Without demand there can be no supply.

HIPNEY. Theres a powerful demand just now, if demand is what you are looking for.

SIR ARTHUR. Can you point out exactly where, Mr Hipney?

HIPNEY. In our children's bellies, Srarthur. And in our own.

SIR ARTHUR. That is not an effective demand, Mr Hipney. I wish I had time to explain to you the inexorable laws of political economy. I—

HIPNEY [interrupting him confidentially] No use, Srarthur. That game is up. That stuff you learnt at college, that gave you such confidence in yourself, wont go down with my lot.

SIR ARTHUR [smiling] What is the use of saying that economic science and natural laws wont go down, Mr Hipney? You might as well say that the cold of winter wont go down.

HIPNEY. You see, you havnt read Karl Marx, have you?

SIR ARTHUR. Mr Hipney, when the Astronomer Royal tells me that it is twelve o'clock by Greenwich time I do not ask him whether he has read the nonsense of the latest flat earth man. I have something better to do with my time than to read the ravings of a half-educated German Communist. I am sorry you have wasted your own time reading such stuff.

HIPNEY. Me read Marx! Bless you, Srarthur, I am like you: I talk about the old doctor without ever having read a word of him. But I know what that man did for them as did read him.

SIR ARTHUR. Turned their heads, eh?

HIPNEY. Just that, Srarthur. Turned their heads. Turned them right round the other way to yours. I dont know whether what Marx said was right or wrong, because I dont know what he said. But I know that he puts into every man and woman that does read him a conceit that they know all about political economy and can look down on the stuff you were taught at college as ignorant old-fashioned trash. Look at that girl Aloysia Brollikins! Her father was a basket maker in Spitalfields. She's full of Marx. And as to examinations and scholarships and certificates and gold medals and the like, she's won enough of them to last your whole family for two generations. She can win them in her sleep. Look at Blee! His father was a cooper. But he managed to go through Ruskin College. You start him paying out Marx, and proving by the materialist theory of history that Capitalism is bound to develop into Communism, and that whoever doesnt know it is an ignorant nobody or a half-educated college fool; and youll realize that your college conceit is up against a Marxist conceit that beats anything you ever felt for cocksureness and despising the people that havnt got it. Look across Europe if you dont believe me. It was that conceit, sir, that nerved them Russians to go through with their Communism in 1917.

SIR ARTHUR. I must read Marx, Mr Hipney. I knew I had to deal with a sentimental revolt against unemployment. I had no idea that it had academic pretensions.

HIPNEY. Lord bless you, Srarthur, the Labor movement is rotten with book learning; and your people dont seem ever to read anything. When did an undersecretary ever sit up half the night after a hard day's work to read Karl Marx or anyone else? No fear. Your hearts are not in your education; but our young people lift themselves out of the gutter with it. Thats how you can shoot and you can ride and you can play golf; and some of you can talk the hind leg off a donkey; but when it comes to book learning Aloysia and Blee can wipe the floor with you.

SIR ARTHUR. I find it hard to believe that the Mayor ever burnt the midnight oil reading Marx.

HIPNEY. No more he didnt. But he has to pretend to, same as your people have to pretend to understand the gold standard.

SIR ARTHUR [laughing frankly] You have us there, Mr Hipney. I can make neither head nor tail of it; and I dont pretend to.

HIPNEY. Did you know the Mayor well, Srarthur? You called him your old friend Tom.

SIR ARTHUR. He took the chair for me once at an election meeting. He has an artificial tooth that looks as if it were made of zinc. I remembered him by that. [Genially—rising]. What humbugs we Prime Ministers have to be, Mr Hipney! You know: dont you? [He offers his hand to signify that the conversation is over].

MR HIPNEY [rising and taking it rather pityingly] Bless your innocence, Srarthur, you dont know what humbug is yet. Wait til youre a Labor leader. [He winks at his host and makes for the door].

SIR ARTHUR. Ha ha! Ha ha ha! Goodbye, Mr Hipney: goodbye. Very good of you to

have given me so much of your time.

HIPNEY. Youre welcome to it, Srarthur. Goodbye. [He goes out].

Sir Arthur presses a button to summon Hilda. Then he looks at his watch, and whistles, startled to find how late it is. Hilda comes in quickly through the masked door.

SIR ARTHUR. Do you know how late it is? To work! Work! work! work! Come along.

HILDA. I am afraid you cant do any work before you start for the Church House lunch. The whole morning is gone with those people from the Isle of Cats.

SIR ARTHUR. But I have mountains of work to get through. With one thing and another I havnt been able to do a thing for the last three weeks; and it accumulates and accumulates. It will crush me if I dont clear it off before it becomes impossible.

HILDA. But I keep telling you, Sir Arthur, that if you will talk to everybody for half an hour instead of letting me get rid of them for you in two minutes, what can you expect? You say you havnt attended to anything for three weeks; but really you havnt attended to anything since the session began. I hate to say anything; but really, when those Isle of Cats people took themselves off your hands almost providentially, to let that ridiculous old man talk to you for an hour—! [She sits down angrily].

SIR ARTHUR. Nonsense! he didnt stay two minutes; and I got a lot out of him. What about the letters this morning?

HILDA. I have dealt with them: you neednt bother. There are two or three important ones that you ought to answer: I have put them aside for you when you have time.

Flavia and David dash into the room through the masked door even more excited and obstreperous than before, Flavia to her father's right, David to his left.

FLAVIA. Papa: weve been to a meeting of the unemployed with Aloysia and Toffy.

DAVID. Such a lark!

FLAVIA. We saw a police charge. David was arrested.

SIR ARTHUR. Do you mean to say that you went with those people who were here?

FLAVIA. Yes: theyve come back to lunch with us.

SIR ARTHUR. To lunch!!!

DAVID. Yes. I say: Aloysia's a marvellous girl.

SIR ARTHUR [determinedly] I dont mind the

girl; but if that young whelp is coming to lunch here he must and shall change his clothes.

DAVID. He's gone home to change and shave: he's dotty on Flavia.

SIR ARTHUR. Why am I afflicted with such children? Tell me at once what you have been doing. What happened?

DAVID. The police brought the Chancellor of the Exchequer to make a speech to the unemployed to quiet them. The first thing we heard him say was "Gentlemen: be patient. I promise you you will soon see the one thing that can revive our industries and save our beloved country: a rise in prices." The mob just gave one howl and went for him. Then the police drew their batons and charged.

FLAVIA. Davy couldnt stand the way the people were knocked about. He screamed to them to stand. The inspector collared him.

SIR ARTHUR. Of course he did. Quite right. Such folly! [*To David*] How do you come to be here if you were arrested? Who bailed you?

DAVID. I asked the inspector who in hell he thought he was talking to. Then Flavia cut in and told him who we were and that old Basham was like a father to us. All he said was "You go home, sir; and take your sister with you. This is no place for you." So as I was rather in a funk by that time we collected Aloysia and Toffy and bunked for home.

SIR ARTHUR. I have a great mind to have that inspector severely reprimanded for letting you go. Three months would have done you a lot of good. Go back to the drawing room, both of you, and entertain your new friends. You know you are not allowed to come in here when I am at work. Be off with you. [*He goes back to his seat*].

FLAVIA. Well, what are we to do? Mamma sends us in on purpose to interrupt you when she thinks you have done enough.

DAVID. She says it's all we're good for.

SIR ARTHUR. A Prime Minister should have no children. Will you get out, both of you; or must I ring for Burton to throw you out?

FLAVIA. Mamma says you are to lunch, Hilda. She wants another woman to make up the party.

HILDA. Oh dear! [*rising*] You must excuse me, Sir Arthur: I must telephone to put off some people who were coming to lunch with me at The Apple Cart. And I must change my frock.

FLAVIA [*squabbling*] You neednt dress up for Brollikins, need you?

DAVID. You let Aloysia alone. You dont want Hilda to dress up for Barking, I suppose.

SIR ARTHUR [*out of patience*] Get out. Do you hear? Get out, the lot of you.

HILDA. Do come, Miss Chavender. Your father is very busy.

SIR ARTHUR [*furious*] Get OUT.

They retreat precipitately through the masked door. Sir Arthur, left alone, rests his wearied head on the table between his arms.

SIR ARTHUR. At last, a moment's peace.

The word rouses the orator in him. He raises his head and repeats it interrogatively; then tries its effect sweetly and solemnly again and again.

SIR ARTHUR. Peace? . . . Peace. Peace. Peace. Peace. Peace. [*Now perfectly in tune*] "Yes, your Grace, my lords and gentlemen, my clerical friends. We need peace. We English are still what we were when time-honored Lancaster described us as 'This happy breed of men.' We are above all a domestic nation. On occasion we can be as terrible in war as we have always been wise and moderate in counsel. But here, in this Church House, under the banner of the Prince of Peace, we know that the heart of England is the English home. Not the battle-field but the fireside—yes, your Grace, yes, my lords and gentlemen, yes, my clerical friends, the fire—"

He starts violently as his eye, sweeping round the imaginary assembly, lights on a woman in grey robes contemplating him gravely and pity-ingly. She has stolen in noiselessly through the masked door.

SIR ARTHUR. Ffffff!!! Who is that? Who are you? Oh, I beg your pardon. You gave me such a—Whew!! [*He sinks back into his chair*] I didnt know there was anyone in the room.

The lady neither moves nor speaks. She looks at him with deepening pity. He looks at her, still badly scared. He rubs his eyes; shakes himself; looks again.

SIR ARTHUR. Excuse me; but are you real?

THE LADY. Yes.

SIR ARTHUR. I wish youd do something real. Wont you sit down?

THE LADY. Thank you. [*She sits down, very uncannily as it seems to him, in Basham's chair*].

SIR ARTHUR. Will you be so good as to introduce yourself? Who are you?

THE LADY. A messenger.

SIR ARTHUR. Please do not be enigmatic. My nerves are all in rags. I did not see you come in. You appeared there suddenly looking like a messenger of death. And now you tell me you are a messenger.

THE LADY. Yes: a messenger of death.

SIR ARTHUR. I thought so. [*With sudden misgiving*] You mean my death, I hope. Not my wife nor any of the children?

THE LADY [*smiling kindly*] No. Your death.

SIR ARTHUR [*relieved*] Well, thats all right.

THE LADY. You are going to die.

SIR ARTHUR. So are we all. The only question is, how soon?

THE LADY. Too soon. You are half dead already. You have been dying a long time.

SIR ARTHUR. Well, I knew I was overworking: burning the candle at both ends: killing myself. It doesnt matter. I have made my will. Everything is provided for: my wife will be comfortably off; and the children will have as much as is good for them.

THE LADY. You are resigned?

SIR ARTHUR. No; but I cannot help myself.

THE LADY. Perhaps I can help you. I am not only a messenger. I am a healer.

SIR ARTHUR. A what?

THE LADY. A healer. One who heals the sick. One who holds off death until he is welcome in his proper time.

SIR ARTHUR. You cannot help me. I am caught in the wheels of a merciless political machine. The political machine will not stop for you. It has ground many men to pieces before their time; and it will grind me.

THE LADY. My business is with life and death, not with political machinery.

SIR ARTHUR. In that case I am afraid you can be of no use to me; so will you think it very uncivil of me if I go on with my work?

THE LADY. Shall I vanish?

SIR ARTHUR. Not unless you have something else to do. As you are a ghost, and therefore not in time but in eternity, another ten minutes or so wont cost you anything. Somehow, your presence is helping me. A presence is a wonderful thing. Would you mind sitting there and reading The Times while I work?

THE LADY. I never read the newspapers. I read men and women. I will sit here and read you. Or will that make you self-conscious?

SIR ARTHUR. My dear ghost, a public man is so accustomed to people staring at him that he very soon has no self to be conscious of. You wont upset me in the least. You may even throw in a round of applause occasionally; so that I may find out the effective bits to work up.

THE LADY. Go on. I will wait as long as you like.

SIR ARTHUR. Thank you. Now let me see where I was when you appeared. [*He takes up a scrap of paper on which he has made a memorandum*]. Ah yes: Ive got it. Peace. Yes: peace. [*Trying to make out a word*] Ence— ence—what? Oh, ensue! Of course: a good word. "My friends, lay and clerical, we must ensue peace. Yes, ensue peace. Peace. Disarmament." A burst of Pacifist applause there, perhaps. "Who says that we need a hundred battleships, gentlemen? Christian brotherhood is a safer defence than a thousand battleships. You have my pledge that the Government will be quite content with —with—" oh, well, my secretary will fill that in with whatever number of ships the Japanese are standing out for. By the way, do you think battleships are any real use now? Kenworthy says theyre not: and he was in the navy. It would be such a tremendous score for us at Geneva if we offered to scrap all our battleships. We could make up for them in aeroplanes and submarines. I should like to have the opinion of an impartial and disinterested ghost.

THE LADY. As I listen to you I seem to hear a ghost preparing a speech for his fellow ghosts, ghosts from a long dead past. To me it means nothing, because I am a ghost from the future.

SIR ARTHUR. Thats a curious idea. Of course if there are ghosts from the past there must be ghosts from the future.

THE LADY. Yes: women and men who are ahead of their time. They alone can lead the present into the future. They are ghosts from the future. The ghosts from the past are those who are behind the times, and can only drag the present back.

SIR ARTHUR. What an excellent definition of a Conservative! Thank Heaven I am a Liberal!

THE LADY. You mean that you make speeches about Progress and Liberty instead of about King and Country.

SIR ARTHUR. Of course I make speeches: that is the business of a politician. Dont you like speeches?

THE LADY. On the Great Day of Judgment the speechmakers will stand with the seducers and the ravishers, with the traffickers in maddening drugs, with those who make men drunk and rob them, who entice children and violate them.

SIR ARTHUR. What nonsense! Our sermons and speeches are the glories of our literature, and the inspired voices of our religion, our patriotism, and—of course—our politics.

THE LADY. Sermons and speeches are not religion, not patriotism, not politics: they are only the gibbering of ghosts from the past. You are a ghost from a very dead past. Why do you not die your bodily death? Is it fair for a ghost to go about with a live body?

SIR ARTHUR. This is too personal. I am afraid I cannot get on with my speech while you are there ordering my funeral. Oblige me by vanishing. Go. Disappear. Shoo!

THE LADY. I cannot vanish. [*Merrily changing her attitude*]. Shall we stop playing at ghosts, and accept one another for convenience sake as real people?

SIR ARTHUR [*shaking off his dreaminess*] Yes, lets. [*He rises and comes to her*]. We have been talking nonsense. [*He pulls out a chair. They sit close together*]. You had me half hypnotized. But first, shake hands. I want to feel that you are real.

He offers his right hand. She seizes both his hands and holds them vigorously, looking straight into his eyes.

SIR ARTHUR [*brightening*] Well, I dont know whether this is real or not; but it's electric, and very soothing and jolly. Ah-a-a-ah! [*a deep sighing breath*]. And now, my dear lady, will you be good enough to tell me who the devil you are?

THE LADY [*releasing him*] Only your wife's lady doctor. Did she not tell you to expect me?

SIR ARTHUR. Of course, of course. How stupid of me! Yes,yes,yes,yes,yes, to be sure. And now I am going to be frank with you. I dont believe in doctors. Neither does my wife; but her faith in quacks is unlimited. And as I am on the verge of a nervous breakdown, she is planting every possible variety of quack on me—you will excuse the expression?—

THE LADY. I excuse everything from my patients. Go on.

SIR ARTHUR. Well, I receive them all as I am receiving you, just to gratify her, or rather to prevent her from making my life miserable. They all say the same obvious thing: and they are none of them of the slightest use. You are going to say it all over again. Can you forgive me for saying flatly that I will not pay you twenty guineas for saying it: not if you said it twenty times over?

THE LADY. Not even if I shew you how to cure yourself? The twenty guineas is an important part of the cure. It will make you take it seriously.

SIR ARTHUR. I know perfectly well how to cure myself. The cure is as simple as a b c. I am Prime Minister of Great Britain. That is, I am an overworked, overworried, overstrained, overburdened, overdriven man, suffering from late hours, irregular snatched meals, no time for digestion nor for enough sleep, and having to keep my mind at full stretch all the time struggling with problems that are no longer national problems but world problems. In short, I am suffering acutely from brain fag.

THE LADY. And the cure?

SIR ARTHUR. A fortnight's golf: thats the cure. I know it all by heart. So suppose we drop it, and part friends. You see, I am really frightfully busy.

THE LADY. That is not my diagnosis. [*She rises*]. Goodbye.

SIR ARTHUR [*alarmed*] Diagnosis! Have you been diagnosing me? Do you mean that there is something else the matter with me?

THE LADY. Not something else. Something different.

SIR ARTHUR. Sit down, pray: I can spare another two minutes. Whats wrong?

THE LADY [*resuming her seat*] You are dying of an acute want of mental exercise.

SIR ARTHUR [*unable to believe his ears*] Of—of—of WHAT, did you say?

THE LADY. You are suffering from that very common English complaint, an underworked brain. To put it in one word, a bad case of frivolity, possibly incurable.

SIR ARTHUR. Frivolity! Did I understand you to say that frivolity is a common English failing?

THE LADY. Yes. Terribly common. Almost a national characteristic.

SIR ARTHUR. Do you realize that you are utterly mad?

THE LADY. Is it you or I who have piloted

England on to the rocks?

SIR ARTHUR. Come come! No politics. What do you prescribe for me?

THE LADY. I take my patients into my retreat in the Welsh mountains, formerly a monastery, now much stricter and perfectly sanitary. No newspapers, no letters, no idle ladies. No books except in the afternoon as a rest from thinking.

SIR ARTHUR. How can you think without books?

THE LADY. How can you have thoughts of your own when you are reading other people's thoughts?

SIR ARTHUR [groaning] Oh, do talk sense. What about golf?

THE LADY. Games are for people who can neither read nor think. Men trifle with their business and their politics; but they never trifle with their games. Golf gives them at least a week-end of earnest concentration. It brings truth home to them. They cannot pretend that they have won when they have lost, nor that they made a magnificent drive when they foozled it. The Englishman is at his best on the links, and at his worst in the Cabinet. But what your country needs is not your body but your mind. And I solemnly warn you that unless you exercise your mind you will lose it. A brain underexercised is far more injurious to health than an underexercised body. You know how men become bone lazy for want of bodily exercise. Well, they become brain lazy for want of mental exercise; and if nature meant them to be thinkers the results are disastrous. All sorts of bodily diseases are produced by half used minds; for it is the mind that makes the body: that is my secret, and the secret of all the true healers. I am sorry you will not allow me to take you a little on the way back to health with me. Good morning. [She rises].

SIR ARTHUR. Must you go?

THE LADY. Well, you are so busy—

SIR ARTHUR [rising] Ah yes: I forgot. I am frightfully busy. Still, if you could spare another minute—

THE LADY. If you wish. [She sits down].

SIR ARTHUR [sitting down] You see, what makes your diagnosis so pricelessly funny to me is that as a matter of fact my life has been a completely intellectual life, and my training the finest intellectual training in the world. First rate preparatory school. Harrow. Oxford. Parliament. An Undersecretaryship.

The Cabinet. Finally the Leadership of the House as Prime Minister. Intellect, intellect, all the time.

THE LADY. At Harrow you wrote Latin verses, did you not?

SIR ARTHUR. Yes, of course.

THE LADY. Do you write any now?

SIR ARTHUR. No, of course not. You dont understand. We learnt to write Latin verses not because the verses are any good—after all, it's only a trick of stringing old tags together—but because it's such a splendid training for the mind.

THE LADY. Have all the boys who made Latin verses at Harrow splendidly trained minds?

SIR ARTHUR. Yes. I unhesitatingly say yes. I dont mean, of course, that they are all geniuses; but if you go into the best society you will see that their minds are far superior to those of persons who have had no classical training.

THE LADY. You mean that they can all be trusted to say the same thing in the same way when they discuss public affairs.

SIR ARTHUR. Precisely. They are an educated class, you see.

THE LADY [coldly, rising] Yes: I see. I have really nothing more to say, Sir Arthur. [She takes a card from her bag and puts it on the table] That is the address of my retreat in Wales.

SIR ARTHUR [rising, rather disappointed at having produced no effect] But surely you cannot deny that a man is the better for having been put through the mill of our great educational system.

THE LADY. If a man is born with a hopelessly bad set of teeth I think it is better for him, and kinder to him, to pull them all out and replace them with a good set of artificial teeth. If some of your political colleagues had not been provided with artificial political minds in the manner you describe they would have been left without any political minds at all. But in that case they would not have meddled in politics; and that, I think, would have been a public advantage. May I reserve a bedroom and a private study for you?

SIR ARTHUR. Pooh! I am not going to your retreat.

THE LADY [steadfastly] I think you are.

SIR ARTHUR. I give you up. You are fact-proof. I am lazy; I am idle; and I am breaking down from overwork. How logical!

THE LADY. All the idlest and laziest of my patients slave from morning to midnight trifling and tittle-tattling about great things. To a retreat, Sir Arthur: get thee to a retreat. I am never mistaken in my diagnosis. I shall telephone to ask whether my number one suite, with private bath and meditation parlor, is vacant.

SIR ARTHUR. No: I wont be rushed. Do you hear? I wont be rushed. [*She is quite unshaken; and he proceeds, much less resolutely*] Of course I shall have to go somewhere for a rest; and if you could really recommend it as a bracing place—

THE LADY. Bracing? What for?

SIR ARTHUR. Well, bracing, you know. Bracing.

THE LADY. Curious, how idle people are always clamoring to be braced! Like trousers.

SIR ARTHUR. Idle people! How you stick to your point! And what a humbug you are! Dont think you can impose on me with your meditation parlor and your dignified airs: I do that sort of thing myself occasionally; and you know it's no use giving tracts to a missionary. But I feel somehow that you are good for me. You are a dear delightful big-hearted wrongheaded half-educated crazy-boots; but a woman may be all that and yet have the right instinct as to how to flirt intellectually with a tired thinker. Will you promise to talk to me if I come?

THE LADY. I will even let you talk to me. I guarantee that in a fortnight you will begin to think before you talk. Your dead mind will come to life. I shall make a man of you. Goodbye. [*She goes out quickly through the main door*].

SIR ARTHUR [*calling after her gaily*] Ha ha! Incorrigible, incorrigible. [*He takes her card from the table, and contemplates it*]. Oh! I forgot to ask her how much a week she wants for that meditation parlor. [*He looks tragic*].

HILDA [*emerging from her office*] Anything the matter, Sir Arthur?

SIR ARTHUR. I am going into a retreat. Because my brain is underworked. Do you grasp that idea? Have you ever heard of a retreat for the mentally underworked?

HILDA. There is a very nice one at Sevenoaks that my aunt was sent to. But that is for inebriates.

SIR ARTHUR. The one I'm going to is for the mentally underworked, the thoughtless and brainless, the inveterately lazy and frivolous. Yes: the frivolous: your ears do not deceive you.

HILDA [*going to her desk*] Oh, well, theyll amuse you: you always get on well with people of that sort. Shall I pack your usual holiday books? some detective stories and Wordsworth?

SIR ARTHUR. No. You will procure all the books you can find by a revolutionary German Jew named Harry Marks—

HILDA. Dont you mean Karl Marx?

SIR ARTHUR. Thats the man. Karl Marx. Get me every blessed book by Karl Marx that you can find translated into English; and have them packed for the retreat.

HILDA. There are much newer books by Marxists: Lenin and Trotsky and Stalin and people like that.

SIR ARTHUR. Get them all. Pack the lot. By George, I'll teach Alderwoman Aloysia Brollikins to give herself airs. I'll teach her and her rabble of half-baked half-educated intellectual beggars-on-horseback that any Oxford man can beat them at their own silly game. I'll just turn Karl Marx inside-out for them. [*The household gong sounds*]. Lunch! Come on: that woman's given me an appetite. [*He goes out impetuously through the masked door*].

HILDA [*rushing after him*] No, no, Sir Arthur: the Church House! the Church House! youve forgotten that you have to lunch at [*her voice is lost in the distance*].

ACT II

The same scene on the 10th November at 9.30 in the morning. There is a generous fire in the grate; and the visitors wear winter clothes. Basham is on the hearthrug, warming his back and reading The Daily Herald.

BASHAM [*amazed by what he reads*] Gosh! [*He reads further*] Wh-e-e-ew!! [*He reads still further*] Well I'll be dashed!!!

Hilda enters through the main door, and announces an explosive elderly gentleman, evidently a person of consequence, who follows her.

HILDA. Sir Dexter Rightside.

SIR DEXTER [*joining Basham on the hearth*] Ah! That you, Basham? Have you come to arrest him?

BASHAM. You may well ask. He isnt up yet. Miss Hanways: is there any sign of his getting a move on?

HILDA [*much worried*] Lady Chavender wont allow him to be disturbed. She says his speech last night at the Guildhall banquet quite tired him out. People have been ringing up and calling all the morning; but she just puts her back to his door and says that anyone who makes noise enough to waken him leaves her service that minute.

SIR DEXTER. Nonsense! He must see me. Does Lady Chavender suppose that a Prime Minister can stand the country on its head without a word of warning to his colleagues and then go to bed as if he was tired out by a day's fishing?

HILDA [*desperate*] Well, what can *I* do, Sir Dexter? [*She goes to her bureau*].

SIR DEXTER. Basham: go and break open his bedroom door.

BASHAM. I cant. I'm a policeman: I mustnt do it without a warrant. Go and do it yourself.

SIR DEXTER. I have a devilish good mind to. Can you conceive anything more monstrous, Basham? [*He sits down in the chair next the end chair*]. But I said that this would happen. I said so. When we made this damned coalition that they call a National Government I was entitled to the Prime Ministership. I was the Leader of the Conservative Party. I had an enormous majority in the country: the election proved that we could have done quite well without Chavender. But I had to give way. He humbugged us. He pretended that without his old guard of Liberals and his ragtag and bobtail of Labor men and Socialists and lawyers and journalists-on-the-make and used-up trade union secretaries, and all the rest of the democratic dregs of human society, we couldnt be sure of a majority. His golden voice was to do the trick. He was the popular man, the safe man: I was the unpopular Die Hard who couldnt be trusted to keep my temper. So I stood down. I sacrificed myself. I took the Foreign Secretaryship. Well, what price your safe man now? How do you like your Bolshy Premier? Who was right? the funkers and compromisers or the old Die Hard?

BASHAM. It's amazing. I could have sworn that if there was a safe man in England that could be trusted to talk and say nothing, to thump the table and do nothing, Arthur Chavender was that man. Whats happened to him? What does it mean? Did he go mad at the sanatorium, do you think? Or was he mad before that woman took him there?

SIR DEXTER. Mad! Not a bit of it. But you had better look up that woman's record: there may be money from Moscow behind this.

BASHAM. Arthur take money! Thats going too far.

SIR DEXTER. The woman took the money. It would be waste of money to bribe Chavender: you could always trust him to say whatever he thought would please his audience without being paid for it: damned mountebank.

BASHAM. But he didnt try to please his audience at the Guildhall. They wanted some of his best soothing syrup about law and order after the attack on the Lord Mayor's Show in the afternoon by the unemployed; but according to The Daily Herald here he gave them a dose of boiling Socialism instead.

SIR DEXTER [*nervously*] By the way, Basham, I hope you have the unemployed well in hand today.

BASHAM. Quiet as lambs. Theyre all reading the papers. New editions every half-hour. Like 1914 over again.

Sir Arthur's voice is heard, singing scales. Hilda looks in.

HILDA. I think I hear Sir Arthur singing. He must have got up.

SIR DEXTER. Singing! Is this a moment for minstrelsy?

HILDA. He always sings scales after his bath [*she vanishes*].

After a final burst of solfeggi the masked door is opened vigorously and Chavender enters beaming.

SIR ARTHUR. Ah, here you are, Dexy [*he proffers his hand*].

SIR DEXTER [*like a baited bull*] Dont attempt to shake hands with me. Dont dare call me Dexy.

SIR ARTHUR. What on earth's the matter? Got out at the wrong side of the bed this morning, eh? Frightfully sorry to have kept you waiting, Basham. Whats wrong with the Foreign Secretary this time?

SIR DEXTER. This time! What do you mean by this time?

SIR ARTHUR. Well theres nothing very novel about your turning up before breakfast in a blazing rage, is there? What is it, Basham?

BASHAM. Oh come, P.M.! If you were too drunk last night at the Guildhall to know what you were saying, youd better read the papers [*he offers his paper*].

SIR ARTHUR [*keeping his hands behind his back to warm them*] I remember perfectly well what I said last night. And I drank nothing but barley water.

BASHAM [*insisting*] But look at it, man. [*Quoting the headlines*] New program for winter session. Nationalization of ground rents. Nationalization of banks. Nationalization of collieries. Nationalization of transport.

SIR DEXTER [*moaning*] Nationalization of women. Why omit it? Why omit it?

BASHAM. No: nothing about women. Municipalization of urban land and the building trade, and consequent extinction of rates.

SIR DEXTER. Apostate!

BASHAM. No: nothing about the Church. Abolition of tariffs and substitution of total prohibition of private foreign trade in protected industries. State imports only, to be sold at State regulated prices.

SIR DEXTER. Rot! Incomprehensible and unheard-of rot.

BASHAM. Compulsory public service for all, irrespective of income, as in war time.

SIR DEXTER. Slavery. Call it by its proper name. Slavery.

BASHAM. Restoration of agriculture. Collective farming. Nationalization of fertilizer industries. Nitrogen from the air. Power from the tides. Britain self-supporting and blockade proof.

SIR DEXTER. Madness. Ruin to our foreign trade.

BASHAM. Ruthless extinction of parasitism.

SIR DEXTER. You dont even know the present law. You have the Verminous Persons Act. What more do you want?

BASHAM. Doubling of the surtax on unearned incomes.

SIR DEXTER. Yes: take our last penny! And when the little that the present ruinous taxation has left us is gone; when we have closed our accounts with the last tradesman and turned the last servant into the streets, where are they to find employment? Who is to pay their wages? What is to become of religion when nobody can afford pewrents or a penny to put in the plate? Even sport will not be safe: our breed of horses will be doomed; our packs of hounds sold or slaughtered; and our masters of hounds will be caddies on motor bicycles. That is to be England's future!

SIR ARTHUR. But is that all the papers have reported?

SIR DEXTER. All!!!

BASHAM. Oh come! All! Isnt that about enough?

SIR ARTHUR. But have they said nothing about our promise to restore the cuts made in the pay of the army and navy and police?

SIR DEXTER. Our promise! Whose promise?

BASHAM [*interested*] What was that you said? Are you going to put my men's wages up to the old figure?

SIR ARTHUR. We shall give you another five thousand men; pay the old wages with a rise of ten per cent; and double your salary.

BASHAM. Whew! That alters the case a bit.

SIR DEXTER [*rising*] Basham: you are not going to allow yourself to be corrupted like this! Are you such a dupe as to imagine that free Englishmen will tolerate such a monstrous waste of public money?

BASHAM. If I have another five thousand men and a rise on the old wages, I'll answer for the free Englishmen. If they dont like it they can lump it.

SIR DEXTER. You really believe he can keep all the monstrous promises he has made?

BASHAM. No: of course he cant. But he can keep this one. He can raise the pay of the ranks and double my salary; and that is all that concerns me. I'm a policeman, not a politician.

SIR DEXTER. Youre a mercenary gangster and a damned fool: thats what you are. [*He flings himself into the end chair*].

BASHAM [*calmly*] You seem ruffled, Sir Dexter.

Before Sir Dexter can reply, Hilda returns and announces a new visitor.

HILDA. Admiral Sir Bemrose Hotspot. [*She goes out*].

Sir Bemrose is a halfwitted admiral; but the half that has not been sacrificed to his profession is sound and vigorous.

SIR BEMROSE [*in the breeziest spirits*] Morning, Dexy. Morning, Basham. [*Slapping Sir Arthur on the back*] Splendid, Arthur! Never heard you in better form. Thats the stuff to give em. [*They shake hands cordially*].

SIR DEXTER [*sobered by his astonishment*] Rosy: have you gone mad too? Have you forgotten that you are a Conservative, and that it was as a Conservative that you were made First Lord of the Admiralty, at my personal suggestion and insistence, in this so-called National Government, which now, thank

Heaven, wont last one day after the next meeting of Parliament?

SIR BEMROSE. Wont it, by Jove! It's safe for the next five years. What the country wants is straight orders, discipline, character, pluck, a big navy, justice for the British sailor, no sham disarmaments, and absolute command of the sea. If that isnt Conservatism what is Conservatism? But mind, Arthur, I must have twelve new aeroplane-carrying battleships. I have my eye on Japan. And theres America. And, of course, Russia.

SIR ARTHUR. You shall have them, Rosy. Twentyfour if you say the word.

SIR BEMROSE. Good! Then I'll answer for the House of Commons.

SIR DEXTER. Dont be silly. What can you do with the House of Commons, except empty it whenever you get up to speak?

SIR BEMROSE. I leave the speaking to Arthur: it's his job, not mine. But if there is any further attempt to starve the navy it can give you a little surprise at Westminster. How will you feel when you see a submarine come to the surface off the terrace, and the commander sends in word that he gives you just five minutes before he torpedoes the whole damned Front Bench?

SIR DEXTER. You are talking ridiculous nonsense. Do you suppose for a moment that the navy would be allowed to interfere in politics?

SIR BEMROSE. Who's to stop it? Where would Lenin and Stalin and Trotsky and all that Bolshy lot have been without the Baltic fleet and the Kronstadt sailors? Do you suppose the British navy, with its discipline and its respectable Conservative commanders, couldnt do what these Communist scoundrels did?

SIR DEXTER. How long would the British navy survive the abolition of property in this country? tell me that.

SIR BEMROSE. Dont talk to the navy about property. We dont live by property: we live by service. [*He takes the chair next to the presidential one, and pursues his personal grievance angrily*]. You and your confounded property owners grudge us a clerk's salary for commanding a battleship, and then dock a quarter off it for income tax. We cant set foot on shore without being rented and rated until we can hardly afford to educate our children. Thanks to Arthur, you are pledged now to give us our pay honestly free of income tax and make these lazy idle lubbers

of landlords sweat for it. I call that the essence of Conservatism. Thats the way to dish these Labor chaps and Red flaggers and all the rest of the scum you have been pandering to ever since you gave them the vote. Give them whats good for them; and put their ballot papers behind the fire: thats what this country needs.

SIR ARTHUR. You see, Dexy: we have the navy and the police on our side.

SIR DEXTER. May I ask who are "we"?

SIR ARTHUR. Why, the National Government, of course. You and I, Dexy: you and I.

SIR DEXTER. It makes me sick to hear you couple my name with yours. It always did.

HILDA [*announcing*] The President of the Board of Trade. Mr Glenmorison.

Glenmorison is an easy mannered Scottish gentleman, distinctly the youngest of the party.

SIR ARTHUR. Hallo, Sandy. Sit down. Lets all sit down and have it out.

They settle themselves at the table with their backs to the fire, Sir Arthur in the middle, Glenmorison on his left, Sir Bemrose on his right, and Sir Dexter and Basham right and left respectively.

GLENMORISON. Well, Sir Arthur, when you were letting yourself go so recklessly you might have said a word about Home Rule for Scotland. We may as well be hanged for a sheep as for a lamb.

SIR DEXTER. We! we! we! Who are we? If you mean the Cabinet, it is not responsible for the Prime Minister's frantic proceedings. He acted without consulting us. Do you suppose that if I had heard a word of this outburst of Bolshevism I should have consented to it?

SIR ARTHUR. That was why I didnt consult you.

SIR DEXTER. Psha!

SIR ARTHUR. The responsibility is mine and mine alone.

SIR BEMROSE. Not at all. I claim my share, Arthur. You got the part about the navy from me.

GLENMORISON. Same here, Sir Dexter. I claim at least two items.

SIR DEXTER. Much good may they do you. Arthur's seat is safe: anybody named Chavender can get in unopposed in his constituency because his cunning old father-in-law has every voter in the place bribed up to the neck. But your majority at the last election was seventeen: there were three recounts. Your seat's gone, anyhow.

GLENMORISON. On the contrary, Sir Dexter, it's safe for the first time in the history of Scotland.

SIR DEXTER. Safe! How? You will get the boot as a crazy Bolshevik unless you come out with me and repudiate Chavender promptly and decisively.

GLENMORISON. Oh, I'm afraid I cant do that, Sir Dexter. You see, the balance is held in my constituency by the tradesmen and shopkeepers. Their great grievance is the heavy rates. And though they are all doing middling well they think they could do better if they could raise enough capital to extend their businesses a bit. But the financiers and promoters wont look at small businesses. They are thinking in millions while my people are thinking in thousands, and mostly in only four figures at that. It's easy enough to get a couple of hundred thousand pounds if you are willing to call it a quarter of a million and pay interest on that sum. But what good is that to a man in the High Street in my constituency who wants from five to twenty thousand to extend his little business?

SIR DEXTER. Nonsense! The bank will give him an overdraft if his credit is good.

GLENMORISON. Yes; and call it in at the next slump and panic on the Stock Exchange. I can shew you half a dozen men who were forced into bankruptcy in the last panic, though they were as solvent as you or I. But Sir Arthur's proposal of panic-proof national and municipal banks, as ready and eager to find five thousand for the five thousand man as the financiers are to find a million on condition that enough of it sticks to their own fingers, is just the thing for my people. I darent say a word against it. It's an inspiration as far as my constituents are concerned. Theyre a canny lot, my people: theyd vote for the devil if he'd promise to abolish the rates and open a municipal bank. My majority fell to seventeen last time because I went to them with empty hands and a bellyful of advice to economize and make sacrifices. This bank nationalization is good business for them: theyll just jump at it.

SIR DEXTER. In short, you will make Utopian promises that you know very well will never be carried out.

GLENMORISON. You made a lot of Utopian promises, Sir Dexter. when you formed this National Government. Instead of carrying them out you told the voters to tighten their belts and save the Bank of England. They tightened their belts; and now the Bank of England is paying twelve and sixpence in the pound. Still, I admit, you pulled down my Liberal majority over my Conservative opponent from four thousand to seventeen. Ive got to pull that up again. I say nothing about the rest of the program; but I represent the small man; and on this bank business I am with Sir Arthur all the time.

HILDA [announcing] Sir Jafna Pandranath. [She withdraws].

This announcement creates a marked sensation. All five gentlemen rise as if to receive a royal personage. Sir Jafna is an elderly Cingalese plutocrat, small and slender to the verge of emaciation, elegantly dressed, but otherwise evidently too much occupied and worried by making money to get any fun out of spending it. One guesses that he must make a great deal of it; for the reverence with which he is received by the five Britons, compared with their unceremonious handling of one another, is almost sycophantic.

SIR JAFNA. Hallo! Am I breaking into a Cabinet meeting?

SIR ARTHUR. No: not a bit. Only a few friendly callers. Pray sit down.

SIR DEXTER [offering the end chair to the visitor] You are welcome, Sir Jafna: most welcome. You represent money; and money brings fools to their senses.

SIR JAFNA. Money! Not at all. I am a poor man. I never know from one moment to another whether I am worth thirteen millions or only three. [He sits down. They all sit down].

SIR BEMROSE. I happen to know, Sir Jafna, that your enterprises stand at twenty millions today at the very least.

GLENMORISON. Fifty.

SIR JAFNA. How do you know? How do you know? The way I am plundered at every turn! [To Sir Dexter] Your people take the shirt off my back.

SIR DEXTER. My people! What on earth do you mean?

SIR JAFNA. Your land monopolists. Your blackmailers. Your robber barons. Look at my Blayport Docks reconstruction scheme! Am I a public benefactor or am I not? Have I not enough to live on and die on without troubling myself about Blayport? Shall I be any the happier when it has ten square miles of docks instead of a tuppeny-hapeny fishing harbor? What have I to gain except the satisfaction of seeing a big publicly useful thing well done, and the knowledge that without me it could not be done? Shall I not be half ruined if it fails?

SIR BEMROSE. Well, whats wrong with it, old chap?

SIR JAFNA. Rosy: you make me puke. What is wrong with it is that the owners of all the miles of land that are indispensable to my scheme, and that without it would not be worth fifteen pounds an acre, are opening their mouths so wide that they will grab sixty per cent of the profit without lifting a finger except to pocket the wealth that I shall create. I live, I work, I plan, I shatter my health and risk all I possess only to enrich these parasites, these vampires, these vermin in the commonwealth. [Shrieking] Yes: vermin! [Subsiding] You were quite right at the Guildhall last night, Arthur: you must nationalize the land and put a stop to this shameless exploitation of the financiers and entrepreneurs by a useless, idle, and predatory landed class.

SIR ARTHUR [chuckling] Magnificent! I have the support of the City.

SIR JAFNA. To the last vote, to the last penny. These pirates think nothing of extorting a million an acre for land in the city. A man cannot have an address in London for his letters until he has agreed to pay them from five hundred to a thousand a year. He cant even die without paying them for a grave to lie in. Make them disgorge, Arthur. Skin them alive. Tax them twenty shillings in the pound. Make them earn their own living, damn them. [He wipes his brow and adds, rather hysterically] Excuse me, boys; but if you saw the Blayport estimates—! [he can no more].

SIR DEXTER. May I ask you to address yourself to this question not as an emotional oriental [Sir Jafna chokes convulsively] but as a sane man of business. If you destroy the incomes of our landed gentry where will you find the capital that exists solely through their prudent saving—their abstinence?

SIR JAFNA. Bah pooh! Pooh bah! I will find it where they find it, in the product of the labor I employ. At present I have to pay exorbitant and unnecessary wages. Why? Because out of those wages the laborer has to pay half or quarter as rent to the landlord. The laborer is ignorant: he thinks he is robbed by the landlord; but the robbed victim is me —ME! Get rid of the landlord and I shall have all the capital he now steals. In addition I shall have cheap labor. That is not oriental emotion: it is British commonsense. I am with you, Arthur, to the last drop of my oriental blood. Nationalized land: compulsory labor: abolition of rates: strikes made criminal: I heartily endorse them all in the name of Capital and private enterprise. I say nothing about the rest of your program, Arthur; but on these points no true Liberal can question your magnificent statesmanship.

SIR ARTHUR [delighted] You hear that, Dexy. Put that in your pipe and smoke it.

HILDA [announcing] His Grace the Duke of Domesday. [She goes out].

An elderly delicately built aristocrat comes in. Well preserved, but nearer 70 than 60.

THE DUKE [surprised to see so many people] Do I intrude, Arthur? I thought you were disengaged.

SIR ARTHUR. Not at all. Only a talk over last night. Make yourself at home.

SIR DEXTER. You come in the nick of time. Sir Jafna here has just been qualifying you as a bloodsucker, a pirate, a parasite, a robber baron and finally as vermin. Vermin! How do you like it?

THE DUKE [calmly taking the end chair nearest the window, on Basham's left] I wonder why the epithet robber is applied only to barons. You never hear of robber dukes; yet my people have done plenty of robbery in their time. [With a sigh of regret] Ah, thats all over now. The robbers have become the robbed. I wish you would create some intermediate class of honest folk. I dislike your calling me vermin, Arthur.

SIR ARTHUR. I didnt. It was Jafna.

THE DUKE. Ungrateful Jafna! He is buying up my Blayport estate for next to nothing.

SIR JAFNA. Next to nothing! Holy Brahma!

THE DUKE [continuing] He will make millions out of it. After paying off the mortgages I shall get three and a half per cent on what is left to me out of the beggarly price he offers; and on that three and a half I shall be income-taxed and surtaxed. Jafna's grandsons will go to Eton. Mine will go to a Polytechnic.

SIR BEMROSE. Send them to Dartmouth, old chap. Theres a career for them in the navy now that Arthur is at the helm.

SIR DEXTER. A lieutenant's pay and pension

for the future Duke of Domesday! Thats the proposition, is it?

THE DUKE. He will be lucky to have any pay at all. But I shall support you in any case, Arthur. You have at last publicly admitted that the death duties are unsound in principle, and promised to abolish them. That will save us from utter extinction in three generations; and the landed classes are with you to the last man for it. Accept the humble gratitude of a pauperized duke.

SIR DEXTER. And the rest of the program. Do you swallow that too?

THE DUKE. I doubt if the rest of the program will come off. Besides, I dont pretend to understand it. By the way, Sir Jafna, I wish you would take Domesday Towers off my hands for a while. I cant afford to live in it. I cant afford even to keep it dusted. You can have it for a hundred a year.

SIR JAFNA. Too far from town.

THE DUKE. Not by aeroplane. Do think it over.

Sir Jafna shrugs his shoulders and intimates that it is hopeless. The Duke resigns himself to the expected.

SIR ARTHUR. Dexy: you are in a minority of one. The landlords are on my side. The capitalists, big and little, are on my side. The fighting services are on my side. The police are on my side. If you leave us you go out into the wilderness alone. What have you to say?

SIR DEXTER. I have to say that you are a parcel of blind fools. You are trying to scuttle the ship on the chance of each of you grabbing a share of the insurance money. But the Country will deal with you. The Country does not want change. The Country never has wanted change. The Country never will want change. And because I will resist change while I have breath in my body I shall not be alone in England. You have all deserted me and betrayed your party; but I warn you that though I am utterly alone in this room . . .

HILDA [*reappearing*] The deputation, Sir Arthur. Theyve come back. [*She vanishes*].

The deputation enters. Hipney is not with them. Barking, shaved, brilliantly dressed, and quite transfigured, is jubilant. Aloysia glows indignation. Blee and the Mayor, doggedly wearing their hats and overcoats, are gloomy, angry, and resolute. They group themselves just inside the door, glowering at the Prime Minister and his colleagues.

SIR ARTHUR [*beaming*] Gentlemen: a Labor deputation from the Isle of Cats. The one element that was lacking in our councils. You have heard the voice of the peerage, of the city, of the King's forces. You will now hear the voice of the proletariat. Sit down, ladies and gentlemen.

THE MAYOR [*rudely*] Who are you calling the proletariat? Do you take us for Communists? [*He remains standing*].

ALOYSIA. What you are going to hear, Sir Arthur, is the voice of Labor. [*She remains standing*].

BLEE. The verdict of democracy. [*He remains standing*].

EARL OF BARKING. The bleating of a bloody lot of fools. I am with you, Chavender. [*He detaches himself from the group and flings himself into Hilda's chair with intense disgust*].

SIR ARTHUR [*surprised*] Am I to understand that your colleagues are against me?

THE MAYOR. Of course we're against you. Do you expect me to go back to my people and tell them they should vote for compulsory labor and doing away with strikes?

BLEE. Arnt the workers enslaved enough already without your depriving them of that last scrap of their liberty? the only weapon they have against the capitalists?

SIR ARTHUR. My dear Mr Mayor, what is the right to strike? The right to starve on your enemy's doorstep and set the whole public against you. Which of you starves first when it comes to the point?

THE MAYOR. I am not going to argue. You can beat me at that. But if you think that the British workingman will listen to compulsory labor and putting down strikes you dont know the world youre living in; and thats all about it.

SIR ARTHUR. But we need not compel the workers to work: they are working already. We shall compel the idlers. Not only your idlers but our idlers: all the idle young gentlemen who do nothing but waste their own time and your labor.

BLEE. We know. Keep all the soft jobs for your lot and the hard ones for us. Do you take us for fools?

BARKING. He does. And you are fools.

SIR ARTHUR. I am glad to have your lordship's support.

ALOYSIA. Support your grandparents! He wants to marry your daughter.

BARKING [*springing up*] Oh! You can hit below the belt, Aloysia. But as a matter of fact, I do want to marry your daughter, Chavender.

SIR ARTHUR. Hardly the moment to go into that now, is it?

BARKING. It was Aloysia and not I who let the cat out of the bag. Being a cat herself she had a fellow-feeling for the animal. [*He resumes his seat*].

BLEE. Youre an aristocrat, young-fellow-me-lad. I always said that when things got serious youd turn on us and side with your own.

BARKING. Rot! Youre always bragging that you are descended from the Blee of Blayport, whoever he may have been. I shouldnt have tuppence in my pocket if my grandfather hadnt made a fortune in pork pies and bought my father's Norman title for his daughter with it. The blue blood is in your skimpy little veins: the proletarian red's in mine.

ALOYSIA. Youve too much money, Toffy.

BARKING. I havnt had all the pluck taken out of me by poverty, like you chaps. And what good will it do me to have a lot of money when I have to work like anyone else?

SIR DEXTER. Why should a man work like anyone else if he has money?

BARKING. My brother had heaps of money; but he had to go into the trenches and fight like anyone else in the war. Thats how I came into the property.

BLEE. So we're all to be slaves for the sake of setting a few loafers to work. The workers will die sooner than put up with it. I want my liberty—

BARKING. Liberty to work fourteen hours a day and bring up three children on thirty-four shillings a week, like your brother the shopman. To hell with your filthy liberty!

BLEE [*hotly*] I—

THE MAYOR. Order! order! Dont argue with him, Blee. No good ever comes of arguing with college men. I'm not arguing with Sir Arthur: I'm telling him. The long and the short of it is that if he dont withdraw that silly new program he'll lose every vote in the Isle of Cats. And what the Ise of Cats thinks today, all England thinks tomorrow.

SIR JAFNA. May I speak to this gentleman? Will you introduce me, Arthur?

SIR ARTHUR [*introducing*] Sir Jafna Pandranath. The Mayor of the Isle of Cats.

SIR JAFNA. You have heard of me, Mr Mayor. You know that I am a man who knows what he is talking about. Well, I tell

you that the fundamental question is not the Labor question but the Land Question.

THE MAYOR. Yes: we all know that.

SIR JAFNA. Then you will vote for Sir Arthur because he will nationalize the land for you.

BLEE [*scornfully*] Yes, with compensation! Take the land with one hand and give back its cash value to the landlords with the other! Not likely. I ask again, do you take us for fools?

SIR ARTHUR [*introducing*] Mr Alderman Blee.

THE DUKE. Enchanted. I happen to be a landlord—a duke, in fact—and I can assure you, Mr Alderman, that as the compensation will come out of my own pocket and that of my unfortunate fellow landlords in the form of income tax, surtax, and estate duties— what you call death duties—you will get all your cash back and the land as well.

THE MAYOR. Blee: I tell you, dont argue. Stick to your point. No compensation.

BLEE. Not a penny, by God.

THE DUKE. You believe in God, Mr Alderman. I am charmed to hear it.

Here the Duke is astonished to find Aloysia towering over him and pointing an accusing finger at him. At the moment of his introduction of himself as a duke, her eyes lighted up; and she has moved menacingly across the hearth towards him until she is now standing behind the vacant chair between him and Basham.

ALOYSIA. Have you ever heard of the Domesday Clearances?

THE DUKE. Clearances? Which clearances do you refer to? The latest cleared me out of Domesday Towers. I can no longer afford to live there.

ALOYSIA. Dont prevaricate. You know very well what I mean. It is written in blood and tears on the pages of working class history.

SIR ARTHUR [*introducing*] Alderwoman Aloysia Brollikins. The Duke of Domesday.

THE DUKE [*rising courteously*] Wont you sit down?

ALOYSIA [*sternly*] You shall not put me out by these tricks and ceremonies. My Lord Duke: I would rather touch the hand of the most degraded criminal in London than touch yours.

THE DUKE [*collapsing into his chair*] Great heavens! Why?

ALOYSIA. Do you forget how your family drove a whole countryside of honest hardworking Scotch crofters into the sea, and turned their little farms into deer forests because you could get more shooting rents out of them in that way? Do you forget that women in childbirth were carried out by your bailiffs to die by the roadside because they clung to their ancient homesteads and ignored your infamous notices to quit? Would it surprise you to learn that I am only one of thousands of young women who have read the hideous story of this monstrous orgy of housebreaking and murder, and sworn to ourselves that never, if we can help it, will it again be possible for one wicked rich man to say to a whole population "Get off the earth."

SIR JAFNA. Admirable! What did I tell you? Hear hear!

ALOYSIA. I thank you, Sir Jafna, for shewing this man that even hardened capitalist millionaires shudder when that story is told. You will not find it in your school histories; but in the new histories, the histories of the proletariat, it has been written, not by the venal academic triflers you call historians, but by the prophets of the new order: the men in whom the word is like a burning fire shut up in their bones so that they are weary of forbearing and must speak.

THE MAYOR. Aye: in the Bible, that is.

ALOYSIA. The Domesday Clearances filled your pockets with gold to console you for the horror and remorse of your dreams; but the vengeance they cried to God for in vain is upon you now that Labor is coming to its own; and it is your turn now to get off the earth.

BLEE. And in the face of all this, you come whining for compensation! Compensation!! Compensation from us to you! From the oppressed to the oppressor! What a mockery!

ALOYSIA. It is from you that we shall exact compensation: aye, to the uttermost farthing. You are conspiring here with these capitalist bloodsuckers to rob us again of the value of what you have already stolen—to make us give you gilt edged securities in exchange for the land that no longer brings you in shooting rents; and you think we cannot see through the plot. But in vain is the net spread in sight of the bird. We shall expose you. We shall tell the story of the Domesday Clearances until the country rings with it if you dare to lift your dishonored head again in English politics. Your demand for compensation is dismissed, turned down: we spit back in your face. The crofters whom you drove from their country to perish in a foreign land would turn in their graves at the chink of a single penny of public money in your hungry pockets. [*She tears out a chair from under the table and flops into it, panting with oratorical emotion*].

BLEE   ⎫ Good for you, Brolly!
SIR JAFNA   ⎪ [*enthused*] Hear hear! [*They*
SIR BEMROSE   ⎪ *hammer on the table with their*
GLENMORISON ⎭ *knuckles*].

THE DUKE [*very appreciative*] What a magnificent speech, Miss Brollikins! I really must insist on your shaking hands with me before we part.

ALOYSIA. Never. How dare you ask me? [*She sweeps away from him and sits down in the opposite chair at the other side of the table*].

THE DUKE [*taking the armchair*] May I not have the privilege of telling my grandchildren how I once met and shook hands with the greatest orator of my time? I assure you all these shocking things happened before I was born.

BLEE [*bawling at him*] Yes; but you still pocket the shooting rents.

THE DUKE [*brusquely*] Of course I do; and so would you too if you were in my place. [*Tenderly, to Aloysia*] I assure you, Miss Brollikins, the people make much more money out of my shooting tenants than they could as crofters: they would not go back to croftering for worlds. Wont you let bygones be bygones —except when you are exercising your wonderful gift of eloquence on the platform? Think of what your ancestors were doing in those ruthless old days!

BARKING. Grabbing all they could get, like yours or mine. Whats the good of tubthumping at these johnnies, Brolly? Theyve been doing it themselves all their lives. Cant you see that compensation makes them share the loss fairly between them?

SIR BEMROSE. It's no use. These damned Liberals cant understand anything but virtuous indignation.

THE MAYOR. Who are you calling a Liberal? I represent the Labor Party.

SIR BEMROSE. Youre a No Compensation man, arnt you?

THE MAYOR. Of course I am.

SIR BEMROSE. Then youre a Liberal.

THE MAYOR. Call me what you like. I'm not arguing. I'm telling you that the Labor Party of the Isle of Cats puts down its foot and says No Compensation. Is that plain?

SIR DEXTER. I am glad we have arrived at the same conclusion from our opposite points of view, Mr Mayor. The Party I represent, the Conservative Party, will withdraw from the Coalition if there is the slightest wobbling on this point. We shall defend our property —and yours: yours, Mr Mayor, to the last drop of our blood.

BASHAM [*incisively re-entering the conversation; they had forgotten him, and now turn to him in some surprise*] Our blood, you mean, dont you?

SIR DEXTER [*puzzled*] Whose blood?

BASHAM. The police's blood. You landed gentlemen never do a thing yourselves: you only call us in. I have twenty thousand constables, all full of blood, to shed it in defence of whatever the Government may decide to be your property. If Sir Arthur carries his point theyll shed it for land nationalization. If you carry yours theyll stand by your rent collectors as usual.

BLEE. The police come from the ranks of labor: dont forget that.

BASHAM. Thats not how they look at it, Blee. They feel that theyve escaped from the ranks of labor; and theyre proud of it. They have a status which they feel to be a part of the status of the Duke here.

THE DUKE. I suppose that is why they are always so civil to me.

BASHAM. In short, Mister Blee, the police are what you Socialists call class-conscious. You will find that out if you are foolish enough to fall out with them.

BLEE. Who cut their pay? Tell me that.

SIR ARTHUR. I shall restore the cuts, Mr Alderman, with a premium.

THE MAYOR. There! Now you see what comes of arguing, Blee. It only gives him his chance.

ALOYSIA. You need not warn us, Sir Broadfoot Basham, D.S.O., K.C.M.G., O.B.E. In the Class War your myrmidons will be well paid.

THE DUKE. Myrmidons!

ALOYSIA. We know too well what we have to expect from your Janissaries.

BLEE. Your bludgeoning Bashi-Bazouks.

ALOYSIA. The Class War is a fact. We face it. What we want we shall have to take; and we know it. The good of the community is nothing to you: you care only for surplus value. You will never give up your privileges voluntarily. History teaches us that: the history you never read.

THE DUKE. I assure you, my dear Héloïse—

ALOYSIA. Héloïse! Who are you calling Héloïse?

THE DUKE. Pardon. I could not resist the French form of your charming name.

ALOYSIA [*interjects*] The cheek!

THE DUKE [*continuing*] I was merely going to point out, as between one student of history and another, that in the French Revolution it was the nobility who voluntarily abolished all their own privileges at a single sitting, on the sentimental principles they had acquired from reading the works of Karl Marx's revolutionary predecessor Rousseau. That bit of history is repeating itself today. Here is Sir Arthur offering us a program of what seems to me to be first rate Platonic Communism. I, a Conservative Duke, embrace it. Sir Jafna Pandranath here, a Liberal capitalist whose billions shame my poverty, embraces it. The Navy embraces it with the sturdy arms of Sir Bemrose Hotspot. The police are enthusiastic. The Army will be with Sir Arthur to the last man. He has the whole propertied class on his side. But the proletariat rises against him and spews out his Socialism through the eloquent lips of its Aloysia. I recall the warning my dear old father gave me when I was five years old. Chained dogs are the fiercest guardians of property; and those who attempt to unchain them are the first to be bitten.

ALOYSIA. Your Grace calls us dogs. We shall not forget that.

THE DUKE. I have found no friends better than faithful dogs, Miss Brollikins. But of course I spoke figuratively. I should not dream of calling you a dog.

ALOYSIA. No. As I am a female dog I suppose you will call me something shorter when my back is turned.

THE DUKE. Oh! Think of the names you have called me!

THE MAYOR. Well, if you will argue, Alderwoman Brollikins, there's no use my staying here. I wish I could stop your mouth as easy as I can stop my ears. Sir Arthur: youve planked down your program and weve planked down our answer. Either you drop compulsory labor and drop compensation or never shew your face in the Isle of Cats again. [*He goes out resolutely*].

BLEE. Take this from me. I am no Communist: I am a respectable Labor man, as law abiding as any man here. I am what no of you has mentioned yet: a democrat. I am just as much against Cabinet dictatorship as individual dictatorship. What I want done is the will of the people. I am for the referendum. I am for the initiative. When a majority of the people are in favor of a measure then I am for that measure.

SIR BEMROSE. Rot! The majority is never in favor of any measure. They dont know what a measure is. What they want is their orders, and as much comfort as they are accustomed to. The lower deck doesnt want to give orders, it looks to the bridge for them. If I asked my men to do my job theyd chuck me overboard; and serve me jolly well right! You just know nothing about it, because youve never had to command; and you havnt sense enough to obey and be thankful to those who have saved you the trouble of thinking for yourself and keeping you off the rocks.

BLEE. You havnt kept us off the rocks. We're on the rocks, the whole lot of us. So long, Rosy. [*He goes out*].

BARKING. Silly swine! When they are offered what they want they wont have it just because you fellows want it too. They think there must be a catch in it somewhere.

THE DUKE. There generally is. That is how you feel, Miss Brollikins, isnt it?

ALOYSIA. You dont know how I feel; and you never will. We are going to save ourselves and not be saved by you and your class. And I prefer Sir Dexter Rightside's downright outspoken opposition to your silly-clever cynicism and your sickening compliments.

THE DUKE. It is only in middle class books, Miss Brollikins, that noblemen are always cynical and insincere. I find you a most brilliant and delightful woman. May I not tell you so? And WHAT a speaker! Will you spend a quiet week-end with me in some out-of-the-way place in the country, and let me try to convince you that a duke is a human being like yourself?

ALOYSIA [*rearing*] Are you trying to seduce me?

THE DUKE. That would be exquisite, Miss Brollikins; but I am an old and very poor man. You are young, beautiful, and probably opulent. Can you find anything seductive about me?

ALOYSIA. Yes. Youre a duke. And you have the charm of a majestic ruin, if you understand me.

BARKING [*rising*] Come on out of this, Brolly: youre only making a fool of yourself listening to that old bird buttering you up. You just dont know when to go.

ALOYSIA [*moving to the hearthrug, behind Sir Arthur*] You can go if you like. I have some business with Sir Arthur that doesnt concern you. Get out.

SIR ARTHUR. Some business with me! Public business?

ALOYSIA. Not exactly.

SIR ARTHUR. Oh! Private business?

ALOYSIA. I dont care who knows it. But perhaps you would.

BARKING. She means to marry your son David. One below the belt for you, Brolly. Ha ha! Ha ha ha ha ha! [*He goes out roaring with laughter*].

SIR ARTHUR [*after a moment of shock*] I congratulate David, Miss Brollikins. Have you arranged the date?

ALOYSIA. I havnt mentioned it to him yet. I hope all you gentlemen will remember that I was not the one that blurted this out: it was your noble viscount. However, now it's out, I stand by it: David is a good boy; and his class is not his fault. Goodbye all. [*She goes to the door*].

THE DUKE [*rising*] And that week-end, Miss Brollikins? Or has David cut me out?

ALOYSIA. Right you are, Your Grace! I will call for you at Domesday House on Friday at half past four. As I shall bring a few friends we shall hire an omnibus from the London Transport; so you neednt trouble about a car. You wont mind my publishing an account of what happens as a special interview: you know that we Labor intelligentsia have to live by our brains. Au revoir. [*She goes out*].

THE DUKE. There is a frightful unexpectedness about these people. Where on earth shall I borrow the money to pay for the omnibus and entertain them all? [*He goes back to his chair at the end of the table and sits down*].

BASHAM. Your share will only be a few shillings, Duke; and she will reckon on having to pay for you. What girl in her class wouldnt foot the bill if she had a duke to walk out with?

THE DUKE. You reassure me, Sir Broadfoot. Thank you.

SIR DEXTER [*triumphant*] Well, Chavender? What have you to say now? When these people came in I was saying that though I was alone in this room, the people of England were on my side and always would be when it came to the point. Was I right or wrong?

SIR BEMROSE. We never meant to desert you, Dexy. You mustnt think that.

SIR ARTHUR. As you have no more intention of consulting the people of England than I have, the situation is unaltered.

SIR DEXTER. Than you have! What do you mean? Do you think you can govern in this country without the consent of the English people?

SIR ARTHUR. No country has ever been governed by the consent of the people, because the people object to be governed at all. Even you, who ought to know better, are always complaining of the income tax.

THE DUKE. But five shillings in the pound, Arthur! Five shillings in the pound!!

SIR DEXTER. Never mind my income tax. If what you said just now means anything it means that you are going to play fast and loose with democracy: that is, you think you are going to do something that both the people and the governing class of this country are determined you shall not do. The Conservative Party, which is ten times more really democratic than you Liberals have ever been, will carry the people with it against you. How do you propose to get over that? What are you banking on? Put your cards on the table if you really have any.

SIR ARTHUR. Well, here is my ace of trumps. The people of this country, and of all the European countries, and of America, are at present sick of being told that, thanks to democracy, they are the real government of the country. They know very well that they dont govern and cant govern and know nothing about Government except that it always supports profiteering, and doesnt really respect anything else, no matter what party flag it waves. They are sick of twaddle about liberty when they have no liberty. They are sick of idling and loafing about on doles when they are not drudging for wages too beggarly to pay the rents of anything better than overcrowded one-room tenements. They are sick of me and sick of you and sick of the whole lot of us. They want to see something done that will give them decent employment. They want to eat and drink the wheat and coffee that the profiteers are burning because they cant sell it at a profit. They want to hang people who burn good food when people are going hungry.

They cant set matters right themselves; so they want rulers who will discipline them and make them do it instead of making them do the other thing. They are ready to go mad with enthusiasm for any man strong enough to make them do anything, even if it is only Jew baiting, provided it's something tyrannical, something coercive, something that we all pretend no Englishman would submit to, though weve known ever since we gave them the vote that theyd submit to anything.

SIR DEXTER [impatiently] Yes, yes: we know the cant of all the tuppeny-hapeny dictators who think themselves Mussolinis. Come down to tin tacks. How are you going to get it through Parliament?

SIR ARTHUR. I am not going to get it through Parliament: I am going to prorogue Parliament and then do it. When it is done I shall call a meeting of Parliament to pass an Act of Indemnity for all my proceedings.

SIR DEXTER. You cannot prorogue Parliament. Only the King can prorogue Parliament.

SIR ARTHUR. Precisely. Kings always have prorogued Parliament and governed without them until money ran short.

GLENMORISON. But, man alive, it is not His Majesty alone that you have to consider. The law courts will not enforce your decisions if they are illegal. The civil servants will sabotage you even if they dont flatly disobey you.

SIR ARTHUR. We shall sidetrack them quite easily by setting up new tribunals and special commissions manned by officials we can depend on.

SIR DEXTER. That was how Cromwell cut off King Charles's head. His commissioners found out afterwards that they were doing it with ropes round their rascally necks.

SIR ARTHUR. A rope round a statesman's neck is the only constitutional safeguard that really safeguards. But never fear the rope. As long as we give the people an honest good time we can do just what seems good to us. The proof of the pudding will be in the eating. That will be really responsible government at last.

SIR DEXTER. So that is your game, is it? Has it occurred to you that two can play at it? What can you do that I cannot do if you drive me to it: tell me that.

SIR ARTHUR. Nothing, if you are willing to take on my job. Are you?

SIR DEXTER. The job of ruining the country and destroying the empire? My job is to prevent you from doing that. And I will prevent you.

SIR ARTHUR. Your job is to prevent me or anybody else from doing anything. Your job is to prevent the world from moving. Well, it is moving; and if you dont get out of the way something will break; and it wont be the world.

SIR DEXTER. Nothing has broken so far except the heads of the unemployed when they are encouraged by your seditious rot to rebel against the laws of nature. England is not breaking. She stands foursquare where she always stood and always will stand: the strongest and greatest land, and the birthplace of the noblest imperial race, that ever God created.

SIR ARTHUR. Loud and prolonged cheering. Come! let us both stop tubthumping and talk business. The real master of the situation is Basham here, with his fifteen thousand police.

BASHAM. Twenty thousand.

SIR ARTHUR. Well, twenty thousand. They dont stop functioning when Parliament is prorogued, do they?

BASHAM. No. At Scotland Yard we look to the Home Secretary as far as we look to anybody.

SIR ARTHUR. I can make myself Home Secretary. So that will be all right.

SIR DEXTER. Will it, by George? If you and Basham dare to try your twenty thousand police on me, do you know what I will do?

SIR ARTHUR. What?

SIR DEXTER. I will put fifty thousand patriotic young Londoners into Union Jack shirts. You say they want discipline and action. They shall have them. They shall have machine guns and automatic pistols and tear gas bombs. My Party has the money. My Party has the newspapers. My Party has the flag, the traditions, the glory that is England, the pluck, the breed, the fighting spirit. One of us is worth ten of your half starved guttersnipes and their leaders that never could afford more than a shilling for a dinner until they voted themselves four hundred a year out of our pockets.

SIR BEMROSE [*carried away*] Thats the stuff, Dexy. Now you are talking, by Jiminy.

BASHAM [*taking command of the discussion coolly*] You are all talking through your hats. The police can do nothing unless the people are on the side of the police. The police cant be everywhere: there arnt enough of them. As long as the people will call the police when anything goes wrong, and stop the runaway criminal and give evidence against him, then twenty thousand constables can keep eight million citizens in order. But if the citizens regard the policeman as their enemy—if the man who snipes a policeman in the back is not given in charge by the bystanders—if he is helped to get away—if the police cannot get a single citizen to go into the box and witness against him, where are you then? You have to double your force because the police must patrol in pairs: otherwise the men will be afraid to patrol at all. Your twenty thousand have to be reinforced up to forty thousand for their own protection; but that doesnt protect you. You would have to put two policemen standing over every able-bodied man and woman in the town to see that they behaved themselves as you want them to behave. You would need not thousands of constables but millions.

SIR DEXTER. My Union Jack men would keep order, or theyd know the reason why.

BASHAM. And who would keep them in order, I should like to know: silly amateurs. And let me remind you of one thing. It seems easy to buy a lot of black shirts, or brown shirts, or red shirts, and give one to every hooligan who is out for any sort of mischief and every suburban out-of-work who fancies himself a patriot. But dont forget that the colored shirt is a uniform.

GLENMORISON. What harm is there in that? It enables a man to recognize his friends.

BASHAM. Yes; but it marks him out as an enemy in uniform; and to kill an enemy in uniform at sight is not murder: it's legitimate warfare.

SIR DEXTER. Monstrous! I should give no quarter to such an outrageous piece of sophistry.

BASHAM. In war you have to give quarter because you have to ask for it as often as to give it. It's easy to sit here and think of exterminating your opponents. But a war of extermination is a massacre. How long do you think a massacre would last in England today? Just as long as it takes a drunken man to get sick and sober.

GLENMORISON. Easy, Sir Broadfoot, easy, easy. Who is talking of extermination? I dont think you will ever induce respectable Britons to wear red-white-and-blue shirts; but surely you can have volunteers, special constables, auxiliary forces—

BASHAM [*flinching violently*] Auxiliary forces! I was in command of them in Ireland when you tried that game on the Irish, who were only a little handful of peasants in their cabbage patch. I have seen these things. I have done them. I know all about it: you know nothing about it. It means extermination; and when it comes to the point you cant go through with it. I couldnt. I resigned. You couldnt: you had to back down. And I tell you, Dexy, if you try any colored shirt hooliganism on me, I'll back the P.M. and shew you what Scotland Yard can do when it's put to it.

SIR DEXTER. Traitor!

BASHAM. Liar! Now weve called one another names how much farther has it got us?

GLENMORISON. Easy, easy: dont let us quarrel. I must support the Prime Minister, Sir Dexter, to secure my seat in Parliament. But I am a Liberal, and, as such, bound by Liberal principles. Whatever we do must be done through Parliament if I am to be a party to it. I am all for the new program; but we must draw up a parliamentary timetable for it. To carry out the program will involve the introduction of at least twelve bills. They are highly controversial bills: every one of them will be resisted and obstructed to the very last clause. You may have to go to the country on several of them. The committee stages will last for weeks and weeks, no matter how hard you work the guillotine: there will be thousands of amendments. Then, when you have got through what is left of your Bill and carried it, the House of Lords will turn it down; and you will have to wait two years and go through the whole job again before you can get your Bill on the statute book as an Act of Parliament. This program is not a matter of today or tomorrow. I calculate that at the very least it will take fifty years to get it through.

SIR ARTHUR. And you think the world will wait for that, Sandy?

GLENMORISON [*naïvely*] What else can it do?

SIR ARTHUR. It wont wait. Unless we can find a shorter way, the program will be fought out in the streets.

SIR DEXTER. And you think that in the streets you will win? You think the mob will be on your side? "Ye are many: they are few" eh? The Class War! Well, you will find out your mistake.

SIR ARTHUR. I dont believe in the Class War any more than you do, Dexy. I know that half the working class is slaving away to pile up riches, only to be smoked out like a hive of bees and plundered of everything but a bare living by our class. But what is the other half doing? Living on the plunder at second hand. Plundering the plunderers. As fast as we fill our pockets with rent and interest and profits theyre emptied again by West End tradesmen and hotel keepers, fashionable doctors and lawyers and parsons and fiddlers and portrait painters and all sorts, to say nothing of huntsmen and stablemen and gardeners, valets and gamekeepers and jockeys, butlers and housekeepers and ladies' maids and scullery maids and deuce knows who not.

THE DUKE. How true, Arthur! how profoundly true! I am with you there to the last drop of my blood.

SIR ARTHUR. Well, these parasites will fight for the rights of property as they would fight for their own skins. Can you get a Labor member into Parliament in the places where they are in a majority? No: there is no class war: the working class is hopelessly divided against itself. But I will tell you what there is. There is the gulf between Dexy's view of the world and mine. There is the eternal war between those who are in the world for what they can get out of it and those who are in the world to make it a better place for everybody to live in.

SIR DEXTER [*rising*] I will not sit here listening to this disgusting ungentlemanly nonsense. Chavender: the coalition is dissolved. I resign. I shall take with me three quarters of the Cabinet. I shall expose the shamelessly corrupt motives of those who have supported you here today. Basham: you will get the sack the day after the King sends for me. Domesday: you have gone gaga: go home to bed and drivel where your dotage can do no harm. Rosy: you are a damned fool; and you ought to know it by this time. Pandranath: you are only a silly nigger pretending to be an English gentleman: you are found out. Good afternoon, gentlemen.

He goes out, leaving an atmosphere of awe behind him, in which the Indian is choking with indignation, and for the moment inarticulate.

SIR BEMROSE. This is awful. We cannot do without him.

SIR JAFNA [*finding his tongue*] I am despised. I am called nigger by this dirty faced barbarian whose forefathers were naked savages worshipping acorns and mistletoe in the woods whilst my people were spreading the highest enlightenment yet reached by the human race from the temples of Brahma the thousandfold who is all the gods in one. This primitive savage dares to accuse me of imitating him: me, with the blood in my veins of conquerors who have swept through continents vaster than a million dogholes like this island of yours. They founded a civilization compared to which your little kingdom is no better than a concentration camp. What you have of religion came from the east; yet no Hindu, no Parsee, no Jain, would stoop to its crudities. Is there a mirror here? Look at your faces and look at the faces of my people in Ceylon, the cradle of the human race. There you see Man as he came from the hand of God, who has left on every feature the unmistakeable stamp of the great original creative artist. There you see Woman with eyes in her head that mirror the universe instead of little peepholes filled with faded pebbles. Set those features, those eyes, those burning colors beside the miserable smudged lumps of half baked dough, the cheap commercial copies of a far away gallery of masterpieces that you call western humanity, and tell me, if you dare, that you are the original and I the imitation. Do you not fear the lightning? the earthquake? the vengeance of Vishnu? You call me nigger, sneering at my color because you have none. The jackdaw has lost his tail and would persuade the world that his defect is a quality. You have all cringed to me, not for my greater nearness to God, but for my money and my power of making money and ever more money. But today your hatred, your envy, your insolence has betrayed itself. I am nigger. I am bad imitation of that eater of unclean foods, never sufficiently washed in his person or his garments, a British islander. I will no longer bear it. The veil of your hypocrisy is rent by your own mouths: I should dishonor my country and my race by remaining here where both have been insulted. Until now I have supported the connection between India and England because I knew that in the course of nature and by the justice of Brahma it must end in India ruling England just as I, by my wealth and my brains, govern this roomful of needy imbeciles. But I now cast you off. I return to India to detach it wholly from England, and leave you to perish in your ignorance, your vain conceit, and your abominable manners. Good morning, gentlemen. To hell with the lot of you. [*He goes out and slams the door*].

SIR ARTHUR. That one word nigger will cost us India. How could Dexy be such a fool as to let it slip!

SIR BEMROSE [*very serious—rising solemnly*] Arthur: I feel I cannot overlook a speech like that. After all, we are white men.

SIR ARTHUR. You are not, Rosy, I assure you. You are walnut color, with a touch of claret on the nose. Glenmorison is the color of his native oatmeal: not a touch of white on him. The fairest man present is the Duke. He's as yellow as a Malayan headhunter. The Chinese call us Pinks. They flatter us.

SIR BEMROSE. I must tell you, Arthur, that frivolity on a vital point like this is in very bad taste. And you know very well that the country cannot do without Dexy. Dexy was at school with me before I went to Dartmouth. To desert him would be for me not only an act of political bad faith but of personal bad feeling. I must go and see him at once. [*He goes very sadly to the door*].

SIR ARTHUR. Make my apologies to Sir Jafna if you overtake him. How are we to hold the empire together if we insult a man who represents nearly seventy per cent of its population?

SIR BEMROSE. I dont agree with you, Arthur. It is for Pandy to apologize. Dexy really shares the premiership with you; and if a Conservative Prime Minister of England may not take down a heathen native when he forgets himself there is an end of British supremacy.

SIR ARTHUR. For Heaven's sake dont call him a native. You are a native.

SIR BEMROSE [*very solemnly*] Of Kent, Arthur: of Kent. Not of Ceylon. [*He goes out*].

GLENMORISON. I think I'd better clear out too. I can make allowances for Sir Dexter: he is an Englishman, and has not been trained to use his mind like us in Scotland. But that is just what gives him such a hold on the Country. We must face it: he's indispensable. I'll just go and assure him that we have no intention of breaking with him. Ta ta. Good morning, Duke. [*He goes out*].

SIR ARTHUR [*rising and strolling round to the other side of the table like a cleaned-out gambler*] That finishes me, I'm afraid.

He throws himself into the middle chair. Basham rises moodily and goes to the window to contemplate the street. The Duke comes sympathetically to Sir Arthur and sits down beside him.

THE DUKE. Oh Arthur, my dear Arthur, why didnt you play golf on your holiday instead of thinking? Didnt you know that English politics wont bear thinking about? Didnt you know that as a nation we have lost the trick of thinking? Hadnt you noticed that though in our great British Constitution there is a department for everything else in the world almost—for agriculture and health and fisheries, for home affairs and foreign affairs and education, for the Exchequer and the Treasury and even the Chiltern Hundreds and the Duchy of Lancaster—we have no department for thinking? The Russians have a special Cabinet for it; and it has knocked the whole place to pieces. Where should you and I be in Russia today? [*He resumes his seat with a hopeless shrug*].

SIR ARTHUR. In our proper place, the dustbin. Yet they got their ideas from us. Karl Marx thought it all out in Bloomsbury. Lenin learnt his lesson in Holford Square, Islington. Why can we never think out anything, nor learn any lessons? I see what has to be done now; but I dont feel that I am the man to do it.

THE DUKE. Of course not. Not a gentleman's job.

SIR ARTHUR. It might be a duke's job, though. Why not have a try at it?

THE DUKE. For three reasons, Arthur. First, I'm not built that way. Second, I'm so accustomed as a duke to be treated with the utmost deference that I simply dont know how to assert myself and bully people. Third, I'm so horribly hard up for pocket money without knowing how to do without it that Ive lost all my self-respect. This job needs a man with nothing to lose, plenty of hard driving courage, and a complete incapacity for seeing any side of a question but his own. A mere hereditary duke would be no use. When Domesday Towers is sold to an American I shall have no family seat left, and must fall back on my political seat, which is at present on the fence. From that eminence I shall encourage the dictator when he arrives as far as I can without committing myself dangerously. Sorry I can be of no use to you, my dear Arthur.

SIR ARTHUR. What about you, Basham? You are a man of action.

BASHAM. I have a jolly good mind to go to the King and make him take the bit between his teeth and arrest the lot of you.

SIR ARTHUR. Do, Basham, do. You couldnt make a worse hash of things than we have.

THE DUKE. Theres nothing to prevent you. Look at Kemal Pasha! Look at Mussolini! Look at Hitler! Look at De Valera! Look at Franklin Roosevelt!

BASHAM. If only I had ambition enough I'd think very seriously over it. As it is, I'll go back quietly to Scotland Yard. [*He is going out when he is confronted in the doorway by Hipney*] Hallo! What the devil are you doing here?

SIR ARTHUR. I am afraid you are late, Mr Hipney. The deputation has been here. They have all gone.

HIPNEY [*seating himself beside Sir Arthur with his usual calm*] I came with them, Srarthur. I been listening on the quiet as you might say. I just come in to tell you not to mind that parliamentary lot. Theyre all the same, west end or east end, parkside or riverside. Theyll never do anything. They dont want to do anything.

BASHAM [*sitting down again in Hilda's chair*] Hipney: I may as well tell you that I have had my eye on you for some time. Take care. I have no objection to your calling yourself a revolutionary Socialist: they all do that. But I suspect you of really meaning business.

HIPNEY. I do, Sir Broadfoot: I do. And if Srarthur means business, then let him come out of Parliament and keep out. It will take the life out of him and leave him a walking talking shell of a man with nothing inside. The only man that ever had a proper understanding of Parliament was old Guy Fawkes.

SIR ARTHUR. But even if he had blown that Parliament up, they would just have elected another.

HIPNEY. Yes; but it was a sort of gesture as you might say. Symbolic, I call it. Mark my words: some day there will be a statue to old Guy in Westminster on the site of the present House of Commons.

THE DUKE. Democracy, Arthur, democracy. This is what it ends in.

SIR ARTHUR [*introducing*] His Grace the Duke of Domesday, Mr Hipney.

HIPNEY. Bless you, I know his Grace. About town, as you might say, though weve never been introduced.

THE DUKE. Very much honored, Mr Hipney.

HIPNEY. No great honor, your Grace. But old Hipney can tell you something about Democracy at first hand. Democracy was a great thing when I was young and we had no votes. We talked about public opinion and what the British people would stand and what they wouldnt stand. And it had weight, I tell you, sir: it held Governments in check: it frightened the stoutest of the tyrants and the bosses and the police: it brought a real reverence into the voices of great orators like Bright and Gladstone. But that was when it was a dream and a vision, a hope and a faith and a promise. It lasted until they dragged it down to earth, as you might say, and made it a reality by giving everybody votes. The moment they gave the working men votes they found that theyd stand anything. They gave votes to the women and found they were worse than the men; for men would vote for men—the wrong men, but men all the same—but the women wouldnt even vote for women. Since then politics have been a laughing stock. Parliamentary leaders say one thing on Monday and just the opposite on Wednesday; and nobody notices any difference. They put down the people in Egypt, in Ireland, and in India with fire and sword, with floggings and hangings, burning the houses over their heads and bombing their little stores for the winter out of existence; and at the next election theyd be sent back to Parliament by working class constituencies as if they were plaster saints, while men and women like me, that had spent their lives in the service of the people, were booted out at the polls like convicted criminals. It wasnt that the poor silly sheep did it on purpose. They didnt notice: they didnt remember: they couldnt understand: they were taken in by any nonsense they heard at the meetings or read in the morning paper. You could stampede them by crying out that the Russians were coming, or rally them by promising them to hang the Kaiser, or Lord knows what silliness that shouldnt have imposed on a child of four. That was the end of democracy for me; though there was no man alive that had hoped as much from it, nor spoke deeper from his heart about all the good things that would happen when the people came to their own and had votes like the gentry. Adult suffrage: that was what was to save us all. My God! It delivered us into the hands of our spoilers and oppressors, bound hand and foot by our own folly and ignorance. It took the heart out of old Hipney; and now I'm for any Napoleon or Mussolini or Lenin or Chavender that has the stuff in him to take both the people and the spoilers and oppressors by the scruffs of their silly necks and just sling them into the way they should go with as many kicks as may be needful to make a thorough job of it.

BASHAM. A dictator: eh? Thats what you want.

HIPNEY. Better one dictator standing up responsible before the world for the good and evil he does than a dirty little dictator in every street responsible to nobody, to turn you out of your house if you dont pay him for the right to exist on the earth, or to fire you out of your job if you stand up to him as a man and an equal. You cant frighten me with a word like dictator. Me and my like has been dictated to all our lives by swine that have nothing but a snout for money, and think the world is coming to an end if anybody but themselves is given the power to do anything.

SIR ARTHUR. Steady, Mr Hipney, steady! Dont empty the baby out with the bath. If the people are to have no voice in the government and no choice of who is to govern them, it will be bad for the people.

HIPNEY. Let em have a voice. Let em have a choice. Theyve neither at present. But let it be a voice to squeal with when theyre hurt, and not to pretend they know more than God Almighty does. Give em a choice between qualified men: theres always more than one pebble on the beach; but let them be qualified men and not windbags and movie stars and soldiers and rich swankers and lawyers on the make. How are they to tell the difference between any cheap Jack and Solomon or Moses? The Jews didnt elect Moses: he just told them what to do and they did it. Look at the way they went wrong the minute his back was turned! If you want to be a leader of the people, Srarthur, youve got to elect yourself by giving us a lead. Old Hipney will follow anyone that will give him a good lead; and to blazes with your elections and your Constitution and your Democracy and all the rest of it!

THE DUKE. The police wont let him, Mr Hipney.

BASHAM [*rising and planting himself between Hipney and Sir Arthur*] Ha ha ha! Dont be too sure of that. I might come down on your side, Arthur, if I spotted you as a winner. Meanwhile, Hipney, I have my eye on you as a dangerous character.

SIR ARTHUR. And on me?

BASHAM. You dont matter: he does. If the proletariat comes to the top things will be more comfortable for Hipney; but they wont be more comfortable for you. His heart is in the revolution: you have only your head in it. Your wife wouldnt like it: his would, if he has one.

HIPNEY. Not me. I'm under no woman's thumb. She's dead; and the children are grown up and off my hands. I'm free at last to put my neck in a noose if I like.

BASHAM. I wonder should I find any bombs in your house if I searched it.

HIPNEY. You would if you put them there first, Sir Broadfoot. What good would a police chief be if he couldnt find anything he wanted to find?

BASHAM. Thats a suggestion, Hipney, certainly. Isnt it rather rash of you to put it into my head?

HIPNEY. There's plenty to put it into your head if I didnt. You could do it if you liked; and you know it, Sir Broadfoot. But perhaps your conscience wouldnt let you.

BASHAM. Perhaps.

HIPNEY [*rising with a chuckle*] Aha! [*Impressively*] You take it from me, you three gentlemen: all this country or any country has to stand between it and blue hell is the consciences of them that are capable of governing it.

THE DUKE [*rising*] Mr Hipney: I find myself in complete agreement with you. Will you lunch with me at the Carlton?

HIPNEY. No: them big clubs is too promiscuous for the like of you and me. You come and lunch with me: I know a nice little place where the cooking's good and the company really select. You wont regret it: come along. Morning, Srarthur. Morning, Boss. [*He goes out, greatly pleased*].

SIR ARTHUR AND BASHAM [*simultaneously*] Morning. Morning.

THE DUKE. You would never have got rid of him, Arthur, if I hadn't made that move. Goodbye. Goodbye, Sir Broadfoot. *He goes to the door*].

BASHAM. Goodbye. I wish you joy of your host.

THE DUKE. You dont appreciate him. He is absolutely unique.

BASHAM. In what way, pray?

THE DUKE. He is the only politician I ever met who had learnt anything from experience [*he goes out*].

BASHAM [*making for the door*] Well, I must be off to the Yard. The unemployed are going to have a general election to amuse them. I suppose youll be off to your constituency right away.

SIR ARTHUR [*rising*] No. I am not going to stand.

BASHAM [*returning to him in amazement*] Not stand! What do you mean? You cant chalk up a program like that and then run away.

SIR ARTHUR. I am through with parliament. It has wasted enough of my life.

BASHAM. Dont tell me you are going to take your politics into the street. You will only get your head broken.

SIR ARTHUR. Never fear: your fellows wont break my head: they have too much respect for an ex-Prime Minister. But I am not going into the streets. I am not a man of action, only a talker. Until the men of action clear out the talkers we who have social consciences are at the mercy of those who have none; and that, as old Hipney says, is blue hell. Can you find a better name for it?

BASHAM. Blackguardocracy, I should call it.

SIR ARTHUR. Do you believe in it? I dont.

BASHAM. It works all right up to a point. Dont run your head against it until the men of action get you past that point. Bye bye.

SIR ARTHUR. Bye bye. I wont.

Basham goes out through the main door. Sir Arthur drops into his chair again and looks rather sick, with his elbows on his knees and his temples on his fists. Barking and Miss Brollikins break into the room simultaneously by the private door, struggling for precedence. Sir Arthur straightens up wearily.

BARKING. I was here first. You get out and wait for your turn.

ALOYSIA. Ladies first, if you please. Sir Arthur—

BARKING [*barring her way with an arm of iron*] Ladies be damned! youre no lady. [*He comes past the table to Sir Arthur's right*] Sir Arthur: I have proposed for the hand of your daughter Flavia; and all I can get out of her is that she is not a gold digger, and wouldnt be seen at a wedding with a lousy viscount. She wants to marry a poor man. I said I'd go over her head straight to you. You cant let her miss so good a match. Exert your authority. Make her marry me.

SIR ARTHUR. Certainly. I'll order her to marry you if you think that will get you any further. Go and tell her so, like a good boy. I'm busy.

BARKING. Righto! [*he dashes out through the masked door*].

SIR ARTHUR. Sit down, Miss Brollikins. [*She comes round to Hipney's chair; and Sir Arthur takes the Duke's chair*]. Have you consulted David?

ALOYSIA [*sitting down rather forlornly*] Of course I have. But he's obstinate. He wont look at it the right way.

SIR ARTHUR. Did he object? He should have jumped at it.

ALOYSIA. Its very nice of you to say so if you really mean it, Sir Arthur. But he has no sense. He objects to my name. He says it's ridiculous.

SIR ARTHUR. But your marriage will change it.

ALOYSIA. Yes; but he says it would be in The Times in the births marriages and deaths: Chavender and Brollikins. My name's not good enough for him. You should have heard what he said about it.

SIR ARTHUR. I hope he did not use the adjective his sister applied to poor young Barking's title.

ALOYSIA. Yes he did. The language you West End people use! I'm sure I dont know where you pick it up.

SIR ARTHUR. It doesnt mean anything, Miss Brollikins. You mustnt mind.

ALOYSIA. Would you mind calling me Aloysia, Sir Arthur? You can call me Brolly if you like; but I prefer Aloysia.

SIR ARTHUR. Certainly, Aloysia.

ALOYSIA. Thank you. I wish I could get rid of Brollikins. I'd never stoop to be ashamed of my name; but I cant deny there's something funny about it. I'm not to blame for that, am I?

SIR ARTHUR. But you can get rid of it quite easily. You can take a new name: any name you like, by deed poll. It costs only ten pounds; and David would have to pay it if it was on his account you changed. What about Bolingbroke [*he pronounces it Bullingbrook*]?

Bolingbroke would be rather a nice name for The Times; and you wouldnt have to change your initials. No bother about your clothes at the laundry, for instance.

ALOYSIA. Thank you, Sir Arthur: thats a practical suggestion. At any rate it will shut David up if he talks about my name again.

SIR ARTHUR. Well, now you can run off and marry him.

ALOYSIA. But thats not all, Sir Arthur. He's such a queer boy. He says he's never loved anyone but his sister, and that he hates his mother.

SIR ARTHUR. He had no right to tell you that he hates his mother, because as a matter of fact he doesnt. Young people nowadays read books about psycho-analysis and get their heads filled with nonsense.

ALOYSIA. Of course I know all about psycho-analysis. I explained to him that he was in love with his mother and was jealous of you. The Edipus complex, you know.

SIR ARTHUR. And what did he say to that?

ALOYSIA. He told me to go to Jericho. But I shall teach him manners.

SIR ARTHUR. Do, Aloysia. Did he make any further objection?

ALOYSIA. Well, he says his people couldnt stand my relatives.

SIR ARTHUR. Tut! the young snob! Still, snobbery is a very real thing: he made a point there, Aloysia. How did you meet it?

ALOYSIA. I said my people couldnt stand his relatives; and no more they could. I said I wasnt asking him to marry my relatives; nor was I proposing to marry his.

SIR ARTHUR. And what did he say to that?

ALOYSIA. He told me to go to hell. He's like that, you know.

SIR ARTHUR. Yes, a hasty boy.

ALOYSIA. He is, just that. But I shall cure him of it.

SIR ARTHUR [*gravely*] Take care, Aloysia. All young women begin by believing they can change and reform the men they marry. They cant. If you marry David he will remain David and nobody else til death do you part. If he tells you to go to hell today instead of trying to argue with you, he will do the same on the morning of your silver wedding.

ALOYSIA [*grimly*] We shall see.

SIR ARTHUR. May I ask whether this match is your idea or David's? So far I do not gather that he has expressed any strong feeling of

—of—shall I say devotion?—to you.

ALOYSIA. We have discussed all that.

SIR ARTHUR. Satisfactorily?

ALOYSIA. I suppose so. You see, Sir Arthur, I am not like David. I am a reading thinking modern woman; and I know how to look at these things objectively and scientifically. You know the way you meet thousands of people and they mean nothing to you sexually: you wouldnt touch one of them with a barge pole. Then all of a sudden you pick out one, and feel sexy all over. If he's not nice you feel ashamed of yourself and run away. But if he is nice you say "Thats the man for me." You have had that experience yourself, havnt you?

SIR ARTHUR. Quite. The moment I saw Lady Chavender I said "Thats the woman for me."

ALOYSIA. Well, the moment I laid eyes on David I went all over like that. You cant deny that he is a nice boy in spite of his awful language. So I said—

SIR ARTHUR. "David's the man for me"?

ALOYSIA. No. I said "Evolution is telling me to marry this youth." That feeling is the only guide I have to the evolutionary appetite.

SIR ARTHUR. The what??

ALOYSIA. The evolutionary appetite. The thing that wants to develop the race. If I marry David we shall develop the race. And thats the great thing in marriage, isnt it?

SIR ARTHUR. My dear Aloysia, the evolutionary appetite may be a guide to developing the race; but it doesnt care a rap for domestic happiness. I have known the most remarkable children come of the most dreadfully unsuitable and unhappy marriages.

ALOYSIA. We have to take our chance of that, Sir Arthur. Marriage is a lottery. I think I can make David as happy as anybody ever is in this—

SIR ARTHUR. In this wicked world. Ah yes. Well, I wont press that.

ALOYSIA. I was about to say "in the capitalist phase of social development." I dont talk like your grandmother, if you will excuse me saying so.

SIR ARTHUR. I beg your pardon. I suppose I do. Have you explained this evolutionary view of the situation to David?

ALOYSIA. Of course I have. I dont treat him as a child.

SIR ARTHUR. And what did he say?

ALOYSIA. He told me to go and— Oh, I really cannot repeat what he told me to go and do. But you see how familiar we are together. I couldnt bear his being distant with me. He talks just as if we were married already.

SIR ARTHUR. Quite. But does he feel about you as you feel about him? Has he picked you out from among the thousand ladies to whom he is indifferent? To use your own expression, does he come all over like that in your presence?

ALOYSIA. He does when I get hold of him. He needs educating in these matters. I have to awaken David. But he's coming along nicely.

SIR ARTHUR. Well, if it must be it must be. I shall not withhold my blessing. That is all I can say. [He rises: she does the same and prepares to go]. You see, Aloysia, the effete society in which I move is based on the understanding that we shall all speak and behave in the manner in which we are expected to behave. We are helpless when this understanding is violated. We dont know what to say or what to do. Well, you have violated it recklessly. What you have said has been unexpected to the last possible degree—

ALOYSIA. It has been true.

SIR ARTHUR. That is the climax of unexpectedness in polite society. Therefore I am at a loss. Apparently my son was not at a loss. He knows how to deal with you: I do not. I must really refer you back to him for further consideration and report.

They are about to shake hands when Lady Chavender comes in through the masked door.

LADY CHAVENDER. Still here, Miss Brollikins! I thought you had gone. [She comes past the table to Sir Arthur's right].

SIR ARTHUR. She wants to marry David, my dear.

LADY CHAVENDER [calmly] Very naturally. I think if I were in Miss Brollikins' position I should want to marry David.

ALOYSIA. I know your class point of view, Lady Chavender. You think it would be a big catch for me and a come-down for him.

LADY CHAVENDER. We both know that point of view, Miss Brollikins; but it is you, not I, that have mentioned it. Wont you sit down? [She sits down herself in the nearest chair].

ALOYSIA [murmurs] I was just going. [She resumes her seat].

Sir Arthur also sits.

LADY CHAVENDER. I daresay a match with

you might be a very good thing for David. You seem to have all the qualities in which he is deficient. And he has been declaring for some months past that if he ever marries he will marry a factory girl.

ALOYSIA. Well, I have been a factory girl. I started as a school teacher; but when they cut my salary I went into the factory. I organized the girls there, and became a trade union secretary. Wherever I went I rose because I couldnt keep down. But I am proletarian, bone and blood, if thats what David wants.

LADY CHAVENDER. Nobody is that in England, Miss Brollikins. We have never had a noble caste: our younger sons have always been commoners.

SIR ARTHUR. Yes, Aloysia: all British blood is blue.

ALOYSIA. Well, call it what you like. All I say is that I belong to the common working people and am proud of it; and that is what David wants, isnt it?

LADY CHAVENDER. What I said was that he wants to marry a factory girl. But I do not know what his attitude will be when a factory girl wants to marry him. Have you proposed to him?

SIR ARTHUR. Yes. He told her to go to hell.

LADY CHAVENDER. David has rather a habit of telling people to go to hell when he is too lazy to think of anything better to say. Miss Brollikins is a resolute and successful young woman. David is an irresolute and unsuccessful young man. If she has made up her mind to marry him she will probably succeed. She will have to support him; but I daresay she can do that as easily as she can support herself.

ALOYSIA. I shall expect him to work for his living.

LADY CHAVENDER. Marriage seldom fulfils all our expectations. You dont know David yet.

ALOYSIA. I will find him a job and see that he does it. I will interest him in it.

SIR ARTHUR. Splendid!

ALOYSIA [puzzled] But I cant make out you two. You havnt flared up as I thought you might; but are you for me or against me?

LADY CHAVENDER. Miss Brollikins: I am sorry; but there are two things that I cannot bring myself to take the smallest interest in: parliamentary affairs and love affairs. They both bore me to distraction.

ALOYSIA [to Sir Arthur] Well, dont you take an interest in David?

SIR ARTHUR. David is at the age at which young men have to break loose from their fathers. They are very sensitive about being interfered with at that age. He would regard my taking an interest in him as parental tyranny. Therefore I am particularly careful not to take any interest in him.

ALOYSIA [rising] Well, you preach at me because my conversation is unexpected; but you two are the most unexpected lot I have ever been up against. What am I to understand? Will you play fair and let David take his own way?

SIR ARTHUR [rising] We will even let him take your way if he wishes, Aloysia.

LADY CHAVENDER [rising] You may leave me out of the question, Miss Brollikins. It is not my business, but my son's. I am neither his enemy nor yours.

ALOYSIA [perplexed] But do you think I ought to marry him?

LADY CHAVENDER. Nobody ought to marry anybody, Aloysia. But they do.

ALOYSIA. Well, thank you for calling me Aloysia, anyhow. It's about all the satisfaction I have got here.

She is about to go when David breaks in obstreperously through the masked door, and strides between the table and the window to Aloysia's left.

DAVID. Look here, Aloysia. What are you up to here? If you think you can get round me by getting round my parents, youre very much mistaken. My parents dont care a damn what I do as long as I take myself off their hands. And I wont be interfered with. Do you hear? I wont be interfered with.

ALOYSIA. Your parents are too good for you, you uncivilized lout. Youve put me right off it by talking that way in front of your mother. If I was your mother I'd smack some manners into you.

DAVID [appalled and imploring] Aloysia! [He tries to take her in his arms].

ALOYSIA. Take your dirty hands off me [she flings him off]. It's off, I tell you, off. Goodbye all. [She storms out through the main door].

DAVID [in loud lament to his mother] Youve ruined my whole life. [He goes in pursuit, crying] Aloysia, Aloysia, wait a moment. [With anguished intensity] Aloysia. [His cries recede in the distance].

LADY CHAVENDER ⎱ *simultan-* ⎰ He might do worse.
SIR ARTHUR ⎰ *eously* ⎱ He might do worse.

LADY CHAVENDER. I beg your pardon. What did you say?

SIR ARTHUR. I said he might do worse.

LADY CHAVENDER. That is what I said. David is overbred: he is so fine-drawn that he is good for nothing; and he is not strong enough physically. Our breed needs to be crossed with the gutter or the soil once in every three or four generations. Uncle Theodore married his cook on principle; and his wife was my favorite aunt. Brollikins may give me goose flesh occasionally; but she wont bore me as a lady daughter-in-law would. I shall be always wondering what she will say or do next. If she were a lady I'd always know. I am so tired of wellbred people, and party politics, and the London season, and all the rest of it.

SIR ARTHUR. I sometimes think you are the only really revolutionary revolutionist I have ever met.

LADY CHAVENDER. Oh, lots of us are like that. We were born into good society; and we are through with it: we have no illusions about it, even if we are fit for nothing better. I dont mind Brollikins one bit.

SIR ARTHUR. What about Barking?

LADY CHAVENDER. I——

Barking enters through the masked door, jubilant. He comes between the pair as they rise, and claps them both on the shoulders right and left simultaneously. They flinch violently, and stare at him in outraged amazement.

BARKING. Good news, old dears! It's all right about Flavia. We may put up the banns. Hooray! [*He rubs hands gleefully*].

SIR ARTHUR. May I ask how you have got over her craze for marrying a poor man?

BARKING. Oh, that was a girlish illusion. You see, she had a glimpse today, at the unemployed meeting, of what poor men are really like. They were awfully nice to her. That did the trick. You see, what she craved for before was their rough manners, their violence, their brutality and filthy language, their savage treatment of their women folk. That was her ideal of a delightful husband. She found today that the working man doesnt realize it. I do. I am a real he-man. I called her the foulest names until she gave in. She's a dear. We shall be perfectly happy.

Good old mother-in-law. [*He kisses Lady Chavender, who is too astounded to resist or speak*]. Tootle loo, Chavender. [*He slaps him on the shoulder*]. I am off to buy her a lot of presents. [*He dashes out through the main door*].

SIR ARTHUR. So thats that.

LADY CHAVENDER. The brute! How dare he kiss me? [*She rubs the place with her handkerchief*].

SIR ARTHUR. Do you realize that we two are free at last? Free, dearest: think of that! No more children. Free to give up living in a big house and to spend the remainder of our lives as we please. A cottage near a good golf links seems to be indicated. What would you like?

LADY CHAVENDER. But your political career? Are you really going to give up that?

SIR ARTHUR. It has given me up, dearest. Arnt you glad?

LADY CHAVENDER. Arthur: I cant bear this.

SIR ARTHUR. Cant bear what?

LADY CHAVENDER. To see you discouraged. You have never been discouraged before: you have always been so buoyant. If this new departure is to do nothing for you but take away your courage and high spirits and selfconfidence, then in Heaven's name go back to your old way of life. I will put up with anything rather than see you unhappy. That sort of unhappiness kills; and if you die I'll die too. [*She throws herself into a chair and hides her face on the table*].

SIR ARTHUR. Dont fuss, dearest: I'm not unhappy. I am enjoying the enormous freedom of having found myself out and got myself off my mind. That looks like despair; but it is really the beginning of hope, and the end of hypocrisy. Do you think I didnt know, in the days of my great speeches and my roaring popularity, that I was only whitewashing the slums? I did it very well—I dont care who hears me say so—and there is always a sort of artistic satisfaction in doing a thing very well, whether it's getting a big Bill through the House, or carrying a big meeting off its feet, or winning a golf championship. It was all very jolly; and I'm still a little proud of it. But even if I had not had you here to remind me that it was all hot air, I couldnt help knowing as well as any of those damned Socialists that though the West End of London was chockful of money and nice people all calling oneanother by their Christian names, the lives of the millions of people whose labor was keeping the whole show going were not worth living. I knew it quite well; but I was able to put it out of my mind because I thought it couldnt be helped and I was doing the best that could be done. I know better now: I know that it can be helped, and how it can be helped. And rather than go back to the old whitewashing job, I'd seize you tight round the waist and make a hole in the river with you.

LADY CHAVENDER [*rising*] Then why, dearest love, dont you—

SIR ARTHUR. Why dont I lead the revolt against it all? Because I'm not the man for the job, darling; and nobody knows that better than you. And I shall hate the man who will carry it through for his cruelty and the desolation he will bring on us and our like.

Shouting, as of an excited mob suddenly surging into the street; and a sound of breaking glass and police whistling.

LADY CHAVENDER. What on earth is that?

Hilda comes from her office and runs to the window.

LADY CHAVENDER [*joining her*] What is going on, Hilda?

HILDA. The unemployed have broken into Downing Street; and theyre breaking the windows of the Colonial Office. They think this side is only private houses.

SIR ARTHUR [*going to see*] Yes: they always break the wrong windows, poor devils!

HILDA. Oh! here come the mounted police.

SIR ARTHUR. Theyve splendid horses, those fellows.

HILDA. The people are all running away. And they cant get out: theyre in a cul-de-sac. Oh, why dont they make a stand, the cowards?

LADY CHAVENDER. Indeed I hope they wont. What are you thinking of, Hilda?

SIR ARTHUR. Men are like that, Hilda. They always run away when they have no discipline and no leader.

HILDA. Well, but cant the police let them run away without breaking their heads? Oh look: that policeman has just clubbed a quite old man.

SIR ARTHUR. Come away: it's not a nice sight. [*He draws her away, placing himself between her and the window*].

HILDA. It's all right when you only read about it in the papers; but when you actually see it you want to throw stones at the police.

Defiant singing through the tumult.

LADY CHAVENDER [*looking out*] Someone has opened the side gate and let them through into the Horse Guards Parade. They are trying to sing.

SIR ARTHUR. What are they singing? The Red Flag?

LADY CHAVENDER. No. I dont know the tune. I caught the first two words. "England, arise."

HILDA [*suddenly hysterical*] Oh, my God! I will go out and join them [*she rushes out through the main door*].

LADY CHAVENDER. Hilda! Hilda!

SIR ARTHUR. Never mind, dear: the police all know her: she'll come to no harm. She'll be back for tea. But what she felt just now other girls and boys may feel tomorrow. And just suppose—!

LADY CHAVENDER. What?

SIR ARTHUR. Suppose England really did arise!

Unemployed England, however, can do nothing but continue to sing, as best it can to a percussion accompaniment of baton thwacks, Edward Carpenter's verses

f Eng-land, a-rise! the long, long night is o-ver,

Faint in the east be-hold the dawn ap-pear;

Out of your e-vil dream of toil and sor-row—

A-rise, O Eng-land, for the day is here;

p From your fields and hills, Hark! the an-swer swells—

f A-rise, O Eng-land, for the day is here.

THE END